"New Reading Room at the Imperial Library, Paris"

BOOKMAN'S
PRICE INDEX

BOOKMAN'S PRICE INDEX

A Guide to the Values of
Rare and Other Out-of-Print Books

VOLUME 11

DANIEL F. McGRATH

GALE RESEARCH COMPANY • BOOK TOWER • DETROIT, MICHIGAN

Library of Congress Catalog Card Number 64-8723
ISBN 0-8103-0611-5
Copyright © 1976 by Gale Research Company
Printed in the United States of America

CONTENTS

HOW TO USE THIS BOOK

All listings in this volume of BOOKMAN'S PRICE INDEX are based on descriptions of books offered for sale by leading dealers in their catalogs published in 1973 and 1974.

Dealer's descriptions have been followed closely, although extensive details not essential to establishing condition or determining price have been condensed or omitted. In any case, however, there has been no addition to or revision of the content of the dealer's description, even in the few cases where a description might have been in error.

Every effort has been made to report prices and other details accurately; the user should keep in mind, however, that the possibility of typographical error--for which the publisher assumes no responsibility--does exist, and, furthermore, that an individual dealer's evaluation of a book may not represent a professional consensus.

ARRANGEMENT--listings are alphabetical according to name of author, or, if no author is mentioned, according to the first word not an article in the title.

Names under which entries appear in BPI have been standardized as much as possible, and therefore are not always given in the exact form in which they appear on some title pages, or in the catalogs of some dealers. Familiar and common forms of names have been preferred. Various editions of a single work have been brought together, even though alphabetical order is in some cases violated thereby. (See the discussion of the handling of such editions in the introduction to Volume 4.)

ORDER OF INFORMATION--Within each entry, the following information is given in this order:

1. Author's name
2. Title
3. Place and date of publication
4. Description of the book, including its condition when offered by the dealer
5. Name of dealer publishing catalog
6. Number of catalog in which offered, and item number within the catalog
7. Year date (or year of receipt) of catalog in which book is offered
8. Price at which offered

DEALERS REPRESENTED

IN THIS VOLUME

WILLIAM H. ALLEN
2031 Walnut Street
Philadelphia, Pennsylvania 19103

AUSTIN BOOK SHOP
P.O. Box 36
Kew Gardens, New York 11415

BALLINGERS BOOK SERVICE
P.O. Box 1013
Englewood Cliffs, New Jersey 07632

BIBLO & TANNEN
63 Fourth Avenue
New York, New York 10003

BOW WINDOWS BOOK SHOP
128 High Street
Lewes, Sussex, BN 7 1 X L, England

VAN ALLEN BRADLEY
Box 578
Lake Zurich, Illinois 60047

C. K. BROADHURST & CO. LTD.
5-7 Market Street
Southport, PR 8 1 Hd, England

ROGER BUTTERFIELD, INC.
White House Route 205
Hartwick, New York 13348

COVENT GARDEN BOOKSHOP
80 Long Acre
London, WC2E 9NG, England

CRANE BOOKSHOP, LTD.
70a High Street
Haslemere, Surrey, England

THE CURRENT COMPANY
Box 46 - 17 Burnside Street
Bristol, Rhode Island 02809

DAWSONS BOOK SHOP
535 North Larchmont Boulevard
Los Angeles, California 90004

DAWSONS OF PALL MALL
16 Pall Mall
London, SW1Y, 5 NB, England

JEFF DYKES/WESTERN BOOKS
Box 38
College Park, Maryland 20740

PETER EATON, LTD.
80 Holland Park Avenue
London, W11, England

EMERALD ISLE BOOKS
539 Antrim Road
Belfast, BT15 3 BU, N. Ireland

W. FORSTER
83 A Stamford Hill
London, N 16, England

DORIS FROHNSDORFF
P.O. Box 831
Gaithersburg, Maryland 20760

GEORGE'S
89 Park Street
Bristol, BS 1 5 PW, England

GILHOEFER & RANSCHBURG
Haldenstrasse 9
Luzerne, Switzerland

LUCIEN GOLDSCHMIDT
1117 Madison Avenue
New York, New York 10028

GOODSPEED'S BOOK SHOP INC.
18 Beacon Street
Boston, Massachusetts 02108

KATHERINE GREGORY
222 East 71st Street
New York, New York 10021

R. D. GURNEY LTD.
23 Campden Street
Kensington Church Street
London W8, England

FRANK HAMMOND
67 Birmingham Road
Sutton Coldfield
Warwickshire, England

LATHROP C. HARPER
22 East 40th Street
New York, New York 10016

ROBERT G. HAYMAN
REDI
Carey, Ohio 43316

PETER MURRAY HILL, LTD.
73 Sloane Avenue - Chelsa
London S.W. 3, England

DORA HOOD'S BOOK ROOM, LTD.
34 Ross Street
Toronto, 2-B, Canada

HOWES BOOKSHOP, LTD.
3 Trinity Street
Hastings, Sussex, England

DOUGLAS M. JACOBS
Box 363
Bethel, Connecticut 06801

THE JENKINS COMPANY
912 Congress Avenue
Austin, Texas

H. P. KRAUSS
16 East 46th Street
New York, New York 10017

GEORGE S. MAC MANUS CO.
1317 Irving Street
Philadelphia, Pennsylvania 19107

MARLBOROUGH RARE BOOKS
35 Old Bond Street
London W1X 4PT, England

FRANCIS MARSDEN
59 Kings Road Chelsea
London S.W. 3, England

ARTHUR H. MINTERS BOOKSELLERS
84 University Place
New York, New York 10003

PUTNAM BOOKSHOP
304 West Jefferson Street
Bloomington, Illinois 61701

BERNARD QUARITCH, LTD.
5-8 Lower John Street
Golden Square
London W1V 6AB, England

EDWARD P. RICH
Box 295
Haverford, Pennsylvania 19041

RITTENHOUSE
1706 Rittenhouse Square
Philadelphia, Pennsylvania 19103

ROBERT H. ROSS
3 Allen Street
Hanover, New Hampshire 03755

BERTRAM ROTA
4,5, & 6 Savile Row
London, W1, England

SADDLEBACK COLLEGE BOOK STORE
28000 Marguerite Parkway
Mission Viejo, California 92675

CHARLES J. SAWYER, LTD.
12 & 13 Grafton Street
London, W1, England

JORG SCHAFFER
Hottingerstrasse 5
8032 Zurich, Switzerland

HENRY SCHUMAN, LTD.
2211 Broadway
New York, New York 10024

HELLMUT SCHUMANN AG
25 Raemistrasse
Zurich, Switzerland

WILLIAM SMITH, LTD.
35-41 London Street
Reading, Berks, England

ALAN G. THOMAS
c/o Westminster Bank
300 Kings Road
London SW 3, England

CHARLES W. TRAYLEN
49-50 Quarry Street
Guildford, Surrey, England

WHELDON & WESLEY, LTD.
Lytton Lodge Codicote
Nr. Hitching, Herts, SG4 8TE England

JEFF WILSON
Box 33
Newton Square, Pennsylvania 19073

XIMINES RARE BOOKS
24 West 45th Street
New York, New York 10036

ZEITLIN & VER BRUGGE
815 North LaCienega Boulevard
Los Angeles, California 90069

A

AAGAARD, B.   Fangst og Forskning I Sydishavet. Oslo, 1930. 2 vols., roy. 8vo., cloth, illus., maps. Wheldon 128-77 1973 £10

AAGARD, C. J.   The Common Birds of Bangkok. Copenhagen, 1930. Roy 8vo., orig. cloth, illus., scarce. Wheldon 129-408 1974 £7.50

AARONSOHN, MICHAEL   Broken Lights. Cincinnati, 1946. Austin 62-1 1974 $12.50

ABBE, FRANK B.   San Juan Bautista. N.P., 1897. Oblong, 16mo., wrapper. Saddleback 14-19 1974 $20

ABBEY, CHARLES J.   The English Church in the 18th Century. 1878. 2 vols., thick 8vo. Howes 185-888 1974 £6.50

ABBOT, ABIEL   Genealogical Register of the Descendants of George Abbot. Boston, 1847. Orig. cloth, first edition. Bradley 35-149 1974 $16

ABBOT, GEORGE   The Case of Impotency as Debated in England. London, 1715. 8vo., contemporary calf, rebacked, gilt, first edition. Dawsons PM 251-159 1974 £120

ABBOT, HENRY G.   Abbotts American Watchmaker and Jeweller. Chicago, n.d. Illus., first edition. Covent 55-849 1974 £6.50

ABBOT, J.   The Natural History of the Rarer Lepidopterous Insects of Georgia. 1797. Folio, contemporary straight grain morocco, gilt, plates. Wheldon 129-1698 1974 £2,600

ABBOT, J.   The Natural History of the Rarer Lepidopterous Insects of Georgia. 1797. Folio, contemporary straight grain morocco gilt, plates, nice copy. Wheldon 131-1 1974 £2,600

ABBOTT, CHARLES D.   A Selection of Books & Manuscripts in the Lockwood Memorial Library. New York, 1935. 8vo., orig. buckram gilt, plates, calf vack, fine, limited. Dawsons PM 10-4 1974 £9

ABBOTT, EDITH   Immigration. 1924. 809 pages. Austin 57-2 1974 $17.50

ABBOTT, EDITH   The Tenements of Chicago, 1908-1935. Chicago, 1936. Orig. ed. Biblo & Tannen 210-1022 1973 $12.50

ABBOTT, EDWIN   Concordance to the Works of Alexander Pope. New York, 1875. 8vo., cloth. Dawsons PM 11-2 1974 £8.25

ABBOTT, GEORGE   Contributions Towards a Bibliography of the Civil War in the United States. Philadelphia, 1886. Wrapper. Jenkins 61-497 1974 $25

ABBOTT, GEORGE   Coquette. Longmans, Green, 1928. 137p. Austin 51-1 1973 $7.50

ABBOTT, GEORGE   Mister Abbott. Random House, 1963. 279p. Austin 51-2 1973 $6.50

ABBOTT, JACOB   Ellen Linn. New York, n.d. 12mo., orig. cloth, frontispiece, engravings. Covent 55-1 1974 £7.50

ABBOTT, JACOB   Rollo At Work. Boston, 1838. 16mo., cloth covers detached and badly worn, illus. Frohnsdorff 16-2 1974 $7.50

ABBOTT, JACOB   Rollo In Naples. Boston, 1858. 12mo., embossed cloth, gilt spine; illus., lst ed. Frohnsdorff 16-1 1974 $15

ABBOTT, JACOB   Rollo in Naples. Boston, 1862. 12mo., illus., orig. purple cloth, spine faded. Current BW9-142 1974 $10

ABBOTT, JACOB   The Young Christian. New York, 1832. Sm. 8vo., cloth, leather spine gilt, corners rubbed; light foxing. Frohnsdorff 16-3 1974 $20

ABBOTT, JOHN STEVENS CABOT 1805-1877   The History of the Civil War in America. New York, 1863-66. 2 vols., illus., tissue guards, rubbed, maps, marbled edges and endpapers, front cover vol. 1 detached. Wilson 63-355 1974 $19.75

A'BECKETT, GILBERT ABBOTT   Comic History of England. n.d. 8vo., plates, half red morocco, gilt, woodcuts. Quaritch 936-266 1974 £18

A'BECKETT, GILBERT ABBOTT   The Comic History of England. 1847. Vol. 1 of 2 vols., orig. cloth gilt, woodcuts, plates. Smith 193-305 1973 £9.50

A'BECKETT, GILBERT ABBOT   The Comic History of Rome. London, 1851. Orig. cloth gilt, colored plates, woodcuts, fine, first edition, later issue with the addition to the imprint the words "and Co.". MacManus 224-1 1974 $75

ABEEL, DAVID   Journal of a Residence in China . . . From 1829-1833. New York and Boston, 1834. Backstrip slightly chipped, orig. binding. Butterfield 10-45 1974 $10

ABEL, O.   Grundzuge der Palaebiologie der Wirbetiere. Stuttgart, 1912. Roy 8vo., orig. cloth. Wheldon 129-800 1974 £10

ABERCROMBIE, JOHN   Inquiries Concerning the Intellectual Powers. Edinburgh, 1831. 8vo., purple cloth, orig. paper label, uncut, fine, second edition. Dawsons PM 249-1 1974 £18

ABERCROMBIE, JOHN 1726-1806   The British Fruit-Gardener. 1779. 8vo., contemporary sheep, rebacked, rare. Wheldon 130-1464 1974 £25

ABERCROMBIE, JOHN 1726-1806   The British Fruit Gardener. 1779. 8vo., modern boards antique style, rare. Wheldon 131-1482 1974 £25

ABERCROMBIE, LASCELLES   The Sale of Saint Thomas. London, 1931. 8vo., orig. cloth, book-plate, first edition. Bow Windows 62-3 1974 £20

ABERCROMBIE, W. R.   Alaska, 1899, Copper River Exploring Expedition. Washington, 1900. Plates, folding map, orig. buckram, fine. Jenkins 61-35 1974 $27.50

ABERCROMBY, PATRICK   The Martial Atchievements of the Scots Nation. Edinburgh, 1711. 2 vols., folio, contemporary calf. Traylen 79-125 1973 £60

ABERDEEN AND TEMAIR, ISHBEL MARIA (MARJORBANKS) GORDON, MARCHIONESS OF, 1857-   Through Canada With a Kodak. Edinburgh, 1893. Illus., intricately designed covers. Hood's 102-546 1974 $25

ABERNETHY, JOHN   Surgical Observations. London, 1806. 8vo., orig. boards, rebacked, uncut, first edition. Dawsons PM 249-4 1974 £15

ABERNETHY, JOHN   Surgical Observations. London, 1824. 8vo., contemporary half calf, worn, seventh edition. Dawsons PM 249-2 1974 £5

ABERNETHY, JOHN   Surgical Observations. London, 1826. 8vo., orig. boards, uncut, rebacked, eighth edition. Dawsons PM 240-3 1974 £6

ABERNETHY, JOHN   Surgical Observations on Diseases Resembling Syphilis; and on Diseases of the Urethra. London, 1810. 8vo., orig. boards, rebacked, uncut, first edition. Gurney 66-2 1974 £15

ABERNETHY, JOHN   Surgical Observations on the Constitutional Origin and Treatment of Local Diseases; and on Aneurisms. London, 1809. 8vo., quarter parchment, uncut, first edition. Gurney 66-1 1974 £25

ABERNETHY, JOHN R.   Catch Em Alive Jack. New York, 1936. First edition, illus., orig. binding. Wilson 63-117 1974 $13.50

ABINGDON, T.   The Antiquities of the Cathedral Church of Worcester. 1717. 8vo., buckram. Quaritch 939-581 1974 £12.50

ABLES, W. E. VAN   Unsere Wichtigeren Giftgewachse. Esslingen, 1874. Small folio, orig. cloth backed boards, plates. Wheldon 129-1680 1974 £15

ABRAHAM WALEH BAR CHASDAI   Ben Ha'melech Ve'hanazir. Mantua, 1557. Second edition, some waterstaining, small 8vo., morocco backed boards. Thomas 32-52 1974 £175

ABRAHAM, JAMES JOHNSTON   Lettsom, His Life, Friends and Descendants. London, 1933. Rittenhouse 46-1 1974 $15

ABRAHAMS, ETHEL B.   Greek Dress. 1908. New Buckram, plates. Allen 213-4 1973 $10

ABSE, DANNIE   After Every Green Thing. n.d. Boards, spine rubbed, nice copy. Covent 51-2087 1973 £10

ABSTRACT of the Answers and Returns Made Pursuant to an Act. 1812. Folio, buckram. Quaritch 939-197 1974 £20

ABSTRACT of the Answers and Returns Made Pursuant to an Act. 1833. 3 vols., folio, modern boards, cloth backs. Quaritch 939-198 1974 £45

ACCADEMIA DEL CIMENTO   Saggi di Naturali Esperienze. Florence, 1666. Folio, engravings, half calf, gilt, very rare first edition. Gilhofer 61-11 1974 sFr. 3,000

ACCADEMIA Del Cimento. 1684. 4to., contemporary calf, ex-library, frontispiece. Zeitlin 235-250 1974 $975

AN ACCOUNT of the Convincement, Exercises . . . of the Lord Richard Davies. 1928. 8vo., buckram, uncut, limited edition. Broadhurst 23-1036 1974 £36

ACCOUNT of the Larch Plantations on the Estates of Atholl & Dunkeld, Executed by the Late John, Duke of Atholl. Perth, 1832. 8vo., disbound, very scarce, first edition. Ximenes 37-83 1974 $20

ACCOUNT OF the Trial of Warren Hastings. London, 1788. Boards, calf, worn. Dawson's 424-315 1974 $20

AN ACCOUNT of the Visit of His Royal Highness the Prince Regent. (1815). Folio, half calf. Quaritch 939-458 1974 £10

AN ACCOUNT of the Visit of . . . . the Prince Regent with. . . . c.1815. 2 works in 1 vol., folio, contemporary diced russia. Howes 186-2114 1974 £18

ACCUM, FRIEDRICH CHRISTIAN   Chemical Re-Agents, or Tests. London, 1828. 12mo., old sheep, very worn but firm, plates. Gurney 66-4 1974 £30

ACCUM, FRIEDRICH CHRISTIAN   A Practical Treatise on Gas-Light. London, 1815. 8vo., modern boards, uncut, plates, first edition. Dawsons PM 245-2 1974 £55

ACCUM, FRIEDRICH CHRISTIAN   A Practical Treatise on Gas-Light. 1818. Roy. 8vo., plates, orig. boards, rebacked, new paper label, uncut, second edition. Quaritch 940-489 1974 £75

ACE, GOODMAN   The Book of Little Knowledge. S & S, 1955. 183p. Austin 51-3 1973 $7.50

ACHARIYAR, R. B. K. R.   A Handbook of Some South Indian Grasses. Madras, 1921. Roy 8vo., cloth. Wheldon 129-1034 1974 £5

ACHESON, SAM HANNA   Joe Bailey: The Last Democrat. New York, 1932. Inscribed by author. Jenkins 61-178 1974 $20

ACKERLEY, J. R.   The Prisoners of War. 1925. Dust wrapper, fine, English first edition. Covent 56-2 1974 £12.50

ACKERMAN, A.   First Book of Natural History. New York, 1846. 12mo., illus. bdg. worn. Biblo & Tannen 213-843 1973 $9.50

ACKERMANN, JAKOB FIDELIS   Infantis Androgyni Historia et Ichnographia. Jena, 1805. Folio, contemporary half calf, plates, first edition. Schuman 37-1 1974 $110

ACKERMANN, RUDOLPH   Ackerman's Repository of Arts, Literature, Commerce, Manufactures, Fashions and Politics. 1809-28. 40 vols., roy. 8vo., plates, half brown morocco, gilt. Quaritch 940-429 1974 £5,000

ACKERMANN, RUDOLPH   History of the Abbey Church of St. Peter's Westminster. 1812. 2 vols., roy. 4to., plates, half blue morocco gilt. Quaritch 939-474 1974 £290

ACKERMANN, RUDOLPH   The History of the Colleges of Winchester, Eton, and Westminster. 1816. Roy. 4to., contemporary half calf, plates. Quaritch 939-25 1974 £1250

ACKERMANN, RUDOLPH   History of the University of Cambridge. 1815. 2 vols., imp. 4to., contemporary half russia. Quaritch 939-313 1974 £1000

ACKERMANN, RUDOLPH   A History of the University of Cambridge. 1815. Coloured aqauatint views, coloured plates, engraved portrait, 4to., half red levant morocco gilt, top edges gilt, others uncut, tear page 199/200 neatly repaired, good copy. Sawyer 293-106 1974 £2,100

ACKERMANN, RUDOLPH   History of the University of Oxford. 1814. 2 vols., roy. 4to., half red morocco, plates. Quaritch 939-513 1974 £650

ACKERMANN, RUDOLPH   A History of the University of Oxford. 1814. Coloured exterior & interior views, coloured plates, portrait, 2 vols., 4to., orig. boards, paper labels, entirely uncut, fine, coloured portraits, rare in uncut state. Sawyer 293-107 1974 £825

ACKERMANN, RUDOLPH   A History of the University of Oxford. London, 1814. 2 vols., large 4to., full blue crushed levant morocco, gilt, plates. Traylen 79-373 1973 £650

ACKERMANN, RUDOLPH   Microcosm of London. 1808-10. Orig. edition, engraved titles, vignettes, coloured views & plates, portraits, 3 vols., 4to., red levant morocco, gilt tooled, very fine copy, rare. Sawyer 293-108 1974 £2750

ACKERMANN, RUDOLPH   The Microcosm of London. London, 1904. 3 vols., 4to., vellum, paper labels, boards, illus., uncut, foxing. Traylen 79-350 1973 £21

ACKLAND, RODNEY   The Celluloid Mistress. Wingate, 1954. 264p., illus. Austin 51-4 1973 $7.50

ACOSTA, JOSEPH DE   De Natura Novi Orbis, Libri Duo. Cologne, 1596. Small 8vo., old calf, worn. Thomas 28-25 1972 £65

ACOSTA, JOSEPH DE   De Natura Novi Orbis, Libri Duo. Cologne, 1596. Small 8vo., old calf, little worn but sound. Thomas 32-1 1974 £65

ACOSTA, JOSEPH DE   The Natvrall and Morall Historie of the East and West Indies. 1604. 4to., contemporary calf, first edition in English. Bow Windows 64-357 1974 £850

ACROSS Niagara's Gorge. 1905. Suede binding, photos tipped in. Hood's 102-581 1974 $30

AN ACT Relating to Bills of Exchange, Cheques, and Promissory Notes, Assented to May 16th, 1890. Ottawa, 1886. Hood's. 104-588 1974 $12.50

AN ACT To Incorporate the Trustees of the Missionary Society of Connecticut. Hartford, 1803. 8vo., fine, first edition. Ximenes 33-316 1974 $45

ACTA Apostolicae Sedis. Rome, 1924-26. 3 vols., roy. 8vo., half morocco. Howes 185-891 1974 £10.50

ACTA Sanctorum Quotquot toto Orbe Coluntur. 1863-1925. 68 vols., thick folio, plates, half calf. Howes 185-892 1974 £1400

ACTON, ELIZA   The English Bread Book for Domestic Use. 1857. Small 8vo., cloth, first edition. Quaritch 939-26 1974 £35

ACTON, HAROLD   An Indian Ass. 1925. Presentation, inscribed, book-plate. Covent 55-4 1974 £10.50

ACTON, HAROLD   The Last of the Medici. Florence, 1930. One of 364 copies on handmade paper, numbered & signed by author, plates, orig. boards, leather label, fine copy, worn d.w. Covent 51-2313 1973 £25

ACTORS EQUITY ASSOCIATION   Players Guide, 1955 (13th ed.). 1955. 862p., illus. Austin 51-5 1973 $37.50

ACTORS EQUITY ASSOCIATION   Players Guide, 1956 (14th ed.). 1956. 936p., illus. Austin 51-6 1973 $37.50

ACTORS EQUITY ASSOCIATION   Players Guide, 1957 (15th ed.). 1957. 983p., illus. Austin 51-7 1973 $37.50

ACTS of Court of the Mercers' Company. 1936. Thick roy. 8vo., orig. buckram, gilt, scarce. Howes 186-1443 1974 £21

ACTS of the Lords Auditors of Causes & Complaints. 1839. Folio, half calf. Howes 186-1159 1974 £20

THE ACTS of the Lords of Council in Civil Causes. 1839. Folio, stamp, cloth back, boards. Quaritch 939-19 1974 £10

ACTS of the Privy Council of England. 1890-95. 11 vols., roy. 8vo., cloth. Quaritch 939-16 1974 £115

ACTS of the Privy Council of England. 1890-1932. 37 vols., roy. 8vo., cloth. Quaritch 939-15 1974 £400

ACTS Relative to the Delaware and Raritan Canal Company. N.P., 1832. 8vo., disbound. Ximenes 35-4 1974 $45

ADAM, G. MERCER   Canada's Patriot Statesman, Life and Career of Rt. Hon. Sir John A. MacDonald. Toronto, 1891. Revised edition, rebound. Hood's 102-219 1974 $12.50

ADAM, G. MERCER   The Canadian North-West, Its History and Its Troubles. Toronto, 1855. Illus. Hood's 102-789 1974 $30

ADAM, G. MERCER   Illustrated Toronto, "The Queen City of the West", 1791-93 to 1891-93. Toronto, 1891. Photos, dec. hard cover. Hood's 102-582 1974 $25

ADAM, JAMES   Practical Essays on Agriculture. London, 1789. 8vo., 2 vols., contemporary half calf, gilt, first edition. Hammond 201-3 1974 £35

ADAM, JULIETTE   Mes Sentiments et nos Idees Avant 1870. Paris, 1905. 12mo., orig. wrapper, uncut, first edition. L. Goldschmidt 42-137 1974 $30

ADAM, L. S.   Recueil de Sculptures Antiques Greques et Romaines. 1754. 4to., contemporary calf, gilt, first edition. Hammond 201-2 1974 £12.50

ADAM, MAGISTER   Summula. Cologne, 1500. 4to., straight grained purple morocco, gilt, fine, sixth edition. Harper 213-1 1973 $625

ADAM, ROBERT   The Decorative Work of. London, 1901. Atlas folio, plates, orig. vellum backed boards. Bow Windows 62-6 1974 £10

ADAM, ROBERT   The Decorative Work of Robert and James Adam. 1901. Roy. folio, quarter vellum, boards, plates. Broadhurst 23-3 1974 £10

ADAM, ROBERT   The Decorative Work of Robert and James Adam, Being a Reproduction of the Plates Illustrating Decorations and Furniture from Their "Works in Architecture". London, n.d. (1902). Folio, plates, spine slightly rubbed top & bottom, orig. binding, small water spots on front cover, fine, scarce. Ross 87-187 1974 $75

ADAM, ROBERT   Ruins of the Palace of the Emperor Diocletian at Spalatro in Dalmatia. 1764. Imp. folio, plates, half russia, newly rebacked. Quaritch 940-488 1974 £250

ADAM, W.   On the Osteological Symmetry of the Camel. 1832. 4to. Wheldon 128-300 1973 £5

ADAMS, ANDY   The Log of a Cowboy. Boston, New York, 1903. Colored pic. cloth, illus. Dykes 24-168 1974 $35

ADAMS, ANDY   The Log of a Cowboy. Boston, 1903. First edition, illus., pict. cloth. Jenkins 61-10 1974 $27.50

ADAMS, ANDY   The Outlet. Boston and New York, 1905. Pic. cloth, illus., 1st ed. Dykes 24-170 1974 $20

ADAMS, ANDY   The Ranch on the Beaver. Boston and New York, 1927. Decor. cloth, illus., 1st ed., one small orig. pen and ink drawing. Dykes 24-137 1974 $100

ADAMS, ANDY   A Texas Matchmaker. Boston and New York, 1904. Pic. cloth, illus., 1st ed. Dykes 24-169 1974 $20

ADAMS, ARTHUR   The Syntax of the Temporal Clause In Old English Prose. 1907. Ex-library, sturdy library binding, folded tables. Austin 61-1 1974 $17.50

ADAMS, BROOKS   The Law of Civilization and Decay. New York, 1910. Biblo & Tannen 213-641 1973 $7.50

ADAMS, C. B.   Catalogue of Shells Collected at Panama. New York, 1852. 8vo., half calf, worn. Wheldon 129-726 1974 £15

ADAMS, CHARLES   Producing and Directing for Television. Holt, 1953. 282p., illus. Austin 51-8 1973 $10

ADAMS, CHARLES FOLLEN   Yawcob Strauss. 1910. Illus., 311 pages. Austin 57-15 1974 $12.50

ADAMS, CHARLES FRANCIS   Charles Francis Adams. Boston, 1916. Orig. blue cloth, frontispiece, first edition. Bradley 35-1 1974 $15

ADAMS, CHARLES FRANCIS   Studies Military and Diplomatic, 1775-1865. New York, 1911. First edition, orig. binding. Butterfield 10-1 1974 $10

ADAMS, E. D.   British Diplomatic Correspondence Concerning the Republic of Texas. Austin, 1917. Wrapper, near mint. Jenkins 61-12 1974 $85

ADAMS, ELIZABETH CHALLIS   The Street Car and the Star. Marcus, 1926. 43p., limited to 500 copies. Austin 54-1 1973 $10

ADAMS, F. COLBURN   The Story of a Trooper. New York, 1865. Repaired. Jenkins 61-13 1974 $17.50

ADAMS, FRANKLIN P.   Among Us Mortals. Houghton, 1917. Austin 54-2 1973 $6.50

ADAMS, FRANKLIN P.   By and Large. Doubleday, Page, 1914. 148p. Austin 54-3 1973 $7.50

ADAMS, FRANKLIN P.   The Melancholy Lute. Viking, 1956. 191p. Austin 54-4 1973 $7.50

ADAMS, FRANKLIN P.   Nods and Becks. Whittlesey, 1944. 246p. Austin 54-5 1973 $6

ADAMS, FRANKLIN P.   Something Else Again. Doubleday, Page, 1920. 123p. Austin 54-6 1973 $7.50

ADAMS, GEORGE   An Essay on Electricity. London, 1787. Engraved title and 9 plates, contemp. green mor., gilt; gilt spine. Jacobs 24-152 1974 $150

ADAMS, GEORGE   An Essay on Electricity. London, 1799. 8vo., contemporary calf, frontispiece, plates. Dawsons PM 245-3 1974 £15

ADAMS, GEORGE   Essays on the Microscope. 1787. 4to and Oblong 4to., 2 vols., modern half calf, first edition. Wheldon 130-87 1974 £75

ADAMS, GEORGE   Essays On the Microscope. 1787. 4to., modern quarter calf antique, plates, first edition. Wheldon 131-139 1974 £60

ADAMS, GEORGE   Essays On the Microscope. 1798. 2 vols., 4to., modern quarter calf antique, plates, second edition. Wheldon 131-140 1974 £60

ADAMS, GEORGE   Geometrical and Graphical Essays. 8vo., orig. boards, 2 vols., uncut. Broadhurst 23-1203 1974 £36

ADAMS, GEORGE   Lectures On Natural and Experimental Philosophy. London, 1794. 5 vols., 8vo., old calf, worn. Traylen 79-193 1973 £52

ADAMS, H.   The Genera of Recent Mollusca. (1853-)1858. Roy 8vo., publisher's cloth, 3 vols., plates. Wheldon 129-727 1974 £75

ADAMS, HARRIET ISABEL   Wild Flower of the British Isles. 1907-10. 4to., 2 vols., cloth, scarce. Wheldon 130-1072 1974 £10

ADAMS, HARRIET ISABEL   Wild Flowers of the British Isles. 1910. 2 vols., 4to., cloth, coloured plates, scarce. Wheldon 128-1182 1973 £7.50

ADAMS, HENRY   A Letter to American Teachers of History. Washington, 1910. Green cloth, fine, first edition, autographed by author. Jenkins 61-14 1974 $185

ADAMS, HENRY   Letters of . . . (1858–1891) & (1892–1918).
Boston & New York, 1930. 2 vols., orig. cloth, paper labels, fine, boxed, first
editions. MacManus 224-2 1974 $55

ADAMS, HENRY   Mont-Saint-Michel & Chartres. 1927. 4to.,
plates. Allen 213-1234 1973 $12.50

ADAMS, HENRY GARDINER   Humming Birds. (1872). Crown 8vo., orig.
dec. cloth, plates. Wheldon 131-528 1974 £15

ADAMS, HENRY GARDINER   The Smaller British Birds. 1874. 8vo., orig.
dec. cloth, gilt, plates. Wheldon 131-529 1974 £10

ADAMS, HERBERT B.   Johns Hopkins University Studies in Historical and
Political Science. Baltimore, 1885. 8vo., orig. bindings. Butterfield 8-220
1974 $15

ADAMS, J. P.   Shakespearean Playhouses. n.d. 8vo., cloth,
illus., ex-library, orig. edition. Quaritch 936-548 1974 £4

ADAMS, JAMES TRUSLOW   Atlas of American History. London, 1943.
8vo., cloth. Dawsons PM 11-4 1974 £8.30

ADAMS, JAMES TRUSLOW   Dictionary of American History. London, 1940.
6 vols., 8vo., cloth. Dawsons PM 11-5 1974 £57

ADAMS, JAMES TRUSLOW   Dictionary of American History. New York,
1940. 1st ed., 7 vols. Jacobs 24-1 1974 $60

ADAMS, JOEY   The Curtain Never Falls. Fell, 1949. Austin
54-7 1973 $6.50

ADAMS, JOEY   From Gags to Riches. Fell, 1946. 336p.,
illus. Austin 54-8 1973 $6.50

ADAMS, JOEY   Joey Adams Joke Book. Fell, 1952. 250p.
Austin 54-9 1973 $6

ADAMS, JOEY   The Joey Adams Joke Dictionary. Citadel,
1962. 343p. Austin 54-10 1973 $7.50

ADAMS, JOHN   The Flowers of Ancient History. Dublin,
1789. 12mo., contemporary full calf. Emerald 50-241 1974 £15

ADAMS, JOHN fl. 1680   Index Villaris. London, 1680. Folio, half
calf, first edition. Quaritch 939-27 1974 £50

ADAMS, JOHN fl. 1680   Index Villaris. 1690. Folio, old calf, stained,
rebacked. Quaritch 939-28 1974 £40

ADAMS, JOHN QUINCY   The Duplicate Letters. Washington, 1822.
Orig. boards, uncut, paper label, first edition. Bradley 35-2 1974 $20

ADAMS, JOHN QUINCY   Oration on the Life and Character of Gilbert
Motier de Lafayette. Washington, 1835. New blue wrappers, first edition.
Bradley 35-3 1974 $10

ADAMS, JOSEPH   Observations On Morbid Poisons, Chronic and
Acute. London, 1807. 4to., contemporary half calf, illus., second edition.
Schuman 37-2 1974 $85

ADAMS, KATHERINE   A Display of Heraldrie. 1638. Folio, contemporary calf, third edition. Quaritch 936-268 1974 £20

ADAMS, KATHERINE   Poems. 1873. Small 8vo., white pigskin, gilt.
Quaritch 936-269 1974 £55

ADAMS, LEONIE   Those Not Elect. New York, 1925. First
U. S. edition, boards, very nice copy. Covent 51-4 1973 £12.50

ADAMS, MORLEY   Omar's Interpreter. 1909. Plates, foxed,
faded, first edition. Covent 55-675 1974 £12.50

ADAMS, NATHANIEL   Annals of Portsmouth Comprising a Period of Two
Hundred Years from the First Settlement of the Town; With Biographical Sketches.
Portsmouth, 1825. First edition, 8vo., ex-library, some binding wear, firm.
Current BW9-398 1974 $25

ADAMS, PERCY WALTER LEWIS   A History of the Adams Family of North
Staffordshire. London, 1914. Crown 4to., plates, illus., orig. cloth, rubbed,
first edition. Bow Windows 62-5 1974 £25

ADAMS, PERCY WALTER LEWIS   A History of the Douglas Family of Morton in
Nithsdale, and Fingland and Their Descendants. Bedford, 1921. 8vo., orig.
cloth, frontis., plates, rebacked. Bow Windows 66-188 1974 £21

ADAMS, ROBERT   The Narrative of Robert Adams. 1816. 4to.,
contemporary calf, first edition. Bow Windows 64-359 1974 £75

ADAMS, SAMUEL HOPKINS   Revelry. New York, 1926. 1st ed. Biblo &
Tannen 213-488 1973 $10

ADAMS, W.   The Old Man's Home. 1847. 12mo., orig.
cloth, faded. Bow Windows 64-360 1974 £4.75

ADAMS, W. H. D.   The Eastern Archipelago. 1880. Crown 8vo.,
cloth, illus., map. Wheldon 129-232 1974 £7.50

ADAMS, WILLIAM DAVENPORT   Dictionary of English Literature. London,
(1880). 4to., orig. cloth, worn, second edition. Dawsons PM 10-5 1974 £5

ADAMS, WILLIAM TAYLOR   Vine and Olive. Boston, 1876. 12mo., first
edition. Biblo & Tannen 213-554 1973 $12.50

ADAMSON, JOHN   Memoirs of the Life and Writings of Luis de Cam-
oens. 1820. 8vo., 2 vols., full calf gilt, frontispieces. Hill 126-34 1974 £32

ADAMSON, R. S.   The Vegetation of South Africa. 1938. 8vo.,
cloth, plates, scarce. Wheldon 131-1256 1974 £7.50

ADAMSON, ROBERT   The Development of Modern Philosophy. 1903.
2 vols., half morocco, orig. cloth. Howes 185-1800 1974 £5.25

ADANSON, MICHEL 1726-1806   Familles des Plantes. Paris, 1763. 8vo.,
2 vols., contemporary calf. Wheldon 130-987 1974 £100

ADANSON, MICHEL 1727-1806   Familles des Plantes. Paris, 1763. 2 vols.,
8vo., contemporary calf, folding plate. Wheldon 128-1072 1973 £100

ADANSON, MICHEL 1727-1806   A Voyage to Senegal, the Isle of Goree, and
the River Gambia. London, 1759. 8vo., contemporary calf. Traylen 79-445
1973 £98

ADDAMS, JANE   The Second Twenty Years at Hull House.
Macmillan, 1930. Austin 62-6 1974 $12.50

ADDISON, AGNES   Romanticism and the Gothic Revival. New
York, 1938. 1st ed. Biblo & Tannen 213-137 1973 $9.50

ADDISON, ALEXANDER   The Trial of... Lancaster, 1803. Marbled
wrappers, uncut, unopened, second edition. Dawson's 424-314 1974 $45

ADDISON, JOSEPH   Days with Sir Roger de Coverley. 1886. 8vo.,
orig. cloth, illus. Bow Windows 64-361 1974 £5.50

ADDISON, JOSEPH   A Discourse on Ancient and Modern Learning.
1739. 4to., orig. blue paper wrapper, uncut, scarce, fine, first edition. Quaritch 936-2 1974 £55

ADDISON, JOSEPH   Remarks on Several Parts of Italy . . . in the
Years 1701-03. 1726. New buckram, blind stamp, third edition. Allen
216-1867 1974 $12.50

ADDISON, JOSEPH   The Spectator. London, 1744. Small 8vo., 8
vols., contemporary sprinkled calf, gilt. Hammond 201-288 1974 £10

ADDISON, JOSEPH   The Spectator. 1775. 8vols., contemporary
calf, gilt, leather labels. Smith 194-119 1974 £10

ADDISON, JOSEPH   The Works of. London, 1721. 4 vols.,
4to., portrait, contemporary speckled calf, first edition. Bow Windows 62-7
1974 £85

ADDISON, JOSEPH   The Works of. 1721. 4 vols., 4to., portrait,
plates, contemporary calf, rebacked, first edition. Bow Windows 66-2 1974 £95

ADDISON, JOSEPH   The Works Of.   London, 1722. 12mo., 2 vols., contemporary calf, plates, scarce. Hill 126-2 1974 £35

ADDISON, JOSEPH   Miscellaneous Works. 1726. 12mo., 3 vols., contemporary panelled calf. Hill 126-1 1974 £12.50

ADDISON, JOSEPH   Miscellaneous Works in Verse and Prose. 1751, 1753, 1756. Small 8vo., 7 vols., contemporary polished calf, gilt, plates. Quaritch 936-1 1974 £20

ADDISON, JOSEPH   Works. Birmingham, 1761. Roy 4to., 4 vols., contemporary dark green morocco, gilt, plates. Quaritch 936-14 1974 £800

ADDISON, JOSEPH   The Works of. Birmingham, 1761. 4 vols., 4to., contemporary speckled calf, plates. Dawsons PM 252-1 1974 £160

ADDISON, JOSEPH   The Miscellaneous Works. London, 1766-67. 4 vols., 12mo., contemporary calf, plates. Dawsons PM 252-2 1974 £20

ADDISON, JOSEPH   The Works of the Right Honourable. London, 1811. 6 vols., 8vo., plates, foxing, contemporary half calf, new edition. Bow Windows 62-8 1974 £24

ADDISON, MRS. JULIA DE WOLF (GIBBS) Arts and Crafts in the Middle Ages. 1908. Orig. dec. buckram, plates. Smith 194-79 1974 £6.50

ADDISON, MRS. JULIA DE WOLF (GIBBS) The Boston Museum of Fine Arts. Boston, 1910. Biblo & Tannen 210-1 1973 $8.50

ADDLEPATE, ERASMUS G.   How to Read Two Books. Stokes, 1940. 107p., illus. Austin 54-11 1973 $6.50

AN ADDRESS of Members of the House of Representatives of The Congress of the United States On the Subject of the War With Great Britain. Alexandria, 1812. 8vo., old wrappers, scarce, first edition. Ximenes 35-458 1974 $30

AN ADDRESS of the Members of the House of Representatives of the Congress of the United States On the Subject of the War With Great Britain. Hartford, 1812. 8vo., unopened. Ximenes 35-459 1974 $20

AN ADDRESS To the Artisans and Operatives of the United Kingdom, On the Present Distress. 1830. 8vo., modern quarter calf, first edition. Dawsons PM 247-1 1974 £40

ADE, GEORGE   Artie. Chicago, 1896. 193p., illus., orig. Lakeside Press ed. Austin 54-13 1973 $7.50

ADE, GEORGE   Breaking Into Society. Harper, 1904. 208p. Austin 54-12 1973 $6.50

ADE, GEORGE   Doc' Horne. Stone, 1899. 292p., illus., orig. Lakeside Press ed. Austin 54-14 1973 $8.50

ADE, GEORGE   Fables in Slang. Stone, 1899. 201p. Austin 54-15 1973 $5

ADE, GEORGE   Fables in Slang. Chicago, 1900. 12mo., 1st ed. Biblo & Tannen 210-698 1973 $20

ADE, GEORGE   George Ade--Warmhearted Satirist. Bobbs, 1947. 282p., illus. Austin 54-20 1973 $7.50

ADE, GEORGE   In Babel--Stories of Chicago. McClure, 1903. 358p. Austin 54-16 1973 $7.50

ADE, GEORGE   In Pastures New. McClure, 1906. 309p., orig. ed. Austin 54-17 1973 $5.75

ADE, GEORGE   The Old Time Saloon. Long, Smith, 1931. 174p., orig. ed. Austin 54-18 1973 $7.50

ADE, GEORGE   People You Know. Russell, 1903. 224p., illus. Austin 54-19 1973 $6.50

ADKIN, R.   The Butterflies of Eastbourne. Eastbourne, 1928-34. 8vo., illus., cloth-bound, orig. wrappers, book-plate. Bow Windows 64-2 1974 £8.50

ADKINS, NELSON FREDERICK   Fitz-Greene Halleck, an Early Knickerbocker Wit and Poet. New Haven and London, 1930. Orig. binding, d.j. Butterfield 10-2 1974 $15

ADLER, ALFRED   Die Individualpsychologie. Bologna, 1914. 8vo., orig. printed wrappers, very scarce first edition. Gilhofer 61-81 1974 sFr. 650

ADLER, ALFRED   Praxis und Theorie der Individualpsychologie. Munchen & Wiesbaden, 1920. 8vo., orig. printed boards, cloth box, first edition. Gilhofer 61-85 1974 sFr. 600

ADLER, ALFRED   Studie Uber Minderwertigkeit Von Organen. Berlin, 1907. 8vo., orig. printed wrappers bound in cloth, first edition. Gilhofer 61-73 1974 sFr. 750

ADLER, ALFRED   Ueber den Nervosen Charakter. Wiesbaden, 1912. 8vo., orig. cloth, first edition. Gilhofer 61-78 1974 sFr. 600

ADLER, CYRUS   American Intercession on Behalf of Jews in the Diplomatic Correxpondence of the U. S. 1943. Austin 57-19 1974 $27.50

ADLER, CYRUS   I Have Considered the Days. 1941. Austin 62-3 1974 $7.50

ADLER, CYRUS   Jacob H. Schiff. 1929. 2 vols., illus., orig. edition. Austin 57-16 1974 $17.50

ADLER, CYRUS   The Jewish Theological Seminary of America. 1939. Illus. Austin 57-17 1974 $12.50

ADLER, CYRUS   Jews in the Diplomatic Correspondence of the U. S. Austin 57-18 1974 $12.50

ADLER, MORTIMER J.   Art and Prudence. Longmans, 1937. 686p. Austin 51-10 1973 $17.50

ADLER, SELIG   From Ararat to Suburbia. 1960. Austin 62-5 1974 $12.50

ADOLPHUS, JOHN   The History of England. 1840-45. 7 vols., full polished fawn calf, gilt. Howes 186-562 1974 £40

The Adventurer
Please turn to
HAWKESWORTH, JOHN

ADVENTURES of Henny Penny and Her Friends. New York, (c. 1890). 8vo., full page full color illus., pictorial front cover, very good. Current BW9-98 1974 $18.75

THE ADVENTURES of Hsi Men Ching. N.p., 1927. Ltd. to 750 copies, bound in 3/4 saffron pigskin and batik bds., hand-colored illus. Jacobs 24-56 1974 $25

ADYE, E. H.   Reports on the Economic Geology of the Porbandar State in the Province of Kathiawar, India. Bombay, 1917. Roy. 8vo., cloth, plates, coloured maps. Wheldon 128-935 1973 £5

AEGERTER, EMMANUEL   Guillaume Apollinaire. Paris, 1943. 8vo., wrappers, uncut. Minters 37-259 1973 $15

AELIANUS, CLAUDIUS   The Tacticks of. London, n.d. (1616). Folio, old vellum, first edition, plates, few minor tears, ex-library, very good copy. Ximenes 36-1 1974 $250

AEPINUS, FRANZ ULRICH THEODOR   Tentamen Theoriae Electricitatis et Magnetismi. (1759). 4to., contemporary boards, worn, plates, first edition. Dawsons PM 245-4 1974 £30

THE AERO CLUB OF AMERICA   Navigating the Air. 1907. Ex-library, illus. Howes 186-1680 1974 £5.50

AESCHYLUS   Oresteia. (London, 1904). Small 4to., unopened, orig. linen-backed boards, inscribed. Bow Windows 62-9 1974 £12.50

AESCHYLUS   Tragedies of Aeschylus. Bohn's Classical Library, 1849. 234p. Austin 51-11 1973 $6.50

AESCHYLUS   Tragoediae Sex. 1518. Vellum, morocco label, stains, first edition. Thomas 30-44 1973 £300

AESOPUS   Aesop's Fables Illustrated by Nora Fry. Philadelphia, n.d. Sm. 4to., 8 color plates. Frohnsdorff 16-9 1974 $7.50

AESOPUS　　　　　　Aesop's Fables: A New Version.　Philadelphia,
n.d. 8vo., illus.　Frohnsdorff 16-8　1974　$7.50

AESOPUS　　　　　　The Fables of.　Roy. 8vo., 2 vols., contemporary
tree calf, rebacked, plates, Stockdale's fine edition.　Quaritch 936-3　1974　£30

AESOPUS　　　　　　Fables of.　Edinburgh, n.d.　Small 8vo.,
orig. dec. cloth, plates, frontispiece, foxing.　Bow Windows 62-10　1974　£4.50

AESOPUS　　　　　　Fables of Aesop and Others.　Boston, n.d.
130 engravings.　Biblo & Tannen 213-726　1973　$8.50

AESOPUS　　　　　　Select Fables of Aesop and Other Fabulists.
1761.　8vo., frontis., plates, contemporary gilt framed calf, worn, rebacked.
Bow Windows 62-67　1974　£45

AESOPUS　　　　　　The Fables of Aesop, with a Life of the Author.
London, 1793.　2 vols., 4to., contemp. tree calf rebacked with morocco, gilt;
marbled endpapers; 112 plates.　Frohnsdorff 16-12　1974　$125

AESOPUS　　　　　　Aesop's Fables.　Philadelphia, 1839.　16mo.,
full roan (badly worn and peeled), gilt, outer hinges cracked.　Frohnsdorff 16-10
1974　$12.50

AESOPUS　　　　　　Fables.　1840.　Folio, green roan gilt, rare.
Hill 127-3　1974　£38

AESOPUS　　　　　　The Fables of Aesop.　New York, 1931.　8vo.,
illus.　Frohnsdorff 16-11　1974　$10

AESOPUS　　　　　　Fables.　1931.　Coloured plates, illus. by
Arthur Rackham, 8vo., orig. dec. cloth.　George's 610-8　1973　£5

AESOPUS　　　　　　Fables.　1936.　8vo., full vellum, gilt, uncut,
signed, limited.　Broadhurst 23-737　1974　£115

L'AFFAIRE Dreyfus.　Le Proces Zola Devant la Cour d'Assises de la Seine et la
Cour de Cassation.　Paris, 1898.　2 vols., 8vo., plates, blue cloth, first edition.
Schafer 10-145　1974　sFr 350

THE AFFECTING History of the Duchess of C - - - -, Who Was Confined Nine
Years in a Horrid Dungeon.　Derby, n.d.　12mo., half roan, frontispiece.
Ximenes 33-26　1974　$27.50

AGARDH, C. A.　　　　　Essai de Reduire la Physiologie.　Lund, (1828).
Small 8vo., old wrappers, fine, first edition.　Gurney 64-1　1974　£15

AGARDH, J. G.　　　　　Recensio Specierum Generis Pteridis.　Lund,
1839.　8vo., modern boards.　Wheldon 128-1331　1973　£5

AGAS, R.　　　　　Civitas Londinum Ano.　(1863).　8vo., map,
paper covers.　Quaritch 939-432　1974　£10

AGASSIZ, ALEXANDER　　　The Coral Reefs of the Maldives.　Cambridge,
1903.　2 vols., 4to., orig. wrappers.　Wheldon 131-296　1974　£10

AGASSIZ, ALEXANDER　　　The Coral Reefs of the Tropical Pacific.　Cambridge, 1903.　4to., 4 vols., orig. wrappers, plates.　Wheldon 129-214　1974
£15

AGASSIZ, ALEXANDER　　　The Coral Reefs of the Tropical Pacific.
Cambridge, 1903.　4 vols., 4to., orig. wrappers, plates.　Wheldon 131-295
1974　£20

AGASSIZ, ELIZABETH C.　　　Seaside Studies in Natural History.　Boston,
1865.　8vo., orig. bindings.　Butterfield 8-221　1974　$20

AGASSIZ, LOUIS　　　　Iconographie des Coquilles Tertiaires.
Neuchatel, 1845.　4to., plates.　Wheldon 128-937　1973　£16

AGASSIZ, LOUIS　　　　A Journey In Brazil.　1868.　8vo., orig.
cloth, plates, woodcuts.　Wheldon 131-328　1974　£25

AGASSIZ, LOUIS　　　　Louis Agassiz and His Life and Work.　1893.
8vo., cloth, plates.　Wheldon 131-209　1974　£7.50

AGASSIZ, LOUIS　　　　Monographie des Poissons Fossiles du Vieux
Gres Rouge ou Systeme Devonien.　Neuchatel, 1844-45.　2 vols., 4to., folio,
contemporary half calf, plates, very rare.　Wheldon 131-3　1975　£120

AGASSIZ, LOUIS　　　　Monographie des Poissons Fossiles.　1844-45.
4to., folio, contemporary half calf.　Wheldon 129-802　1975　£120

AGASSIZ, LOUIS　　　　Nomenclator Zoologicus.　Soleure, 1842-46.
4to., half morocco, complete copy, rare.　Wheldon 128-254　1973　£50

AGASSIZ, LOUIS　　　　Outlines of Comparative Physiology.　Bohn,
1851.　8vo., cloth, frontispiece.　Wheldon 131-405　1974　£7

AGASSIZ, LOUIS　　　　Recherches sur les Poissons Fossiles.　1833-43
(-1844).　4to. and folio, contemporary half calf.　Wheldon 129-801　1974　£985

AGASSIZ, LOUIS　　　　Recherches sur les Poissons Fossiles.　Neuchatel,
1833-43.　10 vols., oblong folio, contemporary half calf, plates, rare.　Wheldon
131-2　1974　£985

AGASSIZ, LOUIS　　　　Recherches sur les Poissons Fossiles.　Neuchatel,
1833-43.　4to., 5 vols., contemporary half calf, plates, rare.　Wheldon 130-1
1974　£875

AGASSIZ, LOUIS　　　　Runner of the Mountain Tops.　New York, 1939.
8vo., cloth, plates.　Wheldon 130-140　1974　£5

AGASSIZ, LOUIS　　　　The Works of.　Boston, 1886.　6 vols., small
8vo., blue cloth, fine, woodcut illus.　Current BW9-445　1974　$17.50

AGATE, JAMES　　　　Bad Manners.　1938.　Fine, scarce, first edition,
defective d.w.　Covent 51-2089　1973　£5.25

AGATE, JAMES　　　　Kingdoms for Horses.　London, 1936.　4to.,
cloth, illus.　Minters 37-171　1973　$18.50

AGERSBORG, H. P.　　　　A Future American.　Mitre Press, n.d.　177p.,
illus.　Austin 62-7　1974　$12.50

AGGIUNTA Alle Rime.　Venetia, 1585.　12mo., full morocco, gilt, portrait.
Bow Windows 62-15　1974　£25

AGGIUNTI, NICCOLO　　　Oratio de Mathematicae Lavdibvs.　1627.　4to.,
modern green dec. paper boards, uncut, first edition.　Zeitlin 235-1　1974　$125

AGLIONBY, WILLIAM　　　Painting Illustrated In Three Dialogues,
Containing Some Choice Observations Upon the Art.　London, 1685.　4to.,
contemporary panelled calf, rebacked, rubbed, first edition, rare.　Quaritch
940-1　1974　£160

AGRESTI, OLIVA ROSSETTI　　　David Lubin.　1922.　372 pages, orig. edition.
Austin 57-21　1974　$15

AGRESTI, OLIVA ROSSETTI　　　David Lubin.　1941.　Illus., second edition.
Austin 57-22　1974　$12.50

AGRESTI, OLIVIA ROSSETTI　　　David Lubin.　Univ. of Calif., 1941.　372p.,
illus.　Austin 62-8　1974　$12.50

AGRICOLA, GEORG　　　De Animantibus Subterraneis Liber.　Wittemberg,
1614.　8vo., old vellum, rare.　Gurney 64-2　1974　£90

AGRICOLA, GEORG　　　De Animantibus Subterraneis Liber.　Wittemberg,
1614.　8vo., old vellum, very rare, main body of text browned.　Gurney 66-6
1974　£90

AGRICOLA, GEORG　　　De Ortu & Causis Subterraneorum Lib. V.　1546.
Sm. folio, marbled boards, fine, first edition.　Dawsons PM 245-10　1974　£1,400

AGRICOLA, GEORG　　　De Re Metallica.　London, 1912.　Folio, woodcuts, orig. vellum, uncut, first edition in English.　Dawsons PM 245-14　1974
£120

AGRICOLA, GEORG　　　De Re Metallica Libri XII.　1556.　Folio, woodcuts, morocco, first edition.　Dawsons PM 245-11　1974　£1,950

AGRICOLA, GEORG　　　De re Metallica Libri XII.　Basle, 1556.
Folio, plates, inscribed, morocco, illus., water-stained, first edition.
Dawsons PM 250-1　1974　£2850

AGRICOLA, GEORG　　　De Re Metallica Libri XII.　1561.　Folio, woodcuts, contemporary blind-stamped pigskin, boards, fine, second edition in Latin.
Dawsons PM 245-12　1974　£550

AGRICOLA, GEORG   De re Metallica Libri XII. Basle, 1561.
Second edition, large woodcuts, folio, contemporary vellum, little rubbed, lacks
ties, but sound. Thomas 32-305 1974 £1,000

AGRICOLA, GEORG   De Re Metallica Libri XII. 1621. Folio, woodcuts, vellum, third edition in Latin. Dawsons PM 245-13 1974 £235

AGRICOLA, GEORG   Vom Bergkwerck. Basel, 1557. First German
edition, woodcut illus., folio, contemporary German pigskin, elaborate blind
tooling on sides, binding worn, corners neatly repaired, no subscriber's list,
good copy. Sawyer 293-13 1974 £950

AGRICULTURAL SOCIETY OF LEGIGH COUNTY, PENNSYLVANIA   Report of
the Mangers of. Allentown, 1855. Wrapper. Jenkins 61-2172 1974 $10

AGRICULTURE In the Twentieth Century. Oxford, 1939. 8vo., cloth, portrait.
Wheldon 128-1636 1973 £5

AGRICULTURE In the Twentieth Century. Oxford, 1939. 8vo., cloth, portrait.
Wheldon 131-1768 1974 £5

AGRIPPA VON NETTESHEIM, HEINRICH CORNELIUS   De Incertitudine et
Vanitate Scientiarum Declamatio Invectiva. (Cologne, 1540/1550?). 8vo.,
author's portrait, contemporary blind stamped pigskin over wooden boards, good
copy. Schafer 10-114 1974 sFr 850

AGRIPPA VON NETTESHEIM, HEINRICH CORNELIUS   De Occulta Philosophia
Libri Tres. (Cologne), 1533. Folio, half vellum, woodcuts, first edition.
Schuman 37-3 1974 $650

AGRIPPA VON NETTESHEIM, HEINRICH CORNELIUS   The Philosophy of
Natural Magic. Chicago, 1913. Text illus., spine faded, corners little bumped,
bookplate. Covent 51-2489 1973 £10

AGUADO, PADRE F. J. L.   Florido Huerto de las Delicias de Dios. 1738.
Small 4to., disbound. Thomas 28-27 1972 £15.75

AGUCCHIA, LATTANZIO   Il Computista Pagato. 1765. 4to., contemporary vellum. Dawsons PM 245-15 1974 £15

AGUECHEEK. Shepard, Clark, Brown, 1859. 336p. Austin 54-43 1973 $12.50

AHLES, W. E. VON   Unsere Wichtigeren Giftgewachse. Esslingen,
1874. Small folio, orig. cloth backed boards, plates, third edition. Wheldon
131-1802 1974 £15

AHRENS, H.   Cours de Psychologie. Paris, 1836(-8). 8vo.,
contemporary green half calf, worn. Dawsons PM 249-6 1974 £26

AIKEN, CONRAD   Among the Lost People. New York, 1934.
First U. S. edition, with Scribner's seal & "A" label, presentation copy, inscribed
by author, covers marked, nice copy. Covent 51-3236 1973 £25

AIKEN, CONRAD   The Coming Forth by Day of Osiris Jones.
New York, 1921. First U. S. edition, covers faded, inscription, first issue with
printer's error on p. 37. Covent 51-2091 1973 £20

AIKEN, CONRAD   Costumes by Eros. New York, 1928. First U. S.
edition, nice copy. Covent 51-2092 1973 £10.50

AIKEN, CONRAD   The Pilgrimage of Festus. n.d. Very good
copy, cloth backed boards. Covent 51-2093 1973 £15

AIKEN, CONRAD   Priapus and the Pool. Cambridge, 1922.
Boards, inscribed presentation. Covent 55-13 1974 £45

AIKEN, CONRAD   A Reviewer's ABC. Meridian, 1958. 414p.,
1st ed. in d/w. Austin 54-21 1973 $8.50

AIKEN, CONRAD   Selected Poems. New York, 1929. Orig.
cloth backed boards, numbered & signed by author, boxed, first edition.
MacManus 224-3 1974 $75

AIKIN, JOHN   Annals of the Reign of George the Third.
London, 1825. 2 vols., 3/4 calf, bdgs. worn. Biblo & Tannen 213-673 1973
$32.50

AIKIN, JOHN   A Description of the Country from Thirty to
Forty Miles Round Manchester. (1795). 4to., half calf. Quaritch 939-416
1974 £160

AIKIN, JOHN   A Description of the Country from Thirty to
Forty Miles Round Manchester. London, 1795. Thick 4to., plates, leather
label, very fine, contemporary mottled calf. Traylen 79-346 1973 £85

AIKIN, JOHN   Essays on Song-Writing With a Collection of
Such English Songas as Are Most Eminent for Poetical Merit. Warrington, 1774.
Second edition, f'cap. 8vo., contemporary full calf, panelled backs, gilt borders,
skilfully rebacked with orig. spine and covers, scarce, fine. Broadhurst 24-514
1974 £25

AIKIN, JOHN   Evenings at Home. 1798-1800. 6 vols. in 3,
12mo., contemporary tree calf, good ex-libris copy, vols. 1-3 fourth editions,
vols. 4-8 third editions. George's 610-11 1973 £10.50

AIKIN, JOHN   Evenings at Home. 1823. 6 vols. in 2,
12mo., contemporary straight grained morocco gilt, labels. Howes 186-284
1974 £18

AIKEN, JOHN   Evenings At Home. Chicago, ca. 1869.
12mo., orig. cloth, gilt; bevelled edges; eight fine chromolithograph plates.
Frohnsdorff 16-13 1974 $7.50

AIKMAN, DUNCAN   The Taming of the Frontier. New York, 1925.
Orig. green cloth, frontispiece, first edition. Bradley 35-6 1974 $12.50

AILLY, PIERRE D'   Tractatus Super Libros Meteororum. Cracow,
1506. 4to., boards, leather spine, second edition, Georg Tannstetter's copy.
Kraus 137-1 1974 $1,850

AINSLEE, KATHLEEN   Me and Catharine Susan. London, ca. 1905.
24mo., illus. Frohnsdorff 16-14 1974 $12.50

AINSLIE, DOUGLAS   Chosen Poems. 1926. 8vo., orig. marbled
boards. Covent 55-388 1974 £6.30

AINSWORTH, WILLIAM HARRISON   Beau Nash. (1879). Orig. cloth, 3 vols.,
first English edition. Covent 56-8 1974 £45

AINSWORTH, WILLIAM HARRISON   Cardinal Pole. 1863. Small 8vo., 3 vols.,
orig. cloth, first edition. Quaritch 936-271 1974 £60

AINSWORTH, WILLIAM HARRISON   Jack Sheppard. 1839. 3 vols., half
dark brown levant morocco, plates, fine, first edition. Howes 185-1 1974 £75

AINSWORTH, WILLIAM HARRISON   Merry England. London, 1874. 3 vols.,
8vo., orig. cloth, scarce, fine, first edition. Dawsons PM 252-4 1974 £95

AINSWORTH, WILLIAM HARRISON   Novels. London, (n.d.). 12 vols.,
8vo., red half morocco, plates. Dawsons 252-5 1974 £60

AINSWORTH, WILLIAM HARRISON   The Novels and Romances of. 1867.
8 vols., full morocco, gilt spines, each vol. signed and dated by author, some
spotting and dust marks, new edition. Bow Windows 66-4 1974 £65

AINSWORTH, WILLIAM HARRISON   The Novels of. 1902. Illus., 20 vols.,
f'cap 8vo., publisher's leather, marbled boards, top edges gilt, little uniform
fading of spines, limited to 2000 copies, Windsor edition, fine. Broadhurst
24-1705 1974 £20

AINSWORTH, WILLIAM HARRISON   Old Saint Paul's. Orig. cloth boards.
Bow Windows 62-11a 1974 £30

AINSWORTH, WILLIAM HARRISON   Old Saint Paul's. London, 1841. 3 vols.,
8vo., plates, orig. cloth, worn, first edition. Bow Windows 62-11 1974 £32

AINSWORTH, WILLIAM HARRISON   Rookwood. London, 1836. 8vo., contemporary full levant morocco, gilt, fine, plates. Hammond 201-480 1974 £10

AINSWORTH, WILLIAM HARRISON   Saint James's. 1844. 3 vols., crown 8vo.,
half dark brown levant morocco, fine, plates, first edition. Howes 185-2 1974
£50

AINSWORTH, WILLIAM HARRISON   The Star Chamber. 1854. 2 vols., crown
8vo., full buff calf, gilt, labels, fine, first edition. Howes 186-1 1974 £25

AINSWORTH, WILLIAM HARRISON   Tower of London. 1840. 2 vols., half calf, plates, foxed, illus. by G. Cruikshank. Allen 216-1312 1974 $15

AINSWORTH, WILLIAM HARRISON   The Tower of London. 1840. 8vo., orig. cloth, foxing, illus., first edition. Bow Windows 64-364 1974 £45

AIRY, G. B.   Account of the Northumberland Equatoreal and Dome Attached to the Cambridge Observatory. Cambridge, 1844. 4to., plates, some foxing, orig. limp cloth covers, faded. Bow Windows 66-5 1974 £8.50

AITCHINSON, J. E. T.   The Botany of the Afghan Delimitation Commission. 1888. 4to., cloth boards, maps. Wheldon 130-1123 1974 £10

AITKEN, R. G.   New General Catalogue of Double Stars within 120° of the North Pole. Washington, 1932. 4to., 2 vols., orig. stiff paper wrappers. Bow Windows 64-365 1974 £20

AITON, WILLIAM   A Treatise on the Origin, Qualities, and Cultivation of Moss-Earth. 1811. 8vo., orig. boards, uncut, first edition. Hammond 201-4 1974 £10.50

AJALBERT, JEAN   En Auvergne. Paris, 1893. 12mo., uncut, contemporary three quarter cloth, orig. wrapper, first edition. L. Goldschmidt 42-138 1974 $12.50

A KEMPIS, THOMAS
Please turn to
THOMAS A KEMPIS

AKEN, F. J.   Kurze Abhandlung. Berlin, 1798. 8vo., boards, plates. Gurney 64-3 1974 £30

AKEN, F. J.   Kurze Abhandlung von der Bessten Weise der Feuerloschung mit Dazu Eingerichtetem Feuer-Gerathe un Nothiger Feuer-Ordnung. Berlin, 1798. 8vo., boards, folding plates. Gurney 66-7 1974 £30

AKENSIDE, MARK   An Epistle to Curio. London, 1744. 4to., modern boards, first edition. Dawsons PM 252-6 1974 £25

AKENSIDE, MARK   The Pleasures of Imagination. 1754. 8vo., contemporary sheep, fifth edition. Quaritch 936-5 1974 £5

AKENSIDE, MARK   The Pleasures of Imagination. London, 1796. 8vo., contemporary calf, plates. Dawsons PM 252-8 1974 £10

AKENSIDE, MARK   Poems. 1772. 4to., rebound, first edition. Quaritch 936-4 1974 £30

AKENSIDE, MARK   The Poems of. London, 1772. 4to., worn, contemporary diced calf, first collected edition. Dawsons PM 252-7 1974 £44

AKENSIDE, MARK   Poetical Works. 1854. Orig. edition. Austin 61-2 1974 $12.50

AKERMAN, JOACHIM   Forelasningar I Kemisk Technologi. Stockholm, 1832. Thick 8vo., 2 vols., contemporary half calf. Zeitlin 235-251 1974 $67.50

AKERS, FLOYD   The Boy Fortune Hunters in Egypt. Chicago, 1908. 8vo., lst ed., illus. Frohnsdorff 16-80 1974 $35

AKIN, WILLIAM H.   The Realty Blue Book of California. Los Angeles, c.1924. 8vo., cloth. Saddleback 14-21 1974 $15

ALADDIN, or, the Wonderful Lamp. London, ca. 1840. 16mo., illus. Frohnsdorff 16-15 1974 $17.50

ALAIN FOURNIER, HENRI
Please turn to
FOURNIER, ALAIN

ALAMANNI, LUIGI   La Coltivazione di Luigi Alamanni e Le Api di Giovanni Rucellai. Padua, 1718. 4to., calf, portrait, scarce. Wheldon 131-1769 1974 £15

ALAN, A. J.   Great Unsolved Crimes. London, n.d. lst ed. Biblo & Tannen 210-403 1973 $10

ALANUS DE INSULIS   Distinctiones Dictionum Theologicalium. (Strassburg, c. 1474). Folio, half leather, fine, rare, first and only edition. Harper 213-2 1973 $1350

THE ALASKA-YUKON Gold Book. Seattle, 1930. Pict. wrapper, illus. Jenkins 61-36 1974 $22.50

ALASTAIR   Fifty Drawings. New York, 1925. 4to., cloth-backed boards, rubbed. Covent 55-875 1974 £75

ALBAN, SAINT   De Incliti et Gloriosi Protomartyris. (Cologne, 1502). Small 4to., polished calf gilt by F. Bedford, rare. Thomas 32-263 1974 £450

ALBAREDA, ANSELM M.   Bibliografia de la Regla Benedictina. Montserrat, 1933. 4to., orig. cloth, rubbed. Dawsons PM 10-30 1974 £15

ALBEE, FRED HOUDLETT   Bone-Graft Surgery. Philadelphia and London, 1915. 8vo., orig. red cloth, first edition. Dawsons PM 249-7 1974 £55

ALBEE, FRED HOUDLETT   Bone-Graft Surgery. Philadelphia & London, 1917. 8vo., orig. cloth, illus. Schuman 37-4 1974 $65

ALBEE, FRED HOUDLETT   Surgery of the Spinal Column. Philadelphia, 1945. Rittenhouse 46-690 1974 $10

ALBERT, THOMAS   Histoire du Madawaska. Quebec, 1920. Hood's 102-675 1974 $25

ALBERTI, GUISEPPE ANTONIO   Tratto della Misura delle Fabbriche. Venice, 1757. 8vo., frontispiece, plates, contemporary vellum, first edition. Quaritch 940-490 1974 £80

ALBERTI, LEON BATTISTA   Opuscoli Morali. Venice, 1568. Small 4to., 18th century mottled calf, gilt, woodcuts, rubbed. Thomas 30-139 1973 £50

ALBERTINA   Handzeichnungen Alter Meister aus der Albertina und Anderen Sammlungen. Vienna, (1896-1908). 12 vols., folio, plates, half morocco. Quaritch 940-2 1974 £300

ALBERTOLLI, GIOCONDO   Ornamenti Diversi Inventati. Alcune Decorazioni di Nobili Sale ed Altri Ornamenti. Fregi Trovati Negli Scavi del Foro Trajano con Altri Esistenti in Roma ed in Diverse Altre Citta. Milan, 1843-38. 3 vols. in 1, roy. folio, plates, half morocco, rubbed. Quaritch 940-491 1974 £150

ALBERTON, CHARLES CARROLL   Lyra Mystica. 1932. 496 pages. Austin 61-3 1974 $12.50

ALBERTUS, LEANDER   De Viris Illustribus Ordinis Praedicatorum Libri Sex. Bologna, 1517. Small folio, modern vellum, woodcuts. Thomas 28-273 1972 £200

ALBERTUS MAGNUS   Paradisus Animae, seu de Virtutibus. (Cologne, 1473). Folio, boards, fine, first edition. Harper 213-3 1973 $1100

ALBERTUS MAGNUS   De Secretis Mulierum cum Commento. Venice, 1508. Small 4to., modern half vellum, rare edition, good copy. Schafer 10-113 1974 sFr 1,300

ALBERTUS MAGNUS   Scriptum Primum... Basle, 1506. 2 vols., folio, contemporary blind stamped pigskin over oak boards. Thomas 28-274 1972 £125

ALBIN, ELEAZAR   A Natural History of English Insects. 1720. 4to., nineteenth century half calf, plates, illus., first edition. Wheldon 130-2 1974 £425

ALBIN, ELEAZAR   A Natural History of Spiders. 1736. 4to., contemporary tree calf, rebacked, plates. Wheldon 131-4 1974 £300

ALBRECHT, PAUL   Beitrag zur Torsionstheorie. Kiel, 1875-76. 4to., illus., quarter morocco. Bow Windows 64-3 1974 £4.50

ALBRECHT, PAUL   Collection of Seven Papers on Vertebrate Anatomy. 1883-34. 8vo., half calf. Wheldon 131-406 1974 £5

ALBUM OF 50 Cartes de Visite. Brown morocco, gilt, portraits. Dawson's 424-323 1974 $50

ALBUM OF 96 Tiny Tintype Portraits. n.d. Red leather, gilt. Dawson's 424-324 1974 $50

AN ALBUM of Original Water Colour Views. 1860-87. 4to., cloth, worn. Quaritch 939-276 1974 £80

ALBUM OF 21 Cartes de Visite. 1860's Leather bound, gilt. Dawson's 424-325 1974 $35

ALBUMASAR   De Magnis Coniunctionibus; Annorum Revolutionibus; ac Eorum Profectionibus; Octo Continens Tractatus. Augsburg, 1489. 4to., contemporary half brown leather over wooden boards, rebacked, first edition, woodcuts, contemporary marginalia in ink, small pieces cut out of 2 leaves, Georg Tannstetter's copy. Kraus 137-2 1974 $1,450

ALCIATI, ANDREA   Emblemata. Lyons, 1614. 8vo., brown levant morocco, gilt, woodcuts. Quaritch 940-3 1974 £75

ALCIATI, ANDREA   Paradoxorum Dispunctionum. Basle, 1531. Small folio, old vellum, sound copy. Thomas 32-217 1974 £30

ALCOCK, ALFRED WILLIAM 1859-   Materials for a Carcinological Fauna of India. Calcutta, 1895-1900. 8vo., cloth, plates. Wheldon 129-762 1973 £30

ALCOCK, RANDAL HIBBERT   Botanical Names for English Readers. 1876. 8vo., cloth. Wheldon 131-1108 1974 £5

ALCOTT, AMOS BRONSON   Table-Talk. Boston, 1877. 12mo., cloth, autograph "Mrs. Daniel Lothrop", first edition. Goodspeed's 578-3 1974 $75

ALCOTT, LOUISA MAY   Little Men. Boston, 1871. 12mo., cloth, gilt, illus; 1st ed. Frohnsdorff 16-17 1974 $25

ALCOTT, LOUISA MAY   Little Men. Boston, 1871. 12mo., 1st ed; marginal hole affecting some text. Frohnsdorff 16-18 1974 $10

ALCOTT, LOUISA MAY   Little Women. Boston, 1869. 2 vols., terra cotta coth, vol. 1 is seconed issue, vol. 2 is first edition, fourth state, nice condition, internally excellent. Ross 86-10 1974 $60

ALCOTT, LOUISA MAY   Jo's Boys, and How They Turned Out. Boston, 1886. Green cloth stamped in gold; spine ends and corners rubbed. Frohnsdorff 16-16 1974 $20

ALCOTT, LOUISA MAY   Three Proverb Stories. Boston, (1870). 16mo., illus., spine ends worn, binding askew. Current BW9-202 1974 $8.50

ALDA, FRANCES   Men, Women and Tenors. Houghton, Mifflin, 1937. 307p., illus. Austin 51-9 1973 $7.50

ALDEN, ISABELLA, M.   Twenty Minutes Late. Toronto, 1893. Illus. Hood's 102-488 1974 $10

ALDEN, W. L.   Domestic Explosives. Lovell, Adam, Wesson, 1877. 334p. Austin 54-22 1973 $12.50

ALDERSON, RALPH   A Chemical Analysis and Medical Treatise On the Shap Spaw. Kendal, (1828). 8vo., orig. boards, uncut, paper label. Traylen 79-195 1973 £7

ALDIN, CECIL   Black Beauty. London, (n.d.). Large 8vo., illus., orig. cloth, gilt, foxing. Bow Windows 62-14 1974 £10.50

ALDIN, CECIL   Dogs of Character. London & New York, 1927. First edition, 8vo., illus., pictorial front cover, minor interior foxing, near fine. Current BW9-148 1974 $14

ALDIN, CECIL   Farm Yard Puppies. New York, n.d. Square 4to., pictorial boards, cloth spine, color plates. Frohnsdorff 16-21 1974 $20

ALDIN, CECIL   Old Manor Houses. London, 1923. 4to., cloth stamped in blue and gold, 12 color plates; 1st ed. Frohnsdorff 16-21 1974 $15

ALDIN, CECIL   The Romance of the Road. 1928. Large folio, plates, vellum gilt, map, limited edition de luxe. Quaritch 940-4 1974 £45

ALDIN, CECIL   The Romance of the Road. London, 1928. Folio, orig. dust wrapper, illus. Traylen 79-283 1973 £12

THE ALDINE EDITION of the British Poets. 1830-49. 12mo., 52 vols., orig. issues, portraits, full maroon polished calf, gilt, fine. Quaritch 936-318 1974 £350

ALDINGTON, RICHARD   All Men are Enemies. 1933. Quarter buckram, signed, English first edition. Covent 56-1398 1974 £30

ALDINGTON, RICHARD   All Men are Enemies. London, 1933. No. 17 of 110 copies of a special edition of the first edition, signed, lacking d.w., fine, in heavy protective dec. paper wrapper. Ross 86-12 1974 $50

ALDINGTON, RICHARD   Artifex: Sketches and Ideas. 1935. Ex-library, first American edition. Austin 61-5 1974 $12.50

ALDINGTON, RICHARD   At All Costs. 1930. 8vo., orig. cloth, worn, signed, first edition. Rota 190-4 1974 £6

ALDINGTON, RICHARD   At All Costs. London, 1930. No. 218 of an edition limited to 275 copies, signed, orig. binding, near fine. Ross 86-13 1974 $30

ALDINGTON, RICHARD   Balls. Westport, 1932. 12mo., stapled as issued, covers detached & split at joint, nice copy, very scarce. Covent 51-8 1973 £22.50

ALDINGTON, RICHARD   A Book of Characters. (1924). 599 pages. Austin 61-4 1974 $12.50

ALDINGTON, RICHARD   The Colonel's Daughter. London, 1931. Dust wrapper somewhat smudged, first edition, heavy dec. paper wrapper, fine. Ross 87-7 1974 $15

ALDINGTON, RICHARD   The Colonel's Daughter. 1931. 8vo., orig. cloth, uncut, signed, limited edition. Broadhurst 23-552 1974 £20

ALDINGTON, RICHARD   The Colonel's Daughter. 1931. Limited edition, demy 8vo., top edges gilt, others uncut, orig. cloth, fine, limited to 200 copies, signed by author. Broadhurst 24-517 1974 £20

ALDINGTON, RICHARD   The Colonel's Daughter. London, 1931. First edition, d.w. somewhat smudged, heavy protective dec. paper wrapper, fine. Ross 86-15 1974 $17.50

ALDINGTON, RICHARD   D. H. Lawrence. 1930. 8vo., cloth-backed boards, signed, limited, first edition. Quaritch 936-461 1974 £50

ALDINGTON, RICHARD   Death of a Hero. 1929. Fine, d.w., first edition. Covent 51-2094 1973 £6.30

ALDINGTON, RICHARD   Death of a Hero. London, 1929. First edition, orig. binding, d.w. slightly rubbed, near mint, scarce thus. Ross 86-16 1974 $30

ALDINGTON, RICHARD   Death of a Hero. 1929. Orig. cloth, first English edition. Rota 188-5 1974 £5

ALDINGTON, RICHARD   A Dream in the Luxembourg. London, 1930. Orig. cloth backed boards, numbered, signed by author, fine, first English edition. ManManus 224-3B 1974 $35

ALDINGTON, RICHARD   A Dream in the Luxembourg. London, 1930. Orig. binding, first English edition, near mint. Ross 87-8 1974 $10

ALDINGTON, RICHARD   The Eaten Heart. 1929. One of 200 numbered copies, signed by author, cloth backed boards, very good, first edition. Covent 51-946 1973 £20

ALDINGTON, RICHARD   The Eaten Heart. Chapelle-Reanville, 1929. Limited, no. 42 of 200 copies, signed, lacking d.w., orig. binding, fine. Ross 86-17 1974 $70

ALDINGTON, RICHARD   Euripides Alcestis. 1930. 8vo., orig. cloth, dec. boards, uncut, signed, limited edition. Broadhurst 23-551 1974 £12

ALDINGTON, RICHARD   Euripides Alcestis. 1930. Limited to 250 copies, signed by author, demy 8vo., dec. boards, linen spine, top edges gilt, others uncut. Broadhurst 24-516 1974 £12

ALDINGTON, RICHARD   Exile and Other Poems. London, (1923). Orig. cloth, about fine, first edition. MacManus 224-3C 1974 $25

ALDINGTON, RICHARD   Fifty Romance Lyric Poems. New York, 1928.
One of 900 copies, signed by author, quarter crimson morocco, handsome copy.
Covent 51-3238 1973 £10.50

ALDINGTON, RICHARD   Fifty Romance Lyric Poems. New York, 1928.
One of 900 copies, signed by author, spine faded, covers little marked, nice copy.
Covent 51-9 1973 £15

ALDINGTON, RICHARD   Fifty Romance Lyric Poems. New York, 1928.
First edition, signed by translator, spine dull, on all-rag paper, fine. MacManus
224-3D 1974 $30

ALDINGTON, RICHARD   Images Old and New. Boston, 1916. Orig.
boards, minor waterstaining in margins, first American edition. MacManus
224-3E 1974 $50

ALDINGTON, RICHARD   Images, Poems. n.d. Fine, signed, English
first edition. Covent 56-10 1974 £35

ALDINGTON, RICHARD   Last Straws. Paris, 1930. Roy 8vo., bookplate,
signed, English first edition. Covent 56-11 1974 £25

ALDINGTON, RICHARD   Last Straws. Paris, 1930. Edition limited to
700 copies, 200 signed, of which this is no. 94, printed on Haut Vidalon paper,
tattered dust wrapper, fine copy. Ross 87-9 1974 $25

ALDINGTON, RICHARD   Life for Life's Sake. New York, 1941. 1st
Amer. ed. Biblo & Tannen 210-825 1973 $8.50

ALDINGTON, RICHARD   Literary Studies and Reviews. 1924. 8vo.,
orig. cloth, faded, first edition. Rota 190-2 1974 £6

ALDINGTON, RICHARD   Love and the Luxembourg. New York, 1930.
Orig. cloth, first edition, numbered, signed by the author & designer, very fine.
MacManus 224-3F 1974 $40

ALDINGTON, RICHARD   Roads to Glory. London, 1930. First edition,
corners little bumped, nice copy, d.w., orig. cloth. Crane 7-1 1974 £5

ALDINGTON, RICHARD   Roads to Glory. London, 1930. Orig. cloth
backed boards, one of 360 numbered copies, signed by author, about fine, first
edition. MacManus 224-3G 1974 $30

ALDINGTON, RICHARD   Roads to Glory. 1930. 8vo., boards, first edition. Quaritch 936-272 1974 £25

ALDINGTON, RICHARD   Soft Answers. London, 1932. Orig. binding,
dust wrapper chipped at bottom, else near mint. Ross 87-12 1974 $10

ALDINGTON, RICHARD   Stepping Heavenward. Florence, 1931. No.
200 of edition limited to 808 copies, signed, d.w. slightly rubbed, mint, heavy
protective dec. paper wrapper. Ross 86-22 1974 $75

ALDINGTON, RICHARD   Stepping Heavenward; A Record. Florence,
1931. Orig. binding, no. 200 of edition limited to 808 copies, signed, dust
wrapper slightly rubbed, else mint, heavy protective dec. paper wrapper. Ross
87-13 1974 $55

ALDINGTON, RICHARD   Two Stories. London, 1930. Orig. cloth
backed boards, first edition, one of 530 numbered copies, signed by author, about
fine. MacManus 224-3H 1974 $30

ALDINGTON, RICHARD   Two Stories: "The Deserter" and "The Lads of
the Two Stories". London, 1930. Orig. binding, no. 444 of edition limited to
530 copies, signed, mint in dust wrapper, protective heavy dec. paper wrapper.
Ross 87-15 1974 $25

ALDINGTON, RICHARD   War and Love (1915-1918). Boston, 1919.
Orig. paper covered boards, paper labels, first edition, fine. MacManus
224-3i 1974 $45

ALDINGTON, RICHARD   Collected Poems. New York, 1928. First
edition, shelf wear top & bottom of spine, one inch tear top of spine, very good,
scarce, orig. binding. Ross 86-14 1974 $30

ALDINI, JEAN   Essai Theorique et Experimental sur le Galvanisme.
Paris, 1804. 8vo., 2 vols., contemporary marbled boards, uncut, gilt, fine, first
edition in French. Dawsons PM 245-18 1974 £95

ALDINI, TOBIA   Exactissima Descriptio Rariorum Quarundam
Plantarum, Quae Contientur Romae in Horto Farnesiano. Rome, 1625. Folio,
contemporary red morocco, engravings, woodcuts, Nicolas Claude Fabri de
Peiresc's copy, bound in are orig. drawings & water colors assembled by Peiresc.
Kraus 137-3 1974 $6,800

ALDRICH, HERBERT L.   Arctic Alaska and Siberia. New Bedford,
1937. Wrappers, illus., inscribed, scarce. Rinsland 58-945 1974 $20

ALDRICH, LILIAN (WOODMAN)   Crowding Memories. Houghton, 1920.
Austin 54-26 1973 $5

ALDRICH, RICHARD S.   Gertrude Lawrence as "Mrs. A". Greystone,
1954. 414p., illus., orig. ed. Austin 51-12 1973 $8.25

ALDRICH, THOMAS BAILEY   The Bells. Derby, c. 1854, 1855. Backstrip
worn, otherwise good condition. Austin 54-23 1973 $25

ALDRICH, THOMAS BAILEY   Daisy's Necklace. 1857. Spine chewed,
first edition. Allen 216-16 1974 $10

ALDRICH, THOMAS BAILEY   Daisy's Necklace: And, What Came of It. New
York, 1857. First edition, orig. red cloth, plus erratum and adverts., lacks front
fly, corner wear. Wilson 63-478 1974 $20

ALDRICH, THOMAS BAILEY   Marjorie Daw and Other People. Boston, 1873.
First edition, orig. binding. Wilson 63-479 1974 $10

ALDRICH, THOMAS BAILEY   Marjorie Daw. Houghton, Mifflin, 1908.
124p. Austin 54-24 1973 $7.50

ALDRICH, THOMAS BAILEY   Marjorie Daw. Boston, 1908. 1st illus. ed.,
3/4 mor., binding rubbed. Biblo & Tannen 213-489 1973 $10

ALDRICH, THOMAS BAILEY   The Poems Of. Boston, 1882. Contemporary
three quarter morocco, gilt, autographed, fine. Jenkins 48-7 1973 $45

ALDRICH, THOMAS BAILEY   The Poems of Thomas Bailey Aldrich. Houghton,
Mifflin, 1886. 286p., illus., "Household ed." Austin 54-25 1973 $10

ALDRICH, THOMAS BAILEY   The Shadow of the Flowers from the Poems of.
Boston, 1912. Illus., first edition, 8vo., mint, publisher's box. Current BW9-
203 1974 $18.50

ALDRICH, THOMAS BAILEY   The Stillwater Tragedy. Boston, 1880. First
edition, 12mo., presentation copy from author. Current BW9-204 1974 $18.50

ALDRICH, THOMAS BAILEY   The Story of a Cat. Boston, 1879. 8vo.,
1st ed., illus. Frohnsdorff 16-25 1974 $12.50

ALDRIDGE, HENRY R.   The Case for Town Planning. London, 1915.
4to., orig. cloth, gilt, illus., first edition. Hammond 201-963 1974 £15

ALDRIDGE, JOHN W.   In Search of Heresy. McGraw, Hill, 1956.
208p. Austin 54-27 1973 $10

ALDROVANDUS, ULYSSES   Monstrorvm Historia. (Bologna), 1642. Folio,
half calf, rebacked, first edition. Dawsons PM 249-8 1974 £450

ALEMAN, MATHEO   The Rogve. London, 1622. 2 parts in 1 vol.,
folio, contemporary calf, first English edition. Dawsons PM 252-9 1974 £95

ALEMAN, MATHEO   The Rogue. 1924. 4 vols., orig. buckram
backed boards, gilt, limited. Howes 185-533 1974 £20

ALEMBERT, JEAN LE ROND D'   Recherches sur la Precession des Equinoxes.
Paris, 1749. 4to., contemporary mottled calf, gilt, plates, first edition. Dawsons
PM 245-199 1974 £85

ALEMBERT, JEAN LE ROND D'   Sur la Destruction des Jesuites en France.
N.P., 1765. 12mo., full sheep, gilt, first edition. L. Goldschmidt 42-1
1974 $100

ALEMBERT, JEAN LE ROND D'   Traite de Dynamique. Paris, 1743. 4to., gilt,
contemporary French calf, plates, fine, first edition. Dawsons PM 250-18 1974
£320

ALEMBERT, JEAN LE ROND D'   Traite de Dynamique. Paris, 1743. 4to.,
contemporary French calf, gilt, fine, first edition. Dawsons PM 245-196 1974
£265

ALEMBERT, JEAN LE ROND D'   Traite de Dynamique. Paris, 1796. 4to.,
contemporary mottled calf, gilt, plates. Dawsons PM 245-197 1974 £35

ALEMBERT, JEAN LE ROND D'   Traite de l'Equilibre et du Mouvement des
Fluides. Paris, 1744. 4to., contemporary mottled calf, rebacked, plates, first
edition. Dawsons PM 245-198 1974 £80

ALESSIO PIEMONTESE PSEUD.
Please turn to
RUSCELLI, GIROLAMO

ALEXANDER, ARCHIBALD   The Canon of the Old and New Testaments Ascertained. 1826. 8vo., orig. boards, rebacked, uncut. Butterfield 8-383 1974
$10

ALEXANDER, E. H.   A Bibliography of John Ferguson. 1920-(1935)-
34. 2 vols., plates, folding tables, crown 4to., orig. wrappers, signed
presentation inscriptions by author. Forster 98-220 1974 £10

ALEXANDER, JAMES E.   L'Acadie; or, Seven Years Explorations in British
America. London, 1849. 2 vols., marbled boards, three quarter leather, spine
worn on vol. 1. Hood's 102-174 1974 $125

ALEXANDER, JAMES E.   Bush Fighting. 1873. 8vo., orig. cloth,
engraved frontispiece, plates. Bow Windows 64-366 1974 £50

ALEXANDER, JAMES E.   Incidents of the Maori War. 1863. Crown 8vo.,
new bound half calf, boards, first edition. Broadhurst 23-1607 1974 £36

ALEXANDER, JOANNES   A Synopis of Algebra. 1709. 8vo., woodcut
diagrams, contemporary panelled calf, first edition. Dawsons PM 245-19 1974
£15

ALEXANDER, JOHN HENRY   Model Balloons and Flying Machines. 1910.
Illus., English first edition. Covent 56-1532 1974 £21

ALEXANDER, S.   Space, Time & Deity. London, 1927.
2 vols., orig. cloth. Smith 194-847 1974 £5.50

ALEXANDER, S.   Space, Time and Deity. 1934. 2 vols., 8vo.,
orig. cloth. Howes 185-1802 1974 £6.50

ALEXANDER, W. J.   The University of Toronto and Its Colleges,
1827-1906. Toronto, 1906. Illus. Hood's 102-400 1974 $20

ALEXANDER, W. J.   The University of Toronto and Its Colleges,
1827-1906. Toronto, 1906. Illus. Hood's 104-387 1974 $20

ALEXANDER, WILLIAM 1767-1816   The Costume of China. London, 1805.
Large 4to., contemporary half smooth red morocco, rubbed, plates. Traylen 79-
511 1973 £90

ALEXANDER, WILLIAM 1767-1816   Picturesque Representations of the Dress and
Manners of the Austrians. London, (1813). Finely coloured full page engravings,
4to., contemporary half red morocco, fresh copy. Schumann 499-1 1974
sFr 1,800

ALEXANDER, WILLIAM 1767-1816   Picturesque Representations of the Dress and
Manners of the Chinese. n.d. Green half morocco, gilt, illus., marbled boards.
Covent 55-528 1974 £65

ALEXANDER, WILLIAM HARDY   These Twenty-Five Years, A Symposium.
Toronto, 1933. Hood's 104-386 1974 $20

ALEXANDER OF APHRODISAEUS   In Tropica Aristotelis Commentarii. 1513.
Folio, old calf, rebacked, first edition. Thomas 30-23 1973 £85

ALEXANDRE, ARSENE   Emile Friant et Son Oeuvre. Braun, n.d.
Large 4to., soiled wrappers, plates. Minters 37-91 1973 $25

ALEXIS OF PIEDMONT PSEUD.
Please turn to
RUSCELLI, GIROLAMO

ALFORD, MARIAN M.   Needlework as Art. 1886. Imp. 4to., gilt,
plates, Japanese vellum, scarce, large paper. Quaritch 940-743 1974 £48

ALFORD, MARIAN M.   Needlework as Art. 1886. Thick roy. 8vo.,
plates, orig. buckram gilt. Smith 193-79 1973 £10

ALFORD, MICHAEL   Fides Regia Britannica Sive Annales Ecclesiae
Britannicae. 1663. 4 vols., folio, contemporary calf, rebacked, rare.
Howes 185-900 1974 £85

ALFRAGANUS   Compilatio Astronomica. Ferrara, 1493. 4to.,
boards, leather spine, first printed edition, woodcut diagrams, full page woodcut
on verso of title, Georg Tannstetter's copy. Kraus 137-4 1974 $2,250

ALFRED, H. JERVIS   The Modern Angler. London, (1876). New
edition, 16mo., three quarter green leather, marbled boards, scuffed & worn at
extremities, else fine, library stamp. Current BW9-182 1974 $18

ALFRED THE GREAT, KING   Memorials of..., Being Essays on the History and
Antiquities of England During the Ninth Century. 1858. Coloured frontis.,
plates. Bow Windows 66-7 1974 £15

ALFRED THE GREAT, KING   The Whole Works. Oxford & Cambridge,
1852-53. 3 vols., roy. 8vo., orig. cloth gilt, plates, scarce, jubilee edition.
Howes 186-564 1974 £45

ALGER, WILLIAM R.   Life of Edwin Forrest, American Tragedian.
1877. 2 vols., 4to., plates. Allen 216-2117 1974 $17.50

ALGREN, NELSON   Never Come Morning. New York, 1942.
First edition, orig. binding, some staining of last leaves, rumpled dust wrapper,
not a collector's copy. Ross 87-17 1974 $17.50

ALIPRANDI   Patris Laurentii de Brundusio ex Capuccinorum
Ordine. Verona, 1627. 4to., disbound, illus. Harper 213-4 1973 $150

ALKEN, HENRY   Illustrations for Landscape Scenery. 1821.
Oblong 4to., 19th century half red morocco, rubbed, plates, scarce, fine, first
edition. Quaritch 940-5 1974 £300

ALKEN, HENRY   The National Sports of Great Britain. New
York, 1904. Folio, half red morocco, uncut, plates, new edition. Traylen
79-284 1973 £155

ALKINDUS   De Pluviis Imbribus et Ventis. Venice, 1507.
4to., boards, leather spine, first printed edition, Georg Tanstetter's copy. Kraus
137-5 1974 $950

ALL About the Little Small Red Hen. New York, 1917. 24mo., boards. Frohnsdorff 16-27 1974 $10

ALL About the Three Bears. New York, 1914. 24mo., mint copy., illus.
Frohnsdorff 16-29 1974 $12.50

ALL About the Three Pigs. New York, 1914. 24mo., mint copy, illus. Frohnsdorff
16-30 1974 $12.50

ALL The Year Round. 1859-71. 19 vols., roy. 8vo., half calf, orig. cloth.
Howes 186-3 1974 £45

ALLAIRE, J. B. A.   Histoire de la Paroisse de Saint-Denis-sur-
Richelieu, Canada. St. Hyacinthe, 1905. Wrappers neatly mended. Hood's
102-676 1974 $15

ALLAN, A.   History of Channelkirk. Edinburgh, 1900.
Orig. buckram, ends os spine and corners worn, plates. Bow Windows 66-8
1974 £14

ALLAN, WILLIAM   Songs of Light and Shade. 1901. Presentation
copy inscribed from author, portrait frontis., small 4to., orig. dec. cloth gilt,
all edges gilt, very nice copy, bookplate, first edition. Covent 51-1656 1973
£7.50

ALLAND, ALEXANDER   American Counterpoint. 1943. 158 pages,
photographs. Austin 57-24 1974 $12.50

ALLARD, PAUL   Histoire des Persecutions. Paris, 1885-90.
5 vols., half calf. Howes 185-901 1974 £38

ALLARD, PAUL   La Persecution de Diocletien et le Triomphe de L'Eglise. Paris, 1908. 2 vols., rebound. Biblo & Tannen 214-585 1974 $19.50

ALLEINE, JOSEPH 1634-1668   An Alarme to Unconverted Sinners. London, 1672. 8vo., contemporary calf. Smith 194-120 1974 £40

ALLEINE, JOSEPH 1634-1668   Vindiciae Pietatis. London, 1665. Foxing, contemporary calf. Smith 194-121 1974 £21

ALLEMAGNE, HENRY RENE D'   Les Cartes a Jouer du XIVe au XXe Siecle. Paris, 1906. 2 vols., roy. 4to., half morocco, orig. wrappers, plates. Quaritch 940-441 1974 £500

ALLEMAGNE, HENRY RENE D'   Jeux. Musee Retrospectif de la Classe 100 a l'Exposition de 1900 a Paris. 2 vols., very large 8vo., orig. grey wrappers, plates. Gregory 44-85 1974 $225

ALLEMAGNE, HENRY RENE D'   Les Jouets. Paris, n.d. Large thick 4to., orig. green cloth, illus. plain & colored. Gregory 44-86 1974 $215

ALLEMAGNE, HENRY RENE D'   Les Jouets a la World's Fair en 1904 a Saint Louis. Paris, 1908. Small folio, orig. stiff wrappers, illus. Gregory 44-87 1974 $55

ALLEN, CHARLES DEXTER   American Bookplates. 1895. Plates, new buckram. Allen 216-160 1974 $10

ALLEN, E. W.   North Pacific, Japan, Siberia, Alaska, Canada. New York, 1936. Illus. Hood's 104-841 1974 $12

ALLEN, F. M.   Brayhard. 1890. Orig. pictorial cloth gilt, English first edition. Covent 56-695 1974 £5.25

ALLEN, FRED   Much Ado About Me. Little, 1956. 380p., illus. Austin 51-13 1973 $6

ALLEN, FRED   Treadmill to Oblivion. Little, Brown, 1954. 240p., illus. Austin 51-14 1973 $6

ALLEN, GRANT   The Attis of Caius Valerius Catullus. 1892. Orig. cloth, stiff wrappers, first edition. Rota 188-7 1974 £12.50

ALLEN, GRANT   The Woman Who Did. 1895. Orig. dec. green cloth, English first edition. Covent 56-12 1974 £15

ALLEN, HARRISON 1841-1897   A Monograph of the Bats of North America. Washington, 1893. 8vo., cloth, plates. Wheldon 129-356 1974 £10

ALLEN, HERVEY   Anthony Adverse. 1933. Inscribed, first edition, first issue. Allen 216-1239 1974 $25

ALLEN, HERVEY   Earth Moods and Other Poems. New York & London, 1925. Orig. cloth, first edition, earliest printing with C-Z on copyright page, fine, dust jacket. MacManus 224-4 1974 $25

ALLEN, HERVEY   Israfel: The Life and Times of Edgar Allan Poe. New York, 1926. Cloth, illus., first edition, first issue. Dawson's 424-244 1974 $40

ALLEN, HERVEY   New Legends. New York, 1929. Orig. cloth backed boards, first edition, one of 175 numbered copies, signed by author, fine, dust jacket. MacManus 224-5 1974 $30

ALLEN, JAMES LANE   Aftermath--Part second of the "Kentucky Cardinal." Harper, 1895. 135p. Austin 54-28 1973 $7.50

ALLEN, JAMES LANE   The Bride of the Mistletoe. Macmillan, 1909. 190p. Austin 54-29 1973 $6.50

ALLEN, JAMES LANE   The Bride of the Mistletoe. New York, 1909. First edition, small stamp rear blank endpaper. Wilson 63-480 1974 $10

ALLEN, JAMES LANE   The Choir Invisible. New York, 1897. Orig. fawn cloth, rubbed, first edition. Rota 188-8 1974 £5

ALLEN, JAMES LANE   The Choir Invisible. Macmillan, 1898. 364p., illus. Austin 54-30 1973 $7.50

ALLEN, JAMES LANE   The Choir Invisible. Macmillan, 1900. 361p., orig. ed. Austin 54-31 1973 $6

ALLEN, JAMES LANE   The Doctor's Christmas Eve. New York, 1910. First edition, 8vo., very good. Current BW9-1 1974 $12.75

ALLEN, JAMES LANE   A Kentucky Cardinal. Harper, 1894. 147p., illus. Austin 54-32 1973 $7.50

ALLEN, JAMES LANE   The Mettle of the Pasture. Macmillan, 1903. 448p., orig. ed. Austin 54-33 1973 $6.50

ALLEN, JAMES LANE   The Reign of Law. Macmillan, 1900. 385p. Austin 54-34 1973 $6.50

ALLEN, JOHN HOUGHTON   San Juan. N. P., 1945. Illus. by Harold Bugbee, boards, limited to 420 copies. Jenkins 61-255 1974 $27.50

ALLEN, JOSIAH (Mrs.)   Josiah Allen's Wife as a P.A. and P.I.--Samantha at the Centennial. American, 1878. 580p., illus. Austin 54-498 1973 $8.50

ALLEN, JOSIAH (Mrs.)   Samantha Among the Brethren. Funk, Wagnall, 1892. 437p., illus. Austin 54-500 1973 $8.50

ALLEN, JOSIAH (Mrs.)   Samantha at Coney Island. Herald, 1911. 349p., illus. Austin 54-501 1973 $10

ALLEN, JOSIAH (Mrs.)   Samantha at Saratoga. Hubbard, 1887. 583p., illus. Austin 54-502 1973 $7.50

ALLEN, JOSIAH (Mrs.)   Samantha at the St. Louis Exposition. Dillingham, 1904. 312p., illus. Austin 54-503 1973 $12.50

ALLEN, JOSIAH (Mrs.)   My Wayward Partner. American, 1880. 490p., illus. Austin 54-499 1973 $12.50

ALLEN, LEWIS A.   American Cattle: Their History, Breeding and Management. New York, 1868. Jenkins 61-112 1974 $12

ALLEN, R. P.   The Roseate Spoonbill. New York, 1942. Roy. 8vo., orig. wrappers, plates, text-figures. Wheldon 128-363 1973 £5

ALLEN, ROWLAND H.   The New England Tragedies. Nichols, Noyes, 1868. 156p. Austin 54-36 1973 $10

ALLEN, THOMAS   The Commerce and Navigation of the Valley of the Mississippi. St. Louis, n.d. 8vo., disbound, first edition. Ximenes 37-2 1974 $75

ALLEN, WILKES   The History of Chelmsford, from Its Origin in 1653, to the Year 1820 . . . to Which is Added, A Memoir of the Pawtuckett Tribe of Indians. Haverhill, 1820. 8vo., contemporary sheep, scuffed, front hinge tender, first edition, some foxing, sound copy. Ximenes 36-3 1974 $45

ALLEN, WILLIAM   A Narrative of the Expedition sent by Her Majesty's Government to the River Niger, in 1841. London, 1848. 2 vols., 8vo., orig. blue cloth, spines faded, first edition, wood engravings, plates, maps, library stamps, very good. Ximenes 36-4 1974 $175

ALLEN, WILLIAM   Picturesque Views in the Island of Ascension. 1835. Fine coloured lithographs, India paper, small oblong folio, modern half brown morocco, gilt title on spine, good copy, very rare. Sawyer 293-109 1974 £375

ALLENDORF Kulturpraxis der Kalt, und Warmhauspflanzen. Berlin, 1916. 8vo., cloth. Wheldon 131-1483 1974 £5

ALLERTON, JAMES M.   Hawk's Nest, or the Last of the Cahoonshees. Port Jervis, (1892). Printed wrapper, chipped, very scarce. Butterfield 10-9 1974 $75

ALLESTREE, RICHARD   The Causes of the Decay of Christian Piety. London, 1669-90. 2 items in 1 vol., 8vo., contemporary calf, worn. Traylen 79-163 1973 £15

ALLESTREE, RICHARD   The Government of the Tongue. 1674. 8vo., contemporary panelled calf, fine, first edition. Dawsons PM 252-10 1974 £85

ALLEY, GEORGE   Observations on the Hydrargyria. London, 1810.
4to., half calf, worn, plates, first edition. Dawsons PM 249-10 1974 £32

ALLEYN, EDWARD   The Alleyn Papers. Shakespeare Soc., 1843.
110p. Austin 51-199 1973 $15

ALLHANDS, J. L.   Gringo Builders. (Iowa City), 1931.
Scarce, illus., orig. cloth, first edition. Bradley 35-369 1974 $26

ALLHANDS, J. L.   Gringo Builders. N. P., 1933. Autographed.
Jenkins 61-113 1974 $22.50

ALLIBONE, SAMUEL AUSTIN   Critical Dictionary of English Literature and
British and American Authors. 1872-1908. 5 vols., new buckram. Allen 216-a
1974 $50

ALLIES, THOMAS W.   The Formation of Christendom. 1865-75.
3 vols., demy 8vo., orig. cloth. Howes 185-902 1974 £6

ALLIES, THOMAS W.   Per Crucem ad Lucem. 1879. 2 vols., orig.
cloth. Howes 185-906 1974 £5

ALLINGHAM, JOHN TILL   Hearts of Oak. London, 1804. 8vo.,
modern boards, first edition. Dawsons PM 252-12 1974 £15

ALLINGHAM, JOHN TILL   The Marriage Promise. London, 1803. 8vo.,
modern boards, second edition. Dawsons PM 252-13 1974 £12

ALLINGHAM, WILLIAM   The Ballad Book. London, 1887. 8vo.,
cloth boards. Emerald 50-8 1974 £5

ALLIONI, C.   Rariorum Pedemontii Stirpium. Turin, 1755.
4to., old half roan, plates. Wheldon 129-1036 1974 £35

ALLISON, JAMES MURRAY   Travel Notes on a Holiday Tour in France.
1931. Cloth-backed boards, inscription. Covent 55-195 1974 $8.50

ALLISON, JAMES MURRAY   Travel Notes on a Holiday Tour in France.
1931. Orig. cloth, scarce, first edition. Rota 188-83 1974 £15

ALLISON, NATHANIEL   Diagnosis In Joint Disease. New York, 1931.
Rittenhouse 46-11 1974 $10

ALLMAN, G. J.   A Monograph of the Gymnoblastic. 1871-72.
Folio, half morocco, plates. Wheldon 129-763 1974 £50

ALLMAN, HERBERT D.   A Unique Institution. 1935. 222 pages,
illus. Austin 57-26 1974 $15

ALLOM, T.   Westmorland. 1847. 4to., contemporary
green morocco gilt, plates. Quaritch 939-574 1974 £50

ALLOM, THOMAS   China. London, n.d. 4 vols., 4to., half
green morocco gilt, engravings. Traylen 79-512 1973 £58

ALLOWAY, MARY W.   Famous Firesides of French Canada. Montreal,
1899. Illus., cover stamped with gold lettering. Hood's 102-677 1974 $10

ALLSTON, WASHINGTON   Monaldi. Boston, 1841. Orig. cloth,
first edition, very good copy. MacManus 224-6 1974 $45

ALMACK, EDWARD   A Bibliography of the King's Book. 1896.
4to., orig. cloth, plates, scarce. Howes 185-573 1974 £14

ALMANACH des Spectacles. Paris, 1822. 32mo., orig. grey boards, matching
case, color plates. Gregory 44-84 1974 $45

ALMANACH of Letter-Geschenk Voor de Leergrage Jeugd. Amsterdam, 1906.
Square 16mo., orig. printed boards, colored figures, spine & front hinge repaired.
Gregory 44-33A 1974 $75

ALMANACH Royal M.DCC.LVIII. Paris, 1758. 8vo., French citron morocco
gilt, raised bands, corners little worn, generally good condition. Thomas 32-75
1974 £100

ALMANACK for 1854. Frontispiece, gold tooled white vellum, matching case
worn, 2 3/8 X 1 1/2 inches. Gregory 44-334 1974 $35

ALONG Quebec Highways. Quebec, 1930. Illus. Hood's 102-679 1974
$10

ALONG Shore at Buzzards Bay. Harwickport, 1890. Wrapper, photographs.
Jenkins 61-1483 1974 $12.50

ALONNIER, DECEMBRE   Typographes et Gens de Lettres. Paris, 1864.
Small 8vo., brown half leather, gilt back. Kraus B8-284 1974 $35

ALPERT, HOLLIS   The Dreams and the Dreamers. Macmillan,
1962. 258p. Austin 51-15 1973 $8.50

ALPHABETISCHES Verzeichniss der in Kloss' Bibliographie der Freimaurerei und
Taute's Maurerischer Bucherkunde Angefuhrten Anonyman Schriften mit
Hinweisung auf die Laufenden Nummern in Beiden Werken. Munchen, 1898.
Med. 8vo., orig. wrappers, slightly chipped. Forster 98-259 1974 £3

ALPHERAKY, SERGIUS   The Geese of Europe and Asia. 1905. 4to.,
orig. cloth, plates. Wheldon 129-1 1974 £70

ALPHERAKY, SERGIUS   The Geese of Europe and Asia. 1905. 4to.,
new half green levant morocco gilt, plates, scarce, fine. Wheldon 131-5
1974 £100

ALPHONSUS LIGUORI   Concessionis Tituli Doctoris. Rome, 1870.
4to., contemporary half vellum. Howes 185-907 1974 £10

ALPHONSUS LIGUORI   Theologia Moralis. Rome, 1905-12. 4 vols.,
thick 4to., half morocco, cloth. Howes 185-909 1974 £15

ALPINI, PROSPER   De Medicina Aegyptiorum Libri Quatuor. Ven-
ice. 4to., full page woodcuts, contemporary limp vellum, first edition, fine, some
marginal brownings. Schafer 10-115 1974 sFr 1,600

ALPINI, PROSPER   Medicina Aegyptiorum. Paris, 1645. 4 books
in 1, 2 vols. bound together. Rittenhouse 46-626 1974 $110

ALPINI, PROSPER   De Medicina Aegyptorum Libri Quator and
Jacobi Bontii. Paris, 1645. Woodcuts, dampstain, limp vellum. Rittenhouse
46-675 1974 $125

ALSOP, VINCENT   Anti-Sozzo, Sive Sherlocismus Enervatus.
London, 1676. 8vo., contemporary sheep, rubbed, library stamp, second edition.
Ximenes 37-4 1974 $45

ALSTON, J. W.   Hints to Young Practitioners. (1804). 8vo.,
orig. boards, plates, third edition. Hammond 201-707 1974 $18.50

ALTENA, J. Q.   Van Regteren. New York, 1949. Illus.
Biblo & Tannen 213-261 1973 $12.50

ALTHAUS, JULIUS   On Failure of Brain Power. London, 1894.
Small 8vo., orig. green cloth, fourth edition. Dawsons PM 249-12 1974 £7

ALUNNO, FRANCESCO   Le Ricchezze Della Lingua Volgare. 1543.
Folio, brown calf over wooden boards, gilt, worn, first edition. Thomas 30-78
1973 £125

AMADIS DE GAULE   Le Premier Livre. Paris, 1918. 2 vols.,
12mo., half morocco, uncut. L. Goldschmidt 42-2 1974 $12.50

AMANN, J.   Bryogeographie de la Suisse. Zurich, 1928.
4to., new buckram, plates. Wheldon 130-1224 1974 £10

AMANN, J.   Flore des Mousses de la Suisse. Zurich, 1912-
33. 4to., new buckram, plates. Wheldon 130-1225 1974 £25

AMANN, J.   Mes Chasses aux Champignons. Lausanne, 1925.
Crown 8vo., half blue levant morocco gilt. Wheldon 129-1140 1974 £5

THE AMBULATOR, or Pocket Companion in a Tour Round London. 1807. Small
8vo., plates, old calf, rebacked. Quaritch 939-433 1974 £8

AMBURGH, F. D. VAN   The Silent Partner Scrap Book. New York,
1915. First edition, 12mo., green flexible covers, publisher's box, mint.
Current BW9-447 1974 $11.50

AMEGHINO, F.   Recherches de Morphologie Phylogenetique.
Buenos Aires, 1904. Roy 8vo., half cloth. Wheldon 129-357 1974 £10

AMEGHINO, F.   Recherches de Morphologie Phylogenetique sur les Molaires Superieures des Ongules. Buenos Aires, 1904. Roy. 8vo., half cloth. Wheldon 131-470 1974 £10

AMELLER, CARLOS FRANCISCO   Elementos de Geometria. 1778. 8vo., contemporary Spanish sheep, gilt, fine, plates, first edition. Dawsons PM 245-20 1974 £25

AMERICA: Or, An Exact Description of the West-Indies. London, 1657. 8vo., full brown morocco, exceedingly rare second edition. Ximenes 37-153 1974 $650

AMERICA As Americans See It. New York, 1932. Plates, fine, first edition. Covent 55-20 1974 £6.30

AMERICAN ACADEMY IN ROME   Memoirs. 1917. Vol. 1, 4to., illus. Allen 213-39 1973 $10

THE AMERICAN Academy of Compliments; or, The Complete American Secretary. Philadelphia, 1796. 12mo., contemporary calf, worn but sound, very good copy, some stains, first edition. Ximenes 37-48 1974 $125

AMERICAN Almanac and Repository of Useful Knowledge--for the year 1834. Boston, 1833. Biblo & Tannen 213-4 1973 $15

THE AMERICAN Anti-Slavery Almanac, for 1839. New York, (1839). Vol. 1 no. 4, pictorial wrapper, woodcuts. Butterfield 10-89 1974 $15

THE AMERICAN Anti-Slavery Almanac, for 1844. New York, (1843). Self wrappers. Hayman 59-20 1974 $25

AMERICAN BATTLE MONUMENTS COMMISSION   American Armies and Battlefields in Europe. (Washington), 1938. Profusely illus., maps, large folding colored maps in rear pocket, orig. binding. Wilson 63-463 1974 $13.75

THE AMERICAN Catholic Who's Who. Herder, 1910. Austin 62-749 1974 $17.50

AMERICAN Citizens Captured Near Santa Fe. Washington, 1842. Scarce. Jenkins 61-116 1974 $30

AMERICAN Guide Series--Connecticut. Boston, 1938. 1st ed. dw., illus. Biblo & Tannen 213-5 1973 $15

AMERICAN Guide Series--Maine. Boston, 1937. 1st ed. dw., illus. Biblo & Tannen 213-6 1973 $15

AMERICAN Guide Series--Massachusetts. Boston, 1937. 1st ed. dw., illus. Biblo & Tannen 213-7 1973 $15

AMERICAN Guide Series--New Hampshire. Boston, 1938. 1st ed. dw., illus. Biblo & Tannen 213-8 1973 $15

AMERICAN Guide Series--The Ocean Highway. New York, 1938. 1st ed. Biblo & Tannen 213-9 1973 $8.50

AMERICAN Guide Series--Rhode Island. Boston, 1937. 1st ed. dw., illus. Biblo & Tannen 213-10 1973 $15

AMERICAN Guide Series--U. S. One. New York, 1938. 1st ed. Biblo & Tannen 213-11 1973 $7.50

AMERICAN Guide Series--Vermont. Boston, 1937. 1st ed. dw. Biblo & Tannen 213-12 1973 $15

AMERICAN INSTITUTE OF GRAPHIC ARTS   Printing for Commerce. New York, 1927. 4to., illus. Biblo & Tannen 214-2 1974 $12.50

THE AMERICAN Jewish Conference. New York, 1944. Austin 62-10 1974 $12.50

AMERICAN JEWISH HISTORICAL SOCIETY   Publications. 1903. 238 pages. Austin 57-28 1974 $12.50

AMERICAN JEWISH HISTORICAL SOCIETY   Publications. 1907. 230 pages, ex-library. Austin 57-29 1974 $12.50

AMERICAN JEWISH HISTORICAL SOCIETY   Publications. 1917. 240 pages, ex-library. Austin 57-30 1974 $12.50

AMERICAN JEWISH HISTORICAL SOCIETY   Publications. 1918. 362 pages. Austin 57-31 1974 $15

AMERICAN JEWISH HISTORICAL SOCIETY   Publications. 1920. 618 pages. Austin 57-32 1974 $17.50

THE AMERICAN Navy: Cuba and Hawaii. Chicago, 1898. 10 parts, loose wrapper, folio, photos. Jenkins 61-117 1974 $37.50

AMERICAN One Cent Primer. New York, n.d. 16mo., mint copy. Frohnsdorff 16-40 1974 $7.50

AMERICAN Ornithology, Fifty Years Progress, 1883-1933. Lancaster, 1933. 8vo., frontispiece, orig. wrappers. Wheldon 131-201 1974 £5

AMERICAN Poetry. New York, 1922. Cloth-backed boards, dust wrapper, fine, first American edition. Covent 55-33 1974 £5.25

AMERICAN Poetry, 1925. New York, 1925. First U. S. edition, spine little faded, very good copy. Covent 51-2101 1973 £5.25

AMERICAN SOCIETY OF LANDSCAPE ARCHITECTS   Illustrations of Work of Members. New York, 1931. 4to., photos, landscape plans, bookplate, limited to 500 numbered copies, cloth. Wilson 63-307 1974 $18.75

AMERICAN SOCIETY OF LANDSCAPE ARCHITECTS   Illustrations of Work of Members. New York, 1932. 4to., photos, landscape plans, bookplate, limited to 500 numbered copies, cloth. Wilson 63-308 1974 $18.75

AMERICAN TECHNICAL SOCIETY   Automobile Engineering. Chicago, 1920. 6 vols., limp simulated morocco, engravings. Wilson 63-429 1974 $42.75

AMERICAN Writer's Congress. International Pub., 1935. 192p. Austin 54-466 1973 $17.50

AMERICAN Writers on American Literature. New York, 1931. First American edition. Covent 55-34 1974 £7.50

AMERICANS in Process. Houghton, Mifflin, 1902. 389p., orig. ed., illus. Austin 62-696 1974 $17.50

AMHERST, W. J.   The History of Catholic Emancipation. 1886. 2 vols., orig. cloth, scarce. Howes 185-911 1974 £8

AMHURST, NICHOLAS   An Argument Against Excises. 1733. 2 parts in 1 vol., 8vo., modern boards, roan back. Quaritch 939-30 1974 £35

AMHURST, NICHOLAS   The Craftsman. 1731-37. 12mo., 14 vols., contemporary calf, frontispieces, gilt. Quaritch 936-6 1974 £70

AMHURST, NICHOLAS   A Letter to Caleb D'Anvers. London, 1729. 8vo., old marbled paper wrappers, first edition. Dawsons PM 247-2 1974 £45

AMHURST, NICHOLAS   Protestant Popery. 1718. 8vo., cloth, uncut. Quaritch 936-7 1974 £30

AMHURST, NICHOLAS   Terrae-Filius. 1726. Small 8vo., calf gilt, frontispiece, second edition. Quaritch 936-8 1974 £15

AMICI, DOMENICO   Raccolta delle Principali Vedute di Roma. Rome, 1832-41. Oblong 4to., half morocco, plates. Traylen 79-564 1973 £48

AMICI, DOMENICO   Raccolta Delle Principali Vedute di Roma. Rome, 1835-39. 2 vols. in 1, oblong 4to., boards, vellum back, plates. Quaritch 940-8 1974 £75

AMICUS COSENTINUS, IOANNES BAPTISTA   De Motibus Corporum Coelestium Iuxta Principia Peripatetica Sine Eccentricis & Epicyclis. Paris, 1540. 4to., modern vellum, illus. Dawsons PM 245-21 1974 £250

AMMAN, DESCHAMPS, ABBE C. F.   Cours Elementaire d'Education. Paris, 1779. 12mo., contemporary calf, plates. Gurney 64-5 1974 £30

AMMAN, JO CONRAD   Dissertatio de Loquela. Amsterdam, 1700. 8vo., old calf, rebacked, first edition. Gurney 64-4 1974 £60

AMMAN, JOBST Kunstbuchlin, Darinnen Neben Furbildung Vieler. (Frankfurt-am-Main, 1599). 4to., contemporary vellum, woodcuts, incomplete, lacking leaves, other leaves are cout out and mounted. Schumann 499-3 1974 sFr 1,100

AMMAN, JOBST Von Ankunfft und Ursprung dess Romischen Reichs, der Alten Romer Herkommen. Frankfurt, 1568. Folio, contemporary blind stamped pig skin over wooden boards, first German edition illus. by Amman, woodcuts, good copy, some minor marginal stains. Schumann 499-2 1974 sFr 2,200

AMMAN, P. Character Plantarum Naturalis. Frankfurt and Leipzig, 1685. 12mo., contemporary calf, worn. Wheldon 129-883 1974 £25

AMMONIUS, HERMEAE In Quinque Voces Porphyrii Commentarius. 1546. Old vellum, woodcut diagram. Thomas 30-85 1973 £15

THE AMORES of P. Ovidius Naso. 1932. 8vo., contemporary half morocco, limited edition. Dawsons PM 252-763 1974 £35

AMORY, THOMAS C. Daniel Sullivan's Visits, May and June, 1781, to General John Sullivan, in Philadelphia to Explain Declarations in Sir Henry Clinton's Secret Journal. Cambridge, 1884. Wrapper. Jenkins 61-2133 1974 $15

AMOS, ANDREW The Great Over of Poisoning. London, 1846. 8vo., contemporary calf, gilt, portraits. Hammond 201-180 1974 £6

THE AMOURS of Messalina, Late Queen of Albion. London, 1689. 2 vols., small 8vo., contemporary calf, rare. Ximenes 33-12 1974 $375

AMPERE, ANDRE-MARIE Memories sur l'Action Mutuelle de Deux Courans Electriques. (Paris, 1820-22). 8vo., quarter morocco, folding plates, exceedingly rare. Gurney 66-8 1974 £350

AMPERE, ANDRE MARIE Sur les Experiences Electro-Magnetiques de MM. Paris, 1820. Orig. blue wrappers, uncut, 4to., first separate edition, offprint with reset pagination, rare. Kraus 137-6 1974 $1,250

AMPERE, ANDRE-MARIE Theorie des Phenomenes Electro-Dynamiques. Paris, 1826. 4to., full calf, plates, first edition. Dawsons PM 245-22 1974 £950

AMPHLETT, J. The Botany of Worcestershire. Birmingham, 1909. 8vo., new cloth, very scarce. Wheldon 131-1215 1974 £15

AMPHORA A Collection of Prose and Verse Chosen by the Editor of the Bibelot. Portland, 1919. 8vo., inscription, orig. boards, label, limited third edition. Bow Windows 62-19 1974 £9.50

AMUSING and Instructive Fables in French and English. 1738-36. 2 parts in 1, 12mo., half roan, raded, copperplate illus., part 1 second edition, part 2 first edition. George's 610-20 1973 £7.50

ANACREONTIS Carmina cum Sapphois et Alcaei Fragmentis. Glasgow, 1751. Full old calf, 3 1/2 X 2 inches. Gregory 44-337 1974 $110

ANACREONTIS Carmina cum Sapphonis et Alcaei Fragmentis. Glasgow, 1761. Orig. old calf, inscribed, 3 1/8 X 2 inches. Gregory 44-336 1974 $95

ANACREONTIS Opera Graece: Cum Latina Versione, Notis and Indice. 1725. 4to., contemporary mottled calf, joints cracked, very good copy. Bow Windows 66-12 1974 £30

ANALECTA JURIS PONTIFICII Dissertations sur Divers Sujets de Droit Canonique, Liturgie et Theologie. Rome & Paris, 1855-77. 8 vols., thick folio, half morocco. Howes 185-912 1974 £50

ANALYTICUS Jews Are Like That. 1928. 231 pages, illus. Austin 57-33 1974 $10

ANALYTICUS Jews Are Like That! Brentano's, 1928. Austin 62-12 1974 $10

ANAND, MULK RAJ The Indian Theatre. Roy, 1951. 60p., illus. Austin 51-16 1973 $6.50

ANBUREY, THOMAS Travels Through the Interior Parts of America. London, 1789. 2 vols., rebound leather spine & corners, folding maps, some mis-paging, folding maps. Hood's 102-547 1974 $385

ANBUREY, THOMAS Travels Through the Interior Parts of America. Boston, 1923. 2 vols., limited to 525 numbered copies, 8vo., map frontis., orig. green paper covered boards. Current BW9-342 1974 $40

ANCESCHI, LUCIANO Mario Sironi. Milan, 1944. Large 4to., plates, boards, limited edition. Minters 37-438 1973 $26

THE ANCESTOR. 1902-05. 12 vols., roy. 8vo., plates, buckram. Quaritch 939-704 1974 £30

ANCIENT and Modern Sculpture. London, (n.d.). Large 8vo., frontispiece, plates, foxing, half morocco, rubbed. Bow Windows 62-821 1974 £6.75

ANCIENT Laws and Institutes of England. 1840. 2 vols., 8vo., cloth, gilt. Quaritch 939-1 1974 £55

ANCIENT Laws and Institutes of England. 1840. Folio, cloth. Quaritch 939-2 1974 £52.50

ANCIENT LAWS and Institutes of Wales. 1841. Folio, orig. cloth. Broadhurst 23-1576 1974 £80

ANCIENT Laws and Institutes of Wales . . . Laws Supposed to be Enacted by Howel the Good . . . and Anomalus Laws . . . With Indexes and Glossary. 1841. Demy folio, orig. cloth, fine. Broadhurst 24-1545 1974 £80

ANCIENT Laws and Institutes of Wales. 1841. 2 vols., 8vo., cloth. Quaritch 939-22 1974 £55

ANCIENT Laws and Institutes of Wales. 1841. Folio, cloth. Quaritch 939-23 1974 £52.50

ANCILLON, CHARLES Eunuchism Displayed. 1718. 8vo., contemporary panelled calf. Quaritch 936-9 1974 £55

ANCILLON, CHARLES Traite des Eunuques, Dans Lequel. (Paris, 1701). 12mo., old morocco backed boards, joints tender, armorial bookplate of Edwin Hanson Freshfield. Bow Windows 66-14 1974 £18

ANDERS, KARL Worterbuch des Flugwesens. Leipzig, 1937. 8vo., orig. printed cloth, first edition. Dawsons PM 245-23 1974 £12

ANDERSEN, HANS CHRISTIAN A Christmas Greeting. New York, Boston, 1848. 16mo., embossed cloth, spine pict. gilt, woodcut frontispiece, spine faded, fine copy, first American edition. Frohnsdorff 15-4 1974 $40

ANDERSEN, HANS CHRISTIAN A Christmas Greeting. New York, 1848. 16mo., embossed cloth, gilt-decorated spine. Frohnsdorff 16-41 1974 $45

ANDERSEN, HANS CHRISTIAN Contes D'Andersen Traduits Du Danois par D. Soldi. Paris, 1896. 12mo., cloth stamped in gold, all edges gilt. Frohnsdorff 16-42 1974 $7.50

ANDERSEN, HANS CHRISTIAN Fairy Tales. London, n.d. Orig. dec. cloth boards, illus. Covent 55-29 1974 £10.50

ANDERSEN, HANS CHRISTIAN Fairy Tales. 1932. Signed, illus., full vellum, numbered, fine. Covent 55-1230 1974 £185

ANDERSEN, HANS CHRISTIAN Fairy Tales and Legends. London, 1935. Illus. by Rex Whistler, superlatively fine copy, very scarce issue of 200 copies on special paper, signed by artist, pristine state, with acetate protective jacket, first edition. Covent 51-1963 1973 £125

ANDERSEN, HANS CHRISTIAN Fairy Tales and Legends. 1935. Dec. green wrappers, illus., proof copy. Covent 55-1528 1974 £65

ANDERSEN, HANS CHRISTIAN Fairy Tales. New York, c. 1945. Color illus and endpapers, pict. cloth. Wilson 63-481 1974 $15

ANDERSEN, HANS CHRISTIAN Fairy Tales From Hans Andersen Told to the Children by Mary Macgregor. London, n.d. 16mo., 8 color plates, very good copy. Frohnsdorff 16-43 1974 $7.50

ANDERSEN, HANS CHRISTIAN   Forty Stories. 1930. Dust wrapper, plates, English first edition. Covent 56-1401 1974 £15

ANDERSEN, HANS CHRISTIAN   The Ice-Maiden, and Other Tales. Philadelphia, 1863. 16mo., embossed cloth. Frohnsdorff 16-46 1974 $30

ANDERSEN, HANS CHRISTIAN   Later Tales. 1869. Plates, text illus., orig. dec. cloth gilt, covers somewhat age-darkened, spine chafed, nice copy, publisher's slip tipped in. Covent 51-27 1973 £10.50

ANDERSEN, HANS CHRISTIAN   Little Maia. New York, n.d. 16mo., woodcuts. Frohnsdorff 16-44 1974 $45

ANDERSEN, HANS CHRISTIAN   The Little Mermaid. New York, 1935. Gilt Pict. cloth, 12mo., 1st ed., illus. Frohnsdorff 16-104 1974 $10

ANDERSEN, HANS CHRISTIAN   Little Rudy, and Other Stories. New York, 1865. 12mo., embossed cloth, gilt-decorated spine, illus. Frohnsdorff 16-45 1974 $20

ANDERSEN, HANS CHRISTIAN   The Nightingale. Boston, 1896. Illus., boards, wrappers. Ballinger 1-66 1974 $17.50

ANDERSEN, HANS CHRISTIAN   Out of the Heart. 1868. 12mo., orig. cloth gilt, English first edition. Covent 56-1402 1974 £10.50

ANDERSEN, HANS CHRISTIAN   The Red Shoes. Bristol, 1928. One of 400 numbered copies, boards, very nice copy, engraved bookplate, coloured wood engravings. Covent 51-28 1973 £15

ANDERSEN, HANS CHRISTIAN   The Red Shoes. 1928. Boards, fine, English first edition. Covent 56-1403 1974 £25

ANDERSEN, HANS CHRISTIAN   A Series of Letters to Horace Scudder, His American Editor. 1942. Presentation copy, inscribed to Jean Hersholt from the translator on tipped in slip, with Hersholt's bookplate, quarter buckram, fine. Covent 51-2099 1973 £25

ANDERSEN, HANS CHRISTIAN   The Snow Queen. London, n.d. 4to., glazed pictorial boards, 8 color plates. Frohnsdorff 16-49 1974 $8.50

ANDERSEN, HANS CHRISTIAN   The Snow Queen and Other Fairy Tales. London, 1894. 8vo., all edges gilt. Frohnsdorff 16-48 1974 $10

ANDERSEN, HANS CHRISTIAN   The True Story of My Life. 1847. Wood engraved frontispiece, plate, post 8vo., orig. ptd. boards, trifle rubbed, spine defective at head, good internally. George's 610-21 1973 £5

ANDERSEN, HANS CHRISTIAN   The Will-O'-The-Wisp and other Stories. London, ca. 1869. 12mo., gilt, illus. Frohnsdorff 16-50 1974 $7.50

ANDERSEN, HANS CHRISTIAN   Works. New York, 1876. Orig. cloth gilt, bookplates, English first edition. Covent 56-1404 1974 £30

ANDERSON, A.   Aucassin and Nicolete. London, 1911. Crown 4to., illus., plates, gilt, orig. dec. cloth. Bow Windows 62-20 1974 £6.50

ANDERSON, ADAM   An Historical and Chronological Deduction of the Origin of Commerce. London, 1764. 2 vols., folio, contemporary polished calf, fine, fist edition. Dawsons PM 247-3 1974 £160

ANDERSON, ALEX D.   The Silver Country. New York, 1877. Folding map, first edition. Jenkins 61-120 1974 $25

ANDERSON, DAVID   Canada. London, 1814. 8vo., old half calf, leather label. Traylen 79-461 1973 £65

ANDERSON, FLORENCE BENET   Through the Hawse-Hole. New York, 1932. Dust jacket, illus. Rinsland 58-930 1974 $20

ANDERSON, ISABEL   The Spell of the Hawaiian Islands and the Philippines. Boston, (1916). 8vo., orig. bindings, dust jacket. Butterfield 8-130 1974 $15

ANDERSON, JAMES   The New Practical Gardener. (1874). Roy 8vo., half roan, plates. Wheldon 130-1371 1974 £15

ANDERSON, JAMES   The New Practical Gardener. (1874). Roy. 8vo., half roan, plain and coloured plates. Wheldon 128-1438 1973 £15

ANDERSON, JAMES 1739-1808   Observations on the Means of Exciting a Spirit of National Industry. Edinburgh, 1777. 4to., contemporary speckled calf, fine, first edition. Quaritch 939-642 1974 £160

ANDERSON, JOHN   Box Office. Cape & Smith, 1929. 121p. Austin 51-17 1973 $10

ANDERSON, JOHN REDWOOD   The Curlew Cries. 1940. Dust wrapper, fine, English first edition. Covent 56-1405 1974 £5.25

ANDERSON, JOHN REDWOOD   The Vortex. 1928. Bookplate, presentation copy, inscribed, English first edition. Covent 56-1407 1974 £5.25*

ANDERSON, JOSEPH   The Town and City of Waterbury . . . From the Aboriginal Period to the Year 1895. New Haven, 1896. 3 vols., ex-library, sahken, orig. binding. Butterfield 10-201 1974 $27.50

ANDERSON, MARGARET   My Thirty Years' War. 1930. Plates, orig. lacquered cloth, bookplate, fine, scarce. Covent 51-3239 1973 £10.50

ANDERSON, MARY   A Few Memories. Harper, 1896. 262p. Austin 51-18 1973 $6.50

ANDERSON, MAXWELL   Joan of Arc. Sloane, 1948. 170p., illus. Austin 51-19 1973 $10

ANDERSON, MAXWELL   Off Broadway. Sloane, 1947. 91p., 1st ed. Austin 51-20 1973 $10

ANDERSON, MAXWELL   Off Broadway. New York, 1947. 1st ed. Biblo & Tannen 213-889 1973 $8.50

ANDERSON, MAXWELL   Three American Plays. Harcourt, Brace, 1926. 263p. Austin 51-21 1973 $15

ANDERSON, R.   Den Danske Kirke Og Episkopalkirken. Brooklyn, 1920. Austin 62-13 1974 $27.50

ANDERSON, SHERWOOD   Alice and the Lost Novel. London, 1929. 12mo., orig. wrappers, lower one third of spine torn, first edition, one of 530 copies, numbered & signed by author. MacManus 224-7 1974 $40

ANDERSON, SHERWOOD   Beyond Desire. New York, (1932). Limited to 165 copies signed by author, glassine d.j., handsome folder and box with black leather backstrip, gilt label. Butterfield 10-51 1974 $75

ANDERSON, SHERWOOD   Dark Laughter. Boni, Liveright, 1925. 319p., orig. ed. Austin 54-35 1973 $6

ANDERSON, SHERWOOD   Dark Laughter. Grosset, Dunlap, 1925. 319p. Austin 54-37 1973 $4

ANDERSON, SHERWOOD   Dark Laughter. New York, 1925. 8vo., orig. cloth, first edition. Rota 189-17 1974 £5

ANDERSON, SHERWOOD   Hello Towns! New York, 1929. First printing with "fingers" misspelled p. 35. Butterfield 10-52 1974 $15

ANDERSON, SHERWOOD   Hello Towns! New York, 1929. Orig. cloth, fine in dust jacket, first issue, with "fingers" misspelled. MacManus 224-8 1974 $25

ANDERSON, SHERWOOD   Letters of Sherwood Anderson. Little, Brown, 1953. 478p. Austin 54-42 1973 $15

ANDERSON, SHERWOOD   Many Marriages. Heubsch, 1923. 264p. Austin 54-38 1973 $10

ANDERSON, SHERWOOD   A New Testament. New York, 1927. Orig. half vellum, first edition, one of 265 large paper copies, signed by author, fine. MacManus 224-9 1974 $60

ANDERSON, SHERWOOD   No Swank. Philadelphia, 1934. Limited to 1000 copies, d.j., orig. binding. Butterfield 10-53 1974 $35

ANDERSON, SHERWOOD   Poor White. 1920. Bookplate, first edition.
Allen 216-1240 1974 $25

ANDERSON, SHERWOOD   Poor White. New York, 1920. Orig. cloth,
spine faded, first edition, signed by author. MacManus 224-10 1974 $35

ANDERSON, SHERWOOD   Sherwood Anderson's Notebook. Boni,
Liveright, 1926. 230p. Austin 54-39 1973 $12.50

ANDERSON, SHERWOOD   A Story Teller's Story. Huebsch, 1922. 442p.,
orig. ed. Austin 54-40 1973 $8.50

ANDERSON, SHERWOOD   A Story Teller's Story. New York, 1927. Orig.
binding, d.j., fourth printing, inscribed by author. Butterfield 10-54 1974 $25

ANDERSON, SHERWOOD   Tar. (New York), 1926. Orig. vellum backed
boards, label on spine, first edition, one of 350 numbered copies, signed by
author, about fine. MacManus 224-11 1974 $60

ANDERSON, SHERWOOD   Tar--A midwest childhood. Boni, 1926.
345p., paper. Austin 54-41 1973 $7.50

ANDERSON, SHERWOOD   The Triumph of the Egg. New York, 1921.
First issue, covers dull, orig. binding. Butterfield 10-55 1974 $10

ANDERSON, SHERWOOD   Winesburg-en-Ohio. Paris, 1927. Wrappers,
fine, first French edition. Covent 55-31 1974 £21

ANDERSON, T.   Volcanic Studies. 1903. Roy. 8vo., cloth,
plates. Wheldon 131-959 1974 £5

ANDERSON, W.   Second Report of the Geological Survey of
Natal and Zululand. 1904. Small folio, orig. boards, plates, folding maps.
Wheldon 128-940 1973 £5

ANDERSON, WILLIAM   Japanese Wood Engravings. 1895. Orig.
cloth gilt, plates, illus., fine. Covent 55-79 1974 £15

ANDERSON, WILLIAM   The Pictorial Arts of Japan. 1886. Folio,
cloth, morocco spine, plates, gilt. Quaritch 940-365 1974 £45

ANDERSSON, N. J.   Cyperaceae Scandinaviae. Stockholm, 1849-52.
8vo., cloth, scarce. Wheldon 129-1039 1974 £7.50

ANDERSSON, N. J.   Plantae Scandinaviae. Stockholm, 1840-52.
2 vols., 8vo., boards, scarce, plates. Wheldon 128-1235 1973 £5

ANDERSSON, N. J.   Salices Lapponiae. Upsala, 1845. 8vo.,
boards, plates. Wheldon 130-1539 1974 £5

ANDERTON, BASIL   Catalogue of the Bewick Collection. (Newcastle, 1904). Orig. wrappers, rebacked, illus. Dawson's 424-34 1974 $45

ANDRADE, EDWARD NEVILLE DA COSTA 1887-   The Structure of the Atom.
1923. First edition. Covent 55-1288 1974 £10.50

ANDRAL, GABRIEL   Cours de Pathologie Interne. Paris, 1836. 8vo.,
3 vols., contemporary marbled boards, first edition. Dawsons PM 249-13 1974
£22

ANDRE, EUGENE   Species des Hymenopteres d'Europe. Paris,
1879-1913. 13 vols., plates, green half morocco. Bow Windows 64-6 1974
£285

ANDRE, MARIUS   Columbus. New York, 1928. Illus. Jenkins
61-550 1974 $10

ANDREE, JULIUS   Der Eiszeitliche Mensch. Stuttgart, 1939.
Tables, cloth, orig. wrappers. Bow Windows 64-7 1974 £4.50

ANDREE, S. A.   Andree's Story: The Complete Record of His
Polar Flight, 1897. New York, 1930. Hood's 104-70 1974 $35

ANDREEV, LEONID NIKOLAEVICH 1871-1919   Savva. 1914. Austin 51-
22 1973 $10

ANDREEV, LEONID NIKOLAEVICH 1871-1919   To the Stars. 1907. Austin
51-23 1973 $12.50

ANDREWES, LANCELOT   Ninety-Six Sermons. Oxford, 1841. 5 vols.,
orig. cloth, worn, best edition. Howes 185-914 1974 £20

ANDREWES, LANCELOT   Opuscula Quaedam Posthuma. Oxford, 1852.
Orig. cloth. Howes 185-915 1974 £5

ANDREWS   The Sei Whale. New York, 1916. Folio,
illus., wrappers, disbound. Rinsland 58-67 1974 $30

ANDREWS, B.   Facts About the Canidate. Chicago, 1904.
2 1/8 X 1 3/4 inches, orig. wrappers, one edge of spine torn. Gregory 44-332
1974 $27.50

ANDREWS, C. C.   Minnesota and Dacotah . . . A Tour Through
the Northwest in the Autumn of 1856. Washington, 1857. Jenkins 61-122
1974 $60

ANDREWS, C. W.   Catalogue of the Tertiary Vertebrata of the
Fayum, Egypt. 1906. 4to., new cloth, plates, text-figures. Wheldon 128-941
1973 £10

ANDREWS, C. W.   A Descriptive Catalogue of the Marine Reptiles
of the Oxford Clay. 1913. Vol. 2, 4to., cloth, plates. Wheldon 131-960
1974 £15

ANDREWS, HENRY   The Botanist's Repository for New and Rare
Plants. 1797-1814. 10 vols., 4to., newly bound in half green morocco gilt,
fine hand-coloured engraved plates, complete copy. Wheldon 128-1439 1973
£1,500

ANDREWS, HENRY   Coloured Engravings of Heaths. 1802-09.
3 vols., folio, contemporary half calf, joints weak, hand-coloured plates, nice
clean copy. Wheldon 128-1696 1973 £1,200

ANDREWS, HENRY   Geraniums. 1805 (-1823?). 4to., modern
half polished red morocco, hand coloured plates, rare. Wheldon 128-1440 1973
£375

ANDREWS, ISRAEL W.   Washington County and the Early Settlement of
Ohio. Cincinnati, 1877. Wrapper. Jenkins 61-1994 1974 $22.50

ANDREWS, JOHN   Elements of Logick. Philadelphia, 1807.
Leather, disbound, worn, second edition. Rinsland 58-911 1974 $15

ANDREWS, JOHN   History of the War With America, France, Spain,
and Holland, Commencing in 1775 and ending in 1783. London, 1785-6. Full
calf, red labels, plates, complete fine. Butterfield 10-35 1974 $250

ANDREWS, JOHN   History of the War With America, France, Spain,
and Holland; Commencing in 1775 and ending in 1783. London, 1785. 4 vols.,
portraits, maps, charts, full leather, leather spines new. Hood's 102-88 1974
$400

ANDREWS, JOHN   History of the War With America, France,
Spain and Holland. London, 1785. 4 vols., portraits, maps, full leather.
Hood's 104-90 1974 $400

ANDREWS, MATTHEW PAGE   Virginia. New York, 1937. Biblo & Tannen,
213-96 1973 $5

ANDREWS, MILES PETER   The Mysteries of the Castle. London, 1795.
8vo., modern boards, first edition. Dawsons PM 252-14 1974 £15

ANDREWS, ROY CHAPMAN   The California Grey Whale. New York,
1914. Large folio, illus., wrappers, disbound, fine. Rinsland 58-66 1974 $25

ANDREWS, THOMAS   The Bakerian Lecture. 1876. 4to., green paper
wrappers. Dawsons PM 245-25 1974 £6

ANDREWS, W. D. 1853-   The Lifeboat, and Other Poems. Toronto, n.d.
Illus. Hood's 104-747 1974 $15

ANDREWS, WILLIAM   Bygone Punishments. London, 1899. Illus.
Rittenhouse 46-15 1974 $15

ANDREWS, WILLIAM 1848-1908   The Church Treasury of History, Custom and
Folk-Lore. London, 1898. 8vo., illus., orig. cloth. Bow Windows 62-22 1974
£5

ANDREWS, WILLIAM 1848-1908   Old Church Lore. 1891. 8vo., orig. quarter roan, illus. Bow Windows 64-370 1974 £6.50

ANDREWS, WILLIAM LORING   A Prospect of the Colleges in Cambridge in New England. New York, 1897. Thin 4to., limited to 115 copies, frontis., full page engravings, very fine. Current BW9-369 1974 $38.50

ANDRIEU, ANTOINE   Avis Aux Citoyens. Paris, 1780. 8vo., uncut, orig. paper wrappers. Dawsons PM 249-14 1974 £30

ANDRY DE BOISREGARD, NICOLAS   An Account of the Breeding of Worms in Human Bodies. London, 1701. 8vo., old calf, rebacked, gilt, plates, first edition in English. Dawsons PM 249-15 1974 £110

ANDRY DE BOISREGARD, NICOLAS   De la Generation des Vers dans le Corps de l'Homme. Amsterdam, 1701. 12mo., half calf, gilt, plates, first Amsterdam edition. Hammond 201-529 1974 £58

ANECDOTES of Mary; or, The Good Governess. 1795. First edition, soiling in text, few minor tears, 12mo., contemporary sheep, lacks part of spine, rare, lacks half title. George's 610-23 1973 £20

ANECDOTES, Poetry and Incidents of the War: North and South. New York, 1866. 3/4 calf., bdg. rubbed. Biblo & Tannen 213-24 1973 $20

ANGEL, MYRON   History of Nevada. Oakland, 1881. Large 4to., part black calf, plates. Putnam 126-324 1974 $125

ANGEL, MYRON   History of San Luis Obispo County. Oakland, 1883. Small folio, orig. bindings, plates, inscribed, fine, rare. Butterfield 8-34 1974 $275

ANGELL, J. B.   Report of the United States Deep Waterways Commission, Accompanied by the Report on Technical Work and Several Topical Reports and Drawings Pertaining Thereto. Washington, 1897. Folding charts, maps. Hood's 102-783 1974 $20

ANGELO, HENRY   The Reminiscences of Henry Angelo. London, 1904. 28 plates, 2 vols., orig. cl., ltd. to 1000 copies. Jacobs 24-57 1974 $50

ANGELUS DE CLAVASIO   Summa Angelica Casus Coscietie & Vitioru Remedia Cotines. Lyons, 1519. 8vo., contemporary blind stamped calf, rebacked, worn, almost split in two. Thomas 32-218 1974 £31.50

ANGEVINE, D. M.   Atlas of Orthopedic Pathology. N.P., 1943. Rittenhouse 46-692 1974 $10

ANGHIERA, PIETRO MARTIRE D'   The Historie of the West-Indies. London, n.d. Small 4to., full brown morocco gilt. Traylen 79-462 1973 £175

ANGHIERA, PIETRO MATIRE D'   De Nuper sub D. Carolo Repertis Insulis, Simulque Incolarum Moribus. Basel, 1521. Small 4to., vellum, first edition, rare. Schumann 499-69 1974 sFr 9,500

ANGLERIUS, PETER MARTYR
Please turn to
ANGHIERA, PIETRO MARTIRE D'

ANGLICUS, BARTHOLOMAEUS
Please turn to
BARTHOLOMAEUS ANGLICUS

AN ANGLO-SAXON Homily. 1709. 8vo., contemporary calf, gilt, worn, rebacked, frontispiece. Thomas 28-169 1972 £30

ANGSTROM, ANDERS JONAS   Washington, 1915. 8vo., orig. green cloth, gilt, illus., fine. Dawsons PM 245-27 1974 £10

ANIMAL Life and The World of Nature. Philadelphia, (c. 1910). 4to., illus., colored plates, 2 pages loose, back cover creased, else very good. Current BW9-449 1974 $12

ANKETELL, JOHN   Poems on Several Subjects. Dublin, 1793. 8vo., full calf, presentation. Emerald 50-11 1974 £18

ANLEY, CHARLOTTE   Influence. 1822. First edition, 2 vols., 12mo., half russia, gilt, trifle rubbed, good copy. George's 610-24 1973 £10

ANNA COMNENA   Alexias, sive de rebus ab Alexio imperatore vel eius tempore gestis, libri quindecim. 1651. Folio, full contemporary calf, rubbed, fine. Howes 186-658 1974 £40

ANNALES Des Sciences Naturelles: Zoologie, a Series Complete from 1854-1884. Paris, 1854-84. 58 vols., roy. 8vo., 40 vols. in 20 in half cloth, 18 vols. in 37 parts in orig. wrappers. Wheldon 128-255 1973 £200

ANNALS of British Geology. 1891-95. 4 vols., 8vo., cloth, scarce. Wheldon 131-202 1974 £12

ANNALS of Philadelphia and Pennsylvania. N. P., 1850. 2 vols. in 1, three quarter morocco, rubbed. Jenkins 61-2134 1974 $10

ANNALS of the Kingdom of Ireland by the Four Masters. Dublin, 1856. 7 vols., 4to., orig. cloth, second edition. Quaritch 939-608 1974 £175

ANNALS of Ulster. Dublin, 1887-1901. 4 vols., 8vo., roxburghe, rubbed. Quaritch 939-7 1974 £50

ANNESLEY, ARTHUR   A Letter. London, 1681. 8vo., modern boards, first edition. Dawsons PM 251-160 1974 £34

ANNO Regni Annae Reginae. 1711. 34 items in 1 vol., folio, old calf, gilt, rubbed. Quaritch 939-476 1974 £40

ANNO Regni Annae Reginae Anglia, Scotia, Francia & Hibernia. London, 1705. Folio, contemporary panelled calf. Bow Windows 62-4 1974 £48

ANNO Regni Caroli II. London, 1673. Folio, old calf. Quaritch 939-475 1974 £30

ANNONI, AMBROGIO   Renzo Gerla. Geneva, 1931. 8vo., gold stamped cloth, plates. Minters 37-534 1973 $24

ANNUAL Customes & Festivals In Peking. 1936. Roy. 8vo., plates, illus., orig. cloth. Smith 194-602 1974 £6.50

ANNUAL of Book Making. 1938. 4to., plates, spine slightly stained. Allen 216-147 1974 $10

AN ANNUAL of New Poetry; 1917. 1917. Boards, cover somewhat soiled by dust and marked, very good copy. Covent 51-36 1973 £6.30

THE ANNUAL Register. 1759-1861. 102 vols. in 104, 8vo., calf gilt, rubbed. Quaritch 939-32 1974 £325

ANNUAL Report of the Adjutant General of Pennsylvania for the Year 1863. Harrisburg, 1864. Jenkins 61-2138 1974 $12.50

ANNUAL Reports: Harbor at Philadelphia, Pa., 1888-1894. Washington, (1894). Three quarter morocco. Jenkins 61-2139 1974 $10

ANNUAL Reports: Key West Harbor, Florida, 1889-1894. Washington, (1894). Three quarter leather, large folding maps. Jenkins 61-885 1974 $12.50

ANNUAL Reports, St. John's River, Florida, 1879-94. Washington, (1894). Repaired, three quarter morocco. Jenkins 61-884 1974 $22.50

ANOUILH, JEAN   The Waltz of the Toreadors. Coward-McCann, 1957. 126p. Austin 51-24 1973 $8.50

ANQUETIL, M.   A Summary of Universal History. 1800. 9 vols., contemporary tree calf, joints cracked, spines and corners worn, light foxing, library labels. Bow Windows 66-16 1974 £12

ANSART   Philotecte. Paris, 1737. Small 8vo., full contemporary marbled calf, gilt, illus. L. Goldschmidt 42-3 1974 $50

ANSBACHER Ratschlag. Nurnberg, 1525. Small 4to., modern half vellum, very fine copy, rare, first edition. Schafer 10-92 1974 sFr 1,600

ANSKY, S.   The Dybbuk. 1927. English first edition. Covent 56-1408 1974 £10.50

ANSTED, DAVID THOMAS   Scenery, Science and Art. London, 1854. 8vo., orig. blind-stamped green cloth, gilt, uncut, plates, illus., first edition. Dawsons PM 245-28 1974 £18

ANSTEY, CHRISTOPHER   The New Bath Guide. 1766-1927. 4to and 8vo., contemporary calf, half calf, orig. cloth, 28 vols., fine, illus. Hammond 201-290 1974 £375

ANSTEY, F. PSEUD.
Please turn to
GUTHRIE, THOMAS ANSTEY

Caution: There is a Real Frank Anstey, 1865-

AN ANSWER To the Tears of the Foot Guards, In Which That Respectable Corps are Vindicated from the Charges of Puppism and Cowardice. London, 1776. 4to., modern cloth, rare, first edition. Ximenes 37-177 1974 $100

ANTAR, a Bedoueen Romance. London, 1820. 4 vols., 8vo., later half calf, foxing, first English edition. Ximenes 33-13 1974 $65

ANTE-NICENE Christian Library. Edinburgh, 1867-72. 24 vols., 8vo. Traylen 79-164 1973 £40

ANTHEIL, GEORGE   Bad Boy of Music. Doubleday, 1945. 378p. Austin 51-25 1973 $7.50

ANTHOLOGIE DE LA Nouvelle Poesie Americaine. Paris, 1928. Wrappers, English first edition. Covent 56-1409 1974 £35

ANTHOLOGIE de la Nouvelle Prose Francaise. Paris, 1926. One of 575 copies on velin, wrappers, spine chafed, covers slightly detached, very good uncut copy, first edition. Covent 51-728 1973 £7.50

ANTHOLOGIA in Regis Exanthemata. 1632. 4to., modern stiff vellum, fine, gilt, first edition. Dawsons PM 252-110 1974 £95

ANTHOLOGY of American Ballads, Sailors' Songs, Cowboy Songs, etc. 1927. 4to. Allen 216-88 1974 $12.50

ANTHOLOGY of Magazine Verse for 1923. Boston, 1923. Cloth backed boards, first American edition. Covent 55-35 1974 £8.50

ANTHOLOGY of Magazine Verse for 1923. Boston, 1923. lst ed. Biblo & Tannen 214-676 1974 $8.50

ANTHON, CHARLES   Classical Dictionary. 1873. New buckram. Allen 213-56 1973 $13.50

ANTHONY, G.   Ballet, Camera Studies. London, (1937). Large 4to., edge of front cover faded, orig. cloth. Gregory 44-3 1974 $18.50

ANTHONY, HAROLD G.   A True Romance Revealed by a Bag of Old Letters. New York, (1902). Cloth, little rubbed. Hayman 59-284 1974 $15

ANTI-SEMITISM. New York, 1946. Biblo & Tannen 213-994 1973 $9.50

THE ANTI-TEXAS Legion: Protest of Some Free Men States and Presses Against the Texas Rebellion Against the Laws of Nature and of Nations. Albany, 1845. Very rare. Jenkins 61-123 1974 $225

ANTIN, BENJAMIN   The Gentleman from the 22nd. 1927. 301 pages. Austin 57-42 1974 $10

ANTIN, MARY   They Who Knock At Our Gates. Houghton, 1914. Austin 62-19 1974 $7.50

THE ANTIQUARY'S Books. London, n.d. 8vo., 16 vols., orig. red cloth gilt. Dawsons PM 251-1 1974 £50

THE ANTIQUARY'S Books. 1904-11. 16 vols., 8vo., plates, cloth, illus. Quaritch 939-36 1974 £65

ANTONINI, DA CARLO   Manuale di Varj Ornamenti Componenti la Serie de Vasi Antichi si' di Marmo che di Bronzo Esistenti in Roma e Fuori. Rome, 1821. 3 vols. in 1, folio, plates, fine clean copy, contemporary vellum, gilt. Quaritch 940-287 1974 £200

ANTONINUS, P.   Iter Britanniarum. Cambridge, 1799. 4to., maps, half calf. Quaritch 939-38 1974 £35

ANTONINUS, P.   Iter Britanniarum. 1709. 4to., old calf, rebacked, plates, map. Quaritch 939-37 1974 £20

ANTONINUS, SAINT   Quarta Pars. Venice, 1503. Small 4to., old vellum, worn, stains. Thomas 30-140 1973 £30

ANTONIO, NICOLAUS   Bibliotheca Hispana Vetus. Madrid, 1783. 4 vols., folio, contemporary speckled calf, morocco labels, worn. Dawsons PM 10-11 1974 £85

ANTONIUS DE VERCELLIS   Sermones Quadragesimales de XII Mirabilibus Christianae Fidei Excellentiis. Venice, 1492-93. 4to., contemporary blind tooled calf, wooden boards, rubbed, fine, first edition. Harper 213-5 1973 $750

ANTONINUS, MARCUS AURELIUS   The XII Books of. 1898. 4to., full dec. calf, gilt, uncut. Broadhurst 23-886 1974 £15

ANVILLE, JEAN BAPTISTE BOURGIGNON D'   Proposition d'une Mesure de la Terre. Paris, 1735. 12mo., contemporary calf, rebacked, gilt, first edition. Dawsons PM 245-29 1974 £40

APENSZLAK, JACOB   The Black Book of Polish Jewry. 1943. 343p., illus. Austin 62-725 1974 $17.50

APIANUS, PETRUS   Cosmographia. Antwerp, 1550. 4to., illus., folding woodcut map, diagrams, exceptionally fine. Schafer 10-117 1974 sFr 3,500

APIANUS, PETRUS   Libro de la Cosmographia. Antwerp, 1548. 4to., contemporary limp vellum, woodcuts, rare, first edition in Spanish. Harper 213-6 1973 $425

APLIN, O. V.   The Birds of Oxfordshire. 1889. 8vo., orig. blue cloth, hand-coloured frontispiece, folding map, scarce. Wheldon 128-366 1973 £5

APLIN, O. V.   The Birds of Oxfordshire. Oxford, 1889. 8vo., orig. blue cloth, presentation copy. Wheldon 130-434 1974 £10

APOLLINAIRE, GUILLAUME   L'Oeuvre de Crebillon le Fils. Paris, 1921. Small 4to., wrappers, uncut. Minters 37-258 1973 $28

APOLLONIUS, PERGAEUS   Apollonii Pergaei de Sectione Rationis Libri duo ex Arabico msto Latine versi. Oxford, 1706. 8vo., modem boards, first edition. Dawsons PM 245-30 1974 £115

APOLLONIUS PERGAEUS   Conicorum Libri Quattuor. Bologna, 1566. Small folio, early 17th century polished brown morocco, woodcut diagrams, few stains, some contemporary marginal notes. Kraus 137-8 1974 $3,500

APOLLONIUS, PERGAEUS   Locorum Planorum Libri II. Glasgow, 1749. 4to., contemporary marbled calf, diagrams, first edition. Schuman 37-5 1974 $95

APOLLONIUS RHODIUS   Argonauticorum Libri Quatuor. Basle, 1550. Small 8vo., contemporary blind tooled calf, first edition in Latin. Thomas 28-275 1972 £35

APPERLEY, CHARLES JAMES   Hunting Reminiscences. London, 1843. Roy. 8vo., plates, first edition. Traylen 79-285 1973 £18

APPERLEY, CHARLES JAMES   Memoirs of the Life of the Late John Mytton. London, 1835. 8vo., full red morocco gilt, plates, first edition. Traylen 79-286 1973 £110

APPERLEY, CHARLES JAMES   Nimrod's Hunting Tours. 1903. 4to., coloured plates, rebacked. Allen 216-35 1974 $15

APPIAN   Delle Guerre Civili et Esterne de Romani. 1545. 3 parts in 2 vols., 19th century blue calf gilt, rubbed. Thomas 30-83 1973 £40

APPIER HANZELET, JEAN   Recveil de Plusieurs Machines Militaires. 1620. Small 4to., contemporary calf, gilt, first edition. Zeitlin 235-5 1974 $1,250

APPLEGATE, FRANK G.   Native Tales of New Mexico. 1932. Illus. Austin 57-46 1974 $15

APPLER, AUGUSTUS   Bank and Train Robbers of the West. Chicago, 1882. 2 vols. in 1, three quarters morocco. Jenkins 61-124 1974 $75

APULEIUS BARBARUS   The Herbal of. Oxford, 1925. 4to., half morocco, top edges gilt, collotype illus. some in color. Thomas 32-295 1974 £175

APULEIUS, LUCIUS   Cupid and Psyches. 1924. Buckram, limited, orig. dec. parchment boards, uncut, fine. Howes 186-213 1974 £21

APULEIUS, LUCIUS   The XI Bookes of the Golden Asse. Golden Cockerel Press, 1923. Printed in blue and black, extra crown 4to., blue Michallet boards, linen spine, paper printed label, uncut, limited to 450 copies, fine. Broadhurst 24-979 1974 £25

APULEIUS, LUCIUS   The XI Bookes of the Golden Asse. 1923. Extra crown 4to., boards, uncut, limited. Broadhurst 23-997 1974 £25

APULEIUS, LUCIUS   The XI Bookes of the Golden Asse. Golden Cockerel Press, (Waltham St. Lawrence, 1923). Orig. cloth backed boards, paper label, one of 450 numbered copies, printed in blue & black, fine. MacManus 224-185 1974 $60

APULEIUS, LUCIUS   The XI Bookes of the Golden Asse. Chelsea, 1924. Small folio, fine, orig. holland backed boards, label, uncut. Bow Windows 62-33 1974 £240

APULEIUS, LUCIUS   The XI Bookes of the Golden Asse. 1924. Folio, orig. cloth. Bow Windows 64-371 1974 £500

APULEIUS, LUCIUS   The XI. Bookes of the Golden Asse. 1923. 4to., holland backed boards, limited edition. Bow Windows 66-287 1974 £34.50

APULEIUS, LUCIUS   The XI Bookes of the Golden Asse. Chelsea, 1924. Folio, chinese silk brocade, fine. Dawsons PM 252-17 1974 £500

APULEIUS, LUCIUS   The XI Bookes of the Golden Asse. 1924. Small folio, orig. patterned boards, canvas spine, printed label, internally very good copy, covers slightly discoloured, edges little rubbed, limited to 165 copies. Sawyer 293-36 1974 £220

APULEIUS, LUCIUS   The Golden Asse of Lucius Apuleius. London, 1923. Ltd. to 3000 numbered copies, illus. Jacobs 24-58 1974 $15

APULEIUS, LUCIUS   Les Metamorphoses. 1787. 2 vols., calf, worn. Allen 213-60 1973 $12.50

APULEIUS, LUCIUS   The Metamorphosis. London, 1822. Full leather, rubber; scarce. Biblo & Tannen 213-450 1973 $47.50

APULEIUS, LUCIUS   Metamorphoseos Siue Lusus Asini Libri XI. 1521. Old red morocco gilt, first Aldine edition. Thomas 30-54 1973 £65

AQUARONI, ANTONIO   Album. Rome, n.d. (c. 1830.) Engraved title and plates, oblong 4to., contemporary quarter sheep, bit rubbed, clean and sound within. Thomas 32-345 1974 $75

AQUINAS, THOMAS
Please turn to
THOMAS AQUINAS

ARABIAN NIGHTS   Stories from the Arabian Nights. 1907. Frontis., illus., full vellum. Covent 55-618 1974 £95

ARABIAN NIGHTS   The Arabian Nights. (London, c. 1930). Illus. by W. H. Robinson, full page full color plates, woodcut text illus., bright pictorial covers, orange shelf back, fine. Current BW9-453 1974 $25

ARABIAN NIGHTS   The Book of the Thousand Nights and a Night. London, 1892-97. 12 vols., 8vo., illus., half morocco. Bow Windows 62-24 1974 £40

ARABIAN NIGHTS   The Book of the Thousand Nights and One Night. 1923. 16 vols., quarter vellum, gilt, first edition. Howes 185-5 1974 £32

ARABIAN NIGHTS   Far-Famed Tales from the Arabian Night's Entertainments. 1883. Orig. pictorial cloth gilt, ownership inscription, nice copy, ads at end, first edition. Covent 51-2109 1973 £5.25

ARAGO, M.   Historical Eloge of James Watt. London and Edinburgh, 1839. Large 4to., orig. green cloth, first edition. Dawsons PM 245-756 1974 £16

ARAGON, LOUIS   La Diane Francaise. Paris, 1945. Square 12mo., orig. wrapper, uncut, first edition. L. Goldschmidt 42-141 1974 $10

ARBEIDERKUNST   Kultur og Politik. Copenhagen, (1932). 8vo., wrappers, illus. Minters 37-30 1973 $15

ARBER, AGNES   The Gramineae. Cambridge, 1934. 8vo., cloth. Wheldon 130-988 1974 £12

ARBER, AGNES   Herbals. Cambridge, 1912. 8vo., cloth, plates, text-figures. Wheldon 128-81 1973 £7.50

ARBER, AGNES   Herbals. Cambridge, (1938). 8vo., cloth, plates, scarce, enlarged new edition. Wheldon 128-82 1973 £15

ARBER, AGNES   Monocotyledons. Cambridge, 1925. Roy. 8vo., orig. cloth, scarce orig. issue. Wheldon 131-1110 1974 £7.50

ARBER, AGNES   Water Plants, a Study of Aquatic Angiosperms. Cambridge, 1920. 8vo., orig. cloth, very scarce orig. issue. Wheldon 131-1109 1974 £7

ARBER, EDWARD   An English Garner. London, 1877-1896. 8 vols., 8vo., orig. dec. cloth, uncut. Dawsons PM 252-18 1974 £25

ARBER, EDWARD   The Story of the Pilgrim Fathers. London, 1897. 1st ed., frontis. Jacobs 24-6 1974 $16

ARBLAY, FRANCES BURNEY D'   Camilla. London, 1796. 5 vols., 12mo., contemporary quarter calf, first edition. Dawsons PM 252-100 1974 £95

ARBLAY, FRANCES BURNEY D'   Cecilia. London, 1782. 8vo., 5 vols., tree calf, gilt, first edition. Hammond 201-293 1974 £95

ARBLAY, FRANCES BURNEY D'   Cecilia, or, Memoirs of an Heiress. 1782. 5 vols., 18th century calf, worn, sev. joints cracked, first edition. Allen 216-1969 1974 $125

ARBLAY, FRANCES BURNEY D'   Diary and Letters 1778-1840. 1904. 6 vols. Austin 61-169 1974 $95

ARBLAY, FRANCES BURNEY D'   Diary and Letters of Madame d'Arblay. London, 1842-46. 7 vols., 8vo., orig. brown cloth, first edition. Dawsons PM 252-101 1974 £45

ARBLAY, FRANCES BURNEY D'   Diary and Letters. 1902. 2 vols., half morocco, slightly scuffed. Allen 216-1970 1974 $25

ARBLAY, FRANCES BURNEY D'   Diary and Letters of Frances Burney. 1902. 2 vols., limited edition. Austin 61-170 1974 $27.50

ARBLAY, FRANCES BURNEY D'   Diary and Letters. 1904-05. 6 vols., plates. Allen 216-1971 1974 $60

ARBLAY, FRANCES BURNEY D'   Evelina. London, 1779. 3 vols., 12mo., contemporary calf, trifle rubbed, third edition, very good copy. Ximenes 36-43 1974 $60

ARBLAY, FRANCES BURNEY D'   Evelina. London, 1821. 8vo., full green morocco, gilt, new edition. Hammond 201-348 1974 £75

ARBLAY, FRANCES BURNEY D'   Evelina. London, 1898. Full page drawings by Arthur Rackham, first edition thus, very nice copy, orig. cloth. Crane 7-273 1974 £15

ARBLAY, FRANCES BURNEY D'   The Wanderer. 1814. 5 vols., small 8vo., contemporary half calf, foxing, first edition. Howes 186-61 1974 £50

ARBLAY, FRANCES BURNEY D'   The Wanderer. London, 1814. 5 vols., 12mo., contemporary half calf, rebacked, first edition. Dawsons PM 252-103 1974

ARBUTHNOT, JOHN   The Miscellaneous Works of.   Glasgow, 1751.
2 vols., 8vo., contemporary calf, first edition.   Dawsons PM 252-19 1974 £50

ARBUTHNOT, JOHN   Tables of Ancient Coins.   London, 1727. 4to.,
contemporary panelled calf gilt. Dawsons PM 247-4 1974 £25

ARCANGELI, G.   Compendio della Flora Italiana.   Turin, 1882.
Crown 8vo., half leather. Wheldon 129-1040 1974 £7.50

ARCHER, JOHN WYKEHAM   Vestiges of Old London.   London, 1851. Folio,
contemporary half roan, fine, first edition. Dawsons PM 251-85 1974 £65

ARCHER, THOMAS   Pictures and Royal Portraits.   London, 1880.
4to., 2 vols., orig. cl., gilt dec., inner hinges cracked. Jacobs 24-38 1974
$25

ARCHER, THOMAS   Pictures and Royal Portraits.   London, 1884.
2 vols., 4to., frontispiece, plates, red half morocco. Bow Windows 62-25
1974 £13.50

ARCHER, THOMAS   William Ewart Gladstone and His Contemporaries.
1883. 4 vols. in 2, contemporary cloth, plates, fine. Covent 55-836 1974
£15.75

ARCHER, WILLIAM   Play Making. Small, 1912. 219p., orig. ed.
Austin 51-26 1973 $6.50

ARCHER, WILLIAM   The Theatrical World for 1893-1897.   London.
5 vols., 8vo., orig. quarter cloth. Bow Windows 62-918 1974 £15

ARCHIBALD, NORMAN   Heaven High--Hell Deep, 1917-18.   New
York, 1935. Biblo & Tannen 213-720 1973 $9.50

ARCHIMEDES   Archimedis Quae Sunt Omnia...   Oxford, 1792.
Large folio, quarter calf, uncut. Gurney 64-7 1974 £40

ARCHIMEDES   Archimedis Quae Supersunt Omnia Cum Eutocii
Ascalonitae Commentarius.   Oxford, 1792. Large folio, quarter calf, cloth
sides, uncut. Gurney 66-10 1974 £40

ARCHIMEDES   Archimedis Syracusani Philosophi ac
Geometrae Excellentissimi Opera.   Basle, 1544. 4 parts in 1 vol., folio,
diagrams, modern half calf, first edition. Gilhofer 61-5 1974 sFr. 8,000

ARCHIMEDES   Archimeds Zwey Bucher Uber Kugel und Cylinder
Ebendesselben Kreismessung. 1798. 8vo., contemporary boards, plates. Dawsons PM 245-32 1974 £16

ARCHIMEDES   De Insidentibus Aquae. 1565. 4to., boards,
first edition. Dawsons PM 245-31 1974 £55

THE ARCHITECTURAL Antiquities and Village Churches of Denbighshire. 1872.
Oblong folio, orig. cloth. Broadhurst 23-1451 1974 £30

ARCHITECTURAL LEAGUE OF NEW YORK   Year Book of . . . ; and,
Catalogue of the Thirty-First Annual Exhibition. (New York), 1916. Illus., orig.
binding. Wilson 63-286 1974 $10

ARCHITECTURE GENERALE.   Amsterdam, 1681. 12mo., contemporary vellum,
new edition. Dawsons PM 251-101 1974 £55

ARCHITECTURE, Modern Cottage and Villa.   London, n.d. Oblong folio, orig.
red cloth gilt, worn, stained. Dawsons PM 251-86 1974 £120

ARCHIVES DE FLORE   Journal Botanique Redige Par F. Schultz.
Wissembourg, 1854-69. Vol. 1, 8vo., half roan, plates, scarce. Wheldon
131-1111 1974 £5

ARCHIVUM Zoologicum.   Budapest, 1909-10. 4to., wrappers, plates. Wheldon
131-409 1974 £5

ARCOS, RENE   Le Bien Commun.   Geneva, 1919. Small 8vo.,
woodcuts, uncut, limited edition. Minters 37-472 1973 $18

ARDMORE, JANE   The Self-Enchanted. McGraw-Hill, 1959.
252p., illus. Austin 51-27 1973 $7.50

ARGUS, ARABELLA   The Adventures of a Donkey.   London, 1823.
16mo., marbled boards (rebacked), engraved presentation leaf and frontis.
Frohnsdorff 16-60 1974 $22.50

ARGUS, ARABELLA   Further Adventures of Jemmy Donkey. 1821.
First edition, engraved plates, 12mo., orig. boards, roan spine, ads at end.
George's 610-26 1973 £6

ARGUS, ARABELLA   Juvenile Spectator. 1810. First edition, half
title, copperplates, 12mo., contemporary tree calf, upper cover almost detached,
ads at end. George's 610-27 1973 £7.50

ARGYLL, GEORGE DOUGLAS CAMPBELL, 8TH DUKE OF, 1823-1900   The
Philosophy of Belief or Law in Christian Theology.   London, 1896. 8vo., library
stamp, presentation, red half morocco, gilt. Bow Windows 62-27 1974 £10.50

ARIAS MONTANO, BENEDICTO   Natvrae Historia. 1601. 4to., contemporary limp vellum, ex-library, rare. Zeitlin 235-8 1974 $325

ARIETTES   Journal d'Ariettes.   Paris, 1780-81. 27 items
in 1 vol., folio, contemporary boards. Quaritch 940-804 1974 £40

ARIOSTO, LODOVICO   Accademia Della Crusca. 1586. Modern
dec. boards. Thomas 28-256 1972 £25

ARIOSTO, LODOVICO   Orlando Furioso.   Venetia, 1556. Modern
panelled blind tooled calf gilt, plates. Smith 193-100 1973 £35

ARIOSTO, LODOVICO   Orlando Furioso.   Birmingham, 1773. 4 vols.,
large 8vo., contemporary tree calf, plates. Dawsons PM 252-20 1974 £100

ARIOSTO, LODOVICO   Orlando Furioso.   Jena, 1805. 5 vols., 8vo.,
marbled orig. boards with labels, uncut. Schumann 499-4 1974 sFr 80

ARIS, ERNEST   Duckling o' the Cosy Corner.   London, n.d.
8vo., 6 color plates. Frohnsdorff 16-61 1974 $7.50

ARISTARCHUS   De Magnitudinibus, et Distantiis Solis, et
Lunae.   Pesaro, 1572. 4to., Spanish Pergamino, first independent edition in
Latin. Schuman 37-7 1974 $210

ARISTOPHANES   Comoediae Novem. 1656. Small folio, 19th
century pigskin, first edition. Thomas 30-1 1973 £650

ARISTOPHANES   Comoediae Novem Cum Commentariis
Antiquis.   Basle, 1547. Folio, late 17th century green morocco, gilt, rare,
very fine. Schafer 8-98 1973 sFr. 1,200

ARISTOPHANES   The Eleven Comedies.   New York, 1928.
2 vols., ltd. to 2000 copies, illus. Jacobs 24-59 1974 $30

ARISTOPHANES   Frogs. 1937. 4to., boxed, wood-engravings.
Allen 213-75 1973 $12.50

ARISTOPHANES   Lysistrata. 114p., n.d., illus. Austin 51-28
1973 $7.50

ARISTOPHANES   Lyristrata. 1926. Illus., one of 300 numbered
copies, signed by translator, bookplate, very good copy, half morocco. Covent
51-667 1973 £50

ARISTOTELES   Aristotelis ad Nicomachum Filium de Moribus.
Paris, 1547. 4to., roan-backed boards. Harper 213-7 1973 $65

ARISTOTELES   Aristotle Compleat Master Piece . . . Displaying
the Secrets of Nature in the Generation of Man . . . to which is added, A
Treasure of Health. (London), 1745. 12mo., contemporary sheep, woodcuts,
twenty-third edition. Gurney 66-11 1974 £25

ARISTOTELES   Contenta, Politicorum Libri Octo.   Paris,
1506. Small folio, 17th century sprinkled calf, gilt panels, rubbed and lacks
label, reasonably sound, woodcut title border. Thomas 32-219 1974 £85

ARISTOTELES   Histoire des Animaux d' Aristote.   Paris,
1783. 2 vols., 4to., contemporary calf, scarce. Wheldon 131-410 1974 £20

ARISTOTELES   Mechanica Graece Emendata, Latine Facta &
Commentariis Illustrata ab Henrico Monantholio.   Paris, 1599. 4to., gilt edges,
gilt back, contemporary vellum, very fine copy, first separate Greek-Latin
edition. Schafer 10-116 1974 sFr 2,200

ARISTOTELES   On Fallacies. 1866. Buckram. Allen 213-
100 1973 $10

ARISTOTELES   Poetica D'Aristotle. Vienna, 1570. 4to.,
orig. vellum, shaky, first edition of this translation, wwodcut device on title page,
very good copy. MacManus 224-12 1974 $150

ARISTOTLES   Poetics. 1775. 8vo., 19th century quarter calf,
fine. Hill 126-10 1974 £30

ARISTOTELES   Politics. 1855. Buckram. Allen 213-97
1973 $10

ARISTOTLES   Problemata Aristotelis. Frankfurt, 1551.
Woodcut. Schuman 37-8 1974 $95

ARISTOTELES   Theory of Conduct. 1906. Allen 213-88
1973 $10

ARISTOTLES   Opera. Venica, 1497. Folio, early 19th
century panelled calf, gilt, fine. Dawsons PM 245-33 1974 £475

ARISTOTLES   Works. 1551-52-53. 6 vols., nineteenth
century olive straight grained morocco gilt, raised bands. Thomas 30-95 1973
£500

ARIZONA: A State Guide. New York, 1941. Illus. Jenkins 61-126 1974
$12.50

ARLAND, MARCEL   Etapes, Avec un Portrait de l'Auteur par
Chagall. Paris, 1927. 8vo., wrapper, limited edition. Minters 37-61 1973
$32

ARLAND, MARCEL   L'Ordre. Paris, 1929. 3 vols., 12mo., orig.
wrapper, inscription, first edition. L. Goldschmidt 42-143 1974 $10

ARLAND, MARCEL   Ou le Coeur se Partage. Paris, 1929.
12mo., orig. wrapper, uncut, revised second edition. L. Goldschmidt 42-144
1974 $12.50

ARLDT, T.   Die Entwicklung der Kontinente und Ihrer
Lebewelt, Ein Beitrag zur Vergleichenden Erdgeschichte. Leipzig, 1907. Roy.
8vo., cloth, maps. Wheldon 131-961 1974 £12

ARLDT, T.   Die Entwicklung der Kontinente und Ihrer
Lebewelt. Leipzig, 1907. Roy. 8vo., cloth, scarce, maps. Wheldon 128-942
1973 £12

ARLEN, MICHAEL   The Acting Version of the Green Hat. New
York, 1925. Hand made paper, signed. Ballinger 1-1 1974 $17.50

ARLEN, MICHAEL   The Ghoul of Golders Green. n.d. Wrappers,
faded covers. Covent 55-77 1974 £7.50

ARLEN, MICHAEL   London Venture. 1919. Dust jacket torn,
browned, first edition. Allen 216-37 1974 $10

ARLISS, GEORGE   Up the Years From Bloomsbury. Little, Brown,
1927. 321p., illus. Austin 51-29 1973 $7.50

ARLISS, GEORGE   Up the Years From Bloomsbury. Blue Ribbon,
1927. 321p. Austin 51-30 1973 $6

ARMER, LAURA ADAMS   Waterless Mountain. New York, 1931.
8vo., cloth; 1st ed., illus. Frohnsdorff 16-62 1974 $17.50

ARMFIELD, MRS. ANNA CONSTANCE (SMEDLEY) Crusaders. 1929. Illus.,
one of 70 copies, signed by author, frontis., nice copy, first edition. Covent
51-2110 1973 £10.50

ARMFIELD, MAXWELL   An Artist in Italy. 1926. Square 8vo., cloth-
backed boards, English first edition. Covent 56-1822 1974 £5.25

ARMITAGE, MERLE   Post Caviar. Longmans, 1939. 210p. Austin
51-31 1973 $8.50

ARMOR, SAMUEL   History of Orange County, California. Los
Angles, 1911. 4to., leather. Saddleback 14-26 1974 $100

ARMOR, SAMUEL   History of Orange County, California. Los
Angeles, 1921. 4to., cloth. Saddleback 14-27 1974 $125

ARMOUR, J.   To the Honourable House of Commons in
Parliament Assembled. (1711). Folio, disbound. Quaritch 939-40 1974 £15

ARMOUR, MARGARET   The Eerie Book. London, 1898. 1st ed.
Biblo & Tannen 210-552 1973 $27.50

ARMOURERS & BRASIERS COMPANY A Short Dexcription of the Ancient
Silver Plate. 1892-1910. 2 vols., 4to., orig. printed boards. Quaritch
939-434 1974 £12.50

ARMROYD, GEORGE   A Connected View of the Whole Internal
Navigation of the United States, Natural and Artificial, Present and Prospective.
Philadelphia, 1826. First edition, maps in excellent condition, recently new
cloth, uncut, excellent copy, rare. Wilson 63-3 1974 $100

ARMSTRONG, EDWARD   The Emperor Charles V. 1910. 2 vols.,
800 pages. Howes 186-702 1974 £7.50

ARMSTRONG, G. H.   The Origin and Meanings of Place-Names in
Canada. Toronto, 1930. First edition. Hood's 102-2 1974 $35

ARMSTRONG, J. M.   The Biographical Encyclopedia of Kentucky.
Cincinnati, 1878. 4to., leather. Saddleback 14-441 1974 $75

ARMSTRONG, JOHN 1709-1779 The Art of Preserving Health. London,
1744. 4to., contemporary calf gilt, first edition. Dawsons PM 252 1974 £75

ARMSTRONG, JOHN 1709-1779 The Art of Preserving Health. Dublin, 1756.
12mo., disbound, wrappers. Schuman 37-9 1974 $35

ARMSTRONG, JOHN 1758-1843 Notices of the War of 1812. New York,
1840. 2 vols., cloth covers bright. Butterfield 10-521 1974 $35

ARMSTRONG, LOUISE V.   We Too Are People. Little, Brown, 1938.
Austin 62-20 1974 $8.50

ARMSTRONG, MOSES K.   Early Empire Builders of the Great West. St.
Paul, 1901. Illus. Jenkins 61-165 1974 $15

ARMSTRONG, R. W.   The Salt of the Earth, a Study in Rural Life and
Social Progress. Ottawa, 1930. Illus. Hood's 102-359 1974 $10

ARMSTRONG, THOMAS ELMER History of the Armstrong Family from 980 to
1939. Pittsburgh, 1939. 8vo., cloth. Saddleback 14-773 1974 $20

ARMSTRONG, WALTER   Gainsborough and His Place in English Art.
1898. Folio, cloth. Quaritch 940-114 1974 £25

ARMSTRONG, WALTER   Turner. 1902. Folio, illus., plates, full
green morocco, gilt, numbered, limited. Quaritch 940-264 1974 £35

ARMY MEMOIRS of Lucius W. Barber. Chicago, 1894. 8vo., cloth. Putman
126-61 1974 $50

THE ARMY Reunion. Chicago, 1869. Green dec. cloth, illus., presentation,
fine, scarce, first edition. Bradley 35-85 1974 $25

ARNALL, WILLIAM   A Letter to the Reverend Dr. Codex. London,
1734. 8vo., modern boards. Dawsons PM 251-161 1974 £12

ARNIM, ACHIM D'   Contes Bizarres. 1933. Roy. 8vo., orig.
wrappers, illus., uncut. Thomas 28-213 1972 £5.50

ARNO, PETER   Sizzling Platter. New York, 1949. 4to.,
1st ed. Biblo & Tannen 214-54 1974 $12.50

ARNOLD, BENJAMIN F.   History of Whittier. Whittier, 1933. 12mo.,
cloth. Saddleback 14-29 1974 $25

ARNOLD, CHANNING   The American Egypt. 1909. Map, plans, illus.,
covers marked. Bow Windows 66-18 1974 £6.50

ARNOLD, CHARLES HENRY   The New and Impartial Universal History of
North and South America, and of the Present Trans-Atlantic War. London,
(1781). Contemporary leather, mended neatly, no foxing, ads at end. Hood's
102-548 1974 $175

ARNOLD, E. C.   British Waders. Cambridge, 1924. 4to., cloth, plates, scarce. Wheldon 130-435 1974 £15

ARNOLD, EDWIN   The Light of Asia. Boston, 1892. Biblo & Tannen 213-909 1973 $5

ARNOLD, ELLIOTT   Deep In My Heart. 1949. Austin 62-21 1974 $10

ARNOLD, FRIEDRICH   Icones Nervorum Capitis. Heidelberg, 1860. Folio, orig. boards, plates, second edition. Dawsons PM 249-16 1974 £52

ARTHUR, J. C.   The Plant Rusts. New York, 1929. 8vo., cloth, scarce. Wheldon 129-1142 1974 £7.50

ARNOLD, MATTHEW   Alaric at Rome. 1893. Orig. cloth, rubbed, parchment boards, first edition. Rota 188-45 1974 £25

ARNOLD, MATTHEW   Culture and Anarchy. New York, 1883. 3/4 lea., rubbed. Biblo & Tannen 210-826 1973 $12.50

ARNOLD, MATTHEW   Empedocles on Etna. 1852. First edition, with half title and ad. leaf at end, 8vo., green levant morocco gilt, top edges gilt, fine copy, rare. Sawyer 293-23 1974 £110

ARNOLD, MATTHEW   Essays in Criticism. London & Cambridge, 1865. 8vo., orig. red brown cloth, portrait, first edition. Ximenes 37-6 1974 $45

ARNOLD, MATTHEW   Essays in Criticism. 1924-10. 3 vols. Allen 216-41 1974 $12.50

ARNOLD, MATHEW   Friendship's Garland: Being the Coversations, Letters and Opinions of the late Baron von Thunder-Ten-Tronckh. 1871. First edition, crown 8vo., very fine copy, orig. cloth. Broadhurst 24-519 1974 £10

ARNOLD, MATTHEW   Higher Schools and Universities in Germany. London, 1882. 8vo., orig. dark blue cloth, fine copy. Ximenes 37-7 1974 $20

ARNOLD, MATTHEW   Literature and Dogma. London, 1873. 1st ed., good copy. Jacobs 24-60 1974 $35

ARNOLD, MATTHEW   Literature and Dogma. New York, 1883. 3/4 lea., rubbed. Biblo & Tannen 210-827 1973 $12.50

ARNOLD, MATTHEW   Literature & Dogma. 1883. Popular edition, G. K. Chesterton's copy with an unpublished 16 line holograph poem & numerous pencil sketches by him, covers worn, sewing weak, bookplate. Covent 51-2252 1973 £75

ARNOLD, MATTHEW   Merope. 1858. 8vo., orig. cloth, book plate, first edition. Bow Windows 64-375 1974 £25

ARNOLD, MATTHEW   Mixed Essays. London, 1879. 8vo., orig. cloth, inscribed, presentation, first edition. Dawsons PM 252-22 1974 £45

ARNOLD, MATTHEW   New Poems. London, 1867. 8vo., green cloth, fine, first edition. Rich Summer-14 1974 $15

ARNOLD, MATTHEW   On the Study of Celtic Literature. London, 1867. Orig. chocolate brown cloth, bookplate, W. P. Ker's copy, very good copy, first edition. Covent 51-2111 1973 £15.75

ARNOLD, MATTHEW   On the Study of Celtic Literature. London, 1867. 8vo., contemporary calf, first edition. Dawsons PM 252-23 1974 £12

ARNOLD, MATTHEW   On the Study of Celtic Literature. London, 1867. 8vo., orig. brown cloth, fine copy, first edition. Ximenes 37-8 1974 $35

ARNOLD, MATTHEW   On the Study of Celtic Literature and on Translating Homer. New York, 1898. Biblo & Tannen 210-828 1973 $6

ARNOLD, MATTHEW   Poems. London, 1853. 8vo., green cloth, scarce, new edition. Rich Summer-13 1974 $27.50

ARNOLD, MATTHEW   Poems. 1881. 8vo., 2 vols., cloth. Quaritch 936-273 1974 £50

ARNOLD, MATHEW   Poems of Wordsworth. 1879. Full green vellum, fine. Covent 55-78 1974 £55

ARNOLD, MATTHEW   St. Paul and Protestantism. London, 1870. 8vo., orig. brown cloth, very good copy, first edition. Ximenes 37-9 1974 $30

ARNOLD, MATTHEW   Selected Poems. 1885. 8vo., full vellum, gilt. Broadhurst 23-885 1974 £10

ARNOLD, MATTHEW   The Strayed Reveller, and Other Poems. London, 1849. 8vo., orig. green cloth, first edition, very good copy. Ximenes 36-6 1974 $200

ARNOLD, MATTHEW   Works. 1903. 15 vols., med. 8vo., orig. blue silk cloth, tooled gilt, spines faded, edition de Luxe, limited to 750 sets. Broadhurst 24-1706 1974 £125

ARNOLD, MATTHEW   The Works Of. 1903-04. 15 vols., portrait, frontispiece, some foxing, mostly unopened set, gilt backs faded, limited, edition de luxe. Bow Windows 66-19 1974 £164

ARNOLD, RICHARD   Chronicle of London. (Southwark, 1521). Small folio, 18th century calf, rare, rebacked, second edition. Dawsons PM 252-24 1974 £1150

ARNOLD, THOMAS   History of Rome. London, 1838-43. 8vo., bound calf, morocco labels, first and second editions. Dawsons PM 251-163 1974 £15

ARNOLD, THOMAS W.   The Preaching of Islam. 1913. Revised & enlarged second edition. Howes 186-1779 1974 £6.50

ARNOLD, WILLIAM HARRIS   Books and Letters Collected by . . . Auction Catalogue, May 7 and 8, 1901, by Banks and Co. New York, 1901. Three quarter morocco, illus. Kraus B8-2 1974 $12.50

ARNOLD, WILLIAM HARRIS   Catalogue of the . . . Collection of Manuscripts, Books and Autograph Letters. New York, 1924. Large paper copy, portraits, facsimiles, wrappers. Kraus B8-3 1974 $15

ARNOLD-FORSTER, FRANCES   Studies in Church Dedications. 1899. 3 vols., large 8vo., orig. buckram, faded. Howes 185-925 1974 £10.50

ARNOLDUS DE VILLA NOVA   Incipit Tractatus de Virtutibus Herbarum. 1520. Small 4to., woodcut illus., stain, vellum bound. Bow Windows 62-30 1974 £450

ARNOTT, NEIL   On the Smokeless Fire-Place, Chimney-Valves, and Other Means, Old and New, of Obtaining Healthful Warmth and Ventilation. 1855. First edition, demy 8vo., good copy, scarce, orig. cloth, text illus. Broadhurst 24-1189 1974 £36

ARNOTT, NEIL   On Warming and Ventilating. 1838. 8vo., woodcuts, orig. limp cloth, good copy. Quaritch 940-493 1974 £48

ARNOTT, NEIL   On Warming and Ventilating. London, 1838. 8vo., cloth, first edition. Hammond 201-784 1974 £16.50

ARONSON, RUDOLPH   Theatrical and Musical Memoirs. McBride, 1913. 283p., illus. Austin 51-32 1973 $10

ARQUITECTURA Colonial de Salta. Buenos Aires, 1926. Drawings, 4to., illus., fine. Current BW9-454 1974 $18

ARRHENIUS, SVANTE   Conferences sur Quelques. Paris, 1912. 8vo., orig. wrappers. Gurney 64-10 1974 £15

ARRILLAGA, BASILIO JOSE   Cuartas Observaciones Sobre el Opusculo Intitulado el Imperio y el Clero Mexicano del Senor Abate Testory. San Luis, 1866. Pict. wrapper. Jenkins 61-169 1974 $45

ARRILLAGA, BASILIO JOSE   Recopilacion de Leyes, Decretos, Bandos . . . 1828-40. Mexico, 1834-52. 13 vols., Thomas Streeter's set, pencilled notations in his hand. Jenkins 61-170 1974 $1,875

ARRILLAGA, BASILIO JOSE   Recopilacion de Leyes, Decretos, Bandos. Mexico, 1834-42. 13 vols., quarto. Jenkins 48-490 1973 $1,875

ART D'AIMER, L.   Chez les Anciens. Paris, 1929. Roy. 8vo.,
half blue morocco. Howes 186-1780 1974 £5

L'ART de Peindre et d'Imprimer les Toiles en Grand et en Petit Teint. Paris,
1800. 8vo., contemporary quarter calf, rare. Gurney 66-13 1974 £35

ART DE VERIFIER LES DATES   L'Art de Verifier les Dates des Faits Historiques,
des Chartes, des Chroniques et Autres Anciens Monumens Depuis la Naissance de
Notre Seigneur. Paris, 1783-87. 3 vols., folio, old calf, rubbed, rebacked.
Quaritch 940-289 1974 £50

ART In the Nursery. Boston, 1879. Oblong 16mo., cloth spine, illus. Frohnsdorff
16-63 1974 $7.50

THE ART Journal Illustrated Catalogue to the Great Exhibition. 1851. Illus.,
half contemporary hard grained morocco, gilt, rubbed. Smith 193-85 1973 £20

THE ART of Preserving the Feet. London, 1818. Contemporary calf, rubbed,
worn corners. Rittenhouse 46-692 1974 $150

ART Treasures in the U.S.S.R. Moscow, 1938. Mounted color plates; in cloth
portfolio, spine torn. Biblo & Tannen 214-38 1974 $12.50

ART Work on Hamilton, Canada and Its Environs. Toronto, 1899. 12 parts
bound together, cloth, mottled endpapers, photo plates. Hood's 102-145 1974
$250

ART Work on Toronto, Canada. Toronto, 1898. 12 parts bound together, full
leather, gilt tooling, mottled endpapers, photo plates. Hood's 102-146 1974
$300

ARTALOITIA, JULIAN   Fundicion Tipografica. Sevilla, 1863-65.
2 parts in 1 vol., illus., folding plates, 8vo., orig. boards, cloth back, light
damp stain. Kraus B8-285 1974 $150

ARTAUD DE MONTOR, ALEXIS F.   The Lives and Times of the Popes. New
York, 1911. 10 vols., large 8vo., illus., orig. cloth. Howes 185-926 1974
£15

ARTEDI, PETER   Ichthyologia. Leyden, 1738. 8vo., vellum.
Wheldon 129-1700 1974 £135

ARTEDI, PETER   Ichthyologia. Leyden, 1738. 5 parts in 1
vol., 8vo., vellum, very rare orig. edition. Wheldon 131-730 1974 £135

ARTHUR, GEORGE   Life of Lord Kitchener. 1920. 3 vols., orig.
cloth, plates. Howes 186-973 1974 £7.50

ARTHUR, TIMOTHY SHAY   Friends and Neighbours. Peck, Bliss, 1858.
Austin 54-46 1973 $12.50

ARTHUR, TIMOTHY SHAY   The Strike at Tivoli Mills; and Waht Came of
It. Philadelphia, 1879. 16mo., orig. cloth, fine, first edition. MacManus
224-15 1974 $50

ARTHUR, TIMOTHY SHAY   Ten Nights in a Bar-Room, and What I Saw
There. Philadelphia, 1854. Orig. cloth, frontis., first edition, variant imprint,
bright copy. MacManus 224-16 1974 $40

ARTHUR, TIMOTHY SHAY   Ten Nights in a Bar Room-And What I Saw There.
Winston. Austin 54-47 1973 $6.50

ARTHUR, TIMOTHY SHAY   The True Path. Philadelphia, 1866. 300p.
Austin 54-48 1973 $12.50

ARTHUR, TIMOTHY SHAY   Woman to the Rescue. Philadelphia, (1874).
Cloth. Hayman 57-169 1974 $10

ARTICLES of Impeachment Against M. E. Trapp, Lt. Governor, Oklahoma. N.P.,
1919. Wrapper. Jenkins 61-2018 1974 $10

ARTICLES of Incorporation, Constitution, By-Laws, Officers and Members of the
Cuyamaca Club, San Diego, California. (San Diego), 1907. 16mo., cloth.
Saddleback 14-260 1974 $10

ARTISTS On Art. New York, 1945. Illus. Biblo & Tannen 210-211 1973 $7

ARTS & Crafts. 1905-1906. Plates, green cloth, bindings. Marsden 37-13
1974 £30

ARTSCHWAGER E.   Dictionary of Biological Equivalents. 1930.
8vo., cloth. Wheldon 129-64 1974 £7.50

ARTURO Onofri (1885-1928). Florence, 1930. 16mo., wrappers. Minters
37-199 1973 $18

ARVIN, NEWTON   American Pantheon. Delacorte, 1966. 251p.
Austin 54-45 1973 $6

ARTIS, E. T.   Antediluvian Phytology. 1925. 4to., orig.
boards, rebacked in calf, uncuts, lithographed plates, rare orig. edition.
Wheldon 128-943 1973 £20

ARTIS, E. T.   The Durobrivae of Antoninus. 1828. Roy.
folio, half morocco, plates, worn. Quaritch 939-500 1974 £70

ARTIS, E. T.   The Durobrivae of Antoninus. 1828. Folio,
plates, half morocco, rubbed. Quaritch 939-501 1974 £60

ASBJORNSEN, PETER CHRISTEN   Folk and Fairy Tales. New York, 1883.
8vo., profuse engravings; rebound. Frohnsdorff 16-64 1974 $25

ASBURY, HERBERT   The French Quarter. New York - London, 1936.
8vo., orig. bindings, first edition. Butterfield 8-393 1974 $15

ASCH, SHOLEM   Three Novels. 1938. 3 vols. in 1. Austin
57-51 1974 $17.50

ASCHAM, ROGER   The Scholemaster. London, 1573. 4to.,
full dark blue levant morocco, gilt, woodcut, third edition. Dawsons PM
250-2 1974 £800

ASCHERSON, P.   Flora des Nordostdeutschen. Berlin, 1898-99.
Crown 8vo., cloth, leather back. Wheldon 129-1042 1974 £5

ASCHOFF, L.   Hundert Jahre Zellforschung. Berlin, 1938.
8vo., cloth. Wheldon 129-122 1974 £5

ASH, J. E.   Atlas of Otolaryngic Pathology. Omaha, 1942.
Revised third edition. Rittenhouse 46-694 1974 $10

ASHBEE, E. W.   Occasional Fac-Simile Reprints. n.d. Crown
4to., morocco, scarce, signed, limited edition. Broadhurst 23-235 1974 £45

ASHBEE, E. W.   Occasional Fac-Simile Reprints of Rare and
Curious Tracts of the 16th and 17th Centuries. n.d. (c. 1880). 2 vols. in 1,
crown 4to., morocco, binding little rubbed, scarce, woodcut illus., limited to
100 copies, fine. Broadhurst 24-232 1974 £45

ASHBEE, HENRY SPENCER   An Iconography of Don Quixote. 1895. 8vo.,
half morocco, uncut, plates. Broadhurst 23-236 1974 £40

ASHDOWN, CHARLES HENRY   Arms & Armour. n.d. Engravings, plates.
Allen 213-1252 1973 $15

ASHDOWN, CHARLES HENRY   British and Foreign Arms and Armour. 1909.
8vo., orig. cloth. Bow Windows 64-306 1974 £10.50

ASHE, THOMAS   History of the Azores, or Western Islands.
1813. 4to., frontispiece, engraved plates, engraved maps, quarter calf, corners
of boards worn. Bow Windows 66-21 1974 £65

ASHE, THOMAS   History of the Azores, or Western Islands.
London, 1813. 4to., contemporary half calf, plates. Traylen 79-414 1973 £36

ASHE, THOMAS   The Spirit of "The Book", or, Memoirs of
Caroline Princess of Hasburgh. London, 1811. 3 vols., 12mo., orig. grey
boards, printed paper labels, first edition, fine. Ximenes 36-7 1974 $90

ASHFORD, DAISY   The Young Visiters. London, 1919. 8vo.,
orig. boards, presentation inscription, portrait, rubbed, first edition. Bow
Windows 62-38 1974 £18.50

ASHMOLE, ELIAS   The Antiquities of Berkshire. 1719. 3 vols.,
small 8vo., half calf. Quaritch 939-297 1974 £45

ASHMOLE, ELIAS   The Antiquities of Berkshire. 1723. 3 vols.,
small 8vo., old panelled calf, gilt. Quaritch 939-298 1974 £50

ASHTON, DORE   Pol Bury. Paris, 1970. Sq. 4to., color plates., artist's sgd. pres. Biblo & Tannen 214-470 1974 $42.50

ASHTON, JOHN   Chapbooks of the 18th Century. 1882. New buckram. Allen 216-1973 1974 $10

ASHTON, JOHN   A History of English Lotteries. London, 1893. Illus. Rinsland 58-99 1974 $20

ASHTON, JOHN 1834-   Curious Creatures in Zoology. 1890. Roy. 8vo., illus., orig. calf backed cloth boards, limited edition. Smith 193-731 1973 £6.50

ASHTON, LEIGH   An Introduction to the Study of Chinese Sculpture. 1924. 4to., map, plates, orig. pigskin, gilt, uncut. Quaritch 940-368 1974 £36

ASHTON, LEIGH   Samplers. 1926. Crown 4to., orig. cloth, fine, plates in colour & monochrome. Broadhurst 24-6 1974 £8

ASKEW, JOHN   A Voyage to Australia and New Zealand. 1857. 8vo., orig. grey cloth boards, first edition. Bow Windows 64-376 1974 £125

ASKINSON, G. W.   Die Parfumerie-Fabrikation. Vienna, 1895. Figures, light foxing, spine faded. Bow Windows 66-22 1974 £6.50

ASPECTS of Ethical Religion. 1926. Austin 62-151 1974 $15

ASPECTS of Jewish Power in the United States. 1922. 246 pages. Austin 57-170 1974 $12.50

ASPIN, J.   Cosmorama. 1834. New edition, hand coloured plates, engravings, small square 8vo., yellow buckram, good clean copy, Pub. catalogue at end. George's 610-30 1973 £12.50

ASQUITH, CYNTHIA   This Mortal Coil. Sauk City, 1947. 1st ed., ltd. Biblo & Tannen 210-557 1973 $32.50

ASQUITH, CYRIL   Versions from 'A Shropshire Lad'. Oxford, 1929. Fine, slightly dusty wrappers. Covent 51-2371 1973 £6.50

ASQUITH, MARGOT   Margot Asquith, an Autobiography. New York, 1920. 2 vols., fine. Ballinger 1-234 1974 $10

ASSHETON, R.   Studies in the Development of the Rabbit and the Frog. 1895. 8vo., half cloth, plates. Wheldon 130-334 1974 £5

ASSIGNY, MARIUS D'   History of Earls & Earldom of Flanders, to Death of King Charles II of Spain. 1734. Second edition. Allen 213-1254 1973 $10

ASSISI, FRANCIS OF
Please turn to
FRANCESCO D'ASSISI, SAINT

ASSOCIATION FOR PROMOTING THE DISCOVERY OF THE INTERIOR PARTS OF AFRICA. Proceedings. London, 1790. Large 4to., orig. boards, uncut, later cloth spine. Traylen 79-446 1973 £98

ASSOCIATED VETERANS OF THE MEXICAN WAR   History of the Celebration of the Fiftieth Anniversary of the Taking Possession of California. Oakland, 1896. 8vo., wrappers. Saddleback 14-30 1974 $20

ASTAIRE, FRED   Steps In Time. Harper, 1959. 338p., illus. Austin 51-33 1973 $7.50

ASTELL, MARY   An Essay in Defence of the Female Sex. London, 1696. 8vo., contemporary speckled calf, fine, first edition. Dawsons PM 252-25 1974 £175

ASTELL, MARY   A Further Essay Relating to the Female Sex. London, 1696. 8vo., contemporary sheep, first edition. Dawsons PM 252-26 1974 £150

ASTELL, MARY   A Serious Proposal to the Ladies. London, 1694. 12mo., contemporary calf, rare, first edition. Dawsons PM 252-27 1974 £580

ASTLE, THOMAS   The Origin and Progress of Writing. London, 1784. 4to., boards, plates. Kraus B8-286 1974 $85

ASTLE, THOMAS   The Origin and Progress of Writing. London, 1784. Full calf, plates, frontispiece. Dawson's 424-350 1974 $75

ASTLEY, CONSTANCE   Catalogue of the Library of Constance Astley. (1938). Folio, half vellum, fine. Quaritch 939-385 1974 £25

ASTON, J.   Curious Creatures in Zoology. 1890. Roy 8vo., orig. half calf, uncut, illus. Wheldon 129-123 1974 £10

ASTOR, MARY   My Story. Doubleday, 1959. 332p. Austin 51-32 1973 $6.50

ASTORIA and Clatsop County, Oregon. Astoria, 1911. 12mo., wrapper. Saddleback 14-644 1974 $10

ASTOUNDING Science Fiction. 1953-1958. 8vo. Biblo & Tannen 210-1023 1973 $150

AT The Fireside: One Hundred Original Stories for Young People. Chicago and Phila., 1891. 4to., 12 color plates, cloth spine. Frohnsdorff 16-65 1974 $7.50

ATHEARN, WALTER SCOTT   Religious Education and American Democracy. Pilgrim, 1917. Austin 62-22 1974 $10

ATHENAEUS   Deipnosophistae. 1858-67. 4 vols. Allen 213-1056 1973 $25

ATHENAGORAS   Della Risurettione de Morti. 1556. Small 4to., old vellum, morocco labels. Thomas 30-105 1973 £40

ATHERSTONE, E.   A Midsummer Day's Dream. 1824. 8vo., orig. boards, illus. Bow Windows 64-378 1974 £5

ATHERTON, CHARLES   The Capability of Steamships. Woolwich, 1854. Tall 8vo., cloth, gilt, second edition. Putman 126-48 1974 $12

ATHERTON, GERTRUDE   Adventures of a Novelist. Liveright, 1932. 598p. Austin 54-49 1973 $8.50

ATHERTON, GERTRUDE   American Wives and English Husbands. New York, 1898. Cloth, first edition. Dawson's 424-245 1974 $12.50

ATHERTON, GERTRUDE   American Wives and English Husbands. Int'l Assoc. of Newspapers and Authors, 1901. 339p. Austin 54-51 1973 $6.50

ATHERTON, GERTRUDE   American Wives and English Husbands. Dodd, Mead, 1909. 339p. Austin 54-50 1973 $7.50

ATHERTON, GERTRUDE   Ancestors. Harper, 1907. 709p. Austin 54-52 1973 $7.50

ATHERTON, GERTRUDE   Ancestors. New York, 1907. Gilt, cloth, first edition. Dawson's 424-246 1974 $10

ATHERTON, GERTRUDE   The Aristocrats. Lane, 1902. 308p., orig. ed. Austin 54-53 1973 $6

ATHERTON, GERTRUDE   The Avalanche. Stokes, 1919. 229p. Austin 54-54 1973 $6.50

ATHERTON, GERTRUDE   Black Oxen. Burt, 1923. 346p. Austin 51-35 1973 $7.50

ATHERTON, GERTRUDE   Black Oxen. New York, 1923. Orig. cloth, first edition, one of 250 numbered copies, signed by author, fine, dust jacket. MacManus 224-17 1974 $30

ATHERTON, GERTRUDE   The Californians. Lane, 1898. 351p., orig. ed. Austin 54-55 1973 $6

ATHERTON, GERTRUDE   Golden Gate Country. Duell, Sloan, Pearce, 1945. 256p. Austin 54-56 1973 $8.50

ATHERTON, GERTRUDE   The Gorgeous Isle. New York, 1908. Orig. pictorial cloth, plates, first American edition. Covent 55-133 1974 £8.50

ATHERTON, GERTRUDE   The Gorgeous Isle. New York, 1908. Cloth, gilt, illus., first edition. Dawson's 424-247 1974 $12.50

ATHERTON, GERTRUDE   The House of Lee. Appleton, 1940. 302p. Austin 54-57 1973 $6

ATHERTON, GERTRUDE   The Immortal Marriage. Boni, Liveright, 1927. 466p. Austin 54-58 1973 $5

ATHERTON, GERTRUDE   Julia France--and her times. Macmillan. 533p. Austin 54-59 1973 $6

ATHERTON, GERTRUDE   Mrs. Balfame. Stokes, 1916. 335p. Austin 54-60 1973 $6

ATHERTON, GERTRUDE   Patience Sparhawk and Her Times. Lane, 1900. 488p. Austin 54-61 1973 $7.50

ATHERTON, GERTRUDE   Perch of the Devil. Stokes, 1914. 373p. Austin 54-62 1973 $6

ATHERTON, GERTRUDE   Rulers of Kings. Harper, 1904. 413p. Austin 54-63 1973 $6

ATHERTON, GERTRUDE   Senator North. Lane, 1900. 367p., orig. ed. Austin 54-64 1973 $6

ATHERTON, GERTRUDE   Sleeping Fires. Stokes, 1922. 299p. Austin 54-65 1973 $6

ATHERTON, GERTRUDE   Tower of Ivory. Macmillan, 1910. 466p. Austin 54-66 1973 $7.50

ATHERTON, GERTRUDE   The Travelling Thirds. Harper, 1905. 294p. Austin 54-67 1973 $8.50

ATHERTON, GERTRUDE   The White Morning. Stokes, 1918. 195p. Austin 54-68 1973 $5

ATHERTON, GERTRUDE   The White Morning. McCleland, Goodchild, Stewart, 1918. 195p. Austin 54-69 1973 $8.50

ATKEY, BERTRAM   Easy Money. 1908. 8vo., orig. cloth, first edition. Rota 190-173 1974 £10

ATKINSON, BROOKS   Broadway Scrapbook. Theatre Arts, 1947. 312p., illus. Austin 51-36 1973 $7.50

ATKINSON, C. T.   A History of Germany. 1908. Thick 8vo., maps, scarce. Howes 186-579 1974 $7.50

ATKINSON, G. F.   Studies of American Fungi. Ithaca, 1900. 8vo., orig. cloth, plates, scarce. Wheldon 128-1332 1973 £10

ATKINSON, G. F.   Studies of American Fungi. Ithaca, 1901. 8vo., cloth, second edition. Wheldon 129-1143 1974 £10

ATKINSON, JOHN   A Compendium of British Ornithology. (182-). 8vo., new cloth. Wheldon 129-414 1974 £7.50

ATKINSON, JOHN   A Compendium of the Ornithology of Great Britain. 1820. Spotting, old boards, new cloth spine, uncut. Bow Windows 64-11 1974 £12.50

ATKINSON, JOHN   A Compendium of the Ornithology of Great Britain With a Reference to the Anatomy and Physiology of Birds. 1820. 8vo., new cloth. Wheldon 128-370 1973 £7.50

ATKINSON, JOHN   A Compendium of the Ornithology of Great Britain. 1820. 8vo., new cloth. Wheldon 130-436 1974 £7.50

ATKYNS, ROBERT   The Ancient and Present State of Glostershire. London, 1768. Thick folio, contemporary panelled calf, plates, second & best edition. Traylen 79-329 1973 £120

THE ATLAS of Nature. London, 1823. Folio, plates, excellent condition. Smith 193-732 1973 £20

ATTERBURY, FRANCIS   An Account and Defence of the Protestation made by the Lower-House of Convocation. 1707. Small 4to., cloth, uncut, first edition. Quaritch 936-10 1974 £15

ATWOOD, GEORGE   An Analysis of a Course of Lectures on the Principles of Natural Philosophy. London, 1784. 8vo., first edition. Dawsons PM 245-35 1974 £25

ATWOOD, WILLIAM   Jani Anglorum Facies Nova. London, 1680. 8vo., contemporary calf, first edition. Dawsons PM 251-2 1974 £20

AUBE, BENJAMIN   Histoire des Persecutions de l'Eglise jusqu'a la fin des Antonins. Paris, 1875-78. 2 vols., crown 8vo., contemporary half calf. Howes 186-580 1974 £5

AUBERY DU MAURIER, LOUIS   The Lives of the Princes of Orange. 1693. Contemporary calf, rebacked, stains, sole English edition. Howes 186-581 1974 £25

AUBREY, JOHN   The Natural History and Antiquities of the County of Surrey. London, 1719. 5 vols., 8vo., contemporary calf, leather labels, plates, rare. Traylen 79-389 1973 £160

AUBREY, JOHN   The Natural History and Antiquities of the County of Surrey. 1723. 5 vols., small 8vo., old calf, plates. Quaritch 939-559 1974 £110

AUBREY, W. H. S.   The Rise and Growth of the English Nation. 1896. 3 vols., some pencilled notes and underlining, end papers foxed. Bow Windows 66-23 1974 £8.50

AUCASSIN ET NICOLETTE   Of Aucassin and Nicolette. 1925. 8vo., orig. boards, fine, limited edition. Quaritch 936-420 1974 £10

AUDEBERT, J. B.   Histoire Naturelle des Singes et des Makis. Paris, (1799-1800). Roy. folio, contemporary calf, gilt, coloured plates, very rare. Wheldon 128-301 1973 £750

AUDEBERT, J. B.   Histoire Naturelle des Singes et des Makis. Paris, (1799-1800). Roy. folio, contemporary calf, rubbed, plates, very rare. Wheldon 131-8 1974 £1,000

AUDEN, WYSTAN HUGH   Another Time. 1940. Dust wrapper, fine, English first edition. Covent 56-1525 1974 £15

AUDEN, WYSTAN HUGH   Another Time. (1940). 8vo., cloth, frayed dust wrappers, first English edition. Quaritch 936-275 1974 £7

AUDEN, WYSTAN HUGH   The Ascent of F6. 1936. First edition, demy 8vo., fine, d.w., uncut. Broadhurst 24-527 1974 £15

AUDEN, WYSTAN HUGH   The Ascent of F. 6. London, 1936. Lacking d.w., owner's name in pencil, covers lightly worn, very nice copy, orig. binding. Ross 86-36 1974 $30

AUDEN, WYSTAN HUGH   The Dance of Death. 8vo., boards, dust wrappers, worn, first edition. Quaritch 936-276 1974 £15

AUDEN, WYSTAN HUGH   The Dog Beneath the Skin. 1935. First edition, demy 8vo., orig. cloth, fine, loosely inserted ad for first production of this play. Broadhurst 24-526 1974 £16

AUDEN, WYSTAN HUGH   The Dog Beneath the Skin. London, 1935. First edition, name in ink on fly, fine, orig. binding. Ross 86-39 1974 $40

AUDEN, WYSTAN HUGH   The Dog Beneath the Skin. London, 1935. Orig. binding, first edition, name in ink on fly leaf, fine. Ross 87-37 1974 $35

AUDEN, WYSTAN HUGH   For the Time Being. (1945). Signature on fly, first English edition. Bow Windows 66-25 1974 £15

AUDEN, WYSTAN HUGH   For the Time Being. 1945. Orig. cloth, first English edition. Rota 188-47 1974 £7.50

AUDEN, WYSTAN HUGH   A Handbook to York and District. 1906. Illus., maps. Covent 55-143 1974 £25

AUDEN, WYSTAN HUGH   Journey to a War. 1939. Frontispiece, cloth, plates. Covent 55-139 1974 £10

AUDEN, WYSTAN HUGH   Journey to a War. New York, 1939. Orig. buckram, frontispiece, plates. Smith 194-382 1974 £8.50

AUDEN, WYSTAN HUGH   Letters from Iceland. 1937. First edition, illus., very good copy. Covent 51-149 1973 £8.50

AUDEN, WYSTAN HUGH   Letters from Iceland. 1937. Plates, folding map, fine, d.w., first edition. Covent 51-2140 1973 £10

AUDEN, WYSTAN HUGH   Letters from Iceland. 1937. Illus., faded covers. Covent 55-141 1974 £7.50

AUDEN, WYSTAN HUGH   Letters from Iceland. 1937. 8vo., cloth, dust wrapper, plates, first edition. Quaritch 936-279 1974 £12

AUDEN, WYSTAN HUGH   Letters from Iceland. 1937. Orig. cloth, illus., first edition. Rota 188-49 1974 £8

AUDEN, WYSTAN HUGH   Letters from Iceland. 1937. Orig. buckram, plates, diagram. Smith 193-311 1973 £9

AUDEN, WYSTAN HUGH   Letters from Iceland. New York, 1937. First American edition, d.w. stained & chipped, not a collector's copy, orig. binding. Ross 86-41 1974 $12

AUDEN, WYSTAN HUGH   Letters from Iceland. New York, 1937. Orig. cloth, label, first American edition. Rota 188-50 1974 £7

AUDEN, WYSTAN HUGH   Letters from Iceland. New York, 1937. Orig. binding, first American edition, dust wrapper dust-stained & chipped, not a collector's copy. Ross 87-38 1974 $12.50

AUDEN, WYSTAN HUGH   Letters from Iceland. New York, 1937. First U. S. edition, illus., author's presentation inscription, very good copy. Covent 51-2136 1973 £20

AUDEN, WYSTAN HUGH   Maupassant Stories. 1927. Signature, English first edition. Covent 56-74 1974 £25

AUDEN, WYSTAN HUGH   On the Frontier. 1938. First edition. Covent 55-140 1974 £10

AUDEN, WYSTAN HUGH   On the Frontier. Random House, 1938. 120p., lst ed. Austin 51-37 1973 $17.50

AUDEN, WYSTAN HUGH   On the Frontier. 1938. First edition, demy 8vo., mint, d.w., uncut, unopened, orig. cloth. Broadhurst 24-528 1974 £20

AUDEN, WYSTAN HUGH   On This Island. New York, 1937. First U. S. edition, signed by author, nice copy. Covent 51-2137 1973 £21

AUDEN, WYSTAN HUGH   The Orators. 1932. Fine, signature, dust wrapper. Covent 55-136 1974 £60

AUDEN, WYSTAN HUGH   The Orators. (1932). 8vo., cloth, dust wrapper, worn, first edition. Quaritch 936-277 1974 £8

AUDEN, WYSTAN HUGH   The Orators: An English Study. 1932. Very good copy, first edition, George Barker's copy with his signature and a holograph poem in his hand. Covent 51-2138 1973 £50

AUDEN, WYSTAN HUGH   Three Poems. 1932. Covers faded, English first edition. Covent 56-1528 1974 £12.50

AUDEN, WYSTAN HUGH   Poems. London, 1930. Orig. blue paper wrappers, fine, first edition. Ross 87-39 1974 $250

AUDEN, WYSTAN HUGH   The Collected Poetry. New York, 1945. First U.S. edition. Covent 56-1526 1974 £6.30

AUDIGUIER, VITAL D'   A Tragi-Comicall History of Ovr Times, Vnder the Borrowed Names of Lisander, and Calista. 1627. Title defective towards edges, one blank corner cut away, small folio, old calf, rebacked. Thomas 32-157 1974 £50

AUDIGUIER, VITAL D'   A Tragi-Comicall History of Our Times, Vinder the Borrowed Names of Lisander, and Calista. 1627. Small folio, old calf, rebacked. Thomas 28-214 1972 £50

AUDOUIN, J. V.   Recherches Pour Servir a l'Histoire Naturelle du Littoral de la France. Paris, 1834. 8vo., orig. boards, plates, rare. Wheldon 131-915 1974 £15

AUDOUIT, M. E.   L'Herbier des Demoiselles. Paris, 1847. Half calf, colored figures. Gregory 44-1 1974 $18.50

AUDRAN, GIRARD   Les Proportions du Corps Humain. Paris, 1683. Folio, contemporary calf, gilt, plates, first edition. Dawsons PM 249-17 1974 £185

AUDSLEY, GEORGE ASHDOWN   Keramic Art of Japan. 1881. Roy. 8vo., orig. dec. cloth, gilt, plates, English first edition. Covent 56-40 1974 £25

AUDSLEY, GEORGE ASHDOWN   Keramic Art of Japan. 1881. Roy. 8vo., plates, illus., orig. dec. cloth gilt. Quaritch 940-369 1974 £26

AUDUBON, JOHN JAMES   The Birds of America. 1937. Roy 4to., orig. buckram, plates. Wheldon 129-415 1974 £30

AUDUBON, JOHN JAMES   The Birds of America. London, 1937. 4to., orig. buckram, gilt, plates. Hammond 201-628 1974 £22.50

AUDUBON, JOHN JAMES   The Birds of America. New York, 1937. Plates, first trade edition. Ballinger 1-235 1974 $40

AUDUBON, JOHN JAMES   The Birds of America. New York, 1942. 4to., orig. binding, color plates. Wilson 63-383 1974 $22.50

AUDUBON, JOHN JAMES   Delineations of American Scenery and Character. New York, 1926. Frontis., very good cond. Jacobs 24-8 1974 $12

AUDUBON, JOHN JAMES   Ornithological Biography. Edinburgh, 1831-39. 5 vols., roy. 8vo., new buckram, rare, library stamp. Wheldon 128-371 1973 £200

AUDUBON, JOHN JAMES   Ornithological Biography. Edinburgh, 1831. Vol. 1, roy. 8vo., contemporary half calf, weak joints, back strip defective at top. Wheldon 128-372 1973 £50

AUDUBON, JOHN JAMES   Ornithological Biography. Edinburgh, 1831. Roy 8vo., contemporary half calf. Wheldon 130-437 1974 £50

AUERBACH, FRANK L.   Immigration Laws of the U. S. Bobbs, Merrill, 1955. Austin 62-24 1974 $17.50

AUGUSTINUS, AURELIUS, SAINT, BP. OF HIPPO   The Confessions of St. Augustine. 1909. Roy. 8vo., full dec. vellum gilt, English first edition. Covent 56-671 1974 £25

AUGUSTINUS, AURELIUS, SAINT, BP. OF HIPPO   Expositio in Euangelium Secundum Johannem. Basle, (Not after 1491). Small folio, 19th century sprinkled boards, calf spine, good clean sound condition. Thomas 32-220 1974 £375

AUGUSTINUS, AURELIUS, SAINT, BP. OF HIPPO   Libri XIII Confessionum. Venice, 1752. 12mo., contemporary full calf, very fine clean copy, engraved title. Schumann 499-6 1974 sFr 85

AUGUSTINUS, AURELIUS, SAINT, BP. OF HIPPO   Of the Citie of God. 1610. Small folio, 19th century half blind tooled calf, first edition in English. Thomas 28-82 1972 £65

AUGUSTINUS, AURELIUS, SAINT, BP. OF HIPPO   Of the Citie of God. 1620. Folio, contemporary calf, stains. Howes 185-930 1974 £55

AUGUSTINE, AURELIUS, SAINT, BP. OF HIPPO   Primvs Tomvs. Basel, 1569 10 vols. and index vol. in 5, folio, contemporary pigskin blindstamped over wooden boards, some clasps wanting, orig. edition. Schumann 499-7 1974 sFr 8,000

AUGUSTINUS AURELIUS, SAINT, B.P. OF HIPPO   Libri XIII Confessionum. Venice, 1752. 12mo., contemporary full calf, very fine clean copy, engraved title. Schumann 499-6 1974 sFr 85

AUGUSTINUS, AURELIUS, SAINT, BP. OF HIPPO   Works. Edinburgh, 1871-72. 13 vols., orig. cloth, soiled, best English edition. Howes 185-931 1974 £28

AULL, WILLIAM F.   The Aull and Martin Genealogy. N. P., n.d. Illus., fine copy. Wilson 63-21 1974 $27.50

AULNOY, MARIE CATHERINE JUMELLE DE BERNEVILLE, COMTESSE OF Temple of the Fairies. 1804. Vol. 2 only, engraved plates, woodcut vignettes, small 8vo., half morocco, gilt. George's 610-33 1973 £8

AUNT Laura. Buffalo, 1863. Orig. gold stamped cloth, lacks rear endpaper, 1 1/2 X 1 1/4 inches. Gregory 44-335 1974 $25

AUNT Louisa's London Toy Books, Sea Side. London, (c. 1870). 8vo., very good, pictorial paperboard covers, rebacked. Current BW9-101 1974 $16.50

AUNT Louisa's Sunday Books, Joseph and His Brethren. London, (c. 1890). 8vo., colored pictures, dec. covers, very good. Current BW9-102 1974 $14

AUNT Louisa's Toy Books, Lily Sweet-Briar's Birthday. London, (c. 1890). 8vo., colored pictures, dec. covers, rebacked, very good. Current BW9-103 1974 $17.50

AURIA, VINCENZO La Sicilia Inventrice. 1704. Small 4to., orig. vellum, inscriptions, first edition. Zeitlin 235-12 1974 $675

AURNER, C. R. History of Education in Iowa. 1914. 4 vols., red buckram, fine. Putnam 126-182 1974 $22

AUSCHER, E. S. A History and Description of French Porcelain. 1905. Roy. 8vo., plates, orig. cloth, gilt, limited edition. Quaritch 940-622 1974 £15

AUSCHER, E. S. A History and Description of French Porcelain. London, 1905. Large 8vo., plates, foxing, orig. cloth, uncut, limited. Bow Windows 62-48 1974 £16

AUSLANDER, JOSEPH My Uncle Jan. 1948. Austin 62-25 1974 $8.50

AUSONIUS, DECIMUS MAGNUS Opera. 1517. 19th century russia, rubbed. Thomas 30-37 1973 £50

AUSONIUS, DESIUS MAGNUS Opera. Amstelodami, 1671. Frontispiece, contemporary calf, worn spine. Smith 194-124 1974 £5

AUSTEN, E. E. Illustrations of African Blood-Sucking Flies. 1909. Crown 4to., orig. cloth. Broadhurst 23-1086 1974 £20

AUSTEN, E. E. Illustrations of African Blood-Sucking Flies Other than Mosquitoes and Tsetse-Flies. 1909. Crown 4to., plates, orig. cloth, fine. Broadhurst 24-1045 1974 £20

AUSTEN, E. E. Illustrations of British Blood-Sucking Flies. 1906. Roy 8vo., cloth, plates, scarce. Wheldon 129-603 1974 £6

AUSTEN, E. E. Illustrations of British Blood-Sucking Flies. 1906. Roy. 8vo., cloth, plates. Wheldon 131-781 1974 £6

AUSTEN, JANE Emma. 1816. Small 8vo., 3 vols., modern half green calf, labels, first edition. Quaritch 936-281 1974 £350

AUSTEN, JANE Pride and Prejudice. London, 1894. 8vo., gilt dec. blue cloth, illus., small splits in cloth, spot on back cover, else fine. Current BW9-206 1974 $12.50

AUSTEN, JANE The Novels Of. Edinburgh, 1906-12. 12 vols., orig. buckram. Smith 193-261 1973 £40

AUSTEN, JOHN Everyman and Other Plays. 1925. Roy. 8vo., plates, orig. buckram. Smith 194-712 1974 £5.50

AUSTEN, JOHN The Infernal Marriage. 1929. Quarter vellum gilt, plates, English first edition. Covent 56-1823 1974 £15

AUSTEN, JOHN Perrault. 1922. Small 4to., illus., signed. Rota 188-51 1974 $7.50

AUSTEN LEIGH, AUGUSTUS Augustus Austen Leigh: A Record of College Reform. 1906. Nice copy, portraits, first edition. Covent 51-339 1973 £5.25

AUSTEN LEIGH, MARY AUGUSTA James Edward Austen Leigh: A Memoir. 1911. Very good copy, first edition, presentation slips inscribed from author loosely inserted. Covent 51-152 1973 £15.75

AUSTIN, CYRIL F. Little Blue Rabbit and His Adventures. New York & London, n.d. (c. 1910). Square 16mo., pictorial boards, cloth spine, full color plates. Frohnsdorff 16-505 1974 $15

AUSTIN, F. B. My Best Thriller. London, 1933. lst ed. Biblo & Tannen 210-411 1973 $7.50

AUSTIN, HORACE Annual Message of Governor Austin to the Legislature of Minnesota, January, 1871. St. Paul, 1871. Wrapper. Jenkins 61-1657 1974 $15

AUSTIN, MARY California. New York, London, 1914. lst ed., 32 mounted color plates, colored pic. cloth. Dykes 24-4 1974 $25

AUSTIN, MARY Everyman's Genius. Indianapolis, 1925. Biblo & Tannen 213-945 1973 $7.50

AUSTIN, MARY The Land of Little Rain. Boston, 1903. Illus., orig. pictorial green cloth, first edition. Bradley 35-18 1974 $30

AUSTIN, O. L. The Birds of Newfoundland Labrador. Cambridge, 1932. 4to., cloth. Wheldon 130-439 1974 £7.50

AUSTIN, SARAH Characteristics of Goethe. 1833. 3 vols., orig. cloth-backed boards, uncut, first edition. Howes 186-211 1974 £32

AUSTIN, THOMAS GEORGE The Straw Plaitting and Straw Hat and Bonnet Trade. 1871. 4to., 19th century half-morocco, gilt, first edition. Dawsons PM 247-5 1974 £15

AUSTIN, WALTER A Forgotten Duel Fought in Rhode Island Between William Austin, of Charlestown, and James Henderson Elliot of Boston. N.P., 1914. Orig. binding. Butterfield 10-70 1974 $20

AUSTIN, WILLIAM Devotionis Augustinianae Flamma. 1637. Folio, contemporary sheep, rebacked. Howes 185-935 1974 £35

AUSTRALASIAN Antarctic Expedition 1911-14 Under the Leadership of Sir Douglas Mawson, Scientific Reports. Sydney, 1916-47. 94 parts in 91, 4to., orig. wrappers, complete set. Wheldon 128-171 1973 £165

AUTHENTIC ADVENTURES of the Celebrated Countess de La Motte. 1787. 12mo., wrappers, rare. Hill 126-188 1974 £50

AUTHORS CLUB, NEW YORK Liber Scriptorum. 1893. Folio, new buckram, first book of the Authors Club. Allen 216-73 1974 $50

THE AUTOBIOGRAPHY of Gurdon Saltonstall Hubbard. Chicago, 1911. 8vo., orig. bindings. Butterfield 8-58 1974 $10

THE AUTOBIOGRAPHY of Lord Alfred Douglas. 1929. 4to., orig. cloth, first edition. Broadhurst 23-532 1974 £6

AUTOLYCUS Ulug Beg. New York, 1923. Ltd. to 250 copies. Biblo & Tannen 210-699 1973 $12.50

AUTON, C. Recollections of Auton House. Boston, 1881. Wide 8vo., full page frontis., text illus., colored pictorial covers, interior fine, soiled exterior with minor rubbing. Current BW9-139 1974 $18.75

AVEBURY, JOHN LUBBOCK Monograph of the Collembola and Thysanura. 1873. 8vo., orig. cloth, plates (some coloured), extremely scarce. Wheldon 128-760 1973 £20

AVELING, J. H. English Midwives. London, 1872. 8vo., cloth. Dawsons PM 11-28 1974 £10

AVENA, F. La Natura, e Coltura de Fiori Fisicamente Eposta in Due Trattati con Nuovo Ragioni, Osservazioni, e Sperienze. Palermo, 1767-68. 2 vols., 4to., half calf, scarce. Wheldon 131-1486 1974 £10

AVILER, AUGUSTIN CHARLES, D' Cours d'Architecture Qui Comprend les Ordres de Vignole. 1720. 2 vols., 4to., plates, contemporary calf, gilt. Quaritch 940-507 1974 £50

AVILOV, LYDIA Chekhov. Harcourt, 1950. 159p., illus. Austin 51-38 1973 $10

AXTELL, SAMUEL B. Message to the Legislative Assembly of New Mexico. Santa Fe, 1878. Printed wrappers, ex-library, rare, presentation copy. Jenkins 61-1832 1974 $75

AYMAR, G. C.   Bird Flight. 1936. Roy. 8vo., cloth.
Wheldon 131-537 1974 £7.50

AYRTON, MAXWELL   Wrought Iron and Its Decorative Use. 1929.
4to., quarter buckram gilt, illus., fine. Covent 55-80 1974 £15

AYRTON, MAXWELL   Wrought Iron and Its Decorative Use. 1929.
4to., orig. cloth, rubbed. Marsden 39-13 1974 £14

AZEVADO FORTES, MANOEL DE   O Engenheiro Portuguez. Lisbon, 1728-9.
4to., 2 vols., calf, gilt, plates, first edition. Gurney 64-11 1974 £60

AZEVADO FORTES, MANOEL DE   O Engenheiro Portuguez. Lisbon, 1728-29.
4to., 2 vols., calf, gilt backs, folding plates, some dampstaining in vol. 2, very
rare. Gurney 66-14 1974 £60

B

B., A.   A Letter to the Craftsmen. London, 1734.
8vo., modern morocco, gilt, first edition. Dawsons PM 247-6 1974 £20

B., H.   A Reply to the Excellent and Elegant Speech
Made by Sir Thomas Player. (London, 1679). Small folio, disbound, first
edition. Dawsons PM 247-7 1974 £25

B., M.   The Thunderer. New York, The Derrydale
Press, 1933. Limited to 950 copies, illus., drawings, red buckram, dulled, fine
interior. Current BW9-173 1974 $22.50

B., W.   The Elephant's Ball and Grande Fete Champetre.
1883. 8vo., printed wrapper, plates. Hammond 201-91 1974 £8

BAAS, JOHANN HERMANN   William Harvey, der Entdecker des Blutkreislaufs
und Dessen Anatomischexperimentelle Studie Uber die Herz-und Blutbewegung Bei
den Thieren. Stuttgart, 1878. 8vo., boards. Gurney 66-81 1974 £15

BABAULT, G.   Mission Guy Babault dans les Provinces
Centrales de l'Inde. Paris, 1920. 4to., wrappers, plates, maps. Wheldon
131-538 1974 £6

BABB, THEODORE A.   In the Bosom of the Comanches. Dallas, 1923.
Nice copy. Jenkins 61-177 1974 $35

BABBAGE, CHARLES   On the Economy of Machinery and
Manufactures. London, 1832. 8vo., engraved, foxing, contemporary half
calf, worn, first edition. Bow Windows 62-49 1974 £85

BABBAGE, CHARLES   Observations Addressed. London, 1856. 8vo.,
disbound, marbled wrappers, first edition. Zeitlin 235-13 1974 $37.50

BABBAGE, CHARLES   On the Economy of Machinery and Manufactures.
London, 1832. 8vo., contemporary calf gilt, fine, first edition. Dawsons PM
247-8 1974 £85

BABBAGE, CHARLES   On the Economy of Machinery and Manufactures.
London, 1832. 8vo., contemporary calf, gilt, very fine, first edition. Gilhofer
61-37 1974 sFr. 1,000

BABBAGE, CHARLES   On the Economy of Machinery and Manufacturers.
London, 1833. Small 8vo., boards, third edition. Hammond 201-786 1974 £21

BABBIT, FRANK COLE   A Grammar of Attic and Ionic Greek. New
York, 1902. Biblo & Tannen 214-587 1974 $7.50

BABCOCK, HAROLD L.   The Turtles of New England. Boston, 1919.
4to., buckram, plates. Wheldon 129-557 1974 £20

BABCOCK, W. H.   The Brides of the Tiger. Chicago, 1892. Cloth.
Hayman 57-171 1974 $20

BABELON, ERNEST   Manual of Oriental Antiquities. 1889.
Illus., fine. Covent 55-421 1974 £12.50

BABELON, JEAN   La Bibliotheque Francaise de Fernand Colomb.
Paris, 1913. 8vo., half morocco, illus. Kraus B8-41 1974 $28.50

THE BABES In the Wood. New York, n.d. 16mo., 6 color plates. Frohnsdorff
16-66 1974 $7.50

BABINGTON, C. C.   Manual of British Botany. 1843. Crown 8vo.,
orig. cloth, first edition. Wheldon 130-1075 1974 £5

BABINGTON, GERVAISE   Certaine Plaine, Briefe, and Comfortable Notes,
Vpon Euery Chapter of Genesis. 1596. Mainly black letter, dec. initials,
slight marginal stains, else excellent condition, small 4to., modern calf, has
final blank. Thomas 32-31 1974 £100

BABINGTON, JOHN   Pyrotechnia. London, 1635. 3 parts in 1
vol., folio, old calf, leather label, engravings. Traylen 79-196 1973 £70

BABINSKI, JOSEPH FRANCOIS FELIX   Demembrement de l'Hysterie Traditionelle
Pithiatisme. Paris, 1909. 8vo., orig. printed wrappers, first edition. Dawsons
PM 249-19 1974 £85

BABO, F. VON UND   Handbuch des Weinbaues und der Kellerwirtschaft.
Berlin, 1921-22. 1 vol. in 2, first part orig. cloth, second part orig. clothbacked
boards. Bow Windows 66-26 1974 £8

THE BABY'S Black Beauty. New York, 1908. 4to., illus. Frohnsdorff 16-68
1974 $8.50

BACCHANELLI, GIOVANNI BATTISTA   De Consensu Medicorum. Venice,
1553. 8vo., contemporary Flemish calf, very fine, first edition. Schafer 8-143
1973 sFr 800

BACCANELLI, GIOVANNI BATTISTA   De Consensv Medicorvm in Cvrandis
Morbis. 1556. Small 8vo., contemporary limp vellum, second edition. Dawsons PM 249-20 1974 £50

BACCI, ANDREA   De Venenis et Antidotis. Romae, 1586. 4to.,
sprinkled calf, gilt, first edition. Dawsons PM 249-21 1974 £115

BACHE, ALEXANDER DALLAS   Report on Education in Europe, to the Trustees
of the Girard College. 1839. New buckram, blind stamp. Allen 216-510
1974 $10

BACHE, JULES S.   A Catalogue of Paintings in the Collection Of.
New York, 1929. 4to., buckram, plates, frontispiece. Quaritch 940-10
1974 £15

BACHELDER, JOHN B.   Bachelder's Illustrated Tourist's Guide of the
United States. Boston, 1873. Folding pictorial map torn but complete, illus.,
maps, small joint split, orig. binding. Wilson 63-356 1974 $16.75

BACHELLER, IRVING   Charge It. Harper, 1912. 192p., illus.
Austin 54-71 1973 $6.50

BACHELLER, IRVING   Darrel of the Blessed Isles. Grosset, Dunlap,
1903. 411p., illus. Austin 54-72 1973 $6

BACHELLER, IRVING   D'Ri and I. Lothrop, 1901. 362p., illus.
Austin 54-73 1973 $6

BACHELLER, IRVING   Eben Holden. Lothrop, 1900. 432p., orig.
ed. Austin 54-74 1973 $5.50

BACHELLER, IRVING   Father Abraham. Bobbs, Merrill, 1925. 419p.
Austin 54-75 1973 $6.50

BACHELLER, IRVING   The Handmade Gentleman. Grosset, Dunlap,
1909. 332p. Austin 54-76 1973 $6.50

BACHELLER, IRVING   In the Days of Poor Richard (Benjamin Franklin).
Bobbs, 1922. 414p. Austin 54-77 1973 $7.50

BACHELLER, IRVING   In Various Moods. Harper, 1910. 78p.
Austin 54-78 1973 $10

BACHELLER, IRVING   Keeping Up With Lizzie. Harper, 1911. 159p.
Austin 54-79 1973 $6.50

BACHELLER, IRVING   A Man For the Ages. Bobbs, Merrill, 1919.
416p., illus. Austin 54-80 1973 $6.50

BACHELLER, IRVING   Opinions of a Cheerful Yankee. Bobbs, Merrill,
1926. 225p. Austin 54-81 1973 $10

BACHELLER, IRVING   Silas Strong. Grosset, Dunlap, n.d. 339p.
Austin 54-82 1973 $6

BACHELLER, IRVING   A Tale of the Coming Christ. Harper, 1904.
278p. Austin 54-83 1973 $7.50

BACHMEYER, ARTHUR C.   The Hospital IN Modern Society. New York,
1943. Rittenhouse 46-24 1974 $10

BACK, GEORGE   Narrative of the Arctic Land Expedition.
London, 1836. 8vo., old half calf, rebacked, plates, first edition. Traylen
79-506 1973 £85

BACK, GEORGE   Narrative of the Arctic Land Expedition to the
Mouth of the Great Fish River, and Along the Shores of the Arctic Ocean in the
Years, 1833-35. 1836. Engraved frontispiece, plates, folding map, first
edition, demy 8vo., half light brown calf by Bayntun, panelled back, marbled
boards, fine. Broadhurst 24-1578 1974 £82

BACKHOUSE, JAMES   A Narrative of a Visit to the Australian Colonies. 1843. First edition, maps, engraved plates, woodcut illus., 8vo., orig. green cloth, slight browning, slightly rubbed, good copy, scarce. Sawyer 293-51 1974 £75

BACLER D'ALBE, LOUIS-ALBERT-GHISLAIN, BARON DE   Description des Tableaux du Haute-Faucigny. Sallenches, (1824). Full page etched views, all colored by hand, orig. grey pictorial front wrapper bound in, oblong folio, dark red morocco. Schumann 499-8 1974 sFr 7,800

BACON, EDWARD R.   Memorial Catalogue of Paintings by Old and Modern Masters Collected by. New York, 1919. 4to., boards, cloth spine, plates. Quaritch 940-11 1974 £50

BACON, FRANCIS   A Conference of Pleasure. London, 1870. 4to., book-plate, orig. cloth. Bow Windows 62-50 1974 £7.50

BACON, FRANCIS   De Dignitate et Augmentis Scientiarum. Strassburg, 1654. 8vo., old vellum, fine. Dawsons PM 245-39 1974 £38

BACON, FRANCIS   The Essayes. London, 1639. 4to., old calf, morocco label, fifth edition. Dawsons PM 252-30 1974 £75

BACON, FRANCIS   The Essays. London, 1696. 8vo., morocco label, contemporary panelled calf, gilt. Dawsons PM 252-31 1974 £60

BACON, FRANCIS   The Essays. 1840. 8vo., old diced calf, worn, orig. cloth. Bow Windows 64-380 1974 £8

BACON, FRANCIS   The Historie of the Raigne of King Henry The Seventh. London, 1622. Folio, contemporary calf, first edition. Dawsons PM 251-164 1974 £150

BACON, FRANCIS   Instauratio Magna. 1620. Folio, contemporary vellum, fine, first edition, second issue. Dawsons PM 245-38 1974 £950

BACON, FRANCIS   Letters, Speeches, Charges, Advices. London, 1763. Contemporary calf gilt. Smith 193-101 1973 £5

BACON, FRANCIS   The Miscellaneous Writings of. 1827. 8vo., frontis., orig. cloth backed boards, torn, uncut. Bow Windows 64-381 1974 £10

BACON, FRANCIS   Nevf Livres de la Dignite et de L'Accroissement des Sciences. Paris, 1632. 4to., contemporary gilt-ruled calf. Zeitlin 235-14 1974 $750

BACON, FRANCIS   The Philosophical Works. London, 1733. 3 vols., 4to., contemporary calf gilt, first edition. Dawsons PM 252-32 1974 £45

BACON, FRANCIS   The Works Of. 1765. 5 vols., 4to., contemporary calf, frontispieces. Bow Windows 66-27 1974 £105

BACON, FRANCIS   The Works of. London, 1819. 10 vols., 8vo., portrait, plates, contemporary calf, gilt. Bow Windows 62-51 1974 £85

BACON, FRANCIS   Works. London, 1853. 2 vols., roy. 8vo., contemporary polished calf. Schuman 37-10 1974 $85

BACON, JOHN   Liber Regis, vel Thesaurus Rerum Ecclesiasticarum. 1786. Thick 4to., text little browned, contemporary calf, rebacked. Bow Windows 66-28 1974 £28

BACON, LEONARD   Guinea-Fowl and Other Poultry. Harper, 1927. 12lp. Austin 54-84 1973 $6.50

BACON, LEONARD   Semi-Centennial. Harper, 1939. 273p. Austin 54-85 1973 $7.50

BACON, M. A.   Winged Thoughts. 1851. Orig. blind-stamped calf, gilt, plates. Dawson's 424-110 1974 $95

BACON, NATHANIEL   The Continuation of an Historical Discourse. London, 1651. Small 4to., contemporary calf, rebacked, first edition. Dawsons PM 251-413 1974 £35

BACON, PEGGY   Cat-Calls. McBride, 1935. 87p. Austin 54-86 1973 $6.50

BACON, R. N.   The Report on the Agriculture of Norfolk. 1844. 8vo., new cloth, portraits, plates, plans, very scarce. Wheldon 128-1638 1973 £15

BACON, R. N.   The Report on the Agriculture of Norfolk. 1844. 8vo., new cloth, plates, very scarce. Wheldon 131-1770 1974 £15

BACON, ROGER   Liber Alberti Magni de Duabus Sapientiis et de Recapitulatione Omnium Librorum Astronomie. (Nuremberg, 1493-96). 4to., boards, leather spine, first edition, Georg Tannstetter's copy. Kraus 137-10 1974 $3,250

BACON, ROGER   Opus Majus ad Clementem Quartum. London, 1733. Folio, old panelled calf, rebacked, leather label, plates, first edition. Traylen 79-197 1973 £120

BADCOCK, F. J.   The History of the Creeds. New York, 1930. Biblo & Tannen 214-588 1974 $12.50

BADCOCK, WILLIAM   A New Touch-Stone for Gold and Silver Wares. London, 1679. 2 parts in 1 vol., 8vo., full calf antique, second edition. Dawsons PM 247-9 1974 £150

BADCOCK, WILLIAM   A Touchstone for Gold and Silver Wares. 1677. Post 8vo., modern half calf antique, rare first edition. Wheldon 131-962 1974

BADDELEY, J. J.   Guide to the Guildhall of the City of London. 1898. Photographic illus., covers damp stained. Bow Windows 66-29 1974 £6.50

BADEN-POWELL, R.   The Downfall of Prempeh. 1896. Orig. cloth gilt, plates. Covent 55-151 1974 £35

BADEN-POWELL, R.   Rovering to Success. 1922. Drab wrappers, illus. Covent 55-152 1974 £15

BADENOCH, L. N.   Romance of the Insect World. 1906. Small 8vo., half green crushed levant morocco, gilt tooled and panelled spine, illus., attractive vol. Sawyer 293-52 1974 £12.60

BADESLADE, THOMAS   The History of the Ancient and Present State of the Navigation of the Port of King's-Lyn. 1766. Folio, buckram. Quaritch 939-41 1974 £70

BADESLADE, THOMAS   The History of the Ancient and Present State of the Navigation of the Port of King's-Lyn. London, 1766. Folio, contemporary panelled calf, gilt, plates. Hammond 201-838 1974 £145

BADHAM, CHARLES DAVID   A Treatise on the Esculent Funguses of England. 1847. Roy. 8vo., orig. cloth, gilt, plates. Wheldon 129-1144 1974 £25

BADHAM, CHARLES DAVID   A Treatise on the Esculent Funguses of England. 1863. 8vo., cloth, scarce, plates, second edition. Wheldon 130-1231 1974 £18

THE BADIANUS Manuscript. Baltimore, 1940. 4to., plates in color. Biblo & Tannen 213-844 1973 $85

BADIN, M. JULES   La Manufacture de Tapisseries de Beauvais Depuis ses Origines jusq'a nos Jours. 1909. 4to., plates, calf backed boards, orig. wrappers, limited, numbered. Quaritch 940-745 1974 £45

BAEDECKER, KARL   The Dominion of Canada With Newfoundland and on Excursion to Alaska. Leipzig, 1907. Third edition. Hood's 104-4 1974 $20

BAEDEKER, KARL   Greece. Leipsic, 1889. 12mo., 1st Eng. ed. Biblo & Tannen 213-647 1973 $20

BAEDEKER, KARL   Italie Septentrionale . . . Jusqu's Livourne, Florence et Ravenne. Leipzig, Paris, 1899. French text, flex cloth, maps, some colored and folding, light pencil notes. Wilson 63-583 1974 $10

BAEDEKER, KARL   Norway and Sweden and Denmark. Leipsic, 1892. Flex cloth, English text, maps, some colored and folding. Wilson 63-585 1974 $10

BAEDEKER, KARL   The Rhine. Leipzig, 1926. 12mo. Biblo & Tannen 213-648 1973 $8.50

BAEDEKER, KARL   Switzerland. Leipsic, 1895. Maps, some colored and folding, illus., orig. binding, English text, very good copy. Wilson 63-584 1974 $10

BAER, KARL ERNST VON   Welche Auffassung der Lebenden Natur ist die Richtige? Und Wie is Diese Auffassung auf die Entomologie Anzuwenden? Berlin, 1862. 8vo., half cloth, orig. wrappers bound in. Gurney 66-15 1974 £30

BAER, KARL ERNST VON   Welche Auffassung der Lebenden Naturist. Berlin, 1862. 8vo., half cloth, orig. wrappers. Gurney 64-12 1974 £30

BAGBY, GEORGE W.   The Old Virginia Gentleman and Other Sketches. Scribners, 1910. 312p., 1st ed. Austin 54-87 1973 $12.50

BAGEHOT, WALTER   The Works. Hartford, 1891. 5 vols., large 8vo., orig. cloth, first collected edition. Howes 186-1342 1974 £21

BAGLIVI, GIORGIO   Canones de Medicina Solidorum ad Rectum Statices Usum. (Leyden), 1707. 8vo., half calf, gilt. Hammond 201-530 1974 £55

BAGLIVI, GIORGIO   De Praxi Medica. 1704. Browning, cracking. Rittenhouse 46-26 1974 $95

BAGNALL, JAMES E.   The Flora of Warwickshire. 1891. 8vo., map, cloth, scarce, limited edition. Wheldon 130-1076 1974 £10

BAGNALL, JAMES E.   The Flora of Warwickshire. 1891. 8vo., cloth, scarce, signed by author, numbered, limited edition. Wheldon 128-1183 1973 £10

BAGNOLD, ENID   The Chalk Garden. Random House, 1956. 165p., illus. Austin 51-39 1973 $6.50

BAGSHAW, SAMUEL   History, Gazetteer and Directory of the County of Kent. Sheffield, (n.d.). 8vo., 2 vols., orig. brown blind-stamped cloth. Dawsons PM 251-3 1974 £60

BAGSHAWE, W. H. G.   A Memoir Of. 1887. 4to., orig. cloth. Broadhurst 23-1302 1974 £6

BAHR, A. W.   Early Chinese Paintings from the A. W. Bahr Collection. 1938. Roy. folio, plates, buckram, limited edition. Quaritch 940-371 1974 £50

BAHR, A. W.   Old Chinese Porcelain and Works in Art in China. 1911. Roy. 8vo., plates, illus., cloth. Quaritch 940-370 1974 £25

BAIF, JEAN ANTOINE DE   Les Amours. Paris, 1572. Small 8vo., full crimson morocco, gilt, enlarged second edition. L. Goldsmidt 42-4 1974 $1,000

BAIGENT, F. J.   A History of the Ancient Town & Manor of Basingstoke In the County of Southampton. Basingstoke, 1889. Very thick demy 8vo., plates, orig. buckram gilt, first edition. Smith 193-189 1973 £10

BAIKIE, JAMES   A Century of Excavation in the Land of the Pharaohs. (n.d. c. 1922). Illus., name on fly. Bow Windows 66-31 1974 £6

BAILEY, ALICE WARD   Mark Hefron. New York, 1896. First edition, orig. binding. Wilson 63-482 1974 $12.50

BAILEY, C. T. P.   Knives and Forks. 1927. 4to., plates, dust wrapper, English first edition. Covent 56-1639 1974 £15.75

BAILEY, DANA R.   History of Minnehaha County, South Dakota. Sioux Falls, 1899. 8vo., leather, rebacked, presentation. Saddleback 14-685 1974 $75

BAILEY, E. B.   The Geology of Ben Nevis and Gleu Coe. 1916. 8vo., cloth, plates. Wheldon 131-963 1974 £5

BAILEY, F. M.   Birds of New Mexico. Santa Fe, 1928. Roy 8vo., orig. buckram, plates, scarce. Wheldon 130-445 1974 £30

BAILEY, H. C.   Case for Mr. Fortune. 1932. 8vo., orig. cloth, first edition. Rota 190-176 1974 £6

BAILEY, H. C.   Clue for Mr. Fortune. 1936. 8vo., orig. cloth, first edition. Rota 190-177 1974 £5

BAILEY, H. C.   Mr. Fortune Speaking. 1929. 8vo., orig. cloth, first edition. Rota 190-175 1974 £5

BAILEY, H. C.   Mr. Fortune's Case Book. 1936. Inscribed presentation, fine. Covent 55-573 1974 £12.50

BAILEY, H. C.   Mr. Fortune's Practice. 1923. 8vo., orig. cloth, first edition. Rota 190-174 1974 £8.50

BAILEY, H. C.   The Roman Eagles. n.d. Pictorial cloth, gilt, fine, English first edition. Covent 56-81 1974 £6.30

BAILEY, HENRY TURNER   Yankee Notions. Washburn, Thomas, 1929. 243p. Austin 54-88 1973 $7.50

BAILEY, JAMES BLAKE   The Diary of a Resurrectionist, 1811-1812. London, 1896. Rittenhouse 46-27 1974 $75

BAILEY, LIBERTY HYDE   The Standard Cyclopedia of Horticulture. New York, 1927. 3 vols., 4to., illus. with color plates, engravings, leather. Wilson 63-309 1974 $50

BAILEY, PERCIVAL   Intracranial Tumors. London, 1933. 8vo., orig. red cloth, faded, first English edition. Dawsons PM 249-22 1974 £12

BAILEY, T.   Annals of Nottinghamshire. (1853-55). 4 vols., 8vo., half calf, illus. Quaritch 939-511 1974 £15

BAILEY, WILLIAM   The Advancement of Arts, Manufactures, and Commerce. London, 1772. 4to., folio, 2 vols., nineteenth century green morocco, gilt, first edition. Dawsons PM 245-40 1974 £460

BAILLIE-GROHMAN, WILLIAM ADOLPH   Sport in the Alps in the Past and Present. New York, 1896. First edition, 8vo., full page illus., text illus., some cover wear, good. Current BW9-152 1974 $22.50

BAILLON, H.   Histoire des Plantes. Paris, 1867-80. Roy 8vo., halt vellum. Wheldon 129-886 1974 £50

BAILLY, GASPARD   Traite des Laods, et Trezeins. (1741). 3 parts in 1 vol., 12mo., full red morocco, gilt. L. Goldsmidt 42-5 1974 $45

BAILLY, JEAN SYLVAIN   Histoire de l'Astronomie Ancienne. 1781. 4to., plates, contemporary mottled calf, worn, second edition. Bow Windows 62-53 1974 £42

BAILLY-MAITRE, J.   Expose des Divers Systemes de Coloration des Pigeons Domestiques et Description des Principales Races de Pigeons de Couleur. Paris, 1909. 8vo., wrappers, scarce, plates. Wheldon 128-376 1973 £5

BAILY, THOMAS   Witty Apophyhegms. London, 1669. 12mo., contemporary calf, frontispiece. Dawsons PM 252-34 1974 £55

BAIN, J. ARTHUR   Life and Adventures of Nansen. London & New York, n.d. Map, illus. Hood's 103-47 1974 $17.50

BAIN, J. ARTHUR   Life and Explorations of Fridtjof Nansen. (n.d.). 8vo., orig. cloth, illus., covers marked and little rubbed. Bow Windows 66-494 1974 £6.50

BAINBRIDGE, JOHN   Garbo. Doubleday, 1955. 256p., illus. Austin 51-40 1973 $6.50

BAINES, EDWARD   The Cotton Trade. Blackburn and London, 1857. 8vo., cloth, first edition. Hammond 201-812 1974 £10

BAINES, EDWARD   History of the Cotton Manufacture in Great Britain. (1835). 8vo., orig. cloth, plates, first edition. Hammond 201-811 1974 £48

BAINES, EDWARD   History of the Cotton Manufacture in Great Britain. (1835). 8vo., cloth, engravings. Quaritch 939-833 1974 £60

BAINES, EDWARD   History of the County Palatine and Duchy of Lancaster. 1836. 4 vols., 4to., half calf. Quaritch 939-417 1974 £80

BAINES, EDWARD   History of the County Palatine and Duchy of
Lancaster. 1868-70. 2 vols., roy. 4to., half maroon morocco gilt. Quaritch
939-418 1974 £35

BAINES, EDWARD   Letters to the Right Hon. Lord John Russell.
London, 1847. 8vo., orig. dark green blind-stamped cloth, gilt, fine. Dawsons
PM 247-10 1974 £16

BAINES, EDWARD   The Social, Educational, and Religious State of
the Manufacturing Districts. London and Leeds, 1843. 8vo., orig. cloth, gilt,
first edition. Hammond 201-788 1974 £15

BAINES, F. E.   Records of the Manor, Parish, and Borough of
Hampstead. 1890. 8vo., frontispiece, orig. cloth. Bow Windows 64-382
1974 £28

BAINES, PETER A.   Theologia Dogmatica et Moralis ad Usum
Seminarii Montis Crucis. 1840. 2 vols., orig. cloth backed boards, paper
labels. Howes 185-936 1974 £5

BAINES, T.   Greenhouse and Stove Plants. 1894. 8vo.,
cloth, plates. Wheldon 131-1489 1974 £7.50

BAINES, THOMAS   History and Commerce and Town of Liverpool.
London and Liverpool, 1852. 8vo., contemporary roan, gilt, first edition. Dawsons PM 251-4 1974 £32

BAINES, THOMAS   Lancashire and Cheshire, Past and Present.
(1867). 2 vols. in 4, 4to., orig. pictorial cloth. Quaritch 939-42 1974 £40

BAINES, THOMAS   Yorkshire, Past and Present. 2 vols., worn,
orig. cloth, stains, gilt. Bow Windows 62-54A 1974 £20

BAINES, THOMAS   Yorkshire, Past and Present. n.d. 4to., 4
vols., orig. cloth, fine. Broadhurst 23-1303 1974 £10

BAINES, THOMAS   Yorkshire, Past and Present. London, n.d.
4 vols., 4to., cloth gilt, faded, plates. Traylen 79-409 1973 £10.50

BAINES, THOMAS   Yorkshire Past and Present. London, (c.1875).
2 vols., 4to., portraits, map, orig. cloth, gilt. Bow Windows 62-54 1974
£25

BAIRD, CHARLES W.   History of the Huguenot Emigration to
America. 1885. Illus., orig. edition. Austin 57-55 1974 $12.50

BAIRD, LEWIS C.   Baird's History of Clark County, Indiana.
Indianapolis, 1909. 8vo., leather, illus. Saddleback 14-399 1974 $75

BAIRD, SPENCER FULLERTON   A History of North American Birds. Boston,
1874. 4to., 3 vols., new buckram, plates. Wheldon 129-419 1974 £80

BAIRD, SPENCER FULLERTON   A History of North American Birds. Boston,
1874. 3 vols., 4to., buckram, woodcuts, plates. Wheldon 131-539 1974
£80

BAIRD, W.   Tabular View of the Orders and Families of
Mammalia. n.d. Roy 8vo., orig. limp boards. Wheldon 130-381 1974 £5

BAIRNSFEATHER, BRUCE   Bullets and Billets. 1917. 4to., quarter
buckram, plates, illus. Covent 55-878 1974 £15.75

BAKER, BLANCHE M.   Dramatic Bibliography. New York, 1933.
Very good copy. Covent 51-239 1973 £15

BAKER, BLANCHE M.   Dramatic Bibliography. New York, 1933.
8vo., buckram. Goodspeed's 578-421 1974 .$10

BAKER, CARLOW   A Friend in Power. Scribner, 1958. 312p.
Austin 54-89 1973 $6.50

BAKER, CHARLES HENRY COLLINS   British Painting. Boston, 1933. Biblo &
Tannen 213-203 1973 $25

BAKER, CHARLES HENRY COLLINS   English Painting of the 16th and 17th
Centuries. Florence, 1930. Roy. 4to., plates, cloth. Quaritch 940-12
1974 £40

BAKER, CHARLOTTE ALICE   True Stories of New England Captives. Cambridge, 1897. 8vo., orig. bindings, uncut, plates. Butterfield 8-339 1974 $50

BAKER, DAVID ERSKIN   The Companion to the Play-House. 1764. Small
8vo., 2 vols., wrappers, rebacked, uncut, first edition. Quaritch 936-12 1974
£75

BAKER, DOROTHY   ·Cassandra at the Wedding. Houghton, 1962.
226p. Austin 54-90 1973 $6

BAKER, DOROTHY   Our Gifted Son. Houghton,, Mifflin, 1948.
243p. Austin 54-91 1973 $6.50

BAKER, DOROTHY   Trio. Sun Dial, 1945. 234p. Austin 54-92
1973 $5

BAKER, DOROTHY   Young Man with a Horn. Houghton, Mifflin,
1938. 243p., orig. ed. Austin 54-93 1973 $6.50

BAKER, EDWARD CHARLES STUART   Cuckoo Problems. 1942. 8vo., cloth,
plates, scarce. Wheldon 130-450 1974 £5

BAKER, EDWARD CHARLES STUART   Ducks and Their Allies. 1921. Plates,
fine, half morocco, gilt. Bow Windows .64-15 1974 £32

BAKER, EDWARD CHARLES STUART   The Game-Birds of India, Burma and Ceylon.
1921. Roy. 8vo., orig. half morocco, plates, scarce. Wheldon 130-448 1974
£15

BAKER, EDWARD CHARLES STUART   The Game Birds of the Indian Empire.
Bombay, 1926-35. Roy. 8vo., half morocco, plates. Wheldon 130-449 1974 £25

BAKER, EDWARD CHARLES STUART   The Indian Ducks. 1908. Roy. 8vo.,
orig. half morocco. Wheldon 130-447 1974 £35

BAKER, EDWARD CHARLES STUART   Indian Pigeons and Doves. 1913.
Roy. 8vo., orig. half morocco, plates. Wheldon 131-540 1974 £40

BAKER, EDWARD CHARLES STUART   Indian Pigeons and Doves. 1913. Roy.
8vo., orig. cloth, scarce. Wheldon 130-446 1974 £35

BAKER, EDWARD CHARLES STUART   An Outline of a Grammar of the Madagascar
Language, as Spoken by the Hovas. Mauritius, 1845. 12mo., orig. marbled
wrappers, spine worn, printed paper side label, first edition, rare. Ximenes 36-
8 1974 $125

BAKER, ELLIOT   A Fine Madness. Putnam, 1964. 319p.
Austin 54-94 1973 $6.50

BAKER, ERNEST A.   A Guide to Historical Fiction. London, 1914.
4to., orig. cloth, first edition. Dawsons PM 10-21 £6

BAKER, GEORGE   The History and Antiquities of the County of
Northampton. London, 1822-41. 2 vols., large thick folio, full green morocco,
gilt, leather labels, illus. Traylen 79-369 1973 £160

BAKER, GEORGE   Medical Tracts, Read at the College Of
Physicians Between the Years 1767 and 1785. London, 1818. Roy. 8vo., gilt,
contemporary half calf, presentation. Traylen 79-198 1973 £60

BAKER, H. F.   Principles of Geometry. Cambridge, 1929-34.
6 vols., signature on fly leaves, prize label in 1 vol. Bow Windows 66-32 1974
£25

BAKER, HENRY   Employment for the Microscope. 1753. 8vo.,
contemporary calf, rebacked, plates, very scarce, first edition. Wheldon 128-4
1973 £30

BAKER, HENRY   Essai sur l'Historie Naturelle du Polype, Insecte.
Paris, 1744. Small 8vo., contemporary calf, scarce, plates. Wheldon 128-869
1973 £15

BAKER, HENRY   Essai su l'Histoire Naturelle du Polype, Insecte.
Paris, 1744. Small 8vo., contemporary calf, plates, scarce. Wheldon 130-848
1974 £15

BAKER, HENRY   The Microscope Made Easy. 1744. Rubbed,
contemporary calf gilt, foxing, copperplates. Smith 194-125 1974 £30

BAKER, HENRY   The Microscope Made Easy. 1769. 8vo.,
contemporary calf, rebacked, plates, fifth edition. Wheldon 128-5 1973 £20

BAKER, J. G.   Handbook of the Fern-Allies. 1887. 8vo.,
cloth, scarce. Wheldon 129-1384 1974 £7.50

BAKER, JAMES H.   History of Colorado. Denver, 1927. 5 vols.,
fine, three quarter morocco, gilt. Jenkins 61-507 1974 $85

BAKER, MOSELEY   To the Hon. John Quincy Adams, and the Other
Twenty Members of Congress Who . . . Remonstrated Against the Annexation of
Texas to the American Union. Washington, 1843. Signed by Adams, extremely
rare. Jenkins 61-183 1974 $450

BAKER, R. ST. B.   Among the Trees. Dorset, 1935-41. 2 vols.,
4to., orig. half parchment, frontispieces, plates, very scarce, limited editions.
Wheldon 128-1580 1973 £15

BAKER, RUSSELL   An American in Washington. Knopf, 1961.
242p. Austin 54-95 1973 $6

BAKER, SAMUEL WHITE   The Albert N'Yanza. London, 1866. 2 vols.,
8vo., illus., orig. green cloth, plates, first edition. Dawsons PM 250-3
1974 £80

BAKER, SAMUEL WHITE   Exploration of the Nile Tributaries of Abyssinia.
Hartford, 1868. Illus., maps. Jacobs 24-135 1974 $45

BAKER, SAMUEL WHITE   Ismailia: A Narrative of the Expedition to
Central Africa for the Suppression of the Slave Trade. 1874. Demy 8vo., first
edition, 2 vols., orig. cloth, plates, frontispiece, fine. Broadhurst 24-1575
1974 £60

BAKER, SAMUEL WHITE   The Nile Tributaries of Abyssinia. London,
1867. 8vo., plates, orig. pictorial cloth, worn, first edition. Dawsons PM
250-4 1974 £40

BAKER, T. THORNE   Wireless Pictures and Television. 1926.
Illus., fine. Covent 55-1292 1974 £25

BAKER, THOMAS   History of the College of St. John the
Evangelist. 1869. 2 vols., orig. cloth. Howes 186-1977 1974 £10

BAKER, THOMAS   The Fine Lady's Airs. (n.d.). 4to., modern
boards, first edition. Dawsons PM 252-35 1974 £20

BAKER, WILLIAM   Life and Labors of Rev. Daniel Baker. Philadelphia, c., 1860. Orig. cloth, worn, third edition. Putnam 126-346 1974
$20

BAKER, WILLIAM SPOHN   The Origin and Antiquity of Engraving.
Philadelphia, 1872. 8vo., orig. green cloth, very fine copy, first edition.
Ximenes 37-14 1974 $27.50

BAKEWELL, FREDERICK S.   Electric Science. 1853. Orig. patterned cloth,
English first edition. Covent 56-1151 1974 £15

BAKEWELL, ROBERT   An Introduction to Geology. 1813. 8vo.,
contemporary half roan, plates, rare, first edition. Wheldon 130-906 1974 £45

BAKEWELL, ROBERT   An Introduction to Geology. 1815. 8vo.,
contemporary calf, plates, scarce, second edition. Wheldon 130-907 1974 £30

BAKEWELL, ROBERT   An Introduction to Geology. 1838. 8vo., orig.
cloth, plates. Wheldon 129-804 1974 £15

BAKST, LEON   The Decorative Art Of. 1913. Folio, plates,
rebound in half red morocco gilt. Quaritch 940-431 1974 £160

BAKST, LEON   Programme for Bakst's Production of 'The Sleeping
Princess' at the Alhambra Theatre, London. n.d. (1921). First edition, fine,
wrappers, coloured designs. Covent 51-162 1973 £12

BAKUNIN, MICHAEL   God and the State. 1893. Wrappers, first
edition. Covent 55-1201 1974 £12.50

BALAU, S.   Histoire de la Seigneurie de Modave. 1895.
4to., boards, worn, limited. Allen 213-1262 1973 $20

BALBIANI, G.   Lecons sur les Sporozoaires. Paris, 1864.
Roy. 8vo., cloth, coloured plates, text-figures. Wheldon 128-870 1973 £5

BALBIANI, G.   Lecons sur les Sporozoaires. Paris, 1864. Roy.
8vo., cloth, plates. Wheldon 131-916 1974 £5

BALCH, EMILY GREENE   Our Slavic Fellow Citizens. 1910. Illus.,
orig. edition. Austin 57-56 1974 $17.50

BALDINUCCI, FILIPPO   Cominciamento, e Progresso dell' Arte dell'
Intagliare in Rame. Florence, 1686. Large 4to., marbled boards, first edition.
Harper 213-8 1973 $325

BALDINUCCI, FILIPPO   Cominciamento e Progresso dell'Arte Intagliare
in Rame. Florence, 1767. 8vo., contemporary calf, rubbed. Quaritch
940-13 1974 £40

BALDINUCCI, FILIPPO   Raccolta di Alcuni Opuscoli Sopra Varie
Materie di Pittura, Scultura e Architettura. Florence, 1765. Small 4to.,
contemporary vellum, scarce, fine, first collected edition. Harper 213-9
1973 $175

BALDINUCCI, FILIPPO   Vita del Cavaliere Gio. Lorenzo Bernino.
Florence, 1682. 4to., marbled boards, copperplates, fine, orig. edition.
Harper 213-10 1973 $375

BALDINUCCI, FILIPPO   Vocabolario Toscanna dell' Arte del Disegno.
Florence, 1681. Large 4to., fine, contemporary vellum, rare first edition.
Harper 213-11 1973 $285

BALDNER, L.   Das Vogel, Fisch, und Thierbuch des Strassburger
Fischers Leonhard Baldner aus dem Jahre 1666. Ludwigshafen, 1903. 8vo.,
buckram. Wheldon 131-411 1974 £10

BALDRY, ALFRED LYS   The Life and Work of Marcus Stone. 1896.
Rubbed, faded, cloth, limited edition. Marsden 39-430 1974 £6

BALDWIN, ALFRED (Mrs.)   The Shadow on the Blind and Other Ghost
Stories. London, 1895. 1st ed. Biblo & Tannen 210-559 1973 $17.50

BALDWIN, ELMER   History of La Salle County, Illinois. Chicago,
1877. 12mo., cloth, rebound. Saddleback 14-366 1974 $45

BALDWIN, H. I.   Forest Tree Seed of the North Temperate
Regions. Waltham, 1942. Roy. 8vo., buckram. Wheldon 131-1712 1974
£7.50

BALDWIN, LOAMMI   Report on the Subject of Introducing Pure Water
into the City of Boston. Boston, 1834. 8vo., half morocco, rebacked. Dawsons
PM 245-41 1974 £21

BALDWIN, SAMUEL ATKINSON   The Story of the American Guild of Organ-
ists. New York, 1946. Biblo & Tannen 214-809 1974 $9.50

BALDWIN, THOMAS   Airopaidia. Chester, 1786. 8vo., contemporary
half calf, plates, first edition. Dawsons PM 245-42 1974 £175

BALDWIN, W.   Reliquiae Baldwinianae. Philadelphia, 1843.
Post 8vo., orig. cloth, very scarce, nice copy. Wheldon 128-83 1973 £30

BALDWIN, W.   Reliquiae Baldwinianae. Philadelphia, 1843.
Post 8vo., orig. cloth, scarce. Wheldon 130-142 1974 £30

BALESTIER, CHARLES W.   James G. Blaine, a Sketch of His Life With a
Brief Record of the Life of John A. Logan. New York, 1884. Cloth, scarce.
Hayman 59-566 1974 $10

BALESTIER, JOSEPH N.   The Annals of Chicago. Chicago, 1876. Orig.
printed wrappers, fine, second edition. Bradley 35-65 1974 $20

BALET, LEO   Die Verburgerlichung der Deutschen Kunst.
Leipzig, 1936. Biblo & Tannen 214-810 1974 $12.50

BALFOUR, GRAHAM   Life of Robert Louis Stevenson. 1901. Illus.,
first English edition. Austin 61-14 1974 $17.50

BALFOUR, GRAHAM   The Life of Robert Louis Stevenson. 1901.
8vo., 2 vols., orig. cloth, first edition. Bow Windows 64-700 1974 £5

BALFOUR, JAMES   Historical Works. Edinburgh, 1825. 4 vols.,
contemporary half russia gilt, first edition. Howes 186-588 1974 £25

BALFOUR, JOHN HUTTON   The Plants of the Bible. 1885. 8vo., cloth, scarce, new edition. Wheldon 130-990 1974 £5

BALIDON, W. PALEY   A Catalogue of Pamphlets, Tracts, Speeches, Trails . . . from 1506-1700. London, 1908. 8vo., orig. buckram, uncut. Dawsons PM 10-363 1974 £15

BALL, ALICE ELIZA   American Land Birds. New York, 1936. 8vo., plates, cloth, second edition. Wheldon 131-541 1974 £5

BALL, ALICE MORTON   Compounding In the English Language. 1939. Ex-library. Austin 61-15 1974 $17.50

BALL, C. D.   Orange County Medical History. Santa Ana, (1926). 12mo., cloth. Saddleback 14-31 1974 $35

BALL, F. ELDRINGTON   The Judges in Ireland. New York, 1927. 2 vols., orig. cloth, frontispieces, scarce. Howes 186-987 1974 £15

BALL, J.   The Geography and Geology of South-eastern Egypt. Cairo, 1912. Roy 8vo., orig. half cloth. Wheldon 129-805 1974 £10

BALL, J.   The Geography and Geology of South-Eastern Egypt. Cairo, 1912. Roy. 8vo., orig. half cloth, scarce, maps, plates. Wheldon 131-964 1974 £10

BALL, JAMES MOORES   The Sack-'Em-Up Men. Edinburgh, 1928. Rittenhouse 46-31 1974 $60

BALL, RICHARD   Broncho. London, (1930). First edition, 8vo., full page plates, top of spine repaired, fine. Current BW9-480 1974 $18

BALL, T. S.   Church Plate of the City of Chester. Manchester, 1907. Roy. 8vo., plates, cloth. Quaritch 939-329 1974 £6

BALL, TIMOTHY H.   The Lake of the Red Cedars. Crown Point, 1880. Cloth, with ads, very scarce. Hayman 59-285 1974 $25

BALLADS and Broadsides. 1912. Folio, half morocco. Quaritch 939-43 1974 £95

BALLANTYNE, ROBERT MICHAEL   Hudson Bay. London, 1876. Orig. pictorial cloth gilt, illus. Smith 193-473 1973 £7.50

BALLANTYNE, ROBERT MICHAEL   The Iron Horse. London, n.d. Hood's 103-477 1974 $12.50

BALLANTYNE, ROBERT MICHAEL   The Norsemen in the West. London, 1880. Illus. Hood's 102-489 1974 $10

BALLANTYNE, ROBERT MICHAEL   The Pioneers, a Tale of Western Wilderness. London, n.c. (c. 1872). Pages browned. Hood's 102-490 1974 $7.50

BALLANTYNE, ROBERT MICHAEL   The World of Ice. 1862. 8vo., plates, orig. pictorial cloth, gilt, foxed. Covent 55-154 1974 £12.50

BALLARD, ADOLPHUS   The Domesday Inquest. 1906. Plates, illus., scarce. Howes 186-589 1974 £6.50

BALLARD, E. G.   Captain Streeter Pioneer. Chicago, 1914. 12-mo., cloth, illus., scarce, first edition. Putman 126-118 1974 $30

BALLENGER, EDGAR G.   Genito-Urinary Diseases and Syphilis. Atlanta, 1908. Rittenhouse 46-32 1974 $10

BALLERINI, ANTONIO   Opus Theologicum Morale in Busembaum Medullam. 1892. 7 vols., large 8vo., half calf. Howes 185-939 1974 £8.50

BALLINGER, J.   The Bible in Wales. 1906. Roy 8vo., orig. cloth, plates. Broadhurst 23-240 1974 £10

BALLINGER, J.   The Bible in Wales. 1906. Plates, roy. 8vo., orig. cloth, fine. Broadhurst 24-235 1974 £10

BALLOU, MATURIN MURRAY   The New Eldorado. Boston, 1890. Browning, faded covers. Hood's 103-48 1974 $12.50

BALLS, W. L.   The Cotton Plant in Egypt. 1912. 8vo., cloth, plate, text-figures, scarce. Wheldon 128-1639 1973 £5

BALSTON, R. J.   Notes on the Birds of Kent. 1907. 8vo., cloth, frontispiece, map, hand-coloured plates, scarce. Wheldon 128-377 1973 £10

BALSTON, R. J.   Notes on the Birds of Kent. 1907. 8vo., cloth, plates, scarce. Wheldon 130-451 1974 £10

BALZAC, HONORE DE   Le Chef-d'Oeuvre Inconnu. Paris, 1931. 4to., plates, half reddish brown morocco, slipcase, orig. wrappers. Marlborough 70-50 1974 £1,800

BALZAC, HONORE DE   Correspondance Inedite Avec Mme. Zulma Carraud. Paris, 1935. Square 8vo., half blue cloth, gilt, uncut, first edition. L. Goldschmidt 42-147 1974 $12.50

BALZAC, HONORE DE   La Peau de Chagrin. Paris, 1831. 2 vols., 8vo., three quarter straight grain red morocco, gilt, uncut, first edition. L. Goldschmidt 42-146 1974 $1,600

BALZAC, JEAN LOUIS GUEZ, SIEUR DE   The Letters of Mounsieur de Balzac. London, 1638. Small 4to., contemporary calf, fine, second English edition. Ximenes 33-132 1974 $60

BANCROFT, EDWARD   Experimental Researches Concerning the Philosophy of Permanent Colour. London, 1794-1813. 8vo., 2 vols., contemporary calf, first edition. Dawsons PM 245-43 1974 £225

BANCROFT, GEORGE   Martin Van Buren to the End of His Public Career. New York, 1889. Jenkins 61-2490 1974 $20

BANCROFT, HUEBERT HOWE   California Inter Pocula, 1848-56. San Francisco, 1888. Full morocco, gilt. Jenkins 61-273 1974 $25

BANCROFT, HUBERT HOWE   California Pastoral, 1769-1848. San Francisco, 1888. Full morocco, gilt. Jenkins 61-274 1974 $25

BANCROFT, HUBERT HOWE   The History of the Northwest Coast. New York, n.d. 2 vols., illus. Jenkins 61-188 1974 $25

BANCROFT, HUBERT HOWE   History of the Northwest Coast, 1543-1846. San Francisco, 1886. 2 vols., full gilt morocco, fine. Jenkins 61-2572 1974 $65

BANCROFT, HUBERT HOWE   Index to the Chronicles of the Builders of the Commonwealth. San Francisco, 1892. 8vo., cloth. Saddleback 14-797 1974 $10

BANDELLO, MATTEO   Certain Tragical Discourses. 1898. 2 vols., orig. buckram backed boards. Howes 185-534 1974 £10.50

BANDINI, RALPH   Veiled Horizons. New York, The Derrydale Press, 1939. Illus., photos, limited to 950 numbered copies, 8vo., orig. green cloth gilt dec. covers, near mint. Current BW9-175 1974 $60

BANDLER, S. WYLLIS   Vaginal Celiotomy. Philadelphia, 1911. First edition. Rittenhouse 46-35 1974 $10

BANEAT, PAUL   Le Mobilier Breton. Paris, (1925). Three quarters red morocco, cloth, plates. Dawson's 424-220 1974 $135

BANGE, E. F.   Eine Bayerische Malerschule des XI and XII Jahrunderts. Munich, 1923. Half cloth, plates, 4to. Kraus B8-4 1974 $75

BANGS, JOHN KENDRICK   The Booming of Acre Hill. New York, 1900. 12mo., cloth, gilt, first U.S. edition. Covent 56-82 1974 £10.50

BANGS, JOHN KENDRICK   The Dreamers. Harper, 1899. First edition. Austin 54-97 1973 $10

BANGS, JOHN KENDRICK   The Enchanted Type-Writer. New York, 1899. Orig. pictorial cloth, plates, fine, first American edition. Covent 55-1363 1974 £12.50

BANGS, JOHN KENDRICK   The Genial Idiot. New York, 1908. First edition, fine, slightly worn d.w. Wilson 63-483 1974 $16.50

BANGS, JOHN KENDRICK   A House-Boat on the Styx. New York, 1896.
Orig. pictorial cloth, first U.S. edition. Covent 56-1539 1974 £40

BANGS, JOHN KENDRICK   A House-Boat on the Styx. New York, 1896.
Orig. pictorial cloth, first U.S. edition. Covent 56-83 1974 £15.75

BANGS, JOHN KENDRICK   The Idiot at Home. New York, 1900. 8vo.,
dec. cloth, English first edition. Covent 56-84 1974 £12.50

BANGS, JOHN KENDRICK   The Inventions of the Idiot. New York, 1904.
Orig. pictorial cloth, fine, first U.S. edition. Covent 56-85 1974 £10.50

BANGS, JOHN KENDRICK   Mr. Bonaparte of Corsica. New York, 1895.
First edition, orig. binding. Wilson 63-484 1974 $12.75

BANGS, JOHN KENDRICK   Mr. Munchausen. Boston, 1901. Post 8vo.,
orig. pictorial cloth, fine, first U.S. edition. Covent 56-86 1974 £12.50

BANGS, JOHN KENDRICK   Mrs. Raffles. New York, 1905. Plates, orig.
pictorial cloth, foxing, first American edition. Covent 55-848 1974 £21

BANGS, JOHN KENDRICK   New Wagglings of Old Tales. Boston, 1888.
Post 8vo., orig. dec. cloth, first U.S. edition. Covent 56-92 1974 £12.50

BANGS, JOHN KENDRICK   Olympian Nights. New York, 1902. 12mo.,
plates, first U.S. edition. Covent 56-87 1974 £10.50

BANGS, JOHN KENDRICK   Over the Plum-Pudding. New York, 1901.
1st ed. Biblo & Tannen 210-700 1973 $10

BANGS, JOHN KENDRICK   Peeps at People. Harper, 1899. 185 pages,
illus. Austin 54-99 1973 $8.50

BANGS, JOHN KENDRICK   Peeps at People. New York, 1899. 12mo.,
orig. pictorial cloth, fine, first U.S. edition. Covent 56-88 1974 £10.50

BANGS, JOHN KENDRICK   The Pursuit of the House Boat. Harper, 1897.
204 pages, orig. edition. Austin 54-100 1973 $4.50

BANGS, JOHN KENDRICK   The Pursuit of the House-Boat. New York,
1897. 12mo., pictorial cloth, plates, first American edition. Covent 55-1364
1974 £15

BANGS, JOHN KENDRICK   The Pursuit of the House-Boat. New York, 1897.
12mo., orig. pictorial cloth, first U.S. edition. Covent 56-89 1974 £15.25

BANGS, JOHN KENDRICK   R. Holmes & Co. New York, 1906. Orig.
pictorial cloth, frontispiece, first American edition. Covent 55-1365 1974 £25

BANGS, JOHN KENDRICK   A Rebellious Heroine. New York, 1896. 12mo.,
orig. pictorial cloth, inscribed, first U.S. edition. Covent 56-90 1974 £10.50

BANGS, JOHN KENDRICK   Uncle Sam Trustee. New York, 1902. Plates,
first U.S. edition. Covent 56-91 1974 £15.75

BANGS, JOHN KENDRICK   The Worsted Man. New York, 1905. 12mo.,
orig. cloth, first edition. Rota 189-68 1974 £5

BANKHEAD, TALLULAH   Tallulah. Harper, 1952. 335p., illus.
Austin 51-42 1973 $6.50

BANKS, CHARLES EDWARD   The Winthrop Fleet of 1630. Boston, 1930.
Large 8vo., plates, limited to 550 copies, signed by author, blue boards, cloth
back. Butterfield 10-369 1974 $35

BANKS, HOMER   The Story of San Clemente, the Spanish Village.
San Clemente, 1930. 8vo., cloth. Saddleback 14-32 1974 $15

BANKS, JOHN   Vertue Betray'd. London, 1692. 4to.,
modern boards, browned. Dawsons PM 252-38 1974 £35

BANKS, JOHN   Vertue Betray'd. London, 1682. 4to.,
quarter morocco, browned, first edition. Dawsons PM 252-37 1974 £85

BANKS, JOSEPH   Journal of the Right Hon. Sir Joseph Banks
During Captain Cook's First Voyage in H. M. S. Endeavour in 1768-71. 1896.
8vo., cloth, charts, portraits, spine sun-faded, very scarce. Wheldon 128-172
1973 £22

BANKS, POLAN   The Man from Cooks. New York, 1938.
1st ed., author's sgd. pres. Biblo & Tannen 210-701 1973 $10

BANKS, THOMAS C.   Annals of Thomas Banks, Sculptor, Royal
Academician. Cambridge, 1938. 4to., plates, cloth. Quaritch 940-14 1974
£12

BANKS, THOMAS C.   Baronia Anglica Concentrata. 1844-43.
2 vols., 4to., cloth, paper labels, worn. Quaritch 939-705 1974 £10.50

BANKS, THOMAS C.   The Dormant and Extinct Baronage of England.
1807-09. 3 vols., 4to., contemporary half calf. Howes 186-1618 1974 £28

BANKS, W.   Views of the English Lakes. c.1860. Oblong
8vo., plates, foxed, half calf. Quaritch 939-44 1974 £15

BANNATYNE, GEORGE   Ancient Scottish Poems. Edinburgh, 1770. Small
8vo., contemporary tree calf, fine. Quaritch 936-13 1974 £30

BANNATYNE, GEORGE   The Bannatyne Manuscript. 1933-28-30.
4 vols., orig. roxburghe binding. Howes 186-590 1974 £18

BANNERMAN, HELEN   Little Black Sambo. Philadelphia, n.d.
16mo., boards, cloth spine, illus. Frohnsdorff 16-71 1974 $20

BANNERMAN, HELEN   The Story of Little Black Sambo. London,
1903. Orig. cloth, engravings. Frohnsdorff 16-69 1974 $50

BANNERMAN, HELEN   The Story of Little Black Sambo. Chicago, 1905.
32mo., colored illus., pictorial paper covered boards, cloth spine. Current
BW9-3 1974 $60

BANNERMAN, HELEN   The Story of Little Black Sambo. Chicago,
1908. 16mo., illus; pictorial boards. Frohnsdorff 16-72 1974 $15

BANNERMAN, HELEN   The Story of Little Black Sambo. London,
1932. 16mo., illus. Frohnsdorff 16-70 1974 $10

BANNERMAN, HELEN   Little Black Sambo. Sandusky, 1943. Large
4to., boards; 6 color plates. Frohnsdorff 16-73 1974 $9.50

BANNERS, Standards, and Badges from a Tudor Manuscript in the College of Arms.
1904. Roy. 4to., frontispiece, illus., buckram. Quaritch 939-717 1974 £7

BANNISTER, HARRY   The Education of a Broadcaster. Simon and
Schuster, 1965. 351p. Austin 51-43 1973 $7.50

THE BANQUET of Wit. Edinburgh, 1802. 12mo., contemporary half calf,
scarce, rebacked, first edition. Ximenes 33-388 1974 $65

BAPST, GERMAIN   Le Marechal Canrobert. Paris, 1899-1904.
3 vols., maps, half morocco gilt. Howes 186-683 1974 £15

BARATTIERI, GIOVANNI BATTISTA   Trattato Teorico-Pratico. 1783. 4to.,
contemporary half mottled calf, gilt, worn, uncut. Zeitlin 235-15 1974 $90

BARBAULD, ANNA LETITIA   The British Novelists. 1820. 50 vols., 12mo.,
contemporary green straight grained morocco, covers and spines gilt panelled, some
foxing and stains, new edition. Bow Windows 66-34 1974 £188

BARBAULD, ANNA LETITIA   Lecons Pour les Enfans de Trois a Huit Ans.
Paris, 1817. 4 vols. in 2, full tan calf, color plates. Gregory 44-34 1974 $175

BARBAULT, JEAN   Nouveaux Recueil de Vues des Principales Eglises
Places, Rues et Palais de Rome Moderne et des Plus Beaux Monuments de Rome
Ancienne. Rome, 1763. Folio, 19th century half red morocco, rubbed but sound,
double page plates. Thomas 32-343 1974 £450

BARBEAU, MARIUS   Quebec, Where Ancient France Lingers.
Toronto, 1936. Leather spine, raised bands, gold stamping, illus. Hood's
102-680 1974 $35

BARBEAU, MARIUS   Quebec, Where Ancient France Lingers.
Toronto, 1936. Illus., leather spine, raised bands. Hood's 104-909 1974 $35

BARBER, E.   Memorials of Old Cheshire. 1910. 8vo., orig.
cloth, illus. Bow Windows 64-384 1974 £6.50

BARBER, EDWIN ATLEE   Artificial Soft Paste Porcelain.   New York, 1907. Plates, cloth backed boards, gilt, near fine. Covent 51-2265 1973 £5.25

BARBER, JOHN WARNER   Historical Collections of the State of New Jersey ...Geographical Descriptions of Every Township in the State.   Newark, 1860. Handsomely rebound in three quarter morocco, green leather labels. Butterfield 10-435 1974 $50

BARBER, JOHN WARNER   The History and Antiquities of New England, New Jersey, and Pennsylvania. Hartford, 1842. 8vo., orig. bindings, frontispiece, first edition. Butterfield 8-411 1974 $60

BARBER, THOMAS   Barber's Picturesque Guide to the Isle of Wight. 1850. Green half morocco, cloth sides, corners worn, coloured map, frontis., plates. Bow Windows 66-35 1974 £17.50

BARBER & HOWE   New Jersey Historical Collections. 1845. Orig. cloth. Putman 126-85 1974 $11

BARBERIIS, PHILIPPUS DE   Discordantiae Sanctorum Doctorum Hieronymi et Augustini. Oppenheim, (c. 1510). Small 4to., boards, cloth back, woodcuts, fine. Harper 213-12 1973 $950

BARBETTE, PAUL   Chirurgia. Amsterdam, 1693. 12mo., old calf, rebacked. Gurney 64-13 1974 £20

BARBETTE, PAUL   Chirurgia, Notis et Observationibus Rarioribus Illustrata Secundeum Verae Philosophiae Fundamenta ac Recentiorum Inventa. Amsterdam, 1693. 12mo., old calf, rebacked, engraved frontis. Gurney 66-16 1974 £20

BARBETTE, PAUL   The Practice of the Most Successful Physician Paul Barbette. London, 1675. Small 8vo., old calf, worn. Traylen 79-200 1973 £190

BARBETTE, PAUL   Praxis Barbettiana. Leyden, 1669. 12mo., contemporary calf. Schuman 37-11 1974 $145

BARBEY, W.   Florae Sardoae Compendium.   Lausanne, 1884-85. 4to., new cloth, plates. Wheldon 129-1043 1974 £20

BARBEY D'AUREVILLY, JULES AMEDEE   Memoranda. Paris, 1883. 12mo., three quarter light brown cloth, orig. wrapper, uncut, limited, first edition. L. Goldschmidt 42-150 1974 $40

BARBEY D'AUREVILLY, JULES AMEDEE   Weird Women. London and Paris, 1900. 2 vols., orig. silken cloth, gilt. Covent 55-155 1974 £22.50

BARBIER, ANTOINE-ALEXANDRE   Dictionnaire des Ouvrages Anonymes et Pseudonymes Composes. Paris, 1806-09. 4 vols., 8vo., contemporary mottled calf, gilt, first edition. Dawsons PM 10-23 1974 £16

BARBIER, ANTOINE ALEXANDRE   Nouvelle Bibliotheque d'un Homme de Gout Entierement Refondue. Paris, 1808-10. 5 vols., 8vo., contemporary half straight grain morocco, gilt. L. Goldschmidt 42-152 1974 $75

BARBIER DE MONTAULT, X.   Traite Pratique de la Construction de l'Ameublement et de la Decoration des Eglises. Paris, 1878. 2 vols., half black calf. Howes 185-943 1974 £7.50

BARBOSA RODRIGUES, J.   Hortus Fluminensis ou Breve Noticia Sobre as Plantas Cultivadas no Jardin Botanico do Rio de Janeiro. Rio de Janeiro, 1894. Roy. 8vo., plates, orig. wrappers, scarce. Wheldon 131-1490 1974 £5

BARBOUR, F. C. W.   Spelman Genealogy: The English Ancestry and American Descendants of Richard Spelman of Middletown, Connecticut. New York, 1910. Illus., stained. Jenkins 61-680 1974 $20

BARBOUR, T.   Cuban Ornithology. Cambridge, 1943. 4to., cloth, plates. Wheldon 130-454 1974 £5

BARBOUTAU, P.   Collection P. Barboutau. Peintures, Estampes et Objets d'Art du Japon. Amsterdam, 1905. 2 vols., roy. 4to., illus., boards, cloth spines, uncut. Quaritch 940-372 1974 £35

BARBUT, JAMES   The Genera Vermium. 1783. 4to., plates, contemporary red morocco gilt. Wheldon 131-917 1974 £25

BARCELONA INSTITUT D'ESTUDIS CATALANS   Seccio Historico-Arqueologica 1927-31. 1936. Vol. 8 only, folio, sewn, illus. Allen 213-134 1973 $15

BARCIA, ANDRES GONZALEZ   Chronological History of the Continent of Florida. Gainesville, 1951. 4to., orig. bds. Jacobs 24-9 1974 $40

BARCLAY, JAMES   Universal English Dictionary. London, (n.d.). 4to., contemporary half calf, plates. Dawsons PM 252-39 1974 £195

BARCLAY, JOHN 1582-1621   Barclay, His Argenis. 1636. Plates, calf, second edition. Allen 213-1888 1973 $75

BARCLAY, JOHN 1758-1826   The Muscular Motions of the Human Body. Edinburgh, 1808. 8vo., orig. boards, uncut, fine, first edition. Dawsons PM 249-24 1974 £30

BARCLAY, JOHN 1758-1826   A New Anatomical Nomenclature. Edinburgh, 1803. 8vo., contemporary boards, plates, first edition. Schumann 35-360 1974 $110

BARCLAY, JOHN 1758-1826   A New Anatomical Nomenclature. Edinburgh, 1803. 8vo., orig. boards, uncut, first edition. Dawsons PM 249-23 1974 £24

BARD, SAMUEL A. PSEUD.
Please turn to
SQUIER, EPHRAIM GEORGE

BARDE, FREDERICK S.   Life and Adventures of "Billy" Dixon of Adobe Walls, Texas Panhandle. Guthrie, (1914). Rare first edition. Jenkins 61-193 1974 $60

BARDI, P. M.   The Arts in Brazil. Milan, 1956. Sq. 4to., illus. Biblo & Tannen 214-317 1974 $37.50

BARDI, P. M.   La Primavera di Sandro Botticelli. Milan, 1949. 4to., color plates. Biblo & Tannen 210-57 1973 $12.50

BARDSLEY, C. W.   Chronicles of the Town and Church of Ulverston. Ulverston, 1885. 4to., orig. cloth. Broadhurst 23-1306 1974 £20

BARDSLEY, SAMUEL ARGENT   Medical Reports. London, 1807. 8vo., contemporary calf, gilt, first edition. Dawsons PM 249-25 1974 £13

BARDWELL, WILLIAM   Temples, Ancient and Modern. 1837. Small 4to., illus., half calf, gilt, foxed. Covent 55-61 1974 £12.50

BARFIELD, OWEN   History In English Words. 1926. Ex-library. Austin 61-16 1974 $10

BARHAM, RICHARD HARRIS   The Garrick Club. (New York), 1896. 8vo., orig. white cloth gilt, uncut. Dawsons PM 252-40 1974 £15

BARHAM, RICHARD HARRIS   The Ingoldsby Legends. London, 1840-47. 3 vols., full levant morocco, plates, fine, first edition. Dawsons PM 252-41 1974 £120

BARHAM, RICHARD HARRIS   The Ingoldsby Legends. 1852. Full contemporary morocco, gilt, 3 vols., English first edition. Covent 56-1541 1974 £21

BARHAM, RICHARD HARRIS   The Ingoldsby Legends. 1887. 8vo., full crimson morocco, boards, gilt, illus. Quaritch 936-283 1974 £10

BARHAM, RICHARD HARRIS   The Ingoldsby Legends. 1905. 8vo., orig. pictorial cloth gilt, plates, second edition. Howes 185-388 1974 £6.50

BARI, VALESKA   The Course of Empire. New York, 1931. Illus. Jenkins 61-276 1974 $12.50

BARICELLI, JULIUS CAESAR   Hortulus Genialis Sive Rerum Iucundarum. Geneva, 1620. Rebound, boards, spotting, good copy. Rittenhouse 46-39 1974 $75

BARING, FRANCIS   Observations on the Establishment of the Bank of England. London, 1797. 8vo., modern boards, first edition. Dawsons PM 247-11 1974 £30

BARING, MAURICE   Algae: An Anthology of Phrases. 1928. First ordinary edition, wrappers, very good, author's signed presentation inscription. Covent 51-2144 1973 £10.50

BARING, MAURICE   The Black Prince and Other Poems. 1903. Bookplate, fine, author's initialled presentation inscription, first edition. Covent 51-168 1973 £9.50

BARING, MAURICE   The Black Prince and Other Poems. 1903. Presentation copy, inscribed, English first edition. Covent 56-95 1974 £10.50

BARING, MAURICE   Cat's Cradle. 1926. Illus., 720 pages. Austin 61-17 1974 $10

BARING, MAURICE   Cecil Spencer. 1929. 4to., signed, first published edition. Rota 188-59 1974 £8

BARING, MAURICE   In My End Is My Beginning. 1921. 312 pages. Austin 61-18 1974 $10

BARING, MAURICE   Jane's All the World's Aircraft. 1942. Folio, illus., orig. cloth. Smith 193-908 1973 £8

BARING, MAURICE   Landmarks in Russian Literature. 1910. 8vo., orig. cloth, inscription, first edition. Rota 189-72 1974 £5

BARING, MAURICE   Overlooked. 1922. Orig. cloth, dust wrapper, fine. Rota 188-56 1974 £10

BARING, MAURICE   Poems. 1919. Full morocco, presentation copy, inscribed, English first edition. Covent 56-1542 1974 £15

BARING, MAURICE   Poems Translated from Pushkin. 1931. 4to., full morocco gilt, orig. wrappers, fine. Covent 55-156 1974 £25

BARING, MAURICE   R. F. C. H. Q. -1914-18. London, 1920. Orig. buckram, first edition. Smith 193-907 1973 £5

BARING, MAURICE   Sarah Bernhardt. Appleton, Century, 1934. 163p. Austin 51-44 1973 $7.50

BARING, MAURICE   Tinker's Leave. 1927. Orig. cloth, dust wrapper, scarce, fine. Rota 188-57 1974 £7

BARING, MAURICE   Tinker's Leave. 1928. 268 pages. Austin 61-19 1974 $10

BARING, MAURICE   Translations Ancient and Modern. 1925. Handmade paper, presentation copy, inscribed, English first edition. Covent 56-96 1974 £20

BARING, MAURICE   What I Saw In Russia. 1927. 386 pages. Austin 61-20 1974 $12.50

BARING-GOULD, SABINE   Cornish Characters and Strange Event. 1908. Illus. Austin 61-21 1974 $12.50

BARING-GOULD, SABINE   Strange Survivals: Some Chapters in the History of Man. 1892. Illus., library plate, front hinge cracked, contents very good, first edition. Covent 51-170 1973 £6.30

BARKER, ELSA   The C. I. D. of Dexter Drake. New York, 1929. 8vo., orig. cloth, fine, first edition. Rota 190-178 1974 £8

BARKER, EUGENE   The Austin Papers. Washington, 1924-28. 3 vols. Jenkins 61-174 1974 $85

BARKER, FRED F.   Compilation of the Acts of Congress and Treaties Relating to Alaska from March 30, 1867 to March 3, 1905. Washington, 1906. Jenkins 61-90 1974 $27.50

BARKER, GEORGE   Alanna Autumnal. 1933. Cloth backed boards, very nice copy, spine faded, scarce, first edition. Covent 51-172 1973 £10

BARKER, GEORGE   Calamiterror. 1937. First edition, brilliant copy, virtually unmarked d.w. Covent 51-174 1973 £10.50

BARKER, GEORGE   Thirty Preliminary Poems. 1933. First edition, boards, spine little faded, extremely fine copy, scarce. Covent 51-178 1973 £17.50

BARKER, M. H.   Greenwich Hospital. 1826. 4to., woodcuts, half morocco, rubbed, first edition. Howes 185-90 1974 £20

BARKER, M. H.   Greenwich Hospital. 1826. 4to., illus., plates, half calf, foxing. Quaritch 939-834 1974 £110

BARKER, RICHARD THOMAS   A Research on the Eucalypts. Sydney, 1902. 4to., cloth, plates, scarce. Wheldon 129-1593 1974 £15

BARKER, RICHARD THOMAS   A Research on the Eucalypts Especially in Regard to Their Essential Oils. Sydney, 1902. 4to., cloth, scarce, plates. Wheldon 131-1711 1974 £15

BARKSDALE, CLEMENT   A Remembrancer of Excellent Men. London, 1670. 8vo., contemporary sheep, first edition. Dawsons PM 251-102 1974 £60

BARLA, J. B.   Les Champignons de la Province de Nice. Nice, 1859. Oblong 4to., contemporary half morocco, plates, rare first edition. Wheldon 131-12 1974 £250

BARLETT, E.   A Monograph of the Weaver Birds. Maidstone, 1888(-89). Crown 4to., half green morocco, plates. Wheldon 130-5 1974 £185

BARLETTI, CARLO   Analisi D'un Nuovo Fenomeno Del Fulmine. 1780. 4to., modern vellum, fine, uncut, first edition. Dawsons PM 245-44 1974 £40

BARLETTI, CARLO   Nuove Sperienze Elettriche Secondo. 1771. 8vo., orig. gray wrappers, uncut, first edition. Zeitlin 235-16 1974 $45

BARLOW, CRAWFORD   The New Tay Bridge. London, 1889. Folio, plates, orig. pictorial cloth gilt. Smith 193-213 1973 £7.50

BARLOW, EDWARD   Barlow's Journal of his Life. 1934. 8vo., 2 vols., orig. cloth. Broadhurst 23-1609 1974 £20

BARLOW, EDWARD   An Exact Survey of the Tide. London, 1722. 8vo., half calf, gilt, plates, second edition. Hammond 201-791 1974 £45

BARLOW, FREDERICK   The Complete English Dictionary. (1772). 2 vols., recent half calf gilt, frontispiece, plates. Hill 126-70 1974 £48

BARLOW, PETER   An Elementary Investigation of the Theory of Numbers. London, 1811. 8vo., orig. paper-covered boards, uncut, first edition. Dawsons PM 245-45 1974 £15

BARLOW, WILLIAM   The Svmme and Svbstance of the Conference, Which it Pleased His Excellent Majestie to Have with the Lords Bishops, and Others of His Clergie . . . at Hampton Court. 1638. Small 4to., contemporary calf, little waterstained. Thomas 32-43 1974 £45

BARNABEE, HENRY CLAY   Reminiscences of Henry Clay Barnabee. Boston, 1913. 1st ed., illus. Biblo & Tannen 213-890 1973 $10

BARNARD, CAROLINE   The Parent's Offering. 1820. New and Improved edition, engraved plates, 12mo., orig. boards, stained, neatly rebacked, edges uncut, ads and pub. catalogue at end. George's 610-46 1973 £6.50

BARNARD, CAROLINE   The Prize. 1817. First edition, half title, engraved frontispiece, some browning of text, 12mo., contemporary half calf. George's 610-47 1973 £7.50

BARNARD, CAROLINE   The Prize. 1817. First edition, half title, frontispiece, slight soiling, 12mo., contemporary sheep, rubbed, one joint broken. George's 610-48 1973 £6.50

BARNARD, F. P.   Edward IV's French Expedition of 1475. Oxford, 1925. F'cap 4to., double page plates, frontispiece, orig. cloth, fine. Broadhurst 24-236 1974 £12

BARNARD, GEORGE   The Theory and Practice of Landscape Painting in Water Colours. 1855. 8vo., contemporary calf gilt, plates, foxed, first edition. Quaritch 940-15 1974 £40

BARNARD, JOHN   A Present for an Apprentice. London, n.d. 8vo., wrappers, fourth edition. Ximenes 37-16 1974 $27.50

BARNARD, JOHN   Sermons on Several Subjects. London, 1727.
Contemporary calf, quite worn, inscriptions, typed note laid in. Butterfield
10-197 1974 $85

BARNES, ALBERT C.   The Art of Henri Matisse. New York, 1933.
First edition, inscribed, signed by Barnes, orig. binding, bookplate, laid in is
copy of typed speech delivered by Barnes. Wilson 63-291 1974 $25

BARNES, C. M.   The Report of the Governor of Oklahoma for
the Year Ended June 30, 1898. Washington, 1898. Wrapper, illus., large
folding colored map, fine content. Jenkins 61-2019 1974 $15

BARNES, DJUNA   A Book. New York, 1923. 8vo., orig. cloth,
inscribed, rare, first edition. Rota 190-28 1974 $150

BARNES, DJUNA   A Night Among the Horses. New York, 1929.
8vo., frayed, dust wrapper, fine, signed, presentation inscription, scarce, second
edition. Rota 190-29 1974 $100

BARNES, DJUNA   Ryder. New York, 1928. Blue cloth, illus.,
first edition. Dawson's 424-248 1974 $20

BARNES, ERIC W.   The Lady of Fashion. Scribner, 1954. 308p.,
illus. Austin 51-45 1973 $7.50

BARNES, ERIC W.   The Man Who Lived Twice. Scribners, 1956.
367p. Austin 51-46 1973 $7.50

BARNES, JAMES   Naval Actions in the War of 1812. New York,
1896. Illus. Hood's 102-89 1974 $35

BARNES, JULIANA
Please turn to
BERNERS, JULIANA

BARNES, MARY CLARKE   The New America. 1913. 160 pages, illus.
paper. Austin 57-58 1974 $10

BARNES, MARY CLARK   The New America. Revell, 1913. 160p.,
illus., paper. Austin 62-29 1974 $10

BARNES, WILLIAM   Poems of Rural Life In Common English. London,
1868. 8vo., orig. cloth, uncut, first edition. Dawsons PM 252-42 1974 £30

BARNES, WILLIAM   Poems of Rural Life in the Dorset Dialect. 1848.
Revised second edition, signature of William Allingham on title, orig. cloth, spine
defective. Thomas 32-154 1974 £15

BARNETT, JOEL   A Long Trip in a Prairie Schooner. Whittier,
(1928). 8vo., orig. bindings. Butterfield 8-689 1974 $15

BARNEY, ELVIRA STEVENS   The Stevens Genealogy. Salt Lake City, 1907.
8vo., cloth. Saddleback 14-791 1974 $20

BARNEY, JAMES M.   Tales of Apache Warfare. N.P., 1933. First
edition, 8vo., scarce, some water stains in top margins. Current BW9-373 1974
$35

BARNEY, NATALIE CLIFFORD   Actes et Entr'Actes. Paris, 1910. Wrappers,
covers little soiled & upper corner of lower cover eaten away, very good copy,
unopened, scarce. Covent 51-2145 1973 £11.50

BARNEY, NATALIE CLIFFORD   Aventures de l'Esprit. Paris, 1929. Wrappers,
frontispiece, English first edition. Covent 56-99 1974 £45

BARNEY, NATALIE CLIFFORD   Cinq Petits Dialogues Grecs. Paris, 1902.
Wrappers, spine partly split, covers dust soiled, very good, scarce, largely
unopened, first edition. Covent 51-180 1973 £17.50

BARNEY, NATALIE CLIFFORD   Nouvelles Pensees de l'Amazone. Paris, 1939.
8vo., wrappers, fine, first edition. Rota 189-77 1974 £7.50

BARNEY, NATALIE CLIFFORD   The One Who is Legion. 1930. Illus., one
of 560 copies, buckram, top edges gilt, fine, d.w., first edition. Covent
51-2146 1973 £15

BARNEY, NATALIE CLIFFORD   Pensees d'une Amazone. Paris, 1920. Stamp
on title & half title, covers slightly soiled, very nice unopened copy, wrappers.
Covent 51-181 1973 £10

BARNEY, NATALIE CLIFFORD   Poems & Poemes. Paris, 1920. Small 4to.,
wrappers. Covent 55-158 1974 £20

BARNOUW, ADRIAAN J.   The Fantasy of Pieter Brueghel. New York,
1947. Oblong 4to., plates. Biblo & Tannen 214-439 1974 $13.50

BARNOUW, ERIK   Handbook of Radio Writing. Little, Brown,
1939. 306p. Austin 51-47 1973 $8.50

BARNS, T. A.   An African Eldorado. 1926. 8vo., cloth,
illus., scarce. Wheldon 129-237 1974 £10

BARNUM, PHINNEAS TAYLOR   Struggles and Triumphs. 1927. 2 vols.,
plates, good ex-library. Allen 216-2107 1974 $10

BARNUM, SAMUEL W.   Romanism as It Is. 1871. 753 pages, illus.
Austin 57-59 1974 $17.50

BAROLINI, ANTONIO   Our Last Family Countess and Related Stories.
Harper. 201p., illus. Austin 62-30 1974 $10

BARONI, CONSTANTINO   Maioliche di Milano. Milano, 1940. 8vo.,
plates, orig. cloth. Bow Windows 62-62 1974 £50

BARONIO, GIUSEPPE   Saggio Di Naturali Osservazioni Sulla Elettricita
Voltiana. Milan, 1806. 8vo., contemporary Italian boards, gilt, first edition.
Dawsons PM 245-46 1974 £62

BARONIUS, CESARE   Annales Ecclesiastici ex XII Tomis Caesaris
Baronii. 1618. Thick folio, contemporary calf, rebacked. Howes 185-944
1974 £50

BAROZZI, FRANCESCO   Cosmographia in Qvatvor Libros Distribvta. Venice, 1585. 8vo., modern half calf, gilt, plates, first edition. Dawsons PM 245-
47 1974 £65

BARR, ALFRED H.   Picasso, Forty Years of His Art. 1941. 4to.,
wrappers, illus., limited, fourth edition. Minters 37-296 1973 $25

BARR, AMELIA EDITH   The Bow of Orange Ribbon. New York, 1886.
6 engravings, orig. printed wrappers; 8vo. Frohnsdorff 16-75 1974 $10

BARR, E. OSMUN   Flying Men and Medicine. New York & London,
1943. Rittenhouse 46-40 1974 $10

BARR, ROBERT   The Face and the Mask. New York, 1895.
12mo., illus., faded. Covent 55-1366 1974 $25

BARRA, E. I.   A Tale of Two Oceans: From Philadelphia
Around Cape Horn, in the Years 1849-50. San Francisco, 1893. Wrapper, very
fine copy. Jenkins 61-277 1974 $65

BARRANDE, J.   Acephales. Prague, 1881. 8vo., half calf,
plates, scarce. Wheldon 131-965 1974 £7.50

BARREIROS, GASPAR   De Ophyra Regione. Rotterdam, 1616. Small
8vo., disbound. Thomas 32-3 1974 £20

BARRELIER, J.   Plantae per Galliam, Hispaniam et Italiam
Observatae. Paris, 1714. Folio, contemporary calf, plates. Wheldon 129-
1044 1974 £200

BARRELIER, J.   Plantae per Galliam, Hispaniam et Italiam
Observatae. Paris, 1714. Folio, contemporary calf, plates, nice clean copy,
rare. Wheldon 131-1257 1974 £200

BARREME, FRANCOIS   L'Arithmetique. Paris, 1732. 12mo., contemporary calf, gilt. Dawsons PM 245-48 1974 £8

BARRES, MAURICE   Le Mystere en Pleine Lumiere. Paris, 1926.
Half cloth, bookplate, first edition. Covent 56-101 1974 £6.30

BARRETT, A. C.   The Propositions in Mechanics and Hydrostatics.
Cambridge, 1847. 8vo., contemporary half calf, rebacked. Dawsons PM 245-
49 1974 £6.50

BARRETT, CHARLES G.   The Lepidoptera of the British Islands. 1893-1907. 11 vols., roy. 8vo., orig. brown cloth, hand-coloured plates, large paper edition. Wheldon 128-673 1973 £120

BARRETT, CHARLES RAYMOND BOOTH   The History of the Society of Apothecaries of London. London, 1905. Rittenhouse 46-41 1974 $50

BARRETT, JAMES WYMAN   Joseph Pulitzer and His World. Vanguard, 1941. Austin 62-32 1974 $12.50

BARRETT, JOSEPH H.   Life of Abraham Lincoln. Cincinnati, 1860. Wrappers, worn, rare, first edition, first issue. Hayman 57-449 1974 $50

BARRETT, W.   The History and Antiquities of the City of Bristol. Bristol, (1789). 4to., buckram. Quaritch 939-354 1974 £35

BARRETT-HAMILTON, G. E. H.   A History of British Mammals. 1910-21. Parts 1 - 21, roy. 8vo., orig. wrappers, portraits, coloured and plain plates, scarce. Wheldon 128-303 1973 £20

BARRETT-HAMILTON, G. E. H.   A History of British Mammals, Vol. 1, Bats. 1910-11. 6 parts, roy. 8vo., orig. wrappers, coloured and plain plates, scarce. Wheldon 128-304 1973 £5

BARRETT-HAMILTON, G. E. H.   A History of British Mammals. 1910-21. Roy 8vo., wrappers, plates. Wheldon 129-360 1974 £20

BARRIE, JAMES MATTHEW   The Admirable Crichton. n.d. Orig. cloth, plates, illus. Marsden 39-446 1974 £7

BARRIE, JAMES MATTHEW   Auld Light Idylls. London, 1888. First edition, blue buckram, rear hinge beginning to loosen, very nice copy, orig. binding. Ross 86-43 1974 $30

BARRIE, JAMES MATTHEW   Courage. London, n.d. (1922). Large paper edition, fine, orig. binding. Ross 86-44 1974 $25

BARRIE, JAMES MATTHEW   Der Tag. (1914). Small 8vo., cloth backed boards, d.w., first edition. Quaritch 936-285 1974 £25

BARRIE, JAMES MATTHEW   Echoes of the War. 1918. Half calf, second edition. Covent 56-102 1974 £8.50

BARRIE, JAMES MATTHEW   The Entrancing Life. London, 1930. First edition, orig. binding, mint. Ross 86-45 1974 $10

BARRIE, JAMES MATTHEW   Farewell Miss Julie Logan. New York, 1932. First American edition, orig. binding. Wilson 63-486 1974 $10

BARRIE, JAMES MATTHEW   George Meredith. Portland, 1919. Limited to 950 copies printed on Kisogawa hand made paper, full black morocco, mint, glassine wrapper. Ross 86-46 1974 $15

BARRIE, JAMES MATTHEW   Half Hours. (1914). 8vo., orig. cloth, signed, inscription, first edition. Rota 189-79 1974 £5

BARRIE, JAMES MATTHEW   The Kirriemuir Edition of the Works of. 1913. Roy. 8vo., boards, uncut, unopened, limited. Broadhurst 23-562 1974 £30

BARRIE, JAMES MATTHEW   A Lady's Shoe. New York, (1893). 12mo., orig. limp leather, first American edition, Vincent Starrett's copy, blue quarter morocco box. MacManus 224-18 1974 $25

BARRIE, JAMES MATTHEW   The Little Minister. New York, 1891. First illus. & first American edition, very scarce, hinges weak, nice condition, orig. binding, glassine wrapper. Ross 86-47 1974 $45

BARRIE, JAMES MATTHEW   The Little Minister. New York, 1898. Biblo & Tannen 213-491 1973 $7.50

BARRIE, JAMES MATTHEW   The Little White Bird. New York, 1902. 8vo., gilt decorated cloth; top edge gilt. Frohnsdorff 16-76 1974 $7.50

BARRIE, JAMES MATTHEW   Peter Pan. 1928. Dust wrapper, fine. Covent 55-159 1974 £5.25

BARRIE, JAMES MATTHEW   Peter Pan in Kensington Gardens. n.d. Dec. cloth gilt, illus., plates. Marsden 39-360 1974 £10

BARRIE, JAMES MATTHEW   Peter Pan in Kensington Gardens. London, 1906. Illus. by Arthur Rackham, orig. binding, lacking d.w., front hinge slightly tender, fine. Ross 87-468 1974 $100

BARRIE, JAMES MATTHEW   The Plays of. London, 1928. Orig. cloth, first edition, tipped in short A.L.s. from Barrie, fine, dust jacket. MacManus 224-19 1974 $40

BARRIE, JAMES MATTHEW   Quality Street. (1913). 4to., orig. vellum, gilt, illus., plates. Howes 185-520 1974 £7.50

BARRIE, JAMES MATTHEW   Sentimental Tommy. 1896. Bookplate, spine faded, first edition, first issue. Allen 216-95 1974 $10

BARRIE, JAMES MATTHEW   Sentimental Tommy. London, 1896. Orig. blue buckram, very good, first edition. MacManus 224-20 1974 $25

BARRIE, JAMES MATTHEW   Sentimental Tommy. New York, 1896. Orig. binding, newspaper clipping pasted to front cover, unusually fine, bright copy. Ross 86-49 1974 $12.50

BARRIE, JAMES MATTHEW   Tommy and Grizel. 1900. Allen 216-96 1974 $12.50

BARRIE, JAMES MATTHEW   Walker London. London & New York, 1907. Orig. cloth, wrappers, scarce. Rota 188-68 1974 £35

BARRIE, JAMES MATTHEW   When A Man's Single. London, 1888. Orig. blue buckram, first edition, bookplate removed, very fine copy, cloth box. MacManus 224-21 1974 $25

BARRIE, JAMES MATTHEW   A Window in Thrums. London, 1889. First edition, scarce, slight foxing, near fine. Ross 86-50 1974 $30

BARRIE, JAMES MATTHEW   A Window in Thrums. 1892. Limited to 550 numbered copies, large paper, fine, illus., first edition. Covent 51-182 1973 £10.50

BARRIE, JAMES MATTHEW   A Window in Thrums. 1892. 8vo., plates, new edition. Covent 56-103 1974 £12.50

BARRIE, JAMES MATTHEW   A Window in Thrums. London, 1892. 4to., orig. cloth, large paper edition, limited to 550 numbered copies, inscribed presentation copy, quarter morocco box. MacManus 224-22 1974 $60

BARRIE, JAMES MATTHEW   Works. 1913. 10 vols., roy. 8vo., orig. cloth backed boards, gilt, limited, best edition. Howes 186-14 1974 £32

BARRIE, JAMES MATTHEW   Works. 1913. Roy. 8vo., 10 vols., boards, gilt, browned. Quaritch 936-284 1974 £40

BARRINGTON, DAINES   Miscellanies. London, 1781. 4to., old calf, rebacked. Traylen 79-464 1973 £130

BARRINGTON, GEORGE   An Account of a Voyage to New South Wales. London, 1810. 2 vols., 8vo., old tree calf gilt, rebacked, leather labels. Traylen 79-544 1973 £120

BARRINGTON, JOHN SHUTE   A Dissuasive from Jacobitism. London, 1713. 8vo., disbound, uncut, first edition. Dawsons PM 251-488 1974 £18

BARRINGTON, JONAH   Historic Memoirs of Ireland. 1835. 2 vols., 4to., half mottled calf gilt, new edition. Quaritch 939-609 1974 £75

BARRINGTON, JONAH   Personal Sketches of His Own Times. London, 1830-32. 3 vols., 8vo., contemporary tree calf, gilt, morocco labels, revised improved second edition. Bow Windows 62-64 1974 £18.50

BARRINGTON, MRS. RUSSELL   The Life, Letters and Work of Frederic Leighton. 1906. 2 vols., crown 4to., orig. cloth, illus. Marsden 37-289 1974 £15

BARRON, A. F.   Vines and Vine-Culture. 1883. 8vo., orig. cloth, plates, scarce. Wheldon 130-1466 1974 £5

BARRON, T.   The Topography and Geology of the Peninsula of Sinai. Cairo, 1907. Roy 8vo., orig. wrappers. Wheldon 129-806 1974 £10

BARRON, T.   The Topography and Geology of the Peninsula of Sinai. Cairo, 1907. Roy. 8vo., orig. wrappers, plates. Wheldon 131-966 1974 £10

BARROUGH, PHILIP   The Method of Physick. London, 1634. Small 4to., old calf, worn, sevent edition. Traylen 79-201 1973 £80

BARROUGH, PHILIP   The Method of Physick. London, 1652. 4to., contemporary calf, worn. Dawsons PM 249-27 1974 £85

BARROW, FANNY   The Fairy Nightcaps. New York, 1861. 12mo., illus. Biblo & Tannen 213-555 1973 $15

BARROW, ISAAC   Archimedis Opera. 1675. 4to., contemporary vellum, plates, first edition. Dawsons PM 245-50 1974 £40

BARROW, ISAAC   Lectiones Habitae in Scholis Publicis Academiae Cantabrigiensis. 1684. 8vo., contemporary half vellum, worn. Dawsons PM 245-51 1974 £36

BARROW, J.   A New and Universal Dictionary of Arts and Sciences. 1751. Folio, plates, rebound in half calf. Quaritch 940-778 1974 £72

BARROW, JOHN   An Autobiographical Memoir. 1847. Orig. patterned cloth, portrait, English first edition. Covent 56-1961 1974 £21

BARROW, JOHN   A Voyage to Cochinchina. London, 1806. 4to., half calf, plates, first edition. Traylen 79-513 1973 £90

BARROW, K. M.   Three Years in Tristan da Cunha. 1910. Extra crown 8vo., orig. cloth, first edition. Broadhurst 23-1610 1974 £8

BARROW, K. M.   Three Years in Tristan de Cunha. 1910. Extra crown 8vo., illus., small map, first edition, orig. cloth, fine. Broadhurst 24-1576 1974 £8

BARROW, WILLIAM   An Essay on Education. London, 1802-04. Small 8vo., 2 vols., half calf, first edition. Hammond 201-277 1974 £32.50

BARROWS, MARJORIE   Box Office. Ziff-Davis, 1943. 291p. Austin 51-48 1973 $10

BARRUS, CLARA   Life & Letters of John Burroughs. 1924. 2 vols., plates. Allen 216-293 1974 $15

BARRY, DAVID   Recherches Experiemntales sur les Causes du Mouvement du Sang dans les Veines. Paris, 1825. 8vo., boards, plate, first edition. Schuman 37-12 1974 $95

BARRY, IRIS   D. W. Griffith. New York, 1940. lst ed. Biblo & Tannen 213-870 1973 $10

BARRY, JOHN STETSON   The History of Massachusetts, Colonial Period, Provincial Period, and Commonwealth Period. Boston, 1856-57. 3 vols. Jenkins 61-1489 1974 $20

BARRY, PHILIP   Hotel Universe. French, 1930. 166p. Austin 51-49 1973 $8.50

BARRY, PHILIP   In a Garden. Doran, 1926. 159p. Austin 51-50 1973 $10

BARRY, PHILIP   John. French, 1929. 173p. Austin 51-51 1973 $7.50

BARRY, PHILIP   The Joyous Season. French, 1934. 168p. Austin 51-52 1973 $8.50

BARRY, PHILIP   Liberty Jones. Coward-McCann, 1941. 167p. Austin 51-53 1973 $10

BARRY, PHILIP   The Philadelphia Story. French, 1942. 141p., paper. Austin 51-54 1973 $6.50

BARRY, PHILIP   Tomorrow and Tomorrow. French, 1931. 173p. Austin 51-55 1973 $7.50

BARRY, PHILIP   White Wings. French, 1929. 149p. Austin 51-56 1973 $7.50

BARRY, PHILIP   Without Love. Coward-McCann, 1943. 206p. Austin 51-57 1973 $8.50

BARRY, PHILIP   You and I. 1923. 179p. Austin 51-58 1973 $8.50

BARRY, WILLIAM   The Papal Monarchy. New York, 1902. Illus. Biblo & Tannen 214-589 1974 $12.50

BARRYMORE, DIANA   Too Much Too Soon. Holt, 1957. 380p., illus. Austin 51-59 1973 $6.50

BARRYMORE, ETHEL   An Autobiography. Harpers, 1955. 310p., illus. Austin 51-60 1973 $6.50

BARRYMORE, JOHN   Confessions of an Actor. 1926. 128p., illus. Austin 51-61 1973 $10

BARRYMORE, LIONEL   We Barrymores. Appleton-Century, 1951. 371p., illus. Austin 51-62 1973 $6.50

BARSCHAK, ERNA   My American Adventure. 1945. Austin 62-33 1974 $10

BARSKY, ARTHUR JOSEPH   Plastic Surgery. Philadelphia, 1938. Rittenhouse 46-71 1974 $20

BARSTOW, GEORGE   The History of New Hampshire from Its Discovery in 1614, to the Passage of the Toleration Act, in 1819. Concord, 1842. First edition, 8vo., backstrip repaired with most of orig. laid down, corners of boards chewed, ex-library, plates, interior good, tight. Current BW9-399 1974 $27.50

BARSTOW, MARJORIE LATTA   Old Hungarian Fairy Tales. n.d. Illus., fine, orig. pictorial cloth, English first edition. Covent 56-432 1974 £15

BARSTOW, MARJORIE LATTA   Wordsworth's Theory of Poetic Diction. 1917. Ex-library, sturdy library binding. Austin 61-27 1974 $27.50

BARTAS, GUILLAUME DE SALUSTE DU
Please turn to
DU BARTAS, GUILLAUME DE SALUSTE

BARTER, RICHARD   Descriptive Notice of the Rise and Progress of the Irish Graffenberg. C., 1860. 8vo., boards, illus. Hammond 201-555 1974 £8

BARTER, RICHARD   The Turkish Bath. Bradford, 1858. 8vo., boards, first edition. Hammond 201-556 1974 £6

BARTH, HANS   Bibliographie Der Schweizer Geschichte. Basel, 1914-15. 3 vols., 8vo., cloth. Dawsons PM 11-37 1974 £49

BARTHOLDT, RICHARD   From Sterrage to Congress. Philadelphia, 1930. 447 pages. Austin 57-60 1974 $10

BARTHOLIN, THOMAS   Epistolarum Medicinalium a Docits Vel ad Doctos Scriptarum, Centuria I. & II. Copenhagen, 1663. 12mo., contemporary vellum, woodcuts. Schuman 37-13 1974 $185

BARTHOLINUS, CASPAR   Specimen Philosophiae Naturalis. 1724. 12mo., contemporary calf, rebacked. Dawsons PM 245-52 1974 £12

BARTHOLINUS, ERASMUS   De Aere Hafniensi Dissertatio. Frankfurt, 1679. 8vo., boards. Gurney 64-14 1974 £20

BARTHOLINUS, THOMAS   De Angina Puerorum Campaniae Siciliaeque Epidemica Exercitationes. Paris, 1646. Small 8vo., contemporary calf, rebacked, first edition. Dawsons PM 249-28 1974 £300

BARTHOLOMAEUS ANGLICUS   Batman Uppon Bartholome His Booke de Proprietatibus Rerum. 1582. Small folio, modern calf, third English edition, black letter, few neat marginal repairs, slight marginal wormina not touching text, some light stains, very satisfactory condition. Thomas 32-158 1974 £950

BARTHOLOMEW, A. T.   Richard Bentley. Cambridge, 1908. 4to., orig. boards, cloth back, uncut, first edition. Dawsons PM 10-32 1974 £9

BARTHOLOW, ROBERTS   Medical Electricity. London, 1881. 8vo., green cloth, first edition. Dawsons PM 245-53 1974 £7

BARTHOU, LOUIS   Bibliotheque de M. Louis Barthou de l'Academie Francaise. Paris, 1935-36. 4 parts, 4to., plates, orig. printed wrappers, cloth. Dawsons PM 10-24 1974 £24

BARTLETT, A. D.   Wild Animals in Captivity. 1898. 8vo., cloth, illus., plates, frontispiece. Wheldon 129-321 1974 £5

BARTLETT, D. W.   Modern Agitators. New York, 1859. Orig. cloth, illus. Putnam 126-219 1974 $10

BARTLETT, EDWARD EVERETT   The Typographic Treasures in Europe. New York, 1925. Ltd. ed., plates. Biblo & Tannen 210-393 1973 $32.50

BARTLETT, JOHN RUSSELL   Dictionary of Americanisms. 1859. Buckram, slightly browned, ex-library, second edition. Allen 216-1382 1974 $10

BARTLETT, JOHN RUSSELL   Personal Narrative of Explorations and Incidents in Texas, New Mexico, California, Sonora, and Chihuhua. New York, 1854. 1st ed., 2 vols., woodcuts, orig. dec. cl., uncut and unopened. Jacobs 24-10 1974 $350

BARTLETT, JOHN RUSSELL   Personal Narrative of Explorations. 1854. 8vo., 2 vols., orig. cloth, first edition. Bow Windows 64-386 1974 £250

BARTLETT, WILLIAM HENRY   American Scenery. London, n.d. 2 vols., 4to., orig. cloth gilt, plates. Traylen 79-466 1973 £140

BARTLETT, WILLIAM HENRY   American Scenery; or, Land, Lake and River Illustrations of Transatlantic Nature. London, 1840. 4to., 2 vols., full page steel engravings, marbled boards and leather, most plates entirely clean. Butterfield 10-44 1974 $450

BARTLETT, WILLIAM HENRY   Forty Days in the Desert. London, c. 1844. 2 vols., illus. Jacobs 24-39 1974 $35

BARTLETT, WILLIAM HENRY   The Scenery and Antiquities of Ireland. n.d. 2 vols., contemporary morocco, gilt. Broadhurst 23-1310 1974 £60

BARTLETT, WILLIAM HENRY   Walks About the City and Environs of Jerusalem. London, c. 1844. Three quarter morocco, rubbed, marbled boards, plates. Jacobs 24-39 1974 $35

BARTOLI, COSIMO   Del Modo di Misvrare le Distantie. 1564. 4to., illus., orig. limp vellum, plates. Zeitlin 235-17 1974 $250

BARTOLI, COSIMO   Del Modo Di Misurare Le Distantie. Venice, 1589. 4to., contemporary limp vellum, second edition. Dawsons PM 245-54 1974 £55

BARTOLI, COSIMO   Del Modo Di Misurare le Distantie. 1614. 4to., quarter vellum, illus., third edition. Dawsons PM 245-55 1974 £50

BARTOLI, DANIELLO   Del Ghiaccio e Della Coagulatione Trattati. Rome, 1681. 4to., nineteenth century marbled boards, worn, first edition. Dawsons PM 245-58 1974 £65

BARTOLI, DANIELLO   Dell'Istoria della Compagnia di Giesv l'Asia Descritta dal P. Daniello Bartoli della Medesima Compagnia. Roma, 1667. Folio, buckram, some marginal worming, water stain. Bow Windows 66-38 1974 £28

BARTOLI, DANIELLO   La Tensione. Rome, 1677. 12mo., contemporary vellum, fine, first edition. Dawsons PM 245-56 1974 £75

BARTOLI, DANIELLO   La Tensione. Venice, 1678. 12mo., contemporary vellum, fine. Dawsons PM 245-57 1974 £48

BARTOLI, PIETRO SANCTO   Picturae Antiquissimi Virgiliani Codicis Bibliothecae Vaticanae. Rome, 1782. 4to., early 19th century polished russia gilt, rubbed. Quaritch 940-16 1974 £45

BARTOLINI, B.   Catalogo delle Piante che Nascono. Siena, 1776. 4to., old half calf. Wheldon 129-1045 1974 £25

BARTOLINI, B.   Catalogo delle Piante che Nascono Spontaneamente Intorno alla Citta' di Siena. Siena, 1776. 4to., old half calf, rare. Wheldon 131-1258 1974 £25

BARTOLINO, DOMENICO   Acta Sacrorum Solemnium Quibus Sanctissimus Dominis Noster Puis Papa IX. Rome, 1864. Thick large 4to., cloth, faded. Howes 185-1295 1974 £15

BARTOLINO, DOMENICO   Commentarium Actorum Omnium Canonizationis Sanctorum Josaphat Kuncewicz. Rome, 1868. 2 vols., large 4to., cloth. Howes 185-1224 1974 £20

BARTOLOMEO, FRA PAOLINO DA SAN   A Voyage to the East Indies. London, 1800. 8vo., plate, contemporary tree calf, first English edition. Bow Windows 62-65 1974 £54

BARTOLOMEO, FRA PAOLINO DA SAN   A Voyage to the East Indies. London, 1800. 8vo., contemporary mottled calf, first edition in English, plate, old library stamp, very good copy. Ximenes 36-9 1974 $85

BARTON, CLARA   History of the Red Cross. Washington, 1883. Half morocco, author's signed presentation copy. Jenkins 61-201 1974 $195

BARTON, F. T.   Pheasants in Covert and Aviary. 1912. 4to., cloth, plates, illus., scarce. Wheldon 130-457 1974 £10

BARTON, LUCY   Natural History of the Holy Land, and Other Places Mentioned in the Bible. (c. 1850). Frontispiece, engraved plates, 12mo., orig. cloth, expertly recased, new cloth spine. George's 610-49 1973 £5

BARTON, MARGARET   Garrick. Macmillan, 1949. 312p., illus. Austin 51-63 1973 $8.50

BARTON, WILLIAM PAUL CRILLON   Compendium Florae Philadelphicae. Philadelphia, 1818. 2 vols., 8vo., orig. boards, uncut, excellent clean copy. Wheldon 131-1259 1974 £85

BARTRAM, WILLIAM   Travels Through North & South Carolina. Philadelphia, 1791. 8vo., contemporary calf, plates, first edition. Traylen 79-465 1973 £980

BARTSCH, ADAM   Le Peintre Graveur. Vienna, 1803-21. 21 vols. in 19, contemporary half calf, well rebacked, uncut, unpressed, good sound set, bookplate of Lord Northwick. Thomas 32-11 1974 £165

BARTSCH, JACOB   Usus Astronomicus Indicis Aspectuum Veterum et Praecip. Nuremberg, 1661. 4to., modern marbled boards. Dawsons PM 245-59 1974 £75

BARWICK, JOHN   Ieronikes, or the Fight, Victory and Triumph of S. Paul. London, 1660. Small 4to., contemporary red morocco, gilt, morocco label, first edition, presentation copy, inscribed, fine. Ximenes 36-10 1974 $75

BARY, A. DE   Beitrage zur Morphologie und Physiologie der Pilze. Frankfurt, (1864)-82, 1888. 2 vols., 4to., cloth, plates (some coloured), rare. Wheldon 128-1335 1973 £15

BARY, A. DE   Comparative Morphology and Biology of the Fungi. Oxford, 1887. Roy 8vo., orig. half morocco, scarce. Wheldon 130-1233 1974 £10

BARY, A. DE   Morphologie und Physiologie der Pilze, Flechten und Myxomyceten. Leipzig, 1866. 8vo., new cloth, text-figures, plate. Wheldon 128-1334 1973 £10

BARY, A. DE   Morphologie und Physiologie der Pilze, Flechten und Myxomyceten. Leipzig, 1866. 8vo., half morocco, rubbed. Wheldon 131-1372 1974 £20

BARY, A. DE   Vergleichende Morphologie. Leipzig, 1885. 8vo., half morocco. Wheldon 129-1145 1974 £15

BASCOM, JOHN   Aesthetics or the Science of Beauty. Crosby, Nichols, 1862. 256p. Austin 54-101 1973 $12.50

BASHFORD, COLES   The Trial in the Supreme Court of the Information in the Nature of a Quo Warranto Filed...on the Relation of Coles Bashford vs. William A. Barstow Contesting the Right to the Office of Governor of Wisconsin. Madison, 1856. Wrappers. Wilson 63-268 1974 $15

BASIL THE GREAT   Opera Omnia Quae Exstant Opera et Studio Juliani Garnier. Paris, 1839. 6 vols., thick roy. 8vo., half roan, rubbed. Howes 185-946 1974 £28

BASILE, GIAMBATTISTA   The Pentamerone of. London, 1932. 2 vols., crown 4to., frontispiece, illus., orig. cloth, dust wrappers. Bow Windows 62-66 1974 £12

BASILE, GIAMBATTISTA   Stories from the Pentamerone. 1911. Roy 8vo., half brown morocco, gilt, plates. Quaritch 936-286 1974 £15

BASKERVILL, W. M.   Anglo-Saxon Reader. 1900. 239 pages. Austin 61-26 1974 $10

BASLER, ADOLPHE   Maurice Utrillo. Paris, 1931. 4to., illus., plates, wrapper. Minters 37-135 1973 $30

BASLER, ADOLPHE   Modern French Painting. New York, 1931. Biblo & Tannen 213-206 1973 $15

BASSI, ELENA   Canova. Bergamo, 1943. Biblo & Tannen 213-212 1973 $12.50

BASTERRA, FELIX B.   El Crepusculo de los Gauchos. Paris, 1903. Biblo & Tannen 213-53 1973 $10

BASTIAN, HENRY CHARLTON   The Brain as an Organ of Mind. London, 1880. 8vo., orig. red printed cloth, gilt, first edition. Dawsons PM 249-29 1974 £12

BATAILLE, HENRY   Tetes et Pensees. Paris, 1901. Folio, orig. half cloth portfolio, first edition. L. Goldschmidt 42-155 1974 $130

BATCHELDER, MILDRED   Adventures of Chippybobbie and His Friend Mr. Fieldmouse. New York, 1927. 16mo., 24 color plates, very good copy. Frohnsdorff 16-6 1974 $10

BATE, C. SPENCE   Catalogue of Specimens of Amphipodous Crustacea. 1862. 8vo., orig. cloth, plates. Wheldon 129-769 1974 £10

BATE, C. SPENCE   Catalogue of the Specimens of Amphipodous Crustacea in the Collection of the British Museum. 1862. 8vo., cloth, plates. Wheldon 131-918 1974 £15

BATE, C. SPENCE   A History of the British Sessile-Eyed Crustacea. 1863-68. 2 vols., 8vo., cloth, woodcuts, very scarce. Wheldon 131-919 1974 £20

BATE, GEORGE   Elenchi Motuum Nuperorum in Anglia. 1663. 12mo., portraits, old half-vellum. Bow Windows 62-68 1974 £55

BATEMAN, JAMES   A Monograph of Odontoglossum. (1864)-1874. Folio, new half green morocco, gilt, plates. Wheldon 129-2 1974 £750

BATEMAN, JAMES   A Monograph of Odontoglossum. (1864)-1874. Imp. folio, half leather, plates, foxing. Wheldon 131-15 1974 £700

BATEMAN, JAMES   The Orchidaceae of Mexico and Guatemala. (1837)-1843. Large folio, contemporary half brown morocco gilt, plates, rare. Wheldon 131-13 1974 £4,500

BATEMAN, JAMES   A Second Century of Orchidaceous Plants. 1867. Roy. 4to., new half green morocco. Wheldon 129-1701 1974 £320

BATEMAN, THOMAS   Delineations of Cutaneous Diseases. London, 1817. Large 4to., plates, first edition. Schuman 37-14 1974 $135

BATEMAN, THOMAS   Delineations of Cutaneous Diseases. London, 1817. 4to., later quarter morocco, plates, first edition. Traylen 79-202 1973 £60

BATES, MRS. D. B.   Incidents on Land and Water. Boston, 1857. 8vo., orig. bindings, first edition. Butterfield 8-453 1974 $35

BATES, MRS. D. B.   Incidents on Land and Water. Boston, 1858. 8vo., orig. bindings, faded, seventh edition. Butterfield 8-454 1974 $20

BATES, ELY   Rural Philosophy. London, 1804. 8vo., orig. boards, third edition. Hammond 201-81 1974 £5

BATES, HENRY WALTER   The Naturalist On the River Amazon. 1864. 8vo., full red calf, gilt, illus., very scarce, nice copy, second edition. Wheldon 131-330 1974 £20

BATES, HENRY WALTER   The Naturalist on the River Amazons. 1891. 8vo., cloth, illus., sixth edition. Wheldon 130-269 1974 £7.50

BATES, HENRY WALTER   The Naturalist on the River Amazons. 1892. 8vo., cloth. Wheldon 129-239 1974 £10

BATES, HENRY WALTER   The Naturalist On the River Amazon. 1910. Crown 8vo., cloth, illus. Wheldon 131-331 1974 £5

BATES, HERBERT ERNEST   Catherine Foster. 1929. Crown 8vo., orig. cloth, signed, first edition. Broadhurst 23-568 1974 £8

BATES, HERBERT ERNEST   Catherine Foster. London, 1929. First edition, 4 line inscription by author, fine, light glassine wrapper. Ross 87-41 1974 $15

BATES, HERBERT ERNEST   Charlotte's Row. London, 1931. First edition, presentation copy to Edward Garnett, inscription by author, near mint, orig. dust wrapper, heavy outside wrapper. Ross 87-42 1974 $15

BATES, HERBERT ERNEST   Flowers and Faces. Golden Cockerel Press, 1935. One of 325 numbered copies, signed by author, engravings, small 4to., orig. quarter green morocco, marbled cloth sides, fine copy. Covent 51-2353 1973 £25

BATES, HERBERT ERNEST   The Hessian Prisoner. 1930. Frontis., Furnival Book No. 2, one of 550 copies numbered & signed by author, fine, buckram. Covent 51-186 1973 £5.25

BATES, HERBERT ERNEST   The Hessian Prisoner. 1930. Roy 8vo., orig. cloth, uncut, signed, limited edition. Broadhurst 23-570 1974 £8

BATES, HERBERT ERNEST   The Hessian Prisoner. London, 1930. No. 2 of the Furnival Books, no. 408 of 550 copies, signed by author, near mint, first edition, light glassine wrapper. Ross 87-47 1974 $12.50

BATES, HERBERT ERNEST   The Last Bread. 1926. Crown 8vo., paper printed wrapper, signed, first edition. Broadhurst 23-565 1974 £6

BATES, HERBERT ERNEST   The Last Bread: A Play in One Act. London, 1926. First edition, signed, mint in orig. wrapper. Ross 87-48 1974 $12.50

BATES, HERBERT ERNEST   Mrs. Esmond's Life. London, 1931. No. 25 of edition limited to 300 copies, signed, orig. tissue wrappers torn, fine. Ross 87-49 1974 $20

BATES, HERBERT ERNEST   Sally Go Round the Moon. 1932. 8vo., orig. cloth, boards, presentation copy, inscribed, first edition. Broadhurst 23-574 1974 £8

BATES, HERBERT ERNEST   Sally Go Round the Moon. London, 1932. Inscribed & signed by author, orig. binding, first edition, dust wrapper somewhat browned & chipped, internally fine. Ross 87-50 1974 $15

BATES, HERBERT ERNEST   The Seekers. 1926. Crown 8vo., boards, inscribed presentation copy, first edition. Broadhurst 23-566 1974 £6

BATES, HERBERT ERNEST   The Spring Song. 1927. Orig. cloth, first edition. Rota 188-72 1974 £6

BATES, HERBERT ERNEST   A Threshing Day. 1931. 8vo., orig. cloth, uncut, signed, limited. Broadhurst 23-569 1974 £5

BATES, HERBERT ERNEST   A Threshing Day. London, 1931. First edition, limited to 300 copies, signed, fine, somewhat torn tissue wrapper. Ross 87-52 1974 $15

BATES, KATHERINE LEE   America the Beautiful and Other Poems. New York, (1911). Second edition, 8vo., presentation copy signed by author, included are two typed poem manuscripts signed by Bates. Current BW9-482 1974 $55

BATES, MARY   Mediaeval England. New York, 1904. Illus. Biblo & Tannen 214-590 1974 $10

BATES, RALPH   Rainbow Fish. 1937. Dust wrapper, fine, English first edition. Covent 56-104 1974 £10.50

BATES, RALPH   Sierra. 1933. Signed, first edition. Covent 55-161 1974 £6.30

BATES, SAMUEL P.   The Battle of Chancellorsville. Meadville, 1883. Second edition, orig. binding. Butterfield 10-147 1974 $12.50

BATES, SAMUEL P.   History of Crawford County, Pennsylvania. Chicago, 1885. 8vo., three quarter leather, illus. Saddleback 14-662 1974 $65

BATES, SAMUEL P.   Martial Deeds of Pennsylvania. Philadelphia, 1876. Hinges cracked, orig. binding, 4to. Butterfield 10-148 1974 $7.50

BATES, WILLIAM   Considerations of the Existence of God. 1677. Thick small 8vo., contemporary calf, second edition. Howes 185-948 1974 £21

BATESON, E.   History of Northumberland. Newcastle-Upon-Tyne, 1893-1940. 15 vols., demy 4to., orig. cloth, illus., plates, maps, few vols. slightly faded, very fine set. Broadhurst 24-1371 1974 £230

BATESON, W.   Letters from the Steppe. 1928. 8vo., cloth, scarce. Wheldon 129-240 1974 £5

BATESON, WILLIAM   Materials for the Study of Variation. London, 1894. Large 8vo., orig. green cloth, first edition. Dawsons PM 245-60 1974 £70

BATESON, WILLIAM   Materials for the Study of Variation. London, 1894. 8vo., orig. green cloth, illus., first edition. Dawsons PM 249-30 1974 £70

BATESON, WILLIAM   Materials for the Study of Variation Treated With Especial Regard to Discontinuity in the Origin of Species. 1894. 8vo., orig. cloth. Wheldon 131-144 1974 £45

BATESON, WILLIAM   Mendel's Principles of Heredity. Cambridge, 1909. 8vo., orig. green cloth, first edition. Dawsons PM 249-31 1974 £11

BATESON, WILLIAM   Mendel's Principles of Heredity. Cambridge, 1909. Roy. 8vo., orig. cloth. Wheldon 129-65 1974 £10

BATESON, WILLIAM   Mendel's Principles of Heredity. Cambridge, 1913. 8vo., orig. cloth, third edition. Broadhurst 23-1087 1974 £6

BATESON, WILLIAM   Mendel's Principles of Heredity. Cambridge, 1913. Coloured plates, illus., third edition, med. 8vo., orig. cloth, fine. Broadhurst 24-1047 1974 £6

BATESON, WILLIAM   The Methods and Scope of Genetics. Cambridge, 1908. Crown 8vo., orig. cloth, scarce. Wheldon 130-92 1974 £10

BATH, WILLIAM PULTENEY, EARL OF 1684-1764   Considerations on the Present State of Public Affairs. London, 1779. 8vo., disbound, first edition. Dawsons PM 251-317 1974 £15

BATH, WILLIAM PULTENEY, EARL OF 1684-1764   Considerations on the Present State of Public Affairs. London, 1779. 8vo., modern boards, second edition. Dawsons PM 247-233 1974 £15

BATH, WILLIAM PULTENEY, EARL OF, 1684-1764   The Effects to be Expected from the East India Bill. London, 1783. 8vo., modern boards, second edition. Dawsons PM 247-234 1974 £15

BATH, WILLIAM PULTENEY, EARL OF, 1684-1764   A Review of the Excise-Scheme. London, 1733. 8vo., modern half calf, label, first edition. Dawsons PM 247-232 1974 £24

BATH, WILLIAM PULTENEY, EARL OF 1684-1764   Some Considerations on the National Debts. London, 1729. 8vo., boards, first edition. Hammond 201-261 1974 £8.50

BATH, WILLIAM PULTENEY, EARL OF, 1684-1764   Substance of the Speech of. London, 1797. 8vo., modern boards, first edition. Dawsons PM 247-235 1974 £15

BATH, WILLIAM PULTENEY, EARL OF, 1684-1764   A Vindication of the Conduct of a Certain Eminent Patriot. London, 1742. 8vo., modern quarter morocco, gilt, uncut, fine, second edition. Dawsons PM 251-471 1974 £15

BATHE, HENRY DE   The Charter of Romney Marsh. 1686. Small 8vo., contemporary sheep, rebacked. Howes 186-2027 1974 £60

BATHE, HENRY DE   The Charter of Romney-Marsh. 1686. 8vo., contemporary calf, rebacked. Quaritch 939-45 1974 £45

BATSCH, A. J. G. C.   Dissertatio Inauguralis Botanica Sistens Dispositionem Generum Plantarum Jenensium. Jena, 1786. Small 4to., modern boards, scarce. Wheldon 128-1237 1973 £12

BATSCH, A. J. G. C.   Dissertatio Inauguralis Botanica Sistens Dispositionem Generum Plantarum Jenensium. Jena, 1786. Small 4to., modern boards, scarce. Wheldon 130-1127 1974 £12

BATSCH, A. J. G. C.   Taschenbuch fur Mineralogische Excursionen in die Umliegende Gegend von Jena. Weimar, 1802. 12mo., old boards, slightly torn. Gurney 66-17 1974 £20

BATTELY, J.   Antiquitates Rutupinae. Oxford, 1711. 8vo., plates, modern boards, first edition. Quaritch 939-395 1974 £15

BATTELY, J.   Antiquitates Rutupinae. Oxford, 1745. 4to., old calf, rebacked, plates. Quaritch 939-396 1974 £25

BATTEN, H. M.   Habits and Characters of British Wild Animals. (1920). Roy. 8vo., orig. cloth, plates. Wheldon 131-471 1974 £5

BATTEN, H. M.   Inland Birds. 1923. 8vo., illus., cloth. Wheldon 130-458 1974 £5

BATTIE, WILLIAM   A Treatise on Madness. London, 1758. 4to., modern half calf, gilt, first edition. Dawsons PM 249-33 1974 £250

BATTLE, J. H.   History of Bucks County, Pennsylvania. Philadelphia, 1887. 8vo., leather. Saddleback 14-663 1974 $125

BATTLES of the Nineteenth Century. n.d. 7 vols., sup. roy. 8vo., illus., orig. cloth. Smith 193-713 1973 £12

BATTY, E. F.   Italian Scenery. London, 1820. 4to., plates, contemporary green half morocco, rubbed. Bow Windows 62-71 1974 £85

BAUCHART, ERNEST QUENTIN   Les Femmes Bibliophiles de France. Paris, 1886. 2 vols., small folio, contemporary half morocco gilt, plates, uncut, first edition. Dawsons PM 10-28 1974 £95

BAUDELAIRE, CHARLES   Eugene Delacroix, his Life and Work. New York, 1947. 4to., illus. Biblo & Tannen 210-114 1973 $10

BAUDELAIRE, CHARLES   Les Fleurs du Mal. Paris, 1855. Contemporary half morocco, gilt, English first edition. Covent 56-1546 1974 £75

BAUDELAIRE, CHARLES   Letters to His Mother, 1833-66. c. 1927. One of 675 numbered copies, leather backed dec. boards, spine rubbed at head, very good copy, defective d.w., first edition. Covent 51-189 1973 £6.50

BAUDELAIRE, CHARLES   Oeuvres Completes. Paris, 1868-70. 7 vols., 12mo., three quarter red levant morocco, gilt, uncut, first collected edition. L. Goldschmidt 42-156 1974 $1,500

BAUDELOCQUE, JEAN LOUIS   L'Art des Accouchemens. Paris, 1781. 8vo., 2 vols., contemporary calf, folding plates, first edition. Gurney 66-20 1974 £70

BAUDERON, BRICE   Pharmacopee. Lyons, 1670. Thick small 8vo., contemporary calf. Schuman 37-15 1974 $95

BAUDIER, MICHAEL   The History of the Administration of Cardinal Ximenes. London, 1671. 8vo., contemporary sheep, first edition in English. Dawsons PM 251-165 1974 £65

BAUDIER, MICHEL   The History of the Administration of Cardinal Ximenes. London, 1671. 8vo., contemporary calf, first edition. Ximenes 35-606 1974 $100

BAUDOT, A. DE   La Sculpture Francaise au Moyen Age et a la Renaissance. 1884. Folio, plates, second edition. Allen 213-1271 1973 $25

BAUDOUIN, CHARLES   Suggestion and Autosuggestion. London, 1922. 8vo., orig. maroon cloth. Dawsons PM 249-34 1974 £4.50

BAUER, JULIETTE   Lives of the Brothers Humboldt, Alexander and William. New York, 1853. Rittenhouse 46-46 1974 $15

BAUER, MAX   Edelsteinkunde. Leipzig, 1896. 4to., half morocco, plates (some coloured), small library stamps, orig. edition. Wheldon 128-944 1973 £20

BAUER, MAX   Precious Stones. 1904. Imp. 8vo., plates, half morocco gilt, very scarce. Quaritch 940-432 1974 £75

BAUER, MAX   Precious Stones. London, 1904. 4to., contemporary red half morocco gilt, gilt, plates, first edition in English. Dawsons PM 245-61 1974 £85

BAUHIN, G.   Pinax Theatri Botanici. Basle, 1671. 4to., contemporary calf. Wheldon 129-887 1974 £60

BAUM, LYMAN FRANK   Father Goose's Year Book. Chicago, (1907). Illus., green buckram, first edition, fine copy. MacManus 224-24 1974 $75

BAUM, LYMAN FRANK   The Life and Adventures of Santa Claus. Indianapolis, 1902. Orig. pictorial cloth, illus., first edition, very good copy. MacManus 224-25 1974 $100

BAUM, LYMAN FRANK   The Magic of Oz. Chicago, (1919). First edition, large 8vo., illus., pictorial colored front cover, very fine. Current BW9-483 1974 $40

BAUM, LYMAN FRANK   The Master Key. Indianapolis, (1901). Orig. cloth, illus., very good copy, first edition. MacManus 224-26 1974 $35

BAUM, LYMAN FRANK   The New Wizard of Oz. Chicago, 1903. Sm. 4to., illus. Frohnsdorff 16-79 1974 $15

BAUM, LYMAN FRANK   The Patchwork Girl of Oz. Chicago, (1913). First edition, large 8vo., illus. in full color, green and red dec. covers are soiled with minor rubbing at extremities, interior mint. Current BW9-484 1974 $60

BAUM, LYMAN FRANK   The Road to Oz. Chicago, 1909. First edition, large 8vo., illus., orig. green and red dec. cloth, near mint. Current BW9-485 1974 $48.50

BAUM, LYMAN FRANK   The Scarecorw and The Tin Woodman. Chicago, n.d. 16mo., illus. Frohnsdorff 16-83 1974 $20

BAUM, LYMAN FRANK   The Scarecrow of Oz. Chicago, 1915. Orig. cloth, 12 color plates; 1st ed. Frohnsdorff 16-82 1974 $35

BAUM, LYMAN FRANK   The Tin Woodman of Oz. Chicago, (1918). First edition, large 8vo., illus., handsome pictorial colored front cover, near mint. Current BW9-486 1974 $40

BAUM, LYMAN FRANK   The Wonderful Wizard of Oz. Chicago & New York, 1899. Orig. pictorial cloth, first edition, very good copy. MacManus 224-27 1974 $750

BAUM, LYMAN FRANK   The Wonderful Wizard of Oz. Chicago & New York, 1899. Orig. pictorial cloth, repairs to head of spine and joints, first edition. MacManus 224-28 1974 $500

BAUME, ANTOINE   Chymie Experimentale et Raisonnee. Paris, 1773. 8vo., 3 vols., contemporary mottled French calf, gilt, first edition. Dawsons PM 245-62 1974 £120

BAUMGARTNER, ANDREAS   Anfangsgrunde der Naturlehre. 1837. 8vo., illus., orig. gray marbled boards, worn, first edition. Zeitlin 235-18 1974 $25

BAX, CLIFFORD   Florence Farr, Bernard Shaw and W. B. Yeats. Dublin, 1941. 8vo., orig. quarter canvas, limited edition. Bow Windows 66-158 1974 £46

BAX, CLIFFORD   Florence Farr, Bernard Shaw, and W. B. Yeats. Dublin, 1941. No. 45 of 500 copies, unopened, mint, tissue wrapper. Ross 86-488 1974 $110

BAX, CLIFFORD   Florence Farr, Bernard Shaw, and W. B. Yeats. Dublin, 1941. No. 267 of 500 copies, orig. binding, unopened, lacking d.w., fine. Ross 87-596 1974 $90

BAX, CLIFFORD   Inland Far. 1925. Portraits, English first edition. Covent 56-1697 1974 £7.50

BAX, CLIFFORD   Pretty Witty Nell. Morrow, 1933. 294p., illus., orig. ed. Austin 51-64 1973 $6.25

BAX, CLIFFORD   The Venetian. Farrar & Rinehart, 1931. 235p. Austin 51-65 1973 $6.50

BAX, CLIFFORD   Vintage Verse. London, 1948. Biblo & Tannen 210-830 1973 $5

BAX, E. BELFORT   Rise and Fall of the Anabaptists. 1903. Scarce. Howes 186-597 1974 £6

BAXTER, BEVERLEY   Westminster Watchtower. London, 1938. Hood's 102-316 1974 $10

BAXTER, E. V.   The Geographical Distribution and Status of Birds in Scotland. Edinburgh, 1928. 8vo., cloth. Wheldon 131-542 1974 £5

BAXTER, GEORGE   The Pictorial Album. London, n.d. Dark red leather, gilt. Dawson's 424-89 1974 $225

BAXTER, JAMES PHINNEY   Documentary History of the State of Maine. Portland, 1900. 8vo., orig. bindings, ex-library. Butterfield 8-197 1974 $10

BAXTER, JAMES PHINNEY   A Memoir of Jacques Cartier, Sieur de Limoilou, His Voyages to the St. Lawrence. New York, 1906. Edition limited to 300 copies, clean & tight copy, illus. Hood's 102-223 1974 $60

BAXTER, RICHARD   Catholick Theologie. London, 1675. Worn spine, contemporary calf. Smith 194-126 1974 £35

BAXTER, RICHARD   Gildas Salvianus. London, 1656. 8vo., old sheep gilt. Smith 194-127 1974 £15

BAXTER, RICHARD   Jesuit Juggling. New York, 1835. First American edition, cloth covers and text pages stained. Butterfield 10-57 1974 $8

BAXTER, RICHARD   The Life of Faith In Three Parts. London, 1670. Small 4to., frontispiece, contemporary calf, foxing. Smith 194-128 1974 £18

BAXTER, RICHARD   Plain Scripture Proof of Infants Church-Membership and Baptism. London, 1651. 2 vols. in 1, small 4to., old half calf, woodcut border. Smith 194-129 1974 £15

BAXTER, RICHARD   The Saints Everlasting Rest. London, 1652. 4 parts, small 4to., contemporary calf, some marks. Smith 194-130 1974 £15

BAXTER, RICHARD   The Saints Everlasting Rest. London, 1688 Small 4to., half old calf, marbled boards, rubbed, twelfth edition. Smith 194-131 1974 £15

BAXTER, W. G.   Fifty Sloper Cartoons. London, 1888. Oblong 4to. Frohnsdorff 16-198 1974 $27.50

BAXTER, WILLIAM   British Phaenogamous Botany. Oxford, 1834-43. 6 vols., 8vo., new half green morocco, plates. Wheldon 131-16 1974 £150

BAY, JENS CHRISTIAN   The Chalice of the Chipped Ruby.   Chicago, 1922. First edition. Dykes 24-58 1974 $15

THE BAY of San Francisco. Chicago, 1892. 2 vols., 4to., leather, illus. Saddleback 14-265 1974 $50

THE BAY Psalm Book. 1903. Facsimile reprint of first edition, fine. Ballinger 1-238 1974 $25

BAYARD, EMILE   L'Art en Anecdotes.   Paris, (n.d.). Half morocco, illus. Bow Windows 66-40 1974 £15

BAYARD, EMILE   Le Style Louis 14. Paris, ca. 1920. Biblo & Tannen 213-285 1973 $10

BAYARD, RALPH   Lone Star Vanguard: The Catholic Re-Occupation of Texas, 1838-48. St. Louis, 1945. Fine copy, partly uncut. Jenkins 61-205 1974 $20

BAYARD, RALPH   Lone Star Vangaurd: The Catholic Re-Occupation of Texas 1838-48. St. Louis, 1945. Jenkins 61-206 1974 $17.50

BAYE, J. DE   Epoque des Invasions Barbares, Industrie Longobarde. 1888. Folio, plates, new buckram. Allen 213-1274 1973 $15

BAYEN, PIERRE   Recherches Chimiques sur l'Etain. Paris, 1781. 8vo., contemporary half sheep, first edition. Dawsons PM 245-63 1974 £85

BAYER, JOHANNES   Explicatio Characterum Aeneis Uranometrias Imaginum, Tabulis Insculptorum, Addita, & Commodiore Hac Forma Redintegrata. Augsburg, 1654. Small 4to., boards, leather spine, F. X. v. Zach's copy with his stamp on title. Kraus 137-11 1974 $1,500

BAYLDON, J. S.   A Treatise on the Valuation of Property for the Poor's Rate. London, 1834. 8vo., contemporary half calf, second edition. Dawsons PM 247-12 1974 £15

BAYLE, A. GASPARD LAURENT   Recherches sur la Phthisie Pulmonaire. Paris, 1810. 8vo., orig. pink boards, gilt, first edition. Dawsons PM 249-35 1974 £55

BAYLE, PIERRE   Dictionnaire Historique et Critique. Rotterdam, (1696). 4 parts in 2 vols., contemporary calf, cloth box, very rare orig. edition. Gilhofer 61-13 1974 sFr. 1,600

BAYLE, PIERRE   Dictionnaire Historique et Critique. Amsterdam, 1730. 4 vols., contemporary boards, leather backs, uncut. L. Goldschmidt 42-6 1974 $240

BAYLE, PIERRE   Dictionary Historical and Critical. London, 1738. Large folio, rebacked, calf, 5 vols., labels. Rich Summer-19 1974 $400

BAYLEY, HAROLD   Archaic England. 1919. Illus. Allen 213-1275 1973 $15

BAYLEY, HAROLD   The Lost Language of Symbolism. London, 1912. 2v., orig. ed. Biblo & Tannen 210-972 1973 $20

BAYLEY, HAROLD   New Light On the Renaissance, Displayed In Contemporary Emblems. 1909. 4to., illus. Allen 213-1276 1973 $15

BAYLEY, HAROLD   The Shakespeare Symphony. 1906. Small 8vo., half calf, gilt. Quaritch 936-549 1974 £7

BAYLEY, RICHARD   An Account of the Epidemic Fever. New York, 1796. 8vo., contemporary marbled boards, first edition. Dawsons PM 249-36 1974 £180

BAYLY, A. ERIC   The House of Strange Secrets. New York, 1899. 1st ed. Biblo & Tannen 210-420 1973 $20

BAYLY, LEWIS   Praxis Pietatis. Danzig, 1629. Small 8vo., dark brown calf gilt, over oak boards, raised bands. Thomas 28-232 1972 £20

BAYLY, T.   Herba Parietis. London, 1650. Small folio, sprinkled calf gilt, first edition. Quaritch 939-436 1974 £225

BAYNES, T. S.   Shakespeare Studies and Essay on English Dictionaries. 1894. Small 8vo., half green morocco, gilt. Quaritch 936-550 1974 £7

BAYNTON, THOMAS   An Account of a Successful Method of Treating Diseases of the Spine. London, 1813. 8vo., modern half calf, gilt, first edition. Dawsons PM 249-37 1974 £35

BAZIN, P. A. E.   Lecons Theoriques et Cliniques sur la Scrofule. Paris, 1861. 8vo., half calf, rebacked. Gurney 66-21 1974 £20

BEACH, REX   The Miracle of Coral Gables. Coral Gables, (c.1926). 8vo., boards. Saddleback 14-346 1974 $15

BEACH, S. A.   The Apples of New York. Albany, 1905. 8vo., 2 vols., orig. cloth, plates. Wheldon 130-1467 1974 £25

BEACOM, JOHN H.   How the Buffalo Lost His Crown. (New York, 1894). Morocco and cloth, illus. by Russell, slip case, near fine copy, rare, first edition. Dykes 22-58 1973 $400

A BEACON Light to the World: Souvenir of Park College and Parkville, Missouri, The Historic Town and the Sui-Generis Institute. Parkville, 1895. Wrapper, photos. Jenkins 61-1705 1974 $12.50

BEADLES, J. H.   Western Wilds. 1881. 4to., cloth, illus., worn. Putnam 126-274 1974 $10

BEADLE'S Dime Dialogues, No. 13. New York, 1872. 16mo. Frohnsdorff 16-92 1974 $10

BEALE, JOSEPH HENRY   A Bibliography of Early English Law Books. Crown 4to., orig. cloth, scarce. Broadhurst 23-247 1974 £50

BEALE, JOSEPH HENRY   A Bibliography of Early English Law Books. Cambridge, 1926. Crown 4to., scarce, fine, orig. cloth. Broadhurst 24-240 1974 £50

BEAMAN, A. GAYLORD   A Doctor's Odyssey. Baltimore, 1935. Uncut. Rittenhouse 46-49 1974 $12

BEAN, WILLIAM JACKSON   The Royal Botanic Gardens. 1908. Roy. 8vo., cloth, illus., plates. Wheldon 129-1434 1974 £10

BEAN, WILLIAM JACKSON   Trees and Shrubs Hardy in the British Isles. 1914-34. 3 vols., illus., first editions. Bow Windows 64-18 1974 £15

BEAN, WILLIAM JACKSON   Trees and Shrubs Hardy in the British Isles. 1921-33. 8vo., 3 vols., cloth, plates. Wheldon 129-1594 1974 £10

BEAN, WILLIAM JACKSON   Trees and Shrubs Hardy in the British Isles. 1929-33. 3 vols., 8vo., orig. cloth, plates, fifth edition. Wheldon 131-1713 1974 £12

BEARD, THOMAS   A Retractive from the Romish Religion. 1616. Small 4to., orig. calf, bookplate. Thomas 28-83 1972 £25

BEARDSLEY, AUBREY   The Art Of. New York, 1918. 8vo., orig. limp cloth, plates, first edition. Smith 193-57 1973 £5

BEARDSLEY, AUBREY   The Best of Beardsley. London, n.d. 4to. Biblo & Tannen 210-50 1973 $17.50

BEARDSLEY, AUBREY   The Early Works of. London, 1920. 3 vols., 4to., portraits, illus., orig. buckram. Bow Windows 62-73 1974 £120

BEARDSLEY, AUBREY   The Early Work Of. London and New York, 1920. 4to., 2 vols., blue dec. cloth, dust jackets, illus., plates. Rich Summer-21 1974 $12.50

BEARDSLEY, AUBREY   Keynotes Series. 1894-97. 13 vols., cloth, rubbing. Marsden 37-26 1974 £45

BEARDSLEY, AUBREY   The Later Work of. 1901. 4to., orig. cloth, illus. Bow Windows 64-387 1974 £42

BEARDSLEY, AUBREY   Letters to Leonard Smithers. 1937. Very fine, portraits, first edition. Covent 51-2147 1973 £15

BEARDSLEY, AUBREY   Lucian's True History. 1902. Square 8vo.,
cloth backed boards, English first edition. Covent 56-106 1974 £9.50

BEARDSLEY, AUBREY   Nineteen Early Drawings. 1919. 4to., orig.
cloth, plates, portfolio, first edition. Rota 190-34 1974 £30

BEARDSLEY, AUBREY   The Savoy. London, 1896. Orig. boards and
wrappers, plates. Frohnsdorff 16-93 1974 $100

BEARDSLEY, AUBREY   Six Drawings Illustrating Theophile Gautier's
Romance Mademoiselle de Maupin. London, 1898. One of 50 numbered copies,
photogravures, first edition, fine, slightly rubbed portfolio. Covent 51-2148
1973 £40

BEARDSLEY, AUBREY   The Story of Venus and Tannhauser. 1907.
One of 300 copies, first printing, very good copy. Covent 51-2149 1973 £12.50

BEARDSLEY, AUBREY   The Story of Venus and Tannhauser. 1907.
4to., boards, English first edition. Covent 56-1547 1974 £35

BEARDSLEY, AUBREY   Under the Hill and Other Essays. 1904. Full
cream pigskin, gilt, illus., first edition. Marsden 37-27 1974 £24

BEARDSLEY, AUBREY   The Uncollected Work. 1925. 4to., dec.
buckram, English first edition. Covent 56-1428 1974 £20

BEARDSLEY, AUBREY   The Uncollected Work Of. 1925. 4to.,
half green morocco, gilt, uncut. Quaritch 940-17 1974 £65

BEARDSLEY, AUBREY   The Uncollected Work Of. 1925. Thick 4to.,
orig. cloth, plates, first edition. Rota 190-35 1974 £15

BEARDSLEY, AUBREY   Under the Hill. Paris, 1959. Sm. 4to., illus.,
orig. watered-silk bds., gilt, front and bottom edges uncut, ltd. to 3000 numbered
copies. Jacobs 24-61 1974 $45

BEASLEY, NORMAN   Knudsen. Whittlesey, 1947. Austin 62-34
1974 $12.50

BEATON, CECIL   Cecil Beaton's Fair Lady. Holt, Rinehart, and
Winston, 1964. 128p., illus. Austin 51-66 1973 $8.50

BEATON, CECIL   Cecil Beaton's New York. Lippincott, 1938.
267p., illus. Austin 51-67 1973 $12.50

BEATON, CECIL   I Take Great Pleasure. Day, 1956. 214p.,
illus. Austin 51-68 1973 $6.50

BEATON, CECIL   Photobiography. Doubleday, 1951. 255p.,
illus. Austin 51-69 1973 $7.50

BEATTIE, JAMES   The Minstrel. Edinburgh, 1807. 8vo., contemporary calf, gilt. Hammond 201-292 1974 £5

BEATTIE, JESSIE L.   Hill Top. Toronto, 1935. Hood's 102-491
1974 $7.50

BEATTIE, WILLIAM   The Castles and Abbeys of England. (n.d.).
2 vols., portrait, engraved plates, woodcut illus. Bow Windows 66-41 1974
£21

BEATTIE, WILLIAM   Scotland Illustrated in a Series of Views. 1838.
4to., 2 vols., contemporary full calf, gilt. Broadhurst 23-1311 1974 £60

BEATTIE, WILLIAM   Scotland Illustrated in a Series of Views. 1838.
2 vols., 4to., plates, blue calf gilt. Quaritch 939-644 1974 £85

BEATTY, JEROME   Shirley Temple. Saalfield, 1935. Austin
51-956 1973 $12.50

BEATTY Barn Book. Fergus, 1931. Very full illustrations. Hood's 102-362
1974 $10

BEAUCHAMP, MARY ANETTE   The Solitary Summer. 1900. Photographs.
Austin 61-28 1974 $10

BEAUCHAMPS, J. DE   Guide du Libraire-Antiquaire et du Bibliophile.
Paris, 1885. Half cloth, plates. Kraus B8-5 1974 $35

BEAUCHESNE, A. H. DU BOIS DE   La Vie et la Legende de Madame Sainte
Nothburg. 1868. 4to., illus., plates, new buckram. Allen 213-1676 1973
$12.50

BEAUDET, L.   Recensement de la Ville de Quebec Pour 1716.
Quebec, 1887. Hood's 102-681 1974 $17.50

BEAUDET, L.   Recensement de la Ville de Quebec Pour 1716.
Quebec, 1887. Hood's 104-910 1974 $17.50

BEAUFOY, GWENDOLYN   Leaves from a Beech Tree. Oxford, 1930.
Plates. Bow Windows 66-42 1974 £6.50

BEAUFOY, HENRY   The Substance of the Speech. London, 1787.
8vo., modern boards. Dawsons PM 251-414 1974 £15

BEAUFOY, MARK   Nautical and Hydraulic Experiments, With
Numerous Scientific Miscellanies. London, 1834. Vol. 1, large thick 4to., orig.
green diapered cloth, orig. printed paper label, first edition, excellent copy,
unopened, inscribed presentation copy. Ximenes 36-11 1974 $175

BEAUGRAND, HONORE   Six Mois Dans les Montagnes-Rocheuses,
Colorado, Utah, Nouveau-Mexique. Montreal, 1890. Wrappers, illus. Hood's
104-842 1974 $22.50

BEAUMARCHAIS, PIERRE AUGUSTIN CARON DE   La Folle Journee ou le
Mariage de Figaro. (Paris), 1785. 8vo., plates, contemporary patterned
boards, rebacked, calf, fine, orig. edition. Dawsons PM 250-5 1974 £450

BEAUMONT, CYRIL W.   Five Centures of Ballet Design. n.d. Roy 8vo.,
rebound, boards, plates, English first edition. Covent 56-1538 1974 £8.50

BEAUMONT, CYRIL W.   The History of Harlequin. 1926. Small 4to.,
quarter vellum gilt, pictorial boards, plates. Covent 55-813 1974 £38.50

BEAUMONT, FRANCIS   The Loyal Subject. London, (n.d.). 4to.,
modern boards, inscription, first edition. Dawsons PM 252-43 1974 £60

BEAUMONT, FRANCIS   The Works. London, 1711. 7 vols., 8vo.,
contemporary panelled calf, modern boards, first Octavo edition. Dawsons PM
252-44 1974 £70

BEAUMONT, FRANCIS   Works. 1750. 10 vols., buckram, some browning,
stamp of Phillips Library on some vols. Allen 216-c 1974 $60

BEAUMONT, FRANCIS   Works. 1750. 10 vols., contemporary calf,
portrait. Howes 185-15 1974 £35

BEAUMONT, FRANCIS   Dramatic Works. 1778. Vols. 1, 3-10 only,
plates, buckram, soiled, labels on spine defective. Allen 216-d 1974 $75

BEAUMONT, FRANCIS   The Dramatick Works of. London, 1778. 8vo.,
10 vols., illus., old mottled calf, worn. Bow Windows 62-74 1974 £60

BEAUMONT, FRANCIS   Works of. London, 1839. 2 vols. Austin 61-
29 1974 $47.50

BEAUMONT, FRANCIS   Works. 1843-46. 11 vols., ex-library, buckram.
Allen 216-2207 1974 $100

BEAUMONT, FRANCIS   Works. 1843-46. 8vo., 11 vols., tree calf,
portraits, library edition. Quaritch 936-287 1974 £40

BEAUMONT, FRANCIS   Works. 1854. 2 vols., 4to., new buckram,
foxed. Allen 216-1876 1974 $17.50

BEAUMONT, FRANCIS   Works. 1854. 2 vols., 4to., new buckram,
text slightly stained and foxed. Allen 216-1877 1974 $20

BEAUMONT, FRANCIS   Works. 1904-12. Vols. 1-4 only, ex-library,
buckram, variorum edition. Allen 216-2208 1974 $45

BEAUMONT, ROBERTS   Woollen and Worsted. 1915. Thick roy.
8vo., illus., orig. buckram, faded. Howes 186-1352 1974 £10

BEAUMONT, WILLIAM　　Experiments and Observations on the Gastric Juice. Plattsburgh, 1833. 8vo., modern boards, first edition. Dawsons PM 249-38 1974 £450

BEAUMONT, WILLIAM　　Physiology of Digestion. Burlington, 1847. Orig. boards, foxing, excellent copy, second edition. Rittenhouse 46-51 1974 $195

BEAUMONT, WILLIAM　　Physiology of Digestion. Burlington, 1847. Second edition. Rittenhouse 46-50 1974 $190

BEAUTES de l'Histoire D'Amerique. Paris, 1818. 2 vols., quarter roan, marbled boards, frontispieces, vignettes, engravings, 8vo. Gregory 44-35 1974 $95

THE BEAUTIFUL Columbia River. Omaha, (1914). Folio, wrappers, hand colored illus. Jenkins 61-2054 1974 $12.50

THE BEAUTIFUL Page; or, Child of Romance. n.d. (1801). Copperplates, 12mo., orig. boards, roan spine, trifle rubbed, frontispiece. George's 610-51 1973 £8

BEAUTIFUL Pasadena California. Los Angeles, c. 1910. Folio, wrapper, illus. Jenkins 61-282 1974 $10

BEAUTIFUL Pasadena California. Los Angeles, c. 1910. Small folio, wrapper, hand colored illus. Jenkins 61-284 1974 $10

BEAUTIFUL Pasadena California. Los Angeles, c. 1915. Small folio, wrapper, hand colored illus. Jenkins 61-285 1974 $12.50

BEAUTIFUL Tuxedo Park. Tuxedo Park, c. 1905. Wrappers, hand colored illus. Jenkins 61-1863 1974 $10

BEAUVAIS, VINCENT DE
Please turn to
VINCENT DE BEAUVAIS

BEAVER, ALFRED　　Memorials of Old Chelsea. 1892. Rubbed, half green morocco, illus. Marsden 39-77 1974 £18

BEAWES, WYNDHAM　　A Civil, Commercial, Political and Literary History of Spain and Portugal. London, 1793. 2 vols. in 1, folio, rebacked, contemporary calf. Traylen 79-557 1973 £58

BEAZIANO, AGOSTINO　　Lachrymae in Funere Petri Bembi. Venice, 1548. 8vo., modern half vellum over boards, good copy, very rare. Schafer 8-100 1973 sFr. 700

BEAZLEY, SAMUEL　　The Roue. London, 1828. 3 vols., all joints cracked or weak, contemporary half calf, marbled boards, first edition, very clean set, bookplate of Reginald Charles Reed. MacManus 224-29 1974 $65

BECCARI, O.　　Wanderings In the Great Forests of Borneo. 1904. 8vo., cloth, illus., nice copy, very scarce. Wheldon 131-332 1974 £25

BECCARIA, CAESAR BONESANA, MARCHESI DI　　An Essay on Crimes and Punishments. London, 1767. 8vo., contemporary sprinkled calf, rebacked, first English edition. Dawsons PM 250-6 1974 £195

BECCARIA, GIOVANNI BATTISTA　　Dell'Elettricismo Artificiale. 1753. 4to., contemporary vellum, gilt, fine, first edition. Dawsons PM 245-64 1974 £95

BECCARIA, GIOVANNI BATTISTA　　Elettricismo Artificiale. (Torino, 1772). Roy 4to., plates, uncut, orig. boards, red buckram case. Zeitlin 235-19 1974 $450

BECCARIA, GIOVANNI BATTISTA　　Elettricismo Artificiale. (Torino, 1772). 4to., plates, contemporary mottled calf, fine. Zeitlin 235-20 1974 $550

BECCARIA, GIOVANNI BATTISTA　　A Treatise upon Artificial Electricity. London, 1776. 4to., contemporary calf, plates, first and only edition in English. Dawsons PM 245-65 1974 £120

BECHSTEIN, J. W.　　Gemeinnutzige Naturgeschichte Deutschlands Etc., Vols. 2 and 3. Leipzig, 1791-93. 2 vols., crown 8vo., boards, engraved plates, frontispieces, rare, first edition. Wheldon 128-381 1973 £10

BECHSTEIN, J. W.　　The Natural History of Cage Birds. Groombridge, 1881. 8vo., orig. cloth, plates. Wheldon 131-543 1974 £10

BECK, C.　　The Microscope. 1921-1924. 8vo., 2 vols., cloth. Wheldon 130-93 1974 £5

BECK, JOSEPH C.　　Fifty Years in Medicine. Chicago, 1940. Rittenhouse 46-48 1974 $10

BECK, LOUIS J.　　New Yorks Chinatown. 1898. 332 pages, illus. Austin 57-62 1974 $27.50

BECKER, EDNA　　Hugh and Denis, Twelve Tales of Two Boys of the Middle Ages. Caldwell, 1934. Morocco, pic. end sheets, gilt top, illus., numbered, signed by author, fine, plastic dust wrapper, slipcase, first edition. Dykes 22-107 1973 $15

BECKER, W. G.　　Augusteum ou Description des Monumens Antiques qui se Trouvent a Dresde. Leipzig, 1804-11. 3 vols. in 1, folio, plates, half calf. Quaritch 940-290 1974 £25

BECKET, THOMAS　　Vita S. Thomae, ab Auctoribus Contemporaneis. Oxford, 1845-46. 7 vols., orig. cloth. Howes 185-952 1974 £25

BECKETT, E.　　Vegetables for Home and Exhibition. 1908. 8vo., cloth, illus., second edition. Wheldon 130-1374 1974 £5

BECKETT, EDMUND　　A Rudimentary Treatise on Clocks, Watches, and Bells for Public Purposes. London, 1903. 12mo., eighth edition, fold out frontis., illus., very fine. Current BW9-538 1974 $28.50

BECKETT, S.　　Portland Directory 1858-9. Orig. cloth, map. Putman 126-74 1974 $14

BECKETT, SAMUEL　　Poems. 1931. Small 8vo., orig. boards, dust-wrapper, first edition. Quaritch 936-288 1974 £35

BECKETT, SAMUEL　　Proust. 1931. First edition, some wear to head and foot of spine, else very good. Covent 51-2163 1973 £20

BECKETT, SAMUEL　　Proust. 1931. Orig. dec. boards, soiled dust wrapper. Smith 193-313 1973 £15

BECKETT, SAMUEL　　Whoroscope. Paris, 1930. Orig. red printed wrapper, rare, first limited edition. Bow Windows 66-43 1974 £220

BECKFORD, PETER　　Thoughts Upon Hare and Fox Hunting. 1796. 8vo., contemporary calf, plates, new edition. Wheldon 131-473 1974 £12

BECKFORD, PETER　　Thoughts Upon Hunting. 1782. Half morocco, rubbed, lacks frontispiece, new edition. Bow Windows 66-44 1974 £30

BECKFORD, WILLIAM　　The Hamilton Palace Libraries. London, 1882-84. 5 parts in 1 vol., large 8vo., contemporary half calf. Dawsons PM 10-29 1974 £80

BECKFORD, WILLIAM　　Italy; together with: Sketches of Italy of Mrs. Jameson. Frankfort, 1841. 2 works in 1 vol., 12mo., orig. boards, covers rubbed, hinge little sprung. Covent 51-208 1973 £10.50

BECKFORD, WILLIAM　　Vathek. 1928. Boxed, very good copy. Austin 61-31 1974 $12.50

BECKFORD, WILLIAM　　Vathek. 1929. Half vellum, coloured plates. Allen 216-114 1974 $17.50

BECKFORD, WILLIAM　　Vathek. 1929. Orig. parchment backed boards, gilt, illus., plates, limited. Howes 185-351 1974 £7.50

BECKMANN, JOHN　　A History of Inventions and Discoveries. London, 1797. 8vo., 3 vols., contemporary half calf, gilt, fine, first edition in English. Dawsons PM 245-66 1974 £70

BECKMANN, JOHN　　A History of Inventions, Discoveries, and Origins. London, 1846. 8vo., 2 vols., orig. green blind-stamped cloth, gilt, fourth edition in English. Dawsons PM 245-67 1974 £12

BECKWITH, H. W.　　　　Collections of the Illinois State Historical
Library. Springfield, 1903. Ex-library. Jenkins 61-1111 1974 $10

BECLARD, PIERRE AUGUSTIN　　Elemens d'Anatomie Generale. Paris, 1823.
8vo., 19th century half calf, first edition. Dawsons PM 249-39 1974 £14

BECLARD, PIERRE AUGUSTIN　　Elements of General Anatomy. Edinburgh,
1830. 8vo., orig. boards, rebacked, first edition in English. Dawsons PM 249-
40 1974 £12

BECQUEREL, ANTOINE CESAR　　Traite d'Electricite at de Magnetisme. Paris,
1856. 8vo., plates, illus., half brown morocco, gilt, foxed, fine, first edition.
Zeitlin 235-21 1974 $45

BECQUEREL, ANTOINE HENRY　　Eight Papers Relating to the Discovery of
Radioactivity. Paris, 1896. 4to., modern wrappers, uncut. Dawsons PM 245-68
1974 £180

BECQUEREL, ANTOINE HENRY　　Rescherches sur une Propriete Nouvelle de la
Matiere. Paris, 1903. 4to., illus., orig. printed paper wrappers, unopened, fine,
first edition. Dawsons PM 250-7 1974 £125

BECQUEREL, ANTOINE HENRY　　Recherches sur une Propriete Nouvelle de la
Matiere. Paris, 1903. 4to., orig. light blue printed boards, uncut, unopened,
fine, first edition. Dawsons PM 245-69 1974 £125

BECQUEREL, ANTOINE HENRI　　Recherches sur une Propriete Nouvelle de
la Matiere Activite Radiante Spontanee ou Radioactive de la Matiere. Paris,
1903. 4to., illus., orig. printed wrappers, first edition. Schafer 8-144
1973 sFr. 950

BEDA, VENERABILIS 673-735　　The History of the Church in Englande. 1565.
Small 4to., full morocco, gilt, illus., first English edition. Bow Windows 62-75
1974 £475

BEDA, VENERABILIS 673-735　　The Historie of the Church of England. 1622.
Thick small 8vo., panelled sheep. Howes 185-953 1974 £115

BEDA, VENERABILIS 673-735　　The History of the Church of England. 1930.
4to., quarter English calf, dec. boards, uncut. Broadhurst 23-1084 1974 £65

BEDA, VENERABILIS 673-735　　The History of the Church of England.
Shakespeare Head Press, 1930. 4to., quarter English calf, dec. boards, uncut,
one of 475 copies, fine. Broadhurst 24-1042 1974 £65

BEDDOES, THOMAS　　Alexander's Expedition Down the Hydaspes and
the Indus to the Indian Ocean. 1792. 4to., half calf, frontispiece. Hill 126-14
1974 £38

BEDDOME, R. H.　　The Ferns of Southern India. Madras, 1873.
4to., buckram, plates, rare orig. printing, second edition. Wheldon 128-1336
1973 £50

BEDDOME, R. H.　　The Ferns of Southern India. Madras, 1873.
4to., buckram, plates, rare. Wheldon 130-1234 1974 £50

BEDDOME, R. H.　　The Flora Sylvatica for Southern India. Madras,
1869. Parts 1 and 2, 4to., orig. wrappers, lithographed plates, very rare.
Wheldon 128-1582 1973 £5

BEDE　　Ecclesiasticae Historiae Gentis Anglorum Libri
Quinque. Antwerp, 1550. Small folio, vellum, lacks ties, some dampstaining,
sound copy. Thomas 32-107 1974 £36

BEDE, CUTHBERT, PSEUD.
Please turn to
BRADLEY, EDWARD

BEDEL, WILLIAM　　Leabhair an Tsean Tiomna. N.P., 1830.
Small thick 8vo., cloth boards. Emerald 50-29 1974 £5

BEDELLS, PHYLISS　　My Dancing Days. 1954. 224p., illus.
Austin 51-70 1973 $7.50

BEDFORD, W. K. R.　　The Blazon of Episcopacy Being the Arms Borne
by or Attributed to the Archbishops and Bishops of England and Wales. Oxford,
1897. Revised & enlarged second edition, crown 4to., spine faded, illus., orig.
cloth. Broadhurst 24-1372 1974 £12

BEDFORD, W. K. R.　　The Order of the Hospital of St. John of Jerusalem. 1902. 8vo., orig. cloth. Bow Windows 64-388 1974 £8.50

BEDIER, JOSEPH　　Les Legendes Epiques. Paris, 1908-14.
4 vols., 12mo., orig. wrappers, uncut. L. Goldschmidt 42-7 1974 $45

BEDNAR, ALOIS　　Die Krankheiten der Neugebornen und
Sanglinge. Vienna, 1850-53. 4 vols. in 1, 8vo., cloth, rubbed, first edition.
Schuman 37-16 1974 $110

BEDOS DE CELLES, DOM FRANCOIS　　L'Art du Facteur d'Orgues. (Paris),
1766-1778. Folio, 3 vols., plates, half contemporary calf, gilt, uncut. Zeitlin
235-22 1974 $1,500

BEDOS DE CELLES, DOM FRANCOIS　　L'Art du Facteur d'Orgues. (Paris),
1766-78. 4 parts in 2 vols., folio, half calf, plates, very fine, first edition.
Gilhofer 61-24 1974 sFr. 4,500

THE BEDSIDE Esquire. Tudor, 1940. 703p. Austin 54-424 1973 $6.50

BEE, POLLY　　Vagaries of Men. Robertson, 1901. 109p.,
illus. Austin 54-103 1973 $7.50

BEEBE, LUCIUS MORRIS　　Shoot If You Must. Appleton, 1943. 296 pages.
Austin 54-104 1973 $6.50

BEEBE, WILLIAM　　The Arcturus Adventure. 1926 or 1927. 8vo.,
cloth, plates, illus. Wheldon 131-298 1974 £7.50

BEEBE, WILLIAM　　Beneath Tropic Seas. New York, 1928. 8vo.,
cloth, illus. Wheldon 128-136 1973 £7.50

BEEBE, WILLIAM　　Beneath Tropic Seas. New York, 1928. 8vo.,
cloth, illus. Wheldon 130-250 1974 £7.50

BEEBE, WILLIAM　　Edge of the Jungle. New York, 1921. 1st ed.
Biblo & Tannen 213-845 1973 $7.50

BEEBE, WILLIAM　　The Edge of the Jungle. 1922. 8vo., cloth,
plates, scarce. Wheldon 131-334 1974 £5

BEEBE, WILLIAM　　Galapagos, World's End. New York & London,
Colored illus., photos, first edition, small 4to., very good. Current BW9-151
1974 $32.50

BEEBE, WILLIAM　　Half Mile Down. 1935. Full dec. cloth, plates,
scarce. Wheldon 131-297 1974 £7.50

BEEBE, WILLIAM　　Jungle Days. New York, (1923). 1925. 8vo.,
cloth, illus. Wheldon 128-173 1973 £5

BEEBE, WILLIAM　　Jungle Peace. 1919. 8vo., cloth, illus.
Wheldon 128-174 1973 £5

BEEBE, WILLIAM　　Jungle Peace. 1919. 8vo., cloth, illus.
Wheldon 131-333 1974 £5

BEEBE, WILLIAM　　A Monograph of the Pheasants. 1918-1922.
Large 4to., 4 vols., plates, maps, limited edition. Bow Windows 64-19 1974
£860

BEEBE, WILLIAM　　A Monograph of the Pheasants. 1918-22. Folio,
4 vols., orig. cloth, maps. Wheldon 129-3 1974 £975

BEEBE, WILLIAM　　A Monograph of the Pheasants. 1918. 4 vols.,
folio, orig. cloth, scarce, plates. Wheldon 131-17 1974 £975

BEEBE, WILLIAM　　Nonsuch, Land of Water. 1932. 8vo., cloth,
plates. Wheldon 131-299 1974 £5

BEEBE, WILLIAM　　Pheasants. New York, 1926. Small 4to., orig.
cloth, 2 vols., plates, scarce, first edition. Wheldon 130-460 1974 £40

BEEBE, WILLIAM　　Pheasants. New York, 1931. Roy. 8vo., 2 vols.,
cloth, plates. Wheldon 129-426 1974 £30

BEEBE, WILLIAM　　Pheasants. New York, 1931. Small 4to., orig.
cloth, plates, scarce, 2 vols. Wheldon 130-461 1974 £35

BEEBE, WILLIAM   Pheasants, Their Lives and Homes. 1938. Small 4to., 2 vols. in 1, buckram, coloured and plain plates, scarce. Wheldon 128-384 1973 £30

BEEBE, WILLIAM   Tropical Wild Life in British Guiana. New York, 1917. Roy. 8vo., cloth, illus. Wheldon 131-335 1974 £15

BEEBE, WILLIAM   Two Bird-Lovers in Mexico. 1905. 8vo., cloth, illus., scarce. Wheldon 130-459 1974 £7.50

BEEBE, WILLIAM   Zaca Venture. 1938. 8vo., cloth, plates. Wheldon 130-251 1974 £5

BEECHER, EDWARD   Narrative of Riots at Alton. Alton, 1838. Dec. blue gray cloth, gilt, first edition. Bradley 35-21 1974 $60

BEECHER, EDWARD   Narrative of Riots at Alton. Alton, 1838. Corners rubbed, orig. binding. Butterfield 10-92 1974 $35

BEECHING, H. C.   William Shakespeare Player, Playmaker, and Poet. 1909. Small 8vo., green calf, gilt. Quaritch 936-551 1974 £6

BEEDOME, THOMAS   Select Poems. 1928. Crown 8vo., full parchment, uncut, limited edition. Broadhurst 23-1066 1974 £10

BEEDOME, THOMAS   Select Poems: Human and Divine. Nonesuch Press, 1928. Crown 8vo., full parchment, uncut, board slip-in-case, limited to 1250 copies, fine. Broadhurst 24-1027 1974 £10

BEER, GEORG JOSEPH   Art of Preserving the Sight. London, 1822. 12mo., orig. boards, uncut. Dawsons PM 249-41 1974 £16

BEER, GEORG JOSEPH   Pflege Gesunder und Geschwachter Augen. Wien, 1800. 8vo., contemporary wrappers, fine, uncut, rare first edition. Gilhofer 61-29 1974 sFr. 600

BEER, THOMAS   Hanna. New York, 1929. Orig. cloth backed boards, first edition, one of 250 numbered copies, signed by author, uncut, fine. MacManus 224-30 1974 $30

BEER, THOMAS   The Road to Heaven. New York, 1928. Orig. cloth, first edition, one of 210 numbered copies, signed by author, spine faded, boxed. MacManus 224-31 1974 $25

BEER, THOMAS   Stephen Crane: A Study in American Letters. New York, 1923. Orig. cloth backed boards, paper label, first edition one of 165 numbered copies, bookplate removed, otherwise fine. MacManus 224-110 1974 $50

BEER, THOMAS   Stephen Crane: A Study in American Letters. 1924. Cloth backed patterned boards, very fine, partly discoloured d.w., first edition. Covent 51-449 1973 £7.50

BEER, THOMAS   Stephen Crane: A Study in American Letters. London, 1924. Orig. binding, first edition, some foxing, fine. Ross 87-126 1974 $15

BEERBOHM, MAX   And Even Now. Printed label, dust wrapper, fine. Covent 55-179 1974 £15

BEERBOHM, MAX   And Even Now. 1920. Extra crown 8vo., uncut, dust wrapper, first edition. Broadhurst 23-610 1974 £10

BEERBOHM, MAX   And Even Now. 1920. First edition, extra crown 8vo., uncut, d.w., orig. cloth, fine. Broadhurst 24-532 1974 £10

BEERBOHM, MAX   A Book of Caricatures. 1907. Folio, boards, inscribed, plates, first edition. Rota 190-42 1974 £75

BEERBOHM, MAX   The Dreadful Dragon of Hay Hill. 1928. 8vo., boards, cloth, dust wrapper, first edition. Broadhurst 23-611 1974 £8

BEERBOHM, MAX   The Dreadful Dragon of Hay Hill. 1928. English first edition. Covent 56-111 1974 £7.50

BEERBOHM, MAX   The Dreadful Dragon of Hay Hill. London, 1928. 8vo., foxing, orig. cloth-backed boards, first edition. Bow Windows 62-76 1974 £6.50

BEERBOHM, MAX   Fifty Caricatures. 1913. Small 4to., orig. green pictorial cloth, dust wrapper, fine, first edition. Howes 186-20 1974 £22.50

BEERBOHM, MAX   Fifty Caricatures. 1913. Pictorial gilt cover, plates, first edition. Marsden 37-32 1974 £8

BEERBOHM, MAX   Fifty Caricatures. London, 1913. First edition, plates, pict. green cloth, spine slightly faded, unusually bright, near mint copy. Ross 87-54 1974 $45

BEERBOHM, MAX   The Happy Hypocrite. (1918). 4to., orig. cloth, first edition. Rota 190-43 1974 £5

BEERBOHM, MAX   Observations. London, 1925. 4to., vellum, illus. Minters 37-235 1973 $14

BEERBOHM, MAX   A Peep Into the Past. New York, 1923. Pale brown boards, quarter brown cloth, paper labels, near mint, very scarce, limited to 300 copies on Japon vellum, unauthorized first edition. Ross 87-55 1974 $90

BEERBOHM, MAX   The Poet's Corner. 1904. Coloured caricatures, folio, pictorial boards, spine & corners rubbed, nice copy, first edition. Covent 51-212 1973 £15.75

BEERBOHM, MAX   Rossetti and His Circle. 1922. Separately mounted colour plates, name on fly, very good copy, slightly frayed d.w., first edition. Covent 51-213 1973 £15

BEERBOHM, MAX   Rossetti and his Circle. 1922. Roy 8vo., blue cloth, dust wrapper, first edition. Quaritch 936-291 1974 £35

BEERBOHM, MAX   Seven Men. 1919. 8vo., orig. cloth, uncut, first edition. Bow Windows 64-390 1974 £9.50

BEERBOHM, MAX   Seven Men. 1919. Browned dust wrapper, scarce, fine. Covent 55-184 1974 £15

BEERBOHM, MAX   Seven Men. London, 1919. First edition, orig. binding, tattered dust wrapper, internally fine. Ross 87-56 1974 $20

BEERBOHM, MAX   A Survey. Small 4to., frontispiece, dust wrapper, fine, first edition. Howes 186-22 1974 £28

BEERBOHM, MAX   A Survey. 1921. 4to., plates. Allen 216-121 1974 $15

BEERBOHM, MAX   A Survey. 1921. 4to., plates, orig. buckram. Smith 193-315 1973 £28

BEERBOHM, MAX   A Survey. 1921. 4to., orig. cloth, plates, first edition. Rota 190-44 1974 £14

BEERBOHM, MAX   A Survey. London, 1921. 4to., cloth, illus. Minters 37-234 1973 $15

BEERBOHM, MAX   A Survey. London, 1921. Orig. binding, plates, colored frontispiece, first edition, slight foxing, lacking dust wrapper, near fine. Ross 87-57 1974 $30

BEERBOHM, MAX   Tales of Three Nations. 1924. Wrappers, plates, fine. Covent 55-185 1974 £12.50

BEERBOHM, MAX   Things New and Old. 1923. 4to., orig. cream buckram, plates, coloured frontispiece, with extra coloured plate signed by the artist, Limited signed edition. Bow Windows 66-47 1974 £55

BEERBOHM, MAX   Things New and Old. 1923. Mounted plates, demy 4to., orig. cloth, fine, limited to 380 copies, signed by author, in pocket at back additional plate in colour signed by author. Broadhurst 24-533 1974 £50

BEERBOHM, MAX   Things New and Old. 1923. 4to., English first edition. Covent 56-1553 1974 £30

BEERBOHM, MAX   Things New and Old. London, 1923. Large 4to., cloth, shaken. Minters 37-236 1973 $16

BEERBOHM, MAX   Things New and Old. London, 1923. Orig. binding, plates, colored frontis., first edition, lacking d.w., fine. Ross 87-58 1974 $45

BEERBOHM, MAX   Things New and Old. 1923. Frontispiece, plates, faded, first edition. Marsden 37-33 1974 £15

BEERBOHM, MAX   Zuleika Dobson. London, 1911. 8vo., orig. cloth, faded, first edition. Dawsons PM 252-45 1974 £45

BEERBOHM, MAX   Zuleika Dobson. 1912. Orig. American edition. Austin 61-36 1974 $10

BEERBOHM, MAX   The Works. 1922. Cloth, 10 vols., bookplates, English first edition. Covent 56-112 1974 £240

BEETHOVEN, LUDWIG VAN   VII Variazioni dell Quartetto - Kind Willst du Richtig. Vienna, (1799). Oblong folio, unbound, first edition. Quaritch 940-806 1974 £120

BEETON, ISABELLA   The Book of Household Management. 1880. Very thick crown 8vo., plates, half contemporary calf gilt. Smith 193-917 1973 £7.50

BEEVER, W. H.   An Alphabetical Arrangement of the Leading Shorthorn Tribes. (188-). 8vo., cloth, very scarce, second edition. Wheldon 128-1640 1973 £5

BEEVER, W. H.   An Alphabetical Arrangement of the Leading Shorthorn Tribes. (188-). 8vo., cloth, very scarce, second edition. Wheldon 131-1771 1974 £5

BEGBIE, HAROLD   Great Men. London, 1901. Sm. 4to., pictorial boards, cloth spine; 24 color plates. Frohnsdorff 16-94 1974 $10

BEGER, HUGO   Die Geographischen Fragmente des Eratosthenes. Leipzig, 1880. 8vo., modern half blue morocco, first edition. Dawsons PM 251-6 1974 £10

BEGG, ALEX   History of British Columbia from Its Earliest Discovery to the Present Time. Toronto, 1894. Illus., first edition, leather, marbled end pages. Hood's 102-792 1974 $40

BEGG, ALEX   History of British Columbia From Its Earliest Discovery to the Present. Toronto, 1894. Illus., first edition. Hood's 103-794 1974 $40

BEGG, ALEX   "Jot It Down", a Story of Life in the Northwest. Toronto, 1871. First edition, rebound in fabric, pages browned. Hood's 102-791 1974 $25

BEHAINE, RENE   The Survivors. 1938. Dust wrapper, fine, English first edition. Covent 56-464 1974 £10.50

BEHAINE, RENE   The Survivors. London, 1938. First English edition, nice copy, orig. cloth. Crane 7-87 1974 £5

BEHAN, RICHARD J.   Pain, Its Origin, Conduction, Perception and Diagnostic Significance. New York, 1920. Rittenhouse 46-57 1974 $10

BEHAN, RICHARD J.   Pain, Its Origin, Conduction, Perception, and Diagnostic Significance. New York & London, 1922. Illus., excellent. Rittenhouse 46-58 1974 $10

BEHAN, RICHARD J.   Pain, Its Origin, Conduction, Perception and Diagnostic Significance. New York, 1914. Soiled cover. Rittenhouse 46-55 1974 $10

BEHN, APHRA   Plays, Histories & Novels. 1871. 6 vols., half calf, ex-library. Allen 216-E 1974 $50

BEHN, APHRA   Poems Upon Several Occasions. London, 1684. 8vo., modern blue boards, first edition. Dawsons PM 252-46 1974 £105

BEHREND, MOSES   Surgical Diseases of the Gall-Bladder, Liver and Pancreas and Their Treatment. Philadelphia, 1927. Rittenhouse 46-60 1974 $10

BEHRENS, WALTER LIONEL   Catalogue of the Second Portion of the Collection of Japanese Works of Art Formed by the Late. Glendining, 1914. 4to., orig. wrappers, worn. Quaritch 940-373 1974 £7

BEHRMAN, S. N.   Biography. Farrar & Rinehart, 1933. 241p. Austin 51-71 1973 $7.50

BEHRMAN, S. N.   Dunnigan's Daughter. Random House, 1945. 184p. Austin 51-72 1973 $7.50

BEHRMAN, S. N.   Meteor. 1930. 178p. Austin 51-73 1973 $8.50

BEIJERINCK, W.   Calluna, A Monograph on the Scotch Heather. Amsterdam, 1940. Roy. 8vo., orig. wrappers, plates, text-figures, coloured frontispiece, scarce. Wheldon 128-1077 1973 £10

BELA, RERRICH   Rerrich Bela. Geneva, 1930. 8vo., cloth, plates. Minters 37-516 1973 $25

BELCHER, C. F.   The Birds of Nyasaland. 1930. 8vo., cloth, folding map. Wheldon 128-385 1973 £7.50

BELCHER, C. F.   The Birds of Nyasaland Being a Classified List of the Species Recorded for the Nyasaland Protectorate Up to the Year 1930. 1930. 8vo., cloth, map. Wheldon 131-544 1974 £12

BELCHER, J.   Later Renaissance Architecture In England. Folio, plates. Smith 193-49 1973 £5

BELDEN, E. PORTER   New York -- As it Is; Being the Counterpart of the Metropolis of America. New York, 1849. 12mo., later wrappers, first edition, very scarce, folding map, wood engraved plate. Ximenes 36-12 1974 $40

BELDEN, H. M.   Ballads and Songs Collected by the Missouri Folk-Lore Society. Columbia, (1940). 8vo., wrapper. Butterfield 8-316 1974 $15

BELFAST NATURALISTS FIELD CLUB   A Guide to Belfast and the Counties of Down and Antrim. Belfast, 1902. 8vo., cloth, folding coloured maps. Wheldon 128-175 1973 £5

LA BELGIQUE Monumentale 100 Planches an Phototypie Tirees de: Sluyterman, Interieurs Anciens en Belgique et des Documents Classes de l'Art. La Haye, 1915. Folio, plates, orig. portfolio, with ties, some soiling, interior fine. Current BW9-488 1974 $30

BELGRADO, JACOPO   De Analyseos Vulgaris usu in re Physica. 1761-2. 4to., 2 vols., plates, modern vellum, boards, ex-library, first edition. Zeitlin 235-23 1974 $150

BELL, ALEXANDRE GRAHAM   The Mechanism of Speech. New York & London, 1911. Illus., fifth edition. Hood's 103-575 1974 $12

BELL, ANDREW   History of Canada. Montreal, 1862. 2 vols., revised second edition. Hood's 103-520 1974 $50

BELL, MRS. ARTHUR   Representative Painters of the XIX Century. 1899. Dec. cloth, gilt, plates. Marsden 37-34 1974 £10

BELL, CHARLES   The Anatomy of the Brain. London, 1802. 4to., contemporary half calf, plates, first edition. Dawsons PM 249-43 1974 £255

BELL, CHARLES   The Anatomy of the Brain. London, 1802. Large 4to., plates, orig. boards, uncut, rebacked, labels, first edition. Schafer 8-145 1973 sFr. 3,200

BELL, CHARLES   An Exposition of the Natural System of the Nerves of the Human Body. London, 1824. 8vo., contemporary speckled calf, rebacked. Dawsons PM 249-44 1974 £90

BELL, CHARLES   The Hand. 1833. Contemporary half calf, worn, second edition. Bow Windows 64-20 1974 £8.50

BELL, CHARLES   The Hand. Philadelphia, 1835. New edition. Rittenhouse 46-61 1974 $25

BELL, CHARLES   A Series of Engravings, Explaining the Courses of the Nerves. London, 1803. Large 4to., plates, orig. boards, uncut, orig. label, rare, first edition. Schafer 8-146 1973 sFr. 1,600

BELL, CLIVE   Art. 1914. 8vo., orig. cloth, scarce, first edition. Rota 189-93 1974 £5

BELL, CLIVE   Enjoying Pictures. 1934. Small 4to., plates, English first edition. Covent 56-1554 1974 £6.30

BELL, CLIVE   Landmarks in Nineteenth-Century Painting. 1927. Plates, faded spine. Covent 55-187 1974 £35

BELL, CLIVE   The Legend of Monte della Sibilla. 1923. Frontis., dec. boards, covers little dusty, nice copy, scarce, first edition. Covent 51-2169 1973 £27.50

BELL, CLIVE   The Legend of Monte della Sibilla. 1923. Roy 8vo., boards, dust wrapper, English first edition. Covent 56-114 1974 £45

BELL, CLIVE   Poems. 1921. Wrapper, fine copy, first edition. Covent 51-2171 1973 £22.50

BELL, D. C.   Notices of the Historic Persons. London, 1877. 8vo., illus., orig. cloth, frontispiece, bookplate. Bow Windows 62-78 1974 £6.50

BELL, EDWARD   George Bell, Publisher. 1924. Frontispiece, fine. Covent 55-1228 1974 £6

BELL, F. J.   Catalogue of the British Echinoderms in the British Museum. 1892. 8vo., cloth, plates. Wheldon 128-872 1973 £5

BELL, F. J.   Catalogue of the British Echinoderms in the British Museum. 1892. 8vo., cloth, plates. Wheldon 131-920 1974 £7.50

BELL, GERTRUDE   The Letters of. 1927. 2 vols., 791 pages. Austin 61-39 1974 $12.50

BELL, H. C.   Guide to British West Indies Archive. 1926. 8vo., cloth. Dawsons PM 11-45 1974 £9

BELL, I. LOWTHIAN   Principles of the Manufacture of Iron and Steel. London, 1884. 8vo., orig. green cloth, gilt, first edition. Dawsons PM 245-70 1974 £12

BELL, J. MUNRO   The Furniture Designs of Chippendale, Hepplewhite and Sheraton. 1910. 4to., plates, English first edition. Covent 56-1640 1974 £25

BELL, JACOB   Historical Sketch of the Progress of Pharmacy In Great Britain. London, 1880. Rittenhouse 46-63 1974 $20

BELL, JOHN   Travels From St. Petersburg In Russia to Diverse Parts of Asia. Glasgow, 1763. 2 vols., 4to., contemporary calf, leather labels, first & best edition. Traylen 79-514 1973 £55

BELL, LANDON C.   Cumberland Parish Lunenburg County. Richmond, (1930). 8vo., orig. bindings, inscribed. Butterfield 8-670 1974 $25

BELL, M.   Sir Edward Burne-Jones. 1894. Illus., third edition. Marsden 37-103 1974 £5

BELL, R. W.   Canada In War-Paint. London, Toronto, 1917. Hood's 103-91 1974 $10

BELL, STEPHEN   Rebel, Priest and Prophet. 1937. Austin 62-35 1974 $10

BELL, T.   Kologynomia. 1899. Orig. buckram gilt, plates, limited edition. Smith 193-418 1973 £5.50

BELL, THOMAS 1792-1880   A History of British Quadrupeds. (1836)-37. Roy. 8vo., orig. cloth. Wheldon 129-361 1974 £10

BELL, THOMAS 1792-1880   A History of British Quadrupeds, Including the Cetacea. (1836)-37. Roy. 8vo., orig. cloth, woodcuts, large paper issue, nice copy. Wheldon 128-305 1973 £10

BELL, THOMAS 1792-1880   A History of British Quadrupeds. (1836)-37. Roy. 8vo., contemporary full green levant morocco, gilt, wood engravings. Wheldon 131-474 1974 £30

BELL, THOMAS 1792-1880   A History of British Quadrupeds. 1874. 8vo., cloth, woodcuts, second edition. Wheldon 130-382 1974 £10

BELL, THOMAS 1792-1880   A History of British Reptiles. 1849. 8vo., orig. cloth, ex-library. Wheldon 130-662 1974 £7.50

BELL, THOMAS 1792-1880   A History of the British Stalk-Eyed Crustacea. 1853. 8vo., cloth, wood engravings. Wheldon 129-770 1974 £10

BELL, THOMAS 1792-1880   A Monograph of the Fossil Malacostracous Crustacea of Great Britain. 1857-62. Parts 1 and 2 in 1 vol., 4to., half calf, Wheldon 131-967 1974 £7.50

BELL, THOMAS 1792-1880   A Monograph of the Testudinata. 1836-42. Parts 1-8, coloured lithograph plates, folio, contemporary half calf, panelled back, covers to orig. parts bound in, extremely scarce, fine. Broadhurst 24-1048 1974 £600

BELL, WILLIAM   A Dissertation on . . . Trade and Economics. Cambridge, 1756. 4to., unbound, scarce. Hill 126-270 1974 £35

BELL, WILLIAM DIXON   The Moon Colony. Chicago, 1937. First American edition. Covent 55-643 1974 £25

BELLAIR, G.   L'Hybridation en Horticulture Production des Varietes. Paris, 1909. 8vo., half morocco. Wheldon 128-1445 1973 £5

BELLAIR, G.   L'Hybridation en Horticulture Production des Varietes, des Metis, des Hybrides et des Races. Paris, 1909. 8vo., half morocco. Wheldon 131-1491 1974 £5

BELLAMY, GEORGE ANNE   An Apology for the Life of. 1785. Small 8vo., 6 vols., contemporary calf, scarce, first edition. Quaritch 936-15 1974 £35

BELLAMY, THOMAS LUDFORD Lyric Poetry of Glees, Madrigals, Catches, Rounds, Canons and Duets. 1840. Contemporary morocco, gilt spine and borders, bookplate. Bow Windows 66-48 1974 £8.50

BELLAMY, WILLIAMS   A Second Century of Charades. Houghton, Mifflin, 1896. Austin 54-105 1973 $7.50

BELLANGE, HIPPOLYTE   Die Soldaten der Franzosischen. Leipzig, 1843. Orig. boards, gilt, plates. Dawson's 424-91 1974 £95

BELLARDI, L.   I Molluschi dei Tereri Terziarii. Turin, 1872-82. 4to., 3 vols., cloth. Wheldon 129-729 1974 £25

BELLARDI, L.   Quadri Iconographici di Zoologia. Turin & Milan, 1863. Imp. 4to., unbound, cloth portfolio, very scarce. Wheldon 131-18 1974 £90

BELLERS, JOHN   An Essay Towards the Improvement of Physick. London, 1714. 4to., modern quarter morocco, first edition. Dawsons PM 249-47 1974 £55

BELLERS, JOHN   Proposals for Raising a Colledge of Industry. London, 1696. 4to., marbled wrappers, second edition. Dawsons PM 247-13 1974 £230

BELLICARD, M.   Observations Upon the Antiquities of the Town of Herculaneum Discovered at the Foot of Mount Vesuvius. 1756. Plates, contemporary calf gilt, second edition. Smith 193-107 1973 £20

BELLINGERI, CARLO FRANCESCO   Del Peso Assoluto e Relativo die Visceri Negli Animali Vertebrati. (1844-51). Large 4to., boards, unopened. Schuman 37-17 1974 $75

BELLOC, HILAIRE   The Alternative. n.d. (c. 1940). First edition, wrappers, very nice copy, bookplate, scarce. Covent 51-219 1973 £7.50

BELLOC, HILAIRE   The Battle Ground. 1936. Maps, near fine. Covent 55-189 1974 £12.50

BELLOC, HILAIRE   The Book of the Bayeux Tapestry, Presenting the Complete Work in a Series of Colour Facsimiles. 1914. Frontis., coloured illus., first edition, roy. 8vo., very good copy, scarce, orig. cloth, signed by author. Broadhurst 24-538 1974 £25

BELLOC, HILAIRE   The Book of the Horace Club. Oxford, (1901). 8vo., parchment, scarce, first edition. Rota 189-103 1974 £12.50

BELLOC, HILAIRE   Cautionary Verses. New York, 1941. 8vo., illus. Frohnsdorff 16-95 1974 $10

BELLOC, HILAIRE   Characters of the Reformation. 1936. Illus., orig. edition. Auston 61-40 1974 $12.50

BELLOC, HILAIRE   Charles, the First King of England. 1933. Illus. Austin 61-41 1974 $12.50

BELLOC, HILAIRE   The Contrast. 1924. First American edition. Austin 61-42 1974 $10

BELLOC, HILAIRE   A Conversation with an Angel. 1928. Demy 8vo., first edition, orig. cloth, fine. Broadhurst 24-540 1974 £5

BELLOC, HILAIRE   A Conversation With a Cat and Others. (1931). Paper labels intact, spine faded, signautre and date on fly, slight foxing, first edition. Bow Windows 66-49 1974 £8.50

BELLOC, HILAIRE   Cranmer: Archbishop of Canterbury, 1533-56. 1931. 333 pages. Austin 61-43 1974 $12.50

BELLOC, HILAIRE   The Crisis of Our Civilization. 1937. 245 pages. Austin 61-44 1974 $10

BELLOC, HILAIRE   Dànton: A Study. 1902. 440 pages. Austin 61-45 1974 $12.50

BELLOC, HILAIRE   Emmanuel Burden. 1904. Drawings, covers somewhat faded & marked, joints little chafed, signed presentation inscription., first edition. Covent 51-220 1973 £6.30

BELLOC, HILAIRE   Esto Perpetua: Algerian Studies and Impressions. 1906. First edition, crown 8vo., top edges gilt, others uncut, coloured frontispiece and illus. by author, orig. cloth, fine. Broadhurst 24-537 1974 £5

BELLOC, HILAIRE   High Lights of the French Revolution. 1915. Frontispiece, illus. Austin 61-48 1974 $17.50

BELLOC, HILAIRE   A History of England: Vol. 1 – Pagon England, Catholic England, the Dark Ages B. C. 55 to A. D. 1066. 1925. Austin 61-49 1974 $12.50

BELLOC, HILAIRE   A History of England: Vol. 2 – Catholic England, The Early Middle Ages A. D. 1066 to 1348. 1927. Maps. Austin 61-50 1974 $15

BELLOC, HILAIRE   James the Second. 1928. 298 pages. Austin 61-51 1974 $12.50

BELLOC, HILAIRE   The Jews. 1922. Faded, first edition. Howes 186-23 1974 £5

BELLOC, HILAIRE   Lambkin's Remains. Oxford, 1900. 12mo., scarce, fine, mint dust wrapper. Covent 55-191 1974 £30

BELLOC, HILAIRE   Lambkin's Remains. Oxford, 1900. Orig. cloth, scarce, first edition. Rota 188-82 1974 £5

BELLOC, HILAIRE   Lambkin's Remains. 1900. Darkened spine, first edition. Covent 55-192 1974 £10

BELLOC, HILAIRE   The Man Who Made Gold. 1931. 296 pages. Austin 61-53 1974 $10

BELLOC, HILAIRE   Marie Antoinette. 1909. Illus., orig. American edition. Austin 61-54 1974 $12.50

BELLOC, HILAIRE   Miniatures of French History. (1925). 8vo., orig. cloth, signature, first edition. Rota 189-96 1974 £10

BELLOC, HILAIRE   The Missing Masterpiece. 1929. Illus. Austin 61-56 1974 $10

BELLOC, HILAIRE   A Moral Alphabet. 1899. Small 4to., orig. pictorial boards, buckram, illus., first edition. Howes 186-24 1974 £15

BELLOC, HILAIRE   A Moral Alphabet. 1899. Small 4to., illus., cloth backed pictorial boards, front joint weak, first edition, very good copy. Covent 51-224 1973 £6.30

BELLOC, HILAIRE   The Old Road. 1904. Folding map, illus., foxing throughout, very good copy, first edition. Covent 51-2173 1973 £12.60

BELLOC, HILAIRE   The Old Road. (1904). Illus., 296 pages. Austin 61-57 1974 $12.50

BELLOC, HILAIRE   The Path to Rome. 1902. 8vo., orig. cloth, ex-library, first edition. Rota 190-46 1974 £8

BELLOC, HILAIRE   The Pyrenees. 1909. Sketches, maps. Austin 61-60 1974 $17.50

BELLOC, HILAIRE   The Road. 1923. 8vo., frontis., illus., cloth. Quaritch 939-213 1974 £6

BELLOC, HILAIRE   Robespierre: A Study. 1901. First edition, demy 8vo., uncut, top edges gilt, very good copy, first issue in blue buckram, ads at end and errata slip. Broadhurst 24-536 1974 £10

BELLOC, HILAIRE   St. Thomas of Canterbury. 1933. Wrappers, fine, English first edition. Covent 56-115 1974 £5.25

BELLOC, HILAIRE   The Servile State. 1913. Second edition. Austin 61-62 1974 $10

BELLOC, HILAIRE   A Shorter History of England. 1934. 437 pages. Austin 61-63 1974 $12.50

BELLOC, HILAIRE   Sonnets and Verse. London, (1923). 8vo., fine, orig. cloth, d.w., limited, first edition. Bow Windows 62-79 1974 £15

BELLOC, HILAIRE   Survivals and New Arrivals. 1929. Ex-library. Austin 61-65 1974 $10

BELLOC, HILAIRE   Sussex. 1906. Large 8vo., orig. pictorial cloth, gilt, plates, map, first edition. Howes 186-25 1974 £10

BELLOC, HILAIRE   Verses. 1910. Dust wrapper, book-plate, fine, scarce. Covent 55-194 1974 £20

BELLOC, HILAIRE   Verses. 1910. Rubbed, foxing, English first edition. Covent 56-119 1974 £6.30

BELLOC, HILAIRE   Wolsey. 1930. 324 pages. Austin 61-66 1974 $12.50

BELLOC, HILAIRE   Wolsey. 1930. Plated, faded, torn, English first edition. Covent 56-120 1974 £5.25

BELLOSTE, AUGUSTIN   Le Chirurgien d'Hopital. Paris, 1696. 12mo., contemporary calf, first edition. Schuman 37-18 1974 $90

BELLOVACENSIS, VICENTIUS
Please turn to
VINCENT DE BEAUVAIS

BELMORE, SOMERSET RICHARD LOWRY-CORRY, 4TH EARL OF 1835-1913
A Catalogue of the Earl of Belmore's Ancient Deeds. Dublin, 1882. 8vo., cloth boards, wrappers. Emerald 50-56 1974 £5.50

BELOE, WILLIAM   Anecdotes of Literature and Scarce Books. London, 1807-11. 6 vols., half leather. Kraus B8-7 1974 $65

BELOE, WILLIAM   Anecdotes of Literature & Scarce Books. 1814-1811. 6 vols., new buckram. Allen 216-156 1974 $50

BELON, PIERRE   L'Histoire de la Nature des Oyseaux. Paris, 1555. Folio, modern half calf antique, woodcuts, rare. Wheldon 131-545 1974 £250

BELON, PIERRE   Les Observations de Plusieurs Singularitez et Choses Memorables. Paris, 1553. 3 parts in 1 vol., 4to., contemporary limp vellum, woodcut illus., very fine, rare first edition. Schafer 8-147 1973 sFr. 4,500

BELON, PIERRE   Les Remonstrances sur le Default du Labour et Culture des Plantes. Paris, 1558. 8vo., contemporary vellum, extremely rare. Wheldon 131-1714 1974 £140

BELT, THOMAS   The Naturalist in Nicaragua. 1874. 8vo., orig. blue cloth, illus., very scarce, nice copy, first edition. Wheldon 128-176 1973 £20

BELTRAMI, J. C.   A Pilgrimage In Europe and America. London, 1828. 2 vols., 8vo., orig. boards, paper labels, uncut. Traylen 79-467 1973 £21

BEMAN, DAVID   The Mysteries of the Trade. Boston, 1825. 8vo., contemporary tree calf, very nice copy. Ximenes 37-18 1974 $125

BEMBO, PIETRO   Gli Asolani. 1505. Small 4to., old mottled calf, worn, stains, rare, first edition, first issue. Thomas 30-17 1973 £100

BEMBO, PIETRO   Le Prose. Napoli, 1714. 4to., vellum, 3 parts in 1 vol. Schumann 499-9 1974 sFr 180

BEMBO, PIETRO   Prose, Nelle Quali si Ragione Della Volgra Lingua. Venice, 1525. Small folio, old vellum over boards, good copy, rare first edition. Schafer 8-99 1973 sFr. 1,200

BEMELMANS, LUDWIG   Are You Hungry Are You Cold. World, 1960. 245p. Austin 54-106 1973 $6

BEMELMANS, LUDWIG   The Blue Danube. Viking, 1945. 153p., illus. Austin 54-107 1973 $7.50

BEMELMANS, LUDWIG   The Donkey Inside. Viking, 1941. 224p., illus. Austin 54-108 1973 $6.50

BEMELMANS, LUDWIG   The Eye of God. Viking, 1949. 312p., colored end papers by the author. Austin 54-109 1973 $7.50

BEMELMANS, LUDWIG   Father Dear Father. Viking, 1953. 247p., illus. Austin 54-110 1973 $6.50

BEMELMANS, LUDWIG   Hotel Bemelmans. New York, 1946. 1st ed. Biblo & Tannen 213-494 1973 $7.50

BEMELMANS, LUDWIG   Hotel Bemelmans. Viking, 1946. 380p., illus. Austin 54-111 1973 $6

BEMELMANS, LUDWIG   How to Travel Incognito. Little, Brown, 1951. 244p., illus. Austin 54-112 1973 $6.50

BEMELMANS, LUDWIG   Life Class. Viking, 1938. 260p., illus. Austin 54-113 1973 $7.50

BEMELMANS, LUDWIG   My War With the U. S. 1937. 151 pages, illus. Austin 57-64 1974 $10

BEMELMANS, LUDWIG   Now I Lay me Down to Sleep. New York, 1943. Cloth, slipcase, illus., first edition. Dawson's 424-249 1974 $25

BEMELMANS, LUDWIG   Now I Lay Me Down to Sleep. Viking, 1944. 245p. Austin 54-114 1973 $6

BEMELMANS, LUDWIG   On Board Noah's Ark. Viking, 1962. 186p., illus. Austin 54-115 1973 $8.50

BEMELMANS, LUDWIG   The Street Where the Heart Lies. World, 1863. 236p., illus. Austin 54-116 1973 $6.50

BEMELMANS, LUDWIG   Sunshine. New York, 1950. Large 4to., 1st ed., illus. Frohnsdorff 16-97 1974 $15

BEMELMANS, LUDWIG   To the One I Love the Best. Viking, 1955. 254p., illus. Austin 54-117 1973 $6.50

BEMELMANS, LUDWIG   The World of Bemelmans. Viking, 1955. 502p., illus. Austin 54-118 1973 $12.50

BEMENT, A. J.   The Mystery Unveiled. De Witt, 1874. 8vo., printed wrapper. Butterfield 8-290 1974 $10

BEMIS, GEORGE   Report of the Case of John W. Webster, Indicted for the Murder of George Parkman, Before the Supreme Judicial Court of Massachusetts. Boston, 1850. Boards. Rittenhouse 46-64 1974 $75

BENCHLEY, NATHANIEL   Catch a Falling Spy. McGraw, Hill, 1963. 247p. Austin 54-129 1973 $6.50

BENCHLEY, NATHANIEL   The Off-Islanders. McGraw, Hill, 1961. 238p. Austin 54-130 1973 $6.50

BENCHLEY, NATHANIEL   One to Grow On. McGraw, Hill, 1958. 241p. Austin 54-131 1973 $6.50

BENCHLEY, NATHANIEL   The Visitors. McGraw, Hill, 1965. 248p. Austin 54-132 1973 $6.50

BENCHLEY, NATHANIEL   A Winter's Tale. McGraw, Hill, 1964. 214p. Austin 54-133 1973 $6.50

BENCHLEY, ROBERT   After 1903--What? Harpers, 1938. 271p. Austin 54-119 1973 $6.50

BENCHLEY, ROBERT   The Benchley Roundup. Harper, 1954. 333p. Austin 54-128 1973 $5

BENCHLEY, ROBERT   Chips Off the Old Benchley. Harpers, 1949. 360p. Austin 54-120 1973 $6

BENCHLEY, ROBERT   The Early Worm. Holt, 1927. 263p., illus. Austin 54-121 1973 $6.50

BENCHLEY, ROBERT   From Bed to Worse. Harpers, 1934. 286p., illus. Austin 54-122 1973 $8.50

BENCHLEY, ROBERT   Inside Benchley. Harper, 1942. 316p., illus. Austin 54-123 1973 $6.50

BENCHLEY, ROBERT   My Ten Years in a Quandary. Harper, 1940. 361p., illus. Austin 54-124 1973 $6

BENCHLEY, ROBERT   Of All Things. Garden City, 1921. Illus. Austin 54-125 1973 $6.50

BENCHLEY, ROBERT   Pluck and Luck. Holt, 1925. 295p. Austin 54-126 1973 $6.50

BENCHLEY, ROBERT   The Treasurer's Report. Harper, 1930. 345p. Austin 54-127 1973 $6.50

BENDA, C.   An Atlas of Practical Histology. Cleveland, (n.d.). Plates. Rittenhouse 46-65 1974 $10

BENDER, P.   Old and New Canada, 1753-1844. Montreal, 1882. Inscribed by author. Hood's 102-224 1974 $25

BENDER, P.   Old and New Canada, 1753-1844. Montreal, 1882. Inscribed. Hood's 104-242 1974 $25

BENDZ, G.   Die Echtheitsfrage des 4. Buches der Frontinschen Strategemata. 1938. Sewn, inscribed. Allen 213-404 1973 $10

BENEDETTI, ALESSANDRO   Collectiones Medicinae. (Venice, c. 1493). 4to., boards, leather spine, first and only separate edition, Georg Tannstetter's copy. Kraus 137-12 1974 $1,500

BENEDETTI, GIAMBATTISTA   De Gnomonvm Vmbrarvmq. 1574. Folio, contemporary limp vellum, ex-library, first edition. Zeitlin 235-24 1974 $950

BENEDICTINA Sive Constitutiones Benedicti Duo-Decimi Pape ad Monachos Nigros Cunctis Cenobitis. Paris, 1517. Small 4to., contemporary deerskin, lacks one tie, excellent condition. Thomas 32-221 1974 £40

BENET, STEPHEN VINCENT   The Ballad of the Duke's Mercy. New York, 1939. 12mo., orig. cloth, first edition, one of 250 numbered copies, signed by author, bookplate removed, otherwise fine. MacManus 224-32 1974 $37.50

BENET, STEPHEN VINCENT   James Shore's Daughter. 1934. Orig. edition. Austin 54-134 1973 $5.50

BENET, STEPHEN VINCENT   James Shore's Daughter. New York, 1934. Orig. boards, first edition, one of 307 numbered copies, signed by author, very good copy. MacManus 224-33 1974 $37.50

BENET, STEPHEN VINCENT   John Brown's Body. New York, 1928. First trade edition. Ballinger 1-71 1974 $10

BENET, STEPHEN VINCENT   Spanish Bayonet. 1926. 268 pages. Austin 54-135 1973 $7.50

BENET, STEPHEN VINCENT   Western Star. 1943. 181 pages. Austin 54-136 1973 $5

BENET, WILLIAM ROSE   The Dust Which is God. 1945. 559 pages. Austin 54-137 1973 $8

BENEZET, ANTHONY   A Short Account of That Part of Africa, Inhabited by the Negroes. Philadelphia, 1762. 8vo., contemporary wrappers, second edition. Ximenes 36-14 1974 $125

BENEZET, ANTHONY   Some Historical Account of Guinea. London, 1772. 8vo., contemporary calf, rebacked, first London edition. Traylen 79-449 1973 £58

BENEZET, ANTHONY   Some Observations on the Situation, Disposition, and Character of the Indian Natives of this Continent. Philadelphia, 1784. 12mo., disbound, first edition. Ximenes 36-15 1974 $75

BENHAM, DANIEL   Reflections on the Genealogy of Our Lord and Saviour Jesus Christ. 1836. Large 4to., orig. patterned cloth. Hill 126-16 1974 £10.50

BENHAM, W.   Short History of the Episcopal Church in the United States. London, 1884. Spine worn. Hood's 102-273 1974 $7.50

BENHAM, WILLIAM GURNEY   Playing Cards. London, (1931). 8vo., orig. cloth, illus., fine, d.w. Gregory 44-238 1974 $12.50

BENIVIENI, GIROLAMO   Opere. Venice, 1522. Small 8vo., vellum, woodcut border. Thomas 32-222 1974 £65

BENJAMIN, GILBERT G.   The Germans in Texas. 1909. 155 pages, maps. Austin 57-81 1974 $27.50

BENJAMIN, JUDAH P.   Correspondence of the Department of State in Relation to the British Consuls Resident in the Confederate States. Richmond, 1863. Printed wrappers, rare. Jenkins 61-577 1974 $25

BENJAMIN, L. S.   Life of William Makepeace Thackeray. 1899. 2 vols., portraits, foxed, large paper copy. Allen 216-1663 1974 $15

BENNETT, A. W.   The Flora of the Alps. 1900. 2 vols., 8vo., cloth, scarce, coloured plates. Wheldon 128-1238 1973 £5

BENNET, ABRAHAM   New Experiments on Electricity. 1789. 8vo., black half morocco, plates, first edition. Dawsons PM 245-71 1974 £45

BENNETT, ARNOLD   Anna of the Five Towns. 1903. 297 pages. Austin 61-69 1974 $10

BENNETT, ARNOLD   The Clayhanger Family. 1925. One of 200 copies on India Paper, numbered & signed by author, buckram gilt, very nice copy. Covent 51-3244 1973 £21

BENNETT, ARNOLD   Don Juan de Marana. 1923. Dust wrapper, signed, numbered, fine. Covent 55-198 1974 $7.50

BENNETT, ARNOLD   Don Juan de Marana. 1923. Orig. parchment backed boards, dust wrapper, uncut, portrait, numbered, signed by author, limited edition. Bow Windows 66-50 1974 £12

BENNETT, ARNOLD   Don Juan de Marana. 1923. 8vo., boards, signed. Quaritch 936-293 1974 £6

BENNETT, ARNOLD   Elsie and the Child. London, (1924). 8vo., orig. cloth, first edition. Bow Windows 62-80 1974 £5.50

BENNETT, ARNOLD   From the Log of the Velsa. London, 1920. 8vo., orig. cloth, illus., signed, limited, special edition. Bow Windows 62-81 1974 £35

BENNETT, ARNOLD   The Gates of Wrath. n.d. 253 pages. Austin 61-74 1974 $10

BENNETT, ARNOLD   The Glimpse. New York, 1909. Inscribed presentation, near fine, first American edition. Covent 55-199 1974 £15

BENNETT, ARNOLD   Hugo. 1906. Crown 8vo., orig. blue cloth, first edition. Howes 185-18 1974 £7.50

BENNETT, ARNOLD   Introduction to 'London Town'. 1926. First edition, pictorial wrappers, very good copy, slightly frayed d.w. Covent 51-230 1973 £5.25

BENNETT, ARNOLD   The Journals of 1896-1928. 1932-33. 3 vols., orig. buckram, dust wrapper, first edition. Smith 194-631 1974 £5

BENNETT, ARNOLD   Mr. Prohack. 1922. Orig. cloth, first edition. Howes 185-19 1974 £5

BENNETT, ARNOLD   The Old Wives' Tale. 1927. Limited to 500 copies, 2 vols., very good set, vellum backed cloth boards. Covent 51-2174 1973 £21

BENNETT, ARNOLD   The Old Wives' Tale. London, (1927). 2 vols., large quarto, orig. half vellum, fine, signed, limited, special edition. Jenkins 48-49 1973 $17.50

BENNETT, ARNOLD   The Old Wives Tale. 1940. 729 pages, illus. Austin 61-81 1974 $10

BENNETT, ARNOLD   Riceyman Steps. 1923. Crown 8vo., orig. cloth, first edition. Howes 186-28 1974 £6

BENNETT, ARNOLD   The Roll-Call. 1918. Orig. cloth, faded, first edition. Rota 188-88 1974 £5

BENNETT, ARNOLD   The Sinews of War. n.d. English first edition. Covent 56-124 1974 £7.50

BENNETT, ARNOLD   These Twain. 1916. Crown 8vo., orig. cloth, first edition. Howes 186-29 1974 £7.50

BENNETT, ARNOLD   Things That Have Interested Me. 1921. 332 pages. Austin 61-87 1974 $10

BENNETT, ARNOLD   The Woman Who Stole Everything. 1927. 345 pages. Austin 61-91 1974 $12.50

BENNETT, ARNOLD   Your United States. New York, 1912. 1st Amer. ed., illus. Biblo & Tannen 213-14 1973 $7.50

BENNETT, CHARLES H.   The Surprising, Unheard of and Never-To-Be Surpassed Adventures of Young Munchausen. London, 1865. 4to., gilt-pictorial cloth (worn); 1st ed. Frohnsdorff 16-98 1974 $27.50

BENNETT, EDWARD TURNER   The Gardens and Menageries of the Zoological Society of London Delineated. 1835. 2 vols., 8vo., contemporary grained calf gilt, second edition. Wheldon 131-412 1974 £20

BENNETT, ENOCH ARNOLD   Journalism for Women. 1898. Square 12mo., orig. pictorial cloth, fine, English first edition. Covent 56-746 1974 £15

BENNETT, ENOCH ARNOLD   A Man from the North. London & New York, 1898. 8vo., orig. cloth, fine, first edition, first issue. Dawsons PM 252-47 1974 £350

BENNETT, G. M.   The Art of the Bone-Setter. (1884). Plates, portrait, inscription on fly-leaf. Bow Windows 66-51 1974 £6.50

BENNETT, JOHN   The Doctor to the Dead. Rinehart, 1946. 260p. Austin 54-138 1973 $10

BENNETT, JOHN WHITCHURCH   A Selection from the Most Remarkable and Interesting Fishes Found on the Coast of Ceylon. 1830. 4to., new half scarlet morocco gilt, plates, rare, first edition. Wheldon 131-19 1974 £400

BENNETT, RICHARD   Catalogue of the Collection of Old Chinese Porcelains. (n.d.). Crown 4to., coloured plates, buckram, fine. Bow Windows 66-52 1974 £22

BENNETT, RICHARD   Catalogue of the Collection of Old Chinese Porcelains Formed By. Gorer, (1910). Roy. 4to., plates, cloth. Quaritch 940-374 1974 £15

BENOIS, A.   Tresors d'Art en Russie. St. Petersburg, 1901-07. 7 vols., 4to., plates, half calf, orig. wrappers, rare. Quaritch 940-779 1974 £850

BENSON, ADOLPH BURNETT   Swedes in America: 1638-1938. Yale University, 1938. Austin 62-39 1974 $22.50

BENSON, ADOLPH BURNETT   Swedes in America. 1938. Illus., orig. edition. Austin 57-66 1974 $22.50

BENSON, ARTHUR CHRISTOPHER   The Book of the Queen's Dolls' House. 1924. One of 1500 numbered copies, plates, 2 vols., 4to., linen backed boards, edges untrimmed, very fine, partly unopened, dust wrappers, slipcase, first edition. Covent 51-2195 1973 £75

BENSON, ARTHUR CHRISTOPHER   Everybody's Book of the Queen's Dolls' House. 1924. Imp. 8vo., plates, illus., cloth. Quaritch 940-473 1974 £5

BENSON, E. F.   The Outbreak of War. 1933. Illus., fine, dust wrapper, English first edition. Covent 56-127 1974 £7.50

BENSON, E. F.   Spook Stories. London, ca. 1928. 1st ed. Biblo & Tannen 210-562 1973 $17.50

BENSON, E. F.   The Money Market. 1898. Wrappers, English first edition. Covent 56-126 1974 £8.50

BENSON, E. F.   More Spook Stories. London, 1934. Biblo & Tannen 210-561 1973 $10

BENSON, E. M.   John Marin. Washington, 1935. Illus. Biblo & Tannen 213-327 1973 $15

BENSON, ROBERT HUGH   A Mirror of Shalott. New York, 1907. 1st ed., scarce. Biblo & Tannen 210-563 1973 $25

BENSON, STELLA   Christmas Formula and Other Stories. 1932. Full buckram, English first edition. Covent 56-128 1974 £5.50

BENSON, STELLA   Hope Against Hope. 1931. 8vo., orig. buckram backed boards, uncut, signature. Bow Windows 64-392 1974 £7

BENT, ARTHUR CLEVELAND   Life Histories of North American Gulls and Terns. Washington, 1921. 8vo., cloth, plates, rare. Wheldon 130-462 1974 £10

BENT, ARTHUR CLEVELAND   Life Histories of North American Gallinaceous Birds. Washington, 1932. 8vo., orig. wrappers, uncut. Wheldon 129-428 1974 £7.50

BENTHAM, GEORGE   Flora Hongkongensis. 1861-72. 8vo., new buckram. Wheldon 129-1047 1974 £40

BENTHAM, GEORGE   Handbook of the British Flora. 1858. 8vo., orig. cloth, first edition. Wheldon 128-1184 1973 £5

BENTHAM, GEORGE   Handbook of the British Flora. 1858. 8vo., orig. cloth, first edition. Wheldon 131-1218 1974 £5

BENTHAM, GEORGE   Handbook of the British Flora. 1865. 8vo., 2 vols., buckram, second edition. Wheldon 129-983 1974 £5

BENTHAM, GEORGE   Handbook of the British Flora. 1866. 8vo., cloth, new edition. Wheldon 130-1078 1974 £5

BENTHAM, GEORGE   Handbook of the British Flora. 1937-44. Post 8vo., cloth, 3 vols. Wheldon 129-984 1974 £5

BENTHAM, JAMES   The History and Antiquities of the Conventual Cathedral Church. Cambridge & Norwich, 1771-1817. 2 vols., 4to., half morocco, first edition. Quaritch 939-314 1974 £60

BENTHAM, JAMES   The History and Antiquities of the Conventual and Cathedral Church. 1812. 4to., plates, contemporary calf, second edition. Quaritch 939-315 1974 £45

BENTHAM, JEREMY   Defence of Usury. London. 3 works in 1 vol., small 8vo., old half calf, worn, first editions. Bow Windows 62-83 1974 £128

BENTHAM, JEREMY   The Elements of the Art of Packing, as Applied to Special Juries, Particularly in Cases of Libel Law. 1821. First edition, med. 8vo., orig. boards, paper printed label, all edges uncut, remarkably fine copy. Broadhurst 24-1201 1974 £50

BENTHAM, JEREMY   Plan of Parliamentary Reform. London, 1817. 8vo., modern boards. Dawsons PM 247-17 1974 £16

BENTHAM, JEREMY   A Protest Against Law Taxes. Dublin, 1793. 8vo., modern boards. Dawsons PM 252-14 1974 £15

BENTHAM, JEREMY   Supply Without Burthen. London, 1795. 8vo., modern half calf, inscribed, presentation, first edition. Dawsons PM 247-15 1974 £165

BENTHAM, JEREMY   Traites de Legislation Civile et Penale. Paris, 1802. 3 vols., 8vo., contemporary mottled calf, gilt, fine, first edition. Dawsons PM 247-16 1974 £350

BENTHAM, JEREMY   Traites de Legislation Civile et Penale. Paris, 1802. 8vo., 3 vols., contemporary green half morocco gilt, first edition. Dawsons PM 251-166 1974 £75

BENTLEY, EDMUND C.   The Woman in Black. Toronto, 1913. Orig. black cloth gilt, first Canadian edition. Howes 185-20 1974 £5

BENTLEY, ELIZABETH   Genuine Poetical Compositions on Various Subjects. Norwich, 1791. 12mo., frontispiece, contemporary tree calf, gilt, first edition. Bow Windows 62-84 1974 £20

BENTLEY, ERIC   In Search of Theatre. Knopf, 1953. 411p., illus. Austin 51-75 1973 $12.50

BENTLEY, R.   Designs by. 1753. Folio, contemporary calf, rebacked, first edition. Quaritch 936-94 1974 £120

BENTLEY, RICHARD 1662-1742   A Letter to the Reverend Master of Trinity College in Cambridge. 1721. 4to., sewed, uncut, first edition. Quaritch 936-16 1974 £8

BENTLEY, RICHARD 1708-1782   Patriotism, a Mock-Heroic. London, 1763. 4to., old half calf, worn, first edition, ex-library, some soiling towards end. Ximenes 36-16 1974 $50

BENTLEY, RICHARD 1708-1782   A Second Letter from a Gentleman in Town, to His Friend in the Country, on Account of the Late Dreadful Earthquake. London, 1750. Folio, disbound, first edition. Ximenes 36-17 1974 $60

BENTLEY, THOMAS   A View of the Advantages of Inland Navigations. London, 1765. 8vo., quarter calf, first edition. Hammond 201-843 1974 £36

BENTON, F. WEBER   Semi-Tropic California. Los Angeles, 1915. 4to., leather, second edition. Saddleback 14-36 1974 $15

BENTON, FRANK   Cowboy Life on the Sidetrack. Denver, (1903). Orig. pictorial cloth, illus., first edition. Bradley 35-109 1974 $50

BENTON, G. M.   The Church Plate of the County of Essex. Colchester, 1926. Demy 4to., orig. cloth, photos, fine. Broadhurst 24-11 1974 £5

BENTON, WALTER   Never a Greater Need. New York, 1948. 1st ed., dw. Biblo & Tannen 213-496 1973 $10

BENYOWSKY, MAURITIUS AUGUSTUS   Memoirs and Travels. London, 1790. 2 vols., 4to., contemporary half calf, plates, first English edition. Traylen 79-515 1973 £175

BENYOWSKY, MAURITIUS AUGUSTUS   Memoirs and Travels. London, 1790.
2 vols., 4to., contemporary calf, spine bit rubbed, morocco labels, first edition,
fine, maps, plates. Ximenes 36-18 1974 $350

BEOWULF. New York, 1952. Ltd. ed. Biblo & Tannen 210-761 1973 $17.50

BERALDI, HENRI   Bibliotheque Henri Beraldi. Paris, 1934.
Vols. 2 & 3 only on 5, plates, thick 4to. Kraus B8-8 1974 $60

BERALDI, HENRI   Bibliotheque Henri Beraldi. Paris, 1934-35.
5 vols., plates, inscriptions. Dawsons PM 10-33 1974 £30

BERANGER, PIERRE JEAN DE   Chansons. Paris, 1829. 2 vols. in 1, 18mo.,
contemporary long grain morocco, gilt. L. Goldschmidt 42-158 1974 $45

BERANGER, PIERRE JEAN DE   Deroieres Chansons de...1834 a 1851. Paris,
1857. Morocco boards, light foxing, raised bands, bookplate, note tipped in,
French text. Wilson 63-487 1974 $15

BERCE, E.   Faune Entomologique Francaise. Paris, 1867-
68. 2 vols., small 8vo., half red morocco, plates. Wheldon 131-784 1974
£10

BERCHTOLD, LEOPOLD   An Essay to Direct and Extent the Inquiries of
Patriotic Travellers . . . to Which is Annexed a List of English and Foreign Works
. . . & a Catalogue of the Most Interesting European Travels. London, 1789.
2 vols., orig. pink boards, 8vo., cloth spines, uncut, first vol. unopened.
Kraus B8-9 1974 $250

BERCOVICI, KONRAD   Main Entrance. Covici, Friede, 1932.
Austin 62-40 1974 $8.50

BERCOVICI, KONRAD   On New Shores. 1925. 302 pages, illus.
Austin 57-67 1974 $10

BERCOVICI, KONRAD   On New Shores. Century, 1925. 302p.,
illus. Austin 62-41 1974 $10

BERCOVICI, KONRAD   The Volga Boatman. Grosset & Dunlap, 1926.
233p., illus. Austin 51-76 1973 $7.50

BERENSON, BERNARD   The Study and Criticism of Italian Art. London,
1920-27. 3 vols., first, second and third series, illus., orig. bindings. Wilson
63-293 1974 $32.50

BERENSON, BERNARD   Three Essays in Method. Oxford, 1927. Roy.
4to., cloth, plates, scarce. Quaritch 940-18 1974 £20

BERESFORD, WILLIAM   A Voyage Round the World. London, 1789.
Full leather, maps, plates, first edition. Hood's 103-49 1974 $450

BEREZNIAK, LEON A.   The Theatrical Counselor. 1923. 223p.
Austin 51-77 1973 $7.50

BERG, BENGT   Gypaetus, den Flygande Draken i Himalaya.
Stockholm, 1931. Roy. 8vo., cloth, illus. Wheldon 131-546 1974 £7.50

BERGAMO, JACOBO FILIPPO
Please turn to
FORESTI DA BERGAMO, JACOBO FILIPPO

BERGE, F.   Schmetterlings-Buch. Stuttgart, 1870. 4to.,
orig. pictorial boards, plates, revised edition, fourth edition. Wheldon 131-785
1974 £25

BERGER, ALWIN   Die Agaven, Beitrage zu Einer Monographie.
Jena, 1915. Roy. 8vo., art leather, illus. Wheldon 131-1640 1974 £7.50

BERGER, ALWIN   Hortus Mortolensis. 1912. 8vo., cloth, plates.
Wheldon 131-1492 1974 £7.50

BERGER, ALWIN   Mesembrianthemen und Portulacaceen.
Stuttgart, 1908. Crown 8vo., cloth. Wheldon 131-1641 1974 £7.50

BERGER, ALWIN   Stapelieen und Kleinien, Einschliesslich Einiger
Anderer Verwandter Sukkulenten. Stuttgart, 1910. 8vo., cloth. Wheldon 131-
1642 1974 £10

BERGER, FRANCESCO   97. 1931. Portrait, boards, fine, dust
wrapper. Covent 55-591 1974 £5.25

BERGH, J. A.   Den Norsk Lutherske Kirkes Historie I
Amerika. Minneapolis, 1914. 528 pages. Austin 57-69 1974 $17.50

BERGH, J. A.   Den Norsk Lutherske Kirkes Historie I Amerika.
Minneapolis, 1914. Austin 62-42 1974 $17.50

BERGHAM, G.   Catalogue Raisonne des Impressions Elzeviriennes
de la Bibliotheque Royale de Stockholm. Stockholm, 1911. Portrait, plate, roy.
8vo., half morocco, orig. wrappers bound in, fine. Forster 98-163 1974 £23

BERGHAUS, H. K. W.   Hand Atlas of Physical Geography. 1850. Roy.
8vo., orig. cloth, plates, maps. Wheldon 128-8 1973 £10

BERGIUS, PETRUS JONAS   A Description of a Rare American Plant. (1773).
4to., new boards, plates. Wheldon 129-1049 1974 £5

BERGIUS, PETRUS JONAS   A Description of a Rare American Plant of the
Brownaeae Kind With Some Remarks on this Genus. (1773). 4to., new boards,
plates. Wheldon 131-1261 1974 £5

BERGIUS, PETRUS JONAS   Descriptiones Plantarum ex Capite Bonae Spei.
Stockholmiae, 1767. First edition, folding plates, 8vo., contemporary mottled
calf, somewhat browned, rare. Sawyer 293-75 1974 £525

BERGMAN, RAY   Just Fishing. New York, (1940). Illus.,
plates, special edition, 8vo., cover somewhat soiled, excellent interior, signed
by author. Current BW9-153 1974 $14.75

BERGMAN, RAY   Trout. New York, 1944. 8vo., plates in full
color, spine trifle faded, front inner hinge sprung, photos. Current BW9-154
1974 $12.50

BERGMAN, S.   In Korean Wilds and Villages. 1938. 8vo.,
cloth, map, plates. Wheldon 128-177 1973 £5

BERGMAN, TORBERN OLOF   Afhandling Om Blasroret. 1781. Small 8vo.,
boards. Zeitlin 235-254 1974 $150

BERGMAN, TORBERN OLOF   Aminnelse-tal ofver Framledne Theol. 1765.
8vo., disbound. Zeitlin 235-256 1974 $37.50

BERGMAN, TORBERN OLOF   Aminnelse-tal Ofver Kongl. 1778. 8vo.,
disbound. Zeitlin 235-257 1974 $37.50

BERGMAN, TORBERN OLOF   Aminnelse-tal over Framledne. 1768. 8vo.,
disbound. Zeitlin 235-255 1974 $37.50

BERGMAN, TORBERN OLOF   Dissertatio Chemica de Acido Sacchari. (1776).
Small 4to., disbound, fine, first edition. Zeitlin 235-258 1974 $77.50

BERGMAN, TORBERN OLOF   Dissertatio Chemica de Analysi Lithomargae.
(1782). Small 4to., disbound, rare, first edition. Zeitlin 235-259 1974 $62.50

BERGMAN, TORBERN OLOF   Dissertatio Chemica de Arsenico. (1777). Small
4to., disbound, fine, rare, first edition. Zeitlin 235-260 1974 $65

BERGMAN, TORBERN OLOF   Disquisitio Chemica de Calce. (1769). Small
4to., disbound, rare, first edition. Zeitlin 235-261 1974 $72.50

BERGMAN, TORBERN OLOF   Dissertatio Chemica de Mineris Zinci. (1779).
Small 4to., disbound, rare, first edition. Zeitlin 235-262 1974 $62.50

BERGMAN, TORBERN OLOF   Dissertatio Chemica de Nicolo. (1775). Small
4to., disbound, rare, first edition. Zeitlin 235-263 1974 $65

BERGMAN, TORBERN OLOF   Dissertatio Chemica de Terra Asbestina. (1782).
Small 4to., disbound, rare, first edition. Zeitlin 235-264 1974 $62.50

BERGMAN, TORBERN OLOF   Dissertatio Chemica de Terra Silicea. (1779).
Small 4to., disbound, rare, first edition. Zeitlin 235-265 1974 $72.50

BERGMAN, TORBERN OLOF   Dissertatio Gradualis Sistens. (1782). Small
4to., disbound, foxing, rare, first edition. Zeitlin 235-266 1974 $62.50

BERGMAN, TORBERN OLOF   Dissertatio Metallurgica de Minerarum. (1780). Small 4to., disbound, rare, first edition. Zeitlin 235-267 1974 $77.50

BERGMAN, TORBERN OLOF   A Dissertation on Elective Attractions. London, 1785. 8vo., contemporary gilt-ruled calf, rebacked. Zeitlin 235-253 1974 $250

BERGMAN, TORBERN OLOF   Observationes Chemicae de Antimonialibus Sulphuratis. (1782). Small 4to., disbound, rare, first edition. Zeitlin 235-268 1974 $65

BERGOMENSIS, JACOBUS PHILIPPUS
Please turn to
FORESTI DA BERGAMO, JACOBO FILIPPO

BERGSON, HENRI   Einfuhrung in die Metaphysik. Jena, 1909. Boards, English first edition. Covent 56-1563 1974 £7.50

BERGSON, HENRI   Das Lachen. 1914. Cloth-backed boards, English first edition. Covent 56-1562 1974 £5.25

BERIGARDUS, CLAUDE   Dubitationes in Dialogorum Galilaei Galilaei. Florence, 1632. Woodcut diagram, small 4to., half morocco, first edition, exlibris of Pietro Ginori Conti. Schumann 500-25 1974 sFr 4,500

BERINGTON, JOSEPH   The History of the Lives of Abeillard and Heloisa. Birmingham, 1788. 4to., contemporary quarter calf, worn, second edition. Hammond 201-82 1974 £9

BERINGTON, JOSEPH   History of Reign of Henry II, and of Richard & John, His Sons. 1790. 4to., new buckram. Allen 213-1286 1973 $25

BERINGTON, JOSEPH   A Literary History of the Middle Ages. London, 1814. 4to., orig. boards, fine, first edition. Dawsons PM 252-48 1974 £20

BERJEAU, J. P.   Catalogue Illustre des Livres Xylographiques. 1865. New buckram. Allen 216-158 1974 $17.50

BERKELEY, GEORGE   The Analyst. London, 1734. 8vo., contemporary calf, rebacked, first edition. Dawsons PM 245-72 1974 £175

BERKELEY, GEORGE   Siris. 1744. 8vo., disbound, uncut. Gurney 64-16 1974 £10

BERKELEY, GEORGE   Siris: A Chain of Philosophical Reflexions and Inquiries Concerning the Virtures of Tar Water, and Divers Other Subjects. Dublin, 1744. Second edition, 8vo., disbound, uncut. Gurney 66-22 1974 £10

BERKELEY, GEORGE CHARLES GRANTLEY FITZHARDINGE 1800-1881 Reminiscences of a Huntsman. 1854. Orig. cloth, plates, rebacked, signed. Covent 54-765 1974 £8.50

BERKELEY, MILES JOSEPH   Handbook of British Mosses. 1863. 8vo., cloth, hand coloured plates. Wheldon 128-1338 1973 £8

BERKELEY, MILES JOSEPH   Handbook of British Mosses. 1895. 8vo., cloth, hand coloured plates, second edition. Wheldon 128-1339 1973 £6

BERKELEY, MILES JOSEPH   Introduction to Cryptogamic Botany. 1857. 8vo., cloth, scarce. Wheldon 129-1385 1974 £5

BERKELEY, MILES JOSEPH   Outlines of British Fungology. 1860. 8vo., half calf, plates. Wheldon 129-1147 1974 £10

BERKELEY, MILES JOSEPH   Outlines of British Fungology. 1891. 8vo., cloth. Wheldon 129-1148 1974 £7.50

BERKENHOUT, JOHN   Dissertatio Medica Inauguralis. Leiden, 1765. 4to., disbound, presentation copy. Gurney 64-17 1974 £20

BERKENHOUT, JOHN   Outlines of the Natural History of Great Britain and Ireland. 1769-72. 3 vols., 8vo., contemporary calf, rare. Wheldon 131-338 1974 £50

BERKENHOUT, JOHN   Synopsis of the Natural History of Great-Britain and Ireland. 1789. 2 vols., 8vo., contemporary calf. Wheldon 128-178 1973 £30

BERKENHOUT, JOHN   Synopsis of the Natural History of Great Britain and Ireland. 1789. 8vo., contemporary calf. Wheldon 130-270 1974 £30

THE BERKSHIRE Jubilee, Celebrated at Pittsfield, Massachusetts, August 22 & 23, 1844. Albany, 1845. 8vo., cloth. Saddleback 14-473 1974 $12.50

BERLAGE, H. P.   Mijn Indische Reis. Rotterdam, 1931. 4to., boards, cloth spine. Minters 37-517 1973 $18.50

BERLESE, A.   Le Cocciniglie Italiane Viventi Sugli Agrumi. 1893-96. 8vo., buckram, plates. Wheldon 129-608 1974 £25

BERLYN, MRS. ALFRED   Sunrise-Land. 1894. Orig. pictorial cloth, English first edition. Covent 56-1840 1974 £15

BERMANN, R. A.   The Mahdi of Allah. 1931. First edition, demy 8vo., fine, slightly soiled d.w., plates, maps, orig. cloth. Broadhurst 24-1577 1974 £5

BERNAL, RALPH   Catalogue of the Celebrated Collection of Works of Art. 1855. Roy. 8vo., plates, orig. cloth, stained. Smith 194-83 1974 £8

BERNALDEZ, ANDRES   The Voyages of Christopher Columbus. 1930. 4to., orig. vellum backed buckram gilt, on jap. vellum, limited edition. Smith 193-308 1973 £20

BERNARD, FRANCIS   Select Letters on the Trade and Government of America. London, 1774. 8vo., cloth bound, gilt, first edition. Bow Windows 62-85 1974 £58

BERNARD, G.   Champignons Observes a La Rochelle. La Rochelle, 1882. 8vo., 2 vols., new cloth. Wheldon 129-1149 1974 £20

BERNARD, GEORGE S.   War Talks of Confederate Veterans . . . Addresses Delivered Before S. P. Hill Camp of Confederate Veterans of Petersburg, Va. Petersburg, 1892. Orig. binding. Butterfield 10-149 1974 $15

BERNARD, SAINT, ABBOT OF CLAIRVAUX   Opera Omnia. 1632. Rebacked in morocco, contemporary calf. Smith 194-132 1974 £35

BERNARD, SAINT, ABBOT OF CLAIRUAUX   Opuscula. 1495. Small 8vo., contemporary vellum over wooden boards. Thomas 28-278 1972 £150

BERNARD, SAINT, ABBOT OF CLAIRVAUX   Opuscula. Venice, 1495. Small 8vo., contemporary calf over oak boards. Thomas 28-277 1972 £150

BERNARD, SAINT, ABBOT OF CLAIRVAUX   Speculum de Honestate Vitae. Rome, c. 1485. Small 4to., 19th century boards, bookplate. Thomas 28-279 1972 £65

BERNARD, CLAUDE   Critique Experimentale sur la Fonction. 1877. 8vo., modern marbled boards. Dawsons PM 249-51 1974 £250

BERNARD, CLAUDE   Critique Experimentale sur la Formation. 1876. 8vo., modern marbled boards. Dawsons PM 249-50 1974 £250

BERNARD, CLAUDE   Lecons de Pathologie Experimentale. Paris, 1880. 8vo., orig. grey printed wrappers, uncut, unopened, second edition. Dawsons PM 249-53 1974 £30

BERNARD, CLAUDE   Lecons de Physiologie Operatoire. Paris, 1879. 8vo., quarter vellum, first edition. Dawsons PM 249-52 1974 £85

BERNARD, CLAUDE   Lecons sur les Effets des Substances Toxiques. Paris, 1857. 8vo., blue quarter roan, first edition. Dawsons PM 249-48 1974 £60

BERNARD, CLAUDE   Lecons sur les Proprietes des Tissus Vivants. Paris, 1866. 8vo., purple cloth, torn, first edition. Dawsons PM 249-49 1974 £60

BERNARD, CLAUDE   Lecons sur les Proprietes des Tissus Vivants. Paris, 1866. 8vo., half red morocco. Wheldon 129-322 1974 £35

BERNARD, CLAUDE   La Science Experimentale. Paris, c. 1885. Second edition. Rittenhouse 46-70 1974 $50

BERNARD, CLAUDE   Sur le Mecanisme de la Formation du Sucre dans la Foie. Paris, 1855. Large 4to., half cloth. Schafer 8-148 1973 sFr. 600

BERNARD, EDWARD   Catalogi Librorum Manuscriptorum Angliae et Hiberniae. Oxford, 1697. 2 vols. in 1, folio, contemporary calf, rebacked. Dawsons PM 10-35 1974 £110

BERNARD, PIERRE JOSEPH   Oeuvres. Paris, 1797. 4to., three quarter red levant morocco, gilt, uncut, illus., foxing. L. Goldschmidt 42-8 1974 $180

BERNARD, THOMAS   Case of the Salt Duties. London, 1817. Small 8vo., orig. boards, illus., first edition. Hammond 201-212 1974 £9.50

BERNARD DE CLAIRVAUX, SAINT 1091-1153   Incipit Speculum Beati Bernhardi Abbatis de Honestate Vite. (Basel, 1472-74). First edition, boards, 4to. Schumann 499-108 1974 sFr 4,000

BERNARD DE CLAIRVAUX, SAINT 1091-1153   Life and Works of. London, (n.d.). 2 vols., 8vo., contemporary red half morocco, rubbed, frontis., foxing, second edition. Bow Windows 62-794 1974 £7.50

BERNARD OF LUTZENBURG   Catalogus Hereticorum. (Cologne), 1526. 8vo., modern half vellum, third enlarged edition, good copy. Schafer 10-93 1974 sFr 1,100

BERNARDETE, M. J.   And Spain Sings! New York, 1937. First U. S. edition, chipped d.w., very good copy. Covent 51-1731 1973 $15.75

BERNARDONI, GIOVANNI
Please turn to
FRANCESCO D'ASSISI, SAINT

BERNERS, JULIANA   A Jewell for Gentrie. London, 1614. 4to., modern crushed brown morocco, engravings. Quaritch 939-47 1974 £650

BERNIER, FRANCIS   Travels in the Mogul Empire. London, 1826. 2 vols., rebound. Biblo & Tannen 210-990 1973 $15

BERNOULLI, JEAN 1667-1748   Recueil pour les Astronomes. Berlin, 1771-76. 8vo., 3 vols., old boards, plates. Gurney 64-18 1974 £40

BERNOULLI, JOHANN   A Sexcentenary Table. London, 1779. Large 4to., contemporary tree calf, gilt, first edition. Dawsons PM 245-74 1974 £20

BERNOULLI, JOHANN   Opera Omnia. 1742. 4to., 4 vols., contemporary mottled calf, rebacked, plates. Dawsons PM 245-73 1974 £160

BERNSTEIN, ALINE   Three Blue Suits. New York, 1933. Ltd. ed., sgd. Biblo & Tannen 213-497 1973 $42.50

BEROALDE DE VERVILLE, FRANCOIS   Le Moyen de Parvenir. Paris, n.d. 3 vols., 12mo., three quarter tan glazed calf, morocco labels, gilt, uncut, excellent copy. L. Goldschmidt 42-9 1974 $45

BEROALDO, FILIPPO   De Felicitate Opusculum. Bologna, 1495. Small 4to., new blind stamped calf, very fine, first edition. Harper 213-12A 1973 $625

BERON, PIERRE   Atlas Meteorologique. Paris, 1860. 4to., orig. paper wrppers, unopened, uncut. Zeitlin 235-25 1974 $75

BERQUIN, ARNAUD   Le Livre de Famille, ou Journal des Enfans. Paris, 1825. 16mo., plates, contemporary mottled calf, worn, stains. Bow Windows 62-86 1974 £5.25

BERQUIN, ARNAUD   Looking-Glass for the Mind. 1817. 12mo., contemporary calf, woodcuts, fourteenth edition. George's 610-58 1973 £6

BERQUIN, ARNAUD   Looking-Glass for the Mind. 1830. 12mo., orig. boards, roan spine, lower cover almost detached, woodcuts, eighteenth edition. George's 610-59 1973 £5

BERQUIN, ARNAUD   The Looking-Glass for the Mind. Philadelphia, 1832. Worn leather (covers detached); over 60 engravings on wood. Frohnsdorff 16-99 1974 $35

BERRETTINI, PIETRO DA CORTONA   Tabulae Anatomicae. Romae, 1741. Large folio, half vellum, fine, first edition. Dawsons PM 249-54 1974 £1,850

BERRETTINI, PIETRO DA CORTONA   Tabulae Anatomicae ex Archetypis Egregii Pictoris. Rome, 1788. Large folio, old boards, new cloth back, second edition. Schuman 37-19 1974 $950

BERRICHON, PATERNE   La Vie de Jean-Arthur Rimbaud. Paris, 1897. 12mo., half cloth, orig. wrapper. L. Goldschmidt 42-351 1974 $15

BERRY, ARTHUR   A Short History of Astronomy. London, 1898. 8vo., orig. red cloth, gilt. Dawsons PM 245-75 1974 £5

BERRY, MARY   Extracts of the Journals and Correspondence Of. Longmans, 1865. 8vo., half red morocco gilt, first edition. Bow Windows 64-393 1974 £78

BERRY, WILLIAM   County Genealogies. 1830. Folio, illus., buckram. Quaritch 939-804 1974 £50

BERRY, WILLIAM   County Genealogies. 1833. Folio, half green morocco, gilt. Quaritch 939-801 1974 £80

BERRY, WILLIAM   County Genealogies. 1837. 3 vols. in 1, folio, half green morocco, gilt. Quaritch 939-800 1974 £100

BERRY, WILLIAM   County Genealogies. (1844). Folio, half green morocco, gilt. Quaritch 939-802 1974 £80

BERRY, WILLIAM   County Genealogies. (1844). Folio, half roan. Quaritch 939-803 1974 £40

BERRY, WILLIAM   Encyclopaedia Heraldica. London, c., 1840. Large 4to., 3 vols., contemporary crimson half morocco, gilt, plates. Hammond 201-410 1974 £60

BERRY, WILLIAM   The History of the Island of Guernsey. 1815. 4to., plates, half calf, rebacked. Quaritch 939-326 1974 £50

BERRYMAN, JOHN   Poems. 1942. Wrappers, fine, English first edition. Covent 56-131 1974 £15.75

BERT, E.   Bert's Treatise of Hawks and Hawking. 1891. Small 4to., orig. Roxburghe binding. Wheldon 128-389 1973 £55

BERT, E.   Bert's Treatise of Hawks and Hawking. 1891. Small 4to., orig. Roxburghe binding, reprinted from the orig. edition. Wheldon 131-548 1974 £55

BERT, JOURDANET, D.   Influence de la Pression. Paris, 1875. Large 8vo., 2 vols., half leather, wom, plates, first edition. Gurney 64-23 1974 £30

BERT, PAUL   Lecons de Zoologie. Paris, 1881. 8vo., buckram, orig. wrappers, illus., first edition. Gumey 64-19 1974 £25

BERT, PAUL   Lecons de Zoologie. Paris, 1881. 8vo., half leather, rubbed, illus., first edition. Schuman 37-21 1974 $95

BERT, PAUL   Lecons de Zoologie Professees a la Sorbonne. Paris, 1881. 8vo., buckram, orig. wrappers bound in, first edition, illus. Gurney 66-23 1974 £25

BERT, PAUL   Lecons sur la Physiologie. Paris, 1870. 8vo., cloth, illus., first edition. Gurney 64-20 1974 £35

BERT, PAUL   Notes d'Anatomie. Paris, 1867. 8vo., orig. wrappers. Gurney 64-21 1974 £20

BERT, PAUL   La Pression Barometrique. Paris, 1878. 8vo., orig. cloth, worn, illus., first edition. Gumey 64-22 1974 £135

BERT, PAUL   La Pression Barometrique. Paris, 1878. Thick roy. 8vo., cloth, rebound, first edition. Schuman 37-20 1974 $500

BERTHELOT, MARCELLIN   Introduction a l'Etude de la Chimie des Anciens et du Moyen Age. Paris, 1889. Large 8vo., half morocco, first edition. Schuman 37-22 1974 $95

BERTHELOT, MARCELIN   La Synthese Chimique. Paris, 1876. 8vo., orig.
cloth, gilt. Dawsons PM 245-76 1974 £8

BERTHOLLET, CLAUDE LOUIS   Elements de l'Art de la Teinture. Paris, 1791.
2 vols., 8vo., contemporary calf, first edition. Schuman 37-23 1974 $165

BERTHOLLET, CLAUDE LOUIS   Elements of the Art of Dyeing; With a
Description of the Art of Bleaching by Oxymuriatic Acid. London, 1824. 8vo.,
2 vols., old half calf repaired, second edition, plates. Gurney 66-24 1974 £40

BERTHOLLET, CLAUDE LOUIS   Essai de Statique Chimique. Paris, 1803. 8vo.,
2 vols., half calf, gilt, first edition. Dawsons PM 245-77 1974 £225

BERTHOLON, NICOLLE PIERRE   De l'Electricite des Meteores. Lyon, 1787.
8vo., 2 vols., contemporary calf, first edition. Gurney 64-24 1974 £36

BERTHOLON, NICOLLE PIERRE   De l'Electricite des Meteores. 1787. 8vo.,
2 vols., contemporary mottled calf, first edition. Zeitlin 235-26 1974 $165

BERTHOLON, NICOLLE PIERRE   De l'Electricite des Vegetaux. Paris, 1783.
8vo., contemporary French calf, gilt, first edition. Dawsons PM 245-78 1974
£85

BERTHOLON, NICOLLE PIERRE   De l'Electricite du Corps Humain Dans l'Etat.
Paris, 1786. 8vo., 2 vols., contemporary half calf, plates, second edition.
Dawsons PM 245-79 1974 £35

BERTIN, LOUIS EMILE   Chaudieres Marines. Paris, 1896. 8vo., calf,
gilt, illus. Dawsons PM 245-81 1974 £36

BERTIN, T. P.   Le Passe-Temps de la Jeunesse, ou Contes
Moraux, Amusans et Instructifs. Paris, 1804. Copperplate frontispiece, 2 vols.
in 1, each with half title, 12mo., contemporary calf, rubbed, spine & hinges
detached, errata leaf to both vols. at end. George's 610-61 1973 £10

BERTRAM, J. G.   Language and Sentiment of Flowers. London,
1846. Orig. green cloth, colored frontis. Gregory 44-17 1974 $18.50

BERTRAM, JAMES   The Starlit Mire. London & New York, 1911.
4to., orig. cloth, plates, limited, first edition. Dawsons PM 252-49 1974 £15

BERTRAM, JAMES GLASS   The Harvest of the Sea. 1865. 8vo., cloth,
illus. Wheldon 130-252 1974 £5

BERTRAND, ALEXANDRE   Du Magnetisme Animal. Paris, 1826. 8vo.,
old calf. Gurney 64-127 1974 £20

BERTRAND, ALOYSIUS   Gaspard de la Nuit. Paris, 1920. 12mo.,
half morocco, gilt, orig. wrapper, uncut, illus. L. Goldschmidt 42-159
1974 $12.50

BERTRAND, GEORGES   Guide des Imprimeurs, Protes, Libraires et
Publicistes, Contenant le Tarif des Prix de Paris. Paris, 1879. Third edition,
wrappers. Kraus B8-289 1974 $12

BERVE, H.   Griechische Geschichte. 1931-33. 2 parts
in 2 vols. Allen 213-150 1973 $10

BERZELIUS, JONS JACOB   Forelasningar I Djurkemien. Stockholm, 1806-
1808. 8vo., 2 vols., orig. blue paper wrappers, uncut, rare, first edition. Dawsons PM 245-82 1974 £165

BERZELIUS, JONS JACOB   Theorie des Proportions Chimiques. Paris, 1835.
8vo., orig. printed wrappers, uncut. Gurney 64-25 1974 £25

BESANT, ANNIE   Marriage: As It Was, As It Is, and As It Should
Be. New York, n.d. (1879). 8vo., orig. bright blue printed wrappers, trifle
worn, very good, scarce. Ximenes 36-19 1974 $30

BESANT, WALTER   All in a Garden Fair. 1883. 3 vols., orig.
pictorial cloth. Covent 55-202 1974 £30

BESANT, WALTER   St. Katharine's by the Tower. 1891. 8vo.,
3 vols., orig. cloth, plates, first edition. Bow Windows 64-394 1974 £45

BESANT, WALTER   Westminster. 1895. Frontispiece etching,
illus. Bow Windows 66-53 1974 £5.50

BESKOW, ELSA   Aunt Green, Aunt Brown and Aunt Lavender.
New York, 1929. Oblong 4to., pict. boards, cloth spine; 16 color plates.
Frohnsdorff 16-100 1974 $40

BESKOW, ELSA   Olle's Ski Trip. New York, n.d. Folio,
pict. boards, cloth spine; color plates. Frohnsdorff 16-101 1974 $35

BESKOW, ELSA   Olle's Ski Trip. New York, n.d. Folio,
pict. boards, cloth spine. Frohnsdorff 16-102 1974 $20

BESLER, MICHAEL RUPERT   Observatio Anatom. N.P., n.d. 4to., boards.
Dawsons PM 249-55 1974 £85

BESLEY, HENRY   Views in Devonshire. Exeter, n.d. (c. 1854).
Oblong, contemporary half calf, engraved plates in very fine state and free from
foxing. Broadhurst 24-1373 1974 £20

BESSARION, JOANNES   In Calumniatore Platonis Libri Quatuor. 1516.
2 parts in 1 vol., small folio, early 19th century russia, excellent copy, second
Aldine edition. Thomas 30-33 1973 £120

BESSEL, FRIEDRICH WILHELM   Recensionen von Friedrich Wilhelm Bessel. Leipzig, 1878. 8vo., half calf, first edition. Dawsons PM 245-83 1974 £10

BESSIE, ALVAH   Inquisition in Eden. Macmillan, 1965. 278p.
Austin 51-78 1973 $8.50

BESSON, FRANCOIS   Le Cosmolabe, ou Instrument Universel.
Paris, 1567-69. 3 parts in 1 vol., small 4to., old limp vellum, woodcuts,
rare. Traylen 79-205 1973 £425

BESSON, JACQUES   Theatre des Instrvmens Mathematiques and Mechaniques. 1578. Folio, old calf, gilt. Dawsons PM 245-84 1974 £650

BESSON, JACQUES   Il Theatro de Gl'Instrumenti & Machine.
Lyons, 1582. Large folio, contemporary limp vellum, engravings. Traylen
79-204 1973 £350

BEST, ELSDON   Maori Agriculture. Wellington, 1925. 4to.,
wrappers, illus. Wheldon 131-1772 1974 £10

BEST, R. I.   Bibliography of Irish Philology and Manuscript
Literature Publications. Dublin, 1942. 8vo., cloth, scarce. Emerald 50-58
1974 £18

THE BEST American Humor. G. C. Pub., 1924. 401p. Austin 54-404 1973 $7.50

BEST Detective Stories. London, 1941. Biblo & Tannen 210-412 1973 $7.50

BEST Murder Stories. London, 1935. 1st ed. Biblo & Tannen 210-407 1973
$8.50

THE BEST of Emphasis. National Broadcasting Co. Newman, 1962. 358p.,
paper. Austin 51-289 1973 $6.50

BEST Plays of 1960-61. Dodd. 436p. Austin 51-120 1973 $7.50

BEST Plays of 1959-60. Dodd. 435p. Austin 51-119 1973 $7.50

BEST Plays of 1958-59. Dodd. 405p. Austin 51-118 1973 $7.50

BEST Plays of 1957-58. Dodd. 402p. Austin 51-117 1973 $7.50

BEST Plays of 1956-57. Dodd. 446p. Austin 51-116 1973 $7.50

BEST Plays of 1955-56. Dodd. 472p. Austin 51-115 1973 $7.50

BEST Plays of 1954-55. Dodd. 490p. Austin 51-114 1973 $7.50

BEST Plays of 1953-54. Dodd. 433p. Austin 51-113 1973 $7.50

BEST Plays of 1952-53. Dodd. 374p. Austin 51-112 1973 $7.50

BEST Plays of 1951-52. Dodd. 387p. Austin 51-111 1973 $7.50

BEST Plays of 1950-51. Dodd. 429p. Austin 51-110 1973 $7.50

BEST Plays of 1949-50. Dodd. 437p. Austin 51-109 1973 $7.50

BEST Plays of 1948-49. Dodd. 486p. Austin 51-108 1973 $7.50

BEST Plays of 1947-48. Dodd. 494p. Austin 51-107 1973 $7.50

BEST Plays of 1946-47. Dodd. 482p. Austin 51-106 1973 $7.50

BEST Plays of 1945-46. Dodd. 515p. Austin 51-105 1973 $7.50

BEST Plays of 1944-45. Dodd. 501p. Austin 51-104 1973 $7.50

BEST Plays of 1943-44. Dodd. 548p. Austin 51-103 1973 $7.50

BEST Plays of 1942-43. Dodd. 543p. Austin 51-102 1973 $7.50

BEST Plays of 1941-42. Dodd. 508p. Austin 51-101 1973 $7.50

BEST Plays of 1940-41. Dodd. 482p. Austin 51-100 1973 $7.50

BEST Plays of 1939-40. Dodd. 524p. Austin 51-99 1973 $7.50

BEST Plays of 1938-39. Dodd. 545p. Austin 51-98 1973 $7.50

BEST Plays of 1937-38. Dodd. 527p. Austin 51-97 1973 $7.50

BEST Plays of 1936-37. Dodd. 549p. Austin 51-96 1973 $7.50

BEST Plays of 1935-36. Dodd. 561p. Austin 51-95 1973 $7.50

BEST Plays of 1934-35. Dodd. 529p. Austin 51-94 1973 $7.50

BEST Plays of 1933-34. Dodd. 574p. Austin 51-93 1973 $7.50

BEST Plays of 1932-33. Dodd. 475p. Austin 51-92 1973 $7.50

BEST Plays of 1931-32. Dodd. 559p. Austin 51-91 1973 $7.50

BEST Plays of 1930-31. Dodd. 570p. Austin 51-90 1973 $7.50

BEST Plays of 1929-30. Dodd. 584p. Austin 51-89 1973 $7.50

BEST Plays of 1928-29. Dodd. 433p. Austin 51-88 1973 $7.50

BEST Plays of 1927-28. Dodd. 588p. Austin 51-87 1973 $7.50

BEST Plays of 1926-27. Dodd. 563p. Austin 51-86 1973 $7.50

BEST Plays of 1925-26. Dodd. 637p. Austin 51-85 1973 $7.50

BEST Plays of 1924-25. Dodd. 425p. Austin 51-84 1973 $7.50

BEST Plays of 1923-24. Dodd. 482p. Austin 51-83 1973 $7.50

BEST Plays of 1922-23. Dodd. 610p. Austin 51-82 1973 $7.50

BEST Plays of 1921-22. Dodd. 482p. Austin 51-81 1973 $7.50

BEST Plays of 1920-21. Small, Maynard. 471p. Austin 51-80 1973 $7.50

BEST Plays of 1919-20. Small, Maynard. 471p. Austin 51-79 1973 $7.50

BEST Television Plays. Ballantine, 1956. 250p. Austin 51-996 1973 $7.50

THE BEST Television Plays of the Year. Merlin, 1950. 317p., illus. Austin 51-486 1973 $12.50

BESTER, ALFRED   Who He? Dial Press, 1953. 313p. Austin 51-121 1973 $7.50

BESTERMAN, THEODORE   A Bibliography of Sir James George Frazer. London, 1934. Portraits, demy 8vo., orig. cloth, d.w., fine. Forster 98-258 1974 £5

BESTERMAN, THEODORE   The Publishing Form of Cadell and Davies. 1938. Imperial 8vo., boards, uncut, signed. Broadhurst 23-254 1974 £15

BESTON, HENRY   The St. Lawrence. New York, 1942. Illus. Hood's 102-682 1974 $10

BETHUNE, A. N.   Memoir of the Rt. Reverend John Strachan, First Bishop of Toronto. Toronto, 1870. Hood's 102-225 1974 $22.50

BETHUNE, JOHN DRINKWATER 1762-1844   Abraham Lincoln. 1918. Crown 8vo., orig. cloth, signed, presentation copy, first edition. Broadhurst 23-690 1974 £12

BETHUNE, JOHN DRINKWATER 1762-1844   Abraham Lincoln. 1918. First edition, crown 8vo., paper printed wrapper, mint, presentation copy signed by author. Broadhurst 24-641 1974 £12

BETHUNE, JOHN DRINKWATER 1762-1844   Abraham Lincoln. Houghton, Mifflin, 1919. Austin 51-260 1973 $6

BETHUNE, JOHN DRINKWATER 1762-1844   Abraham Lincoln. 1931. Small 8vo., orig. cloth, presentation copy, signed. Quaritch 936-374 1974 £10

BETHUNE, JOHN DRINKWATER 1762-1844   Christmas Poems. 1931. First edition, f'cap 4to., limp boards, dec. paper printed wrappers, uncut, mint, illus., presentation copy inscribed by author. Broadhusrt 24-65 1974 £6

BETHUNE, JOHN DRINKWATER 1762-1844   The Collected Plays of. 1925. 2 vols., 8vo., orig. cloth, hand made paper, limited. Bow Windows 66-190 1974 £15

BETHUNE, JOHN DRINKWATER 1762-1844   The Collected Poems. London, 1923. 2 vols., 8vo., orig. buckram, signed, limited. Dawsons PM 252-310 1974 £25

BETHUNE, JOHN DRINKWATER 1762-1844   The Collected Poems of. London, 1923 and 1937. 3 vols., 8vo., frontis., foxing, orig. buckram. Bow Windows 62-284 1974 £7.50

BETHUNE, JOHN DRINKWATER 1762-1844   Cophetua. 1911. 8vo., wrappers, orig. cloth, first edition. Rota 189-268 1974 £5

BETHUNE, JOHN DRINKWATER 1762-1844   Cotswold Characters. 1921. Crown 8vo., boards, signed, first edition. Broadhurst 23-692 1974 £10

BETHUNE, JOHN DRINKWATER 1762-1844   An English Medley. (Bournville), 1911. 8vo., orig. cloth, wrappers, first edition. Rota 189-269 1974 £5

BETHUNE, JOHN DRINKWATER 1762-1844   A History of the Late Siege of Gibraltar. Dublin, 1791. 8vo., orig. calf, gilt. Dawsons PM 251-374 1974 £20

BETHUNE, JOHN DRINKWATER 1762-1844   Life and Adventures of Carl Laemmle. Putnam, 1931. Illus. Austin 51-261 1973 $8.50

BETHUNE, JOHN DRINKWATER 1762-1844   The Life of Galileo Galilei. London, 1829. 4to., polished calf, gilt, illus. Gurney 66-69 1974 £45

BETHUNE, JOHN DRINKWATER 1762-1844   Lyrical and Other Poems. 1908. One of 300 copies, author's signed presentation inscription, full calf, very good, first edition. Covent 51-599 1973 £10.50

BETHUNE, JOHN DRINKWATER 1762-1844   More About Me. Boston, 1930. 8vo., first edition, illus. Frohnsdorff 16-300 1974 $10

BETHUNE, JOHN DRINKWATER 1762-1844   Oliver Cromwell. 1921. Austin 51-262 1973 $6

BETHUNE, JOHN DRINKWATER 1762-1844   The Outline of Literature. London, (n.d.). 2 vols., 4to., illus., half morocco. Dawsons PM 252-311 1974 £20

BETHUNE, JOHN DRINKWATER 1762-1844   The Outline of Literature. 1923. 3 vols., illus., ex-library, orig. edition. Austin 61-333 1974 $17.50

BETHUNE, JOHN DRINKWATER 1762-1844   Outline of Literature. 1923-24. 3 vols., 4to., plates. Allen 216-496 1974 $10

BETHUNE, JOHN DRINKWATER 1762-1844   Pawns. 1917. Author's signed presentation inscription, very good copy, first edition. Covent 51-600 1973 £10.50

BETHUNE, JOHN DRINKWATER 1762-1844   Robert E. Lee. London, 1923. Inscribed by author. Jacobs 24-83 1974 $10

BETHUNE, JOHN DRINKWATER 1762-1844   The World's Lincoln. New York, 1928. 8vo., part vellum, limited. Putman 126-22 1974 $15

BETHUNE, MAXIMILIEN DE, DUC DE SULLY
Please turn to
SULLY, MAXIMILIEN DE BETHUNE, DUC DE

BETJEMAN, JOHN   Antiquarian Prejudice. 1939. 8vo., wrappers, fine, first edition. Rota 190-51 1974 £5

BETJEMAN, JOHN   Continual Dew. 1937. Signed by author, bookplate, else very good copy, first edition. Covent 51-2176 1973 £30

BETJEMAN, JOHN   Continual Dew. 1937. Orig. cloth gilt, illus., scarce, first edition. Howes 185-23 1974 £18

BETJEMAN, JOHN   Continual Dew. 1937. 8vo., orig. cloth, first edition. Rota 189-122 1974 £20

BETJEMAN, JOHN   Continual Dew. 1937. Fine, gilt motif on upper board, all edges gilt, slightly worn d.w., first edition. Covent 51-2177 1973 £17.50

BETJEMAN, JOHN   Continual Dew. 1937. Illus., fine, all edges gilt, gilt design on upper board, first edition. Covent 51-2178 1973 £17.50

BETJEMAN, JOHN   Continual Dew. 1937. Illus., dec. cloth gilt, dust wrapper, English first edition. Covent 56-132 1974 £15

BETJEMAN, JOHN   Continual Dew. 1937. First edition, illus., small 8vo., orig. gilt embossed cloth, dust wrappers, signed by author. Sawyer 293-57 1974 £57

BETJEMAN, JOHN   Ghastly Good Taste. 1933. Cloth-backed boards, illus. Covent 55-203 1974 £17.50

BETJEMAN, JOHN   Ghastly Good Taste. 1933. 8vo., orig. cloth, first edition, second issue. Rota 189-121 1974 £21

BETJEMAN, JOHN   Ghastly Good Taste. London, 1933. 8vo., orig. cloth backed boards, first edition. Dawsons PM 252-50 1974 £28

BETJEMAN, JOHN   John Piper. Harmondsworth, 1944. Oblong 8vo., wrappers, plates. Minters 37-162 1973 $10

BETJEMAN, JOHN   Vintage London. 1942. Colour plates, text illus., very good copy, signed by author, first edition. Covent 51-236 1973 £8.50

BETJEMAN, JOHN   Vintage London. 1942. 4to., plates, illus., signed. Covent 55-207 1974 £10

BETTERTON, THOMAS   The Amorous Widow. London, 1706. Small 4to., 19th century half morocco, first edition. Dawsons PM 252-51 1974 £60

BETTINI, MARIO   Apiaria Vniversae Philosophiae Mathematicae. 1645. Folio, frontispiece, contemporary mottled calf, gilt panelled, fourth edition. Zeitlin 235-27 1974 $550

BETTS, A. D.   Practical Bee Anatomy. 1923. 8vo., orig. boards, plates. Wheldon 129-702 1974 £5

BETTS, ERNEST   Inside Pictures. Cresset, 1960. 161p., illus. Austin 51-122 1973 $10

BETZ, MAURICE   Rilke a Paris & Les Cahiers de Malte Laurids Brigge. Paris, 1941. Small 4to., orig. pictorial wrapper, first edition. L. Goldschmidt 42-161 1974 $15

BEUGHEM, CORNELIUS VAN   Bibliographia Mathematica et Artificiosa Novissima. 1688. 12mo., calf antique, gilt, first edition. Dawsons PM 245-85 1974 £85

BEURMANN, C. L. DE   Les Sporotrichoses. Paris, 1912. Roy 8vo., buckram, plates. Wheldon 129-1152 1974 £12

BEVAN, W. L.   Mediaeval Geography. London, 1873. 8vo., calf, plates. Traylen 79-296 1973 £8

BEVERIDGE, ALBERT J.   Abraham Lincoln, 1809-1858. Boston, 1928. First printing of this Standard Library edition, 4 vols., top edges gilt, others uncut, orig. binding. Wilson 63-204 1974 $25

BEVERIDGE, ALBERT J.   The Life of John Marshall. Boston, c. 1916. 4 vols., Standard Library edition, illus., orig. binding, top edges gilt, others uncut. Wilson 63-211 1974 $25

BEVERIDGE, ALBERT J.   The Life of John Marshall. (1919). 4 vols., Standard Library Edition, virtually new. Butterfield 10-86 1974 $25

BEVERIDGE, ERSKINE   A Bibliography of Works Relating to Dunfermline and the West of Fife. Dunfermline, 1901. 4to., orig. cloth gilt, uncut, limited. Dawsons PM 10-199 1974 £12

BEVERIDGE, ERSKINE   A Bibliography of Works Relating to Dunfermline and the West of Fife, Including Publications of Writers Connected with the District. Dunfermline, 1901. Limited to 300 copies for presentation, crown 4to., orig. cloth, fine, top edges gilt. Forster 98-118 1974 £15

BEVERIDGE, HENRY   A Comprehensive History of India, Civil, Military and Social. 1862. 3 vols., contemporary gilt framed calf, worn, maps, joints beginning to crack, illus., foxing. Bow Windows 66-54 1974 £10.50

BEVERIDGE, WILLIAM   Theological Works. Oxford, 1842. 12 vols., orig. cloth, best edition. Howes 185-964 1974 £65

BEVERLEY-GIDDINGS, A. R.   Broad Margins. New York, 1945. 1st ed., author's sgd. pres. Biblo & Tannen 210-702 1973 $10

BEVIS, JOHN   An Experimental Enquiry Concerning the Contents, Qualities and Medicinal Virtues, of the two Mineral Waters. London, 1760. 8vo., cloth-backed marbled boards, first edition. Hammond 201-558 1974 £12

BEVIS, JOHN   An Experimental Enquiry Concerning the Contents, Qualities, and Medicinal Virtues, of the Two Mineral Waters. London, 1767. 8vo., wrappers, second edition. Hammond 201-559 1974 £10

BEWARE After Dark. New York, 1929. Inscription, first U.S. edition. Covent 56-434 1974 £7.50

BEWICK, J.   Geological Treatise on the District of Cleveland, in North Yorkshire. 1861. Roy. 8vo., cloth, coloured plans, large folding coloured map, very scarce. Wheldon 128-946 1973 £15

BEWICK, THOMAS   Alnwick Picture Book for the Use of Children. Alnwick, (c. 1815). 12mo., orig. printed wrappers, frayed, engravings. Quaritch 940-22 1974 £35

BEWICK, THOMAS   Bewick Memento. London, n.d. Cloth, plates, illus. Dawson's 424-36 1974 $75

BEWICK, THOMAS   Bewick Memento. London, (1884). 4to., orig. half cloth, plates. Hammond 201-469 1974 £20

BEWICK, THOMAS   Bewick's Select Fables of Aesop and Others. (1871). 4to., orig. half roan, woodcuts, inscribed. Wheldon 131-145 1974 £25

BEWICK, THOMAS   The Dance of Death. Newcastle, 1789. Brown cloth, woodcuts, illus. Dawson's 424-41 1974 $100

BEWICK, THOMAS   The Fables of Esop. Newcastle, 1818. Roy 8vo., beige half morocco, gilt, illus., signed, first edition. Hammond 201-470 1974 £125

BEWICK, THOMAS   A General History of Quadrupeds. Newcastle, 1790. Full marbled calf, first edition. Dawson's 424-2 1974 $235

BEWICK, THOMAS   A General History of Quadrupeds. Newcastle, 1791. Full calf, rebound, second edition. Marsden 37-44 1974 £25

BEWICK, THOMAS   A General History of Quadrupeds. Newcastle, 1792. Marbled boards, third edition. Dawson's 424-3 1974 $175

BEWICK, THOMAS   A General History of Quadrupeds. Newcastle, 1800. Full morocco, fourth edition. Dawson's 424-4 1974 $250

BEWICK, THOMAS   A General History of Quadrupeds. Newcastle, 1807. 8vo., contemporary half calf, rebacked, illus., fifth edition. Hammond 201-466 1974 £32

BEWICK, THOMAS   A General History of Quadrupeds. Newcastle-Upon-Tyne, 1811. 8vo., contemporary calf, rebacked, scarce, nice copy, sixth edition. Wheldon 131-475 1974 £30

BEWICK, THOMAS   A General History of Quadrupeds. Newcastle, 1824. Leather, gilt, inscription, eighth edition. Dawson's 424-5 1974 $125

BEWICK, THOMAS   A General History of Quadrupeds. Newcastle, 1824. 8vo., contemporary polished calf, gilt, eighth edition. Hammond 201-467 1974 £20

BEWICK, THOMAS   A General History of Quadrupeds. Newcastle Upon Tyne, 1824. 8vo., orig. boards, uncut, woodcuts, eighth edition. Wheldon 128-307 1973 £18

BEWICK, THOMAS   History of British Birds. Newcastle, 1797-1804. 2 vols., roy. 8vo., half morocco, illus. Wheldon 131-548A 1974 £75

BEWICK, THOMAS   A History of British Birds. Newcastle, 1805. Full calf, gilt, 2 vols., bookplates. Dawson's 424-6 1974 $200

BEWICK, THOMAS   A History of British Birds. Newcastle, 1809-21. Full diced calf, 2 vols., gilt, rebacked. Dawson's 424-7 1974 $135

BEWICK, THOMAS   A History of British Birds. Newcastle, 1821. Full morocco, gilt, 2 vols. Dawson's 424-9 1974 $250

BEWICK, THOMAS   A History of British Birds. Newcastle, 1826. 2 vols., illus., half calf, labels, sixth edition. Bow Windows 64-22 1974 £65

BEWICK, THOMAS   A History of British Birds. Newcastle, 1826. Cloth, labels, 2 vols. Dawson's 424-10 1974 $125

BEWICK, THOMAS   History of British Birds. Newcastle, 1826. 8vo., 2 vols., contemporary cloth. Wheldon 130-464 1974 £20

BEWICK, THOMAS   A History of British Birds. Newcastle, 1826. Vol. 1, imp. 8vo., contemporary cloth. Wheldon 131-549 1974 £20

BEWICK, THOMAS   A History of British Birds. Newcastle, 1826. 2 vols., demy 8vo., orig. boards, worn, uncut. Quaritch 940-23 1974 £30

BEWICK, THOMAS   A Memoir. London and Newcastle, 1862. Orig. cloth, gilt, bookplate. Dawson's 424-35 1974 $85

BEWICK, THOMAS   A Memoir Of. Newcastle-on-Tyne & London, 1862. 8vo., orig. blind stamped cloth, wood engravings. Quaritch 940-24 1974 £30

BEWICK THOMAS   A Memoir Of. Newcastle, 1887. Roy 8vo., orig. cloth, frontispiece, woodcuts. Wheldon 130-144 1974 £10

BEWICK, THOMAS   A Memoir of Thomas Bewick. London, 1862. 8vo., contemporary calf, rebacked, engravings, first edition. Bow Windows 62-87 1974 £30

BEWICK, THOMAS   A Natural History of British Quadrupeds, Foreign Quadrupeds, British Birds . . . Alnwick, 1809. Small 8vo., half green morocco, wood engravings. Quaritch 940-20 1974 £200

BEWICK, THOMAS   Select Fables. Newcastle, 1820. Roy 8vo., beige half morocco, gilt, woodcuts, first edition. Hammond 201-468 1974 £65

BEWICK, THOMAS   A Supplement to the History of British Birds. Newcastle, 1821. Orig. boards, rebacked, first edition. Dawson's 424-8 1974 $125

BEWICK, THOMAS   The Works Of. Newcastle, 1822. 5 vols., demy 8vo., full green morocco, gilt, woodcuts, very scarce. Wheldon 131-20 1974 £180

BEWS, J. W.   The Grasses and Grasslands of South Africa. Pietermaritzburg, 1918. 8vo., cloth, map, figures, very scarce. Wheldon 128-1641 1973 £7.50

BEWS, J. W.   Plant Forms and their Evolution in South Africa. 1925. 8vo., cloth, scarce. Wheldon 129-1050 1974 £7.50

BEYER, JOHANN HARTMANN   Stereometriae Inanium Nova et Facilis Ratio. Frankfurt, 1603. 4to., vellum, first edition. Dawsons PM 245-86 1974 £95

BEYER, JOHANN MATTHIAS   Theatrum Machinarum Molarium. Leipzig and Rudelstadt, 1735. Folio, plates, contemporary half vellum, first edition. Dawsons PM 245-87 1974 £185

BEYLE, MARIE HENRI   La Chartreuse de Parme. Paris, 1921. 2 vols., 8vo., half sheep, gilt, limited. L. Goldschmidt 42-380 1974 $240

BEYLE, MARIE HENRI   Oeuvres Completes. Paris, 1913-34. 2 vols., roy. 8vo., three quarter blue morocco, gilt, uncut, limited. L. Goldschmidt 42-381 1974 $950

BEZOUT, ETIENNE   Theorie Generale des Equations Algebriques. Paris, 1779. 4to., quarter calf, gilt, first edition. Dawsons PM 245-88 1974 £15

BIANCANI, GIUSEPPE   Papere Sopra la Cagione. Rome, 1758. 8vo., old vellum. Gurney 64-26 1974 £12

BIANCHINI, GIOVANNI   Tabule Joa Bianchini Bononiensis. Venice, 1526. 4to., eighteenth century half vellum, second edition. Dawsons PM 245-89 1974 £320

BIANCO, MARGERY WILLIAMS   The House That Grew Smaller. New York, 1931. 8vo., green cloth with pict. label, illus. in color, very good copy, frayed dust jacket, first edition. Frohnsdorff 15-7 1974 $15

BIANCO, MARGERY WILLIAMS   The Little Wooden Doll. New York, 1936. 16mo., illus; sgd. by P. Bianco (illus.) Frohnsdorff 16-105 1974 -$17.50

BIANCO, MARGERY WILLIAMS   Winterbound. New York, 1936. 8vo., first edition. Frohnsdorff 16-103 1974 $7.50

BIANCONI, C.   Esemplare di Alcuni Ornati per la Gioventu Amante del Disegno. Bologna, (c. 1785). Oblong 4to., plates, loose in new boards folder. Quaritch 940-433 1974 £30

BIBER, E.   Henry Pestalozzi. 1831. Orig. cloth, uncut, label, worn, first edition. Howes 186-364 1974 £32

BIBIENA, FERDINANDO GALLI DA
Please turn to
GALLI DA BIBIENA, FERDINANDO

BIBLE   Gospels In Arabic and Latin. Rome, 1591. Folio, 18th century calf, rubbed, woodcuts, first edition of Gospels in Arabic. Harper 213-13 1973 $475

BIBLE   Psalterium Hebreum Grecum Arabicum and Chaldeum cum Tribus Latinis Interpretatonibus and Glossis. Genoa, 1516. Folio, contemporary vellum, tall copy, title in red and black within arabesque woodcut border. Thomas 32-24 1974 £850

BIBLE   Bible In Armenian. Venice, 1733. Small folio, calf, rubbed. Thomas 28-75 1972 £36

BIBLE   The New Testament Printed in Chinese. Shanghai, 1894. 4to., contemporary citron morocco, blind stamped, light brown cloth box, fine copy. Sawyer 293-62 1974 £95

BIBLE   Biblia Det er Den Gantske Hellige Scrifft. Copenhagen, 1589-88. Folio, 18th century Danish black calf gilt, raised bands, rubbed. Thomas 28-52 1972 £90

BIBLE　　　　　　　　A New Hieroglyphic Bible.　Boston, n.d.
(c. 1840's).　Square 16mo., orig. pictorial wrappers, some chipping of spine.
Frohnsdorff 16-434 1974 $60

BIBLE　　　　　　　　The Holy Bible.　Glasgow, n.d.　Full orig. red
morocco, magnifying glass inside pocket in back cover, 1 1/4 X 1 1/4 inches.
Gregory 44-349 1974 $17.50

BIBLE　　　　　　　　Holy Bible, Containing Portions of the New
Testament.　Chicago, n.d.　Orig. green cloth, 1 1/2 X 1 1/16 inches.　Gregory
44-395 1974 $9.50

BIBLE　　　　　　　　The New Testament.　London, n.d.　Orig. dark
morocco, 2 1/8 X 1 3/4.　Gregory 44-434 1974 $13.50

BIBLE　　　　　　　　Geneva Version.　Geneva, 1560.　Large 4to.,
old calf, worn, maps, woodcuts, rebacked, first edition.　Thomas 28-49 1972
£75

BIBLE　　　　　　　　The Boke of Psalmes, Geneva Version.　1576.
16mo., 17th century brown morocco, gilt, little rubbed, lacks ties, very rare,
reasonable copy.　Thomas 32-27 1974 £225

BIBLE　　　　　　　　The New Testament . . . Translated Faithfully
into English out of the Authentical Latin.　Rheims, 1582.　First edition, 4to.,
18th century calf gilt, little worn, copper plates coloured by a contemporary hand,
rather used and soiled throughout.　Thomas 32-28 1974 £180

BIBLE　　　　　　　　The Holy Bible, Bishops' Version.　1585.
Folio, 19th century quarter calf, worn, rebacked.　Thomas 28-51 1972 £40

BIBLE　　　　　　　　New Testament.　London, 1596.　Small 8vo.,
contemporary brown calf gilt, worn, rebacked.　Thomas 28-53 1972 £200

BIBLE　　　　　　　　Geneva Version.　1599.　Small 4to., sheep,
worn.　Thomas 28-55 1972 £18

THE BIBLE.　London, 1602.　Thick small 4to., half calf, stains, Geneva Version.
Howes 185-971 1974 £35

BIBLE　　　　　　　　The Holy Bible.　1611-17.　Folio, old
blind-stamped calf, rubbed, rebacked.　Thomas 28-57 1972 £300

BIBLE　　　　　　　　Authorized Version.　1614-13.　4to., old
calf, rebacked, worn.　Thomas 28-58 1972 £18

BIBLE　　　　　　　　The Holy Bible.　London, 1616.　Thick folio,
rebound, half calf, woodcut, staining.　Howes 185-966 1974 £50

BIBLE　　　　　　　　Authorized Version.　1617.　Folio, old calf
backed boards, worn.　Thomas 28-60 1972 £35

BIBLE　　　　　　　　Authorized Version.　1628.　4to., old calf,
woiled, worn.　Thomas 28-63 1972 £18

BIBLE　　　　　　　　Authorized Version.　London, 1631-30.
Small 8vo., old blind-stamped calf, worn, soiled.　Thomas 28-64 1972 £18

BIBLE　　　　　　　　New Testament.　1633.　4to., old calf, plates,
fourth edition.　Thomas 28-65 1972 £12

BIBLE　　　　　　　　Authorized Version.　1648.　3 vols. in 1,
4to., 18th century dark green calf gilt.　Thomas 28-68 1972 £21

BIBLE　　　　　　　　The Holy Bible.　1658.　2 vols., 24mo., full
19th century russia, gilt, staining.　Howes 185-967 1974 £25

BIBLE　　　　　　　　New Testament.　1684.　2 vols., small 8vo.,
modern buckram, gilt.　Thomas 28-72 1972 £5.50

BIBLE　　　　　　　　Authorized Version.　4 works in 1 vol., 18th
century dark olive morocco gilt, worn.　Thomas 28-66 1972 £36

BIBLE　　　　　　　　The Holy Bible.　1700.　Thick 12mo., early 19th
century black straight grain morocco, gilt.　Howes 185-968 1974 £25

BIBLE　　　　　　　　A Paraphrase On the New Testament.　1701.
Old calf, rebacked, third edition.　Thomas 28-73 1972 £30

BIBLE　　　　　　　　New Testament.　Brussels, 1702.　4 vols. in
2, small 8vo., modern cloth boards, brown crushed levant morocco spines, labels.
Thomas 28-74 1972 £5.50

BIBLE　　　　　　　　Authorized Version.　1704.　Small folio,
late 18th century or early 19th century quarter calf.　Thomas 28-59 1972 £70

BIBLE　　　　　　　　New Testament.　1707.　12mo., raised bands,
contemporary English black morocco gilt.　Thomas 28-140 1972 £35

BIBLE　　　　　　　　Biblia, or, A Practical Summary of Ye Old and
New Testaments.　1727-28.　Engraved frontispiece, engraved titles, plates, size
1 1/2 by 1 inches, dark brown blind stamped polished calf, raised bands, lower
edge rubbed, good copy, scarce.　Sawyer 293-218 1974 £195

BIBLE　　　　　　　　The Holy Bible Containing the Old Testament
and the New.　Oxford, 1735.　Contemporary straight grained red morocco.
Bow Windows 66-56 1974 £60

BIBLE　　　　　　　　Mr. Whiston's Primitive New Testament.
Stamford & London, 1745.　Contemporary sprinkled calf, gilt, excellent
condition.　Thomas 28-76 1972 £30

BIBLE　　　　　　　　Bible in Miniature, or a Concise History of the
Old and New Testament.　1774.　Engraved plates, contemporary black calf, good
copy 52 X 32 mm. in size.　George's 610-525 1973 £65

BIBLE　　　　　　　　Bible in Miniature, or A Concise History of the
Old and New Testaments.　1775.　Engraved plates, contemporary calf, raised
bands, 44 X 30 mm. in size.　George's 610-526 1973 £50

BIBLE　　　　　　　　The Bible in Miniature.　1780.　First Newbery
edition, engraved titles, engraved plates, 1 6/10 X 1 1/10 inches, rare, orig.
green morocco gilt, scarce, good copy.　Sawyer 293-217 1974 £130

BIBLE　　　　　　　　Bible in Miniature.　London, 1780.　Full green
morocco, gilt, engravings, neat, sound copy, 1 3/4 X 1 1/8 inches.　Gregory
44-338 1974 $125

BIBLE　　　　　　　　The Holy Bible.　Bath, 1785.　3 vols., 4to., full
contemporary navy straight grained morocco gilt, fine.　Howes 185-970 1974 £60

BIBLE　　　　　　　　The Bible in Miniature.　London, (c. 1790).
Contemporary full calf, engravings, 1 3/4 X 1 3/4 inches.　Gregory 44-339
1974 $125

BIBLE　　　　　　　　The Holy Bible.　Worcester, 1791.　Large 4to.,
orig. brown calf, frontispiece.　Putman 126-3 1974 $250

BIBLE　　　　　　　　A Translation of the New Testament from the
Original Greek Humbly Attempted by Nathaniel Scarlett.　London, 1798.　8vo.,
orig. black straight grain morocco, first edition of this translation.　Goodspeed's
578-269 1974 $25

BIBLE　　　　　　　　Bible in Miniature, or A Concise History of Both
Testaments.　London, (c. 1802).　Dark leather, gilt band on spine, 1 15/16 X
1 1/4 inches.　Gregory 44-340 1974 $115

BIBLE　　　　　　　　New and Complete Hieroglyphical Bible.　1820.
Woodcut frontispiece, 12mo., orig. ptd. boards, spine defective.　George's
610-371 1973 £5

BIBLE　　　　　　　　Epistle of Paul the Apostle to the Ephesians.
Birminghan, (c. 1831).　Full bright red roan, small ink mark on cover, fine, 2 1/2
x 2 inches.　Gregory 44-372 1974 $35

BIBLE　　　　　　　　The Holy Bible.　1833.　Thick 4to., orig. half
morocco, gilt.　Howes 185-969 1974 $25

BIBLE　　　　　　　　The English Bible.　London, 1836.　Frontispiece,
front inner hinge repaired, orig. cloth.　Gregory 44-367 1974 $20

BIBLE　　　　　　　　Isaish.　New York, 1839.　Small 8vo., cloth,
first edition.　Hill 126-17 1974 £20

BIBLE   The Holy Bible, Old & New Testaments. Oxford, 1851. Thick 8vo., contemporary black morocco, gilt. Smith 193-817 1973 £6

BIBLE   The Illustrated Family Bible. c. 1865. Thick 4to., 2 vols., plates, orig. morocco, boards. Howes 185-976 1974 £8.50

BIBLE Forget Me Nots. London, c. 1884. Full orig. brown leather, illus., 2 13/16 X 2 13/16 inches. Gregory 44-342 1974 $22.50

BIBLE   The Song of Songs. 1886. 4to., etchings, half contemporary morocco gilt, etchings, limited. Smith 194-747 1974 £13

BIBLE   The Holy Bible Containing Old and New Testaments. 1896. Full red morocco in case, magnifying glass inset, 1 5/8 X 1 1/8 inches. Gregory 44-348 1974 $22.50

BIBLE   A Book of Songs and Poems from the Old Testament and the Apocrypha. 1904. Printed in black & red, 8vo., orig. limp vellum, fine, limited to 150 copies. Sawyer 293-37 1974 £145

BIBLE   The Holy Bible. London & New York, 1924-27. 5 vols., folio, orig. parchment gilt, slipcase, fine. Dawsons PM 252-52 1974 £150

BIBLE   The Twenty-Third Psalm. Rome, 1927. Large square 4to., hand-painted vellum, gilt, fine. Rich Summer-23 1974 $45

BIBLE   The New Testament. (1934-36). 8vo., orig. cloth, 4 vols., first edition. Bow Windows 64-518 1974 £7.50

BIBLE   The New Testament Translated by William Tyndale. Cambridge, 1938. 4to., buckram, soiled. Howes 185-975 1974 £12.50

BIBLE   The Parables told to the People by Jesus of Nazareth. New York, 1942. Large 4to., cloth, plates, illus. Rich Summer-22 1974 $25

BIBLE   Biblia Germanica. Augsburg, 1477. Folio, 18th century half calf, woodcuts, fine, entirely uncolored copy, woodcuts, good, very clean copy, from the Prince of Liechtenstein Library. Schumann 499-10 1974 sFr 85,000

BIBLE   Ein Kurtzer Zeiger der Furnemsten Historien und Gemeinsten Articklen im Alten und Nuwen Testament. Zurich, 1546. 8vo., modern boards, fine, very rare. Schafer 8-103 1973 sFr. 750

BIBLE   Psalms In Greek. Paris, 1618. 12mo., contemporary calf gilt, worn. Thomas 28-61 1972 £15

BIBLE   Old and New Testament in Greek. Sedan, 1628. Full red morocco, gilt, 3 1/8 X 1 7/8, fine. Gregory 44-437 1974 $165

BIBLE   Vetus Testamentum Graecum. 1653. Large 8vo., modern calf, rebacked, first edition. Thomas 28-69 1972 £45

BIBLE   Libri Historici, Graec & Lat. Perpetuo Commentario. 1653. 1 vol. bound in 2, old calf, rebacked in morocco, worn, morocco labels. Thomas 28-70 1972 £30

BIBLE   Novum Testamentum Graecum e Codice MS Alexandrino. 1786. Folio, rebacked, contemporary half calf. Howes 185-1075 1974 £20

BIBLE   Novum Testamentum Graecum. Hartford, 1822. 8vo., contemporary calf, leather label. Harper 213-14 1973 $75

BIBLE   Novum Testamentum Graece. Leipzig, 1869-94. 3 vols., cloth, labels, best edition. Howes 185-1725 1974 £35

BIBLE   Novum Testamentum Graece. Leipzig, 1869-72. 2 vols., contemporary divinity calf, best edition. Howes 185-1726 1974 £22.50

BIBLE   Il Nuovo Testamento. Lyons, 1547. 16mo., 19th century calf, rebacked, first Italian New Testament to be printed in Lyons, possibly in France, title worn and little defective, else clean and sound. Thomas 32-25 1974 £100

BIBLE   Biblia Latina. Venice, 1498. Thick small 4to., 19th century quarter red roan, rubbed. Thomas 28-280 1972 £200

BIBLE   New Testament. Novum Instrumentum Omne Diligenter ab Erasmo Roterodamo Recognitum & Emendatum. Basle, 1516. Small folio, calf, rebacked, woodcut borders, slight worming, sound condition, first edition. Thomas 32-23 1974 £3,000

BIBLE   Sacrae Scripturae Veteris. 1518. Small folio, 18th century brown morocco gilt, raised bands, rare. Thomas 30-43 1973 £1,250

BIBLE   Textus Biblia. Lyon, 1526. 2 parts in 1 vol., thick 8vo., contemporary blind-stamped sheep. Thomas 28-46 1972 £50

BIBLE   Biblia Sacrosancta Testamenti Veteris et Novi. Zurich, 1543. Folio, contemporary German Blind-stamped pigskin over oak boards. Thomas 28-47 1972 £260

BIBLE   Novum Testamentum. 1567. New buckram, worn, stained text. Allen 213-154 1973 $15

BIBLE   Novum Testamentum. Basle, 1570. Folio, contemporary German blind-stamped pigskin over oak boards. Thomas 28-50 1972 £12.50

BIBLE   Biblia Sacra. Venice, 1576. Folio, 19th century russia, blind tooled borders, edges gilt, soundly rebacked, presentation inscription. Thomas 32-26 1974 £85

BIBLE   Novi Testamenti Libri Omnes. London, 1622. Allen 213-153 1973 $35

BIBLE   Psalmi Davidis Regis, & Prophetae Lingua Syriaca. Leyden, 1625. Small 4to., 19th century half tree calf, rubbed, first European edition. Thomas 28-62 1972 £60

BIBLE   Sive Novum Foedus. 1642. Folio, old panelled calf, rebacked. Thomas 28-67 1972 £19

BIBLE   Liber Jobi in Versiculos Metrice Divisus. 1742. Old calf, rebacked, London library stamps and disposal stamps, else clean and sound. Thomas 32-30 1974 £30

BIBLE   Ko te Kawenata hou o to Tatou Ariki o te Kai Whakaora o Ihu Karaiti. Ranana, 1852. 8vo., old calf, badly worn, fifth edition of the New Testament in Maori. Kraus B8-413 1974 $25

BIBLE   Biblia Polyglota. 1514-22. 6 vols., full red-brown goatskin, rare. Thomas 28-45 1972 £8500

BIBLE   Novum Testamentum Syriace. Hamburg, 1663-64. Small 8vo., contemporary calf, rebacked, good condition. Thomas 28-71 1972 £30

BIBLE   Psalterium Syriacum Recensuit et Latine Vertit. Halle, 1768. Old half calf, gilt. Thomas 28-78 1972 £5.50

BIBLE   New Testament In Syriac. 1816. 4to., blind stamped calf. Thomas 28-79 1972 £7.50

BIBLIA, das ist die Ganze Heil Schrift. 1761. Thick small 8vo., contemporary blue vellum gilt. Howes 185-972 1974 £25

BIBLIA Sacra, Cum Duplici Translatione. 1584-85. 2 vols., small folio, orig. limp vellum, morocco backed cloth boxes. Thomas 28-28 1972 £1000

BIBLIANDER, THEODOR   Institutionum Grammaticarum de Lingua Hebraea Liber Unus. Zurich, 1535. 8vo., modern boards, first edition. Schafer 8-104 1973 sFr. 420

THE BIBLIOGRAPHER, A Journal of Book-Lore. London, 1882-84. 6 vols., orig. quarter roan, rubbed, worn. Dawsons PM 10-38 1974 £25

BIBLIOGRAPHICA: Papers on Books, Their History and Art. London, 1895-97. 3 vols., 4to., illus., orig. wrappers, quarter morocco. Dawsons PM 10-39 1974 £150

A BIBLIOGRAPHICAL Catalogue of the First Loan Exhibition of Books and Manuscripts Held By the First Edition Club. London, (1922). 8vo., orig. cloth-backed boards, uncut, limited. Dawsons PM 10-222 1974 £7

BIBLIOGRAPHIE der Rezensionen und Referate. Leipzig, 1901-44. 77 vols., cloth. Dawsons PM 11-62 1974 £1160

BIBLIOGRAPHIE Geographique de l'Egypte Publiee sous la Direction de Henri Lorin. London, 1928-9. 2 vols., roy. 8vo., half morocco, orig. wrappers bound in, fine. Forster 98-150 1974 £35

BIBLIOGRAPHIE Hispanique. New York, 1909-19. 13 vols., cloth. Dawsons PM 11-63 1974 £87

A BIBLIOGRAPHY of the Writings of William Somerset Maugham. London, 1931. 8vo., orig. cloth. Dawsons PM 10-398 1974 £8

BIBLIOPHILE SOCIETY   Letters and Poems of Queen Elisabeth. Boston, 1920. 2 vols., rubbed slip cases. Ballinger 1-239 1974 $10

BIBLIOTECA Dell Economista. Roy. 8vo., orig. wrappers. Howes 186-1354 1974 £5

BIBLIOTHECA Parisiana: A Catalogue of A Collection of Books by a Gentleman in France. London, 1791. 8vo., contemporary boards, first English edition. Dawsons PM 10-47 1974 £72

BIBLIOTHECA Sunderlandiana. London, 1881-1883. 5 vols., small folio, red half morocco, rubbed. Dawsons PM 10-589 1974 £65

BICAISE, HONORE   Manuale Medicorum. London, 1659. 16mo., old French calf, very rare, misbound. Gurney 66-25 1974 £28

BICHAT, MARIE FRANCOIS XAVIER   General Anatomy, Applied to Physiology and to the Practice of Medicine. London, 1824. 8vo., 2 vols., half morocco, uncut, vol. 1 mainly unopened. Gurney 66-26 1974 £75

BICK, EDGAR M.   Source Book of Orthopaedics. Baltimore, 1937. First edition. Rittenhouse 46-73 1974 $10

BICKERSTAFFE, ISAAC   The Capitive. London, 1769. 8vo., modern boards, first edition. Dawsons PM 252-54 1974 £15

BICKERSTAFFE, ISAAC   The Hypocrite. London, 1769. 8vo., modern boards, first edition. Dawsons PM 252-55 1974 £15

BICKERSTAFFE, ISAAC   Love in a Village. London, 1763. 8vo., frayed, modern boards, second edition. Dawsons PM 252-56 1974 £12

BICKERSTAFFE, ISAAC   Love in the City. London, 1767. 8vo., modern boards, first edition. Dawsons PM 252-57 1974 £15

BICKERSTAFFE, ISAAC   The Maid of the Mill. London, 1765. 8vo., modern boards, first edition. Dawsons PM 252-58 1974 £15

BICKERSTAFFE, ISAAC   The Padlock. London, (n.d.). 8vo., modern boards, vignette, new edition. Dawsons PM 252-59 1974 £12

BICKERSTAFFE, ISAAC   Thomas and Sally. London, 1763. 8vo., modern boards, second edition. Dawsons PM 252-60 1974 £10

BICKHAM, GEORGE   The Musical Entertainer. n.d. Engravings, fine, English first edition. Covent 56-969 1974 £15.75

BICKNELL, C.   Flowering Plants and Ferns of the Riviera. 1885. Imp. 8vo., modern half morocco, gilt, nice copy, scarce. Wheldon 128-1239 1973 £40

BIDDLE, ALEXANDER   The Alexander Biddle Papers American Historical Autographs...Catalogues of Public Sale, Held at Parke-Bernet Galleries, Inc., New York, May 24-25, Oct. 12-13, and November 16-17, 1943. 3 parts in patterned boards and leather, orig. wrappers bound in. Butterfield 10-34 1974 $25

BIDDLE, RICHARD   A Memoir of Sebastion Cabot. 1915. Half calf, rebacked in buckram. Allen 213-1321 1973 $10

BIDLAKE, L.   Eugenio. 1799. First edition, lacks half title, 12mo., later straight grained morocco, gilt. George's 610-65 1973 £5.50

BIE, OSCAR   Der Architekt Oskar Kaufmann. Berlin, 1928. 4to., cloth, plates. Minters 37-546 1973 $32

BIERBAUM, OTTO JULIUS   Samalio Pardulus. Munchen, 1911. Limited to 600 copies, plates by Alfred Kubin, 8vo., dark red morocco gilt, uncut, top edges gilt, good copy. Sawyer 293-195 1974 £48

BIERCE, AMBROSE   Cobwebs from an Empty Skull. London, 1874. 8vo., orig. brown dec. cloth, scarce, first edition, illus. Ximenes 36-21 1974 $50

BIERCE, AMBROSE   The Eyes of the Panther. Cape, 1928. 252p. Austin 54-140 1973 $7.50

BIERCE, AMBROSE   In the Midst of Life. New York, 1898. Orig. cloth, first edition of this edition, fine. MacManus 224-34 1974 $40

BIERCE, AMBROSE   The Monk and the Hangman's Daughter. Heritage Press, 1907 (1906). 80p. Austin 54-142 1973 $6.50

BIERCE, AMBROSE   The Monk and the Hangman's Daughter and Fantastic Fables. Cape, Smith, 1911. 264p. Austin 54-141 1973 $7.50

BIERCE, AMBROSE   The Shadow of the Dial and Other Stories. San Francisco, 1909. Orig. cloth, first edition, fine in tattered dust jacket. MacManus 224-35 1974 $50

BIERCE, AMBROSE   A Son of the Gods & A Horseman in the Sky. San Francisco & New York, 1907. 12mo., quarter vellum gilt, fine. Covent 55-214 1974 £26.50

BIERCE, AMBROSE   Tales of Soldiers and Civilians. New York, (1891). 12mo., cloth, second edition. Goodspeed's 578-24 1974 $10

BIERCE, AMBROSE   Tales of Soldiers and Civilians. San Francisco, 1891. Orig. cloth, first edition, very good copy. MacManus 224-36 1974 $110

BIERCE, AMBROSE   Collected Writings of Ambrose Bierce. Citadel, 1946. 810p. Austin 54-139 1973 $12.50

BIGEARD, R.   Flore des Champignons Superieurs de France. 8vo., 2 vols., half calf, plates. Wheldon 129-1154 1974 £30

BIGELOW, HENRY JACOB   Ether and Chloroform. Boston, 1848. 8vo., orig. blue printed wrappers, uncut. Dawsons PM 249-67 1974 £95

BIGELOW, JACOB   Brief Expositions of Rational Medicine. Boston, 1858. Small 12mo., cloth, first edition. Rittenhouse 46-75 1974 $25

BIGELOW, JACOB   Discourse on Self-Limited Diseases. Boston, 1835. 8vo., orig. boards, very rare first edition. Gilhofer 61-39 1974 sFr. 1,200

BIGELOW, JACOB   The Wars of the Gulls. New York, 1812. 8vo., sewn, first edition, excellent uncut copy. Ximenes 36-22 1974 $175

BIGELOW, JOHN   The Mystery of Sleep. New York, 1896. Rittenhouse 46-76 1974 $10

BIGELOW, T.   Journal of a Tour to Niagara Falls in the Year 1805. Boston, 1867. Hood's 102-583 1974 $40

BIGGAR, P. E.   Diesel Engines. Toronto, 1936. Photographs, drawings. Hood's 104-810 1974 $15

BIGGERS, DON H.   From Cattle Range to Cotton Patch. Bandera, 1944. Wrapper. Jenkins 61-215 1974 $17.50

BIGLAND, JOHN   A Natural History of Birds, Fishes, Reptiles, and Insects. Philadelphia, 1828. 12mo., publisher's half roan, worn, colored illus. Goodspeed's 578-25 1974 $50

BIGNELL, EFFIE   Saint Anne of the Mountains, the Story of a Summer in a Canadian Pilgrimage Village. Toronto, 1912. Illus. Hood's 102-683 1974 $7.50

BIJOU Illustrations of Christ's Life. London, (c. 1840). Full orig. red morocco, gold stamped, engravings, 1 1/8 X 1 inch. Gregory 44-343 1974 $55

BIJOU Picture of London. London, (c. 1850). Full maroon morocco gilt, views, 1 1/8 X 1 inch. Gregory 44-344 1974 $55

BIJOU Pictures of Paris. London, (c. 1840). Full black morocco, gilt, full page plates, 1 1/4 X 1 inch. Gregory 44-345 1974 $60

BILDER Zum Anschauungs-Unterricht fur die Jugend. Stuttgart, (c. 1850). Vols. 1 and 3 only, plates some defective and torn, (hand coloured), small folio, cloth backed boards. George's 610-66 1973 £10

BILLING, ARCHIBALD   First Principles of Medicine. London, 1831. 8vo., orig. cloth, presentation copy, first edition. Gurney 66-27 1974 £10

BILLINGHURST, PERCY J.   Beasts Shown to the Children. London, n.d. 16mo., cloth, gilt, illus. Frohnsdorff 16-107 1974 $7.50

BILLINGS, ANNA HUNT   A Guide to the Middle English Metrical Romances Dealing With English and Germanic Legends. 1901. Ex-library, sturdy library binding, orig. edition. Austin 61-111 1974 $10

BILLINGS, JOSH   Farmer's Allminax for 1872. Carleton, 1872. Illus., paper. Austin 54-143 1973 $6.50

BILLINGS, ROBERT WILLIAM   The Baronial and Ecclesiastical Antiquities of Scotland. Edinburgh and London, n.d. 4to., 4 vols., full purple morocco, gilt, plates, first edition. Dawsons PM 251-7 1974 £120

BILLINGS, ROBERT WILLIAM   Illustrations of the Architectural Antiquities of the County of Durham. Durham, 1846. 4to., half morocco, plates, rubbed. Quaritch 939-345 1974 £30

BILLINGTON, WILLIAM   Movable Kidney. 1929. 8vo., orig. green cloth, gilt. Dawsons PM 249-68 1974 £8

BILLQUIST, FRITIOF   Garbo. 1960. 255p., illus. Austin 51-123 1973 $7.50

BILLROTH, CHRISTIAN ALBERT THEODOR   General Surgical Pathology and Therapeutics. London, 1871. 8vo., full calf, illus., first London edition. Schuman 37-24 1974 $110

BILLY, ANDRE   Apollinaire Vivant. Paris, 1923. Small 8vo., wrappers, illu. Minters 37-260 1973 $32

BINDER, JACOB   All in a Lifetime. Hackensack, 1942. Signed. Ballinger 1-240 1974 $15

BINDING, RUDOLF G.   Vom Leben der Plastik. Berlin, 1933. 4to., cloth, plates. Minters 37-465 1973 $15

BINDING, RUDOLF G.   Vom Leben der Plastik. c. 1934. Boards, cloth spine, plates, third edition. Minters 37-465A 1973 $16.50

BING, ROBERT   Compendium of Regional Diagnosis In Lesions of the Brain and Spinal Cord. St. Louis, 1940. Eleventh edition. Rittenhouse 46-678 1974 $10

BINGHAM, CLIFTON   Magic Moments. London, n.d. (c. 1890). Square 4to., pictorial boards, cloth spine, very good copy, pen & ink illus. by Florence Hardy. Frohnsdorff 16-592 1974 $200

BINGHAM, JOSEPH   The Works. 1855. 10 vols., orig. cloth, printed labels, best edition. Howes 185-978 1974 £40

BINGHAM, MRS. KATE (BOYLES)   Langford of the Three Bars. Chicago, 1907. 12mo., buckram, very fine, illus., first edition. Goodspeed's 578-412 1974 $75

BINGLEY, WILLIAM   Musical Biography. London, 1814. 2 vols. in 1, 8vo., stain, half calf. Bow Windows 62-89 1974 £9.50

BINNING, ARTHUR CECIL   British Regulation of the Colonial Iron Industry. Philadelphia & London, 1933. Butterfield 10-198 1974 $12.50

BINNS, HENRY BRYAN   A Life of Walt Whitman. 1905. Plates, very good copy. Covent 51-1972 1973 £6.30

BINNS, L. ELLIOTT   The History of the Decline and Fall of the Medieval Papacy. London, 1934. 1st ed. Biblo & Tannen 214-591 1974 $15

BINNS, RICHARD WILLIAM   Catalogue of a Collection of Worcester Porcelain. Worcester, 1884. 8vo., illus., orig. boards. Bow Windows 62-90 1974 £6.50

BINNS, RICHARD WILLIAM   Catalogue of a Collection of Worcester Porcelain. Worcester, 1884. Illus., cloth back, boards. Marsden 39-32 1974 £5

BINNS, W. MOORE   The First Century of English Porcelain. 1906. 4to., plates, dec. cloth, scarce. Quaritch 940-623 1974 £28

BINYON, LAURENCE   Catalogue of the Loan Collection of English Water Colour Drawings Held at the Institute of Art Research, Uneo, Tokyo, Oct. 10-24, 1929. Tokyo, (1930). Roy. folio, plates, Jap. style limp cloth, presentation copy. Quaritch 940-26 1974 £20

BINYON, LAURENCE   The Idols. 1928. Small 4to., orig. buckram backed boards, first edition. Howes 186-32 1974 £6.50

BINYON, LAURENCE   Lyric Poems. 1894. One of 300 copies, covers little dull, very good copy, first edition. Covent 51-249 1973 £8.50

BINYON, LAURENCE   The Sirens. 1925. Small 4to., orig. buckram backed boards, first trade edition. Howes 186-33 1974 £15

BINYON, LAURENCE   The Winnowing-Fan. 1914. Orig. cloth, wrappers, signature, first edition. Rota 188-105 1974 £6.50

BINZ, CARL   Lectures on Pharmacology. London, 1895-1897. 8vo., 2 vols., orig. brown cloth, gilt. Dawsons PM 249-69 1974 £6

A BIOGRAPHICAL Album of Prominent Pennsylvanians. Philadelphia, 1889. Thick 4to., embossed dec. leather, gilt, excellent. Rinsland 58-95 1974 $60

THE BIOGRAPHICAL Cyclopedia and Portrait Gallery With an Historical Sketch of the State of Ohio. Cincinnati, 1883-84. 3 vols., full morocco, nice set, fine steel engravings. Hayman 59-426 1974 $50

BIOGRAPHICAL Dictionary. 1761-67. 8vo., 12 vols., contemporary calf, gilt. Quaritch 936-18 1974 £30

BIOGRAPHICAL History of Cherokee County, Iowa. Chicago, 1889. 4to., leather. Saddleback 14-408 1974 $35

BIOGRAPHICAL Review . . . Life Sketches of Leading Citizens of Sagadahoc, Lincoln, Knox, and Waldo Counties Maine. Boston, 1897. Large thick 4to., portraits, index, orig. binding. Butterfield 10-363 1974 $40

BIOGRAPHICAL Sketches of Some of the Early Settlers of Chicago. Chicago, 1876. Printed wrappers, illus., first editions. Bradley 35-66 1974 $20

BIOLOGIA Centrali-Americana. Insecta. Coleoptera Vol. 5. Longicornia. 1879-86. 4to., new buckram, plates. Wheldon 131-786 1974 £50

BION, NICOLAS   Neu-eroffnete Mathematische Werck-Schule. Nurnberg, 1741. 4to., contemporary sheep, gilt, plates. Dawsons PM 245-90 1974 £40

BIONDI, GIOVANNI FRANCESCO   An History of the Civill Wares of England. 1641-46. 2 vols. in 1, folio, full 18th century mottled calf, first English edition. Howes 186-612 1974 £40

BIOT, J. B.   Relation d'un Voyage. Paris, 1803. 4to., boards, first edition. Gurney 64-27 1974 £16

BIOT, J. B.   Relation d'un Voyage fait dans le Departement de l'Orne, pour Constater la Realite d'un Meteore Observe a l'Aigle le 26 Floreal an II. Paris, 1803. 4to., boards, folding plate, first edition. Gurney 66-28 1974 £16

BIRCH, GEORGE W. F.   Our Church and Our Village.   New York, 1899.
8vo., orig. bindings, plates.   Butterfield 8-466   1974 $15

BIRCH, JOHN GRANT   Travels in North and Central China.   1907.
8vo., orig. cloth, first edition.   Broadhurst 23-1613   1974   £10

BIRCH, S.   History of Ancient Pottery, Egyptian, Assyrian,
Greek, Etruscan and Roman.   1873. 8vo., half morocco, gilt, plates, new and
revised edition.   Quaritch 940-624   1974   £10

BIRCH, THOMAS   The Life of Robert Boyle.   London, 1744. 8vo.,
contemporary speckled calf, gilt, first edition.   Dawsons PM 245-122   1974   £58

BIRCKWOOD, JOHN   A Plan for Reducing the Capital.   (N.P., n.d.)
8vo., unbound, first edition.   Dawsons PM 252-23   1974   £15

BIRD, ANNIE LAURIE   Boise: The Peace Valley.   Caldwell, 1934.
12mo., cloth.   Saddleback 14-357   1974 $35

BIRD, GOLDING   Lectures on Electricity and Galvanism.   London,
1849. 8vo., orig. cloth, illus., first edition.   Gurney 64-28   1974   £25

BIRD, H. E.   Chess Novelties and Their Latest Developments.
London, 1895. 12mo., 1st ed.   Biblo & Tannen 213-1003   1973 $15

BIRD, ROBERT MONTGOMERY   Calavar; or, The Knight of the Conquest.
Philadelphia, 1834. 2 vols., orig. cloth, spines faded, ex-library set, some
foxing, first edition, very good set.   MacManus 224-37   1974 $100

BIRD, ROBERT MONTGOMERY   The Hawks of Hawk-Hollow.   Philadelphia,
1835. 2 vols., orig. cloth, paper label, first edition, very good set.   MacManus
224-38   1974 $125

BIRD, ROBERT MONTGOMERY   The Infidel.   Philadelphia, 1835. 2 vols.,
orig. cloth, stained, paper labels, first edition, foxed, good set.   MacManus
224-39   1974 $100

BIRD-CATCHING: or, The Northern Adventurers.   1823. Plates, copperplate
illus., 12mo., orig. boards, roan spine, trifle rubbed, ads at end.   George's
610-67   1974   £5

BIRDS of Paradise.   1871-97. 1 vol., 8vo., cloth, coloured plates.   Wheldon
128-391   1973   £20

BIRDSALL, RALPH   The Story of Cooperstown.   Cooperstown,
(1917). Cloth, cover little discolored, second printing.   Hayman 59-412   1974
$10

BIRINGUCCIO, VANNOCCIO   Pirotechnia.   1559. 8vo., half sheep, fourth
edition, woodcuts.   Dawsons PM 245-91   1974   £130

BIRINGUCCI, VANNUCCIO   Pirotechnia.   1943. 4to., half vellum,
woodcuts, limited edition.   Allen 213-1294   1973 $25

BIRINGUCCIO, VANNOCCIO   La Pyrotechnie ou Art du Feu.   1627. 4to.,
contemporary limp vellum, fine, woodcuts.   Dawsons PM 245-92   1974   £95

BIRKBECK, GEORGE   A Lecture on the Preservation of Timber by Kyan's
Patent for Preventing Dry Rot.   London, (1835). 8vo., wrappers, plates, fine,
first edition.   Dawsons PM 245-93   1974   £8

BIRKBECK, MORRIS   Letters from Illinois.   Philadelphia, 1818. Printed boards, rebacked, scarce, first edition.   Hayman 57-311   1974 $85

BIRKENHEAD, FREDERICK EDWIN SMITH, 1ST EARL OF   Famous Trials of
History.   London, c. 1928). 2 vols., 8vo., illus., foxing, orig. cloth.   Bow
Windows 62-91   1974   £5.50

BIRKENHEAD, SHEILA   Against Oblivion.   London, 1943. 8vo.,
cloth, plates, foxed.   Minters 37-164   1973 $11.50

BIRKENHEAD, SHELIA   Against Oblivion: Life of Joseph Severn.
1944. Austin 61-114   1974 $10

BIRKETT, JOHN   The Diseases of the Breast.   London, 1850.
8vo., orig. green cloth, plates.   Dawsons PM 249-70   1974   £14

BIRMINGHAM, GEORGE A. PSEUD.
Please turn to
HANNAY, JAMES OWEN

BIRNBAUM, MARTIN   Oscar Wilde.   1920. Cloth-backed boards,
English first edition.   Covent 56-1328   1974   £5.25

BIRNEY, HOFFMAN   Vigilantes.   Philadelphia, (1929). 8vo., orig.
bindings, dust jacket, first edition.   Butterfield 8-323   1974 $15

BIRRELL, AUGUSTINE   Collected Essays.   London, 1902. 2 vols.,
8vo., orig. cloth, faded, rubbed, second edition.   Bow Windows 62-92   1974
£5

BIRRELL & Garnett Ltd., Booksellers, Catalogue.   London, 1938. 4to., orig.
printed wrappers, soiled, limited.   Dawsons PM 10-53   1974   £25

BIRT, HENRY N.   The Elizabethan Religious Settlement.   1907.
Plates, faded, scarce, orig. edition.   Howes 185-980   1974   £10

BISBY, G. R.   The Fungi of Manitoba.   1929. 8vo., cloth,
map, scarce.   Wheldon 131-1373   1974   £5

BISCHOFF, GOTTLIEB W.   Worterbuch der Beschreibenden Botanik.   Stuttgart, 1857. 8vo., cloth, second edition.   Wheldon 129-888   1974   £5

BISHOP, G. W.   Barry Jackson and the London Theatre.   1933.
Small 4to., quarter buckram, fine, plates.   Covent 55-1439   1974   £10.50

BISHOP, GEORGE   Observations, Remarks, and Means, to Prevent
Smuggling.   Maidstone, 1783. 8vo., unbound.   Hill 126-250   1974   £10.50

BISHOP, GLENN A.   Chicago's Accomplishments and Leaders.
Chicago, (c.1932). 8vo., cloth.   Saddleback 14-368   1974 $15

BISHOP, HARRIET E.   Minnesota.   St. Paul, 1869. Pictorial wrappers.
Hayman 57-503   1974 $20

BISHOP, ISABELLA LUCY (BIRD), MRS. J. F.   A Lady's Life in the Rocky
Mountains.   New York & London, 1890. Ex-library, illus.   Hood's 104-843   1974
$12.50

BISHOP, ISABELLA LUCY (BIRD) MRS. J. F.   The Yangtze Valley and Beyond.
New York, 1900. Cloth, 2 vols, gilt, illus.   Dawsons 424-336   1974 $50

BISHOP, J. G.   "A Peep into the Past".   Brighton, 1892.
8vo., illus., orig. cloth, portrait.   Bow Windows 62-885   1974   £8.50

BISHOP, JOHN   Researches into the Pathology and Treatment of
Deformities of the Human Body.   London, 1852. 8vo., orig. black cloth.   Dawsons PM 249-71   1974   £28

BISHOP, JOHN PEALE   Act of Darkness.   New York, 1935. 8vo.,
orig. cloth, fine, first edition.   Rota 190-58   1974   £10

BISHOP, JOHN PEALE   Selected Poems.   New York, 1941. 8vo., orig.
cloth, first edition.   Rota 189-137   1974   £5

BISHOP, RICHARD E.   Bishop's Birds.   1936. Roy 4to., orig. cloth,
limited edition.   Broadhurst 23-1088   1974   £42

BISHOP, WILLIAM AVERY   Winged Peace.   Toronto, 1944. Maps, illus.
Hood's 103-92   1974 $10

BISHOP, WILLIAM AVERY   Winged Warfare.   Toronto, 1918. Rebound,
illus.   Hood's 104-93   1974 $20

BISHOPE, GEORGE   New-England Judged, by the Spirit of the Lord.
London, 1703. 2 parts, 8vo., full panelled calf, gilt, second edition, fine, extra-
illus.   Ximenes 36-23   1974 $200

BISLAND, ELIZABETH   The Life and Letters of Lafcadio Hearn.   Boston
and New York, 1906. Cloth, 2 vols., first edition.   Dawson's 424-270   1974
$175

BISLAND, ELIZABETH   The Life and Letters of Lafcadio Hearn.   1911.
Plates, 2 vols., gilt tops, fine, first edition.   Covent 51-889   1973   £15

BISMARCK, OTTO VON　　Memoirs. 1898. 2 vols., portraits, orig. edition. Howes 186-613 1974 £9.50

BISNO, BEATRICE　　Tomorrow's Bread. 1938. 328 pages. Austin 57-76 1974 $10

BISSELL, RICHARD　　Good Bye Ava. Brown, 1960. 241p. Austin 54-144 1973 $6.50

BISSELL, RICHARD　　Still Circling Moose Jaw. McGraw, Hill, 1965. 260p. Austin 54-145 1973 $6.50

BISSELL, RICHARD　　A Stretch on the River. Little, Brown, 1950. 242p. Austin 54-146 1973 $6.50

BISSELL, RICHARD　　You Can Always Tell a Harvard Man. McGraw, Hill, 1962. 280p. Austin 54-147 1973 $6.50

BISSET, CHARLES　　An Essay on the Medical Constitution of Great Britain. London, 1762. 8vo., rebound, modern half calf, first edition. Dawsons PM 249-72 1974 £135

BISSET, HABAKKUK　　Rolment of Courtis. 1920-26. 3 vols., orig. half roan. Howes 186-615 1974 £12.50

BITTIO, A. DE　　A Series o Plates Representing the Most Extraordinary and Interesting Basaltic Mountains, Caverns and Causeways. 1825. Folio, orig. half morocco, plates. Traylen 79-78 1973 £35

BJERKE-PETERSEN, VILH　　Erik Olson. Copenhagen, 1935. 32mo., wrappers. Minters 37-358 1973 $12.50

BJERRE, ANDREAS　　The Psychology of Murder. London, 1927. Rittenhouse 46-81 1974 $15

BJORK, KENNETH　　Saga In Steel and Concrete. 1947. 504p., illus. Austin 62-46 1974 $17.50

BJORNSON, BJORNSTJERNE　　Plays. Scribner, 1914. 284p. Austin 51-124 1973 $10

BLAAUW, W. H.　　The Baron's War. London & Lewes, 1844. Small 4to., plates, woodcuts. Traylen 79-393 1973 £5

BLACK, ALEXANDER　　Time and Chance. Farrar, 1937. 338p., illus. Austin 51-125 1973 $8.50

BLACK, CARL E.　　Names of Surgical Operations. St. Paul, 1935. Rittenhouse 46-82 1974 $10

BLACK, ELEANORA　　The Gold Rush Song Book. San Francisco, 1940. 8vo., orig. bindings, dust jacket. Butterfield 8-36 1974 $15

BLACK, G. V.　　The Formation of Poisons by Micro-Organisms. Philadelphia, 1884. Rittenhouse 46-83 1974 $15

BLACK, JEAN FERGUSON　　Penny Wise. 1937. 154p., paper. Austin 51-126 1973 $7.50

BLACK, JOHN H.　　Forty Years in the Medical Profession, 1858-1898. Philadelphia, 1900. Stained cover. Rittenhouse 46-84 1974 $10

BLACK, LIBBIE　　The Hills of Beverly. Doubleday, 1957. 357p. Austin 51-127 1973 $6.50

BLACK, SAMUEL　　Dissertatio Physica Inauguralis de Ascensu Vaporum Spontaneo. 1786. 8vo., contemporary tree calf, gilt. Dawsons PM 245-95 1974 £8

BLACK, SAMUEL F.　　San Diego County, California. Chicago, 1913. 2 vols., 4to., half leather, rebacked. Saddleback 14-38 1974 $40

BLACK, WILLIAM　　Green Pastures and Piccadilly. 1877. 3 vols., orig. blue cloth. Covent 55-215 1974 £40

BLACK, WILLIAM　　A Princess of Thule. 1899. Illus., 505 pages. Austin 61-116 1974 $10

BLACK, WILLIAM HENRY　　Catalogue of the Arundel Manuscripts in the Library of the College of Arms. (London), 1829. 8vo., contemporary polished calf, gilt, rebacked. Dawsons PM 10-14 1974 £64

THE BLACK Book of Carmarthen. 1906. Imperial 8vo., half black morocco, gilt, limited edition. Broadhurst 23-1340 1974 £10

THE BLACK Book of Warwick. (1898). Square 8vo., plates, 500 pages. Howes 186-1297 1974 £7.50

BLACKALL, JOHN　　Observations of the Nature and Cure of Dropsies. Philadelphia, 1820. First American edition. Rittenhouse 46-85 1974 $23

BLACKBURN, ISAAC WRIGHT　　Illustrations of the Gross Morbid Anatomy of the Brain In the Insane. Washington, 1908. Roy. 8vo., orig. cloth, first edition. Schuman 37-25 1974 $110

BLACKBURN, JANE　　Birds from Moidart. Edinburgh, 1895. 8vo., cloth, plates. Wheldon 130-468 1974 £5

BLACKFORD, MRS.　　The Eskdale Herd-Boy. 1819. First edition, 12mo., contemporary sheep, engraved frontispiece, spine rubbed, upper cover almost detached. George's 610-68 1973 £6

BLACKMORE, RICHARD　　King Arthur. London, 1697. Folio, first edition, contemporary panelled calf. Ximenes 36-24 1974 $85

BLACKMORE, RICHARD DODDRIDGE　　Cradock Nowell. 1893. New edition revised, very nice copy. Covent 51-253 1973 £5

BLACKMORE, RICHARD DODDRIDGE　　Dariel. Edinburgh & London, 1897. 8vo., orig. cloth, illus., fine, first edition. Dawsons PM 252-61 1974 £45

BLACKMORE, RICHARD DODDRIDGE　　Fringilla. 1895. Small 4to., orig. pictorial gilt vellum, illus., limited. Smith 193-322 1973 £12

BLACKMORE, RICHARD DODDRIDGE　　Lorna Doone. London, 1883. 8vo., orig. blind stamped cloth, twenty first edition. Dawsons 252-62 1974 £15

BLACKMORE, RICHARD DODDRIDGE　　Tales from the Telling-House. 1896. Orig. dec. cloth, top edges gilt, very good copy, first edition. Covent 51-254 1973 £5.25

BLACKMUR, R. P.　　Dirty Hands. Cambridge, 1930. Wrappers, English first edition. Covent 56-1611 1974 £15

BLACKSTONE, WILLIAM　　Commentaries of the Laws of England. Oxford, 1765-66-68-69. 4 vols., 4to., contemporary calf, plates, first editions. Dawsons PM 250-8 1974 £1150

BLACKSTONE, WILLIAM　　Commentaries on the Laws of England. Oxford, 1765-66-68-69. 4 vols., 4to., plates, contemporary calf, first editions. Dawsons PM 247-18 1974 £950

BLACKSTONE, WILLIAM　　Commentaries on the Laws of England. 1765-69. 4 vols., 4to., half morocco, first edition. Quaritch 939-48 1974 £950

BLACKSTONE, WILLIAM　　The Great Charter and Charter of the Forest. Oxford, 1759. 4to., contemporary reversed calf, rebacked, fine, first edition. Dawsons PM 247-19 1974 £95

BLACKSTONE, WILLIAM　　Dissertation on the Accounts of All Souls College. 1898. 4to., quarter roan, top edges gilt. Thomas 32-289 1974 £40

BLACKWALL, ANTHONY　　An Introduction to the Classics. London, 1728. 12mo., contemporary Cambridge style calf, worn, inscription, fourth edition. Bow Windows 62-93 1974 £7.50

BLACKWALL, J.　　A History of the Spiders of Great Britain and Ireland. London, 1860-(64). Folio, new buckram, plates, very scarce, nice copy. Wheldon 131-921 1974 £75

BLACKWELL, J.　　A History of the Spiders of Great Britain & Ireland. 1861-64. 2 vols., 4to., plates, orig. linen backed boards, very scarce. Smith 194-802 1974 £45

BLACKWALL, J.   A History of the Spiders of Great Britain and
Ireland. London, 1861-64. Folio, half red morocco, hand-coloured plates,
nice copy, very scarce. Wheldon 128-874 1973 £65

BLACKWALL, J.   Researches in Zoology. 1873. 8vo., cloth,
scarce, second edition. Wheldon 128-256 1973 £5

BLACKWALL, J.   Researches in Zoology. 1873. 8vo., cloth,
scarce, second edition. Wheldon 130-335 1974 £5

BLACKWOOD, ALGERNON   The Dance of Death and Other Tales. New
York, 1928. 12mo., 1st ed. Biblo & Tannen 210-565 1973 $15

BLACKWOOD, ALGERNON   Full Circle. London, 1929. 1st ed., ltd. to
530 copies., sgd. by author, scarce. Biblo & Tannen 210-565 1973 $37.50

BLACKWOOD, ALGERNON   The Human Chord. London, 1910. 1st ed.
Biblo & Tannen 210-566 1973 $17.50

BLACKWOOD, ALGERNON   Incredible Adventures. London, 1914. 1st
ed. Biblo & Tannen 210-567 1973 $18.50

BLACKWOOD, ALGERNON   The Listener and Other Stories. 1907. 8vo.,
orig. cloth, first edition. Rota 190-59 1974 £5

BLACKWOOD, ALGERNON   The Promise of Air. London, 1918. 1st ed.
Biblo & Tannen 210-568 1973 $20

BLACKWOOD, ALGERNON   Strange Stories. London, 1929. 1st ed.
Biblo & Tannen 210-569 '1973 $20

BLACKWOOD, ALGERNON   The Wave. 1916. Dust wrapper, dec. cloth
gilt, fine. Covent 55-217 1974 £12.50

BLADES, WILLIAM   The Pentateuch of Printing With a Chapter on
Judges. Chicago, 1891. 4to., orig. cloth, illus. Dawsons PM 10-58 1974
£11

BLAEU, G. J.   Geographiae Blavianae. Amsterdam, 1662.
Large folio, full brown morocco, gilt, fine. Traylen 79-380 1973 £1,150

BLAEU, J.   Vectis Insula. (Amsterdam, 1648). Map.
Quaritch 939-368 1974 £50

BLAEU, JOANNES   Le Theatre du Monde. 1654. 8vo., folio,
orig. cloth. Bow Windows 64-395 1974 £1,600

BLAEU, W.   Buckinghamiensis Comitatus. (Amsterdam,
1648). Maps. Quaritch 939-50 1974 £50

BLAEU, W.   Comitatus Nottinghamiensis. (Amsterdam,
1648). Map. Quaritch 939-512 1974 £50

BLAEU, W.   Ducatus Eboracensis Pars Borealis. (Amsterdam,
1648). Map. Quaritch 939-590 1974 £50

BLAEU, W.   Surria Vernacule Surrey. (Amsterdam, 1648).
Map. Quaritch 939-560 1974 £50

BLAEU, WILLIAM   Le Grand Atlas ou Cosmographie Blaviane en
Laquelle est Exactement Descritte la Terre. Amsterdam, 1667. 12 vols., large
folio, contemporary Dutch vellum, gilt, morocco labels, illus. Traylen
79-577 1973 £10,5000

BLAIKIE, T.   Diary of a Scotch Gardener at the French Court
at the End of the 18th Century. 1931. 8vo., cloth, plates. Wheldon 131-204
1974 £5

BLAINE, DELABERE   Canine Pathology. 1841. Frontispiece, stains,
fourth edition. Bow Windows 64-26 1974 £10.50

BLAINVILLE, H. M. D. DE   Manul de Malacologie et de Conchyliologie.
Paris, 1825. 2 vols., med. 8vo., contemporary French half dark green morocco,
panelled backs, raised bands, top edges gilt, others uncut, rare, coloured & plain
plates, fine. Broadhurst 24-1051 1974 £100

BLAIR, EMMA H.   Annotated Catalogue of Newspaper Files in the
Library of the State Historical Society of Washington. Madison, 1898. Front
wrapper missing. Jenkins 61-2662 1974 $22.50

BLAIR, EMMA H.   The Indian Tribes of the Upper Mississippi and
the Region of the Great Lakes. Cleveland, 1911-12. 2 vols., first English
translation, portraits, maps. Jenkins 61-218 1974 $87.50

BLAIR, H. M.   Pictures of the Past, Memories of Old Toulon.
(1906). 8vo., wrappers, illus. Putnam 126-159 1974 $15

BLAIR, HUGH   Lectures on Rhetoric and Belles Lettres. 1790.
8vo., 3 vols., contemporary marbled calf, gilt, fourth edition. Quaritch 936-19
1974 £6

BLAIR, HUGH   Lectures on Rhetoric and Belles Letters. 1804.
2 vols., new buckram, margin of text stained. Allen 216-1979 1974 £12.50

BLAIR, ROBERT   The Grave. London, 1813. Cloth, rebacked,
second edition. Dawson's 424-92 1974 $300

BLAIR, ROBERT   The Grave. 1813. Engraved title and plates
by Schiavonetti after William Blake, large 4to., uncut in orig. boards, paper
label, rebacked. Thomas 32-86 1974 £80

BLAIR, VILRAY PAPIN   Surgery and Diseases of the Mouth and Jaws.
St. Louis, 1913. Faded, worn, second edition. Rittenhouse 46-679 1974 $10

BLAIR, WILLIAM L.   Pasadena Community Book. Pasadena, c.1943.
4to., leather. Saddleback 14-39 1974 $20

BLAKE, EDWARD   Exzema and Its Congeners. Philadelphia, 1902.
Rittenhouse 46-86 1974 $10

BLAKE, J. F.   A Monograph of the British Fossil Cephalopoda,
Part 1. 1882. 4to., boards, plates. Wheldon 131-969 1974 £10

BLAKE, J. P.   Little Books About Old Furniture. 1926-14-13.
4 vols., frontispiece, plates, orig. buckram. Smith 194-75 1974 £8

BLAKE, JOHN H.   Tea Hints for Retailers. Denver, 1903. Orig.
cloth, illus., scarce. Covent 55-699 1974 £7.50

BLAKE, WILLIAM   The Book of Job. 1927. 4to., cloth, dust wrapper, plates. Quaritch 936-298 1974 £30

BLAKE, WILLIAM   The Book of Job. 1927. 4to., facsimile of
engravings. Thomas 32-91 1974 £8.50

BLAKE, WILLIAM   The Book of Job. London, 1927. 4to.,
illus., orig. cloth, gilt, rubbed. Bow Windows 62-94 1974 £18

BLAKE, WILLIAM   The Engraved Designs Of. 1926. 4to.,
dec. boards, cloth back, dust wrapper, plates. Quaritch 940-31 1974 £60

BLAKE, WILLIAM   Etchings from His Works. 1878. Folio,
plates, boards, cloth back, bookplate. Quaritch 940-29 1974 £35

BLAKE, WILLIAM   The Illustrations for Thornton's Virgil. 1937.
English first edition. Covent 56-1565 1974 £8.50

BLAKE, WILLIAM   Illustrations of the Book of Job. London & New
York, 1902. Orig. cloth backed wrappers, plates. Smith 194-716 1974 £25

BLAKE, WILLIAM   Illustrations of the Book of Job. 1903.
Orig. buckram backed boards, plates, limited edition. Smith 193-58 1973 £5

BLAKE, WILLIAM   Illustrations of the Book of Job. New York, 1935.
Imperial 4to., cloth, illus., plates. Quaritch 936-299 1974 £600

BLAKE, WILLIAM   Illustrations to the Divine Comedy of Dante.
1922. Limited to 250 copies, unbound as issued in the orig. portfolio. Thomas
32-88 1974 £100

BLAKE, WILLIAM   Illustrations to the Divine Comedy of Dante.
1922. Folio, boards, plates. Quaritch 936-300 1974 £90

BLAKE, WILLIAM   Illustrations to Young's Night Thoughts.
Cambridge, 1927. Plates in colour and monotone, unbound as issued in orig.
portfolio. Thomas 32-90 1974 £85

BLAKE, WILLIAM   The Land of Dreams. Northampton, 1928.
8vo., unopened copy; No. 138 of 350 copies printed on Normandy Vellum paper;
sgd. and numbered by the artist (P. Bianco). Frohnsdorff 16-110 1974 $25

BLAKE, WILLIAM   The Marriage of Heaven and Hell. 1911. Post
8vo., linen-backed, fine, English first edition. Covent 56-144 1974 £5.25

BLAKE, WILLIAM   Pencil Drawings by. 1927. 4to., orig. half
canvas, illus., limited. Bow Windows 62-679 1974 £65

BLAKE, WILLIAM   Pencil Drawings By. 1927. 4to., plates, half
buckram. Quaritch 940-32 1974 £60

BLAKE, WILLIAM   The Poems of. Pickering, 1874. First edition,
light brown cloth boards, stamped in gilt and blind, nice copy. Crane 7-22
1974 £15

BLAKE, WILLIAM   Poetical Sketches. London, 1868. 8vo.,
orig. brown cloth, printed paper label, bookplate, second edition. Ximenes
37-20 1974 $70

BLAKE, WILLIAM   Poetical Sketches. 1926. English first edition.
Covent 56-145 1974 £7.50

BLAKE, WILLIAM   Poetical Works. Oxford, 1905. 8vo., full
levant morocco, plates, gilt. Broadhurst 23-624 1974 £25

BLAKE, WILLIAM   The Prophetic Writings. 1926. 2 vols., cloth
gilt, fine, worn dust wrapper. Covent 55-219 1974 £17.50

BLAKE, WILLIAM   The Songs of Experience. n.d. Orig. pictorial
cloth, drawings. Covent 55-220 1974 £15

BLAKE, WILLIAM   Songs of Innocence. 1926. Dec. cloth gilt,
rubbed, facsimile edition. Covent 55-221 1974 £8.50

BLAKE, WILLIAM   Songs of Innocence and Experience, With
Other Poems. London, 1866. 8vo., orig. brown cloth, printed paper label.
Ximenes 37-21 1974 $60

BLAKE, WILLIAM   Songs of Innocence and Experience. 1866.
Small 8vo., contemporary green straight grained morocco gilt. Thomas 32-87
1974 £55

BLAKE, WILLIAM   Visions of the Daughters of Albion. 1932. Fine,
dust wrapper, English first edition. Covent 56-147 1974 £7.50

BLAKE, WILLIAM   The Writings of. 1925. 3 vols., 4to., limited
edition, parchment spines, marbled boards, collotype plates. Thomas 32-89
1974 £100

BLAKE, WILLIAM   The Writings Of. 1925. 3 vols., 4to.,
parchment spines, limited edition. Thomas 28-154 1972 £100

BLAKENEY, R. P.   Popery in Its Social Aspects. Toronto,
(ca. 1854). 326 pages. Austin 57-78 1974 $12.50

BLANC, LOUIS   The History of Ten Years, 1830-1840. 1844.
2 vols., thick 8vo., full buff calf, gilt, fine, first English edition. Howes
186-616 1974 £15

BLANCANUS, JOSEPHUS
Please turn to
BIANCANI, GIUSEPPE

BLANCARD, STEPHEN   A Physical Dictionary. London, 1684. 8vo.,
contemporary calf, first edition in English. Dawsons PM 249-74 1974 £195

BLANCARD, STEPHEN   The Physical Dictionary. London, 1708. 8vo.,
contemporary panelled calf, rebacked, gilt, fifth edition. Hammond 201-531
1974 £25

BLANCHAN, N.   Bird Neighbours. New York, 1904. Roy.
8vo., half morocco, coloured and plain plates. Wheldon 128-392 1973 £10

BLANCHAN, N.   Birds That Hunt and Are Hunted. New York,
1904. Roy. 8vo., half morocco, coloured and plain plates. Wheldon 128-393
1973 £10

BLANCHARD, C. E.   La Zoologie Agricole. (1854-56). 4to.,
orig. wrappers, uncut, plates. Wheldon 129-4 1974 £50

BLANCHARD, C. E.   La Zoologie Agricole. Paris, (1854-56).
15 parts, 4to., orig. wrappers, uncut, plates, scarce. Wheldon 131-21
1974 £50

BLANCHARD, E.   L'Organisation du Regne Animal. Paris,
(1852-64). Parts 1 - 38, imp. 4to., orig. wrappers, plates, rare. Wheldon
131-413 1974 £75

BLANCHARD, E.   L'Organisation du Regne Animal Arachnides.
Paris, (c.1852-64). 18 parts, imp. 4to., orig. wrappers, plates, rare. Wheldon
131-922 1974 £15

BLANCHARD, E.   Les Poissons des Eaux Douces de la France.
Paris, 1866. Roy 8vo., half morocco, illus. Wheldon 130-664 1974 £8

BLANCHARD, E.   Les Poissons des Eaux Douces de la France.
Paris, 1866. Roy 8vo., half morocco, plates, illus. Wheldon 130-665 1974
£12

BLANCHARD, E.   Les Poissons des eaux Douces. Paris, 1880.
Roy 8vo., half calf. Wheldon 129-562 1974 £5

BLANCHARD, EDWARD LYTTON   The Life of George Barnwell. (c., 1830).
8vo., old half calf, frontispiece, illus. Hill 126-189 1974 £12.50

BLANCHARD, P.   Le Voyageur de la Jeunesse dans les Quatre
Parties du Monde. Paris, 1804. First edition, copperplates, 6 vols., half calf,
12mo., little rubbed, each vol. with half titles. George's 610-69 1973 £20

BLANCHE, JACQUES EMILE   Aymeris, Roman. Paris, 1922. Square 8vo.,
orig. wrapper, numbered, first edition. L. Goldschmidt 42-162 1974 $30

BLANCHERE, H. DE LA   La Peche et les Poissons. Paris, 1926. Roy.
8vo., half cloth, coloured plates, text-figures. Wheldon 128-615 1973 £7.50

BLANCHINUS, FRANCISCUS   De Tribus Generibus Instrumentorum Musicae
Veterum Organicae Dissertatio. Rome, 1742. 8vo., plates, contemporary
boards, leather back, worn, first edition. Quaritch 940-807 1974 £95

BLANCO, M.   Flora de Filipinas. Manila, 1837. Small 4to.,
contemporary vellum. Wheldon 129-1051 1974 £90

BLANCO Y FERNANDEZ, A.   Introduccion al Estudio de las Plantas. Madrid,
1845-46. 8vo., contemporary calf, rare. Wheldon 130-992 1974 £30

BLANCOURT, JEAN HAUDICQUER DE
Please turn to
HAUDICQUER DE BLANCOURT, JEAN

BLANDIN, PHILIPPE FREDERIC   Traite d'Anatomie Topographique. Paris, 1826.
8vo and 4to., 2 vols., contemporary quarter calf, first edition. Dawsons PM
249-75 1974 £55

BLANDIN, PHILIPPE-FREDERIC   A Treatise on Topographical Anatomy. New
York, 1834. Plates, stained. Rittenhouse 46-87 1974 $10

BLANE, GILBERT   Elements of Medical Logick. London, 1819.
8vo., orig. boards, uncut, first edition. Dawsons PM 249-76 1974 £24

BLANE, GILBERT   Inquiry into the Causes and Remedies of the Late
and Present Scarcity and High Price of Provisions. London, 1800. 8vo., wrapper,
signed, first edition. Hammond 201-214 1974 £9.50

BLANE, WILLIAM   Cynegetica. London, 1788. 8vo., contemporary calf, gilt, frontispiece, new edition. Hammond 201-83 1974 £24

BLANSCH, H. L.   Beknopte en Volledige Handleiding tot het
Overslaan van Drukvormen. The Hague, 1844. Oblong 8vo., orig. wrappers.
Kraus B8-290 1974 $65

BLANSHARD, PAUL   American Freedom and Catholic Power.
Beacon, 1949. Austin 62-726 1974 $5

BLANTON, WYNDHAM B.   Medicine In Virginia In the 18th Century.
1931. Numbered. Rittenhouse 46-88 1974 $60

BLARRU, PIERRE DE   Naceidos. Opus de Bello Nanceiano. St.
Nicolas du Port, 1518. Folio, fine woodcuts, contemporary limp vellum with ties,
first edition, first issue, splendid copy. Schafer 10-85 1974 sFr 12,000

BLASHILL, T.   Sutton-In-Holderness. 1896. 4to., illus.,
orig. morocco backed cloth boards. Smith 193-227 1973 £8.50

BLASIUS, GERARD   Anatome Animalium. Amsterdam, 1681.
4to., old boards, rubbed, engravings, morocco label, first edition. Gilhofer
61-12 1974 sFr. 1,900

BLATCHFORD, ROBERT   The Sorcery Shop. 1907. English first edition.
Covent 56-1740 1974 £6.30

BLATCHLEY, W.   Orthoptera of Northeastern America.
Indianapolis, 1920. 8vo., cloth, stained, plates. Wheldon 128-677 1973 £7.50

BLATTER, E.   Beautiful Flowers of Kashmir. (1928). Vol. 1
only, 8vo., cloth, plates. Wheldon 131-1263 1974 £7.50

BLATTER, E.   Some Beautiful Indian Trees. 1937. Roy. 8vo.,
cloth, coloured and plain plates. Wheldon 128-1583 1973 £5

BLATZ, W. E.   Collected Studies On the Dionne Quintuplets.
Toronto, 1937. Plates, illus. Hood's 103-579 1974 $15

BLATZ, W. E.   The Five Sisters. Toronto, 1938. Faded,
illus. Hood's 103-578 1974 $10

BLAVATSKY, H. P.   Nightmare Tales. 1892. Frontispiece, illus.,
English first edition. Covent 56-435 1974 £35

BLEAKLEY, WILLIAM   Moral and Religious Poems. Belfast, 1840.
8vo., cloth boards, wrappers. Emerald 50-68 1974 £16

BLEDSOE, ALBERT TAYLOR   An Essay On Liberty and Slavery. Philadelphia,
1856. First edition, 12mo., substantial foxing, covers dull with bit of soiling,
binding firm, generally good. Current BW9-436 1974 $55

BLEECKER, ANN ELIZA   The Posthumous Works of. New York, 1793.
Orig. roan, rubbed, upper cover detached, first edition, some staining. MacManus
224-44 1974 $50

BLEEKER, P.   Atlas. Amsterdam, 1862-7. 8 vols., folio,
half cloth, plates. Wheldon 129-5 1974 £1,350

BLEGEN, THEODORE C.   Norwegian Emigrant Songs and Ballads. 1936.
350 pages. Austin 57-84 1974 $17.50

BLEGEN, THEODORE C.   Norwegian Migration to America: 1825-1860.
1931. 413p., orig. ed. Austin 62-47 1974 $12.50

BLEGEN, THEODORE C.   Norwegian Migration to America. 1931. Orig.
edition. Austin 57-85 1974 $12.50

BLEGEN, THEODORE C.   Norwegian Migration to America. 1940. Orig.
edition, illus. Austin 57-86 1974 $15

BLEGEN, THEODORE C.   Norwegian Migration to America. 1940.
655p., illus., orig. ed. Austin 62-48 1974 $15

BLENHEIM PALACE   Catalogue of the Collection of Limoges Enamels
From. 1883. Roy. 8vo., plates, cloth, wrappers, scarce. Quaritch 940-434
1974 £25

BLENKINSOP, ADAM   A Transport Voyage to the Mauritius and Back;
Touching at the Cape of Good Hope and St. Helena. London, 1851. 8vo., orig.
blue cloth, first edition, very good copy. Ximenes 36-25 1974 $50

BLENMAN, JONATHAN   Remarks on Several Acts of Parliament Relating
More Especially to the Colonies Abroad. London, 1742. 8vo., disbound, first
edition. Ximenes 36-26 1974 $75

BLESSINGTON, MARGUERITE (POWER) FARMER GARDINER, COUNTESS OF
1789-1849   Strathern. London, 1845. 4 vols., 8vo., half roan, marbled
boards, black labels. Emerald 50-70 1974 £21

BLEW, WILLIAM C. A.   Brighton and Its Coaches. 1894. Roy. 8vo.,
plates, orig. cloth. Quaritch 939-214 1974 £45

BLISS, DOUGLAS PERCY   The Devil in Scotland. 1934. Marbled boards,
cloth back, wood engravings. Marsden 39-46 1974 £7

BLISS, DOUGLAS PERCY   A History of Wood-Engraving. London, 1928.
4to., orig. buckram, illus., fine, first edition. Dawsons PM 10-60 1974 £18

BLISS, WILLIAM ROOT   Colonial Times on Buzzard's Bay. Boston and
New York, 1888. Pictorial boards, inscribed by author. Butterfield 10-370
1974 $20

BLISS, WILLIAM ROOT   The Old Colony Town and Other Sketches.
Boston and New York, 1893. Inscribed by author, pictorial boards. Butterfield
10-371 1974 $15

BLOCH, CHAYIM   The Golem. 1925. Illus., fine, first English
edition. Covent 56-157 1974 £25

BLOCH, IWAN   Ethnological and Cultural Studies of the Sex
Life in England Illustrated as Revealed in Its Erotic and Obscene Literature and
Art With Nine Private Cabinets of Illustrations by the Greatest Masters of Erotic
Art. New York, (1934). Tall 8vo., fine, limited to 3000 copies. Current
BW9-491 1974 $40

BLOCH, IWAN   Das Sexualleben Unserer Zeit. Berlin, 1907.
8vo., orig. blue cloth, gilt. Dawsons PM 249-77 1974 £13

BLOCH, MARC LEOPOLD BENJAMIN   Rois et Serfs. Paris, 1920. Roy. 8vo.,
buckram, rebound. Howes 186-619 1974 £7.50

BLOCH, MARCUS   Abhandlung von der Erzeugung der Einweide-
Wurmer und den Mittein Wider Dieselben. Berlin, 1782. 4to., old boards, back
worn, plates, firt edition. Gurney 66-29 1974 £48

BLOCIUS, JOHANN   Historaie per Saturamex Novi Orbis Scriptoribus.
1627. 12mo., vellum, second edition. Dawsons PM 251-170 1974 £55

BLOCK, ETTA   One Act Plays from the Yiddish. 1923.
165 pages. Austin 57-87 1974 $12.50

BLOCK, ETTA   One Act Plays from the Yiddish. 1929.
123 pages. Austin 57-88 1974 $10

BLOCK, HERBERT   The Herblock Book. Beacon, 1952. 244p.,
illus. Austin 54-148 1973 $6.50

BLOCK, HERBERT   Herblock's--Special for Today. Simon,
Schuster, 1958. 255p. Austin 54-149 1973 $7.50

BLODGET, LORIN   Climatology of the United States. Philadelphia,
1857. Tall 8vo., orig. purple pebbled cloth, gilt, uncut, bookplate, scarce, first
edition. Zeitlin 235-28 1974 $75

BLOK, ALEXANDER   Les Douze. Paris, 1923. Small 8vo., illus.,
wrappers. Minters 37-214 1973 $18

BLOME, RICHARD   The Art of Heraldry. London, 1685. Small
8vo., modem calf, morocco, gilt, first edition. Dawsons PM 251-104 1974
£70

BLOMEFIELD, FRANCIS   An Essay Towards a Topographical History of the
County of Norfolk. London, 1805. 8vo., nineteenth century half calf, gilt, 11
vols., uncut. Dawsons PM 251-8 1974 £200

BLONDEL, J. A.   The Strength Of Imagination In Pregnant
Women Examin'd. London, 1727. Small 8vo., new boards, calf spine.
Traylen 79-206 1973 £75

BLONDEL, JACQUES-FRANCOIS   De la Distribution des Maisons. Paris, 1737-
38. 4to., 2 vols., contemporary speckled calf, fine, first edition. Dawsons PM
251-90 1974 £145

BLOOMFIELD, ROBERT   The Banks of Wye. London, 1811. 8vo.,
contemporary marbled calf gilt, first edition. Dawsons PM 252-64 1974 £15

BLOOMFIELD, ROBERT   The Farmer's Boy. 1800, 1802. 4to., speckled calf, gilt, illus., frontispiece, 1 vol. Quaritch 936-310 1974 £35

BLOOMFIELD, ROBERT   The Farmer's Boy. New York, 1801. 16mo., wood engravings, lacks covers. Frohnsdorff 16-109 1974 $15

BLOOMFIELD, ROBERT   Rural Tales, Ballads and Songs. 1802. 8vo., orig. boards, uncut, scarce. Broadhurst 23-625 1974 £20

BLOOMFIELD, ROBERT   Wild Flowers. Small 8vo., contemporary calf, gilt, woodcuts, first edition. Quaritch 936-311 1974 £15

BLOOMFIELD, ROBERT   Wild Flowers. 1806. Contemporary tree calf gilt, wood engravings. Smith 193-324 1973 £20

BLORE, E.   The Monumental Remains of Noble and Eminent Persons. 1826. Roy. 4to., plates, morocco gilt. Quaritch 939-51 1974 £25

BLORE, T.   The History and Antiquities of the County of Rutland. (1811). Roy. folio, half morocco. Quaritch 939-529 1974 £45

BLOSSFELDT, CHARLES   La Plante. Berlin, n.d. 4to., photo plates, French text, bookplate, orig. binding. Wilson 63-310 1974 $25

BLOUNT, CHARLES   The Two First Books. London, 1680. Folio, contemporary calf, label, first English edition. Dawsons PM 252-65 1974 £50

BLOUNT, CHARLES   The Two First Books of Philostratus. 1680. Small folio, modern boards, some browning, light pencil marks in margin, title neatly repaired, else clean and sound. Thomas 32-159 1974 £25

BLOUNT, THOMAS   Boscobel. Worcester, 1769. Small 8vo., plates, half calf. Quaritch 939-583 1974 £20

BLOUNT, THOMAS   De re Poetica. London, 1694. 4to., 18th century tree calf, label, fine, first edition. Dawsons PM 252-66 1974 £140

BLOUNT, THOMAS   Fragmenta Antiquitatis. 1679. Contemporary calf, signature. Thomas 28-171 1972 £30

BLOUNT, THOMAS   Fragmenta Antiquitatis Antient Tenures of Land and Jocular Customs of Some Mannors. 1679. Contemporary calf, upper joint repaired. Thomas 32-108 1974 £30

BLOW, JOHN   Amphion Anglicus. London, 1700. Folio, contemporary calf, rebacked, gilt. Hammond 201-84 1974 £75

BLOXAM, M. H.   Rugby, the School and Neighbourhood. 1889. 8vo., plates, orig. cloth. Quaritch 939-568 1974 £8

BLOXHAM, JOHN FRANCIS   The Priest and the Acolyte. c., 1895. Square 8vo., orig. wrappers, English first edition. Covent 56-1571 1974 £35

BLUEN, H.   Poems. 1937. 8vo., orig. cloth, first edition. Bow Windows 64-396 1974 £4.50

BLUET D'ARBERES, BERNARD DE   L'Intitulation & Recueil de Toutes les Oeuvres. Paris, 1604. 12mo., contemporary French red morocco, woodcuts, bookplates. Schumann 499-12 1974 sFr 8,500

BLUM, ANDRE   The Origin and Early History of Engraving in France. New York & Frankfurt, 1930. 4to., half morocco, uncut, limited, revised enlarged edition. Dawsons PM 10-61 1974 £58

BLUM, DANIEL   Great Stars of the American Stage. Greenberg, 1952. Illus. Austin 51-128 1973 $12.50

BLUM, DANIEL   A Pictorial History of the American Theatre. Greenberg, 1951. 304p., illus., orig. ed. Austin 51-129 1973 $10

BLUM, DANIEL   A Pictorial History of the American Theatre. Bonanza Books, 1960. 384p., illus. Austin 51-130 1973 $7.50

BLUM, DANIEL   A Pictorial History of the Talkies. G & D., 1958. 318p., illus. Austin 51-131 1973 $12.50

BLUM, DANIEL   Theatre World. Chilton, 1959. 256p., illus. Austin 51-132 1973 $12.50

BLUME, CARL LUDWIG   Rumphia. Leyden, 1848. Folio, new buckram, plates. Wheldon 129-1568 1974 £65

BLUME, CARL LUDWIG   Rumphia. 1835-48. Folio, new half morocco, plates, 4 vols. in 3. Wheldon 129-6 1974 £600

BLUME, CARL LUDWIG   Rumphia. Leyden, 1848. Folio, plates, new buckram. Wheldon 131-1608 1974 £65

BLUME, CARL LUDWIG   Rumphia. Leyden, 1835-48. 4 vols. in 3, folio, new half morocco, plates, rare. Wheldon 131-22 1974 £600

BLUME, CARL LUDWIG   Collection des Orchidees les Plus Remarquables de l'Archipel Indien et du Japon. Amsterdam, 1858. Folio, half green morocco gilt, leather label, plates. Traylen 79-2 1973 £390

BLUMENBACH, JOHANN FRIEDRICH   De Generis Humani Varietate Nativa. Gottingen, 1795. Small 8vo., half calf, rubbed, plates. Schuman 37-26 1974 $45

BLUMENFELD, SIMON   The Iron Garden. 1936. 210 pages. Austin 57-90 1974 $10

BLUMNER, H.   Die Roemischen. 1911. Buckram, worn spine. Allen 213-160 1973 $20

BLUNDELL, JAMES   Observations On Transfusion of Blood. London, 1828-29. 8vo., cloth, illus., first edition. Schuman 37-27 1974 $145

BLUNDEN, EDMUND   De Bello Germanico. 1930. 8vo., orig. cloth, signed, first edition. Rota 189-144 1974 £50

BLUNDEN, EDMUND   The Bonadventure: A Roman Journal of an Atlantic Holiday. 1922. First edition, crown 8vo., uncut, mint, dust wrapper, orig. cloth. Broadhurst 24-549 1974 £10

BLUNDEN, EDMUND   Charles Lamb: His Life Recorded by His Contemporaries. 1934. First edition, spine little faded, very good, soiled d.w. Covent 51-269 1973 £6.30

BLUNDEN, EDMUND   Christ's Hospital. n.d. (1923). First edition, illus., crown 8vo., mint, faded d.w., scarce, orig. cloth. Broadhurst 24-550 1974 £15

BLUNDEN, EDMUND   Christ's Hospital. (1923). 8vo., cloth, illus., first edition. Quaritch 936-313 1974 £30

BLUNDEN, EDMUND   Dead Letters, Poems. 1922. One of 50 copies, wrappers, very good copy, this copy unnumberd. Covent 51-2188 1973 £12.50

BLUNDEN, EDMUND   English Poems. New York, 1926. Linen backed boards, first American edition. Covent 55-230 1974 £7.50

BLUNDEN, EDMUND   Fall In, Ghosts. 1932. One of 50 numbered copies, signed by author. Covent 51-2189 1973 £25

BLUNDEN, EDMUND   Fall in, Ghosts. London, 1932. First edition, first issue, with comma on cover misplaced, mint, orig. yellow paper wrappers. Ross 86-63 1974 $30

BLUNDEN, EDMUND   Great Short Stories of the War. 1930. Orig. cloth backed boards, on India paper, numbered, signed, limited, first edition. Bow Windows 66-59 1974 £6

BLUNDEN, EDMUND   Great Short Stories of the War. 1930. Demy 8vo., dec. boards, cloth spine, limited to 250 copies, numbered and signed by Blunden, printed on India paper. Broadhurst 24-559 1974 £10

BLUNDEN, EDMUND   Halfway House. 1932. Bow Windows 66-60 1974 £6.50

BLUNDEN, EDMUND   The Harbingers. 1916. Paper printed wrapper, presentation copy, inscribed, first edition. Broadhurst 23-626 1974 £150

BLUNDEN, EDMUND   The Harbingers. Uckfield, 1916. First edition,
paper printed wrapper, presentation copy, inscribed by author, very good copy,
scarce. Broadhurst 24-547 1974 £160

BLUNDEN, EDMUND   Leigh Hunt. 1930. Med. 8vo., orig. cloth,
portrait, first edition. Broadhurst 24-556 1974 £5

BLUNDEN, EDMUND   Leigh Hunt's "Examiner" Examined. 1928.
8vo., orig. cloth, first edition. Rota 189-142 1974 £5

BLUNDEN, EDMUND   Masks of Time. 1925. 8vo., dec. boards,
uncut. Broadhurst 23-627 1974 £9

BLUNDEN, EDMUND   Masks of Time. 1925. Illus., limited edition,
demy 8vo., dec. boards, linen spine, uncut, fine. Broadhurst 24-551 1974 £9

BLUNDEN, EDMUND   Near and Far. 1929. Fine, unopened, dust
wrapper, English first edition. Covent 56-160 1974 £7.50

BLUNDEN, EDMUND   Near and Far. 1929. Buckram, signed, English first edition. Covent 56-1573 1974 £25

BLUNDEN, EDMUND   Near and Far, New Poems. London, 1929.
Edition limited to 160 copies, printed on hand made paper, this is copy no. 118,
signed, lacking d.w., spine faded, else fine, orig. binding. Ross 86-64 1974
$40

BLUNDEN, EDMUND   On the Poems of Henry Vaughan. 1927.
Frontispiece, inscribed, presentation, fine. Covent 55-231 1974 £20

BLUNDEN, EDMUND   Pastorals. 1916. 12mo., wrappers, scarce,
first edition. Rota 189-140 1974 £25

BLUNDEN, EDMUND   Poems, 1914-1930. First edition, med. 8vo.,
slightly faded, orig. cloth, limited to 200 copies, signed by author. Broadhurst
24-557 1974 £18

BLUNDEN, EDMUND   Poems, 1914-1930. 1930. Ordinary first
edition, orig. cloth, fine, faded d.w. Broadhurst 24-558 1974 £9

BLUNDEN, EDMUND   Poems, 1914-1930. London, 1930. Orig.
binding, inscription by author, unusually bright copy, near mint, lacking d.w.
Ross 86-65 1974 $55

BLUNDEN, EDMUND   Poems. 1930. 8vo., orig. cloth, signed, first
limited edition. Broadhurst 23-632 1974 £18

BLUNDEN, EDMUND   Retreat. 1928. One of 112 numbered copies,
hand made paper, signed by author, fine, full buckram, d.w. Covent 51-2190
1973 £28

BLUNDEN, EDMUND   Retreat. 1928. 8vo., cloth, first edition.
Quaritch 936-314 1974 £25

BLUNDEN, EDMUND   Retreat. 1928. Hand-made paper, signed,
buckram, fine. Covent 55-232 1974 £17.50

BLUNDEN, EDMUND   The Shepherd and Other Poems of Peace and
War. 1922. First edition, demy 8vo., uncut, mint, dust wrapper, orig. cloth.
Broadhurst 24-548 1974 £10

BLUNDEN, EDMUND   A Summer's Fancy. 1930. One of 80 numbered
copies on handmade parchment vellum, signed by author & artist, fine, vellum
backed boards. Covent 51-2191 1973 £25

BLUNDEN, EDMUND   A Summer's Fancy. London, 1930. Orig.
vellum backed boards, first edition, parchment vellum, signed by author & artist,
fine. MacManus 224-45 1974 $65

BLUNDEN, EDMUND   To Nature: New Poems. London, 1923. Fine,
lacking d.w., no. 240 of edition limited to 390 copies, orig. binding. Ross
86-67 1974 $17.50

BLUNDEN, EDMUND   To Themis. 1931. 8vo., dec. boards, uncut,
first edition. Broadhurst 23-635 1974 £9

BLUNDEN, EDMUND   To Themis: Poems on Famous Trials. 1931.
Illus., first edition, demy 8vo., dec. boards, linen spine, uncut, mint, limited
to 325 copies. Broadhurst 24-562 1974 £9

BLUNDEN, EDMUND   To Themis. Poems on Famous Trials. With Other
Pieces. London, 1931. Orig. vellum backed boards, first edition, parchment
vellum, signed by artist & author, fine. MacManus 224-46 1974 $60

BLUNDEN, EDMUND   Undertones of War. 1928. First edition, demy
8vo., mint, slightly faded d.w., orig. cloth. Broadhurst 24-552 1974 £15

BLUNDEN, EDMUND   Undertones of War. 1928. Orig. cloth, dust
wrapper, bookplate, first edition. Rota 188-109 1974 £12

BLUNDEN, EDMUND   Undertones of War. London, 1928. D.w.
somewhat stained, else fine, orig. binding. Ross 86-68 1974 $35

BLUNDEN, EDMUND   Votive Tablets. n.d. 8vo., orig. cloth, signed,
first limited edition. Broadhurst 23-634 1974 £35

BLUNDEN, EDMUND   Votive Tablets: Studies Chiefly Appreciative of
English Authors and Books. n.d. (1931). First edition, limited to 50 copies,
numbered and signed by author, demy 8vo., orig. cloth, fine. Broadhurst 24-561
1974 £35

BLUNDEN, EDMUND   The Waggoner and Other Poems. 1920. Fine,
dust wrapper, English first edition. Covent 56-161 1974 £50

BLUNDEN, EDMUND   Winter Nights: A Reminiscence. London, 1928.
No. 405 of large paper edition limited to 500 copies, signed, bright, near
pristine copy, orig. binding. Ross 86-69 1974 $22.50

BLUNT, ANTHONY   The French Drawings in the Collection of His
Majesty the King at Windsor Castle. Oxford and London, 1945. 4to., orig. cl.,
illus. Jacobs 24-40 1974 $15

BLUNT, DAVID ENDERBY   Elephant. 1933. Orig. cloth, plates, very
scarce, first edition. Smith 193-749 1973 £25

BLUNDEN, EDMUND   The Poems of. London, 1930. 8vo., orig. cloth,
d.w., first edition. Bow Windows 62-96 1974 £5

BLUNT, GERALD   Memoirs of. 1911. Dec. cloth gilt, illus.,
worn, rare. Marsden 39-49 1974 £12

BLUNT, J.   A Scheme for Raising Two Millions Upon
Standing Orders in the Exchequer. (1711). Large folio, disbound. Quaritch
939-52 1974 £18

BLUNT, WILFRID SCAWEN   In Vinculis. 1889. Portrait, name on fly,
fine, first edition. Covent 51-273 1973 £7.50

BLUNT, J.   A Supplement to the Scheme for Raising
1,500,00 1. Upon Talleys and Orders. (1711). Folio, disbound. Quaritch
939-53 1974 £18

BLUNT, WILFRED SCAWEN   In Vinculis. 1889. 8vo., frontispiece, orig.
cloth, first edition. Bow Windows 64-397 1974 £10.50

BLUNT, WILFRED SCAWEN   The Love-Lyrics and Songs of Proteus.
Kelmscott Press, 1892. Woodcut borders and initials, printed in black and red,
8vo., orig. stiff vellum with ties, good copy, limited to 300 copies. Sawyer
293-177 1974 £135

BLUNT, WILFRID SCAWEN   A New Pilgrimage and Other Poems. London,
1889. Small 8vo., orig. cloth, first edition. Bow Windows 62-97 1974 £8.50

BLUNT, WILFRID SCAWEN   A New Pilgrimage and Other Poems. 1889.
Very good copy, inscribed by author. Covent 51-274 1973 £25

BLUNT, WILFRID SCAWEN   The Poetical Works. 1914. 2 vols., very nice
copies, presentation copies inscribed by author, first edition. Covent 51-2192
1973 £21

BLUNT, WILFRID SCAWEN   The Poetry of. 1898. Very nice copy, first
edition, booklabel. Covent 51-275 1973 £5.25

BLUNT, WILFRID SCAWEN   Satan Absolved.   1899.   Square 8vo., buckram, English first edition.   Covent 56-1574 1974 £21

BLYTH, HARRY   Magic Morsels!   n.d. Boards, rubbed, foxing, first edition.   Covent 55-687 1974 £8.50

BLYTON, ENID   The Play's the Thing!   London, (c.1935). 4to., soiled, orig. cloth.   Bow Windows 62-98 1974 £6.50

BLYTT, A.   Haandbog i Norges Flora.   1902-06.   Crown 8vo., cloth, illus.   Wheldon 130-1128 1974 £7.50

BOADEN, JAMES   Fontainville Forest.   London, 1794.   8vo., modern boards, first edition.   Dawsons PM 252-67 1974 £12

BOADEN, JAMES   An Inquiry Into the Authenticity of Various Pictures and Prints . . . . Offered As Portraits of Shakespeare.   London, 1824. Illus., orig. leather binding.   Austin 61-119 1974 $47.50

BOADEN, JAMES   Memoirs of the Life of John Philip Kemble. 1825. 2 vols., 19th century cloth, first edition.   Howes 185-510 1974 £12

BOADEN, JAMES   Mrs. Sarah Siddons.   Athenoeum Press, n.d. 326p., illus.   Austin 51-133 1973 $9

BOAG, JOHN   Imperial Lexicon of the English Language Exhibiting the Pronunciation, Etymology and Explanation of Every Word. 2 vols.   Austin 61-120 1974 $47.50

BOARD, ANDREW   Scogin's Jests.   London, 1796.   8vo., half morocco trifle rubbed, very scarce, frontis.   Ximenes 36-124 1974 $70

BOAS, FRANZ   Materials For the Study of Inheritance in Man. Columbia Univ., 1928. 540p., orig. ed.   Austin 62-50 1974 $25

BOAS, FRANZ   Materials for the Study of Inheritance in Man. 1928. Orig. edition.   Austin 57-92 1974 $25

BOAS, W. S.   Canada In World War II.   Montreal, 1945. Illus., first edition.   Hood's 103-93 1974 $12.50

BOASE, HENRY   Guineas.   London, 1803.   8vo., blue paper wrappers, second edition.   Dawsons PM 247-20 1974 £20

BOAZ, HERMAN   The Angler's Progress.   1820-27.   8vo., half green morocco, gilt.   Hammond 201-73 1974 £45

BOB, the Spotted Terrier; or, Memoirs of the Dog of Knowledge.   (c. 1815). 12mo., orig. boards, roan spine, little rubbed, stiching loose at end, woodcuts. George's 610-72 1973 £6

BOBALI SORDO, SAVINO DE   Rime Amorose.   1589.   Small 4to., old vellum gilt.   Thomas 30-123 1973 £25

BOCCACCIO, GIOVANNI   Ameto.   Venice, 1558.   Light foxing on first few and last few leaves, cut a bit close at top, generally quite nice copy, early 19th century diced calf, rebacked.   Thomas 32-144 1974 £30

BOCCACCIO, GIOVANNI   Ameto.   Venice, 1558.   Early 19th century diced calf, rebacked, foxing.   Thomas 28-257 1972 £30

BOCCACCIO, GIOVANNI   Il Corbaccio.   Paris, 1569.   Small 8vo., old calf, worn, fine, rare 174 pages issue.   Harper 213-15 1973 $175

BOCCACCIO, GIOVANNI   The Decameron of.   (n.d.).   8vo., orig. cloth, 2 vols.   Bow Windows 64-398 1974 £7.50

BOCCACCIO, GIOVANNI   The Decameron of.   (N.P., n.d.).   8vo., illus., 2 vols., portrait, orig. cloth.   Bow Windows 64-399 1974 £6

BOCCACCIO, GIOVANNI   The Decameron.   London, n.d.   2 vols., orig. cl., gilt.   Jacobs 24-63 1974 $20

BOCCACCIO, GIOVANNI   The Decameron.   London, 1741.   8vo., 19th century dark green morocco gilt, plates.   Dawsons PM 252-68 1974 £70

BOCCACCIO, GIOVANNI   Il Decamerone.   (Lucca), 1761.   Thick 4to., wrappers, portraits.   Harper 213-16 1973 $150

BOCCACCIO, GIOVANNI   The Decameron.   1903.   2 vols., plates, some spotting, illus. by Louis Chalon.   Bow Windows 66-63 1974 £7.75

BOCCACCIO, GIOVANNI   The Decameron.   1909.   4 vols., square 8vo., orig. buckram backed boards.   Howes 185-535 1974 £20

BOCCACCIO, GIOVANNI   The Decameron.   New York, 1930.   Thick crown 4to., half crimson levant morocco, gilt, fine.   Howes 185-27 1974 £15

BOCCACCIO, GIOVANNI   La Geneologia de Gli Dei.   Venetia, 1569. 4to., contemporary limp vellum.   Schumann 499-13 1974 sFr 160

BOCCALINI, TRAJANO   De Ragguagli de Parnaso.   Venetia, 1618. 3 parts in 1 vol., 8vo., contemporary limp vellum, fine.   Schumann 499-14 1974 sFr 200

BOCK, F. S.   Versuch Einer Vollstandigen.   Konigsberg, 1769. 8vo., half calf, rare.   Wheldon 129-563 1974 £5

BODDAERT, M.   Table des Planches Enluminees d'Histoire Naturelle de M. D'Aubenton.   1874.   Roy. 8vo., wrappers.   Wheldon 131-550 1974 £7.50

BODE, WILHELM   The Complete Works of Rembrandt.   Paris, 1897-1906. 8 vols., 4to., orig. limp buckram wrappers, dust wrappers, limited edition.   Bow Windows 62-760 1974 £120

BODE, WILHELM   The Complete Work of Rembrandt.   Paris, 1897-1906. Large folio, 8 vols., plates, three quarter leather.   Kraus B8-416 1974 $400

BODELSEN, M.   Emil Hannover Bibliografi 1884-1923. Copenhagen, 1942.   16mo., boards, very good copy.   Minters 37-218 1973 $14

BODENHEIM, MAXWELL   Duke Herring.   Liveright, 1931.   242p. Austin 54-150 1973 $6.50

BODENHEIM, MAXWELL   George May.   Boni, Liveright, 1928.   272p. Austin 54-151 1973 $5

BODENHEIM, MAXWELL   My Life and Loves in Greenwich Village. Bridgehead, 1954.   255p.   Austin 54-152 1973 $10

BODENHEIM, MAXWELL   Naked on Roller Skates.   Liveright, 1930. 277p.   Austin 54-153 1973 $6

BODENHEIM, MAXWELL   Ninth Avenue.   Liveright, 1926.   267p. Austin 54-154 1973 $6.50

BODENHEIM, MAXWELL   A Virtuous Girl.   Liveright, 1930.   260p. Austin 54-155 1973 $6.50

BODIN, JEAN   De la Demonomanie des Sorciers.   1593.   8vo., calf.   Gurney 64-29 1974 £60

BODKIN, THOMAS   May It Please Your Lordships.   Dublin, 1917. Vellum-backed boards, English first edition.   Covent 56-1576 1974 £5.25

BODKIN, THOMAS   The Paintings of Jan Vermeer.   New York, 1940. Folio, color plates.   Biblo & Tannen 214-551 1974 $27.50

BODMER, JOHANN JACOB   Noah.   1767.   12mo., 2 vols., contemporary calf, gilt, fine, first edition.   Hill 126-21 1974 £45

BOECKESSEN, JOHANN GOTHARD   Tractatio Synoptica Juridico-Politica de Jure Hospitiorum.   1677.   4to., modern cream cloth boards.   Dawsons PM 251-172 1974 £12

BOECKH, AUGUSTUS   Corpus Inscriptionum Graecarum.   Berlin, 1828-53. 3 vols. in 4, roy. folio, half calf.   Quaritch 940-291 1974 £100

BOECKH, AUGUSTUS   The Public Economy of Athens.   London, 1828. 8vo., half calf, boards, fine.   Dawsons PM 251-171 1974 £10

BOECKLER, GEORG ANDREAS   Architectura Curiosa Nova.   Nuremberg, (1664). 4 parts in 1 vol., engraved plates, folio, contemporary vellum, first edition.   Kraus 137-13 1974 $1,400

BOEHME, JAKOB   Aurora. 1656. Thick small 4to., contemporary calf, rebacked, first English edition.   Howes 186-1787 1974 £85

BOEHN, M. VON   Modes and Manners. 1932-5. 8vo., orig. cloth, illus., plates.   Broadhurst 23-24 1974 £21

BOEHN, M. VON   Modes and Manners. 1932-35. 4 vols., demy 8vo., 3 vols. in dust wrappers, coloured & plain plates, mint.   Broadhurst 24-20 1974 £30

BOERHAAVE, HERMANN   Elementa Chemiae. 1759. Small 4to., plates, contemporary vellum.   Zeitlin 235-270 1974 $185

BOERHAAVE, HERMANN   Methodus Studii Medici.   Amsterdam, 1751. 2 vols., large 4to., contemporary marbled calf, plates, best edition.   Schuman 37-28 1974 $165

BOERHAAVE, HERMAN   Opera Omnia Medica.   Venice, 1766. 4to., old calf.   Gurney 64-30 1974 £22

BOERIUS, NICOLAUS   Decisiones Aureae.   Lyons, 1544. Folio, contemporary blind stamped calf, worn, large woodcut.   Thomas 32-223 1974 £15

BOETHIUS, ANICIUS MANLIUS SEVERINUS   Arithmetica. Augsburg, 1488. 4to., boards, leather spine, woodcut diagrams, Georg Tannstetter's copy.   Kraus 137-14 1974 $2,850

BOETHIUS, ANICIUS MANLIUS SEVERINUS   Boetius de Philosophico Consolatu Sive de Consolatione Philosophiae.   Strassburg, 1501. Folio, woodcut illus., old half vellum, very rare, first fully illus. edition.   Schafer 8-89 1973 sFr. 4,500

BOETHIUS, ANICIUS MANILIUS SEVERINUS   De Consolatione Philosophiae. (Westminster, c. 1478). Purple morocco gilt, brown morocco case, fine, first English edition.   Dawsons PM 1974 $37,500

BOETTIGER, JOHN   Jake Lingle or Chicago on the Spot.   New York, (1931). Cloth, illus., fine, first edition.   Bradley 35-67 1974 $50

BOGARDUS, EMORY S.   Essentials of Americanization. 1919. 303p.   Austin 62-51 1974 $12.50

BOGARDUS, EMORY S.   Immigration and Race Attitudes. 1928. Orig. edition.   Austin 57-93 1974 $10

BOGG, E.   Two Thousand Miles of Wandering.   Leeds, 1898. 4to., illus., orig. quarter roan, rubbed, frayed.   Bow Windows 62-100 1974 £8.50

BOHMER, HEINRICH   Kirche und Staat in England und in der Normandie im XI und XII.   Leipzig, 1899. Rebound, buckram.   Howes 186-623 1974 £8.50

BOHN, J.   Circulus Anatomico-Physiologicus, seu Oeconomia Corporis Animalis.   Leipzig, 1697. 4to., old vellum, second edition, small piece torn from corner of title.   Gurney 66-30 1974 £48

BOHR, NIELS   The Theory of Spectra and Atomic Constitution. Cambridge, 1922. 8vo., orig. cloth, gilt, first edition in English.   Dawsons PM 245-97 1974 £15

BOHUN, EDMUND   An Address to the Free-Men and Free-Holders of the Nation.   London, 1682. 4to., modern boards, first edition.   Dawsons PM 247-21 1974 £15

BOHUN, EDMUND   The Character of Queen Elizabeth.   London, 1693. 8vo., contemporary sprinkled calf, gilt, first edition.   Dawsons PM 251-173 1974 £75

BOHUN, WILLIAM   Cursus Cancellariae. 1723. 8vo., contemporary calf, rebacked.   Dawsons PM 251-174 1974 £16

BOILEAU-DESPREAUX, NICHOLAS   Poesies.   Paris, 1781. 2 vols., 16mo., contemporary green long grain morocco, gilt.   L. Goldschmidt 42-10 1974 £40

BOIN, A.   Memoire sur la Maladie qui Regna en 1809 Chez les Espagnols Prisonniers de Guerre a Bourges.   Paris, 1815. 8vo., uncut, inscribed.   Rittenhouse 46-91 1974 $22.50

BOINE, GIOVANNI   La Ferita non Chiusa.   Florence, 1921. 8vo., wrappers, frontispiece, foxed.   Minters 37-378 1973 $16

BOINE, GIOVANNI   Frantumi Seguiti da Plausi e Botte.   Florence, 1921. 8vo., wrappers, unopened, second edition.   Minters 37-377 1973 $18

BOINE, GIOVANNI   Il Peccato ed Altre Cose.   Florence, 1914. 8vo., orig. wrapper, covers soiled.   Minters 37-376 1973 $18

BOIS, L. E.   Le Colonel Dambourges.   Quebec, 1866. Rebound, stamped in gold.   Hood's 102-684 1974 $30

BOIS, L. E.   Ile d'Orleans, Avec une Carte par M. de Villeneuve.   Quebec, 1895.   Hood's 102-685 1974 $15

BOISDUVAL, J. A.   Histoire Naturelle des Insectes.   Paris, 1836-74. 8vo., 8 vols., half leather, scarce.   Wheldon 130-724 1974 £75

BOISSIER, E.   Icones Euphorbiarum.   Paris, 1866. Folio, orig. wrappers, plates, scarce.   Wheldon 131-1645 1974 £50

BOISSIER, E.   Pugillus Plantarum Novarum Africae Borealis Hispaniaeque Australis.   Geneva, 1852. 8vo., orig. printed boards, scarce.   Wheldon 128-1241 1973 £5

BOISSONNET, VICTOR DANIEL   Dictionnaire Alphabetico-Methodique des Ceremonies et des Rites Sacres. 1864-65. 3 vols., imp. 8vo., half cloth.   Howes 185-985 1974 £15

BOIT, C.   Proposals for Raising a Supply to Her Majesty. (1711). Folio, disbound.   Quaritch 939-54 1974 £20

BOITARD, PIERRE   Botanique des Demoiselles.   Paris, 1835. Blue cloth, 2 vols.   Dawson's 424-99 1974 $135

BOITARD, PIERRE   Les Pigeons de Voliere et de Colombier.   Paris, 1824. 8vo., orig. wrappers, plates, scarce.   Wheldon 130-469 1974 £60

BOITARD, PIERRE   Traite des Prairies Naturelles et Artificielles. Paris, 1827. 8vo., half morocco, plates, scarce.   Wheldon 130-1583 1974 £10

BOIVIN, M. A. V.   Memorial de l'Art.   Paris, 1812. 8vo., calf, frontispiece, plates, first edition.   Gurney 64-31 1974 £40

BOK, EDWARD W.   The Americanization of.   New York, 1923. 8vo., cloth, plates.   Minters 37-6 1973 $20

BOK, EDWARD W.   Twice Thirty. 1925.   Austin 57-95 1974 $10

BOLDREWOOD, ROLF   A Colonial Reformer. 1890. Creased covers, first edition.   Covent 55-235 1974 £5

BOLDREWOOD, ROLF   The Miner's Right. 1890. Marked covers, first edition.   Covent 55-236 1974 £5

BOLDREWOOD, ROLF   Robbery Under Arms. 1891. Rubbed, stained.   Covent 55-237 1974 £5

BOLDREWOOD, ROLF   The Squatter's Dream. 1890. Covers marked.   Covent 55-238 1974 £5

BOLDREWOOD, ROLF   A Sydney-Side Saxon. 1891. Covers marked.   Covent 55-239 1974 £5

BOLINGBROKE, HENRY ST. JOHN 1678-1751   A Dissertation Upon Parties. 1735. Contemporary calf gilt, third edition.   Smith 194-133 1974 £7.50

BOLINGBROKE, HENRY ST. JOHN 1678-1751   A Final Answer to the Remarks on the Craftsman's Vindication; And to All the Libels . . . Against the Person Last Mentioned in the Craftsman of 22 May. 1731. Demy 8vo., disbound, dust stained.   Broadhurst 24-1318 1974 £5

BOLINGBROKE, HENRY ST. JOHN 1678-1751   A Letter to Sir William Windham. London, 1753. 8vo., contemporary tree calf, first edition.   Ximenes 35-101 1974 $25

BOLINGBROKE, HENRY ST. JOHN 1678-1751   Letters on the Spirit of Patriotism. London, 1749. 8vo., contemporary calf, first authorized edition. Dowsons PM 252-70 1974 £40

BOLINGBROKE, HENRY ST. JOHN 1678-1751   Letters on the Study and Use of History. 1752. 2 vols., contemporary calf, morocco labels, spines trifle rubbed, first published edition. Bow Windows 66-67 1974 £35

BOLITHO, HECTOR   The Reign of Queen Victoria. New York, 1948. Biblo & Tannen 213-714 1973 $8.50

BOLITHO, WILLIAM   Overture. Simon and Schuster, 1931. 136p. Austin 51-134 1973 $7.50

BOLOGNA, JOSEPH   At the Feet of the Mighty. ca. 1936. 39p., illus. Austin 62-53 1974 $17.50

BOLT, ROBERT   Brother and Sister. n.d. 4to., wrappers, English first edition. Covent 56-162 1974 £10

BOLTON, ARTHUR T.   The Architecture of Robert and James Adam, 1758-1794. 1922. Profusely illus. with photos., 2 vols., folio, cloth, fine copy, scarce. Sawyer 293-24 1974 £115

BOLTON, CHARLES K.   Brookline: The History of a Favored Town. Brookline, 1897. 12mo., cloth, mad, illus., limited. Saddleback 14-474 1974 $12.50

BOLTON, CHARLES KNOWLES   Scotch Irish Pioneers in Ulster and America. 1910. Maps, illus., orig. edition. Austin 57-96 1974 $12.50

BOLTON, CHARLES KNOWLES   Scotch Irish Pioneers in Ulster and America. 1910. 398p., illus., orig. ed. Austin 62-54 1974 $12.50

BOLTON, GUY   Adam and Eva. French, 1947. 133p., paper. Austin 51-135 1973 $7.50

BOLTON, GUY   The Light of the World. Holt, 1920. 205p. Austin 51-136 1973 $7.50

BOLTON, HERBERT EUGENE   The Black Robes of New Spain. Washington, 1935. Inscribed and signed by author. Jenkins 61-220 1974 $12.50

BOLTON, HERBERT EUGENE   Guide to Materials for the History of the United States. 1913. Dawsons PM 11-93 1974 £11

BOLTON, HERBERT EUGENE   The Opening of North America. N.P., 1942. 4to., orig. mimeographed typescript, buckram, charts. Jenkins 61-222 1974 $125

BOLTON, HERBERT EUGENE   Rim of Christendom, a Biography of Eusebio Francisco Kino, Pacific Coast Pioneer. New York, 1936. Autographed by author, first edition. Jenkins 61-1321 1974 $40

BOLTON, J.   An History of Funguses Growing About Halifax. Halifax & Huddersfield, 1788-89. 3 vols., 4to., half morocco, plates. Wheldon 131-23 1974 £200

BOLTON, JOHN   Geological Fragments. Ulverston and London, 1869. 8vo., orig. cloth, gilt, plates, first edition. Hammond 201-360 1974 £7.50

BOLTON, JOHN   Geological Fragments Collected Principally from Rambles Among the Rocks of Furness and Cartmel. Ulverston, 1869. 8vo., orig. cloth, illus. Wheldon 131-972 1974 £12

BOLTON, JOHN   Geological Fragments Collected Principally from Rable Among the Rocks of Furness and Cartmel. Ulverston, 1869. 8vo., orig. cloth, illus. Wheldon 128-947 1973 £12

BOLTON, JOHN   Harmonia Ruralis. (1824). 4to., contemporary half green morocco, plates. Wheldon 130-6 1974 £250

BOLTON, ROBERT   A History of the County of Westchester, from its First Settlement to the Present Time. New York, 1848. 2 vols., med. 8vo., first edition, illus., orig. cloth, vol. 1 worn at hinges. Broadhurst 24-1580 1974 £40

BOLUS, H.   The Orchids of the Cape Peninsula. Cape Town, 1888. 8vo., orig. cloth, plates, rare. Wheldon 131-1609 1974 £45

BOLZANIO, URBANO   Grammaticae Institutiones. 1560. 19th century calf gilt, rubbed. Thomas 30-113 1973 £35

BONACINA, MARTIN   Opera Omnia. Venice, 1694. 3 vols., folio, foxing, contemporary vellum. Howes 185-986 1974 £30

BONALD, LOUIS GABRIEL AMBROISE   Legislation Primitive. Paris, 1817. 3 vols., 8vo., orig. wrapper, uncut, second edition. L. Goldschmidt 42-163 1974 $75

BONANNI, FILIPPO
Please turn to
BUONANNI, FILIPPO

BONAPARTE, C. L.   A Geographical and Comparative List of the Birds of Europe and North America. 1838. 8vo., cloth. Wheldon 131-551 1974 £5

BONAPARTE, C. L.   Monographie des Loxiens. Leyden & Dusseldorf, 1850. 4to., contemporary full red morocco, gilt, plates, rare. Wheldon 131-24 1974 £700

BONAPARTE, ROLAND PRINCE   Notes Pteridologiques. Paris, 1915-25. 8vo., orig. wrappers, complete set. Wheldon 131-1374 1974 £75

BONAPARTE, ROLAND PRINCE   Notes Pteridologiques. Paris, 1915-25. 8vo., orig. wrappers. Wheldon 129-1387 1974 £75

BONAVENTURA, SAINT   Expositio Super Regulam Fratrum Minorum. (Italy, c.1400-20). Small 8vo., old vellum, fine. Harper 213-17 1973 $1200

BONAVENTURA, SAINT   Meditationes Vitae Christi. Pavia, 1490. 8vo., wrappers, fine, pocket edition. Harper 213-18 1973 $550

BONAVENTURA, SAINT   Speculum Disciplinae et Profectus Religiosorum. Antwerp, 1591. Small 8vo., contemporary blind-stamped pigskin, very fine. Harper 213-19 1973 $135

BONAVIA, E.   Studies in the Evolution of Animals. 1895. Small 4to., cloth, illus., scarce. Wheldon 130-385 1974 £5

BOND, BEVERLEY W.   The Civilization of the Old Northwest. New York, 1934. First edition, ex-library, orig. binding. Wilson 63-162 1974 $10

BOND, FRANCIS   Gothic Architecture in England. 1906. Crown 4to., buckram, illus., worn. Marsden 37-73 1974 £6

BOND, J.   A Complete Guide for Justices of Peace. London, 1685. 8vo., contemporary calf. Quaritch 939-55 1974 £60

BOND, J. WESLEY   Minnesota and Its Resources. New York, 1853. Rebound, block fabric. Hood's 103-795 1974 $45

BOND, J. WESLEY   Minnesota and Its Resources. Chicago-Philadelphia, 1856. 8vo., orig. bindings. Butterfield 8-300 1974 $15

BOND, JOHN   In the Pillory. 1927. Austin 62-55 1974 $10

BONE, ALEXANDER H.   Bowsprit Ashore. 1933. Woodcuts, first American edition. Austin 61-123 1974 $10

BONE, GERTRUDE   Children's Children. 1908. Limited to 215 copies signed by illus., drawings, japanese vellum, 4to., blue morocco gilt, presentation inscription from author, fine copy. Sawyer 293-73 1974 £75

BONE, GERTRUDE   This Old Man. London, 1925. Cloth, labels, first edition. Dawson's 424-250 1974 $7.50

BONER, CHARLES   Chamois Hunting in the Mountains of Bavaria. 1853. 8vo., orig. cloth, first edition. Broadhurst 23-1616 1974 £6

BONES, JAMES   London Perambulator. 1925. Illus. Austin 61-125 1974 $12.50

BONESANA, CESARE, MARCHESE DI BECCARIA
Please turn to
BECCARIA, CESARE BONESANA, MARCHESE DI

BONGARS, JACQUES   Gesta Dei per Francos. Hanau, 1611.
2 vols. in 1, very thick folio, contemporary calf, worn, stains, maps, fine.
Harper 213-20 1973 $275

BONHOTE, J. L.   Birds of Britain. 1907. 8vo., orig. cloth,
plates. Wheldon 131-552 1974 £10

BONHOTE, J. L.   Birds of Britain and Their Eggs. 1923. 8vo.,
cloth, plates, new edition. Wheldon 130-470 1974 £5

BONIFACIUS VIII, POPE   Liber Sextus Decretalium. Speier, 1481.
Folio, contemporary Augsburg brown calf, wooden boards, worn. Harper
213-21 1973 $850

BONMARIAGE, SYLVAIN   Solgane Schaal et Son Oeuvre. Paris, 1932.
4to., wrappers, plates. Minters 37-130 1973 $18.50

BONNAFOX-DEMALET, JULIEN   Traite sur la Nature et le Traitement de la
Phthisie Pulmonaire. Paris, 1804. 8vo., orig. boards, gilt, first edition. Dawsons PM 249-78 1974 £32

BONNARDOT, ALFRED   Essai sur l'Art de Restaurer les Estampes et les
Livres. Paris, 1858. 16mo., half morocco, second edition. Kraus B8-15
1974 $12

BONNATERRE, J. P.   Tableau Encyclopedique et Methodique des
Trois Regnes de la Nature. Paris, 1790. 4to., modern boards, engraved plates.
Wheldon 128-617 1973 £20

BONNER, EUGENE   The Club in the Opera House. New York,
1949. Biblo & Tannen 210-955 1973 $8.50

BONNER, SHERWOOD   Dialect Tales. New York, 1883. 8vo.,
pict. cloth, spine ends worn, lst ed., illus. Frohnsdorff 16-347 1974 $15

BONNET, CHARLES   Essai Analytique sur les Facultes de l'Ame.
Copenhagen, 1760. 4to., contemporary marbled calf, gilt, leather labels, first
edition. L. Goldschmidt 42-11 1974 $150

BONNET, CHARLES   Recherches sur l'Usage des Feuilles des
Plantes. Gottingen & Leyden, 1754. 4to., folding-plates, contemporary
boards, rubbed, fine, uncut, first edition. Gilhofer 61-19 1974 sFr. 900

BONNET, CHARLES   Recherches sur l'Usage des Feuilles dans les
Plantes. Leyden, 1754. 4to., contemporary half calf gilt, first edition. Wheldon
130-994 1974 £60

BONNIE AND CLYDE. Dallas, 1934. Frontispiece, fine, worn, dust wrapper,
first U.S. edition. Covent 56-163 1974 $15

BONIFACE, ELEANOR   Welsh Ways and Days. 1935. Wrappers, English first edition. Covent 56-1138 1974 £12.50

BONNAT, L.   Les Dessins de la Collection Leon Bonnat au
Musee de Bayonne. Paris, 1925-26. 2 vols., 4to., orig. portfolios, plates.
Quaritch 940-34 1974 £75

BONOMI, J.   Nineveh and Its Palaces. 1853. 8vo., illus.,
calf gilt, plates, frontispiece, revised second edition. Quaritch 940-292 1974
£25

BONNYCASTLE, JOHN   An Introduction to Astronomy. London, 1786.
8vo., contemporary half calf, rebacked, plates, first edition. Hammond 201-793
1974 £22.50

BONNYCASTLE, JOHN   An Introduction to Astronomy. London, 1803.
8vo., contemporary mottled calf, gilt, plates, fourth edition. Hammond 201-794
1974 £12.50

BONNYCASTLE, R. H.   The Canadas in 1841. London, 1841. 2 vols.,
orig. binding. Hood's 102-549 1974 $175

BONTEMPELLI, MASSIMO   Piero Antonio Gariazzo. Milan, Rome,
n.d. 4to., cloth, plates, illus. Minters 37-187 1973 $11.50

BONTIUS, JACOBUS   De Medicina Indorv Lib. 1642. 12mo., vellum, first edition. Dawsons PM 249-79 1974 £145

BONZELET, HONORATUS   Mixed Marriages and Prenuptial Instructions.
1942. 164 pages. Austin 57-97 1974 $10

THE BONZO Book. London, 1922. Folio, 16 color plates. Frohnsdorff 16-119
1974 $20

BONZO'S Star Turns. London, 1922. Folio, 16 color plates. Frohnsdorff 16-120
1974 $20

A BOOK About Animals. London, ca. 1875. 12mo., gilt pict. cloth, all edges
gilt; 6 chromolothograph plates. Frohnsdorff 16-114 1974 $35

THE BOOK Craftsman. 1934-1935. Orig. blue stiff wrappers, illus. Dawson's
424-80 1974 $60

THE BOOK of a Thousand Thrills. London, n.d. Biblo & Tannen 210-408 1973
$12.50

THE BOOK of Accidents. New Haven, n.d. Orig. printed wrappers, 4 woodcuts.
Frohnsdorff 16-116 1974 $17.50

BOOK of Bertram the Priest. London, 1686. 12mo., old calf, staining.
Traylen 79-168 1973 £8

THE BOOK of Birds, Beasts and Fishes. Philadelphia & Baltimore, ca. 1860.
4to., hand-colored engravings. Frohnsdorff 16-117 1974 $22.50

THE BOOK of British Ballads. London, 1842. Sm. 4to., lst ed., engravings.
Biblo & Tannen 213-774 1973 $20

BOOK OF COMMON PRAYER
Please turn to
CHURCH OF ENGLAND

THE BOOK of Games; or, A History of Juvenile Sports, Practised at a
Considerable Academy Near London. 1812. 12mo., orig. boards, roan spine,
rare, little rubbed. George's 610-75 1973 £25

BOOK OF HAWKING, HUNTING AND HERALDRY
Please turn to
BERNERS, JULIANA

BOOK of Instructions for the Guidance of Carriers in Making Annual Reports to
the Railroad Commission of Dakota. Washington, 1889. Wrapper. Jenkins
61-737 1974 $12.50

BOOK of Instructions for the Guidance of Carriers in Making Annual Reports to
the Railroad Commission of the State of Florida. Washington, 1889. Wrapper.
Jenkins 61-887 1974 $12.50

BOOK of Instructions for the Guidance of Carriers in Making Annual Reports to
the Railroad Commission of the State of Georgia. Washington, 1889. Wrapper.
Jenkins 61-929 1974 $12.50

BOOK of Instructions for the Guidance of Carriers in Making Annual Reports to
the Railroad Commission of the State of Kentucky. Washington, 1889. Wrapper.
Jenkins 61-1305 1974 $12.50

BOOK of Kells, Described by Sir Edward Sullivan. 1933. 4to., plates, fourth
edition. Allen 213-1299 1973 $17.50

BOOK OF KELLS   Celtic Ornaments from the Book of Kells. 1895.
4to., plates, half green morocco gilt. Quaritch 939-611 1974 £60

BOOK OF MORMON   The Book of Mormon. New York, 1869.
Boards. Hayman 59-402 1974 $50

THE BOOK of Old English Songs and Ballads. London, 1915. 4to., orig. cloth
gilt, dust-wrapper, plates. Hammond 201-476 1974 £5

A BOOK of Pictured Carols. London, 1893. First edition, 8vo., illus., orig.
covers bit soiled, woodcuts, presentation copy from Sir Arthur Quiller-Couch.
Current BW9-8 1974 $48.50

THE BOOK of Rhode Island. (Providence), 1930. 4to., cloth, illus. Saddleback 14-682 1974 $15

BOOK Of Riddles. 1816. Square 8vo., contemporary straight grained blue morocco, gilt, inscribed. Quaritch 940-35 1974 £60

BOOK OF ST. ALBANS
Please turn to
BERNERS, JULIANA

THE BOOK of the Labour Party. c.1925. 3 vols., roy. 8vo., plates. Howes 186-1357 1974 £7.50

A BOOK of the Valuations of all the Ecclesiastical Preferments in England and Wales. 1680. 12mo., old calf. Quaritch 939-56 1974 £15

BOOK of the Victorian Era Ball, Toronto, 28th of December, MDCCCXCVII. Toronto, 1898. Illus., limited, numbered. Hood's 104-157 1974 $45

THE BOOK of Trades. n.d. (1870). First edition, f'cap 8vo., text illus., orig. cloth, fine. Broadhurst 24-1339 1974 £5

BOOK of Trades; or, Library of the Useful Arts, Part 2. 1815. 12mo., orig. boards, rubbed, roan spine, stitching weak in places, cooperplates and text stained, sixth edition. George's 610-78 1973 £6

BOOK of Trades; or, Library of the Useful Arts, Part 3. 1805. First edition, copperplates, 12mo., orig. boards, roan spine, little rubbed, rare, good copy internally. George's 610-79 1973 £20

THE BOOK of Trinity College Dublin. Belfast, 1892. 4to., illus., cloth boards. Emerald 50-954 1974 £6

THE BOOK-FINISHERS' Friendly Circular. London, 1845. 12mo., illus., fine, contemporary gilt-framed calf, scarce. Dawsons PM 10-221 1974 £200

BOOKER, M. Embroidery Design. 1935. Roy. 8vo., plates, illus., orig. cloth backed boards. Quaritch 940-746 1974 £8

BOOKSTABER, PHILIP D. Judaism and the American Mind. Bloch, 1939. Austin 62-56 1974 $8.50

BOORDE, ANDREW The Breviary of Healthe. 1557. 4to., modern brown morocco, third edition. Dawsons PM 249-80 1974 £1,800

BOOTH, CHARLES Life and Labour of the People in London. 1902. 2 vols., orig. parchment binding. Howes 186-1358 1974 £8.50

BOOTH, E. T. Rough Notes on Birds. 1881-87. Folio, half green morocco, 3 vols., maps, plates. Wheldon 129-7 1974 £550

BOOTH, HENRY The Theory and Practice of Propelling through Water. Liverpool, 1842. 8vo., boards, plates, first edition. Hammond 201-839 1974 £32

BOOTH, MARY L. History of the City of New York. New York, 1859. 1st ed., engravings. Biblo & Tannen 213-73 1973 $30

BOOTH, WILLIAM In Darkest England and the Way Out. 1890. Demy 8vo., first edition, orig. cloth, folding colour frontispiece, fine. Broadhurst 24-1206 1974 £6

BOOTH, WILLIAM In Darkest England and the Way Out. 1890. 8vo., orig. cloth, first edition. Broadhurst 23-1212 1974 £6

BOOTH, WILLIAM In Darkest England and the Way Out. London, (1890). 8vo., orig. cloth gilt, worn, first edition. Dawsons PM 250-9 1974 £30

BOOTH, WILLIAM In Darkest England and the Way Out. London, (1890). 8vo., orig. black cloth gilt, first edition. Dawsons PM 251-417 1974 £10

BOOTH, WILLIAM In Darkest England and the Way Out. (1890). 8vo., cloth, first edition. Quaritch 939-57 1974 £17.50

BOOTH, WILLIAM STONE Subtle Shing Secrecies Writ in the Margents of Books. 8vo., frontispiece, orig. cloth-backed boards, label, first edition. Bow Windows 62-106 1974 £6.50

BOOTHBY, BROOKE Sorrows. 1796. Folio, contemporary boards, uncut, plates. Quaritch 936-20 1974 £28

BOOTHBY, GUY Dr. Nikola's Experiment. 1899. 8vo., orig. pictorial cloth, first edition. Rota 190-185 1974 £10

BOOTHBY, GUY Farewell, Nikola. 1901. 8vo., orig. pictorial cloth, illus., worn, first edition. Rota 190-186 1974 £6

BOOTHE, CLARE Margin for Error. Random House, 1940. 198p. Austin 51-137 1973 $10

BOOTHE, CLARE The Women. Random House, 1937. 215p. Austin 51-138 1973 $8.50

BOOTHE, CLARE The Women. 1937. 224p., illus., acting ed., paper. Austin 51-139 1973 $7.50

BOOTHE, CLARE The Women. 1937. 92p., paper. Austin 51-140 1973 $6.50

BORCHGRAVE D'ALTENA, J. DE Het Werk Van Onze Romaansche & Gothische Beeldenaars. n.d. Folio, plates, half calf. Allen 213-1300 1973 $37.50

BORDA, JEAN CHARLES DE Description et Usage. Paris, 1787. 4to., old quarter calf, plates, first edition. Gurney 64-32 1974 £50

BORDENAVE, TOUSSAINT Essai sur la Physiologie. Paris, 1764. 12mo., contemporary mottled calf, second edition. Dawsons PM 249-81 1974 £12

BOREAU, A. Flore du Centre de la France et du Bassin de la Loire. Paris, 1857. 2 vols., 8vo., half morocco, third edition. Wheldon 131-1265 1974 £12

BORELLI, GIOVANNI ALFONSO De Motu Animalium. Leyden, 1685. 2 vols. in 1, 4to., contemporary calf, frontis., engraved plates, revised second edition. Wheldon 128-257 1973 £98

BORELLI, GIOVANNI ALFONSO Euclides Restitutus siue Prisca Geometricae Elementa. 1695. 12mo., orig. vellum. Zeitlin 235-70 1974 $37.50

BORELLI, GIOVANNI ALFONSO De Motu Animalium. Leyden, 1685. 2 vols. in 1, 4to., contemporary calf, plates, revised second edition. Wheldon 131-414 1974 £98

BORENIUS, TANCRED Florentine Frescoes. n.d. 4to., orig. dec. cloth, English first edition. Covent 56-1429 1974 £15

BORENIUS, TANCRED The Picture Gallery of Andrea Vendramin. 1923. Roy. 8vo., plates, illus., buckram, scarce, limited, nice copy. Quaritch 940-36 1974 £15

BORETIUS, F. Europas Bekannteste Schmetterlinge. n.d. Orig. picture boards, cloth back, plates. Wheldon 129-609 1974 £10

BORLASE, EDMUND The History of the Execrable Irish Rebellion. 1680. Folio, contemporary calf, rebacked, first edition. Howes 186-629 1974 £48

BORLASE, EDMUND The History of the Execrable Irish Rebellion. 1680. Folio, old calf, rebacked. Quaritch 939-612 1974 £80

BORLASE, W. C. The Dolmens of Ireland. 1897. 3 vols., roy. 8vo., orig. buckram, illus. Quaritch 939-613 1974 £75

BORN, ESTHER The New Architecture in Mexico. New York, 1937. Tall 4to., illus., cloth. Minters 37-851 1973 $27.50

BORN, MAX Der Aufbau der Materie. Berlin, 1920. 8vo., orig. pictured wrappers, illus., first edition. Schuman 37-29 1974 $75

BORN, MAX Optik. Berlin, 1933. 8vo., orig. cloth. Dawsons PM 245-99 1974 £10

BORN, MAX Probleme der Atomdynamik. Berlin, 1926. 8vo., orig. printed wrappers. Dawsons PM 245-98 1974 £10

BORNMULLER, J.   Symbolae ad Floram Anatolicam. Berlin, 1940. 8vo., wrappers. Wheldon 129-1052 1974 £7.50

BORRADAILE, L. A.   The Animal and Its Environment. 1923. 8vo., cloth, scarce, plates. Wheldon 131-416 1974 £7.50

BORROW, G.   The Bible in Spain. London, 1843. 3 vols., 12mo., half calf, gilt, morocco labels, first edition. Bow Windows 62-107 1974 £24

BORROW, G.   The Bible in Spain. London, 1843. 3 vols., 8vo., orig. cloth, worn, third edition. Bow Windows 62-108 1974 £8

BORROW, GEORGE   The Bible in Spain. 1843. 3 vols., rebound, buckram, labels, third edition. Covent 55-245 1974 £15

BORROW, GEORGE   Celtic Bards, Chiefs and Kings. 1928. Demy 8vo., first edition, fine, orig. cloth. Broadhurst 24-1378 1974 £6

BORROW, GEORGE   Lavengro. 1851. 3 vols., new half calf, first edition. Allen 216-217 1974 $35

BORROW, GEORGE   Lavengro. 1851. 3 vols., orig. cloth, foxing, rebacked. Covent 55-246 1974 £35

BORROW, GEORGE   Lavengro. 1851. 3 vols., orig. cloth, spines faded, printed labels rubbed, nice copy, ads at end of vols. 1 & 3, first edition. Covent 51-2198 1973 £45

BORROW, GEORGE   Lavengro; The Scholar-The Gypsy-The Priest. London, 1851. 3 vols., 12mo., half calf, frontispiece protrait, first edition. Goodspeed's 578-27 1974 $35

BORROW, GEORGE   Lavengro; The Scholar – The Gypsy – The Priest. London, 1851. 3 vols., orig. blue cloth, paper labels, good set, first edition. MacManus 224-47 1974 $55

BORROW, GEORGE   Lavengro. New York, 1937. Biblo & Tannen 210-832 1973 $7.50

BORTHWICK, J. D.   The Gold Hunters. New York, 1929. Blue cloth, fine, dust wrapper. Bradley 35-24 1974 $15

BOSANQUET, B.   The Principle of Individuality and Value. 1927. Scarce. Howes 185-1819 1974 £5.75

BOSANQUET, EUSTACE F.   English Printed Almanacks and Prognostications. London, 1917. 4to., orig. holland-backed boards, first edition. Dawsons PM 10-71 1974 £26

BOSANQUET, HELEN   The Strength of the People. 1903. Scarce, second revised edition. Howes 186-1359 1974 £5.75

BOSANQUET, THEODORA   Paul Valery. 1933. 12mo., portrait, soiled. Covent 55-1486 1974 £5.25

BOSCOVICH, RUDJER JOSIP   De Cycloide et Logistica. Rome, 1745. 8vo., dec. boards, first edition. Dawsons PM 245-101 1974 £120

BOSCOVICH, RUDJER JOSIP   De Iride et Aurora Boreali Carmina. 1747. Small 4to., contemporary vellum, boards, inscription, rare, first edition. Zeitlin 235-29 1974 $250

BOSCOVICH, RUDJER JOSIP   Theoria Philosophiae Naturalis. Venice, 1763. 4to., contemporary half sheep, gilt, fine, first Venetian Edition. Dawsons PM 245-102 1974 £260

BOSCOVICH, RUDJER JOSIP   A Theory of Natural Philosophy. Chicago and London, 1922. Folio, orig. cloth, first English edition, fine. Gurney 66-32 1974 £65

BOSCOVICH, RUDJER JOSIP   A Theory of Natural Philosophy. London and Chicago, 1922. Folio, orig. cloth, first English edition. Gurney 64-33 1974 £65

BOSCOVICH, RUDJER JOSIP   Trigonometria Sphaerica. Rome, 1745. 8vo., printed boards, presentation copy, inscribed. Dawsons PM 245-100 1974 £160

BOSE, JAGADIS CHUNDER   Comparative Electro-Physiology. London, New York, 1907. 8vo., orig. black buckram, presentation copy, inscribed, first edition. Dawsons PM 245-103 1974 £12

BOSE, JAGADIS CHUNDER   The Physiology of the Ascent of Sap. 1923. 8vo., buckram, scarce. Wheldon 131-1116 1974 £5

BOSE, JAGADIS CHUNDER   Plant Autographs and Their Revelations. 1927. 8vo., cloth, portrait. Wheldon 128-1080 1973 £5

BOSE, JAGADIS CHUNDER   Researches on Irritability of Plants. 1913. 8vo., cloth, scarce. Wheldon 131-1117 1974 £5

BOSE, JAGADIS CHUNDER   Response in the Living and Non-Living. London, 1922. 8vo., orig. blue buckram. Dawsons PM 249-82 1974 £4

BOSQ, JACQUES DU   The Accomplish'd Woman. London, 1753. 2 vols., 12mo., contemporary mottled calf. Dawsons PM 252-73 1974 £95

BOSSCHERE, JEAN DE   Christmas Tales of Flanders. London, 1917. Large 4to., cloth, illus. Minters 37-491 1973 $16

BOSSCHERE, JEANE DE   The Enclosed Door. London, 1927. 8vo., cloth, illus., orig. dust wrappers. Minters 37-490 1973 $12

BOSSE, ABRAHAM   Traicte des Manieres de Graver en Taille Douce Sur l'Airin. Paris, 1645. 8vo., contemporary mottled calf, gilt, plates, first edition. Dawsons PM 10-73 1974 £200

BOSSE, ABRAHAM   Traicte des Manieres de Graver en Taille Douce sur l'Airin. Paris, 1645. 8vo., contemporary limp vellum, plates, first edition. Harper 213-23 1973 $900

BOSSERT, HELMUTH THEODOR   The Art of Ancient Crete. London, 1937. Crown 4to., orig. buckram, scarce, illus. Smith 194-87 1974 £15

BOSSEWELL, JOHN   Workes of Armorie. 1572. Small 4to., illus., early full calf, rebacked, first edition. Howes 186-1620 1974 £210

BOSSLER, ULRICH   Ain Schoner Dialogus Oder Gesprech des Appostolicums. (Augsburg, 1521). Small 4to., modern dark blue morocco, gilt, slip case, very fine, rare. Schafer 8-105 1973 sFr. 1,300

BOSSUET, JACQUES-BENIGNE   Histoire des Variations des Eglises Protestantes. Paris, 1760. 3 vols., 8vo., full leather, gilt spine, occasional stains, else fine. Schumann 499-15 1974 sFr 240

BOSSUET, LOUIS AUGUST NAPOLEON   Catalogue des Livres Relatifs a l'Histoire de la Ville de Paris et de ses Environs. Paris, 1888. 8vo., wrappers, uncut, unopened. Kraus B8-17 1974 $35

BOSTON, THOMAS   Human Nature. New York, 1811. Leather, worn, first New York edition. Hayman 57-42 1974 $15

BOSTON ATHENAEUM   A Catalogue of the Library of. 1845-51. 8vo., 2 vols., roxburghe. Quaritch 939-435 1974 £20

THE BOSTON Common. Boston, 1838. Orig. cloth, frontispiece, blindstamped. Dawson's 424-190 1974 $25

BOSTON, One Hundred Years a City. Boston, 1922. First edition, photos, 8vo., illus., fine. Current BW9-383 1974 $14

BOSWELL, JAMES   An Account of Corsica. Glasgow, 1768. 8vo., map, first edition. Quaritch 936-21 1974 £50

BOSWELL, JAMES   Boswelliana. London, 1874. 8vo., orig. blue cloth, portrait, first edition. Dawsons PM 252-572 1974 £6.25

BOSWELL, JAMES   The Journal of a Tour to the Hebrides. London, 1785. 8vo., contemporary calf, second edition. Dawsons PM 252-558 1974 £35

BOSWELL, JAMES   The Journal of a Tour to the Hebrides. London, 1786. 8vo., contemporary tree calf, third edition. Dawsons PM 252-559 1974 £18

BOSWELL, JAMES   The Journal of a Tour to the Hebrides. London, 1807. 8vo., new half calf, fourth edition. Dawsons PM 252-560 1974 £15

BOSWELL, JAMES   The Journal of a Tour to the Hebrides. London, 1813. 8vo., contemporary calf, sixth edition. Dawsons PM 252-561 1974 £12

BOSWELL, JAMES   Journal of a Tour to the Hebrides with Samuel Johnson. 1936. 4to., plates, boxed, limited edition. Allen 216-1983 1974 $15

BOSWELL, JAMES   Letters of. London, 1857. 8vo., orig. cloth, first edition. Dawsons PM 252-571 1974 £5

BOSWELL, JAMES   Life of Samuel Johnson. 4to., 2 vols., contemporary half calf, first edition. Quaritch 936-22 1974 £350

BOSWELL, JAMES   The Life of Samuel Johnson. London, 1791. 2 vols., 4to., contemporary tree calf, fine. Dawsons PM 252-563 1974 £820

BOSWELL, JAMES   The Life of Samuel Johnson. Dublin, 1792. 3 vols., 8vo., contemporary mottled calf, scarce, first Dublin edition. Dawsons PM 252-564 1974 £45

BOSWELL, JAMES   The Life of Samuel Johnson. London, 1804. 4 vols., contemporary tree calf, fourth edition. Dawsons PM 252-565 1974 £27.50

BOSWELL, JAMES   The Life of Samuel Johnson. Boston, 1807. First American edition, 3 vols., portrait frontis., old sheep bindings heavily rubbed, ex-library, hinges weak. Current BW9-207 1974 $17.50

BOSWELL, JAMES   The Life of Samuel Johnson. London, 1819. 4 vols., 12mo., contemporary tree calf, new edition. Dawsons PM 252-566 1974 £25

BOSWELL, JAMES   The Life of Samuel Johnson. London, 1827. 8vo., contemporary half morocco, illus. Dawsons PM 252-567 1974 £7

BOSWELL, JAMES   The Life of Samuel Johnson. 1831. 5 vols., full rose calf gilt, labels, new edition. Howes 186-278 1974 £31

BOSWELL, JAMES   The Life of Samuel Johnson. 1831. 8vo., 5 vols., half hard grained morocco, gilt, frontis. Quaritch 936-315 1974 £20

BOSWELL, JAMES   Life of Johnson, Including Journal of Tour to Hebrides. 1887. 6 vols., plates, spines worn. Allen 216-2034 1974 $25

BOSWELL, JAMES   The Life of Samuel Johnson. London, 1888-89. 3 vols., 8vo., frontis., orig. cloth, second edition. Bow Windows 62-109 1974 £10

BOSWELL, JAMES   The Life of Samuel Johnson. 1907. 4to., 2 vols., cloth gilt, plates, illus., English first edition. Covent 56-740 1974 £15

BOSWELL, JAMES   The Life of Samuel Johnson. 1925. Cloth, gilt, 2 vols., plates, illus., English first edition. Covent 56-741 1974 £15

BOSWELL, JOHN   A Method of Study. London, 1738-43. 2 parts in 2 vols., first edition, 8vo., contemporary calf. Ximenes 36-27 1974 $65

BOSWELL, PEYTON, JR.   Modern American Painting. New York, 1940. 4to., 89 full color plates. Biblo & Tannen 214-45 1974 $12.50

BOSWORTH, JOSEPH   A Compendious Anglo-Saxon and English Dictionary. London, 1849. Orig. cl., very good copy. Jacobs 24-64 1974 $15

BOSWORTH, NEWTON   Hochelaga Depicta. Montreal, 1839. Map, illus., faded. Hood's 103-760 1974 $150

BOSWORTH, T. O.   Geology of the Mid-Continent Oilfields Kansas, Oklahoma and North Texas. New York, 1920. 8vo., cloth, illus. Wheldon 131-973 1974 £5

BOSWORTH, T. O.   Geology of the Tertiary and Quaternary Periods. 1922. 8vo., cloth, plates, scarce. Wheldon 130-908 1974 £10

THE BOTANICAL Keepsake. London, 1846. 8vo., contemporary morocco, gilt, plates, prize label. Smith 193-4 1973 £15

BOTKIN, BENJAMIN ALBERT   The American Play-Party Song with a Collection of Oklahoma Texts and Tunes. Lincoln, 1937. 8vo., wrapper. Butterfield 8-443 1974 $20

BOTSFORD, G. W.   Hellenic Civilization. New York, 1920. Rear inner hinge split. Biblo & Tannen 214-592 1974 $12.50

BOTT, ALAN   This was England. New York, 1931. 4to., black cloth, illus., first edition. Rich Summer-104 1974 $10

BOTT, ALAN   This Was England - Manners and Customs of the Ancient Victorians. 1931. Illus. Austin 61-126 1974 $12.50

BOTTARI, G.   Dialoghi Sopra le Tre Art del Disegno. Lucca, 1754. 8vo., contemporary boards. Quaritch 940-37 1974 £25

BOTTOMLEY, GORDON   Gruach & Britain's Daughter. 1921. One of 50 numbered copies signed by author, fine, full buckram, first edition. Covent 51-2200 1973 £12.60

BOTTOMLEY, GORDON   Grauch and Britain's Daughter. London, 1921. No. 7 of edition limited to 60 copies, white cloth, pict. gilt design on front cover & backstrip, small damp stain on cover, nice. Ross 87-78 1974 $85

BOTTOMLEY, GORDON   Gruach & Britain's Daughter. 1922. New edition, author's signed presentation inscription, very good copy. Covent 51-2201 1973 £10.50

BOTTOMLEY, GORDON   Scenes and Plays. 1929. Plates, presentation copy, inscribed, English first edition. Covent 56-1580 1974 £35

BOTTOMLEY, GORDON   A Vision of Giorgione. 1922. One of 50 numbered copies signed by author, nice copy, full buckram. Covent 51-2202 1973 £10

BOTTOMLEY, GORDON   A Vision of Giorgione. London, 1922. First collected English edition, green cloth, front cover blind stamped, some staining inside covers, slight foxing, nice. Ross 87-79 1974 $40

BOTTOMLEY, HORATIO   Songs of the Cell. 1928. Presentation copy inscribed by author, boards, covers little worn, very good copy, scarce, first edition. Covent 51-570 1973 £5.25

BOTTONE, S. R.   Galvanic Batteries, Their Theory, Construction and Use. 1902. Illus. Covent 55-1294 1974 £5.25

BOUCHARD, MADDALENA   Recueil de Cent-Trent-Trois Oiseaux. Rome, 1775. Very large 4to., contemporary boards, worn, stains, rare. Traylen 79-102 1973 £3,750

BOUCHARLAT, JEAN LOUIS   An Elementary Treatise on the Differential and Integral Calculus. Cambridge, 1828. 8vo., contemporary half calf, fine, first edition. Dawsons PM 245-104 1974 £10

BOUCHER, ANTHONY   The Case of the Crumpled Knave. New York, 1939. 8vo., orig. cloth, first edition. Rota 190-187 1974 £5

BOUCHER, F.   Les Boiseries du Musee Carnavalet. Paris, n.d. Roy. folio, plates, unbound in linen backed folder, second edition. Quaritch 940-572 1974 £20

BOUCHETTE, JOSEPH   A Topographical Description of the Province of Lower Canada. London, 1815. New green cloth, orig. leather label, scarce, first edition. Bradley 35-52 1974 $330

BOUCHETTE, JOSEPH   A Topographical Description of the Province of Lower Canada. London, 1815. Roy. 8vo., plates, orig. card cover. Hood's 103-761 1974 $175

BOUCHETTE, JOSEPH   Topographical Dictionary of the Province of Lower Canada. London, 1831. Marbled boards, frontispiece. Hood's 103-762 1974 $175

BOUCHOTTE   Les Regles du Dessein et du Lavis. 1754. 8vo., plates, contemporary calf. Quaritch 940-495 1974 £35

BOUCICAULT, DION   Foul Play. Ticknor & Fields. 1868. 136p., illus. Austin 51-141 1973 $15

BOUCICAULT, DION   Foul Play. London, 1868. 8vo., half roan, first edition. Emerald 50-75 1974 £5

BOUDIER, E.   Icones Mycologicae ou Iconographie des Champignons de France. Paris, 1905-11. 4 vols., roy. 4to., full contemporary morocco, plates, rare. Wheldon 131-25 1974 £1,250

BOUDOU, ADRIEN   Le Saint-Siege et La Russie. Paris, 1922-25. 2 vols., roy. 8vo., buckram, scarce. Howes 185-992 1974 £20

BOUE, AMI   Essai Geologique sur l'Ecosse. Paris, (1820). 8vo., sprinkled calf, red morocco label, gilt, fine, scarce, first edition. Zeitlin 235-30 1974 $250

BOUGARD, LE SIEUR R.   The Little Sea Torch. London, 1801. Folio, orig. vellum-backed marbled boards, plates, maps, first edition. Hammond 201-695 1974 £425

BOUGAUD, L. E.   History of St. Vincent de Paul. 1899. 2 vols., orig. cloth, labels, frontispieces. Howes 185-1746 1974 £8

BOUGEANT, GUILLAUME HYACINTHE   A Philosophical Amusement Upon the Language of Beasts. 1739. 8vo., unbound. Hill 126-22 1974 £12.50

BOUGHTON, JAMES   A Genealogy of the Families of John Rockwell, of Stamford, Conn., 1641, and Ralph Keeler, of Hartford, Conn., 1639. New York, 1903. Orig. binding. Butterfield 10-268 1974 $50

BOUGHTON, RUTLAND   The Immortal Hour. 1920. 4to., label, orig. wrappers, signed. Smith 194-392 1974 £5

BOUGUER, PIERRE   Optice de Diversis Lvminis Gradibvs. (1762). 4to., contemporary marbled paper boards, plates. Zeitlin 235-31 1974 $125

BOUGUER, PIERRE   Traite d'Optique sur la Gradation de la Lumiere. Paris, 1760. 4to., contemporary mottled calf, gilt, first edition. Dawsons PM 245-105 1974 £80

BOUHOURS, DOMINIQUE   The Life of St. Ignatius. 1686. Small 8vo., contemporary calf, rebacked, sole English edition. Howes 185-1285 1974 £35

BOUILHET, LOUIS   Helene Peyron. Paris, 1858. 12mo., orig. wrapper. L. Goldschmidt 42-164 1974 $15

BOUILLE, FRANCOIS CLAUDE AMOUR, MARQUIS DE   Memoirs. 1797. 8vo., contemporary tree calf, rebacked, first edition in English. Dawsons PM 251-175 1974 £25

BOUILLET, MARIE NICOLAS   Dictionnaire Universel des Sciences. Paris, 18-54. 4to., 2 vols., dark green quarter calf, first edition. Dawsons PM 245-106 1974 £18

BOUILLY, JEAN NICOLAS   Contes a ma Fille. Paris, 1818. 2 vols., 12mo., contemporary calf, spines gilt, slightly rubbed, engraved plates, ads at end. George's 610-83 1973 £12.50

BOUISSON, E. F.   Traite Theorique et Pratique. Paris, 1850. 8vo., old quarter roan, illus., first edition. Gurney 64-34 1974 £35

BOULAY, J. N.   Flore Pliocene du Mont Dore. Paris, 1892. 4to., orig. wrappers, plates. Wheldon 128-948 1973 £7.50

BOULENGER, E. G.   Apes and Monkeys. 1936. 8vo., cloth, illus., scarce. Wheldon 131-476 1974 £7.50

BOULENGER, G. A.   Catalogue of Fishes in the British Museum, Vol. 1, Perciform Fishes. 1895. 8vo., orig. cloth, plates, very scarce, second edition. Wheldon 128-621 1973 £10

BOULENGER, G. A.   Catalogue of the Fresh-Water Fishes of Africa. 1909-1916. 4 vols., signatures, cloth bound. Bow Windows 64-32 1974 £55

BOULENGER, G. A.   Catalogue of the Lizards in the British Museum. 1885-87. 3 vols., 8vo., orig. cloth, plates, extremely scarce, second edition. Wheldon 128-619 1973 £55

BOULENGER, G. A.   The Snakes of Europe. 1913. 8vo., cloth, text-figures, plates, very scarce. Wheldon 128-620 1973 £7.50

BOULESTIN, X. MARCEL   Herbs, Salads, Seasonings. London, 1930. 1st ed. Biblo & Tannen 213-846 1973 $10

BOULGER, D. C.   The Battle of the Boyne . . . . the War in Ireland. London, 1911. 8vo., cloth boards. Emerald 50-76 1974 £7.50

BOULGER, D. C.   The History of China. London, 1898. 2 vols., 8vo., map, orig. cloth, plates, frayed, new and revised edition. Bow Windows 62-110 1974 £10.50

BOULGER, G. S.   Familiar Trees. n.d. Crown 8vo., 3 vols., cloth, plates, illus. Wheldon 130-1543 1974 £5

BOULTBEE, R.   Pilgrimages and Personalities. London, 1924. Frontis., illus. Hood's 102-3 1974 $10

BOULTING, WILLIAM   Woman in Italy. Plates, scarce. Howes 186-632 1974 £6

BOULTON, A. C. F.   Adventures, Travels and Politics. London, 1939. Hood's 104-244 1974 $10

BOULTON, W. B.   The History of White's. 1892. 2 vols., 4to., plates, cloth, limited numbered edition. Quaritch 939-491 1974 £20

BOURDALOUE, LOUIS   A Collection of Sermons and Other Works. 1773. 15 vols., contemporary calf, gilt. Howes 185-994 1974 £25

BOURDEILLE, PIERRE DE, SEIGNEUR DE BRANTOME
Please turn to
BRANTOME, PIERRE DE BOURDEILLE, SEIGNEUR DE

BOURDET, M.   Soins Faciles Pour la Proprete de la Bouche et Pourla Conservation des Dents. Lausanne, 1782. Modern boards. Rittenhouse 46-696 1974 $155

BOURDILLON, F. W.   The Early Editions of the Roman de la Rose. London, 1906-13. 2 works in 1 vol., 4to., contemporary blue half morocco, fine, gilt, uncut. Dawsons PM 10-74 1974 £43

BOURDOT, H.   Hymenomycetes de France. Sceaux, 1927. Roy 8vo., half buckram. Wheldon 129-1156 1974 £15

BOURGERY, D. M. P.   A Treatise on Lesser Surgery. Philadelphia, 1834. Staining. Rittenhouse 46-94 1974 $10

BOURGET, PAUL   Essais. Paris, 1883-86. 2 vols., 12mo., three qurter dark blue morocco, gilt, uncut, first edition. L. Goldschmidt 42-166 1974 $90

BOURGOING, J. DE   English Miniatures. 1928. 4to., plates, cloth, gilt, limited, numbered. Quaritch 940-38 1974 £45

BOURINOT, A. S.   Rhymes Of the French Regime. Toronto, 1937. Hood's 103-704 1974 $15

BOURINOT, A. S.   Under the Sun, Poems. Toronto, 1939. Hood's 103-706 1974 $12.50

BOURINOT, J. G.   Cape Breton and Its Memorials of the French Regime. 1891. Illus., folding plans, card cover. Hood's 102-177 1974 $25

BOURKE, ULICK J.   The College Irish Grammar. Dublin, 1856. 8vo., cloth boards. Emerald 50-77 1974 £5

BOURNE, EDWARD G.   A Two Years' Journal in New York and Part of Its Territories in America. Cleveland, 1902. 8vo., boards, limited. Saddleback 14-571 1974 $20

BOURNE, H. R. FOX   English Newspapers. 1887. 2 vols., thick 8vo., orig. cloth, orig. edition. Howes 186-38 1974 £12.50

BOURNE, H. R. FOX   A Memoir of Sir Philip Sidney. 1862. Spine worn, hinges weak, bookplate, first edition. Covent 51-1696 1973 £5.25

BOURNE, JOHN   The History and Description of the Great Western Railway. 1846. Imp. folio, buckram, fine, plates. Quaritch 939-74 1974 £500

BOURNE, JOHN   A Treatise on the Screw Propeller. London, 1855.
4to., orig. cloth, recased, plates, second edition. Hammond 201-795 1974 £25

BOUSFIELD, H. T. W.   The God With Four Arms and Other Stories.
London, 1942. 1st ed. Biblo & Tannen 210-570 1973 $15

BOUSSINGAULT, J. B.   Memoires de Chimie Agricole et de Physiologie.
Paris, 1854. 8vo., half calf, folding plates, scarce. Wheldon 128-1642 1973
£30

BOUSSUET, FRANCOIS   De Natura Aquatilium Carmen, in Universam
Gulielmi Rondeletii . . . Quam de Piscibus Marinis Scripsit Historiam. Lyons,
1558. 2 parts in 1, 4to., woodcuts, late 17th century half calf, richly gilt back,
first edition, fine, rare. Schafer 10-119 1974 sFr 2,200

BOUTCHER, WILLIAM   A Treatise On Forest Trees. Edinburgh, 1775.
4to., old calf, rebacked, scarce, first edition. Traylen 79-6 1973 £40

BOUTELL, CHARLES   Heraldry. London, 1864. 8vo., half morocco,
plates, third edition. Hammond 201-412 1974 £7.50

BOUTET DE MONVEL, MAURICE   Chansons de France Pour Les Petits Francais.
Paris, n.d. Oblong 4to., illus. Frohnsdorff 16-112 1974 $20

BOUTET DE MONVEL, MAURICE   Joan of Arc. Philadelphia, 1918. Oblong
4to., illus. Frohnsdorff 16-113 1974 $15

BOUVIER, L.   Flore des Alpes de la Suisse et de la Savoie.
Paris, 1882. Crown 8vo., scarce, second edition. Wheldon 130-1130 1974
£5

BOVILL, M.   'Roddy Owen'. 1897. Demy 8vo., first
edition, scarce, portraits, maps, orig. cloth, fine. Broadhurst 24-1581 1974 £8

BOWDICH, THOMAS EDWARD   Taxidermy. 1821. Post 8vo., orig. boards,
rebacked, plates, rare, second edition. Wheldon 130-337 1974 £10

BOWDITCH, N. I.   An Argument for a Catholic Church on the
Jail Lands. Wilson, 1853. Austin 62-728 1974 $17.50

BOWEN, ALICE M.   The Story of Savanna Early Settlement.
Savanna, 1928. 12mo., cloth. Saddleback 14-369 1974 $12.50

BOWEN, CHARLES S. C.   The "Alabama" Claims and Arbitration
Considered from a Legal Point of View. London, 1868. Quarter red morocco,
marbled boards scuffed, interior fine. Current BW9-351 1974 $17.50

BOWEN, E.   A Complete System of Geography. London,
1747. Vol. 1 of 2 vols., contemporary vellum. Smith 193-103 1973 £100

BOWEN, ELIZABETH   The Death of the Heart. 1938. English first
edition. Covent 56-170 1974 £5.25

BOWEN, ELIZABETH   The Fothergill Omnibus for Which Seventeen
Eminent Authors Have Written Short Stories Upon One and the Same Plot.
London, 1931. Orig. green leather, spine faded, first edition, one of 250
numbered copies, signed by all contributors, fine. MacManus 224-48 1974 $75

BOWEN, ELIZABETH   The Hotel. New York, 1928. First American
edition, very nice copy, orig. cloth, partially defective d.w. Crane 7-23 1974
£6

BOWEN, ELIZABETH   The Hotel. New York, 1928. 8vo., orig.
cloth, first American edition. Rota 190-63 1974 £7.50

BOWEN, ELIZABETH   The Last September. 1929. Dust wrapper,
fine. Covent 55-252 1974 £25

BOWEN, ELIZABETH   The Last September. 1929. Orig. cloth,
scarce, faded, first edition. Rota 188-113 1974 £15

BOWEN, ELIZABETH   Seven Winters. Dublin, 1942. One of 450
numbered copies, cloth backed boards, title label missing from spine, else very
good. Covent 51-2203 1973 £20

BOWEN, ELIZABETH   Seven Winters. Dublin, 1942. Orig. cloth,
bookplate, first edition. Rota 188-114 1974 £25

BOWEN, FRANCIS   Sir William Phipps. New York, 1845. 12mo.,
text foxed. Biblo & Tannen 213-84 1973 $7.50

BOWEN, I.   The Statues of Wales. 1908. Demy 8vo., orig.
cloth, fine. Broadhurst 24-1380 1974 £8

BOWEN, JAMES C.   Dissertatio Inauguralis de Sanguine Mittendo.
Edinburgh, 1809. 8vo., orig. wrappers, chipped & torn, text clear and uncut.
Current BW9-574 1974 $20

BOWEN, L. P.   The Days of Makemie. Philadelphia, (1885).
8vo., orig. bindings. Butterfield 8-210 1974 $10

BOWEN, MARJORIE   The Bishop of Hell and Other Stories. London,
1949. 1st ed. Biblo & Tannen 210-571 1973 $10

BOWEN, MARJORIE   The Cockney's Mirror. New York, 1936.
32 plates. Biblo & Tannen 213-302 1973 $15

BOWEN, MARJORIE   Ethics in Modern Art. 1939. 12mo., wrappers,
spine browned. Covent 51-2545 1973 £5.25

BOWEN, STELLA   Drawn from Life: Reminiscences. c. 1942.
Plates, hinges weak, very good copy, torn d.w., scarce, first edition. Covent
51-2204 1973 £7.50

BOWEN'S Automobile and Sportsmen's Guide for Michigan.   Indianapolis, (1916).
Suede, moderate wear, maps. Hayman 59-379 1974 $10

BOWER, F. O.   The Origin of a Land Flora. 1908. 8vo.,
cloth, scarce. Wheldon 130-995 1974 £7.50

BOWERS, CLEMENT GRAY   Rhododendrons and Azaleas. New York, 1936.
4to., color plates, fine, d.w., orig. edition, orig. cloth. Gregory 44-23
1974 $20

BOWERS, D. N.   Seventy Years in Norton County. Norton, 1942.
Cloth, fine, first edition. Putnam 126-306 1974 $20

BOWES, ROBERT   A Catalogue of Books Printed at or Relating to
the University Town & County of Cambridge from 1521 to 1893 With
Bibliographical and Biographical Notes. Cambridge, 1894. Roy. 8vo., three
quarter morocco. Kraus B8-31 1974 $65

BOWKER, B.   Lancashire under the Hammer. 1928. English
first edition. Covent 56-632 1974 £15

BOWKER, R. R.   The Arts of Life. Boston & New York, 1900.
Vellum back. Ballinger 1-3 1974 $10

BOWLES, CARINGTON   The Artist's Assistant in the Study and Practice
of Mechanical Sciences. London & Birmingham, (c. 1800). 8vo., contemporary
sheep, rebacked, plates. Quaritch 940-39 1974 £50

BOWLES, CARINGTON   Bowles's Principles of Drawing. (c. 1810).
Folio, orig. wrappers, buckram, plates, improved seventh edition. Quaritch
940-40 1974 £120

BOWLES, CAROLINE   The Birth-Day, a Poem in Three Parts. 1836.
First edition, f'cap. 8vo., half red calf, fine. Broadhurst 24-570 1974 £5

BOWLES, CAROLINE   Chapters on Churchyards. 1829. First edition,
2 vols., f'cap. 8vo., half red calf, fine. Broadhurst 24-569 1974 £10

BOWLES, E. A.   My Garden in Spring. 1914. 8vo., orig. dec.
cloth, coloured and plain plates, very scarce. Wheldon 128-1444 1973 £10

BOWLES, J. L.   Japanese Enamels. 1886. Imp. 8vo.,
plates, cloth, recased, limited edition. Quaritch 940-376 1974 £30

BOWLES, W.   Introduccion a la Historia Natural y a la Geo-
grafia Fisica de Espana. Madrid, 1789. Contemporary calf, scarce, third edition. Wheldon 130-271 1974 £20

BOWLES, WILLIAM LISLE   The Life of Thomas Ken. 1830. 2 vols., orig.
boards, plates, uncut, first edition. Howes 185-29 1974 £14

BOWLKER, CHARLES   The Art of Angling. Birmingham, 1792. 8vo., half calf, gilt, illus. Hammond 201-74 1974 £38

BOWMAN, I.   Desert Trails of Atacama. New York, 1924. Roy. 8vo., cloth, frontispiece, map, illus. Wheldon 128-181 1973 £7.50

BOWMAN, ISAIAH   Limits of Land Settlements. 1937. Orig. ed. Austin 62-57 1974 $12.50

BOWMAN, ISAIAH   Limits of Land Settlement. 1937. Maps, orig. edition. Austin 57-100 1974 $12.50

BOWMAN, ISAIAH   The Pioneer Fringe. New York, 1931. 8vo., orig. bindings. Butterfield 8-691 1974 $20

BOWMAN, SAMUEL MILLARD   Sherman and His Campaigns. New York, 1865. First edition, three quarter calf, inner hinge split. Biblo & Tannen 213-25 1973 $15

BOWMAN, SAMUEL MILLARD   Sherman and His Campaigns. New York, 1865. Three quarter calf, marbled boards, first edition. Bradley 35-342 1974 $24

BOWMAN, W. D.   Bristol and America. n.d. 4to., orig. cloth, plates, mint. Broadhurst 23-1323 1974 £12

BOWMAN, W. D.   Bristol and America: A Record of the First Settlers in the Colonies of North America, 1654-1685. nd. (c. 1925). Demy 4to., plates, mint, orig. cloth. Broadhurst 24-1381 1974 £12

BOWRING, J.   Minor Morals for Young People. 1834-35. Vols. 1 and 2 only in 1, 12mo., half calf, slightly soiled and rubbed, plates, frontispiece. George's 610-84 1973 £7.50

BOWRING, JOHN 1792-1872 The Decimal System. London, 1854. 8vo., orig. brown cloth, plates, first edition. Dawsons PM 245-108 1974 £20

BOWYER, WILLIAM   The Origin of Printing. London, 1776. 8vo., orig. boards, uncut, second edition. Dawsons PM 10-75 1974 £70

BOY SCOUTS OF AMERICA   Handbook For Scout Masters. 1913. Illus., first edition. Rinsland 58-900 1974 $42

BOYAJIAN, ZABELLE C.   Gilgamesh. 1924. 4to., orig. buckram gilt, plates, inscribed presentation, first edition. Howes 186-39 1974 £18

BOYARS, ARTHUR   Poems. 1944. Fine, dust wrapper, English first edition. Covent 56-172 1974 £5.25

BOYCE, ANNE OGDEN   Records of a Quaker Family. 1889. Roy. 8vo., orig. cloth, portraits. Howes 186-1648 1974 £6

BOYCE, ROBERT   Mosquito or Man. London, 1909. 8vo., orig. green cloth gilt, uncut, first edition. Dawsons PM 249-83 1974 £5

BOYD, A. S.   A Versailles Christmas-Tide. London, 1901. First edition, 8vo., pen and ink illus. by author, contents fine, minor cover wear and soiling. Current BW9-5 1974 $18.50

BOYD, ERNEST A.   Appreciations and Depreciations. 1918. First edition. Austin 61-128 1974 $12.50

BOYD, ERNEST A.   Ireland's Literary Renaissance. 1916. Roy. 8vo., first edition. Covent 55-911 1974 £15

BOYD, ERNEST A.   Ireland's Literary Renaissance. New York, 1922. 8vo., cloth boards. Emerald 50-82 1974 £6.50

BOYD, ERNEST A.   Literary Blasphemes. New York, 1927. Binding poor. Biblo & Tannen 213-730 1973 $9.50

BOYD, JAMES   Long Hunt. New York, 1930. Orig. cloth, first edition, one of 260 numbered copies, signed by author, boxed, fine, inscribed by author to John Stuart Groves with his bookplate. MacManus 224-49 1974 $30

BOYD, JOHN   Sir George Etienne Cartier, Bart, His Life and Times. Toronto, 1914. Inscribed by author. Hood's 102-227 1974 $45

BOYD, JOHN   A Summary of Canadian History from the Time of Cartier's Discovery to the Present Day. Toronto, 1869. Hood's 102-550 1974 $10

BOYD, JULIA   Bewick Gleanings. Newcastle, 1886. Black morocco, plates, signed. Dawson's 424-31 1974 $165

BOYD, LOUISE A.   Polish Countrysides. 1937. Austin 62-58 1974 $27.50

BOYD, THOMAS   Mad Anthony Wayne. New York, 1929. Small bookplate, deluxe edition, limited to 530 copies, signed by author, first edition, orig. binding. Butterfield 10-36 1974 $15

BOYEL, ROBERT   The Sceptical Chymist. London, 1661. Small 8vo., old (probably orig.) brown calf, rebacked, mended, half morocco case, first edition. Kraus 137-15 1974 $20,000

BOYER, ABEL   Boyer's Royal Dictionary Abridged: 1 French & English. 2 English & French. 1755. Old calf, corrected ninth edition. Allen 216-462 1974 $12.50

BOYER, ABEL   Dictionnaire Royal Francois. Lyon, 1768. 2 vols., 4to., contemporary speckled calf gilt. Smith 194-134 1974 £12

BOYER, ALEXIS   The Lectures of Boyer Upon Diseases of the Bones. London, 1804. 2 vols., 8vo., old-style boards, first edition in English. Schuman 37-30 1974 $145

BOYER, L.   Les Champignons Comestibles. Paris, 1891. Roy 8vo., orig. cloth, plates. Wheldon 129-1157 1974 £30

BOYER, MARY G.   Arizona in Literature: A Collection of the Best Writings of Arizona Authors from the Early Spanish Days to the Present Time. Glendale, 1935. Jenkins 61-128 1974 $15

BOYLE, CHARLES 4TH EARL OF ORRERY
Please turn to
ORRERY, CHARLES BOYLE, 4TH EARL OF

BOYLE, ELEANOR V.   Child's Play. Boston, 1860. 12mo., embossed cloth, gilt; all edges gilt., plates. Frohnsdorff 16-115 1974 $35

BOYLE, F.   About Orchids. 1893. 8vo., orig. cloth. Broadhurst 23-1091 1974 £6

BOYLE, F.   The Culture of Greenhouse Orchids. 1902. 8vo., cloth, illus., plates, scarce. Wheldon 129-1569 1974 £5

BOYLE, F.   The Culture of Greenhouse Orchids, Old System and New. 1902. 8vo., cloth, plates, illus., scarce. Wheldon 131-1610 1974 £5

BOYLE, JOHN   Proceedings of a Meeting of the Friends of Civil and Religious Liberty . . . at The City Hall In Washington City. Washington, 1826. Sewed, uncut, wrapper. Butterfield 10-317 1974 $12.50

BOYLE, JOHN F.   The Irish Rebellion of 1916. 1916. Name on fly, else fine, d.w., first edition. Covent 51-981 1973 £7.50

BOYLE, JOHN, 5TH EARL OF ORRERY
Please turn to
CORK AND ORRERY, JOHN BOYLE, 5TH EARL OF

BOYLE, ROBERT   A Discourse of Things Above Reason. London, 1681. Small 8vo., calf antique, fine, first edition, second issue. Dawsons PM 245-119 1974 £240

BOYLE, ROBERT   Experiments and Considerations Touching Colours. London, 1664. 8vo., vellum, gilt, first edition. Hammond 201-797 1974 £125

BOYLE, ROBERT   Experimenta et Considerationes de Coloribus. Geneva, 1680. 4to., modern cloth. Quaritch 940-41 1974 £30

BOYLE, ROBERT   General Heads for the Natural History of a Country. London, 1692. 12mo., contemporary sprinkled calf, rebacked. Zeitlin 235-303 1974 $775

BOYLE, ROBERT   Medicinal Experiments. London, 1692. 12mo., blind calf antique, first edition. Dawsons PM 249-85 1974 £195

BOYLE, ROBERT   Memoirs for the Natural History of the Humane Blood. London, 1683. 8vo., mottled calf, rebacked, gilt, first edition, second issue. Dawsons PM 249-84 1974 £750

BOYLE, ROBERT   New Experiments and Observations Made Upon the Icy Noctiluca. London, 1681/2. 8vo., crimson morocco, gilt, first edition. Dawsons PM 245-120 1974 £600

BOYLE, ROBERT   Origo Formarvm et Qvalitatvm. 1688. 4to., disbound, rare. Zeitlin 235-271 1974 $200

BOYLE, ROBERT   The Sceptical Chymist. London, 1661. Half morocco labels, contemporary calf, worn, fine, first edition. Dawsons PM 250-10 1974 £10,500

BOYLE, ROBERT   The Sceptical Chymist. Oxford, 1680. 8vo., contemporary sheep, second edition. Dawsons PM 245-110 1974 £725

BOYLE, ROBERT   The Works Of. London, 1772. Large 4to., 6 vols., contemporary calf, fine, gilt, second collected edition. Dawsons PM 245-121 1974 £285

BOYLE, WILLIAM   The Building Fund. Dublin, 1905. Wrappers, fine. Covent 55-253 1974 £6.30

BOYLES, KATE
Please turn to
BINGHAM, MRS. KATE (BOYLES)

BOYLESVE, RENE   Les Nouvelles Lecons d'Amour dans un Parc. Paris, 1924. 8vo., orig. wrapper, uncut, limited edition. L. Goldschmidt 42-167 1974 $12.50

BOYS, JOHN   General View of the Agriculture of the County of Kent. Brentford, 1794. 4to., boards, first edition. Hammond 201-5 1974 £35

BOYS, JOHN   Workes Of. 1629. Folio, old calf. Allen 213-1892 1973 $25

BOYS, THOMAS SHOTTER   Picturesque Architecture in Paris. London, 1839. Large folio, plates, orig. half red morocco gilt. Marlborough 70-40 1974 £550

BOYS, W.   Collections for an History of Sandwich in Kent. Canterbury, 1792. 4to., buckram. Quaritch 939-397 1974 £40

BOYS, W. F. A.   A Practical Treatise on the Office and Duties of Coroners. Toronto, 1864. Flyleaves & pages browned, spine mended. Hood's 102-4 1974 $30

BOYSE, JOSEPH   Vox Populi. London, 1690. 4to., modern boards, uncut, first edition. Dawsons PM 251-176 1974 £15

BOZMAN, JOHN LEEDS   History of Maryland. Baltimore, 1837. 2 vols., calf, ex-library. Putman 126-75 1974 $32

BOZMAN, JOHN LEEDS   A Sketch of the History of Maryland, During the First Three Years After Its Settlement. Baltimore, 1811. 12mo., leather. Saddleback 14-465 1974 $35

BRACCIOLINI, POGGIO-
Please turn to
POGGIO-BRACCIOLINI

BRACHET DE LA MILITIERE, THEOPHILE   The Victory of Truth for the Peace of the Church, to the King of Great Britain. The Hague, 1654. Second edition, clean and sound, lacks final blank, small 8vo., old vellum. Thomas 32-32 1974 £45

BRACKENRIDGE, H. M.   History of the Late War Between the United States and Great Britain. Baltimore, 1817. Plates, orig. binding, third revised edition. Hood's 102-90 1974 $70

BRACKENRIDGE, H. M.   History of the Late War Between the United States and Great Britain. Baltimore, 1817. Orig. binding, illus., revised third edition. Hood's 104-94 1974 $70

BRACKETT, F. P.   History of Pomona Valley, California. Los Angeles, 1920. 4to., half leather, illus., rebacked. Saddleback 14-42 1974 $65

BRACQ, J. C.   The Evolution of French Canada. New York, 1924. Hood's 104-911 1974 $10

BRADBECK, EMIL E.   Handbook of Basic Motion Picture Techniques. McGraw-Hill, 1950. 311p., illus., orig. unrev. ed. Austin 51-150 1973 $10

BRADBEER, B. M.   A Catalogue of the Valuabel Collection of Fine Old Porcelain. Yarmouth, 1873. Square 8vo., cloth, wrappers. Quaritch 940-625 1974 £25

BRADBURY, JOHN   Travels in the Interior of America in the Years, 1809-11. Liverpool, 1817. Three quarter leather, errata. Jenkins 61-232 1974 $137.50

BRADDON, MARY ELIZABETH
Please turn to
MAXWELL, MARY ELIZABETH (BRADDON)

BRADFORD, A. J.   History of Woodford County. Peoria, 1877. 12mo., black cloth, scarce. Putnam 126-162 1974 $90

BRADFORD, ALEXANDER W.   American Antiquities and Researches Into the Origin and History of the Red Race. New York and Boston, 1841. Orig. binding. Butterfield 10-6 1974 $25

BRADFORD, GAMALIEL   Early Days in Wellesley. Wellesley, 1929. 12mo., cloth. Saddleback 14-475 1974 $10

BRADFORD, ROARK   John Henry. Harper, 1939. 91p., illus. Austin 51-142 1973 $12.50

BRADFORD, SARAH H.   Scenes in the Life of Harriet Tubman. Auburn, 1869. Frontis. portrait, corners rubbed, orig. binding, scarce first edition. Butterfield 10-93 1974 $50

BRADFORD, WILLIAM   Bradford's History of Plymouth Plantation. Boston, 1900. 8vo., orig. cloth. Broadhurst 23-1617 1974 £12

BRADFORD, WILLIAM   Bradford's History "Of Plymouth Plantation". Boston, 1900. Med. 8vo., plates, orig. cloth, fine. Broadhurst 24-1582 1974 £12

BRADFORD, WILLIAM   Sketches of the Country, Character, and Costume, in Portugal and Spain. London, n.d. Folio, contemporary maroon morocco gilt, plates. Traylen 79-557A 1973 £200

BRADFORD, WILLIAM   Sketches of the Country, Character and Costume in Portugal and Spain, Made During the Campaign. (1813). Folio, plates, green morocco. Quaritch 940-42 1974 £420

BRADFORD, WILLIAM J. A.   Notes on the Northwest; of, The Valley of the Upper Mississippi. New York, 1846. First edition. slight wear, orig. cloth. Jenkins 61-234 1974 $47.50

BRADLEY, A. C.   Oxford Lectures on Poetry. 1934. Ex-library, second edition. Austin 61-129 1974 $12.50

BRADLEY, A. G.   Canada In the Twentieth Century. Westminster, 1903. Map, illus. Hood's 103-521 1974 $10

BRADLEY, A. G.   The Fight With France for North America. Westminster, 1900. Illus. Hood's 104-95 1974 $20

BRADLEY, C.   Good Sport Seen With Some Famous Packs 1885-1910. (n.d.). Plates, illus., corners and joints worn. Bow Windows 66-75 1974 £7.50

BRADLEY, DANIEL H.   Alameda County, California. N.P., c.1915. 12mo., wrapper. Saddleback 14-43 1974 $12.50

BRADLEY, EDWARD   The Adventures of the Mr. Verdant Green. Carleton, 1875. 3 vols. in 1, illus. Austin 54-102 1973 $12.50

BRADLEY, F. H.   The Principles of Logic. London, 1883. Biblo & Tannen 213-947 1973 $7.50

BRADLEY, JOHN H.   The Visitor's Guide to Knole. 1839. 8vo., orig. cloth. Broadhurst 23-1326 1974 £9

BRADLEY, KATHERINE HARRIS, d. 1914
Joint Author with Edith Cooper
Please turn to
FIELD, MICHAEL, PSEUD.

BRADLEY, RICHARD   The History of Succulent Plants: Historia Plantarum Succulentarum, Decades 1 and 2. 1716-17. 4to., contemporary calf backed boards, plates. Wheldon 131-1646 1974 £60

BRADLEY, RICHARD   The History of Succlent Plants. 1739. 4to., contemporary calf, plates, corrected second edition. Wheldon 131-1647 1974 £200

BRADLEY, RICHARD   Improvements of Planting & Gardening. 1731. Contemporary calf, copperplates, sixth edition. Smith 194-135 1974 £12

BRADLEY, RICHARD   New Improvements of Planting and Gardening. 1739. 3 parts in 1 vol., 8vo., contemporary calf, plates. Wheldon 131-1495 1974 £30

BRADLEY, RICHARD   A Philosophical Account of the Works of Nature. 1721. 4to., modern half calf, plates. Wheldon 129-69 1974 £65

BRADLEY, RICHARD   A Philosophical Account of the Works of Nature. 1721. 4to., contemporary calf, worn, rebacked in morocco, plates, scarce. Wheldon 128-11 1973 £65

BRADLEY, WILL   A Portfolio of Printing. Springfield, n.d. Wrappers. Dawson's 424-141 1974 $125

BRADLEY, WILLIAM ASPENWALL   Amicitia Amorque. New York, 1901. 12mo., printed boards, limited, first edition. Goodspeed's 578-28 1974 $25

BRADSHAW, G.   Maps of the Canals. Manchester, 1829-32. 4to., contemporary calf slipcases, first editions. Quaritch 939-75 1974 £325

BRADSHAW, GEORGE   Bradshaw's Railway Manual. 1865. 8vo., orig. cloth. Broadhurst 23-1213 1974 £8

BRADSHAW, JOHN   Concordance to Poetical Works of John Milton. 1894. Ex-library, buckram. Allen 216-1934 1974 $17.50

BRADSHAW, JOHN   A Concordance to the Poetical Works of John Milton. 1894. 8vo., orig. cloth. Broadhurst 23-266 1974 £5

BRADSHAW, R.   A Catalogue of the Bradshaw Collection of Irish Books. Cambridge, 1916. 3 vols., 8vo., cloth boards. Emerald 50-84 1974 £25

BRADY, CYRUS TOWNSEND   A Christmas When the West was Young. Chicago, 1913. Cloth and boards, marbled end sheets, gilt top, illus., 1st ed., autographed by author. Dykes 24-59 1974 $15

BRADY, G. S.   A Monograph of the Free and Semi-Parasitic Copepoda of the British Islands. 1878-80. 3 vols., 8vo., cloth, plates (some coloured), scarce. Wheldon 128-875 1973 £18

BRADY, G. S.   A Monograph of the Free and Semi-Parasitic Copepoda of the British Islands. 1878-80. 8vo., cloth, plates, scarce. Wheldon 130-850 1974 £18

BRADY, G. S.   A Monograph of the Post-Tertiary Entomostraca of Scotland. 1874. 4to., wrappers, plates. Wheldon 130-909 1974 £5

BRADY, G. S.   A Monograph of the Post-Tertiary Entomostraca of Scotland Including Species from England and Ireland. 1874. 4to., half calf, plates. Wheldon 131-974 1974 £15

BRADY, H. B.   A Monograph of Carboniferous and Permian Foraminifera. 1876. 4to., half morocco, plates. Wheldon 131-975 1974 £10

BRADY, JOHN G.   Report of the Governor of the District of Alaska to the Secretary of the Interior, 1897. Washington, 1897. Wrapper, large folding map. Jenkins 61-39 1974 $12.50

BRAGG, WILLIAM H.   The Crystalline State. London, 1933. Large 8vo., orig. cloth, gilt, first edition. Dawsons PM 245-123 1974 £10

BRAGG, WILLIAM H.   Studies in Radioactivity. London, 1912. 8vo., orig. cloth, first edition. Gurney 64-35 1974 £20

BRAGHT, TIELEMAN J. VAN   Het Bloedigh Tooneel der Doops-Gesinde en Weereloose Christenen. Dordrecht, 1660. 2 parts in 1 vol., very thick folio, contemporary blind-stamped calf, oak boards, raised bands, rare orig. edition. Harper 213-24 1973 $750

BRAID, JAMES   Neurypnology. London, 1843. 8vo., orig. cloth, first edition, fine. Gurney 66-33 1974 £275

BRAIKENRIDGE, WILLIAM   Exercitatio Geometrica de Descriptione Linear um Curvarum. London, 1733. 4to., contemporary calf, rebacked, stains. Bow Windows 62-115 1974 £18

BRAINERD, C. N.   My Diary; or, Three Weeks on the Wing. New York, 1868. Orig. printed wrappers, boxed. Jenkins 61-237 1974 $75

BRAITHWAITE, RICHARD   The British Moss-Flora. 1887-1895. 2 vols., plates, stains. Bow Windows 64-33 1974 £8.50

BRAITHWAITE, RICHARD   Some Rules and Orders for the Government of the House of an Earle. 1821. 4to., half roan. Quaritch 939-59 1974 £10.50

BRAITHWAITE, RICHARD   The Sphagnaceae. 1880. 8vo., cloth, plates. Wheldon 130-1240 1974 £12

BRAITHWAITE, RICHARD   The Sphagnaceae. 1880. Roy 8vo., orig. cloth, plates. Wheldon 129-1388 1974 £7.50

BRAMAH, ERNEST PSEUD.
Please turn to
SMITH, ERNEST BRAMAH

BRAMHALL, JOHN   Works. Oxford, 1842-45. 5 vols., orig. cloth, damp stained, standard edition. Howes 185-997 1974 £32.50

BRAMLEY, CHARLES   Adventures of a Social Detective. n.d. Cloth, illus., English first edition. Covent 56-313 1974 £10.50

BRAMSTON, JAMES   The Art of Politicks. London, 1729. 8vo., frontispiece, modern boards, first edition. Dawsons PM 252-74 1974 £36

BRANCH, ANNA H.   Sonnets from a Locked Box. Houghton, Mifflin, 1929. 126p. Austin 54-157 1973 $8.50

BRAND, FRANKLIN M.   The Wade Family: Monogalia County, Virginia, Now West Virginia. Morgantown, 1927. 8vo., cloth. Saddleback 14-793 1974 $35

BRAND, JOHN   The History and Antiquities of the Town and County of the Town of Newcastle upon Tyne. London, 1789. 4to., 2 vols., contemporary calf, gilt, first edition. Dawsons PM 251-9 1974 £160

BRAND, JOHN   Observations on the Popular Antiquities of Great Britain. 1849. 3 vols., orig. edition. Austin 61-132 1974 $17.50

BRAND, JOHN   Observations on Popular Antiquities. 1813. 2 vols., 4to., some foxing, contemporary half calf, gilt spines, black morocco labels. Bow Windows 66-76 1974 £22

BRAND, MAX   Brothers On the Trial. 1935. Dust wrapper, faded. Covent 55-1519 1974 £6.30

BRANDANE, JOHN   The Treasure, Rory Aforesaid, The Happy War. Houghton, Mifflin, 1928. 248p. Austin 51-143 1973 $10

BRANDE, W. T.   Outlines of Geology. 1829. 8vo., orig. boards, uncut, rare. Wheldon 130-910 1974 £25

BRANDENBURG, BROUGHTON   Imported Americans. Stokes, 1904. 303p., illus. Austin 62-59 1974 $12.50

BRANDENBURG, HANS   Der Moderne Tanz. Munich, 1921. 247p., illus. Austin 51-144 1973 $17.50

BRANDES, GEORGE   Main Currents in 19th Century Literature.
1906. 6 vols., portraits, contemporary half morocco gilt, orig. and best edition.
Howes 186-41 1974 £40

BRANDES, GEORGE   Main Currents in 19th Century Literature.
1924. 6 vols., plates. Allen 216-227 1974 $50

BRANDFORD, VICTOR   Interpretations and Forecasts. 1914. Thick
8vo., orig. cloth, scarce. Howes 186-1363 1974 £5

BRANDIS, D.   The Forest Flora of North West and Central
India. 1874. 8vo., half morocco, very scarce. Wheldon 128-1242 1973 £10

BRANDIS, D.   The Forest Flora of North West and Central
India. 1874. 8vo., new cloth, very scarce. Wheldon 128-1586 1973 £10

BRANDON, BRUCE   On the Bridge at Midnight. French, 1909.
132p., paper. Austin 51-145 1973 $8.50

BRANDON, RAPHAEL   An Analysis of Gothic Architecture. 1903.
2 vols., plates, illus., new edition. Marsden 37-79 1974 £8

BRANDT, H.   Alaska Bird Trails. Cleveland, 1943. Crown
4to., cloth, plates, scarce. Wheldon 130-473 1974 £20

BRANGWYN, F.   Belgium. 1916. 4to., orig. linen backed
boards, uncut, illus. Bow Windows 64-403 1974 £10

BRANGWYN, FRANK   A Book of Bridges. London, 1915. 4to.,
cloth, library stamp, plates, illus. Minters 37-493 1973 $28

BRANGWYN, FRANK   The Bridge, a Chapter in the History of Building.
1926. Plates, illus., faded. Marsden 37-80 1974 £10

BRANGWYN, FRANK   Catalogue of the Etched Work of. 1912.
Plates, cloth, buckram back. Marsden 39-57 1974 £24

BRANGWYN, FRANK   The Last Fight of the Revenge. (1908). Roy.
8vo., orig. cloth gilt, uncut, illus., plates, first edition. Howes 186-42
1974 £7.50

BRANK, MCDONOUGH & CO.   History of Macoupin County. Philadelphia,
1879. Folio, new red leather, gilt, fine. Putman 126-137 1974 $85

BRANN, W. C.   Brann, the Iconoclast. Texas 1905. 464p.,
in 2 vols. Austin 54-158 1973 $12.50

BRANNER, J. L.   Bibliography of Clays and the Ceramic Arts.
Washington, 1896. 8vo., half morocco. Quaritch 940-626 1974 £16

BRANNON, GEORGE   Brannon's Graphic Delineations. (1857).
Oblong 8vo., plates, orig. cloth, gilt. Quaritch 939-369 1974 £35

BRANNON, GEORGE   Brannon's Picture of the Isle of Wight. (1856).
8vo., orig. pictorial limp boards, cloth back. Quaritch 939-370 1974 £25

BRANNON, GEORGE   Vectis Scenery. Isle of Wight, 1848. 4to.,
contemporary half morocco, rubbed, plates. Traylen 79-339 1973 £40

BRANSON, ANN   Journal of Ann Branson. Philadelphia, 1892.
Cloth, fine. Hayman 57-370 1974 $12.50

BRANT, F. B.   Byways and Boulevards in and About Historic
Philadelphia. Philadelphia, 1926. Orig. drawings, illus., photos, first edition,
8vo., fine. Current BW9-407 1974 $22.50

BRANT, SEBASTIAN   Stultifera Nauis. London, 1570. Folio, 18th
century calf, fine, second English edition. Dawsons PM 252-75 1974 £1200

BRANTOME, PIERRE BOURDEILLE   Memoires. Leyden, 1666. 6 vols.,
small 12mo., tan hardgrain morocco, gilt. L. Goldschmidt 42-12 1974 $150

BRASAVOLA, ANTONIO MUSA   Examen Omnium Syruporum. Venice, 1545.
Modern boards, booklabel of Lord Westbury. Thomas 32-333 1974 £60

BRASSEY, THOMAS BRASSEY, 1ST EARL 1836-   Voyages and Travels. 1895.
2 vols., orig. cloth, English first edition. Covent 56-1265 1974 £12.50

BRASSINGTON, W. SALT   Historic Worcestershire. Birmingham, (1895).
Roy. 8vo., orig. cloth gilt, illus. Howes 186-2225 1974 £7.50

BRATHWAITE, RICHARD   A Strappado for the Diuell. Boston, 1878.
8vo., orig. cloth, faded, limited edition. Bow Windows 62-116 1974 £18

BRAUN, F.   Thermoelektrizitat. Leipzig, 1905. 8vo.,
printed wrappers. Dawsons PM 245-124 1974 £7

BRAUN, LUDWIG   Ueber Herzbewegung und Herzstoss. Jena, 1898.
8vo., orig. wrappers, plates, first edition. Gurney 64-36 1974 £20

BRAUN, MARCUS   Immigration Abuses. New York, 1906.
Austin 62-60 1974 $22.50

BRAUNE, WILHELM   The Position of the Uterus and Foetus at the end
of Pregnancy. Leipzig, 1872. Large folio, buckram. Gurney 64-37 1974 £25

BRAY, CHARLES   The Education of the Feelings. London, 1838.
8vo., orig. maroon cloth, first edition, very good copy. Ximenes 36-29 1974
$65

BRAYBROOKE, PATRICK   Some Catholic Novelists: Their Art and
Outlook. 1931. Illus., ex-library, orig. edition. Austin 61-133 1974 $10

BRAYBROOKE, RICHARD   The History of Audley End. 1836. 4to.,
illus., orig. cloth-back boards, plates. Howes 186-2005 1974 £25

BRAYBOOKE, RICHARD   The History of Audley End. 1836. Folio,
plates, orig. boards, limited. Quaritch 939-349 1974 £85

BRAYLEY, E. W.   The Ancient Castles of England and Wales.
1825. 2 vols., 8vo., plates, contemporary half morocco gilt. Quaritch
939-60 1974 £70

BRAYLEY, E. W.   A Concise Account, Historical and Descriptive,
of Lambeth Palace. London, 1806. 4to., modern gilt-framed diced calf, fine.
Dawsons PM 251-88 1974 £75

BRAYLEY, E. W.   The History of the Ancient Palace and Late
Houses of Parliament. 1836. 8vo., half calf. Quaritch 939-477 1974 £15

BRAYLEY, E. W.   London and Middlesex. 1810-16. 4 vols. in
5, 8vo., plates, half red morocco, plates. Quaritch 939-437 1974 £45

BRAYLEY, E. W.   Topographical History of Surrey. 1850.
5 vols., 4to., half calf, foxed. Quaritch 939-561 1974 £80

THE BRAZEN Nose. Oxford, 1909-19. 6 vols., 8vo., plates, cloth. Quaritch
939-514 1974 £15

BRAZIER, MARION H.   Stage and Screen. Brazier, 1920. 130p.,
illus. Austin 51-146 1973 $12.50

BREBEUF, GUILLAUME DE   Poesies Diverses. Paris, 1658. 4to.,
contemporary limp vellum, good copy, first edition. L. Goldschmidt 42-13
1974 $275

BREBEUF, JEAN DE   The Travels & Sufferings of. 1938. Folio,
buckram, linen, leather label, limited edition. Howes 185-198 1974 £95

BREBNER, JOHN BARTLET   The Neutral Yankees of Nova Scotia, a Marginal
Colony During the Revolutionary Years. New York, 1937. Hood's 102-178
1974 $35

BREBNER, JOHN BARTLET   New England's Outpost Acadia Before the
Conquest of Canada. New York & London, 1927. Orig. binding. Butterfield
10-135 1974 $35

BREBNER, PERCY JAMES   Christopher Quarles. New York, 1914. 8vo.,
orig. cloth, first edition. Rota 190-189 1974 £10

BREBNER, PERCY JAMES   The Master Detective. New York, 1916. 8vo.,
orig. cloth, faded, first edition. Rota 190-190 1974 £10

BRECHT, BERTOLT   Hauspostille. Berlin, 1927. Orig. wrappers, fine, first edition. Covent 55-255 1974 £30

BREDER, C. M.   Field Book of Marine Fishes of the Atlantic Coast. 1929. 8vo., cloth, plates. Wheldon 130-668 1974 £7.50

BREE, C. R.   A History of the Birds of Europe. 1863, 1860-63. Roy 8vo., 4 vols., orig. cloth, plates. Wheldon 130-7 1974 £90

BREE, C. R.   A History of the Birds of Europe. 1863-64. 4 vols., roy. 8vo., orig. cloth, gilt, plates, scarce. Wheldon 131-26 1974 £90

BREE, C. R.   A History of the Birds of Europe Not Observed in the British Isles. 1875-76. 5 vols., roy. 8vo., orig. cloth, coloured plates, revised second edition. Wheldon 128-399 1973 £60

BREE, ROBERT   A Practical Inquiry into Disordered Respiration. London, 1803. 8vo., modern half calf. Dawsons PM 249-87 1974 £15

BREES, S. C.   Pictorial Illustrations of New Zealand. 1849. Large 4to., 19th century red half morocco, first edition. Bow Windows 64-404 1974 £180

BREESE, EDWARD   Kalendors of Gwynedd. 1873. 4to., orig. cloth. Broadhurst 23-1327 1974 £8

BREESE, EDWARD   Kalendors of Gwynedd. 1873. Demy 8vo., good copy, coloured frontis., best edition, fine, orig. cloth. Broadhurst 24-1546 1974 £8

BREHM, A. E.   Cassell's Book of Birds. (1869-73). 4 vols., 4to., orig. green cloth, gilt, wood engravings. Wheldon 131-553 1974 £35

BREHM, A. E.   Merveilles de la Nature. Paris, (n.d.). Small 4to., 3 vols., orig. morocco backed boards. Bow Windows 64-34 1974 £8.50

BREISLAK, SCIPIONE   Saggio di Osservazioni Mineralogiche Sulla Tolfa, Oriolo, e Latera. Rome, 1786. 8vo., old half vellum, back torn, first edition, inner margin lightly wormed. Gurney 66-34 1974 £32

BREIT, HARVEY   The Writer Observed. World, 1956. 285p. Austin 54-160 1973 $8.50

BREMER, FREDERIKA   The Novels. 1844-45. 9 vols., 16mo., contemporary half calf gilt. Howes 186-43 1974 £10.50

BREMNER, ARCHIE   City of London, Ontario, Canada. London, 1897. First edition. Hood's 102-584 1974 $35

BRENDEL, JOHANN GOTTFRIED   Opusculorum Mathematici et Medici Argumenti. 1769. 4to., contemporary calf, worn, first edition. Dawsons PM 245-125 1974 £12

BRENNAN, FREDERICK H.   The Wookey. Knopf, 1941. 249p. Austin 51-147 1973 $7.50

BRENNECKE, ERNEST   The Life of Thomas Hardy. New York, 1925. First U. S. edition, illus., frontis. portrait, bookplate, else fine. Covent 51-862 1973 £15

BRENTANO, LUJO   Eine Geschichte der Wirtschaftlichen Entwicklung Englands. 1927-29. 2 vols. in 3, buckram. Howes 186-1364 1974 £12.50

BRENTON, E. P.   The Naval History of Great Britain. 1823-25. 8vo., contemporary half roan, first edition. Bow Windows 64-405 1974 £21

BRERETON, JOHN LE GAY   The Turkish Bath in Health and Disease. Sheffield, (1859). 8vo., boards. Hammond 201-560 1974 £5

BRESADOLA, G.   Fungi Tridentini. Tridenti, 1881. 8vo., half calf, plates. Wheldon 129-1159 1974 £25

BRESADOLA, G.   Iconographia Mycologica. Milan, 1927-30. Orig. portfolio, buckram. Wheldon 129-1158 1974 £120

BRESCIANI-TURRONI, COSTANTINO   Le Vicende del Marco Tedesco. Milan, 1931. Small 4to., orig. wrappers. Howes 186-1365 1974 £5

BRETON, ANDRE   L'Amour Fou. Paris, 1937. Orig. wrappers, English first edition. Covent 56-1581 1974 £15

BRETON, ANDRE   Anthologie de l'Humour Noir. 1940. Orig. wrappers, portraits, first edition. Thomas 28-217 1972 £25

BRETON, ANDRE   Les Champs Magnetiques. Paris, 1920. Square 12mo., orig. wrapper, uncut, first edition. L. Goldschmidt 42-168 1974 $35

BRETON, ANDRE   Young Cherry Trees Secured Against Hares. n.d. Drawings, fine, d.w., first edition. Covent 51-2208 1973 £6

BRETON, NICHOLAS   No Whippinge, Nor Trippinge. 1601. Calf, orig. edition. Thomas 28-218 1972 £31.50

BRETONNE, RESTIF DE LA   Monsieur Nicolas. 1930. 4to., 6 vols., cloth, parchment backs, gilt, plates, limited edition. Quaritch 936-317 1974 £40

BRETSCHNEIDER, E.   Die Pekinger Ebene. Gotha, 1876. 4to., new boards, rare. Wheldon 130-272 1974 £10

BRETSCHNEIDER, E.   History of European Botanical Discoveries in China. London, 1898. 2 vols., 8vo., cloth. Dawsons PM 11-104 1974 £29

BRETT, EDWIN JOHN   A Pictorial and Descriptive Record of the Origin and Development of Arms and Armour. 1894. Roy. 4to., illus., half morocco, scarce. Quaritch 940-693 1974 £110

BREUIL, HENRI 1877-   Rock Paintings of Southern Andalusia. Oxford, 1929. 4to., orig. buckram, plates, first edition. Smith 193-60 1973 £10

BREVAL, J.   History of Most Illustrious House of Nassau. 1714. Plates, new buckram. Allen 213-1665 1973 $15

LE BREVIAIRE Grimani. Leyden, 1903-10. 13 vols. in 7, roy. folio & 4to., half levant morocco gilt, orig. wrappers, plates, fine. Quaritch 940-128 1974 £750

BREVIARIUM Novissimum Monasticum. 1677. Thick folio, 19th century buff calf, boards, fine. Howes 185-1001 1974 £45

BREVIARUM Sanctae Lugdunensis Ecclesiae, Primae Galliarum Sedis. Paris, 1780. 4 vols., contemporary French red morocco gilt, raised bands. Thomas 28-128 1972 £150

THE BREVIATE: In the Boundary Dispute Between Pennsylvania and Maryland. Harris, 1891. First edition, half morocco, marbled boards, top of backstrip worn, frontispiece maps in fine state. Wilson 63-66 1974 $16.50

BREVIS Notitia Urbis Veteris Vindobonae ex Variis Documentis Collecta. Vienna, 1764. 4to., contemporary light brown calf, richly gilt covers, first edition, fine, engraved frontis. Schumann 499-116 1974 sFr 520

BREWER, DANIEL CHAUNCEY   The Conquest of New England By the Immigrant. Putnam, 1926. Austin 62-61 1974 $15

BREWER, GRIFFITH   Aeronautics. London, 1893. 8vo., orig. blue cloth, gilt, fine, first edition. Dawsons PM 245-126 1974 £30

BREWER, J.   Flora of Surrey. 1863. Post 8vo., cloth, maps. Wheldon 129-985 1974 £10

BREWER, J.   Flora of Surrey. 1863. Post 8vo., maps, cloth, very scarce. Wheldon 131-1216 1974 £10

BREWER, JAMES NORRIS   Descriptive and Historical Account of Various Palaces and Public Buildings, English and Foreign. 1821. 4to., contemporary diced russia gilt, rebacked. Quaritch 940-496 1974 £28

BREWER, LUTHER A.   Some Lamb and Browning Letters to Leigh Hunt. 1924. One of 300 copies, plates, quarter vellum, fine. Covent 51-961 1973 £5.25

BREWER, ROBERT W. A.   The Art of Aviation. 1910. Frontispiece, plates, text-figures, covers trifle rubbed, front fly-leaf missing. Bow Windows 66-79 1974 £10

BREWERTON, GEORGE DOUGLAS   Overland With Kit Carson.   New York, 1930. Illus. in line by author, first printing in book form, folded map.   Butterfield 10-122 1974 $17.50

BREWERTON, GEORGE DOUGLAS   The War in Kansas.   New York, Cincinnati, 1856. 8vo., orig. bindings.   Butterfield 8-173 1974 $25

BREWSTER, DAVID   Memoirs of the Life, Writings, and Discoveries of Sir Isaac Newton.   Edinburgh, 1855. 8vo., 2 vols., orig. brown cloth, uncut, illus.   Dawsons PM 245-561 1974 £55

BREWSTER, DAVID   Memoirs of the Life, Writings, and Discoveries of Sir Isaac Newton.   Edinburgh, 1855. 8vo., 2 vols., orig. brown cloth, woodcuts, second edition.   Dawsons PM 245-562 1974 £40

BREWSTER, DAVID   Optics.   1831. 8vo., orig. cloth, faded, Smith 194-393 1974 £30

BREWSTER, DOROTHY   Dead Reckonings in Fiction.   1924. Cover dull, else very good, inscribed presentation copy, first edition.   Covent 51-1143 1973 £7.50

BRICE, ANDREW   A Universal Geographical Dictionary.   London, 1759. 2 vols. in 1, maps, thick folio, contemporary calf, leather label.   Traylen 79-419 1973 £45

BRIDGE, BEWICK   A Treatise on the Elements of Algebra.   London, 1821. 8vo., orig. green cloth, fifth edition.   Dawsons PM 245-127 1974 £6

BRIDGE, WILLIAM   A Sermon.   London, 1642. 4to., disbound, first edition.   Dawsons PM 251-490 1974 £10

BRIDGER, CHARLES   Am Index to Printed Pedigrees, Contained in County and Local Histories.   1867. Demy 8vo., half contemporary calf by Zaehnsdorf, rubbed, hinge weak.   Broadhurst 24-1208 1974 £6

BRIDGES, ROBERT   Eros and Psyche.   1885. Vellum-backed cloth, scarce, English first edition.   Covent 56-175 1974 £25

BRIDGES, ROBERT   Eros and Psyche.   1894. Author's signed presentation inscription, nice copy, first edition.   Covent 51-2209 1973 £15.75

BRIDGES, ROBERT   Eros & Psyche.   London, 1894. Orig. cloth, gilt, fine, uncut, inscribed, first edition.   Jenkins 48-66 1973 $50

BRIDGES, ROBERT   Eros and Psyche.   1935. 4to., white pigskin, gilt, limited edition.   Broadhurst 23-1052 1974 £120

BRIDGES, ROBERT   Eros and Psyche.   1935. 4to., full white pigskin, gilt, illus.   Hammond 201-769 1974 £185

BRIDGES, ROBERT   The Feast of Bacchus.   Oxford, 1889. One of 105 numbered copies, bookplate, inscription, very good copy, vellum backed boards.   Covent 51-2210 1973 £40

BRIDGES, ROBERT   John Keats.   1895. 8vo., orig. buckram gilt, faded, limited edition.   Smith 194-394 1974 £7.25

BRIDGES, ROBERT   New Verse, Written in 1921, With the Other Poems of That Year and a Few Earlier Pieces.   Oxford, 1925. Frontis., one of 100 numbered copies signed by author, small stain at foot of covers, very nice copy, full vellum, worn d.w.   Covent 51-2211 1973 £12.50

BRIDGES, ROBERT   Now in Wintry Delights.   Oxford, 1903. 4to., wrappers, torn, first edition.   Rota 189-155 1974 £15

BRIDGES, ROBERT   Overhead in Arcady.   Scribners, n.d. 133p. Austin 54-161 1973 $10

BRIDGES, ROBERT   The Poems of Digby Mackworth Bolben.   1911. Plates, cloth backed boards, bookplate, very good copy.   Covent 51-2212 1973 £7.50

BRIDGES, ROBERT   Poems Written in the Year MCMXIII.   1914. Printed in black red and blue, 8vo., orig. Holland backed boards, fine copy, limited to 85 copies.   Sawyer 293-38 1974 £225

BRIDGES, ROBERT   Poetical Works.   1898-1905. 6 vols., covers little faded, very nice set, 4 vols. unopened.   Covent 51-291 1973 £10.50

BRIDGES, ROBERT   Sonnet XLIV of Michelangelo Buonarroti. 1912. One of 5 copies on Japanese vellum, very fine, unopened copy, wrappers.   Covent 51-2213 1973 £35

BRIDGES, ROBERT   Suppressed Chapters and Other Bookishness.   New York, 1895. Orig. red cloth, gilt, fine, inscription, first edition.   Jenkins 48-67 1973 $45

BRIDGES, ROBERT   The Testament of Beauty.   Oxford, 1929. Nice copy, publishers note on the text tipped in, first edition.   Covent 51-2214 1973 £10.50

BRIDGES, ROBERT   The Testament of Beauty.   Oxford, 1929. 4to., orig. green cloth, uncut, boards, fine.   Dawsons PM 252-76 1974 £55

BRIDGES, ROBERT   Collected Essays, Papers, Etc.   1927-32. 6 parts in 1 vol., buckram, gilt top, fine, orig. wrappers preserved at end.   Covent 51-290 1973 £5.25

BRIDGES, ROBERT   Collected Poetical Works.   Oxford, 1898-1905. 6 vols., crown 8vo., orig. blue cloth.   Howes 185-31 1974 £12

BRIDGMAN, E. C.   A Chinese Chrestomathy in the Canton Dialect. 1841. Crown 4to., buckram, rebound, scarce, illus.   Howes 186-1790A 1974 £10

BRIDGMAN, HOWARD ALLEN   New England in the Life of the World.   Boston - Chicago, (1920). 8vo., orig. bindings.   Butterfield 8-341 1974 $15

BRIDGMAN, JOHN   An Historical and Topographical Sketch of Knole.   London, 1817. Contemporary half roan, plates, rubbed, first edition.   Howes 186-2028 1974 £25

BRIDGMAN, L. J.   The Santa Claus Club.   New York and Boston, 1907. 8vo., pict. cloth, illus.   Frohnsdorff 16-121 1974 $8.50

A BRIEF Account of a Boston Way.   Boston, (1906). First edition, 8vo., full page illus., orig. wrappers, fine.   Current BW9-384 1974 $20

BRIEUX, EUGENE   La Foi, Piece en Cinq Actes.   Paris, 1912. 12mo., three quarter hard grain morocco, gilt, orig. wrapper, uncut, first edition.   L. Goldschmidt 42-171 1974 $20

BRIEUX, EUGENE   "Woman On Her Own," "False Gods," "Red Robes."   Brentano's, 1916. 330p.   Austin 51-148 1973 $7.50

BRIFFAULT, ROBERT   The Mothers.   New York, 1927. 3 vols. Jacobs 24-138 1974 $50

BRIGGS, CLARE   Selected Drawings of Clare Briggs.   Wise, 1930. Austin 54-162 1973 $7.50

BRIGGS, HENRY   Arithmetica Logarithmica.   1628. Folio, old panelled calf, gilt, first edition.   Dawsons PM 245-128 1974 £300

BRIGGS, HENRY   Trigonometria Britannica.   1633. Folio, contemporary calf, illus., first edition.   Dawsons PM 245-129 1974 £385

BRIGGS, L. VERNON   Arizona and New Mexico 1882; California 1886; Mexico 1891.   Boston, 1932. 8vo., cloth.   Saddleback 14-4 1974 $12

BRIGGS, T. R. A.   Flora of Plymouth.   1880. Crown 8vo., map, cloth.   Wheldon 128-1186 1973 £5

BRIGHOUSE, HAROLD   Hobson's Choice.   Doubleday, Page, 1916. 136p.   Austin 51-149 1973 $8.50

BRIGHT, BENJAMIN HEYWOOD   Catalogue of the Valuable Library of.   London, 1845. 8vo., orig. printed wrappers, uncut.   Dawsons PM 10-78 1974 £5

BRIGHT, JAMES W.   Bright's Anglo Saxon Reader.   1935. 395 pages.   Austin 61-134 1974 $10

BRIGHT, P. M.   A Monograph of the British Aberrations of the Chalk-Hill Blue Butterfly.   Bournemouth, 1938. 4to., niger morocco, gilt, plates.   Hammond 201-630 1974 £18

BRIGHT, RICHARD   Clinical Memoirs on Abdominal Tumours and Intumescence. 1860. 8vo., orig. cloth. Dawsons PM 249-89 1974 £15

BRIGHT, RICHARD   Clinical Memoirs On Abdominal Tumours and Intumescence. London, 1860. 8vo., orig. cloth, illus., first book form edition. Schuman 37-31 1974 $95

BRIGHT, RICHARD   Reports of Medical Cases. London, 1827. 4to., modern half calf, uncut, fine, first edition. Dawsons PM 249-88 1974 £1,250

BRIGHT, ROBERT   The Life and Death of Little Jo. Doubleday, Doran, 1944. Austin 62-62 1974 $10

BRIGHTON BEACH MUSIC HALL   Brighton Beach Programmes. Eagle Press, 1891. 10 programmes, for season of 1891. Austin 51-149 1973 $12.50

BRIGHTWELL, T.   Sketch of a Fauna Infusoria for East Norfolk. Norwich, 1848. Small 4to., orig. cloth, plates, rare. Wheldon 130-851 1974 £10

BRIGHTY, ISABEL MC COMB   A Pilgrimage Through the Historic Niagara District, Including a List of Place Names. St. Catharines, 1932. Card cover, folding map. Hood's 102-585 1974 $15

BRILLAT-SAVARIN, JEAN ANTHELME   A Handbook of Gastronomy. Boston, 1915. Illus., unopened copy, ltd. to 375 copies. Jacobs 24-66 1974 $10

BRILLAT-SAVARIN, JEAN ANTHELME   Physiologie du Gout. Paris, 1826. 2 vols., 8vo., contemporary quarter leather, worn, first edition. Traylen 79-213 1973 £195

BRINDLEY, W.   Ancient Sepulchral Monuments. 1887. Folio, plates, cloth, scarce. Quaritch 940-298 1974 £18

BRINE, MARY D.   Christmas Rhymes and New Year's Chimes. New York, 1883. First edition, oblong 8vo., illus., covers with some soiling, interior very good. Current BW9-6 1974 $18.75

BRINKELOW, HENRY   The Coplaint of Roderyck Mors. n.d. Small 8vo., brown morocco gilt, fine, first edition. Dawsons PM 251-420 1974 £650

BRINLEY, G.   Away to Cape Breton. New York, 1936. Illus., coloured frontis. Hood's 102-179 1974 $12.50

BRINLEY, G.   Away to Cape Breton. New York, 1936. Illus., frontispiece. Hood's 104-192 1974 $12.50

BRINLEY, G.   Away to the Canadian Rockies and British Columbia. New York, 1938. Ex-library, illus. Hood's 103-796 1974 $12.50

BRIOT, C.   Theorie des Fonctions Abeliennes. Paris, 1879. 4to., brown cloth, gilt, first edition. Dawsons PM 245-130 1974 £7

BRISBANE, J.   The Anatomy of Painting. 1769. Folio, contemporary boards, plates, new vellum spine, rare. Quaritch 940-44 1974 £60

BRISBIN, JAMES S.   Red Wing and Its Advantages. Red Wing, 1891. 16mo., boards. Saddleback 14-513 1974 $10

BRISSON, MATHURIN JACQUES 1723-1806   Ornithologie ou Methode Contenant. 1760. 4to., 6 vols., contemporary half calf. Bow Windows 64-35 1974 £460

BRISSON, MATHURIN JACQUES 1723-1806   Ornithologia. Paris, 1760. 4to., 6 vols., contemporary boards, leather backs, uncut, plates. Wheldon 131-27 1974 £350

BRISTED, JOHN   America and Her Resources. 1818. Modern quarter calf, morocco label, first London edition. Bow Windows 66-81 1974 £56

BRISTED, JOHN   The Resources of the Unites States. New York, 1818. First edition, old calf, sound. Butterfield 10-124 1974 $65

BRISTOL, GEORGE DIGBY, LORD   Letters Between...and Sir Kenelm Digby. London, 1651. 8vo., modern calf, first edition, first issue. Dawsons PM 252-290 1974 £110

BRISTOL, WALTER W.   The Story of the Ojai Valley. Ojai, (c.1945). 12mo., cloth. Saddleback 14-44 1974 $15

BRITISH AND FOREIGN SCHOOL SOCIETY   Manual of the System of Primary Instruction. 1834. 8vo., orig. green cloth, slightly soiled, fine clean copy internally, engraved plates. George's 610-94 1973 £15

BRITISH and Foreign Trade and Industry. 1903-04. 2 vols., folio, half buckram. Howes 186-1366 1974 £12

THE BRITISH Classics. London, 1903-10. 29 vols., small 8vo., contemporary blue straight grained morocco, plates, gilt. Dawsons PM 252-77 1974 £290

THE BRITISH Coleoptera Delineated. London, 1861. 8vo., plates, orig. quarter roan, worn. Bow Windows 62-862 1974 £6

BRITISH Curiosities in Art and Nature. 1721. Small 8vo., half calf. Quaritch 939-62 1974 £15

BRITISH LEGION   Legion: The Book of the British Legion By Britain's Foremost Writers in Prose and Verse. 1939. Illus., first edition. Austin 61-135 1974 $12.50

BRITISH MUSEUM   Catalogue of Birds, Vol. II. 1886. 8vo., cloth, plates. Wheldon 131-555 1974 £25

BRITISH MUSEUM   Catalogue of Birds, Vol. 14. 1888. 8vo., cloth, plates. Wheldon 131-556 1974 £20

BRITISH MUSEUM   Catalogue of Birds, Vol. 15. 1890. 8vo., cloth, plates. Wheldon 131-557 1974 £25

BRITISH MUSEUM   Catalogue of the Fifty Manuscripts and Printed Books Bequeathed to the ... by Alfred H. Huth. 1912. Folio, orig. buckram, plates. Howes 185-609 1974 £12.50

BRITISH MUSEUM   Illuminated Manuscripts in the British Museum. 1903. Folio, plates, orig. printed paper wrapper. Bow Windows 62-491 1974 £10

BRITISH MUSEUM   List of the Specimens of British Animals In the Collection of the British Museum. 1848-56. 18 parts, 12mo., orig. wrappers, complete set. Wheldon 131-339 1974 £15

BRITISH MUSEUM   Nomenclature of Coleopterous Insects in the Collection of the British Museum. 1847-56. 9 parts in 2 vols., 12mo., half calf and orig. wrappers. Wheldon 128-680 1973 £20

BRITISH MUSEUM   Nomenclature of Coleopterous Insects in the Collection of the British Museum. 1847-56. 9 parts in 2 vols., 12mo., half calf. Wheldon 131-787 1974 £20

BRITISH MUSEUM, DEPT. OF BRITISH & MEDIAEVAL ANTIQUITIES   Catalogue of Engraved Gems of Post-Classical Periods. 1915. 4to., plates. Allen 213-1302 1973 $35

BRITISH MUSEUM - DEPT. OF MANUSCRIPTS   A Catalogue of the Harleian Manuscripts. London, 1808. Folio, 3 vols., orig. quarter buckram, uncut, rubbed. Dawsons PM 8-266 1973 £30

BRITISH MUSEUM - DEPT. OF ORIENTAL ANTIQUITIES AND OF ETHNOGRAPHY   Catalogue of the Frank Lloyd Collection of Worcester Porcelain. London, 1923. 4to., plates, quarter cloth, boards, faded. Bow Windows 62-461 1974 £18

BRITISH MUSEUM - DEPT. OF ORIENTAL ANTIQUITIES AND OF ETHNOGRAPHY   Catalogue of the Frank Lloyd Collection of Worcester Porcelain of the Wall Period. 1923. Covent 55-452 1974 £12.50

BRITISH MUSEUM, DEPT. OF PRINTED BOOKS   Catalogue of Books Printed in the 15th Century, Now in the British Museum. 1908-24. Vols. 1-5, folio, ex-library. Allen 216-171 1974 $40

BRITISH MUSEUM - (NAT. HIST.) - DEPT. OF ZOOLOGY   Lord Walsingham and Sir G. Hampson, Illustrations of Typical Specimens of Lepidoptera Heterocera. 1877-93. 9 vols., 4to., cloth, coloured plates, small library stamps, scarce. Wheldon 128-687 1973 £65

BRITISH Museum Reproductions. London, 1923-28. 4 vols., 4to., plates, cloth backed, slip cases. Bow Windows 62-490 1974 £18

BRITISH Ornithologist's Union Expedition and the Wollaston Expedition in Dutch New Guinea, 1910-13, Reports on the Collections. 1916. 2 vols., roy. 4to., orig. wrappers, uncut, limited, very scarce. Wheldon 131-340 1974 £100

BRITISH Poetry of the Eighteen-Nineties. New York, 1937. Biblo & Tannen 210-851 1973 $8.50

THE BRITISH POETS. Edinburgh, 1773-76. 12mo., 44 vols., contemporary vellum, gilt. Hammond 201-289 1974 £125

BRITISH SCHOOL AT ATHENS Annual, Sessions 1927-30. 1932. Vols. 29 & 30, plates, illus., orig. cloth-backed boards, rubbed. Bow Windows 66-15 1974 £10.50

BRITISH THEATRE. Tragedies, Comedies, Operas and Farces, From Most Classic Writers, With Notes. 1850. Allen 216-2102 1974 $10

BRITNELL, J. Books and Booksellers in Ancient and Modern Times. Toronto, 1923. Card cover. Hood's 103-392 1974 $17.50

BRITON-JONES, H. R. The Diseases and Curing of Cacao. 1934. 8vo., cloth, scarce. Wheldon 129-1645 1974 £5

BRITTAINE, GEORGE Irishmen and Irishwomen. Dublin, 1831. 8vo., half calf, third edition. Emerald 50-87 1974 £7.50

BRITTEN, JAMES European Ferns. (1881-82). 4to., cloth, coloured plates. Wheldon 128-1344 1973 £10

BRITTEN, NATHANIEL LORD An Illustrated Flora of the Northern United States. New York, 1896-98. 3 vols., roy. 8vo., cloth, first edition. Wheldon 128-1243 1973 £10

BRITTON, BELLE Belle Brittan on a Tour at Newport and Here and There. Derby, Jackson, 1858. 359p. Austin 54-163 1973 $17.50

BRITTON, F. Souvenir of Gananoque and Thousand Islands. N.P., (1901). Illus. Hood's 104-671 1974 $10

BRITTON, J. Illustrations of Fonthill Abbey. 1823. Small folio, orig. boards, rebacked. Thomas 28-216 1972 £30

BRITTON, JOHN The Architectural Antiquities of Great Britain. 1807-14. 4 vols. in 2, 4to., full brown calf, covers gilt, plates, frontispieces, attractive copy. Bow Windows 66-82 1974 £85

BRITTON, JOHN The Architectural Antiquities of Great Britain. London, 1807-14. 4 vols., large 4to., half morocco, uncut, worn. Traylen 79-297 1973 £30

BRITTON, JOHN The Architectural Antiquities of Great Britain. 1807-26. 5 vols., 4to., contemporary polished calf. Quaritch 939-63 1974 £85

BRITTON, JOHN Bath and Bristol. 1829. Plates, half green morocco, worn. Marsden 37-92 1974 £115

BRITTON, JOHN The Beauties of England and Wales. 1801-26. 26 vols. in 33, 8vo., cloth, plates. Quaritch 939-64 1974 £350

BRITTON, JOHN The Beauties of England and Wales. 1808. 8vo., plates, illus., contemporary morocco gilt. Quaritch 939-65 1974 £30

BRITTON, JOHN Descriptive Sketches of Tunbridge Wells and the Calverley Estate. 1832. 8vo., cloth, plates. Quaritch 939-398 1974 £27.50

BRITTON, JOHN The Fine Arts of the English School. 1812. Folio, plates, contemporary blue straight-grained morocco, gilt, rubbed. Quaritch 940-780 1974 £50

BRITTON, KARL Communication: A Philosophical Study of the Language. 1939. Ex-library, orig. edition. Austin 61-137 1974 $10

BRITTON, N. L. The Bahama Flora. New York, 1920. 8vo., cloth. Wheldon 129-1053 1974 £5

BRITTON, N. L. North American Trees. 1908. Crown 4to., cloth, text-figures, rare. Wheldon 128-1587 1973 £18

BRITTON, NAN The President's Daughter. White and blue d.j., lacking blurb by Mencken. Butterfield 10-126 1974 $10

BRITTON, NAN The President's Daughter. New York, 1927. First or early printing, black and yellow d.j., pamphlet about book laid in, orig. binding. Butterfield 10-125 1974 $25

BRITWELL COURT LIBRARY Sale Catalogues. 1916-27. 21 vols., 4to., orig. wrappers, illus., plates. Thomas 28-110 1972 £85

BROAD, C. LEWIS Dictionary to the Plays & Novels of Bernard Shaw. 1929. Frontispiece, faded. Covent 55-1358 1974 £7.50

A BROADSIDE for June 1908. Dundrum, 1908-15. Small folio, orig. blue cloth folders, illus., limited. Dawsons PM 252-222 1974 £575

BROADUS, EDMUND KEMPER The Story of English Literature. 1931. Illus. Austin 61-138 1974 $12.50

BROCK, H. M. Ballads. 1934. 4to., crimson leather, gilt, illus., limited, special edition. Howes 185-33 1974 £14

BROCK, H. M. A Book of Old Ballads. 1934. 4to., orig. cloth, plates. Bow Windows 64-407 1974 £15

BROCK, R. A. The Richmond, Virginia, Fire Department. Richmond, 1894. 8vo., cloth. Saddleback 14-737 1974 $15

BROCK, SAMUEL Injuries of the Brain and Spinal Cord and Their Coverings. Baltimore, 1939. Third edition. Rittenhouse 46-98 1974 $12.50

BROCKE, H. C. VAN Beobachtungen Von Einigen Blumen. Leipzig, 1769. Post 8vo., boards. Wheldon 128-1446 1973 £5

BROCKE, H. C. VAN Beogachtungen von Einigen Blumen, Deren bau und Zubereitung der Erde. Leipzig, 1769. Post 8vo., boards. Wheldon 131-1496 1974 £5

BROCKETT, J. T. Hints on the Propriety of Establishing a Typographical Society. Newcastle, 1818. 8vo., contemporary half morocco, first edition. Ximenes 35-405 1974 $90

BROCKETT, L. P. Woman's Work in the Civil War. Philadelphia, 1867. 8vo., contemporary calf, rubbed, first edition. Dawsons PM 247-24 1974 £20

BROCKLEHURST, H. C. Game Animals of the Sudan. 1931. Roy. 8vo., plates, orig. buckram gilt, first edition. Smith 193-762 1973 £18

BROCQ, LOUIS Traitement des Maladies de la Peau. Paris, 1890. 8vo., modern quarter calf, uncut. Dawsons PM 249-90 1974 £13

BRODERICK, GERTRUDE Radio and Television Bibliography. G.P.O., 1948. 33p., paper. Austin 51-151 1973 $10

BRODERICK, GERTRUDE Radio and Television Bibliography. 1952. 48p., paper. Austin 51-152 1973 $10

BRODIE, B. C. An Experimental Inquiry on the Action of Electricity on Gases. 1872. 4to., disbound. Dawsons PM 245-131 1974 £7.50

BRODIE, BENJAMIN Lectures. London, 1846. 8vo., orig. cloth, first edition. Gurney 64-38 1974 £20

BRODIE, WALTER Remarks on the Past and Present State of New Zealand. 1845. 8vo., orig. cloth, first edition. Bow Windows 64-408 1974 £75

BRODRICK, JAMES The Life & Work of Cardinal Bellarmine. 1928. 2 vols., orig. cloth gilt, plates. Howes 185-955 1974 £7.50

BRODZKY, HORICE   Henri Gaudier-Brzeska, 1891-1915. London, 1933. Very nice copy, illus., first edition, orig. cloth. Crane 7-98 1974 £5

BROGLIE, LOUIS VICTOR   L'Electron Magnetique. Paris, 1934. 8vo., orig. printed wrappers, fine, first edition. Dawsons PM 245-134 1974 £18

BROGLIE, LOUIS VICTOR   Ondes et Mouvements. Paris, 1926. 8vo., orig. green wrappers, first edition. Dawsons PM 245-132 1974 £65

BROGLIE, LOUIS-VICTOR   Ondes et Mouvements. Paris, 1926. 8vo., orig. printed green wrappers, cloth folder, first edition. Gilhofer 61-93 1974 sFr. 1,400

BROGLIE, LOUIS VICTOR   Untersuchungen zur Quantentheorie. Leipzig, 1927. 8vo., grey printed wrappers. Dawsons PM 245-133 1974 £8

BROKAW, H. CLIFFORD   Putnam's Automobile Handbook. New York and London, 1918. Orig. binding. Butterfield 10-71 1974 $12.50

BROKENSHIRE, NORMAN   This is Norman Brokenshire. McKay, 1954. 307p., illus. Austin 51-153 1973 $7.50

BROME, J.   An Historical Account of Mr. Roger's Three Years Travels. 1694. Small 8vo., half calf. Quaritch 939-66 1974 £40

BROMFIELD, LOUIS   Awake and Rehearse. New York, 1929. Orig. paper-backed boards, first edition, one of 500 numbered copies, signed by author, boxed. MacManus 224-50 1974 $25

BROMFIELD, LOUIS   Out of the Earth. New York, (1940). First edition, 8vo., note in author's hand laid in, illus., very nice. Current BW9-208 1974 $20

BROMFIELD, WILLIAM   Thoughts arising from Experience. London, 1767. 8vo., disbound, first edition. Dawsons PM 249-91 1974 £21

BROMLEY, HENRY   A Catalogue of Engraved British Portraits. London, 1793. 4to., contemporary diced calf, label. Dawsons PM 10-82 1974 £28

BROMLEY, THOMAS   The Way to the Sabbath of Rest. 1759. 8vo., contemporary sheep. Hill 126-114 1974 £21

BROMWELL, WILLIAM J.   History of Immigration to the United States. Redfield, 1856. 225p., 1st ed. Austin 62-63 1974 $27.50

BROMWICH, T. J. I'A.   An Introduction to the Theory of Infinite Series. London, 1908. 8vo., black half morocco, first edition. Dawsons PM 245-135 1974 £10

BRONDSTED, P. O.   The Bronzes of Siris now in the British Museum. 1836. Roy. folio, plates, boards, cloth spine. Quaritch 940-299 1974 £25

BRONGNIART, ALEX   Traite des Arts Ceramiques ou des Poteries. Paris, 1877. Oblong 4to., plates, orig. cloth. Bow Windows 62-120 1974 £7.50

BRONSON-HOWARD, GEORGE   The Black Book. New York, 1920. 8vo., orig. cloth, first edition. Rota 190-193 1974 £8

BRONSON-HOWARD, GEORGE   Norroy, Diplomatic Agent. New York, 1907. 8vo., orig. dark blue dec. cloth, first edition. Rota 190-191 1974 £12

BRONSON-HOWARD, GEORGE   Slaves of the Lamp. New York, 1917. 8vo., orig. cloth, illus., first edition. Rota 190-192 1974 £8

BRONTE, ANNE   The Life and Works of Charlotte Bronte and her Sisters. 1899-1900. Small 8vo., 7 vols., half morocco, gilt, plates. Quaritch 936-319 1974 £80

BRONTE, CHARLOTTE   The Four Wishes. 1918. 8vo., sewn, paper printed wrapper, gilt, first edition. Broadhurst 23-643 1974 £35

BRONTE, CHARLOTTE   Jane Eyre. 1847. Small 8vo., 3 vols., contemporary half calf, first edition. Quaritch 936-320 1974 £200

BRONTE, CHARLOTTE   Life and Works of Charlotte Bronte and Her Sisters. 1891-89. 7 vols., crown 8vo., contemporary half morocco gilt, plates, illus., portraits. Howes 186-47 1974 £55

BRONTE, CHARLOTTE   Novels of Sisters Bronte. 1905-07. 11 vols. Allen 216-F 1974 $60

BRONTE, CHARLOTTE   Poems. London, 1846. 8vo., orig. green blind-stamped cloth, first edition, second issue. Dawsons PM 252-78 1974 £110

BRONTE, EMILY   Wuthering Heights. New York, 1931. Wood engravings, 4to., orig. cloth, one of 450 numbered copies, signed by author. MacManus 224-51 1974 $25

BRONTE, CHARLOTTE   Works. 1893. 12 vols., orig. buckram gilt, plates, portraits, limited large paper edition. Howes 186-48 1974 £30

BRONTE, CHARLOTTE   Works. Edinburgh, 1924. 8vo., 12 vols., orig. cloth, uncut, fine. Broadhurst 23-644 1974 £45

BRONTE, CHARLOTTE   Works. Edinburgh, 1924. 12 vols., demy 8vo., uncut, fine, dust wrappers, orig. cloth. Broadhurst 24-571 1974 £50

BRONTE, PATRICK BRANWELL   "And the Weary Are At Rest". London, 1924. 4to., orig. wrappers, first edition. Goodspeed's 578-31 1974 $50

BROOK, ABRAHAM   Miscellaneous Experiments and Remarks on Electricity. London, 1789. 4to., half calf, first edition. Dawsons PM 245-136 1974 £25

BROOK, HARRY E.   The Land of Sunshine. Los Angeles, 1893. Orig. pictorial wrappers. Hayman 57-64 1974 $25

BROOK, R.   New Cyclopaedia of Botany and Complete Book of Herbs. London & Huddersfield, (1854). 2 vols., 8vo., orig. dec. cloth, plates, very scarce. Wheldon 131-1803 1974 £25

BROOK, THOMAS   A Catalogue of the Manuscripts and Printed Books Collected By. London, 1891. 2 vols., 8vo., orig. boards, plates, uncut, limited. Dawsons PM 10-84 1974 £42

BROOKE, ARTHUR DE CAPELL   Winter Sketches in Lapland. London, 1827. Atlas 4to., plates, contemporary half calf. Marlborough 70-37 1974 £165

BROOKE, CHARLOTTE   Receipt Book of. Small 4to., stained, half calf. Quaritch 939-555 1974 £23.50

BROOKE, FRANCES   The History of Lady Julia Mandeville. London, 1763. 2 vols., 8vo., contemporary speckled calf, first edition. Dawsons PM 252-79 1974 £75

BROOKE, FULKE GREVILLE, BARON 1554-1628   Caelica. Gregynog Press, 1937. Demy 8vo., broad dark green basis leather spine, top edges gilt, others uncut, limited to 210 copies, complete with prospectus, printed in red & black, fine. Broadhurst 24-1011 1974 £80

BROOKE, FULKE GREVILLE, BARON 1554-1628   Caelica. 1937. 8vo., orig. cloth, uncut, limited edition. Broadhurst 23-1053 1974 £75

BROOKE, FULKE GREVILLE, BARON 1554-1628   Certaine Learned and Elegant Workes of. London, 1633. Folio, red morocco gilt, fine, first edition. Dawsons PM 252-418 1974 £380

BROOKE, HENRY   A Collection of the Pieces. 1778. 8vo., 4 vols., half green calf. Quaritch 936-24 1974 £10

BROOKE, HENRY   Fool of Quality. Baltimore, 1810. 2 vols., old calf, joints broken, foxed. Allen 216-1986 1974 $12.50

BROOKE, J.   Poems Dedicated to My Country, Canada. Toronto, 1882. Hood's 103-707 1974 $10

BROOKE, JOHN ARTHUR   Cat. of the Valuable and Extensive Library. London, 1921. Plates, crown 4to., orig. wrappers, spine slightly defective. Forster 98-190 1974 £4

BROOKE, JOHN ARTHUR   Catalogue of the Valubale...Library of... John Arthur Brooke. 1921. Plates. Kraus B8-249 1974 $15

BROOKE, RICHARD   Observations Illustrative of the Historical Accounts of the Battle of Stoke Field. Liverpool, (1847). Orig. boards, spine cracked and worn, presentation inscription by author, bookplate of William Garnett. Bow Windows 66-84 1974 £7.50

BROOKE, RUPERT   A Letter to the Editor of the 'Poetry Review'. 1929. One of 50 copies, marbled wrappers, morocco label, fine, first edition. Covent 51-294 1973 £17.50

BROOKE, RUPERT   Letters from America. New York, 1916. 12mo., cloth, first edition. Goodspeed's 578-32 1974 $35

BROOKE, RUPERT   Lithuania. 1915. One of 200 copies, nice, scarce, wrappers. Covent 51-2216 1973 £35

BROOKE, RUPERT   Lithuania. Chicago, 1915. Dec. paper covers, slightly chipped, fine copy, quarter blue morocco slip case, scarce thus. Ross 86-168 1974 $200

BROOKE, RUPERT   New Poems. 1914. Vols. 1 - 4, crown 4to., paper printed wrappers, immaculate condition. Broadhurst 24-575 1974 £40

BROOKE, RUPERT   1914. 1915. 16mo., limp wrappers, first edition. Allen 216-236 1974 $15

BROOKE, RUPERT   1914 and Other Poems. 1915. Orig. buckram, inscription, paper label. Smith 194-397 1974 £8.50

BROOKE, RUPERT   1914 and Other Poems. London, 1915. First edition, frontis. portrait, covers worn, spine darkened, orig. binding. Ross 86-169 1974 $80

BROOKE, RUPERT   "1914" Five Sonnets. 1915. First edition, small 4to., mint, orig. printed envelope, envelope dust stained. Broadhurst 24-576 1974 £5

BROOKE, RUPERT   "1914" Five Sonnets. London, 1915. Thin small 4to., orig. wrappers, very scarce. Smith 193-325 1973 £5

BROOKE, RUPERT   "1914" Five Sonnets. London, 1915. First seperate edition, paper wrappers, notice of other Brooke books for sale laid in, fine. Ross 86-170 1974 $45

BROOKE, RUPERT   The Old Vicarage Grantchester. London, 1916. Woodcut, gray paper wrappers, first separate edition, very nice copy. Ross 86-171 1974 $45

BROOKE, RUPERT   Poems. 1911. Inscription, nice copy, first edition. Covent 51-2217 1973 £27.50

BROOKE, RUPERT   Collected Poems. 1933. Full blue calf, gilt, labels. Covent 55-258 1974 £10.50

BROOKE, STOPFORD A.   Notes on the Liber Studiorum of J. M. W. Turner. 1885. Illus., fine. Covent 55-83 1974 £10.50

BROOKE, STOPFORD A.   On Ten Plays of Shakespeare. 1914. 8vo., half polished calf, gilt. Quaritch 936-552 1974 £8

BROOKE, STOPFORD A.   Ten More Plays of Shakespeare. 1913. 8vo., half calf, gilt. Quaritch 936-553 1974 £7

BROOKE, STOPFORD A.   A Treasury of Irish. 1932. Revised and enlarged. Austin 61-144 1974 $12.25

BROOKER, B.   Yearbook of the Arts In Canada, 1928-29. Toronto, 1929. Illus., limited edition. Hood's 103-138 1974 $17.50

BROOKES, R.   The Art of Angling, Rock and Sea-Fishing. 1740. 12mo., contemporary calf, first edition. Quaritch 939-67 1974 £80

BROOKES, R.   A New and Accurate System of Natural History. 1763. 8vo., 6 vols., orig. boards, uncut, scarce. Wheldon 129-70 1974 £20

BROOKES, RICHARD   The Art of Angling. London, 1740. 8vo., half calf, gilt, first edition. Hammond 201-75 1974 £45

BROOKS, CHARLES   Chimney-Pot Papers. Yale, 1919. 184p., illus. Austin 54-164 1973 $6.50

BROOKS, CHARLES   Frightful Plays. Harcourt, 1922. 214p. Austin 54-165 1973 $7.50

BROOKS, CHARLES   History of the Town of Medford, Middlesex County, Massachusetts. Boston, 1855. 8vo., cloth. Saddleback 14-476 1974 $17.50

BROOKS, CHARLES   History of the Town of Medford, Middlesex County . . . 1630 to the Present Time. Boston, 1855. Engraved views and portraits, woodcuts, newly rebound green buckram, clean crisp copy. Butterfield 10-372 1974 $22.50

BROOKS, CHARLES   An Italian Winter. Harcourt, 1933. 350p. Austin 54-166 1973 $6.50

BROOKS, CHARLES   Journeys to Bagdad. Yale, 1915. 140p., illus. Austin 54-167 1973 $6.50

BROOKS, CHARLES   Luca Sarto. Harcourt, Brace, 1924. 186p. Austin 54-168 1973 $7.50

BROOKS, CHARLES   Prologue. Harcourt, 1931. 335p., illus. Austin 54-169 1973 $7.50

BROOKS, CHARLES   There's Pippins and Cheese to Come. Yale, 1917. 139p., illus. Austin 54-170 1973 $7.50

BROOKS, CHARLES   A Thread of English Road and Roads to the North. Harcourt, 1924. 374p. Austin 54-171 1973 $8.50

BROOKS, J. S.   First Administration of Oklahoma. (1908). Crimson leather, portraits. Putnam: 126-330 1974 $14

BROOKS, JAMES J.   Whiskey Drips. Philadelphia, (1873). Cloth, fine. Hayman 57-50 1974 $15

BROOKS, NOAH   First Across the Continent. New York, 1901. Pictorial green cloth, illus., first edition. Bradley 35-221 1974 $15

BROOKS, SHIRLEY   Sooner or Later. London, 1868. 2 vols., large 8vo., orig. blue cloth, first edition, fine. Ximenes 36-30 1974 $90

BROOKS, THOMAS   London's Lamentations. 1670. 4to., some browning and stains, calf antique, morocco label. Bow Windows 66-85 1974 £58

BROOKS, VAN WYCK   The Times of Melville and Whitman. New York, 1947. 1st ed. Biblo & Tannen 210-833 1973 $7.50

BROOKS, W. K.   The Foundations of Zoology. New York, 1899 or 1915. 8vo., cloth. Wheldon 130-148 1974 £7.50

BROOKS, WALTER R.   Freddy and the Baseball Team from Mars. New York, 1955. 8vo., cloth, illus; 1st ed. Frohnsdorff 16-125 1974 $7.50

BROOKS, WILLIAM ALEXANDER   Treatise on the Improvement of the Navigation of Rivers. London, 1841. 8vo., orig. cloth, gilt, first edition. Hammond 201-841 1974 £12

BROOKSHAW   Strawberries. 1812. Large folion, fine, orig. cloth. Gregory 44-25A 1974 $145

BROOM, R.   The Mammal-like Reptiles of South Africa. 1932. Roy 8vo., cloth, scarce. Wheldon 130-669 1974 £30

BROSNAN, CORNELIUS J.   Jason Lee Prophet of the new Oregon. New York, 1932. 8vo., orig. bindings, dust jacket. Butterfield 8-449 1974 $20

BROSS, WILLIAM   The Rail-Roads, History and Commerce of Chicago. Chicago, 1854. Disbound, woodcut, second edition. Bradley 35-68 1974 $75

BROSSE, PIERRE LE LOYER, SIEUR DE LA
Please turn to
LE LOYER, PIERRE, SIEUR DE LA BROSSE

BROTERO, F. A.   Compendio de Botanica. Paris, 1788. 8vo.,
2 vols., contemporary calf, plates. Wheldon 129-889 1974 £60

BROTERO, F. A.   Compendio de Botanica. Paris, 1788. 2 vols.,
8vo., contemporary calf, plates, rare. Wheldon 131-1120 1974 £60

BROTERO, F. A.   Compendio de Botanica. Lisbon, 1837-39.
2 vols., 8vo., contemporary half calf, plates, rare, second edition. Wheldon
128-1084 1973 £40

BROTERO, F. A.   Compendio de Botanica. Lisbon, 1837-39.
8vo., 2 vols., contemporary half calf, rare, second edition. Wheldon 130-996
1974 £40

BROTERO, F. A.   Flora Lusitanica. Lisbon, 1804. 2 vols.,
8vo., contemporary mottled calf, rare. Wheldon 128-1244 1973 £60

BROTERA, F. A.   Historia Natural dos Pinheiros. Lisbon, 1827.
Small 4to., contemporary calf, rare. Wheldon 128-1588 1973 £30

BROUGH, ROBERT B.   Shadow and Substance. London, 1860. Illus.,
contemporary half calf, marbled boards, gilt back, fine copy, first edition.
MacManus 224-52 1974 $35

BROUGHAM, HENRY   Albert Lunel; or, The Chateau of Languedoc.
London, 1844. 3 vols., 12mo., mid 19th century half calf, first edition, inscribed
presentation copy. Ximenes 36-31 1974 $150

BROUGHAM, HENRY   Lives of Men of Letters and Science. 1845.
First American edition. Austin 61-145 1974 $27.50

BROUGHAM, HENRY   Lives of Men of Letters of the Time of George
III. 1855. Orig. dec. cloth, English first edition. Covent 56-178 1974 £5

BROUGHAM, JOHN   The Demon Lover. French, 1856. 26p.
Austin 51-154 1973 $8.50

BROUGHTON, RHODA   "Good-Bye, Sweetheart!" 1929. One of
50 copies, marbled wrappers, morocco label, fine copy, first edition. Covent
51-295 1973 £6.30

BROUGHTON, RICHARD   A True Memorial. 1650. 8vo., half antique
calf, boards, first edition. Broadhurst 23-1217 1974 £20

BROUGHTON, THOMAS   The Mottoes of the Spectators, Tatlers, and
Guardians. London, 1737. 12mo., contemporary calf, worn, second edition.
Bow Windows 62-122 1974 £7.50

BROUGHTON, U. H. R.   The Dress of the First Regiment of Life Guards in
Three Centuries. 1925. Plates in colour and monochrome, limited to 300 copies,
very fine, full brown pig skin, roy. 4to., lettered gilt, top edges gilt, others
uncut. Broadhurst 24-578 1974 £50

BROUN, A. F.   Sylviculture in the Tropics. 1912. 8vo.,
cloth, scarce. Wheldon 131-1718 1974 £7.50

BROUN, HEYWOOD   The Boy Grew Older. Putnam, 1922. 291p.
Austin 54-172 1973 $7.50

BROUN, HEYWOOD   Our Army at the Front. New York, 1918.
1st ed., illus. Biblo & Tannen 213-721 1973 $8.50

BROUN, HEYWOOD   Our Army at the Front. Scribner, 1919.
332p., illus. Austin 54-173 1973 $7.50

BROUSSAIS, FRANCOIS   Examen des Doctrines Medicales. Paris, 1829-
1834. 8vo., 4 vols., orig. boards, gilt. Dawsons PM 249-92 1974 £28

BROWER, J. V.   The Missouri River and Its Utmost Source.
St. Paul, 1897. Limited to 500 numbered copies, illus., mint. Jenkins 61-248
1974 $65

BROWN, A. A.   A Dryad In Nanaimo. Toronto, 1934. Hood's
103-709 1974 $10

BROWN, A. A.   The Tree of Resurrection. Toronto, 1937.
Hood's 103-710 1974 $17.50

BROWN, A. V.   Report on the Oregon Territory and the
Advisability of Extending Government and Laws to the Territory. Washington,
1844. Jenkins 61-2055 1974 $15

BROWN, ALEXANDER   By-Laws of the County of Wentworth, Revised
and Consolidated By Order of the Council, 1862. Dundas, 1863. Faded spine.
Hood's 104-672 1974 $40

BROWN, ALEXANDER   By-Laws of the County of Wentworth. Dundas,
1863. Title faded off spine, slight water stain on fly leaf. Hood's 102-586
1974 $40

BROWN, ALEXANDER   A Practical Treatise on the Construction of the
Power-Loom and the Art of Weaving. Dundee, 1896. Small 8vo., orig. cloth,
gilt. Hammond 201-798 1974 £5

BROWN, C. B.   Canoe and Camp Life In British Guiana.
1876. 8vo., cloth, plates, good copy, very scarce. Wheldon 131-341 1974
£20

BROWN, CARLETON   A Register of Middle English & Didactic Verse.
Oxford, 1916-20. 2 vols., 4to., orig. hollan-backed boards, uncut. Dawsons
PM 10-86 1974 £48

BROWN, CARLETON   A Register of Middle English Religious &
Didactic Verse. Oxford, 1916-20. 2 vols., small 4to., orig. holland backed
boards. Dawsons PM 252-80 1974 £48

BROWN, CHARLES BROCKDEN   Edgar Huntly: Or, Memoirs of a Sleep-Walker.
Philadelphia, 1801. 3 vols., 12mo., contemporary calf, worn, sound copy.
Ximenes 37-23 1974 $175

BROWN, CHARLES BROCKDEN   Ormond, or the Secret Witness. London,
1839. 8vo., half calf, apparently second English edition, unopened. Ximenes
36-32 1974 $45

BROWN, D. DENNY   Selected Writings of Sir Charles Sherrington.
London, 1939. Rittenhouse 46-101 1974 $10

BROWN, DAVID PAUL   The Prophet of St. Paul's. Philadelphia, 1836.
Orig. cloth, first edition, fine copy, written top of title page "Presented by the
Author". MacManus 224-53 1974 $65

BROWN, EDWARD   An Account of Several Travels. London, 1677.
4to., calf, plates, first edition. Gurney 64-39 1974 £50

BROWN, EDWARD   An Account of Several Travels Through a Great
Part of Germany; In Four Journeys. London, 1677. 4to., calf, plates, first
edition, some minor staining. Gurney 66-35 1974 £50

BROWN, FRANK C.   Letters and Lettering. Boston, 1918.
Biblo & Tannen 210-351 1973 $8.50

BROWN, FRANK P.   London Buildings, Paintings and Sculpture.
London, 1933-34. 3 vols. in 1, 8vo., fold out maps, interior fine. Current BW9-
517 1974 $30

BROWN, G. B.   The Art of the Cave Dweller. 1928. 8vo.,
illus., cloth, maps. Quaritch 940-302 1974 £6

BROWN, G. M.   Ponce De Leon Land and Florida War Record.
St. Augustine, 1902. Pictorial wrappers, eighth edition. Putnam 126-237 1974
$25

BROWN, GEORGE   Arithmetica Infinita. 1717-18. Oblong small
4to., contemporary panelled calf, fine, first edition. Dawsons PM 245-139 1974
£35

BROWN, GEORGE   A Compendious, But a Compleat System of Decimal Arithmetick. Edinburgh, (1701). Small 4to., orig. unlettered calf, rebacked,
first edition. Dawsons PM 245-138 1974 £150

BROWN, GLENN   History of the United States Capitol. Washington,
1900-03. Folio, 2 vols., full page plates, inscribed by author. Butterfield
10-62 1974 $90

BROWN, GOOLD   The Grammar of English Grammars. New York, 1851. Unbound sheets. Biblo & Tannen 213-757 1973 $7.50

BROWN, H. R.   Butterflies and Moths at Home and Abroad. 1912. Roy. 8vo., cloth, plates. Wheldon 131-789 1974 £5

BROWN, HARRY   A Sound of Hunting. Knopf, 1945. 176p., illus. Austin 51-155 1973 $8.50

BROWN, HORATIO F.   John Addington Symonds. 1903. Portrait, second edition. Covent 56-1232 1974 £7.50

BROWN, HORATIO F.   John Addington Symonds. London, 1908. Biblo & Tannen 213-824 1973 $10

BROWN, HORATIO F.   Studies in the History of Venice. 1907. 2 vols., thick 8vo., orig. cloth, orig. edition. Howes 186-639 1974 £8.50

BROWN, IVOR   Theatre. Reinhart, 1956. 200p., illus. Austin 51-156 1973 $8.50

BROWN, J. H.   Spectropia. London, 1864. 4to., orig. cloth-backed dec. boards, plates, second edition, first series. Hammond 201-85 1974 £20

BROWN, JAMES BARRETT   Skin Grafting of Burns, Primary Care, Treatment, Repair. Philadelphia, 1943. Mint. Rittenhouse 46-103 1974 $20

BROWN, JOHN   A Dissertation on the Rise, Union, and Power, the Progressions, Separations, and Corruptions, of Poetry and Music. 1763. 4to., contemporary calf, fine, first edition. Quaritch 940-808 1974 £70

BROWN, JOHN   History of San Bernardino and Riverside Counties. (Chicago), 1922. 3 vols., 4to., cloth. Saddleback 14-46 1974 $125

BROWN, JOHN   Letters Upon the Poetry and Music of the Italian Opera. Edinburgh, 1789. 8vo., disbound, old library blindstamp, very good copy, first edition. Ximenes 37-24 1974 $75

BROWN, JOHN   Spare Hours. Boston, 1897. Rittenhouse 46-105 1974 $10

BROWN, JOHN MASON   The World of Robert E. Sherwood, Mirror of His Times. Harper & Row, 1962. 409p. Austin 51-157 1973 $6

BROWN, JONATHAN   The History and Present Condition of St. Domingo. Philadelphia, 1837. 2 vols., 12mo., orig. green cloth, early library stickers on spines, nice copy, first edition. Ximenes 37-25 1974 $125

BROWN, MOSES TRUE   The Synthetic Philosophy of Expression. Houghton, 1886. 297p. Austin 51-158 1973 $12.50

BROWN, N. E.   Mesembryanthema. 1931. 4to., cloth, illus., coloured plates, scarce. Wheldon 128-1447 1973 £6.50

BROWN, N. E.   Mesembryanthema. 1931. 4to., cloth, scarce. Wheldon 130-1377 1974 £7.50

BROWN, N. E.   Stapelieae, from Hooker's Icones Plantarum Third Series, Vol. 10, Part 1. 1890. 8vo., half morocco, plates. Wheldon 131-1649 1974 £5

BROWN, NATHAN   De Histori ov Magnus Maha'rba and de Blak Dragun. Nu-York, 1866. 12mo., orig. light blue printed wrappers, first edition, very good copy. Ximenes 36-33 1974 $45

BROWN, O. PHELPS   The Complete Herbalist. Jersey City, 1867. Biblo & Tannen 214-346 1974 $17.50

BROWN, P. HUME   History of Scotland. Cambridge, 1909. 3 vols., small 8vo., cloth. Quaritch 939-646 1974 £8.50

BROWN, P. HUME   History of Scotland, to the Present Time. 1911. 3 vols., large 8vo., buckram, plates, maps, best library edition. Howes 186-640 1974 £15.50

BROWN, R.   Miscellaneous Botanical Works. 1866-68. Folio, orig. boards, 3 vols., plates. Wheldon 129-890 1974 £30

BROWN, R.   Prodromus Florae Novae Hollandiae et Insulac Van-Diemen. Nuremberg, 1827. 8vo., contemporary calf, second edition. Wheldon 130-1131 1974 £75

BROWN, R.   Supplementum Primum Prodromi Florae Novae Hollandiae. 1830. 8vo., sewed, rare. Wheldon 130-1132 1974 £20

BROWN, R. C.   History of Butler County, Pennsylvania. (Chicago), 1895. 8vo., cloth, illus. Saddleback 14-664 1974 $135

BROWN, R. N. R.   The Polar Regions. 1927. 8vo., cloth, maps, scarce. Wheldon 129-251 1974 £5

BROWN, RICHARD   A History of Accounting and Accountants. Edinburgh, 1905. Large 8vo., orig. cloth, illus., first edition. Dawsons PM 10-87 1974 £10

BROWN, SYDNEY MAC GILLVARY.   Medieval Europe. New York, 1935. Biblo & Tannen 214-596 1974 $8

BROWN, T.   The Zoologists Text-Book. Glasgow, 1832-33. 2 vols., post 8vo., orig. cloth, plates, rare. Wheldon 128-258 1973 £15

BROWN, T.   The Zoologists Text-Book. Glasgow, 1832-33. 2 vols., 8vo., orig. cloth, plates, rare. Wheldon 131-417 1974 £15

BROWN, THOMAS   A Legacy for the Ladies. 1705. 8vo., contemporary panelled calf, rebacked, scarce, first edition. Quaritch 936-25 1974 £100

BROWN, THOMAS, CAPTAIN   An Atlas of the Fossil Conchology of Great Britain and Ireland. 1889. 4to., cloth. Wheldon 129-734 1974 £15

BROWN, THOMAS, CAPTAIN   Illustrations of the Land and Fresh Water Conchology of Great Britain and Ireland. 1845. Roy. 8vo., orig. cloth, plates. Wheldon 131-890 1974 £18

BROWN, THOMAS, CAPTAIN   Illustrations of the Land and Fresh Water Conchology of Great Britain and Ireland. 1845. Roy. 8vo., cloth, coloured plates, scarce. Wheldon 128-833 1973 £18

BROWN, THOMAS, CAPTAIN   Illustrations of the Land and Fresh Water Conchology of Great Britain and Ireland. 1845. Roy. 8vo., orig. cloth, plates. Wheldon 129-733 1974 £5

BROWN, THOMAS, CAPTAIN   Illustrations of the Recent Conchology of Great Britain and Ireland. (1844). 4to., plates, half calf, second edition. Bow Windows 64-37 1974 £60

BROWN, W. J.   The Gods Had Wings. London, 1936. Cloth, dust wrapper, woodcuts. Dawson's 424-100 1974 $15

BROWN, W. M.   The Queen's Bush, a Tale of the Early Days of Bruce County. London, 1932. Folding map. Hood's 102-587 1974 $25

BROWN, W. N.   A Descriptive and Illustrated Catalogue of Miniature Paintings of the Jaina Kalpasutra as Executed in the Early Western Indian Style. Washington, 1934. Folio, plates, wrappers, soiled. Quaritch 940-377 1974 £7

BROWN, WILLIAM   New Zealand and its Aborigines. 1845. 8vo., green cloth, first edition. Bow Windows 64-409 1974 £60

BROWN, WILLIAM ADAMS   The Church. Scribner, 1935. Austin 62-729 1974 $10

BROWN, WILLIAM H.   The History of the First Locomotives in America. New York, 1871. Plates, first edition, orig. binding. Butterfield 10-474 1974 $85

BROWN, WILLIAM WELLS   My Southern Home. Boston, 1880. Fine copy, first edition, orig. binding. Butterfield 10-95 1974 $35

BROWNE, EDWARD   A Brief Account of Some Travels In Divers Parts of Europe. London, 1685. Folio, old half calf, plates, second edition. Traylen 79-558 1973 £45

BROWNE, G. F.   King Alfred's Books. 1920. Roy. 8vo., map, scarce. Howes 186-565 1974 £7.50

BROWNE, GEORGE WALDO 1851-   The New America and the Far East. Boston, c. 1913. 10 vols., 4to., cloth, illus., plates. Rinsland 58-927 1974 $35

BROWNE, GEORGE WALDO 1851-   The St. Lawrence River. New York, 1905. Cloth, plates, fine. Hayman 57-54 1974 $15

BROWNE, H. K.   Sir Gudy de Guy. London, 1864. First edition, 8vo., illus., orig. gilt dec. red cloth, top and bottom of spine chipped, interior very fine. Current BW9-583 1974 $42.50

BROWNE, JAMES 1793-1841   A History of the Highlands. Edinburgh, (c. 1875). 4 vols. in 2, 8vo., calf, illus., fine. Quaritch 939-647 1974 £45

BROWNE, JOHN ROSS 1821-1875   Adventures in the Apache Country. New York, 1869. Orig. cloth, illus., first edition. Bradley 35-351 1974 $150

BROWNE, JOHN ROSS 1821-1875   Report...on the Mineral Resources of the States and Territories West of the Rocky Mountains and Report...on the Minearl Resources of the U. S. East of the Rocky Mountains. Washington, 1868. Jenkins 61-249 1974 $10

BROWNE, M.   Artistic and Scientific Taxidermy and Modelling. 1896. 8vo., cloth, faded, text-figures, plates. Wheldon 128-259 1973 £5

BROWNE, M.   The Vertebrate Animals of Leicestershire and Rutland. 1889. 4to., cloth, plates, scarce. Wheldon 130-273 1974 £10

BROWNE, MATTHEW   Chaucer's England. 1869. 8vo., 2 vols., frontispiece, marbled boards, gilt, first edition. Quaritch 936-338 1974 £6

BROWNE, MATTHEW   Little Ben Bute. Philadelphia, 1884. 4to., pict. boards, cloth spine. Frohnsdorff 16-126 1974 $10

BROWNE, PATRICK   The Civil and Natural History of Jamaica. 1756. Engraved plates, map, chart, first edition, folio, contemporary morocco spine, some light foxing, very good copy, scarce. Broadhurst 24-1059 1974 £250

BROWNE, T. A.   In Memoriam 1841-1919. Ottawa, 1919. Card cover, illus., second edition. Hood's 103-201 1974 $10

BROWNE, THOMAS   Christian Morals. London, 1756. 8vo., contemporary calf, first edition. Dawsons PM 252-543 1974 £85

BROWNE, THOMAS   Hydriotaphia. 1927. Post 8vo., full vellum, English first edition. Covent 56-180 1974 £12.50

BROWNE, THOMAS   Posthumous Works of the Learned Sir Thomas Browne. London, 1712. 8vo., contemporary panelled calf, rebacked, plates, portrait, some foxing, minor tears, first edition. Ximenes 37-26 1974 $125

BROWNE, THOMAS   Pseudodoxia Epidemica. 1646. Small folio, new calf antique, first edition, tall copy. Thomas 32-308 1974 £250

BROWNE, THOMAS   Pseudoxia Epidemica. London, 1658. 4to., contemporary calf, rebacked, plates. Gurney 64-40 1974 £36

BROWNE, THOMAS   Religio Medici. Philadelphia, 1844. Foxing. Rittenhouse 46-106 1974 $45

BROWNE, THOMAS   Religio Medici and Other Writings. New York, 1906. Rittenhouse 46-107 1974 $10

BROWNE, THOMAS   La Religion du Medecin. N.P., 1668. 12mo., contemporary vellum, first French edition. Schuman 37-32 1974 $115

BROWNE, THOMAS   The Works. London, 1686. Folio, fine, contemporary panelled calf, first collected edition. Dawsons PM 252-81 1974 £155

BROWNE, THOMAS   Works. 1836-35. 4 vols., new buckram, blind stamp. Allen 216-1880 1974 $45

BROWNE, THOMAS   Works. 1836. 4 vols., roy. 8vo., orig. brown cloth, rebacked, plates, limited, portrait. Howes 186-52 1974 £30

BROWNE, THOMAS   The Works of. London, 1928. 6 vols., 8vo., frontispiece, orig. blue buckram, faded. Dawsons PM 252-83 1974 £40

BROWNE, THOMAS   The Works of. London, 1928-31. 6 vols. in 3, 8vo., half morocco, fine, limited, signed. Dawsons PM 252-82 1974 £60

BROWNE, WALTER   Who's Who On the Stage. Dodge, 1908. 467p., illus. Austin 51-159 1973 $15

BROWNE, WILLIAM   Britannia's Pastorals. London, 1616. 2 books in 1 vol., small folio, modern full morocco, plates, first & second editions. Dawsons PM 252-84 1974 £300

BROWNELL, HENRY H.   The People's Book of Ancient and Modern History. Boston, 1854. 2 vols. in 1 as issued, coloured illus., leather, lacks spine, plates in color. Hayman 59-73 1974 $12.50

BROWNELL, W. C.   American Prose Masters. Scribner, 1909. 400p., orig. ed. Austin 54-175 1973 $7.50

BROWNELL, W. C.   French Traits. Scribner, 1889. 316p. Austin 54-176 1973 $6

BROWNELL, W. C.   The Genius of Style. Scribners, 1924. 226p. Austin 54-177 1973 $7.50

BROWNING, ELIZABETH BARRETT   Aurora Leigh. 1857. Orig. patterned cloth, English first edition. Covent 56-181 1974 £21

BROWNING, ELIZABETH BARRETT   Casa Guidi Windows. 1851. First edition, half title, 33 page Publisher's Catalogue at end, small 8vo., orig. embossed cloth, faded, good copy. Sawyer 293-77 1974 £15.75

BROWNING, ELIZABETH BARRETT   Casa Guidi Windows. 1851. 8vo., orig. cloth, first edition. Broadhurst 23-645 1974 £25

BROWNING, ELIZABETH BARRETT   Elizabeth Barrett Browning and Her Scorcer Books. 1896. 8vo., frontis., orig. white boards, first edition. Bow Windows 64-410 1974 £25

BROWNING, ELIZABETH BARRETT   The Greek Christian Poets and the English Poets. London, 1863. 12mo., orig. green cloth, very good copy, first edition. Ximenes 37-27 1974 $35

BROWNING, ELIZABETH BARRETT   Poems Before Congress. London, 1860. 8vo., uncut, orig. cloth, first edition. Dawsons PM 252-85 1974 £8

BROWNING, ELIZABETH BARRETT   Poetical Works. London, 1866. 5 vols., 8vo., engraved, orig. green cloth, first edition. Bow Windows 62-124 1974 £48

BROWNING, ELIZABETH BARRETT   Sonnets from the Portuguese. London, 1904. Purple morocco, gilt, fine, 2 3/4/ X 2 inches. Gregory 44-346 1974 $22.50

BROWNING, ELIZABETH BARRETT   Two Poems. London, 1854. Orig. printed wrappers, first edition. Dawson's 424-251 1974 $100

BROWNING, ELIZABETH BARRETT   Two Poems. 1854. Small 8vo., orig. printed wrapper, fine, first edition. Quaritch 936-321 1974 £18

BROWNING, OSCAR   The Life of Bartolomeo Colleoni of Anjou. 1891. Roy. 8vo., cloth, rebound, plates. Covent 55-259 1974 £5.20

BROWNING, ROBERT   Aristophanes' Apology. 1875. Thick small 8vo., orig. dark green cloth, first edition. Howes 185-40 1974 £5

BROWNING, ROBERT   Christmas Eve. London, n.d. Gilt, excellent. Rinsland 58-925 1974 $12.50

BROWNING, ROBERT   Christmas Eve and Easter Day. London, 1850. First edition, orig. cloth, small library stamp & inked inscription, covers lightly worn, nice. Ross 86-78 1974 $12.50

BROWNING, ROBERT   Dramatis Personae. 1910. 8vo., limp vellum. Hammond 201-747 1974 £150

BROWNING, ROBERT   Dramatis Personae. Doves Press, 1910. Printed in black and red, 8vo., orig. limp vellum, fine, limited to 250 copies on paper, presentation copy inscribed. Sawyer 293-125 1974 £138

BROWNING, ROBERT   Fifine at the Fair. London, 1872. 8vo., orig. brown cloth, first edition. Bow Windows 62-125 1974 £8.50

BROWNING, ROBERT   Fifine at the Fair. London, 1872. 8vo., orig. brown cloth, book-plate, first edition. Dawsons PM 252-87 1974 £8

BROWNING, ROBERT   The Letters 1845-46. 1899. 2 vols., crown 8vo., orig. cloth, portraits, first edition. Howes 186-55 1974 £5

BROWNING, ROBERT   The Letters. New York, 1899. 2 vols., cloth gilt, portraits, English first edition. Covent 56-183 1974 £11

BROWNING, ROBERT   Men & Women. Hammersmith, 1908. 2 vols., 8vo., orig. limp vellum, limited. Bow Windows 62-273 1974 £225

BROWNING, ROBERT   Pacchiarotto and How He Worked in Distemper. 1876. Library stamp, first edition. Bow Windows 66-86 1974 $32.50

BROWNING, ROBERT   Parleyings with Certain People. 1887. 8vo., orig. cloth, rubbed. Covent 55-260 1974 £8

BROWNING, ROBERT   Pauline. 1886. Orig. boards, paper label, rubbed, uncut, limited. Thomas 28-220 1972 £10.50

BROWNING, ROBERT   The Pied Piper of Hamelin. London, n.d. 4to., orig. glazed pictorial boards, first edition, about fine, illus. by Kate greenaway. MacManus 224-193 1974 $50

BROWNING, ROBERT   The Pied Piper of Hamelin. (1888). First edition, coloured illus. by Kate Greenaway, light foxing, 4to., orig. cloth backed pictorial boards, good copy. George's 610-332 1973 £25

BROWNING, ROBERT   The Pied Piper of Hamelin. (1888). First edition, coloured illus. by Kate Greenaway, 4to., orig. cloth backed pictorial boards, little light spotting. George's 610-333 1973 £20

BROWNING, ROBERT   The Pied Piper of Hamelin. Chicago, 1910. 4to., color plates. Frohnsdorff 16-127 1974 $15

BROWNING, ROBERT   The Pied Piper of Hamelin. 1935. Roy 8vo., full limp vellum, signed, limited edition. Broadhurst 23-167 1974 £70

BROWNING, ROBERT   Poems. London, 1849. 2 vols., new edition, 8vo., orig. olive green cloth, first collected edition, very nice copy. Ximenes 36-34 1974 $100

BROWNING, ROBERT   Poems. New York, 1924. 2 vols., demy 4to., morocco spines, fine. Broadhurst 24-295 1974 £35

BROWNING, ROBERT   The Poetic and Dramatic Works. 1890. 6 vols. Austin 61-150 1974 $37.50

BROWNING, ROBERT   Poetical Works. 1868-75. 6 vols., small 8vo., orig. brown bevelled cloth. Howes 185-39 1974 £7.50

BROWNING, ROBERT   Poetical Works. 1907. 2 vols., crown 8vo., full prize calf gilt, portraits. Howes 186-53 1974 £7.50

BROWNING, ROBERT   Prince Hohenstiel-Schwangau. London, 1871. 8vo., orig. cloth, fine, first edition. Dawsons PM 252-88 1974 £15

BROWNING, ROBERT   Prince Hohenstiel-Schwangau: Saviour of Society. 1871. Spine & corners rubbed, library label, very good copy, first edition. Covent 51-297 1973 £20

BROWNING, ROBERT   Red Cotton Night-Cap Country. London, 1873. First edition, hinges somewhat loose, good copy, orig. binding. Ross 86-79 1974 $10

BROWNING, ROBERT   The Ring and the Book. New York, 1949. Biblo & Tannen 210-735 1973 $7.50

BROWNING, ROBERT   La Saisiaz: The Two Poets of Croisic. London, 1878. First edition, fine, tight copy, orig. binding. Ross 86-80 1974 $10

BROWNLOW, KEVIN   The Parade's Gone By. Knopf, 1968. 577p., orig. hard cover ed., illus. Austin 51-160 1973 $12.50

BROWNRIG, RALPH   Fourty Sermons. 1661. Folio, contemporary calf, rebacked. Howes 185-1008 1974 £22.50

BROWNSON, ORESTES AUGUSTUS   A Discourse on the Wants of the Times. Boston, 1836. 8vo., orig. printed wrappers, fine, first edition. Goodspeed's 578-35 1974 $25

BROWNSON, ORESTES AUGUSTUS   The Spirit-Rapper. Detroit, 1884. Cloth, fine. Hayman 57-55 1974 $12.50

BROWNSON, ORESTES AUGUSTUS   Uncle Jack and His Nephew. Detroit, 1888. Cloth, fine. Hayman 57-56 1974 $12.50

BRUCE, HAROLD   William Blake. 1925. Plates, inscription, frayed dust wrapper, fine. Covent 55-222 1974 £8.50

BRUCE, I. M.   The History of the Aberdeenshire Shorthorn. Aberdeen, 1923. 8vo., cloth, illus. Wheldon 129-363 1974 £10

BRUCE, I. M.   The History of the Aberdeenshire Shorthorn. Aberdeen, 1923. 8vo., cloth, plates, illus. Wheldon 131-477 1974 £10

BRUCE, J.   Select Specimens of Natural History. Edinburgh, 1790. 4to., orig. boards, plates. Wheldon 129-252 1974 £35

BRUCE, J. C.   A Descriptive Catalogue of Antiquities. Newcastle, 1880. 4to., plates, cloth. Quaritch 939-507 1974 £20

BRUCE, J. C.   Roman Wall: Historical, Topographical & Descriptive Account. 1851. Half morocco, lithograph. Allen 213-182 1973 $15

BRUCE, JOHN   Annals of the Honourable East-India Company. London, 1810. 3 vols., 4to., tree calf, rebacked, foxing. Traylen 79-516 1973 £190

BRUCE, R.   Fifty Years Among Shorthorns. 1907. 8vo., cloth, scarce. Wheldon 129-364 1974 £7.50

BRUCE, R.   Fifty Years Among Shorthorns. 1907. 8vo., cloth, plates, scarce. Wheldon 131-478 1974 £6

BRUCKMANN, F. E.   Magnalis Dei in Locis Subterraneis Oder Unterirdische Schatz-Cammer. Braunschweig, 1727. Folio, old boards, worn, copperplates, very rare. Harper 213-25 1973 $650

BRUCKNER, FERDINAND   Races. Knopf, 1934. 139p. Austin 51-161 1973 $8.50

BRUDZEWO, ALBERTUS DE   Commentum in Theoricas Planetarum Georgii Purbachii. Milan, 1495. 4to., boards, leather spine, woodcut diagrams, enlarged second edition, neat contemporary marginalia, Georg Tannstetter's copy. Kraus 137-17 1974 $1,650

BRUEGHEL, PIETER   Pieter Brueghel the Elder. (c. 1938). Roy. 4to., plates, canvas. Quaritch 940-45 1974 £10

BRUETTE, WILLIAM   American Duck, Goose, and Brant Shooting. New York, 1934. 8vo., d.j. soiled, full color plates, very good. Current BW9-157 1974 $12.50

BRUEYS, D. A.   Histoire du Fanatisme de Nostre Temps. Paris, 1692. Small 8vo., old calf, worn, first edition. Goodspeed's 578-36 1974 $10

BRUGMAN, KARL   Griechische und Lateinische.   1890.   New buckram.   Allen 213-184 1973 $15

BRULLER, JEAN   21 Delightful Ways of Committing Suicide. 1930.   Austin 54-178 1973 $10

BRUMPT, E.   Les Mycetomes.   Paris, 1906.   Roy 8vo., buckram, plates.   Wheldon 130-1244 1974 £5

BRUN, MARCELIN   Manuel Pratique et Abrege de la Typographie Francaise.   Brussels, 1826.   Second edition, cloth.   Kraus B8-294 1974 $30

BRUN, ROBERT   Le Livre Illustre en France en France Au XVIe Siecle.   Paris, 1930.   4to., plates, contemporary purple half morocco, fine. Dawsons PM 10-91 1974 £40

BRUNEL, ADRIAN   Film Script.   Burke, 1948.   192p., illus. Austin 51-162 1973 $8.50

BRUNETTI, E.   Oriental Diptera.   Calcutta, 1907-25.   Roy. 8vo., wrappers, plates.   Wheldon 128-682 1973 £15

BRUNETTI, E.   Oriental Diptera.   Calcutta, 1907-25.   Roy. 8vo., wrappers, plates.   Wheldon 131-790 1974 £15

BRUNHOFF, JEAN DE   Histoire de Babar.   London, 1949.   4to., music of Francis Poulenc.   Biblo & Tannen 214-898 1974 $20

BRUNI, DOMENICO   Opera Intitolato Difese Delle Donne, Nella Quale si Contengano le Difese loro, Dalle Calumnie Dategli per Gli Scrittori, & Insieme le Lodi di Quelle.   Florence, 1552.   Vellum, title little soiled and mounted, first few leaves trifle used, else clean & sound.   Thomas 32-145 1974 £35

BRUNIUS, JACQUES B.   Idolatry & Confusion.   (c.1943).   4to., orig. cloth, scarce, first edition.   Rota 188-873 1974 £5

BRUNNICH, M. T.   Dyrenes Historie og Dyre-Samlingen udi Universitetetes Natur-Theater.   Copenhagen, 1782.   4to., old half calf, plates, very rare.   Wheldon 131-479 1974 £200

BRUNNOW, F.   Lehrbuch der Spharischen Astronomie.   Berlin, 1862.   8vo., half calf.   Dawsons PM 245-140 1974 £5

BRUNSCHWIG, HIERONYMUS   Liber De Arte Distillandi.   1500.   Folio, contemporary blind-stamped calf, boards, worn, rebacked, woodcuts, first edition. Dawsons PM 245-141 1974 £2,750

BRUNSCHWIG, HIERONYMUS   Liber de Arte Distillandi.   Strassburg, 1500. Folio, woodcuts, contemporary blind-stamped calf, wooden boards, worn, rebacked, dampstain, first edition.   Dawsons PM 250-11 1974 £3750

BRUNSCHWIG, HIERONYMUS   The Noble Experyence of the Vertuous Handy Warke of Surgeri.   London, 1525.   Woodcuts, folio, calf, from the collection of the Earl of Dysart, Ham House, first edition in English, splendidly preserved. Kraus 137-19 1974 £32,500

BRUNSCHWIG, HIERONYMUS   Thesaurus Pauperum.   Frankfurt, 1537.   Small 4to., woodcut title border, woodcuts, modern brown morocco, rare first edition, very fine, some occasional foxing.   Schafer 10-121 1974 sFr 3,900

BRUNSCHWIG, HIERONYMUS   The Vertuose Boke of Distyllacyon of the Waters.   London, 1427, (i.e., 1527?).   Folio, calf, first edition, from the collection of Earl of Dysart, Hame House, complete in magnificent condition. Kraus 137-18 1974 £28,500

BRUNSCHWIG, HIERONYMUS   The Vertuose Boke of Distyllacyon of the Waters of All Maner of Herbes . . . .   London, 1527.   Small folio, woodcuts, blind-panelled leather.   Traylen 79-207 1973 £85

BRUNTON, MARY   Self Control.   Edinburgh & London, 1811. 2 vols., 12mo., contemporary half calf, first edition.   Dawsons PM 252-89 1974 £30

BRUNTON, T. LAUDER   Collected Papers on Physical and Military Training.   London, 1887-1915.   8vo., blue half morocco, gilt, presentation copy, inscribed, first edition.   Dawsons PM 249-93 1974 £12

BRUNTON, T. LAUDER   On Disorders of Digestion, Their Consequences and Treatment.   London, 1888.   Rittenhouse 46-110 1974 $11

BRUNUS, ARETINUS, LEONARDUS   Aquila Volante.   Milan, 1518.   Italian 18th century mottled boards, woodcut.   Thomas 28-281 1972 £50

BRUNUS ARETINUS, LEONARDUS   Aquila Volante.   Milan, 1518.   Italian 18th century mottled boards, some browning, somewhat used and worn.   Thomas 32-224 1974 £50

BRUSH, KATHARINE   The Boy from Maine.   Farrar, Rinehart, 1949. 340p.   Austin 54-179 1973 $6

BRUSH, KATHARINE   Don't Ever Leave Me.   1935.   311p.   Austin 54-180 1973 $6.50

BRUSH, KATHARINE   You Go Your Way.   Farrar, 1941.   240p. Austin 54-181 1973 $6.50

BRUSH, KATHARINE   Young Man of Manhatten.   Farrar, 1930. 325p.   Austin 54-182 1973 $7.50

BRUUN, H. G.   Cytological Studies in Primula.   Uppsala, 1932.   Roy. 8vo., orig. wrappers, uncut.   Wheldon 131-1121 1974 £5

BRUYN, CORNELIS DE   Conference de Monsieur Le Brun.   Amsterdam, and Paris, 1698.   12mo., plates, stains, contemporary calf.   Quaritch 940-163 1974 £30

BRY, JOHANN THEODOR DE   Nova Alphati Effictio Historiis ad Singulas Literas Correspondantibus.   Frankfurt, 1595.   4to., plates, polished calf gilt, rare. Quaritch 940-430 1974 £1,000

BRYAN, DANIEL   The Mountain Muse, Comprising the Adventures of Daniel Boone.   Harrisonburg, 1813.   12mo., contemporary sheep, bit rubbed, but sound, first edition.   Ximenes 36-35 1974 $80

BRYAN, MARGARET   Lectures on Natural Philosophy.   London, 1806. 4to., half morocco, presentation copy, plates, first edition.   Dawsons PM 245-142 1974 £10

BRYAN, MICHAEL   A Biographical and Critical Dictionary of Painters & Engravers.   1816.   2 vols., foxed.   Covent 55-84 1974 £25

BRYAN, MICHAEL   Bryan's Dictionary of Painters and Engravers. 1919-21.   5 vols., 4to., illus., plates, cloth.   Quaritch 940-46 1974 £70

BRYAN, MICHAEL   Dictionary of Painters and Engravers.   1902. 2 vols., 4to., revised & enlarged new edition.   Marsden 37-95 1974 £12

BRYAN, WILLIAM S.   Our Islands and Their People.   St. Louis, 1899. 2 vols., folio, photos, color plates, maps.   Wilson 63-6 1974 $25

BRYANT, CHARLES   Flora Diaeteica.   London, 1783.   8vo., first edition, contemporary calf, joints cracked.   Gurney 66-109 1974 £35

BRYANT, CHARLES   An Historical Account of Two Species of Lycoperdon.   (1782).   8vo., orig. wrappers, uncut, folding plate.   Wheldon 128-1346 1973 £12

BRYANT, EDWIN   What I Saw In California.   Santa Ana, 1936. 8vo., quarter leather.   Saddleback 14-47 1974 $60

BRYANT, G. E.   The Chelsea Porcelain Toys.   1925.   Roy. 4to., plates, cloth, limited edition.   Quaritch 939-441 1974 £50

BRYANT, JACOB   A New System.   1807.   6 vols., roy. 8vo., full polished calf gilt, plates, labels.   Howes 186-1793 1974 £42

BRYANT, JACOB   Observations Upon the Plagues Inflicted Upon the Egyptians.   London, 1810.   Half leather, marbled boards, new edition. Rittenhouse 46-95 1974 $55

BRYANT, MARGARET M.   Psychology of English.   1940.   Ex-library. Austin 61-154 1974 $27.50

BRYANT, WILLIAM CULLEN   Picturesque America.   New York, c. 1872.
2 vols., large 4to., embossed morocco, beveled edges, fine engraved plates, text
illus., lightly rubbed.   Wilson 63-7 1974 $75

BRYANT, WILLIAM CULLEN   Picturesque America.   Appleton, 1873.
46 parts, illus., soiling.   Rinsland 58-936 1974 $25

BRYANT, WILLIAM CULLEN   Poems.   Boston, 1821. 16mo., contemporary
half roan, first edition.   Goodspeed's 578-37 1974 $125

BRYANT, WILLIAM CULLEN   Poems.   New York, 1947. 4to., ltd ed.,
lea., rubbed.   Biblo & Tannen 210-760 1973 $12.50

BRYANT, WILLIAM CULLEN   Prose Writings.   1884. 2 vols., ex-library.
Allen 216-271 1974 $15

BRYANT, WILLIAM CULLEN   The United States Review and Literary Gazette.
N.P. (New York?), 1826. 8vo., disbound, very rare.   Ximenes 36-36 1974
$100

BRYCE, G.   The Siege and Conquest of the North Pole.
London, 1910. Maps.   Hood's 103-50 1974 $20

BRYCE, JAMES   The American Commonwealth.   1888. 3 vols.,
nice set, very largely unopned, first edition.   Covent 51-2095 1973 £15

BRYCE, JAMES   The American Commonwealth.   New York,
1910. 2 vols., revised & enlarged edition, as new.   Jenkins 61-253 1974
$13.50

BRYCE, JAMES   Geology of Arran and Clydesdale.   Glasgow,
1865. Crown 8vo., cloth, plates, maps.   Wheldon 129-809 1974 £5

BRYCE, JAMES   Modern Democracies.   New York, 1921.
2 vols., mint.   Jenkins 61-254 1974 $12.50

BRYCE, JAMES   Practical Observations On the Inoculation of
Cowpox.   Edinburgh, 1802. 8vo., contemporary tree calf, rebacked, plates,
first edition.   Traylen 79-208 1973 £48

BRYCE, JAMES   South America.   1912. 8vo., maps, cloth.
Wheldon 129-253 1974 £7.50

BRYCE, JAMES   Studies In Contemporary Biography.   1903.
Ex-library.   Austin 61-155 1974 $10

BRYCE, WILLIAM MOIR   The Scottish Grey Friars.   (1909). 2 vols.,
thick roy. 8vo., orig. cloth, scarce, plates.   Howes 185-1009 1974 £18

BRYCE'S English Dictionary.   Glasgow, n.d. Orig. limp cloth, stained covers.
Smith 194-361 1974 £9.50

BRYCE'S Thumb Dictionary.   Glasgow, (before 1894). Orig. black stamped russet
cloth, 2 1/8 X 1 3/4 inches.   Gregory 44-353 1974 $12.50

BRYCE'S Thumb Dictionary.   Glasgow, (c. 1900). Full red morocco, rounded
corners, all edges gilt, fine, 2 1/8 X 1 3/4 inches.   Gregory 44-354 1974
$16.50

BRYCE'S Thumb English Dictionary.   Glasgow, n.d. Orig. black roan, gilt,
fine, 2 1/4 X 1 7/8 inches.   Gregory 44-355 1974 $17.50

BRYDEN, H. A.   Great and Small Game of Africa.   1899. 4to.,
orig. cloth, hand-coloured plates, text-figures, numbered, very scarce, limited
edition.   Wheldon 128-1697 1973 £200

BRYDEN, H. A.   Hare Hunting and Harriers, With Notices of
Beagles and Basset Hounds.   (c. 1900). First edition, illus., 8vo., orig. red
cloth gilt, fine.   Sawyer 293-269 1974 £5.25

BRYDGES, SAMUEL EGERTON   Censura Literaria.   London, 1805-09.
10 vols., 8vo., old quarter calf, marbled boards, first edition.   Dawsons PM
252-90 1974 £110

BRYDGES, SIR SAMUEL EGERTON   Letters from the Continent.   Kent, 1821.
8vo., contemporary calf, gilt, rubbed but sound, first edition.   Ximenes 36-37
1974 $65

BRYDGES, SIR SAMUEL EGERTON   Letters on Character and Poetical Genius of
Lord Byron.   1824. Half morocco, first edition.   Allen 216-297 1974 $15

BRYDGES, SAMUEL EGERTON   Polyanthea Librorum Vetustiorum.   Geneva,
1822. 8vo., contemporary half morocco, uncut, scarce.   Dawsons PM 10-93
1974 £40

BRYDGES, SIR SAMUEL EGERTON   The Population and Riches of Nations.   Paris,
1819. 8vo., modern quarter cloth, first edition, very good.   Ximenes 36-38 1974
$55

BRYDGES, SAMUEL EGERTON   Restituta.   London, 1814-16. 4 vols., 8vo.,
contemporary gilt-framed polished calf gilt, first edition.   Dawsons PM 10-94
1974 £95

BRYDGES, SAMUEL EGERTON   Restituta.   London, 1814-16. 4 vols., 8vo.,
contemporary gilt framed polished calf, first edition.   Dawsons PM 252-91
1974 £110

BRYDGES, THOMAS   A Burlesque Translation of Homer.   London,
1797. Illus., 19th cent. 3/4 mor. and marbled bds.   Jacobs 24-97 1974 £35

BRYDGES, THOMAS   A Burlesque Translation of Homer.   1797. 8vo.,
2 vols., half red morocco, gilt, plates.   Quaritch 936-26 1974 £25

BUCELIN, GABRIEL   Annales Benedictini.   1656. 2 parts in 1 vol.,
folio, contemporary vellum.   Howes 185-1010 1974 £25

BUCH, CHRISTIAN LEOPOLD VON   Essai d'une Description Mineralogique.
Paris, 1805. 8vo., orig. wrappers.   Zeitlin 235-272 1974 $125

BUCHAN, JOHN   The Courts of the Morning.   London, 1929.
1st ed.   Biblo & Tannen 210-704 1973 $8.50

BUCHAN, JOHN   Essays and Apothegms of Francis Lord Bacon.
n.d. (c. 1894). Gilt top, spine faded, very good copy, first edition.   Covent
51-2218 1973 £10.50

BUCHAN, JOHN   A History of English Literature.   1929. Illus.
Austin 61-156 1974 $12.50

BUCHAN, JOHN   The Island of Sheep.   1936. Dust wrapper,
English first edition.   Covent 56-1586 1974 £7.50

BUCHAN, JOHN   The King's Grace 1910-1935.   1935. Coloured
portrait, illus., first edition.   Bow Windows 66-89 1974 £5.50

BUCHAN, JOHN   The Moon Endureth.   New York, 1912.
Biblo & Tannen 210-573 1973 $15

BUCHAN, JOHN   Prester John.   1910. Orig. cloth, map.
Smith 194-399 1974 £5

BUCHAN, WILLIAM   Domestic Medicine.   London, 1786. 8vo., contemporary calf, ninth edition.   Hammond 201-532 1974 £12

BUCHANAN, A.   Wild Life in Canada.   1920. 8vo., cloth, map,
illus.   Wheldon 128-183 1973 £5

BUCHANAN, A.   Wild Life In Canada.   1920. 8vo., cloth,
illus.   Wheldon 131-342 1974 £5

BUCHANAN, GEORGE   My Mission to Russia and Other Diplomatic
Memories.   1923. 2 vols., large 8vo., plates.   Howes 186-644 1974 £5.50

BUCHANAN, GEORGE   Poemata Omnia Innumeris Pene Locis, ex Ipsius
Autographo Castigata and Aucta.   Edinburgh, 1615. 12mo., contemporary calf,
somewhat worn, lacks clasps.   Thomas 32-160 1974 £45

BUCHANAN, GEORGE   Rerum Scoticarum Historia.   Edinburgh, 1582.
Small folio, contemporary vellum, fine, first edition.   Dawsons PM 252-92
1974 £190

BUCHANAN, ISAAC   First Series of Five Letters Against the Baldwin
Faction By an Advocate of Responsible Government.   Toronto, 1844. Orig.
wrappers.   Hood's 104-673 1974 $95

BUCHANAN, ISAAC   First Series of Five Letters Against the Baldwin Faction by an Advocate of Responsible Government and of the New College Bill. Toronto, 1844. Orig. wrappers, good condition. Hood's 102-588 1974 $95

BUCHANAN, J. Y.   Accounts Rendered of Work Done and Things Seen. Cambridge, 1919. 8vo., cloth. Wheldon 131-301 1974 £12

BUCHANAN, JAMES   Mr. Buchanan's Administration on the Eve of the Rebellion. New York, 1866. Orig. cloth, backstrip faded. Butterfield 10-128 1974 $27.50

BUCHANAN, JOHN   Manual of the Indigenous Grasses of New Zealand. Wellington, 1880. Roy 8vo., half calf, gilt, plates, second edition. Hammond 201-631 1974 £8.50

BUCHANAN, R. E.   General Systematic Bacteriology. Baltimore, 1925. 8vo., cloth. Wheldon 130-1245 1974 £5

BUCHANAN, ROBERT   The Fleshly School of Poetry. 1872. Orig. dec. wrappers, cloth slip-case, rare. Covent 55-262 1974 £130

BUCHANAN, ROBERT   North Coast and Other Poems. 1868. Small 4to., orig. dec. cloth gilt, foxing. Covent 55-263 1974 £25

BUCHANAN, ROBERT   The Piper of Hamelin. 1893. Plates, orig. dec. cloth, English first edition. Covent 56-1587 1974 £25

BUCHANAN, ROBERT   The Wandering Jew. 1893. Orig. cloth gilt, second edition. Covent 55-264 1974 £7.50

BUCHANAN, ROBERTSON   Practical and Descriptive Essays on the Economy of Fuel, and Management of Heat. Glasgow, 1810. 8vo., plates, scarce, contemporary half calf. Quaritch 940-498 1974 £75

BUCHEN, GUSTAVE WILLIAM   Historic Sheboygan County. (Sheboygan, c.1944). 8vo., cloth, autographed. Saddleback 14-756 1974 $35

BUCHLER, SAMUEL   Cohen Comes First and Other Cases. Vanguard, 1933. Austin 62-65 1974 $12.50

BUCHOZ, M.   The Toilet of Flora. London, 1772. 12mo., old sheep, inscription. Bow Windows 62-126 1974 £44

BUCHWALD, ART   ...And Then I Told the President. Putnam, 1965. 243p., illus. Austin 54-183 1973 $5

BUCHWALD, ART   The Brave Coward. Harper, 1957. 211p., illus. Austin 54-184 1973 $6.50

BUCHWALD, ART   How Much is That In Dollars. World, 1961. Austin 54-185 1973 $6.50

BUCHWALD, ART   I Chose Capital Punishment. World, 1963. 249p., illus. Austin 54-186 1973 $6.50

BUCHWALD, ART   Is It Safe to Drink the Water? World, 1962. 253p., illus. Austin 54-187 1973 $6

BUCHWALD, ART   Son of the Great Society. Putnam, 1966. 242p., illus. Austin 54-188 1973 $5

BUCK, GEORGE   The History of the Life and Reigne of Richard the Third. London, 1646. Small folio, 18th century panelled calf gilt, rebacked, first edition. Dawsons PM 251-179 1974 $45

BUCK, GERTRUDE   The Social Criticism of Literature. Yale Univ., 1916. 60p. Austin 54-189 1973 $8.50

BUCK, KATHERINE M.   The Wayland-Dietrich Saga. London, 1924-29. 9 vols., illus., orig. green cloth, uncut. Bow Windows 62-127 1974 £15

BUCK, PEARL S.   The Good Earth. New York, c. 1931. First edition, first state with "flees" for "fleas", dull, orig. binding. Wilson 63-491 1974 $15

BUCK, PEARL S.   The Good Earth. New York, (1931). Orig. cloth, early issue, with "flees" for "fleas", top edges stained green, fine, dust jacket. MacManus 224-54 1974 $35

BUCK, SAMUEL   Proposals for Publishing by Subscription, Six Prespective Views Viz. of the Cities of Canterbury, Rochester, and Chichester. London, 1736. Folio, broadside. Ximenes 36-169 1974 $40

BUCK, SAMUEL   Proposals for Publishing by Subscription, Twenty Four Perspective Views of the Present State of the Most Noted Abbies, Religious Foundations, Castles, and Other Remains of Antiquity, in Norfolk, Suffolk and Essex. London, 1737. Folio, broadside. Ximenes 36-170 1974 $40

BUCK, SAMUEL   Yanaguana's Successors. San Antonio, TX, 1949. Austin 62-66 1974 $17.50

BUCKBEE, EDNA B.   Pioneer Days of Angel's Camp. Angel's Camp, c.1932. 12mo., wrapper. Saddleback 14-48 1974 $20

BUCKE, CHARLES   On the Life, Writings and Genius of Akenside. London, 1832. 8vo., cloth, first edition. Dawsons PM 252-94 1974 £10

BUCKE, RICHARD MAURICE   Cosmic Consciousness. New York, 1923. Sq. 8vo., portrait, fourth edition. Covent 56-187 1974 £12.50

BUCKELY, FRANCIS   A History of Old English Glass. 1925. 4to., plates, dust wrapper, English first edition. Covent 56-1641 1974 £21

BUCKINGHAM, JAMES SILK   Canada, Nova Scotia, New Brunswick, and the Other British Provinces in North America. London, n.d. Folding map, three quarter leather, no plates. Hood's 102-551 1974 $35

BUCKINGHAM, NASH   Blood Lines. Tales of Shooting and Fishing. New York, 1938. Illus., red buckram, limited to 1250 copies, presentation copy, inscription of owner. Current BW9-159 1974 $100

BUCKLAND, F. T.   Curiosities of Natural History. 1882-83. 4 vols., 12mo., orig. cloth. Wheldon 131-147 1974 £10

BUCKLAND, F. T.   Curiosities of Natural History. London, 1900. 4 vols., 8vo., illus., contemporary half calf, morocco labels. Bow Windows 62-129 1974 £18.50

BUCKLAND, W.   Geology and Mineralogy. 1836. 8vo., 2 vols., modern cloth, plates. Wheldon 129-810 1974 £15

BUCKLAND, W.   Geology and Mineralogy Considered With Reference to Natural Theology. 1837. 2 vols., 8vo., contemporary calf, joints broken, covers detached, second edition. Wheldon 128-950 1973 £7

BUCKLAND, WILLIAM   Relinquiae Diluvianae. 1820-23. 4to., half calf, gilt. Hammond 201-362 1974 £60

BUCKLAND, WILLIAM   Reliquiae Diluvianae. 1824. 4to., plates, contemporary green morocco, nice copy, second edition. Wheldon 131-976 1974 £40

BUCKLER, J.   Views of Eaton Hall in Cheshire. 1826. Imp. folio, plates, russia back, contemporary boards. Quaritch 939-330 1974 £60

BUCKLER, W.   The Larvae of the British Butterflies and Moths. 1886. 8vo., orig. cloth, hand coloured plates. Wheldon 128-684 1973 £7.50

BUCKLER, W.   The Larvae of the British Butterflies and Moths, Vols. 2 and 3, Sphinges or Hawk-Moths and Bombyces. 1887-89. 2 vols., 8vo., orig. cloth, hand coloured plates. Wheldon 128-685 1973 £10

BUCKLEY, F.   A History of Old English Glass. 1925. 4to., plates, pigskin, gilt, uncut, limited. Quaritch 940-614 1974 £65

BUCKLEY, W. E.   Partonope of Blois. 1862. 4to., roan spine, some foxing else clean and sound. Thomas 32-286 1974 £50

BUCKMAN, S. S.   Type Ammonites. (1909-30). Roy 8vo., cloth. Wheldon 129-811 1974 £75

BUCKMAN, S. S.   Type Ammonites. (1909-30). 7 vols. in 3, roy. 8vo., cloth, plates. Wheldon 131-977 1974 £75

BUCKMASTER, J. C.   A Village Politician. London, 1897. 8vo., foxing, inscription, orig. green cloth. Bow Windows 62-133 1974 £6.50

BUCKNALL, T. S. D.   The Orchardist. 1805. 8vo., modern boards, second edition. Wheldon 131-1497 1974 £7.50

BUCKSTONE, JOHN B.   A Kiss In the Dark. Taylor, 1840. 20p. Austin 51-163 1973 $7.50

BUCKTON, G. B.   Monograph of the British Aphides. 1876-83. 4 vols., 8vo., cloth, hand coloured and plain plates, scarce. Wheldon 128-686 1973 £25

BUCKTON, G. B.   Monograph of the British Aphides. 1876-83. 8vo., 4 vols., cloth, plates. Wheldon 129-614 1974 £30

BUCKTON, G. B.   Monograph of the British Cicadae. 1890-1891. 2 vols., plates, half morocco, uncut. Bow Windows 64-39 1974 £17.50

BUCKTON, G. B.   Monograph of the British Cicadae. 1890-91. 8vo., 2 vols., orig. wrappers, scarce. Wheldon 129-613 1974 £15

THE BUD. Philadelphia, 1844. 24mo., pict. wrappers, 8 woodcuts. Frohnsdorff 16-129 1974 $5

BUDD, ALFRED   The Oxford Circus. 1922. Illus., English first edition. Covent 56-188 1974 £8.50

BUDDEN, LIONEL B.   The Book of the Liverpool School of Architecture. Liverpool & London, 1932. Plates, worn, limited edition. Marsden 37-99 1974 £10

BUDDEN, MARIA E.   True Stories from Modern History. London, 1824. 16mo., orig. marbled boards, roan back (gilt), 22 engravings on 11 plates. Frohnsdorff 16-130 1974 $30

BUDGE, ERNEST ALFRED THOMPSON WALLIS   Baralam and Yewasef. Cambridge, 1923. First edition, plates. Biblo & Tannen 210-992 1973 $37.50

BUDGE, ERNEST ALFRED THOMPSON WALLIS   Book of the Dead. 1890. Folio, coloured plates, orig. half roan, worn, small wormholes. Bow Windows 66-91 1974 £36

BUDGE, ERNEST ALFRED THOMPSON WALLIS   The Book of the Dead. 1895. 4to., library stamps, some spotting, damp stain, contemporary half morocco, rubbed. Bow Windows 66-90 1974 £27.50

BUDGE, ERNEST ALFRED THOMPSON WALLIS   By Nile and Tigris. London, 1920. 2 vols., illus. Biblo & Tannen 210-993 1973 $47.50

BUDGE, ERNEST ALFRED THOMPSON WALLIS   From Fetish to God in Ancient Egypt. Oxford, 1934. Roy. 8vo., orig. cloth. Broadhurst 23-1619 1974 £20

BUDGE, ERNEST ALFRED THOMPSON WALLIS   From Fetish to God in Ancient Egypt. Oxford and London, 1934. 8vo., orig. green cloth, gilt, first edition. Dawsons PM 251-12 1974 £35

BUDGE, ERNEST ALFRED THOMPSON WALLIS   From Fetish to God in Ancient Egypt. Oxford, 1934. 8vo., orig. cloth. Bow Windows 64-425 1974 £22.50

BUDGE, ERNEST ALFRED THOMPSON WALLIS   From Fetish to God in Ancient Egypt. Oxford, 1934. Illus., roy. 8vo., orig. cloth, fine. Broadhurst 24-1585 1974 £20

BUDGE, ERNEST ALFRED THOMPSON WALLIS   The Mummy. 1925. Illus., second edition. Covent 56-402 1974 £15

BUDGE, ERNEST ALFRED THOMPSON WALLIS   The Mummy. Cambridge, 1925. Large 8vo., orig. cloth, plates, second edition. Dawsons PM 251-10 1974 £25

BUDGE, ERNEST ALFRED THOMPSON WALLIS   Osiris and the Egyptian Resurrection. London, 1911. Large 8vo., 2 vols., orig. red pictorial cloth, gilt, uncut, first edition. Dawsons PM 251-11 1974 £50

BUDGE, ERNEST ALFRED THOMPSON WALLIS   The Sarcophagus of Anchnesraneferab, Queen of Ahmes 2, King of Egypt. London, 1885. 4to., rebound. Biblo & Tannen 210-994 1973 $22.50

BUDGE, ERNEST ALFRED THOMPSON WALLIS   Some Account of the Collection of Egyptian Antiquities in the Possesion of Lady Meux. 1896. 4to., half morocco, plates, limited, rubbed. Quaritch 940-304 1974 £25

BUDGE, ERNEST ALFRED THOMPSON WALLIS   Syrian Anatomy, Pathology and Therapeutics. Oxford, 1913. 2 vols. Rittenhouse 46-112 1974 $87.50

BUDGELL, EUSTACE   A Short History of Prime Ministers in Great Britain. London, 1733. 8vo., modern boards, first edition. Dawsons PM 251-105 1974 £12

BUDGEN, FRANK   James Joyce and the Making of 'Ulysses'. New York, 1934. First U. S. edition, portrait, drawings by author, very good copy. Covent 51-1024 1973 £7.50

BUFF, MARY   Dash and Dart. New York, 1942. Tall 8vo., cloth, illus; lst ed., a mint copy. Frohnsdorff 16-131 1974 $10

BUFF, MARY   Kobi, a Boy of Switzerland. New York, 1939. 4to., cloth, color plates; lst ed. Frohnsdorff 16-132 1974 $15

BUFFON, GEORGE LOUIS LECLERC, COMTE DE   Histoire Naturelle, Generale et Particuliere, Avec la Description du Cabinet du Roi. Paris, 1749. Vols. 2 and 3 only, 4to., contemporary mottled calf gilt, first issues of first editions. Wheldon 128-14 1973 £20

BUFFON, GEORGE LOUIS LECLERC, COMTE DE   Histoire Naturelle, Generale et Particuliere, Avec la Description du Cabinet du Roi. Paris, 1749-1804. 44 vols., 4to., contemporary calf, rebacked, plates, rare, first edition. Wheldon 128-13 1973 £600

BUFFON, GEORGE LOUIS LECLERC COMTE DE   Buffon's Natural History. 1797-1816. 16 vols., 8vo., boards, cloth backs, plates. Wheldon 131-148 1974 £48

BUFFON, GEORGES LOUIS LECLERC, COMTE DE   The Natural History of Insects. Perth, 1792. 8vo., contemporary calf, plates. Schuman 37-33 1974 $75

BUGENHAGEN, JOHANN   Eine Christliche Predigt, Uber der Leich und Begrebnis, des Ehrwirdigen D. Martini Luthers. Wittenberg, 1546. 4to., boards. Harper 213-203 1973 $225

BULL, GEORGE   Works. Oxford, 1844-55. 5 vols., orig. cloth, faded, standard edition. Howes 185-1012 1974 £15

BULL, H. G.   Notes on the Birds of Herefordshire. 1888. 8vo., cloth, portrait. Wheldon 129-436 1974 £5

BULL, W. PERKINS   Spadunk; or, From Paganism to Davenport United. Toronto, 1935. Illus., some in colour. Hood's 102-277 1974 $17.50

BULLAR, JOHN   An Historical and Picturesque Guide to the Isle of Wight. Southampton, 1806. 12mo., contemporary half calf, joints cracked, some spotting and stains, worn. Bow Windows 66-93 1974 £7

BULLEIN, WILLIAM   Bvlleins Bulwarke of Defence Against all Sicknesse. 1562. Small folio, 18th century sprinkled calf, gilt, second edition. Dawsons PM 249-94 1974 £1,950

BULLEN, A. H.   Elizabethans. 1924. English first edition. Covent 56-1874 1974 £5.25

BULLEN, FRANK THOMAS   The Cruise of the Cachalot. New York, 1928. Plates, illus. Rinsland 58-80 1974 $15

BULLEN, FRANK THOMAS   The Cruise of the Cachalot Round the World After Sperm Whales. 1898. Illus., inscription, nice copy, first edition. Covent 51-2220 1973 £32.50

BULLEN, FRANK THOMAS   The Cruise of the "Cachalot" Round the World After Sperm Whales. 1898. Plates, map, frontispiece, first edition. Bow Windows 66-94 1974 £18

BULLEN, FRANK THOMAS   The Log Of a Sea-Waif. New York, 1899. 8vo., orig. cloth, illus., first American edition. Rinsland 58-90 1974 $25

BULLEN, GEORGE   Caxton Celebration, 1877. London, 1877. 8vo., orig. cloth, book-plate, third issue. Dawsons PM 10-95 1974 £10

BULLER, A. H. R.   Essays on Wheat. 1919. 8vo., cloth, illus., scarce. Wheldon 129-1646 1974 £5

BULLER, A. H. R.   Researches on Fungi. 1909-34. Vols. 1-6, roy. 8vo., orig. cloth, very scarce orig. issue. Wheldon 128-1345 1973 £45

BULLER, WALTER LAWRY   A History of the Birds of New Zealand. London, 1873. 4to., half maroon morocco, gilt, plates, first edition. Hammond 201-632 1974 £375

BULLET, P.   Architecture Pratique . . . Avec une Explication de Trente-Six Articles de la Coutume de Paris. 1788. 8vo., plates, contemporary calf, worn. Quaritch 940-500 1974 £36

BULLETT, GERALD   Helen's Lovers. 1932. Dust wrappers, fine, inscibed presentation. Covent 55-267 1974 £10

BULLETT, GERALD   The History of Egg Pandervil. Knopf, 1929. 335p. Austin 54-191 1973 $8.50

BULLETT, GERALD   Mr. Godley Beside Himself. Boni, Liveright, 1925. 255p. Austin 54-190 1973 $7.50

BULLETT, GERALD   The Quick and the Dead. 1933. Inscribed, presentation, faded. Covent 55-268 1974 £10.50

BULLEY, E.   Life of Edward VII. 1901. Orig. cloth, plates, inscription, 2 15/16 X 2 3/8 inches. Gregory 44-356 1974 $17.50

BULLFINCH, THOMAS   Legends of Charlemagne. (New York), 1924. 8vo., full page full color Wyeth illus., near mint, d.j. soiled & torn.   Current BW9-209 1974 $30

BULLINGER, HEINRICH   The Decades. 1849-52. 5 vols. in 4, orig. cloth, best English edition. Howes 185-1531 1974 £15

BULLION, T.   Internal Management of a County Bank. Toronto, 1876. Hood's 102-363 1974 $10

BULLOCK, WILLIAM   A Companion to Mr. Bullock's Museum. London, 1811. 12mo., orig. boards, uncut, frontispiece, tenth edition. Hill 126-23 1974 £5.50

BULLOCK, WILLIAM   The History of Bacteriology. London, 1938. 8vo., plates, illus., orig. cloth, first edition. Dawsons PM 10-96 1974 £7

BULMER, HOBSON   The Gate Theatre Dublin. Dublin, 1934. One of 650 copies, illus., cloth backed boards, very good copy, this copy unnumbered. Covent 51-2387 1973 £12.50

BULWER, JAMES   Views In the Madeiras Executed On Stone. London, 1827. Folio, boards, vignettes, uncut. Traylen 79-420 1973 £150

BULWER-LYTTON, EDWARD GEORGE EARLE OF LYTTON, 1ST BARON LYTTON 1803-1873
Please turn to
LYTTON, EDWARD GEORGE EARLE LYTTON BULWER-LYTTON, 1ST BARON 1803-1873

BUMKE, OSWALD   Handbuch der Neurologie. Berlin, 1935-37. 17 vols. in 18, large 8vo., orig. cloth, illus., first edition. Schuman 37-34 1974 $1450

BUNBURY, CHARLES J. F.   Journal of a Residence at the Cape of Good Hope. London, 1848. Small 8vo., foxing, plates, rare, first edition. Traylen 79-450 1973 £40

BUNGAY, GEORGE W.   Off-Hand Takings or Crayon Sketches. Dewitt, 1854. 408p., 20 portraits on steel. Austin 54-195 1973 $15

BUNIM, MIRIAM SCHILD   Space in Medieval Painting and the Forerunners of Perspective. New York, 1940. 4to., 1st ed., illus. Biblo & Tannen 213-220 1973 $17.50

BUNIN, I. A.   The Gentleman from San Francisco and Other Stories. 1922. Fine copy, boards, first edition. Covent 51-1101 1973 $15

BUNKLEY, JOSEPHINE M.   Miss Bunkley's Book. New York, 1855. 12mo., half calf, frontispiece. Hill 126-24 1974 £10.50

BUNN, ALFRED   The Stage. 1840. Orig. patterned cloth, 3 vols., English first edition. Covent 56-1243 1974 £45

BUNNELL, LAFAYETTE H.   Discovery of the Yosemite, and the Indian War of 1851, Which led to That Event. Chicago, (1880). New cloth, first edition, attractively rebound. Hayman 59-77 1974 $20

BUNNER, H. C.   Airs from Arcady and Elsewhere. New York, 1884. Orig. binding. Butterfield 10-130 1974 $10

BUNNER, H. C.   More "Short Sixes". Keppler, Schwarzmann, 1894. 229p., illus., orig. ed. Austin 54-192 1973 $7.50

BUNNER, H. C.   The Stories of H. C. Bunner. Scribner, 1925. 434p., 1st series. Austin 54-194 1973 $10

BUNNER, H. C.   The Suburban Sage. Keppler, Schwarzmann, 1896. 114p., illus. Austin 54-193 1973 $7.50

BUNSEN, ROBERT   Gasometrische Methoden. Brunswick, 1877. 8vo., marbled boards, contemporary continental quarter calf, illus., second edition. Dawsons PM 245-145 1974 £30

BUNT, CYRIL G. E.   A History of Russian Art. London, 1946. Biblo & Tannen 210-59 1973 $15

BUNTING, BASIL   First Book of Odes. n.d. One of 175 copies, numbered, fine, boards. Covent 51-2221 1973 £20

BUNTING, R. H.   Gold Coast Plant Diseases. (1925). 8vo., boards, plates, scarce. Wheldon 129-1647 1974 £5

BUND, J. W. WILLIS   The Celtic Church of Wales. 1897. Scarce, worn. Howes 185-1015 1974 £5.50

BUNYAN, JOHN   The Church Book of the Bunyan Meeting, 1650-1821. 1928. Folio, parchment gilt, slipcase, limited edition. Thomas 28-233 1972 £12

BUNYAN, JOHN   Divine Emblems. 1802. Contemporary sheep, woodcuts. Thomas 28-227 1972 £25

BUNYAN, JOHN   The Doctrine of the Law and Grace Unfolded. 1760. 12mo., orig. canvas, sixth edition. Thomas 28-230 1972 £20

BUNYAN, JOHN   Eines Christen Reise. 3 vols. in 1, small 8vo., sheep, rubbed. Thomas 28-223 1972 £65

BUNYAN, JOHN   Eines Christen Reise nach der Seeligen Ewigkeit. Ephrata, 1754. 2 vols. in 1, contemporary calf, first American edition. Bradley 35-299 1974 $200

BUNYAN, JOHN   Grace Abounding. Leeds, 1798. Tall 6mo., modern sheep, good condition. Thomas 28-229 1972 £20

BUNYAN, JOHN   The Holy War. 1682. Small 8vo., gilt, contemporary dark olive green morocco, first edition. Thomas 28-225 1972 £350

BUNYAN, JOHN   The Jerusalem-Sinner Saved. 1728. 12mo., orig. calf, woodcuts, worn, tenth edition. Thomas 28-228 1972 £35

BUNYAN, JOHN   The Pilgrim's Progress. n.d. Small 8vo., dark green crushed levant morocco gilt. Thomas 28-221 1972 £80

BUNYAN, JOHN   The Pilgrim's Progress and Other Works. Glasgow, n.d. Thick 4to., half calf gilt, plates, woodcut illus. Smith 194-856 1974 £5

BUNYAN, JOHN   The Pilgrim's Progress. London, 1681. 12mo., orig. sheep, portrait, rare, sixth edition. Dawsons PM 250-12 1974 £1200

BUNYAN, JOHN   The Pilgrims Progress. 1755-57. 3 vols. in 1,
12mo., contemporary calf, rebacked. Thomas 28-222 1972 £55

BUNYAN, JOHN   The Pilgrim's Progress. Dublin, 1795. First
edition of this version, plates, mottled calf, gilt, rubbed. Thomas 32-161 1974
£18

BUNYAN, JOHN   The Pilgrim's Progress. Cincinnati, 1813. Leather, worn. Hayman 57-549 1974 $20

BUNYAN, JOHN   The Pilgrim's Progress. New Haven, 1821.
16mo., full calf (worn), foxed, 10 woodcut illustrations. Frohnsdorff 16-134
1974 $40

BUNYAN, JOHN   The Pilgrim's Progress. 1830. 8vo., red morocco
gilt, plates, woodcuts. Hill 126-25 1974 £12.50

BUNYAN, JOHN   The Pilgrim's Progress. 1861. Leather, illus.
Austin 61-165 1974 $25

BUNYAN, JOHN   The Pilgrim's Progress. (1874). Thick 4to.,
orig. black morocco gilt, plates. Howes 186-58 1974 £7.50

BUNYAN, JOHN   The Pilgrim's Progress. 1875. 2 vols. in 1,
crown 8vo., illus., full morocco, first edition. Howes 185-48 1974 £7.50

BUNYAN, JOHN   The Pilgrim's Progress. 1895. 8vo., orig.
brown cloth, etchings. Quaritch 940-249 1974 £40

BUNYAN, JOHN   The Pilgrim's Progress. 1903. Thick roy.
8vo., orig. cloth, plates, illus., limited numbered edition. Howes 186-121
1974 £14.50

BUNYAN, JOHN   A Relation of the Imprisonment of. 1765. 12mo.,
contemporary sheep, rebacked, first edition. Hill 126-26 1974 £25

BUNYAN, JOHN   Solomon's Temple Spiritualised. Edinburgh,
1760. 6mo., quarter sheep, ninth edition. Thomas 28-226 1972 £30

BUNYAN, JOHN   The Works Of. London, 1767-68. 2 vols.,
folio, contemporary calf, copperplates, third edition. Smith 193-104 1973 £15

BUNYAN, JOHN   The Complete Works of. Philadelphia, 1856.
2 vols. in 1, illus. Austin 61-164 1974 $17.50

BUNYARD, EDWARD ASHDOWN   The Epicure's Companion. London, 1937.
12mo., illus. Biblo & Tannen 214-779 1974 $6.50

BUNYARD, EDWARD ASHDOWN   Old Garden Roses. London, 1936. 4to.,
plates, fine, orig. cloth. Gregory 44-27 1974 $35

BUONANNI, FILIPPO   Recreatio Mentis et Oculi in Observatione
Animalium Testaceorum. Rome, 1684. 4to., contemporary calf, plates, rare.
Wheldon 131-891 1974 £120

BUONANNI, FILIPPO   Ricreatione dell' Occhio e della Mente Nell'
Osservation' delle Chiocciole. Rome, 1681. 4to., contemporary calf, engraved
plates, nice clean copy, rare first edition. Wheldon 128-834 1973 £150

BURBERRY, H. A.   The Amateur Orchid Cultivators' Guide Book.
Liverpool, 1895. 8vo., orig. cloth, plates, second edition. Wheldon 131-1613
1974 £5

BURBIDGE, F. W.   Cultivated Plants. 1877. 8vo., orig. cloth,
scarce. Wheldon 128-1448 1973 £5

BURBIDGE, F. W.   The Narcissus. 1875. Roy 8vo., new half
green morocco gilt, plates, scarce. Wheldon 130-8 1974 £75

BURCHARDUS, JOHANNES   Historia Arcana. Hanover, 1697. Small
4to., modern marbled boards, green crushed levant morocco spine. Thomas
28-173 1972 £21

BURCHARDUS, JOHANNES   Historia Arcana Sive de Vita Alexandri VI.
Hanover, 1697. Small 4to., modern marbled boards, green crushed levant morocco
spine, woodcut monogram on title. Thomas 32-109 1974 £21

BURCHIELLO, DOMENICO   Rime. 1597. Old vellum, gilt, browned.
Thomas 30-132 1973 £30

BURCKHARDT, JACOB   The Civilization of the Renaissance in Italy.
1929. Crown 4to., illus., coloured plates, orig. cloth, fine. Broadhurst 24-25
1974 £6

BURCKHARDT, JOHN LEWIS   Travels in Nubia. London, 1822. 4to., half
russia leather, gilt, second edition. Traylen 79-451 1973 £64

BURDEN, W. D.   Dragon Lizards of Komodo. 1927. 8vo.,
cloth, illus., scarce. Wheldon 130-671 1974 £7.50

BURDETT, MRS. C. D.   English Fashionables Abroad. 1827. 3 vols.,
crown 8vo., contemporary calf, first edition. Howes 185-49 1974 £35

BURDETT, OSBERT   The Very End and Other Stories. 1929. 8vo.,
orig. cloth, dust wrapper, signed, first edition. Rota 189-165 1974 £5

BURDETT, OSBERT   William Blake. New York, 1926. Biblo &
Tannen 210-831 1973 $5

BURDICK, WILLIAM   An Oration on the Nature and Effects of the Art
of Printing. Delivered in Franklin-Hall, July 5, 1802. Boston, 1802. 8vo.,
sewn as issued, first edition. Ximenes 36-39 1974 $100

BUREAU, L.   L'Age des Perdrix. Nantes, 1911-13. Roy
8vo., wrappers, 2 vols., illus. Wheldon 129-437 1974 £5

BURET, F.   Syphilis In the Middle Ages and In Modern
Times. Philadelphia, 1895. 2 vols. in 1. Rittenhouse 46-115 1974 $10

BURGASSI, A. C.   Serie Dell 'Edizioni Aldine Per Ordine.
Florence, 1803. Small 8vo., contemporary marbled boards, third edition.
Dawsons PM 10-9 1974 £14

BURGEFF, H.   Die Wurzelpilze der Orchideen. 1909-11. Roy
8vo., buckram. Wheldon 129-1571 1974 £10

BURGESS, E. S.   History of Pre-Clusian Botany In Its Relation to
Aster. 1902. 8vo., new cloth. Wheldon 128-87 1973 £7.50

BURGESS, FRED W.   Antique Jewelry & Trinkets. 1937. Allen
213-190 1973 $15

BURGESS, GELETT   The Burgess Nonsense Book. New York, 1901.
8vo., pict. boards, 1st ed., illus. Frohnsdorff 16-135 1974 $15

BURGESS, GELETT   The Goop Directory. New York, 1913.
12mo., cloth spine, 1st ed., illus. Frohnsdorff 16-136 1974 $17.50

BURGESS, GELETT   The Goop Encyclopedia. New York, 1916.
8vo., pict. cloth, gilt, front innter hinge cracked and tear on title, otherwise
good; 1st ed. Frohnsdorff 16-137 1974 $10

BURGESS, GELETT   The Goop Encylopedia. New York, (1916).
Orig. pictorial cloth, illus. by author, first edition, fine, on front free-endpaper
Burgess has drawn a "Goop" in ink and signed & dated it. MacManus 224-55
1974 $75

BURGESS, GELETT   Lady Machante. Stokes, 1909. 393p., illus.
Austin 54-196 1973 $8.50

BURGESS, GELETT   The Lark. San Francisco, 1896. 8vo., illus.
Frohnsdorff 16-138 1974 $100

BURGESS, GELETT   The Maxims of Methuselah. New York, 1907.
12mo., 1st ed., illus., orig. dec. bds., with autographed postcard enclosed.
Jacobs 24-67 1974 $35

BURGESS, GELETT   More Goops and How Not To Be Them. New
York, 1903. 4to., pict. cloth, illus. Frohnsdorff 16-139 1974 $40

BURGESS, JOSHUA   The Medical and Legal Relations of Madness.
London, 1858. 8vo., orig. cloth, rare, first edition. Gurney 64-41 1974 £25

BURGESS, THOMAS HENRY   Eruptions of the Face Head and Hands. London,
1849. 8vo., orig. black cloth, first edition. Dawsons PM 249-95 1974 £26

BURGESS, THORNTON W.   The Adventures of Bobby Coon. Boston, 1918. 12mo., pict. cloth, illus, lst ed.   Frohnsdorff 16-140 1974 $15

BURGESS, THORNTON W.   The Adventures of Paddy the Beaver. Boston, 1917. 12mo., pict. cloth, illus, lst ed.   Frohnsdorff 16-141 1974 $15

BURGESS, THORNTON W.   Bowser the Hound. Boston, 1920. 8vo., 8 color plates, lst ed.   Frohnsdorff 16-142 1974 $20

BURGESS, THORNTON W.   Grandfather Frog Stays in the Smiling Pool. New York, 1928. 4to., illus.   Frohnsdorff 16-143 1974 $8.50

BURGESS, THORNTON W.   Mrs. Peter Rabbit. Boston, 1919. 8vo., cloth, 8 color plates, lst ed.   Frohnsdorff 16-144 1974 $20

BURGESS, THORNTON W.   Unc' Billy Possum Has a Fright. New York, 1928. 4to., illus.   Frohnsdorff 16-145 1974 $8.50

BURGHER, G. A.   Leonora. 1796. Folio, half calf, plates, rubbed.   Marsden 37-31 1974 £15

BURGOYNE, JOHN   The Maid of the Oaks. London, 1774. 8vo., modern boards, first edition.   Dawsons PM 252-95 1974 £15

BURGOYNE, JOHN   A State of the Expedition from Canada, As Laid Before the House of Commons . . . London, 1780. Fold out maps, orig. heavy grey card, fawn spine, perfect condition, large, first edition.   Hood's 102-91 1974 $500

BURGOYNE, JOHN   A State of the Expedition from Canada. London, 1780. 4to., contemporary calf, rebacked, gilt, leather label, first edition.   Traylen 79-468 1973 £280

BURGOYNE, JOHN   A State of the Expedition From Canada, As Laid Before the House of Commons. London, 1780. Orig. heavy card, second edition.   Hood's 104-96 1974 $400

BURKE, BERNARD   A Genealogical and Heraldic Dictionary of the Landed Gentry of Great Britain and Ireland. London, 1868. Roy 8vo., 2 vols., half morocco, gilt, fourth edition.   Hammond 201-413 1974 £7.50

BURKE, BERNARD   A Genealogical and Heraldic History of the Landed Gentry of Ireland. London, 1912. 8vo., cloth boards, new edition.   Emerald 50-93 1974 £12.50

BURKE, BERNARD   The Romance of the Aristocracy. 1855. 3 vols., small 8vo., half red calf, new revised edition.   Quaritch 939-707 1974 £12.50

BURKE, BERNARD   Works. 1855-73. Crown 8vo., 7 vols., full contemporary calf, gilt.   Broadhurst 23-1218 1974 £25

BURKE, BILLIE   With a Feather On My Nose. 1949. 272p., illus.   Austin 51-164 1973 $8.50

BURKE, EDMUND   An Appeal from the New to the Old Whigs. London, 1791. 8vo., modern quarter morocco, fine, first edition.   Dawsons PM 247-32 1974 £125

BURKE, EDMUND   Articles of Charge of High Crimes and Misdemeanors. London, 1786. 8vo., contemporary sprinkled calf, gilt, fine.   Bow Windows 62-137 1974 £48

BURKE, EDMUND   The Epistolary Correspondence of the Right Hon. Edmund Burke and Dr. French Laurence. London, 1827. 8vo., contemporary calf, spine gilt, first edition, nice copy.   Ximenes 36-40 1974 $30

BURKE, EDMUND   A Letter from Mr. Burke to a Member of the National Assembly. Paris, 1791. 8vo., cloth, gilt, first English edition, second issue.   Dawsons PM 247-33 1974 £10

BURKE, EDMUND   A Letter . . . to His Grace the Duke of Portland, on the Conduct of the Minority in Parliament. London, 1797. 8vo., half morocco, very good uncut copy.   Ximenes 37-28 1974 $35

BURKE, EDMUND   Mr. Burke's Speech. London, 1785. 8vo., modern boards, rare, first edition.   Dawsons PM 247-28 1974 £40

BURKE, EDMUND   A Philosophical Enquiry Into the Origin of Our Ideas of the Sublime and Beautiful. London, 1757. 8vo., contemporary calf, rebacked, scarce, first edition.   Ximenes 37-29 1974 $175

BURKE, EDMUND   A Philosophical Enquiry into the Origin of our Ideas of the Sublime and Beautiful. London, 1793. 8vo., contemporary tree calf, gilt, fine, new edition.   Hammond 201-86 1974 £10

BURKE, EDMUND   Reflections on the Revolution in France. London, 1790. 8vo., contemporary mottled calf, fine, uncut, third edition.   Dawsons PM 247-30 1974 £30

BURKE, EDMUND   Reflections on the Revolution in France. London, 1790. 8vo., orig. wrappers, uncut, fine, first edition, first issue.   Dawsons PM 247-29 1974 £220

BURKE, EDMUND   A Speech of. 1780. 8vo., boards, leather label.   Quaritch 939-355 1974 £7

BURKE, EDMUND   Speech of Edmund Burke, to the House of Commons, 11th day of February, 1780. London, 1780. Contemporary mottled card.   Hood's 103-396 1974 $95

BURKE, EDMUND   Substance of the Speech . . . . On the Army Estimates in the House of Commons. London, 1790. 8vo., modern boards, fourth edition.   Dawsons PM 247-31 1974 £15

BURKE, EDMUND   Substance of the Speeches. London, 1779. 8vo., uncut, unopened, fine, fist edition.   Dawsons PM 247-27 1974 £20

BURKE, EDMUND   A Third Letter to a Member of the Present Parliament. London, 1797. 8vo., modern half calf, first edition, first issue.   Dawsons PM 247-36 1974 £22

BURKE, EDMUND   Thoughts and Details on Scarcity. London, 1800. 8vo., modern boards, first edition.   Dawsons PM 247-37 1974 £26

BURKE, EDMUND   Thoughts on the Cause of Present Discontents. London, 1770. 4to., modern cloth boards, gilt, fine, first edition.   Dawsons PM 247-26 1974 £50

BURKE, EDMUND   Thoughts on the Prospect of a Regicide Peace. London, 1796. 8vo., modern half calf, first pirated edition.   Dawsons PM 247-35 1974 £25

BURKE, EDMUND   Two Letters Addressed to a Member of the Present Parliament. London, 1796. London, 1796. 8vo., modern half calf, first authorized edition, first issue.   Dawsons PM 247-34 1974 £25

BURKE, EDMUND   Works. 1808. 8 vols., contemporary calf gilt, new edition.   Howes 186-59 1974 £38

BURKE, EDMUND   The Works Of. 1808-27. 16 vols., contemporary mottled calf gilt, leather labels.   Smith 193-267 1973 £45

BURKE, EMILY P.   Reminiscences of Georgia. N.P. (Oberlin), 1850. 12mo., orig. brown cloth, spine gilt, first edition, very good copy.   Ximenes 36-41 1974 $80

BURKE, FRANCIS   Loch Ce and Its Annals. Dublin, 1895. 8vo., cloth boards.   Emerald 50-94 1974 £6

BURKE, JACKSON   Prelum to Albion. San Francisco, 1940. Unopened, uncut, illus.   Dawson's 424-144 1974 $35

BURKE, JOHN   A Genealogical and Heraldic History. 1838. Orig. cloth, rebacked, woodcuts, first edition.   Howes 186-1624 1974 £7.50

BURKE, JOHN   A Genealogical and Heraldic Dictionary of the Landed Gentry of Great Britain and Ireland. London, 1847. Roy 8vo., 2 vols., contemporary half calf, gilt, first edition.   Hammond 201-414 1974 £10

BURKE, JOHN   A General Armory of England, Scotland and Ireland. 1843. Thick roy. 8vo., half morocco, revised edition.   Howes 186-1625 1974 £10

BURKE, S. H.　　　　Historical Portraits of the Tudor Dynasty & Reformation Period.　1880-83.　Vols. 1 - 3 only of four, new buckram.　Allen 213-1315　1973　$30

BURKE, THOMAS　　　　City of Encounters.　Little, Brown, 1932. 373p.　Austin 51-165　1973　$8.50

BURKE, THOMAS　　　　Dark Nights.　n.d.　English first edition. Covent 56-194　1974　£5.25

BURKE, THOMAS　　　　The London Spy.　1922.　Presentation copy, inscribed, English first edition.　Covent 56-195　1974　£7.50

BURLEY, WALTER　　　　Das Buch von Dem Leben und Sitten der Heydnischen Maister.　Augsburg, 1490.　4to., red crushed morocco, armorial bookplate, good copy, excellent internally.　Schumann 499-16　1974　sFr 3,700

BURLINGAME, ANNE ELIZABETH　　The Battle of the Books in its Historical Setting.　New York, 1920.　lst ed., author's sgd. pres., bdg. rubbed.　Biblo & Tannen 213-733　1973　$9.50

BURLINGAME, ROGER　　　　Of Making Many Books.　New York, 1946. lst ed.　Biblo & Tannen 213-735　1973　$15

BURLINGHAM, R.　　　　Instructions to Prevent the Blight.　1802. 8vo., wrappers, uncut, rare.　Wheldon 129-1443　1974　£12

BURLINGTON FINE ARTS CLUB　　Exhibition of Bookbindings.　1891.　Roy. 4ao., frontispiece, plates, half green levant morocco gilt.　Quaritch 940-596 1974　£125

BURMANN, JOHANNES　　　Rariorium Africanarum Plantarum.　Amsterdam, 1738-9.　4to., plates, contemporary sprinkled calf, gilt.　Bow Windows 64-40 1974　£450

BURMANN, JOHANNES　　　Thesaurus Zeylanicus.　Amsterdam, 1737.　4to., contemporary vellum, engraved plates, rare, good copy.　Wheldon 128-1245 1973　£80

BURMEISTER, H.　　　　A Manual of Entomology.　1836.　8vo., claf, plates.　Wheldon 129-615　1974　£7.50

BURMEISTER, H.　　　　The Organisation of Trilobites.　1846.　Folio, boards, plates.　Wheldon 130-913　1974　£7.50

BURN, A. R.　　　　Alexander the Great and the Hellenistic Empire.　New York, 1948.　12mo.　Biblo & Tannen 214-584　1974　$7.50

BURN, J. S.　　　　A History of Henley-On-Thames in the County of Oxford.　1861.　Orig. cloth, plates, very scarce, first edition.　Smith 193-208　1973　£10

BURN, ROBERT SCOTT　　　The Steam Engine.　London, c., 1856.　8vo., orig. cloth, gilt, illus., seventh edition.　Hammond 201-802　1974　£6

BURNABY, WILLIAM　　　The Ladies Visiting-Day.　London, 1701. 4to., modern boards, first edition.　Dawsons PM 252-97　1974　£20

BURNABY, WILLIAM　　　The Reform'd Wife.　London, 1700.　4to., buckram backed boards, first edition.　Dawsons PM 252-98　1974　£75

BURNAT, E.　　　　Les Roses des Alpes Maritimes.　Geneva, 1879-83.　8vo., half cloth, scarce.　Wheldon 129-1055　1974　£5

BURNE, PETER　　　　The Teetotaler's Companion.　1847.　Orig. cloth, plates, bookplate, worn.　Covent 55-709　1974　£15

BURNE-JONES, EDWARD　　　Memorials of.　1904.　Plates, bookplate, faded, rubbed.　Marsden 37-102　1974　£12

BURNET, GILBERT　　　The Abridgement of the History of the Reformation of the Church of England.　1705.　8vo., contemporary mottled calf, plates, fourth edition.　Hill 126-26a　1974　£8.50

BURNET, GILBERT　　　An Abridgement of His History of the Reformation of the Church of England.　Oxford, 1808.　Full contemporary calf, portrait. Howes 185-1018　1974　£8.50

BURNET, GILBERT　　　Bishop Burnet's History of His Own Time.　London, 1818.　8vo., 4 vols., contemporary tree calf, gilt.　Hammond 201-450　1974 £12

BURNET, GILBERT　　　Dr. Burnet's Travels.　Amsterdam, 1687.　Small 8vo., old calf, rebacked.　Thomas 32-340　1974　£21

BURNET, GILBERT　　　Four Discourses Delivered to the Clergy of the Diocese of Sarum.　1694.　Contemporary sheep.　Howes 195-1016　1974　£15

BURNET, GILBERT　　　History of His Own Time.　1724-34.　2 vols., folio, vol. 1 old panelled calf, rebacked, vol. 2 modern calf, not uniform, but sound working set.　Thomas 32-109A　1974　£20

BURNET, GILBERT　　　The History of the Reformation of the Church of England.　1830.　4 vols., roy. 8vo., full crushed brown morocco gilt.　Howes 185-1017　1974　£25

BURNET, GILBERT　　　The Last Confession.　London, 1682.　Small folio, disbound, first edition.　Dawsons PM 252-99　1974　£12

BURNET, GILBERT　　　The Last Confession, Prayers and Meditations of Lieuten. John Stern.　London, 1682.　Small folio, disbound, first edition.　Dawsons PM 251-180　1974　£15

BURNET, GILBERT　　　The Life and Death of Sir Matthew Hale.　London, 1682.　8vo., contemporary sheep, second edition.　Dawsons PM 251-106 1974　£15

BURNET, GILBERT　　　Some Passages.　London, 1805.　12mo., contemporary half calf, worn.　Dawsons PM 252-544　1974　£6.50

BURNET, GILBERT　　　Some Passages in the Life of John, Earl of Rochester.　1787.　Portrait, contemporary calf, spine rubbed, joints broken, internally sound.　Covent 51-2547　1973　£10

BURNET, JOHN　　　Practical Hints on Colour in Painting.　London, 1843.　Fifth edition, orig. boards, worn, dust stained, bottom corner of outsided cover missing, internally very sound, good copy.　Ross 86-24　1974　$60

BURNET, JOHN　　　Practical Hints on Light and Shade in Painting. 1838.　Plates, cloth back, boards, fifth edition.　Marsden 39-65　1974　£5

BURNET, JOHN　　　A Practical Treatise on Painting.　1827.　4to., orig. cloth, English first edition.　Covent 56-1433　1974　£35

BURNET, JOHN　　　A Practical Treatise on Painting.　1830.　4to., half vellum, gilt, plates, new edition.　Hammond 201-709　1974　£10.50

BURNET, JOHN　　　A Treatise on Painting.　1880.　Plates, cloth sides, morocco back, worn.　Marsden 39-66　1974　£15

BURNET, PETER H.　　　Recollections and Opinions of an Old Pioneer. New York, 1880.　First edition, slight wear.　Jenkins 61-260　1974　$50

BURNET, THOMAS　　　Archaeologiae Philosophicae.　London, 1692. 4to., contemporary mottled calf, rebacked, gilt, first edition.　Dawsons PM 251-181　1974　£35

BURNET, THOMAS　　　A Certain Information of a Certain Discourse. London, 1712.　8vo., uncut, disbound, first edition.　Dawsons PM 251-182 1974　£35

BURNET, THOMAS　　　De Fide & Offic is Christianorum.　London, 1727.　Contemporary mottled calf gilt.　Smith 194-136　1974　£7.50

BURNETT, FRANCES HODGSON　　Editha's Burglar.　Boston, 1888.　First edition, first state, corner wear, orig. binding, front free endpaper removed, very good copy.　Wilson 63-492　1974　$25

BURNETT, FRANCES HODGSON　　Editha's Burglar.　Boston, 1925.　8vo., cloth, illus., lst ed.　Frohnsdorff 16-146　1974　$8.50

BURNETT, FRANCES HODGSON　　Little Lord Fauntleroy.　1886.　Plates, first edition, first issue.　Allen 216-285　1974　$50

BURNETT, FRANCES HODGSON   Little Lord Fauntleroy. New York, 1886. 8vo., pict. cloth, illus., lst ed. Frohnsdorff 16-147 1974 $25

BURNETT, FRANCES HODGSON   Little Saint Elizabeth and other Stories. New York, 1890. 8vo., pict. cloth, illus., lst ed. Frohnsdorff 16-148 1974 $20

BURNETT, FRANCES HODGSON   The Pretty Sister of Jose. New York, 1889. 8vo., pict. cloth, illus., lst ed. Frohnsdorff 16-149 1974 $10

BURNETT, FRANCES HODGSON   Racketty-Packetty House As Told by Queen Crosspatch. New York, 1906. 16mo., 20 color plates. Frohnsdorff 16-150 1974 $12.50

BURNETT, FRANCES HODGSON   Sara Crewe. New York, 1891. 4to., orig. pict. cl., illus., sgd. by author. Jacobs 24-68 1974 $60

BURNETT, FRANCES HODGSON   Surly Tim. New York, 1877. First edition, first state, corner wear, front free endpaper removed, very good, orig. binding. Wilson 63-493 1974 $18.75

BURNETT, FRANCES HODGSON   Surly Tim and Other Stories. New York, 1877. First edition, orig. binding. Butterfield 10-10 1974 $12.50

BURNETT, FRANCES HODGSON   Two Little Pilgrim's Progress. New York, 1895. 8vo., pict. cloth, gilt, lst ed., illus. Frohnsdorff 16-151 1974 $10

BURNETT, GEORGE   Specimens of English Prose-Writers, From Earliest Times to Close of the 17th Century. 1807. 3 vols., buckram, ex-library. Allen 216-289 1974 $15

BURNETT, H. L.   History of the Ohio Society of New York, 1885-1905. New York, 1906. Limited edition, illus. Jenkins 61-1866 1974 $15

BURNETT, H. L.   History of the Ohio Society of New York, 1885-1905. New York, 1906. Illus., limited edition. Jenkins 61-1995 1974 $15

BURNETT, M. A.   Plantae Utiliores. London, 1842-45. 4to., 2 vols., contemporary half morocco, plates, gilt, first edition. Hammond 201-633 1974 £85

BURNETT, M. A.   Plantae Utiliores. London, 1842-45. 4 vols., 4to., full polished calf, gilt, leather labels, fine, plates. Traylen 79-8 1973 £250

BURNETT, WHIT   Great Stories of the Human Spirit. Garden City, 1944. Austin 61-168 1974 $10

BURNETT, WHIT   Story. New York, 1949. lst ed. Biblo & Tannen 210-705 1973 $7.50

BURNEY, CHARLES   An Account of the Musical Performances In Westminster Abbey and the Pantheon. London, 1785. 4to., contemporary marbled boards, foxing, plates. Smith 194-401 1974 £15

BURNEY, FANNY
Please turn to
ARBLAY, FRANCES BURNEY D'

BURNEY, JAMES   A Chronological History of the Discoveries In the South Sea. London, 1803-17. 5 vols., 4to., half calf, mottled boards. Traylen 79-546 1973 £850

BURNEY, SARAH HARRIET   The Romance of Private Life. London, 1839. 3 vols., 12mo., contemporary half calf, first edition. Dawsons PM 252-104 1974 £70

BURNHAM, FREDERICK RUSSELL   Scouting On Two Countinents. Garden City, 1926. First edition, illus. Wilson 63-8 1974 $14.50

BURNHAM, JOSEPHINE MAY   Concessive Constructions In Old English Prose. 1911. Ex-library, sturdy library binding. Austin 61-171 1974 $22.50

BURNHAM, MARY   United States Catalog, Books in Print, Jan. 1, 1928. 1928. 4to., new buckram, fourth edition. Allen 216-S 1974 $50

BURNHAM, R.   Hymns. 1803. 8vo., contemporary black straight-grain morocco gilt. Thomas 28-129 1972 £7.50

BURNHAM, SMITH   The Making of Our Country. Philadelphia, 1921. Illus. Biblo & Tannen 213-16 1973 $8.50

BURNLEY, JAMES   The History of Wool and Woolcombing. London, 1889. Cloth, illus., plates. Dawson's 424-221 1974 $30

BURNS, A. R.   Money and Monetary Policy in Early Times. New York, 1927. Illus. Biblo & Tannen 214-597 1974 $10

BURNS, ALLAN   Observations on the Surgical Anatomy of the Head and Neck. Edinburgh, 1811. 8vo., contemporary half calf, rebacked, first edition. Dawsons PM 249-96 1974 £110

BURNS, ALLAN   Observations on the Surgical Anatomy of the Head and Neck. Glasgow, 1824. 8vo., contemporary marbled boards, half calf, second edition. Dawsons PM 249-97 1974 £24

BURNS, B. H.   Recent Advances in Orthopaedic Surgery. London, 1937. 8vo., orig. red cloth, first edition. Dawsons PM 249-98 1974 £5

BURNS, R.   The Land of Burns. 1840. 2 vols., 4to., plates, half morocco gilt. Quaritch 939-649 1974 £30

BURNS, R.   Memorial Catalogue of the Burns Exhibition. Glasgow, 1898. 4to., cloth, plates, limited. Quaritch 939-648 1974 £25

BURNS, R.   The Poems, Epistles, Songs, Epigrams, and Epitaphs. 1896. Small 8vo., 2 vols., half morocco, gilt. Quaritch 936-323 1974 £5

BURNS, ROBERT   His Life and Character. 1886. 8vo., orig. cloth. Bow Windows 64-426 1974 £5

BURNS, ROBERT   Illustrated Songs of. 1861. Folio, engravings, frontispiece. Bow Windows 66-96 1974 £8.50

BURNS, ROBERT   The Merry Muses. 1827. 12mo., English first edition. Covent 56-1589 1974 £10.50

BURNS, ROBERT   Poems. Edinburgh, 1787. 8vo., contemporary half calf, gilt, first Edinburgh edition. Hammond 201-291 1974 £55

BURNS, ROBERT   Poems and Songs. Glasgow, 1889. Roy. 8vo., good copy, orig. cloth. Broadhurst 24-296 1974 £10

BURNS, ROBERT   Poems Chiefly in the Scottish Dialect. Edinburgh, 1787. 8vo., full morocco, uncut, fine, second edition, second issue. Dawsons PM 252-106 1974 £170

BURNS, ROBERT   Poems Chiefly in the Scottish Dialect. London, 1927. 8vo., orig. wrappers, slip case. Bow Windows 62-139 1974 £10.75

BURNS, ROBERT   The Poetical Works of. Alnwick, 1808. 2 vols., marbled boards, gilt. Dawson's 424-42 1974 $100

BURNS, ROBERT   The Poetry. Edinburgh, 1896-97. 4 vols., 4to., orig. buckram gilt, limited. Howes 185-51 1974 £20

BURNS, ROBERT   The Poetry of Robert Burns. Edinburgh, 1896. 4 vols., ltd. ed., uncut. Biblo & Tannen 210-706 1973 $47.50

BURNS, ROBERT   The Prose Works Of. Edinburgh, 1839-38-40-38-41. 7 vols. in 1, roy. 8vo., half contemporary calf gilt. Smith 193-297 1973 £9.50

BURNS, ROBERT   Scots Ballads. (1939). 8vo., orig. holland backed boards. Bow Windows 64-427 1974 £12.50

BURNS, ROBERT   Tam O'Shanter. 1884. 4to., rebound, illus., English first edition. Covent 56-1827 1974 £5.25

BURNS, ROBERT   Views in North Britain. 1811. 4to., orig. boards, rebacked, uncut, rubbed, plates, some foxing. Bow Windows 66-98 1974 £8.50

BURNS, ROBERT   Works. Philadelphia, 1851. Ex-library.
Austin 61-167 1974 $17.50

BURNS, ROBERT   The Life and Works of. Edinburgh and London,
1896. 4 vols., fine half tone plates, signed by publishers, top edges gilt, other
edges uncut, numbered, limited. Bow Windows 66-97 1974 £38

BURNS, ROBERT E.   I am a Fugitive from a Georgia Chain Gang!
New York, 1932. 1st ed. Biblo & Tannen 213-17 1973 $10

BURPEE, L. J.   Among the Canadian Alps. London, New York,
and Toronto, 1914. Photos, maps, illus. in colour. Hood's 102-795 1974 $25

BURPEE, L. J.   An Historical Atlas of Canada. Toronto,
1927. Charts. Hood's 103-6 1974 $30

BURPEE, L. J.   Jungling in Jasper. Ottawa, 1929. Hood's
104-844 1974 $20

BURPEE, L. J.   The Search for the Western Sea, The Story of
the Exploration of North-Western America. London, 1908. Rebound, rare
folding-map. Hood's 104-845 1974 $60

BURR, ANNA ROBESON   Weir Mitchell. New York, 1929. First edition,
illus., orig. binding. Wilson 63-74A 1974 $15

BURR, F.   The Elements of Practical Geology. 1838.
Post 8vo., orig. cloth, plates. Wheldon 130-914 1974 £7.50

BURRARD, S. G.   A Sketch of the Geography and Geology of
the Himalaya Mountains and Tibet. Calcutta, 1907. Parts 1-3 only of 4, 4to.,
wrappers. Wheldon 131-343 1974 £7.50

BURRELL, H.   The Platypus. Sydney, 1927. 8vo., cloth,
plates. Wheldon 128-310 1973 £15

BURRIEL, ANDRES MARCOS   Paleografia Espanola, Que Contiene Todos los
Modos Conocidos, Que ha Habido de Escribir en Espana. Madrid, 1758. 4to.,
contemporary limp vellum, plates. Kraus B8-28 1974 $65

BURROUGH, EDWARD   The Memorable Works of a Son of Thunder and
Consolation: Namely, that True Prophet, and Faithful Servant of God, and
Sufferer for the Testimony of Jesus. 1672. Thick folio, full modern hardgrain
morocco, amateur but sound binding. Thomas 32-33 1974 £40

BURROUGHES, J.   Moses His Self-Denyall. London, 1614.
Contemporary calf. Smith 194-137 1974 £14.50

BURROUGHS, EDGAR RICE   Carson of Venus. 1939. Illus., first U. S.
edition, very good copy. Covent 51-2223 1973 £15

BURROUGHS, EDGAR RICE   The Gods of Mars. New York, 1918. Frontispiece, first U.S. edition. Covent 56-1590 1974 £6.30

BURROUGHS, EDGAR RICE   Land of Terror. Tarzana, 1944. First American
edition. Covent 55-272 1974 $25

BURROUGHS, EDGAR RICE   Tarzan and the Jewels of Opar. Chicago,
1918. Illus., first edition. Ballinger 1-102 1974 $15

BURROUGHS, JOHN   Waiting. (Boston, c. 1910). Authographed
by author. Goodspeed's 578-42 1974 $25

BURROUGHS, JOHN   Winter Sunshine. New York, 1877. 16mo.,
orig. binding. Wilson 63-493A 1974 $10

BURROUGHS, MARIE   Art Portfolio of 280 Stage Celebrities. c. 1900.
4to., buckram, spine rubbed. Allen 216-2104 1974 $10

BURROWES, ALEXANDER   The Humble Representation made to the King's
Majesty. 1720. 8vo., cloth, uncut. Quaritch 936-27 1974 £8

BURROWS, GEORGE MAN   Commentaries on the Causes . . . of Insanity.
London, 1828. 8vo., half calf, gilt, first edition. Dawsons PM 249-100 1974
£65

BURROWS, GEORGE MAN   An Inquiry into Certain Errors Relative to Insanity.
London, 1820. 8vo., orig. paper boards, uncut, first edition. Dawsons PM 249-
99 1974 £115

BURROWS, RAYMOND   Symphony Themes. New York, 1942. Biblo
& Tannen 214-824 1974 $7.50

BURRUS, CLARA   Whitman and Burroughs, Comrades. Boston and
New York, 1931. Cloth, slipcase, illus. Dawson's 424-310 1974 $45

BURSTEIN, ABRAHAM   The Ghetto Messenger. 1928. 302 pages.
Austin 57-107 1974 $10

BURT, A. L.   The Old Province of Quebec. Toronto &
Minneapolis, 1933. Maps, illus. Hood's 103-763 1974 $35

BURT, E. A.   The Thelephoraceae of North America. St.
Louis, 1914-26. Roy 8vo., cloth, plates. Wheldon 130-1246 1974 £30

BURT, KATHARINE NEWLIN   Strong Citadel. Scribner, 1949. Austin
62-67 1974 $6.50

BURT, MARY   The Eugene Field Book. Scribner, 1898.
136p. Austin 54-205 1973 $10

BURT, STRUTHERS   Powder River: Let 'Er Buck. New York, 1938.
Illus. Jenkins 61-2701 1974 $10

BURTON, EDWIN H.   The Life and Times of Bishop Challoner. 1909.
2 vols., thick 8vo., scarce, orig. & best edition. Howes 185-1054 1974 £10.50

BURTON, G. W.   Burton's Book on California and Its Sunlit Skies
of Glory. Los Angeles, 1909. 3 vols. in 1, 8vo., cloth. Saddleback 14-50
1974 $12.50

BURTON, HENRY   The Grand Impostor Unmasked. London, n.d.
4to., modern boards, first edition. Dawsons PM 251-492 1974 £20

BURTON, JOHN HILL   The Book Hunter. Edinburgh, 1862. First
edition, 12mo., cloth, rebacked. Kraus B8-29 1974 $15

BURTON, JOHN HILL   The Book-Hunter Etc. Edinburgh & London,
1882. 4to., orig. cloth gilt, uncut, limited, new edition. Dawsons PM 10-99
1974 £8

BURTON, JOHN HILL   Political and Social Economy. Edinburgh,
1849. 8vo., orig. blind-stamped cloth, first edition. Dawsons PM 247-38
1974 £25

BURTON, KATHERINE   Lily and Sword and Crown. Chicago, 1958.
Austin 62-68 1974 $10

BURTON, R.   A New View and Observations on the Ancient
and Present State of London. 1730. Small 8vo., old calf, woodcuts. Quaritch
939-442 1974 £20

BURTON, RICHARD   Men of Progress. Boston, 1898. 4to., three
quarter leather, rehinged. Saddleback 14-332 1974 $25

BURTON, RICHARD, 17TH CENT., PSEUD.
Please turn to
CROUCH, NATHANIEL

BURTON, RICHARD FRANCIS   The City of the Saints and Across the Rocky
Mountains to California. 1861. Orig. cloth, plates, illus. Smith 193-327
1973 £58

BURTON, RICHARD FRANCIS   First Footsteps in East Africa. 1856. Plates,
contemporary cloth, English first edition. Covent 56-202 1974 £75

BURTON, RICHARD FRANCIS   The Kasidah of Haji Abdu El-Yezdi. New
York, (c. 1910). 8vo., publisher's leather, spine rubbed, good copy. Sawyer
293-78 1974 $15.75

BURTON, RICHARD FRANCIS   The Sotadic Zone. New York, (c. 1920).
8vo., limited edition, orig. violet cloth gilt, uncut, top edges gilt, fine copy.
Sawyer 293-79 1974 $45

BURTON, ROBERT   Admirable Curiosities, Rarities and Wonders. London, 1737. 12mo., frontispiece, half calf, antique, tenth edition. Bow Windows 62-141 1974 £10.50

BURTON, ROBERT   The Anatomy of Melancholy. 1925. 2 vols., small folio, orig. quarter parchment, limited. Bow Windows 66-511 1974 £125

BURTON, ROBERT   The Anatomy of Melancholy. 1945. 1036 pages. Austin 61-172 1974 $17.50

BURTON, W. E.   Bibliotheca Dramatica. New York, 1860. Large paper copy, roy. 8vo., lacks wrappers, stitching coming loose, else good. Thomas 32-66 1974 £25

BURTON, WILLIAM 1575-1645   The Description of Leicestershire. London, (1622). Small folio, contemporary speckled calf, gilt, first edition. Dawsons PM 251-13 1974 £100

BURTON, WILLIAM 1575-1645   The Description of Leicester Shire. (1622). Small folio, half calf, first edition. Quaritch 939-427 1974 £60

BURTON, WILLIAM 1609-1657   A Commentary on Antoninus, His Itinerary. 1658. Small folio, old calf, rebacked. Quaritch 939-39 1974 £45

BURTON, WILLIAM 1863-   A General History of Porcelain. 1921. Crown 4to., 2 vols., orig. cloth, plates. Broadhurst 23-30 1974 £20

BURTON, WILLIAM 1863-   A History and Description of English Earthenware and Stoneware. 1904. Roy. 8vo., plates. Covent 55-430 1974 £8.50

BURTON, WILLIAM 1863-   Porcelain. 1906. 8vo., orig. cloth, plates. Bow Windows 64-428 1974 £7.50

BURTON, WILLIAM E.   Encyclopedia of Wit and Humor of America, Ireland, Scotland and England. 1858. 2 vols., buckram, ex-library. Allen 216-796 1974 $15

BURWASH, N.   The History of Victoria College. Toronto, 1927. Hood's 103-323 1974 $25

BURY, A.   The Case of Exeter-Colledge. London, 1691. 4to., paper wrappers, frayed. Quaritch 939-515 1974 £30

BURY, CHARLOTTE   Conduct is Fate. Edinburgh, 1822. 3 vols., 12mo., contemporary half roan, bit rubbed, first edition, very good copy, very scarce. Ximenes 36-44 1974 $125

BURY, E.   A Selection of Hexandrian Plants. 1831-34. Atlas folio, contemporary green morocco, neatly rebacked, hand coloured plates, very rare. Wheldon 128-1449 1973 £1,500

BURY, P. S.   Polycystins. (1869). 4to., cloth, plates, rare. Wheldon 130-915 1974 £10

BURY, T. T.   Six Coloured Views on the Liverpool and Manchester Railway. 1831. Roy. 4to., half morocco, first edition. Quaritch 939-76 1974 £400

BUSBECQ, OGIER GHISLAIN DE   A. Gislinii Busbequii Omnia Quae Extant cum Privilegio. 1660. 12mo., contemporary calf, rebacked. Bow Windows 66-100 1974 £9.50

BUSBY, RICHARD   Graecae Grammatices Rudimenta. London, 1671. 8vo., contemporary sheep, worn, fourth edition. Dawsons PM 251-144 1974 £20

BUSBY, T. L.   Costumes of the Lower Orders in Paris. (c. 1820). 12mo., mounted to small 4to., plates, boards, cloth back. Quaritch 940-707 1974 £60

BUSCH, WILHELM   Hans Huckebein, der Unglucksrabe. Stuttgart and Leipzig, n.d. 4to., pict. boards, cloth spine, illus. Frohnsdorff 16-152 1974 $20

BUSCH, WILHELM   Max und Moritz. Munchen, n.d. 8vo., pict. boards, cloth spine, illus. Frohnsdorff 16-153 1974 $7.50

BUSCH, WILHELM   Plish and Plum. Boston, 1883. 8vo., pict. cloth, illus., 1st ed. Frohnsdorff 16-154 1974 $15

BUSEE, JEAN   De Statibus Hominum. 1613. Thick small 4to., contemporary calf, rubbed. Howes 185-1020 1974 £10

BUSGEN, M.   The Structure and Life of Forest Trees. 1929. Roy. 8vo., cloth, very scarce, third edition. Wheldon 131-1720 1974 £20

BUSHE, GERVAIS P.   A Digested Abridgement of the Laws Relating to the Linen and Hempen Manufactures of Ireland. Dublin, 1808. 8vo., half cloth boards. Emerald 50-97 1974 £5

BUSHNELL, HORACE   Women's Suffrage. New York, 1870. 12mo., orig. brown cloth, uncut, second edition. Dawsons PM 251-423 1974 £12.50

BUSK, G.   Catalogue of the Cyclostomatous Polyzoa in the Collection of the British Museum. 1875. 8vo., cloth, plates, scarce. Wheldon 128-880 1973 £5

BUSK, G.   Catalogue of the Marine Polyzoa in the British Museum. 1852-75. 3 parts, plates. Wheldon 131-923 1974 £7.50

BUSK, G.   Monograph of the Fossil Polyzoa of the Crag. 1859. 4to., half calf, plates. Wheldon 131-978 1974 £15

BUTCHER, R.   Survey and Antiquity of the Towns of Stamford. 1717-18. Small 8vo., half calf, rubbed. Quaritch 939-68 1974 £65

BUTEO, IOANNES   Logistica. 1559. 8vo., contemporary vellum, first edition. Dawsons PM 245-147 1974 £70

BUTLER, ALBAN   The Lives of the Fathers, Martyres and Other Principal Saints. n.d. 6 vols., imp. 8vo., plates, orig. cloth gilt. Smith 194-859 1974 £7.50

BUTLER, ALBAN   The Lives of the Fathers, Martyrs, and Other Principal Saints. New York, 1846. 4 vols., roy. 8vo., contemporary half calf. Howes 185-1022 1974 £7.50

BUTLER, ALBAN   The Lives of the Fathers, Martyrs and Other Principle Saints. London, (1928). 4 vols., large 8vo., plates, foxing, orig. cloth. Bow Windows 62-142 1974 £5.50

BUTLER, ARTHUR GARDNER   Birds' Eggs of the British Isles. (1907). 4to., orig. cloth, coloured plates, scarce. Wheldon 128-407 1973 £5

BUTLER, ARTHUR GARDNER   British Birds, Their Nest & Eggs. n.d. 6 vols., 4to., plates, orig. pictorial cloth. Smith 193-736 1973 £18

BUTLER, ARTHUR GARDNER   British Birds and Their Nests and Eggs. Hull and London, (n.d.). 4to., 6 vols., plates. Bow Windows 64-42 1974 £12

BUTLER, ARTHUR GARDINER   Catalogue of Diurnal Lepidoptera Described by Fabricius. 1869. 8vo., cloth, plates, scarce. Wheldon 131-791 1974 £5

BUTLER, ARTHUR GARDNER   Foreign Birds for Cage and Aviary. (1908-10). Crown 4to., cloth, 2 vols., illus. Wheldon 129-439 1974 £7.50

BUTLER, ARTHUR GARDNER   Foreign Birds for Cage and Aviary. (1908-10). 2 vols., crown 4to., cloth, illus. Wheldon 131-559 1974 £10

BUTLER, ARTHUR GARDNER   Foreign Finches in Captivity. 1899. Roy. 8vo., orig. half buckrom, coloured plates, second edition. Wheldon 128-406 1973 £20

BUTLER, ARTHUR GARDNER   Foreign Finches in Captivity. 1899. Roy. 8vo., orig. half morocco, plates, second edition. Wheldon 129-438 1974 £25

BUTLER, ARTHUR GARDINER   Monograph of the Genus Callidryas. 1873. 4to., orig. cloth, plates. Wheldon 130-726 1974 £7.50

BUTLER, CUTHBERT   The Life and Times of Bishop Ullathorne. 1926. 2 vols., orig. cloth, plates. Howes 185-1735 1974 £7.50

BUTLER, CUTHBERT   The Vatical Council. 1930. 2 vols., label, scarce. Howes 185-1023 1974 £8.50

BUTLER, E. J.   The Fungi of India. 1931-38. Roy 8vo., 2 vols., cloth. Wheldon 129-1161 1974 £7.50

BUTLER, ELLIS PARKER   Mike Flannery. Doubleday, Page, 1909. 101p., illus. Austin 54-197 1973 $6

BUTLER, FRANCES ANNE KEMBLE
Please turn to
KEMBLE, FRANCES ANNE

BUTLER, H.   South African Sketches. 1841. Frontispiece, plates, drawings (some colored), folio, half red calf, scarce. Sawyer 293-2 1974 £135

BUTLER, JAMES DAVIE   Deficiencies in Our History. Montpelier, 1846. 8vo., printed yellow wrapper. Butterfield 8-657 1974 $10

BUTLER, JOHN OLDING   Questions in Roman History. 1827. 12mo., contemporary tree sheep, maps. Hill 126-27 1974 £5.50

BUTLER, JOSEPH   The Analogy of Religion. London, 1736. 4to., contemporary calf, worn, first edition. Bow Windows 62-143 1974 £36

BUTLER, JOSEPH   The Analogy of Religion. 1736. 4to., calf rebacked, first edition. Hill 126-28 1974 £35

BUTLER, JOSEPH   The Analogy of Religion, Natural and Revealed. 1791. 8vo., contemporary calf, new edition. Hill 126-29 1974 £12.50

BUTLER, M. B.   My Story of the Civil War. Huntington, 1914. Cloth. Hayman 57-91 1974 $35

BUTLER, PIERCE   A Check List of 15th Century Books in the Newberry Library and In Other Libraries of Chicago. Chicago, 1933. Cloth. Kraus B8-30 1974 $10

BUTLER, R.   The New London and Country Cook. (c.1770). 8vo., 19th century marbled boards, morocco back. Quaritch 939-69 1974 £20

BUTLER, SAMUEL   On the Trapanese Origin of the Odyssey. Cambridge, 1893. First edition, frontispiece, demy 8vo., orig. paper printed wrapper, fine, presentation copy inscribed by author. Broadhurst 24-580 1974 £150

BUTLER, SAMUEL   Samuel Butler. Cambridge, 1903. Orig. wrappers, half morocco. Covent 55-277 1974 £15.75

BUTLER, SAMUEL 1612-1680   Hudibras. 1704. 8vo., early panelled calf, rebacked. Quaritch 936-28 1974 £5

BUTLER, SAMUEL 1612-1680   Hudibras. London, 1772. 2 vols., engraved plates, full contemporary calf, one cover detached, others worn, internally very good. Jacobs 24-69 1974 $35

BUTLER, SAMUEL 1612-1680   Hudibras. 1819. Rebound, buckram, 3 vols., English first edition. Covent 56-204 1974 £15.75

BUTLER, SAMUEL 1612-1680   Hudibras. 1819. Large paper copy, coloured aquatint plates, 2 vols., 8vo., crimson crushed levant morocco, gilt inside borders, top edges gilt, fine, scarce. Sawyer 293-80 1974 £42.50

BUTLER, SAMUEL 1612-1680   Hudibras. 1819. 3 vols., full morocco, first U.S. edition. Covent 56-1592 1974 £65

BUTLER, SAMUEL 1612-1680   Hudibras. Hartford, 1852. 16mo. Biblo & Tannen 213-740 1973 $6

BUTLER, SAMUEL 1835-1902   Butleriana. 1932. 8vo., orig. calf backed marbled boards, uncut, first edition. Dawsons PM 10-100 1974 £12

BUTLER, SAMUEL 1835-1902   Erewhon. 1933. 8vo., full sheepskin, limited. Broadhurst 23-1045 1974 £40

BUTLER, SAMUEL 1835-1902   Ex Voto. 1888. Plates, orig. cloth, inscribed, English first edition. Covent 56-203 1974 £175

BUTLER, SAMUEL 1835-1902   The Humour of Homer and Other Essays. 1913. Portrait, first edition. Bow Windows 66-101 1974 £6

BUTLER, SAMUEL 1835-1902   The Note Books of Samuel Butler. 1912. Small 8vo., cloth, frontis., first edition. Quaritch 936-324 1974 £9

BUTLER, W. F.   The Great Lone Land. 1886. Half morocco gilt, rubbed, plates. Smith 194-599 1974 £5.50

BUTLER, W. F.   The Lombard Communes. 1906. Thick 8vo., plates, maps, scarce. Howes 186-655 1974 £8.50

BUTLER, W. F. T.   Confiscation in Irish History. Dublin, 1918. 8vo., cloth boards, second & best edition. Emerald 50-95 1974 £8.50

BUTLER, WILLIAM ALLEN   Two Millons. Appleton, 1858. 93p. Austin 54-198 1973 $10

BUTLIN, HENRY T.   Diseases of the Tongue. London, 1885. Rittenhouse 46-118 1974 $20

BUTLIN, HENRY T.   Diseases of the Tongue. London, 1900. Second edition. Rittenhouse 46-119 1974 $25

BUTT, MARY MARTHA
Please turn to
SHERWOOD, MRS. MARY MARTHA (BUTT)

BUTTEL-REEPEN, H. VON   Leben und Wesen der Bienen. Braunschweig, 1915. 8vo., orig. cloth. Wheldon 129-704 1974 £7.50

BUTTERFIELD, CONSUL WILLSHIRE   History of Dane County, Wisconsin. Chicago. 8vo., three quarter leather, illus. Saddleback 14-757 1974 $40

BUTTERFIELD, CONSUL WILLSHIRE   History of George Rogers Clark's Conquest. Columbus, 1904. Cloth, fine. Hayman 57-62 1974 $15

BUTTERFIELD, CONSUL WILLSHIRE   History of the . . . Girty Brothers . . . and . . . of the Part Taken by Them in Lord Dunmore's War, In the Western Border War of the Revolution, and in the Indian War of 1790-95. Cincinnati, 1890. First edition, with errata, orig. binding. Butterfield 10-131 1974 $55

BUTTERFIELD, W. H.   A Book of House Plans. New York, 1912. 4to., bdg. dull. Biblo & Tannen 214-11 1974 $15

BUTTERWORTH, ADELINE M.   William Blake, Mystic. Liverpool, 1911. Roy. 8vo., boards, cloth back, dust wrapper, frontispiece. Quaritch 940-30 1974 £20

BUTTS, MARY   The Crystal Cabinet. 1937. Dust wrapper, fine, frontispiece. Covent 55-278 1974 £22.50

BUTTS, MARY   The Crystal Cabinet, My Childhood at Salterns. London, 1937. Frontispiece, first edition, back cover little stained, very good copy, frayed d.w., orig. cloth. Crane 7-33 1974 £6

BUTTS, MARY   Scenes from the Life of Cleopatra. 1935. Fine, d.w., first edition. Covent 51-2224 1973 £15

BUTTS, MARY   Scenes from the Life of Cleopatra. 1935. Dust wrapper, fine. Covent 55-279 1974 £15

BUTTS, MARY   Several Occasions. 1932. Very good copy, scarce, first edition. Covent 51-2225 1973 £12.50

BUTTS, MARY   Several Occasions. 1932. Dust wrapper, scarce. Covent 55-280 1974 £35

BUTTS, MARY   Traps for Unbelievers. 1932. Very good copy, rubber review stamp on title page, rather scarce, first edition. Covent 51-2226 1973 £15.75

BUXTON, THOMAS FOWELL   The African Slave Trade. London, 1839. Fine folding map, first edition, very scarce. Jenkins 61-264 1974 $60

BUXTON, THOMAS FOWELL   The African Slave Trade.   London, 1839. 8vo.,
green cloth, first edition.   Dawsons PM 251-424 1974 £55

BUXTON, THOMAS FOWELL   The Remedy.   London, 1840. 8vo., green cloth,
first edition.   Dawsons PM 251-425 1974 £45

BUXTON Diamonds; or, Grateful Ellen.   (1823). First edition, copperplates,
12mo., orig. boards, roan spine, good internally.   George's 610-112 1973 £7.50

BUXTORF, JOHANNES   Lexicon Chaldaicum Talmudicum et Rabbinicum
nunc Primum in Lucem Editum.   Basel, 1639-40. Thick large folio, contemporary
calf, very worn, first edition.   Harper 213-26 1973 $175

BUZZARD, THOMAS   Clinical Lectures on Diseases of the Nervous
System.   London, 1882. 8vo., orig. cloth, slightly stained, illus., first edition.
Gurney 66-36 1974 £15

BUZZI, PAOLO   Carmi Degli Augusti e dei Consolari.   Milan,
1920. Small 8vo., wrappers, worn covers, uncut.   Minters 37-379 1973
£13.50

BUZZI, PAOLO   Poema dei Quarantanni.   Milan, 1922. 8vo.,
wrappers, frontispiece.   Minters 37-381 1973 $26

BUZZI, PAOLO   Poema di Radio-Onde.   Florence, 1940. 8vo.,
wrappers, uncut.   Minters 37-380 1973 $12

BYERLY, WILLIAM ELWOOD   An Elementary Treatise on Fourier's Series.   Boston, New York, (1893). 8vo., orig. blue cloth, fine, first edition.   Dawsons PM
245-148 1974 £10

BYFORD, WILLIAM H.   A Treatise On the Chronic Inflammation and
Displacements of the Unimpregnated Uterus.   Philadelphia, 1871. Second
edition.   Rittenhouse 46-120 1974 £10

BYNNER, WITTER   An Ode to Harvard, and Other Poems.   Boston,
1907. Presentation copy inscribed from author, full morocco, gilt top, spine worn
at head, some damp staining throughout, very good copy.   Covent 51-323 1973
£12.60

BYNNER, WITTER   Spectra.   New York, 1916. 8vo., orig. cloth,
inscribed, scarce, first edition.   Rota 189-167 1974 £40

BYNNER, WITTER   Tiger.   New York, 1913. Presentation copy
inscribed by author, very good copy, first U. S. edition.   Covent 51-324 1973
£8.50

BYNNER, WITTER   Tiger.   New York, 1913. Presentation copy,
inscribed, first U.S. edition.   Covent 56-206 1974 £10

BYNNER, WITTER   Tiger.   1914. First edition, boards, fine, d.w.
Covent 51-325 1973 £5.25

BYNUM, LINDLEY   The Record Book of the Rancho Santa Ana Del
Chino.   Los Angeles, 1935. 8vo., wrapper.   Saddleback 14-53 1974 $10

BYRD, RICHARD EVELYN   Little America Aerial Exploration in the
Antarctic.   New York and London, 1930. Author's autograph edition, limited to
1000 copies, large 8vo., maps, illus.   Butterfield 10-76 1974 $35

BYRD, RICHARD EVELYN   Skyward.   New York, 1928. 8vo., illus., maps,
orig. cloth, portrait, first edition.   Bow Windows 62-144 1974 £6.50

BYRNE, D.   An Untitled Story.   n.d. Orig. cloth, dust
wrapper, signed presentation.   Smith 194-403 1974 £5

BYRNE, DESMOND   Australian Writers.   1896. English first edition.
Covent 56-1529 1974 £15

BYRNE, DONN   Crusade.   Boston, 1928. 12mo., cloth, dust
wrapper, first edition.   Goodspeed's 578-45 1974 $15

BYRNE, DONN   Crusade.   Boston, 1928. Limited to 365 copies,
signed by author, 8vo., bellum back, near fine.   Current BW9-210 1974 $20

BYRNE, DONN   Crusade.   Boston, 1928. First U. S. edition,
one of 15 lettered copies signed by author, with author's signed presentation
inscription, very good copy, vellum backed boards.   Covent 51-2227 1973
£10.50

BYRNE, DONN   Field of Honor.   New York, (1929). 12mo.,
cloth, dust wrapper, first edition.   Goodspeed's 578-46 1974 $15

BYRNE, DONN   Messer Marco Polo.   New York, 1921. First
edition, first state, cloth cover lightly freckled with small stain.   Wilson 63-494
1974 $15

BYROM, JOHN   The Universal English Short Hand.   1767.
Covent 55-1370 1974 £15

BYRON, GEORGE GORDON   Bibliographical Catalogue of First Editions,
Proof Copies and Manuscripts of Books by Lord Byron.   (London), 1925. 4to.,
orig. cloth gilt, uncut, first edition.   Dawsons PM 10-103 1974 £20

BYRON, GEORGE GORDON   The Bride of Abydos.   London, 1813. 8vo.,
full mottled calf, first edition, second issue.   Dawsons PM 252-108 1974 £95

BYRON, GEORGE GORDON   Cain.   1822. 8vo., orig. boards.   Quaritch
936-328 1974 £30

BYRON, GEORGE GORDON   Childe Harold's Pilgrimage.   1814. Orig.
cloth backed boards, uncut, eighth edition.   Howes 185-56 1974 £5

BYRON, GEORGE GORDON   Childe Harold's Pilgrimage.   1816-19.
3 vols. in 1, contemporary calf gilt, rubbed.   Smith 194-404 1974 £18.50

BYRON, GEORGE GORDON   Childe Harold's Pilgrimage.   1818. Orig.
cloth backed boards, first edition, fourth issue.   Howes 185-57 1974 £10

BYRON, GEORGE GORDON   The Corsair.   London, 1814. 8vo., modern
boards, first edition, second issue.   Dawsons PM 252-109 1974 £9

BYRON, GEORGE GORDON   The Corsair.   London, 1814. Modern morocco,
second issue, without the words "The End" and the printer's imprint on page 100,
fine.   MacManus 224-57 1974 $30

BYRON, GEORGE GORDON   A Descriptive Catalogue of an Exhibition of
Manuscripts and First Editions of Lord Byron.   Austin, 1924. Large 8vo., orig.
cloth, plates.   Dawsons PM 10-102 1974 £18

BYRON, GEORGE GORDON   Don Juan.   London, 1822. Thick 12mo.,
contemporary half calf.   Ximenes 36-45 1974 $22.50

BYRON, GEORGE GORDON   Don Juan.   London, 1828. 2 vols., 12mo.,
frontispieces, inscription, contemporary half roan.   Bow Windows 62-146
1974 £4.75

BYRON, GEORGE GORDON   Don Juan.   New York, (1926). 8vo., illus.,
plates, cloth, d.j., uncut.   Rich Summer-48 1974 $17.50

BYRON, GEORGE GORDON   Don Juan.   London, 1926. Orig. white, dec.
cl., illus.   Jacobs 24-70 1974 $15

BYRON, GEORGE GORDON   Don Juan.   New York, 1943. Illus.   Biblo &
Tannen 214-730 1974 $7.50

BYRON, GEORGE GORDON   The Drawing-Room Edition of the Poetical Works
Of.   (n.d.). 4to., 2 vols., half morocco.   Bow Windows 64-429 1974 £12.50

BYRON, GEORGE GORDON   The Giaour, A Fragment of a Turkish Tale.
London, 1813. Modern half morocco, fine, first published edition.   MacManus
224-58 1974 $35

BYRON, GEORGE GORDON   Hebrew Melodies.   London, 1815. 8vo.,
half calf, marbled boards, stains, first edition.   Bow Windows 62-147 1974
£28

BYRON, GEORGE GORDON   Hebrew Melodies.   London, 1815. Modern
morocco, fine, first edition.   MacManus 224-59 1974 $50

BYRON, GEORGE GORDON   Lara.   1814. 8vo., contemporary calf gilt,
label.   Howes 185-58 1974 £30

BYRON, GEORGE GORDON   Lara.   1814. Small 8vo., orig. drab boards,
first edition.   Quaritch 936-329 1974 £50

BYRON, GEORGE GORDON   Marino Faliero, Doge of Venice.   1821. Orig.
boards, uncut, label, first edition, first issue.   Howes 185-59 1974 £21

BYRON, GEORGE GORDON   Marino Faliero, Doge of Venice. The Prophecy of Dante. London, 1821. Modern morocco, first issue, portrait. MacManus 224-60 1974 $50

BYRON, GEORGE GORDON   Mazeppa. London, 1819. Orig. drab wrappers, uncut, second issue, 4 leaves of ads, folding box. MacManus 224-61 1974 $85

BYRON, GEORGE GORDON   Poems. First edition, first issue, 8vo., plain blue calf, spine gilt, gilt inside border, good copy, rare. Sawyer 293-82 1974 £55

BYRON, GEORGE GORDON   The Prisoner of Chillon, and Other Poems. London, 1816. Orig. wrappers, first issue, with recto of E8 blank, fine, slip case. MacManus 224-62 1974 $175

BYRON, GEORGE GORDON   Sardanapalus. 1821. Calf antique, uncut edges browned, first edition. Bow Windows 66-103 1974 £30

BYRON, GEORGE GORDON   Sardanapalus. 1821. Contemporary half black calf gilt, foxing, first edition. Howes 186-65 1974 £21

BYRON, GEORGE GORDON   The Siege of Corinth. London, 1816. 8vo., contemporary sheep, stains, worn, second edition. Bow Windows 62-148 1974 £9.50

BYRON, GEORGE GORDON   The Siege of Corinth. Parisina. London, 1816. Modern half morocco, first edition, lacks half title and the ads. MacManus 224-63 1974 $35

BYRON, GEORGE GORDON   Werner. 1823. Half calf, marbled boards, fine. Covent 55-283 1974 £10.50

BYRON, GEORGE GORDON   Werner, a Tragedy. London, 1823. Later half calf, marbled boards, first issue, without the concluding imprint, has the half title, internally clean. MacManus 224-64 1974 $30

BYRON, GEORGE GORDON   Works. 8vo., 6 vols., half morocco, gilt, fine. Quaritch 936-327 1974 £60

BYRON, GEORGE GORDON   The Works Of. Edinburgh & London, n.d. 2 vols., roy. 8vo., half contemporary calf gilt, plates. Smith 194-718 1974 £12

BYRON, GEORGE GORDON   The Works of Lord Byron. London, 1818. 2 vols. Biblo & Tannen 213-738 1973 $10

BYRON, GEORGE GORDON   Works. 1832-33. 12mo., 17 vols., illus., half morocco, plates. Quaritch 936-325 1974 £50

BYRON, GEORGE GORDON   Works. 1838. Roy. 8vo., contemporary half calf, rubbed, portrait. Howes 185-54 1974 £5.50

BYRON, GEORGE GORDON   Works. 1898-1901. 13 vols., orig. blue cloth gilt, plates, revised, best edition. Howes 185-55 1974 £65

BYRON, GEORGE GORDON   Works. 1898-1904. 8vo., 13 vols., cloth, portraits, illus. Quaritch 936-326 1974 £70

BYRON, GEORGE GORDON   Complete Works. 1898-1930. 13 vols., demy 8vo., fine set, several vols. in dust wrappers, vol. 1 rebound uniformly to match set. Broadhurst 24-265 1974 £40

BYRON, R.   The Birth of Western Painting. 1930. 4to., half morocco, gilt, plates. Broadhurst 23-32 1974 £30

BYTHNER, VICTORINUS   Lyra Prophetica Davidis Regis. Zurich, 1670. 8vo., contemporary stiff vellum. Dawsons PM 251-145 1974 £20

C

C., H.   Abbrege de l'Histoire Francoise. Paris, 1599.
Small folio, quarter calf, rebacked. Thomas 28-176 1972 £40

C., L. D.   The Right Spirit. Buffalo, 1885. Orig.
binding. Butterfield 10-15 1974 $35

C. & G. COOPER CO.   Traction Engines, Common Farm Engines . . .
Manufactured by. Mt. Vernon, 1881. 12mo., wrappers, illus. Putman 126-49
1974 $22

CABANES, J. F. M. CABIRAN   Apercu sur Quelques. Paris, 1805. 4to.,
disbound. Gurney 64-42 1974 £15

CABANIS, PIERRE JEAN GEORGES   Coup d'Oeil sur les Revolutions. Paris,
1804. 8vo., quarter shagreen, first edition. Gurney 64-43 1974 £20

CABANIS, PIERRE JEAN GEORGES   Coup d'Oeil sur les Revolutions et sur la
Reforme de la Medecine. Paris, 1804. 8vo., quarter shagreen, first edition,
some worming. Gurney 66-37 1974 £20

CABASSUT, JEAN   Notitia Ecclesiastica Historiarum, Conciliorum
& Canonum Invicem Collatorum. 1754. Thick folio, contemporary calf,
rubbed. Howes 185-1024 1974 £25

CABEL, NICCOLO   Philosophia Magnetica in qua Magnetis Natura.
1629. Folio, contemporary calf, rebacked, first edition. Dawsons PM 245-149
1974 £450

CABELL, JAMES BRANCH   The Eagle's Shadow. New York, 1904. Orig.
cloth gilt, plates, fine, first American edition, first issue. Covent 55-284
1974 £75

CABELL, JAMES BRANCH   The Eagle's Shadow. New York, 1904. Orig.
cloth, first issue, with the dedication "M.L.P.B.", very good copy. MacManus
224-65 1974 $40

CABELL, JAMES BRANCH   The Eagle's Shadow. New York, 1904. Orig.
cloth, fine copy. MacManus 224-66 1974 $35

CABELL, JAMES BRANCH   Jurgen. 1921. Roy. 8vo., illus., plates,
limited, first English edition. Howes 185-62 1974 £7.50

CABELL, JAMES BRANCH   The Line of Love. New York, 1905. Orig.
dec. cloth, illus. in color, first edition, fine, orig. publisher's box. MacManus
224-67 1974 $35

CABELL, JAMES BRANCH   Preface to the Past. New York, 1936. Dust
wrapper, fine, first American edition. Covent 55-285 1974 £15

CABELL, JAMES BRANCH   The Silver Stallion. New York, 1926.
Numbered, signed, large paper edition. Ballinger 1-103 1974 $12.50

CABELL, JAMES BRANCH   Something About Eve. New York, 1927.
Half vellum, numbered, autographed, special limited edition. Jenkins 48-82
1973 $25

CABELL, JAMES BRANCH   Something About Eve. New York, 1927.
First trade edition, orig. binding. Wilson 63-496 1974 $10

CABELL, JAMES BRANCH   Sonnets from Antan. New York, 1929. First
edition, demy 8vo., dec. boards, linen spine, paper printed label, uncut, signed
by author, limited to 676 copies. Broadhurst 24-582 1974 £8

CABELL, JAMES BRANCH   Straws and Prayer-Books. New York, 1924.
First American edition. Covent 55-287 1974 £6.30

CABELL, JAMES BRANCH   The White Robe. 1928. Illus., first U. S.
edition, limited to 3290 copies, fine, leather backed boards, slipcase. Covent
51-333 1973 £15

CABINET of Useful Arts and Manufactures. New York, 1827. 16mo., rebound,
leather label on spine, engravings. Frohnsdorff 16-156 1974 $100

CABLE, GEORGE   Bonaventure. 1901 (1888). 314p. Austin
54-199 1973 $5

CABLE, GEORGE   Bylow Hill. Scribner, 1902. 215p., illus.,
orig. ed. Austin 54-200 1973 $6

CABLE, GEORGE   The Cavalier. Scribner, 1901. 311p., illus.,
orig. ed. Austin 54-201 1973 $4.75

CABLE, GEORGE   Kincaid's Battery. Scribner, 1908. 396p.,
illus., orig. ed. Austin 54-202 1973 $6

CABLE, GEORGE   Posson Jone and Pere Raphael. Scribner, 1909.
162p., illus., orig. ed. Austin 54-203 1973 $7.50

CABLE, GEORGE   Strong Hearts. Scribner, 1899. 214p., orig.
ed. Austin 54-204 1973 $6

CABLE, GEORGE WASHINGTON   The Grandissimes. New York, 1880. Cloth,
first edition. Hayman 57-175 1974 $17.50

CABLE, GEORGE WASHINGTON   Old Creole Days. New York, 1879. 12mo.,
cloth, first edition. Goodspeed's 578-47 1974 $85

CABLE, GEORGE WASHINGTON   Old Creole Days. New York, 1879. 12mo.,
cloth, second printing. Goodspeed's 578-48 1974 $15

CABLE, GEORGE WASHINGTON   Old Creole Days. New York, 1879. Orig.
illus. cloth, spine sun darkened, ends of spine chipped, first printing, bookplate
of C. W. Barrett, very good copy. MacManus 224-68 1974 $50

CABOT, ELIZABETH   Letters of. Boston, 1905. 8vo., 2 vols., orig.
bindings. Butterfield 8-27 1974 $20

CABOT, ELLA LYMAN   A Course in Citizenship. 1914. 386 pages.
Austin 57-108 1974 $10

CABOT, HUGH   Modern Urology In Original Contributions By
American Authors. Philadelphia, 1936. 2 vols. Rittenhouse 46-121 1974 $15

CABRERA, A.   Los Maniferos de Marruecos. Madrid, 1932.
8vo., half calf, plates. Wheldon 130-387 1974 £15

CACTUSSEN en Vetplanten Maandblad van de Nederl. Amsterdam, 1936-43.
Vols. 2 - 9, part 1, 8vo., cloth & in parts as issued. Wheldon 131-1651
1974 £25

CADILLAC MOTOR CAR COMPANY   Cadillac Participation In the World War.
Detroit, 1919. First edition, 4to., photos, green suede covers spotted & soiled,
interior mint. Current BW9-459 1974 $35

CADOGAN, W. B.   Liberty & Equality. London, n.d. 7 items in
1 vol., contemporary calf backed marbled boards, third edition. Smith
193-340 1973 £20

CADWALLADER, D.   A Vindication of the Steam-Boat Right Granted by
the State of New York. New York, 1819. 8vo., tree calf. Putman 126-45
1974 $50

CAESAR, GAIUS JULIUS   Commentariorum de Bello Gallico. 1519.
Contemporary Italian black morocco, gilt, woodcuts, bookplates. Thomas
30-50 1973 £250

CAESAR, GAIUS JULIUS   Commentariorum de Bello Gallico. 1519.
18th century vellum gilt, stains, morocco label. Thomas 30-51 1973 £60

CAESAR, GAIUS JULIUS   Les Commentaires et les Annotations de Blaise
de Vigenere. 1625. 4to., old calf, worn, stains, woodcut illus. Allen
213-199 1973 £25

CAESAR, GAIUS JULIUS   Commentaries. Amsterdam, 1661. 24mo.,
engraved title, plates, full contemporary vellum, wallet edges. Jacobs 24-71
1974 $35

CAESAR, GAIUS JULIUS   The Complete Captain. Cambridge, 1640.
8vo., contemporary vellum, first edition. Dawsons PM 251-370 1974 £125

CAESAR, GAIUS JULIUS   Ivlli Caesaris Quae Extant ex Emedatione los
Scaligeri. 1635. 24mo., maps, illus., stains, contemporary vellum. Bow
Windows 62-305 1974 £8.50

CAESAR, GAIUS JULIUS   Quae Exstant Opera. 1755. 2 vols., 16mo.,
new buckram, maps. Allen 213-198 1973 $12.50

CAFFIN, CHARLES H.   Art for Life's Sake. New York, 1913. 1st
ed., author's sgd. pres. Biblo & Tannen 210-60 1973 $15

CAGE-BIRD CLUB   Transactions of the. 1893-96. 2 vols., 8vo.,
cloth, extremely scarce. Wheldon 131-560 1974 £10

CAGNAT, R.   L'Armee Romaine d'Afrique et l'Occupation
Militaire de l'Afrique sous les Empereurs. 1892. 4to., new buckram. Allen
213-209 1973 $50

CAGNAT, R.   Manuel d'Archeologie Romaine. 1916-20.
2 vols., browned. Allen 213-210 1973 $30

CAHEN, E.   Elements de la Theorie des Nombres. Paris, 19-
00. 8vo., grey printed wrapper, first edition. Dawsons PM 245-150 1974 £6

CAHN, WILLIAM   Goodnight, Mrs. Calabash. 1963. 191p.,
illus. Austin 51-166 1973 $7.50

CAHN, WILLIAM   The Laugh Makers. Putnam, 1957. 192p.,
illus. Austin 51-167 1973 $7.50

CAHUN, LEON   Les Pilotes d'Ango. Paris, 1878. Gravures,
8vo., orig. highly gilt dec. red cloth, interior with moderate foxing. Current
BW9-497 1974 $22.50

CAILLIE, RENE   Travels Through Central Africa to Timbuctoo.
London, 1830. 2 vols., 8vo., contemporary half calf, plates. Traylen 79-452
1973 £68

CAIN, JAMES M.   The Butterfly. New York, 1947. 1st ed.
Biblo & Tannen 214-677 1974 $7.50

CAINE, CAESAR   The Martial Annals of the City of York.
York, 1893. Imp. 8vo., orig. cloth, illus. Howes 186-2228 1974 £5.50

CAINE, CLARENCE J.   How to Write Photoplays. McKay, n.d.
269p. Austin 51-168 1973 $10

CAINE, HALL   The Bondman. 1890. Orig. cloth,
presentation inscription, first 1 vol. edition. Rota 188-141 1974 £5

CAINE, HALL   The Eternal City. 1901. Orig. cloth, faded,
inscribed, first edition. Rota 188-143 1974 £5

CAINE, HALL   Recollections of Rossetti. 1928. Dust wrapper,
English first edition. Covent 56-1105 1974 £7.50

CAINE, LOU S.   North American Fresh Water Sport Fish.
New York, 1949. 1st ed. Biblo & Tannen 213-1004 1973 $10

CAIRD, EDWARD   The Critical Philosophy of Immanuel Kant.
Glasgow, 1889. 2 vols., orig. cloth. Smith 194-881 1974 £15

CAIRD, EDWARD   The Evolution of Theology in the Greek
Philosophers. Glasgow, 1904. 2 vols., stain. Howes 185-1828 1974 £6

CAIRD, JAMES   The Plantation Scheme. Edinburgh, 1850.
8vo., uncut, cloth boards. Emerald 50-103 1974 £12

CAIRNCROSS, DAVID   The Origin of the Silver Eel. London, 1862.
8vo., orig. green cloth, printed side-label, frontispiece, very good copy, first
edition. Ximenes 37-31 1974 $35

CAIUS, JOHANNES   De Antiquitate Cantabrigiensis Academiae
Libri Duo. 1568. 2 parts in 1 vol., small 8vo., old vellum, first edition.
Quaritch 939-316 1974 £85

CALAMUS   A Quarterly Journal. London, Dublin &
Chatham, 1929-34. Orig. wrappers, illus. Howes 186-1797 1974 £12.50

CALAMY, EDMUND   An Abridgement of Mr. Baxter's History of His
Life and Times. 1727. 4 vols., modern buckram. Thomas 28-86 1972 £35

CALASIO, F. MARIO DE   Concordantiae Sacrorum Bibliorum Hebraicorum.
London, 1747-49. 4 vols., contemporary leather backed marbled boards.
Smith 194-138 1974 £30

CALDECOTT, ANDREW   Fires Burn Blue. New York, 1948. Biblo &
Tannen 210-575 1973 $8.50

CALDECOTT, RANDOLPH   The Babes in the Wood. London, n.d. 1st ed.,
all edges gilt, 8 color plates. Frohnsdorff 16-160 1974 $40

CALDECOTT, RANDOLPH   Breton Folk. London, 1880. 4to., cloth,
gilt; bevelled edges; all edges gilt. Frohnsdorff 16-159 1974 $30

CALDECOTT, RANDOLPH   Come Lasses and Lads. London, 1884.
Oblong 4to., 6 color plates, 1st ed. Frohnsdorff 16-161 1974 $15

CALDECOTT, RANDOLPH   The Complete Collection of Randolph Caldecott's
Contributions to the "Graphic". 1888. Imp. 4to., uncut, illus. in colour and
b.w., orig. cloth, limited to 1250 copies, signed by Edmund Evans, fine.
Broadhurst 24-26 1974 £45

CALDECOTT, RANDOLPH   An Elegy on the Death of a Mad Dog. London,
n.d. All edges gilt, 8 color plates, 1st ed. Frohnsdorff 16-164 1974 $25

CALDECOTT, RANDOLPH   An Elegy on the Glory of Her Sex. London,
1885. Oblong 4to., 6 color plates, 1st ed. Frohnsdorff 16-165 1974 $12.50

CALDECOTT, RANDOLPH   The Farmer's Boy. London, 1881. 4to.,
8 color plates, 1st ed. Frohnsdorff 16-166 1974 $20

CALDECOTT, RANDOLPH   The Fox Jumps Over the Parsons Gate. (1883).
4to., orig. glazed wrapper, illus., first edition. Hammond 201-96 1974 £5

CALDECOTT, RANDOLPH   Hey Diddle Diddle and Baby Bunting. (1882).
4to., orig. glazed wrapper, illus. Hammond 201-95 1974 £5

CALDECOTT, RANDOLPH   Last Graphic Pictures. 1888. Oblong 4to.,
coloured illus., orig. cloth backed pictorial boards, very good copy, first edition.
Covent 51-336 1973 £5.25

CALDECOTT, RANDOLPH   The Panjandrum Picture Book. (1885). 4to.,
orig. cloth, first edition. Hammond 201-97 1974 £15

CALDECOTT, RANDOLPH   The Panjandrum Picture Book. London, (c.1890).
Square 8vo., illus. in full color, spine darkened with ends missing, pictorial
front cover soiled, hinges loose, interior very good. Current BW9-126 1974
$17.50

CALDECOTT, RANDOLPH   A Personal Memoir of His Early Career.
London, 1886. Crown 4to., illus., orig. cloth, first edition. Bow Windows
62-150 1974 £9.50

CALDECOTT, RANDOLPH   Picture Books. n.d. 14 vols., coloured &
plain illus., crown 4to., and oblong roy. 8vo., orig. coloured pictorial wrappers,
spines rubbed. George's 610-114 1973 £12

CALDECOTT, RANDOLPH   The Queen of Hearts. London, 1881. 4to.,
color plates, first edition. Frohnsdorff 16-167 1974 $25

CALDECOTT, RANDOLPH   Randolph Caldecott's Painting Book. c., 1919.
4to., orig. coloured pictorial boards, plates, first series. Hammond 201-98 1974
£10

CALDECOTT, RANDOLPH   R. Caldecott's Picture Book. c., 1890. 4to.,
orig. cloth, illus., first edition. Hammond 201-99 1974 £10

CALDECOTT, RANDOLPH   R. Caldecott's Picture Book. c., 1890. 4to.,
orig. cloth, illus., first edition. Hammond 201-100 1974 £10

CALDECOTT, RANDOLPH   Randolph Caldecott's Sketches. London, n.d.
4to., cloth, illus. Frohnsdorff 16-169 1974 $12.50

CALDECOTT, RANDOLPH   Some of Aesop's Fables. 1883. 4to., orig.
pictorial cloth, English first edition. Covent 56-681 1974 £21

CALDECOTT, RANDOLPH   Some of Aesop's Fables with Modern Instances
Shwen in Designs. London, 1883. Pict. cloth, top edge gilt, 1st ed., engravings.
Frohnsdorff 16-170 1974 $20

CALDECOTT, RANDOLPH   Three Jovial Huntsmen. London, 1880. 4to., 8 color plates. Frohnsdorff 16-171 1974 $20

CALDELAR, ADELE   Nouvelles Fables Morales et Religieuses. Paris, 1862. Large 8vo., orig. wrapper, inscribed, woodcuts. L. Goldschmidt 42-174 1974 $20

CALDERA DE HEREDIA, CASPAR   Tribvnalis Medici Illvstrationes et Observationes Practicae. 1663. Folio, elaborately tooled panelled calf, first edition. Dawsons PM 249-101 1974 £55

CALDICOTT, J. W.   The Values of Old English Silver and Sheffield Plate From the XVth to the XIXth Centuries. 1906. Large crown 4to., plates. Bow Windows 66-105 1974 £18.50

CALDWELL, CHARLES   Medical and Physical Memoirs. Philadelphia, 1801. 8vo., modern calf, boards, gilt, first edition. Dawsons PM 249-102 1974 £70

CALDWELL, D. S.   Incidents of War. Dayton, 1864. Printed wrappers, rare. Hayman 57-84 1974 $75

CALDWELL, ERSKINE   All Night Long. 1942. 283p. Austin 54-206 1973 $6

CALDWELL, ERSKINE   All-Out On the Road to Smolensk. Duell, 1942. 230p. Austin 54-207 1973 $6

CALDWELL, ERSKINE   American Earth. Scribner, 1931. 314p., orig. ed. Austin 54-208 1973 $10

CALDWELL, ERSKINE   Around About America. Farrar, Straus, 1964. 224p., illus. Austin 54-209 1973 $7.50

CALDWELL, ERSKINE   Call It Experience. Duell, 1951. 239p. Austin 54-210 1973 $10

CALDWELL, ERSKINE   Claudelle Inglish. Little, Brown, 1958. 208p. Austin 54-211 1973 $6

CALDWELL, ERSKINE   Georgia Boy. Grosset, Dunlap, 1943. 239p. Austin 54-212 1973 $6.50

CALDWELL, ERSKINE   God's Little Acre. Viking, 1933. 303p., orig. ed. Austin 54-213 1973 $7.50

CALDWELL, ERSKINE   A House In the Uplands. 1946. 238p., 1st ed. Austin 54-214 1973 $7.50

CALDWELL, ERSKINE   In Search of Bisco. Farrar, 1965. 219p. Austin 54-215 1973 $6.50

CALDWELL, ERSKINE   Jenny By Nature. Farrar, Straus, 1961. 215p., 1st ed. Austin 54-216 1973 $6

CALDWELL, ERSKINE   Journeyman. New York, 1935. First U. S. edition, one of 1475 numbered copies, very nice copy, worn slip case. Covent 51-2230 1973 £15

CALDWELL, ERSKINE   Kneel to the Rising Sun. Viking, 1935. 246p. Austin 54-217 1973 $7.50

CALDWELL, ERSKINE   A Lamp for Nightfall. Duell, 1952. 211p. Austin 54-218 1973 $6.50

CALDWELL, ERSKINE   Place Called Estherville. Duell, 1949. 244p. Austin 54-219 1973 $6

CALDWELL, ERSKINE   Some American People. New York, (1935). Blind-stamped rough linen, mint, first edition. Bradley 35-30 1974 $36

CALDWELL, ERSKINE   Summertime Island. World, 1968. 183p. Austin 54-220 1973 $6

CALDWELL, ERSKINE   The Sure Hand of God. Grosset, Dunlap, 1947. 243p. "The Autograph Ed." Austin 54-222 1973 $6.50

CALDWELL, ERSKINE   The Sure Hand of God. Duell, 1947. 243p. Austin 54-221 1973 $6

CALDWELL, ERSKINE   This Very Earth. Duell, 1948. 254p. Austin 54-223 1973 $7

CALDWELL, ERSKINE   Tragic Ground. Duell, Sloan, Pearce, 1944. 237p., hard cover ed. Austin 54-224 1973 $6.50

CALDWELL, ERSKINE   Trouble in July. Duell, Sloan, Pearce, 1940. 241p. Austin 54-225 1973 $6.50

CALDWELL, ERSKINE   Trouble In July. New York, (1940). Wrappers, uncorrected proof copy of first edition. Jenkins 48-86 1973 $30

CALDWELL, GUY A.   Treatment of Fractures. New York, 1943. First edition. Rittenhouse 46-122 1974 $10

CALDWELL, J. E.   Songs of the Pines. Toronto, 1895. Marbled boards, leather spine. Hood's 103-712 1974 $15

CALDWELL, H. R.   South China Birds. Shanghai, 1931. 8vo., cloth, plates, scarce. Wheldon 130-480 1974 £50

CALEF, ROBERT   The Wonders of the Invisible World Displayed. Boston, 1828. 18mo., orig. boards, cloth back, paper label, new edition. Butterfield 10-534 1974 $25

CALENDAR of Entries In the Papal Registers Relating to Great Britain and Ireland. 1921-33. 2 vols., thick roy. 8vo., orig. cloth. Howes 185-1587 1974 £20

CALENDAR of Entries in the Papal Registers Relating to Great Britain and Ireland. 1896. Roy. 8vo., cloth. Quaritch 939-12 1974 £15

CALENDAR of Inquisitions Post Mortem and Other Analogous Documents. 1898. Roy. 8vo., cloth. Quaritch 939-6 1974 £12.50

CALENDAR of Letter-Books Preserved Among the Archives of the City of London. 1899-1912. 11 vols. Howes 186-2122 1974 £25

CALENDAR of Letter-Books Preserved Among the Archives of the Corporation of the City of London. 1899-1915. 11 vols., 8vo., cloth. Quaritch 939-459 1974 £20

CALENDAR of the College for Presbyterian Assemblys College. Belfast, 1912-42. 9 vols., 8vo., orig. boards. Emerald 50-798 1974 £9

A CALENDAR of the Crown Prisoners. Lancaster, 1821. 4to., half green morocco. Quaritch 939-420 1974 £21

CALENDAR of the Laing Charters A. D. Edinburgh, 1899. Thick roy. 8vo., orig. cloth, scarce. Howes 186-976 1974 £18

CALENDAR of the Justiciary Rolls or Proceedings in the Court of the Justiciar of Ireland. Dublin, 1905-14. 2 vols., roy. 8vo., cloth. Quaritch 939-8 1974 £30

CALENDAR of the Proceedings of the Committee for Compounding. 1889-92. 5 vols., thick imp. 8vo., cloth. Quaritch 939-5 1974 £70

CALENDAR of Treasury Papers. 1874-89. 5 vols., roy. 8vo., cloth. Quaritch 939-21 1974 £47.50

CALENDARIO Del Reale Osservatorio del 1863. Palermo. 16mo., embossed white black and gold binding, slip case. Gregory 44-27A 1974 $47.50

CALENDARIUM Rotulorum Patentium in Turri Londinensi. 1802. Folio, half russio. Quaritch 939-14 1974 £12

CALENDARS of the Proceedings in Chancery, in the Reign of Queen Elizabeth. 1832. Folio, cloth. Quaritch 939-3 1974 £9.50

CALHOUN, S. F.   Fifteen Years in the Church of Rome. Lowell, 1886. 192 pages. Austin 57-112 1974 $15

CALIFORNIA: A Guide to the Golden State. New York, 1939. Green cloth, illus., first edition. Bradley 35-33 1974 $16

CALIFORNIA Illustrated in Photogravure. San Francisco, 1894. Boards, illus., spine weak. Jenkins 61-291 1974 $15

CALIFORNIA in 1846. San Francisco, 1934. Cloth, dec. boards, illus., fine, quite scarce. Dykes 22-184 1973 $45

CALIFORNIA MID-WINTER INTERNATIONAL EXPOSITION   Souvenir. San Francisco, 1894. Photogravures, fine. Jenkins 61-430 1974 $27.50

CALITRI, ANTONIO   Canti Del Nord-America. 1925. 278 pages. Austin 57-114 1974 $27.50

CALKINS, G. N.   The Biology of the Protozoa. 1926. 8vo., cloth, scarce. Wheldon 130-855 1974 £7.50

CAII Sallustii Crispi Quae Extant. Londini, 1713. 12mo., frontispiece, portrait, contemporary vellum. Bow Windows 62-801 1974 £9

CALLAHAN, CHARLES H.   Washington: The Man and the Mason. N. P., 1913. Illus., folding map. Jenkins 61-2597 1974 $10

CALLENDER, JAMES H.   Yesterdays on Brooklyn Heights. New York, 1927. 8vo., cloth, limited, autographed. Saddleback 14-572 1974 $15

CALLIMACHUS CYRENAEUS   Hymni, cum Scholiis Nunc Primum Aeditis. Basle, 1532. Small 4to., modern half scored calf, title cleaned, stains. Thomas 32-225 1974 £35

CALLISON, JOHN   Bill Jones of Paradise Valley Oklahoma. Chicago, 1914. Illus., scarce. Jenkins 61-1243 1974 $75

CALLISON, JOHN   Bill Jones of Paradise Valley Oklahoma. Chicago, 1914. Scarce, illus. Jenkins 61-2021 1974 $75

CALMEIL, LOUIS FLORENTIN   Traite des Maladies Inflammatoires du Cerveau. Paris, 1859. 2 vols., orig. wrappers, unopened, first edition. Schuman 37-36 1974 $145

CALMET, AUGUSTINE   Commentarius Literalis in Omnes Libros Novi Testamenti. 1787. 4 vols., 4to., contemporary calf. Howes 185-1028 1974 £7.50

CALMET, AUGUSTINE   Dictionnaire Historique, Archeologique, Philologique, Chronologique. Paris, 1846-59. 4 vols., roy. 8vo., orig. leather, rebacked. Howes 185-1029 1974 £8.50

CALNEK, W. A.   History of the County of Annapolis. Toronto, 1897. 2 vols., first editions. Hood's 103-169 1974 $85

CALONNE, CHARLES ALEXANDRE DE   De L'Etat de la France. Londres, 1790. 8vo., orig. wrappers, uncut. Dawsons PM 247-39 1974 £30

CALTHROP, DION CLAYTON   The Charm of Gardens. London, 1910. First edition, color plates, bookplate, orig. binding. Wilson 63-312 1974 $12.50

CALTHORP, DION CLAYTON   English Costume. Loneon, 1926. Biblo & Tannen 210-98 1973 $12.50

CALTHROP, HENRY   The Liberties, Usages, and Customes of the City of London. 1642. Small 4to., calf back. Quaritch 939-443 1974 £42.50

CALVER, EDWARD KILLWICK   The Conservation and Improvement of Tidal Rivers. London, 1853. 8vo., orig. cloth, gilt, illus. Hammond 201-842 1974 £14

CALVERT, ALBERT FREDERICK   Daffodil Growing for Pleasure and Profit. 1929. 8vo., cloth, plates, coloured frontis., scarce. Wheldon 128-1450 1973 £10

CALVERT, ALBERT FREDERICK   Daffodil Growing for Pleasure and Profit. 1929. 8vo., cloth, plates, scarce. Wheldon 130-1379 1974 £10

CALVERT, ALBERT FREDERICK   The Discovery of Australia. n.d. Second edition revised, plates, small 4to., title foxed, nice copy, first edition. Covent 51-2142 1973 £7.50

CALVERT, ALBERT FREDERICK   Goya, an Account of His Life and Works. London, 1908. 8vo., plates, foxing, orig. cloth, rubbed. Bow Windows 62-392 1974 £7.50

CALVERT, ALBERT FREDERICK   Spain: An Historical and Descriptive Account of Its Architecture, Landscape, and Art. 1924. Demy 4to., 2 vols., illus., coloured plates, orig. cloth, fine. Broadhurst 24-1586 1974 £10

CALVERT, BRUCE   Thirty Years on the Open Road. New York, 1941. 1st ed. Biblo & Tannen 213-741 1973 $7.50

CALVERT, F.   The Isle of Wight Illustrated. 1846. Dec. cloth gilt, frontispiece, inscription. Marsden 37-111 1974 £115

CALVIN, JEAN 1509-1564   Institutio Christianae Religionis. Strassburg, 1545. Folio, contemporary calf over wooden boards, very rare, fourth Latin edition. Schafer 8-107 1973 sFr 4,200

CALVIN, JEAN 1509-1564   Institutio Christianae Religionis. (Strassburg), 1561. Folio, contemporary blind stamped calf, wooden boards, rubbed, rare. Harper 213-27 1973 $500

CALVIN, JEAN 1509-1564   Institutio Christianae Religionis. Geneva, 1618. Thick small 8vo., contemporary vellum, early edition. Howes 185-1030 1974 £15

CALVIN, JEAN 1509-1564   The Institution of the Christian Religion in Four Books. Glasgow, 1722. Thick crown 4to., contemporary calf. Howes 185-1031 1974 £7.50

CALVIN, JEAN 1509-1564   Opera Omnia Theologica. Geneva, 1617. Contemporary calf, worn. Smith 194-139 1974 £6.50

CALVIN, JEAN 1509-1564   The Psalmes of David and Others. 1571. Thick small 4to., quarter modern hardgrain morocco, marbled boards, first English edition. Thomas 28-87 1972 £80

CALWER, C. G.   Kaferbuch. Struttgart, 1858. 8vo., boards, plates. Wheldon 129-617 1974 £10

CALWER, C. G.   Kaferbuch. Struttgart, (1884). 8vo., orig. cloth backed boards, fourth edition. Wheldon 129-618 1974 £10

CALZA, G.   La Necropoli del Porto di Roma nell 'Isola Sacra. 1940. 4to., illus. Allen 213-213 1973 $30

CAMBELL, DONALD   A Journey Over Land to India. Philadelphia, 1807. 8vo., old calf, worn. Butterfield 8-565 1974 $35

THE CAMBRIAN Journal. 1854-64. 8vo., boards, labels, uncut, scarce. Broadhurst 23-1577 1974 £50

THE CAMBRIAN Tourist. 1821. Large 12mo., contemporary half calf, rebacked, fifth edition. Smith 193-222 1973 £15

THE CAMBRIDGE Ancient History. 1928. 8vo., uncut, orig. red-brown cloth gilt, second edition. Dawsons PM 251-183 1974 £150

THE CAMBRIDGE Directory for 1861. Cambridge, 1861. 12mo., cloth, map. Saddleback 14-478 1974 $12.50

CAMBRIDGE Essays. 1855. 8vo., contemporary calf. Hill 126-33 1974 £16

THE CAMBRIDGE History of American Literature. New York, 1944. 3 vols. in 1. Biblo & Tannen 210-926 1973 $7.50

CAMBRIDGE History of British Foreign Policy 1783-1919. 1922-23. 3 vols., thick roy. 8vo., scarce. Howes 186-670 1974 £40

CAMBRIDGE Medieval History. 1911-26. 5 vols., thick 8vo., orig. buckram, faded, maps. Howes 186-672 1974 £25

THE CAMBRIDGE Medieval History. 1911. 8vo., orig. green cloth, 8 vols., first edition. Dawsons PM 251-184 1974 £50

THE CAMBRIDGE Modern History. 1902. 14 vols., atlas, orig. black buckram, orig. & best edition. Howes 186-675 1974 £50

THE CAMBRIDGE Modern History. 1934. 8vo., 13 vols., orig. green cloth, new edition. Dawsons PM 251-185 1974 £90

CAMBRIDGE Natural History. London, 1906. 10 vols., 8vo., maps, folding plans, library stamps, complete set, orig. edition. Traylen 79-65 1973 £40

THE CAMBRIDGE Songs: A Goliard's Song Book of the XIth Century. 1915. 4to., half morocco gilt, fine. Covent 55-1129 1974 £25

THE CAMBRIDGE Tart: Epigrammatic and Satiric-Poetical Effusions. London, 1823. 8vo., orig. quarter cloth and boards, printed paper label, frontispiece, nice copy, first edition. Ximenes 37-175 1974 $27.50

CAMDEN, WILLIAM　Britannia. London, 1695. Folio, plates, illus., calf back, marbled boards. Quaritch 939-835 1974 £500

CAMDEN, WILLIAM　Britannia. 1722. Folio, 2 vols., contemporary panelled calf. Bow Windows 64-433 1974 £480

CAMDEN, WILLIAM　Britannia. London, 1753. 2 vols., folio, contemporary calf, gilt, plates, fine. Traylen 79-298 1973 £350

CAMDEN, WILLIAM　Britannia. 1789. 3 vols., folio, old calf, rebacked. Quaritch 939-72 1974 £250

CAMDEN, WILLIAM　Britannia Sive Florentissorum Regnorum Angliae. Londini, 1607. Folio, contemporary panelled calf, fine, sixth & last Latin edition. Dawsons PM 250-13 1974 £1600

CAMDEN Society. 1838-1885. 81 vols., demy 8vo., orig. cloth, exceptional state. Broadhurst 24-1387 1974 £250

CAMDEN SOCIETY　John of Gaunt's Register, 1379-83. 1911. 2 vols. Allen 213-1343 1973 $15

CAMDEN SOCIETY　Ministers' Accounts of Earldom of Cornwall, 1296-97. 1942-45. 2 vols. Allen 213-1348 1973 $15

CAMDEN SOCIETY　Plumpton Correspondence: Series of Letters, Chiefly Domestick, Written in Reigns of Edward IV, et al. 1839. Allen 213-1324 1974 $1839

CAMDEN SOCIETY　Promptorium Parvulorum Sive Clericorum, Dictionarius, Anglo - Latinus Princeps. 1865. Vols. 1 - 2 only. Allen 213-1330 1973 $12.50

CAMERARIUS, JOACHIM　Astrologica. Quorum Titulos . . . ex Hephaestione Aliisque Antiquis. Nuremberg, 1532. Small 4to., half vellum, rare first edition, marginal waterstains towards end. Schafer 10-118 1974 sFr 800

CAMERARIUS, JOACHIM　De Philippi Melanchthonis Ortu, Totius Vitae Curriculo et Morte. Leipzig, 1566. 8vo., contemporary pigskin over boards, fine, rare first edition. Schafer 8-132 1973 sFr. 900

CAMERON, DONALD CLOUGH　Grave Without Grass. New York, 1940. 8vo., orig. cloth, dust wrapper, fine, first edition. Rota 190-195 1974 £5

CAMERON, K.　History of No. 1 General Hospital, Canadian Expeditionary Force, 1914-19. Sackville, 1938. Illus. Hood's 104-97 1974 $22.50

CAMERON, P.　A Monograph of the British Phytophagous Hymenoptera. 1882-93. 4 vols., 8vo., orig. cloth, plates coloured, scarce. Wheldon 128-689 1973 £25

CAMERON, P.　A Monograph of the British Phytophagous Hymenoptera. 1882-93. 4 vols., 8vo., orig. cloth, plates, scarce. Wheldon 131-792 1974 £25

CAMERON, S.　No Matter How Thin You Slice It. Calgary, n.d. Card covers. Hood's 103-139 1974 $10

CAMILLO, GIULIO　L'Idea del Theatro. Florence, 1550. Small 4to., contemporary limp vellum, soiled, very scarce, first edition. Harper 213-28 1973 $385

CAMINADA, JEROME　Twenty-Five Years of Detective Life. Manchester & London, 1895. Cloth gilt, illus. Covent 55-546 1974 £15

CAMINTA, LUDOVICO, SR.　Obici. New York, 1943. Austin 62-69 1974 $27.50

CAMM, BEDE　Forgotten Shrines. 1910. Small 4to., orig. buckram gilt, illus., orig. & best edition. Howes 185-1033 1974 £6.50

CAMM, BEDE　Forgotten Shrines. 1910. 4to., rubbed. Allen 213-1354 1973 $12.50

CAMOES, LUIZ DE　Ignez de Castro. Lisbon, 1862. Folio, gilt and blind tooled dark purple morocco, wood engravings, steel engraved author's portrait. Kraus B8-295 1974 $45

CAMP, WADSWORTH　The Communicating Door. New York, 1923. 8vo., orig. cloth, dust wrapper, first edition. Rota 190-196 1974 £7.50

CAMP, WALTER　The Substitute, A Football Story. New York, 1908. First edition, 8vo., illus., very good. Current BW9-158 1974 $25

CAMPANELLA, TOMMASO　Apologia pro Galileo, Mathematico Florentino, ubi Disquiritur. Frankfort, 1622. Small 4to., vellum, engraved title border, first edition. Schumann 500-20 1974 sFr 12,000

CAMPANELLA, TOMMASO　Compendium Librorum Politicorum de Papana & Hispanica Monarchia. N.P., 1628. Small 4to., wrappers. Schumann 499-17 1974 sFr 825

CAMPANELLA, TOMMASO　Von der Spannischen Monarchy. N.P., 1623. Small 4to., wrappers, first complete edition. Schumann 499-18 1974 sFr 1,300

CAMPBELL, A. J.　Nests and Eggs of Australian Birds. Sheffield, 1901. Roy. 8vo., orig. dec. cloth, map, coloured and photo plates, nice copy, very scarce. Wheldon 128-409 1973 £100

CAMPBELL, D. H.　The Evolution of Land Plants. Stanford, 1940. 8vo., cloth. Wheldon 129-892 1974 £7.50

CAMPBELL, D. H.　Lectures on the Evolution of Plants. 1899. 8vo., cloth. Wheldon 130-997 1974 £5

CAMPBELL, D. H.　An Outline of Plant Geography. 1926. 8vo., cloth, illus. Wheldon 129-893 1974 £7.50

CAMPBELL, D. H.　The Structure and Development of Mosses and Ferns. New York, (1918). 8vo., cloth, scarce, revised third edition. Wheldon 131-1379 1974 £7.50

CAMPBELL, F. R.　The Language of Medicine. New York, 1888. Rittenhouse 46-123 1974 $25

CAMPBELL, J. F.　Geology. Edinburgh, 1865. Boards, 2 vols., foxing, bookplates, English first edition. Covent 56-505 1974 £21

CAMPBELL, J. G.　Witchcraft and Second Sight in the Highlands and Islands of Scotland. Glasgow, 1902. Bow Windows 66-107 1974 £8

CAMPBELL, JOHN　Alfred and Galba. 1831. 16mo., contemporary roan-backed boards, frontispiece, illus. Hammond 201-102 1974 £6.50

CAMPBELL, JOHN　A Political Survey of Britain. London, 1774. 2 vols., 4to., contemporary calf, first edition. Dawsons PM 247-40 1974 £85

CAMPBELL, LANG　The Dinky Ducklings. Joliet, 1928. 12mo., pict. boards, cloth spine, illus., 1st ed. Frohnsdorff 16-172 1974 $8.50

CAMPBELL, LANG　Merry Murphy. New York, 1929. 12mo., 1st ed., illus. Frohnsdorff 16-173 1974 $8.50

CAMPBELL, MARIOUS R.　Guidebook of the Western United States Part A. Washington, 1915. 8vo., orig. bindings. Butterfield 8-693 1974 $15

CAMPBELL, NORMAN ROBERT　Modern Electrical Theory. Cambridge, 1907. 8vo., green cloth. Dawsons PM 245-154 1974 £7

CAMPBELL, R.　The London Tradesman. London, 1757. 8vo., contemporary calf, gilt, third edition. Hammond 201-216 1974 £60

CAMPBELL, RICHARD L.   Historical Sketches of Colonial Florida.
Cleveland, 1892. First edition, orig. binding, light uniform browning of text.
Wilson 63-109 1974 $48.75

CAMPBELL, ROY   Adamastor. 1930. Crown 8vo., orig. cloth,
presentation copy, inscribed, first edition. Broadhurst 23-646 1974 £25

CAMPBELL, ROY   Adamastor. 1930. First edition, crown 8vo.,
frayed d.w., inscribed presentation copy from author. Broadhurst 24-586 1974
£25

CAMPBELL, ROY   Adamastor. 1930. Limited first edition, 8vo.,
orig. red cloth, top edges gilt, others uncut, slip-in case, fine copy, limited to
90 copies on hand made paper, signed by author. Sawyer 293-83 1974 £60

CAMPBELL, ROY   The Flaming Terapin. 1924. First edition,
crown 8vo., dec. boards, cloth spine, fine, frayed d.w., loosely inserted A.L.s.
from the author. Broadhurst 24-583 1974 £42

CAMPBELL, ROY   The Georgiad. 1931. Oatmeal linen,
apparently one of 15 unnumbered copies for presentation, fine copy. Covent
51-2232 1973 £21

CAMPBELL, ROY   The Georgiad. 1931. First edition, limited to
170 copies, signed by author, 8vo., orig. cloth backed printed boards, top edges
gilt, others uncut, fine. Sawyer 293-84 1974 £62

CAMPBELL, ROY   Poems. Paris, 1930. First edition, demy 4to.,
orig. dec. boards, morocco spine, uncut, very good copy, limited to 200 copies,
signed by author. Broadhurst 24-585 1974 £35

CAMPBELL, ROY   Poems. 1930. 4to., orig. dec. boards, uncut,
signed, first limited edition. Broadhurst 23-647 1974 £5

CAMPBELL, ROY   Pomegranates. 1932. Limited to 99 copies on
hand made paper signed by author, first edition, 8vo., orig. cloth, fine copy,
illus. Sawyer 293-85 1974 £58

CAMPBELL, ROY   The Wayzgoose. 1928. Dust wrapper, fine.
Covent 55-288 1974 £8.50

CAMPBELL, ROY   The Wayzgoose: A South African Satire.
1928. First edition, extra crown 8vo., mint, d.w., scarce. Broadhurst 24-584
1974 £12

CAMPBELL, RUTH   The Cat Whose Whiskers Slipped. Joliet, 1925.
Tall 8vo., illus. Frohnsdorff 16-174 1974 $7.50

CAMPBELL, THOMAS   Gertrude of Wyoming. 1809. 4to., half morocco, rubbed, bookplate, English first edition. Covent 56-209 1974 £11.50

CAMPBELL, THOMAS   Gertrude of Wyoming. 1819-21. 2 vols.,
small 8vo., plates, full contemporary russia, gilt. Howes 186-72 1974 £12

CAMPBELL, THOMAS   The Pleasures of Hope. Edinburgh, 1802. 8vo.,
contemporary calf, gilt, plates, sixth edition. Hammond 201-294 1974 £5

CAMPBELL, THOMAS   Poetical Works of. 1854. 427 pages. Austin
61-175 1974 $12.50

CAMPBELL, THOMAS   Poetical Works. (1854). 2 vols. in 1.
Austin 61-176 1974 $12.50

CAMPBELL, THOMAS   Complete Poetical Works of. Boston, 1857.
Austin 61-174 1974 $12.50

CAMPBELL, THOMAS JEFFERSON   Records of Rhea. Dayton, 1940. 12mo.,
cloth. Saddleback 14-695 1974 $27.50

CAMPBELL, W.   The Beauty, History, Romance and Mystery of
the Canadian Lake Region. Toronto, 1910. Illus., worn. Hood's 103-613
1974 $15

CAMPBELL, W. J.   The Collection of Franklin Imprints in the
Museum of the Curtis Publishing Company. Philadelphia, 1918. Limited to 425
copies, demy 4to., orig. cloth. Forster 98-257 1974 £21

CAMPBELL, W. W.   Annals of Tryon County. New York, 1831.
8vo., leather, rebound, map. Saddleback 14-573 1974 $25

CAMPBELL, WALTER   The Old Forest Ranger. New York, 1859.
12mo., cloth, frontispiece. Goodspeed's 578-136 1974 $10

CAMPBELL, WALTER DOUGLAS   Beyond the Border. 1898. Orig. pictorial
cloth gilt, illus., fine. Covent 55-640 1974 £7.50

CAMPBELL'S NEW ATLAS of the State of Illinois. Chicago and Philadelphia, 1871.
Folio, orig. binding, rubbed, maps. Butterfield 8-143 1974 $65

CAMPE, JOACHIM HEINRICH   Polar Scenes, Exhibited in the Voyages of
Heemskirk and Barenz to the Northern Regions. 1821. First edition, plates,
12mo., orig. ptd. boards, roan spine, soiled & rubbed. George's 610-125 1973
£5

CAMPEAU, F. R. E.   Illustrated Guide to the House of Commons of
Canada. Ottawa, 1875. Portraits, diagram, ads at end. Hood's 102-6 1974
$25

CAMPEAU, F. R. E.   Illustrated Guide to the House of Commons of
Canada. Ottawa, 1875. Hood's 104-7 1974 $25

CAMPLIN, JOHN M.   Diabetes, and Its Successful Treatment. New
York, 1861. Rittenhouse 46-680 1974 $15

CAMPOS, EMMANUEL DE   Synopse Trigonometrica dos Casos que Commum-
mente. 1737. Small 4to., contemporary calf, gilt, first edition. Dawsons PM
245-155 1974 £30

CAMPOS, JULES   Jose de Creeft. New York, 1945. Large 4to.,
cloth, plates, limited edition. Minters 37-495 1973 $20

CAMUS, JEAN PIETTE   Nature's Paradox. London, 1652. 4to.,
19th century calf, first English edition. Dawsons PM 252-111 1974 £200

CANADA   Canadian Dualism. Toronto, 1960. Biblo &
Tannen 213-20 1973 $22.50

CANADA   Manitoba Essays. Toronto, 1937. Biblo &
Tannen 213-18 1973 $9.50

CANADA - COMMISSION OF CONSERVATION   Annual Reports, 1-10.
1910-1919. Bound. Hood's 102-846 1974 $75

CANADA - DEPT. OF MARINE AND FISHERIES   Port Directory of Principal
Canadian Ports and Harbours. Ottawa, 1909. Photos, large folding maps.
Hood's 102-752 1974 $10

CANADA - GEOGRAPHIC BOARD   Place Names of Alberta. Ottawa, 1928.
Stiff card cover, folding map. Hood's 102-796 1974 $7.50

CANADA - HOUSE OF COMMONS   Rules, Orders, and Forms of Proceedings
of the. Ottawa, 1868. Bi-lingual. Hood's 102-7 1974 $40

CANADA - NATIONAL ART GALLERY   Catalogue. Ottawa, 1913. Hood's
103-135 1974 $15

CANADA PUBLIC ARCHIVES   Index to Reports from 1872 to 1908. 231 pages.
Hood's 104-10 1974 $12.50

CANADA In the Great World War, An Authentic Account of the Military History
of Canada From the Earliest Days. Toronto, 1918-21. 6 vols., leather.
Hood's 104-99 1974 $75

THE CANADIAN Agricultural Reader. Niagara, 1845. Leather, cover mended.
Hood's 102-402 1974 $40

THE CANADIAN Agricultural Reader. Niagara, 1845. Leather cover, mended.
Hood's 104-390 1974 $40

CANADIAN Book of Printing. Toronto, 1940. Illus., very fine. Covent
55-1225 1974 $7.50

CANADIAN Crafts in Industry. Toronto, n.d. 4 booklets, illus. Hood's
104-145 1974 $17.50

CANADIAN Exploxives Limited.   Montreal, 1911. Card cover, illus. Hood's 102-8 1974 $10

CANADIAN Explosives Limited. Montreal, 1911. Illus., 116 pages. Hood's 104-12 1974 $10

CANADIAN Guide Book, With a Map of the Province. Montreal, 1849. Hood's 102-553 1974 $75

CANADIAN Guide Book, With a Map of the Province. Montreal, 1849. Hood's 104-628 1974 $75

CANADIAN KODAK COMPANY, LTD.   How to Make Good Pictures. Toronto, n.d. Illus., card covers. Hood's 102-9 1974 $17.50

CANADIAN MILITARY INSTITUTE   The Golden Book. Toronto, 1927. Hood's 104-101 1974 $15

CANADIAN MILITARY INSTITUTE   Selected Papers, No. 35 and 50th Annual Metting. Toronto, 1940-41. Card cover. Hood's 102-92 1974 $10

CANADIAN Painters from Paul Kane to the Group of Seven. 1945. Small folio, plates, dust wrapper, scarce, fine. Covent 55-85 1974 £20

CANADIAN Political Science Association Proceedings. (1930-34). Ex-library. Hood's 104-892 1974 $80

CANADIAN Writer's Market Survey. Ottawa, 1931. Hood's 102-11 1974 $12.50

CANBY, HENRY SEIDEL   Elements of Composition for Secondary Schools. Macmillan, 1915. 593p. Austin 54-226 1973 $12.50

CANBY, HENRY SEIDEL   Thoreau. Houghton, 1939. 508p., illus., orig. ed. Austin 54-227 1973 $12.50

CANBY, HENRY SEIDEL   Thoreau. Boston, (1939). First edition, 8vo., nice plates, fine. Current BW9-211 1974 $14.50

CANDEE, H. C.   The Tapestry Book. New York, 1935. 8vo., plates, cloth. Quaritch 940-747 1974 £8

CANDOLLE, AUGUSTIN PYRAMUS DE   Memoire sur la Famille des Crassulacees. Paris, 1828. 4to., orig. wrappers, plates, rare. Wheldon 131-1652 1974 £20

CANDOLLE, AUGUSTIN PYRAMUS DE   Memoire sur Quelques Especes de Cactees Nouvelles ou Peu Connues. Paris, 1834. 4to., wrappers, plates, rare. Wheldon 131-1653 1974 £15

CANDOLLE, AUGUSTIN PYRAMUS DE   Organographie Vegetale. Paris, 1827. 2 vols., 8vo., contemporary half calf, plates. Wheldon 131-1124 1974 £25

CANDOLLE, AUGUSTIN PYRAMUS DE   Physiologie Vegetale ou Exposition des Forces et des Fonctions Vitales des Vegetaux. Paris, 1832. 3 vols., 8vo., half leather, folding tables, scarce. Wheldon 128-1086 1973 £25

CANDOLLE, AUGUSTIN PYRAMUS DE   Physiologie Vegetale. Paris, 1832. 3 vols., 8vo., half leather, scarce. Wheldon 131-1125 1974 £25

CANDOLLE, AUGUSTIN PYRAMUS DE   La Phytographie. Paris, 1880. 8vo., half calf neat, nice copy, scarce. Wheldon 128-1085 1973 £15

CANDOLLE, AUGUSTIN PYRAMUS DE   Plantarum Succulentarum Historia. Paris, (1797-1837) 2 vols., folio, new half morocco, plates, rare. Wheldon 131-28 1974 £850

CANESTRINI, G.   Prospetto dell' Acarofauna Italiana. Padua, 1885-99. 8vo., half morocco. Wheldon 129-1702 1974 £100

CANGIULLO, FRANCESCO   Poesia Innamorata 1911-1940. Naples, 1943. 8vo., wrapper, unopened. Minters 37-382 1973 $22

CANINA, L.   Indicazione Topografica di Roma Antica Distribuita Nelle XIV Regioni. Rome, 1841. 8vo., plates, cloth, gilt. Quaritch 940-501 1974 £40

CANISIUS, HENRY   Thesaurus Monumentorum Ecclesiasticorum et Historicorum. Antwerp, 1725. 7 parts in 4 vols., thick folio, contemporary blind stamped vellum. Howes 185-1036 1974 £50

CANISIUS, PETRUS   Catechismus. Dillingen, 1563. 8vo., unusually fine copy, contemporary blind stamped calf over wooden boards, revised second edition. Schafer 10-95 1974 sFr 3,300

CANIVELL, FRANCISCO   Tratado de Vendages. Barcelona, 1763. 4to., old vellum, plates, illus. Gurney 64-44 1974 £35

CANIVELL, FRANCISCO   Tratado de Vendages, y Apositos Para el Uso de los Reales Colegios de Cirugia. Barcelona, 1763. 4to., old vellum, folding plates. Gurney 66-38 1974 £35

CANNIFF, W.   History of the Province of Ontario. Toronto, 1872. Faded spine. Hood's 103-614 1974 $75

CANNING, ELIZABETH   Genuine and Impartial Memoirs Of. 1754. 12 mo., old calf, worn. Hill 126-35 1974 £10.50

CANNINGS, THOMAS   Detached Pieces. Cork, (n.d.). 8vo., modern boards. Dawsons PM 252-112 1974 £15

CANNON, CHARLES L.   Tales of Old New York. 1896. 364 pages. Austin 57-116 1974 $10

CANNON, CORNELIA JAMES   Red Rust. Little, Brown, 1928. Austin 62-70 1974 $10

CANNON, W. A.   Physiological Features of Roots. Washington, 1925. Roy 8vo., orig. wrappers. Wheldon 129-896 1974 £5

CANNON, WALTER BRADFORD   The Way of an Investigator. New York, 1945. First edition. Rittenhouse 46-124 1974 $10

CANNON, WALTER BRADFORD   The Wisdom of the Body. New York, 1939. Biblo & Tannen 213-838 1973 $9.50

CANONES et Decreta. 1564. Russia gilt, woodcut initials. Thomas 30-119 1973 £15

CANONGE, JULES   Le Tasse a Sorrente, Terentia, le Monge des iles d'or. Paris, 1839. 8vo., contemporary half sheep, gilt, first edition. L. Goldschmidt 42-175 1974 $15

CANOT, THEODORE   Adventures of an African Slaver . . . His Own Story as Told in the Year 1854 to Brantz Mayer. New York, 1928. Large 8vo., first printing, illus., orig. binding. Butterfield 10-96 1974 $15

CANOT, THEODORE   Adventures of an African Slaver . . . His Own Story as Told in the Year 1854 to Brantz Mayer. New York, 1928. Large 8vo., illus., orig. binding, second printing. Butterfield 10-97 1974 $7.50

CANTABRIGIENSES Graduati: Sive Catalogus, Exhibens Nomina Eorum, Quos ab Anno 1659. Cambridge, 1800. 4to., contemporary half calf. Traylen 79-314 1973 $7.50

CANTILLON, C. E.   Traite Complet sur la Fabrication des Etoffes de Soie. Lyon, 1859. Large 8vo., orig. cloth, folding tables. Gurney 10-39 1974 £15

CANTILLON, C. E.   Traite complet sur la Fabrication. Lyon, 1859. Large 8vo., orig. cloth. Gurney 64-45 1974 £15

CANTON, WILLIAM   The True Annals of Fairy-Land. London, n.d. Orig. binding, illus. by Charles Robinson, gilt, inscription, front hinge tender, near fine. Ross 87-476 1974 $12.50

CANTOR, EDDIE   Take My Life. Doubleday, 1956. 288p., illus. Austin 51-169 1973 $10

CANTWELL, ROBERT   Nathaniel Hawthorne. Rinehart, 1948. 499p., orig. ed. Austin 54-228 1973 $12.50

CANU, F.   North American Early Tertiary Bryozoa. Washington, 1920. 4to., 2 vols., plates, orig. wrappers, tom. Bow Windows 64-44 1974 £8.50

THE CANYONS of Colorado. Denver, (1876). Cloth album, photographs. Jenkins 61-512 1974 $50

CANZIO, ISRAELE THEOPH   Philosophiae Leibnitianae et Wolffianae Usus in Theologia. 1733. Small 8vo., contemporary sprinkled calf, rebacked, gilt, first edition. Zeitlin 235-32 1974 $125

CAPART, JEAN   Histoire de l'Orient Ancien. Paris, 1936. Biblo & Tannen 214-935 1974 $10

CAPART, JEAN   Lectures on Egyptian Art. Chapel Hill, 1928. Roy. 8vo., illus., half morocco, gilt. Quaritch 940-305 1974 £18

CAPART, JEAN   Thebes. Brussels, 1925. 4to., illus., half niger morocco. Quaritch 940-306 1974 £25

CAPEFIGUE, JEAN BAPTISTE   Jacques II a Saint-Germain. Paris, 1833. 2 vols., 12mo., contemporary half calf, gilt. L. Goldschmidt 42-176 1974 $17.50

CAPELLA, GALEAZZO   Commentarii delle Cose Fatte per la Restitutione di Francesco Sforza. Venetia, 1539. 4to., contemporary limp vellum, fine. Schumann 499-19 1974 sFr 450

CAPET, G.   Gabrielle Capet, 1761-1818. Paris, 1934. Folio, buckram, orig. wrappers, scarce. Quaritch 940-47 1974 £15

CAPGRAVE, JOHN   Chronicle of England. 1858. 4to. Allen 213-1356 1973 $12

CAPGRAVE, JOHN   The Chronicle of England. 1858. Roy. 8vo., orig. roxburgh binding, frontispiece. Howes 186-1174 1974 £6.50

CAPGRAVE, JOHN   Liber de Illustribus Henricis. 1858. Roy. 8vo., orig. half roan, frontispiece. Howes 186-1175 1974 £6.50

CAPICIUS, SCIPIO   De Principiis Rerum. 1546. 19th century russia gilt, excellent condition. Thomas 30-90 1973 £40

CAPITAINE, LOUIS   Carte Chorographique de la Belgique. Paris, n.d. Large folio, half leather, cloth, plates. Harper 213-30 1973 $155

CAPITO, WOLFGANG   Das die Pfaffhait Schuldig sey Burgerlichen Ayd Zuthun. (Augsburg), 1525. Small 4to., modern half vellum, fine, rare. Schafer 8-108 1973 sFr. 1,300

CAPPON, JAMES   Bliss Carman: and the Literary Currents and Influences of His Time. Toronto, 1930. Spine faded, else very good copy. Covent 51-342 1973 £6

CAPRON, GEORGE   New England Popular Medicine. Boston, 1847. Detached front cover, interior excellent. Rittenhouse 46-681 1974 $15

CARABOO   A Narrative of a Singular Imposition, Practised Upon the Benevolence of a Lady. Bristol, 1817. Roy. 8vo., half green morocco, worn, frontispiece. Traylen 79-330 1973 £18

CARADJA, A. VON   Rumanian Lepidoptera. Bucharest, (1905). 8vo., cloth, map. Wheldon 131-793 1974 £5

CARADOG OF LLANCARVAN d. 1152?   The Historie of Cambria. 1584. Small 4to., modern red morocco, fine. Quaritch 939-679 1974 £250

CARADOG OF LLANCARVAN d. 1152?   The History of Wales. London, 1774. 8vo., old calf, worn. Traylen 79-401 1973 £8

CARAVELLI, VITO   Trattati del Calcolo Differenziale. Naples, 1786. 8vo., contemporary half calf, gilt, plates, first edition. Dawsons PM 245-156 1974 £12

CARCAT, AUGUSTIN   La Vie de Saincte Fare, Fondatrice et Premiere Abbesse de Fare-Monstier en Brie. Paris, 1629. 8vo., contemporary limp vellum, gilt. L. Goldschmidt 42-14 1974 $45

CARCO, FRANCIS   M. de Vlaminck. Paris, n.d. 16mo., plates, wrapper. Minters 37-142 1973 $10

CARCOPINO, JEROME   Autour des Gracques. Paris, 1928. Biblo & Tannen 214-599 1974 $10

CARCOPINO, JEROME   Points de Vue sur l'Imperialisme Romain. Paris, 1934. Biblo & Tannen 214-600 1974 $7.50

CARCOPINO, JEROME   Sylla ou la Monarchie Manquee. Paris, 1931. Rebound. Biblo & Tannen 214-662 1974 $9.50

CARDANO, GIROLAMO 1501-1576   Opera Omnia Tam Hactenus Excusa. 1663. Folio, contemporary half white vellum. Zeitlin 235-33 1974 $1,000

CARDANO, GIROLAMO 1501-1576   Opvs Novvm de Proportionibvs Nvmerorvm. 1570. Folio, half vellum, first edition. Dawsons PM 245-157 1974 £180

CARDANO, GIROLAMO 1501-1576   Somniorum Synesiorum Omnis Generis Insomnia Explicantes. Basel, 1585. 2 parts in 1 vol., 4to., vellum. Schuman 37-37 1974 $225

CARDONA   Lo Studio di Giovanni Boldini. Milan, 1937. Folio, cloth, drawings, rare. Minters 37-174 1973 $125

CARDONELL, A. DE   Numismata Scotiae. Edinburgh, 1786. 4to., plates, contemporary tree calf gilt. Quaritch 939-651 1974 £35

CARE, HENRY   English Liberties. Providence, 1774. 8vo., old leather, sixth edition. Butterfield 8-574 1974 $60

CAREME, A.   Le Patissier Pittoresque. Paris, 1828. Half linen, revised & augmented third edition, 8vo., engravings. Gregory 44-71 1974 $225

CARERIUS, LUDOVICUS   Practica Causarum Criminalium. Venice, 1566. 8vo., contemporary limp vellum, rare, browning. Harper 213-31 1973 $275

CAREW, R.   The Survey of Cornwall. London, 1602. Small 4to., old calf, rebacked, first edition. Quaritch 939-333 1974 £50

CAREW, R.   The Survey of Cornwall. London, 1602. Small 4to., contemporary calf, rebacked. Smith 193-328 1973 £75

CAREW, R.   The Survey of Cornwall. 1769. Small 4to., half calf, new edition. Quaritch 939-334 1974 £40

CAREW, R.   The Survey of Cornwall. 1811. 4to., old calf, rebacked, portrait. Quaritch 939-335 1974 £40

CAREW, THOMAS   A Rapture. Golden Cockerel Press, 1927. Engraved plates, one of 375 numbered copies, J. R. Abbey's copy, full green niger morocco, top edges gilt, bookplate, exceptionally elegant. Covent 51-2354 1973 £75

CAREWS OF CROWCOMBE   Library Catalogue. (c.1740). Folio, orig. vellum. Quaritch 939-537 1974 £35

CAREY, A. E.   Tidal Lands. 1918. 8vo., cloth, plates, scarce. Wheldon 129-215 1974 £7.50

CAREY, A. E.   Tidal Lands. 1918. 8vo., cloth, plates, scarce. Wheldon 131-302 1974 £7.50

CAREY, AL   Clovernook. Radfield, 1852. 342p. Austin 54-229 1973 $12.50

CAREY, MATHEW   The Olive Branch. Philadelphia, 1815. Leather. Hayman 57-74 1974 $15

CARLEN, EMILIE   The Magic Goblet. 1845. 2 vols., square 12mo., contemporary half calf gilt, first English edition. Howes 186-74 1974 £5

CARLEN, EMILIE   The Rose of Tisteldon. 1844. 2 vols., square 12mo., contemporary half calf gilt. Howes 186-73 1974 £5

CARLETON, WILL   City Festivals. Harper, 1898. 177p., illus., new ed. from new plates. Austin 54-230 1973 $6.50

CARLETON, WILL   Farm Ballads. Harper, 1873. 159p., orig. ed., illus. Austin 54-231 1973 $7.50

CARLETON, WILL   Farm Ballads. Harper, 1882. 159p., rev. ed., illus. Austin 54-232 1973 $6

CARLETON, WILL   Farm Festivals. New York, 1881. Illus. Hood's 103-714 1974 $15

CARLETON, WILL   Farm Legends. Harper, 1875. 131p., illus., orig. ed. Austin 54-233 1973 $7.50

CARLETON, WILL   Farm Legends. Harper, (1875) 1887. 187p., illus. Austin 54-234 1973 $6

CARLETON, WILL   New York, 1886. 1st ed. Biblo & Tannen 210-707 1973 $7.50

CARLETON, WILLIAM   The Black Baronet. Dublin, 1858. Half green leather, frontispiece. Emerald 50-113 1974 £9

CARLETON, WILLIAM   The Clarionet, the Dead Boxer, and Barney Branagan. London, 1850. 8vo., half leather. Emerald 50-112 1974 £7.50

CARLETON, WILLIAM   Farforougha the Miser. London, n.d. 8vo., cloth boards. Emerald 50-116 1974 £5

CARLETON, WILLIAM   One Way Out. 1911. Austin 62-73 1974 $10

CARLETON, WILLIAM   Traits and Stories of the Irish Peasantry. London, n.d. 2 vols. in 1, thick 8vo., blue cloth, gilt, illus. Emerald 50-115 1974 £10

CARLETON, WILLIAM   Traits and Stories of the Irish Peasantry. London, n.d. 8vo., red cloth, stained. Emerald 50-117 1974 £5

CARLETON, WILLIAM   Traits and Stories of Irish Peasantry. 1854. 2 vols., half morocco gilt, illus. Howes 185-63 1974 £21

CARLETON, WILLIAM   Traits and Stories of the Irish Peasantry. 1911. 4 vols., illus. Austin 61-177 1974 $47.50

CARLETON, WILLIAM   Valentine McClutchy. London, (1846). 8vo., orig. cloth, gilt, engravings. Emerald 50-111 1974 £12.50

CARLETON, WILLIAM   Valentine M'Clutchy. Dublin, 1847. 8vo., illus., 19th century calf gilt, morocco label. Dawsons PM 252-114 1974 £20

CARLIER, AUGUSTE   Marriage in the United States. Boston, 1867. Orig. cloth, fine. Hayman 57-75 1974 $15

CARLIN, GEORGE A.   He Who Gets Slapped. G & D, 1925. 273p., illus. Austin 51-170 1973 $10

CARLIN, THOMAS   Letter from the Governor, Enclosing a Communication from Richard M. Young, as Agent of the State of Illinois, for Negotiating Lasons for the Illinois and Michigan Canal. (Springfield, 1841). Disbound. Hayman 59-252 1974 $10

CARLISLE, NICHOLAS   A Concise Description of the Endowed Grammar School in England and Wales. London, 1818. 2 vols., thick 8vo., orig. grey boards, spines rubbed but sound, wood-engraved coats of arms, first edition. Ximenes 37-32 1974 $50

CARLL, L. B.   A Treatise on the Calculus of Variations. London, 1885. 8vo., orig. blue cloth. Dawsons PM 245-158 1974 £6

CARLONI, M.   Bassirilievi Volsci in Terra Cotta Dipinti a Varii Colori Trovati Nella Citta di Velletri. Rome, 1785. Roy. folio, plates, contemporary boards, vellum spine. Quaritch 940-307 1974 £30

CARLS, CARL DIETRICH   Ernst Barlach. Berlin, 1931. 4to., wrappers, foxed, plates. Minters 37-445 1973 $20

CARLSTADT, ANDREAS BODENSTEIN VON   Predig . . . Von Emphahung des Heiligen Sacraments. Wittenberg, 1522. Small 4to., boards, woodcut title border, good copy, first edition. Schafer 8-109 1973 sFr. 1,300

CARLYLE, ALEXANDER   Autobiography of. 1861. Orig. American edition. Austin 61-178 1974 $12.50

CARLYLE, JANE WELSH   Letters & Memorials. 1883. 2 vols., buckram, ex-library. Allen 216-310 1974 $10

CARLYLE, JANE WELSH   New Letters & Memorials. 1903. 2 vols., plates. Allen 216-311 1974 $12.50

CARLYLE, THOMAS   Carlyle's Unpublished Lectures. 1892. 8vo., orig. cloth. Bow Windows 64-437 1974 £6.50

CARLYLE, THOMAS   Critical & Miscellaneous Essays. 1840. 5 vols., 8vo., brown calf, gilt. Howes 186-75 1974 £8.50

CARLYLE, THOMAS   Critical and Miscellaneous Essay, Kings of Norway. 1907. 8 vols. in 1. Austin 61-179 1974 $27.50

CARLYLE, THOMAS   The French Revolution. London, 1837. 3 vols., 8vo., orig. boards, blue cloth box, orig. paper labels, first edition. Dawsons PM 250-14 1974 £220

CARLYLE, THOMAS   The French Revolution, a History. 1898. 3 vols., half crimson morocco gilt, centenary edition. Howes 186-687 1974 £7.50

CARLYLE, THOMAS   Jocelin of Brakelond. New York, 1923. 12mo., cloth, uncut, numbered, fine. Ballinger 1-7 1974 $15

CARLYLE, THOMAS   Love Letters. 1909. 2 vols., plates. Allen 216-314 1974 $12.50

CARLYLE, THOMAS   Montaigne and Other Essays. 1897. English first edition. Covent 56-216 1974 £11

CARLYLE, THOMAS   Occasional Discourse on the Nigger Question. London, 1853. 8vo., orig. green printed paper wrappers, uncut, first separate edition. Dawsons PM 251-426 1974 £60

CARLYLE, THOMAS   Oliver Cromwell. New York, 1860. 2 vols. Biblo & Tannen 210-1024 1973 $15

CARLYLE, THOMAS   Past and Present. London, 1843. Orig. cloth, first edition, light spotting, hines tender, spine faded & chipped. MacManus 224-70 1974 $30

CARLYLE, THOMAS   Reminiscences of My Irish Journey. 1882. Unopened, foxed. Covent 55-290 1974 £7.50

CARLYLE, THOMAS   Sartor Resartus. Hammersmith, 1907. 8vo., orig. limp vellum, limited. Bow Windows 62-274 1974 £110

CARMAN, BLISS   Later Poems. Toronto, 1921. Hood's 103-715 1974 $12.50

CARMAN, BLISS   Sanctuary. New York, 1929. One of 20 numbered copies, with author's last photograph & his signature tipped in, drawings, covers little dusty, very nice copy, hinged to end-leaf is an orig. MS poem, not included in the book. Covent 51-348 1973 £42.50

CARMANNE, J. G.   Notions Pratiques de Typographie. Liege, 1870. Folding plates, contemporary cloth. Kraus B8-296 1974 $22.50

CARMER, CARL   Dark Trees to the Wind. Sloane, 1949. 370p., illus. hard cover ed. Austin 54-235 1973 $6.50

CARMER, CARL   Genessee Fever. Farrar, 1941. 360p. Austin 54-236 1973 $6

CARMER, CARL   Listen for a Lonesome Drum. Sloane, 1950. 430p., illus. Austin 54-237 1973 $6

CARMER, CARL   Stars Fell on Alabama. Farrar, 1934. 294p., illus. Austin 54-238 1973 $6

CARMICHAEL, J. W.   Views on the Type. (c.1832). 4to., contemporary half calf. Quaritch 939-508 1974 £48

CARMINA DE Vrinarvm Ivdicus. 1529. Small 8vo., contemporary panelled calf, worn, rebacked. Dawsons PM 249-5 1974 £120

CARMINA Quadragesimalia ab Aedis Christi Oxon. Oxford, 1723. Tallish 8vo., contemporary calf gilt, panelled sides, on good paper, handsome copy. Thomas 32-309 1974 £30

CARNAGEY, DALE The Art of Public Speaking. Springfield, Mass., 1915. 512p. Austin 51-171 1973 $10

CARNARVON, GEORGE EDWARD STANHOPE MOLYNEUX HERBERT, 5TH EARL OF Catalogue of Books Selected from the Library of an English Amateur. London, 1893. 2 vols., large 8vo., orig. wrappers, limited. Dawsons PM 10-109 1974 £25

CARNEGIE, ANDREW An American Four-In-Hand in Britain. Scribner, 1886. 338p., orig. ed. Austin 62-74 1974 $12.50

CARNEGIE, ANDREW An American Four-In-Hand in Britain, Doran, 1933. Austin 62-75 1974 $10

CARNEGIE, ANDREW Autobiography of Andrew Carnegie. Doubleday, Doran, 1933. Austin 62-76 1974 $6

CARNEGIE, ANDREW The Empire of Business. Doubleday, Doran, 1933. Austin 62-77 1974 $7.25

CARNEGIE, ANDREW The Gospel of Wealth. Doubleday, Doran, 1933. Austin 62-78 1974 $6.50

CARNEGIE, ANDREW James Watt. New York, 1908. 8vo., cloth, first edition. Schuman 37-38 1974 $45

CARNEGIE, ANDREW `` James Watt. Doubleday, Doran, 1933. Austin 62-79 1974 $10

CARNEGIE, ANDREW Miscellaneous Writings of Andrew Carnegie. Doubleday, Doran, 1933. Orig. ed. Austin 62-80 1974 $12.25

CARNEGIE, ANDREW Problems of Today. 1933. Austin 62-81 1974 $10

CARNEGIE, ANDREW Round the World. Doubleday, Doran, 1933. Austin 62-82 1974 $10

CARNEGIE, ANDREW Triumphant Democracy. Scribner, 1886. Orig. ed. Austin 62-83 1974 $10

CARNEGIE, ANDREW Triumphant Democracy. Doubleday, Doran, 1933. Austin 62-84 1974 $8.50

CARNET Mandain, 1883. Paris, (1882). 12mo., dec. cloth gilt, fine, illus., plates. Covent 55-881 1974 £32.50

CARNOT, LAZARE NICOLAS MARGUERITE De la Correlation des Figures de Geometrie. Paris, 1801. 8vo., quarter roan, gilt, boards, plates, first edition. Dawsons PM 245-159 1974 £85

CARNOT, LAZARE NICOLAS MARGUERITE Geometrie de Position. Paris, 1803. 4to., contemporary calf gilt, first edition. Dawsons PM 245-160 1974 £65

CARNOT, LAZARE NICOLAS MARGUERITE Memoire sur La Relation qui Existe Entre les Distances. Paris, 1823. 4to., contemporary quarter sheep, first edition. Dawsons PM 245-161 1974 £65

CARNOT, LAZARE NICOLAS MARGUERITE Principes Fondamentaux. Paris, 1803. 8vo., orig. blue wrappers, uncut, second edition. Zeitlin 235-34 1974 $85

CAROLIS, ADOLFO DE Esposizione Romana Delle Opere di Adolfo de Carolis. 1929. Square 4to., wrapper, illus., limited edition. Minters 37-181 1973 $15

CAROLSFELD, SCHNORR VON Sammlung Darmstaedter Berlin. Berlin, 1933. Large 4to., plates, illus., orig. half vellum. Bow Windows 62-152 1974 £72

CARPENTER, EDWARD Towards Democracy. 1883. Inscribed by author, nice copy, first edition. Covent 51-2234 1973 £10.50

CARPENTER, ESTHER BERNON South County Studies of Some 18th Century Persons, Places and Conditions in That Portion of Rhode Island Called Narragansett. Boston, 1924. First edition, 8vo., spine with few spots and rubbed a bit, else fine. Current BW9-432 1974 $15.50

CARPENTER, F. B. Six Months at the White House with Abraham Lincoln. New York, 1866. Cloth, first edition. Dawson's 424-252 1974 $20

CARPENTER, F. G. Alaska, Our Northern Wonderland. New York, 1923. Illus., maps. Hood's 104-75 1974 $17.50

CARPENTER, HELEN GRAHAM The Reverend John Graham of Woodbury, Connecticut, and His Descendants. Chicago, 1942. 4to., cloth. Saddleback 14-784 1974 $32.50

CARPENTER, MATILDA GILRUTH The Crusade; Its Origin and Development at Washington Court House and Its Results. Columbus, 1893. Cloth, laid in is a typewritten letter. Hayman 59-429 1974 $10

CARPENTER, W. H. The History of Connecticut. Philadelphia, 1854. 8vo., orig. bindings. Butterfield 8-81 1974 $10

CARPENTER, W. H. The History of New Jersey. Philadelphia, 1854. 8vo., orig. bindings. Butterfield 8-369 1974 $10

CARPENTER, W. H. The History of Ohio. Philadelphia, 1854. 8vo., orig. bindings. Butterfield 8-413 1974 $10

CARPENTER, WILLIAM Introduction to the Study of the Foraminifera. 1862. Folio, orig. boards, plates, scarce. Wheldon 129-776 1974 £15

CARPENTER, WILLIAM Introduction to the Study of the Foraminifera. 1862. Folio, buckram, plates. Wheldon 128-881 1973 £18

CARPENTER, WILLIAM The Microscope and Its Revelations. London, 1868. 8vo., plates, cloth bound, fourth edition. Bow Windows 62-153 1974 £7.50

CARPENTER, WILLIAM The Microscope and Its Revelations. New York, 1883. 2 vols., sixth edition. Rittenhouse 46-128 1974 $12.50

CARPENTER, WILLIAM The Microscope and Its Revelations. 1901. 2 vols., 8vo., cloth, plates, eighth edition. Wheldon 128-15 1973 £7.50

CARPENTER, WILLIAM The Microscope and Its Revelations. 1901. 2 vols. in 1, 8vo., cloth. Wheldon 131-149 1974 £12

CARR, EMILY The Book of Small. Toronto, 1942. Hood's 104-248 1974 $15

CARR, FRANCES SUSANNA Genevive: A Tale. Isabella: An Historical Sketch. London, 1826. 12mo., orig. grey boards, printed paper label, fine, first edition. Ximenes 37-33 1974 $85

CARR, HENRY The West is Still Wild. Boston, 1932. Tan cloth, illus., paper labels, first edition. Bradley 35-35 1974 $20

CARR, JOHN A Northern Summer. 1805. Crown 4to., contemporary half calf, boards, first edition. Broadhurst 23-1622 1974 £50

CARR, JOHN A Northern Summer. 1805. Sepia aquatints, 4to., contemporary calf gilt, top edges gilt, joints weak, good copy, scarce. Sawyer 293-262 1974 £50

CARR, JOHN A Northern Summer; or, Travels Round the Baltic Through Denmark, Sweden, Russia, Prussia and Part of Germany in the Year 1804. 1805. Engraved plates in sepia, first edition, crown 4to., contemporary half calf worn, boards. Broadhurst 24-1588 1974 £45

CARR, JOHN Pioneer Days in California. Eureka, 1891. Blind-stamped cloth, faded, gilt, first edition. Bradley 35-34 1974 $100

CARR, JOHN DICKSON It Walks by Night. New York, 1930. First American edition. Covent 55-576 1974 £6.30

CARR, WILLIAM G. John Swett. Santa Ana, 1933. 8vo., cloth. Saddleback 14-62 1974 $20

CARRA, CARLO   Ettore Cosomati.   Milan, 1923. 8vo.,
wrappers, plates. Minters 37-183 1973 $20

CARRICK, ALICE VAN LEER   Shades of Our Ancestors. Boston, 1928. Illus.,
fine, d.w., orig. cloth, 8vo.   Gregory 44-270 1974 $27.50

CARRICK, G. L.   Koumiss. 1881. Crown 8vo., orig. cloth,
scarce, first edition. Broadhurst 23-1219 1974 £10

CARRICK, G. L.   Koumiss. 1881. Scarce, first edition, crown
8vo., good copy, orig. cloth, publisher's presentation copy. Broadhurst 24-1214
1974 £10

CARRICK, J. J.   Hall of Fame. Toronto, 1943. Photos,
cartoons, sketches. Hood's 102-12 1974 $7.50

CARRIERI, RAFFAELE   Campigli. Venice, (1945). Large 4to.,
cloth, illus., plates, limited edition. Minters 37-179 1973 $45

CARRIERI, RAFFAELE   Il Disegno Italiano Contemporaneo. Milan,
1945. Folio, cloth, plates, limited. Quaritch 940-48 1974 £20

CARRIGAN, WILLIAM   The History and Antiquities of the Diocese of
Ossory. Dublin, 1905. 3 vols., small 4to. Emerald 50-121 1974 £18

CARRINGTON, FITZROY   Prints and Their Makers Essays on Engravers and
Etchers Old and Modern. London, 1913. 8vo., orig. cloth gilt, first edition.
Dawsons PM 10-110 1974 £8

CARRINGTON, GEORGE   Our West Indian Colonies. 1898. Roy 8vo.,
printed wrapper. Hammond 201-217 1974 £14.50

CARROLL, LEWIS PSEUD.
Please turn to
DODGSON, CHARLES LUTWIDGE

CARROLL, MARY B.   Ten Years in Paradise. San Jose, c.1903.
8vo., cloth. Saddleback 14-63 1974 $25

CARROLL, PAUL VINCENT   Shadow and Substance. Random House, 1937.
176p. Austin 51-172 1973 $10

CARROLL, PAUL VINCENT   The White Steed and Coggerers. Random
House, 1939. 190p. Austin 51-173 1973 $10

CARRUTHERS, JOHN   Political Economy of Socialism. n.d. Fine,
wrappers, first edition. Covent 51-1723 1973 £9.50

CARRUTHERS, JOHN   Socialism & Radicalism. 1894. Fine, first
edition. Covent 51-1724 1973 £9.50

CARRYL, CHARLES E.   The River Syndicate. New York, 1899. Orig.
pictorial cloth, plates, English first edition. Covent 56-315 1974 £25

CARSEL, WIFRED   A History of the Chicago Ladies' Garment
Workers' Union. 1940. 323p., illus. Austin 62-85 1974 $15

CARSON, HAMPTON L.   History of the Celebration of the One Hundredth
Anniversary of the Promulgation of the Constitution of the United States.
Philadelphia, 1889. 2 vols., 4to., top edges gilt, others uncut, portraits,
beveled edges. Wilson 63-11 1974 $40

CARSON, HAMPTON L.   The History of the Supreme Court of the United
States . . . With Biographys of all Chief and Associate Justices. Philadelphia,
1902. 2 vols., full calf, gilt seal, illus., marbled endpapers, gilt dentelles,
edge wear, rubbed. Wilson 63-169 1974 $28.75

CARSON, HAMPTON L.   Unique Collection of Engraved Portraits of
Signers of the Declaration of Independence. Philadelphia, (1904). 4to., three
quarter vellum, uncut, plates. Kraus B8-33 1974 $15

CARSON, JOSEPH   A History of the Medical Department of the
University of Pennsylvania. Philadelphia, 1869. Rittenhouse 46-682 1974
$25

CARSTARPHEN, J. E.   My Trip to California in '49. Louisiana,
1914. Wrapper. Jenkins 61-296 1974 $75

CARSWELL, CATHERINE   The Savage Pilgrimage. 1932. Frontispiece,
scarce, first edition. Howes 185-292 1974 £5

CARTAE et alia Munimenta quae ad Dominium de Glamorgancia Pertinent.
1910. 6 vols., 4to., buckram. Quaritch 939-684 1974 £45

CARTARI, VINCENZO   Imagines Deorum, Qui ab Antiquis Colebantur.
Lyons, 1581. 4to., contemporary pigskin over boards, woodcuts. Schafer
8-90 1973 sFr. 1,200

CARTE, THOMAS   An History of the Life of James, Duke of
Ormonde. London, 1736-5. 3 vols., folio, contemporary panelled calf, spines
gilt, minor wear, first edition, handsome set. Ximenes 36-46 1974 $100

CARTER, FREDERICK   D. H. Lawrence and the Body Mystical.
London, 1932. Signed artist's proof of engraved portrait of Lawrence, no. 15 of
edition limited to 75 copies, covers warped, glassine wrapper, slight foxing,
fine. Ross 86-304 1974 $60

CARTER, FREDERICK   Gold Like Glass. 1932. One of 20 numbered
copies with signed frontis. etching by author, fine, full buckram, first edition.
Covent 51-2240 1973 £12.50

CARTER, FREDERICK   Gold Like Glass. 1932. Full buckram, fine,
numbered, inscribed. Covent 55-1484 1974 £25

CARTER, G. WOODSON   Free Negro Heads of Families in the United
States in 1830, together with A Brief Treatment of the Free Negro. Washington,
(1925). Large 8vo., d.j., orig. binding. Butterfield 10-119 1974 $27.50

CARTER, HORACE E.   Reports of Cases Argued and Determined in the
Supreme Court of Judicature of the State of Indiana, Being an Official
Continuation of Blackford's Reports. Indianapolis, 1852. Vol. 1, leather.
Hayman 59-288 1974 $12.50

CARTER, HOWARD   The Tomb of Tut-Ankh-Amen, Discovered by the
Late Earl of Carnarvon and Howard Carter. London, 1923-27-33. 3 vols., large
8vo., illus., plates, orig. brown cloth, first edition. Schafer 10-143 1974
sFr 480

CARTER, J.   Some Account of the Cathedral Church of
Gloucester. 1809-13. Imp. folio, half leather. Quaritch 939-92 1974 £18

CARTER, J. SMYTH   The Story of Dundas. Iroquois, 1905. First
edition, portraits, illus. Hood's 102-590 1974 $55

CARTER, MATTHEW   Honor Redivivus. London, 1660. 8vo.,
frontispiece, old calf, rubbed, worn, second edition. Bow Windows 62-157
1974 £21

CARTER, MATTHEW   Honor Redivivus. London, 1673. 8vo., contemporary calf, plates. Dawsons PM 251-107 1974 £30

CARTER, N. H.   Letters from Europe . . . Journal Of a Tour
Through Ireland, England, Scotland, France, Italy and Switzerland. New York,
1827. 2 vols., orig. boards, paper labels, worn. Butterfield 10-46 1974 $20

CARTER, R.   A Scheme for Preventing the Exportation of
Wool. 1713. 4to., disbound, uncut. Quaritch 939-283 1974 £20

CARTER, RUSSEL GORDON   A Patriot Lad of Old Rhode Island. Philadelphia,
(1930). First edition, 8vo., d.j., illus. Current BW9-349 1974 $9.75

CARTER, SUSANNA   The Frugal Housewife. London, (c., 1800).
12mo., calf antique, gilt, illus. Hammond 201-157 1974 £85

CARTER, T. J. P.   King's College Chapel. 1867. 8vo., cloth,
frontispiece, presentation. Quaritch 939-318 1974 £35

CARTER, W. N.   Harry Tracy the Desperate Western Outlaw. Chicago, (1902). Orig. cloth, illus., wrappers. Putnam 126-282 1974 $20

CARTMELL, VAN H.   Amateur Theatre. 1961. 220p. Austin 51-174
1973 $4

CARTWRIGHT, C. E.   Life and Letters of the Late Hon. Richard
Cartwright. Toronto, 1876. Black cloth. Hood's 102-229 1974 $20

CARTWRIGHT, JOHN   Give Us Our Rights. London, n.d. 8vo., modern boards. Dawsons PM 251-427 1974 £15

CARTWRIGHT, JULIA   The Life & Work of Sir E. Burne-Jones Bart. 1894. Dec. cloth gilt, scarce, worn. Marsden 37-104 1974 £10

CARTWRIGHT, JULIA   The Pilgrim's Way From Winchester to Canterbury. 1893. Illus. Austin 61-181 1974 $12.50

CARTWRIGHT, THOMAS   Commentarii . . . In Proverbia Salomonis. Amsterdam, 1632. Thick small 4to., old calf, first part of book printed on poor paper which is bit browned the rest on good paper. Thomas 32-34 1974 £18

CARTWRIGHT, WILLIAM   Comedies Tragi-Comedies. London, 1651. 8vo., contemporary calf, first edition. Dawsons PM 252-116 1974 £300

CARUEL, T.   Prodromo della Flora Toscana. 1860-71. 8vo., new cloth, rare. Wheldon 130-1133 1974 £20

CARUEL, T.   Statistica Botanica Della Toscana Ossia Saggio di Studi Sulla Distribuzione Geografica Della Piante Toscane. Florence, 1871. 8vo., cloth, folding coloured plate. Wheldon 128-1247 1973 £5

CARUEL, T.   Statistica Botanica Della Toscana Ossia Saggio di Studi Sulla Distribuzione Geografica Delle Piante Toscane. Florence, 1871. 8vo., cloth, plate. Wheldon 131-1270 1974 £5

CARUS, CARL GUSTAV   Anleitung zu dem Studium. Leipzig, 1823. 4to., plates, foxing, orig. boards. Bow Windows 64-46 1974 £12.50

CARUS, CARL GUSTAV   Psyche. Pforzheim, 1846. 8vo., engraved portrait frontis., modern boards, first edition, fine copy. Schafer 10-122 1974 sFr 1,200

CARUS, CARL GUSTAV   Ueber Grund und Bedeutung. Stuttgart, 1846. 4to., half cloth, plates, first edition. Gurney 64-46 1974 £45

CARVER, CHARLES   Brann and the Iconoclast. Univ. of Texas, 1957. 196p., hard cover ed. Austin 54-159 1973 $7.50

CARVER, JONATHAN   Travels Through the Interior Parts of North America. Boston, 1797. Three quarter leather. Jenkins 61-469 1974 $75

CARY, ELIZABETH LUTHER   Browning: Poet and Man, A Survey. 1899. Illus., orig. edition. Austin 61-182 1974 $10

CARY, ELISABETH LUTHER   The Novels of Henry James. New York, 1905. Plates, cloth backed boards, gilt top, very good copy. Covent 51-993 1973 £6.50

CARY, ELIZABETH LUTHER   The Rossettis: Dante Gabriel and Christina. 1900. Illus. Austin 61-183 1974 $15

CARY, FALKLAND L.   Practical Playwriting. 1941. 180p. Austin 51-176 1973 $7.50

CARY, JOHN   Cary's New Map of England and Wales With Part of Scotland. 1794. 4to., contemporary calf, first edition. Wheldon 131-344 1974 £75

CARY, JOHN   Cary's New Universal Atlas. London, 1808. Oblong 4to., old half leather, boards, rubbed, maps, scarce. Traylen 79-416 1973 £150

CARY, JOHN   Cary's Reduction of His Large Map of England and Wales. 1805. 8vo., orig. case, label. Quaritch 939-77 1974 £15

CARY, JOHN   New Itinerary. London, 1817. Thick 8vo., contemporary leather, maps, seventh edition. Traylen 79-299 1973 £15

CARY, JOHN   New Itinerary. London, 1821. Thick 8vo., old calf, rebacked, staining, ninth edition. Traylen 79-300 1973 £10

CARY, JOYCE   The African Witch. 1935. Drab wrappers, worn covers. Covent 55-295 1974 £22.50

CARY, JOYCE   The African Witch. 1936. Dust wrapper, fine, signed. Covent 55-296 1974 £15

CARY, JOYCE   The African Witch. 1936. Worn dust wrapper. Covent 55-297 1974 £8

CARY, JOYCE   The African Witch. London, 1936. Orig. binding, signed by author, lacking d.w., protected by heavy dec. paper wrapper, fine. Ross 87-91 1974 $25

CARY, JOYCE   The African Witch. 1936. First edition, crown 8vo., orig. cloth, fine, faded d.w. Broadhurst 24-589 1974 £10

CARY, JOYCE   The African Witch. 1936. Crown 8vo., orig. cloth, faded dust wrapper, first edition. Broadhurst 23-648 1974 £25

CARY, JOYCE   The African Witch. 1936. Orig. cloth, dust wrapper, first edition. Rota 188-151 1974 £5

CARY, JOYCE   Aissa Saved. 1932. Rubber stamps, very good copy, very scarce, first edition. Covent 51-358 1973 £15

CARY, JOYCE   Aissa Saved. 1932. Scarce, first edition. Covent 55-298 1974 £75

CARY, JOYCE   An American Visitor. 1933. Covers little faded, else fine copy, very good d.w., scarce in this condition, first edition. Covent 51-2241 1973 £21

CARY, JOYCE   An American Visitor. 1933. Worn dust wrapper, fine. Covent 55-301 1974 £45

CARY, JOYCE   An American Visitor. 1933. 8vo., orig. cloth, scarce, first edition. Rota 189-180 1974 £20

CARY, JOYCE   The Case for African Freedom. 1941. Very good copy, wrappers, first edition. Covent 51-1394 1973 £6.50

CARY, JOYCE   The Case for African Freedom. 1941. Fine, wrappers, dust wrapper. Covent 55-308 1974 £12.50

CARY, JOYCE   The Case for African Freedom. 1944. Maps, dust wrapper, fine, revised & enlarged edition. Covent 55-309 1974 £7.50

CARY, JOYCE   Castle Corner. 1937. Advance proof copy, drab wrappers. Covent 55-310 1974 £30

CARY, JOYCE   Charley is My Darling. New York, n.d. Dust wrapper, fine, first American edition. Covent 55-312 1974 £7.50

CARY, JOYCE   Charley is My Darling. 1940. First edition. Covent 55-311 1974 £15

CARY, JOYCE   The Horse's Mouth. 1944. Orig. drawing, inscribed, fine, worn dust wrapper. Covent 55-321 1974 £110

CARY, JOYCE   The Horse's Mouth. 1944. Uncorrected proof copy, drab wrappers. Covent 55-322 1974 £25

CARY, JOYCE   The Horse's Mouth. 1944. Worn dust wrapper, fine. Covent 55-325 1974 £5

CARY, JOYCE   The Horse's Mouth. London, 1944. Orig. binding, first edition, d.w., heavy dec. paper wrapper, mint. Ross 87-95 1974 $40

CARY, JOYCE   The Horse's Mouth. 1944. 8vo., orig. cloth, fine, first edition. Rota 189-181 1974 £6

CARY, JOYCE   A House of Children. New York, n.d. Fine, dust wrapper, first American edition. Covent 55-331 1974 £5.25

CARY, JOYCE   A House of Children. 1941. Worn dust wrapper, fine. Covent 55-329 1974 £10

CARY, JOYCE   A House of Children. 1941. First edition. Covent 5-330 1974 £6

CARY, JOYCE   Marching Soldier. 1945. Fine, dust wrapper, inscribed. Covent 55-333 1974 £45

CARY, JOYCE   Marching Soldier. 1945. Booklabel, dust wrapper, inscribed, presentation. Covent 55-334 1974 £30

CARY, JOYCE   Marching Soldier. 1945. Presentation, inscribed, fine, worn dust wrapper. Covent 55-335 1974 £25

CARY, JOYCE   Power in Men. 1939. Soiled covers, signed. Covent 55-345 1974 £15

CARY, JOYCE   Power in Men. First edition. Covent 55-346 1974 £10.50

CARY, JOYCE   Power in Men. London, 1939. Fine copy, orig. cloth, first edition, chipped d.w. Crane 7-36 1974 £6

CARY, JOYCE   To be a Pilgrim. 1942. 8vo., orig. cloth, first edition. Rota 190-93 1974 £6

CARY, M.   A History of Rome Down to the Reign of Constantine. London, 1938. Orig. ed., inner hinges sprung. Biblo & Tannen 214-601 1974 $6.50

CARY, SETH C.   John Cary, the Plymouth Pilgrim. Boston, 1911. Frontispiece, illus., olive cloth. Bradley 35-150 1974 $16

CARYL, J.   An Exposition With Practicall Observations. 1649. Small 4to., contemporary calf. Thomas 28-89 1972 £21

CARYL, J.   An Exposition With Practical Observations Upon the Three First Chapters of the Book of Job. 1651. Small 4to., contemporary calf. Thomas 28-88 1972 £21

CASALI, GIOVANNI BATTISTA, d. 1648   Romani de Profanis et Sacris Veteribus Titibus Opus Tripartitum, Cujus Prima Pars. 1681. 4to., old calf, woodcuts on plates, some foxing, stains, joints broken, worn, scarce. Bow Windows 66-109 1974 £9.50

CASANOVA DI SEINGALT, GIACOMO GIROLAMO   Le Duel ou Essai sur la Vie de J. C. Venitien / Le Messager de Thalie. Paris, 1925. 2 vols., 12mo., three quarter hard grain morocco, gilt, uncut, orig. wrapper. L. Goldschmidt 42-16 1974 $12.50

CASANOVA DI SEINGALT, GIACOMO GIROLAMO   Memoirs of. 1922. 12 vols., crown 4to., boards, parchment spines, uncut, one of 1000 numbered sets, fine. Broadhurst 24-1709 1974 £25

CASANOVA DI SEINGALT, GIACOMO GIROLAMO   The Memoirs. London, 1922. 12 vols., 4to., orig. parchment backed boards, frontis., limited. Dawsons PM 252-117 1974 £28

CASANOVA DI SEINGALT, GIACOMO GIROLAMO   The Memoirs of. 1922. 12 vols., 4to., parchment backed boards, limited to 1000 sets, illus. Thomas 32-276 1974 £25

CASANOVA DI SEINGALT, GIACOMO GIROLAMO   The Memoirs of. London, 1922. 12 vols., 8vo., quarter vellum, cloth boards, limited. Bow Windows 62-158 1974 £30

CASANOVA DI SEINGALT, GIACOMO GIROLAMO   Memoires Ecrits par Lui-Meme Suivis de Fragments des Memoires du Prince de Ligne. Paris, (1880). 8 vols., roy. 8vo., three quarter burgundy hard grain morocco, gilt, uncut, very fine. L. Goldschmidt 42-15 1974 $50

CASAS, BARTHOLOME DE LAS, BISHOP OF CHIAPA   A Complete Set of His 9 Celebrated Tracts in Defence of the Indians of America. 1552. 9 tracts in 2 vols., 8vo., 19th century Spanish half calf and full green morocco gilt, excellent condition, complete set of first editions. Ximenes 37-30 1974 $1,750

CASE, ARTHUR E.   A Bibliography of English Poetical Miscellanies 1521-1750. 1935. Small 4to., orig. linen backed boards, scarce. Howes 185-631 1974 £25

CASE, ARTHUR E.   A Bibliography of English Poetical Miscellanies. Oxford, 1935. 4to., orig. boards, uncut. Dawsons PM 10-114 1974 £55

CASE, LEONARD   Early Settlement of Warren, Trumbull County, Ohio. Cleveland, 1876. Wrappers. Hayman 59-517 1974 £10

A CASE Humbly Offer'd to the Honourable House of Commons. (1713). Folio, disbound. Quaritch 939-284 1974 £10

THE CASE of Dorothy Petty. (1711). Folio, disbound. Quaritch 939-146 1974 £18

THE CASE of John Nicholson. (1711). Folio, disbound. Quaritch 939-218 1974 £10

THE CASE of Salt Exported for Ireland. (1711). Folio, disbound. Quaritch 939-231 1974 £12

THE CASE of the Book-Binders of Great Britain. (N.P., 1711). Folio broadside, fine, plastic folder. Dawsons PM 247-22 1974 £140

THE CASE of the Creditors of the Office of Ordance. (1711). Folio, disbound. Quaritch 939-183 1974 £12

THE CASE of the Importers of Linnen and Linnen Drapers, and Packers, in London. (1714). Folio, disbound, second expanded edition. Quaritch 939-71 1974 £12

THE CASE of the Inhabitants of St. Mary Rotherhith. (1711). Folio, disbound. Quaritch 939-469 1974 £10

THE CASE of the Leather-Sellers. (1711). Folio, disbound. Quaritch 939-157 1974 £12

THE CASE of the Manufacturers of British Sail-Cloth. (1713). Folio, disbound. Quaritch 939-230 1974 £12

THE CASE of the Manufacturers of Gilt and Silver Wire. (1713). Folio, disbound. Quaritch 939-281 1974 £10

THE CASE of the Packers, Concerned in the Woollen Manufactures. (1714). Folio, disbound. Quaritch 939-285 1974 £10

THE CASE of the Parish of St. Giles Criplegate. (1713). Folio, disbound. Quaritch 939-282 1974 £10

THE CASE of the Pursers of Her Majesties Navy. (1711). Folio, disbound. Quaritch 939-184 1974 £15

THE CASE of the Thread-Makers of Great Britain. (1714). Folio, disbound. Quaritch 939-265 1974 £14

THE CASE of the United States, to be Laid Before the Tribunal of Arbitration, to Be Convened at Geneva. Washington, 1872. 8vo., fine fold out map. Current BW9-352 1974 $17.50

CASEMENT, ROGER   Sir Roger Casement's Diaries. Munich, 1922. Orig. cloth, illus., presentation inscription. Rota 188-154 1974 £25

CASEMENT, ROGER   Some Poems. Dublin, 1918. Frontis., very good copy, wrappers. Covent 51-2243 1973 £12

CASEY, C.   Riviera Nature Notes. 1903. 8vo., orig. dec. cloth, plates, frontispiece, second edition. Wheldon 128-184 1973 £7.50

THE CASE of the Poor Children Belonging to the Charity-School of Saint Sepulchres. (1711). Folio, disbound. Quaritch 939-466 1974 £10

CASEY, SILAS   Infantry Tactics, for the Instruction, Exercise, and Manoeuvers of the Soldier, A Company, Line of Skirmishers, Battalion, Brigade, or Corps D'Armee. New York, 1862. 3 vols., 32mo., plates, spine ends worn and chipped, green cloth. Current BW9-353 1974 $45

CASLON, WILLIAM   Caslon Old Face. 1924. Roy 4to., limp boards, mint. Broadhurst 23-285 1974 £6

CASLON, WILLIAM   Caslon Old Face. 1924. Roy. 4to., limp boards, mint. Boardhurst 24-280 1974 £6

CASLON, WILLIAM   A Specimen of Printing Types. (London, 1785). Folio, modern marbled boards, fine. Dawsons PM 10-115 1974 £50

CASOTTI, GIOVAMBATISTA   Memorie Istoriche della Miracoloso Imagine di Maria Vergine dell' Impruneta. Florence, 1714. 3 parts in 1, 4to., plates, frontispiece, contemporary vellum, fine. Harper 213-33 1973 $450

CASPER, JOHANN LUDWIG   A Handbook of the Practice of Forensic Medicine. 1861-5. 8vo., 4 vols., orig. cloth, first edition in English.   Dawsons PM 249-103 1974 £10

CASPER, JOHANN LUDWIG   A Handbook of the Practice of Forensic Medicine. London, 1861-65. 4 vols., 8vo., half calf, first edition in English. Schuman 37-39 1974 $145

CASPER, LEOPOLD   A Textbook of Genito-Urinary Diseases. Philadelphia, 1906. Weak cover. Rittenhouse 46-130 1974 $10

CASSELLA, ALBERTA   Death Takes a Holiday. French, 1930. 151p., paper. Austin 51-177 1973 $7.50

CASSELLA, LEOPOLD & COMPANY   The Dyeing of Cotton and Other Vegetable Fibres with the Dyestuffs of. Frankfurt, 1902. 8vo., fabric samples, illus., orig. half cloth. Quaritch 940-748 1974 £35

CASSELLA, LEOPOLD & COMPANY   The Dyeing of Wool Including Wool-Printing with the Dyestuffs of. Frankfurt, 1905. 8vo., samples, orig. half cloth. Quaritch 940-749 1974 £35

CASSELL'S History of the Russo-Japanese War. n.d. 5 vols. in 3, 4to., plates, maps, orig. cloth. Smith 193-722 1973 £10

CASSELL'S History of the War Between France & Germany, 1870-71. n.d. 2 vols., 4to., illus., half contemporary calf gilt, leather labels. Smith 194-769 1974 £6

CASSELL'S Popular Natural History. n.d. 4 vols., 4to., illus., half contemporary calf gilt. Smith 193-744 1973 £6

CASSELMAN, A. C.   Richardson's War of 1815. Toronto, 1902. Inscribed by Casselman, limited to 1000 copies. Hood's 102-94 1974 $40

CASSELMAN, A. C.   Richardson's War of 1812. Toronto, 1902. Inscribed, numbered, limited edition. Hood's 104-103 1974 $40

CASSIANUS, JOANNES   De Institutis Coenobiorum. Basel, 1485. Folio, half calf, very fine, woodcut, first edition. Harper 213-34 1973 $1150

CASSINI, GIOVANNI DOMENICO   La Meridiana Del Tempio. Bologna, 1695. Small folio, contemporary vellum, boards. Zeitlin 235-35 1974 $375

CASSINI, JACQUES   Elements d'Astronomie. Paris, 1740. 4to., contemporary calf, gilt, first edition. Zeitlin 235-36 1974 $75

CASSINI, JACQUES   Tables Astronomiques du Soleil, de la Lune, des Plantes, des Etoiles Fixes, et des Satellites de Jupiter et de Saturne. Paris, 1740. Large 4to., contemporary vellum, plates, first edition. Schuman 37-40 1974 $110

CASSINI, JACQUES   Tables Astronomiques du Soleil. Paris, 1740. 4to., contemporary mottled calf, gilt, first edition. Zeitlin 235-37 1974 $175

CASSINI DE THURY, CESAR FRANCOIS   La Meridienne de l'Observatoire. Paris, 1744. 4to., contemporary calf, gilt, worn. Zeitlin 235-38 1974 $85

CASSINI DE THURY, JACQUES DOMINIQUE   Extrait des Observations Astronomiques et Physiques. Paris, 1786. 4to., orig. wrappers, uncut, slipcase, fine. Zeitlin 235-39 1974 $1,175

CASSIUS DIO COCCEIANUS   Neruae & Traiani. 1519. Old vellum, stains. Thomas 30-48 1973 £25

CASSON, STANLEY   Rupert Brooke and Skyros. 1921. Orig. cloth, illus., first separate edition. Rota 188-130 1974 £5

CASSOU, JEAN   Couleurs des Maitres. Paris, 1939. 4to., cloth, plates. Minters 37-106 1973 $12.50

CASTAGNA, GIOVANNI   De Beneficio Deducto ne Egeat Tractatus. Rome, 1656. Small folio, contemporary Roman brown morocco, gilt. Thomas 28-130 1972 £50

CASTANEDA, CARLOS E.   Communications Between Santa Fe and San Antonio in the 18th Century. N.P., n.d. Wrapper, inscribed, signed by author. Jenkins 61-474 1974 $10

CASTEL-BLAZE   La Danse et les Ballets Depuis Bacchus Jusqu'a Mlle. Taglioni. Paris, (c. 1832). Half red morocco. Gregory 44-7 1974 $85

CASTELLANI, SIR ALDO 1875-   Fungi and Fungous Diseases. 1928. 8vo., cloth, illus. Wheldon 131-1380 1974 £5

CASTELLANI, ALESSANDRO   Cat. d'un Recueil Choisi d'Estampes Anciennes, et Modernes des plus Celebres Aristes. Milano, 1822. Crown 8vo., orig. wrappers. Forster 97-13 1974 £5

CASTELLI, BENEDETTO   Della Misura dell' Acque Correnti. Rome, 1628. Small 4to., orig. boards, first edition. Schumann 500-22 1974 sFr 6,000

CASTELLI, BENEDETTO   Della Misvra Dell'Acqve Correnti. 1660. Small 4to., modern half mottled calf, labels, gilt. Zeitlin 235-40 1974 $175

CASTELLI, BENEDETTO   Risposta Alle Opposizioni Del S. Lodovico delle Colombe, e del S. Vincenzo di Grazia, Contra al Trattato. Florence, 1615. Small 4to., leather, first edition, exlibris of Giuseppe Martini and Prince Pietro Ginori Conti. Schumann 500-17 1974 sFr 2,200

CASTELNAU, F. DE   Animaux Nouveaux ou Rares Recueillis. Leipzig, 1922. 4to., new cloth, plates. Wheldon 130-481 1974 £25

CASTELNAU, F. DE   Histoire Naturelle des Animaux Articules. Paris, 1840. 8vo., 4 vols., cloth, plates. Wheldon 130-727 1974 £25

CASTIGLIONE, BALDASSARE   Il Libro Del Cortegiano. 1528. Small folio, 18th century mottled calf gilt, rubbed, first edition. Thomas 30-68 1973 £350

CASTIGLIONE, BALDASSARE   Il Libro del Cortegiano. 1547. 19th century English brown hard grain morocco gilt, raised dec. bands. Thomas 30-91 1973 £75

CASTIGLIONI, CAMILLO DE VIENNE   Cat. des Tableaux-Sculptures-Meubles-Orfevreries-Bijoux-Tapisseries-Tapis-Etoffes-Porcelaine de la Cluve etc. Amsterdam, 1925-26. Parts 1 and 3, plates, folio, orig. wrappers dust soiled. Forster 97-58 1974 £10

CASTIGLIONI, CAMILLO DE VIENNE   Die Sammlung . . . Gemalde, Skulpturen, Mobel, Keramik, Textilien. Berlin, 1930. Roy. 4to., orig. wrappers, plates. Forster 97-59 1974 £3

CASTILLO, BERNAL DIAZ DEL
Please turn to
DIAZ DEL CASTILLO, BERNAL

CASTILLON, M.   Nouvelle Chasse aux Papillons. Paris, (1858). Roy. 8vo., orig. half morocco, plates, scarce. Wheldon 131-794 1974 £20

CASTLE, AGNES   The Bath Comedy. 1900. 243 pages. Austin 61-188 1974 $10

CASTLE, AGNES   Our Sentimental Garden. (1914). Coloured plates and other illus. by Charles Robinson. Bow Windows 66-110 1974 £6.75

CASTLE, EGERTON   English Book-Plates Ancient and Modern. London & New York, 1894. 8vo., morocco gilt, fine, illus., new enlarged edition. Dawsons PM 10-116 1974 £12

CASTLE, HENRY JAMES   A Treatise on Land Surveying and Levelling. London, 1845. 8vo., orig. cloth, gilt, illus., plates. Hammond 201-803 1974 £9.50

CASTLE, LEWIS   Cactaceous Plants. 1884. Crown 8vo., cloth, scarce. Wheldon 131-1654 1974 £5

CASTLE, THOMAS   An Introduction to Systematical and Physiological Botany. 1829. Small 8vo., new boards, hand-coloured figures. Wheldon 128-1087 1973 £10

CASTLE, MRS. VERNON   My Husband. Scribner, 1919. 264p., illus. Austin 51-178 1973 $8.50

CASTLEHAVEN, JAMES TOUCHET   The Earl of Castlehaven's Revievv. London, 1684. Small 8vo., modern calf, gilt, fine. Dawsons PM 252-118 1974 £95

CASTORANI, RAPHAEL   De la Keratite. Paris, 1856. 8vo., contemporary boards, gilt, inscribed.   Dawsons PM 249-104 1974 £19

CASTRACANE, A. F.   Challenger Voyage, Report on the Diatomaceae. 1886. 4to., orig. cloth, plates, orig. printing, very scarce.   Wheldon 128-1347 1973 £35

CASTRACANE, A. F.   Challenger Voyage, Report on the Diatomaceae. 1886. 4to., cloth, very scarce, plates.   Wheldon 131-1380 1974 £5

CASTRACANE, A. F.   Report on the Diatomaceae, Challenger Voyage. 1886. 4to., cloth, very scarce, orig. printing.   Wheldon 131-1383 1974 £35

CASTRO, JOAO DE   Roteiro em Que se Contem a Viagem Que Fizeram os Portuguezes no Anno de 1541. Paris, 1833. 8vo., half calf, map, very scarce.   Harper 213-35 1973 $75

THE CAT and the Fiddle. London, ca. 1890. Cloth spine, 4 color plates, glazed pictorial boards.   Frohnsdorff 16-199 1974 $15

CATALA, R.   Variatious Experimentales de Chrysiridia Madagascariensis Less. Paris, 1940. 4to., wrappers, plates.   Wheldon 130-728 1974 £10

CATALLUS, GAIUS VALERIUS   Catullus et in Eum Commentarius M. Antoni Mureti. 1554. Contemporary limp vellum, worn.   Thomas 30-102 1973 £30

CATALOGUE and Book of Specimens of Type Faces and Printing, Material and Machinery of the Cleveland Type Foundery. Cleveland, n.d. 8vo., orig. green cloth.   Ximenes 35-404 1974 $35

CATALOGUE and Price List of Type and Material of the Cleveland Type Foundery. (Cleveland, 1893). 8vo., orig. red cloth, illus.   Ximenes 35-403 1974 $40

CATALOGUE de Reliures du XVe AU XIXe Siecle. Paris, (1930-31?). 4to., orig. printed wrappers, uncut, limited, plates.   Dawsons PM 10-259 1974 £48

CATALOGUE of a Collection of Italian Sculpture and Other Plastic Art of the Renaissance. 1913. Roy. 4to., plates, buckram, gilt.   Quaritch 940-147 1974 £50

CATALOGUE of a Collection of Printed Broadsides. London, 1866. Large 8vo., orig. cloth, worn, stained.   Dawsons PM 10-10 1974 £15

CATALOGUE of an Exhibition of Florentine Painting Before 1500. 1920. 4to., buckram, faded, plates.   Quaritch 940-101 1974 £25

CATALOGUE of Contemporary Paintings and Sculpture. Buffalo, 1949. Sm. 4to., plates.   Biblo & Tannen 214-215 1974 $12.50

CATALOGUE of Early English Books. New York, 1926. 8vo., orig. cloth, morocco labels, book-plate, fine.   Dawsons PM 252-1055 1974 £10

CATALOGUE of Early English Books, Chiefly of the Elizabethan Period. New York, 1926. 8vo., orig. cloth, fine.   Dawsons PM 10-652 1974 £10

CATALOGUE of Italian Pictures. London, 1914. Crown 4to., illus., faded, contemporary buckram.   Bow Windows 62-31 1974 £7.50

THE CATALOGUE of Old and New England, an Exhibition of American Painting of Colonial and Early Republican Days together With the English Painting of the Same Time. Providence, 1945. First edition, 4to., illus., errata slip laid in, very fine, 19 pages of catalogue.   Current BW9-406 1974 $17.50

CATALOGUE of Parliamentary Papers. (c.1905). 4to., buckram.   Quaritch 939-486 1974 £30

CATALOGUE Of the Library Of the Writers To His Majesty's Signet. Edinburgh, 1805. 4to., contemporary calf.   Dawsons PM 10-555 1974 £18

CATALOGUE of the Luttrell Psalter and the Bedford Horae. 1929. 4to., orig. printed wrappers, coloured plates, illus.   Bown Windows 66-111 1974 £5.75

CATALOGUE of the Officers and Pupils of Friend's Boarding School, Providence, Rhode Island, for the Year Ending Fourth Month, 1842. Providence, 1842. 16mo., bottom right corner chewed away not affecting text.   Current BW9-418 1974 $14.50

CATALOGUE of the Paintings and Sculpture in the Permanent Collection. Buffalo, 1949. Sm. 4to., plates.   Biblo & Tannen 214-216 1974 $10

A CATALOGUE of the Printed Books Bequethed by John Forster, With Index. London, 1888. Roy. 8vo., orig. cloth, morocco back.   Forster 98-247 1974 £15

CATALOGUE Raisonne. 1911. Roy 8vo., orig. limp vellum.   Howes 186-165 1974 £35

CATANEO, PIETRO   L'Architettura. 1567. Folio, old vellum, woodcut illus., first complete edition.   Thomas 30-121 1973 £180

CATCOTT, GEORGE SYMES   A Descriptive Account of a Descent Made into Penpark-Hole, in the Parish of Westbury-upon-Trin, in the County of Gloucester, in the Year 1775. Bristol, 1792. 8vo., disbound, first edition, rare.   Ximenes 36-47 1974 $100

CATEL, GUILLAUME   Histoire des Comtes de Tolose. 1623. Folio, old calf, foxed.   Allen 213-1360 1973 £90

CATESBY, M.   The Natural History of Carolina, Florida and the Bahama Islands. Folio, roy, plates.   Wheldon 129-8 1974 £205

CATESBY, M.   The Natural History of Carolina, Florida and the Bahama Islands. Roy folio, portfolio, plates, limited edition.   Wheldon 130-9 1974 £205

CATHARINE OF SIENA, SAINT.   Epistole Devotissime. 1500. Folio, French 19th century calf, gilt, woodcut.   Thomas 30-4 1973 £650

CATHER, WILLA   Alexander's Bridge. Boston & New York, 1912. Orig. cloth, later issue, with title alone in rectangular box on front cover.   MacManus 224-71 1974 $50

CATHER, WILLA   April Twilights. New York, 1923. Quarter parchment-vellum, dec. boards, fine, slip-case, first American edition.   Covent 55-361 1974 £35

CATHER, WILLA   April Twilights and Other Poems. New York, 1923. Orig. binding, first edition, dust stained d.w., nice.   Ross 87-99 1974 $15

CATHER, WILLA   Death Comes for the Archbishop. n.d. 4to., buckram, bookplate, fine, drawings.   Covent 55-362 1974 £5.25

CATHER, WILLA   Death Comes for the Archbishop. New York, 1929. Folio, orig. vellum, drawings, first edition, one of 170 numbered copies, signed by author, very fine, boxed.   MacManus 224-72 1974 $135

CATHER, WILLA   December Night. New York, 1933. Orig. binding, first edition in this format, mint.   Ross 87-100 1974 $15

CATHER, WILLA   Lucy Grayheart. New York, 1935. Orig. binding, first edition, fine, d.w.   Ross 87-101 1974 $12.50

CATHER, WILLA   My Mortal Enemy. New York, 1926. First trade edition, orig. binding, spine faded, else fine.   Ross 87-102 1974 $12.50

CATHER, WILLA   Obscure Destinies. New York, 1932. First U. S. edition, beautiful copy, perfect d.w.   Covent 51-378 1973 £10.50

CATHER, WILLA   Obscure Destinies. New York, 1932. First edition, 8vo., spine faded.   Current BW9-212 1974 $12.50

CATHER, WILLA   Obscure Destinies. New York, 1932. Orig. binding, first edition, no. 117 of 260 copies, on Nihon Japan vellum, signed, lacking d.w., near mint.   Ross 87-103 1974 $60

CATHER, WILLA   Sapphira and the Slave Girl. New York, 1940. Orig. cloth backed boards, first edition one of 520 numbered copies, signed by author, boxed, very fine, dust jacket.   MacManus 224-73 1974 $60

CATHER, WILLA   Sapphira and the Slave Girl. New York, 1940. Near mint, slightly darkened d.w., first edition, orig. binding.   Ross 87-105 1974 $10

CATHER, WILLA   Shadows on the Rock.   New York, 1931. Full orange vellum, no. 199 of 199 signed copies, numbered, boxed. Jenkins 61-478 1974 $135

CATHER, WILLA   Shadows on the Rock.   New York, 1931. No. 181 of 619 copies, printed on Croxley hand made paper, signed, box & dust wrapper torn, else fine. Ross 87-106 1974 $80

CATHER, WILLA   Works. 1937-41. Limited to 970 copies, this being no 189, signed by author, portraits, blue & beige buckram, gilt tops, other edges untrimmed, handsome set. Butterfield 10-139 1974 $325

CATHERINE CHARLOTTE, LADY JACKSON   Complete Works. Paris & Boston, c. 1910. 14 vols., edition deLuxe limited to 1000 copies, spines soiled with some wear, paper labels. Current BW9-213 1974 $22.50

CATHEY, JAMES   Truth is Stranger than Fiction. (1899). Cloth, fine, first edition. Putman 126-21 1974 $20

CATHOLIC Builders of the Nation. 1923. 428p., illus. Austin 62-395 1974 $15

CATHOLIC CHURCH   Bullarii Romani Continuatio Summorum Pontificum Benedicti XIV, Clementis XIII, Clementis XIV, Pii VI, Pii VII, Leonis XII, Pii VIII. 1843-56. 6 vols. in 10, 4to., orig. boards. Howes 185-1013 1974 £45

CATHOLIC CHURCH. LITURGY & RITUAL. CEREMONIAL OF BISHOPS. Nouissime Reformatum. Rome, 1600. Woodcut illus., occasional light browning, else clean and sound, 4to., sprinkled sheep, rebacked. Thomas 32-33a 1974 £120

THE CATHOLIC Encyclopedia. 1913-14. 15 vols., orig. ed. Austin 62-732 1974 $95

THE CATHOLIC Encyclopaedia. 1913-22. 17 vols., large roy. 8vo., illus., plates, orig. cloth, special edition. Howes 185-1047 1974 £35

THE CATHOLIC Layman. Dublin, (1852-58). 7 vols., 4to. Emerald 50-768 1974 £20

THE CATHOLIC Miscellany. (1886). Unusual color plates, 251 pages. Austin 57-121 1974 $17.50

CATLIN, GEORGE   Anglo-Saxony and Its Traditions. 1939. Ex-library. Austin 61-189 1974 $10

CATLIN, GEORGE   Letters and Notes on the Manners, Customs, and Condition of the North American Indians. London, 1841. 2 vols., illus., rebound, red fabric, second edition. Hood's 104-512 1974 $95

CATLIN, GEORGE   Letters and Notes on the Manners, Customs and Condition of the North American Indians. 1841. 2 vols., illus., second edition, rebound in red fabric, some slight foxing. Hood's 102-444 1974 $95

CATLIN, GEORGE   North American Indians. Edinburgh, 1926. 2 vols., pictorial cloth, dust jacket, fine, illus. Bradley 35-61 1974 $250

CATLOW, A.   Popular Field Botany. 1852. Square post 8vo., plates, third edition. Wheldon 130-1081 1974 £5

CATLOW, A.   Popular Greenhouse Botany. 1857. Small 8vo., orig. cloth, plates, scarce. Wheldon 131-1498 1974 £10

CATO, MARCUS PORCIUS   Praeter Librum de re Rustica Quae Extant. 1860. Buckram. Allen 213-230 1973 $10

CATT, HENRI DE   Frederick the Great. 1916. 2 vols., portrait. Howes 186-830 1974 £7.50

CATTERMOLE, RICHARD   The Great Civil War of the Times of Charles I and Cromwell. (1846). 4to., plates, buckram, rebound, label. Howes 186-694 1974 £6

CATULLUS, GAIUS VALERIUS   Carmina. 1928. Allen 213-232 1973 $10

CATULLUS, GAIUS VALERIUS   Opera. 1502. 19th century calf gilt, raised bands, first Aldine edition, second issue. Thomas 30-15 1973 £95

CATULLUS, GAIUS VALERIUS   Opera. 1515. 19th century russia gilt, raised bands, faded. Thomas 30-29 1973 £50

CATULLUS, GAIUS VALERIUS   The Carmina of. 1894. Brown half morocco, frontis., fine hand made paper, limited, very good copy. Bow Windows 66-112 1974 £15

CATULLUS, GAIUS VALERIUS   Properti Carmina Quae Extant Omnia Cura. Londini, 1911. 8vo., orig. holland backed boards, uncut, limited. Bow Windows 62-763 1974 £7.50

CAULFIELD, JAMES   The High Court of Justice. 1820. 4to., orig. cloth, illus., first edition. Broadhurst 23-1220 1974 £10

CAULFIELD, JAMES   The High Court of Justice, Comprising Memoirs of the Principal Persons Who Sat in Judgment on King Charles the First. 1820. First edition, demy 4to., good copy, binding dull, internally fine, orig. cloth, illus. Broadhurst 24-1216 1974 £10

CAULFIELD, JAMES   Memoirs of the Political and Private Life of James Caulfield. London, 1810. 4to., frontispiece, foxed, contemporary tree calf, worn, first edition. Bow Windows 62-159 1974 £14

CAULFIELD, JAMES   Portraits, Memoirs and Characters of Remarkable Persons. 1819-20. 4 vols., 8vo., contemporary half green morocco, uncut. Quaritch 940-49 1974 £20

CAULFIELD, S. F. A.   The Dictionary of Needlework. (1882). 6 vols., 4to., orig. red cloth, gilt. Quaritch 940-750 1974 £50

CAULKINS, FRANCES MANWARING   History of New London. New London, 1852. 8vo., orig. bindings. Butterfield 8-82 1974 $35

CAUTHORN, HENRY S.   A History of the City of Vincennes, Indiana. (Terre Haute), 1902. 12mo., cloth. Saddleback 14-400 1974 $12.50

CAVAIGNAC, EUGENE   Histoire Generale de l'Antiquite. Paris, 1946. Biblo & Tannen 214-602 1974 $12.50

CAVALIERI, BONAVENTURA   Lo Specchio Ustorio overo Trattato Delle Settioni Coniche. Bologna, 1650. 4to., contemporary calf, gilt, second edition. Dawsons PM 245-164 1974 £55

CAVALLERII, J. B. DE   Ecclesiae Anglicane Tropaea. Rome, 1584. Small folio, modern quarter hard grain morocco, plates. Thomas 28-175 1972 £10.50

CAVALLO, TIBERIUS   A Complete Treatise on Electricity. London, 1795. 8vo., contemporary half calf, fourth edition. Dawsons PM 245-165 1974 £30

CAVE, H. W.   Golden Tips. 1901. 8vo., orig. cloth, illus. Bow Windows 64-439 1974 £10.50

CAVE, H. W.   The Ruined Cities of Ceylon. 1897. 4to., plates, illus., half roan. Quaritch 940-308 1974 £25

CAVE, WILLIAM   Antiquitates Apostolicae. London, 1677. Folio, old calf, gilt, engraved plates. Jacobs 24-139 1974 $75

CAVE, WILLIAM   Apostololi. London, 1677. Engraved plates, old calf, gilt. Jacobs 24-140 1974 $75

CAVE, WILLIAM   The Lives of the Fathers in the Primitive Church. 1732. Small 4to., contemporary panelled calf, rebacked. Howes 185-1048 1974 £10

CAVENDISH, GEORGE   The Life of Thomas Wolsey. Hammersmith, 1893. Small 4to., orig. limp vellum. Dawsons PM 252-119 1974 £175

CAVENDISH, GEORGE   The Life of Thomas Wolsey. Kelmscott Press, 1893. Limited to 250 copies, vellum, printed in Golden Type. Thomas 32-277 1974 £130

CAVENDISH, GEORGE   The Life of Thomas Wolsey, Cardinal Archbishop of York. Kelmscott Press, 1893. 8vo., orig. limp vellum, yellow silk ties, fine copy, woodcut borders and initials, limited to 250 copies, presentation copy from the editor. Sawyer 293-178 1974 £130

CAVENDISH, HENRY   Government of Canada. London, 1839.
Maps, inscribed. Hood's 103-522 1974 $125

CAVENDISH, WILLIAM, DUKE OF NEWCASTLE
Please turn to
NEWCASTLE, WILLIAM CAVENDISH, DUKE OF

CAVERLY, R. C.   Heroism of Hannah Duston. Boston, 1874. Orig.
cloth, first edition. Putman 126-71 1974 $12

CAVICCHIOLI, GIOVANNI   Filippo de Pisis. Venice, 1932. 8vo., plates,
wrapper. Minters 37-431 1973 $15

CAVICEO, GIACOME   Dialogue Treselegant Intitule le Peregrin . . .
Traduit de Vulgarei Italien. Paris, 1527. Small folio, woodcuts, mid 19th
century olive straight grained morocco with blind stamped and gilt dec., first
edition. Schumann 499-21 1974 sFr 3,875

CAVOUR, GUSTAVE DE   Fragmens Philosophiques. Turin, 1841.
8vo., contemporary tan calf, gilt, label. L. Goldschmidt 42-21 1974 $15

CAWSE, J.   Introduction to the Art of Painting in Oil
Colours. 1822. 8vo., plates, contemporary roan backed boards, scarce.
Quaritch 940-50 1974 £60

CAXTON, WILLIAM   The Fables of Esope. 1932. Folio, full sheepskin, uncut, limited edition. Broadhurst 23-1042 1974 £75

CAXTON, WILLIAM   William Caxton's Prologues and Epilogues.
1927. Orig. vellum. Bow Windows 66-113 1974 £14.50

CAYLEY, N. W.   Budgerigars in Bush and Aviary. Sydney, 1933.
8vo., cloth, illus., scarce. Wheldon 129-442 1974 £10

CAZENAVE, P. L. ALPHEE   Traite des Maladies du Cuir Chevelu Suivi de
Conseils Hygieniques sur les Soins a Donner a la Chevelure. Paris, 1850. 8vo.,
old quarter shagreen, coloured plates, first edition, library stamps. Gurney
10-40 1974 £18

CAZENOVE D'ARLENS   Henriette et Emma, ou l'Education de l'Amitie.
Paris, 1796. 8vo., half leather, labels. Schumann 499-22 1974 sFr 100

CAZOTTE, JACQUES   Le Diable Amoureux. Paris, 1921. 8vo.,
orig. wrapper, uncut, numbered, illu., limited edition. L. Goldschmidt
42-23 1974 $40

CAZOTTE, JACQUES   Ollivier. Paris, (1798). 2 vols., 12mo.,
contemporary glazed green boards, uncut, very fine. L. Goldschmidt 42-22
1974 $125

CEBOLLERO, PEDRO A.   La Politica Linguistico-Escolar de Puerto Rico.
1945. Austin 62-86 1974 $27.50

CECIL, ALGERNON   A House In Bryanston Square. (1944).
Ex-library. Austin 61-191 1974 $10

CECIL, E.   A History of Gardening In England. 1910.
8vo., cloth, illus., scarce, enlarged third edition. Wheldon 131-207 1974 £15

CECOF, ANTON   Racconti. Florence, 1910. 16mo., wrappers,
good copy. Minters 37-385 1973 $15

CEDRENUS, GEORGE   Compendium Historiarum. 1647. 2 vols.,
folio, half calf, frayed, first edition. Howes 186-659 1974 £60

CEILLIER, REMY   Histoire Generale des Auters Sacres et
Ecclesiastiques. Paris, 1863-69. 16 vols., thick roy. 8vo., half maroon calf,
rubbed. Howes 185-1050 1974 £50

CELEBRATED & Historical Speeches; an Anthology of Ancient & Modern Oratory.
1933. Plates, covers faded, very good copy. Covent 51-47 1973 £6.30

CELEBRATION of the 86th Anniversary of the Independence of the United States,
in Chicago. Chicago, 1862. Printed wrappers, first edition. Bradley 35-76
1974 $14

CELESIA, DOROTHEA   Almida. London, 1771. 8vo., fine, modern
boards, first edition. Dawsons PM 252-120 1974 £15

CELESTINA   The Spanish Bawd. London, 1631. Folio, fine,
full red crushed levant morocco, first English edition. Dawsons PM 252-121
1974 £300

CELIDE   Ou Histoire de la Marquise de Bliville. n.d.
2 vols. in 1, 8vo., contemporary morocco backed marbled boards. Smith
193-105 1973 £5

CELIERE, PAUL   The Startling Exploits of Dr. J. B. Quies.
New York, 1887. Orig. pictorial cloth, first American edition. Covent
55-644 1974 £8.50

CELIZ, FRAY FRANCISCO   Diary of the Alarcon Expedition into Texas,
1718-1719. Los Angeles, 1935. Limited to 600 numbered copies, first
publication in book form. Jenkins 61-483 1974 $85

CELLARIUS   La Danse des Salons. Paris, 1847. 8vo.,
boards, morocco back, fine, plates, first edition. Quaritch 940-809 1974 £40

CELLINI, BENVENUTO   Due Trattati, uno Intorno Alle Otto Principali
Arti Dell' Oreficeria. Florence, 1568. 4to., 19th century morocco, good
large copy, first edition. Quaritch 940-669 1974 £980

CELLINI, BENVENUTO   Memoirs. London, 1822. 2 vols., orig. cloth
boards, worn. Covent 55-87 1974 £15

CELLINI, BENVENUTO   Vita di Benvenuto Cellini Orefice e Scultore
Fiorentino. (Naples, 1728). 4to., 18th century mottled calf, very good copy.
Quaritch 940-670 1974 £350

CELLINI, BENVENUTO   Vita di Benvenuto Cellini. (Florence, 1792).
4to., half calf antique, counterfeit edition. Quaritch 940-671 1974 £40

CELSUS, AURELIUS CORNELIUS   In Hoc Volvmine Haec Continentvr. 1528.
8vo., seventeenth century French red morocco. Dawsons PM 249-105 1974
£375

CELSUS, AURELIUS CORNELIUS   Medicina Libri Octo. 1786. Rittenhouse
46-131 1974 $15

CELSUS, AURELIUS CORNELIUS   De Medicina Libri Octo. Edinburgi, 1809.
8vo., contemporary half calf, rebacked. Dawsons PM 249-106 1974 £12

CENDRARS, BLAISE   Dix-neuf Poemes Elastiques. Paris, 1919.
12mo., orig. wrapper, uncut, first edition. L. Goldschmidt 42-180 1974 $100

CENSUS 1821. 1822. Thick folio, rebound, uncut, fine, label, scarce.
Howes 186-1381 1974 £38

CENSUS of Canada, 1880-1881. Ottawa, 1882. 4 vols. Hood's 104-895
1974 $60

CENTENARY Celebration of the Battle of Lundy's Lane, July 25, 1914. Niagara
Falls, 1919. Linen spine, plain heavy card cover, inscribed & signed by editor,
illus. Hood's 102-591 1974 $15

A CENTENNIAL Biographical History of Crawford County, Ohio. Chicago,
1902. New cloth. Hayman 59-449 1974 $55

CENTENNIAL of the Province of Upper Canada, 1792-1892. (Toronto), 1893.
Card cover. Hood's 102-593 1974 $15

THE CENTENNIAL of the Settlement of Upper Canada By the United Empire
Loyalists, 1764-1884. Toronto, 1885. Hood's 104-674 1974 $125

THE CENTENNIAL of the Settlement of Upper Canada by the United Empire
Loyalists, 1784-1884. With Appendix. Toronto, 1885. Hood's 102-594 1974
$125

CENTLIVRE, SUSANNA   The Beau's Duel. London, 1702. Small 4to.,
19th century red morocco gilt, first edition. Dawsons PM 252-122 1974 £80

A CENTURY of Canadian Art. London, 1938. Illus., stained. Hood's
104-146 1974 $15

A CENTURY of Detective Stories. London, n.d. Biblo & Tannen 210-435 1973
$10

A CENTURY of French Romance. 1902. 12 vols., turquoise pigskin gilt, illus., plates, library edition. Howes 185-65 1974 £48

A CENTURY of Thrillers. London, 1935. Biblo & Tannen 210-545 1973 $10

CERCEAU, PERE DU   Recueil de Poesies Diverses. Paris, 1733. 8vo., frontispiece, contemporary speckled calf, worn. Bow Windows 62-161 1974 £6.15

CERCLE DE LA LIBRAIRIE   Premiere Exposition. Paris, 1880. 2 parts in 1, 8vo., orig. tooled cloth, uncut. Kraus B8-35 1974 £45

CERDAN, JEAN PAUL DE   Europe a Slave. London, 1681. 12mo., contemporary sheep, first edition. Dawsons PM 251-493 1974 £75

THE CEREMONIES For the Healing. London, 1686. 8vo., disbound. Gurney 64-47 1974 £8.50

CERRI, GIUSEPPE.   Trattato Teorico. 1854. Oblong 8vo., orig. cloth, frontispiece, plates. Bow Windows 64-316 1974 £12.50

CERTANI, ABBOTE D. GIACOMO   La Santita Prodigiosa, Vita dis Brigida Ibernese. Bologna, 1695. Contemporary calf gilt. Smith 193-106 1973 £10

CERVANTES SAAVEDRA, MIGUEL DE   The History of Don Quixote. London, n.d. 4to., contemporary half morocco, gilt, plates, illus. Hammond 201-481 1974 £5

CERVANTES SAAVEDRA, MIGUEL DE   The History and Adventures of the Renowned Don Quixote. 1755. 4to., 2 vols., quarter calf. Hill 126-36 1974 £60

CERVANTES-SAAVEDRA, MIGUEL DE   El Ingenioso Hidalgo Don Quixote De La Mancha. Madrid, 1780. 4 vols., 4to., contemp. marbled calf, gilt, 4 engraved titles, portrait frontis, plates. Jacobs 24-72 1974 $800

CERVANTES SAAVEDRA, MIGUEL DE   The History of the Ingenious Gentleman. Edinburgh, 1822. Small 8vo., 5 vols., orig. boards, uncut. Quaritch 936-331 1974 £15

CERVANTES SAAVEDRA, MIGUEL DE   Don Quixote de la Mancha. 1840. Orig. cloth, 3 vols., gilt, English first edition. Covent 56-221 1974 £18

CERVANTES SAAVEDRA, MIGUEL DE   The History of the Ingenious Gentleman Don Quixote of La Mancha. 1892. 4 vols., large 8vo., cloth, plates. Howes 185-66 1974 £6

CERVANTES SAAVEDRA, MIGUEL DE   The History of Don Quixote of the Mancha. 1896. 4 vols., square 8vo., orig. buckram backed boards. Howes 185-536 1974 £21

CERVANTES SAAVEDRA, MIGUEL DE   El Ingenioso Hidalgo Don Quixote de la Mancha. (New York, 1909). Thick small 4to., orig. vellum gilt, slipcase, uncut, limited, fine. Howes 186-82 1974 £50

CERVANTES SAAVEDRA, MIGUEL DE   The History of Don Quixote. 1922. 4to., cloth gilt, plates, illus., foxing. Covent 55-879 1974 £20

CERVANTES SAAVEDRA, MIGUEL DE   The History of the Valorous and Wittie Knight-Errant Don Quixote. Chelsea, 1927. 2 vols., folio, full dark green morocco, uncut, limited. Bow Windows 62-34 1974 £600

CERVANTES SAAVEDRA, MIGUEL DE   Don Quixote. 1930. 2 vols., orig. full leather, plates, fine. Covent 55-1142 1974 £45

CERVANTES-SAAVEDRA, MIGUEL DE   The Ingenious Gentleman Don Quixote de la Mancha. New York, 1949. 2 vols., 1st ed., fine. Jacobs 24-73 1974 $18

CESALPINUS, ANDREA   De Plantis Libri XVI. Florence, 1583. 4to., contemporary mottled vellum, old gilt label, signatures, first edition. Dawsons PM 250-15 1974 £2100

CESCINSKY, HERBERT   Chinese Furniture. 1922. Small folio, plates, illus., cloth. Quaritch 940-379 1974 £25

CESCINSKY, HERBERT   Early English Furniture and Woodwork. 1922. Roy. 4to., 2 vols., orig. cloth, illus. Broadhurst 23-45 1974 £35

CESCINSKY, HERBERT   Early English Furniture and Woodwork. 1922. 2 vols., roy. 4to., publisher's binding, morocco spine, top edges gilt, illus., fine. Broadhurst 24-39 1974 £42

CESCINSKY, HERBERT   Early English Furniture and Woodwork. 1922. 2 vols., small folio, black quarter morocco, gilt, fine. Quaritch 940-574 1974 £40

CESCINSKY, HERBERT   English Furniture of the Eighteenth Century. (1909-11). 3 vols., 4to., plates, orig. wrappers, half morocco. Quaritch 940-573 1974 £60

CESCINSKY, HERBERT   The Old World House. 1924. Crown 4to., red morocco, illus., 2 vols. Broadhurst 23-44 1974 £20

CESCINSKY, HERBERT   The Old World House. 1924. 2 vols., illus., fine. Covent 55-62 1974 £15

CESCINSKY, HERBERT   The Old World House. 1924. 2 vols., large 8vo., quarter red morocco, illus. Quaritch 939-93 1974 £10

CESI, F.   Phytosophicarum Tabularum. (Rome, 1904). 4to., limp boards. Wheldon 129-897 1974 £5

CESI, F.   Phytosophicarum Tabularum. Rome, 1904. 4to., orig. limp boards. Wheldon 131-1126 1974 £15

CEZANNE, P.   Le Maitre Paul Cezanne. Paris, 1923. 4to., plates, half morocco, orig. wrappers. Quaritch 940-51 1974 £75

CHABANNES, MARQUIS DE   Appendix to the Marquis de Chabannes' Publication, On Conducting By Forced Ventilation. (1818). 8vo., plates, new boards. Quaritch 940-502 1974 £50

CHABRAEUS, D.   Omnium Stirpium Sciagraphia et Icones. Geneva, 1678. Folio, old leather backed boards, woodcuts. Wheldon 129-898 1974 £50

CHADWICK, EDWIN   Report to Her Majesty's Principal Secretary. London, 1842 & 1843. 2 vols., 8vo., plates, orig. boards, engravings, first edition. Dawsons PM 250-16 1974 £300

CHADWICK, EDWIN   Report to Her Majesty's Principal Secretary of State. London, 1842. 8vo., orig. cloth, plates. Gurney 64-48 1974 £50

CHADWICK, H. MUNRO   The Growth of Literature. 1932-40. 3 vols., large thick 8vo., orig. cloth, inscribed, presentation, orig. and best edition. Howes 186-83 1974 £28

CHADWICK, JOHN W.   Book of Poems. Roberts, 1878. 209p. Austin 54-239 1973 $7.50

CHADWICK, WILLIAM   A Practical Treatise on Brewing. 1835. 12mo., new paper wrappers. Bow Windows 64-50 1974 £14

CHAFFERS, WILLIAM   Gilda Aurif Abrorum. London, 1883. 8vo., orig. cloth gilt, illus. Dawsons PM 10-119 1974 £10

CHAFFERS, WILLIAM   Hall Marks on Gold & Silver Plate. 1865. Embossed cloth, second edition. Covent 55-432 1974 £7.50

CHAFFERS, WILLIAM   Hall Marks On Gold and Silver Plate. London, 1875. 8vo., orig. dec. cloth gilt, fifth edition. Dawsons PM 10-120 1974 £10

CHAFFERS, WILLIAM   Hall Marks On Gold and Silver Plate. London, 1891. 8vo., orig. cloth gilt, revised seventh edition. Dawsons PM 10-121 1974 £18

CHAFFERS, WILLIAM   Hall Marks on Gold and Silver Plate...to which is now added, A History of l'Orfevrerie Francaise. London, 1896. Folding plate, illus., roy. 8vo., orig. cloth, frontis., eighth edition. Forster 97-15 1974 £3

CHAFFERS, WILLIAM   Marks and Monograms on European and Oriental Pottery and Porcelain. 1886. 8vo., orig. cloth, illus., slight foxing, bookplate, seventh edition. Bow Windows 66-115 1974 £7.50

CHAFFERS, WILLIAM   Marks and Monograms on Pottery and Porcelain of the Renaissance and Modern Periods. 1876. 8vo., orig. cloth, illus., covers worn, revised sixth edition. Bow Windows 66-116 1974 £6

CHAFFERS, WILLIAM   The New Keramic Gallery. London, 1926. 2 vols., 8vo., plates, orig. gilt dec. cloth, worn, third edition. Bow Windows 62-162 1974 £14.50

CHAFFERS, WILLIAM   The New Keramic Gallery. 1926. 2 vols., roy. 8vo., illus., coloured plates, orig. cloth, mint, dust wrappers, enlarged third edition. Broadhurst 24-40 1974 £15

CHAFFIN, WILLIAM L.   History of Rboert Chaffin and His Descendants. New York, (1913). 8vo., cloth. Saddleback 14-777 1974 $35

CHAGALL, BELLA   Brenendicke Licht. New York, 1945. First U. S. edition, drawings by Marc Chagall, nice copy. Covent 51-2244 1973 £15

CHAGALL, BELLA   Burning Lights. New York, 1946. 1st ed. Biblo & Tannen 213-216 1973 $15

CHAGALL, MARC   Ma Vie. Trad de Russe par Bella Chagall. Paris, 1931. 8vo., wrapper, drawings, limited edition. Minters 37-59 1973 $32

CHAGALL, MARC   Poeme de Fernand Marc. Avec un Dessin de Marc Chagall. Paris, 1934. Oblong 8vo., wrapper, scarce, limited edition. Minters 37-74 1973 $20

CHAIR, SOMERSET DE   The First Crusade. Golden Cockerel Press, 1945. Half vellum, fine, one of 500 copies. Broadhurst 24-991 1974 £60

CHAIR, SOMERSET DE   The First Crusade. Golden Cockerel Press, 1945. Engravings, folio, full vellum, tooled gilt, by Sangorski & Sutcliffe, uncut, fine, one of 100 signed copies. Broadhurst 24-990 1974 £90

CHAIR, SOMERSET DE   The Golden Carpet. 1943. Crown 4to., full dark green morocco, signed, limited edition. Broadhurst 23-1009 1974 £80

CHAIR, SOMERSET DE   The Golden Carpet. Golden Cockerel Press, 1943. Frontispiece, crown 4to., full dark green morocco, panelled back, top edges gilt, others uncut, fine, limited to 30 copies, signed by author. Broadhurst 24-987 1974 £80

CHAIR, SOMERSET DE   Napoleon's Memoirs. Golden Cockerel Press, 1945. Engraved plates, 2 vols., folio, orig. cloth, top edges gilt, others uncut, one of 500 copies, fine. Broadhurst 24-992 1974 £70

CHAIR, SOMERSET DE   The Silver Crescent. 1943. Crown 4to., full blue morocco, signed, limited edition. Broadhurst 23-1010 1974 £80

CHAIR, SOMERSET DE   The Silver Crescent. Golden Cockerel Press, 1943. Crown 4to., full blue morocco, panelled back, top edges gilt, others uncut, photos, limited to 30 copies, signed by author, fine. Broadhurst 24-988 1974 £80

CHAIR, SOMERSET DE   The Silver Crescent. Golden Cockerel Press, 1943. Crown 4to., quarter blue morocco, panelled back, top edges gilt, others uncut, one of 500 copies, fine. Broadhurst 24-989 1974 £25

CHALFANT, W. A.   Tales of the Pioneers. Stanford, c.1942. 8vo., cloth. Saddleback 14-66 1974 $15

CHALIAPIN, FEODOR   Man and Mask. Knopf, 1932. 358p., illus. Austin 51-179 1973 $8.50

CHALKHILL, JOHN   Thealma and Clearchus. London, 1683. 8vo., modern red half morocco, first edition. Dawsons PM 252-125 1974 £125

CHALLIS, JAMES   An Essay on the Mathematical Principles of Physics. Cambridge, London, 1873. 8vo., brown cloth, gilt, presentation copy. Dawsons PM 245-166 1974 £7

CHALMERS, ALEX   A History of the Colleges, Halls, and Public Buildings Attached to the University of Oxford. Oxford, 1810. 2 vols., 8vo., contemporary polished calf, plates. Traylen 79-375 1973 £12

CHALMERS, CHARLES   Notes, Thoughts, and Inquiries. 1852. 8vo., orig. cloth, first edition, first series. Hammond 201-218 1974 £8.50

CHALMERS, GEORGE   The Arrangements with Ireland Considered. London, 1785. 8vo., modern boards. Dawsons PM 247-42 1974 £18

CHALMERS, GEORGE   Banking. Edinburgh, 1762. 8vo., unbound, rare, second edition. Hill 126-12 1974 £15

CHALMERS, GEORGE   A Short View of the Proposals. London, 1785. 8vo., modern boards. Dawsons PM 247-41 1974 £18

CHALMERS, PATRICK REGINALD   Birds Ashore and A-Foreshore. (1935). Crown 4to., bookplate. Bow Windows 64-51 1974 £12

CHALMERS, PATRICK REGINALD   Birds Ashore and A-Foreshore. London, 1935. 4to., half dark green morocco, orig. box, signed, de luxe limited edition. Traylen 79-104 1973 £20

CHALMERS, PATRICK REGINALD   Birds Ashore and A-Foreshore. 1935. 4to., cloth, plates. Wheldon 129-443 1974 £6

CHALMERS, PATRICK REGINALD   Birds Ashore and A-Foreshore. 1935. 4to., new cloth, plates. Wheldon 131-562 1974 £7.50

CHALMERS, PATRICK REGINALD   Birds Ashore ond A-Foreshore. London, 1935. 4to., cloth, gilt, plates, illus., first edition. Hammond 201-634 1974 £10.50

CHALMERS, PATRICK REGINALD   A Dozen Dogs or So. 1928. Roy. 8vo., fine, plates, quarter vellum, signed, numbered. Covent 55-876 1974 £10.50

CHALMERS, PATRICK REGINALD   The Horn, a Lay of the Grassington Fox-Hounds. 1937. 4to., plates, orig. cloth, first edition. Howes 185-143 1974 £5

CHALMERS, PATRICK REGINALD   Rhymes of Flood and Field. London, 1931. 4to., orig. cloth, illus. Hammond 201-465 1974 £5.50

CHALMERS, THOMAS   On the Power, Wisdom and Goodness of God. 1839. 8vo., 2 vols., calf fully gilt. Hill 126-37 1974 £18.50

CHALMERS, THOMAS   Statement in Regard to the Pauperism of Glasgow. Glasgow, 1823. 8vo., boards, first edition. Hammond 201-219 1974 £22.50

CHALON, J. J.   Scenes In Paris. 1820-22. Folio, boards, roan spine, rubbed, plates. Thomas 28-315 1972 £85

CHAMBERLAIN, ALLEN   Beacon Hill. Boston, 1925. Edition limited to 475 numbered copies, illus., orig. binding, uncut, slipcase. Wilson 63-54 1974 $25

CHAMBERLAIN, C. J.   Gymnosperms, Structure and Evolution. Chicago, 1935. 8vo., cloth, figures, rare orig. issue. Wheldon 128-1089 1973 £8

CHAMBERLAIN, MARY STUART   We Inheritors. Furman, 1937. Austin 62-88 1974 $10

CHAMBERLAIN, SAMUEL   Open House in New England. Brattleboro, 1937. Sm. 4to., 1st ed. Biblo & Tannen 213-138 1973 $10

CHAMBERLAIN, THOMAS   The Minister Preaching His Own Funeral Sermon. Deerfield, 1821. Self wrapper. Butterfield 10-141 1974 $15

CHAMBERLAYNE, JOHN   A Family-Herbal. London, 1689. Small 8vo., old calf gilt, leather labels, rare second edition. Traylen 79-9 1973 £125

CHAMBERLEN, HUGH   A Few Proposals. Edinburgh, 1700. 4to., marbled boards, first edition. Dawsons PM 247-43 1974 £120

CHAMBERS, EDMUND K.   Early English Lyrics. London, 1926. 12mo. Biblo & Tannen 210-838 1973 $6.50

CHAMBERS, EDMUND K.   The Elizabethan Stage. Oxford, 1923. 8vo., 4 vols., orig. issue, frontispiece, buckram. Quaritch 936-332 1974 £10

CHAMBERS, EDMUND K.   English Literature at the Close of the Middle Ages. New York, 1947. Biblo & Tannen 210-837 1973 $6.50

CHAMBERS, EDMUND K.   William Shakespeare; Study of Facts and Problems. 1930. 2 vols., plates. Allen 216-2164 1974 $11.50

CHAMBERS, G. F.   East Bourne Memories of the Victorian Period
1845-1901. East-Bourne, 1910. 8vo., orig. cloth, plates, some spotting.
Bow Windows 66-671 1974 £12

CHAMBERS, HENRY E.   Mississippi Valley Beginnings. New York - London, 1922. 8vo., orig. bindings. Butterfield 8-310 1974 $17.50

CHAMBERS, JOHN   A General History of Worcester. Worcester
and London, 1820. 8vo., orig. boards, buckram, first edition. Dawsons PM
251-17 1974 £30

CHAMBERS, R.   Vestiges of the Natural History of Creation.
1847. Small 8vo., half morocco. Wheldon 129-812 1974 £7.50

CHAMBERS, R.   Vestiges of the Natural History of Creation.
1860. Post 8vo., cloth, eleventh edition. Wheldon 129-813 1974 £7.50

CHAMBERS, ROBERT   The Book of Days. 1864-66. 2 vols., thick
crown 4to., woodcut illus., contemporary red morocco, first edition. Smith
194-341 1974 £7

CHAMBERS, ROBERT   Book of Days. 1886. 2 vols., illus., new
library binding, orig. edition. Austin 61-196 1974 $27.50

CHAMBERS, ROBERT   The Maker of Moons. New York, 1896. Orig.
dec. cloth gilt, frontispiece, first U.S. edition. Covent 56-436 1974 £25

CHAMBERS, ROBERT W.   Garden-Land. New York, 1907. 4to.,
pict. boards, cloth spine, 8 color plates, lst ed. Frohnsdorff 16-158 1974 $10

CHAMBERS, ROBERT W.   The King in Yellow. Chicago & New York,
1895. 12mo., orig. pictorial cloth, scarce, first American edition. Covent
55-645 1974 £35

CHAMBERS, WILLIAM   Traite des Edifices, Meubles, Habits,
Machines et Ustensiles des Chinois, Graves sur les Originaux Dessines a la Chine.
1776. 4to., plates, 19th century boards, cloth spine, very rare. Quaritch
940-438 1974 £65

CHAMBERS' Edinburgh Journal. London, 1834-39. 7 vols., folio, foxing,
contemporary half calf, worn. Bow Windows 62-163 1974 £15

CHAMBERS'S Cyclopaedia of English Literature. n.d. 3 vols., 4to., orig.
cloth, new edition. Smith 193-272 1973 £6.50

CHAMBERS'S Cyclopaedia of English Literature. 1901-03. 3 vols., 4to.,
half contemporary morocco gilt. Smith 193-271 1973 £7.50

CHAMBERS'S Cyclopaedia of English Literature. 1903-06. 3 vols., imp. 8vo.,
illus., orig. cloth gilt. Smith 194-340 1974 £6

CHAMBLAIN DE MARIVAUX, PIERRE CARLET DE
Please turn to
MARIVAUX, PIERRE CARLET DE CHAMBLAIN DE

CHAMFORT, SEBASTIEN ROCH NICOLAS   Oeuvres. Paris, 1808. 2 vols.,
8vo., contemporary calf, gilt, second edition. L. Goldschmidt 42-24 1974
$40

CHAMPION, F. W.   The Jungle in Sunlight and Shadow. (1933).
Roy. 8vo., cloth, plates. Wheldon 128-188 1973 £7.50

CHAMPION, F. W.   The Jungle In Sunlight and Shadow. (1933).
Roy. 8vo., cloth, plates. Wheldon 131-345 1974 £7.50

CHAMPION, F. W.   With A Camera in Tiger-land. 1927. Roy 8vo.,
plates, cloth. Wheldon 129-255 1974 £7.50

CHAMPION, F. W.   With a Camera in Tiger-Land. (1927). Roy
8vo., cloth, plates. Wheldon 130-275 1974 £5

CHAMPION, F. W.   With a Camera in Tiger-Land. 1934. Plates,
crown 4to., orig. cloth, frontispiece, binding trifle faded. Broadhurst 24-1589
1974 £6

CHAMPION, H. G.   Manual of Indian Silviculture, Part 1 General
Silviculture, Part 2 Silvicultural Systems. Calcutta, 1938. Roy. 8vo., cloth,
plates. Wheldon 131-1721 1974 £7.50

CHAMPION, H. G.   Over on the Island. Toronto, 1939. Hood's
104-197 1974 $10

CHAMPION, HELEN J.   Over on the Island. Toronto, 1939. Hood's
102-181 1974 $10

CHAMPION, PIERRE   Francois Villon. Paris, 1913. 2 vols., 8vo.,
orig. wrapper, plates. L. Goldschmidt 42-130 1974 $32.50

CHAMPION, PIERRE   Histoire Poetique du Quinzieme Siecle. Paris,
1923. 2 vols., large 8vo., three quarter green morocco, gilt, uncut, plates.
L. Goldschmidt 42-25 1974 $55

CHAMPION, PIERRE   Louis XI. Paris, 1927. 2 vols., roy. 8vo.,
three quarter brown levant morocco, gilt, plates, uncut, first edition.
L. Goldschmidt 42-26 1974 $35

CHAMPION, S. G.   Racial Proverbs. 1928. Allen 216-2217
1974 $15

CHAMPION, T. E.   The Methodist Churches of Toronto. Toronto,
1899. Illus. Hood's 102-281 1974 $20

CHAMPLIN, J. D.   Cyclopedia of Painters and Paintings. New
York, 1888. 4 vols., imp. 8vo., plates, half green levant morocco. Quaritch
940-52 1974 £60

CHAMPNEY, ELIZABETH W.   Paddy O'Learey and his Learned Pig. New
York, 1895. 12mo., lst ed., illus. Frohnsdorff 16-200 1974 $7.50

CHAMPOLLION LE JEUNE, JEAN FRANCOIS   L'Egypte Sous les Pharaons.
Paris, 1814. 8vo., 2 vols., old wrappers, fine, uncut, first edition. Gilhofer
46-32 1974 sFr. 700

CHAMPOLLION LE JEUNE, JEAN FRANCOIS   Grammaire Egyptienne ou
Principes Generaux de l'Ecriture Sacree Egyptienne. Paris, 1836. Folio, orig.
printed wrappers, stained, first edition. Gilhofer 61-41 1974 sFr. 800

CHANCE, E.   The Cuckoo's Secret. 1922. 8vo., cloth,
scarce. Wheldon 130-483 1974 £5

CHANCE, E.   The Truth About the Cuckoo. 1940. 8vo.,
cloth, plates. Wheldon 130-484 1974 £5

CHANCELLOR, E. BERESFORD   The History of the Squares of London. 1907.
Crown 4to., plates. Howes 186-2096 1974 £7.50

CHANCELLOR, E. BERESFORD   The Lives of the British Sculptors. 1911.
Plates, dust soiled. Marsden 37-121 1974 £6

CHANCELLOR, E. BERESFORD   The Lives of the Rakes. 1924-25. 8vo., 6
vols., half red morocco, gilt, portraits, limited edition. Quaritch 936-333 1974
£55

CHANCELLOR, E. BERESFORD   Picturesque Architecture in Paris, Ghent,
Antwerp, Rome. 1928. 4to., plates. Covent 55-63 1974 £18

CHANDLER, FRANK W.   Modern Continental Playwrights. New York,
1931. English first edition. Covent 56-1876 1974 £6.30

CHANDLER, J. A. C.   Colonial Virginia. Richmond, 1907. Signed
by author. Jenkins 61-2521 1974 $10

CHANDLER, JOHN   A Treatise of the Disease called a Cold. London,
1761. 8vo., boards, gilt, first edition. Hammond 201-533 1974 £36

CHANDLER, LLOYD H.   A Summary of the Work of Rudyard Kipling.
New York, 1930. 2 vols., large 8vo., orig. canvas-backed boards, uncut.
Dawsons PM 10-338 1974 £45

CHANDLER, RAYMOND   Farewell My Lovely. New York, 1940. Mint,
wrappers, first American edition. Covent 55-369 1974 £135

CHANDLER, RAYMOND   Farewell My Lovely. New York, 1940.
Dust wrapper, near fine, first American edition. Covent 55-370 1974 £40

CHANDLER, RAYMOND   The Simple Art of Murder. Boston, 1950. First
edition. Biblo & Tannen 210-429 1973 $20

CHANDLER, RICHARD   The Life of William Wayneflete. 1811. Contemporary calf gilt, plates. Howes 185-1782 1974 £9

CHANNING, MARK   White Python. (1934). Presentation, inscribed, near fine. Covent 55-377 1974 £7.50

CHANNING, WILLIAM ELLERY   Discourses, Reviews and Miscellanies. Boston, 1830. Large 8vo., contemporary cloth, uncut. Hill 126-38 1974 £12.50

CHANNING, WILLIAM ELLERY   Eliot. Boston, 1885. 64mo., cloth, presentation inscription, first edition. Goodspeed's 578-51 1974 $35

CHANNING, WILLIAM ELLERY   John Brown and the Heroses of Harper's Ferry. Boston, 1886. 64mo., cloth, first edition. Goodspeed's 578-52 1974 $25

CHANNING, WILLIAM ELLERY   A Sermon Preached, August 20, 1812, in Consequence of the Declaration of War Against Great Britain. Boston, 1812. Three quarter morocco. Jenkins 61-2563 1974 $35

CHANNING, WILLIAM ELLERY   A Sermon Preached in Boston, August 20, 1812. Boston, 1812. Unbound. Hood's 103-523 1974 $25

CHANNING, WILLIAM ELLERY   Thoreau the Poet-Naturalist. Boston, 1902. 8vo., boards, cloth back, leather label, hand made paper, worn binding, foxed, enlarged new edition. Goodspeed's 578-378 1974 $20

CHANNING, WILLIAM ELLERY   Thoreau the Poet-Naturalist With Memorial Verses. Boston, 1902. 8vo., boards, cloth back, paper label, enlarged new edition. Goodspeed's 578-379 1974 $20

CHANSONS   Recueil de Trois Cent Chansons Francoises. Londres, 1737. 8vo., contemporary calf, gilt. Bow Windows 62-164 1974 £12

CHANTER, CHARLOTTE   Ferny Combes: A Ramble after Ferns in the Glens and Valleys of Devonshire. 1857. F'cap 8vo., scarce, coloured plates, orig. cloth, fine. Broadhurst 24-1060 1974 £5

CHAPBOOK, The Irish Comic Melodist. Glasgow, 1856. 8vo., cloth boards, orig. wrappers. Emerald 50-134 1974 £5

CHAPBOOK, The Irish Comic Song Book. Glasgow, 1856. 16mo., cloth boards, orig. wrappers. Emerald 50-135 1974 £5

CHAPIN, G.   Tales of the St. Lawrence. Montreal, 1874. Illus., mended spine. Hood's 103-764 1974 $10

CHAPIN, HENRY   Leifsaga. Farrar, 1934. Austin 62-89 1974 $10

CHAPIN, HOWARD M.   The Seal, The Arms and the Flag of Rhode Island. Providence, 1913. First edition, 8vo., illus., cover spotted, water stain at page bottoms in margins only, else very good, author's inscription. Current BW9-350 1974 $14.50

CHAPLIN, CHARLES, JR.   My Father, Charles Chaplin. Random House, 1960. 369p., illus. Austin 51-180 1973 $7.50

CHAPLIN, CHARLIE   My Wonderful Visit. n.d. Plates, boards, worn. Covent 55-405 1974 £5.25

CHAPLIN, LITA GREY   My Life With Chaplin. Geis, 1966. 325p., illus. Austin 51-181 1973 $6.50

CHAPLIN, RALPH   Bars and Shadows. New York, c. 1922. First edition, orig. binding, inscription and signature of author. Wilson 63-170 1974 $12.50

CHAPMAN, A. R. F.   Catalogue of Fine Oriental Manuscripts and Miniatures...The Property of A. R. F. Chapman. 1930. Plates. Kraus B8-250 1974 $20

CHAPMAN, ABEL 1851-1929   Bird-Life of the Borders. 1889. 8vo., cloth, plates. Wheldon 131-563 1974 £6

CHAPMAN, ABEL 1851-1929   The Borders and Beyond. 1924. 8vo., cloth, plates. Wheldon 129-256 1974 £5

CHAPMAN, ABEL 1851-1929   First Lessons in the Art of Wild Fowling. 1896. 8vo., orig. cloth, very scarce, only edition. Wheldon 131-564 1974 £12

CHAPMAN, ABEL 1851-1929   On Safari. 1908. 8vo., binders cloth, illus., very scarce, rebound. Wheldon 131-347 1974 £12

CHAPMAN, ABEL 1851-1929   On Safari. 1908. 8vo., orig. cloth, illus., scarce, first edition. Wheldon 130-276 1974 £22

CHAPMAN, ABEL 1851-1929   On Safari. 1908. 8vo., half green morocco, gilt, illus., scarce. Wheldon 128-189 1973 £22

CHAPMAN, ABEL 1851-1929   Unexplored Spain. 1910. Roy. 8vo., orig. cloth, first edition. Broadhurst 23-1623 1974 £16

CHAPMAN, ABEL 1851-1929   Unexplored Spain. 1910. Roy. 8vo., first edition, illus., orig. cloth, fine. Broadhurst 24-1590 1974 £16

CHAPMAN, ABEL 1851-1929   Unexplored Spain. 1910. Roy. 8vo., orig. cloth, illus. Wheldon 131-348 1974 £30

CHAPMAN, ABEL 1851-1929   Wild Norway. 1897. 8vo., half morocco, frontis., plates, text figures. Wheldon 128-190 1973 £12.50

CHAPMAN, ABEL 1851-1929   Wild Norway. 1897. 8vo., orig. cloth, illus., plates. Wheldon 131-346 1974 £18

CHAPMAN, ABEL 1851-1929   Wild Spain. 1893. Roy. 8vo., cloth, scarce, plates. Wheldon 130-277 1974 £30

CHAPMAN, E. J.   The Minerals and Geology of Central Canada. Toronto, 1888. Third edition. Hood's 103-354 1974 $12.50

CHAPMAN, F. M.   Camps and Cruises of an Ornithologist. 1908. 8vo., cloth, scarce. Wheldon 129-444 1974 £7.50

CHAPMAN, F. M.   The Distribution of Bird Life in Colombia. New York, 1917. 8vo., cloth, plates. Wheldon 130-485 1974 £20

CHAPMAN, F. M.   Life in an Air Castle. New York, 1938. 8vo., cloth, plates. Wheldon 129-258 1974 £5

CHAPMAN, F. M.   My Tropical Air Castle. New York, (1929). 8vo., cloth, illus. Wheldon 129-257 1974 £7.50

CHAPMAN, F. SPENCER   Lhasa: The Holy City. 1938. Med. 8vo., first edition, coloured and monochrome plates, orig. cloth, fine. Broadhurst 24-1592 1974 £5

CHAPMAN, GEORGE   Hints on the Education of the Lower Ranks of the People. Edinburgh, 1801. 8vo., wrappers, first edition. Ximenes 37-35 1974 $25

CHAPMAN, GEORGE   Works. 1875. 3 vols., ex-library. Allen 216-1890 1974 $20

CHAPMAN, HARVEY W.   An Index to the Old English Glosses of the Durham Hymnarium. 1905. Ex-library, sturdy library binding. Austin 61-197 1974 $27.50

CHAPMAN, J.   A Map of the County of Essex. 1777. Roy. folio, half calf, rebacked. Quaritch 939-350 1974 £265

CHAPMAN, JOHN JAY   Notes on Religion. Letters and Religion. New York, 1915 and Boston, 1924. 2 vols., 12mo., boards, cloth, first edition. Goodspeed's 578-53 1974 $25

CHAPMAN, R. W.   Cancels. London & New York, 1930. 8vo., orig. parchment-backed boards, plates, limited. Dawsons PM 10-122 1974 £32

CHAPMAN, R. W.   Cancels. London, 1930. 8vo., plates, orig. parchment backed boards, fine, limited. Dawsons PM 252-126 1974 £32

CHAPMAN, WILLIAM   Report on the Improvement of the Harbour of Arklow. Dublin, 1793. 8vo., disbound, first edition. Ximenes 37-36 1974 $45

CHAPONE, MRS. HESTER (MULSO) 1727-1801   Letters on the Improvement of the Mind, Addressed to a Young Lady. 1787. 2 vols., small 8vo., contemporary mottled calf, spines gilt, ex-libris copy, new edition. George's 610-146 1973 £7.50

CHAPONE, MRS. HESTER (MULSO) 1727-1801   Letters on the Improvement of the Mind Addressed to a Young Lady. 1809. 12mo., orig. ptd. boards, spine rubbed, good copy internally, woodcut frontis. George's 610-147 1973 £5

CHAPONE, MRS. HESTER (MULSO) 1727-1801   Letters on the Improvement of the Mind Addressed to a Young Lady. 1811. New edition, engraved frontis., 12mo., contemporary tree calf, joints cracked, occasional browning. George's 610-148 1973 £5

CHAPONE, MRS. HESTER (MULSO) 1727-1801   Letters on the Improvement of the Mind. 1822. 12mo., contemporary straight grained morocco, gilt spine, some foxing, engravings by Charles Rolls, leather label. Bow Windows 66-119 1974 £7.50

CHAPOT, VICTOR   The Roman World. New York, 1928. Plates. Biblo & Tannen 214-603 1974 $15

CHAPPELL, EDWARD   Narrative of a Voyage to Hudson's Bay In His Majesty's Ship Rosamond. London, 1817. 8vo., old calf, rebacked, leather label, foxed, plates. Traylen 79-469 1973 £68

CHAPPELL, EDWARD   Narrative of a Voyage to Hudson's Bay in His Majesty's Ship Rosamond. London, 1817. Orig. boards, rebacked cloth. Hood's 103-52 1974 $150

CHAPPELL, EDWARD   Voyage of His Majesty's Ship Tosamond to Newfoundland and the Southern Coast of Labrador. London, 1818. 8vo., old calf, rebacked, plates, foxing. Traylen 79-470 1973 £65

CHAPPELL, EDWIN 1883-   Eight Generations of the Pepys Family. London, 1936. 8vo., orig. cloth, faded, limited, first edition. Bow Windows 62-713 1974 £6.50

THE CHARACTER of Eusebius. Philadelphia, 1767. Modern half calf, two fore edges slightly cropped, little browned, else clean and sound. Thomas 32-7 1974 £18

CHARAS, M.   Nouvelles Experiences sur la Vipere. Paris, 1672. 8vo., contemporary calf, frontispiece, plates, rare, nice copy. Wheldon 128-623 1973 £45

CHARAS, M.   Nouvelles Experiences sur la Vipere. Paris, 1672. 8vo., contemporary calf, plates, rare. Wheldon 130-675 1974 £45

CHARCOT, JEAN   The Voyage of the "Why Not?" in the Antarctic. New York, n.d. Rittenhouse 46-134 1974 $15

CHARCOT, JEAN MARTIN   Expose des Titres du Docteur J.-M. Charcot. Paris, 1866. 4to., orig. pictured wrappers. Schuman 37-41 1974 $75

CHARCOT, JEAN MARTIN   Expose de Titres Scientifiques. Paris, 1872. Large 4to., orig. pictured wrappers. Schuman 37-42 1974 $125

CHARD, J. S. R.   British Animal Trucks. 1936. 8vo., cloth, scarce. Wheldon 130-388 1974 £5

CHARDIN, J. B. S.   Art et Artistes Francais, J. B. S. Chardin. 1932. 4to., plates, half morocco, rubbed, orig. pictorial wrapper. Quaritch 940-53 1974 £15

CHARENSOL, GEORGES   Georges Rouault. Paris, 1926. 4to., plates, wrappers, inscribed. Minters 37-125 1973 $35

CHARKE, CHARLOTTE   A Narrative of the Life Of. 1755. 12mo., eighteenth century half morocco, scarce. Hill 126-262 1974 £105

CHARLEMONT, JAMES CAULFIELD   Memoirs of the Political and Private Life of. 1810. 4to., half calf gilt, fine, first editon. Quaritch 939-614 1974 £20

CHARLES I, KING OF ENGLAND   Eikon Basilike. 1903. Folio, portrait, orig. buckram backed boards, limited, label, gilt. Howes 186-84 1974 £6.50

CHARLES I, KING OF ENGLAND   The Papers Which Passed at New-Castle Betwixt His Sacred Majestie and Mr. Al. Henderson, Concerning the Change of Church Government. London, 1649. Small 8vo., later leather, first edition. Traylen 79-372 1973 £15

CHARLES I, KING OF ENGLAND   The Workes Of. (1658). Thick small 8vo., 19th century half calf. Thomas 28-178 1972 £20

CHARLES II, KING OF ENGLAND   The Royal Charter of Confirmation Granted By. (1680). Small 8vo., old calf. Quaritch 939-444 1974 £40

CHARLES II, KING OF ENGLAND   The Royal Charter of Confirmation Granted by King Charless II, to the City of London. London, n.d. old sheep, browning. Smith 193-116 1973 £28

CHARLES III, KING OF SPAIN   Don Carlos, Por la Gracia de Dios, Rey de Castilla . . . Por Quanto desde el Reynado del Senor Phelipe Segundo hon Estado los Religiosos del Escorial en la Posesion de ser les Distribuidores de los Libros de Rezo. N.P., n.d. (Madrid, 1764). Folio, modern boards. Kraus B8-297 1974 $275

CHARLES V, EMPEROR   Romischer Kayserlicher Maiestat Regiment. (Mainz, 1521). Folio, boards, woodcuts, extremely rare. Harper 213-36 1973 $455

CHARLES V, EMPEROR   Statibus Ecclesiasticis. Mainz, (1548). Folio, boards, fine, woodcut. Harper 213-37 1973 $375

CHARLES, ROBERT   A Roundabout Turn. London and New York, 1930. 8vo., pict. cloth, gilt; 4 color plates; ltd. ed. to 65 copies, sgd. by illus. (L. Brooke). Frohnsdorff 16-123 1974 $50

CHARLES LENTZ AND SONS   Illustrated Catalogue and Price List of Surgical Instruments. Philadelphia, 1906. Seventh edition. Rittenhouse 46-698 1974 $10

CHARLES' Wain, A Miscellany of Short Stories. London, 1933. First edition, frontispiece, limited to 99 numbered copies on japon vellum, signed by each contributor, very fine, slipcase. Crane 7-4 1974 £40

CHARLETON, RICE   A Chymical Analysis of the Bath Waters. Bath, 1776. 8vo., boards, second edition. Hammond 201-561 1974 £12

CHARLETON, WALTER   Enquiries into Human Nature. London, 1680. 4to., contemporary calf, rebacked, first edition. Dawsons PM 249-110 1974 £95

CHARLEVOIX, PIERRE FRANCOIS XAVIER DE   Journal of a Voyage to North America. London, 1761. 2 vols., full leather, first English edition. Hood's 104-629 1974 $650

CHARLEVOIX, PIERRE FRANCOIS XAVIER DE   Journal of a Voyage to North America. London, 1761. First English edition, beautiful condition, full leather, large folding map, 2 vols. Hood's 102-554 1974 $650

CHARLEVOIX, PIERRE FRANCOIS XAVIER DE   Letters to the Duchess of Lesdiguieres. London, 1763. Colf, orig. boards, map, fine. Hood's 103-524 1974 $375

CHARLTON, LIONEL   The History of Whitby. York, 1779. 4to., rebound boards, uncut, plates. Broadhurst 23-1345 1974 £20

CHARLTON, LIONEL   The History of Whitby and Whitby Abbey. York, 1799. 4to., plates, modern boards. Quaritch 939-592 1974 £20

CHARLTON, R. M.   Charlton's General Street and Business Directory of West Toronto Junction, 1890-92. Toronto, 1890. Orig. hard card covers, mended, title faded from spine. Hood's 102-13 1974 $65

CHARPENTIER, J. DE   Essai Sur les Glaciers. 1841-43. 8vo., boards. Wheldon 130-931 1974 £110

CHARPENTIER, JOHN   Coleridge: The Sublime Somnambulist. 1929. Austin 61-199 1974 $10

CHARPENTIER, T. DE   Libellulinae Europaeae Descriptae ac Depictae. Leipzig, 1840. 4to., modern boards, uncut, hand coloured plates, rare. Wheldon 128-694 1973 £60

CHARPENTIER, T. DE   Libellulinae Europaeae Descriptae ac Depictae. Leipzig, 1840. 4to., modern boards, uncut, plates. Wheldon 130-729 1974 £60

CHARRIERES, MME DE   Caliste ou Suite des Lettres Ecrites de Lausonne. Geneva, 1788. 8vo., three quarter tan morocco, gilt, first edition. L. Goldschmidt 42-27 1974 $12.50

CHARRON, PIERRE   Toutes les Oeuvres. Paris, 1635. 5 parts in 1 vol., very thick 4to., contemporary calf, rubbed, fine, first collected edition. Harper 213-38 1973 $275

CHART, D. A.   The Drennan Letters. Belfast, 1931. 8vo., illus. Emerald 50-137 1974 £10

CHARTER For the City and County of San Francisco Proposed By the Board of Freeholders. San Francisco, 1883. Disbound. Bradley 35-331 1974 $24

CHARTER of the Delaware Rail Road Company. Dover, 1837. 8vo., orig. blue printed boards, map. Ximenes 35-5 1974 $30

CHARTERIS, FRANCIS   Some Authentick Memoirs of. London, 1730. 8vo., full calf, scarce, first edition. Dawsons PM 252-127 1974 £120

CHARTRES   Monographie de la Cathedrale de Chartres. (n.d.). 4to., plates, cloth bound, gilt. Bow Windows 62-166 1974 £6.50

CHASE, FRANCIS, JR.   Sound and Fury. Harper, 1942. 303p. Austin 51-183 1973 $10

CHASE, ILKA   Elephants Arrive at Half-Past Five. Doubleday, 1963. 269p. Austin 54-241 1973 $6.50

CHASE, ILKA   Free Admission. Doubleday, 1948. 319p. Austin 54-242 1973 $6.50

CHASE, ILKA   In Bed We Cry. Doubleday, Doran, 1943. 308p. Austin 54-243 1973 $6

CHASE, ILKA   I Love Miss Tilli Bean. Doubleday, 1946. 400p. Austin 54-244 1973 $6.50

CHASE, ILKA   The Island Players. Doubleday, 1956. 314p. Austin 54-245 1973 $6

CHASE, MARY   Mrs. McThing. Oxford Univ. Press, 1952. 126p., illus. Austin 51-184 1973 $10

CHASE, ROBERT H.   The Ungeared Mind. Philadelphia, 1919. Rittenhouse 46-137 1974 $10

CHASE, SAMUEL P.   Letter . . . On the Subject of Relations With Northwest British America. Washington, 1862. Folding map. Jenkins 61-488 1974 $12.50

CHASE County Historical Sketches. (Emporia), 1940. 8vo., cloth, 448 pages. Saddleback 14-424 1974 $17.50

CHASSEROT   Le Vicomte de Le-Plessy des Tours. Paris, 1840. 2 vols., 8vo., contemporary half polished calf, gilt. L. Goldschmidt 42-182 1974 $22.50

CHATEAUBRIAND, F. R.   Atala. Rene. Les Aventures du Dernier Abencerage. Paris, 1830. 8vo., contemporary tan polished calf, gilt, illus. L. Goldschmidt 42-183 1974 $45

CHATEAUBRIAND, F. R.   Memories d'Outre Tombe. Paris, 1849-50. 12 vols., 8vo., contemporary half hard grain morocco, first edition. L. Goldschmidt 42-184 1974 $150

CHATEAUBRIAND, F. R.   Reflexions Politiques sur Quelques Ecrits du Jour et sur les Interets de Tous les Francais. Paris, 1814. 8vo., orig. wrapper, uncut, first edition. L. Goldschmidt 42-185 1974 $37.50

CHATHAM, WILLIAM PITT, 1ST EARL OF, 1708-1778
Please turn to
PITT, WILLIAM, 1ST EARL OF CHATHAM, 1708-1778

CHATIN, A.   La Truffe. 1892. 8vo., plates, half morocco, scarce. Wheldon 129-1164 1974 £5

CHATTERTON, EDWARD KEBLE   Captain John Smith. New York, 1927. First edition, orig. binding. Wilson 63-344 1974 $12.75

CHATTERTON, EDWARD KEBLE   Old Sea Paintings. 1928. 4to., orig. cloth, spine faded, coloured and black and white illus. Bow Windows 66-120 1974 £48

CHATTERTON, EDWARD KEBLE   Old Ship Prints. 1927. 4to., orig. cloth, plates. Broadhurst 23-48 1974 £30

CHATTERTON, EDWARD KEBLE   Old Ship Prints. 1927. Demy 4to., very good copy, plates, orig. cloth. Broadhurst 24-42 1974 £30

CHATTERTON, EDWARD KEBLE   Old Ship Prints. 1927. 4to., orig. cloth gilt, illus., plates, first edition. Howes 186-1702 1974 £28

CHATTERTON, THOMAS   Miscellanies in Prose and Verse. London, 1778. 8vo., half calf, first edition. Dawsons PM 252-128 1974 £70

CHATTERTON, THOMAS   Poems. London, 1777. 8vo., modern dark red half calf, faded, plate, first edition. Dawsons PM 252-129 1974 £70

CHATTERTON, THOMAS   Poems. London, 1782. Marbled boards, re-backed, calf. Dawson's 424-191 1974 $75

CHATTERTON, THOMAS   Poems, Supposed to Have Been Written at Bristol, by Thomas Rowley and Others in the 15th Century. Cambridge, 1794. Large paper edition, bookplate, very good, half calf, marbled boards, first edition. Covent 51-2246 1973 $47.50

CHATTERTON, THOMAS   Poems, Supposed to Have Been Written at Bristol, by Thomas Rowley, and Others, in the 15th Century. Cambridge, 1794. 8vo., later half calf, spine gilt, engraved title-page, very good copy, first edition. Ximenes 37-38 1974 $60

CHATTO, WILLIAM ANDREW   Facts and Speculations on the Origin and History of Playing Cards. London, 1848. Blue binder's cloth, red label, 8vo. Gregory 44-240 1974 $37.50

CHATTO, WILLIAM ANDREW   Facts and Speculations on the Origin and History of Playing Cards. London, 1848. 8vo., orig. cloth, plates, first edition. Hammond 201-87 1974 £28

CHAUCER, GEOFFREY   The Canterbury Tales of. London, 1741. 3 vols., 8vo., contemporary sprinkled calf, first edition. Dawsons PM 252-131 1974 £120

CHAUCER, GEOFFREY   The Canterbury Tales. New York, 1904. 4to., 6 color plates. Frohnsdorff 16-202 1974 $12.50

CHAUCER, GEOFFREY   The Canterbury Tales. 1913. 4to., full limp vellum, uncut, d.w., 3 vols. Broadhurst 23-72 1974 £130

CHAUCER, GEOFFREY   The Canterbury Tales of . . . Together With a Version in Modern English Verse. New York, 1930. 2 vols., folio, orig. cloth, one of 999 numbered copies, signed by the artist, fine. MacManus 224-74 1974 $135

CHAUCER, GEOFFREY   The Minor Poems. Oxford, 1896. Biblo & Tannen 210-839 1973 $7.50

CHAUCER, GEOFFREY   Modern Reader's Chaucer. 1912. 4to., coloured plates by Warwick Goble. Allen 216-2221 1974 $15

CHAUCER, GEOFFREY   Workes. 1542. Folio, brown crushed levant morocco, raised bands, woodcuts. Thomas 28-234 1972 £300

CHAUCER, GEOFFREY   The Workes . . . With Dyvers Workes Whiche Were Never in Print Before. (c. 1545). Third collected edition, black letter, upper and fore margins of title defective and repaired, some stains, sound reasonable copy, folio, contemporary calf, rebacked, rubbed. Thomas 32-164 1974 £1,050

CHAUCER, GEOFFREY   The Workes of. London, 1687. Folio, fine, contemporary blind stamped calf, eighth edition. Dawsons PM 252-132 1974 £150

CHAUCER, GEOFFREY   Works. 1721. Large folio, contemporary calf, rebacked, illus. Quaritch 936-29 1974 £70

CHAUCER, GEOFFREY   The Works of. Hammersmith, 1896. Folio, illus., orig. holland-backed boards. Dawsons PM 252-1095 1974 £4200

CHAUCER, GEOFFREY   Complete Works. 1899. Vols. 1-6 only, ex-library, second edition. Allen 216-1776 1974 $30

CHAUCER, GEOFFREY   Complete Poetical Works. New York, 1912. Roy 8vo., half blue morocco, gilt, plates. Quaritch 936-336 1974 £20

CHAUCER, GEOFFREY   The Works. Oxford, 1928. 8 vols., small folio, illus., orig. boards, fine, uncut. Dawsons PM 252-133 1974 £280

CHAUCER, GEOFFREY   The Works Of. 1928-29. Small folio, 8 vols., orig. holland backed boards. Bow Windows 64-681 1974 £300

CHAUNCY, HENRY   The Historical Antiquities of Hertfordshire. 1700. Folio, full russia, plates, first edition. Howes 186-2014 1974 £120

CHAUNDY, LESLIE   A Bibliography of the First Editions of the Works of R. B. Cunninghame. 1924. Fine, wrappers, English first edition. Covent 56-289 1974 £7.50

CHAUSSIER, FRANCOIS   Exposition Sommaire de la Structure. Paris, 1807. 8vo., old boards, torn, plates. Gurney 64-50 1974 £35

CHAUVET, JACQUES   Methodiques Institutions de la Vraye et Parfaicte Arithmetique. 1645. 8vo., contemporary yapped vellum. Dawsons PM 245-169 1974 £70

CHAUVIN, ESTIENNE   Lexicon Rationale, Sive Thesaurus Philosophicus Ordine Alphabeticus Digestus. Rotterdam, 1692. Folio, contemporary vellum, first edition, folding engraved plates, Prince Liechtenstein's copy. Kraus 137-20 1974 $150

CHAVANNES, HERMINIE DE   Albert de Haller . . . . Biographie. Lausanne, 1840. 8vo., quarter morocco, rubbed, first edition. Schuman 37-119 1974 $65

CHAYEFSKY, PADDY   The Goddess. S & S, 1957. 167p. Austin 51-185 1973 $10

CHAYEFSKY, PADDY   The Tenth Man. Random House, 1960. 154p., illus. Austin 51-186 1973 $7.50

CHEATLE, G. LENTHAL   Tumours of the Breast. Philadelphia, n.d. Stained cover. Rittenhouse 46-138 1974 $15

CHEDWORTH, JOHN   Notes Upon Some of the Obscure Passages in Shakespeare's Plays. 1805. Orig. boards, printed label, spine defective, nice copy, first edition. Covent 51-1663 1973 £18.90

CHEESEMAN, T. F.   Manual of the New Zealand Flora. Wellington, 1925. Rubbed, pencillings, second edition. Bow Windows 64-52 1974 £40

CHEESEMAN, T. F.   Manual of the New Zealand Zora. Wellington, 1925. Roy 8vo., cloth, scarce, second edition. Wheldon 129-1056 1974 £30

CHEESMAN, R. E.   Lake Tana and the Blue Nile. 1936. 8vo., cloth, illus., maps, scarce. Wheldon 128-191 1973 £7.50

CHEETHAM, F. H.   Cartmel Fell Chapel. Manchester, 1912. 8vo., quarter morocco. Broadhurst 23-1346 1974 £8

CHEETHAM, JAMES   An Answer to Alexander Hamilton's Letter. 1800. Disbound. Dawson's 424-192 1974 $30

CHEEVER, JOHN   The Way Some People Live. New York, 1943. 1st ed. Biblo & Tannen 210-708 1973 $10

THE CHELSEA Historical Pageant. Chelsea, 1908. Crown 4to., contemporary half vellum gilt, morocco label, presentation. Howes 186-2101 1974 £7.50

CHELUCCI, PAOLINO   Institutiones Arithmeticae. Rome, 1743. 8vo., contemporary vellum, fine, first edition. Dawsons PM 245-170 1974 £12

CHENAYE-DES-BOIS, A. A. DE LA   Systeme Naturel du Regne Animal. Paris, 1754. 2 vols., 8vo., portraits, contemporary calf. Wheldon 128-261 1973 £50

CHENAYE-DES-BOIS, A. A. DE LA   Systeme Naturel du Regne Animal. Paris, 1754. 2 vols., 8vo., contemporary calf. Wheldon 131-420 1974 £50

CHENEY, EDNA DOW   Reminiscences of. Boston, 1902. Illus. Jenkins 61-489 1974 $10

CHENEY, O. H.   Economic Survey of the Book Industry, 1930-31. 1931. Allen 216-173 1974 $10

CHENEY, SHELDON   Expressionism in Art. New York, 1934. Illus., rubbed, first American edition. Covent 55-88 1974 £12.50

CHENEY, SHELDON   The New Movement in the Theatre. Kennerley, 1914. 309p., illus., orig. ed. Austin 51-187 1973 $10

CHENEY, SHELDON   A World History of Art. New York, 1943. Biblo & Tannen 214-71 1974 $8.50

CHENIER, MARIS JOSEPH   Epitre a Voltaire. Paris, 1806. 8vo., three quarter red morocco, gilt, uncut, first edition. L. Goldschmidt 42-186 1974 $15

CHENU, J. C.   Encyclopedie d'histoire Naturelle Papillons. Paris, (1874). Imperial 8vo., half calf. Wheldon 129-620 1974 £7.50

CHENU, J. C.   Manuel de Conchydiologie et de Palaeontologie Conchyliologique. Paris, 1859-62. 2 vols. in 1, roy. 8vo., half morocco. Wheldon 128-835 1973 £30

CHERBURY, EDWARD HERBERT, BARON HERBERT OF
Please turn to
HERBERT, EDWARD HERBERT, BARON

CHERRY, ANDREW   The Travellers. London, 1806. 8vo., modern boards, second edition. Dawsons PM 252-134 1974 £8

CHERRY-GARRARD, APSLEY
Please turn to
GARRARD, APSLEY CHERRY

CHERVILLE, GASPARD GEORGES   Les Oiseaux de Chasse. Paris, n.d. Small 4to., orig. wrappers, neatly rebacked, portrait, coloured plates, fourth edition. Wheldon 128-413 1973 £7.50

CHESAPEAKE & OHIO CANAL CO.   Fifteenth Annual Report of the President and Directors of . . . June, 5, 1843. Baltimore, 1843. Printed wrappers. Hayman 59-101 1974 $10

CHESELDEN, WILLIAM   The Anatomy of the Human Body. Boston, 1795. Half calf, boards, first American edition. Dawson's 424-88 1974 $100

CHESELDEN, WILLIAM   Osteographia. London, (1733). Plates, rebound handsomely. Rittenhouse 46-139 1974 $225

CHESHIRE HOUSE   The Vigil of Venus as rendered into English Rhyme by Joseph Auslander. New York, 1931. 4to., ltd. to 895 copies. Biblo & Tannen 210-709 1973 $17.50

CHESNEY, LIEUT. COL.   The Military Resources of Prussia and France and Recent Changes in the Art of War. 1870. 8vo., orig. cloth, some dust marks, covers soiled and rubbed. Bow Windows 66-122 1974 £7.50

CHESTER, GEORGE RANDOLPH   Wallingford and Blackie Daw. Indianapolis, 1913. 8vo., orig. cloth, fine, first edition. Rota 190-215 1974 £8

CHESTER, GEORGE RANDOLPH   Wallingford in His Prime. Indianapolis, 1913. 8vo., orig. cloth, first edition. Rota 190-214 1974 £8

CHESTER, GEORGE RANDOLPH   Young Wallingford. 1910. 8vo., orig. blue cloth, illus., fine, first edition. Rota 190-213 1974 £10

CHESTER An Act. 1772. Crown 8vo., binder's cloth. Broadhurst 23-1348 1974 £16

CHESTERFIELD, PHILIP DORMER STANHOPE   The Case of the Hanover Forces. London, 1743. 8vo., modern quarter calf, gilt, first edition. Dawsons PM 247-277 1974 £18

CHESTERFIELD, PHILIP DORMER STANHOPE   A Farther Vindication of the Case of the Hanover Troops. London, 1743. 8vo., modern quarter calf, first edition. Dawsons PM 247-278 1974 £18

CHESTERFIELD, PHILIP DORMER STANHOPE   The Fine Gentleman's Etiquette. London, 1776. 4to., disbound, engraved vignette, very good copy, first edition. Ximenes 37-176 1974 $75

CHESTERFIELD, PHILIP DORMER STANHOPE   Letters. Dublin, 1774. 2 vols., 8vo., full calf, first Dublin edition. Emerald 50-244 1974 £40

CHESTERFIELD, PHILIP DORMER STANHOPE   Letters to Several Celebrated Individuals of the Time of Charles II. 1829. Contemporary half calf, portrait. Howes 186-706 1974 £7.50

CHESTERFIELD, PHILIP DORMER STANHOPE   The Letters of. 1845. 4 vols., boards, rebacked, English first edition. Covent 56-226a 1974 £15

CHESTERFIELD, PHILIP DORMER STANHOPE   Letters. 1926. 3 vols. Allen 216-1992 1974 $12.50

CHESTERFIELD, PHILIP DORMER STANHOPE   Letters to His Son. London, 1776. 4 vols., 8vo., full tree calf, gilt, foxing, fine. Ballinger 1-244 1974 $50

CHESTERTON, ARTHUR KENNETH   Adventures in Dramatic Appreciation. n.d. Austin 61-200 1974 $12.50

CHESTERTON, GILBERT KEITH   Appreciations and Criticisms of the Works of Charles Dickens. 1911. 8vo., orig. cloth, portraits, first edition. Bow Windows 64-480 1974 £7.50

CHESTERTON, GILBERT KEITH   Autobiography. 1936. 360 pages. Austin 61-204 1974 $10

CHESTERTON, GILBERT KEITH   The Ball and the Cross. Orig. edition. Austin 61-205 1974 $10

CHESTERTON, GILBERT KEITH   The Ballad of St. Barbara and Other Verses. 1922. 8vo., orig. linen backed boards, first edition. Bow Windows 64-443 1974 £6

CHESTERTON, GILBERT KEITH   The Ballad of the White Horse. London, (1911). 8vo., orig. cloth, uncut, foxed, first edition. Bow Windows 62-170 1974 £6.50

CHESTERTON, GILBERT KEITH   The Ballad of the White Horse. New York, 1911. First American edition, orig. binding. Wilson 63-499 1974 $10

CHESTERTON, GILBERT KEITH   The Ballad of the White Horse. 1928. Cloth gilt, foxing, bookplate, first illus. edition. Covent 56-1615 1974 £6

CHESTERTON, GILBERT KEITH   The Book of Job. 1907. Orig. boards, English first edition. Covent 56-1616 1974 £5.25

CHESTERTON, GILBERT KEITH   The Book of Job. (1916). 4to., orig. parchment backed cloth boards, plates, first edition. Bow Windows 64-444 1974 £10

CHESTERTON, GILBERT KEITH   Charles Dickens: A Critical Study. 1906. Orig. hard cover edition. Austin 61-206 1974 $10

CHESTERTON, GILBERT KEITH   The Church and Agorophobia. Liverpool, 1933. Covent 55-381 1974 £5.50

CHESTERTON, GILBERT KEITH   The Club of Queer Trades. New York, 1905. First American edition. Biblo & Tannen 210-431 1973 $15

CHESTERTON, GILBERT KEITH   The Coloured Lands. New York, 1938. 4to., cloth, illus., first edition. Frohnsdorff 16-203 1974 $7.50

CHESTERTON, GILBERT KEITH   The Coloured Lands. 1938. 4to., illus., orig. buckram backed boards. Smith 194-408 1974 £5.50

CHESTERTON, GILBERT KEITH   The Crimes of England. London, 1915. 126 pages. Austin 61-208 1974 $12.50

CHESTERTON, GILBERT KEITH   The Defendant. 1901. Buckram, faded. Covent 55-382 1974 £10

CHESTERTON, GILBERT KEITH   The Defendant. 1901. 8vo., orig. cloth, scarce, first edition. Rota 190-101 1974 £10

CHESTERTON, GILBERT KEITH   The End of the Armistice. 1940. Dust wrapper, fine, first American edition. Covent 55-383 1974 £5.25

CHESTERTON, GILBERT KEITH   Five Types. London, 1910. First edition, mint, orig. box & wrappers. Ross 87-107 1974 $15

CHESTERTON, GILBERT KEITH   Five Types: A Book of Essays. 1910. First edition. Austin 61-210 1974 $12.50

CHESTERTON, GILBERT KEITH   The Flying Inn. New York, 1914. Biblo & Tannen 210-432 1973 $10

CHESTERTON, GILBERT KEITH   George Bernard Shaw. New York, 1910. Orig. binding, unusually bright copy, lacking d.w. Ross 87-108 1974 $15

CHESTERTON, GILBERT KEITH   Gloria in Profundis. (1927). Slim crown 8vo., orig. wrappers, wood engravings. Smith 193-330 1973 £5

CHESTERTON, GILBERT KEITH   The Grave of Arthur. 1930. Boards, signed, bookplate, English first edition. Covent 56-1617 1974 £8.50

CHESTERTON, GILBERT KEITH   Ian Hamilton's March. 1900. Illus., maps, plans, nice copy, first edition. Covent 51-2256 1973 £45

CHESTERTON, GILBERT KEITH   The Incredulity of Father Brown. New York, 1926. Fine, first American edition. Covent 55-385 1974 £5

CHESTERTON, GILBERT KEITH   Irish Impressions. 1919. 222 pages. Austin 61-213 1974 $10

CHESTERTON, GILBERT KEITH   Magic: A Fantastic Comedy. 1913. 88 pages. Austin 61-214 1974 $12.50

CHESTERTON, GILBERT KEITH   The Man Who Knew Too Much, and Other Stories. 1922. Orig. brown cloth, nice copy, unrecorded variant binding, first edition, very scarce. Covent 51-2250 1973 £10

CHESTERTON, GILBERT KEITH   Manalive. 1912. 8vo., blue cloth, fine, first edition. Rota 190-103 1974 £6

CHESTERTON, GILBERT KEITH   Manalive. New York, 1912. Biblo & Tannen 210-433 1973 $8.50

CHESTERTON, GILBERT KEITH   Masters of Literature. London, 1909. First edition. Austin 61-216 1974 $12.50

CHESTERTON, GILBERT KEITH   My African Journey. 1908. Photos, maps, inscribed, nice copy, orig. pictorial cloth, first edition. Covent 51-2257 1973 £45

CHESTERTON, GILBERT KEITH   The Napoleon of Notting Hill. 1904. Plates, orig. dec. linen, covers loose & little dusty, bookplate, signed, first edition. Covent 51-2251 1973 £7.50

CHESTERTON, GILBERT KEITH   The Return of Don-Quixote. 1927. 302 pages. Austin 61-220 1974 $12.50

CHESTERTON, GILBERT KEITH   The Return of Don Quixote. London, 1927. Orig. binding, first edition, slightly torn d.w., else near mint. Ross 87-111 1974 $15

CHESTERTON, GILBERT KEITH   The Scandal of Father Brown. 1935. Fine, d.w., newspaper clippings tipped in, first edition. Covent 51-390 1973 £6.50

CHESTERTON, GILBERT KEITH   Sidelights On New London and Newer York. 1932. Ex-library. Austin 61-222 1974 $10

CHESTERTON, GILBERT KEITH   Sidelights on New London and Newer York and Other Essays. New York, 1932. Biblo & Tannen 210-844 1973 $6.50

CHESTERTON, GILBERT KEITH   Step by Step. 1939. Maps, very good copy, first edition. Covent 51-2258 1973 £15

CHESTERTON, GILBERT KEITH   The Story of the Malakand Field Force.   1901.
Frontis., portrait, maps, plans, author's signature pasted on title page, good
copy, Colonial Library green & black dec. cloth, first edition.   Covent 51-2259
1973 £55

CHESTERTON, GILBERT KEITH   The Superstition of Divorce.   1920.   First
American edition.   Austin 61-223 1974 $12.50

CHESTERTON, GILBERT KEITH   The Supersitions of the Critic.   Cambridge,
1925.   Wrappers, scarce.   Covent 55-386 1974 £7.50

CHESTERTON, GILBERT KEITH   The Sword of Wood.   1928.   Dec. boards, fine,
signed, English first edition.   Covent 56-1618 1974 £21

CHESTERTON, GILBERT KEITH   Tales of the Long Bow.   New York, 1925.
Biblo & Tannen 210-434 1973 $10

CHESTERTON, GILBERT KEITH   Tremendous Trifles.   1909.   325 pages.
Austin 61-225 1974 $10

CHESTERTON, GILBERT KEITH   Tremendous Trifles.   New York, 1909.   Biblo
& Tannen 210-710 1973 $7.50

CHESTERTON, GILBERT KEITH   Utopia of Usurers.   New York, 1917.   Biblo &
Tannen 214-678 1974 $7.50

CHESTERTON, GILBERT KEITH   The Wisdom of Father Brown.   1914.   8vo.,
orig. cloth, first edition.   Rota 190-216 1974 £8

CHETHAM SOCIETY   Remains Historical and Literary, Connected
With the Palatine Counties of Lancaster and Chester.   Manchester, 1845.
Rittenhouse 46-140 1974 $25

CHETWIND, CHARLES   A Narrative of the Depositions of Robert Jeni-
son.   London, 1679.   Folio, disbound, first edition.   Dawsons PM 251-188
1974 £10

CHEVALIER, MAURICE   With Love.   Little, Brown, 1960.   424p.,
illus.   Austin 51-188 1973 $7.50

CHEVALIER, MICHEL   On the Probable Fall in the Value of Gold.
London, 1859.   8vo., orig. blind-stamped cloth, uncut, second English edition.
Dawsons PM 247-44 1974 £15

CHEVALLIER, JEAN GABRIEL AUGUSTIN   Le Conservateur de la Vue.   Paris,
1810.   8vo., orig. wrappers, uncut, plates.   Gurney 64-51 1974 £20

CHEVALLIER, JEAN GABRIEL AUGUSTIN   Le Conservateur De La Vue.   1815.
Thick 8vo., contemporary green boards, worn, third edition.   Zeitlin 235-43
1974 $125

CHEVE, C. F.   Dictionnaire des Apologistes Involontaires.
Paris, 1853.   2 vols., roy. 8vo., orig. leather.   Howes 185-1062 1974 £5.50

CHEVE, C. F.   Dictionnaire des Papes.   Paris, 1857.   Thick
roy. 8vo., half buckram, foxing.   Howes 185-1064 1974 £5

CHEVEY, P.   Iconographie Ichthyologique de l'Indochine.
Saigon, 1932.   4to., buckram, plates, scarce.   Wheldon 130-676 1974 £40

CHEVREAU, URBAIN   La Tableau de la Fortune.   Paris, 1651.
Small 12mo., half sheep.   L. Goldschmidt 42-28 1974 $20

CHEVREUL, MICHEL EUGENE   The Laws of Contrast of Colour.   Routledge,
1868.   Small 8vo., orig. cloth, gilt, plates.   Hill 126-49 1974 £16

CHEVREUL, MICHEL EUGENE   The Laws of Contrast of Colour and Their
Application to the Arts.   1858.   Small 8vo., plates, cloth, scarce.   Quaritch
940-54 1974 £15

CHEVRIER, FRANCOIS ANTOINE   Le Colporteur.   London, n.d. 12mo.,
silk brocade, leather label, gilt.   L. Goldschmidt 42-29 1974 $25

CHEVROLAT, A.   Coleopteres de l'Ile de Cuba.   1862-70.
8 parts in 1 vol., 8vo., wrappers.   Wheldon 128-695 1973 £5

CHEYNE, GEORGE   An Essay On Regimen.   1740.   Contemporary
calf gilt, rubbed.   Smith 193-332 1973 £20

CHEYNE, GEORGE   The Natural Method of Cureing the Diseases of
the Body, and the Disorders of the Mind Depending On the Body.   London, 1742.
8vo., contemporary calf, rubbed, first edition.   Schuman 37-43 1974 $145

CHEYNE, T. K.   Encyclopaedia Biblica.   1899.   4 vols., thick
roy. 8vo.   Howes 185-1065 1974 £6.50

CHEYNE, W. W.   Lister and His Achievement.   1925.   Portriat
frontispiece.   Covent 55-1090 1974 £6.50

CHIARI, G.   Statue di Firenze.   Florence, c. 1800.
3 parts in 1 vol., 8vo., plates, contemporary half calf, dust soiled, scarce.
Quaritch 940-55 1974 £75

CHICAGO   Two Years After the Fire.   Chicago, 1873.
Plates, folio, pictorial wrapper, illus. ads, remarkably good condition.   Butterfield
10-144 1974 $100

THE CHICAGO Record's Book for Gold Seekers.   Cloth, rubbed, variant without
illus. on title-page, with imprint of "Imperial Publishing Co. . . . . Philadelphia".
Hayman 59-5 1974 $10

THE CHICAGO Record's Book for Gold Seekers.   (Chicago, 1897).   Cloth,
with ads, covers somewhat worn.   Hayman 59-4 1974 $10

CHICAGO Und Sein Deutschthum.   Cleveland, Ohio, 1901.   512p., illus.
Austin 62-195 1974 $47.50

CHICHORIUS, C.   Untersuchungen zu Lucilius.   1908.   Buckram.
Allen 213-653 1973 $10

CHICKEN Little.   Chicago, 1919.   12mo., illus., cloth.   Frohnsdorff 16-204
1974 $7.50

CHIDLAW, B. W.   The Story of My Life.   Philadelphia, (1890).
Cloth.   Hayman 57-374 1974 $10

CHILD, C. M.   Physiological Foundations of Behaviour.   New
York, 1924.   8vo., cloth.   Wheldon 129-325 1974 £7.50

CHILD, HAMILTON   Gazetteer and Business Directory of Rutland
County, Vermont.   Syracuse, 1881.   8vo., cloth, map.   Saddleback 14-734
1974 $20

CHILD, IRVIN L.   Italian or American.   1943.   Orig. edition.
Austin 57-125 1974 $10

CHILD, L. MARIA   Letters from New York.   New York & Boston,
1844.   Second edition, backstrip chipped, orig. binding.   Butterfield 10-99
1974 $10

CHILD, PHILIP   Day of Wrath.   Toronto, 1945.   First edition.
Hood's 102-493 1974 $12.50

CHILD, STEPHEN   Landscape Architecture.   Stanford, 1927.   First
edition, 4to., illus., plans, some folding.   Wilson 63-313 1974 $10

THE CHILD'S Life of Christ.   New York, Paris, London, 1887.   First edition,
orig. illus., 4to., very good, fresh gilt edges.   Current BW9-10 1974 $15

CHILDE, CROMWELL   Trolley Exploring, the Pioneer Electric Railway
Guide.   Brooklyn, (1913).   16mo., printed wrapper, maps, photos, fine,
nineteenth edition.   Butterfield 10-513 1974 $15

CHILDE, WILFRED ROWLAND   Dream English: A Fantastical Romance.   1917.
106 pages.   Austin 61-233 1974 $12.50

CHILDREN as They Are; or, Tales and Dialogues.   1830.   Plates, half calf, spine
gilt, trifle rubbed, goo copy.   George's 610-154 1973 £6

THE CHILDREN in the Wood.   Cooperstown, 1839.   18mo., pictorial wrapper,
quaint woodcuts, nice copy.   Butterfield 10-145 1974 $25

THE CHILDREN in the Wood.   Cooperstown, 1844.   Little chipped, added
stitching on spine.   Butterfield 10-146 1974 $15

THE CHILDREN In the Wood Restored.   (c. 1835).   Orig. printed wrappers.
Gregory 44-36 1974 $14.50

THE CHILDREN's Art Book. n.d. 4to., cloth-backed pictorial boards, plates, fine, English first edition. Covent 56-1622 1974 £12.50

CHILDREN'S Friend. London, 1886. Sm. 4to., cloth, illus. Frohnsdorff 16-205 1974 $15

CHILDREN'S Library. (Boston, 1838). 12mo., orig. blue printed wrappers, very good copy, woodcut. Ximenes 36-139 1974 $40

CHILDS, FRANCIS SERGEANT   French Refugee Life in the United States. 1940. 229p., illus. Austin 62-91 1974 $27.50

CHILDS, GEORGE W.   Recollections of General Grant. Philadelphia, 1890. Printed wrappers, scarce. Hayman 57-80 1974 $10

THE CHILD'S Cabinet of Stories. Troy, ca. 1851. 16mo., orig. pictorial boards, cloth spine; 54 fine woodcuts. Frohnsdorff 16-206 1974 $15

THE CHILD'S Delight. Philadelphia, 1845. 16mo., pict. boards, cloth spine, 6 hand-colored plates. Frohnsdorff 16-207 1974 $15

THE CHILD'S Magazine. London, 1836. Orig. boards, roan spine (worn), engravings. Frohnsdorff 16-208 1974 $20

THE CHILD'S Primer. York, n.d. 16mo., woodcuts. Frohnsdorff 16-209 1974 $20

CHILLINGWORTH, WILLIAM   The Works. 1838. 3 vols., large 8vo., full contemporary calf, gilt, best edition. Howes 185-1066 1974 £18

CHINESE DRAWINGS on Rice-Paper. (Canton, c., 1820). Roy 8vo., orig. binding. Hammond 201-153 1974 £30

CHINESE EXHIBITION   A Commemorative Catalogue of the International Exhibition of Chinese Art, Royal Academy of Arts, November 1935 – March 1936. 1936. 4to., frontispiece, plates, cloth. Quaritch 940-381 1974 £28

CHINIQUY, CHARLES PASCHAL TELESPHORE 1809-1899   Fifty Years in the Church of Rome. 1886. Illus., orig. edition. Austin 57-127 1974 $12.50

CHINQUY, CHARLES PASCHAL TELESPHORE 1809-1899   The Priest, The Women and the Confessional. London, n.d. Austin 57-128 1974 $12.50

CHIOVENDA, E.   Angiospermae. Rome, 1939. Roy 8vo., illus., sewed. Wheldon 130-1135 1974 £5

CHIPPENDALE, THOMAS   The Gentleman and Cabinet-Maker's Director. 1894. Folio, half mottled calf. Marsden 37-123 1974 £25

CHIPPENDALE, THOMAS   The Gentlemen and Cabinet Maker's Director. New York, 1938. Large folio, illus. Ballinger 1-245 1974 $30

CHIPPENDALE, THOMAS   Ornaments and Interior Decorations in the Old French Style. (c. 1850). Folio, plates, binders' cloth, large paper. Quaritch 940-575 1974 £18

CHIRICO, GIORGIO DE   Hebdomeros. Paris, 1929. 8vo., wrappers, first edition. Minters 37-386 1973 $65

CHISENHALL, EDWARD   A Journal of the Siege of Lathom House. 1823. Crown 8vo., morocco. Broadhurst 23-1352 1974 £10

CHISENHALL, EDWARD   A Journal of the Siege of Lathom House. 1823. Orig. boards, paper printed label. Broadhurst 23-1353 1974 £6

CHISHOLM, BELLE V.   Stephen Lyle. Cincinnati, 1891. Cloth. Hayman 57-179 1974 $12.50

CHISLETT, R.   Northward Ho. 1933. Roy 8vo., cloth, map, photographs. Wheldon 129-446 1974 £5

CHISLETT, R.   Northward Ho! 1933. Roy. 8vo., cloth. Wheldon 131-565 1974 £10

CHITTENDEN, HIRAM M.   The American Fur Trade of the Far West. New York, 1935. 2 vols., illus., cloth. Bradley 35-142 1974 $85

CHIZHOVA, A.   "Beryozka" Dance Company. USSR, n.d. Biblo & Tannen 213-876 1973 $12.50

CHLADNI, ERNST FLORENS FRIEDRICH   Die Akustik. Leipzig, 1802. 4to., half calf, boards, gilt, plates, first edition. Dawsons PM 245-171 1974 £300

CHLADNI, ERNST FLORENS FRIEDRICH   Beytrage zur Praktischen Akustik. Leipzig, 1821. 8vo., contemporary mottled boards, gilt, plates, first edition. Dawsons PM 245-172 1974 £75

CHLADNI, ERNST FLORENS FRIEDRICH   Neue Beytrage zur Akustik. Leipzig, 1817. 4to., contemporary marbled boards, rebacked, plates, first edition. Dawsons PM 245-173 1974 £175

CHOATE, RUFUS   Speech of . . . On the Question of Annulling the Convention for the Common Occupation of Oregon. Washington, 1844. Uncut, inscribed & signed by Choate. Jenkins 61-2056 1974 $12.50

CHODZKO, A.   Legendes Slaves du Moyen Age, 1169-1237. 1858. 4to., new buckram. Allen 213-1379 1973 $15

CHOISEUL-GOUFFIER, GABRIEL AUGUSTE FLORENT COMTE DE 1752-1817 Voyage Pittoresque de la Grece. 1824. Folio, English mid 19th century red morocco, gilt. Marlborough 70-26 1974 £480

CHOIX de Farces, Soties & Moralites des XVe et SVIe Siecles, Recueillies sur les Manuscrits Originaux et Publies par Emile Mabille. Nice, 1872-73. 2 vols., 16mo., contemporary straight grain royal blue morocco, limited edition. L. Goldschmidt 42-31 1974 $290

CHOLDWIG OF HOHENLOHE-SCHILLINGSFUERST, PRINCE   Memoirs of. New York, 1906. 2 vols., orig. binding, top edges gilt, illus. Wilson 63-592 1974 $10

CHOQUET, DR.   Hygiene Professionnelle: Le Compositeur Typographe. Paris, 1882. 8vo., wrappers. Kraus B8-298 1974 $25

CHORLEY, HENRY FOTHERGILL   The Lion. 1839. 12mo., 3 vols., contemporary calf, gilt, first edition. Hill 126-190 1974 £35

CHORLEY, HENRY FOTHERGILL   Modern German Music. 1854. Crown 8vo., full calf, 2 vols., first edition. Broadhurst 23-50 1974 £6

CHORLEY, HENRY FOTHERGILL   Thirty Years' Musical Recollections. 1862. 8vo., 2 vols., orig. orange cloth, frontis. Hill 126-177 1974 £32

CHORON, FREDERIC   Theorie des Atomes et des Equivalents. Paris, 1839. 8vo., old boards. Gurney 64-52 1974 £15

CHOULES, JOHN OVERTON   The Cruise of the Steam Yacht North Star. Boston, 1854. Biblo & Tannen 213-660 1973 $15

CHOUX, P.   Les Didiereacees, Xerophytes de Madagascar. 1934. 4to., wrappers, plates. Wheldon 131-1655 1974 £5

CHOUX, P.   Thesis; Etudes Biologiques sur les Asclepiadacees de Madagascar. Marseilles, 1914. Plates. Wheldon 131-1127 1974 £7.50

CHRESTIEN, JEAN ANDRE   De la Methode Iatraleptique. Paris, 1811. 8vo., contemporary calf, rubbed, first edition. Schuman 37-44 1974 $95

CHRIST, HERMANN 1833-   La Flore de la Suisse. Basel, 1883. 8vo., cloth, plates, coloured maps. Wheldon 128-1248 1973 £6

CHRIST, HERMANN 1833-   La Flore de la Suisse, et ses Origines. Basel, 1883. 8vo., cloth, plates. Wheldon 131-1271 1974 £10

CHRIST-JANER, ALBERT   Eliel Saarinen. Chicago, 1948. 4to., 1st ed. Biblo & Tannen 214-32 1974 $47.50

CHRISTAIN, LINDA   Linda. Crown, 1962. 380p., illus. Austin 51-189 1973 $8.50

THE CHRISTIAN Examiner and Church of Ireland Magazine. Dublin, 1826-34. 16 vols., 8vo., half calf. Emerald 50-120 1974 £45

THE CHRISTIAN Garland. London, (c. 1860). 12mo., plates, orig. cloth, fine. Gregory 44-67 1974 $27.50

THE CHRISTIAN Irishman. Dublin, 1888-1893. 6 vols. in 2, 8vo. Emerald 50-769 1974 £7.50

THE CHRISTIAN Offering for MDCCCXXXII. Boston, 1832. 12mo., plates, orig. blind-stamped morocco. Ximenes 33-79 1974 $17.50

THE CHRISTIAN Year. London, n.d. Full black morocco, fine, 2 1/4 X 1 7/8 inches. Gregory 44-358 1974 $25

CHRISTIE, GRACE "MRS. A. H. CHRISTIE Samplers and Stitches. London, (1920). 4to., plates, drawings, orig. cloth. Gregory 44-68 1974 $15

CHRISTIE, AGATHA The Regatta Mystery and Other Stories. New York, 1939. 8vo., orig. cloth, first edition. Rota 190-224 1974 £10

CHRISTIE, H. KENRICK Technique and Results of Grafting of Skin. New York, 1930. Rittenhouse 46-141 1974 $10

CHRISTIE, GRACE "MRS. A. H. CHRISTIE" Embroidery. 1909. 4to., cloth, plates, illus. Quaritch 940-751 1974 £12

A CHRISTMAS and New Year's Gift. Boston, 1846. 16mo., engraved illus., fine. Current BW9-2 1974 $38.75

CHRISTMAS Carol of the Year 1695. New York, 1882. 16mo., chromolithograph illustrations, fine copy. Frohnsdorff 16-210 1974 $10

CHRISTMAS in Art and Song. New York, 1879. First edition, square 8vo., orig. blue gilt and black dec. Victorian cloth, minor corner wear, else fine & bright, drawings. Current BW9-11 1974 $22.50

CHRISTMAS in the Heart. New York, (c. 1910). 16mo., full color tipped in illus., pictorial covers bit soiled, interior fine. Current BW9-13 1974 $8

CHRISTOPHE, J. B. Histoire de la Papaute Pendant le 14e Siecle. 1855. 3 vols., new buckram. Allen 213-1380 1973 $27.50

CHRISTY, M. The Birds of Essex. Chelmsford, 1890. 8vo., cloth, frontispiece, text-figures. Wheldon 128-414 1973 £5

CHRISTY, ROBERT Proverbs, Maxims and Phrases of All Ages. 1888. 8vo., 2 vols., half morocco, gilt, first edition. Quaritch 936-340 1974 £14

CHRISTY'S Panorama Songster. New York, n.d. 12mo., orig. yellow pictorial wrappers, woodcut. Ximenes 35-244 1974 $10

THE Chromolithograph. London, 1867-1868. Green cloth, gilt, plates. Dawson's 424-128 1974 £60

CHRONICLES and Memorials of Great Britain and Ireland During the Middle Ages. 1858-97. 232 vols., roy. 8vo., roxburghe & half calf, orig. issue. Quaritch 939-94 1974 £1800

THE CHRONICLES of America. 1918-21. 50 vols., crown 8vo., plates, maps, orig. cloth gilt, Abraham Lincoln edition. Howes 186-709 1974 £25

CHRONICON Monasterii de Abingdon. 1858. 2 vols., roy. 8vo., orig. roxburgh binding, frontispieces. Howes 186-1176 1974 £15

CHRONICUM Scotorum, Chronicle of Irish Affairs. 1866. Allen 213-1381 1973 $25

CHRYSOSTOM
Please turn to
CHRYSOSTOMUS, JOANNES

Caution: Do not confuse with Chrysostom, John, Brother

CHRYSOSTOMUS, JOANNES, SAINT Opera Graece, Octo Voluminibus. 1612-13. 8 vols., folio, contemporary calf. Howes 185-1303 1974 £145

CHRYSOSTOMUS, JOANNES, SAINT Opera Omnia Quae Exstant. 1863. Vol. 1, part 1 only, 4to., torn spine. Allen 213-1382 1973 $12.50

CHRYSOSTOMUS, JOANNES, SAINT Quartus Tomus Operum Divi. 1530. Thick folio, dark calf, damp staining, fraying, woodcut initials. Howes 184-229 1973 $25

CHUBB, RALPH A Fable of Love and War. 1925. Crown 8vo., sewn, paper printed wrapper, first limited edition. Broadhurst 23-651 1974 £5

CHUBB, RALPH A Fable of Love and War. 1925. Woodcuts, first edition, crown 8vo., sewn, paper printed wrapper, limited to 200 copies, fine. Broadhurst 24-592 1974 £8

CHUBB, RALPH A Fable of Love and War. 1925. One of 200 numbered copies, initialled by author, woodcuts, wrappers, near fine, first edition. Covent 51-396 1973 £10

CHUBB, RALPH A Fable of Love and War. 1925. Fine, wrappers, English first edition. Covent 56-231 1974 £15

CHUDLEIGH, ELIZABETH An Authentic Detail of Particulars Relative To. 1788. 8vo., unbound, new edition. Hill 126-53 1974 £8.50

CHUN, W. Y. Chinese Economic Trees. Shanghai, (1921). 8vo., cloth, scarce. Wheldon 130-1544 1974 £15

THE CHUNKIES' Adventures. Springfield, n.d. 4to., 6 color plates. Frohnsdorff 16-211 1974 $15

CHURCH, A. H. Botanical Memoirs. Oxford, 1919-25. Roy 8vo., orig. wrappers. Wheldon 129-900 1974 £7

CHURCH, A. H. Josiah Wedgwood, Master-Potter. London, 1903. Roy 8vo., cloth, gilt, plates, new edition. Hammond 201-991 1974 £7.50

CHURCH, A. J. With the King at Oxford. 1886. 8vo., contemporary tree calf, illus. Bow Windows 64-445 1974 £5

CHURCH, JOHN A Cabinet of Quadrupeds. 1805. 2 vols. in 1, roy. 4to., contemporary calf gilt, gilt borders, engraved plates. Wheldon 128-311 1973 £60

CHURCH, JOHN A Cabinet of Quadrupeds. 1805. 4to., 2 vols., plates, contemporary half calf, worn. Bow Windows 64-53 1974 £48

CHURCH, RICHARD The Solitary Man. London, 1941. Edition limited to 900 copies, unopened, d.w. very lightly foxed, near mint. Ross 86-85 1974 $20

CHURCH, RICHARD Twentieth Century Psalter. London, 1943. Name in ink on fly, fine, d.w., orig. binding. Ross 86-86 1974 $15

CHURCH, THOMAS The History of Philips War. Exeter, 1829. Illus., full leather, repaired. Jenkins 61-495 1974 $25

CHURCH OF ENGLAND An Abstract of Certain Acts of Parliament: of Certaine Her Majesties Iniunctions: of Certaine Canons, Constitutions, and Synodalles Prouinciall: Established and in Force, for the Peaceable Gouernment of the Church, With Her Majesties Dominions and Countries. 1583. Small 4to., modern quarter levant morocco, Sir Thomas Phillipps copy. Thomas 32-35 1974 £50

CHURCH OF SCOTLAND The Booke of Common Prayer, with, The Psalter or Psalms of David. Edinburgh, 1637. Printed in Black Letter, woodcut borders, 2 vols. in 1, folio, contemporary calf, gilt borders, fine unpressed copy. Sawyer 293-249 1974 £165

CHURCH OF ENGLAND Book of Common Prayer. 1706. Folio, contemporary English red morocco gilt. Thomas 28-132 1972 £100

CHURCH OF ENGLAND The Book of Common Prayer...According to the Church of England Together With the Psalter of Psalms of David. Cambridge, 1762. Contemporary straight grained red morocco, corners little rubbed. Bow Windows 66-39 1974 £32

CHURCH OF ENGLAND Book of Common Prayer. Dublin, 1832. 8vo., old leather. Emerald 50-74 1974 £8

CHURCH OF ENGLAND Book of Common Prayer. London, 1845. 8vo., full red morocco, illus., gilt, foxing. Bow Windows 62-105 1974 £28

CHURCH OF ENGLAND Book of Common Prayer. 1891. Folio, orig. cloth, 550 pages. Howes 185-988 1974 £21

CHURCH OF ENGLAND   Book of Common Prayer in Irish. London, 1825. 8vo., contemporary cloth boards. Emerald 50-73 1974 £7.50

CHURCHILL, AWNSHAM   A Collection of Voyages and Travels. 1704. Folio, 4 vols., contemporary panelled calf, first edition. Bow Windows 64-447 1974 £350

CHURCHILL, AWNSHAM   A Collection of Voyages and Travels. London, 1732-47. 8 vols., folio, old calf, rebacked, leather labels. Traylen 79-421 1973 £385

CHURCHILL, C.   The Duellist. 1764. 4to., modern calf-backed boards, first edition. Quaritch 936-31 1974 £30

CHURCHILL, CHARLES   Poetical Works. 1854. 3 vols. Austin 61-234 1974 $27.50

CHURCHILL, CLEMENTINE   My Visit to Russia. (1945). 8vo., wrappers, fine, frontispiece. Covent 55-399 1974 £5.25

CHURCHILL, WINSTON LEONARD SPENCER   Arms and the Covenant. London, 1938. Lacking d.w., slight water spotting bottom front cover, fine, orig. binding. Ross 86-88 1974 $65

CHURCHILL, WINSTON LEONARD SPENCER   Arms and the Covenant. 1938. Orig. cloth, d.w., first edition. Rota 188-167 1974 £25

CHURCHILL, WINSTON LEONARD SPENCER   Arms and the Covenant. 1938. Portrait, inscription, first edition. Howes 185-73 1974 £7.50

CHURCHILL, WINSTON LEONARD SPENCER   Charles IXth Duke of Marlborough, K. G. London, 1934. First edition, mint, orig. binding. Ross 86-89 1974 $50

CHURCHILL, WINSTON LEONARD SPENCER   The Crisis. New York, 1901. First edition. Biblo & Tannen 210-711 1973 $10

CHURCHILL, WINSTON LEONARD SPENCER   Dictatorship on Trail. 1930. Portraits, d.w., fine, English first edition. Covent 56-1624 1974 £21

CHURCHILL, WINSTON LEONARD SPENCER   Great Contemporaries. 1937. Orig. cloth, faded, first edition. Rota 188-166 1974 £25

CHURCHILL, WINSTON LEONARD SPENCER   Great Contemporaries. London, 1937. Lacking d.w., spine slightly faded, name in ink on fly, very nice, orig. binding. Ross 86-90 1974 $80

CHURCHILL, WINSTON LEONARD SPENCER   Great Contemporaries. 1938. Plates, revised edition. Covent 56-232 1974 £10.50

CHURCHILL, WINSTON LEONARD SPENCER   Great Contemporaries. 1938. Orig. cloth. Smith 194-412 1974 £5

CHURCHILL, WINSTON LEONARD SPENCER   The Great War. n.d. 3 vols., roy. 8vo., orig. cloth gilt, fine, drawings. Covent 55-400 1974 £10.50

CHURCHILL, WINSTON LEONARD SPENCER   The Great War. (1933). 3 vols., 8vo., red half morocco, maps, drawings, illus. from photos. Bow Windows 66-128 1974 £16.50

CHURCHILL, WINSTON LEONARD SPENCER   The Great War. 1933-34. 3 vols., sup. roy. 8vo., illus., orig. blue cloth gilt, first edition. Smith 193-333 1973 £8

CHURCHILL, WINSTON LEONARD SPENCER   Ian Hamilton's March. 1900. First edition, portrait frontispiece, map, plans, 8vo., red levant morocco, gilt line border, gilt edges, good copy. Sawyer 293-89 1974 £95

CHURCHILL, WINSTON LEONARD SPENCER   Ian Hamilton's March. London, 1900. 8vo., orig. red cloth, first edition. Dawsons PM 252-135 1974 £30

CHURCHILL, WINSTON LEONARD SPENCER   India. 1931. Orig. wrappers, orig. cloth, faded, rare, first edition. Rota 188-164 1974 £135

CHURCHILL, WINSTON LEONARD SPENCER   Into Battle. 1941-46. 7 vols., orig. cloth, inscription, first edition. Rota 188-168 1974 £22.50

CHURCHILL, WINSTON LEONARD SPENCER   The Legion Book. 1929. 4to., orig. cloth, illus., signed, first edition. Rota 188-174 1974 £25

CHURCHILL, WINSTON LEONARD SPENCER   Liberalism and the Social Problem. London, 1909. First edition, armorial bookplate, fine, scarce, orig. binding. Ross 86-91 1974 $240

CHURCHILL, WINSTON LEONARD SPENCER   Liberalism and the Social Problem. 1909. Orig. cloth, scarce, first edition. Rota 188-162 1974 £95

CHURCHILL, WINSTON LEONARD SPENCER   London to Ladysmith Via Pretoria. 1900. Orig. dec. cloth, foxing, first edition. Howes 185-74 1974 £28

CHURCHILL, WINSTON LEONARD SPENCER   London to Ladysmith via Pretoria. 1900. First edition, maps, folding and plans, ads. at end, 8vo., orig. illus. cloth, slightly fingerstained, good copy. Sawyer 293-90 1974 £55

CHURCHILL, WINSTON LEONARD SPENCER   Marlborough. 1933-38. 8vo., 4 vols., orig. cloth, first edition. Rota 190-108 1974 £35

CHURCHILL, WINSTON LEONARD SPENCER   Marlborough. 1933-8. 8vo., 4 vols., half brown morocco, gilt, plates, first edition. Quaritch 936-341 1974 £75

CHURCHILL, WINSTON LEONARD SPENCER   Marlborough. 1933-38. 4 vols., large 8vo., orig. buckram gilt, plates, first edition. Howes 185-75 1974 £42

CHURCHILL, WINSTON LEONARD SPENCER   Marlborough. 1933-38. Fine in dust wrappers, scarce in this state. Sawyer 293-92 1974 £65

CHURCHILL, WINSTON LEONARD SPENCER   Marlborough. 1933-38. First edition, portraits, maps, 4 vols., 8vo., orig. buckram gilt, top edges gilt, buckram slip-in case, each vol. with signed presentation inscription by author to Bertram Romilly, good set. Sawyer 293-91 1974 £675

CHURCHILL, WINSTON LEONARD SPENCER   Marlborough, His Life & Times. 1933-38. 4 vols., roy. 8vo., plates, orig. buckram gilt. Smith 193-334 1973 £15

CHURCHILL, WINSTON LEONARD SPENCER   Marlborough, His Life and Times. 1938. Vol. 4 only, orig. buckram, plates, maps. Smith 194-414 1974 £5

CHURCHILL, WINSTON LEONARD SPENCER   The Munitions Miracle. n.d. (1918). Scarce, very good, wrappers, first edition. Covent 51-398 1973 £65

CHURCHILL, WINSTON LEONARD SPENCER   My African Journey. London, 1908. 8vo., maps, illus., orig. red pictorial cloth, first edition. Bow Windows 62-178 1974 £52

CHURCHILL, WINSTON LEONARD SPENCER   My African Journey. 1908. 8vo., cloth, illus., first edition. Bow Windows 66-127 1974 £48

CHURCHILL, WINSTON LEONARD SPENCER   My African Journey. 1908. First edition, maps, illus., 8vo., orig. pictorial cloth, spine faded, fine copy, scarce. Sawyer 293-87 1974 £85

CHURCHILL, WINSTON LEONARD SPENCER   My Early Life. 1930. 8vo., orig. cloth, first edition. Rota 190-107 1974 £25

CHURCHILL, WINSTON LEONARD SPENCER   My Early Life. 1930. First edition, maps, illus., 8vo., orig. cloth, spine faded, good copy, scarce. Sawyer 293-88 1974 £65

CHURCHILL, WINSTON LEONARD SPENCER   The People's Rights. (1910). Orig. cloth, wrappers, first edition. Rota 188-163 1974 £100

CHURCHILL, WINSTON LEONARD SPENCER   Proceedings at the Unveiling of the Memorial to Lawrence of Arabia, 3 October, 1936. Oxford, 1937. First edition, frontis., 4to., orig. wrappers, good copy, scarce. Sawyer 293-99 1974 £35

CHURCHILL, WINSTON LEONARD SPENCER   The River War. 1933. Orig. light mauve cloth, worn, second cheap edition. Rota 188-165 1974 £5

CHURCHILL, WINSTON LEONARD SPENCER   A Speech. 1940. 8vo., first edition, wrappers. Rota 189-195 1974 £5

CHURCHILL, WINSTON LEONARD SPENCER   A Speech by the Prime Minister in the House of Commons, August 20th, 1940. Wrappers slightly dust stained. Sawyer 293-95 1974 £25

CHURCHILL, WINSTON LEONARD SPENCER   A Speech by the Prime Minister in the House of Commons, August 20th, 1940. 1940. First edition, 8vo., orig. wrappers, fine. Sawyer 293-94 1974 £28

CHURCHILL, WINSTON LEONARD SPENCER   Speech in the House of Commons. London, 1940. 8vo., orig. printed paper wrappers, fine. Dawsons PM 251-190 1974 £30

CHURCHILL, WINSTON LEONARD SPENCER   A Speech in the House of Commons, 20, August, 1940. London, 1940. 8vo., orig. printed wrappers, first edition. Gilhofer 61-99 1974 sFr 250

CHURCHILL, WINSTON LEONARD SPENCER   Strike Nights in Printing House Square. 1926. 8vo., orig. cloth, illus., scarce, first edition. Rota 189-197 1974 £5

CHURCHILL, WINSTON LEONARD SPENCER   Thoughts and Adventures. 1932. 8vo., half red morocco, photo. frontispiece, maps, top edges gilt, signed presentation inscription from author, fine copy. Sawyer 293-97 1974 £140

CHURCHILL, WINSTON LEONARD SPENCER   Thoughts and Adventures. 1932. 8vo., orig. grey green cloth, gilt, first edition. Hammond 201-154 1974 £25

CHURCHILL, WINSTON LEONARD SPENCER   Thoughts and Adventures. 1932. Orig. cloth gilt. Smith 193-337 1973 £20

CHURCHILL, WINSTON LEONARD SPENCER   The War by Land and Air and Sea. New York, 1917. Wrappers. Covent 55-402 1974 £21

CHURCHILL, WINSTON LEONARD SPENCER   "What Kind of People do They Think We Are?" (1942). 4to., scarce, first edition. Rota 188-169 1974 £8

CHURCHILL, WINSTON LEONARD SPENCER   "What Kind of People do They Think We Are?" 1942. First edition, 4to., orig. printed wrappers, good copy, rare. Sawyer 293-98 1974 £35

CHURCHILL, WINSTON LEONARD SPENCER   Winston Churchill and Harrow. n.d. Plates, cloth gilt, near fine. Covent 55-404 1974 £6.30

CHURCHILL, WINSTON LEONARD SPENCER   The World Crisis 1911-1918. n.d. 2 vols., thick demy 8vo., orig. blue cloth, first edition. Smith 194-417 1974 £5

CHURCHILL, WINSTON LEONARD SPENCER   The World Crisis 1911-1914. London, 1923-31. 8vo., 6 vols., orig. blue cloth, first edition. Dawsons PM 251-189 1974 £60

CHURCHILL, WINSTON LEONARD SPENCER   The World Crisis. 1923-31. Orig. blue cloth, maps, illus., first editions. Howes 186-711 1974 £42

CHURCHILL, WINSTON LEONARD SPENCER   The World Crisis. New York, 1931. First American edition. Biblo & Tannen 213-661 1973 $15

CHURCHILL, WINSTON LEONARD SPENCER   The World Crisis. (1923-31). 4 vols., 8vo., orig. cloth, bookplates, library stamps, first editions. Bow Windows 66-129 1974 £65

CHURTON, RALPH   Life of Alexander Nowell. 1809. New buckram. Allen 213-1677 1973 $15

CHURTON, RALPH   The Life of Alexander Nowell. Oxford, 1809. Contemporary half calf, plates. Howes 185-1504 1974 £8

CHYLINSKI, D.   The Beekeeper's Manual. 1845. Small 8vo., orig. cloth, frontispiece, plates. Wheldon 129-705 1974 £7.50

CIACCONIUS, PETRUS   De Triclinio Sive de Modo Convivandi apud Priscos Romanos. Amsterdam, 1689. Small 8vo., 19th century panelled calf, plates, engraved title, almost new condition. Thomas 32-334 1974 £21

CIBBER, COLLEY   An Apology for the Life of. 1740. 8vo., new quarter calf, first edition. Hill 126-263 1974 £95

CIBBER, COLLEY   An Apology for the Life of. London, 1740. 4to., contemporary mottled calf, first edition. Dawsons PM 252-136 1974 £145

CIBBER, COLLEY   The Provok'd Husband. London, 1728. 8vo., modern boards, first edition. Dawsons PM 252-137 1974 £40

CIBBER, THEOPHILUS   The Lives of the Poets of Great Britain and Ireland. London, 1753. 5 vols., 12mo., contemporary half calf, spines very worn, first edition. Ximenes 37-39 1974 $50

CICERO, MARCUS TULLIUS   Les Aratea. 1941. Sewn. Allen 213-246 1973 $10

CICERO, MARCUS TULLIUS   Defensiones Contra Celii Calcagnini. 1546. Roan-backed boards, fine. Thomas 30-88 1973 £35

CICERO, MARCUS TULLIUS   Epistolarum ad Atticum. 1513. 18th century vellum. Thomas 30-21 1973 £75

CICERO, MARCUS TULLIUS   Epistolarum ad Atticum. 1513. Contemporary blind-stamped English calf, raised bands, first Aldine edition. Thomas 30-20 1973 £125

CICERO, MARCUS TULLIUS   Epistolarum ad Atticum ad Brutum. 1521. 19th century calf gilt, rubbed, second Aldine edition. Thomas 30-57 1973 £35

CICERO, MARCUS TULLIUS   Le Epistole Famigliare. 1545. Vellum gilt, morocco labels. Thomas 30-82 1973 £30

CICERO, MARCUS TULLIUS   Epistolae ad Atticum. 1549. 19th century russia, worn, rubbed. Thomas 30-93 1973 £25

CICERO, MARCUS TULLIUS   In Epistolas ad. Atticum. 1547. 19th century russia gilt, rubbed, worn. Thomas 30-92 1973 £30

CICERO, MARCUS TULLIUS   The Familiar Epistles Of. (1620). 12mo., contemporary calf, first edition. Dawsons PM 251-192 1974 £110

CICERO, MARCUS TULLIUS   De Finibus Malorum Et Bonorum. 1471. Small folio, 17th century English red morocco. Bow Windows 64-448 1974 £1,450

CICERO, MARCUS TULLIUS   De Legibus Libri tres. 1824. New buckram. Allen 213-248 1973 $10

CICERO, MARCUS TULLIUS   De Officiis Libri Tres. 1552. 19th century calf, worn. Thomas 30-98 1973 £12

CICERO, MARCUS TULLIUS   De Officiis, Libri Tres, cum Indice Auctorum, Adagiorumque suo loco Citatorum. Strassburg, 1512. Small 4to., cased boards, rare, fine. Schumann 499-23 1974 sFr 750

CICERO, MARCUS TULLIUS   Officiorum Lib. 1519. 19th century calf, rubbed, rare, excellent condition. Thomas 30-47 1973 £40

CICERO, MARCUS TULLIUS   In Omnes de Arte Rhetorica. 1551. Small folio, boards backed with sheep, gilt, rubbed. Thomas 30-97 1973 £40

CICERO, MARCUS TULLIUS   Orationem Volumen Primum. 1519. 3 vols., 19th century polished calf gilt, rubbed. Thomas 30-46 1973 £60

CICERO, MARCUS TULLIUS   Orationum. Venice, 1554-65-46. 3 vols., old vellum, vol. 1 in excellent state, vols. 2 & 3 have titles mounted with blank portions cut away. Thomas 32-206 1974 £36

CICERO, MARCUS TULLIUS   Orationes. 1546. 3 vols., contemporary Venetian dark brown morocco, raised bands, gilt. Thomas 30-86 1973 £125

CICERO, MARCUS TULLIUS   On Oratory and Orations. 1855. 522 pages. Austin 51-190 1973 $6.50

CICERO, MARCUS TULLIUS   De Philosophia. 1523. 2 vols., 19th century russia gilt, rubbed. Thomas 30-63 1973 £45

CICERO, MARCUS TULLIUS   De Philosophia. 1546. 3 vols., old calf, rubbed. Thomas 30-87 1973 £21

CICERO, MARCUS TULLIUS   De Philosophia. 1555-56. 2 vols., 18th century vellum, browned. Thomas 30-103 1973 £35

CICERO, MARCUS TULLIUS　　Le Pistole di Cicerone ad Attico.　Venice, (1555?).　18th century vellum, reasonable copy, counterfeit edition with the Aldine anchor on the title.　Thomas 32-207　1974　£40

CICERO, MARCUS TULLIUS　　Respublica Sive Statvs Regni Scotiae et Hiberniae.　1627.　16mo., contemporary gilt framed calf, worn, engraved. Bow Windows 62-307　1974　£7

CICERO, MARCUS TULLIUS　　Rhetorica.　1546.　Vol. 2 only of 2, calf. Thomas 30-84　1973　£8.50

CICERO, MARCUS TULLIUS　　Rhetorica.　1550.　Vol. 2 only of 2, old calf, gilt, rubbed.　Thomas 30-94　1973　£8.50

CICERO, MARCUS TULLIUS　　Rhetorica.　1559.　Vol. 2 of 2, 18th century vellum gilt, morocco labels.　Thomas 30-111　1973　£8.50

CICERO, MARCUS TULLIUS　　Rhetoricorum.　1521.　Vellum, stains.　Thomas 30-56　1973　£31.50

CICERO, MARCUS TULLIUS　　Rhetoricorum ad C. Herennium.　Venice, 1521. Contemporary blind stamped calf, rebacked, lacks ties.　Thomas 32-205　1974 £75

CICERO, MARCUS TULLIUS　　Rhetoricorum ad C. Herennium.　1521. Contemporary Italian black morocco, gilt, raised bands, worn.　Thomas 30-55 1973　£85

CICERO, MARCUS TULLIUS　　Select Orations.　1777.　2 vols., calf, worn. Allen 213-254　1973　£10

CICERO, MARCUS TULLIUS　　M. Tvllii Ciceronis Epistolae ad Atticum. Venetiis, 1540.　2 works in 1 vol., 8vo., contemporary calf, rebacked.　Bow Windows 62-16　1974　£60

CICERO, MARCUS TULLIUS　　Tvllii Ciceronis Orationvm Tomvs I.　1642. 12mo., bookplate, contemporary calf, worn.　Bow Windows 62-306　1974　£9

CICERO, MARCUS TULLIUS　　Opera Philosophica.　Paris, 1521-22.　Folio, 2 parts in 1 vol., contemporary brown calf, rebacked.　Schumann 499-24　1974 sFr 1,600

CICERO, MARCUS TULLIUS　　Opera.　Paris, 1531.　Small folio, 18th century calf, rubbed.　Thomas 28-282　1972　£40

CICERO, MARCUS TULLIUS　　Opera.　Venice, 1537-34.　4 vols., small folio, early 19th century diced brown russia gilt, raised bands, joints cracked, excellent internally.　Thomas 32-226　1974　£80

CICERO, MARCUS TULLIUS　　Opera.　Paris, 1539.　Folio, calf over wooden boards, bookplate.　Thomas 28-131　1972　£100

CICERO, MARCUS TULLIUS　　Opera Omnia . . . ex Vulgata Dion.　Lyons, 1594.　Thick large 8vo., contemporary blind-stamped pigskin, scarce, excellent copy.　Harper 213-39　1973　$155

CICOGNINI, JACOPO　　Alla Sacra Maesta Cesarea dell' Imperatore in Lode del Famoso Signor Galileo Galilei.　Florence, 1631.　4to., contemporary limp vellum, extremely rare.　Schumann 500-23　1974　sFr 12,800

CIGALINUS, FRANCISCUS　　Coelum Sydereum.　1655.　4to., contemporary vellum, fine, first edition.　Dawsons PM 245-175　1974　£45

CINCINNATUS　　War! War! War!　N.P., 1940.　292 pages. Austin 57-131　1974　$10

CINDERELLA.　Chicago, n.d.　8vo., 24 color plates, cloth.　Frohnsdorff 16-217 1974　$7.50

CINDERELLA.　New York, n.d.　24mo., pict. boards, cloth spine, fine copy. Frohnsdorff 16-221　1974　$10

CINDERELLA.　New York, ca. 1850.　16mo., 8 hand-colored woodcuts; spine restitched, margins frayed.　Frohnsdorff 16-222　1974　$30

CINDERELLA.　Ca. 1850.　8vo., 16 hand-colored cuts.　Frohnsdorff 16-224 1974 $35

CINDERELLA.　Philadelphia, ca. 1850.　8vo., 4 hand-colored plates, each page of text has floral engraved boarders, also hand-colored.　Frohnsdorff 16-213　1974 $35

CINDERELLA.　Glasgow, 1852.　16mo., engravings.　Frohnsdorff 16-223　1974 $15

CINDERELLA.　Ca. 1890.　Sm. 4to., 4 color plates.　Frohnsdorff 16-218　1974 $7.50

CINDERELLA.　New York, 1907.　Sm. 4to., 4 color plates.　Frohnsdorff 16-214 1974　$10

CINDERELLA.　Chicago, 1908.　16mo., illus., spine chipped.　Frohnsdorff 16-220 1974　$10

CINDERELLA.　Chicago, 1909.　8vo., illus.　Frohnsdorff 16-219　1974　$17.50

CINDERELLA.　New York, 1934.　4to., illus.　Frohnsdorff 16-216　1974　$15

CISCAR Y CISCAR, GABRIEL　　Curso de Estudios Elementales de Marina.　1811. 4to., modern green half calf, plates.　Dawsons PM 245-176　1974　£32

CIST, CHARLES　　Sketches and Statistics of Cincinnati.　Cincinnati, 1851.　8vo., orig. bindings.　Butterfield 8-72　1974　$20

CITY of Hamilton Directory, 1858.　Hamilton, 1858.　Folding map.　Hood's 102-14　1974　$105

CITY of Hamilton Directory, 1858.　Hamilton, 1858.　Map.　Hood's 104-17 1974　$105

CITY OF MANCHESTER ART GALLERY　　Loan Exhibition Catalogue.　1911. Plates, wrappers, second edition.　Marsden 37-126　1974　£10

CIULI, E.　　Composizioni di Ettore Ciuli Rappresentanti Varii Costumi di Roma e Suoi Dintorni.　(c. 1830).　Folio, plates, orig. lithographed wrapper.　Quaritch 940-708　1974　£75

CLADEL, JUDITH　　Rodin.　New York, 1937.　1st ed., dw. Biblo & Tannen 213-404　1973　$12.50

CLADEL, LEON　　Petits Cahiers.　Paris, 1885.　8vo., orig. wrapper, uncut, illus.　L. Goldschmidt 42-188　1974　$15

CLAFLIN, TENNIE C.
Please turn to
COOK, TENNESSEE CELESTE

CLAGHORN, CHARLES EUGENE　　The Mocking Bird, The Life and Diary of Its Author.　Philadelphia, 1937.　First edition, d.j., limited to 300 copies, orig. binding.　Butterfield 10-428　1974　$7.50

CLAGHORN, KATE HOLLADAY　　The Immigrant's Day in Court.　1923. Orig. edition.　Austin 57-133　1974　$10

CLAGHORN, KATE HOLLADAY　　The Immigrant's Day in Court.　Harper, 1923. Orig. edition.　Austin 62-95　1974　$10

CLAIR, SAINT　　Vita di Santa Chiara Vergine Composta per Ugolino Verino Cittadino Florentino.　1921.　Printed in black, red and blue, 8vo., orig. limp vellum, fine copy, limited to 236 copies on paper, with facsimile of the first four pages of the orig. manuscript.　Sawyer 293-39　1974　£135

CLAIRMONT, J.　　Der Hochleistungs-Steilrohrkessel.　Wiesbaden, (n.d.).　Oblong folio, yellow printed boards.　Dawsons PM 245-177　1974　£8

CLAIRVILLE, J. P. DE　　Manuel d'Herborisation en Suisse.　1811.　8vo., calf-backed boards, scarce.　Wheldon 130-1136　1974　£15

CLANVOWE, THOMAS　　The Floure and the Leafe.　1896.　Small 4to., orig. holland backed boards, limited.　Bow Windows 62-530　1974　£85

CLAPHAM, JOHN　　The Bank of England.　1944.　2 vols., plates, buckram, dust wrappers, first edition.　Howes 186-1384　1974　£5.50

CLAPHAM, JOHN　　The Bank of England.　Cambridge, 1944. 2 vols., illus.　Jacobs 24-141　1974　$25

CLAPHAM, JOHN   An Economic History of Modern Britain. Cambridge, 1926-38. 3 vols., thick roy. 8vo., orig. buckram, first edition. Smith 194-678 1974 £15

CLAPHAM, JOHN   An Economic History of Modern Britain. 1926-38. 3 vols., roy. 8vo., maps. Howes 186-1385 1974 £13.50

CLAPHAM, JOHN   An Economic History of Modern Britain. 1930. Large 8vo., 3 vols., orig. green cloth gilt, fine, second edition. Dawsons PM 251-193 1974 £12

CLAPIERS DE VAUVENARGUES, LUC DE
Please turn to
VAUVENARGUES, LUC DE CLAPIERS DE

CLAPP, H. AUSTIN   Reminscences of a Dramatic Critic. Cambridge, 1902. Orig. boards, portraits, limited edition. Smith 194-205 1974 £5

CLAPPERTON, GEORGE   Practical Paper-Making. London, 1894. 12mo., cloth. Goodspeed's 578-440 1974 $15

CLAPPERTON, HUGH   Journal of a Second Expedition into the Interior of Africa, from the Bight of Benin to Soccatoo. 1829. First edition, portrait frontispiece, map, 4to., full Spanish calf, joints neatly repaired, spine slightly worn, fine copy. Sawyer 293-4 1974 £64

CLAPPERTON, R. H.   Paper, an Historical Account of Its Making By Hand. Oxford, 1934. Folio, plates, illus., orig. half morocco. Dawsons PM 10-664 1974 £260

CLAPPERTON, R. H.   Paper and its Relationship to Books. London and Tronto, (1934). Marbled boards. Dawson's 424-182 1974 $10

CLAPPERTON, R. H.   Paper-Making. 1929. Crown 4to., orig. cloth, illus. Broadhurst 23-1221 1974 £5

CLARE, JOHN   Madrigals & Chronicles. 1924. Orig. floral boards, buckram backed, uncut, engravings, limited. Howes 186-92 1974 £21

CLARE, JOHN   Poems. 1901. Boards, English first edition. Covent 56-1635 1974 £32.50

CLARE, JOHN   Poems. 1920. Dust wrapper, portrait, fine, English first edition. Covent 56-243 1974 £15

CLARE, JOHN   Poems. 1920. Portrait, English first edition. Covent 56-1634 1974 £21

CLARE, JOHN   Poems. London, 1920. 8vo., cloth, dustwrapper, first edition. Hammond 201-155 1974 £24

CLARE, JOHN   Poems. 1920. Portrait, fine, dust wrapper, first edition. Howes 186-93 1974 £5.50

CLARE, JOHN   The Village Minstrel. London, 1821. 2 vols. in 1, 12mo., contemporary red blind-stamped cloth, gilt, first edition. Dawsons PM 252-138 1974 £50

CLARE, M.   Youth's Introduction to Trade and Business. London, 1769. 8vo., contemporary sheep. Dawsons PM 247-45 1974 £30

CLARE, MARTIN   The Motion of Fluids. London, 1737. 8vo., contemporary calf, gilt, second edition. Zeitlin 235-44 1974 $75

CLARE College 1326-1926. University Hall 1326-1346. Clare Hall 1346-1856. Cambridge, 1928-30. 2 vols., folio, illus. Quaritch 939-319 1974 £7.75

CLARENDON, EDWARD HYDE, 1ST EARL OF   A Brief View and Survey of the Dangerous and Pernicious Errors to Church. 1676. 4to., frontis., woodcut, old gilt framed calf, rebacked, second edition. Bow Windows 63-104 1974 £56

CLARENDON, EDWARD HYDE, 1ST EARL OF   The History of the Rebellion and Civil Wars in England. Oxford, 1702-04. 3 vols., folio, contemporary calf gilt, rebacked, first edition. Howes 186-713 1974 £80

CLARENDON, EDWARD HYDE, 1ST EARL OF   The History of the Rebellion and Civil Wars in England. Oxford, 1707-05-06. 7 vols., 8vo., plates, stains, old calf, rebacked. Bow Windows 63-105 1974 £42

CLARENDON, EDWARD HYDE, 1ST EARL OF   The History of the Rebellion and Civil Wars in England. 1888. 6 vols., crown 8vo., full Prussian blue morocco, gilt, fine, best modern edition. Howes 186-714 1974 £45

CLARENDON, EDWARD HYDE, 1ST EARL OF   The History of the Rebellion and Civil Wars in Ireland. London, 1720. 8vo., contemporary panelled calf, morocco label, gilt, portrait, first edition. Beeleigh 18-521 1974 £12

CLARENDON, EDWARD HYDE, 1ST EARL OF   The History of the Rebellion and Civil Wars in Ireland. London, 1720. 8vo., portrait, old calf, rebacked. Bow Windows 63-106 1974 £15

CLARENDON, EDWARD HYDE, 1ST EARL OF   The Life of. Oxford, 1759. 3 vols., 8vo., foxing, stains, old calf, rebacked. Bow Windows 63-107 1974 £22

CLARENDON, EDWARD HYDE, 1ST EARL OF   The Life. Oxford, 1827. 3 vols., orig. labels, contemporary calf, new edition. Howes 186-715 1974 £18

CLARENDON, EDWARD HYDE, 1ST EARL OF   Religion and Policy. Oxford, 1811. 8vo., 2 vols., contemporary calf. Bow Windows 64-449 1974 £8

CLARETIE, L.   Les Jouets. Paris, (1880). Large 8vo., plates, vignettes, small label removed from spine, recased upside down in cover, clean copy. Gregory 44-89 1974 $30

CLARIDGE, R. T.   Hydropathy. London, 1842. Demy 8vo., frontispiece, boards, inscribed, scarce. Covent 55-1091 1974 £21

CLARIDGE, R. T.   Hydropathy. 1942. Rebound, first edition. Covent 55-1295 1974 £15

CLARK, A. HOBART   A Monograph of the Existing Crinoids. Washington, 1915-21-31. 4to., 3 vols., plates, orig. wrappers. Bow Windows 64-54 1974 £20

CLARK, A. J.   The Mode of Action of Drugs on Cells. 1933. 8vo., cloth, figures, scarce. Wheldon 128-1675 1973 £5

CLARK, A. J.   The Mode of Action of Drugs on Cells. 1933. 8vo., cloth, scarce. Wheldon 131-1805 1974 £5

CLARK, BADGER   Sun and Saddle Leather. Boston, 1922. Jenkins 61-498 1974 $13.50

CLARK, BARRETT   Eugene O'Neill. McBride, 1926. 110p. Austin 51-191 1973 $5

CLARK, BARRETT   Great Short Biographies of the World. 1928. Austin 61-235 1974 $15

CLARK, BARRETT   An Hour of American Drama. Lippincott, 1930. 159p. Austin 51-192 1973 $6

CLARK, BARRETT   How to Produce Amateur Plays. Little, Brown, 1917. 144p. Austin 51-193 1973 $8.50

CLARK, CHARLES T.   Opdycke Tigers 125th O.V.I. Columbus, 1895. Orig. binding. Butterfield 10-150 1974 $25

CLARK, DANIEL KINNEAR   Railway Machinery. Glasgow, 1855. Roy 4to., 2 vols., three quarter polished calf, gilt, first edition. Zeitlin 235-45 1974 $325

CLARK, G.   Which We Did. Toronto, 1936. Illus. Hood's 103-398 1974 $10

CLARK, G. H.   Farm Weeds of Canada. Ottawa, 1909. Roy 8vo., orig. buckram, plates, second edition. Wheldon 129-1057 1974 £7.50

CLARK, HUGH   A Short and Easy Introduction to Heraldry. London, 1776. 8vo., boards, plates, second edition. Hammond 201-416 1974 £14

CLARK, HUGH   A Short and Easy Introduction to Heraldry. London, 1827. 8vo., contemporary calf, plates, tenth edition. Hammond 201-417 1974 £14

CLARK, J. H.   The Rose and the Lily. Halifax, 1858. Orig. stiff wrappers, fine, colored frontis. Gregory 44-69 1974 $32.50

CLARK, J. S.   Rand and the Micmacs. Charlottetown, 1899. Three quarter leather, inscribed by author. Hood's 102-446 1974 $22.50

CLARK, J. PATTERSON   A New System of Treating the Human Teeth. London, 1830. 8vo., old cloth. Gurney 64-53 1974 £25

CLARK, JAMES   The Sanative Influence of Climate. London, 1841. 8vo., contemporary half calf, rebacked, third edition. Dawsons PM 249-111 1974 £6.50

CLARK, JOHN   Observations On the Diseases In Long Voyages to Hot Countires. London, 1773. 8vo., contemporary calf, first edition. Schuman 37-45 1974 $75

CLARK, JOSEPH G.   Lights and Shadows of Sailor Life. Boston, 1847. Jenkins 61-499 1974 $18.50

CLARK, KENNETH   The Drawings of Leonardo da Vinci in the Collection of His Majesty the King at Windsor Castle. Cambridge, 1935. 2 vols., demy 4to., plates, orig. cloth, fine. Broadhurst 24-31 1974 £40

CLARK, L. GAYLORD   Knick-Knacks. Appleton, 1853. 335p. Austin 54-247 1973 $15

CLARK, LILLIAN   Federal Textbook on Citizenship Training. 1935. 159 pages. Austin 57-134 1974 $10

CLARK, NATHANIEL G.   A Scale of Prices for Job Work. London, 1825. 8vo., contemporary half calf, gilt. Hammond 201-696 1974 £21

CLARK, R. S.   Through Shen-Kan. 1912. 4to., orig. cloth, coloured and other plates, frontispiece, map. Bow Windows 66-130 1974 £38

CLARK, SAMUEL   The Marrow of Ecclesiastical Historie. London, 1650. Small 4to., old calf, rebacked, portraits. Traylen 79-170 1973 £12

CLARK, SOLOMON   Antiquities, Historicals and Graduates of Northampton. Northampton, 1882. Orig. binding, index & errata. Butterfield 10-373 1974 $15

CLARKE, A.   A Bibliographical Dictionary; and, The Bibliographical Miscellany. Liverpool, Manchester & London, 1802-06. 8 vols. in 4, folding frontis., crown 8vo., contemporary straight grained morocco, bit rubbed, text fine. Forster 98-78 1974 £30

CLARKE, ALEXANDER ROSS   Ordnance Trigonometrical Survey of Great Britain and Ireland. London, 1858. 4to., orig. cloth, gilt, plates. Hammond 201-804 1974 £38

CLARKE, ARTHUR   An Essay on Warm, Cold and Vapour Bathing. Dublin, 1816. 8vo., orig. boards, rebacked, third edition. Hammond 201-563 1974 £12

CLARKE, AUSTIN,   The Fires of Baal. Dublin, 1921. Fine copy, worn, d.w., upper board very slightly faded, first edition. Covent 51-408 1973 £15

CLARKE, C. B.   Handbook of British Fungi. 1871. 2 vols., 8vo., orig. cloth, plates, coloured frontispiece, scarce. Wheldon 128-1350 1973 £10

CLARKE, C. B.   Illustrations of Cyperaceae. 1909. Roy 8vo., cloth, plates. Wheldon 129-901 1974 £20

CLARKE, C. B.   A Review of the Ferns of Northern India. 1880. 3 parts, 4to., wrappers, plates, rare orig. printing. Wheldon 128-1348 1973 £15

CLARKE, CHARLES   Architectura Ecclesiastica Londini. 1820. Folio, plates, contemporary half maroon morocco. Howes 186-2102 1974 £55

CLARKE, CHARLES 1826-   Sixty Years in Upper Canada. Toronto, 1908. Illus. Hood's 103-615 1974 $20

CLARKE, CHARLES KIRK   A History of the Toronto General Hospital. Toronto, 1913. Illus. Hood's 103-584 1974 $35

CLARKE, E. D.   A Tour Through the South of England, Wales and Part of Ireland. 1793. 8vo., contemporary half calf, plates, rare. Quaritch 939-95 1974 £60

CLARKE, EDWARD   Letters Concerning the Spanish Nation. 1763. 4to., uncut in contemporary boards, paper spine torn, first edition. Bow Windows 66-131 1974 £36

CLARKE, ERIC   Music in Everyday Life. New York, 1935. lst ed. Biblo & Tannen 214-828 1974 $7.50

CLARKE, FRANCIS L.   The Life of the Most Noble Arthur, Marquis and Earl of Wellington. (1813-14). 2 vols., full contemporary diced russia gilt, plates, morocco labels, rubbing. Howes 186-1769 1974 £15

CLARKE, G.   Pompeii. 1831-32. 12mo., half calf, 2 vols., morocco labels. Bow Windows 64-450 1974 £12.50

CLARKE, G. R.   The History and Description of the Town and Borough of Ipswich. (n.d.). 8vo., frontispiece, half calf, worn. Bow Windows 64-451 1974 £20

CLARKE, HEWSON   The History of the War. 1816. 3 vols., 4to., contemporary calf, plates. Howes 186-1707 1974 £15

CLARKE, HUGH   The Grave of O'Neill. Dublin, 1823. 8vo., cloth boards. Emerald 50-143 1974 £12.50

CLARKE, J. M.   Fosseis Devonianos do Parana. Rio de Janeiro, 1913. 4to., wrappers, plates. Wheldon 128-953 1973 £5

CLARKE, J. M.   The Gaspe, Including an Account of l'Ile Percee the Finial of the St. Lawrence. New Haven, 1935. Illus. Hood's 102-691 1974 $10

CLARKE, J. M.   The Heart of Gaspe; Sketches in the Gul of St. Lawrence. New York, 1913. Illus. Hood's 102-692 1974 $7.50

CLARKE, J. M.   The Heart of Gaspe. New York, 1937. Illus. Hood's 102-182 1974 $15

CLARKE, JOHN   Commentaries on Some of the Most Important Diseases of Children. London, 1815. 8vo., half calf, rebacked, first edition. Dawsons PM 249-112 1974 £90

CLARKE, JOHN   Erasmi Colloquia Selecta. 1789. 12mo., contemporary cloth, twenty-second edition. Bow Windows 62-310 1974 £7.50

CLARKE, L. C.   Objects for the Microscope. 1863. 8vo., orig. cloth, second edition. Wheldon 128-17 1973 £5

CLARKE, MARY   Sadler's Wells Ballet. Macmillan, 1955. 336p., illus. Austin 51-194 1973 $12.50

CLARKE, MARY ANN   The Rival Princes. London, 1810. 8vo., 2 vols., orig. boards, uncut, second edition. Dawsons PM 251-194 1974 £30

CLARKE, MARY COWDEN   The Girlhood of Shakespeare's Heroines. 1881. 2 series in 1, illus. Austin 61-236 1974 $17.50

CLARKE, ROBERT   Sierra Leone. London, n.d. (1843). 8vo., orig. purple cloth, printed paper label, first edition, very good copy. Ximenes 36-49 1974 $125

CLARKE, S.   A Reply to the Objections of Robert Nelson. London, 1714. Contemporary panelled calf, worn, rubbed. Smith 194-140 1974 £5.50

CLARKE, SAMUEL   A Discourse Concerning the Being and Attributes of God. 1725. 8vo., contemporary calf, sixth edition. Hill 126-56 1974 £8.50

CLARKE, SAMUEL   A Geographical Description Of All the Countries In the Known World. London, 1671-70. 3 parts in 1 vol., folio, 18th century panelled calf, rebacked, leather label. Traylen 79-422 1973 £115

CLARKE, SAMUEL   A Paraphrase on the Four Evangelists. Dublin, 1756. 2 vols., contemporary calf. Thomas 28-77 1972 £15.75

CLARKE, SAMUEL   Three Practical Essays. Dublin, 1730. 8vo., contemporary calf. Hill 126-57 1974 £10.50

CLARKE, SIDNEY W.   The Bibliography of Conjuring and Kindred Deceptions. 1920. 8vo., orig. cloth-backed boards. Bow Windows 66-132 1974 £7.50

CLARKE, T. WOOD   Emigres in the Wilderness. Macmillan, 1941. 247p., illus. Austin 62-97 1974 $17.50

CLARKE, W. W.   Clarke's History of the Earliest Railways in Nova Scotia. (Windsor, 1925?). Card cover, illus. Hood's 102-754 1974 $17.50

CLARKE, WILLIAM   Repertorium Bibliographicum. 1819. New buckram, rubber stamp on all plates. Allen 216-174 1974 $35

CLARKE, WILLIAM FRANCIS   The Folly of Bigotry. 1940. Austin 62-96 1974 $10

CLARKSON, L.   Indian Summer. New York, 1881. 4to., orig. cloth, gilt, plates. Wheldon 130-1137 1974 £7.50

CLARKSON, R. E.   Magic Gardens. New York, 1939. 8vo., cloth. Wheldon 130-1380 1974 £10

CLARKSON, THOMAS   An Essay on the Slavery and Commerce of the Human Species. London, 1786. 8vo., orig. boards, uncut, fine, first edition. Dawsons PM 250-17 1974 £320

CLARKSON, THOMAS   An Essay on the Slavery and Commerce of the Human Species. 8vo., 19th century calf, first edition. Dawsons PM 247-46 1974 £95

CLARKSON, THOMAS   The History of the Rise, Progress and Accomplishment of the Abolition of the African Slave-Trade, by the British Parliament. Wilmington, 1816. Leather, slight wear at bottom of spine, very good copy overall. Hayman 59-126 1974 $30

CLARKSON, THOMAS   A Portraiture of Quakerism. New York, 1806. Leather, 3 vols., attractive set. Hayman 59-127 1974 $25

CLASEN, K. H.   German Architecture. Berlin, (1939). Fine photographs. Rich Summer-10 1974 $17.50

CLAUDE LE LORRAINE   Claude Lorrain. Berlin, 1921. Small 4to., plates, illus., half morocco. Quaritch 940-57 1974 £25

CLAUDE LE LORRAINE   Liber Veritatis. (1777-1819). 3 vols., roy. folio, plates, contemporary russia, gilt, very clean copy. Quaritch 940-56 1974 £1,500

CLAUDEL, PAUL   Cette Heure Qui Est Entre le Printemps et l'Ete. Paris, 1913. Folio, orig. wrapper, uncut, first edition. L. Goldschmidt 42-189 1974 $50

CLAUDIANUS, CLAUDIUS   Opera. 1523. 19th century blind stamped russia, rubbed, only Aldine edition. Thomas 30-62 1973 £35

CLAUDIANUS, CLAUDIS   Opera Omnia. Amsterdam, 1760. Thick large 4to., contemporary vellum, gilt, fine. Harper 213-40 1973 $145

CLAUDIANUS, CLAUDIUS   Works. 1817. 2 vols. in 1, new buckram, first complete English translation. Allen 213-269 1973 $12.50

CLAUDIANUS, CLAUDIUS   Opera Omnia ex Optimis Codd. Paris, 1824. 2 vols., large 8vo., contemporary half leather, richly gilt spines & labels. Schumann 499-25 1974 sFr 75

CLAUDIN, A.   The First Paris Press. London, 1898. 4to., orig. printed wrappers, uncut. Dawsons PM 10-126 1974 £20

CLAUS, C.   Die Halocypriden des Atlantischen Oceans und Mittlemeeres. Vienna, 1891. Folio, half morocco, plates. Wheldon 128-883 1973 £10

CLAUSIUS, RUDOLF   Abhandlungen uber die Mechanische Warme-Theorie. 1864. 8vo., modern unlettered half calf, first edition. Dawsons PM 245-178 1974 £120

CLAUSS Primer. Fremont, ca. 1900. 8vo., illus; fine copy. Frohnsdorff 16-31 1974 $10

CLAVERS, MARY PSEUD.
Please turn to
KIRKLAND, CAROLINE MATILDA

CLAVIUS, CHRISTOPHORUS   In Sphaeram Ioannis de Sacro Bosco. 1606. Small 4to., contemporary limp vellum, woodcuts. Zeitlin 235-46 1974 $250

CLAY, C.   Swampy Cree Legends. Toronto, 1938. Worn, signed, presentation. Hood's 103-449 1974 $20

CLAY, HENRY   The Speeches . . . Delivered in the Congress of the United States; to which is prefixed A Biographical Memoir. Philadelphia, 1827. Uncut, orig. boards, paper label, shaken. Butterfield 10-190 1974 $25

CLAY, J. W.   Dugdal's Visitation of Yorkshire. 1899-1917. Imperial 8vo., 3 vols., half morocco, labels, uncut, scarce. Broadhurst 23-1222 1974 £90

CLAY, J. W.   Dugdale's Visitation of Yorkshire. Exeter, 1899-1917. 3 vols., imp. 8vo., half light brown morocco, panelled backs, orig. wrappers bound in, scarce, top edges gilt, others uncut, very fine set. Broadhurst 24-1217 1974 £90

CLAY, ROTHA M.   The Hermits and Anchorites of England. 1914. Illus. Howes 185-1069 1974 £5.50

CLAY, S.   The Present-Day Rock Garden. 1937. 8vo., cloth, plates. Wheldon 131-1499 1974 £20

CLAY, THOMAS   Briefe, Easie and Necessary Tables. London, 1624. 2 parts in 1 vol., 8vo., calf antique, rare, third edition. Dawsons PM 247-47 1974 £175

CLEARK, C. F.   The Mechanic's Book of Reference. (c. 1845). 8vo., orig. printed wrappers in cloth case. Quaritch 940-439 1974 £50

CLEARY, JAMES   Rhetoric and Public Address. Univ. of Wis., 1964. 487p. Austin 51-195 1973 $10

CLEAVELAND, ELIZABETH WHITTLESEY   A Study of Tindale's Genesis Compared With the Genesis of Coverdale and Of the Authorized Version. 1911. Ex-library, sturdy library binding, orig. edition. Austin 61-238 1974 $10

CLEGG, S.   Clegg's Patent Atmospheric Railway. 1839. Large 8vo., orig. cloth, scarce. Quaritch 939-78 1974 £30

CLELAND, J. B.   Toadstools and Mushrooms. Adelaide, 1934-35. 8vo., 2 vols., buckram, plates. Wheldon 129-1168 1974 £7.50

CLELAND, JOHN   Memoirs of a Coxcomb. Fortune Press, 1926. Demy 8vo., quarter antique calf, marbled boards, uncut, unopened, limited to 575 copies, fine. Broadhurst 24-977 1974 £10

CLELAND, JOHN   Memoirs of a Coxcomb. 1926. 8vo., quarter antique calf, marbled boards, uncut, unopened, limited edition. Broadhurst 23-995 1974 £10

CLEMENS, CLARA   My Husband Gabrilowitsch. 1938. Illus., photographs. Austin 57-136 1974 $10

CLEMENS, CYRIL   An Evening With A. E. Housman. 1937. Portraits, first American edition. Covent 55-854 1974 £10

CLEMENS, CYRIL   Mark Twain and Mussolini. Webster Grove, 1934. Orig. cloth, first edition, presentation copy, inscribed by author, fine. MacManus 224-86 1974 $55

CLEMENS, SAMUEL LANGHORNE   Adventures of Huckleberry Finn. New York, 1885. Illus., bright copy, orig. green gilt cloth, portrait frontis. Butterfield 10-192 1974 $300

CLEMENS, SAMUEL LANGHORNE   The Adventures of Huckleberry Finn. New York, 1933. Orig. illus., Limited Editions Club, signed by designer, fine, boxed, limited edition. MacManus 224-76 1974 $40

CLEMENS, SAMUEL LANGHORNE   Adventures of Huckleberry Finn.   New York, Limited Editions Club, 1942. Limited edition, signed by the artist, sepia illus. by Thomas Hart Benton, roy. 8vo., orig. cloth, fine.   Sawyer 293-206 1974 £40

CLEMENS, SAMUEL LANGHORNE   The Adventures of Tom Sawyer.   New York, 1930. Crown 4to., illu., printed cloth boards, limited.   Howes 185-531 1974 £5.50

CLEMENS, SAMUEL LANGHORNE   American Claiment.   1892. First edition.   Allen 216-335 1974 $10

CLEMENS, SAMUEL LANGHORNE   The American Claimant.   New York, 1892. 8vo., illus., orig. cloth, d.w., first edition.   Bow Windows 62-951 1974 £18

CLEMENS, SAMUEL LANGHORNE   A Connecticut Yankee In King Arthur's Court.   New York, 1889. Light green, blue and gold pictorial cloth, good copy, first edition.   Butterfield 10-193 1974 $25

CLEMENS, SAMUEL LANGHORNE   Conversation As It Was by The Social Fireside In the Time of the Tudors.   Chicago, 1939. Signed, buckram cover, leather labels, orig. glassine wrappers.   Ballinger 1-218 1974 $17.50

CLEMENS, SAMUEL LANGHORN   A Double Barrelled Detective Story.   n.d. Fine, English first edition.   Covent 56-2092 1974 £5.25

CLEMENS, SAMUEL LANGHORNE   A Double Barrelled Detective Story. New York, 1902. Plates, cloth gilt, first American edition.   Covent 55-1479 1974 £20

CLEMENS, SAMUEL LANGHORNE   English as She is Taught.   London, 1887. First edition, small square 8vo., orig. patterned cloth, top edges gilt, others uncut, buckram box, fair copy, very rare.   Sawyer 293-278 1974 £135

CLEMENS, SAMUEL LANGHORNE   Eve's Diary.   London & New York, 1906. Cloth, illus., fading.   Dawson's 424-254 1974 $15

CLEMENS, SAMUEL LANGHORNE   Following the Equator.   Hartford, 1897. First trade edition, orig. edition.   Wilson 63-502 1974 $65

CLEMENS, SAMUEL LANGHORNE   The Gilded Age.   Hartford, 1875. Thick 8vo., profusely illus., some wear at extremities.   Current BW9-215 1974 $22.50

CLEMENS, SAMUEL LANGHORNE   The Innocents Abroad.   Hartford, 1869. Cloth, first edition.   Hayman 57-112 1974 $10

CLEMENS, SAMUEL LANGHORNE   Life On the Mississippi.   1883. Half contemporary calf gilt, woodcut illus., first English edition.   Smith 193-338 1973 £9.50

CLEMENS, SAMUEL LANGHORNE   Life On the Mississippi.   1904. Orig. cloth, illus., fine, signed, new edition.   Covent 55-1480 1974 £17.50

CLEMENS, SAMUEL LANGHORNE   Mark Twain's Autobiography.   1924. 2 vols., plates.   Allen 216-337 1974 $15

CLEMENS, SAMUEL LANGHORNE   Mark Twain's Autobiography.   Harper, 1924. 2 vols., 368p., 365p., unabridged ed.   Austin 54-1018 1973 $15

CLEMENS, SAMUEL LANGHORNE   Mark Twain's Autobiography.   New York, 1924. 2 vols., 8vo., cloth, first edition.   Goodspeed's 578-64 1974 $10

CLEMENS, SAMUEL LANGHORNE   Mark Twain's Autobiography and First Romance.   New York, (1871). Self wrapper, chipped, first edition.   Butterfield 10-194 1974 $10

CLEMENS, SAMUEL LANGHORNE   Mark Twain's Autobiography and First Romance.   New York, (1871). Orig. cloth, second issue, very fine.   MacManus 224-77 1974 $35

CLEMENS, SAMUEL LANGHORNE   The Mysterious Stranger.   New York, (1916). Orig. cloth, illus., first edition, about fine.   MacManus 224-78 1974 $27.50

CLEMENS, SAMUEL LANGHORNE   The 1,000,000 Bank Note.   New York, 1893. Cloth, first edition.   Dawson's 424-253 1974 $50

CLEMENS, SAMUEL LANGHORNE   The 1,000,000 Pound Bank-Note and Other Stories.   New York, 1893. Orig. cloth, fine, first edition.   MacManus 224-79 1974 $32.50

CLEMENS, SAMUEL LANGHORNE   Personal Recollections of Joan of Arc. 1902. Orig. pictorial cloth gilt, illus., inscribed, presentation, new edition.   Covent 55-1481 1974 £22.50

CLEMENS, SAMUEL LANGHORNE   The Prince and the Pauper.   Boston, 1882. Orig. dec. cloth, first American edition.   MacManus 224-81 1974 $65

CLEMENS, SAMUEL LANGHORNE   The Prince and the Pauper.   Boston, 1892. Illus., first American edition, sheep.   Current BW9-216 1974 $35

CLEMENS, SAMUEL LANGHORNE   Pudd'nhead Wilson.   1894. 8vo., orig. cloth, illus., first edition.   Bow Windows 66-715 1974 £15

CLEMENS, SAMUEL LANGHORNE   Punch, Brothers, Punch! And Other Sketches.   New York, 1878. 16mo., orig. cloth, second edition, very fine copy.   MacManus 224-82 1974 $50

CLEMENS, SAMUEL LANGHORNE   Roughing It.   Hartford, 1872. 8vo., cloth, considerably worn, first edition.   Goodspeed's 578-59 1974 $10

CLEMENS, SAMUEL L.   Roughing It.   Hartford, 1900. 8vo., orig. bindings, illus., fine.   Butterfield 8-331 1974 $10

CLEMENS, SAMUEL LANGHORNE   1601 or Social Fireside Conversation in Ye Time of Ye Tudors.   Louisville, 1929. Orig. boards, limited to 1,000 copies, fine.   MacManus 224-83 1974 $27.50

CLEMENS, SAMUEL LANGHORNE   To the Person Sitting in Darkness.   1901. Stapled, first separate printing, scarce.   Butterfield 10-195 1974 $100

CLEMENS, SAMUEL LANGHORNE   The Tragedy of Pudd'nhead Wilson and the Comedy of Those Extraordinary Twins.   Hartford, 1894. Marginal illus., first edition, publisher's calf, worn and chipped, front cover attached only by cords.   Butterfield 10-196 1974 $17.50

CLEMENS, SAMUEL LANGHORNE   The Tragedy of Pudd'nhead Wilson and the Comedy Those Extraordinary Twains.   Hartford, 1894. Orig. cloth, first American edition, first issue, fine bright copy.   MacManus 224-84 1974 $65

CLEMENS, SAMUEL LANGHORNE   A Tramp Abroad.   London, 1880. 8vo., orig. red illus. cloth, illus., bookplate, first English edition.   Bow Windows 62-952 1974 £20

CLEMENS, SAMUEL LANGHORNE   A Tramp Abroad.   1884. Orig. pictorial yellow boards, English first edition.   Covent 56-2095 1974 £5.25

CLEMENS, SAMUEL LANGHORNE   The Washoe Giant in San Francisco.   San Francisco, 1938. Orig. cloth backed boards, first edition, very fine, dust jacket.   MacManus 224-85 1974 $30

CLEMENT XIV, POPE   Breve de Nuestro Muy Santo Padre Clemente XIV.   Madrid, 1773. Folio, disbound, woodcut.   Harper 213-41 1973 $275

CLEMENT OF ALEXANDRIA   Opera Quae Exstant Omnia.   1857. 2 vols., thick roy. 8vo., cloth.   Howes 185-1070 1974 £12.50

CLEMENT-JANIN   Les Imprimeurs et les Libraires dans la Cote-d'Or.   Dijon, 1883. Contemporary brown half leather, gilt, engraved frontispiece, second edition.   Kraus B8-299 1974 $30

CLEMENTS, EDITH S.   Flowers of Coast and Sierra.   New York, 1928. First edition, orig. binding, color plates.   Wilson 63-128 1974 $15

CLEMENTS, F. E.   The Genera of Fungi.   New York, 1931. Roy 8vo., buckram, plates, second edition.   Wheldon 129-1169 1974 £6.50

CLENDENING, LOGAN   A Handbook to Pickwick Papers.   1936. Illus., limited, first edition.   Austin 61-237 1974 $12.50

CLENNELL, LUKE   Recreations in Natural History.   1815. Roy. 8vo., plates, woodcuts, contemporary red straight grained morocco, gilt.   Quaritch 940-58 1974 £60

CLERK, JOHN   An Essay on Naval Tactics. London, 1790-97. Large 4to., contemporary tree calf, worn, first edition. Dawsons PM 251-371 1974 £50

CLERK-MAXWELL, JAMES
Please turn to
MAXWELL, JAMES CLERK

CLERKE, RICHARD   Sermons Preached By. 1637. Folio, rebacked, contemporary calf. Howes 185-1072 1974 £14

CLERMONT, CHARLES   De Aere, Locis, & Aquis Terrae Angliae. London, 1672. 12mo., 19th century calf. Gumey 64-54 1974 £95

CLEVELAND, GROVER   Letters of 1850-1908. Boston, 1933. First edition, orig. binding, sound ex-library. Wilson 63-172 1974 $10

CLEVELAND, H. W. S.   Hints to Riflemen. New York, 1864. Illus., pebbled blue cloth, frontispiece, first edition. Bradley 35-160 1974 $16

CLEVELAND, HORACE GILLETTE   A Genealogy of Benjamin Cleveland. Chicago, 1879. 8vo., cloth. Saddleback 14-778 1974 $25

CLEVELAND, JOHN   Clievelandi Vindiciae. London, 1677. 8vo., modern half calf, portrait. Dawsons PM 252-139 1974 £130

CLEVELAND, JOHN   The Works. London, 1687. 8vo., modern calf, first collected edition. Dawsons PM 252-140 1974 £110

CLEVELAND. Cleveland, c. 1910. Small folio, pict. wrappers, photographs. Jenkins 61-1998 1974 $10

THE CLEVELAND Directory for the Year Ending August, 1909, Comprising an Alphabetical List of All Business Firms and Private Citizens and Complete Street Guide. Cleveland, 1908. Cloth. Hayman 59-440 1974 $15

CLEVENGER, SHOBAL VAIL   Fun In a Doctor's Life. Atlantic City, 1909. Rittenhouse 46-146 1974 $12.50

CLIAS, PETER HEINRICH   An Elementary Course of Gymnastic Exercises. London, 1825. 8vo., orig. blue-green cloth, printed paper label, engraved folding plates, fourth edition. Ximenes 37-41 1974 $30

CLICHTOVEUS, JOSSE   Antilutherus. Paris, 1524. Folio, rubbed, rebacked, contemporary blind-stamped brown calf, rare, fine, first edition. Harper 213-42 1973 $650

CLIFFORD, C.   How to Lower Ships' Boats. London, 1855. 8vo., unbound, plates, second edition. Hammond 201-697 1974 £12

CLINCH, GEORGE   Bloomsbury and St. Giles's. London, 1890. 4to., orig. half red morocco, worn, limited edition. Dawsons PM 251-18 1974 £10

CLINCH, GEORGE   Bloomsbury and St. Gile's Past and Present. 1890. 4to., plates, maps, limited edition. Howes 186-2103 1974 £8.50

CLINT, M. B.   Our Bit. Montreal, 1934. Hood's 102-97 1974 $10

CLINTON, DE WITT   An Indtroductory Discourse Delivered. New York, 1815. 8vo., orig. boards, first edition. Dawsons PM 252-141 1974 £45

CLINTON, HENRY   Authentic Copies of Letters. London, 1793. 8vo., unopened, half roan, first edition. Dawsons PM 247-48 1974 £15

CLINTON, HENRY   Memorandums, . . . Respecting the Unprecedented Treatment Which the Army Met With Respecting Plunder Taken After a Siege, and of Which Plunder the Navy Serving with the Army Divided More than Ample Share, Now Fourteen Years Since. London, 1794. 8vo., recent half morocco, first edition, very nice unopened copy. Ximenes 36-51 1974 $150

CLINTON-BAKER, H.   Illustrations of Conifers. 1909-1935. 4to., 4 vols., frontispiece, plates, uncut. Bow Windows 64-55 1974 £148

CLIO and Euterpe, or British Harmony: A Collection of Celebrated Songs and Cantatas. 1758-62. First editions, 3 vols., med. 8vo., full crimson levant morocco by Zaehnsdorf, panelled backs, raised bands, richly tooled gilt, all edges gilt, choice item. Broadhurst 24-588 1974 £320

CLOQUET, H.   Faune des Medecins. Paris, 1822-28. 8vo., orig. wrappers, plates. Wheldon 130-339 1974 £25

CLOSE, LISSIE E.   Home Poems. Chicago and Cleveland, 1876. 8vo., orig. bindings. Butterfield 8-75 1974 $10

CLOSE Rolls of the Reign of Henry III Preserved in the Public Record Office. 1902-16. 4 vols., roy. 8vo., cloth. Quaritch 939-4 1974 £30

CLOUD, VIRGINIA WOODWARD   Down Durley Lane. New York, 1898. Gilt pict. cloth, illus; author's pres. copy. Frohnsdorff 16-108 1974 $10

CLOUGH, ARTHUR HUGH   Poems. 1862. Inscribed, contents a little loose, first edition. Covent 51-2263 1973 £25

CLOUSTON, K. WARREN   The Chippendale Period in English Furniture. 1897. 4to., English first edition. Covent 56-1645 1974 £7.50

CLOUSTON, R. S.   English Furniture and Furniture Makers of the 18th Century. London, 1906. 8vo., illus., orig. cloth. Bow Windows 62-182 1974 £7.50

CLOWES, WILLIAM LAIRD   The Royal Navy. London, 1897-1903. 7 vols., thick roy. 8vo., half blue morocco, gilt, illus. Traylen 79-129A 1973 £150

CLUB Cameos: Portraits of the Day. London, 1879. 8vo., orig. blue cloth, illus., first edition. Ximenes 33-304 1974 $12.50

THE CLUMBER LIBRARY   Catalogue of the Magnificent Library, the Property of the Late Seventh Duke of Newcastle. 1937. 3 vols. in 2, roy. 8vo., half morocco, lettered gilt, top edges gilt, plates in colour & monochrome, fine. Broadhurst 24-282 1974 £25

CLURMAN, HAROLD   Lies Like Truth. Macmillan, 1958. 300p. Austin 51-196 1973 $8.50

CLUSIUS, CAROLUS
Please turn to
L'ECLUSE, CHARLES DE

CLUVERIUS, PHILIPPUS   Sicilia Antiqua. Leiden, 1619. Engraved double page maps, excellent condition within, folio, mid 19th century calf, raised gilt bands, large gilt armorial stamp of J. Gomez de la Cortina in centre of each cover. Thomas 32-76 1974 £150

COATES, C.   The History and Antiquities of Reading. 1802-10. 2 vols., 4to., half morocco, plates. Quaritch 939-299 1974 £55

COATES, G.   The General Short-Horned Herd Book. Otley, 1822. 8vo., orig. boards, plates, scarce. Wheldon 130-389 1974 £20

COATS, W. A.   Catalogue of the Collection of Pictures of the French, Dutch, British and Other Schools Belonging to W. A. Coats. Glasgow, 1904. Folio, olive green morocco, gilt, plates, uncut. Quaritch 940-59 1974 £45

COBB, ELIJAH   A Cape Cod Skipper. New Haven, 1925. Frontispiece, first edition, orig. binding. Wilson 63-408 1974 $12.50

COBB, ELIJAH   Elijah Cobb. New Haven, 1925. Illus., red-brown cloth, first edition. Bradley 35-94 1974 $12.50

COBB, HUMPHREY   Paths of Glory. New York, 1935. Cloth, dust wrapper, first edition. Dawson's 424-255 1974 $15

COBB, IRVIN S.   Alias Ben Alibi. Doran, 1925. 345p. Austin 54-249 1973 $6

COBB, IRVIN S.   The Escape of Mr. Trimm. Doran, 1913. 279p. Austin 54-250 1973 $6.50

COBB, IRVIN S.   Exit Laughing. Bobbs, Merrill, 1941. 572p.
Austin 54-251 1973 $8.50

COBB, IRVIN S.   Fibible, D. D. Doran, 1916. 279p., illus.
Austin 54-252 1973 $6.50

COBB, IRVIN S.   From Place to Place. Doran, 1920. 407p.
Austin 54-253 1973 $6.50

COBB, IRVIN S.   Glory, Glory Hallelujah. Bobbs, Merrill,
1941. 6lp., illus. Austin 54-254 1973 $6

COBB, IRVIN S.   Here Comes the Bride. Doran, 1925. 340p.
Austin 54-255 1973 $6.50

COBB, IRVIN S.   Irvin Cobb At His Best. Sun Dial, 1923. 34lp.
Austin 54-256 1973 $5

COBB, IRVIN S.   Local Color. Doran, 1916. 460p. Austin
54-257 1973 $8.50

COBB, IRVIN S.   Many Laughs For Many Days. Doran, 1925.
243p. Austin 54-258 1973 $6.50

COBB, IRVIN S.   On An Island That Cost $24.00. Doran, 1926.
347p. Austin 54-259 1973 $6

COBB, IRVIN S.   Red Likker. Cosmopolitan, 1929. 339p.
Austin 54-260 1973 $6.50

COBB, IRVIN S.   Roll Call. Bobbs, Merrill, 1942. 48p.,
illus. Austin 54-261 1973 $6.50

COBB, IRVIN S.   Speaking of Operations. Doran, 1915. 64p.,
illus. Austin 54-262 1973 $5

COBB, IRVIN S.   Sundry Accounts. Doran, 1922. 435p.
Austin 54-263 1973 $6

COBB, JAMES   Songs, Duets, Trios, Chorusses. London,
1791. 8vo., modern boards, first edition. Dawsons PM 252-142 1974 £12

COBB, SANFORD H.   The Rise of Religious Liberty in America.
New York, 1902. Frayed, orig. edition. Howes 185-1073 1974 £5

COBBE, HENRY   Luton Church. Bedford & London, 1899.
8vo., orig. cloth, presentation inscription. Howes 186-1972 1974 £7.50

COBBETT, WILLIAM   Cobbett's Genuine Two-Penny Trash. London,
1831. 8vo., first edition. Dawsons PM 247-52 1974 £15

COBBETT, WILLIAM   Cobbett's Gridiron. London, 1822. 8vo.,
uncut, modern boards. Dawsons PM 247-49 1974 £25

COBBETT, WILLIAM   Cobbett's Legacy to Labourers. 1834. 12mo.,
contemporary red straight-grained morocco. Quaritch 939-96 1974 £30

COBBETT, WILLIAM   Cobbett's Paper Against Gold. (1817). 8vo.,
contemporary boards, rebacked. Quaritch 939-97 1974 £45

COBBETT, WILLIAM   Cobbett's Poor Man's Friend. London, 1826.
8vo., modern boards, first edition. Dawsons PM 247-50 1974 £28

COBBETT, WILLIAM   The Emigrant's Guide. London, 1829. 12mo.,
19th century half calf, first edition, nice copy. Ximenes 36-52 1974 $50

COBBETT, WILLIAM   The English Gardener. Andover, 1829. 8vo.,
orig. boards, illus., uncut, first edition. Hammond 201-6 1974 £30

COBBETT, WILLIAM   The English Gardener. 1838. Demy 8vo.,
orig. cloth backed boards, early edition. Howes 185-76 1974 £10

COBBETT, WILLIAM   The English Gardnener. 1845. Small 8vo.,
orig. boards, new edition. Wheldon 130-1381 1974 £7.50

COBBETT, WILLIAM   A Grammar of the English Language. 1826.
12mo., contemporary half calf, rebacked. Bow Windows 64-453 1974 £28

COBBETT, WILLIAM   A Grammar of the English Language. London,
1829. 12mo., reversed calf, uncut. Dawsons PM 252-143 1974 £55

COBBETT, WILLIAM   A History of the Protestant "Reformation", in
England and Ireland. London, 1824. 8vo., contemporary calf, gilt, first edition.
Hammond 201-156 1974 £7.50

COBBETT, WILLIAM   The Life of. London, 1835. 12mo., orig.
blue cloth, paper label, first edition. Dawsons PM 247-53 1974 £10

COBBETT, WILLIAM   A Treatise on Cobbett's Corn. London, 1828.
12mo., contemporary boards, plates, first edition. Dawsons PM 247-51 1974
£65

COBBETT, WILLIAM   The Woodlands. 1825. Orig. boards, uncut,
rebacked, first edition. Bow Windows 64-57 1974 £28

COBBETT, WILLIAM   The Woodlands. 1825. First edition, crown
8vo., contemporary half calf, marbled boards, scarce, fine. Broadhurst 24-1062
1974 £25

COBBETT, WILLIAM   The Woodlands. London, 1825. 8vo., orig.
cloth-backed boards, first edition. Hammond 201-7 1974 £28

COBBETT, WILLIAM   A Year's Residence, in the United States of
America. London, 1818-19. 3 vols., 8vo., orig. blue boards, first English
edition. Ximenes 36-53 1974 $125

COBBOLD, T. SPENCER   Human Parasites. London, 1882. Small 8vo.,
orig. cloth, first edition. Schuman 37-46 1974 $85

COBDEN, RICHARD   The Political Writings of. London, 1868.
2 vols., 8vo., unopened, orig. cloth, second edition. Bow Windows 62-183
1974 £12.75

COBDEN SANDERSON, T. J.   Imantium Irae. 1914. 8vo., limp vellum, frontispiece. Hammond 201-749 1974 £110

COBLENTZ, STANTON A.   The Planet of Youth. 1932. Dust wrapper,
fine, English first edition. Covent 56-1158 1974 £7.50

COCHRANE, CHARLES NORRIS   Christianity and Classical Culture. New York,
1944. Biblo & Tannen 214-605 1974 $8.50

COCKAYNE, T. O.   Leechdoms, Wortcunning and Starcraft of
Early England. London, 1864-66. 3 vols., 8vo., cloth. Dawsons PM 11-185
1974 £16.80

COCKBURN, A. P.   Political Annals of Canada. Toronto, 1905.
Hood's 103-526 1974 $12.50

COCKERELL, SIR SYDNEY CARLYLE 1867   Friends of a Lifetime. 1940. 8vo.,
cloth, d.j., plates, first edition. Quaritch 936-343 1974 £8

COCKERELL, SIR SYDNEY CARLYLE 1867   Laudes Beatae Mariae Virginis.
Kelmscott Press, 1896. Hand coloured borders, hand coloured initials, large 4to.,
orig. holland backed boards, uncut, cloth folder, slip in case, limited to 250
copies, first book from Kelmscott printed in red, blue and black. Sawyer 293-181
1974 £110

COCKERELL, SIR SYDNEY CARLYLE 1867-   Some German Woodcuts of the
Fifteenth Century. 1898. Folio, full brown pigskin, gilt, illus. Hammond 201-
742 1974 £185

COCKERELL, SIR SYDNEY CARLYLE 1867-   Some German Woodcuts of the 15th
Century. Kelmscott Press, 1898. Printed in red and black, large 4to., orig.
Holland backed boards, uncut, fine, limited to 225 copies. Sawyer 293-180
1974 £250

COCKERELL, SIR SYDNEY CARLYLE 1867   The Work of W. de Brailes. 1930.
Folio, plates, half morocco. Quaritch 939-58 1974 £110

COCKRANE, CHARLES N.   Christianity and Classical Culture. New York,
1944. Biblo & Tannen 213-458 1973 $7.50

COCKSHOTT, WINNIFRED   The Pilgrim Fathers, Their Church and Colony.
1909. Plates, map faded. Howes 186-725 1974 £5

COCKTON, HENRY   The Life and Adventures of George St. Julian,
The Prince of Swindlers. London, 1844. 8vo., full page plates, full purple calf,
gilt dec. corded spine. Current BW9-217 1974 $40

COCKTON, HENRY   The Life and Adventures of Valentine Vox. London, 1846. 8vo., orig. cloth, plates. Dawsons PM 252-144 1974 £12

COCLES, BARTHOLOMAEUS   Chiromantia. Venice, 1525. Small 8vo., modern limp vellum, woodcut border. Thomas 32-227 1974 £45

COCLES, BARTHOLOMAEUS   Chiromantia. Venice, 1525. Small 8vo., modern limp vellum, stains. Thomas 28-283 1972 £45

COCTEAU, JEAN   A Call to Order. 1926. Self-portrait frontis., very good copy, with holograph letter in author's hand laid in, first edition. Covent 51-414 1973 £25

COCTEAU, JEAN   A Call to Order. 1926. 8vo., cloth, first edition in English. Quaritch 936-344 1974 £5

COCTEAU, JEAN   Eloge de l'Imprimerie. Prague, 1930. Blue wrappers. Dawson's 424-145 1974 $20

COCTEAU, JEAN   Escales. Paris, 1920. 4to., orig. pictorial wrapper, uncut, limited, first edition. L. Goldschmidt 42-192 1974 $80

COCTEAU, JEAN   The Infernal Machine. 1936. Fine, faded, dust wrapper, English first edition. Covent 56-1637 1974 £7.50

COCTEAU, JEAN   La Machine Infernale. Paris, 1934. Illus. by author, first French edition, one of 1180 numbered copies on alfa, fine, wrappers. Covent 51-416 1973 £17.50

COCTEAU, JEAN   Portraits - Souvenir, 1900-1914. Paris, 1935. 12mo., orig. wrapper, illus. L. Goldschmidt 42-191 1974 $10

COCTEAU, JEAN   The Typewriter. London, 1947. 1st English ed. Biblo & Tannen 213-505 1973 $10

CODMAN, E. A.   The Shoulder. Boston, 1934. Rittenhouse 46-151 1974 $25

CODY, WILLIAM F.   The Life of. Hartford, (1879). Full tan leather, scarce, illus., first edition. Putnam 126-284 1974 $40

COETLOGON, DENIS DE   An Universal History of Arts and Sciences. 1745. 2 vols., thick folio, plates, contemporary calf, rebacked. Quaritch 940-782 1974 £85

COFFEY, P.   The Science of Logic. 1912. 2 vols., faded, scarce. Howes 185-1833 1974 £7.75

COFFIN, GEORGE   A Pioneer Voyage to California and Round the World, 1849-1852. Chicago, 1908. First edition, inscribed & signed by author's son. Jenkins 61-506 1974 $45

COFFIN, HAYDEN   Hayden Coffin's Book. 1930. Presentation, inscribed, illus. Covent 55-1436 1974 £5.25

COFFIN, JOSHUA   An Account of Some of the Principal Slave Insurrections . . . In the United States and Elsewhere, During the Last Two Centuries. New York, 1860. Sewed. Butterfield 10-100 1974 $20

COFFIN, JOSHUA   A Sketch of the History of Newbury. Boston, 1845. 8vo., orig. bindings, plates. Butterfield 8-229 1974 $20

COFFIN, ROBERT P. TRISTRAM   John Dawn. 1936. Austin 54-264 1973 $8.50

COFFIN, ROBERT P. TRISTRAM   Primer for America. New York, 1943. 1st ed., illus. Biblo & Tannen 214-679 1974 $7.50

COFFIN, ROBERT P. TRISTRAM   Yankee Coast. 1947. Illus. Austin 54-265 1973 $8.50

COFFIN, ROBERT P. TRISTRAM   The Yoke of Thunder. 1932. Austin 54-266 1973 $10

COFFIN, W. F.   1812, The War and Its Moral, a Canadian Chronicle. Montreal, 1864. Hood's 102-98 1974 $25

COHAUSEN, JOHANN HEINRICH   Hermippus Redivivus. London, 1749. 8vo., half calf, gilt, second edition in English. Traylen 79-211 1973 £25

COHEN, CHARLES J.   Memoir of Rev. John Wiley Faires. (Philadelphia), 1926. Thick 8vo., orig. bindings. Butterfield 8-540 1974 $25

COHEN, GEORGE   The Jews in the Making of America. 1924. 274 pages. Austin 57-137 1974 $12.50

COHEN, HENRI   Guide de l'Amateur de Livres a Gravures de XVIIIe Siecle. Paris, 1912. 2 parts in 1 vol., large 8vo., contemporary brown half morocco, limited. Dawsons PM 10-129 1974 £95

COHEN, MORRIS RAPHAEL   A Dreamer's Journey. 1949. Austin 62-98 1974 $12.50

COHEN, MORRIS RAPHAEL   Reason and Nature. New York, 1931. First edition. Biblo & Tannen 213-951 1973 $12.50

COHEN, MORRIS RAPHAEL   Reason and Nature. New York, 1931. Thick 8vo., orig. cloth. Howes 185-1834 1974 £5

COHEN, ROBERT   La Grece et l'Hellenisation du Monde Antique. Paris, 1934. Rebound. Biblo & Tannen 214-606 1974 $10

COHEN, ROSE   Out of the Shadow. Doran, 1918. Austin 62-99 1974 $12.50

COHEN, SAMUEL H.   Transplanted. 1937. Austin 62-100 1974 $12.50

COHN, ART   The Nine Lives of Michael Todd. Random House, 1958. 396p., illus. Austin 51-197 1973 $6.50

COHN, LOUIS HENRY   A Bibliography of the Works of Ernest Hemingway. New York, 1931. Frontis., first U. S. edition, one of 500 numbered copies, fine. Covent 51-895 1973 £15

COHN, TOBIAS   The Works of Tobias. (Venice, 1708). Small 4to., contemporary sprinkled calf, illus., rare, first edition. Zeitlin 235-48 1974 $1,275

COHN, WILLIAM   Buddha in der Kunst des Ostens. Leipzig, 1925. 4to., plates and illus., orig. cloth, light damp staining. Bow Windows 66-134 1974 £12

COHNHEIM, JUL   Neue Untersuchungen. Berlin, 1873. 8vo., old boards, first edition. Gurney 64-55 1974 £65

COIFFIER DE VERSEUX, HENRI-LOUIS   Dictionnaire Biographique Et Historique des Hommes Marquans. London, 1800. 3 vols., 8vo., contemporary speckled calf, labels, first edition. Dawsons PM 10-130 1974 £35

COKAYNE, G. E.   Complete Peerage of England, Scotland, Ireland, Great Britain and the United Kingdom. 1887-98. 8 vols., 8vo., half morocco. Quaritch 939-711 1974 £30

COKE, HENRY R.   A Ride Over the Rocky Mountains to Oregon and California. London, 1852. 8vo., orig. pink cloth, gilt, foxed. Traylen 79-471 1973 £75

COKE, ROGER   A Detection of the Court and State of England during the Four Last Reigns. London, 1694. 8vo., contemporary speckled calf, first edition. Dawsons PM 251-195 1974 £40

COKER, JOHN   A Survey of Dorsetshire. London, 1732. Small folio, nineteenth century half calf, plates, first edition. Dawsons PM 251-19 1974 £175

COKER, W. C.   The Clavarias of the United States and Canada. Chapel Hill, 1923. Roy 8vo., cloth, plates. Wheldon 129-1171 1974 £10

COKER, W. C.   The Gasteromycetes. Chapel Hill, 1928. Imperial 8vo., cloth, plates. Wheldon 129-1172 1974 £15

COKER, W. C.   The Saprolegniaceae. Chapel Hill, 1923. 4to., cloth, plates. Wheldon 129-1170 1974 £7.50

COLBY, C. C.   Parliamentary Government in Canada. Montreal, 1886. Hood's 104-18 1974 $10

COLE, F. J.   Early Theories of Sexual Generation. Oxford,
1930. 8vo., orig. blue cloth gilt, first edition. Dawsons PM 249-113 1974
£15

COLE, H. E.   Baraboo, Dells, and Devil's Lake Region.
Baraboo, c.1921. 8vo., wrapper, illus., new enlarged edition. Saddleback
14-758 1974 $10

COLE, H. E.   Stagecoach and Tavern Days in the Baraboo
Region. Baraboo, c.1923. 8vo., wrapper, illus. Saddleback 14-759 1974
$15

COLE, HENRY   Alphabet of Quadrupeds. 1844. Crown 8vo.,
orig. cloth, loose in case due to perishing gutta-percha binding, plates ptd. in
colour. George's 610-168 1973 £5

COLE, HERBERT   Heraldry and Floral Forms as Used in Decoration.
London, 1922. 4to., 1st ed., illus. Biblo & Tannen 210-192 1973 $8.50

COLE, J.   The History and Antiquities of Ecton.
Scarborough, 1825-26. 3 items in 2 vols., 8vo., fine, morocco gilt, limited
editions. Quaritch 939-502 1974 £90

COLE, R. V.   British Trees. 1907. 4to., half calf, 2 vols.
Wheldon 130-1545 1974 £10

COLE, T. H.   The Antiquities of Hastings and the
Battlefield. 1884. 8vo., orig. cloth, maps and plans, revised enlarged new
edition. Bow Windows 66-673 1974 £5

COLE, V.   The Life and Paintings of Vicat Cole, R. A.
1896. 3 vols., folio, illus., cloth. Quaritch 940-60 1974 £10

COLE, W.   Index Nominum in Libris Dictis Cole's
Escheats. 1852. Small 8vo., cloth. Quaritch 939-774 1974 £35

COLE, W. RUSSELL   Sonoma County, California. San Francisco,
1915. 8vo., wrapper. Saddleback 14-75 1974 $12.50

COLEMAN, A. P.   Ice Ages Recent and Ancient. 1926. 8vo.,
cloth, illus., maps, scarce. Wheldon 128-954 1973 £7.50

COLEMAN, EMMA LEWIS   New England Captives Carried to Canada, Between
1677 and 1760.... Portland, 1925. 2 vols., illus., cloth covers. Hood's 102-
183 1974 $75

COLEMAN, EMMA LEWIS   New England Captives Carried to Canada
Between 1677 and 1760. Portland, 1925. 2 vols. Jenkins 61-909 1974
$67.50

COLEMAN, JOHN   Players and Playwrights I Have Known. 1890.
2 vols., plates, ex-library, spines slightly worn. Allen 216-2112 1974 $12.50

COLEMAN, SATIS N.   Bells. Chicago, 1928. Illus. Biblo & Tannen
214-813 1974 $8

COLENSO, WILLIAM   Fifty Years Ago in New Zealand. 1888. 8vo.,
orig. printed paper wrappers, first edition. Bow Windows 64-457 1974 £40

COLERIDGE, HARTLEY   Poems: Vol. 1. Leeds, 1833. Well rebound
in buckram, gilt lettering, library stamp, very good copy, first edition. Covent
51-2264 1973 £21

COLERIDGE, HARTLEY   Poems By. 1851. 8vo., 2 vols., orig. cloth,
second edition. Bow Windows 64-456 1974 £8.50

COLERIDGE, SAMUEL TAYLOR   Aids to Reflection. 1854. Sixth edition,
spine worn, very good copy. Covent 51-421 1973 £6.50

COLERIDGE, SAMUEL TAYLOR   Aids to Reflection. 1872. 324 pages.
Austin 61-239 1974 $17.50

COLERIDGE, SAMUEL TAYLOR   Aids to Reflection and The Confessions of an
Inquiring Spirit. London, 1890. Biblo & Tannen 213-743 1973 $7

COLERIDGE, SAMUEL TAYLOR   Autograph Letter Signed. 1830. 12mo.,
3 1/4 pages. Dawsons PM 252-145 1974 $360

COLERIDGE, SAMUEL TAYLOR   The Devil's Walk. London, (n.d.). 8vo.,
illus., orig. wrappers, first edition, first issue. Dawsons PM 252-146 1974
£125

COLERIDGE, SAMUEL TAYLOR   The Evil Genius. 1886. 3 vols., orig.
dec. cloth, library label, first edition. Howes 186-101 1974 £30

COLERIDGE, SAMUEL TAYLOR   The Friend. (1809-10). 8vo., half calf,
contemporary boards, first edition. Dawsons PM 252-147 1974 £475

COLERIDGE, SAMUEL TAYLOR   The Friend: À Series of Essays. London, 1863.
2 vols., new revised edition, nice set, orig. cloth. Covent 51-422 1973
£10.50

COLERIDGE, SAMUEL TAYLOR   Kubla Khan. New York, 1933. 1st ed.
Biblo & Tannen 210-168 1973 $7.50

COLERIDGE, SAMUEL TAYLOR   Letters. 1895. 2 vols., new buckram,
blind stamp. Allen 216-343 1974 $15

COLERIDGE, SAMUEL TAYLOR   Literary Remains. 1836-39. 4 vols., new
buckram, blind stamp. Allen 216-344 1974 $40

COLERIDGE, SAMUEL TAYLOR   Omniana. 1812. Small 8vo., boards, half
calf, first edition. Quaritch 936-345 1974 £55

COLERIDGE, SAMUEL TAYLOR   Osorio. London, 1873. 8vo., orig. boards,
uncut, first edition. Dawsons PM 252-148 1974 £45

COLERIDGE, SAMUEL TAYLOR   Osorio a Tragedy. London, 1873. 8vo.,
paper boards, label, worn, first edition. Bow Windows 62-187 1974 £40

COLERIDGE, SAMUEL TAYLOR   Poems. London, 1797. 8vo., blue morocco
gilt, uncut, second edition. Dawsons PM 252-149 1974 £110

COLERIDGE, SAMUEL TAYLOR   The Poetical and Dramatic Works. n.d.
8vo., contemporary brown morocco, gilt. Smith 193-246 1973 £5

COLERIDGE, SAMUEL TAYLOR   Poetical and Dramatic Works. 1847.
3 vols., small 8vo., half crimson levant morocco, gilt. Howes 185-78 1974
£16.50

COLERIDGE, SAMUEL TAYLOR   Poetical and Dramatic Works. 1880. 4 vols.,
very nice set. Covent 51-425 1973 £9.50

COLERIDGE, SAMUEL TAYLOR   Poetical Works. 1840. 3 vols., small 8vo.,
contemporary full buff calf, gilt. Howes 186-98 1974 £15

COLERIDGE, SAMUEL TAYLOR   The Poetical Works. London, 1885. 2 vols.,
8vo., orig. cloth, frontispiece, uncut. Dawsons PM 252-150 1974 £20

COLERIDGE, SAMUEL TAYLOR   The Rime of the Ancient Mariner. London, n.d.
4to., orig. dec. cloth, gilt, dust-wrapper, fine, illus. Hammond 201-492 1974
£15

COLERIDGE, SAMUEL TAYLOR   The Rime of the Ancient Mariner. 1899.
Woodcut border, light blue gray boards, bookplate, nice, scarce. Ross 86-451
1974 $75

COLERIDGE, SAMUEL TAYLOR   Rime of the Ancient Mariner. (London,
1903). Orig. blind stamped vellum, one of 150 numbered copies on vellum,
woodcut frontispiece, fine. MacManus 224-155 1974 $85

COLERIDGE, SAMUEL TAYLOR   The Rime of the Ancient Mariner. 1944.
Folio, orig. morocco backed boards, by Sangorski and Sutcliffe, one of 18 sets
of proofs of an abandoned edition. Thomas 32-279 1974 £60

COLERIDGE, SAMUEL TAYLOR   The Rime of the Ancient Mariner. New York,
1945. 4to. Biblo & Tannen 210-738 1973 $7.50

COLERIDGE, SAMUEL TAYLOR   Selected Poems of. (N.P.), 1935. Large
8vo., hand made paper, orig. vellum, limited. Bow Windows 62-680 1974
£35

COLERIDGE, SAMUEL TAYLOR   Selected Poems of. 1935. Small folio, orig.
vellum, gilt, uncut, limited. Broadhurst 23-1076 1974 £30

COLERIDGE, SAMUEL TAYLOR   Selected Poems of. Nonesuch Press, 1935. Wood engravings, small folio, orig. orange stained vellum gilt, top edges gilt, others uncut, limited to 500 copies, on Auvergne hand made paper, fine. Broadhurst 24-1037 1974 £30

COLERIDGE, SAMUEL TAYLOR   Seven Lectures on Shakespeare and Milton. London, 1856. 8vo., orig. cloth, uncut, first edition. Dawsons PM 252-151 1974 £45

COLERIDGE, SAMUEL TAYLOR   Specimens of the Table Talk. 1835. 2 vols. in 1, foxed, first American edition. Allen 216-345 1974 $15

COLETTE   Trois-Six-Neuf. Paris, 1945. 4to., worn wrappers, illus., limited edition. Minters 37-83 1973 $25

COLEY, HENRY   Merlinus Anglicus Junior. 1702. Contemporary roan, some leaves cropped at foot. Thomas 32-306 1974 £15

COLGATE, WILLIAM   Canadian Art, Its Origin and Development. Toronto, 1943. Hood's 104-159 1974 $85

COLGATE, WILLIAM   Canadian Art, Its Origin and Development. Toronto, 1943. Hood's 102-150 1974 $85

COLGRAVE, BERTRAM   Two Lives of St. Cuthbert. 1940. 390 pages. Howes 185-1099 1974 £7.50

COLIN, A.   Historical Illustrations of Lord Byron's Works. London, 1833. 3/4 red. mor. and marbled bds., orig. wraps., bound in. Jacobs 24-41 1974 $18

COLIN, GABRIEL-CONSTANS   Traite de Physiologie Comparee des Animaux Domestiques. Paris, 1854-56. 2 vols., 8vo., contemporary half calf, illus., first edition. Schuman 37-47 1974 $75

COLLECTANEA Archaeologica. 1862-71. 2 vols., 4to., plates, half morocco gilt. Quaritch 939-61 1974 £12

COLLECTION of Catholic Pamphlets, Chiefly Relating to Ireland. 7 items in 1 vol. Emerald 50-149 1974 £21

A COLLECTION of Cookery and Medical Receipts. 4to., old sheep. Quaritch 939-207 1974 £20

A COLLECTION of Fashion Prints from the Series Costume Parisien and Modes de Paris. (Paris, 1823-25. Hand coloured engraved plates, 8vo., contemporary green straight grained morocco gilt tooled, fine binding. Sawyer 293-139 1974 £390

A COLLECTION of Interesting Biography. Dublin, 1792. 8vo., contemporary calf, plates. Emerald 50-246 1974 £15

A COLLECTION of Louisiana Folk Tales Gumbo Ya-Ya. Boston - New York, (1945). 8vo., orig. bindings, dust jacket. Butterfield 8-192 1974 $15

A COLLECTION of New American Writing. New York, 1944. Dust wrapper, fine, first American edition. Covent 55-37 1974 £10

A COLLECTION of Nineteenth Century Culinary Receipts. (c.1840). Small 8vo., marbled wrappers. Quaritch 939-208 1974 £10

A COLLECTION of Oaths, Grants, relating to Heraldic Offices. Folio, calf back, boards. Quaritch 939-733 1974 £40

COLLECTION of Pamphlets, relating to the Church and State of Ireland. 8vo., 12 items in 1 vol. Emerald 50-150 1974 £30

A COLLECTION of Poems. 1701. 8vo., orig. calf, worn, signature. Quaritch 936-186 1974 £50

A COLLECTION of Poems. 1702. 8vo., contemporary calf, fine, second edition. Quaritch 936-187 1974 £40

COLLECTION Of Poems. 1782. 6 vols., contemporary calf, ex-library. Austin 61-307 1974 $47.50

A COLLECTION of Poems by Several Hands. London, 1693. 8vo., inscription, contemporary calf, rebacked, first edition. Dawsons PM 252-152 1974 £125

A COLLECTION of Reports and Notices of the Committee of Management of the Kennet and Avon Canal Navigation. 1807-89. 24 items, folio. Quaritch 939-80 1974 £200

A COLLECTION of the Dresses of Different Nations. (1757-72). 4 vols., 4to., plates, tree calf, rubbed. Quaritch 940-720 1974 £650

A COLLECTION of the Epistles from the Yearly Meeting of Friends in London, to the Quarterly Meetings in Great Britain, Ireland and Elsewhere, 1675 to 1820. New York, 1821. Leather, cover worn. Hayman 59-578 1974 $10

A COLLECTION of the Most Reputed Tragedies. London, (1824). 4 vols., 8vo., illus., foxing, contemporary half roan, frontispieces. Bow Windows 62-928 1974 £21

A COLLECTION of the Most Reputed Tragedies, Comedies, Operas, Melodramas, Farces and Interludes. (1824-27). 4 vols., contemporary half black calf gilt. Howes 186-462 1974 £25

A COLLECTION of the Parliamentary Debates in England. 1741-42. 15 vols., contemporary calf, stained. Howes 186-1125 1974 £42

A COLLECTION of Works Having Reference to Coaching. 1861-93. 11 vols., 8vo., half red morocco, plates. Quaritch 939-215 1974 £115

COLLECTORUM Medicinalium Libri XVII. Venice, n.d. 8vo., old vellum. Gurney 64-165 1974 £50

COLLES, RAMSAY   The History of Ulster. London, 1919. 4 vols., 8vo., illus., maps. Emerald 50-151 1974 £15

COLLETT, HENRY   Flora Simlensis. Calcutta and Simla, 1902. Frontispiece, faded, first edition. Bow Windows 64-58 1974 £7.50

COLLETT, HENRY   Flora Simlensis. Calcutta, 1902 or 1921. 8vo., cloth, illus., map, scarce. Wheldon 128-1249 1973 £6

COLLETT, HENRY   Flora Simlensis. Calcutta, 1902. 8vo., cloth, illus., scarce. Wheldon 131-1275 1974 £10

COLLETT, R.   Norges Hvirveldyr, II Fugle. Kristiania, 1921. 3 vols., 8vo., half calf, illus. Wheldon 131-569 1974 £45

COLLIDGE, MARY ROBERTS   Chinese Immigration. Holt, 1909. 531p., orig. ed. Austin 62-108 1974 $12.50

COLLIER, JEREMY   A Defence of the Short View of the Profaneness and Immorality of the English Stage. London, 1699. 8vo., modern half calf, first edition. Dawsons PM 252-156 1974 £65

COLLIER, JEREMY   An Ecclesiastical History of Great Britain. 1852. 9 vols., orig. cloth. Howes 185-1078 1974 £35

COLLIER, JEREMY   Essays upon Several Moral Subjects. 1722-20-25. 8vo., 3 vols., contemporary panelled calf, rebacked. Quaritch 936-32 1974 £35

COLLIER, JEREMY   A Short View of the Immorality. London, 1698. 8vo., modern morocco, first edition. Dawsons PM 252-155 1974 £85

COLLIER, JOHN   The Devil and All. (1935). 8vo., orig. cloth, signed, inscription, first edition. Rota 190-128 1974 £6.50

COLLIER, JOHN   No Traveller Returns. 1931. One of 210 numbered copies on handmade paper, signed by author, fine, velvet boards, gilt design, first edition. Covent 51-430 1973 £12.50

COLLIER, JOHN   No Traveller Returns. 1931. 8vo., full black velvet, gilt, signed, first edition. Rota 190-127 1974 £10

COLLIER, JOHN PAYNE   Illustrations of Early English Literature. London, 1867-70. 17 parts in 3 vols., 4to., contemporary citron half morocco, uncut. Dawsons PM 252-154 1974 £90

COLLIER, JOHN PAYNE   Illustrations of Old English Literature.   London, 1866. 24 parts in 3 vols., 4to., orig. wrappers, contemporary green half morocco. Dawsons PM 252-153 1974 £110

COLLIER, JOHN PAYNE   Notes and Emendations.   Whitaker, 1853. Austin 51-198 1973 $25

COLLIER, JOHN PAYNE   Notes and Emendations to the Text of Shakespeare's Plays.   1853. 8vo., calf, second edition.   Hill 126-240 1974 £16

COLLIER, JOHN PAYNE   Notes and Emendations to the Text of Shakespeare's Plays.   1853. 8vo., polished calf, gilt.   Quaritch 936-555 1974 £15

COLLIER, JOHN PAYNE   Poetical Decameron.   1820. 2 vols., new buckram, blind stamp.   Allen 216-1785 1974 $15

COLLIER, JOHN PAYNE   Punch and Judy.   New York, 1929. 8vo., boards, cloth spine, unopened, ltd. ed. to 376 copies, illus.   Frohnsdorff 16-251 1974 $30

COLLIER, JOHN PAYNE   Reprints of Early English Literature.   1870. 4to., straight grained morocco, gilt, uncut.   Quaritch 936-346 1974 £15

COLLIER, JOHN PAYNE   Shakespeare's Library.   (1843). 8vo., 2 vols., binders cloth.   Quaritch 936-556 1974 £12

COLLIER'S Photographic History of the European War.   New York, 1915. Grey boards, pictorial cover, rubbed.   Ballinger 1-246 1974 $12.50

COLLIGNON, CHARLES   The Miscellaneous Works Of.   Cambridge, 1786. 4to., orig. wrappers, uncut, scarce.   Hill 126-58 1974 £25

COLLIN, E.   Des Rhubarbes.   Paris, 1871. 4to., sewed, plates.   Wheldon 128-1676 1973 £5

COLLIN, E.   Des Rhubarbes.   Paris, 1871. 4to., sewed, plates.   Wheldon 130-1610 1974 £5

COLLIN, HEINRICH JOSEPH   Camphorae Vires.   Vienna, 1773. 8vo., contemporary calf, first edition.   Schuman 37-48 1974 $85

COLLINGWOOD, C.   Rambles of a Naturalist.   1868. 8vo., orig. cloth, plates, scarce.   Wheldon 129-259 1974 £25

COLLINGWOOD, FRANCIS   The Universal Cook.   London, 1792. 8vo., half calf, gilt, plates, first edition.   Hammond 201-159 1974 £85

COLLINGWOOD, STUART DODGSON   The Life and Letters of Lewis Carroll. Toronto, n.d. Illus., small tear in spine which is somewhat darkened & shelf rubbed, owner's name in ink on free fly, orig. binding, very good copy.   Ross 87-90 1974 $10

COLLINGWOOD, STUART DODGSON   Life and Letters of Lewis Carroll. 1899.   Austin 61-240 1974 $10

COLLINGWOOD, W. G.   Life and Work of John Ruskin.   1893. 2 vols., plates.   Allen 216-1544 1974 $17.50

COLLINGWOOD, W. G.   Thorstein of the Mere.   1895. Dec. cloth gilt, fine, wood-engravings.   Covent 55-494 1974 £5.25

COLLINS, ANTHONY   A Discourse of Free-Thinking.   1713. 8vo., unbound.   Hill 126-59 1974 £25

COLLINS, ANTHONY   A Discourse of Free-Thinking, Occasion'd by the Rise and Growth of a Sect Call'd Free-Thinkers.   London (in fact, the Hague), 1713. 8vo., contemporary calf, front cover loose, spine gilt.   Ximenes 36-54 1974 $45

COLLINS, ANTHONY   A Philosophical Inquiry Concerning Human Liberty.   Birmingham, 1790. 8vo., boards.   Hammond 201-526 1974 £20

COLLINS, ARTHUR 1682-1760   Collin's Peerage of England.   London, 1812. 8vo., 9 vols., contemporary diced calf, gilt.   Hammond 201-418 1974 £35

COLLINS, ARTHUR 1682-1760   Proceedings, Precedents and Arguments.   1734. Folio, old calf.   Quaritch 939-712 1974 £30

COLLINS, DAVID   An Account of the English Colony in New South Wales.   1798. 4to., 2 vols., contemporary calf, rebacked, fine, first edition. Bow Windows 64-458 1974 £650

COLLINS, DAVID   An Account of the English Colony in New South Wales.   1804. 4to., contemporary calf, rebacked, second edition.   Broadhurst 23-1625 1974 £225

COLLINS, DAVID   An Account of the English Colony in New South Wales.   1804. Engraved plates, second edition, 4to., contemporary calf, rebacked, fine, complete with ad leaf.   Broadhurst 24-1597 1974 £250

COLLINS, FREDERICK L.   The Christmas Trail.   Mt. Vernon, 1928. First book edition, limited to 600 copies, illus. in grey tones, red gilt dec. covers, publisher's box, very fine.   Current BW9-22 1974 $14.50

COLLINS, HERMAN LEROY   Philadelphia.... A Story of Progress.   New York, c. 1941. 4 vols., 4to., illus., orig. binding.   Wilson 63-89 1974 $45

COLLINS, J. C.   Studies in Shakespeare.   1904. Small 8vo., half calf, gilt.   Quaritch 936-557 1974 £6

COLLINS, J. E.   The Private Book of Useful Alloys and Memoranda for Goldsmiths, Jewellers, etc.   (1872). 8vo., cloth, scarce. Quaritch 940-672 1974 £28

COLLINS, JOHN   Commercium Epistolicum.   1712. 4to., calf antique, first edition, first issue.   Dawsons PM 245-179 1974 £245

COLLINS, JOHN   The Sector On a Quadrant.   London, 1658. Small 4to., contemporary calf, fine, plates, first edition.   Traylen 79-212 1973 £270

COLLINS, MORTIMER   The Vivian Romance.   London, 1870. 3 vols., 8vo., orig. cloth, first edition.   Dawsons PM 252-157 1974 £55

COLLINS, PETE   No People Like Show People.   Muller, 1957. 258p., illus.   Austin 51-200 1973 $8.50

COLLINS, S.   Paradise Retriev'd.   1717. 8vo., modern boards, plates, rare.   Wheldon 130-1469 1974 £35

COLLINS, WILKIE
Please turn to
COLLINS, WILLIAM WILKIE

COLLINS, WILLIAM 1721-1759   Poetical Works of.   Austin 61-242 1974 $12.50

COLLINS, WILLIAM 1721-1759   The Poetical Works of.   London, 17998. 8vo., contemporary crimson morocco, gilt.   Hammond 201-296 1974 £15

COLLINS, WILLIAM 1721-1759   The Poetical Works.   London, 1798. 8vo., contemporary calf, rubbed, first edition.   Dawsons PM 252-545 1974 £21

COLLINS, WILLIAM WIEHE 1862-   Cathedral Cities of Italy.   New York, 1911. Biblo & Tannen 210-15 1973 $7.50

COLLINS, WILLIAM WIEHE 1862-   Cathedral Cities of Italy.   New York, 1911. Biblo & Tannen 210-14 1973 $7.50

COLLINS, WILLIAM WIEHE 1862-   Cathedral Cities of Spain.   New York, 1912. Biblo & Tannen 210-16 1973 $7.50

COLLINS, WILLIAM WILKIE   Antonina.   1840. 3 vols., spine worn, binding trifle soiled, first edition.   Allen 216-350 1974 $100

COLLINS, WILLIAM WILKIE   Armadale.   New York, 1866. Apparently true first edition, fading of spine, unusually fine, tight copy, rare thus, orig. binding. Ross 86-95 1974 $150

COLLINS, WILLIAM WILKIE   The Moonstone.   Leipzig, 1868. 2 vols. in 1, calf backed boards, very good copy, first edition.   Covent 51-431 1973 £10.50

COLLINS, WILLIAM WILKIE   A Rogue's Life.   New York, n.d. Orig. wrappers, English first edition.   Covent 56-319 1974 £10.50

COLLINS, WILLIAM WILKIE   The Woman in White. New York, 1861. Orig. cloth, engravings, first American edition. Covent 55-495 1974 £110

COLLINS, WILLIAM WILKIE   The Works of. London, 1875-89. 23 vols., 8vo., frontispiece, illus., orig. cloth. Bow Windows 62-190 1974 £75

COLLINSON, JOHN   The History and Antiquities of the County of Somerset. 1791. 4to., 3 vols., contemporary diced russia, rebacked, first edition. Dawsons PM 251-20 1974 £170

COLLYNS, CHARLES PALK   Notes on the Chase of the Wild Red Deer in the Counties of Devon and Somerset. London, 1862. 8vo., orig. green cloth, plates, very nice copy, first edition. Ximenes 37-44 1974 $27.50

COLMAN, GEORGE   The Battle of Hexham. Dublin, 1790. 12mo., old stiff wrappers, very good uncut copy, some foxing, scarce, first edition. Ximenes 37-46 1974 $27.50

COLMAN, GEORGE   The Comedies of Terence. 1765. 4to., contemporary calf, frontispiece, plates. Hill 126-261 1974 £21

COLMAN, GEORGE   The Comedies of Terence. 1768. 2 vols., 8vo., contemporary calf, joints cracked, frontispiece, second edition. Bow Windows 66-691 1974 £10

COLMAN, GEORGE   Critical Reflections on the Old English Dramatick Writers. London, 1761. 8vo., disbound, first edition. Ximenes 37-45 1974 $80

COLMAN, GEORGE   The Iron Chest. London, 1808. 8vo., modern boards, fourth edition. Dawsons PM 252-160 1974 £6

COLMAN, GEORGE   The Jealous Wife. London, 1761. 8vo., modern boards, second edition. Dawsons PM 252-158 1974 £15

COLMAN, GEORGE   John Bull. London, 1805. 8vo., modern boards, first authorised edition. Dawsons PM 252-161 1974 £13

COLMAN, GEORGE   Man and Wife. Dublin, 1770. 12mo., modern boards, first Dublin edition. Dawsons PM 252-159 1974 £15

COLMAN, GEORGE   The Mountaineers. London, 1805. 8vo., modern boards, new edition. Dawsons PM 252-162 1974 £12

COLMAN, GEORGE   The Surrender of Calais. London, 1808. 8vo., modern boards, first authorised edition. Dawsons PM 252-163 1974 £13

COLMAN, GEORGE   Who Wants a Guinea? London, 1805. 8vo., modern boards, new edition. Dawsons PM 252-164 1974 £12

COLMAN, J.   Hybridization of Orchids. 1932. Small 4to., orig. cloth, plates, rare. Wheldon 131-1614 1974 £15

COLMEIRO, M.   Enumeracion Y Revision de las Plantas de la Peninsula Hispano-Lusitana e Isles Baleares. Madrid, 1885-89. 5 vols., roy. 8vo., new cloth, very scarce. Wheldon 128-1250 1973 £90

COLOM, J. A.   The Lighting Colomme or Sea-Mirrour. Amsterdam, 1668. 2 parts in 1 vol., folio, new half calf, diagrams, rare. Traylen 79-576 1973 £980

COLOMBE, LODOVICO   Risposte Piacevoli. 1808. Small 4to., contemporary limp vellum, first edition. Zeitlin 235-91 1974 $775

COLOMBO, CRISTOFORO   Codice Diplomatico Colombo-Americano Ossia Raccolta di Documenti Originali a Inediti. Genova, 1823. 4to., half blue calf, leather label, plates. Traylen 79-472 1973 £15

COLONNA, FRANCESCO   Hypnerotomachia Poliphili. 1904. Folio, orig. holland backed boards, label, illus., limited, scarce. Howes 186-104 1974 £40

COLONNE, GUIDO DELLE   Historia Trojana. Strassburg, 1494. Small folio, modern marbled boards, clean and sound. Thomas 32-228 1974 £225

COLORADO   A Guide to the Highest State. New York, 1941. 8vo., orig. bindings. Butterfield 8-77 1974 $10

COLQUHOUN, PATRICK   A Treatise on the Wealth, Power and Resources of the British Empire. 1815. 4to., contemporary gilt framed calf, neatly rebacked, some spotting, second edition. Bow Windows 66-135 1974 £64

COLTMAN-ROGERS, C.   Conifers and Their Characteristics. 1920. 8vo., cloth, plates, scarce. Wheldon 130-1546 1974 £5

COLTON, CALVIN   Annexation of Texas. New York, 1844. Very scarce. Jenkins 61-549 1974 $30

COLTON, WALTER   Three Years in California. New York, 1850. Orig. cloth, rubbed, first edition. Hayman 57-65 1974 $15

COLUM, PADRAIC   Anthology of Irish Verse. New York, 1922. 8vo., cloth boards. Emerald 50-155 1974 £5

COLUM, PADRAIC   Balloon. Macmillan, 1929. 123p. Austin 51-201 1973 $12.50

COLUM, PADRAIC   Castle Conquer. New York, 1923. 8vo., cloth boards, first edition. Emerald 50-156 1974 £6.50

COLUM, PADRAIC   Creatures. 1927. Illus., first edition. Austin 61-243 1974 $17.50

COLUM, PADRAIC   The Land. Dublin, 1905. Wrappers, fine. Covent 55-497 1974 £8.50

COLUM PADRAIC   The Road Round Ireland. New York, 1926. First U. S. edition, illus., very good copy, with author's signed presentation inscription. Covent 51-435 1973 £21

COLUM, PADRAIC   The Road Round Ireland. New York, 1926. 8vo., cloth boards, illus., first edition. Emerald 50-157 1974 £7.50

COLUM, PADRAIC   Three Plays. Boston, 1916. 8vo., cloth boards. Emerald 50-153 1974 £7.50

COLUM, PADRAIC   Wild Earth. Dublin, 1907. 8vo., foxing, fine, linen-backed boards. Covent 55-499 1974 £10.50

COLUMBIA BROADCASTING SYSTEM   Radio and Television Bibliography. 89p. Austin 51-202 1973 $17.50

COLUMBIA River Highway: America's Greatest Scenic Drive. Portland, c. 1920. Small folio, wrappers, hand colored illus. Jenkins 61-2059 1974 $12.50

THE COLUMBIAN Muse. New York, 1794. 12mo., later half morocco, spine gilt, first edition, very good copy. Ximenes 36-165 1974 $125

COLUMBUS, CHRISTOPHER   Discovery of America. Dublin, 1824. 16mo., full calf, worn, hinges weak, fine woodcuts. Frohnsdorff 16-292 1974 $40

COLUMBUS, CHRISTOPHER   The Voyages of Christopher Columbus. London, 1930. 4to., vel. back, orig. bds., illus., unopened, uncut, ltd. to 1050 copies. Jacobs 24-12 1974 $85

COLUMBUS CITIZENS COMMITTEE   Columbus Day Celebration: 1951. Austin 62-282 1974 $17.50

COLUMNA, GUIDO DE
Please turn to
COLONNE, GUIDO DELLE

COLVIN, IAN   The Life of Jameson. 1922. 2 vols., maps, plates. Howes 186-959 1974 £6.50

COLVIN, S.   The Letters of Robert Louis Stevenson. 1899. 8vo., orig. cloth, 2 vols. Bow Windows 64-701 1974 £5

COMAN, KATHARINE   The Industrial History of the United States. New York, 1917. Biblo & Tannen 213-28 1973 $7.50

COMBA, EMILIO   History of the Waldenses of Italy. 1889. Orig. cloth. Howes 186-728 1974 £5.50

COMBA, ERNESTO   Storia Dei Valdesi. 1937. Austin 62-103 1974 $27.50

COMBE, JAMES SCARTH   History of a Case of Anaemia. 1824. 8vo.,
contemporary boards, new cloth back, unopened. Schuman 37-49 1974 $750

COMBE, WILLIAM   The Dance of Life. London, 1903. 12mo.,
color engravings. Biblo & Tannen 210-162 1973 $8.50

COMBE, WILLIAM   The Diabo-Lady. London, 1777. 4to.,
modern boards, first edition. Dawsons PM 252-165 1974 £15

COMBE, WILLIAM   The English Dance of Death. London, 1815-16.
2 vols., 8vo., modern calf, first edition. Dawsons PM 252-166 1974 £235

COMBE, WILLIAM   The First, Second and Third Tours of Dr. Syntax.
1813-21. 3 vols., large 8vo., contemporary calf, half calf gilt, plates. Howes
185-81 1974 £85

COMBE, WILLIAM   An Interesting Letter to the Duchess of Devonshire. 1778. Small 8vo., contemporary calf, worn. Hill 126-61 1974 £16

COMBE, WILLIAM   The Tour of Doctor Syntax In Search of the
Picturesque. n.d. Contemporary diced calf, plates, fifth edition. Smith
193-680 1973 £19.50

COMBE, WILLIAM   The Tour of Doctor Syntax in Search of the
Picturesque. London, 1838. Orig. cloth, first edition with these illus. by
Alfred Crowquill, presentation copy. MacManus 224-87 1974 $40

COMBER, H. F.   Field Notes of Tasmanian Plants. n.d. Small
8vo., cloth. Wheldon 130-1498 1974 £5

COMBS, H. C.   Concordance to English Poems of John Donne.
1940. 4to. Allen 216-1903 1974 $10

COMENIUS, JOHANN AMOS   Orbis Pictualium Pictus. London, 1777.
12mo., full calf, spine ends & corners worn. Frohnsdorff 16-228 1974 $200

COMENIUS, JOHANN AMOS   Orbis Sensualium Pictus. London, 1777.
12mo., full calf, spine ends and corners worn, woodcuts, back free endpaper
creased, very nice copy. Frohnsdorff 15-15 1974 $200

COMENIUS, JOHANN AMOS   Orbis Sensualium Pictus. New York, 1810.
12mo., full calf, worn, joints partially cracked, lacking 9 leaves, woodcuts,
first American edition. Frohnsdorff 15-16 1974 $50

COMFORT, ALEX   No Such Liberty. 1941. Dust wrapper, English first edition. Covent 56-246 1974 £7.50

THE COMIC ADVENTURES of Old Mother Hubbard and Her Dog. London, 1806.
Orig. wrappers, 2 vols. Dawson's 424-217 1974 $115

COMIC Grammar. Ca. 1830. Orig. cloth, 16mo., gilt-lettered, 20 hand-colored
plates mounted on cloth. Frohnsdorff 16-229 1974 $45

COMINES, PHILIPPE DE   The Historie of. London, 1596. Folio, contemporary calf, rebacked, gilt, first edition in English. Hammond 201-451 1974 £48

COMMANVILLE, CAROLINE   Souvenirs sur Gustave Flaubert. Paris, 1895.
8vo., orig. wrapper, illus. L. Goldschmidt 42-224 1974 $17.50

COMMELIN, J.   Horti Medici Amstelodamensis. Amsterdam,
1697-1701. 2 vols., folio, contemporary vellum, plates, rare first edition.
Wheldon 131-31 1974 £650

COMMEMORATIVE Biographical Record of Northeastern Pennsylvania. Chicago,
1900. 4to., leather, rebacked. Saddleback 14-674 1974 $110

COMMEMORATIVE Biographical Record of the Counties of Sandusky and Ottawa,
Ohio. Chicago, 1896. 4to., leather, illus. Saddleback 14-625 1974 $65

COMMEMORATIVE Catalogue of the Exhibition of Dutch Art Held in the
Galleries of the Royal Academy, Burlington House, London, Jan.-March, 1929.
1930. Large 4to., cloth, full page plates, many in colour. Eaton Music-575
1973 £12

COMMERCIAL-RATING Reference Book and Mercantile, Law and Bank Directory.
Toronto, 1891. Hood's 104-58 1974 $20

COMMISSION of Conservation of Canada Annual Reports. 1910-19. Hood's
104-896 1974 $75

COMMONS, JOHN R.   Races and Immigrants in America. Macmillan,
1907. 242p., orig. ed. Austin 62-106 1974 $7.50

COMMONS, JOHN R.   Races and Immigrants in America. 1920.
Ex-library, new edition. Austin 57-145 1974 $10

COMPANION to Hungarian Studies. Budapest, 1943. Thick roy. 8vo.,
maps, illus. Howes 186-731 1974 £7.50

COMPARATIVE Account of the Population of Great Britain. 1831. Folio,
boards, cloth back. Quaritch 939-199 1974 £17.50

COMPENDIUM Maleficarum. London, 1929. 4to., orig. cloth, uncut.
Dawsons PM 252-1069 1974 £18

THE COMPLEAT FAMILY Companion. London, 1753. 8vo., full calf, gilt.
Hammond 201-160 1974 £115

COMPLEAT Planter and Cyderist. 1685. 8vo., 19th century mottled calf gilt,
rare, first edition. Wheldon 128-1644 1973 £50

THE COMPLEAT Tutor for the German Flute. (1771). 8vo., frontispiece, sewed,
cloth case. Quaritch 940-810 1974 £110

THE COMPLETE Florist; Or, the Lady and Gentleman's Recreation in the Flower
Garden. n.d. Small 8vo., modern boards, second edition. Wheldon
131-1501 1974 £20

COMPOSING Room Lectures: A Manual for Young Printers. London, 1881.
Small 8vo., orig. printed wrappers, third edition. Kraus B8-359 1974 $18

COMPTON, R. H.   Our South African Flora. Cape Town, n.d.
Roy. 8vo., boards, illus. Wheldon 131-1276 1974 £5

COMPTON, T.   The Northern Cambrian Mountains. 1820.
Roy. 4to., half red roan. Quaritch 939-680 1974 £765

COMPTON-BURNETT, IVY   Daughters and Sons. 1937. Nice copy, first
edition. Covent 51-2267 1973 £10

COMPTON-BURNETT, IVY   Elders and Betters. 1944. Nice copy, first
edition, Roger Senhouse's copy. Covent 51-2268 1973 £15.75

COMPTON-BURNETT, IVY   Men and Wives. 1931. Small mark on front
cover, very nice copy, first edition. Covent 51-441 1973 £8.40

COMPTON-BURNETT, IVY   Men and Wives. 1931. English first edition.
Covent 56-247 1974 £10

COMPTON-BURNETT, IVY   More Women than Men. 1933. Covers faded
and marked, very good copy, first edition. Covent 51-2269 1973 £10

COMPTON-BURNETT, IVY   More Women than Men. 1933. Spine faded,
English first edition. Covent 56-248 1974 £10.50

COMPTON-BURNETT, IVY   Pastors and Masters. 1925. Orig. cloth, dust
wrapper, scarce, first edition. Rota 188-183 1974 £7.50

COMRIE, JOHN D.   History of Scotish Medicine. London, 1932.
2 vols., second edition. Rittenhouse 46-154 1974 $35

COMSTOCK, J. L.   History of the Greek Revolution. 1828.
Old calf, rubbed, frontispiece, foxed. Allen 213-705 1973 $12.50

COMTE, AUGUSTE   Cours de Philosophie Positive. Paris, 1830-42.
6 vols., 8vo., contemporary half calf, rebacked, morocco labels, fine, first
edition. Gilhofer 61-35 1974 sFr. 3,000

CONANT, THOMAS   Upper Canada Sketches. Toronto, 1898.
Portraits, map, illus. Hood's 103-616 1974 $165

CONARD, A.   Sur le Mecanisme de la Division Cellulaire.
Brussels, 1939. 8vo., plates. Wheldon 130-99 1974 £5

CONCILIUM CONSTANTIENSE   Acta et Decreta. Hagenau, 1500. 4to., modern brown morocco, only 15th century edition. Gilhofer 61-3 1974 sFr. 4,500

CONDER, F. R.   Personal Recollections of English Engineers. London, 1868. 8vo., contemporary calf, gilt, first edition. Hammond 201-906 1974 £6

CONDILLAC, ETIENNE BONNOT DE   La Langue des Calcules. Paris, (1798). 2 vols. in 1, 8vo., half calf, first edition. Gilhofer 61-28 1974 sFr. 1,100

CONFALONIERI, FEDERICO   Dell'Elettricita Trattato Fisico-Sperimentale. 1805. 4to., pink silk boards, fine, first edition. Dawsons PM 245-181 1974 £45

THE CONDUCT of His Grace the Duke of Ormonde. London, 1715. Small 4to., browned, old paper wrappers. Bow Windows 62-699 1974 £9.75

CONFEDERATE STATES OF AMERICA   A Bill Making Further Regulations for the Taxation of Banks and Bank Notes, and for the Confiscation of Such Notes Held by Alien Enemies. Richmond, 1865. Jenkins 61-583 1974 $10

CONFEDERATE STATES OF AMERICA   A Bill Requiring Suit to be Brought Against Persons Connected With the Cotton Bureau and Cotton Office in Texas. Richmond, 1865. Jenkins 61-585 1974 $12.50

CONFEDERATE STATES OF AMERICA   A Bill to Provide for the Establishment of a Bureau of Special and Secret Service. Richmond, 1864. Jenkins 61-612 1974 $12.50

CONFEDERATE STATES OF AMERICA   A Bill to Provide for Organizing, Arming and Disciplining the Militia of the Confederate States . . . and for Calling Them Forth to Execute the Laws of the Confederate States, Suppress Insurrections, and Repel Invasions. Richmond, 1864. Jenkins 61-610 1974 $17.50

CONFEDERATE STATES OF AMERICA   Special Report of the Secretary of the Treasury on the Subject of the Finances. Richmond, 1865. Jenkins 61-674 1974 $12.50

CONFESSION of Faith and Covenant of the Second Church in Hartford. (Hartford), 1860. Wrapper. Jenkins 61-684 1974 $15

CONFUCIUS   The Morals of. 1691. 12mo., recent half calf antique, gilt, frontis. Hill 126-62 1974 £25

CONGRES ORNITHOLOGIQUE INTERNATIONAL   IXme Congres Ornithologique International, Rouen, 1938. Rouen, 1938. 8vo., orig. wrappers. Wheldon 131-570 1974 £10

CONGREVE, WILLIAM   The Birth of the Muse. London, 1698. Folio, modern wrappers, fine, first edition. Dawsons PM 252-167 1974 £120

CONGREVE, WILLIAM   The Doubler-Dealer. London, 1694. 4to., 19th century marbled wrappers, first edition. Dawsons PM 252-168 1974 £150

CONGREVE, WILLIAM   The Works. Birmingham, 1761. 3 vols., 8vo., modern polished mottled calf gilt. Dawsons PM 252-1093 1974 £200

CONGREVE, WILLIAM   The Complete Works. Soho, 1923. 4 vols., 4to., orig. boards, uncut, limited edition. Dawsons PM 252-169 1974 £60

CONIFERS in Cultivation - Report of the Conifer Conference 1931. 1932. 8vo., wrappers, illus., scarce. Wheldon 128-1591 1973 £7.50

CONIFERS in Cultivation - Report of the Conifer Conference 1931. 1932. Roy. 8vo., buckram, illus. Wheldon 128-1592 1973 £10

CONINGSBY, T.   Collections Concering the Manor of Marden. (1722). Folio, russia, uncut. Quaritch 939-381 1974 £40

CONKLIN, EDWIN GRANT   Heredity and Environment In the Development of Men. Princeton & London, 1915. Library plate. Rittenhouse 46-155 1974 $10

CONMAGER, HENRY S.   Civil Liberties Under Attack. Univ. of Penn., 1951. 155p. Austin 51-203 1973 $7.50

CONNANT, M.   Urim and Thummim. London, 1669. Small 4to., later calf, rubbed. Traylen 79-394 1973 £15

CONNECTICUT   Acts and Laws of His Majesty's English Colony of Connecticut. New-Haven & New-London, 1769. Small folio, old calf, bookplate, rubbed, stains. Thomas 28-26 1972 £80

CONNECTICUT   Acts and Laws of His Majesty's English Colony of. New London, 1769. Small folio, old calf, little rubbed & stained, orig. blue grey wrappers, armorial bookplate of Earl of Rosebery. Thomas 32-2 1974 £80

CONNECTICUT, A Guide to Its Roads, Lore and People. Boston, 1938. First edition, 8vo., illus., maps, d.j. with some tears, else very fine. Current BW9-359 1974 $24.50

THE CONNECTICUT Register: Being a State Calendar of Public Officers and Institutions in Connecticut, for 1856. Hartford, (1856). Jenkins 61-685 1974 $10

CONNELL, BRIAN   Knight Errant. Doubleday, 1955. 255p., illus. Austin 51-204 1973 $7.50

CONNELL, FRANCIS J.   Morals in Politics and Professions. Newman, 1946. Austin 62-735 1974 $12.50

CONNELLAN, OWEN   The Annals of Ireland. Dublin, 1846. 4to., cloth boards, rebound. Emerald 50-164 1974 £35

CONNELLEY, WILLIAM E.   History of Kansas Newspapers. Topeka, 1916. Near mint. Jenkins 61-1256 1974 $10

CONNELLEY, WILLIAM ELSEY   Quantrill and the Border Wars. Cedar Rapids, 1910. Large 8vo., orig. bindings, fine. Butterfield 8-174 1974 $65

CONNER'S SONS, JAMES, NEW YORK   Abridged Specimens of Printing Types. 1888. 4to., worn. Allen 216-2222 1974 $25

CONNETT, EUGENE V.   American Big Game Fishing. New York, 1935. Plates, roy. 4to., one of 850 copies, fine, orig. cloth. Broadhurst 24-1063 1974 £50

CONNOLD, E. T.   British Vegetable Galls. 1901. Roy. 8vo., cloth, plates, text-figures. Wheldon 128-700 1973 £6

CONNOLD, E. T.   British Vegetable Galls. 1901. Roy 8vo., plates, cloth. Wheldon 130-731 1974 £6

CONNOLLY, CYRIL   The Condemned Playground: Essays, 1927-44. London, 1945. Orig. binding, first edition, near mint. Ross 87-112 1974 $15

CONNOLLY, CYRIL   Enemies of Promise. London, 1938. 8vo., orig. cloth, inscribed, presentation, first edition. Dawsons PM 252-170 1974 £50

CONNOLLY, CYRIL   Enemies of Promise. 1938. Dust wrapper, first edition. Howes 186-107 1974 £14

CONNOLLY, CYRIL   The Unquiet Grave. London, 1945. Orig. binding, revised edition, lacking d.w., fine. Ross 87-114 1974 $15

CONNOLLY, JAMES B.   Jeb Hutton. New York, 1902. Cloth, fine, dust jacket. Hayman 57-122 1974 $50

CONNOLLY, T. W. J.   The History of the Corps of Royal Sappers and Miners. London, 1855. 2 vols., orig. red cloth, plates. Dawson's 424-101 1974 $50

CONOLLY, JOHN   The Construction and Government of Lunatic Asylums. London, 1847. 8vo., orig. cloth, first edition. Dawsons PM 249-115 1974 £160

CONOLLY, JOHN   The Construction and Government of Lunatic Asylums and Hospitals for the Insane. London, 1847. 8vo., orig. cloth, first edition. Gurney 64-56 1974 £75

DE CONQUESTU Angliae per Hispanos. 1869. Folio, boards. Quaritch 939-775 1974 £15

CONRAD, EARL   Billy Rose. World, 1968. 272p., illus.
Austin 51-205 1973 $7.50

CONRAD, JESSIE   Joseph Conrad and His Circle. London, 1935.
8vo., illus., orig. cloth. Bow Windows 62-194 1974 £8.50

CONRAD, JESSIE   Joseph Conrad and His Circle. 1935. Near
fine, plates, first edition. Covent 51-453 1973 £7.50

CONRAD, JESSIE   Joseph Conrad As I Knew Him. London, 1926.
Orig. binding, first edition, near mint, d.w. Ross 87-127 1974 $15

CONRAD, JOSEPH   Almayer's Folly. 1895. First American edition.
Allen 216-353 1974 $75

CONRAD, JOSEPH   Almayer's Folly. 1895. Small 8vo., cloth, first
American edition. Quaritch 936-349 1974 £10

CONRAD, JOSEPH   The Arrow of Gold. London, 1919. 8vo.,
orig. green cloth, first English edition. Dawsons PM 252-171 1974 £12

CONRAD, JOSEPH   The Arrow of Gold. London, 1919. First
English edition, second issue, lacking d.w., fine copy, orig. binding. Ross
86-96 1974 $12.50

CONRAD, JOSEPH   The Arrow of Gold. 1919. Orig. cloth.
Smith 194-419 1974 £5

CONRAD, JOSEPH   Chance: A Tale in Two Parts. London, 1925.
Orig. binding, Medallion edition, owner's name in ink, fine. Ross 87-115
1974 $10

CONRAD, JOSEPH   Conrad to a Friend: 150 Selected Letters from
. . . to Richard Curle. London, 1928. First edition, inscription of owner, fine,
orig. binding. Ross 86-97 1974 $30

CONRAD, JOSEPH   Des Souvenirs. Paris, 1924. Small 4to., mint,
unopened, wrappers. Covent 55-502 1974 £42.50

CONRAD, JOSEPH   La Fleche d'Or. Paris, 1928. Small 4to.,
fine, wrappers. Covent 55-503 1974 £42.50

CONRAD, JOSEPH   Le Frere-de-la-Cote. Paris, 1928. Small
4to., fine, wrappers. Covent 55-504 1974 £42.50

CONRAD, JOSEPH   Gaspar Ruiz. Paris, 1927. Small 4to., fine,
wrappers. Covent 55-505 1974 £42.50

CONRAD, JOSEPH   Jeunesse, Suivi du Coeur des Tenebres. Paris,
1925. Small 4to., mint, unopened, wrappers. Covent 55-506 1974 £42.50

CONRAD, JOSEPH   John Galsworthy: An Appreciation. 1922.
Fine, wrappers. Covent 51-2271 1973 £15

CONRAD, JOSEPH   John Galsworthy, an Appreciation.
Canterbury, 1922. Orig. wrappers, sewn, first edition, fine. MacManus
224-89 1974 $50

CONRAD, JOSEPH   Last Essays. London, 1926. First edition, fine,
lacking d.w., orig. binding. Ross 86-100 1974 $20

CONRAD, JOSEPH   Laughing Anne & One Day More. 1924.
Dust wrapper, fine. Covent 55-507 1974 £10.50

CONRAD, JOSEPH   Laughing Anne and One Day More. London,
1924. Owner's name in ink, fine, d.w., orig. binding. Ross 86-101 1974 $15

CONRAD, JOSEPH   Letters From. 1928. 8vo., orig. cloth, uncut,
limited edition. Broadhurst 23-654 1974 £16

CONRAD, JOSEPH   Letters From. 1928. Portraits, English first
edition. Covent 56-250 1974 £12.50

CONRAD, JOSEPH   Letters from Conrad, 1895-1924. 1928.
Demy 8vo., uncut, limited to 925 copies, fine unfaded copy, orig. cloth, portrait.
Broadhurst 24-596 1974 £18

CONRAD, JOSEPH   Letters from Conrad; 1895-1924. 1928. First
edition, one of 925 numbered copies, portraits, buckram, gilt top spine faded
very good copy. Covent 51-450 1973 £7.50

CONRAD, JOSEPH   Letters from Joseph Conrad, 1895-1924.
Indianapolis, 1928. First American edition, illus., orig. binding, owner's name
in ink on fly leaf, fine. Ross 87-118 1974 $15

CONRAD, JOSEPH   Letters from Conrad, 1895-1924. London, 1928.
No. 515 of edition limited to 925 copies, lacking d.w., near mint. Ross 86-99
1974 $50

CONRAD, JOSEPH   Letters from Conrad, 1895-1924. London,
1928. Orig. binding, edition limited to 925 copies, this one out of series for
presentation to Francis Meynell with his bookplate, fine. Ross 87-117 1974
$100

CONRAD, JOSEPH   Letters of . . . to Richard Curle. New York,
1928. Frontis., first U. S. edition, one of 850 copies on rag paper, nice copy,
cloth backed dec. boards. Covent 51-2272 1973 £15.75

CONRAD, JOSEPH   The Nature of a Crime. London, 1924. First
edition, orig. binding, bookplate, nice, orig. d.w. Ross 87-119 1974 $15

CONRAD, JOSEPH   The Nigger of the Narcissus. 1898. Fine,
scarce. Covent 55-509 1974 £65

CONRAD, JOSEPH   Nostromo. New York & London, 1904. 8vo.,
orig. green dec. cloth, first American edition. Dawsons PM 252-172 1974 £12

CONRAD, JOSEPH   Nostromo, a Tale of the Seaboard. London,
1904. 12mo., cloth, first edition. Goodspeed's 578-65 1974 $75

CONRAD, JOSEPH   Notes on Life and Letters. London, 1921.
1st ed. Biblo & Tannen 210-712 1973 $12.50

CONRAD, J.   Notes on Life & Letters. London, 1921.
8vo., green cloth, first edition. Bow Windows 62-195 1974 £6.50

CONRAD, JOSEPH   Notes on Life and Letters. 1921. Crown 8vo.,
orig. cloth, first edition. Broadhurst 23-653 1974 £10

CONRAD, JOSEPH   Notes on Life and Letters. 1921. First edition,
crown 8vo., mint, d.w., orig. cloth. Broadhurst 24-595 1974 £10

CONRAD, JOSEPH   Notes on Life and Letters. London, 1925. Orig.
binding, Medallion edition, fine. Ross 87-120 1974 $10

CONRAD, JOSEPH   Notes on My Books. 1921. Vellum-backed
boards, numbered, signed. Covent 55-510 1974 £45

CONRAD, JOSEPH   An Outcast of the Islands. London, 1896.
8vo., orig. cloth, rubbed, first edition. Bow Windows 62-196 1974 £38

CONRAD, JOSEPH   An Outcast of the Islands. London, 1896.
First edition, good copy, bookplate, scarce, orig. cloth. Crane 7-52 1974 £21

CONRAD, JOSEPH   The Rescue. London and Toronto, 1920. 8vo.,
orig. cloth, first English published edition. Bow Windows 64-460 1974 £6.50

CONRAD, JOSEPH   The Rescue. London & Toronto, 1920. 8vo.,
orig. cloth, fine, first published English edition. Dawsons PM 252-173 1974
£7.50

CONRAD, JOSEPH   The Rescue: A Romance of the Shallows.
London, 1925. Orig. binding, Medallion edition, fine. Ross 87-121 1974 $10

CONRAD, JOSEPH   Romance. 1903. 428 pages, illus. Austin
61-248 1974 $12.50

CONRAD, JOSEPH   Rover. 1923. First edition. Allen 216-358
1974 $10

CONRAD, JOSEPH   The Rover. London, 1923. 1st ed. Biblo &
Tannen 210-713 1973 $30

CONRAD, JOSEPH   The Rover. New York, 1923. 8vo., uncut,
parchment boards, dust wrapper, first edition. Bow Windows 62-197 1974 £55

CONRAD, JOSEPH   The Rover. 1923. Scarce, dust wrapper, fine. Covent 55-512 1974 £30

CONRAD, JOSEPH   The Rover. 1923. Dust wrapper, advance proof copy, fine. Covent 55-511 1974 £110

CONRAD, JOSEPH   The Rover, 1923. 8vo., orig. green cloth, first edition. Dawsons PM 252-174 1974 £7

CONRAD, JOSEPH   The Rover. New York, 1923. Orig. vellum boards, first edition, one of 377 numbered copies, signed by author, fine, dust jacket. MacManus 224-90 1974 $125

CONRAD, JOSEPH   The Rover. London, 1923. Clipping of review laid in, first edition, bookplate, some foxing, nice, orig. d.w., orig. binding. Ross 86-102 1974 $35

CONRAD, JOSEPH   The Rover. 1923. 8vo., orig. cloth, dust-wrapper, first English edition. Rota 190-135 1974 £5

CONRAD, JOSEPH   The Rover. London, 1923. Orig. binding, first English edition, front hinge weak, spine torn at top, nice. Ross 87-122 1974 $20

CONRAD, JOSEPH   The Secret Agent. 1907. English first edition. Covent 56-1666 1974 £12.50

CONRAD, JOSEPH   The Secret Agent. London, 1923. Half vellum and boards, label, dust jacket, near mint, autographed, special limited edition. Jenkins 48-109 1973 $125

CONRAD, JOSEPH   The Secret Agent. London, 1923. No. 132 of edition limited to 1000 copies, signed, quarter vellum, mint, orig. d.w. Ross 86-103 1974 $100

CONRAD, JOSEPH   A Set of Six. London, 1908. Orig. binding, label inside front cover, some foxing, very good, first edition, second issue. Ross 87-123 1974 $25

CONRAD, JOSEPH   A Set of Six, Stories. 1908. 8vo., orig. dark blue cloth, scarce, first edition, second issue. Rota 189-200 1974 £30

CONRAD, JOSEPH   The Shadow Line. New York, 1917. 8vo., orig. cloth, first American edition. Rota 189-202 1974 £5

CONRAD, JOSEPH   Some Reminiscences. 1912. Orig. cloth. Smith 194-421 1974 £7.50

CONRAD, JOSEPH   Sous les Yeux d'Occident. Paris, 1920. Small 4to., mint, unopened, wrappers. Covent 55-514 1974 £42.50

CONRAD, JOSEPH   Suspense. 1925. Worn, dust wrapper, English first edition. Covent 56-1667 1974 £12.50

CONRAD, JOSEPH   Suspense. London, 1925. 12mo., cloth, first edition. Goodspeed's 578-66 1974 $10

CONRAD, JOSEPH   Suspense. London, 1925. Frontispiece, first English edition, d.w. chipped & slightly torn, some foxing, nice. Ross 86-104 1974 $25

CONRAD, JOSEPH   Tales of Hearsay. London, 1925. lst ed. Biblo & Tannen 210-714 1973 $15

CONRAD, JOSEPH   Tales of Hearsay. 1925. Dust wrapper, worn, English first edition. Covent 56-252 1974 £11

CONRAD, JOSEPH   Tales of Hearsay. 1925. Stained dust wrapper. Covent 55-515 1974 £17.50

CONRAD, JOSEPH   Tales of Hearsay. New York, 1925. 8vo., orig. cloth, presentation inscription, first edition. Rota 190-137 1974 £5

CONRAD, JOSEPH   Tales of Unrest. n.d. Pictorial dust wrapper, worn, new edition. Covent 56-253 1974 £5

CONRAD, JOSEPH   The Tremoine. New York, 1942. Edition limited to 1000 copies, this is one of 500 copies specially bound, mint, orig. binding. Ross 86-105 1974 $30

CONRAD, JOSEPH   Twixt Land & Sea. 1912. 8vo., orig. cloth, faded, first edition. Rota 190-133 1974 £10

CONRAD, JOSEPH   Typhoon and Other Stories. 1903. English first edition. Covent 56-1668 1974 £45

CONRAD, JOSEPH   Under Western Eyes. 1911. Orig. cloth gilt, worn covers. Covent 55-516 1974 £8.50

CONRAD, JOSEPH   Under Western Eyes. 1911. Crown 8vo., orig. scarlet cloth, first edition. Howes 185-83 1974 £21

CONRAD, JOSEPH   Victory. (1915). 8vo., orig. cloth, first English edition. Bow Windows 64-462 1974 £6

CONRAD, JOSEPH   Une Victoire. Paris, 1923. 2 vols., small 4to., mint, unopened, wrappers. Covent 55-517 1974 £42.50

CONRAD, JOSEPH   Victory, an Island Tale. 1915. First American edition. Allen 216-359 1974 $10

CONRAD, JOSEPH   Within the Tides. London & Toronto, 1915. 8vo., orig. cloth, first edition. Bow Windows 62-199 1974 £10.50

CONRAD, JOSEPH   Within the Tides. 1915. Faded, English first edition. Covent 56-255 1974 £10

CONRAD, JOSEPH   Within the Tides. London, 1915. First edition, lacking d.w., very nice, slight foxing, orig. binding. Ross 86-106 1974 $40

CONRAD, JOSEPH   Within the Tides. 1915. Orig. cloth. Smith 194-424 1974 £7.50

CONRAD, JOSEPH   Works. Garden City, 1920-25. 20 vols., 8vo., uncut, linen-backed boards, limited, Sun Dial edition. Ballinger 1-111 1974 $250

CONRAD, JOSEPH   The Works of Joseph Conrad. 1921. 20 vols., demy 8vo., boards, linen spines, uncut, mainly unopened, limited to 750 sets, signed by author, fine. Broadhurst 24-593 1974 £350

CONRAD, JOSEPH   Works. 1921-27. 8vo., 20 vols., boards, fine, unopened, limited edition. Quaritch 936-348 1974 £200

CONRAD, JOSEPH   The Works Of. 1925. 8vo., orig. cloth, 20 vols., illus., fine. Broadhurst 23-652 1974 £45

CONRAD, JOSEPH   The Works of. 1925. 20 vols., illus., demy 8vo., very fine, unfaded, the unlimited edition, orig. cloth. Broadhurst 24-594 1974 £50

CONRAT VON ULM, JOHANN   Geodaisia. 1580. Small 8vo., modem calf. Dawsons PM 245-182 1974 £120

CONRY, FLORENCE   Tractatus de Statu Parvulorum Sine Baptismo Decedentium Ex Hac Vita. 1624. New buckram. Allen 213-1396 1973 $15

LE CONSEILLER des Graces. Paris, 1817. Full green morocco, 1 1/8 X 3/4 inches. Gregory 44-359 1974 $85

CONSETT, MATTHEW   A Tour Through Sweden. London, 1789. Marbled boards, calf, illus. Dawson's 424-43 1974 $150

CONSETT, THOMAS   The Present State and Regulations of the Church of Russia. 1729. 8vo., contemporary calf, gilt. Hill 126-231 1974 £30

CONSTANS, L. A.   Guide Illustre des Campagnes de Cesar en Gaule. Paris, 1929. Plates. Biblo & Tannen 214-607 1974 $6

CONSTANTINI, ANGELO   The Birth, Life and Death of Scaramouch. 1924. Orig. parchment-backed boards, uncut, limited. Howes 186-18 1974 £12.50

CONSTITUTION of the Anti Bell-Ringing Society, Instituted, Oct. 26, 1838. Boston, 1839. 16mo., orig. marbled wrappers, nice copy. Ximenes 36-13 1974 $40

CONTEMPORARY American Biography. New York, 1893. Full morocco, full page plates, portraits on steel, Daniel Agnew's copy with his signature. Hayman 59-131 1974 $15

CONTINENT'S End. San Francisco, 1925. Quarter vellum gilt, boards, rubbed. Covent 55-241 1974 £15

CONVERSIO et Passio SS. Martyrum Afrae, Hilariae, Dignae, Evnomiae, Evtropiae. Venice, 1591. 4to., calf, spine somewhat worn, three page priced catalogue of Aldine books at end. Thomas 32-208 1974 £90

CONWAY, MONCURE DANIEL   Barons of the Potomack and the Rappahannock. New York, 1892. Large 8vo., orig. bindings, limited edition. Butterfield 8-673 1974 $45

CONWAY, MONCURE DANIEL   Life of Nathaniel Hawthorne. Scott, n.d. Orig. edition. Austin 54-267 1973 $7.50

CONYBEARE, JOHN   Calumny Refuted. 1735. 8vo., cloth, uncut, first edition. Quaritch 936-34 1974 £10

CONYBEARE, WILLIAM DANIEL   Outlines of the Geology of England and Wales, Part 1. 1822. 8vo., contemporary calf, map, rare. Wheldon 131-981 1974 £35

CONYBEARE, WILLIAM DANIEL   Outlines of the Geology of England and Wales. London, 1822. 8vo., orig. boards. Hammond 201-363 1974 £32

CONYNGHAM, D. P.   The Irish Brigade and Its Campaigns. Glasgow, (1866). 8vo., new cloth. Emerald 50-163 1974 £5

COOCH, FRANCIS A.   Little Know History of Newark, Dela. Newark, 1936. Orig. cloth, illus., d.w. Putman 126-72 1974 $12.50

COOCH, FRANCIS A.   Little Known History of Newark, Delaware. Newark, 1936. 8vo., cloth. Saddleback 14-340 1974 $12.50

COOK, ALBERT STANBURROUGH   Some Accounts of the Bewcastle Cross. 1914. Ex-library, sturdy library binding. Austin 61-249 1974 $37.50

COOK, EDWARD T.   Life of John Ruskin. 1911. 2 vols., plates, spine slightly worn. Allen 216-1545 1974 $15

COOK, EDWARD T.   Studies In Ruskin. 1890. 4to., drawings, portrait, first edition. Howes 185-411 1974 £7.50

COOK, JAMES   The Explorations of Captain James Cook In the Pacific. n.d. Illus., fine, worn box. Austin 61-250 1974 $10

COOK, JAMES H.   Fifty Years on the Old Frontier as Cowboy, Hunter, Guide, Scout, and Ranchman. New Haven, 1923. Jenkins 61-712 1974 $25

COOK, JOEL   The Siege of Richmond. Philadelphia, 1862. Ballinger 1-247 1974 $27.50

COOK, JOHN R.   The Border and the Buffalo. 1938. Dec. cloth, gilt top, frontispiece, very good copy. Dykes 22-138 1973 $10

COOK, MARC   "Vandyke-Brown" Poems. Boston, 1883. Orig. cloth, fine, first American edition. Covent 55-735 1974 £30

COOK, SAMUEL F.   Drummond Island. Lansing, 1896. Folding map, printed wrappers. Hayman 59-381 1974 $12.50

COOK, TENNESSEE CELESTE   Constitutional Equality, a Right of Woman. New York, 1871. Orig. binding. Butterfield 10-537 1974 $75

COOKE, A. H.   The Early History of Maple-Durham. Oxford, 1925. Orig. cloth, plates. Smith 194-271 1974 £6.50

COOKE, A. O.   A Book of Dovecotes. 1920. Crown 8vo., modern half morocco, uncut, plates. Wheldon 131-575 1974 £7.50

COOKE, A. O.   A Book of Dovecotes. 1920. Crown 8vo., orig. boards, illus., scarce. Wheldon 128-417 1973 £5

COOKE, G. A.   Topographical and Statistical Description of the County of Derby. n.d. 3 vols. in 1, thick 8vo., contemporary roan backed marbled boards, maps. Smith 193-232 1973 £15

COOKE, JAMES   Mellificium Chirurgiae. London, 1662. 12mo., contemporary calf, second edition. Dawsons PM 249-118 1974 £210

COOKE, JAMES   Under a New Patent. (London, 1789). 8vo., orig. plain blue wrappers, frontispiece engraving, nice copy, very scarce, first edition. Ximenes 37-47 1974 $45

COOKE, JOHN ESTEN   Hammer and Rapier. New York, 1870. Orig. cloth, rubbed, first printing, hinges repaired. MacManus 224-91 1974 $27.50

COOKE, LAYTON   Practical Observations on the Importation of Foreign Cron. 1826. 8vo., modern marbled paper wrappers, first edition. Bow Windows 66-136 1974 £6.50

COOKE, M. C.   British Edible Fungi. 1891. 8vo., cloth, plates. Wheldon 129-1179 1974 £5

COOKE, M. C.   British Fresh-Water Algae. 1882-84. 8vo., 2 vols., new cloth, plates. Wheldon 130-1257 1974 £25

COOKE, M. C.   British Fresh-Water Algae. 1882-84. 8vo., 2 vols., new cloth, plates. Wheldon 130-1256 1974 £30

COOKE, M. C.   Fungi Australiani. Melbourne, 1883. 8vo., sewed, plates, scarce. Wheldon 130-1259 1974 £5

COOKE, M. C.   Illustrations of British Fungi. 1881-91. 8vo., 8 vols., plates, orig. cloth. Wheldon 129-1173 1974 £400

COOKE, M. C.   Illustrations of British Fungi. 1881-91. 8vo., half calf, 10 vols. Wheldon 129-9 1974 £500

COOKE, M. C.   Plain and Easy Account of British Fungi. 1866. 12mo., cloth, plates. Wheldon 129-1175 1974 £5

COOKE, M. C.   A Plain and Easy Account of British Fungi. London, 1884. Small 8vo., orig. cloth, gilt, illus., plates, fifth edition. Hammond 201-636 1974 £10.50

COOKE, M. C.   Rust, Smut, Mildew and Mould. 1870. Post 8vo., cloth, plates, second edition. Wheldon 129-1176 1974 £5

COOKE, M. C.   Rust Smut, Mildew and Mould. 1902. Crown 8vo., cloth, plates, sixth edition. Wheldon 129-1177 1974 £3.50

COOKE, M. C.   Rust, Smut, Mildew, and Mould. 1865. Small 8vo., orig. cloth, plates, scarce first edition. Wheldon 131-1385 1974 £7.50

COOKE, ROSE TERRY   The Deacon's Week. Boston, (1894). 64mo., wrappers, first edition. Goodspeed's 578-67 1974 $15

COOKE, S.   The Complete English Gardener. n.d. Small 8vo., contemporary leather-backed boards, rare, first edition. Wheldon 130-1383 1974 £50

COOKE, WILLIAM   The Life of Samuel Johnson. Dublin, 1785. 12mo., contemporary sheep, scarce, first Dublin edition. Dawsons PM 252-574 1974 £14

COOKE, WILLIAM BRYAN   The Seize Quartiers of the Family of. 1857. 4to., cloth. Hammond 201-419 1974 £8.50

COOLEY, JEROME E.   Recollections of Early Days in Duluth. Duluth, 1925. 12mo., cloth. Saddleback 14-515 1974 $17.50

COOLIDGE, CALVIN   Have Faith In Massachusetts. Boston, 1919. Inscribed. Jenkins 48-371 1973 $70

COOLIDGE, CALVIN   Have Faith in Massachusetts: A Collection of Speeches and Messages. Boston, 1919. Inscribed & signed by author. Jenkins 61-714 1974 $60

COOMARASWAMY, ANANDA   Buddha and the Gospel of Buddhism. (1928).
8vo., orig. cloth, coloured and photo. plates. Bow Windows 66-137 1974
£8.50

COOMES, OLIVER   The Giant Rifleman. New York, 1880. Self
wrappers. Hayman 57-485 1974 $10

COOPER, ASTLEY PASTON   A Series of Lectures, On the Most Approved
Principles and Practice of Modern Surgery. Boston, 1823. 8vo., contemporary
calf. Schuman 37-50 1974 $110

COOPER, ASTLEY PASTON   A Treatise on Dislocations. London, 1823.
4to., new half calf, uncut, second edition. Dawsons PM 249-119 1974 £60

COOPER, C. H.   Athenae Cantabrigienses. Cambridge, 1858-
61. 2 vols., 8vo., cloth, orig. edition. Quaritch 939-759 1974 £20

COOPER, C. S.   The Outdoor Monuments of London. London,
(1928). 8vo., illus., orig. cloth, first edition. Bow Windows 62-580 1974
£5.75

COOPER, C. S.   Trees and Shrubs of the British Isles. 1909.
4to., cloth, plates, 2 vols. Wheldon 130-1547 1974 £5

COOPER, D.   Flora Metropolitana or Botanical Rambles
Within Thirty Miles of London. (1837). Post 8vo., cloth, second edition.
Wheldon 128-1188 1973 £5

COOPER, DOUGLAS   Paul Klee. London, 1949. Biblo & Tannen
213-310 1973 $7.50

COOPER, EDWARD H.   Wyemarke and the Sea-Fairies. 1899. Roy.
8vo., orig. pictorial cloth, plates, Japanese vellum. Covent 55-892 1974
£12.50

COOPER, J. A.   Men of Canada, a Portrait Gallery. Montreal
& Toronto, 1901-2. Re-spined. Hood's 104-19 1974 $25

COOPER, J. F.   The Jack O'Lantern. 1842. 3 vols., 8vo.,
quarter cloth, some foxing, first English edition. Bow Windows 66-138 1974
£35

COOPER, JAMES FENIMORE   The American Democrat. Cooperstown, 1838.
Covers rubbed, text foxed, orig. binding. Butterfield 10-203 1974 $25

COOPER, JAMES FENIMORE   The American Democrat. Cooperstown, 1838.
Bright copy, perfect label, minimum foxing. Butterfield 10-202 1974 $35

COOPER, JAMES FENIMORE   The Borderers. Paris, 1829. 3 vols., labels,
rebound, buckram, first edition. Covent 55-522 1974 £42.50

COOPER, JAMES FENIMORE   The Bravo. London, 1831. 3 vols., later half
morocco, first edition, fine set. MacManus 224-92 1974 $100

COOPER, JAMES FENIMORE   Correspondence. 1922. 776 pages, 2 vols.
Austin 54-268 1973 $25

COOPER, JAMES FENIMORE   Correspondence of. New Haven, 1922. Orig.
cloth, 2 vols., first edition, one of 250 sets on rag paper, unnumbered. MacManus
224-93 1974 $40

COOPER, JAMES FENIMORE   The Deerslayer. Philadelphia, 1841. 2 vols.,
modern half morocco, first edition, lacks flyleaves front and rear of each vol.
MacManus 224-94 1974 $100

COOPER, JAMES FENIMORE   England. With Sketches of Society in the
Metropolis. Paris, 1837. Half calf, first French edition in English, light foxing.
MacManus 224-95 1974 $35

COOPER, JAMES FENIMORE   The History of the Navy of the United States.
Philadelphia, 1839. 2 vols., first edition, nice set. Butterfield 10-204 1974
$65

COOPER, JAMES FENIMORE   The History of the Navy of the United States of
America. London, 1839. 2 vols., orig. cloth, extremities worn, first English
edition, frontispieces. MacManus 224-97 1974 $55

COOPER, JAMES FENIMORE   The History of the Navy of the United States of
America. Philadelphia, 1839. 2 vols., orig. cloth, rebacked, orig. spines laid
down, first edition, foxed, maps. MacManus 224-96 1974 $75

COOPER, JAMES FENIMORE   History of the Navy of the U. S. A. Putnam,
1854. 3 vols. in 1, illus. Austin 54-269 1973 $27.50

COOPER, JAMES FENIMORE   The Lake Gun. New York, 1932. Orig.
cloth backed boards, paper label, first separate edition, one of 450 numbered
copies, boxed, fine. MacManus 224-98 1974 $25

COOPER, JAMES FENIMORE   Last of the Mohicans. 1932. Half calf,
coloured plates, in case, bookplate, limited editions. Allen 216-367 1974 $15

COOPER, JAMES FENIMORE   Mercedes of Castile: or, The Voyage to
Cathay. Philadelphia, 1840. 2 vols., orig. cloth, spines faded, paper labels,
first edition, bookplate, rubber stamp, fine. MacManus 224-99 1974 $75

COOPER, JAMES FENIMORE   Ned Myers; or, A Life Before the Mast.
Philadelphia, 1843. Contemporary quarter leather, rubbed, first American edition,
foxed, lacks ads at rear. MacManus 224-100 1974 $50

COOPER, JAMES FENIMORE   New York. New York, 1930. Orig. cloth
backed boards, frontispiece, first edition, one of 765 numbered copies, fine,
boxed. MacManus 224-101 1974 $25

COOPER, JAMES FENIMORE   The Two Admirals. London, 1842. 8vo., orig.
maroon cloth-backed boards, first English edition. Hammond 201-297 1974 £25

COOPER, JAMES FENIMORE   The Two Admirals. Philadelphia, 1842. 2 vols.,
orig. cloth, paper labels, first edition, about fine, bookplate of C. W. Barrett in
each vol., quarter morocco box. MacManus 224-102 1974 $85

COOPER, JAMES FENIMORE   The Water Witch. London, 1830. 3 vols.,
12mo., contemporary half calf, first edition. Dawsons PM 252-176 1974 £35

COOPER, JOHN   Commonplace Book Containing Poems.
(c.1613-1647). Folio, contemporary vellum boards, signed, worn. Dawsons PM
252-177 1974 £1000

COOPER, S. M.   Life in the Forest; or, The Trials and
Sufferings of a Pioneer. Philadelphia, 1854. 12mo., orig. cloth, first edition.
MacManus 224-103 1974 $45

COOPER, SAMUEL   Concise System of Infantry Instructions and
Regulations for the Militia and Volunteers. . . Philadelphia, 1836. Cloth
measurably stained, faded, minimal edge wear, illus., marginal ink notes.
Wilson 63-14 1974 $28.50

COOPER, SAMUEL   A Dictionary of Practical Surgery. New York,
1843. Rittenhouse 46-156 1974 $45

COOPER, THOMAS   Lectures on the Elements of Political Economy.
London, 1831. Contemporary calf, second edition. Howes 186-1390 1974 £15

COOPER, THOMAS   A Reply to Mr. Burke's Invective Against Mr.
Cooper and Mr. Watt. Manchester, 1792. 8vo., modern boards. Dawsons PM
247-56 1974 £15

COOPER, WILLIAM   Trina. London, 1934. First edition, very good
copy, extremely scarce, orig. cloth. Crane 7-53 1974 £10

COOPER, WILLIAM   Wootton Wawan: Its History and Records. 1936.
Crown 4to., orig. cloth, illus. Broadhurst 23-1356 1974 £5

COOPER-PRICHARD, A. H.   Conversations with Oscar Wilde. 1931. English first edition. Covent 56-1329 1974 £8.50

COOPER, WILLIAM M.
Please turn to
BERTRAM, JAMES GLASS

CO-OPERATIVE BEES'   Catalogue of Herbaceous Plants. (1905).
8vo., half roan. Wheldon 131-1504 1974 £5

COOTE, CHARLES   Statistical Survey of the County of Armagh.
Dublin, 1804. 8vo., cloth boards, faded. Emerald 50-168 1974 £21

COPE, W. H. Bramshill. (n.d.). 4to., orig. cloth, illus., photos., bookplates. Bow Windows 66-140 1974 £8

COPELAND, A. B. The Society and Club Register of Southern California. Los Angles, c.1925. 8vo., cloth. Saddleback 14-77 1974 $10

COPELAND, EDWIN BINGHAM Natural Conduct. Stanford, 1928. Biblo & Tannen 213-952 1973 $7.50

COPINGER, W. A. The Bible and Its Transmission. London, 1897. Folio, cloth. Dawsons PM 11-191 1974 £27.50

COPINGER, W. A. Heraldry Simplified. Manchester, 1910. Roy. 8vo., orig. buckram, illus., scarce. Howes 186-1627 1974 £12.50

COPLAND, SAMUEL A History of the Island of Madagascar. 1822. 8vo., contemporary maroon half morocco, map, slightly rubbed, minor foxing, good copy, very scarce. Sawyer 293-5 1974 £88

COPLEY, ESTHER The Cook's Complete Guide. London, n.d. 8vo., half calf, gilt, plates, first edition. Hammond 201-161 1974 £55

COPPARD, ALFRED EDWARD The Black Dog and Other Stories. New York, 1923. Biblo & Tannen 210-578 1973 $10

COPPARD, ALFRED EDWARD Count Stefan. Golden Cockerel Press, 1928. One of 600 numbered copies, signed by author, woodcuts, buckram backed dec. boards, fine. Covent 51-2274 1973 £12.50

COPPARD, ALFRED EDWARD Count Stefan. 1928. Orig. cloth, faded, patterned boards, faded, first edition. Rota 188-201 1974 £6.50

COPPARD, ALFRED EDWARD Crotty Shinkwin and the Beauty Spot. 1932. Quarter leather, numbered, limited, fine. Covent 55-523 1974 £15.75

COPPARD, ALFRED EDWARD Dunky Fitlow. 1933. 8vo., full vellum, signed, first edition. Rota 190-146 1974 £10

COPPARD, ALFRED EDWARD Easter Day. Inscribed, cloth backed boards, card slipcase faded. Covent 51-2275 1973 £15

COPPARD, ALFRED EDWARD Easter Day. N.P., 1931. Boards, boxed, autographed, limited edition. Jenkins 48-117 1973 $20

COPPARD, ALFRED EDWARD Emergency Exit. 1934. Signed, first American edition. Allen 216-374 1974 $10

COPPARD, ALFRED EDWARD Emergency Exit. New York, 1934. One of 350 copies, signed by author, fine. Covent 51-2276 1973 £18.50

COPPARD, ALFRED EDWARD Fearful Pleasures. Sauk City, 1946. lst ed., ltd. Biblo & Tannen 210-579 1973 $15

COPPARD, ALFRED EDWARD The Field of Mustard. New York, 1927. Biblo & Tannen 210-580 1973 $7.50

COPPARD, ALFRED EDWARD Fishmonger's Fiddle, Tales. London, 1925. First edition, nice copy, d.w., orig. cloth. Crane 7-54 1974 £5

COPPARD, ALFRED EDWARD Hips & Haws. 1922. Dust jacket, limited, first edition. Allen 216-375 1974 $10

COPPARD, ALFRED EDWARD The Hundredth Story of. 1931. 8vo., dec. boards, uncut, limited edition. Broadhurst 23-998 1974 £25

COPPARD, ALFRED EDWARD The Hundredth Story. Golden Cockerel Press, 1931. Woodcuts, med. 8vo., dec. boards, morocco spine, top edges gilt, others uncut, limited to 1000 copies, fine. Broadhurst 24-980 1974 £25

COPPARD, ALFRED EDWARD The Man from Kilsheelan. 1930. Woodcut, limited to 550 copies, signed by author and inscribed by him, roy. 8vo., orig. cloth, uncut, mint. Broadhurst 24-597 1974 £20

COPPARD, ALFRED EDWARD The Man from Kilshellan. 1930. Woodcut frontis., Furnival Book No. 3, one of 550 numbered copies, signed by author, fine, buckram. Covent 51-459 1973 £6.30

COPPARD, ALFRED EDWARD Nixey's Harlequin. 1931. Hand-made paper, signed, full vellum, English first edition. Covent 56-257 1974 £15

COPPARD, ALFRED EDWARD Pink Furniture. 1930. Illus., one of 260 numbered copies, signed by author, fine, full vellum. Covent 51-2277 1973 £17.50

COPPARD, ALFRED EDWARD Ring the Bells of Heaven. 1933. One of 150 copies, presentation copy inscribed from author, frontis., nice copy, first edition. Covent 51-462 1973 £10.50

COPPARD, ALFRED EDWARD Yokohama Garland. 1926. 4to., signed by author & Illus., vignettes by Wharton Esherick, limited edition. Allen 216-377 1974 $20

COPPARD, ALFRED EDWARD Yokohoma Garland and Other Poems. Philadelphia, (1926). Vignettes, orig. cloth backed boards, paper label, first edition one of 500 numbered copies, signed by author & illus., boxed, fine. MacManus 224-104 1974 $35

COPPEE, HENRY A Gallery of Famous English and American Poets. Philadelphia, 1859. Large 8vo., full calf, morocco gilt label, first edition. Dawsons PM 252-178 1974 £10

COPPINGER, R. W. Cruise of the "Alert", Four Years In Patagonian, Polynesian, and Mascarene Waters, 1878-82. 1883. 8vo., prize calf, plates. Wheldon 131-349 1974 £15

CORAM, ROBERT Political Inquiries; to Which is Added, a Plan for the General Establishment of Schools Throughout the United States. Wilmington, 1791. 8vo., disbound, first edition, very rare. Ximenes 36-57 1974 $400

CORBETT, ELIZABETH Walt. Stokes, 1928. 33lp. Austin 54-270 1973 $8.50

CORBETT, MRS. GEORGE Secrets of a Private Enquiry Office. 1891. 8vo., orig. cloth, first edition. Rota 190-236 1974 £12

CORBETT, J. Sir Frances Drake. London, 1902. 8vo., frontispiece, contemporary calf, gilt. Bow Windows 62-205 1974 £5

CORBIERE, L. Nouvelle Flore de Normandie. 1893. Crown 8vo., cloth. Wheldon 130-1140 1974 £7.50

CORDA, A. C. J. Ueber Spiralfaserzellen in dem Haargeflechte der Trichien. Prague, 1837. 4to., orig. wrappers, rare. Wheldon 130-1262 1974 £5

CORDEAUX, J. Birds of the Humber District. 1872. 8vo., cloth, frontispiece. Wheldon 131-576 1974 £5

CORDIALE Quattuor Novissimorum. (Paris, c.1499.) 8vo., vellum, extremely rare. Harper 213-43 1973 $650

CORDIER, F. S. Les Champignons. Paris, 1876. Very large 8vo., color plates, quarter morocco. Gregory 44-210 1974 $100

CORDIER, F. S. Les Champignons de la France. Paris, 1870. Imperial 8vo., half calf, plates. Wheldon 129-1180 1974 £60

CORELLI, ARCANGELO Opera Prima XII Sonatas. (n.d.). 3 vols., 4to., 18th century quarter roan, worn, some damp stains. Bow Windows 66-142 1974 £18.50

CORELLI, MARIE Holy Orders. 1908. 8vo., orig. cloth, inscription, first edition. Rota 190-147 1974 £5

CORELLI, MARIE The Mighty Atom. 1896. 8vo., orig. cloth, uncut. Bow Windows 64-463 1974 £8.50

CORELLI, MARIE "Temporal Power". 1902. Cloth gilt, fine, inscription. Covent 55-524 1974 £7.50

CORELLI, MARIE Wormwood. London, 1890. 3 vols., 8vo., orig. dark green cloth, little worn, first edition, very scarce. Ximenes 36-58 1974 $80

CORELLI, MARIE   Ziska. London, 1897. 8vo., inscription, uncut, orig. cloth, gilt, first edition. Bow Windows 62-208 1974 £7.50

CORINTH, LOVIS   Das Leben Walter Leistikows. Berlin, 1910. 8vo., illus. Minters 37-856 1973 $35

CORIOLIS, GASPARD GUSTAVE, MARQUIS DE   Theorie Mathematique Des Effets du Jeu de Billard. Paris, 1835. 8vo., contemporary half green morocco, plates. Zeitlin 235-50 1974 $115

CORK AND ORRERY, JOHN BOYLE, 5TH EARL OF   Remarks on the Life and Writings of Dr. Jonathan Swift. London, 1752. 12mo., contemporary calf, fifth edition. Dawsons PM 252-934 1974 £8

CORMACK, ALEXANDER A.   Teinds and Agriculture. 1930. Scarce, 217 pages. Howes 186-735 1974 £7.50

CORNEILLE, PIERRE   Oeuvres de Pierre Corneille Precedees d'Une Notice sur sa Vie et Ses Ouvrages. Paris, c. 1900. Thick 8vo., full page steel engravings with heavy foxing on white borders only, else fine, spine rubbed. Current BW9-218 1974 $18

CORNEILLE, THOMAS   Theatre de Pierre et de. Paris, 1868. 2 vols., 8vo., contemporary mottled calf, portrait, slight foxing, morocco labels. Bow Windows 66-144 1974 £7

CORNELIUS, NEPOS   Vitae Excellentium Imperatorum. Leyden, 1734. 4to., contemporary vellum, first edition, engravings. Schumann 499-26 1974 sFr 100

CORNELIUS, PETER   Ausgewahlte Schriften und Briefe. Berlin, 1938. Biblo & Tannen 214-829 1974 $15

CORNELL University and Ithaca. Ithaca, c. 1910. Pict. wrapper, back wrapper missing, photos. Jenkins 61-1873 1974 $10

CORNELY, RUDOLPH   Historica et Critica Introductio in U.T. Libros Sacros. Paris, 1885. 3 vols., roy. 8vo., contemporary half calf. Howes 185-1081 1974 £5

CORNER, E. J. H.   Wayside Trees of Malaya. Singapore, 1940. Profusley illus., 2 vols., globe 4to., very fine copy, orig. edition, orig. cloth. Broadhurst 24-1066 1974 £16

CORNER, J.   A Gift to Young Friends. Loncon, (c. 1840). Square 16mo., color plates, orig. cloth, fine. Gregory 44-39 1974 $22.50

CORNER, JULIA   Plays. (c. 1875). Text illus., slight pencil scoring, 4 items in 1, large crown 8vo., binder's cloth. George's 610-177 1973 £6

CORNEVIN, C.   Des Plantes Veneneuses et des Empoisonnements. Paris, 1887. 8vo., half morocco, scarce. Wheldon 129-1684 1974 £12.50

CORNEVIN, C.   Des Plantes Veneneuses et des Empoisonnements Qu'elles Determinent. Paris, 1887. 8vo., half morocco, scarce. Wheldon 131-1806 1974 £12.50

CORNFORD, L. COPE   The Designers of Our Buildings. 1921. Illus. Covent 55-64 1974 £10.50

CORNIL, ANDRE-VICTOR   Les Bacteries. Paris, 1890. 8vo., 2 vols., red half morocco, plates. Dawsons PM 249-122 1974 £10

CORNISH, C. J.   Life at the Zoo. 1895. 8vo., cloth, plates. Wheldon 128-266 1973 £5

CORNISH, C. J.   The Living Animals of the World. (n.d.). 4to., 2 vols., plates, illus. Bow Windows 64-61 1974 £5.25

CORNISH, G. A.   Social Studies for Canadians. Toronto, 1938. Hood's 103-327 1974 £10

CORNWALL, BARRY   Portraits of British Poets from Chaucer to Cowper & Beatie. 1824. 2 vols., folio, full morocco, richly dec, engraved plates, large paper edition. Allen 216-379 1974 $75

CORNWALL Domesday Book. 1861-72. 2 vols., thin folio, orig. cloth gilt. Smith 194-255 1974 £10

CORNWALLIS, KINAHAN   A Panorama of the New World. London, 1859. 2 vols., 8vo., first edition. Traylen 79-423 1973 £20

CORNWALLIS, MARY   Scrapbook. c.1790-1820. Folio, vellum. Dawsons PM 252-179 1974 £75

COROT, JEAN BAPTISTE CAMILLE   Corot. 1930. 4to., half morocco, plates. Quaritch 940-66 1974 £35

COROT, JEAN BAPTISTE CAMILLE   Corot. Berlin, 1930. Roy. 4to., half vellum, plates. Quaritch 940-67 1974 £75

COROT, JEAN BAPTISTE CAMILLE   Corot and His Work. Glasgow, 1905. 2 vols., roy. 4to., plates, quarter morocco, limited edition. Quaritch 940-65 1974 £65

CORPE, JOHN   Some Very Remarkable Facts. London, 1758. 8vo., modern green half morocco, first edition. Dawsons PM 251-494 1974 £15

CORPUS Juris Canonici. Leipzig, 1839. 2 vols., 4to., cloth. Howes 185-1082 1974 £12.50

CORPUS Vasorum Antiquorum. Yugoslavia, Fascicules 1-3. 1933-38. 3 vols., small folio, plates, in portfolios. Quaritch 940-309 1974 £10

CORREVON, H.   The Alpine Flora. Geneva, 1911. Orig. buckram, plates. Smith 193-7 1973 £5

CORREVON, H.   Flora Alpina Tascabile per i Touristi Nelle Montagne dell Alta Italia della Svizzera della Savoja. Turin, 1898. Small 8vo., cloth, coloured plates. Wheldon 128-1251 1973 £5

CORREVON, H.   La Flore Alpine. Geneva, n.d. 8vo., orig. picture boards, plates, second edition. Wheldon 130-1141 1974 £5

CORREVON, H.   Flore Coloriee de Poche a L'Usage du Touriste dans les Montagnes de la Suisse. Paris, 1898. Post 8vo., cloth, plates. Wheldon 131-1277 1974 £5

CORRY, JOHN   The Life of Joseph Priestley. Birmingham, 1804. 12mo., half calf, rebacked, first edition. Dawsons PM 245-615 1974 £40

CORSON, HUAM   The Voice and Spiritual Education. Macmillan, 1896. 198p. Austin 51-206 1973 $6.50

CORTES, HERNANDO   De Insulis Nuper Inventis Ferdinandi Cortesi . . . Narrationes. Cologne, 1532. Folio, extremely rare, unusually fine condition, from the collection of Sir Thomas Phillips. Jenkins 61-717 1974 $1,750

CORTISSOZ, ROYAL   An Introduction to the Mellon Collection. Boston, 1937. 12mo., illus. Biblo & Tannen 210-135 1973 $15

CORTISSOZ, ROYAL   Monograph of the Work of Charles A. Platt. New York, 1913. Folio, cloth, plates, ex-library. Minters 37-564 1973 $25

CORTISSOZ, ROYAL   The Works of Edwin Howland Blashfield. New York, 1937. Large 4to., cloth, plates, frontispiece. Minters 37-4 1973 $27

CORTLANDT, F. BISHOP   History of Elections in the American Colonies. New York, 1893. Orig. binding. Butterfield 10-199 1974 $25

CORVO, FREDERICK BARON, <u>PSEUD.</u>
Please turn to
ROLFE, FREDERICK WILLIAM

CORWIN, NORMAN   More By Corwin. Holt, 1944. 412p. Austin 51-207 1973 $8.50

CORWIN, NORMAN   On a Note of Triumph. Simon and Schuster, 1945. 71p. Austin 51-208 1973 $4.75

CORWIN, NORMAN   The Plot to Overthrow Christmas. Holt, 1942. 32p. Austin 51-209 1973 $6.50

CORWIN, NORMAN   Thirteen by Corwin. Holt, 1942. 338p.
Austin 51-210 1973 $8.50

CORWIN, NORMAN   Untitled and Other Radio Dramas. Holt, 1947.
558p. Austin 51-211 1973 $10

CORY, C. B.   The Birds of Haiti and San Domingo. Boston,
1885. 4to., half polished green morocco, gilt, plates, rare, limited edition.
Wheldon 130-12 1974 £260

CORY, HARPER   Grey Owl and the Beaver. London, 1935.
Hood's 102-320 1974 $7.50

CORY, R.   The Horticultural Record. 1914. 4to., illus.,
plates, buckram. Wheldon 131-1505 1974 £20

CORY, WILLIAM   Ionica. 1891. 8vo., orig. cloth, English first
edition. Covent 56-258 1974 £35

CORYAT, T.   Thomas Coriate Traveller for the English Wits.
1616. Small 4to., calf, rebacked. Quaritch 936-350 1974 £25

COSMETICS for My Lady and Good Fare for My Lord. Golden Cockerel Press,
1934. Limited to 300 copies, med. 8vo., uncut, fine, orig. cloth. Broadhurst
24-981 1974 £15

COSNETT, THOMAS   The Footman's Directory and Butler's
Remembrancer. London, 1825. 12mo., orig. printed boards, fourth edition, very
fine, rare. Ximenes 36-59 1974 $75

COSSIO, JOSE MARIA DE   Los Toros. Madrid, 1943-47-43. 3 vols.,
4to., illus., inscription, orig. quarter sheep. Bow Windows 62-209 1974 £40

COSSLEY-BATT, JILL L.   The Last of the California Rangers. New York
and London, 1928. Morocco and marbled boards, illus., gilt top, slip case,
signed by author, Deluxe limited edition. Dykes 22-142 1973 $35

COSSMAN, M.   Catalogue Illustre des Coquilles Fossiles de
l'Eocene des Environs de Paris. Appendices 1 - 5. Brussels, 1886-1913. 9 vols.
in 8, uniform half morocco, plates, very rare, special limited edition. Wheldon
131-893 1974 £120

COSSON, E.   Flore des Environs de Paris. Paris, 1861.
8vo., half brown morocco, map, scarce, nice copy, second edition. Wheldon
128-1252 1973 £10

COSSON, E.   Flore des Environs de Paris. Paris, 1861. 8vo.,
half brown morocco, scarce, second edition. Wheldon 130-1142 1974 £100

COSTA, EMANUEL MENDES DA   Historia Naturalis Testaceorum Britanniae.
1778. 4to., contemporary cloth, rebacked, rare. Wheldon 130-821 1974 £55

COSTA DE MACEDO, JOAQUIM JOSE   Discurso Lido em 15 de Maio de 1838
na Sessao Publica da Academia Real das Sciencias de Lisboa. Lisbon, 1838.
Small 4to., wrappers, uncut, unopened. Kraus B8-42 1974 $10

COSTANTIN, J.   Atlas en Couleurs des Orchidees Cultivees.
Paris, (1913-26). 4to., cloth, very scarce, coloured plates. Wheldon 128-1553
1973 £30

COSTANTIN, J.   Materiaux pour l'histoire des Champignons.
Paris, 1888. 8vo., buckram. Wheldon 129-1181 1974 £5

COSTARD, GEORGE   The History of Astronomy. London, 1757.
Large 4to., polished half calf, gilt, diagrams, second edition. Schuman 37-51
1974 $225

COSTE, JEAN-FRANCOIS   De Antiqua Medico-Philosophia . . . Oratio
Habita in Capitolio Gulielmopolitani. (Leyden), 1783. Orig. marbled front
wrapper, dusty on margins, sewed, uncut. Butterfield 10-37 1974 $200

COSTELLO, D.   Piedmont and Italy, From the Alps to the Tiber.
1861. 2 vols., 4to., contemporary full morocco, engraved vignette titles,
portrait frontispieces, maps, gilt spines, raised bands. Bow Windows 66-146
1974 £165

COSTER, F.   Enchiridion Controuersiarum. Cologne,
1599. Small 8vo., contemporary stamped calf, gilt. Thomas 28-133 1972
£10.50

COTCHETT, L. E.   The Evolution of Furniture. 1938. Crown
4to., frontispiece, plates, orig. cloth, fine. Broadhurst 24-45 1974 £5

COTES, ROGER   Harmonia Mensurarum. 1722. Large 4to., contemporary calf, worn, first edition. Dawsons PM 245-184 1974 £90

COTGREAVE, A.   A Contents-Subject Index to General and
Periodical Literature. 1900. Demy 8vo., half morocco, marbled boards, inscribed
by author, fine. Broadhurst 24-303 1974 £6

COTGREAVE, A.   Views & Memoranda of Public Libraries.
1901. New buckram, illus. Allen 216-175 1974 $10

COTTAFAVI, GAETANO   Raccolta delle Principali Vedute di Roma e
Suoi Contorne. Rome, 1843. Oblong small folio, plates, half morocco. Quaritch
940-68 1974 £120

COTTALAMBERGIUS, JOANNES FRANCISCUS   Eccius Dedolatus Autore
Ioannefrancisco Cottalambergio Poeta Laureato. (Basel, 1520). 4to., boards,
woodcut, fine. Harper 213-44 1973 $675

COTTE, LOUIS   Traite de Meteorologie. Paris, 1774. 4to.,
contemporary half calf, first edition. Zeitlin 235-51 1974 $95

COTTE, P.   Traite de Meteorolgie. Paris, 1774. 4to.,
old quarter calf, worn, plates, first edition. Gurney 64-57 1974 £32

COTTERELL, H. H.   Old Pewter. 4to., orig. cloth, plates, mint.
Broadhurst 23-54 1974 £10

COTTERILL, HENRY BERNARD   A History of Art. 1922-24. Profusely illus.,
2 vols., 8vo., half brown morocco, gilt line panelled backs, uncut, top edge gilt,
slightly rubbed on spine, fine, scarce. Sawyer 293-25 1974 £15

COTTERILL, HENRY BERNARD   Italy from Dante to Tasso 1300-1600. New
York, (1919). 8vo., maps, plans, full page illus., very good. Current BW9-
505 1974 $20

COTTIN, MARIE (RISTEAU)   Amelie Mansfield. Paris, 1835. 2 vols. in 1,
small 12mo., contemporary half green calf, gilt, worn. L. Goldschmidt 42-194
1974 $12.50

COTTIN, MARIE (RISTEAU)   Elizabeth. 1814. 12mo., half calf, frontis.
George's 610-183 1973 £6.50

COTTIN, MARIE (RISTEAU)   Elizabeth. 1821. 12mo., orig. boards, roan
spine, engraved frontis. George's 610-184 1973 £5

COTTIN, MARIE (RISTEAU)   Mathilde; ou, Memoires Tires de l'Histoire des
Croisades. 1809. 12mo., contemporary calf, little rubbed. George's 610-185
1973 £5

COTTLE, JOSEPH   Poems. Bristol, 1796. 8vo., contemporary calf,
gilt, spine gilt, morocco labels, second edition. Ximenes 36-60 1974 $45

COTTON, CHARLES   The History and Antiquities of the Church and
Parish of St. Laurence. 1895. 4to., orig. half roan, signed. Howes
186-2032 1974 £14.50

COTTON, CLEMENT   A Complete Concordance to the Bible. 1631.
Small folio, old calf, rebacked and repaired, tears amateurly repaired, generally
clean and sound. Thomas 32-38 1974 £30

COTTON, CLEMENT   A Large Concordance to the Bible. 1635.
Small folio, calf spine, cloth sides, enlarged second edition. Thomas 28-90
1972 £15

COTTON, J.   The Song Birds of Great Britain. 1836. Roy
8vo., modern half calf, plates. Wheldon 130-13 1974 £175

COTTON, ROBERT   An Abstract Out of the Records of the Tower.
London, (n.d.). Small 4to., uncut, modern grey boards, first edition. Dawsons
PM 247-57 1974 £35

COTTON, ROBERT   A Choice Narrative of Count Gondamor's
Transactions. London, 1820. 8vo., later quarter morocco. Ximenes 35-218
1974 $17.50

COTTON, ROBERT   An Exact Abridgement of the Records in the
Tower of London. London, 1657. Folio, contemporary calf. Quaritch 939-445
1974 £35

COTTON, ROBERT   The Histories of the Lives and Raignes of Henry
the Third and Henry the Fourth. London, 1642. 12mo., contemporary calf, rebacked, first edition. Dawsons PM 251-201 1974 £55

COTUGNO, DOMENICO   De Sedibus Variolarum. Vienna, 1771. 8vo.,
old-style half calf, boards, plate, second edition. Schuman 37-52 1974 $95

COUCH, JONATHAN   A History of the Fishes of the British Isles.
1862-65. Coloured plates, first edition, 4 vols., roy. 8vo., orig. cloth, fine,
unfaded. Broadhurst 24-1067 1974 £175

COUCH, JONATHAN   A History of the Fishes of the British Islands.
1877. 8vo., 4 vols., orig. cloth. Bow Windows 64-774 1974 £120

COUCH, JONATHAN   A History of the Fishes of the British Islands.
London, 1877. 4 vols., 8vo., plates, illus., orig. cloth, foxing, bookplate.
Bow Windows 62-211 1974 £120

COUCH, JONATHAN   A History of the Fishes of the British Islands.
1877. 4 vols., roy. 8vo., orig. blue cloth, coloured plates. Wheldon 128-624
1973 £65

COUCH, JONATHAN   A History of the Fishes of the British Islands.
1862-67. Roy. 8vo., 4 vols., contemporary blue full morocco, plates. Wheldon
129-10 1974 £100

COUES, ELLIOTT   Birds of the Northwest. Washington, 1874.
8vo., new cloth. Wheldon 131-577 1974 £7.50

COUES, ELLIOTT   The Expeditions of Zebulon Montgomery Pike.
New York, 1895. 3 vols., near mint, folding maps, one of 150 sets on laid
paper, uncut, best edition. Jenkins 61-719 1974 $135

COUES, ELLIOTT   The Fur-Bearing Animals of North America.
Boston, 1877. 8vo., cloth, plates. Wheldon 128-312 1973 £7.50

COUES, ELLIOTT   Handbook of Field and General Ornithology.
1890. 8vo., cloth. Wheldon 129-448 1974 £5

COUES, ELLIOTT   Key to North American Birds. New York,
1874. Roy. 8vo., orig. cloth. Wheldon 131-578 1974 £5

COUGHLIN, CHARLES E.   Driving Out the Moneychangers. 1933.
Austin 62-736 1974 $10

COUGHLIN, CHARLES E.   Eight Discourses on the Gold Standard.
1932-33. 80p., paper. Austin 62-737 1974 $10

COUGHLIN, CHARLES E.   Father Coughlin's Radio Discourses. 1931-32.
Austin 62-738 1974 $6.50

COUGHLIN, CHARLES E.   The New Deal in Money. 1933. 133p.
Austin 62-739 1974 $7.50

COUGHLIN, CHARLES E.   Series of Lectures on Social Justice. 1935-36.
Austin 62-741 1974 $8.50

COUGHLIN, CHARLES E.   Sixteen Radio Lectures. Michigan, 1938.
Austin 62-742 1974 $10

COULON, MARCEL   Le Probleme de Rimbaud, Poete Maudit.
Paris, 1923. 12mo., orig. wrapper, limited edition. L. Goldschmidt 42-352
1974 $12.50

COULTAS, HARLAND   The Plant. Philadelphia, 1855. Rittenhouse
46-158 1974 $10

COULTER, J. M.   Preliminary Revision of the N. American Species
of Cactus, Anhalonium, Lophophora, Echinocactus Cereus and Opuntia. 1894-96.
2 parts in 1 vol., 8vo., half cloth, scarce. Wheldon 131-1657 1974 £5

COULTER, JOHN   The Complete Story of the Galveston Horror.
1900. Rubbed, good condition. Ballinger 1-319 1974 $12.50

COULTON, G. G.   Art and the Reformation. Oxford, 1928.
Thick 8vo., plates, illus. Howes 186-737 1974 £5.50

COULTON, G. G.   From St. Francis to Dante. 1906. 370 pages.
Howes 186-739 1974 £5

COULTON, G. G.   Medieval Panorama. 1939. Thick 8vo.,
illus., plates. Howes 186-741 1974 £5

COULTON, G. G.   The Medieval Village. 1931. Plates, illus.,
scarce. Howes 186-742 1974 £7.50

COUNTRY Pets. London, ca. 1890. Square 12mo., cloth spine, illus. Frohnsdorff
16-230 1974 $7.50

THE COUNTY of Stafford. 1897. 4to., orig. cloth, limited edition. Broadhurst 23-1546 1974 £20

COURBOIN, FRANCOIS   La Gravure Francaise. 1927-28. 3 vols., roy.
8vo., orig. wrappers, limited. Quaritch 940-69 1974 £50

COURBOIN, FRANCOIS   La Gravure Francaise Essai de Bibliographie.
Paris, 1927-28. 2 vols., 4to., orig. wrappers, uncut, fine. Dawsons PM
10-139 1974 £33

COURIER, PAUL LOUIS   Oeuvres Completes. Paris, 1878. Small
4to., contemporary half red hard grain morocco, illus. L. Goldschmidt 42-195
1974 $15

COURNOT, ANTOINE AUGUSTIN   Essai sur les Fondements de Nos
Connaissances et Sur les Caracteres de la Critique Philosophique. Paris, 1851.
8vo., 2 vols., contemporary half calf, rubbed, first edition. Gilhofer 61-47
1974 sFr. 550

COURT, LEWIS H.   Untarnished Gold and Other Poems. Taunton,
1938. Plates, English first edition. Covent 56-1677 1974 £5.25

COURTHION, PIERRE   Images Continentales. Paris, 1936. Oblong
16mo., wrappers, plates, limited edition. Minters 37-350 1973 $30

COURTHION, PIERRE   Raoul Dufy. Paris, 1929. Large 4to.,
wrappers, plates, limited edition. Minters 37-85 1973 $35

COURTHOPE, W. J.   A History of English Poetry. 1922-26. 6 vols.,
orig. cloth. Howes 186-112 1974 £32

LE COURTISAN   Sans Art ou Les Complimens sans Fard. Paris,
1777. Engraved plates, 16mo., contemporary red morocco gilt, orig. lead stylus,
gilt edges, slight stains, some spotting. Sawyer 293-115 1974 £25

COURT Jobbery: Or, the Black Book of the Palace, a Detailed Account of
Pensions Granted by Queen Victoria. London, 1848. 12mo., orig. printed
wrappers, spine chipped, first edition. Ximenes 37-168 1974 $22.50

COURTNEY, MARGUERITE   Laurette. Rinehart, 1955. 433p., illus.
Austin 51-212 1973 $7.50

THE COURTSHIP, Marriage, and Death of a Pretty Robin Redbreast. London,
1812. Orig. printed brown wrappers, full page engravings, fine. Gregory
44-40 1974 $60

THE COURTSHIP, Merry Marriage, and Feast of Cock Robin and Jenny Wren.
New York, 1935. 24mo., boards, cloth spine, illus. Frohnsdorff 16-226 1974
$10

COUSIN, CHARLES   Racontars Illustres d'un Vieux Collectionneur.
Paris, 1887. Large 4to., red brown three quarter morocco, faded at back, illus.,
color plates, on Japan paper. Kraus B8-43 1974 $150

COUSIN FANNIE   Uncle Curioso's Tales for Youths and Maidens.
Boston, 1858. First edition, 12mo., full color illus., very good, orig. red blind
and gilt stamped covers. Current BW9-145 1974 $27.50

COUSINS, FRANK   The Colonial Architecture of Philadelphia.
Boston, 1920. First edition, limited to 975 numbered copies, 8vo., illus., mint.
Current BW9-408 1974 $32.50

COUSINS, FRANK   The Wood-Carver of Salem. Boston, 1916.
First edition, limited to 920 copies, 8vo., plates, extremities rubbed, ex-library
copy, interior fine. Current BW9-562 1974 $40

COUSINS, HENRY   Hastings of Bygone Days. Hastings, 1911.
Large 8vo., illus., orig. buckram, scarce. Howes 186-2198 1974 £8.50

THE COUT de Santerre. Bath, 1797. 2 vols., 12mo., 19th century green
morocco rubbed, first edition. Ximenes 36-87 1974 $150

COUTS, J.   A Practical Guide to the Tailor's Cutting-Room.
Glasgow, (1848). 4to., plates, contemporary half calf, rebacked. Quaritch
940-709 1974 £160

COUVRAY, JEAN BAPTISTE LOUVET DE
Please turn to
LOUVET DE COUVRAY, JEAN BAPTISTE

COVARRUBIAS, M.   Island of Bali. 1937. 8vo., orig. cloth.
Broadhurst 23-1628 1974 £5

COVELLO, LEONARD   The Italians in America. 1934. Maps,
charts. Austin 57-153 1974 $12.50

COVENTRY, FRANCIS   The History of Pompey the Little. 1751. 12mo.,
contemporary calf, rebacked, frontispiece, first edition. Quaritch 936-35 1974
£55

COVENTRY, GEORGE   A Critical Enquiry Regarding the Real Author of the
Letters of Junius. London, 1825. 8vo., orig. boards, presentation copy, first edition. Hammond 201-298 1974 £6.50

COWAN, FRANK   South-Western Pennsylvania. 1878. Orig.
green cloth, gilt, English first edition. Covent 56-14 1974 £25

COWAN, ROBERT ERNEST   A Bibliography of the History of California,
1510-1930. San Francisco, 1933. 3 vols., exceptionally valuabel set of fine
work. Jenkins 61-305 1974 $145

COWAN, ROBERT ERNEST   Forgotten Characters of Old San Francisco,
1850-70. San Francisco, 1938. Limited to 500 copies. Jenkins 61-306 1974
$17.50

COWAN, ROBERT ERNEST   The Library of William Andrews Clark, Jr.
San Francisco, 1921. 4to., orig. cloth-backed boards, uncut, fine. Dawsons
PM 10-140 1974 £30

COWARD, NOEL   Bitter Sweet. Secker, 1929. 110p. Austin
51-213 1973 $7.50

COWARD, NOEL   Home Chat. 1927. 8vo., orig. cloth, dust-
wrapper, fine, first edition. Rota 189-211 1974 £5

COWARD, NOEL   Peace In Our Time. Austin 51-214 1973 $7.50

COWARD, NOEL   Play Parade. Doubleday, 1933. 576p.
Austin 51-215 1973 $7.50

COWARD, NOEL   Post Mortem. Doubleday, Doran, 1931. 111p.
Austin 51-216 1973 $7.50

COWARD, NOEL   Present Indicative. Doubleday, 1937.
371p. Austin 51-217 1973 $6

COWARD, NOEL   Present Laughter. Doubleday, 1946. 222p.
Austin 51-218 1973 $7.50

COWARD, NOEL   Private Lives. Doubleday, Doran, 1930. 88p.
Austin 51-219 1973 $6.50

COWARD, NOEL   Sirocco. 1927. 8vo., orig. cloth, dust wrapper,
fine, first edition. Rota 189-212 1974 £5

COWARD, NOEL   This Happy Breed. Doubleday, 1947. 223p.
Austin 51-220 1973 $7.50

COWARD, NOEL   We Were Dancing. French, 1935. 28p., paper.
Austin 51-221 1973 $7.50

COWARD, NOEL   Weather Wise. 1925. 4to., frontispiece,
plates, wrappers. Covent 55-534 1974 £7.50

COWARD, T. A.   The Vertebrate Fauna of Cheshire and Liverpool
Bay. 1910. 8vo., 2 vols., cloth, illus. Wheldon 129-262 1974 £5

COWDEN-CLARKE, MARY   Complete Concordance to Shakespeare. 1886.
New buckram, new revised edition. Allen 216-2165 1974 $17.50

COWDRY, E. V.   Special Cytology. New York, 1932.
3 vols., second edition. Rittenhouse 46-159 1974 $25

COWELL, J.   The Curious and Profitable Gardener. 1730.
8vo., contemporary panelled calf, rebacked, rare, first edition. Wheldon 130-
1384 1974 £75

COWEN, PHILIP   Memories of an American Jew. 1932. Austin
62-115 1974 $17.50

COWLEY, ABRAHAM   Anacreon. 1923. 8vo., orig. boards, uncut,
limited edition. Broadhurst 23-732 1974 £21

COWLEY, ABRAHAM   Poems. London, 1656. Small folio, worn,
contemporary calf, first edition. Dawsons PM 252-180 1974 £80

COWLEY, ABRAHAM   The Works. London, 1674. Folio, fine,
blind-stamped calf, frontispiece, first edition. Dawsons PM 252-181 1974 £30

COWLEY, ABRAHAM   Works, in Prose and Verse. 1809. 3 vols.,
16mo., old calf, joints cracked. Allen 216-1892 1974 $10

COWLEY, ABRAHAM   The Works Of. London, 1672. Small folio,
contemporary calf, third edition. Smith 194-141 1974 £8.50

COWLEY, CHARLES   A Hand Book of Business in Lowell. Lowell,
1856. 8vo., cloth. Saddleback 14-479 1974 $15

COWLEY, HANNAH   The Belle's Stratagem. London, 1782. 8vo.,
modern boards, first authorised edition. Dawsons PM 252-182 1974 £15

COWLEY, HANNAH   A Bold Stroke for a Husband. London, 1784.
8vo., modern boards, first edition. Dawsons PM 252-183 1974 £15

COWLEY, HANNAH   The Fate of Sparta. London, 1788. 8vo.,
modern boards, stains, first edition. Bow Windows 62-212 1974 £15

COWLEY, HANNAH   The Fate of Sparta. Dublin, 1788. 12mo.,
modern boards. Dawsons PM 252-184 1974 £12

COWLEY, HANNAH   Which is the Man? London, 1784. 8vo.,
modern boards, first edition. Dawsons PM 252-185 1974 £8

COWLEY, HANNAH   Who's the Dupe? London, 1780. 8vo.,
modern boards, fourth edition. Dawsons PM 252-186 1974 £8

COWLEY, MALCOLM   Exile's Return. New York, 1934. First U. S.
edition, ownership inscription, very good copy. Covent 51-479 1973 $7.50

COWLEY, MALCOLM   Blue Juniata. New York, 1929. Orig. cloth,
presentation inscription, first edition. Rota 188-207 1974 £12.50

COWLEY, MALCOLM   Exiles Returns. Viking, 1951. 332p., hard
cover ed. Austin 54-271 1973 $7.50

COWPER, J. MEADOWS   The Names of Them that Were Crystened,
Maryed, and Buryed in the Paryshe of Saint Mary. 1890. Roy. 8vo., orig.
cloth. Howes 186-2034 1974 £8.50

COWPER, J. MEADOWS   Our Parish Books. Canterbury, 1884-85.
2 vols., crown 8vo., orig. cloth. Howes 186-2033 1974 £6.50

COWPER, J. MEADOWS   Our Parish Books, and What They Tell Us.
Canterbury, 1884-85. 2 vols., 8vo., orig. cloth, uncut, fine. Dawsons PM
10-142 1974 £6

COWPER, WILLIAM   Correspondence. 1904. 4 vols., spines worn,
ex-library. Allen 216-1996 1974 $25

COWPER, WILLIAM   The Diverting History of John Gilpin.   New York and London, (c. 1895). Heavy paper, full page colored illus., orig. paper boards, scuffed, faded & worn, interior good, rebacked.   Current BW9-110 1974 $13.50

COWPER, WILLIAM   Life and Posthumous Writings.   Boston, 1803. 3 vols., new buckram, plates.   Allen 216-1997 1974 $15

COWPER, WILLIAM   Poems.   London, 1782-85. 2 vols., 8vo., full brown levant, gilt, spines gilt, first editions.   Ximenes 37-49 1974 $250

COWPER, WILLIAM   Poems.   London, 1821. Small 8vo., 2 vols., contemporary brown straight-grained morocco, gilt.   Hammond 201-349 1974 £38.50

COWPER, WILLIAM   The Poetical Works Of.   London, n.d. Tall post 8vo., plates, contemporary red morocco.   Smith 193-248 1973 £5

COWPER, WILLIAM   Poetical Works of.   1853. 3 vols.   Austin 61-252 1974 $17.50

COWPER, WILLIAM   Private Correspondence.   London, 1824. 2 vols., 8vo., old half morocco, first edition.   Dawsons PM 252-187 1974 £32

COWPER, WILLIAM   The Task.   1855. Orig. green cloth, illus., signed.   Smith 194-726 1974 £9.50

COWPER, WILLIAM   Works.   1835. 8 vols., small 8vo., foxed, frontispieces, contemporary morocco gilt.   Howes 185-88 1974 £18

THE COWSLIP, or More Cautionary Stories in Verse.   Philadelphia, 1939. Square 16mo., woodcut illus., full page woodcut frontis., spine faded, attractive book.   Current BW9-109 1974 $12.50

COWTAN, R.   Memories of the British Museum.   1872. 8vo., cloth, presentation inscription, portrait.   Quaritch 939-440 1974 £25

COX, CHARLES   Sir Charles Cox's Case.   (1711). Folio, disbound.   Quaritch 939-98 1974 £10

COX, E. H. M.   Plant Hunting in China.   1945. 8vo., cloth, plates, maps, scarce, orig. issue.   Wheldon 131-1598 1974 £7.50

COX, E. M.   A Remedy for Sedition Which Rare and Witty Book is Now Reprinted for the First Time.   1933. Roy. 8vo., full pigskin, uncut, fine, limited to 100 copies.   Broadhurst 24-601 1974 £15

COX, E. N. M.   New Flora and Silva.   1929-40. Vols. 1-12, roy. 8vo., in parts as issued.   Wheldon 128-1513 1973 £35

COX, E. W.   Our Common Insects.   1864. Crown 8vo., cloth.   Wheldon 131-795 1974 £5

COX, E. W. (Mrs.)   Twilight Tales.   London, 1855. 12mo., embossed cloth with gilt lettering, all edges gilt, lst ed.   Frohnsdorff 16-252 1974 $125

COX, I. E. B.   Facts and Useful Hints Relating to Fishing and Shooting.   1874. 8vo., orig. cloth.   Bow Windows 64-464 1974 £6

COX, J. C.   Memorials of Old Surrey.   London, 1911. 8vo., frontispiece, plates, illus., orig. cloth, faded.   Bow Windows 62-214 1974 £5

COX, J. C.   The Sanctuaries and Sanctuary Seekers of Mediaeval England.   1911. 8vo., orig. cloth, coloured frontispiece, plates, illus., slight spotting, spine faded.   Bow Windows 66-149 1974 £7

COX, JAMES   A Descriptive Inventory of the Several Exquisite and Magnificent Pieces of Mechanism and Jewellery.   1774. 4to., contemporary boards, frontispiece, new leather spine, rare.   Quaritch 940-440 1974 £65

COX, JAMES   My Native Land.   St. Louis, 1895. Blue cloth, gilt, first edition.   Bradley 35-111 1974 $20

COX, JOHN HARRINGTON   Folk-Songs of the South.   Harvard, 1925. 8vo., orig. bindings.   Butterfield 8-582 1974 $22.50

COX, PALMER   Bomba, the Merry Old King, and Other Stories.   New York, 1902. Sm. 4to., pict. boards, cloth spine, illus.   Frohnsdorff 16-231 1974 $12.50

COX, PALMER   The Brownies and the Lovers.   1895. 4to., Flexible pictorial boards.   Frohnsdorff 16-232 1974 $35

COX, PALMER   Queer People Such as Goblins, Giants, Merry-Men and Monarchs.   Philadelphia, 1888. 4to., illus., lst ed.   Frohnsdorff 16-235 1974 $30

COX, PALMER   Queer People With Paws and Claws and Their Kweer Kapers.   Philadelphia, 1888. 4to., lst ed., illus.   Frohnsdorff 16-236 1974 $25

COX, PALMER   Rhyme and Reason.   ca. 1890. 16mo., mint copy, illus.   Frohnsdorff 16-237 1974 $15

COX, RICHARD   Hibernia Anglicana.   London, 1689. 2 vols. in 1, folio, half calf, map.   Emerald 50-177 1974 £55

COX, RICHARD   The Proceedings of the Honourable House of Commons of Ireland.   Dublin, 1754. 8vo., boards, third edition.   Hammond 201-224 1974 £12

COX, ROSS   Adventures on the Columbia River.   1831. 8vo., contemporary half calf, 2 vols., first edition.   Bow Windows 64-465 1974 £310

COX, SANDFORD C.   Recollections of the Early Settlement of the Wabash Valley.   Lafayette, 1860. Cloth.   Hayman 57-346 1974 $50

COX, SIDNEY   Robert Frost: Original Ordinary Man.   New York, 1929. Orig. binding, no. 877 of edition limited to 1,000 copies, signed, dust wrapper slightly torn at top, else mint, thus scarce.   Ross 87-224 1974 $25

COX, WILLIAM D.   Boxing in Art and Literature.   New York, 1935. Limited to 200 numbered copies and signed by editor, illus. with tipped in plates, half morocco, marbled endpapers, top edges gilt, others uncut, raised bands, very good to fine.   Wilson 63-416 1974 $50

COX, WILLIAM V.   Celebration of the One Hundredth Anniversary of the Establishment of the Seat of Government in the District of Columbia.   Washington, 1901. 4to., illus., maps, engraved plan, orig. binding.   Wilson 63-107 1974 $22.50

COXE, JOHN REDMAN   The Writings of Hippocrates and Galen.   Philadelphia, 1846. Loose front cover, first edition.   Rittenhouse 46-683 1974 $50

COXE, PETER   Social Day.   1823. 4to., engraved plates, new buckram, frontispiece.   Allen 213-391 1974 $35

COXE, W.   A View of the Cultivation of Fruit Trees.   Philadelphia, 1817. 8vo., contemporary sheep, rebacked, plates, rare.   Wheldon 130-1470 1974 £100

COXE, WILLIAM   An Historical Tour of Monmouthshire.   1801. 4to., 2 vols., full contemporary calf.   Broadhurst 23-1358 1974 £36

COXE, WILLIAM   A Historical Tour Through Monmouthshire Illustrated With Views by Sir. R. C. Hoare and Other Engravings.   Brecon, 1904. Roy. 4to., publisher's half morocco, illus., fine.   Broadhurst 24-1396 1974 £24

COXE, WILLIAM   Memoirs of John Duke of Marlborough.   London, 1819. 4to., 3 vols., half calf, gilt, first edition.   Hammond 201-612 1974 £35

COXWELL, C. FILLINGHAM   Siberian and Other Folk-Tales.   1924. Thick 8vo., orig. cloth, scarce.   Howes 186-1804 1974 £8.50

COYNE, J. E.   The Talbot Papers.   (1907-09). Full leather.   Hood's 103-617 1974 $45

COYNE, W. P.   Ireland Industrial and Agricultural.   Dublin, Cork & Belfast, 1902. Roy. 8vo., illus., cloth.   Quaritch 939-615 1974 £8

COZENS, JOHN ROBERT   Drawings By.   1922-23. 4to., plates, buckram.   Quaritch 940-70 1974 £25

COZZENS, FREDERICK S.   Sayings, Wise and Otherwise.   New York, 1880. Covers damped. Butterfield 10-205 1974 $10

COZZENS, FREDERICK S.   The Sparrow Grass Papers. Derby, Jackson, 1854. 328p. Austin 54-272 1973 $10

COZZENS, J. G.   Ask Me To-Morrow.   1940. Fine, dust wrapper, English first edition. Covent 56-262 1974 $7.50

COZZENS, JAMES GOULD   S. S. San Pedro. 1931. First edition, fine, d.w. Covent 51-481 1973 £5.25

COZZENS, JAMES GOULD   S. S. San Pedro. New York, 1931. Dust wrapper, fine, first American edition. Covent 55-536 1974 £12.60

CRABB, GEORGE   Universal Technological Dictionary.   London, 1823. 2 vols. in 1, full calf, gilt, plates. Covent 55-1461 1974 £25

CRABB, JAMES   The Gipsies' Advocate. 1832. 12mo., orig. cloth, third edition. Bow Windows 64-529 1974 £15

CRABBE, GEORGE   The Borough. London, 1810. 8vo., foxing, contemporary half calf, first edition. Dawsons PM 252-188 1974 £35

CRABBE, GEORGE   The Library. London, 1781. 4to., disbound, very good copy, first edition. Ximenes 37-49 1974 $150

CRABBE, GEORGE   The Poetical Works. London, 1823. 8vo., 5 vols., contemporary full calf, gilt, plates, fine. Hammond 201-299 1974 £35

CRABBE, GEORGE   Tales. 1820. 2 vols., 8vo., full contemporary fawn calf, labels. Howes 186-114 1974 £14

CRABBE, GEORGE   The Tales and Miscellaneous Poems. London, 1847. Small 8vo., contemporary green morocco, gilt. Hammond 201-300 1974 £6.50

CRABBE, GEORGE   The Village. London, 1783. 4to., disbound, very scarce, very good copy, first edition. Ximenes 37-51 1974 $250

CRABBE, GEORGE   The Works. London, 1823. 5 vols., 8vo., contemporary calf, rubbed. Dawsons PM 252-189 1974 £12.50

CRABITES, PIERRE   Clement VII and Henry VIII. 1936. Howes 185-1087 1974 £5

CRABTREE, A. D.   The Funny Side of Physic. Hartford, 1880. Inner hinges split, good, used. Biblo & Tannen 213-910 1973 $15

CRABTREE, J.   Concise History of the Parish and Vicarage of Halifax. 1836 and 93. 8vo., half calf, gilt. Broadhurst 23-1359 1974 £10

CRACKANTHORPE, HUBERT   Vignettes. 1896. 8vo., orig. boards, fine. Covent 55-537 1974 £10

CRACKANTHORPE, HUBERT   Wreckage. 1893. Orig. dec. cloth, faded, English first edition. Covent 56-263 1974 £10

CRADDOCK, SAMUEL   The Harmony of the Four Evangelists. 1670. Small folio, old calf, worn. Thomas 28-91 1972 £25

CRAFTS, E. P. R.   Pioneer Days in the San Bernardino Valley. Redlands, 1906. 12mo., cloth. Saddleback 14-78 1974 $45

CRAFTS, W. A.   The Southern Rebellion. Boston, 1868. 4to., 2 vols., part morocco, illus. Putman 126-56 1974 $22

CRAFTS, WILLIAM   A Selection, in Prose and Poetry. Charleston, 1828. 8vo., orig. quarter green cloth and pink boards, printed paper label, nice copy, orig. condition, first edition. Ximenes 37-52 1974 $75

CRAIG, ALEC   The Banned Books of England. 1937. Fine, d.w., first edition. Covent 51-713 1973 £8

CRAIG, EDWARD   Nothing. 1925. Separately mounted bookplates, cloth backed boards, very good, scarce. Covent 51-2280 1973 £10.50

CRAIG, EDWARD GORDON   Ellen Terry and Her Secret Self. (1931). Orig. buckram, fine, first edition. Howes 185-515 1974 £6

CRAIG, EDWARD GORDON   Henry Irving. Longman's, 1930. 232p., illus. Austin 51-222 1973 $12.50

CRAIG, EDWARD GORDON   Henry Irving. 1938. 8vo., cloth, dust wrapper, presentation copy. Quaritch 936-351 1974 £140

CRAIG, EDWARD GORDON   On the Art of the Theatre. 1911. 294p. Austin 51-221a. 1973 $15

CRAIG, EDWARD GORDON   On the Art of the Theatre. London, 1912. 8vo., soiled boards, cloth spine, foxed, illus. Minters 37-496 1973 $24

CRAIG, EDWARD GORDON   A Production. 1930. Roy 4to., cloth, slipcase, plates, limited edition. Quaritch 936-352 1974 £90

CRAIG, EDWARD GORDON   Towards a New Theatre. London, 1913. Black cloth, gilt, dust wrapper. Dawson's 424-102 1974 $65

CRAIG, EDWARD GORDON   Woodcuts and Some Words. Boston, 1925. Cloth, boards. Dawson's 424-103 1974 $20

CRAIG, J.   Forty Years Among the Telugus. Toronto, 1908. Hood's 104-297 1974 $10

CRAIG, ROBERT   An Inquiry into the Justice and Necessity of the Present War with France. N.P., 1785. 8vo., nineteenth century half calf, first edition. Dawsons PM 251-202 1974 £10

CRAIK, DINAH MARIA (MULOCK)   John Halifax, Gentleman. London, 1856. 3 vols., 8vo., orig. brown cloth, first edition. Dawsons PM 252-734 1974 £290

CRAIK, DINAH MARIA (MULOCK)   John Halifax, Gentleman. 1856. First edition, 3 vols., 8vo., orig. earth brown cloth, publisher's catalogue at end of Vol. 1, spines slightly chipped, good copy, rare. Sawyer 293-116 1974 £130

CRAIK, DINAH MARIA (MULOCK)   A Life for a Life. London, 1859. 3 vols., 8vo., orig. cloth, first edition. Dawsons PM 252-735 1974 £55

CRAIK, DINAH MARIA (MULOCK)   The Little Lame Prince and His Traveling Cloak. New York, (1900). 12mo., red pictorial cloth, illus. in color. Frohnsdorff 16-597 1974 $10

CRAIK, GEORGE LILLIE 1798-1866   The Romance of the Peerage. 1848-50. 4 vols., 8vo., orig. cloth, endpapers & frontis. damp marked. Bow Windows 66-150 1974 £8

CRAIK, GEORGE LILLIE 1798-1866   A Compendious History of English Literature and of the English Language from the Norman Conquest. 1878. 2 vols., full crimson calf, gilt, rubbed. Howes 186-115 1974 £5

CRAIK, GEORGE LILLIE 1798-1866   English of Shakespeare. 1886. Austin 51-223 1973 $7.50

CRAM, JACOB   Journal of a Missionary Tour of... Rochester, 1909. Square 12mo., orig. binding, handwritten label, limited. Butterfield 8-346 1974 $150

CRAM, MILDRED   Old Seaport Towns of the South. New York, 1917. Boxed, orig. binding. Butterfield 10-206 1974 $15

CRAM, RALPH ADAMS   Church Building. Boston, 1924. Third edition, 8vo., near mint, some soiling of d.j. Current BW9-455 1974 $16

CRAM, RALPH ADAMS   The Ruined Abbeys of Great Britain. New York, (1905). First edition, 8vo., illus., very good. Current BW9-527 1974 $18.75

CRAMER, JOHN ANTONY   A Geographical and Historical Description of Ancient Italy. Oxford, 1826. 8vo., 2 vols., contemporary diced calf, rebacked first edition. Dawsons PM 251-21 1974 £10

CRAMER, JOHN ANTHONY   A Geographical and Historical Description of Ancient Italy. Oxford, 1827. 8vo., 2 vols., contemporary diced russia, first edition. Dawsons PM 251-203 1974 £10

CRAMP, J. M.   Textbook of Popery. Appleton, 1831. Austin 62-747 1974 $17.50

CRAN, MARION   Wind-harps. London, 1929. Biblo & Tannen 213-848 1973 $7.50

CRANACH, LUCAS   Das Symbolum Oder Gemeine Bekentnis der Zwelff Apsteln. Wittenberg, 1539. Folio, contemporary blind-stamped calf, woodcuts, rebacked, first edition. Harper 213-45 1973 $3500

CRANACH, LUCAS   Werke Moderner Goldschmiedekunst von W. Lucas Von Cranach. Leipzig, (c. 1905). Folio, plates, unbound in orig. cloth portfolio. Quaritch 940-673 1974 £21

CRANAGE, D. H. S.   An Architectural Account of the Churches of Shropshire. 1901-12. 2 vols., 4to., illus., half red morocco. Quaritch 939-531 1974 £60

CRANCH, CHRISTOPHER P.   Ariel and Caliban With Other Poems. Boston, 1887. 12mo., cloth, first edition. Goodspeed's 578-71 1974 $10

CRANDALL, ARTHUR G.   New England Joke Lore. Davis, n.d. 293p., illus. Austin 54-273 1973 $12.50

CRANDALL, CHARLES H.   Representative Sonnets by American Poets. Houghton, 1891. 363p. Austin 54-274 1973 $10

CRANE, L. H.   Flowers and Folk-Lore from Far Korea. Tokyo, (1932). 4to., orig. cloth, rare, plates. Wheldon 130-1144 1974 £30

CRANE, LUCY   Art and the Formation of Taste. 1882. 8vo., illus., dec. cloth, soiled, scarce. Quaritch 940-71 1974 £7

CRANE, LUCY   Art and the Formation of Taste. 1882. Orig. dec. cloth, English first edition. Covent 56-1681 1974 £15

CRANE, NATHALIA   Lava Lane. New York, 1925. Presentation, inscribed, foxed, first American edition. Covent 55-540 1974 £8.50

CRANE, R. S.   A Census of British Newspapers and Periodicals 1620-1800. Chapel Hill, 1927. 8vo., buckram, orig. edition. Goodspeed's 578-445 1974 $10

CRANE, STEPHEN   Active Service. 1899. Orig. cloth, almost fine. Covent 51-2281 1973 £10.50

CRANE, STEPHEN   George's Mother. London and New York, 1896. Cloth, first edition. Dawson's 424-257 1974 $25

CRANE, STEPHEN   The Little Regiment. 1897. English first edition. Covent 56-266 1974 £10.50

CRANE, STEPHEN   The Little Regiment and Other Episodes of the American Civil War. New York, 1896. Orig. cloth, soiled, joints worn, good copy, first edition, second printing. MacManus 224-105 1974 $30

CRANE, STEPHEN   Maggie. 1896. Orig. cloth gilt, very nice copy, ads at end. Covent 51-2282 1973 £20

CRANE, STEPHEN   Maggie. 1896. 12mo., orig. dec. cloth gilt, first edition. Covent 55-541 1974 £25

CRANE, STEPHEN   Maggie, a Girl of the Streets. New York, 1896. 1st ed. to acknowledge Crane's authorship; bdg rubbed. Biblo & Tannen 210-715 1973 $25

CRANE, STEPHEN   Maggie, A Girl of the Streets. New York, 1896. Orig. cloth, second edition, second state, about fine. MacManus 224-106 1974 $40

CRANE, STEPHEN   The Monster and Other Stories. New York & London, 1899. Orig. cloth, first edition, very good copy. MacManus 224-107 1974 $35

CRANE, STEPHEN   The O'Ruddy. New York, (1903). Orig. illus. cloth, first edition, frontispiece portrait, about fine. MacManus 224-108 1974 $35

CRANE, STEPHEN   The O'Ruddy. 1921. 12mo., cheap edition. Covent 55-542 1974 £5.25

CRANE, STEPHEN   Pictures of War. 1898. Inscription, English first edition. Covent 56-267 1974 £25

CRANE, STEPHEN   The Third Violet. New York, 1897. Buckram, first edition. Dawson's 424-258 1974 $35

CRANE, STEPHEN   Whilomville Stories. New York & London, 1900. Orig. cloth, illus., first edition, fine copy. MacManus 224-109 1974 $45

CRANE, STEPHEN   Wounds in the Rain. New York, (1900). Cloth, first edition. Dawson's 424-259 1974 $40

CRANE, STEPHEN   The Work of Stephen Crane. New York, 1925. 12 vols., ltd. to 750 sets. Jacobs 24-74 1974 $200

CRANE, THOMAS   Abroad. London, ca. 1882. Sm. 4to., cloth spine, edges rubbed; illus. Frohnsdorff 16-4 1974 $15

CRANE, W.   Flowers from Shakespeare's Garden. London, 1906. 4to., orig. pictorial boards, attractive color plates. Gregory 44-41 1974 $35

CRANE, W. J. E.   Bookbinding for Amateurs. New York & London, 1903. Engravings, 12mo., very fine except for some page browning. Current BW9-495 1974 $10

CRANE, WALTER   An Artist's Reminiscences. 1907. Plates, text illus., orig. dec. cloth, near fine. Covent 51-2284 1973 £20

CRANE, WALTER   The Baby's Bouquet. New York, n.d. Square 8vo., pict. boards, cloth spine. Frohnsdorff 16-238 1974 $27.50

CRANE, WALTER   The Baby's Opera. London and New York, n.d. Square 8vo., pict. boards, cloth spine, 1st ed. Frohnsdorff 16-239 1974 $40

CRANE, WALTER   The Baby's Opera. New York, n.d. 4to., pict. boards, cloth spine, rear endpaper cracked at hinge. Frohnsdorff 15-19 1974 $15

CRANE, WALTER   The Baby's Opera, a Book of Old Rhymes With New Dresses. (1877). First edition, coloured illus., slight spotting, oblong 8vo., orig. cloth backed pictorial boards. George's 610-190 1973 £5

CRANE, WALTER   The Baby's Own Aesop. London, n.d. Square 8vo., pictorial boards, cloth spine. Frohnsdorff 16-240 1974 $17.50

CRANE, WALTER   Beauty and the Beast. London & New York, n.d. 4to., pictorial wrappers, fine color plates engraved, very good copy, stitching weak. Frohnsdorff 15-18 1974 $20

CRANE, WALTER   "Carrots". 1910. Marked cover, illus., first edition. Covent 55-543 1974 £7.50

CRANE, WALTER   Chattering Jack's Picture Book. Routledge, n.d. 4to., orig. pictorial boards, first collected edition. Smith 194-426 1974 £10

CRANE, WALTER   A Floral Fantasy In an Old English Garden. 1899. Crown 4to., illus., orig. pictorial cloth. Smith 193-341 1973 £9.60

CRANE, WALTER   Line and Form. 1900. Dec. cloth gilt, illus., worn, first edition. Marsden 39-99 1974 £10

CRANE, WALTER   Molesworth. 1887. Orig. pictorial cloth, illus., plates, English first edition. Covent 56-269 1974 £6.30

CRANE, WALTER   Of the Decorative Illustration of Books Old and New. 1896. Plates, illus., buckram, first edition. Marsden 37-142 1974 £7

CRANE, WALTER — Of the Decorative Illustration of Books Old and New. 1901. Orig. dec. buckram, engravings, second edition. Smith 194-720 1974 £7.50

CRANE, WALTER — Of the Decorative Illustration of Books, Old & New. 1905. Illus. Allen 216-176 1974 $10

CRANE, WALTER — Red Riding Hood's Picture Book. n.d. 4to., orig. pictorial cloth, illus. Smith 194-721 1974 £5

CRANE, WALTER — Renascence. London, 1891. Large 8vo., vellum spine (gilt-lettered), one of 15 copies for the U.S. printed on Japanese Vellum; sgd. and numbered by author. Frohnsdorff 16-243 1974 $125

CRANE, WALTER — Rumbo Rhymes. London and New York, 1911. Pale grey green cloth, plates. Dawson's 424-211 1974 $40

CRANE, WALTER — The Shepheard's Calender. London and New York, 1898. Pictorial binding, plates, first edition. Dawson's 424-104 1974 $45

CRANE, WALTER — The Sleeping Beauty and Blue Beard. London, 1914. Pict. boards, 14 color plates. Frohnsdorff 16-244 1974 $15

CRANE, WALTER — Spenser's Faerie Queene. 1897. 4to., 6 vols., orig. dec. buckram, gilt, English first edition. Covent 56-683 1974 £185

CRANE, WALTER — Time's Garland for the Year. n.d. 12mo., fine, scarce. Covent 51-2285 1973 £10.50

CRANE, WALTER — William Morris to Whistler. 1911. Full blue buckram gilt, illus., fine. Covent 55-544 1974 £45

CRANE, WALTER — William Morris to Whistler. 1911. Dec. cloth, illus., plates, first edition. Marsden 39-102 1974 £10

CRANE, WALTER — A Wonder Book for Girls and Boys. Boston, 1893. Small 4to., dec. cloth, full page color plates, very good copy, first edition. Frohnsdorff 15-17 1974 $25

CRANE, WALTER — The Work of. 1898. Plates, illus., worn. Marsden 37-143 1974 £10

CRANFIELD, S. W. — Houses for the Working Classes. London, 1904. Folio, orig. cloth, gilt, plates, second edition. Hammond 201-964 1974 £12

CRANMER, THOMAS — A Defence of the True and Catholike Doctrine of the Sacrament of the Body and Blood of Our Saviour Christ. London, 1550. Small 4to., 19th century calf, rare. Howes 185-1088 1974 £90

CRANMER, THOMAS — The Remains. 1833. 4 vols., contemporary calf, labels. Howes 185-1089 1974 £15

CRANTZ, H. J. N. — Stirpium Austriacarum. Vienna, 1769. 4to., contemporary half leather, plates. Wheldon 129-1060 1974 £10

CRASHAW, RICHARD — The Complete Works Of. 1858. 8vo., orig. cloth. Bow Windows 64-466 1974 £6.50

CRATER Lake National Park. Medford, c. 1900. Wrappers, folio, hand colored photos. Jenkins 61-2060 1974 $12.50

CRAVEN, FRANK — The First Year. French, 1921. 107p., paper. Austin 51-224 1973 $7.50

CRAVEN, THOMAS — Cartoon Cavalcade. Chicago, 1944. Sm. 4to., illus. Biblo & Tannen 214-55 1974 $8.50

CRAVEN, THOMAS — Men of Art. New York, 1940. Plates. Biblo & Tannen 210-105 1973 $8.50

CRAVEN, THOMAS — The Story of Painting. New York, 1943. 4to., color plates., 1st ed. Biblo & Tannen 210-106 1973 $8.50

CRAWFORD, ALEXANDER WILLIAM CRAWFORD LINDSAY, 25TH EARL OF — Bibliotheca Lindesiana: Catalogue of English Broadsides 1505-1897. Aberdeen, 1898. Demy 4to., good copy, limited to 100 copies, orig. cloth. Broadhurst 24-305 1974 £30

CRAWFORD, ALEXANDER WILLIAM CRAWFORD LINDSAY, 25TH EARL OF — Bibliotheca Lindesiana. 1890. Crown 4to., half vellum, board sides, uncut, limited, one of 100 copies, inscribed presentation copy, fine. Broadhurst 24-304 1974 £35

CRAWFORD, ALEXANDER WILLIAM CRAWFORD LINDSAY, 25TH EARL OF — Sketches of the History of Christian Art. 1847. 3 vols., 8vo., cloth worn. Quaritch 940-793 1974 £10

CRAWFORD, F. MARION — Khaled. London, 1891. 1st ed. Biblo & Tannen 214-680 1974 $15

CRAWFORD, JACK R. — What to Read In English Literature. 1928. Ex-library. Austin 61-256 1974 $12.50

CRAWFORD, LEWIS F. — Badlands and Broncho Trails. Bismark, 1922. Scarce. Jenkins 61-720 1974 $22.50

CRAWFORD, LEWIS F. — Rekindling Camp Fires. Bismarck, (1926). Cloth, stains, first edition. Bradley 35-113 1974 $24

CRAWFORD, LEWIS F. — Rekindling Camp Fires. Bismarck, (1926). Blue cloth, gilt, plates, scarce, first edition. Bradley 35-112 1974 $44

CRAWFORD, LEWIS F. — Rekindling Camp Fires. Bismarck, (1926). 8vo., orig. bindings. Butterfield 8-697 1974 $35

CRAWFURD, G. — A General Description of the Shire of Renfrew. 1818. 4to., plates, contemporary diced calf. Quaritch 939-652 1974 £30

CRAWFURD, G. — The Peerage of Scotland. Edinburgh, 1716. Folio, old calf, rebacked, gilt. Quaritch 939-713 1974 £20

CRAWFURD, OSWALD — The Revelations of Inspector Morgan. Toronto, 1907. Orig. pictorial cloth, first Canadian edition. Covent 56-321 1974 £45

CRAWFURD, OSWALD — A Year of Sport and Natural History. 1895. 4to, illus., contemporary inscription, foxing, stains. Bow Windows 64-62 1974 £6.50

CRAWLEY, ERNEST — The Mystic Rose. 1927. 2 vols., revised & enlarged new edition. Howes 186-1805 1974 £5

CRAWLEY, ERNEST — The Mystic Rose. 1927. 2 vols., orig. cloth, second edition. Smith 193-772 1973 £6.50

CRAWSHAY, R. — The Birds of Tierra del Fuego. 1907. Imp. 8vo., half morocco, hand-colored plates by Keulemans, limited edition. Wheldon 128-418 1973 £75

CRAWSHAY, R. — The Spore Ornamentation of the Russules. (1930). 8vo., half blue morocco, plates. Wheldon 129-1182 1974 £12

CREAGER, LEWIS — An Inaugural Essay On the Dysentery. Philadelphia, 1806. Disbound. Rittenhouse 46-160 1974 $23

CREAMER, JOSEPH — Radio Sound Effects. 1945. 61p., illus. Austin 51-225 1973 $10

CREBILLON, PROSPER JOLYOT DE — Oeuvres. Paris, 1797. 2 vols., 8vo., contemporary full red long grain morocco, gilt. L. Goldschmidt 42-33 1974 $100

CREED, JAMES — An Impartial Examination of a Pamphlet. London, 1752. 8vo., old marbled wrappers. Gurney 64-58 1974 £20

CREIGHTON, C. — Shakespeare's Story of His Life. 1904. 8vo., half brown morocco, gilt. Quaritch 936-558 1974 £8

CREIGHTON, J. H. — Central Banking in Canada. Vancouver, 1933. Hood's 102-368 1974 $10

CREIGHTON, J. H. — Central Banking in Canada. Vancouver, 1933. Hood's 104-340 1974 $10

CREIGHTON, M. — A History of the Papacy. 1901. 6 vols., crown 8vo., new edition. Howes 185-1093 1974 £18

CREPIN, F.   Manuel de la Flore de Belgique. Brussels, 1874. Crown 8vo., cloth, third edition. Wheldon 130-1145 1974 £5

CRESPEL, LOUIS   Voiages du R. P. Emmanuel Crespel dans le Canada et son Naufrage en Revenant en France. (Quebec, 1884). Hood's 102-694 1974 $30

CRESPIN, JEAN   The Estate of the Church. London, 1602. 4to., contemporary calf, worn, rebacked, first edition in English. Dawsons PM 251-109 1974 £40

CRESWICKE, LOUIS   South Africa and the Transvaal War. 1900-(03). 7 vols., roy. 8vo., orig. pictorial cloth, maps, plates, illus. Howes 186-1706 1974 £14

CRESY, EDWARD   An Encyclopaedia of Civil Engineering. London, 1846. 8vo., contemporary sheep, gilt, illus., first edition. Hammond 201-815 1974 £28

CRETINEAU-JOLY, JACQUES   Histoire Religieuse, Politique et Litteraire de la Compagnie de Jesus. Paris & Lyons, 1844-46. 6 vols., contemporary half calf, first edition. Howes 185-1094 1974 £25

CREUTZBERGER, HANS   Wahrhafftige und Eygentliche Contrafactur vnd Formen der Zeumung vnd Gebisz. Augsburg, 1562. Folio, illus., rare, fine, contemporary pigskin, wooden boards, first edition. Harper 213-46 1973 $3500

CREVECOEUR, JEAN HECTOR ST. JOHN DE
Please turn to
CREVECOEUR, MICHEL GUILLAUME ST. JEAN DE

CREVECOEUR, MICHEL GUILLAUME ST. JEAN DE   Sketches of Eighteenth Century America. New Haven, 1925. Cloth, illus., scarce, mint, first edition. Bradley 35-114 1974 $26

CREVEL, RENE   La Mort Difficile. Paris, 1926. 12mo., orig. wrapper, uncut. L. Goldschmidt 42-196 1974 $12.50

CREVEL, RENE   Paul Klee. Paris, 1930. 16mo., wrappers, plates. Minters 37-591 1973 $15

CRICHTON, ALEXANDER   An Inquiry into the Nature and Origin of Mental Derangement. London, 1798. 8vo., 2 vols., modern half calf, boards, first edition. Dawsons PM 249-126 1974 £160

CRICHTON, KYLE   The Marx Brothers. Doubleday, 1950. 310p., illus. Austin 51-226 1973 $6.50

CRICK, W. F.   A Hundred Years of Joint Stock Banking. 1936. Thick roy. 8vo., plates, contemporary blue crushed levant morocco, limited, presentation edition. Smith 194-676 1974 £7.50

CRILE, GEORGE W.   Anemia and Resuscitation. New York, 1914. Rittenhouse 46-165 1974 $10

CRILE, GEORGE W.   Diagnosis and Treatment of Diseases of the Thyroid Gland. Philadelphia, 1942. Rittenhouse 46-161 1974 $10

CRILE, GEORGE W.   Hemorhage and Transfusion. New York, 1909. Rittenhouse 46-166 1974 $15

CRILE, GEORGE W.   Problems In Surgery, University of Washington Graduate Medical Lectures, 1927. Philadelphia, 1928. First edition. Rittenhouse 46-167 1974 $10

CRILE, GEORGE W.   Surgical Shock and the Shockless Operation Through Anoci-Association. Philadelphia, 1920. Second edition. Rittenhouse 46-170 1974 $10

CRILE, GEORGE W.   The Thyroid Gland, Clinics Of. Philadelphia, 1922. First edition. Rittenhouse 46-168 1974 $10

CRIME and Its Detection. 1931. 2 vols., roy. 8vo., plates, faded covers. Covent 55-547 1974 £10.50

THE CRIME of Christmas Day. 1885. 12mo., orig. wrappers, English first edition. Covent 56-1714 1974 £27.50

CRINGLE, TOM   Jottings of an Invalid In Search of Health. Bombay, 1865. Rittenhouse 46-171 1974 $18.50

CRINOLINE in Our Parks and Promenades. 1864. Oblong 4to., orig. wrappers, illus., rebound. Covent 55-529 1974 £18

CRIPPS, ERNEST C.   Plough Court. London, 1927. Rittenhouse 46-172 1974 $12

CRIPPS, HARRISON   On Diseases of the Rectum and Anus. Chicago, 1907. Third edition. Rittenhouse 46-173 1974 $10

CRIPPS, WILFRED J.   Old English Plate. London, 1926. Biblo & Tannen 210-72 1973 $22.50

THE CRISIS; or, the Briton's Advocate. London, 1733. 8vo., uncut. Quaritch 939-99 1974 £30

CRISP, FRANK   Mediaeval Gardens. (1924). 4to., 2 vols., illus., stained. Bow Windows 64-63 1974 £40

CRISP, FREDERICK ARTHUR   Armorial China. 1907. Large 4to., orig. half vellum, coloured plates, very good copy, number 48 of 150 copies, limited edition. Bow Windows 66-154 1974 £72

CRISP, FREDERICK ARTHUR   Armorial China. 1907. Roy. 4to., half vellum, plates, uncut, limited. Broadhurst 23-57 1974 £45

CRISP, FREDERICK ARTHUR   Calendar of Wills at Ipswich, 1444-1600. 1895. Imp. 4to., half green morocco, panelled back, raised bands, fine, one of 100 copies, signed by author. Broadhurst 24-1399 1974 £15

CRISP, FREDERICK ARTHUR   Visitation of England and Wales. 1893-1921. 4to., orig. vellum-backed boards. Dawsons PM 251-110 1974 £10

CRISP, SAMUEL   Virginia. London, 1754. 8vo., modern boards, first edition. Dawsons PM 252-190 1974 £16

CRIST, JUDITH   The Private Eye, The Cowboy and the Very Naked Girl. 1968. 291p., hard cover ed. Austin 51-227 1973 $7.50

CRIVELLI, GIOVANNI   Elementi di Fisica. Venice, 1744. 4to., contemporary mottled calf, gilt, fine, plates. Dawsons PM 245-187 1974 £45

CROCKER, HENRY RADCLIFFE   Atlas of Diseases of the Skin. London, 1903. Folio, orig. printed board, unbound, second edition. Dawsons PM 249-127 1974 £35

CROCKETT, DAVID   An Account of Col. Crockett's Tour to the North and Down East. Philadelphia, 1835. Tan cloth, portrait, foxing. Rinsland 58-968 1974 $50

CROCKETT, DAVID   A Narrative of the Life of David Crockett of the State of Tennessee. Philadelphia, 1837. Jenkins 61-725 1974 $40

CROCKETT, S. R.   Kit Kennedy. 1899. Dec. cloth gilt, portrait, signed, English first edition. Covent 56-272 1974 £15

CROCKETT, S. R.   The Surprising Adventures of Sir Toady Lion with Those of General Napoleon Smith. London, 1897. 8vo., pict. cloth, top edge gilt, 1st ed., illus. Frohnsdorff 16-247 1974 $15

CROCKETT, W. S.   Footsteps of Scott. 1909. Illus., 219 pages. Austin 61-257 1974 $12.50

CROCKETT, W. S.   The Scott Country. 1902. 8vo., orig. cloth, illus. Bow Windows 66-155 1974 £5.85

CROCKETT, W. S.   The Scott Originals. 1932. Illus., 431 pages. Austin 61-258 1974 $10

CROFF, E.   Nos Ancetres a l'Oeuvre a la Riviere-Ouelle. Montreal, 1931. Wrappers, signed. Hood's 102-695 1974 $7.50

CROFT, HERBERT   The Literary Fly. London, 1779. Small folio, contemporary half calf, first edition. Dawsons PM 252-191 1974 £55

CROFTS, FREEMAN WILLS   Man Overboard. 1936. 8vo., orig. cloth, dust wrapper, first edition. Rota 190-239 1974 £5.50

CROFTS, THOMAS   Bibliotheca Croftsiana. London, 1783. Large 8vo., contemporary calf, morocco label. Dawsons PM 10-148 1974 £45

CROGHAN, JOHN   Rambles in the Mannoth Cave, During the Year 1844, By a Vistor. Louisville, 1845. Fine folded map, errata slip, lithograph plates, nice, orig. cloth, one plate was never bound in. Butterfield 10-140 1974 $25

CROIL, JAMES   Dundas; or, A Sketch of Canadian History. Montreal, 1861. Inscribed by author. Hood's 102-595 1974 $40

CROIL, JAMES   Steam Navigation, and Its Relation to the Commerce of Canada and the United States. Toronto, 1898. Illus., portraits. Hood's 102-755 1974 $40

CROISET, ALFRED   Abridged History of Greek Literature. 1904. Shaken. Allen 213-301 1973 $15

CROISSANDEAU, J.   Scydmaenidae Europeens et Circa-Mediterran-eens. Paris, 1893-1900. 8vo., plates, rare. Wheldon 130-732 1974 £5

CROKER, J. WILSON   Johnsoniana. 1842. 529 pages. Austin 61-506 1974 $12.50

CROKER, THOMAS CROFTON   Fairy Legends and Traditions of South of Ireland. 1826-28. 3 vols., 8vo., contemporary half calf, plates, illus. Howes 186-1806 1974 £65

CROLY, GEORGE   The Life and Times of His Late Majesty, George the Fourth. London, 1830. 8vo., half calf gilt, first edition. Dawsons PM 251-204 1974 £12

CROLY, GEORGE   May Fair in Four Cantos. 1827. Small 8vo., orig. blue boards, first edition. Quaritch 936-357 1974 £40

CROLY, GEORGE   Tales of the Great St. Bernard. 1828. 3 vols., full contemporary calf, gilt, inscribed presentation, first edition. Howes 186-118 1974 £30

CROME, J.   Crome. 1921. Roy. 4to., plates, buckram, gilt, dust jacket. Quaritch 940-72 1974 £125

CROMIE, ROBERT   Chicago. Chicago, 1948. 4to., photos. Biblo & Tannen 210-280 1973 $7.50

CROMPTON, F. C. B.   Glimpses of Early Canadians. Toronto, 1925. Illus., maps. Hood's 102-231 1974 $12.50

CROMPTON, RICHARD   The Copie of a Letter to the Right Honourable the Earle of Leycester. 1586. Small 4to., full red morocco, first edition. Dawsons PM 251-205 1974 £320

CROMWELL, T. K.   Excursions in the County of Kent. 1822. 8vo., plates, calf, rebacked. Quaritch 939-399 1974 £35

CRONAU, RUDOLF   German Achievements in America. Cronau, 1916. Austin 62-117 1974 $12.50

CRONAU, RUDOLF   German Achievements in America. 1916. Illus., 233 pages. Austin 57-155 1974 $12.50

CRONIN, A. J.   Investigations in First-Aid Organization at Collieries in Great Britain. 1927. Wrappers, fine, illus. Covent 55-548 1974 $12.50

CROOKES, WILLIAM   The Mechanical Action of Light. London, 1876. 8vo., illus., orig. printed wrappers. Zeitlin 235-52 1974 $45

CROOKSHANK, EDGAR M.   Manual of Bacteriology. New York, 1887. Plate, library mark, second edition. Rittenhouse 46-174 1974 $10

CROS, L. J. M.   Histoire de Notre-Dame de Lourdes, d'Apres les Documents et les Temonis. Paris, 1925-27. 3 vols., orig. wrappers, plates. Howes 185-1095 1974 £7.50

CROSBY, HARRY   Transit of Venus. Paris, 1929. 12mo., fine, wrappers, slip-case, English first edition. Covent 56-1685 1974 £32.50

CROSBY, JOHN   Out of the Blue. Simon & Schuster, 1952. 301p. Austin 51-228 1973 $7.50

CROSBY, P. A.   Lovell's Gazetteer of British North America. Montreal, 1873. Leather, spine mended. Hood's 102-16 1974 $45

CROSFIELD, ROBERT   Truth Brought to Light. London, 1694. 4to., old calf, rebacked, first edition. Dawsons PM 251-432 1974 £50

CROSLAND, T. W. H.   The First Stone. 1912. Boards, English first edition. Covent 56-2122 1974 £7.50

CROSLAND, T. W. H.   The Flying Horse, No. 1. 1923. Fine, unopened copy, wrappers. Covent 51-2287 1973 £5

CROSS, A. F.   The People's Mouth. Toronto, 1943. Inscribed by author. Hood's 102-15 1974 $10

CROSS, C. F.   A Text-Book of Paper-Making. London, 1920. Plates, illus., fifth edition. Goodspeed's 578-446 1974 $15

CROSS, E. F. H.   Fire and Frost, Stories, Dialogues, Satires, Essays, Poems. Toronto, 1898. Hood's 103-399 1974 $10

CROSS, J. W.   George Eliot's Life as Related in Her Letters and Journals. 1885. 4 vols. in 2, crown 8vo., contemporary half maroon morocco gilt. Howes 186-174 1974 £5

CROSS, M. I.   Modern Microscopy. 1912. 8vo., cloth, plates, fourth edition. Wheldon 129-73 1974 £5

CROSS, T.   The Autobiography of a Stage Coachman. 1904. 2 vols., imp. 8vo., red crushed levant morocco, limited, plates. Quaritch 393-216 1974 £350

CROSS, W. L.   The History of Henry Fielding. New Haven, 1918. 3 vols., plates, demy 8vo., orig. cloth. Forster 98-223 1974 £25

CROSS, W. L.   The Life and Times of Laure ce Stone. 1925. 8vo., 2 vols., half morocco, plates. Broadhurst 23-321 1974 £35

CROSSLEY, F. H.   English Church Monuments. 1921. Crown 4to., illus., faded. Marsden 37-148 1974 £6

CROTHERS, RACHEL   Let Us Be Gay. French, 1929. 172p., paper. Austin 51-229 1973 $7.50

CROTHERS, RACHEL   Three Plays. Brentano, 1923. 297p. Austin 51-230 1973 $10

CROTHERS, SAMUEL MC CHORD   By the Christmas Fire. Boston & New York, 1908. Illus., author's copy. Ballinger 1-10 1974 $17.50

CROTHERS, SAMUEL MC CHORD   Oliver Wendell Holmes. Boston & New York, 1909. Very good copy. Ballinger 1-14 1974 $12

CROUCH, EDMUND A.   An Illustrated Introduction to Lamarck's Conchology. London, 1827. Large 4to., buckram, coloured plates. Gurney 66-97 1974 £60

CROUCH, HENRY   A Complete View of the British Customs. London, 1738. 8vo., modern half morocco, third edition. Dawsons PM 247-58 1974 £30

CROUCH, HENRY   A Complete View of the British Customs. London, 1738. 8vo., contemporary calf, gilt, third edition. Hammond 201-225 1974 £16.50

CROUCH, NATHANIEL   The Unfortunate Court Favourites of England. London, 1706. 12mo., modern half morocco, second edition. Dawsons PM 251-206 1974 £25

CROUSAZ, JEAN PIERRE   Commentaire sur l'Analyse des Infiniment Petits. Paris, 1721. 4to., contemporary calf, gilt, first edition. Dawsons PM 245-189 1974 £45

CROUSE, RUSSELL   Mr. Currier and Mr. Ives, a Note on Their Lives and Times. New York, 1936. Small 4to., illus., front cover with some spots, else fine. Current BW9-508 1974 $13.50

CROW, G. H.   William Morris Designer. 1934. Wrappers, illus., scarce. Marsden 39-316 1974 £10

CROWE, J. A.   A History of Painting In North Italy. 1912. 3 vols., plates, orig. cloth gilt. Smith 194-88 1974 £6

CROWLEY, ABRAHAM   Works in Prose and Verse. 1809. Orig. full diced calf gilt, 3 vols., English first edition. Covent 56-1679 1974 £55

CROWLEY, ALEISTER   Ahab. London, 1903. 4to., orig. Japanese vellum wrapper, uncut, first edition. Dawsons PM 252-192 1974 £40

CROWLEY, ALEISTER   Alice. 1903. Wrappers, English first edition. Covent 56-273 1974 £25

CROWLEY, ALEISTER   Alice. 1905. 8vo., orig. Japanese vellum wrapper, uncut, second edition. Dawsons PM 252-193 1974 £20

CROWLEY, ALEISTER   Ambergris. 1910. Portrait, boards, English first edition. Covent 56-274 1974 £12.50

CROWLEY, ALEISTER   Berashith. Paris, (n.d.). 4to., paper wrapper, uncut, first edition. Dawsons PM 252-194 1974 £80

CROWLEY, ALEISTER   The Book of the Goetia of Solomon the King. 1904. 4to., orig. camel-hair wrapper, first edition. Dawsons PM 252-195 1974 £60

CROWLEY, ALEISTER   Carmen Saeculae. 1901. 4to., wrappers, English first edition. Covent 56-1688 1974 £30

CROWLEY, ALEISTER   Carmen Saeculare. London, 1901. 4to., orig. blue wrapper, second edition. Dawsons PM 252-196 1974 £20

CROWLEY, ALEISTER   The City of God. London, 1943. 8vo., orig. paper wrappers, frontispiece, first edition. Dawsons PM 252-197 1974 £25

CROWLEY, ALEISTER   The Diary of a Drug Fiend. London, 1922. 8vo., orig. cloth, stained, first edition. Dawsons PM 252-199 1974 £45

CROWLEY, ALEISTER   Eight Lectures on Yoga. London. 4to., orig. grey buckram, uncut, first edition. Dawsons PM 252-200 1974 £45

CROWLEY, ALEISTER   The Fun of the Fair. Barstow & London, 1942. Wrappers, portrait, inscribed presentation. Covent 55-549 1974 £95

CROWLEY, ALEISTER   The Fun of the Fair. 1942. 8vo., orig. paper wrapper, uncut, first edition. Dawsons PM 252-201 1974 £25

CROWLEY, ALEISTER   Gargoyles. 1906. 8vo., orig. grey buckram, uncut, first edition. Dawsons PM 252-202 1974 £50

CROWLEY, ALEISTER   The High History of Good Sir Palamedes. 1912. 8vo., orig. buckram, first edition. Dawsons PM 252-203 1974 £50

CROWLEY, ALEISTER   Household Gods. 1912. Square 8vo., orig. white buckram, scarce, English first edition. Covent 56-278 1974 £45

CROWLEY, ALEISTER   Jephthah. London, 1899. 8vo., cloth-backed boards, inscription, first edition. Dawsons PM 252-204 1974 £50

CROWLEY, ALEISTER   Jephthah and Other Mysteries Lyrical and Dramatic. 1899. Covers faded & worn, else good copy, cloth backed boards. Covent 51-2289 1973 £35

CROWLEY, ALEISTER   Liber XXI. London, 1939. Folio, signed, half buckram, first limited edition. Dawsons PM 252-206 1974 £125

CROWLEY, ALEISTER   Liber CCCXXXIII. London, 1913. 8vo., orig. buckram, plates, first edition. Dawsons PM 252-207 1974 £90

CROWLEY, ALEISTER   Magick in Theory & Practice. New York, n.d. Smith 193-774 1973 £6.50

CROWLEY, ALEISTER   Moonchild. 1929. Covers little marked, very good copy. Covent 51-2291 1973 £6

CROWLEY, ALEISTER   Moonchild. 1929. First edition, nice copy. Covent 51-493 1973 £6.50

CROWLEY, ALEISTER   Moonchild. London, 1929. 8vo., orig. green cloth, book-plate, first edition. Dawsons PM 252-209 1974 £44

CROWLEY, ALEISTER   Moonchild. 1929. Orig. cloth, dust wrapper, first edition. Howes 186-119 1974 £12.50

CROWLEY, ALEISTER   Mortadello. London, 1912. 8vo., orig. red buckram, inscription, first edition. Dawsons PM 252-210 1974 £40

CROWLEY, ALEISTER   The Mother's Tragedy. 1907. 8vo., orig. blue cloth, uncut, second edition. Dawsons PM 252-211 1974 £20

CROWLEY, ALEISTER   Seven Lithographs. London, 1907. 4to., orig. buckram, plates, uncut, first edition. Dawsons PM 252-212 1974 £90

CROWLEY, ALEISTER   777 vel Prolegomena Symbolica. London, 1909. 8vo., orig. buckram, uncut, first limited edition. Dawsons PM 252-214 1974 £40

CROWLEY, ALEISTER   Songs of the Spirit. London, 1898. 8vo., orig. paper wrappers, first limited edition. Dawsons PM 252-215 1974 £60

CROWLEY, ALEISTER   The Soul of Osiris a History. London, 1901. 8vo., orig. cloth-backed boards, uncut, first edition. Dawsons PM 252-216 1974 £32

CROWLEY, ALEISTER   The Spirit of Solitude. 1929. Roy 8vo., 2 vols., orig. pictorial white buckram, gilt, English first edition. Covent 56-1695 1974 £35

CROWLEY, ALEISTER   The Star & the Garter. London, 1903. 4to., orig. camel-hair wrapper, first edition. Dawsons PM 252-217 1974 £20

CROWLEY, ALEISTER   The Stratagem. London, (n.d.). 8vo., orig. cloth-backed boards, first edition. Dawsons PM 252-218 1974 £12

CROWLEY, ALEISTER   Thumbs Up! 1941. 4to., orig. paper wrapper, signed, frontispiece, first limited edition. Dawsons PM 252-219 1974 £36

CROWLEY, ALEISTER   The Winged Beetle. (London), 1910. 8vo., orig. buckram, handmade paper, first limited edition. Dawsons PM 252-220 1974 £45

CROWLEY, MARY C.   A Daughter of New France. Boston, 1909. Hood's 102-496 1974 $7.50

CROWNE, JOHN   Darius King of Persia. London, 1688. 4to., calf antique, first edition. Dawsons PM 252-221 1974 £120

CROWQUILL, ALFRED   Absurdities. London, 1827. 12mo., orig. blue printed boards, spine little chipped, first edition, fine, very scarce in this condition. Ximenes 36-63 1974 $90

CROWQUILL, ALFRED   Seymour's Humorous Sketches. 1878. Etchings, plates, orig. dec. cloth gilt, sewing weak, very good copy, first edition. Covent 51-495 1973 £8.50

CROWTHER, BOSLEY   Hollywood Rajah. Holt, 1960. 339p., illus. Austin 51-231 1973 $7.50

CROWTHER, BOSLEY   The Lion's Share. Dutton, 1957. 320p., illus. Austin 51-232 1973 $7.50

CROXALL, S.   Fables of Aesop. 1846. Tall 8vo., orig. cloth. Smith 193-646 1973 £5

CROY, HOMER   Our Will Rogers. Duell, Sloan, Pearce, 1953. 377p. Austin 54-873 1973 $6.50

CRUCHLEY, G. F.   Cruchley's New Map of the Railways of England. 1857. Small 8vo., orig. cloth. Howes 186-2154 1974 £7.50

CRUIKSHANK, E. A.   Harrison and Proctor, the River Raisin. 1910.
Hood's 102-99 1974 $10

CRUIKSHANK, E. A.   Harrison and Proctor, the River Raisin. 1910.
Initialled. Hood's 104-105 1974 $10

CRUIKSHANK, E. A.   A Study of Disaffection in Upper Canada, 1812-
15. 1912. Hood's 102-100 1974 $10

CRUIKSHANK, E. A.   A Study of Disaffection in Upper Canada,
1812-15. 1912. 55 pages. Hood's 104-106 1974 $10

CRUIKSHANK, GEORGE   The Bachelor's Own Book. Glasgow, c., 1890.
Small 4to., orig. linen-backed printed wrapper, plates. Hammond 201-105 1974
£5

CRUIKSHANK, GEORGE   The Comic Almanack and Diary, London, 1850.
16mo., pictorial gilt cloth, hand-colored folding frontis, 6 engraved plates.
Frohnsdorff 16-249 1974 $25

CRUIKSHANK, GEORGE   George Cruikshank: The Artist, the Humorist
and the Man. 1879. 4to., plates, illus., cloth, rebacked. Quaritch 940-73
1974 £25

CRUIKSHANK, GEORGE   George Cruikshank's Omnibus. 1842.
Contemporary half calf, gilt, plates. Covent 55-552 1974 £20

CRUIKSHANK, GEORGE   The History of Jack and the Bean-Stalk.
London, n.d. Etchings, covers slightly worn and soiled, first edition, very good,
wrappers. Covent 51-496 1973 £20

CRUIKSHANK, GEORGE   The Horkey. 1882. 4to., cloth-backed pictorial boards, English first edition. Covent 56-684 1974 £21

CRUIKSHANK, GEORGE   Lady Arabella. London, ca. 1856. 8vo.,
pictorial gilt cloth, 4 engraved plates, full crushed morocco, gilt, lst ed.
Frohnsdorff 16-250 1974 $150

CRUIKSHANK, GEORGE   The Memoirs of Joseph Grimaldi. London,
1846. Illus., frontis. portrait, new edition, orig. red cloth, gilt design, good
copy. Covent 51-2293 1973 £25

CRUIKSHANK, GEORGE   Punch and Judy. London, 1828. 8vo., cloth,
rebacked, paper label on spine, light foxing, clean state, engraved plates, first
edition, first issue. Frohnsdorff 15-20 1974 $60

CRUIKSHANK, GEORGE   Tales of Humour, Gallantry, & Romance.
1824. Orig. boards, plates, uncut, label, first edition, second issue. Howes
186-120 1974 £18

CRUIKSHANK, GEORGE   Uncle Tom's Cabin. London, 1852. Full
tan calf, illus., leather labels, first English book edition. Bradley 35-115
1974 $100

CRUIKSHANK, ROBERT   A bound volume of several small booklets.
16mo., spine gilt, half-leather. Frohnsdorff 16-254 1974 $40

CRUISE, F. R.   Thomas a. Kempis. 1887. Binding rubbed.
Allen 213-1817 1973 $10

CRULL, J.   The Antiquities of St. Peter's. 1742. 2 vols.,
8vo., plates, modern boards, fifth edition. Quaritch 939-481 1974 £20

CRUM, L. H.   Kingston City Directory for the Years 1883-4.
Newburgh, 1883. 8vo., quarter cloth. Saddleback 14-574 1974 $17.50

CRUMPE, SAMUEL   An Essay on the Best Means of Providing
Employment for the People. Dublin, 1793. 8vo., contemporary calf, fine,
first edition. Dawsons PM 247-59 1974 £56

CRUMPE, SAMUEL   An Essay on the Best Means of Providing Employment for the People. Dublin, 1793. 8vo., contemporary calf, gilt, first edition.
Hammond 201-226 1974 £24

CRUSO, JOHN   Militarie Instructions for the Cavallrie. Cambridge, 1632. Folio, contemporary calf, rebacked. Zeitlin 235-304 1974
$975

CRUNDEN, JOHN   Convenient and Ornamental Architecture. 1788.
4to., plates, contemporary calf, worn. Quaritch 940-503 1974 £95

CRUSE, AMY   The Englishman and His Books. New York, n.d.
Cloth, dust wrapper, foxing, illus., fine. Dawson's 424-204 1974 $30

CRUSE, AMY   The Englishman and His Books in the Early 19th
Century. New York, (n.d.). 8vo., plates, orig. buckram. Dawsons PM
10-149 1974 £6

CRUSO, J.   The Complete Captain. Cambridge, 1640.
8vo., old sheep, leather label. Traylen 79-130 1973 £70

CUBITT, WILLIAM   Description of a Plan for a Central Union Canal.
London, 1833. 8vo., boards, first edition. Hammond 201-846 1974 £32

CUBBON, WILLIAM   A Bibliographical Account of Works Relating
to the Isle of Man. 1933-39. 2 vols., thick 8vo., buckram, fine, scarce.
Howes 185-648 1974 £20

CUBBON, WILLIAM   A Bibliographical Account of Works Relating to
the Isle of Man. Oxford, 1933-39. 2 vols., 8vo., plates, buckram. Quaritch
939-392 1974 £35

CUBBON, WILLIAM   A Bibliographical Account of Works Relating to
the Isle of Man; With Biographical Memoranda and Copious Literary References.
1933. 2 vols., demy 8vo., orig. cloth, mint. Broadhurst 24-306 1974 £10

CUBBON, WILLIAM   A Bibliographical Account of Works Relating
to the Isle of Man. London, 1933-39. 2 vols., 8vo., blue cloth, fine, illus.
Dawsons PM 10-302 1974 £40

CUCHULAIN OF MUIRTHEMNE   Story of the Men of the Red Branch of Ulster,
1934. Allen 216-853 1974 $15

CUDWORTH, RALPH   The Intellectual System of the Universe. London, 1678. Folio, contemporary calf, rebacked, first edition. Gurney 64-59
1974 £60

CUDWORTH, RALPH   The True Intellectual System of the Universe.
1820. 4 vols., full tree calf, rebacked, new edition. Howes 185-1840 1974
£30

CULL, GEORGE SAMUEL   The Youthful Travels and Adventures of.
Toronto, 1863. Orig. paper cover. Hood's 102-232 1974 $55

CULL, GEORGE SAMUEL   The Youthful Travels and Adventures of.
Toronto, 1863. Orig. paper cover. Hood's 104-251 1974 $55

CULLEN, CHARLES   The History of Mexico, Collected from Spanish
and Mexican Historians. London, 1737. 2 vols., calf, repaired, maps repaired.
Jenkins 61-728 1974 $45

CULLEN, COUNTEE   Copper Sun. New York, 1927. First U. S.
edition, nice copy, cloth backed boards. Covent 51-2296 1973 £12.50

CULLEN, THOMAS S.   Adenomyoma of the Uterus. Philadelphia,
1908. Rittenhouse 46-175 1974 $35

CULLEN, THOMAS S.   Cancer of the Uterus. New York, 1900.
Some marking. Rittenhouse 46-176 1974 $22.50

CULLEN, THOMAS S.   Early Medicine in Maryland. 1927. Spine
chipped. Rittenhouse 46-702 1974 $10

CULLEN, WILLIAM   Synopsis Nosologiae Methodicae. Zurich,
1790. 8vo., contemporary half calf. Schuman 37-54 1974 $95

CULLEN, WILLIAM   A Treatise of the Materia Medica. Edinburgh,
4to., 2 vols., half calf, first edition, some water staining. Gurney 66-43 1974
£65

CULLEN, WILLIAM   A Treatise of the Materia Medica. Edinburgh,
1789. 4to., 2 vols., half calf, first edition. Gurney 64-60 1974 £65

CULLEN, WILLIAM   A Treatise of the Materia Medica. Edinburgh,
1789. 2 vols., 4to., old boards, new leather spine. Traylen 79-218 1973 £68

CULLUM, GEORGE W.   Biographical Register of the Officers and
Graduates of the U. S. Military Academy, 1802 to 1866-67. New York, 1868.
2 vols., shaken, backstrips chipped and partly loose. Butterfield 10-529 1974
$27.50

CULLUM, GEORGE W.   Register of the Officers and Graduates of the
U. S. Military Academy at West Point, 1802-1850. New York, 1850. Pict.
boards. Jenkins 61-729 1974 $75

CULPEPER, NICHOLAS   Culpeper's Complete Herbal. Philadelphia, n.d.
Biblo & Tannen 213-849 1973 $12.50

CULPEPER, NICHOLAS   Culpeper's Complete Herbal. 1814. 4to.,
contemporary half calf, plates, foxing. Covent 55-1138 1974 £35

CULPEPER, NICHOLAS   Culpeper's Complete Herbal. London, (c. 1830).
4to., color plates, orig. cloth. Gregory 44-77 1974 $125

CULPEPER, NICHOLAS   Culpeper's English Physician and Complete Herbal. (1798). 4to., 2 vols., portrait, plates, 19th century half calf, worn.
Bow Windows 64-64 1974 £52

CULPEPER, NICHOLAS   The English Physician Enlarged. 1799.
Contemporary calf gilt. Smith 193-108 1973 £12

CULPEPER, NICHOLAS   Pharmacopoeia Londinensis. London, 1683.
8vo., old sheep worn, rebacked. Gurney 64-61 1974 £45

CULVERWEL, N.   An Elegant and Learned Discourse of the Light of
Nature With Several Other Treatises. London, 1652. Small 4to., half 19th
century calf, woodcut borders. Smith 194-142 1974 £20

CUMBERLAND, G.   Reliquiae Conservatae. Bristol, 1826. Roy.
8vo., orig. boards, plates, rare. Wheldon 131-982 1974 £12

CUMBERLAND, GEORGE   An Essay on the Utility of Collecting the Best
Works of the Ancient Engravers of the Italian School. 1827. 4to., old boards,
cloth backed, uncut, plates. Hill 126-65 1974 £35

CUMBERLAND, RICHARD   An Essay Towards the Recovery of the Jewish
Measures & Weights. London, 1686. 8vo., contemporary mottled calf, fine,
first edition. Dawsons PM 247-60 1974 £110

CUMBERLAND, RICHARD   An Essay Towards the Recovery of the Jewish
Measures & Weights. London, 1686. 8vo., contemporary calf, first edition.
Schuman 37-55 1974 $165

CUMBERLAND, RICHARD   First Love. London, 1795. 8vo., modern
boards, first edition. Dawsons PM 252-223 1974 £18

CUMBERLAND, RICHARD   The Note of Hand. London, 1774. 8vo.,
modern boards, fine, first edition. Dawsons PM 252-224 1974 £20

CUMBERLAND, RICHARD   The Posthumous Dramatick Works. 1813.
2 vols., contemporary half calf, first edition. Howes 186-122 1974 £15

CUMBERLAND, RICHARD   The Summer's Tale. London, 1765. 8vo.,
modern boards, browned, first edition. Dawsons PM 252-225 1974 £14

CUMBERLAND, RICHARD   The Wheel of Fortune. London, 1795. 8vo.,
modern boards, first edition. Dawsons PM 252-226 1974 £13

CUMMING, JAMES   A Manual of Electro Dynamics. London, 1827.
8vo., orig. cloth, plates, first edition. Dawsons PM 245-190 1974 £10

CUMMINGS, E. E.
Please turn to
CUMMINGS, EDWARD ESTLIN

CUMMINGS, EDWARD ESTLIN   Eimi. (New York, 1933). Orig. cloth,
first edition, one of 1,381 copies, signed by author, fine, somewhat soiled &
worn dust jacket. MacManus 224-115 1974 $75

CUMMINGS, EDWARD ESTLIN   The Enormous Room. New York, 1922. First
U. S. edition, owner's notes in pen on one page, very good copy. Covent
51-2297 1973 £25

CUMMINGS, EDWARD ESTLIN   The Enormous Room. New York, 1922. First
edition, ex. lib., name in ink inside front cover, orig. binding, not collector's
copy, but good copy of scarce book. Ross 87-138 1974 $55

CUMMINGS, EDWARD ESTLIN   The Enormous Room. New York, 1922. First
edition with word inked out on p. 219, ex-library copy with loan envelope, not
a collector's copy but good, scarce. Ross 86-111 1974 $65

CUMMINGS, EDWARD ESTLIN   The Enormous Room. 1928. Inscription,
very good copy, first edition. Covent 51-2298 1973 £12.60

CUMMINGS, EDWARD ESTLIN   XLI Poems. New York, 1925. Faded.
Ballinger 1-120 1974 $50

CUMMINGS, EDWARD ESTLIN   Is 5. New York, 1926. 8vo., orig. cloth
backed boards, d.w., first edition. Dawsons PM 252-227 1974 £32

CUMMINGS, EDWARD ESTLIN   No Thanks. New York, 1935. First U. S.
trade edition, one of 900 copies, fine, d.w. Covent 51-500 1973 £20

CUMMINGS, EDWARD ESTLIN   Tulips and Chimneys. 1922. Quarter vellum,
fine, English first edition. Covent 56-283 1974 £25

CUMMINGS, EDWARD ESTLIN   Tulips and Chimneys. Mount Vernon, 1937.
Orig. vellum backed boards, first edition, with 84 added poems, one of 481
numbered copies, fine, dust jacket. MacManus 224-116 1974 $55

CUMMINGS, EDWARD ESTLIN   W. New York, 1931. Nice copy, dust jacket.
Ballinger 1-119 1974 $75

CUMMINGS, G. A.   Oakland: A History. Oakland, c.1942.
8vo., quarter cloth. Saddleback 14-80 1974 $10

CUMMINGS, H.   The College Stamps of Oxford and Cambridge.
(c.1890). 8vo., illus., cloth. Quaritch 939-100 1974 £5

CUMMINGS, J. A.   First Lessons in Geography and Astronomy.
Boston, 1823. 16mo., foxed, rebacked with leather. Frohnsdorff 16-255 1974
$17.50

CUMMINS, HARLE OREN   Welsh Rarebit Tales. Boston, 1902. 1st ed.,
rare. Biblo & Tannen 210-582 1973 $27.50

CUMMINS, SARAH J.   Autobiography and Reminiscences of. N. P.,
(Walla Walla, 1914). Wrappers, little worn. Hayman 59-142 1974 $10

CUMMINS, WILLIAM J.   The Turkish Bath. Dublin, 1860. 8vo., boards.
Hammond 201-565 1974 £5.50

CUMSTON, CHARLES GREENE   An Introduction to the History of Medicine.
London, 1926. Rittenhouse 46-177 1974 $22

CUNARD, NANCY   Black Man and White Ladyship. 1931. Orig.
wrappers, English first edition. Covent 56-284 1974 £20

CUNARD, NANCY   Black Man and White Ladyship. 1931.
Orig. cloth, wrappers, scarce, first edition. Rota 188-215 1974 £8

CUNARD, NANCY   Outlaws. London, 1921. First edition, very
good copy, author's signed presentation inscription. Covent 51-504 1973 £30

CUNDALL, F.   Reminiscences of the Colonial and Indian
Exhibition. London, 1886. 4to., illus., orig. dec. cloth. Bow Windows
62-227 1974 £5.50

CUNDALL, JOSEPH   Bookbinding. 1881. Small 4to., plates, foxing,
English first edition. Covent 56-164 1974 £32.50

CUNDALL, JOSEPH   A Brief History of Wood-Engravings From Its
Invention. Green cloth, pictorial board, foxing. Covent 55-91 1974 £7.50

CUNLIFFE, J. W.   English Literature During the Last Century.
1923. Revised and enlarged second edition. Austin 61-259 1974 $10

CUNLIFFE, J. W.   English Literature In the Twentieth Century.
1933. Ex-library. Austin 61-260 1974 $12.50

CUNNINGHAM, C. D.   The Pioneers of the Alps. 1887. 4to., illus., photographs, English first edition. Covent 56-1946 1974 $35

CUNNINGHAM, EUGENE   Famous in the West. El Paso, 1926. Pict. wrapper, exceedingly rare. Jenkins 61-731 1974 $60

CUNNINGHAM, EUGENE   Triggernometry. New York, 1934. Illus., black-stamped blue cloth, first edition. Bradley 35-116 1974 $56

CUNNINGHAM, G. H.   Fungous Diseases of Fruit-Trees in New Zealand and Their Remedial Treatment. Auckland, 1925. 8vo., cloth, photographs, scarce. Wheldon 128-1352 1973 £7.50

CUNNINGHAM, G. H.   Fungous Diseases of Fruit-Trees in New Zealand and Their Remedial Treatment. Auckland, 1925. 8vo., cloth, very scarce. Wheldon 131-1386 1974 £7.50

CUNNINGHAM, G. H.   The Gasteromycetes of Australia and New Zealand. Dunedin, 1944. 8vo., cloth, plates. Wheldon 129-1184 1974 £7.50

CUNNINGHAM, G. H.   The Rust Fungi of New Zealand. Dunedin, 1931. Roy 8vo., cloth, plate. Wheldon 129-1185 1974 £10

CUNNINGHAM, JOHN   Poems. 1766. 8vo., old boards, scarce, frontispiece, first edition. Quaritch 936-36 1974 £45

CUNNINGHAM, JOHN   Poems, Chiefly Pastoral. Newcastle, 1771. 12mo., old half calf, little rubbed, some spotting and stains, second edition. Bow Windows 66-161 1974 £12

CUNNINGHAM, JOSEPH DAVEY   A History of the Sikhs. London, 1849. 8vo., orig. brown blind-stamped cloth, first edition. Dawsons PM 251-207 1974 £30

CUNNINGHAM, T.   A New Treatise on the Laws Concerning Tithes. London, 1768. 8vo., contemporary calf, third edition. Dawsons PM 247-61 1974 £18

CUNNINGHAM, W.   The Growth of English Industry and Commerce. Cambridge, 1915-21. 2 vols. in 3, 8vo., orig. cloth, illus., fifth & sixth editions. Dawsons PM 247-62 1974 £10

CUNNINGHAME-GRAHAM, ROBERT BONTINE
Please turn to
GRAHAM, ROBERT BONTINE CUNNINGHAME

CUPID'S Annual Charter. London, ca. 1825. 16mo., hand-colored frontis. Frohnsdorff 16-256 1974 $30

CUPID'S Catechism, or Guide to Matrimony. London, (c. 1845). Orig. dark morocco, gold stamped, fine, 2 X 1 1/4 inches. Gregory 44-360 1974 $65

CUPPY, WILL   How to Get From January to December. Holt, 1951. 279p. Austin 54-275 1973 $6.50

CURETON, WILLIAM   Corpus Ignatianum. 1849. Roy. 8vo., orig. cloth. Howes 185-1097 1974 £6

CURIE, MARIE SKLODOWSKA   Conference Faite le 7 Mars 1920 sur les Radio-Elements et Leurs Applications. Paris, 1920. 12mo., orig. wrappers, rebacked. Gurney 66-44 1974 £15

CURIE, MARIE SKLODOWSKA   L'Isotopie et les Elements Isotopes. Paris, 1924. 8vo., grey cloth. Dawsons PM 245-192 1974 £15

CURIE, MARIE SKLODOWSKA   Rayons Emis par les Composes de l'Uranium et du Thorium. Paris, 1898. 4to., uncut, modern wrappers. Dawsons PM 245-191 1974 £140

CURIE, MARIE SKLODOWSKA   Traite de Radioactivite. Paris, 1910. 2 vols., 8vo., half calf, illus., scarce first edition. Gilhofer 61-76 1974 sFr. 1,600

CURIE, P.   Principles of Homoeopathy. London, 1837. Rittenhouse 46-179 1974 $10

CURIONE, CELIO SECONDO   Der Verzucket Pasquinus. (Augsburg), 1543. 8vo., modern boards, very rare first German edition, fine despite light waterstains, several wormholes at end. Schafer 10-97 1974 sFr 1,800

CURIONE, CELIO SECONDO   Pasquillus Ecstaticus, una cum Aliis Etiam Aliquot Sanctis Pariter & Lepidis Dialogis. (Basle, c. 1544). 8vo., contemporary limp vellum, first edition, very fine copy. Schafer 10-96 1974 sFr 1,400

CURLE, RICHARD   Collecting American First Editions. Indianapolis, 1930. First U. S. edition, illus., one of 1250 numbered copies, signed by author, rubber stamp, else fine. Covent 51-2181 1973 £12.50

CURLE, RICHARD   Into the East: Notes on Burma & Malaya. 1923. One of 125 copies on large paper, linen backed boards, small 4to., fine, defective d.w. Covent 51-2273 1973 £25

CURLE, RICHARD   Joseph Conrad: A Study. 1914. Author's signed lengthy inscription, very good copy, first edition. Covent 51-455 1973 £7.50

CURLE, RICHARD   Robert Browning and Julia Wedgwood. Orig. edition. Austin 61-261 1974 $10

CURRAN, C. H.   Insects of the Pacific World. New York, 1945. 8vo., cloth, text-figures. Wheldon 128-703 1973 £5

CURRAN, MARY DOYLE   The Parish and the Hill. Houghton, Mifflin, 1948. Austin 62-118 1974 $8.50

CURRAN, W. T.   In Canada's Wonderful Northland. New York & London, 1917. Maps, illus. Hood's 103-53 1974 $15

CURRIE, BARTON   Fishers of Books. Boston, 1931. First U. S. edition, presentation copy, inscribed by author, profusely illus., spine faded, very good copy. Covent 51-281 1973 £8.50

CURRIE, E. A.   The Story of Laura Secord, and Canadian Reminiscences. Toronto, 1900. First edition. Hood's 102-233 1974 $20

CURRIE, GILBERT E.   History of the Wesley Methodist Episcopal Church of Brooklyn. New York, 1876. 12mo., cloth. Saddleback 14-575 1974 $12.50

CURRIE, JAMES   Medical Reports On the Effects of Water, Cold and Warm, as a Remedy In Fever and Other Diseases. London, 1805. 2 vols., 8vo., enlarged second edition. Rittenhouse 46-180 1974 $50

CURRIE, WILLIAM   Observations On the Causes and Cure of Remitting of Bilious Fevers. Philadelphia, 1798. 8vo., contemporary calf, dampstained. Rittenhouse 46-181 1974 $75

CURRIEHILL, JOHN SKENE   De Verborum Significatione. 1681. Folio, cloth backed boards. Bow Windows 64-470 1974 £21

CURRIER, CHARLES WARREN   Carmel in America. Baltimore, 1890. Orig. cloth, plates. Howes 185-1098 1974 £5

CURSON, HENRY   The Theory of Sciences Illustrated. London, 17-02. 8vo., contemporary panelled calf, first edition. Dawsons PM 245-193 1974 £45

CURTIN, JEREMIAH   Myths and Folk Tales of the Russians. Boston, 1890. Cloth, gilt, first edition. Dawson's 424-260 1974 $12.50

CURTIS, CHARLES HENRY   Orchids for Everyone. London, 1910. 4to., color plates, orig. cloth, fine. Gregory 44-80 1974 $47.50

CURTIS, CHARLES M.   Old Swedes Church, Wilmington, Delaware. 1698-1938. Wilmington, 1938. First edition, small 8vo., illus., map, mint, d.j. soiled & chipped. Current BW9-361 1974 $22.50

CURTIS, DAVID A.   Stand Pat: CR, Poker Stories from the Mississippi. Boston, 1906. Illus. by Henry Roth. Jenkins 61-1683 1974 $25

CURTIS, E.   History of Mediaeval Ireland from 1110 to 1513. 1923. Allen 213-1409 1973 $12.50

CURTIS, GEORGE W.   Literary and Social Essays. Harper, 1894. 293p., orig. ed. Austin 54-276 1973 $7.50

CURTIS, GEORGE W.   Trumps. New York, 1861. Illus., first edition,
8vo., interior very fine, spine chipped at ends and faded, else very good.
Current BW9-219 1974 $17.50

CURTIS, H.   The Beauties of the Rose. Bristol, 1850-53.
New half red levant morocco, plates, foxing. Wheldon 130-14 1974 £250

CURTIS, HENRY   Pedigree of Joyce of Boxford. 1917. Crown
4to., full red morocco gilt, illus. Howes 186-2047 1974 £25

CURTIS, JOHN   British Etomology. 1823-40. Roy. 8vo., half
morocco gilt, 8 vols., plates. Wheldon 129-11 1974 £500

CURTIS, JOHN   British Entomology. 1824-1839. 16 vols.,
green half morocco, plates. Bow Windows 64-65 1974 £625

CURTIS, JOHN   British Entomology: Coleoptera. 1862.
2 vols., roy. 8vo., contemporary half morocco, plates, scarce. Wheldon
131-34 1974 £120

CURTIS, JOHN   Farm Insects. Edinburgh, 1860. Royal 8vo.,
contemporary half calf, gilt, illus., plates, first edition. Hammond 201-637
1974 £38

CURTIS, JOHN   Farm Insects. 1860. Roy. 8vo., orig. cloth,
hand-coloured plates by author. Wheldon 128-705 1973 £15

CURTIS, JOHN   The Genera of British Lepidoptera. 1858. Small
4to., orig. half roan, plates. Wheldon 129-624 1974 £25

CURTIS, JOHN HARRISON   A Treatise on the Physiology and Diseases of
the Eye. London, 1833. 8vo., marbled boards, worn, first edition. Dawsons
PM 249-130 1974 £12

CURTIS, JOSEPH S.   Silver-Lead Deposits of Eureka, Nevada.
Washington, 1884. Leather, plates. Hayman 59-143 1974 $10

CURTIS, M. M.   The Book of Snuff and Snuff Boxes. New York,
1935. Fine. Covent 55-435 1974 $12.50

CURTIS, W.   Fundamenta Entomologiae. London, 1772.
Thin 8vo., binder's cloth, copperplates. Traylen 79-71 1973 £25

CURTIS, WILLIAM   Flora Londinensis. 1777-98. 2 vols. in 4,
folio, contemporary half calf, plates. Wheldon 131-35 1974 £1,500

CURTIS, WILLIAM   Flora Londinensis. 1817-28. Folio, modern
buckram-backed boards, 5 vols., plates, worn, uncut. Wheldon 130-15 1974
£1,350

CURTIS, WILLIAM   Lectures on Botany. 1803-1804. 2 vols., contemporary green half morocco, plates, signature. Bow Windows 64-66 1974 £65

CURTIS, WILLIAM   Lectures on Botany. 1803-04. 3 vols. in 2,
8vo., modern half calf antique, plates, rare, first edition. Wheldon 131-36
1974 £75

CURTIS, WILLIAM   Lectures on Botany. London, 1805. 8vo., 2
vols., half calf, gilt, plates, first edition. Hammond 201-639 1974 £75

CURTIS, WILLIAM   Practical Observations on the British Grasses.
1804. 8vo., modern boards, plates, first issue, fourth edition. Wheldon
131-1773 1974 £10

CURTIS, WILLIAM   Practical Observations on the British Grasses.
1805. 8vo., orig. boards, uncut, rebacked, plates. Wheldon 131-1774
1974 £12

CURTIS, WILLIAM   Practical Observations on the British Grasses.
1805. 8vo., orig. boards, uncut, hand coloured plates. Wheldon 128-1645
1973 £10

CURTIS, WILLIAM   Practical Observations on the British Grasses.
London, 1812. 8vo., boards, plates, fifth edition. Hammond 201-8 1974 £25

CURTIS, WILLIAM   Practical Observations on the British Grasses.
1812. 8vo., orig. boards, plates. Wheldon 129-1650 1974 £5

CURTIS, WILLIAM ELEROY   The Yankees of the East. New York, 1896.
2 vols., orig. binding. Butterfield 10-208 1974 $25

CURTIS'S Botanical Magazine Dedications. 1931. 8vo., cloth, portraits.
Wheldon 131-210 1974 £10

DER CURTISAN Vnnd Pfrunden Fresser / Wurde ich Billich Genant. (Augsburg,
1521-22). Small 4to., modern red half morocco, good copy. Schafer 10-98
1974 sFr 2,200

CURTISS, DANIEL S.   Western Portaiture and Emigrant's Guide. New
York, 1852. Large folding map, worn, expert repairs. Jenkins 61-733 1974
$15

CURTISS-WEDGE, FRANKLYN   History of Wabasha County, Minnesota.
Winona, 1920. 8vo., three quarter leather, illus. Saddleback 14-516 1974
$65

CURTIUS, ERNST 1814-1896   History of Greece. 1897. 5 vols. Allen 213-
304 1973 $15

CURTIUS, ERNST ROBERT   Marcel Proust. Paris, 1928. Square 12mo.,
full cloth, gilt, uncut, orig. wrapper, limited edition. L. Goldschmidt 42-339
1974 $12.50

CURWEN, HENRY   A History of Booksellers. n.d. Illus., English
first edition. Covent 56-166 1974 £7.50

CURWEN, HENRY   A History of Booksellers, the Old and the New.
London, 1873. 8vo., plates, orig. cloth gilt. Dawsons PM 10-152 1974 £7

CURZON, S. A.   Laura Secord, the Heroine of 1812, a Drama;
and Other Poems. Toronto, 1887. Hood's 102-647 1974 $10

CUSACK, M. F.   The History of Ireland. Edinburgh, (1876).
4to., illus., worn leather. Emerald 50-197 1974 £5

CUSHING, HARVERY   The Harvey Cushing Collection of Books and
Manuscripts. New York, 1943. Large 8vo., orig. cloth gilt. Dawsons PM
10-154 1974 £30

CUSHING, HARVEY   From a Surgeon's Journal 1915-18. Boston,
1936. 8vo., cloth, presentation copy, first edition. Goodspeed's 578-73
1974 $50

CUSHING, HARVEY   The Harvey Cushing Collection of Books and
Manuscripts. New York, 1943. Rittenhouse 46-182 1974 $65

CUSHING, HARVEY   The Pituitary Body and Its Disorders. Philadelphia and London, (1912). 8vo., orig. red cloth, first edition. Dawsons PM 249-
131 1974 £36

CUSHING, JOHN T.   Vermont in the World War. (Burlington),
1928. 8vo., cloth. Saddleback 14-735 1974 $12.50

CUSHING, TOM   Barely Proper. Farrar, Rinehart, 1931.
93p. Austin 51-233 1973 $7.50

CUSHING, WILLIAM   Initials & Pseudonyms. 1886-88. 2 vols.,
4to., good ex-library. Allen 216-154 1974 $20

CUSHING, WILLIAM   Initials and Pseudonyms: A Dictionary of
Literary Disguises. New York, 1885. 4to., cloth. Kraus B8-44 1974 $15

CUSHY Cow. Philadelphia, ca. 1850. 8 hand-colored illus., orig. pictorial
wrappers. Frohnsdorff 16-257 1974 $17.50

CUSICK, DAVID   Sketches of Ancient History of the Six Nations.
Lockport, 1848. Third edition, rare, full page engravings, orig. binding. Butterfield 10-311 1974 $75

CUSSANS, J. E.   History of Hertfordshire. 1870-81. 3 vols.,
folio, half morocco, plates, limited edition. Quaritch 939-386 1974 £120

CUSSLER, MARGERET   Not By a Long Shot. Exposition, 1951.
200p. Austin 51-234 1973 $7.50

CUSTER, ELIZABATH B. "Boots and Saddles". New York, 1885. 8vo., orig. bindings, first edition, second issue. Butterfield 8-699 1974 $10

CUSTER, ELIZABETH B. "Boots and Saddles" or Life in Dakota with General Custer. New York, 1885. Tipped in A.L.s. from author, related clipping pasted to front endpaper. Butterfield 10-209 1974 $35

CUSTER, ELIZABETH B. Following the Guidon. New York, 1890. Illus., cloth, first edition. Bradley 35-119 1974 $18

CUSTER, ELIZABETH B. Following the Guidon. New York, 1890. Illus., dec. green cloth, fine, first edition. Bradley 35-118 1974 $24

CUSTER, ELIZABETH B. Following the Guidon. New York, 1890. Cloth, fine, first edition. Hayman 57-131 1974 $10

CUSTER, ELIZABETH B. Tenting On the Plains. New York, 1889. 8vo., cloth, illus., engravings. Rinsland 58-961 1974 $65

CUSTOMS and Privileges of the Manors of Stepney and Hackney in the County of Middlesex. 1736. Small 8vo., old sheep. Quaritch 939-472 1974 £15

CUTHBERT, G. A. Freshwater: A History and a Narrative of the Great Lakes. Toronto, 1931. Coloured plates, illus., first edition, med. 8vo., limited to 200 copies signed by author, orig. cloth, fine. Broadhurst 24-1600 1974 £10

CUTHBERTSON, CATHERINE Rosabella. London, 1817. 5 vols., 8vo., orig. boards, uncut, first edition. Dawsons PM 252-228 1974 £275

CUTLER, B. D. Modern British Authors. London, (1930). Med. 8vo., limited to 300 copies, orig. cloth. Forster 97-115 1974 £10

CUTLER, B. D. Modern British Authors: Their First Editions. 1930. Med. 8vo., mint, dust wrapper, orig. cloth, limited to 300 copies. Broadhurst 24-307 1974 £12

CUTLER, M. An Account of Some of the Vegetable Productions Naturally Growing In this Part of America. Cincinnati, 1903. Small 4to., orig. wrappers. Wheldon 131-1278 1974 £6

CUTTER, CHARLES The Gem Souvenir of Hot Springs, Arkansas. (Hot Springs, c.1906). Oblong 12mo., quarter cloth, rebound. Saddleback 14-14 1974 $10

CUVIER, GEORGES The Animal Kingdom. New York, 1831. 8vo., 4 vols., orig. green cloth, uncut, plates. Wheldon 129-329 1974 £35

CUVIER, GEORGES The Animal Kingdom. New York, 1931. 4 vols., 8vo., orig. green cloth, leather labels, uncut, plates, very scarce. Wheldon 131-426 1974 £35

CUVIER, GEORGES The Animal Kingdom. (1833-) 1834-37. 8 vols., 8vo., contemporary half calf gilt, portraits, plates, complete copy, scarce. Wheldon 128-268 1973 £90

CUVIER, GEORGES The Animal Kingdom. (1833-)1837. 8vo., 8 vols., orig. half leather, plates. Wheldon 129-328 1974 £60

CUVIER, GEORGES Discours sur les Revolutions de la Surface du Globe. Paris, 1825. 8vo., orig. pictured wrappers, plates. Schuman 37-56 1974 $195

CUVIER, GEORGES Discours sur les Revolutions de la Surface du Globe. Paris, 1830. 8vo., orig. wrappers, uncut, plates, sixth edition. Wheldon 131-986 1974 £15

CUVIER, GEORGES Essai sur la Geographie. Paris, 1811. 4to., contemporary boards, plates. Gurney 64-66 1974 £80

CUVIER, GEORGES Essay on the Theory of the Earth. Edinburgh, London, 1813. 8vo., modern half calf, gilt, first edition in English. Dawsons PM 245-194 1974 £30

CUVIER, GEORGES Essay on the Theory of the Earth. Edinburgh, 1813. 8vo., modern half morocco, uncut. Wheldon 129-815 1974 £35

CUVIER, GEORGES Essay on the Theory of the Earth. Edinburgh & London, 1827. 8vo., half calf, plates, fifth edition. Wheldon 131-984 1974 £20

CUVIER, GEORGES Essay on the Theory of the Earth. Edinburgh, 1827. 8vo., orig. quarter cloth, uncut. Gurney 64-65 1974 £12.50

CUVIER, GEORGES Histoire des Progres des Sciences Naturelles Depuis 1789. Paris, 1834-36. 5 vols., 8vo., modern half morocco, very scarce. Wheldon 128-90 1973 £50

CUVIER, GEORGES Histoire des Progres des Sciences Naturelles Depuis 1789 Jusqu'a ce Jour. Paris, 1826-28. 4 vols., 8vo., contemporary half calf, scarce. Wheldon 128-91 1973 £40

CUVIER, GEORGES Histoire des Progres des Sciences. Paris, 1826-28. 8vo., 4 vols., contemporary half calf, scarce. Wheldon 130-153 1974 £40

CUVIER, GEORGES Histoire des Sciences Naturelles. Paris, 1841-45. 3 parts in 5 vols., 8vo., new cloth, library stamp, good copy, scarce. Wheldon 128-92 1973 £50

CUVIER, GEORGES Lecons d'Anatomie Comparee. 1805. 8vo., 5 vols., contemporary half calf, rebacked, first edition. Dawsons PM 249-133 1974 £185

CUVIER, GEORGES Lecons d'Anatomie Comparee. Paris, 1835-46. 8vo., new cloth, scarce, second edition. Wheldon 130-349 1974 £80

CUVIER, GEORGES Quadro Elementar da Historia dos Animaes. London, n.d. 8vo., 2 vols., orig. boards, uncut. Gurney 64-62 1974 £12.50

CUVIER, GEORGES Quadro Elementar da Historia dos Animaes. London, n.d.-1815. 8vo., 2 vols., orig. boards, uncut, plates, folding tables, few minor stains. Gurney 66-47 1974 $12.50

CUVIER, GEORGES Quadro Elementar da Historia Natural dos Animaes. London, 1815. 2 vols., 8vo., half calf, plates, folding tables. Wheldon 128-270 1973 £30

CUVIER, GEORGES Quadro Elementar da Historia Natural dos Animaes. London, 1815. 8vo., 2 vols., modern boards, uncut. Wheldon 130-348 1974 £30

CUVIER, GEORGES Quadro Elementar da Historia Natural dos Animaes. London, 1815. 2 vols., 8vo., half calf, plates. Wheldon 131-425 1974 £30

CUVIER, GEORGES Quadroelementar da historia Natural dos Animaes. London, 1815. 8vo., 2 vols., modern boards, uncut. Wheldon 129-330 1974 £30

CUVIER, GEORGES Rapport sur un Memoire de M. Dutrochet. Paris, 1817. 4to., modern boards. Wheldon 129-331 1974 £10

CUVIER, GEORGES Recherches sur les Ossemens Fossiles. Paris, 1834-36. 4to., 2 vols., new cloth. Wheldon 129-814 1974 £250

CUVIER, GEORGES Recherches sur les Ossemens Fossiles. Paris, 1834-36. 11 vols., 8vo., & 2 vols., 4to., new cloth, plates. Wheldon 131-983 1974 £250

CUVIER, GEORGES Le Regne Animal. Paris, 1817. 8vo., 4 vols., contemporary half calf, plates, rare, first edition. Wheldon 130-344 1974 £140

CUVIER, GEORGES Le Regne Animal. Paris, 1817. 8vo., 4 vols., contemporary half leather, plates. Wheldon 129-327 1974 £130

CUVIER, GEORGES Le Regne Animal. Paris, 1817. 8vo., half cloth. Wheldon 129-777 1974 £25

CUVIER, GEORGES Le Regne Animal Distribue d'Apres son Organisation. Paris, 1817. 4 vols., 8vo., contemporary calf, gilt, engravings, first edition. Gilhofer 61-33 1974 sFr 2,400

CUVIER, GEORGES Le Regne Animal Distribue d'Apres Son Organisation. Paris, 1817. 4 vols., 8vo., contemporary half calf, plates, rare first edition. Wheldon 128-267 1973 £140

CUVIER, GEORGES   Le Regne Animal Distribue D'Apres son Organisation. Paris, 1817. 4 vols., 8vo., contemporary half leather, worn, plates. Wheldon 131-423 1974 £130

CUVIER, GEORGES   Le Regne Animal. Paris, 1829-30. 8vo., 5 vols., new cloth, plates, rare, second edition. Wheldon 130-345 1974 £45

CUVIER, GEORGES   Le Regne Animal. Paris, (1836-49). Imp. 8vo., 2 vols., half red morocco, plates. Wheldon 129-12 1974 £100

CUVIER, GEORGES   Le Regne Animal. Paris, (1836-49). 3 vols., roy. 8vo., half calf, plates. Wheldon 131-482 1974 £80

CUVIER, GEORGES   Le Regne Animal. Paris, (1836-49). 2 vols., imp. 8vo., new half red morocco, plates, very scarce. Wheldon 131-38 1974 £100

CUVIER, GEORGES   Le Regne Animal Distribue d'Apres son Organisation. Paris, (1836-49). 22 vols. in 20, imp. 8vo., orig. half red morocco gilt, hand-coloured and plain plates, nice set. Wheldon 128-269 1973 £500

CUVIER, GEORGES   Le Regne Animal, per une Reunion de Disciples de Cuvier. Insectes Coleopteres. Paris, (1836-49). 2 vols., roy. 8vo., half morocco, plates. Wheldon 131-796 1974 £20

CUVIER, GEORGES   Le Regne Animal, Atlas. Paris, (1849). Imp. 8vo., orig. half red morocco, plates. Wheldon 131-483 1974 £50

CUVIER, GEORGES   Le Regne Animal. Paris, (1849). Imperial 8vo., boards, cloth backs, plates, scarce. Wheldon 130-822 1974 £20

CUVIER, GEORGES   Le Regne Animal. Paris, (1849). Imperial 8vo., cloth backed boards, plates. Wheldon 129-739 1974 £50

CUVIER, GEORGES   Le Regne Animal. Les Annelides. Paris, (1849). Imp. 8vo., half red morocco, plates. Wheldon 131-926 1974 £10

CUVIER, GEORGES   Le Regne Animal. Les Annelides. Paris, (1849). 2 vols. in 1, imp. 8vo., new cloth, plates. Wheldon 131-925 1974 £15

CUVIER, GEORGES   Recueil des Eloges Historiques lus dans les Seances Publiques de l'Institut Royal de France. Strasbourg and Paris, 1819-27. 8vo., boards, 3 vols., first edition, lacks half titles, rare complete with vol 3. Gurney 66-45 1974 £45

CUVIER, GEORGES   Recueil des Eloges Historiques lus Dans les Seances Publiques de l'Institut Royal de France. Paris, 1819-27. 3 vols., 8vo., new cloth, library stamp, scarce, first edition. Wheldon 128-93 1973 £30

CUVIER, GEORGES   Recueil des Eloges Historiques. Strasbourg and Paris, 1819-27. 8vo., 3 vols., boards, first edition. Gurney 64-63 1974 £45

CUVIER, GEORGES   Tableau Elementaire de l'Histoire Naturelle des Animaux. Paris, (1798). 8vo., contemporary sheep, worn, plates. Wheldon 131-424 1974 £75

CUVIER, GEORGES   Tableau Elementaire de l'Histoire Naturelle des Animaux. Paris, (1798). 8vo., contemporary quarter calf, plates, first edition. Gurney 64-64 1974 £60

CUVIER, GEORGES   Tableau Elementaire de l'Histoire Naturelle des Animaux. Paris, (1798). 8vo., contemporary quarter calf, vellum corners, first edition, slightly rubbed, library stamp. Gurney 66-46 1974 £60

CUVIER, GEORGES   Tableau Elementaire de l'Histoire Naturelle des Animaux. Paris, (1798). 8vo., modem half morocco, plates. Wheldon 130-347 1974 £75

CUVIER, GEORGES   Das Thierreich Geordnet nach Seiner Organisation. Leipzig, 1831-43. 8vo., 6 vols., contemporary boards, scarce. Wheldon 130-346 1974 £35

CUVILLIES, FRANCOIS DE   A Collection of 112 Architectural and Ornamental Plates. (Paris, c. 1750-70). Roy. folio album, plates, 19th century half morocco, worn corners. Quaritch 940-504 1974 £290

CUYPERS, FIRMIN   James Ensor. Paris, 1925. 16mo., wrappers, uncut, foxed, plates, limited edition. Minters 37-244 1973 $15

CYCLOPAEDIA of American Biography. 1887-89. 6 vols., plates, lacks supp. vol. 7. Allen 216-B 1974 $50

CYCLOPAEDIA of Botany. London, c. 1840. 2 vols., half calf, color plates, fine, 8vo. Gregory 44-82 1974 $165

THE CYCLOPEDIA of Wit and Humor. New York, 1858. 2 vols., 24 portraits on steel and many wood engravings. Biblo & Tannen 213-736 1973 $27.50

CYCLOPAEDIA of Wit and Humor. New York, 1875. I vol ed., bdg. worn. Biblo & Tannen 213-737 1973 $15

CYNTHIA; With the Tragical Account of the Unfortunate Loves of Almerin and Desdemona. London, n.d. 12mo., old calf, worn, rare, corrected tenth edition. Ximenes 33-14 1974 $75

CYNWAL, WILLIAM   In Defence of Woman. London, (n.d.). Tall 8vo., illus., orig. cloth, limited. Bow Windows 62-381 1974 £12.50

CYNWAL, WILLIAM   In Defence of Woman. n.d. Fine, English first edition. Covent 56-530 1974 £12.50

CYPRESS, J. JR. PSEUD.
Please turn to
HERBERT, HENRY WILLIAM

CYPRIANUS, CAECILIUS   Opera. 1520. 4to., modern buckram, rebound, woodcut border. Smith 194-151 1974 £20

CYPRIANUS, CAECILIUS   Opera Omnia. Paris, 1865. 2 vols., roy. 8vo., half vellum, morocco labels. Howes 185-1100 1974 £9

CZAPEK, F.   Biochemie der Pflanzen. 1920-22. Roy 8vo., 3 vols., orig. half buckram. Wheldon 129-908 1974 £10

CZAPEK, F.   Biochemie der Pflanzen. Jena, 1922. Vol. 1 only, roy. 8vo., orig. half buckram. Wheldon 131-1130 1974 £10

CZERNY, KARL   Letters to Young Ladies on the Art of Playing the Pianoforte. Ditson, n.d. 56p., illus. Austin 51-235 1973 $10

CZIZEK, J.   Erlauterungen zur Geognostischen Karte. Vienna, 1849. 8vo., half calf. Wheldon 129-816 1974 £10

CZUBER, EMANUEL   Einfuhrung in die Hohere Mathematik. Leipzig and Berlin, 1909. 8vo., blue cloth, first edition. Dawsons PM 245-195 1974 £5

CZVITTINGER, DAVID   Specimen Hungariae Literatae. Frankfurt, 1711. 4to., old boards, vellum back, fine. Harper 213-48 1973 $195

D

D., H. PSEUD.
Please turn to
DOOLITTLE, HILDA

DAFFODIL Stories. New York, n.d. 16mo., illus. Frohnsdorff 16-258 1974 $7.50

DAFOE, J. W.   Laurier, A Study in Canadian Politics. Toronto, 1922. Hood's 103-205 1974 $15

DAFYDD AP GWILYM   Barddoniaeth. Lundian, 1789. 12mo., 19th century full morocco, gilt. Jacobs 24-75 1974 $20

DAFYDD AP GWILYM   Selected Poems. Dublin, 1944. Orig. bds. Jacobs 24-76 1974 $30

DAGLEY, R.   A Compendium of the Theory and Practice of Drawing and Painting. 1822. 4to., orig. boards, old cloth back, uncut, second edition. Quaritch 940-74 1974 £20

DAGLISH, ERIC FITCH   The Smaller Beasts. New York, 1928. Square 8vo., pict. boards, cloth spine, illus. Frohnsdorff 16-259 1974 $7.50

DAHL, NISSER WILHELM   Michael Dahl and the Contemporary Swedish School of Painting in England. 1927. Plates, boards, de Luxe edition. Marsden 37-153 1974 £21

DAHLBERG, EDWARD   Bottom Dogs. 1929. One of 520 numbered copies, fine copy, first edition. Covent 51-506 1973 £30

DAHLBERG, ERIC J.   Suecia Antiqua et Hodierna. Stockholm, c. 1691-1715. Thick oblong folio, modern calf, gilt, morocco label, plates. Traylen 79-559 1973 £800

DAHLBERG, ERIC J.   Suecia Antiqua et Hodernia. (Stockholm, 1693-1714). 3 vols. in 1, oblong folio, polished calf, plates, slip case, rare first edition. Quaritch 940-75 1974 £3,500

DAHN, FELIX   A Struggle for Rome. 1878. 3 vols. in 1, thick 8vo., orig. blue cloth, first edition, second issue. Howes 186-123 1974 £8.50

DAILY Food for Christians. 1845. Fifth American edition, 2 X 2 1/2 inches. Gregory 44-361 1974 $15

DAILY Verses. London, (1840-45). Full red roan, wallet flap, 1 1/4 X 2 inches. Gregory 44-363 1974 $30

THE DAISY. C., 1909. 4to., orig. cloth-backed boards, gilt, plates, illus., dust-jacket. Hammond 201-106 1974 £5

DALBY, W. B.   Lectures on Diseases and Injuries of the Ear. London, 1885. Small 8vo., orig. black cloth, rebacked, third edition. Dawsons PM 249-134 1974 £6.50

DALCHO, FREDERICK   An Historical Account of the Protestant Episcopal Church. Charleston, 1820. 8vo., old calf, worn. Butterfield 8-586 1974 $37.50

DALE, EDGAR   The Content of Motion Pictures. Macmillan, 1935. 230p., orig. ed. Austin 51-236 1973 $10

DALE, EDWARD EVERETT   The Range Cattle Industry. Norman, 1930. Illus., rare. Jenkins 61-756 1974 $55

DALE, ELIZABETH   The Scenery and Geology of the Peak of Derbyshire. London and Buston, 1900. 8vo., orig. cloth, gilt, illus., first edition. Hammond 201-366 1974 £10

DALE, HARRISON CLIFFORD   The Ashley-Smith Explorations. Glendale, 1941. Plates, frontispiece, orig. cloth. Bradley 35-143 1974 $40

DALE, R.   An Exact Catalogue of the Nobility of England. London, 1697. 8vo., half calf, frontispiece. Quaritch 939-714 1974 £25

DALE, T. C.   The Inhabitants of London in 1638. 1931. 2 vols., roy. 8vo. Quaritch 939-766 1974 £7.50

D'ALEMBERT, JEAN LEROND
Please turn to
ALEMBERT, JEAN LEROND D'

DALGADO, D. G.   Flora de Goa e Savantradi. Lisbon, 1898. Roy. 8vo., orig. wrappers, scarce. Wheldon 128-1255 1973 £10

DALGLIESH, ALICE   The Little Wooden Farmer. New York, 1930. Oblong 8vo., pictorial cloth, lst ed., illus. Frohnsdorff 16-260 1974 $15

DALI, SALVADOR   La Conquete de l'Irrationnel. Paris, 1935. 16mo., orig. pictorial wrapper, first edition. L. Goldschmidt 42-198 1974 $75

DALI, SALVADOR   50 Secrets of Magic Craftsmanship. New York, 1948. 4to., lst ed. Biblo & Tannen 210-109 1973 $75

DALL, C. H.   What We Really Know About Shakespeare. Boston, 1886. Small 8vo., half calf, gilt. Quaritch 936-559 1974 £6

DALL, WILLIAM HEALEY   Spencer Fullerton Baird. Philadelphia, 1915. Rittenhouse 46-185 1974 $15

DALLA BELLA, J. A.   Memorias sobre o Modo de Aperfeicoar. Lisbon, 1784. 4to., contemporary calf, gilt, first edition. Gurney 64-67 1974 £25

DALLAS, FRANCIS GREGORY   The Papers of. New York, 1917. Boxed, top edge gilt, limited, numbered edition. Jenkins 61-757 1974 $20

DALLAWAY, JAMES   Anecdotes of the Arts in England. 1800. Contemporary calf, rebacked, illus., bookplate of C. W. H. Sotheby. Eaton Music-565 1973 £15

DALLAWAY, JAMES   A Series of Discourses Upon Architecture in England from the Norman Era to the Close of the Reign of Queen Elizabeth. London, 1833. 8vo., later half calf, spine gilt, attractive unopened copy, first edition. Ximenes 37-57 1974 $45

D'ALLEMAGNE, HENRY RENE
Please turn to
ALLEMAGNE, HENRY RENE D'

DALLIMORE, W.   Holly, Yew and Box, With Notes on Other Evergreens. 1908. 8vo., cloth, illus., very scarce. Wheldon 131-1724 1974 £10

DALLWITZ, R. WEGNER VON   Hilfsbuch fur den Luftschiff. 1910. 8vo., orig. black printed cloth, illus., first edition. Dawsons PM 245-200 1974 £25

DALMAN, J. W.   Analecta Entomologica. Stockholm, 1823. 4to., half brown morocco, plates, rare. Wheldon 131-797 1974 £30

DALRYMPLE, ALEXANDER   An Historical Collection of the Several Voyages and Discoveries In the South Pacific Ocean. London, 1770-71. 2 vols., 4to., full calf antique, gilt, plates, first edition. Traylen 79-424 1973 £420

DALRYMPLE, JOHN 1726-1810   The Address of the People of Great Britain. London, 1775. 8vo., wrappers, first edition. Dawsons PM 247-63 1974 £28

DALRYMPLE, JOHN 1726-1810   The Address of the People of Great Britain to the Inhabitants of America. London, 1775. White wrappers, first edition. Bradley 35-120 1974 $150

DALRYMPLE, JOHN 1726-1810   Memoirs of Great Britain and Ireland. 1771-73. 4to., contemporary calf, gilt, second edition. Hammond 201-452 1974 £12.50

DALRYMPLE, JOHN, 1726-1810   Rights of Great Britain
Please turn to
MAC PHERSON, JAMES

DALRYMPLE, L.   Diane of the Green Van. Toronto, 1914. Illus.,
presentation note from author included. Hood's 102-498 1974 $15

DALTON, C. A.   Flame and Adventure. Toronto, 1924. Illus.
Hood's 102-648 1974 $10

DALTON, JOHN   A New System of Chemical Philosophy. London,
1808-10-27. 8vo., contemporary half calf, cloth, first edition. Dawsons PM
245-201 1974 £1,200

DALTON, JOHN   Two Epistles. London, 1745. 4to., disbound,
first edition. Dawsons PM 252-229 1974 £22

DALTON, JOHN C.   Human Physiology. Philadelphia, 1867.
Orig. leather cover, library stamp, fourth edition. Rittenhouse 46-186
1974 $10

DALTON, JOHN C.   Human Physiology. Philadelphia, 1871.
Orig. leather covers, fifth edition. Rittenhouse 46-187 1974 $10

DALTON, JOHN C.   A Treatise On Human Physiology. Philadelphia,
1882. Seventh edition. Rittenhouse 46-188 1974 $10

DALTON, M.   The Countrey Justice. London, 1677. Folio,
contemporary ledger calf, stained. Quaritch 939-101 1974 £30

DALTON, M.   Officium Vicecomitum. London, 1682.
Folio, half mottled calf. Quaritch 939-102 1974 £40

DALTON, O. M.   Franks Bequest. 1912. Clothbound, plates.
Covent 55-436 1974 £20

DAMANIANT, M.   The Midnight Hour. 1787. 8vo., cloth, signature. Quaritch 936-37 1974 £5

THE DAME and Her Donkeys Five. 1888. 8vo., wrappers, engravings, worn
covers. Covent 55-996 1974 £15.75

DAME Trot and Her Comical Cat. Albany, ca. 1850. 16mo., 8 hand-colored
engravings. Frohnsdorff 16-261 1974 $20

DAME Trot and Her Comical Cat. New York, 1903. 12mo., illus. Frohnsdorff
16-263 1974 $10

DAMIRON, CHARLES   La Faience de Lyon Premiere Epoque Le XVI
Siecle. Paris, (1926). 2 vols. in 1, large 4to., plates, illus., cloth bound,
orig. wrappers. Bow Windows 62-230 1974 £150

DAMMERMAN, K. W.   The Agricultural Zoology of the Malay Archipelago. Amsterdam, 1929. 4to., cloth, plates. Wheldon 129-263 1974 £15

DAMON, S. FOSTER   William Blake. 1924. Roy 8vo., cloth, plates,
scarce, presentation copy, signed. Quaritch 936-301 1974 £30

DAMPIER, WILLIAM   A Collection of Voyages. London, 1698-1709.
4 vols. in 3, 8vo., contemporary calf, rebacked, illus., morocco labels,
scarce. Traylen 79-425 1973 £120

DAMPIER, WILLIAM   A History of Science and Its Relations With
Philosophy & Religion. New York, 1932. Reprint. Rittenhouse 46-189
1974 $10

DAMPIER, WILLIAM   A History of Science and its Relations with
Philosophy and Religion. Cambridge, 1944. Biblo & Tannen 213-857 1973 $10

DAMPIER, WILLIAM   A New Voyage Round the World. 1927. 4to.,
maps, illus., orig. quarter vellum, cloth sides, uncut, jap vellum, limited
edition. Bow Windows 66-162 1974 £21

DAMPIER, WILLIAM   Voyages and Discoveries. London, 1931.
4to., parchment backed cloth, uncut, maps, limited edition. Traylen 79-426
1973 £22

DAMROSCH, WALTER   My Musical Life. Scribner, 1923. 376p.,
illus., orig. ed. Austin 51-237 1973 $10

DAN, ADAM   Sommerlov. Cedar Falls, Iowa, 1903.
Austin 62-120 1974 $17.50

DANA, CHARLES A.   The Life of Ulysses S. Grant, General of the
Armies of the United States. Springfield, 1868. Cloth. Hayman 59-560 1974
$10

DANA, H. W. L.   Handbook on Soviet Drama. Amer. Russ. Inst.,
1938. 158p. Austin 51-238 1973 $12.50

DANA, JAMES D.   Characteristics of Volcanoes. New York, 1890.
8vo., orig. bindings, maps, plates. Butterfield 8-132 1974 $17.50

DANA, MALCOLM   The Annals of Norwich, New London County,
Connecticut in the Great Rebellion of 1861-65. Norwich, 1873. Chipped,
illus. Jenkins 61-688 1974 $10

DANA, RICHARD HENRY 1815-1882   To Cuba and Back. Boston, 1859.
Bright clean copy, orig. binding. Butterfield 10-211 1974 $15

DANA, RICHARD HENRY 1815-1882   Two Years Before the Mast. London,
1841. Very good copy, rebound in cloth backed marbled boards, upper wrapper
not bound in, first edition. Covent 51-507 1973 £30

DANA, RICHARD HENRY 1815-1882   Two Years Before the Mast. New York,
1936. Illus., 8vo., full cream colored morocco, gilt, slipcase, limited to 1000
copies, fine. Ross 86-213 1974 $70

DANBY, HENRY   A Commonplace Book Containing Two Quotations
from Shakespeare's Othello. (Yorkshire). 4to., orig. vellum wrappers, green
quarter calf box. Dawsons PM 252-230 1974 £1850

DANBY, WILLIAM   Extracts from Young's Night Thoughts with
Observations Upon Them. 1832. 2 works in 1 vol., orig. cloth, uncut,
inscribed presentation, first editions. Howes 186-124 1974 £7.50

THE DANCES OF Death Through the Various Stages of Human Life. London, 1803.
Small 4to., contemporary half roan, gilt, plates. Hammond 201-487 1974 £35

DANCES of Our Pioneers. Barnes, 1930. Austin 51-813 1973 $7.50

DANDIEU, ARNAUD   Marcel Proust: Sa Revelation Psychologique.
Pairs, 1930. Front hinge little weak, contents browned, very good copy, wrappers.
Covent 51-1529 1973 £5.25

DANDOLO, VINCENZO   De l'Art d'Elever les Vers-a-Soie. Paris, 1819.
8vo., contemporary green quarter morocco, first edition in French. Dawsons PM
245-202 1974 £10

DANDURAND, J. M.   Nos Travers. Montreal, 1901. Hood's 102-
696 1974 $7.50

DANE, CLEMENCE   Broome Stages. 1931. Presentation, inscribed,
fine. Covent 55-559 1974 £5.25

DANET, PIERRE   The Complete Dictionary of the Greek and
Roman Antiquities. London, 1700. 4to., contemporary panelled calf, spine gilt,
fine crisp copy. Ximenes 36-64 1974 $75

DANGEARD, P. A.   Etudes sur la Cellule. Paris, 1899. Roy 8vo.
Wheldon 129-910 1974 £5

DANGERFIELD, THOMAS   A Particular Narrative. London, 1679. Folio,
disbound, first edition. Dawsons PM 251-496 1974 £18

DANIEL, GABRIEL   The Discourses of Cleander and Eudoxe. 1704.
Small 8vo., contemporary sheep, fine, first English edition. Quaritch 936-38
1974 £45

DANIEL, GEORGE　　　The Poems of. 1878. 4 vols., 4to., orig. mauve cloth, uncut, fine, limited edition. Dawsons PM 252-231 1974 £95

DANIEL, I. J. E.　　　A History of the Canadian Knights of Columbus Catholic Army Huts. N.P., 1922. Plates, charts. Hood's 103-98 1974 $12.50

DANIEL, W.　　　A Voyage Round Great Britain. 1814-25. 8 vols. in 4, folio, half red morocco, plates. Quaritch 939-837 1974 £6500

DANIEL, WILLIAM B.　　　Rural Sports. 1807. 3 vols. Austin 61-262 1974 $75

DANIELE, F.　　　Le Forche Caudine Illustrate. Caserta, 1778. Large folio, contemporary boards, leather back, plates, first edition. Harper 213-49 1973 $375

DANIELL, WILLIAM　　　Devon, 1814-1825. London, 1825. Oblong 4to., contemporary half red morocco, leather label. Traylen 79-321 1973 £160

DANIELSON, RICHARD E.　　　Martha Doyle and Other Sporting Memories. New York, The Derrydale Press, 1938. Illus., limited to 1250 copies, red cloth, red leather labels, very good to fine. Current BW9-168 1974 $37

DANNAY, FREDERIC
Please turn to
QUEEN, ELLERY PSEUD.

DANTE, ALIGHIERI　　　Divina Comedia. Venice, 1564. Folio, old vellum, woodcut, foxing, first edition. Schafer 8-91 1973 sFr. 1,900

DANTE, ALIGHIERI　　　La Divina Commedia. (London), 1928. Folio, orig. orange parchment gilt, presentation, plates. Dawsons PM 252-232 1974 £100

DANTE, ALIGHIERI　　　La Divina Commedia. 1928. Small folio, orange stained parchment gilt, top edges gilt, spine faded, else mint, limited edition, drawings. Thomas 32-284 1974 £100

DANTE ALIGHIERI　　　Illustrations and Notes. Edinburgh, 1890. Engraved plates, binding little worn, plates on Japanese vellum, first edition. Covent 51-508 1973 £5.25

DANTE, ALIGHIERI　　　Le Terze Rime. 1502. 19th century dark green morocco gilt, first Octavo edition. Thomas 30-10 1973 £300

DANTE, ALIGHIERI　　　Le Terze Rime. 1502. 18th century Italian vellum, first Octavo edition. Thomas 30-9 1973 £450

DANTE, ALIGHIERI　　　Le Terze Rime. 1502. 19th century blue calf gilt, morocco label, raised bands, first Aldine edition. Thomas 30-11 1973 £450

D'ANVERS, CALEB　　　A Proper Reply to a Late Scurrilous Libel. 1731. 8vo., disbound. Broadhurst 23-1225 1974 £6

D'ANVILLE, J. B. B.　　　Proposition d'une Mesure de la Terre. Paris, 1735. 12mo., contemporary calf, first editions. Gurney 64-6 1974 £20

DARBY, WILLIAM　　　A Tour From the City of New York to Detroit in 1818. New York, 1819. Orig. boards, ex-library, foxing. Hood's 103-528 1974 $155

DARBY, WILLIAM　　　A Tour from the City of New York to Detroit in the Michigan Territory. New York, 1819. Contemporary calf, foxed, folding maps, errata slip, exceptional copy, Laurence Washington's copy, signed and with corrections by him throughout. Jenkins 61-758 1974 $85

DARCET, J. P. J.　　　Rapport sur la Fabrication des Savons. Paris, (1795). 4to., wrappers. Gurney 64-68 1974 £25

D'ARCONVILLE, G. C. THIROUX　　　Essai pour Servir a l'Histoire. Paris, 1766. 8vo., old calf, worn, first edition. Gurney 64-9 1974 £25

DARDIENNE, PIERRE DENIS　　　Traite d'Osteologie. 1725. 4to., old calf, gilt. Dawsons PM 249-136 1974 £55

DARE, M. P.　　　Unholy Relics and Other Uncanny Tales. London, 1947. 1st ed. Biblo & Tannen 210-584 1973 $15

DARELL, W.　　　The History of Dover Castle. 1786. 4to., plates, modern boards. Quaritch 939-400 1974 £14

DARELL, W.　　　The History of Dover Castle. 1797-1811. 2 vols. in 1, folio, diced russia, new edition. Quaritch 939-103 1974 £30

DAREMBERG, C.　　　La Medecine dans Homere ou Etudes d'Arch- eologie sur les Medecins, l'Anatomie, la Physiologie, la Chirurgie et la Medecine dans les Poemes Homeriques. Paris, 1865. 8vo., cloth, wrappers bound in, plate. Gurney 66-48 1974 £15

DARESTE, C.　　　Recherches sur la Production. Paris, 1891. 8vo., cloth, plates, second edition. Wheldon 129-332 1974 £10

DARK, SIDNEY　　　Paris. 1926. Illus., 139 pages. Austin 61-263 1974 $10

DARKER, G. D.　　　The Hypodermataceae of Conifers. 1932. 8vo., buckram, plates. Wheldon 129-1187 1974 £7.50

DARKER, G. D.　　　The Hypodermataceae of Conifers. 1932. 8vo., buckram. Wheldon 131-1387 1974 £7.50

DARLEY, FELIX O. C.　　　Illustrations of the Legend of Sleepy Hollow. 1849. Oblong 4to., orig. pictorial wrappers, 6 engraved plates. Frohnsdorff 16-265 1974 $35

DARLEY, GEORGE　　　Sylvia, or the May Queen. London, 1892. 8vo., orig. brown buckram cloth, very rare, first edition. Ximenes 36-65 1974 $25

DARLINGTON, C. D.　　　Recent Advances In Cytology. 1932. 8vo., cloth, plates. Wheldon 131-151 1974 £5

DARLOW, T. H.　　　Historical Catalogue of the Printed Editions of the Holy Scriptures in the Library of the British and Foreign Bible Society. 1911. Vols. 2, 3 & 4, 4to., buckram, new and unopened. Thomas 32-22 1974 £60

DARMON, J. E.　　　Dictionnaire des Estampes et Livres Illustres sur les Ballons & Machines. Montpellier, 1929. 8vo., orig. wrappers, limited, first edition. Dawsons PM 10-159 1974 £40

DARNELL, A. W.　　　Orchids for the Outdoor Garden. Ashford, 1930. 4to., cloth, illus., scarce. Wheldon 131-1617 1974 £20

DARRAS, JOSEPH-EPIPHANE　　　Histoire Generale de l'Eglise Depuis Creation Jusqu'a Nos Jours. Paris, 1875-88. 44 vols., half calf, morocco labels. Howes 185-1102 1974 £65

DARROW, CLARENCE　　　The Prohibition Mania. New York, 1927. Ma- roon cloth, first edition. Dawson's 424-261 1974 $12.50

DARROW, CLARENCE　　　The Story of My Life. New York and London, 1932. Cloth, dust wrapper, illus., first edition. Dawson's 424-262 1974 $25

DART, J.　　　History and Antiquities of the Cathedral Church of Canterbury. 1726. Folio, old russia, plates. Quaritch 939-401 1974 £60

DARTON, F. J. HARVEY　　　Dickens. London, 1933. Plates, demy 8vo., orig. boards, cloth back. Forster 98-57 1974 £5

DARTON, F. J. HARVEY　　　Modern Book Illustration in Great Britain and America. 1931. 4to., plates, illus., orig. wrappers, first edition. Quaritch 936-358 1974 £20

DARTON, F. J. HARVEY　　　Tales of the Canterbury Pilgrims. 1904. Orig. dec. black cloth, illus. Howes 185-521 1974 £6.50

DARTON, N. H.   Guidebook of the Western United States Part C.
Washington, 1915. 8vo., orig. bindings. Butterfield 8-603 1974 $15

DARTON'S Leading Strings. London, 1901. 4to., pictorial boards, cloth spine,
illus. Frohnsdorff 16-266 1974 $10

DARWIN, CHARLES   Charles Darwin. 1902. 8vo., cloth, portrait.
Wheldon 130-244 1974 £5

DARWIN, CHARLES   Charles Darwin and the Voyage of the "Beagle".
1945. 8vo., cloth, plates, scarce. Wheldon 131-290 1974 £5

DARWIN, CHARLES   Ch. Darwin's Gesammelte Werke. Stuttgart,
1875-78. Vols. 1 - 12, 8vo., orig. cloth. Wheldon 128-22 1973 £75

DARWIN, CHARLES   Charles Darwin, His Life Told in a
Autobiographical Chapter and In a Selected Series of His Published Letters.
1892. 8vo., cloth. Wheldon 131-289 1974 £5

DARWIN, CHARLES   Darwin and Modern Science. 1909. Buckram,
plates, English first edition. Covent 56-1152 1974 £15.75

DARWIN, CHARLES   Darwin and Modern Science. Cambridge,
1910. 8vo., buckram, plates. Wheldon 128-28 1973 £5

DARWIN, CHARLES   Darwin and Modern Science. Cambridge, 1910.
8vo., buckram, plates. Wheldon 130-242 1974 £10

DARWIN, CHARLES   De la Variation des animaux et des Plantes.
Paris, 1868. 8vo., 2 vols., orig. cloth. Wheldon 129-201 1974 £15

DARWIN, CHARLES   De la Variation des Animaux et des Plantes Sous
l'Action de la Domestication. Paris, 1868. 2 vols., 8vo., orig. cloth, scarce,
woodcuts. Wheldon 131-277 1974 £15

DARWIN, CHARLES   The Descent of Man. London, 1871. 8vo., 2
vols., orig. green cloth, worn, uncut, illus. Dawsons PM 245-206 1974 £12

DARWIN, CHARLES   The Descent of Man. London, 1871. 8vo., contemporary half calf, gilt, illus., first edition. Dawsons PM 245-205 1974 £50

DARWIN, CHARLES   The Descent of Man. London, 1871.
2 vols., 8vo., orig. green cloth, gilt, rebacked, first edition, first issue.
Gilhofer 61-56 1974 sFr. 900

DARWIN, CHARLES   The Descent of Man. 1871. 8vo., 2 vols.,
cloth, woodcuts. Wheldon 129-200 1974 £20

DARWIN, CHARLES   The Descent of Man. 1871. 8vo., orig. green
cloth, 2 vols., woodcuts. Wheldon 130-223 1974 £40

DARWIN, CHARLES   The Descent of Man. 1877. Crown 8vo., orig.
cloth, revised second edition. Wheldon 128-26 1974 £10

DARWIN, CHARLES   The Descent of Man. 1883. Orig. cloth,
illus., second edition. Smith 194-798 1974 £8

DARWIN, CHARLES   The Descent of Man, and Selection in Relation
to Sex. 1871. 2 vols., orig. cloth, rubbed, first edition, second issue. Smith
194-430 1974 £28

DARWIN, CHARLES   The Descent of Man, and Selection in Relation
to Sex. 1871. 2 vols., 8vo., cloth, good copy. Wheldon 131-272 1974 £10

DARWIN, CHARLES   The Descent of Man, and Selection in Relation
to Sex. 1871. 2 vols., 8vo., cloth, good copy. Wheldon 131-271 1974 £20

DARWIN, CHARLES   The Descent of Man, and Selection in Relation
to Sex. 1871. 2 vols., 8vo., orig. green cloth, woodcuts. Wheldon 128-25
1973 £30

DARWIN, CHARLES   The Different Forms of Flowers on Plants of the
Same Species. 1877. 8vo., orig. cloth, text-figures, tables, first edition.
Wheldon 128-1101 1973 £18

DARWIN, CHARLES   Des Differentes Formes de Fleurs dans les
Plantes de la Meme Espece. Paris, 1878. 8vo., cloth, figures. Wheldon
128-1098 1973 £5

DARWIN, CHARLES   Des Differentes Formes de Fleurs dans les Plantes.
Paris, 1878. 8vo., cloth. Wheldon 130-235 1974 £5

DARWIN, CHARLES   The Effects of Cross and Self-Fertilisation In
the Vegetable Kingdom. 1878. 8vo., orig. cloth, second edition. Wheldon
131-285 1974 £20

DARWIN, CHARLES   Des effets de la Fecondation Croisee. Paris,
1877. 8vo., cloth. Wheldon 129-204 1974 £8

DARWIN, CHARLES   Des Effets de la Fecondation Croisee et de la
Fecondation Directe Dans le Regne Vegetal. Paris, 1877. 8vo., cloth.
Wheldon 131-286 1974 £8

DARWIN, CHARLES   The Expression of the Emotions in Man and Animals. 1872. Crown 8vo., orig. cloth, plates, first edition. Broadhurst 23-
1099 1974 £25

DARWIN, CHARLES   The Expression of the Emotions in Man and Animals. 1873. 8vo., orig. green cloth, plates. Wheldon 130-224 1974 £10

DARWIN, CHARLES   The Expression of the Emotions in Man and
Animals. 1890. 8vo., orig. cloth, plates, text-figures, second edition.
Wheldon 128-271 1973 £7.50

DARWIN, CHARLES   The Expression of the Emotions in Man and Animals. 1890. 8vo., orig. cloth, plates, second edition. Wheldon 130-225
1974 £7.50

DARWIN, CHARLES   The Formation of Vegetable Mould. 1881.
8vo., cloth. Wheldon 129-207 1974 £5

DARWIN, CHARLES   The Formation of Vegetable Mould. 1881.
8vo., cloth. Wheldon 129-206 1974 £7.50

DARWIN, CHARLES   The Formation of Vegetable Mould. 1882.
Crown 8vo., orig. green cloth, woodcuts. Wheldon 130-236 1974 £10

DARWIN, CHARLES   The Formation of Vegetable Mould. 1888.
8vo., cloth. Wheldon 130-237 1974 £7.50

DARWIN, CHARLES   The Formation of Vegetable Mould Through the
Action of Worms. 1881. 8vo., cloth. Wheldon 131-283 1974 £7.50

DARWIN, CHARLES   The Formation of Vegetable Mould Through
the Action of Worms With Observations On Their Habits. 1882. Crown 8vo.,
orig. green cloth, woodcuts. Wheldon 128-1100 1973 £5

DARWIN, CHARLES   Geological Observations on the Volcanic Islands.
London, 1876. 8vo., orig. cloth, presentation copy, inscribed, second edition.
Gurney 64-69 1974 £40

DARWIN, CHARLES   Geological Observations on the Volcanic Islands.
1876. 8vo., orig. cloth, plates, worn. Wheldon 129-202 1974 £12

DARWIN, CHARLES   Geological Observations on the Volcanic
Islands. London, 1891. 8vo., orig. cloth, plates, map, third edition. Bow
Windows 62-234 1974 £10

DARWIN, CHARLES   Gesammelte Werke. Stuttgart, 1875-78. 8vo.,
orig. cloth, 12 vols. Wheldon 130-221 1974 £75

DARWIN, CHARLES   God or Natural Selection? Glasgow & London,
(189-). 8vo., orig. cloth, scarce. Wheldon 128-29 1973 £7.50

DARWIN, CHARLES   Insectivorous Plants. New York, 1875. 8vo.,
orig. brown cloth, first American edition. Wheldon 130-234 1974 £10

DARWIN, CHARLES   Insectivorous Plants. 1875. 8vo., orig. cloth.
Wheldon 130-233 1974 £15

DARWIN, CHARLES   Insectivorous Plants. 1875. 8vo., cloth.
Wheldon 130-232 1974 £15

DARWIN, CHARLES　　　　Insectivorous Plants. 1875. 8vo., text-figures, cloth. Wheldon 128-1099 1973 £15

DARWIN, CHARLES　　　　Journal of Researches. 1845. 8vo., new half calf, second edition. Wheldon 129-197 1974 £30

DARWIN, CHARLES　　　　Journal of Researches Into the Natural History and Geology of the Countries Visited During the Voyage of H.M.S. Beagle Round the World. 1845. 8vo., half calf, second edition. Wheldon 131-273 1974 £30

DARWIN, CHARLES　　　　Journal of Researches into the Natural History and Geology. London, 1882. 8vo., signature, orig. cloth. Bow Windows 62-235 1974 £10

DARWIN, CHARLES　　　　Journal of Researches Into the Natural History and Geology of the Countries Visited During the Voyage of H. M. S. Beagle Round the World. 1890. 8vo., half morocco, illus., ninth edition. Wheldon 131-274 1974 £5

DARWIN, CHARLES　　　　Journal of Researches into the Natural History and Geology. 1890. Portrait. Bow Windows 62-235A 1974 £7

DARWIN, CHARLES　　　　Journal of Researches Into the Natural History & Geology of the Countries Visited During the Voyage Round the World of H.M.S. Beagle Under the Command of Captain Fitzroy. 1890. Large demy 8vo., illus., orig. cloth, first illus. edition. Smith 194-431 1974 £12

DARWIN, CHARLES　　　　Letters on Geology to Henslow. 1835. 8vo., boards, first edition. Dawsons PM 245-204 1974 £1,400

DARWIN, CHARLES　　　　Life and Letters. London, 1887. 3 vols., 8vo., cloth, plates, third edition. Traylen 79-69 1973 £9

DARWIN, CHARLES　　　　Life and Letters Of. 1887 or 1888. 3 vols., 8vo., cloth. Wheldon 128-95 1973 £15

DARWIN, CHARLES　　　　Life and Letters Of. 1887 or 1888. 8vo., 3 vols., cloth, portraits. Wheldon 130-243 1974 £15

DARWIN, CHARLES　　　　Life and Letters Of. 1888. 8vo., 3 vols., cloth. Wheldon 129-210 1974 £15

DARWIN, CHARLES　　　　Life and Letters of. 1888. 3 vols., 8vo., cloth, portraits, foxed. Wheldon 131-288 1974 £15

DARWIN, CHARLES　　　　A Monograph of the Fossil Lepadidae. and A Monograph of the Fossil Balanidae and Verrucidae of Great Britain. London, 1851 & 1854. 4to., 2 vols. in 1, half morocco, plates, first and only edition, very rare. Gurney 66-49 1974 £125

DARWIN, CHARLES　　　　More Letters of. New York, 1903. 2 vols., cloth gilt, plates, fine, first American edition. Covent 55-560 1974 £25

DARWIN, CHARLES　　　　The Movements and Habits of Climbing Plants. 1875. 8vo., orig. cloth, figures, revised second edition. Wheldon 128-1097 1973 £15

DARWIN, CHARLES　　　　The Movements and Habits of Climbing Plants. 1875. 8vo., orig. cloth, second edition. Wheldon 129-208 1974 £25

DARWIN, CHARLES　　　　The Movements and Habits of Climbing Plants. 1875. 8vo., cloth, second edition. Wheldon 130-230 1974 £25

DARWIN, CHARLES　　　　The Movements and Habits of Climbing Plants. 1882. 8vo., orig. cloth. Wheldon 129-209 1974 £7.50

DARWIN, CHARLES　　　　The Movements and Habits of Climbing Plants. 1882. 8vo., cloth. Wheldon 131-281 1974 £10

DARWIN, CHARLES　　　　The Movements and Habits of Climbing Plants. 1888. 8vo., orig. cloth. Wheldon 131-282 1974 £5

DARWIN, CHARLES　　　　The Movements and Habits of Climbing Plants. 1906. 8vo., cloth. Wheldon 130-231 1974 £5

DARWIN, CHARLES　　　　A Naturalist's Voyage. 1888. Bow Windows 64-68 1974 £8

DARWIN, CHARLES　　　　On the Origin of Species. 1861. Bow Windows 64-69 1974 £35

DARWIN, CHARLES　　　　On the Origin of Species. 1866. 8vo., orig. cloth. Wheldon 129-198 1974 £25

DARWIN, CHARLES　　　　On the Origin of Species. 1869. 8vo., orig. cloth, fifth edition. Wheldon 130-222 1974 £50

DARWIN, CHARLES　　　　On the Various Contrivances by Which British and Foregin Orchids are Fertilized by Insects. 1862. 8vo., orig. brown cloth, woodcuts, first edition. Wheldon 128-1554 1973 £30

DARWIN, CHARLES　　　　The Origin of Species. 1872. Crown 8vo., orig. cloth, sixth edition, third issue. Wheldon 128-24 1973 £15

DARWIN, CHARLES　　　　The Origin of Species. 1876. 8vo., orig. cloth, sixth edition. Wheldon 129-199 1974 £15

DARWIN, CHARLES　　　　The Origin of Species. London, 1892. 8vo., diagram, orig. cloth, sixth edition. Bow Windows 62-236 1974 £6.50

DARWIN, CHARLES　　　　The Origin of Species. 1895. Orig. cloth, sixth edition. Bow Windows 62-236A 1974 £6

DARWIN, CHARLES　　　　The Origin of Species. 1897. Orig. cloth, inscription, sixth edition. Bow Windows 62-236B 1974 £6

DARWIN, CHARLES　　　　The Origin of the Species. London, 1901. 8vo., orig. green paper wrappers. Dawsons PM 245-207 1974 £5

DARWIN, CHARLES　　　　On the Origin of Species by Means of Natural Selection. London, 1859. 8vo., contemporary green half calf, gilt, morocco labels, plate, first edition. Dawsons PM 250-19 1974 £850

DARWIN, CHARLES　　　　On the Origin of Species By Means of Natural Selection. 1860. 8vo., orig. green cloth. Wheldon 128-23 1973 £40

DARWIN, CHARLES　　　　On the Origin of Species By Means of Natural Selection. 1860. 8vo., orig. green cloth, second edition. Wheldon 131-269 1974 £60

DARWIN, CHARLES　　　　On the Origin of Species By Means of Natural Selection. 1902. 8vo., cloth, sixth edition. Wheldon 131-270 1974 £5

DARWIN, CHARLES　　　　On the Structure and Distribution of Coral Reefs. Glasgow, n.d. 8vo., cloth, maps. Wheldon 131-280 1974 £5

DARWIN, CHARLES　　　　On the Structure and Distribution of Coral Reefs. 1890. 8vo., cloth, maps, plates. Wheldon 131-279 1974 £5

DARWIN, CHARLES　　　　Order of the Proceedings at the Darwin Celebrations Held at Cambridge, June 22-24, 1909. Cambridge, 1909. 4to., orig. half canvas, portraits, plates. Wheldon 131-291 1974 £10

DARWIN, CHARLES　　　　Les Plantes Insectivores. Paris, 1877. 8vo., cloth. Wheldon 129-203 1974 £8

DARWIN, CHARLES　　　　Les Recifs de Corail. Paris, 1878. 8vo., half leather, plates. Wheldon 130-239 1974 £10

DARWIN, CHARLES　　　　Les Recifs de Corail, leur Structure et Leur Distribution. Paris, 1878. 8vo., half leather, plates. Wheldon 128-958 1973 £10

DARWIN, CHARLES　　　　Role des Vers de Terre dan la Formation de la Terre Vegetale. Paris, 1882. 8vo., orig. cloth. Wheldon 130-238 1974 £8

DARWIN, CHARLES　　　　The Structure and Distribution of Coral Reefs. 1874. 8vo., orig. cloth, coloured charts, text-figures, revised second edition. Wheldon 128-141 1973 £30

DARWIN, CHARLES   Uber den Bau und die Verbreitung. Stuttgart, 1877. 8vo., orig. dec. cloth, woodcuts. Wheldon 130-240 1974 £7.50

DARWIN, CHARLES   The Variation of Animals and Plants Under Domestication. London, 1868. 2 vols., 8vo., illus., orig. green cloth, first edition, good copy, second issue, with catalogue at end of vol. 1, ads at end of vol. 2. Schafer 10-123 1974 sFr 350

DARWIN, CHARLES   The Variation of Animals and Plants Under Domestication. 1868. 2 vols., 8vo., orig. green cloth, nice copy, first edition, second issue. Wheldon 128-27 1973 £25

DARWIN, CHARLES   The Variation of Animals and Plants Under Domestication. 1890. 2 vols., 8vo., cloth, second edition. Wheldon 131-275 1974 £10

DARWIN, CHARLES   The Variation of Animals and Plants Under Domestication. 1905. 2 vols., 8vo., cloth. Wheldon 131-276 1974 £7.50

DARWIN, CHARLES   Die Wirkungen der Kreuz. Stuttgart, 1877. 8vo., orig. dec. cloth. Wheldon 129-205 1974 £7.50

DARWIN, CHARLES   Die Wirkungen der Kreuz-Und Selbst-Befruchtung im Pflanzenreich. Stuttgart, 1877. 8vo., orig. dec. cloth. Wheldon 131-287 1974 £7.50

DARWIN, ERASMUS   The Botanic Garden. 1791-94. 2 vols. in 1, 4to., contemporary tree calf, frontispieces, plates. Wheldon 128-1102 1973 £50

DARWIN, ERASMUS   The Botanic Garden. 1791-94. 2 vols. in 1, 4to., contemporary tree calf, plates, frontispieces. Wheldon 131-1131 1974 £50

DARWIN, ERASMUS   The Botanic Garden. 1795 and 1794. 4to., contemporary russia, frontispiece, third and fourth editions. Quaritch 936-302 1974 £280

DARWIN, ERASMUS   Phytologia. 1800. 4to., modern half calf antique style, plates. Wheldon 128-1103 1973 £50

DARWIN, FRANCIS   The Life and Letters of Charles Darwin. London, 1888. 8vo., 3 vols., orig. green cloth. Dawsons PM 245-208 1974 £12

DARYLISH, ELIZABETH   The Last Man and Other Verses. 1936. Fine copy, textual corrections in author's hand, first edition. Covent 51-510 1973 £15

DARZENS, RODOLPHE   La Nuit. Paris, 1885. 12mo., half morocco, gilt, uncut, orig. wrapper, first edition. L. Goldschmidt 42-199 1974 $15

DASENT, ARTHUR I.   John Thadeus Delane. 1908. 2 vols., plates, frayed, library labels. Howes 186-766 1974 £5

DASYPODIUS, CONRAD   Heron Mechanicus. Strassburg, 1580. Small 4to., old calf, first edition. Dawsons PM 245-209 1974 £420

DAUBENY, CHARLES   A Description of Active and Extinct Volcanos. 1826. 8vo., orig. boards, uncut, plate, maps. Wheldon 131-987 1974 £20

DAUBENY, CHARLES   Journal of a Tour Through the United States and Canada, 1837-38. Oxford, 1843. Inscribed. Hood's 103-529 1974 $450

D'AUBIGNE, J.-H. MERLE   Histoire de la Reformation en Europe au Temps de Calvin. Paris, 1863-69. 5 vols., English half calf, library edition. Howes 185-1103 1974 £21

DAUBREE, GABRIEL AUGUSTE   Recherches sur la Presence de l'Arsenic. 1851. 8vo., wrappers, presentation copy, inscription. Zeitlin 235-274 1974 $75

DAUDET, ALPHONSE   Tartarin of Tarascon. New York, Limited Editions Club, 1930. Limited to 1500 numbered copies, 16mo., 2 vols., paper dec. covered boards, cloth back, publisher's slip case, books mint, case a bit dull, illus. & signed by W. A. Dwiggins. Current BW9-220 1974 $42.50

DAUGHERTY, CHARLES M.   Let 'Em Roll. Viking, 1950. 188p., illus. Austin 51-239 1973 $7.50

DAUGHERTY, HARRY M.   The Inside Story of the Harding Tragedy. New York, 1932. First edition, illus., covers stained, orig. binding. Wilson 63-177 1974 $10

DAUGHERTY, SONIA   Ten Brave Men. Philadelphia, 1951. 8vo., lst ed., illus. Frohnsdorff 16-268 1974 $7.50

DAUGHERTY, JAMES   Daniel Boone. New York, 1939. 4to., cloth, orig. lithographs. Frohnsdorff 16-267 1974 $10

DAUGHTERS of Eve. Schenectady, 1826. 12mo., orig. blue printed wrappers, first edition, fine uncut copy. Ximenes 36-166 1974 $45

DAUGHTERS OF THE AMERICAN REVOLUTION   The Valley of San Fernando. (N.P., c.1924). 8vo., cloth. Saddleback 14-81 1974 $50

D'AULNOY, MARIE CATHERINE JUMELLE DE BERNEVILLE, COMTESSE
Please turn to
AULNOY, MARIE CATHERINE JUMELLE DE BERNEVILLE, COMTESSE D'

DAUDET, LEON   Memoirs. 1926. Roy 8vo., English first edition. Covent 56-1702 1974 £5.25

DAUMIER, HONORE   Honore Daumier. Munich, 1923. Imp. 8vo., plates, boards, cloth spine. Quaritch 940-77 1974 £8

DAUMIER, HONORE   Hunting and Fishing. New York, n.d. 24 Lithographs. Biblo & Tannen 210-111 1973 $25

DAUMIER, HONORE   Der Maler Daumier. Munich, 1927-30. 2 vols., large folio, plates, illus., cloth. Quaritch 940-78 1974 £65

DAUMIER, HONORE   240 Lithographs. New York, 1946. Folio. Biblo & Tannen 210-112 1973 $25

DAUNOU, PIERRE CLAUDE FRANCOIS   Analyses des Opinions Diverses sur l'Origine de l'Imprimerie. Paris, (1803). 8vo., half leather. Kraus B8-304 1974 $42.50

DAUNT, W. J. O'NEILL   Eighty Five Years of Irish History. London, 1886. 2 vols., 8vo., cloth boards, second edition. Emerald 50-199 1974 £10

DAUPELEY-GOUVERNEUR, G.   Le Compositeur et le Correcteur Typographes. Paris, 1880. 8vo., cloth. Kraus B8-305 1974 $20

DAVAINE, C.   De l'incubation des Maladies Charbonneuses. 1868-70. 8vo., full green morocco. Wheldon 129-1651 1974 £30

DAVAINE, C.   Traite des Entozoaires et des Maladies Vermineuses de l'Homme et des Animaux Domestiques. Paris, 1860. 8vo., half morocco, rare, text-figures. Wheldon 128-889 1973 £20

DAVANNE, ALPHONSE   Recherches Theoriques et Pratiques sur la Formation des Epreuves Photographiques Positives. Paris, 1864. 8vo., leather backed boards, first edition. Schuman 37-57 1974 $110

DAVENANT, CHARLES   Discourses on the Publick Revenues. London, 1698. 2 vols., 8vo., contemporary panelled calf, first edition. Dawsons PM 247-64 1974 £150

DAVENANT, CHARLES   The True Picture of a Modern Whig. London, 1701. 8vo., uncut, fourth edition. Dawsons PM 251-434 1974 £30

D'AVENANT, CHARLES   Works. 1695-1701. 6 vols. in 5, 8vo., old calf, stained, worn. Quaritch 939-104 1974 £220

DAVENANT, WILLIAM   Gondibert. London, 1651. 4to., stains, contemporary calf. Bow Windows 62-239 1974 £105

DAVENANT, WILLIAM   The Man's the Master. London, 1775. 8vo., modern boards. Dawsons PM 252-233 1974 £6

DAVENANT, WILLIAM   Works. 1673. Folio, portrait, full tooled morocco, nice copy. Allen 216-1894 1974 $150

DAVENANT, WILLIAM   The Works. London, 1673. 19th century green blind-stamped calf, first folio edition. Dawsons PM 252-234 1974 £195

DAVENPORT, BISHOP   A New Gazetteer or Geographical Dictionary of North America and the West Indies. Philadelphia, c. 1838. Contemporary calf, rubbed, folding map, text maps, illus., marginal damp stain. Wilson 63-15 1974 $30

DAVENPORT, CYRIL   English Embroidered Bookbindings. 1899. Plates, full buckram, book-plate. Covent 55-240 1974 £45

DAVENPORT, CYRIL   English Embroidered Bookbindings. London, 1899. Small 4to., plates, orig. cloth, uncut. Dawsons PM 10-160 1974 £40

DAVENPORT, CYRIL   English Heraldic Book Stamps. London, 1909. 8vo., orig. cloth, illus. Dawsons PM 10-161 1974 £30

DAVENPORT, CYRIL   English Heraldic Book-Stamps. 1909. Roy. 8vo., illus., cloth, gilt. Quaritch 940-598 1974 £30

DAVENPORT, CYRIL   The English Regalia. 1897. Roy. 4to., plates, buckram, limited. Quaritch 939-715 1974 £15

DAVENPORT, CYRIL   Mezzotints. 1904. 8vo., red morocco by Bumpus, plates, dust spots. Bow Windows 66-167 1974 £16

DAVENPORT, CYRIL   Mezzotints. 1904. Japanese paper, fine. Covent 55-92 1974 £18

DAVENPORT, CYRIL   Roger Payne. Chicago, 1929. 4to., orig. cloth, uncut, plates, scarce, limited edition. Broadhurst 23-326 1974 £45

DAVENPORT, CYRIL   Royal English Bookbindings. London, 1896. 8vo., orig. red cloth gilt, illus., plates. Dawsons PM 10-162 1974 £30

DAVID, ERNEST   Erudes Historiques sur la Poesie et la Musique dans la Cambrie. Paris, 1884. Roy. 8vo., contemporary half calf, boards, orig. paper printed wrapper bound in, binding little rubbed, scarce, text illus. Broadhurst 24-1403 1974 £20

DAVID, HENRY   The History of the Haymarket Affair. New York, (1936). 8vo., orig. bindings. Butterfield 8-59 1974 $12.50

DAVID, HERMINE   Le Silence de la Mer. N.P., n.d. Square 8vo., inscribed, wrappers, English first edition. Covent 56-685 1974 £5.25

DAVID, SIR PERCIVAL VICTOR   A Catalogue of Chinese Pottery and Porcelain in the Collection of. 1934. Folio, worn cloth, portfolio, plates, silk binding, limited. Quaritch 940-384 1974 £450

DAVIDIS, HENRIETTE   Praktisches Kochbuch fur die Deutschen in Amerika. Milwaukee, (1879). Cloth, second American edition. Hayman 59-132 1974 $12.50

DAVIDMAN, JOY   Letter to a Comrade. New Haven, 1938. 1st ed. Biblo & Tannen 213-508 1973 $20

DAVIDSON, D.   A Connected History of Early Egypt, Babylonia, and Central Asia. Leeds, 1927. 4to. Biblo & Tannen 210-997 1973 $17.50

DAVIDSON, D.   The Great Pyramid. 1941. Roy. 8vo., plates, diagrams. Howes 186-1813 1974 £6.50

DAVIDSON, EDITH B.   Bunnikins-Bunnies in Camp. Boston and New York, 1909. 16mo., pict. boards, cloth spine; 4 color plates. Frohnsdorff 16-133 1974 $9.50

DAVIDSON, GABRIEL   Our Jewish Farmers and the Story of the Jewish Agriculture Society. Fischer, 1943. Austin 62-123 1974 $12.50

DAVIDSON, JOHN   Fleet Street Eclogues. 1893. Presentation copy, inscribed from author, buckram, gilt top, very nice copy, second edition. Covent 51-511 1973 £20

DAVIDSON, JOHN   The Great Men and A Practical Novelist. 1891. Illus., very good copy, orig. embossed cloth, scarce, first edition. Covent 51-2302 1973 £12.50

DAVIDSON, JOHN   An Investigation of the Native Rights of British Subjects. 1784. 8vo., unbound. Hill 126-67 1974 £5.50

DAVIDSON, JOHN   Notes Taken During Travels in Africa. London, 1839. 4to., orig. cloth, plates, foxed. Traylen 79-453 1973 £60

DAVIDSON, JOHN   Self's the Man. 1901. Library-label. Covent 55-561 1974 £6.50

DAVIDSON, NORA FONTAINE M.   Cullings from the Confederacy. Washington, 1903. Orig. wrapper bound in marbled boards and leather. Butterfield 10-152 1974 $20

DAVIDSON, T.   British Fossil Brachiopoda. 1851-86. 6 vols., 4to., half calf, rare, complete copy. Wheldon 131-988 1974 £130

DAVIDSON, T.   A Monograph of Recent Brachiopoda. 1886-88. 4to., boards, plates, scarce. Wheldon 130-859 1974 £20

DAVIE, JOHN CONSTANSE   Letters from Paraguay. London, 1805. 8vo., contemporary diced russia gilt, stained. Traylen 79-473 1973 £24

DAVIE, MAURICE R.   A Constructive Immigration Policy. 1923. 46 pages. Austin 57-164 1974 $10

DAVIE, MAURICE R.   World Immigration. 1936. 588 pages. Austin 57-165 1974 $10

DAVIE, MAURICE R.   World Immigration. Macmillan, 1936. Austin 62-125 1974 $10

DAVIE, W. G.   Architectural Studies in France. (c. 1877). Imp. folio, plates, half morocco rebacked. Quaritch 940-506 1974 £24

DAVIE, W. G.   Old Cottages, Farm-Houses and Other Stone Buildings in the Cotswold District. 1905. Dec. cloth gilt, plates, faded. Marsden 39-117 1974 £8

DAVIE, W. G.   Old English Doorways. 1903. Inscription, plates, orig. cloth. Marsden 39-118 1974 £6

DAVIES, ACTON   Maud Adams. Stokes, 1901. 110p., illus. Austin 51-240 1973 $10

DAVIES, E.   Celtic Researches on the Origin, Traditions and Language of the Ancient Britons. 1804. 8vo., half calf, plates. Quaritch 939-105 1974 £17.50

DAVIES, G. R.   Collection of Old Chinese Porcelains Formed By. 1913. Imp. 4to., plates, buckram. Quaritch 940-386 1974 £12

DAVIES, G. S.   Hans Holbein the Younger. 1903. Large folio, plates, buckram, dust wrapper. Quaritch 940-142 1974 £8

DAVIES, J.   The Ancient Rites and Monuments of the Monastical & Cathedral Church. 1672. Small 8vo., half calf, signature. Quaritch 939-346 1974 £25

DAVIES, J. C.   Life, Travels and Reminiscences of. 1927. 4to., plates, illus., cloth, limited, signed. Quaritch 939-681 1974 £50

DAVIES, J. N.   Souvenir, Eureka Volunteer Fire Department. Eureka, 1914. 8vo., wrapper. Saddleback 14-82 1974 $25

DAVIES, R.   Extracts from the Municipal Records of the
City of York. 1843. 8vo., cloth, worn. Quaritch 939-593 1974 £5

DAVIES, RANDALL   Thomas Girtin's Watercolours. 1924. Fine,
plates, vellum back, boards, gilt. Marsden 37-209 1974 £27

DAVIES, RHYS   Arfon, a Story. London, (1931). Limited to
400 numbered copies, signed by author, buckram, fine, d.w., inscribed. Crane
7-62 1974 £8.50

DAVIES, RHYS   A Bed of Feathers. London, (1929). First
edition, boards, fine, d.w., insribed by author, orig. cloth. Crane 7-59
1974 £6

DAVIES, RHYS   Count Your Blessings. London, 1932. First
edition, very nice copy, d.w., inscribed by author, orig. cloth, loosely inserted
A.L.s. from author. Crane 7-63 1974 £7.50

DAVIES, RHYS   Daisy Matthews and Three Other Tales. 1932.
Dec. cloth, morocco back, signed, limited edition. Marsden 37-362 1974 £21

DAVIES, RHYS   Honey and Bread. London, 1935. First edition,
very nice copy, d.w., inscribed by author, orig. cloth. Crane 7-66 1974 £6

DAVIES, RHYS   Jubilee Blues. London, 1938. First edition,
fine copy, d.w., orig. cloth, inscribed by author. Crane 7-68 1974 £6.50

DAVIES, RHYS   Love Provoked. London, 1933. First edition,
fine, worn d.w., inscribed by author, orig. cloth. Crane 7-65 1974 £6

DAVIES, RHYS   The Red Hills. London, 1932. First edition,
very nice copy, d.w., inscribed by author, orig. cloth. Crane 7-64 1974 £6

DAVIES, RHYS   Rings on Her Fingers. (1930). 8vo., orig.
cloth, limited, signed by author, first collectors edition. Bow Windows 66-169
1974 £7.50

DAVIES, RHYS   Rings on Her Fingers. London, 1930. First
edition, very fine, d.w., orig. cloth, inscribed by author. Crane 7-60 1974
£6.50

DAVIES, RHYS   Rings On Her Fingers. London, 1930. Ltd. to
175 copies, sgd. by author. Jacobs 24-78 1974 $10

DAVIES, RHYS   The Stars, the World, and the Women. 1930.
Frontis., Furnival Book no. 4, one of 550 copies, numbered & signed by author,
fine, buckram. Covent 51-519 1973 £5.25

DAVIES, RHYS   A Time to Laugh. London, 1937. First edition,
fine copy, d.w., inscribed by author, orig. cloth. Crane 7-67 1974 £5

DAVIES, RICHARD   An Account of the Convincement, Exercises,
Services and Travels of that Ancient Servant of the Lord. Golden Cockerel Press,
1928. Demy 8vo., buckram, uncut, fine, limited to 150 copies. Broadhurst
24-1007 1974 £36

DAVIES, RICHARD   An Account of the Convincement, Exercises, Services, and Travels of that Antient Servant of the Lord. 1928. 8vo., buckram,
gilt. Hammond 201-759 1974 £45

DAVIES, T.   Dramatic Miscellanies. 1784. 3 vols., boards,
labels defective, ex-library. Allen 216-2166 1974 $15

DAVIES, WILLIAM HENRY   The Autobiography of a Super-Tramp. New
York, 1925. 12mo. Biblo & Tannen 210-852 1973 $5

DAVIES, WILLIAM HENRY   Beggars. 1909. First edition, crown 8vo., orig.
cloth, exceptionally fine. Broadhurst 24-605 1974 £6

DAVIES, WILLIAM HENRY   The Bird of Paradise and Other Poems. Cloth
backed boards, fine, signed, presentation copy, English first edition. Covent 56-
297 1974 £10

DAVIES, WILLIAM HENRY   Forty New Poems. 1918. Small 8vo., cloth,
faded, first edition. Quaritch 936-359 1974 £8

DAVIES, WILLIAM HENRY   Forty-Nine Poems, Selected and Illustrated by
Jacynth Parsons. 1928. Coloured illus., demy 8vo., mint, d.w., orig. cloth,
board slip-in-case, limited special edition of 110 copies, signed by author & artist.
Broadhurst 24-611 1974 £10

DAVIES, WILLIAM HENRY   In Winter. 1931. First edition, med. 8vo.,
boards, paper printed labels, fine, one of 290 numbered copies, signed by author.
Broadhurst 24-613 1974 £5

DAVIES, WILLIAM HENRY   The Lovers' Song-Book. 1933. Cloth-backed
marbled boards, rubbed. Covent 55-784 1974 £40

DAVIES, WILLIAM HENRY   The Poems. 1934. First edition. Howes
185-98 1974 £5.50

DAVIES, WILLIAM HENRY   Raptures. 1918. 8vo., patterned boards, bookplate, first edition. Rota 189-224 1974 £5

DAVIES, WILLIAM HENRY   Selected Poems. 1928. 8vo., buckram, marbled
boards, frontispiece. Hammond 201-760 1974 £40

DAVIES, WILLIAM HENRY   Selected Poems. 1928. Marbled boards, canvas
spine and fore edges, portrait engraved, 310 copies on Jap. vellum. Thomas
32-281 1974 £40

DAVIES, WILLIAM HENRY   Selected Poems Of. 1928. 8vo., dec. boards,
uncut, limited edition. Broadhurst 23-1037 1974 £30

DAVIES, WILLIAM HENRY   The Song of a Life and Other Poems. London,
1920. First edition. Biblo & Tannen 213-510 1973 $8.50

DAVIES, WILLIAM HENRY   The True Traveller. 1912. First edition, crown
8vo., orig. cloth, exceptionally fine. Broadhurst 24-606 1974 £6

D'AVILER, AUGUSTIN CHARLES
Please turn to
AVILER, AUGUSTIN CHARLES D'

DAVIS, A.   History of New Amsterdam: Or, New York As
It Was. New York, 1854. Orig. cloth, gilt. Jenkins 61-1876 1974 $10

DAVIS, A.   History of New Amsterdam: or, New York as it
Was Then. New York, 1854. Orig. cloth, gilt. Jenkins 61-2145 1974 $10

DAVIS, ANDREW JACKSON   The Diakka, and Their Earthly Victims. Boston,
(1873). Cloth. Dawson's 424-263 1974 $10

DAVIS, JR., ARTHUR KYLE   Traditional Ballads of Virginia. Cambridge,
1929. 8vo., orig. bindings. Butterfield 8-674 1974 $22.50

DAVIS, B. P.   The Davis Family and the Leather Industry.
Toronto, 1934. Full calf. Hood's 102-372 1974 $22.50

DAVIS, BETTE   The Lonely Life. Putnam, 1962. 254p., illus.
Austin 51-241 1973 $7.50

DAVIS, BRITTON   The Truth About Geronimo. New Haven,
1929. Jenkins 61-935 1974 $12.50

DAVIS, C. H.   Narrative of the North Polar Expedition.
Washington, 1876. Engravings, maps, staining. Hood's 104-77 1974 $65

DAVIS, CHARLES F.   The Monrovia Blue Book. Monrovia, 1943.
4to., cloth. Saddleback 14-83 1974 $35

DAVIS, E. A.   Commemorative Review of the Methodist,
Presbyterian and Congregational Churches in British Columbia. Vancouver,
1925. Hood's 104-300 1974 $10

DAVIS, E. A.   Commemorative Review of the Methodist,
Presbyterian and Congregational Churches in British Columbia. Vancouver, 1925.
Some wear. Hood's 102-282 1974 $10

DAVIS, ELMER   Friends of Mr. Sweeney. McBride, 1925.
282p. Austin 54-277 1973 $7.50

DAVIS, FREDERIK   The History of Luton. 1855. Orig. cloth,
plates, map, worn. Howes 186-1973 1974 £5

DAVIS, GEORGE   Report of the Attorney General. Richmond,
1864. Jenkins 61-623 1974 $12.50

DAVIS, H. W. C.   Mediaeval England. Oxford, 1924. Demy
8vo., illus., orig. cloth, fine. Broadhurst 24-1223 1974 £6

DAVIS, HUGH   Welsh Botanology. London, 1813. 8vo.,
orig. boards, uncut, plate. Traylen 79-12 1973 £10

DAVIS, J. R. A.   The Natural History of Animals. 1903-04.
4 vols. in 8, 4to., cloth, plates. Wheldon 131-427 1974 £5

DAVIS, JAMES   Selective Immigration. St. Paul, MN, 1925.
Austin 62-126 1974 $12.50

DAVIS, JEFFERSON   Information Respecting the Purchase of Camels
for the Purpose of Military Transportation. Washington, 1857. Orig. cloth,
fine illus. Jenkins 61-759 1974 $60

DAVIS, JEFFERSON   Message from the President . . . Relative to
the Amount of Money Forwarded to the Trans-Mississippi Department. Richmond,
1864. Jenkins 61-624 1974 $12.50

DAVIS, JEFFERSON   President's Message. Richmond, 1863. Sewn.
Jenkins 61-632 1974 $22.50

DAVIS, JEFFERSON   Regulations for the U. S. Military Academy at
West Pint. New York, 1853. Very scarce. Jenkins 61-761 1974 $25

DAVIS, JOHN FRANCIS   The Fortunate Union. London, 1829. 2 vols.,
8vo., orig. boards, first English edition. Dawsons PM 252-235 1974 £45

DAVIS, MARY GOULD   Randolph Caldecott. Philadelphia, 1946.
4to., cloth, illus. Frohnsdorff 16-168 1974 $15

DAVIS, N.   Carthage and Her Remains. 1861. 8vo.,
maps, plates, half calf. Quaritch 940-311 1974 £20

DAVIS, OSCAR KING   Some Inside Political History of Theodore
Roosevelt and His Times, 1898-1918. Boston, 1925. Biblo & Tannen 213-94
1973 $8.50

DAVIS, OWEN   I'd Like To Do It Again. Farrar, Rinehart,
1931. 233p., illus. Austin 51-242 1973 $7.50

DAVIS, OWEN   Mr. and Mrs. North. French, 1941. 161p.,
paper. Austin 51-243 1973 $7.50

DAVIS, PHILIP   Immigration and Americanization. 1920.
770 pages. Austin 57-166 1974 $15

DAVIS, PHILIP   Immigration and Americanization. 1920. Austin
62-127 1974 $17.50

DAVIS, RICHARD HARDING   Our English Cousins. New York, 1894. First
edition, first state, illus., former owner's rubber stamp, orig. binding, very good
copy. Wilson 63-503C 1974 $10

DAVIS, RICHARD HARDING   The Novels and Stories of. New York, 1920.
12 vols., illus., orig. binding. Wilson 63-505 1974 $37.50

DAVIS, RICHARD HARDING   The Red Cross Girl. New York, 1912. 1st ed.
Biblo & Tannen 213-509 1973 $15

DAVIS, RICHARD HARDING   Vera the Medium. New York, 1908. First
edition, orig. binding. Wilson 63-504 1974 $15

DAVIS, RICHARD HARDING   West from a Car-Window. 1892. Illus. by
Remington, worn. Allen 216-412 1974 $15

DAVIS, RICHARD HARDING   With the Allies. 1915. Plates, faded.
Covent 55-1566 1974 £7.50

DAVIS, ROBERT TYLER   Native Arts of the Pacific Northwest.
Stanford, 1949. 4to., color plates., scarce. Biblo & Tannen 213-271 1973
$42.50

DAVIS, SAM P.   The History of Nevada. Reno, 1913. 2 vols.,
8vo., three quarter leather. Saddleback 14-537 1974 $200

DAVIS, THOMAS   General View of the Agriculture of the County of
Wilts. London, 1794. 4to., boards, first edition. Hammond 201-9 1974 £26

DAVIS, THOMAS   General View of the Agriculture of Wiltshire.
1813. 8vo., orig. boards, rebacked. Hammond 201-10 1974 £18

DAVIS, W. M.   The Coral Reef Problem. New York, 1928.
Roy. 8vo., cloth, scarce. Wheldon 131-306 1974 £15

DAVIS, W. W. H.   El Gringo. New York, 1857. Orig. cloth,
worn, first edition. Putnam 126-325 1974 $20

DAVIS, WARREN B.   Development and Anatomy of the Nasal
Accessory Sinuses in Man. Philadelphia, 1914. Rittenhouse 46-703 1974 $10

DAVIS, WILLIAM   Seventy Five Years in California. San
Francisco, 1929. Maps, plates, top edge gilt, limited edition. Jenkins 61-308
1974 $60

DAVIS-DU BOIS, RACHEL   Adventures in Intercultural Education.
1938. Austin 62-128 1974 $17.50

DAVIS-DU BOIS, RACHEL   Know Your Neighbors. 1955. Austin 62-129
1974 $12.50

DAVISON, ARCHIBALD T.   Historical Anthology of Music. Cambridge,
Mass., 1949. 4to. Biblo & Tannen 214-833 1974 $10

DAVISON, CHARLES   Autoplastic Bone Surgery. Philadelphia,
1916. Rittenhouse 46-199 1974 $15

DAVISON, FRANCIS   Poetical Rhapsody. 1826. 2 vols. Allen
216-1896 1974 $17.50

DAVISON, PHINEAS   Evangelical Poems. (Palmer) & Greenwich,
1810. 16mo., orig. calf over wooden boards, first edition. Goodspeed's
578-76 1974 $100

DAVY, HUMPHREY   Elements of Agricultural Chemistry. London, 18-
14. 8vo., contemporary half calf, gilt, plates, second edition. Hammond 201-11
1974 £18

DAWKINS, W. BOYD   Early Man In Britain and His Place In the
Tertiary Period. London, 1880. Rittenhouse 46-200 1974 $25

DAWSON, CHARLES   History of Hastings Castle. 1909. Imperial
8vo., 2 vols., orig. cloth, fine. Broadhurst 23-1367 1974 £10

DAWSON, CHARLES   History of Hastings Castle. 1909. 2 vols.,
imp. 8vo., orig. cloth, illus., scarce. Howes 186-2199 1974 £15

DAWSON, K.   Marsh and Mudflat. 1931. Roy. 8vo., cloth,
plates. Wheldon 128-420 1973 £5

DAWSON, K.   Marsh and Mudflat. 1931. Roy 8vo., cloth,
plates. Wheldon 130-494 1974 £5

DAWSON, LIONEL   Sport in War. 1936. 4to., plates, orig.
buckram, illus., first edition. Howes 185-144 1974 £5

DAWSON, LUCY   Lucy Dawson's Dogs. Racine, 1938. 4to., illus. Frohnsdorff 16-269 1974 $5

DAWSON, S. E.   A Study, With Critical and Explanatory Notes, of Lord Tennyson's Poem, The Princess. Montreal, 1884. Second edition. Hood's 103-403 1974 $10

DAWSON, SAMUEL EDWARD   The St. Lawrence, Its Basin & Borderlands. New York, (1905). Maps, illus., orig. binding. Butterfield 10-136 1974 $17.50

DAWSON, W. J.   The Father of a Soldier. Toronto, 1918. Hood's 102-101 1974 $7.50

DAWSON, WARREN   The Beginnings Egypt & Assyria. New York, 1930. Ex-library. Rittenhouse 46-201 1974 $10

DAWYDOFF, C.   Traite d'Embryologie Comparee des Invertebres. Paris, 1928. Roy. 8vo., buckram, text-figures, rare orig. printing. Wheldon 128-891 1973 £20

DAY, CLARENCE   After All. Knopf, 1936. 316p., illus. Austin 54-278 1973 $6

DAY, CLARENCE   The Crow's Nest. Knopf, 1921. 222p., illus. Austin 54-279 1973 $6

DAY, CLARENCE   God and My Father. Knopf, 1932. 83p. Austin 54-280 1973 $5

DAY, CLARENCE   This Simian World. Knopf, 1920. 95p., illus. Austin 54-281 1973 $5

DAY, DONALD   Will Rogers. McKay, 1962. 370p., illus. Austin 54-874 1973 $6

DAY, F.   The Fishes of India. n.d. 4to., orig. cloth portfolio, worn, plates. Wheldon 130-679 1974 £15

DAY, J. W.   The Modern Fowler. 1934. 8vo., plates, cloth, illus. Quaritch 939-106 1974 £7.50

DAY, LEWIS F.   Ornament and Its Application. London, 1904. lst ed., illus. Biblo & Tannen 210-116 1973 $10

DAY, LILLIAN   Death Comes on Friday. New York, 1937. lst ed., author's sgd. pres. Biblo & Tannen 210-441 1973 $12.50

DAY, MRS. FRANK R.   The Princess of Manoa and Other Romantic Tales. San Francisco and New York, (1906). Tall 8vo., orig. bindings. Butterfield 8-134 1974 $15

DAY, ST. JOHN V.   The Prehistoric Use of Iron and Steel. 1877. 8vo., plates, cloth, presentation copy, scarce. Quaritch 940-312 1974 £12

DAY, THOMAS   The History of Sandford and Merton. London, 1808. 12mo., contemporary sheep. Dawsons PM 252-236 1974 £15

DAY, THOMAS   The History of Sandford and Merton. 1829. 12mo., plates, contemporary purple calf, faded. Howes 186-285 1974 £5

DAY, THOMAS   Reflexions Upon the Present State of England. London, 1782. 8vo., uncut, second edition. Dawsons PM 247-65 1974 £80

DAYOT, A.   Grands et Petits Maitres Hollandais. 1912. Imp. 4to., plates, illus., half morocco, rubbed, orig. wrapper, uncut, limited edition. Quaritch 940-79 1974 £28

DAYTON, KATHERINE   First Lady. Random House, 1935. 194p. Austin 51-244 1973 $8.50

DAY-LEWIS, CECIL   Anatomy of Oxford. 1938. Small stain on lower cover, very good copy, first edition. Covent 51-2304 1973 £10

DAY-LEWIS, CECIL   Child of Misfortune. 1939. Fine, worn d.w., first edition. Covent 51-521 1973 £12.50

DAY, C. L.   English Song-Books, 1651-1702. London, 1940. F'scap 4to., orig. boards, holland back, fine. Forster 98-7 1974 £40

DAY-LEWIS, CECIL   Noah and the Waters. 1936. One of 100 numbered copies, signed by author, very fine copy, d.w., first edition. Covent 51-522 1973 £45

DAY LEWIS, CECIL   Orion. London, 1945. Vol. 2, fine, orig. binding, without d.w. Ross 86-116 1974 $12.50

DAY-LEWIS, CECIL   Poems in Wartime. 1940. One of 250 numbered copies, fine, scarce, first edition. Covent 51-523 1973 £25

DAY LEWIS, CECIL   Ten Singers, an Anthology. London, 1925. Unopened, very slight rubbing of covers, mint, orig. binding. Ross 86-118 1974 $35

DAY-LEWIS, CECIL   Transitional Poem. 1929. Orig. boards. Smith 193-387 1973 £6

DAY LEWIS, C.   We're Not Going to do Nothing. 1936. Wrappers, English first edition. Covent 56-299 1974 £6.30

DEACON, THOMAS   The History of the Village of Willoughby. London, 1828. 8vo., half calf, gilt, first edition. Hammond 201-567 1974 £15

DEAKIN, R.   Flora of the Colosseum of Rome. Groombridge, 1855. Crown 8vo., orig. cloth, worn, plates. Wheldon 131-1280 1974 £7.50

DEALINGS With the Dead. Boston, 1856. Frontis., well rebound 19th century cloth backed boards, nice copy. Covent 51-2494 1973 £12

DEAN, ALEXANDER   Fundamentals of Play Directing. Farrar & Rinehart, 1941. 428p., illus. Austin 51-245 1973 $10

DEAN, H. H.   Canadian Dairying. Toronto, 1920. Fifth edition, revised, illus. Hood's 102-373 1974 $7.50

DEAN, HOWARD   The Iron Hand. New York, (1898). Cloth. Hayman 59-174 1974 $12.50

DEANE, ETHEL   The Collector. 1903. Frontispiece, illus., buckram. Covent 55-437 1974 £5.50

DEANE, JOHN   A Narrative of the Shipwreck of the Nottingham Galley. (London), 1738. 8vo., modern boards, very uncommon. Ximenes 36-66 1974 $150

DEANE, SAMUEL   The New-England Farmer. Worcester, 1790. 8vo., contemporary speckled calf, first edition. Dawsons PM 247-66 1974 £70

DE ANGELI, MARGUERITE   Copper-Toed Boots. New York, 1939. Small 4to., cloth, illus., lst ed. Frohnsdorff 16-270 1974 $10

DE ANGELI, MARGUERITE   The Door in the Wall. New York, 1949. 8vo., lst ed., illus. Frohnsdorff 16-271 1974 $10

DE ANGELI, MARGUERITE   Elin's Amerika. New York, 1941. Large Square 8vo., cloth, illus., mint, dust jacket, first edition. Frohnsdorff 15-23 1974 $10

DE ANGELI, MARGUERITE   Elin's Amerika. New York, 1941. Small 4to., cloth, lst ed., illus. Frohnsdorff 16-272 1974 $10

DE ANGELI, MARGUERITE   Henner's Lydia. New York, 1936. Small 4to., cloth, lst ed., illus. Frohnsdorff 16-273 1974 $15

DE ANGELI, MARGUERITE   Henner's Lydia. New York, 1936. Square 8vo., pict. boards, cloth spine, illus., very fine copy, dust jacket, first edition, autographed by author. Frohnsdorff 15-24 1974 $20

DE ANGELI, MARGUERITE   Skippack School. New York, 1939. Small 4to., cloth, lst ed., illus. Frohnsdorff 16-275 1974 $7.50

DE ANGELI, MARGUERITE   A Summer Day With Ted and Nina. New York, 1940. Square 8vo., pictorial boards, illus. by author, mint copy, dust jacket, first edition. Frohnsdorff 15-22 1974 $10

DE ANGELI, MARGUERITE   Thee, Hannah. New York, 1940. Cloth, illus., very good copy, dust jacket, first edition. Frohnsdorff 15-25 1974 $10

DE ANGELI, MARGUERITE   Thee, Hannah! New York, 1940. Small 4to., cloth, lst ed., illus. Frohnsdorff 16-274 1974 $10

DE ANGELI, MARGUERITE   Yonie Wondernose. New York, 1944. 4to., cloth, lst ed., illus. Frohnsdorff 16-276 1974 $7.50

DEARBORN INDEPENDENT   The International Jew. Vol l., 1920. Austin 62-132 1974 $12.50

DEARBORN INDEPENDENT   Jewish Influences in American Life. 1921. Austin 62-133 1974 $12.50

DEARN, MAY   A Real Ghost and Other Christmas Stories. 1892. 8vo., orig. cloth, first edition. Rota 190-827 1974 £10

DEASE, EDMUND F.   A Complete History of the Westmeath Hunt from Its Foundation. Dublin, 1898. 4to., illus. Emerald 50-204 1974 £10

DEBAYE, J.   The Industrial Arts of the Anglo-Saxons. 1893. 4to., plates, dec. cloth gilt. Covent 55-93 1974 £15.75

DEBEAUX, O.   Synopsis de la Flore de Gilbraltar. Bordeaux, 1889. Roy 8vo., half calf, plate, map. Wheldon 129-1063 1974 £5

DE BEER, G. R.   Early Travellers in the Alps. 1930. 8vo., cloth, plates, scarce. Wheldon 129-137 1974 £5

DE BEER, G. R.   Growth. 1924. 8vo., cloth, plates, scarce. Wheldon 130-350 1974 £5

DE BELLOY, A.   Christophe Colomb et la Decouverte du Nouveau Monde. Paris, n.d. Illus., pict. cloth, gilt edges. Jenkins 61-553 1974 $10

DE BIASI, AGOSTINO   La Batlaglia Dell'Italia Negli Stati Uniti. 1927. 408 pages. Austin 57-172 1974 $37.50

DEBIERRE, CHARLES   Malformations of the Genital Organs of Woman. Philadelphia, 1905. Illus. Rittenhouse 46-203 1974 $15

DEBORAH Dent and Her Donkey. 1887. Square 8vo., engravings, wrappers, dust-stained. Covent 55-997 1974 £15.75

DE BOTELLA, D. FEDERICO   Descripcion Geologica-Minera de las Provincais de Murcia y Albacete. Madrid, 1868. Folio, old quarter leather, plates, rubbed, presentation copy. Traylen 79-80 1973 £18

DEBRAW, J.   Discoveries on the Sex of Bees Explaining the Manner in Which Their Species is Propagated. 1777. 8vo. Wheldon 131-798 1974 £5

DE BREE, JOHN   Pay Table for the Use of Pursers and Others of the United States Navy. Washington, 1846. Rittenhouse 46-204 1974 $12

DE BRUNHOFF, JEAN   Babar and Father Christmas. New York, (1940). Small folio, binding bit loose, few pencil scratches. Current BW9-25 1974 $10

DE BRY, JOHANN THEODOR
Please turn to
BRY, JOHANN THEODOR DE

DEBSON, AUSTIN   Horace Walpole: A Memoir. 1927. Fourth edition revised, plates, buckram, very nice copy, spare title label tipped in. Covent 51-1912 1973 £5

DEBURE, GUILLAUME FRANCOIS   Bibliographie Instructive. Paris, 1763-82. 10 vols., post 8vo., contemporary mottled calf, bit rubbed, spines gilt. Forster 98-11 1974 £75

DEBURE, GUILLAUME FRANCOIS   Bibliographie Instructive. 10 vols., one of 50 large paper copies on papier de Hollande, f'scap 4to., contemporary calf, bit rubbed but sound, text fine. Forster 98-12 1974 £95

DEBURE, GUILLAUME FRANCOIS   Bibliographie Instructive: ou Traite de la Connoissance des Livres Rares et Singuliers. Paris, 1763-68. 7 vols., calf, contemporary mottled calf. Kraus B8-47 1974 $125

DE BURE, J. J.   Catalogue des Livres Rares et Precieux. Paris, 1853. 8vo., contemporary blue cloth. Dawsons PM 10-166 1974 £10

DE CASSERES, BENJAMIN   The Anatomy of America's Voltaire and England's Other John Bull. New York, (1930). Scarce, d.j., orig. binding. Butterfield 10-406 1974 $20

DE CAUZONS, THOMAS   La Magie et la Sorcellerie en France. Paris, n.d. Cracking. Rittenhouse 46-205 1974 $35

DE CHAIR, SOMERSET   The Silver Crescent. Golden Cockerel Press, (1943). Limited to 500 copies, illus., large 8vo., white cloth sides, blue morocco backs, uncut, top edges gilt, good copy, presentation copy by author. Sawyer 293-148 1974 £18.90

DE CHAIR, SOMERSET   The Silver Crescent. 1943. Crown 4to., quarter blue morocco, uncut. Broadhurst 23-1011 1974 £25

DE CHAIR, SOMERSET   The Silver Crescent. (1943). 4to., full dark blue morocco, slip case, maps, fine, signed by author. Bow Windows 66-289 1974 £68

DE CIERLYKE Voorsnydinge aller Tafel-Gerechten. Amersterdam, (1644?). Oblong 8vo., vellum, fine, plates, complete copy. Harper 213-32 1973 $475

DECISIONS of the General Land Office . . . On Keystone Mining Co., Original Armidor Mining Co., et. al, Versus the State of California. Washington, 1873. Wrapper. Jenkins 61-312 1974 $10

DECISION of the General Land Office Upon the Surveys of the Ranchos Lampoc, La Purisma, Mission Viego of La Purisma, Santa Ritaand Canada de Salsipuedes. Washington, 1872. Wrapper. Jenkins 61-1655 1974 $10

DECIUS, PHILIPPUS   De Regulis Iuris. Lyon, 1521. Small 8vo., contemporary limp vellum, some stains and browning. Thomas 32-229 1974 £36

DECKER, MATTHEW   Serous Considerations on the Several High Duties. London, 1743. 8vo., uncut. Quaritch 939-107 1974 £18

DECKER, MATHEW   Serious Considerations of the Several High Duties. London, 1743. 8vo., modern boards, first edition. Dawsons PM 247-67 1974 £40

A DECLARATION of His Majesties Royall Pleasure. 1619. 4to., modem grey boards, second edition. Dawsons PM 251-215 1974 £45

A DECLARATION of the Just Causes of His Majesties Proceeding Against Those Ministers Attainted of High Treason. London, 1606. Small 4to., disbound, first edition. Ximenes 35-132 1974 $45

DECORATOR'S Assistant, Vol. 1. 1847. Cloth, worn, engravings. Eaton Music-568 1973 £15

DE COSTER, CHARLES   Contes Brabancons. Paris, 1861. 8vo., contemporary tan three quarter hard grain morocco, excellent copy, first edition. L. Goldschmidt 42-201 1974 $80

DE COURSEY, ELBERT   Atlas of Ophthalmic Pathology. Omaha, 1942. Rittenhouse 46-704 1974 $10

THE DEDICATION of the Bennington Battle Monument, and Celebration of the Hundredth Anniversary of the Admission of Vermont as a State, at Bennington, August 19, A.D., 1891. Bennington, 1892. Wrapper, chipped, illus. Jenkins 61-2501 1974 $10

THE DEED Of Settlement of the Society for Equitable Assurances On Lives and Survivorships. London, 1801. 8vo., uncut, plain boards. Dawsons PM 247-274 1974 £13

A DEFENCE of Southern Slavery, Against the Attacks of Henry Clay and Alex'r Campbell. Hamburg, 1851. Self wrapper, stitched as issued. Butterfield 10-101 1974 $35

DEFOE, DANIEL   An Account of the Conduct of Robert Earl of Oxford. London, 1715. 8vo., half calf antique, first edition. Dawsons PM 247-80 1974 £85

DEFOE, DANIEL   Advice to all Parties. 1705. Small 4to., uncut, first edition. Quaritch 936-40 1974 £50

DEFOE, DANIEL   Advice to the People of Great Britain. 1714. 8vo., fine, uncut, cloth, first edition. Quaritch 936-41 1974 £50

DEFOE, DANIEL   An Answer to the Late K. James's Last Declaration. London, 1693. 4to., calf antique, fine, uncut, first edition. Dawsons PM 252-237 1974 £110

DEFOE, DANIEL   An Appeal to Honour and Justice. 1715. 8vo., cloth, uncut, inscription, rare, first edition. Quaritch 936-42 1974 £110

DEFOE, DANIEL   Armageddon. London, n.d. 8vo., modern boards, first edition. Dawsons PM 247-73 1974 £150

DEFOE, DANIEL   A Brief State of the Question. London, 1719. 8vo., calf antique, fine, first edition. Dawsons PM 247-84 1974 £230

DEFOE, DANIEL   The Chimera. London, 1720. 8vo., label, contemporary calf, first edition. Dawsons PM 247-85 1974 £285

DEFOE, DANIEL   The Conduct of the Parties in England. 1712. 8vo., modern boards, first edition. Dawsons PM 252-238 1974 £150

DEFOE, DANIEL   Conjugal Lewdness. London, 1727. 8vo., full morocco gilt, fine, first edition. Dawsons PM 252-239 1974 £275

DEFOE, DANIEL   The Consolidator. London, 1705. 8vo., contemporary panelled calf, first edition. Dawsons PM 247-71 1974 £130

DEFOE, DANIEL   The Dyet of Poland. Dantzick, (1705). 4to., modern boards, stained, first edition. Dawsons PM 252-240 1974 £170

DEFOE, DANIEL   The Dyet of Poland. 1705. 4to., full red levant morocco, first edition. Quaritch 936-44 1974 £260

DEFOE, DANIEL   An Elegy on the Author of the True Born English-Man. London, 1704. 4to., disbound, stained, first edition. Dawsons PM 252-241 1974 £180

DEFOE, DANIEL   Eleven Opinions. London, 1711. 8vo., mocern marbled boards, first edition. Dawsons PM 252-242 1974 £55

DEFOE, DANIEL   An Enquiry into Occasional Conformity. 1702. Small 4to., cloth, first edition. Quaritch 936-45 1974 £70

DEFOE, DANIEL   The Evident Advantages to Great Britain and Its Allies from the Approaching War. London, 1727. 8vo., paper wrappers, first edition. Dawsons PM 247-88 1974 £150

DEFOE, DANIEL   An Essay at a Plain Exposition of that Difficult Phrase a Good Peace. 1711. 8vo., uncut, cloth, first edition. Quaritch 936-46 1974 £65

DEFOE, DANIEL   An Essay on the South-Sea Trade. London, 1712. 8vo., calf antique, first edition. Dawsons PM 247-74 1974 £325

DEFOE, DANIEL   The Four Years Voyages of Capt. George Roberts. London, 1726. 8vo., 19th century panelled calf, gilt, first edition. Dawsons PM 252-243 1974 £220

DEFOE, DANIEL   The Fortunes and Misfortunes of the Famous Moll Flanders. 1929. Roy 8vo., orig. dec. buckram gilt, presentation copy, inscribed, English first edition. Covent 56-672 1974 £15.75

DEFOE, DANIEL   A Friendly Rebuke to One Parson Benjamin. London, 1719. 8vo., modern quarter calf, first edition. Dawsons PM 252-244 1974 £80

DEFOE, DANIEL   A General History of Discoveries and Improvements. London, n.d. 8vo., contemporary calf, first edition. Dawsons PM 247-87 1974 £475

DEFOE, DANIEL   The Great Law of Subordination Consider'd. London, 1724. 8vo., panelled calf antique, first edition. Dawsons PM 247-86 1974 £95

DEFOE, DANIEL   The History of the Great Plague in London. London, 1754. 8vo., modern quarter calf, modern boards, second edition. Dawsons PM 252-245 1974 £75

DEFOREST, JOHN W.   History of the Indians of Connecticut from the Earliest Known Period to 1850. Hartford, 1851. Illus., map. Jenkins 61-690 1974 $65

DEFOE, DANIEL   The History of the Union Between England and Scotland. London, 1786. 4to., contemporary half calf, fine, gilt. Dawsons PM 252-246 1974 £60

DEFOE, DANIEL   The History of the Wars. London, 1715. 8vo., contemporary calf, fine, first edition. Dawsons PM 252-247 1974 £80

DEFOE, DANIEL   An Impartial Account of the Late Famous Siege of Gibraltar. 1728. Small 8vo., orig. wrappers, first edition. Quaritch 936-47 1974 £90

DEFOE, DANIEL   An Impartial Enquiry. London, 1717. 8vo., modern quarter morocco, first edition. Dawsons PM 252-248 1974 £75

DEFOE, DANIEL   Jure Divino. London, 1706. Folio, label contemporary panelled calf, first edition. Dawsons PM 252-249 1974 £120

DEFOE, DANIEL   King William's Affection to the Church of England. London, 1703. 4to., half calf antique, first edition. Dawsons PM 252-250 1974 £55

DEFOE, DANIEL   A Letter from Captain Tom to the Mobb. (London, 1710). 8vo., old half calf, first edition. Dawsons PM 252-251 1974 £300

DEFOE, DANIEL   A Letter from a Member of the House of Commons to His Friend in the Country. London, 1713. 8vo., modern boards, first edition. Dawsons PM 247-76 1974 £115

DEFOE, DANIEL   A Letter from Captain Tom to the Mobb. 1710. Small 8vo., disbound, first edition. Quaritch 936-48 1974 £200

DEFOE, DANIEL   The Life and Adventures of Robinson Crusoe. 1864. Crown 4to., illus., orig. purple morocco grained cloth. Smith 193-650 1973 £7.50

DEFOE, DANIEL   The Life and Strange Surprizing Adventures of Robinson Crusoe. London, 1719 & 1720. 8vo., olive green morocco gilt, bookplate, frontispiece, first edition. Dawsons PM 250-20 1974 £4800

DEFOE, DANIEL   The Life and Strange Surprising Adventures of Robinson Crusoe of York, Mariner. New York, Limited Editions Club, 1930. Illus., orig. cloth, limited, signed by illus., boxed, fine. MacManus 224-188 1974 $40

DEFOE, DANIEL   The Life and Suprizing Adventures of Robinson Crusoe of York, Mariner. London, 1929. Rag paper, illus., fine, blue cloth. Ballinger 1-123 1974 $12.50

DEFOE, DANIEL   Lives and Adventures of the Most Celebrated Highwaymen. London, n.d. 8vo., finely bound red morocco. Dawsons PM 251-111 1974 £95

DEFOE, DANIEL   Madagascar. London, 1729. 8vo., plates, contemporary calf gilt, first edition.   Dawsons PM 252-252 1974 £200

DEFOE, DANIEL   Memoirs of Capt. George Carleton. Edinburgh & London, 1809. 8vo., contemporary half calf, fourth edition. Dawsons PM 252-253 1974 £25

DEFOE, DANIEL   Memoirs of Count Tariff. London, 1713. 8vo., modern quarter calf, first edition. Dawsons PM 247-75 1974 £110

DEFOE, DANIEL   Memoirs of the Church of Scotland. 1717. 8vo., contemporary panelled calf, first edition.   Hill 126-68 1974 £60

DEFOE, DANIEL   Memoirs of the Church of Scotland. London, 1717. 8vo., modern marbled boards, first edition. Dawsons PM 252-254 1974 £110

DEFOE, DANIEL   Memoirs of the Conduct of Her Late Majesty and Her Last Ministry. 1715. 8vo., modern half calf, gilt, first edition. Quaritch 936-49 1974 £90

DEFOE, DANIEL   Minutes of the Negotiations of Monsr. Mesnager. London, 1717. 8vo., contemporary panelled calf, first edition. Dawsons PM 252-255 1974 £70

DEFOE, DANIEL   A New Test of the Church of England's Loyalty. 1702. 4to., modern marbled paper wrappers, first edition. Dawsons PM 252-256 1974 £65

DEFOE, DANIEL   A New Voyage Round the World. London, 1725. 2 parts in 1 vol., 8vo., plates, contemporary panelled calf, first edition. Dawsons PM 252-257 1974 £145

DEFOE, DANIEL   No Queen. London, 1712. 8vo., modern quarter morocco, first edition. Dawsons PM 252-258 1974 £85

DEFOE, DANIEL   Novels and Miscellaneous Works. Oxford, 1840-41. 12mo., 20 vols., half calf, gilt. Quaritch 936-39 1974 £100

DEFOE, DANIEL   The Novels and Miscellaneous Works of. London, 1871. 7 vols., 8vo., frontispiece, contemporary half calf. Dawsons PM 252-272 1974 £28

DEFOE, DANIEL   Novels and Selected Writings. Oxford, 1927-28. 14 vols., 8vo., fine, orig. cloth, limited edition. Dawsons PM 252-273 1974 £245

DEFOE, DANIEL   A Plan of the English Commerce. London, 1728. 8vo., modern quarter calf, gilt, first edition. Dawsons PM 247-89 1974 £240

DEFOE, DANIEL   The Political History of the Devil. London, 1726. 8vo., contemporary panelled calf, frontispiece, first edition. Dawsons PM 252-259 1974 £85

DEFOE, DANIEL   The Present State of Jacobitism Considered. London, 1701. 4to., modern sprinkled half calf, fine, first edition. Dawsons PM 252-260 1974 £210

DEFOE, DANIEL   The Pretences of the French Invasion Examined. London, 1692. 4to., marbled paper wrappers, first edition. Dawsons PM 252-261 1974 £165

DEFOE, DANIEL   Reasons Against a War With France. London, 1701. 4to., unbound, fine, first edition. Dawsons PM 247-70 1974 £95

DEFOE, DANIEL   Reasons for Impeaching the Lord High Treasurer. (1714). Small 4to., half calf, first edition. Quaritch 936-51 1974 £80

DEFOE, DANIEL   Reformation of Manners. 1702. First edition, small 4to., disbound, slightly browned, little dampstained, very scarce. Broadhurst 24-615 1974 £35

DEFOE, DANIEL   Reformation of Manners. 1702. Small 4to., disbound, first edition. Broadhurst 23-658 1974 £40

DEFOE, DANIEL   Reformation of Manners. 1702. Small 4to., cloth, gilt, first edition.   Quaritch 936-52 1974 £60

DEFOE, DANIEL   A Reply to a Pamphlet. London, 1706. 4to., modern quarter morocco, first edition. Dawsons PM 247-72 1974 £80

DEFOE, DANIEL   The Re-Representation. 1711. 8vo., cloth, first edition.   Quaritch 936-54 1974 £50

DEFOE, DANIEL   Robinson Crusoe. London, ca. 1890. Large 4to., pict. wrappers, 8 chromolithograph plates. Frohnsdorff 16-278 1974 $7.50

DEFOE, DANIEL   The Adventures of Robinson Crusoe. New York, (c. 1890). 8vo., full page full color illus., spine rebacked, else fine. Current BW9-99 1974 $15.75

DEFOE, DANIEL   Robinson Crusoe Arranged in Words of One Syllable for Young Children by Mary Godolphin. 1904. Small 4to., orig. illus. cloth, spine little worn, illus. Bow Windows 66-170 1974 £6.15

DEFOE, DANIEL   A Second Letter from a Country Whig. London, 1715. 8vo., modern boards, first edition. Dawsons PM 247-81 1974 £35

DEFOE, DANIEL   The Secret History of State Intrigues in the Management of the Scepter. 1715. Small 8vo., modern marbled boards. Quaritch 936-55 1974 £80

DEFOE, DANIEL   The Secret History of the White-Staff. London, 1714. 8vo., modern quarter morocco, uncut, first edition. Dawsons PM 247-77 1974 £90

DEFOE, DANIEL   Secret Memoirs of a Treasonable Conference. London, 1717. 8vo., modern boards, first edition. Dawsons PM 247-83 1974 £65

DEFOE, DANIEL   The Secrets of the Invisible World Disclos'd. London, 1729. 8vo., frontispiece, contemporary calf gilt, second edition. Dawsons PM 252-262 1974 £60

DEFOE, DANIEL   Some Considerations On a Law for Triennial Parliaments. London, 1716. 8vo., modern quarter calf, fine, first edition. Dawsons PM 247-82 1974 £90

DEFOE, DANIEL   Some Reasons Offered by the Late Ministry in Defence of Their Administration. London, 1715. 8vo., modern quarter morocco, gilt, first edition. Dawsons PM 247-79 1974 £65

DEFOE, DANIEL   Some Reflections on a Pamphlet Lately Publish'd. London, 1697. 4to., quarter calf, second edition. Dawsons PM 247-68 1974 £50

DEFOE, DANIEL   A Spectators Address to the Whigs. 1711. 8vo., modern marbled boards, first edition. Dawsons PM 252-263 1974 £80

DEFOE, DANIEL   A Speech for Mr. Dundasse. London, 1711. 8vo., modern marbled boards, first edition. Dawsons PM 252-264 1974 £100

DEFOE, DANIEL   A Speech Without Doors. London, 1710. 8vo., old half calf, first edition. Dawsons PM 252-265 1974 £100

DEFOE, DANIEL   The Storm. London, 1704. 8vo., 19th century calf, fine, gilt, first edition. Dawsons PM 252-266 1974 £85

DEFOE, DANIEL   The Succession to the Crown of England, Considered. 1701. Small 4to., cloth, uncut. Quaritch 936-56 1974 £40

DEFOE, DANIEL   A Supplement to the Faults on Both Sides. London, 1710. 8vo., modern boards, first edition. Dawsons PM 252-267 1974 £50

DEFOE, DANIEL   A System of Magick. 1727. 8vo., contemporary calf, frontispiece, first edition. Quaritch 936-57 1974 £40

DEFOE, DANIEL   A System of Magick. London, 1727. 8vo., modern quarter morocco, first edition. Dawsons PM 252-268 1974 £110

DEFOE, DANIEL   A Tour Thro' London About the Year 1725.
London, 1929. Folio, calf gilt, slip case, limited edition. Traylen 79-355
1973 £50

DEFOE, DANIEL   A Tour Thro' the Whole Island of Great Britain.
1762-61. 4 vols., 12mo., calf antique, orig. labels, sixth edition. Dawsons
PM 252-269 1974 £70

DEFOE, DANIEL   A Tour thro' the Whole Island of Great Britain.
1927. Roy 8vo., 2 vols., marbled boards. Broadhurst 23-1368 1974 £40

DEFOE, DANIEL   A Tour Thro' the Whole Island of Great
Britain. 1927. 2 vols., orig. buckram backed cold boards, limited edition.
Smith 193-233 1973 £40

DEFOE, DANIEL   A Tour Thro' the Whole Island of Great Britain.
1927. Maps, 2 vols., roy. 8vo., marbled boards, cloth spine, limited to 1000
sets, fine. Broadhurst 24-1406 1974 £42

DEFOE, DANIEL   Treason Detected. London, 1715. 8vo.,
modern marbled wrappers, first edition. Dawsons PM 247-78 1974 £160

DEFOE, DANIEL   A True Collection of the Writings of the Author
of the True Born English-Man. London, 1703. 8vo., mottled calf antique,
calf labels, first authorised edition. Dawsons PM 252-270 1974 £75

DEFOE, DANIEL   The Two Great Questions Consider'd. London,
1700. 4to., modern quarter calf, first edition. Dawsons PM 247-69 1974 £85

DEFOE, DANIEL   A Vindication. London, 1711. 8vo., fine,
modern quarter brown morocco, first edition. Dawsons PM 252-271 1974 £80

DE FONATINE, FELIX G.   Marginalia; or, Gleanings from an Army
Note-Book. Columbia, 1864. Leather, front cover detached, back cover
missing, scarce, some foxing. Hayman 59-102 1974 $50

DE FOREST, ROBERT W.   A Walloon Family in America, Lockwood de
Forest and His Forebears 1500-1848; together with A Voyage to Guiana Being the
Journal of Jesse de Forest. 1914. Large 8vo., 2 vols., gilt tops, orig. binding.
Butterfield 10-269 1974 $35

DE FORNARO, CARLO   Carranza and Mexico. New York, 1915.
Author's Sgd. Pres. Biblo & Tannen 213-54 1973 $10

DEFOUR, THEOPHILE   Recherches Bibliographiques sur les Oeuvres
Imprimees de J. J. Rousseau. Paris, 1925. 2 vols., 8vo., orig. wrappers,
fine. Dawsons PM 10-523 1974 £15

DE GABALIS   Continuation of, Or New Discourses Upon the
Secret Sciences. Bath, 1897. Rittenhouse 46-272 1974 $25

DEGAS, EDGAR   Degas. 1923. 4to., black and white plates.
Eaton Music-569 1973 £8

DEGAS, EDGAR   Degas . . . Peintres, Pastels, Dessins et
Estampes. 1914. Folio, plates, quarter cloth, leather labels, orig. wrappers.
Quaritch 940-80 1974 £28

DEGAS, EDGAR   Degas. Quatre-Vingt-Dix-Huit
Reproductions Signees par Degas. Paris, 1918. 4to., plates, half sheep,
rubbed, illus., limited edition. Quaritch 940-81 1974 £68

DE GASPE, P. AUBERT   Les Anciens Canadiens. Ottawa, 1925. Nealty
mended, wrappers. Hood's 102-698 1974 $10

DE GAULLE, CHARLES   La France et Son Armee. Paris, 194a. Orig.
binding, illus., first edition, small tear in paper cover, unopened, fine. Ross
87-139 1974 $10

DEGENHARD, WILLIAM   The Regulators. New York, 1943. 1st ed.
Biblo & Tannen 210-717 1973 $5

DEGEORGE, LEON   Historique de l'Imprimerie E. Guyot. Brussels,
1880. 8vo., orig. printed wrappers, large folding plates. Kraus B8-336 1974
$28

DEGEORGE, LEON   Le Maison Plantin a Anvers. Paris, 1886.
8vo., portrait, cloth. Dawsons PM 11-227 1974 £7.50

DEGLAND, C. D.   Ornithologie Europeene ou Catalogue. Paris
and Lille, 1849. 8vo., 2 vols., half leather. Wheldon 129-450 1974 £10

DEGLAND, C. D.   Ornithologie Europeene ou Catalogue
Analytique et Raisonne des Eiseaux Observees en Europe. Paris & Lille, 1849.
2 vols., 8vo., orig. wrappers. Wheldon 128-422 1973 £10

DEGLAND, C. D.   Ornithologie Europeene ou Catalogue Descriptif.
Paris, 1867. 2 vols., 8vo., orig. wrappers, second edition. Wheldon
131-579 1974 £10

DE GOURMONT, REMY   Le Vieux Roi. Paris, 1897. Full morocco, gilt,
signed, English first edition. Covent 56-300 1974 £65

DE GOUY, E. L.   The Derrydale Cookbook of Fish and Game.
New York, Derrydale Press, 1937. 2 vols., first edition limited to 1250 numbered
copies, orig. red buckram, rare, mint. Current BW9-163 1974 $185

DEGUERLE, J. M. N.   Eloge des Perruques. (1799). 8vo., gilt,
contemporary calf. Quaritch 940-710 1974 £9

DE HAAS, JACOB   Louis D. Brandeis. 1929. 296 pages.
Austin 57-174 1974 $10

DE HAVILLAND, OLIVIA   Every Frenchman Has One. Random House,
1962. 202p. Austin 51-246 1973 $6.50

DEI Delitti E Delle Pene. Paris, 1786. Small 8vo., contemporary mottled calf,
rebacked, bookplate. Smith 193-110 1973 £5

DEIDIER, ABBE 1696-1746   La Mesure des Surfaces et des Solides. Paris,
1740. 4to., contemporary calf, gilt, plates, first edition. Dawsons PM 245-
212 1974 £35

DE JACZ, G.   Raphael Colours. London, 1937. Sm. 4to.,
mounted color plates. Biblo & Tannen 214-453 1974 $17.50

DEJEAN, M.   Traite des Odeurs. Paris, 1764. 8vo., contemporary French mottled calf, gilt, first edition. Hammond 201-894 1974 £16

DE JUBAINVILLE, H. D'ARBOIS   Le Cycle Mythologique Irlandais et la
Mythologie Celtique. Paris, 1884. 8vo., cloth boards. Emerald 50-211
1974 £10

DE JUBAINVILLE, H. D'ARBOIS   Introduction a l'etude de la Litterature
Celtique. Paris, 1883. 8vo., cloth boards. Emerald 50-210 1974 £10

DE KAY, J. E.   Natural History of New York. Albany, 1842.
4to., 2 vols., contemporary full red roan, rebacked, plates, scarce. Wheldon
130-680 1974 £40

DE KAY, J. E.   Zoology of New York. Albany, 1844. 4to.,
orig. black cloth, plates, scarce. Wheldon 130-16 1974 £150

DE KAY, J. E.   Zoology of New-York, or the New-York Fauna,
Part II, Birds. Albany, 1844. 4to., orig. black cloth, hand-coloured plates,
very scarce. Wheldon 128-421 1973 £150

DEKKER, THOMAS   Dramatic Works. 1873. 8vo., 4 vols., orig.
boards. Quaritch 936-361 1974 £35

DE KIRILINE, L.   The Loghouse Nest. Toronto, 1945. Inscribed
& signed by author. Hood's 102-499 1974 $15

DEKKER, THOMAS   Dramatic Works. 1873. 4 vols., new buckram.
Allen 216-1897 1974 $45

DE KROYFT, S. H.   A Place in Thy Memory. New York, 1854.
Frontis., portrait, orig. binding. Butterfield 10-540 1974 $7.50

DE LA BLETERIE, L'ABBE   Histoire de L'Empereur Jovien. Amsterdam,
1750. 12mo., engraved frontis., contemp. mottled calf, 2 vols. Jacobs 24-170
1974 $20

DE LA CAILLE, M. L'ABBE NICOLAS LOUIS   Journal Historique de Voyage Fait au Cap de Bonne-Esperance. Paris, 1763. 12mo., contemporary French mottled calf, folding map, some damp and other stains, inscription and signatures on title. Bow Windows 66-172 1974 £78

DE LA CASA, GIOVANNI   Galateo. London, 1774. 8vo., contemporary tree calf, gilt. Hammond 201-196 1974 £5

DELACOUR, J.   Les Oiseaux de l'Indochine Francaise. Paris, 1932. 4 vols., 4to., half blue morocco, coloured plates, maps, very scarce, orig. wrappers bound in. Wheldon 128-423 1973 £175

DELACROIX, EUGENE   Delacroix: Peintre, Graveur, Ecrivain. 1926-29. 3 vols., imp. 8vo., plates, orig. wrappers. Quaritch 940-83 1974 £65

DELACROIX, EUGENE   Dictionnaire Historique des Cultes Religieux Etablis dans le Monde Depuis son Origine Jusqu'a Present. Paris, 1777. 3 vols., 8vo., contemporary marbled calf, gilt. L. Goldschmidt 42-34 1974 $55

DELAFIELD, JOHN R.   An Inquiry Into the Origin of the Antiquities of America. New York, 1839. Rittenhouse 46-705 1974 $15

DELAFOND, O.   Traite Sur La Maladie de Poitrine du Gros Detail. Paris, 1844. Orig. covers, library copy. Rittenhouse 46-208 1974 $10

DELAGE, CYRILLE F.   Conferences, Discours, Lettres. Quebec, 1927. Hood's 102-404 1974 $7.50

DELAGE, Y.   Annee Biologique, Comptes Annuels des Travaux de Biologie Generale. Paris, 1897-99. 3 vols., roy. 8vo., half red morocco. Wheldon 128-2 1973 £6

DELAMAIN, RICHARD   The Making, Description, and Use of a Small Portable Instrument for ye Pocket. London, 1632. Small 8vo., contemporary vellum, plates, first edition. Traylen 79-219 1973 £285

DE LA MARE, WALTER   Arabia. n.d. English first edition. Covent 56-1705 1974 £6.30

DE LA MARE, WALTER   Broomsticks and Other Tales. 1925. 8vo., boards, uncut, signed, limited edition. Broadhurst 23-670 1974 £32

DE LA MARE, WALTER   Broomsticks and Other Tales. 1925. Illus., limited to 278 copies, signed by author, illus., med. 8vo., boards, linen spine, uncut, fine. Broadhurst 24-620 1974 £32

DE LA MARE, WALTER   Come Hither. 1923. Bookplate, English first edition. Covent 56-302 1974 £10.50

DE LA MARE, WALTER   Come Hither: A Collection of Rhymes and Poems for the Young of all Ages. London, 1923. Orig. binding, first edition, fine. Ross 87-140 1974 $17.50

DE LA MARE, WALTER   The Connoisseur and Other Stories. 1926. Quarter buckram gilt, fine, signed, English first edition. Covent 56-303 1974 £15

DE LA MARE, WALTER   Desert Islands and Robinson Crusoe. London, 1930. First trade edition, spine faded, orig. binding, nice copy. Ross 86-174 1974 $15

DE LA MARE, WALTER   Desert Island and Robinson Crusoe. 1930. Roy 8vo., orig. cloth, uncut, signed, limited edition. Broadhurst 23-674 1974 £45

DE LA MARE, WALTER   Desert Island and Robinson Crusoe. 1930. Illus. by Rex Whistler, limited to 650 copies, signed by author, roy. 8vo., uncut, mint, orig. cloth. Broadhurst 24-624 1974 £45

DE LA MARE, WALTER   Desert Islands and Robinson Crusoe. 1930. Signed first edition, limited to 650 copies, 8vo., cloth gilt, slipcase, fine. Thomas 32-280 1974 $55

DE LA MARE, WALTER   Ding Dong Bell. London, 1924. First edition, unusually fine copy, dust wrappers are mint, orig. binding. Ross 86-175 1974 $12.50

DE LA MARE, WALTER   Ding Dong Bell. 1924. Unusually fine copy, d.w., author's signature, first edition. Covent 51-525 1973 £12.50

DE LA MARE, WALTER   Early One Morning in the Spring. London, 1935. First edition, d.w. somewhat torn at top, fine, orig. binding. Ross 86-176 1974 $12.50

DE LA MARE, WALTER   Early One Morning in the Spring. (1935). 8vo., orig. cloth, illus., first edition. Bow Windows 66-173 1974 £9.75

DE LA MARE, WALTER   The Eighteen-Eighties: Essays. Lacking d.w., near fine. Ross 86-144 1974 $20

DE LA MARE, WALTER   The Fleeting and Other Poems. London, 1933. Orig. binding, first edition, spine slightly faded, else fine. Ross 87-141 1974 $15

DE LA MARE, WALTER   Henry Brocken. 1904. Crown 8vo., orig. cloth, fine, first edition, first issue. Broadhurst 23-659 1974 £6

DE LA MARE, WALTER   Henry Brocken. 1904. 8vo., orig. cloth, first edition, first issue. Quaritch 936-363 1974 £9

DE LA MARE, WALTER   Henry Brocken. London, n.d. (1924). No. 183 of edition limited to 250 copies, signed, lacking d.w., fine, orig. binding. Ross 87-143 1974 $30

DE LA MARE, WALTER   Henry Brocken: His Travels and Adventures in the Rich, Strange, Scarce-Imaginable Regions of Romance. 1904. Unusually fine copy, rubber stamp, first edition. Covent 51-526 1973 £15

DE LA MARE, WALTER   Lewis Carroll. 1932. Fine crisp copy, dust wrapper, first edition. Covent 51-355 1973 £6.50

DE LA MARE, WALTER   The Listeners and Other Poems. 1912. 12mo., orig. cloth, scarce, first edition. Rota 188-232 1974 £18

DE LA MARE, WALTER   The Listeners and Other Poems. London, 1912. First edition, unusually bright fine copy, inscribed, rare thus, orig. binding. Ross 86-177 1974 $75

DE LA MARE, WALTER   The Listeners and Other Poems. New York, 1916. Orig. cloth, spine dull, first American edition. MacManus 224-119B 1974 $25

DE LA MARE, WALTER   The Lord Fish. n.d. Plates, illus., cloth gilt, inscribed, English first edition. Covent 56-304 1974 £5.25

DE LA MARE, WALTER   Motley and Other Poems. 1922. Boards, illus., orig. vignettes. Covent 55-565 1974 £15

DE LA MARE, WALTER   News. 1930. 8vo., boards, uncut, mint, signed, limited edition. Broadhurst 23-676 1974 £5

DE LA MARE, WALTER   News. London, 1930. Orig. binding, large paper edition, hand made paper, limited, no. 42 of 500 copies, hardcover, fine, signed. Ross 87-144 1974 $25

DE LA MARE, WALTER   The Old Men. n.d. Illus., foxed, English first edition. Covent 56-305 1974 £7.50

DE LA MARE, WALTER   On the Edge. London, 1930. Orig. cloth, wood-engravings, first edition, one of 300 numbered copies, signed by author, boxed, fine. MacManus 224-120 1974 $25

DE LA MARE, WALTER   On the Edge. 1930. Fine, dust wrapper, English first edition. Covent 56-306 1974 £12.50

DE LA MARE, WALTER   On the Edge. 1930. 4to., orig. cloth, uncut, signed, limited edition. Broadhurst 23-675 1974 £35

DE LA MARE, WALTER   On the Edge: Short Stories. 1830. Limited to 300 copies, signed by author, med. 4to., uncut, orig. cloth, fine, wood engravings. Broadhurst 24-625 1974 £35

DE LA MARE, WALTER   On the Edge: Short Stories. London, 1930. First edition, wood engravings, orig. binding, torn d.w., else fine. Ross 87-145 1974 $15

DE LA MARE, WALTER   Peacock Pie. 1913. 8vo., cloth, fine, book-plate, first edition. Quaritch 936-364 1974 £9

DE LA MARE, WALTER   Peacock Pie. London, 1913. First edition, some dust staining on spine, nice copy, orig. binding. Ross 86-178 1974 $25

DE LA MARE, WALTER   Peacock Pie. 1924. 8vo., boards, uncut, signed, limited edition. Broadhurst 23-667 1974 £21

DE LA MARE, WALTER   Poems. 1906. Very fine, Roger Senhouse's signature, first edition. Covent 51-527 1973 £20

DE LA MARE, WALTER   Poems. London, (1920). 2 vols., 8vo., foxing, orig. cloth, uncut, first edition. Bow Windows 62-243 1974 £6.50

DE LA MARE, WALTER   Poems. 1920. 8vo., 2 vols., orig. cloth, signed, first edition. Rota 189-233 1974 £15

DE LA MARE, WALTER   Poems. n.d. (about 1938). Buckram backed boards, gilt top, near fine, printed by Carlow on his private press and given as presents to his friends. Covent 51-529 1973 £25

DE LA MARE, WALTER   Poems 1901 to 1918. London, (1920). 2 vols., orig. cloth backed boards, leather labels, first edition, limited to 210 numbered sets, signed in each vol. by author, uncut. MacManus 224-121 1974 £40

DE LA MARE, WALTER   Poems, 1901-1918. 1920. One of 210 copies, numbered & signed by author, linen backed boards, morocco labels, bookplate, fine, unopened copy, first edition. Covent 51-528 1973 £21

DE LA MARE, WALTER   Poems 1901 to 1918. 1920. First edition, 2 vols., med. 8vo., boards, linen spine, uncut, limited to 210 copies, fine. Broadhurst 24-616 1974 £25

DE LA MARE, WALTER   Poems 1919 to 1934. 1935. First edition, crown 8vo., orig. cloth, d.w., fine. Broadhurst 24-630 1974 £5

DE LA MARE, WALTER   The Return. 1922. 8vo., boards, uncut, signed, limited edition. Broadhurst 23-664 1974 £12

DE LA MARE, WALTER   The Riddle and Other Stories. 1923. Dust wrapper, fine, English first edition. Covent 56-1708 1974 £8.50

DE LA MARE, WALTER   Rupert Brooks and the Intellectual Imagination. 1919. Crown 8vo., dust wrapper, first edition. Broadhurst 23-661 1974 £5

DE LA MARE, WALTER   Rupert Brooke and the Intellectual Imagination. 1919. 8vo., orig. cloth, first edition, first issue. Rota 189-232 1974 £6

DE LA MARE, WALTER   Rupert Brooke and the Intellectual Imagination. London, 1919. First edition, first issue, fine, orig. binding. Ross 86-172 1974 $30

DE LA MARE, WALTER   Seven Short Stories. 1931. 8vo., orig. cloth, uncut, first edition. Broadhurst 23-677 1974 £6

DE LA MARE, WALTER   Seven Short Stories Chosen from 'The Connoisseur' 'Broomsticks' and 'The Riddle'. 1931. Coloured woodcuts, first edition, med. 8vo., uncut, orig. cloth, fine. Broadhurst 24-627 1974 £8

DE LA MARE, WALTER   Songs of Childhood. 1923. 8vo., boards, plates, signed. Quaritch 936-365 1974 £55

DE LA MARE, WALTER   Stories from the Bible. London, 1929. Orig. vellum backed boards, first edition, one of 300 numbered copies, signed by author, uncut, fine. MacManus 224-122 1974 $37.50

DE LA MARE, WALTER   Thus Her Tale. 1923. First edition, large paper copy, demy 4to., paper printed wrapper, sewn, uncut, illus. Broadhurst 24-617 1974 £5

DE LA MARE, WALTER   To Lucy. London, 1931. Orig. binding, large paper edition, drawings, hand made paper, no. 35 of edition limited to 275 copies, hardcover, mint. Ross 87-147 1974 $25

DE LA MARE, WALTER   Two Tales. I. The Green Room. II. The Connoisseur. London, (1925). Orig. vellum backed boards, first edition, one of 250 copies, numbered & signed by author, fine. MacManus 224-123 1974 $30

DE LA MARE, WALTER   The Veil. 1921. Cloth-backed boards. Covent 55-570 1974 £12.50

DE LA MARE, WALTER   The Veil and Other Poems. London, 1921. First edition, dec. boards, usual dust staining, fine copy. Ross 86-179 1974 $15

DE LA MARE, WALTER   The Veil and Other Poems. 1921. Orig. buckram backed boards, dust wrapper. Smith 194-435 1974 £9.50

DE LA MARE, WALTER   The Veil and Other Poems. London, (1921). Orig. cloth backed boards, leather label, first edition, one of 250 numbered copies signed by author, uncut. MacManus 224-124 1974 $30

DE LAMARTINE, A.   Graziella. 1929. Crown 8vo., orig. cloth, uncut, limited edition. Broadhurst 23-1067 1974 £10

DELAMOTTE, F.   Primer of the Art of Illumination. London, 1860. Orig. brown cloth, gilt, plates. Dawson's 424-129 1974 $35

DE LA MOTTE, PHILIP   The Principal, Historical, and Allusive Arms, borne by Families of the United Kingdom of Great Britain and Ireland. London, 1803. 4to., contemporary half calf, gilt, first edition. Hammond 201-420 1974 £28

DE LA MOTTE FOUQUE, FRIEDRICH
Please turn to
LA MOTTE FOUQUE, FRIEDRICH DE

DELAND, MARGARET   Old Chester Tales. New York, (c. 1900). 8vo., illus., spine browned & faded, good. Current BW9-221 1974 $10

DELANEY, PATRICK   Reflections upon Polygamy. 1737. 8vo., contemporary calf, gilt, first edition. Quaritch 936-61 1974 £40

DELANEY, PATRICK   Twenty Sermons on Social Duties. London, 1747. 8vo., full calf. Emerald 50-212 1974 £7.50

DELANGE, C.   Recueil de Toutes les Pieces Connues Jusqu'a ce Jour de la Faience Francaise. 1861. Imp. folio, plates, half morocco, worn. Quaritch 940-627 1974 £95

DELANGE, C.   Recueil des Fayences Francaises Dites de Henri II. Paris, 1861. Folio, plates, contemporary half morocco, limited, worn. Bow Windows 62-245 1974 £85

DE LA RAMEE, PIERRE
Please turn to
LA RAMEE, PIERRE DE

DELAROCHE, F.   Eryngiorum nec non Generis Novi Alepidae Historia. Paris, 1808. Folio, new half calf, engraved plates. Wheldon 128-1104 1973 £50

DE LA ROCHE, MAZO   Finch's Fortune. 1931. 443 pages, first edition. Austin 61-269 1974 $10

DE LA ROCHE, MAZO   Whiteoaks of Jalna. 1929. 423 pages, first edition. Austin 61-273 1974 $10

DE LARONDE, A.   Instructions en Sauteux sur Toute la Doctrine Catholique. Montreal, (1911). Hood's 103-450 1974 $30

DE LA TORRE, LILLIAN   Elizabeth is Missing. New York, 1945. 1st ed., illus. Biblo & Tannen 210-444 1973 $8.50

DE LA TORRE, LILLIAN   Villainy Detected. New York, 1947. 1st ed.
Biblo & Tannen 210-445 1973 $10

DELATTRE, C.   Recherches Chimiques et Medicales sur les
Huiles de Foies de Morue. Dieppe, 1859. 8vo., orig. wrappers. Wheldon
131-735 1974 £5

DE LAUNE, THOMAS   A Plea for the Non-Conformists. London,
1712. 2 vols. in 1, 16mo., contemporary calf. Goodspeed's 578-80 1974 $25

DELAUNEY, H. F.   Origine de la Tapisserie de Bayeux. Caen,
1824. 8vo., disbound, dogeared, uncut. Quaritch 940-752 1974 £10

DELAVAL, EDWARD HUSSEY   An Experimental Inquiry into the Causes of the
Changes of Colours in Opake and Coloured Bodies. London, 1777. 4to., contemporary calf, first edition. Dawsons PM 245-213 1974 £105

DELAWARE Tercentenary Almanack & Historical Repository. (Wilmington), 1938.
First edition, thin 8vo., illus., maps, plans, very good. Current BW9-360 1974
$20

DELAWARE Water Gap. Delaware Water Gap, c. 1900. Small folio, pict.
wrappers, photos. Jenkins 61-2146 1974 $10

DELEAU, NICOLAS   Traite du Catheterisme de la Trompe d'Eustachi.
Paris, 1838. 8vo., contemporary boards, rubbed, plates, first edition. Schuman
37-58 1974 $75

DELEBOE, FRANCISCI   Opera Medica. Paris, 1679. Foxing, binders
cloth on boards. Rittenhouse 46-206 1974 $175

DELEBOE, FRANCISCI   Opera Medica. Amstelodami, 1697. Worn
spine. Rittenhouse 46-207 1974 $275

DELEGORGUE, A.   Voyage dans l'Afrique Australe Notamment dans
le Territoire de Natal. Paris, 1847. 2 vols., 8vo., modern buckram, plates,
portrait, maps, very scarce. Wheldon 128-195 1973 £50

DELEUZE, JOSEPH PHILIPPE FRANCOIS   Histoire Critique du Magnetisme
Animal. Paris, 1813. 8vo., 2 vols., old calf, worn, first edition. Gurney 64-70
1974 £25

DELEUZE, JOSEPH PHILIPPE FRANCOIS   Histoire Critique du Magnetisme
Animal. Paris, 1813. 8vo., 2 vols. in 1, first edition. Gurney 66-50 1974
$25

DELGADO, J. F. N.   Etudes sur les Bilobites et Autres Fossiles des
Quartzites de la Base du Systeme Silurique de Portugal. Lisbon, 1886. 4to.,
wrappers, plates, scarce. Wheldon 131-990 1974 £10

DE LILLE, ALAIN   The Complaint of Nature. 1908. 96 pages.
Austin 61-274 1974 $17.50

DELISLE, LEOPOLD   Les Collection de Bastard D'Estang a la
Bibliotheque Nationale. 1885. Cloth, orig. wrappers bound in. Kraus B8-48
1974 $35

DELL, FLOYD   The Briary-Bush. Knopf, 1921. 425p.
Austin 54-282 1973 $7.50

DELL, FLOYD   Homecoming. Farrar, Rinehart, 1933. 368p.,
orig. ed. Austin 54-283 1973 $10

DELL, FLOYD   King Arthur's Socks. Knopf, 1912. 238p.
Austin 51-247 1973 $12.50

DELL, FLOYD   Moon-Calf. Knopf, 1920. 394p. Austin
54-284 1973 $6

DELL, FLOYD   Runaway. Doran, 1925. 304p. Austin 54-285
1973 $7.50

DELOLME, J. L.   The History of the Flagellants. London, 1783.
8vo., contemporary calf, gilt, plates, second edition. Hammond 201-195 1974
£15

DE LOMENIE, LOUIS   Beaumarchais and His Times. New York,
1857. Bdg. worn. Biblo & Tannen 213-650 1973 $8.50

DELPRAT, G. H. M.   Verhandeling Over de Broederschap Van G.
Groote en Over den Invloed der Fraterhuizen. 1856. New buckram. Allen
213-1518 1973 $22.50

DELTEIL, LEO   Annuaire des Ventes de Livres. Guide du
Bibliophile et du Libraire. 1re Annee-5e, 7e Annee. Paris, (1920-6). 6 vols.,
roy. 8vo., first 4 cloth, seventh boards with calf back, fifth orig. wrappers.
Forster 98-22 1974 £10

DELTEIL, LEO   Henri de Toulouse-Lautrec. Paris, 1920. 4to.,
illus., rebound. Biblo & Tannen 214-533 1974 $97.50

DELTEIL, LEO   Manuel de l'Amateur d'Estampes des XIXe et
XXe Siecles (1801-1924). Paris, 1925. 2 vols., roy. 8vo., orig. cloth. Forster
98-24 1974 £30

DELTEIL, LEO   Manuel de l'Amateur d'Estampes des XIXe et
XXe Siecles (1801-1924). 1925. 2 vols., large 8vo., plates, orig. wrappers,
cloth, uncut. Quaritch 940-84 1974 £20

DELTEIL, LEO   Manuel de l'Amateur d'Estampes du XVIIIe
Siecle. Paris, (1910). Plates, med. 8vo., marbled boards, straight grained
morocco back. Forster 98-23 1974 £25

DELTEIL, LEO.   Manuel de l'Amateur d'Estampes des XIXe et
XXe Siecles. Paris, (1925). 2 vols., large 8vo., buckram, plates, orig.
wrappers, fine. Dawsons PM 10-171 1974 £28

DE LUC, JEAN ANDRE   Recherches sur les Modifications de l'Atmosphere.
Geneve, 1772. 4to., 2 vols., contemporary sprinkled calf, first edition. Zeitlin
235-54 1974 $450

DE LUC, JEAN ANDRE   Recherches sur les Modifications de l'Atmosphere.
Geneve, 1772. 4to., engraved folding plates, contemporary polished calf, richly
gilt back, morocco title label, very fine, first edition. Schafer 10-126A 1974
sFr 2,500

DELVAU, ALFRED   Les Cytheres Parisiennes. Paris, 1864.
12mo., half calf, gilt, orig. wrapper, illus., first edition. L. Goldschmidt
42-202 1974 $60

DE MADARIAGA, SALVADOR   Don Quixote. 1934. 8vo., boards, uncut,
limited edition. Broadhurst 23-1049 1974 $45

DE MAISSE, ANDRE HURAULT   A Journal Of All That Wast Accomplished By.
1931. Orig. buckram, uncut. Howes 185-352 1974 £5.25

DE MAISSE, ANDRE HURAULT   A Journal of all that was Accomplished by. 1931.
8vo., orig. buckram, gilt, dust-wrapper. Hammond 201-776 1974 £8

DE MAUPASSANT, GUY   Clair de Lune. Leipzig, 1916. 4to., full
morocco, gilt, foxing, English first edition. Covent 56-1711 1974 £65

DE MAUPASSANT, GUY   Yvette. New York, 1916. First U.S. edition.
Covent 56-256 1974 £15.75

DE-MAURI, L.   Vinovo and Its Porcelain. Milan, (1925).
8vo., orig. paper boards, plates, spines little torn. Bow Windows 66-174 1974
£8

DEMELIUS, P.   Beitrag zur Kenntnis der Cystiden. Vienna,
1911-13. 8vo., buckram, plates. Wheldon 129-1188 1974 £5

DEMIDOFF, A. DE   Voyage dans la Russie Meridionale et la
Crimee. Paris, 1842. Folio, new half morocco, plates, maps, rare. Wheldon
131-39 1974 £200

DEMING, HENRY C.   Eulogy of Abraham Lincoln. Hartford, 1865.
Wrappers. Hayman 57-450 1974 $15

DEMING, HENRY C.   The Life of Ulysses S. Grant, General United
States Army. Hartford, 1868. Cloth. Hayman 59-561 1974 $10

DEMING, LEONARD   A Collection of Useful . . . Events, Original and Selected, from Ancient and Modern Authorities. Middlebury, 1825. 8vo., orig. bindings. Butterfield 8-659 1974 $12.50

DEMING, P.   Adirondack Stories. Houghton, Mifflin, 1880. 192p. Austin 54-286 1973 $10

DEMING, THERESE O.   American Animal Life. New York, 1916. Oblong 4to., pict. cloth, lst ed., 24 color plates. Frohnsdorff 16-279 1974 $30

DEMING, THERESE O.   Indian Child Life. New York, 1899. Oblong 4to., pict. boards, cloth spine, lst ed., color plates. Frohnsdorff 16-280 1974 $60

DEMOCRITUS. London, n.d. 12mo., contemporary calf, frontispiece, worn. Ximenes 33-389 1974 $75

DE MOIVRE, ABRAHAM
Please turn to
MOIVRE, ABRAHAM DE

DE MORGAN, AUGUSTUS   A Budget of Paradoxes. Chicago, 1915. 2 vols., demy 8vo., cloth, gilt, second edition. Covent 55-1139 1974 £15

DE MORGAN, SOPHIA E.   Memoir of Augustus de Morgan. 1882. New buckram, rubber stamp. Allen 216-423 1974 $10

DEMOSTHENES   Opera. Paris, 1570. Greek text, folio, 18th century diced calf, gilt and blind tooling, somewhat worn and faded. Thomas 32-231 1974 £35

DEMOSTHENES   Orationes. 1554. 2 vols., 19th century panelled calf, gilt. Thomas 30-101 1973 £20

DEMPWOLFF, AUGUST FRIEDRICH   De Origine, Progressu et Hodierno Statu Pharmaciae. Gottingen, 1807. 8vo., old-style boards, unopened. Schuman 37-59 1974 $95

DEMOUSTIER, CHARLES ALBERT   Lettre a Emilie sur la Mythologie. Paris, 1801. 6 parts in 1 vol., engraved portrait, engravings, 16mo., contemporary half calf, slight browning & some foxing throughout. Schumann 499-27 1974 sFr 100

DEMSON, MURIEL   Susannah of the Mounties. Random, 1936. Austin 51-957 1973 $10

DE MUSSET, PAUL   Mr. Wind and Madam Rain. New York, 1864. 12mo., gilt pictorial cloth, illus. Frohnsdorff 16-281 1974 $25

DE MUSSET, PAUL   Voyage Pittoresque en Italie Partie Meridionale et en Sicile. Paris, 1865. New edition, 8vo., full page engravings, orig. brown cloth, generally very good to fine. Current BW9-510 1974 $30

DENDY MARSHALL, C. F.   A History of the Southern Railway. London, 19-36. 4to., orig. cloth, gilt, plates, illus., first edition. Hammond 201-935 1974 £16

DENHAM, DIXON   Narrative of Travels and Discoveries in Northern and Central Africa in the Years 1822-1824. 1826. Engraved plates, maps, folding map, 4to., contemporary diced russia, rebacked morocco, hinges rubbed, fine. Broadhurst 24-1601 1974 £120

DENHAM, DIXON   Narrative of Travels and Discoveries in Northern and Central Africa. 1826. 4to., contemporary mottled calf, uncut, first edition. Bow Windows 64-475 1974 £100

DENHAM, JOHN   Poems and Translations. 1703. 8vo., contemporary calf, fourth edition. Quaritch 936-62 1974 £24

DENING, CHARLES FREDERICK WILLIAM   The Eighteenth-Century Architecture of Bristol. 1923. 4to., plates, illus., orig. cloth, first edition. Smith 193-53 1973 £14

DENIS, M.   Einleitung in die Bucherkunde. Wien, 1777-8. 2 vols. in 1, copperplate illus., folding table, crown 4to., contemporary half calf, rubbed. Forster 98-27 1974 £65

DENISON, G. T.   The Struggle for Imperial Unity. London, 1909. Hood's 104-630 1974 $20

DENISON, MARY ANDREWS   Out of Prison. Boston, 1864. Cloth, worn. Hayman 57-183 1974 $10

DENISON, MERRILL   Klondike Mike, an Alaskan Odyssey. New York, 1943. Hood's 102-500 1974 $8.50

DENMAN, JOSEPH   Observations on Buxton Waters. London, 1801. 8vo., orig. wrappers, second edition. Hammond 201-566 1974 £15

DENMAN, THOMAS   An Introduction to the Practice of Midwifery. London, 1832. 8vo., half calf, seventh edition. Gurney 64-71 1974 £20

DENNING, DAVID   Wood-Carving for Amateurs. London, 1905. Wrappers, cloth, illus., second edition. Dawson's 424-224 1974 $20

DENNIS, CLARA G.   Cuddly Kitty and Busy Bunny. New York, 1927. 16mo., 24 color plates. Frohnsdorff 16-52 1974 $9.50

DENNIS, J.   The Landscape Gardener. 1835. 8vo., cloth, plates, scarce. Wheldon 131-1508 1974 £7.50

DENNIS, JOHN   The Advancement and Reformation of Modern Poetry. London, 1701. 8vo., later calf, spine gilt, bit rubbed but sound, very scarce, first edition. Ximenes 36-67 1974 $275

DENNIS, JOHN   Appius and Virginia. London, (n.d.). 4to., full calf antique, first edition. Dawsons PM 252-274 1974 £90

DENNIS, JOHN   The Grounds of Criticism in Poetry, Contain'd in Some New Discoveries Never Made Before, Requisite for the Writing and Judging of Poems. London, 1704. 8vo., contemporary calf, rebacked, first edition, very rare. Ximenes 36-68 1974 $375

DENNIS, JOHN   Letters Upon Several Occasions. London, 1696. 8vo., 19th century blue morocco gilt, first edition. Dawsons PM 252-275 1974 £125

DENNIS, JOHN   Letters Upon Several Occasions. London, 1696. 8vo., contemporary calf, hinges worn, first edition. Ximenes 36-69 1974 $375

DENNIS, JOHN   Liberty Asserted. London, 1704. 4to., modern boards, first edition. Dawsons PM 252-276 1974 £12

DENNIS, JOHN   Original Letters, Familiar, Moral and Critical. London, 1721. 2 vols. in 1, 8vo., modern half calf, large paper copy, good copy, scarce, first edition. Ximenes 37-58 1974 $200

DENNIS, JOHN   A Plot, and No Plot. London, n.d. Small 4to., modern cloth, large copy, some foxing, first edition. Ximenes 37-59 1974 $150

DENNIS, JOHN   Remarks on a Play, Call'd, The Conscious Lovers, a Comedy. London, 1723. 8vo., wrappers, very rare, first edition. Ximenes 37-60 1974 $275

DENNIS, JOHN   Remarks Upon Cato, a Tragedy. London, 1713. Small 4to., half morocco, gilt, very good large copy, foxed, very rare, first edition. Ximenes 37-61 1974 $275

DENNIS, JOHN   Rinaldo and Armida. London, 1699. Small 4to., old half calf, spine worn, first edition, good copy. Ximenes 36-70 1974 $175

DENNIS, JOHN   The Select Works. London, 1718. 2 vols., 8vo., old calf, worn, very scarce, first edition. Ximenes 37-62 1974 $150

DENNY, HENRY   Monographia Anoplurorum Britanniae. 1842. 8vo., new cloth, plates, scarce. Wheldon 129-626 1974 £20

DENNY, NORMAN   The Yellow Book. n.d. 372 pages, illus. Austin 61-1097 1974 $10

DENOUVRAY, MME.   Nouveaux Contes. Paris, (c. 1845). 12mo., orig. green boards, little rubbed, engravings, plates, frontispiece. George's 610-209 1973 £5

DENOVAN, A.   Joshua Denovan. Toronto, 1901. Hood's 104-252 1974 $10

DENSLOW, W. W.   Fairbank's History of the United States. Chicago, 1911. Oblong 16mo., wrappers, illus. Frohnsdorff 15-176 1974 $30

DENSLOW, W. W.   Fairbank's Juvenile History of the United States. Chicago, 1911. Oblong 16mo., illus. Frohnsdorff 16-282 1974 $30

DENT, HUGH   The House of Dent. 1938. 8vo., quarter morocco, inscribed. Broadhurst 23-328 1974 £6

DENT, HUGH   The House of Dent. 1938. Plates, demy 8vo., quarter morocco, fine. Broadhurst 24-316 1974 £6

DENT, J. C.   The Story of the Upper Canadian Rebellion. Toronto, 1885. 2 vols., three quarter leather, gilt. Hood's 103-99 1974 $75

DENT, J. M.   My Memoirs, 1849-1921. London, 1921. Post 8vo., plates, orig. cloth, linen back, dust soiled. Forster 98-30 1974 £4

DENT, JOHN   The Candidate. London, 1782. 8vo., modern boards, staining, second edition. Dawsons PM 252-277 1974 £7

DENT, JOHN   Too Civil By Half. 1783. 8vo., contemporary boards, first edition. Quaritch 936-63 1974 £20

DENT, JOHN CHARLES   The Gerrard Street Mystery and Other Weird Tales. Toronto, 1888. Half leather, with gold design. Hood's 102-596 1974 $35

DENT, ROBERT K.   Historic Staffordshire. 1896. Crown 4to., illus., half black calf, plates. Howes 186-2188 1974 £14

DENTON, S. F.   Moths and Butterflies. Boston, 1900. 4to., 2 vols., morocco, plates, limited edition. Putman 126-33 1974 $60

DENTON, V. L.   The Far West Coast. Toronto, 1924. Illus., maps, inside cover mended. Hood's 102-803 1974 $10

DENYSE, JEAN   La Nature Expliquee par le Raisonnement et par l'Experience. Paris, 1719. 8vo., orig. continental speckled boards, uncut, unopened, fine, first edition. Dawsons PM 245-214 1974 £25

DEONA, W.   Catalogue du Musee Ariana. Geneve, (n.d.). Crown 4to., illus., cloth bound. Bow Windows 62-247 1974 £10

DEPONS, FRANCOIS   Travels In Parts of South America, 1801-04. London, 1806. 8vo., polished brown calf, rebacked, uncut, first edition. Traylen 79-474 1973 £20

DEPONS, FRANCOIS   A Voyage to the Eastern Part of Terra Firma. New York, 1806. 3 vols., 8vo., contemporary tree calf, map. Ximenes 33-334 1974 $275

DE PRADT, M.   The Colonies, and the Present American Revolutions. London, 1817. Leather, fine. Hood's 103-530 1974 $300

DE QUATREFAGES, ARMAND
Please turn to
QUATREFAGES DE BREAU, ARMAND DE

DE QUILLE, DAN PSEUD.
Please turn to
WRIGHT, WILLIAM

DE QUINCEY, THOMAS   Autobiography Sketches. 1853. 383 pages. Austin 61-278 1974 $10

DE QUINCEY, THOMAS   The Autograph Manuscript of "The Dark Interpreter". (c.1843-46). 4to., 4 pages. Dawsons PM 252-278 1974 £730

DE QUINCEY, THOMAS   The Avenger. 1859. Ex-library, 332 pages. Austin 61-279 1974 $10

DE QUINCEY, THOMAS   The Ceasars. 1854. Ex-library, 284 pages. Austin 61-281 1974 $10

DE QUINCEY, THOMAS   The Confessions of an English Opium Eater. 1822. First edition, f'cap. 8vo., orig. boards, new back strip, uncut, fine, complete with half title & ad leaf, scarce in uncut state. Broadhurst 24-634 1974 £200

DE QUINCEY, THOMAS   The Confessions of an English Opium-Eater. 1930. Roy. 8vo., dec. cloth gilt, fine. Covent 55-906 1974 £12.50

DE QUINCEY, THOMAS   Confessions of an English Opium-Eater. Oxford, 1930. Limited Editions Club. Folio, lithographs, orig. cloth backed marbled boards, one of 1520 numbered copies, signed by artist & printer, fine. MacManus 224-391 1974 $35

DE QUINCEY, THOMAS   Essays On Philisophical Writers and Other Men of Letters. 1854. 2 vols., ex-library. Austin 61-283 1974 $17.50

DE QUINCEY, THOMAS   Historical and Critical Essays. 2 vols., ex-library. Austin 61-285 1974 $17.50

DE QUINCY, THOMAS   Klosterheim. Edinburgh, 1832. Small 8vo., orig. cloth, first edition. Broadhurst 23-684 1974 £30

DE QUINCEY, THOMAS   Klosterheim. London, 1832. Small 8vo., orig. cloth-backed boards, worn, uncut, first edition. Hill 126-193 1974 £45

DE QUINCEY, THOMAS   Klosterheim. Edinburgh, 1832. 8vo., orig. quarter green cloth and boards, little scuffed, printed paper label, rubbed, cloth case, first edition, very good copy. Ximenes 36-72 1974 $100

DE QUINCEY, THOMAS   Letters to a Young Man and Other Papers. 1854. Ex-library. Austin 61-286 1974 $10

DE QUINCEY, THOMAS   Literary Reminiscences. 1851. 2 vols., ex-library. Austin 61-288 1974 $17.50

DE QUINCEY, THOMAS   The Logic of Political Economy, and Other Papers. 1859. Ex-library. Austin 61-289 1974 $10

DE QUINCEY, THOMAS   Memorials and Other Papers. 1868. 2 vols. Austin 61-290 1974 $12.50

DE QUINCEY, THOMAS   Miscellaneous Essays. 1851. 276 pages. Austin 61-291 1974 $10

DE QUINCEY, THOMAS   Narrative and Miscellaneous Papers. 1853. 2 vols., ex-library. Austin 61-292 1974 $17.50

DE QUINCEY, THOMAS   A Substantial Collection of Autograph Manuscripts. 4to., 21 pages, stains, frayed. Dawsons PM 252-279 1974 £295

DE QUINCEY, THOMAS   Theological Essays and Other Papers. 1854. 2 vols., ex-library. Austin 61-294 1974 $17.50

DE QUINCEY, THOMAS   Toilette of the Hebrew Lady. Hartford, 1926. Biblo & Tannen 210-853 1973 $7.50

DE QUINCEY, THOMAS   Works. Edinburgh, 1862. 15 vols., crown 8vo., contemporary half calf, gilt, frontispieces. Howes 186-129 1974 £50

DE QUINCEY, THOMAS   Works. Edinburgh, 1862. 15 vols., crown 8vo., half calf, panelled backs, contrasting leather labels, gilt extra, engraved frontispiece, portrait. Broadhurst 24-635 1974 £60

DE QUINCEY, THOMAS   Works. 1862-72. 16 vols., buckram, lower margins stained, ex-library. Allen 216-G 1974 $65

DE QUINCEY, THOMAS   The Works Of. Edinburgh, 1880. 16 vols., orig. cloth gilt, portraits, plates. Smith 194-344 1974 £20

DERBY, E. H.   The Catholic Letters. Boston, 1856. Austin 62-134 1974 $17.50

DERCUM, FRANCIS X.   A Clinical Manual of Mental Diseases. Philadelphia, 1913. Rittenhouse 46-211 1974 $10

DERCUM, FRANCIS X.   A Clinical Manual of Mental Diseases. Philadelphia, 1913. Spotted cover. Rittenhouse 46-706 1974 $10

DERCUM, FRANCIS X.   Rest, Suggestion and Other Therapeutic Measures in Nervous and Mental Diseases. Philadelphia, 1917. Second edition. Rittenhouse 46-707 1974 $10

DERHAM, WILLIAM   The Artificial Clock-Maker. London, 1700. 12mo., contemporary panelled calf, plates, second edition. Dawsons PM 245-215 1974 £265

DERHAM, WILLIAM   The Artificial Clock-Maker. London, 1714. 12mo., contemporary speckled sheep, rebacked, third edition. Dawsons PM 245-216 1974 £150

DERHAM, WILLIAM   Physico-Theology. London, 1714. Third edition corrected, contemporary calf, bookplate, lacks endpapers, rubbed. Wilson 63-593 1974 $27.50

DE RICCI, SEYMOUR   The Book Collectors Guide. New York, 1921. 8vo., cloth, limited edition. Dawsons PM 10-176 1974 £10

DE RICCI, SEYMOUR   The Book Collector's Guide. Philadelphia, 1921. 8vo., cloth, first edition. Goodspeed's 578-447 1974 $35

DE RICCI, SEYMOUR   A Catalogue of Early English Books in the Library of John L. Clawson. Philadelphia & New York, 1924. 4to., orig. blue cloth, fine. Dawsons PM 10-173 1974 £42

DE RICCI, SEYMOUR   A Hand-List of a Collection of Books and Manuscripts Belonging to The Right Hon. Lord Amherst. Cambridge, 1906. 4to., orig. printed wrappers. Dawsons PM 10-174 1974 £10

DE RIVAS, DAMASO   Clinical Parasitology and Tropical Medicine. Philadelphia, 1935. First edition. Rittenhouse 46-212 1974 $10

DEROME, L.   La Reliure de Luxe, le Livre et l'Amateur. Paris, 1888. Roy. 8vo., plates, buckram. Quaritch 940-599 1974 £45

DERRICK, CHARLES   Memoirs of the Rise and Progress of the Royal Navy. London, 1806. 4to., contemporary mottled calf, rebacked, presentation copy, first edition. Hammond 201-698 1974 £48

DERRICKE, JOHN   The Image of Irelande With a Discouerie of Woodkarne. Edinburgh, 1883. 4to., orig. quarter roan, cloth sides, plates, library stamp, limited. Bow Windows 66-176 1974 £48

DERRIEY, CHARLES   Specimen Album. Paris, 1862. Unbound, portfolio, untrimmed. Dawson's 424-146 1974 $675

DERRYDALE PRESS   A Decade of American Sporting Books & Prints, 1927-1937. New York, Derrydale Press, 1937. Plates, limited to 950 numbered copies, mint. Current BW9-162 1974 $85

DERWENTWATER, JAMES RADCLIFFE   A Report from the Committe. London, 1732. Folio, uncut. Quaritch 939-814 1974 £10

DERYS, GASTON   Gaites et Curiosities Gastronomiques. Paris, 1933. Biblo & Tannen 214-780 1974 $10

DE SACY   A Discourse of Friendship. London, 1707. 8vo., contemporary English morocco, gilt. Bow Windows 62-248 1974 £68

DESAGUILIERS, JOHN THEOPHILUS   A Course of Experimental Philosophy. London, 1745, 44. 4to., contemporary calf, plates. Dawsons PM 245-217 1974 £65

DE SAVITSCH, EUGENE   In Search of Complications. 1940. Austin 62-135 1974 $10

DESBORDES-VALMORE, MARCELINE   Lettres de Marceline Desbordes a Prosper Valmore. Paris, 1924. 2 vols., roy. 8vo., orig. wrapper, uncut, plates. L. Goldschmidt 42-203 1974 $20

DESCAMPS, J. B.   La Vie des Peintres Flamands. 1753-64. 4 vols., 8vo., leather labels, contemporary calf, gilt, fine. Quaritch 940-85 1974 £120

DESCAMPS, J. B.   Voyage Pittoresque de la Flandre et du Brabant, Avec des Reflexions Relativement aux Arts & Quelques Gravures. Paris, 1769. Contemporary calf, worn, lacks map, engravings. Eaton Music-572 1973 £20

DESCAMPS-SCRIVE, RENE   Bibliotheque. Paris & Lille, 1925. 3 parts, 4to., orig. wrappers, uncut. Dawsons PM 10-177 1974 £26

DESCARTES, RENE   Discovrs De La Methode. Paris, 1668. 4to., woodcuts, contemporary calf, rebacked. Zeitlin 235-56 1974 $650

DESCARTES, RENE   Discours de la Methode Pour Bien Conduire sa Raison & Chercher la Verite dans les Sciences. Leyden, 1637. Small 4to., first edition, contemporary (probably orig.) brown calf, half morocco case, woodcut diagrams, illus., with unpublished emendations. Kraus 137-22 1974 $25,000

DESCARTES, RENE   Epistolae. London, 1668. 4to., nineteenth century half calf, first London edition. Dawsons PM 245-223 1974 £85

DESCARTES, RENE   Epistolae. Amsterdam, 1668. 4to., 2 vols., contemporary calf, gilt, fine, first Latin edition. Dawsons PM 245-222 1974 £85

DESCARTES, RENE   La Geometrie. Paris, 1664. Small 4to., contemporary calf, gilt, worn. Zeitlin 235-57 1974 $750

DESCARTES, RENE   Lettres de Mr. Descartes. Paris, 1657. 4to., contemporary calf gilt, gilt, first edition. Dawsons PM 245-221 1974 £400

DESCARTES, RENE   Meditationes de Prima Philosophia. London, 1664. 8vo., contemporary calf. Gurney 64-73 1974 £105

DESCARTES, RENE   Le Monde de Mr. Descartes ou le Traite de la Lumiere. Paris, 1664. 8vo., contemporary calf, gilt, fine, first edition. Dawsons PM 245-220 1974 £185

DESCARTES, RENE   Musicae Compendium. Amsterdam, 1656. 4to., quarter sheep, second edition. Gurney 64-72 1974 £65

DESCARTES, RENE   Musicae Compendium. Amsterdam, 1656. 4to., quarter sheep, second edition. Gurney 66-51 1974 £65

DESCARTES, RENE   Opera Philosophica. 1692. 4to., contemporary vellum, plates, illus. Dawsons PM 245-224 1974 £45

DESCARTES, RENE   Principia Philosophiae. Amsterdam, 1644. 4to., contemporary vellum, first edition. Dawsons PM 245-218 1974 £265

DESCARTES, RENE   Principia Philosophiae. Amsterdam, 1644. Small 4to., contemporary vellum, foxing, first edition. L. Goldschmidt 42-35 1974 $850

DESCARTES, RENE   Principia Philosophiae. Amsterdam, 1650. 4to., full calf antique, second edition. Dawsons PM 245-219 1974 £110

DESCARTES, RENE   Principia Philosophiae. Amsterdam, 1656. 4to., contemporary calf, worn, woodcuts. Schuman 37-60 1974 $225

DESCARTES, RENE   Traite de la Mechanique . . . de plus l'Abrege de Musique . . . mis en Francois Avec les Eclaircissemens Necessaires. Paris, 1668. 4to., woodcut figures, modern vellum over thin boards, vignettes, very fine, rare, first edition. Schafer 10-126 1974 sFr 2,600

DES CAURRES, JEAN   Oeuvres Morales, et Diversifiees en Histoires, Pleines de Beaux Exemples. Paris, 1575. Thick 8vo., 17th century calf, gilt, worn, first edition. Harper 213-50 1973 $350

DESCHAMPS, EUSTACHE   Poesies Morales et Historiques. Paris, 1832.
Roy. 8vo., orig. boards, uncut, first edition. L. Goldschmidt 42-36 1974 $50

DES CHARMES, PAJOT   The Art of Bleaching Piece-Goods. London, 17-
99. 8vo., contemporary half calf, gilt, plates, first edition in English. Hammond
201-816 1974 £75

DE SCHWEINITZ, EDMUND   The Life and Times of David Zeisberger the Western
Pioneer and Apostle of the Indians. Philadelphia, 1870. First edition, orig.
binding. Butterfield 10-213 1974 $50

DESCOT, PIERRE-JULES   Dissertation sur les Affections Locales des
Nerfs. Paris, 1825. 8vo., morocco-backed cloth, frontispiece, best edition.
Schuman 37-61 1974 $75

DESCOURTILZ, J. T.   Ornitologia Brasileira ou Historia Natural. Rio
de Janeiro and Sao Paulo, (1944). Orig. wrappers, illus. Dawson's 424-316
1974 $40

A DESCRIPTION of Ithiel Town's Improvement in the Construction of Wood and
Iron Bridges. New Haven, 1821. 8vo., wrappers, rare, plates, first edition.
Ximenes 35-363 1974 $125

A DESCRIPTIVE Bibliography of the Books Printed at the Ashendene Press.
Chelsea, 1935. Folio, plates, full cowhide, limited. Dawsons PM 10-16
1974 £260

DESCRIPTIVE Catalogue of a Collection of Rare Minerals. New York, 1829.
8vo., sewn as issued, light waterstains, very good copy, rare. Ximenes 37-34
1974 $40

DESCRIPTIVE CATALOGUE of Shetland Ponies. Detroit, 1892. 8vo., stiff wrapper, portraits. Butterfield 8-280 1974 $25

DESCRIZIONE DELLE Vedute di Roma. Rome, 1817. Folio, contemporary half
calf, worn, plates. Dawsons PM 251-97 1974 £300

DESFONTAINES, R.   Flora Atlantica, Sive Historia Plantarum Quae
in Atlante, Agro Tunetano et Algeriensi Crescunt. Paris, (1797-98). 2 vols.,
4to., contemporary mottled calf neatly rebacked in morocco, engraved plates,
rare. Wheldon 128-1256 1973 £250

DESFORETS, B.   Un Sillon dans la Foret. Montreal, 1936.
Wrappers, unopened. Hood's 104-546 1974 $10

DESFORETS, B.   Un Silon dans la Foret. Montreal, 1936.
Wrappers, pages uncut. Hood's 102-501 1974 $10

DESFORGES, E. D.   Porte-Feuille Vole, Contenant: 1. Le Paradis
Perdu, Poeme en Quatre Chants; 2. Les Deguisements de Venus, Tableaux Imites
du Grec; 3. Les Galanteries de la Bible, Sermon en Vers. Paris, 1805. 12mo.,
orig. marbled wrappers bound in contemporary vellum. Schumann 499-28 1974
sFr 150

DESHAYES, G. P.   Description des Coquilles Fossiles des Environs
de Paris. Paris, 1824-37. 2 vols., 4to., new buckram, plates, very rare.
Wheldon 128-838 1973 £100

DESHAYES, G. P.   Description des Coquilles Fossiles des Environs
de Paris. Paris, 1824-37. 4to., new buckram, plates, rare. Wheldon 130-
919 1974 £100

DESIGNERS in Britain, Vol. 2. New York, 1949. 4to., illus. Biblo & Tannen
210-117 1973 $17.50

DESJARDINS, MARIE CATHERINE HORTENSE DE   Exiles at Court of Augustus
Caesar. 1726. Old calf, quite worn, joints broken. Allen 216-2225 1974 $15

DESJARDINS, MARIE CATHERINE HORTENSE DE   The Unfortunate Heroes.
1679. 8vo., contemporary sheep, first English edition. Dawsons PM 252-1094
1974 £95

DESLANDES, ANDRE FRANCOIS BOUREAU   Essay Sur La Marine et Sur Le
Commerce. (Paris), 1743. 12mo., contemporary continental mottled calf,
fine, first edition. Dawsons PM 247-90 1974 £70

DE SMET, PIERRE JEAN
Please turn to
SMET, PIERRE JEAN DE

DESNOIRESTERRES, GUSTAVE   Voltaire et la Societe au XVIIIe Siecle.
Paris, 1867-78. 8 vols., 8vo., three quarter red hard grain morocco, orig.
wrapper. L. Goldschmidt 42-132 1974 $200

DESNOS, ROBERT   Deuil Pour Deuil. Paris, 1924. Square
12mo., orig. wrapper, uncut, fine, first edition. L. Goldschmidt 42-204
1974 $20

DES PERIERS, BONAVENTURE   Cymbalum Mundi. 1712. 8vo., wrappers,
scarce, first English edition. Hill 126-69 1974 £18

DESPIAU, L.   Select Amusements in Philosophy and Mathematics. 1801. 12mo., orig. boards, uncut, fine. Hill 126-63 1974 £25

DESPORTES, PHILIPPE   Les CL. Pseaumes de David Mis en vers Fracois.
Paris, 1603. 2 parts in 1, small 8vo., 19th century boards. L. Goldschmidt
42-38 1974 $150

DESPORTES, PHILIPPE   Les Premieres Oeuvres. Rouen, 1600.
4 parts in 1, 12mo., contemporary limp vellum. L. Goldschmidt 42-37 1974
$250

DESPRETZ, CESAR MANSUETTE   Recherches sur la Prolagation de la Chaleur.
(1838). 8vo., orig. blue wrappers, fine, unopened, uncut. Zeitlin 235-275
1974 $35

DESROCHES DE PARTHENAY, JEAN BAPTISTE   The History of Poland under
August II. 1734. 8vo., contemporary calf, first edition in English. Hill 126-
217 1974 £22.50

DESSALINES D'ORBIGNY, ALCIDE
Please turn to
ORBIGNY, ALCIDE DESSALINES D'

DESSUBRE, M.   Bibliographie de L'Ordre des Templiers.
Paris, 1928. Buckram, numbered. Covent 55-965 1974 £12.50

DESTOMBES, C.-J. L'ABBE   La Persecution Religieuse en Angleterre Sous
Elisabeth et les Premiers Stuarts. 1883. 3 vols., contemporary half calf,
plates, illus. Howes 185-1110 1974 £15

DESTOUCHES, JEAN-LOUIS   Principles Fondamentaux de Physique Theorique.
8vo., 3 vols., orig. printed wrappers, uncut, first edition. Dawsons PM 245-227
1974 £15

DE TABLEY, J. B. L. W.   Guide to Study of Book-Plates. 1900. Plates,
binding time darkened. Allen 216-161 1974 $10

DE THOU, JACQUES AUGUSTE DE
Please turn to
THOU, JACQUES AUGUSTE DE

DE THOU, POTHERAT   Recherches sur l'Origine de l'Impot en France.
Paris, 1838. 8vo., rebound, modern calf, first edition. Dawsons PM 247-91
1974 £25

DE TIVOLI, J.   A Guide to the Falls of Niagara. New York,
1846. Cover worn, lithographic view. Hood's 102-597 1974 $75

DE TIVOLI, J.   A Guide to the Falls of Niagara. New York,
1846. Worn cover. Hood's 104-678 1974 $75

DE TOCQUEVILLE, ALEXIS
Please turn to
TOCQUEVILLE, ALEXIS DE

DEUEL, WALLACE R.   People Under Hitler. New York, 1942.
Biblo & Tannen 213-663 1973 $8.50

DEUTCHE Amerikaner. Cleveland, Ohio, 1892. 316p. Austin 62-194 1974
$17.50

DEUTSCH, HELEN   The Psychology of Women. New York, 1944.
2 vols. Biblo & Tannen 213-963 1973 $12.50

DEUTSCH, O. E.   Handel: Selection from The Messiah. London, 1945. Oblong 4to. Biblo & Tannen 214-856 1974 $17.50

DEVAL, JACQUES   Tovarich. Random House, 1937. 159p. Austin 51-248 1973 $8.50

DE VAYNES, JULIA H. L.   The Kentish Garland. 1881. 2 vols., thick 8vo., illus., scarce. Howes 186-2035 1974 £38

DEVENTER, HENRY   The Art of Midwifery Improv'd. London, 1746. 8vo., old calf, rebacked, gilt. Dawsons PM 249-138 1974 £40

DE VERE, AUBREY   Legends of the Saxon Saints. London, 1879. 8vo., orig. cloth, inscribed, first edition. Dawsons PM 252-280 1974 £42

DE VERE, AUBREY   St. Thomas of Canterbury. London, 1876. 8vo., orig. cloth gilt, inscribed, first edition. Dawsons PM 252-281 1974 £26

DE VERE, AUBREY   A Song of Faith. 1842. Small 8vo., orig. cloth, printed label, first edition. Howes 185-104 1974 £30

DE VERE, M. S.   Americanisms; English of the New World. 1872. new buckram. Allen 216-1387 1974 $12.50

DEVERE, WILLIAM   Jim Marshall's New Pianner. Witmack, 1897. 130p., illus. Austin 54-287 1973 $10

DEVIL Stories, an Anthology. New York, 1921. 1st ed. Biblo & Tannen 210-665 1973 $12.50

DE VILLAMIL, R.   Newton: The Man. London, 1931. 8vo., orig. cloth, portrait, first edition. Dawsons PM 10-452 1974 £7

DEVILLE, ETIENNE   La Reliure Francaise, 1: Des Origines a la Fin du XVIIe Siecle. Paris, 1930. Small 4to., plates, wrappers, uncut. Kraus B8-50 1974 $30

DEVINE, E. J.   Historic Caughnawaga. Montreal, 1922. Map, illus. Hood's 103-768 1974 $45

DE VINNE, THEODORE LOW   Brilliants: A Setting of Humorous Poetry in Brilliant Types. New York, 1895. Presentation copy, inscribed from editor & printer, full crimson morocco gilt, exceptionally fine. Covent 51-3251 1973 £195

DE VINNE, THEODORE LOW   Printing in the Nineteenth Century. New York, 1924. Ltd. ed. Biblo & Tannen 213-443 1973 $12.50

DE VOGUE, E. M.   The Russian Novelists. Boston, 1887. Biblo & Tannen 210-854 1973 $8.50

DE VOTO, BERNARD   The Chariot of Fire. Macmillan, 1926. 356p. Austin 54-288 1973 $10

DE VOTO, BERNARD   The Easy Chair. Houghton, 1955. 356p., orig. ed. Austin 54-289 1973 $6.75

DE VOTO, BERNARD   Mountain Time. Little, Brown, 1947. 313p. Austin 54-290 1973 $6

DEVOY, JOHN   Recollections of an Irish Rebel. New York, 1929. 8vo., cloth boards, illus. Emerald 50-214 1974 £7.50

DE VRIES, HUGO
Please turn to
VRIES, HUGO DE

DE VRIES, PETER   The Cat's Pajamas and Witch's Milk. Little, Brown, 1962. 303p. Austin 54-293 1973 $5

DE VRIES, PETER   The Blood of the Lamb. Little, Brown, 1961. 346p. Austin 54-292 1973 $5

DE VRIES, PETER   Let Me Count the Ways. Little, Brown, 1965. 307p. Austin 54-294 1973 $5

DE VRIES, PETER   The Mackerel Plaza. Little, Brown, 1958. 260p. Austin 54-295 1973 $5

DE VRIES, PETER   No But I Saw the Movie. Little, Brown, 1952. 249p. Austin 54-296 1973 $7.50

DE VRIES, PETER   Reuben, Reuben. Little, Brown, 1964. 435p. Austin 54-297 1973 $5

DE VRIES, PETER   The Tents of Wickedness. Little, Brown, 1959. 276p. Austin 54-298 1973 $6

DE VRIES, PETER   Through the Fields of Clover. Little, Brown, 1961. 275p. Austin 54-299 1973 $5

DE VRIES, PETER   The Tunnel of Love. Little, Brown, 1954. 246p. Austin 54-300 1973 $5

DE VRIES, PETER   The Vale of Laughter. Little, Brown, 1967. 352p. Austin 54-301 1973 $5

DEWAR, W.   The Making of Species. 1909. 8vo., cloth, plates. Wheldon 130-351 1974 £5

DEWART, E. H.   Songs of Life. Toronto, 1869. Hood's 103-718 1974 $20

DEWITT, DAVID M.   The Assassination of Abraham Lincoln. New York, 1909. Cloth, scarce. Hayman 57-451 1974 $15

DE WITT, MARY BREWERTON   Kansas City, 1922. 8vo., illus., fine, each page with dec. borders. Current BW9-112 1974 $11

DE WITT, S. A.   Where Are the Snows? Parnasus Press, 1941. 94p., limited 140 copies on Victorian laid paper; this copy inscribed by author. Austin 51-249 1973 $15

DE WITT, SUSAN   The Pleasures of Religion. New York, 1820. 12mo., orig. tan boards, printed paper label, fine copy, first edition. Ximenes 37-63 1974 $45

DEWOLFF, J. H.   Pawnee Bill. N.P., 1902. New cloth, first edition. Hayman 57-137 1974 $15

DEWSBURY, WILLIAM   The Word of the Lord to All Children Born Again of the Immortal Seed. (London), 1665. Small 4to., half morocco, very good copy, first edition. Ximenes 37-64 1974 $40

DE WULF, MAURICE   History of Mediaeval Philosophy. 1935. 2 vols., third edition. Howes 185-1845 1974 £8.50

DEXHEIMER, FLORENCE CHAMBERS   Sketches of Wisconsin Pioneer Women. (Fort Atkinson, n.d.). Tan cloth. Bradley 35-405 1974 $10

DEXTER, R. C.   Social Adjustment. New York & London, 1927. Hood's 103-586 1974 $12.50

DEZALLIER D'ARGENVILLE, A. J.   L'Histoire Naturelle. Paris, 1755. 4to., contemporary calf gilt, plates. Wheldon 130-920 1974 £40

DHETEL, P.   L'Abbaye de Notre-Dame-de-Lone et ses Succursales. 1864. Orig. wrappers, scarce. Howes 185-1112 1974 £8

DHU, HELEN   Stanhop Burleigh. 1855. Frontispiece, 406 pages. Austin 57-179 1974 $15

DHU, HELEN   Stanhope Burleigh. 1855. Austin 62-137 1974 $15

DIALECT Play-Reading. French, 1937. 128p. Austin 51-324 1973 $7.50

DIALOGUES Between Three Little Girls, On Subjects Calculated to Facilitate Their Progress in Knowledge and Virtue. 1821. Small square 8vo., orig. ptd. boards, rare. George's 610-210 1973 £10

DIAZ, ABBY MORTON   King Grimalkum and Pussyanita. Boston, 1881. 8vo., pictorial boards, 1st ed., illus. Frohnsdorff 16-283 1974 $15

DIAZ, PORFIRIO   Por Nemesio Garcia Naranjo. San Antonio, 1930. Biblo & Tannen 213-56 1973 $7.50

DIAZ DEL CASTELLO, BERNAL   The Discovery and Conquest of Mexico. (Mexico City), 1942. Orig. leather labels, illus., fine. Bradley 35-434 1974 $140

DIAZ DEL CASTILLO, BERNAL   The True History of the Conquest of Mexico. (1927). 2 vols., plates, orig. buckram. Howes 186-771 1974 £6.50

DIAZ INFANTE, JOSE   Compendio de Artilleria. 1762. 4to., modern boards, plates, second edition. Dawsons PM 245-229 1974 £24

DIBDIN, CHARLES   The Songs Of. 1884. 2 vols., roy. 8vo., half contemporary calf gilt, rubbed. Smith 194-206 1974 £5

DIBDIN, CHARLES   The Wedding Ring. London, 1773. 8vo., modern boards, first edition. Dawsons PM 252-282 1974 £15

DIBDIN, CHARLES 1745-1814   The Professional Life of Mr. Dibdin. 1803. 4 vols., rebacked panelled calf, front cover missing from vol. 2. Eaton Music-518 1973 £20

DIBDIN, THOMAS FROGNALL   Aedes Althorpianae. London, 1822. 2 vols. in 1, folding plan, plates, many illus., roy. 8vo., calf gilt. Forster 98-48 1974 £40

DIBDIN, THOMAS FROGNALL   A Bibliographical Antiquarian and Picturesque Tour in France and Germany. London, 1829. 3 vols., 8vo., plates, illus., contemporary half calf, second edition. Bow Windows 62-249 1974 £45

DIBDIN, THOMAS FROGNALL   A Bibliographical, Antiquarian and Picturesque Tour in France and Germany. London, 1831. 3 vols. including supp., plates, illus., med. 8vo., contemporary panelled calf, armorial bookplates. Forster 98-45 1974 £50

DIBDIN, THOMAS FROGNALL   A Bibliographical Antiquarian and Picturesque Tour in the Northern Counties of England and Scotland. London, 1838. 2 vols., 8vo., contemporary morocco, plates. Dawsons PM 10-178 1974 £100

DIBDIN, THOMAS FROGNALL   The Bibliographical Decameron. London, 1817. 3 vols., large 8vo., contemporary straight-grained morocco, first edition. Dawsons PM 10-179 1974 £190

DIBDIN, THOMAS FROGNALL   A Bibliographical Decameron. London, 1817. 3 vols., plates, some foxing, roy. 8vo., orig. boards, spines bit defective, text fine and uncut, bookplates. Forster 98-44 1974 £95

DIBDIN, THOMAS FROGNALL   The Bibliomnaia. London, 1809. First edition, med. 8vo., orig. boards, spine defective. Forster 98-43 1974 £35

DIBDIN, THOMAS FROGNALL   Bibliomania. London, 1811. 8vo., faded, contemporary calf-backed cloth boards, second edition. Dawsons PM 10-180 1974 £50

DIBDIN, THOMAS FROGNALL   Bibliomania. London, 1876. Large 8vo., illus., modern half morocco. Dawsons PM 10-181 1974 £40

DIBDIN, THOMAS FROGNALL   The History of Cheltenham and Its Environs. Cheltenham, 1803. 8vo., cloth back. Quaritch 939-357 1974 £8

DIBDIN, THOMAS FROGNALL   An Introduction to the Knowledge of Rare and Valuable Editions of the Greek and Latin Classics. 1808. 8vo., contemporary half calf. Bow Windows 64-476 1974 £26

DIBDIN, THOMAS FOGNALL   Library Companion. 1824. Half calf. Allen 216-177 1974 $17.50

DIBDIN, THOMAS FROGNALL   The Library Companion. 1824. First edition, demy 8vo., newly bound boards, leather title label, slight foxing of title page, Broadhurst 24-319 1974 £20

DIBDIN, THOMAS FROGNALL   The Library Companion. London, 1824. First edition, 2 vols. in 1, demy 8vo., half calf, lacks spine, covers detached. Forster 98-50 1974 £6

DIBDIN, THOMAS FROGNALL   The Library Companion. London, 1824. 2 parts in 1 vol., 8vo., contemporary calf, rebacked. Dawsons PM 10-182 1974 £35

DIBDIN, THOMAS FROGNALL   The Library Companion. 1824. 8vo., recent half calf, first edition. Bow Windows 64-477 1974 £38

DIBDIN, THOMAS FROGNALL   The Library Companion. 1824. 2 vols., roy. 8vo., half dark blue crushed levant morocco. Thomas 30-134 1973 £45

DIBDIN, THOMAS FROGNALL   The Library Companion. London, 1825. 8vo., orig. boards, label, second edition. Dawsons PM 10-183 1974 £24

DIBDIN, THOMAS FROGNALL   The Library Companion. 1825. 2 vols. in 1, large 8vo., contemporary green morocco gilt, second edition. Thomas 28-111 1972 £31.50

DIBDIN, THOMAS FROGNALL   The Old Paths. London, 1844. 8vo., cloth, orig. printed wrappers bound in, first edition, very rare. Ximenes 36-73 1974 $40

DIBDIN, THOMAS FROGNALL   Typographical Antiquities. London, 1810-19. 4 vols., 4to., contemporary half pigskin, third edition. Dawsons PM 10-184 1974 £300

DIBDIN, THOMAS FROGNALL   Typographical Antiquities. London, (1810)-19. 4 vols., large paper copy, plates, many foxed, folio, contemporary half vellum, soiled, uncut, tipped in vol. 1 is an A.L.s. from Dibdin. Forster 98-52 1974 £300

DIBDIN, THOMAS FROGNALL   Venetian Printers. Mt. Vernon, 1924. Roy. 8vo., orig. wrappers. Kraus B8-309 1974 $20

DIBDIN, THOMAS FROGNALL   Voyage Bibliographique, Archeologique et Pittoresque, en France et en Allemagne. Paris, 1821. Roy. 8vo., orig. boards, uncut. Forster 98-46 1974 £10

DIBDIN, THOMAS FROGNALL   Voyage Pittoresque en France et en Allemagne, Relatif a la Bibliographie et aux Antiquites. Paris, 1821. Roy. 8vo., orig. boards, spine defective, text fine, uncut. Forster 98-47 1974 £9

DIBDIN, THOMAS JOHN 1771-1841   Two Faces Under a Hood. London, (1807). 8vo., modern boards, first edition. Dawsons PM 252-283 1974 £15

DIBDIN, THOMAS JOHN 1771-1841   The Will for the Deed. London, 1805. 8vo., modern boards, first edition. Dawsons PM 252-284 1974 £15

DICK, ROBERT   Robert Dick, Baker of Thurso, Geologist and Botanist. 1878. 8vo., cloth, illus., maps, foxed. Wheldon 131-213 1974 £5

DICK Whittington and His Cat. New York, 1937. 16mo., boards, cloth spine, colored wood engravings. Frohnsdorff 16-290 1974 $10

DICK-LAUDER, MRS.   Pen and Pencil Sketches of Wentworth Landmarks. Hamilton, 1897. Card cover. Hood's 103-619 1974 $20

DICKENS, CHARLES   American Notes for General Circulation. 1842. 2 vols., crown 8vo., half green calf, gilt, morocco labels, third edition. Howes 185-111 1974 £25

DICKENS, CHARLES   American Notes for General Circulation. 1842. 2 vols., full crushed morocco, gilt, uncut, second edition. Howes 186-132 1974 £35

DICKENS, CHARLES   Barnaby Rudge. Philadelphia, 1842. First American edition, small 4to., cover worn stained & soiled, labels on spine missing, foxing on interior. Current BW9-222 1974 $22.50

DICKENS, CHARLES   La Bataille de la Vie. Paris, 1853. Orig. wrappers, foxing, first French edition. Covent 56-350 1974 £21

DICKENS, CHARLES   The Battle of Life. 1846. 8vo., half contemporary red morocco gilt, illus. Smith 193-343 1973 £7.50

DICKENS, CHARLES   Bentley's Miscellany. 1837-39. Vols. 1-5, illus. by George Cruikshank, large 8vo., half red levant morocco, gilt backs, uncut, choice set, loosely inserted in vol. 1 is an A.L.s. by Dickens. Sawyer 293-121 1974 £250

DICKENS, CHARLES   Bleak House. 1853. Thick 8vo., foxing, contemporary half green calf gilt, plates, label. Howes 186-133 1974 £22.50

DICKENS, CHARLES   Bleak House. 1853. Illus. by H. K. Browne, first edition, lacks half title, plates little browned, else clean & sound, full calf, raised bands, good binding in fine state, morocco labels. Thomas 32-165 1974 £35

DICKENS, CHARLES   Bleak House. 1938. Plates. Allen 216-428 1974 $10

DICKENS, CHARLES   Captain Boldheart and Other Stories. New York, 1930. 12mo., cloth, 4 color plates. Frohnsdorff 16-285 1974 $10

DICKENS, CHARLES   Character Sketches. 1924. 4to., full lambskin binding, fine, portraits, English first edition. Covent 56-348 1974 £35

DICKENS, CHARLES   The Children's Pickwick. London, n.d. 12mo., cloth, 4 color plates. Frohnsdorff 16-286 1974 $10

DICKENS, CHARLES   A Child's History of England. 1854-53-54. 3 vols., square crown 8vo., orig. brown cloth, ads at end of each vol., vols. 2 & 3 first editions. George's 610-215 1973 £5.25

DICKENS, CHARLES   A Child's History of England. 1852-53-54. First edition, frontispieces, 3 vols., square crown 8vo., orig. brown cloth, spine vols. 1 worn and defective at foot. George's 610-214 1973 £20

DICKENS, CHARLES   The Chimes. New York, 1845. 8vo., foxed. Frohnsdorff 16-287 1974 $15

DICKENS, CHARLES   The Chimes. London, Limited Editions Club, 1931. Limited to 1500 copies, tall 4to., illus. by Rackham, very fine, copy no. 653, signed by illus. Current BW9-27 1974 $140

DICKENS, CHARLES   The Christmas Books. 1843-48. 5 vols., 12mo., orig. cloth, morocco box, first editions. Howes 185-112 1974 £195

DICKENS, CHARLES   Christmas Books. New York, 1867. 8vo., steel engravings, interior fine, exterior bit soiled. Current BW9-28 1974 $32.50

DICKENS, CHARLES   A Christmas Carol. London, n.d. Square 8vo., illus. by Arthur Rackham, d.j. with some splits and tears, else very fine. Current BW9-32 1974 $55

DICKENS, CHARLES   A Christmas Carol. 1849. 8vo., illus., orig. crimson cloth gilt, plates, early edition. Howes 185-113 1974 £5

DICKENS, CHARLES   A Christmas Carol. London, (c. 1900). Small 4to., embossed 'Presentation Copy', illus., very fine. Current BW9-31 1974 $24.50

DICKENS, CHARLES   A Christmas Carol. 1915. Full vellum, fine, illus., numbered, signed. Covent 55-1232 1974 £135

DICKENS, CHARLES   A Christmas Carol. London, 1961. 4to., gilt pictorial cloth, illus, mint copy. Frohnsdorff 16-284 1974 $15

DICKENS, CHARLES   A Christmas Carol in Prose. Philadelphia, 1938. Small 4to., pictorial cloth, illus. Frohnsdorff 16-288 1974 $10

DICKENS, CHARLES   A Christmas Carol in Prose, Being a Ghost Story of Yuletide. East Aurora, 1902. 8vo., moire silk doublures and orig. suede covers, mint. Current BW9-34 1974 $45

DICKENS, CHARLES   Dickens's Dictionary of London. 1879. Maps. Covent 55-593 1974 £7.50

DICKENS, CHARLES   Doctor Marigold's Prescriptions. 1865. 8vo., contemporary cloth binding, first edition. Quaritch 936-367 1974 £10

DICKENS, CHARLES   Dombey and Son. 1848. Thick 8vo., orig. green cloth, frayed, plates. Howes 186-134 1974 £30

DICKENS, CHARLES   Dombey and Son. 1848. Thick 8vo., illus., contemporary navy morocco, plates, first edition. Howes 185-115 1974 £38

DICKENS, CHARLES   Drawn from Life. New York, 1875. 1st Amer. ed., bdg. rubbed., illus. Biblo & Tannen 213-531 1973 $27.50

DICKENS, CHARLES   Exhibition Catalogue of the Sawyer Collection of the Works of Charles Dickens... London, 1936. Plates, illus., crown 4to., orig. wrappers. Forster 98-60 1974 £4

DICKENS, CHARLES   Gone Astray. 1912. Illus., English first edition. Covent 56-1722 1974 £5.25

DICKENS, CHARLES   Hard Times for These Times. 1854. Crown 8vo., half green calf, gilt, first edition. Howes 185-116 1974 £25

DICKENS, CHARLES   The Haunted Man and the Ghost's Bargain. 1848. 8vo., illus., half contemporary red morocco gilt. Smith 193-344 1973 £7.50

DICKENS, CHARLES   The Haunted Man and the Ghost's Bargain. London, 1848. First edition, second issue without broken type on p. 166, illus., interior good. Current BW9-35 1974 $25

DICKENS, CHARLES   The Holly Tree & The Seven Poor Travellers. Philadelphia, 1900. 12mo., photogravure & text illus., covers bit soiled, interior very good. Current BW9-36 1974 $14

DICKENS, CHARLES   Household Words. 1850-59. 19 vols., half calf, worn. Howes 186-143 1974 £65

DICKENS, CHARLES   The Lazy Tour of Two Idle Apprentices. 1890. Illus., orig. cloth, English first edition. Covent 56-351 1974 £8.50

DICKENS, CHARLES   The Life and Adventures of Martin Chuzzlewit. London, 1844. 8vo., frontispiece, plates, foxing, contemporary red half morocco, gilt, first edition. Bow Windows 62-250 1974 £15

DICKENS, CHARLES   The Life and Adventures of Martin Chuzzlewit. 1844. Thick 8vo., contemporary half green calf gilt, plates, rebacked, first edition. Howes 186-135 1974 £25

DICKENS, CHARLES   The Life and Adventures of Nicholas Nickleby. 1839. Half contemporary calf, gilt, plates. Smith 193-345 1973 £12

DICKENS, CHARLES   The Life and Adventures of Nicholas Nickleby. 1839. 2 vols., half calf, morocco labels, plates, foxed, first edition. Howes 186-136 1974 £32

DICKENS, CHARLES   The Life and Adventures of Nicholas Nickleby. 1839. Plates, half olive morocco gilt, first edition. Howes 185-120 1974 £40

DICKENS, CHARLES   The Life and Adventures of Nicholas Nickleby. New York, 1931. Small 4to., gilt pictorial cloth, 16 color plates, unopened, 1st ed. thus. Frohnsdorff 16-289 1974 $15

DICKENS, CHARLES   The Life of Our Lord. New York, 1934. 12mo., boards, in publisher's box, first edition. Goodspeed's 578-86 1974 $10

DICKENS, CHARLES   Little Dorrit. London, 1855-1857. 8vo., orig. printed wrappers, plates, first edition. Hammond 201-301 1974 £250

DICKENS, CHARLES   Little Dorrit. 1857. 8vo., contemporary half roan, worn, first edition. Bow Windows 64-478 1974 £9.50

DICKENS, CHARLES   Little Dorrit. 1857. Thick 8vo., plates, contemporary buff calf gilt, first edition. Howes 185-117 1974 £22.50

DICKENS, CHARLES   Little Dorrit. 1857. Thick 8vo., foxing, contemporary half green calf, plates, label, first edition. Howes 186-137 1974 £22.50

DICKENS, CHARLES   Master Humphrey's Clock. 1840-41. 3 vols., roy. 8vo., half green calf, gilt, illus., first edition. Howes 185-118 1974 £30

DICKENS, CHARLES   Master Humphrey's Clock. 1840-41. Roy 8vo., 3 vols., illus., calf gilt back, first edition. Quaritch 936-368 1974 £40

DICKENS, CHARLES   Memoirs of Joseph Grimaldi. 1838. 2 vols.,
half olive morocco gilt, plates, first edition, rare first issue. Howes 185-119
1974 £28

DICKENS, CHARLES   Mr. Pickwick's Christmas. New York &
London, 1906. 8vo., illus. in color and line, gilt dec. pictorial front cover,
binding fine. Current BW9-37 1974 $20

DICKENS, CHARLES   The Mystery of Edwin Drood. 1870. Plates,
half navy calf gilt, morocco label, first edition. Howes 186-138 1974 £21

DICKENS, CHARLES   The Mystery of Edwin Drood. 1870. In the
orig. six monthly parts, engraved portrait frontispiece, engraved plates, with the
orig. ads., green cloth box rubbed, some parts neatly rebacked, fair copy, scarce.
Sawyer 293-122 1974 £95

DICKENS, CHARLES   The Mystery of Edwin Drood. Brattleboro,
1873. 8vo., cloth. Goodspeed's 578-85 1974 $10

DICKENS, CHARLES   The Nonesuch Dickens. Bloomsbury, 1937-38.
24 vols., large 8vo., buckram, illus., fine. Dawsons PM 252-288 1974 £1375

DICKENS, CHARLES   Oliver Twist. 1838. Small 8vo., 3 vols., illus.,
early half calf, first edition, first issue. Quaritch 936-369 1974 £70

DICKENS, CHARLES   Oliver Twist. 1839-38. 3 vols., gilt, full
levant morocco, plates, first & second editions. Howes 185-121 1974 £60

DICKENS, CHARLES   Oliver Twist. London, 1840. 3 vols., 8vo.,
frontispiece, plates, contemporary half calf, gilt, worn. Bow Windows 62-251
1974 £25

DICKENS, CHARLES   Our Mutual Friend. London, 1865. 2 vols.,
8vo., contemporary half morocco, plates, first edition. Dawsons PM 252-285
1974 £60

DICKENS, CHARLES   Our Mutual Friend. 1865. 2 vols., half
green calf gilt, plates, first edition. Howes 185-122 1974 £30

DICKENS, CHARLES   Perkin Warbeck, and Some Other Poems. 1897.
Quarter vellum, top edges gilt, fine, first edition. Covent 51-2310 1973 £15

DICKENS, CHARLES   The Personal History of David Copperfield. London, n.d. 4to., orig. cloth, gilt, plates. Hammond 201-493 1974 £5

DICKENS, CHARLES   The Personal History of David Copperfield.
1850. Plates, contemporary half maroon morocco gilt, foxing, first edition.
Howes 186-140 1974 £30

DICKENS, CHARLES   The Personal History of David Copperfield.
1910. 2 vols., thick roy. 8vo., dust wrappers, fine, illus. Howes 186-141
1974 £12.50

DICKENS, CHARLES   Pictures from Italy. 1846. Small 8vo., half
green calf, gilt, first edition. Howes 185-123 1974 £25

DICKENS, CHARLES   The Posthumous Papers of the Pickwick Club.
London, n.d. 4to., orig. cloth, gilt, plates. Hammond 201-494 1974 £5

DICKENS, CHARLES   The Posthumous Papers of the Pickwick Club.
Philadelphia, 1836-37. 5 vols. in 2, 12mo., half roan, first American edition.
Goodspeed's 578-84 1974 $25

DICKENS, CHARLES   The Posthumous Papers of the Pickwick Club.
London, 1837. 8vo., frontispiece, foxed, contemporary red half morocco,
worn. Bow Windows 62-252 1974 £18

DICKENS, CHARLES   The Posthumous Papers of the Pickwick Club.
London, 1837. 8vo., modern quarter calf, first book form edition. Dawsons
PM 252-286 1974 £45

DICKENS, CHARLES   The Posthumous Papers of the Pickwick Club.
1837. Thick 8vo., plates, full polished tree calf, first edition, early issue.
Howes 185-124 1974 £75

DICKENS, CHARLES   The Posthumous Papers of The Pickwick Club.
London, 1910. 2 vols., illus. Biblo & Tannen 210-855 1973 $12.50

DICKENS, CHARLES   The Posthumous Papers of the Pickwick Club.
1910. 2 vols., imp. 8vo., plates, illus., orig. buckram gilt. Smith 193-651
1973 £7.50

DICKENS, CHARLES   Selections From "Household Words". 1858-59.
Austin 61-295 1974 $47.50

DICKENS, CHARLES   Sketches by Boz. 1836-37. 2 series in 3
vols., crown 8vo., half green calf, plates, first & second editions. Howes
185-125 1974 £55

DICKENS, CHARLES   Sketches by Boz. Philadelphia, 1839. 1st
Amer. ed., illus. Biblo & Tannen 210-719 1973 $47.50

DICKENS, CHARLES   Sketches by Boz. 1839. Plates, half tan
calf, gilt, labels, uncut, new edition. Howes 186-142 1974 £50

DICKENS, CHARLES   The Strange Gentleman. 1928. Drawings,
frontis., one of 50 numbered copies, handmade paper, plates coloured, 4to., half
imitation vellum, fine, bookplate. Covent 51-2307 1973 £21

DICKENS, CHARLES   A Tale of Two Cities. London, 1859. 8vo.,
plates, foxing, contemporary half calf, worn, first edition. Bow Windows
62-253 1974 £16

DICKENS, CHARLES   The Uncommercial Traveller. 1861. Crown
8vo., contemporary half calf gilt, third edition. Howes 185-126 1974 £7.50

DICKENS, CHARLES   Works Of. (n.d.). 8vo., wine coloured
leather, 23 vols. Bow Windows 64-479 1974 £45

DICKENS, CHARLES   Works. London, (n.d.). 30 vols., 8vo.,
illus., fine, orig. cloth, illus. library edition. Dawsons PM 252-287 1974 £75

DICKENS, CHARLES   The Works of. 1874-76. 30 vols., red half
morocco, marbled sides, gilt spines, illus. library edition. Bow Windows 66-177
1974 £188

DICKENS, CHARLES   Works. c.1890. 21 vols. in 15, crown 8vo.,
plates, half crimson morocco, gilt. Howes 186-131 1974 £48

DICKENS, CHARLES   Works. c.1910. 22 vols. in 17, crown 8vo.,
half calf, gilt, fireside edition. Howes 185-109 1974 £75

DICKENS, CHARLES   The Works Of. 1913-14. 22 vols., orig.
cloth, illus. Smith 193-278 1973 £15

DICKENS, CHARLES   Works. 1929. 20 vols., crown 8vo., orig.
cloth, illus. Howes 185-110 1974 £20

DICKENS PARODY. n.d. Wrappers, illus., English first edition. Covent 56-
354 1974 £15

DICKERSON, EDWARD N.   Joseph Henry and the Magnetic Telephone. New
York, 1885. 8vo., orig. printed wrappers, first edition. Hammond 201-817 1974
£7.50

DICKES, W. F.   The Norwich School of Painting. (1906).
Roy. 4to., plates, cloth, scarce. Quaritch 939-495 1974 £180

DICKEY, D. R.   The Birds of El Salvador. Chicago, 1938.
8vo., cloth, plates. Wheldon 130-500 1974 £20

DICKEY, PAUL   The Lincoln Highwayman. French, 1931.
36p., paper. Austin 51-250 1973 $6.50

DICKIE, G.   The Botanists Guide. 1860. Post 8vo., cloth,
maps, scarce. Wheldon 129-991 1974 £5

DICKIE, G.   Flora Abredonensis. Aberdeen, 1838. Post
8vo., orig. printed boards. Wheldon 129-990 1974 £10

DICKINSON, EDWARD H.   The Medicine of the Ancients. Liverpool,
1875. Rittenhouse 46-216 1974 $12.50

DICKINSON, EDWARD R.   Poems of the Dance. Knopf, 1921. 263p.,
illus. Austin 51-251 1973 $10

DICKINSON, EMILY   Further Poems. Boston, 1929. Orig. cloth, paper label, first edition, one of 465 numbered copies, boxed, fine, bookplate of John Stuart Groves. MacManus 224-125 1974 $40

DICKINSON, EMILY   Poems. Boston, 1896. 12mo., orig. cloth, first edition, fine. MacManus 224-127 1974 $90

DICKINSON, G. LOWES   The International Anarchy. 1926. Dust wrapper, fine. Covent 55-595 1974 £7.50

DICKINSON, G. LOWES   Jacob's Ladder. n.d. (1890). Wrappers, very good copy, bookplate, first edition. Covent 51-553 1973 £22.50

DICKINSON, H. W.   Matthew Boulton. Cambridge, 1937. 8vo., fine, orig. cloth, gilt, plates, first edition. Dawsons PM 245-107 1974 £10

DICKINSON, H. W.   A Short History of the Steam Engine. 1938. 8vo., orig. cloth, plates, illus., first edition. Hammond 201-818 1974 £8.50

DICKINSON, JONATHAN   The True Scripture-Doctrine. Elizabeth Town, 1793. 8vo., old calf. Butterfield 8-385 1974 $10

DICKINSON, ROBERT LATOU   Control of Conception. Baltimore, 1931. Illus. Rittenhouse 46-217 1974 $10

DICKINSON, W. HOWSHIP   Diabetes. London, 1877. Rittenhouse 46-218 1974 $10

DICKINSON, W. HOWSHIP   Diabetes. London, 1877. 8vo., orig. brown cloth, uncut. Dawsons PM 249-140 1974 £11

DICKSON, ADAM   A Treatise on Agriculture. Edinburgh, 1765. 8vo., contemporary calf, labels, plates, gilt, second edition. Hammond 201-12 1974 £35

DICKSON, ROBERT   Annals of Scottish Printing. Cambridge, 1890. 4to., orig. buckram, limited. Dawsons PM 10-186 1974 £30

DICTIONARIUM Graecum Cum Interpretatione Latina. 1524. Small folio, old boards backed with sheep, morocco labels, stains. Thomas 30-66 1973 £21

A DICTIONARY of Quotations. 1798. 8vo., half calf. Hill 126-71 1974 £8.50

DICTIONNAIRE Apologetique de la Foi Catholique. Paris, 1925-31. 5 vols., crown 4to., orig. half morocco. Howes 185-1113 1974 £18

DICTIONNAIRE des Ecrivains Belges et Catalogue. Brussels, 1886-1910. 4 vols., cloth. Dawsons PM 11-64 1974 £61

DICTIONNAIRE Historique. 1786. 8 vols., crown 8vo., contemporary calf, worn. Howes 186-773 1974 £20

DICTIONNAIRE Liliput. Leipzig, n.d. Orig. red cloth, 1 7/8 X 1 1/4 inches. Gregory 44-364 1974 $8.50

DICTIONNAIRE Universel d'Histoire Naturelle. Paris, 1842-49. 13 vols., roy. 8vo., orig. printed wrappers, uncut, slipcases, scarce. Wheldon 131-40 1974 £280

DIDAY, CHARLES J.   A Treatise on Syphilis. 1859. 8vo., orig. cloth, first edition in English. Dawsons PM 249-142 1974 £5

DIDEROT, DENIS   Encyclopedie. Paris, 1751. 35 vols., folio, contemporary French mottled calf, fine, plates, first & best editions. Dawsons PM 250-21 1974 £4200

DIDEROT, DENIS   Encyclopedie. (c. 1755). 3 parts in 1 vol., folio, paper wrapper, torn, cloth spine. Quaritch 940-443 1974 £40

DIDEROT, DENIS   Encyclopedie, ou Dictionnaire Raisonne des Sciences, des Arts et des Metiers. Paris, Neufchastel & Amsterdam, 1751-80. 35 vols., roy. folio, plates, old calf, rubbed, gilt leather labels, very nice clean set. Quaritch 940-442 1974 £3,000

DIDEROT, DENIS   Encyclopedie ou Dictionnaire Raisonne des Sciences, des Arts et des Metiers. Paris, Neufchatel & Amsterdam, 1751-80. 35 vols., folio, contemporary French mottled calf, plates, fine, first edition, first issue. Wheldon 131-41 1974 £4,750

DIDEROT, DENIS   Encyclopedie, ou Dictionnaire Raissonne des Sciences. Geneve, 1777. 39 vols., large 4to., contemporary French mottled calf, plates, fine, first quarto edition. Dawsons PM 250-22 1974 £1600

DIDEROT, DENIS   Correspondance Inedite. Paris, 1931. 2 vols., 8vo., three quarter brown levant morocco, gilt, uncut, numbered. L. Goldschmidt 42-40 1974 $20

DIDEROT, DENIS   Memoires sur Differens Sujets de Mathematiques. Paris, 1748. 8vo., contemporary marbled calf, gilt, illus., first edition. L. Goldschmidt 42-41 1974 $120

DIDEROT, DENIS   Le Neveu de Rameau. Paris, 1821. 8vo., orig. wrapper, uncut, first French edition. L. Goldschmidt 42-42 1974 $175

DIDEROT, DENIS   Le Pere de Famille, Drame. Paris, 1772-71. 2 vols. in 1, 8vo., contemporary full tree calf, gilt, morocco label. L. Goldschmidt 42-43 1974 $20

DIDEROT, DENIS   La Religieuse. Paris, 1804. 2 vols., 8vo., contemporary tree calf, gilt, morocco labels, plates, second edition. L. Goldschmidt 42-44 1974 $90

DIDEROT, DENIS   Oeuvres Completes. Paris, 1875-77. 20 vols., large 8vo., contemporary half cloth, labels, uncut, excellent copy. L. Goldschmidt 42-39 1974 $700

DIELITZ, THEO   The Hunters of the World. Philadelphia, 1854. 12mo., gilt pictorial cloth, 4 hand-colored lithographs. Frohnsdorff 16-291 1974 $40

DIERBACH, J. H.   Repertorium Botanicum. Lemgo, 1831. Boards. Wheldon 129-912 1974 £5

DIEREVILLE, SIEUR DE   Relation du Voyage du Port Royal de l'Acadie ou de la Nouvelle France. Vellum. Hood's 103-172 1974 $500

DIETRICH, D. N. F.   Forstflora Oder Abbildung und Beschreibung der fur den Forstmann Wichtigen Baume und Straucher. Jena, 1838-40. 4to., contemporary boards, rare, plates, second edition. Wheldon 131-1726 1974 £75

DIETTERLIN, WENDEL   Architectura. Nuremburg, 1598. Folio, nineteenth century diced russia gilt, second edition. Dawsons PM 251-91 1974 £1,500

DIGBY, GEORGE LORD BRISTOL
Please turn to
BRISTOL, GEORGE DIGBY LORD

DIGBY, KENELM   The Broad Stone of Honour. 1877-76. 5 vols., small 8vo., frontis., cloth. Quaritch 939-718 1974 £10.50

DIGBY, KENELM   Choice and Experimental Receipts in Physick and Chirurgery. London, 1668. Small 8vo., contemporary calf, rebacked, first edition. Dawsons PM 249-144 1974 £295

DIGBY, KENELM   Two Treatises. Paris, 1644. Folio, modern panelled calf, black morocco label, gilt, first edition. Zeitlin 235-59 1974 $950

DIGBY, KENELM   Two Treatises. London, 1645. 4to., old calf, rebacked, second edition. Dawsons PM 249-143 1974 £165

A DIGEST of the Acts of Assembly and of the Ordinances of the Inhabitants and Commissioners of the District of Spring Garden. Philadelphia, 1841-46. 2 vols. in 1, 8vo., contemporary sheep. Ximenes 35-265 1974 $22.50

DIGGES, DUDLEY   The Compleat Ambassador. London, 1655. Folio, contemporary sheep, first edition. Dawsons PM 251-208 1974 £95

DIGGES, DUDLEY   The Compleat Ambassador. 1665. Folio, contemporary calf, rebacked. Howes 18-774 1974 £75

DIGGES, LEONARD   An Arithmeticall Militare Treatise. 1579. 4to., calf antique, fine, rare, first edition. Dawsons PM 251-373 1974 £1,000

DIGGES, LEONARD   An Arithmeticall Militare Treatise, named Stratioticos. London, 1579. 4to., calf antique, fine, illus., first edition. Dawsons PM 245-783 1974 £850

DIGGES, LEONARD   A Geometrical Practical Treatize Named Pantometria. London, 1591. Folio, old vellum, woodcuts, second edition. Traylen 79-220 1973 £585

DIGGES, LEONARD   A Geometrical Practical Treatize Named Pantometria, Divided into Three Bookes. London, 1591. Contemporary (probably orig.) calf, Thomas Digges' own copy with his inscription, enlarged second edition, rebacked. Kraus 137-26 1974 $2,800

DIGGES, LEONARD   A Geometrical Practise, named Pantometria. London, 1571. 4to., contemporary calf, first edition. Dawsons PM 245-232 1974 £750

DIGGES, LEONARD   A Geometrical Practice Treatize named Pantometria, Divided into Three Bookes. London, 1591. Folio, 19th century calf, new edition, woodcut illus. & diagrams. Kraus 137-25 1974 $2,400

DIGGES, LEONARD   A Geometrical Practise, Named Pantometria, Divided into Three Bookes. London, 1571. Small 4to., modern niger morocco, stamp of the Royal Engineers Library, first edition, printed partly in black letter. Kraus 137-24 1974 $2,750

DIGGES, THOMAS   Englands Defence. 1680. Folio, crimson label, 19th century vellum. Howes 186-2036 1974 £55

DILKE, CHARLES W.   Greater Britain. 1869. 4 parts in 1, 8vo., cloth, illus., library stamps, fourth edition. Bow Windows 66-179 1974 £9.50

DILL, SAMUEL   Roman Society from Nero to Marcus Aurelius. London, 1920. Biblo & Tannen 214-608 1974 $7.50

DILL, W. S. PSEUD.
Please turn to
MAC BETH, MADGE HAMILTON LYONS

DILLENIUS, JOHANN JAKOB   The Dillenian Herbaria. Oxford, 1907. 8vo., cloth, portrait. Wheldon 129-139 1974 £10

DILLENIUS, JOHANN JAKOB   Historia Muscorum. Oxford, 1741. 4to., very rare first edition, modern half calf antique, engraved plates. Wheldon 128-1354 1973 £100

DILLENIUS, JOHANN JAKOB   Historia Muscorum. 1768. 4to., plates, contemporary calf, rebacked. Bow Windows 64-79 1974 £95

DILLENIUS, JOHANN JAKOB   Historia Muscorum. 1768. 4to., new half calf, plates. Wheldon 129-1391 1974 £50

DILLENIUS, JOHANN JAKOB   Historia Muscorum. 1768. 4to., contemporary calf, plates. Wheldon 131-1391 1974 £50

DILLER, J. S.   Guidebook of the Western United States Part D. Washington, 1915. 8vo., wrapper. Butterfield 8-455 1974 $15

DILLER, THEODORE   Credulity As It Concerns the Medical Man. Chicago, 1930. Rittenhouse 46-219 1974 $10

DILLER, THEODORE   Pioneer Medicine In Western Pennsylvania. New York, 1927. Presentation, signed. Rittenhouse 46-220 1974 $20

DILLON, E.   Porcelain. 1904. Roy. 8vo., plates, cloth, rebacked. Quaritch 940-628 1974 £7

DILLON, E. J.   The Eclipse of Russia. 1918. Inscribed. Covent 55-837 1974 £6.50

DILLON, JOHN B.   A History of Indiana. Indianapolis, 1859. 8vo., leather, rebacked. Saddleback 14-401 1974 $25

DILLON, PHILIP R.   American Anniversaries. New York, 1918. Biblo & Tannen 213-30 1973 $7.50

DILLON, WENTWORTH   Poems By. London, 1717. 8vo., contemporary panelled calf, first edition. Dawsons PM 252-291 1974 £65

DILLWYN, L. W.   British Confervae. (1802-)1809. 4to., contemporary boards, uncut, plates. Wheldon 129-1392 1974 £50

DILLWYN, L. W.   British Confervae. (1802-) 09. 4to., rare, contemporary calf, joints weak, coloured plates. Wheldon 128-1355 1973 £85

DIMAND, M. S.   A Handbook of Mohammedan Decorative Arts. New York, 1930. Illus. and color plates., bds., spine missing. Biblo & Tannen 214-368 1974 $10

DIMOND, WILLIAM   The Foundling of the Forest. London, 1809. 8vo., wrappers, first edition. Dawsons PM 252-292 1974 £12

DIMSDALE, BARON T.   Tracts on Inoculation. London, 1781. 8vo., boards, first edition. Gurney 64-74 1974 £30

DINELEY, THOMAS   The Account of the Official Progress of His Grace Henry the First Duke of Beaufort Through Wales in 1684. 1888. Crown 4to., photo-lithographed from the orig. MS. Broadhurst 24-1409 1974 £10

DINET, E.   The Life of Mohammad. Paris, c., 1925. 4to., cloth, gilt, Japanese vellum, limited edition. Hammond 201-197 1974 £9

DINGLEY, R.   The Spirituall Tast Described. London, 1649. 19th century linen backed boards, faded spine. Smith 194-143 1974 £18

DINGWELL, WILBUR   The Handbook Annual of the Theatre. Coward, McCann, 1941. 201p. Austin 51-252 1973 $10

DINSMOOR, ROBERT   Incidental Poems Accompanied With Letters . . . With a Preface and Sketch of the Author's Life. Haverhill, 1828. 12mo., boards, cloth back, paper label, uncut, Wallace copy with his bookplate, first edition. Goodspeed's 578-402 1974 $50

DIO CASSIUS   De' Fatti de'Romani Dalla Guerra di Candia. 1566. Sheep. Allen 213-324 1973 $15

DIO CHRYSOSTOMUS PRUSENSIS
Please turn to
DIO COCCEIANUS, CHRYSOSTOMUS, OF PRUSA

DIO COCCEIANUS, CHRYSOSTOMUS, OF PRUSA   Orationes LXXX. n.d. 19th century calf gilt, rubbed. Thomas 30-96 1973 £75

DIODATI, GIOVANNI   La Bibbia. Geneva, 1607. Large 4to., orig. limp vellum, soiling, clasps wanting, first edition, binding worn, else very well preserved and fresh copy. Schumann 499-11 1974 sFr 680

DIODORUS SICULUS   Bibliotheca Historica. 1888-93. Vols. 1 - 3. Allen 213-1066 1973 $15

DION CASSIUS COCCEIANUS
Please turn to
CASSIUS DIO COCCEIANUS

DION CHRYSOSTOMUS
Please turn to
DIO COCCEIANUS, CHRYSOSTOMUS, OF PRUSA

DION COCCEIANUS, CHRYSOSTOMUS, OF PRUSA
Please turn to
DIO COCCEIANUS, CHRYSOSTOMUS, OF PRUSA

DIONIS DU SEJOUR, ACHILLE PIERRE   Essai sur les Cometes en General. Paris, 1775. 8vo., contemporary quarter calf, rebacked, fine. Dawsons PM 245-233 1974 £28

DIONIS DU SEJOUR, ACHILLE PIERRE   Essai sur les Phenomenes. Paris, 1776. 8vo., contemporary French mottled calf, gilt, first edition. Dawsons PM 245-234 1974 £15

DIONNE, C. E.   Les Oiseaux de la Province de Quebec. Quebec, 1906. First edition, 8vo., full page plates, marbled boards, red morocco spine faded, very good. Current BW9-180 1974 $18

DIONYSIUS HALICARNASSUS   Antiquitatum Romanarum Quae Supersunt. 1885-91. Vols. 1 - 3 only. Allen 213-1067 1973 $25

DIONYSIUS HALICARNASSUS   De Thvcydidis Historia Ivdicivm. 1560. Small 4to., 19th century straight grain olive morocco gilt. Thomas 30-114 1973 £50

DIONYSIUS PERIEGETES   Cosmographia Sive De Situ Orbis. 1477. 4to., woodcut, red half roan, gilt, first edition. Bow Windows 62-256 1974 £850

DIOSCORIDIS Libri Octo Graece et Latine. Paris, 1549. 8vo., contemporary calf over boards, very fine. Schafer 8-149 1973 sFr. 650

DIRCKS, H.   A Biographical Memoir of Samuel Hartlib. London, c., 1865. 8vo., cloth. Hammond 201-830 1974 £5

A DISCOURSE Upon Honour and Peerage. London, 1719. Small 4to., uncut. Quaritch 939-669 1974 £10

THE DISCOVERIE of Witchcraft. (London), 1930. Folio, illus., orig. cloth, uncut, limited. Dawsons PM 252-1070 1974 £35

DISCURSUS Eines Weitberiembten . . . Italianer, so Etwan Koniglicher Mayest. N.P., 1620. 4to. Schumann 499-29 1974 sFr 600

DISNEY, A. N.   Origin and Development of the Microscope. 1928. 8vo., cloth, plates, scarce. Wheldon 128-97 1973 £12

DISNEY, WALT   Animals from Snow White and the Seven Dwarfs. c., 1938. Roy 8vo., orig. pictorial wrappers, English first edition. Covent 56-235 1974 £45

DISNEY, WALT   Mickey Mouse and His Friends. c., 1936. 4to., orig. pictorial wrappers, English first edition. Covent 56-236 1974 £40

DISNEY, WALT   Pinocchio. c., 1940. Roy 8vo., orig. pictorial wrappers, fine, English first edition. Covent 56-238 1974 £35

DISNEY, WALT   Story of Minnie Mouse. 1938. Illus., 12mo., pictorial boards, illus., first U.S. edition. Covent 56-237 1974 £25

A DISPASSIONATE Remonstrance of the Nature and Tendency of the Laws Now in Force for the Reduction of Interest. London, 1751. 8vo., modern boards, first edition. Dawsons PM 247-92 1974 £18

DISRAELI, BENJAMIN   The Bradenham Edition of the Novels and Tales. London, 1926-27. 12 vols., 8vo., inscription, bookplate, orig. black buckram, dust wrappers. Bow Windows 62-257 1974 £75

DISRAELI, BENJAMIN   Endymion. London, 1880. 3 vols., 8vo., orig. red cloth, uncut, first edition. Dawsons PM 252-294 1974 £18

DISRAELI, BENJAMIN   An Inquiry into the Plans, Progress and Policy of the American Mining Companies. 1825. First edition, 8vo., modern cloth, title slightly spotty and stained, good copy, rare. Sawyer 293-15 1974 £175

DISRAELI, BENJAMIN   The Letters of . . . to Lady Bradrod and Lady Chesterfield. 1929. Plates, 2 vols., med 8vo., orig. cloth, fine. Broadhurst 24-324 1974 £6

DISRAELI, BENJAMIN   The Letters of Disraeli to Lady Bradford and Lady Chesterfield. 1929. 8vo., 2 vols., orig. cloth. Broadhurst 23-337 1974 £6

DISRAELI, BENJAMIN   Lothair. 1870. 3 vols., 8vo., contemporary half morocco, rubbed, second edition. Bow Windows 66-180 1974 £8.50

DISRAELI, BENJAMIN   Lothair. 1870. 3 vols., first edition. Allen 216-104 1974 $45

DISRAELI, BENJAMIN   Novels. London, n.d. 8vo., contemporary half polished calf, gilt. Hammond 201-302 1974 £10

DISRAELI, BENJAMIN   Novels and Tales. London, 1881. 11 vols., 8vo., contemporary half morocco. Dawsons PM 252-293 1974 £55

DISRAELI, BENJAMIN   Novels and Tales. 1926-27. 12 vols., orig. black buckram gilt, dust wrappers, uncut, library edition. Howes 186-152 1974 £68

DISRAELI, BENJAMIN   Works. New York & London, 1904-05. 20 vols., plates, half crushed morocco gilt, uncut, fine. Howes 186-151 1974 £150

D'ISRAELI, ISAAC   Curiosities of Literature. London, 1794. 2 vols., 8vo., labels, fourth edition. Dawsons PM 252-295 1974 £15

D'ISRAELI, ISAAC   Curiosities of Literature. 1866. 3 vols., orig. cloth, worn, portraits, new edition. Howes 186-153 1974 £5

A DISSERATION Upon Drunkenness. London, (n.d.). 8vo., modern wrappers, book-plate. Dawsons PM 252-296 1974 £75

DISTANT, W. L.   Insecta Transvaaliensia. 1900-11. 4to., half green morocco, plates, very rare. Wheldon 131-799 1974 £75

THE DISTILLER of London. London, 1639. Small folio, contemporary calf, rare, rebacked, boards, first edition. Dawsons PM 247-93 1974 £450

DISTURNELL, J.   A Trip Through the Lakes of North America. New York, 1857. Worn cover. Hood's 103-620 1974 $30

DITCHFIELD, P. H.   Cathedrals of Great Britain. London, 1916. 12mo., illus. Biblo & Tannen 214-17 1974 $7.50

DITCHFIELD, P. H.   The City Companies of London and Their Good Works. 1904. 4to., illus., full morocco, fine. Howes 186-1439 1974 £21

DITCHFIELD, P. H.   Memorials of Old London. 1908. 2 vols., illus., plates, orig. cloth gilt. Howes 186-2110 1974 £5

DITMARS, R. L.   Reptiles of the World. New York, (1933). 8vo., cloth, plates. Wheldon 130-684 1974 £5

DITMARS, R. L.   Snake-Hunters' Holiday. New York, 1935. 8vo., cloth, illus. Wheldon 131-350 1974 £10

DITMARS, R. L.   Snakes of the World. New York, (1931). Roy 8vo., cloth, plates. Wheldon 130-685 1974 £6

DITTE, ALFRED   Recherches sur les Proprietes et les Applications de l'Aluminium. 1900. 8vo., orig. printed green wrappers, first edition. Dawsons 245-236 1974 £5

DIVERS Works of Early Masters in Christian Decoration. London, 1846. 2v., in 1, folio, color plates, engravings and woodcuts, orig. half morocco. Biblo & Tannen 210-210 1973 $75

DIVES AND PAUPER
Please turn to
PARKER, HENRY

DIVINAE Scripturae. Frankfurt, 1597. Thick folio, old reversed calf, damp staining. Howes 185-973 1974 £35

DIVINE, JAMES   Irish Legends, Fairy Tales, Love Stories and Comic Compositions. Clifton, 1859. 8vo., contemporary dark green morocco, rubbed. Smith 194-475 1974 £8

THE DIVISION of the County of Essex into Severall Classes. 1648-58. 2 items in 1 vol., small 4to., half calf, rare. Quaritch 939-351 1974 £90

DIXIE, FLORENCE   Across Patagonia. 1880. 8vo., contemporary half red calf, gilt. Broadhurst 23-1631 1974 £8

DIXON, C.   Birds' Nests. London and New York, 1902. 8vo., cloth, plates. Wheldon 130-504 1974 £5

DIXON, C.   Lost and Vanishing Birds. 1898. 8vo., cloth,
plates. Wheldon 130-502 1974 £5

DIXON, F.   The Geology and Fossils of the Teritary and
Cretaceous Formations of Sussex. 1850. 4to., orig. cloth, somewhat worn,
plates. Wheldon 128-959 1973 £15

DIXON, F.   The Geology and Fossils of the Tertiary and
Cretaceous Formations of Sussex. 1850. 4to., orig. cloth, plates, worn.
Wheldon 131-991 1974 £20

DIXON, F.   The Geology of Sussex. Brighton, 1878. 4to.,
buckram, coloured folding map, plain and coloured plates, scarce, revised
second edition. Wheldon 128-960 1973 £22

DIXON, F.   The Geology of Sussex. Brighton, 1878. 4to.,
buckram, scarce, plates, revised second edition. Wheldon 131-992 1974 £25

DIXON, GEORGE   A Voyage Round the World. 1789. 4to., contemporary diced calf, second edition. Bow Windows 64-481 1974 £250

DIXON, GEORGE   A Voyage Round the World; But More Particularily
to the North West Coast of America. London, 1789. Second edition, boards and
leather. Butterfield 10-214 1974 $200

DIXON, J. M.   Centennial History of Polk County. Des Moines,
1876. Cloth. Putnam 126-181 1974 $50

DIXON, THOMAS   The Black Hood. Appleton, 1924. 336p.
Austin 54-302 1973 $7.50

DIXON, THOMAS   The Clansman. Grosset, 1905. 374p., illus.
Austin 54-303 1973 $7.50

DIXON, THOMAS   Comrades. Grosset, 1909. 319p. Austin
54-304 1973 $6

DIXON, THOMAS   The Foolish Virgin. Grosset, Dunlap, 1915.
353p., illus. Austin 54-305 1973 $6.50

DIXON, THOMAS   The Love Complex. Boni, 1925. 287p.
Austin 54-306 1973 $10

DIXON, THOMAS   The Man in Gray. Appleton, 1921. 427p.
Austin 54-307 1973 $7.50

DIXON, THOMAS   The One Woman. Grosset, Dunlap, 1903.
350p. Austin 54-309 1973 $6

DIXON, THOMAS   The One Woman. Doubleday, Page, 1903.
350p., illus. Austin 54-308 1973 $7.50

DIXON, THOMAS   The Root of Evil. Grosset, Dunlap, 1911.
407p., illus. Austin 54-311 1973 $6

DIXON, THOMAS   The Root of Evil. Doubleday, Page, 1911.
407p., illus. Austin 54-310 1973 $7.50

DIXON, THOMAS   The Traitor. Grosset, Dunlap, 1907. 331p.,
illus. Austin 54-313 1973 $6

DIXON, THOMAS   The Traitor. Doubleday, Page, 1907. 331p.
Austin 54-312 1973 $7.50

DIXON, WILLIAM HEPWORTH   New America. London, 1867. 1st ed., illus.,
2 vols., orig. 3/4 lea. and marbled bds. Jacobs 24-14 1974 $45

DOANE, A. SIDNEY   Surgery Illustrated. New York, 1836.
Woodcuts. Rittenhouse 46-221 1974 $15

DOBELL, BERTRAM   Catalogue of Books Printed for Private Circulation.
London, 1906. Med. 8vo., orig. cloth. Forster 98-87 1974 £15

DOBELL, BERTRAM   Rosemary and Pansies. Orig. cloth,
inscription. Bow Windows 62-261A 1974 £6

DOBELL, BERTRAM   Rosemary and Pansies. London, 1904. 8vo.,
orig. paper wrappers, first edition. Bow Windows 62-261 1974 £6.50

DOBELL, C.   Antony Van Leeuwenhoek and His "Little
Animals". 1932. Roy. 8vo., cloth, plates, dust jacket, nice copy, scarce orig.
issue. Wheldon 128-115 1973 £15

DOBELL, P. J.   The Popish Plot and the Religious and Political
Intrigues of the Last Quarter of the 17th Century. London, 1918-20. Orig.
wrappers. Forster 98-89 1974 £5

DOBELL, PETER   Travels In Kamtchatka. London, 1839.
2 vols., 8vo., boards, orig. paper labels, uncut. Traylen 79-518 1973 £50

DOBIE, J. FRANK   A Corner Forever Texas. Austin, 1938.
Wrapper. Jenkins 61-797 1974 $12.50

DOBIE, J. FRANK   Coronado's Children: Tales of Lost Mines and
Buried Treasure of the Southwest. Dallas, 1930. First edition, first issue, dust
jacket, first issue dedication and endpapers. Jenkins 61-798 1974 $45

DOBIE, J. F.   Legends of Texas. 1924. Orig. cloth, ex-library, second edition. Putnam 126-344 1974 $15

DOBIE, J. FRANK   Foller de Drink' Gou'd. Austin, 1928. First
edition, near mint. Jenkins 61-835 1974 $22.50

DOBIE, J. FRANK   Follow de Drinkin' Gou'd. Austin, 1928. First
edition, wrapper. Jenkins 61-803 1974 $22.50

DOBIE, J. FRANK   Guide to Life and Literature of the Southwest.
Austin, 1943. Orig. wrappers, fine, first edition. Jenkins 61-805 1974 $35

DOBIE, J. FRANK   John C. Duval: First Texas Man of Letters.
Dallas, 1939. First edition, limited, illus. by Tom Lea. Jenkins 61-808 1974
$115

DOBIE, J. FRANK   Spur-of-the-Cock. Austin, 1933. First edition,
mint. Jenkins 61-836 1974 $20

DOBIE, J. FRANK   A Texan in England. Boston, 1945. Fine,
red-stamped tan cloth, presentation inscription. Bradley 35-127 1974 $50

DOBIE, J. FRANK   Toungues of the Monte. New York, 1935.
Orig. dec. cloth, first edition. Jenkins 61-821 1974 $35

DOBIE, R.   The History of the United Parishes. London,
1829. 8vo., map, uncut, cloth covers. Bow Windows 62-262 1974 £15

DOBSON, AUSTIN   At the Sign of the Lyre. 1885. 239 pages.
Austin 61-303 1974 $10

DOBSON, AUSTIN   A Bibliography of the First Editions of
Published and Privately Printed Books and Pamphlets by. 1925. 8vo., orig. cloth,
fine, limited to 500 numbered copies. Broadhurst 24-325 1974 £6

DOBSON, AUSTIN   Coridon's Song and Other Verses. London,
1894. 1st ed. Biblo & Tannen 210-166 1973 $10

DOBSON, AUSTIN   Eighteenth Century Vignettes. 1892-96.
Crown 8vo., orig. buckram, gilt, frontispiece, first editions. Howes 186-154
1974 £12.50

DOBSON, AUSTIN   Horace Walpole. 1890. Roy. 8vo., plates,
cloth backed boards, limited, first edition. Howes 185-541 1974 £7.50

DOBSON, AUSTIN   Poems on Several Occasions. New York, 1895.
8vo., orig. cloth, 2 vols., gilt, illus., new edition. Rota 189-255 1974 £7.50

DOBSON, AUSTIN   Proverbs In Procelain. London, 1893. Signed.
Jenkins 48-145 1973 $10

DOBSON, AUSTIN   The Story of Rosina and Other Verses.
London, 1895. Biblo & Tannen 213-533 1973 $15

DOBSON, AUSTIN   Thomas Bewick and His Pupils. 1899. 8vo.,
orig. binding, rubbed. Marsden 39-29 1974 £6

DOBSON, G. E.   Monograph of the Asiatic Chiroptera.
Calcutta, 1876. 8vo., cloth, rare. Wheldon 131-484 1974 £25

DOBSON, MATTHEW   A Medical Commentary On Fixed Air.
London, 1787. Third edition. Rittenhouse 46-223 1974 $50

DOBSON, AUSTIN   The Story of Rosina and Other Verses. 1895.
8vo., orig. cloth, gilt, illus., first edition. Hammond 201-108 1974 £5

DOBZHANSKY, THEODOSIUS   Genetics and the Origin of Species.   New
York, 1941. Second edition. Rittenhouse 46-224 1974 $10

DOCUMENTS Connected with the History of Ludlow. 1841. 4to., half morocco,
boards, foxing, illus., plates. Broadhurst 23-1541 1974 £15

DOCUMENTS and Records Illustrating the History of Scotland. 1837. Roy. 8vo.,
cloth. Quaritch 939-18 1974 £20

DOCUMENTS Relating to the Settlement of the Church of England By the Act of
Uniformity of 1662. 1862. Cloth, rebound. Howes 185-890 1974 £7.50

DODD, LAMAR   Charlot Murals In Georgia. Atlanta, 1945.
4to., cloth, shaken, plates. Minters 37-8 1973 $15

DODD, LEE WILSON   The Changelings. Dutton, 1924. 155p.
Austin 51-253 1973 $7.50

DODD, LORING HOLMES   A Glossary of Wulfstan's Homilies. 1908.
Ex-library, sturdy library binding. Austin 61-305 1974 $27.50

DODD, LORING HOLMES   The Golden Age of American Sculpture.
Boston, 1936. 1st ed., illus. Dykes 24-11 1974 $25

DODD, WILLIAM   A Sermon on St. Mathew. London, 1759-62.
4to., boards. Hammond 201-527 1974 £38

DODDRIDGE, JOHN   The Lawes Resolutions of Womens Rights. London, 1632. Contemporary calf, rebacked. Dawson's 424-337 1974 £150

DODDRIDGE, PHILIP   The Rise and Progress of Religion in the Soul.
Paris, Ky., 1815. 8vo., orig. bindings. Butterfield 8-189 1974 $25

DODDRIDGE, PHILIP   The Rise and Progress of Religion in the Soul.
1810. 8vo., contemporary red straight grained morocco, richly gilt tooled, one
hinge little rubbed, very good state. Sawyer 293-64 1974 £78

DODDRIDGE, PHILIP   Some Remarkable Passages in the Life of.
Edinburgh, (n.d.). 12mo., misbound, inscription, old sheep, worn. Bow
Windows 62-263 1974 £16

DODDRIDGE, PHILIP   Some Remarkable Passages in the Life of . . .
Col. James Gardiner, Slain at . . . Preston-Pans, 21st Sept., 1745. 1776.
Modern calf spine, marbled boards, some stains. Thomas 32-115 1974 £8.50

DODDS, JOHN W.   American Memoir. Holt, Rinehart, Winston,
1961. 176p. Austin 54-314 1973 $8.50

DODGE, C. W.   Medical Mycology. (St. Louis, 1935). Roy.
8vo., cloth. Wheldon 131-1393 1974 £10

DODGE, HENRY IRVING   Skinner Steps Out. G & D, 1916. 165p.,
illus. Austin 51-254 1973 $8.50

DODGE, MARY ABIGAIL   Chips, Fragments and Vestiges. Boston, 1902.
Partly unopened, frontis. portrait, silk covers thumbed. Butterfield 10-539
1974 $8.50

DODGE, MARY ABIGAIL   Gala-Days. 1863. 12mo., orig. cloth, first
edition. Bow Windows 64-482 1974 £15

DODGE, MARY ABIGAIL   A New Atmosphere. Boston, 1865. First
edition, orig. binding. Butterfield 10-538 1974 $15

DODGE, MARY MAPES   St. Nicholas Songs. New York, 1913. Large
4to., pictorial boards, cloth spine. Frohnsdorff 16-293 1974 $20

DODGE, RICHARD IRVING   Our Wild Indians. Hartford, 1882. 8vo., orig.
bindings. Butterfield 8-700 1974 $20

DODGE, T. A.   Alexander. 1890. 2 vols. Allen 213-29
1973 $12.50

DODGE, T. A.   Hannibal, History of Art of War Among the
Carthaginians & Romans to Battle of Pydna, 168 B. C. 1891. 2 vols. Allen
213-467 1973 $12.50

DODGSON, CAMPBELL   The Etchings of James McNeill Whistler.
1922. Plates, vellum back, boards, fine. Marsden 37-517 1974 £15

DODGSON, CAMPBELL   An Iconography of the Engravings of Stephen
Gooden. London, 1944. 4to., cloth, illus., limited edition. Minters 37-149
1973 $30

DODGSON, CHARLES LUTWIDGE   Alice in Wonderland. Mount Vernon, n.d.
8vo., illus. Frohnsdorff 16-180 1974 $7.50

DODGSON, CHARLES LUTWIDGE   Alice's Adventures in Wonderland. N.P.,
n.d. Gilt pictorial cloth, fine. Frohnsdorff 16-182 1974 $30

DODGSON, CHARLES LUTWIDGE   Alice's Adventures in Wonderland. New
York, 1866. 8vo., rebound, full maroon straight grain morocco, first American
edition. Rota 189-177 1974 £350

DODGSON, CHARLES LUTWIDGE   Alice's Adventures in Wonderland. Boston,
1871. 8vo., gilt pictorial green pebbled cloth, illus. Frohnsdorff 16-177 1974
$35

DODGSON, CHARLES LUTWIDGE   Alice's Adventures in Wonderland. Boston,
1872. 8vo., gilt. pictorial blue pebbled cloth, illus., spine ends worn.
Frohnsdorff 16-178 1974 $17.50

DODGSON, CHARLES LUTWIDGE   Alice's Adventures in Wonderland. Boston,
1872. 8vo., gilt pictorial rust pebbled cloth, spine ends worn, illus., inner
hinges cracked. Frohnsdorff 16-179 1974 $12.50

DODGSON, CHARLES LUTWIDGE   Alice's Adventures Under Ground. London,
1886. Illus. by author, 8vo., orig. red cloth, first edition, fine, inscription from
author. Schumann 499-20 1974 sFr 3,145

DODGSON, CHARLES LUTWIDGE   Alice's Adventures in Wonderland. New
York, 1893. 12mo., three quarter cloth, gilt and floral dec. boards, illus.
Frohnsdorff 16-176 1974 $12.50

DODGSON, CHARLES LUTWIDGE   Alice's Adventures in Wonderland. London
and New York, 1907. Small 4to., special limited edition, one of 550 copies, illus.
Biblo & Tannen 213-588 1973 $150

DODGSON, CHARLES LUTWIDGE   Alice in Wonderland. New York, 1917.
16mo., illus., printed in Gregg Shorthand. Frohnsdorff 16-184 1974 $45

DODGSON, CHARLES LUTWIDGE   Alice's Adventures in Wonderland. New
York, 1929. 8vo., gilt pictorial cloth, first edition. Frohnsdorff 16-175 1974
$17.50

DODGSON, CHARLES LUTWIDGE   Alice's Adventures in Wonderland. London,
1932. 12mo., gilt pictorial cloth. Frohnsdorff 16-181 1974 $35

DODGSON, CHARLES LUTWIDGE   Alice's Adventures Underground. New York,
1932. 8vo., plates. Frohnsdorff 16-185 1974 $10

DODGSON, CHARLES LUTWIDGE   Christmas Greetings. n.d. Fine, English
first edition. Covent 56-1598 1974 £21

DODGSON, CHARLES LUTWIDGE   Feeding the Mind. 1907. Cloth backed
boards, English first edition. Covent 56-1600 1974 £12.50

DODGSON, CHARLES LUTWIDGE   Feeding the Mind. London, 1907. Orig. binding, first edition, unusually fine copy of fragile book, near mint. Ross 87-88 1974 $30

DODGSON, CHARLES LUTWIDGE   For the Train. 1932. Illus., English first edition. Covent 56-1601 1974 £15

DODGSON, CHARLES LUTWIDGE   The Formulae of Plane Trigonometry Printed With Symbols to Express the "Goniometrical Ratios". Oxford, 1861. Stitched without wrappers, uncut, folded at center, near fine, rare. Covent 51-2236 1973 £85

DODGSON, CHARLES LUTWIDGE   The Formulae of Plane Trigonometry. Oxford, 1861. Fine. Covent 55-292 1974 £85

DODGSON, CHARLES LUTWIDGE   Further Nonsense Verse and Prose. New York, 1926. 4to., illus. Frohnsdorff 16-187 1974 $10

DODGSON, CHARLES LUTWIDGE   The Game of Logic. London, 1886. 8vo., gilt lettered cloth, first edition, limited. Frohnsdorff 16-188 1974 $200

DODGSON, CHARLES LUTWIDGE   The Lewis Carroll Picture Book. London, 1899. 8vo., orig. cloth, illus., uncut, first edition. Dawsons PM 252-115 1974 £20

DODGSON, CHARLES LUTWIDGE   The Nursery "Alice". 1890. First edition, corner of cover trifle worn, excellent condition, presentation inscription to Frances Raymond Barker from the author. Thomas 32-162 1974 £85

DODGSON, CHARLES LUTWIDGE   Rhyme? and Reason? London, 1883. Orig. green cloth, illus., gilt, first edition, frontispiece, fine copy. MacManus 224-129 1974 $45

DODGSON, CHARLES LUTWIDGE   Some Popular Fallacies About Vivisection. Oxford, 1875. First edition, stiched, fine, preserved in cloth folding case. Thomas 32-163 1974 £120

DODGSON, CHARLES LUTWIDGE   Sylvie and Bruno. London, 1889. 8vo., illus., orig. cloth, faded, first edition. Bow Windows 62-156 1974 £6.50

DODGSON, CHARLES LUTWIDGE   Sylvie and Bruno. 1889. Cloth, gilt, illus., English first edition. Covent 56-1604 1974 £15

DODGSON, CHARLES LUTWIDGE   Sylvie and Bruno. London, 1889. 8vo., gilt pictorial cloth, first edition. Frohnsdorff 16-190 1974 $15

DODGSON, CHARLES LUTWIDGE   Sylvie and Bruno. London, 1889-1893. 2 vols., 8vo., gilt pictorial cloth, all edges gilt, first edition, illus. Frohnsdorff 16-189 1974 $75

DODGSON, CHARLES LUTWIDGE   Sylvie and Bruno Concluded. 1893. Orig. cloth gilt, illus., English first edition. Covent 56-1606 1974 £45

DODGSON, CHARLES LUTWIDGE   Sylvie and Bruno Concluded. 1893. Illus., half title foxed, fine bright copy, ads tipped in, first edition. Covent 51-2237 1973 £20

DODGSON, CHARLES LUTWIDGE   Sylvie and Bruno Concluded. 1893. Cloth gilt, illus., English first edition. Covent 56-1605 1974 £27.50

DODGSON, CHARLES LUTWIDGE   Sylvie and Bruno Concluded. London, 1893. Orig. binding, first edition, illus., presentation copy with inscription by author, laid in also the scarce ad by Carroll regarding faulty copies of the Sixtieth thousand of Through the Looking Glass (thus rare). Ross 87-89 1974 $90

DODGSON, CHARLES LUTWIDGE   Symbolic Logic. London, 1896. 12mo., first edition. Frohnsdorff 16-191 1974 $50

DODGSON, CHARLES LUTWIDGE   A Tangled Tale. 1885. Orig. dec. cloth gilt, illus., English first edition. Covent 56-1607 1974 £15

DODGSON, CHARLES LUTWIDGE   A Tangled Tale. London, 1885. 12mo., cloth, covers soiled, trifle worn, first edition. Goodspeed's 578-87 1974 $15

DODGSON, CHARLES LUTWIDGE   A Tangled Tale. London, 1885. Orig. cloth, illus., first edition, fine copy. MacManus 224-130 1974 $45

DODGSON, CHARLES LUTWIDGE   Through the Looking-Glass. 1872. Orig. cloth gilt, illus., English first edition. Covent 56-1608 1974 £8.50

DODGSON, CHARLES LUTWIDGE   Through the Looking-Glass and What Alice Found There. London, 1872. 8vo., gilt pictorial cloth, first edition, illus. Frohnsdorff 16-193 1974 $150

DODGSON, CHARLES LUTWIDGE   Through the Looking-Glass, and What Alice Found There. Boston, 1872. 8vo., three quarter navy morocco. Frohnsdorff 16-194 1974 $85

DODGSON, CHARLES LUTWIDGE   Through the Looking Glass and What Alice Found There. New York, 1899. 8vo., red cloth, gilt, illus. Rich Summer-55 1974 $17.50

DODGSON, CHARLES LUTWIDGE   Complete Works. 1939. Buckram, English first edition. Covent 56-1599 1974 £10.50

DODGSON, R. W.   Report on Mussel Purification. 1928. Roy 8vo., cloth, plates. Wheldon 130-823 1974 £7.50

DODICI Opere di Picasso. Florence, 1914. 4to., wrapper, illus., scarce. Minters 37-300 1973 $16

DODINGTON, GEORGE BUBB   The Diary of. London, 1785. 8vo., half calf, gilt, third edition. Hammond 201-198 1974 £10

DODOENS, REMBERT   Frumentorum, Leguminum, Palustrium et Aquatilium Herbarum. Antwerp, 1566. Small 8vo., 18th century marbled boards, more recent vellum spine, remarkably good within, woodcuts. Thomas 32-313 1974 £150

DODOENS, REMBERT   A Niewe Herball. 1578. Small folio, 19th century calf, rubbed, first English edition. Thomas 28-261 1972 £40

DODOENS, REMBERT   A Nevv Herball. London, 1619. Small folio, inscription, half calf, red morocco label. Bow Windows 62-265 1974 £120

DODOENS, REMBERT   A Nevv Herball. 1619. Small folio, half calf, inscription, stains. Bow Windows 64-775 1974 £120

DODOENS, REMBERT   A New Herbal. 1619. Small folio, 19th century quarter green morocco. Thomas 28-262 1972 £50

DODOENS, REMBERT   A Niewe Herball. London, 1578. Folio, half calf, woodcuts, first edition in English. Schuman 37-62 1974 $1275

DODRIDGE, JOHN   The History of the Ancient and Modern Estate of the Principality of Wales, Dutchy of Cornwall and Earldom of Chester. 1630. First edition, small 4to., newly bound half antique calf by Bayntun, panelled back, raised bands, marbled boards, fine. Broadhurst 24-1411 1974 £40

DODSLEY, J.   A Select Collection of Old Plays. 1780. Small 8vo., 12 vols., calf, gilt, frontispiece, second edition. Quaritch 936-64 1974 £125

DODSLEY, R.   Cleone. 1758. 8vo., cloth, first edition. Quaritch 936-66 1974 £7

DODSLEY, R.   The Economy of Human Life. 1806., 12mo., contemporary calf, gilt, morocco labels. Bow Windows 64-483 1974 £10

DODSLEY, ROBERT   A Collection of Poems by Several Hands. 1748. 12mo., 3 vols., contemporary calf, first edition. Quaritch 936-65 1974 £70

DODSLEY, ROBERT   Collection of Poems, By Several Hands. 1775, 1783. 10 vols., old calf, joints cracked, one cover detached. Allen 216-H 1974 $75

DODSLEY, ROBERT   A Collection of Poems in Six Volumes. London, 1782. 6 vols., 8vo., contemporary calf, fine. Dawsons PM 252-297 1974 £60

DODSLEY, ROBERT   The King and the Miller of Mansfield. 1737.
8vo., half calf, first edition. Hill 126-73 1974 £21

DODSLEY, ROBERT   Select Collection of Old Plays. 1825. 12 vols.,
half calf, joints very tender, ex-library. Allen 216-1 1974 £65

DODSON, JAMES   The Calculator. London, 1747. Small folio,
contemporary calf, gilt, first edition. Dawsons PM 245-237 1974 £58

DODWELL, EDWARD   A Classical and Topographical Tour Through
Greece, During the Years, 1801, 1805 and 1806. 1819. Engraved plates, first
edition, 2 vols., contemporary full diced calf, binding little rubbed, text & plates
fine, complete with 2 erratas. Broadhurst 24-1602 1974 £125

DODWELL, HENRY   Dissertationes Cyprianicae. 1684. 8vo.,
contemporary calf, very good copy. Bow Windows 66-184 1974 £20

DODWELL, HENRY   De Veteribus Graecorum Romanorumque Cyclis.
1701. 4to., contemporary calf, joints little cracked, small wormholes. Bow
Windows 66-183 1974 £12.50

DOERING, HEINRICH U.   Old Peruvian Art. 1936. 4to., plates, cloth,
book-plate, fine. Covent 55-96 1974 £42.50

DOESTICTS, P.   Doesticts. Livermore, 1855. 330p., illus.,
orig. ed. Austin 54-989 1973 $10

DOESTICTS, P.   Nothing to Say. Rudd, 1857. 60p., illus.
Austin 54-990 1973 $7.50

DOESTICTS, P.   Plu-Ri-Bus-Tah. Peterson, 1856. 264p.
Austin 54-992 1973 $10

DOESTICTS, P.   Plu-Ri-Bus-Tah. Livermore, 1856. 264p.,
illus. Austin 54-991 1973 $12.50

DOEVEREN, WALTHER VAN   Specimen Observationum Academicarum. 1765.
4to., speckled calf, rebacked, first edition. Dawsons PM 249-145 1974 £75

THE DOG'S Dinner Party. New York, n.d. 8vo., 8 color plates. Frohnsdorff
16-294 1974 $10

DOHERTY, HUGH   The Discovery. 1807. 12mo., new half morocco, uncut, third edition. Hill 126-74 1974 £10.50

DOHERTY, WILLIAM JAMES   Inis-Owen and Tirconnell, Notes Antiquarian
and Topographical. Dublin, 1891. 8vo., cloth boards, limited, scarce.
Emerald 50-226 1974 £15

DOHERTY, WILLIAM JAMES   Inis-Owen and Tirconnell. Dublin, 1895.
8vo., cloth boards. Emerald 50-227 1974 £12.50

DOLBEN, DIGBY MACKWORTH   The Poems. London, 1911. 8vo., orig.
boards, cloth back, plates, fine, first edition. Dawsons PM 252-298 1974 £25

DOLCE, LODOVICO   Delle Osservationi Libri III. Venice, 1566.
8vo., contemporary limp vellum, early edition. Harper 213-51 1973 $150

DOLCE, LODOVICO   I Quattro Libri Delle Osservationi. Venice,
1558. Small 8vo., contemporary vellum. Thomas 32-147 1974 £18

DOLCE, LODOVICO   L'Ulisse. Venice, 1573. 4to., woodcuts,
early 18th century calf, gilt, first edition. Schafer 8-92 1973 sFr. 750

DOLGE, ALFRED   Pianos and Their Makers. Covina, 1911.
Orig. buckram, fine, scarce, first edition. Bradley 35-427 1974 $40

DOLLARD, J. B.   Poems. Toronto, 1910. Hood's 103-720
1974 $10

DOLLFUS, CHARLES   Historie de l'Aeronautique. Paris, 1938.
Folio, cloth-backed boards, illus., plates. Schuman 37-63 1974 $110

DOLLINGER, JOHN J. I.   Geschichte der Moralstreitigkeiten in der
Romisch-Katholischen Kirche. 1889. 2 vols., half calf, rebacked, scarce.
Howes 185-1118 1974 £15

DOLLY'S Diary. New York & London, n.d. (c. 1900). Oblong 5 1/4" X
3 3/4", pict. boards, color illus. Frohnsdorff 15-28 1974 $10

DOLMETSCH, H.   Ornamental Treasures. n.d. Plates, fine.
Covent 55-438 1974 £45

DOMASZEWSKI, A. VON   Die Rangordnung des Roemischen Heeres.
1908. Sewn. Allen 213-325 1973 $10

DOMENECH, EMMANUEL   Journal d'un Missionairre au Texas, et au
Mexique. Paris, 1857. Contemporary three quarter mottled calf, very fine, first
edition, excellent color folding map. Jenkins 61-841 1974 $150

DOMENECH, EMMANUEL   Seven Years Residence in the Great Deserts of
North America. London, 1860. 2 vols., fine, half morocco slipcase, first
edition, folding map, plates. Jenkins 61-842 1974 $135

DOMENICHI, LUDOVICO   Historia Varia. Venice, 1564. Small 8vo.,
vellum, lacks colophon leaf. Thomas 32-5 1974 £25

DOMESDAY Book. 1863. 4to., orig. cloth, plates, rebacked. Howes
186-2016 1974 £8.50

DOMINIAN, LEON   The Frontiers of Language and Nationality
in Europe. 1917. Maps. Austin 57-184 1974 $37.50

"DOMINO" PSEUD.
Please turn to
BRIDLE, AUGUSTUS

DOMVILLE, MRS.   Arabella's Letters, Together With the Contents of
Her Small Diary, 1823-1828. Toronto, 1927. Cover worn. Hood's 102-234
1974 $17.50

DON, G.   A General History of the Dichlamydeous Plants.
1831-38. 4 vols., 4to., orig. cloth, worn. Wheldon 131-1133 1974 £20

DON, G.   A General History of the Dichlamydeous Plants.
1832-38. 4to., 4 vols., cloth, scarce. Wheldon 129-913 1974 £25

DON, G.   A General History of the Dichlamydeous Plants.
1831-38. 4 vols., 4to., buckram, scarce. Wheldon 131-1132 1974 £30

DONAGHY, LYLE   Into the Light. Dublin, 1934. Orig. linen
backed boards, signed, limited, first edition. Howes 185-92 1974 £30

DONCK, ADRIAEN VAN DER   Beschryvinghe Van Nieuw-Nederlandt.
Amsterdam, 1655. Small 4to., modern orange morocco, fine, first edition.
Harper 213-52 1973 $9500

DONDERS, FRANS CORNELIUS   On the Anomalies of Accommodation and
Refraction of the Eye. 1864. 8vo., orig. cloth, first edition. Dawsons PM
249-146 1974 £18

DONDERS, FRANS CORNELIUS   On the Anomalies of Accomodation and
Refraction of the Eye. London, 1864. 12mo., cloth, first edition. Goodspeed's
578-88 1974 $50

DONK, M. A.   Revisie van de Nederlandse. 1931-33. 8vo.,
buckram. Wheldon 129-1189 1974 £10

DONNADIEU, A.   Catalogue of Highly Interesting and Valuable
Autograph Letters, Being the Well-Known Collection of Mons. A. Donnadieu.
(London), 1851. 4to., plates, cloth, large paper copy. Kraus B8-51 1974
$38.50

DONNAY, MAURICE   Lysistrata. Paris, 1896. 12mo., full levant
morocco, gilt, uncut, orig. wrapper. L. Goldschmidt 42-206 1974 $50

DONNE, JOHN   Complete Poetry and Selected Prose. 1929.
Blue hardgrain morocco, limited to 675 copies on Pannekoek paper. Thomas
32-282 1974 £40

DONNE, JOHN   A Declaration of that Paradoxe. London,
1648. 4to., contemporary sheep, first edition, second issue. Dawsons PM
252-299 1974 £375

DONNE, JOHN   Donne's Sermon of Valediction. 1932. Small folio, boards, uncut, limited. Broadhurst 23-1071 1974 £20

DONNE, JOHN   The Holy Sonnets of. London, 1938. Tall 8vo., engravings, orig. cloth, limited. Dawsons PM 252-300 1974 £10

DONNE, JOHN   Letters to Severall Persons of Honour. New York, 1910. Ltd. ed., uncut. Biblo & Tannen 210-720 1973 $15

DONNE, JOHN   Letters to Severall Persons of Honour. 1651. Small 8vo., 19th century half red morocco, worn, first edition. Thomas 28-235 1972 £18

DONNE, JOHN   Paradoxes and Problems. 1923. 8vo., dec. boards, uncut, limited edition. Broadhurst 23-1060 1974 £12

DONNE, JOHN   Paradoxes and Problems. Nonesuch Press, 1923. Demy 8vo., dec. boards, uncut, limited to 645 copies, fine. Broadhurst 24-1021 1974 £15

DONNE, JOHN   Poems. London, 1633. Small 4to., rebacked, contemporary panelled calf, first edition. Dawsons PM 252-301 1974 £875

DONNE, JOHN   Poems by . . . With Elegies on the Author's Death. To Which is Added, Divers Copies Under His Own Hand Never Before in Print. London, 1650. 8vo., full brown crushed levant, fourth edition, second issue, nice copy. Ximenes 36-75 1974 $450

DONNE, T. E.   The Maori Past and Present. London, 1927. 8vo., illus., orig. cloth, first edition. Bow Windows 62-267 1974 £7.50

DONNELLY, IGNATIUS   Atlantis. New York, 1882. Illus., orig. cloth gilt, covers worn, contents shaken, 2 gatherings loose. Covent 51-2495 1973 £6.30

DONNELLY, IGNATIUS   The Great Cryptogram: Francis Bacon's Cipher in the So-Called Shakespeare Plays. 1888. 2 vols., med. 8vo., illus., orig. cloth, fine. Broadhurst 24-326 1974 £12

DONNELLY, J.   Behind the Curtains. 1896. 225 pages. Austin 57-185 1974 $12.50

DONNISON, A.   Winning a Wife In Australia. London, 1894. Crown 8vo., half leather. Traylen 79-548 1973 £5

DONOVAN, EDWARD   The Natural History of British Birds. 1799. Vols. 1 and 2 in 1 vol., 8vo., old half calf, worn, broken joints, hand-coloured plates. Wheldon 128-424 1973 £50

DONOVAN, EDWARD   The Natural History of British Fishes. 1802-08. Roy 8vo., new half blue levant morocco gilt, plates, fine, rare. Wheldon 130-18 1974 £450

DONOVAN, EDWARD   The Natural History of British Insects. 1792-1801. 8vo., 10 vols., contemporary calf, rebacked, plates, first editions, first issues. Wheldon 130-19 1974 £450

DONOVAN, EDWARD   The Natural History of British Shells. 1799-1081. 8vo., contemporary calf, rebacked, plates. Wheldon 129-740 1974 £70

DONOVAN, EDWARD   The Natural History of British Shells. 1799-1801. Vols. 1 - 3 in 1 vol., 8vo., contemporary calf, rebacked. Wheldon 131-896 1974 £70

DONOVAN, EDWARD   The Natural History of British Shells. 1804. Roy 8vo., contemporary half calf, rebacked, plates. Wheldon 130-20 1974 £150

DONOVAN, EDWARD   The Natural History of British Shells. 1804. 5 vols. in 2, roy. 8vo., contemporary half calf, hand-coloured plates. Wheldon 128-839 1973 £150

DONOVAN, JOHN   Thoughts on the Necessity and Means of Educating the Poor of Ireland. Dublin, 1795. 8vo., wrapper, first edition. Hammond 201-279 1974 £9.50

DONOVAN, M.   Chemistry. 1832. 8vo., wood engravings, orig. cloth, rebacked, rubbed. Smith 194-441 1974 £5

DOOLITTLE, HILDA   Palimpsest. Paris, 1926. 8vo., orig. wrappers, unopened, first edition. Quaritch 936-371 1974 £40

DOORNINCK, J. I. VAN   Bibliotheek van Nederlandsche Anonymen en Pseudonymen. 18--. New buckram, rubber stamp on title. Allen 216-155 1974 $12.50

DOPPET, F. A.   Traite du Fouet et de ses Effets sur le Physique de l'Amour, ou Aphrodisiaque Externe. N.P., 1788. Small octavo, boards. Rittenhouse 46-225 1974 $50

DORAN, JOHN   "Their Majesties' Servants". London, 1864. 2 vols., 8vo., contemporary half calf, rubbed, signature. Bow Windows 62-921 1974 £15

DORAN, JOHN   "Their Majesties' Servants." 1888. 3 vols., large 8vo., orig. buckram gilt, best edition. Howes 185-504 1974 £14

DORAT, CLAUDE JOSEPH   Les Deux Reines. Paris, 1770. 8vo., gilt, contemporary mottled sheep. L. Goldschmidt 42-45 1974 £20

DORAT, CLAUDE JOSEPH   Lettres d'une Chanoinesse de Lisbonne a Melcour. Paris, 1771. Small 8vo., full red morocco, cover detached, engravings, second edition. Goodspeed's 578-89 1974 $10

D'ORBIGNY, ALCIDE DESSALINES
Please turn to
ORGIBNY, ALCIDE DESSALINES D'

DORE, GUSTAVE   The Fables of La Fontaine. (n.d.) Thick 4to., illus., 19th century half morocco. Bow Windows 64-485 1974 £9

DORE, GUSTAVE   Histoire de l'Intrepide Capitaine Castagnette Par Quatrelles. Paris, 1890. 4to., illus., foxing, orig. cloth-backed boards. Bow Windows 62-268 1974 £6.50

DORE, GUSTAVE   A Pilgrimage. London, 1872. Folio, plates, contemporary half red morocco, gilt. Marlborough 70-43 1974 £50

DORE, GUSTAVE   Rabelais. London, 1882. Good used copy, rebacked. Biblo & Tannen 213-259 1973 $7.50

DORE, GUSTAVE   The Vision of Hell. 1866. Large 4to., plates, contemporary half crimson morocco gilt, foxing, portrait. Howes 186-157 1974 £21

DORE, GUSTAVE   Vivien, Together with Guinevere. 1867. Large folio, orig. dec. cloth gilt, English first edition. Covent 56-688 1974 £25

DOREAU, DOM VICTOR MARIE   Les Ephemerides de l'Ordre des Chartreux d'Apres les Documents. Montreuil, 1897. 4 vols., 8vo., orig. wrapper. L. Goldschmidt 42-46 1974 £20

DORIVAL, BERNARD   Rouault. Paris, 1942. 4to., wrappers, plates, scarce, limited edition. Minters 37-126 1973 $27.50

D'ORLEANS, LOUIS PHILLIPE   History of the Civil War in America. Philadelphia, 1875-88. 4 vols., orig. binding. Butterfield 10-151 1974 $25

DORNHOFFER, FRIEDRICH   Hortulus Animae. Frankfurt A/M, 1907. Cloth, 3 vols., large folio, lacks text vol., photomechanical reproductions in color. Kraus B8-52 1974 $100

DORRANCE, GEORGE M.   The Operative Story of Cleft Palate. Philadelphia, 1933. Rittenhouse 46-226 1974 $50

DORSET, CATHERINE A.   The Peacock "At Home." London, 1883. Square 12mo. Frohnsdorff 16-298 1974 $15

DORSET, CATHERINE A.   The Peacock "At Home." London, 1824. 16mo., orig. printed wrappers (rebacked), 8 hand-colored engravings. Frohnsdorff 16-297 1974 $60

DORSEY, SARAH A.   Panola. Philadelphia, (1877). Cloth, rubbed. Hayman 57-184 1974 $12.50

DORVAL, MARCELLE   Le Coeur sur la Main. New York, 1943. Large 4to., faded cloth, illus. Minters 37-56 1973 $12.50

DOS PASSOS, JOHN   Airways, Inc.   New York, (1928). First edition, signed, d.j., orig. binding.   Butterfield 10-217 1974 $25

DOS PASSOS, JOHN   Chosen Country.   Houghton, 1951. 485p. Austin 54-315 1973 $4.75

DOS PASSOS, JOHN   Facing the Chair.   Boston, 1927. First U. S. edition, very good copy, slightly worn wrappers.   Covent 51-557 1973 £12.60

DOS PASSOS, JOHN   The 42nd Parallel.   New York, 1930. First U. S. edition, fine, cloth backed dec. boards.   Covent 51-558 1973 £10.50

DOS PASSOS, JOHN   The Garbage Man, A Parade With Shouting. London, 1929. First English edition, wrapper.   Butterfield 10-219 1974 $10

DOS PASSOS, JOHN   The Grand Design.   Houghton, 1949. 440p. Austin 54-316 1973 $5

DOS PASSOS, JOHN   The Ground We Stand on.   New York, (1941). First edition, orig. binding, d.j.   Butterfield 10-220 1974 $15

DOS PASSOS, JOHN   In All Countries.   New York, (1934). First edition, orig. binding.   Butterfield 10-221 1974 $8.50

DOS PASSOS, JOHN   Manhatten Transfer.   Houghton, Mifflin (1925) ca 1945. 404p.   Austin 54-318 1973 $7.50

DOS PASSOS, JOHN   Manhatten Transfer.   Somerset Books, 1925. 404p.   Austin 54-319 1973 $7.50

DOS PASSOS, JOHN   Manhatten Transfer.   Harper, 1925. 404p., orig. ed., illus.   Austin 54-317 1973 $8.50

DOS PASSOS, JOHN   Men Who Made the Nation.   Doubleday, 1957. 469p.   Austin 54-320 1973 $5

DOS PASSOS, JOHN   Mid Century.   Houghton, 1961. 496p., hard cover ed.   Austin 54-321 1973 $4.75

DOS PASSOS, JOHN   Most Likely to Succeed.   Prentice Hall, 1954. 310p., orig. ed.   Austin 54-322 1973 $6

DOS PASSOS, JOHN   Most Likely to Succeed.   Houghton, Mifflin, 1966. 316p., 1st printing of this ed.   Austin 54-323 1973 $7.50

DOS PASSOS, JOHN   One Man's Initiation - - 1917.   New York, 1922. Orig. binding.   Butterfield 10-223 1974 $8.50

DOS PASSOS, JOHN   Orient Express.   New York & London, 1927. Illus. in color, first edition, orig. binding.   Butterfield 10-224 1974 $10

DOS PASSOS, JOHN   The Prospect Before Us.   Lehman, London, 1951. 288p.   Austin 54-324 1973 $8.50

DOS PASSOS, JOHN   Prospects of a Golden Age.   Prentice-Hall, 1959. 271p., illus.   Austin 54-325 1973 $12.50

DOS PASSOS, JOHN   A Pushcart at the Curb.   New York, (1922). First edition, orig. binding.   Butterfield 10-225 1974 $12.50

DOS PASSOS, JOHN   Rosinante to the Road Again.   New York, (1922). First state, thumb marks on title page and cover, orig. binding.   Butterfield 10-226 1974 $15

DOS PASSOS, JOHN   Three Soldiers.   New York, 1921. First U. S. edition, very nice copy, defective d.w.   Covent 51-559 1973 £10.50

DOS PASSOS, JOHN   Three Soldiers.   New York, 1921. Jacobs 24-79a. 1974 $20

DOS PASSOS, JOHN   Three Soldiers.   New York, 1921. 1st issue. Jacobs 24-79 1974 $30

DOS PASSOS, JOHN   Three Soldiers.   New York, 1921. Orig. cloth, first issue, with "signing" p. 213 line 7 from bottom, fine, dust jacket (extremities worn).   MacManus 224-131 1974 $40

DOS PASSOS, JOHN   Tour Duty.   Houghton, 1946. 335p.   Austin 54-326 1973 $10

DOSSIE, ROBERT   The Elaboratory Laid Open.   London, 1768. 8vo., half roan, second edition.   Gumey 64-76 1974 £45

DOSSIE, ROBERT   The Handmaid to the Arts.   London, 1764. 2 vols., full brown calf.   Dawson's 424-183 1974 $275

DOSSIE, ROBERT   The Handmaid to the Arts.   1764. 2 vols., 8vo., contemporary tree calf, very scarce, second edition.   Quaritch 940-86 1974 £80

DOSIO, GIOVANNI ANTONIO   Urbis Romae Aedificiorum Illustrium.   1569. Oblong 4to., modem boards.   Marlborough 70-6 1974 £480

DOSTOEVSKY, FEDOR MIKHAILOVICH   The Grand Inquisitor.   (London), 1930. 8vo., orig. printed vellum boards, boxed, numbered, nice copy, first edition.   Ximenes 37-127 1974 $50

DOSTOEVSKY, FEDOR MIKHAILOVICH   Poor Folk.   1894. Orig. pictorial yellow cloth, English first edition.   Covent 56-361 1974 £21

DOTTIN, P.   Robinson Crusoe Examin'd and Criticis'd. London, 1923. Med. 8vo., orig. wrappers, limited to 200 copies.   Forster 98-14 1974 £3

DOUBLEDAY, E.   List of the Specimens of Lepidopterous Insects. 1844-48. 3 parts in 2 vols., 12mo., half calf.   Wheldon 131-800 1974 £5

DOUBLEDAY, RUSSELL   Cattle-Ranch to College.   New York, 1899. Cloth, scarce, first edition.   Hayman 57-149 1974 $15

DOUCE, FRANCIS   Illustrations of Shakespeare.   Tegg, 1839. 631p.   Austin 51-255 1973 $20

DOUCET, JACQUES   Collection Jacques Doucet.   1912. 3 vols., roy. 4to., plates, wrappers, slip case.   Quaritch 940-784 1974 £20

DOUGALL, J.   The Young Man's Companion and Guide to Useful Knowledge.   1815. Contemporary calf gilt, rubbed, plates.   Smith 194-346 1974 £5

DOUGHTY, ARTHUR GEORGE   Cheadle's Journal of a Trip Across Canada, 1862-63.   Ottawa, 1931. Drawings.   Hood's 103-802 1974 $35

DOUGHTY, ARTHUR GEORGE   The Cradle of New France.   Montreal, 1908. Illus., first edition.   Hood's 103-769 1974 $12.50

DOUGHTY, ARTHUR GEORGE   A Daughter of New France.   Ottawa, 1916. Full leather, illus.   Hood's 103-206 1974 $25

DOUGHTY, ARTHUR GEORGE   Guide to the Model of Quebec Made By Lieut. Jean Baptiste Duberger.   Ottawa, 1926. Illus.   Hood's 103-770 1974 $30

DOUGHTY, ARTHUR GEORGE   Quebec of Yester-Year.   Toronto, 1932. Illus. Hood's 102-700 1974 $12.50

DOUGHTY, ARTHUR GEORGE   Quebec Under Two Flags.   Quebec, 1903. Hood's 102-701 1974 $20

DOUGHTY, CHARLES M.   Wanderings in Arabia.   1923. Frontis., folding map, 2 vols., covers of vol. 2 somewhat cockled, very good copies.   Covent 51-560 1973 £5.25

DOUGHTY, OSWALD   English Lyric in the Age of Reason.   1922. Orig. edition.   Howes 185-135 1974 £5.50

DOUGLAS, ALFRED BRUCE   The City of the Soul.   1899. Covers somewhat faded & marked, bookplate, good copy, vellum backed boards, first edition. Covent 51-564 1973 £12.50

DOUGLAS, ALFRED BRUCE   The Collected Satires.   1926. One of 550 copies, roy. 8vo., quarter morocco, spine rubbed & worn, corners bumped, ownership inscription, very good copy, first edition.   Covent 51-565 1973 £5.25

DOUGLAS, ALFRED BRUCE   The Collected Satires of. London, 1926. Orig. binding, edition limited to 550 copies on Verge de Mongolfier a la Forme, Marie Carmichael Stopes' copy with her bookplate & signature, lacking d.w., fine. Ross 87-149 1974 $40

DOUGLAS, ALFRED BRUCE   In Excelsis. 1924. One of 100 numbered copies, signed by author, bookplate, very fine, slightly worn d.w., first edition. Covent 51-566 1973 £25

DOUGLAS, ALFRED BRUCE   Lyrics. London, 1935. No. 20 of edition limited to 50 copies, signed, bound in full vellum, near fine. Ross 87-150 1974 $35

DOUGLAS, ALFRED BRUCE   Lyrics. London, 1935. 2 vols., 8vo., frontispiece, orig. parchment boards, uncut, first editions. Bow Windows 62-270 1974 £20

DOUGLAS, ALFRED BRUCE   Poems. Paris, 1896. 8vo., rare, foxed, full niger morocco, uncut, firest edition. Bow Windows 62-271 1974 £35

DOUGLAS, ALFRED BRUCE   Poemes. Paris, 1896. Cloth, bookplate, portrait, English first edition. Covent 56-1727 1974 £10.50

DOUGLAS, ALFRED BRUCE   The Principles of Poetry. London, 1943. Orig. paper wrappers, inscribed by author, near mint. Ross 87-151 1974 $25

DOUGLAS, ALFRED BRUCE   The Rossiad. London, 1916. Wrappers, near fine, scarce, small holes in front cover, first edition. Covent 51-568 1973 £25

DOUGLAS, ALFRED BRUCE   Sonnets. 1909. Orig. boards, uncut, second edition. Howes 185-136 1974 £6

DOUGLAS, ALFRED BRUCE   Sonnets. London, 1935. No. 20 of edition limited to 50 copies, signed, full vellum, fine. Ross 87-152 1974 $35

DOUGLAS, ALFRED BRUCE   The True History of Shakespeare's Sonnets. 1933. Frontis., author's signed presentation inscription, very good copy, first edition. Covent 51-569 1973 £25

DOUGLAS, HENRY KYD   I Rode With Stonewall. (Chapel Hill, 1940). Second printing, small 4to., orig. binding, d.j. Butterfield 10-153 1974 $10

DOUGLAS, HOWARD   Observations on Modern Systems of Fortification. London, 1859. 8vo., contemporary polished calf, gilt, illus. Hammond 201-606 1974 £12.50

DOUGLAS, J. W.   The British Hemiptera. 1865. 8vo., cloth, plates. Wheldon 129-629 1974 £7.50

DOUGLAS, JAMES   Myographiae Comparatae Specimen. London, 1707. Rittenhouse 46-227 1974 $82.50

DOUGLAS, JAMES   New England and New France. Toronto & New York, 1913. Maps, illus., first edition. Hood's 103-531 1974 $35

DOUGLAS, JAMES   Old France In the New World. Cleveland & London, 1905. Maps, illus., photographs. Hood's 103-771 1974 $45

DOUGLAS, JOHN   The Criterion. 1754. Crown 8vo., 19th century half roan, first edition. Howes 185-1122 1974 £7.50

DOUGLAS, JOHN   A Letter Addressed to Two Great Men. London, 1760. 8vo., modern quarter calf, first edition. Dawsons PM 247-94 1974 £18

DOUGLAS, JOHN   A Letter Addressed to Two Great Men, On the Prospect of Peace. London, 1760. Second printing, beautifully rebound, three quarter leather, mottled boards. Hood's 102-555 1974 $90

DOUGLAS, JOHN   A Letter Addressed to Two Great Men, On the Prospect of Peace. London, 1760. Three quarter leather, mottled boards, rebound. Hood's 104-631 1974 $90

DOUGLAS, LLOYD C.   Disputed Passage. Boston, 1939. First edition, inscribed, signed by author, d.w., orig. binding. Wilson 63-507 1974 $10

DOUGLAS, NORMAN   Birds and Beasts of the Greek Anthology. London, 1928. Orig. binding, mint, d.w. Ross 87-153 1974 $25

DOUGLAS, NORMAN   Birds and Beasts of the Greek Anthology. 1929. Austin 61-308 1974 $10

DOUGLAS, NORMAN   Birds and Beasts of the Greek Anthology. New York, 1929. 1st Amer. ed., illus. Biblo & Tannen 214-609 1974 $10

DOUGLAS, NORMAN   Birds and Beasts of the Greek Anthology. 1927. 8vo., orig. boards, uncut, signed, limited, first edition. Broadhurst 23-685 1974 £20

DOUGLAS, NORMAN   Birds and Beasts of the Greek Anthology. (Florence), 1927. Orig. paper covered boards, label on spine, first edition, one fo 500 copies numbered & singed by author, fine, dust jacket. MacManus 224-132 1974 $25

DOUGLAS, NORMAN   Capri. Florence, 1930. 4to., linen over boards, morocco label, illus., first edition. Howes 185-137 1974 £68

DOUGLAS, NORMAN   Experiments. (Florence), 1925. One of 300 copies, numbered & signed by author, roy. 8vo., boards, top of spine chipped and slightly defective, fine, with remains of d.w. Covent 51-2311 1973 £17.50

DOUGLAS, NORMAN   Experiments. 1925. Orig. cloth, stained, inscription, first English edition. Rota 188-254 1974 £7.50

DOUGLAS, NORMAN   Experiments. N. P., 1925. Orig. paper covered boards, first edition, one of 300 numbered copies, signed by author. MacManus 224-133 1974 $40

DOUGLAS, NORMAN   How About Europe. 1929. Crown 8vo., dec. boards, uncut, signed, limited edition. Broadhurst 23-686 1974 £21

DOUGLAS, NORMAN   How About Europe. 1929. Limited to 550 copies, signed by author, crown 8vo., dec. boards, uncut, mint, d.w., paper printed label. Broadhurst 24-637 1974 £21

DOUGLAS, NORMAN   How About Europe. (Florence), 1929. 8vo., orig. cloth, signed, fine, first edition. Rota 189-259 1974 £20

DOUGLAS, NORMAN   How About Europe? (Florence), 1929. Orig. paper covered boards, label on spine, first edition, numbered & signed by author, fine, dust jacket. MacManus 224-134 1974 $25

DOUGLAS, NORMAN   In the Beginning. (Florence), 1927. 8vo., orig. boards, fine, limited, first edition. Dawsons PM 252-302 1974 £30

DOUGLAS, NORMAN   In the Beginning. 1927. Signed, label slightly rubbed, first edition. Allen 216-473 1974 $25

DOUGLAS, NORMAN   In the Beginning. Florence, 1927. One of 700 copies, numbered & signed by author, patterned boards, morocco label, exceptionally fine copy. Covent 51-2312 1973 £20

DOUGLAS, NORMAN   In the Beginning. New York, 1928. Orig. designed boards, first trade edition. Smith 194-346 1973 £5

DOUGLAS, NORMAN   London Street Games. London, 1916. First edition, buckram, lacking d.w., unusually fine, bright copy, scarce. Ross 87-156 1974 $65

DOUGLAS, NORMAN   Looking Back. London, 1934. Orig. binding, front hinge weak, nice, single vol. edition. Ross 87-157 1974 $12.50

DOUGLAS, NORMAN   Looking Back. 1934. Plates, faded, first ordinary edition. Covent 56-363 1974 £5

DOUGLAS, NORMAN   Nerinda 1901. Florence, 1929. Orig. paper covered boards, first edition, one of 475 numbered copies, signed by author. MacManus 224-135 1974 $37.50

DOUGLAS, NORMAN   Old Calabria. 1915. Plates, cloth gilt. Covent 55-598 1974 £25

DOUGLAS, NORMAN   Paneros. London, 1931. Orig. cloth backed boards, corners rubbed, first edition, one of 650 numbered copies. MacManus 224-136 1974 $25

DOUGLAS, NORMAN   Paneros. 1931. 8vo., dec. boards, uncut, limited edition. Broadhurst 23-687 1974 £20

DOUGLAS, NORMAN   Paneros: Some Words on Aphrodisiacs and the Like. 1931. Frontis., limited to 650 numbered copies, med. 8vo., dec. boards, linen spine, uncut. Broadhurst 24-638 1974 £20

DOUGLAS, NORMAN   Siren Land. London, 1911. 8vo., plates, orig. cloth, uncut, fine, first edition. Dawsons PM 252-304 1974 £48

DOUGLAS, NORMAN   South Wind. 1929. 2 vols., illus. by John Austen. Allen 216-474 1974 $17.50

DOUGLAS, NORMAN   South Wind. Harmondsworth, 1942. 8vo., orig. cloth, first edition. Rota 189-261 1974 £15

DOUGLAS, NORMAN   Summer Islands. 1931. Frontispiece, dust wrapper. Covent 55-599 1974 £7.50

DOUGLAS, NORMAN   Summer Islands. New York, 1931. Sm. 4to., illus., ltd. to 550 copies, sgd. by author. Jacobs 24-80 1974 $22.50

DOUGLAS, NORMAN   Summer Islands. 1931. Orig. cloth, faded, first trade edition. Rota 188-256 1974 £5

DOUGLAS, NORMAN   Summer Islands: Ischia and Ponza. 1931. Fine, d.w., spare printed label tipped in at end, first edition. Covent 51-573 1973 £5.25

DOUGLAS, R. LANGTON   Piero di Cosimo. Chicago, 1946. 87 plates. Biblo & Tannen 214-85 1974 $15

DOUGLAS, STEPHEN A.   Speech of . . . In the Senate, Jan. 30, 1859 on the Nebraska Territory. Washington, 1854. Disbound, double col. text. Wilson 63-130 1974 $10

DOUGLAS, STEPHEN A.   Speech of . . . on Kansas Territorial Affairs. Washington, 1856. Self wrappers, unopened as issued. Wilson 63-131 1974 $10

DOUGLAS, W. S.   Cromwell's Scotch Campaigns. 1898. Orig. cloth, scarce. Howes 186-748 1974 £6.50

DOUGLASS, BEN   History of Wayne County, Ohio. Indianapolis, 1878. 8vo., leather, rebacked. Saddleback 14-614 1974 $75

DOUGLASS, FREDERICK   My Bondage and My Freedom. Part 1 - Life as a Slave. Part 2 - Life as a Freeman. New York, 1855. First edition, 12mo., very good, frontis., spine ends chipped away, covers spotted. Current BW9-362 1974 $60

DOUGLASS, FREDERICK   Narrative of the Life of. Boston, 1845. First edition. Jenkins 61-849 1974 $75

DOUGLASS, WILLIAM   A Summary . . . . . of the British Settlements in North-America. London, 1755. 2 vols., 8vo., contemporary calf, red morocco labels, first English edition. Traylen 79-475 1973 £120

DOURNEL, JULES   Histoire Generale de Peronne. 1879. Thick 8vo., rebound, buckram, leather label. Howes 186-784 1974 £6

DOW, A.   Sethona. 1774. 8vo., cloth, first edition. Quaritch 936-67 1974 £5

DOW, A.   Zingis. 1769. 8vo., cloth, first edition. Quaritch 936-68 1974 £6

DOW, ANN ELIZA   The Life and Adventures of. Burlington, 1845. 8vo., orig. pink printed wrappers, first edition, woodcut illus. Ximenes 36-89 1974 $125

DOW, C. M.   Anthology and Bibliography of Niagara Falls. Albany, 1921. 2 vols., illus. Hood's 103-13 1974 $30

DOW, GEORGE FRANCIS   Slave Ships and Slaving. Salem, 1927. Cloth, marbled boards, limited edition. Dawson's 424-106 1974 $125

DOW, JOSEPH   History of the Town of Hampton, New Hampshire. Salem, 1893. 2 vols. in 1, 8vo., map, cloth. Saddleback 14-545 1974 $45

DOW, LORENZO   History of Cosmopolite. Cincinnati, 1849. New cloth, sixth edition. Hayman 57-377 1974 $10

DOWDEN, EDWARD   Poems. 1876. Orig. dec. cloth gilt, some foxing of text, very good copy, first edition. Covent 571 1973 £5.25

DOWELL, STEPHEN   A History of Taxation and Taxes in England. London, 1884. 4 vols., 8vo., modern green calf gilt, fine, first edition. Dawsons PM 247-95 1974 £60

DOWER, JOHN   A New General Atlas of the World. London, 1831. Folio, modern buckram, maps. Traylen 79-417 1973 £65

DOWLING, A. E.   The Flora of the Sacred Nativity. 1900. Small 4to., cloth. Wheldon 128-98 1973 £5

DOWLING, A. E.   The Flora of the Sacred Nativity. 1900. Small 4to., cloth. Wheldon 131-214 1974 £5

DOWLING, HENRY G.   A Survey of British Industrial Arts. Essex, England, 1935. 4to., illus. Biblo & Tannen 214-106 1974 $32.50

DOWN & Connor Historical Society Journal. Belfast, (1928-30). 3 vols., 4to., orig. wrappers, scarce. Emerald 50-770 1974 £10

DOWNES, JOHN   Roscitus Anglicanus. London, (n.d.). 8vo., orig. vellum, uncut, limited. Dawsons PM 252-305 1974 £48

DOWNEY, E.   Charles Lever: His Life In His Letters. 1906. 2 vols., plates. Allen 216-2250 1974 $12.50

DOWNEY, FAIRFAX   Indian-Fighting Army. New York, 1941. 1st ed., edges worn, illus, very good copy. Dykes 24-275 1974 $40

DOWNEY, STEPHEN W.   The Play of Destiny, As Played by Actors From the Kingdom of the Dead in the Theatre of the Universe. New Creek, 1867. 8vo., contemporary half calf, library bookplate, very good copy, very rare, first edition. Ximenes 37-130 1974 $250

DOWNING, A. J.   The Fruits and Fruit Trees of America. New York, 1872. 8vo., 2 vols., orig. cloth. Wheldon 130-1472 1974 £10

DOWNING, A. J.   The Fruits and Fruit Trees of America. London, 1845. Roy 8vo., half polished green morocco gilt, first edition. Wheldon 130-1471 1974 £25

DOWS, OLIN   Franklin Roosevelt at Hyde Park. New York, 1949. Sm. 4to., 1st ed., author's sgd. pres. Biblo & Tannen 210-156 1973 $15

DOWSON, ERNEST   Adrian Rome. 1899. Covers slightly faded, very good copy, first edition. Covent 51-578 1973 £10.50

DOWSON, ERNEST   The Pierrot of the Minute. San Francisco, 1932. 12mo., boards, cloth back. Goodspeed's 578-90 1974 $25

DOWSON, ERNEST   La Pucelle the Maid of Orleans. 1899. 2 vols., one of 500 numbered copies, very good. Covent 51-577 1973 £21

DOWSON, ERNEST   Voltaire, La Pucelle, the Maid of Orleans. 1899. 2 vols., small 4to. Covent 55-601 1974 £21

DOYLE, ARTHUR CONAN   The Adventures of Sherlock Holmes. London, 1892. Large 8vo., orig. cloth, first edition. Dawsons PM 252-306 1974 £130

DOYLE, ARTHUR CONAN   The Adventures of Sherlock Holmes. 1892. Roy. 8vo., illus., orig. cloth, faded, gilt. Howes 186-166 1974 £65

DOYLE, ARTHUR CONAN   The Annotated Sherlock Holmes. New York, 1967. 2 vols., 4to. Biblo & Tannen 210-446 1973 $35

DOYLE, ARTHUR CONAN   Arsene Lupin Versus Sherlock Holmes. Chicago, 1910. Austin 61-330 1974 $10

DOYLE, ARTHUR CONAN   The British Campaign In France and Flanders, 1914-1918. London, (1920). 6 vols., 8vo., maps. Traylen 79-132 1973 £5

DOYLE, ARTHUR CONAN   Conan Doyle's Stories for Boys. New York, 1938. Biblo & Tannen 213-516 1973 $7.50

DOYLE, ARTHUR CONAN   Conan Doyle's Stories for Boys. New York, 1938. Faded, illus. Covent 55-602 1974 £7.50

DOYLE, ARTHUR CONAN   The Crome of the Congo. 1909. 126 pages. Austin 61-313 1974 $15

DOYLE, ARTHUR CONAN   The Croxley Master. New York, 1907. First U. S. edition, frontis., nice copy, scarce book. Covent 51-579 1973 £65

DOYLE, ARTHUR CONAN   The Doings of Raffles Haw. New York, 1919. Fine, first American edition. Covent 55-603 1974 £15

DOYLE, ARTHUR CONAN   The Doings of Raffles Haw. 1892. Nice copy, top edges gilt, first edition, ads at end. Covent 51-2315 1973 £25

DOYLE, ARTHUR CONAN   A Duet: With an Occasional Chorus. 1899. Austin 61-314 1974 $12.50

DOYLE, ARTHUR CONAN   The Exploits of Brigadier Gerard. New York, 1896. First American edition, bookplate, fine. Ross 86-126 1974 $15

DOYLE, ARTHUR CONAN   The Exploits of Brigadier Gerard. 1896. Illus. Austin 61-315 1974 $10

DOYLE, ARTHUR CONAN   The Fate of Fenella. New York, 1892. First American edition. Covent 55-604 1974 £35

DOYLE, A. CONAN   Five Sherlock Holmes Detective Stories. n.d. Orig. wrappers, English first edition. Covent 56-366 1974 £12.50

DOYLE, A. CONAN   The Great Shadow. 1892. Orig. wrappers, worn, English first edition. Covent 56-367 1974 £45

DOYLE, A. CONAN   The Gully of Bluemansdyke and Other Stories. (1893). 8vo., orig. cloth, second edition. Rota 189-263 1974 £7.50

DOYLE, A. CONAN   The Hound of the Baskervilles. New York, 1902. Faded, first U.S. edition. Covent 56-368 1974 £17.50

DOYLE, A. CONAN   The Hound of the Baskervilles. 1902. Orig. dec. cloth gilt, plates, English first edition. Covent 56-1729 1974 £95

DOYLE, ARTHUR CONAN   The Maracot and Other Stories. 1929. First American edition. Austin 61-317 1974 $12.50

DOYLE, ARTHUR CONAN   Memoirs of Sherlock Holmes. 1902. Illus., new and revised edition. Austin 61-318 1974 $10

DOYLE, A. CONAN   The Memoirs of Sherlock Holmes. 1894. Roy 8vo., illus., orig. cloth, gilt, first edition. Quaritch 936-373 1974 £80

DOYLE, ARTHUR CONAN   Profile By Gaslight. 1944. 312 pages. Austin 61-331 1974 $10

DOYLE, ARTHUR CONAN   Rodney Stone. London, 1896. Illus., dark blue cloth, first edition, front hinge slightly loose, else fine. Ross 86-127 1974 $45

DOYLE, ARTHUR CONAN   Round the Red Lamp. London, 1894. First edition, spine somewhat faded, nice copy, orig. binding. Ross 86-128 1974 $45

DOYLE, A. CONAN   Round the Red Lamp. 1894. 8vo., orig. cloth, first edition. Rota 189-264 1974 £6

DOYLE, ARTHUR CONAN   The Sign of Four. n.d. 171 pages. Austin 61-322 1974 $10

DOYLE, A. CONAN   The Sign of Four. Leipzig, 1891. Contemporary cloth, orig. wrappers, English first edition. Covent 56-369 1974 £7.50

DOYLE, ARTHUR CONAN   The Sign of Four. n.d. Orig. cloth, first shorthand edition. Rota 188-259 1974 £5

DOYLE, ARTHUR CONAN   The Speckled Band. 1912. 124 pages. Austin 61-323 1974 $10

DOYLE, ARTHUR CONAN   The Stark Munro Letters. London, 1895. 8vo., frontispiece, orig. cloth, gilt, first edition. Bow Windows 62-279 1974 £15

DOYLE, A. CONAN   The Stark Munro Letters. 1895. Frontispiece, English first edition. Covent 56-370 1974 £6.30

DOYLE, ARTHUR CONAN   The Stark Munro Letters. 1895. Orig. buckram gilt, waterstain. Smith 194-443 1974 £8.50

DOYLE, ARTHUR CONAN   Uncle Bernac. 1897. Orig. cloth, worn, inscribed, first edition. Rota 188-258 1974 £25

DOYLE, ARTHUR CONAN   The Valley of Fear. New York, 1914. Plates, first American edition. Covent 55-608 1974 £10.50

DOYLE, ARTHUR CONAN   The Vital Message. 1919. 160 pages. Austin 61-326 1974 $10

DOYLE, ARTHUR CONAN   The White Company. 1903. Bookplate, illus., signed, limited. Covent 55-609 1974 £25

DOYLE, A. CONAN   The White Company. 1903. Illus., signed, fine, authors edition. Covent 56-371 1974 £25

DOYLE, ARTHUR CONAN   The White Company. Doves Press, 1891. First edition, 3 vols., 8vo., orig. dark green cloth, complete with half titles and blank preliminaries in vols. 2 & 3, corner cut off page 75/76 in vol. 1, no ads, else fine copy. Sawyer 293-132 1974 £135

DOYLE, HELEN M.   Mary Austin. Gotham, 1939. 302p. Austin 54-70 1973 $7.50

DOYLE, J. E.   Official Baronage of England, 1066-1885. 1886. 3 vols., half calf, illus., rubbed. Allen 213-1430 1973 $25

DOYLE, JOSEPH B.   In Memoriam. Steubenville, 1911. Cloth, limited edition. Hayman 57-151 1974 $12.50

DOYLE, LYNN   Ballygullion. Dublin, 1918. Illus., very good copy, first edition. Covent 51-587 1973 £10.50

DOYLE, M.   A Cat. of Books . . . In Various Languages . . . to be sold . . . for Ready Money. London, 1818. Post 8vo., disbound. Forster 98-100 1974 £3

DOYLE, M.   The Irish Farmer's and Gardener's Magazine. Dublin, 1834. 8vols., 8vo., half calf. Emerald 50-771 1974 £25

DOYLE, RICHARD   A Journal Kept By. Dec. cloth gilt, illus., second edition. Marsden 37-169 1974 £10

DOYLE, RICHARD   Manners and Customs of Ye Englyshe. (1849). Oblong 4to., orig. half morocco, gilt, English first edition. Covent 56-689 1974 £35

DOYLEY, CHARLES   The Costume and Customs of Modern India. London, n.d. Folio, contemporary half maroon morocco, plates. Traylen 79-519 1973 £70

DRAGONETTE, JESSICA   Faith Is a Song. McKay, 1951. 288p. Austin 51-256 1973 $6.50

DRAKE, FRANCIS   Eboracum. 1736. 2 vols., folio, plates, full contemporary calf, rubbed. Covent 55-1459 1974 £65

DRAKE, FRANCIS S.   Dictionary of American Biography. 1874. Half calf, rebacked in buckram. Allen 216-483 1974 $15

DRAKE, FRANCIS S.   Dictionary of American Biography . . . Boston, 1876. Jenkins 61-852 1974 $15

DRAKE, JAMES   The History of the Last Parliament. 1702. 8vo., contemporary panelled calf, second edition. Hill 126-75 1974 £10.50

DRAKE, JOSEPH RODMAN   Croakers. 1860. Half calf, worn, limited, first complete edition. Allen 216-484 1974 $50

DRAKE, NATHAN   Literary Hours, or Sketches Critical and Narrative. Sudbury, 1798. 8vo., contemporary tree calf, neatly rebacked, orig. spine laid down, first edition. Ximenes 36-76 1974 $85

DRAKE, NATHAN   Mornings in Spring. 1828. 8vo., 2 vols., gilt, polished calf, faded. Hill 126-76 1974 £25

DRAKE, NATHAN   Shakespeare and His Times, Including a Biography of the Poet. 1817. 2 vols., demy 4to., contemporary full calf, first edition, portrait, fine. Broadhurst 24-328 1974 £24

DRAKE, ST. CLAIR   Black Metropolis: A Study of Negro Life in a Northern City. New York, 1945. First edition, 809 pages. Jenkins 61-853 1974 $10

DRAKE, SAMUEL ADAMS   Historic Fields and Mansions of Middlesex. Boston, 1874. 8vo., orig. bindings, illus., fine. Butterfield 8-233 1974 $25

DRAKE, SAMUEL ADAMS   Nooks and Corners of the New England Coast. New York, 1875. 8vo., orig. bindings. Butterfield 8-342 1974 $17.50

DRAPER, JOHN S.   Shams. Thomson, Thomas, 1887. 42lp., illus. Austin 54-327 1973 $12.50

DRAPER, JOHN W.   History of the Intellectual Development of Europe. New York, 1903. 2 vols. Biblo & Tannen 213-954 1973 $9.50

DRAPER, MURIEL   Music At Midnight. Harper, 1929. 237p., illus. Austin 51-257 1973 $6

DRAUGHTSMEN: Edna Clarke Hall, Henry Rushbury, Randolph Schwabe, Leon Underwood. 1924. First edition, plates, cloth backed boards, fine, d.w. Covent 51-121 1973 £5.25

DRAWING Room Album and Companion for the Budoir, an Elegant Literary Miscellany. Mid 19th century. Pictorial cloth, engravings on steel. Eaton Music-574 1973 £5

DRAYTON, MICHAEL   Mortimeriados. London, 1596. Small 4to., contemporary parchment, rare, first edition. Dawsons PM 252-307 1974 £4500

DRAYTON, MICHAEL   The Muses Elizivm. London, 1630. 4to., modern morocco, gilt, first edition. Dawsons PM 252-308 1974 £985

DRAYTON, MICHAEL   Poems. London, (n.d.). Folio, morocco gilt, fine, first edition, second issue. Dawsons PM 252-309 1974 £650

DRAYTON, MICHAEL   Poems. London, 1637. 12mo., full morocco, gilt, half morocco slipcase, very nice copy. Ximenes 37-65 1974 $250

DRAYTON, MICHAEL   The Complete Works of. London, 1876. 3 vols., small 8vo., portrait, orig. cloth, rubbed. Bow Windows 62-282 1974 £12.50

DREISER, THEODORE   American Tragedy. 1925. 2 vols., first issue. Allen 216-485 1974 $25

DREISER, THEODORE   An American Tragedy. New York, 1925. 1st issue, 2 vols. Jacobs 24-82 1974 $25

DREISER, THEODORE   An American Tragedy. New York, 1925. 2 vols., orig. cl., uncut, ltd. to 792 numbered and sgd. copies. Jacobs 24-81 1974 $75

DREISER, THEODORE   The Bulwark. Doubleday, 1946. 337p. Austin 54-328 1973 $4

DREISER, THEODORE   Chains. New York, 1927. 8vo., orig. cloth, boards, signed, first edition. Rota 190-383 1974 £12.50

DREISER, THEODORE   Chains. New York, 1927. Orig. cloth backed boards, label on spine, first limited edition, one of 440 numbered copies, signed by author, fine. MacManus 224-137 1974 $50

DREISER, THEODORE   The Color of a Great City. New York, (1923). First edition, backstrip faded, orig. binding. Butterfield 10-227 1974 $10

DREISER, THEODORE   Color of a Great City. 1923. Faded spine, first edition. Allen 216-486 1974 $12.50

DREISER, THEODORE   Dawn. 1931. Binding scratched, first edition. Allen 216-487 1974 $17.50

DREISER, THEODORE   Dreiser Looks at Russia. New York, 1928. First edition, d.j. torn, orig. binding. Butterfield 10-228 1974 $7.50

DREISER, THEODORE   Epitaph. New York, (1929). 4to., orig. calf, first edition, one of 200 numbered copies, printed on VanGelder paper, signed by author, fine. MacManus 224-138 1974 $55

DREISER, THEODORE   The Financier. 1912. Bookplate, spine worn, first edition. Allen 216-488 1974 $10

DREISER, THEODORE   The Financier. Harper, 1912. 786p., orig. ed. Austin 54-329 1973 $12.50

DREISER, THEODORE   The Financier. New York, 1912. First edition, with publisher's code letters K-M on copyright page, some foxing, orig. binding, fine. Ross 87-159 1974 $20

DREISER, THEODORE   A Gallery of Women. New York, 1929. 2 vols., box split, both vols. fine, orig. d.w.'s, first edition, orig. binding. Ross 87-160 1974 $25

DREISER, THEODORE   The Genius. Boni, Liveright, 1923. 736p., orig. hard cover ed. Austin 54-330 1973 $6.50

DREISER, THEODORE   The "Genius". New York, London & Toronto, 1915. Shaken and covers spotted, first edition, earliest issue with p. 497 numbered, orig. binding. Butterfield 10-229 1974 $15

DREISER, THEODORE   The Hand of the Potter. New York, 1918. First edition, shaken, orig. binding. Butterfield 10-230 1974 $10

DREISER, THEODORE   Hey Rub-A-Dub-Dub. New York, 1920. First edition, owner's name in ink on fly leaf, lacking d.w., fine. Ross 87-161 1974 $20

DREISER, THEODORE   A Hoosier Holiday. New York, 1916. 8vo., orig. cloth, illus., first edition. Rota 189-267 1974 £6

DREISER, THEODORE   A Hoosier Holiday. New York and London, 1916. Large 8vo., covers dull and rubbed, first edition. Butterfield 10-232 1974 $35

DREISER, THEODORE   A Hoosier Holiday. New York, 1916. Orig. cloth backed boards, illus., fine copy, first issue, with "The war! The war!" last paragraph p. 173. MacManus 224-139 1974 $40

DREISER, THEODORE   Hoosier Holiday. 1916. Bookplate, illus. by Franklin Booth, second issue. Allen 216-490 1974 $20

DREISER, THEODORE   Jennie Gerhardt. 1911. Bookplate, spine worn, first edition, second issue. Allen 216-491 1974 $10

DREISER, THEODORE   Letters of Theodore Dreiser. Penn, 1959. 3 vols. Austin 54-332 1973 $17.50

DREISER, THEODORE   Moods Cadenced and Declaimed. New York, 1926. Large 8vo., ornate marbled boards and cloth, glassine wrapper, limited to 550 signed copies. Butterfield 10-234 1974 $40

DREISER, THEODORE   My City. New York, 1929. Illus., folio, orig. cloth backed boards, corners worn, first edition, one of 275 numbered copies, signed by author, fine. MacManus 224-140 1974 $65

DREISER, THEODORE   Plays of the Natural and the Supernatural.   New York, 1916. First U. S. edition, lower corners worn, very fine copy, Publisher's complimentary copy blind stamped on title page.   Covent 51-593 1973 £10

DREISER, THEODORE   Sister Carrie. New York, 1939. Orig. binding, first edition, illus., mint, orig. box. Ross 87-278 1974 $25

DREISER, THEODORE   The Titan. New York, 1914. First edition, first state binding, lacking d.w., owner's name lightly in pencil on fly leaf, fine. Ross 87-162 1974 $30

DREISER, THEODORE   Tragic America . Liveright, 1931. 435p. Austin 54-333 1973 $15

DREISER, THEODORE   Tragic America. New York, (1931). Cloth covers rubbed, first edition, early issue. Butterfield 10-235 1974 $35

DREISER, THEODORE   A Traveller at Forty. New York, 1913. Drawings, first American edition. Covent 55-614 1974 £10.50

DREISER, THEODORE   A Traveller At Forty. Century, 1920. 526p., illus. Austin 54-331 1973 $15

DREISER, THEODORE   Twelve Men. Boni, Liveright, 1919. 360p., orig. ed. Austin 54-334 1973 $7.25

DREISER, THEODORE   Twelve Men. 1919. Names on endpaper, first edition. Allen 216-493 1974 $15

DREISER, THEODORE   Twelve Men. New York, (1928). Early issue of Modern Library Edition, orig. binding. Butterfield 10-236 1974 $7.50

DREPPERD, CARL W.   Early American Prints. New York, c. 1930. First edition, illus., orig. binding. Wilson 63-296 1974 $22.50

DRESSER, HENRY EELES   Eggs of the Birds of Europe. (1905)-1910. 2 vols., roy. 4to., new buckram, plates. Wheldon 131-43 1974 £100

DRESSER, HENRY EELES   A History of the Birds of Europe. 1871-96. Roy 4to., 9 vols., half maroon morocco, plates. Wheldon 129-13 1974 £1,800

DRESSER, HENRY EELES   A History of the Birds of Europe. London, 1871-96. 9 vols., plates, half contemporary green crushed levant morocco gilt. Smith 193-737 1973 £900

DRESSER, HENRY EELES   A Monograph of the Coraciidae. 1893. Imp. 4to., new half morocco, gilt, plates. Wheldon 131-42 1974 £1,100

DRESSLER, ALBERT   California's Pioneer Mountaineer of Rabbit Creek. San Francisco, 1930. 8vo., cloth, limited. Saddleback 14-88 1974 $25

DRESSLER, MARIE   The Life Story of an Ugly Duckling. McBride, 1924. 234p., illus. Austin 51-258 1973 $7.50

DREUX DU RADIER, JEAN FRANCOIS   Dictionnaire d'Amour. 1741. 12mo., contemporary calf. Hill 126-77 1974 £25

DREW, ANDREW   A Narrative of the Capture and Destruction of the Steamer "Caroline" and Her Descent Over the Fall of Niagara on the Night of the 29th of December, 1837. London, 1864. Marbled boards, linen spine. Hood's 102-598 1974 $95

DREW, JOHN   My Years On the Stage. Dutton, 1922. 242p., illus. Austin 51-259 1973 $7.50

DREWITT, F. DAWTREY   The Romance of the Apothecaries' Garden at Chelsea. London, 1924. Second edition. Rittenhouse 46-229 1974 $10

DREXEL, JEREMIAS 1581-1638   Aloe Amari Sed Salubris Succi IEIVNIVM. Munich, 1638. Narrow 32mo., full old brown calf, excellent. Rittenhouse 46-230 1974 $40

DREY, A. S.   Aus Dem Besitz der Firma. Berlin, 1936. 4to., plates, illus., cloth. Bow Windows 62-283 1974 £5.25

DRIEDO, JAN   Joannis Driedonis. 1533. Folio, contemporary blind stamped calf, boards, first edition. Howes 185-1124 1974 £55

DRIEU LA ROCHELLE, PIERRE   Fond de Cantine. Paris, 1920. 12mo., orig. wrapper, uncut. L. Goldschmidt 42-207 1974 $10

DRING, THOMAS   A Catalogue of the Lords. London, 1655. 12mo., modern calf, first edition. Dawsons PM 247-96 1974 £45

DRINKER, CECIL K.   Lane Medical Lectures.   Stanford, 1942. Rittenhouse 46-231 1974 $10

DRINKWATER, JOHN, 1762-1844
Please turn to
BETHUNE, JOHN DRINKWATER, 1762-1844

DRISCOLL, C. B.   Country Jake. Macmillan, 1946. 256p. Austin 54-335 1973 $6.50

DRISCOLL, C. B.   The Life of O. O. McIntyre. Greystone, 1938. 344p. Austin 54-336 1973 $7.50

DRISCOLL, LUCY   Chinese Calligraphy. Chicago, 1935. 4to. Biblo & Tannen 214-369 1974 $9.50

DRISKO, GEORGE W.   Narrative of the Town of Machias. Machias, 1904. 12mo., cloth, 589 pages. Saddleback 14-456 1974 $17.50

DROUET, L.   God Save the King. Paris, (c. 1815). Small folio, contemporary French imitation morocco gilt, cloth box, morocco labels. Thomas 28-134 1972 £150

DRUCE, G. C.   The Comital Flora of the British Isles. Arbroath, 1932. 8vo., cloth, map. Wheldon 129-994 1974 £5

DRUCE, G. C.   The Flora of Berkshire. Oxford, 1897. 8vo., cloth, scarce. Wheldon 129-992 1974 £7.50

DRUCE, G. C.   The Flora of Oxfordshire. 1886. 8vo., cloth, map, scarce. Wheldon 129-993 1974 £5

DRUCKER, C.   Physikalische Methoden der Analytischen Chemie. Leipzig, 1933-9. 8vo., 3 vols., cloth. Dawsons PM 245-239 1974 £12

DRUECK, CHARLES J.   Fistula of the Anus and Rectum. Philadelphia, 1927. Rittenhouse 46-232 1974 $15

DRUERY, C.   Choice British Ferns. 1888. 8vo., cloth, plates. Wheldon 131-1395 1974 £5

DRUJON, FERNAND   Catalogue des Ouvrages, Ecrits et Dessins de Toute Nature Poursuivis, Supprimes ou Condamnes Depuis le 21 Octobre 1814, Jusqu' au 31 Juillet 1877. Paris, 1879. Roy. 8vo., marbled boards, morocco back, gilt. Forster 98-103 1974 £20

DRUJON, FERNAND   Les Livres a Clef. Etude de Bibliographie Critique et Analytique pour Servir a l'Histoire Litteraire. Paris, 1888. 2 vols. in 1, limited to 600 copies, med. 8vo., cloth, morocco back, orig. wrappers bound in, top edges gilt, others uncut. Forster 98-104 1974 £30

DRUMMOND, HENRY   A Letter to Captain Fitzroy on Rifle Corps. London, 1852. 8vo., boards, first edition. Hammond 201-507 1974 £6

DRUMMOND, JAMES   Ancient Scottish Weapons. Edinburgh and London, 1881. Folio, orig. dark red half morocco, limited edition. Dawsons PM 251-375 1974 £50

DRUMMOND, JAMES   Ancient Scottish Weapons. Edinburgh, 1881. Folio, plates, half morocco, gilt, rubbed, limited edition. Quaritch 940-694 1974 £55

DRUMMOND, WILLIAM 1585-1649   A Cypress Grove. Glasgow, 1751. Small 8vo., 19th century half morocco, first edition. Hill 126-78 1974 £8.50

DRUMMOND, WILLIAM HAMILTON   Bruce's Invasion of Ireland. Dublin, 1826. 8vo., orig. grey boards, printed paper label, first edition, very fine, unopened. Ximenes 36-77 1974 $45

DRUMMOND, WILLIAM HENRY   Complete Poems. Toronto, 1926. Biblo and
Tannen 213-748 1973 $7.50

DRUMMOND, WILLIAM HENRY   Thoughts on the Study of Natural History.
Belfast, 1820. 8vo., orig. boards, worn. Emerald 50-239 1974 £7.50

DRURY, ANNA HARRIET   Friends and Fortune. 1849. Orig. cloth, English first edition. Covent 56-375 1974 £7.50

DRURY, D.   Illustrations of Natural History. 1770-73.
Vols. 1 and 2, 4to., contemporary calf-backed boards, worn, broken joints,
plain and hand-coloured plates, uncut. Wheldon 128-704 1973 £150

DRURY, HENRY   A Catalogue of the Extensive and Valuable
Library of. London, 1827. 8vo., contemporary half blue calf, marbled boards,
gilt, fine. Dawsons PM 10-194 1974 £45

DRUSIANO DAL LEONE   Elqual Tratta Delle Battaglie Dapo la Morte di
Paladini. Venice, 1553. Small 8vo., brown morocco, gilt, woodcuts, rare.
Schumann 499-30 1974 sFr 675

DRYDEN, JOHN   All for Love. 1692. 4to., modern boards,
second edition. Dawsons PM 252-312 1974 £55

DRYDEN, JOHN   All for Love. London, 1776. 12mo.,
disbound, wrappers, frontispiece. Dawsons PM 252-313 1974 £15

DRYDEN, JOHN   Amboyna. London, 1673. 4to., modern
panelled vellum, gilt, first edition. Dawsons PM 252-314 1974 £150

DRYDEN, JOHN   The Annual Miscellany. London, 1694. 8vo.,
contemporary mottled calf, first edition. Dawsons PM 252-315 1974 £95

DRYDEN, JOHN   The Dramatic Works. Nonesuch Press, 1931-23.
6 vols., roy. 8vo., half vellum, marbled boards, top edges gilt, others uncut,
mint, one of 50 sets, on Van Gelder paper. Broadhurst 24-1030 1974 £250

DRYDEN, JOHN   The Dramatic Works. London, 1931. 6 vols.,
8vo., orig. buckram-backed boards, fine, limited edition. Dawsons PM
252-320 1974 £170

DRYDEN, JOHN   The Dramatic Works. Nonesuch Press, 1931-32.
6 vols., roy. 8vo., linen spines, marbled boards, top edges gilt, others uncut,
limited to 750 sets, fine. Broadhurst 24-1031 1974 £90

DRYDEN, J.   The Dramatic Works. 1931-32. 6 vols.,
8vo., quarter buckram, limited. Bow Windows 62-681 1974 £145

DRYDEN, JOHN   Dramatick Works. 1717. 12mo., 6 vols., mot-
tled calf, gilt, frontispiece, first collected edition. Quaritch 936-69 1974 £95

DRYDEN, JOHN   The First Part of Miscellany Poems. London,
1716. 6 parts in 3 vols., 12mo., 18th century straight-grained morocco gilt,
fourth edition. Dawsons PM 252-316 1974 £120

DRYDEN, JOHN   The History of the League. London, 1684.
8vo., contemporary calf, fine, first edition. Dawsons PM 252-317 1974 £60

DRYDEN, JOHN   The Miscellaneous Works. 1760. 8vo., 4 vols.,
contemporary calf, gilt. Hill 126-79 1974 £42

DRYDEN, JOHN   The Miscellaneous Works of. London, 1767.
4 vols., 12mo., contemporary calf, gilt tooling on spines, morocco labels,
fine set, internally clean. MacManus 224-141 1974 £50

DRYDEN, JOHN   Oedipus. London, 1701. 4to., modern boards,
inscription, sixth edition. Dawsons PM 252-321 1974 £25

DRYDEN, JOHN   Of Dramatick Poesie. 1928. One of 580
numbered copies, quarter buckram, marbled boards, roy. 8vo., very good copy,
signed presentation copy from publisher. Covent 51-635 1973 £15

DRYDEN, JOHN   Of Dramatick Poesie. London, 1928. One of
580 numbered copies, very fine, d.w., first edition. Covent 51-634 1973 £20

DRYDEN, JOHN   The Poetical Works of. Edinburgh, 1793.
8vo., contemporary half calf, morocco label. Dawsons PM 252-323 1974 £15

DRYDEN, JOHN   The Poetical Works Of. London, 1833.
5 vols., ex-library. Austin 61-338 1974 £37.50

DRYDEN, JOHN   Poetical Works Of. 1854. 5 vols. Austin
61-339 1974 $27.50

DRYDEN, JOHN   The Poetical Works Of. 1862. 8vo., sup.
roy. 8vo., contemporary cerise polished calf, gilt. Smith 193-250 1973 £5.50

DRYDEN, JOHN   Prologue to His Royal Highness. London,
(1682). Dawsons PM 252-319 1974 £120

DRYDEN, JOHN   The Second Part of Absalom and Achitophel.
1682. Folio, modern half calf, first edition. Dawsons PM 252-322 1974 £85

DRYDEN, JOHN   Works. Edinburgh, 1821. 18 vols., illus.,
contemporary calf, rebacked. Howes 185-140 1974 £48

DRYDEN, JOHN   The Works Of. 1808. 8vo., 18 vols., contemporary green half morocco. Bow Windows 64-487 1974 £125

DRYDEN, JOHN   The Works Of. 1808. 18 vols., 8vo.,
full green morocco, engraved portrait, frontispiece, little foxed, bookplate in
each vol. of John Deacon. Bow Windows 66-191 1974 £168

DRYER, SHERMAN   Radio In Wartime. Greenberg, 1942. 384p.
Austin 51-265 1973 $12.50

DU BARTAS, GUILLAUME DE SALUSTE   Du Bartas, His Devine Weekes and Workes
Translated. London, n.d. Thick small 4to., contemporary calf, fine, third
collected edition. Ximenes 35-108 1974 $350

DU BARTAS, GUILLAUME DE SALUSTE   Du Bartas, His Devine Weekes and
Workes Translated. London, n.d. Thick small 4to., later calf, fine, fourth
collected edition. Ximenes 35-109 1974 $225

THE DUBLIN Directory. Dublin, (n.d.). 2 directories in 1, 8vo., full red
morocco, gilt, rare, first edition. Dawsons PM 247-97 1974 £75

DUBOIS, CARDINAL   Memoirs of. London, 1899. 2 vols., 8vo.,
frontispiece, foxing, orig. cloth. Bow Windows 62-285 1974 £7.50

DUBOIS, CARDINAL   Memoirs of Cardinal Dubois. New York,
1929. Ltd. ed., 2 vols. Biblo & Tannen 213-664 1973 $22.50

DUBOIS, FELIX   The Anarchist Peril. 1894. Text illus., orig.
dec. cloth, cover stained, very good copy. Covent 51-26 1973 £6.30

DUBOIS, FELIX   The Anarchist Peril. 1894. Orig. dec. cloth,
illus., worn. Covent 55-27 1974 £15

DUBOIS, JACQUES   In Linguam Gallicam Isagoge. Paris,
1530-31. 4to., full red morocco, rare. Harper 213-53 1973 $950

DU BOIS, JACQUES   Novissima Idea de Febribus et Earunden
Dogmatica, ac Rationalis Cura. Dublin, 1694. 12mo., old pasteboards, back
defective. Gurney 66-181 1974 £20

DU BOIS, PAUL   The Psychic Treatment of Nervous Disorders.
New York, 1907. Rittenhouse 46-233 1974 $10

DU BOIS, WILLIAM PENE   Otto At Sea. New York, 1936. Square 16mo.,
pictorial boards, illus., 1st ed., mint copy. Frohnsdorff 16-302 1974 $25

DU BOIS-REYMOND, EMIL   Gedachtnissrede auf Johannes Muller. Berlin,
1860. 4to., orig. boards, rebacked. Gurney 64-77 1974 £15

DUBOIS-REYMOND, EMIL   Gesammelte Abhandlungen zur Allgemeinen
Muskelund Nervenphysik. Leipzig, 1875-77. 2 vols., large 8vo., plates,
orig. printed wrappers, uncut, first edition. Schafer 8-151 1973 sFr. 450

DUBOIS-REYMOND, EMIL   Gesammelte Abhandlungen zur Allgemeinen
Muskelund Nervenphysik. Leipzig, 1875-77. 2 vols., large 8vo., orig. printed
wrappers, uncut, text figures, plates, first edition. Schafer 10-124 1974
sFr 450

DUBOIS-REYMOND, EMIL   Der Physiologische Unterricht Sonst und Jetzt.
Berlin, 1878. Large 8vo., orig. printed wrappers, first edition. Schafer 10-125
1974 sFr 180

DU BOIS-REYMOND, EMIL   Uber Thierische Bewegung. Berlin, 1851. 8vo.,
orig. wrappers, first edition. Gurney 64-78 1974 £10

DU BOISGOBEY, FORTUNE   "The Golden Tress". Philadelphia, 1876.
Orig. dec. cloth gilt, first American edition. Covent 55-577 1974 £35

DUBOURDIEU, JOHN   Statistical Survey of the County of Down.
Dublin, 1802. 8vo., fine, orig. boards, uncut. Emerald 50-254 1974 £30

DUBOURG, MATTHEW   Views of the Remains of Ancient Buildings in
Rome. London, 1820. Folio, 19th century half morocco. Marlborough 70-34
1974 £280

DUBOURG, MATTHEW   Views of the Remains of Ancient Buildings in
Rome. 1844. Imp. 4to., plates, orig. cloth, roan back, gilt. Quaritch
940-88 1974 £250

DUBRAY, JEAN-PAUL   Eugene Carriere. Paris, 1931. Small 4to.,
wrappers, plates. Minters 37-240 1973 $20

DU BUS DE GISIGNIES, B. L.   Esquisses Ornithologiques. Brussels, 1845-(50).
5 parts, imp. 4to., orig. wrappers, uncut, hand-coloured lithographed plates,
cloth book-box, very rare. Wheldon 128-426 1973 £175

DU BUS DE GISIGNIES, B. L.   Esquisses Ornithologiques. Brussels, 1845.
5 parts, imp. 4to., orig. wrappers, uncut, plates, very rare. Wheldon
131-44 1974 £175

DUBUISSON, A.   Richard Parkes Bonington: His Life and Work.
(1924). 4to., coloured and other plates, orig. quarter cloth, limited. Bow
Windows 66-70 1974 £45

DUBUISSON, J. R. J.   Des Vesanies. Paris, 1816. 8vo., half calf,
rebacked. Dawsons PM 249-147 1974 £70

DU CANE, FLORENCE   The Flowers and Gardens of Japan. 1908.
F'cap 4to., coloured plates, orig. cloth, fine. Broadhurst 24-1604 1974 £5

DU CANE, FLORENCE   Flower Gardens of Japan. London, 1908.
8vo., orig. cloth, color plates, fine. Gregory 44-111 1974 $12.50

DU CANN, C. G. L.   The Loves of George Bernard Shaw. Funk,
1963. 300p., illus. Austin 51-266 1973 $7.50

DUCASSE, CURT JOHN   The Philosophy of Art. 1929. 314 pages.
Austin 61-340 1974 $10

DUCASSE, ISIDORE LUCIEN   Les Chants de Maldoror. Buenos Aires, 1944.
One of 1500 numbered copies, wrappers, covers faded, first edition. Covent
51-736 1973 £5

DUCASSE, ISIDORE LUCIEN   The Lay of Maldoror. 1924. 8vo., full parchment, first edition. Rota 189-738 1974 £15

DUCATEL, J. T.   Manual of Practical Toxicology Condensed
from Dr. Christison's Treatise on Poisons. Baltimore, 1833. Detached front
and back covers. Rittenhouse 46-235 1974 $17

DUCATUS Lancastriae. 1823-34. 3 vols., folio, modern boards, cloth backs.
Quaritch 939-10 1974 £40

DUCATUS Lancastriae. 1834. Folio, cloth sides, stained. Quaritch 939-11
1974 £9.50

DU CHAILLU, PAUL B.   Explorations and Adventures in Equatorial
Africa, and a Journey to Ashango-Land. 1861 and 1867. 2 vols., illus., maps,
first editions, demy 8vo., newly bound binder's cloth, fine. Broadhurst 24-1605
1974 £60

DU CHAILLU, PAUL B.   The Land of the Midnight Sun. New York,
1882. 2 vols., map, illus. Hood's 103-55 1974 $22.50

DU CHAILLU, PAUL B.   Viking Age. 1889. 2 vols., illus. Allen
213-1432 1973 $12.50

DUCHARTRE, PIERRE L.   The Italian Comedy. Day, 1929. 330p.,
illus., orig. ed. Austin 51-267 1973 $27.50

DUCHAUSSOIS, PIERRE   Apotres Inconnus. Paris, 1924. Wrappers.
Hood's 102-283 1974 $15

DUCHAUSSOIS, PIERRE   Apotres Inconnus. Paris, 1924. Wrappers.
Hood's 104-303 1974 $15

DUCHE, J.   Les Actinomyces. Paris, 1934. Roy 8vo.,
cloth, plates. Wheldon 129-1190 1974 £5

DUCHENE, MAURICE   The Mechanics of the Aeroplane. 1917. 8vo.,
orig. red cloth. Dawsons PM 245-240 1974 £5

DU CHESNE, ANDREAS   Historiae Normannorum Scriptores Antiqui.
Paris, 1619. Folio, half calf, first edition. Goodspeed's 578-92 1974 $45

DUCLOS, CHARLES PINEAU   Histoire de Louis XI. The Hague, 1745.
2 vols., 12mo., contemporary full marbled tan calf, gilt, illus. L. Goldschmidt
42-47 1974 $125

DUCLOS, R.   Dictionnaire Bibliographique. Paris, 1790-
1802. 4 vols., 8vo., contemporary gilt-framed mottled calf. Dawsons PM
10-195 1974 £50

DUCLOS, R.   Dictionnaire Bibliographique, Historique et
Critique des Livres Rares. Paris, 1802. 4 vols., half calf, binding defective,
text fine. Forster 98-107 1974 £20

DU CLOS, S. C.   Dissertation sur les Principes des Mixtes Naturels.
Amsterdam, 1680. 12mo., boards, first edition. Gurney 64-79 1974 £30

DUCRAY-DUMINIL, FRANCOIS GUILLAUME   Lolotte et Fanfan. Paris,
(1795). 4 vols., bound in 2, small 12mo., contemporary burgundy red morocco,
gilt, plates. L. Goldschmidt 42-48 1974 $30

DUCREST, CHARLES LOUIS   Essais sur les Machines Hydrauliques. Paris, 17-
77. 8vo., contemporary French calf, gilt, plates, fine, first edition. Dawsons
PM 245-241 1974 £35

DUDEVANT, MME.
Please turn to
SAND, GEORGE

DUDLEY, ROBERT
Please turn to
LEICESTER, ROBERT DUDLEY

DUER, EDWARD R.   Bluebeard in Bologna. 1929. 55p. Austin
51-268 1973 $8.50

DUER, WILLIAM   Speech of . . . In the House of Representatives
August 15, 1850, On the President's Message of August 6, 1850 Concerning
Texas and New Mexico. N. P., n.d. (1850). Disbound, foxed, double col.
text. Wilson 63-179 1974 $10

DUERER, ALBRECHT   Albrecht Durer Kupferstiche. Munich, 1920.
Folio, plates, cloth backed portfolio, unbound. Quaritch 940-90 1974 £10

DUERER, ALBRECHT   Handzeichnungen. 1923. 4to., plates. Allen
213-1436 1973 $12.50

DUERER, ALBRECHT   Institutionum Geometricarum Libri Quatuor.
1605. Small folio, old vellum, stains, inscription. Thomas 28-37 1972 £185

DUERER, ALBRECHT   The Little Passion. 1894. Crown 8vo., orig.
silk cloth, faded, plates, frontis. Howes 186-170 1974 £5

DUEVARA, DON ANTONIO DE   The Praise and Happiness of the Countrie-Life.
Gregynog Press, 1938. Crown 8vo., quarter morocco, boards, paper printed label,
mint, orig. d.w., limited to 380 copies, complete with prospectus. Broadhurst
24-1013 1974 £65

DUFAULT, JAMES ERNEST NEPHTALI   The American Cowboy.   New York, 1942. Cloth, ilus., first edition.   Dykes 24-161 1974 $10

DUFAULT, JAMES ERNEST NEPHTALI   Cow Country.   New York, London, 1927. Pic. cloth, illus., autographed.   Dykes 24-158 1974 $25

DUFAULT, JAMES ERNEST NEPHTALI   Scorpion, A Good Bad Horse.   New York, London, 1936. Cloth, illus., 1st ed.   Dykes 24-160 1974 $10

DU FAY, CHARLES JEROME DE CISTERNAY   Bibliotheca Fayana.   Paris, 1725. 8vo., contemporary mottled calf, gilt.   Dawsons PM 10-196 1974 £30

DUFF, CHARLES   Handrail and the Wampus.   1931. 4to., orig. cloth, wrappers, first edition.   Rota 189-273 1974 £5

DUFF, CHARLES   James Joyce and the Plain Reader.   1932. Faded, dust wrapper.   Covent 55-947 1974 £7.50

DUFF, CHARLES   Mind Products Limited.   The Hague, 1932. 8vo., orig. cloth, wrappers, first edition.   Rota 189-275 1974 £5

DUFF, EDWARD GORDON   The English Provincial Printers, Stationers and Bookbinders to 1557.   Cambridge, 1912. 8vo., orig. blue cloth, first edition. Dawsons PM 10-197 1974 £11

DUFF, EDWARD GORDON   The Printers, Stationers and Bookbinders of Westminster and London.   Cambridge, 1906. 8vo., orig. cloth, plates, fine, first edition.   Dawsons PM 10-198 1974 £13

DUFF, EDWARD GORDON   The Printers, Stationers and Bookbinders of Westminster and London from 1476-1535.   Cambridge, 1906. Plates, 12mo., orig. cloth, bookplate.   Forster 98-111 1974 £12

DUFF, L. B.   Burnaby.   Welland, 1926. Inscribed, illus., limited edition.   Hood's 103-621 1974 $20

DUFFERIN   A Yacht Voyage.   New York, 1878. Plates, illus.   Hood's 104-57 1974 $12.50

DUFFIELD, BRAINERD   The Lottery.   1953. 26p., paper.   Austin 51-269 1973 $7.50

DUFFIELD, KENNETH GRAHAM   Four Little Pigs That Didn't Have Any Mother. Philadelphia, 1919. 16mo., pict. boards, cloth spine, illus.   Frohnsdorff 16-335 1974 $10

DUFFIELD, KENNETH GRAHAM   The Little Puppy that Wanted to Know Too Much.   Philadelphia, (1920). 16mo., boards, cloth spine, color plates, very good copy.   Frohnsdorff 16-510 1974 $10

DUFFIELD, KENNETH GRAHAM   The Old, Old Story of Poor Cock Robin. Philadelphia, 1920. 24mo., pict. boards, cloth spine; 29 color plates.   Frohnsdorff 16-227 1974 $7.50

DUFFUS, R. L.   The Tower of Jewels.   Norton, 1960. 250p. Austin 54-337 1973 $6.50

DUFFY, CHARLES G.   Conversations with Carlyle.   London, 1892. 8vo., cloth boards, illus., scarce, first edition.   Emerald 50-257 1974 £10

DUFFY, CHARLES G.   Young Ireland.   London, 1880-83. 2 vols., 8vo., cloth boards, signed, second edition.   Emerald 50-255 1974 £20

DUFOUR, L.   Recherches Anatomiques et Physiologiques sur les Hemipteres.   Paris, 1833. 4to., wrappers, plates, very scarce.   Wheldon 128-710 1973 £15

DUFOUR, ROGER   Etude Clinique sur l'Oculo-Reaction.   Geneve, 1908. 8vo., orig. paper wrappers, signed.   Dawsons PM 249-149 1974 £6

DUFRESNE, FRANK   Alaska's Animals and Fishes.   New York, 1946. Illus.   Jacobs 24-2 1974 $10

DU FRESNOIS, ANDRE   Une Etape de la Conversion de Huysmans. Paris, n.d. Portrait, wrappers, very nice largely unopened copy, first edition. Covent 51-735 1973 £5

DU FRESNOY, C. A.   The Art of Painting.   1716. Small 8vo., contemporary panelled calf, rebacked, enlarged second edition.   Quaritch 940-89 1974 £65

DUFY, RAOUL   Croquis de Modes.   Paris, 1920. Rare, fine, coloured lithographs in folder.   Covent 51-604 1973 £40

DUGANNE, AUGUSTINE   The Poetical Works of.   Philadelphia, 1855. Full brown morocco, gilt.   Dawsons 424-53 1974 $175

DUGDALE, BLANCHE E. C.   Arthur James Balfour.   1936. 2 vols., plates.   Howes 186-587 1974 £5.75

DUGDALE, RICHARD   A Narrative of the Wicked Plots.   London, 1679. Folio, disbound, first edition.   Dawsons PM 251-501 1974 £25

DUGDALE, WILLIAM   The Antiquities of Warwickshire.   London, 1656. Folio, contemporary panelled calf, first edition.   Dawsons PM 251-22 1974 £250

DUGDALE, WILLIAM   The Antiquities of Warwickshire.   1656. Folio, diced russia gilt, plates, first edition.   Quaritch 939-569 1974 £200

DUGDALE, WILLIAM   The Antiquities of Warwickshire.   Birmingham, 1891. Folio, half morocco, illus., limited.   Quaritch 939-570 1974 £15

DUGDALE, WILLIAM   The Antiquities of Warwickshire.   London, 1730. 2 vols., folio, contemporary calf gilt, leather labels, illus., second edition.   Traylen 79-402 1973 £180

DUGDALE, WILLIAM   The Baronage of England.   1675-76. 3 vols. in 1, thick folio, full 18th century calf, gilt, label, first edition.   Howes 186-1630 1974 £75

DUGDALE, WILLIAM   The History of Imbanking and Draining of divers Fens and Marshes.   London, 1772. Folio, half calf, gilt, maps, second edition. Hammond 201-847 1974 £165

DUGDALE, WILLIAM   The History of Imbanking and Drayning of Divers Fenns and Marshes.   1772. Folio, old calf gilt, maps.   Quaritch 939-108 1974 £175

DUGDALE, WILLIAM   The History of St. Paul's Cathedral in London. 1818. Thick folio, full contemporary panelled russia, rebacked, best edition. Howes 186-787 1974 £40

DUGDALE, WILLIAM   Monasticon Anglicanum.   1817-30. 6 vols. in 8, folio, buckram, half morocco.   Quaritch 939-109 1974 £160

DUGDALE, WILLIAM   A Perfect Copy of All Summons of the Nobility to the Great Councils.   1685. Folio, full contemporary diced russia, worn. Howes 186-1631 1974 £45

DUGDALE, WILLIAM   A Short View of the Late Troubles in England. Oxford, 1681. Folio, diced calf, gilt, first edition.   Hammond 201-199 1974 £28.50

DUGDALE, WILLIAM   A Short View of the Late Troubles in England. Oxford, 1681. Folio, russia.   Quaritch 939-110 1974 £35

DUGES, A.   Recherches sur l'Osteologie et la Myologie des Batraciens.   Paris, 1835. 4to., orig. wrappers, plates, uncut, scarce.   Wheldon 130-687 1974 £21

DUGGER, SHEPPERD M.   The Balsam Groves of the Grandfather Mountain. Banner Elk, 1934. 8vo., orig. bindings.   Butterfield 8-400 1974 $15

DUGMORE, A. A. RADCLYFFE   Bird Homes.   New York, 1904. Color plates. Biblo & Tannen 214-347 1974 $8.50

DUGMORE, A. A. RADCLYFFE   Camera Adventures in the African Wilds.   1910. Imp. 8vo., orig. cloth.   Broadhurst 23-1632 1974 £10

DUGMORE, A. A. RADCLYFFE   Camera Adventures in the African Wilds.   1910. Imp. 8vo., orig. cloth, fine, photos.   Broadhurst 24-1606 1974 £10

DUGMORE, A. A. RADCLYFFE   The Romance of the Newfoundland Caribou. Philadelphia, 1913. Illus., blue cloth, gilt, frontispiece, first edition. Bradley 35-132 1974 $36

DUGMORE, A. A. RADCLYFFE   The Romance of the Newfoundland Caribou. Philadelphia & London, 1913. Illus., worn. Hood's 104-199 1974 $30

DUGMORE, A. A. RADCLYFFE   The Wonderland of Big Game Being an Account of Two Trips Through Tanganyika and Kenya. 1925. Crown 4to., photos, map, orig. cloth, fine. Broadhurst 24-1607 1974 £8

DUGMORE, A. A. RADCLYFFE   The Wonderland of Big Game. 1925. Crown 4to., orig. cloth. Broadhurst 23-1633 1974 £8

DU HALDE, JEAN BAPTISTE   The General History of China. London, 1736. 8vo., 4 vols., contemporary red morocco, gilt, rebacked, plates, first English edition. Gurney 66-52 1974 £115

DUHAMEL, GEORGES   Les Plaisirs. Paris, 1930. 8vo., orig. wrapper, numbered, illus. L. Goldschmidt 42-209 1974 $27.50

DU HAMEL, JEAN BAPTISTE   De Meteoris et Fossilibus. 1660. 4to., old half vellum, first edition. Dawsons PM 245-242 1974 £95

DU HAMEL, JEAN BAPTISTE   Regiae Scientiarum Academiae Historia. 1698. 4to., modern quarter calf, first edition. Dawsons PM 245-243 1974 £45

DUHAMEL DU MONCEAU, HENRI LOUIS   De l'Exploitation des Bois. Paris, 1764. 2 vols. in 1, 4to., contemporary calf, plates, rare. Wheldon 131-1727 1974 £50

DUHAMEL DU MONCEAU, HENRI LOUIS   De l'Exploitation des Bois. Paris, 1764. 4to., contemporary calf, plates. Wheldon 129-1598 1974 £50

DUHAMEL DU MONCEAU, HENRI LOUIS   De l'Expoitation des Bois. Paris, 1764. 4to., 2 vols., contemporary calf, plates. Wheldon 130-1553 1974 £45

DUHAMEL DU MONCEAU, HENRI LOUIS   De l'Exploitation des Bois. Paris, 1764. 2 vols., 4to., contemporary calf, engraved folding plates. Wheldon 128-1593 1973 £45

DUHAMEL DU MONCEAU, HENRI LOUIS   La Physique des Arbres. Paris, 1758. 2 vols., 4to., contemporary calf, engraved plates. Wheldon 128-1594 1973 £45

DUHAMEL DU MONCEAU, HENRI LOUIS   A Practical Treatise on Husbandry. London, 1759. 4to., contemporary half calf, first edition. Dawsons PM 247-98 1974 £40

DUHRING, LOUIS A.   Cutaneous Medicine. Philadelphia, 1895. 2 vols. Rittenhouse 46-236 1974 $35

DUJARDIN, EDOUARD   Les Lauriers Sont Coupes. Paris, 1897. 12mo., orig. wrapper, second edition. L. Goldschmidt 42-211 1974 $15

DUJARRIC DE LA RIVIERE, R.   Les Champignons Toxiques. Paris, 1938. 4to., wrappers, plates. Wheldon 131-1396 1974 £7.50

DUJARRIC DE LA RIVIERE, R.   Le Poison des Amanites Mortelles. Paris, 1933. Roy 8vo., buckram, plates. Wheldon 129-1192 1974 £7.50

DUKE, THOMAS S.   Celebrated Criminal Cases of America. San Francisco, 1910. 1st ed., illus. Biblo & Tannen 210-450 1973 $42.50

DUKE, VERNON   Passport to Paris. Little, Brown, 1955. 502p. Austin 51-270 1973 $6.50

DUKES, ASHLEY   The Man With a Load of Mischief. French. 82p., paper. Austin 51-271 1973 $7.50

DULAC, EDMUND   Rubaiyat of Omar Khayyam. n.d. Orig. buckram gilt, inscribed, plates. Smith 193-653 1973 £10

DU LAC, FRANCOIS MARIE PERRIN
Please turn to
PERRIN DU LAC, FRANCOIS MARIE

DULEEP SINGH, FREDERICK   Portraits in Norfolk Houses. Norwich, (1927). 2 vols., 4to., plates, half morocco, limited edition. Quaritch 939-496 1974 £40

DUMAS, ALEXANDRE   Affaire Clemenceau. Paris, 1909. 4to., orig. wrapper, cloth portfolio, numbered. L. Goldschmidt 42-212 1974 $20

DUMAS, ALEXANDRE   Celebrated Crimes. 1895. 8vo., 8 vols., illus., cloth. Quaritch 936-375 1974 £15

DUMAS, ALEXANDRE   La Question du Divorce. Paris, 1880. contemporary half cloth, leather label, uncut, first edition. L. Goldschmidt 42-213 1974 $15

DUMAS, ALEXANDER   Les Trois Mousquetaires. Paris, 1886. 2 vols., rebound in wide red morocco backstrips and marbled boards, French text. Wilson 63-507B 1974 £10

DUMAS, ALEXANDRE   The Waverley Dumas. (n.d.). 8vo., 25 vols., orig. cloth. Bow Windows 64-489 1974 £12.50

DUMAS, ALEXANDRE   Works. c.1912. 20 vols., orig. cloth, plates, Aramis edition. Howes 185-142 1974 £15

DU MAURIER, GEORGE   A Legend of Camelot. 1898. Oblong 4to., orig. cloth gilt, all edges gilt, spine chafed at foot, few leaves loose at begining and end of text, very good copy, illus., first edition. Covent 51-606 1973 £15

DU MAURIER, GEORGE   Peter Ibbetson. 1892. 2 vols., pictorial cloth, illus., fine. Marsden 37-170 1974 £6

DU MAURIER, GEORGE   Peter Ibbetson. 1892. 2 vols., orig. cloth, drawings, worn, scarce, first edition. Rota 188-261 1974 £15

DU MAURIER, GEORGE   Social Pictorial Satire. New York, 1898. Plates, first U.S. edition. Covent 56-376 1974 £10.50

DU MAURIER, GEORGE   Trilby. 1894. 3 vols., orig. cloth, scarce, inscription, seventh edition. Rota 188-262 1974 £35

DU MAURIER, GEORGE   Trilby. London, 1895. Spine torn, illus. Biblo & Tannen 214-696 1974 $15

DU MAURIER, GUY   An Englishman's Home. Harper, 1909. 131p. Austin 51-272 1973 $8.50

DU-MAY, LEWIS   The Estate of the Empire. London, 1676. 8vo., contemporary mottled calf, rebacked. Dawsons PM 251-211 1974 £30

DUMBRILLE, D.   All This Difference. Toronto, 1945. Illus. Hood's 104-548 1974 $12.50

DUMEE, P.   Nouvel Atlas de Poche des Champignons. Paris, 1911-12. Post 8vo., 2 vols., cloth, plates. Wheldon 129-1193 1974 £7.50

DUMERIL, A. M. C.   Considerations Generales sur le Classe des Insectes. Paris, 1823. 8vo., half morocco, plates. Wheldon 131-801 1974 £20

DUMERIL, A. M. C.   Considerations Generales sur la Classe des Insectes. Paris, 1823. 8vo., contemporary half morocco, plates. Wheldon 129-630 1974 £20

DUMESNIL, J. B. GARDIN   Latin Synonyms. 1809. 8vo., contemporary calf. Hill 126-80 1974 £7.50

DUMESNIL, RENE   Le Realisme. Paris, 1936. 8vo., orig. wrapper. L. Goldschmidt 42-215 1974 $17.50

DU MONCEL   The Telephone, the Microphone and the Phonograph. 1879. Woodcuts. Covent 55-1296 1974 £35

DUMONT, ETIENNE   Recollections of Mirabeau. London, 1832. 8vo., contemporary half calf, second edition. Dawsons PM 247-99 1974 £15

DUMONT, JEAN   Les Soupirs de l'Europe &c. 1713. 8vo., cloth, uncut. Quaritch 936-70 1974 £10

DUMONT, JEAN   Vade-Mecum du Typographe. Brussels, 1891. 8vo., orig. printed wrappers, bound in cloth, gilt back. Kraus B8-311 1974 $35

DUMONT, JEAN   Vade-Mecum du Typographe. Brussels, 1915. 8vo., orig. printed wrappers, fourth edition. Kraus B8-312 1974 $35

DU MORTIER, M. B.   Opuscules de Botanique. Brussels, 1873. 8vo., half vellum, scarce. Wheldon 130-1006 1974 £10

DUNAL, M. F.   Considerations sur la Nature. Paris and Mont-pelier, 1829. 4to., wrappers, uncut, plates. Wheldon 130-1007 1974 £5

DUNANT, JEAN HENRY   La Charite sur les Champs de Bataille Suites du Souvenir. Geneva, 1864. 4to., old cloth, first edition. Gurney 64-80 1974 £60

DUNANT, JEAN HENRY   Un Souvenir de Solferino. Geneve, 1862. 8vo., full red morocco, inscribed, first edition. Dawsons PM 249-150 1974 £465

DUNANT, JEAN HENRY   Un Souvenir de Solferino. Geneva, 1862. 4to., contemporary calf, rebacked, orig. wrappers, cloth box, fine, rare first edition. Gilhofer 61-53 1974 sFr. 2,800

DUNANT, JEAN HENRY   Un Souvenir de Solferino. Geneve, 1862. 8vo., full red morocco, rebound, inscribed, first edition. Dawsons PM 250-23

DUNBAR, ELIZABETH   Talcott Williams, Gentleman of the Fourth Estate. (New York), c. 1936. First edition, 2 A.L.s laid in. Wilson 63-105 1974 $16.50

DUNBAR, JANET   Mrs. G. B. S. Harper, 1963. 303p., illus. Austin 51-273 1973 $6.50

DUNBAR, PAUL LAURENCE   Candle Lightin' Time. New York, 1903. Fine copy, slightly worn d.w., orig. binding, top edges gilt, photos. Wilson 63-508A 1974 $10

DUNBAR, PAUL LAURENCE   Lyrics of Lowly Life. New York, 1898. Orig. binding, gilt dec. on cover & spine, name in ink on fly, portrait, frontis., first edition, fine. Ross 87-164 1974 $12.50

DUNBAR, PAUL LAURENCE   Lyrics of Lowly Life. Dodd, Mead, 1899 (1896) 208p., orig. ed. Austin 54-339 1973 $7.50

DUNBAR, PAUL LAURENCE   Lyrics of the Hearthside. Dodd (1899) 1911. 227p., orig. ed. Austin 54-338 1973 $8.50

DUNBAR, PAUL LAURNECE   Lyrics of the Hearthside. New York, 1899. Frontispiece portrait, orig. binding, first edition, name in ink on fly leaf, backstrip slightly faded, fine. Ross 87-163 1974 $15

DUNBAR, PAUL LAURENCE   Lyrics of the Hearthside. New York, 1899. First edition, 16mo., top edges gilt, others uncut, portrait, orig. binding. Wilson 63-509 1974 $17.50

DUNBAR, PAUL LAURENCE   Poems of Cabin and Field. New York, 1904. Fine copy, slightly worn d.w., photos, orig. binding. Wilson 63-509A 1974 $15

DUNBAR, PAUL LAURENCE   The Uncalled. Dodd, Mead, 1898. 255p., 1st ed. Austin 54-340 1973 $12.50

DUNBAR, SEYMOUR   A History of Travel in America. Indianapolis, 1915. Blue cloth, 4 vols., plates, illus. Dawson's 424-107 1974 $60

DUNBAR, SEYMOUR   A History of Travel in America. New York, 1937. 8vo., orig. cloth, maps, plates, illus. Bow Windows 64-490 1974 £9.50

DUNCAN, ANDREW   Observations On the Structure of Hospitals for the Treatment of Lunatics. Edinburgh, 1809. 4to., half calf, plates, orig. edition. Schuman 37-64 1974 $550

DUNCAN, D. A.   Some Letters and Other Writings. Halifax, 1945. Hood's 102-236 1974 $12.50

DUNCAN, DANIEL   Wholesome Advice Against the Abuse of Hot Liquors, Particularly of Coffee, Chocolate, Tea, Brandy and Strong-Waters. London, 1706. 8vo., old panelled calf, rebacked, very rare, some browning. Gurney 66-53 1974 £90

DUNCAN, DOROTHY   Bluenose, a Portrait of Nova Scotia. New York and London, 1942. First edition. Hood's 102-185 1974 $17.50

DUNCAN, EDMONDSTOUNE   The Story of the Carol. London, 1911. 12mo., illus. Biblo & Tannen 214-838 1974 $7.50

DUNCAN, HANNIBAL GERALD   Immigration and Assimilation. Heath, 1933. Austin 62-144 1974 $27.50

DUNCAN, HENRY   William Douglas. Edinburgh, 1826. 8vo., 3 vols., contemporary half calf, first edition. Hammond 201-303 1974 £8

DUNCAN, ISADORA   My Life. Boni, Liveright, 1927. 359p. Austin 51-274 1973 $5

DUNCAN, JAMES   Beetles. Edinburgh, 1835. 8vo., half morocco gilt, rubbed, plates. Smith 194-803 1974 £7.50

DUNCAN, JAMES   Beetles. Edinburgh, 1835. Post 8vo., cloth, plates. Wheldon 130-738 1974 £7.50

DUNCAN, JAMES   British Moths, Sphinxes. Edinburgh, 1836. 8vo., plates, half morocco gilt. Smith 194-804 1974 £7.50

DUNCAN, JAMES   The History of Guernsey. 1841. 8vo., cloth, rebacked. Quaritch 939-327 1974 £30

DUNCAN, JAMES   Introduction to Entomology. Edinburgh, 1840. Post 8vo., calf, plates. Wheldon 129-631 1974 £5

DUNCAN, JAMES   The Natural History of British Butterflies. Edinburgh, 1835. Post 8vo., cloth, coloured vignette, coloured plates, portrait. Wheldon 128-711 1973 £7.50

DUNCAN, JAMES   The Natural History of British Butterflies. Edinburgh, 1835. 8vo., half calf gilt, plates. Smith 194-805 1974 £6.50

DUNCAN, JAMES   The Natural History of British Butterflies. Edin-burgh, 1835. Post 8vo., cloth, plates. Wheldon 130-739 1974 £7.50

DUNCAN, JAMES   The Natural History of British Moths. Edin-burgh, 1836. Post 8vo., cloth, plates. Wheldon 130-740 1974 £7.50

DUNCAN, JAMES   The Naturalist's Library. Edinburgh and London, c., 1830. 8vo., contemporary half roan, gilt, plates. Hammond 201-641 1974 £5

DUNCAN, JOHN   Travels In Western Africa In 1845 & 1846. London, 1847. 2 vols., 8vo., half green morocco, gilt, plates. Traylen 79-454 1973 £80

DUNCAN, JOHN   Travels in Western Africa, in 1845 & 1846. London, 1847. 2 vols., 12mo., orig. green cloth, first edition, plates, fine copy. Ximenes 36-78 1974 $150

DUNCAN, JOHN M.   A Reply to Dr. Miller's Letter to a Gentleman of Baltimore. Baltimore, 1826. 8vo., orig. printed boards, uncut. Butterfield 8-215 1974 $12.50

DUNCAN, L. L.   History of the Borough of Lewisham. London, 1908. 8vo., illus., orig. cloth. Bow Windows 62-288 1974 £6

DUNCAN, LELAND L.   The Register of all the Marriages, Christenings and Burials in the Church of S. Margaret. 1888. Roy. 8vo. Howes 186-2037 1974 £8.50

DUNCOMBE, CHARLES   Doctor Charles Duncombe's Report Upon the Subject of Education, Made to the Parliament of Upper Canada, 25th February, 1836. Toronto, 1836. Orig. boards, spine taped. Hood's 102-406 1974 $135

DUNCOMBE, CHARLES   Doctor Charles Duncombe's Report Upon the Subject of Education. Toronto, 1836. Orig. boards. Hood's 104-392 1974 $135

DUNCUMB, J.   Collections Towards the History and Antiquities of the County of Hereford. 1804-82. 3 vols., 4to., half calf. Quaritch 939-382 1974 £150

DUNGLISON, ROBLEY   A Dictionary of Medical Science. Philadelphia, 1852. Revised ninth edition. Rittenhouse 46-237 1974 $10

DUNGLISON, ROBLEY   The Practice of Medicine. Philadelphia, 1848. 2 vols., third edition. Rittenhouse 46-238 1974 $20

DUNHAM, GEORGE C.   Military Preventative Medicine. Harrisburg, 1940. Third edition. Rittenhouse 46-708 1974 $10

DUNHAM, MABEL   Grand River. Toronto, 1945. Illus. Hood's 104-680 1974 $22.50

DUNHAM, MABEL   Grand River. Toronto, 1945. Illus. Hood's 102-599 1974 $20

DUNHAM, MABEL   Toward Sodom. Toronto, 1927. Ex-library. Hood's 104-549 1974 $10

DUNHILL, ALFRED   The Pipe Book. 1924. 8vo., plates, cloth, scarce. Quaritch 940-444 1974 £20

DUNIWAY, CLYDE A.   The Development of the Freedom of the Press in Massachusetts. New York - London - Bombay, 1906. 8vo., orig. bindings, inscribed. Butterfield 8-235 1974 $22.50

DUNKIN, ALFRED JOHN   The Chronicles of Kent. Dover, 1844. 2 parts in 1 vol., 8vo., cloth, limited. Quaritch 939-402 1974 £60

DUNKIN, ALFRED JOHN   Corpus Juris Cantici. (Dover, 1873?). 8vo., presentation inscription, limited. Quaritch 939-403 1974 £30

DUNKIN, ALFRED JOHN   History of the County of Kent. 1856. 2 vols., 4to., orig. cloth, plates, rare, inscribed. Howes 186-2038 1974 £80

DUNLAP, GEORGE T.   Lest We Forget! 1948. 12mo., ltd. to 250 copies, author's sgd. pres. Biblo & Tannen 213-535 1973 $7.50

DUNLAP, GEORGE T.   The Players at the Chess. New York, 1927. 12mo., ltd. to 250 copies, author's sgd. pres., 1/4 morocco. Biblo & Tannen 213-536 1973 $10

DUNLAP, WILLIAM   A History of the American Theatre. New York, 1832. 8vo., contemporary half calf, marbled boards, rubbed but sound, spine gilt, first edition. Ximenes 36-79 1974 $70

DUNLAP, WILLIAM   The Voice of Nature. New York, 1807. 12mo., disbound, second edition. Ximenes 37-66 1974 $65

DUNLOP, JOHN COLIN   The History of Fiction. London, 1814. 3 vols., 8vo., contemporary half calf, gilt, first edition. Ximenes 37-67 1974 $65

DUNLOP, JOHN COLIN   History of Prose Fiction. 1911. 2 vols., new edition. Allen 216-1215 1974 $15

DUNLOP, O. JOCELYN   English Apprenticeship and Child Labour. 1912. Faded, English first edition. Covent 56-1196 1974 £10.50

DUNN, ARTHUR   Monterey County, California. San Francisco, 1915. 8vo., wrapper. Saddleback 14-89 1974 $12.50

DUNN, ARTHUR   Yolo County, California. San Francisco, 1915. 8vo., wrapper. Saddleback 14-90 1974 $12.50

DUNN, J. P.   Massacres of the Mountains. New York, 1886. Illus., pictorial cloth, fine, first edition. Bradley 35-133 1974 $100

DUNN, WALDO H.   The Life of Donald G. Mitchell. 1922. Austin 54-341 1973 $12.50

DUNNE, FINLEY PETER   Dissertations. Harper, 1906. Orig. edition. Austin 54-342 1973 $7.50

DUNNE, FINLEY PETER   Mr. Dooley in Peace and War. Small, Maynard, 1898. Orig. edition. Austin 54-343 1973 $4.75

DUNNE, FINLEY PETER   Mr. Dooley on Making a Will and Other Necessary Evils. 1919. Austin 54-344 1973 $10

DUNNE, FINLEY PETER   Mr. Dooley Says. 1910. 239 pages. Austin 54-346 1973 $7.50

DUNNE, FINLEY PETER   Mr. Dolley's Opinions. Russell, 1901. Orig. edition. Austin 54-345 1973 $6.50

DUNNE, FINLEY PETER   Mr. Dooley's Philosophy. Russell, 1900. Orig. edition, 263 pages. Austin 54-347 1973 $5.25

DUNNE, JOHN G.   The Studio. Farrar, 1968. 255p. Austin 51-275 1973 $5

DUNNE, WILLIAM H.   Captain Jolly on the Picturesque St. Croix. St. Paul, 1880. 16mo., orig. bindings, illus., scarce, first edition. Butterfield 8-301 1974 $25

DUNNING, ALBERT E.   Congregationalists in America. Boston, 1894. Bdg. worn, inner hinges split. Biblo & Tannen 213-31 1973 $12.50

DUNNING, PHILIP   Broadway. Doran, 1927. 236p. Austin 51-276 1973 $8.50

DUNNING, WILLIAM A.   History of Political Theories. 1913. 2 vols., spotted spines. Allen 213-337 1973 $15

DUNSANY, EDWARD JOHN MORETON DRAX PLUNKETT   The Charwoman's Shadow. New York, 1926. First American edition. Biblo & Tannen 214-697 1974 $7.50

DUNSANY, EDWARD JOHN MORETON DRAX PLUNKETT   Fifty-One Tales. 1915. Linen backed boards, foxed, English first edition. Covent 56-378 1974 £7.50

DUNSANY, EDWARD JOHN MORETON DRAX PLUNKETT   Fifty Poems. 1929. Near fine, English first edition. Covent 56-379 1974 £35

DUNSANY, EDWARD JOHN MORETON DRAX PLUNKETT   Five Plays. 1914. Frontis., foxing, English first edition. Covent 56-380 1974 £6.30

DUNSANY, EDWARD JOHN MORETON DRAX PLUNKETT   Five Plays. Kennerley, 1914. 116 pages. Austin 51-277 1973 $8.50

DUNSANY, EDWARD JOHN MORETON DRAX PLUNKETT   The Fourth Book of Jorkens. Sauk City, 1948. First edition, limited. Biblo & Tannen 210-595 1973 $15

DUNSANY, EDWARD JOHN MORETON DRAX PLUNKETT   The Fourth Book of Jorkens. Sauk City, 1948. First edition. Biblo & Tannen 214-698 1974 $12.50

DUNSANY, EDWARD JOHN MORETON DRAX PLUNKETT   If. Putnam, 1929. 185 pages. Austin 51-278 1973 $7.50

DUNSANY, EDWARD JOHN MORETON DRAX PLUNKETT   The Last Book of Wonder. 1916. Illus. Austin 61-344 1974 $10

DUNSANY, EDWARD JOHN MORETON DRAX PLUNKETT   A Night at an Inn. New York, 1916. First U. S. edition, very good, wrappers. Covent 51-611 1973 £8.50

DUNSANY, EDWARD JOHN MORETON DRAX PLUNKETT   A Night at an Inn. New York, 1916. Wrappers, first U.S. edition. Covent 56-381 1974 £10

DUNSANY, EDWARD JOHN MORETON DRAX PLUNKETT   The Old Folk of the Centuries. n.d. Cloth backed boards, English first edition. Covent 56-382 1974 £8.50

DUNSANY, EDWARD JOHN MORETON DRAX PLUNKETT   Plays of Gods and Men. Boston, 1917. Cloth backed boards, first U. S. edition. Covent 56-1730 1974 £10.50

DUNSANY, EDWARD JOHN MORETON DRAX PLUNKETT   Tales of Three Hemispheres. 1920. Cloth backed boards, English first edition. Covent 56-384 1974 £8.50

DUNSANY, EDWARD JOHN MORETON DRAX PLUNKETT   Tales of War. Boston, 1918. Faded, first U.S. edition. Covent 56-385 1974 £7.50

DUNSANY, EDWARD JOHN MORETON DRAX PLUNKETT   Unhappy Far-Off Things. 1919. Linen backed boards, bookplate, English first edition. Covent 56-386 1974 £12.50

DUNSANY, EDWARD JOHN MORETON DRAX PLUNKETT   Unhappy Far-Off Things. Boston, 1919. First American edition. Biblo & Tannen 214-699 1974 $7.50

DUNSANY, EDWARD JOHN MORETON DRAX PLUNKETT   Unhappy Far Off Things. 1919. Austin 51-280 1973 $7.50

DUNSANY, EDWARD JOHN MORETON DRAX PLUNKETT   While the Sirens Slept. London, (1944). 8vo., orig. cloth, first edition. Bow Windows 62-290 1974 £7.50

DUNSFORD, MARTIN   Historical Memoirs of the Town and Parish of Tiverton. 1790. 4to., contemporary half russia, first edition. Howes 186-1995 1974 £30

DUNSTAR, S.   Anglia Rediviva. London, 1699. Small 8vo., calf. Quaritch 939-111 1974 £35

DUNTHORNE, GORDON   Flower & Fruit Prints of the 18th and Early 19th Centuries. Washington, 1938. Folio, orig. cloth, case, subscriber's copy, large folding plate listing names, fine. Gregory 44-114 1974 $200

DUNTON, JOHN   Athenian Sport. London, 1707. 8vo., contemporary panelled calf, first edition. Dawsons PM 252-325 1974 £120

DUNTON, JOHN   Athenian Sport. 1707. 8vo., contemporary calf, first edition. Quaritch 936-71 1974 £20

DUPIRE, NOEL   Etude Critique des Manuscrits et Editions des Poesies de Jean Molinet. Paris, 1932. Wrappers, uncut, unopened. Kraus B8-54 1974 $12.50

DU PLEIX, SCIPION   Les Causes de la Veille et du Sommeil des Songes, & de la Vie & de la Mort. Paris, 1631. Small 8vo., old-style vellum. Schuman 37-65 1974 $75

DUPLESSIS, GEORGES   Essai Bibliographique sur les Differentes Editions des Oeuvres d'Ovide . . . Publiees aux XVe et SVI Siecles. Paris, 1889. Orig. wrappers. Kraus B8-55 1974 $25

DUPLESSIS, GEORGES   Histoire de la Gravure en France. Paris, 1861. 8vo., printed wrappers, uncut. Kraus B8-56 1974 $28

DUPLESSIS, GEORGES   The Wonders of Engraving. n.d. Faded, wood-engravings, rubbed, English first edition. Covent 56-1737 1974 £5.50

DUPLESSIS, GEORGES   The Wonders of Engraving. New York, 1886. Biblo & Tannen 213-377 1973 $10

DUPLESSIS-MORNAY, PHILIPPE
Please turn to
MORNAY, PHILIPPE DE

DU PONCEAU, PETER S.   A Dissertation on the Nature and Extent of the Jurisdiction of the Courts of the U. S. Philadelphia, 1824. 254p., orig. boards. Austin 62-145 1974 $150

DU PONCEAU, PETER S.   A Dissertation on the Nature and Extent of the Jurisdiction of the Courts of the U. S. Philadelphia, 1824. Orig. boards. Austin 57-187 1974 $150

DUPONT, ELEUTHERE IRENEE   Life of . . . From Contemporary Correspondence, 1778-1791. 1923-27. 11 vols. plus index, blue boards, parchment backs stamped with gold, each vol. boxed, limited to 250 sets. Butterfield 10-237 1974 $200

DUPONT, PAUL   Histoire de l'Imprimerie. Paris, n.d. (1869). 8vo., orig. printed wrappers. Kraus B8-313 1974 $30

DUPONT, PAUL   Notice Historique sur l'Imprimerie. Paris, 1849. 4to., orig. printed wrappers, bound in half cloth. Kraus B8-314 1974 $50

DUPONT, PAUL   Notice sur les Etablissements de M. Paul Dupont Imprimeur a Paris. Paris, 1867. 4to., orig. printed wrappers. Kraus B8-315 1974 $65

DUPPA, RICHARD   The Classes and Orders of the Linnean System of Botany. 1816. 3 vols., plates, contemporary half calf. Bow Windows 64-81 1974 £85

DUPPA, RICHARD   A Journal of the Most Remarkable Occurrences that Took Place in Rome, Upon the Subversion of the Ecclesiastical Government in 1798. 1799. 8vo., old tree calf, neatly rebacked, first edition. Bow Windows 66-195 1974 £10

DUPRAT, FRANCOIS ANTOINE   Histoire de l'Imprimerie Imperiale de France, Suivi des Specimens des Types Etrangers et Francais de cet Etablissement. Paris, 1861. 4to., orig. printed wrappers bound in half leather. Kraus B8-316 1974 $57.50

DUPUIS, C. F.   Origine de tous les Cultes. Paris, 1835-36. 10 vols. in 5, thick 8vo., half calf gilt. Howes 186-1819 1974 £10

DUPUYTREN, GUILLAUME   On the Injuries and Diseases of Bones. London, 1847. 8vo., orig. green blind stamped cloth, uncut. Dawsons PM 249-152 1974 £23

DURAND, CHARLES   Reminiscences of. Toronto, 1897. Hood's 102-237 1974 $20

DURAND, EDWARD DANA   The Finances of New York City. New York, 1898. First U. S. edition, blind stamp 'Presentation copy' on title page, else very good copy. Covent 51-2096 1973 £12.60

DURAND, JEAN BAPTISTE LEONARD   A Voyage to Sengal. 1806. 8vo., old half calf, rebacked, worn. Hill 126-4 1974 £10.50

DURAND, JEAN BAPTISTE LEONARD   A Voyage to Senegal. London, 1806. 8vo., old calf, rebacked, uncut, plates, first edition. Traylen 79-455 1973 £20

DURAND, T.   Index Generum Phanerogamorum Usque ad Finem anni 1887 Promulgatorum in Benthami et Hookeri. Brussels, 1888. Roy. 8vo., cloth. Wheldon 128-1105 1973 £10

DURANTY, E.   John Everett Millais. (1882). Orig. cloth, etchings, disbound, illus. Marsden 37-306 1974 £15

D'URBAN, W. S. M.   The Birds of Devon. 1892. Roy. 8vo., orig. cloth, plates, maps. Wheldon 131-588 1974 £7.50

D'URBAN, W. S. M.   The Birds of Devon. 1895. 8vo., orig. dec. cloth, plates, second edition. Wheldon 129-455 1974 £12

DURER, ALBRECHT
Please turn to
DUERER, ALBRECHT

DURFEE, JOB   Whatcheer. Cranston, Hammond, 1832. 200p. Austin 54-348 1973 $27.50

D'URFEY, THOMAS 1653-1723   Collin's Walk Through London and Westminster. London, 1690. 8vo., contemporary mottled calf, rare. Quaritch 939-446 1974 £100

D'URFEY, THOMAS 1653-1723   Tales Tragical and Comical. London, 1704. 8vo., half calf, spine gilt, first edition. Ximenes 37-68 1974 $150

D'URFEY, THOMAS 1653-1723   Wit and Mirth. (1874). Small 8vo., 6 vols., half red morocco, gilt, frontis. Quaritch 936-376 1974 £30

DURHAM, JAMES   A Practical Exposition of the Ten Commandments With a Resolution. Glasgow, 1676. Small 4to., quarter morocco, rare. Howes 185-1128 1974 £22.50

DURHAM, JOHN GEORGE LAMBTON, 1ST EARL OF 1792-1840   Report on the Affairs of British North America. Toronto, 1839. Three quarter leather. Hood's 103-532 1974 $85

DURKEN, B.   Lehrbuch der Experimental-Zoologie. Berlin, 1928. Roy 8vo., buckram, second edition. Wheldon 130-352 1974 £6

DURKIN, D.   The Lobstick Trail. Toronto, 1921. Hood's 102-504 1974 $7.50

DURNING-LAWRENCE, EDWIN   Bacon is Shakespeare. Gay, Hancock, 1910. 286p., illus. Austin 51-281 1973 $10

DURRANT, C. S.   A Link Between Flemish Mystics and English Martyrs. 1925. Plates. Howes 185-1129 1974 £5

DURRELL, LAWRENCE   The Black Book. Paris, n.d. (1938). First edition, 4to., orig. wrappers, uncut and partly unopened, signed by Durrell. Thomas 32-166 1974 £100

DURRELL, LAWRENCE   The Black Book. Paris, 1938. 8vo., orig. cloth, wrappers, scarce, first edition. Rota 190-390 1974 £90

DURRELL, LAWRENCE   The Black Books. Paris, 1938. First edition, wrappers, small tears in covers, margins little browned, last leaf carelessly opened, very good copy, scarce. Covent 51-616 1973 £85

DURRELL, LAWRENCE   Prospero's Cell. 1945. 8vo., orig. cloth, illus., first edition. Rota 190-391 1974 £10

DURRIEU, PAUL   La Miniature Flamande, au Temps de la Cour de Bourgogne (1415-1530). Brussels, 1921. Folio, reproductions of miniatures, three quarter morocco. Kraus B8-57 1974 $58.50

DURU, H.   Mythologie Illustree. Paris, (c. 1835). 16mo., orig. boards, coloured illus. on upper cover, lithograph plates rather roughly hand coloured. George's 610-229 1973 £6

DUSEJOUR, DIONIS   The Origin of the Graces. London, n.d. Tall 8vo., illus., contemporary crushed morocco, fine, limited. Dawsons PM 252-328 1974 £15

DU SOMMERARD, A.   Les Arts au Moyen Age. 1838-46. 5 vols., roy. 8vo., 11 vols. in 3, imp. folio, half crimson morocco, raised boards, gilt, plates. Quaritch 940-445 1974 £500

D'USSEAU, ARNAUD   Deep Are the Roots. 1946. 96p., paper. Austin 51-283 1973 $7.50

D'USSEAU, ARNAUD   Deep Are the Roots. Scribner, 1946. 205p. Austin 51-282 1973 $10

DUTENS, LOUIS   An Enquiry into the Origin of the Discoveries Attributed to the Moderns. 1769. 8vo., calf. Wheldon 131-215 1974 £20

DUTENS, LOUIS   Recherches sur l'Origine des Decouvertes Attributees aux Moderns. Paris, 1766. 2 vols. in 1, 8vo., contemporary mottled calf, first edition. Schuman 37-66 1974 £110

DU TERTRE, DU PORT   Histoire des Conjurations. Paris, 1757. 12mo., old calf, some foxing. Biblo & Tannen 213-32 1973 $47.50

DUTHY, J.   Sketches of Hampshire. Winchester, (1839). 8vo., cloth, plates. Quaritch 939-371 1974 £15

DU TOIT, A. L.   Physical Geography for South African Schools. Cambridge, 1912. Crown 8vo., orig. cloth, illus. Wheldon 131-351 1974 £7.50

DUTROCHET, M. H.   Recherches Anatomiques et Physiologiques sur la Structure. Paris, 1824. 8vo., modern half calf, foxing, first edition. Dawsons PM 249-153 1974 £85

DUTT, W. A.   A Guide to the Norfolk Broads Being Part 1 to "The Norfolk Broads". 1923. 8vo., cloth, map, illus. Wheldon 128-196 1973 £5

DUTT, W. A.   A Guide to the Norfolk Boards. 1923. 8vo., cloth, illus. Wheldon 131-352 1974 £5

DUTTON, R.   The English Garden. 1937. 8vo., cloth, illus., frontispiece. Wheldon 131-1510 1974 £5

DUTUIT, E.   La Collection Dutuit. Paris, 1899. Limited to 350 copies, plates, illus., med. folio, dec. boards, vellum back, uncut. Forster 98-123 1974 £55

DUVAL, ELIZABETH W.   T. E. Lawrence. New York, 1938. Linen-backed boards, English first edition. Covent 56-1868 1974 £15

DUVAL, JACQUES   Methode Novvelle de Gvarir les Catarrhes. 1611. Small 8vo., vellum, first edition. Dawsons PM 249-154 1974 £90

DUVAL, M.   Etudes sur l'embryologie des Cheiropteres. Paris, 1899. 4to., wrappers, plates. Wheldon 129-369 1974 £5

DUVAL, M.   Le Placenta des Carnassiers. Paris, 1895. 4to., 2 vols., wrappers, plates. Wheldon 129-370 1974 £5

DUVEEN, EDWARD J.   Colour in the Home. n.d. 4to., presentation inscription, plates, English first edition. Covent 56-311 1974 £12.50

DUVERGER, EUGENE   Histoire de l'Invention de l'Imprimerie par les Monuments. Paris, 1840. 4to., illus., contemporary boards, rebacked, worn. Dawsons PM 10-200 1974 £40

DUVERGER, EUGENE   Histoire de l'Invention de l'Imprimerie par les Monuments. Paris, 1840. Half buckram. Kraus B8-318 1974 $65

DUVERGER, EUGENE   Histoire de l'Invention de l'Imprimerie par les Monuments. Paris, 1840. Small folio, red half morocco, plates, illus., portrait. Kraus B8-317 1974 $95

DU VERNET, THEOPHILE IMARIGEON   La Vie de Voltaire par M. Geneva, 1787. 8vo., three quarter red hard grain morocco, gilt. L. Goldschmidt 42-134 1974 $20

DUVERNOY, G. L.   Fragments sur les Organes. Paris, 1850. 4to., sewed, plates. Wheldon 130-353 1974 £5

DUYCKINCK, EVERT A.   Cyclopaedia of American Literature. Philadelphia, 1875. 2 vols., 4to., publisher's half morocco, illus. Goodspeed's 578-451 1974 $50

DUYCKINCK, EVERT A.   Portrait Gallery of Eminent Men and Women of Europe and America. Wilson, 1878. Vol 1-640p., vol 2-638p., illus. with steel engravings. Austin 54-349 1973 $27.50

DWIGGINS, W. A.   22 Printers' Marks and Seals. New York, 1929. Black cloth, unopened, signed. Dawson's 424-148 1974 $45

DWIGHT, H. G.   Art Parade. New York, 1943. 4to., color plates. Biblo & Tannen 210-128 1973 $15

DWIGHT, THEODORE   History of the Hartford Convention, With a Preview of the Policy of the United States Government Which Led to the War of 1812. New York, 1833. Jenkins 61-691 1974 $10

DWIGHT, TIMOTHY   The Conquest of Canaan.   Hartford, 1785.
Orig. leather, rubbed, first edition, without the leaf of errata, internally
clean.   MacManus 224-142 1974 $85

DWYER, PHILIP   The Diocese of Killaloe From the Reformation.
Dublin, 1878. 8vo., cloth boards, map. Emerald 50-268 1974 £8.50

DYCE, A.   Glossary to Works of William Shakespeare.
1902. Allen 216-2168 1974 $12.50

DYE, EVA EMERY   The Conquest. Chicago, 1902. Pictorial
charcoal cloth, first edition. Bradley 35-222 1974 $15

DYE, EVA EMERY   McLoughlin and Old Oregon. Chicago, 1913.
Hood's 102-238 1974 $10

DYE, EVA EMERY   McLoughlin and Old Oregon. Chicago, 1913.
Hood's 104-254 1974 $10

DYER, G.   History of the University and College of
Cambridge. 1814. 2 vols., 8vo., buckram. Quaritch 939-320 1974 £30

DYER, G.   The Privileges of the University of Cambridge.
1824. 2 vols., 8vo., buckram. Quaritch 939-321 1974 £17.50

DYER, HENRY   Dai Nippon. 1904. Cloth gilt, faded, foxed,
first edition. Covent 55-925 1974 £6.30

DYER, JOHN   Poems. London, 1761. 8vo., contemporary
calf, plates, first collected edition. Dawsons PM 252-329 1974 £40

DYER, T. F. THISELTON   Church-lore Gleanings. London, 1892.
1st ed. Biblo & Tannen 214-573 1974 $12.50

DYKES, WILLIAM RICKATSON   The Genus Iris. 1913. Folio, cloth, scarce,
coloured plates. Wheldon 128-1457 1973 £35

DYKES, WILLIAM RICKATSON   The Genus Iris. 1913. Folio, cloth, plates,
scarce. Wheldon 130-1388 1974 £35

DYKES, WILLIAM RICKATSON   A Handbook of Garden Irises. 1924. Plates.
Bow Windows 64-82 1974 £6.50

DYKES, WILLIAM RICKATSON   Handbook of Garden Irises. London, 1924.
Illus., fine, 8vo., orig. cloth. Gregory 44-117 1974 $22.50

DYKES, WILLIAM RICKATSON   A Handbook of Garden Irises. 1924. 8vo.,
cloth, plates. Wheldon 130-1389 1974 £7.50

DYKES, WILLIAM RICKATSON   Notes on Tulip Species. 1930. Folio, orig.
green buckram, coloured plates. Wheldon 128-1458 1973 £20

DYKES, WILLIAM RICKATSON   Notes on Tulip Species. (1930). Large 4to.,
plates, bookplate. Bow Windows 64-83 1974 £24.50

DYKES, WILLIAM RICKATSON   Notes On Tulip Species. London, 1930.
Folio, plates, illus. Traylen 79-13 1973 £28

DYKES, WILLIAM RICKATSON   Notes on Tulip Species. 1930. Folio, orig.
green buckram, plates. Wheldon 131-1511 1974 £15

DYMENT, CLIFFORD   First Day. 1935. Boards, signed, English first
edition. Covent 56-395 1974 £5.25

DYMOCK, W.   Pharmacographia Indica. Bombay, 1890-93.
3 vols., 8vo., buckram, very rare. Wheldon 128-1677 1973 £45

E

E., A. PSEUD.
Please turn to
RUSSELL, GEORGE WILLIAM

E., J.　　　Glas und Keramik Sammlung J. E., Berlin and Berliner Privatbestiz. Berlin, 1929. Small folio, plates, cloth, orig. wrapper. Quaritch 940-446 1974 £10

EADMER　　　Historiae Nouorum Siue Sui Saeculi Libri VI. 1623. First edition, lacks first and last blanks, small folio, modern half sheep, marbled boards. Thomas 32-111 1974 £25

EAMES, WILBERFORCE　　　The First Year of Printing in New York, May 1693 to April, 1694. 8vo., wrappers. Kraus B8-319 1974 $10

EAREE, ROBERT BRISCO　　　Album Weeds, or, How to Detect Forged Stamps. (1905). Third and best edition, illus., 2 vols., orig. green cloth, good copy, scarce. Sawyer 293-245 1974 £35

EARHART, AMELIA　　　Twenty Hours and Forty Minutes, Our Flight in the Friendship. New York & London, 1928. Author's autograph edition, limited to 150 copies, large paper, uncut, large 8vo., laid on front endpaper is small silk U.S. flag "taken by Miss Earhart Across the Atlantic in the Friendship". Butterfield 10-77 1974 $50

EARHART, JOHN F.　　　The Harmonizer. Cincinatti, 1897. Orig. grey cloth. Dawson's 424-130 1974 $135

EARL, HENRY H.　　　A Centennial History of Fall River. New York, 1877. Folio, pictorial cloth, plates. Butterfield 8-236 1974 $35

EARLAND, ADA　　　John Opie and His Circle. 1911. Orig. cloth, plates, faded. Marsden 37-349 1974 £5.50

EARLE, ALICE MORSE　　　Old Time Gardens. New York, 1901. First edition, large paper, limited to 350 copies, full page photogravures, text illus., 8vo., orig. green boards, vellum back, interior fine. Current BW9-512 1974 $22.50

EARLE, AUGUSTUS　　　A Narative Of. 1832. 8vo., contemporary half calf, plates, first edition. Bow Windows 64-493 1974 £90

EARLE, C. W.　　　Pot-Pourri from a Surrey Garden. 1901-2. 2 vols., illus., faded. Bow Windows 64-84 1974 £5.50

EARLE, CYRIL　　　The Earle Collection of Early Staffordshire Pottery. (1915). Roy. 4to., plates, rebound in half calf, gilt, limited edition. Quaritch 940-629 1974 £90

EARLE, HENRY　　　Practical Observation in Surgery. London, 1823. 8vo., half calf, plates, first edition. Schuman 37-67 1974 $95

EARLE, JOHN　　　The Philology of the English Tongue. Oxford, 1879. Biblo & Tannen 213-758 1973 $7.50

EARLY Illinois. Chicago, 1889. 4 parts, printed yellow wrappers, illus., uncut, first editions. Bradley 35-176 1974 $40

EARLY Missionaries. Paris, 1781. Old calf. Biblo & Tannen 213-33 1973 $20

EARLY Venetian Pictures and Other Works of Art. 1912. 4to., buckram, uncut, plates. Quaritch 940-269 1974 £30

EARNEST, ERNEST　　　S. Weir Mitchell. Univ of Penna., 1950. 279p. Austin 54-781 1973 $12.50

EARNSHAW, T.　　　Explanations of Time-Keepers Constructed By. 1806. 4to., plates, contemporary half calf. Quaritch 940-447 1974 £70

EARWAKER, J. P.　　　East Cheshire. 1877. 2 vols., thick 4to., orig. green cloth, plates, illus. Howes 186-1989 1974 £45

EARWAKER, J. P.　　　East Cheshire: Past and Present. 1877-80. 2 vols., roy. 4to., good copy, scarce, plates, illus. Broadhurst 24-1412 1974 £42

EARWAKER, J. P.　　　The History of the Church and Parish of St. Mary-on-the-Hill. 1898. 4to., orig. cloth. Broadhurst 23-1372 1974 £15

EASTLAKE, CHARLES L.　　　Hints on Household Taste in Furniture, Upholstery and Other Details. Boston, 1872. Binding worn, illus. Biblo & Tannen 213-286 1973 $10

EASTLAKE, CHARLES L.　　　Hints on Household Taste in Furniture. 1872. Illus., blind stamped cloth, third revised edition. Marsden 37-172 1974 £10

EASTMAN, MARY H.　　　Chicora and Other Regions of the Conquerors and the Conquered. Philadelphia, 1854. Red leather. Hood's 102-450 1974 $100

EASTMAN, MAX　　　Enjoyment of Laughter. Simon, 1936. 367p. Austin 54-350 1973 $8.50

EASTMAN, MAX　　　Enjoyment of Living. Harper, 1948. 603p., illus. Austin 54-351 1973 $7.50

EASTMAN, MAX　　　Enjoyment of Poetry. Scribner, 1926. 254p. Austin 54-352 1973 $7.50

EASTMAN, MAX　　　Poems of Five Decades. Harper, 1954. 249p. Austin 54-353 1973 $10

EASTMAN, MAX　　　The Sense of Humor. Scribner, 1921. 257p. Austin 54-354 1973 $8.50

AN EASY Introduction to the Game of Chess. 1813. 12mo., contemporary boards, uncut, folding plate, inscription, new edition. Bow Windows 66-123 1974 £5

EATON, A.　　　An Index to the Geology of the Northern States. Troy, 1820. 12mo., orig. sheep worn, rare. Wheldon 129-818 1974 £20

EATON, A. E.　　　A Revisional Monograph of Recent Ephemeridae. 1883-88. 4to., full morocco gilt, plates. Wheldon 129-632 1974 £25

EATON, ALLEN H.　　　Immigrant Gifts to American Life. 1932. 185p., illus., orig. ed. Austin 62-148 1974 $10

EATON, ALLEN H.　　　Immigrant Gifts to American Life. 1932. Illus., orig. edition. Austin 57-191 1974 $10

EATON, E. H.　　　The Birds of New York. New York, 1910-14. 4to., 2 vols., orig. cloth, plates. Wheldon 130-506 1974 £25

EATON, EDWARD SEYMOUR　　　Charles Dickens. Philadelphia, 1900. Cloth backed portfolio, wrappers, limited edition. Covent 56-352 1974 £25

EATON, S. J. M.　　　History of the Presbytery of Erie. New York, 1868. 8vo., orig. bindings. Butterfield 8-475 1974 $12.50

EATON, SEYMOUR　　　Shakespeare Rare Print Collection. (New York), 1900. 12 parts, plates, stains. Rinsland 58-74 1974 $40

EATON, WALTER P.　　　The Actor's Heritage. 1924. 294p., illus. Austin 51-284 1973 $7.50

EATON, WALTER P.　　　The Theatre Guild. Brentano, 1929. 299p., illus., orig. ed. Austin 51-285 1973 $12.50

EBER, PAUL　　　Calendarium Historicum. Basle, 1550. 8vo., rebound, first edition. Dawsons PM 251-212 1974 £90

EBERHART, RICHARD　　　Poems New and Selected. Norfolk, 1944. 8vo., wrappers, signature, fine, first edition. Rota 189-287 1974 £12.50

EBERLEIN, HAROLD DONALDSON　　　The Colonial Homes of Philadelphia and Its Neighborhood. Philadelphia, 1912. First edition, thick 8vo., illus., spine browned and faded, else perfect. Current BW9-409 1974 $32.50

EBERLEIN, HAROLD DONALDSON　　　Colonial Interiors. New York, 1938. Blue cloth, plates. Dawson's 424-223 1974 $35

EBERLEIN, HAROLD DONALDSON　　　The Practical Book of Interior Decoration. Philadelphia, 1919. Plates, d.w. Covent 55-910 1974 £12.50

EBERLEIN & RICHARDSON   The English Inn Past and Present. Philadelphia, 1926. First edition, large 8vo., full page photo plates, text drawings, maps, fine bright covers. Current BW9-513 1974 $37.50

EBERLIN VON GUNZBURG, JOHANN   Ein Newe Ordnung Weltliche Standts das Psitacus Anzeigt Hat in Wolfaria Beschriben. N.P., n.d. 4to., marbled boards, red morocco back, first and only edition. Harper 213-54 1973 $1100

EBERMAYER, J. M. VON   Gemmarum Affabre Sculptarum Thesaurus. 1720. Folio, new buckram, plates, illus. Allen 213-340 1973 $40

EBERS, G.   Egypt: Descriptive, Historical, and Picturesque. (1878). 2 vols., 4to., orig. cloth, minor spotting, illus. Bow Windows 66-197 1974 £9.25

EBERT, FREDERIC ADOLPHUS   A General Bibliographical Dictionary. Oxford, 1837. 4 vols., orig. blue cloth, first English edition. Dawsons PM 10-202 1974 £48

EBERT, FREDERIC ADOLPHUS   A General Bibliographical Dictionary. Oxford, 1837. 4 vols., first English edition, demy 8vo., half cloth. Forster 98-127 1974 £50

EBNER, ADALBERT   Quellen und Forschungen zur Geschichte und Kunstgeschichte des Missale Romanum im Mittelalter. Freiburg, 1896. 8vo., cloth, illus. Kraus B8-59 1974 $45

EBSWORTH, J. W.   Cavalier Lyrics. London and Hertford, 1887. 8vo., illus., numbered, signed by author, orig. well preserved paper wrappers, inscription signed by author. Bow Windows 66-197 1974 £15

ECK, JOHANN   Enchiridion Locorum Communium Aduersus Lutherum & Alios Hostes Ecclesiae. Antwerpen, 1545. Small 8vo., newly bound in old leather, gilt on spine, fine. Schumann 499-31 1974 sFr 340

ECKART, DIETRICH   Lorenzaccio. (1920). 8vo., new quarter morocco, wrappers, rare. Rich Summer-57 1974 $100

ECKEL, JOHN C.   The First Editions of the Writings of Charles Dickens and Their Values. 1913. Orig. buckram, gilt, illus., limited edition. Howes 185-661 1974 $12.50

ECKEL, JOHN C.   Prime Pickwick in Parts. New York, 1928. Limited to 440 copies, signed by Eckel, illus., med. 8vo., orig. cloth, bookplate. Forster 98-62 1974 £8

ECKER, ALEXANDER   On the Convolutions of the Human Brain. London, 1873. 8vo., orig. brown cloth. Dawsons PM 249-153 1974 £21

ECKHEL, L'ABBE   Choix des Pierres Graves du Cabinet Imperial des Antiques. Vienna, 1788. Folio, contemporary diced russia, rebacked with morocco gilt, engravings. Quaritch 940-313 1974 £50

ECKSTEIN, O.   Potash Deficiency Symptoms. Berlin, 1937. Roy. 8vo., half leather, plates, scarce. Wheldon 131-1775 1974 £5

THE ECLECTIC and General Dispensatory. Philadelphia, 1827. Orig. binding. Rittenhouse 46-241 1974 $30

EDDINGTON, A. S.   The Mathematical Theory of Relativity. 1923. Ex-library. Covent 55-1297 1974 £8.50

EDDIS, WILLIAM   Letters from America. London, 1792. 8vo., contemporary half calf, leather label, very fine. Traylen 79-476 1973 £90

EDDISON, E. R.   Mistress of Mistresses. 1935. Dust wrapper, fine, English first edition. Covent 56-1744 1974 £15

EDDISON, E. R.   Poems, Letters and Memories of Philip Sidney Nairn. London, 1916. First edition, orig. cloth, very nice copy. Crane 7-77 1974 £10

EDDISON, E. R.   Poems, Letters, and Memoirs of Philip Sidney Nairn. 1916. Plates, English first edition. Covent 56-1731 1974 £15

EDDISON, E. R.   Poems, Letters and Memories of Philip Sidney Nairn. 1916. Frontispiece, near fine. Covent 55-624 1974 £17.50

EDDISON, E. R.   The Worm Ouroboros. 1926. Illus., first American edition. Austin 61-347 1974 $12.50

EDDY, MARY BAKER   Science and Health. Boston, 1875. 8vo., orig. printed cloth, rebacked, first edition. Gilhofer 61-60 1974 sFr. 2,500

EDE, H. S.   Savage Messiah. New York, 1931. Sm. 4to., plates, lst ed. Biblo & Tannen 210-205 1973 $8.50

EDE, H. S.   Savage Messiah. 1931. Illus., unusually fine copy, first edition. Covent 51-763 1973 £10

EDE, H. S.   Savage Messiah. London, 1931. 8vo., cloth, illus., plates. Minters 37-279 1973 $15

EDEBOHLS, GEORGE M.   Movable Kidney. 1893. 8vo., contemporary half calf. Dawsons PM 249-159 1974 £16

EDEN, F. SYDNEY   Ancient Stained and Painted Glass. 1933. Illus. Covent 55-439 1974 £5.25

EDEN, WILLIAM   The Substance of a Speech. London, 1799. 8vo., disbound, new edition. Dawsons PM 247-100 1974 £10

EDEN, WILLIAM   Substance of the Speeches of Lord Auckland. London, 1846. 8vo., boards. Hammond 201-181 1974 £6.50

EDGAR, A. T.   Manual of Rubber Planting. 1937. Roy 8vo., cloth, illus. Wheldon 129-1652 1974 £7.50

EDGAR. M. G.   A Treasury of Verse. New York, 1926. 8vo., 8 color plates. Frohnsdorff 16-54 1974 $7.50

EDGAR, MATILDA   Ten Years of Upper Canada in Peace and War, 1805-1815, Being the Ridout Letters. Toronto, 1890. Hood's 102-600 1974 $60

EDGAR, MATILDA   Ten Years of Upper Canada in Peace and War, 1805-1815. Toronto, 1890. Hood's 104-681 1974 $60

EDGAR, P.   The Art of the Novel, From 1700 to the Present Time. New York, 1933. Hood's 103-404 1974 $12.50

EDGARTON, SARAH C.   The Rose of Sharon. Boston, 1841. 8vo., orig. blind-stamped morocco, wron, plates. Ximenes 33-78 1974 $17.50

EDGE, A. B. BROUGHTON   The Principles and Practices of Geophysical Prospecting. Cambridge, 1931. 4to., frontispiece map, diagrams, book-plate. Bow Windows 64-85 1974 £6

EDGE, EDWARD   Edgiana. 1910. Fine, rebound, orig. wrappers, English first edition. Covent 56-401 1974 £15

EDGEWORTH, F. Y.   Papers Relating to Political Economy. 1925. 3 vols., English first edition. Covent 56-398 1974 £9

EDGEWORTH, M. P.   Descriptions of Unpublished Species of Plants from N.-W. India. 1845. 4to., plate. Wheldon 131-1282 1974 £5

EDGEWORTH, MARIA   Comic Dramas. London, 1817. 12mo., contemporary mottled half calf, first edition. Dawsons PM 252-330 1974 £15

EDGEWORTH, MARIA   Frank. London, 1825. 16mo., contemp. marbled boards, roan spines (worn), 3 vols. Frohnsdorff 16-304 1974 $45

EDGEWORTH, MARIA   Harrington. 1817. 3 vols., crown 8vo., hlaf calf, foxing, labels, gilt, first edition. Howes 186-171 1974 £35

EDGEWORTH, MARIA   Harry and Lucy Concluded; Being the Last Part of Early Lessons. 1827. Corrected second edition, 4 vols., 12mo., contemporary roan backed boards, slightly rubbed, each vol. with half title. George's 610-233 1973 £7.50

EDGEWORTH, MARIA   The Parent's Assistant; or, Stories for Children. 1831. 3 vols., 12mo., contemporary roan backed boards, stitching weak in places, ex-libris copy, new edition. George's 610-235 1973 £5

EDGEWORTH, MARIA   Patronage. London, 1814. 4 vols., 12mo., contemporary half calf, somewhat worn, one hinge weak, first edition, inscribed presentation copy from author. Ximenes 36-80 1974 $175

EDGEWORTH, MARIA   Tales. London, 1825. 14 vols., 8vo., uncut, contemporary cloth, scarce, inscription, first collected edition. Dawsons PM 252-331 1974 £250

EDGEWORTH, MARIA   Tales, and Miscellaneous Pieces. London, 1825. Small 8vo., contemporary diced calf, gilt, first collected edition. Hammond 201-304 1974 £60

EDGEWORTH, MARIA   Works. 1832-33. Engraved frontispiece, 18 vols., f'cap 8vo., half green morocco, panelled backs, by Zaehsdorf, marbled boards, fine. Broadhurst 24-1710 1974 £80

EDGEWORTH, RICHARD LOVELL   Poetry Explained for the Use of Young People. 1809. 12mo., half calf. Hill 126-83 1974 £30

EDINBURGH BIBLIOGRAPHICAL SOCIETY   Papers, Vol. XI, Part 2; XII-XV. Edinburgh, 1918-35. 9 parts, illus., post 8vo., orig. wrappers. Forster 98-132 1974 £16

EDINBURGH Musical Miscellany. Collection of Most Approved Scotch, English and Irish Songs, Set to Music. 1804. New buckram, some pencillings, second edition. Allen 216-2009 1974 $15

EDINBURGH UNIVERSITY LIBRARY   Catalogue of the Printed Books In. Edinburgh, 1918-23. 3 vols., 4to., orig. cloth gilt. Dawsons PM 10-203 1974 £26

EDINBURGH UNIVERSITY LIBRARY   Catalogue of the Printed Books in... Edinburgh, 1918-23. 3 vols., 4to., buckram. Quaritch 939-653 1974 £15

EDINBURGH UNIVERSITY LIBRARY   Catalogue of the Printed Books in the Library of. (Edinburgh), 1918-23. 3 vols., demy 4to., orig. buckram. Forster 98-131 1974 £25

EDINBURGH ZOOLOGICAL GARDENS   The Visitor's Companion to. n.d. Small 8vo., orig. pictorial boards, woodcuts. Wheldon 131-428 1974 £5

EDINGER, LUDWIG   Twelve Lectures On the Structure of the Central Nervous System for Physicians and Students. Philadelphia, 1891. Revised second edition. Rittenhouse 46-242 1974 $12.50

EDINGER, LUDWIG   Zehn Vorlesungen uber den Bau der Nervosen Centralorgane. Leipzig, 1885. 8vo., half morocco, illus., first edition. Schuman 37-68 1974 $65

EDMOND, J. P.   Guide to the Exhibition of Manuscripts, Printed Books, Pictures and Exhibits in the Art Gallery and Museum. Aberdeen, 1885. 8vo., orig. quarter roan, marbled boards. Dawsons PM 10-204 1974 £6

EDMONDS, H.   Zweite Auflage im Altertum. 1941. Sewn. Allen 213-343 1973 $12.50

EDMONDS, J. E.   Military Operations France & Belgium. 1914. 2 vols., maps, orig. cloth. Smith 193-728 1973 £5

EDMONDS, RANDOLPH   Six Plays for a Negro Theatre. Boston, 1934. 12mo. Biblo & Tannen 213-537 1973 $15

EDMONDS, WALTER D.   The Big Barn. Boston, 1930. 1st ed. Biblo & Tannen 213-538 1973 $10

EDMONDSON, J.   Complete Body of Heraldry. 1780. 2 vols., folio, plates, old calf. Quaritch 939-719 1974 £45

EDMONSTON, ARTHUR   Observations on the Nature and Extent of the Cod Fishery. Edinburgh, 1820. 8vo., wrappers, very scarce, first edition. Ximenes 37-70 1974 $30

EDMUNDS, W. H.   Pointers and Clues to the Subjects of Chinese and Japanese Art as Shewn in Drawings, Prints, Carvings and the Decoration of Porcelain and Lacquer. (1934). 4to., cloth. Quaritch 940-387 1974 £28

EDMUNDSON, WILLIAM   A Journal of the Life, Travels, Sufferings, and Labour of Love in the Work of the Ministry Of. Dublin, 1715. 4to., buckram. Hill 126-84 1974 £36

EDWARD, THE CONFESSOR   Lives of. 1858. Roy. 8vo., rebound, vellum, gilt. Howes 186-1177 1974 £5

EDWARD I, KING OF ENGLAND   Liber Quotidianus Contrarotularis Garderobae. London, 1787. 4to., buckram. Allen 213-1440 1973 $22.50

EDWARD III, KING OF ENGLAND   Lives of Edward the Confessor. 1858. New buckram, plates. Allen 213-1443 1973 $12.50

EDWARD III, KING OF ENGLAND   Le Second Part de les Reports des Cases en Ley, Que Surent Argues en le Temps de le tres Haut & Puissant Prince, Roy Edward le Tierce. London, 1679. Folio, disbound. Bow Windows 66-198 1974 £20

EDWARDS, A.   My Native Land. 1928. 8vo., orig. cloth. Broadhurst 23-1634 1974 £6

EDWARDS, BRYAN   The History, Civil and Commercial, of the British Colonies In the West Indies. London, 1793. 2 vols., 4to., foxing, contemporary tree calf, first edition. Traylen 79-477 1973 £65

EDWARDS, CYRIL   Seven Sonnets. 1934. Plates, orig. full tree calf gilt, uncut, unopened, limited, first edition. Howes 186-172 1974 £15

EDWARDS, E.   Lives of the Founders of the British Museum. 1870. 8vo., cloth, illus., frontispiece. Wheldon 130-159 1974 £10

EDWARDS, E.   Personal Recollections of Birmingham and Birmingham Men. Birmingham, 1877. 8vo., frontispiece, illus., portraits, orig. cloth. Bow Windows 62-297 1974 £7.50

EDWARDS, F. E.   A Monograph of the Eocene Cephalopoda. 1849-77. 4to., half green morocco. Wheldon 129-819 1974 £15

EDWARDS, F. E.   A Monograph of the Eocene Cephalopoda and Univalves of England, Vol. 1. 1849-77. 4to., half calf, plates, scarce. Wheldon 131-994 1974 £12

EDWARDS, G.   A Discourse on the Emigration of British Birds. (1814). 8vo., wrappers. Wheldon 129-456 1974 £10

EDWARDS, G.   A Discourse on the Emigration of British Birds. (1814). 8vo., wrappers. Wheldon 131-589 1974 £15

EDWARDS, GEORGE   The Pioneer Work of the Presbyterian Church in Montana. Helena, n.d. (c. 1906). Cloth. Hayman 59-158 1974 $10

EDWARDS, GEORGE WHARTON   Belgium Old and New. Philadelphia, 1920. First edition, small 4to., illus., very fine, gilt dec. cloth cover. Current BW9-487 1974 $20

EDWARDS, GERARD NOEL   Letter From . . . . to the Secretary of the Newtown Society. London, 1793. 8vo., modern boards. Dawsons PM 247-101 1974 £15

EDWARDS, JAMES   The Hemiptera-Homoptera. 1896. 8vo., orig. cloth, plates. Bow Windows 64-776 1974 £45

EDWARDS, JOHN   Beronice. n.d. 4to., 19th century half roan. Dawsons PM 252-332 1974 £75

EDWARDS, JOHN   Calliclea. n.d. 4to., 19th century half roan. Dawsons PM 252-333 1974 £75

EDWARDS, JOHN   A Free Discourse Concerning Truth and Error. 1701. 8vo., contemporary panelled calf. Hill 126-94 1974 £12.50

EDWARDS, JOHN   Periander. n.d. 4to., 19th century half roan. Dawsons PM 252-334 1974 £75

EDWARDS, JOHN   The Whole Concern of Man. Boston, 1725. Second edition. Rinsland 58-92 1974 $100

EDWARDS, JONATHAN   An Account of the Life of the Late Reverend Mr. David Brainerd. Edinburgh, 1765. Contemporary sheep, worn. Smith 194-145 1974 £9.50

EDWARDS, PHILIP L.   California in 1837. Sacramento, 1890. Orig. cloth, very fine copy. Jenkins 61-318 1974 $125

EDWARDS, JONATHAN   Life and Character. Edinburgh, 1799. Small 8vo., old boards, uncut. Traylen 79-478 1973 £7

EDWARDS, LIONEL   Sketches in Stable and Kennel. 1935. One of 110 copies, numbered & signed by artist, coloured plates, drawings, 4to., gilt top, very nice copy. Covent 51-625 1973 £12.50

EDWARDS, PHILIP L.   California in 1837, Diary of Col. Philip Edwards Containing an Account of a Trip to the Pacific Coast. Sacramento, 1890. Orig. cloth, very fine. Jenkins 61-861 1974 $125

EDWARDS, R.   Georgian Cabinet-Makers. (1944). Crown 4to., orig. cloth, illus., inscription on fly-leaf. Bow Windows 66-199 1974 £6.50

EDWARDS, RICHARD   Industries of New Jersey. New York, 1883. 8vo., wrapper. Saddleback 14-552 1974 $10

EDWARDS, SYDENHAM   The New Botanic Garden. 1812. 4to., 2 vols., contemporary half morocco, rubbed, worn. Bow Windows 64-86 1974 £520

EDWARDS, W. A.   Plagiarism. Cambridge, 1933. Stiff wrappers, English first edition. Covent 56-841 1974 £12.50

EDWARDS, WILLIAM FREDERICK   Des Caracteres Physiologiques des Races. Paris, 1829. 8vo., half calf, first edition. Gurney 64-81 1974 £20

EDWARDS, WILLIAM FREDERICK   Des Caracteres Physiologiques des Races Humaines Consideres dans Leurs Rapports avec l'Histoire. Paris, 1829. 8vo., half calf, first edition. Gurney 66-54 1974 £20

EDWARDS, WILLIAM FREDERICK   On the Influence of Physical Agents on Life. London, 1832. 8vo., modern half calf, first edition in English. Dawsons PM 249-160 1974 £70

EDWARDS, Z. I.   The Ferns of the Axe and Its Tributaries. 1862. Crown 8vo., orig. cloth, plates. Wheldon 130-1272 1974 £5

EDWARD'S Botanical Register. 1815-47. 34 vols. in 33, roy. 8vo., modern cloth, hand-coloured and plain plates, complete set. Wheldon 128-1698 1973 £2,000

E'EXIDEUIL, PIERRE   The Human Pair in the Work of Thomas Hardy. 1929. Spine slightly faded, else fine, first edition. Covent 51-865 1973 £8.50

EFROSS, A.   Die Kunst Marc Chagalls. Potsdam, 1921. Cloth spine. Minters 37-64A 1973 $26

EFROSS, A.   Die Kunst Marc Chagalls. Potsdam, 1921. 4to., wrappers, illus., plates. Minters 37-64 1973 $30

EGAN, PIERCE   Life in London. 1821-30. 2 vols., roy 8vo., red crushed levant morocco gilt, plates, first editions. Quaritch 939-112 1974 £200

EGAN, PIERCE   Life of an Acotr. 1892. Coloured plates, half calf, rubbed. Allen 216-2114 1974 $15

EGAN, PIERCE   Tom and Jerry. London, 1821. Biblo & Tannen 210-155 1973 $45

EGAS, MONIZ, ANTONIO CAETANO DE ABREU FREIRE
Please turn to
MONIZ, EGAS, 1874-

EGERTON, D. T.   The Melange of Humour. (1824). Folio, half roan, gilt, rubbed. Quaritch 940-92 1974 £500

EGERTON, M.   Here and There Over the Water. London, 1825. 4to., contemporary half calf gilt, plates. Smith 194-444 1974 £75

EGGLESTON, EDWARD   The Circuit Rider. New York, 1874. 12mo., cloth, first edition, first state. Goodspeed's 578-93 1974 $15

EGGLESTON, EDWARD   The Faith Doctor. New York, 1891. Orig. dec. cloth, first edition, tight copy. MacManus 224-144 1974 $27.50

EGGLESTON, GEORGE CARY   A Carolina Cavalier. Lothrop, 1901. 448p., illus. Austin 54-357 1973 $8.50
EGGLESTON, GEORGE CARY   Two Gentlemen of Virginia. Grosset, Dunlap, 1908. 456p., illus. Austin 54-356 1973 $6.50

EGGLESTON, GEORGE CARY   Two Gentlemen of Virginia. Lothrop, Lee, Shepard, 1908. 456p., illus, orig. ed. Austin 54-355 1973 $8.50

EGLE, WILLIAM   An Illustrated History of the Commonwealth of Penna. 1876. 4to., new red cloth, fine. Putman 126-92 1974 $40

EGNATIUS, JOANNES BAPTISTA   De Exemplis Illustrium Virorum Venete Ciuitatis. Paris, 1554. 16mo., old vellum gilt, morocco labels. Thomas 30-127 1973 £30

EGRI, LAJOS   The Art of Dramatic Writing. Simon, Schuster, 1946. 308p., hard cover. Austin 51-287 1973 $6

EHRENBERG, C. G.   Symbolae Physicae. Berlin, 1828-30(-33). Folio, orig. printed portfolios, unbound. Wheldon 129-371 1974 £50

EHRENBERG, C. G.   Symbolae Physicae seu Icones et Descriptiones Mammalium. Berlin, 1828. Roy folio, unbound, orig. printed boards, plates, rare. Wheldon 130-390 1974 £20

EHRLICH, PAUL   Beitrage zur Experimentellen Pathologie und Chemotherapie. Leipzig, 1909. 8vo., orig. cloth, first edition. Gilhofer 61-75 1974 sFr. 350

EHRLICH, PAUL   Die Experimentelle Chemotherapie der Spirillosen. Berlin, 1910. Large 8vo., illus., folding tables, orig. wrappers, first edition. Gilhofer 61-77 1974 sFr. 700

EHRLICH, PAUL   Die Experimentelle Chemotherapie der Spirillosen. Berlin, 1910. 8vo., orig. green cloth, first edition. Dawsons PM 249-161 1974 £85

EHRLICH, PAUL   Die Experimentelle Chemotherapie der Spirillosen. Berlin, 1910. 8vo., plates, orig. green cloth, very fine, first edition. Schafer 8-150 1973 sFr. 750

EHRLICH, PAUL   Die Werbemessung. Jena, 1897. 8vo., orig. wrappers. Gurney 64-82 1974 £40

EHRMANN, HERBERT B.   The Untried Case. London, 1934. Black cloth, plates, dust jacket, first edition. Bradley 35-328 1974 $36

EHRMANN, THEOPHIL FRIEDRICH   Nueste Kunde Van Afrika, nach Quellen Bearbetet. Prague, 1810. Folding engraved maps, mostly coloured, copper plates, some folding, 2 vols., 8vo., half morocco gilt, slip-in case, one plate torn in inner margin, slight browning, good copy, scarce. Sawyer 293-6 1974 £95

EIFFEL, ALEXANDRE GUSTAVE   La Resistance de l'Air et l'Aviation. Paris, 1911. Roy 4to., orig. grey cloth, illus. Zeitlin 235-60 1974 $75

EIGHT Oxford Poets. 1941. Wrappers, signature, fine. Covent 55-38 1974 £10

EIMMART, GEORG CHRISTOPH   Ichnographia Nova Contemplationum de Sole. 1701. Folio, contemporary boards, uncut. Zeitlin 235-61 1974 $250

EINSTEIN, ALBERT   Aether und Relativitatstheorie. Berlin, 1920. 8vo., orig. printed wrappers, perfect copy, first edition. Gilhofer 61-86 1974 sFr. 300

EINSTEIN, ALBERT   Ather and Relativitatstheorie. Berlin, 1920. Small 8vo., orig. buff printed wrappers, first edition. Zeitlin 235-63 1974 $45

EINSTEIN, ALBERT   Bemerkungen zu Unserer Arbeit.   Leipzig, 1909. 8vo., orig. pictured wrappers, first separate edition.   Schuman 37-70 1974 $110

EINSTEIN, ALBERT   Eine Theorie der Grundlagen der Thermodynamik. Leipzig, 1903. 8vo., sewn, orig. front printed wrappers, first edition, from the library of Ernst Mach.   Kraus 137-27 1974 $900

EINSTEIN, ALBERT   Entwurf einer Verallgemeinerten Relativitatstheo- rie.   Leipzig and Berlin, 1913. 8vo., orig. pale green printed paper wrappers, first separate edition.   Dawsons PM 245-248 1974 £150

EINSTEIN, ALBERT   Geometrie und Erfahrung.   Berlin, 1921. 8vo., orig. printed wrappers, uncut, first separate edition.   Dawsons PM 245-252 1974 £75

EINSTEIN, ALFRED   Greatness in Music.   New York, 1941. 1st ed.   Biblo & Tannen 214-839 1974 $7.50

EINSTEIN, ALBERT   Die Grundlage der Allgemeinen.   Leipzig, 1916. 8vo., orig. printed wrappers, fine, first edition.   Zeitlin 235-64 1974 $650

EINSTEIN, ALBERT   Die Grundlage der Allemeinen Relativitatstheorie. Leipzig, 1916. Marbled bds. and cloth back.   Jacobs 24-178 1974 $825

EINSTEIN, ALBERT   Die Grundlage der Allgemeinen Relativitatstheorie.   (Leipzig, 1916). 8vo., cloth box.   Schafer 8-152 1973 sFr. 2,500

EINSTEIN, ALBERT   Die Grundlage der Allgemeinen Relativitaets-Theo- rie.   Leipzig, 1916. 8vo., orig. printed paper wrappers, fine, first separate edi- tion.   Dawsons PM 245-250 1974 £180

EINSTEIN, ALBERT   Die Grundlage der Allgemeinen Relativitats-Theo- rie.   Leipzig, 1916. 4to., black half morocco.   Dawsons PM 245-249 1974 £220

EINSTEIN, ALBERT   The Meaning of Relativity.   1945. 8vo., grey cloth, gilt, dust jacket, second edition.   Dawsons PM 245-254 1974 £6

EINSTEIN, ALBERT   Relativity, the Special and the General Theory. 1920. Illus.   Covent 55-1298 1974 £7.50

EINSTEIN, ALBERT   Relativity the Special and the General Theory. London, 1921. 8vo., orig. red cloth, fourth edition.   Dawsons PM 245-253 1974 £7.50

EINSTEIN, ALBERT   Uber die Spezielle und die Allgemeine Relativi- tatstheorie.   1917. 8vo., orig. yellow printed wrappers, first edition.   Dawsons PM 245-251 1974 £105

EINSTEIN, ALBERT   Vier Vorlesungen uber Relativitatstheorie. Braunschweig, 1922. 8vo., orig. wrappers, first edition.   Schafer 8-153 1973 sFr. 300

EINSTEIN, ALBERT   Zur Einheitlichen Feldtheorie.   Berlin, 1929. 4to., orig. orange printed wrappers, first edition.   Gilhofer 61-96 1974 sFr. 450

EINSTEIN, ALBERT   Zur Einheitlichen Feldtheorie.   1929. Tall 8vo., orig. printed orange wrappers, fine.   Zeitlin 235-65 1974 $75

EISLER, MAX   De Bouwmeester H. P. Berlage.   Vienna, n.d. 8vo., wrapper, plates.   Minters 37-518 1973 $15

EINSTEIN, ALBERT   Zur Elektrodynamik Bewegter Koerper.   Leipzig, 1905. 8vo., binder's cloth, plates.   Dawsons PM 245-247 1974 £450

EINSTEIN, ALBERT   Zur Electrodynamik Bewegter Korper.   Leipzig, 1905. 1st printing of this paper, and others.   Jacobs 24-177 1974 $1,650

EINSTEIN, ALBERT   Zur Elektrodynamik Bewegter Korper. (Leipzig), 1905. Boards, red morocco labels, first edition.   Gilhofer 61-71 1974 sFr. 2,800

EINSTEIN, ALBERT   Zur Theorie der Lichterzeugung und Lichtabsorption.   Leipzig, 1906. 8vo., half leather, illus., plates.   Schuman 37-69 1974 $225

EINSTEIN, CARL   Georges Braque.   Paris, 1934. Large 4to., wrappers, uncut, plates, limited edition.   Minters 37-267 1973 $60

EISLER, HANNS   Composing For the Films.   Oxford Univ. Press, 1947. 165p., orig. ed.   Austin 51-288 1973 $8.50

EISLER, ROBERT   Orpheus the Fisher.   1921. Roy. 8vo., plates, scarce.   Howes 186-1821 1974 £10

EITEL, ERNEST J.   Feng-Shui.   Hong Kong, 1873. 8vo., orig. cloth, presentation copy.   Gurney 64-83 1974 £20

EKINS, JEFFERY   Poems.   1810. Half morocco, worn, limited. Allen 213-346 1973 $10

EKONOMIDOU, MARIA SARANDOPULOU   The Greeks of America Observed. New York, 1916. 249p., illus.   Austin 62-149 1974 $27.50

ELBOGEN, ISMAR   Geschichte der Juden in Deutschland. Berlin, 1935.   Biblo & Tannen 213-620 1973 $12.50

ELDER, WILLIAM   Biography of Elisha Kent Kane.   Philadelphia, London, 1858. First edition, orig. binding.   Butterfield 10-327 1974 $7.50

ELDER-DUNCAN, J. H.   Country Cottages and Week-End Homes. London, Paris, n.d. Large 4to., illus., plates, worn wrappers.   Minters 37-523 1973 $10

ELDER-DUNCAN, J. H.   Country Cottages and Week-end Homes.   New York, 1907. 4to., illus.   Biblo & Tannen 214-18 1974 $15

ELDRED, WILLIAM   The Gvnners Glasse.   London, 1646. Small 4to., old calf, rubbed, illus., very rare, very good copy, first edition. Traylen 79-221 1973 £465

ELDREDGE, ZOETH S.   History of California.   New York, (1915). 5 vols., 8vo., cloth, rebound.   Saddleback 14-96 1974 $65

ELDREDGE, ZOETH S.   History of California.   New York, (1915). 5 vols., 8vo., three quarter leather.   Saddleback 14-95 1974 $85

ELDRIDGE, LEMUEL B.   The Torrent.   Middlebury, 1831. 8vo., old calf. Butterfield 8-643 1974 $35

ELECTRICAL Tables and Memoranda.   London, 1902. Full red morocco, ads at begining & end, 1 3/4 X 2 5/8 inches.   Gregory 44-365 1974 $55

ELEGANT Epistles, or, Copious Collection of Familiar & Amusing Letters.   1790. New buckram, rubber stamp.   Allen 216-523 1974 $15

ELEGANT Extracts: Selection of Instructive, Moral and Entertaining Passages From the Most Eminent British Poets.   London, (n.d.). 18 vols., contemporary straight-grained morocco gilt.   Dawsons PM 252-335 1974 £125

ELEGANT Extracts, or, Useful and Entertaining Pieces of Prose.   1808. Buckram. Allen 216-524 1974 $10

ELEGY On the Death of Miss Caroline Campbell.   (N.P., n.d.). 4to., fine, wrappers, first edition.   Dawsons PM 252-1032 1974 £32

THE ELEPHANT'S Ball.   London, 1883. Square 8vo., pict. wrappers, illus. Frohnsdorff 16-305 1974 $15

EL GRECO   Loan Exhibition for the Benefit of the Greek War Relief Association.   New York, 1941. 4to., ltd. ed., illus.   Biblo & Tannen 210-138 1973 $9.50

ELIAS, SOL P.   Stories of Stanislaus.   Modesto, c.1924. 12mo., cloth.   Saddleback 14-97 1974 $17.50

ELIESER BEN HURKANOS   Yakov Heilperin.   Venice, 1623. Small 8vo., limp boards, fifth edition, woodcut border.   Thomas 32-54 1974 £65

ELIOT, GEORGE   Adam Bede.   New York, 1859. Orig. cloth, first U.S. edition.   Covent 56-406 1974 £10

ELIOT, GEORGE   Adam Bede. Edinburgh & London, 1859. 3 vols., 8vo., modern half calf, fine, first edition. Dawsons PM 252-336 1974 £40

ELIOT, GEORGE   Adam Bede. 1859. 3 vols., crown 8vo., contemporary polished calf gilt, uncut. Howes 185-145 1974 £35

ELIOT, GEORGE   Bourl'Honne. Paris, 1933. Roy 8vo., English first edition. Covent 56-407 1974 £10.50

ELIOT, GEORGE   Daniel Deronda. Edinburgh & London, 1876. 4 vols., 8vo., orig. red cloth bit rubbed & shaken, first edition. Ximenes 36-81 1974 $325

ELIOT, GEORGE   Daniel Deronda. 1876. 4 vols., crown 8vo., contemporary half calf, gilt, first edition. first issue. Howes 185-146 1974 £60

ELIOT, GEORGE   Daniel Deronda. Edinburgh & London, 1876. Contemporary half calf, marbled boards (scuffed), first issue, with all half-titles, lacking erratum slip in Vol. 3 & final leaf of ads in Vol. 4, very good copy. MacManus 224-145 1974 $45

ELIOT, GEORGE   Felix Holt. Edinburgh & London, 1866. 3 vols., 8vo., orig. cloth, first edition. Dawsons PM 252-337 1974 £32

ELIOT, GEORGE   Impressions of Theophrastus Such. 1879. Top of spine frayed, bookplate, first edition. Allen 216-525 1974 $12.50

ELIOT, GEORGE   Life, as Related in Her Letters and Journals. n.d. Allen 216-526 1974 $10

ELIOT, GEORGE   Middlemarch. 1871-72. 4 vols., crown 8vo., contemporary half calf, first edition. Howes 185-147 1974 £65

ELIOT, GEORGE   The Mill on the Floss. Edinburgh & London, 1860. 3 vols., 8vo., orig. cloth, cloth box, first edition. Dawsons PM 252-338 1974 £95

ELIOT, GEORGE   The Novels of. Edinburgh & London, (c. 1895). 8 vols., 8vo., illus., orig. cloth, labels, stained. Bow Windows 62-298 1974 £10

ELIOT, GEORGE   Novels. Edinburgh & London, (n.d.). 8 vols. in 7, 8vo., contemporary half calf, new edition. Dawsons PM 252-339 1974 £45

ELIOT, GEORGE   Romola. 1863. 3 vols., crown 8vo., gilt, labels, scarce, first edition. Howes 185-148 1974 £75

ELIOT, GEORGE   Scenes of Clerical Life. 1858. 2 vols., crown 8vo., contemporary half calf, uncut, first edition. Howes 185-149 1974 £65

ELIOT, GEORGE   Silas Marner, the Weaver of Raveloe. New York, 1861. 8vo., orig. slate brown cloth, fine, first American edition. Ximenes 37-71 1974 $45

ELIOT, GEORGE   Works & Life. n.d. 24 vols., plates, tops of spines chipped, illus. Cabinet edition. Allen 216-J 1974 $75

ELIOT, JOHN   An Anology for Socrates and Negotium Posterorum. 1881-82. 4 vols., full tree calf, gilt, illus., fine, rare. Howes 186-795 1974 £100

ELIOT, THOMAS STEARNS   After Strange Gods. New York, 1934. 1st Amer. ed. Biblo & Tannen 214-700 1974 $17.50

ELIOT, THOMAS STEARNS   After Strange Gods. London, (1934). First edition, demy 8vo., orig. cloth marked. Forster 97-118 1974 £8.50

ELIOT, THOMAS STEARNS   After Strange Gods. 1934. First edition, med. 8vo., d.w., orig. cloth, fine. Broadhurst 24-660 1974 £20

ELIOT, T. S.   After Strange Gods. 1934. 8vo., orig. cloth, dust wrapper, first edition. Broadhurst 23-707 1974 £20

ELIOT, THOMAS STEARNS   After Strange Gods. London, 1934. 8vo., orig. cloth, rubbed, first edition. Dawsons PM 252-340 1974 £32

ELIOT, THOMAS STEARNS   Anabasis. London, 1930. Numbered, slip case, dust jacket, signed. Ballinger 1-129 1974 $97.50

ELIOT, THOMAS STEARNS   Animula. London, 1929. Wood engravings, large paper edition, limited to 400 copies, of which this is no. 272, signed, yellow boards, mint, additional protective heavy dec. paper wrapper. Ross 86-139 1974 $120

ELIOT, THOMAS STEARNS   Ash Wednesday. London, 1930. First ordinary edition, small booksellers' stickers, mint copy, heavy dec. paper wrapper. Ross 86-140 1974 $35

ELIOT, THOMAS STEARNS   Collected Poems. New York, 1936. 1st Amer. ed. Biblo & Tannen 210-722 1973 $10

ELIOT, THOMAS STEARNS   Collected Poems. London, (1944). Orig. cloth, uncut, hand made paper, rare. Bow Windows 62-299 1974 £5

ELIOT, THOMAS STEARNS   Collected Poems, 1909-1935. New York, 1936. Yellow d.w. printed in dark blue, inscribed by author, author has corrected text in his own hand and initialed each correction, mint, heavy protective dec. paper wrapper. Ross 87-165 1974 $150

ELIOT, THOMAS STEARNS   Collected Poems, 1909-1935. 1936. Near fine copy, first edition. Covent 51-632 1973 £8.50

ELIOT, T. S.   Collected Poems. 1936. 8vo., orig. cloth, first edition. Rota 189-293 1974 £5

ELIOT, THOMAS STEARNS   Dante. London, 1929. First edition, edges of d.w. snipped, near mint, orig. binding, additional heavy dec. paper wrapper. Ross 86-142 1974 $50

ELIOT, THOMAS STEARNS   Dante By. London, (1929). 8vo., orig. boards, inscription, first edition. Bow Windows 62-300 1974 £6

ELIOT, THOMAS STEARNS   The Dry Salvages. London, 1941. 8vo., orig. wrappers, uncut, first edition. Dawsons PM 252-341 1974 £12

ELIOT, THOMAS STEARNS   The Dry Salvages. London, 1941. First edition, blue wrapper, covers somewhat chipped & faded, very good copy. Ross 86-143 1974 $20

ELIOT, THOMAS STEARNS   The Dry Salvages. London, 1941. First edition, blue paper covers somewhat spotted & faded, good copy, Clifford Dyment's copy with his name in ink on half title & his notes. Ross 87-169 1974 $20

ELIOT, THOMAS STEARNS   The Dry Salvages. London, 1941, First edition, orig. blue paper covers protected by heavy board case, mint, thus rare. Ross 87-168 1974 $35

ELIOT, THOMAS STEARNS   The Family Reunion. 1939. First edition, demy 8vo., d.w., orig. cloth, fine. Broadhurst 24-662 1974 £5

ELIOT, THOMAS STEARNS   The Family Reunion. 1939. Dust wrapper, first edition. Howes 185-152 1974 £8.50

ELIOT, THOMAS STEARNS   For Lancelot Andrewes, Essays. 1928. 8vo., orig. cloth, scarce, first edition. Rota 189-290 1974 £10.50

ELIOT, THOMAS STEARNS   For Lancelot Andrewes. (1928). 8vo., orig. cloth, spine faded, first edition. Bow Windows 66-207 1974 £10.50

ELIOT, THOMAS STEARNS   For Lancelot Andrewes. 1928. Small 8vo., orig. cloth, printed label, first edition. Howes 185-151 1974 £21

ELIOT, THOMAS STEARNS   Homage to John Dryden. 1924. Orig. cloth, wrappers, foxing, scarce, first edition. Rota 188-274 1974 £21

ELIOT, THOMAS STEARNS   The Idea of a Christian Society. 1939. First edition, med. 8vo., faded d.w., orig. cloth, fine. Broadhurst 24-661 1974 £5

ELIOT, T. S.   The Idea of a Christian Society. 1939. 8vo., orig. cloth, first edition. Broadhurst 23-708 1974 £5

ELIOT, THOMAS STEARNS   The Idea of a Christian Society. 1939. Very fine, soiled and torn d.w., first edition. Covent 51-637 1973 £5.25

ELIOT, THOMAS STEARNS   Introducing James Joyce. (1942). 8vo., orig. cloth, first edition. Bow Windows 66-209 1974 £9.50

ELIOT, THOMAS STEARNS   Little Gidding. London, 1942. First edition, orig. paper wrappers, additional heavy dec. paper wrapper, pristine, rare thus. Ross 86-145 1974 $25

ELIOT, THOMAS STEARNS   Little Gidding. 1942. Orig. wrappers, first edition. Howes 186-175 1974 £5

ELIOT, THOMAS STEARNS   Little Gidding. London, 1942. First edition, paper wrappers, pages somewhat darkened, name in ink on fly leaf, wrappers soiled, nice. Ross 87-171 1974 $17.50

ELIOT, THOMAS STEARNS   Murder in the Cathedral. Canterbury, 1935. Small 8vo., stiff grey paper wrappers, first edition. Quaritch 936-377 1974 £25

ELIOT, THOMAS STEARNS   Old Possum's Book of Practical Cats. New York, 1939. 8vo., cloth. Frohnsdorff 16-306 1974 $10

ELIOT, THOMAS STEARNS   Poems, 1909-1925. New York, 1932. First American edition, lacking d.w., spine & parts of covers somewhat faded, very nice. Ross 86-146 1974 $17.50

ELIOT, THOMAS STEARNS   Prufrock and Other Observations. London, 1917. 8vo., orig. wrappers, first edition. Bow Windows 62-301 1974 £340

ELIOT, THOMAS STEARNS   The Rock. 1934. Boards, fine, d.w., English first edition. Covent 56-413 1974 £21

ELIOT, THOMAS STEARNS   The Sacred Wood. 1920. Small 8vo., orig. blue cloth, first edition. Howes 185-153 1974 £25

ELIOT, THOMAS STEARNS   The Sacred Wood. 1920. First edition, orig. cloth, f'cap. 8vo., name neatly erased from fly leaf, else fine. Broadhurst 24-657 1974 £20

ELIOT, THOMAS STEARNS   The Sacred Wood. 1920. Very good copy, first edition. Covent 51-641 1973 £17.50

ELIOT, THOMAS STEARNS   The Sacred Wood. London, 1920. First edition, first issue, cover somewhat shelf rubbed at bottom, three slight worm holes along hinges, good working copy. Ross 87-173 1974 $25

ELIOT, THOMAS STEARNS   The Sacred Wood. 1920. 8vo., orig. cloth, inscription, scarce, first edition. Rota 190-400 1974 £20

ELIOT, THOMAS STEARNS   The Sacred Wood. 1920. 8vo., orig. cloth, fine, first edition. Broadhurst 23-706 1974 £20

ELIOT, THOMAS STEARNS   Selected Essays 1917-1932. 1932. 8vo., orig. cloth, marginal pencilling, slight spotting, spine faded, covers stained, first edition. Bow Windows 66-210 1974 £6

ELIOT, THOMAS STEARNS   Selected Essays. 1934. Dust wrapper, fine, revised second edition. Howes 185-154 1974 £5

ELIOT, THOMAS STEARNS   Sweeney Agonistes: Fragments of an Aristophanic Melodrama. London, 1932. Blue boards, first edition, d.w. somewhat faded, near fine. Ross 86-148 1974 $60

ELIOT, THOMAS STEARNS   The Use of Poetry and the Use of Criticism. 1933. 8vo., orig. cloth, inscription, first edition. Rota 189-292 1974 £6.50

ELIOT, THOMAS STEARNS   The Use of Poetry and the Use of Criticism. 1933. First edition, med. 8vo., uncut, orig. cloth, fine. Broadhurst 24-659 1974 £10

ELIOT, THOMAS STEARNS   The Use of Poetry and the Use of Criticism. 1933. Dust wrapper, first edition. Howes 186-176 1974 £18.50

ELIOT, THOMAS STEARNS   What is a Classic? London, 1945. Ordinary issue, d.w. somewhat chipped & rumpled, nice copy, orig. binding. Ross 86-149 1974 $17.50

ELIZABETH I, QUEEN OF ENGLAND   A Proclamation for the Dearth of Corne. London, 1596. Folio, uncut, buckram folder, rare. Dawsons PM 247-229 1974 £240

ELLACOMBE, HENRY NICHOLSON   A Memoir, 1822-1916. 1919. 8vo., cloth, illus. Wheldon 131-216 1974 £5

ELLEN, or The Naughty Girl Reclaimed. London, 1811. Square 16mo., orig. grey boards in case, latter has seam at bottom split, book fine. Gregory 44-43 1974 $350

ELLENBOROUGH, EDWARD LAW, EARL OF 1790-1871   A Biography of. Cambridge, 1939. Biblo & Tannen 213-665 1973 $8.50

ELLET, ELIZABETH F.   The Women of the American Revolution. New York, 1849. Second edition, 2 vols., 8vo., spine ends heavily chipped, plates. Current BW9-341 1974 $13.50

ELLIOT, D. G.   The Life and Habits of Wild Animals. 1874. Folio, contemporary full green morocco gilt, plates. Wheldon 131-429 1974 £50

ELLIOT, D. G.   A Monograph of the Bucerotidae. (1877-)1882. Imperial 4to., new cloth. Wheldon 129-457 1974 £15

ELLIOT, HUGH   A Memoir of the Right Honourable Hugh Elliot. Edinburgh, 1868. 8vo., orig. cloth. Bow Windows 62-302 1974 £5

ELLIOT, KATHLEEN MORROW   Riema, Little Brown Girl of Java. New York, 1937. 8vo., cloth spine, pict. boards, illus., lst ed. Frohnsdorff 16-303 1974 $7.50

ELLIOT, ROBERT   Specimens of Plants. (Essex), 1815. Oblong 8vo., contemporary tree calf, drawings. Traylen 79-14 1973 £240

ELLIOTT, DAVID   The Life of the Rev. Elisha Macurdy. Allegheny and Philadelphia, 1848. 8vo., orig. bindings. Butterfield 8-529 1974 $10

ELLIOTT, HENRY W.   A Report Upon the Condition of Affairs in the Territory of Alaska. Washington, 1875. Wrapper missing. Jenkins 61-66 1974 $20

ELLIOTT, ISAAC H.   Record of the Services of Illinois Soldiers in the Black Hawk War. Springfield, 1882. Scarce, first edition. Bradley 35-229 1974 $20

ELLIOTT, J. S.   Outlines of Greek and Roman Medicine. 1914. 8vo., orig. cloth, plates. Bow Windows 64-494 1974 £6.50

ELLIOTT, MARY BELSON   Confidential Memoirs. London, 1821. 16mo., 1/2 calf and marbled boards, 4 engraved copperplates, lst ed. Frohnsdorff 16-307 1974 $75

ELLIS, A. J.   On Early English Pronunciation. 1869-75. 4 parts in 2 vols., 8vo., half green morocco gilt, faded. Quaritch 939-113 1974 £15

ELLIS, ARTHUR M.   Historical Review. Los Angeles, c.1929. 8vo., cloth. Saddleback 14-99 1974 $15

ELLIS, BENJAMIN   Medical Formulary. Philadelphia, 1834. Orig. covers, fourth edition. Rittenhouse 46-685 1974 $15

ELLIS, D.   Sulphur Bacteria. 1932. 8vo., cloth, scarce. Wheldon 129-75 1974 £5

ELLIS, DANIEL   An Inquiry into the Changes Induced on Atmospheric Air. Edinburgh, London, 1807. 8vo., contemporary boards, worn, first edition. Dawsons PM 245-255 1974 £60

ELLIS, EDWARD S.   Low Twelve . . . Incidents Illustrative of the Fidelity of Free Masons to One Another in Times of Distress and Danger. New York, 1907. Orig. binding. Butterfield 10-368 1974 $12.50

ELLIS, EDWIN   The Works of William Blake, Poetic, Symbolic and Critical. London, 1893. 3 vols., large paper edition limited to 150 copies, brown imitation leather, leather spine & corners, signs of shelf wear at top and bottom, unusually bright, no foxing, nice set, rare. Ross 87-605 1974 $700

ELLIS, EDWIN   The Works of William Blake, Poetic, Symbolic and Critical. London, 1893. 3 vols., large paper edition, limited to 150 copies, brown imitation leather, some signs of shelf wear top & bottom, nice set, extremely rare. Ross 86-497 1974 $650

ELLIS, F. S.   Catalogues 1-6, 10, 13. n.d. 8 cats. in 1 vol., demy 8vo., cloth, bookplate. Forster 98-156 1974 £3.50

ELLIS, F. S.   The History of Reynard the Fox. 1894. Small 4to., untrimmed, presentation copy, inscribed, English first edition. Covent 56-268 1974 £12.50

ELLIS, F. S.   The Order of Chivalry. Kelmscott Press, 1893. Woodcut frontispiece, borders and initials, printed in black and red, 8vo., orig. limp vellum with silk ties, fine copy, limited to 225 copies. Sawyer 293-186 1974 £220

ELLIS, GEORGE   Specimens of Early English Metrical Romances. 1805. 3 vols., full green calf, dec. raised bands, morocco labels, slight spotting, very good set, first edition. Bow Windows 66-212 1974 £38

ELLIS, GEORGE   Specimens of Early English Metrical Romances. 1811. 8vo., contemporary diced calf, 3 vols., second edition. Bow Windows 64-495 1974 £28

ELLIS, GEORGE   Specimens of Early English Metrical Romances. London, 1848. Bdg. worn, good copy. Biblo & Tannen 213-752 1973 $7.50

ELLIS, H. D.   Catalogue of a Remarkable Collection of 16th and 17th Century Provincial Silver Spoons Incorporating the Entire Collection Left By. 1935. 8vo., illus., orig. wrappers, dust soiled. Quaritch 940-674 1974 £11

ELLIS, HAVELOCK   Chapman. 1934. Paper boards, orig. covers, label. Broadhurst 23-1074 1974 £18

ELLIS, HAVELOCK   Chapman. Nonesuch Press, 1934. Paper boards, orig. covers, paper printed labels, cloth slip-in-case, one of 700 copies, fine. Broadhurst 24-1035 1974 £20

ELLIS, HAVELOCK   Chapman. 1934. Mint, no. 25 of 75 copies, niger goat skin tooled spine, top edges gilt, on Van Gelder paper. Thomas 32-283 1974 £25

ELLIS, HAVELOCK   Chapman. 1934. Roy 8vo., full niger morocco, uncut. Broadhurst 23-1073 1974 £40

ELLIS, HAVELOCK   Chapman. Nonesuch Press, 1934. Roy. 8vo., full niger morocco, top edges gilt, others uncut, one of 75 copies. Broadhurst 24-1034 1974 £40

ELLIS, HAVELOCK   The Dance of Life. Boston, 1923. Bdg. dull. Biblo & Tannen 213-955 1973 $6

ELLIS, HAVELOCK   My Confessional. 1934. Orig. edition. Austin 61-352 1974 $10

ELLIS, HAVELOCK   The World of Dreams. London, 1911. 1st ed. Biblo & Tannen 213-957 1973 $15

ELLIS, HENRY   Journal of the Proceedings of the Late Embassy to China. 1817. 4to., plates, maps, buckram backed boards. Smith 193-349 1973 £50

ELLIS, HENRY   Original Letters Illustrative of English History. London, 1825-1846. 8vo., contemporary calf, gilt. Dawsons PM 251-213 1974 £40

ELLIS, HENRY   Original Letters of Eminent Literary Men. 1843. Orig. cloth, boards, illus., English first edition. Covent 56-417 1974 £10.50

ELLIS, HENRY   A Voyage to Hudson's Bay. 1748. 8vo., old calf gilt, rebacked, first edition. Bow Windows 64-496 1974 £300

ELLIS, J. B.   The North American Pyrenomycetes. Newfield, 1892. Roy 8vo., orig. cloth, plates. Wheldon 129-1194 1974 £20

ELLIS, JOHN   An Essay Towards a Natural History of the Corallines. 1755. 4to., contemporary calf, plates, rare. Wheldon 131-928 1974 £60

ELLIS, JOHN   Essai sur l'Histoire Naturelle des Corallines. The Hague, 1756. 4to., modern half calf, plates, rare. Wheldon 130-863 1974 £35

ELLIS, JOHN   Essai sur l'Histoire Naturelle des Corallines. The Hague, 1756. 4to., calf, frontispiece, plates. Wheldon 128-894 1973 £22

ELLIS, JOHN   An Historical Account of Coffee. London, 1774. 4to., contemporary calf, rebacked, very good large copy, rare, hand coloured folding plate, first edition. Ximenes 37-72 1974 $250

ELLIS, JOHN E.   Free Love and Its Votaries. New York, (1870). 8vo., illus., orig. cloth, first edition. Putman 126-34 1974 $35

ELLIS, JOHN S.   Our County: Its History and Early Settlement By Townships. (Muncie, 1898). 8vo., cloth. Saddleback 14-402 1974 $37.50

ELLIS, MRS. SARAH (STICKNEY) 1812-1872   The Daughters of England. New York, 1842. Ballinger 1-254 1974 $10

ELLIS, T. P.   The Welsh Benedictines of the Terror. Newtown, (1936). Roy. 8vo., plates, soiled. Howes 185-1136 1974 £5.50

ELLIS, W. H.   Wayside Weeds. Toronto, 1914. Leather, limited edition. Hood's 103-723 1974 $10

ELLIS, WILLIAM   Agriculture Improv'd. London, 1746. 2 vols., 8vo., contemporary calf gilt, first edition. Dawsons PM 247-103 1974 £35

ELLIS, WILLIAM   Chiltern and Vale Farming. London, 1745. 8vo., contemporary calf gilt. Dawsons PM 247-104 1974 £30

ELLIS, WILLIAM   The Modern Husbandman. London, 1744. 4 vols., 8vo., contemporary calf gilt. Dawsons PM 245-106 1974 £70

ELLIS, WILLIAM   New Experiments in Husbandry. London, 1736. 8vo., modern boards, first edition. Dawsons PM 247-102 1974 £25

ELLIS, WILLIAM   The Parks and Forest of Sussex. 1885. Orig. cloth, illus. Howes 186-2195 1974 £6.50

ELLIS, WILLIAM   The Timber-Tree Improved. London, 1738. 8vo., modern half calf, first edition. Dawsons PM 247-105 1974 £30

ELLIS, WILLIAM   The Timber-Tree Improved. 1745 and 1747. 2 parts in 1 vol., contemporary calf, worn, fourth edition. Bow Windows 64-87 1974 £38

ELLIS & ELVEY   General Catalogue of Rare Books. 1894. Plates, orig. cloth. Howes 185-669 1974 £5

ELLIS & ELVEY'S   General Catalogue of Rare Books & MSS. London, 1894. Plates, med. 8vo., orig. cloth. Forster 98-159 1974 £3

ELLISON, ROBERT S.   Fort Bridger, Wyoming, A Brief History. (Sheridan), 1938. 8vo., wrapper, map, revised enlarged edition. Saddleback 14-770 1974 $15

ELLMS, CHARLES   The Pirates Own Book. Salem, 1924. Illus., black cloth, fine, trade edition. Bradley 35-302 1974 $34

ELLSBERRY, GEORGE W.   Ordinances of Mason City. Bloomington, 1873. 12mo., leather, boards, scarce. Putman 126-141 1974 $35

ELLSWORTH, H. L.   Illinois in 1837. Philadelphia, 1837. Printed boards, folded map, very good. Butterfield 10-310 1974 $25

ELOESSER, ARTHUR   Vom Ghetto Nach Europa. Berlin, 1936. Biblo & Tannen 213-621 1973 $12.50

ELSASSER, CARL LUDWIG   Der Weiche Hinterkopf. Stuttgart, 1843. 8vo.,
orig. grey printed wrappers, uncut, first edition. Dawsons PM 249-162 1974 £9

ELSON, J. M.   The Scarlet Sash. Toronto & London, 1925.
Frontispiece. Hood's 104-550 1974 $10

ELSON, J. M.   The Scarlet Sash, a Romance of the Old Niagara
Frontier. Toronto & London, 1925. Coloured frontispiece. Hood's 102-506
1974 $10

ELSTOBB, W.   An Historical Account of the Great Level of the
Fens. Lynn, 1793. 8vo., half morocco, gilt, scarce, fine, first edition. Hammond 201-848 1974 £75

ELTON, CHARLES ISAAC   An Account of Shelley's Visit to France,
Switzerland and Savoy, in the Years 1814 and 1816. 1894. 12mo., cloth, first
edition. Goodspeed's 578-323 1974 $10

ELTON, CHARLES ISAAC   A Catalogue of a Portion of the Library of.
London, 1891. Large 8vo., plates, orig. cloth, gilt, uncut, fine. Dawsons PM
10-207 1974 £14

ELTON, CHARLES ISAAC   A Catalogue of a Portion of the Library of.
London, 1891. Plates, roy. 8vo., orig. cloth, roan back, rubbed, text fine.
Forster 98-160 1974 £16

ELTON, CHARLES ISAAC   The Great Book Collectors. 1893. 8vo., orig.
buckram, faded, illus. Howes 185-670 1974 $7.50

ELTON, CHARLES ISAAC   The Great Book Collectors. London, 1893.
Plates, med. 8vo., orig. buckram, spine faded. Forster 98-161 1974 £6

ELTON, CHARLES ISAAC   The Great Book-Collectors. London, 1893.
8vo., orig. cloth, uncut. Dawsons PM 10-206 1974 £8

ELTON, C. T.   The Tenures of Kent. 1867. Roy. 8vo.,
soiled, scarce. Howes 186-2039 1974 £9

ELUARD, PAUL   La Barre d'Appui. Paris, 1936. 8vo., full
black polished calf, first edition. L. Goldschmidt 42-218 1974 $12,500

ELUARD, PAUL   Capitale de la Douleur. Paris, 1926. 12mo.,
orig. wrapper, uncut, first edition. L. Goldschmidt 42-219 1974 $25

ELUARD, PAUL   Poetry and Truth. 1942. Dust wrapper, English
first edition. Covent 56-419 1974 £15.75

ELVIN, C. N.   Dictionary of Heraldry. (1889). Roy. 8vo.,
illus., cloth, plates, orig. edition. Quaritch 939-720 1974 £10

ELWELL, J. B.   The Principles, Rules and Laws of Auction
Bridge. New York, 1910. 12mo., 1st ed. Biblo & Tannen 213-1007 1973 $15

ELWES, HENRY JOHN   A Monograph of the Genus Lilium. London, 1877-
80. Large folio, contemporary half morocco, gilt, fine, rare, plates. Traylen
79-15 1973 £675

ELWES, HENRY JOHN   A Monograph of the Genus Lilium. 1933-40.
7 parts, imp. folio, orig. wrappers, hand coloured plates. Wheldon 128-1459
1973 £120

ELWES, HENRY JOHN   The Trees of Great Britain and Ireland.
Edinburgh, 1906-13. 7 vols., 4to., printed wrappers, plates. Traylen 79-16
1973 £200

ELWES, HENRY JOHN   The Trees of Great Britain and Ireland.
Edinburgh, 1906-13. 7 vols., 4to., new half green morocco, gilt, plates,
scarce. Wheldon 131-45 1974 £350

ELWORTHY, FREDERICK T.   Horns of Honour. 1900. Illus., scarce.
Howes 186-1824 1974 £6.50

ELWORTHY, FREDERICK T.   Horns of Honour. 1900. Orig. buckram, gilt,
first edition. Smith 193-775 1973 £5.50

ELWORTHY, FREDERICK T.   Horns of Honour. 1900. Coloured frontis.,
little loose in case. Bow Windows 66-214 1974 £7.50

ELY, ALFRED   Journal of . . . a Prisoner of War in Richmond.
New York, 1862. Orig. binding. Butterfield 10-154 1974 $27.50

ELYOT, THOMAS   The Boke, Named the Governovr. London,
1580. 8vo., contemporary sheep. Dawsons PM 252-342 1974 £280

ELYOT, THOMAS   The Castel of Helth. 1541. Small 4to., modern brown morocco, gilt. Dawsons PM 249-163 1974 £1,250

EMANUEL, HARRY   Diamonds and Precious Stones. London, 1867.
Small 8vo., contemporary half calf, worn, illus., plates, second edition. Hammond 201-820 1974 £8.50

EMANUEL, WALTER   A Dog Day. London, 1902. 4to., cloth spine,
color plates, first edition. Frohnsdorff 16-19 1974 $20

EMANUEL, WALTER   A Dog Day. 1902. 4to., orig. cloth-backed
pictorial boards, plates. Hammond 201-109 1974 £9

EMANUEL, WALTER   The Dog Who Wasn't What He Thought He Was.
London, ca. 1918. 4to., 24 color plates. Frohnsdorff 16-22 1974 $7.50

EMBLEMS for Youth. (c. 1795). Small Square 8vo., new yellow buckram, illus.,
copperplates. George's 610-247 1973 £10

EMBREY, ALVIN T.   History of Fredericksburg, Virginia. Richmond,
1937. 8vo., cloth. Saddleback 14-739 1974 $25

EMBROIDERY, a Collection of Articles on Subjects Connected with the Study of
Fine Needlework. 1909. 4to., covers slightly soiled, coloured plates, illus.
Eaton Music-576 1973 £5

EMDEN, R.   Thermodynamik der Himmelskorper. Leipzig and
Berlin, 1926. 8vo., orig. green cloth, gilt, first edition. Dawsons PM 245-256
1974 £6

EMERSON, B.   The Causes and Effects of War. Salem, 1812.
Hood's 103-533 1974 $25

EMERSON, CAROLINE D.   Old New York for Young New Yorkers.
New York, 1932. 1st ed., illus. Biblo & Tannen 213-74 1973 $7.50

EMERSON, GEORGE B.   A Report on the Trees and Shrubs Growing
Naturally in the Forests of Massachusetts. Boston, 1875. 2 vols., illus., plates,
fine, expanded edition. Jenkins 61-1500 1974 $35

EMERSON, G. D.   The Niagara Frontier Landmarks Association.
Buffalo, 1906. Wrappers, illus. Hood's 103-624 1974 $60

EMERSON, JOSEPH   The Evangelical Primer. Boston, ca. 1811.
16mo., marbled wrappers, 72 woodcuts. Frohnsdorff 16-308 1974 $17.50

EMERSON, RALPH WALDO   The Conduct of Life. Edinburgh, (n.d.).
Small 4to., orig. parchment backed boards, dust marked, uncut. Bow Windows
66-216 1974 £7.50

EMERSON, RALPH WALDO   The Conduct of Life. Boston, 1860. 12mo.,
cloth, first edition, first issue. Goodspeed's 578-94 1974 $15

EMERSON, RALPH WALDO   The Conduct of Life. Boston, 1860. Orig.
cloth, first printing, about fine. MacManus 224-146 1974 $50

EMERSON, RALPH WALDO   English Traits. 1856. 8vo., contemporary half
calf, English first edition. Covent 56-420 1974 £11

EMERSON, RALPH WALDO   English Traits. Boston, 1856. Orig. cloth,
one small stain on lower cover, first edition, fine, tight copy. MacManus
224-147 1974 $55

EMERSON, RALPH WALDO   Essays. 1906. Royal 8vo., limp vellum. Hammond 201-744 1974 £120

EMERSON, RALPH WALDO   Fortune of the Republic. Boston, 1878. Post
8vo., orig. cloth, first U.S. edition. Covent 56-421 1974 £11

EMERSON, RALPH WALDO   Journals of Ralph Waldo Emerson, 1820-24. 1909. 10 vols.   Austin 54-359 1973 $95

EMERSON, RALPH WALDO   Letters and Social Aims.   Boston, 1876. First edition, probable second state, hinges cracked internally, orig. binding.   Wilson 63-510 1974 $10

EMERSON, RALPH WALDO   Miscellanies; Embracing Nature, Addresses, and Lectures.   Boston, 1856. Orig. cloth, first collected edition, tight copy, fine.   MacManus 224-148 1974 $50

EMERSON, RALPH WALDO   Nature. (1929). 4to., numbered, hand made paper, orig. dec. boards, parchment spine, uncut.   Bow Windows 66-78 1974 £38

EMERSON, RALPH WALDO   Oration, Delivered Before the Literary Societies of Dartmouth College, July 24, 1838.   1838. Buckram, wrapper not bound in, library bookplate.   Allen 216-548 1974 $20

EMERSON, RALPH WALDO   Representative Men.   Boston, 1850. Orig. cloth, ends of spine chipped, first printing, fine.   MacManus 224-149 1974 $40

EMERSON, RALPH WALDO   Society and Solitude.   Boston, 1870. Orig. cloth, first printing, fine.   MacManus 224-150 1974 $35

EMERSON, RALPH WALDO   The Complete Works of.   Cambridge, 1903-14. 22 vols., orig. cloth, paper labels, autograph centenary edition, one of 600 numbered sets signed by publishers, fine, inserted is a portion of manuscript in Emerson's hand in fine condition.   MacManus 224-151 1974 $450

EMERSON, W. R.   Poems.   1847. Orig. cloth, gilt, worn, signed by William Allingham on title & half title.   Thomas 32-155 1974 £15

EMERY, WALTER B.   Mission Archeologique de Nubie 1929-1934. The Excavations and Survey Between Wadi Es-Sebua and Adindan 1929-1931.   Cairo, 1935. 2 vols., 4to., plates, illus., cloth, morocco backs.   Quaritch 940-347 1974 £50

EMERY, WALTER B.   Mission Archeologique de Nubie 1929-1934. The Royal Tombs of Ballana and Qustul.   Cairo, 1938. 2 vols., 4to., half morocco, orig. wrappers, plates.   Quaritch 940-348 1974 £40

EMINENT Women of the Age.   Hartford, 1869. First edition, thick 8vo., steel engravings, some foxing and waterstaining, orig. green gilt dec. cloth, very nice.   Current BW9-618 1974 $17.50

EMMONS, NATHANAEL   A Sermon, Delivered at Salem, in New Hampshire, January 4, 1797, at the Ordination of the Rev. John Smith to the Work of the Ministry in That Place.   Concord, 1797. First edition, 12mo., mild foxing, else very good.   Current BW9-516 1974 $16.75

EMMONS, NATHANAEL   A Sermon Preached Before His Excellency, Increase Sumner, Governor.   Boston, 1798. First edition, 12mo., very good, new blue grey wrappers.   Current BW9-515 1974 $20

EMMONS, RICHARD   The Fredoniad.   Boston, 1827. 4 vols., 8vo., orig. quarter cloth, printed paper labels, very good copy, first edition.   Ximenes 37-73 1974 $75

EMMONS, RICHARD   The Fredoniad: Independence Preserved. Boston, 1827. 4 vols., orig. cloth backed boards, paper labels, first edition, ex-library set, fine, uncut.   MacManus 224-152 1974 $80

EMMONS, W. H.   Geology of Petroleum.   New York, 1931. Cloth, second edition.   Wheldon 130-921 1974 £5

EMORY, WILLIAM HENSLEY   United States and Mexican Boundary Survey. Washington, 1857-59. 2 vols. in 3, 4to., half brown morocco, illus., plates. Wheldon 131-397 1974 £50

EMORY, WILLIAM HENSLEY   United States and Mexican Boundary Survey. Washington, 1857-58. 4 parts, plates, lithographs, folding maps, foxed, rare. Jenkins 61-865 1974 $275

EMPSON, WILLIAM   Seven Types of Ambiguity.   London, 1930. First edition, nice copy, name on fly, scarce, orig. cloth.   Crane 7-78 1974 £15

EMPSON, WILLIAM   Seven Types of Ambiguity.   1930. 8vo., orig. cloth, dust wrapper, presentation copy, first edition.   Quaritch 936-378 1974 £50

EMPSON, WILLIAM   Some Versions of Pastoral.   London, 1935. First edition, nice copy, front hinge cracked, scarce, neat pencillings, orig. cloth. Crane 7-79 1974 £18

EMPSON, WILLIAM   Some Versions of Pastoral.   1935. Orig. cloth, scarce, first edition.   Rota 188-282 1974 £20

ENCHIRIDION Medicum oft Medicyn-Boeksken.   Antwerp, 1757¢ Leather, worn upper cover.   Rittenhouse 46-245 1974 $20

ENCYCLOPAEDIA Britannica.   1910-22. 32 vols., square 8vo., orig. full morocco binding, plates, illus., maps.   Howes 186-178 1974 £60

ENCYCLOPAEDIA Britannica.   1926. 24 vols., 4to., orig. half dark blue morocco, fourteenth edition.   Howes 185-164 1974 £40

AN ENCYCLOPAEDIA of Ironwork.   1927. 4to., plates, fine, first edition. Covent 55-106 1974 £21

THE ENCYCLOPAEDIA of Sport.   1900. 4 vols., imp. 8vo., plates, rubbed. Smith 194-944 1974 £7.50

ENCYCLOPAEDIA Britannica.   Edinburgh, 1875-89. 25 vols., 4to., illus., orig. quarter roan, ninth edition, plates.   Dawsons PM 252-343 1974 £40

ENCYCLOPAIDIA Britannica.   1910-11. 29 vols., large 8vo., orig. half morocco, plates, illus., eleventh edition.   Howes 185-163 1974 £45

ENCYCLOPEDIA Britannica.   New York, c. 1910, c. 1911, c. 1922. Cloth, 4to., 16 double vols. containing the 29 vols. of the much sought 11th edition and the three "New Vols.", which added to the 11th edition, constitute the 12th

ENCYCLOPEDIA Metropolitana.   1848. 4to., engravings, plates, stitching weak. Eaton Music-579 1973 £15

THE ENCYCLOPEDIA Of Health and Physical Culture.   New York, 1937. 8vols.   Ballinger 1-255 1974 $15

AN ENCYCLOPEDIC Lexicon of the English Language.   London, 1899. 11 vols. in 10., 4to., half leather.   Dawsons PM 252-123 1974 £20

AN ENCYCLOPEDIC Lexicon of the English Language.   London, 1900. 16 vols., 4to., illus., orig. half roan, rubbed.   Dawsons PM 252-124 1974 £20

ENCYCLOPEDIE Methodique, Botanique.   Paris, 1783-1823. 20 vols. in 33, 4to., contemporary boards, uncut, engraved plates, nice complete copy. Wheldon 128-1106 1973 £320

ENDLICHER, STEPHAN LADISLAUS   Enchiridion Botanicum Exhibens Classes et Ordines Plantarum.   Leipzig & Vienna, 1841. 8vo., half morocco, scarce. Wheldon 131-1135 1974 £15

ENDLICHER, STEPHEN LADISLAUS   Enchiridion Botanicum Exhibens Classes et Ordines Plantarum.   Leipzig & Vienna, 1841. 8vo., half morocco, scarce. Wheldon 128-1107 1973 £10

ENFANTINES.   Paris, (c. 1830). Orig. white glazed boards, spine worn, front inner hinge repaired, 2 1/8 X 1 5/16 inches.   Gregory 44-362 1974 $25

ENGELHARDT, F. ZEPHYRIN   The Holy Man of Santa Clara.   San Francisco, 1909. 16mo., cloth.   Saddleback 14-100 1974 $12.50

ENGELHARDT, F. ZEPHYRIN   San Francisco Or Mission Dolores.   Chicago, 1924. Cloth, front cover illus. in gilt, illus., fine, scarce, first edition.   Dykes 22-37 1973 $20

ENGELHARDT, F. ZEPHYRIN   San Gabriel Mission and the Beginnings of Los Angeles.   San Gabriel, 1927. Cloth with front cover illus. in gilt, first edition. Dykes 24-138 1974 $17.50

ENGELHARDT, F. ZEPHYRIN   San Gabriel Mission and the Beginnings of Los Angeles.   San Gabriel, 1927. Cloth, front cover illus. in gilt by Borein, illus., fine, scarce, first edition.   Dykes 22-38 1973 $17.50

ENGELHARDT, F. ZEPHYRIN   Santa Barbara Mission.   San Francisco, 1923. Cloth, front cover illus. in gilt by Borein, illus., scarce, first edition.   Dykes 22-36 1973 $17.50

ENGELHARDT, H.   Die Tertiarflora des Jesuitengrabens Bei Kundratitz in Nordbohem.   Halle, 1885.   4to., half calf, tinted plates. Wheldon 128-962 1973 £10

ENGELHARDT, H.   Ueber die Flora der Uber den Braunkohlen Befindichen Tertiarschichten von Dux.   Halle, 1891.   4to., plates.   Wheldon 128-963 1973 £5

ENGELHARDT, N. L.   Planning School Building Programs.   New York, 1930.   8vo., cloth, illus., maps.   Minters 37-526 1973 $15

ENGELMANN, W.   Bibliotheca Scriptorum Classicorum.   Leipzig, 1880-82.   2 vols., 8vo., orig. buckram, eighth edition.   Dawsons PM 10-209 1974 £20

ENGLAND, J. F.   The Life of Joseph G. E. Petter.   London, n.d. Inscription, orig. blue cloth, gold stamped, 2 X 1 3/4 inches.   Gregory 44-366 1974 $32.50

ENGLAND, JOHN   Letters Concerning the Roman Chancery. 1840.   276 pages.   Austin 57-193 1974 $15

ENGLAND   England Yesterday & Today.   London, 1949. Biblo & Tannen 213-830 1973 $8.50

ENGLAND and Wales, a Coloured Map.   (c.1840).   Roy. 4to., calf worn. Quaritch 939-114 1974 £45

ENGLEFIELD, HENRY   Vases from the Collection by H. Moses. (1820).   4to., contemporary cloth, faded, plates, large paper.   Quaritch 940-317 1974 £35

ENGLER, A.   Die Naturlichen Pflanzenfamilien.   Leipzig, 1887-1915.   Roy 8vo., new buckram, 18 vols.   Wheldon 130-1009 1974 £250

ENGLER, A.   Die Pflanzenwelt Afrikas.   Leipzig, 1925.   Roy 8vo., cloth, map.   Wheldon 129-1065 1974 £12

ENGLISCH, PAUL   Sittengeschichte Des Orients.   Berlin, c. 1932. First edition, illus., few light cover stains, German text, orig. binding.   Wilson 63-596 1974 $40

ENGLISCH, PAUL   Sittengeschichte Europas.   Berlin, c. 1931. First edition, illus., orig. binding, cover slightly stained, German text.   Wilson 63-597 1974 $42.50

ENGLISH, HARRIET   Conversations and Amusing Tales.   1799.   First edition, engraved frontispiece, plates, 4to., half calf, rubbed, joints broken. George's 610-249 1973 £15

ENGLISH, HARRIET   Conversations and Amusing Tales.   1799.   4to., contemporary diced russia gilt, plates.   Hill 126-95 1974 £25

ENGLISH, S. M.   Only a Fisherman's Daughter.   N.P., 1899. Card cover.   Hood's 103-480 1974 $17.50

ENGLISH Bijou Almanack.   London, 1837.   Emerald green wrappers, nice copy, orig. leather box, 3/4 X 1/2 inch.   Gregory 44-368 1974 $100

ENGLISH Bijou Almanack.   London, 1837.   Red morocco back, white covers, 3/4 X 1/2 inch.   Gregory 44-369 1974 $125

ENGLISH Bijou Almanack.   London, 1838.   Orig. white and gold, red onlay, fine, matching case little dull.   Gregory 44-370 1974 $95

ENGLISH Bijou Almanacs for 1838-1843.   Schloss, (1837-42).   Engraved portraits, 6 vols., size 8/10 by 6/10 inches, orig. wrappers, slip in cases, fine set.   Sawyer 293-219 1974 £450

ENGLISH Bijou Almanac for 1840.   Schloss, (1839).   Engraved portraits, size 8/10 by 6/10 inches, orig. red wrappers gilt, gilt edges, slip in case, fine copy. Sawyer 293-220 1974 £65

ENGLISH Bijou Almanack.   London, 1841.   Orig. green wrappers, matching case, orig. leather case containing book & magnifying glass, 3/4 X 5/8 inches. Gregory 44-371 1974 $145

THE ENGLISH Dialect Dictionary Being the Complete Vocabulary of all Dialect Words Still in Use.   Oxford, 1898-1905.   6 vols., thick med. 4to., half morocco by Fazakerley, pannelled backs, raised bands, fine.   Broadhurst 24-317 1974 £60

ENGLISH Embroidery Executed Prior to the Middle of the XVIth Century.   1905. Roy. 4to., plates, buckram.   Quaritch 940-753 1974 £30

ENGLISH Forests and Forest Trees.   1853.   8vo., orig. cloth, frontispiece, engravings.   Wheldon 128-1595 1973 £7.50

ENGLISH Forests and Forest Trees.   1853.   8vo., orig. cloth, frontispiece, engravings.   Wheldon 131-1728 1974 £7.50

THE ENGLISH Hexapla.   1841.   Thick 4to., cloth, rebacked, scarce.   Howes 185-1137 1974 £15

THE ENGLISH Hexapla.   London, 1841.   Grey buckram, labels.   Dawson's 424-206 1974 $85

ENGLISH Landscape Scenery.   1855.   Folio, half dark red morocco, plates, gilt.   Marsden 39-87 1974 £70

ENGLISH Mezzotint Portraits from Circa 1750 to Circa 1830.   1902.   Roy. 4to., plates, buckram, unopened.   Quaritch 940-93 1974 £25

ENGLISH Place Name Society.   Cambridge, 1924-31.   9 vols., 8vo., maps, orig. cloth, faded.   Bow Windows 62-309 1974 £34

ENGLISH Sacred Lyrics· An Anthology.   1883.   Vellum, 269 pages.   Austin 61-358 1974 $10

ENNEMOSER, JOSEPH   History of Magic.   London, 1854.   2 vols., some wear.   Rittenhouse 46-246 1974 $25

ENNIUS, QUINTUS   Annalium Libb. XIIX, Quae Apud Varios Auctores Superant.   1595.   Limp vellum, second printed edition.   Allen 213-350 1973 $30

ENNODIUS, B.   Ennodii Episc. Ticinensis Poemata Sacra Vitae SS.   Tornaci, 1610.   8vo., contemporary calf, worm-holes, upper joint cracked, worn.   Bow Windows 66-219 1974 £7.50

AN ENQUIRY into the Causes of the Miscarriage of the Scots Colony at Darien. Glasgow, 1700.   8vo., modern boards, first edition.   Dawsons PM 247-110 1974 £110

ENRICO BENEDETTO CARDINALE DUCA DI YORCK   Diario per L'Anno MDCCLXXXVIII.   1876.   4to., full red levant morocco, gilt spine, top edges gilt, others uncut, presentation inscription.   Thomas 32-113 1974 £40

ENSCHEDE EN ZONEN, J.   Die Hochdeutschen Schriften aus dem 15ten bis Zum 19ten Jahrhundert der Schriftgiesserei und Druckerei J. Enschede en Zonen.   Haarlem, 1919.   4to., orig. wrappers.   Kraus B8-321 1974 $27.50

ENSLIN, T. C. F.   Bibliothek der Forst-und Jagd Wissenschaft. Leipzig, 1843.   Med. 8vo., orig. wrappers.   Forster 98-187 1974 £4

EOBANUS, HELIUS   De Tvenda Bona Valetvdine.   Paris, 1555. 16mo., contemporary blind-stamped vellum, corners worn, trifle wormed.   Thomas 32-337 1974 £45

EPICTETUS   The Discourses Of.   London, 1902.   2 vols., handmade paper, orig. dust jackets, fine.   Ballinger 1-256 1974 $25

EPICTETUS   Epictetus His Morals.   London, 1704.   12mo., mor. and marbled bds., rubbed.   Jacobs 24-169 1974 $25

EPICTETUS   The Works of Epictetus.   Boston, 1891. 3/4 calf & bds., 2 vols.   Biblo & Tannen 213-461 1973 $17.50

EPIGRAMMATUM Delectus, Ex. Omnibus Tum Veteribus, tum Recentioribus Poetis Accurate Decerptus cum Dissertatione. 1732. 12mo., contemporary sheep, rebacked, pencilled marginalia. Bow Windows 66-221 1974 £7.75

EPISTOLA Luciferi ad Malos Principes Ecclesiasticos Parisius Primum Impressa Ubi est fons Optimorum Studiorum. (Strassburg, c. 1507-10). Small 4to., boards, scarce, first edition. Harper 213-56 1973 $850

EPISTOLAE Diuersorum Philosophorum Graecorum. 1499. Small 4to., rebacked, blind-stamped russia. Thomas 30-3 1973 £350

EPSTEIN, JULIUS J. Chicken Every Sunday. French, 1946. 150p., paper. Austin 51-290 1973 $6.50

ERASMUS, DESIDERIUS Adagiorvm Opvs. Basle, 1526. Folio, old calf, very worn, upper cover almost detached, clean and sound. Thomas 32-233 1974 £60

ERASMUS, DESIDERIUS Antiquitatum Iudaicarum Libri XX. Basel, 1540. Folio, 18th century full vellum, good copy. Schumann 499-32 1974 sFr 1,230

ERASMUS, DESIDERIUS Apophthegmes. 1542. Thick small 8vo., contemporary blind stamped calf, worn, first edition in English. Thomas 28-241 1972 £65

ERASMUS, DESIDERIUS Collectanea Adagiorum Veterum. Strassburg, 1520. 4to., wrappers, woodcut border. Harper 213-57 1973 $225

ERASMUS, DESIDERIUS Colloquia Nunc Emendatiora. Amstelodami, 1662. 12mo., old vellum, dust soiled. Smith 194-147 1974 £10

ERASMUS, DESIDERIUS Das Theur vnd Kunstlich Buchlin Morie Encomion. (Ulm, 1534). Small 4to., half vellum, first edition in German. Harper 213-60 1973 $750

ERASMUS, DESIDERIUS De Utraq Verborum Acrerum Copia Lib II. Amsterdam, 1645. 12mo., contemporary calf. Smith 194-149 1974 £6.50

ERASMUS, DESIDERIUS Epistolae ad Diversos, & Aliquot Aliorum ad Illum. Basel, 1521. Folio, full red morocco, very fine, most complete edition. Harper 213-58 1973 $685

ERASMUS, DESIDERATUS Erasmus in Praise of Folly. (c., 1725). 12mo., contemporary calf, rebacked, first edition. Hill 126-96 1974 £40

ERASMUS, DESIDERIUS Paraphrase Upon the Newe Testament. 1551-49. 2 vols., small folio, modern sheep, first & second editions. Thomas 28-48 1972 £85

ERASMUS, DESIDERIUS Witt Against Wisdom. Oxford, 1683. 8vo., contemporary sheep, fine, first edition. Dawsons PM 252-344 1974 £160

ERASMUS AB HULDEBURG, DANIEL Opuscula iuventutis Mathematica Curiosa. 1710. 4to., contemporary calf, third edition. Dawsons PM 245-257 1974 £45

ERASMUS Against the War. Boston, 1907. 8vo., boards, linen back, leather label, uncut. Goodspeed's 578-96 1974 $20

ERDMANN, J. E. A History of Philosophy. 1922-24-21. 3 vols., orig. cloth. Smith 194-868 1974 £9.50

EREINOFF, NICOLAS The Theatre in Life. Brentano, 1927. 296p., illus. Austin 51-291 1973 $10

ERHEITERUNGEN und Belehrungen aus dem Natur, Kunst- und Volkerleben, fur die Reifere Jugend Bearb. Mainz, (c. 1850). Coloured lithograph plates, large crown 8vo., orig. red boards, dull, spine worn. George's 610-251 1973 £5

ERHLICH, PAUL Die Experimentelle Chemotherapie der Spirillosen. Berlin, 1910. 8vo., plates, orig. green cloth, library stamp, first edition. Dawsons PM 250-24 1974 £85

ERICHSEN, JOHN ERIC On Consussion of the Spine, Nervous Shock. New York, 1882. New revised edition. Rittenhouse 46-248 1974 $20

ERICHSEN, JOHN ERIC "Science & Art of Surgery." Philadelphia, 1860. Full leather, wood engravings, very good. Rittenhouse 46-249 1974 $15

ERIKSSON, J. Fungous Diseases of Plants. 1930. Roy 8vo., cloth, illus., second edition. Wheldon 129-1197 1974 £5

ERLANDE, ALBERT The Life of John Keats. 1929. 244 pages. Austin 61-359 1974 $12.50

ERMATINGER, C. O. The Talbot Regime. St. Thomas, 1904. Orig. covers, rebound, special edition. Hood's 104-682 1974 $40

ERMATINGER, C. O. The Talbot Settlement Centenary Celebration. St. Thomas, 1910. Wrappers. Hood's 103-625 1974 $17.50

ERMATINGER, E. Life of Colonel Talbot and the Talbot Settlement, Its Rise and Progress. St. Thomas, 1859. First edition, with errata sheet. Hood's 102-240 1974 $60

ERNST, A. Bastardierung als Ursache der Apogamie im Pflanzenreich. Jena, 1918. Roy. 8vo., half morocco, plates, text-figures, scarce. Wheldon 128-1108 1973 £5

ERNST, BERNARD M. Houdini and Conan Doyle. 1932. Orig. edition. Austin 61-329 1974 $10

ERNST, MARGARET S. In a Word. Knopf, 1939. 249p., illus., 1st ed. Austin 54-1010 1973 $10

ERNST, MARGARET S. In a Word. Channel, 1960. 239p., illus. Austin 54-1011 1973 $7.50

ERNST, MAX La Femme 100 Tetes. Paris, 1929. One of 900 numbered copies on velin teinte, 4to., buckram, orig. wrappers preserved, very nice copy. Covent 51-2324 1973 £105

ERNST, MORRIS The Censor Marches On. Doubleday, 1940. 346p., paper. Austin 51-294 1973 $10

ERNST, MORRIS Censored. Cape, Smith, 1930. 199p., illus. Austin 51-292 1973 $15

ERNST, MORRIS The First Freedom. Macmillan, 1946. 316p. Austin 51-293 1973 $7.50

ERNST, MORRIS To the Pure. Viking, 1928. 336p., orig. ed. Austin 51-295 1973 $7

ERSKINE, JAMES Reasons Against the Bill Before the House of Lords. London, 1737. 8vo., modern boards, second edition. Dawsons PM 247-111 1974 £8

ERSKINE, THOMAS Letters. Edinburgh, 1877. 2 vols., full brown morocco, gilt, portrait. Howes 186-180 1974 £15

ERSKINE, THOMAS Observations on the Prevailing Abuses in the British Army. London, 1775. 8vo., modern boards. Dawsons PM 247-112 1974 £15

ERSKINE, THOMAS A View of the Causes and Consequences of the Present War With France. London, 1797. 8vo., modern half calf, first edition. Dawsons PM 247-113 1974 £20

ERVINE, SAINT JOHN G. Anthony and Anna. Macmillan, 1925. 92p. Austin 51-296 1973 $6.50

ERVINE, SAINT JOHN G. The First Mrs. Fraser. Allen, Unwin, 1929. 88p. Austin 51-297 1973 $6.50

ERVINE, SAINT JOHN G. John Ferguson. Macmillan, 1915. 122p. Austin 51-298 1973 $6.50

ERVINE, ST. JOHN G. The Lady of Belmont. London, 1923. 8vo., orig. boards, signed, first edition. Dawsons PM 252-345 1974 £15

ERVINE, SAINT JOHN G. Robert's Wife. Allen, Unwin, 1938. 101p. Austin 51-299 1973 $7.50

ESAR, EVAN　　　　　Esar's Comic Dictionary. Harvest House, 1943. 3l3p. Austin 54-360 1973 $8.50

ESAR, EVAN　　　　　Esar's Joke Dictionary. Harvest House, 1945. 49lp. Austin 54-361 1973 $8.50

ESCHENBURG, J. J.　　　　　Handbuch der Klassischen Literatur. Berlin & Stettin, 1808. Quarter sheep, mottled boards, browned, fifth edition. Thomas 28-113 1972 £8.50

ESDAILE, ARUNDELL　　　　　A List of English Tales. London, 1912. 4to., orig. cloth backed boards, first edition. Dawsons PM 252-346 1974 £40

ESDAILE, ARUNDELL　　　　　A List of English Tales and Prose Romances Printed Before 1740. London, 1912. 4to., orig. cloth-backed boards, uncut, first edition. Dawsons PM 10-210 1974 £35

ESDAILE, ARUNDELL　　　　　National Libraries of the World. London, 1934-37. 2 vols. Biblo & Tannen 213-753 1973 $32.50

ESHER, VISCOUNT　　　　　The Modern Library Collected by . . . at Watlington Park. London, 1930. Limited to 100 copies, lacks back endpaper, small 4to., orig. buckram, faded. Forster 98-193 1974 £25

ESMARCH, JOHANN FRIEDRICH AUGUST VON　　Die Erste Hulfe bei Vertelzungen. Hannover, 1875. 8vo., orig. pictured wrappers, illus., first edition. Schuman 37-71 1974 $85

ESMARCH, JOHANN FRIEDRICH AUGUST VON　　Verbandplatz und Feldlazareth. Berlin, 1868. 8vo., old style boards, plates, first edition. Schuman 37-72 1974 $110

ESNAULT-PELTERIE, ROBERT　　Considerations sur les Resultats d'un Allegement. Paris, 1913. 8vo., orig. paper wrappers, rare first edition. Zeitlin 235-67 1974 $250

ESNAULT-PELTERIE, ROBERT　　L'Exploration Par Fusees de la Tres Haute Atmosphere. Paris, 1928. 8vo., orig. printed wrappers, uncut. Zeitlin 235-68 1974 $450

ESNAULT-PELTERIE, ROBERT　　L'Exploration par Fusees de la Tres Haute Atmosphere et la Possibilite des Voyages Interplanetaires. Paris, 1928. 8vo., diagrams, orig. wrappers, uncut, presentation, rare first edition. Gilhofer 61-95 1974 sFr. 1,400

ESPEY, JOHN J.　　　　　Minor Heresies. Knopf, 1945. 202p. Austin 54-362 1973 $6.50

ESPEY, JOHN J.　　　　　Tales Out of School. Knopf, 1947. 204p. Austin 54-363 1973 $6.50

ESPOUY, HENRI D'　　　　100 Selected Plates from Fragments d' Architecture Antique. 1923. Folio, plates. Allen 213-1898 1973 $15

ESQUIE, PIERRE　　　　　The Five Orders of Architecture. New York, (ca., 191-). 4to., printed boards, plates. Rich Summer-8 1974 $17.50

ESQUIROL, JEAN ETIENNE DOMINIQUE　　Des Maladies Mentales. Paris, 1838. 8vo., 2 vols., calf, labels, first edition. Dawsons PM 249-165 1974 £185

ESSAI de Traduction en vers Burlesques d'une Piece de Poesie Latine Intitulee Excidium Augi. Rouen, 1887. 4to., orig. wrappers, uncut, limited edition. Harper 213-61 1973 $30

AN ESSAY How to Raise Above One Million Sterling Per Ann. (1711). Folio, disbound. Quaritch 939-258 1974 £18

AN ESSAY on the Improvement of the Woollen Manufacture. London, 1741. 8vo., modern boards, first edition. Dawsons PM 247-114 1974 £30

AN ESSAY On the Inequality of Our Present Taxes. London, 1746. 8vo., modern boards, first edition. Dawsons PM 247-115 1974 £20

AN ESSAY on the Influence of Welsh Tradition Upon European Literature. n.d. Lacks backstrip, very good copy, worn wrappers, first edition. Covent 51-1153 1973 £6.30

AN ESSAY Upon the Original Authority of the King's Council. 1834. 8vo., cloth, gilt. Quaritch 939-9 1974 £8.50

ESSAYS IN Honour of Gilbert Murray. 1936. 8vo., levant morocco, gilt. Broadhurst 23-880 1974 £20

ESSAYS on Romanism. 1841. 407p., lst Am. ed. Austin 62-541 1974 $17.50

ESSEX FIELD CLUB　　　　　Transactions and Proceedings, Vols. 1 - 4, Continued as Essex Naturalist, Vols. 1 - 17. Buckhurst Hill & Stratford, 1881-1913. 21 vols., 8vo., cloth. Wheldon 128-30 1973 £25

ESSLINGER, F.　　　　　Catalogue des Nouveautes . . . Foire de St. Michel. 1799. 18mo., unbound as issued. Forster 98-194 1974 £5

ESTAMPAS de la Revolucion Espanola. Barcelona, n.d. Oblong 4to., color plates, lst ed. Biblo & Tannen 210-339 1973 $12.50

ESTCOURT, E. E.　　　　　The Question of Anglican Ordinations Discussed. 1873. Plates. Howes 185-1141 1974 £6

ESTIENNE, CHARLES　　　　　La Guide des Chemins de France de 1553. Paris, 1936. 2 vols. in 1, large 8vo., full cloth, orig. wrapper, folding maps. L. Goldschmidt 42-49 1974 $35

ESTIENNE, HENRI　　　　　Avertissement. 1860. 8vo., roan backed boards, limited. Thomas 28-114 1972 £35

ESTIENNE, HENRI　　　　　Parodiae Morales. 1575. Vellum, little worn but sound, printed on one side of the leaf only, alternate pages blank, fair copy. Thomas 32-264 1974 £25

ESTIENNE, HENRI　　　　　Parodiae Morales. 1575. Vellum, worn, stains. Thomas 28-310 1972 £25

ESTIENNE, HENRI　　　　　Traicte de la Conformite du Language Francois Avec le Grec. N.P. (Geneva), n.d. 8vo., full purple morocco, first edition, very good copy, rare. Ximenes 36-82 1974 $300

ESTIUS, WILLEM HESSELS　　Asolutissima in Omnes Beati Pauli et Septem Catholicas Apostolorum Epistolas Commentaria. Paris, 1679. 3 vols. in 2, folio, contemporary vellum. Howes 185-1143 1974 £18

ETHEREGE, GEORGE　　　　　The Man of Mode; or, Sir Fopling Flutter. London, 1693. Small 4to., disbound, third edition, scarce. Ximenes 36-83 1974 $65

ETHERIDGE, R.　　　　　Fossils of the British Islands. Oxford, 1888. 4to., orig. cloth, scarce. Wheldon 131-995 1974 £10

ETHERIDGE, R.　　　　　Fossils of the British Islands. Oxford, 1888. 4to., gilt. Bow Windows 64-91 1974 £12

ETRENNES a l'Innocence. Paris, (c. 1825). Full red morocco, gilt, fine, 1 X 3/4 inches. Gregory 44-373 1974 $95

ETRENNES Lyriques Almanach Portatif Pour l'An. Paris, 1804. Full dark brown morocco, tan cloth box, 1 1/4 X 3/4 inches. Gregory 44-374 1974 $175

ETS, MARIE HALL　　　　　Mister Penny. New York, 1935. Oblong 4to., boards, cloth spine, lst ed., illus. Frohnsdorff 16-311 1974 $10

ETTERIDGE, R.　　　　　Monograph of the Silurian and Devonian Corals of New South Wales. Sydney, 1904-07. 2 parts, 4to., boards. Wheldon 128-964 1973 £15

ETTINGSHAUSEN, C. VON　　Bericht uber das Werk Physiotypia Plantarum Austriacarum. Vienna, 1856. 8vo., cloth, plates. Wheldon 130-1150 1974 £5

ETTINGSHAUSEN, C. VON　　Die Fossile Flora von Leoben in Steiermark. Vienna, 1889. 2 parts, plates. Wheldon 128-965 1973 £5

ETTMULLER, MICHEL　　　　　Nouvelle Pratique de Chirurgie. Amsterdam, 1691. 12mo., half calf, gilt. Hammond 201-537 1974 £38

EUCLIDES   Delle Scientie Mathematice. Venice, 1543. Folio, old vellum, fine, first edition in Italian. Dawsons PM 245-264 1974 £335

EUCLIDES   Elementa Geometrica. 1678. 12mo., new half calf, gilt. Dawsons PM 245-261 1974 £35

EUCLIDES   Elementorum Libros XIII ... Venice, 1510. Folio, vellum, fine. Dawsons PM 245-258 1974 £650

EUCLIDES   Elementorum Libri XV . . . 1659. 8vo., contemporary vellum. Dawsons PM 245-260 1974 £20

EUCLIDES   Euclidis Elementorum Libri XV. London, 1678. 8vo., contemporary calf, rebacked. Dawsons PM 245-262 1974 £40

EUCLIDES   Euclidis Elementorum Libri XV. 1687. 8vo., contemporary calf. Dawsons PM 245-263 1974 £35

EUCLIDES   Euclidis Elementorum Libri XV Breviter Demonstrati. 1678. Small 8vo., quarter calf, gilt. Hammond 201-821 1974 £21

EUCLIDES   Habent in Hoc Volumine . . . Elementorum Libros XIII Cum Expositione Theonis. Venice, 1505. Folio, modern vellum over boards, fine, rare, first collective edition. Schafer 8-154 1973 sFr. 8,500

EUCLIDES   Elementorvm Geometricorvm Libri Tredecim. Rome, 1594. Contemporary vellum, folio, first edition in Arabic, diagrams, lacking 3 of the preliminary leaves, from the Prince Liechtenstein Library. Kraus 137-31 1974 $650

EUCLIDES   Elementorum Libri XV. Londini, 1678. 2 works in 1 vol., small 8vo., staining, contemporary calf, rebacked. Bow Windows 62-311 1974 £16.50

EUCLIDES   Euclide Megarense Acutissimo Philosopho, Solo Introduttore delle Scientie Mathematice. Venice, 1569. 4to., contemporary limp vellum. Schuman 37-73 1974 $165

EUCLIDES   La Perspectiva y Especularia de Euclides. Madrid, 1585. Small 4to., nineteenth century blue morocco, fine, first edition in Spanish. Dawsons PM 245-265 1974 £550

EUCLIDES   La Prospettiva di Euclide . . . 1773. 4to., contemporary vellum. Dawsons PM 245-266 1974 £45

EUDES-DESLONGCHAMPS, J. A.   Essai sur les Plicatules Fossiles des Terrains du Calvados et sur Quelques Autres Genres Voisins ou Demembres de ces Coquilles. Caen, 1858. 4to., boards, folding table, plates. Wheldon 128-966 1973 £7.50

EUGENE, PRINCE OF SAVOY   Memoirs. 1811. Contemporary half calf, crimson label, portrait. Howes 186-809 1974 £12.50

EUGENICS SOCIETY OF THE U.S.A.   Second and Third Report of the Committee on Selective Immigration of the Eugenics Society of the U. S. of America. New Haven, CT, 1925. Austin 62-152 1974 $12.50

EULENBERG, HERBERT   Fritz August Breuhaus de Groot. Berlin, 1929. 4to., cloth, plates. Minters 37-519 1973 $24.50

EULENBERG, HERMANN   Handbuch des Offentlichen Gesundheitswesens. Berlin, 1881. 8vo., 2 vols., old quarter cloth. Gumey 64-84 1974 £15

EULENBURG-WIENER, RENEE VON   Fearfully and Wonderfully Made. New York, 1938. Biblo & Tannen 213-860 1973 $9.50

EULER, LEONHARD   Institutiones Calculi Differentialis. 1755. 4to., contemporary calf, rebacked, first edition. Dawsons PM 245-269 1974 £200

EULER, LEONHARD   Introductio in Analysin Infinitorum. 1748. 4to., 2 vols., contemporary mottled calf, fine, first edition. Dawsons PM 245-268 1974 £425

EULER, LEONHARD   Introductio in Analysin Infinitorum. Lausanne, 1748. 2 vols., 4to., plates, contemporary boards, very fine, uncut, first edition. Gilhofer 61-16 1974 sFr. 3,000

EULER, LEONHARD   Introductio in Analysin Infinitorum. Lausanne, 1748. 2 vols., 4to., contemporary (publisher's?) card-boards, engraved frontis. and plates, first edition, fine clean copy, complete with often missing portrait of J. J. Dortous de Mairan. Schafer 10-128 1974 sFr 3,300

EULER, LEONHARD   Opvscvla Analytica. 1783-1785. 4to., half red morocco, rubbed, fine. Zeitlin 235-74 1974 $350

EULER, LEONHARD   Opuscula Varii Argumenti. 1746. Small 4to., contemporary half calf, plates. Zeitlin 235-75 1974 $250

EULER, LEONHARD   Theoria Motuum Planetarum et Cometarum. Berlin, (1744). 4to., contemporary calf, rebacked, gilt, first edition. Dawsons PM 245-267 1974 £195

EULLER, LEONHARD   Introductio In Analysin Infinitorum. Lusanne, 1748. 2 vols., large 4to., leather-backed boards, plates, first edition. Schuman 37-74 1974 $1500

EURIPIDES   Alcestis. London, 1930. Orig. cloth backed boards, numbered, signed by translator, first edition. MacManus 224-3A 1974 $35

EURIPIDES   Euripidis Quae Extant Omnia. 1694. Folio, contemporary calf, gilt, rubbed, bookplate, portrait, rare. Bow Windows 62-312 1974 £85

EURIPIDES   The Plays. 1931. Folio, 2 vols., cloth, gilt, illus. Hammond 201-764 1974 £145

EURIPIDES   The Plays of Euripides. 1931. 2 vols., folio, orig. cloth, uncut, fine. Bow Windows 62-398 1974 £115

EURIPIDES   Tragedies of Euripides. 1863. 2 vols. Austin 51-300 1973 $10

EURIPIDES   Tragoediae. 1602. Greek text, somewhat worn, lacks ties, 4to., contemporary stamped vellum. Thomas 32-234 1974 £25

EURIPIDES   Tragoediae Septdecim. 1503. 2 vols., 17th century French dark green morocco gilt, morocco labels, first complete edition. Thomas 30-16 1973 £500

EURIPIDES   Tragoediae XVIII. Frankfurt, (1557). Thick 8vo., contemporary blind-stamped pigskin, wooden boards, rare, fine. Harper 213-62 1973 $350

EURIPIDES   The Plays of. 1931. 2 vols., folio, immaculate, limited. Covent 55-786 1974 £90

EUROPEAN Civilization: Its Origin and Development. 1934-39. 7 vols., buckram, very fine set. Covent 51-3249 1973 £85

EUROPEAN Enamels from the Earliest Date to the End of the XVIIth Century, Exhibited in 1897. 1897. Roy. 4to., plates, buckram. Quaritch 940-448 1974 £50

EUROPEAN History. London, 1898-1928. 8 vols., 8vo., signature, orig. cloth. Bow Windows 62-313 1974 £9.50

EUROPEAN Magazine. Parchment back, pink boards, engravings, label, staining. Marsden 37-177 1974 £12

EUSEBIUS PAMPHILI   Presbyter. Milan, 1818. 2 parts in 1 vol., 4to., vellum, morocco labels. Howes 185-1145 1974 £25

EUSTACCHI, BARTOLOMMEO   Bernardi Siegfried Albinus Explicatio. 1761. Folio, old half calf, worn. Dawsons PM 249-166 1974 £135

EUSTACCHI, BARTOLOMMEO   Tabulae Anatomicae Clarissimi Viri. Amstelaedami, 1722. Folio, old roan backed boards, engraved plates, uncut, spine rubbed. Bow Windows 66-223 1974 £225

EUSTACE, G. W.   Arundel: Borough and Castle. 1922. Illus. Howes 186-2196 1974 £5

EUSTIS, MORTON   B'Way Inc.! Dodd, Mead, 1934. 356p. Austin 51-301 1973 $10

EUSTIS, MORTON   Players At Work. Theatre Arts, 1937. 127p., orig. ed.   Austin 51-302 1973 $7.50

EUSTRATIUS   Commentaria In Libros Decem Aristotelis de Moribus ad Nicomachum.   1536.   Small folio, late 18th century vellum gilt, raised bands, morocco labels.   Thomas 30-75 1973 £60

EUTROPIUS   Breviarium Historiae Romanae. Parisiss, 1754. Engr. frontis., 12mo., Old French red mor., gilt, silk linings.   Jacobs 24-142 1974 $50

EUTROPIUS   Eutropii Breviarium Historiae Romanae. Oxonii, (1703). 8vo., 18th century calf, small worm hole.   Bow Windows 66-224 1974 £10.50

EVANS, A.   The Palace of Minos. 1921-30. 3 vols. in 4, 4to., illus., plates, orig. buckram gilt.   Smith 193-35 1974 £45

EVANS, A. H.   Turner on Birds.   Cambridge, 1903. 8vo., orig. cloth, gilt.   Hammond 201-643 1974 £5

EVANS, ARTHUR BENONI   The Cutter.   London, 1808. 8vo., orig. boards, plates, uncut, first edition.   Dawsons PM 252-347 1974 £40

EVANS, BERGEN   Natural History of Nonsense. Knopf, 1946. 275p., hard cover ed.   Austin 54-364 1973 $6

EVANS, BERGEN   The Spoor of Spooks and Other Nonsense. Joseph, London, 1955. 288p.   Austin 54-365 1973 $7.50

EVANS, CARADOC   Capel Sion. n.d. (c. 1917). Covers little worn, front hinge weak, library label, very good copy, first edition.   Covent 51-659 1973 £5.25

EVANS, CARADOC   Wasps.   n.d. Fine, dust wrapper, English first edition.   Covent 56-426 1974 £7.50

EVANS, C. S.   The Sleeping Beauty. 1920. Illus. by Arthur Rackham, edition de Luxe, with additional colour-plate, limited to 625 copies, numbered & signed by artist, 4to., orig. parchment backed boards, top edges gilt, others uncut.   George's 610-836 1973 £65

EVANS, C. S.   The Sleeping Beauty. 1920. Numbered, illus., fine, parchment-backed boards.   Covent 55-1233 1974 £115

EVANS, E. C.   Cofiant a Phregethau Y Diweddar Barchedig William Roberts, D. D.   New York, 1890. Austin 62-153 1974 $22.50

EVANS, EDWARD   Catalogue of a Collection of Engraved Portraits. London, n.d. 2 vols., 8vo., orig. boards, paper labels.   Dawsons PM 10-212 1974 £18

EVANS, H. W.   The Menace of Modern Immigration. 1923. Austin 62-154 1974 $22.50

EVANS, H. W.   The Rising Storm. 1930. 345 pages. Austin 57-196 1974 $10

EVANS, JAMES W.   Autobiography of Samuel S. Hildebrand. Jefferson City, 1870. Rare.   Jenkins 61-1709 1974 $85

EVANS, JAMES W.   The Autobiography of Samuel S. Hildebrand. Jefferson City, 1870.   Jenkins 61-1062 1974 $85

EVANS, JOE M.   A Corral Full of Stories. El Paso, (1939). First edition, 12mo., illus., pictorial wrappers, some edge chipping, pristine, presentation copy from author.   Current BW9-363 1974 $32.50

EVANS, JOHN   The Christian Temper. 1761. 8vo., contemporary sheep.   Hill 126-98 1974 £7.50

EVANS, LADY   Lustre Pottery.   New York, (c. 1920). Folio, plates, orig. cloth.   Gregory 44-119 1974 $15

EVANS, MARY ANN
Please turn to
ELIOT, GEORGE

EVANS, MAURICE   The Aegis of England. 1817. Full polished calf, gilt.   Howes 186-1712 1974 £10

EVANS, NATHANIEL   Poems on Several Occasions With Some Other Compositions.   Philadelphia, 1772. Contemporary calf, rubbed, first edition, browned, few stains, lacks leaf of errata.   MacManus 224-156 1974 $75

EVANS, NELSON W.   A History of Scioto County, Ohio. Portsmouth, 1903. 8vo., cloth.   Saddleback 14-616 1974 $65

EVANS, NELSON W.   A History of Scioto County, Ohio, Together With a Pioneer Record of Southern Ohio. Portsmouth, 1903. Cloth, scarce.   Hayman 59-502 1974 $57.50

EVANS, W. H.   The Identification of Indian Butterflies. Bombay, 1922-26. Roy. 8vo., half green levant morocco, plates.   Wheldon 131-803 1974 £10

EVANS, WALKER   American Photographs. New York, 1938. Small 4to., rubbed, plates.   Covent 55-1188 1974 £35

EVANS, WILLIAM DAVIES   Dros Gyfanfor a Chyfandir. 1883. 8vo., orig. cloth, first edition.   Broadhurst 23-1636 1974 £21

EVANS, WILLIAM SLOANE   A Grammar of British Heraldry.   London, 1847. 8vo., orig. cloth, plates, first edition.   Hammond 201-421 1974 £8.50

EVELYN, JOHN   A Devotionarie Book. 1936. Buckram backed boards, English first edition.   Covent 56-427 1974 £7.50

EVELYN, JOHN   Diary. 1879. 4 vols., thick 8vo., half brown morocco, plates, portraits, new edition.   Howes 186-183 1974 £42

EVELYN, JOHN   The Diary. 1906. Illus., 3 vols., blue three quarter polished calf, English first edition.   Covent 56-428 1974 £36

EVELYN, JOHN   Diary of. 1906. 4 vols., 8vo., orig. cloth, plates, spines slightly faded, uncut.   Bow Windows 66-225 1974 £24

EVELYN, JOHN   Extracts from the Diaries and Correspondence Of. 1915. Square 8vo., cloth-backed boards, English first edition.   Covent 56-429 1974 £7.50

EVELYN, JOHN   The Life of Mrs. Godolphin. 1847. Small 8vo., binder's cloth, first edition.   Hill 126-99 1974 £16.50

EVELYN, JOHN   Memoirs. 1819. 2 vols., 4to., contemporary half calf gilt, labels, plates, second edition.   Howes 186-182 1974 £28

EVELYN, JOHN   Memoirs.   London, 1819. 4to., 2 vols., half green morocco, gilt, plates, second edition.   Hammond 201-305 1974 £48

EVELYN, JOHN   Memoirs.   London, 1819, 1825. Large heavy 4to., plates, contemporary polished gilt calf.   Rich Summer-59 1974 $100

EVELYN, JOHN   Memoirs Of. 1827. 8vo., half calf, 5 vols., portraits, plates.   Bow Windows 64-501 1974 £44

EVELYN, JOHN   The Miscellaneous Writings Of. 1825. 4to., contemporary diced calf, foxing, first edition.   Bow Windows 64-502 1974 £55

EVELYN, JOHN   Sylva, or a Discourse of Forest Trees. 1664. Folio, modern calf antique style, woodcuts, rare first edition.   Wheldon 128-1596 1973 £175

EVELYN, JOHN   Sylva. 1664. Folio, contemporary calf, first edition.   Wheldon 130-1554 1974 £150

EVELYN, JOHN   Sylva. 1670. Small folio, contemporary calf.   Thomas 28-263 1972 £45

EVELYN, JOHN   Sylva. 1679. Small folio, contemporary calf. Wheldon 129-1599 1974 £50

EVELYN, JOHN   Sylva, Or a Discourse of Forest-Trees. London, 1679. Folio, later half calf, gilt, third edition.   Traylen 79-17 1973 £32

EVELYN, JOHN   Silva. 1706. Folio, portrait, illus., old calf repaired, fourth edition. Bow Windows 64-92 1974 £60

EVELYN, JOHN   Silva, or a Discourse of Forest Trees. 1706. Small folio, contemporary panelled calf gilt, fourth edition. Wheldon 131-1729 1974 £30

EVELYN, JOHN   Silva. 1706. Small folio, contemporary panelled calf gilt, portrait, fourth edition. Wheldon 128-1597 1973 £30

EVELYN, JOHN   Sylva, Or a Discourse of Forest-Trees. London, 1729. Folio, half calf, gilt, labels, engravings, good copy, fifth edition. Traylen 79-18 1973 £20

EVELYN, JOHN   Sylva. (1908). Roy. 8vo., 2 vols., cloth. Wheldon 129-1600 1974 £15

EVELYN, JOHN   Terra. 1778. 8vo., modern half calf, uncut, new edition. Wheldon 130-1391 1974 £25

THE EVELYNS In America. Oxford, 1881. Small 4to., portraits, maps, limited edition. Traylen 79-480 1973 £5

EVERARD, EDMUND   The Depositions and Examinations Of. London, 1679. Folio, disbound, first edition. Dawsons PM 251-502 1974 £30

EVERETT, EDWARD   An Oration Delivered at Charlestown. Boston, 1850. 80 pages. Bradley 35-134 1974 $40

EVERETT, EDWARD   Uses of Astronomy. Boston, 1856. 8vo., disbound, presentation, inscription, first edition. Zeitlin 235-76 1974 $37.50

EVERETT, MARSHALL   Complete Life of William McKinley and a Story of His Assassination. N.P., 1901. First edition, 8vo., full page plates, rubbed at extremities, interior fine. Current BW9-380 1974 $12.50

EVERETT, MARSHALL   Exciting Experiences in Our War With Mexico. Chicago, 1914. Illus. Jenkins 61-1582 1974 $17.50

THE EVERGREEN Tales, Series I. New York, 1949-1952. Folio, 3 vols., sgd. by editor. Frohnsdorff 16-312 1974 $35

THE EVERGREEN Tales, Series II. New York, 1949-1952. Folio, 3 vols., illus., sgd. Frohnsdorff 16-312 1974 $30

THE EVERGREEN Tales, Series III. New York, 1949-1952. Folio, 3 vols., illus. Frohnsdorff 16-312 1974 $35

THE EVERGREEN Tales, Series IV. New York, 1949-1952. Folio, 3 vols., illus., sgd. Frohnsdorff 16-312 1974 $35

EVERITT, GRAHAM   English Caricaturists and Graphic Humourists of the 19th Century. 1893. Illus., rubbed, second edition. Covent 55-97 1974 £21

EVERITT, N.   Broadland Sport. 1902. 4to., orig. half vellum, illus. Wheldon 130-280 1974 £7.50

EVERSFIELD, C.   A Journal Kept on a Journey From Bassora to Bagdad. Horsham, 1784. 8vo., contemporary half calf, first edition. Ximenes 37-75 1974 $75

EVERSON, WILLIAM   San Joaquin. Los Angeles, 1939. Boards. Dawson's 424-264 1974 $35

EVERY-DAY English. 1922. Photographs, 80 pages. Austin 57-113 1974 $12.50

EVES, REGINALD G.   The Art Of. 1940. Cloth, morocco spine, signed by Eves, limited edition. Eaton Music-582 1973 £5

EVJEN, JOHN O.   The Life of J. H. W. Stuckenberg. 1938. Austin 62-155 1974 $20

EVJEN, JOHN O.   Scandinavian Immigrants in New York, 1630-1674. Minneapolis, 1916. 8vo., cloth, illus. Saddleback 14-576 1974 $25

EVJEN, JOHN O.   Scandinavian Immigrants in New York. 1916. Illus. Austin 57-197 1974 $27.50

EVJEN, JOHN O.   Scandinavian Immigrants in New York. Minneapolis, 1916. Austin 62-156 1974 $27.50

EVOLUTION In the Light of Modern Knowledge. 1925. 8vo., cloth, plates, map. Wheldon 131-152 1974 £7.50

EWALD, CARL   The Queen Bee. 1907. Dec. cloth gilt, plates. Covent 55-884 1974 £8.50

EWART, A. J.   The Weeds, Poisonous Plants and Naturalized Aliens of Victoria. Melbourne, 1909. 8vo., orig. cloth, plates. scarce. Wheldon 131-1284 1974 £15

EWART, WILFRID   When Armageddon Came. 1933. Orig. cloth, signed, first edition. Rota 188-286 1974 £7

EWING, J. A.   Magnetic Induction in Iron and Other Metals. London, (1900). 8vo., purple calf, gilt, third edition. Dawsons PM 245-272 1974 £7

EWING, J. A.   The Steam-Engine and Other Heat-Engines. Cambridge, 1910. 8vo., orig. cloth, folding plate, large folding diagrams, signature on fly, third edition. Bow Windows 66-226 1974 £7.50

EWING, J. H.   A Collection of the Works of. London, 1871. 14 vols., 8vo., illus., orig. quarter cloth, worn. Bow Windows 62-314 1974 £35

EWING, JOHN   A Plain Elementary and Practical System of Natural Experimental Philosophy. Philadelphia, 1809. 8vo., contemporary mottled calf gilt, worn, plates. Rittenhouse 46-250 1974 $75

EWING, JULIANA HORATIA   Daddy Darwin's Dovecot. London, ca. 1884. 8vo., engravings. Frohnsdorff 16-162 1974 $10

EWING, JULIANA HORATIA   Daddy Darwin's Dovecot. (1884). 8vo., orig. pictorial boards, illus. Hammond 201-110 1974 £5

EWING, JULIANA HORATIA   The Peace Egg and a Christmas Mumming Play. (1887). 8vo., orig. pictorial boards, illus. Hammond 201-113 1974 £5

EWING, THOMAS   Memorial of. New York, 1873. Cloth, slight wear. Hayman 59-455 1974 $10

EX GESTIS Romanorum Hystorie Notabiles Collecte de Vicijs Virtutibusque Tractantes Cum Applicationbus. Germany?, 1507. Small 8vo., English 16th century calf, rebacked. Thomas 28-137 1972 £80

AN EXACT Collection of the Most Considerable Debates in the Honourable House of Commons. 1681. Small 8vo., contemporary calf. Quaritch 939-485 1974 £30

AN EXACT SURVEY of the Grand Affairs of France. London, 1686. 8vo., contemporary sheep, worn, first edition. Dawsons PM 251-140 1974 £85

AN EXAMEN of Witches. (London), 1929. 8vo., orig. cloth, faded, limited. Dawsons PM 252-1071 1974 £7.50

AN EXAMINATION and Explanation of the South-Sea Company's Scheme. London, 1720. 8vo., half calf, first edition. Ximenes 35-250 1974 $60

EXCURSION in Eastern Quebec and the Maritime Provinces. Ottawa, 1913. 2 parts, part 1 paper cover, part 2 cloth, illus., maps. Hood's 102-186 1974 $15

EXHIBIT of Condition, Resources, and Prospective Business, of the Fort Wayne and Southern Railroad. Indianapolis, 1854. Orig. wrappers, map. Bradley 35-192 1974 $50

EXHIBITION Illustrative of Early English Portraiture. 1909. Roy. 4to., plates, buckram. Quaritch 940-204 1974 £25

EXHIBITION of a Collection of Silversmiths'. London, 1901. Thick 4to., plates, orig. cloth, stained. Bow Windows 62-138 1974 £28

THE EXHIBITION of Art-Industry in Dublin. London, 1853. Large 4to., cloth boards, illus. Emerald 50-251 1974 £7.50

EXHIBITION Of Early English Earthenware. 1914. 4to., buckram, plates, frontispiece. Quaritch 940-630 1974 £50

EXPLANATION of the Proceedings of the Loyal and Patriotic Society of Upper Canada. Toronto, 1841. Cloth. Hood's 102-601 1974 $90

EXPLANATION of the Proceedings of the Loyal and Patriotic Society of Upper Canada. Toronto, 1841. Cloth. Hood's 104-683 1974 $90

AN EXTENSIVE Collection of the Publications of the Belfast Religious Tract Society. Belfast, c.1816. 8vo., uncut. Emerald 50-36 1974 £35

EXTRACTS From a Pilgrim's Log, or A Journal Through Canada and the United States. Demerara, 1881. Small 4to., orig. printed boards, cloth spine, nice copy, first edition. Ximenes 37-22 1974 $75

THE EXTRAORDINARY Black Book. London, 1831. 8vo., modern black calf, frontispiece, first edition. Dawsons PM 250-25 1974 £65

EYB, ALBRECHT VON   Margarita Poetica. (Venice), 1493. Folio, full blind-stamped red morocco. Harper 213-63 1973 $450

EYGES, THOMAS B.   Beyond the Horizon. 1844. Austin 62-157 1974 $12.50

EYN NEWE Badenfart. Strassburg, (c. 1537). Small 4to., half vellum, very fine copy, full page woodcuts, extremely rare. Schafer 10-120 1974 sFr 4,800

EYRE, EDWARD   European Civilization. 1935-39. 7 vols., thick 8vo., orig. buckram, faded, maps, very scarce. Howes 186-810 1974 £75

EYRE, HENRY   A Brief Account of the Holt Waters . . . to Which are added, Directions for Drinking the Holt Waters, and Some Experimental Observations on the Several Wells. London, 1731. 12mo., boards, frontis., folding plate. Gurney 66-56 1974 £20

EYRE, HENRY   A Brief Account of the Holt Waters. London, 17-31. 8vo., half calf, gilt, first edition. Hammond 201-568 1974 £22.50

EYSTER-BLESSING, NELLIE   A Chinese Quaker. 1902. 377 pages, illus. Austin 57-198 1974 $12.50

EYTON, R. W.   Antiquities of Shropshire. 1854-60. 12 vols. in 11, roy. 8vo., illus., buckram. Quaritch 939-532 1974 £130

EYTON, ROBERT W.   Domesday Studies. 1881. Crown 4to., orig. cloth, fine, with list of subscribers. Broadhurst 24-1415 1974 £6

EYTON, T. C.   A History of the Oyster. 1858. 8vo., cloth, scarce, plates. Wheldon 129-741 1974 £5

EYTON, T. C.   A History of the Rarer British Birds. 1836. 8vo., cloth, worn, woodcuts. Wheldon 131-590 1974 £15

EYTON, T. C.   A History of the Rarer British Birds. 1836. 8vo., cloth. Wheldon 129-458 1974 £15

EYTON, T. C.   A History of the Rarer British Birds. 1836. 8vo., cloth, woodcuts. Wheldon 128-433 1973 £15

EYTON, T. C.   A History of the Rarer British Birds. 1836. Roy. 8vo., contemporary cloth, woodcuts, large paper edition. Wheldon 128-434 1973 £20

EYTON, T. C.   A History of the Rarer British Birds. 1836. Large 8vo., contemporary half calf, worn, woodcuts. Wheldon 131-591 1974 £20

EYTON, T. C.   A History of the Rarer British Birds. 1836. Large 8vo., orig. cloth. Wheldon 129-459 1974 £20

EYTON, T. C.   A History of the Rarer British Birds. 1836. 8vo., orig. cloth, woodcuts. Wheldon 130-509 1974 £20

EYTON, T. C.   A History of the Rarer British Birds. London, 18-36. 8vo., orig. cloth, first edition. Hammond 201-644 1974 £28

F

FABER, REGINALD STANLEY   Bibliotheque de la Providence. London, 1890.
Folio, uncut, blue half morocco, orig. wrappers, limited. Dawsons PM 10-214
1974 £15

FABER, REGINALD STANLEY   Bibliotheque de la Providence. London, 1890.
Limited to 300 copies, demy 8vo., orig. wrappers. Forster 98-202 1974 £3

FABES, GILBERT   The Autobiography of a Book. 1926. First
edition, fine, presentation copy inscribed by author. Covent 51-282 1973 £5.25

FABES, GILBERT H.   Modern First Editions: Points and Values. First,
Second and Third Series. London, 1929-32. 3 vols., on handmade paper, demy
8vo., orig. buckram, vol. 3 spotted, complete sets of 3 vols, limited to 750
copies, scarce. Forster 98-203 1974 £15

A FABLE for Critics; or Better . . . A Glance at a Few of Our Literary Progenies
from the Tub of Diogenes. New York, 1848. Second edition, 12mo., top &
bottom of spine chipped, minor foxing, good. Current BW9-205 1974 $15

FABRE, J. H.   Fabre's Book of Insects. c., 1935. 4to., orig.
white cloth, plates. Wheldon 130-743 1974 £7.50

FABRE, J. H.   Souvenirs Entomologiques. Paris, 1920-24.
Roy 8vo., uniform cloth. Wheldon 129-637 1974 £40

FABRETTI, RAPHAEL   Bellum et Excidium Trojanum, ex Antiquitatum.
1699. 8vo., bent at corners, vellum, engravings. Eaton Music-583 1973 £35

FABRI, OTTAVIO   L'Uso del La Squadra Mobile. Venice, 1598.
4to., contemporary limp vellum, first edition. Dawsons PM 245-273 1974 £65

FABRI, OTTAVIO   L'Vso del la Sqvadra Mobile. 1615. Small
4to., old paper boards. Zeitlin 235-77 1974 $200

FABRICIUS, JOHANN ALBERT   Bibliographia Antiquaria. 1716. F'scap 4to.,
contemporary calf. Forster 98-205 1974 £25

FABRICIUS, JOHANN ALBERT   Bibliotheca Graeca, Sive Notita Scriptorum
Veterum Graecorum. Hamburgi, 1790-1809. 12 vols., 4to., contemporary calf,
fourth edition. Dawsons PM 10-216 1974 £150

FABRONI, ANGELO   Lettere Inedite di Uomini Illustri. 1773-75.
8vo., 2 vols., half calf, first edition. Dawsons PM 245-274 1974 £25

FACSIMILE Of the Black Letter Prayer Book. 1871. Folio, orig. cloth. Howes
185-989 1974 £10

FACSIMILES of National Manuscripts, from William the Conqueror to Queen
Anne. Southampton, 1865-68. 4 vols., roy. 4to., cloth, worn. Quaritch
939-182 1974 £60

FACTUMS, et Arrest Du Parlement de Paris, Contre des Bergers Sorciers. Paris,
1695. 12mo., half calf, rebacked, armorial bookplate. Schuman 37-272
1974 $110

FADEN, WILLIAM   Le Petit Neptune Francais. 1793. 4to., contemporary half calf, gilt, fine, first edition. Hammond 201-699 1974 £165

FAHEY, DERRIS   The Mystical Body of Christ in the Modern
World. 1938. Second edition. Austin 57-199 1974 $12.50

FAHEY, DERRIS   The Mystical Body of Christ in the Modern
World. 1938. Austin 62-158 1974 $12.50

FAHEY, DERRIS   The Rulers of Russia. 1939. Austin 62-159
1974 $10

FAHRINGER, J.   Opuscula Braconologica. Vienna, 1925-38.
8vo., wrappers. Wheldon 129-639 1974 £31

FAIRBAIRN, JAMES   Book of Crests of the Families of Great Britain
and Ireland. London, 1905. 2 vols., 4to., plates. Jacobs 24-145 1974 $85

FAIRBAIRN, JAMES   Fairbairn's Crests of the Families of Great
Britain and Ireland. 2 vols., plates, orig. edition. Austin 61-361 1974
$37.50

FAIRBAIRN, WILLIAM   An Experimental Inquiry into the Strength of
Wrought-Iron Plates. 1850. 4to., brown paper wrapper, illus. Dawsons PM
245-275 1974 £15

FAIRBAIRN, WILLIAM   Iron. Edinburgh, 1861. 8vo., orig. green
cloth, uncut, plates, first edition. Dawsons PM 245-276 1974 £35

FAIRBANKS, LORENZO SAYLES   Genealogy of the Fairbanks Family in
America, 1633-1897. Boston, 1897. 8vo., cloth, dampstained. Saddleback
14-782 1974 $75

FAIRBRIDGE, D.   Gardens of South Africa. 1924. 8vo., cloth,
coloured plates, scarce first edition. Wheldon 128-1460 1973 £5

FAIRCHILD, D.   Exploring for Plants, From Notes of the Allison
Vincent Armour Expeditions for the U. S. Dept. of Agriculture, 1925-27. New
York, 1930. Roy. 8vo., cloth, illus., extremely scarce orig. issue. Wheldon
131-1599 1974 £15

FAIRCHILD, D.   Garden Islands of the Great East. New York,
1943. 8vo., cloth, illus., extremely scarce orig. issue. Wheldon 131-1601
1974 £15

FAIRCHILD, D.   The World Was My Garden, Travels of a Plant
Explorer. New York, (1938), 1944. Roy. 8vo., cloth, illus., scarce. Wheldon
131-1600 1974 £10

FAIRCHILD, HENRY PRATT   Immigration. 1913. 455 pages. Austin 57-200
1974 $10

FAIRCHILD, HENRY PRATT   Immigration. Macmillan, 1925. Rev. ed.
Austin 62-160 1974 $10

FAIRCHILD, HENRY PRATT   The Melting Post Mistake. 1926. 266 pages.
Austin 57-201 1974 $12.50

FAIRCHILD, T.   The City Gardener. 1722. 8vo., modern
calf, frontispiece. Wheldon 129-1457 1974 £120

FAIRCHILD, T.   The City Gardener. 1722. 8vo., contemporary calf, rare. Wheldon 130-1392 1974 £120

FAIRFAX, H.   An Impartial Relation . . . Against St. Mary
Magdalen Colledge. 1688. 3 items in 1 vol., small 4to., cloth, morocco
back. Quaritch 939-516 1974 £60

FAIRFAX, THOMAS   A Declaration from His Excellence. London,
1647. 4to., modern half morocco, gilt, first edition. Dawsons PM 251-380
1974 £30

FAIRFIELD, EDMUND B.   Wickedness in High Places. Mansfield, 1874.
Sewed, second edition. Hayman 57-162 1974 $12.50

FAIRLESS, MICHAEL   The Roadmender. 1920. 4to., full limp vellum.
Broadhurst 23-720 1974 £65

FAIRLEY, JOHN   Lauriston Castle. 1925. Roy. 8vo., plates,
buckram, limited, signed. Howes 186-811 1974 £5.50

FAIRLEY, M.   Spirit of Canadian Democracy. Toronto,
1945. Hood's 103-406 1974 $12.50

FAIRMAN, CHARLES E.   Art and Artists. Washington, 1927. Cloth, fine,
plates. Hayman 57-163 1974 $10

FAIRPLAY, FRANCIS   The Canadas As They Now Are. Dublin,
1833. Marbled boards, leather spine. Hood's 104-633 1974 $225

FAIRYLAND Tales and A.B.C's. Sm. 4to., illus. Frohnsdorff 16-32 1974 $12.50

FAITS MEMORABLES des Empereurs de la Chine. Paris, n.d. 4to., contemporary polished calf, first edition. Dawsons PM 251-122 1974 £85

FALCONER, H.   Fauna Antiqua Sivalensis. 1845-49. Roy 8vo.,
orig. printed wrappers, plates. Wheldon 130-922 1974 £80

FALCONER, ROBERT   Idealism In Natural Character, Essays and
Addresses. London, 1920. Hood's 104-473 1974 $15

FALCONER, WILLIAM   An Account of the Efficacy of the Aqua Mephiti-
ca Alkalina. London, 1789. 8vo., boards, uncut, third edition. Dawsons PM
249-168 1974 £10

FALCONER, WILLIAM   An Essay on Bath Waters. London, 1770. 12-
mo., contemporary calf, gilt, first edition. Dawsons PM 249-167 1974 £38

FALCONER, WILLIAM   Poetical Works of. 1854. 236 pages. Austin
61-362 1974 $12.50

FALCONER, WILLIAM   The Shipwreck. London, 1811. 8vo., contemporary calf, gilt, plates. Hammond 201-306 1974 £8

FALDA, GIOVANNI BATTISTA   Li Giardini di Roma Disegnate da Giovanni
Battista Falda Nuovamento Dati alle Stampe con Direttione di Giov. Giacomo de
Sandrart. Nuremburg, (1695). Folio, plates, contemporary mottled calf, worn,
crisp copy. Quaritch 940-509 1974 £350

FALKENER, EDWARD   The Museum of Classical Antiquities. London,
1860. 2 vols. in 1, 8vo., illus., plates, foxing, orig. cloth. Bow Windows
62-316 1974 £6.50

FALKENSTEIN, KARL   Geschichte der Buchdruckerkunst. Leipzig,
1840. Plates, boards, cloth. Dawson's 424-149 1974 $85

FALKNER, WILLIAM   Two Treatises. 1684. Crown 4to., fine, full
contemporary morocco, gilt. Howes 185-1147 1974 £48

FALKNER, WILLIAM C.   The Fall of Fort Sumter. New York, (1867).
Butterfield 10-12 1974 $35

FALL, MARCUS   London Town. London, 1896. New ed.,
inner hinges split. Biblo & Tannen 213-668 1973 $7.50

FALLE, PHILLIP   An Account of the Island of Jersey. Jersey,
1837. 8vo., old calf, rebacked, illus. Quaritch 939-838 1974 £20

FALLE, PHILLIP   Caesarea. London, 1797. 4to., modern half
calf, plates, second edition. Dawsons PM 251-23 1974 £95

FALLETTI, GIROLAMO   De Bello Sicambrico Libri IIII. 1557. Small
4to., calf, rubbed. Thomas 30-108 1973 £25

FALLOPPIO, GABRIELE   Opuscula. 1566. 4to., vellum, first edition.
Gurney 64-85 1974 £200

FALQUI, ENRICO   Ragguaglio Sulla Prosa d'Arte con un'Appendice
Dannunziana. Florence, 1944. 8vo., wrappers, limited edition. Minters
37-184 1973 $16

A FAMILIAR Introduction to Botany. London, 1801. Orig. boards, green label,
rebacked with quarter morocco, color plates. Gregory 44-22 1974 $55

FAMILLE Nau. Paris, 1894. Roy. 8vo., full polished maroon calf, gilt.
Howes 186-1645 1974 £7.50

FAMOUS Fantastic Mysteries. 1941-1953. Biblo & Tannen 210-1025 1973 $175

FAMOUS Horses of the British Turf. 1924-33. 11 vols., 4to., orig. cloth,
gilt. Quaritch 939-115 1974 £30

FAMOUS Plays of Crime and Detection. Blakiston, 1946. 910p. Austin 51-175
1973 $8.50

FANATICISM and Treason. London, 1780. 8vo., disbound, dust-stained, first
edition. Dawsons PM 247-117 1974 £10

FANATICISM AND Treason. London, 1780. 8vo., modern boards, gilt, first
edition. Dawsons PM 251-503 1974 £10

FANNING, EDMUND   Voyages Round the World . . . With the Report
of the Commander of the First American Exploring Expedition. New York, 1833.
Lithographed plates, orig. boards, paper label, specially made slipcase and box.
fine. Butterfield 10-238 1974 $200

FARADAY, MICHAEL   Chemical Manipulation. London, 1827. 8vo.,
modern boards, illus., first edition. Dawsons PM 245-278 1974 £75

FARADAY, MICHAEL   Chemical Manipulation. Philadelphia, 1831.
8vo., orig. wrappers, rebound, first American edition. Dawsons PM 245-279
1974 £95

FARADAY, MICHAEL   Experimental Researches in Electricity.
London, 1839. 3 vols., 8vo., orig. green cloth, gilt, fine, first edition in
book form. Dawsons PM 250-26 1974 £110

FARADAY, MICHAEL   Faraday's Diary. London, 1932-36. 8 vols.,
8vo., plates, illus., cloth. Dawsons PM 11-271 1974 £52.50

FARADAY, MICHAEL   Lectures on the Various Forces of Matter. London, 1863. 8vo., orig. green cloth, gilt, illus. Dawsons PM 245-280 1974 £7

FARADAY, MICHAEL   On the Practical Prevention of Dry Rot in Timber.
London, 1836. 8vo., boards. Gurney 66-57 1974 £25

FARAL, EDMOND   Le Manuscrit 19152 du Fonds Francais de la
Bibliotheque Nationale. Paris, 1934. 4to., tan cloth. Kraus B8-62 1974 $45

FARALICQ, RENE   The French Police from Within. 1933. English
first edition. Covent 56-1682 1974 £6.30

FARBENS, JOSEPH WARREN   In the Tropics. New York, 1863. 12mo.,
orig. cloth, fine, first edition. Ximenes 33-1 1974 $27.50

FARGO, F. F.   Memorial of the City and County Hall Opening
Ceremonies, Buffalo, New York. Buffalo, 1876. 8vo., cloth. Saddleback
14-577 1974 $12.50

FARGUS, FREDERICK JOHN   Dark Days. Bristol, 1884. 8vo., vellum, first
edition, presentation copy, inscribed. Ximenes 36-56 1974 $50

FARIS, JOHN T.   Old Roads Out of Philadelphia. Philadelphia,
1917. Map, illus., first edition, 8vo., spine faded, binding little soiled, contents
fine. Current BW9-410 1974 $25

FARIS, JOHN T.   The Romance of Forgotten Towns. New York,
1924. First edition, illus. Wilson 63-17 1974 $14.50

FARIS, JOHN T.   The Romance of Old Philadelphia. Philadelphia,
1918. Frontis. in color, illus., first edition, 8vo., fine. Current BW9-411
1974 $25

FARIS, JOHN T.   The Romance of the Boundaries. New York &
London, 1926. First edition, profusely illus., orig. binding. Butterfield 10-121
1974 $12.50

FARIS, JOHN T.   Seeing Pennsylvania. Philadelphia, 1919.
Frontis. in color, doubletones, maps, first edition, 8vo., mint. Current BW9-
412 1974 $30

FARISH, THOMAS E.   History of Arizona. Phoenix, 1915. 2 vols.,
fine and near mint. Jenkins 61-131 1974 $75

FARJEON, ELEANOR   Dream-Songs for the Beloved. 1911. Cloth
backed boards. Covent 55-655 1974 £12.50

FARJEON, ELEANOR   Heroes and Heroines. New York, n.d. Small
4to., pict. boards, illus., 1st ed. Frohnsdorff 16-313 1974 $10

FARJEON, ELEANOR   Nursery Rhymes of London Town. London,
1916. 8vo., gilt-lettered cloth, illus., 1st ed. Frohnsdorff 16-314 1974 $20

FARJEON, ELEANOR   Pan-Worship. 1908. Boards, first edition.
Covent 55-657 1974 £12.50

FARJEON, ELEANOR   Panny chis. Shaftesbury, 1933. Boards, presentation copy, inscribed, English first edition. Covent 56-445 1974 £25

FARJEON, ELEANOR   Sonnets and Poems. Oxford, 1918. Dec.
wrappers, spine somewhat rubbed, very nice copy, scarce. Covent 51-2327
1973 £8.50

FARJEON, ELEANOR   Sonnets and Poems. Oxford, 1918. Dec.
wrappers, scarce, English first edition. Covent 56-446 1974 £10

FARJEON, ELEANOR   The Tale of Tom Tiddler. London, (1929).
8vo., cloth, pict. gilt, snag on spine, illus., first edition. Frohnsdorff 15-36
1974 $12.50

FARLEIGH, JOHN   Fifteen Craftsmen on Their Crafts. London,
1945. Frontis., plates, fine paper, demy 8vo., orig. cloth. Forster 98-224
1974 £3

FARLEIGH, JOHN   Graven Image. 1940. Pictorial boards, fine,
dust wrapper, scarce. Marsden 39-146 1974 £8

FARLEY, HARRIET   Fancy's Frolics. New York, 1880. First
edition, 8vo., full page illus., red cloth covers soiled, interior fine. Current
BW9-41 1974 $25

FARLEY, JOHN   The London Art of Cookery. London, 1785. 8vo.,
contemporary calf, plates, third edition. Hammond 201-162 1974 £50

FARLEY, JOHN   The London Art of Cookery. London, 1796. 8vo.,
half calf, gilt, plates, eighth edition. Hammond 201-163 1974 £60

FARLEY, JOHN   The London Art of Cookery. London, (c., 1805).
8vo., half calf, gilt, plates, tenth edition. Hammond 201-164 1974 £60

FARLOW, W. G.   Icones Farlowianae. Cambridge, 1929. Imperial 4to., buckram, plates. Wheldon 130-1274 1974 £35

FARMER, J. S.   Dictionary of Slang and Its Analogues Past and
Present. London, 1890-1904. 7 vols. in 3, 8vo., cloth. Dawsons PM
11-273 1974 £41.50

FARMER, MARGUERITE (POWER), COUNTESS OF BLESSINGTON
Please turn to
BLESSINGTON, MARGUERITE (POWER) FARMER GARDINER, COUNTESS OF

FARMER, MRS. P.   The Captives. Laporte, 1856. 8vo., orig.
cloth, scarce, paper label, first edition. Ximenes 33-2 1974 $55

FARMER, S.   On the Shores of Scugog. Port Perry, 1934.
Drawings, illus., revised, enlarged edition. Hood's 103-628 1974 $22.50

FARMER, S.   On the Shores of Scugog. Port Perry, 1934.
Illus., drawings, revised edition. Hood's 104-684 1974 $22.50

FARMER, T. D. J.   The Parish of St. John's Church, Ancaster.
Guelph, 1924. Hood's 102-287 1974 $25

THE FARMER Restored. London, 1739. 4to., uncut. Quaritch 939-116
1974 £12.50

THE FARMER'S Almanac, for 1829. Blairsville, (1828). Pict. wrappers, only
known copy? Hayman 59-8 1974 $30

THE FARMER'S Almanac, for . . . 1841. Cincinnati, (1840). Pict. wrappers,
presumably the only recorded copy. Hayman 59-17 1974 $27.50

FARNBOROUGH, CHARLES LONG   A Temperate Discussion of the Causes
Which Have Led to the Present High Price of Bread. London, 1880. 8vo.,
blue paper wrappers. Dawsons PM 247-118 1974 £15

FARNOL, JEFFERY   A Jade of Destiny. Boston, 1931. Dust wrapper,
presentation copy, inscribed, first U.S. edition. Covent 56-447 1974 £10.50

FARNOL, JEFFERY   Some War Impressions. n.d. Presentation copy,
inscribed, English first edition. Covent 56-448 1974 £15

FARQUHAR, GEORGE   The Beaux Stratagem. Bristol, 1929. One of
527 numbered copies, copper engravings, buckram backed boards, gilt top, fine,
first edition. Covent 51-670 1973 £7.50

FARQUHAR, GEORGE   The Constant Couple. London, 1704. 4to.,
modern boards, fourth edition. Dawsons PM 252-350 1974 £20

FARQUHAR, GEORGE   Dramatic Works. 1892. 2 vols., new buckram,
blind stamp. Allen 216-2011 1974 $25

FARQUHAR, GEORGE   The Complete Works of. London, 1930.
2 vols., cloth backed boards, corners worn, paper labels, one of 900 sets, fine.
MacManus 224-158 1974 $100

FARRELL, JAMES T.   The Road Between. Vanguard, 1949. 463p.
Austin 54-375 1973 $6.50

FARRELL, JAMES T.   No Star is Lost. World, 1938. 637p.
Austin 54-374 1973 $6

FARRELL, JAMES T.   My Days of Anger. World, 1947. 403p.
Austin 54-373 1973 $6

FARRELL, JAMES T.   My Baseball Diary. Barnes, 1957. 276p.
Austin 54-372 1973 $7.50

FARRELL, JAMES T.   Gas-House McGinty. World, 1942. 250p.
Austin 54-371 1973 $7.50

FARRELL, JAMES T.   Father and Son. Vanguard, 1940. 616p.
Austin 54-369 1973 $7.50

FARRELL, JAMES T.   Father and Son. World, 1947. 616p.
Austin 54-370 1973 $6

FARRELL, JAMES T.   Ellen Rogers. Sun Dial, 1942. 439p.
Austin 54-368 1973 $6

FARRELL, JAMES T.   Bernard Clare. New York, 1946. First edition.
Biblo & Tannen 210-723 1973 $7.50

FARRELL, JAMES T.   Bernard Clare. Vanguard, 1946. 367p.
Austin 54-366 1973 $6

FARRAR, GERALDINE   Such Sweet Compulsion. Greystone, 1938.
303p., illus. Austin 51-303 1973 $6

FARRAR, F. W.   The Life and Work of St. Paul. c.1880.
2 vols., thick 8vo., full prize vellum gilt. Howes 185-1150 1974 £5

FARRAR, F. W.   Eric, or, Little by Little. 1858. First edition,
with half title, large crown 8vo., new binder's cloth, rare. George's 610-275
1973 £20

FARR, SAMUEL   A Philosophical Enquiry Into the Nature, Origin
and Extent, of Animal Motion. London. 8vo., contemporary calf, worn, first
edition. Schuman 37-76 1974 $125

FARQUHAR, GEORGE   The Complete Works. 1930. 2 vols., 4to.,
orig. buckram backed boards, limited. Dawsons PM 252-351 1974 £60

FARRELL, JAMES T.   The Silence of History. Doubleday, 1963.
372p. Austin 54-376 1973 $6.50

FARRELL, JAMES T.   Studs Lonigan. New York, (1938). Inscribed,
d.j., orig. binding, clippings laid in. Butterfield 10-245 1974 $25

FARRELL, JAMES T.   To Whom It May Concern. Sun Dial, 1944.
204p. Austin 54-377 1973 $7.50

FARRELL, JAMES T.   World I Never Made. Vanguard, 1936. 508p.
Austin 54-378 1973 $7.50

FARRELL, JAMES T.   World I Never Made. World, 1936. 308p.
Austin 54-379 1973 $6

FARRELL, JAMES T.   Yet Other Waters. Vanguard, 1942. 414p.
Austin 54-380 1973 $7.50

FARRELL, JAMES T.   Collected Poems. Fleet, 1965. 82p. Austin
54-367 1973 $4

FARRELL, WALTER   A Companion To the Summa. New York,
1939-42. 4 vols., damp-stained. Howes 185-1716 1974 £12.50

FARRENC, EDMUND   Carlotina. 1853. 432 pages. Austin
57-203 1974 $12.50

FARRENC, EDMUND   Carlotina and the Sanfedesti. New York,
1853. 8vo., orig. blue cloth, first edition. Ximenes 33-5 1974 $17.50

FARRER, REGINALD JOHN   Alpines and Bog Plants. 1908. 8vo., orig.
cloth, uncut, plates. Wheldon 129-1459 1974 £10

FARRER, REGINALD JOHN   Alpines and Bog Plants. 1908. 8vo., orig.
cloth, plates. Wheldon 130-1394 1974 £7.50

FARRER, REGINALD JOHN   Among the Hills. (1911). 8vo., orig. cloth,
plates. Wheldon 129-1558 1974 £7.50

FARRER, REGINALD JOHN   The English Rock Garden. (1919). Roy. 8vo.,
2 vols., cloth, plates. Wheldon 130-1393 1974 £25

FARRER, REGINALD JOHN   In Old Ceylon. 1908. 8vo., orig. cloth, very
scarce. illus., first and only edition. Wheldon 128-198 1973 £7.50

FARRER, REGINALD JOHN   In a Yorkshire Garden. 1909. 8vo., orig.
cloth, illus. Wheldon 129-1460 1974 £6

FARRER, REGINALD JOHN   My Rock-Garden. 1907. 8vo., orig. cloth,
uncut, illus. Wheldon 129-1461 1974 £10

FARRER, REGINALD JOHN   My Rock Garden. 1907. 8vo., orig. cloth,
scarce, first edition. Wheldon 131-1513 1974 £12

FARRER, REGINALD JOHN   On the Eaves of the World. 1917. 8vo., orig.
blue cloth, 2 vols., illus., map. Wheldon 129-1555 1974 £28

FARRER, REGINALD JOHN   On the Eaves of the World. 1926. 8vo., orig.
blue cloth, 2 vols., illus., map. Wheldon 129-1556 1974 £25

FARRER, REGINALD JOHN   On the Eaves of the World. London, 1926.
2 vols., second impression, fine. Gregory 44-120 1974 $65

FARRER, REGINALD JOHN   The Rainbow Bridge. 1926. 8vo., orig. blue
cloth, illus. Wheldon 129-1557 1974 £10

FARRINGTON, B.   Samuel Butler and the Odyssey. 1929. English
first edition. Covent 56-1593 1974 £7.50

FARRINGTON, J.   Views of the Lakes. 1789. Oblong folio,
plates, half calf, foxed. Quaritch 939-118 1974 £95

FARRINGTON, S. KIP   Atlantic Game Fishing. New York, 1937.
4to., color plates, 1st ed., author's sgd. pres; intro. by Ernest Hemingway.
Biblo & Tannen 214-727 1974 $97.50

FARROW, G. E.   Zoo Babies. C., 1910. 4to., orig. green boards, illus., plates, inscribed. Hammond 201-114 1974 $8

THE FATAL Caress...and other Accounts of English Murders from 1551 to 1888.
New York, 1947. 1st ed. Biblo & Tannen 210-418 1973 $8.50

FATHER Clement. Newark, NJ, 1851. Austin 62-17 1974 $10

FAUJAS DE SAINT-FOND, B.   Recherches sur la Pouzzolane. Grenoble and
Paris, 1778. 8vo., stitched, uncut. Gurney 64-86 1974 £18

FAULDS, HENRY   Guide to Finger-Print Identification. 1905.
8vo., printed wrapper, plates. Hammond 201-182 1974 £5

FAULKNER, T.   An Historical and Topographical Account of
Fulham. 1813. 4to., half calf, illus. Quaritch 939-447 1974 £30

FAULKNER, T.   An Historical and Topographical Description
of Chelsea. 1829. 2 vols., 8vo., half calf, illus. Quaritch 939-448
1974 £35

FAULKNER, T.   The History and Antiquities of the Parish of
Hammersmith. 1839. 8vo., cloth, illus. Quaritch 939-449 1974 £25

FAULKNER, WILLIAM   Absalom, Absalom! New York, 1936. First
trade edition, good, d.j., orig. binding. Butterfield 10-249 1974 $45

FAULKNER, WILLIAM   As I Lay Dying. New York, 1930. First U.S.
edition, very fine, in very good d.w. Covent 51-3245 1973 £22.50

FAULKNER, WILLIAM   Doctor Martino and Other Stories. New York,
1934. Fine, first U. S. edition, defective d.w. Covent 51-671 1973 £35

FAULKNER, WILLIAM   Light in August. New York, 1932. 1st ed.
Biblo & Tannen 214-701 1974 $35

FAULKNER, WILLIAM   Light in August. (New York, 1932). Orig.
cloth, first edition, fine, dust jacket. MacManus 224-160 1974 $90

FAULKNER, WILLIAM   Light in August. New York, 1932. First
printing, first issue with "Jefferson" line 1 p. 340, tan cloth, heavy dec. paper
wrapper, mint copy, near pristine d.w., thus rare. Ross 87-178 1974 $125

FAULKNER, WILLIAM   Mosquitoes. New York, 1927. Orig. cloth,
first edition, fine, in somewhat worn & defective dust jacket. MacManus
224-161 1974 $80

FAULKNER, WILLIAM   Mosquitoes. New York, 1927. Blue cloth,
fine, well preserved d.w., heavy dec. paper wrapper, scarce in d.w. Ross
87-179 1974 $175

FAULKNER, WILLIAM   The Portable Faulkner. New York, 1946.
Biblo & Tannen 210-724 1973 $7.50

FAULKNER, WILLIAM   Pylon. New York, 1935. 1st printing. Jacobs
24-87 1974 $30

FAULKNER, WILLIAM   Pylon. New York, 1935. First U. S. edition,
nice copy, d.w. (lacking front) laid in. Covent 51-672 1973 £17.50

FAULKNER, WILLIAM   Pylon. New York, 1935. First printing, first
trade edition, blue cloth, fine, slightly chipped d.w., heavy dec. paper wrapper.
Ross 87-180 1974 $115

FAULKNER, WILLIAM   Sherwood Anderson and Other Famous Creoles.
New Orleans, 1926. 1st ed., sgd. by several of the subjects drawn, ltd. to 250
copies., board covers spotted; unique. Biblo & Tannen 213-539 1973 $275

FAULKNER, WILLIAM   Soldier's Pay. New York, 1926. Orig.
cloth, first edition, fine. MacManus 224-162 1974 $75

FAULKNER, WILLIAM   These Thirteen. New York, 1931. 1st ed.
Biblo & Tannen 210-725 1973 $40

FAULKNER, WILLIAM   These 13. New York, 1931. First trade
edition, blue & gray cloth, heavy dec. paper wrapper, tight, mint copy, d.w.
slightly darkened along spine. Ross 87-182 1974 $110

FAULKNER, WILLIAM   The Unvanquished. New York, 1938. 1st ed.,
illus. Jacobs 24-86 1974 $25

FAULKNER, WILLIAM   The Unvanquished. New York, 1938. Drawings,
first printing, first trade edition, gray cloth, heavy dec. paper wrapper, mint,
tight, near pristine d.w. Ross 87-183 1974 $75

FAULKNER, WILLIAM   Wild Palms. New York, 1939. First printing,
orig. binding, fine, dust wrapper. Ross 87-185 1974 $60

FAULKNER, WILLIAM   The Wild Palms. New York, 1939. First
printing, veavy dec. paper wrappers, orig. binding, mint copy, pristine d.w.,
thus rare. Ross 87-184 1974 $75

FAULL, J. H.   The Natural History of the Toronto Region.
Toronto, 1913. Maps. Hood's 103-356 1974 $20

FAUQUIER, FRANCIS   An Essay on Ways and Means for Raising
Money for the Support of the Present War. London, 1756. 8vo., modern boards,
first edition. Dawsons PM 247-119 1974 £20

FAURE, ELIE   Histoire de l'Art. 1924-27. 5 vols., 8vo.,
illus., half morocco, scarce. Quaritch 940-785 1974 £18

FAURE, ELIE   Soutine. Paris, 1929. 16mo., wrappers,
plates. Minters 37-131 1973 $12

FAUSSET, B.   Inventorum Sepulchrale. 1856. 4to., plates,
half morocco, woodcuts, plates. Quaritch 939-404 1974 £55

FAUST, ALBERT BERNHARDT   The German Element in the U. S. Houghton,
1909. Orig. ed. Austin 62-161 1974 $25

FAUST, ALBERT BERNHARDT   The German Element in the United States.
New York, 1927. 2 vols. in one, illus. Biblo & Tannen 213-34 1973 $17.50

FAUST, ALBERT BERNHARDT   The German Element in the U. S. 1927.
2 vols. in 1, illus., new edition. Austin 57-204 1974 $22.50

FAUSTO, SEBASTIANO   Delle Nozze, Trattato. Venice, 1554. Small
4to., modern boards, woodcut border, rare, first (sole?) edition. Schafer
8-110 1973 sFr. 700

FAUSTUS, VICTORIUS   Orationes Quinque. Venice, 1551. First
Aldine edition, 4to., 18th century marbled calf, fine copy with wide margins.
Thomas 32-209 1974 £40

FAUTEAUX, J. N.   Essai sur l'Industrie au Canada sous le Regime
Francais. Quebec, 1927. 2 vols. Hood's 102-375 1974 $40

FAUTEUX, AEGIDIUS   The Introduction of Printing Into Canada.
Montreal, 1929. Illus. card cover. Hood's 103-145 1974 $150

FAVA, D.   Modena-Reggio Emilia, Scandano. 1943. Vol.
1, limited to 1000 copies, illus., f'scap 4to., orig. wrappers, unopened. Forster
98-212 1974 £5

FAVORITE Fairy Tales. Philadelphia, 1930. Small 4to., gilt-lettered cloth,
20 color plates. Frohnsdorff 16-315 1974 $15

FAVARO, ANTONIO   Documenti Inediti. 1886. Tall 4to., orig. blue
printed wrappers, unopened, uncut. Zeitlin 235-92 1974 $27.50

FAVES, GILBERT H.   Modern First Editions: Points and Values.
Second Series. London, 1931. Limited to 1000 copies on hand made paper, demy
8vo., orig. buckram, d.w. torn, fine. Forster 98-204 1974 £3

FAWCETT, EDGAR   The Confessions of Cloud. Ticknor, 1887.
395p. Austin 54-381 1973 $10

FAWCETT, H. S.   Citrus Diseases and Their Control. New York,
1926. 8vo., cloth. Wheldon 129-1654 1974 £5

FAWCETT, H. S.   Citrus Diseases and Their Control. New York,
1936. 8vo., cloth, scarce, revised second edition. Wheldon 131-1777 1974
£10

FAWCETT, H. S.   Citrus Diseases and Their Control. New York,
1936. 8vo., cloth, scarce, second edition. Wheldon 129-1655 1974 £10

FAWCETT, J. M.   Notes on the Transformations of Some South-
African Lepidoptera. 1901-03. 2 parts in 1 vol., 4to., half morocco, coloured
plates. Wheldon 128-719 1973 £5

FAWCETT, WILLIAM   An Elucidation. 1798. 8vo., modern half blue
morocco, uncut, first edition. Dawsons PM 251-381 1974 £50

FAY, ELIZABETH   Original Letters from India. 1925. Faded,
English first edition. Covent 56-475 1974 £10

FAY, THEODORE SEDGWICK   Norman Leslie. New York, 1835. 2 vols.,
12mo., orig. blue cloth, first edition. Ximenes 33-6 1974 $75

FAYOD, V.   Prodrome d'une Histoire Naturelle des Agaricines.
Paris, 1889. Roy 8vo., half calf, plates. Wheldon 129-1200 1974 £12

FAYRER, J.   On the Poison of Venomous Snakes. 1909.
8vo., cloth. Wheldon 131-738 1974 £10

FEA, ALLAN   Some Beauties of the Seventeenth Century.
London, 1907. Spine worn, frontis. loose. Biblo & Tannen 213-670 1973 $10

FEARING, KENNETH   The Big Clock. New York, 1946. 1st ed.
Biblo & Tannen 213-518 1973 $7.50

FEARON, HENRY BRADSHAW   Sketches of America. London, 1818. Orig.
boards, rebacked with vellum, printed label, nice, slipcase and leather backed
box. Butterfield 10-250 1974 $50

FEASTS and Fasts of the Church of England. 1732. Contemporary calf, plates,
rubbed. Howes 185-1152 1974 £7.50

FEATHERSTONHAUGH, GEORGE WILLIAM   Geological Report of an
Examination Made in 1834. Washington, 1835. Orig. wrappers, fine, first edition.
Bradley 35-135 1974 $50

FEATHERSTONHAUGH, GEORGE WILLIAM   Geological Report of an
Examination Made in 1834, of the Elevated Country between the Missouri and
Red Rivers. Washington, 1835. Disbound, folding plate is not present.
Hayman 59-165 1974 $12.50

FEATHERSTONHAUGH, GEORGE WILLIAM   Geological Report an an
Examination Made in 1834 of the Elevated Country Between the Missouri and Red
Rivers. Washington, 1835. Cloth, foxed. Jenkins 61-873 1974 $35

FECHNER, GUSTAV THEODOR   Einige Ideen zur Schopfungs und
Entwickelungsgeschichte der Organismen. Leipzig, 1873. 8vo., half cloth,
first edition. Schuman 37-77 1974 $85

FECHNER, GUSTAV THEODOR   In Sachen der Psychophysik. Leipzig, 1877.
8vo., orig. cloth, first edition. Gurney 64-87 1974 £15

FECHNER, GUSTAV THEODOR   Massbestimmungen uber die Galvanische Kette.
Leipzig, 1831. 4to., contemporary pebbled cloth, first edition. Zeitlin 235-
80 1974 $250

FEDERAL WRITERS' PROJECT   The Idaho Encyclopedia. Caldwell, 1938.
4to., orig. binding. Butterfield 10-308 1974 $35

THE FEDERALIST. Philadelphia, 1826. New edition, rebound, fly leaves missing.
Biblo & Tannen 213-36 1973 $7.50

THE FEDERALIST. Morisania, 1864. 2 vols., limited to 250 copies, numbered,
recently new cloth. Wilson 63-31 1974 $35

THE FEDERALIST. New York, 1945. 2 vols., boards, leather, boxed. Bradley
35-224 1974 $50

FEDERN, R.   Repertoire Bibliographique de la Litterature
Francaise des Origines a nos Jours. Leipzig and Berlin, 1913. 2 vols. in 1, med.
8vo., half morocco. Forster 98-213 1974 £15

FEE, A. L. A.   Cryptogames Vasculaires. Paris, 1872-73.
4to., sewed, plates, scarce. Wheldon 130-1275 1974 £10

FEE, NORMAN   Catalogue of Pamphlets, Journals and Reports in
the Public Archives of Canada, 1611-1867, with Index. Ottawa, 1916. Second
edition. Hood's 102-19 1974 $35

FEIBLEMAN, JAMES K.   Aesthetics. New York, 1949. Biblo & Tannen
210-173 1973 $7.50

FEIFFER, JULES   Pictures At a Prosecution. Grove, 1971
Austin 54-382 1973 $10

FEIGERLE, I.   Historia Vitae Sanctorum Thomae a Villanova.
1839. New buckram. Allen 213-1458 1973 $12.50

FEINAIGLE, GREGOR VON   The New Art of Memory. London, 1813. 8vo.,
orig. boards, plates, second edition. Hammond 201-824 1974 £32

FEISTMANTEL, O.   Geological and Palaentological Relations of the
Coal and Plant-Bearing Beds of Palaeozoic and Mesozoic Age in Eastern Australia
and Tasmania. Sydney, 1890. 4to., orig. boards, plates, scarce. Wheldon
128-968 1973 £15

FELD, ROSE C.   Sophie Halenczik, American. Little, Brown,
1943. Austin 62-162 1974 $8.50

FELICIANO DA LAZESIO, FRANCESCO   Libro di Arithmetica and Geometria. 1563. 4to., contemporary limp vellum, illus. Dawsons PM 245-281 1974 £255

FELL, H. GRANVILLE   The Fairy Gifts and Tom Hickathrift. London, 1895. 16mo., gilt pictorial cloth with silk ties, top edge gilt, illus. Frohnsdorff 16-316 1974 $40

FELLOWES, ROBERT   The History of Ceylon. London, 1817. 4to., contemporary diced calf, rebacked, plates, map, foxing, portrait. Bow Windows 62-317 1974 £120

FELS, FLORENT   Chana Orloff. Paris, 1925. 4to., wrappers, uncut, plates. Minters 37-117 1973 $17.50

FELS, FLORENT   Edzard. Paris, 1929. 4to., wrappers, uncut, shaken, plates. Minters 37-90 1973 $24

FELT, JOSEPH B.   History of Ipswich, Essex, and Hamilton. Cambridge, 1834. 8vo., orig. bindings, fine, first edition. Butterfield 8-237 1974 $35

FELTHAM, OWEN   Resolves. London, 1634. 4to., recased, contemporary limp vellum. Dawsons PM 252-352 1974 £50

FELTON, S.   Gleanings on Gardens. 1897. 8vo., cloth, second edition. Wheldon 129-1462 1974 £7.50

FEMALE Friendship, or the Innocent Sufferer. Hallowell, 1797. 2 vols. in one, 12mo., contemporary sheep, scarce, first American edition. Ximenes 33-15 1974 $75

FEMALE LIFE Among the Mormons. New York, 1855. Orig. brown cloth, first edition. Dawson's 424-338 1974 $25

THE FEMALE Politician. London, n.d. 8vo., disbound, rare, first edition. Ximenes 33-16 1974 $250

LES FEMMES de Walter Scott. Bruxelles, 1842. Roy. 8vo., half contemporary roan gilt, plates, foxing. Smith 194-736 1974 £5

FENELON, FRANCOIS DE SALIGNAC DE LA MOTHE   The Adventures of Telemachus. 1776. 12mo., 2 vols., contemporary calf. Quaritch 936-217 1974 £15

FENELON, FRANCOIS DE SALIGNAC DE LA MOTHE   Les Aventures de Telemaque, fils d'Ulysse. Paris, 1790. Large 8vo., engraved portrait and plates, contemporary full brown polished calf, well preserved copy. Schumann 499-34 1974 sFr 750

FENELON, FRANCOIS DE SALIGNAC DE LA MOTHE   Extracts from the Writings of. 1805. 12mo., tree calf. Hill 126-101 1974 £10.50

FENELON, FRANCOIS DE SALIGNAC DE LA MOTHE   The Tales and Fables of the Late Archbishop and Duke of Cambray. London, 1736. 8vo., fine, rare, contemporary half calf, first edition. Ximenes 35-106 1974 $150

FENICHEL, OTTO   The Psychoanalytic Theory of Neurosis. New York, 1945. Biblo & Tannen 210-1026 1973 $15

FENNELL, J. H.   Drawing-Room Botany. London, 1840. Orig. cloth, plates in color, 8vo. Gregory 44-122 1974 $22.50

FENNER, C. W. H.   De Anatomia Comparata et Naturali Philosophia Commentatio Sistens Descriptionem et Significationem Cranii Encephali et Nervorum Encephali in Piscibus. Jena, 1820. 8vo., boards, plates. Wheldon 131-739 1974 £5

FENTON, R.   Historical Tour Through Pembrokeshire. 1811. 4to., plates, modern boards, foxing. Quaritch 939-682 1974 £35

FENTON, R.   Tour in Quest of Genealogy. 1811. 8vo., plates, modern boards. Quaritch 939-722 1974 £17.50

FENWICK, ELIZA   Infantine Stories. 1819. Copperplates, 12mo., orig. boards, roan spine, slightly rubbed, fifteenth edition. George's 610-285 1973 £6

FENWICK, ELIZA   Lessons for Children. 1813. Woodcuts, 4 parts in 1, 12mo., orig. boards, roan spine, slightly rubbed, new edition. George's 610-286 1973 £6

FENWICK, ELIZA   Rays from the Rainbow. 1812. 12mo., orig. ptd. boards, spine defective, second edition. George's 610-287 1973 £15

FENWICK, THOMAS FITZROY   A Catalogue of the Phillipps Manuscripts, Numbers 1388 to 2010. Cheltenham, 1886. 8vo., orig. printed wrappers. Kraus B8-208 1974 $85

FERBER, EDNA   Old Man Minick. Doubleday, Page, 1924. 271p. Austin 51-304 1973 $8.50

FERBER, EDNA   A Peculiar Treasure. New York, 1939. Orig. cloth backed boards, first edition, one of 351 copies, numbered & signed by author, boxed, very fine. MacManus 224-163 1974 $30

FERBER, EDNA   Saratoga Trunk. New York, 1941. 1st ed., ltd. to 545 copies, sgd. Biblo & Tannen 210-726 1973 $20

FERE, CHARLES   The Pathology of Emotions. London, 1899. 8vo., cloth, rubbed, illus., first edition in English. Schuman 37-78 1974 $75

FERET, C. J.   Fulham Old and New. 1900. 3 vols., 4to., illus., cloth. Quaritch 939-450 1974 £15

FERGUSON, ADAM   Essay on the History of Civil Society. London, 1773. Both covers detached but present, contemporary calf, rubbed, worn, lacks front and rear blanks and half of a single leaf, revised and corrected fourth edition. Wilson 63-597B 1974 $10

FERGUSON, ADAM   The History of the Proceedings In the Case of Margaret. (London), 1761. 8vo., later calf, gilt, second edition. Ximenes 33-7 1974 $75

FERGUSON, ADAM   Institutes of Moral Philosophy. Edinburgh, 1769. 12mo., contemporary calf, first edition. Ximenes 37-76 1974 $125

FERGUSON, CHARLES D.   The Experiences of a Forty-Niner. Cleveland, 1888. Cloth, rubbed, fine. Hayman 57-167 1974 $25

FERGUSON, E. S.   Bibliotheca Chemica. Glasgow, 1906. 2 vols., handmade paper, crown 4to., orig. buckram, soiled. Forster 98-217 1974 £24

FERGUSON, E. S.   Transactions of the Glasgow Archaeological Society, Vol. 2. Glasgow, 1883. Plates, illus., post 8vo., half morocco, spine gilt. Forster 98-219 1974 £4

FERGUSON, HENRY LEE   The English Springer Spaniel in America. New York, The Derrydale Press, 1932. Illus., limited to 850 copies, brown & gilt cover, fine, scarce. Current BW9-164 1974 $100

FERGUSON, J. C.   Outlines of Chinese Art. Chicago, 1920. 8vo., illus., cloth. Quaritch 940-390 1974 £16

FERGUSON, J. C.   Survey of Chinese Art. Shanghai, 1939. 4to., orig. cloth, illus. Bow Windows 64-504 1974 £40

FERGUSON, JAMES   Astronomy Explained Upon Sir Isaac Newton's Principles. London, 1772. 8vo., contemporary calf, leather label, plates, fifth edition. Traylen 79-223 1973 £18

FERGUSON, JAMES   An Introduction to Electricity. London, 1778. 8vo., contemporary calf, gilt, plates, third edition. Hammond 201-825 1974 £22

FERGUSON, JAMES   Lectures on Select Subjects. 1760. 8vo., contemporary calf, plates, fine, first edition. Hill 126-102 1974 £75

FERGUSON, JAMES   Select Mechanical Exercises. London, 1773. 8vo., contemporary calf, leather label, plates, good copy, first edition. Traylen 79-224 1973 £25

FERGUSON, RICHARD   The Fiery-Flying Serpent Slander. Winchester, 1814. 12mo., contemporary sheep, first edition. Ximenes 33-8 1974 $17.50

FERGUSON, RICHARD   The Fiery-Flying Serpent Slander. Winchester, 1814. 8vo., orig. bindings, first edition. Butterfield 8-684 1974 $35

FERGUSON, ROBERT   A Just and Modest Vindication of the Scots Design. (Edinburgh), 1699. 8vo., contemporary panelled calf, first edition. Dawsons PM 247-120 1974 £185

FERGUSON, ROBERT   The Social Pipe. London, 1826. 12mo., half dark green morocco, gilt, spine gilt, nice copy, first edition. Ximenes 37-77 1974 $40

FERGUSON, SAMUEL   The Cromlech on Howth. London, 1861. Folio, embossed cloth, gilt. Emerald 50-291 1974 £25

FERGUSSON, ERNA   Dancing Gods. New York, 1931. 1st ed., illus. Dykes 24-182 1974 $12.50

FERGUSSON, JAMES   Observations on the Present State of the Art of Navigation. London, 1787. 8vo., orig. marbled wrappers, first edition. Hammond 201-700 1974 £28.50

FERISHTAH, MAHOMET 1550-1611   Ferishta's History of Dekkan from the First Mahummedan Conquests. Shrewsbury, 1794. 2 vols., 4to., contemporary polished tree calf, leather label. Traylen 79-520 1973 £60

FERLET, E.   Eloge de l'Imprimerie. Nancy, 1771. Small 8vo., half leather. Kraus B8-322 1974 $28.50

FERMIN, PHILIPPE   Description Generale, Historique, Geographique et Physique de la Colonie de Surinam. Amsterdam, 1769. 2 vols., 8vo., worn, contemporary mottled calf, first edition. Ximenes 33-9 1974 $150

FERNALD, JAMES C.   Connectives of English Speech. 1904. Illus. Austin 61-364 1974 $17.50

FERNANDEZ, DIEGO   Primera y Segunda Parte de la Historia del Peru. Seville, 1571. Rare first edition, woodcuts, 2 vols. in 1, folio, 18th century vellum, small hole in sig. S9, very fine large copy, rare. Sawyer 293-16 1974 £575

FERNANDEZ, JUSTINO   Joes Clemente Orozco. Mexico, 1942. Large 4to., cloth, plates, limited, first edition. Minters 37-25 1973 $20

FERNEL, JEAN FRANCOIS   Monalosphaerium, Partibus Constans Quatuor. 1526. Small folio, calf antique, first edition. Dawsons PM 245-283 1974 £625

FERNEL, JEAN FRANCOIS   De Morbis Universalibus et Particularibus. Leyden, 1644. 3 works in 1 vol., old calf. Schuman 37-79 1974 $165

FERNIE, W. T.   Animal Simples Approved for Modern Uses of Cure. Bristol, 1899. 8vo., cloth, scarce. Wheldon 129-333 1974 £5

FERRAND, JACQUES PHILIPPE   L'Art du Feu ou de Peindre en Email. 1721. 12mo., contemporary calf, gilt. Quaritch 940-95 1974 £52

FERRARIS, LUCIO   Bibliotheca Canonica Juridica Moralis Theologia. Rome, 1885-92-99. 9 vols., thick imp. 8vo., half calf, rubbed, best edition. Howes 185-1153 1974 £35

FERRARIUS, PHILLIPUS   Novum Lexicon Geographicum. 1677. Folio, contemporary vellum, first edition. Dawsons PM 251-146 1974 £25

FERRARO, GIOVANNI BATTISTA   Cavallo Frenato. Venice, 1620. 2 parts in 1 vol., woodcuts, folio, contemporary limp vellum, fine. Harper 213-65 1973 $650

FERRERO, G.   Greatness & Decline of Rome. 1908. 5 vols. Allen 213-386 1973 $25

FERRERO, LEO   Leonard de Vinci ou l'Oeuvre d'Art. Paris, 1929. 12mo., orig. wrapper, uncut, limited, first edition. L. Goldschmidt 42-401 1974 $15

FERREY, B.   Antiquities of the Priory of Christ-Church. 1834. 4to., plates, orig. boards. Quaritch 939-372 1974 £10

FERRIAR, JOHN   Illustrations of Sterne. London, 1798. 8vo., old tree calf, first edition. Gurney 64-210 1974 £30

FERRIER, A. D.   Reminiscences of Canada and the Early Days of Fergus, Being Three Lectures Delivered to the Farmers' and Mechanics' Institute. Fergus, 1923. Card cover, second edition. Hood's 102-602 1974 $60

FERRIER, DAVID   The Croonian Lecture on Cerebral Localisation. London, 1890. 8vo., orig. cloth, illus., first edition, few library stamps, some notes in pencil. Gurney 66-58 1974 £50

FERRIER, SUSAN EDMONSTONE   Destiny. Edinburgh, 1831. 3 vols., 8vo., orig. boards, paper labels, first edition. Dawsons PM 252-353 1974 £55

FERRIER, SUSAN EDMONSTONE   The Inheritance. Edinburgh & London, 1824. 3 vols., small 8vo., contemporary half calf, first edition. Howes 186-186 1974 £18

FERRIER, SUSAN EDMONSTONE   The Inheritance. London, 1824. 3 vols., 8vo., contemporary half calf, first edition. Dawsons PM 252-354 1974 £60

FERRIER, SUSAN EDMONSTONE   Marriage. Edinburgh, 1818. 3 vols., 12mo., contemporary half calf, first edition. Dawsons PM 252-355 1974 £50

FERRIER, SUSAN EDMONSTONE   Marriage. Edinburgh, 1819. 3 vols., crown 8vo., contemporary half crimson morocco gilt, second edition. Howes 185-167 1974 £15

FERRISS, EDWIN   The Plain Restitutionist. 1827. 8vo., orig. bindings. Butterfield 8-530 1974 $15

FERRY, GABRIEL   Vagabond Life in Mexico. 1856. Crown 8vo., contemporary half morocco, first edition. Broadhurst 23-1637 1974 £14

FERTE-SENECTERE, F. DE LA   Monographie des Anthicus et Genres Voisins. Paris, 1848. 8vo., plates. Wheldon 128-720 1973 £5

FESSENDEN, THOMAS GREEN   Democracy Unveiled. New York, 1806. 2 vols., 12mo., modern half calf, foxed, third edition. Ximenes 33-10 1974 $60

FESSENDEN, THOMAS GREEN   Terrible Tractoration! New York, 1804. 12mo., contemporary calf, worn first American edition. Ximenes 33-11 1974 $25

FESTSKRIFT Til Den Norske Synodes Jubilaeum. 1903. 456 pages, illus. Austin 57-477 1974 $27.50

FETHERSTONHAUGH, R. C.   The Royal Canadian Mounted Police. New York, 1938. Maps, illus. Hood's 103-104 1974 $17.50

FEUCHTWANGER, LION   Two Anglo Saxon Plays. 1927. 241p. Austin 51-305 1973 $8.50

FEULNER, ADOLF   Bayerisches Rokoko. Munich, 1923. Roy. 4to., plates, cloth. Quaritch 940-786 1974 £50

FEULNER, ADOLF   O. O. Kurtz und E. Herbert. Berlin, Vienna, Leipzig, 1927. 4to., boards, cloth spine, plates. Minters 37-550 1973 $30

FEVRE, JUSTIN L. P.   Histoire Apologetique de la Papaute Depuis St. Pierre Jusqu'a Pie X. Paris, 1878-82. 7 vols., thick 8vo., half calf. Howes 185-1154 1974 £18

FEWKES, J. W.   Certain Antiquities of Eastern Mexico. Washington, 1907. 4to., orig. cloth, plates, covers marked. Bow Windows 66-229 1974 £6

FEYDEAU, GEORGES   Monsieur Chasse! Paris, 1896. Square 12mo., contemporary three quarter orange hard grain morocco, gilt, uncut, excellent copy, first edition. L. Goldschmidt 42-220 1974 $45

FEYERABEND, SIEGMUND   Theatrum Diabolorum. Frankfurt, 1587. 2 vols., folio, contemporary vellum, from the Prince of Liechtenstein library. Schumann 499-35 1974 sFr 1,500

FFOULKE, CHARLES M.   The Ffoulke Collection of Tapestries. 1913. Folio, full dark blue morocco gilt, cloth slip case, plates, limited. Quaritch 940-754 1974 £75

FFOULKES, CHARLES JOHN   Armour and Weapons. Oxford, 1909. Illus.,
fine, scarce. Covent 55-440 1974 £6.50

FFOULKES, CHARLES JOHN   The Armourer and His Craft. 1912. Roy. 4to.,
plates, cloth, scarce, orig. edition. Quaritch 940-695 1974 £60

FFOULKES, CHARLES JOHN   The Gun-Founders of England. 1937. 4to.,
illus., plates, orig. & best edition. Howes 186-1670 1974 £12.50

FFOULKES, CHARLES JOHN   Inventory and Survey of the Armouries of the
Tower of London. 1916. 2 vols., 4to., cloth. Quaritch 939-451 1974 £45

FFRANGCON-DAVIES, MARJORIE   David Ffrangcon-Davies: His Life and
Book. London, 1938. Illus., spine torn. Biblo & Tannen 214-842 1974 $8.50

FICHTE, JOHANN GOTTLIEB   Grundlage des Naturrechts nach Principien der
Wissen-Schaftslehre. Jena & Leipzig, 1796. 2 parts in 1 vol., 8vo., first
edition, contemporary boards. Schumann 499-37 1974 sFr 570

FICHTE, JOHANN GOTTLIEB   Das System der Sittenlehre Nach den Principien
der Wissen-Schaftslehre. Jena & Leipzig, 1798. 8vo., contemporary boards,
first edition. Schumann 499-36 1974 sFr 820

FICHTE, JOHANN GOTTLIEB   Die Staatslehre Oder Uber das Verhaltniss des
Urstaates zum Vernunftreiche. Berlin, 1820. 8vo., contemporary boards,
fine, unopened, first edition. Gilhofer 61-34 1974 sFr. 600

FIDANZA, GIOVANNI
Please turn to
BONAVENTURA, SAINT

FIEDLER, WILHELM   Analytische Geometrie der Kegelschnitte. Leipzig, 1887. 8vo., contemporary half calf. Dawsons PM 245-285 1974 £8

FIELD, AL. G.   Watch Yourself Go By. Columbus, Ohio,
1912. 1st ed., illus. Biblo & Tannen 213-875 1973 $15

FIELD, B.   An Analysis of Blackstone's Commentaries on the
Laws of England. 1811. 8vo., first edition. Quaritch 939-49 1974 £15

FIELD, BARRON   Geographical Memoirs On New South Wales.
London, 1825. 8vo., plates, half brown morocco. Traylen 79-549 1973 £110

FIELD, DAVID D.   Centennial Address . . . With Historical
Sketches of Cromwell. Middletown, 1853. 12mo., orig. cloth, scarce, first
edition. Ximenes 33-27 1974 $35

FIELD, EUGENE   Echoes From the Sabine Farm. Scribner, 1895.
14lp. Austin 54-384 1973 $7.50

FIELD, EUGENE   A Little Book of Nonsense. Mutual, 1901
28p. Austin 54-383 1973 $10

FIELD, EUGENE   A Little Book of Profitable Tales. Chicago,
1889. Orig. half cloth, first edition, one of 250 numbered copies, very good
copy, in half morocco slipcase, presentation copy inscribed by author. MacManus
224-164 1974 $60

FIELD, EUGENE   Little Willie. San Francisco, 1921. 4to., orig.
boards, paper label, one of 200 copies, fine. MacManus 224-165 1974 $25

FIELD, EUGENE   The Love Affairs of a Bibliomaniac. New
York, 1896. Orig. half parchment boards, first edition, one of 150 numbered
copies, very fine clean copy, quarter morocco slipcase. MacManus 224-166
1974 $85

FIELD, EUGENE   Lullaby Land. Scribner, 1894. 229p., illus.
Austin 54-385 1973 $7.50

FIELD, EUGENE   The Model Primer. Brooklyn, (1882). 12mo.,
orig. wrappers, quarter morocco slipcase. MacManus 224-167 1974 $75

FIELD, EUGENE   My Book. 1919. 2 letters laid in, full blue
morocco, gilt, very near mint. Ross 86-150 1974 $100

FIELD, EUGENE   My Book. 2 letters laid in, full blue morocco,
gilt, very near mint. Ross 86-151 1974 $100

FIELD, EUGENE   Penn-Yann Bill's Wooing. 1914. Backstrip
missing, text loose in covers, first edition. Covent 51-682 1973 £6

FIELD, EUGENE   Second Book of Tales. New York, 1896.
12mo., 1st ed. Biblo & Tannen 214-703 1974 $10

FIELD, EUGENE   Sharps and Flats. New York, 1900. 2 vols.,
first edition, inscription, orig. binding. Butterfield 10-251 1974 $15

FIELD, EUGENE   The Tribune Primer. Boston, 1900. 16mo.,
orig. grey wrappers, page edges curled. Current BW9-224 1974 $18.50

FIELD, EUGENE   With Trumpet and Drum. New York, 1892.
Orig. half parchment, first edition, one of 250 numbered copies, signed by
publishers, about fine. MacManus 224-168 1974 $40

FIELD, EUGENE   Wynken, Blynken and Nod. New York, n.d.
Illus. Frohnsdorff 16-318 1974 $9.50

FIELD, GEORGE   Chromatography. n.d. Frontispiece, illus.,
new improved edition. Marsden 39-152 1974 £8

FIELD, GEORGE   Chromatography. 1841. 8vo., orig. cloth,
frayed, scarce, improved new edition. Quaritch 940-96 1974 £18

FIELD, GEORGE   A Grammar of Colouring Applied to
Decorative Painting and the Arts. 1877. Small 8vo., plates, woodcuts, cloth.
Quaritch 940-97 1974 £12

FIELD, H.   Memoirs of the Botanic Garden. 1878. 8vo.,
cloth, plate, scarce, second edition. Wheldon 130-160 1974 £10

FIELD, H.   Memoirs of the Botanic Garden at Chelsea
Belonging to the Society of Apothecaries of London. 1878. 8vo., cloth, plans,
plate, scarce, revised enlarged second edition. Wheldon 128-100 1973 £10

FIELD, MICHAEL   The Tragic Mary. 1890. Small 4to., orig.
cloth, first edition. Rota 189-305 1974 £8

FIELD, RACHEL   All Through the Night. New York, 1940.
24mo., pict. boards, illus., 1st ed. Frohnsdorff 16-319 1974 $5

FIELD, RACHEL   An Alphabet for Boys and Girls. New York,
1926. 16mo., cloth, 1st ed., illus. Frohnsdorff 16-320 1974 $20

FIELD, RACHEL   Calico Bush. New York, 1931. 8vo., cloth,
wood engravings. Frohnsdorff 16-321 1974 $10

FIELD, RACHEL   Eliza and the Elves. New York, 1926. 8vo.,
gilt-lettered cloth, color plates, 1st ed., sgd. and dated by author along with a
small orig. ink sketch. Frohnsdorff 16-322 1974 $25

FIELD, RACHEL   Hepatica Hawks. New York, 1932. 8vo.,
cloth, 1st ed., wood engravings. Frohnsdorff 16-323 1974 $10

FIELD, RACHEL   Hitty, Her First Hundred Years. New York,
1929. 8vo., dec. cloth, illus., fine copy, orig. dust jacket, third printing.
Frohnsdorff 15-43 1974 $10

FIELD, RACHEL   A Little Book of Days. New York, 1927. 16mo.
cloth, 1st ed., illus. Frohnsdorff 16-324 1974 $20

FIELD, RACHEL   Little Dog Toby. New York, 1928. 12mo.,
cloth, 4 color plates, 1st ed. Frohnsdorff 16-325 1974 $20

FIELD, RACHEL   Patchwork Plays. New York, 1930. 8vo.,
cloth, 1st ed., illus. Frohnsdorff 16-326 1974 $8.50

FIELD, RACHEL   Polly Patchwork. New York, 1928. 16mo.,
cloth, little worn, illus in color by author, first edition. Frohnsdorff 15-46
1974 $10

FIELD, RACHEL   Polly Patchwork. New York, 1928. 16mo.,
cloth, 1st ed., illus. Frohnsdorff 16-327 1974 $20

FIELD, RACHEL   Time Out of Mind. New York, 1935. 1st ed., inscribed to critic Franklin P. Adams. Jacobs 24-88 1974 $37.50

FIELD, RACHEL   The Yellow Shop. New York, 1934. 16mo., cloth, 1st ed., illus. Frohnsdorff 16-328 1974 $20

FIELD, RICHARD   Of the Church, Five Bookes. Oxford, 1635. Folio, contemporary calf, third edition. Howes 185-1155 1974 £36

FIELD, ROSWELL   The Bondage of Ballinger. Revell, 1903. 214p. Austin 54-386 1973 $10

FIELD, SAMUEL   The Miscellaneous Productions in Poetry and Prose, of the Late . . . Greenfield, 1818. 12mo., contemporary calf, bit rubbed but sound, first edition, good copy. Ximenes 36-92 1974 $60

FIELDING, HENRY   The Adventures of Joseph Andrews. 1929. Roy. 8vo., frontispiece, first edition. Covent 55-662 1974 £5.25

FIELDING, HENRY   Amelia. London, 1752. 4 vols., 12mo., modern polished calf, first edition. Dawsons PM 252-356 1974 £140

FIELDING, HENRY   Amelia. 1884. 8vo., half calf, frontispiece. Bow Windows 64-506 1974 £8

FIELDING, HENRY   Avventure di Gioseffo Andrews Fratello di Pamela. 1752-3. 12mo., 2 vols., orig. paper boards, fine, uncut, frontispiece, plates. Hill 126-103 1974 £42

FIELDING, HENRY   Collection of First Editions of the Major Works. 1742-55. 8vo., small 8vo., 16 vols., crimson morocco, gilt. Quaritch 936-72 1974 £850

FIELDING, HENRY   An Enquiry into the Causes of the Late Increase of Robbers. London, 1751. 8vo., modern sprinkled calf, fine, first edition. Dawsons PM 247-121 1974 £135

FIELDING, HENRY   An Enquiry into the Causes of the Late Increase of Robbers. London, 1751. 8vo., modern sprinkled calf, fine, first edition. Dawsons PM 252-357 1974 £135

FIELDING, HENRY   The History and Adventures of Joseph Andrews. London, 1929. 1st ed., 3/4 lea., rubbed. Biblo & Tannen 210-727 1973 $27.50

FIELDING, HENRY   The History of the Adventures of Joseph Andrews and His Friend Mr. Abraham Adams. 1929. Roy. 8vo., illus., plates, dust wrapper, fine. Howes 186-188 1974 £5

FIELDING, HENRY   The History of Tom Jones. London, 1749. 6 vols., 12mo., contemporary calf gilt, fine, first edition. Dawsons PM 252-358 1974 £360

FIELDING, HENRY   The History of Tom Jones. 1782. 4 vols., contemporary calf, frontispieces. Smith 194-150 1974 £8

FIELDING, HENRY   The History of Tom Jones, a Foundling. 1930. Thick roy. 8vo., plates, illus., dust wrapper, fine. Howes 186-189 1974 £5.50

FIELDING, HENRY   The Journal of a Voyage to Lisbon. London, 17-55. Small 8vo., contemporary calf, gilt, first edition. Hammond 201-307 1974 £100

FIELDING, HENRY   A Journey From This World to the Next. 1930. Ballinger 1-136 1974 $27.50

FIELDING, HENRY   The Miser. London, 1761. 8vo., wrappers, fourth edition. Ximenes 33-28 1974 $25

FIELDING, HENRY   Pasquin. 1736. 8vo., modern half calf, first edition. Quaritch 936-73 1974 £40

FIELDING, HENRY   The Tragedy of Tragedies. 1731. 8vo., modern cloth, frontispiece, first complete edition. Quaritch 936-74 1974 £50

FIELDING, HENRY   Works. n.d. 8vo., 12 vols., fine, English first edition. Covent 56-451 1974 £22.50

FIELDING, HENRY   Works. 1859. Thick 8vo., plates, calf, rebacked. Howes 185-168 1974 £6.50

FIELDING, HENRY   The Works of. 1806. 10 vols., contemporary diced calf, several joints breaking, portrait, some foxing, new edition. Bow Windows 66-231 1974 £60

FIELDING, HENRY   Works. 1902-03. 11 vols., half calf, labels, portrait, rebacked. Howes 186-187 1974 £40

FIELDING, HENRY   The Works Of. 1903. 12 vols., orig. buckram, frontispieces. Smith 193-282 1973 £25

FIELDING, HOWARD   Col. Evans from Kentucky and Other Humorous Sketches. New York, 1889. Pictorial wrapper. Butterfield 10-20 1974 $35

FIELDING, SARAH   Familiar Letters Between Principal Characters in David Simple. London, 1747. 2 vols., 8vo., contemporary calf gilt, fine, first edition. Dawsons PM 252-360 1974 £250

FIELDING, THEODORE HENRY ADOLPHUS   Cumberland, Westmorland and Lancashire. 1822. Folio, plates, contemporary half straight grained morocco. Quaritch 939-118 1974 £500

FIELDING, THEODORE HENRY ADOLPHUS   A Picturesque Tour of the English Lakes. 1821. Roy. 4to., plates, fine, contemporary red straight grained morocco gilt. Quaritch 939-119 1974 £550

FIELDING, THEODORE HENRY ADOLPHUS   A Picturesque Tour of the English Lakes. London, 1821. Roy. 4to., full blue morocco, raised bands, gilt, large paper copy. Traylen 79-342 1973 £350

FIELDING, THEODORE HENRY ADOLPHUS   Synopsis of Practical Perspective, Lineal and Aerial. 1836. 8vo., plates, orig. cloth, rebacked, scarce, enlarged second edition. Quaritch 940-98 1974 £25

FIELDS, ANNIE   Asphodel. Boston, 1866. 8vo., orig. brick cloth, first edition. Ximenes 33-29 1974 $12.50

FIELDS, ANNIE   Authors and Friends. Houghton, 1896. 355p., orig. ed. Austin 54-387 1973 $6

FIELDS, ANNIE   Nathaniel Hawthorne. Small, Maynard, 1899. 136p. Austin 54-388 1973 $8.50

FIELDS, JAMES T.   Yesterdays with Authors. Houghton, 1871. 419p., orig. ed. Austin 54-389 1973 $5.50

FIELDS, JAMES T. (Mrs.)   Whittier. Harper, 1893. 103p. Austin 54-390 1973 $7.50

FIELDS, JOSEPH   Wonderful Town. Random, 1953. 173p. Austin 51-306 1973 $8.50

FIERENS, PAUL   Filippo de Pisis. Paris & Milan, 1937. 4to., wrapper, plates. Minters 37-430 1973 $18

FIFE, AUSTIN & ALTA   Saints of Sage and Saddle. Indiana Univ., 1956. 367p. Austin 54-391 1973 $10

FIFTH Annual Review of the Commerce, Manufactures, and the Public and Private Improvemtns of Chicago, for the Year 1856. Chicago, 1857. Printed wrapper, illus. ads, fine copy. Butterfield 10-142 1974 $45

FIFTY Queries Concerning the Present Oxfordshire Contest. Oxford, 1754. 8vo., dust soiled. Quaritch 939-517 1974 £7.50

FIFTY Reasons Why the Catholic Religion Ought To Be Preferred To All Others. Cincinnati, n.d., ca. 1850. Austin 62-18 1974 $12.50

FIFTY Years of Ghost Stories. London, ca. 1935. Spine torn. Biblo & Tannen 210-548 1973 $8.50

FIGUIER, LOUIS   L'Homme Primitif. Paris, 1870. 8vo., some foxing, contemporary quarter sheep, rubbed. Bow Windows 66-232 1974 £6.50

FIGUIER, LOUIS   Vies des Savants Illustres . . . Jean Gutenberg,
Fust et Schoeffer. Paris, 1867. Small 8vo., orig. printed wrappers. Kraus
B8-323 1974 $35

FIGURES OF BIRDS, Quadrupeds, and Vignettes. Newcastle, 1891. Vellum,
boards, woodcuts, leather back. Dawson's 424-11 1974 $100

FILIAL Duty, Recommended and Enforced, By a Variety of Instructive and
Entertaining Stories. (1798). 12mo., orig. boards, soiled & badly defective,
lacks frontispiece. George's 610-289 1973 £5

FILLEBROWN, THOMAS   A Text-Book of Operative Dentistry.
Philadelphia, 1889. Illus. Rittenhouse 46-254 1974 $10

FILLION, L. C.   Histoire d'Israel. Paris, 1927-28. 2 vols.,
large 8vo., illus. Howes 185-1156 1974 £6

FILLION, L. C.   The Life of Christ. St. Louis & London, 1931-
29. 3 vols., thick large 8vo., stamp. Howes 185-1157 1974 £12

FILLMORE, MILLARD   Message from the President of the United States
Inviting the Attention of Congress to the Condition of Things in the Territory of
Oregon. Washington, 1852. Jenkins 61-2064 1974 $11.50

FILLMORE, MILLARD   Message from the President to the Two Houses of
Congress, Dec. 2, 1850, With the Accompanying Documents. Washington, 1850.
Parts 1 and 2 complete, plates, charts, marbled boards, leather back, tight copy.
Butterfield 10-528 1974 $65

FILLMORE, MILLARD   Message from the President . . . Dec. 6, 1852.
Washington, 1852. Part 1, fine large folded maps, binding sound. Butterfield
10-332 1974 $17.50

FILLMORE, MILLARD   Message of the President in Reference to
Conditions in Utah. Washington, 1852. Jenkins 61-2468 1974 $10

FILON, AUGUSTIN   The English Stage. Dodd, Mead, 1897.
319p., orig. ed. Austin 51-308 1973 $10

FINAN, P.   Journal Of a Voyage to Quebec in the Year
1825. Newry, 1828. Leather. Hood's 103-534 1974 $400

FINCH, DANIEL   Observations Upon the State of the Nation.
London, 1713. 8vo., modern boards, second edition. Dawsons PM 247-122
1974 £10

FINCH, GEORGE ENGLE   The Making of a Mountaineer. (1924). 8vo.,
orig. cloth, photo illus., slight foxing, plates. Bow Windows 66-233 1974
£6.75

FINCH, ROBERT   Plays of the American West. Greenberg, 1947.
247p. Austin 51-309 1973 $10

FINCHAM, HENRY W.   Artists and Engravers of British and American Book
Plates. 1897. Folio, plates, spine slightly frayed. Allen 216-163 1974 $25

FINCHAM, HENRY W.   Artists and Engravers of British and American
Book Plates. London, 1897. 4to., orig. cloth, first edition. Dawsons PM
10-220 1974 £16.50

FINCK, WILLIAM J.   Lutheran Landmarks and Pioneers in America.
1917. Austin 62-167 1974 $12.50

FINDEN, E.   The Ports, Harbours, and Watering-Places and
Coast Scenery of Great Britain. 1842. 2 vols., 4to., plates, half morocco gilt.
Quaritch 939-120 1974 £130

FINDLATER, RICHARD   Banned. Macgibbon & Kee, 1967. 238p.
Austin 51-310 1973 $10

FINDLAY, WILLIAM   Robert Burns and the Medical Profession. 1898.
Square 4to., half morocco, portraits, first edition. Rittenhouse 46-256 1974
$60

FINDLEY, PALMER   Priests of Lucina. Boston, 1939. Library
stamp. Rittenhouse 46-255 1974 $12.50

FINE, ORONCE   Protomathesis. 1532. Folio, contemporary
mottled calf, woodcuts, gilt. Zeitlin 235-81 1974 $1,850

FINEBERG, SOLOMAN ANDHIL   Overcoming Anti-Semitism. Harper, 1943.
Austin 62-168 1974 $10

FINGER, CHARLES J.   The Affair at the Inn. Westport, 1931.
Wrappers, paper title label, faded, text fine, scarce. Dykes 22-124 1973 $15

FINEMAN, IRVING   Hear, Ye Sons. Longmans, 1933. Austin
62-169 1974 $10

FINEMAN, IRVING   Woman of Valor. Simon and Schuster, 1961.
448p., illus. Austin 62-170 1974 $8.50

FINESSE. London, 1835. 2 vols., 8vo., green calf half, gilt, morocco gilt
labels, first edition. Dawsons PM 252-361 1974 £48

FINET, JOHN   Finetti Philoxenis. London, 1656. 8vo., contemporary sheep, rebacked, first edition. Dawsons PM 251-221 1974 £100

FINGER, CHARLES J.   An Affair at the Inn. 1937. Signed.
Ballinger 1-140 1974 $10

FINGER, CHARLES J.   The Affair at the Inn. Chicago, 1938. Cloth,
paper label, illus. in color, fine, inscribed by author. Dykes 22-126 1973
$12.50

FINGER, CHARLES J.   The Affair at the Inn. Chicago, 1938. Illus.,
limited ed. of 210 copies, inscribed by author. Dykes 24-61 1974 $15

FINGER, CHARLES J.   Highwaymen. n.d. Illus., fine, English first
edition. Covent 56-271 1974 £6.50

FINK, B.   The Lichen Flora of the United States. Ann
Arbor, 1935. 8vo., cloth, plates. Wheldon 129-1394 1974 £7.50

FINK, B.   The Lichen Flora of the United States. Ann
Arbor, 1935. 8vo., cloth, plates, scarce. Wheldon 131-1399 1974 £10

FINK, LEO GREGORY   Monsignor Heinen. 1937. 75 pages.
Austin 57-210 1974 $12.50

FINKELSTEIN, LOUIS   The Jews. Philadelphia, 1949. Author's sgd.
pres. Biblo & Tannen 214-790 1974 $10

FINLAY, IAN HAMILTON   Art in Scotland. London, 1948. Illus. Biblo
& Tannen 214-243 1974 $15

FINLAY, IAN HAMILTON   Glasgow Beasts, an an Burd. Edinburgh, n.d.
Presentation copy, inscribed from author, fine, wrappers. Covent 51-684 1973
£6.30

FINN, F.   Birds of Our Country. (1923). 4to., cloth
2 vols., illus., plates. Wheldon 129-462 1974 £7.50

FINN, F.   Indian Sporting Birds. 1915. Roy. 8vo.,
buckram, coloured plates, scarce. Wheldon 128-437 1973 £10

FINN, F.   The Wild Beasts of the World. 1909. 4to.,
2 vols., orig. dec. cloth. Wheldon 130-392 1974 £7.50

FINNEY, CHARLES G.   Circus of Dr. Lao. Abramson (1935) 1945.
154p., illus. Austin 54-392 1973 $8.50

FIRBANK, ARTHUR ANNESLEY RONALD   Odette. 1916. Orig. pictorial
wrappers, worn, English first edition. Covent 56-453 1974 $15

FIRBANK, ARTHUR ANNESLEY RONALD   Odette d'Antrevernes and a Study in
Temperament. London, 1905. Very nice partly unopened copy, orig. wrappers,
scarce first issue in pink wrappers. Covent 51-686 1973 £55

FIRBANK, ARTHUR ANNESLEY RONALD   Sorrow in Sunlight. c. 1925. One
of 1000 numbered copies, nice copy, worn d.w., first edition. Covent 51-687
1973 £15

FIRMIN, GILES   Separation Examined. London, 1652. Small
4to., boards, first edition. Ximenes 33-30 1974 $125

FIRMIN DIDOT, AMBROISE   Essai Typographique et Bibliographique sur l'Histoire de la Gravure sur Bois . . . Pour Faire Suite aux Costumes Anciens et Modernes de Cesar Vecellio. Paris, 1863. 8vo., orig. printed wrappers, fine wood engraved title page border. Kraus B8-325 1974 $37.50

FIRMIN DIDOT, AMBROISE   Les Estienne. Paris, (1856). 8vo., wrappers, inscribed. Kraus B8-324 1974 $25

FIRST Annual Report of the Board of Directors of the Pittsburgh, Ft. Wayne & Chicago Railway Company. Pittsburgh, 1863. 8vo., modern quarter red morocco, fine. Ximenes 35-6 1974 $20

FIRST Annual Report of the Chief Enginner of the Pennsylvania Railroad Company. Philadelphia, 1848. 8vo., orig. wrappers, first edition. Ximenes 35-7 1974 $17.50

FIRST Book of Arithmetic. Toronto, 1857. Spine mended, slight staining. Hood's 102-408 1974 $25

FIRST Book of Arithmetic. Toronto, 1857. Staining, mended spine, revised. Hood's 104-393 1974 $25

FIRST Circular of the State University of Iowa. N.P., 1855. 8vo., disbound, rare. Ximenes 33-322 1974 $50

FIRST EDITION CLUB   A Bibliographical Catalogue of the First Loan Exhibition of Books and Manuscripts. London, 1922. Limited to 500 copies, demy 8vo., orig. boards, buckram back, soiled & string marked, text fine, signed. Forster 98-225 1974 £5

FIRTH, RAYMOND   Art and Life in New Guinea. London, 1936. Sm. 4to., plates. Biblo & Tannen 214-247 1974 $17.50

FISCH, MAX   Nicolaus Pol, Doctor, 1494. New York, 1947. Illus. Jacobs 24-153 1974 $15

FISCHEL, O.   Die Mode, Menschen und Moden im Neunzehnten Jahrhundert. Munich, 1925. 4 vols., 8vo., plates, illus., cloth. Quaritch 940-711 1974 £16

FISCHER, EDWARD 1861-   Biologie der Pflanzenbewohnenden. Jena, 1929. Roy. 8vo., buckram. Wheldon 129-1202 1974 £5

FISCHER, FRANZ   Die Umwandlung der Kohle in Oele. Berlin, 1924. 8vo., orig. printed cloth, illus., first edition. Gilhofer 61-91 1974 sFr. 350

FISCHER, FRIEDRICH ERNST LUDWIG VON 1782-1854   Specimen de Vegetabilium. Halle, 1804. 8vo., boards, rare. Wheldon 130-1277 1974 £10

FISCHER, M.   New Mexico Territorial Bureau of Immigration. Socorro, 1881. 12mo., wrapper. Saddleback 14-559 1974 $75

FISCHER, MARTIN   Christian R. Holmes, Man and Physician. Springfield, 1937. Rittenhouse 46-257 1974 $10

FISCHER, P.   Manuel de Conchyliologie. Paris, (1880-)1887. Roy 8vo., half morocco, plates. Wheldon 130-824 1974 £45

FISHER, A. HUGH   Frolics With Uncle Yule. Boston, 1928. 4to., pict. boards, cloth spine, lst ed., illus. Frohnsdorff 16-329 1974 $10

FISHER, CHARLES   The Columnists. Howell, Soskin, 1944. 317p. Austin 54-393 1973 $7.50

FISHER, CLARENCE S.   The Excavation of Armageddon. Chicago, 1929. Biblo & Tannen 210-998 1973 $15

FISHER, GEORGE   The Instructor. London, 1755. 12mo., contemporary calf, scuffed, thirteenth edition revised, engraved frontis., illus. Ximenes 36-93 1974 $30

FISHER, H. D.   The Gun and the Gospel. Kansas City, (1902). 8vo., orig. bindings. Butterfield 8-175 1974 $15

FISHER, H. H.   America and the New Poland. Macmillan, 1928. Austin 62-171 1974 $15

FISHER, H. H.   America and the New Poland. 1928. 403 pages. Austin 57-211 1974 $15

FISHER, VARDIS   April. New York, 1937. Orig. morocco, first edition, one of 50 numbered copies, signed by author, fine, extremities rubbed. MacManus 224-169 1974 $50

FISHER, VARDIS   Children of God. New York, 1939. Orig. cloth, fine, first edition. Rota 188-300 1974 £5

FISHER, VARDIS   Children of God. Caldwell, 1939. Morocco, numbered, signed by author, fine, slip case, very scarce, first edition. Dykes 22-111 1973 $50

FISHER, VARDIS   City of Illusion. New York, 1941. Orig. cloth, fine, first edition. Rota 188-301 1974 £5

FISHER, VARDIS   Darkness and the Deep. Caldwell & New York, 1943. Dec. morocco, numbered, signed by author, fine, slip case, first edition. Dykes 22-112 1974 $40

FISHER, VARDIS   In Tragic Life. Caldwell, 1932. Morocco, gilt top, little worn, slip case, numbered, signed by author, fine, first edition. Dykes 22-108 1973 $50

FISHER, VARDIS   No Villain Need Be. New York, 1936. Orig. morocco, top of spine chipped, first edition, one of 75 numbered copies, signed by author, fine. MacManus 224-170 1974 $40

FISHER, VARDIS   Passions Spin the Plot. Caldwell, 1934. Morocco, numbered, fine, slip case, Ingle Barr's copy with his bookplate and inscribed to him by author, first edition. Dykes 22-109 1973 $37.50

FISHER, VARDIS   We Are Betrayed. New York, (1935). Orig. morocco, first edition, one of only 75 numbered copies, signed by author, fine. MacManus 224-171 1974 $40

FISHER, VARDIS   We Are Betrayed. Caldwell & Garden City, (1935). Morocco, numbered, Ingle Barr's copy with his bookplate and inscribed by author, fine, slip case, first edition. Dykes 22-110 1973 $40

THE FISHER-BOY of Weymouth, to which is added, The Pet Donkey and The Sisters. 1819. Engraved frontis., some light foxing, orig. boards, 12mo., later spine, edges uncut, rare. George's 610-294 1973 £10

FISHWICK, HENRY   A History of Lancashire. 1894. First edition, demy 8vo., orig. cloth, fine. Broadhurst 24-1417 1974 £5

FISHWICK, HENRY   The History of the Parish of Preston. 1900. 4to., morocco spine. Broadhurst 23-1377 1974 £15

FISHWICK, HENRY   The History of the Parish of Preston in the Amounderness of the County of Lancashire. Rochdale, 1900. Demy 4to., illus., morocco spine, fine. Broadhurst 24-1418 1974 £15

FISK, EARL E.   Lovely Laughter. 1932. 137 pages. Austin 61-367 1974 $12.50

FISK, EARL E.   Persuasions to Joy. 1927. 104 pages, illus. Austin 61-368 1974 $10

FISK, MAY ISABEL   Monologues. Harper, 1903. 190p. Austin 51-311 1973 $6.50

FISKE, JOHN   The American Revolution. Boston & New York. 2 vols., fine. Ballinger 1-258 1974 $10

FISKE, JOHN   The Beginnings of New England. Boston, 1889. Biblo & Tannen 213-66 1973 $6

FISKE, JOHN   The Beginnings of New England or the Puritan Theocracy in Its Relations to Civil and Religious Liberty. Boston, 1898. 8vo., illus., fold out maps, neatly rebound in red buckram, black leather spine label. Current BW9-364 1974 $35

FISKE, JOHN   The Dutch and Quaker Colonies in America. 1902. Illus. Austin 57-212 1974 $10

FISKE, JOHN   Essays, Historical and Literary. 1902. 2 vols. in 1. Allen 216-598 1974 $10

FISKE, JOHN   Essays Historical and Literary. New York, 1922. 2 vols. in 1. Biblo & Tannen 213-35 1973 $10

FISKE, JOHN   Life Everlasting. Boston & New York, 1901. 12mo., boards, paper label, wrappers, fine, limited edition. Ballinger 1-16 1974 $15

FISKE, JOHN   The Mississippi Valley In the Civil War. Boston & New York. Fine. Ballinger 1-263 1974 $10

FISKE, JOHN   The Mississippi Valley in the Civil War. Boston, 1900. Fine, first edition. Jenkins 61-882 1974 $17.50

FISKE, JOHN   Old Virginia and Her Neighbors. Boston, 1897. 2 vols. Biblo & Tannen 213-97 1973 $10

FISKE, JOHN   Old Virginia and Her Neighbours. Boston & New York. 2 vols., fine. Ballinger 1-265 1974 $10

FISKE, JOHN   Unpublished Orations. Boston, 1909. 8vo., orig. quarter vellum, boards, first edition. Ximenes 33-31 1974 $10

FISKE, STEPHEN   Off Hand Portrait of Prominent New Yorkers. Lockwood, 1884. 247p. Austin 51-312 1973 $15

FITCH, CLYDE   Beau Brummel. Lane, 1908. 142p., illus. Austin 51-313 1973 $10

FITCH, CLYDE   Plays by Clyde Fitch. Little, Brown, 1919. 636p. Austin 51-314 1973 $17.50

FITTON, E.   Conversations on Botany. 1817. Post 8vo., orig. boards, plates, first edition. Wheldon 130-1016 1974 £10

FITTON, E.   Conversations on Botany. 1818. Post 8vo., modern cloth, uncut, engraved plates, scarce, second edition. Wheldon 128-1109 1973 £5

FITTON, E.   Conversations on Botany. London, 1823. Small 8vo., contemporary half calf, gilt, illus., plates, fourth edition. Hammond 201-645 1974 £16

FITTON, W. H.   An Account of Some Geological Specimens from the Coasts of Australia. 1826. 8vo., cloth, plates, rare. Wheldon 130-924 1974 £35

FITTON, W. H.   An Account of Some Geological Specimens from the Coasts of Australia. 1826. 8vo., orig. boards, plates, folding map, very rare. Wheldon 128-969 1973 £40

FITZGERALD, E. A.   The Highest Andes. 1899. 8vo., cloth, maps, illus. Wheldon 129-267 1974 £7.50

FITZGERALD, EDWARD   Agamemnon. London, 1876. Small 4to., orig. quarter roan, slightly rubbed, first published edition. Ximenes 37-80 1974 $30

FITZGERALD, EDWARD   Letters and Literary Remains. 1889. 3 vols., frontispieces. Covent 55-666 1974 £6.30

FITZGERALD, EDWARD   Letters and Literary Remains. 1902-03. One of 775 sets, frontispieces, 7 vols., russet silken cloth gilt, some joints weak, attractive set. Covent 51-2331 1973 £35

FITZGERALD, EDWARD   Letters to Bernard Quaritch. 1926. Plates, buckram, rebound, library label. Covent 55-667 1974 £20

FITZGERALD, EDWARD   Rubaiyat of Omar Khayyam. n.d. Orig. designed buckram, dust wrapper, plates, fine. Smith 194-741 1974 £5.50

FITZGERALD, EDWARD   The Ruba'iyat of Omar Khayyam. 1872. Small 4to., quarter roan, gilt, rubbed, third edition. Covent 55-670 1974 £17.50

FITZGERALD, EDWARD   Ruba'iyat of Omar Khayyam. 1879. Quarter roan, frontispiece, rubbed, fourth edition. Covent 55-669 1974 £15

FITZGERALD, EDWARD   Ruba'iyat of Omar Khayyam. 1890. Dust soiled, parchment vellum, new edition. Covent 55-671 1974 £7.50

FITZGERALD, EDWARD   The Ruba'iyat of Omar Khayyam. 1901. Handmade paper, numbered, bookplate. Covent 55-672 1974 £35

FITZGERALD, EDWARD   The Rubaiyat of Omar Khayyam. London, 1903. Full tan calf, blind stamped, 2 5/8 X 1 5/8 inches. Gregory 44-376 1974 $8.50

FITZGERALD, EDWARD   The Rubaiyat of Omar Khayyam. New York, 1909. Illus., nice copy, orig. binding. Ross 86-31 1974 $17.50

FITZGERALD, EDWARD   The Rubaiyat of Omar Khyayam. 1916. 12mo., orig. dec. boards, plates, English first edition. Covent 56-679 1974 £10.50

FITZGERALD, EDWARD   Salaman and Absal. London, 1856. 8vo., orig. blue cloth, very good copy, first edition. Ximenes 37-81 1974 $35

FITZGERALD, EDWARD   Six Dramas of Calderon. London, 1853. 8vo., orig. rose cloth, first edition, scarce. Ximenes 37-82 1974 $40

FITZGERALD, FRANCIS SCOTT KEY   All the Sad Young Men. New York, 1926. First printing, orig. binding. Butterfield 10-256 1974 $12.50

FITZGERALD, FRANCIS SCOTT KEY   Babylon Revisited. 1932. Presentation copy, inscribed, English first edition. Covent 56-455 1974 £7.50

FITZGERALD, FRANCIS SCOTT KEY   The Beautiful and Damned. New York, 1922. First printing, orig. binding. Butterfield 10-257 1974 $15

FITZGERALD, FRANCIS SCOTT KEY   The Beautiful and Damned. New York, 1922. Orig. cloth, rubbed, hinges shaky, first edition, good copy. MacManus 224-172 1974 $25

FITZGERALD, FRANCIS SCOTT KEY   The Beautiful and Damned. New York, 1922. First U. S. edition, front hinge slightly cracked, very good copy. Covent 51-690 1973 £15

FITZGERALD, FRANCIS SCOTT KEY   Flappers and Philosophers. New York, 1920. First edition, second printing. Ballinger 1-132 1974 $15

FITZGERALD, FRANCIS SCOTT KEY   Flappers and Philosophers. New York, 1920. First edition, orig. binding. Butterfield 10-258 1974 $20

FITZGERALD, FRANCES SCOTT KEY   The Great Gatsby. New York, 1925. First printing, orig. binding. Butterfield 10-259 1974 $35

FITZGERALD, FRANCIS SCOTT KEY   Tales of the Jazz Age. New York, 1922. First edition, orig. binding. Butterfield 10-260 1974 $17.50

FITZGERALD, FRANCIS SCOTT   Tales of the Jazz Age. New York, 1922. Orig. cloth, inscription, bookplate, first edition. Rota 188-303 1974 £12

FITZGERALD, FRANCIS SCOTT KEY   Tales of the Jazz Age. New York, 1922. First edition, with "Published Sept., 1922" and Scribner's seal on copyright page, dark green cloth, lacking d.w., partially unopened, fine tight copy. Ross 87-204 1974 $65

FITZGERALD, FRANCIS SCOTT KEY   Tender Is the Night. New York, 1934. First edition, second printing. Ballinger 1-133 1974 $15

FITZGERALD, FRANCIS SCOTT KEY   Tender is the Night. New York, 1934. First edition, first issue, with the "A" and the Scribner seal on verso of title page, lacking d.w., orig. binding, some dust staining, nice, Richard Hofstadter's copy with his signature on fly leaf. Ross 87-205 1974 $110

FITZGERALD, FRANCIS SCOTT KEY   Tender is the Night. New York, 1934. First edition, first issue, with "A" and the Scribner seal on verso of title page, lacking d.w., nice copy, Richard Hofstadter's copy with his signature. Ross 86-154 1974 $125

FITZGERALD, FRANCIS SCOTT KEY   The Vegetable, or From President to Postman. New York, 1923. Hinge cracked, lacks fron free endpaper, orig. binding. Butterfield 10-261 1974 $7.50

FITZGERALD, PERCY   The History of Pickwick. 1891. Orig. dec. cloth, illus., gilt, bookplate, English first edition. Covent 56-1723 1974 £12.50

FITZGERALD, PERCY   Life and Adventures of Alexander Dumas. 1873. 2 vols., orig. dec. cloth, spine of vol. 1 torn at head, very good, largely unopened copy, first edition. Covent 51-605 1973 £6.50

FITZGERALD, PERCY   London City Suburbs. 1893. 4to., orig. cloth, English first edition. Covent 56-1261 1974 £7.50

FITZGERALD, PERCY   An Output. London, n.d. Small 4to., cloth boards, illus. Emerald 50-299 1974 £5.25

FITZGERALD, R. D.   Australian Orchids. Sydney, 1875-77. Vol. 1, parts 1 - 3, full morocco & orig. printed wrappers, plates, rare. Wheldon 131-1620 1974 £70

FITZGIBBON, MARY AGNES   A Veteran of 1812, the Life of John Fitzgibbon. Toronto, 1898. Second edition. Hood's 102-241 1974 $25

FITZGIBBON, MARY AGNES   A Veteran of 1812, the Life of James Fitzgibbon. Toronto, 1898. Second edition. Hood's 104-255 1974 $25

FITZHARYS'S Last Sham Detected. London, 1681. Small folio, first edition. Ximenes 33-32 1974 $30

FITZPATRICK, H. M.   The Lower Fungi: Phycomycetes. New York, 1930. 8vo., cloth, illus. Wheldon 131-1400 1974 £6.50

FITZPATRICK, J. P.   The Transvaal from Within: A Private Record of Public Affairs. 1899. Demy 8vo., first trade edition enlarged, orig. cloth, fine. Broadhurst 24-1608 1974 £10

FITZPATRICK, J. P.   The Transvaal from Within. 1899. 8vo., orig. cloth. Broadhurst 23-1638 1974 £12

FITZPATRICK, W. J.   Correspondence of Daniel O'Connell. London, 1888. 2 vols., 8vo., cloth boards. Emerald 50-302 1974 £7.50

FITZPATRICK, W. J.   Life of Charles Lever. 1879. 2 vols., new buckram. Allen 216-872 1974 $15

FITZPATRICK, W. J.   Secret Service Under Pitt. London, 1892. 8vo., cloth boards, enlarged second edition. Emerald 50-303 1974 £7.50

FITZSIMONS, F. W.   The Monkey Folk of South Africa. 1911. 8vo., cloth, plates, frontispiece. Wheldon 129-374 1974 £5

FIVE Bad Chunkies. Springfield, 1929. 4to., 8 color plates. Frohnsdorff 16-212 1974 $15

FIVE Centuries of Sport. New York, 1945. Large 8vo., orig. printed wrappers, illus. Dawsons PM 10-577 1974 £5

THE FIVE Little Pigs. New York, n.d. 12mo., spine restitched, 6 color plates on linen. Frohnsdorff 16-330 1974 $10

FLACOURT, ETIENNE DE   Petit Catechisme Avec les Prieres du Matin et du Soir. Paris, 1657. Small 8vo., frontispiece portrait, contemporary vellum, binding repaired, library stamp on title. Kraus B8-407 1974 $250

FLAGG, J. F. B.   Ether and Chloroform. Philadelphia, 1851. Sound, foxing. Rittenhouse 46-259 1974 $45

FLAGG, J. F. B.   Ether and Chloroform. Philadelphia, 1851. Rittenhouse 46-710 1974 $65

FLAGG, WILSON   The Woods and By-Ways of New England. Boston, 1872. 8vo., orig. bindings, illus. Butterfield 8-343 1974 $20

FLAHAULT, C.   Nouvelle Flore Coloriee de Poche des Alpes et des Pyrenees. Paris, 1906-12. 3 vols., 8vo., cloth, coloured plates, very scarce. Wheldon 128-1257 1973 £15

FLAHERTY, ROBERT   The Captains Chair. 1938. Presentation copy, inscribed, English first edition. Covent 56-456 1974 £5.25

FLAMANK, JAMES   A Treatise on Happiness. 1832. 12mo., 2 vols., full green calf, gilt. Hill 126-104 1974 £18.50

FLAMINIUS, M. ANTONIUS   In Librum Psalmorum Brevis Explanatio. Venice, 1564. 18th century vellum, blank portions of title mended, clean and sound. Thomas 32-210 1974 £21

FLATMAN, THOMAS   On the Death of Our Late Sovereign Lord King Charles II. London, 1685. Folio, disbound, first edition. Ximenes 33-33 1974 $125

FLATT, W. D.   The Making of a Man. Toronto, 1918. Illus. Hood's 102-511 1974 $12.50

FLAUBERT, GUSTAVE   Bouvard and Pecuchet. London, 1896. 8vo., illus., orig. cloth, fine, first English edition. Dawsons PM 252-362 1974 £23

FLAUBERT, GUSTAVE   Correspondance. Paris, 1926-33. 9 vols., 8vo., orig. wrapper. L. Goldschmidt 42-221 1974 $90

FLAUBERT, GUSTAVE   L'Education Sentimentale. Paris, 1870. 2 vols., 8vo., orig. wrapper, uncut, first edition. L. Goldschmidt 42-223 1974 $375

FLAUBERT, GUSTAVE   Herodias. 1901. One of 226 copies, frontis., 12mo., linen backed boards, very nice copy, booklabel of Roger Senhouse & signed by him in pencil, first edition. Covent 51-2323 1973 £35

FLAUBERT, GUSTAVE   Madame Bovary. 1928. Dec. cloth gilt, illus. Marsden 39-11 1974 £5

FLAUBERT, GUSTAVE   Salammbo. Paris, 1863. Panelled calf, marbled boards, rubbed, presentation copy. Jenkins 48-183 1973 $165

FLAUBERT, GUSTAVE   Salammbo. London, 1886. 8vo., red calf gilt, fine, first English edition. Dawsons PM 252-363 1974 £20

FLAUBERT, GUSTAVE   Salambo. Golden Cockerel Press, Waltham St. Lawrence, (1931). Orig. cloth backed boards, leather label, engravings on wood, one of 500 numbered copies, some off-setting from illus., fine. MacManus 224-187 1974 $45

FLAUBERT, GUSTAVE   Sentimental Education. London, 1898. 2 vols., 8vo., orig. cloth, plates, fine, first English edition. Dawsons PM 252-364 1974 £20

FLAVEL, JOHN   Divine Conduct. 1727. Modern sheep, few stains, clean and sound. Thomas 32-40 1974 £18.50

FLAVELL, JOHN   Pneumatologia. 1698. Small 4to., half calf, second edition. Howes 185-1161 1974 £30

FLECHIER, ESPRIT   Histoire du Cardinal Ximenes. Amsterdam, 1693. 2 vols. in 1, 12mo., contemporary blind stamped calf. Ximenes 35-607 1974 $50

FLECKER, JAMES ELROY   The Bridge of Fire. 1907. Wrappers, English first edition. Covent 56-457 1974 £17.50

FLECKER, JAMES ELROY   Don Juan. London, 1926. No. 204 of 385 copies on hand made paper, limited, d.w. slightly torn, fine, orig. binding. Ross 86-183 1974 $15

FLECKER, JAMES ELROY   Don Juan. 1926. Orig. cloth, dust wrapper, fine, first edition. Rota 188-306 1974 £8.50

FLECKER, JAMES ELROY   The Golden Journey to Samarkand. London, 1913. First edition, somewhat rubbed but skillfully repaired d.w., presentation inscription from Edward Marsh to Edmund Gosse, laid in A.L.s. from Marsh to Gosse, orig. binding. Ross 86-181 1974 $250

FLECKER, JAMES ELROY   Hassan. Heinemann, 1922. 183p. Austin 51-315 1973 $6.50

FLECKER, JAMES ELROY   The King of Alsander. 1914. First edition, crown 8vo., mint, first issue in red cloth. Broadhurst 24-673 1974 £8

FLECKER, JAMES ELROY   The Old Ships. (1915). 8vo., wrappers, scarce, first edition. Rota 189-313 1974 £8

FLECKER, JAMES ELROY   The Old Ships. London, n.d. (1915). Paper covers, nice copy, covers slightly worn & chipped. Ross 86-182 1974 $35

FLECKER, JAMES ELROY   Thirty Six Poems. 1910. Very scarce, first edition. Covent 51-692 1973 £25

FLECKER, JAMES ELROY   The Collected Poems of James E. Flecker. London, 1923. Sm. 4to., orig. cl., Ltd. to 500 copies. Jacobs 24-89 1974 $15

FLEET, C.   Glimpses of Our Ancestors in Sussex. Brighton, 1878. 8vo., orig. cloth, faded, first edition. Bow Windows 62-887 1974 £5.25

FLEETWOOD, WILLIAM   Chronicon Preciosum. London, 1707. 8vo., contemporary panelled calf. Dawsons PM 247-123 1974 £48

FLEISCHER, M.   Die Musci der Flora von Buitenzorg. Leyden, 1900-22. Roy 8vo., 4 vols., buckram. Wheldon 129-1395 1974 £40

FLEISCHMANN, HECTOR   Marie-Antoinette Libertine. Paris, 1911. 8vo., modem half brown morocco, fine, limited edition. Dawsons PM 251-114 1974 £30

FLEMING, ALEXANDER   On the Antibacterial Action of Cultures of a Penicilium. London, 1929. 4to., plates, cloth. Dawsons PM 250-28 1974 £1200

FLEMING, ALEXANDER   On the Antibacterial Action of Cultures of a Penicillium. (1944). 4to., as issued, fine, quarter morocco slip-case. Dawsons PM 249-170 1974 £245

FLEMING, ALEXANDER   On the Antibacterial Action of Cultures of a Penicillium. (1944). 4to., photographs, quarter morocco slip-case, fine. Dawsons PM 250-29 1974 £245

FLEMING, AMBROSE   The Wireless Telegraphist's Pocket Book of Notes. London, 1915. 8vo., orig. cloth, gilt, fine. Dawsons PM 245-290 1974 £8

FLEMING, GEORGE T.   Fleming's Views of Old Pittsburgh. Pittsburgh, 1932. 4to., wrapper. Saddleback 14-667 1974 $10

FLEMING, GEORGE T.   History of Pittsburgh and Enviorons. New York, 1922. 4 vols., 4to., cloth. Saddleback 14-668 1974 $25

FLEMING, JAMES   The Lakes of Scotland. Glasgow, 1834. 4to., half calf, plates, uncut. Quaritch 939-654 1974 £45

FLEMING, JAMES   Trial of. London, 1825. 8vo., boards, plates, first edition. Hammond 201-183 1974 £12.50

FLEMING, MAY AGNES   Sharing Her Crime.. New York, 1883. Cloth. Hayman 59-176 1974 $17.50

FLEMING, SANDFORD   Expedition to the Pacific, With a Brief Reference to the Voyages of Discovery in Seas Contiguous to Canada. 1889. Folding map, unbound. Hood's 102-556 1974 $25

FLEMMING, J. M.   Old Violins. 1883. Crown 8vo., orig. cloth, illus., frontispiece. Broadhurst 23-71 1974 £8

FLEMWELL, G.   Sur l'Alpe Fleurie. Paris, 1914. Roy 8vo., orig. wrappers, plates, illus. Wheldon 130-1151 1974 £43

FLEMYNG, MALCOLM   Neuropathia: Sive, de Morbis. Amsterdam, 1741. 8vo., contemporary boards. Schuman 37-80 1974 $75

FLENLEY, R.   A History of Montreal, 1640-72. London, 1928. Limited edition. Hood's 102-704 1974 $35

FLETCHER, ALEXANDER   Scripture History. London, 1839. Thick 16mo., full leather, pictorial-gilt, all edges gilt, 242 engravings, 2 vols. Frohnsdorff 16-331 1974 $50

FLETCHER, ANDREW   A Discourse of Government with Relation to Militia's. Edinburgh, (1698). 8vo., disbound, first edition. Dawsons PM 247-124 1974 £50

FLETCHER, HENRY   The Perfect Politician. London, 1660. 8vo., contemporary sheep, rebacked, first edition. Dawsons PM 251-115 1974 £80

FLETCHER, J. S.   Green Ink and Other Stories. 1926. 8vo., orig. cloth, first edition. Rota 190-253 1974 £5

FLETCHER, J. S.   The Ivory God and Other Stories. 1907. 8vo., orig. cloth, first edition. Rota 190-252 1974 £7.50

FLETCHER, JAMES THOMAS   John Singleton Copley. Boston, 1948. 4to., illus. Biblo & Tannen 214-96 1974 $32.50

FLETCHER, JOHN   A Comparative View of the Grounds of the Catholic and Protestant Churches. 1826. Orig. boards, uncut, first edition. Howes 185-1162 1974 £5

FLETCHER, JOHN   The Works Of. 1836-1818. 8 vols., contemporary cloth gilt. Smith 193-813 1973 £15

FLETCHER, JOHN GOULD   Paul Gauguin. New York, 1921. Plates, foxed, cloth-backed boards, first American edition. Covent 55-682 1974 £7.50

FLETCHER, PHINEAS   The Purple Island. 1633. 4to., old calf gilt, morocco labels, first edition. Dawsons PM 252-365 1974 £195

FLETCHER, PHINEAS   The Purple Island. 1816. Rebound, English first edition. Covent 56-459 1974 £15

FLETCHER, R. A.   Steam Ships. 1910. Thick crown 4to., orig. navy cloth gilt, plates, illus., first edition. Howes 186-1715A 1974 £10.50

FLETCHER, RALPH   Medico-Chirurgical Notes and Illustrations. London, 1831. 4to., modern boards, first edition. Dawsons PM 249-172 1974 £45

FLETCHER, T. B.   Birds of an Indian Garden. Calcutta, 1924. Roy 8vo., orig. cloth, plates. Wheldon 130-515 1974 £5

FLETCHER, T. B.   Birds of an Indian Garden. Calcutta, 1936. Roy 8vo., cloth, plates, second edition. Wheldon 130-516 1974 £7.50

FLETCHER, WILLIAM YOUNGER   Bookbinding in England and France. 1897. 2 parts in 1 vol., roy. 8vo., plates, orig. cloth, gilt. Howes 185-678 1974 £10

FLETCHER, WILLIAM YOUNGER   English Book Collectors. London, (1902). Green buckram, plates, illus. Dawson's 424-208 1974 $25

FLETCHER, WILLIAM YOUNGER   English Bookbindings in the British Museum. London, 1895. Folio, cloth, faded and bit worn, plates. Goodspeed's 578-458 1974 $125

FLETCHER, WILLIAM YOUNGER   English Bookbindings in the British Museum. London, 1895. Folio, color plates, full brown morocco, top edges gilt, others uncut, bookplate of M. C. D. Borden, limited to 500 copies. Kraus B8-63 1974 $250

FLEURS Emblematques. Paris, 1832. Full olive calf, 4 1/4 X 2 1/2, color plates. Gregory 44-124 1974 $30

FLEURY, CLAUDE   Les Moeurs des Israelites. Brussels, 1769. 2 vols. in 1, 12mo., contemporary sheep, gilt. L. Goldschmidt 42-50 1974 $25

FLEXNER, ABRAHAM   Universities American English German. Oxford, 1930. Inscribed by author, d.j., orig. binding. Butterfield 10-262 1974 $7.50

FLEXNER, SIMON   William Henry Welch and the Heroic Age of American Medicine. New York, 1941. Rittenhouse 46-711 1974 $10

FLICHE, AUGUSTIN   La Querelle des Investitures. Paris, 1946. Biblo & Tannen 214-610 1974 $8.50

FLINT, F. S.   Otherworld. 1920. Boards, fine, first edition. Covent 51-693 1973 £6.50

FLINT, J. M.   Recent Foraminifera. Washington, 1899. 8vo., cloth, plates, scarce. Wheldon 128-896 1973 £5

FLINT, TIMOTHY   Recollections of the Last Ten Years . . . From Pittsburg and the Missouri to the Gulf of Mexico, and From Florida to the Spanish Border. Boston, 1826. First edition, later three quarter morocco, spine restored. Jenkins 61-883 1974 $95

FLINT, WILLIAM RUSSELL   The Book of Tobit and the History of Susanna. 1929. Plates, signed, boards, gilt, English first edition. Covent 56-460 1974 £55

FLINT, WILLIAM RUSSELL   Famous Water-Colour Painters II. London, 1928. 4to., plates, orig. boards. Bow Windows 62-321 1974 £5.75

FLINT, WILLIAM RUSSELL   Judith. 1928. Plates, no. 2 of 12 numbered copies on vellum, signed by artist, fine, orig. silk ties, limp vellum, slipcase. Covent 51-695 1973 £125

FLITCROFT, JOHN E.   The Novelist of Vermont. Cambridge, 1929. 8vo., orig. bindings. Butterfield 8-644 1974 $10

FLOCHIA, seu Gedichtum Versicale de Flochis, Schwartzis illis Thiericulis. N.P., n.d. 4to., new calf, fine. Harper 213-67 1973 $375

FLORAL Poetry and the Language of Flowers. London, 1877. 4to., color plates, orig. cloth. Gregory 44-125 1974 $25

FLORAL Poetry and the Language of Flowers. 1877. Large square 8vo., plates, orig. designed cloth. Smith 193-657 1973 £5

FLORENCE, P. SARGANT   Economics of Fatigue and Unrest. New York, 1924. 8vo., orig. cloth, fine, first edition. Dawsons PM 247-125 1974 £12

FLORIAN, JEAN PIERRE CLAVIS DE   Eleazar and Naphtaly. London, 1827. 12mo., 19th century morocco, first edition. Ximenes 33-34 1974 $25

FLORIAN, JEAN PIERRE CLARIS DE   Gonzalve de Cordoue. Paris, 1791. 2 vols., 8vo., contemporary tree calf, gilt, first edition. L. Goldschmidt 42-51 1974 $20

FLORIDA   Proceedings of the Florida Convention. Washington, 1868. Jenkins 61-892 1974 $12.50

FLORILEGIUM Omnium Veterum Graecorum Postarum Epigrammatum in Septem Libros. 1604. Small 4to., old speckled calf gilt. Smith 194-152 1974 £5

FLORIO e Biancofiore - Questa sie la Historia de lo Inamoramento de Florio & Biancefiore. (Venice, c. 1530). Small 4to., modern limp vellum, rare edition, fine copy. Schafer 10-99 1974 sFr 2,600

FLORIST, Fruitist and Garden Miscellany. London, 1848-65. 18 vols., half morocco, color plates, 8vo. Gregory 44-127 1974 $525

FLORIST'S Manual, or Hints for the Construction of a Gay Flower Garden. London, 1822. Orig. pink boards, folding frontis., color plates, 8vo. Gregory 44-128 1974 $135

FLORUS, LUCIUS ANNAEUS   Annotationum in Lucium Florum. Vienna, 1511. Small 4to., boards. Harper 213-68 1973 $185

FLORUS, LUCIUS ANNAEUS   The Roman Histories of. London, 1636. 12mo., half calf, third edition. Dawsons PM 251-223 1974 £30

THE FLOURE and the Leafe. Hammersmith, 1896. Blue boards, linen back. Dawson's 424-76 1974 $275

FLOWER, WILLIAM HENRY   Diagrams of the Nerves of the Human Body. London, 1881. Large octavo, plates, third edition. Rittenhouse 46-261 1974 $10

FLOWER, WILLIAM HENRY   Fashion in Deformity as Illustrated in the Customs of Barbarous & Civilized Races. London, 1881. Small octavo, illus. Rittenhouse 46-262 1974 $15

FLOWER, WILLIAM HENRY   Recent Memoirs on the Cetacea. 1866. Folio, orig. boards, plates. Wheldon 128-313 1973 $15

FLOWER Emblems, or The Seasons of Life. London, 1871. Large 8vo., color plates, orig. cloth. Gregory 44-129 1974 $22.50

FLOWERS, MONTAVILLE   The Japanese Conquest of American Opinion. Doran. Austin 62-173 1974 $17.50

FLOWERS From the Holy Land. London, (c. 1845). Hand colored bouquets, orig. brown cloth, 8vo. Gregory 44-131 1974 $30

FLOYER, JOHN   The Ancient Psychrolusia Revived. London, 1702. 8vo., contemporary panelled calf. Gurney 64-88 1974 £50

FLOYER, JOHN   The Physician's Pulse-Watch. London, 1710. 8vo., contemporary panelled calf, first edition. Dawsons PM 249-173 1974 £850

FLUCKIGER, F. A.   Pharmacographia. London, 1874. Rittenhouse 46-263 1974 $20

FLUGGE, CARL G. F. W.   Micro-Organisms. 1890. 8vo., orig. cloth. Dawsons PM 249-174 1974 £9

FLYNT, WILLARD   The Powers That Prey. New York, 1900. 8vo., orig. green pictorial cloth, inscription, first edition. Rota 190-255 1974 £10

FOAKES-JACKSON, FREDERICK JOHN   The Beginnings of Christianity. 1920-33. 5 vols., fine, d.w.s, very scarce. Howes 185-1292 1974 £35

FOCILLON, H.   Peintures Romanes des Eglises de France. 1938. 4to., illus. Allen 213-1470 1973 $17.50

FOCKE, G. W.   Physiologische Studien. Bremen, 1847-54. 4to., orig. wrappers, plates. Wheldon 129-1396 1974 £10

FOESIUS, ANUTIO   Oeconomia Hippocratis. 1588. Folio, old half calf, gilt, first edition. Dawsons PM 249-175 1974 £85

FOETHE, JOHANN WOLFGANG VON   Faust. London, 1925. 4to., orig. vellum-backed bds., illus., ltd. to 1000 copies. Jacobs 24-90 1974 $100

FOGLIETTA, UBERTO   Ex Universa Historia Rerum Europae Suorum Temporum. Naples, 1571. Small 4to., contemporary vellum over thin boards, fine, first edition. Schafer 8-111 1973 sFr. 600

FOLEY, EMILY HOWARD   The Language of the Northumbrian Gloss to the Gospel of Saint Matthew. 1903. Ex-library, sturdy library binding. Austin 61-369 1974 $17.50

FOLEY, HENRY   Records of the English Province of the Society of Jesus. 1877-83. 6 vols., thick 8vo., orig. cloth. Howes 185-1164 1974 £60

FOLEY, P. K.   American Authors 1795-1895. 4to., binder's buckram, large paper, used copy. Goodspeed's 578-459 1974 $25

FOLK-LORE Society. 1879-1946. 47 vols., 8vo., orig. cloth. Quaritch 939-121 1974 £250

FOLKES, MARTIN   Tables of English, Silver & Gold Coins. London, 1763. 4to., contemporary diced russia, gilt, plates. Bow Windows 62-329 1974 £32.50

FOLLIE, LOUIS GUILLAUME DE LA
Please turn to
LA FOLLIE, LOUIS GUILLAUME DE

FOMON, SAMUEL   The Surgery of Injury and Plastic Repair. Baltimore, 1939. Dust jacket. Rittenhouse 46-686 1974 $25

FONTAINAS, A.   Histoire Generale de l'Art Francais de la Revolution a nos Jours. 1922. 3 vols., 4to., plates, illus., half morocco, gilt. Quaritch 940-787 1974 £25

FONTAINE, AUGUSTE   Cat. de Livres Anciens et Modernes, Rares et Curieux. Paris, 1878-9. Med. 8vo., half calf, slightly rubbed, top edges gilt. Forster 98-241 1974 £5

FONTAINE, NICOLAS   The History of the Old and New Testament.
1791. 8vo., old calf, rebacked, scarce. Thomas 28-92 1972 £65

FONTANA, BARTOLOMEO   The Musical Manual. 1847. 8vo., orig. cloth,
uncut. Hill 126-179 1974 £13.50

FONTANA, FELICE   Traite sur le Venin de la Vipere. Florence,
1781. 4to., 2 vols. in 1, old boards, first French edition, back slightly worn,
library stamps. Gurney 66-59 1974 £65

FONTANA, MARIANO   Della Dinamica libri Tre. 1790-95. 8vo., 3
vols., contemporary wrappers, rebacked, fine, uncut, first edition. Dawsons PM
245-291 1974 £25

FONTENELLE, BERNARD LE BOVIER DE   Entretiens sur la Pluralite des Mondes.
Paris, (1804). 12mo., contemporary calf gilt, rebacked. Dawsons PM 245-292
1974 £8

FONTENELLE, BERNARD LE BOVIER DE   Entretiens sur la Pluralite des Mondes.
Paris, 1811. 12mo., plate, contemporary mottled calf, morocco label, rubbed.
Nouvelle edition. Bow Windows 62-330 1974 £18.50

FONTENELLE, BERNARD LE BOVIER DE   Entretiens sur la Pluralite des Mondes.
Paris, 1820. 8vo., contemporary full long grain blue morocco, gilt, illus.
L. Goldschmidt 42-52 1974 $130

THE FOOLISH Fox. Philadelphia, 1904. 16mo., pictorial boards, illus.
Frohnsdorff 16-333 1974 $10

THE FOOLISH Fox. Philadelphia, 1904. 16mo., pict. cloth, 1st ed., illus.
Frohnsdorff 16-334 1974 $15

FOORD, A. H.   Catalogue of Fossil Cephalopoda in the British
Museum. 1888-1934. 5 vols., 8vo., orig. cloth, complete set. Wheldon
131-997 1974 £25

FOORD, A. H.   Monograph on the Carboniferous Cephalopoda
of Ireland. 1897-1903. 4to., half calf, plates. Wheldon 131-996 1974 £20

FOOT, PETER   General View of the Agriculture of the County of
Middlesex. London, 1794. 4to., boards, first edition. Hammond 201-14 1974
£25

FOOTE, HORTON   Harrison, Texas. Harcourt, Brace, 1956.
266p. Austin 51-316 1973 $10

FOOTE, SAMUEL   The Author. London, 1757. 8vo., modern
boards, first edition. Dawsons PM 252-366 1974 £15

FOOTE, SAMUEL   The Cozeners. London, 1778. 8vo., disbound,
first authorized edition. Ximenes 33-35 1974 $20

FOOTE, SAMUEL   The Englishman in Paris. London, 1753.
8vo., modern boards, first edition. Dawsons PM 252-367 1974 £15

FOOTE, SAMUEL   The Englishman Return'd from Paris. London,
1756. 8vo., modern boards, first edition. Dawsons PM 252-368 1974 £15

FOOTE, SAMUEL   The Maid of Bath. London, 1778. 8vo., rare,
disbound, first authorized edition. Ximenes 33-36 1974 $20

FOOTE, SAMUEL   The Maid of Bath. London, 1778. 8vo.,
contemporary marbled boards, first edition. Dawsons PM 252-369 1974 £24

FOOTE, SAMUEL   The Mayor of Garratt. 8vo., disbound, new
edition. Ximenes 33-37 1974 $10

FOOTE, SAMUEL   The Minor. London, 1760. 8vo., disbound,
first edition. Ximenes 33-38 1974 $27.50

FOOTE, SAMUEL   The Orators. London, 1752. 8vo., modern
boards, first edition. Dawsons PM 252-370 1974 £15

FOOTE, SAMUEL   The Patron. London, 1764. 8vo., wrappers,
first edition. Ximenes 33-39 1974 $27.50

FOOTE, SAMUEL   The Patron. London, 1764. 8vo., modern
boards, first edition. Dawsons PM 252-371 1974 £15

FOOTE, SAMUEL   Taste. London, 1753. 8vo., modern boards,
frontispiece, second edition. Dawsons PM 252-372 1974 £12

FOOTNER, HULBERT   The Almost Perfect Murder. Philadelphia, (19-
37). 8vo., orig. cloth, first edition. Rota 190-257 1974 £6.50

FOPPENS, J. F.   Bibliotheca Belgica, Sive Virorum in Belgio
Vita. Brussels, 1739. 2 vols., 4to., contemporary calf, worn. Dawsons PM
10-224 1974 £85

FOPPENS, J. F.   Bibliotheca Belgica, Sive Virorum in Belgio
Vita. Bruxellis, 1739. 2 vols., portraits, crown 4to., contemporary calf, text
fine. Forster 98-243 1974 £115

FOR Love of the King. 1922. Handmade paper, buckram gilt, dust wrapper,
fine. Covent 55-1543 1974 £12.50

FORAIN, J. L.   J. L. Forain, Aquafortiste. 1912. 2 vols.,
imp. 8vo., plates, cloth, gilt, orig. wrappers, limited. Quaritch 940-102
1974 £250

FORAN, J. K.   Jeanne Mance, or the "Angel of the Colony".
Montreal, 1931. Illus. Hood's 102-242 1974 $10

FORBES, ABNER   The Rich Men of Massachusetts. Boston, 1851.
Scarce, sewed signatures, orig. binding. Butterfield 10-476 1974 $75

FORBES, ALLAN   Boston and Some Noted Emigris. 1938.
Illus. paper. Austin 57-215 1974 $12.50

FORBES, ALLAN   Boston and Some Noted Emigres. Boston, 1938.
98p., illus. Austin 62-175 1974 $12.50

FORBES, ALLAN   Towns of New England and Old England, Ireland,
and Scotland. New York & London, 1921. 4to., 2 vols., gilt stamped cloth.
Butterfield 10-433 1974 $27.50

FORBES, E.   Memoir Of. 1861. 8vo., cloth, scarce.
Wheldon 130-161 1974 £10

FORBES, EDWARD   A History of British Mollusca. 1853. 4 vols.,
plates, dust marks, foxing, rebacked. Bow Windows 64-96 1974 £140

FORBES, EDWARD   A History of British Mollusca and Their Shells.
1853. 4 vols., 8vo., half calf, plates, small paper issue. Wheldon 128-840
1973 £50

FORBES, EDWARD   A History of British Starfishes. 1841. 8vo.,
cloth, woodcuts. Wheldon 128-898 1973 £10

FORBES, EDWARD   A Monograph of the British Naked-Eyed Medusae.
1848. Folio, coloured plates, orig. boards, scarce. Wheldon 128-897 1973
£7.50

FORBES, HENRY OGG   A Hand Book to the Primates. 1896-97.
2 vols., crown 8vo., cloth, coloured plates, folding maps, scarce. Wheldon
128-314 1973 £10

FORBES, HENRY OGG   A Hand Book to the Primates. 1896-97. Crown
8vo., 2 vols., cloth, scarce. Wheldon 130-393 1974 £10

FORBES, HENRY OGG   A Hand Book to the Primates. 1896-97.
2 vols., crown 8vo., cloth, plates. Wheldon 131-487 1974 £10

FORBES, HENRY OGG   A Naturalist's Wanderings In the Eastern
Archipelago. 1885. 8vo., cloth, illus., very scarce. Wheldon 131-353
1974 £20

FORBES, J. D.   Norway and Its Glaciers Visited in 1851.
Edinburgh, 1853. Roy. 8vo., orig. cloth, maps, coloured plates, scarce.
Wheldon 128-970 1973 £20

FORBES, J. D.   Norway and Its Glaciers. Edinburgh, 1853.
Roy 8vo., orig. cloth, plates, scarce. Wheldon 130-926 1974 £20

FORBES, JAMES G.   Report of the Trial of Brig. General William Hull.
New York, 1814. 8vo., marbled boards. Butterfield 8-112 1974 $65

FORBES, JOHN   Instructiones Historico Theologicae de
Doctrina Christiana. 1680. Folio, illus., contemporary calf, second edition.
Bow Windows 62-331 1974 £22.50

FORBES, JOHN   A Manual of Select Medical Bibliography.
London, 1835. Tall 8vo., cloth, first edition. Rittenhouse 46-265 1974 $125

FORBES, JOHN   Original Cases with Dissections and Observations. London, 1824. 8vo., orig. boards, worn, first edition. Dawsons PM
249-176 1974 £280

FORBES, LEITH, WILLIAM   The Scots Men-at-Arms and Life-Guards in
France. Edinburgh, 1882. 2 vols., 4to., plates, presentation, limited edition.
Traylen 79-134 1973 £15

FORBES, R. J.   Short History of the Art of Distillation.
Leiden, 1948. Biblo & Tannen 213-861 1973 $32.50

FORBES, ROBERT   Jacobite Memoirs of the Rebellion of 1745.
1834. Contemporary calf gilt, rubbed. Howes 186-821 1974 £8.50

FORBES, WILLIAM ALEXANDER   Collected Scientific Papers. 1885. Illus.,
new buckram, uncut, unopened, plates. Covent 55-1299 1974 £18

FORBUSH, EDWARD HOWE   Birds of Massachusetts and Other New England
States. 1925. 4to., 3 vols., orig. cloth. Gregory 44-134 1974 $145

FORBUSH, EDWARD HOWE   Useful Birds and Their Protection. Boston,
1908. Illus., plates, third edition, frontispiece, lacking d.w., bookplate, fine,
orig. binding. Ross 87-430 1974 $15

FORCELLINI, EGIDIO   Totius Latinitatis Lexikon. Padua, 1805.
Second edition, 4 vols., engraved portrait frontispiece, folio, contemporary half
calf, uncut. Kraus B8-65 1974 $95

FORCHHAMMER, OLAF   Byplan. Copenhagen, 1939. 4to., plates,
maps, illus., orig. wrapper. Minters 37-532 1973 $18.50

FORD, CHARLES HENRI   The Mirror of Baudelaire. Norfolk, 1942. Tall
8vo., dust jacket. Minters 37-855 1973 $25

FORD, CHARLES HENRI   The Overturned Lake. 1941. Limited to 400
copies, signed presentation copy from author, first U. S. edition, defective d.w.,
very good copy, with inscribed typescript by author tipped in. Covent 51-698
1973 £50

FORD, E.   Can You Top This? Blue Ribbon, 1945. 237p.
Austin 54-394 1973 $6

FORD, E.   Cream of the Crop. Grosset, Dunlap, 1947.
271p. Austin 54-395 1973 $6

FORD, FORD MADOX   Antwerp. n.d. Sewn, English first edition.
Covent 56-461 1974 £42.50

FORD, FORD MADOX   Between St. Dennis and St. George. 1915.
Near fine, first edition. Covent 51-699 1973 £10

FORD, FORD MADOX   The Brown Owl. London, 1892. Illus., covers
somewhat marked & worn, rubber stamps, frontis., else good copy, first edition.
Covent 51-700 1973 £16

FORD, FORD MADOX   The Cinque Ports. 1900. 4to., orig. buckram,
illus., plates, first edition. Howes 186-2045 1974 £25

FORD, FORD MADDOX   The Good Soldier. New York, 1927. Orig.
binding, front hinge somewhat weak, nice copy, Avignon edition. Ross 87-206
1974 $20

FORD, FORD MADOX   The Heart of the Country. 1906. Buckram
gilt, faded, first edition. Covent 55-715 1974 £7.50

FORD, FORD MADOX   Homage To. Norfolk, 1942. Dust wrapper,
fine, English first edition. Covent 56-465 1974 £25

FORD, FORD MADOX   It Was the Nightingale. 1934. Fine, d.w., first
edition. Covent 51-701 1973 £10.50

FORD, FORD MADOX   The Last Post. 1928. First U. S. edition, fine.
Covent 51-702 1973 £6.30

FORD, FORD MADOX   A Man Could Stand Up. 1926. Edges of text
spotted, very nice copy, scarce. Covent 51-703 1973 £10

FORD, FORD MADOX   A Mirror to France. 1926. Frontispiece,
first edition. Covent 55-716 1974 £5.25

FORD, FORD MADOX   No More Parades. 1925. 8vo., orig. cloth,
scarce, first edition. Rota 189-321 1974 £12

FORD, FORD MADOX   On Impressionism in Poetry and Drama. 1914.
Wrappers, English first edition. Covent 56-462 1974 £10.50

FORD, FORD MADOX   Return to Yesterday. 1932. Ex-library, first
edition. Austin 61-373 1974 $12.50

FORD, FORD MADOX   The Soul of London. 1905. English first edition. Covent 56-463 1974 £11

FORD, FORD MADOX   The Spirit of the People. London, 1907. First
edition, slight foxing, orig. binding, unusually fine copy. Ross 87-207 1974
$25

FORD, FORD, MADOX   When Blood is Their Argument. 1915. 8vo.,
orig. cloth, first edition. Rota 189-320 1974 £10

FORD, HENRY   The International Jew. n.d. 231 pages.
Austin 57-216 1974 $10

FORD, HORACE   The Theory and Practice of Archery. London,
1887. 8vo., orig. green cloth, illus., fine, new edition. Ximenes 33-40
1974 $27.50

FORD, PAUL LEICESTER   A Checked Love Affair. Dodd, Mead, 1903.
112p., illus. Austin 54-396 1973 $8.50

FORD, PAUL LEICESTER   The Great K. and A. Train Robbery. New York,
1897. 8vo., orig. dec. cloth, frontis., first edition. Bow Windows 66-242 1974
£12.50

FORD, PAUL LEICESTER   The Great K. & A. Robbery. New York,
1897. Orig. cloth, first printing, very fine, dust jacket. MacManus 224-173
1974 $75

FORD, PAUL LEICESTER   His Version of It. Dodd, Mead, 1905. 109p.,
illus. Austin 54-397 1973 $6.50

FORD, PAUL LEICESTER   Janice Meredith. Dodd, 1899. 2 vols., illus.
Austin 54-398 1973 $10

FORD, PAUL LEICESTER   Love Finds a Way. Dodd, Mead, 1904.
108p., illus. Austin 54-399 1973 $7.50

FORD, PAUL LEICESTER   The Story of an Untold Love. Boston & New
York, 1897. Ballinger 1-17 1974 $11

FORD, PAUL LEICESTER   The Story of an Untold Love. Houghton,
Mifflin, 1897. 348p. Austin 54-400 1973 $6.50

FORD, PAUL LEICESTER   Wanted--A Chaperon. Dodd, 1902. 109p.,
illus. Austin 54-401 1973 $7.50

FORD, PAUL LEICESTER   Wanted--A Matchmaker. Dodd, Mead, 1900.
111p., illus. Austin 54-402 1973 $6.50

FORD, PAUL LEICESTER   Webster Genealogy. Brooklyn, 1876. Folio,
orig. plain wrappers, fine, first edition. Ximenes 33-42 1974 $90

FORD, SIMON   A Discourse Concerning Gods Judgements.
London, 1678. 2 works in 1 vol., 12mo., contemporary speckled calf, first
edition. Schuman 37-81 1974 $95

FORD, WORTHINGTON CHAUNCEY   Journals of the Continental Congress. Washington, 1904-1922. 25 thick quarto vols., orig. bindings, only 2000 sets issued. Butterfield 10-40 1974 $500

FORDER, A.   Petra: Perea: Phoenicia. London, (1923). Crown 4to., illus., stain, orig. cloth. Bow Windows 62-334 1974 £6

FORDHAM, HERBERT GEORGE   John Cary, Engraver, Map, Chart and Print Seller. Cambridge, 1925. Small 4to., orig. cloth, uncut. Dawsons PM 10-113 1974 £32

FORDHAM, HERBERT GEORGE   Une Piraterie Litteraire au 18me Siecle. Cambridge, 1922. Limited to 200 copies signed by author, plates, full page illus., post 8vo., orig. wrappers. Forster 98-244 1974 £5

FORDYCE, GEORGE   A Dissertation on Simple Fever. London, 1880. 8vo., orig. wrappers, second edition. Dawsons PM 249-177 1974 £10

FORDYCE, GEORGE   A Second Dissertation on Fever. London, 1802. 8vo., orig. wrappers, uncut, unopened, second edition. Dawsons PM 249-178 1974 £8

FORDYCE, GEORGE   A Third Dissertation on Fever. London, 1799. 8vo., 2 vols., orig. wrappers, first edition. Dawsons PM 249-179 1974 £10

FORDYCE, GEORGE 1762-1802   Elements of Agriculture and Vegetation. 1771. 8vo., sewed, plates, uncut, scarce. Wheldon 130-1585 1974 £7.50

FORDYCE, WILLIAM   A History of Coal, Coke, Coal Fields . . . 18-60. Folio, full crimson morocco, gilt, plates, presentation copy, inscribed. Hammond 201-807 1974 £225

FORDYCE, WILLIAM   A Reveiw of the Verneral Disease and Its Remedies. London, 1777. Fourth edition, 8vo., boards. Gurney 66-60 1974 £10

FOREL, AUGUSTE   Le Monde Social des Fourmis. Geneva, 1921-23. 5 vols., 8vo., illus., orig. printed wrappers, fine, unopened, first edition. Gilhofer 61-87 1974 sFr. 400

FOREL, AUGUSTE   The Social World of the Ants. 1928. 8vo., 2 vols., cloth, plates, scarce. Wheldon 130-750 1974 £15

FOREL, F. A.   Le Leman, Monographie Limnologique. Lausanne, 1892-1904. 3 vols., roy. 8vo., half calf, illus., maps, extremely scarce. Wheldon 128-145 1973 £100

FOREL, F. A.   Le Leman. Lausanne, 1892-1904. Roy 8vo., half calf, 3 vols., scarce. Wheldon 130-255 1974 £100

FOREMAN, CAROLYN THOMAS   Oklahoma Imprints, 1835-1907: A History of Printing In Oklahoma Before Statehood. Norman, 1936. Jenkins 61-2023 1974 $25

FOREST, LOUIS EFFINGHAM DE   The Journals and Papers of Seth Pomeroy. (New Haven), 1926. New copy, orig. binding. Butterfield 10-267 1974 $15

FORESTER, C. S.   Death to the French. 1932. Fine, scarce, first edition. Covent 55-718 1974 £17.50

FORESTER, C. S.   The General. 1936. Orig. cloth, faded, first edition. Rota 188-311 1974 £5

FORESTER, C. S.   The Happy Return. 1937. Fine, worn dust wrapper, signed. Covent 55-719 1974 £12.50

FORESTER, C. S.   Josephine. 1925. Plates, faded, English first edition. Covent 56-467 1974 £10.50

FORESTER, C. S.   Napoleon and His Court. 1924. Plates, slight foxing, fine, presentation inscription from author. Covent 51-705 1973 £21.50

FORESTER, C. S.   Napoleon and His Court. 1924. Plates, fine, d.w. Covent 51-2337 1973 £8.50

FORESTER, C. S.   Victor Emmanuel II and the Union of Italy. 1927. Plates, map, spine trifle marked, nice copy, scarce, first edition. Covent 51-706 1973 £8.50

FORESTER, FRANK   Sporting Scenes and Sundry Sketches. New York, 1842. 2 vols., orig. binding. Butterfield 10-298 1974 $20

FORESTI DA BERGAMO, JACOPO FILIPPO   Novissime Historiarum. Venice, 1506. Folio, parchment covers, woodcuts. Traylen 80-85 1974 £350

FORESTIDA BERGAMO, JACOBO FILIPPO   Novissime Hystoria 4 Omniu. Venice, 1503. Thick folio, contemporary blind stamped pigskin over wooden boards. Thomas 28-276 1972 £300

FORESTI DA BERGAMO, JACOPO FILIPPO   Supplementum Chronicorum. Paris, 1535. Folio, 19th century buff calf, rebacked, orig. label, boards, fine, woodcut. Howes 184-172 1973 £145

FORESTUS, PETRUS   Observationum et Curationum Medicinalium Libri Tres. Leyden, 1589. 8vo., limp vellum. Dawsons PM 249-180 1974 £42

FORGET, AMEDEE   De la Trepanation de l'Apophyse Mastoide. 1860. 8vo., black cloth. Dawsons PM 249-181 1974 £16

FORKEL, J. N.   Life of John Sebastian Bach. 1820. 8vo., orig. boards, paper label, first English edition. Quaritch 940-805 1974 £40

THE FORM and Order of the . . . Coronation of their Majesties King George II and Queen Caroline. 1727-61. 2 items in 1 vol., 4to., modern boards. Quaritch 939-726 1974 £17.50

FORMAN, CHARLES   Mr. Forman's Letter to the Right Honourable William Pulteney. London, 1725. Small 4to., old wrapper, first edition. Hammond 201-232 1974 £8.50

FORMAN, HENRY JAMES   Our Movie Made Children. Macmillan, 1933. 288p. Austin 51-317 1973 $7.50

FORMAN, J. G.   The Western Sanitary Comission. St. Louis, 1864. Cloth, chipped. Jenkins 61-900 1974 $25

FORMULES de Medicamens Usitees dans les Differens Hopitaux de Paris. Paris, 1780. New edition. Rittenhouse 46-266 1974 $38

FORNEY, JOHN W.   Letters from Europe. Philadelphia, 1867. Inscribed, signed & dated by author. Jenkins 61-901 1974 $17.50

FORREST, CHARLES RAMUS   A Picturesque Tour Among the Rivers Ganges and Jumna in India. 1824. Coloured aquatint plates, folio, half maroon morocco, panelled back, fine tall uncut copy. Broadhurst 24-1609 1974 £450

FORREST, E. W.   Ned Fortescue. Ottawa & Toronto, 1869. Foxing. Hood's 104-554 1974 $15

FORREST, E. W.   Ned Fortescue; or, Roughing it Through Life. Ottawa & Toronto, 1869. Some light foxing. Hood's 102-512 1974 $15

FORREST, F. L. S.   The Atlantean Continent. 1935. 8vo., cloth, maps, plates, second edition. Wheldon 131-998 1974 £7.50

FORREST, H. E.   The Vertebrate Fauna of North Wales. 1907. 8vo., buckram, leather label. Broadhurst 23-1114 1974 £9

FORREST, H. E.   The Vertebrate Fauna of North Wales. 1907. 8vo., cloth, plates. Wheldon 131-354 1974 £7.50

FORREST, H. E.   The Vertebrate Fauna of North Wales. 1907. 8vo., cloth, plates, coloured map. Wheldon 128-199 1973 £7.50

FORREST, SAMUEL   Variety of Miscellania. New York, 1939. Author's sgd. pres. Biblo & Tannen 213-894 1973 $15

FORRESTER, A.   The Object, Benefits and History of Normal Schools. Halifax, 1855. Hood's 104-203 1974 $22.50

FORRESTER-BROWN, M. F.   Diagnosis and Treatment of Deformities in Infancy and Early Childhood.   New York, 1929.   Rittenhouse 46-267 1974 $10

FORSTER, C. F.   Handbuch der Cacteenkunde in Ihrem Ganzen Umfange.   Leipzig, 1886.   8vo., orig. half leather, scarce, revised second edition.   Wheldon 131-1660 1974 £35

FORSTER, C. S.   The Happy Return.   London, 1937.   First edition, fine copy, d.w., orig. cloth.   Crane 7-88 1974 £5

FORSTER, EDWARD MORGAN   Abinger Harvest.   1936.   8vo., orig. cloth, first edition.   Rota 189-329 1974 £5

FORSTER, EDWARD MORGAN   Alexandria, A History and a Guide.   Alexandria, 1938.   Second edition revised, illus., orig. boards, scarce, very good copy.   Crane 7-92 1974 £5

FORSTER, EDWARD MORGAN   Anonymity.   1925.   8vo., orig. cloth, presentation inscription, first edition.   Rota 190-429 1974 £15

FORSTER, EDWARD MORGAN   Aspects of the Novel.   1927.   Crown 8vo., orig. cloth, first edition.   Broadhurst 23-721 1974 £8

FORSTER, EDWARD MORGAN   Aspects of the Novel.   1927.   8vo., orig. cloth, first edition.   Rota 190-430 1974 £5.50

FORSTER, EDWARD MORGAN   Aspects of the Novel.   1927.   First edition, sewing little weak, very good copy, signature.   Covent 51-708 1973 £5

FORSTER, EDWARD MORGAN   The Development of English Prose Between 1918 and 1939.   Glasgow, 1945.   First edition, demy 8vo., paper printed wrapper, fine.   Broadhurst 24-674 1974 £6

FORSTER, EDWARD MORGAN   The Development of English Prose.   Glasgow, 1945.   8vo., orig. cloth, wrapppers, fine, first edition.   Rota 190-432 1974 £5

FORSTER, EDWARD MORGAN   The Eternal Moment.   1928.   Crown 8vo., orig. cloth, first edition.   Broadhurst 23-722 1974 £14

FORSTER, EDWARD MORGAN   The Eternal Moment, and Other Stories.   1928.   Fin, frayed d.w., covers blocked in gilt, first edition.   Covent 51-709 1973 £8.40

FORSTER, EDWARD MORGAN   The Eternal Moment and Other Stories.   New York, 1928.   8vo., orig. cloth, signature, first American edition.   Rota 190-431 1974 £35

FORSTER, EDWARD MORGAN   The Eternal Moment and Other Stories.   1928.   Small 8vo., cloth, d.j, first edition.   Quaritch 936-379 1974 £20

FORSTER, EDWARD MORGAN   Goldsworthy Lowes Dickinson.   1934.   Plates, first edition.   Howes 186-195 1974 £6.50

FORSTER, EDWARD MORGAN   Goldsworthy Lowes Dickinson.   1934.   Orig. cloth, illus., first edition.   Rota 188-316 1974 £5

FORSTER, EDWARD MORGAN   The Ivory Tower.   Boston, 1939.   Wrappers, English first edition.   Covent 56-1766 1974 £5.25

FORSTER, EDWARD MORGAN   The Longest Journey.   Edinburgh & London, 1907.   8vo., orig. cloth, first edition.   Dawsons PM 252-373 1974 £38

FORSTER, EDWARD MORGAN   A Passage to India.   1924.   Orig. cloth, first edition, presentation copy.   Howes 185-178 1974 £18.50

FORSTER, EDWARD MORGAN   Pharos and Pharillon.   1923.   First American edition.   Allen 216-611 1974 $10

FORSTER, EDWARD MORGAN   Programme of England's Pleasant Land.   1938.   Wrappers, presentation copy, inscribed, English first edition.   Covent 56-471 1974 £75

FORSTER, EDWARD MORGAN   A Room With a View.   1908.   Crown 8vo., half maroon levant morocco, gilt, uncut, orig. cloth covers, fine.   Howes 186-196 1974 £32

FORSTER, EDWARD MORGAN   Sinclair Lewis Interprets America.   n.d.   One of 100 copies, numbered & signed by Harvey Taylor, stapled as issued, mint.   Covent 51-2338 1973 £20

FORSTER, EDWARD MORGAN   What I Believe.   1939.   Orig. cloth, wrappers, first edition.   Rota 188-317 1974 £5

FORSTER, GEORGE   A Voyage Round the World In His Britannic Majesty's Sloop.   London, 1777.   2 vols., 4to., contemporary calf, leather labels, first edition.   Traylen 79-427 1973 £215

FORSTER, JOHN   The Life and Times of Oliver Goldsmith.   London, 1877.   2 vols. in 1, full red calf.   Emerald 50-310 1974 £5

FORSTER, JOHN   Life of Charles Dickens.   (1911).   2 vols., portraits, illus., best edition.   Austin 61-377 1974 $27.50

FORSTER, JOHN   The Life of Charles Dickens.   New York, 1911.   2 vols., poor set.   Biblo & Tannen 210-856 1973 $15

FORSTER, JOHN   Life of Jonathan Swift.   1876.   Vol. 1, new buckram, blind stamp.   Allen 216-2072 1974 $15

FORSTER, NATHANIEL   A Dissertation upon the Account Suppos'd to have been given of Jesus Christ by Josephus.   Oxford, 1749.   8vo., unbound.   Hill 126-107 1974 £6.50

FORSTER, THOMAS IGNATIUS MARIA   Observations on the Natural History of Swallows, to Which is added, A General Catalogue of British Birds.   1817.   8vo., boards, uncut, plates, enlarged sixth edition.   Wheldon 128-440 1973 £5

FORSTER, THOMAS IGNATIUS MARIA   Researches About Atmospheric Phaenomena.   London, 1815.   8vo., orig. half calf, gilt.   Zeitlin 235-83 1974 $125

FORSTER, THOMAS IGNATIUS MARIA   Researches About Atmospheric Phaenomena.   London, 1823.   8vo., contemporary calf, rebacked.   Dawsons PM 245-293 1974 £26

FORSTER, THOMAS IGNATIUS MARIA   Researches About Atmospheric Phaenomena.   1823.   8vo., orig. cloth, plates, third edition.   Wheldon 129-77 1974 £10

FORSTER, THOMAS IGNATIUS MARIA   Researches About Atmospheric Phaenomena.   1823.   8vo., orig. cloth, plates.   Wheldon 131-153 1974 £10

FORSTER, WALTER O.   Zion on the Mississippi.   1953.   606p., illus.   Austin 62-178 1974 $27.50

FORSTER, WESTGARTH   A Treatise on a Section of the Strata.   1821.   Roy 8vo., quarter calf, orig. boards, illus., gilt, uncut, second edition.   Hammond 201-364 1974 £48

FORSYTH, ANDREW RUSSELL   Lectures Introductory to the Theory of Functions of Two Complex Variables.   1914.   8vo., blue cloth, gilt, first edition.   Dawsons PM 245-295 1974 £5

FORSYTH, ANDREW RUSSELL   Theory of Functions of a Complex Variable.   Cambridge, 1900.   8vo., blue cloth gilt, second edition.   Dawsons PM 245-294 1974 £9

FORSYTH, JAMES   The Sporting Rifle and its Projectiles.   1867.   8vo., orig. cloth, frontispiece.   Bow Windows 64-318 1974 £9

FORSYTH, JOSEPH   Remarks On Antiquities, Arts & Letters During Excursion in Italy, 1802-03.   1818.   New buckram.   Allen 213-393 1973 $10

FORSYTH, WILLIAM   Observations on the Diseases, Defects, and Injuries in all Kinds of Fruit and Forest Trees.   1791.   8vo., modern half calf.   Wheldon 129-1601 1974 £26

FORSYTH, WILLIAM   Observations on the Diseases, Defects and Injuries in all Kinds of Fruit and Forest Trees.   1791.   8vo., modern half calf, rare.   Wheldon 131-1730 1974 £26

FORSYTH, WILLIAM   A Treatise on the Culture and Management of Fruit Trees.   1802.   4to., contemporary diced calf, first edition.   Bow Windows 64-777 1974 £36

FORSYTH, WILLIAM   A Treatise on the Culture and Management of Fruit-Trees. 1802. 4to., contemporary diced calf, plates. Wheldon 129-1602 1974 £12

FORSYTH, WILLIAM   A Treatise on the Culture and Management of Fruit-Trees. 1802. 4to., modern half calf, plates, first edition. Wheldon 130-1473 1974 £25

FORSYTH, WILLIAM   A Treatise on the Culture and Management of Fruit-Trees. 1802. 4to., contemporary diced calf, plates, scarce. Wheldon 131-1731 1974 £12

FORSYTH, WILLIAM   A Treatise on the Culture and Management of Fruit-Trees. 1818. 8vo., modern half buckram, uncut, plates, sixth edition. Wheldon 130-1474 1974 £10

FORSYTH, WILLIAM   A Treatise on the Culture and Management of Fruit-Trees. 1803. 8vo., contemporary half calf, gilt, plates, second edition. Hammond 201-15 1974 £24

FORSYTHE, ROBERT   Reading from Left to Right. Covici, Friede, 1938. 255p., illus. Austin 54-403 1973 $10

FORT, CHARLES   Wild Talents. New York, 1932. 1st ed. Biblo & Tannen 214-708 1974 $12.50

FORT Snelling and Minnehaha Falls. Brooklyn, 1898. Wrapper, illus. Jenkins 61-1660 1974 $12.50

FORT Sumter Memorial: The Fall of Fort Sumter. New York, 1915. Foxed, limited to 750 copies. Jenkins 61-2371 1974 $12.50

FORTESCUE, J. W.   History of the British Army. London, 1910-35. 20 vols., 8vo., orig. cloth gilt, faded. Traylen 79-135 1973 £185

FORTESCUE, THOMAS CLERMONT   The History of the Family Fortescue. 1880. Roy 4to., orig. cloth, uncut. Broadhurst 23-1380 1974 £10

FORTESCUE-ALAND, JOHN   The Difference Between an Absolute and Limited Monarchy. London, 1714. 8vo., contemporary calf, first edition. Ximenes 37-84 1974 $65

FORTESQUE, J. W.   The Story of a Red-Deer. 1935. Roy 8vo., gilt, cloth. Hammond 201-770 1974 £65

FORTESQUE, JOHN   De Laudibus Legum Angliae. 1672. 16mo., old calf, torn spine. Allen 213-1474 1973 $50

FORTESQUE, JOHN   De Laudibus Legum Anglie. 1942. Allen 213-1475 1973 $12.50

FORTIA D'URBAN, AGRICOLE JOSEPH   Nouveau Sisteme Bibliographique. Paris, 1821. Small 8vo., orig. wrappers, uncut, scarce. Dawsons PM 10-226 1974 £10

FORTSON, JOHN   Pott Country and What Has Come of It. (Shawnee), 1936. 12mo., cloth, 90 pages. Saddleback 14-635 1974 $17.50

FORTUNE   The Fortune Anthology: Stories, Criticism and Poems. n.d. Fine, largely unopened, cloth backed boards. Covent 51-2102 1973 £10.50

FORTUNE, R.   A Residence Among the Chinese. 1857. 8vo., orig. cloth, illus., plates, scarce. Wheldon 130-1500 1974 £30

FORTUNE, R.   Three Years' Wanderings in the Northern Provinces of China. 1847. 8vo., orig. cloth, illus., second edition. Wheldon 129-1559 1974 £25

FORTUNES Made in Business. 1884. 2 vols., full crimson morocco, gilt. Covent 55-500 1974 £35

FORTY of Boston's Historic Houses. Boston, (1912). First edition, 8vo., illus., fine. Current BW9-386 1974 $8.50

FORTY Years of Struggle for a Principle. Bloch, 1928. 403p., illus. Austin 62-214 1974 $15

FOSBROKE, THOMAS D.   British Monachism. 1843. Orig. cloth, illus., plates, rebacked, third edition. Howes 185-1166 1974 £8.50

FOSBROKE, THOMAS DUDLEY   The Economy of Monastic Life. Glocester, (n.d.). 4to., old half calf, first edition. Dawsons PM 252-374 1974 £25

FOSDICK, WILLIAM WHITEHEAD   Ariel, and Other Poems. New York, (1855). Woodcut designs, orig. binding. Butterfield 10-263 1974 $12.50

FOSSOMBRONI, VITTORIO   Saggio di Richerche. 1781. 4to., orig. boards, uncut, fine, first edition. Zeitlin 235-84 1974 $85

FOSSUM, ANDREW   The Norse Discovery of America. 1918. Illus. Austin 57-220 1974 $12.50

FOSTER, A. H.   High Days and Holidays in Canada. Toronto, 1938. Card covers. Hood's 102-20 1974 $7.50

FOSTER, BIRKET   Birket Foster. 1910. Pictorial cloth gilt, fine. Covent 55-100 1974 £5

FOSTER, BIRKET   Brittany. 1878. Folio, orig. buckram gilt, plates. Smith 193-659 1973 £15

FOSTER, BIRKET   The Illustrated Book of Songs for Children. New York, 1854. Orig. dec. cloth, foxing, English first edition. Covent 56-1829 1974 £21

FOSTER, BIRKET   Milton's L'Allegro and Il Penseroso. 1855. 8vo., illus., orig. cloth, gilt. Quaritch 936-380 1974 £35

FOSTER, C. L.   Letters From the Front. Toronto, 1920-21. 2 vols., illus. Hood's 103-105 1974 $17.50

FOSTER, CHARLES H. W.   The Eastern Yacht Club Ditty Box. Norwood, 1932. 8vo., orig. bindings. Butterfield 8-239 1974 $15

FOSTER, GEORGE C.   New York By Gas-Light. New York, 1850. 8vo., old half morocco, little rubbed, first edition, scarce. Ximenes 36-94

FOSTER, HANNAH   The Coquette. Charlestown, 1802. 12mo., contemporary sheep rubbed, second edition, some stains and signs of use, but sound copy. Ximenes 36-95 1974 $75

FOSTER, J. E.   An Illustrated Catalogue of the Loan Collection of Plate. Cambridge, 1896. 4to., illus., cloth, scarce, limited. Quaritch 939-322 1974 £12

FOSTER, J. J.   French Art from Watteau to Prud'hon. 1905-07. 3 vols., large folio, plates, half vellum, gilt, fine, limited edition de luxe. Quaritch 940-104 1974 £75

FOSTER, J. J.   Miniature Painters: British and Foreign. 1903. 2 vols., folio, plates, vellum, soiled. Quaritch 940-103 1974 £65

FOSTER, J. J.   The Stuarts. 1902. 2 vols., folio, orig. buckram gilt, plates, limited deLuxe edition. Howes 186-1243 1974 £18

FOSTER, JOSEPH   The Peerage of the British Empire for 1882. (18-82). Roy 8vo., orig. cloth, gilt. Hammond 201-422 1974 £18

FOSTER, JOSEPH   Some Feudal Coats of Arms. Oxford and London, 1902. 4to., orig. cloth, gilt, illus., first edition. Hammond 201-423 1974 £18

FOSTER, MICHAEL   A Report of Some Proceedings on the Commission for the Trial of the Rebels. 1776. 8vo., half calf, second edition. Quaritch 939-562 1974 £12.50

FOSTER, MYLES B.   A Day in a Child's Life. 1881. 4to., orig. cloth-backed glazed pictorial boards, first edition. Hammond 201-118 1974 £30

FOSTER, SAMUEL   The Art of Dialling. London, 1638. Small 4to., woodcuts, later wrappers, first edition. Traylen 79-226 1973 £210

FOSTER, T. C.   Letters on the Condition of the People of Ireland. London, 1846. Thick 8vo., cloth boards. Emerald 50-312 1974 £15

FOSTER, W.   The East India House, Its History and Associations. (1924). 8vo., brown half morocco, illus., presentation inscription. Bow Windows 66-244 1974 £7.50

FOSTER, WILLIAM   Hoplocrismaspongus. London, 1631. Small 4to., disbound, rare, first edition. Ximenes 33-44 1974 $250

FOTHERGILL, JOHN   An Account of the Sore Throat. London, 1748. 8vo., later marbled boards. Dawsons PM 249-182 1974 £25

FOTHERGILL, JOHN   An Account of the Sore Throat Attended With Ulcers. London, 1754. 8vo., boards, fourth edition. Gurney 66-62 1974 £20

FOTHERGILL, JOHN   Hortus Uptonensis. 1784. 8vo., modern boards, plate. Wheldon 128-1464 1973 £15

THE Fothergill Omnibus. 1931. Crown 8vo., full green morocco, gilt, mint, signed, limited edition. Broadhurst 23-727 1974 £45

FOTTORUSSO, J.   Wonders of Italy. Florence, 1928. Bdg. worn. Biblo & Tannen 213-669 1973 $10

FOUCHER D'OBSONVILLE   Essais Philosophiques sur les Moeurs de Divers Animaux Etrangers. Paris, 1783. 8vo., contemporary marbled sheep, gilt, morocco label, first edition. L. Goldschmidt 42-53 1974 $95

FOULCHE-DELBOSC, R.   Manuel de l'Hispanisant. New York, (1920-25). 2 vols., bound, reprint. Kraus B8-67 1974 $45

FOULD, LOUIS   Description des Antiquites et Objets d'Art Composant le Cabinet de Louis Fould. 1861. Roy. folio, illus., marbled boards, linen spine. Quaritch 940-318 1974 £32

FOUNTAIN, PAUL   The Great Deserts and Forests of North America. London - New York - Bombay, 1901. 8vo., orig. bindings. Butterfield 8-701 1974 $12.50

FOUQUE, FRIEDRICH DE LA MOTTE
Please turn to
LA MOTTE FOUQUE, FRIEDRICH DE

FOURCROY, ANTOINE FRANCOIS   Elements of Chemistry and Natural History. to which is prefixed, The Philosophy of Chemistry. Edinburgh, 1800. Fifth edition, 8vo., 3 vols., old half calf, vellum corners. Gurney 66-63 1974 £48

FOURCROY, ANTOINE FRANCOIS   Elements of Chemistry and Natural History. 1800. 8vo., 3 vols., contemporary mottled calf, labels. Zeitlin 235-276 1974 $200

FOURCROY, ANTOINE FRANCOIS   Systeme des Connaissances Chimiques. Paris, (1800-1801). Contemporary continental mottled calf, gilt, first edition. Dawsons PM 245-296 1974 £250

FOURCROY, ANTOINE FRANCOIS   Systeme des Connaissances Chimiques. (1801-1802). 4to., contemporary tree calf, labels, gilt. Zeitlin 235-277 1974 $385

FOURIER, JEAN BAPTISTE JOSEPH   Theorie Analytique de la Chaleur. 1883. 4to., half calf. Dawsons PM 245-297 1974 £15

FOURNET, JULES   Recherches Cliniques sur l'Auscultation des Organes Respiratoires. Paris, 1839. 8vo., 2 vols., modern quarter calf, first edition. Dawsons PM 249-184 1974 £55

FOURNIER, ALAIN 1886-1914   The Wanderer. (1929). Orig. cloth, first complete English edition. Rota 188-4 1974 £6

FOURNIER, ALFRED   Syphilis Secondaire Tardive. Paris, 1911. 8vo., half morocco, plates. Schuman 37-82 1974 $85

FOURNIER, DENIS   L'Anatomie Pacifique Nouvelle et Curieuse. Paris, 1678. 4to., contemporary calf, cloth case, only edition. Schuman 37-83 1974 $485

FOURNIER, EDOUARD   L'Art de la Reliure en France aux Derniers Siecles. Paris, 1864. 8vo., three quarter light blue morocco, orig. wrappers bound in, no. 130 of 300 copies on laid paper. Kraus B8-68 1974 $25

FOURNIER, F. I.   Nouveau Dictionnaire Portatif de Bibliographie. Paris, 1809. Contemporary gilt framed speckled calf, gilt, revised second edition. Dawsons PM 10-227 1974 £20

FOURNIER, HENRI   Traite de la Typographie. Brussels, 1826. 8vo., green half morocco, slight foxing. Kraus B8-326 1974 $75

FOURNIER, HENRI   Traite de la Typographie. Tours, 1854. 8vo., half leather, gilt back, revised second edition. Kraus B8-327 1974 $40

FOURNIER, HENRI ALBAN
Please turn to
FOURNIER, ALAIN

FOURNIER, JEAN ALFRED
Please turn to
FOURNIER, ALFRED

FOURNIER, P.   Voyages et Decouvertes. Paris, 1932. 8vo., cloth, portraits. Wheldon 129-143 1974 £10

FOURTH Antimasonic State Convention . . . of Massachusetts, Held at Boston, 1833, for the Nomination of Governor. Boston, 1833. Wrapper, almost new copy. Butterfield 10-60 1974 $15

FOURTY Four Queries to the Life of Queen Dick. (London), 1659. Small 4to., wrappers, very scarce, first edition. Ximenes 37-55 1974 $75

FOWKE, GERARD   Archaeological History of Ohio. Columbus, n.d. Cloth, scarce. Hayman 57-564 1974 $25

FOWLER, EDWARD   A Discourse of Offences. London, 1683. 4to., modern boards, first edition. Dawsons PM 251-504 1974 £12

FOWLER, EDWARD   A Vindication of an Undertaking of Certain Gentlemen, in Order to the Suppressing of Debauchery and Profaneness. London, 1692. Small 4to., disbound, first edition. Ximenes 36-96 1974 $45

FOWLER, GENE   Father Goose. Covici, Friede, 1934. 407p., illus. Austin 51-318 1973 $8.50

FOWLER, GENE   The Mighty Barnum. Covici, Friede, 1934. 240p., illus. Austin 51-319 1973 $10

FOWLER, H. W.   Contributions to the Biology of the Philippine Archipelago. Washington, 1928-43. 8vo., cloth. Wheldon 129-1703 1974 £50

FOWLER, H. W.   Contribution to Biology of Philippine Archipelago, Fishes of Families Banjosidae to Enopiosidae. Washington, 1933. 8vo., scarce. Wheldon 128-628 1973 £6

FOWLER, H. W.   Fishes of Families Banjosidae to Enoplosidae. Washington, 1933. 8vo. Wheldon 131-741 1974 £10

FOWLER, HENRY   The American Pulpit. New York, 1856. Portraits on steel, orig. binding. Butterfield 10-33 1974 $12.50

FOWLER, JAMES K.   A History of Beaulieu Abbey. (1911). 8vo., orig. cloth, maps, plates, bookplate. Bow Windows 66-246 1974 £8.50

FOWLER, NATHANIEL C.   How to Obtain Citizenship. 1914. 167 pages. Austin 57-222 1974 $10

FOWLER, WILLIAM CHAUNCEY   History of Durham. Hartford, 1866. 8vo., orig. bindings. Butterfield 8-85 1974 $45

FOWLER, WILLIAM WARDE   The City-State of the Greeks and Romans. London, 1908. 12mo., orig. edition. Biblo & Tannen 214-611 1974 $6

FOWLER, WILLIAM WEEKES   The Coleoptera of the British Islands. 1887-1891. and 1913. Roy. 8vo., 6 vols., plates, illus., frayed, cloth. Bow Windows 64-97 1974 £210

FOWLER, WILLIAM WORTHINGTON   Ten Years in Wall Street. Hartford, 1870. Illus., first edition, 8vo., plates, near fine, scarce. Current BW9-607 1974 $37.50

FOWLIE, WALLACE   Pantomime. Regnery, 1951. 246p. Austin 51-320 1973 $10

FOWNES, G.   An Essay on the Food of Plants. 1843. 8vo., calf. Wheldon 131-1138 1974 £5

FOX, CAROLINE   Memories of Old Friends. 1882. Large 8vo., portrait, quarter vellum, scarce, English first edition. Covent 56-476 1974 £10

FOX, CAROLINE   Memories of Old Friends. 1882. Presentation copy, inscribed from editor, portrait, large 8vo., quarter vellum, very nice copy, scarce, first edition. Covent 51-720 1973 £8.50

FOX, CHARLES JAMES   A History of the Early Part of the Reign of James the Second. London, 1808. 4to., early 19th century straight-grained morocco, gilt, first edition. Ximenes 33-45 1974 $70

FOX, CHARLES JAMES   A History of the Early Part of the Reign of James the Second. 1808. 4to., contemporary diced calf, portrait. Bow Windows 64-508 1974 £6.50

FOX, CHARLES JAMES   A History of the Early Part of the Reign of James the Second. 1808. 4to., calf, gilt. Quaritch 936-381 1974 £10

FOX, CHARLES JAMES   History of the Old Township of Dunstable. Nashua, 1846. 8vo., orig. bindings, plates, fine. Butterfield 8-350 1974 $75

FOX, CHARLES JAMES   Memoirs of the Latter Years Of. 1811. 8vo., old half calf, rebacked. Hill 126-108 1974 £15

FOX, CHARLES JAMES   The Speeches. 1815. 6 vols., half calf gilt, labels, rubbed, sole edition. Howes 186-824 1974 £25

FOX, CLARA MASON   A History of El Toro. N.P., (1939). 4to., wrapper. Saddleback 14-103 1974 $50

FOX, FRANK   The Royal Inniskilling Fusiliers in the World War. London, (1938). 8vo., cloth boards, illus., maps. Emerald 50-316 1974 £6.50

FOX, GEORGE   A Journal. London, 1694. Sm. folio, 1st ed., old blind-stamped calf, rebacked and repaired, clasps missing; a very good copy. Jacobs 24-143 1974 $325

FOX, JOHN   The Little Shepherd of Kingdom Come. New York, 1931. Illus. and signed by N. C. Wyeth, 4to., limited to 512 copies, pages uncut, partly unopened, glassine wrapper, very fine, orig. binding. Butterfield 10-264 1974 $75

FOX, HELEN MONTAGU   Patio Gardens. New York, 1929. First edition, illus., bookplate, orig. binding. Wilson 63-316 1974 $15

FOX, R.   The History of Godmanchester. 1831. 8vo., buckram, foxing. Quaritch 939-391 1974 £6

FOX, R. M.   The Triumphant Machine. 1928. First edition. Covent 55-841 1974 £8.50

FOX, RALPH   The Novel and the People. 1937. Ex-library. Austin 61-378 1974 $10

FOX, W. S.   Letters of William Davies, Toronto, 1854-1861. Toronto, 1945. Hood's 104-634 1974 $17.50

FOX, WILLIAM F.   Regimental Losses in the American Civil War. Albany, 1889. 4to., front hinge cracked, firm, errata slip, orig.binding. Butterfield 10-155 1974 $65

FOX-DAVIES, ARTHUR CHARLES   Armorial Families. 1929-30. 2 vols., imp. 8vo., illus., buckram, seventh edition. Quaritch 939-723 1974 £30

FOX-DAVIES, ARTHUR CHARLES   The Book of Public Arms. 1915. Imp. 8vo., orig. cloth, illus. Broadhurst 23-74 1974 £25

FOX-DAVIES, ARTHUR CHARLES   The Book of Public Arms. 1915. Imp. 8vo., illus., orig. cloth, good copy. Broadhurst 24-68 1974 £20

FOX-DAVIES, ARTHUR CHARLES   A Complete Guide to Heraldry. c. 1930. Thick large 8vo., orig. buckram, illus. Howes 186-1634 1974 £7.50

FOX-DAVIES, ARTHUR CHARLES   The Mauleverer Murders. 1907. Orig. pictorial cloth, English first edition. Covent 56-236 1974 £15

FOXE, JOHN   Acts and Monuments. 1641. 2 vols., folio, old calf, worn. Thomas 28-93 1972 £18

FOXE, IOHN   Book of Martyrs. 1589. 2 parts in 1 vol., first abridged edition, woodcut illus., small 4to., contemporary calf, rebacked. Thomas 32-41 1974 £105

FRACASTORIUS, HIERONYMUS   Liber Vnvs, de Sympathia and Antipathia Rerum. 1554. 12mo., contemporary panelled calf, third edition. Dawsons PM 249-185 1974 £145

FRACASTORO, GIROLAMO   La Sifilide. Parma, 1829. Small folio, quarter calf, uncut, excellent condition. Thomas 28-317 1972 £18

FRACASTORO, GIROLAMO   De Sympathia & Antipathia Rerum. Lyons, 1550. Small 8vo., contemporary limp vellum, second edition. Schuman 37-84 1974 $265

FRACASTORO, GIROLAMO   Syphilis Sive Morbvs Gallicvs. Verona, 1530. 4to., 19th century vellum, early cryptographic inscription, first edition, fine and large copy of orig. edition. Kraus 137-32 1974 $2,600

FRADRYSSA, G. V.   Roman Catholicism Capitulating Before Protestantism. Mobile, 1908. 359 pages. Austin 37-223 1974 $10

FRAENKEL, G. S.   The Orientation of Animals. Oxford, 1940. 8vo., cloth, plates. Wheldon 130-354 1974 £7.50

FRAENKEL, MICHAEL   Death in a Room. New York, 1936. One of 200 copies on Satin Paper, presentation copy inscribed by author, stiff wrappers, fine. Covent 51-2339 1973 £21

FRAETAS, JOSIAH A.   Ethan Allen. New York, 1846. 8vo., orig. brick printed wrappers, fine, rare, first edition. Ximenes 33-46 1974 $125

FRAGONARD, J. H.   J. H. Fragonard, 1732-1806. Paris, 1906. 4to., plates, half morocco, worn, limited. Quaritch 940-105 1974 £50

FRAGOSO, R. G.   Flora Iberica: Uredales. Madrid, 1924-25. 2 vols., 8vo., cloth, text-figures. Wheldon 128-1358 1973 £7.50

FRAMSTAENDE Man Och Qvinnor I Var Tid. Chicago, 1890. Austin 62-425 1974 $27.50

FRANCATELLI, CHARLES ELME   The Cook's Guide. London, 1888. 8vo., orig. cloth, gilt, illus. Hammond 201-165 1974 £5.50

FRANCE, ANATOLE   Le Petit Pierre. Paris, (1918). 12mo., orig. wrapper, first edition. L. Goldschmidt 42-226 1974 $25

FRANCE, ANATOLE   Works of. New York, 1924. 30 vols., orig. cloth backed boards, paper labels, autograph edition, singed by author in vol. 1, fine set. MacManus 224-174 1974 $65

FRANCE, ANATOLE   Oeuvres Completes Illustrees. Paris, 1925-34. Small 4to., orig. wrapper, uncut, only complete edition. L. Goldschmidt 42-225 1974 $150

FRANCESCO D'ASSISI, SAINT   I Fioretti del Glorioso Poverello. 1922. 8vo.,
orig. limp vellum, woodcut illus., green silk ties, fine copy, limited to 240
copies, printed in black, red and blue.   Sawyer 293-40 1974 £120

FRANCHERE, GABRIEL   Narrative of a Voyage to the Northwest Coast
of America, 1811, 1812, 1813, and 1814. New York, 1854. Library binding.
Rittenhouse 46-687 1974 $75

FRANCHET, A.   Plantae Davidianae ex Sinarum Imperio.
Paris, 1884-88. 2 vols. in 1, roy. 4to., half morocco, plates, very rare.
Wheldon 128-1258 1973 £120

FRANCIS, G.   Chemical Experiments. London, 1842 & 1844.
2 works in 1 vol., 8vo., old half roan, worn, stains. Bow Windows 62-339
1974 £12

FRANCIS, GEORGE G.   Charters Granted to Swansea. 1867. Crown
folio, contemporary full morocco, gilt. Broadhurst 23-1383 1974 £30

FRANCIS, GEORGE G.   Charters Granted to Swansea, the Chief
Borough of the Seignory of Gower. 1867. Illus., maps, crown folio, contemporary
full morocco, panelled back, edges gilt, fine. Broadhurst 24-1420 1974 £30

FRANCIS, J. G.   A Book of Cheerful Cats and Other Animated
Animals. New York, 1911. Oblong 8vo., pict. boards, spine ends rubbed, illus.
Pres. copy. Frohnsdorff 16-336 1974 $75

FRANCIS, J. G.   The Joyous Aztecs, Pictures and Verse. New
York, 1929. Oblong 8vo., pictorial boards (spine and corners repaired).
Frohnsdorff 16-337 1974 $10

FRANCIS, JOHN   History of the Bank of England. 1847. Rebound
cloth, 2 vols., second edition. Covent 56-1540 1974 £42.50

FRANCIS, PHILIP   Constantine. London, 1754. 8vo., disbound,
first edition. Ximenes 33-47 1974 $30

FRANCIS, PHILLIP   Eugenia. 1752. 8vo., cloth, first edition.
Quaritch 936-81 1974 £10

FRANCIS, PHILIP   The Francis Letters. (1901). 2 vols., orig.
buckram gilt. Howes 185-181 1974 £7.50

FRANCIS, SALLY R.   "Scat, Scat." New York, 1940. Color plates.
Frohnsdorff 16-338 1974 $7.50

FRANCIS OF ASSISI
Please turn to
FRANCESCO D'ASSISI, SAINT

FRANCIS OF SALES   Oeuvres Completes. Paris, 1879. 12 vols.,
half morocco, rubbed, portrait. Howes 185-1173 1974 £16

FRANCIS OF SALES   Oeuvres. 1892-1932. 26 vols., thick large
8vo., cloth, best edition. Howes 185-1172 1974 £85

FRANCKE, KUNO   German Ideal of Today. 1907. 341 pages.
Austin 57-224 1974 $12.50

FRANCKE, KUNO   German Ideal of Today. Houghton, Mifflin,
1907. Austin 62-180 1974 $12.50

FRANCKENAU, GERHARDI ERNESTI DE   Bibliotheca Hispanica Historico-
Genealogico-Heraldica. Leipzig, 1724. 4to., contemporary calf, raised bands.
Dawsons PM 10-228 1974 £26

FRANCKLIN, THOMAS   The Earl of Warwick. Dublin, 1767. Small 8vo.,
cloth. Quaritch 936-82 1974 £6

FRANCKLIN, THOMAS   Matilda. 8vo., cloth, first edition. Quaritch
936-83 1974 £10

FRANCKLIN, THOMAS   Matilda. London, 1775. 8vo., modern
boards, first edition. Dawsons PM 252-376 1974 £15

FRANCKLIN, THOMAS   Matilda. London, 1775. 8vo., disbound,
first edition. Ximenes 33-48 1974 $25

FRANCO, GIACOMO   Descrittione di Quello che i Turchi Possedono
in Europa. (Venice, 17th century). Oblong 4to., old vellum backed boards,
first edition. Harper 213-69 1973 $450

FRANCOEUR, L. B.   Astronomie Pratique. Paris, 1830. 8vo., rebound, blue cloth, plates. Dawsons PM 245-299 1974 £5.50

FRANK, A. B.   Die Krankheiten der Pflanzen. Breslau, 1895-
96. 8vo., 3 vols., half calf, second edition. Wheldon 130-1280 1974 £5

FRANK, BRUNO   Sturm im Wasserglas. Munchen, 1930. Wrappers, first German edition. Covent 56-477 1974 £7.50

FRANK, GERALD   Zsa Zsa Gabor. World, 1960. 308p., illus.
Austin 51-321 1973 $6.50

FRANK, WALDO   City Block. Darien, 1922. Orig. cloth
backed boards, first edition, presentation copy from author to John Stuart Groves,
with his bookplate, fine, cloth slipcase. MacManus 224-175 1974 $25

FRANK, WALDO   Holiday. New York, 1923. Ist ed. Biblo &
Tannen 213-542 1973 $7.50

FRANK, WALDO   The Jew in Our Day. New York, 1944. Dust
wrapper, first U.S. edition. Covent 56-479 1974 £5.25

FRANK, WALDO   The Jew In Our Day. Duell, 1944. Austin
62-181 1974 $6.50

FRANK, WALDO   The Unwelcome Man. Boston, 1917. Orig.
cloth, first edition, very good copy, Stephen Vincent Benet's copy with his
signature. MacManus 224-176 1974 $60

FRANK, WALDO   Virgin Spain. 1926. Dust wrapper, English
first edition. Covent 56-1767 1974 £5.25

FRANK, WALTER   Nationalismus und Demokratie im Frankreich
der Dritten Republik. Hamburg, 1933. Nazi rubber stamp on Copyright page.
Biblo & Tannen 210-1027 1973 $15

FRANKAU, JULIA   William Ward, A.R.A. and James Ward, R.A.,
Their Lives and Works. 1904. Photogravures. Eaton Music-685 1973 £6

FRANKEN, ROSE   Soldier's Wife. French, 1945. 167p., illus.
Austin 51-322 1973 $7.50

FRANKEN, ROSE   Soldier's Wife. French, 1945. 167p., paper.
Austin 51-323 1973 $6.50

FRANKENBERG, LLOYD   The Red Kite. New York, 1939. First U. S.
edition, one of 500 numbered copies, numbered & signed by author, very good,
remains of d.w. loosely inserted. Covent 51-722 1973 £7.50

FRANKLIN, ARTHUR E.   Records of the Franklin Family and Collaterals.
1935. Crown 4to., second edition. Howes 186-1634A 1974 £8.50

FRANKLIN, BENJAMIN   The Autobiography. 1906. Limited to 1000
copies, photogravure illus., 4to., all edges untrimmed. Butterfield 10-265 1974
$15

FRANKLIN, BENJAMIN   The Autobiography of Benjamin Franklin.
Chicago, 1903. Decor. cloth, gilt. Dykes 24-75 1974 $25

FRANKLIN, BENJAMIN   The Collection of Franklin Imprints in the
Museum of the Curtis Publishing Company. Philadelphia, 1918. Demy 4to., fine.
Broadhurst 24-283 1974 £14

FRANKLIN, BENJAMIN   Experiences et Observations sur l'Electricite Faites
a Philadelphia en Amerique. Paris, 1752. Small 8vo., contemporary calf,
rebacked, plate. Gurney 66-64 1974 £50

FRANKLIN, BENJAMIN   Experiences et Observations sur l'Electricite.
Durand, 1752. Small 8vo., contemporary calf, rebacked. Gurney 64-90 1974
£50

FRANKLIN, BENJAMIN   Experiments and Observations on Electricity.
London, 1774. 4to., contemporary half calf, rebacked, gilt, uncut, plates, fifth
edition. Dawsons PM 245-300 1974 £145

FRANKLIN, BENJAMIN   Experiments and Observations on Electricity.
London, 1774. 4to., half calf, uncut, fifth edition. Gurney 64-89 1974 £115

FRANKLIN, BENJAMIN   Experiments and Observations on Electricity,
Made at Philadelphia in America . . . to which is added, Letters and Papers on
Philosophical Subjects. With, Political, Miscellaneous, and Philosophical
Pieces. London, 1774 & 1779. 2 vols., 4to., contemporary calf, gilt, fine,
some scattered foxing. Ximenes 36-97 1974 $500

FRANKLIN, BENJAMIN   The Ingenious Dr. Franklin . . . Selected
Scientific Letters of. Philadelphia, 1931. First edition, orig. binding, dust
wrapper. Wilson 63-91 1974 $10

FRANKLIN, BENJAMIN   Memoires. Paris, 1828. 12mo., 2 vols., orig.
printed wrappers, worn, foxed. Dawsons PM 251-118 1974 £10

FRANKLIN, BENJAMIN   Memoirs of the Life and Writings. London,
1833. 8vo., 6 vols., contemporary tree calf, gilt, rebacked, orig. spines
preserved, nice set, plates. Gurney 66-65 1974 £42

FRANKLIN, BENJAMIN   New Experiments and Observations on Electricity.
London, 1760. 4to., modern wrappers, third edition. Dawsons PM 245-301 1974
£60

FRANKLIN, BENJAMIN   La Science du Bonhomme Richard, due Moyen
Facile de Payer les Impots. 1777. Full vellum. Jenkins 61-902 1974 $45

FRANKLIN, BENJAMIN   Works. London, 1793. 2 vols., 8vo.,
contemporary polished calf, first edition. Schuman 37-86 1974 $165

FRANKLIN, BENJAMIN   Works. London, 1793. 2 vols., 8vo.,
contemporary half calf, first English edition. Dawsons PM 252-377 1974 £55

FRANKLIN, HAROLD B.   Sound Motion Pictures. Doubleday, Doran,
1929. 401p., illus. Austin 51-325 1973 $12.50

FRANKLIN, WILLIAM SUDDARDS   Electric Waves. New York, 1909. 8vo.,
cloth, first edition. Dawsons PM 245-302 1974 £6

FRANKS, ROBERT S.   A History of the Doctrine of the Work of Christ.
(1918). 2 vols. Howes 185-1176 1974 £5.50

FRANZ, J. C. A.   A Treatise on Mineral Waters. London, 1842.
8vo., orig. cloth, gilt, fine, first edition. Hammond 201-569 1974 £24

FRANZ-JOSEPH, EMPEROR   Cortege Historique de la Ville de Vienne a
l'Occasion des Noces d'Argent de leurs Majestes Francois-Joseph I et Elisabeth.
Paris, (c. 1880). Roy. folio, plates, three quarter levant morocco, gilt,
limited. Quaritch 940-106 1974 £50

FRANZIUS, W.   Historia Animalium. Amsterdam, 1665. 12mo.,
old calf, scarce. Wheldon 130-355 1974 £10

FRASER, ALEXANDER   Brock Centenary, 1812-1912, Account of the
Celebration at Queenston Heights, Ontario, October 12, 1912. Toronto, 1913.
Letter from Fraser tipped in. Hood's 102-603 1974 $35

FRASER, ALEXANDER   Toronto, Historical, Descriptive and Pictorial.
Toronto, 1899. Wrappers. Hood's 103-631 1974 $10

FRASER, CHARLES MC LEAN   Hydroids of the Pacific Coast. Toronto, 1937.
8vo., cloth, plates, scarce. Wheldon 129-780 1974 £7.50

FRASER, CLAUDE LOVAT   Claude Lovat Fraser. 1923. Roy. 4to.,
plates, buckram, limited edition. Quaritch 940-107 1974 £15

FRASER, CLAUD LOVAT   The Luck of the Bean-Rows. London, 1921.
8vo., cloth spine, 1st ed., illus. Frohnsdorff 16-340 1974 $15

FRASER, CLAUD LOVAT   The Luck of the Bean-Rows. London, 1921.
8vo., dec. boards, cloth spine, 1st ed., illus. Frohnsdorff 16-341 1974 $15

FRASER, CLAUD LOVAT   Nurse Lovechild's Legacy. London, 1922.
8vo., pict. boards, cloth spine, illus. Frohnsdorff 16-342 1974 $15

FRASER, CLAUD LOVAT   Nursery Rhymes with Pictures. London, 1919.
4to., pict. boards, cloth spine, 1st ed., illus. Frohnsdorff 16-343 1974 $40

FRASER, CLAUD LOVAT   The Woodcutter's Dog. London, 1921. 8vo.,
boards, 1st ed., illus. Frohnsdorff 16-344 1974 $15

FRASER, J.   Canadian Pen and Ink Sketches. Montreal, 1890.
Three Quarter leather, marbled covers. Hood's 102-557 1974 $25

FRASER, J.   Fraser's Panoramic Plan of London. (c.1830).
8vo., cloth case, map. Quaritch 939-839 1974 £20

FRASER, J.   A Tale of the Sea. Montreal, 1870. Illus.,
ex-library. Hood's 103-724 1974 $12.50

FRASER, JAMES   Major Fraser's Manuscript. Edinburgh, 1889.
Small 8vo., 2 vols., frontispieces, half polished red calf, gilt. Quaritch 936-
382 1974 £10

FRASER, JAMES BAILLIE   Allee Neemroo. London, 1842. 3 vols.,
12mo., contemporary half calf, first edition, very good copy. Ximenes 36-98
1974 $70

FRASER, JAMES BAILLIE   The Persian Adventurer. London, 1830. 3
vols., 12mo., contemporary half calf, first edition, very good. Ximenes 36-
99 1974 $75

FRASER, JOHN FOSTER   The Conquering Jew. Funk and Wagnall,
1915. Austin 62-182 1974 $12.50

FRASER, R.   A Letter to the Rt. Hon. Charles Abbot. 1803.
8vo., half calf, map, rubbed. Quaritch 939-655 1974 £50

FRASER, THOMAS R.   On the Physiological Action of the Calabar
Bean. Edinburgh, 1867. 4to., inscription, disbound. Bow Windows 62-1034
1974 £6

FRASER, WILLIAM ALEXANDER   Thoroughbreds. Toronto, 1925. Inscribed and
signed by author. Hood's 102-513 1974 $12

FRASER, WILLIAM AUGUSTUS   Poems By the Knight of Morar. London, 1867.
4to., orig. blue cloth, scarce, first edition. Ximenes 33-50 1974 $65

FRAUNHOFER, JOSEPH VON   Gesammelte Schriften. Munich, 1888. Large
4to., old-style half morocco, orig. wrappers, plates, first collected edition.
Schuman 37-87 1974 $285

FRAY, EDMUND   Pantographia. London, 1799. Large 8vo.,
contemporary calf, gilt, first edition. Dawsons PM 10-229 1974 £110

FRAZER, JAMES GEORGE   Adonis Attis Osiris. 1906. Orig. buckram,
signed. Smith 194-825 1974 £8

FRAZER, JAMES GEORGE   Anthologia Anthropologica. 1939. 4to.,
double column, map. Bow Windows 64-98 1974 £15

FRAZER, JAMES GEORGE   The Belief in Immortality and the Worship of
the Dead. 1913, 1922 and 1924. 3 vols., demy 8vo., orig. cloth, fine.
Broadhurst 24-1236 1974 £12

FRAZER, JAMES GEORGE   The Belief in Immortality and the Worship of the
Dead. 1913-22. 2 vols., orig. cloth. Smith 193-776 1973 £6

FRAZER, JAMES GEORGE   Folk-Lore in the Old Testament. 1918. 3 vols.,
orig. cloth, first edition. Smith 193-777 1973 £7.50

FRAZER, JAMES GEORGE   Folk Lore in the Old Testament. 1919.
3 vols., 8vo., orig. cloth, spines faded. Bow Windows 66-252 1974 £12

FRAZER, JAMES GEORGE   Folk-Lore in the Old Testament. 1919. Demy
8vo., orig. cloth, 3 vols., fine. Broadhurst 24-1237 1974 £10

FRAZER, JAMES GEORGE   Folk-Lore in the Old Testament. 1919. 3 vols.,
large 8vo., faded. Howes 186-1829 1974 £12.50

FRAZER, JAMES GEORGE   The Golden Bough. 1900. 3 vols., 8vo.,
orig. cloth, frontispiece, inscription on fly-leaf, covers marked, revised second
edition. Bow Windows 66-253 1974 £10

FRAZER, JAMES GEORGE   The Golden Bough. 1890. 2 vols., roy. 8vo.,
first edition. Smith 193-778 1973 £6

FRAZER, JAMES GEORGE   Totemism and Exogamy. 1910. 4 vols.,
thick 8vo., orig. & best edition. Howes 186-1832 1974 £32

FREART, ROLAND   A Parallel of the Ancient Architecture. 1654.
Folio, half morocco, gilt, plates. Broadhurst 23-75 1974 £130

FRECULPHUS, BISHOP   Chronicorum Tomi II. Cologne, 1539. Folio,
modern half vellum, very fine, first edition. Schafer 8-112 1973 sFr. 900

FREDERIC, HAROLD   March Hares. New York, 1896. Orig. dec.
cloth, fine, first American edition. Covent 55-734 1974 £15

FREDERIC and George; or, The Utility of Play-Ground Sports, as Conducive to
Health, Hilarity, and Hardihood. (c. 1810). Copperplates, 12mo., contemporary
stiff wrappers, spine defective, rare. George's 610-299 1973 £7.50

FREDERICK, CHARLES   Fox-hunting. London, 1947. 4 color plates.
Biblo & Tannen 213-1010 1973 $17.50

FREEDGOOD, MORTON   The Wall-to-Wall Trap. Simon, Schuster,
1957. 243p. Austin 51-326 1973 $7.50

FREEDLEY, EDWIN T.   Philadelphia and Its Manufactures. Philadelphia,
1859. 8vo., orig. bindings. Butterfield 8-545 1974 $25

FREELING, ARTHUR   The Railway Companion. London, 1838. 8vo.,
map. Traylen 79-308 1973 £30

FREEMAN, DOUGLAS SOUTHALL   Lee's Dispatches. New York and London,
1915. Orig. binding. Butterfield 10-156 1974 $35

FREEMAN, DOUGLAS SOUTHALL   R. E. Lee. New York, 1934-35. 4 vols.,
full brown morocco, gilt, first edition. Bradley 35-140 1974 $250

FREEMAN, DOUGLAS SOUTHALL   R. E. Lee: A Biography. 1934-35. 4 vols.,
large 8vo., plates, illus. Howes 186-1733a 1974 £18

FREEMAN, EDWARD A.   The History of the Norman Conquest of England.
1870-79. 6 vols., thick 8vo., orig. cloth. Howes 186-832 1974 £55

FREEMAN, EDWARD A.   History of the Norman Conquest of England, Its
Causes & Its Results. 1870-79. 6 vols. Allen 213-1482 1973 $45

FREEMAN, EDWARD A.   The Reign of William Rufus and the Accession
of Henry the First. Oxford, 1881. 2 vols., contemporary plum calf, maps,
first edition. Smith 194-697 1974 £13

FREEMAN, H. W.   Down in the Valley. 1930. Fine, quarter
buckram, signed. Covent 55-736 1974 £5.25

FREEMAN, JOHN   Fifty Poems. 1911. Orig. wrappers, fine,
limp morocco, English first edition. Covent 56-481 1974 £5.25

FREEMAN, JOHN   The Grove and Other Poems. 1924. Fine,
signature, English first edition. Covent 56-482 1974 £5.25

FREEMAN, JOHN   Memories of Childhood. 1918. Illus., wrappers, signature, English first edition. Covent 56-484 1974 £6.30

FREEMAN, JOHN   A Portrait of George Moore in a Study Of His
Work. 1922. Orig. half parchment, uncut, limited, special edition. Howes
185-338 1974 £7.50

FREEMAN, JOHN   Presage of Victory and Other Poems. 1916.
Wrappers, signature, English first edition. Covent 56-486 1974 £7.50

FREEMAN, JOHN   The Red Path. Cambridge, 1921. 8vo., orig.
holland backed boards, hand made paper, numbered, signed by author, first
ordinary edition. Bow Windows 66-254 1974 £5

FREEMAN, JOHN   Two Poems. Cambridge, 1921. Rubbed.
Ballinger 1-18 1974 $17

FREEMAN, L. R.   On the Roof of the Rockies. London, 1926.
Photographs, mended spine. Hood's 104-853 1974 $12.50

FREEMAN, LYDIA   Pet of the Met. New York, 1953. Oblong
4to., cloth, illus., lst ed., mint copy. Frohnsdorff 16-345 1974 $10

FREEMAN, M. B.   Herbs for the Mediaeval Household. New York,
1943. 4to., illus., fine, orig. cloth, d.w. Gregory 44-135 1974 $8.50

FREEMAN, NATHANIEL C.   Parnassus in Philadelphia. Philadelphia,
1854. 12mo., orig. boards, first edition. Ximenes 33-51 1974 $17.50

FREEMAN, R. AUSTIN   The Cat's Eye. London, ca. 1923. lst ed.
Biblo & Tannen 210-455 1973 $17.50

FREEMAN, R. AUSTIN   Dr. Thorndyke Intervenes. 1933. 8vo., orig.
cloth, dust wrapper, first edition. Rota 190-264 1974 £10

FREEMAN, R. AUSTIN   Dr. Thorndyke Intervenes. New York, 1933.
Biblo & Tannen 210-457 1973 $8.50

FREEMAN, R. AUSTIN   Dr. Thorndyke's Case-book. London, n.d.
lst ed. Biblo & Tannen 210-456 1973 $17.50

FREEMAN, R. AUSTIN   Dr. Thorndyke's Case-Book. (1923). 8vo.,
orig. cloth, first edition. Rota 190-262 1974 £10

FREEMAN, R. AUSTIN   The Great Portrait Mystery. (1918). 8vo.,
orig. cloth, scarce, first edition. Rota 190-261 1974 £10

FREEMAN, R. AUSTIN   The Magic Casket. (1927). 8vo., orig. cloth,
presentation inscription, first edition. Rota 190-263 1974 £20

FREEMAN, R. AUSTIN   Mr. Polton Explains. New York, 1940.
lst Amer. ed. Biblo & Tannen 210-458 1973 $7.50

FREEMAN, R. AUSTIN   Mr. Pottermack's Oversight. New York,
1930. lst Amer. ed. Biblo & Tannen 210-459 1973 $10

FREEMAN, R. AUSTIN   The Mystery of Angelina Frood. New York,
1925. lst Amer. ed. Biblo & Tannen 210-460 1973 $10

FREEMAN, R. AUSTIN   The Mystery of 31 New Inn. London, 1939.
Biblo & Tannen 210-461 1973 $7.50

FREEMAN, R. AUSTIN   Pontifex, Son and Thorndyke. New York,
1931. lst Amer. ed. Biblo & Tannen 210-462 1973 $7.50

FREEMAN, R. AUSTIN   The Unconscious Witness. New York, 1942.
lst Amer. ed. Biblo & Tannen 210-463 1973 $8.50

FREEMAN, R. AUSTIN   The Uttermost Farthing. Philadelphia, 1914.
lst ed. Biblo & Tannen 210-464 1973 $25

FREEMAN, W. G.   The World's Commercial Products. 1908. 4to.,
cloth, photographic illus., coloured plates. Wheldon 128-1649 1973 £6

FREEMAN, W. G.   The World's Commercial Products. 1908. 4to.,
cloth, illus., plates. Wheldon 130-1586 1974 £6

FREEMANTLE, W. T.   A Bibliography of Sheffield and Vicinity.
Sheffield & London, 1911. 4to., plates, orig. buckram. Dawsons PM 10-553
1974 £15

THE FREEMEN'S Glee Book. New York, 1856. 12mo. Biblo & Tannen 214-844
1974 $20

FREESTON, CHARLES L.   Motoring on the Continent. London, n.d.
Maps, illus., orig. binding. Butterfield 10-73 1974 $10

FREIBURG IM BREISGAU   Nuwe Stattrechten und Statuten der Loblichen
Statt Fryburg in Pryszgow Gelegen. Basel, 1520. Folio, old boards, vellum
back, very fine, rare. Harper 213-70 1973 $2500

FREILIGRATH, FERDINAND   Rose, Thistle and Shamrock. Stuttgart, 1874.
Illus. Austin 61-380 1974 $10

FREIND, JOHN   Emmenologia. Oxford, 1703. 8vo., contemporary full morocco, gilt, first edition. Broadhurst 23-1232 1974 £200

FREIND, JOHN   The History of Physick. London, 1725-6. 8vo.,
2 vols., contemporary calf, rebacked, second edition. Gurney 64-91 1974 £75

FREKE, JOHN   An Essay on the Art of Healing. London, 1748.
8vo., old calf, rebacked, first edition. Dawsons PM 249-186 1974 £48

FRELINGHUYSEN, THEODORUS JACOBUS   Sermons of Theodorus Jacobus
Frelinghuysen. 1856. 422p. Austin 62-183 1974 $37.50

FREMONT, JESSIE BENTON   The Story of the Guard: A Chronicel of the
War. Boston, 1863. Orig. cloth, gilt, very fine copy. Jenkins 61-907 1974
$13.50

FREMONT, JOHN CHARLES   Narrative of the Exploring Expedition to the
Rocky Mountains in 1842; and to Oregon and North California in 1843-44.
Syracuse, 1846. First Syracuse edition, orig. binding. Butterfield 10-266 1974
$25

FREMONT and Sandusky County. Fremont, (1940). Folding map. Hayman
59-458 1974 $10

FRENCH, B. B.   "The Changes of Earth". N. P., c. 1850.
12mo., half roan, first edition. Goodspeed's 578-104 1974 $10

FRENCH, C.   A Handbook of the Destructive Insects of Victoria. Melbourne, 1891-1911. 8vo., 5 vols., orig. cloth. Wheldon 129-642 1974 £15

FRENCH, G. D.   The Life & Times of Samuel Crompton.
Manchester & London, 1860. Frontispiece, illus. Covent 55-1300 1974 £18

FRENCH, HIRAM T.   History of Idaho. Chicago, 1914. 3 vols.,
4to., three quarter leather, illus. Saddleback 14-360 1974 $100

FRENCH, J.   Sermons Delivered on the 20th of August, 1812.
Exeter, (1812?). Hood's 103-535 1974 $25

FRENCH, JAMES   Clongibbon. Dublin, 1845. 8vo., cloth
boards, rebacked, scarce. Emerald 50-319 1974 £18

FRENCH, LAURA M.   History of Emporia and Lyon County. Emporia,
1929. 12mo., cloth, presenatation. Saddleback 14-425 1974 $35

FRENCH, WILLIAM LESLIE   The Psychology of Handwriting. New York,
1922. Bdg. rubbed. Biblo & Tannen 213-959 1973 $12.50

FRENCH Art of the 18th Century. 1914. 4to., plates, buckram. Quaritch
940-788 1974 £30

FRENCH Master Drawings of the 18th Century. New York, 1949. Biblo & Tannen
214-114 1974 $7.50

FRENCH Painting from David to Toulouse-Lautrec. New York, 1941. Biblo &
Tannen 210-139 1973 $6.50

FRENCH VIRTUOSI   Another Collection of Philosophical Conferences
of the French Virtuosi. London, 1665. Folio, contemporary calf, stain.
Traylen 79-227 1973 £38

FRENEAU, PHILIP   The Miscellaneous Works. Philadelphia,
1788. 12mo., contemporary sheep, first edition. Ximenes 33-52 1974 $80

FRENEAU, PHILIP   Poems Relating to the American Revolution.
New York, 1865. Marbled boards & leather. Butterfield 10-26 1974 $15

FRENILLY, AUGUSTE FRANCOIS FAUVEAU, MARQUIS DE 1768-1848
Recollections. 1909. 8vo., vellum, gilt, frontis. Quaritch 936-354 1974 £45

FRERE, JOHN HOOKAM   Works, In Verse and Prose. 1874. 3 vols.,
half morocco, revised second edition. Allen 216-2012 1974 $25

FRERICHS, FRIEDRICH THEODORE   Traite Pratique des Maladies du Foie. Paris,
1866. 8vo., contemporary marbled boards. Dawsons PM 249-187 1974 £15

FRESH Flowers for My Children. Boston, 1842. 16mo., embossed cloth, gilt,
fine engravings, lst ed. Frohnsdorff 16-346 1974 $10

FRESNEL, AUGUSTIN   Memoire sur un Nouveau Systeme d'Eclairage
des Phares . . . lu a l'Academie des Sciences. Paris, 1822. 4to., orig. wrapper,
uncut, unopened, plates, first edition, very rare. Gurney 66-66 1974 £70

FRESNEL, AUGUSTIN   Oeuvres Completes. Paris, 1866-70. 4to., 3
vols., contemporary morocco, gilt, first collected edition. Dawsons PM 245-303
1974 £85

FREUCHEN, P.   Ice Floes and Flaming Water. London, n.d.
Hood's 103-60 1974 $10

FREUD, SIGMUND   Aus der Geschichte einer Infantilen Neurose.
Leipzig, Vienna and Zurich, 1924. 8vo., orig. boards, first separate edition.
Dawsons PM 249-190 1974 £18

FREUD, SIGMUND   Beyond the Pleasure Principle. London, 1922.
8vo., cloth, first edition in English. Schuman 37-90 1974 $45

FREUD, SIGMUND   Das Ich und das Es. Leipzig, 1923. 8vo.,
wrappers, first edition. Gilhofer 61-89 1974 sFr. 250

FREUD, SIGMUND   Das Ich und das Es. Leipzig, Vienna and
Zurich, 1923. 8vo., boards, wrappers in, first edition. Gurney 66-67 1974
£30

FREUD, SIGMUND   Die Traumdeutung. Leipzig, 1900. 8vo.,
modern full red morocco, library stamp, fine, first edition. Dawsons PM
250-30 1974 £1750

FREUD, SIGMUND   Die Traumdeutung. 1900. 8vo., modern full
red morocco, fine, first edition. Dawsons PM 249-188 1974 £1,750

FREUD, SIGMUND   Dream Psychology. New York, 1921. 1st
Amer. ed. Biblo & Tannen 213-960 1973 $10

FREUD, SIGMUND   The Ego and the Id. London, 1927. 8vo.,
cloth, first edition in English. Schuman 37-91 1974 $75

FREUD, SIGMUND   The Future of an Illusion. London, 1928. 8vo.,
orig. green cloth, uncut. Dawsons PM 249-191 1974 £8

FREUD, SIGMUND   Group Psychology and the Analysis of the Ego.
London, 1922. 8vo., cloth, worn, first edition in English. Schuman 37-92
1974 $75

FREUD, SIGMUND   Hemmung, Symptom und Angst. Wien, 1926.
Large 8vo., orig. cloth, first edition. Gilhofer 61-92 1974 sFr. 400

FREUD, SIGMUND   Leonardo da Vinci. New York, 1947.
Biblo & Tannen 213-961 1973 $6.50

FREUD, SIGMUND   Massenpsychologie und Ich-Analyse. Leipzig,
1921. First edition, some pencil scoring, very good copy. Covent 51-744
1973 £15

FREUD, SIGMUND   Three Contributions to the Sexual Theory.
New York, 1910. 8vo., orig. pictured wrappers, unopened, first edition in
English. Schuman 37-94 1974 $110

FREUD, SIGMUND   Totem and Tabu. Leipzig & Vienna, 1913.
4to., boards, first edition. Gilhofer 61-80 1974 sFr. 800

FREUD, SIGMUND   Totem and Taboo. London, 1919. 8vo.,
cloth, dust jacket, first English edition. Schuman 37-93 1974 $75

FREUD, SIGMUND   Uber Psychoanalyse. Leipzig & Vienna, 1910.
8vo., cloth-backed boards, first edition. Schuman 37-88 1974 $145

FREUD, SIGMUND   Zur Geschichte der Psychoanalytischen
Bewegung. Leipzig, Vienna, Zurich, 1924. 8vo., cloth-backed boards, first
separate edition. Schuman 37-89 1974 $50

FREUNDLICH, ERWIN   Die Grundlagen der Einsteinschen Gravitations
Theorie. Berlin, 1917. Wrappers, enlarged second edition. Covent 55-1301
1974 £5.25

FREWER, G. D.   Frewer's Handbook for Lake Shipmasters and
Officers. Toronto, 1925. Leather. Hood's 103-15 1974 $10

FREWIN, LESLIE   Blond Venus. Roy, 1956. 159p., illus.
Austin 51-327 1973 $7.50

FREWIN, LESLIE   The Story of a Star. Stein, Day, 1967.
191p., illus. Austin 51-328 1973 $6.50

FREY-WYSSLING, A.   Submikroscopische Morphologie des Protoplasmas.
Berlin, 1938. 8vo., cloth. Wheldon 130-105 1974 £5

FREYER, P. J.   Clinical Lectures On Enlargement of the
Prostate. New York, 1906. Third edition. Rittenhouse 46-270 1974 $10

FREYGANG, JOSEPH E.   Twenty Years in the Church of Rome.
Cincinnati, 1843. Cloth, minor internal damp stains, rare. Hayman 59-196
1974 $20

FREYTAG, GEORG WILHELM FRIEDRICH   Lexicon Arabico-Latinum ex Opere suo
Maiore in Usum Tironum Excerptum. Halle, 1837. Large thick 4to., cloth backed
boards, rebacked, excellent condition, uncut, unpressed. Thomas 30-10 1974
£21

FREYTAG, GUSTAV   The Technic of the Drama. Foresman, 1894.
395p., orig. ed. Austin 51-329 1973 $6.50

FREZIER, A. E.   A Voyage to the South-Sea, and Along the
Coasts of Chili and Peru, 1712-14. London, 1717. 4to., modern panelled
calf antique, gilt, plates, first English edition. Traylen 79-428 1973 £175

FREZIER, AMEDEE FRANCOIS   Traite des Feux D'Aritifice. 1741. 12mo.,
modern paper boards, plates. Zeitlin 235-86 1974 $85

THE FRICK Collection. New York, 1935. 12mo., illus. Biblo & Tannen 210-140
1973 $8.50

FRIDRICH, CARL   Rechenbuch Worin Zu Ersehen Ist. Wien, 1821.
8vo., contemporary marbled wrappers, first edition. Dawsons PM 247-127
1974 £10

FRIEDBERG, EMIL   Lehrbuch des Katholischen und Evangelischen
Kirchenrechts. Leipzig, 1909. Roy. 8vo., orig. cloth. Howes 185-1178
1974 £7.50

FRIEDENTHAL, H.   Tierhaaratlas. Jena, 1911. Folio, coloured
and plain plates, cloth-backed boards, rare. Wheldon 128-315 1973 £22

FRIEDENTHAL, H.   Tierhaaratlas. Jena, 1911. Folio, cloth backed boards, plates, rare. Wheldon 130-394 1974 £22

FRIEDENWALD, HERBERT   A Calendar of Washington Manuscripts in the
Library of Congress. Washington, 1901. Cloth, uncut. Jenkins 61-2598
1974 $12.50

FRIEDLANDER, GERALD   Laws and Customs of Israel. London, 1949.
Biblo & Tannen 214-791 1974 $12.50

FRIEDMAN, BRUCE J.   A Mother's Kisses. S & S, 1964. 286p., lst
ed. Austin 54-405 1973 $7.50

FRIEDMAN, HERBERT 1900-   Birds Collected by the Childs Frick Expedition.
Washington, 1930. 8vo., wrappers, scarce. Wheldon 129-466 1974 £5

FRIEDMAN, LEE M.   Jewish Pioneers and Patriots. 1942.
430 pages. Austin 57-228 1974 $10

FRIEDMAN, LEE M.   Jewish Pioneers and Patriots. 1942. 430p.,
illus. Austin 62-184 1974 $10

FRIEDMAN, LEE M.   Jewish Pioneers and Patriots. Philadelphia,
1942. Biblo & Tannen 213-623 1973 $8.50

FRIEDMAN, LEE M.   Jewish Pioneers and Patriots. New York, 1943.
Illus. Jenkins 61-910 1974 $12.50

FRIEDMAN, LEE M.   Pilgrims In a New Land. 1948. 471p., illus.
Austin 62-185 1974 $12.50

FRIEDMANN, HERBERT 1900-   Birds Collected by the Childs Frick Expedition.
Washington, 1930-37. 8vo., 2 vols., cloth, plates, scarce. Wheldon 130-519
1974 £10

FRIEDREICH, A.   Traite des Maladies du Coeur. Paris, 1873.
8vo., blue half calf. Dawsons PM 249-194 1974 £8

FRIEDRICH, P.   Beitrage zur Kenntniss der Tertiarflora der
Provinz Sachsen. Berlin, 1883. 2 vols., roy. 8vo., and 4to., map, atlas of
plates. Wheldon 128-971 1973 £7.50

FRIEL, BRIAN   Philadelphia Here I Come. 1965. 110p.
Austin 51-330 1973 $4

FRIEND, H.   Flowers and Flower Lore. 1884. 2 vols., wom,
stained, frayed, foxing. Bow Windows 64-99 1974 £6.50

FRIEND, H.   Flowers and Flower Lore. 1884. 8vo., orig.
cloth, second edition. Wheldon 130-162 1974 £5

FRIEND, JOHN   Chymical Lectures. 1712. 8vo., contemporary
panelled sheep, rebacked, rare, first edition in English. Hill 126-109 1974
£135

FRIENDSHIPS'S Offering: A Christmas, New Year, and Birthday Present, for
MDCCCLIV. Philadelphia, 1854. Red leather, rubbed, engraved plates.
Hayman 59-197 1974 $10

FRIES, E. M.   Epicrisis Systematis Mycologici. Uppsala, 1836-
38. 8vo., half calf gilt. Wheldon 129-1206 1974 £35

FRIES, E. M.   Hymenomycetes Europaei. Ippsala, 1874. 8vo.,
half calf. Wheldon 129-1205 1974 £40

FRIES, E. M.   Icones Selectae Hymenomycetum. 1867-84.
Folio, 2 vols., contemporary half morocco, plates. Wheldon 129-15 1974 £500

FRIES, E. M.   Novitae Florae Suecicae. Lund, 1828. 8vo.,
half leather, worn, second edition. Wheldon 128-1259 1973 £7.50

FRIES, E. M.   Novitiae Florae Suecicae. Lund, 1828.
8vo., half leather, worn. Wheldon 131-1288 1974 £7.50

FRIES, E. M.   Novitiae Florae Suecicae. 1828-42. 8vo.,
2 vols., cloth, boards, second edition. Wheldon 129-1070 1974 £20

FRIES, E. M.   Summa Vegetabilium Scandinaviae. Leipzig
& Stockholm, 1846. Part 1 only, 8vo., half calf, rubbed. Wheldon 131-1290
1974 £5

FRIES, E. M.   Summa Vegetabilium Scandinaviae. Stockholm,
1846-49. 8vo., half calf. Wheldon 129-1207 1974 £15

FRIES, E. M.   Sveriges Atliga och Giftiga Svampar. Stockholm, 1860. Folio, orig. half morocco, plates. Wheldon 129-16 1974 £180

FRIES, E. M.   Sveriges Atliga Och Giftiga Svampar.
Stockholm, 1860. Folio, orig. half morocco, plates, rare. Wheldon 131-48
1974 £180

FRIES, E. M.   Systema Mycologicum. 1821-30. 8vo., 5
vols., modern buckram. Wheldon 129-1204 1974 £100

FRIES, JOHANN JACOB   Bibliotheca Philosophorum Classicorum Authorum
Chronologica. Zurich, 1592. Small 4to., cloth, carefully restored, very well
preserved & fresh copy. Schumann 499-38 1974 sFr 255

FRIES, LORENZ   Epitome Opusculi de Curandis Pusculis Ulceribus.
Basileae, 1532. 4to., full calf antique, gilt. Hammond 201-538 1974 £125

FRIES, LORENZ   Spiegel der Artzney. Strassburg, 1529. Folio,
vellum, woodcut. Schuman 37-96 1974 $1700

FRIPP, E. I.   Shakespeare, Man & Artist. Oxford, 1938.
2 vols., orig. cloth, plates, dust wrappers. Smith 194-231 1974 £5.50

FRISBIE, A. L.   The Siege of Calais. Des Moines, 1880. 8vo.,
orig. green cloth, inscribed, first edition. Ximenes 33-53 1974 $15

FRISCH, K. VON   Der Farbensinn und Formensinn der Biene.
1914. 8vo., cloth, plates. Wheldon 129-710 1974 £6

FRISCH, K. VON   Uber die "Sprache" der Bienen. 1923. 8vo.,
cloth, plates. Wheldon 129-713 1974 £5

FRISCH, K. VON   Uber die "Sprache" der Bienen. Jena, 1923.
8vo., cloth, plates. Wheldon 131-806 1974 £5

FRISCH, VICTOR   Auguste Rodin. New York, 1939. Biblo &
Tannen 213-405 1973 $15

FRISIUS, JOHANNES   Dictionarium Latinogermanicum. Zurich, 1541.
Folio, contemporary calf over wooden boards, first edition, good copy despite
some waterstains. Schafer 10-100 1974 sFr 1,300

FRISWELL, J. H.   Essays on English Writers. London, 1869.
8vo., contemporary calf, gilt. Bow Windows 62-349 1974 £5

FRITSCH, A.   Evropske Ptactvo. Prague, 1871. Folio, orig.
morocco backed cloth, embossed sides, chromolithographic plates, fine clean
copy. Wheldon 128-441 1973 £50

FRITSCH, F. E.   The Structure and Reproduction of the Algae.
1935-45. 8vo., 2 vols., cloth. Wheldon 130-1281 1974 £15

FRITSCH, F. E.   The Structure and Reproduction of the Algae.
Cambridge, 1935-45. 2 vols., 8vo., cloth, maps, frontispieces, text-figures,
scarce orig. printing. Wheldon 128-1359 1973 £15

FRITSCH, G.   Untersuchungen uber den Feineren. Berlin,
1878. Folio, new boards, plates. Wheldon 129-570 1974 £15

FRITSCH, J.   Traite de la Distillation. Paris, 1890. 8vo.,
red cloth. Dawsons PM 245-305 1974 £6

FROBENIUS, LEO   Prehistoric Rock Pictures in Europe and Africa.
New York, 1937. 1st ed., illus. Biblo & Tannen 213-113 1973 $10

FROGGATT, W. W.   Some Useful Australian Birds. Sydney, 1921.
Roy. 8vo., cloth, good copy. Wheldon 131-596 1974 £12

FROHAWK, FREDERICK WILLIAM   Natural History of British Butterflies. (1914).
Folio, 2 vols., cloth, plates, scarce. Wheldon 129-644 1974 £35

FROHAWK, FREDERICK WILLIAM   Natural History of British Butterflies.
(1914). 2 vols., folio, cloth, plates, scarce. Wheldon 131-807 1974 £45

FROHAWK, FREDERICK WILLIAM   Varieties of British Butterflies. 1938.
Roy. 8vo., plates. Wheldon 131-808 1974 £12

FROHMAN, DANIEL   Daniel Frohman Presents. Forman, 1937.
397p., illus. Austin 51-331 1973 $7.50

FROHMAN, DANIEL   Daniel Frohman Presents. New York, 1937.
Biblo & Tannen 210-961 1973 $8.50

FROISSART, JEAN   Chronicles of England, France, Spain. London,
1852. 4to., red half morocco, boards. Dawsons PM 251-226 1974 £150

FROISSART, JEAN   Chronicles of England, France, Spain and the
Adjoining Countries from the Latter Part of the Reign of Edward II to the
Coronation of Henry IV. 1857. 2 vols., 8vo., cloth, illus. Bow Windows
66-256 1974 £9.50

FROISSART, JEAN   Chronicles of England, France, Spain, etc.
1862. 2 vols., half calf, worn. Allen 213-1485 1973 $15

FROISSARTS Cronycles. Shakespeare Head Press, 1927-28. Hand coloured coats
of arms, 8 vols., boards, linen spines, paper printed labels, uncut, limited to
350 sets, exceptionally fine. Broadhurst 24-1040 1974 £250

FROM Niagara to the Sea, Official Guide, 1898. Montreal, 1898. Illus.,
pictorial wrappers. Hood's 102-604 1974 $20

FROMMES Wiener Porte-Monnaie Kalender fur 1873. Vienna. Orig. printed
wrappers, crisp & sound, 2 X 1 3/16 inches. Greogry 44-397 1974 $30

FROMMES Wiener Porte-Monnaie Kalender. Vienna, 1874. Gilt metal cover,
2 X 1 3/16. Gregory 44-398 1974 $30

FROMONDUS, LIBERTUS   Meteorologicorum Libri Sex. 1639. Small 8vo.,
eighteenth century speckled calf, rebacked, first English edition. Dawsons PM
245-306 1974 £95

FRONSPERGER, LEONHARD   Besatzung. Frankfort, 1564. Small folio, half
leather, rare, woodcuts. Schumann 499-39 1974 sFr 750

FRONTINUS, SEXTUS JULIUS   Strategematicon. Leyden and Amsterdam, 1675.
12mo., contemporary vellum, fine. Dawsons PM 251-382 1974 £12

FRORIEP, ROBERT   De Lingua Anatomica Quaedam et Semiotica.
Bonn, 1828. Large 4to., orig. boards, uncut. Gurney 64-92 1974 £16

FRORIEP, ROBERT   De Lingua Anatomica Quaedam et Semiotica.
Bonn, 1828. Large 4to., orig. boards, joint weak, uncut, coloured engravings.
Gurney 66-68 1974 £16

FROST, A. B.   A Book of Drawings by A. B. Frost. 1904, n.p.
Austin 54-465 1973 $12.50

FROST, DANIEL LEE   Ten Years in Oregon. New York, 1844. 8vo.,
cloth, worn, frontispiece. Butterfield 8-459 1974 $20

FROST, F.   Sketches of Indian Life. Toronto, 1904.
Stained cover. Hood's 104-519 1974 $10

FROST, JOHN   The Mexican War and Its Warriors. New Haven,
1848. Color frontispiece. Jenkins 61-1585 1974 $15

FROST, ROBERT   A Book of Yale Review Verse. New Haven,
1917. Nice copy, orig. binding. Ross 86-156 1974 $10

FROST, ROBERT   Book Six. 1937. Foxing, first English edition.
Howes 185-182 1974 £10

FROST, ROBERT   A Boy's Will. New York, 1915. First U. S.
edition, very fine, crisp copy, first state with uncorrected text. Covent 51-745
1973 £25

FROST, ROBERT   A Boy's Will. New York, 1934. Biblo &
Tannen 214-709 1974 $6.50

FROST, ROBERT   Collected Poems. New York, 1930. Orig.
buckram, signed, uncut, limited edition. Dawsons PM 252-378 1974 £60

FROST, ROBERT   Collected Poems. New York, 1930. First
traded edition, fine copy, orig. binding. Ross 86-157 1974 $12.50

FROST, ROBERT   Collected Poems. New York, 1939. Orig.
binding, first edition, signed, mint. Ross 87-212 1974 $60

FROST, ROBERT   From Snow to Snow. New York, 1936. Green
cloth, somewhat dust stained d.w., near mint. Ross 86-158 1974 $20

FROST, ROBERT   A Further Range. New York, 1936. One of
803 copies, numbered & signed by author, orig. linen, leather label, fine copy.
Covent 51-2341 1973 £25

FROST, ROBERT   A Further Range. New York, 1936. Cloth,
dust wrapper, fine, first edition. Dawson's 424-267 1974 $25

FROST, ROBERT   A Further Range. New York, 1936. Orig.
binding, not a first printing, dust stained d.w., fine. Ross 87-213 1974 $10

FROST, ROBERT   A Further Range. New York, 1936. First printing, near mint, fine d.w., orig. binding. Ross 86-159 1974 $17.50

FROST, ROBERT   A Further Range. 1937. 8vo., orig. cloth,
fine, first English edition. Rota 189-340 1974 £6

FROST, ROBERT   The Lone Striker. New York, (1933). 8vo.,
orig. wrappers, inscribed, presentation, first edition. Dawsons PM 252-379
1974 £120

FROST, ROBERT   The Lone Striker. (New York, 1933). Orig.
wrappers, sewn, first edition, fine. MacManus 224-177 1974 $40

FROST, ROBERT   A Masque of Reason. New York, 1945. First
printing, orig. binding, fine, d.w. Ross 87-216 1974 $15

FROST, ROBERT   A Masque of Reason. New York, 1945. No.
389 of edition limited to 800 copies, signed, mint, boxed, orig. binding. Ross
86-162 1974 $65

FROST, ROBERT   Mountain Interval. New York, 1916. First
issue with duplicated line on p. 88, orig. binding, owner's name & address in ink
on free fly leaf, portrait of Frost pasted inside cover, newspaper clipping pasted
inside rear cover, nice. Ross 87-217 1974 $50

FROST, ROBERT   Mountain Interval. New York, 1916. First
issue, with duplicated line on p. 88, lacking d.w., orig. binding, fine. Ross
86-163 1974 $75

FROST, ROBERT   Mountain Interval. New York, 1921. Frontis.,
first U. S. edition, fine, cloth backed boards, worn d.w. Covent 51-2343
1973 £12.50

FROST, ROBERT   New Hampshire. New York, 1923. Boards,
cloth, dust wrapper, fine, first edition. Dawson's 424-265 1974 $30

FROST, ROBERT   North of Boston. London, 1914. Small 4to.,
orig. cloth, presentation inscription, fine, first edition. Dawsons PM 252-380
1974 £450

FROST, ROBERT   North of Boston. New York, 1915. Orig.
binding, second American edition, fourth reprinting, address in ink & small
presentation card pasted to free fly, spine somewhat worn, very good. Ross
87-218 1974 $25

FROST, ROBERT   The Pilgrim Spirit. Boston, 1921. Wrappers,
English first edition. Covent 56-491 1974 £12.60

FROST, ROBERT   Selected Poems. 1923. 8vo., orig. cloth,
first English edition. Rota 189-339 1974 £5

FROST, ROBERT   Selected Poems. New York, 1928. Orig.
binding, first printing, bookplate, inscription in ink on fly leaf, good working
copy. Ross 87-219 1974 $10

FROST, ROBERT   A Way Out. New York, 1929. One of 485
copies, numbered & signed by author, cloth backed boards, mint, unopened copy.
Covent 51-2344 1973 £35

FROST, ROBERT   West-Running Brook. New York, 1928. First
U. S. edition, drawings, cloth backed boards, fine. Covent 51-746 1973 £7.50

FROST, ROBERT   West-Running Brook. New York, (1928).
Cloth, boards, dust wrapper, fine, first edition. Dawson's 424-266 1974 $25

FROST, ROBERT   West Running Brook. New York, 1928. First
edition, with misprint p. 44, inscribed by author, dust-stained d.w., fine copy,
orig. binding. Ross 86-166 1974 $75

FROST, ROBERT   West Running Brook. New York, 1928. No.
125 of edition limited to 1000 copies, signed, woodcuts signed, fine, near mint,
lacking d.w., orig. binding. Ross 86-165 1974 $90

FROST, ROBERT   A Witness Tree. New York, 1942. Orig.
binding, first printing, d.w., very good copy. Ross 87-223 1974 $20

FROST, ROBERT   A Witness Tree. New York, 1942. No. 40 of
edition limited to 735 copies, boxed, signed, mint, orig. binding. Ross 86-167
1974 $100

FROTHINGHAM, RICHARD   History of the Siege of Boston, and of the
Battles of Lexington, Concord and Bunker Hill. Boston, 1849. Folding maps,
plates, cloth covers slightly worn, first edition. Butterfield 10-38 1974 $25

FROUDE, JAMES ANTHONY   The Divorce of Catherine of Aragon. 1891.
Orig. cloth, frayed. Howes 186-834 1974 £5

FROUDE, JAMES ANTHONY   The English in Ireland in the 18th Century.
1872-74. 3 vols., thick demy 8vo., orig. cloth, frayed, first edition. Howes
186-835 1974 £15

FROUDE, JAMES ANTHONY   History of England from the Fall of Wolsey to
the Death of Elizabeth. 1856-70. 12 vols., demy 8vo., half calf, labels,
library edition. Howes 186-836 1974 £60

FROUDE, JAMES ANTHONY   History of England from the Fall of Wolsey to
the Death of Elizabeth. London, 1858-70. 8vo., calf, gilt, first edition.
Dawsons PM 251-225 1974 £58

FROUDE, JAMES ANTHONY   History of England. London, 1872-77.
12 vols., 8vo., label, half morocco, gilt, marbled boards. Bow Windows
62-350 1974 £35

FROUDE, JAMES ANTHONY   Life and Letters of Erasmus. 1894. Orig.
cloth, first edition. Howes 186-807 1974 £5

FROUDE, JAMES ANTHONY   Short Studies on Great Subjects. 1901-03. Small
8vo., 4 vols., half blue calf, gilt. Quaritch 936-383 1974 £10

FROUDE, JAMES ANTHONY   Short Studies On Great Subjects. 1909.
4 vols., contemporary green calf gilt. Smith 193-613 1973 £10

FROUDE, JAMES ANTHONY   Thomas Carlyle. 1882-85. 4 vols., plates,
damp-stained, library edition. Howes 186-688 1974 £10

FROUDE, JAMES ANTHONY   Thomas Carlyle. New York, 1885. 2 vols.,
illus. Biblo & Tannen 210-836 1973 $6.50

FROUT DE FONTPERTUIS, A.   Le Canada. Paris, 1867. Hood's 102-706
1974 $10

FROWDE, PHILIP   The Fall of Sagantum. London, 1727. 8vo.,
quarter morocco, first edition. Ximenes 33-54 1974 $50

FRUIT of the Valley. Los Angeles, 1942. One of 600 numbered copies. Jenkins
61-321 1974 $12.50

FRY, CHARLES BURGESS   The Book of Cricket. London, (c. 1898). 4to.,
illus., contemporary half roan, rubbed, worn. Bow Windows 62-351 1974 £7.50

FRY, CHRISTOPHER   The Boy With a Cart. 1950. Austin 51-332
1973 $7.50

FRY, CHRISTOPHER   The Firstborn. Oxford, 1950. 101p. Austin
51-333 1973 $6

FRY, FREDERICK   Fry's Traveler's Guide and Descriptive Journal
of the Great North-Western Territories of the United States of America.
Cincinnati, 1865. Orig. cloth, fine half morocco slipcase, first edition, rare.
Jenkins 61-912 1974 $450

FRY, H.   The History of North Atlantic Steam Navigation
With Some Account of Early Ships and Shipowners. London, 1896. Illus. Hood's
102-756 1974 $40

FRY, JOHN   Bibliographical Memoranda. Bristol, 1816.
4to., contemporary half morocco, first edition. Ximenes 33-55 1974 $125

FRY, JOHN   An Essay on Conduct and Education. London,
1738. 8vo., boards, first edition. Hammond 201-280 1974 £9.50

FRY, JOHN   Select Poems. (New York), 1805. 12mo.,
contemporary sheep, scarce. Ximenes 33-56 1974 $17.50

FRY, ROGER   The Artist and Psycho-Analysis. 1924. 8vo.,
wrappers, first edition. Rota 189-344 1974 £8.50

FRY, ROGER   Cezanne. London, 1927. 4to., dec. boards,
cloth spine. Minters 37-272 1973 $30

FRY, ROGER   Chinese Art. (1935). 8vo., orig. cloth, coloured plates, illus., revised new edition. Bow Windows 66-258 1974 £10.75

FRY, ROGER   English Handwriting. 1926. Plates, very good in wrappers. Covent 51-2345 1973 £6.30

FRY, ROGER   Georgian Art (1760-1820). 1929. 4to., orig. cloth, plates, dust wrapper. Bow Windows 66-259 1974 £18

FRY, ROGER   Last Lectures. 1939. Fine, illus., first edition. Covent 55-745 1974 £8.50

FRY, ROGER   Last Lectures. Cambridge, 1939. Large 8vo., illus., buckram. Quaritch 940-108 1974 £15

FRY, ROGER   Vision and Design. 1920. 4to., orig. cloth, inscription, rubbed, first edition. Rota 188-329 1974 £18

FRYER, JANE EAYRE   The Mary Francis Cook Book. Philadelphia, 1912. 8vo., cloth, illus. Frohnsdorff 16-349 1974 $27.50

FRYER, JANE EAYRE   The Mary Francis Garden Book. Philadelphia, 1916. 8vo., cloth, illus. Frohnsdorff 16-350 1974 $35

FRYER, MICHAEL   The Trial and Life of Eugene Aram. Richmond, 1832. 8vo., orig. quarter cloth, boards, fine, first edition. Ximenes 33-57 1974 $25

FUCHS, E.   L'Element Erotique dans la Caricature. Vienna, 1906. Imp. 8vo., plates, illus., boards, new cloth. Quaritch 940-109 1974 £45

FUCHS, LEONHARD   De Historia Stirpium Commentarii Insignes. Basle, 1542. Folio, contemporary blind tooled calf over wooden boards, tall copy, lacks 29 leaves, woodcuts by V. R. Speckle, first edition, remarkably clean fresh condition. Thomas 32-314 1974 £500

FUERTES, LOUIS AGASSIZ   Album of Abyssinian Birds and Mammals. Chicago, 1930. 4to., orig. card box, plates. Wheldon 131-597 1974 £80

FUERTES, LOUIS AGASSIZ   Artist and Naturalist in Ethiopia. New York, 1936. 4to., cloth, plates, scarce. Wheldon 130-281 1974 £50

FUERTES, LOUIS AGASSIS   The Book of Dogs. Washington, (1919). First book edition, 8vo., natural color portraits, mint. Current BW9-511 1974 $20

FUERTES, LOUIS AGASSIZ   Portraits of New England Birds. Boston, 1932. 4to., orig. cloth, plates. Wheldon 130-521 1974 £10

FUERTES, LOUIS AGASSIZ   Portraits of New England Birds, Drawn for "Birds of Massachusetts". Boston, 1932. 4to., cloth, coloured plates, scarce. Wheldon 128-443 1973 £10

FUGITIVE Pieces, on Various Subjects. 1771. 12mo., 2 vols., contemporary calf, gilt, third edition. Hill 126-72 1974 £28

FUHRMANN, F.   Vorlesungen uber Technische Mykologie. Jena, 1913. Roy 8vo., cloth. Wheldon 129-1208 1974 £4

FUKUKITA, YASUNOSUKE   Cha-No-Yu. Tokyo, 1932. Plates, dec. cloth, bookplate, slip-case. Covent 55-1165 1974 £12.50

FULKE, WILLIAM   A Defense of the Sincere and True Translations of the Holie Scriptures into the English Tong. 1583. Old sprinkled calf, gilt on vellum, monogram of Sir Mark Masterman Sykes on both covers, with his armorial bookplate, first edition. Thomas 32-42 1974 £250

FULKE, WILLIAM   Meteors. London, 1670. Small 8vo., contemporary sheep. Dawsons PM 245-309 1974 £65

A FULL ACCOUNT of the Great Victory. London, 1689. Small folio, disbound, first edition. Dawsons PM 251-520 1974 £40

FULLARTON, JOHN   Historical Memoir of the Family of Eglington and Winton. Ardrossan, 1864. 8vo., cloth, frontispiece, plate, small stain. Bow Windows 66-260 1974 £8.50

FULLER, ANDREW S.   The Illustrated Strawberry Culturist. Brooklyn, 1863. 12mo., orig. salmon printed wrappers, very good copy, first edition. Ximenes 37-85 1974 $25

FULLER, FRANCIS   Medicina Gymanistica. London, 1705. 8vo., contemporary panelled calf, rebacked, first edition. Schuman 37-97 1974 $125

FULLER, HENRY   Adventures of Bill Longley, Captured by Sheriff Milton Mast and Deputy Bill Burrows . . . in 1877. Nacogdoches, n.d. Stiff pict. wrapper. Jenkins 61-913 1974 $75

FULLER, J.   Art of Coppersmithing. New York, 1894. Large 8vo., illus., cloth. Quaritch 940-676 1974 £30

FULLER, J. D. P.   The Movement for the Acquisition of all Mexico, 1846-1848. Baltimore, 1936. Wrapper. Jenkins 61-1586 1974 $45

FULLER, J. F. C.   The Star in the West, A Critical Essay Upon the Works of Aleister Crowley. 1907. Frontis., spine faded, very good copy, scarce, first edition. Covent 51-2292 1973 £10

FULLER, J. F. C.   The Star in the West. 1907. Contemporary signed presentation inscription, buckram, English first edition. Covent 56-279 1974 £35

FULLER, J. F. C.   The Star in the West. 1907. Orig. dec. buckram gilt, fine, English first edition. Covent 56-1698 1974 £65

FULLER, THOMAS   The Church-History of Britain. 1655. Thick folio, contemporary calf, worn, first edition. Howes 185-1179 1974 £60

FULLER, THOMAS   The Church-History of Britain. 1837. 3 vols., orig. cloth, plates. Howes 185-1180 1974 £15

FULLER, THOMAS   The Church-History of Britain. Oxford, 1845. 6 vols., orig. cloth, best edition. Howes 185-1181 1974 £55

FULLER, THOMAS   The Historie of the Holy Warre. Cambridge, 1639. Contemporary calf, labels. Howes 185-1182 1974 £35

FULLER, THOMAS   The History of the Worthies of England. London, 1662. Folio, full calf, gilt, fine, first edition. Ximenes 33-58 1974 $275

FULLER, THOMAS   The History of the Worthies of England. London, 1662. 1 vol. in 3, folio, old calf backed boards, first edition. Quaritch 939-122 1974 £85

FULLER, THOMAS   The History of the Worthies of England. 1662. Folio, old calf, first edition. Quaritch 939-123 1974 £60

FULLER, THOMAS   The History of the Worthies of England. 1840. 3 vols., orig. cloth, scarce, best edition. Howes 185-1184 1974 £20

FULLER, THOMAS   The Holy and the Profane State. 1663. Folio, contemporary calf, gilt, fourth edition. Howes 185-1183 1974 £22.50

FULLER, THOMAS   The Holy State. Cambridge, 1648. Small folio, contemporary calf, rebacked. Thomas 28-242 1972 £15.75

FULLER, WILLIAM   A Brief Discovery of the True Mother of the Pretended Prince of Wales. London, 1696. 8vo., stitched, uncut, first edition. Dawsons PM 251-227 1974 £15

FULLERTON, GEORGINA   Constance Sherwood. 1865. 8vo., orig. cloth, first edition. Bow Windows 64-511 1974 £35

FULTON, D.   New York to Niagara, 1836. New York, 1938. Card cover. Hood's 102-243 1974 $12.50

FULTON, J. F.   Physiology of the Nervous System. London, 1938. First edition, second printing. Rittenhouse 46-714 1974 $10

FULTON, JUSTIN DEWEY 1828-1901   The Way Out. n.d. (1877). Illus. Austin 62-187 1974 $12.50

FULTON, JUSTIN DEWEY 1828-1901   Why Priests Should Wed. 1888. Illus.
Austin 57-232 1974 $15

FULTON, JUSTIN DEWEY 1828-1901   Why Priests Wed. 1888. Ex-library.
Austin 57-40 1974 $12.50

FULTON, ROBERT   Book of Pigeons. 1895. Demy 4to., good
copy, plates, orig. cloth, revised & enlarged new edition. Broadhurst 24-1083
1974 £6

FUMEE, MARTIN SIEUR DE GENILLE   The Historie of the Trovbles of Hvngarie.
London, 1600. Folio, contemporary limp vellum, first edition in English. Dawsons
PM 251-228 1974 £195

FUN for the Fireside, or, Joe Miller Alive Again. London, n.d. 12mo.,
disbound, frontispiece. Ximenes 33-390 1974 $25

FUN On Draught. Ogilvie, n.d., ca. 1910. 328p., illus., paper. Austin
54-803 1973 $7.50

FUNCK, M.   Le Livre Belge a Gravure. Paris et Bruxelles,
1925. Plates, illus., roy. 8vo., orig. wrappers, bit loose. Forster 98-270
1974 £30

FUNK, FRANCIS X.   A Manual of Church History. 1914. 2 vols.,
thick 8vo., scarce. Howes 185-1185 1974 £6.50

FUNK, FRANCIS X.   Patres Apostolici. 1901-13. 2 vols., thick
8vo., half prize green calf gilt. Howes 185-1186 1974 £10

FURLEY, ROBERT   A History of the Weald of Kent. London, 1781.
8vo., orig. green cloth gilt, maps. Dawsons PM 251-25 1974 £60

FURLEY, ROBERT   A History of the Weald of Kent. 1871-74.
2 vols. in 3, orig. cloth, scarce, inscribed. Howes 186-2040 1974 £32

FURLONG, CHARLES WELLINGTON   Let ' er Buck. New York, 1921.
Illus., blue cloth, signed presentation, paper label. Bradley 35-148 1974 $14

FURNAS, ROBERT W.   Nebraska: Her Resources, Advantages, and
Promises. Lincoln, 1885. Sewn, rare. Jenkins 61-1782 1974 $22.50

FURNISS, HARRY   Poverty Bay. 1905. Orig. pictorial cloth,
plates, illus., fine. Covent 55-887 1974 £10

THE FURNITURE of Thomas Chippendale. n.d. 4to., plates, boards, English first
edition. Covent 56-1644 1974 £12.50

FURNIVAL, W. J.   Leadless Decorative Tiles, Faience, and Mosaic.
Staffordshire, 1904. Crown 4to., plates (many coloured), illus., orig. cloth.
Bow Windows 66-261 1974 £21

THE FURNIVAL Books. 1930-32. 8vo., 12 vols., orig. cloth, signed, first edition. Rota 189-345 1974 £60

FURNIVAL BOOKS, Nos. 1-12. 1930-32. Complete set, all limited to 500
copies, numbered & signed by author, all fine, buckram. Covent 51-750 1973
£90

FURSE, CHARLES WELLINGTON   Illustrated Memoir of. 1908. Roy. 4to.,
plates, buckram. Quaritch 940-110 1974 £12

FURST, HERBERT   The Decorative Art of Frank Brangwyn. 1924.
Plates, fine, orig. cloth. Marsden 39-58 1974 £20

FURST, HERBERT   The Modern Woodcut. 1924. 4to., dust wrapper, plates, illus., English first edition. Covent 56-1454 1974 £20

FURST, HERBERT   The Modern Woodcut. London, 1924. 4to.,
plates, orig. dec. cloth, uncut, fine. Dawsons PM 10-231 1974 £20

FURST, HERBERT   The Modern Woodcut. London, (1924). Demy
4to., orig. linen, plates in colour. Forster 98-273 1974 £20

FURST, HERBERT   Original Engraving and Etching. 1931. 4to.,
plates, fine, English first edition. Covent 56-1455 1974 £15

FURSTENBERG, H.   Das Franzosische Buch im Achtzehnten
Jahrhundert und in der Empirezeit. Weimar, 1929. Limited to 1588 copies, demy
4to., orig. wrappers, spine slightly defective, text fine. Forster 98-274 1974
£15

FUSELI, H.   Lectures on Painting, Delivered at the Royal
Academy. 1801-20. 2 parts in 1 vol., 4to., contemporary calf gilt, first
editions. Quaritch 940-111 1974 £120

FUSON, HARVEY H.   Ballads of the Kentucky Highlands. London,
(1931). 8vo., orig. bindings, dust jacket. Butterfield 8-187 1974 $10

FUSSELL, L.   A Journey Round the Coast of Kent. 1818.
Full vellum, plates, illus., leather label. Howes 186-2041 1974 £45

FUTRELLE, JACQUES   Lieutenant What's-his-Name. Indianapolis,
1915. Biblo & Tannen 213-543 1973 $15

FYENS, THOMAS   De Viribus Imaginationis Tractatus. London,
1657. Small 12mo., old boards. Schuman 37-98 1974 $150

FYFE, ANDREW   Plates Illustrative of the Different Parts of the
Human Body. Edinburgh, 1826. 8vo., old boards, new cloth back, plates,
first edition. Schuman 37-99 1974 $110

FYFFE, C. A.   A History of Modern Europe. 1889. 3 vols.,
contemporary dark green polished calf gilt, raised bands. Smith 194-698
1974 £5

FYLEMAN, ROSE   Round the Mulberry Bush. New York, 1928.
4to., cloth, illus. Frohnsdorff 16-351 1974 $7.50

FYNES-CLINTON, O. H.   The Welsh Vocabulary of the Bangor District.
1913. Demy 8vo., orig. cloth, fine. Broadhurst 24-1421 1974 £6

FYSON, P. F.   The Flora of the South Indian Hill Stations.
Madras, 1932. 8vo., 2 vols., cloth, plates. Wheldon 129-1071 1974 £25

G

G., W. L. S. Trial of Anti Christ. Philadelphia, 1858. Second edition. Austin 57-39 1974 $12.50

GABORIAU, EMILE Caught in the Net. New York, 1913. Plates, fine, first American edition. Covent 55-579 1974 £7.50

GABORIAU, EMILE La Degringolade. Paris, 1873. 2 vols., half calf, gilt, labels, English first edition. Covent 56-327 1974 £7.50

GABORY, GEORGES Essai sur Marcel Proust. Paris, 1926. Boards, English first edition. Covent 56-1068 1974 £7.50

GABUCINIUS, HIERONYMUS De Comitiali Morbo Libri III. 1561. Small 4to., 19th century red quarter morocco gilt, first edition. Thomas 30-116 1973 £40

GACHARD, M. Don Carlos et Philippe II. Brussels, 1863. 2 vols., contemporary calf, faded. Howes 186-685 1974 £6.50

GADBURY, JOHN Magna Veritas. London, 1680. Folio, disbound, first edition. Dawsons PM 251-505 1974 £25

GADDIS, MAXWELL P. Foot-Prints of an Itinerant. Cincinnati, 1855. Cloth, first edition. Hayman 57-381 1974 $15

GADEAU DE KERVILLE, H. Voyage Zoologique en Khroumirie. Paris, 1908. Roy. 8vo., wrappers, plates. Wheldon 131-929 1974 £5

GAG, WANDA Nothing At All. New York, (1941). Oblong 8vo., pictorial boards, illus. in color, very good copy, d.j., editor's review copy slip loosely inserted, first edition. Frohnsdorff 16-356 1974 $20

GAGE, A. T. A History of the Linnean Society. 1938. Roy 8vo., half morocco, plates. Wheldon 129-145 1974 £5

GAGE, J. The History and Antiquities of Hengrave in Suffolk. 1822. 4to., cloth, plates. Quaritch 939-556 1974 £15

GAGE, J. The History and Antiquities of Suffolk. 1838. 4to., plates, illus., buckram. Quaritch 939-557 1974 £22.50

GAIGE, CROSBY Footlights and Highlights. Sutton, 1948. 319p. Austin 51-334 1973 $8.50

GAILLIARD, J. Inscriptions Fumeraires et Monumentales de la Flandre Occidentale. 1861-67. 3 parts in 2 vols., 4to., half morocco, illus., plates. Allen 213-1492 1973 $50

GAINES, CHARLES KELSEY Echoes of Many Moods. Mt. Vernon, 1926. Ballinger 1-19 1974 $12.50

GAINES, E. P. A Plan for the Defence of the Western Frontier. Washington, 1838. Very fine folding map. Jenkins 61-915 1974 $75

GAINSBOROUGH, THOMAS The Life of. 1856. Small 8vo., plates, cloth, scarce, second edition. Quaritch 940-113 1974 £28

GAIRDNER, J. Paston Letters, 1422-1509. 1904. 6 vols., ex-library, best edition. Allen 216-1834 1974 $50

GAIRDNER, JAMES Lollardy and the Reformation of England. 1908-13. 4 vols., thick 8vo., scarce, orig. & best edition. Howes 185-1187 1974 £35

GALBRAITH, JR., R. C. The History of the Chillicothe Presbytery. Chillicothe, 1889. 8vo., orig. bindings. Butterfield 8-415 1974 $15

GALBRAITH, WILLIAM Trigonometrical Surveying, Levelling, and Railway Engineering. Edinburgh and London, 1842. 8vo., orig. cloth-backed boards, first edition. Hammond 201-826 1974 £12

GALE, EDWARDS J. Pewter and the Amateur Collector. London, 1910. Demy 8vo., orig. cloth, gilt. Covent 55-441 1974 £7.50

GALE, EDWARDS J. Pewter and the Amateur Collector. London, 1910. Illus., excellent copy, 8vo., orig. cloth. Gregory 44-139 1974 $12.50

GALE, GEORGE Quebec 'Twixt Old and New. Quebec, 1915. Illus. Hood's 102-707 1974 $15

GALE, GEORGE Upper Mississippi. Chicago, 1867. First edition, illus., three quarter morocco. Jenkins 61-916 1974 $85

GALE, R. Registrum Honoris de Richmond. 1722. Folio, old calf, rebacked. Quaritch 939-594 1974 £25

GALE, THOMAS Historiae Poeticae Scriptores Antiqui. London, 1675. Thick 8vo., old blind-tooled red morocco, fine. Harper 213-71 1973 $375

GALEN, CLAUDIUS
Please turn to
GALENUS

GALENUS. De Affectorum Locorum Notitia Libri VI, Guilielmo Copo Basileiensi Interprete. (Venice?), c. 1500-1510. Folio, rare first separate edition, modern half vellum, fine. Schafer 10-130 1974 sFr 1,200

GALENUS De Ossibus. 1535. 4to., full calf antique, gilt. Hammond 201-539 1974 £85

GALENUS Reccettario di Galeno. Venice, 1645. 12mo., contemporary limp vellum. Schuman 36-174 1974 $145

GALERIE RENE DROUIN Kandinsky, Epoque Parisienne 1934-1944. Paris, n.d. 8vo., wrapper, illus. Minters 37-586 1973 $10

GALERIE Theatrale, Ou Collection des Portraits en Pied des Principaux Acteurs des Trois Premiers Theatres de la Capital. Paris, (n.d. 1812-1834). 3 vols., folio, engraved plates, quarter green calf, rubbed, minimal foxing. Bow Windows 66-263 1974 £245

GALIBERTO Il Cavallo da Maneggio. Vienna, 1650. Folio, parchment, very rare, first edition. Harper 213-72 1973 $650

GALILEI, GALILEO Dialogo . . . 1632. 4to., modern brown morocco binding, fine, first edition. Dawsons PM 245-313 1974 £950

GALILEI, GALILEO Dialogo . . . Sopra i due Massimi Sistemi del Mondo, Tolemaico, e Copernicano. Florence, 1632. Large 8vo., old vellum, entirely uncut, woodcut diagrams, very fine, first edition. Schumann 500-24 1974 sFr 8,200

GALILEI, GALILEO Dialogo . . . Sopra i Due Massimi Sistemi del Mondo, Tolemaico, e Copernicano. Florence, 1632. Large 8vo., orig. vellum, woodcut diagrams, engraved title page by Stefano della Bella, Giovanni Battista Baliani's copy, first edition, as new condition. Kraus 137-33 1974 $25,000

GALILEI, GALILEO Difesa . . . Contro Alle Calunnie & Imposture di Baldessar Capra. Venice, 1607. Small 4to., woodcut diagrams, contemporary vellum, first edition. Schumann 500-2 1974 sFr 11,500

GALILEI, GALILEO Discorsi e Demonstrazioni Matematiche Intorno a due Nuove Scienze Attenti alla Mecanica and i Movimenti Locali. Leyden, 1638. Small 4to., vellum, first edition. Schumann 500-30 1974 sFr 8,500

GALILEI, GALILEO Discorso al Serenissimo Don Cosimo II . . . 1612. Small 4to., old quarter calf, worn, first edition. Dawsons PM 245-310 1974 £1,600

GALILEI, GALILEO Discorso al Serenissimo Don Cosimo II. Florence, 1612. Small 4to., vellum, woodcut diagrams, first edition. Schumann 500-10 1974 sFr 11,000

GALILEI, GALILEO Discorso . . . Intorno alle cose, Che Stanno in su l'Acqua. Florence, 1612. Small 4to., vellum, blind stamped Giuccardini exlibris on title, with exlibris of Prince Pietro Ginori Conti, second edition. Schumann 500-11 1974 sFr 4,500

GALILEI, GALILEO   Galileo a Madama Cristina di Lorena. Padua, 1896. Vellum, gilt sides, cloth case, 17 X 10 mm. Schumann 500-36 1974 sFr 500

GALILEI, GALILEO   Istoria E Dimostrazioni Intorno Alle Macchie Solari. 1613. 4to., vellum, fine, plates, first edition, first issue. Dawsons PM 245-311 1974 £450

GALILEI, GALILEO   Istoria e Dimonstrazioni Intorno Alle Macchie Solari. Rome, 1613. Small 4to., vellum, gilt line borders, recased, engraved portrait, full page engravings, woodcuts, first edition, first issue with the supplement. Schumann 500-15 1974 sFr 14,000

GALILEI, GALILEO   Istoria e Dimonstrazioni Intorno Alle Macchie Solari e loro Accidente. Rome, 1613. Full page engraved portrait, full page engravings, woodcut diagrams, small 4to., contemporary vellum, first edition. Schumann 500-16 1974 sFr 6,000

GALILEI, GALILEO   Istoria e Dimonstrazioni Intorno Alle Macchie Solari e Loro Accidenti. Rome, 1613. 4to., misbound, plates, old boards, very fine, uncut, first edition, first issue. Gilhofer 61-7 1974 sFr. 8,000

GALILEI, GALILEO   Mathematical Discourses. London, 1730. 4to., half morocco, boards, gilt, fine, first edition. Dawsons PM 245-315 1974 £450

GALILEI, GALILEO   Les Mechaniques de Galilee . . . Avec Plusieurs Additions Rares, and Nouvelles. Paris, 1634. Small 8vo., vellum, first edition. Schumann 500-26 1974 sFr 14,200

GALILEI, GALILEO 1564-1642   Memorie e Lettere Inedite Finora. 1818-21. 4to., one quarter mottled calf, gilt, boards. Zeitlin 235-94 1974 $175

GALILEI, GALILEO   Nov-Antiqua Sanctissimorum Patrum. 1636. 4to., modern limp vellum, first edition. Zeitlin 235-89 1974 $950

GALILEI, GALILEO   Nov-Antiqua Sanctissimorum Patrum, and Profanorum Theologorum Doctrina. (Strassburg), 1636. Small 4to., vellum, first edition. Schumann 500-29 1974 sFr 6,500

GALILEI, GALILEO   La Operazione del Compasso Geometrico, et Militare. Padua, 1640. Folding engraved plate, woodcut diagrams, small 4to., vellum, third edition. Schumann 500-31 1974 sFr 1,850

GALILEI, GALILEO   Le Operazioni del Compasso Geometrico. Padova, 1606. Small 4to., woodcut diagrams, contemporary vellum, first edition of only 60 copies. Schumann 500-1 1974 sFr 82,000

GALILEI, GALILEO   Il Saggiatore. Rome, 1623. 4to., very fine, contemporary vellum, engravings, first edition, first issue. Gilhofer 61-8 1974 sFr. 8,000

GALILEI, GALIEO   Il Saggiatore Nel Quale Con Bilancia . . . 16-23. 4to., nineteenth century vellum, fine, first edition. Dawsons PM 245-312 1974 £550

GALILEI, GALILEO   Sidereus Nuncius Magna, Longeque Admirabilia Spectacula Pandens. Venice, 1610. Small 4to., morocco, engravings, first edition, woodcuts, very fine condition. Schumann 500-3 1974 sFr 115,000

GALILEI, GALILEO   Systema Cosmicum. 1663. 8vo., undressed sheep. Dawsons PM 245-314 1974 £135

GALILEI, GALILEO   Systema Cosmicum. 1699. Small 4to., contemporary vellum, leather labels. Zeitlin 235-90 1974 $375

GALILEI, GALILEO   Systema Cosmicum . . . Dialogis IV . . . Ejusdem Tractatus de Motu. Leiden, 1699. 2 vols. in 1, engraved portrait and frontispiece, diagrams, 4to., contemporary vellum, rebacked, first Latin edition, fine. Kraus 137-34 1974 $1,250

GALILEI, GALILEO   Trattato della Sfera . . . con Alcune Prattiche Intorno a Quella . . . di Buonardo Savi. Rome, 1656. 12mo., half leather, exlibris of F. M. Pellegrini and Pietro Ginori Conti, first edition. Schumann 500-33 1974 sFr 800

GALILEI, GALILEO   Il Saggiatore Nel Quale Con Bilancia Esquisita e Giusta si Ponderano le Cose Contenute nella Libra Astronomica. Rome, 1623. Small 4to., contemporary vellum, engraved illus. and diagrams, first edition, first issue. Schumann 500-21 1974 sFr 8,000

GALILEI, GALILEO   Opere . . . di Varii Trattati dell'Istesso Autore non Piu Stampato Accresciuto. Bologna, 1655-56. 2 vols., small 4to., engraved portrait, orig. red morocco, elaborate gilt borders, first edition, splendid copy, printed on fine heavy paper. Schumann 500-32 1974 sFr 28,200

GALILEI, GALILEO   Opere. Florence, 1718. 3 vols., engraved portrait, woodcut diagrams, large 8vo., vellum, stamped exlibris of the Secular Library of the Jesuit College in Rome, second edition. Schumann 500-35 1974 sFr 950

GALILEI, GALILEO   Opere . . . Divise in Quattro Tomi. Padua, 1744. 4 vols., 4to., 19th century cloth backed boards, fine. Traylen 79-228 1973 £70

GALILEI, GALILEO   Opere. 1808-11. 8vo., 13 vols., cloth, plates. Dawsons PM 245-317 1974 £75

GALINDO, CATHERINE   Mrs. Galindo's Letter to Mrs. Siddons. London, 1809. 8vo., quarter roan, spine rubbed, front cover loose, first edition, very scarce. Ximenes 36-100 1974 $75

GALITZIN, MICHEL   Catalogue des Livres de la Bibliotheque de Prince Michel Galitzin. Moscou, 1866. Plates, med. 8vo., full contemporary morocco. Forster 98-279 1974 £120

GALL, FRANZ JOSEPH   Sur les Fonctions du Cerveau. Paris, 1825. 6 vols., 8vo., contemporary half calf. Schuman 37-100 1974 $135

GALLANDI, ANDREA   Bibliotheca Veterum Patrum Antiquorumque Scriptorum Ecclesiasticorum. Venice, 1765-81. 14 vols., folio, contemporary half vellum. Howes 185-1189 1974 £160

GALLATIN, ALBERT 1761-1849   Peace With Mexico. New York, 1947. Yellow printed wrappers, fine, first edition, first issue. Jenkins 61-1587 1974 $15

GALLATIN, ALBERT 1761-1849   The Speech of..., In the House of Representatives of the General Assembly of Pennsylvania...on the 14th Day of October, 1794. Philadelphia, 1795. 8vo., sewn, very good copy, rare, first edition. Ximenes 37-86 1974 $75

GALLATIN, ALBERT EUGENE   American Water-Colourists. New York, 1922. Fine, unopened. Ballinger 1-20 1974 $25

GALLATIN, ALBERT EUGENE   Aubrey Beardsley's Drawings. New York, 1903. Illus., limited to 250 numbered copies, very good. Covent 51-2150 1973 £21

A GALLERY of Great Paintings. New York, 1944. Folio, 100 color plates, spine torn. Biblo & Tannen 210-104 1973 $15

GALLI DA BIBIENA, FERDINANDO   L'Architettura Civile. Parma, 1711. Folio, contemporary vellum, plates, rare first edition. Gilhofer 61-14 1974 sFr 7,000

GALLOIS, L.   Les Geographes Allemands de la Renaissance. Paris, 1890. Folding plates, portfolio. Kraus B8-70 1974 $35

GALLONIO, ANTONIO   De S. S. Martyrum Cruciatibus Liber. Entwerp, 1662. 12mo., contemporary vellum, frontispiece, plates. Smith 194-153 1974 £10

GALLOWAY, ELIJAH   History and Progress of the Steam Engine. London, 1832. 8vo., calf gilt, rebacked, leather label, illus. Traylen 79-230 1973 £45

GALLOWAY, JOSEPH   A Reply to the Observations of Lieut. Gen. Sir William Howe. London, 1780. 8vo., modern boards, first edition. Dawsons PM 247-129 1974 £30

GALLUP, JOSEPH A.   Sketches of Epidemic Diseases in the State of Vermont. Boston, 1815. 8vo., contemporary half calf, first edition. Dawsons PM 249-196 1974 £85

GALLWITZ, S. D.   Briefe und Tagebuchblatter von Paula Modersohn-Becker. Berlin, 1920. 8vo., cloth, twelfth edition. Minters 37-476 1973 $12.50

GALPINE, J.   A Synoptical Compend of British Botany. Salisbury, 1806. Small 8vo., contemporary boards, rebacked, frontis., scarce. Wheldon 128-1191 1973 £5

GALPINE, J.   A Synoptical Compend of British Botany. Salisbury, 1806. Small 8vo., contemporary boards, rebacked, scarce. Wheldon 130-1086 1974 £5

GALSWORTHY, JOHN   Awakening. New York, (1920). 8vo., illus., d.j. soiled and chipped, very good. Current BW9-225 1974 $10

GALSWORTHY, JOHN   The Bells Of Peace. 1920. 8vo., wrappers, fine, limited edition. Rinsland 58-974 1974 $15

GALSWORTHY, JOHN   The Burning Spear. London, 1919. 8vo., orig. cloth, rubbed, first edition, first issue. Bow Windows 62-354 1974 £6

GALSWORTHY, JOHN   The Burning Spear. 1919. Orig. cloth, dust wrapper, fine, first edition, first issue. Rota 188-336 1974 £6.50

GALSWORTHY, JOHN   The Burning Spear. London, 1919. Green cloth, first edition. Dawson's 424-193 1974 $25

GALSWORTHY, JOHN   Caravan. 1925. 8vo., orig. cloth, full green leather, signed, first edition. Rota 190-448 1974 £17.50

GALSWORTHY, JOHN   Carmen. 1932. Cloth-backed boards, torn, dust wrapper, English first edition. Covent 56-495 1974 £21

GALSWORTHY, JOHN   Collected Plays. London, 1929. First edition, limited to 1250 numbered copies, handmade paper, signed by author, fine, d.w., orig. cloth. Crane 7-95 1974 £10

GALSWORTHY, JOHN   The Creation of Character in Literature. Oxford, 1931. 8vo., wrappers, signed, first edition. Rota 189-354 1974 £6

GALSWORTHY, JOHN   The Dark Flower. 1913. Verny nice copy, uncommon book, first edition. Covent 51-756 1973 £7.50

GALSWORTHY, JOHN   Five Tales. 1918. 8vo., orig. cloth, fine, first English edition. Rota 189-350 1974 £7.50

GALSWORTHY, JOHN   The Freelands. 1915. Orig. cloth, first edition. Rota 188-335 1974 £8

GALSWORTHY, JOHN   The Freelands. London, 1915. 8vo., orig. cloth, presentation, inscribed, first edition. Dawsons PM 252-381 1974 £20

GALSWORTHY, JOHN   To Let. 1921. 8vo., orig. cloth, inscription, first English edition. Rota 190-446 1974 £10

GALSWORTHY, JOHN   To Let. London, 1921. 8vo., orig. cloth, presentation, first edition. Dawsons PM 252-384 1974 £55

GALSWORTHY, JOHN   Loyalties. 1930. 4to., buckram, illus., first edition. Rota 190-450 1974 £10

GALSWORTHY, JOHN   A Man of Devon. 1901. English first edition. Covent 56-494 1974 £45

GALSWORTHY, JOHN   The Man of Property. 1906. English first edition. Covent 56-1768 1974 £15

GALSWORTHY, JOHN   A Modern Comedy. 1929. Thick 8vo., first edition. Howes 186-200 1974 £5

GALSWORTHY, JOHN   A Modern Comedy. 1929. 8vo., orig. parchment, signed with inscription by author, limited edition. Bow Windows 66-265 1974 £12.50

GALSWORTHY, JOHN   A Modern Comedy. 1929. Orig. vellum gilt, fine, limited, first edition. Howes 185-184 1974 £12.50

GALSWORTHY, JOHN   A Modern Comedy. 1929. 8vo., limp parchment, fine, slipcase, signed, first edition. Rota 189-353 1974 £20

GALSWORTHY, JOHN   Plays. 1935. Thick 8vo., full light tan levant morocco, raised bands, gilt. Howes 186-201 1974 £10

GALSWORTHY, JOHN   The Plays of. 1929. 8vo., orig. cloth, signed by author, first limited edition. Bow Windows 66-266 1974 £12.50

GALSWORTHY, JOHN   Poems of. London, (c.1932). 8vo., orig. cloth, inscribed. Bow Windows 62-355 1974 £6

GALSWORTHY, JOHN   On Forsyte 'Change. 1930. Fine, dust wrapper. Covent 55-750 1974 £5.25

GALSWORTHY, JOHN   On Forsyte 'Change. London, 1930. 8vo., orig. cloth, presentation, first edition. Dawsons PM 252-382 1974 £45

GALSWORTHY, JOHN   The Roof. 1931. 125 pages. Austin 51-335 1973 $7.50

GALSWORTHY, JOHN   Saint's Progress. 1919. Orig. cloth, dust wrapper, scarce, first English edition. Rota 188-337 1974 £10

GALSWORTHY, JOHN   A Sheaf. 1916. 8vo., orig. cloth, first English edition. Rota 189-349 1974 £5

GALSWORTHY, JOHN   The Silver Spoon. London, n.d. (1926). Orig. cloth, spine sun faded, first edition, one of 265 numbered copies, signed by author. MacManus 224-180 1974 $25

GALSWORTHY, JOHN   The Silver Spoon. 1926. 8vo., orig. cloth, signed, first edition. Rota 189-352 1974 £15

GALSWORTHY, JOHN   The Silver Spoon. 1926. 8vo., dust wrapper, cloth, signed, limited edition. Quaritch 936-384 1974 £17

GALSWORTHY, JOHN   Swan Song. London, 1928. First edition, orig. cloth, limited to 525 numbered copies, signed by author, fine, d.w. Crane 7-94 1974 £10

GALSWORTHY, JOHN   Swan Song. London, 1928. 8vo., orig. cloth, presentation, first edition, first issue. Dawsons PM 252-383 1974 £55

GALSWORTHY, JOHN   Two Forsythe Interludes. London, 1927. First edition, limited to 500 numbered copies, signed by author, batik boards, fine copy, d.w. Crane 7-93 1974 £6

GALSWORTHY, JOHN   The White Monkey. London, n.d. Orig. cloth, deLuxe edition, limited to 265 numbered copies, signed by author, fine, d.w. Crane 7-96 1974 £10

GALSWORTHY, JOHN   The White Monkey. 1924. 8vo., cloth, inscribed, first edition. Quaritch 936-385 1974 £18

GALSWORTHY, JOHN   Works. 1929. 8vo., orig. blue lambskin gilt, fine. Howes 186-199 1974 £18

GALT, JOHN   The Ayrshire Legatees. Edinburgh, 1821. 12mo., contemporary half calf, rubbed, inscribed by publisher, first edition. Bow Windows 66-268 1974 £30

GALT, JOHN   The Entail. Edinburgh, 1823. 3 vols., 12mo., contemporary calf, rubbed, first edition. Bow Windows 66-269 1974 £24

GALT, JOHN   The Last of the Lairds. Edinburgh, 1826. 8vo., contemporary straight grained morocco, rubbed, some spotting, first edition. Bow Windows 66-270 1974 £22.50

GALT, JOHN   The Provost. Edinburgh, 1822. 12mo., contemporary cloth, joints torn, some foxing, corners rubbed, first edition. Bow Windows 66-271 1974 £15

GALT, JOHN   Ringan Gilhaize. Edinburgh, 1823. 3 vols., 12mo., contemporary calf, some foxing, rubbed, first edition. Bow Windows 66-272 1974 £25

GALT, JOHN   Sir Andrew Wylie of That Ilk. Edinburgh, 1822. 3 vols., 12mo., contemporary half morocco, gilt spines, second edition. Bow Windows 66-267 1974 £25.50

GALT, JOHN   Sir Andrew Wylie, of that Ilk. Edinburgh, 1822. 3 vols., 8vo., half calf, very good copy, scarce, first edition, with half titles and ad leaf at end of vol. 3. Sawyer 293-144 1974 £60

GALTON, DOUGLAS STRUTT   Observations On the Construction of Healthy Dwellings. Oxford, 1880. Contemporary calf gilt, rubbed, prize label, illus., first edition. Smith 194-48 1974 £8.50

GALTON, FRANCIS   Finger Prints. London, 1892. 8vo., orig. maroon cloth, gilt, plates, first edition. Dawsons PM 250-31 1974 £130

GALTON, FRANCIS   Finger Prints. London, 1892. Large 8vo., orig. cloth, plates, perfect copy, first edition. Gilhofer 61-65 1974 sFr. 1,000

GALTON, FRANCIS   Hereditary Genius. London, 1869. 8vo., orig. purple cloth, gilt, first edition. Dawsons PM 249-197 1974 £120

GALTON, FRANCIS   Hereditary Genius. New York, 1871. 8vo., orig. cloth, second American edition. Schuman 37-101 1974 $45

GALTON, FRANCIS   Inquiries into Human Faculty and its Development. London, 1883. 8vo., modern brown half morocco, gilt, first edition. Dawsons PM 249-198 1974 £70

GALTON, FRANCIS   Probability, the Foundation of Eugenics. Oxford, 1907. 8vo., orig. pictured wrappers, illus., first edition. Schuman 37-102 1974 $50

GALTON, FRANCIS   Vacation Tourists and Notes of Travel in 1860, 1861, 1862-3. Cambridge & London, 1861-62-64. 3 vols., 8vo., orig. cloth, some spotting, joints rubbed. Bow Windows 66-273 1974 £26

GAMA, J. P.   Esquisse Historique de Gutenberg. Paris, 1857. 4to., orig. printed wrappers. Kraus B8-329 1974 $30

GAMBA, B.   Delle Novelle Italiane in Prosa. Venezia, 1833. Limited to 100 copies, portraits, stained, demy 8vo., boards, vellum back. Forster 98-280 1974 £12

GAMBA, CARLO   Michel-Ange et son Ecole. Paris, 1948. Sm. 4to., plates. Biblo & Tannen 214-323 1974 $13.50

GAMBA, PETER   A Narrative of Lord Byron's Last Journey to Greece. London, 1825. 8vo., old half calf, first edition. Ximenes 33-60 1974 $100

GAMBLE, J. S.   Flora of the Presidency of Madras. 1915-36. 8vo., 3 vols., calf. Wheldon 129-1072 1974 £15

GAMBLE, J. S.   Flora of the Presidency of Madras. 1915-36. 3 vols., 8vo., calf, very scarce. Wheldon 131-1291 1974 £15

THE GAMBLER'S Last Throw. n.d. Rebound, cloth, English first edition. Covent 56-346 1974 £12.50

GAMELIN, JACQUES   Nouveau Recueil d'Osteologie et de Myologie. 1779. Large folio, contemporary boards, rebacked, fine, first edition. Dawsons PM 249-199 1974 £3,250

GAMMEL, H. P. N.   The Laws of Texas, 1822-1897. Austin, 1898. 12 vols., half morocco, raised bands, marbled boards, signed. Jenkins 48-480 1973 $1000

GAMMER Curton's Famous Histories of Sir Guy of Warwick, Sir Bevis of Hampton, Tom Hickathrift, Friar Bacon, Robin Hood and the King and the Cobler. New York, 1846. Revised edition, square 12mo., orig. brown cloth embossed covers, gilt titles, woodcut illus., binding firm with no wear. Current BW9-111 1974 $38.50

GAMMER Gurton's Garland. London, n.d. (c. 1840). Pictorial wrappers, fine, unopened copy, frontispiece engraved. Frohnsdorff 16-360 1974 $25

GAND, MICHEL JOSEPH DE   Recherces Historiques et Critiques sur la Vie et les Editions de Thierry Martens. Alost, 1845. Wrappers, illus., uncut. Kraus B8-154 1974 $28.50

GANDEE, B. F.   The Artist or Young Ladies' Instructor in Ornamental Painting, Drawing, etc. 1835. Small 8vo., plates, orig. cloth, gilt. Quaritch 940-449 1974 £25

GANDON, YVES   Imageries Critiques. Paris, 1933. Fine, wrappers, English first edition. Covent 56-843 1974 £10.50

GANNETT, HENRY   On the Arable Pasture Lands of Colorado. Washington, 1878. Rare. Jenkins 61-526 1974 $17.50

GANOT, ADOLPHE   Elementary Treatise on Physics Experimental and Applied. London, 1866. 8vo., half calf, gilt, illus., second edition in English. Dowsons PM 245-319 1974 £11

GANS, RICHARD   Muestrario de Caracteres. Madrid, n.d. Orig. cloth binding, rebacked, gilt. Dawson's 424-150 1974 $75

GANTZ, W. H.   Postal Riders and Raiders. Chicago, 1912. Orig. binding. Butterfield 10-466 1974 $7.50

GARCIA CONDE, PEDRO   Verdadera Albeyteria. Madrid, 1681. Folio, contemporary limp vellum, extremely rare. Harper 213-74 1973 $195

GARCIA DE LA CONCEPCION, JOSEPH   Historia Bethlehemitica. Sevilla, 1723. 4 parts in 1 vol., folio, contemporary limp vellum, first edition. Harper 213-73 1973 $275

GARCIA LORCA, FEDERICO   Poems. London, 1939. Tall 8vo., cloth, first English edition. Minters 37-231 1973 $28

GARCIA ROMERO, FRANCISCO   Catalogo de los Incunables Existentes en la Biblioteca de la Real Academia de la Historia. Madrid, 1921. 8vo., plates, wrappers. Kraus B8-71 1974 $25

GARCIE, PIERRE   Le Grand Routier Pillotage. Rouen, 1632. 4to., full modern red morocco, rare. Harper 213-75 1973 $3500

GARCILASSO DE LA VEGA   Histoire des Yncas, Rois du Perou, Depuis le Premier Ynca Manco Capac. Amsterdam, 1737. 4to., contemporary brown calf, engraved folding maps, very fine. Schumann 499-40 1974 sFr 980

GARCILASO DE LA VEGA   The Royal Commentaries of Peru. London, 1688. Folio, contemporary calf, gilt. Dawsons PM 251-353 1974 £250

GARCON, MAURICE   La Vie Execrable de Guillemette Babin, Sorciere. Paris, 1930. Unbound sheets. Biblo & Tannen 213-911 1973 $12.50

GARD, ANSON   The Real Cobalt. Toronot, 1908. Cloth, first edition. Putnam 126-270 1974 $12

GARD, R. E.   Johnny Chinook, Tall Tales and True From the Canadian West. Toronto, 1945. Drawings, first edition. Hood's 102-806 1974 $7.50

GARD, WAYNE   Sam Bass. Boston, 1936. Jenkins 61-203 1974 $22.50

GARDEN, FRANCIS   Travelling Memorandums Made in a Tour Upon the Continent of Europe in the Years 1786, 1787, and 1788. Edinburgh, 1792. Corrected and enlarged second edition, 2 vols., small 8vo., blue straight grained morocco, gilt line border, with 2 1/2 pages of MS. notes in pencil by William Beckford. Sawyer 293-65 1974 £310

THE GARDEN Manual, or Practical Instructions for the Cultivation of all Kinds of Vegetables, Fruits, and Flowers. n.d. Crown 8vo., cloth. Wheldon 131-1518 1974 £5

THE GARDEN of Caresses. 1934. Small 4to., orig. vellum backed blue cloth, gilt, uncut, dust wrapper, limited, fine. Howes 186-214 1974 £35

GARDENHIRE, SAMUEL M. The Long Arm. New York, 1906. 8vo., orig. dark blue pictorial cloth, first edition. Rota 190-267 1974 £10

GARDENS Old and New. (1900-08). Folio, orig. cloth, illus., scarce. Wheldon 130-1398 1974 £8

GARDINER, C. WREY Cold Moon. 1938. Dust wrapper, signed, presentation copy, English first edition. Covent 56-496 1974 £8.40

GARDINER, C. WREY Evening Silence. 1937. Presentation copy, frontispiece, wrappers, inscribed, English first edition. Covent 56-497 1974 £10.50

GARDINER, DOROTHY English Girlhood at School. 1929. Plates, scarce. Howes 186-1428 1974 £8.75

GARDINER, HAROLD C. Catholic Viewpoint on Censorship. Hanover House, 1958. 192p. Austin 51-336 1973 $10

GARDINER, J. S. Old Silver Work, Chiefly English, from the XVth to the XVIIIth Centuries. 1903. Large 4to., illus. Eaton Music-597 1973 £15

GARDINER, MARGUERITE (POWER) FARMER, COUNTESS OF BLESSINGTON
Please turn to
BLESSINGTON, MARGUERITE (POWER) FARMER GARDINER, COUNTESS OF

GARDINER, R. England's Grievance Discovered in Relation to the Coal Trade. 1796. 8vo., plates, worn. Quaritch 939-509 1974 £45

GARDINER, R. Profitable Instructions for the Measuring, Sowing and Planting of Kitchin Gardens. 1603. 4to., nineteenth century half calf. Wheldon 129-1466 1974 £150

GARDINER, SAMUEL R. History of the Commonwealth and Protectorate. 1897-1901. 3 vols., thick demy 8vo., orig. cloth, maps, best library edition. Howes 186-839 1974 £20

GARDINER, SAMUEL R. History of the Great Civil War. 1886-91. 3 vols., thick demy 8vo., orig. cloth, best library edition. Howes 186-840 1974 £20

GARDINER, STEPHEN De Vera Obediencia. (London), 1553. Small 8vo., calf antique, rare, first English edition. Ximenes 33-60A 1974 £275

GARDINER, W. Twenty Lessons on British Mosses. 1847. Post 8vo., orig. cloth, illus., enlarged third edition. Wheldon 128-1361 1973 £5

GARDINER, W. Twenty Lessons on British Mosses. 1852. Crown 8vo., cloth, fourth edition. Wheldon 130-1283 1974 £5

GARDINI, FRANCESCO GIUSEPPE De Electrici Ignis Natura Dissertatio. 1792. Folio, orig. quarter vellum, first edition. Dawsons PM 245-320 1974 £25

GARDNER, ARTHUR A Handbook of English Medieval Sculpture. Cambridge, 1935. Orig. ed., illus. Biblo & Tannen 213-226 1973 $12.50

GARDNER, CHARLES Vision and Vesture. 1916. 226 pages. Austin 61-383 1974 $10

GARDNER, EDMUND G. The Story of Florence. London, 1903. 12mo., illus. Biblo & Tannen 213-469 1973 $9.50

GARDNER, J. S. A Monograph of the British Eocene Flora. 1879-86. 2 vols. in 1, 4to., half calf, plates. Wheldon 131-999 1974 £25

GARDNER, PERCY New Chapters In Greek History. 1892. New buckram, maps. Allen 213-409 1973 $10

GARGAZ, PIERRE-ANDRE A Project of Universal and Perpetual Peace. New York, 1922. Paper label, fine, rubbed, slip case. Ballinger 1-21 1974 $17

GARGIAREUS, GIOVANNI Tractatus Varii. Bologna, 1643. Large 4to., contemporary full red morocco, gilt, presentation. Harper 213-76 1973 $485

GARGIULD, RAFAELE Raccolta Dei Monumenti Piu Interessanti del re Museo Borbonico. Napoli, 1825. 4to., plates, contemporary cloth. Smith 194-94 1974 £10

GARGUILLE, GAULTIER French Literature. Paris, 1858. Cloth, portrait, English first edition. Covent 56-488 1974 £7.50

GARIMBERTO, GIROLAMO Concetti Divinissimi. 1552. First edition, wrappers, reasonable working copy. Thomas 32-148 1974 £20

GARIS, HOWARD R. The Second Adventures of Uncle Wiggily the Bunny Rabbit Gentleman and His Muskrat Lady Housekeeper. Newark & New York, (1925). 4to., boards with paste label, cloth spine, illus. in full color by Lang Campbell, corners and edges rubbed, nice copy, scarce, first edition. Frohnsdorff 15-52 1974 $20

GARLAND, HAMLIN Afternoon Neighbors. Macmillan, 1934. 584p., orig. ed. Austin 54-406 1973 $12

GARLAND, HAMLIN Ancient Egyptian Metallurgy. London, 1927. Biblo & Tannen 210-256 1973 $15

GARLAND, HAMLIN Cavanagh--Forest Ranger. Harper, 1910. 300p. Austin 54-411 1973 $6.50

GARLAND, HAMLIN Cavanagh Forest Ranger. Harper, 1910. 365p., orig. ed. Austin 54-410 1973 $8.50

GARLAND, HAMLIN The Captain of the Gray-Horse Troop. Harper, 1901. 414p. Austin 54-407 1973 $7.50

GARLAND, HAMLIN The Captain of the Gray-Horse Troop. Harper, 1901, 414p. Austin 54-408 1973 $7.50

GARLAND, HAMLIN The Captain of the Gray-Horse Troop. Grosset, Dunlap, 1902. 415p., "special limited ed." Austin 54-409 1973 $6.50

GARLAND, HAMLIN Companions on the Trail. Macmillan, 1931. 539p., orig. ed. Austin 54-412 1973 $10.50

GARLAND, HAMLIN A Daughter of the Middle Border. Macmillan, 1921. 399p., orig. ed. Austin 54-413 1973 $7.50

GARLAND, HAMLIN The Eagle's Heart. Appleton, 1901. 369p., orig. ed. Austin 54-414 1973 $10

GARLAND, HAMLIN Hesper. Grosset, Dunlap, 1903. 445p. Austin 54-417 1973 $6

GARLAND, HAMLIN Hesper. Harper, 1903. 443p., "Sunset Ed." Austin 54-416 1973 $6.50

GARLAND, HAMLIN Hesper. Harper, 1903. 445p., orig. ed. Austin 54-415 1973 $7

GARLAND, HAMLIN Main-Travelled Roads. Harper, 1899. 299p. Austin 54-419 1973 $7.50

GARLAND, HAMLIN Money Magic. Harper, 1907. 354p. Austin 54-418 1973 $6.50

GARLAND, HAMLIN Roadside Meetings. Macmillan, 1930. 474p., orig. ed. Austin 54-420 1973 $9.75

GARLAND, HAMLIN Trail-Makers of the Middle Border. Grosset, Dunlap (1926) 1927. 426p., illus. Austin 54-422 1973 $6.50

GARLAND, HAMLIN Trail-Makers of the Middle Border. Macmillan, 1926. 426p., orig. ed. Austin 54-421 1973 $7.50

THE GARLAND of Rachel. Portland, 1902. 8vo., orig. cloth, handmade paper, first edition. Rota 189-22 1974 £15

GARMANN, CHRISTIAN FREDERICK   De Miraculis Mortuorum. Dresden & Leipzig, 1709. Thick 4to., contemporary vellum, first edition. Schuman 37-103 1974 $95

GARNER, ROBERT   The Natural History of the County of Stafford. And, Supplement. 1844 and 1860. 2 vols. in 1, demy 8vo., newly bound red buckram, engravings, vignettes, plates, fine. Broadhurst 24-1085 1974 £25

GARNETT, DAVID   Go She Must! Buckram, signed, first edition. Rota 188-352 1974 £5

GARNETT, DAVID   The Grasshoppers Come. London, 1931. Wood engravings, orig. binding, d.w. creased along spine, good copy. Ross 87-229 1974 $10

GARNETT, DAVID   Letters of T. E. Lawrence of Arabia. 1938. Illus. Austin 61-555 1974 $27.50

GARNETT, DAVID   The Letters of T. E. Lawrence. 1939. Illus., first American edition. Austin 61-554 1974 $37.50

GARNETT, DAVID   The Man in the Zoo. London, 1924. Wood engravings, orig. binding, first edition, slight foxing of end papers, else fine. Ross 87-230 1974 $10

GARNETT, DAVID   No Love. 1929. 8vo., orig. cloth, first edition. Howes 185-186 1974 £5

GARNETT, DAVID   The Old Dovecote. London, 1928. No. 8 in the Woburn Books, no. 302 of edition limited to 530 copies, signed unopened, orig. binding, near mint. Ross 87-231 1974 $15

GARNETT, DAVID   Pocahontas, of the Nonpareil of Virginia. London, 1933. Orig. binding, no. 2 of edition limited to 110 copies, signed, lacking d.w., near mint. Ross 87-232 1974 $15

GARNETT, DAVID   A Terrible Day. 1932. Frontispiece, signed, numbered, buckram. Covent 55-752 1974 £7.50

GARNETT, DAVID   A Terrible Day. 1932. Full buckram, signed, English first edition. Covent 56-498 1974 £7.50

GARNETT, DAVID   A Terrible Day. London, 1932. No. 9 of Furnival Books, no. 421 of edition limited to 550 copies, orig. binding, signed, spine darkened & stained, good copy, frontispiece. Ross 87-233 1974 $20

GARNETT, E.   Friday Nights. London, (1922). Orig. boards, linen back rubbed. Forster 97-121 1974 £3

GARNETT, EDWARD   The Breaking Point. 1907. Browned, fine. Covent 55-367 1974 £7.50

GARNETT, EDWARD   Letters From W. H. Hudson, 1901-1922. 1923. Ex-library, orig. edition. Austin 61-484 1974 $12.50

GARNETT, RICHARD   English Literature. 1903. 4 vols., roy. 8vo., half maroon calf gilt, illus. Howes 185-189 1974 £15

GARNETT, RICHARD   English Literature, an Illustrated Record. London, 1903. 4 vols., folding plates, imp. 8vo., orig. cloth, bookplates. Forster 98-282 1974 £10.50

GARNETT, RICHARD   De Flagello Myrteo: Thoughts and Fancies on Love. London, 1905. Orig. binding, inscribed by author, both sides of back fly leaf were used by author to compose additional aphorisms, not included in published text, very slight foxing, near mint. Ross 87-234 1974 $80

GARNETT, RICHARD   The Twilight of the Gods. London, 1888. 8vo., orig. cloth, first edition. Dawsons PM 252-385 1974 £15

GARNETT, THOMAS   Experiments and Observations on the Crescent Water at Harrogate. Leeds, 1791. 8vo., boards, first edition. Hammond 201-570 1974 £11

GARNETT, THOMAS   Facts on the Natural History and Habits of the Salmon. Clitheroe, n.d. 8vo., orig. yellow printed wrappers, first edition. Ximenes 37-87 1974 $45

GARNETT, THOMAS   A Treatise on the Mineral Waters of Harrogate. Knaresborough, 1822. 8vo., boards, seventh edition. Hammond 201-571 1974 £7

GARNIER, C.   Le Nouvel Opera de Paris. Ducher et Cie, 1878-81. 2 vols., roy. 8vo., and 2 vols., roy. folio, orig. half red morocco gilt. Quaritch 940-510 1974 £650

GARNIER, EDOUARD   Dictionnaire de la Ceramique - Faiences - Gres - Poteries. (1893). 8vo., plates, cloth, morocco spine. Quaritch 940-633 1974 £10

GARNIER, EDOUARD   The Soft Porcelain of Sevres. 1892. Folio, plates, full vellum, gilt. Quaritch 940-632 1974 £98

GARRARD, APSLEY CHERRY   The Worst Journey in the World. London, 1922. 2 vols., 8vo., cloth backed boards, paper labels, uncut, illus., first edition. Traylen 79-508 1973 £45

GARRICK, DAVID   A Catalogue of the Library. (London, 1823). 4to., contemporary half morocco. Dawsons PM 252-386 1974 £150

GARRICK, DAVID   A Catalogue of the Library of. (London, 1823). 4to., contemporary half morocco, marbled boards. Dawsons PM 10-233 1974 £150

GARRICK, DAVID   The Country Girl. London, 1766. 8vo., modern boards, first edition. Dawsons PM 252-387 1974 £15

GARRICK, DAVID   Cymon. London, 1767. 8vo., modern boards, first edition. Dawsons PM 252-388 1974 £15

GARRICK, DAVID   The Guardian. London, 1759. 8vo., disbound, first edition. Ximenes 33-61 1974 $30

GARRICK, DAVID   Irish Widow. French, 1807. 24p. Austin 51-338 1973 $8.50

GARRICK, DAVID   Isabella. London, 1757. 8vo., modern boards, first edition. Dawsons PM 252-389 1974 £15

GARRICK, DAVID   A New Dramatic Entertainment. London, 1774. 8vo., half calf, frontispiece, second edition. Ximenes 33-63 1974 $20

GARRICK, DAVID   The Poetical Works. London, 1785. 2 vols., 8vo., contemporary mottled calf, gilt, first edition. Ximenes 33-64 1974 $80

GARRICK, DAVID   The Sick Monkey. London, 1765. 4to., rare, disbound, frontispiece, very good copy, first edition. Ximenes 37-88 1974 $150

GARRISON, ALETHEIA   Impressions of Mexico. New York, 1937. Large 8vo., buckram, first edition. Quaritch 936-386 1974 £6

GARRISON, ALETHEIA   Impressions of Mexico. New York, 1937. Large 4to., illus., inscription, orig. cloth, rubbed. Bow Windows 62-358 1974 £8.50

GARRISON, FIELDING H.   Memorial Meeting in Honor of William Henry Welch. Baltimore, 1935. 1st ed. Biblo & Tannen 213-842 1973 $15

GARRISON, GEORGE P.   Diplomatic Correspondence of the Republic of Texas. Washington, 1908-11. 3 vols. Jenkins 61-923 1974 $35

GARRISON, WILLIAM LLOYD   Sonnets and Other Poems. Boston, 1843. 8vo., orig. green cloth, first edition. Ximenes 33-65 1974 $35

GARRISON, WINFRED ERNEST   Catholicism and the American Mind. Willett, 1928. Austin 62-189 1974 $8.50

GARRY, JAMES   An Easy and Familiar Introduction to the Rudiments of Perspective. 1820. Large folding diagram, orig. boards, loose. Eaton Music-598 1973 £5

GARSAULT, FRANCOIS A. DE   Faites des Causes Celebres et Interessantes, Augumentes de Quelques Causes. Amsterdam, 1757. Small 8vo., calf, hinges, cracked, first edition. Goodspeed's 578-108 1974 $10

GARSAULT, FRANCOIS A. DE   Les Figures des Plantes. (Paris, 1764). 5 vols., plates, contemporary tree calf, gilt, labels, fine, first edition. Bow Windows 64-100 1974 £85

GARSON, BARBARA   Mac Bird. 1966. 56p. Austin 51-337 1973 $6.50

GARSTANG, JOHN   The Burial Customs of Ancient Egypt. 1907. Frontispiece, plates, illus., English first edition. Covent 56-403 1974 £15

GARSTANG, JOHN   The Hittite Empire. 1929. Orig. cloth gilt, plates, illus., maps. Smith 193-37 1973 £5.50

GARTH, SAMUEL   Claremont. London, 1715. Folio, orig. marbled wrappers, worn, scarce, first edition. Ximenes 33-66 1974 $100

GARTSIDE, MARY   An Essay on a New Theory of Colours. London, 1808. 4to., crimson morocco label, gilt, plates, second edition. Hammond 201-710 1974 £75

GARTSIDE, MARY   An Essay on Light and Shade. 1805. 4to., plates, orig. printed boards. Quaritch 940-115 1974 £190

GARVER, WILL L.   Brother of the Third Degree. Chicago, 1930. First U.S. edition. Covent 56-438 1974 £10.50

GARVIN, J. W.   Canadian Poets. Toronto, 1926. Revised edition. Hood's 102-652 1974 $10

GARVIN, VIOLA GERARD   Dedication. 1928. 8vo., orig. cloth, presentation, first edition. Bow Windows 64-512 1974 £5

GARZA Y MELO, TRINIDAD DE LA   Oracion Civica. Monterey, 1845. 8vo., orig. printed self-wrappers, woodcuts, first edition. Ximenes 33-67 1974 $45

GASCOYNE, DAVID   Poems. 1943. Orig. cloth, illus., worn, first edition. Rota 188-359 1974 £6.50

GASCOYNE, DAVID   Poems. 1943. Cloth-backed dec. boards, presentation copy, inscribed, English first edition. Covent 56-499 1974 £15

GASCOYNE, DAVID   Poems 1937-1942. London, 1943. Very nice copy, half tone illus., first edition, orig. cloth. Crane 7-97 1974 £12

GASCOYNE, DAVID   Poems; 1937-1942. London, 1943. Presentation copy, inscribed by author, colour plates, cloth backed dec. boards, spine little faded, nice copy, first edition. Covent 51-762 1973 £15

GASCOYNE, DAVID   Poems. 1943. 4to., orig. cloth, illus., first edition. Broadhurst 23-729 1974 £36

GASCOYNE, DAVID   A Short Survey of Surrealism. 1935. Illus., orig. cloth, scarce, first edition. Rota 188-358 1974 £15

GASCOYNE, DAVID   A Short Survey of Surrealism. 1935. Illus., faded, English first edition. Covent 56-500 1974 £25

GASK, NORMAN   Old Silver Spoons of England. 1926. 4to., plates, cloth. Quaritch 940-677 1974 £30

GASKELL, ELIZABETH CLEGHORN   Cranford. New York, (c. 1855). First American edition, 8vo., orig. green embossed cloth, good copy. Sawyer 293-145 1974 £21

GASKELL, ELIZABETH CLEGHORN   Cranford. 1891. Crown 8vo., orig. plain cloth, foxing, illus., first edition. Howes 185-523 1974 £5

GASKELL, ELIZABETH CLEGHORN   The Life of Charlotte Bronte. 1857. 8vo., 2 vols., old half roan, second edition. Hill 126-111 1974 £10.50

GASKELL, ELIZABETH CLEGHORN   The Life of Charlotte Bronte. London, 1857. 2 vols., 8vo., orig. cloth, first edition. Dawsons PM 252-390 1974 £140

GASKELL, ELIZABETH CLEGHORN   The Works. 1906. 8 vols., crown 8vo., faded, rebacked. Howes 185-192 1974 £22.50

GASKELL, ELIZABETH CLEGHORN   The Works. 1906. 8 vols., crown 8vo., faded, rebacked. Howes 185-192 1974 £22.50

GASKELL, G. A.   A Dictionary of the Sacred Language. New York, 1930. Roy. 8vo., scarce. Howes 186-1835 1974 £9

GASKELL, G. A.   A Dictionary of the Sacred Language of All Scriptures and Myths. 1924. Orig. edition. Austin 61-385 1974 $12.50

GASKELL, W. H.   The Origin of Vertebrates. 1908. 8vo., cloth, text-figures, scarce. Wheldon 128-274 1973 £5

GASPARRINI, G.   Ricerche Sulla Origine dell'Embroine Seminale in Alcune Piante Fanerogama. Naples, 1846. 4to., plates. Wheldon 131-1139 1974 £5

GASPE Peninsula; History, Legends, Resources, Attractions. Quebec, 1930. Illus., card cover. Hood's 102-708 1974 $7.50

GASQUET, FRANCIS AIDAN, CARDINAL 1846-1929   Edward VI and the Book of Common Prayer. 1891. Second edition. Howes 185-1199 1974 £6.50

GASQUET, FRANCIS AIDAN, CARDINAL 1846-1929   Henry VIII and the English Monasteries. 1888. 2 vols., thick 8vo., map. Howes 185-1198 1974 £7.50

GASQUET, FRANCIS AIDAN, CARDINAL 1846-1929   Lord Acton and His Circle. 1906. Thick 8vo., portrait, orig. edition. Howes 186-556 1974 £6

GASQUET, FRANCIS AIDAN, CARDINAL 1846-1929   Parish Life in Mediaeval England. (1929). 8vo., orig. cloth, illus. Bow Windows 66-277 1974 £7.50

GASSENDI, PETRUS   Institutio Astronomica. 1653. 8vo., contemporary panelled calf, rebacked. Dawsons PM 245-322 1974 £95

GASSER, ACHILLES PIRMIN   Catalogus Regum Omnium, Quorum sub Christiana Professione per Europam. (Augsburg), 1554. 4to., marbled boards, red morocco backs, rare, woodcut. Harper 213-77 1973 $425

GASSET, JOSE ORTEGO Y   Velasquez. New York, 1946. Folio. Biblo & Tannen 214-548 1974 $15

GASSNER, JOHN   Dramatic Soundings. Crown, 1968. 716p. Austin 51-340 1973 $7.50

GASSNER, JOHN   Producing the Play. Dryden, 1941. 744p., orig. unrev. ed. Austin 51-339 1973 $10

GASTON, JOSEPH   Portland, Oregon. Chicago, 1911. 3 vols., 8vo., three quarter leather. Saddleback 14-647 1974 $75

GATES, ELEANOR   The Poor Little Rich Girl. Arrow, 1916. 238p. Austin 51-341 1973 $7.50

GATKE, H.   Heligoland as an Ornithological Observatory. Edinburgh, 1895. Roy. 8vo., cloth, portrait, scarce. Wheldon 128-445 1973 £5

GATKE, H.   Heligoland as an Omithological Observatory. Edinburgh, 1895. Roy 8vo., cloth, scarce. Wheldon 130-525 1974 £5

GATTINGER, AUGUSTIN   The Flora of Tennessee. Nashville, 1901. 8vo., orig. bindings. Butterfield 8-611 1974 $15

GATTY, ALFRED   The Bell. London, 1848. 12mo., orig. red cloth, illus., fine, unopened. Ximenes 33-68 1974 $20

GAUDEN, JOHN   A Discourse of Auxiliary Beauty or Artificiall Hansomenesse. (London), 1656. 8vo., contemporary sheep, engraved, first edition. Bow Windows 62-360 1974 £110

GAUDEN, JOHN   The Loosing of St. Peter's Bands. 1660. 4to., modern sheep, scarce. Thomas 28-94 1972 £21

GAUDIN, C. T.   Memoire sur Quelques Gisements de Feuilles Fossiles de la Toscane. Zurich, 1858-64. 6 parts in 1 vol., 4to., half calf. Wheldon 131-1000 1974 £30

GAUDIN, J.   Agrostologia Helvetica. Paris, 1811. 2 vols.
in 1, 8vo., calf. Wheldon 128-1261 1973 £15

GAUDIN, J.   Agrostologia Helvetica. Paris, 1811. 8vo.,
calf, 2 vols. Wheldon 130-1155 1974 £15

GAUGER, NICHOLAS   Fires Improv'd. London, 1715. Small 8vo., contemporary calf, plates, first edition in English. Dawsons PM 245-324 1974 £75

GAUGER, NICHOLAS   La Mechanique du Feu. Amsterdam, 1714. 8vo.,
contemporary sheep, gilt, fine, plates, second edition. Dawsons PM 245-323
1974 £35

GAUGER, NICOLAS   Fires Improved. London, 1715. 12mo.,
contemporary calf, fine, first English edition. Ximenes 33-69 1974 $150

GAUGUIN, PAUL   Intimate Journals. 1923. Buckram, plates,
English first edition. Covent 56-48 1974 £25

GAUGIN, PAUL   Noa Noa. New York, n.d. 4to., color
plates. Biblo & Tannen 210-206 1973 $27.50

GAULD, H. DRUMMOND   Ghost Tales and Legends. London, 1929.
1st ed. Biblo & Tannen 210-599 1973 $10

GAULE, JOHN   Practique Theories. London, 1629. 12mo.,
old half calf, worn, first edition. Ximenes 33-70 1974 $100

GAUMANN, E.   Comparative Morphology of Fungi. New York,
1928. 8vo., cloth, text figures. Wheldon 128-1363 1973 £7.50

GAUMANN, E.   Comparative Morphology of Fungi. New
York, 1928. 8vo., cloth. Wheldon 131-1405 1974 £7.50

GAUNT, WILLIAM   Bandits in a Landscape. 1937. Inscribed, presentation copy, English first edition. Covent 56-1458 1974 £8.50

GAUNTLETT, HENRY   Letters to the Stranger in Reading. London,
1810. 8vo., uncut, orig. boards, first edition. Bow Windows 62-361 1974
£8.50

GAUSE, G. F.   The Struggle for Existence. Baltimore, 1934.
8vo., cloth, scarce. Wheldon 129-79 1974 £5

GAUSS, KARL FRIEDRICH   Dioptrische Untersuchungen. 1841. 4to., modern quarter calf, first edition. Dawsons PM 245-326 1974 £170

GAUSS, KARL FRIEDRICH   Theorematis Fundamentalis in Doctrina de Residuis.
1818. 4to., modern boards, first edition. Dawsons PM 245-325 1974 £70

GAUSS, KARL FRIEDRICH   Untersuchungen Uber Gegenstande der Hohern
Geodaesie. 1844. 4to., modern boards, first separate edition. Dawsons PM
245-327 1974 £25

GAUSS, KARL FRIEDRICH   Untersuchungen Uber Gegenstande der Hohern
Geodasie. 1847. 4to., modern boards, uncut, unopened, first separate edition.
Dawsons PM 245-328 1974 £25

GAUTIER, L. M.   Les Champignons. Paris, (1884). Roy 8vo.,
buckram, plates. Wheldon 129-1214 1974 £15

GAUTIER, LEON 1832-1897   Bibliographie des Chansons de Geste. Paris,
1897. 8vo., orig. wrappers, uncut. Dawsons PM 10-236 1974 £15

GAUTIER, THEOPHILE   Captain Fracasse. 1901. 2 vols., orig. dec.
silken cloth gilt, faded. Covent 55-753 1974 £8.50

GAUTIER, THEOPHILE   Emaux et Camees. Paris, 1892. Portrait,
quarter vellum, nice copy. Covent 51-2592 1973 £15

GAUTIER, THEOPHILE   Jean et Jeanette. Paris, 1894. Limited edition,
engraved illus., 8vo., red levant morocco, spine gilt tooled, slip in case, fine.
Sawyer 293-146 1974 £52

GAUTIER, THEOPHILE   Journeys in Italy. New York, 1902. Inner
hinges split. Biblo & Tannen 213-672 1973 $7.50

GAUTIER, THEOPHILE   Mademoiselle de Maupin. 1938. 4to., vellum,
uncut. Broadhurst 23-1004 1974 £25

GAUTIER, THEOPHILE   The Works Of. 1906. 8vo., orig. cloth, 24
vols. Bow Windows 64-513 1974 £17.50

GAUTIER DE METZ   Image du Monde. Paris, c. 1530. Small
4to., red morocco, gilt stamped border by Chambolle-Duru, woodcut map, from
the Library of Fernando Colon, Baron Pichon, and Charles Fairfax Murray. Kraus
137-35 1974 $3,500

GAVANTI, BARTOLOMMEO   Thesaurus Sacrorum Rituum. Venice, 1769.
3 vols. in 2, folio, contemporary vellum backed boards. Howes 185-1202
1974 £30

GAVER, JACK   Curtain Calls. Dodd, Mead, 1949. 310p.
Austin 51-342 1973 $7.50

GAVER, JACK   There's Laughter In the Air. Greenberg, 1945.
291p. Austin 51-343 1973 $7.50

GAVIN, ANTHONY   The Great Red Dragon. 1854. 408 pages.
Austin 57-237 1974 $15

GAVIT, JOHN PALMER   "Opium". London, 1925. Orig. binding.
Butterfield 10-447 1974 $10

GAWSWORTH, JOHN   Mishka and Madeleine. 1932. English first
edition. Covent 56-503 1974 £12.50

GAWSWORTH, JOHN   Mishka and Madeleine. 1932. Small 4to.,
English first edition. Covent 56-1272 1974 £12.50

GAWSWORTH, JOHN   Ten Contemporaries. 1933. English first edition. Covent 56-1564 1974 £5.25

GAWSWORTH, JOHN   Thrills, Crimes and Mysteries. London, n.d.
Biblo & Tannen 210-466 1973 $15

GAY, C.   Historia Fisica Y Politica de Chile. Paris
& Santiago, 1848. 2 vols., 8vo. & imp. 4to., new cloth, plates, rare.
Wheldon 131-49 1974 £85

GAY, J. H.   Anacreon Chez Polycrate. Paris, 1799.
8vo., modern boards, second edition. Dawsons PM 252-425 1974 £8

GAY, JACQUES   Recherches sur la Famille des Amaryllidacees,
Premier Memoire, Esquisse Monographique des Narcissees a Couronne Rudimentaire.
Paris, 1859. Wheldon 131-1140 1974 £5

GAY, JOHN   The Beggar's Opera. Black buckram, plates,
woodcuts, gilt. Marsden 37-189 1974 £12

GAY, JOHN   The Beggar's Opera. 4to., buckram, handmade
paper, illus., first edition. Rota 189-335 1974 £12.50

GAY, JOHN   The Beggar's Opera. 1922. 8vo., orig. quarter
cloth, illus, plates. Bow Windows 64-514 1974 £10

GAY, JOHN   The Captives. 1724. 8vo., modern half morocco,
first edition. Quaritch 936-84 1974 £50

GAY, JOHN   Fables. London, 1727-38. 2 vols., 4to.,
contemporary sprinkled calf, first edition. Dawsons PM 252-391 1974 £130

GAY, JOHN   Fables. London, 1757. 2 vols. in 1, 8vo.,
illus., contemporary tree calf gilt. Dawsons PM 252-392 1974 £15

GAY, JOHN   Fables. London, 1793. 2 parts in 1 vol.,
8vo., contemporary speckled calf, plates. Dawsons PM 252-393 1974 £18

GAY, JOHN   Fables. 1793. 8vo., 2 vols., straight-grained
red morocco gilt, gilt. Quaritch 936-303 1974 £250

GAY, JOHN   Fables. London, 1793. 8vo., full contemp.
tree calf; gilt spines, leather labels; 70 plates., 2 vols. Frohnsdorff 16-111 1974
$250

GAY, JOHN   Fables. Alnwick, 1842. Faded purple cloth,
bookplate. Dawson's 424-44 1974 $50

GAY, JOHN   Fables By Mr. Gay. London, 1801. 12mo.,
illus., contemporary sheep, worn, rebacked. Bow Windows 62-362 1974 £8

GAY, JOHN   Gay's Chair. London, 1820. 8vo., modern
boards, uncut, first edition. Ximenes 33-71 1974 $50

GAY, JOHN   Poetical Works Of. 1854. 2 vols. Austin
61-388 1974 $15

GAY, JOHN   Polly. London, 1729. 8vo., modern boards,
pirated edition. Dawsons PM 252-394 1974 £50

GAY, JOHN   Trivia. London, n.d. 8vo., half calf, first
edition. Ximenes 33-72 1974 $150

GAY, JOHN   The Wife of Bath. London, 1713. 4to., half
morocco, ex-library, bookplate, very scarce, good copy, first edition. Ximenes
37-89 1974 $275

GAY, JOHN   The Wife of Bath. London, 1713. 4to., full
polished mottled calf, gilt, first edition, fine clean copy, very rare with woodcut
on the half title. Ximenes 36-101 1974 $550

GAY, W. B.   Gazetteer of Hampshire County. Syracuse,
(1886). 8vo., red embossed boards. Butterfield 8-241 1974 $27.50

GAY-LUSSAC, JOSEPH LOUIS   Instruction sur l'essai des Matieres D'Argent.
1832. 4to., orig. blue wrappers. Zeitlin 235-278 1974 $150

GAYA, LOUIS DE   Gaya's Traite des Armes 1678. Oxford, 1911.
8vo., blue cloth. Dawsons PM 245-329 1974 £6

GAYLEY, CHARLES MILLS   Beaumont, the Dramatist. 1914. Illus.,
ex-library, orig. edition. Austin 61-389 1974 $10

GAZETTEER and Directory of the Great Western Railway and Branches, Embracing
a Complete Alphabetical and Classified Directory of Business Firms in . . .
Southern Ontario . . . together With Every Village and Station on the Above
Named Route. Toronto, 1874. Map, ads, bound. Hood's 102-22 1974 $75

GAZOLA, BONAVENTURA   Raccolta di Alcune Recenti Produzioni di
Fr. Bonaventura Gazola Vescovo di Cervia. 1820. 4to., contemporary
Italian red morocco gilt. Thomas 28-135 1972 £30

GEARY, R. W.   Centenary Celebration of the Battle of Lundy's
Lane, July 25, 1914. Niagara Falls, 1919. Illus., inscribed. Hood's 104-685
1974 $17.50

GEBAUER, J. J.   Systematisches Verzeichniss der Seesterne,
Seeigel, Conchylien und Pflanzenthiere Nach Linne Systema Naturae. Halle,
1802. 4to., sewed. Wheldon 131-930 1974 £5

GEBELIN, ANTOINE COURT DE   Histoire Naturelle de la Parole. Paris, 1776.
8vo., contemporary mottled calf, gilt. Dawsons PM 249-200 1974 £135

GEE, DENSON W.   Long Beach in the World War. Long Beach,
c.1921. 4to., cloth. Saddleback 14-110 1974 $25

GEE, G. E.   The Jeweller's Assistant. 1892. 8vo., orig.
cloth. Bow Windows 64-515 1974 £8.50

GEE, HENRY   The Elizabethan Clergy, and the Settlement of
Religion, 1558-1564. 1898. Orig. half roan, rebacked, scarce. Howes
185-1205 1974 £8.50

GEE, JOSHUA   The Trade and Navigation of Great Britain
Considered. London, 1729. 8vo., modern half calf, fine, first edition.
Dawsons PM 247-130 1974 £160

GEE, JOSHUA   The Trade and Navigation of Great Britain Considered. London, 1730. 8vo., boards, second edition. Hammond 201-233 1974
£48

GEER, J. J.   Beyond the Lines. Philadelphia, 1864. 12mo.,
brown cloth, illus., first edition. Putman 126-57 1974 $20

GEFFROY, GUSTAVE   Corot and Millet. New York, 1902. 4to.,
illus. Jacobs 24-42 1974 $10

GEGENBACK, PAMPHILUS   Von Ainem Waldbruder Wie er Underricht Gibt
Bapst Kaiser Kunig Und Allen Standen. (Augsburg), 1522. Woodcut border, rare,
small wormholes throughout affecting text but not too badly, 4to., 19th century
boards. Thomas 32-131 1974 £800

GEHLE, FREDERICK W.   Our Dubbledam Journey. 1941. 50 pages.
Austin 57-238 1974 $10

GEHLE, FREDERICK W.   Our Dubbledam Journey. 1941. Austin
62-191 1974 $10

GEIKIE, ARCHIBALD   The Ancient Volcanoes of Great Britain.
London, 1897. 2 vols., roy. 8vo., maps. Traylen 79-83 1973 £18

GEIKIE, ARCHIBALD   Annals of the Royal Society Club. 1917.
8vo., cloth, portraits, scarce. Wheldon 131-217 1974 £12

GEIKIE, ARCHIBALD   The Founders of Geology. 1905. 8vo., prize
calf, very scarce, second edition. Wheldon 128-102 1973 £7.50

GEIKIE, ARCHIBALD   Geological Sketches. 1882. 8vo., cloth.
Wheldon 130-928 1974 £5

GEIKIE, ARCHIBALD   Geological Sketches at Home and Abroad.
London, 1882. 8vo., faded, first edition. Traylen 79-82 1973 £5

GEIKIE, ARCHIBALD   Geology of Central and Western Fife and
Kinross. Glasgow, 1900. 8vo., cloth. Wheldon 128-973 1973 £10

GEIKIE, ARCHIBALD   Geology of Central and Western Fife and Kinross. Glasgow, 1900. 8vo., cloth. Wheldon 130-927 1974 £10

GEIKIE, ARCHIBALD   Text-Book of Geology. 1882. 8vo., orig.
cloth. Wheldon 130-930 1974 £5

GEIKIE, ARCHIBALD   Text-book of Geology. 1903. 8vo., cloth,
plates, fourth edition. Wheldon 129-824 1974 £7.50

GEIKIE, J.   The Great Ice Age. 1894. 8vo., cloth, maps,
frontispiece. Wheldon 128-974 1973 £7.50

GEILER VON KAISERSBERG, JOHANNES Nauicula Siue Speculum Fatuorum.
Strassburg, 1511. 4to., 19th century blind-tooled brown morocco, woodcuts,
fine, first edition. Harper 213-78 1973 $2150

GEINITZ, H. B.   Die Versteinerungen der Grauwackenformation in
Sachsen und den Angrenzenden Lander-Abtheilungen. Leipzig, 1852-53. 2 parts
in 1 vol., 4to., cloth, plates. Wheldon 128-975 1973 £20

GELL, WILLIAM   Pompeiana: The Topography, Edifices and
Ornaments of Pompeii. 1832. 2 vols., roy. 8vo., plates, fine olivet straight
grained morocco, gilt. Quaritch 940-319 1974 £65

GELLIBRAND, HENRY   An Institution Trigonometricall. London, 1635.
Small 8vo., contemporary sheep rebacked, first edition. Dawsons PM 245-331
1974 £575

GELLIBRAND, HENRY   An Institution Trigonometricall. London, 1652.
Small 8vo., contemporary calf, second edition. Dawsons PM 245-332 1974 £225

GELLIBRAND, HENRY   Trigonometria Britannica. 1633. Folio, old
paper boards, worn. Zeitlin 235-96 1974 $950

GELLIUS, AULUS   Noctes Atticae. Florence, 1513. Small 8vo.,
19th century calf, gilt tooled spine in panels, first and last pages ?washed, else
mint. Thomas 32-235 1974 £50

GELLIUS, AULUS   Noctes Atticae. 1515. Contemporary Venetian
dark brown morocco, book-label, worn, first Aldine edition. Thomas 30-31
1973 £55

GEMALDE-GALERIE, DIE   Alte Meister. Wien, 1896. Biblo & Tannen
213-292 1973 $15

GEMINIANI, FRANCESCO   The Compleat Tutor for the Violin. (c. 1790).
Oblong 8vo., frontispiece, orig. wrappers, sewed. Quaritch 940-811 1974
£55

GEMMA, CORNELIUS   De Naturae Divinis Characterismis. Antwerp,
1575. 2 vols. in 1, 8vo., limp vellum, illus., first edition. Schuman 37-104
1974 $145

GEMMA FRISIUS, REINERUS   Arithmetica Practicae Methodus Facilis. Leipzig, 1558. 8vo., modern half vellum, woodcut diagrams, unrecorded edition.   Schafer 8-155 1973 sFr. 950

THE GENEALOGIST.   London & Exeter, 1877-1922. 45 vols., 8vo., plates, half red morocco.   Quaritch 939-724 1974 £250

A GENERAL Collection of Treatys.   London, 1732. 8vo., 4 vols., contemporary calf gilt, second edition.   Dawsons PM 251-229 1974 £115

THE GENERAL Gazetteer.   Berwick, 1823. 3 vols., half contemporary calf gilt, foxed.   Smith 193-535 1973 £9

THE GENERAL HISTORY of Europe.   London, 1690-1697. 4to., contemporary calf, first editions in English.   Dawsons PM 251-230 1974 £350

DE GENERIBUS Ebriosorum, et Ebrietate Vitanda.   Frankfurt, 1557. 12mo., modern calf, light stains, minor repairs.   Thomas 32-230 1974 £50

GENET, EDMOND CHARLES   Memorial on the Alluvions or Obstructions, at the Head of the Navigation of the River Hudson.   Albany, 1818. 8vo., sewn as issued, first edition, very good uncut copy.   Ximenes 36-102 1974 $100

GENET, JEAN   The Balcony.   Grove, 1958. 118p., hard cover ed.   Austin 51-344 1973 $6.50

GENET, JEAN   The Man Condemned to Death.   n.d. Faded, fine, English first edition.   Covent 56-504 1974 £12.50

GENGA, BERNARDINO   Anatomia per Vso et Intelligenza del Disegno. Roma, 1691. Folio, contemporary mottled boards, first edition.   Dawsons PM 249-202 1974 £475

GENGENBACH, PAMPHILIUS   Der alt und New Bruder Nolhard.   Strassburg, (1544). Small 4to., woodcuts, recent green morocco, good copy.   Schafer 10-87 1974 sFr 5,500

GENGENBACH, PAMPHILIUS   Die. X. Alter Dyser Welt.   Basel, (1515). Small 4to., large woodcuts, modern half red morocco, extremely rare first edition, fine copy.   Schafer 10-86 1974 sFr 16,000

GENIN, THOMAS HEDGES   The Napolead.   St. Clairsville, 1833. 12mo., early boards, first edition.   Ximenes 33-74 1974 $35

THE GENIUS of Britain.   London, 1775. 4to., disbound, nice copy, very scarce, first edition.   Ximenes 37-178 1974 $80

GENLIS, STEPHANIE FELICITE DUCREST DE SAINT AUBIN   Arabesques Mythologiques, ou les Attributs de Toutes les Divinites de la Fable.   Paris, 1810. Quarter tan morocco, marbled boards, few pages misbound but all present. Gregory 44-140 1974 $37.50

GENLIS, STEPHANIE FELICITE DUCREST DE SAINT AUBIN   Mademoiselle de la Fayette, ou le Siecle de Louis XIII.   1813. 2 vols., 12mo., contemporary calf, trifle rubbed, mottled board sides, vellum corners.   George's 610-305 1973 £6

GENLIS, STEPHANIE FELICITE DUCREST DE SAINT AUBIN   Le Siege de la Rochelle.   London, 1808. 3 vols., 12mo., contemporary half citron morocco, gilt. Ximenes 33-75 1974 $17.50

GENEALOGICAL and Biographical Record of Cook County, Illinois.   Chicago, 1894. 8vo., leather, rebacked.   Saddleback 14-371 1974 $30

GENT, THOMAS   The Ancient and Modern History of the Loyal Town of Rippon.   York, 1733. 8vo., full red morocco gilt, raised bands, fine, plates.   Traylen 79-410 1973 £60

GENTHE, ARNOLD   As I Remember.   1936. Photographs. Austin 57-239 1974 $10

GENTHE, ARNOLD   The Book of the Dance.   Kennedy, 1916. Austin 51-345 1973 $25

GENTHE, ARNOLD   Impressions of Old New Orleans.   New York, (1926). 4to., orig. bindings, dust jacket, torn.   Butterfield 8-394 1974 $20

GENTIL, F.   Le Jardinier Solitaire.   Paris, 1704. 12mo., contemporary sheep gilt, rare, first edition.   Wheldon 130-1400 1974 £55

GENTILIS, ALBERICUS   Regales Disputationes Tres.   London, 1605. 4to., contemporary calf, gilt, rebacked, first edition.   Dawsons PM 251-231 1974 £750

THE GENTLEMAN'S Magazine.   1793-97. 5 vols. in 10, thick 8vo., labels, plates, contemporary half calf gilt.   Howes 186-207 1974 £30

GENUINE MEMOIRS of John Murray.   1747. 8vo., unbound.   Hill 126-139 1974 £18

GEOFFROY, E. L.   Histoire Abregee des Insectes Qui se Trouvent aux Environs de Paris.   Paris, 1762. 2 vols., 4to., contemporary calf gilt, engraved plates, nice copy, rare first edition.   Wheldon 128-723 1973 £30

GEOLOGICAL RECORD   An Account of Works of Geology, Mineralogy and Palaeontology Published During the Year, for the Years 1874-1884.   1875-88. 8vo., 8 vols., cloth.   Wheldon 131-1004 1974 £20

GEORGE, DAVID LLOYD-
Please turn to
LLOYD-GEORGE, DAVID

GEORGE, E.   Etchings On the Mosel.   1873. Folio, orig. cloth gilt, plates.   Smith 194-609 1974 £8.50

GEORGE, HENRY   The Complete Works.   New York, 1904. 10 vols., gilt tops, other edges uncut, largely unopened, buckram.   Butterfield 10-274 1974 $75

GEORGE, WALDEMAR   Arturo Tosi.   Paris, 1933. 4to., wrappers, plates.   Minters 37-210 1973 $18

GEORGE, WALDEMAR   Chirico.   Paris, 1928. 4to., plates, drawings, yellow cloth, orig. wrappers.   Covent 55-94 1974 £65

GEORGE, WALDEMAR   Marc Chagall et son Oeuvre.   Paris, 1928. 16mo., boards, illus.   Minters 37-66 1973 $12.50

GEORGE, WILLIAM   An Essay on Angling.   Worcester, 1840. 8vo., orig. limp cloth, scarce, first edition.   Ximenes 33-76 1974 $35

GEORGE OF TREBIZOND   Rhetoricorum Libri.   Basle, 1522. Raised bands, contemporary blind stamped calf, worn.   Thomas 28-285 1972 £31.50

GEORGE II, KING OF ENGLAND   An Act for Encouraging the Making of Indico in the British Plantations in America.   London, 1748. Small folio, disbound, first edition.   Dawsons PM 247-131 1974 £20

GEORGE III, KING OF ENGLAND   An Act for Continuing . . . . and Amending Acts . . . . Made for Encouraging the Making of Indico in America. London, 1770. Small folio, first edition.   Dawsons PM 247-132 1974 £18

GEORGE III, KING OF ENGLAND   An Act for Granting to His Majesty Certain Rates and Duties Upon Letters and Packets Sent by Post Within Ireland.   London, 1803. Folio.   Dawsons PM 247-133 1974 £15

GEORGIAN Poetry, 1920-22.   1922. Boards, covers little faded, very good, defective d.w.   Covent 51-61 1973 £5.25

GERALDINUS, ANTONIUS   Oratio in Obsequio Nomine.   Rome, 1488-1491. 4to., boards, first edition.   Dawsons PM 251-232 1974 £135

GERARD, ALEXANDER   An Essay on Genius.   London, 1774. 8vo., contemporary calf, bit rubbed, first edition, very good copy.   Ximenes 36-105 1974 $75

GERARD, JOHN   A Catalogue of Plants Cultivated in the Garden of John Gerard 1596-1599.   1876. 4to., orig. boards, rare, signed, numbered. Wheldon 128-1466 1973 £20

GERARD, JOHN   The Herball.   1597. Folio, modern half calf, antique style, woodcuts, complete copy, first edition.   Wheldon 128-1678 1973 £350

GERARD, JOHN   The Herball.   1633. Folio, 19th century half pigskin, woodcuts, revised second edition.   Wheldon 131-50 1974 £585

GERARD, JOHN   The Herball.   1633. Folio, modern half calf, woodcuts, second edition.   Wheldon 130-1612 1974 £350

GERARD, JOHN   The Herball. 1633. 8vo., contemporary calf, rebacked, worn, folio   Bow Windows 64-778 1974 £290

GERARD, JOHN   The Herball of Generall Historie of Plantes. London, 1636. Thick folio, modern half morocco, gilt, good copy, third edition.   Traylen 79-21 1973 £200

GERARD, JOHN   The Herball. 1936. Folio, contemporary dark red morocco gilt, hand coloured title, woodcuts, initials and ornaments.   Thomas 32-315 1974 £1,500

GERARD, L.   Flora Gallo-Provincialis. Paris, 1761. 8vo., half calf, weak joints, engraved plates, scarce. Wheldon 128-1262 1973 £20

GERARD, L.   Flora Gallo-Provincialis. Paris, 1761. 8vo., boards, cloth, plates. Wheldon 129-1074 1974 £25

GERARDUS   Tractatus de Spiritualibus Ascensionibus. (Basel, 1489). 8vo., 16th century vellum, recase. Harper 213-79 1973 $600

GERCKE, A.   Einleitung In Die Altertumswissenschaft. 1910-12. 3 vols., one with worn spine. Allen 213-411 1973 $10

GERDES, D.   Florilegium Historico-Oriticum Librorum Rariorum cui Multa Simul Scitu Jucunda Adsperguntur Historiam Omnem Litterariam. London, 1763. Third and last edition, demy 8vo., contemporary quarter calf, spine slightly defective. Forster 98-293 1974 £20

GERENZANO, CARLO GIUSEPPE   L'Armeria d'Esculapio. Milan, 1694. 12mo., old pasteboards. Gurney 64-95 1974 £10

GERHARD, E.   Auserlesene Griechische Vaserbilder, Hauptsachlich Etruskschen Fundorts. Berlin, 1840-47. 3 vols. of 4, roy. 4to., plates, foxing, half morocco. Quaritch 940-320 1974 £20

GERHARD, FRED   Illinois As It Is. Chicago, 1857. Cloth, map, illus., nice copy. Hayman 59-258 1974 $20

GERHARD, FRED   Illinois As It Is. Chicago-Philadelphia, 1857. 8vo., orig. bindings, maps, fine. Butterfield 8-146 1974 $35

GERHARDI, WILLIAM   Pending Heaven. 1930. 8vo., orig. cloth, dust wrapper, inscribed, first edition. Rota 189-361 1974 £6

GERHARDI, WILLIAM   The Romanovs. 1940. Fine copy, worn & marked d.w., illus., first edition. Covent 51-767 1973 £12.50

GERHARDT, HANS   Schone Frag und Antwort. (Augsburg, 1525). Small 4to., woodcuts, modern half vellum, very rare, very fine copy. Schafer 10-101 1974 sFr 1,500

GERHARDT, HANS   Schone Frag und Antwort. (Augsburg), 1525. Small 4to., modern half vellum, woodcuts, very fine, very rare. Schafer 8-113 1973 sFr. 1,600

GERMAN ART from the Fifteenth to the Twentieth Century. Philadelphia, 1937. 4to., blue printed cloth, illus. Rich Summer-67 1974 $15

THE GERMAN ERATO. Berlin, 1800. 4to., contemporary half calf, fine. Hill 126-113 1974 £55

THE GERMAN Reich and Americans of German Origin. Oxford, 1938. Austin 62-193 1974 $7.50

GERMAR, E. F.   Fauna Insectorum Europae, Hemiptera. (Halle, 1817). Small 4to., coloured plates. Wheldon 128-724 1973 £15

GERNOLDT, WOLF   Ein Schoner vnnd Trostlicher Spruch von Dem Menschlichen Leben vnnd Dem Tode. Nuremberg, (c. 1575). Small 4to., boards. Schumann 499-41 1974 sFr 1,150

GERNON, BLAINE BROOKS   Lincoln in the Political Circus. Chicago, 1938. First edition, orig. binding, 1,000 copies printed. Wilson 63-205 1974 $30

GERONVAL, AUDOUIN DE   Manuel de l'Imprimeur, ou Traite Simplifie de la Typographie. Paris, 1826. 16mo., half leather, folding plates, tables, illus., diagrams. Kraus B8-332 1974 $75

GERRARD, E. A.   Elizabethan Drama and Dramatists, 1583-1603. 1928. Allen 216-1801 1974 $10

GERRARD DE NERVAL   Les Cydalises et Autres Poemes. Paris, 1922. Large 8vo., orig. wrapper, numbered. L. Goldschmidt 42-321 1974 $15

GERARD DE NERVAL   The Women of Cairo. 1929. 2 vols., 8vo., orig. cloth, first edition. Bow Windows 66-497 1974 £14.50

GERSHWIN, GEORGE   Song-book. New York, 1932. 1st ed., 4to., illus. Biblo & Tannen 214-848 1974 $15

GERSON, JOANNES   Imitatio Christi
Please turn to
IMITATIO CHRISTI

GERSON, LOUIS L.   The Hyphenate in Recent American Politics and Diplomacy. Univ. of Kansas, 1964. Austin 62-196 1974 $12.50

GERSPACH, M.   Les Tapisseries Coptes. Paris, 1890. 4to., plates, illus., dec. cloth, rare. Quaritch 940-755 1974 £35

GERSTACKER, FREDERICK   Gerstacker's Travels. London, 1854. Red cloth, gilt. Rinsland 58-72 1974 $32

GERSTENBERG, ALICE   Comedies All. Longman's, 1930. 238p. Austin 51-346 1973 $10

GERVAIS, PAUL 1816-1879   Histoire Naturelle des Mammiferes. Paris, 1854-55. 2 vols., imp. 8vo., contemporary half morocco gilt, hand coloured plates, nice copy, usual foxing. Wheldon 128-317 1973 £30

GERVAIS, PAUL 1816-1879   Histoire Naturelle des Mammiferes. Paris, 1854-55. 2 vols., imp. 8vo., new cloth, plates. Wheldon 131-489 1974 £35

GERVAIS, PAUL 1816-1879   Zoologie et Paleontologie Generale. Paris, 1867-76. 2 vols. in 1, 4to., new cloth, plates, scarce. Wheldon 131-430 1974 £40

GERVAIS, PAUL 1816-1879   Zoologie et Paleontologie Generale. Paris, 1876. 4to., orig. wrappers, uncut, plates, scarce. Wheldon 131-431 1974 £10

GERVAISE, NICOLAS   Description Historique de Royaume de Macacar. Ratisbonne, 1700. 12mo., contemporary calf, spine gilt, second edition, very good copy. Ximenes 36-106 1974 $80

GERVASE OF TILBURY   De Imperio Romano, et Gottorum, Lombardorum, Brittonum, Francorum, Anglorumque Regnis. Helmstadt, 1673. 4to., marbled boards, scarce, first edition. Harper 213-80 1973 $295

GERVINUS, G. G.   Shakespeare Commentaries. 1863. 2 vols., large 8vo., orig. plum cloth, first English edition. Howes 185-435 1974 £5

GESAMTKATALOG der Wiegendrucke. Leipzig, 1925-38. Vols. 1 - 7, 4to., orig. cloth, orig. edition. Kraus B8-73 1974 $475

GESAMTKATALOG der Wiegendrucke. Leipzig, 1925-38. Vols. 1-7, all with supps., roy. 4to., orig. buckram, 4 with d.w.'s. Forster 98-294 1974 £175

GESCHICKTER, CHARLES F.   Diseases of the Breast. Philadelphia, 1943. Rittenhouse 46-715 1974 $10

GESCHICKTER, CHARLES F.   Diseases of the Breast, Diagnosis, Pathology, Treatment. Philadelphia, 1945. Second edition. Rittenhouse 46-278 1974 $15

GESCHICKTER, CHARLES F.   Tumors of Bone. New York, 1931. First edition. Rittenhouse 46-279 1974 $15

GESCHICKTER, CHARLES F.   Tumours of Bone. New York, 1931. 8vo., orig. buckram, first edition. Gurney 66-70 1974 £15

GESCHICHTE des Amerikanischen Kriegs Von 1812. Reading, 1817. Plates, foxing, worn. Rinsland 58-94 1974 $50

GESNER, A.   New Brunswick. London, 1847. Worn spine. Hood's 103-175 1974 $45

GESNER, J. M.   Novus Linguae et Eruditionis Romanae
Thesaurus Post R. Stephanum. 1749. 4 vols. in 2, boards, rebacked, worn,
ex-library. Allen 213-412 1973 $50

GESNER, KONRAD 1516-1565   Euonymus...de Remedijs Secretis. (Zurich,
1569). 2 parts in 1 vol., 8vo., illus., contemporary pigskin over boards, very fine,
first edition to contain both ports. Schafer 8-156 1973 sFr 3,400

GESNER, KONRAD 1516-1565   Fischbuch. 1598-1613. Folio, contemporary
calf, woodcuts. Wheldon 129-572 1974 £240

GESNER, KONRAD 1516-1565   Gesneri Tigvrini. 1585. Folio, illus., old
gilt gramed calf, frayed. Bow Windows 64-101 1974 £360

GESNER, KONRAD 1516-1565   Historia Animalium. Frankfurt, 1617-21.
5 vols. in 3, folio, modern vellum, browned. Traylen 79-93 1973 £105

GESNER, KONRAD 1516-1565   Historiae Animalium. Frankfurt, 1617. Folio,
old calf, woodcuts. Wheldon 129-467 1974 £200

GESNER, KONRAD 1516-1565   Historiae Animalium. Frankfurt, 1617-21.
Folio, modern vellum, woodcuts. Wheldon 129-335 1974 £180

GESNER, KONRAD 1516-1565   A New Booke of Destillatyon of Waters.
London, 1565. Small 4to., 19th century calf, woodcuts, stains, second edition in
English. Traylen 79-231 1973 £475

GESPRACH, Ausprachen und Deklamationen. Cleveland, Ohio, 1892.
Austin 62-554 1974 $17.50

GESSI, BERLINGIERO   Pareri Cavalereschi. Bologna, 1675. Small
4to., contemporary Italian red morocco gilt. Thomas 28-136 1972 £80

GESSNER, SALOMON   Gessners Auserlesene Idyllen in Verse Gebracht
von K. W. Ramler. Berlin, 1787. 8vo., wrappers, red labels, corners and back
end slightly damaged, first edition in book form, very well preserved copy.
Schumann 499-43 1974 sFr 270

GESSNER, SALOMON   La Mort d'Abel. Hamburg, 1791. Roy. 8vo.,
orig. wrappers, back damaged, uncut, fresh copy. Schumann 499-42 1974
sFr 240

GETCHELL, F. H.   An Illustrated Encyclopaedia of the Science
and Practice of Obstetrics. Philadelphia, 1890. Large octavo, weak cover,
woodcuts. Rittenhouse 46-280 1974 $20

GEUZE, G.   Cours d'Agriculture Pratique. Paris, 1857.
8vo., half calf, plates. Wheldon 130-1588 1974 £5

GEWOLD, CHRISTOPH   Genealogia Serenissimorum Ducum. Augsburg,
1605. Small folio, engraved portraits, first edition, fine clean copy. Schumann
499-44 1974 sFr 600

GHALIGAI, FRANCESCO   Pratica d'Arithmetica. 1548. 4to., quarter calf.
Dawsons PM 245-334 1974 £90

GHENT, PERCY   John Reade and His Friends. (Toronto), 1925.
Inscribed, signed. Hood's 103-208 1974 $30

GHENT, PERCY   Literary and Historic Fragments of Canadian
Interest. Toronto, 1927. Illus., limited edition. Hood's 103-409 1974 $12.50

GHEUSI, P. B.   Le Blason. (Paris), 1933. 4to., wrappers,
uncut, illus. Kraus B8-74 1974 $35

GHISLAIN DE BUSBECQ, OGIER
Please turn to
BUSBECQ, OGIER GHISLAIN DE

THE GHOST Book. London, n.d. Biblo & Tannen 210-554 1973 $15

THE GHOST Plays of Japan. New York, 1933. Tall 8vo., limited to 1000
copies, fine full page color illus. on heavy paper, pristine. Current BW9-551
1974 $20

GHOST Stories and Other Queer Tales. London, n.d. 1st ed. Biblo & Tannen
210-549 1973 $8.50

GIBB, WILLIAM   A Book of Porcelain. London, 1910. Large
8vo., plates, orig. cloth. Bow Windows 62-366 1974 £8.50

GIBB, WOLCOTT   More In Sorrow. Holt, 1958. 308p. Austin
54-423 1973 $8.50

GIBBES, GEORGE SMITH   A Second Treatise on the Bath Waters. Bath,
1803. 8vo., orig. boards, rebacked, uncut, first edition. Gurney 66-71 1974
£9

GIBBINGS, RICHARD   An Exact Reprint of the Roman Index
Expurgatorius. Dublin, 1887. 12mo., contemporary red half morocco, marbled
boards. Dawsons PM 10-237 1974 £7

GIBBON, C.   The Casquet of Literature. 1886. 6 vols. in
3, large demy 8vo., half contemporary calf gilt, rubbed. Smith 194-348 1974
£7.50

GIBBON, C.   The Casquet of Literature. London, 1896.
6 vols., 8vo., illus., foxing, orig. dec. cloth, rubbed. Bow Windows 62-367
1974 £5

GIBBON, EDWARD   The Autobiographies . . . Printed Verbatim from
Hitherto Unpublished MSS. London, 1896. 8vo., orig. purple cloth, first
edition, fine. Ximenes 36-108 1974 $40

GIBBON, EDWARD   An Essay on the Study of Literature. London,
1764. 8vo., orig. boards, fine, first English edition. Dawsons PM 252-395
1974 £130

GIBBON, EDWARD   The History of the Decline and Fall of the
Roman Empire. London, 1776. 6 vols., 4to., contemporary diced calf, first
edition, first issue. Dawsons PM 250-32 1974 £580

GIBBON, EDWARD   The History of the Decline and Fall of the Roman
Empire. London, 1789(-1788). 4to., contemporary calf gilt. Dawsons PM
251-233 1974 £150

GIBBON, EDWARD   The History of the Decline and Fall of the
Roman Empire. 1797. 12 vols., 19th century half roan, maps. Howes 186-851
1974 £18

GIBBON, EDWARD   The History of the Decline and Fall of the Roman
Empire. London, 1815. 12 vols., 8vo., portrait, maps, contemporary half calf,
rubbed, rebacked, morocco labels. Bow Windows 62-368 1974 £50

GIBBON, EDWARD   The History of the Decline and Fall of the Roman
Empire. London, 1821. 8vo., 8 vols., maps, half calf, rebacked. Bow
Windows 62-369 1974 £32

GIBBON, EDWARD   The History of the Decline and Fall of the Roman
Empire. 1828. 8vo., 8 vols., half calf. Quaritch 936-388 1974 £30

GIBBON, EDWARD   The History of the Decline and Fall of the Roman
Empire. 1838. 8 vols., 8vo., half calf, portrait, folding maps, some foxing,
stains, marbled sides. Bow Windows 66-278 1974 £40

GIBBON, EDWARD   The History of the Decline and Fall of the Roman
Empire. London, 1854-5. 8vo., 8vols., modern half calf, fine. Dawsons PM
251-234 1974 £130

GIBBON, EDWARD   The History of the Decline and Fall of the
Roman Empire. 1906. 7 vols., contemporary calf, leather labels, rubbed,
fourth edition. Smith 194-26 1974 £40

GIBBON, EDWARD   The History of the Decline & Fall of the Roman
Empire. 1909-14. 7 vols., plates, orig. cloth gilt. Smith 193-617 1973 £18

GIBBON, EDWARD   Decline and Fall of the Roman Empire. 1936.
3 vols., fine, illus., boxed. Austin 61-391 1974 $27.50

GIBBON, EDWARD   The Library of. London, 1940. Plates, med.
8vo., orig. buckram, d.w. Forster 98-297 1974 £12

GIBBON, EDWARD   Miscellaneous Works. London, 1796. 2 vols.,
4to., orig. boards, first edition. Dawsons PM 252-396 1974 £150

GIBBON, EDWARD   The Miscellaneous Works of Edward Gibbon.
London, 1837. Bdg. worn. Biblo & Tannen 213-674 1973 $10

GIBBON, EDWARD   Private Letters. 1896. 8vo., 3 vols., buckram, frontispieces. Quaritch 936-389 1974 £10

GIBBON, J.   Introductio ad Latinam Blasoniam. London, 1682. Small 8vo., old calf, rebacked. Quaritch 939-727 1974 £18

GIBBON, JOHN MURRAY   Canadian Folk Songs. Dutton, 1927. 105p. Austin 51-237 1973 $10

GIBBON, JOHN MURRAY   The Romantic History of the Canadian Pacific. Toronto, 1935. Illus. Hood's 103-803 1974 $25

GIBBS, A. HAMILTON   Bluebottles. Boston, 1928. 12mo., 1st ed., author's sgd. pres. Biblo & Tannen 214-710 1974 $13.50

GIBBS, A. HAMILTON   Chances. Boston, 1930. 1st ed. Biblo & Tannen 214-711 1974 $7.50

GIBBS, A. HAMILTON   Gun Fodder. Boston, 1919. 1st Amer. ed., author's sgd. pres. Biblo & Tannen 214-714 1974 $10

GIBBS, A. HAMILTON   A Half Inch of Candle. Boston, 1939. 1st ed., author's sgd. pres. Biblo & Tannen 214-712 1974 $10

GIBBS, A. HAMILTON   Harness. Boston, 1928. 1st ed. Biblo & Tannen 214-713 1974 $7.50

GIBBS, A. HAMILTON   Labels. Boston, 1926. 1st ed., author's sgd. pres. Biblo & Tannen 214-715 1974 $15

GIBBS, A. HAMILTON   The Need We Have. Boston, 1936. 1st ed., author's initialed pres., bdg. faded. Biblo & Tannen 214-716 1974 $10

GIBBS, A. HAMILTON   Rivers Glide On. Boston, 1934. 1st ed., author's sgd. pres. Biblo & Tannen 214-720 1974 $12.50

GIBBS, A. HAMILTON   Undertow. Boston, 1932. 1st ed., author's sgd. pres. Biblo & Tannen 214-721 1974 $12.50

GIBBS, A. HAMILTON   The Young Prince. Philadelphia, 1937. 12mo., 1st ed., author's sgd. pres. Biblo & Tannen 214-722 1974 $12.50

GIBBS, HENRY HUCKS   A Catalogue of Some Printed Books and Manuscripts at St. Dunstan's. London, 1888. Small folio, contemporary quarter roan, uncut, fine. Dawsons PM 10-238 1974 £18

GIBBS, JAMES   A Book of Architecture. 1728. Folio, half brown morocco. worn. Marsden 37-201 1974 £45

GIBBS, JAMES   A Book of Architecture. 1739. Roy. folio, plates, half pigskin. Quaritch 940-511 1974 £150

GIBBS, OLIVER   The St. Croix Valley. N.P., n.d. 8vo., disbound, scarce, first edition. Ximenes 33-77 1974 $30

GIBBS, PHILIP   Across the Frontiers. 1938. Illus., first American edition. Austin 61-393 1974 $10

GIBBS, PHILIP   America Speaks. 1942. First American edition. Austin 61-394 1974 $10

GIBBS, WOLCOTT   Seasons in the Sun. Random, 1950. 168p., illus. Austin 51-348 1973 $7.50

GIBNEY, V. P.   The Hip and Its Diseases. New York, 1884. Rittenhouse 46-281 1974 $15

GIBRAN, KAHLIL   The Wanderer. New York, 1932. 1st ed. Biblo & Tannen 210-728 1973 $15

GIBSON, A. BOYCE   The Philosophy of Descartes. 1932. Orig. edition. Howes 185-1843 1974 £5

GIBSON, A. M.   A Political Crime. New York, 1885. Cloth, with ads, scarce. Hayman 59-214 1974 $15

GIBSON, CHARLES DANA   The Education of Mr. Pipp. New York, 1899. Oblong folio, illus., orig. pictorial buckram backed boards, orig. box. Smith 194-729 1974 £7.50

GIBSON, CHARLES DANA   The Social Ladder. New York, 1902. Oblong folio, illus., orig. pictorial buckram backed boards. Smith 194-730 1974 £7.50

GIBSON, EDMUND   Codex Juris Ecclesiastici Anglicani. Oxford, 1761. 2 vols., folio, contemporary calf, second & best edition. Howes 185-1213 1974 £62

GIBSON, EMILY M.   English Class Plays for New Americans. 1927. Ex-library, 121 pages. Austin 57-242 1974 $12.50

GIBSON, EVA KATHARINE   Zauberlinda the Wise Witch. Chicago, 1901. Sm. 4to., illus. Frohnsdorff 16-89 1974 $15

GIBSON, F.   Six French Artists of the Nineteenth Century. 1925. Roy. 4to., plates, cloth, scarce. Quaritch 940-116 1974 £5

GIBSON, J.   The Fruit-Gardener. 1768. 8vo., modern half calf. Wheldon 130-1477 1974 £35

GIBSON, JOHN   The History of Glasgow. Glasgow, 1777. 8vo., panelled calf, gilt, morocco, first edition. Dawsons PM 251-26 1974 £120

GIBSON, KATHARINE   Goldsmith of Florence. 1929. 4to., plates. Allen 213-1498 1973 $10

GIBSON, O.   The Chinese in America. Cincinnati, 1877. Orig. binding. Butterfield 10-275 1974 $15

GIBSON, ROBERT   A Treatise of Practical Surveying. 1802. 8vo., contemporary mottled calf, label, gilt. Zeitlin 235-99 1974 $48.50

GIBSON, ROBERT   A Treatise on Practical Surveying. Dublin, 1810. 8vo., contemporary calf, sixth edition. Dawsons PM 245-335 1974 £12

GIBSON, S.   A Bibliography of the Works of Thomas Fuller. London, 1936. Portrait, crown 4to., orig. wrappers. Forster 98-268 1974 £3.50

GIBSON, T. A.   Geography of Canada. Montreal & Toronto, 1855. Orig. boards, worn. Hood's 104-396 1974 $15

GIBSON, T. A.   Geography of Canada, for the Use of Schools and Families. Montreal & Toronto, 1855. Orig. boards, slightly worn. Hood's 102-411 1974 $15

GIBSON, WALCOT   Memoirs of the Geological Survey, England and Wales. London, 1905. 8vo., cloth, gilt, plates. Hammond 201-367 1974 £16

GIBSON, WILFRED WILSON 1878- Friends. London, 1916. Inscribed by author to his wife, near mint, orig. brown paper covers. Ross 86-184 1974 $80

GIBSON, WILFRED WILSON 1878- Home. 1920. Small 8vo., boards, first edition, Japanese vellum. Quaritch 936-390 1974 £18

GIBSON, WILFRED WILSON 1878- I Heard a Sailor. London, 1925. Orig. binding, unusually fine, bright copy. Ross 86-185 1974 $10

GIBSON, WILFRED WILSON 1878- Krindlesyke. London, 1922. Bookplate, fine, orig. binding. Ross 86-186 1974 $10

GIBSON, WILFRED WILSON 1878- On the Threshold. 1907. Boards, rubbed, English first edition. Current 56-508 1974 £10

GIBSON, WILFRED WILSON 1878- The Stonefolds. 1907. Edition limited to 500 copies, scarce, near fine, orig. binding. Ross 86-187 1974 $25

GIBSON, WILLIAM   The See Saw Log. Knopf, 1959. 273p. Austin 51-349 1973 $5

GIBSON, WILLIAM MARION   Aliens and the Law. Univ. of North Carolina, 1940. Austin 62-197 1974 $17.50

GIDDINGS, LUTHER   Sketches of the Campaign in Northern Mexico. New York, 1853. First edition. Jenkins 61-1590 1974 $45

GIDE, ANDRE   Le Retour de l'Enfant Prodique. Paris, 1912. 12mo., orig. wrapper, uncut, second edition. L. Goldschmidt 42-231 1974 $40

GIDE, ANDRE   Les Nourritures Terrestres. Paris, 1897. 12mo., half vellum, early 20th century boards, uncut, first edition. L. Goldschmidt 42-228 1974 $150

GIDE, ANDRE   Les Nourritures Terrestres. Paris, 1930. 4to., half brown morocco with morocco corners, no. 150 of edition limited to 300 copies, printed on Verge Creme de Hollande, lacking slip case, sepia engravings, front cover slightly sprung, near mint. Ross 87-237 1974 $75

GIDE, ANDRE   Montaigne. London, 1929. No. 69 of edition limited to 800 copies, orig. binding, signed, fine. Ross 87-236 1974 $50

GIDE, ANDRE   Notes on Chopin. New York, 1949. Biblo & Tannen 214-827 1974 $7.50

GIDE, ANDRE   Numquid et tu? Paris, 1926. Square 8vo., orig. wrapper, first trade edition. L. Goldschmidt 42-229 1974 $17.50

GIDE, ANDRE   Oedipe. Paris, 1931. 8vo., blue cloth, illus., first edition. Rota 190-462 1974 £6

GIDE, ANDRE   Robert. Supplement a l'Ecole des Femmes. Paris, 1930. 16mo., orig. wrapper, first edition. L. Goldschmidt 42-230 1974 $17.50

GIDE, ANDRE   Voyage au Congo. Paris, 1927. Small 4to., wrappers, maps, English first edition. Covent 56-1775 1974 £15.75

GIEBEL, C. G.   Insecta Epizoa. Leipzig, 1874. Folio, half morocco, plates, rare, nice copy. Wheldon 128-725 1973 £60

GIEBEL, C. G.   Insecta Epizoa. Leipzig, 1874. Folio, half morocco, plates, rare. Wheldon 130-751 1974 £60

GIEBEL, C. G.   Odontographie. Leipzig, 1855. 4to., boards, plates, library stamps, rare. Wheldon 128-318 1973 £30

GIERKE, OTTO VON   The Development of Political Theory. 1939. Faded. Howes 186-852 1974 £5

GIESELER, JOHN C. L.   A Compendium of Ecclesiastical History. Edinburgh, 1846-48. 2 vols. in 1, thick 8vo., contemporary half green morocco, revised fourth edition. Howes 185-1216 1974 £5

THE GIFT. Philadelphia, (1845). Plates, full calf, rubbed. Allen 216-638 1974 $35

THE GINGERBREAD Boy. New York, (1943). 8vo., pictorial boards, spiral bound, color illus., animated, very good copy. Frohnsdorff 16-590 1974 $15

GIONO, JEAN   Triomphe de la Vie. Paris, 1942. 12mo., orig. wrapper, uncut, limited, first edition. L. Goldschmidt 42-233 1974 $10

GIORDANI, VITALE   Evclide Restitvto Overo gli antichi Elementi Geometrici Ristaurati. 1680. Small folio, contemporary vellum, boards, foxing. Zeitlin 235-71 1974 $175

GIOSCIA, BARBARA   A Survey of Raritan. 1939. Austin 62-201 1974 $47.50

GIOVIO, PAOLO   Commentarii Delle Cose de Turchi. 1541. 3 parts in 1 vol., very good, 19th century calf gilt, rubbed. Thomas 30-77 1973 £50

GIGOT, F.   Le Pigeon Voyageur. Brussels, n.d. Roy 8vo., cloth, illus. Wheldon 130-527 1974 £15

GIL AYUSO, FAUSTINO   Junta de Incorporaciones. Madrid, 1934. Stiff wrappers. Kraus B8-75 1974 $18

GILBART, JAMES WILLIAM   The Works of. London, 1865. 6 vols., 8vo., contemporary calf gilt, first collected edition. Dawsons PM 247-134 1974 £60

GILBERT, A.   Alfred Gilbert. 1929. 4to., plates, cloth. Quaritch 940-117 1974 £8

GILBERT, ANNE H.   The Stage Reminiscences of Mrs. Gilbert. Scribner, 1901. 248p., illus. Austin 51-350 1973 $10

GILBERT, BERNARD   Bly Market. London, (1924). 4to., limited, orig. holland backed boards, first edition. Bow Windows 62-371 1974 £6.50

GILBERT, J. E.   Le Genre Amanita. 1918. 8vo., half calf. Wheldon 129-1215 1974 £5

GILBERT, J. E.   Les Livres du Mycologie. Paris, 1927-34. Post 8vo., buckram, 4 vols. Wheldon 129-1216 1974 £12

GILBERT, MURRAY   Essays in Honour of. 1936. Very fine, d.w., first edition. Covent 51-1340 1973 £5.50

GILBERT, NATHANIEL   An Answer to Mr. John Slack's Remarks. 1812. 12mo., contemporary quarter calf. Hill 126-115 1974 £8.50

GILBERT, STUART   James Joyce's Ulysses. London, (1930). 8vo., orig. cloth, first edition. Bow Windows 62-372 1974 £12

GILBERT, V. WALTER   Notes on Dental Porcelain. London, 1905. 8vo., orig. fawn cloth. Dawsons PM 249-203 1974 £5.50

GILBERT, WILLIAM   De Mundo Nostro Sublunari Philosophia Nova. Amsterdam, 1651. Small 4to., contemporary vellum, inscribed, first edition. Traylen 79-232 1973 £1,500

GILBERT, WILLIAM   Tractatus sive Physiologia Nova de Magnete. 1628. 4to., nineteenth century continental boards, gilt, fine, plates, second edition. Dawsons PM 245-336 1974 £950

GILBERT, WILLIAM SCHWENCK   The "Bad" Ballads. London, 1869. Illus., all edges gilt, bright stamping of gilt on cover & spine, fine, scarce, orig. binding. Ross 86-201 1974 $65

GILBERT, WILLIAM SCHWENCK   The Midado, or the Town of Titipu. 1928. Colour plates, drawings, fine, d.w. repaired with adhesive tape, first edition. Covent 51-773 1973 £6.30

GILBERT, WILLIAM SCHWENCK   The Mikado. Mt. Vernon, 1940. Limited edition. Biblo & Tannen 210-786 1973 $7.50

GILBERT, WILLIAM SCHWENCK   Princess Ida. 1912. Coloured plates, nice copy, green cloth, gilt, first edition. Covent 51-694 1973 £7.50

GILBERT, WILLIAM SCHWENCK   Savoy Operas. 1909. Plates, orig. cloth, gilt, first edition. Howes 185-174 1974 £12

GILBERT, WILLIAM SCHWENCK   Songs of a Savoyard. London, 1890. 8vo., orig. dec. cloth, gilt, first edition. Hammond 201-483 1974 £12

GILBEY, WALTER   Animal Painters of England from the Year 1650. 1900-1911. 3 vols., 4to., plates, half morocco, gilt, fine. Quaritch 940-118 1974 £250

GILBEY, WALTER   Animal Painters of England from the Year 1650. 1900. Plates, rubbed. Marsden 37-203 1974 £14

GILBEY, WALTER   Small Horses in Warfare. 1900. Orig. cloth, gilt, English first edition. Covent 56-942 1974 £7.50

GILCHRIST, ALEXANDER   Life of William Blake. 1880. 2 vols., cloth gilt, illus. Thomas 28-155 1972 £31.50

GILCHRIST, ALEXANDER   Life of William Blake. 1863. 8vo., 2 vols., cloth, first edition. Quaritch 936-305 1974 £35

GILCHRIST, ALEXANDER   Life of William Blake, With Selections from His Poems and Other Writings. London & Cambridge, 1863. 2 vols., orig. cloth, first edition, illus., very good. MacManus 224-42 1974 $100

GILCHRIST, ALEXANDER   Life of William Blake. 1907. Plates, top of spine frayed, ex-library. Allen 216-1981 1974 $20

GILCHRIST, JOHN   A Collection of Ancient and Modern Scottish Ballads. Edinburgh, 1815. 2 vols., 8vo., contemporary half calf, first edition. Ximenes 33-80 1974 $40

GILCHRIST, MURRAY   Frangipanni. 1893. Orig. boards, limited, uncut, first edition. Howes 186-210 1974 £8.50

GILDAY, JOHN P.   Oklahoma History. Chicago, 1925. 3 vols., 4to., cloth, illus. Saddleback 14-637 1974 $60

GILDER, RICHARD WATSON   The New Day. New York, 1876. Square 12mo., orig. pictorial cloth, first edition, illus., fine. MacManus 224-183 1974 $35

GILDON, CHARLES   Miscellaneous Letters and Essays. London, 1694. 8vo., contemporary morocco gilt, first edition. Dawsons PM 252-397 1974 £215

GILDON, CHARLES   Phaeton. London, 1698. 4to., modern cloth, some foxing, scarce, first edition. Ximenes 37-90 1974 $250

GILDON, CHARLES   The Post-Boy Robb'd of His Mail. London, 1706. 8vo., contemporary panelled calf, second edition. Bow Windows 62-375 1974 £46.50

GILES, E. B.   The History of the Art of Cutting in England. 1887. 8vo., cloth, plates, illus., scarce. Quaritch 940-712 1974 £14

GILES, HENRY   Lectures and Essays. Boston, 1850. 2 vols., 12mo., orig. brown cloth, fine, first edition. Ximenes 33-81 1974 $15

GILES, HERBERT A.   Strange Stories from a Chinese Studio. Shanghai, Singapore, Hongkong, and Yokohama, 1916. 8vo., orig. cloth, third edition. Rota 190-835 1974 £5

GILES, J. A.   History of the Ancient Britons, to Invasion of the Saxons. 1854. 2 vols., new buckram. Allen 213-1500 1973 $15

GILL, A. CLOYD   The Jew In This War. Mullen, 1942. Austin 62-198 1974 $10

GILL, ERIC   Art & Love. Bristol, 1927. 8vo., orig. cloth, limited edition. Bow Windows 64-517 1974 £15

GILL, ERIC   Art Nonsense and Other Essays. 1929. 8vo., buckram, uncut, first edition. Quaritch 936-391 1974 £6

GILL, ERIC   Clothes. 1931. Bookplate, diagrams, faded. Marsden 37-206 1974 £6

GILL, ERIC   Clothes. 1931. 8vo., orig. cloth, signature, first edition. Rota 189-378 1974 £7

GILL, ERIC   The Game. 1922. Quarter linen, plain brown paper boards, fine, first edition. Rota 188-368 1974 £10

GILL, ERIC   Hand und Inschrift-Alphabete fur Schulen und Fachklassen und fur Kunstgewerbliche Werkstatten. Leipzig, 1922. Plates, orig. cloth, first edition. Rota 188-367 1974 £18

GILL, ERIC   Social Justice. 1939. 12mo., boards, faded, English first edition. Covent 56-512 1974 £21

GILL, ERIC   Twenty-Five Nudes Engraved By Eric Gill. London, 1938. Tall 8vo., cloth, plates. Minters 37-148 1973 $20

GILL, ERIC   War Memorial. 1923. Thin 8vo., engravings, orig. pictorial wrappers. Smith 194-516 1974 £7.50

GILL, SAMUEL THOMAS   Victoria Illustrated. Melbourne & Sydney, 1857. Oblong 4to., black half morocco gilt. Traylen 79-550 1973 £420

GILL, W. F.   Lotus Leaves. Original Stories, Essays and Poems. New York, 1882. Large 8vo., gilt & green Victorian dec. binding, some edge wear, woodcut plates with tissue guards, fine. Current BW9-226 1974 $12

GILLE, J. G.   Manuel de l'Imprimerie. Paris, 1817. Orig. wrappers, engraved plates, revised second edition. Kraus B8-333 1974 $85

GILLELAND, J. C.   History of the Late War Between the United States and Great Britain. Baltimore, 1817. Worn leather binding, pages browned. Hood's 102-102 1974 $100

GILLEM, ALVIN C.   Report on the Modoc War. Washington, 1877. Jenkins 61-323 1974 $15

GILLESPIE, C. B.   Illustrated History of South Boston. South Boston, 1900. First edition, 8vo., illus., covers scuffed, else very good. Current BW9-388 1974 $15

GILLETT, CHARLES RIPLEY   Catalogue of the Mcalpin Collection of British History and Theology. New York, 1927. 5 vols., 8vo., cloth. Dawsons PM 10-240 1974 £13.25

GILLETT, CHARLES RIPLEY   Catalogue of the McAlpin Collection of British History and Theology. New York, 1927-30. 5 vols., med. 8vo., orig. cloth. Forster 98-312 1974 £30

GILLETT, JAMES B.   Six Years with the Texas Rangers, 1875-1881. New Haven, 1925. Inscription signed by author, fine, slipcase. Jenkins 61-939 1974 $45

GILLETT, JAMES B.   Six Years with the Texas Rangers, 1875-1881. Chicago, 1943. Decor. cloth, gilt top. Dykes 24-76 1974 $10

GILLIAM, ALBERT M.   Travels over the Table Lands and Cordilleras of Mexico. Philadelphia, 1846. Illus., orig. cloth, spine slightly chipped, first edition. Jenkins 61-940 1974 $125

GILLIAM, TOD D.   A Text-Book of Practical Gynecology. Philadelphia, 1908. Revised third edition. Rittenhouse 46-282 1974 $10

GILLIERS, LE SIEUR   Le Cannameliste Francais. 1751. 4to., contemporary calf, first edition. Bow Windows 64-520 1974 £400

GILLIES, ROBERT PEARSE   Tales of a Voyager to the Arctic Ocean. London, 1826. 3 vols., 12mo., orig. grey boards, rebacked in cloth, first edition. Ximenes 37-91 1974 £65

GILLMORE, PARKER   Prairie and Forest. New York, 1874. Illus. Hood's 104-430 1974 $17.50

GILLMORE, PARKER   Prairie and Forest. London, 1874. Illus., orig. green cloth, scarce, first edition. Bradley 35-152 1974 $30

GILLOW, JOSEPH   A Literary and Biographical History. London & New York, 1885-1902. 5 vols., 8vo., orig. cloth, faded. Dawsons PM 10-241 1974 £45

GILLOW, JOSEPH   A Literary and Biographical History. London, (1885-1902). Demy 8vo., 5 vols., orig. cloth, text fine. Forster 98-314 1974 £50

GILLOW, JOSEPH   A Literary and Biographical History of the English Catholics. (1885-1902). 5 vols., orig. cloth, scarce, orig. edition. Howes 185-692 1974 £60

GILLOW, JOSEPH   A Literary and Biographical History . . . . of the English Catholics. (1885-1902). 5 vols., orig. cloth, scarce, orig. & best edition. Howes 185-1218 1974 £65

GILLY, W. S.   Vigilantius and His Times. 1844. Rubbed, contemporary maroon straight-grained morocco gilt. Howes 185-1744 1974 £5.75

GILMAN, CAROLINE   Recollections of a Southern Matron. New York, 1838. 12mo., orig. brown cloth, first edition. Ximenes 33-82 1974 $27.50

GILMAN, CHARLES   The Illinois Conveyancer. Quincy, 1846. Orig. brown cloth, leather label, first edition. Bradley 35-179 1974 $75

GILMAN, SAMUEL   Memoirs of a New England Village Choir. Boston, 1829. 12mo., orig. quarter cloth, boards, first edition. Ximenes 33-83 1974 $30

GILMORE, JAMES ROBERTS   Among the Guerillas. New York, 1866. 12mo., orig. cloth, first edition. Ximenes 33-84 1974 $15

GILMORE, JAMES ROBERTS   Down in Tennessee. New York, 1864. 12mo., orig. green cloth, first edition. Ximenes 33-85 1974 $15

GILMORE, JAMES ROBERTS   My Southern Friends.   New York, 1863.
12mo., orig. cloth, first edition. Ximenes 33-86 1974 $10

GILMORE, JENE C.   Art for Conservation. Barre, Mass., 1971.
4to., orig. lea.-backed bds., mint in orig. box, ltd. to 300 copies, sgd., with
an orig. etching. Jacobs 24-43 1974 $80

GILPIN, WILLIAM   The Last Work Published of the Rev. W. Gilpin
. . . Representing the Effect of a Morning, a Noon Tide and an Evening Sun.
1810. Folio, plates, orig. boards. Quaritch 940-122 1974 £55

GILPIN, WILLIAM   Observations on the Coasts of Hampshire. Sussex
and Kent, 1804. 4to., half morocco. Quaritch 939-124 1974 £17.50

GILPIN, WILLIAM   Observations on the River Wye. 1782. Plates,
contemporary calf, rebacked, first edition. Marsden 37-205 1974 £21

GILPIN, WILLIAM   Observations, Relative Chiefly to Picturesque
Beauty, Made in Year 1776. 1789. 2 vols., tinted plates and maps, new buckram,
foxed. Allen 216-2014 1974 $50

GILPIN, WILLIAM   Observations, Relative Chiefly to Picturesque
Beauty. 1792. 2 vols., 8vo., plates, contemporary tree calf, gilt, rebacked.
Quaritch 940-120 1974 £45

GILPIN, WILLIAM   Observations, Relative Chiefly to Picturesque
Beauty. 1792. 2 vols., 4to., calf, third edition. Quaritch 939-125 1974 £45

GILPIN, WILLIAM   Practical Hints upon Landscape Gardening. London, 1832. 8vo., contemporary half calf, gilt, plates, first edition. Hammond
201-399 1974 £50

GILPIN, WILLIAM   Remarks on Forest Scenery. 1791. 2 vols.,
8vo., half calf, plates, scarce. Wheldon 131-1732 1974 £35

GILPIN, WILLIAM   Remarks On Forest Scenery and Other
Woodland Views. London, 1794. 2 vols., 8vo., old polished calf, rebacked,
plates. Traylen 79-333 1973 £26

GILPIN, WILLIAM   Remarks on Forest Scenery and Other Woodland
Views. 1794. 2 vols., 8vo., plates, half mottled calf, gilt. Quaritch
940-121 1974 £35

GINGERICH, MELVIN   The Mennonites in Iowa. 1939. Austin
62-199 1974 $27.50

GINZBERG, ELI   Report to American Jews. 1942. 92 pages.
Austin 57-243 1974 $10

GINZBERG, ELI   Report to American Jews. Harper, 1942.
Austin 62-200 1974 $10

GIRARD, ABBE   Synonymes Francois et Traite de la Prosodie
Francoise. Amsterdam, 1766. 12mo., old calf, bdg. broken. Biblo & Tannen
210-863 1973 $9.50

GIRARD, P. J. F.   L'Academie de l'Homme D'Epee. The Hague,
1755. Oblong small folio, contemporary full brown calf, orig. edition, illus.
Schumann 499-45 1974 sFr 3,250

GIRARD, P. S.   Description Generale des Differens Ouvrages
Pour la Distribution des Eaux du Canal de l'Ource dans l'Interieur de Paris.
Paris, 1812. 4to., boards, uncut, unopened, folding plates, first edition. Gurney
66-72 1974 £30

GIRARD, STEPHEN   Bound Collection of Five Pamphlets Relating to
His Will. Philadelphia, 1840-51. 8vo., marbled boards and leather. Butterfield
8-547 1974 $32.50

GIRARDIN, MADAME EMILIE DE   Stories of an Old Maid. New York, 1856.
Cloth, plates, frontispiece. Hayman 57-259 1974 $12.50

GIRAUD, CHARLES JOSEPH BATHELEMY   Catalogue des Livres Rares et
Precieux Composant la Bibliotheque. Paris, 1855. 8vo., cloth. Dawsons PM
10-242 1974 £10

GIRAUD, P. F.   The Campaign of Paris in 1814. London, 1815.
Old calf. Jacobs 24-162 1974 $15

GIRAUDOUX, JEAN   Amphitry on 38. Paris, 1931. 4to., wrappers,
staining, rubbed. Covent 55-737 1974 £5.25

GIRAUDOUX, JEAN   Simon le Pathetique. Paris, 1927. 8vo.,
orig. wrapper, numbered, limited edition. L. Goldschmidt 42-234 1974 $20

GIRTIN, THOMAS   A Selection of Twenty of the Most Picturesque
Views in Paris. London, 1803. Large oblong folio, orig. blue boards, uncut.
Marlborough 70-28 1974 £850

GIRTY, G. H.   The Carboniferous Formations and Faunas of
Colorado. Washington, 1903. 4to., cloth, plates. Wheldon 131-1008 1974
£7.50

GIRVAN, I. WAVENEY   A Bibliography and a Critical Survey of the
Works of Henry Williamson. 1931. One of 420 copies, linen backed patterned
boards, spine browned, some pencil scoring, nice copy, spare printed label tipped
in. Covent 51-2618 1973 £10.50

GISBORNE, THOMAS   An Enquiry into the Duties of the Female Sex.
London, 1797. 8vo., orig. boards, rebacked, second and best edition. Hammond
201-400 1974 £12.50

GISBORNE, THOMAS   An Enquiry Into the Duties of the Female Sex.
London, 1797. 8vo., contemporary tree calf, first edition. Ximenes 33-87
1974 $80

GISBORNE, THOMAS   Poems, Sacred and Moral. 1798. Calf, first
edition, one cover detached. Allen 216-2015 1974 $10

GISBORNE, THOMAS   Poems, Sacred and Moral. London, 1799. 8vo.,
full red straight-grained morocco, gilt, rubbed, frontispiece, plates, second
edition. Ximenes 37-92 1974 $35

GISH, LILLIAN   Lillian Gish. Prentice-Hall, 1969. 401p.,
illus. Austin 51-351 1973 $7.50

GISSING, A. C.   William Holman Hunt. 1936. 8vo., orig.
cloth, illus. Marsden 39-245 1974 £5

GISSING, GEORGE   Charles Dickens. 1903. Dec. cloth gilt, illus.,
revised edition. Covent 56-353 1974 £7.50

GISSING, GEORGE   Demos. London, 1886. 3 vols., 8vo., orig.
brown cloth, uncut, rare, first edition. Dawsons PM 252-398 1974 £160

GISSING, GEORGE   A Life's Morning. n.d. 348 pages. Austin
61-415 1974 $10

GISSING, GEORGE   New Grub Street. 1891. 3 vols., second
edition. Covent 56-522 1974 £27.50

GISSING, GEORGE   New Grub Street. London, 1891. 3 vols.,
8vo., orig. cloth, rubbed, first edition. Ximenes 33-88 1974 $325

GISSING, GEORGE   The Private Papers of Henry Ryecroft. 1903.
Foxing, English first edition. Covent 56-523 1974 £7.50

GISSING, GEORGE   The Private Papers of Henry Ryecroft.
Portland, 1921. Boards, rubbed, hand-made paper. Covent 55-757 1974
£17.50

GISSING, GEORGE   Sins of the Fathers, and Other Tales. Chicago,
1924. One of 550 numbered copies, cloth backed patterned boards, fine.
Covent 51-2349 1973 £12.50

GISSING, GEORGE   The Town Traveller. New York, 1898. Orig.
pictorial cloth, rubbed, first American edition. Covent 55-759 1974 £10

GISSING, GEORGE   Veranilda. London, 1904. 12mo., orig. red
cloth, first edition. Ximenes 33-89 1974 $15

GISSING, GEORGE   Veranilda. New York, 1905. Faded, first
U.S. edition. Covent 56-525 1974 £6.50

GISSING, GEORGE   A Victim of Circumstances. 1927. Near
fine, first edition. Covent 55-760 1974 £7.50

GISSING, GEORGE   A Victim of Circumstances.   1927.   Dust wrapper, fine, English first edition.   Covent 56-526 1974 £21

GISSING, T. W.   The Ferns and Fern Allies of Wakefield.   Wakefield, 1862.   8vo., cloth, plates.   Wheldon 129-1398 1974 £15

GITLER, IRA   Jazz Masters of the 40's.   Macmillan, 1966.   290p.   Austin 51-352 1973 $5

GIUNTINI, F.   Discorso Sopra Quello che Minaccia.   Rome, n.d. 4to., wrappers.   Gurney 64-97 1974 £35

GLACIER National Park: Scenic Marvel of America.   N. P., c. 1920.   Small folio, wrapper, hand colored illus.   Jenkins 61-1746 1974 $10

GLACIER National Park: The Switzerland of America.   N. P., c. 1915.   Folio, wrapper, hand colored illus.   Jenkins 61-1748 1974 $10

GLACIER National Park: Switzerland of America.   Glacier Park, c. 1915.   Folio, pict. wrapper, hand colored illus.   Jenkins 61-1747 1974 $12.50

GLADSTONE, WILLIAM EWART   "Ecce Homo".   1868.   Small 8vo., orig. cloth, gilt, first edition.   Quaritch 936-393 1974 £8

GLAIRE, J. B.   Dictionaire Universelle des Sciences Ecclesiastiques.   Paris, 1868.   2 vols., thick roy. 8vo., half black roan.   Howes 185-1221 1974 £6

GLANVIL, BARTHOLOMAEUS
Please turn to
BARTHOLOMAEUS ANGLICUS

GLANVILL, JOSEPH   Saducismus Triumphatus.   1681.   8vo., calf antique, engraved frontispiece, first edition.   Bow Windows 66-280 1974 £105

GLANVILL, JOSEPH   Saducismus Trumphatus.   1726.   New buckram, plates.   Allen 216-1910 1974 $25

GLANVILL, JOSEPH   Scepsis Scientifica.   1665.   Small 4to., half calf.   Howes 186-1837 1974 £110

GLANVILL, JOSEPH   Scepsis Scientifica.   London, 1665.   4to., orig. calf, rebacked, first edition.   Dawsons PM 245-338 1974 £175

GLAREANUS, HENRICUS   Descriptio de Situ Helvetiae.   Basel, 1519.   4to., boards, fine, rare.   Harper 213-82 1973 $550

GLAREANUS, HENRICUS   De Geographia Liber Unus.   Basel, (1528).   4to., contemporary limp vellum, fine.   Harper 213-81 1973 $500

GLASGOW, ELLEN   The Ancient Law.   Doubleday, Page, 1908.   485p.   Austin 54-425 1973 $8.50

GLASGOW, ELLEN   Barren Ground.   Doubleday, Page, 1925.   511p.   Austin 54-426 1973 $6.50

GLASGOW, ELLEN   The Battleground.   Doubleday, Page, 1902.   512p., illus.   Austin 54-428 1973 $8.50

GLASGOW, ELLEN   The Battleground.   Doubleday, 1929 (1902).   444p.   Austin 54-427 1973 $10

GLASGOW, ELLEN   The Builders.   Doubleday, Page, 1919.   379p., orig. ed.   Austin 54-429 1973 $6.50

GLASGOW, ELLEN   A Certain Measure.   Harcourt, 1938.   272p., orig. ed.   Austin 54-430 1973 $10

GLASGOW, ELLEN   The Deliverance.   Doubleday, 1904.   543p., illus.   Austin 54-431 1973 $6

GLASGOW, ELLEN   The Deliverance.   New York, 1904.   Orig. cloth gilt, plates, presentation copy, inscribed, first U.S. edition.   Covent 56-528 1974 £12.50

GLASGOW, ELLEN   The Deliverance.   Doubleday, 1929.   Austin 54-432 1973 $10

GLASGOW, ELLEN   In This Our Life.   Harcourt, 1941.   467p.   Austin 54-433 1973 $6

GLASGOW, ELLEN   The Miller of Old Church.   Doubleday, Page, 1911.   432p., orig. ed.   Austin 54-435 1973 $7.50

GLASGOW, ELLEN   The Miller of Old Church.   Doubleday, 1933.   394p.   Austin 54-434 1973 $10

GLASGOW, ELLEN   One Man In His Time.   Doubleday, 1922.   379p.   Austin 54-436 1973 $10

GLASGOW, ELLEN   The Romantic Comedians.   Doubleday, 1926.   346p.   Austin 54-437 1973 $4.75

GLASGOW, ELLEN   The Shadowy Third and Other Stories.   New York, 1923.   1st ed.   Biblo & Tannen 210-602 1973 $20

GLASGOW, ELLEN   The Sheltered Life.   Doubleday, 1932.   395p.   Austin 54-438 1973 $5

GLASGOW, ELLEN   They Stooped to Folly.   Doubleday, 1929.   351p.   Austin 54-439 1973 $4.50

GLASGOW, ELLEN   They Stooped to Folly.   Doubleday, 1929.   351p., Old Dominion Ed.   Austin 54-440 1973 $6

GLASGOW, ELLEN   The Voice of the People.   Doubleday, 1900.   444p.   Austin 54-441 1973 $8

GLASGOW, ELLEN   The Wheel of Life.   Doubleday, Page, 1906.   474p.   Austin 54-442 1973 $7.50

GLASGOW, ELLEN   The Women Within.   Harcourt, 1954.   307p.   Austin 54-443 1973 $8.50

GLASGOW BIBLIOGRAPHICAL SOCIETY   Records, Vols. 2-8.1.   Glasgow, 1913-28.   Illus., crown 4to., orig. wrappers, one wrapper detached.   Forster 98-316 1974 £30

GLASIER, J. BRUCE   William Morris and the Early Days of the Socialist Movement.   1921.   Linen back, grey boards, worn, paper label, scarce.   Marsden 39-317 1974 £5

GLASPELL, SUSAN   Ambrose Holt and Family.   Stokes, 1931.   315p.   Austin 54-444 1973 $6.50

GLASPELL, SUSAN   Brook Evans.   Stokes, 1928.   312p.   Austin 54-445 1973 $5

GLASPELL, SUSAN   Cherished and Shared of Old.   Massner, 1940.   n.p., illus.   Austin 54-446 1973 $6

GLASPELL, SUSAN   Cherished and Shared of Old.   New York, (1940).   16mo., illus., very fine, d.j.   Current BW9-43 1974 $12

GLASPELL, SUSAN   Fidelity.   Small, Maynard, 1915.   442p.   Austin 54-447 1973 $7.50

GLASPELL, SUSAN   Fugitives Return.   Stokes, 1929.   324p.   Austin 54-448 1973 $6

GLASPELL, SUSAN   The Glory of the Conquered.   Stokes, 1909.   376p.   Austin 54-449 1973 $7.50

GLASPELL, SUSAN   The Morning is Near Us.   Lit. Guild., 1940.   296p.   Austin 54-450 1973 $5

GLASPELL, SUSAN   Norma Ashe.   Lippincott, 1942.   349p.   Austin 54-451 1973 $6.50

GLASPELL, SUSAN   The Road to the Temple.   Stokes, 1927.   445p., illus.   Austin 54-453 1973 $7.50

GLASPELL, SUSAN   The Road to the Temple.   Stokes, 1941.   445p.   Austin 54-452 1973 $6.50

GLASPELL, SUSAN   The Visioning.   Stokes, 1911.   464p.   Austin 54-454 1973 $6.50

GLASS, MONTAGUE   Potash and Perlmutter. 1911. 419p., illus.
Austin 62-202 1974 $10

GLASSE, HANNAH   The Art of Cookery. London, 1796. 8vo., half
calf, boards, new edition. Hammond 201-166 1974 £42

GLASSE, HANNAH   The Art of Cookery Made Plain and Easy. 1755.
8vo., old calf, rebacked, stains, fifth edition. Bow Windows 66-281 1974 £52

GLASSE, HANNAH   The Art of Cookery Made Plain and Easy. 1788.
8vo., old calf, rebacked. Quaritch 939-126 1974 £45

GLASSE, HANNAH   The Compleat Confectioner. (1760). 8vo.,
old style calf, first edition. Quaritch 939-128 1974 £200

GLASSE, HANNAH   The New Art of Cookery Made Plain and Easy.
Dublin, 1773. Small 8vo., calf gilt. Quaritch 939-127 1974 £60

GLASSMAN, LEO M.   Biographical Encyclopedia of American Jews.
1935. 606 pages. Austin 57-244 1974 $27.50

GLASSMAN, LEO M.   Biographical Encyclopedia of American Jews.
1935. Austin 62-203 1974 $27.50

GLAZEBROOK, G. P. DE T.   Canadian External Relations. London, New
York, & Toronto, 1942. Hood's 104-635 1974 $12.50

GLAZEBROOK, RICHARD   A Dictionary of Applied Physics. London, 1922-
3. 8vo., 5 vols., orig. brown cloth gilt, fine. Dawsons PM 245-339 1974 £34

GLAZIER, WILLARD   Three Years in the Federal Cavalry. New
York, 1874. Orig. binding. Wilson 63-360 1974 $10

GLEANINGS From Books on Agriculture and Gardening. (1802). 8vo., boards,
plates, uncut, rare, enlarged second edition. Wheldon 128-103 1973 £7.50

GLEICHEN, EDWARD   London's Open-Air Statuary. London, 1928.
8vo., inscription, orig. cloth, fine, first edition. Bow Windows 62-581
1974 £6

GLEIG, GEORGE ROBERT   A Narrative of the Campaigns of the British Army
at Washington and New Orleans. 1821. 8vo., half calf, first edition. Bow
Windows 64-522 1974 £38

GLENELG, LORD   Lord Glenelg's Despatches to Sir. F. B. Head,
Bart, During His Administration of the Government of Upper Canada. London,
1839. Three quarter leather. Hood's 102-558 1974 $100

GLENELG, LORD   Lord Glenelg's Despatches to Sir. F. B. Head,
Bart. London, 1839. Three quarter leather. Hood's 104-636 1974 $100

GLENNY, G.   The Culture of Fruit and Vegetables. London,
1860. Hand colored frontis., orig. cloth, rebacked, 8vo. Gregory 44-143
1974 $15

DE GLI ACADEMICI di Banchi di Roma. Parma, 1573. Small 8vo., vellum,
large woodcut device fills verso of first title. Thomas 32-151 1974 £30

GLI ITALIANI Negli Stati Uniti D'America. 1906. 473p., illus. Austin
62-280 1974 $125

GLICK, CARL   Three Times I Bow. Whittlesey, 1943.
259p., illus. Austin 62-204 1974 $8.50

GLIMPSES of California. San Francisco, 1898. Wrapper, photogravures.
Jenkins 61-324 1974 $12.50

GLIMPSES of Norfolk Connecticut. Norfolk, 1900. Wrapper, photographs.
Jenkins 61-693 1974 $12.50

GLIMPSES of the Hawaiian Islands. Honolulu, 1892. Wrapper, photographs.
Jenkins 61-1020 1974 $15

GLISSON, FRANCIS   Anatomia Hepatis. 1654. Small 8vo., contemporary sheep, first edition. Dawsons PM 249-205 1974 £1,500

GLISSON, FRANCIS   De Rachitide sive Morbo Puerili. 1650. Small
8vo., orig. sheep, fine, first edition. Dawsons PM 249-204 1974 £2,450

GLISSON, FRANCIS   De Rachitide, sive Morbo Puerili Qui Vulgo
the Rickets Dicitur, Tractatus. London, 1660. Woodcuts, 12mo., contemporary
blind-panelled calf, from the library of the Royal College of Physicians. Kraus
137-37 1974 $1,450

GLISSON, FRANCIS   Tractatus de Ventriculo et Intestinis. 1677.
12mo., contemporary mottled calf, gilt. Dawsons PM 249-206 1974 £90

GLOAG, JOHN   Time, Taste and Furniture. London, 1925.
Demy 8vo., orig. cloth, illus, uncut. Covent 55-444 1974 £6.50

A GLOSSARY of Terms Used In Grecian, Roman, Italian and Gothic
Architecture. Oxford, 1850. 3 vols., contemporary calf, gilt, morocco labels,
enlarged fifth edition. Thomas 28-41 1972 £18

GLOTZ, GUSTAVE   Ancient Greece at Work. New York, 1926.
Illus. Biblo & Tannen 214-612 1974 $8

GLOVER, J. A.   The Cerebro-Spinal Fever Epidemic. 1918.
Large and small 8vo., red buckram. Dawsons PM 249-207 1974 £15

GLOVER, R.   Nobilitas Politica Vel Civilis. Londini,
1608. Folio, half calf, fine. Quaritch 939-728 1974 £47.50

GLOVER, RICHARD   Boadicia. 1753. 8vo., new quarter calf, first
edition. Hill 126-213 1974 £7.50

GLOVER, RICHARD   Boadicia. London, 1753. 8vo., disbound,
first edition. Ximenes 33-92 1974 $30

GLOVER, RICHARD   Boadicia. London, 1753. 8vo., modern
boards, first edition. Dawsons PM 252-399 1974 £15

GLOVER, RICHARD   Leonidas. London, 1737. 4to., speckled
calf, morocco label, first edition. Dawsons PM 252-400 1974 £55

GLOVER, RICHARD   Leonidas. 1737. 4to., contemporary mottled
calf, gilt, first edition. Quaritch 936-85 1974 £15

GLOVER, T. R.   The Ancient World. New York, 1935. Biblo
& Tannen 214-613 1974 $9.50

GLUCK, GUSTAV   Les Tableaux de Peter Bruegel. Brussels, 1910.
Boards, illu. Eaton Music-600 1973 £5

GMELIN, J. G.   Flora Sibirica. St. Petersburg, 1747-69. 4to.,
buckram, plates. Wheldon 129-1075 1974 £250

GMELIN, J. G.   Flora Sibirica Sive Historia Plantarum Sibiriae.
St. Petersburg, 1747-69. 4 vols. in 5, 4to., buckram, plates. Wheldon
131-1293 1974 £250

GNOLI, UMBERTO   Pittori e Miniatori Nell 'Umbria. Spoleto,
(1923). 4to., illus., cloth, leather labels, uncut. Kraus B8-76 1974 $185

GOAD, CAROLINE   Horace In the English Literature Of the
Eighteenth Century. 1918. Ex-library, sturdy library binding, orig. edition.
Austin 61-417 1974 $17.50

GOAD, JOHN   Astro-Meteorologica. London, 1686. Folio,
contemporary sprinkled calf, rebacked, gilt, first edition. Dawsons PM 245-340
1974 £175

GOBLE, W.   Geologisch-Bergmannische Karten von Idria
Nebst Bildern von den Quecksilber-Lagerstatten. Vienna, 1893. Roy. 8vo.,
plates, portfolio, worn. Wheldon 131-1009 1974 £5

GOBLE, WARWICK   Stories from the Pentamerone. 1911. 4to.,
orig. pictorial cloth gilt, English first edition. Covent 56-696 1974 £12.50

GOBINEAU, JOSEPH ARTHUR, COMTE DE 1816-1882   The Moral and
Intellectual Diversity of Races. Philadelphia, 1856. Orig. cloth, first American
edition. Jacobs 24-15 1974 $25

GOBINEAU, JOSEPH ARTHUR, COMTE DE 1816-1882   La Renaissance. Paris,
1877. 8vo., half red hard grain morocco, gilt, first edition. L. Goldschmidt
42-235 1974 $37.50

GOCHER, W. H.   Wadsworth. Hartford, 1904. 8vo., orig. bindings. Butterfield 8-87 1974 $20

GODAL, ERIC   Nymphs. n.d. Portfolio, signed, slipcase, English first edition. Covent 56-697 1974 £65

GODCHARLES, FREDERIC A.   Pennsylvania . . . Political, Governmental, Military and Civil. New York, c. 1933. 5 vols., 4to., orig. binding, fore edge cover stains. Wilson 63-71 1974 $40

GODEFROY, JACQUES   The History of the United Provinces of Achaia. London, 1673. 4to., modern boards, first edition in English. Dawsons PM 251-235 1974 £20

GODEY'S Ladies Book. 1858-59. 8vo., 2 vols., black quarter morocco, plates, illus., foxing. Rich Summer-71 1974 $27.50

GODFREY, E.   English Children in the Olden Time. (1907). 8vo., orig. cloth, illus., some foxing, inscription on title, second edition. Bow Windows 66-283 1974 £7.50

GODFREY, MASTERS JOHN   Monograph and Iconograph of British Orchidacae. Cambridge, 1933. 4to., orig. cloth. Broadhurst 23-1116 1974 £50

GODFREY, MASTERS JOHN   Monograph and Iconography of Native British Orchidaceoe. 1933. 4to., cloth, plain and coloured plates, portrait, very scarce. Wheldon 128-1556 1973 £50

GODFREY, MASTERS JOHN   Monograph and Iconography of Native British Orchidaceae. 1933. 4to., cloth, plates, very scarce. Wheldon 131-1622 1974 £50

GODFREY, WALTER H.   The English Staircase. 1911. Small 4to., illus., plates. Covent 55-65 1974 £12.50

GODKIN, JAMES   The Land War in Ireland. London, 1870. 8vo., cloth boards. Emerald 50-333 1974 £9

GODLEY, ELIZABETH   Green Outside. London, (1931). Fine copy, frayed d.w., orig. cloth, frontispiece in colour, and other dec. by Rex Whistler, first edition. Crane 7-310 1974 £8.50

GODMAN, F. DU CANE   A Monograph of the Petrels. 1907-10. 4to., half blue morocco, gilt, uncut. Wheldon 129-17 1974 £700

GODON, J.   Painted Tapestry and Its Application to Interior Decoration. 1879. Roy. 8vo., cloth textured paper, unopened. Quaritch 940-756 1974 £21

GODSELL, P. H.   Arctic Trader. New York, 1934. Illus. Hood's 103-62 1974 $12.50

GODSHALK, ABRAHAM   A Description of the New Creature. Doylestown, 1838. 16mo., orig. bindings. Butterfield 8-531 1974 $10

GODWIN, MARY (WOLLSTONECRAFT) 1759-1797   A Vindication of the Rights of Woman. London, 1792. 8vo., black morocco label, contemporary calf, first edition. Dawsons PM 250-84 1974 £175

GODWIN, MARY WOLLSTONECRAFT 1797-1851
Please turn to
SHELLEY, MARY WOLLSTONECRAFT GODWIN

GODWIN, WILLIAM   The Adventures of Caleb Williams. Paris, 1832. 8vo., contemporary half morocco. Dawsons PM 252-401 1974 £30

GODWIN, WILLIAM   Considerations on Lord Grenville's and Mr. Pitt's Bills, Concerning Treasonable and Seditious Practices, and Unlawful Assemblies. London, n.d. (1795). 8vo., disbound, first edition, scarce. Ximenes 36-109 1974 $85

GODWIN, WILLIAM   The Enquirer. London, 1797. 8vo., contemporary calf, gilt, first edition. Hammond 201-401 1974 £50

GODWIN, WILLIAM   The Enquirer. London, 1797. 8vo., morocco label, contemporary tree calf, first edition. Dawsons PM 252-402 1974 £100

GODWIN, WILLIAM   Enquirer; Reflections on Education, Manners, and Literature. Philadelphia, 1797. Old calf, spine worn, one cover detached, stained text, foxed. Allen 216-2016 1974 $35

GODWIN, WILLIAM   Fables Ancient and Modern. (c. 1810). Third edition, plates, 12mo., orig. marbled boards, roan spine, rubbed, plates. George's 610-311 1973 £7.50

GODWIN, WILLIAM   History of Rome: From the Building of the City to the Ruin of the Republic. 1811. Second edition, folding maps, engraved plates, contemporary calf, 12mo., lower cover detached. George's 610-312 1973 £5

GODWIN, WILLIAM   Life of Lady Jane Grey, and of Lord Guildford Dudley, Her Husband. 1806. First edition, engraved frontispiece, 12mo., later half morocco, marbled board sides. George's 610-313 1973 £30

GODWIN, WILLIAM   St. Leon. London, 1799. 4 vols., 12mo., contemporary tree calf, fine, first edition. Ximenes 33-93 1974 $350

GODWYN, FRANCIS   A Catalogue of the Bishops of England. 1601. Small 4to., modern buckram, gilt, first edition. Thomas 28-96 1972 £30

GOEBEL, K.   Outlines of Classification and Special Morphology of Plants. Oxford, 1887. Roy. 8vo., half morocco. Wheldon 131-1143 1974 £10

GOEBEL, K.   Organography of Plants. Oxford, 1900-05. 2 vols., roy. 8vo., orig. half morocco, woodcuts. Wheldon 131-1142 1974 £30

GOEBEL, K.   Pflanzenbiologische Schilderungen. Marburg, 1889-93. 2 vols. in 1, roy. 8vo., binder's cloth, plates. Wheldon 131-1144 1974 £10

GOELICKE, ANDREAS OTTOMAR   Historia Medicinae Universalis Qua Celebriorum Quorumcunque Medicorum. Vitae, 1717. 2 works in 1 vol., 8vo. Rittenhouse 46-289 1974 $75

GOEPPERT, H. R.   Die Tertiare Flora von Schossnitz in Schlesien. Gorlitz, 1855. 4to., orig. boards, plates, scarce. Wheldon 128-978 1973 £7.50

GOES, WILLEM   Rei Agrariae Auctores Legesque Variae. Amsterdam, 1674. 4to., calf, gilt, plates, illus. Hammond 201-16 1974 £26

GOETHALS, F. V.   Catalogue de la Bibliotheque. Bruxelles, 1876. Roy. 8vo., orig. wrappers. Forster 98-318 1974 £6

GOETHE, JOHANN WOLFGANG VON   Aus Meinem Leben: Dichtung und Wahrheit. Frankfurt, 1921-22. Plates, coloured frontispieces, 4 vols., dec. boards, name on fly leaves, very nice set. Covent 51-2350 1973 £10

GOETHE, JOHANN WOLFGANG VON   Faust. Leipzig, 1790. 12mo., dark blue morocco, cloth slip case, fine, first separate edition. Dawsons PM 250-33 1974 £880

GOETHE, JOHANN WOLFGANG VON   Faust. Boston, 1898. 2v. in l. Biblo & Tannen 210-865 1973 $6

GOETHE, JOHANN WOLFGANG VON   Faust. 1906. 8vo., vellum, gilt, fine. Dawsons PM 250-34 1974 £220

GOETHE, JOHANN WOLFGANG VON   Faust. Leipzig, 1917. Full black calf, 2 X 1 1/4 inches. Gregory 44-381 1974 $28.50

GOETHE, JOHANN WOLFGANG VON   Faust. Norfolk, 1941. Bilbo & Tannen 210-158 1973 $10

GOETHE, JOHANN WOLFGANG VON   Goethe's Correspondence With a Child. Lowell, 1841. 2 vols., 12mo., orig. cloth, paper labels, first American edition. Ximenes 33-94 1974 $30

GOETHE, JOHANN WOLFGANG VON   Gotz von Berlichingen. Leipzig, 1910. Tan calf. Gregory 44-382 1974 $28.50

GOETSCHIUS, PERCY   The Homophonic Forms of Musical Composition. New York, 1924. Biblo & Tannen 214-851 1974 $7.50

GOETZ, KARL   John Bruecker. Wuerttemberg, 1957. Austin 62-205 1974 $12.50

GOETZ, RUTH   The Heiress. 1948. 93p., paper. Austin 51-353 1973 $6.50

GOFF, D. W.　　　Divine Protection through Extraordinary
Dangers. London, 1857. 8vo., embossed blue cloth, scarce. Emerald 50-334
1974 £5

GOFFRES, JOSEPH-MARIE-ACHILLE　Considerations sur l'Asthme.
Montpelier, 1835. Wrappers, unopened, soiled, foxing. Rittenhouse 46-290
1974 $27

GOGARTY, OLIVER ST. JOHN　Elbow Room. Dublin, 1930. Edition limited
to 450 copies, unopened, mint, orig. binding. Ross 86-202 1974 $75

GOGARTY, OLIVER ST. JOHN　Going Native. New York, 1940. First
American edition, fine, somewhat worn d.w. Covent 51-2351 1973 £8.50

GOGARTY, OLIVER ST. JOHN　Going Native. New York, 1940. Lacking
d.w., very nice, orig. binding, presentation inscirption by author. Ross 86-203
1974 $35

GOGARTY, OLIVER ST. JOHN　An Offering of Swans. n.d. Portrait,
buckram, cover little faded, very nice copy, bookplate. Covent 51-780 1973
£12.50

GOGARTY, OLIVER ST. JOHN　An Offering of Swans and Other Poems.
London, n.d. (1935). Inscribed, by author, covers somewhat worn & marked,
internally fine. Ross 86-204 1974 $60

GOGARTHY, OLIVER ST. JOHN　Selected Poems. New York, 1933. Orig.
buckram gilt, dust wrapper, foxing. Smith 194-454 1974 £7.50

GOGOL, NIKOLAI　　　The Inspector General. Knopf, 1916. 119p.
Austin 51-354 1973 $6.50

GOHDES, C. B.　　　Does the Modern Papacy Require a New
Evaluation? Burlington, Iowa, 1940. Austin 62-206 1974 $10

GOIFFON, JOSEPH　　Harmonie des Deux Spheres Celeste et
Terrestre. Paris, 1739. 4to., old mottled calf, rebacked, corners worn,
some spotting, second edition. Bow Windows 66-285 1974 £48

GOLBERRY, S. M. XAVIER　Fragmens D'un Voyage en Afrique. Paris,
1802. 2 vols., 8vo., contemporary calf, neatly rebacked, folding maps, plans,
tables, plates, library stamp. Bow Windows 66-286 1974 £48

GOLBORNE, JOHN　　　The Report of . . . Drainage of the North Level
of the Fens. (1769). 4to., orig. wrappers, first edition. Hammond 201-849
1974 £22

GOLD, MICHAEL　　　Jews Without Money. Liveright, 1930.
Austin 62-207 1974 $6.50

GOLD, PLEASANT DANIEL　History of Volusia County, Florida. Deland,
1927. 8vo., cloth, presentation. Saddleback 14-347 1974 $30

GOLDBERG, I.　　　Our People. 1944. Illus., 285 pages.
Austin 57-250 1974 $12.50

GOLDBERG, ISAAC　　The Drama of Transition. Steward, Kidd.
487p. Austin 51-358 1973 $10

GOLDBERG, ISAAC　　Havelock Ellis. 1926. 359 pages, illus.
Austin 61-355 1974 $10

GOLDBERG, ISAAC　　Major Noah. 1938. 316p., illus. Austin
62-209 1974 $10

GOLDBERG, ISAAC　　The Man Menchken. S & S, 1925. 388p.
Austin 54-455 1973 $12.50

GOLDBERG, ISAAC　　Tin Pan Alley. Day, 1930. 341p. Austin
51-355 1973 $12.50

GOLDBERG, MECISLAS　　Lazare le Ressuscite. Paris, 1901. 8vo.,
wrappers. Minters 37-248 1973 $24

GOLDEN, I. J.　　　Precedent. Farrar, Rinehart, 1931. 142p.
Austin 51-360 1973 $7.50

GOLDEN, JOHN　　　7th Heaven. 1924. 278p., illus. Austin
51-356 1973 $7.50

THE GOLDEN Cockerel Greek Anthology. 1937. Folio, quarter morocco, uncut,
limited edition. Broadhurst 23-1002 1974 £55

GOLDEN COCKEREL PRESS　Pertelote. A Sequel to Chanticleer, Being a
Bibliography of the Golden Cockerel Press. London, (1943). Roy. 8vo., orig.
cloth. Forster 98-321 1974 £8

THE GOLDEN Hind. 1922-24. 4to. & folio, illus., cloth backs, dec. boards.
Marsden 37-213 1974 £35

THE GOLDEN Poets. n.d. 12mo., 12 vols., rebound, English first edition.
Covent 56-534 1974 £52.50

GOLDING, ARTHUR　　The XV Bookes of P. Ovidius Naso. London,
1587. 4to., full 19th century dark green morocco, fourth edition. Ximenes
33-95 1974 $750

GOLDING, C. E.　　　A History of Reinsurance With Sidelights on
Insurance. 1931. Illus. Bow Windows 66-291 1974 £10.50

GOLDING, F. Y.　　　Boots and Shoes. 1934-35. 8 vols., crown
8vo., illus. Howes 186-1575 1974 £10

GOLDING, HARRY　　　Zoo Days. London, 1919. Thick 8vo., cloth
with oval pictorial paste label, color plates, pictorial endpapers. Frohnsdorff
15-162 1974 $15

GOLDMARK, JOSEPHINE　　Pilgrims of '48. Yale Univ., 1930. 311p.
Austin 62-210 1974 $17.50

GOLDMARK, JOSEPHINE　　Pilgrims of '48. 1930. Ex-library, 311 pages.
Austin 57-254 1974 $17.50

GOLDMAYER, ANDREAS　　Computus Directionum Astronomicus. 1657. Sm.
4to., dec. tailpiece, disbound, woodcuts. Zeitlin 235-100 1974 $175

GOLDONI, CARLO　　　The Good-Humoured Ladies. Beaumont, 1922.
Quarter vellum, English first edition. Covent 56-1550 1974 £27.50

GOLDSCHMIDT, A.　　　Goethe in Almanach. Leipzig, 1932. Roy.
8vo., illus., dec. boards, cloth back, presentation inscription from author.
Forster 98-319 1974 £15

GOLDSCHMIDT, R.　　　The Mechanism and Physiology of Sex
Determination. 1923. Roy. 8vo., cloth, illus. Wheldon 131-432 1974 £7

GOLDSMITH, OLIVER　　The Art of Poetry On a New Plan. London,
1762. 2 vols., 12mo., contemporary calf, fine, first edition. Ximenes 33-98
1974 $300

GOLDSMITH, OLIVER　　The Citizen of the World. London, 1762.
2 vols., 12mo., full maroon levant, gilt, first edition. Ximenes 37-93 1974
$225

GOLDSMITH, OLIVER　　The Deserted Village. 1899. Buckram,
plates, Japanese Paper, near fine. Covent 55-897 1974 £18.50

GOLDSMITH, OLIVER　　The Deserted Village. 1909. Crown 4to.,
orig. cloth, coloured illus., some foxing. Bow Windows 66-292 1974 £9.50

GOLDSMITH, OLIVER　　An Enquiry into the Present State of Polite
Learning. London, 1759. 8vo., full morocco, gilt, fine, first edition. Dawsons
PM 252-403 1974 £195

GOLDSMITH, OLIVER　　The Good Natur'd Man. 1768. 8vo., full brown
levant morocco, first edition. Quaritch 936-86 1974 £65

GOLDSMITH, OLIVER　　The Good Natur'd Man. London, 1768. 8vo.,
full red morocco, gilt, nice copy, first edition. Ximenes 37-94 1974 $80

GOLDSMITH, OLIVER　　The History of the Earth and Animated
Nature. London, n.d. 2 vols., sup. roy. 8vo., plates, half calf gilt.
Smith 194-809 1974 £18.50

GOLDSMITH, OLIVER　　Le Ministre de Wakefield. 1767. 12mo., contemporary calf, first edition. Hill 126-194 1974 £55

GOLDSMITH, OLIVER　　The Life of Richard Nash. London, 1762.
8vo., contemporary calf, fine, gilt, first edition. Ximenes 33-96 1974 $150

GOLDSMITH, OLIVER　　The Memoirs of a Protestant, Condemned to the Galleys of France, For His Religion. London, 1758. 2 vols., 12mo., mottled calf, gilt, first edition. Ximenes 33-97 1974 $275

GOLDSMITH, OLIVER　　Poems. Bulmer, 1804. 8vo., boards. Quaritch 936-395 1974 £12

GOLDSMITH, OLIVER　　Poems and Plays. Dublin, 1777. 8vo., contemporary calf, large and thick paper copy, very good copy, first edition. Ximenes 37-95 1974 $175

GOLDSMITH, OLIVER　　The Poetical Works Of. 1811. 4to., plates, rebacked boards, worn, scarce. Quaritch 940-7 1974 £50

GOLDSMITH, OLIVER　　Poetical Works Of. 1853. 176 pages. Austin 61-418 1974 $10

GOLDSMITH, OLIVER　　The Roman History from the Foundation of the City of Rome. London, 1769. 2 vols., 8vo., contemporary calf, first edition. Bow Windows 62-386 1974 £40

GOLDSMITH, OLIVER　　She Stoops to Conquer. (1912). 4to., orig. cloth, illus., plates, first edition. Howes 185-524 1974 £15

GOLDSMITH, OLIVER　　She Stoops to Conquer. c.1920. 4to., orig. cloth, faded, illus., plates. Howes 186-475 1974 £8.50

GOLDSMITH, OLIVER　　The Traveller. 1765. 4to., dark green morocco, first edition. Quaritch 936-87 1974 £70

GOLDSMITH, OLIVER　　The Traveller, or a Prospect of Society. London, 1765. 4to., polished calf, gilt, very good copy, first edition. Ximenes 37-96 1974 $250

GOLDSMITH, OLIVER　　The Vicar of Wakefield. Salisbury, 1766. 2 vols., 12mo., contemporary calf, rebacked, first edition. Dawsons PM 252-404 1974 £750

GOLDSMITH, OLIVER　　The Vicar of Wakefield. Worcester, 1795. 2 vols. in 1, 12mo., contemporary calf, very good copy. Ximenes 37-97 1974 $45

GOLDSMITH, OLIVER　　The Vicar of Wakefield. Hereford, 1798. 2 vols. in 1, 8vo., contemporary calf, spine gilt, first edition illus. by Thomas Bewick, fine, woodcuts. Ximenes 36-20 1974 $90

GOLDSMITH, OLIVER　　The Vicar of Wakefield. 1855. Victorian binding, illus., gilt, fine. Covent 55-889 1974 £12.50

GOLDSMITH, OLIVER　　The Vicar of Wakefield. 1890. Crown 8vo., orig. plain cloth, illus., first edition. Howes 185-525 1974 £5

GOLDSMITH, OLIVER　　The Vicar of Wakefield. 1903. Orig. vellum, uncut, limited, first edition. Bow Windows 66-108 1974 £21

GOLDSMITH, OLIVER　　The Vicar of Wakefield. 1926. Roy. 8vo., plates, fine, buckram, dust wrapper. Covent 55-899 1974 £12.50

GOLDSMITH, OLIVER　　The Vicar of Wakefield. London, 1929. 4to., illus., uncut, mint, limited edition. Dawsons PM 252-405 1974 £170

GOLDSMITH, OLIVER　　The Vicar of Wakefield. London, 1929. No. 50 of English issue of limited signed edition of 775 copies, box split down one edge, mint, orig. binding, illus. by Arthur Rackham. Ross 87-469 1974 $250

GOLDSMITH, OLIVER　　The Works. 1854. 4 vols., nice set, full calf, raised panelled spines gilt, engraved frontispieces, slightly rubbed. Covent 51-787 1973 £25

GOLDSMITH, OLIVER　　Works. 1854. 4 vols., demy 8vo., full green levant morocco, panelled backs, raised bands, richly tooled gilt, slight fading of spines, fine. Broadhurst 24-1711 1974 £50

GOLDSMITH, OLIVER　　Works. New York, 1908. 10 vols., orig. cloth, labels, gilt, plates, limited edition. Howes 186-215 1974 £32

GOLDSTEIN, DAVID　　Autobiography of a Campaigner for Christ. Boston, 1936. Austin 62-212 1974 $10

GOLDSTEIN, DAVID　　Bolshevism and Its Cure. Boston, 1919. Austin 62-211 1974 $8.50

GOLDSTEIN, DAVID　　Campaigners for Christ Handbook. Flynn, 1934. Austin 62-213 1974 $8.50

GOLDSTEIN, HERBERT　　Forty Years of Struggle for a Principle. 1928. Illus. Austin 57-256 1974 $15

GOLDWATER, ROBERT　　Rufino Tamayo. New York, 1947. 4to., color plates. Biblo & Tannen 213-419 1973 $42.50

GOLL, CLAIRE　　Diary of a Horse, With Four Original Drawings by Marc Chagall. New York, 1945. Large 4to., boards, signed, numbered, scarce, limited edition. Minters 37-67 1973 $32.50

GOLL, CLAIRE　　Poemes d'Amour. Paris, 1925. 8vo., orig. wrapper, drawings, scarce, limited edition. Minters 37-68 1973 $42

GOLL, IVAN　　Chansons de France. New York, 1940. 8vo., wrapper, uncut, unopened. Minters 37-339 1973 $20

GOLLANCZ, ISRAEL　　The Exeter Book. 1893. 8vo., cloth backed boards, uncut, inscribed, some spotting. Bow Windows 66-293 1974 £8

GOLLANCZ, ISRAEL　　Parlement of the Thre Ages. 1897. Large 4to., roan spine. Thomas 32-288 1974 £50

GOLLERBACH, E.　　La Porcelaine d'Art Russe. Leningrad, 1924. Imp. 8vo., cloth, leather label, orig. wrappers, plates. Quaritch 940-634 1974 £42

GOLLUT, LOUIS　　Les Memoires Historiques de la Republique Sequanoise des Princes de la Franche-Comte de Bourgougne. Dole, 1592. Thick folio, old calf, rubbed, first edition. Harper 213-83 1973 $685

GOLTZIUS, HUBERTUS　　Icones Imperatorum Romanorum. 1645. Folio, contemporary brown morocco, gilt, fine. Marlborough 70-13 1974 £250

GOMEZ, ISAAC　　Selections of a Father for the Use of His Children. 1820. 408 pages. Austin 57-258 1974 $27.50

GOMEZ DE LA SERNA, RAMON　　Echantillons. Paris, 1923. 12mo., contemporary boards, leather label, first edition. L. Goldschmidt 42-270 1974 $25

GOMEZ SICRE, JOSE　　Spanish Drawings. New York, 1949. Biblo & Tannen 213-264 1973 $8.50

GOMME, LAURENCE　　London. 1914. 8vo., orig. cloth, plates, illus. Bow Windows 66-294 1974 £6

GONCHAROV, IVAN　　Oblomov. 1915. Fine copy, scarce, first English translation. Covent 51-788 1973 £5

GONCHAROV, IVAN　　The Precipice. 1915. Fine, first edition. Covent 55-765 1974 £5.25

GONCOURT, EDMOND DE　　Manette Salomon. Paris, 1896. 8vo., uncut, contemporary half sheep, orig. wrapper. L. Goldschmidt 42-236 1974 $25

GONDAR, JACQUES　　Chronicques Francoises de Jacques Gondar, Clerc, Publiees par F. Michel. Paris, (1830). Small 8vo., orig. pink cloth, plates. Harper 213-84 1973 $195

GONELLI, G.　　Monumenti Sepolcrali della Toscana. Florence, 1819. Folio, half red morocco, gilt, plates. Quaritch 940-321 1974 £12

GOOD, JOHN MASON　　The Book of Nature. New York, 1828. Large 8vo., orig. cloth-backed boards, uncut. Hill 126-117 1974 £13.50

A GOOD Joke; or, The History of the Mischievous Tom Freeborn, Who in the End Outwitted Himself, By Being Caught in His Own Trap. New Haven, 1825. Wrappers stained, engravings, 2 3/4 X 5 inches. Frohnsdorff 16-367 1974 $37.50

GOODACRE, J. A.　　Buxton Old & New. Buxton, 1928. Crown 4to., drawings, orig. cloth. Bow Windows 62-387 1974 £7.50

GOODALE, ELAINE   In Berkshire with the Wild Flowers. New York, 1879-80. 8vo., orig. bindings, illus., signed. Butterfield 8-243 1974 $15

GOODALE, ELAINE   Journal of a Farmer's Daughter. New York, 1881. 8vo., orig. bindings. Butterfield 8-242 1974 $10

GOODE, G. B.   Oceanic Ichthyology. Washington, 1895. 4to., buckram, plates. Wheldon 129-573 1974 £45

GOODEN, STEPHEN   The Fables of Jean de la Fontaine. 1931. 2 vols., roy. 8vo., full vellum, uncut, engravings, limited to 525 copies, signed by artist & author, fine. Broadhurst 24-691 1974 £120

GOODEN, STEPHEN   An Iconography of the Engravings of. 1944. Illus., limited to 500 numbered copies, fine, first edition. Covent 51-789 1973 £35

GOODEN, STEPHEN   An Iconography of the Engravings of. London, 1944. Edition limited to 500 copies, no. 94 of 160 copies specially bound & containing an orig. proof engraving signed by artist, quarter vellum spine, light gray buckram box, near mint. Ross 86-206 1974 $200

GOODEN, STEPHEN   Pindar. 1928. Engraved title page, f'cap 8vo., uncut, limited to 1050 copies, orig. cloth, fine. Broadhurst 24-688 1974 £12

GOODENOUGH, IRWIN R.   The Politics of Philo Judea's Practice and Theory. New Haven, 1938. 8vo., buckram. Goodspeed's 578-514 1974 $25

GOODFELLOW, ROBIN   The Fairy Annual. London, 1838. Folded sheets, unbound, 2 X 2 inches. Gregory 44-375 1974 $35

GOODLAND, ROGER   A Bibliography of Sex Rites and Customs. London, 1931. Demy 4to., orig. buckram, d.w. frayed, illus. Forster 98-327 1974 £18

GOODLAND, ROGER   A Bibliography of Sex Rites and Customs. London, 1931. 4to., orig. cloth, illus. Dawsons PM 10-246 1974 £30

GOODLANDER, C. W.   Memoirs and Recollections of the Early Days of Fort Scott, 1858-1870. Ft. Scott, 1900. Orig. boards, very good copy, presentation copy from author. Jenkins 61-944 1974 $22.50

GOODMAN, ABRAM VOSSEN   American Overture. 1947. 264p., illus. Austin 62-216 1974 $12.50

GOODMAN, EZRA   The Fifty Year Decline and Fall of Hollywood. Simon, Schuster, 1961. 465p. Austin 51-361 1973 $5

GOODMAN, JACK   I Wish I'd Said That? S & S, 1935. 130p., illus. Austin 54-456 1973 $7.50

GOODRICH, ARTHUR   Caponsacchi. 1927. 185p. Austin 51-362 1973 $10

GOODRICH, LLOYD   Edward Hopper. London, 1949. Biblo & Tannen 213-305 1973 $8.50

GOODRICH, P. G.   History of Wayne County. Honesdale, 1880. 8vo., rubbed, fine, first edition. Rinsland 58-91 1974 $35

GOODRICH, SAMUEL GRISWOLD   The Balloon Travels of Robert Merry and His Young Friends, Over Various Countries in Europe. New York, 1855. 8vo., embossed cloth, pictorial gilt spine, fine engravings, first edition. Frohnsdorff 16-368 1974 $25

GOODRICH, SAMUEL GRISWOLD   Lives of Celebrated Women. Boston, 1844. 12mo., orig. wrappers, parts 1 & 2 in 2 vols., chipped spines, illus., ex-library stamp, very good copies, first edition. Frohnsdorff 16-369 1974 $20

GOODRICH, SAMUEL GRISWOLD   Personal Recollections of Poets, Philosophers and Statesmen. New York, 1856. Biblo & Tannen 210-866 1973 $7.50

GOODRICH, SAMUEL GRISWOLD   Peter Parley's Method of Telling About Geography to Children. New York, 1836. Square 16mo., orig. wrappers, cloth spine, fine engravings. Frohnsdorff 16-370 1974 $30

GOODRICH, SAMUEL GRISWOLD   Peter Parley's Tales About the Sun, Moon, and Stars. Philadelphia, 1833. Printed boards, engravings. Hayman 57-411 1974 $12.50

GOODRICH, SAMUEL GRISWOLD   Recollections of a Lifetime, or Men and Things I Have Seen. New York, 1856. 2 vols., cloth covers worn. Butterfield 10-276 1974 $25

GOODRICH, SAMUEL GRISWOLD   Robert Merry's Museum. New York, 1846. Vols. 3 & 4, 8vo., embossed cloth, pictorial gilt spine, cloth split along spine edges, illus. Frohnsdorff 16-371 1974 $20

GOODRICH, SAMUEL GRISWOLD   A Tale of Adventure, or the Siberian Sable Hunter. New York, 1843. 12mo., orig. green cloth, first edition, illus., very good copy. Ximenes 36-110 1974 $65

GOODRICH, E. S.   Studies on the Structure and Development of Vertebrates. 1930. 8vo., cloth, scarce orig. issue. Wheldon 131-433 1974 £7.50

GOODRICH-FREER, A.   The Alleged Haunting of B_____ House. London, 1899. Rittenhouse 46-292 1974 $15

GOODRIDGE, JOHN   The Phoenix, an Essay. 1781. 8vo., orig. boards, uncut. Hill 126-118 1974 £15

GOODSIR, JOHN   Anatomical Memoirs. Edinburgh, 1868. 8vo., 2 vols., orig. cloth, little ink stained, plates. Gurney 66-73 1974 £25

GOODSIR, JOHN   Anatomical Memoirs. Edinburgh, 1868. 8vo., 2 vols., orig. cloth, plates. Gurney 64-96 1974 £25

GOODSPEED, E. J.   History of the Great Fires in Chicago and the West. New York, (1871). 8vo., orig. bindings. Butterfield 8-61 1974 $15

GOODSPEED, H. T.   Plant Hunters in the Andes. n.d. 8vo., cloth, plates, scarce. Wheldon 130-1501 1974 £10

GOODSPEED, WESTON A.   Counties of Morgan, Monroe and Brown, Indiana. Chicago, 1884. 8vo., half leather. Saddleback 14-403 1974 $75

GOODWIN, G.   Thomas Watson, James Watson, Elizabeth Judkins. 1904. Plates, gilt. Marsden 37-215 1974 £6

GOODWIN, MAUD WILDER   Historic New York. New York, 1897. Biblo & Tannen 213-75 1973 $17.50

GOODWIN, T.   The Vanity of Thoughts Discovered. London, 1637. 12mo., half early 19th century calf gilt. Smith 194-154 1974 £45

GOODY Two-Shoes. New York, 1888. 4to., pictorial wrappers, piece missing from upper corner of front wrappers, color plates. Frohnsdorff 16-372 1974 $15

GOODYEAR, CHARLES   Decision in the Great India Rubber Case of Charles Goodyear vs. Horace H. Day, Delivered Sept. 28th, 1852. New York, 1852. 8vo., orig. green printed wrappers, spine chipped, first edition. Ximenes 37-98 1974 $27.50

GOOGE, BARNABE   The Popish Kingdome or Reigne of Antichrist. 1880. Crown 4to., full vellum, crimson label. Howes 186-217 1974 £10

GOOLRICK, JOHN T.   Historic Fredericksburg. Richmond, c. 1922. First edition, orig. binding. Wilson 63-114 1974 $17.50

GOOSSENS, EUGENE   Chamber Music. 1930. Very good copy, wrappers, first edition. Covent 51-1017 1973 £10.50

GORDIS, ROBERT   Conservative Judaism. 1945. Austin 62-220 1974 $12.50

GORDON, ALEXANDER   The History, Pathology, and Treatment of Puerperal Fever and Crural Phlebitis. Philadelphia, 1842. 8vo., contemporary calf. Schuman 37-106 1974 $85

GORDON, ALEXANDER   Itinerarium Septentrionale. 1726-32. Folio, plates, calf gilt, fine. Quaritch 939-656 1974 £60

GORDON, ALEXANDER   The Lives of Pope Alexander VI and His Son Caesar Borgia. 1729. 2 parts in 1 vol., folio, contemporary calf, first edition. Thomas 28-172 1972 £25

GORDON, ALFRED   Diseases of the Nervous System. Philadelphia, 1913. Revised & enlarged second edition. Rittenhouse 46-716 1974 $10

GORDON, C. A.   A Concise History of the Ancient and Illustrious House of Gordon. 1890. 8vo., orig. roan backed cloth, limited. Bow Windows 62-389 1974 £5

GORDON, CAROLINE   Aleck Maury Sportsman. New York, 1934. 8vo., orig. cloth, first edition. Rota 189-386 1974 £5

GORDON, CAROLINE   The Garden of Adonis. New York, 1937. 8vo., orig. cloth, first edition. Rota 189-387 1974 £6

GORDON, ELIZABETH   Bird Children. Chicago, 1912. 8vo., illus. Frohnsdorff 16-106 1974 $15

GORDON, GEORGE 1806-1879   The Pinetum. 1858. 8vo., cloth. Wheldon 128-1600 1973 £5

GORDON, GEORGE 1806-1879   The Pinetum. 1858. 8vo., cloth. Wheldon 131-1733 1974 £5

GORDON, GEORGE 1806-1879   The Pinetum. 1858-62. 8vo., 2 vols., cloth. Wheldon 130-1555 1974 £7.50

GORDON, GEORGE 1806-1879   The Pinetum. 1880. Demy 8vo., good copy, orig. cloth. Broadhurst 24-1086 1974 £5

GORDON, GEORGE 1751-1793   The Trial of the Right Honourable George Gordon. London, n.d. 8vo., disbound, first edition. Dawsons PM 251-345 1974 £10

GORDON, GEORGE HAMILTON   An Inquiry Into the Principles of Beauty in Grecian Architecture. 1822. 8vo., contemporary half calf, worn. Hill 126-9 1974 £8.50

GORDON, GEORGE HENRY   Brook From to Cedar Mountain in the War of the Great Rebellion, 1861-62. Boston, 1883. Folded map in front separated at seams, fragment clipped from blank fly, orig. binding. Butterfield 10-157 1974 $15

GORDON, GEORGE HENRY   History of the Campaign of the Army of Virginia, Under John Pope, Brigadier-General U.S.A...From Cedar Mountain to Alexandria, 1862. Boston, 1880. Maps, orig. binding. Butterfield 10-158 1974 $25

GORDON, JAMES F. F.   Ecclesiastical Chronicle for Scotland. London & Dumfries, 1875. Small 4to., half morocco, rubbed, illus. Howes 185-1225 1974 £7.50

GORDON, JOHN B.   Reminiscences of the Civil War by General . . . of the Confederate Army. New York, 1903. Portraits, orig. binding. Butterfield 10-159 1974 $22.50

GORDON, MAX   Max Gordon Presents. Geis, 1965. 314p., illus. Austin 51-363 1973 $7.50

GORDON, PAT   Geography Anatomiz'd. 1749. Folding maps, contemporary calf gilt, rebacked. Smith 193-111 1973 £23

GORDON, RUTH   Years Ago. Viking, 1947. 173p. Austin 51-364 1973 $7.50

GORDON, SETON PAUL 1886-   Days With the Golden Eagle. 1927. Roy. 8vo., cloth, plates, frontis. Wheldon 131-604 1974 £5

GORDON, SETON PAUL 1886-   Days With the Golden Eagle. 1927. Roy. 8vo., cloth, frontis., colour and plain plates, text figures. Wheldon 128-447 1973 £5

GORDON, SETON PAUL 1886-   Hill Birds of Scotland. 1915. 8vo., cloth, plates, frontis. Wheldon 128-448 1973 £5

GORDON, SETON PAUL 1886-   Hill Birds of Scotland. 1930. 8vo., cloth, illus. Wheldon 131-605 1974 £5

GORDON, SETON PAUL 1886-   Wanderings of a Naturalist. 1921. Illus., first edition. Bow Windows 64-104 1974 £3.50

GORDON, T. F.   A Gazetteer Of the State of Pennsylvania. Philadelphia, 1832. 8vo., leather, disbound. Rinsland 58-907 1974 $30

GORDON, W. J.   Englishman's Haven. New York, 1892. Illus. Hood's 102-515 1974 $10

GORDON, W. J.   Our Country's Fishes, and How to Know Them. n.d. 8vo., cloth, plates, scarce. Wheldon 131-744 1974 £5

GORDON, THOMAS   A Cordial for Low-Spirits. 1751. Small 8vo., 3 vols., contemporary speckled calf, second edition. Quaritch 936-89 1974 £55

GORDON, THOMAS   A Learned Dissertation Upon Dumpling. London, 1726. 8vo., modern boards, fine, fifth edition. Dawsons PM 252-406 1974 £40

GORDON, W. EVANS   The Alien Immigrant. 1903. 323 pages, illus. Austin 57-261 1974 $17.50

GORDON, W. J.   Round About the North Pole. London, 1907. Woodcuts, illus. Hood's 103-63 1974 $20

GORDON, WILLIAM   The Plan of a Society for Making Provision for Widows. Boston, 1772. 8vo., half brown morocco, rare, signed, first edition. Ximenes 33-100 1974 $200

GORDON MEMORIAL COLLEGE - WELLCOME RESEARCH LABORATORIES
First to Fourth Reports With Supplements to Third and Fourth Reports. Khartoum, 1904-11. 7 vols., roy. 8vo., orig. cloth, plates. Wheldon 131-878 1974 £15

GORDON'S Map of the South Wales Coalfield. (c.1880). 8vo., canvas backed cloth, map, new edition. Quaritch 939-694 1974 £20

GORE, CATHERINE   Stokeshill Place. London, 1837. 3 vols., 12mo., contemporary half calf, first edition. Dawsons PM 252-407 1974 £35

GORE, THOMAS   Catalogus in Certa Capita, Seu Classes, Alphabetico Ordine Concinnatus. Oxford, 1674. 4to., fine, contemporary mottled sheep, second edition. Dawsons PM 10-247 1974 £55

GORE-BOOTH, EVA   The Three Resurrections & The Triumph of Maeve. 1905. Frontis., orig. lilac cloth, cover somewhat faded, very nice copy, scarce, first edition. Covent 51-793 1973 £6.30

GORELIK, MORDECAI   New Theatres for Old. French, 1947. 533p., illus., hard cover ed. Austin 51-365 1973 $12.50

GORER, E.   Chinese Porcelain and Hard Stones. 1911. 2 vols., roy. 4to., plates, buckram, limited, numbered. Quaritch 940-391 1974 £200

GORGES, RAYMOND   The Story of a Family Through Eleven Centuries. Boston, 1944. 4to., buckram, plates. Howes 186-1638 1974 £14

GORING, C. R.   Microscopic Illustrations of a Few New, Popular and Diverting Living Objects. 1830. Plates. Covent 55-1302 1974 £20

GORING, C. R.   Microscopic Illustrations of Living Objects. 1845. 8vo., orig. cloth, rebacked, plates, third edition. Wheldon 130-106 1974 £10

GORINI, J. M. SAUVEUR   Defense de l'Eglise Contre les Erreurs Historiques de MM. Lyon, 1875. 4 vols., cloth. Howes 185-1226 1974 £6.50

GORKOM, K. W. VAN   De Oost-Indische Cultures, In Betrekking tot Handel en Nijverheid. Amsterdam, 1881. 2 vols., 8vo., orig. wrappers. Wheldon 131-1780 1974 £5

GORKY, MAXIM   Mother. New York, 1930. Plates, faded, inscription, English first edition. Covent 56-537 1974 £7.50

GORMAN, HERBERT S.   James Joyce. New York, 1924. Bookplate, fine, dust wrapper, first American edition. Covent 55-948 1974 £7.50

GORMAN, HERBERT S.   James Joyce. (1926). Cloth-backed boards, portrait, English first edition. Covent 56-1853 1974 £17.50

GORRELL, J. R.   Sins Absolved. Des Moines, 1895. Cloth, author's presentation inscription, John Lacey's copy. Hayman 59-177 1974 $27.50

GORRES, JOHANN J. VON   La Mystique Divine, Naturelle et Diabolique. Paris, 1854-55. 3 parts in 5 vols., half calf. Howes 185-1227 1974 £18

GORRINGE, H. H.   Egyptian Obelisks. New York, (1882). 4to., plates, illus., publisher's morocco gilt. Quaritch 940-322 1974 £65

GOSCHEN, GEORG JOACHIM, VISCOUNT   The Life and Times of. London, 1903. 2 vols., 8vo., orig. cloth gilt, plates. Dawsons PM 10-248 1974 £17

GOSCHEN, GEORG JOACHIM, VISCOUNT   The Life of. 1911. 2 vols., label, portraits. Howes 186-860 1974 £6.50

GOSS, C. W. F.   The London Directories. 1932. 8vo., frontispiece, buckram. Quaritch 939-453 1974 £12.50

GOSS, N. S.   History of the Birds of Kansas. Topeka, 1891. Roy. 8vo., orig. cloth, plates, scarce. Wheldon 128-451 1973 £15

GOSS, N. S.   History of the Birds of Kansas. Topeka, 1891. Roy 8vo., orig. cloth, illus., scarce. Wheldon 130-531 1974 £15

GOSSE, EDMUND WILLIAM 1849-1928   The Autumn Garden. London, 1909. 8vo., orig. linen backed boards, label, inscribed, first edition. Bow Windows 62-390 1974 £8.50

GOSSE, EDMUND WILLIAM 1849-1928   Critical Kit-Kats. 1896. Full buckram, English first edition. Covent 56-538 1974 £6.50

GOSSE, EDMUND WILLIAM 1849-1928   Father and Son. New York, 1908. Biblo & Tannen 210-867 1973 $5

GOSSE, EDMUND WILLIAM 1849-1928   Father and Son. 1913. Illus. Austin 61-422 1974 $12.50

GOSSE, EDMUND WILLIAM 1849-1928   Henrik Ibsen. New York, 1908. Biblo & Tannen 210-883 1973 $7.50

GOSSE, EDMUND WILLIAM 1849-1928   Jeremy Taylor. 1904. 8vo., orig. cloth, first edition. Rota 190-562 1974 £25

GOSSE, EDMUND WILLIAM 1849-1928   Lawrence Alma-Tadema. (1882). Plates, illus., disbound. Marsden 37-9 1974 £8

GOSSE, EDMUND WILLIAM 1849-1928   Life and Letters of John Donne. 1899. 2 vols., ex-library, spines worn. Allen 216-1904 1974 $15

GOSSE, EDMUND WILLIAM 1849-1928   The Life and Letters of John Donne. London, 1899. 2 vols., first edition, orig. cloth, illus. Jacobs 24-91 1974 $30

GOSSE, EDMUND WILLIAM 1849-1928   Portraits and Sketches. 1913. Orig. edition. Austin 61-425 1974 $10

GOSSE, P. H.   Tenby. 1856. 8vo., orig. cloth, plates, first edition. Broadhurst 23-1389 1974 £8

GOSSE, PHILIP HENRY   The Aquarium. 1854. 8vo., cloth, plates, scarce, first edition. Wheldon 130-256 1974 £7.50

GOSSE, PHILIP HENRY   The Aquarium. 1854. 8vo., orig. blue cloth, plates, scarce first edition. Wheldon 131-310 1974 £10

GOSSE, PHILIP HENRY   Evenings at the Microscope. n.d. 8vo., orig. cloth, gilt. Wheldon 131-155 1974 £10

GOSSE, PHILIP HENRY   Evenings at the Microscope. 1884. 8vo., cloth, new edition. Wheldon 130-107 1974 £7.50

GOSSE, PHILIP HENRY   An Introduction to Zoology. n.d. 2 vols., author's presentation inscription, rebound, red cloth. Covent 51-2355 1973 £20

GOSSE, PHILIP HENRY   The Naturalist of the Sea Shore. 1896. 8vo., orig. cloth, scarce, second edition. Wheldon 130-164 1974 £7.50

GOSSE, PHILIP HENRY   A Naturalist's Sojourn in Jamaica. 1851. Plates, spotted, inscription. Bow Windows 64-105 1974 £37.50

GOSSE, PHILIP HENRY   The Ocean. 1854. Crown 8vo., orig. cloth, illus. Wheldon 131-311 1974 £7.50

GOSSE, PHILIP HENRY   Popular British Ornithology. 1849. 16mo., orig. cloth gilt, rare first edition. Wheldon 131-606 1974 £30

GOSTLING, W.   A Walk in and About the City of Canterbury. Canterbury, 1777. 8vo., half calf, second & best edition. Quaritch 939-405 1974 £20

GOTHEIN, MARIE LUISE   A History of Garden Art. London, 1928. 2 vols., 4to., first edition, illus., orig. binding. Wilson 63-317 1974 $50

GOTHEIN, MARIE LUISE   A History of Garden Art. 1928. 2 vols., imp. 8vo., illus., cloth, ex-library, good copy, very scarce, orig. printing. Wheldon 128-105 1973 £25

GOTHEIN, MARIE LUISE   A History of Garden Art. 1928. 2 vols., imp. 8vo., cloth, illus., very scarce orig. printing. Wheldon 128-104 1973 £30

GOTHEIN, MARIE LUISE   A History of Garden Art. 1928. 2 vols., imp. 8vo., cloth, illus. Wheldon 131-219 1974 £25

GOTHEIN, MARIE LUISE   A History of Garden Art. London, (1928). Large 8vo., 2 vols., illus., fine, orig. edition, orig. cloth. Gregory 44-142 1974 £85

GOTHIC Architecture. 1893. 16mo., orig. boards, vellum. Broadhurst 23-1058 1974 £250

GOTT, J.   Bibliotheca Pretiosa. London, 1907. Plates, crown 4to., orig. wrappers. Forster 98-329 1974 £3.50

GOTTINGEN - KIRCHENORDNUNG   Christliche, und in Gottes Wort Altem und Newen Testament. Frankfurt, 1567. Folio, boards, red morocco back, fine, earliest available edition. Harper 213-85 1973 $450

GOUAN, ANTOINE 1733-1821   Flora Monspeliaca. Lyons, 1765. 8vo., contemporary calf, plates. Wheldon 128-1263 1973 £15

GOUAN, ANTOINE 1733-1821   Flora Monspeliaca. Lyons, 1765. 8vo., contemporary calf, plates. Wheldon 131-1295 1974 £15

GOUAN, ANTOINE 1733-1821   Historia Piscium. Histoire des Poissons. Strasburg, 1770. 4to., contemporary boards, plates, scarce. Wheldon 128-630 1973 £30

GOUAN, ANTOINE 1733-1821   Histoire des Poissons. Strasburg, 1770. 4to., contemporary boards, plates, scarce. Wheldon 131-745 1974 £40

GOUBARD, MME.   Madame Goubard's Pillow Lace Patterns, and Instructions in Honiton Lace Making. (c. 1850). Square 8vo., dec. cloth gilt, crisp copy, illus. Quaritch 940-757 1974 £9

GOUDY, FREDERIC W.   The Alphabet. New York, 1918. 4to., orig. cloth, illus., plates, first edition. Howes 185-694 1974 £21

GOUDY, FREDERIC W.   The Alphabet. New York, 1922. 4to., illus., black cloth. Kraus B8-334 1974 $25

GOUDY, FREDERIC W.   The Alphabet. New York, 1922. Nice copy, second edition, upper board slightly marked. Covent 51-799 1973 £20

GOUFFE, JULES   The Book of Preserves. London, 1871. Roy 8vo., orig. cloth, gilt, illus., first edition. Hammond 201-167 1974 £14

GOUFFE, JULES   The Royal Book of Pastry and Confectionery. London, 1874. Roy 8vo., orig. cloth, gilt, plates, first edition. Hammond 201-168 1974 £35

GOUFFE, JULES   Le Livre de Cuisine. Paris, 1884. 4to., boards, plates, sixth edition. Smith 193-919 1973 £8

GOUFFE, JULES   The Royal Cookery Book. London, 1868. Roy 8vo., orig. cloth, gilt, plates, illus., first edition. Hammond 201-169 1974 £32

GOUGE, WILLIAM M.   The Fiscal History of Texas. Philadelphia, 1852. Cloth, leather label. Jenkins 61-945 1974 $85

GOUGH, JOHN   A History of the People Called Quakers. Dublin, 1789. 4 vols., 8vo., full calf. Emerald 50-343 1974 £15

GOUGH, RICHARD   A Comparative View of the Antient Monuments of India. London, 1785. 4to., contemporary half calf, rebacked, first edition. Hammond 201-457 1974 £18.50

GOUGH, W.   Londinum Triumphans. London, 1682. 8vo., half green morocco, gilt. Quaritch 939-454 1974 £60

GOUJET, CLAUDE-PIERRE   Bibliotheque Francoise, ou Histoire de la Litterature Francoise dans Laquelle on Montre l 'Utilite que l'on Peut Retirer des Livres Publies en Francois. . . Paris, 1740-56. 18 vols., plus vols. 1 & 2 in a second revised edition, 20 vols. in all, 12mo., contemporary mottled calf, gilt backs, some vols. slightly rubbed. Kraus B8-81 1974 $180

GOULARD, THOMAS   A Treatise On the Effects and Various Preparations of Lead. London, 1773. Rebacked. Rittenhouse 46-295 1974 $50

GOULARD, THOMAS   A Treatise on the Effects and Various Preparations of Lead. London, 1775. Small 8vo., contemporary calf, rebacked, new edition. Hammond 201-540 1974 £20

GOULD, BENJAMIN APTHORP   The Transatlantic Longitude. Washington, 1869. Folio, orig. pictured wrappers, first edition. Schuman 37-107 1974 $110

GOULD, BENJAMIN APTHORP   Uranometria Argentina. Buenos Aires, 1879. 4to., orig. cloth rebacked, first edition. Dawsons PM 245-341 1974 £28

GOULD, C.   Mythical Monsters. 1886. Roy 8vo., orig. cloth, illus., scarce. Wheldon 130-165 1974 £15

GOULD, GEORGE M.   Concerning Lafcadio Hearn. London and Leipsic, 1908. Cloth, illus. Dawson's 424-271 1974 $17.50

GOULD, GERALD   Monogamy. 1918. Wrappers, English first edition. Covent 56-540 1974 £5

GOULD, JOHN   The Birds of Great Britain. (1862-) 1873. 5 vols., imp. folio, half morocco, hand-coloured plates, nice copy, practically free from foxing. Wheldon 128-452 1973 £8,500

GOULD, JOHN   A Century of Birds from the Himalaya Mountains. (1831)-1832. Large folio, contemporary half morocco, panelled back, raised bands, first issue with backgrounds uncoloured, hand coloured lithographic plates, bound without text, but with title page, dedication and List of Subscribers. Broadhurst 24-1087 1974 £2,250

GOULD, JOHN   A Century of Birds from the Himalaya Mountains. London, 1832. Large folio, contemporary half morocco, plates. Marlborough 70-38 1974 £2,000

GOULD, JOHN   Handbook to the Birds of Australia. London, 1865. 2 vols., roy. 8vo., worn, first edition. Traylen 79-107 1973 £68

GOULD, JOHN   Handbook to the Birds of Australia. 1865. 2 vols., 8vo., orig. green cloth, gilt, scarce, nice copy. Wheldon 128-458 1973 £70

GOULD, JOHN   Handbook to the Birds of Australia. 1865. 2 vols., signature, illus., gilt. Bow Windows 64-106 1974 £80

GOULD, JOHN   Handbook to the Birds of Australia. 1865. 8vo., 2 vols., orig. green cloth, gilt, scarce. Wheldon 130-532 1974 £70

GOULD, JOHN   Icones Avium. 1838. Imp. folio, boards, rubbed, plates, rare. Wheldon 131-51 1974 £750

GOULD, JOHN   An Introduction to the Birds of Great Britain. 1873. 8vo., orig. red cloth. Wheldon 130-533 1974 £15

GOULD, JOHN   An Introduction to the Birds of Great Britain. 1873. 8vo., orig. red cloth, book-plate, inscribed by author, nice copy. Wheldon 128-453 1973 £15

GOULD, JOHN   Monograph of the Pittidae. 1880-81. Folio, orig. printed boards, plates, rare. Wheldon 130-23 1974 £875

GOULD, JOHN   A Monograph of the Ramphastidae. 1834-35. Hand coloured lithographic plates, first edition, large folio, 2 orig. parts, boards, cloth spine. Broadhurst 24-1088 1974 £2,500

GOULD, JOHN   A Monograph of the Trogonidae. 1835-38. Hand coloured lithographic plates, first edition, large folio 3 orig. parts, boards, cloth spines, uncut, fine. Broadhurst 24-1089 1974 £2,500

GOULD, JOHN   A Synopsis of the Birds of Australia. 1837-38. Imperial 8vo., half red levant morocco, plates, rare. Wheldon 130-22 1974 £575

GOULD, ROBERT FREKE   The History of Freemasonry. 1885-87. 4to., 6 vols., orig. cloth, gilt, plates. Hammond 201-358 1974 £14.50

GOULD, ROBERT FREKE   Military Lodges. 1899. 8vo., orig. cloth. Bow Windows 66-295 1974 £6.50

GOULD, RUPERT T.   Enigmas. London, 1929. Rittenhouse 46-297 1974 $15

GOULU, PIERROT   Petite Histoire de Pierrot Gouly. Paris, (c. 1825). Full new brown morocco, gilt, fine, full page engravings, 2 7/16 X 2 3/4 inches. Gregory 44-383 1974 $75

GOURLAY, J. L.   History of the Ottawa Valley. N.P., 1896. Hood's 104-688 1974 $25

GOURLAY, J. L.   History of the Ottawa Valley, a Collection of Facts, Events, and Reminiscences for Over Half a Century. N. P., 1896. Hood's 102-605 1974 $25

GOURLAY, ROBERT FLEMING   The Banished Briton and Neptunian. Boston, 1843. Parts 1 to 12, bound with orig. covers, re-spined, inscribed by author, with a part 32. Hood's 102-244 1974 $700

GOURLAY, ROBERT FLEMING   The Banished Briton and Neptunian. Boston, 1843. Inscribed, re-spined. Hood's 104-259 1974 $700

GOURLAY, ROBERT FLEMING   Statistical Account of Upper Canada Compiled With a View to a Grand System of Emigration. London, 1820-22. 3 vols., leather, mottled boards. Hood's 104-899 1974 $750

GOURMONT, REMY DE   La Latin Mystique. Paris, 1913. Roy. 8vo., three quarter levant morocco, gilt, uncut, limited edition. L. Goldschmidt 42-237 1974 $20

GOURMONT, REMY DE   Lilith. Paris, 1932. 8vo., orig. wrapper, uncut, very fine. L. Goldschmidt 42-238 1974 $15

GOURMONT, REMY DE   Le Puits de la Verite. Paris, 1922. 12mo., orig. wrapper, numbered, limited edition. L. Goldschmidt 42-239 1974 $10

GOURMONT, REMY DE   The Natural Philosophy of Love. 1926. 4to., orig. cloth-backed boards, fine, limited, first edition. Howes 186-372 1974 £18

GOURSAT, EDOUARD   Cours d'Analyse Mathematique. Paris, 1910. Large 8vo., green buckram, gilt, fine. Dawsons PM 245-342 1974 £6

GOUVAN, A.   Flora Monspeliaca. Lyons, 1765. 8vo., new boards, plates. Wheldon 130-1158 1974 £20

GOVER, ROBERT   Here Goes Kitten. Grove Press, 1964. 184p. Austin 54-457 1973 $6.50

GOVER, ROBERT   The Maniac Responsible. Grove Press, 1963. 22p. Austin 54-458 1973 $6.50

GOVONI, CORRADO   Piccolo Veleno Color di Rosa. Florence, 1921. 8vo., wrapper. Minters 37-397 1973 $14

GOVONI, CORRADO   La Strada Sull'Acqua. Milan, 1923. 8vo., wrapper. Minters 37-398 1973 $12.50

GOW, LEONARD 1859-   Catalogue of the Leonard Gow Collection of Chinese Porcelain. 1931. Roy. 4to., plates, full niger morocco, gilt, signed, numbered. Quaritch 940-392 1974 £250

GOW, LEONARD 1859-   Catalogue of the Leonard Gow Collection of Chinese Porcelain. 1931. Roy. 4to., plates, cloth, gilt. Quaritch 940-393 1974 £225

GOW, LEONARD 1859-   Catalogue of the Leonard Gow Collection of Chinese Porcelain. 1931. Roy. 4to., coloured and plain plates, orig. cloth, uncut, limited, one of 243 copies signed by Gow, on hand made paper, fine. Broadhurst 24-97 1974 £220

GOW, LEONARD 1859-   Catalogue of the Leonard Gow Collection of Chinese Porcelain. 1931. Limited edition, hand made paper, coloured plates, 4to., orig. niger morocco gilt, uncut, top edges gilt, cloth box, very scarce, only 300 copies printed and signed by Gow. Sawyer 293-28 1974 £375

GOWER, J.   Illustrations of the Lives and Writings of Gower and Chaucer. 1810. 4to., plates, orig. boards, uncut. Quaritch 936-397 1974 £5

GOWER, JOHN   De Confessione Amantis. London, (1554). Small folio, contemporary panelled calf, third edition. Dawsons PM 252-408 1974 £370

GOWER, JOHN   Confessio Amantis. 1857. 8vo., 3 vols., gilt, polished calf. Quaritch 936-396 1974 £8

GOWER, RONALD SUTHERLAND   Sir Joshua Reynolds, His Life & Art. 1902. Red morocco, photo illus. Eaton Music-668 1973 £8

GOYA, FRANCISCO DE   Francisco de Goya. Munich, 1923. 4to., illus., boards, cloth spine. Quaritch 940-123 1974 £40

GRABE, J. E.   Spicilegium S. S. Patrum. 1714. 2 vols., half calf, ex-library. Allen 213-425 1973 $12.50

GRABNER, DAVID VON   Ephemerides Meteorologicae Vratislavienses. 1723. 4to., contemporary calf, gilt. Zeitlin 235-101 1974 $150

GRACIAN Y MORALES, BALTASAR   The Critick. London, 1681. 8vo., contemporary calf, fine, first English edition. Dawsons PM 252-410 1974 £225

GRADUS ad Cantabrigiam. 1828. 8vo., plates, half calf, uncut, second edition. Quaritch 939-317 1974 £40

GRADY, THOMAS   No. III. Dublin, 1816. 8vo., orig. boards, plates, label, worn, second edition. Ximenes 33-101 1974 $12

GRAELLS, M. DE LA P.   Ramilletes de Plantas Espanolas. Madrid, 1859. Roy 8vo., half morocco, plates. Wheldon 130-1159 1974 £5

GRAEME, BRUCE   Blackshirt. 1925. 8vo., orig. cloth, first edition. Rota 190-279 1974 £6

GRAF, MAX   Legend of a Musical City. New York, 1945. Orig. ed. Biblo & Tannen 214-853 1974 $10

GRAFE, V.   Chemie der Pflanzenzelle. Berlin, 1922. Roy. 8vo., cloth. Wheldon 131-1146 1974 £5

GRAFF, WERNER   Es Kommt der Neue Fotograf. Berlin, 1929. 4to., cloth, illus. Minters 37-608 1973 $50

GRAFF, WERNER   Willi Baumeister. Stuttgart, n.d. 4to., boards, illus., scarce. Minters 37-497 1973 $30

GRAFFIGNY, FRANCOISE DE   Lettres d'Une Peruvienne. Paris, 1797. Large 8vo., full tobacco brown morocco, gilt. L. Goldschmidt 42-54 1974 $95

GRAFFIGNY, FRANCOISE DE   Oeuvres Completes. Paris, 1821. 8vo., contemporary diced tobacco brown calf, gilt, morocco label. L. Goldschmidt 42-55 1974 $80

GRAHAM, A.   Historic St. John's At York Mills, 1816-1843. Toronto, n.d. Illus. Hood's 103-248 1974 $12.50

GRAHAM, D.   Chinese Gardens. (1938). Roy. 8vo., cloth, illus., frontispiece, scarce. Wheldon 131-1520 1974 £15

GRAHAM, E. M.   A Canadian Girl in South Africa. Toronto, 1905. Illus., portraits. Hood's 102-245 1974 $10

GRAHAM, H. G.   Scottish Men of Letters in the 18th Century. 1901. New buckram, blind stamp. Allen 216-2019 1974 $10

GRAHAM, J. D.   Report of Lieut. Col. J. D. Graham on Mason and Dixon's Line. Chicago, 1862. Printed wrappers, fine, folding map, very scarce. Jenkins 61-1480 1974 $35

GRAHAM, JAMES R. G.   A Compendium of the Laws. 1827. 8vo., wrapper, second edition. Hammond 201-236 1974 £6

GRAHAM, JOHN   A History of the Siege of Derry and Enniskillen. Dublin, 1829. 8vo., cloth boards, second edition. Emerald 50-344 1974 £5.50

GRAHAM, MARGARET COLLIER   Do They Really Respect Us? San Francisco, 1912. Biblo & Tannen 210-868 1973 $8.50

GRAHAM, MARIA   Journal of a Residence in Chile, During the Year 1822. London, 1824. 4to., half calf, plates. Traylen 79-482 1973 £98

GRAHAM, MARIA   Journal of a Voyage to Brazil. London, 1824. 4to., half calf, plates. Traylen 79-481 1973 £125

GRAHAM, P. ANDERSON   The Collapse of Homo Sapiens. 1923. Fine, first edition. Covent 55-646 1974 £7.50

GRAHAM, ROBERT BONTINE CUNNINGHAME   Bibi. 1929. 8vo., orig. cloth, signed, fine, first edition. Rota 190-476 1974 £7.50

GRAHAM, ROBERT BONTINE CUNNINGHAME   The Book of Martin Harvey. (1930). 4to., buckram, first edition. Rota 190-477 1974 £5

GRAHAM, ROBERT BONTINE CUNNINGHAME   Cartagena and the Banks of the Sinu. (1921). 8vo., orig. cloth. Bow Windows 64- 524 1974 £6

GRAHAM, ROBERT BONTINE CUNNINGHAME   The Dream of the Magi. 1923. One of 280 copies, numbered & signed by author, this is copy no. 1, cloth backed boards, library labels, very nice copy, discoloured d.w., first edition. Covent 51-505 1973 £10

GRAHAM, ROBERT BONTINE CUNNINGHAME   Inveni Portam: Joseph Conrad. Cleveland, 1924. One of 157 copies, fine, wrappers. Covent 51-454 1973 £25

GRAHAM, ROBERT BONTINE CUNNINGHAME   Inveni Portam. Cleveland, 1924. Fine, numbered, wrappers. Covent 55-519 1974 £45

GRAHAM, ROBERT BONTINE CUNNINGHAME   Success. 1902. First edition. Covent 55-556 1974 £12.50

GRAHAM, SHEILAH   Beloved Infidel. Holt, 1958. 338p., illus. Austin 51-366 1973 $6.50

GRAHAM, STEPHEN   A Private in the Guards. 1919. English first edition. Covent 56-541 1974 £10.50

GRAHAM, STEPHEN   With Poor Immigrants to America. 1914. Illus., 306 pages. Austin 57-262 1974 $12.50

GRAHAM, STEPHEN   With Poor Immigrants to America. Macmillan, 1914. Austin 62-226 1974 $12.50

GRAHAM, VIRGINIA   There Goes What's Her Name. Prentice, 1965. 246p., illus. Austin 51-367 1973 $6.50

GRAHAME, KENNETH   Dream Days. London & New York, n.d. 8vo., pictorial cloth stamped in gold, green, red, black and white, pictorial endpapers, plates, illus., very good copy, partially unopened, illus. by Maxfield Parrish. Frohnsdorff 15-128 1974 $17.50

GRAHAME, KENNETH   Dream Days. London, 1899. 8vo., blue ribbed cloth, slightly worn, inner joints weak, first edition, attached to front flyleaf is an autograph letter by Elspeth Grahame. Frohnsdorff 15-60 1974 $25

GRAHAME, KENNETH   First Whisper of "The Wind in the Willows". Philadelphia, (1945). 12mo., cloth, very good copy, d.j., first edition. Frohnsdorff 16-373 1974 $15

GRAHAME, KENNETH   Fun O' The Fair. London & Toronto, (1929). 8vo., orig. pict. wrappers, illus., mint, first American edition. Frohnsdorff 15-62 1974 $10

GRAHAME, KENNETH   Fun O' The Fair. London & Toronto, (1929). 8vo., orig. pict. wrappers, illus., first edition. Frohnsdorff 15-61 1974 $12.50

GRAHAME, KENNETH   Fun O' the Fair. London & Toronto, (1929). 8vo., pictorial wrappers, first edition, illus. Frohnsdorff 16-374 1974 $15

GRAHAME, KENNETH   Fun O' the Fair. London & Toronto, (1929). 8vo., pictorial wrappers, first American edition. Frohnsdorff 16-375 1974 $15

GRAHAME, KENNETH   The Golden Age. Chicago, 1895. 12mo., gilt lettered cloth, top edge gilt, inscription, nice copy, first American edition. Frohnsdorff 16-376 1974 $15

GRAHAME, KENNETH   The Golden Age. 1900. Pictorial cloth, fine, illus. Covent 55-895 1974 £20

GRAHAME, KENNETH   The Golden Age. London & New York, 1904. 8vo., cloth, illus., good condition. Minters 37-27 1973 $20

GRAHAME, KENNETH   The Golden Age. 1915. Plates, English first edition. Covent 56-1832 1974 £12.50

GRAHAME, KENNETH   The Reluctant Dragon. N. P., (1938). 8vo., pict. cloth, illus., first edition. Frohnsdorff 15-63 1974 $10

GRAHAME, KENNETH   The Wind in the Willows. New York, 1908. 12mo., first American edition, very good to fine. Current BW9-227 1974 $8.50

GRAHAME, KENNETH   The Wind in the Willows. New York, 1908. 8vo., green cloth, faded, top edge gilt, frontispiece, early edition. Frohnsdorff 15-68 1974 $10

GRAHAME, KENNETH   The Wind in the Willows. New York, 1908. 8vo., gilt lettered cloth, spine sunned, top edge gilt, frontispiece by Graham Robertson, nice copy, first American edition. Frohnsdorff 16-377 1974 $40

GRAHAME, KENNETH   The Wind in the Willows. 1908. First edition, frontispiece, crown 8vo., orig. blue cloth, ex-libris. George's 610-321 1973 £30

GRAHAME, KENNETH   The Wind in the Willows. 1908. First edition, frontispiece, bookplate, crown 8vo., orig. blue cloth, top edges gilt, others uncut. George's 610-320 1973 £65

GRAHAME, KENNETH   The Wind in the Willows. New York, 1913. 8vo., pictorial cloth, top edge gilt, full page color plates, very good copy, first edition, illus. by Paul Bransom. Frohnsdorff 16-379 1974 $40

GRAHAME, KENNETH   The Wind in the Willows. New York, 1915. 8vo., gilt lettered cloth, frontispiece by Graham Robertson, top edge gilt, very fine copy. Frohnsdorff 16-378 1974 $15

GRAHAME, KENNETH   The Wind in the Willows. London, (1927). 8vo., cloth, lettered in gilt, illus. in color by Wyndham Payne, first edition thus. Frohnsdorff 15-65 1974 $12.50

GRAHAME, KENNETH   The Wind in the Willows. New York, 1929. 8vo., pict. cloth lettered in gilt, illus. in full clor, illus. endpapers. Frohnsdorff 15-64 1974 $12.50

GRAHAME, KENNETH   The Wind in the Willows. New York, 1933. 8vo., pictorial gilt cloth, illus. by Ernest Shepard, first edition. Frohnsdorff 16-380 1974 $15

GRAHAME, KENNETH   The Wind In the Willows. New York, (1940). Tall 8vo., cloth pict. stamped in gold, color plates by Arthur Rackham, bookplate, very fine copy, pict. slipcase. Frohnsdorff 15-67 1974 $12.50

GRAHAME, KENNETH   The Wind in the Willows. New York, (1940). Tall 8vo., cloth, full page color plates by Arthur Rackham, near mint, orig. dust jacket, pict. slipcase, first trade edition. Frohnsdorff 15-66 1974 $30

GRAHAME, THOMAS   A Letter addressed to Nicholas Wood. Glasgow, 1831. 8vo., boards, first edition. Hammond 201-853 1974 £25

GRAHAME-WHITE, CLAUDE   The Aeroplane in War. (1912). Cloth gilt, plates, English first edition. Covent 56-1533 1974 £25

GRAIN, R. C.   Corney Grain by Himself. 1888. 8vo., contemporary half morocco, little rubbed, first separate edition. Bow Windows 66-296 1974 £6

GRAINGER, RICHARD DUGARD   Observations On the Cultivation of Organic Science. London, 1848. 8vo., disbound, first edition. Schuman 37-108 1974 $75

GRAMBERG, E.   Pilze der Heimat. Leipzig, 1921. 8vo., half calf, plates, third edition. Wheldon 129-1217 1974 £5

GRAMMATICI Latini. 1855-58. 2 vols., new buckram. Allen 213-428 1973 $45

GRAMONDO, GABRIEL BARTHOLOMAEO   Historiarum Galliae, ab Excessv. Amsterdam, 1653. 8vo., contemporary vellum, contemporary annotations on fly. Schumann 499-46 1974 sFr 175

GRAN, H. H.   Die Diatomen der Arktischen Meere, Part 1, Plankton. Jena, 1904. 4to., half cloth, plate. Wheldon 131-1406 1974 £5

GRAND, GORDON   Colonel Weatherford and His Friends. New York, The Derrydale Press, 1933. Drawings, limited to 1450 copies, orig. red cloth, very good to fine. Current BW9-160 1974 $45

GRAND, GORDON   Colonel Weatherford's Young Entry. New York, Derrydale Press, 1935. First edition limited to 1350 copies, 8vo., full page illus., minor wear. Current BW9-161 1974 $47

GRAND, GORDON   Old Man and Other Colonel Weatherford Stories. New York, The Derrydale Press, 1934. Limited to 1150 copies, 8vo., colored frontis., illus., very fine. Current BW9-170 1974 $37.50

GRAND, GORDON   The Silver Horn and Other Sporting Tales of John Weatherford. New York, The Derrydale Press, 1932. Drawings, first edition, 8vo., illus., limited to 950 copies, presentation copy. Current BW9-171 1974 $115

GRAND, SARAH   The Heavenly Twins. London, 1893. 3 vols., 8vo., orig. green cloth, first edition. Ximenes 33-103 1974 $60

THE GRAND Concern of England Explained. London, 1673. 4to., modern half calf, water-stained, first edition. Dawsons PM 247-135 1974 £95

GRAND Rapids, Michigan . . . In Photogravure from Recent Negatives. New York, 1892. Wrappers. Jenkins 61-1623 1974 $12.50

GRAND TRUNK RAILWAY COMPANY   Proceedings of the First Meeting of the Shareholders, Held at Quebec, the 27th of July, 1854. Montreal, 1854. Paper cover. Hood's 102-759 1974 $50

GRANDI, FRANCESCO LUIGI GUIDO   Flores Geometrici ex Rhodonearum. 1728. 4to., contemporary vellum, fine, first edition. Zeitlin 235-102 1974 $75

GRANDI, GUIDO   Geometrica Demonstratio Theorematum Hugenianorum. 1701. 4to., orig. stiff wrappers, uncut, fine, woodcuts, first edition. Dawsons PM 245-343 1974 £55

GRANDI, GUIDO   Instituzioni Meccaniche. 1739. 8vo., contemporary vellum, fine, uncut, plates, first edition. Dawsons PM 245-344 1974 £45

GRANDPRE, L. DE   A Voyage In the Indian Ocean and to Bengal. London, 1803. 2 vols., 8vo., full tree calf, leather labels, plates, fine. Traylen 79-521 1973 £45

GRANDVILLE, JEAN IGNACE ISIDORE GERARD   Scenes de la Vie Privee et Publique des Animaux. Paris, 1842. 2 vols., roy. 8vo., green cloth, gilt, first edition. L. Goldschmidt 42-240 1974 $450

GRANDVILLE, JEAN IGNACE ISIDORE GERARD   Vie Privee et Publique des Animaux. Paris, 1867. Large 8vo., half red hard grain morocco, gilt. L. Goldschmidt 42-241 1974 $45

GRANGER, GIDEON   The Address of Epaminondas to the Citizens of the State of New York. Albany, 1819. 8vo., disbound, first edition. Ximenes 33-102 1974 $17.50

GRANGER, JAMES   Letters Between the Rev. James Granger, and Many of the Most Eminent Literary Men of His Time. London, 1805. 8vo., contemporary tree calf, first edition. Ximenes 33-104 1974 $22.50

GRANGES DE SURGERES, ANATOLE, MARQUIS DE 1850-1902   Les Francaises du XVIIIe Siecle. 1887. Imp. 8vo., plates, half morocco, gilt, wrappers, nice copy, limited. Quaritch 940-251 1974 £20

GRANIER, MICHEL   Conferences upon Homeopathy. 1859. 8vo., orig. green cloth, uncut. Hill 126-166 1974 £8.50

GRANLUND, NILS THOR   Blondes, Brunettes and Bullets. McKay, 1957. 300p. Austin 51-368 1973 $7.50

GRANT, ANNE (MAC VICAR)   Letters from Armageddon. Boston, 1930. Illus. Hood's 104-112 1974 $22.50

GRANT, ANNE (MAC VICAR)   Letters from the Mountains. London, 1896. 3 vols., 12mo., orig. boards, first edition. Dawsons PM 252-411 1974 £60

GRANT, ANNE (MAC VICAR)   Poems on Various Subjects. Edinburgh, 1803. 8vo., contemporary calf, rebacked, first edition. Quaritch 936-398 1974 £25

GRANT, ANNE (MAC VICAR)   Poems on Various Subjects. Edinburgh, 1803. 8vo., orig. boards, first edition. Quaritch 936-399 1974 £30

GRANT, ANNE (MAC VICAR)   Poems on Various Subjects. Edinburgh, 1803. 8vo., contemporary calf, rebacked, some spots and stains, library stamp. Bow Windows 66-297 1974 £36

GRANT, DAVID   Metrical Tales. Sheffield, 1880. Orig. dec. cloth gilt. Covent 55-769 1974 £10.25

GRANT, G. M.   Ocean to Ocean, Sandford Fleming's Expedition Through Canada in 1872. Toronto, 1877. Illus., enlarged & revised edition. Hood's 102-807 1974 $15

GRANT, G. M.   Picturesque Canada. Toronto, 1882. 2 vols., rebound, brown leather, gilt, engravings. Hood's 103-147 1974 $60

GRANT, J. P.   Stray Leaves. Montreal, 1865. Hood's 103-726 1974 $35

GRANT, MADISON   The Conquest of a Continent. 1934. Maps, revised edition. Austin 57-263 1974 $12.50

GRANT, MADISON   The Founders of the Republic on Immigration, Naturalization and Aliens. Scribner, 1928. Austin 62-227 1974 $12.50

GRANT, ROBERT   Jack Hall or the School Days of an American Boy. Boston, 1888. 8vo., pictorial cloth, gilt lettered, first edition, spine ends rubbed. Frohnsdorff 16-383 1974 $20

GRANT, ROBERT   Jack Hall or the School Days of an American Boy. Boston, 1888. 8vo., pictorial cloth, gilt lettered, illus., very good copy, first edition. Frohnsdorff 16-382 1974 $25

GRANT, ULYSSES SIMPSON   Message from the President of the U. S. Communicating the Report and Journal of Proceedings of the Commission Appointed to Obtain Certain Concessions from the Sioux Indians. Washington, 1876. Jenkins 61-949 1974 $10

GRANTHAM, A. E.   Hills of Blue. London, (1927). 8vo., map, portraits, orig. cloth. Bow Windows 62-395 1974 £5.50

GRANVIK, H.   Contributions to the Knowledge of the East African Ornithology. Berlin, 1923. 8vo., full niger morocco, plates, map, author's copy. Wheldon 128-461 1973 £10

GRANVILLE, GEORGE   The She-Gallants. London, 1696. 4to., modern half calf, first edition. Dawsons PM 252-412 1974 £60

GRANVILLE, GEORGE, VISCOUNT LANSDOWNE
Please turn to
LANSDOWNE, GEORGE GRANVILLE, VISCOUNT

Caution: There was also a George Granville who was 1st Marquis Stafford and Duke of Sutherland.

GRASSI, ORAZIO   Libra Astronomica ac Philosophica qua Galilaei Galilaei Opiniones de Cometis a Mario Guidicio. Perugia, 1619. Small 4to., contemporary vellum, woodcut diagrams, first edition. Schumann 500-19 1974 sFr 5,000

GRATAMA, JAN   Religie en Bouwkunst. 1928. 8vo., wrappers, frayed covers, plates. Minters 37-535 1973 $12.50

GRATAROLI, GUGLIELMI   Discours Notables. Lyon, 1586. 16mo., limp vellum. Gurney 64-98 1974 £60

GRATI Falisci Cynegeticon. London, 1654. 12mo., contemporary calf, first edition. Ximenes 33-105 1974 $90

GRATIANUS, BRIXIENSIS   Decretum. Venice, 1525. Thick small 4to., quarter calf, worn. Thomas 30-142 1973 £30

GRATTAN, HENRY   Speeches in the Irish and in the Imperial Parliament. London & Dublin, 1822. 4 vols., contemporary half russia gilt, foxing, first edition. Howes 186-865 1974 £18

GRATTAN, THOMAS COLLEY   The Curse of the Black Lady. London, n.d. 8vo., half calf. Emerald 50-346 1974 £5

GRATZ, REBBECCA   Letters of Rebecca Gratz. 1929. 454 pages. Austin 57-264 1974 $10

GRATZ, REBECCA   Letters of Rebecca Gratz. 1929. Austin 62-228 1974 $10

GRAU, ROBERT   The Business Man in the Amusement World. 1910. 362p., illus. Austin 51-369 1973 $15

GRAU, ROBERT   Forty Years Observation of Music and the Drama. Broadway, 1909. 370p. Austin 51-370 1973 $17.50

GRAUNT, JOHN   Natural and Political Observations. London, 1676. 8vo., contemporary sprinkled calf, fifth edition. Dawsons PM 247-136 1974 £140

GRAUNT, JOHN   Natural and Political Observations. London, 1676. 8vo., calf antique, gilt, fifth edition. Dawsons PM 249-209 1974 £160

GRAUPE, PAUL   Manuscripte/Inkunablen. Cat. 57. Berlin, 1925. Illus., in German. Current BW9-492G 1974 $12.75

GRAVE, CHARLES-JOSEPH DE   Republique des Champs-Elysees ou Monde Ancien. Ghent, 1806. 3 vols., 8vo., contemporary half leather, labels. L. Goldschmidt 42-242 1974 $275

GRAVES, A.   A Century of Loan Exhibitions, 1813-1912. 1913-15. 5 vols., 4to., half leaf green morocco, gilt, limited, orig. issue. Quaritch 940-126 1974 £110

GRAVES, A. J.   Girlhood and Womanhood. Boston, 1844. 12mo., orig. cloth, soiled, first edition. Ximenes 33-106 1974 $40

GRAVES, ALFRED PERCEVAL   Irish Doric in Song and Story. 1926. Faded, portrait, first edition. Covent 55-770 1974 £5

GRAVES, ALFRED PERCEVAL   The Irish Song Book. London, 1895. Small 4to., cloth boards, second edition. Emerald 50-348 1974 £5

GRAVES, ALFRED PERCEVAL   To Return to All That. 1930. Plates, first edition. Covent 55-771 1974 £6.30

GRAVES, ALFRED PERCEVAL   Welsh Poetry: Old and New In English Verse. 1912. Austin 61-426 1974 $15

GRAVES, ALGERNON   Art Sales From the Early 18th Century to Early 20th Century. London, 1918-21. 3 vols. in 1, 8vo., cloth. Dawsons PM 11-328 1974 £18

GRAVES, ALGERNON   The British Institution. London, 1908. 4to., cloth. Dawsons PM 11-329 1974 £7

GRAVES, ALGERNON   A Century of Loan Exhibitions. 1913-15. 5 vols., 8vo. Dawsons PM 11-330 1974 £24

GRAVES, ALGERNON   A Dictionary of Artists Who Have Exhibited Works in London Exhibitions. London, 1901. 4to., cloth. Dawsons PM 11-331 1974 £6

GRAVES, ALGERNON   Royal Academy Exhibitors. London, 1905-06. 8vols. in 4, 8vo., portraits, cloth. Dawsons PM 11-332 1974 £45

GRAVES, ALGERNON   The Society of Artists of Great Britain. London, 1907. 4to., cloth. Dawsons PM 11-333 1974 £5

GRAVES, F. M.   Catalogue of the Loan Exhibition of Relics of Past and Present Wars, Held at South Lodge, Horsham, 7 Aug., 1916. Boards, binding slightly damaged, illu., no. 40 of 250 copies, limited edition. Eaton Music-602 1973 £5

GRAVES, GEORGE   British Ornithology. 1821. Roy 8vo., 3 vols., contemporary half red morocco, rare, second edition. Wheldon 130-24 1974 £720

GRAVES, GEORGE   British Ornithology. 1821. 3 vols., roy. 8vo., contemporary half red morocco, plates, rare. Wheldon 131-53 1974 £720

GRAVES, J.   The History of Cleveland. Carlisle, 1808. 4to., plates, illus., modern boards. Quaritch 939-595 1974 £20

GRAVES, RICHARD   Senilities. 1801. 8vo., contemporary half calf. Hill 126-119 1974 £15

GRAVES, RICHARD   The Spiritual Quixote. 1926. 2 vols. in 1, buckram, portrait. Howes 185-204 1974 £5.25

GRAVES, ROBERT   Another Future of Poetry. 1926. First edition, demy 8vo., dec. limp boards, very good copy. Broadhurst 24-696 1974 £21

GRAVES, ROBERT   But It Still Goes On. 1930. 8vo., orig. cloth, first edition. Rota 189-395 1974 £5

GRAVES, ROBERT   But It Still Goes On. 1930. Fine, soiled d.w., first edition. Covent 51-802 1973 £10

GRAVES, ROBERT   Claudius the God & His Wife. Messalina, 1934. Boxed, dust jacket, first English edition. Allen 213-270 1973 $10

GRAVES, ROBERT   Count Belisarius. London, 1938. First edition, lacking d.w., near fine, orig. binding. Ross 86-219 1974 $12.50

GRAVES, ROBERT   Count Belisarius. London, 1938. First edition, lacking d.w., orig. binding, near fine. Ross 87-249 1974 $15

GRAVES, ROBERT   Country Sentiment. 1920. Orig. cloth, first edition. Rota 188-376 1974 £22

GRAVES, ROBERT   The English Ballad. 1927. Unopened, English first edition. Covent 56-545 1974 £32

GRAVES, ROBERT   Fairies and Fusiliers. 1917. English first edition. Covent 56-546 1974 £45

GRAVES, ROBERT   Fairies and Fusiliers. 1917. Small 8vo., cloth, first edition. Quaritch 936-400 1974 £30

GRAVES, ROBERT   The Feather Bed. 1923. Small 4to., signed, orig. boards, first edition. Quaritch 936-401 1974 £55

GRAVES, ROBERT   Good Bye to All That. 1929. Plates, near fine, dust wrapper, first edition, first issue. Covent 55-772 1974 £35

GRAVES, ROBERT   Good-Bye to All That. London, 1929. First edition, first state, with the Sasson poem, lacking d.w., orig. binding, heavy protective dec. paper wrapper, fine. Ross 87-250 1974 $100

GRAVES, ROBERT   Good-Bye to all That. London, 1929. First edition, first state, with the Sasson poem, lacking d.w., orig. binding, protective heavy dec. paper wrapper, fine. Ross 86-220 1974 $135

GRAVES, ROBERT   Impenetrability, or the Proper Habit of English. 1926. Dec. boards, spine yellowed, very good copy, scarce. Covent 51-2357 1973 £20

GRAVES, ROBERT   Lars Porsena. n.d. 8vo., boards, labels, first edition. Broadhurst 23-742 1974 £6

GRAVES, ROBERT   Lars Porsena. n.d. (1927). First edition, f'cap 8vo., boards, paper printed labels, good copy. Broadhurst 24-698 1974 £6

GRAVES, ROBERT   Lawrence and the Arabian Adventure. 1928. Illus. Austin 61-564 1974 $12.50

GRAVES, ROBERT   Lawrence and the Arabs. 1927. 8vo., orig. cloth, illus., first edition. Rota 190-481 1974 £5

GRAVES, ROBERT   Lawrence and the Arabs. London, 1927. Maps, first edition, nice copy, lacking d.w., ink inscription. Ross 86-221 1974 $25

GRAVES, ROBERT   Lawrence and the Arabs. London, 1927. Illus., maps, first edition, ink inscription of free fly leaf, orig. binding, lacking d.w., spine lightly worn, nice. Ross 87-251 1974 $25

GRAVES, ROBERT   Lawrence and the Arabs. 1941. 288 pages. Austin 61-565 1974 $10

GRAVES, ROBERT   The Left Heresy in Literature and Life. London, 1939. Very good copy, scarce, orig. cloth, first edition. Crane 7-108 1974 £10

GRAVES, ROBERT   The Long Week-End. 1940. Covers slightly dull, else very good copy, first edition. Covent 51-811 1973 £5.25

GRAVES, ROBERT   Mrs. Fisher. 1928. 8vo., boards, first edition. Broadhurst 23-743 1974 £15

GRAVES, ROBERT   Mrs. Fisher or, The Future of Humour. 1928. First edition, f'cap. 8vo., boards, fine. Broadhurst 24-699 1974 £12

GRAVES, ROBERT   Old Soldiers Never Die. 1933. First edition, crown 8vo., very good copy, orig. cloth. Broadhurst 24-702 1974 £12

GRAVES, ROBERT   On English Poetry. 1922. Small 8vo., orig. yellow cloth, fine, first English edition. Quaritch 936-403 1974 £100

GRAVES, ROBERT   On English Poetry. 1922. Crown 8vo., orig. cloth, dust wrapper, first English edition. Broadhurst 23-738 1974 £25

GRAVES, ROBERT   On English Poetry. 1922. Patterned boards, fine, slightly torn d.w., first edition, scarce. Covent 51-806 1973 £25

GRAVES, ROBERT   On English Poetry. 1922. First English edition, extra crown 8vo., fine, d.w., orig. cloth. Broadhurst 24-694 1974 £25

GRAVES, ROBERT   A Pamphlet Against Anthologies. 1928. Crisp copy, exceptionally fine, lightly soiled d.w., very scarce in this condition, first edition. Covent 51-812 1973 £25

GRAVES, ROBERT   The Pier-Glass. (1921). Small 8vo., orig. boards, label, first edition. Howes 185-201 1974 £20

GRAVES, ROBERT   The Pier-Glass. London, n.d. 8vo., orig. dec. boards, worn, first edition. Ximenes 33-107 1974 $22.50

GRAVES, ROBERT   The Pier-Glass. London, 1921. One of 500 copies, d.w. somewhat darkened, fine, orig. binding. Ross 86-223 1974 $65

GRAVES, ROBERT   The Pier-Glass. (1921). Portriat, patterned boards, fine, frayed d.w., scarce, first edition. Covent 51-808 1973 £40

GRAVES, ROBERT   Poems, 1914-26. 1927. First edition, crown 8vo., boards, fine. Broadhurst 24-697 1974 £20

GRAVES, ROBERT   Poems, 1926-1930. London, 1931. First edition, one of 1,000 copies printed, extra spine label tipped in, lacking d.w., near fine, orig. binding. Ross 87-254 1974 $30

GRAVES, ROBERT   Poems, 1914-1926. London, 1927. Lacking d.w., orig. binding, very nice, first impression, owner's name in ink on fly. Ross 86-224 1974 $60

GRAVES, ROBERT   Poems, 1926-30. 1931. Orig. patterned cloth, fine copy, printed spare label tipped in, worn d.w. Covent 51-2358 1973 £12.50

GRAVES, ROBERT   Poems 1926-1930. London, 1931. First edition, nice copy, chipped d.w., orig. cloth, scarce, only 1000 copies. Crane 7-105 1974 £18

GRAVES, ROBERT   Poems, 1926-1930. 1931. First edition, crown 8vo., orig. cloth, fine. Broadhurst 24-701 1974 £20

GRAVES, ROBERT   Poems. 1927. 8vo., boards, uncut, scarce, signed, limited edition. Broadhurst 23-741 1974 £50

GRAVES, ROBERT   Poems. 1931. Orig. cloth, inscription, first edition. Rota 188-377 1974 £10

GRAVES, ROBERT   Poems. 1931. Extra crown 8vo., orig. cloth, first edition. Broadhurst 23-745 1974 £20

GRAVES, ROBERT   Poetic Unreason and Other Studies. 1925. Spine and Covers discoloured, lacks front endpaper, first edition. Covent 51-809 1973 £5

GRAVES, ROBERT   Poetic Unreason and Other Studies. 1925. Crown 8vo., fine, orig. cloth, scarce, first edition. Broadhurst 23-740 1974 £26

GRAVES, ROBERT   The Reader Over Your Shoulder. 1943. 8vo., orig. cloth, first edition. Rota 189-402 1974 £6

GRAVES, ROBERT   The Reader Over Your Shoulder. New York, 1944. Biblo & Tannen 213-772 1973 $7.50

GRAVES, ROBERT   The Real David Copperfield. 1933. Faded, English first edition. Covent 56-550 1974 £12.50

GRAVES, ROBERT   The Real David Copperfield. London, 1933. First edition, very nice copy, torn d.w., orig. cloth. Crane 7-106 1974 £15

GRAVES, ROBERT   Sergeant Lamb of the Ninth. 1940. Fine, dust wrapper, frontispiece, first edition. Howes 185-202 1974 £7.50

GRAVES, ROBERT   The Shout. 1929. Small 4to., orig. boards, signed, limited edition. Broadhurst 23-744 1974 £40

GRAVES, ROBERT   The Shout. 1929. Limited, small 4to., orig. boards, mint, d.w., one of 500 copies, signed by author. Broadhurst 24-700 1974 £42

GRAVES, ROBERT   A Survey of Modernist Poetry. 1927. Cloth-backed boards, English first edition. Covent 56-552 1974 £42.50

GRAVES, ROBERT   Ten Poems More. Paris, 1930. Roy 8vo., quarter leather, English first edition. Covent 56-551 1974 £45

GRAVES, ROBERT   Welchman's Hose. 1925. Crown 8vo., dec. boards, uncut, first edition, limited issue. Broadhurst 23-739 1974 £50

GRAVES, ROBERT   Welchman's Hose. 1925. Wood engravings, first edition, limited to 500 copies, extra crown 8vo., dec. boards, uncut, fine. Broadhurst 24-695 1974 £55

GRAVES, ROBERT   Whipperginny. London, n.d. 8vo., orig. dec. boards, paper label, fine, first edition. Ximenes 33-108 1974 £65

GRAVES, ROBERT EDMUND   The History of Oliver of Castile. 1898. 4to., contemporary green levant morocco, printed on vellum, wide gilt dentelle border, Christie-Miller's own copy, spine slightly faded, fine, possibly the only one printed on vellum. Sawyer 293-260 1974 £750

GRAVES, ROBERT JAMES   A System of Clinical Medicine. Dublin, 1843. 8vo., half calf, first edition. Gumey 64-99 1974 £55

GRAVES, ROBERT JAMES   A System of Clinical Medicine. Dublin, 1843. 8vo., half calf, first edition, old library stamp. Gurney 66-74 1974 £55

GRAVIER, GABRIEL   Decouvertes et Etablissements de Cavelier de la Salle de Rouen Dans L'Amerique du nord. Paris, 1870. Maps, plates, first edition. Jenkins 61-1331 1974 $125

GRAVIS, A.   Recherches Anatomiques et Physiologiques sur le Tradescantia Virginica. Brussels, 1898. 4to., cloth. Wheldon 131-1147 1974 £10

GRAY, A.   Botany for Young People and Common Schools. New York, (1858). Crown 8vo., orig. leather backed dec. boards. Wheldon 129-918 1974 £5

GRAY, A.   Plantae Fendlerianae Novi-Mexicanae. 1849. 4to., boards, rare. Wheldon 131-1296 1974 £15

GRAY, A.   Synoptical Flora of North America. Washington, 1886-88. 2 vols. in 1, 8vo., half morocco, scarce. Wheldon 131-1297 1974 £20

GRAY, B. KIRKMAN   A History of English Philanthropy. 1905. Worn, ex-library. Howes 186-1437 1974 £5

GRAY, GEORGE JOHN   Abstracts from the Wills and Testamentary Documents of Printers. London, 1915. 4to., orig. holland-backed boards, uncut. Dawsons PM 10-250 1974 £8

GRAY, GEORGE ROBERT   The Entomology of Australia. London, 1833. Thin 4to., cloth, plates, rare. Traylen 79-72 1973 £250

GRAY, GEORGE ROBERT   The Genera of Birds. 1844-49. Imperial 4to., 3 vols., contemporary red morocco, plates. Wheldon 129-19 1974 £2,200

GRAY, GEORGE ROBERT   Hand List of Genera and Species of Birds. 1869-71. 8vo., 3 vols., cloth. Wheldon 130-534 1974 £10

GRAY, HAROLD   Little Orphan Annie and the Haunted House. New York, 1928. 8vo., pictorial boards, cloth spine, covers little rubbed, fine copy, first edition. Frohnsdorff 16-386 1974 $15

GRAY, HENRY   Anatomy Descriptive and Surgical. London, 1858. 8vo., orig. cloth, first edition. Dawsons PM 249-210 1974 £160

GRAY, HENRY   Anatomy, Descriptive and Surgical. Philadelphia, 1859. Foxing, restored binding, first American edition. Rittenhouse 46-298 1974 $500

GRAY, HENRY   Anatomy, Descriptive and Surgical. Philadelphia, 1870. New American edition. Rittenhouse 46-299 1974 $12.50

GRAY, HENRY   Anatomy of the Human Body. Philadelphia, 1924. Twenty-first edition. Rittenhouse 46-300 1974 $15

GRAY, HUGH   Letters from Canada. London, 1809. 8vo., calf, gilt, map, first edition. Ximenes 33-110 1974 $125

GRAY, HUGH   Letters from Canada, Written During a Residence There in the Years 1806, 1807 and 1808. London, 1809. Leather spine and corners, marbled boards, large folding map, some wear. Hood's 102-559 1974 $160

GRAY, HUGH   Letters from Canada, Written During a Residence There in the Years, 1806-1808. London, 1809. Marbled boards, map. Hood's 104-639 1974 $175

GRAY, J.   A Text-Book of Experimental Cytology.
Cambridge, 1931. 8vo., cloth, scarce. Wheldon 128-31 1973 £5

GRAY, J. E.   Catalogue of Carnivorous, Pachydermatous and
Edentate Mammalia in the British Museum. 1869. 8vo., cloth, woodcuts,
library stamps, scarce. Wheldon 128-321 1973 £7.50

GRAY, J. E.   Catalogue of Monkeys, Lemurs, and Fruit
Eating Bats in the Collection of the British Museum. 1870. 8vo., cloth, scarce,
woodcuts. Wheldon 128-322 1973 £7.50

GRAY, J. E.   Catalogue of Ruminant Mammalia in British
Museum. 1872. 8vo., boards, scarce, plates. Wheldon 128-323 1973 £5

GRAY, J. E.   Catalogue of the Specimens of Mammalia in the
Collection of the British Museum, Part 1, Cetacea. 1850. 12mo., calf, plates,
Jonathan Couch's copy with his signature. Wheldon 128-324 1973 £7.50

GRAY, J. E.   Handbook of British Water-Weeds or Algae.
1864. 12mo., orig. cloth, presentation copy. Wheldon 128-1364 1973 £5

GRAY, J. E.   Illustrations of Indian Zoology. (1830-35).
Folio, half morocco, plates. Wheldon 130-282 1974 £150

GRAY, J. W.   Shakespeare's Marriage. 1905. 8vo., half calf,
gilt. Quaritch 936-560 1974 £7

GRAY, JOHN   The Long Road. Oxford, 1926. Wrappers,
English first edition. Covent 56-553 1974 £10

GRAY, JOHN HENRY   China. London, 1878. 8vo., 2 vols., orig.
blue cloth gilt, first edition. Dawsons PM 251-236 1974 £12.50

GRAY, LANDON CARTER   A Treatise On Nervous and Mental Diseases.
Philadelphia, 1893. Illus. Rittenhouse 46-301 1974 $10

GRAY, LEWIS CECIL   History of Agriculture in the Southern United
States. Washington, 1933. 8vo., 2 vols., buckram. Butterfield 8-583 1974
$35

GRAY, MRS. HAMILTON   Tour to the Sepulchres of Etruria. London,
1840. 12mo., orig. cloth, fine, first edition. Ximenes 33-109 1974 $40

GRAY, S. O.   British Sea-Weeds. 1867. 8vo., cloth, plates.
Wheldon 131-1407 1974 £5

GRAY, TERENCE   Cuchulainn. Cambridge, 1925. Orig. cloth,
illus., first edition. Rota 188-379 1974 £6.50

GRAY, THOMAS   The Bard. 1837. Rebacked, illus., first
edition. Covent 55-890 1974 £5.25

GRAY, THOMAS   Designs by Mr. R. Bentley. London, 1753.
Large 4to., contemporary calf gilt, illus., fine, first edition, first issue.
Dawsons PM 252-413 1974 £130

GRAY, THOMAS   An Elegy written in a Country Churchyard. London, 1914. 4to., orig. dec. cloth, plates. Hammond 201-491 1974 £6

GRAY, THOMAS   Poems. Glasgow, 1768. 4to., contemporary
boards. Quaritch 936-93 1974 £40

GRAY, THOMAS   Poems. 1768. Small 8vo., contemporary calf,
rebacked, first collected edition. Quaritch 936-92 1974 £50

GRAY, THOMAS   Poems. Parma, 1793. Small 4to., morocco
backed cloth case, orig. wrappers, misbound. Dawsons PM 252-414 1974
£225

GRAY, THOMAS   The Poetical Works of. n.d. 128 pages, illus.
Austin 61-439 1974 $10

GRAY, THOMAS   Poetical Works Of. 1853. Austin 61-438
1974 $12.50

GRAY, THOMAS   Works. 1816. 4to., 2 vols., orig. boards, unopened, frontispiece. Quaritch 936-91 1974 £20

GRAYSON, WILLIAM J.   The Hireling and the Slave. Charleston, 1856.
8vo., orig. cloth, rubbed, first edition. Ximenes 33-111 1974 $15

GRAYSON, WILLIAM J.   The Hireling and the Slave, Chicora, and Other
Poems. Charleston, 1856. Orig. binding. Butterfield 10-104 1974 $35

GRAZIA, VINCENZIO DE   Considerazioni. 1613. 4to., boards, red linen
box. Zeitlin 235-93 1974 $750

GRAZIA, VINCENZO DI   Considerazioni . . . Sopra 'I Discorso di
Galileo Galilei. Florence, 1613. Boards, mends on title not affecting print,
some stains, with the exlibris of Pietro Ginori Conti, first edition. Schumann
500-14 1974 sFr 4,000

GRAZIA, VINCENZO DI   Considerazioni . . . Sopra 'I Discorso di
Galileo Galilei Intorno alle cose che Stanno su I'Acqua. Florence, 1613. First
edition, vellum. Schumann 500-13 1974 sFr 5,800

GRAZZINI, ANTONIO FRANCESCO   The Story of Dr. Manente. Florence,
1929. 8vo., cream coloured parchment boards, fine, slipcase, first edition.
Quaritch 936-462 1974 £18

GREAT BRITAIN   Appendix to Reports from the Commissioners
Appointed by his Majesty. 1819. Folio, half cloth, frayed. Quaritch 939-17
1974 £8.75

GREAT BRITAIN - BOARD OF AGRICULTURE   The Agricultural State of the
Kingdom. 1816. Rebound, buckram, uncut. Howes 186-1355 1974 £25

GREAT BRITAIN - BOARD OF AGRICULTURE   General View of the Agriculture
of the County of Argyll. Edinburgh, 1798. 8vo., contemporary half calf, gilt,
plates, first edition, fine. Dawsons PM 243-423 1973 £25

GREAT BRITAIN - BOARD OF AGRICULTURE   General View of the Agriculture.
Perth, 1799. 8vo., plates, library stamp, contemporary half calf, gilt. Bow
Windows 63-460 1974 £20

GREAT BRITAIN - BOARD OF AGRICULTURE   General View of the Agriculture
of the County of Stafford. London, 1796. 8vo., frontis., contemporary half
morocco, gilt, second edition. Dawsons PM 243-347 1973 £35

GREAT BRITAIN - BOARD OF AGRICULTURE   General View of the Agriculture
of the County of Stafford. 1796. 8vo., contemporary half calf, gilt, plates,
second edition. Hammond 201-41 1974 £38

GREAT BRITAIN - DEPT. OF AGRICULTURE   General View of the Agriculture of
the County of Sussex. London, 1793. 4to., boards, plates, first edition.
Hammond 201-60 1974 £30

GREAT BRITAIN, LAWS   An Act Passed 13th June, 1806, for Granting
to His Majesty, During the Present War . . . Further Additional Rates and Duties
. . . on Profits Arising from Property, Professions, Trades and Offices. 1806.
8vo., contemporary calf, worn, joints broken, some foxing and stains. Bow
Windows 66-685 1974 £6.50

GREAT BRITAIN - PARLIAMENT   The Debate on the Subject of a Regency, in the
House of Commons. London, 1788. 8vo., disbound, first edition. Ximenes 35-
24 1974 $10

GREAT BRITAIN. PARLIAMENT.   The Declaration of the Lords & Commons
Assembled in the Parliament of England, to the Subjects of Scotland. York,
1642. Sewn. Smith 193-109 1973 £15

GREAT BRITAIN - PARLIAMENT   First and Second Reports from the Committees of
the House of Lords...Consumption of Grain. 1814. 8vo., half calf. Quaritch
939-478 1974 £35

GREAT BRITAIN PUBLIC RECORD OFFICE   Acts of the Privy Council of
England. London, 1908-12. 6 vols., cloth. Dawsons PM 11-335 1974 £83

GREAT BRITAIN PUBLIC RECORD OFFICE   Calendar of Charter Rolls Covering
the Years 1226-1516. London, 1903-27. 6 vols., cloth. Dawsons PM
11-343 1974 £99

GREAT BRITAIN PUBLIC RECORD OFFICE   Calendar of Letters and Papers,
Foreign and Domestic, of the Reign of Henry VIII. London, 1862-1932.
37 parts, cloth. Dawsons PM 11-336 1974 £590

GREAT BRITAIN PUBLIC RECORD OFFICE   Calendar of State Papers, Colonial Series. London, 1860-1939. 40 vols., cloth. Dawsons PM 11-337 1974 £690

GREAT BRITAIN PUBLIC RECORD OFFICE   The Close Rolls of Henry III. London, 1902-38. 14 vols., cloth. Dawsons PM 11-346 1974 £220

THE GREAT Delusion, a Study of Aircraft in Peace and War. New York, 1927. lst ed. Biblo & Tannen 213-646 1973 $17.50

GREAT Ghost Stories. London, 1930. lst ed. Biblo & Tannen 210-583 1973 $15

GREAT Lakes Pilot. Washington, 1921. Vols. 1 & 2, library bookplates, else very good set, second edition. Hayman 59-217 1974 $10

THE GREAT Modern American Stories. Boni, Liveright, 1920. 432p. Austin 54-535 1973 $10

THE GREAT Northern Route. Buffalo, 1852. Engravings, maps, cloth. Hood's 102-606 1974 $55

GREAT WESTERN RAILWAY OF CANADA   Statement of Accounts and Report of the Directors of the Great Western Railway of Canada. Quebec, 1854. Some staining. Hood's 102-778 1974 $35

GREAVEN, ALFRED L.   A Cycle of Irish Song. Dublin, n.d. 4to., cloth boards. Emerald 50-351 1974 £5

GREAVES, JOHN   The Origin and Antiquity of Our English Weights and Measures Discover'd. 1745. 12mo., old sheep rebacked, second edition. Hill 126-120 1974 £15

GREAVES, RICHARD N.   Tarquin and the Consulate. Whittaker, 1846. 117p., paper. Austin 51-371 1973 $7.50

GRECO, GIOACHINO   On the Game of Chess. London, 1819. 8vo., contemporary half calf, illus., gilt, first edition. Hammond 201-88 1974 £10.50

THE GREEDY Puppy. London, n.d. (c. 1855). 8vo., embossed boards, gilt, full page engravings. Frohnsdorff 16-387 1974 $35

GREEK POETRY and Life. 1936. 8vo., full morocco, gilt, plates. Broadhurst 23-879 1974 £20

GREELEY, HORACE   Glances at Europe. New York, 1851. lst ed. Biblo & Tannen 213-676 1973 $18.50

GREELY, A. W.   Reminiscences of Adventure and Service. New York, 1927. First edition, illus., orig. binding. Wilson 63-339 1974 $18.75

GREEN, ABEL   Show Biz. Garden City, 1951. 613p. Austin 51-373 1973 $6

GREEN, ALICE STOPFORD   The Making of Ireland and Its Undoing. 1919. Map, scarce, revised, second & best edition. Howes 186-866 1974 £6

GREEN, ANNA KATHARINE   Hand and Ring. London, n.d. Cloth-backed marbled boards, worn. Covent 55-580 1974 £12.50

GREEN, ASHBEL   Memoirs of the Rev. Joseph Eastburn. Philadelphia, 1828. 12mo., contemporary calf, first edition. Ximenes 33-112 1974 $22.50

GREEN, C. T.   The Flora of the Liverpool District. Liverpool, 1902. 8vo., orig. cloth, plates. Wheldon 131-1222 1974 £5

GREEN, C. T.   Flora of the Liverpool District. Liverpool, 1902. Illus., first edition, orig. cloth, demy 8vo., fine. Broadhurst 24-1091 1974 £6

GREEN, CAROLYN   Janus. Random House, 1956. 179p., illus. Austin 51-374 1973 $7.50

GREEN CHARLES R.   Quantrell's Raid on Lawrence. Lyndon, 1899. 12mo., quarter cloth & boards, first edition. Ximenes 36-111 1974 $90

GREEN, DORON   A History of Bristol Borough in the County of Bucks, State of Pennsylvania. Camden, 1911. 8vo., cloth. Saddleback 14-669 1974 $25

GREEN, EMANUEL   Bibliotheca Somersetiensis. Taunton, 1902. 3 vols., 4to., uncut, orig. cloth. Dawsons PM 10-572 1974 £70

GREEN, FITZHUGH   Peary . . . The Man Who Refused to Fail. New York, 1926. First edition, orig. binding, illus. Wilson 63-120 1974 $12.50

GREEN, GEORGE   An Essay on the Application of Mathematical Analysis to the Theories of Electricity and Magnetism. Nottingham, 1828. 4to., orig. wrappers, first edition. Dawsons PM 245-346 1974 £625

GREEN, H. M.   An Outline of Australian Literature. Sydney and Melbourne, 1930. English first edition. Covent 56-1878 1974 £5.25

GREEN, J.   Poetical Sketches of Scarborough. 1813. 8vo., calf, plates, first edition, second issue. Quaritch 939-596 1974 £150

GREEN, J. R.   A History of Botany in the United Kingdom. (1914). 8vo., cloth, portraits, scarce. Wheldon 129-146 1974 £10

GREEN, JACOB   Astronomical Recreations. Philadelphia, 1824. Large 4to., contemporary half leather, plates, first edition. Schuman 37-109 1974 $195

GREEN, JOHN   The Principles and Practices of the Methodists Farther Considered. Cambridge, 1761. 8vo., contemporary marbled wrappers, fine, first edition. Ximenes 33-113 1974 $50

GREEN, JOHN L.   Pioneer Evangelists of the Church of God in the Pacific Northwest. Portland, (1939). 12mo., cloth. Saddleback 14-648 1974 $10

GREEN, JOHN RICHARD   A Short History of the English People. 1892-1894. 4 vols., 8vo., orig. cloth, coloured plates, maps, illus., foxing. Bow Windows 66-299 1974 £8.50

GREEN, JOHN RICHARD   A Short History of the English People. 1892. 4 vols., roy. 8vo., half morocco, illus. library edition. Howes 186-867 1974 £15

GREEN, JULIAN   The Pilgrim of the Earth. 1929. Half vellum, buckram, fine, English first edition. Covent 56-555 1974 £10.50

GREEN, L. W.   Popery and Puseyism. Pittsburgh, 1844. 12mo., orig. cloth, first edition. Ximenes 33-114 1974 $25

GREEN, MATTHEW   The Spleen. London, 1737. 8vo., rebacked, contemporary calf, first edition. Dawsons PM 252-415 1974 £65

GREEN, PAUL   Johnny Johnson. French, 1937. 175p., illus. Austin 51-375 1973 $8.50

GREEN, PAUL   Native Son. Harper. 148p. Austin 51-376 1973 $10

GREEN, RICHARD   The Works of John and Charles Wesley. London, 1906. 8vo., orig. cloth-backed boards, second edition. Dawsons PM 10-643 1974 £40

GREEN, SARAH P.   The Moral Imbeciles. New York, 1898. 8vo., orig. dec. cloth, fine, first edition. Ximenes 33-116 1974 $10

GREEN, THOMAS J.   Journal of the Texian Expedition Against Mier. New York, 1845. Cover reinforced, inscribed by author. Jenkins 61-961 1974 $125

GREEN, THOMAS HILL   Works. 1894-91. 3 vols., thick 8vo., portrait. Howes 185-1865 1974 £20

GREEN, VALENTINE   The History and Antiquities of the City and Suburbs of Worcester. 1796. 2 vols., 4to., plates. Quaritch 939-585 1974 £25

GREEN, VALENTINE   A Survey of the City of Worcester. Worcester, 1764. 8vo., contemporary speckled calf, gilt, first edition. Dawsons PM 251-27 1974 £38

GREEN, W. CURTIS   Old Cottages and Farm-Houses in Surrey.
1908. Small 4to., plates. Howes 186-2192 1974 £7.50

GREEN, WILLIAM   A Description of a Series of Sixty Small Prints.
London & Ambleside, 1814. Plates, contemporary half calf, joints broken, back
strip detached, internally sound, first edition. Covent 51-654 1973 £12.60

GREEN, WILLIAM   A Description of a Series of Sixty Small Prints.
1814. Oblong 8vo., half calf antique. Quaritch 939-129 1974 £75

GREEN, WILLIAM   Plans of Economy. London, 1803. 8vo.,
uncut, orig. boards, fifth edition. Bow Windows 62-397 1974 £10.50

GREENAWAY, KATE   Almanack. 1884. 8vo., white morocco, fine.
Gregory 44-47B 1974 $17.50

GREENAWAY, KATE   Almanack. 1884. 8vo., pictorial wrappers,
fine. Gregory 44-47A 1974 $20

GREENAWAY, KATE   Almanack. 1885. 8vo., white morocco, fine.
Gregory 44-47C 1974 $30

GREENAWAY, KATE   Almanack. 1886. 8vo., white morocco, fine.
Gregory 44-47D 1974 $35

GREENAWAY, KATE   Almanack for 1883. n.d. Illus. coloured and
engraved, small 12mo., orig. cloth backed coloured pictorial boards, fine copy.
George's 610-835 1973 £9

GREENAWAY, KATE   Almanack for 1884. London. 16mo., orig.
imitation morocco gilt, first edition, fine. MacManus 224-189 1974 $40

GREENAWAY, KATE   Almanack for 1886. Pictorial boards, illus.,
gilt, rare, near mint. Rinsland 58-921 1974 $60

GREENAWAY, KATE   Almanack for 1887. n.d. Coloured illus.,
oblong 12mo., orig. cloth backed coloured pictorial boards, trifle soiled, scarce.
George's 610-323 1973 £7.50

GREENAWAY, KATE   Almanack for 1891. (London). 16mo., orig.
imitation morocco dec., first edition, very fine. MacManus 224-190 1974 $45

GREENAWAY, KATE   Almanack for 1893. London. 16mo., orig.
cloth, fine, first edition. MacManus 224-191 1974 $45

GREENAWAY, KATE   Almanack for 1895. 1895. Illus in colour,
clothbacked boards, very nice copy. Covent 51-3246 1973 £12

GREENAWAY, KATE   Alphabet. n.d. 8vo., orig. cloth, very fine.
Gregory 44-45 1974 $22.50

GREENAWAY, KATE   Alphabet. London & New York, n.d. 24mo.,
orig. pictorial boards, first edition, very fine. MacManus 224-192 1974 $35

GREENAWAY, KATE   The April Baby's Book of Tunes. 1900. Illus.,
English first edition. Covent 56-558 1974 £21

GREENAWAY, KATE   The Girl's Own Annual. 1890-91. 4to., dec.
cloth gilt, illus., English first edition. Covent 56-559 1974 £10.50

GREENAWAY, KATE   Language of Flowers. (1884). First edition,
illus., small 8vo., orig. cloth backed pictorial boards, corners rubbed, front
hinge weak. George's 610-326 1973 £5

GREENAWAY, KATE   The Language of Flowers. (1884). Small 4to.,
nice copy, orig. cloth. Gregory 44-48 1974 $35

GREENAWAY, KATE   Language of Flowers. 1884. Small 8vo., orig.
glazed pictorial boards, first edition. Hammond 201-116 1974 £24

GREENAWAY, KATE   Marigold Garden. London, n.d. 8vo., many
colored illus., near mint. Current BW9-120 1974 $38.75

GREENAWAY, KATE   Marigold Garden. n.d. 4to., orig. cloth-
backed glazed pictorial boards. Hammond 201-117 1974 £20

GREENAWAY, KATE   Marigold Garden. (1885). 4to., orig. cloth,
illus., inscription, first edition. Rota 189-410 1974 £30

GREENAWAY, KATE   Mother Goose, or the Old Nursery Rhymes.
(1881). First edition, illus. in colour, crown 8vo., orig. dec. cloth, upper cover
almost detached. George's 610-328 1973 £5

GREENAWAY, KATE   Orient Line Guide. 1889. Large thick 8vo.,
frontispiece, unusually nice copy, orig. cloth. Gregory 44-49 1974 $45

GREENAWAY, KATE   Pictures from Originals Presented by Her to
John Ruskin and Other Personal Friends. 1921. Portrait photo, exceptionally
fine, buckram backed cloth, drawings, first edition. Covent 51-820 1973 £30

GREENAWAY, KATE   Under the Window. (1878). First edition, small
4to., orig. cloth backed pictorial boards, spine & edges slightly rubbed, hinges
weak, coloured illus. George's 610-329 1973 £10

GREENBAUM, FLORENCE KREISLER   The International Jewish Cook Book.
Bloch, 1918. 419p. Austin 62-229 1974 $12.50

GREENE, ALBERT G.   Old Grimes. Providence, 1867. Large 8vo.,
orig. brown cloth, gilt, illus., first edition. Ximenes 33-115 1974 $15

GREENE, CHARLES S.   Sparks from the Campfire, Thrilling Stories of
Heroism, Adventure, Daring and Suffering, retold by the Boys Who Were There ...
and A Truthful Account of the Prison Pens of Dixie. New York, 1889. First
edition, 8vo., full page copper plate engravings on India background, interior
fine, covers with spots and a bit dull. Current BW9-354 1974 $16.75

GREENE, E. L.   Illustrations of West American Oaks. San Francisco, 1889-90. 4to., buckram, scarce. Wheldon 129-1603 1974 £25

GREENE, E. L.   Illustrations of West American Oaks. San
Francisco, 1889-90. 4to., buckram, plates, scarce. Wheldon 131-1734
1974 £25

GREENE, E. L.   Landmarks of Botanical History. Washington,
1909. 8vo., modern buckram. Wheldon 129-147 1974 £10

GREENE, FRANCIS B.   History of Boothbay, Southport and Boothbay Harbor. Portland, 1906. 8vo., orig. bindings, scarce. Butterfield 8-202 1974
$45

GREENE, GRAHAM   British Dramatists. London, 1942. Very nice
copy, d.w., orig. cloth, illus., first edition. Crane 7-115 1974 £5

GREENE, GRAHAM   The Gamesters. 1923. Boards, faded, blind-
stamped, presentation copy, English first edition. Covent 56-562 1974 £25

GREENE, GRAHAM   The Name of Action. 1930. Navy levant
morocco, gilt, fine, scarce, first edition. Howes 185-207 1974 £25

GREENE, GRAHAM   The Name of Action. 1930. Crown 8vo.,
orig. cloth, scarce, first edition. Broadhurst 23-754 1974 £30

GREENE, GRAHAM   The Name of Action. London, 1930. First
edition, exceedingly crisp and bright copy, very scarce, orig. cloth. Crane
7-114 1974 £40

GREENE, GRAHAM   The Power and the Glory. London, 1940.
8vo., orig. cloth, dust wrapper, first edition. Dawsons PM 252-416 1974 £20

GREENE, GRAHAM   The Seed Cake and the Love Lady. 1934.
Wrappers, fine, English first edition. Covent 56-568 1974 £5

GREENE, GRAHAM   Stamboul Train. 1932. Bookplate, English first
edition. Covent 56-1786 1974 £7.50

GREENE, GRAHAME   Stamboul Train. 1932. Front hinge slightly
cracked, very good copy, covers slightly stained & worn, author's signed
presentation inscription, first edition. Covent 51-823 1973 £21

GREENE, GRAHAM   Stepping Stones and Apologia. New York,
1924. Orig. boards, first U.S. edition. Covent 56-569 1974 £25

GREENE, H. I.   Yozonde of the Wilderness. Toronto, 1910.
Hood's 102-517 1974 $10

GREENE, ROBERT   Dramatic and Poetical Works. 1861. New buckram. Allen 216-1804 1974 $15

GREENE, WILLIAM CHASE   The Achievement of Rome. Cambridge, 1933. Illus. Biblo & Tannen 214-614 1974 $12.50

GREENE, WILLIAM THOMAS   Parrots in Captivity. London, 1884-87. 3 vols., roy. 8vo., plates. Traylen 79-108 1973 £200

GREENE, WILLIAM THOMAS   Parrots In Captivity. 1884-87. 3 vols., roy. 8vo., half red morocco, plates, nice copy. Wheldon 131-54 1974 £240

GREENE, WILLIAM THOMAS   Parrots in Captivity. 1884-87. Roy. 8vo., 3 vols., publisher's cloth, gilt, plates. Wheldon 130-25 1974 £220

GREENE, WILLIAM THOMAS   Parrots in Captivity. 1884-87. 3 vols., roy. 8vo., half red morocco neat, plates printed in colours, nice copy. Wheldon 128-463 1973 £240

GREENE, WILLIAM THOMAS   Parrots in Captivity. 1884-87. 3 vols., roy. 8vo., publisher's cloth, gilt, plates printed in colours, scarce. Wheldon 128-462 1973 £220

GREENER, WILLIAM WELLINGTON   The Gun and Its Development. (1881). 8vo., orig. cloth, first edition. Bow Windows 64-323 1974 £28

GREENER, WILLIAM WELLINGTON   The Science of Gunnery. London, 1846. 8vo., orig. blue cloth, gilt, second edition. Dawsons PM 251-383 1974 £40

GREENHILL, ALFRED GEORGE   The Applications of Elliptic Functions. London, 1892. 8vo., blue cloth, first edition. Dawsons PM 245-347 1974 £6

GREENHOUSE Favourites, a Description of Choice Greenhouse Plants With Practical Directions for Their Management and Cultivation. (1880). Roy. 8vo., orig. cloth gilt, plates, scarce. Wheldon 131-1521 1974 £30

GREENHOW, ROBERT   Memoir, Historical and Political on the Northwest Coast of North Ameri. New York, 1840. Three quarter leather, repaired, fine large folding map, cloth backed. Jenkins 61-963 1974 $35

GREENISH, H. G.   The Microscopical Examination of Foods and Drugs. 1923. 8vo., cloth, illus., scarce, third edition. Wheldon 128-1650 1973 £7.50

GREENWOOD, JAMES   The Hatchet Throwers. London, 1866. Small 4to., full red polished calf, raised spine, gilt tooled with leather labels, all edges gilt, marbled endpapers, illus. drawn on wood by Ernest Griset, hand colored, orig. cloth covers bound in, first edition, fine. Frohnsdorff 15-70 1974 $85

GREENWOOD, JAMES   The Hatchet Throwers. London, 1866. Illus. drawn on wood by Ernest Griset, full red polished calf, leather labels, hand colored engravings, fine, first edition. Frohnsdorff 16-395 1974 $85

GREENWOOD, JAMES   Legends of Savage Life. London, 1867. 4to., full red polished calf, raised spine, gilt tooled, leather labels, all edges gilt, marbled endpapers, orig. covers bound in, hand colored wood engravings, fine, first edition. Frohnsdorff 15-72 1974 $85

GREENWOOD, JAMES   Legends of Savage Life. London, 1867. Illus. drawn on wood by Ernest Griset, full red polished calf, 4to., orig. pictorial cloth cover bound in, fine, first edition, hand colored engravings. Frohnsdorff 16-396 1974 $85

GREENWOOD, JAMES   Legends of Savage Life. London, 1869. Illus. drawn on wood by Ernest Griset, 4to., gilt pictorial cloth, bookplates. Frohnsdorff 16-397 1974 $30

GREENWOOD, JAMES   The Purgatory of Peter the Cruel. London, 1868. 4to., full red polished calf, floral gilt designs, raised spine, gilt tooled, orig. covers bound in, hand colored wood engravings by Ernest Griset, first edition. Frohnsdorff 15-73 1974 $85

GREENWOOD, JAMES   The Purgatory of Peter the Cruel. London, 1868. 4to., full red polished calf, illus. drawn on wood by Ernest Griset, all edges gilt, orig. gilt pict. cloth cover bound in, first edition, fine, hand colored engravings. Frohnsdorff 16-398 1974 $85

GREER, HOWARD   Designing Male. Putnam, 1951. 310p., illus. Austin 51-377 1973 $10

A GREETING from Martha's Vineyard. New York, 1895. Stiff wrappers. Jenkins 61-1504 1974 $12.50

GREEVEN, H.   Collection des Costumes des Provinces Septentrionales du Royaume des Pays Bas. Amsterdam & Paris, 1828. 4to., plates, contemporary boards, new morocco spine, orig. label. Quaritch 940-713 1974 £350

GREFFIER, DESIRE   Les Regles de la Composition Typographique. Paris, 1897. Small 8vo., orig. printed wrappers. Kraus B8-335 1974 $10

GREFORY, DAVID   Astronomiae Physicae & Geometricae Elementa. Oxford, 1702. Folio, contemporary calf, diagrams, first edition. Schuman 37-185 1974 $375

GREGG, J.   Thesaurus Poeticus. New York, 1826. 12mo., orig. quarter cloth, boards, first edition. Ximenes 33-117 1974 $25

GREGG, JOSIAH   The Commerce of the Prairies. Chicago, 1926. Cloth. Hayman 59-218 1974 $10

GREGG, JOSIAH   The Commerce of the Prairies. 1926. Dec. cloth, gilt top, frontispiece, map, fine copy. Dykes 22-136 1973 $12.50

GREGG, JOSIAH   The Commerce of the Prairies. Chicago, 1926. Frontis., map. Hood's 102-826 1974 $20

GREGOR, JOSEPH   Weltgeschichte des Theaters. 1933. Illus. Allen 216-2127 1974 $12.50

GREGORIUS IX, POPE   Decretales, Cum Glossa. Venice, 1484. Large folio, wooden boards, contemporary blind-stamped pigskin, rubbed, rare. Harper 213-86 1973 $2500

GREGORY, A.   The White Cockade. Dublin, 1905. 8vo., wrappers, cloth boards, first edition. Emerald 50-354 1974 £10

GREGORY, ANNADORA FOSS   Pioneer Days in Crete, Nebraska. Chadron, (1937). Orig. binding. Butterfield 10-431 1974 $15

GREGORY, DAVID   Astronomiae Physicae and Geometricae Elementa. Oxford, 1702. Folio, contemporary unlettered calf, fine, first edition. Dawsons PM 245-565 1974 £285

GREGORY, DAVID   Astronomiae Physicae and Geometrical Elementa. 1702. Folio, contemporary sprinkled calf, first edition. Dawsons PM 245-564 1974 £385

GREGORY, DAVID   Astronomiae Physicae and Geometricae Elementa. 1726. 4to., 2 vols., contemporary mottled calf, gilt, plates. Dawsons PM 245-348 1974 £80

GREGORY, DAVID   Astronomiae Physicae & Geometricae Elementa. Geneva, 1726. 2 vols., 4to., contemporary calf, plates, fine, rubbed. Traylen 79-233 1973 £85

GREGORY, GEORGE   A Dictionary of Arts and Sciences. London, 18-06-7. 4to., 2 vols., contemporary tree calf, gilt, plates, first edition. Hammond 201-828 1974 £55

GREGORY, GEORGE   The Life of Thomas Chatterton. London, 1789. 8vo., 19th century half calf, first edition. Ximenes 33-118 1974 $55

GREGORY, GEORGE   A New and Complete Dictionary of Arts and Sciences. Charlestown, 1815. 3 vols., thick 4to., contemporary tree calf, fine, first American edition. Ximenes 33-119 1974 $130

GREGORY, HORACE   Chorus for Survival. New York, 1935. 8vo., orig. cloth, first edition. Rota 189-416 1974 £5

GREGORY, HORACE   The Shield of Achilles. New York, 1944. Orig. cloth, presentation inscription, fine, first edition. Rota 188-381 1974 £16

GREGORY, ISABELLA AUGUSTA (PERSSE)   A Book of Saints and Wonders. Dandrum, 1906. 8vo., orig. cloth, scarce, first edition. Rota 190-483 1974 £40

GREGORY, ISABELLA AUGUSTA (PERSSE)   Cuchulain of Muirthemne. London, 1915. 8vo., quarter cloth boards. Emerald 50-355 1974 £10

GREGORY, ISABELLA AUGUSTA (PERSSE)   Gods and Fighting Men. London, 1905. 8vo., cloth boards. Emerald 50-353 1974 £25

GREGORY, ISABELLA AUGUSTA (PERSSE)   Gods and Fighting Men. 1926. Allen 216-860 1974 $12.50

GREGORY, ISABELLA AUGUSTA (PERSSE)   The Kiltarton History Book. 1926. First English edition, f'cap 8vo., inscribed by author to Lennox Robinson. Broadhurst 24-719 1974 £20

GREGORY, ISABELLA AUGUSTA (PERSSE)   The Kiltartan Poetry Book. Dublin, 1918. 8vo., orig. cloth, first edition. Rota 190-484 1974 £40

GREGORY, ISABELLA AUGUSTA (PERSSE)   The Kiltartan Poetry Book. Dublin, 1918. Limited to 400 copies, cover & spine somewhat browned, unopened, fine. Ross 86-236 1974 $85

GREGORY, ISABELLA AUGUSTA (PERSSE)   My First Play. 1930. First edition, crown 8vo., boards, uncut, fine, frayed d.w., limited to 530 copies, signed by author. Broadhurst 24-720 1974 £15

GREGORY, ISABELLA AUGUSTA (PERSSE)   Seven Short Plays. Dublin, 1909. 8vo., orig. holland backed boards, portrait, label missing, corner worn, first edition, signature of Geoffrey Fry on fly. Bow Windows 66-300 1974 £14

GREGORY, ISABELLA AUGUSTA (PERSSE)   Seven Short Plays. Dublin, 1909. First edition. Biblo & Tannen 214-724 1974 $10

GREGORY, ISABELLA AUGUSTA (PERSSE)   The White Cockade. Dublin, 1905. Fine, wrappers, foxed, first edition. Covent 55-783 1974 £15

GREGORY, JAMES   Optica Promota, seu Abdita Radiorum Reflexorum & Refractorum Mysteria, Geometrice Enucleata. London, 1663. 4to., half vellum, first edition, woodcut diagrams, F. X. von Zach's copy. Kraus 137-38 1974 $1,250

GREGORY, J. W.   Catalogue of the Fossil Bryozoa. 1899-1922. 8vo., 4 vols., orig. cloth. Wheldon 129-825 1974 £20

GREGORY, J. W.   Catalogue of the Fossil Bryozoa in the British Museum. The Cretaceous Bryozoa. 1899-1922. 4 vols., 8vo., orig. cloth, scarce. Wheldon 128-981 1973 £18

GREGORY, J. W.   Catalogue of the Fossil Bryozoa in the British Museum. The Cretaceous Bryozoa. 1899-1922. 4 vols., 8vo., cloth. Wheldon 131-1011 1974 £20

GREGORY, ODIN   Caius Gracchus A Tragedy. New York, 1920. 8vo., wrappers, front wrapper detached, first edition. Goodspeed's 578-91 1974 $10

GREGORY, TOM   History of Sonoma County, California. Los Angeles, 1911. 4to., three quarter leather, illus. Saddleback 14-120 1974 $100

GREGORY, W.   International Congresses and Conferences 1840-1937. New York, 1938. Cloth. Dawsons PM 11-354 1974 £24.50

GREGORY, W. K.   In Quest of Gorillas. New Bedford, 1937. First edition, 8vo., illus., very fine. Current BW9-183 1974 $12.50

GREGORY, W. K.   Man's Place Among the Anthropoids. Oxford, 1934. 8vo., cloth, plates. Wheldon 130-399 1974 £5

GREGORY, W. K.   Man's Place Among the Anthropoids. Oxford, 1934. 8vo., cloth, illus. Wheldon 131-490 1974 £7.50

GREGORY, WILLIAM   A Visible Display of Divine Providence. London, n.d. 8vo., contemporary tree calf, worn, covers loose, engraved plates, map, ex-library, first edition. Ximenes 37-99 1974 $150

GRELLMAN, HEINRICH MORITZ GOTTLIEB   Dissertation on the Gipsies. London, 1787. 4to., old half calf, first English edition. Ximenes 33-120 1974 $125

GRELLMANN, HEINRICH MORITZ GOTTLIEB   Dissertation on the Gipsies. London, 1787. 4to., contemporary calf gilt, boards, first edition in English. Dawsons PM 251-237 1974 £55

GRENFELL, WILFRED T.   Yourself and Your Body. New York, 1924. Drawings. Hood's 103-590 1974 $20

GRENIER, ALBERT   The Roman Spirit in Religion, Thought and Art. New York, 1926. 1st Amer. ed., illus. Biblo & Tannen 214-615 1974 $12.50

GRENIER, C.   Flore de la Chaine Jurassique. Paris, 1865-69. 8vo., half morocco, scarce. Wheldon 128-1264 1973 £12

GRENVILLE, GEORGE NUGENT TEMPLE, BARON NUGENT
Please turn to
NUGENT, GEORGE NUGENT GRENVILLE, BARON

GRENVILLE, RICHARD   The Private Diary. London, 1862. 3 vols., 8vo., orig. purple cloth, first edition. Ximenes 33-121 1974 $25

GRENVILLE, WILLIAM WYNDHAM   Substance of the Speech of . . . in the House of Lords, November 30, 1819. 1820. 8vo., boards, first edition. Hammond 201-238 1974 £9.50

GRESLEY, W.   The Siege of Lichfield. 1841. 12mo., illus., contemporary half calf, worn, third edition. Bow Windows 66-301 1974 £6

GRESS, EDMUND G.   The Art and Practice of Typography. New York, 1917. Green cloth, second edition. Dawson's 424-151 1974 $60

GRESSWELL, RONALD KAY   Original Typescript Manuscript of the Geomorphology of the Southport to Liverpool Coastline. 1936. Crown 4to., orig. cloth. Broadhurst 23-1391 1974 £200

GRESWELL, WILLIAM PARR   Annals of Parisian Typography. London, 1818. 8vo., orig. boards, uncut, portrait, plates. Dawsons PM 10-253 1974 £46

THE GRETE Herbal Which Geveth Perfyt Knowledge and Understanding of All Manner of Herbes. London, 1526. Folio, woodcuts, 17th century calf, back mended, magnificnet copy, first English edition, copy of Earl of Dysart, Ham House. Kraus 137-40 1974 $35,000

GRETRY, A. E. M.   Silvain. Paris, (1770). 4to., contemporary vellum, rubbed, first edition. Quaritch 940-812 1974 £35

GREUZE, J. B.   Les Dessins de Greuze Conserves a l'Academie des Beaux-Arts de Saint-Petersbourg. Paris, 1922. Folio, plates. Quaritch 940-127 1974 £40

GREVE, FELIX PAUL   Oscar Wilde. Berlin, 1903. Fine, wrappers, text in German. Covent 51-2616 1973 £5.25

GREVE, FELIX PAUL   Oscar Wilde. Berlin, 1903. Wrappers, English first edition. Covent 56-2123 1974 £8.50

GREVILLE, CHARLES   On the Corundum Stone from Asia. N.P., c., 1798. 4to., boards. Hammond 201-402 1974 £15

GREVILLE, CHARLES CAVENDISH FULKE   The Greville Memoirs. 1874-87. 8vo., 8 vols., half brown morocco, gilt, orig. edition. Quaritch 936-405 1974 £30

GREVILLE, CHARLES CAVENDISH FULKE   Memoirs. 1874-87. First edition, 8 vols., 8vo., half blue morocco gilt, spines gilt tooled, gilt edges, some spotting, good copy. Sawyer 293-158 1974 £85

GREVILLE, FULKE, BARON BROOKE
Please turn to
BROOKE, FULKE GREVILLE, BARON

CAUTION: GREVILLE, FULKE, B. 1717 OR 18
              GREVILLE, CHARLES CAVENDISH FULKE, 1794-1865

GREVILLE, R. K.   Flora Edinensis. Edinburgh, 1824. 8vo., orig. cloth, plates. Wheldon 128-1194 1973 £10

GREVILLE, R. K.   Flora Edinensis. Edinburgh, 1824. 8vo., half calf, plates. Wheldon 129-996 1974 £10

GREVILLE, R. K.   Scottish Cryptogamic Flora. Edinburgh, 1823-28. 6 vols. in 3, roy. 8vo., half morocco, hand-coloured plates. Wheldon 128-1365 1973 £180

GREVILLE, R. K.   Scottish Cryptogamic Flora. Edinburgh, 1823-28. Roy 8vo., 6 vols., half green morocco gilt. Wheldon 129-20 1974 £240

GREW, NEHEMIAH   The Anatomy of Plants. London, 1682. Folio, early 19th century calf, plates, first edition. Traylen 79-23 1973 £160

GREW, NEHEMIAH   The Anatomy of Plants. 1682. 8vo., old calf, folio, plates. Bow Windows 64-779 1974 £250

GREW, NEHEMIAH   The Anatomy of Plants. London, 1682. Folio, contemporary calf, worn, plates, first edition. Schuman 37-110 1974 $500

GREW, NEHEMIAH   The Anatomy of Plants. 1682. Folio, plates, contemporary mottled calf, rare, nice complete copy. Wheldon 131-1148 1974 £280

GREW, NEHEMIAH   The Anatomy of Vegetables Begun. London, 1672. Small 8vo., modern half morocco, plates, first edition. Dawsons PM 250-35 1974 £360

GREW, NEHEMIAH   Musaeum Regalis Societatis. London, 1681. Folio, contemporary calf, worn, plates, first edition. Traylen 79-234 1973 £60

GREY, CHARLES HERVEY   Hardy Bulbs. (1937-1938). 3 vols., plates, drawings, first edition. Bow Windows 64-109 1974 £78

GREY, CHARLES HERVEY   Hardy Bulbs. 1937-38. 3 vols., roy. 8vo., orig. cloth, plates, complete set, extremely scarce, nice clean copy, orig. dust jackets. Wheldon 128-1468 1973 £70

GREY, CHARLES HERVEY   Hardy Bulbs. London, 1938. 3 vols., large 8vo., complete, fine, vol. 3 very scarce, orig. cloth. Gregory 44-145 1974 $150

GREY, GEORGE   Journals of Two Expeditions. London, 1841. 2 vols., 8vo., maps, plates, orig. cloth, unopened, faded, first edition. Bow Windows 62-401 1974 £210

GREY, RICHARD   Dr. R. Grey's Memoria Technica. Oxford, 1833. 12mo., contemporary boards. Bow Windows 66-302 1974 £6.50

GREY, RICHARD   Memoria Technica. London, 1730. Small 8vo., contemporary calf, first edition. Schuman 37-111 1974 $110

GREY, T. DE   The Compleat Horseman. London, 1651. Small 4to., old calf, rebacked. Quaritch 939-130 1974 £200

GREY, ZACHARY   Critical, Historical and Explanatory Notes on Shakespeare. London, 1754. 2 vols., 8vo., contemporary calf, scarce. Ximenes 33-123 1974 $125

GREY, ZANE   The Man of the Forest. New York, 1920. 8vo., orig. cloth, illus., inscription, first edition. Rota 190-486 1974 £6

GREY, ZANE   Tales of Lonely Trails. New York, 1922. First edition, lacking d.w., photos, orig. binding, bright, near pristine gilt, fine, scarce. Ross 87-432 1974 $25

GREY, ZANE   Tales of the Angler's Eldorado. London, 1926. 4to., illus., orig. cloth, plates, first edition. Bow Windows 62-402 1974 £11.50

GREY OWL 1888-1938   Sajo and Her Beaver People. London, 1935. Hood's 102-516 1974 £7.50

GRIER, WILLIAM   The Mechanic's Calculator. Glasgow, 1835. 12mo., orig. green cloth, second edition. Ximenes 33-124 1974 £12.50

GRIESINGER, THEODOR   The Jesuits. 1883. 2 vols., 8vo., orig. cloth, frontispiece, illus., library stamps, corners worn. Bow Windows 66-303 1974 £8.50

GRIESINGER, W.   Mental Pathology and Therapeutics. New York, 1882. Rittenhouse 46-304 1974 $15

GRIEVE, CHRISTOPHER MURRAY   The Islands of Scotland. 1939. Illus., author's signed inscription, fine, d.w., first edition. Covent 51-1208 1973 £12.50

GRIEVE, CHRISTOPHER MURRAY   Lucky Poet. London, 1943. Orig. binding, remarkably good condition. Ross 86-324 1974 $35

GRIEVE, CHRISTOPHER MURRAY   O Wha's Been Here Afore Me, Lass. 1931. One of 100 copies, numbered and signed by author, fine, first edition. Covent 51-1215 1973 £25

GRIEVE, CHRISTOPHER MURRAY   Scottish Scene, or, The Intelligent Man's Guide to Albyn. London, 1934. First edition, nice, orig. cloth. Crane 7-183 1974 £6

GRIEVE, CHRISTOPHER MURRAY   To Circumjack Cencrastus. 1930. English first edition. Covent 56-887 1974 £10.50

GRIEVE, MRS. MAUD   A Modern Herbal. 1931. 8vo., 2 vols., orig. cloth. Broadhurst 23-1127 1974 £18

GRIEVE, ROBERT   An Illustrated History of Pawtucket, Central Falls and Vicinity. Pawtucket, 1897. First edition, 4to., illus., hinges strengthened, binding scuffed, interior very good. Current BW9-421 1974 $32.50

GRIEVE, S.   The Great Auk. 1885. 4to., cloth, folding map, coloured plates, illus. Wheldon 128-464 1973 £20

GRIFFIN, APPLETON PRENTISS CLARK   List of Books Relating to Hawaii. Washington, 1898. Wrapper, scarce. Jenkins 61-1021 1974 $17.50

GRIFFIN, APPLETON PRENTISS CLARK   A List of Books on Samoa and Guam. Washington, 1901. Large 8vo., orig. buckram, uncut. Kraus B8-143 1974 $10

GRIFFIN, APPLETON PRENTISS CLARK   A List of Books . . . On the Philippine Islands in the Library of Congress. Washington, 1903. Large 8vo., orig. buckram, large paper copy, uncut. Kraus B8-142 1974 $56

GRIFFIN, APPLETON PRENTISS CLARK   Select List of Books Relating to the Far East. Washington, 1904. Large 8vo., orig. buckram, uncut. Kraus B8-144 1974 $10

GRIFFIN, GERALD   The Duke of Monmouth. Dublin, 1857. 8vo., embossed green cloth, rubbed. Emerald 50-368 1974 £7.50

GRIFFIN, GERALD   The Invasion. Dublin, n.d. 8vo., cloth boards. Emerald 50-369 1974 £7

GRIFFIN, H.   Alaska and the Canadian Northwest. New York, 1944. Hood's 103-64 1974 $10

GRIFFIN, MARTIN I. J.   Catholics and the American Revolution. 1907. 352 pages, limited. Austin 57-265 1974 $12.50

GRIFFIN, R. B.   The Chemistry of Paper-making. New York, 1894. Dark green cloth, illus. Dawson's 424-185 1974 $45

GRIFFINI, A.   Imenotteri. Milan, 1897. Post 8vo., cloth, scarce. Wheldon 129-646 1974 £7.50

GRIFFIS, WILLIAM ELLIOT   The Story of the Wallons. Houghton, 1923. 299p., illus. Austin 62-230 1974 $12.50

GRIFFIS, WILLIAM ELLIOT   The Story of the Walloons. 1923. 299 pages, illus. Austin 57-266 1974 $12.50

GRIFFITH, ACTON FREDERICK   Bibliotheca Anglo-Poetica. 1815. New buckram, rubber stamp, upper corner missing from first 6 leaves. Allen 216-1806. 1974 $35

GRIFFITH, ACTON FREDERICK   Bibliotheca Anglo-Poetica. London, 1815. 8vo., illus., modern boards, first edition. Dawsons PM 10-254 1974 £30

GRIFFITH, ACTON FREDERICK   Bibliotheca Anglo-Poetica. London, 1815. 8vo., illus., modern boards, first edition.   Dawsons PM 252-419 1974 £30

GRIFFITH, ELIZABETH   The Double Mistake. 1766. 8vo., cloth, first edition. Quaritch 936-95 1974 £10

GRIFFITH, ELIZABETH   The Morality of Shakespeare's Drama Illustrated. Dublin, 1777. 2 vols., 12mo., contemporary calf, gilt, first Dublin edition. Ximenes 33-125 1974 $40

GRIFFITH, ELIZABETH   The Platonic Wife. London, 1765. 8vo., modern boards, first edition.   Dawsons PM 252-420 1974 £15

GRIFFITH, ELIZABETH   The School for Rakes. 1769. 8vo., cloth, first edition. Quaritch 936-96 1974 £10

GRIFFITH, ELIZABETH   The School for Rakes. London, 1769. 8vo., quarter cloth, boards, first edition. Ximenes 33-126 1974 $27.50

GRIFFITH, ELIZABETH   The Times. 1780. 8vo., cloth, first edition. Quaritch 936-97 1974 £10

GRIFFITH, ELIZABETH   The Times. London, 1780. 8vo., wrappers, first edition. Ximenes 33-127 1974 $22.50

GRIFFITH, G. W. E.   My 96 Years in the Great West. (Los Angeles, 1929). Orig. cloth, scarce, first edition. Bradley 35-158 1974 $30

GRIFFITH, GEORGE   The Life and Adventures of George Wilson. 1854. 8vo., orig. cloth, gilt, fine. Hill 126-85 1974 £25

GRIFFITH, GEORGE   Sidelights on Convict Life. 1903. Orig. cloth, illus., English first edition. Covent 56-1683 1974 £15.75

GRIFFITH, J. E.   Flora. Bangor, n.d. 8vo., orig. cloth. Broadhurst 23-1108 1974 £6

GRIFFITH, J. E.   Pedigrees of Anglesey and Caernarvonshire Families. 1914. Roy folio, half calf, scarce. Broadhurst 23-1395 1974 £135

GRIFFITH, J. E.   Pedigrees of Anglesey and Caernarvonshire Families With Their Collateral Branches in Denbighshire, Monmouthshire and Other Parts. 1914. Roy. folio, half calf, rubbed, very scarce. Broadhurst 24-1424 1974 £150

GRIFFITH, J. E.   Portfolio of Photographs. 1900. Oblong folio, orig. cloth. Broadhurst 23-1394 1974 £5

GRIFFITH, J. W.   An Elementary Text-Book of the Microscope. 1864. 8vo., cloth, plates, scarce. Wheldon 130-108 1974 £5

GRIFFITH, J. W.   The Micrographic Dictionary. 1856. Engraved plates, some in colour, illus., demy 8vo., contemporary half morocco, marbled boards, spine rubbed, hinge weak. Broadhurst 24-1092 1974 £8

GRIFFITH, J. W.   The Micrographic Dictionary. 1875. 2 vols., 8vo., cloth, coloured & plain plates, third edition. Wheldon 128-32 1973 £15

GRIFFITH, J. W.   The Micrographic Dictionary. 1875. 2 vols., 8vo., cloth, plates, third edition. Wheldon 131-156 1974 £15

GRIFFITH, MARTHA ELEANOR   The Czechs in Cedar Rapids. 1944. 334 pages. Austin 57-267 1974 $10

GRIFFITH, RICHARD   Variety. 1782. 8vo., cloth, first edition. Quaritch 936-98 1974 £9

GRIFFITH, RICHARD   Variety. London, 1782. 8vo., modern wrappers, first edition. Ximenes 33-128 1974 $17.50

GRIFFITH, W.   Icones Plantarum Asiaticarum Part 4 Dicotyledonous Plants. Calcutta, 1854. Small folio, new cloth, plates. Wheldon 131-1298 1974 £60

GRIFFITHS, ARTHUR   Ford's Folly Ltd. 1900. Frontispice, orig. pictorial cloth. Covent 55-787 1974 £15

GRIFFITHS, ARTHUR   Memorials of Millbank and Chapters in Prison History. 1884. Orig. cloth gilt, illus. Howes 186-2113 1974 £5

GRIFFITHS, ARTHUR   Mysteries of Police and Crime. 1904. 3 vols., 8vo., orig. half roan, cloth sides faded, plates, illus. Bow Windows 66-304 1974 £18

GRIFFITHS, DAVID   Forage Conditions on the Northern Border of the Great Basin. Washington, 1902. Plates, wrapper, 4to., scarce. Jenkins 61-970 1974 $12.50

GRIGGS, F. L.   Modern Masters of Etching. 1926. Oblong 4to., boards, English first edition. Covent 56-1463 1974 £5.25

GRIGGS, W.   147 Examples of Armorial Book Plates. 1892. Crown 4to., orig. cloth backed pictorial boards, plates. Howes 185-698 1974 £10

GRIGORAKI, LEON   Contribution a Petude des Teignes. Lyons, 1928. Roy. 8vo., buckram. Wheldon 129-1219 1974 £5

GRIGORAKI, LEON   Recherches Cytologiques et Taxinomiques. Paris, 1925. Roy. 8vo., half morocco. Wheldon 129-1220 1974 £7.50

GRIGORIEFF, BORIS   Boui Bouis. (Berlin), 1924. Folio, orig. wrapper, uncut, illus. L. Goldschmidt 42-243 1974 $45

GRIGSON, GEOFFREY   The Arts To-Day. London, 1935. First edition, very nice copy, orig. cloth. Crane 7-3 1974 £10

GRIGSON, GEOFFREY   Before the Romantics. London, 1946. Biblo & Tannen 210-869 1973 $6.50

GRIGSON, GEOFFREY   Henry Moore. Harmondsworth, 1943. Oblong 8vo., wrappers, plates. Minters 37-156 1973 $10

GRILLPARZER, F.   Des Meeres un der Liebe Wellen. Leipzig, 1908. Orig. olive morocco, hinge repaired, 2 X 1 3/8 inches. Gregory 44-384 1974 $17.50

GRIMALDI, S.   Origines Genealogicae. 1828. 4to., uncut, boards. Quaritch 939-729 1974 £8.50

GRIMALKIN, or, The Rebel-Cat. London, 1681. Folio, fine, uncut, first edition. Ximenes 33-17 1974 $175

GRIME, J. H.   History of Middle Tennessee Baptists. (Nashville, 1902). Orig. cloth, illus., fine, first edition. Bradley 35-368 1974 $30

GRIMESTON, EDWARD   A Generall Historie of the Netherlands. London, 1608. Folio, contemporary calf, rebacked, first edition. Dawsons PM 251-28 1974 £75

GRIMM, BROTHERS   Household Stories. London, 1922. Biblo & Tannen 213-557 1973 $7.50

GRIMM, BROTHERS   Household Stories from the Collection of the Brothers Grimm. London, 1882. 4to., gilt lettering, illus. Frohnsdorff 16-242 1974 $85

GRIMM, THE BROTHERS   Fairy Tales. 1894. Drawings, second edition, fine, very bright orig. pict. cloth boards, attractive book. Covent 51-662 1973 £8.50

GRIMM, THE BROTHERS   Fairy Tales Translated from the German. New York, Boston, n.d. (c. 1890). Orig. colored plates, pictorial cloth, gilt, one corner bumped, illus., very good copy. Frohnsdorff 16-389 1974 $10

GRIMM, THE BROTHERS   Kinder- und Hausmarchen. Gutersloh, 1890. 16mo., pictorial boards, cloth spine, label, chromolithograph illus., board edges rubbed, very good copy. Frohnsdorff 16-393 1974 $12.50

GRIMWOOD, HERBERT   Introduction to Decorative Woodwork for the Use of Schools. 1936. Illus., cloth, presentation. Covent 55-446 1974 £8.50

GRINDLAY, R. M.   Scenery, Costumes and Architecture Chiefly on the Western Side of India. 1826-(1830). Folio, plates, half morocco gilt, fine. Quaritch 940-394 1974 £900

GRINDON, L. H.   The Manchester Flora.   1859. Crown 8vo.,
cloth, rebound, library stamps. Wheldon 128-1195 1973 £5

GRINKER, ROY R.   Neurology. London, 1937. Large 8vo., orig.
red cloth, second edition. Dawsons PM 249-214 1974 £5.50

GRINNELL, GEORGE BIRD   American Game Bird Shooting. New York,
(1910). Colored plates, full page portraits, first edition, 8vo., spine spotted, good.
Current BW9-184 1974 $20

GRINNELL, GEORGE BIRD   When Buffalo Ran. New Haven, 1920. 8vo.,
orig. bindings. Butterfield 8-702 1974 $10

GRINNELL, JOSEPH   The Game Birds of California. Berkeley, 1918.
Roy 8vo., cloth, gilt, plates. Hammond 201-647 1974 £24.50

GRINNELL, JOSEPH   Gold Hunting in Alaska. Elgin and Chicago,
(1901). Three quarter cloth. Hayman 57-268 1974 $15

GRISAR, H.   Roma Alla Fine del Mondo Antico Secondo le
Fonti Scritte E I Monumenti. 1943. 2 vols., sewn. Allen 213-445 1973 $25

GRISCOM, L.   The Distribution of Bird-Life in Guatemala.
New York, 1932. 8vo., maps, figures. Wheldon 128-465 1973 £7.50

GRISEBACH, A. H. R.   Flora of the West Indian Islands. (1859-)1864.
Roy 8vo., orig. cloth, rare. Wheldon 130-1160 1974 £45

GRISEBACH, A. H. R.   Genera et Species Gentianearum Adjectis
Observationibus Quibus dam Phytogeographicis. Stuttgart and Tubingen, 1839.
8vo., new cloth, rare. Wheldon 128-1111 1973 £15

GRISET, ERNEST   Griset's Grotesques. London, 1867. Tall
4to., full red polished calf, raised spine, gilt tooled, leather labels, marbled
endpapers, all edges gilt, orig. covers bound in, illus. are hand colored.
Frohnsdorff 15-71 1974 $100

GRISET, ERNEST   Griset's Grotesques; or, Jokes Drawn on Wood.
London, 1867. Tall 4to., full red polished calf, leather labels, orig. cloth cover
bound in, hand colored engravings, fine, first edition. Frohnsdorff 16-394
1974 $100

GRISMER, JOSEPH   Way Down East. 1928. Austin 51-378 1973
$10

GRISONS   Arttickel So Die Zwen Pundt. (Augsburg),
1523. Small 4to., modern half vellum, very fine, very rare. Schafer 8-114
1973 sFr. 950

GRISTON, HARRIS JAY   Shaking the Dust From Shakespeare. 1924.
Austin 51-379 1973 $12.50

GRISWOLD, FRANK GRAY   Old Madeiras. New York, 1929. Bds.,
vellum back, ltd. to 200 copies. Biblo & Tannen 213-1011 1973 $17.50

GRISWOLD, RUFUS W.   Poets and Poetry of America. 1877. Revised
edition. Allen 216-1506 1974 $10

GRISWOLD, RUFUS W.   The Republican Court. New York, 1867. New
edition, portraits, full leather, blindstamp on title page. Hayman 59-221 1974
$10

GROBER, KARL   Children's Toys of Bygone Days. London,
(1928). 4to., colored & plain plates, orig. cloth. Gregory 44-98 1974 $47.50

GROBERT, J. F. L.   Machine Pour Mesurer la Vitesse Initiale des
Mobiles de Differens Calibres, Projettes sous yous les Angles. Paris, 1804. 4to.,
orig. wrappers, uncut, unopened, folding plates, signed presentation copy.
Gurney 66-75 1974 £30

GROENWEGEN-FRANKFORT, H. A.   Art of the Ancient World. New York,
n.d. 4to., illus., fine, dust wrapper, English first edition. Covent 56-1462
1974 £6

GROFF, ROBERT A.   Manual of Diagnosis and Management of
Peripheral Nerve Injuries. Philadelphia, 1945. Rittenhouse 46-305 1974 $10

GROLLIER DE SERVIERE, NICOLAS   Recueil d'Onvrages Curieux de
Mathematique et de Mecanique, ou Description du Cabinet de Monsieur Grollier
de Serviere. Paris, 1751. Second edition, 4to., contemporary calf, copper
plates. Gurney 66-77 1974 £150

GROMORT, GEORGES   Jardins d'Espagne. Paris, 1926. 2 portfolios,
plates, folios. Gregory 44-146 1974 $85

GROMORT, GEORGES   Jardins d'Espagne. Paris, 1926. 2 vols., atlas
folio, loose sheets laid in 2 cloth backed marbled board portfolios. Wilson 63-318
1974 $67.50

GROMORT, GEORGES   Jardins d'Itolie. Paris, 1922. 2 vols., atlas
folio, loose sheets in cloth backed marbled boards, fine plates. Wilson 63-319
1974 $95

GRONOVIUS, JACOBUS   Thesaurus Graecarum Antiquitatum, in quo
Continentur Effigies Virorum ac Foeminarum Illustrium. Leyden, 1697-1702.
13 vols. in 12, plates, engravings, folio, contemporary vellum, brown & red
leather labels, plates, engravings. Kraus B8-417 1974 $785

GRONOVIUS, JOANNES FREDERICUS   Flora Orientalis Sive Recensio
Plantarum. Leyden, 1755. 8vo., old half vellum, rare. Wheldon 131-1299
1974 £150

GROOME, FRANCIS HINDES   Edward Fitzgerald. Portland, 1902. Small
4to., cloth-backed patterned boards, fine, unopened. Covent 55-677 1974
£27.50

GROOT, HUGO DE
Please turn to
GROTIUS, HUGO

GROSART, ALEXANDER B.   The Towneley Hall MSS. 1877. 4to., 2 vols.,
orig. blue cloth, fine. Dawsons PM 251-238 1974 £25

GROSE, FRANCIS   The Antiquarian Repertory. London, 1807.
Large 4to., 4 vols., contemporary half calf, boards, second edition. Dawsons
PM 251-29 1974 £110

GROSE, FRANCIS   The Antiquities of England and Wales. London,
(1783-97). Folio, 8 vols., nineteenth century black half morocco and cloth, new
edition. Dawsons PM 251-30 1974 £200

GROSE, FRANCIS   The Antiquities of England, Wales, Scotland and
Ireland. (c. 1790). 12 vols., roy. 4to., contemporary russia gilt, plates.
Quaritch 939-131 1974 £350

GROSE, FRANCIS   The Antiquities of Scotland. London, 1797.
4to., 2 vols., contemporary half calf, boards, worn, third edition. Dawsons
PM 251-31 1974 £35

GROSE, FRANCIS   Classical Dictionary of the Vulgar Tongue.
1796. New buckram, third edition. Allen 216-1396 1974 $15

GROSE, FRANCIS   Lexicon Balatronicum. N.P., 1811. Orig.
leather edition. Austin 61-437 1974 $37.50

GROSE, FRANCIS   Military Antiquities. London, 1786-88. 4to.,
2 vols., contemporary russia, first edition. Dawsons PM 251-384 1974 £90

GROSE, FRANCIS   Military Antiquities. London, 1801. 4to., 2
vols., modern brown buckram, second edition. Dawsons PM 251-385 1974 £85

GROSE, FRANCIS   A Treatise on Ancient Armour and Weapons.
London, 1785. 4to., contemporary tree calf, rebacked, first edition. Dawsons
PM 251-386 1974 £40

GROSE, HOWARD B.   Aliens of Americans? 1906. 337 pages,
illus. Austin 57-269 1974 $12.50

GROSE, HOWARD B.   Aliens or Americans? 1906. 337p., illus.
Austin 62-231 1974 $12.50

GROSS, BEN   I Looked and I Listened. Random House, 1954.
344p. Austin 51-380 1973 $8.50

GROSS, EMANUEL   Hops in Their Botanical, Agricultural and
Technical Aspect. 1900. Illus., scarce. Howes 186-1438 1974 £7.50

GROSS, H.   Die Wichtigeren Handels. Esslingen, 1880.
Small folio, orig. cloth backed dec. boards. Wheldon 129-1656 1974 £12

GROSS, H.   Die Wichtigeren Handelspflanzen in Bild und
Wort. Esslingen, 1880. Small folio, orig. cloth backed dec. boards, plates.
Wheldon 131-1782 1974 £12

GROSS, MILT   De Night in de Front from Chreesmas. New
York, (1927). First edition, 12mo., orig. pictorial cover, profusely illus.
Current BW9-45 1974 $28.50

GROSS, MILT   Dear Dollink. Putnam, 1945. 160p., illus.
Austin 54-459 1973 $6.50

GROSS, MILT   Nize Baby. Doran, 1926. 207p., illus.
Austin 54-460 1973 $6.50

GROSS, SAMUEL DAVID   Autobiography. Philadelphia, 1887. 2 vols.,
thick large 8vo., cloth, gilt. Rittenhouse 46-306 1974 $45

GROSS, SAMUEL DAVID   Lives of Eminent American Physicians and
Surgeons of the 19th Century. Philadelphia, 1861. Thick large 8vo., cloth,
first edition. Rittenhouse 46-308 1974 $65

GROSS, SAMUEL DAVID   A Practical Treatise on Foreign Bodies in the
Air-Passages. Philadelphia, 1854. 8vo., orig. cloth, rebacked, first edition.
Dawsons PM 249-215 1974 £85

GROSS, SAMUEL WEISSELL   A Practical Treatise on Tumors of the Mammary
Gland. New York, 1880. Engravings. Rittenhouse 46-309 1974 $12

GROSS, SIDNEY WILLIAM 1904-   Diagnosis and Treatment of Head Injuries.
New York, 1940. Dust jacket. Rittenhouse 46-310 1974 $10

GROSSER, MICHAEL DE   Phosphorentia Adamantum Novis Experimentis
Illustrata. 1777. 8vo., contemporary grey boards, first edition. Dawsons PM
245-350 1974 £25

GROSSETESTE, ROBERT   Epistolae. 1861. Thick roy. 8vo., orig.
half roan, frontispiece. Howes 186-1178 1974 £9

GROSSI, TOMASO   Marco Visconti. London, 1845. 2 vols. in 1,
12mo., orig. red dec. cloth, gilt, first edition. Ximenes 33-129 1974 $17.50

GROSSMAN, EDWINA B.   Edwin Booth. Century, 1884. 292p., illus.
Austin 51-381 1973 $12.50

GROSSMITH, WEEDON   From Studio to Stage Reminiscences. Lane,
1913. 371p., illus. Austin 51-382 1973 $12.50

GROSVENOR, GILBERT   The Book of Birds. Washington, (1937).
2 vols., illus., orig. cloth, first edition. Bradley 35-431 1974 $25

GROSVENOR, GILBERT   The Book of the Birds. Washington, 1937.
2 vols., photos, plates in color, spines slightly darkened, orig. binding, first
edition, near mint. Ross 87-433 1974 $17.50

GROSVENOR HOUSE   Catalogue of the Pictures at Grosvenor House.
1821. Folio, plates, etchings, contemporary half leather, rubbed. Quaritch
940-129 1974 £16

GROSZ, GEORGE   Abrechnung Folgt! Berlin, 1923. Pictorial
wrappers, nice copy, cartoons. Covent 51-123 1973 £40

GROSZ, GEORGE   Drawings. New York, 1944. 4to., 52 plates,
1st ed. Biblo & Tannen 214-115 1974 $47.50

GROTE, GEORGE   History of Greece to Close of Generation
Contemporary With Alexander the Great. 1884. 12 vols. Allen 213-447
1973 $30

GROTE, HARRIET   Memoir of the Life of Ary Scheffer. London,
1860. 8vo., orig. grey cloth, first edition. Ximenes 33-130 1974 $12.50

GROTH, PAUL HEINRICH VON Physikalische Krystallographie. Leipzig, 1885.
8vo., contemporary half calf, second edition. Dawsons PM 245-351 1974 £15

GROTH, PAUL HEINRICH VON   Physikalische Krystallographie. Leipzig, 1895.
8vo., orig. cloth, third edition. Dawsons PM 245-352 1974 £10

GROTIUS, HUGO   De Iure Belli ac Pacis Libri Tres. Frankfurt-
on-Main, 1626. 8vo., contemporary vellum, woodcut, rare second edition.
Harper 213-87 1973 $475

GROTIUS, HUGO   Hugo Grotius, His Most Choice Discourses.
London, 1669. 12mo., contemporary calf, worn, rare, fourth English edition.
Ximenes 33-131 1974 $75

GROULX, LIONEL   Chez nos Ancetres. Montreal, 1920. Wrappers,
second edition. Hood's 102-710 1974 $12.50

GROULX, LIONEL   La Naissance d'Une Race. Montreal, 1919.
Wrappers. Hood's 102-711 1974 $17.50

GROUT, A. J.   Mosses With Hand-Lens and Microscope. New
York, (1903). 4to., three quarter leather and buckram, drawings, inscribed.
Butterfield 10-425 1974 $45

GROVE, FREDERICK   A Search for America. 1928. 391 pages.
Austin 57-270 1974 $10

GROVE, FREDERICK P.   A Search for America. Carver, 1928.
Austin 62-232 1974 $10

GROVE, GEORGE   Dictionary of Music and Musicians. 1940.
6 vols., large 8vo., plates, orig. half morocco, revised fourth edition. Howes
185-342 1974 £20

GROVE, GEORGE   Grove's Dictionary of Music and Musicians.
1929-40. 6 vols, orig. cloth, plates, fourth edition. Smith 193-143 1973 £15

GROVE, W. B.   The British Rust Fungi. Cambridge, 1913.
8vo., cloth, scarce. Wheldon 129-1221 1974 £5

GROVE, W. B.   British Stem- and Leaf-Fungi. Cambridge,
1935-37. 8vo., 2 vols., cloth. Wheldon 129-1222 1974 £12

GROVES, H.   Toronto Does Her "Bit". Toronto, 1918.
Photographs, card cover. Hood's 103-106 1974 $7.50

GROVES, J.   The British Charophyta. 1920-25. 2 vols.,
8vo., cloth, scarce, plates. Wheldon 131-1411 1974 £20

GROWOLL, ADOLF   The Profession of Book Selling. New York,
1913. 8vo., boards, scarce. Goodspeed's 578-464 1974 $15

GROWOLL, ADOLPH   Three Centuries of English Booktrade
Bibliography. 1903. New buckram, plates. Allen 216-182 1974 $12.50

GRUBE, HERMAN   De Ictu Tarantulae. Frankfurt, 1679. 12mo.,
boards. Gurney 64-100 1974 £20

GRUEL, LEON   Manuel Historique et Bibliographique de
l'Amateur de Reliures. Paris, 1887-1905. 2 vols., 4to., plates, half dark red
morocco, orig. wrappers, limited. Quaritch 940-600 1974 £250

GRUELLE, JOHNNY   The Cruise of the Rickety-Robin. Chicago,
1931. Folio, pictorial paper wrappers, color illus. Frohnsdorff 16-399 1974 $25

GRUELLE, JOHNNY   Johnny Gruelle's Golden Book. Chicago &
New York, (1929). Large 4to., pictorial boards, cloth spine, edges rubbed.
Frohnsdorff 16-400 1974 $10

GRUISEN, N. L. VAN   A Holiday in Iceland. 1879. Demy 8vo.,
plates of orig. mounted photos, orig. cloth, fine. Broadhurst 24-1616 1974 £6

GRUNEBERG, CHRISTIAN   Pandora Mathematicarum Tabularum. Frankfurt,
1684. 12mo., contemporary vellum. Schuman 37-112 1974 $85

GRUNEWALD, MATTHIAS   Le Retable d'Isenheim. 1932. Folio. Allen
213-1905 1973 $10

GRUNPECK, JOSEPH   Ein Spiegel der Naturlichen Himlischen und Prophetischen Sehungen Aller Trubsalen. Nuremberg, 1508. Small folio, old manuscript vellum leaf, woodcuts, first German edition, fine copy. Schafer 10-88 1974 sFr 4,200

GRYLLS, R. GLYNN   Mary Shelley. 1938. Frontispiece, buckram, presentation copy, English first edition. Covent 56-1171 1974 £12.50

GRYLLS, R. GLYNN   Mary Shelley: A Biography. 1938. Coloured frontis., portraits, buckram, fine, d.w., presentation copy from author, bookplate, first edition. Covent 51-1690 1973 £6

GSELL, P.   Auguste Rodin - Die Kunst. Munich, 1920. Large 8vo., boards, plates. Minters 37-122 1973 $10

GUALANDI, DOMENICO   Descriptio duorum non Communium Morborum Corporis. 1839. Large 8vo., orig. wrappers. Dawsons PM 249-216 1974 £15

THE GUARDIAN. Glasgow, 1746. 2 vols., 12mo., contemporary calf, red labels, fine, signature. Dawsons PM 252-423 1974 £24

GUARINI, GIOVANNI BATTISTA   Il Pastor Fido. Venice, 1590. Small 4to., old calf, rebacked, stains, first edition. Thomas 28-258 1972 £75

GUARINI, GIOVANNI BATTISTA   Il Pastor Fido. London, 1676. 8vo., contemporary calf, engraving. Dawsons PM 252-424 1974 £45

GUATTINI, MICHEL ANGELO DE   Relation Curieuse et Nouvelle d'un Voyage de Congo. Lyons, 1680. 12mo., old calf, rebacked, first edition, scarce. Ximenes 36-112 1974 $225

GUBERNATIS, A. DE   Ricordi Biografici. Florence, 1872. 4to., half leather. Kraus B8-84 1974 $25

GUDIO, MARQUARDO   Antiquae Inscriptiones Quum Graecae. 1731. Folio, contemporary vellum, gilt, first edition. Dawsons PM 251-147 1974 £55

GUEGUEN, F.   Les Champignons Parasites. Paris, 1904. 8vo., cloth, plates. Wheldon 129-1223 1974 £10

GUENTHER, K.   Der Darwinismus und die Probleme des Lebens. 1905. 8vo., boards, cloth back. Wheldon 131-292 1974 £5

GUENTHER, K.   A Naturalist in Brazil. 1931. Roy 8vo., cloth, plates, scarce. Wheldon 130-283 1974 £10

GUENTHER, K.   A Naturalist in Brazil. 1931. Roy. 8vo., cloth, plates, scarce. Wheldon 128-201 1973 £10

GUERARD, ALBERT   Art for Art's Sake. Boston, 1936. Biblo & Tannen 210-215 1973 $7.50

GUERANGER, P. L. P.   Sainte Cecile et la Societe Romaine. Paris, 1874. Imp. 8vo., orig. half morocco, gilt, illus. Howes 185-1049 1974 £5

GUERIN, EUGENIE DE   Un Cahier Inedit du Journal d'Eugenie de Guerin. Paris, 1911. 16mo., half brown morocco, gilt, uncut, first edition. L. Goldschmidt 42-245 1974 $15

GUERIN, EUGENIE DE   Lettres. Paris, 1914. 2 vols., 12mo., three quarter dark brown morocco, gilt, uncut. L. Goldschmidt 42-244 1974 $20

GUERIN, PAUL   Les Petits Bollandistes Vies des Saints de l'Ancien et du Nouveau Testament. Paris, 1888-87. 20 vols., thick roy. 8vo., contemporary half calf. Howes 185-893 1974 £75

GUERIN-MENEVILLE, F. E.   Iconographie du Regne Animal. Paris and London, 1829-44. 8vo., 3 vols., half calf, plates. Wheldon 130-26 1974 £100

GUERINIERE, M. DE LA   Elemens de Cavalerie. Bruxelles, 1791. Orig. blank wrappers, plates, uncut. Hayman 57-269 1974 $42.50

GUERNSEY, ORRIN   History of Rock County. Janesville, 1856. Orig. cloth, plates, gilt, scarce, first edition. Bradley 35-407 1974 $80

GUERY, SUZANNE   La Philosophie de Somerset Maugham. Paris, 1933. Wrappers, English first edition. Covent 56-1923 1974 £8.40

GUEST, E.   History of English Rhythms. 1882. Ex-library. Allen 216-1447 1974 $12.50

GUETTARD, M.   Nouvelle Collection de Memoires sur Differentes Parties Interessantes des Sciences et Arts. Paris, 1786. 4to., sewn, plates. Wheldon 131-157 1974 £10

GUEVARA, ANTONIO DE   Le Livre Dore de Marc Aurele Empereur. Paris, 1569. Small 8vo., glazed calf, gilt, labels. L. Goldschmidt 42-56 1974 $175

GUEZ, JEAN LOUIS, SIEVR DE BALZAC
Please turn to
BALZAC, JEAN LOUIS GUEZ, SIEVR DE

GUHL, E.   The Life of the Greeks and Romans. London, n.d. 8vo., illus., diced purple morocco, gilt, first English edition. Dawsons PM 251-32 1974 £10

GUICCIARDINI, FRANCESCO   Della Istoria d'Italia. 1738. Folio, 2 vols., contemporary calf, gilt. Dawsons PM 251-240 1974 £105

GUICCIARDINI, FRANCESCO   The Histoire of Guicciardin. London, 1579. 4to., contemporary vellum, woodcut, first English edition. Dawsons PM 250-36 1974 £290

GUICCIARDINI, FRANCESCO   The Historie of Guicciardin. 1599. 4to., nineteenth century half calf, boards, second English edition. Dawsons PM 251-239 1974 £110

GUICHENOT, A.   Exploration Scientifique de l'Algerie, 1840-42. Histoire Naturelle des Reptiles et des Poissons. Paris, 1850. Imp. 4to., new half morocco, plates, rare. Wheldon 131-746 1974 £50

GUIDE de L'Etranger. Paris, 1827. Small 8vo., contemporary paper boards, plates. Bow Windows 62-959 1974 £6.50

A GUIDE To Hillsboro, Kansas. Hillsboro, 1940. 12mo., wrapper, 91 pages. Saddleback 14-421 1974 $20

GUIDE to Quebec and the Lower St. Lawrence. Quebec, 1882. Wrappers. Hood's 102-713 1974 $15

GUIDE to Quebec and the Lower St. Lawrence. Quebec, 1882. Wrappers. Hood's 104-914 1974 $15

A GUIDE to Zionism. New York, 1920. Biblo & Tannen 213-636 1973 $8.50

GUIDICCI, MARIO   Discorso delle Comete. Florence, 1619. Small 4to., half leather, exlibris of Hans Ludendorff and Prince Pietro Ginori Conti, first edition. Schumann 500-18 1974 sFr 8,000

GUIDOTT, THOMAS   A Collection of Treatises. London, 1725. 8vo., 19th century half calf, plates, second edition. Gurney 64-101 1974 £25

GUIDOTT, THOMAS   A Collection of Treatises Relating to City and Waters of Bath. 1725. 8vo., calf, gilt. Quaritch 939-538 1974 £15

GUIDOTT, THOMAS   A Discourse of Bathe, and the Hot Waters There. London, 1676. 8vo., full panelled calf, gilt, first edition. Hammond 201-573 1974 £80

GUIDOTT, THOMAS   De Thermis Britannicis. London, 1691. 4to., contemporary panelled calf, rebacked, gilt, first edition. Hammond 201-572 1974 £75

GUIFFREY, JULES   Histoire Generale des Arts Appliques a l'Industrie. C., 1905. Folio, half blue morocco, gilt, illus. Hammond 201-403 1974 £18.50

GUIGARD, JOANNIS   Armorial Du Bibliophile. Paris, 1870-73. 2 vols. in 1, large 8vo., contemporary dark green half morocco gilt, orig. wrappers. Dawsons PM 10-257 1974 £50

GUILDAY, PETER   A History of the Councils of Baltimore. 1932. Orig. edition. Austin 57-271 1974 $10

GUILANDINI, MELCHIOR 1520-1589   Melchrois Gvilandini Borvssi. 1558. 2 works in 1 vol., small 4to., calf antique. Bow Windows 62-403 1974 £100

GUILES, FRED L.   Norma Jean. McGraw-Hill, 1969. 373p.,
illus. Austin 51-383 1973 $7.50

GUILLAUME, G.   Architectural Views & Details of Netley Abbey.
Southampton, 1848. Folio, orig. roan backed boards, plates.   Smith 194-259
1974 £12

GUILLAUME, G.   Architectural Views and Details of Netley
Abbey. Southampton, 1848. Small folio, cloth.   Quaritch 939-373 1974 £26

GUILLEMARD, FRANCIS HENRY HILL   The Cruise of the Marchesa to
Kamschatka and New Guinea. 1886. 2 vols., 8vo., orig. cloth, gilt, plates,
maps, scarce. Wheldon 131-358 1974 £40

GUILLEMEAU, JACQUES   Child-Birth, or, the Happy Delivery of Women.
London, 1635. 2 parts in 1 vol., 4to., old boards, woodcuts, rare, second
edition in English. Schuman 37-113 1974 $475

GUILLEMIN, AMEDEE   Electricity and Magnetism. 1891. Orig.
cloth, illus., rubbed, fine. Covent 55-1303 1974 £15

GUILLEMIN, AMEDEE   The Forces of Nature. 1877. Illus., third
edition. Covent 55-1304 1974 £15

GUILLIE, SEBASTIEN   Essai sur l'Instruction des Aveugles. Paris,
1820. 8vo., orig. speckled boards, uncut, fine. Dawsons PM 249-217 1974
£24

GUILLIERMOND, A.   Les Levures. Paris, 1912. Crown 8vo., cloth,
scarce. Wheldon 129-1224 1974 £5

GUILLIERMOND, A.   Recherches Cytologiques sur les Levures et
Quelques Moisissures a Formes Levures. Lyons, 1902. Roy. 8vo., cloth, plates.
Wheldon 131-1412 1974 £5

GUILLIM, JOHN   A Display of Heraldry. London, 1679. Folio,
eighteenth century half calf, gilt, illus., fifth edition. Hammond 201-427 1974
£35

GUILLIM, JOHN   A Display of Heraldry. London, 1724. 6th
ed., folio, rebound in modern cl., illus. Jacobs 24-146 1974 $90

GUILLIM, JOHN   A Display of Heraldry. London, 1724. Folio,
contemporary calf, worn, sixth edition. Dawsons PM 251-119 1974 £85

GUILLIM, JOHN   A Display of Heraldry. 1724. Folio, red
morocco gilt, plates, sixth and best edition. Quaritch 939-730 1974 £35

GUILTY, or not Guilty. The True Story of Manhattan Well. New York, 1870.
Orig. cloth, first edition, fine. MacManus 224-194 1974 $25

GUINEY, LOUIS IMOGEN   The White Sail and Other Poems. Boston,
(1887). Orig. cloth, spine faded, first edition, inscribed copy, very good.
MacManus 224-195 1974 $25

GUINN, J. M.   A History of California and An Extended History
of Its Southern Coast Counties. Los Angeles, 1907. 2 vols., 4to., three
quarter leather. Saddleback 14-123 1974 $45

GUINN, J. M.   A History of California and An Extended History
of Los Angeles and Environs. Los Angeles, 1915. 3 vols., 4to., cloth, illus.,
rebound. Saddleback 14-121 1974 $50

GUINN, J. M.   A History of California and An Extended History
of Los Angeles and Environs. Los Angeles, 1915. 3 vols., 4to., three quarter
leather, illus. Saddleback 14-122 1974 $60

GUIOL   Essai sur la Composition et l'Ornement des
Jardins. Paris, 1818. 12mo., orig. blue printed wrappers, plates. Ximenes
33-133 1974 $85

GUISLAIN, JOSEPH   Traite sur les Phrenopathies. 1833. 8vo., contemporary marbled boards. Dawsons PM 249-218 1974 £24

GUITRY, SACHA 1885-   If I Remember Right. Methuen, 1935. Illus.
Austin 51-385 1973 $7.50

GUITRY, SACHA 1885-   If Memory Serves. 1935. Illus. Austin 51-384
1973 $6.50

GUITRY, SACHA 1885-   Pasteur. Paris, 1919. Wrappers, label, first
edition. Covent 55-789 1974 £5.25

GUIZOT, FRANCOIS   De la Democratie en France. Paris, 1849.
8vo., orig. wrapper, uncut, first edition. L. Goldschmidt 42-247 1974 $35

GUIZOT, FRANCOIS   Histoire de la Revolution d'Angleterre. Paris,
1841. 8vo., 2 vols., black morocco-backed boards, second edition. Dawsons
PM 251-241 1974 £10

GUIZOT, FRANCOIS   The History of Civilization. London, 1851.
Small 8vo., 3 vols., green morocco, labels. Dawsons PM 251-242 1974 £12

GUIZOT, FRANCOIS   The History of Civilization from the Fall of the
Roman Empire to the French Revolution. New York, 1877. 4 vols. in 2,
Biblo & Tannen 213-677 1973 $10

GULICK, SIDNEY L.   The American Japanese Problem. 1914.
Illus. Austin 57-272 1974 $17.50

GULICK, SIDNEY L.   The American Japanese Problem. Scribners,
1914. 349p., illus. Austin 62-234 1974 $22.50

GULIELMINI, DOMINICO   De Salibus Dissertatio Epistolaris. 1705. 8vo.,
contemporary mottled sheep, first edition. Dawsons PM 249-219 1974 £45

GULL, WILLIAM WITHEY   A Collection of the Published Writings. 1864-
96. 8vo., 2 vols., orig. cloth. Dawsons PM 249-220 1974 £10

GUMILLA, J.   El Orinoco Ilustrado. Madrid, n.d. 8vo.,
half calf. Wheldon 129-273 1974 £12.50

GUMMERE, FRANCIS B.   The Popular Ballad. Boston, 1907. First
edition, orig. binding. Wilson 63-519 1974 $18.75

GUMPERT, MARTIN   First Papers. 1941. Austin 62-236 1974
$8.50

GUMUCHIAN AND COMPANY   Catalogue de Reliures du XVe au XUXe
Siecle, en Vente a la Librairie Gumuchian & Cie. Paris, (c. 1929). 4to.,
plates, illus., marbled boards, parchment back. Quaritch 940-601 1974 £55

THE GUN at Home and Abroad. 1913. Roy. 4to., plates, morocco gilt, foxed,
limited. Quaritch 939-132 1974 £35

GUNCKEL, JOHN E.   The Early History of the Maumee Valley. Toledo,
1902. New cloth, rebound. Hayman 57-567 1974 $10

GUNN, EDWIN   Economy in House Design. Westminster, 1932.
4to., cloth, illus. Minters 37-536 1973 $12.50

GUNN, GLENN DILLARD   Music: Its History and Enjoyment. New York,
1939. Biblo & Tannen 214-854 1974 $7.50

GUNSTON, DANIEL   Jemmy Twitcher's Jests. Glasgow, 1798.
12mo., 19th century half morocco, rubbed, very rare, very good copy. Ximenes
36-113 1974 $150

GUNTER, ARCHIBALD CLAVERING   The Ladies Juggernaut. 1895. Orig.
pictorial boards, illus., English first edition. Covent 56-2149 1974 £5.25

GUNTER, EDMUND   The Description and Use of the Sector, Cross-
Staffe, and other Instruments. London, 1636. 4to., contemporary calf, second
edition. Dawsons PM 245-354 1974 £90

GUNTHER, ALBERT   Catalogue of Fishes in the British Museum.
1859-70. 8 vols., 8vo., new cloth, rare, orig. issue. Wheldon 128-632 1973
£45

GUNTHER, ALBERT   Catalogue of the Acanthopterygian Fishes in the
Collection of the British Museum. 1859-1870. 8 vols., foxing, stains, worn.
Bow Windows 64-110 1974 £45

GUNTHER, ALBERT   Catalogue of the Batrachia Salientia in the
British Museum. 1858. 8vo., orig. cloth, plates, scarce. Wheldon 131-747
1974 £7.50

GUNTHER, ALBERT   The Gigantic Land-Tortoises in the Collection of the British Museum. 1877. 4to., new buckram, lithographed plates, rare. Wheldon 128-633 1973 £50

GUNTHER, ALBERT   The Gigantic Land-Tortoises. 1877. 4to., new buckram, plates, rare. Wheldon 130-693 1974 £50

GUNTHER, ALBERT   The Gigantic Land-Tortoises in the Collection of the British Museum. 1877. 4to., new buckram, plates, rare. Wheldon 131-748 1974 £35

GUNTHER, ALBERT   Handbuch der Ichthyologie. Vienna, 1886. 8vo., cloth, scarce. Wheldon 130-695 1974 £7.50

GUNTHER, ALBERT   An Introduction to the Study of Fishes. Edinburgh, 1880. 8vo., modern half calf. Wheldon 131-749 1974 £14

GUNTHER, JOHN   Inside Europe. London, 1936. Half morocco, slipcase. Jenkins 48-224 1973 $200

GUNTHER, ROBERT WILLIAM THEODORE   Early British Botanists. Oxford, 1922. Roy. 8vo., orig. cloth, illus., plates. Wheldon 129-148 1974 £35

GUNTHER, ROBERT WILLIAM THEODORE   Historic Instruments for the Advancement of Science. London, 1925. Paper covers. Rittenhouse 46-313 1974 $10

GUNTHER, ROBERT WILLIAM THEODORE   A History of the Daubeny Laboratory. 1904. 8vo., 3 vols., orig. red cloth gilt. Dawsons PM 245-355 1974 £7

GUNTHER, SIEGMUND   Geschichte der Anorganischen Naturwissenchaften im Neunzehten Jahrhundert. Berlin, 1901. Thick roy. 8vo., contemporary half morocco, rubbed. Schuman 37-114 1974 $55

GUNTON, S.   The History of the Church of Peterburgh. London, 1686. Folio, old calf, illus. Quaritch 939-503 1974 £25

GURLEY, L. B.   Memoir of Rev. William Gurley. Cincinnati, 1861. Cloth. Hayman 57-383 1974 $12.50

GURLEY, P. D.   The Voice of the Rod: A Sermon Preached in the New York Avenue Presbyterian Church, Washington, D. C. Washington, 1865. Wrapper, inscribed & signed by author. Jenkins 61-781 1974 $10

GURLEY, RALPH RANDOLPH   Life of Jehudi Ashmun, Late Colonial Agent in Liberia. Washington, 1835. Shaken, front pages loose, cloth covers spotted, scarce. Butterfield 10-105 1974 $40

GURLEY, RALPH RANDOLPH   Life of Jehudi Ashmun, Late Colonial Agent in Liberia. Washington, 1835. 8vo., contemporary tree calf, fine copy, portrait, first edition. Ximenes 37-100 1974 $85

GURLT, ERNST JULIUS   Leitfaden fur Operationsubungen am Cadaver. Berlin, 1862. Small 8vo., orig. pictured cloth-backed boards, first edition. Schuman 37-115 1974 $35

GURNALL, W.   The Christian In Compleat Armour. London, 1656-58. Small thick 4to., half 19th century calf. Smith 194-155 1974 £25

GURNEY, J. H.   Early Annals of Ornithology. 1921. 8vo., cloth, illus., very scarce. Wheldon 128-107 1973 £7.50

GURNEY, J. H.   Rambles of a Naturalist. (1876). 8vo., cloth. Wheldon 129-474 1974 £7.50

GURNEY, JOSEPH JOHN   Familiar Letters to Henry Clay of Kentucky, Describing a Winter in the West Indies. New York, 1840. Orig. binding. Butterfield 10-106 1974 $35

GURNEY, JOSEPH JOHN   Notes on a Visit Made to See Some of the Prisons. 1819. Small 8vo., contemporary calf. Quaritch 939-840 1974 £45

GURNEY, THOMAS   Brachygraphy. 1825. 8vo., old calf, plates. Bow Windows 64-528 1974 £9.50

GURNEY, THOMAS   Brachygraphy. London, 1835. Small 8vo., half calf, gilt, plates, portrait. Hammond 201-404 1974 £10

GUSSOW, H. T.   Mushrooms and Toadstools. Ottawa, 1927. 4to., cloth, plates, scarce. Wheldon 130-1286 1974 £7.50

GUTHRIE, JAMES   A Biography by. London, 1932. Large 4to., plates, illus., orig. cloth, faded. Bow Windows 62-404 1974 £5

GUTHRIE, JAMES   The Elf. 1904. Linen-backed dec. boards, English first edition. Covent 56-575 1974 £10.50

GUTHRIE, JAMES   The Elf; a Sequence of the Seasons: Summer. 1902. One of 250 copies, drawings & dec. by author, cloth backed dec. boards, fine, first edition. Covent 51-835 1973 £8.50

GUTHRIE, THOMAS   The Traveling Companions. 1892. Illus. Austin 61-440 1974 £12.50

GUTHRIE, THOMAS ANSTEY   A Bayard from Bengal. London, 1902. 8vo., illus., inscribed, orig. cloth, first edition. Dawsons PM 252-15 1974 £18

GUTHRIE, THOMAS ANSTEY   The Brass Bottle. London, 1900. 8vo., orig. cloth, uncut, rubbed, first edition. Dawsons PM 252-16 1974 £20

GUTHRIE, THOMAS ANSTEY   Love Among the Lions. n.d. Orig. pictorial cloth gilt, illus., fine. Covent 55-32 1974 £5.25

GUTHRIE, THOMAS ANSTEY   Vice Versa or a Lesson to Fathers. London, 1882. 12mo., cloth, back faded, first edition. Goodspeed's 578-116 1974 $35

GUTHRIE, THOMAS MABERLY   The Statement of Stella Maberly. 1896. Frontispiece, orig. dec. buckram, English first edition. Covent 56-1794 1974 £25

GUTHRIE, TYRONE   A Life In the Theatre. McGraw, Hill, 1959. 357p. Austin 51-386 1973 $6

GUTHRIE, Oklahoma. Guthrie, 1906. Pict. wrappers. Jenkins 61-2026 1974 $17.50

GUTS-MUTHS, JOHANN CHRISTOPH FRIEDRICH   Anviisning til at Dreie. 1802. Small 8vo., contemporary marbled boards. Zeitlin 235-279 1974 $38.50

GUY, P. L. O.   New Light from Armageddon. Chicago, 1931. Biblo & Tannen 210-1000 1973 $15

GUYOT, ARNOLD   The Earth and Man. 1850. Illus., fine. Covent 55-1305 1974 £6.50

GUYTON DE MORVEAU, L. B.   Rapport Fait au nom d'Une Commission Speciale Chargee de l'Executif, Concernant le Mode d'Affermer le Canal du Midi. (Paris), 1797. 8vo., unbound, uncut, unopened. Gurney 66-78 1974 £16

GWALTHER, RUDOLF   Von der Heiligen Gschrifft und Jrem Ursprung. (Zurich, 1553). 8vo., boards, first edition. Schafer 8-115 1973 sFr. 600

GWIN, W. M.   Speech of Mr. Gwin of California on the Bill to Establish a Railway to the Pacific. Washington, 1853. Jenkins 61-974 1974 $25

GWYNN, DANIEL   Proceedings of a General Court-Martial. Dublin, 1788. 8vo., modern boards, first edition. Dawsons PM 251-387 1974 £15

GWYNN, STEPHEN   Irish Books and Irish People. 1919. 120 pages. Austin 61-441 1974 £10

GWYNN, STEPHEN   The Life of the Rt. Hon. Sir Charles W. Dilke. 1917. 2 vols., orig. cloth, plates. Howes 186-775 1974 £10

GYVENIMAS, JO   Kuningas Vladislavas Dembskis. 1916. Illus. Austin 57-277 1974 $27.50

H

H., B.   The Children's Garden. 1913. Printed in
black and red, 8vo., orig. paper wrappers, fine. Sawyer 293-41 1974 £125

H., D.   The Walls Do Not Fall. 1944. 8vo., orig.
cloth, stiff wrappers, first edition. Rota 189-438 1974 £5

H.D.
Please turn to
DOOLITTLE, HILDA

HAAST, J. VON   Geology of the Provinces of Canterbury and
Westland, New Zealand. 1879. 8vo., half calf, plates, maps. Wheldon
131-1012 1974 £40

HABBEN, F. H.   London Street Names. London, 1896. 1st ed.
Biblo & Tannen 213-678 1973 $15

HABERLY, LOYD   Anne Boleyn and Other Poems. 1934. 4to.,
full morocco, uncut, limited edition. Broadhurst 23-1050 1974 £45

HACHISUKA, M. U.   A Handbook of the Birds of Iceland. 1927.
Roy. 8vo., cloth, map, plates, folding diagram, scarce. Wheldon 128-468
1973 £7.50

HACK, MARIA   Harry Beaufoy. 1821. First edition, engraved
frontispiece, 12mo., orig. boards, roan spine, good copy, trifle rubbed. George's
610-339 1973 £10

HACK, MARIA   Stories of Animals, Intended for Children,
Between Five and Seven Years Old. 1820. First edition, engraved plates, very
rare, square 16mo., orig. marbled boards, roan spine. George's 610-340 1973
£25

HACK, MARIA   Winter Evenings. 1819-20. 4 vols., 12mo.,
orig. boards, roan spine, engraved frontispiece, good, clean internally. George's
610-341 1973 £15

HACK, MARIA   Winter Evenings, or, Tales of Travellers. New
York & Philadelphia, 1851. 12mo., gilt pictorial cloth, spine ends worn, first
American edition, engravings. Frohnsdorff 16-404 1974 $17.50

HACKER, A. E.   Official Souvenir Program, City of Toronto
Diamond Jubilee of Confederation Celebration. Toronto, 1927. Illus.,
112 pages. Hood's 104-689 1974 $15

HACKET, JOHN   Scrina Reserata: A Memorial Offer'd to the
Great Deservings of John Williams. 1693. Folio, contemporary panelled calf
gilt, joints neatly repaired, handsome copy, armorial rococo bookplate of Benj.
Hyett of Painswick House, large paper, portrait, ad leaf at end. Thomas 32-142
1974 £25

HACKETT, FRANCIS   The Green Lion. 1936. 8vo., orig. cloth,
2 vols., wrappers, first edition. Rota 190-488 1974 £7.50

HACKETT, JOHN   Select and Remarkable Epitaphs. London, 1757.
12mo., 2 vols., contemporary calf, first edition. Dawsons PM 251-120 1974
£20

HACKETT, W. T. G.   A Background of Banking Theory. Toronto,
1945. Hood's 104-351 1974 $10

THE HACKNEY Coachmens Case. (1711). Folio, disbound. Quaritch
939-217 1974 £10

HADAMARD, J.   Lecons sur le Calcul des Variations. Paris, 1910.
8vo., blue buckram. Dawsons PM 245-357 1974 £7

HADDEN, J. CUTHBERT   The Operas of Wagner. 1908. Plates, fine.
Covent 55-1350 1974 £6.50

HADDON, A. C.   Actiniaria of Torres Straits. Dublin, 1898.
4to., wrappers, plates. Wheldon 131-932 1974 £7.50

HADER, BERTA   The Cat and the Kitten. New York, 1940.
Square 4to., pictorial cloth, illus., mint, orig. d.j., first edition. Frohnsdorff
16-405 1974 $15

HADFIELD, J. A.   Psychology and Morals. New York, 1929.
Biblo & Tannen 213-966 1973 $7.50

HADFIELD, R. A.   Metallurgy and Its Influence On Modern
Progress. 1925. Presentation, inscribed, plates. Covent 55-1432 1974 £12.50

HADFIELD, R. A.   Metallurgy and Its Influence on Modern
Progress. (1925). Plates, limp morocco. Covent 55-1431 1974 £12.50

HAEBLER, K.   Typenrepertorium der Wiegendrucke. Leipzig,
1905-24. 5 vols. in 3, cloth. Dawsons PM 11-369 1974 £57.50

HAENEL, E.   Der Sachsischen Kurfursten Turnierbucher in
Ihren Hervorragendsten Darstellungen. 1910. Oblong 4to., plates, unbound
in orig. half cloth, portfolio. Quaritch 940-696 1974 £40

HAESAERTS, PAUL   Renoir. New York, 1947. Folio, plates.
Biblo & Tannen 210-328 1973 $12.50

HAFEN, LE ROY R.   Broken Hand. Denver, 1933. 1st revised ed.
Dykes 24-218 1974 $15

HAFEN, LEROY R.   The Overland Mail. Cleveland, 1926. Illus.
Jenkins 61-976 1974 $85

HAFENREFFER, SAMUEL   Aussfuhrlicher Bericht. 1640. Small 4to.,
plates, disbound. Zeitlin 235-104 1974 $85

HAFNER, JEAN-JACQUES   Compositions de Jardins . . . Garden
Compositions. Paris, 1931. First edition, 4to., plates laid in printed boards,
text in French and English, bookplate, orig. binding. Wilson 63-320 1974 $10

HAGAN, JAMES   One Sunday Afternoon. French, 1933. 122p.
Austin 51-387 1973 $6.50

HAGEDOORN, A. L.   The Relative Value of the Processes Causing
Evolution. The Hague, 1921. Roy 8vo., cloth. Wheldon 130-111 1974 £7.50

HAGEM, O.   Untersuchungen uber Norwegische Mucorineen.
1908-10. Roy 8vo., buckram. Wheldon 129-1227 1974 £5

HAGEMAN, G. E.   Sketches From the History of the Church.
n.d., ca. 1920. 289p., illus. Austin 62-240 1974 $15

HAGENBECK, C.   Beasts and Men. 1909. 8vo., cloth, illus.,
portrait, scarce orig. issue. Wheldon 128-278 1973 £5

HAGENBECK, C.   Beasts and Men. 1911. Roy 8vo., cloth, illus.,
frontispiece. Wheldon 130-166 1974 £5

HAGGARD, HENRY RIDER   Allan Quatermain. 1887. Illus., English first
edition. Covent 56-577 1974 £8.50

HAGGARD, HENRY RIDER   Allan Quatermain. London, 1887. 8vo., orig.
cloth, first edition, frontis., plates, illus. Bow Windows 62-407 1974 £25

HAGGARD, HENRY RIDER   Allan's Wife and Other Tales. 1917. Illus.
Austin 61-442 1974 $10

HAGGARD, HENRY RIDER   The Ancient Allan. 1920. Crown 8vo., plates,
first edition. Howes 186-221 1974 £7.50

HAGGARD, HENRY RIDER   Ayesha. 1905. Orig. cloth, first English
edition. Rota 188-386 1974 £5

HAGGARD, HENRY RIDER   Ayesha. 1905. Orig. dec. cloth gilt, plates,
first edition. Howes 186-222 1974 £7.50

HAGGARD, HENRY RIDER   Belshazzar. (1930). Crown 8vo., orig. cloth,
first edition. Howes 186-223 1974 £7.50

HAGGARD, HENRY RIDER   Belshazzar. 1930. 306 pages. Austin
61-443 1974 $10

HAGGARD, HENRY RIDER   Fair Margaret. 1907. Illus., first edition.
Howes 186-225 1974 £5

HAGGARD, HENRY RIDER   Finished. 1917. Crown 8vo., frontis., first edition. Howes 186-226 1974 £8.50

HAGGARD, HENRY RIDER   A Gardener's Year. 1905. Illus., 404 pages. Austin 61-444 1974 $17.50

HAGGARD, HENRY RIDER   A Gardener's Year. 1905. Plates, faded, first edition. Covent 55-794 1974 £12.50

HAGGARD, HENRY RIDER   Heart Of the World. 1894. 347 pages. Austin 61-445 1974 $10

HAGGARD, HENRY RIDER   The Holy Flower. 1915. Plates, orig. cloth gilt, fine, English first edition. Covent 56-584 1974 £25

HAGGARD, HENRY RIDER   King Solomon's Mines. London, 1885. 8vo., orig. cloth, uncut, first edition. Dawsons PM 252-426 1974 £38

HAGGARD, HENRY RIDER   The Lady of Blossholme. 1909. Orig. green pictorial cloth, illus.., first edition. Howes 186-228 1974 £7.50

HAGGARD, HENRY RIDER   The Lady of Blosshome. London, 1909. First edition. Biblo & Tannen 210-604 1973 $17.50

HAGGARD, HENRY RIDER   The Lady of Blossholme. 1909. Illus., near fine, English first edition. Covent 56-585 1974 £15

HAGGARD, HENRY RIDER   The Mahatma and the Hare. 1911. Fine, illus., first U.S. edition. Covent 56-587 1974 £25

HAGGARD, HENRY RIDER   The Mahatma and the Hare. London, 1911. 8vo., plates, orig. cloth, fine, first edition. Dawsons PM 252-427 1974 £95

HAGGARD, HENRY RIDER   Maiwa's Revenge. 1888. Faded, bookplate, first edition. Covent 55-795 1974 £8.50

HAGGARD, HENRY RIDER   Maiwa's Revenge. 1888. Crown 8vo., orig. grey boards, first edition. Howes 186-229 1974 £7.50

HAGGARD, HENRY RIDER   Marie. 1912. Orig. cloth, plates, first edition. Howes 186-230 1974 £7.50

HAGGARD, HENRY RIDER   Mr. Meeson's Will. 1888. Orig. pictorial cloth, plates, first edition. Howes 186-233 1974 £7.50

HAGGARD, HENRY RIDER   Mr. Meeson's Will. 1888. Plates, orig. pictorial cloth gilt, covers little dusty, very nice copy, ads at end, first edition. Covent 51-838 1973 £15

HAGGARD, HENRY RIDER   Mr. Meeson's Will. 1888. Orig. pictorial cloth, illus., faded. Covent 55-796 1974 £15

HAGGARD, HENRY RIDER   Mr. Meeson's Will. 1888. Orig. pictorial cloth, plates, first issue. Covent 56-588 1974 £50

HAGGARD, HENRY RIDER   Montezuma's Daughter. 1893. Crown 8vo., orig. bevelled cloth gilt, plates, first edition. Howes 186-231 1974 £5.50

HAGGARD, HENRY RIDER   Moon of Israel. 1918. Crown 8vo., orig. cloth, first edition. Howes 186-232 1974 £7.50

HAGGARD, HENRY RIDER   Queen of the Dawn. (1925). Crown 8vo., orig. cloth, scarce, first edition. Howes 186-234 1974 £10

HAGGARD, HENRY RIDER   Queen Sheba's Ring. 1910. Crown 8vo., orig. red cloth, frontis., first edition. Howes 186-235 1974 £7.50

HAGGARD, HENRY RIDER   Queen Sheba's Ring. 1909. Illus., 326 pages. Austin 61-446 1974 $10

HAGGARD, HENRY RIDER   Red Eve. (1911). Crown 8vo., orig. pictorial red cloth gilt, plates, first edition. Howes 186-236 1974 £6.50

HAGGARD, HENRY RIDER   Regeneration. London, 1910. 8vo., orig. maroon cloth, fine, inscribed, first edition. Dawsons PM 252-428 1974 £70

HAGGARD, HENRY RIDER   She. 1887. Crown 8vo., orig. cloth gilt, frontis., scarce, first edition. Howes 186-237 1974 £12.50

HAGGARD, HENRY RIDER   She. Paris, 1920. Wrappers, numbered, faded, unopened. Covent 55-793 1974 £35

HAGGARD, HENRY RIDER   Smith and the Pharaohs and Other Tales. 1921. Fine, rubber stamp, English first edition. Covent 56-590 1974 £25

HAGGARD, HENRY RIDER   The Witch's Head. n.d. Orig. cloth, faded, frontis. Covent 55-797 1974 £10.50

HAGGARD, HENRY RIDER   The Wizard. New York, 1896. First American edition. Biblo and Tannen 214-725 1974 $15

HAGGARD, HOWARD W.   Devils, Drugs, and Doctors. London, n.d. 8vo., orig. cloth, gilt, plates, illus. Hammond 201-541 1974 £5

HAGGARD, HOWARD W.   Devils, Drugs, and Doctors. London, (1929). 8vo., orig. orange cloth. Dawsons PM 249-223 1974 £10

HAGGARD, HOWARD W.   The Lame, the Halt, and the Blind. New York and London, 1932. 8vo., orig. red cloth, first American edition. Dawsons PM 249-224 1974 £10

HAGGARD PARODY. 1887. 8vo., English first edition. Covent 56-592 1974 £25

HAGUENOT, HENRI H.   Tractatus de Morbis. Avignon, 1751. 12mo., contemporary limp boards. Schuman 37-116 1974 $85

HAHN-HAHN, IDA VON   Ulrich. 1845. 2 vols., square 12mo., contemporary half calf gilt, first English edition. Howes 186-240 1974 £5

HAHNEMANN, SAMUEL CHRISTIAN FRIEDRICH   Doctrine et Traitement Homoeopathique des Maladies Chroniques. Paris, 1832. 8vo., 2 vols., rebacked, contemporary half calf, first edition in French. Dawsons PM 249-225 1974 £30

HAHNEMANN, SAMUEL CHRISTIAN FRIEDRICH   Etudes de Medecine Homoeopathique. Paris, 1855. 8vo., 2 vols., orig. wrappers, uncut, unopened. Dawsons PM 249-226 1974 £25

HAHNEMANN, SAMUEL CHRISTIAN FRIEDRICH   Fragmenta de Viribus. Leipzig, 1805. 8vo., old boards, calf, rebacked, first edition. Gurney 64-103 1974 £120

HAHNEMANN, SAMUEL CHRISTIAN FRIEDRICH   Organon der Ratio-Nellen Heilkunde. Dresden, 1810. 8vo., old boards, cloth box, very fine, rare first edition. Gilhofer 61-31 1974 sFr. 11,000

HAIG-BROWN, R.   Return to the River. London, 1943. Illus. Hood's 104-555 1974 $10

HAIG BROWN, W.   Charterhouse Past & Present. 1879. Plates, contemporary hard grained morocco, rubbed. Smith 194-280 1974 £5

HAIGHT, C.   Life In Canada Fifty Years Ago. Toronto, 1885. Orig. card covers, plates. Hood's 103-212 1974 $30

HAIGHT, MRS. R. K.   Letters from the Old World. New York, 1840. 2 vols., fine, orig. binding. Butterfield 10-47 1974 $25

HAIGHT, WALTER L.   Racine County in the World War. (Racine, c.1920.) 8vo., cloth, 607 pages. Saddleback 14-762 1974 $25

HAKE, T.   The Life & Letters of Theodore Watts-Dunton. 1916. 2 vols., illus., orig. cloth, scarce. Marsden 37-508 1974 £12

HAKEWILL, 'JAMES   The History of Windsor and its Neighbourhood. 1813. Imp. 4to., half morocco, plates. Quaritch 939-300 1974 £30

HAKEWILL, JAMES   A Picturesque Tour of the Island of Jamaica. 1825. Small folio, morocco gilt, fine, first edition. Bow Windows 64-531 1974 £2,250

HAKLUYT, RICHARD   The Principal Navigations Voyages Traffiques & Discoveries of the English Nation. London, Toronto & New York, 1927-28. 10 vols., 8vo., illus. orig. cloth, fine. Dawsons PM 250-37 1974 £80

HALBLEIB, A. J.   The Autobiography of a Fallen "Christ."
Haltina, 1927. 143p. Austin 62-241 1974 $10

HALDANE, R. B.   Universities and National Life. 1911. Bookplate, second edition. Covent 56-593 1974 £5.25

HALE, EDWARD E.   Kanzas and Nebraska. Boston - New York, 1854.
8vo., orig. bindings. Butterfield 8-177 1974 $35

HALE, G. E.   Magnetic Observations of Sunspots. Washington, 1938. 4to., 2 vols., orig stiff paper wrappers. Bow Windows 64-532
1974 £12.50

HALE, KATHERINE   Legends of the St. Lawrence. (Montreal, 1926).
Pictured in colour. Hood's 102-714 1974 $25

HALE, KATHERINE   Legends of the St. Lawrence. Montreal, 1926.
Illus. Hood's 104-163 1974 $25

HALE, LUCRETIA P.   Fagots for the Fireside. Houghton, 1888.
274p. Austin 54-462 1973 $10

HALE, LUCRETIA P.   The Last of the Peterkins, With Others of Their
Kin. Boston, 1886. 12mo., cloth, illus., very good copy, first edition.
Frohnsdorff 16-412 1974 $30

HALE, LUCRETIA P.   The Peterkin Papers. Boston, 1880. 12mo.,
cloth, illus. by F. G. Atwood, covers little worn, nice copy, first edition.
Frohnsdorff 16-413 1974 $75

HALE, LUCRETIA P.   The Peterkin Papers. Boston & New York,
(1914). 8vo., gilt pictorial cloth, illus. Frohnsdorff 16-414 1974 $15

HALE, LUCRETIA P.   The Peterkin Papers. Boston & New York,
(1924). 8vo., cloth, pictorial cover label, color plates, first edition. Frohnsdorff
16-415 1974 $10

HALE, MATTHEW   A Letter of Advice to His Grand-Children.
1816. First edition, engraved portrait, 12mo., orig. boards, paper label, edges
uncut, good. George's 610-342 1973 £5.25

HALE, MATTHEW   Magnetismus Magnus. London, 1695. 8vo.,
contemporary calf, rebacked, first edition. Dawsons PM 245-359 1974 £125

HALE, MATTHEW   The Primitive Origination of Mankind. London,
1677. Folio, contemporary calf, rebacked, first edition. Dawsons PM 245-358
1974 £95

HALE, MATTHEW   A Short Treatise Touching Sheriffs Accompts.
1683. 2 parts in 1 vol., 8vo., old sheep. Quaritch 939-133 1974 £60

HALE, SALMA   Annals of the Town of Keene. Concord, 1826.
8vo., quarter cloth, first edition. Ximenes 33-135 1974 $35

HALE, SARAH   The Genius of Oblivion. Concord, 1823.
12mo., contemporary sheep, first edition. Ximenes 33-136 1974 $45

HALE, THOMAS   A Compleat Body of Husbandry. London,
1756. Folio, illus., contemporary calf, first edition. Dawsons PM 247-139
1974 £90

HALES, STEPHEN   Haemastatique, ou la Statique des Animaux.
1744. 4to., contemporary mottled sheep, gilt, first edition in French. Dawsons
PM 249-227 1974 £125

HALES, STEPHEN   Statical Essays. London, 1769. 8vo., 2 vols.,
calf, plates. Gurney 64-104 1974 £85

HALES, STEPHEN   Statical Essays. London, 1731-33. 2 vols.,
8vo., contemporary calf, leather labels, plates, first & second editions.
Traylen 79-235 1973 £260

HALES, STEPHEN   Vegetable Staticks. London, 1727. 8vo.,
contemporary panelled calf, plates, fine, first edition. Dawsons PM 250-38
1974 £235

HALES, WILLIAM   Irish Pursuits of Literature. Dublin, 1799.
8vo., half calf. Emerald 50-379 1974 £12.50

HALEY, J. EVETTS   Charles Goodnight, Cowman and Plainsman.
Boston, New York, 1936. Cloth, illus. Dykes 24-142 1974 $50

HALEY, J. EVETTS   Jeff Milton, a Good Man with a Gun. Norman,
1948. Ist ed., cloth, illus; inscribed by Haley and with a small orig. pen and ink
drawing by Bugbee. Dykes 24-143 1974 $85

HALEY, J. EVETTS   A Log of the Texas-California Cattle Trail,
1854. Austin, 1932. Blue printed wrappers, scarce. Jenkins 61-980 1974 $60

HALFORD, F. M.   The Dry-Fly Man's Handbook. 1913. 8vo.,
orig. buckram, plates, first edition. Wheldon 131-751 1974 £20

HALFPENNY, JOSEPH   Fragmenta Vetusta. York, 1807. Imp. 4to.,
half russia, plates. Quaritch 939-597 1974 £30

HALFPENNY, JOSEPH   Fragmenta Vetusta. York, 1807. 4to., full
contemporary diced russia gilt, rebacked, plates, inscribed, presentation. Howes
186-2230 1974 £45

HALFPENNY, JOSEPH   Gothic Ornaments in the Cathedral Church of
York. 1795. Imp. 4to., half calf. Quaritch 939-598 1974 £25

HALFPENNY, WILLIAM   Practical Architecture. (London), 1724.
12mo., contemporary calf, fine, first edition. Ximenes 33-137 1974 $175

HALHED, NATHANIEL BRASSEY   A Grammar of the Bengal Language. Bengal,
1778. 4to., red morocco, worn. Thomas 28-327 1972 £75

HALHED, NATHANIEL BRASSEY   Testimony of the Authenticity of the
Prophecies of Richard Brothers. London, 1795. 8vo., disbound, first edition.
Ximenes 33-138 1974 $25

HALIBURTON, THOMAS CHANDLER   The Clockmaker. 1872. Illus., orig.
edition. Austin 54-463 1973 $12.50

HALIBURTON, THOMAS CHANDLER   The English in America. London, 1851.
2 vols., orig. covers. Hood's 103-536 1974 $150

HALIBURTON, THOMAS CHANDLER   A General Description of Nova Scotia.
Halifax, 1825. New edition, illus., map, three quarter leather, mottled covers,
inscribed. Hood's 102-190 1974 $225

HALIBURTON, THOMAS CHANDLER   An Historical and Statistical Account of
Nova-Scotia. Halifax, 1829. 2 vols., raised bands, illus. Hood's 103-176
1974 $250

HALIBURTON, THOMAS CHANDLER   The Letter Bag of the Great Western.
London, 1840. First edition. Hood's 104-208 1974 $65

HALIBURTON, THOMAS CHANDLER   The Letter Bag of the Great Western.
London, 1840. First edition. Hood's 102-191 1974 $65

HALIBURTON, THOMAS CHANDLER   Traits of American Humour. London,
1852. 3 vols., 8vo., orig. cloth, fine, first edition. Ximenes 33-139 1974
$175

HALIFAX, GEORGE SAVILE, MARQUIS OF   A Character of King Charles the
Second. 1750. Contemporary calf, rubbed, first edition. Howes 186-881
1974 £12

HALIFAX, GEORGE SAVILE, MARQUIS OF   Miscellanies. London, 1700.
8vo., contemporary panelled calf, rebacked, first edition. Dawsons PM 251-
332 1974 £45

HALIFAX, GEORGE SAVILE, MARQUIS OF   Observations on a Late Libel.
London, 1681. Folio, grey green wrappers, first edition. Dawsons PM 251-333
1974 £12

HALL, A. D.   The Book of the Tulip. 1929. 8vo., cloth,
coloured plates, scarce. Wheldon 128-1469 1973 £5

HALL, ANNA MARIA FIELDING   Pilgrimages to English Shrines. London, 1853.
8vo., orig. cloth, illus., fine, first edition. Ximenes 33-140 1974 $22.50

HALL, BASIL   Travels in North America. Edinburgh, 1829. Crown 8vo., quarter calf, boards, first edition. Broadhurst 23-1646 1974 £40

HALL, BASIL   Travels in North America in the Years 1827 and 1828. Edinburgh, 1829. Folding map in colour, first edition, 3 vols., crown 8vo., newly bound quarter calf, marbled boards, with ads at end. Broadhurst 24-1619 1974 £42

HALL, BAYARD RUSH   The New Purchase. New York, 1843. 2 vols., 12mo., orig. boards, first edition. Ximenes 33-141 1974 $75

HALL, E. EDWIN   A Hab and Naboth: or, The United States and Mexico, a Discourse. New Haven, 1847. Jenkins 61-1593 1974 $10

HALL, F.   Travels in Canada and the United States. 1819. 8vo., contemporary straight grained morocco, second edition. Bow Windows 64-533 1974 £54

HALL, FREDERIC   The History of San Jose. San Francisco, 1871. 8vo., cloth. Saddleback 14-124 1974 $95

HALL, G. STANLEY   Adolescence. New York, 1904. 2 vols. Biblo & Tannen 213-967 1973 $15

HALL, H. R.   Babylonian and Assyrian Sculpture in the British Museum. Paris, 1928. 4to., plates, fine. Covent 55-103 1974 £25

HALL, H. R.   A Season's Work at Ur: Al-'Ubaid, Abu Shahrain and Elsewhere. 1930. Illus., maps, crown 4to., orig. cloth, binding slightly spotted. Broadhurst 24-1620 1974 £6

HALL, J. S.   The Book of the Feet. n.d. Small 8vo., orig. cloth, illus., plates, second edition. Quaritch 940-714 1974 £25

HALL, JAMES   A History of the Town and Parish of Nantwich in the County Palatine of Chester. Nantwich, 1883. Plates, illus., limited edition, demy 4to., half brown calf, very fine copy, bevelled marbled boards, with list of subscribers. Broadhurst 24-1425 1974 £35

HALL, JAMES   Legends of the West. New York, 1854. 8vo., orig. bindings, frontispiece, worn. Butterfield 8-295 1974 $15

HALL, JAMES   Notes on the Western States. Philadelphia, 1838. Orig. cloth, slightly foxed. Jenkins 61-982 1974 $45

HALL, JAMES   Sketches of History, Life, and Manners in the West. Philadelphia, 1835. 2 vols., foxed, orig. cloth, chipped. Jenkins 61-983 1974 $100

HALL, JOSEPH   The Great Mysteries of Godliness. London, 1652. 12mo., contemporary calf, first edition. Ximenes 33-142 1974 $75

HALL, JOSEPH   The Works. 1837-39. 12 vols., 8vo., contemporary calf, rubbed. Howes 185-1246 1974 £70

HALL, MANLY PALMER   Healing. Los Angeles, 1944. Biblo & Tannen 213-912 1973 $7.50

HALL, MARSHALL   On the Mimoses. London, 1818. 8vo., contemporary half calf, rebacked, first edition. Dawsons PM 249-228 1974 £50

HALL, MARY BEEBE   Reminiscences of Elyria, Ohio. N.P., 1900. 8vo., cloth. Saddleback 14-617 1974 $15

HALL, PRESCOTT F.   Immigration. 1906. 393 pages. Austin 57-281 1974 $12.50

HALL, PRESCOTT F.   Immigration and its Effect Upon the U. S. Holt, 1906. Austin 62-243 1974 $12.50

HALL, R.   Hope Foundry, Bury. 1853-(1906). 9 vols., illus., dampstaining. Quaritch 939-421 1974 £185

HALL, RADCLYFFE   The Master of the House. London, 1932. 8vo., orig. parchment backed cloth, signed, fine, limited. Bow Windows 62-411 1974 £24

HALL, ROBERT   An Address to the Public . . . the Renewal of the Charter of the East India Company. London, 1813. 8vo., orig. wrappers, fine, first edition. Ximenes 33-143 1974 $30

HALL, ROBERT GREAM   An Essay on the Rights of the Crown. 1830. Roy. 8vo., calf, rebacked, scarce. Howes 186-2183A 1974 £12.50

HALL, S. C.   The Baronial Halls. London, 1858. 2 vols., folio, full contemp. mor., gilt., plates. Jacobs 24-43a 1974 $50

HALL, S. C.   Book of British Ballads. 1853. 4to., new buckram, illus. Allen 216-86 1974 $12.50

HALL, S. C.   The Book of the Thames from Its Rise to Its Fall. n.d. Large square 9vo., wood engraving, orig. cloth gilt. Smith 194-283 1974 £6.50

HALL, S. C.   A Week at Killarney. 1858. Engraved plates, illus., maps, first edition, f'cap 4to., good copy, orig. cloth. Broadhurst 24-1426 1974 £10

HALL, SAM S.   Wild Wolf. New York, 1884. Self wrappers. Hayman 57-706 1974 $12.50

HALL, MRS. SAMUEL CARTER
Please turn to
HALL, ANNA MARIA FIELDING

HALL, T. F.   Has the North Pole Been Discovered? Boston & Toronto, 1917. Maps, diagrams, ex-library. Hood's 103-65 1974 $12.50

HALL, T. Y.   Treatises on Various British and Foreign Coal and Iron Mines and Mining. Newcastle, 1853-54. Roy 8vo., half morocco. Broadhurst 23-1233 1974 £50

HALL, W.   The History of the Glove Trade. 1834. Crown 8vo., cloth, paper label. Quaritch 940-719 1974 £44

HALL, WILLIAM   A Biography of David Cox. 1881. Orig. cloth, worn, portrait. Marsden 39-95 1974 £7.50

HALLACK, CECILY   Candlelight Attic. 1925. 8vo., orig. cloth, fine, dust wrapper, first edition. Rota 190-838 1974 £5

HALLAM, H.   View of the State of Europe During the Middle Ages. London, 1818. 2 vols., 4to., contemporary calf, inscription, worn, first edition. Bow Windows 62-412 1974 £12

HALLAM, HENRY   Introduction to the Literature of Europe. 1839-40. 4 vols., half maroon straight grain morocco, gilt. Howes 186-241 1974 £20

HALLAM, HENRY   Introduction to the Literature of Europe. 1847. 3 vols., full contemporary calf, gilt, labels. Howes 185-209 1974 £24

HALLAM, HENRY   Introduction to Literature of Europe in 15th-17th Centuries. 1873. 3 vols., half morocco, fifth edition. Allen 216-1810 1974 $15

HALLBAUM, FRANZ   Der Lanschaftsgarten . . . Sein Enstehen und Seine Einfuhrung in Deutschland Durch Friedrich Ludwig von Schell, 1750-1823. Munchen, 1927. 4to., illus., orig. binding. Wilson 63-321 1974 $10

HALLE, JEAN-NOEL   Recherches sur la Nature et les Effets du Mephitisme des Fosses d'Aisance. Paris, 1785. 8vo., orig. wrappers, fine, first edition. Dawsons PM 249-230 1974 £16

HALLECK, FITZ-GREENE   Alnwick Castle. New York, 1845. 12mo., orig. quarter violet cloth, boards. Ximenes 33-144 1974 $7.50

HALLECK, FITZ-GREENE   Fanny. New York, 1839. 12mo., orig. brown cloth, worn. Ximenes 33-145 1974 $20

HALLER, ALBRECHT VON   Disputationes ad Morborum. Lausanne, 1757-60. 7 vols., 4to., contemporary mottled calf, plates, first edition. Schuman 37-117 1974 $145

HALLER, ALBRECHT VON   The Poems. London, 1794. 12mo., rebacked, contemporary calf. Gurney 66-79 1974 £20

HALLER, ALBRECHT VON   Versuch Schweizerischer Gedichte. Danzig, 1743. 8vo., wrappers, uncut, frontis. Schumann 499-48 1974 sFr 585

HALLER, ALBRECHT VON   Versuch Schweizerischer Gedichte. Bern, 1772. 12mo., contemporary half calf. Schuman 37-118 1974 $75

HALLERVORDT, JOHANN   Bibliotheca Curiosa in Qua Plurimi Rarissimi a Tque Paucis Cogniti Scriptores. Konigsberg & Frankfurt, 1676. Small 4to., contemporary vellum. Dawsons PM 10-263 1974 £50

HALLEY, EDMOND   Correspondence and Papers. Oxford, 1937. 8vo., plates, cloth. Dawsons PM 11-376 1974 £5

HALLEY, EDMOND   Correspondence and Papers of. London, 1937. 8vo., cloth, frontispiece. Dawsons PM 245-362 1974 £5

HALLEY, EDMOND   Miscellanea Curiosa. London, 1708. 8vo., 3 vols., contemporary calf, gilt, fine. Dawsons PM 245-361 1974 £135

HALLEY, ROBERT   Lancashire. Manchester, 1869. 2 vols., orig. cloth, scarce. Howes 185-1248 1974 £12

HALLGREN, MAURITZ   Landscape of Freedom. 1941. 444 pages. Austin 57-290 1974 $10

HALLIDAY, ANDREW   Observations on Emphysema. London and Edinburgh, 1807. 8vo., orig. boards, uncut, first edition. Dawsons PM 249-231 1974 £42

HALLIWELL-PHILLIPPS, JAMES ORCHARD   An Account of the Only Known Manuscript of Shakespeare's Plays. Smith, 1843. Austin 51-388 1973 $12.50

HALLIWELL-PHILLIPPS, JAMES ORCHARD   Catalogue of Proclamations, Broadsides, Ballads and Poems. 1851. 4to., cloth, rebacked. Quaritch 939-419 1974 £30

HALLIWELL-PHILLIPPS, JAMES ORCHARD   Dictionary of Archaic and Provincial Words. Smith, 1846. Austin 51-389 1973 $47.50

HALLIWELL-PHILLIPPS, JAMES ORCHARD   A Dictionary of Archaic and Provincial Words. 1852. 2 vols., 4to., cloth, limited edition. Quaritch 939-134 1974 £25

HALLIWELL-PHILLIPPS, JAMES ORCHARD   Dictionary of Archaic and Provincial Words, Obsolete Phrases, Proverbs, etc., from the 14th Century. 1878. 2 vols., half calf, worn. Allen 216-1397 1974 $15

HALLIWELL-PHILLIPPS, JAMES ORCHARD   The Merry Tales of the Wise Men of Gotham. London, 1840. 12mo., orig. wrappers, first edition. Ximenes 33-146 1974 $17.50

HALLIWELL-PHILLIPPS, JAMES ORCHARD   Morte Arthure. Brixton Hill, 1847. 4to., orig. violet cloth, first edition. Ximenes 33-147 1974 $45

HALLIWELL-PHILLIPPS, JAMES ORCHARD   Nugae Poeticae. London, 1844. 12mo., orig. purple cloth, first edition. Ximenes 33-148 1974 $35

HALLIWELL-PHILLIPPS, JAMES ORCHARD   Nursery Rhymes and Nursery Tales. (c. 1870). Large paper, med. 8vo., orig. quarter roan, rubbed, cloth sides, faded. George's 610-346 1973 £5.50

HALLIWELL-PHILLIPPS, JAMES ORCHARD   Popular Rhymes and Nursery Tales. 1849. Austin 61-447 1974 $12.50

HALLOCK, CHARLES   The Fishing Tourist. New York, 1873. Orig. binding. Butterfield 10-252 1974 $10

HALLS, JOHN JAMES   Two Months in Arrah in 1857. 8vo., orig. dark green cloth, fine, first edition. Ximenes 33-149 1974 $22.50

HALM UND GOLDMANN   Sales Catalogue Verzeichnis der Radierungen Von E. M. Lilien. n.d. Square 8vo., wrapper, illus. Minters 37-252 1973 $14

HALMA, NICHOLAS B.   Commentaire de Theon d'Alexandrie. Paris, 1822. 4to., contemporary black pebbled cloth, gilt. Zeitlin 235-183 1974 $75

HALMA, NICOLAS B.   Table Chronologique des Regnes. Paris, 1819. Thick 4to., cloth, gilt. Zeitlin 235-182 1974 $100

HALPER, ALBERT   Sons of the Fathers. Harper, 1940. 431p. Austin 62-242 1974 $10

HALPINE, CHARLES GRAHAM   Baked Meats of the Funeral. New York, 1866. 8vo., orig. cloth, first edition. Ximenes 33-150 1974 $12.50

HALPINE, CHARLES GRAHAM   The Life and Adventures . . . . of Miles O'Reilly. New York, 1864. Illus., cloth, first edition. Bradley 35-432 1974 $12.50

HALPINE, CHARLES GRAHAM   The Life and Adventures, Songs, Services and Speeches of Private Miles O'Reilly. New York, 1864. First edition, first printing, blind stamped black cloth, illus. Butterfield 10-189 1974 $35

HALS, FRANS   Frans Hals: Sa Vie et son Oeuvre. Brussels, 1909. 4to., plates, boards, buckram spine. Quaritch 940-130 1974 £15

HALSBEKE, CHARLES-LEON VAN   L'Art Typographique dans les Pays-Bas Depuis 1892. Maestricht, 1929. 4to., orig. wrappers, plates, numbered copy, lacking 4 supplements. Kraus B8-337 1974 $30

HALSTED, WILLIAM STEWART   Surgical Papers. Baltimore, 1924. Large 8vo., 2 vols., orig. cloth, plates, illus., portraits. Gurney 64-105 1974 £25

HALYBURTON, T.   Natural Religion Insufficient. Edinburgh, 1714. Small 4to., contemporary panelled calf. Smith 194-156 1974 £7.50

HAMBIDGE, JAY   Dynamic Symmetry: The Greek Vase. 1920. 4to., plate. Allen 213-461 1973 $12.50

HAMBLEN, EMILY S.   On the Minor Prophecies of William Blake. 1930. Orig. edition. Austin 61-448 1974 $12.50

HAMBLEN, EMILY S.   On the Minor Prophecies of William Blake. 1930. First edition, cover somewhat faded, very good copy, scarce. Covent 51-262 1973 £12.50

HAMBLETON, CHALKLEY J.   A Gold Hunter's Experience. Chicago, 1898. Orig. cloth, signed, presentation, first edition. Bradley 35-163 1974 $150

HAMBLETT, CHARLES   The Hollywood Cage. Hart, 1969. 435p. Austin 51-390 1973 $6

HAMEL, FRED   Das Atlantisbuch der Musik. Berlin, 1934. Spine torn. Biblo & Tannen 214-855 1974 $12.50

HAMEL, GUSTAV   Flying. London, New York, 1914. 8vo., green cloth, gilt, presentation copy, first edition. Dawsons PM 245-363 1974 £15

HAMERTON, PHILIP GILBERT   The Graphic Arts. 1882. 4to., cloth covers, spine gone. Eaton Music-606 1973 £6.50

HAMERTON, PHILIP GILBERT   Landscape. 1885. Orig. vellum gilt, large paper copy, limited edition. Smith 194-96 1974 £9

HAMERTON, PHILIP GILBERT   Man in Art. Studies in Religious and Historical Art. 1892. Large 4to., rebound, cloth. Eaton Music-605 1973 £10

HAMES, GEORGE WHARTON   The Grand Canyon of Arizona. Boston, 1910. Pictorial green cloth, illus., first edition. Bradley 35-154 1974 $20

HAMES, HENRY   The Wings of the Dove. 1902. Thick crown 8vo., orig. blue cloth, first English edition. Howes 186-276 1974 £21

HAMILTON, A.   The Art Workmanship of the Maori Race in New Zealand. 1896-1900. 5 parts complete in 1 vol., 4to., contemporary buckram, plates, illus. Bow Windows 66-309 1974 £180

HAMILTON, ALEXANDER   The Examination of the President's Message. New York, 1802. Disbound. Dawson's 424-194 1974 $25

HAMILTON, ALEXANDER   Letter Concerning the Public Conduct and Character of John Adams.   New York, 1800. Third edition, foxed.   Jenkins 61-17 1974 $22.50

HAMILTON, ALEXANDER   Letter Concerning the Public Conduct and Character of John Adams.   New York, 1800. Third edition.   Jenkins 61-985 1974 $22.50

HAMILTON, ALEXANDER   Letter from Alexander Hamilton, Concerning the Public Conduct and Character of John Adams.   New York, 1800. 8vo., disbound, first edition.   Ximenes 33-152 1974 $60

HAMILTON, ALEXANDER   A New Account of the East Indies.   Edinburgh, 1727. 2 vols., 8vo., full contemporary maroon morocco gilt, rubbed, first edition.   Traylen 79-522 1973 £200

HAMILTON, ALEXANDER   The Works.   New York, 1904. 12 vols., roy. 8vo., orig. red cloth, frontispieces, limited.   Howes 186-882 1974 £48

HAMILTON, ANTHONY   Memoirs of Count Grammont.   London, 1811. 8vo., 2 vols., contemporary half red morocco, new edition.   Dawsons PM 251-121 1974 £10

HAMILTON, ANTHONY   Memoirs of Count Grammont.   London, 1818. Small 8vo., 2 vols., contemporary maroon straight-grained morocco, gilt, new edition.   Hammond 201-350 1974 £42.50

HAMILTON, ANTHONY   Memoirs of Comte de Gramont.   London, 1930. Biblo & Tannen 213-771 1973 $9.50

HAMILTON, CLAYTON   On the Trail of Stevenson.   New York, 1915. Folio, orig. cloth backed boards, paper labels, second edition, censored edition. MacManus 224-411 1974 $25

HAMILTON, CLAYTON   On the Trail of Stevenson.   New York, 1915. Folio, orig. cloth backed boards, corners rubbed, paper labels, first edition. MacManus 224-410 1974 $50

HAMILTON, CLAYTON   Studies in Stagecraft.   Holt, 1914. 298p. Austin 51-391 1973 $6.50

HAMILTON, DAVID   Tractatus Duplex.   1710. 8vo., contemporary panelled calf, rebacked, first edition.   Dawsons PM 249-232 1974 £22

HAMILTON, EDWIN   The Moderate Man.   n.d. Small 4to., orig. pictorial cloth gilt, plates.   Covent 55-886 1974 £10.50

HAMILTON, ELIZABETH   Letters on the Elementary Principles of Education.   Bath, 1803. 2 vols., 8vo., contemporary tree calf, corners worn, third edition.   Bow Windows 66-310 1974 £28

HAMILTON, ELIZABETH   Memoirs of the Life of Agrippina.   Bath, 1804. 3 vols., 8vo., contemporary half calf gilt, first edition.   Dawsons PM 252-429 1974 £55

HAMILTON, ERNEST   Elizabethan Ulster.   London, n.d. 8vo., cloth boards.   Emerald 50-382 1974 £5

HAMILTON, ERNEST   The Irish Rebellion of 1641.   1920. 415 pages. Howes 186-885 1974 £5

HAMILTON, F.   An Account of the Fishes Found in the River Ganges and Its Branches.   Edinburgh, 1822. 2 vols., 4to., oblong 4to., new half morocco, engraved plates, library stamps, rare.   Wheldon 128-634 1973 £100

HAMILTON, GAIL PSEUD.
Please turn to
DODGE, MARY ABIGAIL

HAMILTON, GEORGE ROSTREVOR   The Latin Portrait.   1929. 8vo., orig. cloth, uncut, unopened.   Broadhurst 23-734 1974 £10

HAMILTON, GEORGE ROSTREVOR   The Latin Portrait.   1929. Vignetttes, 8vo., top edges gilt, others uncut, unopened, slip-in-case, illus., fine, orig. cloth.   Broadhurst 24-690 1974 £10

HAMILTON, GEORGE ROSTREVOR   Light in 6 Moods.   1930. Dust wrapper, fine, English first edition.   Covent 56-595 1974 £5.25

HAMILTON, H. R.   Foot Prints.   Chicago, 1927. Cloth, fine, presentation copy.   Hayman 57-323 1974 $17.50

HAMILTON, J. C.   The Georgian Bay, An Account of Its Position, Inhabitants, Mineral Interests, Fish, Timber and Other Resources.   Toronto, 1893. Map, illus.   Hood's 102-607 1974 $25

HAMILTON, JAMES   The Hamilton Manuscripts.   Belfast, (1867). 4to., new cloth.   Emerald 50-383 1974 £12.50

HAMILTON, JOHN   Angelica's Ladies Library.   London, 1794. 8vo., half calf, gilt, first edition.   Ximenes 33-153 1974 $75

HAMILTON, JOHN POTTER   Travels Through the Interior Provinces of Columbia.   London, 1827. 2 vols., 8vo., orig. quarter cloth, fine, first edition. Ximenes 33-154 1974 $150

HAMILTON, LOUIS   Canada.   New York, 1926. Illus.   Hood's 102-152 1974 $20

HAMILTON, P. H.   An Analytical System of Conic Sections.   Cambridge, 1838. 8vo., contemporary sheep, fourth edition.   Bow Windows 64-534 1974 £4.75

HAMILTON, TERRICK   Antar.   London, 1819. 8vo., half calf, gilt, book-plate, first edition.   Dawsons PM 252-430 1974 £28

HAMILTON, W. J.   American Mammals.   New York, 1939. 8vo., cloth.   Wheldon 131-491 1974 £5

HAMILTON, WALTER   French Book-Plates.   London & New York, (1896). 8vo., orig. cloth gilt, uncut, limited, second edition.   Dawsons PM 10-264 1974 £9

HAMILTON, WILLIAM   Campi Phlegraei.   Naples, 1776-79. 3 parts in 1 vol., roy. folio, new blue morocco gilt, plates.   Wheldon 131-55 1974 £2,200

HAMILTON, WILLIAM   Collection of Engravings from Ancient Vases of Greek Workmanship Discovered in Sepulchres in the Kingdom of the Two Sicilies.   Naples, 1791-95. 3 vols., imp. folio, plates, boards, leather spines.   Quaritch 940-323 1974 £150

HAMILTON, WILLIAM   Discussions On Philosophy and Literature. 1853.   Austin 61-449 1974 $37.50

HAMILTON, WILLIAM   Discussions On Philosophy and Literature, Education and University Reform.   1853. Thick 8vo., orig. cloth, enlarged second edition.   Howes 185-1868 1974 £6.50

HAMILTON, WILLIAM   The Eighteenth Epistle of the Second Book of Horacf.   Edinburgh, 1737. 8vo., modern boards, first edition.   Dawsons PM 252-431 1974 £20

HAMILTON, WILLIAM   Outlines from the Figures and Compositions Upon the Greek, Roman and Etruscan Vases.   1814. 8vo., plates, contemporary straight grain green morocco gilt, second edition.   Quaritch 940-324 1974 £30

HAMILTON, WILLIAM   Poems on Several Occasions.   Edinburgh, 1760. 8vo., contemporary calf, first authorized edition.   Ximenes 33-155 1974 $55

HAMILTON, WILLIAM GERARD   Parliamentary Logick.   London, 1808. 8vo., orig. boards, fine, first edition.   Dawsons PM 247-140 1974 £35

HAMILTON, WILLIAM GERARD   Parliamentary Logick.   London, 1808. 8vo., contemporary mottled calf, first edition.   Dawsons PM 252-546 1974 £40

HAMILTON, WILLIAM R.   Supplement to an Essay on the Theory of Systems of Rays.   Dublin, 1830. 4to., orig. wrappers, fine, first edition.   Ximenes 33-156 1974 $150

HAMILTON, WILLIAM R.   Theory of Conjugate Functions. Dublin, 1835. 4to., orig. wrappers, rare, fine, first edition. Ximenes 33-157 1974 $175

HAMLIN, A. D. F.   A History of Ornament, Vol. 2. New York, 1923. Biblo & Tannen 214-255 1974 $13.50

HAMMER, JOHN   Notes and Papers. 1872. 4to., orig. cloth, plate, illus. Broadhurst 23-1399 1974 £12

HAMMER, JOSEPH VON   New Arabian Nights' Entertainments. London, 1826. 3 vols., 12mo., contemporary calf, first edition. Ximenes 33-158 1974 $50

HAMMER, THOMAS   The Garden Book Of. 1933. Small 4to., cloth, portraits, scarce. Wheldon 128-1470 1973 £7.50

HAMMERSHOI, SVEND   Thorvald Bindesboll. Copenhagen, 1918. Large 4to., faded wrappers, illus., signed, limited edition. Minters 37-238 1973 $50

HAMMERSTEIN, OSCAR THE 2nd.   Me and Juliet. Random, 1953. 142p. Austin 51-392 1973 $7.50

HAMMERSTEIN, OSCAR THE 2nd.   Pipe Dream. Viking. 1956. 158p., illus. Austin 51-393 1973 $8.50

HAMMERSTEIN, OSCAR THE 2ND   South Pacific. Random House, 1949. Austin 51-394 1973 $5

HAMMERTON, J. A.   Barrie. 1929. Austin 51-395 1973 $12.50

HAMMERTON, J. A.   Peoples of All Nations. n.d. 7 vols., roy. 8vo., orig. buckram gilt, photographs. Smith 194-627 1974 £8

HAMMERTON, J. A.   The War Illustrated. 1914-19. 9 vols. in 8, 4to., illus., orig. cloth. Smith 193-729 1973 £7

HAMMERTON, J. A.   Wonderful Britain. n.d. Photographs, worn. Marsden 39-201 1974 £12

HAMMERTON, JOHN   The Second Great War. London, n.d. 8 vols., 4to., plates, illus. Traylen 79-137 1973 £10

HAMMETT, DASHIELL   The Continental Op. New York, 1945. Biblo & Tannen 210-474 1973 $15

HAMMETT, DASHIELL   The Creeping Siamese. New York, 1950. 1st ed. Biblo & Tannen 210-475 1973 $15

HAMMETT, DASHIELL   Dead Yellow Women. New York, 1947. 1st ed. Biblo & Tannen 210-476 1973 $12.50

HAMMETT, DASHIELL   The Glass Key. ·London & New York, 1931. Scarce, fine copy, first edition. Covent 51-844 1973 £15

HAMMETT, DASHIELL   Hammett Homicides. New York, 1946. Biblo & Tannen 210-477 1973 $12.50

HAMMETT, DASHIELL   Nightmare Town. New York, 1948. Biblo & Tannen 210-478 1973 $15

HAMMETT, DASHIELL   The Return of the Continental Op. New York, 1945. Biblo & Tannen 210-479 1973 $15

HAMMETT, DASHIELL   They Can Only Hang You Once. New York, 1944. Biblo & Tannen 210-480 1973 $15

HAMMETT, R. C.   A Handbook on Meat and Text Book for Butchers. 1929. Fine, illus., first edition. Covent 55-688 1974 £5.25

HAMMETT, R. W.   Romanesque Architecture of Europe. 1927. 4to., plates. Allen 213-1906 1973 $25

HAMMOND, ALEX   The Book of Chessmen. London, 1950. Sm. 4to., 1st ed., plates. Biblo & Tannen 210-320 1973 $22.50

HAMMOND, H.   The Whole Duty of Man. 1711. 12mo., contemporary black calf, rubbed. Smith 193-112 1973 £12

HAMMOND, J. L.   The Village Labourer. 1911, 17, and 19. 8vo., orig. cloth, first editions. Broadhurst 23-1234 1974 £30

HAMMOND, JOHN WINTHROP   Charles Proteus Steinmetz. Century, 1924. Austin 62-246 1974 $10

HAMMOND, M. O.   Confederation and Its Leaders. Toronto, 1917. Portraits. Hood's 102-24 1974 $20

HAMMOND, M. O.   Canadian Footprints. Toronto, 1926. Inscribed & signed, photos. Hood's 102-560 1974 $25

HAMMOND, WILLIAM A.   Sleep and Its Derangements. Philadelphia, 1869. 12mo., cloth, first edition. Rittenhouse 46-321 1974 $60

HAMON, AUGUSTE   Les Auxiliatrices des Ames du Purgatoire. Paris, 1919-21. 2 vols., cloth, labels. Howes 185-1249 1974 £5

HAMPER, W.   A Topographical Account of Dunster. 1808. 4to., boards, 13 pages. Quaritch 939-539 1974 £15

HAMPSON, G. F.   The Lepidoptera Heterocera of the Nilgiri District. 1891. 4to., cloth, coloured plates. Wheldon 128-729 1973 £7.50

HAMPSON, G. F.   The Lepidoptera Heterocera of the Nilgiri District. 1891. 4to., cloth, plates. Wheldon 131-811 1974 £7.50

HAMPSON, G. F.   The Macrolepidoptera Heterocera of Ceylon. 1893. 4to., cloth, coloured plates. Wheldon 128-730 1973 £7.50

HAMPSON, G. F.   The Macrolepidoptera Heterocera of Ceylon. 1893. 4to., cloth, plates. Wheldon 131-812 1974 £7.50

HAMSUN, KNUT   Hunger. London, 1899. Tight copy, very good, splits at side of spine, first edition. Covent 51-845 1973 £8.50

HAMPTON, MOULTON   The Mirrour of the World. Boston, 1856. Cloth, little wear. Hayman 59-178 1974 $12.50

HANBURY, F. J.   An Illustrated Monograph of the British Hieracia. 1889-98. Parts 1 - 8, folio, cloth, hand coloured plates. Wheldon 128-1196 1973 £15

HANCKE, ERICH   Max Liebermann. Berlin, 1914. Large 4to., worn boards, three quarter rubbed leather, illus. Minters 37-857 1973 $75

HANCOCK, SAMUEL   The Narrative of Samuel Hancock, 1845-1860. New York, 1927. Jenkins 61-993 1974 $12.50

HANCOCK, WINFIELD SCOTT (Mrs.)   Reminiscences of... New York, 1887. 3/4 lea., binding rubbed., illus. Biblo & Tannen 213-23 1973 $17.50

HANDBOOK of Aeronautics. London, 1934. 8vo., 2 vols., blue cloth gilt, illus., second edition. Dawsons PM 245-5 1974 £10

THE HAND-BOOK of Carving. London, 1844. 12mo., orig. cloth, gilt, illus. Hammond 201-158 1974 £7.50

HANDEL, LEO A.   Hollywood Looks At Its Audience. 1950. Austin 51-397 1973 $12.50

HANDEL-MAZZETTI, H.   Symbolae Sinicae. Vienna, 1929-36. 5 parts, roy. 8vo., orig. wrappers. Wheldon 128-1266 1973 £45

HANDEL-MAZZETTI, H.   Symbolae Sinicae. Vienna, 1929-36. Roy 8vo., orig. wrappers, plates. Wheldon 130-1163 1974 £45

HANDLEY, W. SAMPSON   Cancer of the Breast and Its Treatment. New York, 1922. Second edition. Rittenhouse 46-322 1974 $10

HANDLIN, OSCAR   Boston's Immigrants. 1941. First edition. Austin 57-284 1974 $17.50

HANDZEICHNUNGEN Alter Meister der Hollandischen Malerschule. Leipzig, 1913. 6 vols., folio, cloth portfolios, worn. Quaritch 940-91 1974 £35

HANHAM, F. Natural Illustrations of the British Grasses. Bath, 1846. Small folio, modern full calf antique, rare, nice copy, limited edition. Wheldon 131-1223 1974 £35

HANKIN, F. Recovery by Control, c Solution for Canada. Toronto, 1932. Underlined. Hood's 102-378 1974 $7.50

HANKINS, C. Dakota Land. New York, 1868. 8vo., orig. bindings, illus., gilt, worn. Butterfield 8-102 1974 $35

HANKINSON, THOMAS EDWARDS A Collection of 9 Poems. 8vo., full green morocco gilt, first editions. Ximenes 33-159 1974 $60

HANLEY, JAMES Boy. Boriswood, 1931. 8vo., orig. cloth, first edition. Rota 189-422 1974 £5

HANLEY, JAMES Captain Bottell. 1933. Bookplate, English first edition. Covent 56-597 1974 £5.25

HANLEY, JAMES Drift. 1930. 8vo., orig. cloth, inscribed, first edition. Rota 189-421 1974 £12

HANLEY, JAMES Ebb and Flood. 1932. Fine copy, first edition. Covent 51-850 1973 £5

HANLEY, JAMES Ebb and Flood. London, 1932. First edition, slight marks on covers, nice copy, chipped d.w., orig. cloth. Crane 7-121 1974 £6

HANLEY, JAMES Ebb and Flood. 1932. 8vo., half white buckram, signed, first edition. Rota 190-497 1974 £12

HANLEY, JAMES The German Prisoner. n.d. 8vo., buckram, frontispiece, signed, presentation copy, first edition. Quaritch 936-407 1974 £8

HANLEY, JAMES The German Prisoner. n.d. Buckram, signed, fine, English first edition. Covent 56-598 1974 £8.50

HANLEY, JAMES Grey Children. London, 1937. Very nice copy, slightly chipped d.w., orig. cloth, first edition. Crane 7-124 1974 £6

HANLEY, JAMES Grey Children. 1937. Scarce, very good copy, first edition. Covent 51-852 1973 £8.50

HANLEY, JAMES The Last Voyage. 1931. Large 8vo., buckram, frontispiece, signed, limited edition. Quaritch 936-409 1974 £6

HANLEY, JAMES The Lasy Voyage. 1931. One of 550 numbered copies, signed by author, frontis., buckram, gilt top, very good copy, first edition. Covent 51-854 1973 £5.25

HANLEY, JAMES Men in Darkness. London, 1931. Nice copy, orig. cloth, torn d.w, first edition. Crane 7-120 1974 £7.50

HANLEY, JAMES The Secret Journey. 1936. 8vo., orig. cloth, first edition. Bow Windows 64-536 1974 £5

HANLEY, JAMES Stoker Bush. London, 1935. First edition, very nice copy, chipped d.w., orig. cloth. Crane 7-123 1974 £6

HANLEY, JAMES Stoker Haslett. 1932. 8vo., white buckram, signed, first edition. Quaritch 936-408 1974 £7

HANLEY, JAMES Stoker Haslett. 1932. Orig. cloth, signed, first edition. Rota 188-389 1974 £8.50

HANLEY, S. An Illustrated and Descriptive Catalogue of Recent Bivalve Shells. 1842-56. Roy. 8vo., orig. blue cloth, plates, rare. Wheldon 128-841 1973 £40

HANMER, JOHN Notes and Papers to Serve for a Memorial of the Parish of Hanmer in Flintshire. 1872. Frontispiece, coloured plate, med. 4to., orig. cloth, fine. Broadhurst 24-1428 1974 £12

HANNA, CHARLES A. Historical Collections of Harrison County, in the State of Ohio. New York, 1900. Cloth. Hayman 59-465 1974 $40

HANNA, DAVID Ava. Putnam, 1960. Austin 51-396 1973 $7.50

HANNAY, JAMES 1842-1910 History of the War of 1812, Between Great Britain and the United States of America. Toronto, 1905. Illus., maps. Hood's 102-105 1974 $20

HANNAY, JAMES 1842-1910 History of the War of 1812. Toronto, 1905. Illus., maps. Hood's 104-113 1974 $20

HANNAY, JAMES 1842-1910 The Life and Times of Sir Leonard Tilley. St. John, 1897. Stain. Hood's 103-177 1974 $15

HANNAY, JAMES OWEN Irishmen All. 1913. 8vo., green suede, illus., first edition. Quaritch 936-297 1974 £6

HANNAY, JAMES OWEN Irishmen All. London, 1914. 8vo., illus., frontis., cloth boards. Emerald 50-62 1974 £5

HANNAY, ROBERT Defence of the Usuary Laws. 1823. 12mo., orig. boards, uncut, first edition. Broadhurst 23-1235 1974 £25

HANNETONIUS, G. De Jure Feudorum Libri Quatuor. 1564. Vellum. Allen 213-1527 1973 $17.50

HANNOVER, ADOLPH Den Menneskelige Hjernes Bygning ved Cyclopia og Misdannelsens Forhold til Hjerneskallens Primordialbrusk. Copenhagen, 1884. 4to., buckram, engraved plate. Gurney 66-80 1974 £10.50

HANNOVER, EMIL Pottery and Porcelain. 1925. 3 vols., roy. 8vo., plates, illus., orig. cloth. Quaritch 940-635 1974 £80

HANNOVER GALERIE VON GARVENS Ausstellung Willy Baumeister, July 2-August 13, 1922. 8vo., wrapper, plates, scarce. Minters 37-498 1973 $20

HANS, F. M. The Great Sioux Nation. Chicago, (1907). Orig. cloth, illus. Putnam 126-295 1974 $22

HANSARD, GEORGE AGAR The Book of Archery. London, 1841. 8vo., contemporary red gilt-framed calf, plates. Dawsons PM 251-388 1974 £25

HANSEMANN, D. VON Atlas der Boesartigen Geschwuelste. Berlin, 1910. Plates. Rittenhouse 46-323 1974 $10

HANSEN, MARCUS LEE The Atlantic Migration: 1607-1860. Harvard, 1940. Austin 62-249 1974 $15

HANSON, HEZECKIA Diary of. Philadelphia, 1813. Orig. cloth, full red leather. Putman 126-91 1974 $45

HANSON, JOSEPH MILLS Frontier Ballads. Chicago, 1910. 12mo., pict. boards, spine ends and corners worn, full page color plates, illus. by Maynard Dixon, first edition. Frohnsdorff 15-27 1974 $10

HANWAY, JONAS An Historical Account of the British Trade Over the Caspian Sea. London, 1753. 4 vols. in 3, 4to., contemporary calf, worn, hinges weak, folding maps, plates, ex-library, first edition. Ximenes 37-101 1974 $150

HANZELET, JEAN APPIER
Please turn to
APPIER HANZELET, JEAN

HAPGOOD, HUTCHINS The Spirit of the Ghetto. 1909. Illus., revised edition. Austin 57-289 1974 $10

HAPPENINGS. Dutton, 1965. 288p., hard cover ed. Austin 51-507 1973 $7.50

HARBIN, GEORGE The Hereditary Right of the Crown of England. 1713. Folio, contemporary calf, first edition. Howes 186-888 1974 $25

HARCOURT, E. W.   Catalogue of the Library. 1883. 4to.,
half calf, presentation inscription. Quaritch 939-518 1974 £50

HARCOURT, L. V.   An Eton Bibliography. London, 1898. Limited
to 200 copies, crown 8vo., orig. buckram, roan back, spine defective. Forster
98-197 1974 £4

HARCOURT, L. V.   An Eton Bibliography. London, 1902. Small
4to., orig. cloth gilt, uncut, fine. Dawsons PM 10-265 1974 £16

THE HARD-BOILED Omnibus. New York, 1946. 1st ed. Biblo & Tannen 210-524
1973 $15

HARDEN, SAMUEL   Those I Have Met. Anderson, 1888. 8vo.,
orig. bindings. Butterfield 8-163 1974 $20

HARDIE, M.   War Posters. Issued by Belligerent and Neutral
Nations 1914-19. 1920. 8vo., plates, orig. illus. cloth, faded, uncut.
Quaritch 940-451 1974 £40

HARDIN, JOHN WESLEY   The Life of. Seguin, 1896. 8vo., pictorial
wrapper. Butterfield 8-620 1974 $20

HARDING, ALFRED   The Revolt of the Actors. New York, 1929.
Biblo & Tannen 213-896 1973 $15

HARDING, BERTITA   Age Cannot Wither. Lippincott, 1947. 281p.,
illus. Austin 51-398 1973 $8.50

HARDING, E.   The Costume of the Russian Empire. 1803.
Folio, plates, contemporary straight grained red morocco gilt, rubbed, first
edition. Quaritch 940-715 1974 £120

HARDING, E.   The Costume of the Russian Empire. 1811.
Folio, contemporary straight grain red morocco gilt, plates. Quaritch 940-716
1974 £140

HARDING, JAMES DUFFIELD   Lessons on Trees. n.d. 4to., plates, morocco
gilt. Smith 193-663 1973 £5.50

HARDING, JAMES DUFFIELD   The Park and the Forest. 1841. Atlas 4to.,
contemporary morocco backed cloth, plates. Bow Windows 64-537 1974 £45

HARDING, JAMES DUFFIELD   The Principles and Practice of Art. 1845.
Plates, brown cloth, gilt, first edition. Marsden 39-203 1974 £24

HARDING, WARREN G.   Last Speeches of President Warren G. Harding,
June-August, 1923. (Washington), 1923. No. 1 of a limited edition. Jenkins
61-996 1974 $22.50

HARDWICKE, T.   An Account of the Sheep-Eater of Hindustan.
1833. 4to., sewed. Wheldon 131-435 1974 £7.50

HARDY, ARTHUR SHERBURNE   Life and Letters of Joseph Hardy Neesima.
1892. 350 pages. Austin 57-291 1974 $12.50

HARDY, CAMPBELL   Sporting Adventures In the New World.
London, 1855. 2 vols., 8vo., orig. cloth. Traylen 79-483 1973 £48

HARDY, F.   Memoirs of the Political & Private Life of
James Caulfield, Earl of Charlemont. 1812. 2 vols., contemporary calf gilt,
second edition. Smith 193-552 1973 £7

HARDY, FLORENCE E.   The Life of Thomas Hardy. 1840-1928.
4 vols., orig. cloth, dust wrappers. Smith 194-649 1974 £6.50

HARDY, G. H.   A Course of Pure Mathematics. 1908. 8vo.,
red cloth, first edition. Dawsons PM 245-364 1974 £10

HARDY, J.   A Picturesque and Descriptive Tour of the Mountains of the High Pyrenees. 1825. 8vo., orig. cloth, worn. Broadhurst 23-
1647 1974 £100

HARDY, MARY ANNE DUFUS   Through Cities and Prairie Lands. 1881.
8vo., orig. cloth, some spotting, first edition. Bow Windows 66-312 1974
£10.50

HARDY, THOMAS   A. L. S. 1910. 8vo., cloth folder. Bow
Windows 62-417 1974 £78

HARDY, THOMAS   A Changed Man. 1913. 8vo., orig. cloth,
first edition. Rota 189-423 1974 £7.50

HARDY, THOMAS   A Changed Man. London, 1913. 8vo., orig.
cloth, map, presentation, first edition. Bow Windows 62-418 1974 £8.50

HARDY, THOMAS   A Changed Man. 1913. Orig. cloth, English
first edition. Covent 56-1795 1974 £8.50

HARDY, THOMAS   A Changed Man. 1913. Small 8vo., orig. cloth,
gilt, frontispiece, first edition. Quaritch 936-410 1974 £12

HARDY, THOMAS   A Changed Man, The Waiting Supper, and
Other Tales. London, 1913. First edition, green cloth, fine, darkened d.w.,
scarce in d.w. Ross 87-257 1974 $30

HARDY, THOMAS   A Changed Man, The Waiting Supper, and Other
Tales. London, 1913. Green cloth, lacking d.w., very nice. Ross 86-241
1974 $40

HARDY, THOMAS   A Changed Man and Other Tales. 1913.
Orig. cloth gilt, map, foxing. Smith 194-463 1974 £6

HARDY, THOMAS   Desperate Remedies. 1871. 3 vols., finely
bound in full dark green morocco, gilt panelled backs, top edges gilt, very
attractive copy, extremely rare, with A.L.s. by author. Covent 51-856 1973
£420

HARDY, THOMAS   The Duke's Reappearance. New York, 1927.
Boards, very fine, English first edition. Covent 56-601 1974 £55

HARDY, THOMAS   The Dynasts. 1910. Small 8vo., portrait, cloth,
first complete edition. Quaritch 936-411 1974 £8

HARDY, THOMAS   The Dynasts. Macmillan, 1921. Austin 51-400
1973 $12.50

HARDY, THOMAS   The Dynasts. Macmillan, 1931. Austin
51-399 1973 $12.50

HARDY, THOMAS   The Dynasts, an Epic Drama. London, 1910.
Frontis., first 1 vol. edition, orig. binding, fine. Ross 86-242 1974 $35

HARDY, THOMAS   The Famous Tragedy of the Queen of Cornwall.
London, 1923. Orig. cloth, d.w. slightly browned at edges & chipped, first
edition, fine. Ross 87-258 1974 $100

HARDY, THOMAS   Far from the Madding Crowd. 1874. Binding
very slightly worn, first American edition. Allen 216-656 1974 $10

HARDY, THOMAS   A Group of Noble Dames. London, 1891.
First edition, first issue, with yellow end papers, lacking d.w., slight foxing,
remarkably fine tight copy, gilt on cover, spine nearly pristine. Ross 87-259
1974 $45

HARDY, THOMAS   The Hand of Ethelberta. 1876. 2 vols.,
orig. cloth, bookplate, first edition. Rota 188-390 1974 £90

HARDY, THOMAS   Human Shows, Far Fantasies. 1925. Dust
wrapper, fine, first edition. Howes 186-242 1974 £7.50

HARDY, THOMAS   Human Shows, Far Fantasies, and Trifles.
London, 1925. First edition, lacking d.w., very nice, orig. binding. Ross
86-243 1974 $20

HARDY, THOMAS   Human Shows, Far Fantasies, Songs and Trifles.
London, 1925. Orig. binding, first edition, unusually well preserved copy, near
mint, immaculate d.w., thus rare, unopened. Ross 87-260 1974 $40

HARDY, THOMAS   Jude the Obscure. 1896. Orig. cloth gilt,
map, frontispiece. Smith 194-465 1974 £7.50

HARDY, THOMAS   Jude the Obscure. 1896. Frontispiece, orig.
cloth, English first edition. Covent 56-602 1974 £10.50

HARDY, THOMAS   Jude the Obscure. London, 1896. Etching, map, orig. binding, first edition, unusually fine, bright copy. Ross 87-261 1974 $75

HARDY, THOMAS   Jude the Obscure. 1896. Front cover slightly wrinkled, first edition of complete text. Allen 216-657 1974 $90

HARDY, THOMAS   Late Lyrics and Earlier. London, 1922. First edition, orig. green cloth, lacking d.w., nice, ink inscription. Ross 86-244 1974 $25

HARDY, THOMAS   Life's Little Ironies. London, 1894. Orig. binding, first edition, spine faded, near fine. Ross 87-262 1974 $50

HARDY, THOMAS   Life's Little Ironies, a Set of Tales. London, 1894. Slight foxing inside front & rear covers, owner's name in ink, fine copy, scarce, orig. binding. Ross 86-245 1974 $90

HARDY, THOMAS   Moments of Vision and Miscellaneous Verses. 1917. 8vo., orig. cloth, first edition. Bow Windows 66-313 1974 £10.15

HARDY, THOMAS   Old Mrs. Chundle. 1929. Limited edition. Allen 216-658 1974 $15

HARDY, THOMAS   Old Mrs. Chundle. New York, 1929. Orig. cloth-backed boards, first separate appearance, one of 742 numbered copies on hand made paper. MacManus 224-196 1974 $25

HARDY, THOMAS   Old Mrs. Chundle. New York, 1929. Cloth backed patterned boards, fine. Covent 55-806 1974 £15.75

HARDY, THOMAS   The Patriot. Edinburgh, 1793. 8vo., half calf, fine, first edition. Ximenes 33-161 1974 $22.50

HARDY, THOMAS   The Return of the Native. 8vo., half parchment, bookplate, illus., first edition. Rota 189-424 1974 £25

HARDY, THOMAS   The Return of the Native. 1929. Woodcuts, one of 1500 copies, signed by artist, vellum backed patterned boards, gilt top, fine, discoloured plain d.w., first edition. Covent 51-860 1973 £10

HARDY, THOMAS   Tess of the D'Urbervilles. London, 1891. 3 vols., first edition, first issue, with "Chapter XXV" for "Chapter XXXV" and "road" for "load", rebound in half tan morocco, slight foxing, very fine. Ross 87-263 1974 $350

HARDY, THOMAS   Tess of the D'Urbervilles. 1892. 3 vols., orig. buckram, second edition. Smith 193-286 1973 £15

HARDY, THOMAS   Tess of the D'Ubervilles. London, 1892. 3 vols., orig. cloth covers, scarce, slip case, first edition. Ballinger 1-141 1974 $30

HARDY, THOMAS   The Thieves Who Couldn't Help Sneezing. Waterville, 1942. Boards, mint, English first edition. Covent 56-603 1974 £35

HARDY, THOMAS   The Trumpet-Major. 1880. Orig. pictorial cloth, 3 vols., English first edition. Covent 56-1797 1974 £325

HARDY, THOMAS   Under the Greenwood Tree. London, 1872. 2 vols., 8vo., full tan calf, orig. cloth, bookplate, first edition. Ballinger 1-142 1974 $50

HARDY, THOMAS   The Well-Beloved. (London, 1897). 8vo., frontispiece, map, orig. cloth, first edition. Bow Windows 62-419 1974 £10

HARDY, THOMAS   The Well-Beloved. 1897. Frontispiece, map, first edition. Howes 186-243 1974 £10

HARDY, THOMAS   The Well-Beloved. London, 1897. 8vo., orig. cloth, gilt, frontispiece, first edition. Dawsons PM 252-432 1974 £18

HARDY, THOMAS   The Well-Beloved. London, 1897. Etching, map, first edition, small stain on front cover, orig. binding, fine, unusually bright gilt on cover & spine. Ross 87-264 1974 $65

HARDY, THOMAS   Wessex Poems and Other Verses. 1898. Orig. cloth, illus., English first edition. Covent 56-604 1974 £7.50

HARDY, THOMAS   Wessex Poems and Other Verses. London, 1898. First edition, dark green cloth, illus. by author, bright gilt on spine & cover. Ross 87-265 1974 $65

HARDY, THOMAS   Wessex Tales. 1895. First edition, illus. by author, crown 8vo., orig. cloth, fine. Broadhurst 24-721 1974 £30

HARDY, THOMAS   Wessex Tales, Strange, Lively and Commonplace. London, 1888. 2 vols., first edition, green cloth, corners somewhat bumped, spines of both vols. slightly creased, very nice. Ross 87-266 1974 $125

HARDY, THOMAS   Winter Words. 1928. First edition, crown 8vo., slight fading of spine, else fine, d.w., orig. cloth. Broadhurst 24-722 1974 £5

HARDY, THOMAS   Winter Words. 1928. Dust wrapper, first edition. Howes 185-210 1974 £7.50

HARDY, THOMAS   Winter Words. 1928. Dust wrapper, fine, unopened, inscription, English first edition. Covent 56-605 1974 £10

HARDY, THOMAS   Winter Words, In Various Moods and Metres. London, 1928. Lacking d.w., fine, orig. binding. Ross 86-246 1974 $25

HARDY, THOMAS   Winter Words In Various Moods and Metres. London, 1928. Unopened, mint, immaculate d.w., thus rare, orig. binding, first edition. Ross 87-267 1974 $35

HARDY, THOMAS   The Works. London, 1919-20. 37 vols., large 8vo., orig. cloth gilt, limited. Dawsons PM 252-433 1974 `$350

HARDY, W. J.   Book-Plates. 1893. Orig. buckram, faded, illus. Howes 185-703 1974 £6

HARDY, W. J.   Book-Plates. 1893. Orig. buckram gilt, plates, faded. Smith 194-84 1974 £7.50

HARE, AUGUSTUS J. C.   Story of My Life. 1896-1901. 4 vols., small hole in one spine. Allen 216-663 1974 $25

HARE, AUGUSTUS J. C.   Walks in Rome. Philadelphia, n. d. 2 vols. Biblo & Tannen 213-679 1973 $7.50

HARE, KENNETH   Three Poems. 1916. 32mo., wrappers, fine, inscribed, first edition. Rota 189-336 1974 £5

HARE, ROBERT   Overing. New York, 1852. 8vo., orig. dark blue-green cloth, first edition. Ximenes 33-162 1974 $27.50

HARE, THOMAS   A View of the Structure, Functions and Disorders of the Stomach. London, 1821. 8vo., boards, first edition. Dawsons PM 249-233 1974 £18

HARGRAVE, JOHN   The Imitation Man. 1931. Fine, English first edition. Covent 56-1159 1974 £8.50

HARGROVE, HENRY LEE   King Alfred's Old English Version St. Augustine's Soliloquies. 1902. Ex-library, sturdy library binding. Austin 61-452 1974 $22.50

HARGROVE, HENRY LEE   King Alfred's Old English Version of St. Augustine's Soliloquies Turned Into Modern English. 1904. Ex-library, sturdy library binding. Austin 61-453 1974 $27.50

HARINGTON, JOHN   Nugae Antiquae. London, 1804. 8vo., 2 vols., 19th century red straight-grain morocco gilt. Dawsons PM 251-243 1974 £20

HARKER, A.   Natural History of Igneous Rocks. 1909. 8vo., cloth, plates, scarce. Wheldon 128-982 1973 £7.50

HARKER, A.   Natural History of Igneous Rocks. 1909. 8vo., cloth, plates, scarce. Wheldon 130-933 1974 £7.50

HARKINS, E. F.   Little Pilgrimages Among the Men Who Have
Written Famous Books. Boston, 1902. 12mo., lst ed., illus. Biblo & Tannen
210-872 1973 $6.50

HARLAND, HENRY   The Cardinal's Snuff Box. 1903. Dec. cloth
gilt, plates, illus., faded. Covent 55-812 1974 £8.20

HARLAND, HENRY   Grey Roses. 1895. Presentation copy, inscribed
from author in pencil, dec. cloth covers little marked, very good copy. Covent
51-2362 1973 £10.50

HARLAND, JOHN   Ballads and Songs of Lancashire. 1875. F'cap
4to., boards, cloth spine. Broadhurst 24-1430 1974 £5

HARLEY, WILLIAM   The Harleian Dairy System. London, 1829.
8vo., orig. cloth, fine, first edition. Ximenes 33-163 1974 $45

HARLOW, REX   Oklahoma Leaders: Biographical Sketches of
the Foremost Living Men of Oklahoma. Oklahoma City, 1928. Uncut. Jenkins
61-2027 1974 $17.50

HARMAND, ADRIEN   Jeanne d'Arc. Paris, 1929. Folio, ltd. ed.
Biblo & Tannen 210-99 1973 $35

HARMAND, J.   Lichens de France. Epinal & Paris, 1905-13.
5 parts, roy. 8vo., new cloth, plates. Wheldon 131-1414 1974 £25

HARMAND, J.   Lichens de France. Epinal and Paris, 1905-13.
5 parts, roy. 8vo., new cloth, plates. Wheldon 128-1368 1973 £15

HARMER, S. F.   Cambridge Natural History, Vol. 7, Hemichordata
Ascidians and Amphioxus, Fishes. (1904). 8vo., cloth. Wheldon 128-622
1973 £5

HARMER, S. F.   Reports on Cetacea Stranded on the British
Coasts During 1913-1926, Nos. 1 - 10. 1914-27. 4to., orig. wrappers.
Wheldon 128-325 1973 £7.50

HARMON, DANIEL W.   A Journal of Voyages and Travels in the Interior
of North America. Andover, 1820. Orig. calf, morocco label, cracked, portrait,
folding map, first edition. Jenkins 61-997 1974 $375

THE HARMONICON: A Journal of Music. 1823-31. 9 vols., 4to., plates,
contemporary half calf, scarce. Howes 185-343 1974 £95

HARPEL, OSCAR H.   Harpel's Typograph. Cincinnati, 1870. Orig.
green cloth, rebacked, morocco, illus. Dawson's 424-152 1974 $250

HARPENDING, ASBURY   The Great Diamond Hoax and Other Stirring
Incidents in the Life of. San Francisco, 1913. Orig. dec. cloth, fine, first
edition. Bradley 35-38 1974 $28

HARPER, CHARLES GEORGE   The Brighton Road. 1906. 8vo., orig. cloth,
coloured frontispiece, plates, illus., some foxing. Bow Windows 66-675 1974
£14

HARPER, CHARLES GEORGE   Cycle Rides Round London Ridden. 1902.
Extra crown 8vo., profusely illus., orig. cloth, first edition, fine. Broadhurst
24-1431 1974 £10

HARPER, CHARLES GEORGE   The Ingoldsby Country Literary Landmarks
of the "Ingoldsby Legends". 1906. 8vo., orig. cloth, some foxing, illus. Bow
Windows 66-314 1974 £6.50

HARPER, CHARLES GEORGE   Thames Valley Villages. 1910. 2 vols.,
plates, illus., orig. buckram. Smith 194-284 1974 £12

HARPER, GEORGE MC LEAN   William Wordsworth: His Life, Works and
Influence. 1910. 2 vols. Allen 216-1750 1974 $12.50

HARPER, GEORGE MC LEAN   William Wordsworth, His Life, Works, and
Influence. 1916. 2 vols., plates, map. Covent 55-1563 1974 £10

HARPER, HENRY H.   A Journey in Southeastern Mexico. Boston,
1910. Boards, uncut, limited, inscription, first edition. Bradley 35-165 1974
$10

HARPER, THOMAS   The Metaphysics of the School. 1879-84.
3 vols., scarce. Howes 185-1869 1974 £8.50

HARPER'S Monthly Magazine. 1882-1909. 51 vols., thick roy. 8vo., orig.
brown cloth. Howes 186-245 1974 £125

HARRAP, G. G.   Love Lyrics from Five Centuries. 1932.
Crown 4to., orig. blue leatherette, coloured tipped in plates, first edition.
Bow Windows 66-316 1974 £10

HARRIMAN, MARGARET C.   Take Them Up Tenderly. Knopf, 1944. 266p.
Austin 54-464 1973 $6.75

HARRIMAN ALASKA EXPEDITION   Insects. New York, 1904. 2vols., roy.
8vo., cloth. Wheldon 131-813 1974 £8

HARRINGTON, JAMES   The Oceana of James Harrington. Dublin,
1737. Folio, full calf. Emerald 50-248 1974 £26

HARRINGTON, JAMES   The Oceanae and Other Works. 1771. 4to.,
contemporary calf, rebacked, best edition. Howes 185-1869A 1974 £36

HARRINGTON, T.   The History of Orangeism. Dublin, (c.1885).
4to., cloth boards, scarce. Emerald 50-390 1974 £9

HARRIS, A. C.   Alaska and the Klondike Gold Fields.
(Chicago?, 1897). Pictorial cloth, illus. Bradley 35-7 1974 $17.50

HARRIS, A. C.   Alaska and the Klondike Gold Fields. N. P.,
1897. Photos and engravings, folding map, pict. cloth. Jenkins 61-73 1974
$20

HARRIS, A. C.   Alaska and the Klondike Gold Fields. Chicago,
1897. Maps, illus., soiled cover. Hood's 103-67 1974 $22.50

HARRIS, ALEXANDER   A Review of the Political Conflict in America,
from the Commencement of the Anti-Slavery Agitation to the Close of Southern
Reconstruction . . . also, A Resume of the Career of Thaddeus Stevens. New
York, 1876. Cloth. Hayman 59-229 1974 $15

HARRIS, ALICE L.   Eugene Field Reader. New York, 1905. 8vo.,
pict. boards, cloth spine, illus., lst ed. Frohnsdorff 16-317 1974 $12.50

HARRIS, CHARLES T.   Memories of Manhattan in the Sixties and Seven-
ties. New York, 1928. Cloth-backed boards, limited edition. Hayman 57-281
1974 $10

HARRIS, FRANK   Bernard Shaw. S & S, 1931. 430p. Austin
51-4-2 1973 $6

HARRIS, FRANK   Bernard Shaw. 1931. Austin 51-401 1973
$6.50

HARRIS, FRANK   The Bomb. New York, 1909. 12mo., cloth,
first American edition. Goodspeed's 578-120 1974 $25

HARRIS, FRANK   Confessional: Intimate Portraits, Sketches &
Studies. New York, 1930. One of 3010 numbered copies, patterned cloth gilt,
fine. Covent 51-2363 1973 £6.50

HARRIS, FRANK   Contemporary Portraits. New York, 1915.
Front hinge loosened, spine somewhat rubbed, good, but not a collector's copy,
orig. binding. Ross 86-247 1974 $12.50

HARRIS, FRANK   Contemporary Portraits: Fourth Series. 1924.
Author's amusing signed presentation inscription, very good, first edition.
Covent 51-875 1973 £15

HARRIS, FRANK   Elder Conklin and Other Stories. New York,
1894. First American edition, presentation inscription from author, spine worn &
somewhat weak, nice copy, orig. binding. Ross 86-248 1974 $50

HARRIS, FRANK   England Or Germany? New York, 1915.
Inscribed, first edition. Jenkins 48-236 1973 $27.50

HARRIS, FRANK   Joan la Romee. (n.d.). 8vo., orig. cloth,
first edition. Bow Windows 64-538 1974 £10

HARRIS, FRANK   Joan la Romee. n.d. (c. 1926). Nice, author's signed presentation inscription, somewhat worn and soiled wrappers, first edition. Covent 51-877 1973 £10

HARRIS, FRANK   Lies & Libels of. 1929. Allen 216-665 1974 $10

HARRIS, FRANK   My Life and Loves. Paris, 1922. Pirated edition. Allen 216-666 1974 $10

HARRIS, FRANK   My Life and Loves. Paris, 1922 & Nice, 1925-27. Various bindings, limited edition. Allen 216-667 1974 $35

HARRIS, FRANK   Oscar Wilde. Harris, 1918. 610p. Austin 51-403 1973 $15

HARRIS, FRANK   Oscar Wilde. 1930. 463p. Austin 51-404 1973 $6

HARRIS, FRANK   Oscar Wilde. New York, 1930. Biblo & Tannen 210-936 1973 $7.50

HARRIS, FRANK   Unpath'd Waters. London, 1913. First edition, nice copy, orig. binding. Ross 86-251 1974 $15

HARRIS, FRANK   Unpath'd Waters. London, 1913. First edition, inscription from author, nice copy, orig. binding. Ross 86-250 1974 $35

HARRIS, G. F.   Catalogue of the Tertiary Mollusca in the Dept. of Geology, British Museum, Part 1, Australasia. 1897. 8vo., orig. cloth, plates, scarce. Wheldon 128-983 1973 £7.50

HARRIS, G. H.   The President's Book: The Story of the Sun Life Assurance Company of Canada. Montreal, 1928. Three quarter leather, illus. Hood's 104-354 1974 $17.50

HARRIS, H. A.   The Horse Thief. Boston, 1845. 8vo., disbound, first edition. Ximenes 33-164 1974 $100

HARRIS, H. E.   Essays and Photographs. 1901. 8vo., cloth, plates, scarce. Wheldon 130-538 1974 £7.50

HARRIS, JAMES   Hermes. 1771. New buckram, third edition. Allen 216-2024 1974 $15

HARRIS, JAMES   Miscellanies. London, 1775-86. 5 vols. in 4, 8vo., contemporary calf, rare, first & fourth edition. Ximenes 33-165 1974 $200

HARRIS, JAMES   Philosophical Arrangements. London, 1775. 8vo., contemporary calf, fine, first edition. Ximenes 33-166 1974 $100

HARRIS, JAMES   Three Treatises. London, 1744. 8vo., contemporary mottled calf, first edition. Ximenes 33-167 1974 $125

HARRIS, JOEL CHANDLER   Daddy Jake the Runaway. London, 1890. 4to., pict. cloth darkened, bevelled edges, all edges gilt, illus. by Kemble, first English edition. Frohnsdorff 15-74 1974 $47.50

HARRIS, JOEL CHANDLER   Daddy Jake the Runaway and Short Stories Told After Dark. London, 1890. 4to., grey cloth darkened, bevelled edges, corners bumped, illus. by Kemble, all edges gilt, first English edition. Frohnsdorff 16-416 1974 $50

HARRIS, JOEL CHANDLER   Joel Chandler Harris as Seen and Remembered by a Few of His Friends. 4to., cloth back, paper label, front cover soiled, first and only edition. Goodspeed's 578-122 1974 $35

HARRIS, JOEL CHANDLER   New Stories of the Old Plantation. New York, 1905. 8vo., illus., cloth, top edge gilt, first edition. Frohnsdorff 16-417 1974 $10

HARRIS, JOEL CHANDLER   On the Wings of Occasion. 1900. Name on flyleaf. Allen 216-672 1974 $10

HARRIS, JOEL CHANDLER   On the Wing of Occasions. New York, 1900. Nice copy, first edition, orig. binding. Butterfield 10-282 1974 $15

HARRIS, JOEL CHANDLER   Tales of the Home Folks in Peace and War. Boston and New York, 1898. Cloth, first edition. Hayman 57-282 1974 $12.50

HARRIS, JOEL CHANDLER   Uncle Remus. New York, 1881. Orig. illus. cloth, first edition, second state, very good fresh copy. MacManus 224-197 1974 $85

HARRIS, JOEL CHANDLER   Uncle Remus, His Songs and Sayings. New York, 1881. 8vo., pictorial cloth, illus., slight rubbing of spine ends, very good copy, first edition. Frohnsdorff 16-418 1974 $60

HARRIS, JOHN   Lexicon Technicum. 1716,1710. Folio, 2 vols., contemporary panelled sprinkled calf, gilt, ex-library. Zeitlin 235-108 1974 $450

HARRIS, JOHN   Navigantium Atque Itinerantium Bibliotheca. 1744-48. 2 vols., folio, contemporary calf, rebacked, plates. Traylen 79-430 1973 £180

HARRIS, LEWIS BIRDSALL   Journal of. Austin, 1922. Wrapper. Jenkins 61-1003 1974 $12.50

HARRIS, M.   A Catalogue and Index of Old Furniture and Works of Decorative Art from Late Sixteenth Century to Early Nineteenth Century. C., 1930. 4to., 3 vols., cloth-backed boards, gilt. Hammond 201-405 1974 £9

HARRIS, MALCOM H.   History of Louisa County. Richmond, 1936. Cloth, fine, first edition. Putnam 126-258 1974 $25

HARRIS, MARK   Friedman and Son. Macmillan, 1963. 152p. Austin 51-405 1973 $7.50

HARRIS, MATTIE ANSTICE   A Glossary of the West Saxon Gospels. 1899. Ex-library, sturdy library binding. Austin 61-455 1974 $22.50

HARRIS, MIRIAM   Richard Vandermarck. New York, 1871. 12mo., orig. cloth, worn, first edition. Ximenes 33-170 1974 $12

HARRIS, MIRIAM   St. Philip's. New York, 1865. 12mo., orig. cloth, faded, first edition. Ximenes 33-171 1974 $12

HARRIS, MOSES   The Aurelian. London, 1766. Roy. folio, contemporary calf, neatly rebacked, gilt, coloured plates, large paper copy, second edition, first issue. Wheldon 128-1699 1973 £750

HARRIS, MOSES   The Aurelian. London, 1766. Roy. folio, contemporary diced russia, rebacked in morocco, plates, second edition, third issue. Wheldon 131-56 1974 £900

HARRIS, MOSES   An Exposition of English Insects. 1782. 4to., modern quarter morocco, plates, second edition, first issue. Wheldon 131-57 1974 £100

HARRIS, MOSES   An Exposition of English Insects. 1782. 4to., plates, blue half calf, second edition. Bow Windows 64-119 1974 £120

HARRIS, MOSES   An Exposition of English Insects. 1782. 4to., contemporary quarter green roan, uncut, plates. Wheldon 129-22 1974 £100

HARRIS, N. DWIGHT   The History of Negro Servitude in Illinois. Chicago, 1904. 8vo., orig. bindings, first edition. Butterfield 8-147 1974 $20

HARRIS, N. DWIGHT   The History of Negro Servitude in Illinois and of the Slavery Agitation in That State, 1719-1864. Chicago, 1904. First edition, orig. binding. Butterfield 10-107 1974 $20

HARRIS, P. W.   The ABC of Wireless. 1922. Wrappers, illus. Covent 55-1235 1974 £5.25

HARRIS, S. H.   The Art of H. Anglada-Camarasa. London, 1929. 4to., three quarter vellum, plates, limited edition. Minters 37-489 1973 $27.50

HARRIS, THOMAS L.   The Wisdom of Angels. 1857. Gilt, English first edition. Covent 56-608 1974 £10.50

HARRIS, WALTER   De Morbis Acutis Infantum. 1689. Small 8vo., contemporary speckled calf, gilt, first edition. Dawsons PM 249-234 1974 £425

HARRIS Memorial Foundation Reports of Round Tables 1930, On the Foreign Policy of the U.S. 2 vols., cloth, bookplates. Rinsland 58-929 1974 $25

HARRISBURG, Pennsylvania. Harrisburg, 1907. Pict. wrappers, illus. Jenkins 61-2148 1974 $10

HARRISON, MRS. BURTON
Please turn to
HARRISON, CONSTANCE (CARY), MRS. BURTON HARRISON

HARRISON, CONSTANCE (CARY) MRS. BURTON HARRISON   The Old-Fashioned Fairy Book. New York, 1884. 12mo., first edition. Biblo & Tannen 210-745 1973 $15

HARRISON, FLORENCE   Guinevere and Other Poems by Alfred, Lord Tennyson. 1912. Dec. cloth gilt, plates. Marsden 37-235 1974 £7

HARRISON, FLORENCE   Poems by Christina Rosetti. 1911. Cream buckram, gilt, illus. Marsden 39-208 1974 £10

HARRISON, FREDERIC   Annals of an Old Manor House. 1893. Thick 4to., orig. cloth gilt, plates, soiled. Howes 186-2193 1974 £5

HARRISON, FREDERICK   Treasures of Illumination. 1937. 4to., orig. pictorial boards, scarce. Howes 185-704 1974 £20

HARRISON, G.   John Howard Payne, Dramatist, Poet, Actor and Author. 1885. Revised edition. Allen 216-1368 1974 $12.50

HARRISON, G. C.   British, French, Italian, Russian, Belgian Cookery. Canada, 1916. Ist ed. Biblo & Tannen 214-784 1974 $10

HARRISON, H.   Canadian Newspaper Service, Reg'd. Montreal, (1928). Hood's 104-27 1974 $25

HARRISON, JANE ELLEN   Reminiscences of a Student's Life. 1925. 12mo., plates, English first edition. Covent 56-633 1974 £10.50

HARRISON, JENNIE   Autumn Leaves. New York, 1877. 12mo., Ist ed., illus. Biblo & Tannen 210-746 1973 $10

HARRISON, ROBERT   Catalogue of the London Library. London, 1888. 2 vols., large 8vo., orig. buckram gilt, fifth edition. Dawsons PM 10-370 1974 £20

HARRISON, SIDNEY   Music for the Multitude. New York, 1940. Biblo & Tannen 214-857 1974 $8.50

HARRISSE, HENRY   Decouverte et Evolution Cartographique de Terreneuve et des Pays Circonvoisins, 1497 - 1501 - 1769 Essais de Geographie Historique et Documentaire. London & Paris, 1900. 4to., blue buckram, black label, printed wrapper bound in, limited to 380 copies, first French edition. Butterfield 10-283 1974 $75

HARRY'S Story Book. Philadelphia, n.d. 16mo., cloth, gilt lettered spine, hand colored woodcuts, presentation inscription. Frohnsdorff 16-419 1974 $25

HARSHA, WILLIAM JUSTIN   Ploughed Under. New York, 1881. Cloth. Hayman 57-197 1974 $10

HARSHA, WILLIAM JUSTIN   Ploughed Under. New York, 1881. Pictorial cloth, rubbed, with ads. Butterfield 10-313 1974 $35

HART, BASIL HENRY LIDDELL
Please turn to
LIDDELL HART, BASIL HENRY

HART, BERTHA SHEPPARD   Introduction to Georgia Writers. Macon, 1929. Presentation, inscribed, fine. Covent 55-1014 1974 £15

HART, G. E.   The Fall of New France, 1755-1760. Montreal, 1888. Portraits, views, rebound. Hood's 102-716 1974 $35

HART, GEORGE   The Violin. 1875. 8vo., orig. cloth. Bow Windows 66-725 1974 £22.50

HART, HORACE   Bibliotheca Typographica. Rochester, 1933. 12mo., buckram, first edition. Goodspeed's 578-467 1974 $12.50

HART, JAMES   Kainikh. London, 1633. Folio, contemporary calf, rebacked, gilt, first edition. Dawsons PM 249-235 1974 £285

HART, JOHN   Pioneer Days in the Southwest from 1850 to 1879. Guthrie, 1909. Illus., pict. cloth, exceptionally clean & bright. Jenkins 61-1005 1974 $47.50

HART, JOHN S.   Spenser and the Fairy Queen. 1854. Full leather, raised bands, gilt, illus. Austin 61-457 1974 $17.50

HART, JOSEPH C.   Miriam Coffin. New York, 1834. 2 vols., 12mo., orig. grey-brown cloth, orig. publisher's morocco labels, good copy, first edition. Ximenes 37-102 1974 $200

HART, MOSS   Act One. Random House, 1959. 444p. Austin 51-406 1973 $6

HART, MOSS   Christopher Hart. Random, 1946. 115p. Austin 51-407 1973 $8.50

HART, MOSS   Once In a Life Time. Farrar, Rinehart, 1930. 236p. Austin 51-409 1973 $7.50

HART, MOSS   Winged Victory. Random House, 1943. 198p. Austin 51-408 1973 $7.50

HART, SCOTT   The Moon in Waning. New York, The Derrydale Press, 1937. Illus., blue cloth with gold dec., limited to 950 copies, very good. Current BW9-169 1974 $28.50

HART, STEPHEN H.   Zebulon Pike's Arkansas Journal in Search of the Southern Louisiana Purchase Boundary Line. Colorado Springs, 1932. Illus., maps, scarce. Jenkins 61-2199 1974 $40

HART, WILLIAM   My Life East and West. Houghton, Mifflin, 1929. 363p., illus. Austin 51-410 1973 $10

HARTE, BRET   Condensed Novels. Boston, 1871. 8vo., orig. cloth, new edition. Rota 189-428 1974 £6.50

HARTE, BRET   Devil's Ford. 1887. 8vo., orig. cloth, first edition. Rota 189-429 1974 £5

HARTE, BRET   East and West Poems. Boston, 1871. Orig. cloth, first edition, end paper loose, tipped in A.L.s from author to Charles Scribner's Monthly. MacManus 224-198 1974 $50

HARTE, BRET   Excelsior. n.d. Small oblond 8vo., orig. blue printed wrappers, first edition, first issue. Ximenes 33-172 1974 $75

HARTE, BRET   A First Family of Tasajara. 1891. 2 vols., first edition. Covent 55-816 1974 £25

HARTE, BRET   Her Letter. Houghton, 1905. 100p., illus. Austin 54-467 1973 $10

HARTE, BRET   The Luck of Roaring Camp and Other Sketches. Boston, 1870. First edition, first issue, 8vo., green cloth, spine ends worn and cracked, front inner hinge sprung, firm copy. Current BW9-228 1974 $25

HARTE, BRET   The Reveille. London, n.d. 12mo., scarce, first separate printing. Ximenes 33-173 1974 $17.50

HARTE, BRET   Three Partners. London, 1897. 8vo., orig. cloth, illus., inscription, first edition. Bow Windows 62-425 1974 £6.50

HARTE, BRET   The Wild West. Paris, 1930. Limited to 840 copies, coloured plates, 8vo., orig. canvas, good copy. Sawyer 293-159 1974 £12

HARTE, BRET   The Complete Works. 1885-89. 5 vols., crown 8vo., contemporary half calf, gilt. Howes 185-212 1974 £25

HARTE, WALTER   Essays on Husbandry. London, 1770. 8vo., contemporary calf, illus., second edition. Hammond 201-19 1974 £36

HARTENFELSS, GEORG CHRISTOPHORUS PETRUS AB   Elephantographia Curiosa seu Elephanti Descriptio. Nuremberg, 1718. 4to., contemporary vellum, worn, first edition. Thomas 28-264 1972 £80

HARTERT, E.   Aus den Wanderjahren Eines Naturforschers. Aylesbury, 1901-02. Imp. 8vo., cloth, plates, scarce. Wheldon 128-471 1973 £10

HARTFORD, Illustrated: Photogravures. Brooklyn, 1899. Wrapper. Jenkins 61-694 1974 $12.50

HARTIG, T.   Die Aderflugler Deutschlands. Berlin, 1837. 8vo., boards, plates, rare. Wheldon 130-755 1974 £15

HARTING, J. E.   The Birds of Middlesex. 1866. Crown 8vo., cloth, frontispiece, scarce. Wheldon 130-541 1974 £5

HARTING, J. E.   The Birds of Middlesex. 1866. Crown 8vo., orig. cloth. Wheldon 131-616 1974 £10

HARTING, J. E.   The Birds of Shakespeare, Critically Examined, Explained and Illustrated. 1871. 8vo., cloth, portrait, illus., scarce. Wheldon 128-473 1973 £10

HARTING, J. E.   Handbook of British Birds. 1901. 8vo., orig. buckram, plates. Wheldon 130-540 1974 £7.50

HARTING, J. E.   Hints On the Management of Hawks. 1898. 8vo., cloth, plates, scarce. Wheldon 131-615 1974 £25

HARTING, J. E.   Our Summer Migrants. 1875. 8vo., orig. cloth, woodcuts. Wheldon 128-474 1973 £5

HARTING, J. E.   Our Summer Migrants. 1875. 8vo., orig. cloth gilt, woodcuts. Wheldon 131-617 1974 £5

HARTING, J. E.   Rambles in Search of Shells. 1875. 8vo., cloth gilt, plates, scarce. Wheldon 130-827 1974 £5

HARTING, J. E.   Recreations of a Naturalist. 1906. 8vo., new cloth, illus. Wheldon 129-475 1974 £10

HARTLEY, DAVID   Observations on Man. London, 1749. 8vo., 2 vols., contemporary calf, labels, first edition. Dawsons PM 249-236 1974 £145

HARTLEY, DOROTHY   Old Book: A Mediaeval Anthology. 1930. 4to., plates. Allen 213-1529 1973 $15

HARTLEY, JOSEPH   The Wholesale and Retail Wine & Spirit Merchant's Companion. 1835. Quarter leather, gilt, boards. Covent 55-701 1974 £15

HARTLEY, JOSEPH   The Wine and Spirit Merchant's Companion. 1843. Orig. cloth, foxing, second edition. Covent 55-702 1974 £12.50

HARTLEY, L. P.   Night Fears and Other Stories. London, 1924. 1st ed. Biblo & Tannen 210-607 1973 $17.50

HARTLEY, L. P.   Night Fears and Other Stories. London, 1924. First edition, very nice copy, inscribed by author, orig. cloth, rare. Crane 7-129 1974 £60

HARTLEY, L. P.   Three, or Four, for Dinner. 1932. Fine, wrappers, English first edition. Covent 56-609 1974 £5.25

HARTLEY, L. P.   The Traveling Grave and Other Stories. Sauk City, 1948. 1st, ltd. ed. Biblo & Tannen 210-608 1973 $17.50

HARTLEY BOTANICAL LABORATORIES   University of Liverpool Publications Nos. 1 to 6. Liverpool, 1924-29. 1 vol., 4to., cloth. Wheldon 131-1150 1974 £5

HARTLEY BOTANICAL LABORATORIES, UNIV. OF LIVERPOOL   Publications. Liverpool, 1924-29. No. 1 - 6 in 1 vol., 4to., cloth, loose. Wheldon 128-1113 1973 £5

HARTLY House, Calcutta. Dublin, 1789. 12mo., contemporary calf, first Irish edition. Ximenes 33-18 1974 $90

HARTMANN, FRANZ   The Principles of Astrological Geomancy. 1889. Diagrams, orig. dec. cloth, very good copy. Covent 51-2499 1973 £5.25

HARTMUT, WALTER   Alice und andere Novellen. Berlin, 1922. Ltd. ed., with an orig. sgd. etching. Biblo & Tannen 214-274 1974 $25

HARTSHORNE, A.   Old English Glasses. 1897. Folio, plates, dec. half vellum. Quaritch 940-615 1974 £30

HARTSHORNE, C. H.   The Book Rarities in the University of Cambridge. London, 1829. Large 8vo., orig. blue cloth, illus., first edition. Ximenes 33-174 1974 $45

HARTSON, HALL   The Countess of Salisbury. London, 1767. 8vo., disbound, first edition. Ximenes 33-175 1974 $27.50

HARTSON, HALL   Youth. London, 1773. 4to., disbound, first edition. Ximenes 33-176 1974 $90

HARTZENBUSCH, JUAN EUGENIO   The Lovers of Teruel. 1938. Roy 8vo., red niger goatskin, uncut, limited edition. Broadhurst 23-1054 1974 £100

HARTZENBUSCH, JUAN EUGENIO   The Lovers of Teruel. Gregynog Press, 1938. Printed in red, roy. 8vo., red niger goatskin, blind stamp design on covers, top edges gilt, others uncut, limited to 155 copies, complete with prospectus, fine. Broadhurst 24-1012 1974 £120

HARTZENBUSCH, JUAN EUGENIO   The Lovers of Teruel. 1938. Roy 8vo., full morocco, gilt. Hammond 201-773 1974 £150

HARVARD, WILLIAM   King Charles the First. London, 1737. 8vo., modern boards, frontispiece, first edition. Dawsons PM 252-435 1974 £15

HARVARD University and Cambridge. Brooklyn, 1898. Boards, photographs. Jenkins 61-1507 1974 $12.50

HARVEY, E. N.   The Nature of Animal Light. Philadelphia, 1920. Crown 8vo., cloth, scarce. Wheldon 130-356 1974 £5

HARVEY, EDMUND GEORGE   Our Cruise in the Undine. London, 1854. 8vo., orig. gree cloth, plates, first edition. Ximenes 33-177 1974 $25

HARVEY, GIDEON   Casus Medico-Chirirgicus. London, 1678. Small 8vo., speckled calf, rebacked, gilt, first edition. Dawsons PM 249-237 1974 £120

HARVEY, WILLIAM 1578-1657   The Anatomical Exercises of. London, 1653. 8vo., old calf, worn, first English edition. Dawsons PM 250-39 1974 £2400

HARVEY, WILLIAM 1578-1657   Anatomical Exercitations. London, 1653. 8vo., full brown levant morocco, gilt, first edition in English. Dawsons PM 249-238 1974 £950

HARVEY, WILLIAM 1578-1657   Exercitationes Anatomicae. 1654. 12mo., 18th century mottled calf, rebacked. Dawsons PM 249-241 1974 £200

HARVEY, WILLIAM 1578-1657   Exercitationes de Motu Cordis et Sanguinis. 1824. 8vo., contemporary half calf, rebacked. Dawsons PM 249-242 1974 £50

HARVEY, WILLIAM 1578-1657   The Anatomical Exercises of De Motu Cordis. c. 1928. Niger morocco gilt, limited. Smith 193-395 1973 £14.50

HARVEY, WILLIAM 1578-1657   The Anatomical Exercises of. London, (1928). 8vo., niger morocco, uncut, unopened, limited. Dawsons PM 249-243 1974 £54

HARVEY, WILLIAM 1578-1657   Exercitatio Anatomica de Motu Cordis et Sanguinis in Animalibus. 1931. 8vo., orig. stiff wrappers, second edition. Dawsons PM 249-244 1974 £12

HARVEY, WILLIAM 1578-1657   Exercitationes de Generatione Animalivm. 1651. 12mo., modern limp vellum, second edition. Dawson's PM 249-239 1974 £175

HARVEY, WILLIAM 1578-1657   Exercitationes de Generatione Animalium. 1651. 12mo., contemporary calf. Wheldon 129-336 1974 £130

HARVEY, WILLIAM 1578-1657   Preclectiones Anatomiae Universalis. 1886.
4to., modern boards, uncut, first edition. Dawsons PM 249-245 1974 £26

HARVEY, WILLIAM FRYER   The Beast with Five Fingers and Other Tales.
1928. 8vo., orig. cloth, fine, dust wrapper, first edition. Rota 190-839 1974
£7.50

HARVEY, WILLIAM FRYER   Midnight House. 1910. Boards, rubbed, scarce.
Covent 55-647 1974 £25

HARVEY, WILLIAM FRYER   Midnight House and Other Tales. London,
1910. 1st ed. Biblo & Tannen 210-609 1973 $15

HARVEY, WILLIAM FRYER   Moods and Tenses. Oxford, 1933. 1st ed.
Biblo & Tannen 210-610 1973 $17.50

HARVEY, WILLIAM HENRY   Flora Capensis. (1859-1927). 7 vols. in 10,
8vo., cloth. Wheldon 131-1301 1974 £95

HARVEY, WILLIAM HENRY   Flora Capensis. (1859-1927). 8vo., cloth.
Wheldon 129-1079 1974 £50

HARVEY, WILLIAM HENRY   A Manual of the British Marine Algae. 1849.
8vo., orig. cloth, plates, second edition. Wheldon 129-1400 1974 £15

HARVEY, WILLIAM HENRY   A Manual of the British Marine Algae. 1849.
8vo., cloth, plates, scarce, second edition. Wheldon 130-1293 1974 £10

HARVEY, WILLIAM HENRY   Nereis Boreali-Americana. Washington, 1858.
4to., 3 vols., orig. cloth, plates. Wheldon 130-1291 1974 £150

HARVEY, WILLIAM HENRY   Phycologia Australica. 1858-63. Roy. 8vo.,
5 vols., publishers' cloth, plates, rare. Wheldon 130-27 1974 £450

HARVEY, WILLIAM HENRY   Phycologia Britannica. 1846-51. 4 vols., roy.
8vo., orig. brown cloth, coloured plates. Wheldon 128-1369 1973 £75

HARVEY, WILLIAM HENRY   The Sea-Side Book. 1849. Post 8vo., cloth,
new edition. Wheldon 128-146 1973 £5

HARVEY, WILLIAM HENRY   The Sea-Side Book. 1854. Post 8vo., cloth,
third edition. Wheldon 129-219 1974 £5

HARVEY, WILLIAM HENRY   Synopsis of British Seaweeds. 1857. Post 8vo.,
cloth, scarce. Wheldon 131-1415 1974 £5

HARVEY-DARTON, F. J.   Modern Book-Illustration in Great Britain and
America. London & New York, 1931. 4to., plates, orig. printed wrappers.
Dawsons PM 10-269 1974 £6

HARVEY-GIBSON, R. J.   Outlines of the History of Botany. 1919. 8vo.,
cloth, scarce. Wheldon 128-108 1973 £7.50

HARVIE-BROWN, J. A.   Vertebrate Fauna of Scotland. Edinburgh,
1887-1911, 1935. 12 vols., 8vo., orig. cloth, plates, maps. Wheldon 128-244
1973 £75

THE HARWICH Guide. Ipswich, 1808. 8vo., orig. boards, uncut, frontispiece.
Quaritch 939-352 1974 £20

HARWOOD, BUSICK   A System of Comparative Anatomy and Physiology. Cambridge, 1796. 4to., orig. wrappers, uncut, first edition. Gurney
64-106 1974 £25

HARWOOD, JOHN BERWICK   The Bridal and the Bride. London, 1851.
8vo., orig. cloth, first edition. Ximenes 33-179 1974 $22.50

HARWOOD, LEE   The Beautiful Atlas. n.d. Fine, wrappers,
English first edition. Covent 56-611 1974 £5.25

HARWOOD, T.   The History and Antiquities of the Church and
City of Lichfield. Gloucester, 1806. 4to., old calf. Quaritch 939-547
1974 £15

HASELMORE, A.   The Economist. 1824. 8vo., plates, boards,
frontispiece. Quaritch 939-135 1974 £35

HASKELL, ARNOLD L.   Miracle in the Gorbals. Albyn Press, 1946.
163p. Austin 51-411 1973 $10

HASKIN, FREDERIC J.   The Immigrant. Revell, 1913. 251p., illus.
Austin 62-250 1974 $12.50

HASKINS, CHARLES H.   Studies in Mediaeval Culture. 1929.
300 pages, orig. edition. Howes 186-897 1974 £5

HASKOLL, W. D.   Railway Construction. London, 1857. 4to., 2
vols., orig. cloth, gilt, illus., plates, first edition. Hammond 201-910 1974
£35

HASLAM, JOHN   Sound Mind. London, 1819. 8vo., orig.
boards, worn, rebacked, first edition. Dawsons PM 249-254 1974 £115

HASLEM, J.   The Old Derby China Factory. 1876. Imp.
8vo., orig. cloth gilt, worn. Quaritch 939-337 1974 £25

HASLEWOOD, FRANCIS   Memorials of Smarden, Kent. Ipswich, 1886.
Crown 4to., illus., scarce. Howes 186-2042 1974 £16

HASLEWOOD, JOSEPH   The Dialogues of Creatures Moralised. London,
1816. 4to., half calf, rare, illus. Ximenes 33-180 1974 $75

HASSALL, A. H.   A History of British Freshwater Algae. 1845.
2 vols., 8vo., orig. cloth, plates, nice copy. Wheldon 131-1416 1974 £30

HASSALL, ARTHUR HILL   Adulterations Detected. London, 1857. 8vo.,
orig. cloth, back slightly torn, illus. Gurney 66-82 1974 £18

HASSE, ADELAIDE R.   Index of Economic Material in the Documents
of the State of Delaware, 1789-1904. Washington, 1910. Wrapper, folio.
Jenkins 61-769 1974 $17.50

HASSELL, JOHN   The Camera. London, 1823. 8vo., orig. boards,
plates, first edition. Hammond 201-711 1974 £56

HASSELL, JOHN   The Camera. 1823. 8vo., plates, orig.
boards, label, very scarce, first edition. Quaritch 940-131 1974 £70

HASSELL, JOHN   The Camera. (1840). 8vo., cloth gilt, plate,
etching. Quaritch 940-132 1974 £60

HASSELL, JOHN   Picturesque Rides and Walks. 1817-18.
2 vols., 8vo., contemporary calf, plates. Quaritch 939-841 1974 £500

HASSELL, JOHN   Picturesque Rides and Walks. London, 1817-18.
2 vols., small 8vo., polished calf gilt, leather labels, fine, plates. Traylen
79-302 1973 £220

HASSELL, JOHN   Tour of the Grand Junction. 1819. 8vo.,
plates, half calf, gilt. Quaritch 939-79 1974 £325

HASSELL, JOHN   Tour of Isle of Wight. 1790. 2 vols. in 1,
new buckram, rubber stamp, plates. Allen 216-2025 1974 $25

HASSELL, JOHN   Tour of the Isle of Wight. 1790. 2 vols.,
8vo., plates, half roan, rubbed. Quaritch 939-374 1974 £16

HASSELL, JOHN   Tour of the Isle of Wight. London, 1790. 2
vols., 8vo., later green morocco, rubbed, first edition, inscription. Ximenes
36-114 1974 $150

HASSELQUIST, FREDERIC   Voyages and Travels in the Levant; in the Years
1749-52. London, 1766. 8vo., contemporary calf, spine gilt, first edition in
English, nice copy, folding map. Ximenes 36-115 1974 $100

HASTED, EDWARD   The History and Topographical Survey of the
County of Kent. 1797-1801. 12 vols., 8vo., full contemporary tree calf,
illus., plates, labels, second edition. Howes 186-2043 1974 £295

HASTINGS, FRANK S.   A Ranchman's Recollections. Chicago, 1921.
Cloth, presentation copy, first edition. Hayman 57-288 1974 $35

HASTINGS, JAMES   A Dictionary of the Bible. Edinburgh, 1906-09.
5 vols., roy. 8vo., half morocco. Traylen 79-174 1973 £10

HASTINGS, JAMES   Encyclopaedia of Religion and Ethics.
Edinburgh, 1908-27. 13 vols., cloth. Dawsons PM 11-389 1974 £104

HASTINGS, JAMES   Encyclopaedia of Religion and Ethics.
Edinburgh, 1908-26. 13 vols., 4to. Traylen 79-173 1973 £40

HASTINGS, SALLY   Poems on Different Subjects. Lancaster, 1808.
Contemporary sheep, rubbed, morocco label, first editic., some staining &
foxing, lacks last leaf of list of subscribers. MacManus 224-199 1974 $125

HASTINGS, WARREN   The Present State of the East Indies. London,
1786. 8vo., modern boards, third edition. Dawsons PM 247-141 1974 £15

HASTY PUDDING CLUB   The Thirteenth Catalog and a History of the.
Cambridge, 1907. Fine. Ballinger 1-51 1974 $10

HATCH, ALDEN   Full Titl, The Sporting Memoirs of Foxhall Kenne.
New York, The Derrydale Press, 1938. Limited to 950 numbered copies, colored
frontis., illus., orig. blue cloth, very fine. Current BW9-166 1974 $40

HATCH, CHARLES   Genealogy of the Descendants of Anthony
Collomer of Scituate, Massachusetts. Salem, 1915. 8vo., cloth. Saddleback
14-779 1974 $25

HATCH, EDWIN   The Growth of Church Institutions. London,
1895. Biblo & Tannen 214-618 1974 $9.50

HATCH, EDWIN   The Influence of Greek Ideas and Usages Upon
the Christian Church. London, 1907. Poor copy. Biblo & Tannen 214-619 1974
$9.50

HATCH, F. H.   The Gold Mines of the Rand. 1895. Roy 8vo.,
buckram. Broadhurst 23-1648 1974 £21

HATCHER, EDMUND N.   The Last Four Weeks of the War. Columbus, 18-
92. Cloth, rubbed, fine. Hayman 57-86 1974 $10

HATCHER, H.   The Great Lakes. London, 1944. Illus.,
maps. Hood's 104-691 1974 $15

HATCHER, MATTIE AUSTIN   Letters of an Early American Traveller. Dallas,
1933. Jenkins 61-1007 1974 $22.50

HATHAWAY, E. J.   Jesse Ketchum, and His Times. Toronto, 1929.
Hood's 102-246 1974 $30

HATTON, EDWARD   An Intire System of Arithmetic. London, 1721.
4to., contemporary panelled calf, gilt, rebacked, plates, first edition. Hammond
201-832 1974 £35

HATTON, JOSEPH   Henry Irving Impressions of America. 1884.
475p. Austin 51-412 1973 $8.50

HATTON, JOSEPH   Under the Great Seal. n.d. Orig. dec. cloth,
first edition. Covent 55-834 1974 £7.50

HATTON, THOMAS   A Bibliography of the Periodical Works of C.
Dickens. London, 1933. Limited to 50 copies, large paper, illus., crown 4to.,
orig. cloth. Forster 98-64 1974 £45

HATTON, THOMAS   A Bibliography of the Periodical Works of Charles
Dickens. Limited to 750 copies, roy. 8vo., orig. cloth, fine. Forster 98-66
1974 £25

HATTON, THOMAS   A Bibliography of the Periodical Works of
Charles Dickens. 1933. Limited edition, illus., facsimiles, 8vo., orig. green
cloth gilt, fine unopened copy, scarce, limited to 750 copies. Sawyer 293-58
1974 £48

HATTON, THOMAS   A Bibliography of The Periodical Works of
Charles Dickens. London, 1933. Limited to 250 copies, illus., large paper,
signed by author, crown 4to., orig. cloth. Forster 98-65 1974 £35

HATTORI, H.   Myxomycetes of Nasie District. Japan, 1935.
8vo., cloth, plates. Wheldon 129-1230 1974 £5

HATZFIELD, JEAN   La Grece et son Heritage. Paris, 1945.
Biblo & Tannen 214-620 1974 $9.50

HAUDICQUER DE BLANCOURT, JEAN   L'Art de la Varrerie. Paris, 1718.
16mo., 2 vols., full contemporary leather, illus. Jacobs 24-137 1974 $85

HAUDICQUER DE BLANCOURT, JEAN   L'Art de la Verrerie. 1718. 2 vols.,
small 8vo., plates, contemporary calf, gilt. Quaritch 940-612 1974 £45

HAUG, E.   Traite de Geologie. Paris, 1920-21. 4 vols.
in 3, roy. 8vo., cloth. Wheldon 131-1013 1974 £12.50

HAUGEN, NILS P.   Pioneer and Political Reminscences. 1930.
198 pages. Austin 57-293 1974 $10

HAUGEN, NILS P.   Pioneer and Political Reminiscences. 1930.
Austin 62-251 1974 $10

HAUGHTON, JAMES   A Plea for Teetotalism. 1855. Small 8vo.,
bookplate, orig. cloth boards. Covent 55-710 1974 £5

HAUGHTON, SAMUEL   Principles of Animals Mechanics. London,
1873. 8vo., brown cloth, first edition. Dawsons PM 249-256 1974 £60

HAUKSBEE, FRANCIS   Experiences Physico-Mechaniques sur Differens
Sujets. Paris, 1754. 12mo., 2 vols., contemporary mottled calf, gilt, first edition in French. Dawsons PM 245-367 1974 £55

HAUKSBEE, FRANCIS   Physico-Mechanical Experiments on Various Subjects. London, 1709. 4to., contemporary panelled calf, rebacked, first edition.
Dawsons PM 245-366 1974 £245

HAULTAIN, ARNOLD   Hints for Lovers. Boston & New York, 1909.
Numbered, fine, slip case. Ballinger 1-23 1974 $15

THE HAUNTERS and the Haunted. London, 1921. 1st ed. Biblo & Tannen 210-
656 1973 $15

HAUPTMANN, GERHART   Der Ketzer von Soana. Berlin, 1918.
Wrappers, first German edition. Covent 55-756 1974 £6.50

HAUPTMANN, GERHART   The Sunken Bell. Doubleday, Page, 1899.
125p., illus. Austin 51-413 1973 $7.50

HAUPTMANN, GERHART   Von Wilhelm Heise. Leipzig, n.d. 12mo.
Biblo & Tannen 213-776 1973 $8.50

HAUSER, C. A.   Latent Religious Resources in the Public
School Education. 1924. 319 pages. Austin 57-292 1974 $17.50

HAUSER, C. A.   Latent Religious Resources in Public School
Education. Heidelberg Press, 1925. Austin 62-252 1974 $17.50

HAUSER, H.   L'Or: L'Or dans le Laboratoire L'Or dans la
Nature. Paris, (n.d. c. 1908?). 4to., recent cloth, morocco label, maps.
Bow Windows 66-320 1974 £21.50

HAUSER, H.   Les Sources de l'Histoire de France Depuis les
Origines. Paris, 1906-15. 4 vols., 8vo., cloth. Dawsons PM 11-391
1974 £32

HAUSSONVILLE, COMTE D'   Madame de Stael et M. Necker. Paris, 1925.
Large 8vo., contemporary three quarter blue morocco, gilt. L. Goldschmidt
42-377 1974 $10

HAUTEFEUILLE, JEAN   Probleme D'Acoustique. Paris, 1788. 8vo.,
gilt, orig. wrappers, half green morocco, first edition. Zeitlin 235-109 1974
$125

HAUY, M.   Tableau Comparatif Des Resultats. Paris, 1809.
Contemporary half calf, book plate, plates. Bow Windows 64-123 1974 £28

HAUY, RENE JUST   Exposition Raisonnee de la Theorie de l'Electricite
et du Magnetisme. Paris, 1787. 8vo., contemporary French mottled sheep, gilt,
first edition. Dawsons PM 245-368 1974 £85

HAUY, RENE JUST   Instruction sur les Poids et Mesures Republicaines.
Paris, (1794). 8vo., half calf, gilt, second edition. Dawsons PM 245-369 1974
£55

HAUY, RENE JUST   Traite Elementaire de Physique. Paris, 1806.
8vo., 2 vols., contemporary tree calf, gilt, fine. Dawsons PM 245-370 1974
£38

HAVARD, HENRY   The Dead Cities of the Zuyder Zee. London,
1875. 8vo., orig. cloth, illus., first English edition. Ximenes 33-181 1974
$17.50

HAVARD, WILLIAM   King Charles the First. 8vo., cloth, frontispiece,
first edition. Quaritch 936-100 1974 £12

HAVARD, WILLIAM   Regulus. London, 1744. 8vo., old calf,
worn, first edition. Ximenes 33-182 1974 $30

HAVELOCK, ELLIS   Marriage Today and Tomorrow. San Francisco,
1929. First edition, limited to 500 copies, signed by author, orange boards,
black cloth back, top of spine cracked, covers soiled, interior bright. Current
BW9-514 1974 $18.75

HAVEN, PETER VON   Reise in Russland. Copenhagen, 1744.
8vo., contemporary half calf. Harper 213-88 1973 $155

HAVERFORD Verse. Philadelphia, 1908. First edition, orig. binding. Wilson
63-520 1974 $12.50

HAVERHILL, Massachusetts: An Industrial and Commercial Center. Haverhill,
1889. 8vo., wrapper. Saddleback 14-484 1974 $10

HAVERS, CLOPTON   Novae Quaedam Observationes de Ossibus.
1731. Small 8vo., contemporary calf, second Latin edition. Dawsons PM 249-
257 1974 £70

HAVERS, CLOPTON   Novae Quaedam Observationes de Ossibus.
Leyden, 1734. 8vo., contemporary leather-backed boards, plates, worn.
Schuman 37-121 1974 $95

HAVILAND, M. D.   Studies in Animal Environment. Cambridge,
1926. 8vo., cloth, plates, scarce. Wheldon 129-337 1974 £7.50

THE HAWAIIAN Islands: Their Resources Agricultural, Commercial and Financial.
Honolulu, 1896. Pict. wrapper, illus. Jenkins 61-1025 1974 $15

HAWARD, WARRINGTON   Phlebitis and Thrombosis. New York, 1906.
Rittenhouse 46-328 1974 $10

HAWEIS, H. R.   Old Violins. 1898. 8vo., orig. cloth,
plates, covers dull. Bow Windows 66-321 1974 £8

HAWEIS, THOMAS   Siberian Anecdotes. London, 1783. 3 vols.,
12mo., contemporary calf, scarce, first edition. Ximenes 33-183 1974 $200

HAWERS, H. R.   American Humorists. Funk, Wagnall, 1881.
180p. Austin 54-468 1973 $12.50

HAWES, CHARLES BOARDMAN   The Dark Frigate. Boston, (1923). 8vo.,
pictorial cloth, illus., very good copy, first edition. Frohnsdorff 16-421 1974
$35

HAWES, WILLIAM POST   Sporting Scenes and Sundry Sketches. New
York, 1842. 2 vols., 12mo., orig. cloth, fine, first edition. Ximenes 33-185
1974 $80

HAWKER, ROBERT STEPHEN   The Cornish Ballads. Oxford & London, 1869.
8vo., orig. green cloth, fine, first edition. Ximenes 33-186 1974 $40

HAWKER, ROBERT STEPHEN   The Cornish Ballads. Oxford & London, 1869.
8vo., orig. cloth gilt, uncut, first edition. Dawsons PM 252-436 1974 £45

HAWKER, ROBERT STEPHEN   Cornish Ballads and Other Poems. Oxford and
London, 1869. Orig. gilt, english first edition. Covent 56-612 1974 £50

HAWKER, ROBERT STEPHEN   Cornish Ballads and Other Poems. 1908. Orig.
cloth, plates, English first edition. Covent 56-613 1974 £6.50

HAWKER, ROBERT STEPHEN   Ecclesia. Oxford, 1840. 8vo., orig. cloth,
presentation, first edition. Ximenes 33-187 1974 $200

HAWKESWORTH, JOHN   An Account of the Voyages. London, 1773-
77-85. 9 vols., 4to., dark brown half morocco, gilt, plates, first & second
editions. Dawsons PM 250-40 1974 £1600

HAWKESWORTH, JOHN   The Adventurer. London, 1753. 2 vols.,
small folio, contemporary calf, first edition. Dawsons PM 252-547 1974 £240

HAWKESWORTH, JOHN   The Adventurer. London, 1756. 4 vols.,
8vo., contemporary speckled calf, third edition. Dawsons PM 252-548 1974
£22

HAWKESWORTH, JOHN   The Adventurer. London, 1778. 4 vols.,
8vo., contemporary calf, labels, new edition. Dawsons PM 252-549 1974 £28

HAWKESWORTH, JOHN   The Adventurer. London, 1794. 3 vols.,
large 8vo., contemporary tree calf, gilt, new edition. Dawsons PM 252-550
1974 £24

HAWKINS, ALFRED   Hawkins's Picture of Quebec. Quebec, 1834.
Orig. drawings, worn cover. Hood's 103-772 1974 $60

HAWKINS, ANTHONY HOPE   The Chronicles of Count Antonio. 1895.
Spine faded, else very good, first edition. Covent 51-931 1973 £5.25

HAWKINS, EDGAR   Medical Climatology of England and Wales.
London, 1923. Rittenhouse 46-329 1974 $10

HAWKINS, EDWARD   The Church in the Colonies. London, 1850.
4 parts in 1, maps. Hood's 104-306 1974 $250

HAWKINS, FRANCIS   A Narrative. London, 1681. Folio, disbound,
first edition. Dawsons PM 251-244 1974 £20

HAWKINS, J. H.   History of the Worshipful Company of the Art and
Mistery of Feltmakers of London. 1917. Crown 8vo., full morocco. Broadhurst
23-1236 1974 £10

HAWKINS, JOHN   An Essay On the Law of Celibacy Imposed
On the Clergy of the Roman Catholic Church. Worcester, (1782). 8vo., old
rough calf, orig. wrapper. Traylen 79-175 1973 £10

HAWKINS, JOHN   The Life of Samuel Johnson. London, 1787.
8vo., contemporary calf, morocco label, first edition. Dawsons PM 252-575
1974 £50

HAWKINS, R.   A Discourse of the Nationall Excellencies of
England. London, 1658. Small 8vo., calf. Quaritch 939-136 1974 £80

HAWKINS, THOMAS   The Origin of the English Drama. Oxford,
1773. 3 vols., 8vo., contemporary calf, first edition. Dawsons PM 252-437
1974 £17

HAWKSHAW, J. C.   Japanese Sword Mounts. 1910. Folio,
plates, cloth, limited edition. Quaritch 940-396 1974 £150

HAWLEY, JESSE   An Essay on the Enlargement of the Erie Canal,
With Arguments in Favor of Retaining the Present Proposed Sive of Seventy Feet
by Seven. Lockport, 1840. 8vo., orig. plain pink wrappers, first edition, very
good copy, very scarce. Ximenes 36-116 1974 $40

HAWORTH, SAMUEL   The True Method of Curing Consumptions.
London, 1683. 12mo., modern half morocco. Traylen 79-236 1973 £40

HAWSER, HARRY   Buds and Flowers of Leisure Hours.
Philadelphia, 1844. First edition, orig. binding, signature of former owner on
title page. Wilson 63-522 1974 $15

HAWTHORNE, JULIAN   Bressant. New York, 1873. First edition, 8vo.,
cloth on back hinge cracked, extremities worn, interior very good. Current
BW9-229 1974 $12.50

HAWTHORNE, JULIAN   Hawthorne and His Circle. Harper, 1903.
372p., orig. ed. Austin 54-469 1973 $10

HAWTHORNE, JULIAN   Nathaniel Hawthorne and His Wife. Houghton,
1884. 505p., 465p. (2 vols.), orig. ed. Austin 54-470 1973 $17.50

HAWTHORNE, JULIAN   The Secret of Solomon. Julian Hawthorne and Company. Solomon Columbus Rhodes and Company. (N. P.), 1909. 3 vols., 12mo., wrappers, first editions. Goodspeed's 578-125 1974 $17.50

HAWTHORNE, JULIAN   The Trial of Gideon. New York, 1886. Orig. half cloth, first U.S. edition. Covent 56-1715 1974 £25

HAWTHORNE, NATHANIEL   The Blithedale Romance. Boston, 1852. Orig. cloth, ends of spine chipped, first American edition, fine. MacManus 224-204 1974 $35

HAWTHORNE, NATHANIEL   The Blithedale Romance. Boston, 1852. 8vo., orig. cloth, first American edition. Ximenes 33-188 1974 $40

HAWTHORNE, NATHANIEL   The Blithedale Romance. 1852. 2 vols., orig. patterned cloth, first edition. Covent 55-819 1974 £45

HAWTHORNE, NATHANIEL   Doctor Grimshaw's Secret. Harvard Univ., n.d. 305p. Austin 54-572 1973 $15

HAWTHORNE, NATHANIEL   The House of the Seven Gables. Boston, 1851. First edition, cloth covers worn & rubbed, much handled but sound. Butterfield 10-284 1974 $25

HAWTHORNE, NATHANIEL   Life of Franklin Pierce. Boston, 1852. Orig. cloth, first edition, fine. MacManus 224-205 1974 $75

HAWTHORNE, NATHANIEL   Our Old Home. London, 1863. 2 vols., 8vo., orig. green cloth, fine, first London edition. Ximenes 33-189 1974 $100

HAWTHORNE, NATHANIEL   Passages from the English Note-Books. 1870. 2 vols. Allen 216-680 1974 $12.50

HAWTHORNE, NATHANIEL   The Scarlet Letter. London, n.d. 8vo., orig. red dec. cloth, first edition. Ximenes 33-190 1974 $22.50

HAWTHORNE, NATHANIEL   The Scarlet Letter. (1920). 4to., orig. cloth, plates, first edition. Bow Windows 64-542 1974 £18

HAWTHORNE, NATHANIEL   The Scarlet Letter. New York, 1935. Illus., full publisher's lea., blind-stamped, unopened copy. Jacobs 24-93 1974 $12

HAWTHORNE, NATHANIEL   The Snow-Image and Other Twice-Told Tales. Boston, 1852. Orig. cloth, first edition, publisher's catalogue inserted at front, fine. MacManus 224-206 1974 $45

HAWTHORNE, NATHANIEL   Tanglewood Tales. n.d. Half vellum, fine, numbered, illus. Covent 55-617 1974 £65

HAWTHORNE, NATHANIEL   Tanglewood Tales, for Girls and Boys. Boston, 1864. 12mo., embossed cloth, gilt pictorial spine, full page illus., engraved on wood, very good copy. Frohnsdorff 16-422 1974 $15

HAWTHORNE, NATHANIEL   Transformation. Leipzig, 1860. 2 vols., 8vo., contemporary half roan, fine. Ximenes 33-191 1974 $15

HAWTHORNE, NATHANIEL   The Weal-Reaf. N.P., 1860. Small 4to., contemporary quarter roan, marbled boards, book-plate. Ximenes 33-192 1974 $60

HAWTHORNE, NATHANIEL   A Wonder Book. n.d. Illus., numbered, signed, fine. Covent 55-1234 1974 £135

HAWTHORNE, NATHANIEL   A Wonder Book. New York, (1922). 4to., cloth, pictorially stamped in gold, color illus. by Arthur Rackham, sixteen of which are mounted on heavy paper, first American edition. Frohnsdorff 15-148 1974 $50

HAWTHORNE, NATHANIEL   A Wonder Book. (1922). Illus. by Arthur Rackham, one of 600 copies, signed by artist, this copy un-numbered, mounted coloured plates, 4to., new half green calf, top edges gilt, others uncut. George's 610-837 1973 £70

HAWTHORNE, NATHANIEL   Works. 1883-86. Small 8vo., 12 vols., half calf, gilt, frontispiece. Quaritch 936-412 1974 £65

HAWTHORNE, NATHANIEL   The Complete Works of Nathaniel Hawthorne. Houghton, 1912. 13 vols., orig. ed. Austin 54-471 1973 $110

HAWTHORNE, NATHANIEL (Mrs.)   Notes in England and Italy. Putnam, 1875. 549p., illus. ed., steel engravings. Austin 54-473 1973 $17.50

HAY, ARTHUR   The Ornithological Works Of. 1881. Thick 4to., portrait, map, plates, contemporary half morocco, book plate. Bow Windows 64-124 1974 £90

HAWTREY, CHARLES   The Truth at Last. 1924. Hinges weak, plates, covers faded. Covent 51-2465 1973 £5.25

HAY, D. R.   The Laws of Harmonious Colouring. Edinburgh, 1844. 8vo., plates, orig. cloth, fifth edition. Quaritch 940-133 1974 £28

HAY, JOHN   Castillian Days. Boston & New York, 1903. Illus. Ballinger 1-24 1974 $17.50

HAY, JOHN   In Praise of Omar. Portland, 1920. 16mo., boards, fine. Covent 55-1158 1974 £7.50

HAY, JOHN   Jim Bludso of the Prairie Belle, and Little Breeches. Boston, 1871. First edition, small 16mo., full page illus., orig. orange wrappers, very good. Current BW9-230 1974 $38.50

HAY, JOHN   Little-Breeches. New York, 1871. 8vo., orig. pictorial wrappers, illus., first edition. Quaritch 936-413 1974 £10

HAY, JOHN   The Pioneers of Ohio. Cleveland, 1879. Small 4to., orig. wrappers, scarce, first edition. Ximenes 33-193 1974 $50

HAY, WILLIAM   An Essay on Civil Government. London, 1728. 8vo., disbound, first edition. Ximenes 33-194 1974 $40

HAY, WILLIAM   Works. 1794. First collected edition, 2 vols., 4to., contemporary red straight grained morocco gilt, engraved frontispiece, spines slightly faded, fine set. Sawyer 293-162 1974 £50

HAYASHI, T.   Collection Hayashi. Dessins, Estampes, Livres Illustres. Paris, 1902. 4to., illus., cloth, worn. Quaritch 940-397 1974 £30

HAYCRAFT, HOWARD   Murder for Pleasure. New York, 1941. lst ed. Biblo & Tannen 210-481 1973 $15

HAYDEN, A. S.   Early History of the Disciples in the Western Reserve. Cincinnati, 1875. Cloth. Hayman 57-384 1974 $17.50

HAYDEN, ARTHUR   Chats on Old Prints. New York, 1906. Illus., coloured frontsipiece, lacking d.w., library bookplate, front hinge beginning to loosen, very nice copy, orig. binding. Ross 86-26 1974 $7.50

HAYDEN, ARTHUR   Kopenhagener Porzellan. Leipzig, 1924. 4to., plates, illus., cloth. Quaritch 940-637 1974 £30

HAYDEN, ARTHUR   Royal Copenhagen Porcelain. 1911. 4to., cloth, plates. Quaritch 940-636 1974 £35

HAYDEN, ARTHUR   Spode and His Successors. 1925. Illus., dust wrapper, fine. Covent 55-450 1974 £17.50

HAYDEN, ARTHUR   Spode and His Successors. 1925. Small 4to., plates, cloth. Quaritch 939-548 1974 £20

HAYDEN, ARTHUR   Spode and His Successors. 1925. Coloured plates, photos., thick roy. 8vo., cloth, fine, scarce. Sawyer 293-26 1974 £21

HAYDEN, JAMES R.   A Manual of Venereal Diseases. Philadelphia, 1898. Second edition. Rittenhouse 46-330 1974 $10

HAYDEN, STERLING   Wanderer. Knopf, 1963. 434p. Austin 51-414 1973 $6.50

HAYDN, JOSEPH   Lettres Ecrites de Vienne en Autriche sur le Celebre Compositeur Joseph Haydn. Paris, 1814. New binding, calf spine, boards. Eaton Music-608 1973 £20

HAYDN'S Dictionary of Dates and Universal Information. 1910. Thick large 8vo., rebound, cloth, scarce, twenty-fifth & best edition. Howes 186-899 1974 £8.50

HAYES, A. A.   New Colorado and the Santa Fe Trail. New York, 1880. Illus., map. Jenkins 61-1048 1974 $37.50

HAYES, A. M.   A Wreath of Christmas Poems. Norfolk, (1942). First collected edition, 8vo., d.j., mint except for slightly soiled d.j. Current BW9-71 1974 $18.75

HAYES, ALFRED   All Thy Conquests. Howell, Soskin, 1946. 295p. Austin 54-474 1973 $7.50

HAYES, ALFRED   The Big Time. Howell, Soskin, 1944. 101p., illus. Austin 54-475 1973 $12.50

HAYES, CHARLES W.   George Edward Hayes, a Memorial. Buffalo, 1882. Half morocco, rare. Jenkins 61-1049 1974 $150

HAYES, HELEN   On Reflection. Lippincott, 1968. 253p., illus. Austin 51-415 1973 $7.50

HAYES, RICHARD   A New Method for Valuing of Annuities Upon Lives. London, 1746. 4to., half morocco, spine repaired, second edition. Ximenes 37-103 1974 $50

HAYES, RICHARD   Old Irish Links With France. Dublin, 1940. 8vo., cloth boards. Emerald 50-398 1974 £7.50

HAYES, RUTHERFORD B.   Letters and Messages Of. Washington, 1881. Three quarter morocco, signed. Jenkins 48-375 1973 $55

HAYES, S.   A Practical Treatise on Planting. 1822. 8vo., half calf, plates. Wheldon 129-1606 1974 £5

HAYES, THOMAS   A Serious Address on the Dangerous Consequences of Neglecting Common Coughs and Colds. London, 1786. 8vo., boards, third edition. Hammond 201-543 1974 £5.50

HAYES, WILLIAM FOSTER   Sixty Years of Owensboro. Owensboro, (1943). 12mo., cloth. Saddleback 14-446 1974 $25

HAYLEY, WILLIAM   Epistle to a Friend on the Death of John Thornton. London, 1780. 4to., modern boards, second edition. Ximenes 33-195 1974 $27.50

HAYLEY, WILLIAM   A Philosophical, Historical, and Moral Essay on Old Maids. London, 1785. 8vo., 3 vols., contemporary calf, first edition. Hammond 201-309 1974 £35

HAYLEY, WILLIAM   The Triumphs of Temper. Chichester, 1803. 8vo., orig. boards, rebacked, uncut, fine, twelfth edition. Quaritch 936-306 1974 £200

HAYLEY, WILLIAM   The Triumphs of Temper. Chichester, 1805. Twelfth edition corrected, engravings by William Blake, first edition with Blake's plates, slight offsets, else good copy, small 8vo., dark blue crushed levant morocco gilt. Thomas 32-85 1974 £130

HAYM, NICOLA FRANCESCO   Biblioteca Italiana o Sia Notizia de Libri Rari Nella Lingua Italiana. Venice, 1741. 4to., contemporary calf. Kraus B8-85 1974 $65

HAYNES, DOROTHY K.   Thou Shalt Not Suffer a Witch and Other Stories. London, 1949. 1st ed., illus. Biblo & Tannen 210-611 1973 $15

HAYNES, EMORY JAMES   A Wedding in War-Time. Boston, 1889. Orig. cloth, somewhat soiled, hinges tender, first edition. MacManus 224-207 1974 $30

HAYS, ARTHUR   Let Freedom Ring. Boni, Liveright, 1928. 341p. Austin 51-416 1973 $6.50

HAYS, HELEN, "MRS. W. J. HAYS"   The Princess Idleways. New York, 1880. 16mo., illus. Biblo & Tannen 210-747 1973 $15

HAYS, LOUISE FREDERICK   History of Macon County, Georgia. Atlanta, 1933. 8vo., cloth, map. Saddleback 14-353 1974 $50

HAYS, WILL H.   The Memoirs of Will H. Hays. Doubleday, 1955. Austin 51-417 1973 $7.50

HAYS, WILL H.   See and Hear. 1929. Austin 51-418 1973 $7.50

HAYWARD, ABRAHAM   Biographical and Critical Essays. 1873-74. 3 vols., 8vo., full polished calf, gilt, light foxing. Bow Windows 66-324 1974 £30

HAYWARD, C.   The Courtesan. 1926. Crown 4to., orig. cloth backed boards, uncut, slight spotting, leather book plate of W. A. Foyle, limited. Bow Windows 66-325 1974 £12.50

HAYWARD, C.   Courtesan: The Part She has Played in Classic and Modern Literature and Life. 1926. 4to., plates. Allen 216-685 1974 $10

HAYWARD, H. E.   The Structure of Economic Plants. New York, 1918. 8vo., cloth, scarce. Wheldon 129-1658 1974 £7.50

HAYWARD, H. E.   The Structure of Economic Plants. New York, 1938. 8vo., cloth, scarce. Wheldon 131-1784 1974 £7.50

HAYWARD, JOHN   The Rape of the Lock. 1939-43. 8vo., 3 vols., cloth, dust wrappers. Quaritch 936-414 1974 £120

HAYWOOD, C. W.   To the Mysterious Lorian Swamp. London, 1927. 8vo., map, illus., orig. cloth, first edition. Bow Windows 62-430 1974 £5.50

HAYWOOD, ELIZA   Memoirs of a Certain Island Adjacent to the Kingdom of Utopia. 1726. 8vo., 2 vols., contemporary calf, second edition. Hill 126-195 1974 £65

HAZARD, CAROLINE   Anchors of Tradition. New Haven, 1924. First edition, 8vo., small spots on front cover, else very fine. Current BW9-417 1974 $37.50

HAZELTINE'S Almanack for 1886. Orig. pink printed wrappers, fine, 2 X 1 3/8 inches. Gregory 44-387 1974 $13.50

HAZELTINE'S Almanack for 1889. Orig. green pictorial wrapper, fine, 2 X 1 3/8 inches. Gregory 44-388 1974 $13.50

HAZELTINE'S Almanack for 1892. Orig. red pictorial wrapper, fine, 2 X 1 3/8 inches. Gregory 44-389 1974 $13.50

HAZLITT, WILLIAM   An Abridgement of the Light of Nature Pursued. London, 1807. 8vo., contemporary calf, spine rubbed, hinges tender, first edition. Ximenes 37-107 1974 $125

HAZLITT, WILLIAM   Characteristics. London, 1823. 12mo., contemporary half mauve calf, first edition. Dawsons PM 252-439 1974 £32

HAZLITT, WILLIAM   Criticisms on Art. London, 1856. Small 8vo., unopened, orig. cloth, second edition. Bow Windows 62-431 1974 £6.50

HAZLITT, WILLIAM   The Fight. Woodstock, 1929. Edition limited to 1000 numbered copies, signed by publisher, 12mo., fine colored frontis., orig. boards, paper label, some fading, else fine. Current BW9-185 1974 $16.50

HAZLITT, WILLIAM   Lectures on the English Poets, Delivered At the Surrey Institution. 1818. Half calf, label, first edition. Howes 185-214 1974 £38

HAZLITT, WILLIAM   Liber Amoris. London, 1823. 12mo., later 19th century calf, gilt, first edition. Ximenes 33-196 1974 $65

HAZLITT, WILLIAM   Memoirs of the Late Thomas Holcroft. London, 1816. 3 vols., 12mo., orig. light blue boards, printed paper labels, rare, first edition. Ximenes 37-108 1974 $275

HAZLITT, WILLIAM   Miscellaneous Works. 1848. 5 vols., new buckram. Allen 216-687 1974 $35

HAZLITT, WILLIAM   The Plain Speaker. London, 1826. 2 vols., 8vo., modern calf backed boards, first edition. Dawsons PM 252-440 1974 £55

HAZLITT, WILLIAM   A Reply to Z. 1923. One of 300 copies on hand made paper, buckram, gilt top, bookplate, fine, torn d.w., first edition. Covent 51-689 1973 £6.30

HAZLITT, WILLIAM   Sketches and Essays. London, 1839. 8vo., orig. dark green cloth, library bookplate, nice copy, first edition. Ximenes 37-104 1974 $22.50

HAZLITT, WILLIAM   The Spirit of Monarchy. London, n.d. 12mo., disbound, very good copy, second separate edition. Ximenes 37-105 1974 $75

HAZLITT, WILLIAM   The Spirit of the Age. London, 1825. Orig. grey boards, paper label, extremely well preserved, first edition. Covent 51-887 1973 £75

HAZLITT, WILLIAM   Table-Talk. London, 1821-22. 2 vols., 8vo., later half calf, scarce, first edition. Ximenes 37-106 1974 $100

HAZLITT, WILLIAM CAREW 1834-1913   Collections and Notes, 1867-76. 1876. New buckram, rubber stamp. Allen 216-690 1974 $15

HAZLITT, WILLIAM CAREW 1834-1913   Faiths and Folklore. 1905. 8vo., 2 vols., orig. cloth, plates. Broadhurst 23-1735 1974 £8

HAZLITT, WILLIAM CAREW 1834-1913   Leisure Intervals. 1897. 8vo., orig. cloth, uncut, first edition. Bow Windows 66-328 1974 £8.50

HAZLITT, WILLIAM CAREW 1834-1913   Memoirs of. 1867. 8vo., 2 vols., orig. cloth, first edition. Bow Windows 64-544 1974 £16.50

HAZLITT, WILLIAM CAREW 1834-1913   Memoirs of. London, 1867. 2 vols., 8vo., orig. green cloth, fine, first edition. Ximenes 33-197 1974 $35

HEAD, EDITH   The Dress Doctor. Little, Brown, 1959. 249p., illus. Austin 51-419 1973 $6.50

HEAD, SIR FRANCIS BOND   Bubbles from the Brunnens of Nassau. 1834. Vellum, soiled, lithographs, foxed, presentation copy. Allen 216-693 1974 $25

HEAD, SIR FRANCIS BOND   The Emigrant. London, 1846. Orig. pict. boards. Jacobs 24-16 1974 $40

HEAD, SIR FRANCIS BOND   A Faggot of French Sticks. London, 1852. 8vo., 2 vols., orig. blue cloth, fine, first edition. Ximenes 33-198 1974 $20

HEAD, SIR FRANCIS BOND   A Narrative. London, 1839. Orig. green cloth gilt, second edition. Dawsons PM 251-245 1974 £10

HEAD, SIR FRANCIS BOND   A Narrative. London, 1839. Faded, first edition. Hood's 103-537 1974 $30

HEAD, SIR FRANCIS BOND   Rough Notes. 1826. Crown 8vo., contemporary half calf, boards. Broadhurst 23-1649 1974 £18

HEAD, SIR FRANCIS BOND   Rough Notes Taken During Some Rapid Journeys Across the Pampas and Among the Andes. 1826. Crown 8vo., contemporary half calf, marbled boards, fine. Broadhurst 24-1622 1974 £16

HEAD, SIR FRANCIS BOND   Stokers and Pokers. London, 1849. 8vo., first edition, contemporary half calf. Hammond 201-931 1974 £12.50

HEAD, G.   A Home Tour Through the Manufacturing Districts of England. 1836. 8vo., half calf. Quaritch 939-137 1974 £12.50

HEADICAR, B. M.   A London Bibliography of the Social Sciences. London, 1931-4. Vols. 1-5, crown 4to., orig. wrappers. Forster 98-130 1974 £65

HEADLEY, H.   Select Beauties of Ancient English Poetry. 1810. 2 vols. in 1, buckram, ex-library. Allen 216-1508 1974 $12.50

HEADLEY, J. T.   The Parlor Book. New York, 1850. 1st ed. Biblo & Tannen 210-732 1973 $15

HEAL, A.   The London Goldsmiths. Cambridge, 1935. Roy 4to., orig. cloth, uncut, plates, fine, limited edition. Broadhurst 23-96 1974 £40

HEALD, F. D.   Manual of Plant Diseases. New York, 1926. 8vo., cloth. Wheldon 129-920 1974 £5

HEALES, ALFRED   The Records of Merton Priory In the Doctrine of the Mysticol Body. 1898. Crown 4to., orig. cloth, plates. Howes 185-1434 1974 £12.50

HEALEY, CHARLES E. H. CHADWYCK   The History of the Part of West Somerset. 1901. Imp. 8vo., plates, illus., half calf gilt, fine, limited edition. Howes 186-2186 1974 £30

HEALTH and Pleasure on "America's Greatest Railroad". (New York, 1895). Wrappers, photos, drawings, folding maps & charts, minor dampstaining, very good copy. Hayman 59-581 1974 $15

HEALY, M. A.   Report of the Cruise of the Revenue Marine Steamer, Corwin, in the Arctic Ocean, 1885. Washington, 1887. Leather, maps, charts, illus. Hood's 104-83 1974 $55

HEALY, T. M.   Letters and Leaders of My Day. London, n.d. 2 vols., 8vo., illus., cloth, faded. Emerald 50-413 1974 £5

HEARD, JOHN   John Wheelwright, 1592-1679. Boston, 1930. First edition, orig. binding, last 3 leaves very lightly foxed. Wilson 63-346 1974 $12.75

HEARN, GEORGE A.   De Luxe Illustrated Catalogue of the Notable Art Collection Formed by the Late George A. Hearn. New York, 1918. 2 vols., 4to., illus., orig. boards, wrappers. Quaritch 940-789 1974 £10

HEARN, GEORGE A.   The George A. Hearn Collection of Carved Ivories. 1908. 4to., illus., half morocco, gilt. Quairtch 940-452 1974 £17

HEARN, LAFCADIO   Appreciations of Poetry. (1919). Orig. cloth, first English edition. Rota 188-395 1974 £5

HEARN, LAFCADIO   Gombo Zhebes. New York. Binding soiled, first edition. Rich Summer-73 1974 $35

HEARN, LAFCADIO   Karma. New York, 1918. 12mo. Biblo & Tannen 210-873 1973 $6.50

HEARN, LAFCADIO   Kotto. New York, 1902. 1st ed. Biblo & Tannen 210-733 1973 $17.50

HEARN, LAFCADIO   Letters from the Raven, Being the Correspondence of . . . With Henry Watkin. New York, 1907. Orig. binding. Butterfield 10-285 1974 $15

HEARN, LAFCADIO   Letters to a Pagan. Detroit, 1933. Boards, gilt, dust wrapper, slipcase, fine. Dawson's 424-274 1974 $50

HEARN, LAFCADIO   One of Cleopatra's Nights. 1907. Orig. pictorial cloth, English first edition. Covent 56-617 1974 £7.50

HEARN, LAFCADIO   The Romance of the Milky Way and Other Stories. Boston & New York, 1905. Faded spine. Ballinger 1-25 1974 $10

HEARN, LAFCADIO   Sketches and Tales from the French. 1935. Cloth, dust wrapper. Dawson's 424-275 1974 $50

HEARN, LAFCADIO   Some Chinese Ghosts. Boston, 1887. First edition, 12mo., red cloth, some minor soiling & rubbing at corners and edges. Current BW9-231 1974 $20

HEARN, LAFCADIO   Stray Leaves from Strange Literature. 1884. Terracotta binding. Allen 216-697 1974 $50

HEARN, LAFCADIO   Stray Leaves from Strange Literature. Boston, 1884. Orig. cloth, bit rubbed, first edition. MacManus 224-208 1974 $75

HEARN, LAFCADIO   Works. Boston, 1922. Cloth dust wrappers. Dawson's 424-272 1974 $450

HEARNE, SAMUEL   A Journey from Prince of Wale's Fort In Hudson's Bay, to the Northern Ocean. London, 1795. 4to., calf backed boards, uncut, cloth case, plates, first edition. Traylen 79-484 1973 £450

HEARNE, SAMUEL   A Journey From Prince of Wales Fort in Hudsons Bay to the Northern Ocean. London, 1795. First edition, three quarter morocco, small folio, large folding maps and plates. Jenkins 61-1051 1974 $475

HEARNE, T.   Ectypa Varia ad Historiam Britannicam Illustrandum. 1737. Folio, half roan, plates. Quaritch 939-139 1974 £20

HEARNE, THOMAS 1678-1735   A Collection of Curious Discourses. London, 1771. 8vo., 2 vols., red morocco gilt, second edition. Dawsons PM 251-34 1974 £60

HEARNE, THOMAS 1678-1735   Bibliotheca Hearneiana. London, 1848. Large 8vo., orig. boards, worn, scarce. Dawsons PM 10-275 1974 £30

HEARNE, THOMAS 1678-1735   An Extensive Collection of Works by. London and Oxford, 1703-57. 73 vols., 8vo., russia and calf. Quaritch 939-138 1974 £650

HEARNE, THOMAS 1678-1735   Reliquiqe Hearnianae. London, 1869. 3 vols., small 8vo., orig. cloth, second edition. Bow Windows 62-432 1974 £16

HEARNE, THOMAS 1744-1817   Antiquities of Great Britain. London, 1807. Oblong folio, 2 vols., straight grained mauve morocco gilt, fine. Dawsons PM 251-33 1974 £195

HEART Songs. Chapple, 1909. 513p. Austin 54-240 1973 $7.50

HEAT IN THE Mechanical Applications. London, 1885. 8vo., plates, illus., orig. blue wrappers, fine, unopened. Zeitlin 235-117 1974 $75

HEATH, DUDLEY   Miniatures. 1905. Roy. 8vo., plates, cloth, worn. Quaritch 940-134 1974 £7

HEATH, JAMES   The Works of William Hogarth. London, (1835-37). Large folio, contemporary half crimson morocco, gilt, plates. Hammond 201-484 1974 $100

HEATH, JOHN BENJAMIN   Some Account of the Worshipful Comapny of Grocers, of the City of London. 1829. 8vo., contemporary calf, rebacked, corners worn, frontispiece, slight foxing. Bow Windows 66-329 1974 £15

HEATH, JOHN BENJAMIN   Some Account of the Worshipful Company of Grocers. 1854. Thick roy. 8vo., illus., orig. cloth, rebacked. Howes 186-1440 1974 £15

HEATH, JOHN BENJAMIN   Some Account of the Worshipful Company of Grocers of the City of London. 1869. Roy. 8vo., illus., contemporary green morocco, third and best edition. Quaritch 939-455 1975 £30

HEATH, ROBERT SAMUEL   A Treatise on Geometrical Optics. Cambridge, 1887. 8vo., orig. cloth, gilt, first edition. Dawsons PM 245-371 1974 £10

HEATH, SIDNEY   Old English Houses of Alms. London, 1910. 4to., half buckram, gilt, illus. Hammond 201-406 1974 £9.50

HEATH, SIDNEY   The Romance of Symbolism. Orig. cloth, foxing, faded. Bow Windows 62-433A 1974 £4

HEATH, SIDNEY   The Romance of Symbolism. London, 1909. Large 8vo., plates, orig. cloth, rebacked, foxing. Bow Windows 62-433 1974 £5.75

HEATH, THOMAS L.   A History of Greek Mathematics. 1921. 2 vols., 8vo., diagrams, cloth. Dawsons PM 11-396 1974 £7

HEATH, WILLIAM 1737-1814   Heath's Memoirs of the American War. New York, 1904. 8vo., ex-library, good condition. Current BW9-339 1974 $12.50

HEATH ROBINSON, W.   A Song of the English. n.d. Large crown 8vo., plates, orig. pictorial buckram. Smith 194-744 1974 £6

HEATHERLEY, F.   The Peregrine Falcon at the Eyrie. 1913. Imp. 4to., cloth, photographs, scarce. Wheldon 128-476 1973 £7.50

HEATHERLEY, F.   The Peregrine Falcon at the Eyrie. 1913. Roy 8vo., orig. boards. Wheldon 129-476 1974 £7.50

HEATON'S Commercial Handbook of Canada. Toronto, 1934. 29th issue. Hood's 102-379 1974 $7.50

HEAVISIDE, OLIVER   Electrical Papers. London, 1892. 8vo., 2 vols., orig. cloth. Gurney 64-107 1974 £30

HEAVISIDE, OLIVER   Electromagnetic Theory. London, (1893-9). 8vo., 2 vols., orig. cloth, first edition. Gurney 64-108 1974 £45

HEAVISIDE, OLIVER   Electromagnetic Theory. London, (1893-9). Vols. 1 and 2, 8vo., orig. cloth, first edition. Gurney 66-83 1974 £45

HEBERDEN, WILLIAM   Antiohpiaka. N.P., 1745. 8vo., wrappers, first edition. Dawsons PM 249-258 1974 £445

HEBERDEN, WILLIAM   A Collection of the Yearly Bills of Mortality. London, 1759. 4to., contemporary calf, first edition. Dawsons PM 247-142 1974 £195

HEBERDEN, WILLIAM   Commentarii de Morborum Historia et Curatione. Londini, 1802. 8vo., full blue straight-grained morocco, gilt, first edition. Dawsons PM 249-259 1974 £285

HEBRA, FERDINAND   On Diseases of the Skin. 1866-80. 8vo., 5 vols., orig. brown cloth. Dawsons PM 249-260 1974 £11

HEBRAE, Chaldaea, Graeca et Latina Nomina. Antwerp, 1565. 16mo., old quarter red roan. Thomas 28-85 1972 £50

HECHT, BEN   A Book of Miracles. Viking, 1939. 465p. Austin 54-476 1973 $6.50

HECHT, BEN   The Champion From Far Away. Covici Friede, 1931, 323p. Austin 54-477 1973 $10

HECHT, BEN   The Champion from Far Away. New York, 1931. 8vo., orig. cloth, first edition. Rota 189-440 1974 £6.50

HECHT, BEN   A Child of the Century. S & S, 1954. 654p. Austin 54-478 1973 $7.50

HECHT, BEN   Count Bruga. Boni, 1926. 319p. Austin 54-479 1973 $6.50

HECHT, BEN   The Front Page. Covici, Friede, 1928. 189p. Austin 51-422 1973 $8.50

HECHT, BEN   Gaily, Gaily. Doubleday, 1963. 227p. Austin 54-480 1973 $6

HECHT, BEN   Gargoyles. Boni, Liveright, 1922. 346p. Austin 54-481 1973 $6.50

HECHT, BEN   A Guide For the Bedevilled. Scribner, 1944. 276p. Austin 54-482 1973 $4.50

HECHT, BEN   I Hate Actors. Crown, 1944. 221p. Austin 51-420 1973 $6.50

HECHT, BEN   A Jew in Love. Covici, Friede, 1931. 341p. Austin 54-483 1973 $6

HECHT, BEN   Kingdom of Evil. 1924. Plates, limited edition. Allen 216-1264 1974 $15

HECHT, BEN   Letters From Bohemia. Hammond, Lond., 1964.
192p.   Austin 54-484 1973 $8.50

HECHT, BEN   Miracle in the Rain. Knopf, 1943. 52p.
Austin 54-485 1973 $4

HECHT, BEN   1001 Afternoons in Chicago. Covici, Friede,
1927. 289p.   Austin 54-486 1973 $7.50

HECHT, BEN   1001 Afternoons in New York. Viking, n.d.
370p., illus.   Austin 54-487 1973 $7.50

HECHT, BEN   Perfidy. Messner, 1961. 381p.   Austin 54-488
1973 $7.50

HECHT, BEN   The Sensualists. Messner, 1959. 256p.
Austin 54-489 1973 $6

HECHT, BEN   To Quito and Back. Covici, Friede, 1937.
Austin 51-421 1973 $10

HECK, EARL L. W.   Augustine Herrman. Englewood, 1941. 8vo.,
orig. bindings, plates. Butterfield 8-219 1974 $20

HECKER, JUSTUS FRIEDRICH KARL   The Epidemics of the Middle Ages.
London, 1844. Rittenhouse 46-331 1974 $35

HECKEWELDER, JOHN   History, Manners, and Customs of the Indian
Nations Who Once Inhabited Pennsylvania and the Neighbouring States.
Philadelphia, 1876. New & revised edition, covers faded, third edition. Butter-
field. 10-286 1974 $27.50

HECKEWELDER, JOHN   A Narrative of the Mission of the United
Brethren Among the Delaware and Mohegan Indians. Philadelphia, 1820. First
edition, rebound, orig. binding. Butterfield 10-287 1974 $45

HEDIN, SVEN   Through Asia. 1899. 8vo., 2 vols., orig.
cloth. Broadhurst 23-1650 1974 £25

HEDIN, SVEN   Through Asia. 1899. Illus., photos, 2 vols.,
med. 8vo., orig. cloth, fine. Broadhurst 24-1623 1974 £25

HEDIO, CASPAR   Von Dem Zenhenden. (Altenburg), 1525.
Small 4to., half vellum over boards, woodcut border, fine, very rare edition.
Schafer 8-116 1973 sFr. 1,500

HEDRICK, U. P.   The Peaches of New York. Albany, 1917.
4to., orig. buckram, coloured plates. Wheldon 128-1471 1973 £10

HEEBNER, BALTHASAR   Genealogical Record of the Descendants of the
Schwenkfelders Who Arrived in Pennsylvania in 1733, 1734, 1736, 1737.
Manyunk, 1879. Orig. binding, cracked inner hinge, very good to fine copy.
Wilson 63-101 1974 $25

HEER, O.   Beitrage zur Nahern Kenntniss der Sachsisch-
Thuringischen Braunkohlenflora. Berlin, 1861. 4to., contemporary boards,
tinted plates. Wheldon 128-986 1973 £10

HEER, O.   Contributions to the Fossil Flora of North
Greenland. 1869. 4to., half roan, worn, tinted plates. Wheldon 128-988
1973 £5

HEER, O.   The Primaeval World of Switzerland. 1876.
2 vols. in 1, 8vo., half calf, folding coloured map, plates, scarce. Wheldon
128-985 1973 £15

HEER, O.   Recherches sur le Climat et la Vegetation du
Pays Tertiaire. Winterthur, 1861. 4to., orig. boards, coloured map. Wheldon
128-987 1973 £20

HEEREN, A. H. L.   A Manual of the History of the Political System
of Europe and its Colonies. Oxford, 1824. 2 vols., contemporary plum calf,
labels, first English edition. Howes 186-903 1974 £12.50

HEEREN, A. H. L.   A Manual of the History of the Political System
of Europe and Its Colonies. Oxford, 1834. 2 vols., 8vo., contemporary calf.
Bow Windows 66-331 1974 £16

HEERS, HENRICUS A.   Spadacrene. Leiden, 1645. 12mo., old
vellum, worn and mudstained. Thomas 32-310 1974 £8.50

HEFELE, CARL JOSEPH VON   Der Cardinal Ximenes und die Kirchlichen
Zustande Spaniens. 1853. 8vo., contemporary half calf, second edition.
Ximenes 35-610 1974 $15

HEFELE, CHARLES J.   A History of the Christian Councils. Edinburgh,
1871-83. 3 vols. Howes 185-1255 1974 £18

HEGEMANN, WERNER   Hans Herkommer. Berlin, 1929. 4to., cloth,
illus. Minters 37-538 1973 $28

HEGEMANN, WERNER   Werner March. Berlin, Leipzig & Vienna,
1930. 4to., cloth, plates. Minters 37-554 1973 $25

HEGENWALD, ERHARD   Handlung der Versamlung, in der Loblichen
Stat Zurich. Augsburg, 1523. 4to., new half vellum covered with incunabula
paper, rare edition, well preserved. Schumann 499-50 1974 sFr 2,200

HEGETSCHWEILER, J.   Beytrage zu Einer Kritischen Aufzahlung der
Schweizerpflanzen. Zurich, 1831. 8vo., orig. wrappers, uncut, folding table,
scarce. Wheldon 128-1268 1973 £10

HEGETSCHWEILER, J.   Beytrage zu Einer Kritischen Aufzahlung der
Schweizerpflanzen. Zurich, 1831. 8vo., orig. wrappers, uncut, scarce.
Wheldon 131-1302 1974 £10

HEGETSCHWEILER, J.   Die Flora der Schweiz. Zurich, 1840. 12mo.,
half cloth, plates. Wheldon 129-1081 1974 £7.50

HEGI, G.   Illustrierte Flora Von Mitteleuropa. Munich,
1908-31. 9 vols., 4to., orig. cloth, coloured and other plates, orig. editions.
Wheldon 128-1267 1973 £40

HEHN, V.   The Wanderings of Plants and Animals. 1885
or 1888. 8vo., cloth, scarce. Wheldon 131-224 1974 £10

HEIDE, JAN VAN DER   Beschrijving der Nieuwelijks Uitgevonden en
Geoctrojeerde Slang-Brand-Spuiten. Amsterdam, 1690. Folio, orig. limp
vellum, soiled. Traylen 79-237 1973 £350

HEIDHARD, C.   On the Efficacy of Crotalus Horridus in Yellow
Fever. New York, 1860. Rittenhouse 46-728 1974 $30

HEIFETZ, ELIAS   The Slaughter of the Jews in the Ukraine in
1919. 1921. 408 pages. Austin 57-294 1974 $15

HEILBERG, NEILS   White-Ear and Peter. London, 1912. 8vo.,
gilt; 16 color plates. Frohnsdorff 16-24 1974 $7.50

HEILMANN, G.   Danmarks Fugleliv. Copenhagen, 1928-30.
3 vols., 4to., orig. half morocco, gilt, plates, nice copy. Wheldon 131-618
1974 £35

HEILMANN, G.   The Origin of Birds. 1926. 8vo., cloth,
coloured plates, rare orig. issue. Wheldon 128-477 1973 £15

HEILNER, VAN C.   Salt Water Fishing. Philadelphia, 1937. F'cap
4to., coloured plates, plain plates, orig. cloth, fine. Broadhurst 24-1095 1974
£10

HEIM, ARNOLD ALBERT   The Throne of the Gods. 1939. Text illus.,
plates in photogravure, med. 8vo., orig. cloth, fine, d.w. Broadhurst 24-1624
1974 £6

HEIM, R.   Le Genre Inocybe. Paris, 1931. Roy 8vo.,
half morocco, plates. Wheldon 129-1233 1974 £15

HEIM, R.   Les Lactario-Russules du Domaine. Paris, 1937
(-38). Roy 8vo., plates. Wheldon 129-1234 1974 £5

HEIMANN, ROBERT   Tobacco and Americans. New York, 1960.
1st ed., illus., 4to. Jacobs 24-17 1974 $15

HEINE, H.   Pictures of Travel. New York, 1866. Biblo
& Tannen 210-875 1973 $7.50

HEINE, HEINRICH   Die Bader von Lucca. Heidelberg, 1921. 4to., orig. vellum, uncut, top edges gilt, engraved plates, fine copy, limited to 200 copies, signed by the artist.   Sawyer 293-163 1974 £35

HEINE, HEINRICH   Romanzero und letzte Gedichte. Hamburg, 1875. 8vo., disbound, blue wrappers, first edition.   Rota 190-542 1974 £5

HEINE, HEINRICH   Vermischte Schriften. Hamburg, 1854. 3 vols., small 8vo., orig. wrappers, uncut, black cloth guled on the back of each vol. on which a label is written in old hand, first edition, clean copy.   Schumann 499-51 1974 sFr 175

HEINROTH, O.   Die Vogel Mitteleuropas. Berlin, (1924-31). 4 vols., 4to., orig. half morocco, complete copy.   Wheldon 131-619 1974 £75

HEISTER, LORENZ   Institutiones Chirurgicae. Amsterdam, 1739. 3 parts in 1 vol., 4to., frontispiece, plates, contemporary half vellum, first Latin edition.   Schafer 8-158 1973 sFr. 1,900

HEITLAND, W. E.   The Roman Republic. 1909. Vol. 1 only, spotted binding.   Allen 213-477 1973 $10

HEITLAND, W. E.   A Short History of the Roman Republic. Cambridge, 1916.   Biblo & Tannen 214-621 1974 $8.50

HELBIG, H.   Notes et Dissertations Relatives a l'Histoire de l'Imprimerie. Brussels, n.d. (c. 1860). 8vo., orig. printed wrappers torn, uncut, unopened.   Kraus B8-338 1974 $15

HELBIG, J.   De Glasschilderkunst in Belgie. Antwerp, 1943. Roy. 4to., plates, illus., orig. printed wrappers, uncut.   Quaritch 940-616 1974 £15

HELBURN, THERESA   A Wayward Quest. Little, Brown, 1960. 344p., illus.   Austin 51-423 1973 $7.50

HELD, JOHN JR.   Women Are Necessary. Vanguard, 1931. 234p.   Austin 54-490 1973 $8.50

HELFERICH, H.   On Fractures and Dislocations. 1899. 8vo., orig. cloth, fine.   Dawsons PM 249-261 1974 £12

HELIODORUS   The Adventures of Theagenes and Chariclia. London, 1717. 2 vols., 8vo., contemporary calf, first edition.   Ximenes 33-199 1974 $225

HELLER, KARL B.   Das Dioptrische Mikroskop. 1856. 8vo., orig. orange printed and illus. boards, uncut.   Zeitlin 235-110 1974 $65

A HELLISH MURDER Committed by a French Midwife. London, 1688. 4to., maroon half calf, gilt, first edition.   Dawsons PM 251-246 1974 £60

HELLMAN, GEOFFREY   Mrs. Depeyster's Parties. Macmillan, 1963. 42lp.   Austin 54-491 1973 $6.50

HELLMAN, LILLIAN   Another Part of the Forest. Viking, 1947. 134p.   Austin 51-424 1973 $6.50

HELLMAN, LILLIAN   The North Star. Viking, 1943. 118p. Austin 51-425 1973 $10

HELLOT, JEAN   L'Art de la Teinture. Paris, 1786. 12mo., contemporary calf, wom, second edition.   Gurney 64-109 1974 £15

HELLOT, JEAN   L'Art de la Teinture des Laines. Paris, 1750. 12mo., contemporary marbled calf, gilt, fine, very rare first edition.   Gilhofer 61-18 1974 sFr. 1,300

HELLYER, S. STEVENS   The Plumber and Sanitary Houses. 1884. Third edition.   Covent 55-1308 1974 £10.50

HELMAN, JAMES A.   History of Emmitsburg. (Fredrick), 1906. 8vo., orig. bindings.   Butterfield 8-212 1974 $15

HELME, ELIZABETH   The Farmer of Inglewood Forest. London, 1824. 8vo., frontispiece, plates, contemporary half roan, gilt, seventh edition.   Bow Windows 62-434 1974 £7.50

HELMHOLTZ, HERMANN LUDWIG FERDINAND VON   Popular Lectures on Scientific Subjects. London, 1873. 8vo., foxing, orig. cloth, rubbed, first English edition.   Bow Windows 62-435 1974 £8.75

HELMHOLTZ, HERMANN LUDWIG FERDINAND VON   Populare Wissenschaftliche Vortrage. Brunswick, 1865-71-76. 8vo., 3 vols. in 1, old half leather, rubbed, illus., coloured engravings, some foxing.   Gurney 66-84 1974 £25

HELMONT, JEAN BAPTISTE VAN   Deliramenta Catarrhi. London, 1650. 4to., calf antique, first edition in English.   Dawsons PM 249-265 1974 £170

HELMONT, JEAN BAPTISTE VAN   Ortvs Medicinae. 1648. 4to., first edition.   Dawsons PM 249-262 1974 £370

HELMONT, JEAN BAPTISTE VAN   Ortvs Medicinae. Amsterodami, 1648. 4to., contemporary vellum, signatures, first and second editions.   Dawsons PM 250-41 1974 £370

HELMONT, JEAN BAPTISTE VAN   Ortvs Medicinae. Amsterodami, 1648. 4to., contemporary vellum, first and second editions.   Dawsons PM 250-41 1974 £370

HELMONT, JEAN BAPTISTE VAN   Ortvs Medicinae. 1655. Folio, contemporary mottled calf, gilt.   Dawsons PM 249-263 1974 £135

HELPER, HINTON R.   The Impending Crisis of the South: How to Meet It. New York, 1860. Worn, foxed.   Jenkins 61-1052 1974 $12.50

HELPS, ARTHUR   Casimir Maremma. London, 1870. 2 vols., 8vo., orig. cloth, scarce, first edition.   Ximenes 33-200 1974 $75

HELPS, ARTHUR   The Claims of Labour. London, 1844. 8vo., contemporary calf gilt, fine, first edition.   Dawsons PM 247-143 1974 £20

HELPS, ARTHUR   Essays Written in the Intervals of Business. London, 1841. 8vo., orig. boards, first edition.   Hammond 201-721 1974 £5

HELPS, ARTHUR   Friends in Council. 1847-59. 4 vols. in 2, new buckram.   Allen 216-701 1974 $15

HELPS, ARTHUR   Life and Labours of Mr. Brassey. London, 1872. 8vo., orig. cloth, first edition.   Ximenes 33-201 1974 $17.50

HELPS, ARTHUR   The Life of Hernando Cortes. London, 1871. 2 vols., 8vo., orig. cloth, fine, first edition.   Ximenes 33-202 1974 $22.50

HELPS, ARTHUR   Oulita the Serf. 1858. Signed, first edition. Allen 216-1326 1974 $25

HELPS, ARTHUR   Some Talks About Animals and Their Masters. London, 1873. 8vo., orig. cloth, fine, first edition.   Ximenes 33-203 1974 $12.50

HELPS, ARTHUR   The Spanish Conquest in America. 1900-04. 4 vols., crown 8vo., maps, orig. cloth, best edition.   Howes 186-904 1974 £20

HELPS, ARTHUR   The Spanish Conquest in America and Its Relation to the History of Slavery and to the Government of Colonies. 1855-61. 4 vols., 8vo., orig. cloth, maps.   Bow Windows 66-333 1974 £28

HELWICH, CHRISTOPHER   The Historical and Chronological Threatre of. 1687. Folio, contemporary panelled calf, rebacked.   Bow Windows 66-334 1974 £12.50

HELWICH, CHRISTOPHER   The Historical and Chronological Theatre Of. London, 1687. Folio, contemporary panelled calf, first edition in English.   Dawsons PM 251-247 1974 £28

HELWICH, CHRISTOPHER   Theatrum Historicum et Chronologicum. Oxford, 1651. Small folio, contemporary sheep, gilt, fifth edition.   Dawsons PM 251-248 1974 £38

HEMANS, FELICIA   Poems. Liverpool, 1808. 4to., early half morocco, first edition.   Ximenes 33-204 1974 $65

HEMANS, FELICIA   The Restoration of the Works of Art to Italy. Oxford, 1816. 8vo., disbound, second edition.   Ximenes 33-205 1974 $10

HEMANS, FELICIA   Tales and Historic Scenes in Verse. London,
1819. 8vo., contemporary half calf, first edition. Ximenes 33-206 1974
$27.50

HEMING, ARTHUR   The Drama of the Forests. Garden City, 1921.
Illus. by author, first edition, quarter leather spine & corners, gilt on spine,
lacking d.w., fine tight copy. Ross 87-435 1974 $20

HEMING, ARTHUR   The Living Forest. New York, 1925. Illus.,
plates, mended. Hood's 104-166 1974 $12.50

HEMINGHAUS, EDGAR H.   Mark Twain in Germany. New York, 1939.
Inscribed and signed by author, orig. binding. Wilson 63-503 1974 $10

HEMINGWAY, ERNEST   After the Storm. 1932. Wrappers, English first
edition. Covent 56-620 1974 £8.50

HEMINGWAY, ERNEST   All the Brave. New York, (1939). Wrappers,
illus. Dawson's 424-277 1974 $40

HEMINGWAY, ERNEST   Death in the Afternoon. 1932. First edition.
Allen 216-1266 1974 $20

HEMINGWAY, ERNEST   Death in the Afternoon. London, 1932. Nice
copy, frontispiece, photos, orig. cloth, first English edition. Crane 7-130 1974
£12

HEMINGWAY, ERNEST   Death in the Afternoon. New York, 1932.
1st ed., illus. Jacobs 24-95 1974 $25

HEMINGWAY, ERNEST   Death in the Afternoon. New York, 1932.
1st ed., illus. Biblo & Tannen 210-734 1973 $27.50

HEMINGWAY, ERNEST   Death in the Afternoon. New York, 1932.
Colored frontispiece & illus., orig. cloth, first edition, bookplate removed, very
fine. MacManus 224-209 1974 $27.50

HEMINGWAY, ERNEST   Death in the Afternoon. New York, 1932.
First edition, first issue with publisher's "A" on verso of title page, frontis., orig.
d.w., orig. binding, pristine, protected by heavy dec. paper wrapper. Ross
86-253 1974 $70

HEMINGWAY, ERNEST   A Farewell to Arms. 1929. Dust wrapper,
fine, first English edition. Howes 185-217 1974 £12.50

HEMINGWAY, ERNEST   A Farewell to Arms. New York, 1929. Orig.
cloth, first printing, bookplate removed, otherwise as new. MacManus 224-211
1974 $35

HEMINGWAY, ERNEST   A Farewell to Arms. London, 1929. First
English edition, lacking d.w., orig. binding, protective dec. paper wrapper, fine.
Ross 87-270 1974 $45

HEMINGWAY, ERNEST   A Farewell to Arms. New York, (1929).
8vo., inscription, orig. cloth, first published edition, first issue. Bow Windows
62-436 1974 £25.50

HEMINGWAY, ERNEST   A Farewell to Arms. New York, 1929. Orig.
cloth, first printing, fine, worn dust jacket. MacManus 224-210 1974 $50

HEMINGWAY, ERNEST   A Farewell to Arms. London, 1929. First
English edition, lacking d.w., orig. binding, protective dec. paper wrapper, fine.
Ross 86-254 1974 $50

HEMINGWAY, ERNEST   A Farewell to Arms. New York, 1929. First
U. S. edition, fine copy, nice d.w. Covent 51-3247 1973 £30

HEMINGWAY, ERNEST   A Farewell to Arms. New York, 1929. First
edition, first state, without the notice on verso of title page, black cloth, d.w.
somewhat chipped, else very fine, protective dec. paper wrapper. Ross 87-269
1974 $90

HEMINGWAY, ERNEST   A Farewell to Arms. New York, 1929. Cloth,
dust wrapper, first edition, first issue. Dawson's 424-276 1974 $125

HEMINGWAY, ERNEST   A Farewell to Arms. New York, 1929. 8vo.,
orig. cloth, gilt labels, first edition. Dawsons PM 252-442 1974 $65

HEMINGWAY, ERNEST   A Farewell to Arms. New York, 1929. Half
vellum, slipcase, autographed, near mint, special limited edition. Jenkins
48-243 1973 $450

HEMINGWAY, ERNEST   Fiesta. London, 1927. First English edition,
orig. binding, orig. d.w. slightly browned, near mint, thus rare. Ross 87-271
1974 $35

HEMINGWAY, ERNEST   The Fifth Column and the First Forty-Nine
Stories. New York, 1938. Orig. cloth, first edition, bookplate removed, fine,
dust jacket. MacManus 224-212 1974 $40

HEMINGWAY, ERNEST   For Whom the Bell Tolls. 1940. Label slightly
rubbed, first edition. Allen 216-702 1974 $10

HEMINGWAY, ERNEST   For Whom the Bell Tolls. New York, 1940.
First edition. Ballinger 1-143 1974 $10

HEMINGWAY, ERNEST   For Whom the Bell Tolls. New York, 1940.
First printing with publisher's "A" on copyright page, lacking d.w., spine faded,
orig. binding, nice. Ross 87-272 1974 $15

HEMINGWAY, ERNEST   For Whom the Bell Tolls. New York, 1940.
First edition, first issue, with publisher's "A" on verso of title page, near pristine,
orig. d.w., protected by heavy dec. paper wrapper, orig. binding. Ross 86-255
1974 $35

HEMINGWAY, ERNEST   For Who the Bell Tolls. 1941. Fine, worn
d.w., first edition. Covent 51-892 1973 £5.25

HEMINGWAY, ERNEST   For Whom the Bell Tolls. 1942. Cloth-backed
linen, slipcase, limited edition. Covent 56-621 1974 £65

HEMINGWAY, ERNEST   Green Hills of Africa. New York, 1935. Orig.
cloth, spine faded, first edition, bookplate removed, about fine. MacManus
224-213 1974 $20

HEMINGWAY, ERNEST   Green Hills of Africa. New York and London,
1935. First edition in d.j., jacket lacking small fragment in front. Butterfield
10-289 1974 $45

HEMINGWAY, ERNEST   In Our Time. New York, 1925. Orig. dec.
cloth, first American edition, bookplate removed, two leaves scalloped, fine.
MacManus 224-214 1974 $40

HEMINGWAY, ERNEST   In Our Time. New York, 1925. First U. S.
edition, dec. cloth gilt, very nice copy, scarce. Covent 51-3248 1973 £20

HEMINGWAY, ERNEST   In Our Time. Paris, 1932. Orig. cloth,
wrappers. Rota 188-397 1974 £12

HEMINGWAY, ERNEST   In Our Time, Stories. 1925. Top of spine &
lettering slightly worn, binding spotted. Allen 216-704 1974 $50

HEMINGWAY, ERNEST   Marlin off the Morro. 1933. English first
edition. Covent 56-622 1974 £21

HEMINGWAY, ERNEST   Men Without Women. New York, 1927. First
edition, front hinge cracked, orig. binding. Butterfield 10-290 1974 $10

HEMINGWAY, ERNEST   Men Without Women. New York, 1927. 1st
ed. Jacobs 24-94 1974 $15

HEMINGWAY, ERNEST   Men Without Women. New York, 1927.
1st ed., binding dull and rubbed. Biblo & Tannen 213-546 1973 $37.50

HEMINGWAY, ERNEST   Men Without Women. New York, 1927.
8vo., orig. cloth, gilt labels, first edition. Dawsons PM 252-443 1974 £20

HEMINGWAY, ERNEST   Men Without Women. New York, 1927. Orig.
cloth, first printing, as new. MacManus 224-215 1974 $45

HEMINGWAY, ERNEST   Men Without Women. 1928. Dust wrapper,
fine, first English edition. Howes 185-218 1974 £12.50

HEMINGWAY, ERNEST   To Have and Have Not. New York, 1937.
Fine, first printing in d.j., orig. binding. Butterfield 10-291 1974 $25

HEMINGWAY, ERNEST   To Have and Have Not. New York, 1937.
Orig. cloth, first edition, bookplate removed, very fine copy. MacManus
224-216 1974 $25

HEMINGWAY, ERNEST   To Have and Have Not. New York, 1937.
First edition, with publisher's "A" on verso of title page, orig. binding, pristine
in d.w., protective heavy dec. paper wrapper. Ross 87-273 1974 $50

HEMINGWAY, ERNEST   To Have and Have Not. New York, 1937.
First edition, with publisher's "A" on verso of title page, pristine, d.w., orig.
binding, protective heavy dec. paper wrapper. Ross 86-256 1974 $60

HEMINGWAY, ERNEST   The Torrents of Spring. New York, 1926. Dark
green cloth imprinted in orange, glassine wrapper, small stains on last few pages
and endpapers, last 2 leaves roughly opened, first printing, only 1250 copies.
Butterfield 10-292 1974 $75

HEMINGWAY, ERNEST   The Torrents of Spring. New York, 1926.
Orig. cloth, first edition, bookplate removed, fine. MacManus 224-217 1974
$100

HEMINGWAY, ERNEST   The Torrents of Spring. Paris, 1932. Orig.
white and green wrappers, virtually mint copy. Covent 51-2365 1973 £25

HEMINGWAY, ERNEST   Wine of Wyoming. 1930. Wrappers, English
first edition. Covent 56-623 1974 £6.30

HEMINGWAY, ERNEST   Winner Take Nothing. New York, 1933. 8vo.,
orig. cloth, ex-library, first edition. Rota 189-441 1974 £5

HEMINGWAY, ERNEST   Winner Take Nothing. New York, 1933. Orig.
cloth, first edition, bookplate removed, otherwise as new. MacManus 224-218
1974 $30

HEMINGWAY, ERNEST   Winner Take Nothing. New York, 1933.
First edition, first issue, with publisher's "A" on verso of title page, orig.
binding, mint in orig. d.w., protective heavy dec. paper wrapper. Ross 87-275
1974 $85

HEMINGWAY, J.   Panorama of the City of Chester. Chester, 1836.
8vo., orig. cloth, fine. Broadhurst 23-1406 1974 £10

HEMMINGER, SEBASTIAN   Kurtzer Summarischer Bericht Was . . . bey
Legung der Ersten Stein zu dem Vorhabenden Gebaw. Regensburg, 1627. Small
4to., boards covered with early printed paper, orig. edition. Schumann 499-95
1974 sFr 3,200

HEMPEL, CHARLES J.   Jahr's New Manual. New York, 1848. 8vo.,
2 vols. in 4, old half calf, rubbed, some minor stains. Gurney 66-85 1974 $18

HEMPEL, CHARLES J.   Jahr's New Manual. New York, 1848. 8vo.,
old half calf, rubbed. Gurney 64-110 1974 £18

HEMSLEY, R.   Looking Back. Montreal, 1930. Hood's
104-261 1974 $10

HENDERSON, ALEXANDER   Aldous Huxley. 1935. Spine faded, very good
copy, scarce. Covent 51-2385 1973 £6

HENDERSON, ALEXANDER   Aldous Huxley. 1935. English first edition.
Covent 56-1819 1974 £10.50

HENDERSON, C. C.   The Story of Murfreesboro. Mufreesboro, 1929.
8vo., cloth. Saddleback 14-698 1974 $17.50

HENDERSON, CHARLES   Essays in Cornish History. 1935. Plates.
Howes 186-905 1974 £5

HENDERSON, EBENEZER   A Treatise on Astronomy. 1843. 8vo., orig.
brown cloth, illus., gilt, second edition. Dawsons PM 245-372 1974 £6

HENDERSON, G.   Lahore to Yarkand. 1873. Roy. 8vo., new
half morocco, plates, good copy. Wheldon 131-359 1974 £75

HENDERSON, J.   Great Men of Canada. Toronto, 1928-29.
2 vols. Hood's 103-16 1974 $20

HENDERSON, JOHN   Excursions and Adventures in New South Wales.
1851. 2 vols. in 1, 8vo., orig. cloth, frontispiece, plates, some browning, map,
first edition. Bow Windows 66-335 1974 £140

HENDERSON, KEITH   Letters to Helen. 1907. Cloth-backed boards,
English first edition. Covent 56-1833 1974 £5.25

HENDERSON, KEITH   Palm Groves and Humming Birds. 1924. Roy
8vo., full pigskin, uncut, limited edition. Broadhurst 23-1652 1974 £20

HENDERSON, MATTHIAS H.   A History of Lodge of the Craft, No. 433,
F. & A. M., of New Castle, Pa. Philadelphia, 1894. 12mo., cloth.
Saddleback 14-670 1974 $15

HENDERSON, THOMAS   Astronomical Observations. Edinburgh, 1848-9.
4to., half calf. Dawsons PM 245-373 1974 £7

HENDLEY, T. H.   The Rulers of India and the Chiefs of
Rajputana (1550-1897). 1897. Folio, illus., red morocco gilt. Quaritch
940-398 1974 £150

HENDRICKS, BURTON J.   Bullwark of the Republic. Boston, 1937. First
edition, orig. binding. Butterfield 10-293 1974 $10

HENDRICKS, BURTON J.   The Life and Letters of Walter H. Page. Garden
City, 1922-26. 3 vols., orig. binding, trade edition. Wilson 63-222 1974
$12.50

HENDRICKS, BURTON J.   The Life and Letters of Walter H. Page. Garden
City, 1922. First edition, limited to 37 numbered copies, illus., unopened, uncut,
fine, dust wrappers. Wilson 63-221 1974 $30

HENDRY, J. F.   The White Horseman: Prose and Verse of the New
Apocalypse. 1941. Illus., Hendry's copy with T.L.s from him laid in, cloth
backed boards, first edition. Covent 51-1352 1973 £10.50

HENIE, SONJA   Wings On My Feet. Prentice Hall, 1940.
177p., illus. Austin 62-253 1974 $7.50

HENIN DE CUVILLIERS, ETIENNE FELIX   Archives du Magnetisme Animal.
Paris, 1820. 8vo., orig. wrappers, soiled, first edition. Schuman 37-122
1974 $110

HENIN DE CUVILLIERS, ETIENNE FELIX   Le Magnetisme Animal Retrouve dans
l'Antiquite. Paris, 1821. 8vo., contemporary half morocco. Schuman 37-123
1974 $65

HENKEL, J. S.   A Fieldbook of the Woody Plants. Durban,
1934. 8vo., cloth, plates, scarce. Wheldon 129-1083 1974 £7.50

HENLE, FRITZ   Mexico. Chicago, 1945. 4to. Biblo &
Tannen 210-285 1973 $12.50

HENLEY, WILLIAM ERNEST   A Book of Verses. 1888. 8vo., stiff wrappers,
first edition. Rota 189-446 1974 £12

HENLEY, WILLIAM ERNEST   A Book of Verses. London, 1888. Orig. stiff
printed wrappers, signed by publisher, specially made cloth case, unusually fine.
Ross 86-258 1974 $60

HENLEY, WILLIAM ERNEST   Hawthorn and Lavender With Other Verses.
1901. Ex-library. Austin 61-458 1974 $10

HENLEY, WILLIAM ERNEST   A London Garland. 1895. First edition, illus.,
4to., orig. dec. parchment, gilt edges, half morocco book form case, very fine
copy. Sawyer 293-252 1974 £75

HENLEY, WILLIAM ERNEST   Tudor Translations. 1892-1909. 44 vols.,
orig. half buckram, orig. & best edition. Howes 185-532 1974 £220

HENNEBERG, F. A. VON   The Art and Craft of Old Lace. 1931. Roy.
4to., plates, buckram, presentation copy. Quaritch 940-758 1974 £45

HENNEPIN, LOUIS   A New Discovery of a Vast Country in America.
Chicago, 1903. 2 vols., illus., maps. Hood's 102-717 1974 $75

HENNEPIN, LOUIS   Voyage, ou Nouvelle Decouverte d'un
tres-grand Pais dans l'Amerique. Amsterdam, 1712. Red leather, gilt. Hood's
103-538 1974 $500

HENNESSY, WILLIAM M.   The Annals of Loch Ce. London, 1871.
2 vols., roy. 8vo., cloth boards. Emerald 50-415 1974 £22

HENNICKE, C. R.   Die Fange der in Mitteleuropa Vorkommenden Raubvogel. Dresden, 1905. 8vo., cloth, wrappers. Wheldon 131-620 1974 £5

HENNINGSEN, CHARLES FREDERICK   The White Slave. London, 1845. 3 vols., 12mo., contemporary calf, gilt, first edition. Ximenes 33-208 1974 $75

HENOCH, EDUARD   Lectures on Childrens Diseases. 1889. 8vo., 2 vols., orig. cloth. Dawsons PM 249-266 1974 £6

HENOT, GEORGES   The Battles of Life. London, 1884. 3 vols., 8vo., orig. cloth, first English edition. Ximenes 33-209 1974 $22.50

HENRICUS DE HASSIA   Secreta Sacerdotum. Nuremberg, n.d. Modern marbled boards. Thomas 28-286 1972 £80

HENRICUS DE HASSIA   Secreta Sacerdotum que in Missa Teneri Debent Multum. Augsburg, 1511. Small 4to, unbound. Schumann 499-52 1974 sFr 350

HENRIKSSON, FRITZ   Sweden's Participation in the U. S. Celebration of the New Sweden Tercentenary. 1939. Photographs. Austin 57-295 1974 $10

HENRION, DENIS   Les Tables des Directions. Paris, 1625, 1626. 4to., old vellum, rare. Zeitlin 235-187 1974 $175

HENRIOT, EMILE   Les Livres du Second Rayon Irreguliers et Libertins. Paris, 1926. 12mo., orig. wrapper, uncut. L. Goldschmidt 42-248 1974 $10

HENRIOT, GABRIEL   Les Beaux Meubles des Collections Privees. Paris, (n.d.). Folio, plates, cloth. Bow Windows 62-437 1974 £12.50

HENRY, ARNOLD K.   Extensile Exposure Apllied to Limb Surgery. Baltimore, 1935. Rittenhouse 46-333 1974 $10

HENRY, DAVID   An Historical Account of All the Voyages Round the World. London, 1774-1773. 4 vols., 8vo., old speckled calf, rebacked, orig. labels, plates. Traylen 79-431 1973 £68

HENRY, EDWARD RICHARD   Classification and Uses of Finger Prints. London, 1900. 8vo., orig. green cloth, first edition. Dawsons PM 249-267 1974 £30

HENRY, EDWARD RICHARD   Classification and Uses of Finger Prints. London, 1900. 8vo., orig. green cloth, illus., first edition. Dawsons PM 250-42 1974 £30

HENRY, FREDERICK P.   Founders' Week Memorial Volume. Philadelphia, 1909. .Photographs, missing spine. Rittenhouse 46-335 1974 $20

HENRY, FREDERICK P.   Standard History of the Medical Profession of Philadelphia. Chicago, 1897. Rebacked. Rittenhouse 46-336 1974 $25

HENRY, G. M.   Coloured Plates of the Birds of Ceylon. Colombo, 1927-35. Roy 4to., cloth, scarce. Wheldon 130-544 1974 £75

HENRY, G. M.   Coloured Plates of the Birds of Ceylon. Colombo, 1927-35. Parts 1 - 4, roy. 4to., orig. wrappers uncut, cloth portfolio, coloured plates, complete copy, very scarce. Wheldon 128-478 1973 £90

HENRY, G. M.   Coloured Plates of the Birds of Ceylon. Colombo, 1927-35. 4 parts, roy. 4to., orig. wrappers, uncut, very scarce, complete copy. Wheldon 131-58 1974 £90

HENRY, GEORGE ALFRED   Through the Sikah War. London, 1894. 8vo., map, illus., orig. illus. cloth, inscription. Bow Windows 62-444 1974 £6

HENRY, JOHN R.   Some Immigrant Neighbors. Revell, 1912. Austin 62-255 1974 $10

HENRY, O. PSEUD.
Please turn to
PORTER, WILLIAM SYDNEY

HENRY, ROBERT   The History of Great Britain. 1788-89. 12 vols., contemporary tree calf, gilt, plates. Howes 186-907 1974 £50

HENRY, WILLIAM   The Abbess. Baltimore, 1802. 16mo., 3 vols., orig. bindings, fine, second edition. Butterfield 8-217 1974 $25

HENRY II, KING OF FRANCE   Recueil de Diverses Pieces Servants a l'Histoire de Cologne. 1666. 12mo., contemporary speckled calf gilt, bookplate. Smith 193-113 1973 £6.50

HENRY IV, KING OF FRANCE   Interesting Anecdotes of Henry IV of France. (n.d.). 2 vols. in 1, 8vo., old half calf, gilt spine, small stains. Bow Windows 66-337 1974 £10.50

HENRY VIII, KING OF ENGLAND   Assertio Septem Sacramentorum Aduersus Martin Lutheru. 1521. First edition, woodcut border by Hans Holbein, with the blank V3 but lacks final blank V4, else excellent, small 4to., early 18th century sprinkled calf, armorial bookplate of the Earl of Essex, bookplate of Henry Yates Thompson and etched bookplate of O. F. Grazebrook of Stourton Castle. Thomas 32-117 1974 £1,850

HENRY VIII, KING OF ENGLAND   Des . . . Herrn Heinrichs des Achtem. Wittenberg, 1539. Small 4to., modern half vellum, fine, first German edition. Schafer 8-117 1973 sFr. 650

HENSHALL, JAMES A.   Book of the Black Bass. Cincinnati, 1889. Cloth, rubbed. Hayman 57-293 1974 $10

HENSHAW, J. W.   Mountain Wild Flowers of America. Boston, 1906. 8vo., cloth, plates. Wheldon 131-1304 1974 £5

HENSHAW, J. W.   Wild Flowers of the North American Mountains. New York, 1916. 8vo., cloth, plates. Wheldon 130-1165 1974 £5

HENSHEW, T. W.   Cleek of Scotland Yard. 1914. 8vo., orig. cloth, fine, first edition. Rota 190-284 1974 £10

HENSLOW, J. S.   Le Bouquet des Souvenirs. London, 1840. 8vo., contemporary morocco, gilt, plates. Hammond 201-648 1974 £14.50

HENSLOW, J. S.   Flora of Suffolk. (1860). Small 8vo., cloth, scarce. Wheldon 131-1224 1974 £5

HENSLOW, T. G. W.   Ye Sundial Booke. 1935. Roy 8vo., cloth, plates. Wheldon 130-1405 1974 £7.50

HENTY, GEORGE ALFRED   Beric the Briton. 1893. 8vo., orig. cloth, illus., scarce, first edition. Rota 189-454 1974 £7.50

HENTY, GEORGE ALFRED   Colonel Thorndyke's Secret. London, 1899. 8vo., frontispiece, orig. pictorial cloth, presentation. Bow Windows 62-439 1974 £10

HENTY, GEORGE ALFRED   A Final Reckoning. n.d. Orig. pictorial cloth, plates, English first edition. Covent 56-626 1974 £10

HENTY, GEORGE ALFRED   A Knight of the White Cross. London, 1896. 8vo., illus., orig. pictorial cloth, first English edition. Bow Windows 62-441 1974 £8.50

HENTY, GEORGE ALFRED   A March on London. London, 1898. 8vo., orig. dec. blue cloth, first edition. Dawsons PM 252-444 1974 £10

HENTY, GEORGE ALFRED   A March on London. 1898. Orig. cloth, first edition. Rota 188-403 1974 £10

HENTY, GEORGE ALFRED   On the Irrawaddy. 1897. Orig. cloth, illus., foxed, frontispiece, first edition. Rota 188-402 1974 £8

HENTY, GEORGE ALFRED   Our Soldiers. n.d. Frontis., rare, new edition. Covent 56-627 1974 £45

HENTY, GEORGE ALFRED   A Roving Commission. London, 1900. 8vo., plates, orig. pictorial cloth, first edition. Bow Windows 62-443 1974 £35

HENTY, GEORGE ALFRED   Under Wellington's Command. London, 1899. 8vo., plates, orig. cloth, first edition. Dawsons PM 252-445 1974 £16

HENTY, GEORGE ALFRED   Winning His Spurs. 1895. Orig. pictorial cloth, illus., inscription. Covent 55-829 1974 £12.50

HENTY, GEORGE ALFRED   With Buller in Natal. London, 1901. Orig. cloth, plates, illus., rubbed, first edition. Bow Windows 62-445 1974 £12

HENTY, GEORGE ALFRED   With Frederick the Great. London, 1898. 8vo., plates, foxing, orig. pictorial cloth, first edition. Bow Windows 62-446 1974 £10

HENTY, GEORGE ALFRED   With Moore at Corunna. 1898. Orig. cloth, illus., first edition. Rota 188-404 1974 £10

HENTY, GEORGE ALFRED   Yarns on the Beach. n.d. Plates, orig. dec. cloth, ownership inscription, nice copy, ads at end. Covent 51-897 1973 £6.30

HENTY, GEORGE ALFRED   The Young Buglers. London, (n.d.). 8vo., plates, orig. cloth, frontispiece. Dawsons PM 252-446 1974 £10

HENTZ, CAROLINE LEE   Courtship and Marriage. Philadelphia, (1856). Cloth. Hayman 57-198 1974 $12.50

HENWOOD, W. J.   Observations on Metalliferous Deposits. 1871. 2 vols., 8vo., boards, worn, plates. Wheldon 131-1014 1974 £25

HEPBURN, A. BARTON   A History of Currency in the United States. New York, 1924. Jacobs 24-144 1974 $18

HEPBURN, A. BARTON   A History of Currency in the United States With a Brief Description of the Currency Systems of All Commercial Nations. New York, 1915. Orig. binding. Butterfield 10-294 1974 $8.50

HEPBURN, JAMES   Lexicon S. Linguae Succinctum. (Italy, 1580?). 12mo., old limp vellum. Kraus B8-87 1974 $125

HEPPLEWHITE, A.   The Cabinet-Maker and Upholsterer's Guide. 1789. Folio, plates, fine, very clean copy, contemporary polished calf, second edition. Quaritch 940-577 1974 £1,000

HEPPLEWHITE, A.   The Cabinet-Maker and Upholsterer's Guide. (1794) 1897. Folio, plates, cloth, facsimile reprint. Quaritch 940-578 1974 £36

THE HEPTAMERON of the Tales of Margaret. London, 1922. 5 vols., 8vo., orig. buckram, bookplate, engravings. Bow Windows 62-604 1974 £12

HERACLITUS Ridens. London, 1681-82. Folio, old paper wrappers, misbound, fine, rare, first edition. Dawsons PM 252-447 1974 £450

THE HERALD and Genealogist. 1863-74. 8 vols., 8vo., plates, half blue morocco, gilt, woodcuts, fine. Quaritch 939-731 1974 £47.50

HERALDS' Commemorative Exhibition, 1484-1934, Held at the College of Arms. 1936. Plates, large 4to., blue morocco gilt, slip case, limited to 300 copies. Thomas 32-106 1974 £35

HERALDS' Commemorative Exhibition. 1936. 4to., plates, blue morocco, gilt. Quaritch 939-732 1974 £30

HERALDS' COMMEMORATIVE EXHIBITION   Catalogue. 1936. Large 4to., blue morocco gilt, plates, limited. Thomas 28-168 1972 £35

HERAUD, JOHN A.   Voyages up the Mediterranean and in the Indian Seas. 1837. Crown 8vo., contemporary morocco. Broadhurst 23-1653 1974 £8

HERBERT, A. P.   The Bomber Gipsy. 1918. Orig. cloth, gilt, signature, dust wrapper, bookplate. Rota 188-405 1974 £8

HERBERT, A. P.   A Collection of 33 First Editions. 1912-47. Orig. bindings. Bow Windows 62-449 1974 £56

HERBERT, A. P.   The Old Flame. 1925. 8vo., orig. cloth, signed, first edition. Rota 189-455 1974 £5

HERBERT, A. P.   Play Hours With Pegasus. Oxford, n.d. 12mo., orig. wrappers, fine, first edition. Ximenes 33-214 1974 $22.50

HERBERT, A. P.   The Wherefore and the Why. 1921. Cloth-backed pictorial boards, English first edition. Covent 56-1801 1974 £6.50

HERBERT, EDWARD HERBERT, BARON   The Life of Henry VIII. 1683. Engraved portrait, title somewhat browned and mounted, few other stains, generally fair state, lacks final blank, small folio, old calf, worn and rebacked. Thomas 32-118 1974 £25

HERBERT, GEORGE   Herbert's Remains. London, 1652. 12mo., full brown levant, gilt, first edition. Ximenes 33-216 1974 $200

HERBERT, GEORGE   Poems. 1923. 8vo., marbled boards, uncut, limited edition. Broadhurst 23-1032 1974 £35

HERBERT, GEORGE   Poems. 1923. Small 4to., full red morocco, gilt. Hammond 201-754 1974 £145

HERBERT, GEORGE   The Temple. London, 1674. 12mo., full polished calf, gilt, tenth edition. Ximenes 33-217 1974 $80

HERBERT, GEORGE   The Temple. 1927. Roy 8vo., orig. brocade binding, limited edition. Broadhurst 23-1064 1974 £20

HERBERT, G.   The Temple, Sacred Poems and Private Ejaculations. 1904. Small 4to., full brown levant morocco, gilt. Quaritch 936-415 1974 £30

HERBERT, GEORGE   The Temple: Sacred Poems and Private Ejaculations. Nonesuch Press, 1927. Engraved portrait, roy. 8vo., orig. brocade, limited to 1500 copies, fine. Broadhurst 24-1025 1974 £20

HERBERT, HENRY WILLIAM   American Game In Its Seasons. New York, 1853. Illus. by author, plates, orig. binding. Butterfield 10-295 1974 $17.50

HERBERT, HENRY WILLIAM   The Captains of the Old World. New York, 1852. Second printing, engravings, top of backstrip chipped, orig. binding. Butterfield 10-296 1974 $10

HERBERT, HENRY WILLIAM   Field Sports in the United States, and the British Provinces of America. London, 1848. 2 vols., 8vo., purple cloth, spines faded. Goodspeed's 578-131 1974 $25

HERBERT, HENRY WILLIAM   Field Sports of the United States, and the British Provinces of America. London, 1848. 2 vols., 12mo., cloth, cloth case,

HERBERT, HENRY WILLIAM   Frank Forester's Fish and Fishing of the United States and British Provinces of North America. New York, 1864. 1 color plate, orig. dec. cl., gilt. Jacobs 24-5 1974 $25

HERBERT, HENRY WILLIAM   Frank Forester's Fugitive Sporting Sketches. Westfield, 1879. 12mo., cloth, cloth case, presentation inscription, first edition. Goodspeed's 578-137 1974 $50

HERBERT, HENRY WILLIAM   Life and Writings of Frank Forester. New York, 1882. 3 vols., 4to., half morocco, hinges rubbed, extra-illus. copy, first edition. Goodspeed's 578-138 1974 $150

HERBERT, HENRY WILLIAM   Persons and Pictures from the Histories of France and England. New York, 1854. 12mo., cloth, gilt, cloth case, fine copy, first edition. Goodspeed's 578-134 1974 $15

HERBERT, HENRY WILLIAM   Sporting Scenes and Sundry Sketches. New York, 1842. 8vo., cloth, illus., uncut. Goodspeed's 578-129 1974 $35

HERBERT, HENRY WILLIAM   The Warwick Woodlands. New York, 1851. 12mo., cloth, illus. by author, revised new edition. Goodspeed's 578-132 1974 $75

HERBERT, JOSEPH   Theoria Phaenomenorum Electricorum. 1772. 8vo., contemporary mottled sheep, worn. Dawsons PM 245-374 1974 £25

HERBERT, THOMAS   Memoirs of the Two Last Years of the Reign of King Charles I. 1813. 8vo., half calf rebacked, worn. Bow Windows 64-545 1974 £8.75

HERBERT, WILLIAM   History of Twelve Great Livery Companies of London. 1837. 2 vols., new buckram, plates. Allen 213-1542 1973 $22.50

HERBERT, WILLIAM   Musae Etonenses. London, 1795. 3 vols. in 2, large 8vo., contemporary speckled calf, first edition. Dawsons PM 252-448 1974 £15

HERBERT, LADY   Life of Dom Bartholomew of the Martyrs. 1890. Scarce. Howes 185-945 1974 £5

HERBIN, J. F.   The History of Grand-Pre. St. John, n.d. Card cover, illus., fifth edition. Hood's 103-178 1974 $17.50

HERBRUCK, WENDELL   Word Histories. 1941. Ex-library. Austin 61-459 1974 $10

HERE Is My Land: Sketches of Butte County, California. 1940. 8vo., quarter cloth, limited edition. Saddleback 14-51 1974 $20

THE HEREFORDIAN. Hereford & Oxford, 1778-88. 10 vols. in 22, 8vo., sewed. Quaritch 939-383 1974 £15

HEREFORDSHIRE Pomona
Please turn to
HOGG, ROBERT

HERFORD, OLIVER   A Child's Primer of Natural History. New York, 1899. Square 8vo., pictorial boards, full page illus., first edition. Frohnsdorff 16-427 1974 $20

HERFORD, OLIVER   The Deb's Dictionary. Philadelphia, 1931. 1st ed. Biblo & Tannen 214-728 1974 $6.50

HERFORD, OLIVER   Neither Here Nor There. Doran, 1923. 165p. Austin 54-492 1973 $6.50

HERFORD, OLIVER   The Rubaiyat of a Persian Kitten. New York, 1904. 8vo., boards, full page illus. in half tone, first edition. Frohnsdorff 16-428 1974 $15

HERGESHEIMER, JOSEPH   Balisand. New York, 1924. Orig. cloth, signed, fine, slipcase, first edition. Rota 188-415 1974 £12.50

HERGESHEIMER, JOSEPH   Balisand. New York, 1924. Orig. cloth backed boards, spine faded, rubbed, paper label, first edition, one of 175 numbered copies, signed by author. MacManus 224-219 1974 $25

HERGENSHEIMER, JOSEPH   The Bright Shawl. New York, 1922. Half parchment, signed, worn slipcase. Rota 188-413 1974 £12.50

HERGESHEIMER, JOSEPH   Cytherea. New York, 1922. Orig. cloth, signed, first edition. Rota 188-414 1974 £12.50

HERGESHEIMER, JOSEPH   The Party Dress. New York, 1930. Orig. vellum backed boards, first edition, one of 225 numbered copies, signed by author, fine, dust jacket, boxed. MacManus 224-220 1974 $27.50

HERGESHEIMER, JOSEPH   The Party Dress. New York, 1930. Full orange vellum, gilt, first edition. Rota 188-417 1974 £16

HERGESHEIMER, JOSEPH   The Presbyterian Child. 1924. Cloth-backed boards, signed, English first edition. Covent 56-1801A 1974 £5.25

HERGESHEIMER, JOSEPH   Tampico. 1926. Label rubbed, signed, limited edition. Allen 216-719 1974 $15

HERGESHEIMER, JOSEPH   Tampico. New York, 1926. Orig. cloth, signed, first edition. Rota 188-416 1974 £12.50

HERGESHEIMER, JOSEPH   The Three Black Pennys. New York, 1930. 4to., full orange vellum, first illus. edition. Rota 188-412 1974 £15

HERGESHEIMER, JOSEPH   The Three Black Pennys. New York, 1930. Illus., orig. vellum, first edition, with the preface, one of 170 numbered copies, signed by author & illus., boxed, fine. MacManus 224-221 1974 $50

HERGESHEIMER, JOSEPH   Tropical Winter. New York, 1933. Orig. cloth, first edition, one of 210 numbered copies, signed by author, printed on orange paper, dust jacket, boxed, fine. MacManus 224-222 1974 $27.50

HERGESHEIMER, JOSEPH   Wild Oranges. 1918. 128p., illus. Austin 51-426 1973 $7.50

HERIBAUD, J.   Les Muscinees d'Auvergne. 1899. 8vo., cloth, scarce. Wheldon 131-1419 1974 £8

HERING, D. W.   The Lure of the Clock. New York, 1932. 1st ed. Biblo & Tannen 210-225 1973 $20

HERIOT, GEORGE   Travels Through the Canadas. London, 1807. 4to., full red morocco, raised bands, excellent copy, scarce, first edition. Traylen 79-485 1973 £385

HERKOMER, HUBERT   Autobiography. 1890. Imperial 8vo., half vellum, presentation copy, inscribed, English first edition. Covent 56-50 1974 £65

HERMAN, HENRY   The Crime of a Christmas Toy. n.d. (1894). Plates, text illus., cloth backed pictorial boards, hinges weak, covers rubbed, very good copy, first edition. Covent 51-538 1973 £6.50

HERMAN, LEWIS HELMAR 1905-   Manuel of Foreign Dialects. 1943. Austin 51-427 1973 $7.50

HERMANN, BINGER   The Louisiana Purchase. Washington, 1900. Plates, blind gilt stamped cloth. Bradley 35-166 1974 $10

HERMANN, HERMANN JULIUS   Die Illuminierten Handschriften in Tirol. Leipzig, 1905. Folio, cloth, plates, illus. Kraus B8-89 1974 $85

HERMANN, JACOB   Phoronomia. 1716. 4to., contemporary calf, label, gilt, ex-library, first edition. Zeitlin 235-137 1974 $50

HERMANN, P.   Horti Academici Lugduno-Batavi Catalogus Exhibens Plantarum Omnium Nomina Quibus ab Anno MDCLXXXI ad Annum MDCLXXXVI Hortus Fuit Instructus. Leyden, 1687. 8vo., contemporary vellum, engravings, rare. Wheldon 131-1154 1974 £100

HERMANT, GODEFROI   La Vie de Saint Jean Chrysostome. Paris, 1669. 2 vols., contemporary calf. Howes 185-1304 1974 £8.50

HERMITAGE GALLERY   Galerie de l'Hermitage, Gravee au Trait d'Apres les plus Beaux Tableaux, Qui la Composent. Leningrad, 1805. 2 vols., 4to., contemporary red morocco gilt, rubbed. Quaritch 940-135 1974 £45

HERNANDEZ-PACHECO, F.   Fisiografia, Geologia y Paleontologia del Territorio de Valladolid. Madrid, 1930. Roy. 8vo., cloth, plates. Wheldon 131-1015 1974 £8

HERNANDEZ-PACHECO, F.   Fisiografia, Geologia y Paleontologia del Territorio der Valladolid. Madrid, 1930. Roy. 8vo., cloth, coloured map, plates, text-figures. Wheldon 128-990 1973 £8

HERNANDEZ-PACHECO, F.   Geolozia y Paleontologia del Mioceno de Palencia. Madrid, 1915. Roy. 8vo., cloth, plates. Wheldon 128-989 1973 £12.50

HERNANDEZ-PACHECO, F.   Rerum Medicarum Novae Hispaniae Thesaurus. Rome, 1651. Folio, modern full calf antique style, woodcuts, very rare second Latin edition. Wheldon 128-202 1973 £1,500

HERNANDEZ-PACHECO, F.   Rerum Medicarum Novae Hispaniae Thesaurus. Rome, 1651. Folio, vellum, woodcuts, very rare, second Latin edition. Wheldon 131-59 1974 £1,750

HERNDON, SARAH RAYMOND   Days on the Road: Crossing the Plains in 1865. New York, 1902. Jenkins 61-1056 1974 $45

HERNDON, SARAH RAYMOND   Days on the Road. New York, 1902. Orig. cloth, frontispiece, fine, first edition. Bradley 35-167 1974 $100

HERNDON, WILLIAM L.   Exploration of the Valley of the Amazon, Made Under the Direction of the Navy Department. Washington, 1854. 4 vols., 2 of text and 2 of maps, many plates. Jenkins 61-1057 1974 $27.50

HERODIANUS   Historiarum Libri VIII. Venice, 1524. 17th century calf gilt, line borders, very small marginal worming, lacks ties but quite nice. Thomas 32-211 1974 £30

HERODOTUS   The Famous History. New York, 1924. Limited to 1025 copies, 8vo., red paper boards with cloth back, binding scuffed, interior fine. Current BW9-532 1974 $10

HERODOTUS   History. 1737-20. 2 vols., new buckram, rubber stamp, second & third editions. Allen 213-484 1973 $12.50

HERODOTUS   History. 1889. 4 vols., maps, new English version. Allen 213-485 1973 $25

HERODOTUS   The History of Herodotus. New York, 1932. Biblo & Tannen 214-622 1974 $7.50

HERODOTIUS   Herodotius History. 1935. Folio, half blue parchment, uncut, woodcuts, limited. Broadhurst 23-1075 1974 £100

HERON-ALLEN, EDWARD   Barnacles in Nature and Myth. 1928. 8vo., orig. cloth. Bow Windows 64-128 1974 £6

HERR, CHARLOTE B.   Punky Dunk's Friends. Chicago, (1913). 16mo., pictorial boards, illus., fine, first editions, 3 vols., boxed. Frohnsdorff 16-431 1974 $30

HERRERA, ANTONIO DE   The General History of the Vast Continent and Islands of America. 1725-26. 8vo., 19th century red half morocco, 6 vols., first English edition. Bow Windows 64-546 1974 £475

HERRERA, ANTONIO DE   De Rampspoedige Scheeps-Togt van Franciscus Hernandez de Cordua. Leyden, 1706. 8vo., old mottled calf, folding map and plates, very good copy. Ximenes 36-117 1974 $100

HERRICK, C. L.   The Mammals of Minnesota. Minneapolis, 1892. 8vo., cloth, plates, text-figures. Wheldon 128-327 1973 £7.50

HERRICK, C. L.   The Mammals of Minnesota. Minneapolis, 1892. 8vo., orig. bindings. Butterfield 8-302 1974 $15

HERRICK, ROBERT   Complete Poems. 1876. 3 vols., ex-library, tops of spines frayed. Allen 216-1912 1974 $25

HERRICK, ROBERT   Hesperides. London, 1890. 2 vols., small 8vo., portrait, orig. cloth, revised second edition. Bow Windows 62-450 1974 £10

HERRICK, ROBERT   The Hesperides & Noble Numbers. 1891. 2 vols., small 8vo., half olive levant morocco gilt. Howes 186-250 1974 £8.50

HERRICK, ROBERT   Poems Chosen. Hammersmith, 1895. Small 4to., orig. limp vellum, fine, uncut. Dawsons PM 252-449 1974 £280

HERRICK, ROBERT   Poetical Works Of. 1859. 608 pages. Austin 61-460 1974 $21.50

HERRICK, ROBERT   The Poetical Works. 1928. 4 vols., crown 8vo., orig. parchment boards, uncut, one of 750 sets, dec. in colour. Broadhurst 24-723 1974 £25

HERRIMAN, D. C.   Mater Silva. Toronto, 1929. Decorations by author. Hood's 102-654 1974 $10

HERRING, FRANCIS   Mischeefes Mysterie. London, 1617. Small 4to., full straight-grained morocco, gilt, first edition. Ximenes 33-218 1974 $400

HERRINGTON, W. S.   History Of the County Of Lennox and Addington. Toronto, 1913. Illus. Hood's 103-638 1974 $55

HERRINGTON, W. S.   Pioneer Life Among the Loyalists in Upper Canada. Toronto, 1938. Illus. Hood's 102-608 1974 $20

HERSCHEL, JOHN   Account of Observations. 1833. 4to., old half calf, rubbed, plates. Gurney 64-111 1974 £36

HERSCHEL, JOHN FREDERICK WILLIAM   A Collection of Examples of the Applications of the Calculus of Finite Differences, and Examples of the Solutions of Functional Equations by Charles Babbage. Cambridge, 1820. Demy 8vo., orig. boards, first edition, uncut, fine. Broadhurst 24-1246 1974 £45

HERSCHEL, JOHN FREDERICK WILLIAM   Outlines of Astronomy. 1849. Demy 8vo., binding faded, frontispiece, text illus., orig. cloth. Broadhurst 24-1111 1974 £6

HERSHEY, BURNET   The Air Future. New York, 1943. Ist ed. Biblo & Tannen 213-643 1973 $10

HERSHFIELD, HARRY   Laugh Louder Live Longer. Grayson, 1959. 174p., illus. Austin 54-493 1973 $6.50

HERSHFIELD, HARRY   Super City. 1930. Austin 62-257 1974 $8.50

HERTER, G.   Estudios Botanicos en la Region Uraguaya. Montevideo, 1927-28. 2 vols., 8vo., wrappers. Wheldon 131-1305 1974 £5

HERTER, G.   Estudios Botanicos en la Region Uruguaya. Montevideo, 1930. Crown 8vo., sewed, plates, scarce. Wheldon 131-1307 1974 £5

HERTER, G.   Estudios Botanicos en la Region Uruguaya. Montevideo, 1933. Roy. 8vo., boards. Wheldon 131-1306 1974 £5

HERTWIG, O.   Handbuch der Vergleichenden. Jena, 1906. Roy 8vo., orig. half morocco, scarce. Wheldon 130-357 1974 £50

HERTZ, HEINRICH RUDOLF   Miscellaneous Papers. London, 1896. 8vo., orig. blue cloth, gilt, first collected edition in English. Dawsons PM 245-377 1974 £30

HERTZ, HEINRICH RUDOLF   Ueber Sehr Schnelle Electrische Schwingungen. Leipzig, 1887. 8vo., contemporary half vellum, gilt. Schafer 8-159 1973 sFr 2,600

HERTZ, HEINRICH RUDOLPH   Untersuchungen ueber die Ausbrietung der Elektrischen Kraft. Leipzig, 1892. 8vo., orig. green cloth, gilt, uncut, first edition. Dawsons PM 245-376 1974 £110

HERTZ, J. H.   Sermons, Addresses and Studies. 1938. 3 vols., portrait. Howes 185-1258 1974 £10.50

HERTZ, MICHAEL   Bibliotheca Germanica. Erfurt, 1679. Folio, old half vellum, very scarce, fine, first edition. Harper 213-89 1973 $225

HERTZKA, THEODOR   Freeland a Social Anticipation. London, 1891. 8vo., orig. cloth, fine, first edition in English. Dawsons PM 251-441 1974 £30

HERVEY, F.   The Naval History of Great Britain. 1779. 5 vols., plates, half contemporary calf gilt, bookplate. Smith 193-114 1973 £20

HERVEY, JAMES   Meditations and Contemplations. 1759. 2 vols., 8vo., frontispieces, plate, contemporary calf, worn. Bow Windows 62-452 1974 £6.50

HERVEY, JOHN   Memoirs of the Reign of George II. 1848. 2 vols., orig. crimson cloth, first edition. Howes 186-915 1974 £6.50

HERVEY, JOHN   Memoirs of the Reign of George the II. 1884. 3 vols., large 8vo., olive levant morocco. Howes 186-916 1974 £15

HERVEY, JOHN   Miscellaneous Thoughts. London, 1742. 8vo., modern half calf, gilt. Dawsons PM 247-144 1974 £15

HERVEY, JOHN   Racing in America 1922-36. New York, (1937). Folio, boards, cloth, first edition. Bradley 35-168 1974 $60

HERVEY, THOMAS K.   Illustrations of Modern Sculpture. 1834.
Roy. 4to., half russia, plates. Quaritch 940-136 1974 £7

HERVEY, THOMAS K.   The Poetical Sketch-Book. London, 1829.
12mo., orig. cloth, worn, first edition. Ximenes 33-220 1974 $12.50

HERVIEUX DE CHANTELOUP, J. C.   Nouveau Traite des Serins de Canarie.
Paris, 1709. 8vo., contemporary calf gilt, plates, first edition. Wheldon
128-479 1973 £35

HERVIEUX DE CHANTELOUP, J. C.   Nouveau Traite des Serins de Canarie.
Paris, 1709. 8vo., contemporary calf gilt, first edition. Wheldon 130-546
1974 £35

HERWERDEN, H. VAN   Lexicon Graecum Suppletorium et Dialecticum.
1902-04. 2 vols., sewn. Allen 213-488 1973 $17.50

HESELTINE, WILLIAM   Last of the Plantagenets. 1829. 2 vols.,
foxed, labels worn, first American edition. Allen 216-2237 1974 $15

HESELTINE, WILLIAM   The Last of the Plantagnets. London, 1829.
8vo., half calf, first edition. Dawsons PM 252-450 1974 £25

HESS, FJERIL   High Adventure. 1925. Austin 62-258
1974 $12.50

HESS, HEINRICH MARIA VON   Die Fresco-Gemalde der Konigl. Munich,
1837 (-41) (-47). Elephant folio, plates, half leather, gilt. Quaritch 940-137
1974 £2,000

HESSE, A.   Allgemeine Volkswirtschaftslehre. 1927-30.
2 vols., roy. 8vo., half morocco, prize label. Howes 186-1455 1974 £8.50

HESYCHIUS   Hesychii Lexicon cum Notis Doctorum Virorum
Integris, Vel Editis Antexhac Nunc Auctis & Emendatis. 1746-66. 2 vols.,
folio, contemporary calf, rebacked. Bow Windows 66-340 1974 £26

HETHERINGTON, A. J.   Togo and the Demon Cats. London, (1933).
Boards, dust wrapper. Dawson's 424-212 1974 $17.50

HETHERINGTON, A. L.   Chinese Ceramic Glazes. Cambridge, 1937.
Biblo & T nnen 214-376 1974 $18.50

HETHERINGTON, J.   Manuscript Notebook. 1711. 4to., old half
green straight-grained morocco, gilt. Zeitlin 235-111 1974 $75

HETLEY, MRS. CHARLES   The Native Flowers of New Zealand. (1887-)
1888. Imp. 4to., orig. cloth gilt, chromo-lithographed plates. Wheldon
128-1270 1973 £35

HETLEY, MRS. CHARLES   The Native Flowers of New Zealand. (1887-)
1888. Imperial 4to., orig. cloth gilt, plates. Wheldon 130-1166 1974 £35

HETLEY, MRS. CHARLES   The Native Flowers of New Zealand. 1888.
Imperial 4to., orig. cloth, gilt. Broadhurst 23-1146 1974 £50

HETTINGER, J.   Exploring the Ultra-Perceptive Faculty. London,
1941. Biblo & Tannen 210-975 1973 $8.50

HEUDE, P. M.   Etudes sur les Ruminants de l'Asie Orientale.
Shanghai, 1888. 4to., cloth, plates. Wheldon 128-328 1973 £15

HEUDE, P. M.   Etudes sur les Ruminants de l'Asie Orientale.
Shanghai, 1888. 4to., cloth, plates. Wheldon 130-401 1974 £15

HEVELIUS, JOHANNES   Cometographia. 1668. Folio, eighteenth century calf, gilt, first edition. Dawsons PM 245-378 1974 £850

HEVELIUS, JOHANNES   The Illustrated Account given by Hevelius in his
"Machina Celestis". 1882. 8vo., orig. red cloth, illus. Dawsons PM 245-379
1974 £10

HEWARD, CONSTANCE   Ameliaranne and the Green Umbrella. Phila.,
1920. 8vo., color plates. Frohnsdorff 16-36 1974 $15

HEWARD, CONSTANCE   The Twins and Tabiffa. Philadelphia, (1923).
8vo., cloth with pictorial cover label, fine color illus., first edition.
Frohnsdorff 16-432 1974 $15

HEWES, CADY   Women and Children First. Houghton, 1956.
15lp. Austin 54-291 1973 $7.50

HEWITSON, WILLIAM CHAPMAN   British Oology. Newcastle, (1831-38,
1842). Roy. 8vo., contemporary full green morocco, gilt, plates, fine, rare, first
edition. Wheldon 130-547 1974 £85

HEWITSON, WILLIAM CHAPMAN   Coloured Illustrations of the Eggs of
British Birds. 1856. 2 vols., 8vo., contemporary half morocco, plates.
Wheldon 131-621 1974 £20

HEWITT, GRAILY   Lettering. 1930. Edition-de-luxe, 4to., orig.
white buckram, uncut, top edges gilt, very fine, limited to 380 copies, signed by
author. Sawyer 293-27 1974 £35

HEWITT, GRAILY   Lettering; for Students and Craftmen. 1930.
4to., white buckram, illus., signed, fine, first edition. Rota 190-514 1974
£45

HEWITT, J.   Ancient Armour and Weapons in Europe. 1855.
8vo., illus., cloth. Quaritch 940-697 1974 £8

HEWITT, RANDALL H.   Across the Plains and Over the Divide. New
York, 1906. Extra plate, pict. cloth, very nice copy. Jenkins 61-1060 1974
$95

HEWLETT, ESTHER   The Cook's Complete Guide. (1836). 8vo.,
contemporary half calf, rebacked, engraved plates, damp stains. Bow Windows
66-341 1974 £6.50

HEWLETT, MAURICE   An Extensive Collection of 40 Works. 1895-
1924. 41 vols., crown 8vo., orig. cloth, illus. Howes 185-221 1974 £150

HEWLETT, MAURICE   The Fool Errant. 1905. First edition. Austin
61-462 1974 $10

HEWLETT, MAURICE   Letters to Sanchia. New York, 1910. Austin
61-464 1974 $10

HEWLETT, MAURICE   The Little Iliad. 1915. Frontispiece, first
American edition. Austin 61-465 1974 $10

HEWLETT, MAURICE   Pan and the Young Shepherd. 1898. 140
pages. Austin 61-466 1974 $10

HEWLETT, MAURICE   The Road In Tuscany. 1904. 2 vols., illus.,
first American edition. Austin 61-467 1974 $17.50

HEWSON, JOHN   The Doctrine of the New Birth, Exemplified in
the Life and Religious Experience of Onesimus. Philadelphia, 1839. 12mo.,
orig. quarter cloth & boards, rubbed, first edition, woodcuts. Ximenes 36-118
1974 $90

HEWSON, WILLIAM   The Works. London, 1846. 8vo., orig. green
cloth, uncut, first edition. Dawsons PM 249-268 1974 £25

HEY, RICHARD   Three Dissertations. Cambridge, 1812. 8vo.,
orig. quarter cloth, revised. Ximenes 33-221 1974 $27.50

HEY, WILLIAM   Practical Observations in Surgery. London,
1814. 8vo., modern brown buckram. Dawsons PM 249-269 1974 £21

HEYER, GEORGETTE   A Blunt Instrument. 1938. English first edition.
Covent 56-331 1974 $7.50

HEYGATE, JOHN   Decent Fellows. London, 1930. First edition,
wrappers, nice copy, scarce. Crane 7-333 1974 £5

HEYLYN, PETER   Cosmography In Four Books. London, 1703.
Thick large folio, contemporary calf, maps. Traylen 79-432 1973 £95

HEYMANN, WALTHER   Max Pechstein. Munich, 1916. Large 4to.,
boards, illus., scarce first edition. Minters 37-482 1973 $45

HEYWARD, DU BOIS   Brass Ankle. Farrar, Rinehart, 1931. 133p.
Austin 51-429 1973 $7.50

HEYWOOD, RAYMOND   The Greater Love. 1919. Presentation, fine,
dust wrapper, inscribed, boards. Covent 55-1393 1974 £10.50

HEYWOOD, RAYMOND   Roses, Pearls and Tears. 1918. Presentation,
inscribed, pictorial boards, fine. Covent 55-1394 1974 £5.25

HEYWOOD, THOMAS   The Exemplary Lives and Memorable Acts of
Nine the Most Worthy Women. London, 1640. 4to., 19th century half diced
russia, rebacked, first edition. Dawsons PM 252-451 1974 £180

HEYWOOD, THOMAS   The Hierarchie of Angels. London, 1646. Contemporary blind-stamped calf. Dawson's 424-331 1974 $85

HEYWOOD, THOMAS   The Hierarchie of the Blessed Angells. London,
1635. Small folio, old mottled calf, plates, first edition. Dawsons PM
252-452 1974 £170

HEYWOOD, THOMAS   Nine Bookes of Various History Concerning
Women. 1624. First edition, reasonably clean and sound, small folio, 19th
century mottled calf gilt, upper joint repaired. Thomas 32-175 1974 £50

HEYWOOD, THOMAS   Pleasant Dialogues and Drammas. London,
1637. 8vo., full morocco, foxing, first edition. Ximenes 33-222 1974 $275

HEYWOOD, THOMAS   Pleasant Dialogves and Drammas. London,
1637. 8vo., black morocco gilt, first edition. Dawsons PM 252-453 1974
£280

HEYWOODE, THOMAS   Gunaikeion. London, 1624. Marbled boards,
first edition. Dawson's 424-339 1974 $300

HEYWORTH, LAWRENCE   Glimpses at the Origin. London, 1866. 8vo.,
orig. cloth, fine, first edition. Ximenes 33-223 1974 $15

HIBBARD, ADDISON   The Lyric South. New York, 1928. 1st ed.
Biblo & Tannen 210-876 1973 $8.50

HIBBERD, SHIRLEY   The Amateur's Kitchen Garden. 1877. 8vo.,
orig. dec. cloth, coloured plates, text-figures. Wheldon 128-1475 1973 £5

HIBBERD, SHIRLEY   The English Flora of Sir J. E. Smith Class
XXIV Cryptogamia, Vol. 5 Part 2, Comprising the Fungi. 1836. 8vo., boards,
scarce. Wheldon 131-1421 1974 £10

HIBBERD, SHIRLEY   The Fern Garden. Groombridge, 1870.
Crown 8vo., orig. cloth, plates. Wheldon 131-1526 1974 £5

HIBBERD, SHIRLEY   Field Flowers. Groombridge, (1870). Crown
8vo., orig. cloth, plates. Wheldon 130-1089 1974 £5

HIBBERD, SHIRLEY   Field Flowers. London, 1878. 8vo., color
plates, orig. cloth. Gregory 44-154 1974 $8.75

HIBBERD, SHIRLEY   The Ivy. 1893. Small 4to., orig. dec. cloth,
plates, second edition. Wheldon 131-1525 1974 £20

HIBBERD, SHIRLEY   New and Rare Beautiful-Leaved Plants. 1870.
Roy. 8vo., orig. cloth gilt, worn, coloured plates. Wheldon 128-1474 1973
£12

HIBBERD, SHIRLEY   New and Rare Beautiful-Leaved Plants. 1870.
Roy 8vo., new half green morocco gilt. Wheldon 129-1472 1974 £25

HIBBERD, SHIRLEY   New and Rare Beautiful Leaved Plants. 1870.
Roy. 8vo., orig. dec. cloth, plates. Wheldon 131-1527 1974 £25

HIBBERD, SHIRLEY   New and Rare Beautiful Leaved Plants. 1891.
Roy. 8vo., orig. cloth, plates, second edition. Wheldon 131-1528 1974 £25

HIBBERD, SHIRLEY   Rustic Adornments for Homes of Taste. 1870.
8vo., plates, woodcuts, orig. dec. cloth, worn. Quaritch 940-512 1974 £50

HIBBERD, SHIRLEY   The Seaweed Collector. (1872). Crown 8vo.,
orig. cloth, gilt, plates. Wheldon 131-1420 1974 £7.50

HIBBERT, GEORGE   A Catalogue of the Library of George Hibbert.
London, 1829. 8vo., contemporary polished calf, fine. Dawsons PM 10-276
1974 £48

HIBBERT, LUKE   The Engineer's and Mechanic's Encyclopaedia.
London, 1836. 8vo., 2 vols., contemporary half calf, gilt, illus., first edition.
Hammond 201-834 1974 £20

HIBBERT, LUKE   The Engineer's and Mechanic's Encyclopaedia.
London, 1848. 8vo., 2 vols., contemporary half polished calf, gilt, illus., new
edition. Hammond 201-835 1974 £12.50

HIBBERT, S.   History of the Extinct Volcanos of the Basin of
Neuwied. Edinburgh, 1832. 8vo., orig. cloth, plates. Wheldon 130-934
1974 £10

HIBBERT-WARE, SAMUEL   A Description of the Shetland Islands. Edinburgh,
1822. 4to., orig. boards, rebacked, plates. Hammond 201-368 1974 £65

HICHENS, ROBERT   Egypt and Its Monuments. New York, 1908.
Illus. in color, inner hinge cracked, orig. binding. Wilson 63-523 1974 $10

HICHENS, ROBERT   Egypt and Its Monuments. New York, 1909.
Gilt, fine, English first edition. Covent 56-404 1974 £8.50

HICKENLOOPER, FRANK   An Illustrated History of Monroe County, Iowa.
Albia, 1896. 12mo., cloth, map. Saddleback 14-411 1974 $25

HICKES, GEORGE   Institutiones Grammaticae Anglo-Saxonicae.
Oxford, 1689. 4to., contemporary mottled calf, rebacked, first edition. Dawsons PM 251-148 1974 £95

HICKES, GEORGE   Linguarum Vett. Oxford, 1705-03-05.
3 vols. in 2, folio, old panelled calf, plates. Quaritch 939-140 1974 £125

HICKEY, WILLIAM   Memoirs. 1916-25. 4 vols., plates. Howes
186-919 1974 £20

HICKS, F. C.   Men and Books Famous in Law. Rochester,
1921. 12mo., cloth, first edition. Goodspeed's 578-470 1974 $15

HICKS, GRANVILLE   Figures of Transition. New York, 1939.
1st ed. Biblo & Tannen 213-777 1973 $8.50

HICKSON, S. J.   A Naturalist in North Celebes. 1889. 8vo.,
plates, cloth, scarce. Wheldon 129-275 1974 £15

HIELSCHER, KURT   Picturesque Spain. New York, 1925. 4to.,
plates. Biblo & Tannen 210-286 1973 $20

HIERN, W. P.   Monograph of Ebenaceae. 1873. 4to., cloth,
plates, scarce. Wheldon 128-1602 1973 £7.50

HIERONYMUS, SAINT   Epistolae. (Rome, 1470). Vol. 1 of 2,
thick large folio, contemporary blind-stamped calf, wooden boards, worn, very
rare. Harper 213-90 1973 $1500

HIERONYMUS, SAINT   Epistolae. 1566. 2 vols. in 1, contemporary
stained vellum, rubbed. Thomas 30-120 1973 £15

HIERONYMUS, SAINT   Operum. Paris, 1693. 5 vols. in 6, old
mottled calf. Smith 194-158 1974 £25

HIERONYMUS, SAINT   Vita et Transitus. Florence, 1490. Small
4to., old vellum, foxing. Thomas 28-287 1972 £90

HIERONYMUS, SAINT   Opera Omnia. Paris, 1864. 7 vols., roy. 8vo.,
half roan, worn. Howes 185-1299 1974 £15

HIFFERNAN, PAUL   The Heroine of the Cave. 1775. 8vo., cloth,
first edition. Quaritch 936-102 1974 £10

HIGDEN, RANULPH　　　Polychronicon. Westminster, 1495. Folio, modern calf, second edition. Dawsons PM 252-455 1974 £3950

HIGDEN, RANULPH　　　Polycronicon. (Westminster, 1482). Folios, 19th century dark green morocco, gilt, excellent. Dawsons PM 252-454 1974 £24,500

HIGGINS, ANTHONY　　　New Castle, Delaware. Boston, 1939. 4to., cloth, plates, limited. Saddleback 14-341 1974 $17.50

HIGGINS, BRYAN　　　Experiments and Observations Made With the View of Improving the Art of Composing and Applying Calcareous Cements. 1780. 8vo., contemporary boards, paper spine, worn, uncut. Quaritch 940-513 1974 £42

HIGGINS, BRYAN　　　Experiments and Observations. London, 1780. 8vo., contemporary half calf, first edition. Dawsons PM 245-382 1974 £95

HIGGINS, D. W.　　　The Mystic Spring and Other Tales of Western Life. New York, 1908. Fully illus., new revised edition. Hood's 102-809 1974 $15

HIGGINS, D. W.　　　The Passing of a Race and More Tales. Toronto, 1905. 8vo., orig. cloth, illus., first edition. Rota 190-518 1974 £5

HIGGINS, F. R.　　　Arable Holdings. Dublin, 1933. Orig. cloth, label, inscribed, first edition. Rota 188-425 1974 £30

HIGGINS, JOHN　　　A Mirovr for Magistrates. London, 1610. 4 parts in 1 vol., 4to., 19th century panelled calf, gilt, first complete edition. Dawsons PM 252-456 1974 £480

HIGGINSON, THOMAS WENTWORTH　　　Contemporaries. Boston, 1899. First edition. Biblo & Tannen 210-877 1973 $7.50

HIGGINSON, THOMAS WENTWORTH　　　Massachusetts in the Army and Navy During the War of 1861-65. Boston, 1896. 4to., 2 vols., hinges in vol. 1 cracked, orig. binding. Butterfield 10-160 1974 $15

HIGGINSON, THOMAS WENTWORTH　　　Merchants. Newberryport, 1851. 8vo., orig. wrappers, scarce, first edition. Ximenes 33-224 1974 $25

HIGHMORE, A.　　　The History of the Honourable Artillery Company. 1804. 8vo., buckram, plate. Quaritch 939-456 1974 £12.50

HIGHWAYS and Byways Series. 1898-1939. 36 vols., illus., cloth gilt, first editions. Howes 186-2018 1974 £75

HILARIUS, SAINT, BISHOP OF POITIERS　　　Lucubrationes Quotquot Extant. Basle, 1535. Small folio, English 17th century calf gilt, bookplate. Thomas 28-138 1972 £80

HILARIUS, ST. BISHOP OF POITIERS　　　Lucubrationes Quotquot Extant. Basle, 1535. Small folio, English 17th century calf gilt, armorial bookplate of Earl Fitzwilliam, head and foot of spine little worn, else good. Thomas 32-77 1974 £80

HILBERT, DAVID　　　Grundlagen der Geometrie. Leipzig, 1899. 4to., modern boards, first edition. Dawsons PM 245-383 1974 £12

HILDEBRANDT, FREIDRICH　　　Handbuch der Anatomie des Menschen. 1830(-1832). 8vo., 4 vols., contemporary half calf, rebacked. Dawsons PM 249-270 1974 £26

HILDEBRAND, F.　　　Die Lebensverhaltnisse der Oxalisarten. 1884. 4to., orig. wrappers. Wheldon 131-1155 1974 £5

HILDEBRAND, F.　　　Die Lebensverhaltnisse der Oxalisarten. 1884. 4to., orig. wrappers, plates. Wheldon 128-1115 1973 £5

HILDENBURN, CHARLES R.　　　Sketches of Printers and Printing in Colonial New York. New York, 1895. Orig. grey boards, illus. Dawson's 424-153 1974 $50

HILDRETH, RICHARD　　　Archy Moore. New York, 1855. 8vo., orig. cloth, illus., first edition. Ximenes 33-225 1974 $15

HILDRETH, RICHARD　　　A Report of the Trail of the Rev. Ephraim K. Avery, Before the Supreme Judicial Court of Rhode Island, on an Indictment for the Murder of Sarah Maria Cornell. Boston, 1833. Second edition, 8vo., foxed, woodcut map, modern brown cloth. Current BW9-371 1974 $50

HILL, AARON　　　Four Essays. London, 1718. 8vo., modern marbled boards, fine, rare, first edition. Dawsons PM 247-145 1974 £185

HILL, AARON　　　King Henry the Fifth. London, 1723. 8vo., half calf, first edition. Ximenes 33-226 1974 $35

HILL, AARON　　　Works. 1753. 4 vols., half boards, label defective, ex-library. Allen 216-2026 1974 $40

HILL, ALICE P.　　　Tales of Colorado Pioneers. Denver, 1884. New cloth, first edition. Putnam 126-288 1974 $50

HILL, EDWIN B.　　　Range Tales. Boston, (1916). Printed tan wrappers, scarce, frontispiece, first edition. Bradley 35-401 1974 $40

HILL, EDWIN DARLEY　　　The Northern Banking Company Ltd. Belfast, 1925. 4to., illus., cloth boards. Emerald 50-426 1974 £15

HILL, G.　　　A History of English Dress. 1893. 8vo., 2 vols., orig. cloth. Bow Windows 64-547 1974 £15

HILL, GEORGE BIRKBECK　　　Footsteps of Dr. Johnson. London, 1890. 4to., orig. half roan, plates, illus. Dawsons PM 252-577 1974 £17.50

HILL, GEORGE BIRBECK　　　Jonsonian Miscellanies. Oxford, 1897. 2 vols., orig. quarter roan, rubbed. Howes 186-279 1974 £8.75

HILL, GEORGE BIRKBECK　　　Talks About Autographs. 1896. Plates, nice copy, first edition, bookplate. Covent 51-154 1973 £6.30

HILL, GEORGE W.　　　History of Ashland County, Ohio. (Cleveland), 1880. Half leather, illus., professionally rebacked, part of orig. spine laid down, scarce. Hayman 59-425 1974 $57.50

HILL, JOHN　　　Observations on the Greek and Roman Classics. London, 1753. 12mo., contemporary calf, rebacked, first edition. Ximenes 33-228 1974 £70

HILL, JOHN 1716?-1775　　　The British Herbal. 1756. Folio, contemporary mottled calf, rebacked gilt, plates, fine, scarce. Wheldon 130-28 1974 £850

HILL, JOHN 1716?-1775　　　The British Herbal. London, 1756. Folio, plates, contemporary calf gilt, labels, good copy. Traylen 79-25 1973 £700

HILL, JOHN 1716?-1775　　　The British Herbal. 1756. Folio, contemporary mottled calf, neatly rebacked gilt, hand-coloured engraved plates & frontispiece, scarce, fine copy. Wheldon 128-1197 1973 £650

HILL, JOHN 1716?-1775　　　Eden: Or, a Complete Body of Gardening. 1757. Folio, contemporary diced calf gilt, plates, rare. Wheldon 131-60 1974 £750

HILL, JOHN 1716?-1775　　　The Family Herbal. Bungay, (1808). 8vo., modern half calf antique, plates, complete copy. Wheldon 131-1808 1974 £30

HILL, JOHN 1716?-1775　　　The Family Herbal. Bungay, c. 1820. 8vo., cloth, plates. Hammond 201-649 1974 £14

HILL, JOHN 1716?-1775　　　The Family Herbal. 1812. 8vo., old calf, worn. Broadhurst 23-1129 1974 £25

HILL, JOHN 1716?-1775　　　The Family Herbal. Bungay, (1808). 8vo., modern half calf. Wheldon 129-1686 1974 £30

HILL, JOHN 1716?-1775　　　The Family Herbal. Bungay, 1812. 8vo., modern half calf antique style, hand coloured plates. Wheldon 128-1679 1973 £30

HILL, JOHN 1716?-1775　　　The History of Plants. London, 1751. Folio, contemporary calf, leather label, rubbed. Traylen 79-26 1973 £48

HILL, JOHN 1716-1775   The Origin and production of Proliferous Flowers. 1579. 8vo., modern boards, plates, uncut, rare. Wheldon 130-1406 1974 £15

HILL, JOHN 1716?-1775   Virtues of British Herbs. 1770. 8vo., modern boards, engraved plates, third edition. Wheldon 128-1680 1973 £10

HILL, JOHN HARWOOD   The Chronical of the Christian Ages. Uppingham, England, ca. 1859. 2 vols., orig. cl. Jacobs 24-148 1974 $15

HILL, JOSEPH   The Interest of These United Provinces. 1673. 4to., calf-antique, first edition in English. Dawsons PM 251-444 1974 £25

HILL, N. N.   History of Knox County, Ohio. Mt. Vernon, 1881. New cloth. Hayman 59-476 1974 $50

HILL, OLIVER   The Garden of Adonis. London, (1923). 4to., illus., orig. gilt dec. cloth, foxing. Bow Windows 62-455 1974 £5

HILL, T. G.   The Essentials of Illustration. 1915. Roy 8vo., orig. cloth boards, plates, scarce. Wheldon 129-82 1974 £7.50

HILL, WILLIAM H.   Reference Catalogue of Books, Pamphlets and Plans, etc., Relating to Glasgow in the Library at Barlanark. Glasgow, 1905. Crown 4to., good copy, orig. cloth, no. 100 of limited issue, inscribed presentation copy by author. Broadhurst 24-284 1974 £10

HILL, WILLIAM HENRY   Antonio Stradivari: His Life and Work. 1902. 4to., orig. quarter calf, cloth sides, top edges gilt, others uncut, plates, first edition. Bow Windows 66-726 1974 £110

HILL, WILLIAM HENRY   Antonio Stradivari: His Life and Work. 1909. 8vo., orig. cloth, illus., coloured frontispiece. Bow Windows 66-727 1974 £20

HILL, WILLIAM HENRY 1857-1927   Violin-Makers of the Guarneri Family. 1931. Plates in colour, photogravures, text illus., roy. 4to., half vellum, top edges gilt, others uncut, mint, limited to 200 copies. Broadhurst 24-94 1974 £100

HILL, WILLIAM HENRY 1857-1927   The Violin-Makers of the Guarneri Family. 1931. 4to., quarter vellum, colour and photogravure plates, fine. Bow Windows 66-728 1974 £110

HILL-TOUT, C.   British North America. London, 1907. Map, illus., foxing. Hood's 103-454 1974 $22.50

HILLARY, WILLIAM   Observations on the Changes of the Air and the Concomitant Epidemical Diseases. London, 1759. 8vo., contemporary calf, re-backed, first edition. Dawsons PM 249-271 1974 £265

HILLARY, WILLIAM   Observations on the Changes of the Air and the Concomitant Epidemical Diseases. London, 1766. 8vo., orig. boards, rebacked, uncut. Dawsons PM 249-272 1974 £65

HILLEBRAND, W.   Flora of the Hawaiian Islands. Heidelberg, 1888. 8vo., cloth, maps, frontispiece, rare orig. printing. Wheldon 128-1271 1973 £15

HILLHOUSE, JAMES A.   Dramas, Discourses, and Other Pieces. Boston, 1839. 2 vols., 8vo., orig. cloth, fine, first edition. Ximenes 33-229 1974 $45

HILLHOUSE, JAMES A.   Hadad. New York, 1825. 8vo., orig. salmon boards, first edition. Ximenes 33-230 1974 $65

HILLHOUSE, JAMES A.   Sachem's-Wood. New Haven, 1838. 8vo., orig. tan printed wrappers, good copy, first edition. Ximenes 37-109 1974 $35

HILLS, WALLACE H.   The History of East Grinstead. 1906. Scarce. Howes 186-2203 1974 £6.50

HILLYER, R. S.   The Hills Give Promise. Boston, 1923. 8vo., boards, hand-made paper, first edition. Goodspeed's 578-142 1974 $10

HILTON, JAMES   Chronograms 5000 and More in Number. 1882-95. 3 vols., 4to., half roan. Quaritch 939-734 1974 £30

HILTON, JAMES   Contango. 1932. 8vo., orig. cloth, foxed, dust wrapper, first edition. Rota 190-521 1974 £7.50

HILL, JOHN 1716-1775   The Actor. 1750. Small 8vo., contemporary calf, first edition. Quaritch 936-103 1974 £50

HILL, JOHN 1716-1775   The Actor. 1755. Small 8vo., contemporary calf, first edition. Quaritch 936-104 1974 £70

HILL, JOHN 1716-1775   A Method of Producing Double Flowers from Single. 1759. 8vo., modern boards, plates, uncut, rare, second edition. Wheldon 130-1407 1974 £15

HILL, JOHN 1716-1775   The Naval History of Britian. London, 1756. Folio, 19th century calf, blind stamped, first edition. Dawsons PM 251-389 1974 £50

HIMES, CHESTER   Pinktoes. Putnam, 1965. 256p., hard cover ed. Austin 54-494 1973 $6.50

HIMES, JOSHUA V.   Millennial Harp. Boston, 1843. 16mo., orig. binding. Butterfield 10-420 1974 $27.50

HIMES, NORMAN E.   Medical History of Contraception. Baltimore, 1936. 1st ed., illus. Biblo & Tannen 213-839 1973 $12.50

HINCKS, T.   A History of the British Hydroid Zoophytes. 1868. 2 vols., 8vo., orig. cloth, plates, scarce. Wheldon 128-899 1973 £12

HINCKS, T.   A History of the British Hydroid Zoophytes. 1868. 8vo., 2 vols., orig. cloth, plates, scarce. Wheldon 130-869 1974 £15

HINCKS, T.   A History of the British Hydroid Zoophytes. 1868. 2 vols., roy. 8vo., orig. cloth, plates, scarce large paper issue. Wheldon 128-900 1973 £20

HIND, HENRY YOULE   Eighty Years' Progress of British North America. Toronto, 1864. Engravings, orig. leather, illus. Hood's 104-642 1974 $55

HIND, HENRY YOULE   Essay on the Insects and Diseases Injurious To the Wheat Crops. Toronto, 1857. Hood's 104-436 1974 $12.50

HIND, HENRY YOULE   Explorations. 1863. Full contemporary light brown calf, gilt, first edition. Broadhurst 23-1654 1974 £180

HIND, HENRY YOULE   Explorations In the Interior of the Labrador Peninsula. London, 1863. Thick 8vo., green prize calf gilt, leather label, plates. Traylen 79-486 1973 £120

HIND, HENRY YOULE   North-West Territory, Reports of Progress. Toronto, 1859. Wood-cuts, maps. Hood's 104-855 1974 $90

HIND, W.   A Monograph of the British Carboniferous Lamellibranchiata. 1896-1905. 2 vols., 4to., half calf, plates. Wheldon 131-1016 1974 £35

HIND, W.   A Monograph on Carbonicola, Anthracomya, and Naiadites. 1894-96. 4to., half calf, plates. Wheldon 131-1017 1974 £15

HINDE, G. J.   Catalogue of the Fossil Sponges in the Geological Department of the British Museum. 1883. 4to., cloth, plates, rare. Wheldon 128-991 1973 £10

HINDE, G. J.   A Monograph of the British Fossil Sponges. 1887-1912. Vol. 1, 4to., unbound, plates. Wheldon 131-1018 1974 £10

HINDE, G. J.   Report on the Materials from the Borings at the Funafuti Atoll. 1904. 4to., wrappers. Wheldon 128-992 1973 £5

HINDLEY, CHARLES   The History of the Catnach Press. London, 1886. Orig. boards, uncut, worn. Dawsons PM 10-277 1974 £35

HINDLEY, CHARLES   The History of the Catnach Press. 1887. Crown 8vo., orig. cloth, illus. Broadhurst 23-377 1974 £22.50

HINDLEY, CHARLES   A History of the Cries of London. London, n.d. Cloth, illus., soiled. Dawson's 424-108 1974 $25

HINDLEY, CHARLES   The Roxburghe Ballads. 1873-74. 8vo., 2 vols., cloth, orig. woodcuts. Quaritch 936-537 1974 £30

HINDS, JOHN   Conversations on Conditioning. 1829. 8vo.,
orig. boards, first edition. Hammond 201-449 1974 £16

HINDWOOD, K. A.   The Birds of Lord Howe Island. Sydney, 1940.
8vo., cloth, illus. Wheldon 129-479 1974 £15

HINE, REGINALD L.   Hitchin Worthies. 1932. One of 1021 copies,
numbered & signed by author, plates, text illus., orig. cloth. Covent 51-2594
1973 £5.25

HINES, GORDON   Alfalfa Bill. Oklahoma City, 1932. Orig.
cloth, illus., first edition. Putnam 126-297 1974 $10

HINES, GUSTAVUS   Life on the Plains of the Pacific. Buffalo,
1851. Second edition, added portrait, orig. binding. Butterfield 10-448 1974
$35

HINES, H. K.   An Illustrated History of the State of Washington.
Chicago, 1893. 4to., leather, rebacked. Saddleback 14-748 1974 $75

HINES, J.   The Red Indians of the Plains. London, 1915.
Maps, illus. Hood's 102-459 1974 $20

HINGESTON-RANDOLPH, FRANCIS CHARLES   Royal and Historical Letters
During the Reign of Henry the Fourth. 1860. Roy. 8vo., orig. roxburgh binding,
rubbed. Howes 186-1180 1974 £5

HINGSTON, R. W. G.   The Meaning of Animal Colour and Adornment.
1933. 8vo., cloth, scarce. Wheldon 130-358 1974 £5

HINKLEY, LAURA L.   Charlotte and Emily Bronte. New York, c. 1945.
First edition, orig. binding. Wilson 63-489 1974 $10

HINKSON, H. A.   Dublin Verses by Members of Trinity College.
London & Dublin, 1895. Nice copy, first edition. Covent 51-1983 1973 £8.50

HINKSON, KATHERINE TYNAN   The Cabinet of Irish Literature. London,
1908. 4 vols., illus., green cloth, gilt. Emerald 50-946 1974 £7.50

HINKSON, KATHERINE TYNAN   The Wild Harp. London, 1913. 4to., cloth
boards, first edition. Emerald 50-947 1974 £5

HINKSON, KATHERINE TYNAN   Collected Poems. 1930. Cover trifle soiled,
nice copy, first edition. Covent 51-1873 1973 £5.25

HINMAN, WILBUR F.   Corporal Si Klegg and His Pard. Cleveland,
1888. New cloth. Hayman 57-88 1974 $10

HINTON, CHARLES HOWARD   The Fourth Dimension. 1906. First edition.
Covent 55-1309 1974 £7.50

HINTON, CHARLES HOWARD   Scientific Romances. 1886. First edition.
Covent 55-833 1974 £5.25

HINTON, EDWARD M.   Ireland Through Tudor Eyes. Philadelphia,
1935. 8vo., cloth boards, scarce. Emerald 50-428 1974 £5

HINTON, RICHARD J.   Civil War in the Southwest. Chicago, 1865.
8vo., cloth, portraits, rare, first edition. Putman 126-58 1974 $60

HIPKINS, ALFRED JAMES   Musical Instruments, Historic, Rare and Unique.
Edinburgh, 1888. Folio, half morocco, plates, fine, orig. edition. Quaritch
940-813 1974 £150

HIPPISLEY, JOHN COXE   The Substance of Additional Observations
Intended to Have Been Delivered in the House of Commons. London, 1806.
8vo., orig. boards, fine, first edition. Ximenes 33-231 1974 $40

HIPPOCRATES   The Genuine Works of. London, 1849. 8vo.,
2 vols., orig. green cloth, plates. Dawsons PM 249-273 1974 £22

HIRMER, M.   Handbuch der Palaobotanik. Munich, 1927.
Roy 8vo., orig. buckram. Wheldon 130-937 1974 £10

HIRSCH, AUGUST   Handbuch der Historisch-Geographischen
Pathologie. Erlangen, 1859-62-64. 2 vols. in 3, large 8vo., half morocco,
library plates. Rittenhouse 46-340 1974 $75

HIRSCH, G. C.   Form und Stoffwechsel der Golgi Korper. Berlin, 1939. 8vo., cloth. Wheldon 130-359 1974 £5

HIRSCHFELD, ALBERT   Manhattan Oasis. New York, 1932.
Ballinger 1-272 1974 $12.50

HIRSCHFELD, LUDOVIC   Nevrologie. Paris, 1853. Large 8vo., 2 vols.,
green half roan, gilt, first edition. Dawsons PM 249-275 1974 £245

HIRSCHFIELD, ALBERT   Show Business Is No Business. Simon, Schuster,
1951. 141p. Austin 51-430 1973 $8.50

HIRST, F. W.   Early Life and Letters of John Morley. 1927.
2 vols., plates. Allen 216-1154 1974 $10

HIRTH, GEORG   Das Deutsche Zimmer de Gothik und
Renaissance des Barock. Muchen & Leipzig, 1886. 4to., illus., orig. cloth,
gilt, worn. Covent 55-104 1974 £12.50

HIS, WILHELM   Die Anatomische Nomenclatur. Leipzig,
1895. 8vo., plates, orig. printed wrappers, first edition. Schafer 8-160
1973 sFr. 250

HIS MAJESTIES COMMISSION to All the Lords. London, 1611. 4to., modern
grey boards, first edition. Dawsons PM 251-216 1974 £30

HISSEY, JAMES JOHN   A Complete Set of His Celebrated Coaching and
Motoring Works. 1884-1917. Full page illus., 14 vols., 8vo., half crimson
morocco gilt, top edges gilt, binding of one vol. darkened, good set, scarce.
Sawyer 293-166 1974 £165

HISTORIA SANCTAE CRUCIS   Legendary History of the Cross. 1887. Vellum,
woodcuts. Allen 213-1253 1973 $10

AN HISTORICAL and Descriptive Account of the Town of Lancaster. Lancaster,
1807. Thin 8vo., half calf, leather label, fine, plates. Traylen 79-347
1973 £10

THE HISTORICAL Cabinet. Philadelphia, 1838. Illus. with engravings. Biblo &
Tannen 213-682 1973 $15

HISTORICAL SOCIETY OF NEW MEXICO   Charter, Constitution and Bylaws
of . . ., Its Officers and Committees, with the Inaugural Address Delivered by
Hon. W. G. Ritch, President. Santa Fe, 1881. 16mo., orig. printed wrappers,
first edition, scarce, fine. Ximenes 36-155 1974 $50

THE HISTORY and Adventures of Jack, The Giant Killer. London, n.d.
(c. 1830). 16mo., engravings, orig. printed wrappers. Frohnsdorff 15-177
1974 $35

HISTORY and Commerce of New York. New York, (1891). 4to., cloth, illus.,
second edition. Saddleback 14-586 1974 $12.50

HISTORY of a French Louse. London, 1779. 8vo., marbled boards, scarce, first
English edition. Ximenes 33-19 1974 $175

A HISTORY of Animals. Concord, 1843. 24mo., pictorial wrappers, woodcuts.
Frohnsdorff 16-437 1974 $20

THE HISTORY of Autonous. London, 1736. 8vo., half morocco, buckram boards,
first edition. Ximenes 37-78 1974 $175

HISTORY of Dick Whittington, Lord Mayor of London; With the Adventures of His
Cat. Banbury, n.d. (c. 1820.). 24mo., woodcuts, fine, unopened, unstitched
as issued. Frohnsdorff 16-438 1974 $20

HISTORY of Discoveries and Inventions, Chiefly Intended for the Entertainment
and Instruction of Young Persons. 1808. 12mo., orig. marbled boards, roan
spine, trifle rubbed. George's 610-374 1973 £7.50

THE HISTORY of Fish. New York, n.d. (c. 1820's). Orig. floral printed
wrappers, woodcuts, 2 1/2 X 4 inches. Frohnsdorff 16-435 1974 $30

HISTORY of Franklin and Pickaway Counties, Ohio. N. P., 1880. Half
leather, title page reinforced. Hayman 59-457 1974 $55

A HISTORY OF French Influence in the United States. Philadelphia, 1812. 8vo., modern boards, first edition. Dawsons PM 251-249 1974 £20

A HISTORY of Haverford College for the First Sixty Years of Its Existence. Philadelphia, 1892. First edition, large 8vo., illus., blue cloth covers, paper label on spine. Current BW9-370 1974 $28.50

THE HISTORY of Henry County, Illinois. Chicago, 1877. 8vo., cloth, map. Saddleback 14-381 1974 $65

THE HISTORY of Jo Daviess County, Illinois. Chicago, 1878. 8vo., cloth, map, illus. Saddleback 14-384 1974 $60

HISTORY of Marshall County. 1878. Illus., map, part leather. Putnam 126-184 1974 $60

HISTORY of Joseph and His Brethren; and of the Bondage and Miraculous Deliverance of the Israelites. Steubenville, 1829. 8vo, orig. stiff yellow printed wrappers, bit soiled, but sound, hand colored engravings, very good, very rare. Ximenes 36-127 1974 $80

HISTORY of McHenry County, Illinois. Chicago, 1885. 8vo., cloth, illus., map, rebound. Saddleback 14-391 1974 $60

HISTORY of North America. Leeds, 1820. Full leather, excellent condition, some mis-numbering of pages, folding map. Hood's 102-561 1974 $400

HISTORY of North America. Leeds, 1820. 2 vols., plates, maps, full leather. Hood's 104-643 1974 $400

THE HISTORY of Ogle County, Illinois. Chicago, 1878. 8vo., illus., cloth, map. Saddleback 14-392 1974 $65

A HISTORY of Public Buildings Under the Control of the Treasury Department. Washington, 1901. 4to., marbled boards and sheep, rubbed, photos, edges of some text pages dampstained. Butterfield 10-63 1974 $50

HISTORY of Southern California and Los Angeles. (1898?). Oblong 16mo., quarter cloth. Saddleback 14-172 1974 $10

THE HISTORY of Susanna, Taken Out of the Apocrypha and Printed in the Authorised Version. 1923. One of 220 copies on hand made paper, illus., dec. boards, fine, unopened copy, first edition. Covent 51-1742 1973 £7.50

HISTORY of Texas World War Heroes. Dallas, c.1919. 4to., cloth, 608 pages. Saddleback 14-705 1974 $25

HISTORY of Worcester County, Massachusetts. Philadelphia, 1889. 2 vols., three quarter leather, engravings, excellent. Rinsland 58-928 1974 $85

HISTORY of the Affaires of Scotland From the Restauration of King Charles the 2nd . . . to Midsomer, 1690. 1690. Modern sheep, frontispiece, stains. Thomas 28-201 1972 £16

HISTORY of the Affaires of Scotland from the Restauration of King Charles the 2d . . . to Midsomer, 1690. 1690. Engraved frontispiece, some stains not too bad, modern sheep. Thomas 32-138 1974 £16

HISTORY of the Bible. Bridgeport, 1831. Full orig. cal, 2 1/4 X 2 inches, frontis., woodcut, sound, some foxing & staining. Gregory 44-390 1974 $27

HISTORY of the Bible. New-London, 1831. Orig. calf, 2 1/8 X 1 7/8 inches, frontis., woodcuts, hinges cracked. Gregory 44-392 1974 $35

HISTORY of the Bible. New London, 1850. Full leather, superb woodcuts, base of spine chipped, 1 3/4" X 2 1/8". Frohnsdorff 15-179 1974 $20

HISTORY OF THE Bible. Buffalo, 1857. Orig. cloth, 2 1/8 X 1 3/4 inches, frontis., full page portraits, front inner hinge cracked, else fine. Gregory 44-391 1974 $22.50

HISTORY Of the British Dominions in North America. London, 1773. Mottled boards, map, excellent. Hood's 103-539 1974 $475

THE HISTORY of the Devil, Ancient and Modern . . . With a Description of the Devil's Dwelling. n.d. (c. 1780). Full contemporary calf, label, some foxing, nice copy. Covent 51-2500 1973 £10.50

THE HISTORY of the Giants. Philadelphia, 1812. 2 1/2 X 2 inches, orig. wrappers, woodcuts, frontispiece. Gregory 44-392A 1974 $85

A HISTORY of the Island of Anglesey. 1775. 4to., orig. wrappers, waterstain. Smith 194-196 1974 £5

THE HISTORY of the Life and Reign of Edward II. 1713. 8vo., new calf. Hill 126-93 1974 £16

THE HISTORY of the Life of Our Lord Jesus Christ. 1739. 12mo., contemporary calf, scarce. Hill 126-129 1974 £42

HISTORY of the Pennsylvania Hospital Unit (Base Hospital No. 10, U.S.A.) In the Great War. New York, 1921. Rittenhouse 46-342 1974 $10

THE HISTORY of the Royal-Society of London. 1702. 4to., contemporary calf, second edition. Broadhurst 23-1275 1974 £35

HISTORY of the Scandinavians and Successful Scandinavians in the United States. Minneapolis, MN, 1893. Austin 62-445 1974 $37.50

THE HISTORY of the Translation of the Blessed Martyrs of Christ, Marcellinus and Peter. Cambridge, 1926. Dust jacket, unopened, fine. Ballinger 1-26 1974 $14

HISTORY OF THE Welsh in Minnesota. n.d. 8vo., orig. cloth. Broadhurst 23-1579 1974 £8

THE HISTORY of Van Buren County, Iowa. Chicago, 1878. 8vo., three quarter leather, rebacked, illus. Saddleback 14-415 1974 $70

THE HISTORY of Wales. 1697. Crown 8vo., contemporary old calf. Broadhurst 23-1574 1974 £25

THE HISTORY of Wales. 1697. Crown 8vo., contemporary old calf, fine. Broadhurst 24-1543 1974 £25

A HISTORY Of Wilkes-Barre. Wilkes-Barre, 1909. 2 vols., 8vo., red cloth, gilt, illus., map. Rinsland 58-96 1974 $35

HISTORICO-POLITICO-Philologica Curiosa. 1696. Small 8vo., contemporary panelled calf. Dawsons PM 251-168 1974 £50

HISTORICORUM Romanorum Reliquiae. 1914-06. 2 vols., new buckram. Allen 213-492 1973 $37.50

THE HISTORIANS' History of the World. London & New York, (1926). 27 vols. in 15, 8vo., orig. cloth, coloured and monochrome plates, slight foxing, illus., fifth edition. Bow Windows 66-345 1974 £12.50

THE HISTORIE of Cambria Now Called Wales. London, 1584. 4to., polished calf, gilt, first edition. Dawsons PM 251-15 1974 £370

HISTORIC Nova Scotia. (Halifax, 1935). Illus., 116 pages, card cover. Hood's 104-223 1974 $10

AN HISTORICAL and Descriptive Account of the Town of Lancaster. Lancaster, 1807. 8vo., half calf, boards, fine, first edition. Broadhurst 23-1436 1974 £15

A HISTORICAL, Descriptive and Commercial Directory of Owyhee County, Idaho. Silver City, 1898. 8vo., cloth. Saddleback 14-362 1974 $50

THE HISTORICAL Part of the Holy Bible. Oxford, 1724. 4to., portrait, plate, contemporary calf, rebacked, worn. Bow Windows 62-88 1974 £15

HISTORICAL Sketches of the County of Elgin. St. Thomas, 1895. Hood's 102-609 1974 $22.50

HISTOIRE de Tom Pouce. London, 1833. Lithograph plates, slightly faded, 12mo., orig. cloth. George's 610-373 1973 £5

HISTORIA del Valoroso Cavallier Polisman. Venice, 1573. Title torn, defective in blank portion and mounted, some stains, else clean & sound, small 8vo., contemporary vellum, somewhat worn, lacks ties, new endpapers, scarce. Thomas 32-150 1974 $75

THE HISTORIANS of Scotland. Edinburgh, 1871-80. 10 vols., complete set. Howes 186-923 1974 £35

HITCHCOCK, DAVID   The Poetical Works. Boston, 1806. 8vo., contemporary tree calf, first edition. Ximenes 33-232 1974 $27.50

HITCHCOCK, DAVID   The Poetical Works of. Boston, 1806. Contemporary calf, morocco label, first edition, light browning. MacManus 224-223 1974 $40

HITCHCOCK, EDWARD   Elementary Geology. New York, 1847. Foxing, rubbed, eighth edition. Ballinger 1-273 1974 $10

HITCHCOCK, EDWARD   The Religion of Geology. Boston, 1851. Crown 8vo., morocco, frontispiece. Wheldon 129-829 1974 £12

HITCHCOCK, EDWARD   The Religion of Geology and Its Connected Sciences. London and Glasgow, (185-). Post 8vo., orig. cloth, frontispiece, scarce. Wheldon 128-993 1973 £7.50

HITCHCOCK, EDWARD   Report on the Geology, Mineralogy, Botany, and Zoology of Massachusetts. Amherst, 1833. 8vo., orig. cloth, uncut, illus. Butterfield 8-245 1974 $20

HITCHCOCK, HENRY RUSSELL   Rhode Island Architecture. Providence, 1939. First edition, 4to., plates, some staining on fore edges, else very fine. Current BW9-427 1974 $15

HITLER, ADOLPH   Der Fuhrer und der Arbeiter. (1937). Pictorial wrappers, 2 X 1 3/8 inches. Gregory 44-393 1974 $22.50

HITLER, ADOLPH   Des Fuhrers Kampf in Belgien. (1940). Pictorial wrappers, 2 X 1 3/8 inches. Gregory 44-394 1974 $27.50

HITLER, ADOLF   Mein Kampf. n.d. 18 parts, very good copy, slightly worn wrappers, first English illus. edition. Covent 51-916 1973 £15

HITLER, ADOLF   On National Socialism and World Relations. Berlin, 1937. English first edition. Covent 56-1803 1974 £12.50

HITLER, ADOLF   Speech Delivered in the Reichstag. Berlin, 1936. English first edition. Covent 56-1804 1974 £12.50

HITSCHMANN, EDUARD   Freud's Theories of the Neuroses. New York, 1913. 8vo., orig. pictured wrappers, unopened, first edition in English. Schuman 37-95 1974 $75

HITT, THOMAS   The Modern Gardener. London, 1771. 8vo., contemporary calf, rebacked, gilt, plates. Hammond 201-18 1974 £17.50

HOADLY, B.   Midsummer Moon. 1709. 8vo., disbound, first edition. Quaritch 936-106 1974 £35

HOADLY, BENJAMIN   A Defence of the Inquiry into the Reasons of the Conduct of Great Britain. London, 1729. 8vo., modern quarter morocco, gilt, first edition. Dawsons PM 251-446 1974 £18

HOARE, KATHARIN I   The Art of Tatting. London, 1910. Cloth, gilt, plates. Dawson's 424-225 1974 $30

HOARE, PRINCE   No Song no Supper. Dublin, 1792. 12mo., disbound, rare, first edition. Ximenes 33-234 1974 $30

HOBART, BENJAMIN   History of the Town of Abington, Plymouth County, Massachusetts. Boston, 1866. First edition, 8vo., very good and tight, plates, stains, spine recased, orig. covers repaired at spine ends, frontis. Current BW9-387 1974 $32.50

HOBART, NOAH   A Congratulatory Letter From a Gentleman of the West, to His Friend in the East. New Haven, 1755. 8vo., disbound, first edition. Ximenes 33-235 1974 $125

HOBBEMA, M.   Meindert Hobbema (1638-1709). 1838. 4to., plates, wrappers, numbered, limited. Quaritch 940-138 1974 £28

HOBBES, JOHN OLIVER   The Dream and the Business. Buckram, pictorial cover. Marsden 37-28 1974 £7

HOBBES, JOHN OLIVER   The Dream and the Business. 1906. Spine rubbed, front hinge cracked, contents very good, first edition. Covent 51-191 1973 £5.25

HOBBES, THOMAS   Decameron Physiologicum. 1678. 8vo., contemporary straight-grained morocco, ex-library. Zeitlin 235-112 1974 $985

HOBBES, THOMAS   Decameron Physiologicum. London, 1678. 8vo., contemporary black morocco, gilt, first edition. Dawsons PM 245-387 1974 £285

HOBBES, THOMAS   Elementorum Philosophiae Sectio Prima de Corpore. 1655. 8vo., contemporary calf, plates, first edition. Dawsons PM 245-386 1974 £130

HOBBES, THOMAS   The History of the Civil Wars of England. 1679. Small 8vo., calf, first edition. Thomas 28-187 1972 £12.50

HOBBES, THOMAS   Humane Nature. London, 1650. 12mo., woodcut, contemporary calf, first edition. Bow Windows 62-459 1974 £450

HOBBES, THOMAS   A True Ecclesiastical History From Moses. London, 1722. 8vo., contemporary calf, first English edition. Ximenes 33-236 1974 $150

HOBHOUSE, BENJAMIN   The Wonders of a Week at Bath. London, 1811. 8vo., contemporary calf, first edition. Dawsons PM 252-457 1974 £25

HOBHOUSE, L. T.   Development and Purpose. 1927. Thick 8vo., scarce, new revised edition. Howes 185-1877 1974 £6

HOBHOUSE, L. T.   Mind In Evolution. 1915. 8vo., orig. cloth, second edition. Howes 185-1878 1974 £5

HOBHOUSE, L. T.   Morals in Evolution. 1915. Thick 8vo., ex-library, orig. edition. Howes 185-1879 1974 £5

HOBHOUSE, JOHN CAM   Recollections of a Long Life. 1909-10. 4 vols., orig. cloth, frayed, portraits. Howes 186-253 1974 £15

HOBSON, ERNEST WILLIAM   The Theory of Functions of a Real Variable. Cambridge, 1907. 8vo., orig. blue cloth, first edition. Dawsons PM 245-388 1974 £14

HOBSON, GEOFFREY DUDLEY   English Binding Before 1500. Cambridge, 1929. Folio, orig. buckram, illus., limited. Dawsons PM 10-279 1974 £40

HOBSON, GEOFFREY DUDLEY   English Binding Before 1500. 1929. Folio, orig. buckram, fine, illus., plates, first edition. Howes 185-712 1974 £30

HOBSON, GEOFFREY DUDLEY   Maioli, Canevari, and Others. Boston, 1926. Plates, 4to., orig. cloth. Kraus B8-102 1974 $156

HOBSON, J. A.   John Ruskin: Social Reformer. 1898. Nice copy, scarce, portrait, gilt top, inscribed presentation copy, first edition. Covent 51-1616 1973 £6.30

HOBSON, ROBERT LOCKHART   The Art of the Chinese Potter from the Han Dynasty to the End of the Ming. 1923. 4to., plates, pigskin, de luxe edition. Quaritch 940-400 1974 £65

HOBSON, ROBERT LOCKHART   Catalogue of the Collection of English Porcelain. London, 1905. Imp. 8vo., plates, orig. cloth. Bow Windows 62-460 1974 £12

HOBSON, ROBERT LOCKHART   Chinese Pottery and Porcelain. 1915. 2 vols., roy. 8vo., plates, illus., cloth gilt, limited edition. Quaritch 940-399 1974 £80

HOBSON, ROBERT LOCKHART   Handbook of the Pottery and Porcelain of the Far East in the Dept. of Oriental Antiquities. London, 1937. Biblo & Tannen 214-377 1974 $15

HOBSON, ROBERT LOCKHART   Porcelain. 1908. Plates, illus., half green leather and cloth, uncut, second edition. Covent 55-453 1974 £15

HOBSON, ROBERT LOCKHART   Wares of the Ming Dynasty. 1923. 4to., illus., pigskin, gilt, uncut, de luxe edition. Quaritch 940-638 1974 £65

HOBSON, ROBERT LOCKHART   Worcester Porcelain. 1910. Imp. 4to., mint, faded dust wrapper, coloured & collotype plates, orig. cloth. Broadhurst 24-96 1974 £75

HOBSON, THOMAS   Christianity. London, 1745. 4to., modern boards, engraving, first edition. Dawsons PM 252-458 1974 £9

HOCHHUTH, ROLF   The Deputy. Grove, 1964. 352p. Austin 51-432 1973 $6.50

HOCHHUTH, ROLF   Soldiers. n.d. 4to., stapled in wrappers, fine, covers slightly creased, first edition. Covent 51-919 1973 £10.50

HOCHSTETTER, F. VON   The Geology of New Zealand in Explanation of the Geographical and Topographical Atlas of New Zealand. Auckland, 1864. 8vo., orig. cloth, rare. Wheldon 131-1019 1974 £7.50

HOCK VON BRACHENAU, WENDELIN   Mentagra. Lyon, 1529. 8vo., contemporary vellum, rebacked. Gurney 64-112 1974 £105

HOCK VON BRACHENAU, WENDELIN   Mentagra, Sive Tractatus Excellens de Causis Praeservativis, Regimine a Cura Morbi Gallici. Lyon, 1529. 8vo., contemporary vellum, rebacked, third edition, good copy. Gurney 66-86 1974 £105

HODDER, JAMES   Hodder's Arithmetick. London, 1678. 12mo., contemporary sheep. Dawsons PM 245-389 1974 £75

HODDER-WILLIAMS, RALPH   Princess Patricia's Canadian Light Infantry. 2 vols., illus. Jacobs 24-11 1974 $20

HODGE, HIRAM C.   Arizona as It Is: or, The Coming Country. New York, 1877. Inscribed by author. Jenkins 61-139 1974 $40

HODGES, GEORGE   Holderness; An Account of a New Hampshire Town. Boston, 1907. 12mo., cloth. Saddleback 14-547 1974 $15

HODGES, JAMES   A Defence of the Scots Abdicating Darien. 1700. 8vo., modern quarter calf, first edition. Dawsons PM 247-147 1974 £110

HODGES, LEROY   Petersburg, Virginia: Economic and Municipal. Petersburg, 1917. Illus., folding maps. Jenkins 61-2531 1974 $10

HODGES, NATHENIEL   Loimologia. London, 1720. 8vo., contemporary calf, rebacked, first edition in English. Dawsons PM 249-276 1974 £55

HODGES, NATHENIEL   Loimologia. London, 1721. 8vo., sheep. Gurney 64-113 1974 £25

HODGES, RICHARD M.   Practical Dissections. Cambridge, 1858. Rittenhouse 46-344 1974 $10

HODGES, WALTER   Elihu, Or an Inquiry Into the Principal Scope and Design of the Book of Job. 1751. Old calf. Howes 185-1264 1974 £6

HODGES, WILLIAM   Travels in India. London, 1793. 4to., full contemporary straight-grained morocco, gilt, fine, first edition. Ximenes 33-237 1974 $200

HODGINS, J. G.   The Geography and History of British America, and of the Other Colonies of the Empire, to Which is Added a Sketch of . . . Indian Tribes and Biographical Notices of Eminent Persons Connected with the History of Canada. Toronto, 1857. Illus. Hood's 102-562 1974 $12.50

HODGINS, J. G.   History of Canada, and of the Other British Provinces in North America. Montreal, 1866. Engravings. Hood's 102-563 1974 $12.50

HODGINS, J. G.   Lovell's General Geography, for the Use of Schools. Toronto, 1861. Maps, illus. Hood's 102-25 1974 $30

HODGKIN, J. E.   Examples of Early English Pottery. London, 1881. Crown 4to., illus., orig. cloth, rare, inscribed. Bow Windows 62-462 1974 £55

HODGKIN, J. E.   Examples of Early English Pottery. 1891. Roy. 4to., cloth, illus., limited edition. Quaritch 940-639 1974 £30

HODGKIN, JOHN ELIOT   The J. E. Hodgkin Collections. 1914. Plates. Kraus B8-246 1974 $10

HODGKIN, JOHN ELIOT   Rariora. London, (n.d.). 3 vols., 4to., orig. cloth, uncut, illus., plates. Dawsons PM 10-281 1974 £45

HODGKIN, JOHN ELIOT   Rariora. London, (n.d.). 3 vols., 4to., orig. cloth, plates, illus. Dawsons PM 252-459 1974 £55

HODGKIN, JOHN ELIOT   Rariora. 1902. 3 vols., 4to., plates, illus., fine. Covent 55-454 1974 £37.50

HODGKIN, R. H.   A History of the Anglo-Saxons. 1935. 2 vols., roy. 8vo., orig. buckram, illus., first edition. Howes 186-925 1974 £7.50

HODGKIN, THOMAS   Italy and Her Invaders. 1892-99. 8 vols. in 9, orig. cloth, plates, revised second & best edition. Howes 186-926 1974 £52

HODGSON, B. H.   Notice of the Mammals of Tibet. Calcutta, 1842. 8vo., coloured plates. Wheldon 128-331 1973 £5

HODGSON, J. E.   The History of Aeronautics in Great Britain. London, 1924. 4to., orig. buckram, illus., limited. Dawsons PM 10-7 1974 £78

HODGSON, J. E.   The Royal Academy and its Members. 1905. Portraits, illus. Marsden 37-254 1974 £7

HODGSON, JOSEPH   A Treatise on the Diseases of Arteries and Veins. London, 1815. 8vo., small folio, 2 vols., contemporary half calf, rebacked, first edition. Dawsons PM 249-277 1974 £285

HODGSON, JOSEPH   A Treatise on the Diseases of Arteries and Veins, Containing the Pathology and Treatment of Aneurisms and Wounded Arteries. London, 1815. 8vo., old half calf, slightly worn, first edition. Gurney 66-87 1974 £30

HODGSON, RALPH   The Birdcatcher. n.d. Illus., English first edition. Covent 56-1897 1974 £7

HODGSON, RALPH   The Bull. 1913. Wrappers, English first edition. Covent 56-875 1974 £10

HODGSON, RALPH   The Last Blackbird. London, 1907. First edition, top edges gilt, some foxing, bookplate, very nice, bright copy, orig. binding. Ross 86-188 1974 $50

HODGSON, RALPH   The Last Blackbird and Other Lines. 1907. First edition, crown 8vo., uncut, first issue, light spots on front cover, fine copy, orig. cloth. Broadhurst 24-724 1974 £10

HODGSON, RALPH   The Last Blackbird and Other Lines. 1907. Faded, first edition. Covent 55-840 1974 £12.60

HODGSON, RALPH   The Mystery and Other Poems. 1913. Wrappers, English first edition. Covent 56-876 1974 £10

HODGSON, RALPH   Poems. London, 1917. First edition, lacking d.w., near fine, orig. binding. Ross 86-189 1974 $15

HODGSON, RALPH   The Song of Honour. 1913. Wrappers, English first edition. Covent 56-877 1974 £10

HODGSON, SOL   The Hive of Ancient and Modern Literature. Newcastle, 1806. Orig. boards, uncut, unopened, third edition. Dawson's 424-45 1974 $75

HODGSON, W.   The Quest of the Antique. London, 1924. Large 8vo., frontispiece, plates, orig. cloth, stained. Bow Windows 62-463 1974 £9

HODGSON, MRS. WILLOUGHBY   The Quest of the Antique. 1924. Plates, cloth. Covent 55-455 1974 £8.50

HODGSON, MRS. WILLOUGHBY   The Quest of the Antique. 1924. 4to.,
orig. buckram, plates, first edition. Smith 194-97 1974 £8

HODKIN, F. W.   A Textbook of Glass Technology. London, 1925.
8vo., blue cloth, gilt, dust wrapper. Dawsons PM 245-390 1974 £6

HODLER, FERDINAND   Koepfe und Gestalten. Zurich, 1947. Folio,
color plates. Biblo & Tannen 214-283 1974 $42.50

HODNETT, EDWARD   English Woodcuts, 1480-1535. London, 1935.
4to., orig. boards, cloth spine, uncut. Kraus B8-103 1974 $25

HODSON, GEOFFREY   The Science of Seership. London, n.d.
Biblo & Tannen 210-976 1973 $7.50

HODSON, T.   The Cabinet of the Arts. 1805. 4to.,
contemporary calf, misbound, rubbed, plates. Smith 194-98 1974 £9.50

HOEVEN, J. VAN DER   Icones ad Illustrandas Coloris Mutationes in
Chamaeleonte. Leyden, 1831. 4to., orig. printed boards, hand coloured plates,
rare. Wheldon 128-637 1973 £10

HOFF, AUGUST   Emil Fahrenkamp: Ein Ausschnitt Seines
Schaffens Aus Den Jahren 1924-1927. Stuttgart, 1928. Large 4to., wrappers,
plates. Minters 37-528 1973 $24

HOFF, AUGUST   Wilhelm Lehmbruck. Berlin, 1936. 4to.,
cloth, illus. Minters 37-467 1973 $22.50

HOFF, EBBE CURTIS   A Bibliography of Aviation Medicine.
Springfield, Baltimore, 1942. Rittenhouse 46-345 1974 $25

HOFF, EBBE CURTIS   A Bibliography of Aviation Medicine.
Baltimore & Washington, 1942-44. 2 vols., large 8vo., orig. cloth. Dawsons
PM 10-285 1974 £9

HOFF, J. H. VAN T'   The Arrangement of Atoms in Space. London,
New York and Bombay, 1898. 8vo., orig. blue cloth, gilt, second edition. Dawsons PM 245-391 1974 £5

HOFF, URSULA   Charles I Patron of Artists. 1942. 4to., orig.
cloth, mounted coloured plates, illus., spine faded. Bow Windows 66-348
1974 £5.25

HOFFDING, HARALD   A History of Modern Philosophy. 1935.
2 vols., 8vo., orig. cloth. Howes 185-1882 1974 £5

HOFFENSTEIN, SAMUEL   Poems in Praise of Practically Nothing. Boni,
Liveright, 1928. 217p. Austin 54-495 1973 $6

HOFFMAN, BENNEVILLE OTTOMAR   Snarl of a Cynic. Ephrata, 1868.
12mo., orig. quarter cloth, fine, first edition. Ximenes 33-238 1974 $27.50

HOFFMAN, CHARLES FENNO   Greyslayer. New York, 1840. 2 vols., orig.
cloth, spines faded, extremities rubbed, paper labels, first edition, foxed and
water-stained. MacManus 224-224 1974 $85

HOFFMAN, CHARLES FENNO   Greyslaer. London, 1840. 3 vols., 12mo.,
later half morocco, first edition. Ximenes 33-239 1974 $200

HOFFMAN, CHARLES FENNO   Greyslaer. New York, 1849. 12mo., orig.
brown cloth, worn, revised fourth edition. Ximenes 33-240 1974 $25

HOFFMAN, CHARLES FENNO   Wild Scenes in the Forest and Prairie. London,
1839. 2 vols., first edition. Jenkins 61-1067 1974 $95

HOFFMAN, CHARLES FENNO   Winter in the West. New York, 1835.
2 vols., 12mo., orig. cloth, first edition. Ximenes 33-241 1974 $75

HOFFMAN, CHARLES FENNO   A Winter in the West. New York, 1835. Orig.
cloth, slight wear, 2 vols. Jenkins 61-1068 1974 $85

HOFFMAN, FREDERICK L.   The Mortality from Cancer Throughout the
World. Newark, 1915. Inscribed, spine label. Rittenhouse 46-346 1974 $10

HOFFMAN, FRIEDRICH   Observationum Physico-Chymicarum Selectiorum
Libri III. 1722. 4to., contemporary boards, first edition. Dawsons PM 245-392
1974 £125

HOFFMAN, MALVINA   Heads and Tales In Many Lands. New York &
London, 1937. 4to., cloth, shaken, illus. Minters 37-13 1973 $16

HOFFMAN, S. F. W.   Handbuch Zur Buecherkunde Fuer Lehre Und
Studium der Beiden Alten Klass U. Deutschen Sprache. 1838. New buckram,
rubber stamp. Allen 213-494 1973 $15

HOFFMANN, E. T. W.   Weird Tales. New York, 1923. Biblo &
Tannen 210-614 1973 $13.50

HOFFMANN, FRIEDRICH   Volente Archiatro Maximo Positionum
Medicarum Pentas. Jena, 1650. 4to., orig. wrappers. Schuman 37-124
1974 $65

HOFFMANN, G. F.   Descriptio et Adumbratio Plantarum. Leipzig,
1789-92. Folio, old boards. Wheldon 129-1403 1974 £50

HOFFMANN, HEINRICH   The English Struwwelpeter. London, n.d.
4to., pictorial boards, cloth spine, colored illus. Frohnsdorff 16-441 1974
$20

HOFFMANN, HEINRICH   The English Struwwelpeter. London, c., 1869.
4to., orig. printed boards, rebacked, twenty-third edition. Hammond 201-120
1974 £20

HOFFMANN, HEINRICH   The English Struwwelpeter. London, c. 1880.
4to., orig. cloth backed pictorial boards, forty-eighth edition. Hammond 201-
121 1974 £18.50

HOFFMANN, HEINRICH   The English Struwwelpeter. London, c., 1900.
4to., orig. cloth-backed pictorial boards. Hammond 201-122 1974 £16

HOFFMANN, HEINRICH   The Merry Christmas Book. New York, 1854.
12mo., gilt pictorial cloth, worn, four hand colored engravings. Frohnsdorff
16-444 1974 $50

HOFFMANN, HEINRICH   Slovenly Peter. New York, Limited Editions
Club, 1935. Folio, pictorial cloth, leather spine, hand colored illus., mint,
orig. chemise & slipcase, orig. glassine d.j., first edition. Frohnsdorff 16-443
1974 $80

HOFFMANN, HEINRICH   Slovenly Peter or Cheerful Stories and Funny
Pictures for Good Little Folks. Philadelphia, n.d. 4to., gilt pictorial cloth,
fine hand colored illus. Frohnsdorff 16-442 1974 $30

HOFFMANN, HEINRICH   Der Struwwelpeter. Frankfurt, n.d. 4to.,
boards, cloth, color plates, rubbed corners, special issue, extra leaf.
Frohnsdorff 16-440 1974 $20

HOFFMANN, HEINRICH   Der Struwelpeter. Leipzig, c. 1871. Pict.
boards, orig. German text, inscription. Wilson 63-524 1974 $10

HOFFMANN, J. J.   Entomologische Hefte. 1803. 8vo., half calf,
plates. Wheldon 129-647 1974 £20

HOFFMANN, WOLFGANG   Die Rontgendiagnostik und-Therapie in der
Augenheilkunde. Verlag, 1932. Rittenhouse 46-348 1974 $10

HOFFMANN VON FALLERSLEBEN, AUGUST H.   Deutschland uber Alles!
Leipzig, 1859. Small 4to., orig. cloth gilt. Harper 213-91 1973 $75

HOFLAND, BARBARA   The Barbadoes Girl. (c. 1825). Fifth edition,
12mo., orig. boards, roan spine, trifle rubbed. George's 610-379 1973 £5

HOFLAND, BARBARA   The Blind Farmer and His Children. 1816.
First edition, engraved frontis., 12mo., contemporary tree sheep, worn spine
defective. George's 610-380 1973 £6

HOFLAND, BARBARA   Decision, a Tale. 1824. First edition, 12mo.,
new red buckram, spine lettered in gilt, good copy, engraved frontis. George's
610-381 1973 £6.50

HOFLAND, BARBARA   Ellen, the Teacher. 1814. 2 vols., 12mo.,
orig. boards, corners slightly rubbed, engraved frontis., first edition. George's
610-382 1973 £10.50

HOFLAND, BARBARA   The Panorama of Europe. 1813. First edition,
with half title, engraved frontis., 12mo., orig. boards, later parchment spine,
good copy, edges uncut. George's 610-384 1973 £10.50

HOFLAND, BARBARA   The Young Cadet. (1827). First edition, 12mo.,
orig. ptd. boards, roan spine, trifle rubbed, engraved plates. George's 610-386
1973 £6

HOFMANN, F. H.   Altes Bayerisches Porzellan. Munchen,
1909. Small 4to., plates, cloth. Bow Windows 62-464 1974 £8

HOFMANN, F. H.   Geschichte der Bayerischen Porzellan-Manufaktur
Nymphenburg. Leipzig, 1921-23. 3 vols., folio, plates, boards, parchment
spines, rare. Quaritch 940-640 1974 £375

HOFMEISTER, WILHELM   Die Lehre Von der Pflanzenzelle. Leipzig,
1867. 8vo., illus., contemporary half calf, first edition. Gilhofer 61-55
1974 sFr. 250

HOGABOAM, JAMES J.   The Bean Creek Valley. Hudson, 1876.
Wrappers. Hayman 59-385 1974 $20

HOGABOAM, JAMES J.   The Bean Creek Valley. Hudson, 1876.
12mo., wrapper, boards. Saddleback 14-503 1974 $25

HOGAN, J. F.   The Life and Works of Dante Allighieri. 1899.
Frontispiece. Howes 185-95 1974 £5

HOGAN, J. SHERIDAN   Le Canada - Essai. Montreal, 1855. Orig.
colored print wrappers, french text. Wilson 63-9 1974 $20

HOGAN, JOHN   Thoughts About the City of St. Louis. St.
Louis, 1855. Roy. 8vo., orig. printed wrappers, rare, plates. Traylen 79-487
1973 £75

HOGAN, WILLIAM   Popery! 1845. Illus., 654 pages. Austin
57-299 1974 $15

HOGARTH, WILLIAM 1697-1764   L'Analisi della Bellezza. Leghorn, 1761.
8vo., contemporary vellum, plates. Quaritch 940-139 1974 £35

HOGARTH, WILLIAM 1697-1764   Works. 18--. 2 vols., 4to., plates, one
spine torn. Allen 216-2027 1974 $25

HOGARTH, WILLIAM 1697-1764   Works. c. 1850. 2 vols., buckram, engravings. Allen 216-2029 1974 $25

HOGARTH, WILLIAM 1697-1764   The Works of. London, (c. 186-). 4to.,
2 vols., green embossed cloth, gilt. Rich Summer-76 1974 $25

HOGARTH, WILLIAM 1697-1764   Works. 1860. 2 vols. in 1, 4to., new
buckram, plates. Allen 216-2028 1974 $20

HOGBEN, JOHN   The Highway of Hades. Edinburgh, 1919.
Handmade paper, numbered, signed, fine. Covent 55-842 1974 £10.50

HOGG, JABEZ H.   The Microscope. 1898 or 1911. 8vo., cloth,
plates. Wheldon 129-83 1974 £5

HOGG, JAMES   The Jacobite Relics of Scotland. Edinburgh,
1819-21. 8vo., 2 vols., contemporary calf, gilt, first edition. Dawsons PM
251-250 1974 £50

HOGG, JAMES   The Queen's Wake. (London), 1813. 8vo.,
half calf, spine gilt, first edition. Ximenes 37-110 1974 $75

HOGG, JAMES   The Queen's Wake. Edinburgh, 1819. 8vo.,
quarter sheep, sixth edition. Bow Windows 64-548 1974 £8.50

HOGG, ROBERT   The Fruit Manual. 1884. 8vo., new cloth,
fifth edition. Wheldon 130-1479 1974 £12

HOGG, THOMAS   A Concise and Practical Treatise on the Growth
and Culture of the Carnation . . . and Other Flowers. London, 1822. 8vo.,
orig. cloth, second edition. Ximenes 33-242 1974 $40

HOGG, THOMAS   A Concise and Practical Treatise on the Growth
and Culture of the Carnation, Pink, Auricula, Polyanthus, Ranunculus, Tulip,
Hyacinth, Rose and Other Flowers. (1832). Post 8vo., modern boards, plates,
scarce, fifth edition. Wheldon 131-1530 1974 £20

HOGG, THOMAS   A Concise and Practical Treatise on the Growth
and Culture of the Carnation, Pink, Auricula, Polyanthus, Ranunculus, Tulip,
Hyacinth, Rose, and Other Flowers: Including a Dissertation on Soils and Manures.
1823. Fourth edition, coloured engravings, crown 8vo., orig. cloth, uncut, fine.
Broadhurst 24-1113 1974 £20

HOGG, THOMAS   A Supplement to the Practical Treatise on the
Culture of Florists 'Flowers. 1833. Small 8vo., orig. cloth, very scarce.
Wheldon 131-1531 1974 £10

HOGG, WARRINGTON   The Book of Old Sundials and Their Mottoes.
Edinburgh, (1922). Color illus., drawings, 12mo., spine faded, else very good.
Current BW9-535 1974 $15

HOGMANN, G.   Vescovadi Cattolici Della Grecia. 1934-38.
4 vols., sewn, plates. Allen 213-1549 1973 $12.50

HOHMAN, JOHN GEORGE   The Long Lost Friend. Harrisburg, 1850. Leather-backed boards, rubbed. Hayman 57-298 1974 $20

HOKANSON, NELS   Swedish Immigrants in Lincoln's Time. 1942.
259 pages. Austin 57-300 1974 $12.50

HOKANSON, NELS   Swedish Immigrants in Lincoln's Time. Harper,
1942. 259p., illus. Austin 62-260 1974 $12.50

HOLBACH, PAUL HENRY THIRY D'   Systeme de la Nature ou des Louis du
Monde Physique & du Monde Moral. London, 1770. 2 vols. in 1, 8vo., gilt,
contemporary red morocco, superb copy, first edition, first issue. Gilhofer
61-25 1974 sFr. 2,500

HOLBEIN, HANS   The Dance of Death. 1816. Plates engraved,
orig. boards, covers stained, spine defective, joints weak, first edition, very
good copy, uncut. Covent 51-124 1973 £25

HOLBEIN, HANS   The Drawings of Hans Holbein in the Collection
of His Majesty the King at Windsor Castle. 1945. 4to., plates, illus., cloth,
second edition. Quaritch 940-143 1974 £5

HOLBEIN, HANS   Icones Veteris Testamenti. 1830. Illus.,
fine. Covent 55-105 1974 £12.50

HOLBEIN, HANS   Imitations of Original Drawings by Holbein in
the Collection of His Majesty. 1792-1800. Atlas folio, half red morocco, gilt,
marbled board sides, rubbed. Quaritch 940-141 1974 £2,200

HOLBEIN, HANS   Imitations of Original Drawings in the Collection
of His Majesty, for the Portraits of Illustrious Persons of the Court of Henry VIII.
1792-(1800). 2 vols., contemporary red straight grained morocco gilt, good
copy, hinges cracked, spines discoloured, slight browning. Sawyer 293-30
1974 £1,150

HOLBEIN, HANS   Imitations of Original Drawings in the Collection
of His Majesty, for the Portraits of Illustrious Persons of the Court of Henry VIII.
1792-(1800). Orig. edition, coloured engravings by Bartolozzi, atlas folio,
contemporary diced russia, blind tooled borders, good copy, scarce, slight spotting.
Sawyer 293-29 1974 £1,250

HOLBROOK, ALFRED   Reminiscences of the Happy Life of a Teacher.
Cincinnati, 1885. Cloth. Hayman 57-572 1974 $15

HOLBROOK, JOHN EDWARDS   North American Herpetology. Philadelphia,
1842. 4to., 5 vols., cloth, leather labels, fine. Traylen 79-120 1973 £1,150

HOLBROOK, STEWART   Mr. Otis. Macmillan, 1958. 7lp., illus.
Austin 54-496 1973 $7.50

HOLCOMBE, HENRY   A Sermon, Occasioned by the Death of
Lieutenant-General George Washington. N.P., n.d. Small 4to., disbound,
first edition. Ximenes 35-478 1974 $90

HOLCROFT, THOMAS   The Deserted Daughter. London, 1795. 8vo.,
disbound, first edition. Ximenes 33-243 1974 $22.50

HOLCROFT, THOMAS   Hear Both Sides. London, 1803. 8vo.,
modern boards, first edition. Dawsons PM 252-460 1974 £15

HOLCROFT, THOMAS   Knave, or Not? London, 1798. 8vo.,
disbound, first edition. Ximenes 33-244 1974 $22.50

HOLCROFT, THOMAS   The Man of Ten Thousand. London, 1796.
8vo., disbound, first edition. Ximenes 33-245 1974 $22.50

HOLCROFT, THOMAS   Memoirs Of. 1852. 8vo., half calf. Hill
126-130 1974 £8.50

HOLCROFT, THOMAS   The Road to Ruin. London, 1792. 8vo.,
wrappers, first edition. Ximenes 33-246 1974 $22.50

HOLDEN, HAROLD M.   Noses. World, 1950. 252p. Austin 54-497
1973 $7.50

HOLDEN, M. R.   Burlington Bay, Beach and Heights, In History.
Hamilton, 1898. Hood's 103-640 1974 $15

HOLDER, C. F.   The Game Fishes of the World. (1913). Crown
4to., cloth, illus., scarce. Wheldon 128-638 1973 £7.50

HOLDSWORTH, ISRAEL   The Literary Picnic. Leeds, 1872. 8vo.,
orig. red cloth, first edition. Ximenes 33-248 1974 $10

HOLE, CHRISTINA   Witchcraft in England. London, 1945. Line
drawings, plates, first edition, covers marked internally nice, name on fly, orig.
cloth. Crane 7-221 1974 £10

HOLE, CHRISTINA   Witchcraft in England. London, 1945.
Rittenhouse 46-349 1974 $10

HOLGATE, JEROME B.   American Genealogy. Albany, 1848.
Illus., foxed, fine. Ballinger 1-274 1974 $40

HOLINSHED, R.   Holinshed's Chronicles of England, Scotland
and Ireland. 1807-1808. 4to., contemporary diced calf, 6 vols. Bow Windows
64-549 1974 £168

HOLLAND, HENRY   Medical Notes and Reflections. 1840. Orig.
cloth, soiled, second edition. Covent 55-1092 1974 £12.50

HOLLAND, JOHN   Memoirs of the Life and Ministry of the Rev. John
Summerfield. New York, 1846. Cloth. Hayman 57-299 1974 $12.50

HOLLAND, JOSIAH GILBERT   Letters to the Joneses. New York, 1863.
8vo., orig. violet cloth, fine, first edition. Ximenes 33-250 1974 $15

HOLLAND, JOSIAH GILBERT   Miss Gilbert's Career. New York, 1860.
8vo., orig. brown cloth, first edition. Ximenes 33-251 1974 $15

HOLLAND, MARY   The Complete Economical Cook and Frugal
Housewife. 1838. Frontispiece, faded, fourteenth edition. Covent 55-689
1974 £25

HOLLAND, N. M.   Spun-Yarn and Spindrift. London & Toronto,
1918. Inscribed. Hood's 104-759 1974 $10

HOLLAND, W. J.   The Butterfly Book. New York, 1898. Roy.
8vo., orig. cloth, coloured plates, text-figures, rare orig. issue. Wheldon
128-732 1973 £10

HOLLANDER, EUGEN   Die Medizin in der Klassischen Malerei. 1903.
Large 8vo., orig. cloth, first edition. Dawsons PM 249-278 1974 £25

HOLLANDER, EUGEN   Plastik und Medizin. 1912. Large 8vo., orig.
dark blue cloth, first edition. Dawsons PM 249-279 1974 £30

HOLLAR, W.   Civitatis Westmonasteriensis Pars. London,
1647. Orig. cloth, very small margins, right margin defective. Forster 97-250
1974 £20

HOLLAR, W.   On the North Side of London. London, 1665.
Orig. cloth, 3 1/4 X 4 3/4 inches, lower corner very slightly defective. Forster
97-247 1974 £12

HOLLAR, W.   Palatium Archiepiscopi Cantuariensis Propae
Londinum, Vulgo Lambeth House. London, 1647. No margins, orig. cloth.
Forster 97-253 1974 £35

HOLLES, DENZIL   Memoirs Of. London, 1699. 8vo., 18th-cen-
tury panelled sprinkled calf, first edition. Dawsons PM 251-123 1974 £40

HOLLES, DENZIL   A True Relation of the Unjust Accusation of
Certain French Gentlemen. London, 1671. 4to., 19th century half calf,
book-plate, first edition. Dawsons PM 252-461 1974 £18

HOLLEY, GEORGE W.   The Falls of Niagara. 1882. Orig. pictorial
cloth, illus., English first edition. Covent 56-2091 1974 £12.50

HOLLEY, GEORGE W.   The Falls of Niagara and Other Famous
Cataracts. London, 1882. Orig. covers, illus., first edition. Hood's 103-641
1974 $35

HOLLEY, GEORGE W.   Niagara, Its History and Geology, Incidents and
Poetry. New York and Toronto, 1872. Inscribed, illus. Hood's 103-359 1974
$30

HOLLEY, MARIETTA   The Widder Doodle's Love Affair, and Other
Stories. New York, 1893. Wrapper. Butterfield 10-21 1974 $20

HOLLIDAY, ROBERT C.   Men and Books and Cities. Doran, 1920.
263p. Austin 54-504 1973 $6.50

HOLLIDAY, ROBERT C.   Peeps at People. Doran, 1919. 118p. Austin
54-505 1973 $6.50

HOLLIDAY, ROBERT C.   Walking Stick Papers. Doran, 1918. 309p.
Austin 54-506 1973 $6.75

HOLLINGSHEAD, JOHN   Good Old Gaiety. 1903. Orig. pictorial
morocco gilt, frontispiece, plates. Covent 55-1438 1974 £6.30

HOLLISTER, GIDEON HIRAM   Mount Hope. New York, 1851. 12mo., orig.
green cloth, fine, foxing, first edition. Ximenes 33-253 1974 $15

HOLLOWAY, JAMES   The Free and Voluntary Confession and Narrative Of. London, 1684. Folio, disbound, first edition. Dawsons PM 251-
251 1974 £20

HOLLOWAY, LAURA C.   The Ladies of the White House; or In the Home of
the Presidents. Philadelphia, 1881. Thick 8vo., plates, first edition, frontis.,
orig. brown cloth, gilt. Current BW9-372 1974 $25

HOLLOWAY, STANLEY   Wiva Little Bit O'Luck. Stein, 1967. 223p.,
illus. Austin 51-433 1973 $6.50

HOLLYER, FREDERICK T.   Catalogue of Platinotype Reproductions of
Pictures & . . . London, 1900. Small 8vo., plates, orig. printed wrappers.
Kraus B8-339 1974 $45

HOLMAN, ALFRED L.   Blackman and Allied Families. Chicago,
1928. 8vo., cloth. Saddleback 14-776 1974 $15

HOLMAN, ALBERT M.   Pioneering in the Northwest. Sioux City, 1924.
Cloth. Hayman 57-301 1974 $12.50

HOLME, C. G.   Art in the U.S.S.R. London, 1935. 4to.,
plates. Biblo & Tannen 213-303 1973 $17.50

HOLME, CHARLES   The Art of the Book. 1914. Imp. 8vo., orig.
cloth, plates. Smith 194-100 1974 £8

HOLME, CHARLES 1848-1923   The Royal Institute of Painters in Water-Colours.
1906. Plates, rubbed. Marsden 39-233 1974 £5

HOLME, CONSTANCE   The Things Which Belong. 1925. Pictorial
dust wrapper, fine, scarce. Rota 188-437 1974 £6

HOLMES, C. J.   Constable and His Influence on Landscape
Painting. 1902. Imp. 4to., plates, Japanese vellum edition, half green
levant morocco, gilt, limited edition.   Quaritch 940-62 1974 £45

HOLMES, C. J.   Self & Partners. 1936. Orig. cloth, illus.
Marsden 39-235 1974 £5

HOLMES, CHARLES   The National Gallery. 3 vols., plates,
rubbed. Marsden 39-234 1974 £6

HOLMES, E. N.   Illustrations of the New Palace of Westminster.
1865. Folio, woodcuts, orig. cloth, worn spine. Quaritch 940-514 1974 £15

HOLMES, EDWARD   The Life of Mozart, Including His Correspondence.
London, 1845. 8vo., orig. light brown cloth, fine copy, first edition.   Ximenes
37-111 1974 $20

HOLMES, ELMER WALLACE   History of Riverside County, California.
Los Angeles, 1912. 4to., three quarter leather. Saddleback 14-137 1974 $65

HOLMES, FRED L.   Old World Wisconsin. 1944. 368 pages,
photographs. Austin 57-302 1974 $12.50

HOLMES, FRED L.   Old World Wisconsin. Hale, 1944. 368p.,
illus. Austin 62-261 1974 $12.50

HOLMES, GORDON   The Science of Voice Production and Voice
Preservation. Worthington, 1880. 157p. Austin 51-434 1973 $10

HOLMES, JOHN H.   If This Be Treason. Macmillan, 1935.
Austin 51-435 1973 $7.50

HOLMES, M. J.   Maggie Lee! Toronto, 1881. Hood's
103-486 1974 $30

HOLMES, MARY J.   Ethelyn's Mistake. New York, 1869. 8vo.,
orig. green cloth, first edition. Ximenes 33-255 1974 $15

HOLMES, MARY J.   Millbank. New York, 1871. 12mo., orig.
purple cloth, first edition. Ximenes 33-256 1974 $15

HOLMES, MARY J.   West Lawn and the Rector of St. Marks. New
York, 1874. 8vo., orig. cloth, first edition. Ximenes 33-257 1974 $12.50

HOLMES, OLIVER WENDELL   Astraea. Boston, 1850. 1st ed., 12mo., orig.
bds. Jacobs 24-96 1974 $45

HOLMES, OLIVER WENDELL   The Autocrat of the Breakfast Table. Boston,
1858. First edition, second issue, 12mo., spine ends heavily rubbed, covers dull,
illus., very good. Current BW9-232 1974 $32.50

HOLMES, OLIVER WENDELL   The Autocrat of the Breakfast Table. Boston,
1858. First edition, second issue, faded spine with minor chipping, other areas
nearly perfect. Current BW9-234 1974 $32.50

HOLMES, OLIVER WENDELL   The Autocrat of the Breakfast Table. Boston,
1858. First edition, second issue, spine ends chipped & spine faded, binding
firm, interior very good. Current BW9-233 1974 $45

HOLMES, OLIVER WENDELL   The Autocrat of the Breakfast-Table. Boswell,
Houghton, Mifflin, 1891. 321p. Austin 54-507 1973 $6.50

HOLMES, OLIVER WENDELL   The Autocrat of the Breakfast-Table. London,
1893. 2 vols., orig. cloth, illus., first London printing of this edition, bright
set. MacManus 224-225 1974 $25

HOLMES, OLIVER WENDELL   Elsie Venner. Houghton, Mifflin, 1891. 487p.
Austin 54-509 1973 $7

HOLMES, OLIVER WENDELL   The Guardian Angel. 1895. Orig. edition.
Austin 54-510 1973 $7

HOLMES, OLIVER WENDELL   Holmes-Pollock Letters. Cambridge, 1941.
First edition, 8vo., d.j., 2 vols., illus., books mint in faded publisher's slipcase.
Current BW9-536 1974 $16.50

HOLMES, OLIVER WENDELL   The Iron Gate, and Other Poems. Boston,
1880. Orig. cloth, first edition, inscribed presentation copy, fine. MacManus
224-226 1974 $50

HOLMES, OLIVER WENDELL   The Iron Gate and Other Poems. Boston, 1881.
First edition, thin 8vo., with note in authors hand laid in, nice clean copy.
Current BW9-236 1974 $30

HOLMES, OLIVER WENDELL   John Lothrop Motley. Houghton, 1878.
278p. Austin 54-511 1973 $8.50

HOLMES, OLIVER WENDELL   The Latest Poems of the Class of 1829. (N. P.,
1891). 12mo., cloth, first edition. Goodspeed's 578-148 1974 $15

HOLMES, OLIVER WENDELL   Life and Letters. 1896. 2 vols., binding
scratched. Allen 216-2238 1974 $10

HOLMES, OLIVER WENDELL   Mechanism in Thought and Morals. Boston,
1871. Cloth. Dawson's 424-278 1974 $45

HOLMES, OLIVER WENDELL   A Mortal Antipathy. Houghton, Mifflin, 1891.
307p., orig. ed. Austin 54-512 1973 $5.75

HOLMES, OLIVER WENDELL   The New Century and the New Building of the
Harvard Medical School, 1783-1883. Cambridge, 1884. 8vo., cloth, first
edition. Goodspeed's 578-147 1974 $10

HOLMES, OLIVER WENDELL   Our Hundred Days in Europe. Boston & New
York, 1887. Crown 8vo., orig. cloth gilt, inscribed, first edition. Howes
186-254 1974 £7.50

HOLMES, OLIVER WENDELL   Over the Teacups. Houghton, Mifflin, 1891.
319p. Austin 54-513 1973 $6

HOLMES, OLIVER WENDELL   Over the Teacups. Boston & New York, 1891.
Orig. cloth gilt, first printing, second state, presentation copy with six line poem
in author's hand, bookplate. MacManus 224-227 1974 $90

HOLMES, OLIVER WENDELL   Poems. Boston, 1836. 12mo., orig. green
cloth, label, first edition. Ximenes 33-258 1974 $65

HOLMES, OLIVER WENDELL   The Poet at the Breakfast Table. 1900. Orig.
edition. Austin 54-514 1973 $9.60

HOLMES, OLIVER WENDELL   The Pollock-Holmes Letters. Cambridge, 1942.
Demy 8vo., 2 vols., orig. cloth, fine. Broadhurst 24-362 1974 £5

HOLMES, OLIVER WENDELL   Professor at the Breakfast Table. Houghton,
1889. 410p., rev. ed. Austin 54-516 1973 $7.50

HOLMES, OLIVER WENDELL   The Professor at the Breakfast Table. Houghton,
Mifflin, 1891. 332p., rev. ed. Austin 54-517 1973 $7.50

HOLMES, OLIVER WENDELL   Ralph Waldo Emerson. Boston, 1912. Biblo
& Tannen 210-860 1973 $6.50

HOLMES, OLIVER WENDELL   Complete Poetical Works. Houghton, Mifflin,
1887. 357p., illus., half leather, marbilized boards. Austin 54-508 1973 $12.50

HOLT, CAROL M.   The Story of Grand Rapids, Michigan. Grand
Rapids, 1932. 8vo., cloth, revised. Saddleback 14-504 1974 $10

HOLT, EDWARD   The Public and Domestic Life of His Late
Most Gracious Majesty George the Third. 1820. 2 vols., plates, contemporary
calf, gilt, damp-staining. Howes 186-848 1974 £5

HOLT, FRANCIS LUDLOW   A Letter to His Grace the Duke of Wellington.
London, 1828. 8vo., disbound, first edition. Dawsons PM 247-148 1974 £10

HOLT, HAMILTON   Life Stories of Undistinguished Americans.
1906. 299 pages. Austin 57-303 1974 $12.50

HOLT, JOHN   General View of the Agriculture of the County of
Lancaster. London, 1794. 4to., half crimson morocco, gilt, first edition. Hammond 201-20 1974 £25

HOLT, JOHN   General View of the Agriculture of the County of Lancaster. London, 1795. 8vo., contemporary tree calf, rebacked, gilt, illus., second edition. Hammond 201-21 1974 £28

HOLT, JOSEPH   The Fallacy of Neutrality. New York, 1861. Printed wrappers. Hayman 57-426 1974 $12.50

HOLT, L. EMMET   The Diseases of Infancy and Childhood. New York, 1897. Thick 8vo., orig. half morocco, rubbed, illus., first edition. Schuman 37-125 1974 $145

HOLT, ROBERT T.   Radio Free Europe. Univ. of Minn. Press. Austin 51-436 1973 $5

HOLWELL, JOHN ZEPHANIAH   Narrative of the Deplorable Deaths. London, (n.d.). 12mo., illus., frontispiece, marbled paper wrappers. Bow Windows 62-466 1974 £7.50

THE HOLY Land and Egypt. New York, 1927. Nice copy, limited to 490 copies, nice, boards, orig. ties. Covent 51-2330 1973 £8.50

HOLYOAKE, GEORGE JACOB   The Policy of Commercial Co-Operation. London, (n.d.). 8vo., boards. Dawsons PM 247-150 1974 £10

HOLYOAKE, GEORGE JACOB   Sixty Years Of an Agitator's Life. London, 1893. 2 vols., 8vo., orig. cloth, second edition. Dawsons PM 247-151 1974 £15

HOLYOAKE, GEORGE JACOB   The Workman and the Suffrage. London, (n.d.) 8vo., library stamp, boards. Dawsons PM 247-149 1974 £10

HOLZHAUSEN, A.   Odlade Vaxter. Stockholm, 1941. Vol. 3, roy. 8vo., cloth, illus. Wheldon 131-1311 1974 £5

HOLZWORTH, JOHN M.   The Wild Grizzlies of Alaska. New York, 1930. Photos, map, bookplate, orig. binding, slight bubbling of front cover, near fine, first edition. Ross 87-436 1974 $15

HOLZWORTH, JOHN M.   The Wild Grizzlies of Alaska. New York and London, 1930. First edition, 8vo., illus., map, spine faded, else fine. Current BW9-186 1974 $17.50

HOMANS, JAMES E.   Self-Propelled Vehicles. New York, 1909. 8vo., red cloth, illus. Putman 126-5 1974 $12

HOMANS, JAMES E.   Self-Propelled Vehicles. New York, 1909. Illus., diagrams, orig. binding. Butterfield 10-74 1974 $25

HOME, D. M.   Traces in Scotland of Ancient Water-Lines Marine. Edinburgh, 1882. 8vo., cloth. Wheldon 130-939 1974 £7.50

HOME, EVERARD   Collection of Treatises from the Philosophical Transactions. ca. 1800-12. 4to., frayed, disbound. Bow Windows 62-467 1974 £24

HOME, GORDON   Normandy. London, 1905. Color plates, line illus., orig. binding. Wilson 63-598C 1974 £10

HOME, HENRY, LORD KAMES
Please turn to
KAMES, HENRY HOME, LORD

HOME, JOHN   Agis. Dublin, 1758. 12mo., disbound, first Irish edition. Ximenes 33-261 1974 $10

HOME, JOHN   Agis. London, 1758. 8vo., disbound, first edition. Ximenes 33-260 1974 $25

HOME, JOHN   Agis. London, 1758. 8vo., modern boards, first edition. Dawsons PM 252-462 1974 £15

HOME, JOHN   Alonzo. 1773. 8vo., cloth, first edition, second issue. Quaritch 936-107 1974 £8

HOME, JOHN   Alonzo. London, 1773. 8vo., modern boards, first edition. Dawsons PM 252-463 1974 £15

HOME, JOHN   Douglas. London, 1780. 8vo., modern boards. Dawsons PM 252-464 1974 £10

HOME, JOHN   The Fatal Discovery. London, 1769. 8vo., modern boards, first edition. Dawsons PM 252-465 1974 £15

HOME, JOHN   The Siege of Aquileia. London, 1760. 8vo., marbled boards, first edition. Ximenes 33-262 1974 $30

HOME Counties Magazine. 1899-1912. 14 vols., orig. half vellum, illus., plates, worn. Howes 186-2020 1974 £22.50

HOMERUS   Die Homerischen Hymnen. 1886. Half vellum. Allen 213-499 1973 $10

HOMERUS   Ilias. 1517. 2 vols., 19th century dark blue levant morocco, gilt. Thomas 30-36 1973 £150

HOMERUS   Ilias Graece et Latine. London, 1806. 2 vols., old calf, rubbed, leather labels. Jacobs 24-171 1974 $25

HOMERUS   The Iliad. 1865-62. 2 vols., thick crown 8vo., full prize calf, plates, gilt, labels. Howes 186-255 1974 £6

HOMERUS   Ilias. 1894. 2 vols., new buckram. Allen 213-502 1973 $10

HOMERUS   Ilad. London, 1928. 4to., ltd. to 750 copies, 1/2 vellum, uncut. Biblo & Tannen 210-742 1973 $20

HOMERUS   The Odyssey Rendered Into English Prose. 1900. Map, first edition, med. 8vo., uncut, orig. cloth, faded, inscribed, loosely inserted A.L.s. by Samuel Butler. Broadhurst 24-581 1974 £25

HOMERUS   The Odyssey of Homer. London, 1924. Crown 4to., plates, illus., orig. buckram, uncut, unopened. Bow Windows 62-469 1974 £60

HOMERUS   Odyssey. 1930. 4to., illus., plates. Allen 213-514 1973 $25

HOMERUS   Opera. Florence, (1488-89). 2 vols., folio, early 19th century full red morocco gilt, fine, signatures, first edition. Dawsons PM 250-43 1974 £7200

HOMERUS   Opera Omnia. 1759-64. 5 vols. in 3, calf, rubbed. Allen 213-498 1973 $15

HONE, JOSEPH   The Life of George Moore. 1936. Illus., orig. edition. Austin 61-474 1974 $12.25

HONE, N. J.   The Manor and Manorial Records. (1906). 8vo., orig. cloth, illus. Bow Windows 66-352 1974 £7.50

HONE, WILLIAM   Ancient Mysteries Described. n.d. Orig. cloth, illus., plates. Smith 193-782 1973 $5

HONE, WILLIAM   Ancient Mysteries Described. London, 1823. 8vo., orig. boards, worn, first edition. Ximenes 33-263 1974 $17.50

HONE, WILLIAM   The Every-Day Book. London, 1826-27. 5 vols., 8vo., contemporary half calf. Bow Windows 62-470 1974 £16

HONE, WILLIAM   The Every-Day Book. 1826-7. Large 8vo., half morocco, woodcuts, first edition. Hill 126-131 1974 £38

HONE, WILLIAM   Every-day Book. 1832. 4 vols., illus., new buckram. Allen 216-747 1974 $45

HONEY, WILLIAM BOWYER   The Ceramic Art of China and other Countries of the Far East. London, 1945. Sm. 4to., 192 plates, 3 in color. Biblo & Tannen 214-379 1974 $25

HONEY, WILLIAM BOWYER   Corean Pottery. New York, n.d. Illus. Biblo & Tannen 214-380 1974 $16.50

HONIG, PIETER   Science and Scientists in the Netherlands Indies.
New York, 1945. Roy. 8vo., cloth, illus. Wheldon 129-152 1974 £10

HONIG, PIETER   Science and Scientists In the Netherlands
Indies. New York, 1945. Rittenhouse 46-719 1974 $10

HONOURABLE Society of Cymmrodorion. 1893-1916. 8 vols., illus., orig.
wrappers. Howes 186-1852 1974 £10.50

HOOD, THOMAS   The Comic Annual. London, 1837. 12mo.,
orig. publisher's pictorial boards, roan spine, all edges gilt, illus. Frohnsdorff
16-447 1974 $15

HOOD, THOMAS   The Comic Annual. London, 1838. 12mo.,
publisher's orig. pictorial boards, roan spine, gilt lettering, all edges gilt, illus.
Frohnsdorff 16-448 1974 $15

HOOD, THOMAS   The Dream of Eugene Aram. London, 1831.
8vo., disbound, plates, first edition. Ximenes 33-266 1974 $25

HOOD, THOMAS   Poems. London, 1871. 4to., orig. dec. cloth,
gilt, plates. Hammond 201-475 1974 £6

HOOD, THOMAS   Poems Of. 1854. 2 vols. Austin 61-475
1974 $17.50

HOOK, THEODORE EDWARD   The Fortress. London, 1807. 8vo., boards,
uncut, first edition. Ximenes 33-267 1974 $15

HOOK, THEODORE EDWARD   Gilbert Gurney. London, 1836. 3 vols.,
12mo., half calf, first edition. Ximenes 33-268 1974 $30

HOOK, THEODORE EDWARD   Maxwell. London, 1830. 3 vols., rubbed,
contemporary half calf, first edition. Ximenes 33-269 1974 $40

HOOK, THEODORE EDWARD   The Trial by Jury. London, 1811. 8vo.,
modern boards, first edition. Dawsons PM 252-466 1974 £15

HOOK, WALTER F.   Lives of the Archbishops of Canterbury.
1860-76. 12 vols., full contemporary divinity calf, labels. Howes 185-1266
1974 £40

HOOKE, ANDREW   An Essay on the National Debt. London, 1750.
8vo., modern wrappers, fine, first edition. Dawsons PM 247-153 1974 £25

HOOKE, ROBERT   Lectiones Cutlerianae. London, 1679. 4to.,
modern panelled calf, rebacked, gilt, first edition. Dawsons PM 245-395 1974
£1,500

HOOKE, ROBERT   Micrographia. 1665. Folio, contemporary
russia, rebacked, plates, first edition. Broadhurst 23-1147 1974 £950

HOOKE, ROBERT   Micrographia. 1667. Folio, contemporary
calf, rebacked, plates. Wheldon 131-158 1974 £800

HOOKE, ROBERT   Micrographia Restaurata. London, 1745.
Folio, contemporary calf, rebacked, plates. Traylen 79-239 1973 £125

HOOKE, ROBERT   Philosophical Experiments and Observations of.
London, 1726. 8vo., orig. panelled calf, illus., first edition. Dawsons PM 245-
397 1974 £200

HOOKER, JOSEPH DALTON   The Botany of the Antarctic Voyage of H. M.
Discovery Ships Erebus and Terror. (1844-)1847. 2 vols., 4to., half morocco,
plates. Wheldon 131-61 1974 £1,000

HOOKER, JOSEPH DALTON   Flora of British India. (1875-97). 8vo., 7 vols.,
cloth. Wheldon 130-1169 1974 £60

HOOKER, JOSEPH DALTON   Himalayan Journals. 1854. 8vo., 2 vols.,
half calf, plates, illus., first edition. Bow Windows 64-134 1974 £58

HOOKER, JOSEPH DALTON   Introductory Essay. 1853. 4to., boards.
Wheldon 129-1086 1974 £7.50

HOOKER, JOSEPH DALTON   Introductory Essay to the Flora of New Zealand.
1853. 4to., boards. Wheldon 128-1272 1973 £12

HOOKER, JOSEPH DALTON   Introductory Essay to the Flora of New Zealand.
1853. 4to., boards. Wheldon 131-1312 1974 £10

HOOKER, RICHARD   Of the Lawes of Ecclesiastical Politie.
London, 1632. Small folio, contemporary sprinkled calf, rebacked. Dawsons
PM 250-44 1974 £70

HOOKER, RICHARD   The Works. 8vo., 3 vols., contemporary calf,
labels, new edition. Dawsons PM 251-506 1974 £30

HOOKER, RICHARD   The Works. 1825. 2 vols., contemporary
calf gilt, rubbed. Smith 194-875 1974 £7.50

HOOKER, W. S.   The English Flora. 1833-36. 8vo., 2 vols.,
half calf. Wheldon 129-1240 1974 £15

HOOKER, WILLIAM   The Paradisus Londinensis. (1805-08). 4to.,
new half green morocco, plates, extremely rare. Wheldon 131-63 1974 £375

HOOKER, WILLIAM   Pomona Londinensis. 1818. Roy. 4to.,
contemporary half calf, engraved aquatint plates most coloured by hand, fine.
Broadhurst 24-1114 1974 £1,100

HOOKER, WILLIAM   Pomona Londinensis. (1813-)1818. Roy.
4to., contemporary blue grained calf, plates, rare. Wheldon 131-62 1974
£1,250

HOOKER, WILLIAM   Pomona Londinensis. 1818. Roy 4to., contemporary half calf. Broadhurst 23-1148 1974 £600

HOOKER, WILLIAM JACKSON   Botanical Illustrations. Glasgow, 1837. 4to.,
modern boards, plates. Wheldon 130-1024 1974 £30

HOOKER, WILLIAM JACKSON   The British Flora. 1830. 8vo., half
morocco, first edition. Wheldon 131-1226 1974 £5

HOOKER, WILLIAM JACKSON   The British Flora. 1831. 8vo., cloth,
second edition. Wheldon 131-1227 1974 £5

HOOKER, WILLIAM JACKSON   A Century of Ferns. 1854. Roy. 8vo., orig.
half morocco, plates, rare. Wheldon 130-1299 1974 £60

HOOKER, WILLIAM JACKSON   Companion to the Curtis Botanical
Magazine. 1835-36. 2 vols., roy. 8vo., new half morocco, plates, rare.
Wheldon 131-1157 1974 £200

HOOKER, WILLIAM JACKSON   Exotic Flora. Edinburgh, 1823-27. 3 vols.,
8vo., binder's cloth, hand coloured engraved plates, ex-library. Wheldon 128-
1477 1973 £200

HOOKER, WILLIAM JACKSON   Exotic Flora. Edinburgh, 1823-27. 8vo.,
3 vols., binder's cloth, plates, ex-library. Wheldon 130-1409 1974 £200

HOOKER, WILLIAM JACKSON   Flora Scotica. 1821. 2 parts in 1 vol., 8vo.,
new cloth. Wheldon 128-1198 1973 £12

HOOKER, WILLIAM JACKSON   Flora Scotica. 1821. 2 parts in 1 vol.,
8vo., new cloth. Wheldon 131-1225 1974 £12

HOOKER, WILLIAM JACKSON   Hooker's Journal of Botany and Kew Garden
Miscellany. 1851. 8vo., half buckram, plates. Wheldon 128-1116 1973 £10

HOOKER, WILLIAM JACKSON   Journal of a Tour in Iceland in the Summer of
1809. Yarmouth, 1813. 2 vols., 8vo., half morocco, plates, second edition.
Wheldon 131-361 1974 £50

HOOKER, WILLIAM JACKSON   Musci Exotici. 1818-20. 2 vols., 8vo.,
contemporary diced calf, panelled backs, marbled edges, hand coloured engraved
plates, rare. Wheldon 128-1372 1973 £98

HOOKER, WILLIAM JACKSON   Niger Flora. 1849. 8vo., half calf, plates.
Wheldon 129-1087 1974 £70

HOOKER, WILLIAM JACKSON   Synopsis Filicum. 1868. 8vo., orig. cloth, plates. Wheldon 130-1300 1974 £20

HOOKER, WILLIAM JACKSON   Synopsis Filicum. 1883. 8vo., cloth, plates. Wheldon 129-1404 1974 £30

HOOLE, JOHN   Cleonice, Princess of Bithynia. 1775. 8vo., cloth, first edition. Quaritch 936-108 1974 £5

HOOLE, JOHN   Cleonice, Princess of Bithynia. London, 1775. 8vo., disbound, first edition. Ximenes 33-270 1974 $40

HOOLE, JOHN   Cyrus. London, 1768. 8vo., wrappers, first edition. Ximenes 33-271 1974 $25

HOOLE, JOHN   Cyrus. London, 1768. 8vo., modern boards, first edition. Dawsons PM 252-467 1974 £15

HOOLE, JOHN   Timanthes. 1770. 8vo., cloth, first edition. Quaritch 936-109 1974 £7

HOOLE, JOHN   Timanthes. London, 1770. 8vo., disbound, first edition. Ximenes 33-272 1974 $25

HOOLE, JOHN   The Works of Metastasio. London, 1767. 2 vols., 8vo., contemporary mottled calf, gilt, spines gilt, morocco labels, fine copy, first edition. Ximenes 37-112 1974 $70

HOOLE, W. STANLEY   Sam Slick in Texas. San Antonio, (1945). Cloth, illus, dust jacket, fine, first edition. Bradley 35-376 1974 $20

HOOPER, L.   The Lady's Book of Flowers and Poetry. New York, 1860. Orig. cloth, frontispiece, plates in color, 8vo. Gregory 44-176 1974 $22.50

HOOPER, ROBERT   The Morbid Anatomy of the Human Brain. London, 1828. Folio, modern half calf, fine, presentation copy. Dawsons PM 249-280 1974 £310

HOOPER, ROBERT   The Physician's Vade-Mecum. London, 1812. 8vo., orig. boards, rebacked, new edition. Hammond 201-544 1974 £8.50

HOOPER, W. EDEN   The Motor Car in the First Decade of the Twentieth Century. London, New York, 1908. 4to., green morocco, gilt, fine, first edition. Dawsons PM 245-398 1974 £95

HOOVER, HERBERT   American Individualism. New York, 1928. Autographed, cloth. Jenkins 48-376 1973 $60

HOPE, ANTHONY, PSEUD.
Please turn to
HAWKINS, ANTHONY HOPE

HOPE, BOB   This Is On Me. Shakespeare, Lond., n.d. Austin 51-437 1973 $6

HOPE, THOMAS   Anastasius. 1827. 3 vols., contemporary half calf, rubbed, fourth edition. Howes 186-257 1974 £7.50

HOPE, THOMAS   Anastasius. 1836. 2 vols., 16mo., half vellum, map. Allen 213-535 1973 $12.50

HOPE, THOMAS   Costume of the Ancients. 1812. 2 vols., 8vo., engravings, half calf, rubbed, enlarged new edition. Quaritch 940-717 1974 £27

HOPE, THOMAS   Costume of the Ancients. 1841. 2 vols., 8vo., plates, full polished calf, leather labels, enlarged new edition. Quaritch 940-718 1974 £30

HOPE, WILLIAM HENRY ST. JOHN   Heraldry for Craftsmen & Designers. 1913. Illus. Allen 213-1540A 1973 $12.50

HOPE, WILLIAM HENRY ST. JOHN   The Stall Plates of the Knights of the Order of the Garter. 1901. Roy. 4to., cloth. Quaritch 939-735 1974 £45

HOPE-NICHOLSON, HEDLEY   The Mindes Delight. 1928. Illus., boards, gilt top, damp stain on upper cover, nice copy. Covent 51-380 1973 £5.25

HOPKIN-JAMES, LEMUEL J.   The Celtic Gospels. 1934. Frontispiece, plates. Howes 185-1269 1974 £6

L'HOPITAL, WINEFRIDE DE   Westminster Cathedral and Its Architect. New York, (1919). 2 vols., small 4to., illus., covers faded and dull, interiors good, front hinge vol. 1 slightly loose. Current BW9-509 1974 $10

HOPKINS, ALFRED   The English Village Church. New York, (1921). 4to., full page plates, front inner hinge sprung, spine rubbed, plates fine. Current BW9-502 1974 $12

HOPKINS, CHARLES   Boadicea, Queen of Britain. London, 1697. 4to., disbound, first edition. Ximenes 33-273 1974 $125

HOPKINS, CHARLES   Friendship Improv'd. London, 1700. 4to., disbound, first edition. Ximenes 33-274 1974 $125

HOPKINS, CHARLES   Pyrrhus, King of Epirus. London, 1695. 4to., disbound, first edition. Ximenes 33-275 1974 $75

HOPKINS, CHARLES   Pyrrhus King of Epirus. London, 1695. 4to., modern half calf, fine, first edition. Dawsons PM 252-468 1974 £110

HOPKINS, E. WASHBURN   The History of Religions. New York, 1926. Biblo & Tannen 213-117 1973 $6.50

HOPKINS, EVAN   On the Connexion of Geology with Terrestrial Magnetism. London, 1851. 8vo., cloth, plates, fine, presentation copy. Dawsons PM 245-399 1974 £12

HOPKINS, EZELCIEL   The Works of. London, 1919. Contemporary panelled calf gilt, third edition. Smith 194-160 1974 £10

HOPKINS, F. G.   Perspectives in Biochemistry. Cambridge, (1937). 8vo., cloth, plates, scarce. Wheldon 130-113 1974 £5

HOPKINS, G. H. E.   Mosquitoes of the Ethiopian Region. 1936-41. Roy 8vo., 3 vols., cloth, plates, scarce. Wheldon 130-760 1974 £35

HOPKINS, GERARD MANLEY   The Correspondence. 1935-38. 3 vols., illus., nice set, bookplates, slightly worn dust wrappers. Covent 51-932 1973 £15.75

HOPKINS, GERARD MANLEY   Letters to Robert Bridges. 1935. Portraits, fine, d.w., first edition. Covent 51-935 1973 £5.25

HOPKINS, GERARD MANLEY   Poems. 1918. Orig. linen-backed boards, English first edition. Covent 56-641 1974 £45

HOPKINS, J. C.   Chronology of Canadian History from Confederation in 1867 to the End of 1900. 1905. Hood's 102-26 1974 $10

HOPKINS, J. C.   Chronology of Canadian History from Confederation in 1867 to the End of 1900. (1905). Hood's 104-30 1974 $10

HOPKINS, J. C.   French Canada and the St. Lawrence. Philadelphia, 1913. Illus., presentation. Hood's 103-773 1974 $20

HOPKINS, J. C.   Progress of Canada In the 19th Century. Toronto, 1900. Illus. Hood's 103-540 1974 $15

HOPKINS, LEMUEL   The Democratiad. Philadelphia, 1796. 8vo., disbound, good copy, scarce, third edition. Ximenes 37-113 1974 $45

HOPKINS, R. THURSTON   Old Watermills & Windmills. n.d. Roy. 8vo., plates, illus., orig. buckram, scarce. Smith 194-305 1974 £10

HOPKINS, R. THURSTON   Oscar Wilde. 1913. Frontispiece, faded. Covent 55-1542 1974 £7.50

HOPKINS, WILLIAM JOHN   She Blows! Boston, 1922. Dust jacket, illus. Rinsland 58-53 1974 $20

HOPP, JULIUS   Tears. 1904. 78p. Austin 51-438 1973 $10

HOPPE, A. J.   A Bibliography of the Writings of Samuel Butler. (1925). 8vo., orig. cloth, first edition. Rota 189-125 1974 £5

HOPPE, A. J.   A Bibliography of the Writings of Samuel Butler. London, 1925. 4to., orig. cloth, limited. Dawsons PM 10-101 1974 £15

HOPPER, DE WOLF   Reminiscences. 1927. 238p., illus. Austin 51-439 1973 $6.50

HOPPER, EDWARD   One Wife Too Many. Hurd, Houghton, 1867. 262p. Austin 54-519 1973 $15

HOPPER, HEDDA   From Under My Hat. Doubleday, 1952. 311p. Austin 51-440 1973 $7.50

HOPPIN, AUGUSTUS   Carrot-Pomade. New York, 1864. Wide 8vo., full page illus. each with tissue guard, rebound in green paper covered boards and leather spine, orig. paper wrappers bound in with some repairs, some age browning on interior, very good. Current BW9-107 1974 $38.50

HOPPIN, AUGUSTUS   A Fashionable Sufferer or Chapters from Life's Comedy. Boston, 1883. First edition, 8vo., purple and gilt dec. cloth, spine faded, interior very fine. Current BW9-540 1974 $28.50

HOPPIN, AUGUSTUS   Hay Fever. Boston, 1873. Oblong 8vo., first edition, full page pen & ink sketches, binding rebacked, boards with heavy rubbing at extremities. Current BW9-541 1974 $28.50

HOPPIN, AUGUSTUS   Nothing to Wear; an Episode of City Life. New York, 1857. 16mo., full page pen & ink sketches, orig. brown cloth, fine. Current BW9-543 1974 $12

HOPPIN, AUGUSTUS   On the Nile. Boston, 1874. First edition, oblong 8vo., pen and ink sketches, interior fine, gilt dec. red cloth, covers slightly soiled. Current BW9-544 1974 $32.50

HOPPIN, AUGUSTUS   Two Compton Boys. Boston, 1885. Illus. by author, first edition, square 8vo., covers dull, minor wear, interior mint except one ink smudge. Current BW9-144 1974 $25

HOPPIN, AUGUSTUS   Ups and Downs on Land and Water. Boston, 1871. First edition, oblong 8vo., pen and ink sketches, green cloth faded & worn, pictures fine. Current BW9-545 1974 $30

HORACE
Please turn to
HORATIUS FLACCUS, QUINTUS

HORATIUS FLACCUS, QUINTUS   Epistolae ad Pisones et Augustum. 1776. 3 vols., calf, fifth edition. Allen 213-537 1973 $15

HORATIUS FLACCUS, QUINTUS   Odes, Epodes & Carmen Seculare. 1741. 2 vols., old calf, worn. Allen 213-538 1973 $12.50

HORATIUS FLACCUS, QUINTUS   The Odes, Satyrs, and Epistles of. London, 1684. 8vo., contemporary calf, plates, first edition. Dawsons PM 252-469 1974 £45

HORATIUS FLACCUS, QUINTUS   Quinti Horati Flacci Carmina Alcaica. 1903. 8vo., orig. limp vellum, fine copy, limited to 150 copies on Japanese vellum. Sawyer 293-42 1974 £165

HORATIUS FLACCUS, QUINTUS   Quinti Horati Flacci Carmina Sapphica. 1903. Printed in black and red, initials supplied by hand, 8vo., orig. limp vellum, fine copy, limited to 150 copies on Japanese vellum. Sawyer 293-43 1974 £165

HORATIUS FLACCUS, QUINTUS   Opera. 1519. Early 19th century straight grain morocco, rubbed. Thomas 30-49 1973 £25

HORATIUS FLACCUS, QUINTUS   Opera. 1555. 18th century Italian mottled calf gilt. Thomas 30-104 1973 £25

HORATIUS FLACCUS, QUINTUS   Opera Omnia. Paris, 1828. Full green morocco, 2 1/2 X 1 3/4. Gregory 44-455 1974 $165

HORCHKIN, JAMES   A History of the Purchase and Settlement of Western New York. New York, 1848. Orig. cloth. Putman 126-88 1974 $25

HORDEN, J.   A Collection of Psalms and Hymns in the Language of the Cree Indians of North-West America. London, 1934. Revised edition. Hood's 104-522 1974 $25

HORE, J. P.   The History of New Market. London, 1886. 3 vols., illus. Austin 61-476 1974 $47.50

HORETZKY, C.   Some Startling Facts Relating to the Canadian Pacific Railway and the North-West Lands. Ottawa, 1880. Hood's 104-826 1974 $35

HORLEY, ENGELBERT   Sefton. 1893. Roy 8vo., orig. cloth, illus., plates. Broadhurst 23-1412 1974 £10

HORN, ALOYSIUS   The Life and Works of. 1927. Portrait, dust wrapper, faded. Covent 55-751 1974 £7.50

HORN, J.   Horn's Description of Dover. Dover, 1817. 8vo., orig. printed boards, frontispiece. Quaritch 939-406 1974 £30

HORN et Rimenhild. Paris, 1845. 4to., label, uncut, stained, cloth. Howes 186-258 1974 £15

HORNBLOW, ARTHUR   A History of the Theatre in America. Philadelphia, 1919. Ist ed., 2 vols., illus., with a letter from the author presenting the book. Jacobs 24-127 1974 $30

HORNBLOWER, JANE ELIZABETH   Nellie of Truro. New York, 1856. 8vo., orig. cloth, first edition. Ximenes 33-276 1974 $15

HORNBY, ELISHA B.   Under Old Roof Trees. Jersey City, 1908. 12mo., half suede, cloth case, inscribed presentation copy. Goodspeed's 578-139 1974 $15

HORNE, HERBERT P.   The Binding of Books. 1894. 8vo., large paper copy, plates, limited. Quaritch 940-602 1974 £45

HORNE, HERBERT P.   The Binding of Books. 1894. Orig. buckram, plates. Howes 185-715 1974 £7.50

HORNE, RICHARD HENRY   Orion. 1843. First edition, small 8vo., fine copy, rare, binder's cloth. Sawyer 293-168 1974 £95

HORNIBROOK, M.   Dwarf and Slow-Growing Conifers. (1930). 8vo., orig. cloth, fine, second edition. Gregory 44-157 1974 $30

HORNMAN, WILLIAM   Vulgaria. 1926. Small folio, half dark red morocco, top edges gilt. Thomas 32-296 1974 £55

HORNUNG, E. W.   The Crime Doctor. 1914. 8vo., orig. cloth, first edition. Rota 190-289 1974 £7.50

HORNUNG, E. W.   Notes of a Camp-Follower. 1919. English first edition. Covent 56-642 1974 £6.30

HORNUNG, E. W.   Some Persons Unknown. 1898. First edition. Covent 55-847 1974 £7.50

HORODEZKY, S. A.   Leaders of Hassidism. London, 1928. Biblo & Tannen 213-628 1973 $9.50

HORRALL, O. H.   Bile: Its Toxicity and Relation to Disease. Chicago, 1938. Rittenhouse 46-351 1974 $10

HORREBOW, NIELS   The Natural History of Iceland. 1758. Folio, modern half calf, marbled boards. Bow Windows 64-136 1974 £120

HORSBURGH, E. M.   Handbook of the Exhibition of Napier Relics. Edinburgh, 1914. Roy. 8vo., full leather, leather label, plates. Traylen 79-251 1973 £15

HORSEY, E. E.   Kingston a Century Ago. Kingston, 1936.
Hood's 103-642 1974 $12.50

HORSFIELD, T.   A Catalogue of the Lepidopterous Insects in the
Museum of the Hon. East-Indian Company. 1857. 2 vols. in 1, 8vo., orig.
cloth, plates, scarce. Wheldon 128-736 1973 £5

HORSFIELD, T.   Plantae Javanica Rariores. 1838-52. Small
folio, new half green morocco, gilt, plates. Wheldon 129-23 1974 £500

HORSFIELD, T.   Zoological Researches in Java and the
Neighbouring Islands. (1821). 4to., cloth, hand-coloured plates, rare.
Wheldon 128-204 1973 £25

HORSFIELD, T. W.   The History, Antiquites . . . . of Sussex.
Lewes, 1835. 2 vols., 4to., plates, contemporary calf. Quaritch 939-564
1974 £85

HORSLEY, H. S.   The Affectionate Parent's Gift, and the Good
Child's Reward. 1828. 2 vols., small square 8vo., full morocco, engraved
plates. George's 610-390 1973 £15

HORSLEY, J.   Britannia Romana. 1732. Folio, buckram,
plates, maps. Quaritch 939-141 1974 £30

HORSLEY, J. SHELTON   Surgery of the Blood Vessels. St. Louis,
1915. Rittenhouse 46-352 1974 $15

HORST, J.   Herbarium Horstianum. Marburg, 1630. 8vo.,
old calf, rare. Wheldon 128-1682 1973 £35

HORST, J.   Herbarium Horstianum. Marburg, 1630. 8vo.,
old calf. Wheldon 130-1613 1974 £35

HORT, RICHARD   The Embroidered Banner. London, 1850. 8vo.,
orig. green cloth, plates, first edition. Ximenes 33-278 1974 $45

HORT, RICHARD   The Man Who Eloped With His Own Wife.
London, 1850. 8vo., orig. wrappers, first edition. Ximenes 33-279 1974 $30

HORT, W. JILLARD   The New Pantheon. 1809. Second edition,
folding engraved frontis., plates, 12mo., contemporary tree calf, gilt, skilfully
rebacked, new leather labels, good copy, ads at end. George's 610-393 1973
£10.50

HORTICULTURAL SOCIETY OF LONDON   Transactions. (1805)-1815-48.
10 vols. in 12, 4to., contemporary half calf gilt, complete set, plates.
Wheldon 131-64 1974 £850

HORTON, W.   Memoir of the Late Thomas Scatcherd, a Family
Record. London, 1878. Hood's 102-247 1974 $25

HORTON, WILLIAM E.   About Stage Folks. Detroit, 1902. 12mo.,
1st ed. Biblo & Tannen 213-897 1973 $12.50

HORTON, WILLIAM THOMAS   William Thomas Horton. n.d. Plates, linen-
backed boards, English first edition. Covent 56-699 1974 £10

HORWOOD, A. R.   A New British Flora. 1919. 4to., cloth,
6 vols., plates. Wheldon 130-1090 1974 £7.50

HOSE, C.   The Pagan Tribes of Borneo. 1912. 8vo., 2
vols., orig. cloth. Broadhurst 23-1655 1974 £50

HOSE, R. E.   Prohibition or Control? London, New York and
Toronto, 1928. Hood's 102-564 1974 $15

HOSE, C.   The Pagan Tribes of Borneo. 1912. 2 vols.,
demy 8vo., coloured and plain plates, map, orig. cloth, fine. Broadhurst
24-1626 1974 £52

HOSHOUR, SAMUEL KLEINFELTER   Mosheim's Church History. Cambridge
City, 1847. 12mo., orig. cloth, scarce, first edition. Ximenes 33-280 1974
$25

HOSKING, E. J.   Birds of the Day. 1944. Roy. 8vo., cloth,
illus. Wheldon 131-624 1974 £5

HOSKING, E. J.   Birds of the Night. 1945. Roy 8vo., cloth,
scarce. Wheldon 130-550 1974 £5

HOSKING, E. J.   Birds of the Night. 1945. 4to., cloth, illus.,
inscription by author, very scarce. Wheldon 128-483 1973 £6

HOSKINS, G. A.   Travels in Ethiopia. London, 1835. 4to.,
modern half green morocco, first edition. Dawsons PM 251-36 1974 £200

HOSMER, GEORGE L.   An Historical Sketch of the Town of Deer Isle,
Maine, With Notices of Its Settlers and Early Inhabitants. Boston, 1886. Foldout map, orig. binding. Butterfield 10-364 1974 $25

HOSMER, H. L.   Early History of the Maumee Valley. Toledo,
1858. Printed wrappers, lacks back wrapper, rare, very good copy. Hayman
59-471 1974 $200

HOTCHKIN, A.   A Concise History of the Town of Maryland From
Its First Settlement. Schenevus, 1876. Foxed, boards. Jenkins 61-1884 1974
$22.50

HOTSON, J. LESLIE   The Death of Christopher Marlowe. Nonesuch
Press, 1925. Limited edition, illus., demy 8vo., full dark red morocco, lettered
gilt, uncut, fine. Broadhurst 24-1022 1974 £16

HOTSON, J. LESLIE   The Death of Christopher Marlowe. 1925.
Buckram, vellum, illus., fine. Covent 55-1078 1974 £21

HOT Stuff. Rositer, 1903. 96p., illus., paper. Austin 54-461 1973 $7.50

HOUARD, C.   Les Zoocecidies des Plantes d'Europe et du Bassin de la Mediteranee. Paris, 1908-14. Roy 8vo., buckram, plates. Wheldon
130-762 1974 £45

HOUARD, C.   Les Zoocecidies des Plantes l'Amerique de Sud
et de l'Amerique Centrale. Paris, 1933. 8vo., wrappers, text-figures, map.
Wheldon 128-737 1973 £7

HOUCK, GEORGE F.   The Church in Northern Ohio and in the
Diocese of Cleveland. 1887. 166 pages. Austin 57-205 1974 $15

HOUCK, GEORGE F.   The Church in Northern Ohio and in the
Diocese of Cleveland. Benziger, 1887. Austin 62-262 1974 $17.50

HOUDRY, VINCENT   Bibliotheca Concionatoria. Venice, 1761-67.
15 vols. in 8, folio, contemporary mottled calf. Howes 185-1270 1974 £15.75

HOUGH, EMERSON   The Covered Wagon. New York, 1922.
Orig. red cloth, fine, first edition. Bradley 35-438 1974 £30

HOUGH, EMERSON   The Girl at the Halfway House. New York,
1900. Orig. binding. Butterfield 10-301 1974 $12.50

HOUGH, EMERSON   The Mississippi Bubble. Indianapolis, (1902).
First edition, later binding with author's full name on backstrip. Butterfield 10-
302 1974 $7.50

HOUGH, EMERSON   The Singing Mouse Stories. Indianapolis,
(1910). Revised edition, orig. binding, ink underlining on 2 pages. Butterfield
10-303 1974 $10

HOUGH, EMERSON   The Web: Authorized History of the American
Protective League. 1919. Allen 216-751 1974 $10

HOUGH, EMERSON   The Young Alaskans on the Trail. New York &
London, 1911. First printing, pictorial cloth. Butterfield 10-304 1974 $15

HOUGH, FRANKLIN B.   History of Jefferson County In the State of New
York. Albany, 1854. Rubbed, foxing. Ballinger 1-275 1974 $30

HOUGH, S. S.   Christian Newcomer. Dayton, (1941). Orig.
cloth. Putman 126-90 1974 $10

HOUGHTON, CLAUDE PSEUD.
Please turn to
OLDFIELD, CLAUDE HOUGHTON

HOUGHTON, ELIZA P.   The Expedition of the Donner Party.   Chicago, 1911. Brown cloth, illus., scarce, first edition.   Putnam 126-302 1974 $50

HOUGHTON, J.   A Collection for the Improvement of Husbandry and Trade.   1727.   Vol. 2 only, 8vo., contemporary panelled calf.   Wheldon 128-1652 1973 £10

HOUGHTON, J.   Husbandry and Trade Improv'd.   1727-28.   8vo., contemporary calf gilt, 4 vols.   Wheldon 129-1659 1974 £85

HOUGHTON, J.   Husbandry and Trade Improv'd.   1727-28. 4 vols., 8vo., contemporary calf gilt.   Wheldon 131-1785 1974 £85

HOUGHTON, NORRIS   But Not Forgotten.   Sloane, 1951. 346p., illus.   Austin 51-441 1973 $10

HOUGHTON, THOMAS   Rara Avis in Terris.   London, 1681. 12mo., contemporary sheep, rebacked, first edition, second issue.   Gumey 64-114 1974 £145

HOUGHTON, THOMAS   Rara Avis in Terris.   London, 1681. 12mo., contemporary sheep, rebacked, first edition, second issue, rare.   Gurney 66-88 1974 £145

HOUGHTON, WILLIAM   British Fresh-Water Fishes.   London, n.d. 2 vols., folio, cloth, gilt, plates.   Traylen 79-94 1973 £70

HOUGHTON, WILLIAM   British Fresh Water Fishes.   (1879). Folio, orig. dec. cloth, 2 vols.   Wheldon 129-1704 1974 £130

HOUGHTON, WILLIAM   British Fresh-Water Fishes.   (1879). Folio, orig. dec. cloth, 2 vols., gilt, plates, scarce.   Wheldon 130-29 1974 £150

HOUGHTON, WILLIAM   British Freshwater Fishes.   1895. Roy. 8vo., cloth, illus., second edition.   Wheldon 131-754 1974 £7.50

HOUGHTON, WILLIAM   Sketches of British Insects.   1888. Crown 8vo., cloth, plates, frontispiece.   Wheldon 131-814 1974 £5

HOUPPELANDE, GUILLERMUS   De Immortalitate Animae.   Paris, 1499. 8vo., half vellum, fine.   Harper 213-92 1973 $750

HOURWICH, ISAAC   Immigration and Labor.   1912. Orig. edition. Austin 57-306 1974 $10

HOUSE, E. J.   A Hunter's Camp-Fires.   New York & London, 1919. Illus.   Hood's 103-360 1974 $17.50

HOUSE, HOMER D.   Wild Flowers.   New York, 1935. Coloured plates, demy 4to., orig. cloth, fine.   Broadhurst 24-1116 1974 £10

HOUSE, HOMER D.   Wild Flowers.   New York, 1935. 4to., fine, orig. cloth, colored illus.   Gregory 44-158 1974 $12.50

HOUSE, HOMER D.   Wild Flowers of New York.   Albany, n.d. 4to., color plates.   Biblo & Tannen 214-350 1974 $17.50

HOUSE, HOMER D.   Wild Flowers of New York.   Albany, 1918. 4to., orig. cloth, plates, illus.   Bow Windows 64-138 1974 £32

HOUSE, HOMER D.   Wild Flowers of New York.   Albany, 1918-20. First edition, 2 vols., 4to., illus., color plates, bookplates, orig. binding. Wilson 63-63 1974 $57.50

HOUSE Beautiful Building Annual, 1926. Boston, 1926. Folio, illus.   Biblo & Tannen 210-24 1973 $7.50

HOUSE Beautiful Furnishing Annual, 1926. Boston, 1926. Folio, color plates. Biblo & Tannen 210-193 1973 $7.50

HOUSE of Commons Select Committee on the London Streets and Buildings Bill. 1894. 3 vols., folio, cloth.   Howes 186-2126 1974 £25

HOUSE That Jack Built.   New York, n.d. (c. 1870). Oblong 4to., pictorial wrappers, spine overstitched, full page color plates.   Frohnsdorff 16-450 1974 $25

HOUSEHOLD Tales and Fairy Stories.   1893. Orig. pictorial cloth, plates, illus., English first edition.   Covent 56-431 1974 £6.30

HOUSMAN, ALFRED EDWARD   Last Poems.   London, 1922. First edition, first issue, with missing punctuation p. 52., slightly torn d.w., near mint, orig. binding.   Ross 86-260 1974 $30

HOUSMAN, ALFRED EDWARD   More Poems.   London, 1936. First trade edition, d.w. chipped, else fine, orig. binding.   Ross 86-262 1974 $17.50

HOUSMAN, ALFRED EDWARD   More Poems.   London, 1936. Frontis. portrait, large paper edition, no. 249 of 379 copies, limited, quarter niger morocco, very fine.   Ross 86-261 1974 $45

HOUSMAN, ALFRED EDWARD   The Name and Nature of Poetry.   Cambridge, 1933. Slight foxing, fine, orig. binding.   Ross 86-263 1974 $15

HOUSMAN, ALFRED EDWARD   A Shropshire Lad.   1914. One of 1000 numbered copies, on handmade paper, cloth backed boards, fine, first edition. Covent 51-947 1973 £8.50

HOUSMAN, ALFRED EDWARD   A Shropshire Lad.   1914. Cloth backed boards, English first edition.   Covent 56-645 1974 £10

HOUSMAN, ALFRED EDWARD   A Shropshire Lad.   New York, 1922. Orig. cloth, signature, authorised edition.   Rota 188-457 1974 $50

HOUSMAN, ALFRED EDWARD   A Shropshire Lad.   1929. 2 vols., roy. 8vo., boards, linen backs, labels, limited.   Howes 186-259 1974 £30

HOUSMAN, LAURENCE   Green Arras.   London, 1896. Orig. patterned cloth, first edition, with the leaf of errata, fine.   MacManus 224-228 1974 $60

HOUSMAN, LAURENCE   Victoria Regina.   Scribner, n.d. 470p., illus. Austin 51-442 1973 $10

HOUSMAN, LOUISE   Footlights.   Harper, 1935. 218p., illus. Austin 51-443 1973 $7.50

HOUSSAYE, ARSENE   Les Femmes du Temps Passe.   Paris, 1863. Roy. 8vo., gilt, first illus. edition.   L. Goldschmidt 42-249 1974 $20

HOUSSAYE, ARSENE   Histoire du 4ime Fauteuil de l'Academie Francaise. Paris, 1855. 8vo., contemporary half cloth, first edition. L. Goldschmidt 42-250 1974 $17.50

HOUSSAYE, H.   1814 & 1815. Paris, 1915-14. 4 vols., maps, buckram, gilt.   Smith 193-626 1973 £5

HOUSSAYE, J. G.   Monographie du The. Description Botanique, Torrefaction, Composition Chimique, Proprietes Hygieniques de Cette Feuille. Paris, 1843. Roy. 8vo., modern half calf, plates, foxed.   Wheldon 128-1653 1973 £15

HOUSSAYE, J. G.   Monographie du The Description Botanique, Torrefaction, Composition Chimique, Proprietes Hygieniques de Celle Feuille. Paris, 1843. Roy. 8vo., modern half calf, plates.   Wheldon 131-1786 1974 £15

HOUSSER, A.   Canadian Art Movement, the Story of the Group of Seven. Toronto, 1926. Illus., second printing.   Hood's 104-167 1974 $85

HOUSTON: A History and Guide. Houston, 1942. 8vo., cloth, 363 pages. Saddleback 14-720 1974 $15

HOUSTOUN, WILLIAM   Reliquiae Houstounianae.   London, 1781. 2 vols. in 1, 4to., half calf, first edition, plates, rare, fine, first edition. Ximenes 33-283 1974 $325

HOVEY, RICHARD   Along the Trail.   Boston, 1898. 1st ed., 12mo. Biblo & Tannen 214-732 1974 $10

HOVGAARD, WILLIAM   The Voyages of the Norsemen to America. 1914. Maps, illus., orig. edition.   Austin 57-307 1974 $20

HOW To See Niagara. New York, 1899. Patterned card cover, illus., cloth spine. Hood's 103-643 1974 $20

HOWARD, A.   Wheat in India. Calcutta, (1910). Roy 8vo., cloth, scarce, plates, maps. Wheldon 129-1660 1974 £5

HOWARD, CECIL HAMPDEN CUTTS   Genealogy of the Cutts Family in America. Albany, 1892. Orig. binding. Butterfield 10-270 1974 $20

HOWARD, CHARLES   Thoughts, Essays, and Maxims, Chiefly Religious and Political. London, 1768. 8vo., contemporary calf, first edition. Ximenes 33-284 1974 $30

HOWARD, F. E.   English Church Woodwork. n.d. Crown 4to., illus., book-plate. Marsden 39-238 1974 £6

HOWARD, F. E.   English Church Woodwork. 1919. 2 vols., 4to., plates. Allen 213-1911 1973 $15

HOWARD, H. E.   The British Warblers. 1907-15. 10 parts, roy. 8vo., orig. boards, maps, coloured and photogravure plates. Wheldon 128-484 1973 £100

HOWARD, H. E.   The British Warblers. 1907-14. 2 vols., imp. 8vo., half red morocco, plates, very scarce. Wheldon 131-65 1974 £200

HOWARD, H. E.   An Introduction to the Study of Bird Behaviour. 1929. 4to., cloth, plans, plates, scarce. Wheldon 128-485 1973 £10

HOWARD, H. E.   The Nature of a Birds World. 1935. 8vo., cloth. Wheldon 131-625 1974 £5

HOWARD, H. E.   Territory in Bird Life. 1920. 8vo., new half calf, first edition. Wheldon 130-551 1974 £15

HOWARD, HENRY   A Course of Lectures on Painting. 1848. Large 12mo., nineteenth century calf, gilt. Hill 126-11 1974 £18

HOWARD, JOHN   The State of the Prisons In England and Wales. Warrington, 1780. 8vo., contemporary half calf, engraved plates, inscription on endpaper, second edition. Bow Windows 66-353 1974 £80

HOWARD, JOHN   The State of the Prisons in England and Wales. 1784. 4to., contemporary tree calf, third edition. Quaritch 939-142 1974 £80

HOWARD, JOHN   The Works. London, 1792-1. 4to., 2 vols., half sheep, plates. Gurney 64-115 1974 £45

HOWARD, JOSEPH JACKSON   Visitation of England and Wales. 1893-1921. 21 vols., small folio, half parchment, plates, limited. Quaritch 939-763 1974 £58.50

HOWARD, L. O.   A History of Applied Entomology. Washington, 1930. 8vo., plates, sewed. Wheldon 129-153 1974 £5

HOWARD, JOHN TASKER   This Modern Music. New York, 1942. Biblo & Tannen 214-861 1974 $7.50

HOWARD, MARY   His Life Work. n.d. Full morocco, gilt. Broadhurst 23-883 1974 £5

HOWARD, O. O.   Reports of the Assistant Commissioners of Freedmen, and a Synopsis of Laws Respecting Persons of Color in the Late Slave States. Washington, 1867. Jenkins 61-2233 1974 $15

HOWARD, ROBERT   The Duell of the Stags. London, 1668. Small 4to., half green morocco, first edition. Ximenes 33-285 1974 $200

HOWARD, ROBERT   The Great Favourite. 1668. 4to., full calf antique, first edition. Dawsons PM 252-471 1974 £110

HOWARD, ROBERT   Historical Observations. London, 1689. 8vo., contemporary mottled calf, first edition. Dawsons PM 251-252 1974 £70

HOWARD, ROBERT   Historical Observations Upon the Reigns of Edward I, II, III, and Richard II. London, 1689. 8vo., contemporary calf, rubbed, first edition. Ximenes 37-114 1974 $175

HOWARD, SIDNEY   Half Gods. Scribner, 1930. Austin 51-444 1973 $8.50

HOWARD, THOMAS   On the Loss of Teeth. London, 1858. 12mo., orig. cloth, gilt. Hammond 201-535 1974 £9

HOWARD, WALDO   The Mistake of a Life-Time: or, The Robber of the Rhine Valley. Boston, 1850. Large 8vo., contemporary half calf, first edition, fine. MacManus 224-229 1974 $35

HOWARD & CROSSLEY   English Church Woodwork. 1927. Illus., second edition. Eaton Music-610 1973 £5

HOWARD-BURY, CHARLES KENNETH   Mount Everest: The Reconaissance, 1921. 1922. First edition, illus., folding maps, 8vo., orig. dark blue cloth gilt, edges uncut, fine copy, scarce. Sawyer 293-230 1974 £6.50

HOWAY, F. W.   British Columbia, the Making of a Province. Toronto, 1928. Maps, illus. Hood's 103-804 1974 $35

HOWAY, F. W.   Builders of the West, a Book of Heroes. Toronto, 1929. Hood's 102-811 1974 $12.50

HOWAY, F. W.   Zimmerman's Captain Cook. Toronto, 1930. Faded. Hood's 103-541 1974 $50

HOWE, DANIEL WAIT   Political History of Secession to the Beginning of the American Civil War. New York & London, 1914. Orig. binding. Butterfield 10-305 1974 $12.50

HOWE, EDGAR WATSON   Plain People. 1929. Orig. edition, 317 pages. Austin 54-520 1973 $9.50

HOWE, EDGAR WATSON   The Story of a Country Town. Harper, 1917. Orig. edition. Austin 54-521 1973 $8.50

HOWE, GEORGE FREDERICK   Chester A. Arthur. New York, 1934. Large 8vo., orig. binding. Butterfield 10-306 1974 $8.50

HOWE, W. E.   The Ferns of Derbyshire. 1865. 8vo., cloth, plates, scarce. Wheldon 130-1302 1974 £5

HOWE, WINIFRED E.   A History of the Metropolitan Museum of Art. New York, 1913 and 1946. 2 vols., illus., ltd. to 1000 copies. Biblo & Tannen 214-335 1974 $20

HOWELL, ARTHUR H.   Birds of Alabama. Montgomery, 1924. 8vo., wrapper. Butterfield 8-4 1974 $15

HOWELL, JAMES   Dodona's Grove. (London), 1640. Folio, 18th century sheep, first edition. Dawsons PM 252-472 1974 £250

HOWELL, JAMES   Epistolae Ho-Elianae. 1737. New buckram. Allen 216-2029A 1974 $12.50

HOWELL, JOHN   An Essay on the War Galleys of the Ancients. Edinburgh and London, 1824. Marbled boards, wrapper, plates. Dawson's 424-109 1974 $25

HOWELLS, JOHN MEAD   The Architectural Heritage of the Merrimack. New York, (1941). Grey buckram, plates. Dawson's 424-227 1974 $85

HOWELLS, JOHN MEAD   Lost Examples of Colonial Architecture. New York, 1931. Blue cloth, dust wrapper, plates. Dawson's 424-226 1974 $40

HOWELLS, MILDRED   A Little Gril Among the Old Masters. Boston, 1884. Orig. cloth, first edition, very good copy. MacManus 224-230 1974 $45

HOWELLS, WILLIAM DEAN   The Albany Depot. Harper, 1892. 68p. Austin 54-522 1973 $12.50

HOWELLS, WILLIAM DEAN   Between the Dark and the Day Light. Harper, 1907, 185p. Austin 54-524 1973 $12.50

HOWELLS, WILLIAM DEAN   A Boy's Town. Harper, 1890. 247p., illus., orig. ed. Austin 54-523 1973 $8.50

HOWELLS, WILLIAM DEAN   Bride Roses. Houghton, Mifflin, 1900. 48p. Austin 54-525 1973 $12.50

HOWELLS, WILLIAM DEAN   A Chance Acquaintance. Osgood, 1873. 279p. Austin 54-526 1973 $10

HOWELLS, WILLIAM DEAN   Criticism and Fiction. Harper, 1891. 188p., orig. ed. Austin 54-527 1973 $6

HOWELLS, WILLIAM DEAN   The Daughter of the Storage. Harper, 1916. 352p. Austin 54-528 1973 $17.50

HOWELLS, WILLIAM DEAN   Doctor Breen's Practice. Osgood, 1881. 272p. Austin 54-529 1973 $10

HOWELLS, WILLIAM DEAN   The Elevator. Houghton, Mifflin, 1913. 84p. Austin 54-530 1973 $10

HOWELLS, WILLIAM DEAN   Familiar Spanish Travels. New York, 1913. 8vo., cloth, frontispiece, foxed, fine copy, first edition. Goodspeed's 578-155 1974 $10

HOWELLS, WILLIAM DEAN   A Fearful Responsibility. Houghton, Mifflin, (1881) 255p. Austin 54-537 1973 $10

HOWELLS, WILLIAM DEAN   A Fearful Responsibility. Osgood, 1881. 255p. Austin 54-531 1973 $12.50

HOWELLS, WILLIAM DEAN   Fennel and Rue. Harper, 1908. 130p. Austin 54-532 1973 $8.50

HOWELLS, WILLIAM DEAN   A Foregone Conclusion. Houghton, Mifflin, 1899. 256p. Austin 54-533 1973 $8.50

HOWELLS, WILLIAM DEAN   A Foregone Conclusion. Houghton, Mifflin, 1916. 256p. Austin 54-534 1973 $10

HOWELLS, WILLIAM DEAN   A Hazard of New Fortunes. Harper, 1890. Vol. 1-332p., vol. 2-332p. Austin 54-536 1973 $12.50

HOWELLS, WILLIAM DEAN   A Hazard of New Fortunes. Harper, 1911. 575p., illus. Austin 54-538 1973 $10

HOWELLS, WILLIAM DEAN   The Heart of Childhood. Harper, 1906. 286p. Austin 54-539 1973 $6.50

HOWELLS, WILLIAM DEAN   Heroines of Fiction. Harper, 1901. Vol. 1-239p., vol. 2-274p. Austin 54-540 1973 $10

HOWELLS, WILLIAM DEAN   An Indian Giver. Houghton, Mifflin, 1900. 97p. Austin 54-541 1973 $12.50

HOWELLS, WILLIAM DEAN   Italian Journeys. New York, 1867. 8vo., orig. terra cotta cloth, first edition. Ximenes 33-288 1974 $20

HOWELLS, WILLIAM DEAN   Italian Journeys. Osgood, 1877. 398p. Austin 54-542 1973 $7.50

HOWELLS, WILLIAM DEAN   Italian Journeys. Houghton, Mifflin, 1895. 398p. Austin 54-543 1973 $8.50

HOWELLS, WILLIAM DEAN   The Lady of the Aroostook. Houghton, Osgood, 1879. 326p. Austin 54-544 1973 $12.50

HOWELLS, WILLIAM DEAN   The Lady of the Aroostook. Houghton, Mifflin, 1879. 326p. Austin 54-545 1973 $7.50

HOWELLS, WILLIAM DEAN   The Landlord at Lion's Head. Harper, 1911. 408p. Austin 54-546 1973 $10

HOWELLS, WILLIAM DEAN   The Leatherwood God. New York, 1916. 1st ed., illus. Biblo & Tannen 214-733 1974 $10

HOWELLS, WILLIAM DEAN   The Leatherwood God. Century, 1916. 236p., illus. Austin 54-547 1973 $12.50

HOWELLS, WILLIAM DEAN   Letters Home. Harper, 1903. 299p. Austin 54-548 1973 $8.50

HOWELLS, WILLIAM DEAN   Life in Letters of. New York, 1928. 2 vols., orig. cloth, paper labels, illus., first edition, scarce. MacManus 224-231 1974 $40

HOWELLS, WILLIAM DEAN   Literary Friends and Acquaintance. Harper, 1900. 287p., illus., orig. ed. Austin 54-549 1973 $7.50

HOWELLS, WILLIAM DEAN   Literary Friends and Acquaintances. New York, 1900. 8vo., orig. cloth, fine, first edition. Ximenes 33-289 1974 $35

HOWELLS, WILLIAM DEAN   Literary Friends and Acquaintance. New York, 1900. 1st ed., illus. Biblo & Tannen 210-743 1973 $15

HOWELLS, WILLIAM DEAN   Literary Friends and Acquaintance. Harper, 1911. 408p., illus., "lib. ed." Austin 54-550 1973 $12.50

HOWELLS, WILLIAM DEAN   Literature and Life. New York, 1902. 8vo., orig. cloth, illus., fine, first edition. Ximenes 33-290 1974 $35

HOWELLS, WILLIAM DEAN   Lives and Speeches of Abraham Lincoln and Hannibal Hamlin. Columbus, 1860. Cloth, worn. Hayman 57-455 1974 $10

HOWELLS, WILLIAM DEAN   London Films. Harper, 1903. 299p. Austin 54-551 1973 $7.50

HOWELLS, WILLIAM DEAN   London Films and Certain Delightful English Towns. Harper, 1911. 527 pages. Austin 54-552 1973 $12.50

HOWELLS, WILLIAM DEAN   Miss Bellard's Inspiration. Harper, 1905. 224 pages. Austin 54-553 1973 $8.50

HOWELLS, WILLIAM DEAN   A Modern Instance. 1881. Austin 54-555 1973 $6

HOWELLS, WILLIAM DEAN   A Modern Instance. Boston, 1882. First edition, 12mo., good, signature of author on card laid on. Current BW9-237 1974 $25

HOWELLS, WILLIAM DEAN   A Modern Instance. 1909. 514 pages. Austin 54-554 1973 $10

HOWELLS, WILLIAM DEAN   A Modern Instance. 1910. Austin 54-556 1973 $6.50

HOWELLS, WILLIAM DEAN   The Mouse Trap. Harper, 1889. Austin 54-558 1973 $10

HOWELLS, WILLIAM DEAN   The Mouse Trap. Harper, 1894. Illus. Austin 54-557 1973 $12.50

HOWELLS, WILLIAM DEAN   My Literary Passions and Criticism and Fiction. Harper, 1910. Illus. Austin 54-559 1973 $12.50

HOWELLS, WILLIAM DEAN   The Rise of Silas Lapham. 1884. Austin 54-562 1973 $7.50

HOWELLS, WILLIAM DEAN   Questionable Shapes. Harper, 1903. 219 pages, orig. edition. Austin 54-561 1973 $7.50

HOWELLS, WILLIAM DEAN   New Leaf Mills. Harper, 1913. Orig. edition. Austin 54-560 1973 $8.50

HOWELLS, WILLIAM DEAN   The Rise of Silas Lapham. 1912. Austin 54-563 1973 $6

HOWELLS, WILLIAM DEAN   Roman Holidays. 1908. 303 pages. Austin 54-564 1973 $7.50

HOWELLS, WILLIAM DEAN   Seven English Cities. Harper, 1909. Illus. Austin 54-565 1973 $7.50

HOWELLS, WILLIAM DEAN   Seven English Cities. New York, 1909. 8vo., orig. cloth, inscribed, presentation, first edition. Ximenes 33-291 1974 $35

HOWELLS, WILLIAM DEAN   The Smoking Car. 1900. Austin 54-566 1973 $10

HOWELLS, WILLIAM DEAN   Their Silver Wedding Journey. 1899. Austin 54-570 1973 $10

HOWELLS, WILLIAM DEAN   Their Silver Wedding Journey. Harper, 1899. 2 vols. Austin 54-569 1973 $12.50

HOWELLS, WILLIAM DEAN   Their Wedding Journey. Osgood, 1872. Illus. Austin 54-571 1973 $7.50

HOWELLS, WILLIAM DEAN   Their Wedding Journey. 1894. Illus. Austin 54-572 1973 $10

HOWELLS, WILLIAM DEAN   Their Wedding Journey. 1916. Illus. Austin 54-573 1973 $10

HOWELLS, WILLIAM DEAN   Through the Eye of the Neddle. Harper, 1907. Orig. edition. Austin 54-574 1973 $8.50

HOWELLS, WILLIAM DEAN   The Undiscovered Country. 1880. Austin 54-575 1973 $12

HOWELLS, WILLIAM DEAN   The Undiscovered Country. Cambridge, 1880. Orig. cloth, bookplate, fine. Covent 51-949 1973 £5.50

HOWELLS, WILLIAM DEAN   The Undiscovered Country. Boston, 1880. 12mo., orig. cloth, first edition. Ximenes 33-292 1974 $10

HOWELLS, WILLIAM DEAN   The Undiscovered Country. 1908. Austin 54-576 1973 $12.50

HOWELLS, WILLIAM DEAN   The Vacation of the Kelwyns. Harper, 1920. Austin 54-577 1973 $8.50

HOWELLS, WILLIAM DEAN   Venetian Life. 1866. Covers little faded and marked, nice copy, first edition, recased. Covent 51-950 1973 £6

HOWELLS, WILLIAM DEAN   Venetian Life. Boston & New York, 1892. 2 vols., modern half morocco, gilt spines, illus., with a short A.L.s. MacManus 224-232 1974 $75

HOWELLS, WILLIAM DEAN   Venetian Life. 1907. Austin 54-578 1973 $10

HOWELLS, WILLIAM DEAN   The World of Chance. Harper, 1893. Austin 54-579 1973 $12.50

HOWELLS, WILLIAM DEAN   Years of My Youth. Harper, 1916. Austin 54-580 1973 $8.50

HOWES, F. N.   Plants and Beekeeping. 1945. 8vo., cloth, illus. Wheldon 130-764 1974 £5

HOWEY, M. OLDFIELD   The Cat in the Mysteries of Religion and Magic. London, n.d. Illus., bdg. worn. Biblo & Tannen 210-977 1973 $10

HOWEY, M. OLDFIELD   The Cat in the Mysteries of Religion and Magic. Philadelphia, n.d. Illus. Biblo & Tannen 214-575 1974 $12.50

HOWEY, M. OLDFIELD   The Encircled Serpent. n.d. Roy. 8vo., frontispiece, plates, illus., orig. cloth. Smith 194-831 1974 £8.50

HOWISON, NEIL M.   Oregon. Washington, 1848. Jenkins 61-2068 1974 $15

HOWITT, M.   Biographical Sketches of the Queens of Great Britain, from the Norman Conquest to the Reign of Queen Victoria. 1856. Large 8vo., imitation red morocco, portraits on steel. Eaton Music-611 1973 £10

HOWITT, SAMUEL   The British Sportsman. n.d. Oblong 4to., full red straight grained morocco, plates. Marsden 37-265 1974 £325

HOWITT, SAMUEL   Miscellaneous Etchings, Old and New. (1806). Oblong 4to., plates, half red morocco, worn. Marsden 39-240 1974 £18

HOWITT, WILLIAM   German Experiences. 1844. 8vo., red polished calf, second edition. Bow Windows 64-553 1974 £6

HOWITT, WILLIAM   The History of the Supernatural in All Ages and Nations. London, 1863. 2 vols., 8vo., half red morocco, spines gilt, very good copy, first edition. Ximenes 37-115 1974 $27.50

HOWL of the Censor. Nourse, 1961. 144p. Austin 54-358 1973 $10

HOWLAND, LOUIS   Stephen A. Douglas. New York, 1920. 1st ed. Biblo & Tannen 213-64 1973 $8.50

HOWLETT, B.   A Selection of Views in the County of Lincoln. 1805. Roy. 4to., plates, half morocco. Quaritch 939-430 1974 £65

HOWLETT, B.   A Selection of Views in the County of Lincoln. 1805-06. 2 vols., 4to., old calf, half morocco. Quaritch 939-431 1974 £60

HOWORTH, HENRY   Saint Augustine of Canterbury. 1913. Thick 8vo., illus., presentation. Howes 185-929 1974 £5

HOWLETT, R.   The Angler's Sure Guide. 1706. Small 8vo., contemporary calf, rare first edition. Quaritch 939-143 1974 £95

HOY, THOMAS   Agathocles the Sicilian Usurper. London, 1683. Folio, uncut, first edition. Ximenes 33-293 1974 $125

HOYLE, EDMOND　　　Hoyle's Games. Philadelphia, (1845). 16mo., orig. blue cloth gilt, early American edition. Howes 185-230 1974 £6.50

HOYLAND, JOHN　　　A Historical Survey of the Customs, Habits & Present State of the Gypsies. 1816. 8vo., half calf, first edition. Bow Windows 64-530 1974 £48

HOYLAND, FRANCIS　　　Poems and Translations. 1763. 4to., buckram, orig. blue wrappers, first edition. Quaritch 936-111 1974 £20

HOYLE, EDMOND　　　Hoyle's Improved Edition of the Rules for Playing Fashionable Games. Philadelphia, 1842. 12mo., contemporary navy roan gilt, early American edition. Howes 186-203 1974 £6.50

HOYT, EDWIN　　　A Gentleman of Broadway. Little, Brown, 1964. 369p., photos. Austin 54-881 1973 $7.50

HOZIER, H. M.　　　The Invasions of England. 1876. 2 vols., 8vo., orig. cloth, some foxing. Bow Windows 66-355 1974 £5

HRDLICKA, ALES　　　The Old Americans. 1925. Illus., orig. edition. Austin 57-308 1974 $20

HRDLICKA, ALES　　　The Old Americans. 1925. 438p., illus., orig. ed. Austin 62-264 1974 $20

HRDLICKA, ALES　　　Physiological and Medical Observations Among the Indians of Southwestern United States and Northern Mexico. Washington, 1908. Rittenhouse 46-353 1974 $15

HSIUNG, S. I.　　　The Professor from Peking. Methuen, 1939. 198p. Austin 51-279 1973 $6

HU, HSEN-HSU　　　Icones Plantarum Sinicarum. Shanghai, 1927-29. 2 vols., folio, plates, orig. wrappers. Smith 194-801 1974 £10

HUARD, V. A.　　　La Vie et l'Oeuvre de l'Abbe Provancher. Quebec, 1926. Wrappers. Hood's 104-264 1974 $17.50

HUARTE DE SAN JUAN, JUAN　　　Essame de Gl'Ingegni de gli Hvomini. 1582. Small 8vo., 18th century half calf, first edition in Italian. Dawsons PM 249-281 1974 £130

HUARTE DE SAN JUAN, JUAN　　　L'Examen des Esprits povr les Sciences. Paris, 1661. 12mo., contemporary mottled calf, rebacked. Dawsons PM 249-283 1974 £70

HUARTE DE SAN JUAN, JUAN　　　Examen de Ingenios. London, 1604. 4to., contemporary vellum, third edition in English. Schuman 37-126 1974 $450

HUARTE DE SAN JUAN, JUAN　　　Examen de Ingenios. London, 1698. 8vo., modern half calf, fifth edition in English. Dawsons PM 249-282 1974 £85

HUARTE NAVARRO, JUAN DE DIOS
Please turn to
HUARTE DE SAN JUAN, JUAN

HUARTE Y NAVARRO, JUAN
Please turn to
HUARTE DE SAN JUAN, JUAN

HUBBACK, J. H.　　　Jane Austen's Sailor Brothers. 1906. Illus., inscription by authors, loose galley sheets laid in, very good copy, scarce, first edition. Covent 51-2141 1973 £75

HUBBARD, A. J.　　　Neolithic Dew-Ponds and Cattleways. 1907. 8vo., orig. cloth, illus., some spotting, second enlarged edition. Bow Windows 66-356 1974 £5

HUBBARD, ALICE　　　Life Lessons. East Aurora, 1909. Boards, frontispiece. Dawson's 424-340 1974 $40

HUBBARD, E. H.　　　In Making and Collecting Etchings. 1902. 8vo., orig. holland backed boards, plates, diagrams, uncut, partly unopened. Bow Windows 66-357 1974 £6.75

HUBBARD, LUCIUS L.　　　The Valuable Private Library of...Consisting Almost Wholly of Rare Books and Pamphlets Relating to American History. New York, 1914. Cloth. Jenkins 61-2488 1974 $25

HUBBARD, ROBERT　　　Historical Sketches of Roswell Franklin and Family. Dansville, 1839. 12mo., orig. quarter roan, marbled boards, first edition. Ximenes 33-294 1974 $375

HUBBARD, ROSE ELLEN　　　Ornamental Waterfowl. 1907. Crown 8vo., cloth, plates, second edition. Wheldon 130-552 1974 £7.50

HUBBARD, T. O'B.　　　To-Morrow is a New Day. 1934. Cloth back, engravings, bookplate. Marsden 37-266 1974 £10

HUBBARD, WILLIAM　　　A Narrative of the Indian Wars in New England. Worcester, 1801. Recently marbled boards, cloth backstrip, marbled end papers, map, internal stains. Wilson 63-55 1974 $38.75

HUBBELL, MARK H.　　　Buffalo, the City Beautiful. (Buffalo), 1931. Oblong 8vo., cloth. Saddleback 14-579 1974 $20

HUBBELL, RICHARD　　　Television. Rinehart, 1950. 240p., illus. Austin 51-445 1973 $10

HUBER, F.　　　New Observations on the Natural History of Bees. Edinburgh, 1806. Small 8vo., half calf, plates. Wheldon 129-714 1974 £10

HUBER, F.　　　New Observations Upon Bees. Hamilton, 1926. 8vo., rexine, plates. Wheldon 129-715 1974 £5

HUBER, MARIE　　　The World Unmask'd. 1743. 12mo., 2 vols., contemporary sheep, second edition. Hill 126-133 1974 £10.50

HUBER, V. A.　　　The English Universities. 1843. 2 vols. in 3, 8vo., plates, cloth, faded. Quaritch 939-144 1974 £125

HUBERT, EMILE　　　Historique de l'Association Libre des Compositeurs & Imprimeurs Typographes de Bruxelles. Brussels, 1892. 8vo., three quarter vellum, orig. wrappers bound in. Kraus B8-340 1974 $35

HUBERT, EMILE　　　Historique de l'Association Libre des Compositeurs & Imprimeurs Typographes de Bruxelles. Brussels, 1892. 8vo., orig. printed wrappers. Kraus B8-341 1974 $35

HUBIN　　　Machines Nouvellement Executees, et en Partie Inventees. Paris, 1673. 4to., old boards, full page engravings. Gurney 66-89 1974 £55

HUBNER, JOSEPH ALEXANDER VON　　　The Life and Times of Sixtus V. 1872. 2 vols., orig. cloth, sole English edition. Howes 185-1653 1974 £8

HUBSCH, H.　　　Monuments de l'Architecture Chretienne Depuis Constantin Jusqu'a Charlemagne et de Leur Influence sur le Style des Constructions Religieuses aux Epoques Posterieures. Paris, 1866. Imp. folio, plates, half morocco, worn. Quaritch 940-515 1974 £28

HUC, EVARISTE REGIS 1813-1860　　　Souvenirs d'un Voyage dans la Tartarie. Paris, 1925-27. 3 vols., 12mo., three quarter hard grain morocco, orig. wrapper, uncut. L. Goldschmidt 42-251 1974 $17.50

HUC, M.　　　Travels In Tartary, Thibet & China, 1844-46. Chicago, 1900. 2 vols. in 1, orig. pictorial cloth gilt, wood engravings, second edition. Smith 194-597 1974 £6.80

HUCKEL, J. F.   American Indians. Kansas City, 1920. Small folio, fine, plates, scarce, second edition. Bradley 35-200 1974 $30

HUDDESFORD, GEORGE   The Wiccamical Chaplet, a Selection of Original Poetry. London, 1804. 8vo., orig. boards, front hinge worn, first edition, uncut. Ximenes 36-119 1974 $30

HUDDESFORD, WILLIAM   The Lives of Those Eminent Antiquaries. Oxford, 1772. 8vo., 2 vols., contemporary sprinkled calf, first edition. Dawsons PM 251-124 1974 £16

HUDDLESTON, SISLEY   Paris, Salons, Cafes and Studios. 1928. Illus. Austin 61-479 1974 $12.50

HUDLESTON, F. J.   Gentleman Johnny Burgoyne. New York, 1927. Illus. Hood's 102-248 1974 $15

HUDLESTON, F. J.   Gentleman Johnny Burgoyne. Garden City, 1927. Illus. Hood's 104-263 1974 $15

HUDSON, A. P.   Folksongs of Mississippi & Their Background. 1936. Allen 216-87 1974 $12.50

HUDSON, C. T.   The Rotifera. 1886. 4to., contemporary half calf, plates. Wheldon 129-782 1974 £82

HUDSON, C. T.   The Rotifera. 1886-89. 4to., cloth, plates, scarce. Wheldon 130-870 1974 £95

HUDSON, MARIANNE SPENCER   Almack's A Novel. 1826. 8vo., 3 vols., cloth, first edition. Quaritch 936-421 1974 £110

HUDSON, PETER   The French Scholar's Guide. London, 1780. 12mo., contemporary calf, eight edition. Ximenes 33-295 1974 $15

HUDSON, STEPHEN   Celeste, and Other Sketches. 1930. One of 50 copies on Japanese vellum, numbered & signed by author & artist, presentation copy, inscription, wood engravings by John Nash, fine linen binding, fine copy, slipcase, additional set of engravings signed in pencil by artist loose in envelope. Covent 51-2484 1973 £45

HUDSON, STEPHEN   Myrtle. London, 1925. First edition, fine, d.w., orig. cloth. Crane 7-138 1974 £6

HUDSON, STEPHEN   A True Story. 1930. 8vo., orig. cloth, full forel, signed, first edition. Rota 190-541 1974 £5

HUDSON, WILLIAM HENRY   Afoot in England. 1909. 8vo., orig. cloth, foxing, first edition. Bow Windows 64-555 1974 £6.15

HUDSON, WILLIAM HENRY   Birds in a Village. London, 1893. Orig. binding, first edition, second issue, fine. Ross 87-286 1974 $20

HUDSON, WILLIAM HENRY   Birds in London. 1898. 8vo., cloth, plates. Wheldon 129-483 1974 £7.50

HUDSON, WILLIAM HENRY   Birds in London. 1898. Orig. cloth, illus., worn, scarce, first edition. Rota 188-461 1974 £5

HUDSON, WILLIAM HENRY   Birds in London. 1898. 8vo., orig. cloth, plates, scarce, first edition. Wheldon 130-554 1974 £5

HUDSON, WILLIAM HENRY   Birds in London. 1898. First edition, demy 8vo., illus., photos, very good copy, name in ink on fly, orig. cloth. Broadhurst 24-736 1974 £5

HUDSON, WILLIAM HENRY   Birds of La Plata. 1920. 2 vols., roy. 8vo., orig. cloth, plates, scarce. Wheldon 131-627 1974 £25

HUDSON, WILLIAM HENRY   Birds of La Plata. 1920. Coloured plates by H. Gronvold, first edition, 2 vols., roy. 8vo., fine, dust wrappers, orig. cloth, limited to 1500 copies. Broadhurst 24-739 1974 £40

HUDSON, WILLIAM HENRY   British Birds. 1895. 8vo., plates, cloth, scarce, first edition. Wheldon 130-553 1974 £7.50

HUDSON, WILLIAM HENRY   Flora Anglica. 1778. 8vo., 2 vols., modern half morocco, second edition. Wheldon 129-998 1974 £25

HUDSON, WILLIAM HENRY   Hampshire Days. 1903. Orig. cloth, first edition, inscription, bookplate. Rota 188-462 1974 £7.50

HUDSON, WILLIAM HENRY   A Hind In Richmond Park. London, 1922. Orig. binding, first edition, near mint. Ross 87-287 1974 $20

HUDSON, WILLIAM HENRY   A Hind in Richmond Park. London, 1928. Orig. binding, nice copy. Ross 87-288 1974 $10

HUDSON, WILLIAM HENRY   Idle Days in Patagonia. London, 1893. Orig. cloth, illus., spine faded, first edition, some foxing. MacManus 224-233 1974 $25

HUDSON, WILLIAM HENRY   Letters From. 1923. Roy 8vo., buckram, English first edition. Covent 56-648 1974 £9.50

HUDSON, WILLIAM HENRY   A Little Boy Lost. 1905. Illus., first edition, crown 8vo., exceptionally fine copy, orig. cloth, F. H. Evans' copy with his bookplate. Broadhurst 24-737 1974 £15

HUDSON, WILLIAM HENRY   A Little Boy Lost. London, 1905. Orig. cloth, illus., first edition, lightly foxed, fine. MacManus 224-234 1974 $55

HUDSON, WILLIAM HENRY   A Little Boy Lost. New York, 1920. 4to., cloth pictorially gilt, top edge gilt, illus. with color plates and b/w illus. by Dorothy Lathrop, first edition thus. Frohnsdorff 15-178 1974 $35

HUDSON, WILLIAM HENRY   153 Letters from. 1923. One of 1000 copies, numbered, roy. 8vo., buckram, fine, d.w., spare title label tipped in at end, first edition. Covent 51-954 1973 £9.50

HUDSON, WILLIAM HENRY   Osprey. 1896. 8vo., sewn, orig. wrapper, scarce. Broadhurst 23-1149 1974 £5

HUDSON, WILLIAM HENRY   Osprey; or, Egrets and Aigrettes. 1896. Demy 8vo., sewn, orig. printed paper wrapper, scarce, fine. Broadhurst 24-735 1974 £5

HUDSON, WILLIAM HENRY   The Purple Land that England Lost. 1885. 8vo., blue buckram slip-case, 2 vols., first edition. Bow Windows 64-556 1974 £375

HUDSON, WILLIAM HENRY   The Purple Land that England Lost. London, 1885. 2 vols., 8vo., orig. cloth, fine, first edition. Dawsons PM 252-473 1974 £375

HUDSON, WILLIAM HENRY   A Shepherd's Life: Impressions of the South Wiltshire Downs. London, 1924. Sixth edition, orig. binding, near mint, slightly chipped d.w. Ross 87-290 1974 $10

HUDSON, WILLIAM HENRY   The Collected Works Of. 1922-1923. 8vo., 24 vols., portraits, orig. cloth. Bow Windows 64-140 1974 £150

HUDSON, WILLIAM HENRY   The Collected Works of. 1923. 24 vols., demy 8vo., uncut, green cloth, limited to 750 copies, very fine set, plates, illus., several vols. with orig. dust wrappers. Broadhurst 24-740 1974 £220

HUDSON, WILLIAM HENRY   The Collected Works Of. 1923. 8vo., 24 vols., orig. cloth, limited edition. Broadhurst 23-1151A 1974 £200

HUE, E.   Musee Osteologique. Paris, 1907. Roy 8vo., new cloth, plates. Wheldon 129-384 1974 £48

AN HUE And Cry After Dr. Swift; Occasion'd By a True and Exact Copy of Part of His Own Diary. London, 1714. 8vo., disbound, scarce, third edition. Ximenes 35-309 1974 $100

HUEFFER, FORD MADOX
Please turn to
FORD, FORD MADOX

HUEFFER, FRANZ   Richard Wagner and the Music of the Future.
1874. Presentation, inscribed, orig. dec. cloth gilt. Covent 55-1133 1974
£17.50

HUES, ROBERT   A Learned Treatise of Globes. London, 1639.
8vo., contemporary calf, rebacked, second edition in English. Dawsons PM 245-
401 1974 £135

HUES, ROBERT   Tractatus Duo Mathematci. 1651. 12mo.,
inscription, contemporary calf, worn. Bow Windows 62-480 1974 £48

HUET, CHRISTOPHE   Singeries ou Differentes Actions. Paris, n.d.
4to., contemporary calf, gilt. Marlborough 70-24 1974 £290

HUET, J. B.   Collection de Mammiferes du Museum d'Histoire
Naturelle. Paris, 1808. Hand coloured engraved plates, demy 4to., contemporary
half calf, binding rubbed. Broadhurst 24-1117 1974 £350

HUGHES, GEORGE   The Art of Embalming Dead Saints. London,
1642. Small 4to., disbound, first edition. Ximenes 33-296 1974 £17.50

HUGHES, GRIFFITH   The Natural History of Barbados. 1750. Folio,
contemporary gilt, rebacked, first edition. Bow Windows 64-141 1974 £220

HUGHES, JOHN   Letters of Abelard and Eloisa. 1788. 8vo.,
tree calf, rebacked, plates. Hill 126-134 1974 £16

HUGHES, JOHN   Liverpool Banks and Bankers. Liverpool, 1906.
8vo., orig. cloth. Broadhurst 23-1239 1974 £5

HUGHES, JOHN   The Siege of Damascus. London, 1753. 12mo.,
modern boards, frontispiece. Dawsons PM 252-474 1974 £12

HUGHES, JOHN   Complete Works. 1865. 2 vols., ex-library.
Austin 57-310 1974 $37.50

HUGHES, MARY   Aunt Mary's New Year's Gift to Good Little
Boys and Girls Who are Learning to Read. 1822. Second edition revised, 12mo.,
orig. boards, roan spine, slightly rubbed, stitching loose in places, copperplate
frontis., ads at end. George's 610-403 1973 £6

HUGHES, MARY   The Ornaments Discovered. 1819. 12mo.,
orig. boards, roan spine, ads at end, copperplate frontis. George's 610-404
1973 £5

HUGHES, MURIEL JOY   Women Healers in Medieval Life and
Literature. New York, 1943. Paper covers, library copy. Rittenhouse
46-353 1974 $10

HUGHES, RICHARD   Evening Standard Book of Best Short Stories.
London, 1934. lst ed. Biblo & Tannen 210-546 1973 $10

HUGHES, RICHARD   A Moment of Time. 1926. 8vo., orig. cloth,
dust-wrapper, scarce, first edition. Rota 189-478 1974 £6

HUGHES, RICHARD   The Sisters' Tragedy and Three Other Plays.
1924. 8vo., orig. cloth, first English edition. Rota 189-477 1974 £7.50

HUGHES, ROBERT   Coberley Hall. Cheltenham, 1824. 8vo.,
orig. boards, scarce, first edition. Ximenes 33-297 1974 $50

HUGHES, RUPERT   Mrs. Budlong's Christmas Presents. New York,
1912. First edition, 16mo., handsome pictorial front cover, some spots on back
cover, else mint. Current BW9-46 1974 $8

HUGHES, RUPERT   The Patent Leather Kid. 1927. 240p., illus.
Austin 51-446 1973 $7.50

HUGHES, T.   The Stranger's Handbook to Chester and its
Envirous. Chester, 1856. 8vo., orig. cloth. Broadhurst 23-1414 1974 £10

HUGHES, T. E.   History of the Welsh. 1895. 8vo., orig. cloth,
illus. Broadhurst 23-1415 1974 £8

HUGHES, T. E.   History of the Welsh in Minnesota Foreston and
Lime Springs, Ia. 1895. Profusely illus., med. 8vo., orig. cloth, fine.
Broadhurst 24-1436 1974 £8

HUGO, THOMAS   Bewick's Woodcuts. London, 1870. Orig.
cloth, illus. Dawson's 424-33 1974 $225

HUGO, THOMAS   A Descriptive Catalogue of the Works of Thomas
and John Bewick. London, 1866-68. 2 vols., 8vo., orig. cloth gilt, worn.
Dawsons PM 10-36 1974 £85

HUGHES, THOMAS   Rugby, Tennessee. New York, 1881. 12mo.,
cloth. Saddleback 14-699 1974 $25

HUGHES, THOMAS   The Scouring of the White Horse. Boston,
1859. 8vo., embossed cloth, gilt-lettered spine, illus. Frohnsdorff 16-299 1974
$10

HUGHES, THOMAS   The Scouring of the White Horse. Cambridge,
1859. 8vo., orig. cloth, illus., fine, first edition. Ximenes 33-298 1974 $10

HUGHES, THOMAS   Tom Brown at Oxford. Cambridge, 1861.
3 vols., 8vo., orig. cloth, fine, first edition. Dawsons PM 252-475 1974
£145

HUGHES, THOMAS   Tom Brown's School-Days. Philadelphia, n.d.
Biblo & Tannen 213-778 1973 $7.50

HUGHES, THOMAS SMART   The History of England. London, 1836. 8vo.,
7 vols., calf, gilt, fine, third edition. Dawsons PM 251-253 1974 £15

HUGO, HERMAN 1588-1629   Pia Desideria Emblematis. Antwerp, 1628. Small
8vo., woodcuts, contemporary vellum over boards, very fine. Schafer 8-93
1973 sFr 1,200

HUGO, HERMAN 1588-1629   De Prima Scribendi Origine et Universa Rei
Literariae Antiquitate. 1617. 8vo., contemporary calf, rubbed, worn, first
edition. Dawsons PM 10-294 1974 £265

HUGO, VICTOR   Les Contemplations. Paris, 1856. 2 vols.,
8vo., contemporary three quarter brown calf, first edition. L. Goldschmidt
42-252 1974 $55

HUGO, VICTOR   Hernani. 1830. 8vo., leather, gilt, inscribed.
Quaritch 936-422 1974 £10

HUGO, VICTOR   Les Miserables. New York, Limited Editions
Club, 1938. 5 vols., slipcase, limited to 1,500 numbered copies, signed by
illus., small 4to., orig. binding. Wilson 63-530 1974 $50

HUGO, VICTOR   Napoleon le Petit. London, 1852. 12mo.,
contemporary half hard grain morocco. L. Golschmidt 42-253 1974 $30

HUGO, VICTOR   Notre-Dame de Paris. Paris, 1844. 8vo.,
full crimson levant morocco, uncut, first edition. L. Goldschmidt 42-254
1974 $300

HUGO, VICTOR   Paris. Paris, 1867. 8vo., contemporary half
hard grain morocco, gilt, first edition. L. Goldschmidt 42-255 1974 $40

HUGO, VICTOR   So This Then is the Battle of Waterloo. East
Aurora, (1907). Limp red leather. Hayman 59-249 1974 $10

HUGO, VICTOR   Les Travailleurs de la Mer. Paris, 1866.
3 vols., English contemporary half calf, gilt, early edition. Howes 185-233
1974 £12.50

HUGO, VICTOR   Les Travailleurs de la Mer. Paris, 1876.
Large 8vo., three quarter brown morocco, orig. wrapper, uncut, first illus.
edition. L. Goldschmidt 42-256 1974 $95

HUGO DE SANCTO CHARO   Sacrorum Bibliorum Vulgatae Editionis
Concordantiae. Venice, 1741. Thick folio, contemporary calf, gilt. Howes
185-1274 1974 £14

THE HUGUENOT Society of America. Abstract of Proceedings, No. One. 1884.
Austin 62-265 1974 $12.50

THE HUGUENOT Society of America. Proceedings. 1903. Austin 62-266 1974
$12.50

HUHNER, LEON   The Life of Judah Touro. 1946. 192p., illus.
Austin 62-267 1974 $8.50

HUISH, MARCUS B.   Greek Terra-Cotta Statuettes. 1900. Illus.
Covent 55-458 1974 £5.50

HUISH, MARCUS B.   Samplers and Tapestry Embroideries. 1913.
4to., plates, illus., cloth. Quaritch 940-759 1974 £38

HUISH, R.   A Treatise on the Nature, Economy and Practical
Management of Bees. 1817. 8vo., cloth backed boards, uncut. Wheldon 129-
716 1974 £20

HULBERT, ARCHER BUTLER   Forty-Niners. Boston, 1931. Green cloth,
illus., scarce, first edition. Bradley 35-39 1974 $10

HULBERT, ARCHER BUTLER   Frontiers. Boston, 1929. Green cloth, fine,
dust jacket, first edition. Bradley 35-171 1974 $10

HULDSCHINSKY, OSCAR   Die Sammlung Oscar Huldschinsky. Berlin,
1928. Folio, plates, cloth. Quaritch 940-790 1974 £12

HULL, EDWARD   The Coal-Fields of Great Britain. London, 1861.
8vo., orig. blind-stamped brown cloth, frontispiece, second edition. Dawsons
PM 245-402 1974 £7.50

HULL, EDWARD   The Coal-Fields of Great Britain. London, 1873.
8vo., orig. cloth, rebacked, plates, third edition. Hammond 201-808 1974 £10

HULL, J.   The British Flora. Manchester, 1799. 8vo.,
2 vols., contemporary half roan. Wheldon 130-1092 1974 £15

HULL, LINDLEY M.   A History of Central Washington. Spokane,
1929. 8vo., cloth, illus. Saddleback 14-749 1974 $35

HULL, NORA   The Official Records of the Centennial
Celebration, Bath, Steuben County, New York, June 4, 6,7, 1893. (Bath,
1893). 8vo., cloth. Saddleback 14-580 1974 $12.50

HULL, THOMAS   Edward and Eleonora. London, 1775. 8vo.,
disbound, first edition. Ximenes 33-299 1974 $25

HULL, THOMAS   Henry the Second. London, 1774. 8vo.,
wrappers, first edition. Ximenes 33-300 1974 $25

HULL, THOMAS   Henry the Second. London, 1774. 8vo.,
modern boards, first edition. Dawsons PM 252-476 1974 £15

HULL, THOMAS   The Perplexities. London, 1767. 8vo.,
modern boards, first edition. Dawsons PM 252-477 1974 £15

HULL, THOMAS   The Perplexities. London, 1767. 8vo.,
wrappers, first edition. Ximenes 33-301 1974 $27.50

HULL, THOMAS   The Royal Merchant. London, 1768. 8vo.,
modern boards, fine, first edition. Dawsons PM 252-478 1974 £15

HULME, F. EDWARD   Butterflies and Moths of the Country Side. (n.d.)
8vo., orig. cloth, plates. Bow Windows 64-142 1974 £6

HULME, F. EDWARD   Familiar Garden Flowers. n.d. 8vo., cloth,
5 vols., plates. Wheldon 129-1476 1974 £7.50

HULME, F. EDWARD   Familiar Wild Flowers. n.d. 4 vols., 8vo.,
orig. cloth, plates. Wheldon 131-1229 1974 £5

HULME, F. EDWARD   Wild Fruits of the Country-Side. 1902. Large
8vo., cloth, plates. Wheldon 129-999 1974 £5

HULME, F. EDWARD   Wild Fruits of the Country-Side. 1902. Large
8vo., cloth, plates. Wheldon 131-1228 1974 £5

HULME, T. E.   Speculations. 1924. Frontispiece, English
first edition. Covent 56-652 1974 £8.50

HULTON, S. F.   The Clerk of Oxford in Fiction. London,
(1909). 8vo., illus., orig. cloth, foxing, first edition. Bow Windows 62-481
1974 £6.50

HUMBOLDT, ALEXANDER, FREIHERR VON, 1769-1859   Asie Centrale. Paris,
1843. 3 vols., 8vo., contemporary mottled calf, neatly rebacked, folding map.
Wheldon 128-994 1973 £75

HUMBOLDT, ALEXANDER, FREIHERR VON, 1769-1859   Asie Centrale. Paris,
1843. 8vo., 3 vols., contemporary mottled calf, rebacked, rare. Wheldon 130-
940 1974 £75

HUMBOLDT, ALEXANDER VON   Essai Politique sur le Royaume de la
Nouvelle-Espagne. Paris, 1811. 2 large quarto vols. and an elephant folio
atlas, fine set, very little foxing, huge maps are exceptionally fine, extremely
rare. Jenkins 61-1086 1974 $2,250

HUMBOLDT, ALEXANDER VON   Experiences sur le Galvanisme. Paris, 1799.
8vo., contemporary tree calf gilt, first edition. Dawsons PM 245-403 1974 £60

HUMBOLDT, ALEXANDER VON   A Geognostical Essay on the Superposition of
Rocks in Both Hemispheres. 1823. 8vo., contemporary half calf, first English
edition. Wheldon 128-995 1973 £35

HUMBOLDT, ALEXANDER VON   A Geognostical Essay on the Superposition of
Rocks in Both Hemispheres. 1823. 8vo., contemporary half calf, first English
edition. Wheldon 131-1021 1974 £35

HUMBOLDT, ALEXANDER VON   Kosmos. Stuttgart and Tubingen, 1845-58.
8vo., 4 vols., contemporary cloth, scarce, first edition. Wheldon 130-114 1974
£30

HUMBOLDT, ALEXANDER VON   Kosmos. 1845-60. 9 vols., 8vo.,
contemporary half calf, plates, first editions, very rare. Wheldon 131-159
1974 £150

HUMBOLDT, ALEXANDER VON   Kosmos. 1845-60. Oblong 4to., orig.
stamped cloth. Wheldon 129-1705 1974 £150

HUMBOLDT, ALEXANDER VON   Kosmos. Stuttgart & Tubingen, 1845-62.
5 vols. in 6, large 8vo., atlas and oblong folio, plates, contemporary half calf,
good copy, first edition. Schafer 8-161 1973 sFr 1,300

HUMBOLDT, ALEXANDER VON   Political Essay on the Kingdom of New
Spain. New York, 1811. 2 vols., full contemporary calf, first American
edition. Jenkins 61-1087 1974 $125

HUMBOLDT, ALEXANDER VON   Researches, Concerning the Institutions and
Monuments of the Ancient Inhabitants of America. London, 1814. 2 vols., all
edges untrimmed, plates, several hand coloured, neatly rebound in boards and cloth,
orig. labels. Butterfield 10-307 1974 $125

HUMBOLDT, ALEXANDER VON   The Travels and Researches of. Edinburgh,
1832. 12mo., orig. cloth, portrait, map, ilus., scarce. Wheldon 128-205
1973 £7.50

HUMBOLDT, ALEXANDER VON   The Travels and Researches of. Edinburgh,
1836. 12mo., cloth, portrait, third edition. Wheldon 130-286 1974 £10

HUMBOLDT, ALEXANDER VON   Views of Nature. 1850. Post 8vo., cloth,
plate, coloured frontis. Wheldon 128-33 1973 £5

HUMBOLDT, ALEXANDER VON   Volcans des Cordilleres de Quito et du
Mexique. Paris, 1854. Oblong 4to., orig. boards. Wheldon 129-830 1974 £30

HUMBOLDT, ALEXANDER VON   Voyage aux Regions Equinoxiales du Nouveau
Continent fait en 1799-1804. Paris, 1816-31. 13 vols., 8vo., contemporary half
calf. Wheldon 131-362 1974 £180

HUMBOLDT, F. H. A.   Nova Genera et Species Plantarum. Paris,
1817-19. 6 parts, 4to., orig. printed wrappers, uncut, unopened. Wheldon
131-1316 1974 £60

HUME, ALLAN OCTAVIAN   The Game Birds of India, Burmah and Ceylon.
Calcutta, 1879-81. Roy. 8vo., 3 vol., new buckram. Wheldon 129-484 1974
£55

HUME, ALLAN OCTAVIAN   The Game Birds of India, Burmah and Ceylon. Calcutta, 1879-81. Roy. 8vo., 3 vols., orig. green cloth gilt, plates. Wheldon 130-557 1974 £65

HUME, ALLAN OCTAVIAN   The Game-Birds of India, Burmah and Ceylon. Calcutta, 1879-81. 3 vols., roy. 8vo., new buckram, plates, scarce, complete copy. Wheldon 131-630 1974 £55

HUME, ALLAN OCTAVIAN   Nests and Eggs of Indian Birds. 1889-90. Large 8vo., 3 vols., portraits, cloth, scarce, second edition. Wheldon 128-487 1973 £10

HUME, ALLAN OCTAVIAN   Nests and Eggs of Indian Birds, Rought Draft, Part 1. Calcutta, 1873-(1875). Roy. 8vo., half morocco, rare. Wheldon 131-629 1974 £15

HUME, DAVID   Dialogues Concerning Natural Religion. London, 1779. 8vo., contemporary sheep, spine gilt, second edition, very good copy. Ximenes 36-120 1974 $45

HUME, DAVID   Essays and Treatises on Several Subjects. 1772. 8vo., 2 vols., recent boards, new edition. Hill 126-135 1974 £17.50

HUME, DAVID   Essays and Treatises On Several Subjects. 1822. 2 vols., contemporary half morocco, gilt. Howes 185-1887 1974 £15

HUME, DAVID   Essays and Treatises on Several Subjects. 1822. 2 vols., demy 8vo., contemporary half light brown calf, marbled boards, very fine copy. Broadhurst 24-1249 1974 £21

HUME, DAVID   The History of England. n.d. Large 4to., 4 vols., illus., half red morocco, gilt. Dawsons PM 251-255 1974 £15

HUME, DAVID   The History of England. Edinburgh, Glasgow, and London, 1818. 8vo., 8 vols., contemporary tooled calf, gilt, fine. Dawsons PM 251-254 1974 £25

HUME, DAVID   The Life of. London, 1777. 8vo., modern quarter calf, first edition. Ximenes 33-302 1974 $100

HUME, FERGUS   Aladdin in London. Boston & New York, 1892. Orig. cloth, gilt, fine, first American edition. Covent 55-582 1974 £20

HUME, FERGUS   Crazy Quilt. 1919. Frontispiece, fine, first edition. Covent 55-859 1974 £5.25

HUME, FERGUS   Crazy Quilt. 1919. Illus., faded, English first edition. Covent 56-332 1974 £5.25

HUME, FERGUS   The Expedition of Captain Flick. 1896. Faded, first edition. Covent 55-860 1974 £12.50

HUME, FERGUS   The Expedition of Captain Flick. 1896. Orig. dec. cloth gilt. Covent 55-583 1974 £20

HUME, FERGUS   The Lone Inn. 1894. Orig. dec. cloth gilt, faded, bookplate. Covent 55-584 1974 £10.50

HUME, FERGUS   The Mandarin's Fan. 1904. Orig. dec. cloth, foxing. Covent 55-585 1974 £9.50

HUME, FERGUS   The Mystery of a Hansom Cab. London, n.d. Spinal extremeties cracked & rubbed, bookplate, rear hinge little weak, very good, half leather marbled boards, first edition. Covent 51-959 1973 £10.50

HUME, FERGUS   The Mystery of a Hansom Cab. 1896. Revised edition, presentation copy inscribed from author, orig. cloth, gilt stamped design on upper cover, spine discoloured, nice copy, scarce, with 18 line holograph poem by Hume. Covent 51-2374 1973 £75

HUME, FERGUS   The Pagan's Cup. New York, 1902. Orig. dec. cloth, bookplate, first American edition. Covent 55-586 1974 £12.50

HUME, FERGUS   A Son of Perdition. 1912. Orig. cloth gilt, plates. Covent 55-587 1974 £10.50

HUME, FERGUS   The Turnpike House. 1902. Orig. pictorial cloth, worn, English first edition. Covent 56-333 1974 £6.50

HUME, FERGUS   When I Lived in Bohemia. Bristol, n.d. Orig. pictorial cloth, English first edition. Covent 56-653 1974 £7.50

HUME, FERGUS   The Yellow Holly. New York, 1903. Orig. dec. cloth, first American edition. Covent 55-588 1974 £15

HUME, HUGH   The Present Interest of the People of Great Britain. London, (1758?). 8vo., modern quarter calf, gilt. Dawsons PM 247-154 1974 £12

HUME, SOPHIA   An Exhortation to the Inhabitants of the Province of South Carolina to Bring Their Deeds to the Light of Christ. Bristol, 1750. Three quarter leather. Jenkins 61-2373 1974 $55

HUME, W. F.   Geology of Egypt. Cairo, 1925. Vol. 1, roy. 8vo., orig. wrappers, plates. Wheldon 131-1022 1974 £10

HUME, W. F.   Geology of Egypt, Vol. 1, The Surface Features of Egypt, Their Determining Causes and Relation to Geological Structure. Caior, 1925. Roy. 8vo., orig. wrappers, plates, folding map, scarce. Wheldon 128-996 1973 £10

HUME, W. F.   Report on the Oilfields Region of Egypt. Cairo, 1916. Roy. 8vo., new cloth, plates, maps, scarce. Wheldon 128-997 1973 £5

HUMFREVILLE, J. LEE   Twenty Years Among Our Hostile Indians. New York, 1903. Red cloth, illus., presentation, second edition. Rinsland 58-903 1974 $25

HUMOURIST. Collection of Entertaining Tales, Anecdotes, Epigrams, etc. 1892. 4 vols., new buckram, illus. by Cruikshank coloured by hand, limited. Allen 216-812 1974 $50

HUMPHREY, HEMAN   The Promised Land. Boston, 1819. 8vo., wrapper. Butterfield 8-135 1974 $20

HUMPHREY, J. E.   The Saprolegniaceae. 1892. 4to., buckram, plates. Wheldon 129-1242 1974 £5

HUMPHREY, WILLIAM   The Religious State. c.1885. 3 vols., cloth. Howes 185-1684 1974 £12

HUMPHREY, ZEPHINE   The Story of Dorset. Rutland, c.1924. 12mo., cloth, 288 pages. Saddleback 14-736 1974 $12.50

HUMPHREYS, ARTHUR L.   East Hendred. 1923. Thick 4to., frontispiece, map, orig. buckram backed boards. Smith 194-247 1974 £5

HUMPHREYS, ARTHUR L.   A Handbook to County Bibliography. London, 1917. 4to., orig. boards, uncut. Dawsons PM 10-295 1974 £80

HUMPHREYS, ARTHUR L.   Old Decorative Maps and Charts. London, 1926. 4to., cloth, plates. Goodspeed's 578-473 1974 $87.50

HUMPHREYS, DAVID   The Miscellaneous Works. New York, 1804. 8vo., orig. boards, fine, second edition. Ximenes 33-305 1974 $70

HUMPHREYS, HENRY NOEL   Masterpieces of the Early Printers and Engravers. London, 1870. Folio, plates, orig. cloth, gilt, foxing. Bow Windows 62-482 1974 £60

HUMPHREYS, HENRY NOEL   Masterpieces of the Early Printers and Engravers. London, 1870. Orig. Victorian cloth, gilt. Dawson's 424-155 1974 $75

HUMPHREYS, HENRY NOEL   Ocean Gardens. 1857. 2 works in 1 vol., square 8vo., orig. cloth, plates. Wheldon 131-312 1974 £15

HUMPHREYS, HENRY NOEL   The Origin and Progress of the Art of Writing. 1853. Roy. 8vo., orig. cloth gilt, plates, first edition. Howes 185-718 1974 £20

HUMPHREYS, HENRY NOEL   Sentiments and Similes of William Shakespeare. (c. 1871). Small 4to., orig. cloth.   Bow Windows 64-680 1974 £35

HUMPHREYS, JOHN R.   Vandameer's Road. New York, 1946. lst ed., author's sgd. pres. Biblo & Tannen 214-734 1974 $10

HUMPHRIES, SYDNEY   Oriental Carpets, Runners and Rugs and Some Jacquard Reproductions. 1910. 4to., plates, buckram, gilt, presentation copy. Quaritch 940-403 1974 £30

HUMPHRYS-ALEXANDER, A.   Narrative of the Oppressive Law Proceedings . . . . to Overpower the Earl of Stirling. Edinburgh, 1852. Hood's 103-542 1974 $125

HUMPTY Dumpty Magical Changes. Springfield, 1878. 12mo., pictorial wrappers, spine and contents taped to wrappers. Frohnsdorff 16-588 1974 $40

HUNDRED Merry Tales, Earliest English Jestbook. 1887. 4to., new buckram, blind stamp, limited edition. Allen 216-1813 1974 $15

HUNEKER, JAMES   Iconclasts. Scribner, 1921. 430p. Austin 51-447 1973 $10

HUNEKER, JAMES   Old Fogy. Presser, 1913. 195p. Austin 51-448 1973 $12.50

HUNEKER, JAMES   Painted Veils. New York, (1920). Orig. paper backed boards, genuine first edition, paper watermarked, one of 1,200 numbered copies, signed by author, fine, dust jacket, boxed, laid-in two page A.L.s to Willard Huntington Wright. MacManus 224-235 1974 $60

HUNGERFORD, JAMES   The Old Plantation and What I Gathered There in an Autumn Month. New York, 1859. Orig. cloth, spine faded, upper hinge cracked, first edition, presentation copy. MacManus 224-236 1974 $30

HUNNEWELL, JAMES F.   Bibliography of the Hawaiian Islands. Boston, 1869. Uncut, large folio, limited to 100 copies, very rare. Jenkins 61-1026 1974 $75

HUNNEWELL, JAMES F.   The Lands of Scott. 1871. Illus., maps. Austin 61-488 1974 $10

HUNT, ELVID   History of Fort Leavenworth. Leavenworth, 1937. 8vo., cloth, maps. Saddleback 14-426 1974 $25

HUNT, FARRAR   William Holman Hunt. 1893. Orig. cloth, illus., orig. wrappers, frayed. Marsden 37-268 1974 £5

HUNT, H. C.   A Retired Habitation. 1932. 8vo., plates, half calf. Quaritch 939-599 1974 £6.50

HUNT, HENRY   Investigation at Ilchester Gaol. London, 1821. 3 works in 1 vol., 8vo., old tree calf, rubbed, plates, frontispiece. Bow Windows 62-483 1974 £16

HUNT, HOLMAN   Collective Exhibition of the Art of. . . . Catalogue. Liverpool, 1907. One of 80 numbered copies, plates, very good copy, on jap. vellum, dusty wrappers. Covent 51-2537 1973 £10

HUNT, J.   British Ornithology. Norwich, 1815(-22). 3 vols., 8vo., modern half calf, plates, rare. Wheldon 131-66 1974 £750

HUNT, LEIGH   A Book for a Corner. 1849. 8vo., orig. cloth, first edition. Bow Windows 64-558 1974 £18.50

HUNT, LEIGH   Essays. 1891. Vellum-backed cloth, near fine, English first edition. Covent 56-655 1974 £12.50

HUNT, LEIGH   Imagination and Fancy. 1844. Half calf, uncut, first edition. Howes 185-235 1974 £21

HUNT, LEIGH   Imagination and Fancy; or, Selections from the English Poets. London, 1844. Later half morocco, gilt spine, some rubbing, first edition. MacManus 224-237 1974 $27.50

HUNT, LEIGH   The Indicator. London, 1822. 8vo., calf label, mottled half calf, second collected edition. Dawsons PM 252-479 1974 £25

HUNT, LEIGH   The Indicator. 1834. 2 vols., crown 8vo., contemporary half green calf gilt, rubbed, first edition. Howes 186-262 1974 £8.50

HUNT, LEIGH   The Indicator and the Companion. 1834. 2 vols., corwn 8vo., full sprinkled calf, gilt, first edition. Howes 185-236 1974 £25

HUNT, LEIGH   A Jar of Honey from Mount Hybla. 1848. Orig. boards, illus., English first edition. Covent 56-656 1974 £15

HUNT, LEIGH   The Literary Examiner. 1823. Half green calf, first edition. Howes 185-237 1974 £30

HUNT, LEIGH   Men, Women, and Books. New York, 1847. 8vo., 2 vols., orig. cloth, slight foxing, portrait engraved, first American edition. Bow Windows 66-360 1974 £6.50

HUNT, LEIGH   Men, Women, and Books. London, 1847. 2 vols., 8vo., orig. cloth, first edition. Dawsons PM 252-480 1974 £35

HUNT, LEIGH   The Months. 1821. Small 8vo., orig. grey boards, printed label, uncut, first edition. Howes 185-238 1974 £12.50

HUNT, LEIGH   Stories from the Italian Poets, With Lives of the Writers. 1846. 2 vols., new buckram, first edition. Allen 216-2241 1974 $17.50

HUNT, LEIGH   The Town. London, 1848. 2 vols., 8vo., illus., orig. patterned cloth, first edition. Bow Windows 62-484 1974 £52

HUNT, LEIGH   The Town. London, 1848. 2 vols., 8vo., old half morocco, gilt, first edition. Dawsons PM 252-481 1974 £30

HUNT, MABEL LEIGH   Peter Piper's Pickled Peppers. New York, 1942. 16mo., pictorial cloth, illus., fine copy, dust jacket, first edition. Frohnsdorff 16-453 1974 $15

HUNT, ROCKWELL D.   California and Californians. Chicago, 1930. 4 vols., 8vo., cloth, illus. Saddleback 14-141 1974 $35

HUNT, ROCKWELL D.   California and Californians. Chicago, 1932. 4 vols., 8vo., cloth, illus. Saddleback 14-142 1974 $35

HUNT, ROCKWELL D.   Oxcart to Airplane. San Francisco, 1929. Woodcuts. Jenkins 61-339 1974 $20

HUNT, THOMAS FREDERICK   Half a Dozen Hints on Picturesque Domestic Architecture in a Series of Designs for Gate Lodges, Gamekeepers' Cottages, and Other Rural Residences. 1833. 4to., plates, orig. boards. Quaritch 940-516 1974 £28

HUNT, VIOLET   A Hard Woman. 1895. Orig. dec. cloth, bookplate, English first edition. Covent 56-657 1974 £15

HUNT, VIOLET   The Last Ditch. 1918. Orig. cloth, ex-library, signature. Rota 188-469 1974 £15

HUNT, VIOLET   More Tales of the Uneasy. London, 1925. lst ed. Biblo & Tannen 210-615 1973 $15

HUNT, VIOLET   Tales of the Uneasy. London, 1911. lst ed. Biblo & Tannen 210-616 1973 $18.50

HUNT, VIOLET   White Rose of Weary Leaf. 1908. Orig. dec. cloth, spine faded and somewhat chafed, very good copy. Covent 51-2375 1973 £15.75

HUNT, VIOLET   The Wife of Rossetti. 1932. 8vo., orig. cloth, first edition. Quaritch 936-423 1974 £15

HUNT, VIOLET   The Wife of Rossetti. 1932. Dust wrapper, plates, English first edition. Covent 56-1106 1974 £20

HUNT, W. HOLMAN   Notes. (1886). Orig. wrappers, English first edition. Covent 56-53 1974 £21

HUNT, W. HOLMAN   The Triumph of the Innocents. 1885. 4to., orig. wrappers, English first edition. Covent 56-52 1974 £50

HUNT, WILLIAM   The Political History of England. 1906-10. 12 vols., demy 8vo., maps, orig. cloth, fine. Broadhurst 24-1280 1974 £35

HUNTER, A. F.   Lake Simcoe and Its Environs. Barrie, 1893. Illus., orig. covers bound into plain hard cover binding. Hood's 102-611 1974 $25

HUNTER, ADAM   An Essay on Two Mineral Springs Recently Discovered at Harrogate. (Leeds), 1819. 8vo., orig. boards, first edition. Hammond 201-576 1974 £10

HUNTER, ADAM   A Treatise on the Mineral Waters of Harrogate and Its Vicinity. London, 1830. Orig. cloth, first edition. Hammond 201-577 1974 £8.50

HUNTER, ADAM   A Treatise on the Mineral Waters of Harrogate and Its Vicinity. London, 1838. 8vo., orig. cloth, gilt, fifth edition. Hammond 201-578 1974 £6

HUNTER, ADAM   A Treatise on the Mineral Waters of Harrogate and Its Vicinity. London, (c., 1840). 8vo., orig. boards, sixth edition. Hammond 201-579 1974 £6

HUNTER, DARD   Chinese Ceremonial Paper. (Chillicothe), 1937. Boards, illus., slipcase, signed, fine. Dawson's 424-186 1974 $850

HUNTER, DARD   Primitive Papermaking. Chillicothe, 1927. Folio, orig. half canvas, boards, fine. Dawsons PM 10-296 1974 £400

HUNTER, GEORGE LELAND   Tapestries, Their Origin, History and Renaissance. 1912. Roy. 8vo., dec. cloth, illus. Quaritch 940-760 1974 £15

HUNTER, J. MARVIN   The Trail Drivers of Texas. Nashville, 1925. Tan cloth spine, light blue cloth, gilt, signed, limited deluxe edition. Jenkins 48-482 1973 $325

HUNTER, J. MARVIN   The Trail Drivers of Texas: Interesting Sketches of Early Cowboys and Their Experiences on the Range and on the Trail. San Antonio, 1920, 1923, 1924. 3 vols, orig. pictorial cloth, boxed, rare. Jenkins 61-1093 1974 $250

HUNTER, JOHN   A Treatise on the Blood, Inflammation, and Gun-Shot Wounds. London, 1812. 8vo., 2 vols., contemporary half calf, rebacked, second edition. Dawsons PM 249-284 1974 £75

HUNTER, JOHN D.   Memoirs of a Captivity Among the Indians of North America. London, 1823. Orig. boards, uncut, first English edition. Bradley 35-173 1974 $160

HUNTER, JOHN D.   Memoirs of a Captivity Among the Indians of North America, From Childhood to the Age of Nineteen. London, 1823. Marbled boards, leather, attractive copy. Butterfield 10-314 1974 $110

HUNTER, R. E.   A Short Description of the Isle of Thanet. 1799. Small 8vo., half calf, rubbed. Quaritch 939-407 1974 £35

HUNTER, WILLIAM   The Anatomy of the Human Gravid Uterus. London, 1851. Folio, orig. green cloth, gilt. Dawsons PM 249-289 1974 £135

HUNTER, WILLIAM   The Novels and Stories of T. F. Powys. Cambridge, 1930. Orig. cloth, fine. Crane 7-269 1974 £5

HUNTER, WILLIAM   Scrutiny of Cinema. 1932. Cloth-backed boards, plates. Covent 55-406 1974 £35

HUNTER, WILLIAM S.   Hunter's Panoramic Guide from Niagara Falls to Quebec. Montreal & Boston, 1857. Map. Hood's 103-644 1974 $50

HUNTER, WILLIAM S.   Hunter's Ottawa Scenery. Ottawa, 1855. Orig. boards, plates, excellent. Hood's 103-148 1974 $500

HUNTER, WILLIAM S.   Panoramic Guide from Niagara Falls to Quebec. Boston, 1857. Engraved folding view, woodcut views, 8vo., orig. embossed cloth gilt, scarce. Sawyer 293-239 1974 £45

HUNTINGTON, ELEAZER   The American Penman. Hartford, 1824. Orig. tan printed boards, oblong 8vo., numbered full page plates, second edition, handsome copy. Butterfield 10-24 1974 $150

HUNTINGDON, FRANCIS JOHN CLARENCE WESTENRA PLAN TAGENET HASTINGS, 15TH EARL OF 1901   The Golden Octopus. 1929. Crown 4to., orig. dec. cloth backed boards, fine, limited. Howes 185-213 1974 £7.50

HUNTINGTON, WILLIAM   Contemplations On the God of Israel in A Series of Letters to a Friend. 1802-04-12. 3 works in 1 vol., contemporary half calf. Howes 185-1278 1974 £6.50

HUNTINGTON, WILLIAM   Excommunication and the Duty of All Men Who Believe. 1787-92. 4 works in 1 vol., contemporary calf, foxing. Howes 185-1279 1974 £7.50

HUPP, OTTO   Ein Missale Speciale. Munchen-Regensburg, 1898. Orig. wrappers. Kraus B8-342 1974 $12.50

HURD, RICHARD   Dialogues On the Uses of Foreign Travel. London, 1764. 8vo., disbound, first edition. Ximenes 33-307 1974 $45

HURDIS, JAMES   The Village Curate. (c. 1802?). 12mo., contemporary half roan, some stains and spotting. Bow Windows 66-677 1974 £5

HURDON, ELIZABETH   Cancer of the Uterus. London, 1942. Paper covers, library copy. Rittenhouse 46-354 1974 $10

HURE, CHARLES   Dictionnaire Universel de Philologie Sacree. Paris, 1846. 4 vols. in 2, thick roy. 8vo., half calf, rubbed. Howes 185-1281 1974 £7.50

HURLBERT, WILLIAM HENRY   Ireland Under Coercion. Edinburgh, 1888. 2 vols., 8vo., cloth boards. Emerald 50-440 1974 £7.50

HURLBURT, JESSE   The Story of Chautauqua. Putnam, 1921. 429p., illus. Austin 51-449 1973 $12.50

HURLBUTT, FRANK   Bow Porcelain. 1926. Plates, colour & half tone, roy. 4to., orig. cloth, very fine unfaded copy. Broadhurst 24-107 1974 £40

HURLBUTT, FRANK   Bristol Porcelain. 1928. 4to., plates, cloth, gilt, dust jacket. Quaritch 940-641 1974 £50

HURLBUTT, FRANK   Bristol Porcelain. (1928). Crown 4to., orig. cloth, plates, slight spotting, dust wrapper, bookplate. Bow Windows 66-362 1974 £78

HURLBUTT, FRANK   Bristol Porcelain. London, (1928). Crown 4to., orig. cloth, worn, plates. Bow Windows 62-486 1974 £78

HURLBUTT, FRANK   Chelsea China. 1937. Roy. 8vo., plates, cloth, dust wrapper, limited, edition de luxe. Quaritch 940-642 1974 £36

HURLBUTT, FRANK   Chelsea China. 1937. Limited edition-de-luxe, plates (some coloured), errata slip tipped in, 4to., orig. cloth, dust wrapper, fine, scarce, limited to 100 copies, signed by author. Sawyer 293-31 1974 £160

HURLBUTT, FRANK   Old Derby Porcelain and Its Artist-Workmen. 1925. 8vo., plates, half parchment. Quaritch 939-338 1974 £10

HURLEY, DORAN   Monsignor. Longmans, 1936. 305p. Austin 62-268 1974 $10

HURLEY, DORAN   The Old Parish. Longmans, Green, 1939. Austin 62-269 1974 $8.50

HURLEY, DORAN   Says Mrs. Crowley, Says She. Longmans, Green, 1941. Austin 62-270 1974 $10

HUROK, S.   A Memoir of the Dance World. Hermitage, 1953. 336p., illus. Austin 51-450 1973 $8.50

HURON Institute: Papers and Records, Vol. 2. Collingwood, 1914. Bound. Hood's 102-612 1974 $17.50

HURST, ARTHUR F.   Gastric and Duodenal Ulcer. London, 1929. Rittenhouse 46-355 1974 $10

HURST, FANNIE   Lummox. Harper, 1923. Austin 62-271 1974 $6.75

HURST, SIDNEY C.   The Silent Cities. New York, n.d. (c. 1929). Illus., maps, orig. binding. Wilson 63-466 1974 $10

HURT, WALTER   Truth About the Jews. Horton, 1922. 343p. Austin 62-272 1974 $12.50

HUSBANDS, J.   A Miscellany of Poems. Oxford, 1731. 8vo., contemporary calf, first edition. Dawsons PM 252-551 1974 £260

HUSENBETH, F. C.   The Life of John Milner. Dublin, 1862. Orig. cloth. Howes 185-1451 1974 £6

HUSKISSON, WILLIAM   The Question Concerning the Depreciation of Our Currency. London, 1810. 8vo., contemporary wrappers, uncut, first edition. Ximenes 33-308 1974 $60

HUSKISSON, WILLIAM   Shipping Interest. London, 1827. 8vo., modern boards, first edition. Dawsons PM 251-390 1974 £20

HUSNOT, T.   Flore Analytique et Descriptive des Mousses. 1882. 8vo., half leather, plates, second edition. Wheldon 130-1303 1974 £5

HUSNOT, T.   Hepaticolgia Gallica. Cahan, 1922. Roy. 8vo., buckram, plates, rare orig. issue, second edition. Wheldon 128-1373 1973 £5

HUSSEY, A. M.   Illustrations of British Mycology. 1847-55. 2 vols., 4to., new half morocco, hand-coloured plates. Wheldon 128-1700 1973 £250

HUSSEY, CHRISTOPHER   Eton College. 1922. Crown folio, full morocco, uncut, limited edition. Broadhurst 23-1416 1974 £10

HUSSEY, CHRISTOPHER   Eton College. 1922. Plates, crown folio, half morocco, uncut, limited to 1000 copies, fine, special Etonian edition. Broadhurst 24-1437 1974 £10

HUSSEY, CHRISTOPHER   Eton College. 1923. Crown folio, boards, plates, second edition. Broadhurst 23-1417 1974 £6

HUSSEY, CHRISTOPHER   Eton College. 1923. Plates, second edition, crown folio, boards, cloth spine, paper printed label, fine. Broadhurst 24-1438 1974 £6

HUSSEY, CHRISTOPHER   Eton College. 1932. Folio, plates, half green morocco, limited. Quaritch 939-306 1974 £15

HUSSEY, S. M.   The Reminiscences of an Irish Land Agent. London, 1904. Roy. 8vo., cloth boards. Emerald 50-441 1974 £5.50

HUSSON, ARMAND   Etude sur les Hopitaux Considerees sous le Rapport de leur Construction. Paris, 1862. Large 4to., old quarter sheep, plates. Gurney 66-90 1974 £2

HUSUNG, M. J.   Bucheinbande aus der Preussischen Staatsbibliothek zu Berlin. Leipzig, 1925. Folio, plates, orig. boards, cloth back. Quaritch 940-603 1974 £140

HUTCHESON, ARCHIBALD   Computations Relating to the Publick Debts. London, 1717. Folio, disbound, first edition. Dawsons PM 247-155 1974 £20

HUTCHINGS, JAMES MASON   In the Heart of the Sierras. Oakland, (1886). 8vo., orig. bindings, illus. Butterfield 8-747 1974 $35

HUTCHINGS, JAMES MASON   Scenes of Wonder and Curiosity in California. San Francisco, (1860). Orig. dec. red cloth, engravings, first edition. Bradley 35-41 1974 $60

HUTCHINGS, JAMES MASON   Scenes of Wonder and Curiosity in California. New York, 1870. Orig. cloth, engravings, revised edition. Bradley 35-42 1974 $26

HUTCHINGS, THOMAS GIBBONS   The Medical Pilot, or New System. New York, 1855. Rittenhouse 46-356 1974 $15

HUTCHINGS, W. W.   London Town Past and Present. (n.d. c. 1910). 4 vols., 8vo., orig. half morocco, illus., plates. Bow Windows 66-364 1974 £7.50

HUTCHINSON, A. S. M.   If Winter Comes. 1921. 415p., illus. Austin 51-451 1973 $7.50

HUTCHINSON, C. C.   Resources of Kansas. Topeka, 1871. Orig. black cloth, gilt, illus., fine, first edition. Bradley 35-211 1974 $40

HUTCHINSON, FRANK   The Australian Contingent. Sydney, 1885. 8vo., contemporary red half calf. Traylen 79-551 1973 £18

HUTCHINSON, H. N.   Extinct Monsters. 1892. Orig. cloth, scarce, first edition. Wheldon 130-941 1974 £7.50

HUTCHINSON, HORACE G.   Fishing. London, (n.d.) 2 vols., roy. 8vo., plates. Traylen 79-288 1973 £15

HUTCHINSON, J.   The Families of Flowering Plants. 1926-44. 8vo., 2 vols., cloth. Wheldon 129-922 1974 £7.50

HUTCHINSON, W.   Britain Beautiful. n.d. 4 vols., 4to., illus., orig. half leather gilt, rubbed, plates. Smith 194-298 1974 £10

HUTCHINSON, W.   The History and Antiquities of the County Palatine of Durham. Newcastle & Carlisle, 1785-94. 3 vols., 4to., half red morocco, plates. Quaritch 939-347 1974 £80

HUTTING, A. M.   Shrine of the Little Flower. 1936. 150p. Austin 62-743 1974 $7.50

HUTTON, ARTHUR WOLLASTON   Arthur Young's Tour in Ireland. London, 1892. 2 vols., 8vo., cloth boards, map. Emerald 50-442 1974 £8

HUTTON, CHARLES   Elements of Conic Sections. London, 1787. 8vo., orig. paper-backed boards, uncut, first edition. Dawsons PM 245-405 1974 £8

HUTTON, CHARLES   A Mathematical and Philosophical Dictionary. 1796,1795. 4to., 2 vols., contemporary half maroon morocco, marbled boards, ex-library. Zeitlin 235-113 1974 $150

HUTTON, CHARLES   Tracts On Mathematical and Philosophical Subjects. London, 1812. 3 vols., 8vo., orig. cloth, uncut, paper labels, first edition. Traylen 79-241 1973 £48

HUTTON, CHARLES   A Treatise on Mensuration. 1770. 4to., old calf, gilt, first edition. Dawsons PM 245-404 1974 £70

HUTTON, F. W.   Darwinism and Lamarckism Old and New. 1899. 8vo., cloth, portrait. Wheldon 131-228 1974 £5

HUTTON, F. W.   Report on the Geology and Gold Fields of Otago. Dunedin, 1875. 8vo., orig. cloth, plates, scarce. Wheldon 128-998 1973 £15

HUTTON, F. W.   Report on the Geology and Goldfields of Otago. Dunedin, 1875. 8vo., orig. cloth, scarce. Wheldon 131-1023 1974 £15

HUTTON, JAMES   The Theory of Rain. 1788-90. 4to., modern boards. Wheldon 130-942 1974 £25

HUTTON, JAMES   Theory of the Earth. Edinburgh, 1795. 8vo.,
2 vols., nineteenth century cloth backed boards, plates, illus. Wheldon 129-
831 1974 £900

HUTTON, JAMES   Theory of the Earth. Edinburgh, 1795. 2 vols.,
8vo., 19th century cloth backed boards, illus., plates. Wheldon 131-1024
1974 £900

HUTTON, JAMES   Theory of the Earth. Edinburgh, 1795. 2 vols.,
8vo., plates, modern brown half morocco, labels, first edition. Dawsons PM
250-45 1974 £1200

HUTTON, MARY A.   The Tain. Dublin, 1907. 4to., cloth boards,
first edition. Emerald 50-444 1974 £7.50

HUTTON, W.   The History of Derby. 1791. 8vo., plates,
calf back, first edition. Quaritch 939-339 1974 £40

HUXHAM, JOHN   Medical and Chemical Observations on
Antimony. London, 1756. 8vo., boards, first edition. Gurney 66-91 1974
£15

HUXHAM, JOHN   Observationes de Aere et Morbis Epidemicis.
London, 1752. 8vo., contemporary calf. Dawsons PM 249-291 1974 £26

HUXLEY, ALDOUS   After Many a Summer. 1939. First edition,
crown 8vo., mint, orig. cloth, d.w. Broadhurst 24-747 1974 £8

HUXLEY, ALDOUS   Antic Hay. New York, 1923. First U.S. edition. Covent 56-658 1974 £5

HUXLEY, ALDOUS   Antic Hay. New York, 1923. 8vo., orig.
cloth, first American edition. Rota 189-482 1974 £6.50

HUXLEY, ALDOUS   Antic Hay. London, 1923. First edition, yellow
cloth, lacking d.w., nice tight copy. Ross 86-264 1974 $20

HUXLEY, ALDOUS   Arabia Infelix and Other Poems. 1929. Roy
8vo., boards, uncut, signed, limited edition. Broadhurst 23-772 1974 £25

HUXLEY, ALDOUS   Arabia Infelix and Other Poems. 1929. Roy.
8vo., boards, linen spine, uncut, one of 692 copies, handmade paper, signed by
author, fine. Broadhurst 24-744 1974 £26

HUXLEY, ALDOUS   Brave New World. London, 1932. First
edition, nice copy, orig. cloth. Crane 7-143 1974 £6.50

HUXLEY, ALDOUS   Brave New World. 1932. First edition, crown
8vo., fine, dust wrapper, orig. cloth. Broadhurst 24-746 1974 £25

HUXLEY, ALDOUS   Brave New World. London, 1932. 8vo.,
orig. cloth, dust wrapper, first edition. Dawsons PM 252-482 1974 £50

HUXLEY, ALDOUS   Brief Candles. 1930. 324 pages, orig. edition.
Austin 61-490 1974 $10

HUXLEY, ALDOUS   Brief Candles. 1930. Orig. American edition.
Austin 61-491 1974 $10

HUXLEY, ALDOUS   Brief Candles. London, 1930. Orig. binding,
first edition, d.w. slightly darkened, else near mint. Ross 87-295 1974 $20

HUXLEY, ALDOUS   Brief Candles. New York, 1930. Fine copy,
autographed. Jenkins 48-259 1973 $27.50

HUXLEY, ALDOUS   Brief Candles. New York, 1930. First U. S.
edition, one of 842 copies, numbered & signed by author, nice copy. Covent
51-2376 1973 £20

HUXLEY, ALDOUS   Brief Candles. New York, 1930. Signed, first
U.S. edition. Covent 56-659 1974 £30

HUXLEY, ALDOUS   The Cicadas, and Other Poems. 1931. One of
160 copies, numbered & signed by author, buckram backed dec. boards, very
nice copy. Covent 51-2377 1973 £35

HUXLEY, ALDOUS   Crome Yellow. London, 1921. First edition,
yellow cloth, extra spine label tipped in, signed by author, covers somewhat
dust-stained, near fine, scarce. Ross 86-265 1974 $70

HUXLEY, ALDOUS   The Defeat of Youth and Other Poems. Oxford,
1918. Backstrip torn, title label 3/4 missing, bookplate, contents little loose,
else good copy, scarce, wrappers, first edition. Covent 51-966 1973 £17.50

HUXLEY, ALDOUS   The Defeat of Youth and Other Poems. 1918.
Orig. limp boards, label, uncut, rare, first edition. Howes 185-239 1974 £35

HUXLEY, ALDOUS   The Discovery. 1924. Small 8vo., dec. boards,
uncut, limited, first edition. Quaritch 936-424 1974 £14

HUXLEY, ALDOUS   Do What You Will. 1929. One of 260 copies,
numbered & signed by author, cloth backed patterned boards, very nice copy.
Covent 51-2378 1973 £32.50

HUXLEY, ALDOUS   Do What You Will: Essays. 1929. Dust wrapper,
fine, English first edition. Covent 56-1813 1974 £8.50

HUXLEY, ALDOUS   Do What You Will: Essays. 1929. Demy 8vo.,
dec. boards, cloth spine, uncut, limited, one of 260 copies, signed by author.
Broadhurst 24-743 1974 £25

HUXLEY, ALDOUS   Ends and Means. London, 1937. Orig. binding,
first edition, d.w. slightly soiled & torn, else fine. Ross 87-296 1974 $12.50

HUXLEY, ALDOUS   Essays. 1929. 8vo., dec. boards, cloth, uncut,
signed, limited edition. Broadhurst 23-771 1974 £25

HUXLEY, ALDOUS   Eyeless in Gaza. 1936. 8vo., mint, dust-
wrapper, first edition. Broadhurst 23-775 1974 £6

HUXLEY, ALDOUS   Holy Face and Other Essays. 1929. Limited
edition, coloured title illus., coloured illus., large 8vo., orig. cloth, uncut,
top edges gilt, slip in case, very good copy, limited to 300 copies. Sawyer
293-169 1974 £38

HUXLEY, ALDOUS   Jesting Pilate. New York, 1928. Biblo &
Tannen 213-779 1973 $8.50

HUXLEY, ALDOUS   Leda. New York, 1929. Orig. linen, signed,
English first edition. Covent 56-1815 1974 £42.50

HUXLEY, ALDOUS   Mortal Coil. Harper, 1922. 207p. Austin
51-452 1973 $10

HUXLEY, ALDOUS   Music at Night and Other Essays. New York,
1931. First U. S. edition, one of 842 copies, numbered & signed by author,
buckram backed marbled boards, fine, glassine wrapper. Covent 51-2380 1973
£25

HUXLEY, ALDOUS   On the Margin. New York, 1923. 1st Amer.
ed. Biblo & Tannen 210-744 1973 $7.50

HUXLEY, ALDOUS   Pacifism and Philosophy. 1936. Dust wrapper,
fine, English first edition. Covent 56-663 1974 £12.50

HUXLEY, ALDOUS   Point Counter Point. 1928. Half morocco,
gilt. Smith 193-370 1973 £6

HUXLEY, ALDOUS   Point Counter Point. 1928. Red binding,
near fine, first edition. Covent 55-868 1974 £10

HUXLEY, ALDOUS   Point Counter Point. London, 1928. First
trade edition, lacking d.w., covers worn, spine somewhat faded & creased, not
a collector's copy, orig. binding. Ross 86-267 1974 $20

HUXLEY, ALDOUS   Point Counter Point. London, 1928. Cloth,
dust wrapper, inscribed, first edition. Dawson's 424-279 1974 $75

HUXLEY, ALDOUS   Proper Studies. 1927. One of 260 copies,
numbered & signed by author, buckram backed marbled boards, nice copy.
Covent 51-2381 1973 £30

HUXLEY, ALDOUS   Rotunda. London, 1932. 1st ed. Biblo &
Tannen 213-551 1973 $12.50

HUXLEY, ALDOUS   Selected Poems. Oxford, 1925. Orig. patterned boards, English first edition. Covent 56-664 1974 £21

HUXLEY, ALDOUS   Those Barren Leaves. London, 1925. First
edition, rust cloth, printed label, d.w. soiled & slightly torn, very nice copy.
Ross 86-268 1974 $20

HUXLEY, ALDOUS   Time Must Have a Stop. New York, 1944.
First American edition, very slightly torn & soiled d.w., orig. binding, near mint.
Ross 87-298 1974 $10

HUXLEY, ALDOUS   Time Must Have a Stop. London, 1945. First
English edition, d.w. somewhat chipped, very nice, orig. binding. Ross 86-269
1974 $10

HUXLEY, ALDOUS   Vulgarity in Literature. London, 1930. Dec.
boards, lacking d.w., bookplate, nice copy. Ross 86-270 1974 $15

HUXLEY, ALDOUS   The World of Light. London, 1931. First
trade edition, d.w. slightly soiled, orig. binding, near mint. Ross 87-299 1974
$10

HUXLEY, ALDOUS   The World of Light. 1931. One of 160 copies,
numbered & signed by author, buckram backed patterned boards, very nice copy.
Covent 51-2382 1973 £27

HUXLEY, ALDOUS   Young Archimedes and Other Stories. New
York, 1924. Biblo & Tannen 210-881 1973 $7.50

HUXLEY, C. T.   The Crayfish. (1880). Crown 8vo., cloth.
Wheldon 129-784 1974 £5

HUXLEY, JULIAN   If I Were Dictator. 1934. Ex-library.
Austin 61-497 1974 $10

HUXLEY, LEONARD   Life and Letters of Thomas Henry Huxley.
1900. 2 vols., illus. Austin 61-498 1974 $17.50

HUXLEY, LEONARD   Life and Letters of Thomas Henry Huxley. 1900.
8vo., 2 vols., cloth, illus. Wheldon 129-155 1974 £7.50

HUXLEY, THOMAS HENRY   American Addresses. 1877. 8vo., orig.
cloth. Wheldon 131-161 1974 £10

HUXLEY, THOMAS HENRY   American Addresses. 1886. 8vo., cloth.
Wheldon 130-116 1974 £5

HUXLEY, THOMAS HENRY   Collected Essays. (1893-95). 9 vols., crown
8vo., cloth. Wheldon 131-164 1974 £18

HUXLEY, THOMAS HENRY   Critiques and Addresses. 1890. 8vo., cloth.
Wheldon 131-163 1974 £5

HUXLEY, THOMAS HENRY   Diary on the Voyage of H.M.S. Rattlesnake.
1935. Roy 8vo., cloth, plates, scarce. Wheldon 130-288 1974 £15

HUXLEY, THOMAS HENRY   Diary on the Voyage of H.M.S. Rattlesnake.
1935. Roy. 8vo., cloth, plates, scarce. Wheldon 131-363 1974 £10

HUXLEY, THOMAS HENRY   Diary of the Voyage of H. M. S. Rattlesnake.
New York, 1936. Rittenhouse 46-358 1974 $10

HUXLEY, THOMAS HENRY   Evidence as to Man's Place in Nature. New
York, 1863. Frontis., first American edition. Ballinger 1-276 1974 $25

HUXLEY, THOMAS HENRY   Evidence As to Man's Place in Nature. 1863.
8vo., orig. cloth. Wheldon 131-160 1974 £40

HUXLEY, THOMAS HENRY   Evidence as Man's Place In Nature. London,
1863. 8vo., cloth, illus., first edition. Gilhofer 61-54 1974 sFr. 650

HUXLEY, THOMAS HENRY   Evidence as to Man's Place in Nature.
London, 1863. 8vo., orig. green cloth, first edition. Dawsons PM 250-46
1974 £70

HUXLEY, THOMAS HENRY   Evidence as to Man's Place in Nature. 1863.
8vo., new cloth, scarce, first edition. Wheldon 130-117 1974 £30

HUXLEY, THOMAS HENRY   Evidence as to Man's Place in Nature. 1864.
8vo., plate, orig. cloth, text figures. Wheldon 128-35 1973 £10

HUXLEY, THOMAS HENRY   Lay Sermons, Addresses, and Reviews. 1880.
8vo., orig. cloth, new edition. Wheldon 130-115 1974 £5

HUXLEY, THOMAS HENRY   Lay Sermons, Addresses and Reviews. 1883.
8vo., cloth. Wheldon 131-162 1974 £5

HUXLEY, THOMAS HENRY   A Manual of the Anatomy of Vertebrated Animals. 1871. Crown 8vo., cloth. Wheldon 130-360 1974 £15

HUXLEY, THOMAS HENRY   A Manual of the Anatomy of Invertebrated
Animals. 1877. 8vo., cloth. Wheldon 129-783 1974 £7.50

HUXLEY, THOMAS HENRY   The Oceanic Hydrozoa. 1859. Folio, orig.
boards, plates by author, nice copy, slip case, scarce. Wheldon 128-903 1973
£30

HUXLEY, THOMAS HENRY   The Oceanic Hydrozoa. 1859. Folio, orig.
boards, plates, scarce. Wheldon 130-871 1974 £15

HUXLEY, THOMAS HENRY   The Oceanic Hydrozoa. 1859. Folio, orig.
boards, plates. Wheldon 131-933 1974 £30

HUYGENS, CHRISTIAN   Astroscopia Compendiaria, Tubi Optici
Molimine Liberata. The Hague, 1684. 4to., boards, fine, full page engravings,
first edition. Kraus 137-48 1974 $950

HUYGENS, CHRISTIAN   De Circuli Magnitudine Inventa. Leiden,
1654. First edition, 4to., boards, woodcut diagrams. Kraus 137-42 1974
$2,500

HUYGENS, CHRISTIAN   Horologium. The Hague, 1658. Folded
engraved plate, small 4to., half vellum, first edition, with the two added leaves,
from the library of F. X. von Zach. Kraus 137-43 1974 $12,500

HUYGENS, CHRISTIAN   Horologium Oscillatorium. Paris, 1673. Folio,
contemporary sheep, first edition. Dawsons PM 245-406 1974 £1,750

HUYGENS, CHRISTIAN   Horologium Oscillatorium. Paris, 1673. Folio,
illus., contemporary sheep, rubbed, first edition. Dawsons PM 250-47 1974
£1,950

HUYGENS, CHRISTIAN   Horologium Oscillatorium Sive de Motu
Pendulorum ad Horologia Aptata Demonstrationes Geometricae. Paris, 1673. Folio,
contemporary (probably orig.) brown calf, large & thick paper copy, author's own
copy with words of manuscript additions. Kraus 137-47 1974 $25,000

HUYGENS, CHRISTIAN   Kort Onderwys Aengaende het Gebruyck der
Horologien tot het Vinden der Lenghten van Oost en West. N.P., n.d. (The
Hague, 1665). Small 4to., half vellum, first edition, rare, F. X. von Zach's
copy. Kraus 137-46 1974 $16,500

HUYGENS, CHRISTIAN   Kosmotheoros, Sive de Terris Coelestibus. The
Hague, 1698. 4to., contemporary vellum, rebacked, plates, first edition.
Schuman 37-128 1974 $450

HUYGENS, CHRISTIAN   Kosmotheoros Sive de Terris Coelestibus,
Earumque Ornatu. The Hague, 1698. Engraved folding plates, 4to., boards,
first edition, with an extra folding plate. Kraus 137-49 1974 $1,250

HUYGENS, CHRISTIAN   Nouveau Traite de la Pluralite des Mondes.
Amsterdam, 1718. 12mo., modern half calf, plates. Dawsons PM 245-409 1974
£40

HUYGENS, CHRISTIAN   Opera Varia. 1724. 4to., 2 vols., plates, gilt,
contemporary calf, fine, first collected edition. Dawsons PM 245-411 1974
£160

HUYGENS, CHRISTIAN   Opuscula Postuma. 1703. 4to., contemporary vellum, fine, illus., plates, first edition. Dawsons PM 245-410 1974 £145

HUYGENS, CHRISTIAN   Systema Saturnium, Sive de Causis Mirandorum Saturni Phaenomenon, et Comite Ejus Planeta Novo. The Hague, 1659. 4to., boards, engravings, woodcuts, first edition, fine. Kraus 137-44 1974 $1,950

HUYGENS, CHRISTIAN   Traite de L'Horloge a Pendule. (Paris, n.d.). 4to., boards, 2 vols. Zeitlin 235-115 1974 $900

HUYSMANS, JORIS KARL   La Bievre et Saint-Severin. 1898. 12mo., orig. wrappers, uncut, marbled boards, first edition. Bow Windows 64-559 1974 £145

HYAKUZO, KURATA   The Priest and His Disciples. Doran, 1927. 246p., illus. Austin 51-453 1973 $10

HYAMSON, A. M.   A Dictionary of Universal Biography of All Ages and of All People. London, 1916. Crown 4to., orig. cloth, 2 corners bumped, bit warped and dust soiled. Forster 98-79 1974 £3

HYATT, CARL B.   The Gateway to Citizenship. 1943. 153 pages. Austin 57-313 1974 $10

HYATT, CARL B.   The Gateway to Citizenship. 1943. 153p. Austin 62-274 1974 $10

HYDE, DOUGLAS   Abhrain Zraoh Chuize Connacht. 1893. Lacks all binding, inscription. Smith 194-474 1974 £8.50

HYDE, DOUGLAS   Love Songs of Connacht. Dublin, 1905. 8vo., full calf, gilt, fourth edition. Emerald 50-445 1974 £7.50

HYDE, EDWARD
Please turn to
CLARENDON, EDWARD HYDE

HYDE, H.   The Mistakes. 1758. 8vo., cloth, first edition. Quaritch 936-112 1974 £10

HYDE, H. MONTGOMERY   Londonderry House and Its Pictures. London, n.d. (1937). Cloth covers somewhat dust stained, plates, lacking d.w. Ross 87-193 1974 $12.50

HYDE, H. MONTGOMERY   Londonderry House and Its Pictures. London, n.d. (1937). Plates, lacking d.w., cloth covers somewhat dust stained, very nice copy. Ross 86-28 1973 £12.50

HYDE, JAMES   The Science of Cotton Spinning. n.d. Orig. cloth, new revised edition. Covent 55-1310 1974 £8.50

HYDE, NANCY MARIA   The Writings . . . Connected With a Sketch of Her Life. Norwich, 1816. 12mo., contemporary half calf, first edition. Ximenes 33-309 1974 $40

HYDER, ALAN   Vampires Overhead. 1935. Stained covers, first edition. Covent 55-648 1974 £21

HYETT, FRANCIS ADAMS   The Bibliographer's Manual of Gloucestershire Literature. Gloucester, 1895. 3 vols., 8vo., orig. buckram, fine, limited. Dawsons PM 10-243 1974 £65

HYETT, FRANCIS ADAMS   The Bibliographer's Manual of Gloucestershire. Gloucester, 1895-97. 5 vols., 4to., buckram, limited. Quaritch 939-360 1974 £60

HYGINUS, CAIUS JULIUS   Poeticon Astronomicon. Venice, 1485. Small 4to., modern calf, illus., very fine. Schafer 8-94 1973 sFr. 7,800

HYGINUS GROMATICUS   De Castris Romanis, Quae Exstant. 1660. New buckram, plates. Allen 213-558 1973 $25

HYMNI et Collectae, Item Evangelia, Epistolae, Introitvs, Gradvalia, et Seqventiae. Coloniae, 1566. Thick small 8vo., contemporary calf, rebacked with modern morocco, fore-edges rubbed, woodcuts. Thomas 32-351 1974 £100

HYMNS and Prayers for Use at the Marriage of Michael Hornby and Nicolette Ward at St. Margaret's Church, Westminster, November 15, 1928. 1928. 8vo., orig. paper wrappers, fine copy, uncut. Sawyer 293-44 1974 £75

HYMNS and Prayers for Use at the Marriage of Roger Anthony Hornby and Veronica Blackwood at St. Paul's Church, Knightsbridge, December XVII, MCMXXXI. 1931. Printed in red and black, 8vo., orig. paper wrappers, fine copy. Sawyer 293-50 1974 £95

HYMNS for the Sundays & Chief Festivals of the Christian Year. 1861. Small 4to., plates, illus., dark blue morocco. Smith 194-889 1974 £6

HYNDMAN, HENRY MAYERS   The Evolution of Revolution. 1920. Portrait, first edition. Howes 186-1461 1974 £5

HYNDMAN, HENRY MAYERS   The Record of An Adventurous Life. 1911-12. 2 vols., thick 8vo., orig. cloth, first editions. Howes 185-240 1974 £7.50

HYNE, C. J. CUTCLIFFE   The Lost Continent. 1900. Orig. dec. cloth, gilt, fine, English first edition. Covent 56-1747 1974 £15

HYNE, C. J. CUTCLIFFE   The Rev. Captain Kettle. 1925. First edition. Covent 55-874 1974 £6

HYRTL, JOSEPH   Handbuch der Topographischen Anatomie. 1853. 8vo., contemporary blue half roan, second edition. Dawsons PM 249-292 1974 £17

I

IACOBI Hollerii Stempani, Medici. Parissiis, 1582. 12mo., cover loosening at spine. Rittenhouse 46-350 1974 $250

IACOVLEFF, ALEXANDRE Dessins et Peintures d'Afrique. Paris, 1927. Limited edition-de-luxe, 4to., suede backed black satin, plates separate, rare, preserved in leather folder as issued, limited to 750 copies. Sawyer 293-7 1974 £150

IBBETSON, JOHN HOLT Specimens in Eccentric Circular Turning. London, n.d. 8vo., orig. quarter cloth, boards, third edition. Ximenes 33-310 1974 $45

IBN BUTLAN, ABU-L-HASAN AL-MUKHTAR IBN AL-HASAN Tacuini Sanitatis. Schott, 1531-32. 4 works in 2, folio, old calf, rebacked, first editions. Schuman 37-35 1974 $1500

IBSEN, HENRIK Hedda Gabler. Copenhagen, 1890. 8vo., contemporary half calf, fine, first edition. Gilhofer 61-64 1974 sFr. 400

IBSEN, HENRIK Hedda Gabler. 1891. Small 4to., orig. wrappers, English first edition. Covent 56-666 1974 £17.50

IBSEN, HENRIK John Gabriel Borkman. New York, 1906. 12mo. Biblo & Tannen 210-882 1973 $7.50

IBSEN, HENRIK The Master Builder. 1895. Small 4to., orig. wrappers, English first edition. Covent 56-667 1974 £17.50

IBSEN, HENRIK Peer Gynt. New York, 1929. 4to., boards, cloth spine, paper label, boards rubbed & faded, full page color plates, illus., first edition. Frohnsdorff 16-531 1974 $10

IBSEN, HENRIK Peer Gynt. London, 1936. No. 243 of edition limited to 460 signed copies, covers very slightly yellowed, mint, orig. box, light glassine wrapper, illus. by Arthur Rackham. Ross 87-470 1974 $225

IBSEN, HENRICK Collected Works. 1906-09. 11 vols., crown 8vo., orig. cloth gilt, copyright edition. Howes 186-268 1974 £40

IBSEN, HENRIK Collected Works. 1906-12. Small 8vo., 12 vols., cloth, faded. Quaritch 936-426 1974 £40

IBSEN, HENRIK The Collected Works Of. 1910-12. 11 vols., 8vo., orig. cloth, inscription, spines and some sides faded. Bow Windows 66-366 1974 £25

IDAHO - GOVERNOR Report of the...to the Secretary of the Interior. Washington, 1882. Printed wrappers, scarce. Jenkins 61-1099 1974 $17.50

IDAHO - GOVERNOR Report of...to the Secretary of the Interior. Washington, 1884. Green printed wrappers. Jenkins 61-1100 1974 $15

IDAHO - GOVERNOR Report of...to the Secretary of the Interior. Washington, 1887. Green printed wrappers, stamped presentation. Jenkins 61-1101 1974 $15

IDAHO - GOVERNOR Report of...to the Secretary of the Interior. Washington, 1888. Green printed wrappers. Jenkins 61-1102 1974 $13.50

IDAHO - GOVERNOR Report of...to the Secretary of the Interior. Washington, 1889. Jenkins 61-1103 1974 $12.50

IDAHO - GOVERNOR Report of...to the Secretary of the Interior. Washington, 1890. Fine folding map, good contents. Jenkins 61-1104 1974 $12.50

IDEAS On Film. Funk, Wagnalls. Austin 51-917 1973 $12.50

IGNATIUS Epistolae, Cum Genuinae, Tum Dibliae et Supposititiae. 1857. Roy. 8vo., cloth. Howes 185-1283 1974 £5.50

IGUINIZ, J. B. La Imprenta en la Nueva Espana. Mexico, 1938. Illus. Jenkins 61-1109 1974 $25

ILDEFONSO, SAINT De Laudibus Virginis Mariae. Basel, 1557. Small 8vo., contemporary limp vellum, rare, fine, woodcut. Harper 213-93 1973 $450

ILES, GEORGE Flame Electricity, and the Camera. New York, 1901. Rittenhouse 46-359 1974 $15

ILLINGWORTH, CAYLEY A Topographical Account of the Parish of Scampton. 1808. 4to., contemporary red morocco, presentation copy, inscribed. Broadhurst 23-1418 1974 £26

ILLINGWORTH, J. A. A Just Narrative. London, 1678. 2 items in 1 vol., half calf. Quaritch 939-549 1974 £80

ILLINOIS Annual Report of the Adjutant General of the State of Illinois. Springfield, 1863. Jenkins 61-1110 1974 $12.50

ILLINOIS STATE BOARD OF HEALTH Report of the Sanitary Investigations of the Illinois River and Its Tributaries With Special Reference to the Effect of the Sewage of Chicago. Springfield, 1901. Charts, maps. Rittenhouse 46-360 1974 $10

ILLINOIS STATE HISTORICAL SOCIETY Transactions of . . . 1908. Springfield, 1909. Illus. Jenkins 61-1127 1974 $10

ILLUMINATED Manuscripts, Incunabula and Americana From the Famous Libraries of the Marquess of Lothian. New York, 1932. 4to., orig. wrappers, plates. Dawsons PM 10-374 1974 £26

ILLUSTRATED BRITISH Ballads, Old and New. n.d. 4to., illus., English first edition. Covent 56-700 1974 £12.50

ILLUSTRATED Catalogue of MacFarlane's Castings. Glasgow, n.d. Orig. cloth, illus., sixth edition. Marsden 39-289 1974 £30

AN ILLUSTRATED Handbook of the London Theatres. London, 1879-92. 12 vols., 8vo., illus., orig. paper wrappers. Bow Windows 62-922 1974 £10

ILLUSTRATED Historical Atlases of Ontario County. 1875-1906. 32 vols., rare. Hood's 104-1 1974 $8875

AN ILLUSTRATED History of Los Angeles County, California. Chicago, 1889. 4to., leather, illus. Saddleback 14-171 1974 $75

AN ILLUSTRATED History of Southern California. Chicago, 1890. 4to., leather, rebacked. Saddleback 14-284 1974 $75

AN ILLUSTRATED History of the Yellowstone Valley. Spokane, (c.1907). 4to., leather. Saddleback 14-533 1974 $125

ILLUSTRATIONS of the Textile Manufactures of India. 1881. Large folio, plates, orig. cloth gilt. Smith 193-491 1973 £40

IMAGE, SELWYN Letters. 1932. Cloth-backed boards, portrait, fine, dust wrapper, limited. Covent 55-907 1974 £12.50

IMISON, JOHN The School of Arts. London, (1794). 8vo., contemporary half calf, gilt, plates, second edition. Hammond 201-837 1974 £32

IMITATIO CHRISTI De Imitatione Christi. Paris, 1640. Folio, blue boards, leather back, frontis., inscription. Harper 213-94 1973 $475

IMITATIO CHRISTI Of the Imitation of Jesus Christ. London, 1828. 8vo., orig. cloth, paper label, first edition. Traylen 79-162 1973 £6

IMLAY, GEORGE GILBERT A Topographical Description of the Western Territory of North America. London, 1793. 8vo., contemporary tooled calf, second edition. Butterfield 8-297 1974 $200

IMLAY, GEORGE GILBERT A Topographical Description of the Western Territory of North America. London, 1793. Second edition, enlarged, full morocco, title page repaired, maps, large folding map is cloth backed. Jenkins 61-1132 1974 $67.50

THE IMMIGRANTS in America Review. 1915-16. 2 vols., ex-library. Austin 57-315 1974 $72.50

IMMIGRATION: Select Documents and Case Records. Chicago, 1924. Austin 62-2 1974 $17.50

IMPERIAL Fresno: Resources, Industries and Scenery. Fresno, 1897. Oblong 8vo., cloth. Saddleback 14-105 1974 $35

IMRIE, J. Songs and Miscellaneous Poems. Toronto, 1891. Illus. Hood's 104-760 1974 $12.50

IMRIE, N. A Catalogue of Specimens Illustrative of the Geology of Greece and Part of Macedonia. (Edinburgh), 1817. 4to., half leather, plates, large paper copy. Wheldon 128-999 1973 £7.50

IN and About Beautiful Spokane. Spokane, (1913). Small folio, wrapper, illus. Jenkins 61-2574 1974 $10

IN the Shade. 1861. 8vo., orig. apple-green cloth, soiled, first edition. Ximenes 33-20 1974 $10

INCA, EL
Please turn to
GARCILASO DE LA VEGA

INCHBALD, ELIZABETH Appearance is Against Them. London, 1785. 8vo., modern boards, first edition. Dawsons PM 252-483 1974 £15

INCHBALD, ELIZABETH A Collection of Farces and Other Afterpieces. 1809. 4 vols., contemporary calf. Howes 186-270 1974 £7.50

INCHBALD, ELIZABETH I'll Tell You What. London, 1786. 8vo., modern boards, first edition. Dawsons PM 252-484 1974 £15

INCHBALD, ELIZABETH I'll Tell You What. 1786. 8vo., cloth, first edition. Quaritch 936-113 1974 £7

INCHBALD, ELIZABETH Next Door Neighbours. 1791. 8vo., cloth, first edition. Quaritch 936-114 1974 £7

INCHBALD, ELIZABETH Next Door Neighbours. London, 1791. 8vo., modern boards, first edition. Dawsons PM 252-485 1974 £15

INCHBALD, ELIZABETH Such Things Are. 1788. 8vo., cloth, first edition. Quaritch 936-115 1974 £9

INCHBALD, ELIZABETH The Wedding Day. London, 1794. 8vo., disbound, first edition. Ximenes 33-315 1974 $22.50

INCHBALD, ELIZABETH The Wedding Day. London, 1794. 8vo., modern boards, first edition. Dawsons PM 252-486 1974 £15

INCHBALD, ELIZABETH The Widow's Vow. London, 1786. 8vo., modern boards, first edition. Dawsons PM 252-487 1974 £15

INCHBALD, ELIZABETH The Widow's Vow. 1786. 8vo., cloth, first edition. Quaritch 936-116 1974 £7

INDEX Librorum Prohibitorum Sanctissimi Domini Nostri PII Sexti Pontificis Maximi Jussu Editus. Rome, 1806. Small 8vo., contemporary tree calf, morocco label. Dawsons PM 10-485 1974 £18

THE INDEX of Twentieth Century Artists. Vol I, Nos. 1-12. New York, 1933-34. Bdg. worn; scarce. Biblo & Tannen 214-504 1974 $95

INDEX of Wills and Administrations now Preserved in the Probate Registry at Canterbury. 1920. Faded. Howes 186-2049 1974 £7.50

AN INDEX to Dr. Nash's Collections for a History of Worcestershire. Worcester, 1894-95. 2 parts, 4to., buckram. Quaritch 939-589 1974 £12.50

INDEXES of the Great White Book and the Black Book of the Cinque Ports. 1905. 4to., orig. cloth, scarce. Howes 186-2030 1974 £7.50

INDIA, FRANCISCUS De Gvita Podagrica, Chiragrica. 1600. Small 4to., old vellum. Dawsons PM 249-293 1974 £95

INDIAN Arms - an Illustrated Handbook, being a Classified and Descriptive Catalogue of the Arms Exhibited at the India Museum. 1880. 4to., boards, folding map, full page plates, some in colour. Eaton Music-613 1973 £25

INDIANA - GENERAL ASSEMBLY Laws of a General Nature Passed and Published at the 19th Session of. Indianapolis, 1835. Printed wrappers, dust soiled. Hayman 59-298 1974 $15

INDUSTRIES of Canada; Historical and Commercial Sketches of Toronto and Environs. Toronto, 1866. Illus. Hood's 102-27 1974 $50

THE INFLUENCE of Immigration on American Culture. 41p. 1929. Austin 62-107 1974 $17.50

INGALLS, JOHN JAMES A Collection of the Writings. Kansas City, 1902. Rebacked, orig. label, front cover loose. Butterfield 10-328 1974 $10

AN INFORMATION to All Good Christians Within the Kingdome of England. Edinburgh, 1639. Small 4to., disbound, first edition. Ximenes 35-133 1974 $22.50

INGALS, E. FLETCHER Diseases of the Chest, Throat and Nasal Cavities. New York, 1898. Revised third edition. Rittenhouse 46-362 1974 $15

INGELOW, JEAN Poems. London, 1885. 8vo., orig. green cloth gilt, fine, first edition. Dawsons PM 252-488 1974 £45

INGERSOLL, C. M. Catalogue of Connecticut Volunteer Organizations. Hartford, 1869. Foxed. Jenkins 61-696 1974 $13.50

INGERSOLL, C. M. Catalogue of the Connecticut Volunteer Organizations. Hartford, 1869. Foxed, 936 pages. Jenkins 61-697 1974 $15

INGERSOLL, L. A. Ingersoll's Century Annals of San Bernardino County. Los Angeles, 1904. 4to., leather. Saddleback 14-146 1974 $75

INGHAM, ALFRED Altrincham and Bowden, With Historical References of Ashton-on-Mersey, Sale, and Surrounding Townships. 1879. Demy 4to., newly bound in half light brown calf, plates, limited to 200 copies, very fine state, entirely free from foxing. Broadhurst 24-1440 1974 £21

INGHIRAMI, F. Monumenti Etruschi o di Etrusco Nome. 1821-26. 7 vols. in 10, 4to., contemporary quarter dark green roan, leather labels, plates. Quaritch 940-326 1974 £500

INGLEBY, CLEMENT MANSFIELD Shakespeare's Centurie of Prayse. 1879. Roy. 8vo., contemporary hard grained blue morocco gilt, frontispiece, revised second edition. Smith 194-233 1974 £5

INGLEBY, CLEMENT MANSFIELD Shakespeare's Centurie of Prayse. (1879). 4to., orig. buckram, revised second edition. Howes 185-436 1974 £8.50

INGLESIDE, California. Ingleside, n.d. Hand colored illus., wrapper, folio. Jenkins 61-340 1974 $11.50

INGLIS, HENRY DAVID 1795-1835 Rambles in the Footsteps of Don Quixote. 1837. 8vo., contemporary half calf, plates, first edition. Quaritch 936-425 1974 £10

INGLIS, HENRY DAVID 1795-1835 Rambles in the Footsteps of Don Quixote. London, 1837. 12mo., orig. cloth, first edition. Ximenes 33-317 1974 $15

INGLIS, HENRY DAVID 1795-1835 Spain. 1837. Large 12mo., 2 vols., orig. cloth, labels, uncut, second edition. Hill 126-136 1974 £7.50

INGOLDSBY, THOMAS The Ingoldsby Legends. 1855. 3 vols., 8vo., orig. cloth, plates, illus., slight foxing. Bow Windows 66-367 1974 £6

INGOLDSBY, THOMAS The Jackdaw of Theims. London, 1913. Folio, bound in full vellum, bevelled edges, top edge gilt, gilt pictorial cover, 12 color plates; ltd, sgd, ed., ltd. to 100 copies. Frohnsdorff 16-332 1974 $85

INGOUVILLE-WILLIAMS, HERBRAND Three Painters. Dublin, n.d. Large 4to., boards, plates. Minters 37-150 1973 $12.50

INGRAHAM, JOSEPH HOLT Burton. New York, 1838. 2 vols., 12mo., orig. coral patterned cloth, printed paper labels, good copy, first edition. Ximenes 37-116 1974 $110

INGRAHAM, JOSEPH HOLT Captain Kyd. New York, 1839. 2 vols., 12mo., orig. cloth, worn, first edition. Ximenes 33-318 1974 $75

INGRAHAM, JOSEPH HOLT Morris Graeme; or, the Cruise of the Sea-Slipper. Boston, 1843. Folio, orig. wrappers, first edition, fine. MacManus 224-238 1974 $75

INGRAHAM, JOSEPH HOLT   The Pillar of Fire. New York, 1859. 12mo., orig. cloth, frontispiece, first edition. Ximenes 33-319 1974 $20

INGRAHAM, JOSEPH HOLT   The Pirate of the Gulf, or Lafitte. London, 1837. 2 vols., 12mo., disbound, first English edition. Ximenes 33-320 1974 $25

INGRAHAM, PRENTISS   Buckskin Sam, The Texas Trailer, or, the Bandits of the Bravo. New York, 1881. Folio, wrapper, some wear, good copy, rare. Jenkins 61-1180 1974 $75

INGRAHAM, PRENTISS   Seventy Years on the Frontier. Chicago, 1893. Front cover slightly bent. Jenkins 61-1436 1974 $47.50

INGRAM, C.   The Birds of the Riviera. 1926. 8vo., cloth, text-figures, scarce, plates. Wheldon 128-488 1973 £5

INGRAM, C.   The Birds of the Riviera. 1926. 8vo., cloth, plates, scarce. Wheldon 129-485 1974 £7.50

INGRAM, JAMES   Memorials of Oxford. Oxford, 1837. 3 vols., 8vo., full contemporary calf, illus. Howes 186-2163 1974 £75

INGRAM, JAMES   Memorials of Oxford. Oxford, 1837. 3 vols., 4to., contemporary morocco, illus. Bow Windows 66-368 1974 £180

INGRAM, JOHN H.   Christopher Marlowe and His Associates. 1904. Plates, gilt top, fine, first edition. Covent 51-1246 1973 £5.25

INGRAM, T. DUNBAR   A Critical Examination of Irish History from the Elizabethan Conquest to the Act of Union. London, 1900. 2 vols., 8vo., cloth boards. Emerald 50-449 1974 £7.50

INGRES, JEAN AUGUSTE DOMINIQUE   "Les Demi-Dieux". Paris, 1949. 4to., color plates. Biblo & Tannen 210-227 1973 $15

INGRES, JEAN AUGUSTE DOMINIQUE   Ingres, sa Vie & Son Oeuvre (1780-1867). 1911. Folio, illus., full tree leather. Quaritch 940-145 1974 £75

INGRES, JEAN AUGUSTE DOMINIQUE   Ingres. Sein Leben und Sein Stil. Leipzig, 1924. 4to., plates, wrappers, faded, uncut. Quaritch 940-146 1974 £20

INMAN, H. T.   Rome. London, 1912. 12mo. Biblo & Tannen 214-623 1974 $6

INMAN, HENRY   The Great Salt Lake Trail. New York, 1898. Illus., scarce, fine. Jenkins 61-1181 1974 $65

INMAN, HENRY   The Old Santa Fe Trail. New York - London, 1898. 8vo., orig. bindings, illus. Butterfield 8-605 1974 $17.50

INMAN, THOMAS   Ancient Pagan and Modern Christian Symbolism. New York, 1874. 2nd ed., illus. Biblo & Tannen 213-119 1973 $12.50

INMAN, W. S.   An Essay on Symbolic Colours. London, 1845. 4to., orig. cloth, gilt, plates, first edition. Hammond 201-712 1974 £12

INNES, THOMAS   Scot's Heraldry. Edinburgh, 1934. 1st ed., color plates. Biblo & Tannen 214-277 1974 $15

INNIS, H. A.   The Canadian Economy and Its Problems. Toronto, 1934. Hood's 104-359 1974 $17.50

INNIS, H. A.   The Dairy Industry in Canada. Toronto, 1937. Hood's 102-381 1974 $12.50

INNIS, H. A.   Select Documents in Canadian Economic History. Toronto, 1929. Hood's 104-358 1974 $45

INNIS, HAROLD A.   The Diary of Alexander James McPhail. Toronto, 1940. Hood's 103-214 1974 $20

INNES, THOMAS   Critical Essay on the Ancient Inhabitants of Northern Parts of Britain. 1729. 2 vols., 8vo., half calf. Quaritch 939-657 1974 £25

INNOCENT XI, POPE   A Decree Made at Rome, the Second of March, 1679, Condemning Some Opinions of the Jesuits and Other Casuists. London, 1679. Small 4to., unbound. Traylen 79-176 1973 £6

AN INQUIRY Into the Condition and Prospects of the African Race in the United States. Philadelphia, 1839. Orig. binding. Butterfield 10-108 1974 $35

INQUISITIONUM in Officio Rotulorum Cancellariae Hiberniae Asservatarum, Repertorium. Dublin, 1829. Folio, cloth. Howes 186-1156 1974 £8.50

INSCRIPTIONES Antiquae Augustae Vindelicorum. 1590. Small 4to., old calf, rubbed. Thomas 30-124 1973 £18

INSECT Life. Washington, 1888-95. Vols. 1 - 7, 8vo. Wheldon 131-816 1974 £12

INSIGNIA Una Cum Timbris Omnium Baronettorum a Prima Institutione Usque ad Annum. 1641. 8vo., contemporary olive morocco gilt. Thomas 28-165 1972 £100

THE INSTRUCTIVE Picture Book. 1860. Engraved plates finely hand coloured, small folio, orig. cloth backed boards, hinges weak. George's 610-409 1973 £25

THE INTERNATIONAL Code of Signals for the Use of All Nations. Washington, 1879. Tall 8vo., 3 parts in 1 vol., color plates, very good. Current BW9-504 1974 $12

INTERNATIONAL CONGRESS OF ZOOLOGY   Proceedings of the Fourth International Congress of Zoology, Cambridge, August 22-27, 1898. 1898. Roy. 8vo., orig. wrappers, uncut, plates. Wheldon 131-421 1974 £7.50

INTERNATIONAL CONGRESS OF ZOOLOGY   6me Congres International de Zoologie, Berne, 1904. Geneva, 1905. Roy. 8vo., cloth, plates, Wheldon 128-263 1973 £10

INTERNATIONAL CONGRESS OF ZOOLOGY   Verhandlungen des V. Internationalen Zoologen-Congresses Berlin, August, 1901. Jena, 1902. Roy. 8vo., cloth, plates, text figures. Wheldon 128-262 1973 £9

INTERNATIONAL CONGRESS OF ZOOLOGY   Verhandlungen des V. Internationalen Zoologen-Congresses, Berlin, August, 1901. Jena, 1902. Roy. 8vo., cloth, plates. Wheldon 131-422 1974 £9

THE INTERNATIONAL Jew. 1920. 235 pages. Austin 57-167 1974 $12.50

INTERNATIONAL JOINT COMMISSION   Report on the Souris River Investigation, Ottawa-Washington, 1940. Ottawa, 1941. Card cover, folding map. Hood's 102-760 1974 $7.50

INTERNATIONAL MATHEMATICAL CONGRESS   Proceedings of, Toronto, August 11-16, 1924. Toronto, 1928. 2 vols., illus., inscribed by editor. Hood's 102-847 1974 $50

INTERNATIONAL MATHEMATICAL CONGRESS   Proceedings of, Toronto, August 11-16, 1924. Toronto, 1928. 2 vols., illus., inscribed. Hood's 104-898 1974 $50

INTERNATIONAL MATHEMATICAL CONGRESS   Proceedings, Cambridge, August, 22-28, 1912. Cambridge, 1913. 2 vols., roy. 8vo. Traylen 79-225 1973 £8

INTERNATIONAL MOTION PICTURE ANNUAL 1959 International Motion Picture Almanac. Quigley, 1958. 850p., illus. Austin 51-454 1973 $27.50

INTERNATIONAL Theatre Annual No. 4. Grove, 1959. 288p., illus. Austin 51-431 1973 $10

INTERNATIONAL Transfers of Territory in Europe. 1937. Austin 62-564 1974 $12.50

INTRODUCTION to a View of the Works for the Tunnel Under the Thames. New York, 1836. Square 8vo., contemporary marbled wrappers, scarce, illus. Ximenes 35-340 1974 $50

AN INVENTORY of Historical Monuments in Buckinghamshire. 1912-13. 2 vols., 4to., plates, illus., cloth. Quaritch 939-305 1974 £30

AN INVENTORY of the Ancient Monuments. 1921. F'cap folio, illus., orig. cloth, fine. Broadhurst 24-1551 1974 £21

AN INVENTORY of the Historical Monuments in London. 1924-30. 5 vols., 4to., plates, cloth. Quaritch 939-457 1974 £30

IONIDES, C.   A Floating Home. 1918. 8vo., cloth, illus., inscribed, first edition. Quaritch 936-295 1974 £25

IORGA, NICOLAS   Melanges Offerts an. Nicolas Iorga Par ses Amis de France et des Pays de Langue Francaise. 1933. Sewn. Allen 213-1559 1973 $25

THE IOWA Band. Boston, 1870. Portrait, maroon cloth, gilt, illus., foxing, first edition. Bradley 35-204 1974 $10

IOWA - GENERAL ASSEMBLY Revision of 1860, Containing All the Statutes of a General Nature of the State of Iowa, Which are Now in Force, or to Be in Force, as the Result of the Legislation of the Eighth . . . Des Moines, 1860. Leather. Hayman 59-312 1974 $15

IRANAEUS, SAINT   Graeci Scriptoris. Paris, 1570. Small folio, contemporary German Calf, somewhat rubbed. Thomas 32-237 1974 £60

IRBY, L. H. L.   The Ornithology of the Straits of Gilbraltar. 1875. 8vo., orig. cloth, first edition. Wheldon 130-558A 1974 £7.50

IRELAND, ALEXANDER   List of the Writings of William Hazlitt & Leigh Hunt. 1868. Full morocco, fine. Covent 55-824 1974 £10

IRELAND, JOHN d. 1808   Hogarth Illustrated. London, 1793-98. 8vo., 3 vols., 19th century straight grained green morocco, gilt, plates, second edition. Hammond 201-486 1974 £50

IRELAND, JOHN d. 1808   Hogarth Illustrated. 1812. 3 vols., roy. 8vo., plates, half 19th century morocco, corrected third edition. Quaritch 940-140 1974 £38

IRELAND, SAMUEL   Graphic Illustrations of Hogarth. 1794. Contemporary diced calf gilt, engravings, foxing. Smith 194-159 1974 £5

IRELAND, SAMUEL   Mr. Ireland's Vindication of His Conduct, Respecting the Publication of the Supposed Shakespeare MSS. London, 1796. 8vo., half red morocco, rubbed, library sticker, very scarce, bookplate, rubbed, ex-library, first edition. Ximenes 37-117 1974 $100

IRELAND, SAMUEL   Picturesque Views on the River Wye. 1797. 4to., russia, plates, rebacked. Quaritch 939-148 1974 £85

IRELAND, SAMUEL   Works. 1792-97. 7 vols., 4to., russia gilt, rebacked calf, plates. Quaritch 939-147 1974 £2000

IRELAND, WILLIAM HENRY   Chalcographimania. London, 1814. 8vo., contemporary morocco gilt, fine, first edition. Dawsons PM 252-489 1974 £80

IRELAND, WILLIAM HENRY   The Confessions of. London, 1805. 8vo., orig. boards, fine, uncut, first edition. Ximenes 33-328 1974 $125

IRELAND, WILLIAM HENRY   Miscellaneous Papers and Legal Instruments Under the Hand and Seal of William Shakespeare. London, 1796. 8vo., later half calf, second edition. Ximenes 33-329 1974 $65

IRELAND, WILLIAM HENRY   Stultifera Navis. 1807. Old calf, worn. Allen 216-2242 1974 $10

IRELAND, WILLIAM HENRY   Vortigern. London, 1832. 8vo., orig. wrappers, second edition. Ximenes 33-330 1974 $40

IRELAND as a Kingdom and a Colony. London, 1843. 8vo., cloth boards. Emerald 50-450 1974 £6.50

IRELAND Mourns Cromwell. London, 1659. 8vo., cloth boards, old wrappers. Emerald 50-451 1974 £35

IRISH Landlords As They Are, and the Poor Law Bill Accompanied As It Ought To Be. Dublin, 1838. 8vo., orig. wrappers, scarce, first edition. Ximenes 33-326 1974 $50

THE IRISH Naturalist. Dublin, 1903-10. 8 vols., 8vo., cloth boards. Emerald 50-773 1974 £18

THE IRISH Theatre: Lectures Delivered During the Abbey Theatre Festival. 1939. Frontispiece, cloth gilt, fine, worn dust wrapper. Covent 55-913 1974 £12.50

IRONMONGERS' HALL   A Catalogue of the Antiquities and Works of Art, Exhibited at Ironmongers' Hall, London, in the Month of May, 1861. 1869. 2 vols., 4to., plates, half calf, illus., very rubbed. Quaritch 940-791 1974 £12

IRVINE, A.   The London Flora. 1838. Crown 8vo., cloth. Wheldon 129-1001 1974 £5

IRVINE, ALEXANDER   A Fighting Parson. Little, Brown, 1930. Austin 62-276 1974 $8.50

IRVINE, ALEXANDER   From the Bottom Up. Doubleday, 1910. 304p., illus. Austin 62-277 1974 $8.50

IRVINE, LEIGH H.   History of Humboldt County, California. Los Angeles, 1915. 4to., three quarter leather, illus. Saddleback 14-148 1974 $125

IRVINE, LYN   Ten Letter-Writers. 1932. Ownership inscription, very good copy, slightly frayed d.w., first edition. Covent 51-921 1973 £5.25

IRVING, CONSTANCE   A Child's Book of Hours. London, n.d. Folio, text illus., fine full color plates, pictorial boards, very good. Wilson 63-531 1974 $20

IRVING, HENRY   We Saw Him Act. London, 1939. 8vo., illus., inscription, orig. cloth, dust wrapper. Bow Windows 62-924 1974 £10

IRVING, JOHN TREAT   Harry Harson. New York, 1853. 12mo., orig. cloth, first edition. Ximenes 33-332 1974 $30

IRVING, JOHN TREAT   The Hunters of the Prairie. London, 1837. 2 vols., 12mo., half morocco, uncut, first English edition. Ximenes 33-333 1974 $100

IRVING, JOHN TREAT   Indian Sketches, Taken During an Expedition to the Pawnee and Other Tribes of American Indians. 1835. First edition, 2 vols., contemporary half calf, marbled boards, very good copy. Broadhurst 24-1631 1974 £100

IRVING, L. H.   Officers of the British Forces In Canada During the War of 1812-15. Welland, 1908. Card cover, mended. Hood's 103-107 1974 $25

IRVING, R. L. G.   The Romance of Mountaineering. New York, 1935. Bdg. worn. Biblo & Tannen 213-1012 1973 $10

IRVING, RALPH   Experiments on the Red and Quill Peruvian Bark. Edinburgh, 1785. 8vo., contemporary half calf, rebacked, first edition. Dawsons PM 249-295 1974 £65

IRVING, WASHINGTON   An Account of the Funeral Honours Bestowed on the Remains of Capt. Lawrence and Lieut. Ludlow. Boston, 1813. 8vo., contemporary wrappers, first edition, very good copy, uncut. Ximenes 36-121 1974 $100

IRVING, WASHINGTON   The Alhambra: A Series of Tales and Sketches of the Moors and Spaniards. Philadelphia, 1832. 2 vols., orig. cloth backed boards, spines faded, paper labels, first American edition, some foxing & staining, very good set. MacManus 224-239 1974 $70

IRVING, WASHINGTON   Astoria. Philadelphia, 1836. 2 vols., first edition, folded map, brown cloth covers remarkably bright, minimal foxing of text. Butterfield 10-319 1974 $100

IRVING, WASHINGTON   Astoria. London, 1836. 3 vols., 8vo., orig. paper labels, orig. boards, first English edition. Dawsons PM 252-490 1974 £70

IRVING, WASHINGTON   Astoria. 1836. 2 vols., map, new buckram, foxed, marginal stains. Allen 216-899 1974 $15

IRVING, WASHINGTON   The Beauties of. 1825. First edition, 6mo., newly bound in half brown calf, top edges gilt, others uncut, fine, coloured plates. Broadhurst 24-751 1974 £25

IRVING, WASHINGTON   Bracebridge Hall. 1822. 2 vols., buckram, first edition. Allen 216-900 1974 $17.50

IRVING, WASHINGTON   Bracebridge Hall. London, 1877. 8vo., orig. cloth, gilt, plates, illus. Hammond 201-477 1974 £6.50

IRVING, WASHINGTON   A Chronicle of the Conquest of Granada. London, 1829. 2 vols., 8vo., half calf, attractive copy, first English edition. Goodspeed's 578-162 1974 $25

IRVING, WASHINGTON   Companions Of Columbus. London, 1831. Disbound. Rinsland 58-65 1974 $15

IRVING, WASHINGTON   A History of New York. New York, 1809. 2 vols., 12mo., contemporary tree calf, fine, first edition. Ximenes 33-335 1974 $475

IRVING, WASHINGTON   A History of the Life and Voyages of Christopher Columbus. London, 1828. 4 vols., orig. cloth-backed boards, maps, labels, first edition. Howes 186-272 1974 £45

IRVING, WASHINGTON   Knickerbocker's History of New York. New York, 1894. 2 vols., 8vo., pen and ink sketches, blue white and gilt dec. covers, bit soiled, all esle very fine. Current BW9-238 1974 $18

IRVING, WASHINGTON   The Legend of Sleepy Hollow. Philadelphia-London, (1875). 8vo., limp pseudo alligator skin, illus. Rich Summer-77 1974 $5

IRVING, WASHINGTON   Legends of the Alhambra. Philadelphia, 1910. 8vo., full page full color illus., pen and ink marginal sketches, fine. Current BW9-239 1974 $18.50

IRVING, WASHINGTON   Life of George Washington. London, 1859. 3 vols., illus., covers worn, very good, orig. green boards, one cover detached, first edition. Covent 51-983 1973 £15.75

IRVING, WASHINGTON   Life of George Washington. New York, 1858. 4 vols., 3/4 lea., bindings rubbed. Biblo & Tannen 213-1-2 1973 $35

IRVING, WASHINGTON   The Old English Christmas. London and Edinburgh, ca. 1910. 12mo., gilt; 16 color plates. Frohnsdorff 16-122 1974 $10

IRVING, WASHINGTON   The Poems of. New York, 1931. 4to., orig. wrappers bound in quarter cloth, paper label, first edition, one of 28 copies specially bound for presentation, this is copy no. 3, fine. MacManus 224-242 1974 $40

IRVING, WASHINGTON   Rip Van Winkle. New York, 1855. 8vo., orig. pink printed wrappers, nice copy, first edition. Ximenes 37-118 1974 $45

IRVING, WASHINGTON   Rip Van Winkle. New York, (c. 1890). 8vo., full page full color illus., fine, colored pictorial front wrapper. Current BW9-141 1974 $18.75

IRVING, WASHINGTON   Rip Van Winkle. 1893. 8vo., cloth, ilius. Hammond 201-124 1974 $5

IRVING, WASHINGTON   Rip Van Winkle. London, 1905. Orig. binding, lacking d.w., small rubbed spot on front of spine, gilt unusually bright, fine, illus. by Arthur Rackham. Ross 87-471 1974 $75

IRVING, WASHINGTON   The Rocky Mountains. Philadelphia, 1837. 2 vols., orig. cloth, ends of spine worn, first American edition, folding maps, browned & foxed, some bad staining in margins. MacManus 224-243 1974 $40

IRVING, WASHINGTON   A Tour of the Prairies. Philadelphia, 1835. Orig. cloth, paper label, first edition, first issue, slight wear. Jenkins 61-1207 1974 $85

IRVING, WASHINGTON   Works. New York, 1895. 40 vols., new leatherette, top edges gilt, photogravure plates, some by Rackham, special Author's Autograph edition, limited, numbered, handmade paper, fine orig. page of Irving's manuscript bound in, rare. Jenkins 61-1208 1974 $350

IRWIN, D.   Alone Across the Top of the World. Toronto, 1935. Illus. Hood's 103-69 1974 $12.50

IRWIN, GEORGE O'MALLEY   The Illustrated Handbook to the County of Wicklow. London, 1844. 8vo., illus., orig. cloth. Emerald 50-466 1974 £15

IRWIN, V.   The Mountain of Jade. New York, 1926. Hood's 104-559 1974 $10

IRWIN, WALLACE   Seed of the Sun. Doran, 1921. Austin 62-278 1974 $12.50

IRWIN, WILL   The House That Shadows Built. Doubleday, 1928. 293p., illus. Austin 51-455 1973 $8.50

ISABEY, JEAN-BAPTISTE   Voyage en Italie. (Paris, n.d.). Folio, contemporary marbled boards. Marlborough 70-35 1974 £150

ISHERWOOD, CHRISTOPHER   Lions and Shadows. 1938. 8vo., orig. cloth, scarce, first edition. Rota 189-492 1974 £10

ISHERWOOD, CHRISTOPHER   The Memorial: Portrait of a Family. 1932. Rubber stamp, very nice copy, late binding, first edition. Covent 51-984 1973 £10.50

ISHII, HAXON   Twelve Poems. Tokyo, 1925. Wrappers, inscription, dust wrapper, fine. Covent 55-233 1974 £35

THE ISLAND of Palmas Arbitration Before the Permanent Court of Arbitration at the Hague Under the Special Agreement Concluded Between the United States of America and the Netherlands, 1925. Washington, 1925. Fine large folding maps and charts. Jenkins 61-2117 1974 $10

ISLER, C.   Well-Boring for Water, Brine and Oil. 1911. 8vo., orig. cloth, illus., second edition. Bow Windows 64-563 1974 £8

ISOCRATES Nuper Accurate Recognitus, et Auctus. 1534. Small folio, old vellum. Thomas 30-70 1973 £65

ISSUE Roll of Thomas de Brantingham . . . . Containing Payments Made Out of His Majesty's Revenue. 1835. Roy. 8vo., half calf. Quaritch 939-194 1974 £10.50

ISTVANFFI, G.   A Clusius Codex Mykologiai Meltatasa - Etudes et Commentaires sur le Code de l'Escluse. Budapest, (1898-) 1900. Folio, cloth, plates, rare. Wheldon 131-1423 1974 £70

ISTVANFFI, G.   A Clusius Codex Mykologiai Meltatasa. Budapest, (1898)-1900. Folio, cloth, coloured plates, rare. Wheldon 128-1374 1973 £70

ISVARAKRISHNA: Gymnosophista Sive Indicae Philosophiae Documenta Collegit. Bonn, 1832. 4to., wrappers, foxed. Bow Windows 66-372 1974 £6.75

ITALIAN HOSPITALIZATION SOCIETY   Second Annual Dinner-Dance. 1939. Austin 62-285 1974 $22.50

ITALIAN INST. - STAMFORD, CT   Twenty-Five Years of Progress 1910-1935. Stamford, Conn., 1935, n.p. Austin 62-286 1974 $27.50

ITALIAN–American Who's Who. Vigo Press, 1966-67. 366p. Austin 62-281 1974 $27.50

ITALIAN - American Who's Who. 1936. 444 pages. Austen 57-330 1974 $32.50

ITALY In America's Making. 1921. 44p. Austin 62-293 1974 $17.50

ITINERIUM Cambriae seu Laboriosiae Balduini Cantuariensis. 1806. 3 vols., 4to., modern boards, plates. Quaritch 939-683 1974 £50

IVANOFF, NICOLA   Francesco Maffei. Padova, 1942. 4to., cloth covers, soiled, plates. Minters 37-191 1973 $16

IVES, J. MOSS   The Ark and the Dove. Longmans, Green, 1936. 435p., illus. Austin 62-294 1974 $17.50

IVIMEY, JOHN W.   Complete Version of Ye Three Blind Mice.
c.1915. Oblong small 4to., orig. boards, illus.   Howes 185-260 1974 £5

IVORY, JAMES   A New and Universal Solution of Kepler's Problem. 4to., disbound.   Zeitlin 235-118 1974 $47.50

IZACKE, R.   Remarkable Antiquities of the City of Exeter.
1724. 8vo., contemporary calf.   Quaritch 939-341 1974 £17.50

J

J., L. A. M.   Preservatif Contre la Fumee, ou Moyens de Construire les Nouvelles Cheminees et de Reparer les Anciennes, de Maniere a ce Que des Unes ni des Autres il ne Puisse Revenir de Fumee dans les Appartemens. c. 1800. 8vo., half calf. Quaritch 940-517 1974 £15

JACK and the Beanstalk. New York, (c. 1850). 12mo., pictorial wrappers, chromolithograph frontispiece, engravings (some colored by a child), stitching has come loose. Frohnsdorff 16-460 1974 $12.50

JACK and the Beanstalk. New York, 1888. 4to., glazed pictorial wrappers, full page color plates, very good copy. Frohnsdorff 16-455 1974 $15

JACK and the Beanstalk. New York, 1935. 16mo., boards, cloth spine, fine copy. Frohnsdorff 16-457 1974 $10

JACKSON, CHEVALIER   Indications, Technique et Resultats de la Bronchoscopie. (Paris, 1930). 8vo., green half cloth. Dawsons PM 249-296 1974 £25

JACKSON, CHEVALIER   The Nose, Throat, and Ear and Their Diseases In Original Contributions. Philadelphia, 1929. Rittenhouse 46-720 1974 $15

JACKSON, CHEVALIER   The Nose, Throat, and Ear and Their Diseases. Philadelphia, 1930. Rittenhouse 46-721 1974 $15

JAEGER, B.   The Life of North American Insects. New York, 1859. Crown 8vo., orig. cloth, engravings, new edition. Wheldon 131-817 1974 £7.50

JAEGAR, G. F.   Uber die Pflanzenversteinerungen Welche in dem Bausondstein von Stuttgart vor Kommen. Stuttgart, 1827. 4to., old half leather, lithographed plates, rare. Wheldon 128-1275 1973 £10

JAENNICKE, F.   Grundriss der Keramik in Bezug auf das Kunstgewerbe. Stuttgart, 1878-79. 2 vols., large 8vo., illus., half morocco, gilt. Quaritch 940-643 1974 £25

JAFFE, BERNARD   Crucibles. London, 1931. 8vo., cloth, gilt, plates. Dawsons PM 245-416 1974 £6

JAGERSKIOLD, L. A.   Nordens Faglar. Stockholm, 1920. Imp. 4to., buckram, coloured plates. Wheldon 128-490 1973 £30

JAGERSKIOLD, L. A.   Nordens Faglar. Stockholm, 1920. Imp. 4to., buckram, plates. Wheldon 131-632 1974 £30

JAGGARD, WILLIAM   Shakespeare Bibliography. Stratford-on-Avon, 1911. 4to., orig. cloth, fine, limited, first issue. Dawsons PM 10-548 1974 £30

JAGGARD, WILLIAM   Shakespeare Bibliography. Stratford-on-Avon, 1911. 4to., orig. cloth, fine, limited, first issue. Dawsons PM 252-879 1974 £25

JALLABERT, JEAN   Experiences sur l'Electricite Avec Quelques Conjectures sur la Cause de ses Effets. Geneva, 1748. 8vo., contemporary marbled wrappers, folding-plates, rare first edition. Gilhofer 61-17 1974 sFr. 950

THE JAMAICA Quarterly Journal of Literature, Science and Art. Kingston, 1861. 8vo., polished wood boards, bevelled edges, leather spine, excellent condition. Ximenes 36-122 1974 $100

JAMES, HENRY   Confidence. Boston, 1880. 12mo., orig. green cloth, first American edition. Ximenes 33-362 1974 $25

JAMES, G. P. R.   Charles Tyrrell. New York, 1839. 2 vols., 12mo., orig. quarter cloth, first American edition. Ximenes 33-357 1974 $15

JAMES, G. P. R.   Corse de Leon. New York, 1841. 2 vols., 12mo., orig. cloth, first American edition. Ximenes 33-358 1974 $12.50

JAMES, G. P. R.   Delaware. (London), 1833. 3 vols., 8vo., contemporary half calf, gilt, first edition. Ximenes 33-359 1974 $60

JAMES, G. P. R.   The Life and Adventures of John Marston Hall. New York, 1834. 2 vols., 12mo., orig. cloth, first American edition. Ximenes 33-360 1974 $15

JAMES, G. P. R.   The Robber. New York, 1838. 2 vols., 12mo., orig. cloth, first American edition. Ximenes 33-361 1974 $15

JANES, NORMAN   Seventeen Woodcuts. n.d. Post 8vo., portfolio, foxing, English first edition. Covent 56-1836 1974 £35

JANIN, JULES   Deburau. Paris, 1881. 12mo., orig. wrapper, uncut. L. Goldschmidt 42-258 1974 $12.50

JANIS, ELSIE   So Far So Good! Dutton, 1932. 344p., illus. Austin 51-458 1973 $7.50

JANIVER, FRANCIS DE HAES   The Sleeping Sentinel. Philadelphia, 1863. 12mo., orig. wrappers, first edition. Ximenes 33-366 1974 $50

JANNASCH, ADOLF   Hans Meid. Berlin, 1943. 4to., boards, very good copy. Minters 37-475 1973 $18

JANNEAU, GUILLAUME   L'Art Cubiste. Paris, 1929. 4to., wrappers, plates, unopened, English first edition. Covent 56-54 1974 £21

JANNEY, SAMUEL M.   The Last of the Lenape, and Other Poems. Philadelphia & Boston, 1839. Orig. cloth, leather label, first edition, some foxing, fine, ex-library. MacManus 224-253 1974 $30

JANOWSKY, OSCAR   The American Jew. Harper, 1942. 322p., orig. ed. Austin 62-297 1974 $10

JANOWSKY, OSCAR   The J. W. B. Survey. Dial, 1948. 355p. Austin 62-299 1974 $12.50

JANSEN, HENDRIK   Essai sur l'Origine de la Gravure en Bois et en Taille-Douce. Paris, 1808. 2 vols., 8vo., plates, contemporary calf. Dawsons PM 10-320 1974 £40

JANSON, FLORENCE EDITH   The Background of Swedish Immigration: 1840-1930. Chicago, 1931. 517p., orig. ed. Austin 62-300 1974 $17.50

JANSON, J. MELVILLE   Encyclopedia of Comedy. McKay, 1899. Austin 51-459 1973 $12.50

JAPAN, DEPARTMENT OF AGRICULTURE AND COMMERCE   Japan in the Beginning of the 20th Century. Tokyo, 1904. 8vo., cloth, scarce. Wheldon 128-206 1973 £7.50

JAPAN. Described and Illustrated by the Japanese. Boston, 1897. 7 vols., rubbed, limited, Orient edition. Ballinger 1-279 1974 $25

JARDE, A.   The Formation of the Greek People. New York, 1926. 1st Amer. ed. Biblo & Tannen 214-624 1974 $10

JARDINE, WILLIAM   The Natural History of Felinae. Edinburgh, 1834. 8vo., half morocco, plates. Wheldon 131-497 1974 £15

JARDINE, WILLIAM   The Natural History of Monkeys. Edinburgh, 1833. 8vo., half morocco, plates, first edition. Wheldon 131-496 1974 £15

JARDINE, WILLIAM   The Natural History of the Pachydermes. Edinburgh, 1836. Small 8vo., half morocco, plates. Wheldon 131-498 1974 £15

JARDINE, WILLIAM   The Naturalist's Library. Edinburgh, (1845-46) Post 8vo., red cloth, plates. Wheldon 131-499 1974 £10

JARDINE, WILLIAM   The Naturalist's Library. Edinburgh, 1833-43. 40 vols., 8vo., half calf gilt, plates. Wheldon 131-69 1974 £500

JARS, GABRIEL   Voyages Metallurgiques. 1774-1781. 4to., 3 vols., contemporary tree calf, plates, first edition. Dawsons PM 245-417 1974 £365

JARVES, JAMES J.   Kiana. Boston, 1857. 12mo., orig. cloth, illus., first edition. Ximenes 33-368 1974 $17.50

JARVIS, A.   5,000 Miles in a 27-Tonner, Narrative Log of the Schooner Yacht "Haswell". Toronto, 1922. Illus. Hood's 104-268 1974 $10

JARVIS, C. B.   Leaves From Rosedale. Toronto, 1905. Leather, illus. Hood's 103-734 1974 $17.50

JARVIS, JOHN W.   The Glyptic. 1875. Orig. cloth, woodcuts, rubbed. Covent 55-557 1974 £7.50

JARVIS, T. S.   Letters From East Longitudes, Sketches of Travel in Egypt, the Holy Land, Greece, and Cities of the Levant. Toronto, 1875. Hood's 103-412 1974 $10

JARVIS, W. H. P.   Trails and Tales in Cobalt. Toronto, 1908. Hood's 103-362 1974 $12.50

JAY, WILLIAM   An Inquiry Into the Character and Tendency of the American Colonization, and American Anti-Slavery Societies. New York & Boston, 1835. Fine, third edition, orig. binding. Butterfield 10-109 1974 $25

JAY, WILLIAM   A View of the Action of the Federal Government in Behalf of Slavery. Utica, 1844. Blue printed wrappers, fine, rare. Jenkins 61-1219 1974 $40

JAYCOCKS, T. G.   Camera Conversations. Toronto, 1936. Fully illus. Hood's 102-153 1974 $12.50

JAYNE, W. A.   Healing Gods of Ancient Civilizations. 1925. Allen 213-565 1973 $15

JACKMAN, ISAAC   The Divorce. London, 1781. 8vo., disbound, first edition. Ximenes 33-336 1974 $22.50

JACKMAN, ISAAC   The Milesian. London, 1777. 8vo., disbound, first edition. Ximenes 33-337 1974 $20

JACKS, WILLIAM   Robert Burns in Other Tongues. Glasgow, 1896. Portraits, fine, scarce. Covent 55-271 1974 £21

JACKSON, A. B.   Catalogue of the Trees and Shrubs in the Collection of Sir G. L. Holford. Oxford, 1927. 4to., cloth. Wheldon 129-1610 1974 £15

JACKSON, A. B.   Catalogue of the Trees and Shrubs in the Collection of Sir G. L. Holford. Oxford, 1927. 4to., cloth, plates. Wheldon 131-1739 1974 £15

JACKSON, A. B.   Catalogue of the Trees and Shrubs In the Collection of the Late Sir George L. Holford. Oxford, 1927. 4to., buckram, plates, portraits. Traylen 79-27 1973 £15

JACKSON, ANDREW   The Case of the Six Mutineers. Albany, 1828. 8vo., first edition. Ximenes 33-338 1974 $40

JACKSON, ANDREW   Memoirs of. Auburn, 1845. 8vo., plates, contemporary mottled calf, first edition. Ximenes 33-339 1974 $20

JACKSON, ARTHUR S.   Goiter and Other Diseases of the Thyroid Gland. New York, 1926. Rittenhouse 46-363 1974 $10

JACKSON, B. D.   Guide to the Literature of Botany. 1881. Roy 8vo., orig. cloth. Wheldon 129-157 1974 £15

JACKSON, B. D.   Vegetable Technology. 1882. 8vo., cloth. Wheldon 129-158 1974 £12

JACKSON, B. D.   Vegetable Technology. 1882. 8vo., cloth. Wheldon 131-229 1974 £12

JACKSON, CHARLES JAMES   English Goldsmiths and Their Marks. 1921. Imp. 8vo., cloth, revised second edition. Quaritch 940-680 1974 £18

JACKSON, CHARLES JAMES   English Goldsmiths and Their Marks. London, 1921. Demy 4to., very good copy, orig. cloth, revised & enlarged second edition. Broadhurst 24-113 1974 £12

JACKSON, CHARLES JAMES   An Illustrated History of English Plate. 1911. 2 vols., small folio, half green morocco, gilt, plates. Quaritch 940-679 1974 £80

JACKSON, EMILY   Ancestors in Silhouette. London, 1921. 4to., illus., fine, orig. cloth. Gregory 44-273 1974 $47.50

JACKSON, EMILY   History of Silhouettes. London, 1911. 4to., illus., little faded, orig. cloth. Gregory 44-274 1974 $45

JACKSON, EMILY   Silhouette Notes and Dictionary. London, (1938). 4to., color plates & monochrome, orig. cloth. Gregory 44-275 1974 $95

JACKSON, EMILY   Toys of Other Days. London, 1908. 4to., orig. cloth, profusely illus. Gregory 44-101 1974 $65

JACKSON, MRS. F. NEVILL
Please turn to
JACKSON, EMILY

JACKSON, FREDERICK JOHN FOAKES
Please turn to
FOAKES-JACKSON, FREDERICK JOHN

JACKSON, H. J.   European Hand Fire Arms of the 16th, 17th and 18th Centuries. London, 1923. 8vo., illus., cloth. Dawsons PM 11-435 1974 £7.35

JACKSON, HELEN HUNT   A Century of Dishonor. New York, 1881. Fine, first edition. Jenkins 61-1211 1974 $60

JACKSON, HELEN HUNT   Mercy Philbrick's Choice. Boston, 1876. 12mo., cloth, first edition. Goodspeed's 578-164 1974 $10

JACKSON, HOLBROOK   The Anatomy of Bibliomania. 1930. 2 vols., med. 8vo., mint, dust wrappers, one of 1,000 copies, orig. cloth. Broadhurst 24-365 1974 £25

JACKSON, HOLBROOK   The Anatomy of Bibliomania. London, 1930-31. 2 vols., 8vo., orig. buckram, limited, first edition. Dawsons PM 10-304 1974 £45

JACKSON, HOLBROOK   The Anatomy of Bibliomania. London, 1930-31. 2 vols., 8vo., orig. red buckram, limited, first edition. Dawsons PM 252-491 1974 £50

JACKSON, HOLBROOK   The Anatomy of Bibliomania. 1930 and 32. 8vo., full morocco, gilt, uncut. Broadhurst 23-384 1974 £130

JACKSON, HOLBROOK   Anatomy of Bibliomania. 1932. Allen 216-187 1974 $17.50

JACKSON, HOLBROOK   The Anatomy of Bibliomania. 1932. 8vo., orig. cloth, third edition. Broadhurst 23-385 1974 £15

JACKSON, HOLBROOK   The Anatomy of Bibliomania. 1932. Med. 8vo., very good copy, third revised edition, orig. cloth, first issue of work in 1 vol. Broadhurst 24-366 1974 £12

JACKSON, HOLBROOK   Bernard Shaw. 1907. Crown 8vo., orig. cloth, presentation copy, inscribed, first edition. Broadhurst 23-383 1974 £10

JACKSON, HOLBROOK   The Printing of Books. New York, 1939. 8vo., orig. cloth, illus., dust wrapper. Dawsons PM 10-306 1974 £10

JACKSON, HOLBROOK   The Reading of Books. New York, 1947. 1st ed. Biblo & Tannen 210-885 1973 $15

JACKSON, ISAAC R.   A Sketch of the Life and Public Services of William Henry Harrison. New York, 1836. 8vo., orig. wrappers, fine, first edition. Ximenes 33-341 1974 $15

JACKSON, J. W.   Shells as Evidence of the Migrations of Early Culture. Manchester, 1917. 8vo., cloth. Wheldon 129-743 1974 £5

JACKSON, JAMES   Memoir of James Jackson, Jr. M.D. Boston, 1841. 12mo., new cloth. Schuman 37-129 1974 $45

JACKSON, JAMES GREY   An Account of the Empire of Marocco. Philadelphia, 1810. 12mo., contemporary calf, worn, first American edition. Ximenes 33-342 1974 $25

JACKSON, JOHN   A Treatise on Wood Engraving Historical and Practical. London, 1861. Large 8vo., orig. quarter morocco, second edition. Dawsons PM 10-308 1974 £22

JACKSON, JOHN BAPTIST   Titiani Vecelii. Venice, 1745. Large folio, 18th century marbled boards. Marlborough 70-21 1974 £750

JACKSON, MARGARET HASTINGS   Catalogue of the Frances Taylor Pearsons Plimpton Collection of Italian Books and Manuscripts in the Library of Wellesley College. Cambridge, 1929. Tall 8vo., cloth. Kraus B8-112 1974 $18

JACKSON, SHELDON   Alaska, and Missions on the North Pacific Coast. New York, 1880. Illus., folding map, foxed. Jenkins 61-80 1974 $12.50

JACKSON, SHIRLEY   The Birds Nest. Farrar, Strauss, 1954. 276p. Austin 54-582 1973 $7.50

JACKSON, SHIRLEY   Hangsaman. Farrar, 1951. 280p., hard cover ed. Austin 54-583 1973 $6

JACKSON, SHIRLEY   Life Among the Savages. Farrar, 1953. 241p. Austin 54-584 1973 $6

JACKSON, SHIRLEY   Raising Demons. Farrar, Strauss, 1957. 310p. Austin 54-585 1973 $6.50

JACKSON, T. A.   Dialectics. 1936. Faded, English first edition. Covent 56-347 1974 £6.30

JACKSON, T. G.   Six Great Stories. London, 1919. 1st ed. Biblo & Tannen 210-617 1973 $15

JACKSON, WILLIAM   A Lecture on Rail Roads. Boston, 1829. 8vo., half crimson morocco, gilt, second edition. Hammond 201-898 1974 £36.50

JACKSON, WILLIAM   Thirty Letters on Various Subjects. London, 1784. 2 vols. in 1, 12mo., contemporary calf, second edition. Ximenes 33-343 1974 $80

JACOB, E.   Plantae Favershamienses. 1777. 12mo., half calf. Wheldon 129-1706 1974 £30

JACOB, E.   Plantae Favershamienses. 1777. 12mo., half calf, rare. Wheldon 131-1230 1974 £30

JACOB, P. L.   Curiosites des Sciences Occultes. Paris, 1885. Rittenhouse 46-364 1974 $15

JACOB, VIOLET   The Good Child's Year Book. London, n.d. 8vo., boards, paper labels, cloth spine, full page color plates. Frohnsdorff 16-461 1974 $15

JACOB, WILLIAM   An Historical Inquiry into the Production and Consumption of the Precious Metals. London, 1831. 8vo., 2 vols., contemporary polished calf, gilt, first edition. Hammond 201-869 1974 £48

JACOBI, C. G. J.   Fundamenta Nova Theoriae. 1829. 4to., quarter morocco, uncut, first edition. Gurney 64-116 1974 £75

JACOBI, CARL   Revelations in Black. Sauk City, 1947. 1st ed., ltd. Biblo & Tannen 210-618 1973 $15

JACOBI, CHARLES THOMAS   Gesta Typographica. London, 1897. 12mo., orig. boards, uncut, fine, first edition. Dawsons PM 10-310 1974 £9

JACOBI, CHARLES THOMAS   On the Making and Issuing of Books. London, 1891. 8vo., orig. boards, uncut, fine, limited edition. Dawsons PM 10-311 1974 £7

JACOBI, CHARLES THOMAS   On the Making and Issuing of Books. 1891. Quarter vellum, signed, English first edition. Covent 56-1623 1974 £65

JACOBI, CHARLES THOMAS   The Printers' Vocabulary. London, 1888. 8vo., orig. cloth, uncut, fine, first edition. Dawsons PM 10-313 1974 £9

JACOBI, CHARLES THOMAS   Some Notes on Books and Printing. London, 1892. 8vo., orig. buckram, uncut. Dawsons PM 10-312 1974 £7.50

JACOBI, CHARLES THOMAS   Some Notes on Books and Printing. 1912. Fourth edition. Howes 185-721 1974 £6.50

JACOBI, M. H.   Die Galvanoplastik. St. Petersburg, 1840. 8vo., orig. wrappers, uncut. Dawsons PM 245-414 1974 £5

JACOBS, JOSEPH   Jewish Contributions to Civilization. 1919. Austin 62-295 1974 $8.50

JACOBS, JOSEPH   The Most Delectable History of Reynard the Fox. 1895. 8vo., orig. green cloth, gilt, fine. Hammond 201-125 1974 $8.50

JACOBS, W. W.   Sea Urchins. 1898. 8vo., orig. cloth, first edition. Quaritch 936-428 1974 £6

JACOBSON, L.   Lehrbuch der Ohrenheilkunde. Leipzig, 1893. 8vo., orig. brown cloth. Dawsons PM 249-297 1974 £6

JACOBUS DE VARAGINE   The Golden Legend. Westminster, 1493. Folio, brown morocco gilt, illus., third English edition. Dawsons PM 252-1020 1974 £8,750

JACOBUS DE VARAGINE   Leben der Heiligen. (?Augsberg, c. 1500). Folio, modern morocco backed and edged boards, hand coloured woodcuts. Thomas 32-273 1974 £55

JACOBUS DE VORAGINE, O. P.   Legenda Aurea Sanctorum. Cologne, 1483. Folio, contemporary brown morocco, blind tooled, damaged with an old cut, mended, rebacked, brass clasps, good sturdy copy. Schumann 499-54 1974 sFr 3,700

JACOBUS DE VARAGINE   Le Legende Doree. Paris, 1912. 3 vols., 8vo., orig. wrapper. L. Goldschmidt 42-135 1974 $50

JACOBUS FONTANUS BRUGENSIS   De Bello Rhodio. 1527. Small 4to., modern wrappers, second edition. Thomas 28-288 1972 £25

JACOBUS MAGDALIUS GAUDENSIS   Passio Magistralis dni nri Jesu Christi. Cologne, 1505. Small 4to., modern vellum. Thomas 28-289 1972 £31.50

JACOBY, F.   Die Fragmenta der Griechischen Historiker. 1923. Torn spine. Allen 213-563 1973 $10

JACQUEMART, A.   History of the Ceramic Art. London, 1877. 8vo., plates, orig. cloth, rubbed, foxing, second edition. Bow Windows 62-494 1974 £6.50

JACQUEMONT, VICTOR   Letters from India. London, 1834. 2 vols., 8vo., orig. cloth, labels, fine, first English edition. Ximenes 33-344 1974 $50

JACQUEMONT, VICTOR   Lettres de Victor Jacquemont a Jean de Charpentier Avec Introduction et des Notes de L. Bultingaire and P. Maes. Paris, 1933. 8vo., wrappers, portrait. Wheldon 128-110 1973 £5

JACQUET, L. S.   Precis de l'Electricite. Vienne, 1775. 8vo., contemporary calf, plates. Dawsons PM 245-415 1974 £25

JACQUIN, JOSEPH FRANZ ELDEN VON   Beytrage zur Geschichte der Vogel. Vienna, 1784. Med. 4to., contemporary half calf, marbled boards, uncut, very scarce, hand coloured engravings. Broadhurst 24-1120 1974 £775

JACQUIN, N. J.   Miscellanea Austriaca. Vienna, 1778-81. 2 vols., small 4to., new half morocco gilt, plates. Wheldon 131-68 1974 £250

JAFFE, BERNARD   Men of Science in America. New York, 1944. Biblo and Tannen 213-865 1973 $7.50

JAMES I, KING OF ENGLAND   A Declaration . . . . to Enlarge, or Reserve Himselfe in Matter of Bountie. London, 1619. Small 4to., disbound. Ximenes 33-345 1974 $75

JAMES I, KING OF ENGLAND   His Majestys Instructions to His Dearest Sonne, Henry the Prince. 1887. 4to., orig. calf binding, gilt panelling, some spotting, plates.   Bow Windows 66-593 1974 £60

JAMES I, KING OF ENGLAND   His Majesties Speech in the Upper House of Parliament, on 26 of March, 1621. London, 1621. Small 4to., disbound, first edition.   Ximenes 33-346 1974 $35

JAMES I, KING OF ENGLAND   His Majesties Speech In This Last Session of Parliament. London, 1605. Small 4to., disbound, first edition.   Ximenes 33-348 1974 $45

JAMES I, KING OF ENGLAND   His Majesties Speech to Both Houses of Parliament. . . . . the Last Day of March, 1607. London, n.d. Small 4to., disbound, first edition.   Ximenes 33-347 1974 $40

JAMES I, KING OF ENGLAND   Lusus Regius. 1901. Folio, corners bent, spine slightly torn, limited edition.   Allen 216-1913 1974 $12.50

JAMES I, KING OF ENGLAND   A Meditation Upon the Lords Prayer. London, 1619. 8vo., disbound, scarce, first edition.   Ximenes 33-350 1974 $90

JAMES I, KING OF ENGLAND   A Proclamation for Restoring the Ancient Merchants to Their Former Trade and Priviledges. London, 1617. Folio, fine, disbound, red cloth folder.   Dawsons PM 247-156 1974 £105

JAMES I, KING OF ENGLAND   A Publication of His Majesties Edict, and Severe Censure Against Private Combats and Combatants. London, 1613. Small 4to., disbound, first edition.   Ximenes 33-351 1974 $60

JAMES I, KING OF ENGLAND   Speech, as it Was Delivered by Him in the Upper House of Parliament, the 19 Day of March 1603. London, 1604. Small 4to., disbound, first edition.   Ximenes 33-349 1974 $50

JAMES I, KING OF ENGLAND   The True Lawe of Free Monarchies. London, 1603. 8vo., disbound, scarce, first London edition.   Ximenes 33-352 1974 $80

JAMES II, KING OF ENGLAND   The Memoirs Of. London, 1702. Slim 8vo., contemporary calf, rubbed.   Smith 194-169 1974 £5.50

JAMES, C. C.   Agriculture. Toronto, 1898. First edition. Hood's 104-360 1974 $10

JAMES, CHARLES T. C.   A Bird of Paradise. 1889. First edition, 3 vols., half title in each vol., 8vo., orig. cloth, fine copy.   Sawyer 293-172 1974 £80

JAMES, EDITH E. COULSON   Bologna. London, 1909. 8vo., orig. cloth, gilt, uncut.   Dawsons PM 251-37 1974 £10

JAMES, EDWARD   The Bones of My Hand. 1938. Large 8vo., frontis., booklabel, very good copy, first edition.   Covent 51-986 1973 £5.25

JAMES, EDWIN   A Narrative of the Captivity and Adventures of John Tanner, U. S. Interpreter at the Sout de Ste. Marie, During the Thirty Years Residence Among the Indians in the Interior of North America. 1830. 8vo., half calf, portrait, some foxing.   Bow Windows 66-373 1974 £52

JAMES, MRS. EDWIN   Wanderings of a Beauty. New York, 1863. 8vo., orig. cloth, worn, first American edition.   Ximenes 33-353 1974 $10

JAMES, F.   The Growth of Chicago Banks. (1938). Large 8vo., 2 vols., cloth, fine.   Putman 126-114 1974 $17

JAMES, GEORGE PAYNE RAINSFORD   Agincourt. London, 1844. 3 vols., 12mo., old quarter cloth, boards, first edition.   Ximenes 33-354 1974 $20

JAMES, GEORGE PAYNE RAINSFORD   The Ancient Regime. New York, 1841. 2 vols., 12mo., orig. cloth, first American edition.   Ximenes 33-355 1974 $22.50

JAMES, GEORGE PAYNE RAINSFORD   Attila. New York, 1837. 2 vols., 12mo., orig. green cloth, first American edition.   Ximenes 33-356 1974 $22.50

JAMES, GEORGE PAYNE RAINSFORD   The Commissioner. Dublin, 1843. Plates, contemporary half olive morocco, gilt, foxed.   Howes 186-273 1974 £12.50

JAMES, GEORGE PAYNE RAINSFORD   Commissioner. 1846. New buckram, plates, illus. on steel by Phiz.   Allen 216-1327 1974 $12.50

JAMES, GEORGE PAYNE RAINSFORD   Corse de Leon. New York, 1841. 2 vols., stained, first American edition.   Covent 55-914 1974 £15

JAMES, GEORGE PAYNE RAINSFORD   Dark Scenes of History. New York, 1855. Foxing.   Ballinger 1-277 1974 $12.50

JAMES, GEORGE PAYNE RAINSFORD   Eva St. Clair; and Other Collected Tales. Philadelphia, n.d. New boards.   Hayman 57-201 1974 $10

JAMES, GEORGE PAYNE RAINSFORD   The False Heir. London, 1843. 3 vols., large 12mo., contemporary half calf, paper boards, first edition.   Bow Windows 62-495 1974 £20

JAMES, GEORGE PAYNE RAINSFORD   The Fate. New York, 1851. 8vo., half morocco, first edition.   Goodspeed's 578-166 1974 $15

JAMES, GEORGE PAYNE RAINSFORD   The Gentleman of the Old School. London, 1839. 3 vols., 8vo., contemporary half calf, first edition.   Bow Windows 62-496 1974 £22.50

JAMES, GEORGE PAYNE RAINSFORD   The History of Charlemagne. 1832. Orig. boards, foxed.   Smith 194-478 1974 £6

JAMES, GEORGE PAYNE RAINSFORD   The King's Highway. 1840. 8vo., contemporary half roan, 3 vols., first edition.   Bow Windows 64-564 1974 £30

JAMES, GEORGE PAYNE RAINSFORD   The Last of the Fairies. London, (n.d.). 18mo., orig. red cloth gilt, illus.   Dawsons PM 252-492 1974 £20

JAMES, GEORGE PAYNE RAINSFORD   The Vicissitudes of a Life. London, 1853. 8vo., 3 vols., contemporary roan backed marbled boards, first edition.   Hammond 201-310 1974 £15

JAMES, GEORGE WHARTON   The Wonders of the Colorado Desert. Boston, 1907. 2 vols., illus., orig. binding.   Butterfield 10-132 1974 $15

JAMES, HENRY   The Awkward Age. London, 1899. 8vo., orig. cloth, first edition, third issue.   Dawsons PM 252-493 1974 £10

JAMES, HENRY   The Art of the Novel. 1935. Very good copy, spine faded, first edition.   Covent 51-987 1973 £6.30

JAMES, HENRY   The Awkward Age. London, 1899. 8vo., inscription, uncut, orig. blue cloth, unopened, first edition.   Bow Windows 62-497 1974 £16

JAMES, HENRY   The Awkward Age. 1899. Crown 8vo., orig. Cambridge fine ribbed cloth, first edition.   Howes 186-274 1974 £21

JAMES, HENRY   The Awkward Age. London, 1899. First edition, lacking d.w., front hinge beginning to loosen, heavy dec. paper wrapper, nice.   Ross 86-272 1974 $30

JAMES, HENRY   American Scene. 1907. Binding dull, bookplate, first edition.   Allen 216-910 1974 $10

JAMES, HENRY   The Awkward Age. 1899. Orig. patterned cloth, English first edition.   Covent 56-729 1974 £6.30

JAMES, HENRY   The Better Sort. London, 1903. First English edition, lacking d.w., orig. binding, heavy dec. paper wrapper, near fine.   Ross 86-273 1974 $40

JAMES, HENRY   The Better Sort. 1903. 8vo., orig. cloth, first edition.   Rota 190-560 1974 £5

JAMES, HENRY   Charles W. Eliot. Boston, 1930. 2 vols., orig. binding, vol. 1 unopened, heavy dec. paper wrapper, bookplate, ex-library, else mint.   Ross 86-274 1974 $40

JAMES, HENRY   Confidence. Leipzig, 1880. Half calf, first edition.   Covent 55-915 1974 £8.50

JAMES, HENRY   Confidence. Boston, 1880. Orig. cloth, soiled, first American edition, tight copy.   MacManus 224-244 1974 $25

JAMES, HENRY   Daisy Miller. Houghton, 1911. 189p.
Austin 51-457 1973 $8.50

JAMES, HENRY   Embarrassments. New York, 1896. Orig. cloth,
covers slightly soiled, first published American edition. MacManus 224-245
1974 $25

JAMES, HENRY   Essays in London and Elsewhere. 1893.
Orig. pale salmon cloth gilt, first edition. Howes 186-275 1974 £18.50

JAMES, HENRY   The Europeans. Boston, 1879. Orig. cloth,
ends of spine worn, first edition. MacManus 224-246 1974 $25

JAMES, HENRY   The Finer Grain. New York, 1910. First
edition, backstrip faded. Butterfield 10-320 1974 $12.50

JAMES, HENRY   The Finer Grain. New York, 1910. First
edition, first binding, lacking d.w., heavy dec. paper wrapper, fine. Ross
86-275 1974 $20

JAMES, HENRY   The Golden Bowl. New York, 1904. Cloth,
gilt, first edition. Dawson's 424-280 1974 $35

JAMES, HENRY   The Golden Bowl. London, 1905. First English
edition, lacking d.w., front hinge somewhat loosened, protected by heavy dec.
paper wrapper, orig. binding. Ross 86-276 1974 $30

JAMES, HENRY   The Golden Bowl. London, 1923. 2 vols.,
orig. binding, owner's bookplate, slight foxing, nice. Ross 87-301 1974 $20

JAMES, HENRY   Great Streets of the World. 1892. 4to.,
illus., bookplate. Rota 188-476 1974 £12

JAMES, HENRY   Italian Hours. Boston & New York, 1909.
4to., orig. dec. cloth, first American edition, fine. MacManus 224-247 1974
$40

JAMES, HENRY   The Ivory Tower. 1917. First edition, 8vo.,
orig. blue cloth, portrait frontispiece, fine copy. Sawyer 293-173 1974 £15.75

JAMES, HENRY   Julia Bride. New York & London, 1909.
8vo., orig. cloth, illus., first separate edition. Ximenes 33-363 1974 $25

JAMES, HENRY   Le Tour d'Ecrou. Paris, 1929. Orig. wrappers,
numbered, worn, first edition. Covent 55-916 1974 £15

JAMES, HENRY   The Lesson of the Master and Other Stories.
New York, 1892. Orig. binding, first edition, cover soiled, heavy dec. paper
wrapper, nice, Roger Senhouse's copy with his bookplate & notes about book in
pencil inside front cover. Ross 87-302 1974 $60

JAMES, HENRY   The Letters of. London, 1920. 2 vols., fine,
somewhat rumpled d.w.'s, orig. binding. Ross 86-277 1974 $45

JAMES, HENRY   A Little Tour in France. 1900. 8vo., Japanese
vellum, fine, first English edition. Rota 189-495 1974 £25

JAMES, HENRY   A London Life, The Patagonia, The Liar, Mrs.
Temperly. London, 1889. New edition, 1 vol., fine, lacking d.w., orig.
binding, heavy dec. paper wrapper. Ross 86-278 1974 $30

JAMES, HENRY   Master Eustace. New York, 1920. Orig.
cloth, first edition, fine, defective dust jacket. MacManus 224-248 1974 $25

JAMES, HENRY   The Middle Years. New York, 1917. 8vo.,
orig. cloth, first American edition. Ximenes 33-364 1974 $20

JAMES, HENRY   Notes and Reviews. Cambridge, 1921. Orig.
cloth backed boards, little worn, first trade edition, unopened. MacManus
224-249 1974 $25

JAMES, HENRY   Notes on Novelists. 1910. Bookplate, first
edition. Allen 216-918 1974 $10

JAMES, HENRY   The Other House. New York, 1896. Orig.
cloth, little soiled, first published American edition, upper hinge little shaky.
MacManus 224-250 1974 $25

JAMES, HENRY   The Outcry. Book 1. London, 1911. First
edition, lacking d.w., orig. binding, fine, bright copy, heavy dec. paper
wrapper. Ross 86-279 1974 $45

JAMES, HENRY   The Outcry. Book 1. London, 1911. First
edition, lacking d.w., orig. binding, fly leaves slightly browned, two small dents
on front cover, heavy dec. paper wrappers. Ross 87-303 1974 $40

JAMES, HENRY   Picture and Text. New York, 1893. 12mo.,
orig. dec. cloth, first edition. Ximenes 33-365 1974 $22.50

JAMES, HENRY   The Portrait of a Lady. Boston, 1882. First
U. S. edition, orig. dec. cloth gilt, covers somewhat marked, hinges weak,
else very good. Covent 51-989 1973 £20

JAMES, HENRY   The Portrait of a Lady. Boston, 1882. Orig.
dec. cloth ends of spine & joints rubbed, first American edition, second issue.
MacManus 224-251 1974 $30

JAMES, HENRY   The Reverberator. London & New York, 1888.
2 vols., 8vo., orig. cloth, first edition. Dawsons PM 252-494 1974 £48

JAMES, HENRY   The Reverberator. London & New York, 1888.
Orig. cloth, extremities little rubbed, first American edition, fine, tight copy.
MacManus 224-252 1974 $27.50

JAMES, HENRY   The Sacred Fount. 1901. Orig. patterned
cloth, English first edition. Covent 56-730 1974 £7.50

JAMES, HENRY   A Small Boy and Others. London, 1913. First
English edition, lacking d.w., owner's inscription in ink on fly leaf, orig. binding,
heavy dec. paper wrapper, near fine, frontispiece. Ross 87-304 1974 $30

JAMES, HENRY   The Soft Side. London, 1900. First English
edition, some browning of end papers, slight foxing of foredge, orig. binding,
heavy dec. paper wrappers, near fine. Ross 87-305 1974 $30

JAMES, HENRY   The Spoils of Poynton. 1897. Covers slightly
marked, very good copy, first edition. Covent 51-991 1973 £8.40

JAMES, HENRY   The Spoils of Poynton. London, 1897. First
edition with tulip binding, hinges beginning to loosen, spine somewhat shelf
rubbed, heavy dec. paper wrapper, nice. Ross 86-280 1974 $40

JAMES, HENRY   Stories Revived. London, 1885. 2 vols.,
8vo., orig. cloth, frayed. Bow Windows 62-498 1974 £78

JAMES, HENRY   Stories Revived. 1885. 2 vols., frayed,
second edition. Rota 188-474 1974 £12

JAMES, HENRY   Stories Revived. 1885. 8vo., orig. cloth,
second edition. Rota 190-559 1974 £5

JAMES, HENRY   Theatre and Friendship. London, (1932).
8vo., illus., orig. cloth, fine, first edition. Bow Windows 62-925 1974 £6.50

JAMES, HENRY   The Tragic Muse. London, 1890. 3 vols.,
some hinges weak, scarce, very good copy, first edition. Covent 51-992 1973
£95

JAMES, HENRY   The Turn of the Screw. 1940. 8vo., fine,
hand made rag paper, numbered. Ballinger 1-147 1974 $70

JAMES, M. R.   The Book of Tobit and the History of Susanna.
1929. 4to., orig. vellum, coloured plates, jap vellum, slip-case, uncut, signed
by artist, number 13 of 13 copies, first edition. Bow Windows 66-323 1974
£185

JAMES, M. R.   Ghost Stories of an Antiquary. 1904. Orig.
linen, plates, English first edition. Covent 56-1748 1974 £8.50

JAMES, M. R.   Ghost Stories of an Antiquary. New York,
1905. Biblo & Tannen 210-619 1973 $22.50

JAMES, M. R.   More Ghost Stories of an Antiquary. London,
1916. Biblo & Tannen 210-620 1973 $7.50

JAMES, MARQUIS   Biography of a Business, 1792-1942: Insurance Company of North America. Indianapolis, 1942. Illus., top edges gilt, three quarter morocco, first edition. Jenkins 61-1214 1974 $15

JAMES, MARQUIS   Mr. Garner of Texas. Indianapolis, 1939. First edition, signed inscription by author. Jenkins 61-921 1974 $28.50

JAMES, MONTAGUE RHODES   The Bohun Manuscripts. Oxford, 1936. Crown folio, orig. quarter roan, lettered gilt, uncut, plates, very limited issue, hand made paper, exceptionally fine copy. Broadhurst 24-368 1974 £150

JAMES, MONTAGUE RHODES   The Bohun Manuscripts. Oxford, 1936. Folio, orig. quarter roan, gilt, uncut, fine. Broadhurst 23-386 1974 £150

JAMES, MONTAGUE RHODES   A Descriptive Catalogue of the Manuscripts in the Fitzwilliam Museum. Cambridge, 1895. Large 8vo., plates, orig. cloth. Dawsons PM 10-315 1974 £20

JAMES, MONTAGUE RHODES   A Descriptive Catalogue of the Manuscripts in the Library of St. John's College. Cambridge, 1913. Tall 8vo., orig. buckram, library plate. Dawsons PM 10-316 1974 £22

JAMES, MONTAGUE RHODES   A Memoir of. Cambridge, 1939. 8vo., plates, orig. cloth, fine. Dawsons PM 10-317 1974 £6

JAMES, MONTAGUE RHODES   A Peterborough Psalter and Bestiary of the 14th Century Described. Oxford, 1921. Folio, orig. half morocco, fine. Dawsons PM 10-318 1974 £75

JAMES, NORAH C.   Women Are Born to Listen. Leipzig, 1937. Half blue morocco, fine, inscribed. Covent 55-922 1974 £15

JAMES, ROBERT   A Treatise on Canine Madness. London, 1760. 8vo., contemporary sheep, first edition. Gurney 64-117 1974 £20

JAMES, T. S.   The History of the Litigation and Legislation Respecting Presbyterian Chapels and Charities in England and Ireland Between 1816 and 1849. 1867. 8vo., orig. cloth, library stamps, gilt stamp. Bow Windows 66-374 1974 £8.50

JAMES, THOMAS   Bellum Papale. 1600. Small 4to., gilt, contemporary calf, first edition. Howes 185-1293 1974 £75

JAMES, THOMAS   Three Years Among the Indians and Mexicans. St. Louis, 1916. Plates, cloth, boards, second edition. Bradley 35-205 1974 $100

JAMES, THOMAS   A Treatise of the Corruption of Scripture. 1609-14. 3 vols. in 1, small 4to., contemporary calf. Thomas 28-97 1972 £40

JAMES, THOMAS ANDREW   Count Cagliostro. London, 1838. 3 vols., 12mo., orig. grey boards, fine, very scarce. Ximenes 36-123 1974 $100

JAMES, W. T.   Toronto As It Was and Is. Toronto, 1903. Illus. Hood's 103-645 1974 $20

JAMES, WILL   Lone Cowboy: My Life Story. New York, 1930. Illus., signed & dated by author, first edition. Jenkins 61-1215 1974 $22.50

JAMES, WILLIAM   Essays in Radical Empiricism. London, 1912. 1st ed. Biblo & Tannen 213-973 1973 $15

JAMES, WILLIAM   The Letters of William James. Boston, 1920. 1st ed., 2 vols. Jacobs 24-98 1974 $22.50

JAMES, WILLIAM   The Letters of William James. Boston, 1920. 2nd ed., 2 vols. Jacobs 24-99 1974 $20

JAMES, WILLIAM   Memories and Studies. New York, 1912. Biblo & Tannen 213-974 1973 $7.50

JAMES, WILLIAM   The Naval History of Great Britain. London, 1822-4. 8vo., 5 vols., contemporary diced calf, first edition. Dawsons PM 251-391 1974 £55

JAMES, WILLIAM   The Naval History of Great Britain, 1793-1820. London, 1826. 6 vols., marbled boards, three quarter leather. Hood's 103-112 1974 $350

JAMES and Charles, and Other Tales for Children. Providence, 1839. Pictorial wrappers, stitching loose, 3 1/2 X 5 1/2 inches. Frohnsdorff 16-462 1974 $20

JAMESON, A. B.   Sacred and Legendary Art. Boston & New York, n.d. 2 vols. Hood's 103-149 1974 $25

JAMESON, ANNA   Winter Studies and Summer Rambles in Canada. Toronto, 1923. Illus., signed. Hood's 104-696 1974 $17.50

JAMESON, ANNA BROWNELL (MURPHY)   Legends of the Madonna as Represented in the Fine Arts. 1891. 8vo., plates, illus., full morocco gilt, new edition. Quaritch 940-148 1974 £10

JAMESON, E. O.   The Jamesons in America, 1647-1900. Boston, 1901. 4to., cloth, illus. Saddleback 14-785 1974 $65

JAMESON, J. FRANKLIN   Dictionary of United States History, 1492-1898. Boston, (1897). Buckram, portraits. Hayman 59-315 1974 $10

JAMESON, L. S.   The Life of Jameson. 1922. 8vo., 2 vols., plates, orig. cloth, first edition. Bow Windows 64-565 1974 £10.50

JAMESON, MARGARET   Training. 1887. First edition, 3 vols., orig. blue cloth, uncut, joints and corners slightly rubbed, very good copy. Sawyer 293-174 1974 £38

JAMESON, THOMAS   Essays On the Changes of the Human Body. London, 1811. 8vo., orig. boards, uncut, very worn, first edition. Traylen 79-242 1973 £10

JAMIESON, JOHN   An Etymological Dictionary of the Scottish Language. Edinburgh, 1808. 4to., 2 vols., contemporary morocco, first edition. Broadhurst 23-387 1974 £40

JAMIESON, JOHN   An Etymological Dictionary of the Scottish Language. Edinburgh, 1808. First edition, 2 vols., demy 4to., contemporary morocco, spines slightly defective, hinges weak, loosely inserted A.L.s from author. Broadhurst 24-369 1974 £40

JAMIESON, JOHN   An Etymological Dictionary of the Scottish Language. 1879-87. 5 vols., orig. cloth, new edition. Smith 193-216 1973 £10

JAMISON, C. V.   Lady Jane. New York, 1891. Cloth, first edition. Hayman 57-405 1974 $10

JAMISON, DAVID FLAVEL   Life & Times of Bertrand Du Gueschlin. 1864. 2 vols. Allen 213-1435 1973 $12.50

JANOWSKY, OSCAR   The American Jew. 1942. 322 pages, orig. edition. Austin 57-333 1974 $10

JANSON, FLORENCE EDITH   The Background of Swedish Immigration. 1931. Orig. edition. Austin 57-334 1974 $17.50

JANSSEN, JOHANNES 1829-1891   History of the German People at the Close of the Middle Ages. 1896-1910. 17vols., library stamp. Howes 186-960 1974 £105

JANSSON, JAN   Novus Atlas Sive Theatrum Orbis Terrarum. Amsterdam, 1649-50. Folio, contemporary vellum, gilt, maps, rebacked. Traylen 79-575 1973 £5,000

JARDINE, WILLIAM   Bees. Edinburgh, 1852. Crown 8vo., red cloth, plates. Wheldon 130-767 1974 £5

JARDINE, WILLIAM   Illustrations of Ornithology. (1826-43). 4to., 4 vols. in 3, half leather, plates. Wheldon 129-24 1974 £450

JARDINE, WILLIAM   The Natural History of the Pachydermes. Edinburgh, 1836. Post 8vo., cloth, plates, first edition. Wheldon 130-406 1974 £12

JARDINE, WILLIAM   The Natural History of the Ruminating Animals. Edinburgh, 1835. Post 8vo., orig. cloth, plates. Wheldon 130-405 1974 £15

JARDINE, WILLIAM   The Naturalist's Library. Edinburgh, (1845-46). Post 8vo., orig. red cloth, plates. Wheldon 130-407 1974 £10

LE JARDINIER Fleuriste. Paris, (1825). 16mo., orig. pink boards, gilt, matching slip case, color plates, fine. Gregory 44-166A 1974 $185

JARNAC, PHILIPPE FERDINAND AUGUSTE DE ROHAN-CHABOT   Dark and Fair. London, 1857. 3 vols., 8vo., orig. cloth, scarce, first edition. Ximenes 33-367 1974 $75

JARNAC, PHILIPPE FERDINAND AUGUSTE DE ROHAN-CABOT   Le Dernier d'Egmont. Paris, 1851. 2 vols., 8vo., contemporary three quarter calf, first edition. L. Goldschmidt 42-259 1974 $15

JAUME SAINT-HILAIRE, J. H.   Plantes de la France. Paris, 1808-9. 8vo., 4 vols., roan backed marbled boards, plates. Bow Windows 64-148 1974 £140

JEAFFRESON, JOHN CORDY   The Real Lord Byron. 1883. 2 vols., orig. cloth, first edition. Howes 185-60 1974 £6.50

JEAFFRESON, JOHN CORDY   The Real Shelley. 1885. Orig. cloth, 2 vols., English first edition. Covent 56-1173 1974 £50

JEAN-AUBRY, G.   Joseph Conrad: Life and Letters. 1927. 2 vols., illus. Austin 61-501 1974 $22.50

JEANS, JAMES   Science and Music. New York, 1937. Biblo & Tannen 213-866 1973 $9.50

JEAURAT, EDMOND SEBASTIEN   Traite de Perspective a l'Usage des Artistes. Paris, 1750. 4to., contemporary French calf, gilt, fine, first edition. Dawsons PM 245-418 1974 £120

JEBB, JOHN   A Proposal for the Establishment of Public Examinations. London, 1774. 8vo., contemporary marbled wrappers, first edition. Ximenes 33-369 1974 $30

JEDAYA HA'PENINI BEN ABRAHAM   Bechinat Olam. 1484. Small 4to., 16th century South German blind stamped calf. Thomas 28-162 1972 £2,000

JEFFERIES, BRADFORD   The Widow of Nain. Manchester, n.d. 12mo., orig. cloth, first edition. Ximenes 33-370 1974 $12.50

JEFFERIES, RICHARD   The Amateur Poacher. London, 1879. 8vo., orig. cloth, first edition. Ximenes 33-371 1974 $10

JEFFERIES, RICHARD   Bevis. 1882. 3 vols., orig. dec. cloth gilt, exceptionally fine bright copy, vols. 2 & 3 entirely unopened, vol. 1 largely unopened, bindings mint. Covent 51-3250 1973 £85

JEFFERIES, RICHARD   Bevis. 1902. Orig. pictorial cloth, fine, new edition. Covent 55-927 1974 £5.25

JEFFERIES, RICHARD   Field and Hedgerow. (1889). Orig. dec. cloth, some foxing throughout, small hole in front endpaper, very nice copy, ads at end. Covent 51-998 1973 £7.50

JEFFERIES, RICHARD   The Hills and the Vale. 1909. 8vo., orig. cloth, first edition. Bow Windows 64-566 1974 £8.50

JEFFERIES, RICHARD   Hodge and His Masters. 1880. Small 8vo., 2 vols., orig. dark brown cloth, gilt, fine, first edition. Quaritch 936-429 1974 £60

JEFFERIES, RICHARD   Hodge and His Masters. London, 1880. 2 vols., 8vo., orig. cloth, first edition. Ximenes 33-372 1974 $60

JEFFERIES, RICHARD   Hodge and his Masters. London, 1880. 8vo., 2 vols., orig. dec. cloth, gilt, first edition. Hammond 201-311 1974 £20

JEFFERIES, RICHARD   The Life of the Fields. 1884. Blind-stamp, English first edition. Covent 56-734 1974 £17.50

JEFFERIES, RICHARD   Nature Near London. London, 1883. 8vo., orig. pictorial cloth, first edition. Ximenes 33-373 1974 $10

JEFFERIES, RICHARD   The Open Air. 1885. Pictorial cloth, English first edition. Covent 56-735 1974 £17.50

JEFFERIES, RICHARD   The Story of My Heart. 1912. Dec. cloth gilt, plates, English first edition. Covent 56-1848 1974 £6.50

JEFFERIES, RICHARD   The Story of My Heart. 1923. 4to., orig. buckram, leather label, uncut, signed, limited. Howes 186-277 1974 £10

JEFFERIES, RICHARD   The Toilers of the Field. London, 1892. 8vo., orig. cloth, paper label, first edition. Ximenes 33-374 1974 $10

JEFFERS, J. FRITH   History of Canada. Toronto, 1879. Hood's 102-416 1974 $7.50

JEFFERS, ROBINSON   Cawdor and Other Poems. New York, 1928. Cloth, boards, dust wrapper, first edition. Dawson's 424-283 1974 $40

JEFFERS, ROBINSON   Cawdor and Other Poems. New York, 1928. Orig. cloth backed boards, first edition, fine, somewhat worn dust jacket. MacManus 224-254 1974 $25

JEFFERS, ROBINSON   Dear Judas and Other Poems. New York, 1929. Cloth, boards, dust wrapper, first edition. Dawson's 424-284 1974 $45

JEFFERS, ROBINSON   Give Your Heart to the Hawks and Other Poems. New York, 1933. Cloth, dust wrapper, first edition. Dawson's 424-285 1974 $45

JEFFERS, ROBINSON   Medea. Random House, 1946. Austin 51-460 1973 $12.50

JEFFERS, ROBINSON   Roan Stallion, Tamar, and Other Poems. London, 1928. Grey-blue boards. Dawson's 424-282 1974 $27.50

JEFFERS, ROBINSON   Solstice. New York, 1935. Rubbed, first American edition. Covent 55-931 1974 £12.60

JEFFERS, ROBINSON   Solstice and Other Poems. New York, 1935. Cloth, dust wrapper, first edition. Dawson's 424-286 1974 $45

JEFFERS, ROBINSON   Such Counsels You Gave to Me and Other Poems. New York, 1937. Cloth, dust wrapper, first edition. Dawson's 424-287 1974 $40

JEFFERS, ROBINSON   Such Counsels You Gave to Me & Other Poems. New York, (1937). Cloth, dust wrapper, first edition. Dawson's 424-288 1974 $40

JEFFERS, ROBINSON   Thurso's Landing. 1932. Spine stained, portion of wrapper tipped in. Allen 216-939 1974 $20

JEFFERS, ROBINSON   Thurso's Landing. New York, 1932. Cloth backed boards, fine, first U. S. edition. Covent 51-1000 1973 £15.75

JEFFERS, ROBINSON   Thurso's Landing and Other Poems. New York, 1932. First edition, edges of boards little faded, very nice copy, scarce. Crane 7-151 1974 £15

JEFFERS, ROBINSON   The Women at Point Sur. New York, 1927. Boards, dust wrapper, fine, first edition. Dawson's 424-281 1974 $40

JEFFERSON, JOSEPH   The Autobiography of Joseph Jefferson. New York, 1890. Biblo & Tannen 213-898 1973 $7.50

JEFFERSON, JOSEPH   The Autobiography of. New York, 1890. Orig. fine three quarter morocco. Jenkins 61-1220 1974 $12.50

JEFFERSON, S.   The History and Antiquities of Cumberland. 1840-42. 2 vols., roy. 8vo. plates, orig. cloth. Quaritch 939-336 1974 £25

JEFFERSON, THOMAS   Notes on the State of Virginia. London, 1787. Fine large folding map, superb copy, orig. three quarter calf, first edition in English, slipcased, Joseph B. Shea's copy, orig. from the library of Jac. And. Pasteur with his bookplate. Jenkins 61-1221 1974 $300

JEFFERSON, THOMAS   Thomas Jefferson's Garden Book, 1766-1824, With Relevant Extracts from His Other Writings. Philadelphia, 1944. Thick 8vo., d.j. with few tears, full page plates, very good. Current BW9-375 1974 $18.50

JEFFERYS, THOMAS   The County of Huntingdon Surveyed. 1768. Roy. 8vo., map, orig. marbled slip case, first edition. Quaritch 939-842 1974 £150

JEFFERYS, THOMAS   Neptune Occidental. 1778. Folio, contemporary boards, charts. Bow Windows 64-568 1974 £1,550

JEFFREY, E. C.   The Anatomy of Woody Plants. Chicago, 1917. 8vo., cloth, scarce. Wheldon 129-925 1974 £12

JEFFREY, FRANCIS   Contributions to the Edinburgh Review. 1844. 4 vols., full contemporary calf gilt, first collected edition. Howes 185-247 1974 £25

JEFFREY, FRANCIS   Contributions to The Edinburgh Review. 1909. 8vo., orig. cloth. Bow Windows 64-567 1974 £6

JEFFREYS, HAROLD   Theory of Probability. Oxford, 1939. First edition. Covent 55-1311 1974 £6.50

JEFFREYS, KETURAH   The Widowed Missionary's Journal. (London), 1827. 12mo., orig. boards, first edition. Ximenes 33-375 1974 $50

JEFFRIES, DAVID   A Treatise on Diamonds and Pearls. London, 1750. 8vo., contemporary calf, first edition. Dawsons PM 247-157 1974 £55

JEFFRIES, RICHARD   Field and Hedgerow. 1889. Half parchment vellum, worn, numbered. Covent 55-928 1974 £25

JEFFRIES, RICHARD   The Pageant of Summer. Portland, 1905. 16mo., wrappers. Covent 55-929 1974 £7.50

JEFFRIES, RICHARD   The Story of My Heart. Portland, 1905. 8vo., fine, wrappers, vellum, first edition. Covent 55-930 1974 £12.50

JEHAN, L. F.   Dictionnaire Apologetique. Paris, 1863-62. 2 vols., thick roy. 8vo., half maroon calf, rubbed. Howes 185-1298 1974 £5.50

JEHAN, L. F.   Dictionnaire de Philosophie Catholique. Paris, 1860-64. 3 vols., imp. 8vo., half cloth. Howes 185-1297 1974 £7.50

JEKYLL, G.   A Gardener's Testament. London, (1937). Nice, clean copy, 8vo., orig. cloth. Gregory 44-167 1974 £12.50

JEKYLL, G.   Home and Garden. 1900. 8vo., illus., orig. buckram, scarce orig. issue. Wheldon 128-1482 1973 £5

JEKYLL, G.   Wall and Water Gardens. n.d. 8vo., orig. buckram, plates. Wheldon 128-1481 1973 £5

JELAGIN, JURI   Taming of the Arts. Dutton, 1957. 333p. Austin 51-461 1973 $10

JELINEK, J. J.   Padesatilete Jubileaum Ceskeho Narodniho Hrbitova v Chicago, Ill. Chicago, 1927. Austin 62-303 1974 $17.50

JELLICOE, G. A.   Gardens of Europe. 1937. Roy. 8vo., illus., cloth. Wheldon 131-1534 1974 £5

JELUSICH, MIRKO   Caesar. New York, 1930. Biblo & Tannen 214-598 1974 $7.50

JEMMAT, CATHERINE   Miscellanies. London, 1766. 4to., orig. boards, rebacked, first edition. Dawsons PM 252-496 1974 £95

JENINGS, EDMUND   A Translation of the Memorial to the Sovereigns of Europe Upon the Present State of Affairs. London, 1781. 8vo., disbound, first edition. Ximenes 33-376 1974 $85

JENKENS, C. A.   The Story of Pot Hooks. St. Louis, 1892. Cloth. Hayman 57-202 1974 $35

JENKINS, CHARLES F.   Tortola A Quaker Experiment of Long Ago in the Tropics. London, 1923. First edition, 8vo., orig. wrappers, spine pieces missing, interior perfect. Current BW9-442 1974 $22.50

JENKINS, D. E.   Bedd Gelert. 1899. Crown 8vo., orig. cloth, illus. Broadhurst 23-1424 1974 £6

JENKINS, HOWARD M.   Historical Collections Relating to Gynedd, a Township of Montgomery County, Pennsylvania. Philadelphia, 1897. 8vo., cloth. Saddleback 14-672 1974 $35

JENKINS, J. GILBERT   A History of the Parish of Penn. 1935. Roy. 8vo., plates, presentation, inscribed. Howes 186-1976 1974 £6

JENKINS, JAMES   The Martial Achievements of Great Britain and her Allies. London, n.d. Large 4to., nineteenth century red morocco gilt, fine. Dawsons PM 251-392 1974 £710

JENKINS, STEPHEN   The Old Boston Post Road. New York - London, 1914. 8vo., orig. bindings. Butterfield 8-250 1974 $10

JENKINSON, CHARLES   A Treatise on the Coins of the Realm. Oxford, 1805. 4to., library stamp, contemporary sprinkled calf, neatly rebacked. Bow Windows 66-429 1974 £12

JENKINSON, F.   Collected Papers of Henry Bradshaw. Cambridge, 1889. Large 8vo., plates, orig. cloth, uncut. Dawsons PM 10-77 1974 £12

JENKINSON, HILARY   The Later Court Hands in England from the 15th to the 17th Century. Cambridge, 1927. Folio, orig. cloth, plates, first edition. Dawsons PM 10-322 1974 £40

JENKS, ANTON SHREWSBURY   A Dead President Makes Answer to "The President's Daughter". New York, (1928). Limited to 999 copies, orig. binding. Butterfield 10-127 1974 $12.50

JENKS, B.   A Second Century of Meditations. London, 1704. 12mo., contemporary calf, rubbed. Smith 194-163 1974 £12

JENKS, JEREMIAH W.   The Immigration Problem. 1926. Revised and enlarged sixth edition. Austin 57-335 1974 $15

JENKS, STEPHEN   The Delights of Harmony. Dedham, 1805. Oblong 18mo., orig. boards, leather back, index. Butterfield 10-429 1974 $35

JENKYN, WILLIAM   Exodus. London, 1675. Small 4to., disbound, first edition. Ximenes 33-377 1974 $15

JENNER, CHARLES   The Gift of Tongues. Cambridge, 1767. 4to., wrappers, first edition. Quaritch 936-118 1974 £32

JENNER, CHARLES   The Placid Man. London, 1770. 2 vols., 12mo., contemporary calf, scarce, first edition. Ximenes 33-378 1974 $250

JENNER, EDWARD   Instructions for Vaccine Inoculation. (London), n.d. 4to., cloth. Dawsons PM 249-298 1974 £350

JENNER, EDWARD   A Letter to Charles Henry Parry. London, 1822. 4to., modern boards, gilt. Dawsons PM 249-300 1974 £400

JENNEY, WALTER P.   The Mineral Wealth, Climate and Rainfall and Natural Resources of the Black Hills of Dakota. Washington, 1876. Large folded map, sewed, front wrapper loose. Butterfield 10-120 1974 $15

JENNEY, WALTER P.   The Mineral Wealth, Climate . . . of the Black Hills of Dakota. Washington, 1876. 8vo., orig. bindings, sewed. Butterfield 8-103 1974 $20

JENNINGS, G. H.   An Anecdotal History of the British Parliament. 1892. 8vo., orig. cloth, torn, third edition. Bow Windows 64-569 1974 £5

JENNINGS, H. S.   Genetics of the Protozoa. (1929). Roy. 8vo., sewed, text-figures. Wheldon 128-906 1973 £5

JENNINGS, OSCAR   Early Woodcut Initials. London, 1908. Green cloth, gilt, foxing. Dawson's 424-159 1974 $60

JENNINGS, PAYNE   Sun Pictures of the Norfolk Broads. n.d. 4to., orig. cloth. Broadhurst 23-1425 1974 £6

JENNINGS, W.   The Foundling of Belgrade. New York, 1808. 12mo., contemporary sheep, scarce, first English edition. Ximenes 33-379 1974 $85

JENSEN, CARL CHRISTIAN   An American Saga. Little, Brown, 1927. Austin 62-304 1974 $8.50

JENSEN, J. MARINUS   History of Provo, Utah. Provo, 1924. 12mo., cloth. Saddleback 14-727 1974 $20

JENYNS, L.   A Manual of British Vertebrate Animals. Cambridge, 1835. 8vo., half morocco. Wheldon 129-338 1974 £5

JENYNS, SOAME   Thoughts on the Causes and Consequences of the Present High Price of Provisions. London, 1767. 8vo., paper wrappers, fourth edition. Dawsons PM 247-158 1974 £15

JENYNS, SOAME   The Works. London, 1790. 4 vols. in 2, 8vo., contemporary tree calf, fine, first edition. Ximenes 33-380 1974 $100

JENYNS, SOAME   The Works Of. 1793. 8vo., 4 vols., contemporary calf, gilt, frontispiece, second edition. Hill 126-141 1974 £32

JEPHSON, HENRY   The Platform. 1892. 2 vols., large 8vo., scarce, orig. edition. Howes 186-1464 1974 £14

JEPHSON, ROBERT   Braganza. London, 1775. 8vo., modern boards, first edition. Dawsons PM 252-497 1974 £15

JEPHSON, ROBERT   Braganza. 1775. 8vo., cloth, first edition. Quaritch 936-119 1974 £7

JEPHSON, ROBERT   The Count of Narbonne. London, 1781. 8vo., modern boards, first edition. Dawsons PM 252-498 1974 £15

JEPHSON, ROBERT   The Law of Lombardy. London, 1779. 8vo., modern boards, first edition. Dawsons PM 252-499 1974 £15

JEPHSON, ROBERT   The Law of Lombardy. London, 1779. 8vo., wrappers, first edition. Ximenes 33-382 1974 $25

JEPSON, EDGAR   Arsene Lupin. c. 1910. Near fine, first edition. Covent 51-539 1973 £5

JEPSON, EDGAR   Barradine Detects. 1937. 8vo., orig. cloth, dust wrapper, first edition. Rota 190-297 1974 £6

JERABEK, ESTHER   A Bibliography of Minnesota Territorial Documents. St. Paul, 1936. Wrappers, foxed. Jenkins 61-1664 1974 $15

JERDON, T. C.   The Birds of India. Calcutta, 1862-64. 8vo., 3 vols., orig. cloth, scarce. Wheldon 130-560 1974 £30

JERMYN, L.   The Butterfly Collector's Vade Mecum. Ipswich, 1927. Post 8vo., orig. boards, printed label, plates, enlarged second edition. Wheldon 128-743 1973 £10

JERNINGHAM, EDWARD   The Siege of Berwick. London, 1794. 8vo., modern boards, first edition. Dawsons PM 252-500 1974 £15

JERNINGHAM, EDWARD   The Siege of Berwick. London, 1794. 8vo., disbound, first edition. Ximenes 33-384 1974 $20

JERNINGHAM, EDWARD   The Swedish Curate. London, 1773. 4to., 19th century wrappers, first edition. Ximenes 33-385 1974 $80

JEROME, JEROME K.   On the Stage and Off. Scribner. 219p., illus. Austin 51-462 1973 $10

JEROME, JEROME K.   The Passing of the Third Floor Back. Court, 1921. 197p. Austin 51-463 1973 $7.50

JEROME, JEROME K.   Stage-Land. Holt, 1906. 158p., illus. Austin 51-464 1973 $12.50

JEROME, JEROME K.   Told After Supper. London, 1891. 1st ed. Biblo & Tannen 210-621 1973 $25

JEROME, JEROME K.   Told After Supper. London, 1891. 4to., orig. red cloth, illus., first edition. Dawsons PM 252-501 1974 £30

JEROME, SAINT
Please turn to
HIERONYMUS, SAINT

JERRARD, PAUL   Gems for the Drawing Room, Fruit and Flowers. London, n.d. Thin folio, orig. boards, plates, new cloth spine. Traylen 79-29 1973 £50

JERROLD, BLANCHARD   The Best of All Good Company. London, 1871. 8vo., buckram, first edition. Ximenes 33-386 1974 $25

JERROLD, BLANCHARD   Life of George Cruikshank. 1882. 2 vols., ex-library. Allen 216-398 1974 $10

JERROLD, BLANCHARD   Life of Gustave Dore. 1891. Plates, bookplate, scarce, English first edition. Covent 56-687 1974 £35

JERROLD, BLANCHARD   The Threads of a Storm-Sail. London, 1853. 8vo., cloth, gilt, first edition. Hammond 201-245 1974 £8.50

JERROLD, DOUGLAS   The Chronicles of Clovernook. 1846. 8vo., orig. pictorial cloth gilt, frontispiece. Covent 55-933 1974 £5.50

JERROLD, WILLIAM BLANCHARD
Please turn to
JERROLD, BLANCHARD

JERVIS, SWYNFEN   A Dictionary of the Language of Shakespeare. Smith, 1868. 374p., newly rebound. Austin 51-465 1973 $7.50

JERVIS, W. H.   A History of France from the Earliest Times to the Fall of the Second Empire in 1870. London, 1907. Biblo & Tannen 213-685 1973 $8.50

JERVISE, A.   Memorials of Angus & Mearns. 1885. 2 vols. Allen 213-1441 1973 $25

JESSE, E.   An Angler's Rambles. 1836. 8vo., worn, contemporary half green morocco, first edition. Quaritch 939-149 1974 £10

JESSE, JOHN HENEAGE   London. London, 1847. 12mo., orig. dark green cloth, first edition. Ximenes 33-387 1974 $22.50

JESSEL, GEORGE   Jessel, Anyone? Prentice, 1960. 179p. Austin 51-466 1973 $6

JESSEL, GEORGE   So Help Me. World, 1943. 240p. Austin 51-467 1973 $6.50

JESSEL, GEORGE   This Way, Miss. Holt, 1955. 228p., illus. Austin 51-468 1973 $6.50

JESSE, GEORGE R.   Researches into the History of the British Dog. London, 1866. 8vo., 2 vols., contemporary half roan, gilt, plates, first edition. Hammond 201-501 1974 £28

JESSOP, FRANCIS   Propositiones Hydrostaticae. 1687. 4to., gilt, half calf, boards, first edition. Dawsons PM 245-419 1974 £65

JESSOP, FRANCIS   Propositiones Hydrostaticae. (1687). Small 4to., sewn, woodcuts, first edition. Zeitlin 235-119 1974 $125

JEWEL, JOHN   The Apology of the Church of England. 1685. Contemporary calf, worn. Smith 194-164 1974 £12

JEWEL, JOHN   An Exposition Upon the Two Epistles . . . to the Thessalonians. 1584. Black letter, device on title, some stains, has final blank, contemporary calf, rebacked with morocco. Thomas 32-46 1974 £85

JEWEL, JOHN   The Works of. Cambridge, 1845. 8vo., orig. cloth, covers dull. Bow Windows 66-378 1974 £5.50

JEWELL, E. A.   Paul Cezanne. New York, 1944. Folio, boards, shaken, plates. Minters 37-273 1973 $10

JEWETT, CHARLES   Speeches, Poems and Miscellaneous Writings. Boston, 1849. Bookplate, worn. Covent 55-711 1974 £20

JEWETT, CHARLES   Speeches, Poems, and Miscellaneous Writings. Boston, 1849. Cloth, worn. Hayman 57-406 1974 $12.50

JEWETT, JOHN H.   Christmas Stocking Series. New York, (1906). Tall 8vo., color plates, colored pictorial boards with some edge wear, else very good. Current BW9-50 1974 $38.75

JEWETT, SARAH ORNE   Deephaven. Boston, 1877. 12mo., orig. cloth, ends of spine worn, first printing, fine. MacManus 224-255 1974 $40

JEWETT, SARAH ORNE   The King of Folly Island and Other People. Boston & New York, 1888. Orig. cloth, bit rubbed, first editon. MacManus 224-256 1974 $25

JEWETT, SARAH ORNE   The Life of Nancy. Boston & New York, 1896. Orig. cloth, first edition, eleven line segment copied from the work by author, signed & dated by author, very fine. MacManus 224-257 1974 $65

JEWETT, SARAH ORNE   The Tory Lover. Boston & New York, 1901. Orig. cloth, author's signature on title-page, very fine. MacManus 224-258 1974 $30

JEWETT, SUSAN W.   The Old Corner Cupboard. Cincinnati, 1856. 8vo., orig. cloth, first edition. Ximenes 33-395 1974 $17.50

JEWISH Activites in the United States. (1920-21). 255 pages. Austin 57-168 1974 $12.50

JEWISH Book Annual (1948-1949), Vol. 7. New York, 1948. Biblo & Tannen 213-629 1973 $7.50

JEWISH Experiences in America. 1930. 309p. Austin 62-341 1974 $12.50

JEWISH Influences in American Life. (1921). 256 pages. Austin 57-169 1974 $12.50

THE JEWISH Theological Seminary of America. 1939. 134p., illus. Austin 62-4 1974 $12.50

JEWITT, LLEWELLYNN   The Wedgwoods. 1865. 8vo., orig. cloth, portrait, illus., first edition. Hammond 201-992 1974 £12

JEWS In America. Random, 1936. Austin 62-179 1974 $8.50

JOACHIM OF FLORIS   Vaticinia, Sive Prophetiae Abbatis Ioachimi & Anselmi Episcopi Marsicani. Venice, 1589. Small 4to., contemporary limp vellum, engravings, waterstains, fine. Schafer 8-95 1973 sFr. 1,300

JOAD, C. E. M.   The Adventures of the Young Soldier in Search of the Better World. London, 1943. First edition, drawings, very nice copy, d.w., orig. cloth. Crane 7-225 1974 £5

JOAD, C. E. M.   Unorthodox Dialogues on Education and Art. 1930. Dust wrapper, English first edition. Covent 56-738 1974 £6.30

JOAN, NATALIE   Ameliaranne and the Big Treasure. Philadelphia, n.d. 8vo., color plates. Frohnsdorff 16-35 1974 $15

JOANNES SECUNDUS   Basia: The Kisses. New York, 1855. Biblo & Tannen 213-781 1973 $12.50

JOBERT, LOUIS   The Knowledge of Medals. London, 1715. Small 8vo., boards, second edition. Hammond 201-502 1974 £8.50

JOBLOT, LOUIS   Descriptions et Usages de Plusieurs Nouveaux Microscopes. Paris, 1718. 4to., contemporary continental speckled calf, gilt, fine, plates, first edition. Dawsons PM 245-420 1974 £240

JOCELYN, ARTHUR   The Orders, Decorations and Medals of the World. 1934. Roy 4to., orig. cloth, plates. Broadhurst 23-113 1974 £5

JODELLE, ESTIENNE   Les Oeuvres et Meslanges Poetiques. Paris, 1583. 12mo., full dark green levant morocco. L. Goldschmidt 42-58 1974 $775

JOHANNES DE SANCTO GERMINIANO   Summa de Exemplis ac Similitudinibus Rerum. Venice, 1497. Small 4to., contemporary Italian blind stamped calf over wooden boards. Thomas 30-143 1973 £80

JOHANNES XXI, POPE   Treasuri of Helth. n.d. Sewn. Allen 213-1573 1973 $10

JOHN, SAINT   The Boke off the Revelacion off Sanct Jhon the Devine. 1901. Black letter, printed in black and red, small 4to., orig. limp vellum, fine, limited to 54 copies signed by printer. Sawyer 293-45 1974 £450

JOHN, EDMUND   Symphonie Symbolique. London, 1919. First edition, illus., front hinge shaken, very nice copy, orig. cloth. Crane 7-152 1974 £5

JOHN, JASPER   Sinister Stories. London, 1930. 1st ed. Biblo & Tannen 210-622 1973 $12.50

JOHN OF DAMASCUS   Theologia Damasceni. Paris, 1519. Folio, full red morocco gilt, woodcut, fine. Harper 213-95 1973 $850

JOHN, ROMILLY   Poems. 1931. Dust wrapper, frontispiece, fine, English first edition. Covent 56-739 1974 £7.50

JOHN, SAINT   The Revelation of Saint John the Divine. 1932. Folio, embossed brown reversed calf, illus. Hammond 201-766 1974 £125

JOHN, SAINT   The Revelation of Saint John. Gregynog Press, 1933. Wood engravings, f'scap folio, full Hermitage calf, orig. board slip-in-case, mint, limited to 232 copies, on Jap. vellum. Broadhurst 24-1009 1974 £100

JOHN, SAINT   The Revelation of Saint John. 1933. Folio, full calf, limited. Broadhurst 23-1046 1974 £90

JOHNES, E. R.   Briefs by a Barrister. Putnam, 1879. 122p. Austin 54-586 1973 $7.50

JOHNS, C. A.   British Birds In Their Haunts. 1867. 8vo., orig. cloth gilt, second edition. Wheldon 131-633 1974 £7.50

JOHNS, C. A.   The Forest Trees and Britain. 1892. Orig. pictorial cloth gilt, illus. Covent 55-1137 1974 £7.50

JOHNS, JANE M.   Personal Recollections. Decatur, 1912. Cloth, illus. Putman 126-136 1974 $17.50

JOHNSON, A. T.   A Woodland Garden. 1937. 8vo., cloth, illus., scarce. Wheldon 130-1417 1974 £5

JOHNSON, ALFRED FORBES   A Catalogue of Engraved and Etched English Title-Pages. 1691. Plates, linen back, boards. Marsden 39-256 1974 £16

JOHNSON, ALFRED FORBES   A Catalogue of Engraved Etched English Title-Pages. (London), 1934. 4to., orig. holland-backed boards. Dawsons PM 10-324 1974 £34

JOHNSON, ALFRED FORBES   German Renaissance Title-Borders. London, 1929. 4to., plates, orig. cloth-backed boards, fine. Dawsons PM 10-325 1974 £30

JOHNSON, AMANDUS   The Swedes in America. Philadelphia, 1914. 4 vols., illus., maps. Austin 57-337 1974 $12.50

JOHNSON, CHARLES   The Gentleman-Cully. London, 1702. 4to., half morocco, scarce, first edition. Ximenes 33-396 1974 $150

JOHNSON, CHARLES   A Virtually Complete Collection of the Dramatic Writings of. 1702-78. Half cloth, colored boards, rare. Ximenes 33-479 1974 $2600

JOHNSON, CHARLES 1791-1880   British Poisonous Plants. 1861. 8vo., cloth, plates, second edition. Wheldon 130-1614 1974 £28

JOHNSON, CHARLES PLUMTRE   Hints to Collectors of Original Editions of the Works of Charles Dickens. London, 1885. 8vo., orig. parchment, first edition. Ximenes 33-397 1974 $10

JOHNSON, CLIFTON 1865-   Historic Hampshire in the Connecticut Valley. Springfield, (1932). 8vo., orig. bindings, illus. Butterfield 8-251 1974 $10

JOHNSON, CLIFTON 1865-   The Picturesque St. Lawrence. New York, 1910. Illus. Hood's 103-774 1974 $17.50

JOHNSON, CRISFIELD   History of Hillsdale County, Michigan. Philadelphia, 1879. 4to., quarter leather, illus. Saddleback 14-505 1974 $75

JOHNSON, EDGAR   A Treasury of Biography. 1941. Ex-library. Austin 61-503 1974 $12.50

JOHNSON, EDGAR   A Treasury of Satire. 1945. 770 pages. Austin 61-504 1974 $12.50

JOHNSON, EDGAR   A Treasury of Satire. New York, 1945. Biblo & Tannen 210-886 1973 $7.50

JOHNSON, EDWARD   The Domestic Practice of Hydropathy. London, 1856. 8vo., orig. cloth, gilt, fourth edition. Hammond 201-582 1974 £9

JOHNSON, EDWARD   The Domestic Practice of Hydropathy. 1850. Illus., second edition. Covent 55-1312 1974 £15

JOHNSON, EDWARD   Hydropathy. London, 1846. 8vo., orig. mauve cloth, faded. Dawsons PM 249-302 1974 £6

JOHNSON, EDWARD   Letters to Brother John. London, 1837. 8vo., red half roan. Dawsons PM 249-301 1974 £6

JOHNSON, F. H.   Every Man His Own Guide at Niagara Falls. Rochester, 1852. Cloth. Hood's 103-646 1974 $50

JOHNSON, FRANK WOODRUFF   The Octopus. 1940. Austin 62-142 1974 $12.50

JOHNSON, FRANK WOODRUFF   The Octopus. 1940. 256 pages. Austin 57-181 1974 $12.50

JOHNSON, G.   The All-Red Line, the Annals and Aims of the Pacific Cable Project. Ottawa, 1903. Hood's 102-761 1974 $10

JOHNSON, G. T.   True Stories In Easy Verse. London, 1831. 8vo., orig. roan backed boards, woodcuts, first edition. Smith 194-757 1974 £6

JOHNSON, GEORGE   On the Diseases of the Kidney. London, 1852. 8vo., orig. black cloth. Dawsons PM 249-303 1974 £14

JOHNSON, GEORGE LINDSAY   The Weird Adventures of Professor Delapine of the Sorbonne. London, 1916. 1st ed. Biblo & Tannen 210-623 1973 $20

JOHNSON, GERALD W.   Our English Heritage. Lippincott, 1949. Austin 62-305 1974 $10

JOHNSON, GERALD W.   The Sunpapers of Baltimore. New York, 1937. First edition, orig. binding, edges rubbed. Butterfield 10-401 1974 $20

JOHNSON, HENRY LEWIS   Historic Design in Printing. Boston, 1923. Dark red cloth, frontispiece. Dawson's 424-160 1974 $35

JOHNSON, HUBERT REX   A History of Neshannock Presbyterian Church New Wilmington. Washington, D.C., 1925. 8vo., orig. bindings, plates. Butterfield 8-484 1974 $15

JOHNSON, JAMES   An Essay on Morbid Sensibility of the Stomach and Bowels. London, 1827. 8vo., orig. boards, fourth edition. Dawsons PM 249-306 1974 £11

JOHNSON, JAMES   The Influence of Tropical Climates. London, 1813. 8vo., orig. boards, uncut, first edition. Dawsons PM 249-304 1974 £30

JOHNSON, JAMES   A Treatise on Derangement of the Liver, Internal Organs, and Nervous System. London, 1820. 8vo., orig. boards, uncut, third edition. Dawsons PM 249-305 1974 £8.50

JOHNSON, JAMES WELDON   Along This Way. New York, 1933. Orig. binding, d.j. Butterfield 10-110 1974 $15

JOHNSON, JAMES WELDON   The Book of American Negro Spirituals. New York, 1929. 4to. Biblo & Tannen 214-866 1974 $8.50

JOHNSON, JOHN   A Collection of the Laws and Canons of the Church of England. Oxford, 1850. 2 vols., orig. cloth. Howes 185-1311 1974 £10

JOHNSON, JOHN   Collected Works. 1847-51. 4 vols., orig. cloth, scarce. Howes 185-1310 1974 £22.50

JOHNSON, JOHN 1777-1848   The Printer His Customers and His Men. London, (1933). 24mo., marbled boards, d.w., fine, first edition. Goodspeed's 578-480 1974 $15

JOHNSON, JOHN 1777-1848   Typographia. London, 1824. 2 vols., roy. 8vo., contemporary calf gilt, first edition. Dawsons PM 10-326 1974 £85

JOHNSON, JOHN 1777-1848   Typographia. London, 1824. 2 vols., 8vo., old calf, rubbed, large paper, fine internally, first edition. Goodspeed's 578-481 1974 $75

JOHNSON, JOHN 1777-1848   Typographia. London, 1824. 2 vols., 8vo., orig. quarter cloth, boards, first edition. Ximenes 33-398 1974 $100

JOHNSON, JOHN 1829-1907   The Defense of Charleston Harbor. Charleston, 1890. Orig. cloth, illus., worn, second edition. Bradley 35-425 1974 $46

JOHNSON, JOHN, VICAR OF CRANBROOK   The Unbloody Sacrifice. Oxford, 1847. 2 vols., orig. cloth, scarce, best edition. Howes 185-1312 1974 £10

JOHNSON, LIONEL   The Art of Thomas Hardy. 1923. Orig. cloth, dust wrapper, fine, first edition. Smith 194-350 1974 £6

JOHNSON, LIONEL   Poetical Works. 1915. Crown 8vo., orig. green cloth, plates, first edition, rare first issue. Howes 185-248 1974 £7.50

JOHNSON, OLIVER   William Lloyd Garrison and His Times. Boston, 1880. Cloth. Hayman 59-319 1974 $12.50

JOHNSON, OVERTON   Route Across the Rocky Mountains. Princeton, 1932. Jenkins 61-1238 1974 $15

JOHNSON, PAMELA HANSFORD   The Monument. 1938. Presentation, inscribed, scarce. Covent 55-940 1974 £15

JOHNSON, R. BRIMLEY   Some Contemporary Novelists. 1922. Fine. Covent 55-1015 1974 £5.25

JOHNSON, R. W.   A Soldier's Reminiscences in Peace and War. Philadelphia, 1886. Orig. brown cloth, first edition. Bradley 35-89 1974 $40

JOHNSON, R. W.   A Soldier's Reminiscences in Peace and War. Philadelphia, 1886. Inscribed by author. Jenkins 61-1239 1974 $42.50

JOHNSON, RICHARD 1733-1793   A New History of the Grecian States. London, 1807. 12mo., orig. boards, roan back. Gregory 44-38 1974 $30

JOHNSON, ROBERT   Nova Britannia. New York, 1867. 4to., orig. boards, unopened. Ximenes 33-399 1974 $20

JOHNSON, SAMUEL   Debates in Parliament. London, 1787. 2 vols., 8vo., orig. boards, uncut, fine, first collected edition. Dawsons PM 252-502 1974 £250

JOHNSON, SAMUEL   A Diary of a Journey into North Wales. London, 1816. 8vo., panelled calf, gilt, fine, first edition. Dawsons PM 252-503 1974 £70

JOHNSON, SAMUEL   A Diary of a Journey into North Wales. 1816. 8vo., half calf, gilt, first edition. Quaritch 936-431 1974 £55

JOHNSON, SAMUEL   A Diary of a Journey Into North Wales. London, 1816. 8vo., early brown cloth. Ximenes 33-400 1974 $85

JOHNSON, SAMUEL   A Dictionary of the English Language. London, 1755. 2 vols., modern half calf, first edition. Dawsons PM 252-504 1974 £850

JOHNSON, SAMUEL   A Dictionary of the English Language. 1755. Large folio, 2 vols., contemporary calf, rebacked, first edition. Quaritch 936-120 1974 £850

JOHNSON, SAMUEL   A Dictionary of the English Language. London, 1756. 2 vols., 8vo., contemporary calf, first octavo edition. Ximenes 33-401 1974 $300

JOHNSON, SAMUEL   A Dictionary of the English Language. London, 1760. 2 vols., contemporary mottled calf, gilt, second ocatvo edition. Dawsons PM 252-505 1974 £35

JOHNSON, SAMUEL   A Dictionary of the English Language. Dublin, 1775. 2 vols., 4to., contemporary calf, first Dublin edition. Dawsons PM 252-506 1974 £75

JOHNSON, SAMUEL   A Dictionary of the English Language. London, 1775. 2 vols., folio, contemporary mottled calf, gilt, first edition. Dawsons PM 250-48 1974 £950

JOHNSON, SAMUEL   A Dictionary of the English Language. London, 1785. 2 vols., 4to., modern half morocco, fine, sixth edition. Dawsons PM 252-507 1974 £65

JOHNSON, SAMUEL   A Dictionary of the English Language. 1785. 4to., 2 vols., calf, rebacked, sixth edition. Quaritch 936-121 1974 £45

JOHNSON, SAMUEL   A Dictionary of the English Language. London, 1786. 2 vols., 4to., modern half calf, marbled boards, sixth edition. Dawsons PM 252-508 1974 £85

JOHNSON, SAMUEL   A Dictionary of the English Language. 1807. 8vo., contemporary tree calf, worn. Bow Windows 64-571 1974 £7.50

JOHNSON, SAMUEL   A Dictionary of the English Language. Philadelphia, 1813. 8vo., contemporary sheep, sixth edition. Ximenes 33-402 1974 $27.50

JOHNSON, SAMUEL   A Dictionary of the English Language. 1816. 4to., 2 vols., half calf, eleventh edition. Bow Windows 64-572 1974 £48

JOHNSON, SAMUEL   A Dictionary of the English Language. 1877. Very thick roy. 8vo., orig. cloth. Smith 194-354 1974 £6

JOHNSON, SAMUEL   Dr. Johnson's Table-Talk. 1798. 8vo., contemporary tree calf, first edition. Quaritch 936-124 1974 £55

JOHNSON, SAMUEL   Dr. Johnson's Table Talk. 1807. 2 vols., crown 8vo., old leather backed cloth. Howes 185-250 1974 £5

JOHNSON, SAMUEL   The False Alarm. London, 1770. 8vo., contemporary calf, morocco label, first edition. Dawsons PM 252-509 1974 £75

JOHNSON, SAMUEL   The French Journals of Mrs. Thrale and Doctor Johnson. 1932. Austin 61-509 1974 $12.50

JOHNSON, SAMUEL   The History of Rasselas, Prince of Abyssinia. Derby, (n.d.). 2 vols. in 1, 12mo., vignette title, portrait, quarter roan. Bow Windows 66-381 1974 £5

JOHNSON, SAMUEL   The History of Rasselas. London, 1799. 12mo., contemporary morocco-backed marbled boards. Dawsons PM 252-535 1974 £11

JOHNSON, SAMUEL   The History of Rasselas. London, 1818. 12mo., plates, modern quarter morocco. Dawsons PM 252-537 1974 £11

JOHNSON, SAMUEL   The History of Rasselas. 1822. 8vo., panelled calf, gilt, plates. Heffer 38-706 1973 £5

JOHNSON, SAMUEL   The Idler. London, 1761. 2 vols., 8vo., contemporary speckled calf, first collected edition. Dawsons PM 252-510 1974 £65

JOHNSON, SAMUEL   The Idler. London, 1783. 2 vols., 12mo., contemporary calf, fine, fourth edition. Dawsons PM 252-511 1974 £20

JOHNSON, SAMUEL   The Idler. London, 1801. 8vo., marbled boards, contemporary half morocco, new edition. Dawsons PM 252-512 1974 £7.50

JOHNSON, SAMUEL   Irene. London, 1749. 8vo., modern boards, first edition. Bow Windows 62-504 1974 £62

JOHNSON, SAMUEL   Johnsoniana. 1836. 8vo., polished calf, plates. Quaritch 936-432 1974 £30

JOHNSON, SAMUEL   Julian the Apostate. London, 1682. 12mo., old sheep, worn. Traylen 79-177 1973 £6

JOHNSON, SAMUEL   A Journey to the Western Islands of Scotland. Dublin, 1775. 2 vols. in 1, 8vo., contemporary calf, fine, first Dublin edition. Dawsons PM 252-514 1974 £30

JOHNSON, SAMUEL   A Journey to the Western Islands of Scotland. 1775. 8vo., contemporary tree calf, first edition, first issue. Quaritch 936-122 1974 £80

JOHNSON, SAMUEL   A Journey to the Western Islands of Scotland. London, 1775. 8vo., contemporary tree calf, first edition, first issue. Dawsons PM 252-513 1974 £80

JOHNSON, SAMUEL   A Journey to the Western Islands of Scotland. London, 1791. 8vo., contemporary sprinkled calf, third London edition. Dawsons PM 252-515 1974 £10

JOHNSON, SAMUEL   A Journey to the Western Islands of Scotland. 1800. 12mo., contemporary mottled sheep. Hill 126-142 1974 £16

JOHNSON, SAMUEL   Letters. 1892. 2 vols. Allen 216-2031 1974 $12.50

JOHNSON, SAMUEL   Letters of Samuel Johnson. Oxford, 1892. 2 vols. Biblo & Tannen 213-782 1973 $30

JOHNSON, SAMUEL   Letters To and From. Dublin, 1788. 2 vols., 8vo., modern half calf, rare, first Dublin edition. Dawsons PM 252-517 1974 £60

JOHNSON, SAMUEL   Letters To and From. London, 1788. 2 vols., 8vo., contemporary tree calf, first edition. Dawsons PM 252-516 1974 £70

JOHNSON, SAMUEL   Letters To and From. 1788. 8vo., 2 vols., orig. boards, torn, first edition. Quaritch 936-123 1974 £250

JOHNSON, SAMUEL   The Lives of the English Poets. Dublin, 1779. 3 vols., 8vo., contemporary calf, first separate edition. Ximenes 33-403 1974 $150

JOHNSON, SAMUEL   The Lives of the English Poets. 1828. Full calf gilt, frontispiece. Howes 185-251 1974 £5

JOHNSON, SAMUEL   The Lives of the Most Eminent English Poets. London, 1781. 4 vols., 8vo., new half calf, first separate London edition. Dawsons PM 252-518 1974 £78

JOHNSON, SAMUEL   The Lives of the Most Eminent English Poets. London, 1783. 4 vols., 8vo., contemporary calf, second separate London edition. Dawsons PM 252-519 1974 £60

JOHNSON, SAMUEL   The Lives of the Most Eminent English Poets. London, 1806. 3 vols., 8vo., contemporary speckled calf, new edition. Dawsons PM 252-520 1974 £20

JOHNSON, SAMUEL   The Lives of the Most Eminent English Poets. London, 1816. 3 vols., 8vo., contemporary speckled calf, new edition. Dawsons PM 252-521 1974 £20

JOHNSON, SAMUEL   The Lives of the Most Eminent English Poets. Edinburgh, 1818. 4 vols., 12mo., contemporary half calf. Dawsons PM 252-522 1974 £12

JOHNSON, SAMUEL   The Lives of the Most Eminent English Poets. Halifax, 1836. 12mo., 2 vols., half green calf. Hill 126-143 1974 £12.50

JOHNSON, SAMUEL   The Lives of the Poets. 1781. 4 vols., contemporary calf, morocco labels, worn, first separate edition. Thomas 28-244 1972 £35

JOHNSON, SAMUEL   The Lives of the Poets. 1781. First separate edition, portrait, has leaf of ads, but not rare leaf of extra labels, little browning and foxing, else quite good, 4 vols., contemporary calf, morocco labels, somewhat worn. Thomas 32-176 1974 £40

JOHNSON, SAMUEL   London. London, 1830. Folio, orig. boards, paper label, limited. Dawsons PM 252-523 1974 £15

JOHNSON, SAMUEL   London. 1930. One of 300 numbered copies, very good copy, unopened, first edition. Covent 51-638 1973 £30

JOHNSON, SAMUEL   Miscellaneous and Fugitive Pieces. 1774. Small 8vo., 3 vols., old calf. Hill 126-144 1974 £52

JOHNSON, SAMUEL   The Patriot. London, 1774. 8vo., disbound, first edition. Ximenes 36-125 1974 $125

JOHNSON, LIONEL   Poems. 1895. 8vo., brown buckram, gilt, fine, signed, first edition. Rota 189-513 1974 £150

JOHNSON, SAMUEL The Poetical Works. London, 1785. 8vo., contemporary half calf, gilt label, first collected edition. Bow Windows 62-505 1974 £64

JOHNSON, SAMUEL The Poetical Works. London, 1785. 12mo., contemporary sheep, second English edition. Dawsons PM 252-525 1974 £20

JOHNSON, SAMUEL The Poetical Works. London, 1785. 12mo., old boards, first edition, second issue. Dawsons PM 252-524 1974 £60

JOHNSON, SAMUEL The Poetical Works. London, 1789. 8vo., contemporary mottled calf, gilt, new edition. Ximenes 33-403A 1974 $150

JOHNSON, SAMUEL Prayers and Meditations. London, 1796. 8vo., contemporary mottled calf, third edition. Ximenes 33-404 1974 $65

JOHNSON, SAMUEL Prefaces, Biographical and Critical. London, 1779. 8vo., contemporary morocco gilt, first edition. Dawsons PM 252-526 1974 £25

JOHNSON, SAMUEL The Prince of Abissinia. London, 1759. 2 vols., 8vo., full morocco, gilt, trifle rubbed, boxed, first edition. Ximenes 37-122 1974 $225

JOHNSON, SAMUEL The Queeney Letters. 1934. Bookplate, English first edition. Covent 56-1851 1974 £6.30

JOHNSON, SAMUEL The Rambler. (London?), 1772. 4 vols., 12mo., contemporary calf, eighth edition. Dawsons PM 252-527 1974 £30

JOHNSON, SAMUEL The Rambler. London, 1794. 4 vols., 8vo., contemporary mottled calf, morocco labels. Dawsons PM 252-530 1974 £27

JOHNSON, SAMUEL The Rambler. London, n.d. 3 vols., 12mo., contemporary half morocco, boards. Dawsons PM 252-528 1974 £22

JOHNSON, SAMUEL The Rambler. London, 1793-95. 4 vols., 12mo., contemporary calf, plates. Dawsons PM 252-529 1974 £32

JOHNSON, SAMUEL The Rambler. London, 1801. 4 vols., 8vo., 19th century tree calf, fourteenth edition. Dawsons PM 252-531 .1974 £27

JOHNSON, SAMUEL The Rambler. London, 1826. 3 vols., 12mo., orig. cloth-backed boards, new edition. Dawsons PM 252-532 1974 £22

JOHNSON, SAMUEL Rasselas. London, 1816. 12mo., rebacked, contemporary tree calf, frontispiece. Dawsons PM 252-536 1974 £12

JOHNSON, SAMUEL Rasselas. London, 1796. 8vo., plates, contemporary tree calf, gilt, new edition. Dawsons PM 252-534 1974 £13

JOHNSON, SAMUEL Rasselas. London, 1783. 8vo., rebacked, contemporary calf, sixth edition. Dawsons PM 252-533 1974 £12

JOHNSON, SAMUEL Rasselas. Cambridge, 1804. 12mo., rubbed, contemporary calf. Ximenes 33-405 1974 $17.50

JOHNSON, SAMUEL Rassela. Londra, 1823. 12mo., contemporary olive straight-grain morocco gilt. Dawsons PM 252-538 1974 £8.50

JOHNSON, SAMUEL Rasselas, The Prince of Abissinia. 1759. Small 8vo., contemporary calf, gilt, rebacked, scarce, first edition. Quaritch 936-125 1974 £200

JOHNSON, SAMUEL Taxation No Tyranny. London, 1775. Plain blue wrappers, disbound, fine, rare, first edition, first issue. Bradley 35-208 1974 $750

JOHNSON, SAMUEL Thoughts on the Late Transactions Respecting Falkland's Islands. London, 1771. 8vo., modern boards, second edition. Dawsons PM 252-539 1974 £28

JOHNSON, SAMUEL The Triple Wreath. Philadelphia, 1844. 12mo., orig. brown cloth, first edition. Ximenes 33-406 1974 $22.50

JOHNSON, SAMUEL The Works. London, 1806. 12 vols., 8vo., contemporary speckled calf. Dawsons PM 252-540 1974 £80

JOHNSON, SAMUEL The Works of. 1810. 8vo., 12 vols., gilt, contemporary half calf. Bow Windows 64-574 1974 £65

JOHNSON, SAMUEL The Works. London, 1810. 14 vols., 8vo., contemporary straight morocco gilt, foxed. Dawsons PM 252-541 1974 £165

JOHNSON, SAMUEL Works. 1816. 12mo., 12 vols., contemporary straight grained morocco, leather labels, worn, staining. Heffer 38-707 1973 £20

JOHNSON, SAMUEL The Works. London, 1820. 12 vols., 8vo., full contemporary straight-grained morocco, gilt, new edition. Dawsons PM 252-542 1974 £190

JOHNSON, SAMUEL The Works. 1820. 12 vols., contemporary full straight grained morocco, gilt. Howes 185-249 1974 £55

JOHNSON, SAMUEL Works. Oxford, 1825. 8vo., 11 vols., half hard grain morocco, worn, gilt. Quaritch 936-430 1974 £45

JOHNSON, SAMUEL Works. 1825. 9 vols., half calf, ex-library. Allen 216-K 1974 $45

JOHNSON, SAMUEL The Works Of. 1825. 6 vols., 8vo., contemporary calf, some joints cracked, portrait. Bow Windows 66-382 1974 £20

JOHNSON, T. Descriptio Itineris Plantarum. 1849. Small 4to., half vellum, scarce. Wheldon 130-1504 1974 £7.50

JOHNSON, T. Opuscula Omnia Botanica. 1847. Small 4to., orig. boards, plates. Wheldon 131-1231 1974 £25

JOHNSON, THEODORE Illustrations of British Hawk Moths. 1874(-1876). Small 4to., contemporary half red morocco gilt, plates, rare. Wheldon 130-30 1974 £150

JOHNSON, THEODORE Miniature Plays For Stage or Study. Baker, 1940. 159p., paper. Austin 51-469 1973 $7.50

JOHNSON, VIRGINIA W. Travels of an American Owl. Philadelphia, 1871. 8vo., orig. cloth, illus., first edition. Ximenes 33-407 1974 $10

JOHNSON, W. F. History of Cooper County, Missouri. Topeka, 1919. 4to., three quarter leather, illus. Saddleback 14-527 1974 $60

JOHNSON, W. R. History of Rome, in Easy Verse. 1808. Folding map, 12mo., orig. boards, roan spine, trifle rubbed. George's 610-416 1973 £6

JOHNSON, WALTER Gilbert White, Pioneer, Poet and Stylist. 1928. Scarce, illus. Howes 185-555 1974 £5

JOHNSTON, A. Myths and Facts of the American Revolution. Toronto, 1908. Hood's 104-645 1974 $20

JOHNSTON, A. Myths and Facts of the American Revolution, a Commentary on United States History as Is Written. Toronto, 1908. Hood's 102-565 1974 $20

JOHNSTON, ALEXANDER KEITH The Physical Atlas of Natural Phenomena. Edinburgh & London, 1850. Imp. 4to., new cloth, hand coloured maps, second edition. Wheldon 128-36 1973 £25

JOHNSTON, ALEXANDER KEITH The Physical Atlas of Natural Phenomena. Edinburgh, 1850. Small folio, rebound in buckram, maps. Wheldon 131-165 1974 £50

JOHNSTON, ALEXANDER KEITH Royal Atlas of Modern Geography. 1861. Half morocco, maps, worn sides. Smith 193-530 1973 £10

JOHNSTON, ALVA The Great Goldwyn. Random, 1937. 99p., illus. Austin 51-470 1973 $7.50

JOHNSTON, ANNIE F. The Little Colonel. 145p., illus. Austin 51-958 1973 $10

JOHNSTON, CHARLES Chrysal. London, 1760. 2 vols., 12mo., contemporary calf, labels, first edition. Dawsons PM 252-589 1974 £75

JOHNSTON, EDWARD A Carol, and Other Rhymes. Hammersmith, 1916. 12mo., printed in red & black, very nice copy, first edition. Covent 51-1008 1973 £7.50

JOHNSTON, G.　　　　The Botany of the Eastern Borders.　1853.
8vo., cloth, plates, scarce.　Wheldon 131-1233 1974 £10

JOHNSTON, G.　　　　Correspondence.　Edinburgh, 1892.　8vo.,
cloth, portrait.　Wheldon 131-230 1974 £10

JOHNSTON, G.　　　　A Flora of Berwick-upon-Tweed.　Edinburgh,
1829-31.　8vo., new cloth, plates.　Wheldon 129-1003 1974 £12

JOHNSTON, G.　　　　A History of British Sponges and Lithophytes.
Edinburgh, 1842.　8vo., orig. cloth, plates.　Wheldon 130-872 1974 £20

JOHNSTON, G.　　　　A History of the British Zoophytes.　1847.
2 vols., 8vo., new cloth, plates, second edition.　Wheldon 128-907 1973 £10

JOHNSTON, G.　　　　A History of the British Zoophytes.　1847.　8vo.,
2 vols., cloth, plates, scarce, second edition.　Wheldon 130-873 1974 £15

JOHNSTON, G.　　　　A History of the British Zoophytes.　1847.　8vo.,
orig. wrappers, plates, scarce, second edition.　Wheldon 130-874 1974 £20

JOHNSTON, G.　　　　A History of the British Zoophytes.　1847.
2 vols., roy. 8vo., contemporary straight grain morocco, gilt, very scarce,
nice copy.　Wheldon 131-935 1974 £30

JOHNSTON, G.　　　　An Introduction to Conchology.　1850.　8vo.,
cloth.　Wheldon 128-842 1973 £5

JOHNSTON, H.　　　　British Mammals, an Attempt to Describe and
Illustrate the Mammalian Fauna of the British Islands.　1903.　8vo., cloth,
coloured and other illus.　Wheldon 128-332 1973 £5

JOHNSTON, HARRY　　　　Mrs. Warren's Daughter.　1920.　Contemporary
half calf, English first edition.　Covent 56-1350 1974 £7.50

JOHNSTON, HARRY　　　　The Uganda Protectorate.　New York and London,
1902.　Crown 4to., 2 vols., orig. dec. cloth, maps, illus.　Wheldon 129-277
1974 £40

JOHNSTON, HARRY　　　　The Uganda Protectorate.　1904.　4to., 2 vols.,
cloth, illus., maps.　Wheldon 129-278 1974 £38

JOHNSTON, HARRY　　　　The Uganda Protectorate.　1904.　2 vols.,
4to., cloth, plates, second edition.　Wheldon 131-364 1974 £40

JOHNSTON, I. M.　　　　Expedition of the California Academy of
Sciences to the Gulf of California in 1921.　1924.　Roy. 8vo., wrappers.
Wheldon 131-1319 1974 £5

JOHNSTON, J.　　　　Grenfell of Labrador.　Toronto, n.d.　Map,
illus., portrait.　Hood's 103-215 1974 $15

JOHNSTON, MARY　　　　Cease Firing.　Boston, 1912.　First edition,
8vo., full color illus., spine faded, else very good.　Current BW9-240 1974
$12.50

JOHNSTON, MARY　　　　The Long Roll.　Boston, 1911.　1st ed., illus.
Biblo & Tannen 214-735 1974 $12.50

JOHNSTON, NATHANIEL　　　　The Assurance of Abby and Other Church-Lands
in England.　London, 1687.　Small 8vo., modern boards, first edition.　Dawsons
PM 251-507 1974 £25

JOHNSTON, REGINALD FLEMING　　　Buddhist China.　1913.　Plates,
inscription.　Howes 186-1860 1974 £5.50

JOHNSTON, W.　　　　History of the County of Perth, 1825-1902.
Stratford, 1903.　Portraits, illus., mended spine.　Hood's 103-647 1974 $45

JOHNSTONE, CHARLES　　　　Chrysal.　London, 1768 (vols. 1 & 2), 1767
(vols. 3 & 4).　4 vols., 12mo., contemporary calf, rubbed, hinges weak, very
good set, vols. 1 & 2 second editions, vols. 3 & 4 sixth editions.　MacManus
224-259 1974 $25

JOHNSTONE, CHARLES　　　　Chrysal.　1821.　8vo., 3 vols., contemporary
diced calf gilt, plates, fine, scarce, first illustrated edition.　Quaritch 936-436
1974 £60

JOHNSTONE, J.　　　　Historical and Descriptive Account of the Palace
and Chapel-Royal of Holyroodhouse.　Edinburgh, 1825-26.　2 items in 1 vol.,
contemporary morocco gilt.　Quaritch 939-658 1974 £7.50

JOHNSTONE, J.　　　　The Marine Plankton With Special Reference to
Investigations Made at Port Erin, 1907-14.　1924.　8vo., cloth, plates, very
scarce.　Wheldon 128-149 1973 £5

JOHNSTONE, J.　　　　A Treatise on the Malignant Angina.　Worcester, 1779.　8vo., boards, inscribed.　Gurney 64-119 1974 £25

JOHNSTONE, JAMES　　　　The Disbanded Officer.　London, 1786.　8vo.,
modern boards, first edition.　Dawsons PM 252-590 1974 £15

JOHNSTONE, JAMES　　　　Lodbrokar-Quida.　(Copenhagen), 1782.
8vo., contemporary diced russia gilt, first edition.　Dawsons PM 252-591
1974 £48

JOHNSTONE, JAMES　　　　Lodbrokar-Quida.　N.P., 1782.　Small 8vo.,
contemporary calf, rubbed, first edition.　Ximenes 33-409 1974 $35

JOHNSTONE, JAMES JOHNSTONE, CHEVALIER DE 1719-1800　Memoirs of
the Rebellion.　London, 1822.　8vo., foxing, half roan, worn, third edition.
Bow Windows 62-508 1974 £15

JOHNSTONE, JOHN　　　　An Account of the Mode of Draining Land.　London, 1808.　8vo., orig. boards, rebacked, uncut, plates, third edition.　Hammond
201-856 1974 £12.50

JOHNSTONE, JOHN　　　　An Account of the Most Approved Mode of
Draining Land.　Edinburgh & London, 1797.　4to., orig. boards, fine, first
edition.　Dawsons PM 247-159 1974 £65

JOHNSTONE, JOHN　　　　A Systematic Treatise on the Theory and Practice
of Draining Land.　Edinburgh, 1834.　4to., orig. cloth-backed boards, plates,
third edition.　Hammond 201-855 1974 £18.50

JOHNSTONE, W. G.　　　　The Nature Printed British Sea Weeds.　1859.
4 vols., orig. green binding.　Eaton Music-617 1973 £60

JOHNSTONE, W. G.　　　　The Nature-Printed British Sea-Weeds.　1859-
60.　Roy 8vo., 4 vols., contemporary half red morocco gilt, plates.　Wheldon
130-1304 1974 £90

JOHODA, MARIE　　　　Research Method in Social Relations.　Dryden,
1951.　Austin 62-296 1974 $15

JOKAI, MAURICE　　　　The New Landlord.　London, 1868.　2 vols.,
8vo., orig. blue cloth, first English edition.　Ximenes 33-410 1974 $30

JOKAI, MAURICE　　　　Timar's Two Worlds.　Edinburgh & London,
1888.　3 vols., 8vo., orig. pictorial cloth, first English edition.　Ximenes
33-411 1974 $60

JOLAS, EUGENE　　　　The Language of Night.　The Hague, 1932.
Wrappers, English first edition.　Covent 56-742 1974 £10.50

JOLI, GUY　　　　Memoirs.　Dublin, 1777.　2 vols., 12mo.,
contemporary calf, fine, first Dublin edition.　Ximenes 33-412 1974 $27.50

JOLIET Illustrated: Historical, Descriptive and Biographical.　Joliet, 1897.
8vo., cloth.　Saddleback 14-386 1974 $15

JOLLY Mother Goose Annual.　New York & Chicago, (1912).　4to., orig. red
cloth pictorial covers, very good, binding recased, full color illus.　Current
BW9-116 1974 $15

JOLY, HENRY L.　　　　Legend in Japanese Art.　1908.　4to., plates,
orig. dec. cloth.　Quaritch 940-404 1974 £60

JOMARD, EDME FRANCOIS　　　Catalogue des Livres de la Bibliotheque de
M. Jomard.　Paris, 1863.　8vo., wrappers.　Kraus B8-118 1974 $20

JONAS, JUSTUS　　　　Doctor Martin Luters Christlicher Abschid und
Sterben.　(Wittenberg), 1546.　4to., morocco-backed boards, first edition.
Harper 213-204 1973 $350

JONAS, JUSTUS   Vom Christlichen Abschied Aus Diesem Todlichen Leben des Ehrwirdigen Herrn D. Martini Lutheri. Wittenberg, 1546. 4to., boards, rare first edition. Harper 213-205 1973 $350

JONAS, JUSTUS   Zwo Trostliche Predigt, Uber der Leich. Wittenberg, 1546. 4to., boards, first edition. Harper 213-206 1973 $275

JONAS, M.   Notes of an Art Collector. 1907. 4to., plates, orig. cloth backed boards. Smith 194-103 1974 £5

JONES, C. SHERIDAN   Brave Deeds by Brave Men. n.d. Cloth-backed pictorial boards, illus., plates, English first edition. Covent 56-372 1974 £5.25

JONES, CHARLES H.   Appletons' Hand Book of American Travel. New York and London, 1873. Maps, orig. binding. Butterfield 10-490 1974 $20

JONES, CHESTER H.   Ancient Architecture. 1933. Large 8vo., cloth, illus., scarce. Quaritch 940-518 1974 £5

JONES, DAVID   A Compleat History of Europe. 1701. Thick crown 8vo., contemporary calf, third edition. Howes 186-963 1974 £15

JONES, E.   Index to Records Called. 1793-95. 2 vols., folio, contemporary sprinkled calf, rebacked. Quaritch 939-150 1974 £45

JONES, EDWARD ALFRED   Catalogue of the Collection of Old Plate of William Farrer. 1924. 4to., plates, crimson morocco gilt, slip case, limited. Quaritch 940-675 1974 £150

JONES, EDWARD ALFRED   Catalogue of the Collection of Old Pate of William Francis Farrer. London, 1924. Large 4to., frontis., red half morocco, slipcase. Bow Windows 62-509 1974 £105

JONES, EDWARD ALFRED   A Catalogue of the Objects in Gold and Silver and the Limoges Enamels in the Collection of the Baroness James de Rothschild. 1912. Folio, plates, orig. Kelmscott boards, limited edition. Quaritch 940-686 1974 £95

JONES, EDWARD ALFRED   The Gold and Silver and Windsor Castle. 1911. First edition, plates, folio, fine, limited to 285 numbered copies. Covent 51-429 1973 £40

JONES, EDWARD ALFRED   The Gold and Silver Plate of Windsor Castle. 1911. Folio, top edges gilt, others uncut, good copy, monochrome plates, orig. cloth, binding faded, limited to 285 copies. Broadhurst 24-119 1974 £30

JONES, EDWARD ALFRED   The Gold and Silver Plate of Winsor Castle. 1911. Folio, orig. cloth, uncut, limited. Broadhurst 23-115 1974 £35

JONES, EDWARD ALFRED   The Old Church Plate of the Isle of Man. London, 1907. 4to., plates, orig. red cloth. Covent 55-107 1974 £7.50

JONES, EDWARD ALFRED   Old English Gold Plate. 1907. Large 4to., plates. Covent 55-459 1974 £15

JONES, EDWARD ALFRED   The Plate of Eton College. 1938. 4to., plates, buckram, fine, English first edition. Covent 56-1650 1974 £15.75

JONES, ERASMUS   Luxury, Pride, and Vanity, the Bane of the British Nation. London, n.d. 8vo., wrappers, first edition. Ximenes 33-413 1974 $30

JONES, EVANS R.   The Emigrant's Friend. London, 1881. 351p., rev. ed. Austin 62-308 1974 $47.50

JONES, F. M.   The History of Winside, Nebraska. N.P., 1942. 8vo., wrapper. Saddleback 14-536 1974 $15

JONES, F. W.   Man's Place Among the Mammals. 1929. 8vo., cloth, scarce, plates. Wheldon 131-500 1974 £10

JONES, G. H.   Celtic Britain and the Pilgrim Movement. 1912. 8vo., orig. cloth, plates. Broadhurst 23-1427 1974 £5

JONES, G. H.   Celtic Britain and the Pilgrim Movement. 1912. Demy 8vo., plates, orig. cloth, fine. Broadhurst 24-1447 1974 £5

JONES, GRIFFITH   Welch Piety. London, 1758. 8vo., half morocco, trifle rubbed, first edition. Ximenes 37-123 1974 £40

JONES, H. G.   Uganda in Transformation 1876-1926. 1926. 8vo., orig. cloth, maps, illus., some spotting, inscription by author, first edition. Bow Windows 66-384 1974 £6

JONES, HENRY   The Earl of Essex. London, 1753. 8vo., modern boards, first edition. Dawsons PM 252-592 1974 £15

JONES, HENRY   A Sermon of Antichrist, Preached at Christ Church, Dublin. London, 1679. Small 4to., boards, soiled, revised second edition. Thomas 28-98 1972 £5

JONES, HENRY ARTHUR   Saints and Sinners. London, 1891. 8vo., orig. vellum, presentation, first edition. Dawsons PM 252-593 1974 £30

JONES, HENRY D.   The Evangelical Movement. 1933-34. 39p. Austin 62-307 1974 $15

JONES, HENRY FESTING   Diversions in Sicily. 1909. 8vo., 2 vols., wrappers, signed, presentation inscription, first edition. Rota 189-516 1974 £10

JONES, HENRY FESTING   Samuel Butler, a Memoir. 1919. Plates, 2 vols., rebound, cloth, English first edition. Covent 56-205 1974 £15

JONES, J.   Gleanings from God's Acre. 1903. 4to., orig. cloth. Broadhurst 23-1429 1974 £4

JONES, J. B.   A Rebel War Clerk's Diary at the Confederate States Capital. Philadelphia, 1866. 2 vols., orig. binding. Butterfield 10-161 1974 $45

JONES, J. P.   Flora Devoniensis. 1829. 8vo., new cloth, scarce. Wheldon 130-1094 1974 £10

JONES, JAMES ATHEARN   Haverhill. London, 1831. 3 vols., orig. boards, linen spines. Hood's 102-522 1974 $350

JONES, JOHN B.   The Cinque Ports. 1903. Crown 4to., orig. wrappers, cloth, plates, illus. Howes 186-2046 1974 £6

JONES, JOHN FREDERICK D.   A Treatise On the Process Employed by Nature In Suppressing the Hemorrhage. Philadelphia, 1811. 8vo., contemporary calf, plates, first American edition. Schuman 37-130 1974 $85

JONES, L. W.   Miniatures of the MSS. of Terence Prio to the 13th Century. 1930-31. 4to., 2 vols., plates. Allen 213-1051 1973 $45

JONES, LOTTIE   History of Vermilion County, Illinois. Chicago, 1911. 8vo., three quarter leather, illus. Saddleback 14-387 1974 $17.50

JONES, M. C.   Feudal Barons of Powys. 1868. Limited. Allen 213-1721 1973 $12.50

JONES, MARGARET   The Charity School Movement. 1938. Roy. 8vo., plates, illus., orig. edition. Howes 186-1469 1974 £6.50

JONES, MARK M.   Alameda County, California. (Oakland), c.1915. 12mo., wrapper. Saddleback 14-152 1974 $12.50

JONES, MARY   Autobiography of Mother Jones. Chicago, 1925. Blue cloth, illus., first edition. Dawson's 424-341 1974 $12.50

JONES, MARY   Miscellanies in Prose and Verse. Oxford, 1750. 8vo., old calf, first edition. Ximenes 33-414 1974 $200

JONES, OWEN   Examples of Chinese Ornament. London, 1867. 4to., 100 col. plates. Jacobs 24-45 1974 $150

JONES, ROBERT   Artificial Fireworks. London, 1776. 8vo., contemporary calf, morocco label, fine, second edition. Ximenes 33-415 1974 $200

JONES, OWEN   The Grammar of Ornament. London, 1868. Folio, orig. cloth, leaves unsewn, some damp stains, back repaired, colored lithographed plates. Kraus B8-418 1974 $250

JONES, OWEN   The Grammar of Ornament. 1868. Small folio, plates, lacks all binding. Smith 193-668 1973 £6

JONES, OWEN   The Grammar of Ornament. London, 1868.
Folio, color plates. Biblo & Tannen 210-119 1973 $75

JONES, OWEN   The Grammar of Ornament. 1868. Small
folio, woodcuts, half morocco. Quaritch 940-454 1974 £80

JONES, OWEN   The Grammar of Ornament. 1910. Small
folio, orig. cloth, recased, clean copy. Quaritch 940-455 1974 £75

JONES, OWEN   The Grammar of Ornament. London, 1910.
4to., 112 plates, orig. cl., gilt. Jacobs 24-46 1974 $125

JONES, OWEN   Plans, Elevations, Sections and Details of the
Alhambra. 1842-45. 2 vols., atlas folio, large paper, half morocco, plates,
gilt. Quaritch 940-521 1974 £500

JONES, OWEN   The Preacher. 1849. 4to., illuminated in
gold throughout. Smith 194-480 1974 £10

JONES, OWEN   The Psalms of David. (N.P., n.d.). Large
4to., contemporary brown morocco. Bow Windows 62-511 1974 £85

JONES, OWEN   The Psalms of David. 1861-62. Folio, orig.
binding, rubbed. Howes 186-281 1974 £85

JONES, OWEN   The Psalms of David Illuminated. London,
1861. Folio, contemp. leather, elab. blind-tooled, illus. Jacobs 24-44 1974
$100

JONES, RHYS   Gorchestion Beirdd Cymru Neu Flodau
Godidowgrwydd Awen. (Shrewsbury), 1773. Large 4to., new half roan, uncut,
good condition. Thomas 32-199 1974 £21

JONES, ROBERT   A New Treatise on Artificial Fireworks. London,
1765. 8vo., half calf, rebound, gilt, plates, first edition. Dawsons PM 245-
421 1974 £165

JONES, ROBERT   Notes on Military Orthopaedics. New York,
1917. Rittenhouse 46-367 1974 $10

JONES, ROBERT   Orthopaedic Surgery of Injuries. London,
1921. 2 vols., roy. 8vo., orig. cloth, illus., first edition. Schuman 37-131
1974 $95

JONES, S. G.   Introduction to Floral Mechanism. 1945.
8vo., cloth, illus. Wheldon 130-1028 1974 £5

JONES, SYDNEY R.   Posters and Publicity, Fine Printing and Design.
1926. Coloured & other plates, very good copy, first edition. Covent 51-1520
1973 £8.40

JONES, SYDNEY R.   The Village Homes of England. 1912. Orig.
binding, illus., plates. Marsden 39-257 1974 £5

JONES, T. R.   A Monograph of the British Palaeozoic
Phyllopoda. 1888-99. 4to., half calf, plates. Wheldon 131-1028 1974 £15

JONES, T. R.   A Monograph of the Entomostraca of the
Cretaceous Formation of England. 1849. 4to., boards, plates. Wheldon
131-1027 1974 £5

JONES, THEOPHILUS   History of the County of Brecknock. 1805-09.
2 vols., 4to., half library morocco, plates. Quaritch 939-686 1974 £65

JONES, THEOPHILUS   A History of the County of Brecknock. 1909-
1930. Roy 4to., 4 vols., half calf. Broadhurst 23-1430 1974 £40

JONES, THEOPHILUS   A History of the County of Brecknock. Brecknock,
1909-30. Engravings, portraits, maps, 4 vols., roy. 4to., half maroon calf, fine,
top edges gilt, Glanusk edition, scarce vol. 4. Broadhurst 24-1450 1974 £40

JONES, THOMAS   Diseases of the Bones. 1887. 8vo., orig.
cloth, first edition. Broadhurst 23-1241 1974 £10

JONES, W. B.   The History and Antiquities of St. Davids.
1856. 4to., plates, cloth. Quaritch 939-687 1974 £17.50

JONES, WILLIAM   The Catholic Doctrine of a Trinity. Urbana,
1819. 12mo., contemporary quarter calf, boards, scarce. Ximenes 33-417
1974 $25

JONES, WILLIAM   Crowns & Coronations. 1883. Illus. Allen
213-1577 1973 $10

JONES, WILLIAM   Poems. Oxford, 1772. 8vo., contemporary
calf, gilt, fine, first edition. Ximenes 33-416 1974 $85

JONES, WILLIAM   Synopsis Palmiorum Matheseos. London, 1706.
8vo., contemporary calf, plates, first edition. Dawsons PM 245-422 1974 £75

JONSON, BEN   The Alchemist. 1903. Ex-library, sturdy
library binding. Austin 61-510 1974 $17.50

JONSON, BEN   Bartholomew Fair. 1904. Ex-library,
sturdy library binding. Austin 61-511 1974 $17.50

JONSON, BEN   The Case Is Altered. 1917. Ex-library, sturdy
library binding. Austin 61-512 1974 $27.50

JONSON, BEN   Catiline His Conspiracy. 1916. Ex-library,
sturdy library binding. Austin 61-513 1974 $27.50

JONSON, BEN   Cynthia's Revels. 1912. Ex-library, sturdy
library binding. Austin 61-514 1974 $27.50

JONSON, BEN   The Devil Is an Ass. 1905. Ex-library, sturdy
library binding. Austin 61-515 1974 $37.50

JONSON, BEN   The English Grammar Made by . . . for the
Benefit of All Strangers. 1928. F'cap. 8vo., limp boards, mint, slip case, orig.
cloth. Broadhurst 24-372 1974 £6

JONSON, BEN   Every Man in His Humour. 1752. 8vo., modern
quarter morocco. Hill 126-214 1974 £5.50

JONSON, BEN   Every Man In His Humor. 1921. Ex-library,
sturdy library binding, waterstained. Austin 61-517 1974 $17.50

JONSON, BEN   The Magnetic Lady. 1914. Ex-library, sturdy
library binding. Austin 61-518 1974 $27.50

JONSON, BEN   The New Inn, Or the Light Heart. 1908.
Ex-library, sturdy library binding. Austin 61-519 1974 $37.50

JONSON, BEN   Poetaster. 1905. Ex-library, sturdy library
binding. Austin 61-520 1974 $37.50

JONSON, BEN   The Staple of News. 1905. Ex-library, sturdy
library binding. Austin 61-521 1974 $37.50

JONSON, BEN   Volpone. 1898. First edition, illus. by
Aubrey Beardsley, 4to., orig. blue cloth, fine copy, scarce, limited edition.
Sawyer 293-55 1974 £37.50

JONSON, BEN   Volpone, Or the Fox. 1919. Ex-library,
sturdy library binding. Austin 61-522 1974 $17.50

JONSON, BEN   Epicoene, Or the Silent Woman. 1906.
Ex-library, sturdy library binding. Austin 61-516 1974 $27.50

JONSON, BEN   Works. 1860. New buckram. Allen 216-1914
1974 $17.50

JONSON, BEN   Works, With Notes & Memoir. 1875. 9 vols.,
buckram, some labels defective. Allen 216-L 1974 $75

JONSON, BEN   Works. London, 1692. Folio, old panelled
calf, rebacked, first complete collected edition. Goodspeed's 578-171 1974
$250

JONSON, BEN   The English Grammar. 1928. 8vo., limp boards,
slipcase. Broadhurst 23-392 1974 £6

JONSON, BEN   The Works Of. (c., 1879). 8vo., orig. cloth,
3 vols. Bow Windows 64-575 1974 £6.75

JONSON, BEN   The Works of. London, 1838. 8vo., portrait, half calf, rubbed. Bow Windows 62-926 1974 £7.50

JONSON, BENJAMIN   Bartholomew Fayre. London, 1631. Folio, plain pink wrappers, first edition. Dawsons PM 252-594 1974 £25

JONSON, BENJAMIN   The Workes Of. 1640. 2 vols., small folio, contemporary calf. Thomas 28-245 1972 £100

JONSTONUS, JOANNES 1603-1675   Historiae Naturalis de Piscibus et Cetis. 1767. Folio, old calf, worn. Wheldon 130-701 1974 £80

JONSTONUS, JOANNES 1603-1675   Thaumatographia Naturalis. Amsterdam, 1632. 12mo., contemporary calf. Wheldon 129-1707 1974 £70

JONSTONUS, JOANNES 1603-1675   Thaumatographia Naturalis. Amsterdam, 1632. 12mo., contemporary calf, rebacked, rare first edition. Wheldon 131-437 1974 £70

JONSTONUS, JOANNES 1603-1675   Theatrum Universale de Avibus. Heilbronn, 1756. Folio, contemporary calf gilt, plates. Wheldon 130-561 1974 £80

JOPLING, LOUISE   Twenty Years of My Life. 1925. 8vo., cloth, plates, first edition. Quaritch 936-356 1974 £25

JORDAENS, J.   Jordaens: Sa Vie et ses Oeuvres. Amsterdam & Anvers, 1906. Roy. 4to., half morocco, gilt. Quaritch 940-149 1974 £65

JORDAN, A.   Diagnoses d'especes Nouvelles. Paris, 1864. Roy 8vo., buckram. Wheldon 129-1090 1974 £10

JORDAN, A.   Observations sur Plusieurs Plantes Nouvelles. 1846-49. Roy 8vo., half calf. Wheldon 129-1089 1974 £20

JORDAN, CHARLOTTE B.   Discovering Christopher Columbus. New York, 1932. 1st ed., illus. Biblo & Tannen 213-27 1973 $7.50

JORDAN, D. S.   American Food & Game Fishes. New York, 1902. Colored plates, text drawings, photos, first edition, 4to., near fine. Current BW9-187 1974 $40

JORDAN, D. S.   The Fishes of Samoa. Washington, 1906. Imp. 8vo., new cloth, plates. Wheldon 131-758 1974 £25

JORDAN, DONALDSON   Europe and the American Civil War. Boston, 1931. Orig. Binding. Wilson 63-361 1974 $10

JORDAN, HENRY H.   Orthopedic Appliances. New York, 1939. Rittenhouse 46-368 1974 $10

JORDAN, J. A.   The Grosse-Isle Tragedy and the Monument to the Irish Fever Victims. Quebec, 1909. Illus. Hood's 102-719 1974 $17.50

JORDAN, PHILIP   Singin Yankees. 1946. 305p., illus. Austin 51-471 1973 $8.50

JORDAN, W. K.   The Development of Religious Toleration in England. 1936. Scarce. Howes 185-1313 1974 £5.50

JORDEN, EDWARD   A Discourse of Natural Bathes and Mineral Waters. 1673. 8vo., contemporary calf. Dawsons PM 249-307 1974 £95

JORDEN, EDWARD   A Discourse of Natural Bathes, and Mineral Waters. London, 1669. 2 parts in 1 vol., small 8vo., cloth-backed boards, woodcuts. Schuman 37-132 1974 $135

JORET, C.   La Rose dans l'Antiquite. Paris, 1892. 8vo., cloth, scarce. Wheldon 129-1486 1974 £7.50

JORTIN, JOHN   The Life of Erasmus. London, 1758-60. 2 vols., 4to., contemporary sprinkled calf, first edition. Dawsons PM 252-596 1974 £55

JORTIN, JOHN   Remarks On Spenser's Poems. London, 1734. 8vo., contemporary sheep, first edition. Dawsons PM 252-597 1974 £60

JORTIN, JOHN   Sermons on Different Subjects. 1771-72. 7 vols., contemporary tree calf, labels. Howes 185-1314 1974 £7.50

JOSEPH Richmond & Company Ltd. Lifts and Cranes Trade Catalogue. 1906. Illus., fine. Covent 55-1460 1974 £6.50

JOSEPHINE, MATTHEW   The Robber Barons. New York, 1934. 1st ed. Biblo & Tannen 213-45 1973 $8.50

JOSEPHUS, FLAVIUS   Famous & Memorable Workes. 1640. New buckram. Allen 213-572 1973 $75

JOSEPHUS, FLAVIUS   The Genuine Works of. London, 1822. 2 vols., 4to., map, plates, contemporary diced calf, stains. Bow Windows 62-512 1974 £7.50

JOSEPHUS, FLAVIUS   Historici Preclara Opera. Paris, 1513-14. 3 parts in 1 vol., has the final blank, small folio, modern calf, upper borderline of title just shaved, else excellent copy. Thomas 32-238 1974 £120

JOSEPHUS, FLAVIUS   Opeara Quae Extant Omnia. Cologne, 1691. Folio, contemporary calf, damaged. Schumann 499-55 1974 sFr 1,250

JOSEPHUS, FLAVIUS   Works. Philadelphia & New York, 1773-75. 4 vols., first American edition. Allen 213-573 1973 $100

JOSEPHUS, FLAVIUS   The Works Of. London, 1701. 2 vols. in 1, contemporary panelled calf, rubbed, second edition. Smith 194-165 1974 £12

JOSEPHUS, FLAVIUS   The Works of. Glasgow, 1773. Seventh edition, 12mo., 6 books bound in 4, frontis., old calf, hinges weak, rubbed, nice old set, interiors browned with age and foxed. Current BW9-554 1974 $20

JOSLYN, R. WAITE   Elgin, Past and Present, Historical and Biographical. Elgin, (c.1927). 8vo., cloth. Saddleback 14-388 1974 $15

JOUBERT, LAURENT   La Prima Parte de Gli Errori Poplari. Florence, 1592. Small 4to., modern boards, some pages slightly browned, but clean sound copy. Thomas 32-318 1974 £40

JOUET, CHEVALIER H.   Index to the Literature of Thorium 1817-1902. Washington, 1903. 8vo., contemporary boards, gilt, first edition. Dawsons PM 245-423 1974 £10

JOUGUET, PIERRE   Macedonian Imperialism and the Hellenization of the East. New York, 1932. Illus. Biblo & Tannen 214-627 1974 $20

JOUHANDEAU, MARCEL   Astaroth. Paris, 1929. 12mo., orig. wrapper, uncut, first edition. L. Goldschmidt 42-260 1974 $15

JOUHANDEAU, MARCEL   Les Pincengrain. Paris, 1924. Orig. wrapper, signed, first edition. L. Goldschmidt 42-262 1974 $15

JOUHANDEAU, MARCEL   Opales. Paris, 1928. 12mo., orig. wrapper, first edition. L. Goldschmidt 42-261 1974 $10

JOUIN, H.   David D'Angers. Sa Vie, Son Oeuvres, Ses Ecrits et ses Contemporains. Paris, 1878. 2 vols., large 8vo., quarter morocco, gilt spines. Eaton Music-618 1973 £25

JOURDAIN, CHARLES   La Philosophie de Saint Thomas D'Aquin. Paris, 1858. 2 vols., 8vo., book-plate, contemporary half calf. Bow Windows 62-513 1974 £6.50

JOURDAIN, MARGARET   Decoration in England from 1640-1760. 1927. Small folio, cloth, illus., second edition. Quaritch 940-579 1974 £9

JOURDAIN, MARGARET   Decoration in England from 1640-1760. 1927. Folio, photos, cloth, revised second edition. Eaton Music-628 1973 £10

JOURDAIN, MARGARET   The History of English Secular Embroidery. 1910. Cloth, spine torn, illus. Eaton Music-619 1973 £5

JOURDAN, CLAUDE   Zeer Gedenkwaardige en Naaukeurige Reisbeschrijivinge. Leiden, 1700. 4to., contemporary calf, worn but sound, library stamp, frontispiece, copperplates, very scarce, first edition. Ximenes 37-124 1974 $175

JOURDANET, D.   Influence de la Pression de l'Air sur la Vie de l'Homme. Climats d'Altitude et Climats de Montagne. Paris, 1875. Large 8vo., 2 vols., half leather, worn, first edition, profusely illus. Gurney 66-93 1974 £30

JOURNAL Des Demoiselles. Paris, 1876-80. 5 vols., roy. 8vo., plates, half green calf, leather labels. Quaritch 940-721 1974 £600

A JOURNAL Devoted to Home-Life, Agriculture, Commerce, Mines and Other Resources of Washington Territory. New Tacoma, 1880-81. 6 vols., folio, orig. wrappers, scarce. Ximenes 35-479 1974 $100

JOURNAL Of a Lady of Quality: Narrative From Scotland to West Indies, North Carolina & Portugal, 1774-76. New Haven, 1921. Rinsland 58-73 1974 $35

THE JOURNAL OF Hellenic Studies. London, n.d. Folio, plates, quarter calf, first edition. Dawsons PM 251-35 1974 £20

THE JOURNAL of the Cambrian Archaeological Association. 1898-1916. Howes 186-2216 1974 £40

JOURNAL of the Econometric Society. 1936-41. 6 vols. in 20. Howes 186-1402 1974 £21

JOURNAL of the Ex Libris Society. London, 1891-1908. 18 vols., 4to., orig. dec. cloth, orig. wrappers, illus. Dawsons PM 10-69 1974 £100

JOURNALS of the Legislative Assembly of Upper Canada for the Years 1792 to 1824. Toronto, 1909-14. 5 vols., marbled boards, fine. Hood's 104-900 1974 $150

JOUVE, PIERRE JEAN   Gloire 1940. 1944. 4to., wrappers, uncut, very good copy, limited edition. Minters 37-95 1973 $13.50

JOUVE, PIERRE JEAN   Priere. Paris, 1924. 12mo., boards, orig. pcitorial wrapper, first edition. L. Goldschmidt 42-265 1974 $15

JOWETT, WILLIAM   Diary of Sergeant William Jowett. 1856. 8vo., orig. limp cloth, scarce, first edition, second issue. Ximenes 33-418 1974 $15

JOY, HENRY   Historical Collections Relative to the Town of Belfast. Belfast, 1817. Rebound, label. Howes 186-964 1974 £8.50

JOY, N. H.   A Practical Handbook of British Beetles. 1932. Roy 8vo., 2 vols., orig. cloth, plates, scarce. Wheldon 130-768 1974 £50

JOYAU, A.   Catalogue de l'Oeuvre Grave de Amedee Joyau. 1938. Roy. 4to., illus., orig. wrappers, uncut, limited. Quaritch 940-150 1974 £20

JOYCE, GEORGE H.   Christian Marriage. 1933. 645 pages. Howes 185-1318 1974 £5

JOYCE, J.   Scientific Dialogues. 1860. Small 8vo., orig. cloth, illus. Hammond 201-871 1974 £5.50

JOYCE, JAMES   Anna Livia Plurabelle. London, 1930. Biblo & Tannen 213-785 1973 $10

JOYCE, JAMES   Anna Livia Plurabelle. 1930. First English edition, crown 8vo., sewn, orig. stiff paper printed wrapper, mint. Broadhurst 24-752 1974 £6

JOYCE, JAMES   Anna Livia Plurabelle. 1930. Crown 8vo., sewn, orig. paper printed wrapper, mint, first English edition. Broadhurst 23-781 1974 £5

JOYCE, JAMES   Anna Livia Plurabelle. 1930. Dust wrapper, English first edition. Covent 56-747 1974 £5.25

JOYCE, JAMES   Anna Livia Plurabelle. 1930. 8vo., wrappers, first English edition. Rota 189-520 1974 £7.50

JOYCE, JAMES   Chamber Music. New York, 1923. 8vo., boards, uncut. Emerald 50-475 1974 £20

JOYCE, JAMES   Continuation of a Work in Progress. Paris, 1927. Wrappers, English first edition. Covent 56-748 1974 £10

JOYCE, JAMES   Continuation of a Work in Progress. Paris, 1928. Wrappers, English first edition. Covent 56-749 1974 £10

JOYCE, JAMES   Dedalus: Portrait de l'Artiste Jeune par Lui-Meme. Paris, 1924. White wrappers, superlative copy, unopened. Covent 51-2393 1973 £40

JOYCE, JAMES   Exiles. London, 1918. 8vo., orig. cloth backed boards, first English edition. Dawsons PM 252-598 1974 £76

JOYCE, JAMES   Finnegans Wake. 1939. First American edition. Allen 216-864 1974 $25

JOYCE, JAMES   Finnegans Wake. London, 1939. Large 8vo., orig. red cloth, fine, first edition. Dawsons PM 252-599 1974 £68

JOYCE, JAMES   Finnegan's Wake. New York, 1939. First American edition, lacking d.w., name in pencil on free fly, nice, orig. binding. Ross 86-286 1974 $40

JOYCE, JAMES   Finnegans Wake. 1939. Orig. cloth, dust wrapper, foxing, first edition. Rota 188-485 1974 £35

JOYCE, JAMES   From a Banned Writer to a Banned Singer. 1932. Wrappers, illus., English first edition. Covent 56-753 1974 £10.50

JOYCE, JAMES   Haveth Childers Everywhere: Fragment from Work in Progress. Paris, 1930. One of 100 copies, imperial hand made iridescent Japan, signed by author, fine unopened copy, slipcase. Covent 51-1018 1973 £300

JOYCE, JAMES   The Joyce Books. n.d. (c. 1932). One of 500 copies, this copy unnumbered, fine, first edition. Covent 51-1028 1973 £50

JOYCE, JAMES   The Mime of Mick, Nick and the Maggies. 1934. 8vo., wrapper, uncut, limited, first edition. Broadhurst 23-782 1974 £30

JOYCE, JAMES   Pomes Penyeach. Paris, 1927. First edition, pale green boards, very nice copy, scarce & fragile book, with the errata slip. Covent 51-1022 1973 £17.50

JOYCE, JAMES   Pomes Penyeach. Paris, 1927. 16mo., orig. boards, first edition, very good copy. MacManus 224-260 1974 $60

JOYCE, JAMES   Pomes Penyeach. Paris, 1927. Orig. boards, tipped in errata slip, usual fading of spine, very good copy. Ross 86-288 1974 $45

JOYCE, JAMES   Pomes Penyeach. Paris, 1927. 12mo., paper boards, faded, first edition. Rota 188-483 1974 £13.50

JOYCE, JAMES   Pomes Penyeach. London, 1945. First English edition, paper covers lightly worn, nice. Ross 86-289 1974 $7.50

JOYCE, JAMES   Stephen Hero. 1944. First U. S. edition, very good copy, torn & defective d.w. Covent 51-1023 1973 £12.60

JOYCE, JAMES   Stephen Hero. London, 1944. 8vo., orig. black cloth, uncut, first edition. Dawsons PM 252-600 1974 £25

JOYCE, JAMES   Ulysses. Paris, 1922. 4to., modern dark blue half calf, first edition. Dawsons PM 252-601 1974 £375

JOYCE, JAMES   Ulysses. Paris, 1922. 8vo., green cloth, hand-made paper, first edition. Rota 189-519 1974 £450

JOYCE, JAMES   Ulysses. Paris, 1924. Small 4to., orig. wrappers, fourth edition. Covent 56-754 1974 £85

JOYCE, JAMES   James Joyce's Ulysses. 1930. 8vo., cloth, first edition. Quaritch 936-437 1974 £6

JOYCE, JAMES   Ulysses. 1930. 8vo., orig. cloth, inscription, first edition. Rota 190-575 1974 £6

JOYCE, JAMES   Ulysses. Paris, 1930. Small 4to., orig. boards. Smith 193-289 1973 £5

JOYCE, JAMES   Ulysses. New York, 1934. Dust wrapper, first authorized American edition. Covent 55-946 1974 £25

JOYCE, JAMES   Ulysses. New York, 1934. Orig. cloth, bookplate, first authorised American edition. Rota 188-484 1974 £10

JOYCE, JAMES   Ulysses. 1936. Crown 4to., full vellum, gilt, uncut, mint, limited edition. Broadhurst 23-783 1974 £750

JOYCE, JAMES   Ulysses. 1936. Thick crown 4to., orig. green buckram gilt, uncut, fine, first English edition. Howes 186-282 1974 £120

JOYCE, P. W.   Ancient Irish Music. Dublin, 1912. 4to., cloth boards. Emerald 50-482 1974 £8

JOYCE, P. W.   The Origin and History of Irish Names of Places. London, 1910. 2 vols., 8vo., faded. Emerald 50-480 1974 £6

JOYCE, P. W.   A Social History of Ancient Ireland. Dublin, (1903). 2 vols., 8vo., second edition. Emerald 50-478 1974 £18

JOYCE, THOMAS A.   Central American and West Indian Archaeology. 1916. Frontispiece, illus., fine, English first edition. Covent 56-34 1974 £35

JOYFUL Jingles. New York, 1901. 4to., flexible pictorial wrappers, full page color plates, fine copy. Frohnsdorff 16-464 1974 $15

JUBILEE History of Latter-Day Saints Sunday Schools, 1849-1899. Salt Lake City, 1900. 8vo., cloth. Saddleback 14-732 1974 $25

JUBINAL, A.   La Armeria Real, ou Collection des Principales Pieces de la Galerie d'Armes Anciennes de Madrid. Paris, (c. 1840). 2 vols. in 1, roy. folio, plates, full red morocco gilt. Quaritch 940-698 1974 £150

JUDAH, SAMUEL B. H.   Gotham and the Gothamites. New York, 1823. 12mo., orig. printed boards, fine, first edition. Ximenes 33-419 1974 $100

JUDISCHE Welt. Judische Erzahlungen des Auslandes. Berlin, 1937. Biblo & Tannen 213-638 1973 $12.50

JUETTNER, OTTO   Daniel Drake and His Followers. Cincinnati, 1909. Rittenhouse 46-369 1974 $17.50

JUETTNER, OTTO   Daniel Drake and His Followers. Cincinnati, 1909. Rittenhouse 46-370 1974 $19

JUKES, J. BEETE   Memoirs of the Geological Survey of Great Britian and of the Museum of Practical Geology. London, 1859. 8vo., green half morocco, gilt, plates, second edition. Hammond 201-370 1974 £24

JULIA, EMILE-FRANCOIS   Antoine Bourdelle. Paris, 1930. 4to., wrappers, soiled cover. Minters 37-53 1973 $22.50

JULIAN, HESTER   Memorials of Henry Forbes Julian. London and Philadelphia, 1914. Portrait, orig. binding. Butterfield 10-324 1974 $10

JULIAN THE APOSTATE   An Account of the Life Of. 1682. 4to., half red polished crushed levant morocco. Thomas 28-191 1972 £25

JULIAN THE APOSTATE   Some Seasonable Remarks Upon the Deplorable Fall of the Emperour Julian. 1681. Small 4to., half dark blue polished crushed levant morocco, excellent condition. Thomas 28-189 1972 £25

JULIANUS, FLAVIUS CLAUDIUS IMPERATOR   Misopogon et Epistolae. Paris, 1566. 8vo., 19th century half calf, gilt, nice copy. Schafer 8-118 1973 sFr. 850

JULIEN, S.   Histoire et Fabrication de la Porcelaine Chinoise. Paris, 1856. 8vo., plates, illus., boards, cloth spine, leather label. Quaritch 940-405 1974 £20

JUNG, CARL GUSTAV   Der Inhalt der Psychose. Leipzig, 1908. 8vo., orig. printed wrappers, first edition. Gilhofer 61-74 1974 sFr. 250

JUNG, CARL GUSTAV   The Psychology of Dementia Praecox. 1936. 8vo., orig. brown cloth, fine. Dawsons PM 249-309 1974 £5

JUNG, CARL GUSTAV   Ueber das Verhalten der Reaktionszeit Beim Assoziationsexperimente. Leipzig, 1905. 4to., orig. printed wrappers, inscription, first edition. Gilhofer 61-72 1974 sFr. 600

JUNG, CARL GUATAV   Wandlungen und Symbole der Libido. 1912. 8vo., orig. printed wrapper, cloth, fine, first edition. Dawsons PM 249-308 1974 £120

JUNG-STILLUNG, JOHANN HEINRICH   Die Siebenlezten Posaunen Oder Wehen Wann sie Anfangen und Aufhoren und Von Den. Reading, 1820. 12mo., orig. quarter calf, first American edition. Ximenes 33-421 1974 $17.50

JUNIUS   Letters, With Notes and Illustrations. 1801. 2 vols., half calf, plates, slightly worn. Allen 216-2244 1974 $12.50

JUNIUS   The Letters of. Dublin, 1772. 2 vols., 8vo., contemporary calf, first Irish edition. Ximenes 33-422 1974 $35

JURIEU, PETER   The Reflections . . . Upon the Strange and Miraculous Exstasies of Isabel Vincent. London, 1689. 4to., disbound, first English edition. Ximenes 33-423 1974 $30

JUSSERAND, J. J.   English Wayfaring Life in the Middle Ages. London, 1889. 1st Eng. ed., illus., orig. gilt cl. Jacobs 24-150 1974 $25

JUSSERAND, J. J.   A Literary History of the English People. 1925-26. 3 vols., cloth gilt, second and third editions. Covent 56-860 1974 £10.50

JUSSERAND, J. J.   With Americans of Post and Present Days. New York, 1916. Biblo & Tannen 213-46 1973 $8.50

JUSSIEU, ANTOINE LAURENT DE   De Euphorbiacearum Generibus Medecisque Earumdem Viribus Tentamen. Paris, 1824. Demy 4to., boards, plates. Wheldon 131-1663 1974 £20

JUSSIEU, ANTOINE LAURENT DE   Genera Plantarum. Paris, 1789. 8vo., half calf. Wheldon 129-927 1974 £120

JUSSIEU, ANTIONE LAURENT DE   Genera Plantarum Secundum Ordines Naturales Disposita. Paris, 1789. 8vo., half calf, rare first edition. Wheldon 131-1164 1974 £150

JUSSIEU, J. DE   Description de l'Arbre a Quinquina. Paris, 1936. 4to., orig. wrappers. Wheldon 131-1809 1974 £7.50

JUSSIEU, J. DE   Description de l'Arbre a Quinquina. Paris, 1936. 4to., orig. wrappers. Wheldon 128-1683 1973 £7.50

JUSTAMOND, J. O.   An Account of the Methods Pursued In the Treatment of Cancerous and Schirrhous Disorders. London, 1780. Disbound. Rittenhouse 46-371 1974 $12

JUSTICE, JAMES   The British Gardener's Director, Chiefly Adapted to the Climate of the Northern Counties. London, 1775. 8vo., contemporary calf, hinges tender. Ximenes 36-126 1974 $40

JUSTICE, JEAN   Dictionary of Marks and Monograms of Delft Pottery. 1930. 4to., orig. cloth. Broadhurst 23-117 1974 £16

JUSTICE, JEAN   Dictionary of Marks and Monograms of Delft Pottery. 1930. 4to., cloth. Quaritch 940-644 1974 £20

JUSTICE, JEAN   Dictionary of Marks & Monograms of Delft Pottery. 1930. Dust wrapper, illus. Covent 55-460 1974 £20

JUSTIN MARTYR, SAINT   Apologiae Duae et Dialogus Cum Tryphone Judaeo. 1722. Folio, old calf. Howes 185-1321 1974 £12

JUSTINIANUS I, EMPEROR   Cocicis Iustiniani Imperatoris cum Variis Legii Summariis Divina Promulgatio. Paris, 1518. 12mo., full blue morocco, gilt, woodcut, very good copy. Ximenes 37-125 1974 $75

JUSTINUS, MARCUS JUNIANUS   Ex Trogi Pompeii Historiis Externis Libri XXXXIIII. Lyon, 1551. 16mo., late 17th century crimson morocco gilt. Thomas 28-139 1972 £21

JUSTINUS, MARCUS JUNIANUS   Externae Historiae. (Lyons, n.d.). Eighteenth century red morocco gilt, raised bands. Thomas 30-126 1973 £100

JUSTINUS, MARCUS JUNIANUS   Externae Historiae. 1522. 19th century vellum gilt. Thomas 30-61 1973 £45

JUSTINUS, MARCUS JUNIANUS   The Historie of Iustine. London, 1606. Small folio, calf antique, first edition. Dawsons PM 251-346 1974 £120

JUSTINUS, MARCUS JUNIANUS   Ivstini ex Trogo Pompeio Historia, Diligentissime Nunc Quidem Supra Omneis Omnium Hactenus Aeditiones Recognita. Basel, 1539. Small 4to., old vellum over boards, full page maps, with some old manuscript notes and underlinings. Schafer 10-102 1974 sFr 680

JUSTINUS, MARCUS JUNIANUS   Ivstini Historiarum ex Trogo Pompeio. 1640. 12mo., contemporary mottled calf, joints cracking, corners worn. Bow Windows 66-215 1974 £12

JUSTINUS, MARCUS JUNIANUS   Opera. 1686. Folio, vellum, foxed. Allen 213-576 1973 $25

JUVARRA, FILIPPO   Raccolta di Targhe Fatte da Professori Primari in Roma. (Rome, 1732). 4to., contemporary vellum, engravings. Harper 213-96 1973 $150

JUVENALIS, DECIMUS JUNIUS   Decii Junii Juvenalis Satirarum Libri Quinque. 1747. 12mo., contemporary morocco, joints tender, engraved frontispiece. Bow Windows 66-386 1974 £6

JUVENALIS, DECIMUS JUNIUS   Satyrae. Amsterdam, 1684. 8vo., fine copy, nice edition, contemporary vellum, frontis. Schumann 499-56 1974 sFr 120

JUVENALIS, DECIMUS JUNIUS   Satyrae cum Commentariis. Basle, 1551. 2 parts in 1 vol., folio, old Italian vellum. Thomas 28-290 1972 £21

JUVENALIS, DECIMUS JUNIUS   Satyrae Sexdecim. 1603. 4to., buckram. Allen 213-579 1973 $25

JUVENILE Plutarch. 1801. First edition, copperplates, 12mo., orig. marbled boards, morocco spine, good copy. George's 610-419 1973 £15

K

KABUKI. Paris, (1933). Blue cloth, plates, illus. Dawson's 424-111 1974 $275

KAFKA, FRANZ   The Metamorphosis. 1937. First publication in English, cloth backed boards, fine, scarce, first issue. Covent 51-1036 1973 £45

KAHANE, JACK   The Lamb. Paris, 1932. 8vo., orig. cloth, first edition in English. Rota 190-585 1974 £5

KAHN, E. J.   The Merry Partners. Random. 302p. Austin 51-472 1973 $6.50

KAHN, E. J.   The Voice. Harper, 1947. 125p., illus. Austin 51-473 1973 $6

KAHN, GORDON   Hollywood On Trial. Boni, Gaer, 1948. 229p. Austin 51-474 1973 $8.50

KAINS-JACKSON, CHARLES   John Addington Symonds: a Portrait. New York, 1915. First U. S. edition, fine, wrappers. Covent 51-1790 1973 £12.50

KAISER, GEORGE   From Morn to Midnight. Brentano, 1922. 154p. Austin 51-475 1973 $8.50

KALENDER Fur das Schaftjahr 1884. N. P. Full dark green calf, 1 3/4 X 1 1/4, fine. Gregory 44-400 1974 $30

KALLEN, HORACE M.   Of Them That Say They Are Jews. Bloch, 1954. Austin 62-312 1974 $17.50

KALM, PETER   Travels Into North America. London, 1772. 2 vols., orig. full leather, second edition. Hood's 103-543 1974 $325

KAMES, HENRY HOME, LORD   Elements of Criticism. Edinburgh, 1762. 8vo., 3 vols., contemporary calf, scarce, first edition. Broadhurst 23-769 1974 £75

KAMES, HENRY HOME, LORD   Essays Upon Several Subjects Concerning British Antiquities. Edinburgh, 1747. 8vo., contemporary calf, fine, first edition. Ximenes 33-259 1974 $65

KAMES, HENRY HOME, LORD   Six Sketches on the History of Man. Philadelphia, 1776. Old leather, rubbed. Butterfield 10-325 1974 $35

KAMES, HENRY HOME, LORD   Sketches of the History of Man. Edinburgh, 1807. 3 vols., contemporary speckled calf, worn, new edition. Bow Windows 64-133 1974 £9.75

KAMES, HENRY HOME, LORD   Sketches of the History of Man. 1813. 3 vols., new library binding. Austin 61-525 1974 $47.50

KANAVEL, ALLEN B.   Infections of the Hand. Philadelphia, 1921. Revised fourth edition. Rittenhouse 46-722 1974 $10

KANE, ELISHA KENT   Arctic Explorations: The Second Grinnell Expedition in Search of Sir John Franklin, 1853-55. Philadelphia, 1857. 2 vols., nice copy, orig. binding. Butterfield 10-326 1974 $15

KANE, PAUL   Wanderings of an Artist Among the Indians of North America. Toronto, 1925. Illus., bookplate, some fading of d.w., near fine, orig. binding. Ross 86-29 1974 $15

KANE, ROBERT JOHN   Elements of Chemistry. New York, 1843. 8vo., orig. bline-stamped cloth, gilt, illus. Zeitlin 235-280 1974 $50

KANG, YOUNGHILL   East Goes West. Scribners, 1937. 401p. Austin 62-313 1974 $8.50

KANIN, GARSON   Remembering Mr. Maugham. 1966. 313p. Austin 51-476 1973 $6.50

KANSAS Contested Election. Washington, 1856. Uncut, unopened, unbound as issued, light damp stain. Wilson 63-197 1974 $10

KANT, IMMANUEL   Anthropologie in Pragmatischer Hinsicht Abgefasst. 1798. 8vo., modem boards, fine, first edition. Dawsons PM 249-310 1974 £110

KANT, IMMANUEL   Anthropologie in Pragmatischer Hinsicht Abgefasst. Konigsberg, 1798. 8vo., contemporary boards, first edition. Schafer 8-164 1973 sFr. 650

KANT, IMMANUEL   Anthropologie in Pragmatischer Hinsicht. Konigsberg, 1798. 8vo., cloth-backed boards, first edition. Schuman 35-254 1974 $150

KANT, IMMANUEL   Critik der Reinen Vernunft. Riga, 1781. 8vo., contemporary half calf, gilt, fine, first edition. Schafer 8-162 1973 sFr. 7,000

KANT, IMMANUEL   Critik der Urtheilskraft. Berlin & Libau, 1790. 8vo., old-style boards, first edition. Schuman 37-133 1974 $210

KANT, IMMANUEL   Immanuel Kant's Logik, ein Handbuch zu Vorlesungen. Konigsberg, 1800. 8vo., contemporary marbled boards bit worn, first edition, very good copy, scarce. Ximenes 36-128 1974 $175

KANT, IMMANUEL   Immanuel Kant. Konigsberg, 1804. 2 works in 1 vol., small 8vo., foxing, contemporary boards, worn. Bow Windows 62-524 1974 £45

KANT, IMMANUEL   The Philosophy of Law. Edinburgh, 1887. 8vo., orig. cloth, library stamp, slight spotting, first English edition. Bow Windows 66-388 1974 £8

KANT, IMMANUEL   Die Religion Innerhalb der Grenzen der Blossen Vernunft. Frankfurt und Leipzig, 1794. Boards, cover somewhat worn, very good copy. Covent 51-1041 1973 £15

KANT, IMMANUEL   Ueber eine Entdeckung nach der alle neue Critik der Reinen Vernuft. Konigsberg, 1790. 8vo., old-style boards, first edition. Schuman 37-134 1974 $95

KANT, IMMANUEL   Versuch den Begriff der Negativen Grossen in der Weltweisheit Einzufuhren. Konigsberg, 1763. 8vo., orig. wrappers, uncut, second print of first edition. Schumann 499-57 1974 sFr 380

KAPLAN, D. M.   Serology of Nervous and Mental Diseases. Philadelphia, 1914. Rittenhouse 46-723 1974 $15

KAPLAN, MORDICAI M.   The Future of the American Jew. Macmillan, 1948. Austin 62-314 1974 $10

KAPLAN, SIMON   Once Upon a Rebel. Farrar, Rinehart, 1941. Austin 62-315 1974 $10

KAPPEL, A. W.   British and European Butterflies and Moths. n.d. Extra imperial 8vo., orig. cloth, fine. Broadhurst 23-1154 1974 £20

KAPPEL, A. W.   British and European Butterflies and Moths. (1895). 4to., orig. dec. cloth, gilt, coloured plates. Wheldon 128-746 1973 £10

KARAZINE, N.   Du Volga au Nil Dans Les Airs. (c. 1906). 8vo., orig. cloth, illus., little browned, school stamp in gilt. Bow Windows 66-387 1974 £5

KARENINE, WLADIMIR   George Sand, sa vie et ses Oeuvres. Paris, 1899-1926. 4 vols., 8vo., orig. wrapper, uncut, very rare. L. Goldschmidt 42-371 1974 $80

KARLBY, BENT   Bo for to Haandbog i Hjemmets Indretning. Copenhagen, 1942. 8vo., illus., wrapper, plates. Minters 37-544 1973 $15

KARLSON, W.   Bokband och Bokbindare i Lund. Lund, 1939. Roy. 8vo., frontispiece, plates, sewed as issued. Quaritch 940-604 1974 £25

KARSAVINA, TAMARA   Theatre Street. Dutton, 1931. 341p., illus. Austin 51-477 1973 $8.50

KARSTEN, P. A.   Kritisk Ofversigt af Finlands. 1889. 8vo., cloth. Wheldon 129-1248 1974 £10

KARSTEN, P. A.   Mycologia Fennica. 1871-79. 8vo., 4 vols., half morocco. Wheldon 129-1245 1974 £75

KARSTEN, P. A.   Rysslands, Finlands och den Skandinaviska. 1879-82. 8vo., 2 vols., buckram. Wheldon 129-1246 1974 £25

KASTNER, ABRAHAM GOTTHELF   Heschichte der Kunste und Wissenschaften. Gottingen, 1796-1800. 8vo., 4 vols., modern cloth-backed boards, unopened, first edition. Schumann 35-255 1974 $135

KATAEV, VALENTINE   Squaring the Circle. French, 1936. 118p., illus. Austin 51-478 1973 $8.50

KATALOG der Kunstsachen und Antiquitaten. 1904. 4to., plates, orig. wrappers, staining. Bow Windows 62-188 1974 £6.30

KATER, HENRY   An Account of the Re-Measurement of the Cube, Cylinder, and Sphere. London, 1821. 4to., disbound. Dawsons PM 245-425 1974 £6

KATKOV, NORMAN   Eagle At My Eyes. Doubleday, 1948. Austin 62-316 1974 $6.50

KATKOV, NORMAN   The Fabulous Fanny. Knopf, 1953. 337p., illus. Austin 51-479 1973 $6.50

KATKOV, NORMAN   A Little Sleep, a Little Slumber. Doubleday, 1949. Austin 62-317 1974 $6.50

KAUFFER, E. M. K.   The Art of the Poster. 1924. 4to., plates, boards, cloth spine. Quaritch 940-457 1974 £55

KAUFMAN, GEORGE S.   I'd Rather Be Right. Random House, 1937. 124p., illus. Austin 51-484 1973 $7.50

KAUFMAN, GEORGE S.   Let 'Em Eat Cake. Knopf, 1933. 241p., illus. Austin 51-485 1973 $8.50

KAUFMAN, GEORGE S.   Merton of the Movies. French, 1922. 112p. Austin 51-480 1973 $7.50

KAUFMAN, GEORGE S.   The Royal Family. Doubleday, 1928. 380p. Austin 51-481 1973 $8.50

KAUFMAN, GEORGE S.   The Royal Family. French, 1929. 171p., illus. Austin 51-482 1973 $7.50

KAUFMAN, GEORGE S.   Stage Door. Doubleday, Doran, 1936. 230p., illus. Austin 51-483 1973 $7.50

KAUFMAN, SUE   The Headshrinker's Test. Random, 1969. 248p. Austin 54-587 1973 $6.50

KAUFMAN, WILLIAM   How to Write for Television. Hastings, 1955. Austin 51-488 1973 $12.50

KAUFMANN, EMIL   Von Ledoux bis le Corbusier. Vienna, 1933. 4to., wrappers, plates, illus., extremely rare. Minters 37-545 1973 $35

KAVANAGH, BRIDGET   The Pearl Fountain and other Fairy Tales. New York, 1876. 1st ed., illus. Biblo & Tannen 210-748 1973 $27.50

KAVANAUGH, PETER   The Story of the Abbey Theatre. 1950. 243p. Austin 51-489 1973 $12.50

KAWAKAMI, KIYOSHI   Asia At the Door. Revell, 1914. 269p. Austin 62-319 1974 $22.50

KAWRAISKY, F. F.   Die Lachse. Tiflis, 1896. Roy 8vo., plates, orig. boards, scarce. Wheldon 130-702 1974 £5

KAY County, Oklahoma. Ponca City, c.1919. 12mo., cloth, 75 pages. Saddleback 14-638 1974 $25

KAYE, JOHN W.   A History of the Sepoy War in Indian. 1896. 7 vols., med. 8vo., half crimson levant morocco, panelled backs, tooled gilt, fine. Broadhurst 24-1712 1974 £110

KAYE-SMITH, SHEILA   A Wedding Morn. London, 1928. Numbered, signed, dust jacket. Ballinger 1-150 1974 $15

KAYSER, E.   Lehrbuch der Geologie. Stuttgart, 1921-24. 4 vols., roy. 8vo., orig. cloth. Wheldon 131-1029 1974 £15

KAZI, DAWASAMDUP   An English-Tibetan Dictionary. Calcutta, 1919. Roy. 8vo., buckram. Howes 186-1862 1974 £10

KEACH, BENJAMIN   Antichrist Stormed. London, 1689. 12mo., contemporary sheep, first edition. Ximenes 33-427 1974 $80

KEAN, EDMUND   The Life of. London, 1835. 2 vols., 8vo., foxing, frontispiece, contemporary half calf. Bow Windows 62-927 1974 £12.50

KEARNEY, THOMAS H.   Flowering Plants and Ferns of Arizona. Washington, 1942. Large 8vo., orig. bindings. Butterfield 8-17 1974 $10

KEARTON, R.   British Birds Nests. (1907). 8vo., cloth, illus., plates, scarce. Wheldon 131-634 1974 £7.50

KEATE, GEORGE   An Account of the Pelew Islands. London, 1788. 4to., plates, contemporary tree calf, rubbed, uncut, second edition. Bow Windows 62-528 1974 £52

KEATE, GEORGE   An Epistle from Lady Jane Gray to Lord Guilford Dudley. London, 1762. 4to., half calf antique, first edition. Ximenes 33-428 1974 $75

KEATE, GEORGE   Sketches from Nature. London, 1779. Small 8vo., contemporary tree calf, gilt, first edition. Hammond 201-312 1974 £35

KEATE, GEORGE   Sketches from Nature. 1782. 2 vols., 8vo., contemporary sheep, rebacked, third edition. Howes 186-2048 1974 £15

KEATE, GEORGE   Sketches from Nature. London, 1790. Small 8vo., contemporary tree calf, gilt, 2 vols., fourth edition. Hammond 201-313 1974 £25

KEATE, THOMAS   Observations on the Fifth Report of the Commissioners of Military Enquiry. London, 1808. 4to., orig. board. Gurney 66-94 1974 £18

KEATING, G.   The History of Ireland. London, 1902-08-14. 4 vols., 8vo., uncut, green cloth, gilt. Emerald 50-487 1974 £35

KEATING, WILLIAM H.   Narrative of an Expedition to the Source of St. Peter's River, Lake Winnepeek, Lake of the Woods . . . Under the Command of Stephen H. Long. Philadelphia, 1824. 2 vols., rubbed, folding map, illus., first edition. Jenkins 61-1294 1974 $85

KEATON, BUSTER   My Wonderful World of Slapstick. Doubleday, 1960. 282p., illus. Austin 51-490 1973 $7.50

KEATS, JOHN   Endymion. 1818. First edition, second issue, has half title and five line errata leaf, lacks inserted ads, excellent copy, uncut, unpressed, 8vo., modern boards. Thomas 32-177 1974 £800

KEATS, JOHN   Endymion. 1927. Unopened, uncut. Howes 185-265 1974 £5

KEATS, JOHN   Lamia: Isabella: The Eve of St. Agnes and Other Poems. Golden Cockerel Press, 1928. Engravings, one of 500 numbered copies, very fine, leather backed buckram, top edges gilt, first edition. Covent 51-783 1973 £95

KEATS, JOHN   Letters of. London, 1878. 8vo., orig. maroon cloth, first edition. Dawsons PM 252-602 1974 £45

KEATS, JOHN   The Poems. 1904. 2 vols., small 4to., dec. white buckram gilt, orig. dec. cloth wrappers. Covent 55-953 1974 £35

KEATS, JOHN   The Poems. 1915. 2 vols., cloth-backed boards. Covent 55-954 1974 £7.50

KEATS, JOHN   Poems. 1927. Post 8vo., full vellum, English first edition. Covent 56-764 1974 £12.50

KEATS, JOHN   The Poetical Works. London, 1841. 8vo., orig. green cloth, first collected edition. Ximenes 33-429 1974 $30

KEATS, JOHN   The Poetical Works. London, 1851. 8vo., orig. green cloth, worn, new edition. Ximenes 33-430 1974 $20

KEATS, JOHN   The Poetical Works. 1885. Orig. buckram gilt, limited edition. Smith 194-320 1974 £5

KEATS, JOHN   The Poetical Works. 1889. Third augmented and corrected edition, portrait frontispiece, 8vo., red levant morocco gilt, gilt borders, inlaid hand painted miniature portrait of Keats on Ivory, blue morocco backed buckram box, good condition. Sawyer 293-67 1974 £765

KEATS, JOHN   Poetical Works and Other Writings. 1889. 4 vols., 2 vols recased. Allen 216-955 1974 $35

KEATS, JOHN   The Poetical Works of. London, 1880. 8vo., full leather, full blue calf, illus., spine faded, extremely good. Current BW9-241 1974 $25

KEATS, JOHN   Poetry and Prose. 1890. Orig. dec. buckram gilt, frontis., very good, first edition. Covent 51-1042 1973 £5

KEATS, JOHN   Three Essays. 1889. First edition, one of 50 copies, with death mask of Keats as frontispiece, 4to., orig. grey paper printed wrapper, unstitched as issued. Sawyer 293-176 1974 £73.

KEBLE, JOHN   De Poeticae Vi Medica. Oxonii, 1844. 2 vols. in 1, full morocco, gilt spine, some foxing. Bow Windows 66-390 1974 £10

KEELE, K. D.   Leonardo Da Vinci On Movement of the Heart and Blood. Philadelphia, n.d. Dust jacket, limited edition. Rittenhouse 46-375 1974 $30

KEELEY, GERTRUDE   Story of the Birds for Young People with Bird Alphabet. New York, 1914. 8vo., illus. Frohnsdorff 16-33 1974 $9.50

KEELING, WILLIAM   Liturgiae Britannicae. Cambridge, 1851. 8vo., foxing, calf, morocco label, second edition. Bow Windows 62-529 1974 £10.50

KEEN, W. W.   Selected Papers and Addresses. Philadelphia, 1923. Rubbed, library plate. Rittenhouse 46-380 1974 $10

KEESE, JOHN   The Opal
Please turn to
THE OPAL

KEHOE, SIM D.   The Indian Club Exercise. New York, 1866. 4to., orig. black cloth, first edition, wood engravings, fine. Ximenes 36-129 1974 $27.50

KEIGHTLEY, THOMAS   The Life and Writings of Henry Fielding. Cleveland, 1907. Quarter calf gilt, plates, slip-case. Covent 55-663 1974 £12.50

KEIL, HANNA   Renee Sintenis. Berlin, 1935. 4to., illus., wrapper, second edition. Minters 37-486 1973 $20

KEILL, JOHN   The Elements of Plain and Spherical Trigonometry. Dublin, 1726. 8vo., contemporary panelled calf, plates, third edition. Dawsons PM 245-426 1974 £35

KEIM, DE B. RANDOLPH   Sheridan's Troopers on the Borders. Philadelphia, 1870. 8vo., orig. bindings. Butterfield 8-705 1974 $15

KEIR, JAMES   An Account of the Life and Writings of Thomas Day. London, 1791. 8vo., modern boards, first edition. Dawsons PM 252-603 1974 £15

KEITH, AGNES NEWTON   Land Below the Wind. Boston, 1939. First edition, 12mo., included is typed letter from author. Current BW9-242 1974 $22.50

KEITH, ARTHUR   The Antiquity of Man. 1925. 8vo., 2 vols., orig. cloth, illus., new edition. Bow Windows 64-151 1974 £5.25

KEITH, ARTHUR   Human Embryology and Morphology. London, 1902. 8vo., cloth, uncut, first edition. Dawsons PM 249-311 1974 £9

KEITH, R.   A Large New Catalogue of the Bishops. Edinburgh, 1755. 4to., half calf. Quaritch 939-659 1974 £15

KELAART, E. F.   Flora Calpensis. 1846. Lithograph views, extra woodcut views pasted in, ads at end, 8vo., orig. red embossed cloth gilt, binding worn and fingerstained. Sawyer 293-147 1974 £36

KELEHER, WILLIAM A.   The Fabulous Frontier. Santa Fe, (1945). Orig. blue cloth, illus., fine, first edition. Bradley 35-213 1974 $75

KELEMEN, PAUL   Medieval American Art. New York, 1943. 2 vols., 4to., plates., lst ed., author's sgd. pres. Biblo & Tannen 210-177 1973 $62.50

KELLAND, CLARENCE B.   The Cosmic Jest. 1949. Austin 51-491 1973 $12.50

KELLER, ELIZABETH LEAVITT   Wall Whitman in Mickle Street. New York, 1921. Bookplate, first U.S. edition. Covent 56-1321 1974 £12.50

KELLER, ROBERT BROWN   History of Monroe County, Pennsylvania. Stroudsburg, 1927. 12mo., cloth. Saddleback 14-673 1974 $15

KELLER, SANBORN C.   The Murdered Maiden Student. Suncook, 1878. 12mo., orig. dec. cloth, fine, plates, first edition. Ximenes 33-431 1974 $10

KELLER, W.   Die Englishce Literature von der Renaissance bis zur Aufklaerung. 1928. 4to., limp boards, coloured plates, illus. Allen 216-1816 1974 $12.50

KELLISON, MATTHEW   A Survey of the New Religion. Douay, 1603. 8vo., later calf, scarce, first edition. Ximenes 33-432 1974 $175

KELLNER, K. A. HEINRICH   Heortology. 1908. Scarce, 484 pages. Howes 185-1323 1974 £7.50

KELLOCK, HAROLD   Parson Weems of the Cherry-Tree, The Eventful Life of M. L. Weems, Author, Pedlar, Preacher, Biographer. New York and Boston, 1928. First printing, orig. binding. Butterfield 10-527 1974 $12.50

KELLOG, ROBERT H.   Life and Death in Rebel Prisons. Hartford, 1865. First edition, 8vo., illus., plans, much foxing, spine heavily worn at ends and faded, binding askew and soiled, else good. Current BW9-376 1974 $10

KELLOGG, CHARLES W.   Up to the Clouds on Muleback . . . The Terrible Triumvirate. Worcester, 1938. Inscribed by author, orig. binding. Butterfield 10-133 1974 $7.50

KELLOGG, JAY C.   The Broncho Buster Busted. Tacoma, Wash., 1932. lst ed., illus. Dykes 24-263 1974 $50

KELLOGG'S Funny Jungleland Moving-Pictures. Battle Creek, 1909. Small 4to., color illus., wrappers soiled. Frohnsdorff 16-589 1974 $15

KELLOR, FRANCES   Immigration and the Future. Doran, 1920. Austin 62-320 1974 $10

KELLOR, FRANCES   Immigration and the Future. 1920. 276 pages. Austin 57-345 1974 $10

KELLWAYE, SIMON   A Defensative Against the Plague . . . Shewing the Meanes How to Preserve Us from the Dangerous Contaigon Thereof . . . Whereunto is Annexed a Short Treatise of the Small Poxe. London, 1593. Small 4to., light brown half leather boxcase, orig. edition, some headlines shaved, few ink spots, contemporary & later marginalia. Kraus 137-54 1974 $1,850

KELLY, GEORGE   The Show Off. Little, Brown, 1924. 129p. Austin 51-492 1973 $8.50

KELLY, GEORGE   The Torch-Bearers. French, 1924. 190p. Austin 51-493 1973 $7.50

KELLY, HOWARD A.   A Scientific Man and the Bible. Philadelphia, (1925). 12mo., cloth, paper labels, inscription. Rittenhouse 46-384 1974 $65

KELLY, HUGH   The School for Wives. London, 1774. 8vo.,
modern boards, first edition. Dawsons PM 252-604 1974 £15

KELLY, HUGH   The Romance of an Hour. London, 1774.
8vo., wrappers, first edition. Ximenes 33-433 1974 $25

KELLY, HUGH   The School for Wives. London, 1774. 8vo.,
quarter cloth, boards, first edition. Ximenes 33-434 1974 $25

KELLY, J. J.   Poems. Edinburgh, n.d. 8vo., orig. dark
green cloth, first edition. Ximenes 33-435 1974 $12.50

KELLY, LUTHER S.   Yellowstone Kelly. New Haven, 1926. 1st
ed., illus. Jacobs 24-19 1974 $20

KELLY, MICHAEL   Reminiscences of Michael Kelly. Colburn,
Lond., 1826. 2 vols., orig. ed. Austin 51-494 1973 $25

KELLY'S Directory of Buckinghamshire. 1935. 4to., map, covers faded. Bow
Windows 66-393 1974 £7.50

KELLY'S Directory of Sussex. 1930. 8vo., orig. cloth, large folding coloured
map, covers faded. Bow Windows 66-678 1974 £8.50

KELLY'S Directory of Sussex. London, 1938. 4to., map, orig. cloth, faded.
Bow Windows 62-889 1974 £8.50

KELSEY, HENRY   The Kelsey Papers. Ottawa, 1929. Orig.
printed wrappers, map, fine. Bradley 35-55 1974 $84

KELSON, ISAAC   Danger in the Dark. 1855. 300 pages.
Austin 57-348 1974 $12.50

KELTY, MARY ANN   Osmond, a Tale. London, 1822. 3 vols.,
12mo., contemporary half calf, spines gilt, first edition, very good copy.
Ximenes 36-130 1974 $100

KEMBLE, FRANCES ANNE   Journal by. London, 1835. 2 vols., 12mo.,
orig. grey boards, first edition. Ximenes 33-436 1974 $100

KEMBLE, FRANCES ANNE   Journal By Frances Anne Butler. London,
1835. 2 vols., 8vo., orig. boards, paper labels, first edition. Dawsons PM
252-605 1974 £60

KEMBLE, FRANCES ANNE   Journal of a Residence on a Georgia Plantation.
New York, 1863. First edition, first issue, 12mo., interior fine, binding faded.
Current BW9-377 1974 $50

KEMBLE, FRANCES ANNE   Journal of a Residence on a Georgian Plantation.
London, 1863. 8vo., orig. cloth, first edition. Dawsons PM 252-606 1974
£30

KEMBLE, FRANCIS ANNE   Notes Upon Some of Shakespeare's Plays.
London, 1882. 8vo., cloth, first edition. Goodspeed's 578-176 1974 $10

KEMBLE, JAMES   Idols and Invalids. London, 1933.
Rittenhouse 46-386 1974 $10

KEMBLE, JOHN PHILIP   An Authentic Narrative of Mr. Kemble's Retire-
ment from the Stage. 1817. 8vo., contemporary half morocco, uncut, plates.
Hill 126-264 1974 £20

KEMBLE, JOHN PHILIP   Lyra Innocentium. Oxford, 1846. 8vo., full
blind stamped levant, first edition, fine. Ximenes 36-131 1974 $70

KEMBLE, JOHN PHILIP   Macbeth, and King Richard the Third. London,
1817. 8vo., old half calf, second edition. Ximenes 33-437 1974 $30

KEMBLE, JOHN PHILIP   The Pannel. London, (1789). 8vo., modern
boards, second edition. Dawsons PM 252-607 1974 £8

KEMBLE, JOHN PHILIP   Shakespeare's Measure for Measure. London,
1803. 8vo., modern boards, first edition. Dawsons PM 252-608 1974 £15

KEMLER, EDGAR   The Irreverent Mr. Mencken. Little, Brown,
1950. 317p., orig. ed. Austin 54-588 1973 $7.50

KEMPER, J. L.   Message . . . Relative to the Impressment of
Slaves. Richmond, 1865. Jenkins 61-643 1974 $12.50

KENDALL, E. A.   The Swallow. 1800. First edition, engraved
frontis. almost detached, ink scoring on blank verso of title, 12mo., orig. boards,
roan spine, rubbed. George's 610-422 1973 £10

KENDALL, GEORGE WILKINS   Narrative of the Texan Santa Fe Expedition.
Chicago, 1929. 8vo., orig. binding. Butterfield 8-622 1974 $10

KENDALL, GEORGE WILKINS   The War Between the United States and Mexico.
New York, 1851. Elephant folio, orig. cloth covers, stained, color lithographs
by Carl Nebel, very rare. Jenkins 61-1295 1974 $850

KENDALL, NANCY NOON   The New House. Caldwell, 1934. Morocco,
map, gilt top, signed by author, fine, slip case, no. 4 of 10 copies, deluxe
limited edition. Dykes 22-114 1973 $20

KENDRICK, A. F.   English Decorative Fabrics of the 16th - 18th
Centuries. London, (1934). Grey cloth, plates. Dawson's 424-229 1974 $25

KENDRICK, A. F.   English Embroidery. London, ca. 1904.
Color plates. Biblo & Tannen 210-194 1973 $20

KENDRICK, A. F.   English Embroidery. (1913). 8vo., plates,
cloth. Quaritch 940-761 1974 £10

KENDRICK, A. F.   English Needlework. London, 1933. Cloth,
illus. Dawson's 424-228 1974 $12.50

KENDRICK, T. D.   The Drvids. 1927. Orig. cloth, plates,
illus. Smith 194-823 1974 £6.50

KENEALY, EDWARD VAUGHAN   Poetical Works. 1875. 3 vols., ex-library,
spines rather worn, text browned. Allen 216-866 1974 $10

KENLY, JOHN R.   Memoirs of a Maryland Volunteer, War With
Mexico In the Years 1846-48. Philadelphia, 1873. Very good copy. Jenkins
61-1595 1974 $22.50

KENNARD, MRS. EDWARD   The Sorrows of a Golders Wife. 1896. Orig.
pictorial cloth, English first edition. Covent 56-765 1974 £10.50

KENNARD, JOSEPH SPENCER   Some Early Printers. Philadelphia, 1902. Full
vellum, soiled, unopened. Dawson's 424-162 1974 $40

KENNAWAY, JOHN H.   On Sherman's Tract. 1867. Fine, polished
calf, signed, presentation copy, English first edition. Covent 56-15 1974 £25

KENNEDY, A. B. W.   Petra. 1925. 4to., illus., maps, half
buckram. Quaritch 940-327 1974 £45

KENNEDY, CHARLES O'BRIEN   Men, Women and Goats. French, 1931.
Austin 51-495 1973 $7.50

KENNEDY, CHARLES RANN   The Army With Banners. Hubsch, 1919. 149p.
Austin 51-496 1973 $8.50

KENNEDY, CHARLES RANN   The Necessary Evil. Harpers, 1913. 111p.
Austin 51-497 1973 $6.50

KENNEDY, CHARLES RANN   Plays For Three Players. Chicago, 1935.
Austin 51-498 1973 $6.50

KENNEDY, CHARLES RANN   The Servant In the House. Harper, 1908.
152p., illus. Austin 51-499 1973 $10

KENNEDY, CHARLES RANN   Translation of Select Speeches of Demosthenes.
Cambridge, 1841. 8vo., orig. cloth, first edition. Ximenes 33-438 1974
$12.50

KENNEDY, DAVID   The Late History of Europe. Edinburgh, 1698.
8vo., modern half calf, first edition. Dawsons PM 251-259 1974 £75

KENNEDY, GRACE   Dunallan. Edinburgh, 1825. 3 vols., 12mo.,
early 19th century cloth, first edition. Ximenes 33-439 1974 $60

KENNEDY, IDA M.　　　Touring Quebec and the Maritimes.　Toronto, 1929. Signed by author, linen cover.　Hood's 102-720 1974 $7.50

KENNEDY, J.　　　A Description of the Antiquities and Curiosities in Wilton-House.　Salisbury, 1769. 4to., plates, contemporary calf.　Quaritch 939-576 1974 £40

KENNEDY, J.　　　New Description of Pictures, Statues, Bustos, etc. at Earl of Pembroke's House at Wilton.　1771. New buckram, rubber stamp, corrected fifth edition.　Allen 213-812 1973 $12.50

KENNEDY, J. M.　　　English Literature 1800-1905.　1913. 340 pages.　Austin 61-529 1974 $12.50

KENNEDY, JAMES　　　Conversations on Religion, with Lord Byron and Others.　London, 1830. 8vo., orig. green cloth, trifle soiled but sound, first edition, very good copy, scarce.　Ximenes 36-132 1974 $100

KENNEDY, JAMES WILLIAM　　Practical Surgery of the Joseph Price Hospital. Philadelphia, 1928.　Rittenhouse 46-387 1974 $10

KENNEDY, JOHN　　　A Treatise upon Planting, Gardening, and the Management of the Hot-House.　York, 1776. 8vo., contemporary calf, gilt, first edition.　Hammond 201-22 1974 £21

KENNEDY, JOHN　　　A Treatise Upon Planting, Gardening, and the Management of the Hot-House.　London, 1777. 2 vols., 8vo., contemporary calf, hinges worn, second edition.　Ximenes 36-133 1974 $50

KENNEDY, JOHN FITZGERALD　　Why England Slept.　n.d. (1940). Orig. cloth.　Smith 193-373 1973 £5

KENNEDY, JOHN FITZGERALD　　Why England Slept.　(1940). Orig. cloth. Smith 193-374 1973 £5

KENNEDY, JOHN FITZGERALD　　Why England Slept.　n.d. (1940). Scarce, nice copy, spine faded.　Covent 51-1045 1973 £15.75

KENNEDY, JOHN FITZGERALD　　Why England Slept.　London, n.d. 8vo., orig. red cloth, first English edition.　Dawsons PM 247-160 1974 £15

KENNEDY, JOHN FITZGERALD　　Why England Slept.　(1940). English first edition.　Covent 56-766 1974 £25

KENNEDY, JOHN PENDLETON　　Horse-Shoe Robinson.　London, 1839. 8vo., disbound.　Ximenes 33-440 1974 $10

KENNEDY, JOHN PENDLETON　　Quodlibet: Containing Some Annal Thereof. Philadelphia, 1840. Orig. cloth, some rubbing, light foxing, first edition, very good copy.　MacManus 224-262 1974 $75

KENNEDY, JOHN PENDLETON　　A Review of Mr. Cambreleng's Report from the Committee of Commerce.　Baltimore, 1830. 8vo., first edition.　Ximenes 33-441 1974 $40

KENNEDY, JOHN PENDLETON　　Rob of the Bowl: A Legend of St. Inigoe's. Philadelphia, 1838. 2 vols., orig. cloth, rubbed, first edition, some foxing and staining.　MacManus 224-263 1974 $60

KENNEDY, JOHN PITT 1796-1879　　Instruct; Employ.　London, 1835. 8vo., cloth boards, plate.　Emerald 50-490 1974 £10

KENNEDY, M.　　　Notes On Criminal Classes in the Bombay Residency.　Bombay, 1908. Sup. roy. 8vo., plates, orig. cloth.　Smith 193-492 1973 £6

KENNEDY, R. EMMIT　　　Mellows, A Chronicle of Unknown Singers. New York, (1925). First edition, 4to., blue cloth covers, paper label, interior fine.　Current BW9-576 1974 $27.50

KENNEDY, RANKIN　　　The Book of the Motor Car.　London, 1913. 3 vols., 4to., illus.　Covent 55-1463 1974 £18

KENNEDY, WILLIAM SLOANE　　The Plan of Union.　Hudson, 1856. Cloth, scarce.　Hayman 57-388 1974 $25

KENNEDY, WILLIAM SLOANE　　Reminiscences of Walt Whitman.　1896. English first edition.　Covent 56-2117 1974 £5.25

KENNETT, BASIL　　　The Lives and Characters of the Ancient Grecian Poets.　London, 1697. 8vo., contemporary panelled calf, plates, first edition.　Dawsons PM 252-609 1974 £55

KENNETT, BASIL　　　Romae Antiquae Notitia.　1696. Old calf, worn, rebacked, copper-plates.　Thomas 28-331 1972 £9.50

KENNETT, BASIL　　　Romae Antiquae Notitia.　1763. 8vo., contemporary calf, worn, damp and other stains, engraved plates, thirteenth edition.　Bow Windows 66-396 1974 £6

KENNETT, WHITE　　　An Address of Thanks to a Good Prince, Presented in a Panegyrick of Pliny Upon Trajan, the Best of Roman Emperours.　London, 1686. 8vo., contemporary mottled calf, gilt, rebacked, orig. spine laid down, first edition, very good.　Ximenes 36-134 1974 $200

KENNETT, WHITE　　　A Compassionate Enquiry Into the Cause of the Civil War in a Sermon Preach'd in the Church of St. Buttolph Algate, on Jan. XXXI, 1703-4.　London, 1708. Disbound, trimmed but not cropped, slight uniform age browning.　Wilson 63-598F 1974 $25

KENNETT, WHITE　　　Parochial Antiquities.　Oxford, 1695. 4to., contemporary panelled calf, plates, first edition.　Dawsons PM 251-38 1974 £40

KENNETT, WHITE　　　Parochial Antiquities.　Oxford, 1695. 4to., plates, half calf, gilt.　Quaritch 939-152 1974 £40

KENNETT, WHITE　　　Parochial Antiquities.　Oxford, 1818. 2 vols., 4to., plates, orig. boards, new enlarged edition.　Quaritch 939-153 1974 £25

KENNEY, J. F.　　　Catalogue of Pictures, Including Paintings, Drawings and Prints in the Public Archives of Canada. Part 1.　Ottawa, 1925. Hood's 102-28 1974 $17.50

KENNEY, J. F.　　　Catalogue of Pictures, . . . in the Public Archives of Canada.　Ottawa, 1925. Illus.　Hood's 104-169 1974 $17.50

KENNEY, JAMES　　　Ella Rosenberg.　London, 1807. 8vo., modern boards, first edition.　Dawsons PM 252-610 1974 £15

KENNEY, JAMES　　　False Alarms.　London, 1807. 8vo., modern boards, first edition.　Dawsons PM 252-611 1974 £15

KENNEY, JAMES　　　Raising the Wind.　London, 1805. 8vo., modern boards, third edition.　Dawsons PM 252-612 1974 £8

KENNEY, JAMES　　　The World!　London, 1808. 8vo., disbound, first edition.　Ximenes 33-443 1974 $10

KENNEY, JAMES　　　The World.　Longman, 1808. 94p.　Austin 51-500 1973 $12.50

KENNION, EDWARD　　　An Essay on Trees in Landscape.　1815. 4to., half calf, plates.　Wheldon 131-1740 1974 £30

KENNION, EDWARD　　　The Essay on Trees in Landscape.　1844. Super roy 4to., orig. cloth, plates.　Broadhurst 23-1155 1974 £65

KENNY, D. J.　　　Illustrated Cincinnati.　Cincinnati, 1875. New cloth, rebound.　Hayman 59-432 1974 $10

KENNY, NICK　　　How To Write, Sing and Sell Popular Songs. Hermitage, 1946. 255p.　Austin 51-501 1973 $8.50

KENNY, T.　　　The Life and Genius of Shakespeare.　1864. 8vo., dark blue half calf, gilt.　Quaritch 936-561 1974 £6

KENRICK, FRANCIS PATRICK　　The Primacy of the Apostolic See Vindicted. Murphy, 1855.　Austin 62-321 1974 $17.50

KENRICK, JOHN　　　Free Thoughts on Seduction, Adultery, and Divorce.　London, 1771. 8vo., contemporary calf gilt, first edition.　Dawsons PM 251-451 1974 £35

KENRICK, WILLIAM　　　The Duellist.　London, (n.d.). 8vo., modern boards, first edition.　Dawsons PM 252-613 1974 £15

KENRICK, WILLIAM   Falstaff's Wedding. London, 1760. 8vo.,
disbound, first edition. Ximenes 33-444 1974 $60

KENRICK, WILLIAM   The New American Orchardist. Boston, 1833.
New half morocco, first edition. Bradley 35-242 1974 $40

KENRICK, WILLIAM   The Widow'd Wife. London, 1767. 8vo.,
wrappers, first edition. Ximenes 33-446 1974 $27.50

KENRICK, WILLIAM   The Widow'd Wife. London, 1767. 8vo.,
modern boards, first edition. Dawsons PM 252-614 1974 £15

KENT, AGNES SCOTT   Rachel. Toronto, 1930. Illus. with sketches.
Hood's 102-523 1974 $7.50

KENT, AGNES SCOTT   Zonya. Toronto, 1938. 314 pages. Austin
57-350 1974 $12.50

KENT, ELIZABETH   Sylvan Sketches. London, 1831. 8vo., orig.
cloth, frontispiece. Hammond 201-652 1974 £6

KENT, NATHANIEL   General View of the Agriculture of the County of
Norfolk. Norwich, 1796. 8vo., orig. calf-backed boards, plates. Hammond
201-23 1974 £30

KENT, NATHANIEL   Hints to Gentlemen of Landed Property. London,
1775. 8vo., contemporary calf, gilt, plates, first edition. Hammond 201-24
1974 £28

KENT, NATHANIEL   Hints to Gentlemen of Landed Property.
London, 1775. 8vo., half morocco, uncut, first edition. Ximenes 33-447
1974 $75

KENT, ROCKWELL   A Birthday Book. New York, 1931. Orig.
illus. cloth, first edition, limited, signed by artist, fine. MacManus 224-264
1974 $30

KENT, ROCKWELL   N. by E. New York, 1930. 4to., illus.,
1st ed., ltd. to 900 numbered and sgd. copies. Jacobs 24-101 1974 $75

KENT, ROCKWELL   Rockwellkentiana. New York, 1933. First
U. S. edition, 4to., dec. cloth, very good copy. Covent 51-1047 1973 £6.30

KENT, ROCKWELL   Salamina. 1936. Plates, dust wrapper, fine,
English first edition. Covent 56-1838 1974 £5.25

KENT, ROCKWELL   This Is My Own. New York, 1940. 1st ed.,
signed by author. Biblo & Tannen 213-308 1973 $17.50

KENT, ROCKWELL   This Is My Own. New York, 1940. Dust
jacket, fine, inscription, first edition. Ballinger 1-152 1974 $60

KENT, WILLIAM SAVILLE   The Great Barrier Reef of Australia. (1893).
Large 4to., orig. cloth, plates, first edition. Bow Windows 64-239 1974 £48

KENT, WILLIAM SAVILLE   The Great Barrier Reef of Australia. (1893).
Imp. 4to., orig. cloth, coloured and photo plates, folding map, scarce. Wheldon
128-165 1973 £28

KENT, WILLIAM SAVILLE   A Manual of the Infusoria. 1881-82. 3 vols.,
8vo., orig. brown cloth, coloured frontis., plates. Wheldon 128-923 1973 £85

KENT, WILLIAM SAVILLE   A Manual of the Infusoria. 1881-82. Roy. 8vo.,
3 vols., orig. brown cloth, plates, scarce. Wheldon 130-890 1974 £85

KEPLER, JOHANN   Dissertatio cum Nuncio Sidereo. Florence,
1610. Vellum, second edition. Schumann 500-5 1974 sFr 5,000

KEPLER, JOHANN   Dissertatio cum Nuncio Sidereo Nuper ad
Mortales Misso a Galilaeo Galilaeo Mathematico Patavino. Prague, 1610. Small
4to., vellum, first edition, very large copy, many fore and lower edges uncut.
Schumann 500-4 1974 sFr 15,000

KEPLER, JOHANN   Narratio de Observatis a se Quatuor Iovis Satellitibus Erronibus. 1611. 4to., marbled boards, second edition. Dawsons PM
245-431 1974 £550

KEPLER, JOHANN   Narratio de Observatis a se Quatuor Iovis
Satellitibus Erronibus, Quos Galilaeus Galilaeus. Florence, 1611. Small 4to.,
paper mends slightly affecting the print, second edition. Schumann 500-9 1974
sFr 4,000

KEPLER, JOHANN   De Stella Nova in Pede Serpentarii. Prague,
1606. 4 parts in 1 vol., 4to., contemporary calf, gilt, first edition. Schuman
37-135 1974 $3500

KEPPEL, HENRY   A Sailor's Life Under Four Sovereigns. 1899.
3 vols., 8vo., illus., maps, orig. cloth. Bow Windows 62-533 1974 £8.50

KER, HENRY   Travels Through the Western Interior of the
United States, 1808-1816. Elizabethtown, 1816. Full calf, label on spine, first
edition, first issue with list of subscribers. Jenkins 61-1317 1974 $275

KER, JOHN   The Memoirs Of. London, 1726. 8vo., contemporary continental mottled sheep, gilt, first edition. Dawsons PM 251-125
1974 £35

KER, W. P.   Collected Essays. 1925. 2 vols., portrait,
scarce, orig. edition. Howes 186-290 1974 £8

KERCHOVE DE DENTERGHEM, O. DE   Les Palmiers. Paris, 1878. Roy. 8vo.,
half morocco, text-figures, coloured plates, scarce. Wheldon 128-1605 1973
£15

KERGUELEN'S Land and Rodriguez. 1879. 4to., plates, half calf, rare.
Wheldon 131-365 1974 £25

KERN, JEROME   The Library of. New York, 1929. 2 vols.,
4to., limp cloth. Dawsons PM 10-337 1974 £25

KERN der Nederlandsch Historie met Figuurtjes. Amsterdam, 1753. 2 parts in 1,
1 7/8 X 1 1/8, copperplates, old red morocco, gilt. Gregory 44-402 1974 $210

KERNAN, W. F.   History of the 103rd Field Artillery, World War
1917-1919. Providence, (c. 1920). 8vo., illus., folding maps, very fine.
Current BW9-620 1974 $10

KERNAN, WILLIAM C.   Ghost of Royal Oak. 1940. 196p., illus.
Austin 62-744 1974 $8.50

KERNER, JUSTINUS   Geschichte Zweyer Somnambulen. Karlsruhe,
1824. 8vo., contemporary boards, very rare, first edition. Schuman 37-136
1974 $235

KERNER VAN MARILAUN, A.   The Natural History of Plants. (1894-95).
2 vols., imp. 8vo., cloth, coloured plates. Wheldon 128-1118 1973 £8

KERNER VON MARILAUN, A.   The Natural History of Plants. (1894-95).
Imperial 8vo., cloth, 2 vols. Wheldon 129-928 1974 £8

KERNER VON MARILAUN, A.   The Natural History of Plants. 1902. 8vo.,
2 vols., contemporary cloth binding, illus. Bow Windows 64-153 1974 £5

KERNER VAN MARILAUN, A.   The Natural History of Plants. 1902. 2 vols.,
roy. 8vo., half leather, text-figures. Wheldon 128-1120 1973 £6

KERNER VAN MARILAUN, A.   The Natural History of Plants. (1904). 2 vols.,
roy. 8vo., cloth, text-figures. Wheldon 128-1119 1973 £5

KERNER VAN MARILAUN, A.   Zhizn Rastenii. St. Petersburg, 1906.
2 vols., roy. 8vo., half roan, text-figures, coloured plates. Wheldon 128-1121
1973 £7.50

KERR, ANNIE B.   Clear Shining After Rain. 1941. 167p.
Austin 62-322 1974 $12.50

KERR, W. A.   Peat and Its Products. Glasgow, 1905. 8vo.,
orig. cloth, gilt, plates, illus. Hammond 201-25 1974 £5

KERR, WALTER   Pieces of Eight. Simon, Schuster, 1957.
Austin 51-502 1973 $4

KERSEY, JOHN   The Elements of that Mathematical Art Commonly
Called Algebra. 1673-1674. Folio, contemporary sprinkled calf, label, first
edition. Zeitlin 235-121 1974 $675

KERSHAW, J. C.   Butterflies of Hong Kong. Hong Kong, (1905-) 1907. Small folio, cloth, plain and coloured plates, complete, rare. Wheldon 128-749 1973 £30

KERSHAW, J. C.   Butterflies of Hong Kong. Hong Kong, 1907. 4to., plates, binders cloth. Smith 193-754 1973 £25

KERSHAW, J. C.   Butterflies of Hong Kong. Hong Kong, (1905). Small folio, cloth, plates, rare. Wheldon 131-819 1974 £35

KERSHAW, MARK   Colonial Facts and Fictions. London, 1886. Small 8vo., orig. pictorial cloth, first edition. Ximenes 33-449 1974 $12.50

KESSINGER, L.   History of Buffalo County. Alma, 1888. Cloth, fine, map. Putnam 126-352 1974 $65

KETCHUM, JOHN WINSLOW   A Wrecked Institution. Burlington, 1902. 8vo., wrapper. Butterfield 8-645 1974 $15

KETCHUM, WILLIAM   An Authentic and Comprehensive History of Buffalo. Buffalo, 1864, 1865. 2 vols., folding map, appendix. Hood's 102-464 1974 $75

KETCHUM, WILLIAM   An Authentic and Comprehensive History of Buffalo. Buffalo, 1864-65. 2 vols., map. Hood's 104-524 1974 $75

KETHAM, JOHANNES DE   Wundartznei und der Chirurgen Handtwirckung. (1534). 4to., vellum over boards. Dawsons PM 249-313 1974 £325

KETTELL, RUSSELL HAWES   The Pine Furniture of Early New England. Garden City, 1929. Very scarce orig. edition, photos, plates, drawings, beige buckram, boxed, limited to 999 copies. Butterfield 10-329 1974 $75

KETTELL, SAMUEL   Specimens of American Poetry. Boston, 1829. 3 vols., 12mo., old half calf, first edition. Ximenes 33-450 1974 $75

KETTLEWELL, JOHN   Death Made Comfortable. London, 1722. Tall 12mo., contemporary calf backed marbled boards, second edition. Smith 194-168 1974 £6.50

KETTLEWELL, S.   Thomas A Kempis and the Brothers of Common Life. 1882. 2 vols., orig. cloth, scarce. Howes 185-896 1974 £7.75

KEULEMANS, J. G.   A Natural History of Cage Birds, Vol. 1 part 3. 1871. Imp. 8vo., orig. printed wrappers, plates, rare. Wheldon 131-70 1974 £50

KEVERNE, RICHARD   Crook Stuff. 1935. 8vo., orig. cloth, dust wrapper, first edition. Rota 190-303 1974 £6

KEY, ALEXANDER   The Red Eagle. Joliet, (1930). 8vo., pictorial boards, cloth spine, very good copy. Frohnsdorff 16-467 1974 $10

KEY, PIERRE   Music Year Book, 1938 Edition. New York, 1938. Biblo & Tannen 214-867 1974 $15

A KEY to Knowledge. 1820. 12mo., orig. quarter red morocco, frontispiece, third edition. Hill 126-50 1974 £18

KEYES, E. L.   The Tonic Treatment of Syphilis. New York, 1881. Rittenhouse 46-724 1974 $12.50

KEYES, F.   Evan Dale. Boston, 1864. 12mo., orig. green cloth, first edition. Ximenes 33-451 1974 $20

KEYES, HERVEY   The Forest King. New York, 1878. 16mo., pictorial wrapper, chipped. Butterfield 10-14 1974 $12.50

KEYES, S.   Collected Poems. 1945. Small 8vo., cloth, dust wrapper, first edition. Quaritch 936-438 1974 £10

KEYES, SIDNEY KILWORTH   Dartford. Dartford, 1933. Thick roy. 8vo., illus., plates, scarce. Howes 186-2050 1974 £12.50

KEYES, SIDNEY KILWORTH   The Iron Laurel. London, 1942. Wrappers, nice copy, ragged d.w., rubber stamps, neat inscription, first edition, scarce. Crane 7-163 1974 £8.50

KEYES, SIDNEY KILWORTH   The Iron Laurel. 1942. 8vo., wrappers, first edition. Rota 189-529 1974 £7.50

KEYES, SIDNEY KILWORTH   The Iron Laurel. (London, 1942). 8vo., orig. stiff paper wrappers, frayed, first edition. Bow Windows 62-534 1974 £12

KEYNES, GEOFFREY   Bibliography of William Hazlitt. London, 1931. 8vo., orig. boards, limited first edition. Dawsons PM 10-274 1974 £40

KEYNES, GEOFFREY   Bibliography of William Hazlitt. London, 1931. 8vo., orig. boards, limited, first edition. Dawsons PM 252-441 1974 £40

KEYNES, GEOFFREY   Jane Austen: A Bibliography. 1929. Illus., crown 8vo., boards, paper printed label, uncut. Broadhurst 24-374 1974 £25

KEYNES, GEOFFREY   Jane Austen, a Bibliography. London, 1929. 8vo., plates, orig. boards, fine, limited. Dawsons PM 10-17 1974 £40

KEYNES, GEOFFREY   Jane Austen. London, 1929. 8vo., orig. boards, plates, dust wrapper, fine, limited. Dawsons PM 252-29 1974 £40

KEYNES, JOHN MAYNARD   The Economic Consequences of the Peace. London, 1919. 8vo., orig. cloth, rare, first edition. Dawsons PM 250-50 1974 £22

KEYNES, JOHN MAYNARD   The Economic Consequences of the Peace. London, 1919. 8vo., orig. cloth, first edition. Dawsons PM 247-161 1974 £22

KEYNES, JOHN MAYNARD   The Economic Consequences of the Peace. London, 1919. 8vo., orig. cloth, rare first edition. Gilhofer 61- 83 1974 sFr 300

KEYNES, JOHN MAYNARD   The Economic Consequences of Mr. Churchill. 1925. Orig. wrappers, faded, scarce, first edition. Howes 186-1476 1974 £12.50

KEYNES, JOHN MAYNARD   The End of Laissez-Faire. London, 1926. 8vo., orig. half cloth, first edition. Gilhofer 61-94 1974 sFr. 150

KEYNES, JOHN MAYNARD   The End of Laissez-Faire. London, 1927. 8vo., orig. blue boards, faded. Dawsons PM 247-165 1974 £12

KEYNES, JOHN MAYNARD   Essays in Biography. London, 1933. 8vo., orig. green cloth, first edition. Dawsons PM 247-166 1974 £12

KEYNES, JOHN MAYNARD   The General Theory of Employment Interest and Money. London, 1936. 8vo., orig. cloth, first edition. Bow Windows 62-535 1974 £30

KEYNES, JOHN MAYNARD   The General Theory of Employment Interest and Money. London, 1936. 8vo., orig. blue cloth, first edition. Dawsons PM 247-167 1974 £35

KEYNES, JOHN MAYNARD   The General Theory of Employment Interest and Money. London, 1936. 8vo., orig. blue cloth, gilt, dust wrapper, first edition. Dawsons PM 250-49 1974 £35

KEYNES, JOHN MAYNARD   The General Theory of Employment, Interest and Money. London, 1936. 8vo., cloth, first edition. Gilhofer 61-98 1974 sFr. 400

KEYNES, JOHN MAYNARD   How to Pay for the War. 1940. Boards, English first edition. Covent 56-767 1974 £10

KEYNES, JOHN MAYNARD   How to Pay for the War. London, 1940. 8vo., orig. paper boards, fine, first edition. Dawsons PM 247-168 1974 £15

KEYNES, JOHN MAYNARD   A Revision of the Treaty. London, 1922. 8vo., orig. cloth, gilt, first edition. Dawsons PM 247-162 1974 £12

KEYNES, JOHN MAYNARD   A Tract on Monetary Reform. 1923. Rubbed, first edition. Covent 55-959 1974 £20

KEYNES, JOHN MAYNARD   A Tract on Monetary Reform. London, 1923. 8vo., orig. cloth, first edition. Dawsons PM 247-163 1974 £15

KEYNES, JOHN MAYNARD   A Tract On Monetary Reform.   London, 1923.
8vo., orig. cloth, first edition.   Gilhofer 61-90 1974 sFr. 150

KEYNES, JOHN MAYNARD   A Treatise on Money.   London, 1930. 2 vols.,
8vo., orig. cloth, first edition.   Dawsons PM 247-164 1974 £25

KEYNES, JOHN NEVILLE   Studies and Exercises In Formal Logic.   1928.
8vo., orig. cloth, fourth & best edition.   Howes 185-1900 1974 £6.50

KEYS, J.   A Treatise on the Breeding and Management of
Bees.   1814. Small 8vo., orig. boards, uncut.   Wheldon 129-717 1974 £15

KEYS, THOMAS EDWARD   The History of Surgical Anesthesia.   New York,
1945.   Rittenhouse 46-389 1974 $10

KEYSLER, J. G.   Antiquitates Selectae Septentrionales et
Celticae.   Hanover, 1720. 12mo., contemporary vellum, plates.   Quaritch
940-328 1974 £50

KHERDIAN, DAVID   On the Death of My Father.   Fresno, n.d.
Signed, dust jacket.   Ballinger 1-153 1974 $25

KIBBE, GUSTAV   Famous Actors and Actresses and Their Homes.
Little, Brown. 360p.   Austin 51-511 1973 $10

KIDD, D.   The Essential Kafir.   1925. 8vo., orig. cloth,
sketch map, frontispiece, illus., second edition.   Bow Windows 66-399 1974
£7.25

KIDD, JAMES   An Essay on the Doctrine of the Trinity.   London,
1815. Full leather, gilt, front hinge cracked, inscribed by author, James Monroe's
copy.   Butterfield 10-468 1974 $20

KIDDER, EDWARD   E. Kidder's Receipts of Pastry and Cookery.
(n.p., n.d.). 8vo., contemporary panelled calf, plates.   Bow Windows 64
579 1974 £300

KIDDIER, WILLIAM   The Profanity of Paint.   1916. Wrappers, fine,
English first edition.   Covent 56-769 1974 £7.50

KIDGELL, JOHN   The Card.   London, 1755. 2 vols., 12mo.,
contemporary sprinkled calf, first edition.   Dawsons PM 252-615 1974 £130

KIDGELL, JOHN   The Card.   London, 1755. 2 vols., 12mo.,
contemporary calf, gilt, first edition.   Ximenes 33-452 1974 $275

KIDSON, J. R.   Historical Notices of the Leeds Old Pottery.
1892. 4to., plates, cloth, rare, limited.   Quaritch 939-600 1974 £28

KIDSTON, R.   A Monograph of the Calamites of Western
Europe, Part 1, Genus Calamites.   The Hague, 1917. 2 vols., 4to., orig.
wrappers and orig. portfolio, plates.   Wheldon 128-1001 1973 £15

KIDSTON, R.   On the Fossil Osmundaceae.   Edinburgh,
1907-14. 5 parts, 4to., wrappers.   Wheldon 131-1030 1974 £7.50

KIEFFER, J. J.   Das Tierreich.   Berlin, 1926. Orig. wrappers,
torn.   Bow Windows 64-71 1974 £12.50

KIEFFER, J. J.   Hymenoptera.   Berlin 1914. Orig. wrappers,
red half morocco, cloth sides.   Bow Windows 64-72 1974 £12.50

KIENER, L. C.   Species General et Iconographie des Coquilles
Vivantes.   Paris, (1834-50). 7 vols., 8vo., new half morocco, hand-coloured
plates.   Wheldon 128-843 1973 £600

KIERAN, JOHN   The American Sporting Scene.   New York,
1941. 4to., plates, 1st ed., author's sgd. pres.   Biblo & Tannen 210-341 1973
$15

KIERKEGAARD, SOREN AABYE   Enten - Eller.   Copenhagen, 1843. 2 vols.,
8vo., contemporary half calf, fine, rare first edition.   Gilhofer 61-45 1974
sFr. 2,300

KIESLING, BARRETT C.   Talking Pictures.   Johnson, 1937. 332p.,
illus.   Austin 51-503 1973 $10

KILBOURN, JOHN   Columbian Geography.   Chillicothe, 1815.
12mo., orig. quarter calf, first edition.   Ximenes 33-453 1974 $275

KILBURNE, RICHARD   A Brief Survey of the County of Kent.   London,
1657. Oblong folio, contemporary calf, fine, rare, first edition.   Dawsons PM
251-39 1974 £850

KILBURNE, RICHARD   A Topographie.   London, 1659. 4to., eighteenth century half calf, worn, first edition.   Dawsons PM 251-40 1974 £80

KILBURNE, RICHARD   A Topographie.   1659. Small 4to., half calf
gilt, dampstaining.   Quaritch 939-408 1974 £85

KILIAN, HERMANN FRIEDRICH   Armamentarium Lucinae Novum.   Bonn, 1856.
Small oblong folio, orig. cloth-backed boards, illus., plates, first edition.   Schumann 35-256 1974 $135

KILLEN, W. D.   The Ecclesiastical History of Ireland.   London,
1875. 2 vols., 8vo., cloth boards.   Emerald 50-495 1974 £7.50

KILLIGREW, THOMAS   Chit-Chat.   London, n.d. 8vo., disbound,
second edition.   Ximenes 33-454 1974 $27.50

KILLIGREW, THOMAS   Chit-Chat.   (1719). 8vo., cloth, first edition.
Quaritch 936-126 1974 £18

KILLINGTON, F. J.   A Monograph of the British Neuroptera.   1936-
37. 8vo., orig. cloth, 2 vols., plates.   Wheldon 129-651 1974 £7.50

KILLPACK, W. B.   The History and Antiquities of Southwell
Collegiate Church.   1839. Folio, cloth-backed boards, plates.   Howes
186-2120 1974 £8.50

KILMER, JOYCE   The Circus and other Essays and Fugitive
Pieces.   New York, 1921. 1st ed.   Biblo & Tannen 210-754 1973 $10

KILMER, JOYCE   Trees.   New York, (1925). Narrow 8vo.,
pictorial boards, cloth spine, illus., fine copy, slightly worn d.j., first edition.
Frohnsdorff 16-530 1974 $20

KILMER, JOYCE   Trees and Other Poems.   New York, (1914).
Orig. boards, paper labels, first issue, not having "Printed in the United States"
on verso of title-page, fine, laid-in short T.L.s. to Dr. Skrainka, boxed.
MacManus 224-266 1974 $65

KILMER, JOYCE   Trees and Other Poems.   New York, 1914.
Boards, paper labels, first edition.   Rinsland 58-908 1974 $35

KILNER, DOROTHY   Edward the Orphan.   (1825). 12mo., half
calf, trifle rubbed, engraved plates, rare.   George's 610-424 1973 £5

KILNER, J.   The Account of Pythagoras's School of
Cambridge.   (1790). Folio, plates, half calf.   Quaritch 939-323 1974 £8

KILNER, M. J.   Memoirs of a Peg-Top.   (c. 1790). Early
edition, 12mo., orig. Dutch floral boards, bottom edge rubbed, lacks spine, sides
loose, woodcuts, lacking title page & frontis.   George's 610-426 1973 £10

KIMBALL, CHARLES P.   The San Francisco Directory of 1850.   San
Francisco, c. 1890. 32mo., reprint, near mint.   Current BW9-347 1974 $30

KIMBER, E.   The Baronetage of England.   London, 1771. 8vo.,
3 vols., contemporary red straight-grained morocco, gilt, plates, first edition.
Hammond 201-430 1974 £30

KIMBROUGH, EMILY   How Dear to My Heart.   Dodd, Mead, 1944.
276p., illus.   Austin 54-592 1973 $6

KIMBROUGH, EMILY   It Gives Me Great Pleasure.   Dodd, Mead,
1948. 227p., illus., orig. ed.   Austin 54-593 1973 $6.50

KIMBROUGH, EMILY   It Gives Me Great Pleasure.   Harper, n.d.
Illus.   Austin 54-594 1973 $5

KIMBROUGH, EMILY   Floating Island.   Harper, Row, 1968. 243p.
Austin 54-589 1973 $5

KIMBROUGH, EMILY   Forever Old Forever New.   Harper, n.d.
24lp.   Austin 54-590 1973 $5

KIMBROUGH, EMILY   Forty Plus and Fancy Free. Harper, 1954.
240p. Austin 54-591 1973 $6

KIMBROUGH, EMILY   Pleasure By the Busload. Harper, 1961. 276p.,
illus. Austin 54-595 1973 $5

KIMBROUGH, EMILY   So Near and Yet So Far. Harper, 1955. 241p.,
illus. Austin 54-596 1973 $6.50

KIMBROUGH, EMILY   Through Charley's Door. Harper, 1952. 273p.
Illus. Austin 54-597 1973 $6.50

KIMBROUGH, EMILY   Water, Water Everywhere. Harper, 1956.
308p., illus. Austin 54-598 1973 $6.50

KIMBROUGH, EMILY   We Followed Our Hearts to Hollywood. Dodd,
Mead, 1943. 210p., illus. Austin 54-599 1973 $6

KIMMEL, S.   The Mad Booths of Maryland. (1940). Large
8vo., orig. cloth, illus., first edition. Putman 126-17 1974 $15

KINDER, GEORGE D.   History of Putnam County. Indianapolis, 1915.
One half leather, fine. Hayman 57-588 1974 $50

KINDS, EDMOND   Etude sur Marcel Proust. Paris, 1933. One of
1150 copies on Navarre Paper, very good, dusty wrappers. Covent 51-2540
1973 £6.30

KING, ARTHUR WILLIAM   An Aubrey Beardsley Lecture. 1924. F'cap.
4to., limited to 500 copies, illus., contains some unpublished letters & drawings,
orig. cloth, fine. Broadhurst 24-753 1974 £10

KING, ARTHUR WILLIAM   An Aubrey Beardsley Lecture. 1924. First
edition, fine, gilt top morocco label, one of 500 copies, this copy unnumbered.
Covent 51-192 1973 £6.30

KING, BEN   Ben King's Verse. Forbes, 1898. 276p.,
illus. Austin 54-600 1973 $10

KING, BOLTON   A History of Italian Unity. 1899. 2 vols.,
maps. Howes 186-969 1974 £7.50

KING, CHARLES   Cadet Days. New York, 1894. 8vo., cloth,
pictorially stamped, spine ends and corners rubbed, illus., first edition.
Frohnsdorff 16-468 1974 $20

KING, CHARLES   Campaigning With Crook and Stories of Army
Life. New York, 1890. Fine. Jenkins 61-1320 1974 $10

KING, CLARENCE   Mountaineering in the Sierra Nevada. New
York, 1902. Orig. binding, lacking d.w., name in ink on fly, near fine. Ross
87-438 1974 $12.50

KING, DAVID BENNETT   The Irish Question. New York, 1882.
8vo., cloth boards. Emerald 50-496 1974 £8

KING, DOROTHY N.   Find the Animals. (New York, 1941).
Oblong 4to., pictorial boards, color illus., plates, advance review copy, first
edition. Frohnsdorff 16-587 1974 $20

KING, GEORGIANA GODDARD   Way of St. James. 1920. 3 vols., 16mo.,
plates. Allen 213-1583 1973 $15

KING, HENRY   The English Poems Of. 1914. Frontispiece,
ex-library. Austin 61-531 1974 $12.50

KING, JAMES L.   History of Shawnee County, Kansas. Chicago,
1905. 4to., leather. Saddleback 14-428 1974 $75

KING, JOHN   An Essay on Hot and Cold Bathing. London, 17-
37. 8vo., half-calf, gilt. Hammond 201-546 1974 £45

KING, JOHN   The Other Side of the "Story", Being Some
Reviews Criticizing "The Story of the Upper Canadian Rebellion; Also the Letters
on the MacKenzie-Rolph Controversy and a Critique of the New Story. Toronto,
1886. Hood's 102-620 1974 $17.50

KING, JOHN GLEN   The Rites and Ceremonies of the Greek Church
in Russia. London, 1772. 4to., contemporary russia, gilt, first edition.
Ximenes 33-455 1974 $90

KING, L. J.   House of Death and Gate of Hell. Detroit,
1928. Illus. Austin 57-355 1974 $12.50

KING, L. J.   House of Death and Gate of Hell. Detroit,
1928. 112p., illus. Austin 62-325 1974 $12.50

KING, LEONARD W.   A History of Sumer and Akkad. London, 1916.
1st ed., plates. Biblo & Tannen 210-1002 1973 $20

KING, MOSES   King's Handbook of New York City. 1893.
Illus., revised second edition. Rinsland 58-973 1974 $35

KING, MOSES   King's Pocket Book of Providence, Rhode Island.
Providence, (1882). 16mo., extremities little rubbed, interior fine. Current BW9-
423 1974 $8.75

KING, PETER   The History of the Apostles Creed. 1703. 8vo.,
contemporary calf, second edition. Hill 126-150 1974 £6.50

KING, R.   A Primer of the History of the Holy Catholic
Church in Ireland. Dublin, 1858-46-51. 3 vols., 12mo., half calf, third
edition. Quaritch 939-617 1974 £10

KING, T. BUTLER   Report on California. Washington, 1850.
Wrapper, second edition & best, errata leaf. Jenkins 61-346 1974 $75

KING, W.   A Monograph of the Permian Fossils of England.
1850. 4to., half calf, plates. Wheldon 131-1031 1974 £15

KING, W. L. M.   The Secret of Heroism, a Memoir of Henry
Albert Harper. New York, Chicago, Toronto, 1906. Second edition, inscription
by author. Hood's 102-334 1974 $30

KING, WILLIAM   The Art of Cookery. (1708). 8vo., contemporary panelled sheep, first edition. Hill 126-149 1974 £48

KING, WILLIAM   The Art of Cookery. London, (1709). 8vo.,
contemporary calf, gilt, first authorized edition. Hammond 201-170 1974 £70

KING, WILLIAM   Chelsea Porcelain. 1922. 4to., orig. cloth,
plates, illus., first edition. Bow Windows 66-400 1974 £34

KING, WILLIAM   Chelsea Porcelain. 1922. 4to., plates,
pigskin, gilt, limited, signed, edition de luxe. Quaritch 940-645 1974 £45

KING, WILLIAM   English Porcelain Figures of the 18th Century.
1925. 4to., plates, cloth. Quaritch 940-646 1974 £15

KING, WILLIAM   Oratio in Theatro Sheldoniano Habita Idibus
Aprilibus. London, n.d. 4to., disbound, first edition. Ximenes 33-456
1974 $30

KING, WILLIAM   The State of Protestants of Ireland. Dublin,
1730. 8vo., full calf, labels. Emerald 50-498 1974 £15

KING, WILLIAM   The State of the Protestants of Ireland under the
Late King James's Government. Dublin, 1730. 8vo., contemporary panelled
calf. Hill 126-151 1974 £15

KING Albert's Book. (London, 1914). 4to., cloth, one color plate, illus.
Frohnsdorff 15-149 1974 $15

THE KING of Spaines Edict, for the Expulsion and Banishment of More Than Nine
Hundred Thousand Moores Out of His Kingdome. London, 1611. Small 4to.,
red quarter morocco, gilt, first edition. Traylen 79-571 1973 £180

KING'S Classics. London, 1930-11. 32 vols., small 4to., book-plate, orig.
bindings, rubbed. Bow Windows 62-537 1974 £58

THE KING'S Pictures from Buckingham Palace, Windsor Castle & Hampton Court.
n.d. 3 vols., 4to., plates, orig. wrappers, limited edition. Smith 193-65
1973 £10

KINGDON, FRANK   Jacob's Ladder. Fischer, 1943.   Austin 62-326
1974 $10

KINGDOM, JOHN A.   Facsimile of First Volume of MS Archives of
the Worshipful Company of Grocers.   1886. 2 vols., 4to., contemporary half
morocco, gilt, scarce. Howes 186-1442 1974 £50

KINGDON-WARD, F.   The Mystery Rivers of Tibet. 1923. 8vo.,
orig. cloth, illus., scarce, first edition. Wheldon 130-1505 1974 £20

KINGDON-WARD, F.   A Plant Hunter in Tibet. 1934. 8vo., orig.
cloth, scarce, first edition. Wheldon 130-1507 1974 £10

KINGDON-WARD, F.   Plant Hunter's Paradise. 1937. 8vo., orig.
cloth, illus., scarce, first edition. Wheldon 130-1508 1974 £10

KINGDON-WARD, F.   The Riddle of the Tsangpo Gorges.   1926.
8vo., orig. cloth, illus., scarce. Wheldon 130-1506 1974 £20

KINGDON-WARD, F.   The Romance of Gardening. 1935. 8vo.,
cloth, plates, scarce. Wheldon 130-1509 1974 £6

KINGLAKE, ALEXANDER WILLIAM   Eothen. London, 1844. 8vo., orig.
green cloth, first edition. Ximenes 33-457 1974 $90

KINGSBURY, ALLEN ALONZO   The Hero of Medfield. Boston, 1862. Orig.
binding, frontis. portrait, presentation copy. Butterfield 10-162 1974 $20

KINGSBURY, JOHN H.   Kingsbury Sketches. New York, 1875.
12mo., orig. cloth, plates, first edition. Ximenes 33-458 1974 $17.50

KINGSFORD, WILLIAM   The Canadian Canals. Toronto, 1865.
Hood's 103-648 1974 $40

KINGSFORD, WILLIAM   The History of Canada, 1608-1841.   London
& Toronto, 1887-98. 10 vols., map. Hood's 103-839 1974 $125

KINGSFORD-SMITH, C. E.   The Flight of the Southern Cross.   New York,
1929. First edition. Butterfield 10-78 1974 $20

KINGSLEY, ADELAIDE D.   Heart or Purse. Chicago, 1887. Cloth.
Hayman 59-182 1974 $22.50

KINGSLEY, CHARLES   Andromeda. London, 1858. 8vo., orig.
green cloth, uncut, first edition. Dawsons PM 252-616 1974 £15

KINGSLEY, CHARLES   At Last: A Christmas in the West Indies. 1871.
First edition, frontispieces, plates, illus., 2 vols., half titles, ads at rear of each
vol., 8vo., orig. green cloth gilt, uncut, binder's ticket of Burn & Co., binding
slightly worn, very fair copy, scarce. Sawyer 293-190 1974 £115

KINGSLEY, CHARLES   At Last: A Christmas in the West Indies.   New
York, 1871. First American edition, 8vo., covers with some spots, spine ends
rubbed, interior very fresh, author's signature laid in. Current BW9-52 1974
$25

KINGSLEY, CHARLES   Glaucus. Cambridge, 1855. 8vo., orig.
dec. cloth, first edition. Ximenes 33-459 1974 $27.50

KINGSLEY, CHARLES   Glaucus. Cambridge, 1855. Post 8vo., orig.
dec. cloth, frontispiece, first edition. Wheldon 128-151 1973 £10

KINGSLEY, CHARLES   Glaucus. Cambridge, 1859. Post 8vo., orig.
cloth, plates. Wheldon 130-261 1974 £5

KINGSLEY, CHARLES   Glaucus; or, The Wonders of the Shore.   1873.
8vo., contemporary half calf by Mudie, coloured plates, fifth edition. Bow
Windows 66-401 1974 £8

KINGSLEY, CHARLES   Glaucus, or, The Wonders of the Shore.
Cambridge, 1856. Third edition corrected and enlarged, engraved frontispiece,
ads and publisher's catalogue at end, 12mo., orig. cloth gilt, inscribed by
Victoria, Duchess of Kent to Frederick Locker. Sawyer 293-191 1974 £12

KINGSLEY, CHARLES   The Hermits. (London), n.d. 8vo., orig.
blue cloth, first edition. Ximenes 33-460 1974 $17.50

KINGSLEY, CHARLES   Hypatia. 1853. 2 vols., orig. cloth,
worn, faded, first edition. Rota 188-492 1974 £35

KINGSLEY, CHARLES   Miscellanies. 1859. 2 vols., crown 8vo.,
orig. red cloth, labels, first edition. Howes 185-273 1974 £8.50

KINGSLEY, CHARLES   The Roman and the Teuton. Cambridge &
London, 1864. 8vo., foxed, uncut, orig. cloth, first edition. Bow Windows
62-539 1974 £12

KINGSLEY, CHARLES   The Roman and the Teuton. 1864. Orig. cloth,
rubbed. Smith 193-375 1973 £5

KINGSLEY, CHARLES   Town Geology. 1872. Presentation copy,
inscribed by author, orig. cloth, very good copy, first edition. Covent 51-1052
1973 £10.50

KINGSLEY, CHARLES   Town Geology. London, 1873. Crown 8vo.,
re-cased, first edition. Traylen 79-87 1973 £7.50

KINGSLEY, CHARLES   The Water-Babies. 1863. Small 4to., orig.
cloth gilt, illus., English first edition. Covent 56-1857 1974 £65

KINGSLEY, CHARLES   The Water-Babies. London & Cambridge,
1863. 4to., morocco gilt, first edition. Dawsons PM 252-617 1974 £35

KINGSLEY, CHARLES   The Water-Babies: A Fairy Tale for a Land-Baby.
Boston, 1864. 8vo., blue pebbled cloth with pictorial gilt, spine ends frayed,
first American edition. Frohnsdorff 16-469 1974 $25

KINGSLEY, CHARLES   The Water-Babies: A Fairy Tale for a Land-Baby.
London & Cambridge, 1863. 4to., orig. cloth, second issue, lacking the scarce
"L'envoi" leaf, pasted-in on the half-titel is slip of paper with autograph of
author, good copy, cracked hinges. MacManus 224-267 1974 $80

KINGSLEY, CHARLES   The Water-Babies. 1885. 4to., orig. blue
cloth, gilt, illus., new edition. Hammond 201-126 1974 £5

KINGSLEY, CHARLES   Westward Ho! Cambridge, 1855. 3 vols.,
8vo., modern half calf, first edition. Dawsons PM 252-618 1974 £45

KINGSLEY, HENRY   A.L.S. (1867). 8vo., 4 pages. Dawsons
PM 252-619 1974 £65

KINGSLEY, HENRY   Leighton Court. 1866. 2 vols., crown 8vo.,
orig. brown sand grain cloth, first edition. Howes 185-274 1974 £32

KINGSLEY, HENRY   Tales of Old Travel. 1869. First edition,
frontispiece, title vignette, plates, catalogue at end, orig. green cloth gilt, top
edges gilt, scarce. Sawyer 293-192 1974 £62

KINGSLEY, JEFFRIES   County Book of Kildare. Dublin, 1837. 4to.,
orig. cloth, fine, first edition. Ximenes 33-461 1974 $45

KINGSLEY, MARY H.   Travels in West Africa. 1897. Demy 8vo.,
engraved plates, illus., orig. cloth, fine. Broadhurst 24-1632 1974 £6

KINGSLEY, SIDNEY   Detective Story. 1951. Austin 51-504 1973
$6.50

KINGSLEY, Z.   A Treatise on the Patriarchal, or Co-operative
System of Society as it Exists . . . In the United States, Under the Name of
Slavery, With Its Necessity and Advantages. N.P., 1829. Second edition, uncut,
orig. plain wrapper. Butterfield 10-111 1974 $200

KINGSTON, WILLIAM HENRY GILES   The Adventures of Dick Onslow Among
the Red Indians. (n.d.). 8vo., orig. cloth, frontis., illus., dust stains, first
edition. Bow Windows 66-402 1974 £8.50

KINGSTON, WILLIAM HENRY GILES   Snow Shoes and Canoes. Toronto, n.d.
Illus. Hood's 104-858 1974 $22.50

KINGSTON, WILLIAM HENRY GILES   The South Sea Whaler. London,
1885. 8vo., orig. cloth, fine. Ximenes 33-462 1974 $15

KINGSTON, WILLIAM HENRY GILES   The Western World. 1874. 8vo.,
orig. cloth, engravings. Wheldon 131-367 1974 £5

KINLOCH, GEORGE RITCHIE   Ancient Scottish Ballads. London, 1827.
8vo., contemporary half morocco, fine, first edition. Dawsons PM 252-620
1974 £55

KINNEY, J. R.   The Town Dog. Harvill, 1954. 193p., illus.
Austin 54-1012 1973 $7.50

KINNEY, TROY   The Dance. Stokes, 1914. 334p., illus.
Austin 51-505 1973 $10

KINNEY, TROY   The Dance. 1935. 372p., illus. Austin
51-506 1973 $7.50

KINSEY, WILLIAM MORGAN   Portugal Illustrated. 1828. Roy. 8vo.,
plates, contemporary calf, rubbed, second edition. Quaritch 940-722 1974 £90

KINSOLVING, ARTHUR B.   Texas George. Milwaukee-London, 1932. 8vo.,
orig. bindings. Butterfield 8-623 1974 $10

KINZIE, JULIETTE AUGUSTA Narrative of the Massacre at Chicago.
Chicago, 1914. Illus., printed wrappers, fine, second edition. Bradley 35-73
1974 $25

KINZIE, JULIETTE AUGUSTA Wau-bun the "Early Day" in the Northwest.
New York & Cincinnati, 1856. Tall 8vo., pictorial cloth, plates, worn, scarce,
first edition. Butterfield 8-148 1974 $50

KINZIE, JULIETTE AUGUSTA Wau-bun the "Early Day" in the Northwest.
Philadelphia, 1873. 12mo., orig. bindings, third edition. Butterfield 8-149
1974 $10

KIPLING, RUDYARD   The Absent Minded Beggar. N.P., 1899.
Folio, satin, fine, scarce, first edition. Ximenes 33-463 1974 $150

KIPLING, RUDYARD   Ballads and Barrack-Room Ballads. New York,
1893. 12mo., cloth, second American edition. Goodspeed's 578-177 1974 $15

KIPLING, RUDYARD   Barrack Room Ballads, Departmental Ditties,
and Other Ballads and Verses. New York, 1899. Orig. binding, hinges slightly
loose, name in ink on free fly, nice copy. Ross 87-315 1974 $10

KIPLING, RUDYARD   A Book of Words. London, 1928. Orig.
binding, dust wrapper, near mint. Ross 87-316 1974 $10

KIPLING, RUDYARD   Captains Courageous. New York, 1897. Orig.
dec. cloth, gilt, illus., fine, first U.S. edition. Covent 56-770 1974 £8.50

KIPLING, RUDYARD   "Captains Courageous". 1897. Plates, orig.
pictorial cloth gilt, faded, foxed, first English edition. Howes 186-292 1974
£12.50

KIPLING, RUDYARD   Certain Maxims of Hafiz. Boston, 1898. Blue
cloth, lettered in gold, 500 copies printed, pencilled initials & date on title page,
fine, scarce. Ross 87-317 1974 $50

KIPLING, RUDYARD   The Day's Work. London, 1898. Fine, orig.
binding. Ross 87-318 1974 $12.50

KIPLING, RUDYARD   Debits and Credits. London, 1926. Orig.
binding, orig. d.w., the Uniform edition, mint. Ross 87-319 1974 $15

KIPLING, RUDYARD   Doctors: An Address Delivered to the Students
of the Medical School of the Middlesex Hospital, 1st October, 1908. London,
1908. 8vo., orig. cloth wrappers, first edition. Schuman 37-137 1974 $85

KIPLING, RUDYARD   England and the English: Speech at the Festival
Dinner, the Royal Society of St. George, 1920. c. 1920. Half morocco, spine
little faded, bookplate, very nice copy, orig. wrappers preserved. Covent
51-1054 1973 £7.50

KIPLING, RUDYARD   The Five Nations. 1903. Parchment-backed
boards, English first edition. Covent 56-771 1974 £20

KIPLING, RUDYARD   A Fleet in Being. London, 1898. Boards
slightly soiled, spine faded, nice tight copy. Ross 87-320 1974 $40

KIPLING, RUDYARD   From Sea to Sea. New York, 1899. 2 vols.,
first edition, first issue, orig. binding, covers slightly worn, fine. Ross 87-321
1974 $25

KIPLING, RUDYARD   Irish Guards in the Great War. 1923. 2 vols.,
4to., first edition. Allen 216-978 1974 $15

KIPLING, RUDYARD   The Jungle Book. New York, 1894. Orig.
pictorial cloth, gilt, illus., first U.S. edition. Covent 56-772 1974 £10.50

KIPLING, RUDYARD   The Jungle Book. 1894-95. 2 vols., illus.,
orig. blue cloth gilt, foxing, first editions. Howes 186-293 1974 £45

KIPLING, RUDYARD   The Jungle Book. 1894-95. 8vo., orig. cloth
gilt, 2 vols., fine, first editions. Quaritch 936-440 1974 £85

KIPLING, RUDYARD   The Just So Song Book. London, 1911. Folio,
pictorial cloth, corners bumped. Frohnsdorff 16-471 1974 $10

KIPLING, RUDYARD   Just So Stories. London, 1902. 8vo., pictorial
cloth, worn, inner hinges have cracked endpapers, first edition. Frohnsdorff
16-470 1974 $25

KIPLING, RUDYARD   Just So Stories. 1902. Crown 4to., illus.,
orig. pictorial buckram. Smith 194-378 1973 £9.50

KIPLING, RUDYARD   Just So Stories for Little Children. 1902. 4to.,
orig. red cloth, illus., first edition. Hammond 201-127 1974 £20

KIPLING, RUDYARD   Kim. London, 1901. Fine, first English
edition. Ballinger 1-155 1974 $12.50

KIPLING, RUDYARD   Kim. London, 1901. Orig. binding, name in
pencil on flyleaf, fine, the Uniform edition. Ross 87-322 1974 $15

KIPLING, RUDYARD   Life's Handicap. London, 1891. Orig.
binding, first edition, very fine. Ross 87-323 1974 $25

KIPLING, RUDYARD   Pan in Vermont. London, 1902. 16mo.,
dark green paper covers. Dawsons PM 252-621 1974 £110

KIPLING, RUDYARD   Plain Tales from the Hills. London, 1888. 8vo.,
orig. cloth, scarce, first edition. Rota 189-531 1974 £12

KIPLING, RUDYARD   Poems, 1886-1929. New York, 1930.
3 vols., large quarto, bookplate, full vellum, fine, autographed, special limited
edition. Jenkins 48-276 1973 $125

KIPLING, RUDYARD   Puck of Pook's Hill. New York, 1906. First
American edition, coloured plates by Arthur Rackham, 8vo., orig. green embossed
cloth, gilt title, good copy. Sawyer 293-251 1974 £75

KIPLING, RUDYARD   Sea Warfare. London, 1916. Orig. binding,
first edition, fine. Ross 87-324 1974 $12.50

KIPLING, RUDYARD   A Song of the English. London, n.d. 4to.,
plates, illus., royal blue cloth, gilt. Dawsons PM 252-622 1974 £40

KIPLING, RUDYARD   Stalky & Co. London, 1899. First English
edition, orig. binding, the first vol. of the Uniform edition, near mint. Ross
87-325 1974 $30

KIPLING, RUDYARD   The Sussex Edition of the Complete Works.
London, 1937-39. 35 vols., 8vo., mint, orig. full niger morocco, gilt,
signed, limited. Bow Windows 62-542 1974 £1400

KIPLING, RUDYARD   Thy Servant a Dog. 1930. 8vo., orig. cloth,
illus., fine, first edition. Rota 189-540 1974 £10

KIPLING, RUDYARD   "Thy Servant a Dog," Told by Boots. New
York, 1930. 1st ed. Biblo & Tannen 210-755 1973 $8.50

KIPLING, RUDYARD   Traffics and Discoveries. London, 1904. Orig.
binding, the Uniform edition, front cover creased, slight foxing on fore-edge,
very nice. Ross 87-326 1974 $10

KIPLING, RUDYARD   The Two Jungle Books. 1895. Orig.
pictorial buckram gilt, illus. Smith 193-380 1973 £5

KIPLING, RUDYARD   The Two Jungle Books. New York, 1925. 8vo.,
pictorial gilt cloth, first edition. Frohnsdorff 16-472 1974 $15

KIPLING, RUDYARD   The Works. London, 1913-18. 31 vols.,
large 8vo., illus., orig. boards, fine, limited. Dawsons PM 252-623 1974
£450

KIPLING, RUDYARD   Works. 1913-38. Bombay edition, 31 vols.,
complete, med. 8vo., boards, linen spines, paper printed labels, top edges gilt,
others uncut, limited to 1050 copies, signed by author, fine. Broadhurst 24-1713
1974 £275

KIPLING, RUDYARD   The Years Between. 1919. Parchment-backed
boards, hand-made paper, English first edition. Covent 56-775 1974 £17.50

KIPLING, RUDYARD   The Years Between. London, 1919. Orig.
cloth-backed boards, first edition, the deluxe edition, one of 200 copies.
MacManus 224-268 1974 $30

KIPLING, RUDYARD   The Years Between. 1919. Orig. cloth,
faded, signature. Rota 188-495 1974 £10

KIPLING, RUDYARD   The Years Between. London, 1919. First
edition, ads bound in, bookplate, orig. binding, lacking d.w., fine. Ross
87-327 1974 $25

KIPPIS, ANDREW   The Life of Captain James Cook. Dublin, 1824.
12mo., contemporary sheep, frontispiece, woodcuts. Hill 126-51 1974 £18.50

KIRBY, F. V.   In Haunts of Wild Game. 1896. First edition,
med. 8vo., very good copy, map, portrait, illus., orig. cloth. Broadhurst
24-1633 1974 £10

KIRBY, J.   The Suffolk Traveller. 1764. 8vo., modern
boards, second edition. Quaritch 939-558 1974 £20

KIRBY, M.   Beautiful Birds in Far Off Lands. 1872 or 1873.
Crown 8vo., orig. cloth gilt, plates, scarce. Wheldon 130-563 1974 £15

KIRBY, MARY   The Discontented Children and How They Were
Cured. London, 1866. Illus. by Hablot K. Browne, 12mo., cloth, gilt, all
edges gilt, third edition. Frohnsdorff 16-473 1974 £10

KIRBY, W.   Annals of Niagara. Welland, 1896. Hood's
103-649 1974 $30

KIRBY, W.   Monographia Apum Angliae. Ipswich, 1802.
8vo., half morocco, rebacked, plates. Wheldon 130-769 1974 £25

KIRBY, W.   Monographia Apum Angliae. 1802. 8vo., 2
vols., modern boards. Wheldon 129-718 1974 £25

KIRBY, W.   The U.E., a Tale of Upper Canada. Niagara,
1859. Orig. covers, spine faded. Hood's 102-658 1974 $55

KIRBY, WILLIAM FORSELL   The Butterflies and Moths of Europe. (1903).
4to., contemporary half roan, plates. Bow Windows 64-154 1974 £18

KIRBY, WILLIAM FORSELL   The Butterflies and Moths of Europe. (1903).
4to., half blue morocco neat, coloured plates, scarce. Wheldon 128-750 1973
£18

KIRBY, WILLIAM FORSELL   The Butterflies and Moths of Europe. (1903).
2 vols., 4to., half calf, plates, scarce. Wheldon 131-820 1974 £18

KIRBY, WILLIAM FORSELL   European Butterflies and Moths. 1882. 4to.,
2 vols., contemporary half roan. Bow Windows 64-155 1974 £24

KIRBY, WILLIAM FORSELL   European Butterflies and Moths. London, 1889.
4to., orig. dec. cloth, gilt, plates, first edition. Hammond 201-653 1974 £36

KIRBY, WILLIAM FORSELL   A Hand-Book to the Order Lepidoptera. 1896-
97. 5 vols., 8vo., binder's cloth, coloured plates. Wheldon 128-751 1973 £10

KIRBY, WILLIAM FORSELL   An Introduction to Entomology. London, 1822.
4 vols., hand colored plates, full tree calf, gilt. Jacobs 24-149 1974 $50

KIRBY, WILLIAM FORSELL   List of Hymenoptera. 1882. 8vo., orig.
cloth, plates. Wheldon 131-821 1974 £6.50

KIRCH, GOTTFRIED   Hottfried Kirchs Neue Himmels-Zeitung. 1681.
4to., three quarter blind stamped vellum. Zeitlin 235-122 1974 $225

KIRCHER, ATHANASIUS   Ars Magna Lvcis et Vmbrae. 1646. Folio, contemporary vellum, boards, plates. Zeitlin 235-123 1974 $875

KIRCHER, ATHANASIUS   Magnes Sive de Arte Magnetica opvs Tripartitvm.
Cologne, 1643. 4to., panelled and blind tooled calf, plates, second edition.
Dawsons PM 245-432 1974 £195

KIRCHER, ATHANASIUS   Magnes Sive de Magnetica Arte Libri Tres.
1654. Folio, contemporary speckled calf, gilt. Zeitlin 235-124 1974 $385

KIRCHER, ATHANASIUS   Primitiae Gnomonicae Catoptricae. 1635. 4to.,
contemporary calf, first edition. Dawsons PM 245-433 1974 £75

KIRCHER, ATHANASIUS   Scrvtinivm Physico-Medicvm Contagiosae Luis.
1658. 4to., brown half morocco, first edition. Dawsons PM 249-315 1974
£535

KIRCHON, V.   Red Rust. Brentano, 1930. 182p. Austin
51-508 1973 $7.50

KIRK, J. W. C.   A British Garden Flora. 1927. 8vo., cloth.
Wheldon 131-1536 1974 £7.50

KIRK, ROBERT   The Secret Commonwealth of Elves, Fauns and
Fairies. 1893. Crown 8vo., orig. printed wrappers, limited. Howes
186-1866 1974 £7.50

KIRK, T.   The Forest Flora of New Zealand. Wellington,
1889. Small folio, orig. cloth, plates, scarce. Wheldon 128-1606 1973 £30

KIRKCONNELL, W.   European Elegies. Ottawa, 1928. Inscribed &
signed by author. Hood's 102-659 1974 $12.50

KIRKCONNELL, W.   The Flying Bull. Toronto, 1940. Drawings.
Hood's 103-735 1974 $10

KIRKE, HENRY   The First English Conquest of Canada, With Some
Account of the Earliest Settlements in Nova Scotia and Newfoundland. London,
1871. First edition. Hood's 102-567 1974 $35

KIRKES, WILLIAM SENHOUSE   Hand-book of Physiology. London, 1848. 8vo.,
orig. cloth, illus., first edition. Schumann 35-257 1974 $95

KIRKLAND, CAROLINE MATILDA   Forest Life. New York, 1842. 2 vols.,
orig. cloth, ends of spines chipped, first edition, about fine. MacManus
224-269 1974 $50

KIRKLAND, CAROLINE MATILDA   Forest Life. New York, 1842. 12mo., orig.
black cloth, paper labels, first edition. Ximenes 33-465 1974 $70

KIRKLAND, CAROLINE MATILDA   Montacute. London, 1840. 2 vols., 12mo.,
early cloth, scarce, first English edition. Ximenes 33-466 1974 $75

KIRKLAND, JOSEPH   The Story of Chicago. Chicago, 1892. Illus.
Jenkins 61-1120 1974 $20

KIRKLAND, JOSEPH   The Story of Chicago. Chicago, 1892-94.
2 vols., 4to., leather. Saddleback 14-389 1974 $50

KIRKLAND, THOMAS   An Appendix to An Inquiry Into the Present
State of Medical Surgery. London, 1813. 8vo., half calf, first edition.
Schuman 37-138 1974 $45

KIRKMAN, F. B.   The British Bird Book. (1908-12). Imperial
4to., buckram book-box, fine. Wheldon 130-32 1974 £570

KIRKMAN, F. B.   The British Bird Book. 1911-13. 4to., 4 vols.,
orig. buckram, plates. Wheldon 129-487 1974 £20

KIRKMAN, F. B.   The British Bird Book. 1911-13. 4 vols.,
4to., orig. buckram, plates. Wheldon 131-635 1974 £20

KIRKMAN, F. B.   British Sporting Birds. 1924. Roy. 8vo.,
cloth, coloured and other plates. Wheldon 128-495 1973 £5

KIRKMAN, F. B.   British Sporting Birds. London & Edinburgh,
1936. Thick 4to., plates, very good. Current BW9-156 1974 $18

KIRKMAN, F. B.   British Sporting Birds. 1924. Roy. 8vo.,
cloth, plates. Wheldon 131-637 1974 £5

KIRKMAN, F. B.   British Sporting Birds. London, 1924. 4to.,
cloth, gilt, plates. Hammond 201-654 1974 £6.50

KIRKPATRICK, JOHN E.   Timothy Flint. Cleveland, 1911. Cloth, very
good copy, private bookplate. Hayman 59-346 1974 $20

KIRKPATRICK, T. PERCY C.   History of the Medical Teaching in Trinity
College. Dublin, 1912. Demy 8vo., orig. dark blue cloth, plates, scarce.
Covent 55-1094 1974 £12.50

KIRWAN, THOMAS   Memorial History of the 17th Regiment,
Massachusetts Volunteer Infantry in the Civil War, 1861-65. Salem, 1911. Orig.
binding. Butterfield 10-163 1974 $15

KISCH, GUIDO   In Search of Freedom. London, 1949. 373p.,
illus. Austin 62-327 1974 $27.50

KITAIBEL, P.   Diaria Itinerum Pauli Kitaibelii. Budapest,
1945. 2 vols., roy. 8vo., orig. wrappers. Wheldon 128-1122 1973 £15

KITCHIN, GEORGE   A Survey of Burlesque and Parody in English.
1931. Orig. edition. Howes 185-279 1974 £6.50

KITCHINER, WILLIAM   The Art of Invigorating and Prolonging Life.
London, 1824. New edition. Rittenhouse 46-688 1974 $30

KITCHINER, WILLIAM   The Economy of the Eyes. London, 1825. 8vo.,
2 vols., old green half calf, frontispiece. Gurney 64-120 1974 £20

KITCHINER, WILLIAM   The Economy of the Eyes. Part 1 - Of Spectacles,
Opera-Glasses, and Theatres. Part 2 - Of Telescopes. London, 1825-26. 8vo.,
2 vols., old green half calf, frontis. Gurney 66-95 1974 £20

KITCHINER, WILLIAM   The Housekeeper's Oracle. London, 1829.
12mo., old calf, rubbed, first edition. Bow Windows 62-543 1974 £9.50

KITTINGER, CHARLES H.   Seattle, the Queen City of the Pacific.
Seattle, (1889). Oblong 16mo., cloth. Saddleback 14-750 1974 $10

KITTON, F. G.   The Dickens Exhibition Held at the Memorial
Hall, London, March 25-27, 1903. London, (1903). F'scap 4to., half vellum,
orig. wrappers bound in, bookplate. Forster 98-67 1974 £5

KITTON, F. G.   Dickensia. 1886. Allen 216-445 1974
$10

KITTREDGE, GEORGE LYMAN   Anniversary Papers. Boston, 1913. 8vo.,
cloth. Goodspeed's 578-485 1974 $25

KLAPROTH, HEINRICH JULIUS   Lettre a M. Le Baron A. De Humboldt. 1834.
8vo., orig. printed wrapper, uncut, first edition. Zeitlin 235-125 1974 $150

KLEBAHN, H.   Die Wirtswechselnden Rostpilze, Versuch Einer
Gesamtdarstellung Ihrer Biologischen Verhaltnisse. Berlin, 1904. Roy. 8vo.,
scarce. Wheldon 131-1425 1974 £7.50

KLEBS, EDWIN   Handbuch der Pathologischen Anatomie.
Berlin, 1868-70. 3 parts in 1 vol., 8vo., half calf, illus., first edition.
Schuman 37-139 1974 $110

KLEIN, JACOB THEODOR   Setmmato Avivm Qvadraginta Tabvlis Aeneis Ornate. Leipzig, 1759. Large 4to., contemporary calf, plates, first edition. Schumann 35-258 1974 $210

KLEIN, JACOB THEODOR   Stemmata Avium. Leipzig, 1759. 4to.,
contemporary boards, uncut, engraved plates, rare. Wheldon 128-496 1973 £25

KLEIN, LUDWIG GOTTFRIED   Interpres Clinicus. Amsterdam, 1769. 8vo.,
quarter morocco, first Amsterdam edition. Schuman 37-120 1974 $85

KLEINHANS, R.   Album des Mousses des Environs de Paris. Paris,
1869. Small folio, new cloth, plates. Wheldon 130-1307 1974 £10

KLEINSCHMIDT, O.   The Formenkreis Theory and the Progress of the
Organic World. 1930. 8vo., cloth, plates, scarce. Wheldon 128-41 1973 £6

KLEMM, GUSTAV   Die Koniglich Sachsische Porzellan-Sammlung.
Dresden, 1834. 8vo., orig. paper wrappers, neatly rebacked, plates, illus.,
label of George Ticknor. Bow Windows 66-404 1974 £65

KLETKE, C. A.   De Polygonorum Regularium Aequationibus Libros
II. Breslau, 1833. 4to., contemporary half calf, first edition. Dawsons PM
245-434 1974 £8

KLEUTGEN, JOSEPH   La Philosophie Scolastique Exposee et
Defendue. Paris, 1868-70. 4 vols., contemporary half calf, labels. Howes
185-1901 1974 £10

KLEY, HEINRICH   The Drawings of Heinrich Kley. Los Angeles,
1941. Folio, ltd. to 475 copies. Biblo & Tannen 210-230 1973 $57.50

KLEYNE WUNDARZNEI des Hoch Beruembten. Strassburg, 1529. 4to., modern
marbled boards. Dawsons PM 249-330 1974 £455

KLINEBERG, OTTO   Race Differences. Harper, 1935. 367p.
Austin 62-328 1974 $12.50

KLINGSOR, TRISTAN-L.   Cezanne. London, n.d. 8vo., cloth covers,
plates. Minters 37-274 1973 $12

KLINKHARDT, JULIUS   Gesamt-Probe der Schriftgiesserei Julius
Klinkhardt in Leipzig und Wien. Leipzig, 1883. Roy. 8vo., publisher's gilt
stamped cloth, specimens. Kraus B8-343 1974 $85

KLONDIKE: The Chicago Record's Book for Gold Seekers. Chicago, 1897.
Pictorial cloth, illus., first edition, first issue. Bradley 35-8 1974 $17.50

KLOSS, G. F. B.   Catalogue of the Library of. London, 1835.
8vo., orig. boards, cloth, rebacked. Dawsons PM 10-341 1974 £50

KLUVER, H.   Mescal, the "Divine" Plant and Its
Psychological Effects. 1928. Crown 8vo., boards, rare. Wheldon 131-1665
1974 £5

KNAPP, BETINA L.   Louis-Jouret. Columbia Univ. Press, 1957.
345p., illus. Austin 51-509 1973 $7.50

KNAPP, ISAAC   The "Negro Pew": Being an Inquiry Concerning
the Propriety of Distinctions in the House of God, on Account of Color. Boston,
1837. First edition, 16mo., fine, orig. yellow paper cover boards, cloth spine.
Current BW9-556 1974 $65

KNAPP, J. L.   Gramina Britannica. 1804. 2 vols., 4to.,
half morocco, hand-coloured plates, rare first edition. Wheldon 128-1200 1973
£40

KNAPP, J. L.   Gramina Britannica. 1842. 4to., brown
buckram, plates, second edition. Bow Windows 64-156 1974 £38

KNAPP, J. L.   The Journal of a Naturalist. 1829. 8vo.,
half calf, plates, second edition. Wheldon 129-281 1974 £5

KNAPP, J. L.   The Journal of a Naturalist. London, 1830.
8vo., plates, orig. cloth, foxed, third edition. Bow Windows 62-545 1974
£6.50

KNAPP, J. L.   The Journal of a Naturalist. 1830. 8vo., half
morocco, plates, third edition. Wheldon 130-291 1974 £7.50

KNAPP, J. L.   The Journal of a Naturalist. 1838. 8vo.,
cloth, plates, fourth edition. Wheldon 131-167 1974 £5

KNAPP, SAMUEL LORENZO   Lectures on American Literature.   New York, 1829. 12mo., later morocco, first edition.   Ximenes 33-467 1974 $40

KNAPP, SAMUEL LORENZO   Sketches of Public Characters.   New York, 1830. 12mo., contemporary quarter morocco, fine, first edition.   Ximenes 33-468 1974 $40

KNAPP, WILLIAM L.   Life, Writings and Correspondence of George Borrow, 1803-1881.   1899. 2 vols., illus., orig. edition.   Austin 61-537 1974 $12.50

KNATCHBULL, NORTON   Annotations Upon Some Difficult Texts In All the Books of the New Testament.   Cambridge, 1693. Contemporary panelled calf, first English edition.   Howes 185-1333 1974 £15

KNECHT, E.   The Principals and Practice of Textile Painting. 1912. 8vo., plates, orig. cloth, scarce.   Quaritch 940-762 1974 £60

KNEELAND, SAMUEL   An American in Iceland . . . With a Description of Its Millennial Celebration in August, 1874.   Boston, 1876. Map, illus., orig. binding.   Butterfield 10-48 1974 $15

KNELLER, GODFREY   The Kit-Cat Club.   1735. Folio, portraits, full red morocco, gilt, first edition.   Marlborough 70-17 1974 £320

KNIBBS, G. H.   The Commonwealth of Australia.   Melbourne, 1914. Roy. 8vo., cloth, illus., maps.   Wheldon 131-368 1974 £7.50

KNIBBS, HENRY HERBERT   Overland Red.   Boston, 1914. Plates, black stamped red cloth, scarce, fine, first edition.   Bradley 35-215 1974 $20

KNIEP, H.   Die Sexualitat der Niederen Pflanzen.   Jena, 1928. 8vo., wrappers.   Wheldon 131-1426 1974 £7.50

KNIGGE, ADOLF FRANZ FRIEDRICH LUDWIG   Practical Philosophy of Social Life.   1805. Old calf, worn, first American edition.   Allen 216-384 1974 $10

KNIGHT, ARTHUR   The Livliest Art.   Macmillan, 1957. 383p., illus.   Austin 51-510 1973 $8.50

KNIGHT, C. W. R.   Aristocrats of the Air.   1925. 8vo., cloth, illus., frontispiece.   Wheldon 129-489 1974 £5

KNIGHT, CHARLES   Half Hours of English History.   London, 1853. 8vo., contemporary polished calf, gilt, new edition.   Dawsons PM 251-260 1974 £6

KNIGHT, CHARLES   Half Hours With the Best Authors.   1889. 4 vols., crown 8vo., full calf, new revised edition.   Howes 185-280 1974 £16

KNIGHT, CHARLES   Old England.   London, n.d. Folio, 2 vols., orig. half red morocco.   Dawsons PM 251-41 1974 £10

KNIGHT, CHARLES   Old England.   c.1860. 2 vols. in 1, thick folio, plates, illus., cloth, rebacked.   Howes 186-2073 1974 £7.50

KNIGHT, CHARLES   Once Upon a Time.   London, 1854. 2 vols., 8vo., orig. cloth, first edition.   Ximenes 33-470 1974 $35

KNIGHT, ELLIS CORNELIA   Dinarbas.   London, 1811. 12mo., orig. boards, paper label, fine, fifth edition.   Ximenes 33-469 1974 $12.50

KNIGHT, ELLIS CORNELIA   Dinarbas.   Brattleborough, 1813. 18mo., orig. boards, worn, second American edition.   Butterfield 8-664 1974 $10

KNIGHT, FRANCIS   A Relation of Seaven Yeares Slaverie Vinder the Turkes of Argeire.   London, 1640. Small 4to., half morocco slip-case, rare, first edition, first issue.   Dawsons PM 247-169 1974 £385

KNIGHT, GRANT C.   Readings from the American Mercury.   New York, 1926. Covers rubbed.   Butterfield 10-402 1974 $15

KNIGHT, HENRY GALLY   Ilderim.   London, 1816. 8vo., orig. wrappers, first edition.   Ximenes 33-471 1974 $22.50

KNIGHT, LAURA   A Book of Drawings.   1923. Roy 4to., boards, uncut, limited edition.   Broadhurst 23-122 1974 £20

KNIGHT, LAURA   A Book of Drawings.   1923. Roy. 4to., boards, buckram spine, paper printed label, uncut, plates, limited to 400 copies signed by the artist, fine.   Broadhurst 24-123 1974 £20

KNIGHT, RICHARD PAYNE   Analytical Inquiry into Principles of Taste. 1806. Buckram, third edition.   Allen 216-2037 1974 $10

KNIGHT, RICHARD PAYNE   A Discourse on the Worship of Priapus.   1865. 8vo., green quarter morocco, cloth boards, plates, foxing, no. 251 of 500 copies, limited edition.   Bow Windows 66-405 1974 £18

KNIGHT, RICHARD PAYNE   Landscape.   1795. 4to., orig. limp wrappers, engraved plates, second edition.   Allen 216-2038 1974 $35

KNIGHT, RICHARD PAYNE   The Symbolical Language of Ancient Art and Mythology.   New York, 1892. Roy. 8vo., orig. buckram backed cloth.   Smith 193-785 1973 £8.50

KNIGHT, SARAH K.   The Journals of.   New York, 1825. 8vo., old half morocco, first edition.   Ximenes 33-472 1974 $65

KNIGHT, T. A.   Pomona Herefordiensis.   1811. Large 4to., full dark blue scored calf, gilt and blind tooled, full page colour plates, bookplate of Richard Gregory of Coole, fine copy.   Thomas 32-312 1974 £850

KNIGHT, WILBUR C.   The Birds of Wyoming.   Laramie, 1902. 8vo., boards.   Butterfield 8-741 1974 $10

KNIGHTS OF ST. STEPHEN   Statuti, Capitoli, et Constitutioni, dell'Ordine de Cavalieri Di Santo Stefano.   Florence, 1595. 8vo., contemporary limp vellum, fine.   Schuman 37-140 1974 $110

KNISTER, R.   Canadian Short Stories.   Toronto, 1928. Hood's 102-524 1974 $15

KNITTLE, WALTER ALLEN   Early Eighteenth Century Palatine Emigration. Dorrance, 1937. 320p., illus., orig. ed.   Austin 62-329 1974 $15

KNITTLE, WALTER ALLEN   Early Eighteenth Century Palatine Emigration. 1937. Illus., orig. edition.   Austin 57-356 1974 $15

KNOOP, J. H.   Beschryving van de Moes.   Leeuwarden, 1769. 4to., modem cloth-backed boards, rare.   Wheldon 130-1420 1974 £25

KNOOP, J. H.   Beschryving Van de Moes-en Keuken-Tuin. Leeuwarden, 1769. 4to., modern cloth-backed boards, rare.   Wheldon 128-1488 1973 £25

KNORR, G. W.   Recueil des Monumens des Catastrophes.   Nuremberg, 1768-78. Folio, 4 vols., contemporary russia, rebacked, gilt, rare, third edition.   Wheldon 130-33 1974 £800

KNOTT, C. G.   Collected Scientific Papers of John Aitken.   Cambridge, 1923. Large 8vo., grey printed wrapper, portrait, first edition.   Dawsons PM 245-16 1974 £6.50

KNOTT, C. G.   Life and Scientific Work of Peter Guthrie Tait.   Cambridge, 1911. Crown 4to., plates, signature, orig. cloth, rubbed.   Bow Windows 62-902 1974 £10

KNOTT, C. G.   Life and Scientific Work of Peter Guthrie Tait.   Cambridge, 1911. Crown 4to., plates, orig. cloth.   Bow Windows 62-902 1974 £8.50

KNOTT, C. G.   Napier Tercentenary Memorial Volume.   1915. Crown 4to., frontispiece, plates, illus.   Bow Windows 66-495 1974 £21

KNOWER, DANIEL   The Adventures of a Forty-Niner.   Albany, 1894. 8vo., orig. bindings.   Butterfield 8-43 1974 $25

KNOWLES, JAMES SHERIDAN   Love.   London, 1840. 8vo., disbound, first edition.   Ximenes 33-473 1974 $10

KNOWLES, JAMES SHERIDAN   The Love-Chase.   London, 1837. 8vo., disbound, first edition.   Ximenes 33-474 1974 $10

KNOWLES, JAMES SHERIDAN   The Maid of Mariendorpt.   London, 1838. 8vo., disbound, first edition.   Ximenes 33-475 1974 $10

KNOWLES, JAMES SHERIDAN   The Wife. London, 1833. 8vo., modern boards, first edition. Dawsons PM 252-624 1974 £10

KNOWLES, R. E.   The Web of Time. New York, 1908. Signed by author. Hood's 102-525 1974 $10

KNOWLSON, J. C.   The Yorkshire Cattle Doctor and Farrier. 1848. Frontispiece, orig. cloth. Bow Windows 64-157 1974 £6

KNOX, A. E.   Ornithological Rambles in Sussex. 1849. Crown, 8vo., orig. cloth, plates. Wheldon 129-490 1974 £5

KNOX, E. V.   A Little Loot. 1920. Cloth backed boards, covers somewhat spotted, very good copy, first edition. Covent 51-1060 1973 £5.25

KNOX, H. T.   Notes On Early History of Dioceses of Tuam, Killala & Achonry. 1904. Map. Allen 213-1585 1973 $12.50

KNOX, JOHN   An Historical Journal of the Campaigns In North-America, 1757-60. London, 1769. 2 vols., full leather, portraits, excellent. Hood's 103-114 1974 $750

KNOX, JOHN   An Historical Journal of the Campaigns In North-America. London, 1769. 2 vols., 4to., old calf, gilt, leather labels, rubbed. Traylen 79-488 1973 £275

KNOX, RONALD A.   A Book of Acrostics. 1924. Cloth backed boards, very good copy, first edition. Covent 51-1061 1973 £5.25

KNOX, RONALD A.   Essays in Satire. London, 1928. First edition, nice copy, name on fly, bookplate, scarce, orig. cloth. Crane 7-165 1974 £7.50

KNOX, RONALD A.   Juxta Salices. Oxford, 1910. Cover little marked, very good copy, first edition. Covent 51-1062 1973 £7.50

KNOX, RONALD A.   Kyd. Twelve Original Character Illustrations to Vanity Fair. c. 1885. Pen & water-colour drawings, mounted with protective tissues, large folio, half leather, marbled sides, spine lettered in gilt, fine. Covent 51-1063 1973 £90

KNOX, THOMAS W.   The Boy Travellers - Egypt and the Holy Land. New York, 1882. Rubbed. Ballinger 1-282 1974 $12.50

KNOX, THOMAS W.   The Boy Travellers - Russian Empire. New York, 1886. Ballinger 1-283 1974 $12.50

KNOX, THOMAS W.   The Boy Travellers - Siam and Java. New York, 1880. Ballinger 1-284 1974 $12.50

KNOX, VICESIMUS   Winter Evenings. London, 1795. 2 vols., 8vo., orig. boards, fine, third edition. Ximenes 33-476 1974 $20

KOBAYASHI, K.   Eggs of Japanese Birds. Tokyo, 1932-40. Small folio, wrappers, plates. Wheldon 131-638 1974 £75

KOBER, ARTHUR   My Dear Bella. Random, 1941. 239p., illus. Austin 54-602 1973 $6

KOBER, ARTHUR   Having Wonderful Time. Random, 1937. 203p. Austin 51-512 1973 $7.50

KOBER, ARTHUR   Pardon Me For Pointing. S & S, 1939. 251p., illus. Austin 54-603 1973 $7.50

KOBER, ARTHUR   That Man Is Here Again. Random, 1946. 233p. Austin 54-604 1973 $6.50

KOBER, ARTHUR   Thunder Over the Bronx. Simon, Schuster, 1935. 233p., illus. Austin 54-605 1973 $6.50

KOCH, FREDERICK   Carolina Folk Comedies. French, 1931. 311p., illus. Austin 51-514 1973 $12.50

KOCH, HOWARD   In Time To Come. 1942. 95p., paper. Austin 51-513 1973 $7.50

KOCH, L.   Untersuchungen Uber die Entwicklung der Crassulaceen. Heidelberg, 1879. Imp. 4to., orig. wrappers, plates, scarce. Wheldon 131-1666 1974 £7.50

KOCH, ROBERT   Zur Untersuchung von Pathogenen Organismen. Berlin, 1881. Small folio, plates, orig. printed boards, very fine, unopened, very rare first edition. Gilhofer 61-62 1974 sFr. 3,000

KOCH, ROBERT   Zur Untersuchung von Pathogenen Organismen. Berlin, 1881. Large 4to., illus., cloth, orig. front wrapper, plates. Schafer 8-165 1973 sFr. 2,800

KOCH, THEODORE WESLEY   Catalogue of the Dante Collection. Ithaca, 1898-1921. 3 vols., 4to., uncut, orig. wrappers, unopened. Dawsons PM 10-158 1974 £30

KOCH, THEODORE WESLEY   Les Livres a la Guerre. Paris, 1920. 8vo., illus., wrappers. Kraus B8-120 1974 $12.50

KOCH, W. D. J.   Synopsis Florae Germanicae et Helveticae. 1836-38. 8vo., calf, 2 vols. Wheldon 129-1093 1974 £10

KOECHLIN-SCHLUMBERGER, J.   Le Terrain de Transition des Vosges. Strasbourg, 1862. Imperial 4to., new cloth. Wheldon 129-833 1974 £15

KOEHLER, A. E.   New Mexico. Albuquerque, 1915. 4to., wrapper. Saddleback 14-560 1974 $65

KOEHLER, GEORGE FREDERIC   Remarks on Cavalry. London, 1798. 4to., modern half calf, first English edition. Dawsons PM 251-407 1974 £90

KOEHLER, R.   An Account of the Deep-sea Holothurioidea. Calcutta, 1905. 4to., new buckram, plates. Wheldon 129-785 1974 £10

KOEHLER, R.   An Account of the Deep-Sea Holothurioidea. Calcutta, 1905. 4to., new buckram, plates. Wheldon 131-936 1974 £10

KOEHLER, S. R.   American Etchings. Boston, c. 1855. 4to., orig. etchings by Moran mounted on cloth strip, backstrip crudely replaced with modern tape, orig. binding. Wilson 63-298 1974 $18.75

KOENIG, C. D. E.   Tracts Relative to Botany. London, 1805. 8vo., old half calf, plates. Traylen 79-30 1973 £9

KOENIG, ROBERT   Deutsche Litteraturgeschichte. 1895. 8vo., 2 vols., quarter morocco, gilt. Rich Summer-69 1974 $20

KOENIGIL, MARK   Movies in Society. Speller, 1962. 214p., illus. Austin 51-515 1973 $6

KOESTLER, ARTHUR   Twilight Bar. Macmillan, 1945. 104p. Austin 51-516 1973 $7.50

KOHL, JOHANN GEORG   Travels in Canada, and Through the States of New York and Pennsylvania. London, 1861. 2 vols. in 1, cover scuffed. Hood's 102-568 1974 $95

KOHL, JOHANN GEORG   Travels in Canada, and Through the States of New York and Pennsylvania. London, 1861. 2 vols. in 1, revised. Hood's 104-648 1974 $95

KOHLER, MAX J.   Immigration and Aliens in the U. S. 1936. 459 pages. Austin 57-358 1974 $25

KOHLER, W.   The Mentality of Apes. 1925. 8vo., cloth, plates, second edition. Wheldon 129-385 1974 £7.50

KOHLER, W.   The Mentality of Apes. (1927). 8vo., cloth, plates, revised second edition. Wheldon 128-335 1973 £7.50

KOHT, HALVDAN   The Old Norse Sagas. New York, 1931. 1st ed. Biblo & Tannen 214-576 1974 $10

KOHUT, ALEXANDER   The Ethics of the Fathers. 1920. 127p. Austin 62-331 1974 $12.50

KOHUT, REBEKAH   As I Know Them. Doubleday, 1929. 305p. Austin 62-332 1974 $8.50

KOHUT, REBEKAH   My Portion. Seltzer, 1925. Austin 62-333
1974 $8.50

KOKOSCHKA, OSKAR   Die Traeumenden Knaben. Leipzig, 1917.
Oblong 4to., orig. cloth. Marlborough 70-46 1974 £550

KOL, H. VAN   Naar de Antillen en Venezuela. Leiden,
1904. Small 4to., orig. dec. cloth, illus. Wheldon 131-369 1974 £7.50

KOLB, ELLSWORTH L.   Through the Grand Canyon from Wyoming to
Mexico. New York, 1914. 8vo., orig. binding, signed. Butterfield 8-127
1974 $10

KOLB, ELLSWORTH L.   Through the Grand Canyon from Wyoming to
Mexico. New York, 1914. Illus., photos. Jenkins 61-1326 1974 $20

KOLK, J. L. C. S. VAN DER   Memoire sur l'anatomie. Amsterdam, 1845.
4to., contemporary boards, plates. Wheldon 129-652 1974 £10

KOLLWITZ, KAETHE   Das Kathe Kollwitz-Werk. Dresden, 1914.
Sm. 4to., illus. Biblo & Tannen 214-296 1974 $15

KOLODIN, IRVING   The Story of the Metropolitan Opera. Knopf,
1953. 607p., illus., lst ed., signed. Austin 51-517 1973 $7.50

KOLODNY, ANATOLE   Bone Sarcoma. Chicago, 1927. Rittenhouse
46-395 1974 $11

KOL'TSOVA-MASAL'SKAIA, ELENA Switzerland the Pioneer of the Reformation.
1858. 2 vols., 8vo., orig. cloth. Bow Windows 66-181 1974 £16.50

KOMISARJEVSKY, T.   The Costume of the Theatre. 1931. Imp. 8vo.,
plates, cloth. Quaritch 940-723 1974 £26

KONGS-SKUGG-ISO Utlogd a Daunsku og Latinu. 1768. 4to., new buckram.
Allen 213-1584 1973 $175

KONIGLICH Gross-Britannischer und Churfurstlich Braun-Schweig-Luneburgischer
Staats-Kalender auf das Jahr 1801. Lauenburg, 1801. Post 8vo., contemporary
needlework binding of white-gold silk twill, orig. red morocco slip-in case, in
choice state, scarce. Sawyer 293-68 1974 £420

KONINCK, L. G. DE   Descriptions of the Palaeozoic Fossils of New
South Wales. Sydney, 1898. 4to., orig. boards, plates. Wheldon 128-1003
1973 £25

KONINCK, P.   Philips Koninck. Ein Beitrag zur Erforschung
der Hollandischen Malerei des XVII. Berlin, 1936. 4to., illus., plates,
cloth. Quaritch 940-151 1974 £250

KONODY, P. G.   Sir William Orpen, Artist and Man. 1932.
Frontispiece, plates, illus. Marsden 39-338 1974 £6

KOOP, A. J.   Early Chinese Bronzes. 1924. Roy. 4to.,
plates, cloth. Quaritch 940-406 1974 £30

KOORDERS, S. H.   Botanische Untersuchungen Uber Blatter
Bewohnende. Amsterdam, 1907. Roy. 8vo., cloth, plates, text-figures, very
scarce. Wheldon 128-1380 1973 £5

KOORDERS, S. H.   Botanische Untersuchungen. Amsterdam, 1907.
Roy 8vo., buckram, plates. Wheldon 129-1251 1974 £7.50

KOPKINS, G. M.   A Vision of Mermaids. 1929. Small folio, dec.
boards, first complete edition. Quaritch 936-419 1974 £40

KOPP, HERMANN   Geschichte der Chemie. 1843(-7). 8vo., 4
vols., contemporary German boards, first edition. Dawsons PM 245-435 1974
£50

KOPP, HERMANN   Geschichte der Chemie. Braunschweig, 1843-
1847. 8vo., half morocco, first edition. Schumann 35-259 1974 £115

KORAN   Machumatis Saracenorum Principis. (Basle,
1542). 2 parts in 1, contemporary blind-stamped pigskin, wooden boards, very
fine, first printed edition, first issue. Gilhofer 61-4 1974 sFr. 5,500

KORSCHELT, EUGEN   Text-book of the Embryology of Invertebrates.
London, 1895. 8vo., 3 vols., cloth, illus., first English edition. Schumann 35-
260 1974 $95

KORN, GALLUS   Warumb die Kirch Vier Evangelisten hat
Angenomen. (Augsburg, 1524). Small 4to., woodcut border, modern dark green
morocco, gilt, fine, rare. Schafer 8-119 1973 sFr. 950

KORN, GALLUS   Warumb die Kirch Vier Evangelisten hat
Angenomen. (Augsburg, 1524). Small 4to., modern dark green morocco, richly
gilt inside dentelle, rare, fine. Schafer 10-103 1974 sFr 900

KOSSUTH in New England. Boston and Cleveland, 1852. Portrait, green gilt
cloth. Butterfield 10-330 1974 $25

KOSTOFF, D.   Cytogenetics of the Genus Nicotiana. Sofia,
1941-43. Roy 8vo., orig. wrappers. Wheldon 129-930 1974 £10

KOTZEBUE, AUGUST VON   The East Indian. New York, 1800. 8vo.,
modern quarter calf, first American edition. Ximenes 33-477 1974 $40

KOUNTZ, WILLIAM J., JR.   Billy Baxter's Letters. Duguesne, 1899.
90p., illus. Austin 54-606 1973 $10

KOURY, PHIL A.   Yes, Mr. Demille. Putnam, 1959. 319p.
Austin 51-518 1973 $7.50

KOVACS, ERNIE   Zoomar. Doubleday, 1957. 347p. Austin
51-519 1973 $6.50

KOZLOVA, E.   Ptitzui Yughozapadnogho Zabaikalya Severnoi
Mongholii i Tzentralnoi Ghobi. Leningrad, 1930. Roy. 8vo., cloth, map.
Wheldon 128-497 1973 £10

KRAEPLIN, EMIL   Psychiatrie. Leipzig, 1903(-4). 8vo., 2 vols.,
orig. brown cloth. Dawsons PM 249-318 1974 £10

KRAFT-EBING, RICHARD VON   Psychopathia Sexualis. 1906. Roy. 8vo.,
cloth. Smith 194-922 1974 £5

KRAIS, P.   Gewerbliche Materialkunde im Auftrag des
Deutschen Werkbunds, Band1 Die Holzer. Stuttgart, 1910. 8vo., cloth
boards. Wheldon 131-1741 1974 £5

KRAMER, DALE   Ross and the New Yorker. Doubleday, 1952.
306p. Austin 54-607 1973 $4.75

KRAMER, WILHELM   Die Erkenntniss und Heilung der Ohrenkrank-
heiten. Berlin, 1836. 8vo., contemporary German boards. Dawsons PM 249-
319 1974 £40

KRAMERS, HENDRIK ANTHONY   The Atom and the Bohr Theory of its Structure.
London, 1923. 8vo., orig. cloth, gilt. Dawsons PM 245-436 1974 £6

KRAMM, JOSEPH   The Shrike. 1952. Austin 51-520 1973
$6.50

KRANS, HORATIO SHEAFE   William Butler Yeats and the Irish Literary
Revival. New York, 1904. First U. S. edition, presentation copy with
inscription from author, gilt top, portrait, spine faded, nice copy. Covent
51-2072 1973 £7.50

KRANTZ, ALBERT   Wandalia in Qua de Wandalorum Populis, et
Eorum Patrio Solo. Cologne, 1519. Folio, contemporary full brown calf, over
wooden boards, first edition, good copy, clean & firm. Schumann 499-58 1974
sFr 1,850

KRANZFELDER, FRITZ WILHELM Funktenphotographie, Insbesondere die Mehr-
fach-Funkenphotographie. Berlin, 1903. 8vo., orig. wrappers, illus., first edition. Schumann 35-262 1974 $125

KRASINSKI, ZYGMUNT   The Un-Divine Comedy. n.d. English first
edition. Covent 56-1619 1974 £25

KRASSNOFF, P. N.   From Double Eagle to Red Flag. 1928. Dust
wrapper, worn, English first edition. Covent 56-780 1974 £12.50

KRAUS, ADOLF   Reminiscences and Comments. Chicago, 1925.
244p., illus. Austin 62-335 1974 $22.50

KRAUSE, DAVID   Sean O'Casey. Macmillan, 1960. 340p.
Austin 51-522 1973 $10

KRAUSE, WILHELM   Die Terminalen Korperchen der Einfach
Sensiblen Nerven. Hanover, 1860. 8vo., orig. pictured wrappers, plates,
unopened, first edition.   Schuman 37-142 1974 $95

KRAUTHEIMER, RICHARD   Corpus Basilicarum Christianarum Romae.
1937. Sewn, plates. Allen 213-1588 1973 $15

KRETSCHMER, ALBERT   The Costumes of all Nations. London, 1882.
4to., full polished calf, gilt, labels, plates, first edition. Hammond 201-178
1974 £45

KRETSCHMER, ALBERT   Die Trachten der Volker vom Beginn der
Geschichte bis zum 19 Jahrhundert. Leipzig, 1906. Roy. 4to., publisher's
cloth, leather back, plates. Quaritch 940-724 1974 £30

DAS KREUTER Buch Oder Herbarius. Strasburg, 1530. Folio, modern sheep,
some leaves badly defective. Thomas 32-316 1974 £275

KREYMBORG, ALFRED   Plays For Merry Andrews. 1920. Austin
51-523 1973 $17.50

KREYMBORG, ALFRED   Plays for Merry Andrews. New York, 1920.
8vo., orig. quarter cloth, boards, first edition. Ximenes 33-478 1974 $12.50

KREYSIG, GEORGE CHRISTOPH   Bibliotheca Scriptorum Venaticorum
Continens Auctores. Altenburg, 1750. Small 8vo., brown boards, book-plate,
labels. Dawsons PM 10-344 1974 £56

KRIEGEL, GEORG CHRISTOPH   Erb-Huldigung. Vienna, (1742). Folio, contemporary calf, gilt. Dawsons PM 251-261 1974 £555

KRISTELLER, P.   Kupferstich und Holzschnitt in Vier
Jahrhunderten. Berlin, 1911. 4to., illus., boards, calf spine.   Quaritch
940-152 1974 £20

KROEBER, A. L.   Handbook of the Indians of California.
Washington, 1925. Large folding map in pocket, other maps, illus. Jenkins
61-347 1974 $45

KRONSER, VICTOR NICOLAUS   Der Schwefel-Aether. Vienna, 1847. 8vo.,
boards, orig. wrappers. Gurney 64-121 1974 £40

KROWS, ARTHUR E.   Play Production in America. Holt, 1916.
Austin 51-525 1973 $12.50

KRUSENSTERN, ADAM J. VON   Voyage Round the World in the Years, 1803,
1804, 1805 and 1806. 1813. Demy 4to., contemporary half calf, scarce, first
edition, 2 vols. in 1, folding map, coloured aquatint frontispiece. Broadhurst
24-1635 1974 £575

KRUTCH, JOSEPH W.   Comedy and Conscience After the Restoration.
New York, 1924. 1st ed.   Austin 51-526 1973 $7.50

KU KLUX Kismet March. Aransas Pass, 1924. Folio. Jenkins 61-1328 1974
$22.50

KUBINYI, VICTOR DE   As We Are. New York, 1929. 1st ed., illus.
Biblo & Tannen 213-314 1973 $7.50

KUCK, L.   The Art of Japanese Gardens. New York, 1941.
4to., illus., fine, orig. cloth. Gregory 44-174 1974 $15

KUDO, Y.   Labiatarum Sino-Japonicarum Prodromus.
Formosa, 1929. Roy. 8vo., buckram. Wheldon 128-1278 1973 £7.50

KUDO, Y.   Labiatarum Sino-Japonicarum Prodromus.
Taihoku, 1929. Roy. 8vo., buckram. Wheldon 131-1323 1974 £7.50

KUESTER, H. C.   Die Kafer Europas. Nuremberg, 1844-54.
7 vols., small 8vo., half morocco, plates. Wheldon 131-822 1974 £40

KUESTER, H. C.   Die Kafer Europas. Nuremberg, 1902-06.
4 vols., small 8vo., unbound in orig. slipcases. Wheldon 131-823 1974 £12

KUGLER, F.   Handbook of the History of Painting from the
Age of Constantine the Great to the Present Time.   1842. 8vo., quarter red
calf, folding plate. Eaton Music-620 1973 £5

KUGLER, F.   The Schools of Painting in Italy. London,
1851. 2 vols., 8vo., illus., orig. cloth, paper labels, second edition. Bow
Windows 62-548 1974 £7.50

KUHL, H.   Beitrage zur Zoologie. 1820. 4to., old
boards, plates. Wheldon 129-492 1974 £20

KUHNER, R.   Le Genre Galera. Paris, 1935. Roy 8vo.,
half green morocco. Wheldon 129-1255 1974 £6

KUHNER, R.   Le Genre Mycena. Paris, 1938. Roy 8vo.,
half morocco, plates. Wheldon 129-1253 1974 £12

KUIPER, W. E. J.   Grieksche Origineelen en Latijnsche
Navolgingen Zes Komedies Van Menander bij Terentius en Plautus. 1936.
Sewn. Allen 213-693 1973 $10

KULP, GEORGE B.   Families of the Wyoming Valley. Wilkes-Barre,
1885. 2 vols., 8vo., cloth. Saddleback 14-676 1974 $20

KUMMEL, O.   Meisterwerke Chinesischer und Japanischer
Kunst. Stuttgart & Berlin, (c. 1925). Folio, plates, unbound in orig. boards
portfolio. Quaritch 940-407 1974 £10

KUNTH, C. S.   Agrostographia Synoptica. Stuttgart and Tubingen, 1833-35. 8vo., 2 vols., half morocco, plates, scarce. Wheldon 130-
1030 1974 £15

KUNTH, C. S.   Agrostographia Synoptica Sive Enumeratio
Graminearum Omnium Hucusque Cognitarum. Stuttgart and Tubingen, 1833-35.
2 vols., 8vo., half morocco, plates, scarce. Wheldon 128-1123 1973 £15

KUNTZ, ALBERT   A Text-Book of Neuro-Anatomy. Philadelphia,
1945. Rittenhouse 46-397 1974 $10

KUNZ, GEORGE FREDERICK   The Book of the Pearl. 1908. 4to., orig. cloth,
pates, maps. Bow Windows 64-582 1974 £58

KUNZ, GEORGE FREDERICK   The Book of the Pearl. 1908. Imp. 8vo.,
plates, buckram, maps, scarce. Quaritch 940-459 1974 £50

KUNZ, GEORGE FREDERICK   Ivory and the Elephant in Art, in Archaeology,
and in Science. New York, 1916. Roy. 8vo., plates, orig. dec. cloth, gilt.
Quaritch 940-458 1974 £35

KUPPER, WINIFRED   The Golden Hoof. New York, 1945. 8vo.,
orig. bindings, dust jacket, first edition. Butterfield 8-606 1974 $10

KUPPER, WINIFRED   The Golden Hoof. New York, 1945. lst ed.
Dykes 24-53 1974 $15

KURILAS, E.   Historical Bibliography of Natural Science in
Greece. Athens, 1938-41. 2 vols., 8vo., wrappers. Wheldon 128-112 1973
£10

KURODA, N.   A Bibliography of the Ducktribe. Tokyo, 1942.
8vo., orig. cloth boards. Wheldon 129-162 1974 £10

KURR, JOHANN GOTTLOB   The Mineral Kingdom. Edinburgh, 1859. Folio,
orig. green cloth, fine, plates, first edition. Dawsons PM 245-437 1974 £32

KUSTER, E.   Pathologie der Pflanzenzelle. Berlin, 1929.
8vo., cloth. Wheldon 129-932 1974 £7.50

KYD, R.   A Short Account of Colonel Kyd. Calcutta,
1893. 4to., boards, portrait. Wheldon 128-113 1973 £5

KYLE, H. M.   The Biology of Fishes. 1926. 8vo., cloth,
plates, text-figures, scarce. Wheldon 128-646 1973 £7.50

KYLE, T.   A Treatise on the Management of Peach and
Nectarine Trees. 1783. 8vo., wrappers, uncut. Wheldon 129-1489 1974 £12

KYLE, T.   A Treatise in the Management of Peach and
Nectarine Trees. Edinburgh, 1787. 8vo., modern boards, scarce.   Wheldon
130-1481 1974 £12

KYLIN, H.   Entwicklungsgeschichte der Phaeophyceen der
Florideen, der Dellesseriaceen - Marine Red Algae of Friday Harbor, Washington.
Lund, 1924-33. 4to., wrappers. Wheldon 131-1428 1974 £8

KYRBURG, FRITZ VAN DER   Aus Einer Kleinen Garnison. Braunschweig,
1908. Colour illus., size 1 by 12 inches, folded into orig. metal binding size
1 1/2 by 1 inches with title laid in upper cover, good copy, scarce.   Sawyer
293-221 1974 £80

KYTE, E. C.   Impartial Account of Lieut. Col. Bradstreet's
Expedition to Fort Frontenac. Toronto, 1940. Card cover. Hood's 103-650
1974 $17.50

L

THE LA ABRA Silver Mining Company. Washington, 1889. Full calf. Jenkins 61-1329 1974 $37.50

LA BARRE, W.   The Peyote Cult. 1938. 8vo., wrappers, plates. Wheldon 131-1669 1974 £5

LA BILLARDIERE, J. J. H. DE   Novae Hollandiae Plantarum Specimen. (Paris, 1804-06). 4to., cloth, plates. Wheldon 130-1172 1974 £36

LABBE, PHILIPPE   Bibliotheca Bibliothecarum Curis Tertiis Auctior. Leipzig, 1682. 12mo., contemporary vellum, fourth edition. Dawsons PM 10-345 1974 £66

LABBE, PHILIPPE   Sacrosancta Concilia ad Regiam Editionem Exacta. Paris, 1671-72. 15 vols. in 16, folio, contemporary calf, worn. Howes 185-1337 1974 £125

LABE, LOUISE   The Debate Between Folly and Cupid. 1925. Small 4to., buckram, dust wrapper, first edition. Quaritch 936-441 1974 £5

THE LABOR Movement, The Problem of Today. New York, 1888. First edition, thick 8vo., profusely illus., spine & front inner hinge repaired, boards bit scuffed, interior very good. Current BW9-558 1974 $9.50

LABOULBENE, JEAN JOSEPH ALEXANDRE   Recherches Cliniques et Anatomiques sur les Affections Pseudo-Membraneuses. Paris, 1861. 8vo., half shagreen, plates, first edition. Schumann 35-263 1974 $110

LABOURET, J.   Monographie de la Famille des Cactees. Paris, (1858). Post 8vo., half morocco, rare. Wheldon 131-1670 1974 £35

LA BROSSE, PIERRE LE LOYER, SIEUR DE
Please turn to
LE LOYER, PIERRE, SIEUR DE LA BROSSE

LA BRUYERE, JEAN 1645-1696   Oeuvres. Paris, 1865-82. 3 vols., 8vo., and 4to., three quarter levant morocco, gilt, uncut. L. Goldschmidt 42-59 1974 $175

LAC, FRANCOIS MARIE PERRIN DE
Please turn to
PERRIN DU LAC, FRANCOIS MARIE

LA CAILLE, NICOLAS LOUIS DE   Lectiones Elementares Mathematicae. (1762). 4to., orig. boards, uncut. Zeitlin 235-126 1974 $75

LACKINGTON, JAMES   Memoirs of First 45 Years of Life of. 1792. Buckram, corrected new edition. Allen 216-169 1974 $17.50

LACLOS, PIERRE-AMBROISE-FRANCOIS CHOLERLOS DE   Les Liaisons Dangereuses ou Lettres Recueillies dans une Societe. Amsterdam & Paris, 1782. 4 vols., small 12mo., contemporary marbled calf, gilt. L. Goldschmidt 42-30 1974 $300

LACLOS, PIERRE-AMBROISE-FRANCOIS CHOLERLOS DE   Les Liaisons Dangereuses. Paris, 1914. 4to., 2 vols., half levant morocco, English first edition. Covent 56-686 1974 £65

LACOMBE, PAUL   Bibliographie des Travaux de M. Leopold Delisle. Paris, 1902-03. 2 works in 1 vol., 8vo., contemporary quarter morocco, marbled boards. Dawsons PM 10-170 1974 £42

LA CONDAMINE, CHARLES MARIE DE   Journal du Voyage fait Part Ordre du Roi a l'Equateur. Paris, 1751. 2 vols., 4to., contemporary marbled calf, gilt, plates, first edition. Schuman 37-143 1974 $325

LACORDAIRE, HENRI-DOMINIQUE   Conferences de Notre-Dame de Paris: 1835-54. Paris, 1884. 5 vols., 8vo., half calf. Howes 185-1340 1974 £10

LACOUR, P.   Essai sur les Hieroglyphes Egyptiens. Bordeaux, 1821. Binding worn. Biblo & Tannen 213-122 1973 $45

LA COURVEE, J. C. DE   De Nutritione Foetus in Utero Paradoxa. 1655. 4to., contemporary vellum, first edition. Dawsons PM 249-321 1974 £165

LACOUTRE, C.   Repertoire Chromatique. Paris, 1890. 4to., plates, boards, morocco spine, scarce. Quaritch 940-153 1974 £70

LACROIX, JULES   Le Testament de Cesar, Drame. Paris, 1849. Roy. 8vo., full cloth, leather label, first edition. L. Goldschmidt 42-266 1974 $22.50

LACROIX, PAUL   Arts In the Middle Ages and at Period of the Renaissance. (1873). 4to., plates. Allen 213-1591 1973 $10

LACROIX, PAUL   Le Livre d'Or des Metiers. Paris, n.d. Orig. printed wrappers (mounted, back missing), narrow 4to., plates. Kraus B8-345 1974 $37.50

LACROIX, PAUL   Louis XII et Anne de Bretagne. 1882. Half calf, rubbed. Allen 213-1618 1973 $12.50

LACROIX, PAUL   Manners, Customs & Dress During the Middle Ages & During the Renaissance Period. 1876. 4to., illus., new buckram. Allen 213-1592 1973 $15

LACROIX, PAUL   Military and Religious Life in the Middle Ages and at the Period of the Renaissance. 1874. Imp. 8vo., plates, dec. cloth gilt. Quaritch 940-460 1974 £5

LACROIX, PAUL   Military and Religious Life, Science and Literature In Middle Ages and Renaissance. 1874. New buckram. Allen 213-1592A 1973 $12.50

LACROIX, SILVESTRE FRANCOIS   Essais sur l'Enseignement en General. Paris, 1805. 8vo., orig. paper wrappers, first edition. Dawsons PM 245-442 1974 £30

LACROIX, SILVESTRE FRANCOIS   Traite Du Calcul Differentiel. Paris, 1797-1800. 4to., 3 vols., contemporary tree calf, labels, plates, first edition. Dawsons PM 245-439 1974 £55

LACROIX, SILVESTRE FRANCOIS   Traite du Calcul Differentiel. Paris, 1810-14-19. 4to., 3 vols., contemporary calf, rebacked. Dawsons PM 245-440 1974 £25

LACROIX, SILVESTRE FRANCOIS   Traite Elementaire du Calcul des Probabilites. Paris, 1816. 8vo., contemporary continental mottled boards, rebacked, gilt. Dawsons PM 245-443 1974 £15

LACROIX, SILVESTRE FRANCOIS   Traite Elementaire de Calcul Differentiel. Paris, 1837. 8vo., contemporary mauve calf, gilt, plates, fifth edition. Dawsons PM 245-441 1974 £8

LA CROIX CHEVRIERES DE SAINT VALLIER, JEAN BAPTISTE DE
Please turn to
SAINT-VALLIER, JEAN BAPTISTE DE LA CROIX CHEVRIERES DE

LACTANTIUS, LUCIUS COELIUS FIRMIANUS   Divinarum Institutionum Libri Septem. 1515. 18th century vellum gilt, morocco labels. Thomas 30-30 1973 £75

LACTANTIUS, LUCIUS COELIUS FIRMIANUS   Divinarum Institutionum Libri VII. Basel, 1521. 4to., blind stamped calf, wooden boards, rebacked. Harper 213-99 1973 $385

LACTANTIUS, LUCIUS COELIUS FIRMIANUS   Divinarum Institutionum Libri Septem. 1535. Vellum, stains. Thomas 30-72 1973 £8

LACTANTIUS, LUCIUS COELIUS FIRMIANUS   Opera, Accedit Nephytomon. (Venice), 1742. Folio, late 18th century boards, gilt, leather back. Harper 213-98 1973 $2500

LACTANTIUS, LUCIUS COELIUS FIRMINAUS   Opera Omnia. Paris, 1844. 2 vols. in 1, roy. 8vo., buckram, rebound. Howes 185-1341 1974 $12.50

LACY, CHARLES DE LACY   The History of the Spur. c. 1904. 4to., orig. cloth, plates, illus. Bow Windows 66-407 1974 £21

LACY, EDMUND   Liber Pontificalis. 1847. Orig. cloth, worn, scarce. Howes 185-1342 1974 £7.50

LADD, HORATIO O.   Minor Wars of the United States, History of the
War With Mexico.   New York, 1883.   Orig. binding.   Butterfield 10-331 1974
$15

LADD, PARISH B.   Appendix to Hebrew and Christian Mythology.
New York, (1898). Printed wrappers. Hayman 59-347 1974 $10

LADENBURG, ALBERT   Vortrage Uber die Entwicklungsgeschichte der
Chemie. 1887. 8vo., rebound, buckram, gilt, second German edition.   Dawsons PM 245-444 1974 £10

THE LADY'S Valentine Writer. London, (c. 1835). Orig. pict. wrappers, fine,
8vo. Gregory 44-304 1974 $12.50

LAENNEC, RENE THEOPHILE HYACINTHE   De l'Auscultation Mediate.   Paris,
1819. 8vo., 2 vols., contemporary half calf, gilt, first edition.   Dawsons PM
249-323 1974 £400

LAENNEC, RENE-THEOPHILE-HYACINTHE   Propositions sur la Doctrine d'Hip-
pocrate. Paris, (1804). 4to., modern half calf, fine, first edition.   Dawsons
PM 249-322 1974 £1,450

LAENNEC, RENE THEOPHILE HYACINTHE   Traite de l'Auscultation Mediate.
Paris, 1826. 8vo., modern brown cloth.   Dawsons PM 249-324 1974 £120

LAENNEC, RENE THEOPHILE HYACINTHE   A Treatise on Mediate Auscultation,
and on Diseases of the Lungs and Heart.   London, 1846. 8vo., cloth, rebound,
few library stamps, plates dampstained.   Gurney 66-96 1974 £45

LAENNEC, RENE THEOPHILE HYACINTHE   A Treatise On the Diseases of the
Chest.   Rebound, first American edition.   Rittenhouse 46-399 1974 $450

LAENNEC, RENE THEOPHILE HYACINTHE   A Treatise on the Diseases of the
Chest. Philadelphia, 1823. Plates, rebound, library stamp, first American
edition.   Rittenhouse 46-398 1974 $475

LAFAR, F.   Handbuch der Technischen Mykologie.   Jena,
1904-14. 5 vols., roy. 8vo., cloth, plates, scarce.   Wheldon 128-1382
1973 £20

LAFAR, F.   Technical Mycology. 1898-1910. 2 vols. in
3, 8vo., cloth.   Wheldon 128-1383 1973 £7.50

LA FARE, C. A., MARQUIS DE   Poesies. Amsterdam, 1755. 16mo., 2 vols.,
full contemporary vellum, gilt.   Quaritch 936-128 1974 £20

LA FARGE, OLIVER   Laughing Boy. Cambridge, 1929. First edition.
Jenkins 61-1330 1974 $17.50

LAFAYE, GEORGES DE   Principj di Chirurgia. 1751. 12mo., contemporary Italian boards.   Dawsons PM 249-325 1974 £18

LA FAYETTE, MARIE-MADELEINE PIOCHE DE LA VERGNE   The Princess of
Cleves. London, 1679. 8vo., contemporary sheep, rare, first English edition.
Dawsons PM 252-625 1974 £275

LAFENESTRE, GEORGES   The Louvre. Paris, (n.d.). 4to., orig.
boards, book-plate, coloured mounted plates.   Bow Windows 66-408 1974 £6

LA FEUILLE, DANIEL DE   Science Hieroglyphique. The Hague, 1746.
Plates. Dawson's 424-332 1974 $75

LAFLER, HENRY A.   Alameda County. (Oakland), c.1915. 12mo.,
wrapper. Saddleback 14-157 1974 $12.50

LAFON, MARY   Histoire d'un Livre. Paris, 1857. Small 8vo.,
half cloth. Kraus B8-125 1974 $30

LA FONT, CHARLES DE   Dissertationes duae Medicae. Amsterdam, 1671.
12mo., wrappers. Gurney 64-232 1974 £20

LA FONTAINE, JEAN DE   Fables de la. Paris, (n.d.). 4to., 19th century
calf, illus., rubbed. Bow Windows 66-241 1974 £10.15

LA FONTAINE, JEAN DE   Fables. Paris, (1796). 6 vols., small 12mo.,
strictly contemporary morocco, gilt, illus. L. Goldschmidt 42-61 1974 $400

LA FONTAINE, JEAN DE   The Fables of... 1931. Roy. 8vo., 2 vols.,
full vellum, uncut, signed, limited. Broadhurst 23-735 1974 £85

LA FONTAINE, JEAN DE   Fables. Paris, 1838. 2 vols., large 8vo.,
contemporary glazed sheep, woodcuts. L. Goldschmidt 42-62 1974 $120

LA FONTAINE, JEAN DE   The Loves of Cupid and Psyche. London, 1744.
8vo., morocco gilt, plates, first English edition. Dawsons PM 252-626 1974
£45

LA FONTAINE, JEAN DE   Tales. 1814. Extra illus. by the insertion of
portraits, beautiful engravings, one vol. extended to 2 vols., small 8vo., maroon
morocco gilt, spines gilt, fine copy. Sawyer 293-196 1974 £135

LA FONTAINE, JEAN DE   Oeuvres. Paris, 1883-92. 11 vols., 8vo.,
three quarter levant morocco, gilt, uncut, plates. L. Goldschmidt 42-63
1974 $225

LA FONTAINE, SIEUR   The Military Duties of the Officers of
Cavalry. London, 1678. 8vo., modern morocco, fine, rare. Traylen 79-144
1973 £155

LAFORD, MARIAN M.   Needlework as Art. 1886. Thick 8vo., plates,
cloth, gilt. Quaritch 940-744 1974 £20

LAFOREST, NICHOLAS-LAURENT   L'Art de Soigner les Pieds. Paris, 1781.
12mo., orig. boards, first edition. Dawsons PM 249-326 1974 £75

LAFUENTE, ENRIQUE   The Paintings and Drawings of Velazquez.
London, 1943. Folio, color plates. Biblo & Tannen 214-549 1974 $22.50

LAGARENNE, F.   Costumes d'Ivanhoe. (Brussels, 1832). 4to.,
orig. wrapper, olive green straight grained morocco, gilt, very rare. Quaritch
940-725 1974 £175

LAGRANGE, JOSEPH LOUIS   Mecanique Analytique. Paris, 1811, 15. 4to.,
blue half calf, second edition. Dawsons PM 245-445 1974 £35

LAGRANGE, JOSEPH LOUIS   Mecanique Analytique. Paris, 1811-15.
2 vols., large 4to., contemporary polished mottled calf, second edition.
Schuman 37-144 1974 $210

LAGRANGE, JOSEPH LOUIS   De la Resolution des Equations. (1798). 4to.,
contemporary marbled wrappers, uncut, first edition. Zeitlin 235-127 1974
$100

LAGRANGE, JOSEPH LOUIS   Theorie des Fonctions Analytiques. (1797).
4to., contemporary half calf, uncut, first edition. Zeitlin 235-128 1974 $175

LAGRANGE, JOSEPH LOUIS   De la Resolution des Equations Numeriques.
Paris, (1798). 4to., quarter calf, orig. wrappers, first edition. Gurney 64-122
1974 £25

LAGRANGE, JOSEPH LOUIS   Theorie des Fonctions Analytiques, Contenant
les Principes du Calcul Differentiel. Paris, (1797). Large 4to., orig. wrappers,
first edition. Schuman 37-145 1974 $145

LAGRANGE, JOSEPH LOUIS   Traite de la Resolution des Equations Numeriques
de Tous Les Degres. Paris, 1826. 4to., half calf, rebacked. Dawsons PM 245-
446 1974 £10.50

LAHEE, HENRY C.   The Organ and its Masters. Boston, 1927.
Biblo & Tannen 214-871 1974 $10

LAHEY CLINIC, BOSTON, MASSACHUSETTS   Surgical Practice of the Lahey
Clinic. Philadelphia, 1941. Rittenhouse 46-400 1974 $10

LAHONTAN, BARON DE   New Voyages to North America. Chicago, 1905.
2 vols., maps, illus. Hood's 102-721 1974 $100

LAIDLAY, J. C.   The Care and Propagation of Ornamental
Waterfowl. 1933. 8vo., cloth. Wheldon 131-640 1974 £5

LAING, D.   Early Popular Poetry of Scotland and the
Northern Border. London, 1895. 2 vols., 8vo., frontispieces, orig. cloth.
Bow Windows 62-549 1974 £10

LAING, SAMUEL   Pre-Historic Remains of Caithness.   London and Edinburgh, 1866. 8vo., orig. brown cloth, gilt, fine, plates. Dawsons PM 251-42 1974 £8

LA JEUNESSE, ERNEST   Recollections of Oscar Wilde. Boston, 1906. 12mo., first U.S. edition. Covent 56-1333 1974 £15

LAKE, ARTHUR   Sermons, With Some Religious and Divine Meditations. 1629. 4 parts in 1 vol., thick folio, contemporary calf, first edition. Howes 185-1346 1974 £18

THE LAKE Regions of Central Africa. New York, 1881. 1st ed. Biblo & Tannen 213-709 1973 $7.50

LAKING, GUY FRANCIS   The Furniture of Windsor Castle. 1905. Roy. 4to., plates, quarter pigskin. Quaritch 939-301 1974 £25

LAKING, GUY FRANCIS   A Record of European Armour and Arms. 1920-25. Roy 4to., full morocco, gilt. Broadhurst 23-125 1974 £275

LAKING, GUY FRANCIS   A Record of European Armour and Arms Through Seven Centuries. 1920-25. 6 vols. in 3, roy. 4to., bound by Worrall in full brown levant morocco, panelled backs, top edges gilt, others uncut, illus., magnificent copy. Broadhurst 24-127 1974 £300

LALANDE, JOSEPH JEROME LE FRANCOIS DE   Astronomie. Paris, 1764. Thick 4to., 2 vols., contemporary mottled calf, scarce, first edition. Zeitlin 235-129 1974 $225

LALANDE, JOSEPH JEROME LE FRANCOIS DE   Astronomie. Paris, 1771, 1781. Thick 4to., 4 vols., contemporary half calf, marbled boards, plates. Zeitlin 235-130 1974 $150

LA MARCHE, OLIVIER DE   Les Memoires. Louvain, 1645. Small 4to., contemporary full vellum. L. Goldschmidt 42-64 1974 $55

LAMARCK, JEAN BAPTISTE PIERRE ANTOINE DE MONET DE   Flore Francaise. Paris, 1805. 8vo., contemporary half leather, third edition. Wheldon 129-1095 1974 £25

LAMARCK, JEAN BAPTISTE PIERRE ANTOINE DE MONET DE   Flore Francaise. Paris, 1815. 8vo., half morocco, plates, third edition. Wheldon 130-1174 1974 £25

LAMARCK, JEAN BAPTISTE PIERRE ANTOINE DE MONET DE   Flore Francaise. Paris, 1815. 5 vols. in 6, 8vo., half morocco, plates, folding coloured map, third edition. Wheldon 128-1279 1973 £25

LAMARCK, JEAN BAPTISTE PIERRE ANTOINE DE MONET DE   Recueil de Planches des Coquilles Fossiles. Paris, 1823. 4to., contemporary boards, plates, rare. Wheldon 130-943 1974 £35

LAMARCK, JEAN BAPTISTE PIERRE ANTOINE DE MONET DE   Recueil de Planches des Coquilles Fossiles des Environs de Paris. Paris, 1823. 4to., modern boards, plates, rare. Wheldon 131-1034 1974 £35

LAMARCK, JEAN BAPTISTE PIERRE ANTOINE DE MONET DE   Recherches sur les Causes des Principaux Faits Physiques. Paris, (1794). 8vo., 2 vols., first edition, contemporary French boards and calf, gilt, worn. Dawsons PM 245-447 1974 £95

LAMARCK, JEAN BAPTISTE PIERRE ANTOINE DE MONET DE   Les Velins de Lamarck. Paris, n.d. 4to., photographs. Wheldon 131-899 1974 £30

LAMARCK, JEAN BAPTISTE PIERRE ANTOINE DE MONET DE   Zoological Philosophy. 1914. Orig. cloth, scarce. Smith 194-812 1974 £10

LAMARR, HEDY   Ecstasy and Me. 1966. 318p., illus. Austin 51-527 1973 $10

LAMARTINE, ALPHONSE DE   Graziella. Nonesuch Press, 1929. Crown 8vo., uncut, illus., fine, orig. cloth, limited to 1026 copies. Broadhurst 24-1028 1974 £10

LAMARTINE, ALPHONSE DE   Gutenberg, Inventeur de l'Imprimerie, 1400-1469. Paris, 1867. Small 8vo., diced maroon half leather. Kraus B8-346 1974 $25

LAMB, CHARLES   Album Verses. London, 1830. 8vo., orig. boards, uncut, first edition. Dawsons PM 252-627 1974 £48

LAMB, CHARLES   Album Verses. 1830. 8vo., full red straight grained morocco gilt. Quaritch 936-443 1974 £300

LAMB, CHARLES   A Book Explaining the Ranks and Dignities of British Society. London, 1809. Coloured engravings, three quarter blue morocco, top edge gilt, marbled endpapers, armorial bookplate, small hole in spine, very good copy, second edition. Frohnsdorff 15-78 1974 $125

LAMB, CHARLES   Elia and the Last Essays of Elia. 1929. 2 vols., 8vo., buckram, illus., limited. Dawsons PM 252-628 1974 £135

LAMB, CHARLES   The Letters of. 1935. 3 vols., thick 8vo., orig. buckram, best edition. Howes 185-284 1974 £30

LAMB, CHARLES   The Letters of Charles Lamb. (1935). 3 vols., 8vo., orig. cloth, frontispieces, slight spotting. Bow Windows 66-410 1974 £20

LAMB, CHARLES   The Life, Letters, and Writings. 1882. 6 vols., crown 8vo., orig. cloth, illus. Howes 185-282 1974 £12.50

LAMB, CHARLES   The Life Letters & Writings. 1886. 6 vols., orig. morocco backed cloth, gilt. Smith 194-356 1974 £5

LAMB, CHARLES   Life, Letters and Writings. (1924). 6 vols., crown 8vo., orig. cloth, portraits. Howes 186-295 1974 £8.50

LAMB, CHARLES   The Life, Letters and Writings of. London & Philadelphia, 1895. 6 vols., 8vo., contemporary half morocco gilt, plates, collected edition. Dawsons PM 252-630 1974 £60

LAMB, CHARLES   Martin. London, 1891. 4to., illus., orig. cloth, uncut, first edition. Dawsons PM 252-631 1974 £7.50

LAMB, CHARLES   Mrs. Leicester's School. London, 1809. 12mo., full calf, rubbed, leather label, engraved frontispiece by James Hopwood, first edition. Frohnsdorff 15-79 1974 $200

LAMB, CHARLES   Mrs. Leicester's School. London, 1809. 12mo., contemporary tree calf, rubbed, leather label, first edition, first state, some marginal tears, wholly acceptable copy. Frohnsdorff 16-476 1974 $250

LAMB, CHARLES   Poetry for Children. 1872. 8vo., contemporary red straight grained morocco. Bow Windows 64-583 1974 £7.50

LAMB, CHARLES   Specimens of English Dramatic Poets who Lived About the Time of Shakespeare. 1893. 2 vols., limited edition. Allen 216-990 1974 $17.50

LAMB, CHARLES   Tales from Shakespeare. London, 1909. 1st trade ed., color plates. Biblo & Tannen 213-589 1973 $50

LAMB, CHARLES   Tales from Shakespeare. 1909. 4to., full white buckram, plates, signed, mint, limited edition. Broadhurst 23-162 1974 £85

LAMB, CHARLES   Tales From Shakespeare. London, 1928. Illus., boxed, orig. glassine wrappers, fine. Ballinger 1-159 1974 $10

LAMB, CHARLES   The Works. London, 1818. 2 vols., 8vo., contemporary morocco gilt, fine, first edition. Dawsons PM 252-629 1974 £110

LAMB, CHARLES   The Works Of. 1903. 12 vols., 8vo., illus., gilt, vellum spines, unopened, mint, limited. Thomas 28-247 1972 £75

LAMB, CHARLES   Works. 1903-05. 8vo., 7 vols., cloth, illus. Quaritch 936-442 1974 £40

LAMB, GEORGE   Whistle for It. London, 1807. 8vo., modern boards, first edition. Dawsons PM 252-632 1974 £15

LAMB, HORACE   Hydrodynamics. Cambridge, 1906. 8vo., blue cloth, gilt, third edition. Dawsons PM 245-448 1974 £8

LAMB, PATRICK　　　　　Royal Cookery. London, 1710. 8vo., old panelled calf, plates, first edition. Traylen 79-214 1973 £85

LAMBARDE, W.　　　　　A Perambulation of Kent. 1596. Small 4to., contemporary calf, rebacked, inscription. Quaritch 939-409 1974 £170

LAMBERT, ANNE THERESE DE MARGUENAT DE COURCELLES　Oeuvres. Paris, 1751. 2 vols., 12mo., contemporary English red morocco gilt, raised bands, engraved vignette titles, somewhat rubbed & worn. Thomas 32-78 1974 £36

LAMBERT, AYLMER BOURKE　　A Description of the Genus Cinchona. London, 1797. Large 4to., contemporary boards, worn, rebacked, plates, first edition. Schumann 35-265 1974 $165

LAMBERT, JOHN　　　　　Travels Through Canada and the United States, 1806-1808. London, 1816. 2 vols., engravings, fine, third edition. Hood's 103-545 1974 $300

LAMBINET, PIERRE　　　Origine de l'Imprimerie d'Apres les Titres Authentiques. Paris, 1810. 2 vols., 8vo., handsome light brown half calf, gilt, engraved portraits, folding tables. Kraus B8-347 1974 $75

LAME, GABRIEL　　　　Lecons sur la Theorie Mathematique. Paris, 1866. 8vo., half calf, gilt, plate, second edition. Dawsons PM 245-449 1974 £8

LAMEERE, A.　　　　　Revision des Prionides. Brussels, 1902-12. 22 parts in 1 vol., roy. 8vo., half red morocco, very rare. Wheldon 131-824 1974 £50

LAMENNAIS, FELICITE ROBERT DE　　Oeuvres Posthumes. Paris, 1859. 2 vols., 8vo., three quarter brown levant morocco, gilt, uncut, first edition. L. Goldschmidt 42-267 1974 $25

THE LAMENTATIONS of Jeremiah. 1933. Folio, embossed blue reversed calf, illus. Hammond 201-767 1974 £95

LAMONT, JAMES　　　Seasons With the Sea-Horses. 1861. 8vo., half calf, illus., map. Wheldon 128-208 1973 £25

LAMONT, JAMES　　　Seasons With the Sea-Horses. 1861. 8vo., half roan, illus., map. Wheldon 131-293 1974 £20

LAMONT, JAMES　　　Seasons With the Sea-Horses. 1861. 8vo., orig. cloth, illus. Wheldon 130-246 1974 £25

LAMONT, JAMES　　　Seasons With the Sea Horses. New York, 1861. Cloth worn, first U. S. edition, foldout map. Butterfield 10-66 1974 $20

LA MONTE, JOHN L.　　　The World of the Middle Ages. New York, 1949. Biblo & Tannen 214-629 1974 $7.50

LA MOTTE, GUILLAUME MAUQUEST DE　　A General Treatise of Midwifry. London, 1746. 8vo., modern half calf, fine, first edition in English. Dawsons PM 249-327 1974 £80

LAMOTTE-FOUQUE, FRIEDRICH　　Peter Schlemihl. 1824. Small 8vo., full contemporary straight-grained calf gilt, plates, second edition. Howes 185-91 1974 £14

LA MOTTE FOUQUE, FRIEDRICH DE　　Sintram and His Companions. 1908. Fine, illus., frontis. Covent 55-1422 1974 £6.50

LAMOUR, JEAN　　　Recueil des Ouvrages en Serrurerie que Stanislas le Bienfaisant. Paris, (n.d.). Folio, recently bound in half morocco, fine plates, uncut copy. Bow Windows 66-411 1974 £145

LAMOUROUX, J. V. F.　　　Corallina. 1824. 8vo., half morocco, plates, rare. Wheldon 131-937 1974 £20

LAMPE, WILLIAM T.　　　Tulsa County in the World War. Tulsa, 1919. 8vo., cloth. Saddleback 14-639 1974 $20

LAMPELL, MILLARD　　　The Long Way Home. Messner, 1946. Austin 51-528 1973 $10

LAMPSAQUE, ETRENNES AUX RAFFINES　Les Bons Contes. Bruxelles, 1882. 8vo., frontispiece, orig. wrappers, contemporary half morocco, limited. Bow Windows 62-551 1974 £7.50

LAMY, BERNARD　　　Traitez de Mechaniqve. Paris, 1679. 12mo., modern vellum, rare, first edition. Zeitlin 235-131 1974 $75

LAMY, G.　　　Discours Anatomiques. Rouen, 1675. 12mo., contemporary calf, first edition. Gurney 64-123 1974 £35

LAMY DE LA CHAPELLE, E.　　Catalogue Raisonne des Lichens du Mont-Dore et de la Haute-Vienne. (1878). 8vo., wrappers. Wheldon 131-1429 1974 £5

LANA TERZI, FRANCESCO　　Magisterium Naturae, et Artis. 1692. Folio, 3 vols., contemporary vellum, plates, illus., first edition. Dawsons PM 245-450 1974 £850

LANCASHIRE and Cheshire. Manchester, 1875-1878. Crown 4to., wrappers, scarce. Broadhurst 23-1439 1974 £10

LANCEY, S. HERBERT　　The Native Poets of Maine. Bangor, 1854. 8vo., gilt-dec. cloth, gilt. Butterfield 8-206 1974 $25

LANCHESTER, FREDERICK WILLIAM　　The Flying Machine. London, 1915. 8vo., buckram, plates, fine, first edition. Dawsons PM 245-451 1974 £15

LANCHESTER, FREDERICK WILLIAM　　The Flying-Machine from an Engineering Standpoint. 1918. 8vo., cloth. Hammond 201-782 1974 £5

LANCISI, GIOVANNI MARIA　　Opera Quae Hactenus Prodierunt Omnia. Geneva, 1718. 4to., old calf, rebacked. Gurney 64-124 1974 £35

THE LANCING College Magazine. 1922-39. 3 vols., thick roy. 8vo. Howes 186-2205 1974 £5

LANCISI, GIOVANNI MARIA　　Dissertatio de Nativis. 1711. 4to., contemporary vellum, first edition. Dawsons PM 249-328 1974 £75

LANCKORONSKI, KARL GRAF　　Der Dom von Aquileia, Sein Bau und Seine Geschichte. Vienna, 1906. Illus., some in color, large folio, dark blue cloth. Kraus B8-419 1974 $250

LANCOMBE, JEAN DE　　A Compendium of the East. 1937. 4to., dec. cloth covered boards, limited edition. Broadhurst 23-1000 1974 £45

THE LAND of Fun. London & New York, n.d. (c. 1900). 4to., pict. boards, cloth spine, color plates, illus. Frohnsdorff 15-80 1974 $12.50

LAND Owners in Ireland. Dublin, 1876. Large 4to., half calf, scarce. Emerald 50-502 1974 £40

LANDAU, ROM　　　Ignace Paderewski. Crown, 1934. 314p. Austin 51-529 1973 $10

LANDELLS, E.　　　The Boy's Own Toy-Maker. London, (1881). 8vo., orig. pictorial cloth, engravings. Bow Windows 62-552 1974 £6

LANDEN, JOHN　　　Mathematical Memoirs. London, 1780. 4to., contemporary half calf, plates. Dawsons PM 245-452 1974 £16

LANDI, ORTENSIO　　　Consolatorie de Diversi Autori. Venice, 1550. Small 8vo., modern half vellum, fine, rare, first edition. Schafer 8-122 1973 sFr. 550

LANDI, ORTENSIO　　　Forcianae Quaestiones, in Quibus Varia Italorum Ingenia Explicantur. Naples, 1536. Small 8vo., 18th century colored paper boards, first edition. Schafer 8-120 1973 sFr. 600

LANDI, ORTENSIO　　　Oracoli de Moderni Ingegni si d'Huomini Come di Donne. Venice, 1550. Small 8vo., modern half vellum, rare first edition. Schafer 8-121 1973 sFr. 550

LANDI, ORTENSIO　　　Sette Libri de Cathaloghi a Varie Cose Appartenenti. Venice, 1552. Small 8vo., contemporary vellum over boards, rare first edition. Schafer 8-123 1973 sFr. 700

LANDIS, CAROLE   4 Jills In a Jeep. Random, 1944. 180p., illus. Austin 51-530 1973 $7.50

LANDMAN, ISAAC   Christian and Jew. Liveright, 1929. Austin 62-337 1974 $10

LANDMAN, ISAAC   Christain and Jew. 1929. 374 pages. Austen 57-365 1974 $10

LANDON, FRED   Western Ontario and the American Frontier. Toronto, 1941. First edition. Hood's 102-616 1974 $45

LANDON, FRED   Western Ontario and the America Frontier. Toronto, 1941. First edition. Hood's 104-698 1974 $15

LANDON, LETITIA ELIZABETH   Characteristics of the Genius and Writings of. 1841. Orig. patterned cloth, illus. Covent 55-968 1974 £10.50

LANDOR, A. H. SAVAGE   Across Widest Africa. 1907. 8vo., 2 vols., orig. cloth, first edition. Broadhurst 23-1666 1974 £25

LANDOR, WALTER SAVAGE   Andrea of Hungary, and Giovanna of Naples. 1839. Full contemporary tree calf, gilt top, gilt panelled back, upper joint cracked, nice copy, with half title, bookplate, first edition. Covent 51-1065 1973 £25

LANDOR, WALTER SAVAGE   Dry Sticks, Fagoted. Edinburgh, 1858. First edition, 8vo., orig. green boards, spine faded to brown with top & bottom chipped, some spots on covers, interior fine. Current BW9-244 1974 $35

LANDOR, WALTER SAVAGE   Imaginary Conversations. London, 1824. 2 vols. in 1, 8vo., contemporary half calf gilt, first edition. Dawsons PM 252-633 1974 £50

LANDOR, WALTER SAVAGE   Imaginary Conversations. 1883. 5 vols., labels rubbed. Allen 216-997 1974 $25

LANDOR, WALTER SAVAGE   Imaginary Conversation of Literary Men and Statesmen. 1824. 2 vols., new half calf, rare. Howes 186-296 1974 £50

LANDOR, WALTER SAVAGE   Imaginary Conversations of Literary Men and Statesmen. 1826-28. 3 vols., orig. boards, first & second editions. Howes 185-286 1974 £50

LANDOR, WALTER SAVAGE   Pericles and Aspasia. London, 1836. 2 vols., 8vo., contemporary half calf, first edition. Dawsons PM 252-634 1974 £60

LANDOR, WALTER SAVAGE   Pericles and Aspasia. London, 1836. 2 vols., 12mo., orig. grey boards, first edition, inscribed presentation copy from author, very good, booklabels of Lytton Strachey & Roger Senhouse. Ximenes 36-135 1974 $325

LANDOR, WALTER SAVAGE   Pericles and Aspasia. 1890. 2 vols., 8vo., orig. half parchment, etchings by Herbert Railton, India paper, cloth sides, uncut, large paper, library edition limited. Bow Windows 66-412 1974 £10

LANDOR, WALTER SAVAGE   Pericles and Aspasia. 1903. Folio, limited. Allen 216-2248 1974 $15

LANDOR, WALTER SAVAGE   Pericles and Aspasia. 1903. Folio, rebound, quarter leather, English first edition. Covent 56-783 1974 £37.50

LANDOR, WALTER SAVAGE   The Works. London, 1846. 2 vols., 8vo., orig. cloth, uncut, first collected edition. Dawsons PM 252-635 1974 £15

LANDOR, WALTER SAVAGE   The Works. 1868. 2 vols., roy. 8vo., orig. patterned cloth, fine, unopened. Covent 55-969 1974 £35

LANDOR, WALTER SAVAGE   Works. 1895. 2 vols., ex-library. Allen 216-996 1974 $10

LANDOR, WALTER SAVAGE   Works & Life. 1874. 8 vols., full morocco, rubbed, ex-library. Allen 216-M 1974 $50

LANDRETH, HELEN   Dear Darkhead. 1936. Orig. edition. Austin 61-541 1974 $10

LANDRY, BERNARD   L'Idee de Chretiente chez les Scolastiques du 13eme Siecle. Paris, 1929. Biblo & Tannen 214-630 1974 $9.50

LANDRY, ROBERT J.   This Fascinating Radio Business. Bobbs, Merrill, 1946. 343p., illus. Austin 51-531 1973 $10

LANDSBERGER, FRANZ   A History of Jewish Art. Cincinnati, 1946. lst ed., illus. Biblo & Tannen 213-317 1973 $10

LANDSBOROUGH, D.   A Popular History of British Seaweeds. 1857. Post 8vo., orig. cloth, coloured plates, third edition. Wheldon 128-1386 1973 £5

LANDSBOROUGH, D.   A Popular History of British Seaweeds. 1857. Post 8vo., cloth, plates, third edition. Wheldon 131-1430 1974 £5

LANDSEER, E.   Landseer's Works. n.d. 2 vols., plates, full maroon morocco, rubbed, gilt. Marsden 37-280 1974 £25

LANE, JOSEPH   Letter of Hon. Joseph Lane to the People of Oregon. Washington, 1859. Jenkins 61-2071 1974 $15

LANE, MARGARET   Edgar Wallace. London, n.d. lst ed. Biblo & Tannen 210-538 1973 $10

LANE, TAMAR   The New Technique of Screen Writing. McGraw, Hill, 1936. 342p. Austin 51-532 1973 $10

LANE, W. B.   Quinte, Songs and Sonnets. Toronto, 1925. Hood's 104-761 1974 $12.50

LANE, YOTI   Psychology of the Actor. Day, 1960. 224p. Austin 51-533 1973 $7.50

LANE-POOLE, STANLEY   Saladin and the Fall of the Kingdom of Jerusalem. 1898. Crown 8vo., full crimson prize calf gilt, plates. Howes 186-977 1974 £5.50

LANG, A.   Die Experimentelle Vererbungslehre in der Zoologie seit 1900. Jena, 1914. Vol. 1, imp. 8vo., wrappers, plates. Wheldon 131-438 1974 £5

LANG, A.   Die Experimentelle Vererbingslehre in der Zoologie Seit 1900, Vol. 1. Jean, 1914. Imp. 8vo., wrappers, plates, text-figures. Wheldon 128-281 1973 £5

LANG, A.   Lehrbuch der Vergleichenden Anatomie der Wirbellosen Thiere. Jena, 1901. Roy. 8vo., wrappers, second edition. Wheldon 131-938 1974 £5

LANG, ANDREW   Angling Sketches. 1891. Etchings, illus., orig. cloth gilt, bevelled edges, very nice copy. Covent 51-2405 1973 £6.50

LANG, ANDREW   The Animal Story Book. London & New York, 1896. First edition, 12mo., pen & ink sketches, blue cloth front cover gilt dec., fine. Current BW9-100 1974 $18.50

LANG, ANDREW   Ballads and Lyrics of Old France, With Other Poems. 1872. Spine little browned, covers potted, very good copy, bookplate, first edition. Covent 51-1068 1973 £12.60

LANG, ANDREW   Ballades in Blue China. Portland, 1897. 8vo., fine, unopened, orig. wrappers, numbered. Covent 55-970 1974 £12.50

LANG, ANDREW   Ballads of Books. 1888. F'scp. 8vo., orig. cloth, bevelled edges, nice copy, bookplate. Covent 51-2407 1973 £5.25

LANG, ANDREW   Ban and Arriere Ban. 1894. Orig. boards, unopened, English first edition. Covent 56-1860 1974 £15

LANG, ANDREW   The Blue Fairy Book. 1891. Illus., orig. pictorial cloth gilt, all edges gilt, name stamped on fly, very nice copy, first edition. Covent 51-1069 1973 £7.50

LANG, ANDREW   The Blue Poetry Book. 1891. 8vo., orig. cloth, illus., gilt, first edition. Quaritch 936-447 1974 £10

LANG, ANDREW   The Blue Poetry Book. 1891. Roy 8vo., orig. boards, illus., English first edition. Covent 56-1861 1974 £28.50

LANG, ANDREW   The Blue Poetry Book. 1892. Orig. dec. cloth gilt, fine, new edition. Covent 56-784 1974 £5.25

LANG, ANDREW   The Blue Poetry Book. London & New York, 1896. 8vo., illus., gilt dec. blue cloth, fine, excellent pen and ink sketches. Current BW9-243 1974 $16

LANG, ANDREW   Books and Bookmen. London, 1886. Large 8vo., orig. boards, uncut, plates, first edition. Dawsons PM 10-349 1974 £6.50

LANG, ANDREW   The Clyde Mystery. Glasgow, 1905. Plates, foxing, faded. Covent 55-971 1974 £6.50

LANG, ANDREW   Grass of Parnassus. 1888. Orig. boards, English first edition. Covent 56-1862 1974 £12.50

LANG, ANDREW   Grey Fairy Book. 1900. First edition, many illus., crown 8vo., orig. grey cloth, gilt, fine copy. George's 610-449 1973 £7.50

LANG, ANDREW   The Grey Fairy Book. London, 1900. First edition, nice copy, 8vo., orig. cloth. Gregory 44-178 1974 $20

LANG, ANDREW   A History of Scotland. 1907-29. 4 vols., thick 8vo., frontispieces, map. Howes 186-978 1974 £18.50

LANG, ANDREW   Johnny Nut and the Golden Goose. 1887. Illus., large 8vo., orig. dec. cloth gilt, top edges gilt, cover somewhat faded & dust soiled, corners bumped, very good copy, first edition. Covent 51-1072 1973 £6.30

LANG, ANDREW   The Library. London, 1881. 12mo., cloth. Kraus B8-127 1974 $18

LANG, ANDREW   The Mark of Cain. 1886. Numbered edition, parchment wrappers, spine chafed & torn at foot, else nice copy. Covent 51-1073 1973 £6.30

LANG, ANDREW   The Mark of Cain. Bristol, 1886. 1st ed., ltd., uncut. Biblo & Tannen 213-563 1973 $15

LANG, ANDREW   The Miracles of Madame Saint Katherine of Fierbois. 1897. Cloth-backed boards, English first edition. Covent 56-1834 1974 £8.50

LANG, ANDREW   The Miracles of Madame Saint Katherine of Fierbois. Chicago, 1897. Vellum backed boards, first American edition. Covent 55-972 1974 £10.50

LANG, ANDREW   The Most Pleasant and Delectable tale of the Marriage of Cupid and Psyche. 1887. Limited large paper edition to 60 copies, engraved plates, large 8vo., orig. japon wrappers preserved, dark blue levant morocco, uncut, fine copy. Sawyer 293-197 1974 £60

LANG, ANDREW   The Nursery Rhyme Book. London, 1898. 8vo., cloth, gilt, all edges gilt, illus. by L. Leslie Brooke. Frohnsdorff 15-82 1974 $45

LANG, ANDREW   The Nursery Rhyme Book. London, 1898. 8vo., gilt lettered cloth, all edges gilt, illus. by L. Leslie Brooke, very good copy. Frohnsdorff 16-479 1974 $45

LANG, ANDREW   Old Friends. 1890. First edition, limited large paper issue to 150 copies, frontispiece, 8vo., orig. two tone boards, uncut, top edges gilt, good condition, scarce. Sawyer 293-198 1974 £27

LANG, ANDREW   The Orange Fairy Book. 1906. Orange cloth, plates, illus., fine. Covent 55-973 1974 £10.50

LANG, ANDREW   The Pink Fairy Book. London, 1897. Second edition, trifle loose, else good copy, 8vo., orig. cloth. Gregory 44-177 1974 $20

LANG, ANDREW   Prince Charles Edward. London, Paris, New York & Edinburgh, 1900. Large folio, half leather, numbered, illus., fine. Ballinger 1-286 1974 $30

LANG, ANDREW   Prince Charles Edward. 1900. One of 350 numbered copies on Japanese paper, coloured frontis., engraved plates, 4to., wrappers, fine unopened copy, with remains of slipcase. Covent 51-2406 1973 £21

LANG, ANDREW   The Princess Nobody. 1884. 4to., orig. glazed pictorial boards, illus. Hammond 201-130 1974 £45

LANG, ANDREW   The Red Book of Animal Stories. 1899. 8vo., orig. cloth, gilt, fine, illus., first edition. Quaritch 936-448 1974 £10

LANG, ANDREW   The Red True Story Book. London, 1895. 8vo., pictorially gilt cloth, all edges gilt, illus., first edition. Frohnsdorff 15-81 1974 $20

LANG, ANDREW   Religio Loci and Almae Matres. 1911. 4to., orig. dec. cloth gilt, plates, English first edition. Covent 56-786 1974 £7.50

LANG, ANDREW   Yellow Fairy Book. 1894. First edition, crown 8vo., orig. yellow cloth, gilt, spine dull, ads at end. George's 610-454 1973 £5

LANG, ANDREW   Yellow Fairy Book. 1894. First edition, crown 8vo., orig. yellow cloth, gilt, fine, illus. George's 610-453 1973 £7.50

LANG, H. C.   Rhopalocera Europae. London, 1884. 4to., 2 vols., rebound in leatherette, color plates, fine. Gregory 44-179 1974 $65

LANG, JOHN   The Secret Police. n.d. Rebound, half morocco, English first edition. Covent 56-334 1974 £45

LANG, JOHN DUNMORE   An Historical and Statistical Account of New South Wales. London, 1834. 2 vols., 8vo., half calf, leather labels, first edition. Traylen 79-552 1973 £45

LANG, LEONORA BLANCHE, MRS. ANDREW LANG   The Red Book of Heroes. London & New York, 1909. First edition, 8vo., illus., gilt dec. red cloth, spine ends chipped and worn, interior very fine. Current BW9-140 1974 $18.50

LANG, LEONORA BLANCHE, MRS. ANDREW LANG   The Red Book of Heroes. 1909. Orig. pictorial cloth gilt, illus., plates. Covent 55-974 1974 £12.50

LANG, LUCY ROBINS   Tomorrow is Beautiful. Macmillan, 1948. Austin 62-338 1974 $8.50

LANG, PAUL HENRY   Music in Western Civilization. New York, 1941. Biblo & Tannen 214-873 1974 $10

LANGBAINE, GERARD   An Account of the English Dramatick Poets. Oxford, 1691. 8vo., modern calf, morocco label, first edition. Dawsons PM 252-637 1974 £140

LANGE, CHRISTIAN   Opera Omnia. 1688. Thick 4to., modern half vellum, first edition. Schumann 35-266 1974 $145

LANGE, J. E.   Studies in the Agarics of Denmark. Copenhagen, 1914-38. Roy 8vo., half morocco, plates. Wheldon 129-1257 1974 £20

LANGELIER, J. C.   Notes on Gaspesia. N.P., 1885. Wrappers, maps, second edition. Hood's 104-215 1974 $35

LANGELIER, J. C.   A Sketch on Gaspesia. Quebec, 1884. Wrappers, 104 pages. Hood's 104-216 1974 $20

LANGENBECK, CONRAD JOHANN MARTIN   Tractatus Anatomico-Chirurgicus de Nervis Cerebri in Dolore Faciei Consideratis. Gottingen, 1805. 4to., contemporary boards, plates, first edition. Schuman 37-146 1974 $165

LANGER, WILLIAM L.   The Diplomacy of Imperialism. New York, 1935. 2 vols., roy. 8vo. Howes 186-979 1974 £8.50

LANGEVIN, PAUL   Conference Faite a la Sorbonne sur l'Evolution. Paris, n.d. 8vo., orig. wrappers, signed presentation copy. Gurney 64-125 1974 £10

LANGFORD, NATHANIEL PITT   Diary of the Washburn Expedition to the Yellowstone and Firehole Rivers. (St. Paul, 1905). 8vo., orig. bindings, portraits, plates. Butterfield 8-744 1974 $12.50

LANGFORD, T.   Plain and Full Instructions to Raise all Sorts of Fruit Trees. 1681. 8vo., old speckled calf, plates, first edition. Bow Windows 64-160 1974 £50

LANGFORD, T.   Plain and Full Instructions to Raise all Sorts of Fruit Trees. 1699. 8vo., old calf, plates, third edition. Bow Windows 64-161 1974 £38

LANGHAM, WILLIAM   The Garden of Health. London, 1633. 4to., half calf, second edition. Schumann 35-267 1974 $175

LANGL, J.   Griechische Goetter-und Helden Gestalten. 1887. Large folio, illus. Allen 213-609 1973 $17.50

LANGLAND, WILLIAM   The Vision of Pierce Plowman. Small 4to., 18th century calf, fine, fourth edition. Dawsons PM 252-638 1974 £750

LANGLAND, WILLIAM   Vision of William Concerning Piers the Plowman. 1886. 2 vols., ex-library, one spine worn. Allen 216-1817 1974 $12

LANGLE, V.   Album de Fleurs, Fruits, Oiseaux, Insectes et Coquilles. 1843. Oblong 4to., plates, orig. dec. boards, rebacked. Quaritch 940-154 1974 £95

LANGLEY, BATTY   The Builders Compleat Assistant. (1740?). 2 vols., 8vo., contemporary tree calf, plates, rebacked, fourth edition. Quaritch 940-522 1974 £75

LANGLEY, BATTY   The Builder's Jewel. 1757. Small 8vo., plates, contemporary unlettered calf. Quaritch 940-524 1974 £28

LANGLEY, BATTY   Gothic Architecture. 1747. 4to., plates, modern boards, uncut, very clean copy. Quaritch 940-523 1974 £90

LANGLEY, JOHN NEWPORT   On the Histology and Physiology of Pepsin. London, 1882. 4to., disbound. Dawsons PM 249-331 1974 £6

LANGLEY, T.   The History and Antiquities of the Hundred of Desborough. 1797. 4to., plates, morocco. Quaritch 939-308 1974 £32

LANGLEY, T.   The History and Antiquities of the Hundred of Desborough. 1797. 4to., half morocco, plates. Quaritch 939-307 1974 £40

LANGLOIS, E. H.   Essai sur la Calligraphie des Manuscrits du Moyen Age, et sur les Ornements des Premiers Livres d'Heures Imprimes. Rouen, 1841. Engraved plates, 8vo. Kraus B8-129 1974 $45

LANGLOIS, E. H.   Memoire sur la Peinture sur Verre et sur Quelques Vitraux Remarquables des Eglises de Rouen. Notice sur le Tombeau des Enerves de Jumieges, et. Rouen, 1823-25. 2 works in 1 vol., roy. 8vo., marbled boards, calf spine, plates. Quaritch 940-617 1974 £9

LANGNER, LAWRENCE   The Magic Curtain. Dutton, 1951. 498p., illus. Austin 51-534 1973 $12.50

LANGNER, LAWRENCE   The Pursuit of Happiness. French, 1934. Austin 51-535 1973 $7.50

LANGNER, LAWRENCE   Suzanna and the Elders. Random, 1940. Austin 51-536 1973 $7.50

LANGRISHE, HERCULES   Baratariana. Dublin, 1772. 12mo., contemporary calf, first Dublin edition. Hammond 201-458 1974 £8.50

LANGSTONE, R.   Responsible Government in Canada. London, 1931. Hood's 104-649 1974 $12.50

LANGTOFT, P.   Peter Lantoft's Chronicle. Oxford, 1725. 2 vols., 8vo., old calf, first edition. Quaritch 939-155 1974 £40

LANGTON, H. H.   Sir Daniel Wilson, A Memoir. Toronto, 1929. Hood's 104-270 1974 $17.50

LANGTON, J.   University Question. Toronto, 1860. Orig. wrapper. Hood's 104-400 1974 $17.50

LANGUAGE Emblematique des Fleurs. Paris, 1852. 12mo., half brown calf, hand colored flowers. Gregory 44-181 1974 $75

THE LANGUAGE of Flowers. Philadelphia, 1835. 16mo., full tan roan, some foxing, rebacked, color plates, last half of book has small waterstain. Gregory 44-180 1974 $25

LANGUET-CHEVREUL, HENRI   Hubert Languet. Paris, 1856. 8vo., contemporary half hard grain morocco, enlarged second edition. L. Goldschmidt 42-65 1974 $17.50

LANGTRY, J.   Come Home; An Appeal on Behalf of Reunion. Toronto, 1900. Hood's 102-297 1974 $7.50

LANHAM, EDWIN M.   Sailors Don't Care. Paris, 1929. 8vo., orig. cloth, wrappers, first edition. Rota 190-140 1974 £5

LANIER, HENRY W.   A Century of Banking in New York, 1822-1922. New York, 1922. First printing, 8vo., interior very good, spine and covers bit faded. Current BW9-559 1974 $30

LANIER, SIDNEY   Shakespeare and His Forerunners. 1902. 2 vols., buckram, ex-library. Allen 216-2174 1974 $17.50

LANKESTER, E. R.   Extinct Animals. 1905-06. 8vo., cloth, illus., scarce. Wheldon 131-1035 1974 £5

LANKESTER, EDWIN   An Account of Askern and Its Mineral Springs. London, 1842. 8vo., orig. cloth, gilt, first edition. Hammond 201-583 1974 £10.50

LANMAN, CHARLES 1819-1895   Adventures in the Wilds of the United States. Philadelphia, 1856. 2 vols., first enlarged edition, three quarter leather, very fine set. Jenkins 61-1337 1974 $85

LANMAN, CHARLES 1819-1895   The Private Life of Daniel Webster. New York, 1852. Cloth. Hayman 59-351 1974 $12.50

LANMAN, CHARLES ROCKWELL 1850-   A Sanskrit Reader. 1920. Roy. 8vo., orig. buckram. Howes 186-1869 1974 £7.50

LANSBERG, JACOB   Apologia. 1633. Small 4to., disbound. Zeitlin 235-132 1974 $150

LANSDELL, HENRY   The Sacred Tenth. 1906. 2 vols., portrait, illus. Howes 185-1347 1974 £5

LANSDOWNE, GEORGE GRANVILLE, BARON 1667-1735   Poems Upon Several Occasions. London, 1716. 12mo., inscription, dark green morocco, gilt, second edition. Bow Windows 63-314 1974 £60

LANSING, ABRAHAM   Recollections. (NewYork), 1909. Portraits, color plate, limited to 300 copies, orig. binding. Butterfield 10-254 1974 $15

LANTERI, GIACOMO   Due Dialoghi. Venice, 1557. Small 4to., calf, gilt, fine, first edition. Dawsons PM 245-453 1974 £75

LANZI, ABATE LUIGI   The History of Painting in Italy. 1828. 6 vols., full contemporary calf, gilt, English first edition. Covent 56-1475 1974 £45

LAPHAM, ALICE GERTRUDE   The Old Planters of Beverly in Massachusetts. Cambridge, 1930. 8vo., orig. bindings. Butterfield 8-252 1974 $15

LAPHAM, I. A.   The Antiquities of Wisconsin, as Surveyed and Described by. Washington, 1855. Folio, boards, chipped, plates. Jenkins 61-2668 1974 $37.50

LAPIDARIO DEL REY D. ALFONSO X.   Codice Original. Madrid, 1881. Roy 4to., half calf, uncut. Broadhurst 23-784 1974 £18

LAPIDE, CORNELIUS   Commentarii in Scripturam Sacram. Lyons & Paris, 1854. 10 vols., thick roy. 8vo., half vellum morocco labels. Howes 185-1349 1974 £30

LAPIDE, CORNELIUS   Commentaria in Scripturam Sacram. Paris, 1874-77. 26 vols., thick roy. 8vo., half buckram, leather labels. Howes 185-1348 1974 £55

LAPLACE, PIERRE SIMON   Exposition du Systeme du Monde. Paris, (1799). 4to., contemporary wrappers, uncut, second edition. Zeitlin 235-133 1974 $85

LAPLACE, PIERRE SIMON   Exposition du Systeme du Monde. Bruxelles, 1827. 8vo., contemporary half calf, sixth edition. Dawsons PM 245-455 1974 £15

LAPLACE, PIERRE SIMON   Theorie Analytique des Probabilites. Paris, 1820. Library stamp, worn. Covent 55-1314 1974 £25

LAPLACE, PIERRE SIMON   Theorie Analytique des Probabilites. Paris, 1820-(25). 4to., old calf, gilt. Gurney 64-126 1974 £45

LAPLACE, PIERRE SIMON   Theorie Analytique des Probabilites. Paris, 1820-(25). 4to., old calf, gilt, joints little worn, fine. Gurney 66-99 1974 £35

LAPLANCHE, M. C. DE   Dictionnaire Iconographique des Champignons Superieurs. Autun & Paris, 1894. 8vo., orig. wrappers. Wheldon 131-1431 1974 £7.50

LAPOINTE, ARTHUR   Soldier of Quebec, 1916-1919. Montreal, 1931. First English edition. Hood's 103-115 1974 $10

LAPOLIA, GARIBALDI M.   The Fire in the Flesh. Vanguard, 1931. Austin 62-339 1974 $12.50

LAPORTE, J.   The Progress of a Water-Coloured Drawing. (1800-1801). Small oblong folio, plates, orig. grey boards, rebacked, paper label. Quaritch 940-155 1974 £150

LA QUINTINYE, J. DE   Le Parfait Jardinier ou Instruction Pour les Jardins Fruitiers et Potagers. Paris, 1695. 4to., 2 vols., contemporary calf, plates, second edition. Wheldon 130-1421 1974 £60

LA RAMEE, PIERRE DE   Arithmeticae Libri Dvo. 1613. Small 8vo., old half calf. Zeitlin 235-186 1974 $275

LA RAMEE, PIERRE DE   Via Regia ad Geometriam. London, 1636. 4to., orig. sheep, woodcuts, first edition in English. Dawsons PM 245-629 1974 £235

LARBAUD, VALERY   Notes sur Maurice Sceve. Paris, 1926. 16mo., orig. wrapper, uncut, first edition. L. Goldschmidt 42-268 1974 $20

LARBAUD, VALERY   Paul Valery. Paris, 1931. 12mo., orig. wrapper, first edition. L. Goldschmidt 42-269 1974 $15

LARD, REBECCA HAMMOND   Miscellaneous Poems on Moral and Religious Subjects. Woodstock, 1820. Orig. paper covered boards, worn, backstrip chipped away, some browning of text pages. Butterfield 10-27 1974 $50

LARDNER, DIONYSIUS   Hand Book of Natural Philosophy. 1855. 8vo., woodcut engravings, orig. gilt, rebacked in cloth. Smith 194-483 1974 £5

LARDNER, DIONYSIUS   The Museum of Science & Art. 1855. 2 vols. in 1, 8vo., orig. cloth gilt. Smith 194-924 1974 £5.50

LARDNER, DIONYSIUS   The Museum of Science & Art. 1859. 12 vols. in 6, orig. cloth gilt, illus. Smith 194-926 1974 £12

LARDNER, DIONYSIUS   The Museum of Science and Art. 1859. 12 vols. in 6, illus., half contemporary calf gilt. Smith 193-866 1973 £25

LARDNER, DIONYSIUS   A Treatise on Hydrostatics and Pneumatics. 1831. 8vo., contemporary half calf. Bow Windows 66-416 1974 £7.50

LARDNER, DIONYSIUS   Treatise on the Progressive Improvement and Present State of the Manufacture of Porcelain and Glass. 1832. Small 8vo., woodcuts, rebound in half leather. Quaritch 940-647 1974 £35

LARDNER, RING   The Big Town. Bobb, Merrill, 1921. 244p., illus. Austin 54-608 1973 $8.50

LARDNER, RING   The Big Town. Scribner, 1925. 244p. Austin 54-609 1973 $6.50

LARDNER, RING   First and Last. Scribner, 1934. 377p. Austin 54-610 1973 $8.50

LARDNER, RING   Gullible's Travels. Scribner, 1925. 255p., orig. ed. Austin 54-611 1973 $6

LARDNER, RING   Gullible's Travels. 1926. Orig. boards, inscribed. Covent 55-1174 1974 £5.25

LARDNER, RING   How to Write Short Stories. 1924. 359p. Austin 54-612 1973 $6.50

LARDNER, RING   June Moon. New York, 1930. Ballinger 1-160 1974 $27.50

LARDNER, RING   The Love Nest and Other Stories. Scribner, 1926. 232p. Austin 54-613 1973 $7.50

LARDNER, RING W.   My Four Weeks in France. Indianapolis, (1918). First edition, backstrip slightly chipped and spotted, orig. binding. Butterfield 10-333 1974 $15

LARDNER, RING   The Portable Ring Lardner. Viking, 1946. 756p. Austin 54-622 1973 $7.50

LARDNER, RING   Ring Lardner's Best Stories. Garden City, 1938. 563p. Austin 54-621 1973 $7.50

LARDNER, RING   Round Up. Literary Guild, 1929. 467p. Austin 54-615 1973 $6

LARDNER, RING   Round Up. Scribner, 1953. 467p. Austin 54-614 1973 $8.50

LARDNER, RING   The Story of a Wonder Man. Scribner, 1927. 151p., illus. Austin 54-616 1973 $10

LARDNER, RING   Symptoms of Being 35. Bobb, Merrill, 1921. 53p. Austin 54-617 1973 $7.50

LARDNER, RING   Treat 'Em Rough. Bobb, Merrill, 1918. 160p., illus. Austin 54-618 1973 $10

LARDNER, RING   Treat 'Em Rough. Indianapolis, 1918. Rubbed, first issue. Ballinger 1-161 1974 $25

LARDNER, RING   What Of It? Scribner. 220p. Austin 54-619 1973 $6

LARDNER, RING W.   What of It? New York, 1925. Orig. binding. Butterfield 10-335 1974 $10

LARDNER, RING   You Know Me Al. Scribner, 1925. 247p. Austin 54-620 1973 $6.50

LARGE, JOHN   Mischiefs of the Malt Tax. Bath, 1864. 8vo., modern green boards, fine, first edition. Dawsons PM 247-170 1974 £10

LARGUIER, LEO   L'Apres-Midi Chez l'Antiquaire. Paris,
1922. Small 12mo., orig. wrapper, illus. L. Goldschmidt 42-271 1974 $12.50

LARKIN, PHILIP   The North Ship. 1945. Orig. buckram, fine,
first edition. Howes 185-289 1974 £21

LARMOR, JOSEPH   Aether and Matter. Cambridge, 1900. 8vo.,
half morocco, first edition. Schumann 35-269 1974 $165

LARNED, J. N.   The Literature of American History. Boston,
1902. Thick 8vo., library stamp. Howes 185-735 1974 £6.50

LA ROCHEFOUCAULD, FRANCOIS DE   Maxims and Moral Reflections. 1775.
Small 8vo., contemporary English red morocco gilt, raised bands, label, new
edition. Thomas 28-246 1972 £100

LA ROCHEFOUCAULD, FRANCOIS DE   Maxims and Moral Reflections. 1775.
Revised new edition, the dedication copy to David Garrick with his bookplate.
8vo., contemporary English red morocco gilt, raised bands, morocco label.
Thomas 32-178 1974 £100

LA ROCHEFOUCAULD, FRANCOIS DE   Maxims and Moral Reflections. 1802.
Small 8vo., contemporary tree calf, gilt, new edition. Hill 126-154 1974 £7.50

LA ROCHEFOUCAULD, FRANCOIS DE   Oeuvres. Paris, 1868-83. 3 vols.,
8vo. and 4to., three quarter levant morocco, gilt, uncut. L. Goldschmidt
42-66 1974 $125

LA ROCHE LACARELLE, S. DE   Catalogue des Livres Rares et Precieux Manuscrits
et Imprimes. Paris, 1888. Large 4to., half leather, back damaged. Kraus
B8-130 1974 $25

LAROUSSE, PIERRE   L'Ecole Normale. Paris, 1858-64. 13 works
in 4 vols., roy. 8vo., contemporary half dark green calf, gilt, excellent copy,
rare. L. Goldschmidt 42-272 1974 $225

LARPENTEUR, CHARLES   Forty Years a Fur Trader on the Upper Missouri.
Chicago, 1933. Cloth, map, frontispiece. Bradley 35-145 1974 $7.50

LARREY, D. J.   Memoirs of Military Surgery and Campaigns of
the French Armies. Baltimore, 1814. 2 vols., first American edition.
Rittenhouse 46-405 1974 $50

LARROUY, MAURICE   L'Odyssee d'un Transport Torpille. Paris,
1926. 8vo., cloth, uncut, orig. wrapper. L. Goldschmidt 42-273 1974 $12.50

LARSEN, ELLOUISE BAKER   American Historical Views on Staffordshire
China. New York, 1939. 4to., plates, illus., buckram. Quaritch 940-648
1974 £28

LASCARIS, CONSTANTINUS   Grammaticae Compendium. 1557. 19th
century calf gilt, browned. Thomas 30-107 1973 £30

LA SERRE, JEAN PUGET   The Secretary in Fashion. London, 1654.
8vo., contemporary sheep. Dawsons PM 252-639 1974 £140

LASKER, BRUNO   Filipino Immigration. Chicago, 1931. 445p.,
illus., orig. ed. Austin 62-340 1974 $14.50

LASKI, HAROLD J.   The American Democracy. New York, 1948.
Biblo & Tannen 213-52 1973 $10

LASKY, JESSE L., JR.   Naked In a Cactus Garden. Bobbs, Merrill,
1961. 254p. Austin 51-537 1973 $7.50

LASS, A. H.   Plays From Radio. Houghton, Mifflin, 1948.
Austin 51-538 1973 $10

LASSAIGNE, JACQUES   Daumier. Paris, 1938. 4to., plates. Biblo &
Tannen 214-101 1974 $18.50

LASSAIGNE, JACQUES   Daumier. New York, 1938. Folio, color
plates. Biblo & Tannen 210-113 1973 $25

LASSALLE, FERDINAND   Offnes Antwortschreiben an das Central-Comite.
Zurich, 1863. 8vo., speckled paper boards, morocco label, fine, first edition.
Dawsons PM 247-171 1974 £150

LASSELL, WILLIAM   Description of a Machine for Polishing Specula.
1849. 4to., cloth, plates. Dawsons PM 245-456 1974 £15

LASSELS, R.   The Voyage of Italy. 1686. 2 parts in 1,
modern sheep, frontispiece. Thomas 28-329 1972 £55

LASSELS, R.   The Voyage of Italy. 1686. 2 parts in 1,
modern sheep, frontispiece, rather soiled and stained throughout, sound. Thomas
32-341 1974 £55

LASTEYRIE, CHARLES PHILIBERT   Traite sur les Betes-a-Laine d'Espagne.
Paris, (1799). 8vo., orig. pictured wrappers, first edition. Schuman 37-147
1974 $95

LATANE, JOHN HOLLADAY   A History of American Foreign Policy. Garden
City, c. 1934. Orig. binding, second printing of revised edition, maps. Wilson
63-202 1974 $15

LATASSA Y ORTIN, FELIX DE   Bibliotecas Antigua Y Neuva de Escritores.
Saragossa, 1884-86. 3 vols., 4to., contemporary quarter calf, marbled boards.
Dawsons PM 10-351 1974 £52

LATERRIERE, P. DE SALES   A Political and Historical Account of Lower
Canada. London, 1830. Orig. boards, rebacked in cloth, med. 8vo. Hood's
102-722 1974 $450

LATHAM, BALDWIN   Sanitary Engineering. 1878. Woodcuts,
plates, contemporary calf gilt, prize label, second edition. Smith 194-681
1974 £6

LATHAM, C.   In English Homes. 1907. Folio, illus., cloth,
second edition. Quaritch 940-525 1974 £5

LATHAM, C.   In English Homes. 1907. Folio, illus., cloth.
Quaritch 940-526 1974 £6

LATHAM, J.   A General Synopsis of Birds. 1781-1801(-1802).
4to., 10 vols., new three-quarter calf, plates, rare. Wheldon 130-34 1974
£600

LATHAM, PETER MERE   The Collected Works. 1876-8. 8vo., 2 vols.,
orig. cloth. Dawsons PM 249-333 1974 £6

LATHAM, ROBERT GORGON   The English Language. 1850. Revised &
enlarged third edition. Austin 61-543 1974 $17.50

LATHAM, ROBERT GORDON   The Natural History of the Varieties of Man.
London, 1850. 8vo., orig. cloth, illus., first edition. Hammond 201-655 1974
£7.50

LATHBURY, MARY A.   The Birthday Week. New York, 1884. 8vo.,
full page full color pictures on heavy paper, pencil scratches on endpapers, spine
mostly gone and boards soiled, used but attractive. Current BW9-105 1974
$17.50

LATHROP, DOROTHY P.   The Grateful Elephant and Other Stories.
New Haven, 1923. 4to., pictorial cloth, color frontispiece, illus., first edition.
Frohnsdorff 16-482 1974 $10

LATHROP, DOROTHY P.   Puppies for Keeps. New York, 1943. Oblong
4to., cloth, color illus., very fine copy, dust jacket, first edition. Frohnsdorff
16-483 1974 $12.50

LATHROP, DOROTHY P.   The Snail Who Ran. New York, 1934. 16mo.,
cloth, color frontispiece, illus. by author, worn, dust jacket, presentation copy
inscribed by author. Frohnsdorff 15-83 1974 $15

LATHROP, ELSIE   Historic Houses of Early America. New York,
1936. Thick 8vo., pictorial endpapers, illus., nearly fine. Current BW9-356
1974 $14.50

LATHROP, GEORGE P.   A Study of Hawthorne. Houghton, 1876.
350p., orig. ed. Austin 54-623 1973 $7.50

LATHROP, JOSEPH   Christ's Warning to the Churches, to Beware of
False Prophets, Who Come as Wolves in Sheeps Clothing. Springfield, 1789.
Disbound. Hayman 59-350 1974 $15

LATHROP, ROSE H.   Memories of Hawthorne. Houghton, 1897. 482p., orig. ed. Austin 54-624 1973 $12.50

LATHY, THOMAS PIKE   The Angler. 1819. Roy. 8vo., crimson straight-grained morocco, gilt, first edition. Quaritch 939-156 1974 £185

LATILLA, EUGENIO   Cartoons In Outline & Illustrative of the Gospels. Florence, 1848. Folio, plates, large paper. Smith 193-669 1973 £12

LATIMER, HUGH   Original Letters Relative To the English Reformation. Cambridge, 1846-47. 2 vols., orig. cloth. Howes 185-1533 1974 £7.50

LATIMER, RUPERT   Murder After Christmas. London, (1944). First edition, 8vo., d.j., very good. Current BW9-53 1974 $16.50

LA TOUCHE, JEAN CLAUDE HIPPOLYTE MEHEE DE
Please turn to
MEHEE DE LA TOUCHE, JEAN CLAUDE HIPPOLYTE

LATOUCHE, JOHN   The Golden Apple. Random, 1953. 133p. Austin 51-539 1973 $6.50

LA TOUCHE, T. H. D.   A Bibliography of Indian Geology and Physical Geography. Calcutta, 1918. Roy 8vo., orig. wrappers, scarce. Wheldon 129-164 1974 £5

LATREILLE, P. A.   Precis des Caracteres Generiques des Insectes Disposes dans un Ordre Natural. Brive, (1796). 8vo., contemporary tree calf, folding table, nice copy, rare orig. issue. Wheldon 129-753 1973 £68

LAUD, WILLIAM   A Relation of the Conference Betweene William Laud, . . . and Mr. Fisher the Jesuite. 1639. Folio, old calf, spine little defective towards top, else quite good, revised second edition. Thomas 32-44 1974 £21

LAUD, WILLIAM   Works. Oxford, 1847-60. 7 vols. in 9, orig. cloth, scarce, best edition. Howes 185-1352 1974 £38

LAUDER, THOMAS D.   Memorial of the Royal Progress in Scotland. Edinburgh, 1843. 4to., cloth, map. Quaritch 939-660 1974 £10

LAUDER, THOMAS D.   The Miscellany of Natural History, Vol. 1, Parrots. Edinburgh, 1833. Small 8vo., half morocco, coloured plates, rare, first edition. Wheldon 128-501 1973 £35

LAUDERDALE, JAMES MAITLAND   An Inquiry into the Nature and Origin of Public Wealth. London, 1819. 8vo., orig. boards, uncut, fine, second edition. Dawsons PM 247-172 1974 £45

LAUFER, BERTHOLD   The Beginnings of Porcelain in China. Chicago, 1917. Orig. ed., illus. Biblo & Tannen 214-383 1974 $15

LAUFERTY, LILIAN   The Street of Chains. Harper, 1929. 374p. Austin 62-342 1974 $10

LAUGHLIN, J. LAURENCE   Reciprocity. New York, 1903. First edition, bookplate, orig. binding. Butterfield 10-336 1974 $25

LAUGHLIN, JAMES   Poems from the Greenberg Manuscripts. Norfolk, 1939. Orig. cloth, scarce, wrappers. Rota 188-506 1974 £5

LAUGHTON, J. K.   Memoirs of a Life and Correspondence of Henry Reeve. 1898. 2 vols. Allen 216-1524 1974 £10

LAUREDANUS, BERNADINUS   In M. Tullii Ciceronis Orationes de Lege Agraria. 1558. 4to., modern vellum, cloth sides, uncut. Thomas 30-110 1973 £40

LAUREMBERG, P.   Horticultura Libris II Comprehensa. 1631-32. 4to., boards, rare. Wheldon 130-1422 1974 £120

LAURENCE J.   The Clergy-Man's Recreation. 1716. 8vo., modern boards, plates. Wheldon 130-1423 1974 £20

LAURENCE, J.   The Clergy-Man's Recreation. The Fruit Garden Kalendar. The Gentleman's Recreation. 1717-18. 3 works in 1 vol., 8vo., contemporary calf, scarce, plates. Wheldon 131-1537 1974 £20

LAURENCE, J.   The Clergy-Man's Recreation. 1717-18. 8vo., contemporary panelled calf. Wheldon 130-1424 1974 £36

LAURENCIE, SOSTHENES DE LA   Etude Technique. Paris, 1872. 8vo., contemporary roan backed boards, worn. Bow Windows 62-558 1974 £8.50

LAURENT, L.   Flore des Calcaires de Celas. Marseille, 1899. 4to., folding table, plates, maps. Wheldon 128-1004 1973 £7.50

LAURENT, L.   Flore Fossile des Schistes de Menat. Marseilles, 1912. 4to., plates, folding table. Wheldon 128-1007 1973 £5

LAURENT, L.   Flore Plaisancienne des Argiles Cineritiques de Niac. Marseilles, 1908. 4to., plates, folding table. Wheldon 128-1006 1973 £5

LAURENT, L.   Flore Pliocene des Cinerites du Pas-de-la-Mougudo et de Saint-Vincent. Marseille, 1904-05. 2 parts, 4to., plates, folding table. Wheldon 128-1005 1973 £7.50

LAURENT DE PARIS, BROTHER   Le Palais d'Amour Divin de Jesus. Paris, 1603. Oblong 12mo., contemporary full dark blue green morocco, gilt, second edition. L. Goldschmidt 42-67 1974 $250

LAURENT-PICHAT, L.   Chroniques Rimees. Paris, 1856. 8vo., contemporary three quarter morocco, gilt, uncut, first edition. L. Goldschmidt 42-274 1974 $10

LAURENTI, J. N.   Specimen Medicum Exhibens Synopsin, Reptilium Emendatam. Vienna, 1768. 8vo., old calf, worn, plates, rare. Wheldon 128-647 1973 £24

LAURENTIUS, ANDREAS   De Mirabili Strumas Sanandi. Paris, 1609. 8vo., shagreen-backed boards, first edition. Schumann 35-270 1974 $95

LAURENTS, ARTHUR   Anyone Can Whistle. Random, 1965. 186p. Austin 51-541 1973 $6.50

LAURENTS, ARTHUR   Gypsy. Random, 1959. 144p., illus. Austin 51-542 1973 $7.50

LAURENTS, ARTHUR   Invitation to a March. Random, 1958. 134p., illus. Austin 51-540 1973 $7.50

LAURIE, JOE, JR.   Vaudeville. Holt, 1953. 561p., orig. ed. Austin 51-543 1973 $8.75

LAURIE and Whittle's New Sailing Directions for the Mediterranean Sea. London, 1807. 8vo., orig. light blue wrappers, printed paper side label, very scarce, fine, first edition. Ximenes 37-152 1974 $80

LAURIER, WILFRID   Lettres a Mon Pere et a Ma Mere. Arthabaska, 1935. Hood's 104-271 1974 $12.50

LAVAL, ANTOINE JEAN DE   Voyage de la Louisiane . . . Divers Voyages Faits Pour la Correction de la Cote de Provence, et des Reflexions sur Quelques Points du Sisteme de M. Newton. Paris, 1727-28. 3 vols. in 1, half morocco, first edition, maps, tables, diagrams. Jenkins 61-1345 1974 $325

LAVALLEY, GASTON   Catalogue des Ouvrages Normands de la Bibliotheque Municipale de Caen. Caen, 1910-12. 3 vols., large 8vo., cloth, morocco labels. Dawsons PM 10-352 1974 £22

LA VALLIERE, LOUIS CESAR DUC DE   Catalogue des Livres de la Bibliotheque de Feu H. le Duc de la Valliere. Paris, 1784. 6 vols., 8vo., boards. Kraus B8-132 1974 $85

LAVATER, JOHANN CASPAR   Essai sur la Physiognomie, Destine a Faire Connaitre l'Homme et a le Faire Aimer. The Hague, 1781-1803. Full page engraved plates, 4to., contemporary brown half calf, first French edition, fine and clean set. Schumann 499-59 1974 sFr 3,900

LAVATER, JOHANN CASPAR   Essays on Physiognomy. 1792. 3 vols. in 5, roy. 4to., plates, contemporary russia, gilt. Quaritch 940-157 1974 £150

LAVATER, JOHANN HEINRICH   Elemens Anatomiques d'Osteologie et de Myologie. Paris, 1797. 8vo., contemporary half calf, plates, first edition. Schumann 35-271 1974 $85

LA VEGA, GARCILASO DE
Please turn to
GARCILASO DE LA VEGA

LAVER, JAMES   English Costume of the 19th Century.   1929.
Coloured & other drawings, inscription on fly, fine, d.w.   Covent 51-2409 1973
£5

LAVER, JAMES   A Stitch in Time.   1927. Small folio, limp marbled boards, uncut, limited edition.   Broadhurst 23-1065 1974 £6

LAVER, JAMES   A Stitch in Time.   Nonesuch Press, 1927. Small
folio, limp marbled paper covered boards, paper printed label, uncut, limited to
1525 copies, fine.   Broadhurst 24-1026 1974 £6

LAVER, JAMES   A Stitch in Time.   1927. Royal 8vo., paper
boards, fine, limited edition.   Covent 56-991 1974 £7.50

LAVER, JAMES   "Vulgar Society".   1936. Orig. cloth, plates.
Marsden 37-484 1974 £7

LAVERAN, CHARLES L. A.   Paludism.   1893. Large 8vo., orig. cloth gilt,
fine.   Dawsons PM 249-334 1974 £5

LAVERY, EMMET   The First Legion.   French, 1934. 138p.
Austin 51-544 1973 $8.50

LAVISSE, ERNEST   Histoire Generale.   Paris, 1893-c.1905.
12 vols., thick roy. 8vo., half crushed morocco, fine.   Howes 186-985
1974 £72

LAVOISIER, ANTOINE LAURENT   Elements of Chemistry.   Edinburgh, 1790.
8vo., contemporary calf, rebacked, plates, first edition in English.   Dawsons PM
245-459 1974 £145

LAVOISIER, ANTOINE LAURENT   Oeuvres de Lavoisier.   Paris, 1862-1893.
Roy 4to., 6 vols., contemporary half brown morocco.   Zeitlin 235-281 1974
$600

LAVOISIER, ANTOINE LAURENT   Traite Elementaire de Chimie.   Paris, 1789.
8vo., 2 vols., contemporary French calf, gilt, first edition, second issue.   Dawsons PM 245-458 1974 £450

LAVOISIER, ANTOINE LAURENT   Traite Elementaire de Chimie.   Paris,
1789. 2 vols., 8vo., plates, continental boards, worn, first edition, second
issue.   Dawsons PM 250-51 1974 £450

LAVOISIER, ANTOINE-LAURENT   Traite Elementaire de Chimie.   Paris,
1789. 2 vols., 8vo., plates, dark blue half morocco, very fine, rare first
edition.   Gilhofer 61-26 1974 sFr. 4,000

LAVOISIER, ANTOINE LAURENT   Oeuvres.   Paris, 1864-2-93. 4to., 6 vols.,
vols. 1, 3, 4, 5 and 6 in red quarter morocco, vol. 2 in red quarter sheep, plates,
complete, rare, good set.   Gurney 66-100 1974 £250

LAVOISNE'S Complete Genealogical, Historical, Chronological and Geographical
Atlas.   1834. Folio, half cloth, coloured maps, fourth edition.   Bow Windows
66-417 1974 £60

LAW, E.   Van Dyke's Pictures at Windsor Castle.   1899-
1901. 2 vols. in 1, imp. folio, half morocco gilt, rubbed.   Quaritch 940-158
1974 £25

LAW, WILLIAM   An Humble, Earnest, and Affectionate Address
to the Clergy.   1764-69. 2 works in 1 vol., contemporary sheep, rebacked.
Howes 185-1356 1974 £10

LAW, WILLIAM   A Practical Treatise Upon Christian Perfection.
London, 1726. 8vo., new calf spine, old cloth sides, stained, first edition.
Traylen 79-178 1973 £12

LAW, WILLIAM   A Serious Call to a Devout and Holy Life.
London, 1729. 8vo., contemporary blind-tooled calf, gilt, rebacked, first
edition.   Dawsons PM 250-52 1974 £135

LAW, WILLIAM   Works.   London, 1718-1782. 9 vols., 8vo.,
full panelled calf.   Traylen 79-179 1973 £60

LAW, WILLIAM   Collected Works.   1762. 9 vols., full calf,
rebacked, scarce, first collected edition.   Howes 185-1355 1974 £50

LAW, WILLIAM   Works.   London, 1892-93. 9 vols., 8vo.,
orig. quarter leather, complete set.   Traylen 79-180 1973 £30

LAWLER, JOHN   Book Auctions in England in the 17th Century.
London, 1898. 12mo., orig. cloth, uncut, fine.   Dawsons PM 10-353 1974 £6

LAWLER, RAY   Summer of the Seventeenth Doll.   Random,
1957. 142p., illus.   Austin 51-545 1973 $7.50

LAWLOR, H. J.   Chapters on the Book of Mulling.   Edinbrugh,
1897. 8vo., cloth boards.   Emerald 50-513 1974 £8.50

LAWLOR, H. J.   The Fasti of St. Patrick's Dublin.   Dundalk,
1930. 8vo., cloth boards.   Emerald 50-514 1974 £5

LAWRENCE, A. W.   T. E. Lawrence By His Friends.   1937. Illus.,
first American edition.   Austin 61-566 1974 $17.50

LAWRENCE, ADA   Early Life of D. H. Lawrence.   1932. 8vo.,
cloth, first English edition.   Quaritch 936-465 1974 £4

LAWRENCE, ADA   Young Lorenzo.   Florence, 1931. 8vo., parchment, dust-wrapper, fine, plates, first edition.   Quaritch 936-464 1974 £18

LAWRENCE, ADA   Young Lorenzo.   Florence, 1931. Edition
limited to 740 copies, of which this is one of 40 out of series, slightly soiled d.w.,
orig. parchment covers, unopened, fine.   Ross 87-342 1974 $70

LAWRENCE, DAVID HERBERT   Aaron's Rod.   1922. First American edition.
Austin 61-544 1974 $12.50

LAWRENCE, DAVID HERBERT   Amores.   n.d. Orig. blue buckram.   Smith
193-383 1973 £5

LAWRENCE, DAVID HERBERT   Apocalypse.   Florence, 1931. 8vo., boards,
dust wrapper, fine, limited, first edition.   Quaritch 936-450 1974 £20

LAWRENCE, DAVID HERBERT   Apocalypse.   Florence, 1931. 8vo., orig.
boards, leather label, limited, first edition.   Dawsons PM 252-640 1974 £28

LAWRENCE, DAVID HERBERT   Apocalypse.   Florence, 1931. Portrait, fine,
boards, dust wrapper.   Covent 55-977 1974 £45

LAWRENCE, DAVID HERBERT   Assorted Articles.   London, 1930. First
edition.   Ballinger 1-162 1974 $15

LAWRENCE, DAVID HERBERT   Assorted Articles.   London, 1930. Front cover
slightly spotted, else fine, orig. binding.   Ross 86-297 1974 $20

LAWRENCE, DAVID HERBERT   Birds, Beasts and Flowers.   1923. 8vo., boards,
dust wrapper, torn, first English edition.   Quaritch 936-451 1974 £25

LAWRENCE, DAVID HERBERT   Birds, Beasts and Flowers.   London, 1930.
Folio, quarter vellum, corners worn, wood engravings, first edition, one of 500
numbered copies, internally fine.   MacManus 224-271 1974 $50

LAWRENCE, DAVID HERBERT   Birds, Beasts and Flowers.   London, 1930.
Wood engravings, one of 500 numbered copies, corners rubbed, else fine, vellum
backed boards, first edition.   Covent 51-1082 1973 £40

LAWRENCE, DAVID HERBERT   Birds, Beasts and Flowers.   1930. Folio, boards,
gilt, fine, limited edition.   Quaritch 936-452 1974 £50

LAWRENCE, DAVID HERBERT   Birds, Beasts and Flowers.   1930. Folio,
quarter vellum, English first edition.   Covent 56-1863 1974 £65

LAWRENCE, DAVID HERBERT   Birds, Beasts and Flowers.   London, 1930.
Quarter vellum, protective paper wrapper, mint, wood engravings by Blair Hughes-
Stanton, no. 58 of edition limited to 530 copies.   Ross 87-332 1974 $125

LAWRENCE, DAVID HERBERT   Birds, Beasts and Flowers.   London, 1930.
Marbled boards, vellum back.   Dawson's 424-61 1974 $100

LAWRENCE, DAVID HERBERT　The Boy in the Bush. London, 1924. First printing, limited to 2000 copies, name in ink on fly, some foxing, very good copy. Ross 86-298 1974 $15

LAWRENCE, DAVID HERBERT　The Boy in the Bush. 1924. English first edition. Covent 56-809 1974 £6.30

LAWRENCE, DAVID HERBERT　The Captain's Doll. 1923. Orig. American edition. Austin 61-545 1974 $10

LAWRENCE, DAVID HERBERT　A Collier's Friday Night. 1934. Dust wrapper, fine, English first edition. Covent 56-789 1974 £15

LAWRENCE, DAVID HERBERT　England My England. 1924. Trifle foxed, else fine, first edition. Covent 51-1085 1973 £5.25

LAWRENCE, DAVID HERBERT　England, My England. London, 1924. First English edition, slightly soiled & torn d.w., very good, orig. binding. Ross 87-333 1974 $25

LAWRENCE, DAVID HERBERT　England My England. London, 1924. First English edition. Ballinger 1-163 1974 $25

LAWRENCE, DAVID HERBERT　Etruscan Places. New York, 1932. First American issue, lacking d.w., spine faded, near fine, orig. binding. Ross 86-299 1974 $20

LAWRENCE, DAVID HERBERT　Fire and Other Poems. San Francisco, 1940. Blue boards. Dawson's 424-67 1974 $75

LAWRENCE, DAVID HERBERT　Kangaroo. 1923. Orig. American edition. Austin 61-546 1974 $10

LAWRENCE, DAVID HERBERT　Kangaroo. 1923. Small 8vo., orig. cloth, dust-wrapper, first edition. Quaritch 936-453 1974 £10

LAWRENCE, DAVID HERBERT　Lady Chatterley's Lover. 1928. 8vo., orig. boards, rebacked, first edition. Quaritch 936-454 1974 £20

LAWRENCE, DAVID HERBERT　Lady Chatterley's Lover. Florence, 1928. Large 8vo., limited, signed, fine, orig. boards, first edition. Dawsons PM 252-641 1974 £210

LAWRENCE, DAVID HERBERT　Lady Chatterley's Lover. 1929. Red brown cloth boards, third edition, no. 299 of edition limited to 500 copies, very nice copy. Ross 86-300 1974 $35

LAWRENCE, DAVID HERBERT　The Ladybird. 1923. Small 8vo., orig. cloth, first edition. Quaritch 936-455 1974 £6

LAWRENCE, DAVID HERBERT　Last Poems. 1932. Orig. cloth, dust wrapper, fine, first edition. Rota 188-509 1974 £30

LAWRENCE, DAVID HERBERT　The Letters of. 1932. 8vo., orig. cloth, dust wrapper, first edition. Rota 189-553 1974 £8

LAWRENCE, DAVID HERBERT　The Letters. 1932. 893 pages. Austin 61-547 1974 $27.50

LAWRENCE, DAVID HERBERT　The Letters of. London, 1932. 8vo., orig. cloth, illus., first edition. Bow Windows 62-559 1974 £12

LAWRENCE, DAVID HERBERT　The Lost Girl. 1920. Covers marked, first edition. Covent 55-981 1974 £15

LAWRENCE, DAVID HERBERT　The Lost Girl. 1921. Orig. American edition. Austin 61-548 1974 $10

LAWRENCE, DAVID HERBERT　Love Among the Haystacks and Other Pieces. 1930. Dust wrapper, fine, English first edition. Covent 56-794 1974 £15.75

LAWRENCE, DAVID HERBERT　Love Among the Haystacks. 1933. Dust wrapper, worn, near fine, first ordinary edition. Covent 56-795 1974 £8.40

LAWRENCE, DAVID HERBERT　Love Poems and Others. 1913. 8vo., cloth, gilt, first edition. Quaritch 936-456 1974 £40

LAWRENCE, DAVID HERBERT　Love Poems and Others. London, 1913. Cloth, first edition, first issue. Dawson's 424-290 1974 $75

LAWRENCE, DAVID HERBERT　The Lovely Lady. 1932. Fine, d.w., English first edition. Covent 56-796 1974 £12.50

LAWRENCE, DAVID HERBERT　The Man Who Died. London, 1931. First English edition, limited to 2000 copies, tall 8vo., very nice copy, orig. cloth. Crane 7-167 1974 £12

LAWRENCE, DAVID HERBERT　The Man Who Died. London, 1931. 8vo., orig. buckram, dust wrapper, first English edition. Dawsons PM 252-642 1974 £15

LAWRENCE, DAVID HERBERT　The Man Who Died. London, 1931. First English edition, limited to 2,000 copies, orig. binding, some fading, lacking d.w., else fine. Ross 87-335 1974 $40

LAWRENCE, DAVID HERBERT　A Modern Lover. 1934. Dust wrapper, fine, English first edition. Covent 56-798 1974 £10.50

LAWRENCE, DAVID HERBERT　A Modern Lover. 1934. Fine, d.w., small piece missing at head of spine, first edition. Covent 51-1088 1973 £9.50

LAWRENCE, DAVID HERBERT　Mornings In Mexico. 1931. 189 pages. Austin 61-549 1974 $12.50

LAWRENCE, DAVID HERBERT　Nettles. 1930. Wrappers, near fine, English first edition. Covent 56-799 1974 £15

LAWRENCE, DAVID HERBERT　Nettles. 1930. First edition, crown 8vo., paper printed wrapper, uncut, unopened, mint. Broadhurst 24-761 1974 £5

LAWRENCE, DAVID HERBERT　An Original Poem. 1934. 8vo., wrappers, first edition. Quaritch 936-457 1974 £40

LAWRENCE, DAVID HERBERT　The Paintings of. 1929. Colour plates, one of 510 numbered copies on mouldmade paper, very fine, half morocco, first edition. Covent 51-1093 1973 £75

LAWRENCE, DAVID HERBERT　Pansies. 1929. First edition, demy 8vo., dec. boards, cloth spine, uncut, fine. Broadhurst 24-760 1974 £5

LAWRENCE, DAVID HERBERT　Pansies. 1929. One of 500 copies, numbered & signed by author, portrait, stiff wrappers, very fine copy, protective tissue, first edition. Covent 51-1094 1973 £35

LAWRENCE, DAVID HERBERT　Phoenix. 1936. Roy. 8vo., dust wrapper, fine, first English edition. Howes 186-298 1974 £8.50

LAWRENCE, DAVID HERBERT　Phoenix. 1936. 8vo., cloth, first English edition. Quaritch 936-458 1974 £9

LAWRENCE, DAVID HERBERT　The Plays of. 1933. Dust wrapper, fine, worn, English first edition. Covent 56-800 1974 £12.50

LAWRENCE, DAVID HERBERT　The Plays of. (1938). Fine, first edition. Covent 55-982 1974 £5.25

LAWRENCE, DAVID HERBERT　The Plumed Serpent. 1926. First edition, crown 8vo., orig. cloth, fine. Broadhurst 24-756 1974 £16

LAWRENCE, DAVID HERBERT　Pornography and Obscenity. 1929. First edition, extra crown 8vo., sewn, paper printed wrapper, mint. Broadhurst 24-759 1974 £6

LAWRENCE, DAVID HERBERT　Pornography and Obscenity. London, 1929. Fine, orig. binding. Ross 86-301 1974 $12.50

LAWRENCE, DAVID HERBERT　Pornography & Obscenity. 1929. Boards, scarce, very fine. Covent 55-983 1974 £10

LAWRENCE, DAVID HERBERT　Pornography and Obscenity. 1929. Wrappers, worn, English first edition. Covent 56-801 1974 £6.50

LAWRENCE, DAVID HERBERT　Pornography and Obscenity. London, 1929. 8vo., orig. wrappers, first edition. Dawsons PM 252-643 1974 £10.50

LAWRENCE, DAVID HERBERT　The Prussian Officer and Other Stories. London, (1914). Orig. cloth, faded, browning, first edition, second issue. Bow Windows 62-560 1974 £18

LAWRENCE, DAVID HERBERT   The Prussian Officer and Other Stories. 1914. 8vo., orig. cloth, first edition, second issue. Rota 189-548 1974 £20

LAWRENCE, DAVID HERBERT   The Prussian Officer and Other Stories. 1914. 8vo., orig. cloth, first edition, first issue. Rota 190-603 1974 £30

LAWRENCE, DAVID HERBERT   Psychoanalysis and the Unconscious. London, 1923. First English edition, orig. binding, slight foxing, tight copy. Ross 87-338 1974 $20

LAWRENCE, DAVID HERBERT   Rawdon's Roof. 1928. First edition, f'cap. 4to., dec. boards, fine, d.w., limited to 500 copies, signed by author. Broadhurst 24-757 1974 £45

LAWRENCE, DAVID HERBERT   Reflections on the Death of a Porcupine and other Essays. 1925. Small 8vo., boards, slip-case, first edition. Quaritch 936-459 1974 £30

LAWRENCE, DAVID HERBERT   Reflections on the Death of a Porcupine and Other Essays. Philadelphia, 1925. First edition, limited to 925 copies, this copy being unnumbered, orig. patterned boards, extremely nice copy, scarce. Crane 7-166 1974 £40

LAWRENCE, DAVID HERBERT   St. Mawr, Together with the Princess. 1925. English first edition. Covent 56-803 1974 £6.30

LAWRENCE, DAVID HERBERT   Selected Poems. 1934. Fine, dust wrapper, English first edition. Covent 56-804 1974 £7.50

LAWRENCE, DAVID HERBERT   The Spirit of Place. 1935. Fine, first edition. Covent 51-1097 1973 £5.25

LAWRENCE, DAVID HERBERT   The Spirit of Place. 1935. Covers little marked text edges spotted, very good, worn d.w. Covent 51-2410 1973 £6.50

LAWRENCE, DAVID HERBERT   The Story of Doctor Manente. Florence, 1929. Small 8vo., soiled vellum, foxing, illus. Minters 37-153 1973 $75

LAWRENCE, DAVID HERBERT   The Story of Doctor Manente Being the Tenth and Last Story from the Suppers of A. F. Grazzini Called il Lasca. Florence, (1929). Orig. paper boards, first edition, light foxing, fine, orig. dust jacket, 1 of 1,000 numbered copies. MacManus 224-272 1974 $40

LAWRENCE, DAVID HERBERT   The Story of Doctor Manente, Being the Tenth and Last Story from the Suppers of A. F. Grazzini Called II Lasca. Florence, 1929. One of 1000 copies printed on Lombardy paper, boards somewhat warped, d.w., unopened, very fine. Ross 86-302 1974 $45

LAWRENCE, DAVID HERBERT   Studies in Classic American Literature. New York, 1923. Orig. cloth, first edition, fine, dust jacket. MacManus 224-273 1974 $40

LAWRENCE, DAVID HERBERT   Three Poems. 1919. Wrappers, English first edition. Covent 56-806 1974 £15

LAWRENCE, DAVID HERBERT   Touch and Go. 1920. First edition, crown 8vo., orig. orange paper printed boards, blue printed title label, fine, orig. paper d.w., scarce. Broadhurst 24-755 1974 £21

LAWRENCE, DAVID HERBERT   Touch and Go. 1920. 8vo., wrappers, fine, first edition. Rota 189-549 1974 £21

LAWRENCE, DAVID HERBERT   Touch & Go. London, 1920. Stiff paper boards, glassine wrapper, d.w., unopened, near mint. Ross 86-303 1974 $50

LAWRENCE, DAVID HERBERT   Twilight in Italy. 1916. Cloth, rubbed, first edition. Rota 188-507 1974 £15

LAWRENCE, DAVID HERBERT   The Virgin and the Gypsy. 1930. 175 pages. Austin 61-550 1974 $10

LAWRENCE, DAVID HERBERT   The Virgin and the Gipsy. 1930. English first edition. Covent 56-807 1974 £5.25

LAWRENCE, DAVID HERBERT   The Virgin and the Gipsy. London, 1930. First English edition. Ballinger 1-164 1974 $15

LAWRENCE, DAVID HERBERT   The Virgin and the Gypsy. London, 1930. First English edition, covers worn, spine slightly creased, orig. binding, nice. Ross 87-339 1974 $40

LAWRENCE, DAVID HERBERT   The Virgin and the Gipsy. Florence, 1930. Orig. cloth, dust wrapper, first edition. Rota 188-508 1974 £30

LAWRENCE, DAVID HERBERT   The Virgin and the Gipsy. Florence, 1930. lst ed., ltd. to 810 copies. Jacobs 24-102 1974 $85

LAWRENCE, DAVID HERBERT   The Virgin and the Gipsy. Florence, 1930. 8vo., boards, first edition. Quaritch 936-460 1974 £55

LAWRENCE, DAVID HERBERT   The White Peacock. 1911. Crown 8vo., orig. blue cloth, extremely rare, first edition. Howes 185-291 1974 £145

LAWRENCE, DAVID HERBERT   The White Peacock. 1911. English first edition. Covent 56-1866 1974 £21

LAWRENCE, DAVID HERBERT   The White Peacock. 1915. Text little soiled, nice copy, first edition under Duckworth's imprint. Covent 51-2411 1973 £12

LAWRENCE, DAVID HERBERT   The Wilderness of Zin. 1915. 4to., orig. cloth backed boards, plates, illus., fine, first edition. Quaritch 936-470 1974 £110

LAWRENCE, DAVID HERBERT   Women in Love. New York, 1922. Faded, first American trade edition. Covent 55-985 1974 £6.50

LAWRENCE, DAVID HERBERT   Collected Poems. 1928. 8vo., 2 vols., buckram, first edition. Quaritch 936-449 1974 £20

LAWRENCE, DAVID HERBERT   The Collected Poems. 1928. First edition, 2 vols., demy 8vo., very fine, slightly frayed d.w., orig. cloth. Broadhurst 24-758 1974 £25

LAWRENCE, DAVID HERBERT   The Collected Poems. 1928. 8vo., orig. cloth, 2 vols., first edition. Broadhurst 23-785 1974 £25

LAWRENCE, EFFINGHAM   Siege at Chepachet. (Providence, 1842). First edition, 8vo., orig. brown wrappers, very fine. Current BW9-430 1974 $36

LAWRENCE, GERTRUDE   A Star Danced. Garden City, 1946. 238p. Austin 51-546 1973 $6

LAWRENCE, HENRY   Of Our Communion and Warre With Angles. 1646. Small 4to., contemporary sheep, bookplate. Thomas 28-99 1972 £21

LAWRENCE, JOHN   The Farmer's Calendar. London, 1800. 8vo., morocco label, contemporary half calf, first edition. Dawsons PM 247-173 1974 £55

LAWRENCE, ROBERT F.   The New Hampshire Churches. N.P., 1856. 8vo., orig. bindings. Butterfield 8-352 1974 $35

LAWRENCE, ROBERT M.   Primitive Pyscho-Therapy and Quackery. Boston & New York, 1910. Orig. buckram. Howes 186-1871 1974 £5

LAWRENCE, ROSE   The Last Autumn at a Favourite Residence, with Other Poems. Liverpool, 1836. 12mo., orig. light blue cloth gilt, spine little worn, first edition, tipped in letter from author, manuscript corrections and annotations by author. Ximenes 36-136 1974 $60

LAWRENCE, THOMAS EDWARD   Crusader Castles. 1936. 2 vols., crown 4to., orig. half tan morocco, gilt, first edition. Howes 185-199 1974 £160

LAWRENCE, THOMAS EDWARD   A Brief Record of the Advance of the Egyptian Expeditionary Force. Cairo, 1919. 4to., orig. wrappers, maps, scarce, first edition. Rota 189-562 1974 £60

LAWRENCE, THOMAS EDWARD   Crusaders Castles. 1936. Crown 4to., half niger morocco, uncut, 2 vols., limited. Broadhurst 23-999 1974 £185

LAWRENCE, THOMAS EDWARD   Crusader Castles. London, Golden Cockerel Press, 1936. Edition limited to 1,000 copies, this being no. 606, half red morocco by Sangorski & Sutcliffe, orig. tissue wrappers, rare, mint. Ross 87-344 1974 $450

LAWRENCE, THOMAS EDWARD   Crusader Castles. (1936). 2 vols., 4to., niger half morocco, plans, drawings, illus., top edges gilt others uncut, limited edition. Bow Windows 66-290 1974 £250

LAWRENCE, THOMAS EDWARD   Crusader Castles. London, 1936. 2 vols., 4to., orig. half niger morocco, limited, fine, first edition. Dawsons PM 252-644 1974 £375

LAWRENCE, THOMAS EDWARD   Etruscan Places. 1932. Orig. buckram, plates, faded spine. Smith 194-484 1974 £10

LAWRENCE, THOMAS EDWARD   Historical Genealogy of the Lawrence Family, 1635-58. New York, 1858. 8vo., cloth. Saddleback 14-787 1974 $17.50

LAWRENCE, THOMAS EDWARD   Lawrence of Arabia. 1936. 4to., linen backed boards, fine, English first edition. Covent 56-813 1974 £250

LAWRENCE, THOMAS EDWARD   Letters From T. E. Shaw to Bruce Rogers. 1933. Damp-stained. Covent 55-991 1974 £110

LAWRENCE, THOMAS EDWARD   The Letters of. 1938. 8vo., orig. cloth, fine, illus., first edition. Rota 189-561 1974 £10

LAWRENCE, THOMAS EDWARD   The Letters of. 1938. First edition, maps, illus., med. 8vo., orig. cloth, fine. Broadhurst 24-767 1974 £8

LAWRENCE, THOMAS EDWARD   Men in Print. 1940. Crown 4to., quarter niger, uncut, limited. Broadhurst 23-1006 1974 £70

LAWRENCE, THOMAS EDWARD   Oriental Assembly. 1940. Illus., 291 pages. Austin 61-556 1974 $17.50

LAWRENCE, THOMAS EDWARD   Revolt in the Desert. 1927. First edition, illus., med. 8vo., orig. cloth, fine. Broadhusrt 24-765 1974 £6

LAWRENCE, THOMAS EDWARD   Revolt in the Desert. London, 1927. Orig. binding, first edition, fine, tight copy, d.w. Ross 87-349 1974 $40

LAWRENCE, THOMAS EDWARD   Revolt in the Desert. 1927. 8vo., orig. cloth, illus., first edition. Broadhurst 23-790 1974 £6

LAWRENCE, THOMAS EDWARD   Revolt in the Desert. 1927. 8vo., orig. cloth, fine, d.w., first edition. Rota 190-608 1974 £6

LAWRENCE, THOMAS EDWARD   Revolt In the Desert. London, 1927. Illus., first edition. Austin 61-557 1974 $47.50

LAWRENCE, THOMAS EDWARD   Revolt in the Desert. London, 1927. 4to., orig. quarter morocco, plates, fine. Dawsons PM 252-645 1974 £125

LAWRENCE, THOMAS EDWARD   Secret Despatches from Arabia. n.d. Crown 4to., quarter niger, uncut, limited. Broadhurst 23-1005 1974 £85

LAWRENCE, THOMAS EDWARD   Secret Despatches from Arabia. 1939. 4to., orig. quarter morocco, cloth sides, top edges gilt, others uncut, slip case, fine copy, scarce, limited edition, portrait frontispiece. Sawyer 293-202 1974 £130

LAWRENCE, THOMAS EDWARD   Secret Dispatches from Arabia. London, Golden Cockerel Press, (1939). Frontispiece portrait, no. 762 of edition limited to 1,000 numbered copies, quarter niger by Sangorski & Sutcliffe, mint, in box. Ross 87-350 1974 $325

LAWRENCE, THOMAS EDWARD   Seven Pillars of Wisdom. (London), 1926. 4to., morocco, presentation inscription, fine, first edition. Dawsons PM 252-646 1974 £3500

LAWRENCE, THOMAS EDWARD   Seven Pillars of Wisdom. 1935. Illus., first American edition. Austin 61-558 1974 $12.50

LAWRENCE, THOMAS EDWARD   Seven Pillars of Wisdom. 1935. 4to., stain, illus., bookplate, first published edition. Rota 188-513 1974 £6.50

LAWRENCE, THOMAS EDWARD   Seven Pillars of Wisdom a Triumph. (1935). 4to., orig. quarter pigskin, maps, illus., first published edition. Bow Windows 64-584 1974 £85

LAWRENCE, THOMAS EDWARD   Seven Pillars of Wisdom. 1935. First edition for general circulation, crown 4to., uncut, orig. cloth, fine, illus., maps. Broadhurst 24-766 1974 £8

LAWRENCE, THOMAS EDWARD   Seven Pillars of Wisdom. London, 1935. 4to., plates, orig. brown buckram. Dawsons PM 252-647 1974 £10

LAWRENCE, THOMAS EDWARD   Seven Pillars of Wisdom. 1935. Crown 4to., orig. cloth, uncut, first edition. Broadhurst 23-791 1974 £8

LAWRENCE, THOMAS EDWARD   Seven Pillars of Wisdom. Garden City, 1935. First trade edition, orig. binding, lacking d.w., near fine. Ross 87-351 1974 $30

LAWRENCE, THOMAS EDWARD   Shaw-Ede: T. E. Lawrence's Letters to H. S. Ede, 1927-35. Golden Cockerel Press, 1942. Crown 4to., quarter morocco by Sangorski and Sutcliffe, top edges gilt, others uncut, limited to 500 copies, fine. Broadhurst 24-769 1974 £70

LAWRENCE, THOMAS EDWARD   Shaw-Ede. 1942. Crown 4to., quarter morocco, limited. Broadhurst 23-1007 1974 £70

LAWRENCE, THOMAS EDWARD   Sir Thomas Lawrence. 1900. Imp. 4to., half crimson morocco, gilt, plates, illus., limited. Quaritch 940-159 1974 £28

LAWRENCE, THOMAS EDWARD   T. E. Lawrence's Letters to H. S. Ede, 1927-1935. Golden Cockerel Press, 1942. One of 500 numbered copies, small 4to., quarter crushed grain morocco, fine. Covent 51-2415 1973 £40

LAWRENCE, WILLIAM   Lectures on Physiology, Zoology and the Natural History of Man. 1819. 8vo., orig. boards, uncut, plates, rare, first edition. Wheldon 130-361 1974 £150

LAWRENCE, WILLIAM   Lectures On Physiology, Zoology and the Natural History of Man. 1819. 8vo., contemporary half calf, plates, very rare first edition. Wheldon 131-168 1974 £120

LAWRENCE, WILLIAM   A Treatise on Ruptures. London, 1810. 8vo., half calf, gilt, fine. Dawsons PM 249-335 1974 £28

LAWSON, A.   The Kingis Quair and the Quare of Jelusy. London, 1910. 8vo., illus., orig. cloth, presentation copy. Bow Windows 62-563 1974 £6.75

LAWSON, ALEXANDER   A St. Andrew's Treasury of Scottish Verse. 1920. Austin 61-578 1974 $12.50

LAWSON, G.   The Royal Water-Lily of South America. Edinburgh, 1851. 12mo., cloth, coloured plates, rebacked, scarce, library stamp, inscribed, presentation copy. Wheldon 128-1489 1973 £10

LAWSON, JOHN H.   Film In the Battle of Ideas. Mainstream, 1953. Austin 51-547 1973 $10

LAWSON, JOHN H.   The International. Macaulay, 1927. 276p. Austin 51-548 1973 $10

LAWSON, JOHN H.   Theory and Technique of Playwriting. Putnam, 1936. 315p., orig. hard cover ed. Austin 51-549 1973 $8.50

LAWSON, JOHN PARKER   The Book of Perth. Edinburgh, 1847. Orig. cloth, illus., frontispiece, limited edition. Howes 186-2178 1974 £7.50

LAWSON, PETER   The Agriculturalist's Manual. 1836. Orig. cloth-backed boards, printed label. Howes 186-1483 1974 £12.50

LAWTON, MARY   Schumann-Heink. Macmillan, 1928. 390p., illus. Austin 51-550 1973 $8.50

LAYARD, A. H.   Discoveries in the Ruins of Nineveh and Babylon With Travels in Armenia, Kurdistan and the Desert. 1853. 8vo., plates, woodcuts, cloth, fair copy, first edition. Quaritch 940-332 1974 £35

LAYARD, A. H.   Nineveh and Its Remains. 1849. 2 vols., 8vo., calf gilt, illus., first edition. Quaritch 940-331 1974 £40

LAYARD, E. L.   The Birds of South Africa. Cape Town, 1867. 8vo., half calf, rare, first edition. Wheldon 130-567 1974 £50

LAYARD, E. L.   The Birds of South Africa. 1875-84. Roy 8vo., half red morocco, plates, scarce. Wheldon 130-35 1974 £340

LAYARD, GEORGE SOMES   The Life and Letters of Charles Samuel Keene.
1893. Plates, illus., rubbed. Marsden 37-275 1974 £10

LAYARD, GEORGE SOMES   Shirley Brooks of Punch. 1907. Illus.
Austin 61-579 1974 $15

LAYARD, GEORGE SOMES   Suppressed Plates, Wood Engravings Etc. 1907.
Fine, plates, text illus., dec. cloth gilt, first edition. Covent 51-283 1973
£8.40

LAYARD, J.   Stone Men of Malekula Vao. 1942. Roy.
8vo., plates, orig. buckram, first edition. Smith 194-837 1974 £10

LAZARE, BERNARD   Anti-Semitism. 1908. 384 pages. Austin
57-367 1974 $15

LAZARE, BERNARD   Antisemitism. 1908. Austin 62-343 1974
$17.50

LAZARUS, EMMA   Letters to Emma Lazarus. 1939. Austin 57-
368 1974 $12.50

LAZESIO, FRANCESCO FELICIANO DA
Please turn to
FELICIANO DA LAZESIO, FRANCESCO

LEA, HENRY CHARLES   An Historical Sketch of Sacerdotal Celibacy in
the Christian Church. Boston, 1884. Jacobs 24-151 1974 $25

LEA, HENRY CHARLES   A History of the Inquisition of Spain. New
York and London, 1906-1907. 8vo., 4 vols., orig. blue cloth, gilt, fine. Dawsons PM 251-264 1974 £55

LEA, HENRY CHARLES   History of the Inquisition of the Middle Ages.
1922. 3 vols. Allen 213-1599 1973 $25

LEA, JOHN   Donald the Daring. New York, ca. 1930.
16mo., 4 color plates. Frohnsdorff 16-296 1974 $10

LEA, TOM   Peleiu Landing. El Paso, 1945. Marine
herringbone twill, drawings by author, signed by author, fine, slip case, morocco
title label, scarce, no. 151 of 500 copies, first edition. Dykes 22-203 1973
$350

LEACH, J. A.   A Descriptive List of the Birds Native to
Victoria, Australia. Melbourne, n.d. Crown 8vo., orig. wrappers, scarce.
Wheldon 131-641 1974 £7.50

LEACH, W. E.   The Zoological Miscellany. 1814-17.
3 vols., 8vo., contemporary red morocco backed boards, complete copy,
very rare. Wheldon 131-71 1974 £200

LEACOCK, STEPHEN   Back to Prosperity: The Great Opportunity of
the Empire Conference. Toronto, 1932. Hood's 102-384 1974 $7.50

LEACOCK, STEPHEN   Canada. Montreal, 1941. Quarter buckram,
fine, illus., English first edition. Covent 56-1869 1974 £5.25

LEACOCK, STEPHEN   Canada's War at Sea. Montreal, 1944. 2 vols.
in 1, illus. Hood's 104-120 1974 $25

LEACOCK, STEPHEN   Charles Dickens: His Life and Work. 1934.
Illus., first edition. Austin 61-584 1974 $10

LEACOCK, STEPHEN   College Days. Toronto, 1923. Hood's 102-
526 1974 $12.50

LEACOCK, STEPHEN   Literary Lapses. Montreal, 1910. 8vo., orig.
cloth, first edition. Rota 190-613 1974 £10

LEACOCK, STEPHEN   Moonbeams From the Larger Lunacy. New
York & London, 1920. Hood's 103-489 1974 $10

LEACOCK, STEPHEN   My Remarkable Uncle, and Other Sketches.
London, 1944. Hood's 103-490 1974 $17.50

LEACOCK, STEPHEN   Too Much College. New York, 1939. 8vo.,
orig. cloth, first edition. Rota 190-615 1974 £5

LEADBETTER, C.   The Young Mathematician's Companion. 1748.
Second edition, copperplate frontis., woodcut diagrams, 12mo., contemporary
calf. George's 610-459 1973 £20

LEAF, MUNRO   Noodle. New York, 1937. Oblong 4to.,
illus; 1st ed. Frohnsdorff 16-96 1974 $20

LEAHY, EDMUND   A Practical Treatise on Making and Repairing
Roads. London, 1844. 8vo., illus., quarter cloth boards. Emerald 50-516
1974 £5

LEAKE, W. M.   Travels in Northern Greece. 1835. Only
edition, plates, text illus., folding maps, 4 vols., orig. cloth, spines sunfaded,
else mint, largely unopened, armorial bookplate of S. Wegg. Thomas 32-347
1974 £225

LEAL, ANTONIO CASTRO   Twenty Centuries of Mexican Art. New York,
1940. Sm. 4to., illus. Biblo & Tannen 214-318 1974 $15

LEAMY, MARGARET   Parnell's Faithful Few. New York, 1936.
8vo., cloth boards, dust jacket. Emerald 50-517 1974 £5

LEAR, EDWARD   The Book of Nonsense. 1907. Oblong 4to.,
orig. blue cloth, gilt, illus., thirty-eighth authentic edition. Hammond 201-131
1974 £8

LEAR, EDWARD   Journal of a Landscape Painter in Albania.
1857. Roy. 8vo., plates, half calf, scarce. Quaritch 940-160 1974 £95

LEAR, EDWARD   Journal of a Landscape Painter in Corsica.
1870. Orig. brown cloth, plates, first edition. Marsden 39-269 1974 £35

LEAR, EDWARD   Journal of a Landscape Painter in Corsica.
1870. Roy. 8vo., plates, illus., cloth. Quaritch 940-162 1974 £45

LEAR, EDWARD   Journal of a Landscape Painter in Corsica.
1870. Large 8vo., orig. cloth, plates, illus. Covent 55-999 1974 £65

LEAR, EDWARD   Journals of a Landscape Painter In Southern
Calabria. 1852. Demy 8vo., orig. cloth, rebacked, plates. Thomas 28-330
1972 £40

LEAR, EDWARD   Journals of a Landscape Painter in Southern
Calabria. 1852. Roy. 8vo., maps, plates, orig. cloth, worn, scarce.
Quaritch 940-161 1974 £58

LEAR, EDWARD   Laughable Lyrics. London, 1877. 8vo.,
pictorial gilt cloth, bevelled edges, illus. by author, first edition. Frohnsdorff
16-489 1974 $125

LEAR, EDWARD   Laughable Lyrics. London, 1877. 8vo.,
cloth pict. stamped in black and gold, bevelled edges, illus. by author, first
edition. Frohnsdorff 15-87 1974 $125

LEAR, EDWARD   Lear in Sicily. 1938. Line drawings, coloured
frontis., small oblong 4to., fine. Covent 51-2418 1973 £6.30

LEAR, EDWARD   Nonsense Songs. London, n.d. Square 8vo.,
gilt pictorial cloth, bevelled edges, all edges gilt, color plates, drawings by
L. Leslie Brooke. Frohnsdorff 16-491 1974 $50

LEAR, EDWARD   Nonsense Songs, Stories, Botany and Alphabets.
1871. Drawings by author, small 4to., orig. cloth backed dec. boards, 1 leaf
misbound, very nice copy, first edition. Covent 51-1111 1973 £25

LEAR, EDWARD   Nonsense Songs Stories, Botany and Alphabets.
London, 1871. 8vo., boards, cloth spine, illus. by author, first edition.
Frohnsdorff 16-490 1974 $200

LEAVITT, T. W. H.   History of Leeds and Grenville, Ontario,
1749-1879. Brockville, 1879. Illus. Hood's 104-700 1974 $125

LEBERT, HERMANN   Physiologie Pathologique. Paris, 1845. 8vo.,
3 vols., contemporary half morocco, first edition. Schumann 35-272 1974 $135

LEBERT, HERMANN   Traite d'Anatomie Pathologique Generale et
Speciale ou Description et Iconographie Pathologique des Alterations. Paris,
1857. Large folio, 4 vols., old quarter leather, good copy, inscriptions. Gurney
66-101 1974 £185

LEBESON, ANITA LIBMAN   Jewish Pioneers in America. Brentanos, 1931.
372p., illus. Austin 62-344 1974 $17.50

LEBLANC, GEORGETTE   Le Choix de la Vie. Paris, 1904. 12mo.,
full grey-green morocco, uncut, first edition. L. Goldschmidt 42-276 1974
$25

LE BLANC, JEAN BERNARD   Letters on the English and French Nations. Dublin, 1747. 12mo., 2 vols., contemporary calf. Hill 126-155 1974 £12.50

LEBLANC, MAURICE   The Confessions of Arsene Lupin. New York,
1913. Plates, orig. pictorial cloth, first U.S. edition. Covent 56-335 1974
£8.40

LEBLANC, MAURICE   Eight Hundred and Thirteen. n.d. Pictorial
wrappers, English first edition. Covent 56-336 1974 £7.50

LE BLOND, GUILLAUME   L'Artiglieria per Principj. 1772. 8vo., 2 vols.,
orig. vellum, fine, plates, first edition in Italian. Dawsons PM 245-463 1974
£52

LEBOUR, M. V.   The Dinoflagellates of Northern Seas. Plymouth,
1925. Roy 8vo., cloth, plates, scarce. Wheldon 130-876 1974 £10

LE BRAZ, ANATOLE   La Legende de la Mort chez les Bretons
Armoricains. Paris, 1923. 2 vols., wrappers. Emerald 50-520 1974 £7.50

LE BRUN, CORNEILLE
Please turn to
BRUYN, CORNELIS DE

LEBRUN, V.   Vigee-Lebrun, 1755-1842. Her Life, Works,
and Friendships. (1915). 4to., plates, cloth, frontispiece. Quaritch
940-164 1974 £12

LECANU, L'ABBE   Dictionnaire des Propheties et des Miracles.
Paris, 1852-54. 2 vols., roy. 8vo., orig. leather, rebacked. Howes 185-1359
1974 £5

LE CAT, CLAUDE NICOLAS   Traite de la Couleur de la Peau Humaine en General. Amsterdam, 1765. 8vo., contemporary wrappers, worn, first edition. Schumann 35-273 1974 $115

LE CAT, CLAUDE NICOLAS   Traite des Sens. Amsterdam, 1744. 8vo., contemporary marbled calf, plates. Schumann 35-274 1974 $115

LECCHI, ANTONIO   Arithmetica Universalis. Milan, 1752. 8vo.,
3 vols., orig. stiff paper wrappers, uncut, fine, first edition. Dawsons PM 245-
566 1974 £55

LECK, BART VAN DER   Het Hooglied Van Salomo. Amsterdam, 1905.
Folio, dec. boards, half cloth, lithographs. Minters 37-249 1973 $85

LECKY, WILLIAM E. H.   A History of England in the 18th Century.
1878-90. 8 vols., large 8vo., orig. cloth, faded, orig. library edition.
Howes 186-1000 1974 £30

LECKY, WILLIAM E. H.   A History of Ireland in the Eighteenth Century.
London, 1906. 5 vols., 8vo., cloth boards. Emerald 50-521 1974 £20

LECKY, WILLIAM E. H.   A History of Ireland in the Eighteenth Century.
London, 1916. 5 vols., cloth boards. Emerald 50-522 1974 £20

LECKY, WILLIAM E. H.   Poems. 1891. Presentation copy inscribed by
author, bookplate, gilt top, fly leaf removed, nice copy, first edition. Covent
51-1112 1973 £12.50

LECLAIRE, A.   Historical, Legendary and Topographical Guide
Along the St. Lawrence. Montreal, 1906. Engravings, charts. Hood's
104-828 1974 $30

LE CLERC, CHARLES GABRIEL   La Medecine Aisee. Paris, 1719. Small 8vo.,
contemporary calf. Schumann 35-275 1974 $95

LE CLERC, DANIEL   Histoire de la Medecine. 1696. 12mo., contemporary speckled calf, first edition. Dawsons PM 249-337 1974 £95

LE CLERC, DANIEL   Histoire de la Medecine. La Haye, 1729.
4 parts in 1 vol., large 4to., contemporary calf, frontispiece, plates. Schuman
37-148 1974 $115

LECLERC, JEAN   Physica. 1700. 12mo., contemporary panelled
calf, labels, rare. Zeitlin 235-135 1974 $95

LE CLERC, SEBASTIEN   Practical Geometry. 1727. 8vo., calf,
illus with engraved figures. Bow Windows 66-419 1974 £25

LE CLERC, SEBASTIEN   Practical Geometry. London, 1742. Small 8vo.,
contemporary calf gilt, rebacked, worn, fourth edition. Dawsons PM 245-464
1974 £40

LE CLERC, SEBASTIEN   Principles of Design. 1794. Small 8vo.,
plates, modern boards. Quaritch 940-165 1974 £125

L'ECLUSE, CHARLES DE   Exoticorum Libri Decem. Curae Posteriores.
Leyden, 1605-11. 2 works in 1 vol., folio, contemporary vellum, first editions.
Wheldon 131-1129 1974 £350

LE COMPTE, LOUIS   Memoirs and Observations. London, 1697.
8vo., contemporary half calf, plates, first edition in English. Traylen 79-523
1973 £90

LECOMTE, GEORGES   Louis Charlot. Paris, 1926. 4to., wrapper,
unopened, illus., plates. Minters 37-82 1973 $18.50

LE CORBEAU, ADRIEN   The Forest Giant. 1924. Frontis., clothbacked
boards, owner's name & note on endpaper, else fine, worn d.w. Covent 51-2414
1973 £6.50

LE CORBEAU, ADRIEN   The Forest Giant. London, 1935. Fine, frayed
d.w., first illus. edition, wood engravings, orig. cloth. Crane 7-170 1974 £5

LE CORBUSIER, M.   The City of Tomorrow and its Planning. New
York, n.d. Cloth, dust wrapper, illus. Dawson's 424-231 1974 $40

LE CORBUSIER, M.   Towards a New Architecture. New York, n.d.
Cloth, dust wrapper, illus. Dawson's 424-232 1974 $40

LE CORBUSIER, M.   Towards a New Architecture. 1927. Crown
4to., orig. cloth, scarce. Broadhurst 23-127 1974 £20

LECOY DE LA MARCHE, ALBERT   Les Manuscrits et la Miniature. Paris, n.d.
(1884). Cloth, illus. Kraus B8-135 1974 $28

LEDEBOUR, K. F.   Flora Rossica. Stuttgart, 1842-53. 4 vols.,
8vo., buckram, extremely scarce, complete copy. Wheldon 131-1324 1974
£120

LEDEBOUR, K. F.   Flora Rossica. Stuttgart, 1842-53. 8vo.,
4 vols., buckram. Wheldon 129-1096 1974 £120

LEDERMULLER, MARTIN FROBENIUS   Physicalische Beobachtungen derer Saamen-
thiergens. Numberg, 1756. 4to., contemporary boards, first edition. Schumann
35-276 1974 $475

LEDWICH, E.   Antiquitates Sarisburiensis. Salisbury,
1771. 8vo., half calf, plates, first edition. Quaritch 939-577 1974 £8

LEDWICH, E.   Antiquities of Ireland. 1803. 4to., plates,
half russia, second edition. Quaritch 939-618 1974 £17.50

LEE, ANN ELIZABETH   The Fruits of the Valley. 1855. 8vo., contemporary dark blue morocco, gilt. Hill 126-156 1974 £10.50

LEE, CHAUNCEY   The American Accomptant. Lansingburgh,
1797. Full calf, worn, lacks frontis., with appendix, errata and list of subscribers.
Butterfield 10-5 1974 $15

LEE, EDWIN   The Mineral Springs of England. London, 1841.
8vo., orig. cloth, gilt, first edition. Hammond 201-584 1974 £12

LEE, FRANCIS BAZLEY   New Jersey as a Colony and as a State.   New York, 1902. 4 vols., fine.   Ballinger 1-287 1974 $45

LEE, GYPSY ROSE   Gypsy. Harper, 1957.   Austin 51-552 1973 $6.50

LEE, HANNAH FARNHAM   Elinor Fulton. Boston, 1837. 16mo., orig. cloth, first edition, text foxed & stained.   MacManus 224-274 1974 $32.50

LEE, HENRY   Memoirs of the War in the Southern Department of the United States. Philadelphia, 1812. 2 vols., full calf, portrait, foxed.   Jenkins 61-1357 1974 $85

LEE, JAMES   Career. Random, 1955.   Austin 51-551 1973

LEE, JAMES   An Introduction to Botany. 1776. 8vo., contemporary half calf, plates, third edition.   Wheldon 131-1167 1974 £30

LEE, JAMES   An Introduction to Botany. London, 1788. 8vo., contemporary calf, rebacked, gilt, plates, fourth edition.   Hammond 201-656 1974 £14.50

LEE, JAMES   An Introduction to Botany. Edinburgh, 1799. 8vo., contemporary calf, plates, rare, new improved edition.   Wheldon 131-1168 1974 £20

LEE, JOHN   Mormonism Unveiled. St. Louis, 1881. Orig. cloth, illus., worn.   Putnam 126-320 1974 $15

LEE, JOHN EDWARD   Note-Book of an Amateur Geologist. London, 1881. 8vo., orig. cloth, gilt, illus., plates, first edition.   Hammond 201-371 1974 £7.50

LEE, NATHANIEL   Constantine the Great. London, 1684. 4to., calf antique, first edition.   Dawsons 252-648 1974 £120

LEE, NATHANIEL   The Rival Queens. London, 1690. 4to., modern boards.   Dawsons PM 252-649 1974 £40

LEE, NATHANIEL   Theodosius. London, 1692. 4to., modern boards.   Dawsons PM 252-650 1974 £35

LEE, R.   Plants, Trees. London, (1854). Colored plates, 8vo., orig. cloth.   Gregory 44-184 1974 $35

LEE, ROBERT   Memoirs on the Ganglia and Nerves of the Uterus. 1849. 4to., boards, plates, scarce.   Wheldon 131-502 1974 £7.50

LEE, ROBERT   Memoirs of Ganglia and Nerves of the Uterus. 1849. 4to., binder's cloth, first edition.   Broadhurst 23-1243 1974 £12

LEE, SIDNEY   Elizabethan Sonnets, Newly Arranged. 1904. 2 vols.   Allen 216-1820 1974 $10

LEE, MRS. ROBERT
Please turn to
LEE, SARAH (WALLIS) BOWDICH, "MRS. ROBERT LEE"

LEE, SARAH (WALLIS) BOWDICH   Anecdotes of the Habits and Instinct of Animals. Philadelphia, 1856. Illus., orig. binding, signature sprung.   Wilson 63-396 1974 $13.75

LEE, SOPHIA   The Chapter of Accidents. 1780. 8vo., cloth, first edition.   Quaritch 936-129 1974 £20

LEE, SOPHIA   The Recess. Dublin, 1791. 2 vols., full calf, rubbed.   Emerald 50-252 1974 £35

LEE, VERNON PSEUD.
Please turn to
PAGET, VIOLET

LEE, W.   Ancient and Modern History of Lewes and Brighthelmston. Lewes, 1795. 8vo., calf, later rebacking, leather labels.   Traylen 79-395 1973 £15

LEECH, JOHN   Pictures of Life and Character. London, (1858). Oblong folio, pictorial boards, illus.   Rich Summer-81 1974 $22.50

LEECH, JOHN   Pictures of Life and Character; From the Collections of "Mr. Punch". 1886-87. 2 vols., 4to., orig. pictorial cloth gilt, bevelled edges, first edition, handsome set.   Covent 51-1113 1973 £12.50

LEEPER, DAVID R.   The Argonauts of '49. South Bend, 1894. First edition, very fine copy.   Jenkins 61-1359 1974 $75

LEERS, J. D.   Flora Herbornensis. Nassau, 1775. 8vo., new cloth, plates, rare, first edition.   Wheldon 130-1175 1974 £25

LEES, F.   The Art of the Great Masters as Exemplified by Drawings in the Collection of Emile Wauters. 1913. 4to., dec. cloth. Eaton Music-625 1973 $5

LEES, F. R.   An Inquiry Into the Reasons and Results of the Prescription of Intoxicating Liquors. 1866. 8vo., orig. limp cloth, foxing. Covent 55-712 1974 £5.25

LEESON, M. A.   History of Allen County, Ohio. Chicago, 1885. 8vo., illus., three quarter leather.   Saddleback 14-619 1974 $45

LEEUWEN, J. VAN   Prolegomena ad Aristophanem. 1908. New buckram.   Allen 213-80 1973 $12.50

LEEUWENHOEK, ANTHONY VAN   Opera Omnia. Leiden, 1722-1719. 4to., 4 vols., contemporary calf, rebacked, plates.   Dawsons PM 245-465 1974 £265

LE FANU, JOSEPH SHERIDAN   Chronicles of the Golden Friars. London, 1871. 3 vols., 8vo., orig. cloth, first edition.   Dawsons PM 252-653 1974 £75

LE FANU, JOSEPH SHERIDAN   A Chronicle of Golden Friars and Other Stories. London, 1896. First edition, scarce.   Biblo & Tannen 210-624 1973 $30

LE FANU, JOSEPH SHERIDAN   Green Tea and Other Ghost Stories. Sauk City, 1945. Limited to 2000 copies.   Biblo & Tannen 210-625 1973 $17.50

LE FANU, JOSEPH SHERIDAN   The House by the Churchyard. London, 1899. Biblo & Tannen 210-626 1973 $12.50

LE FANU, JOSEPH SHERIDAN   In a Glass Darkly. London, 1844. Biblo & Tannen 210-627 1973 $15

LE FANU, JOSEPH SHERIDAN   Madam Crowl's Ghost and Other Tales of Mystery. London, 1923. First edition.   Biblo & Tannen 210-628 1973 $15

LE FANU, SHERIDAN   The Fortunes of Colonel Torlogh O'Brien. Dublin, 1847. Full polished tree calf, plates, fine, first edition.   Howes 185-296 1974 £55

LE FANU, JOSEPH SHERIDAN   Works. Dublin & London, 1845-96. 50 vols., 8vo., half morocco, gilt, fine.   Dawsons PM 252-652 1974 £1950

LE FANU, T. P.   Memoir of the Le Fanu Family. Small 4to., illus., limited.   Emerald 50-525 1974 £7.50

LE FAURE, GEORGES   Aventures Extraordinaires d'un Savant Russe. Paris, 1889. Large 8vo., red quarter morocco, illus., first edition.   Dawsons PM 245-466 1974 £30

LEFEBVRE, THEODORE   Les Modes de Vie dans les Pyrenees Atlantiques Orientales. Paris, 1933. Roy. 8vo., illus., orig. wrappers, maps.   Howes 186-1484 1974 £7.50

LEFEVRE, RAOUL   The Recuyell of the Historyes of Troye. 1892. 8vo., limp vellum with ties.   Hammond 201-726 1974 £400

LEFEVRE, RAOUL   The Recuyell of the Historyes of Troye. Hammersmith, 1892. 3 parts in 2 vols., folio, orig. limp vellum, fine.   Dawsons PM 252-654 1974 £575

LEFFERTS, SARAH T.   Land of Play Verses-Rhymes-Stories. New York, (1911). Illus., square 8vo., colored frontis., pages browned with age, pictorial colored front cover, rebacked.   Current BW9-117 1974 $16.50

LEFRANCQ, P.   Cartulaire de l'Abbaye de Saint-Cybard.
1930. New buckram.   Allen 213-1602 1973 $10

LEFROY, H. M.   Indian Insect Life. Calcutta, 1909. Small
4to., new cloth, scarce, plates.   Wheldon 130-771 1974 £30

LEFROY, H. M.   Indian Insect Pests. Calcutta, 1906. Roy.
8vo., orig. dec. cloth, very scarce.   Wheldon 128-756 1973 £10

LEFROY, J. H.   Magnetical and Meteorological Observations.
London, 1855. 8vo., orig. brown cloth, uncut, plates, inscribed, first edition.
Dawsons PM 245-467 1974 £20

LEFROY, W. CHAMBERS   The Ruined Abbeys of Yorkshire. 1883. 4to.,
etchings, illus., orig. cloth.   Bow Windows 66-420 1974 £5.25

THE LEGACY of the Exposition, San Francisco, 1915. San Francisco, 1916.
Boards.   Jenkins 61-349 1974 $27.50

LE GALLIENNE, EVA   At 33. Longman, 1934. 262p., illus.
Austin 51-553 1973 $7.50

LE GALLIENNE, RICHARD   The Book-Bills of Narcissus. 1891. Small
paper edition, limited to 250 copies, very good, wrappers, errata slip tipped in,
scarce, first edition.   Covent 51-1116 1973 £10.50

LE GALLIENNE, RICHARD   The Book-Bills of Narcissus. Derby, 1892.
Second edition, presentation copy inscribed, spine somewhat faded, nice, orig.
binding.   Ross 86-309 1974 $25

LE GALLIENNE, RICHARD   The Book-Bills of Narcissus. London, 1895.
Frontis., name in ink on free fly, covers somewhat worn, nice, orig. binding.
Ross 86-310 1974 $10

LE GALLIENNE, RICHARD   English Poems. 1892. Crown 8vo., orig.
boards, uncut, label, foxed, limited, first edition.   Howes 186-301 1974 £10

LE GALLIENNE, RICHARD   English Poems. 1892. Demy 8vo., orig.
boards, limited, first edition.   Howes 185-298 1974 £18

LE GALLIENNE, RICHARD   The Junk-Man and Other Poems. Garden City,
1921. Presentation copy, inscribed by author, fine, orig. binding.   Ross
86-311 1974 $25

LE GALLIENNE, RICHARD   Odes From the Divan of Hafiz. 1903. Austin
61-598 1974 $10

LE GALLIENNE, RICHARD   An Old Country House. 1905. Illus. Austin
61-599 1974 $12.50

LE GALLIENNE, RICHARD   The Quest of the Golden Girl. London &
New York, 1896. 8vo., uncut, orig. cloth, faded, first edition.   Bow
Windows 62-566 1974 £5.50

LE GALLIENNE, RICHARD   The Religion of a Literary Man. London, 1893.
Some dust staining, else fine, orig. binding.   Ross 86-312 1974 $25

LE GALLIENNE, RICHARD   The Romance of Perfume. New York & Paris,
1928. Coloured plates, orig. dec. boards, small hole in upper joint, very fine
copy, illus. prospectus in pocket at end.   Covent 51-2143 1973 £12

LE GALLIENNE, RICHARD   Rudyard Kipling: A Criticism. 1900. Austin
61-601 1974 $12.50

LE GALLOIS, SIEUR   Traitte des Plus Belles Bibliotheques de
l'Europe. Paris, 1685. Small 8vo., calf, rebacked, foxed.   Thomas 28-116
1972 £21

LEGATI, L.   Museo Cospiano Annesso a Quello del Famoso
Ulisse Aldrovandi. Bologna, 1677. Folio, parchment, rare.   Wheldon 128-43
1973 £90

LE GENDRE, LOUIS   Nouvelle Histoire de France. Paris, 1718.
3 vols., folio, contemporary calf, morocco labels, first edition.   Howes
186-1002 1974 £35

LEGG, J. WICKHAM   English Church Life From the Restoration to
the Tractarian Movement. 1914. Frontispiece.   Howes 185-1362 1974 £5

LEGG, J. WICKHAM   Inventories of Christchurch Canterbury. 1902.
Faded, scarce.   Howes 185-1363 1974 £6

LEGG, J. WICKHAM   Inventories of Christchurch Canterbury. 1902.
Presentation, scarce.   Howes 186-2053 1974 £10

LEGGE, C.   A Glance at the Victoria Bridge, and the Men
Who Built It. Montreal, 1860. Paper cover.   Hood's 102-764 1974 $30

LEGGE, W. VINCENT   A History of the Birds of Ceylon. 1878-80.
4to., 2 vols., new half morocco.   Wheldon 129-26 1974 £300

LEGGE, W. VINCENT   A History of the Birds of Ceylon. 1878-80.
4to., 2 vols., contemporary half morocco, plates.   Wheldon 130-36 1974 £500

LEGGE, W. VINCENT   A History of the Birds of Ceylon. 1878-80.
2 vols., 4to., new half morocco, plates.   Wheldon 131-72 1974 £300

LEGH, GERARD   The Accedens of Armory. 1562. 8vo., plates,
contemporary panelled calf, rebacked, first edition.   Dawsons PM 251-126 1974
£195

THE LEGION Book. 1929. 4to., buckram, illus., numbered, signed, fine.
Covent 55-40 1974 £35

LEGOUIS, EMILE   Defense de la Poesie Francaise a l'Usage des
Lecteurs Anglais. New York, 1912. 8vo., cloth, uncut.   L. Goldschmidt
42-278 1974 $10

LEGOUVE, GABRIEL   Le Merite des Femmes et Autres Poesies.
Paris, 1813. 12mo., full cherry red morocco, gilt.   L. Goldschmidt 42-279
1974 $175

LEGRAND, EMILE   Bibliographie Hellenique. 1928. Vol. 2
only.   Allen 213-617 1973 $10

LE GUERCHOIS, MADELEINE D'AGUESSEAU   Avis d'Une Mere a Son Fils.
Paris, 1743. 12mo., contemporary calf, gilt.   L. Goldschmidt 42-68 1974
$15

LEHMAN, C. G.   Physiological Chemistry. London, 1851-54.
8vo., 3 vols., orig. green blind-stamped cloth.   Dawsons PM 245-468 1974 £15

LEHMANN, C.   Novarum et Minus Cognitarum Stirpium Decimus.
Hamburg, 1857. 4to., sewed, rare, presentation copy.   Wheldon 128-1387
1973 £5

LEHMANN, CARL GOTTHELF   Physiological Chemistry. London, 1851-54.
3 vols., 8vo., cloth, rebacked, first English edition.   Schuman 37-149 1974
$135

LEHMANN, H.   Die Kinematographie. Leipzig, 1911. Illus.,
English first edition.   Covent 56-1631 1974 £7.50

LEHMANN, HERMAN   Nine Years Among the Indians, 1870-1879.
Austin, 1927. Near mint.   Jenkins 61-1361 1974 $27.50

LEHMANN, JOHN   New Writings In England. 1939. Austin
61-603 1974 $12.50

LEHMANN, JOHN   Prometheus and the Bolsheviks. n.d. Illus.
Austin 61-605 1974 $17.50

LEHMANN, LOTTE   My Many Lives. New York, 1948. Illus.
Biblo & Tannen 214-874 1974 $10

LEHMANN, W.   The Art of Old Peru. 1924. Roy. 4to., cloth,
faded spine, plates, very scarce.   Quaritch 940-333 1974 £32

LEHMANN, WALTER   Die Chirurgie der Peripheren
Nervenverletzungen. Berlin & Vienna, 1921. Large 8vo., orig. cloth-backed
boards, first edition.   Schuman 37-150 1974 $75

LEIBNIZ, GOTTFRIED WILHELM   Oeuvres Philosophiques & Francoises.
Amsterdam & Leipzig, 1765. 4to., contemporary boards, vellum back, vignette,
rare first edition.   Harper 213-100 1973 $450

LEICESTER, ROBERT DUDLEY   Correspondence During His Government of the Low Countries, 1585-86. 1844. Allen 213-1332 1973 $10

LEICESTER, ROBERT DUDLEY   Secret Memoirs of. London, 1706. 8vo., contemporary calf, gilt. Hammond 201-454 1974 £12

LEIDY, J.   Fresh-Water Rhizopods of North America. Washington, 1879. 4to., cloth, plates, scarce. Wheldon 130-877 1974 £20

LEIDY, J.   Fresh-Water Rhizopods of North America. Washington, 1879. 4to., cloth, coloured plates, scarce. Wheldon 128-910 1973 £20

LEIGH, CHARLES   The Natural History of Lancashire, Cheshire and the Peak in Derbyshire. Oxford, 1700. Folio, engraved plates, nice clean copy, nineteenth century half calf. Wheldon 128-209 1973 £50

LEIGH, CHARLES   The Natural History of Lancashire, Cheshire and the Peak in Derbyshire. Oxford, 1700. Folio, plates 19th century half calf. Wheldon 131-370 1974 £50

LEIGH, CHARLES   The Natural History of Lancashire, Cheshire, and the Peak, in Derbyshire. Oxford, 1700. Folio, contemporary panelled calf, rebacked. Dawsons PM 251-43 1974 £90

LEIGH, J. E. AUSTEN   Recollections of the Early Days of the Vine Hunt. 1865. 8vo., orig. cloth, first edition. Broadhurst 23-1157 1974 £6

LEIGH, J. E. AUSTEN   Recollections of the Early Days of the Vine Hunt and Its Founder, William John Chute, Together with Brief Notices of the Adjoining Hunt. 1865. First edition, 8vo., orig. cloth, fine, inscribed presentation copy. Broadhurst 24-1123 1974 £6

LEIGH, R. A. AUSTEN   By Gone Eton, 1622-1905. Eton, 1906. Orig. buckram backed boards, plates, drawings. Smith 193-183 1973 £5

LEIGHTON, CAROLINE   Life at Puget Sound With Sketches of Travel in Washington Territory, British Columbia, Oregon, and California, 1865-81. Boston, 1884. Ex-library. Jenkins 61-2576 1974 $10

LEIGHTON, G. R.   The Life-History of British Serpents. 1901. 8vo., cloth, illus., scarce. Wheldon 130-703 1974 £5

LEIGHTON, JOHN   The Life of Man. 1866. 4to., full morocco, gilt, fine, English first edition. Covent 56-702 1974 £25

LEIGHTON, R.   Rules and Instructions for a Holy Life. London, 1835. Orig. plum silk, 2 1/2 X 1 5/8. Gregory 44-404 1974 $32.50

LEIGHTON, W. A.   The British Species of Angiocarpous Lichens Elucidated by Their Sporidia. 1851. 8vo., cloth, coloured plates, scarce. Wheldon 128-1388 1973 £7.50

LEIGHTON, W. A.   The Lichen Flora of Great Britain, Ireland and the Channel Islands. Shrewsbury, 1879. 8vo., cloth, third edition. Wheldon 131-1432 1974 £7.50

LEIGHTON, W. A.   The Lichen-Flora of Great Britain. Shrewsbury, 1872. Post 8vo., cloth, rare, second edition. Wheldon 129-1407 1974 £7.50

LEIGHTON, W. A.   The Lichenflora of Great Britain, Ireland and the Channel Islands. Shrewsbury, 1879. 8vo., cloth, third edition. Wheldon 128-1389 1973 £7.50

LEIGHTON, WILLIAM, JR.   At the Court of King Edwin. Lippincott, 1877. 157p. Austin 54-625 1973 $15

LEININGEN-WESTERBURG, KARL EMICH   German Book-Plates. London, 1901. 8vo., orig. cloth gilt, plates, first English edition. Dawsons PM 10-355 1974 £8

LEISERSON, WILLIAM   Adjusting Immigrant and Industry. 1924. Orig. edition. Austin 57-371 1974 $10

LEISTE, CHRISTIAN   Neue Einrichtung der Luft-pumpe. (1770). 4to., modern boards, first edition. Dawsons PM 245-469 1974 £20

LE JAY, GABRIEL FRANCOIS   Le Triomphe de la Religion Sous Louis Le Grand Represente Par des Inscriptions & des Devises. Paris, 1687. 8vo., half vellum, portrait, plates, fine. Harper 213-101 1973 $175

LEJEUNE, A. L. S.   Compendium Florae Belgicae. Liege, 1828-36. Post 8vo., cloth, scarce. Wheldon 130-1176 1974 £15

LEJEUNE, E.   Les Rois et Reines de France en Estampes. (c. 1860). Oblong 4to., plates, gilt, orig. cloth. Quaritch 940-726 1974 £35

LE JEUNE, L.   Dictionnaire General de Biographie Histoire . . . . . du Canada. Ottawa, 1931. 2 vols., three quarter leather, marbled boards. Hood's 104-34 1974 $100

LEKAIN, HENRI LOUIS KAIN   Memoires. Paris, 1825. Contemporary three quarter tan polished calf, gilt. L. Goldschmidt 42-280 1974 $55

LELAND, CHARLES GODFREY   Hans Breitmann's Ballads. Peterson, 1869. Austin 54-643 1973 $12.50

LELAND, CHARLES GODFREY   Hans Breitmann's Ballads. Peterson, 1869. Austin 62-347 1974 $10

LELAND, CHARLES GODFREY   Hans Breitmann's Ballads. 1870. New enlarged and complete edition. Austin 57-372 1974 $12.50

LELAND, CHARLES GODFREY   Hans Breitmann's Ballads. Peterson, 1870. New edition. Austin 62-348 1974 $12.50

LELAND, CHARLES GODFREY   Pidgin-English Sing-Song. London, 1876. 8vo., orig. cloth, inscribed, presentation, fare, first English edition. Dawsons PM 252-655 1974 £20

LELAND, JOHN   A Blow at the Root. New-London, 1801. Orig. binding. Butterfield 10-338 1974 $20

LELAND, JOHN   Commentarii de Scriptoribus Britannicis. 1709. 8vo., 2 vols., sheep rebacked, gilt, first edition. Hill 126-158 1974 £35

LELAND, JOHN   The Itinerary in Wales Of. 1906. 8vo., orig. cloth, uncut. Broadhurst 23-1441 1974 £10

LELAND, JOHN   The Itinerary of. London, 1906-10. Square 8vo., 5 vols., orig. blue cloth, gilt. Dawsons PM 251-44 1974 £50

LELAND, JOHN   De Rebus Britannicis Collectanea. Oxford, 1715. 6 vols. in 3, 8vo., plates, morocco backs. Quaritch 939-159 1974 £40

LELAND, THOMAS   The History of Ireland. 1773. 3 vols., 4to., modern boards. Quaritch 939-619 1974 £15

LELAND, THOMAS   The History of Ireland from the Invasion of Henry II. Dublin, 1773. 3 vols., 4to., full calf. Emerald 50-526 1974 £22

LELAND, THOMAS   Longsword, Earl of Salisbury. 1762. 12mo., 2 vols., contemporary calf, first edition. Quaritch 936-130 1974 £90

LELIEVRE, J. F.   Nouveau Jardinier de la Louisiane. New Orleans, 1838. Boards, worn. Jenkins 61-1400 1974 $15

LELLO, G. LUIGI   Historia Della Chiesa di Monreale. Roma, 1596. 4 parts in 1 vol., 4to., boards, very scarce, fine. Harper 213-102 1973 $275

LELONG, JACQUES   Bibliotheque Historique de la France, Contenant le Catalogue des Ouvrages, Imprimes & Manuscrits, Qui Traitent de l'Histoire de ce Royaume. Paris, 1768-78. 5 vols., folio, contemporary calf, rebacked. Kraus B8-138 1974 $500

LE LOYER, PIERRE, SIEUR DE LA BROSSE   A Treatise of Specters of Straunge Sights. 1605. Small 4to., full calf, inscriptions, sole English edition. Howes 186-1872 1974 £85

LE MAIR, H. WILLEBEEK   Our Old Nursery Rhymes. New York, (1911). Oblong 4to., cloth, color plates engraved, very good copy. Frohnsdorff 16-492 1974 $35

LEMAIRE, C.   Cactearum Aliquot Novarum ac Insuetarum in
Horto Monvilliano Cultarum Accurata Descriptio. Paris, 1838. 4to., orig.
wrappers, rare. Wheldon 131-1672 1974 £10

LEMAIRE, C.   Les Cactees. Les Plantes Grasses. Paris, 1868.
2 works in 1 vol., small 8vo., cloth. Wheldon 131-1673 1974 £7.50

LE MAOUT, E.   Histoire Naturelle des Oiseaux Suivant la
Classification de Geoffroy-Saint-Hilaire. Paris, 1855. Imp. 8vo., half
morocco gilt, coloured and plain plates, second edition. Wheldon 128-503
1973 £15

LE MAOUT, E.   Traite General de Botanique. Paris, 1876.
Small folio, half morocco, text-figures, second edition. Wheldon 128-1124
1973 £7.50

LEMERY, LOUIS   A Treatise of all Sorts of Foods. London, 1745.
8vo., polished calf, gilt. Hammond 201-171 1974 £70

LEMERY, LOUIS   A Treatise of All Sorts of Foods, Both Animal
and Vegetable. 1745. Full panelled calf, gilt, raised bands, first edition.
Covent 55-693 1974 £165

LEMERY, NICOLAS   A Course of Chymistry. London, 1686. 8vo.,
calf, plates. Gurney 64-128 1974 £95

LEMERY, NICOLAS   A Course of Chymistry. London, 1686. 8vo.,
calf, some worming. Gurney 66-103 1974 £95

LE METTRIE, JULIEN OFFRAY DE   Oeuvres Philosophiques. Berlin, 1775.
12mo., 3 vols., contemporary boards, morocco labels, nice set. Gurney 66-98
1974 £90

LEMMON, H. GALLIENNE   Public Rights in the Seashore. 1934. Roy.
8vo., cloth, bookplate. Howes 186-2184 1974 £8.50

LEMNIUS, LEVINUS   De Habitu et Constitutione Corporis. 1551.
Stamped pigskin. Allen 213-1603 1973 $125

LEMNIUS, LEVINUS   An Herbal for the Bible. 1587. 8vo.,
contemporary sheep, neatly rebacked, rare. Wheldon 128-1684 1973 £100

LEMNIUS, LEVINUS   An Herbal for the Bible. 1587. 8vo., contemporary sheep. Wheldon 130-1616 1974 £100

LEMNIUS, LEVINUS   De Occultis Naturae Miraculis. Cologne,
1573. 8vo., contemporary pigskin over boards, nice copy. Schafer 8-166
1973 sFr. 600

LEMOINE, J. M.   Chateau Bigot. Quebec, 1874. Orig.
wrappers, mottled boards. Hood's 103-775 1974 $35

LEMOINE, J. M.   Historical Notes On Quebec and Its Environs.
Quebec, 1887. Bookplate, inscribed, second edition. Hood's 103-776 1974
$17.50

LE MOINE, J. M.   Maple Leaves, 1894. Quebec, 1894.
Hood's 104-651 1974 $17.50

LEMOINE, J. M.   Picturesque Quebec. Montreal, 1882. Maps,
mended spine. Hood's 103-777 1974 $35

LEMON, MARK   Tom Moody's Tales. London, 1864. 8vo.,
orig. red cloth, gilt, spine bit rubbed, first edition, plates. Ximenes 36-137
1974 $25

LEMONNIER, CAMILLE   Constantin Meunier, Sculptre et Peintre. Paris,
1904. 4to., half morocco, English first edition. Covent 56-1480 1974 £21

LEMONNIER, CAMILLE   Un Male. Brussels, (1881). 12mo., uncut,
contemporary full red cloth, first edition. L. Goldschmidt 42-282 1974 $22.50

LEMONNIER, LEON   Histoire du Far-West. Paris, 1948. Biblo &
Tannen 213-63 1973 $7.50

LE MONNIER, PIERRE CHARLES   Description et Usage des Principaux Instruments
d'Astronomie. 1774. Roy folio, orig. blue wrappers, fine, uncut, first edition.
Zeitlin 235-138 1974 $275

LEMPRIERE, J.   Classical Dictionary of Proper Names Mentioned
in Ancient Authors. New York, 1949. Biblo & Tannen 214-631 1974 $12.50

LENARD, PHILIPP   Uber Kathodenstrahlen. Leipzig, 1906.
8vo., orig. pictured wrappers, illus., first edition. Schuman 37-151 1974 $110

LENDNER, A.   Les Mucorinees de la Suisse. Berne, 1908.
8vo., cloth, plates. Wheldon 129-1260 1974 £5

LENGYEL, EMIL   Americans From Hungary. Lippincott, 1948.
Austin 62-350 1974 $12.50

LENIN, VLADIMIR ILYICH   Marxism. London, 1929. 8vo., orig. wrappers,
first separate English edition. Dawsons PM 247-174 1974 £10

LENIN, VLADIMIR IL'ICH   O Gosvdarstue. (Kharkov), 1924. 8vo., orig.
paper wrappers, text in Russian, first collected edition. Bow Windows 66-421
1974 £16

LENIN, VLADIMIR ILYICH   Will the Bolsheviks Maintain Power? London,
1922. Small 8vo., orig. cloth, first English edition. Dawsons PM 247-175
1974 £15

LENNOX, CHARLOTTE   The Female Quixote. London, 1752. 2 vols.,
12mo., contemporary calf, fine, second edition. Dawsons PM 252-552 1974
£55

LENNOX, CHARLOTTE   Shakespear Illustrated. 1753-54. 12mo., 3
vols., speckled calf, first edition. Quaritch 936-131 1974 £25

LE NOIR, ABBE   Dictionnaire des Droits de la Raison dans la Foi.
Paris, 1860. Thick roy. 8vo., half morocco. Howes 185-1364 1974 £5

LE NOIR, ABBE   Dictionnaire des Harmonies de la Raison et de
la Foi. Paris, 1856. Thick roy. 8vo., half roan. Howes 185-1365 1974
£5.50

LENORMAND, H. R.   Failures. Knopf, 1923. 231p. Austin 51-554
1973 $8.50

LE NORMAND, VICTORINE   The Oracle of Human Destiny. London, 1825.
8vo., boards. Hammond 201-357 1974 £14.50

LENSKI, LOIS   Two Brothers and Their Baby Sister. New
York, 1930. Cloth with pict. label, illus., first edition, 7" X 5 3/8".
Frohnsdorff 15-92 1974 $10

LENSKI, LOIS   The Washington Picture-Book. New York,
1930. Oblong 4to., pictorial boards, full color illus. by author, first edition.
Frohnsdorff 16-499 1974 $15

LENT, EDWARD B.   Being Done Good. Brooklyn, 1904.
Rittenhouse 46-408 1974 $10

LENYGON, FRANCIS PSEUD.
Please turn to
JOURDAIN, MARGARET

Note: L. C. Enters under Lenygon
      Weinreb claims it is a Pseud. for Jourdain

LEO, FRIEDRICH   Geschichte der Roemischen. 1913. New
buckram. Allen 213-620 1973 $17.50

LEO, FRIEDRICH   Plautinische Forschungen zur Kritik und
Geschichte der Komoedie. 1912. Worn spine. Allen 213-864 1973 $10

LEON, ACHILLE   Lives of the Saints and Blessed of the Three
Orders of Saint Francis. Taunton, 1885-87. 4 vols. Howes 185-1368 1974
£10

LEON PINELO, ANTONIO DE   Question Moral si el Chocolate Quebranta el
Ayuno Eclesiastico. Madrid, 1636. Small 4to., Spanish mottled calf, first
and only edition. Harper 213-105 1973 $675

LEONARD, C. H.   The Hair, Diseases and Treatment. Detroit,
1881. Broken spine. Rittenhouse 46-409 1974 $12.50

LEONARD, EDDIE   What a Life. 1934. Austin 51-555 1973
$12.50

LEONARD, IRVING A.   The Mercurio Volante of Don Carlos de
Siguenza Y Gongora. Los Angeles, 1932. One of 35 on Rives paper, signed by
the editor. Jenkins 61-1846 1974 $65

LEONARD, IRVING A.   Spanish Approach to Pensacola, 1689-1693.
Albuquerque, 1939. Limited to 550 copies. Jenkins 61-891 1974 $30

LEONARD, LEWIS ALEXANDER   Life of Alphonso Taft. New York, (1920).
8vo., orig. bindings. Butterfield 8-417 1974 $20

LEONARD, R. M.   A Book Of Light Verse. 1910. Orig. edition.
Austin 61-606 1974 $10

LEONARD, WILLIAM ELLERY   The Fragments of Empedocles Translated Into
English Verse. Chicago, 1908. 12mo., boards, cloth back, first edition.
Goodspeed's 578-181 1974 $15

LEONARD, ZENAS   Adventures of Zenas Leonard, Fur Trapper and
Trader, 1831-1836. Cleveland, 1904. Limited to 520 copies. Jenkins
61-1364 1974 $85

LEONARDO DA VINCI   The Drawings of. Cambridge, 1935. 4to.,
2 vols., orig. cloth, plates. Broadhurst 23-39 1974 £45

LEONARDO DA VINCI   The Drawings of Leonardo da Vinci. New York,
1945. 3 vols., orig. cloth. Jacobs 24-47 1974 $35

LEONARDO DA VINCI   The Notebooks of. New York, n.d. Orig.
cloth, 2 vols., illus. Jacobs 24-47 1974 $35

LEONARDO DA VINCI   Trattato della Pittura, Novamente Dato in Luce,
con la Vita dell'Istesso Autore, Scritta dc Rafaelle du Fresne. Paris, 1651. Large
folio, full page engraved portraits, vignettes, contemporary vellum over boards,
first edition, illus., splendid copy. Schafer 10-150 1974 sFr 4,600

LEONARDO DA VINCI   Trattato Della Pittura. Rome, 1817. 2 vols.
in 1, large 4to., contemporary boards, gilt leather back, plates, fine. Harper
213-103 1973 $475

LEONARDO DA VINCI   A Treatise of Painting. 1721. 8vo., half
calf, rebound, plates, clean crisp copy. Quaritch 940-166 1974 £125

LEONARDO DA VINCI   A Treatise on Painting. 1796. 8vo., plates,
contemporary boards, uncut, new edition. Quaritch 940-167 1974 £20

LEONARDUS DE UTINO   Sermones de Sanctis. (Augsburg), 1474.
Thick folio, contemporary wooden boards, blind-stamped calf. Harper 213-104
1973 $850

LEONE, R. P.   Stvdivm Sapientiae Vniversalis. 1657. Folio,
old vellum, woodcuts, maps. Zeitlin 235-139 1974 $350

LEONHARD, KARL CASAR VON   Lehrbuch der Geognosie. Stuttgart, 1835.
Thick 8vo., half contemporary calf. Zeitlin 235-282 1974 $45

LEONHARD, KARL CASAR VON   Naturgeschichte des Mineralreichs. Heidelberg, 1831. 8vo., contemporary half tree calf, gilt. Zeitlin 235-283 1974
$27.50

LEONI, I.   Some Designs for Buildings Both Publick and
Private. 1726. Folio, plates, orig. boards, calf spine. Quaritch 940-527
1974 £75

LEONI, LEONE   Leone Leoni, Sculpteur de Charles. 1887.
Small folio, plates, half red morocco, gilt, fine. Quaritch 940-169 1974 £30

LEONICENUS THOMAEUS, NICOLAUS   Opuscula. 1532. Small folio, new
mottled morocco, gilt. Dawsons PM 249-338 1974 £160

LEONICENUS THOMAEUS, NICOLAUS   Opvsvla Nvper in Lvcem Aedita.
1525. 8vo., 18th century vellum, first edition. Dawsons PM 249-339 1974 £180

LEONICENUS THOMAEUS, NICOLAUS   Opuscula Nuper in Lucem Aedita.
1525. Rittenhouse 46-410 1974 $275

LEONOWENS, MRS. ANNA H.   The Romance of the Harem. Boston, 1873.
Biblo & Tannen 210-1003 1973 $15

LEOTAUD, VINCENT   Magnetologia. 1668. 4to., contemporary paper
boards, uncut, first edition. Dawsons PM 245-470 1974 £235

LE PAUTRE, JEAN   Oeuvres d'Architecture de Jean le Pautre
Dessinateur des Batimens du Roy. Paris, 1751. 3 vols., folio, plates, modern
calf antique. Quaritch 940-528 1974 £500

LE PETIT, JULES   Bibliographie des Principales Editions Originales
d'Ecrivans Francais. Paris, 1888. Large 8vo., contemporary half morocco,
uncut, first edition. Dawsons PM 10-358 1974 £40

LEPSIUS, C. RICHARD   Konigsbuch der Alten Agypter Von. Berlin,
1858. 2 parts in 1 vol., 4to., orig. cloth backed boards, covers worn, uncut,
plates, foxed. Bow Windows 66-422 1974 £22

LE QUEUX, WILLIAM   The Mystery of a Motor-Car. 1906. Orig.
pictorial cloth, bookplate, English first edition. Covent 56-337 1974 £5.25

LE QUEUX, WILLIAM   The Rainbow Mystery. (1917). 8vo., orig.
cloth, presentation inscription, first edition. Rota 190-314 1974 £8

LEREBOULLET, A.   Recherches d'Embryologie Comparee sur le Developpement du Brochet. 1862. 4to., half morocco, plates. Wheldon 130-704
1974 £10

LERNER, ALAN JAY   Paint Your Wagon. Coward-McCann, 1952.
Austin 51-556 1973 $7.50

LEROND D'ALEMBERT, JEAN
Please turn to
ALEMBERT JEAN LEROND D'

LEROQUAIS, ABBE V.   Exposition de Manuscrits a Peintures du VIe au
XVII e Siecle. Lyons, 1920. Loose in wrappers, 4to., plates. Kraus B8-139
1974 $75

LEROQUAIS, ABBE V.   Le Breviaire-Missel du Prieure Clunisien de
Lewes. Paris, 1935. Plates, 4to., wrappers, author's autograph signature &
presentation inscription. Kraus B8-140 1974 $35

LEROQUAIS, ABBE V.   Le Breviaire - Missel Du Prieure Clunisien de
Lewes. Paris, 1935. Small 4to., plates, orig. printed paper wrappers, slight
foxing, bookplate. Bow Windows 66-679 1974 £10

LEROQUAIS, ABBE V.   Un Livre d'Heures Manuscrit a l'Usage de
Macon. Macon, 1935. 8vo., wrappers, unopened, author's autograph signature
and inscription. Kraus B8-141 1974 $20

LE ROSSIGNOL, J. E.   Little Stories of Quebec. Cincinnati, 1908.
Illus. Hood's 102-723 1974 $7.50

LE ROUX, HUGES   Acrobats and Mountebanks. 1890. Illus.,
front hinge cracked, very good copy, first edition. Covent 51-406 1973 £12.50

LE ROY, LOUIS   De la Vicissitude ou Variete des Choses en
l'Univers. Paris, 1575. Folio, modern calf, raised bands, rare first edition.
Schafer 8-124 1973 sFr. 2,200

LE ROY, LOYS   Les Politiques d'Aristote, Esquelles est Monstree
la Science de Gouverner le Genre Humain en Toutes Especes d'Estats Publique.
Paris, 1576. Folio, contemporary calf, gilt, very fine, some occasional stains.
Schafer 10-104 1974 sFr 1,300

LEROY, LOUIS   La Vicissitudine O Mutabile Varieta Delle
Cose Nell' Universo. 1585. Small 4to., roxburghe binding, woodcut title.
Thomas 30-122 1973 £35

LE SAGE, ALAIN RENE   The Adventures of Gil Blas of Santillane. 1792.
12mo., 4 vols., half calf, gilt. Quaritch 936-132 1974 £40

LE SAGE, ALAIN RENE   The Adventures of Gil Blas of Santillane. 1812.
Frontis., contemporary calf, 4 vols. Bow Windows 64-590 1974 £7.50

LE SAGE, ALAIN RENE   Adventures of Gil Blas de Santillane.   London, 1819. 3 vols., cold aquatints, demy 8vo., contemporary diced calf gilt, bit rubbed, some foxing.   Forster 97-210 1974 £10

LE SAGE, ALAIN RENE   Asmodeus.   1841. Roy. 8vo., half crimson levant morocco gilt, fine.   Howes 185-301 1974 £12

LESAGE, P. C.   Deuxieme Recueil de Divers Memoires Extraits de la Bibliotheque Imperiale des Ponts et Chaussees a l'Usage de M. M. les Ingenierus.   1808. Roy. 4to., plates, contemporary half leather, presentation copy.   Quaritch 940-529 1974 £32

LESKY, W. E. H.   A History of England In the Eighteenth Century.   1907. 7 vols., contemporary dark green polished calf gilt.   Smith 194-702 1974 £28

LESLIE   Narrative of Discovery and Adventure In the Polar Seas and Regions.   New York, 1831. Woodcuts, scarce, American first edition.   Rinsland 58-62 1974 $55

LESLIE, CHARLES ROBERT   Handbook for Young Painters.   London, 1870. 8vo., contemporary crimson morocco, gilt, plates, illus., second edition.   Hammond 201-713 1974 £6

LESLIE, CHARLES ROBERT   Life and Letters of John Constable.   1896. 4to., plates, illus., buckram, gilt.   Quaritch 940-61 1974 £25

LESLIE, JOHN   Elements of Geometry, Geometrical Analysis, and Plane Trigonometry.   Edinburgh, 1811. 8vo., contemporary half calf, gilt, second edition.   Hammond 201-873 1974 £6

LESLIE, SHANE   The Hyde Park Pageant.   1930. Wrappers, fine.   Covent 55-1000 1974 £5.25

LESLIE, SHANE   Masquerades.   1924. Author's copy with his bookplate & ex libris label, signed inscription by him, very good.   Covent 51-2419 1973 £12.50

LESLIE, SHANE   Poems.   1928. Small 4to., buckram, unopened, signed, English first edition.   Covent 56-823 1974 £12.50

LESLIE, T. W.   The Legislative Buildings of Manitoba.   Winnipeg, 1925. Illus.   Hood's 104-860 1974 $15

LE SOUEF, A. S.   The Wild Animals of Australasia.   1926. 8vo., cloth, illus., scarce.   Wheldon 129-386 1974 £25

LE SOUEF, A. S.   The Wild Animals of Australasia Embracing the Mammals of New Guinea and the Nearer Pacific Islands.   1926. 8vo., cloth, illus., very scarce, nice copy.   Wheldon 131-503 1974 £25

LESPERANCE, J.   The Bastonnais: A Tale of the American Invasion of Canada in 1775-78.   Toronto, 1877. Hood's 102-527 1974 $25

LESPINASSE, R.   The Great Cataract.   Chicago, 1885. Orig. wrappers, illus.   Hood's 103-654 1974 $25

LESQUEREUX, L.   Contributions to the Fossil Flora of the Western Territories.   Washington, 1874-83. 4to., orig. brown cloth.   Wheldon 130-945 1974 £40

LESSEPS, FERDINAND MARIE DE   Percement de l'Isthme de Suez.   Paris, 1855-57. 4 vols., 8vo., maps, contemporary half calf, fine, first edition.   Gilhofer 61-48 1974 sFr. 550

LESSER, ALLEN   Enchanting Rebel.   1947. 284p., illus.   Austin 62-351 1974 $12.50

LESSER, F. C.   Theologie des Insectes.   The Hague, 1742. 2 vols., 8vo., contemporary calf, plates.   Wheldon 131-826 1974 £30

LESSON, R. P.   Centurie Zoologique. Paris, 1830 - (1832). 4to., boards, leather back, plates, rare.   Wheldon 131-440 1974 £20

LE STRANGE, HAMON   History of Freemasonry in Norfolk, 1724-1895.   Norwich, 1896. 8vo., orig. cloth, frontispiece, bookplate.   Bow Windows 66-255 1974 £8.50

LE TELLIER, C. C.   Le Fabuliste des Demoiselles, Precede d'un Exercice sur l'Apologue.   Paris, 1826. 12mo., contemporary wrappers, faded, fine internally, uncut, partly unopened.   George's 610-467 1973 £5

LE TELLIER, C. C.   Manuel Mythologique de la Jeunesse, ou Instruction sur la Mythologie.   Paris, 1812. Copperplates, 12mo., half calf, slightly rubbed, joints tender.   George's 610-468 1973 £7.50

LETH, H. DE   Het Zegenpralend Kennemerland.   c. 1730. Large folio, half vellum, uncut, engravings.   Quaritch 940-170 1974 £200

LETI, GREGORIO   The Life of Donna Olimpia Maldachini.   London, 1667. 8vo., contemporary sheep, fine.   Dawsons PM 251-508 1974 £55

LETI, GREGORIO   The Life of Pope Sixtus V.   1754. Folio, contemporary half morocco, sole English edition.   Howes 186-1218 1974 £30

LETI, GREGORIO   Il Nipotismo di Roma, or the History of the Popes Nephews.   1669. First edition in English, old calf, joints repaired, sides pitted, else excellent crisp condition, armorial bookplate, Campbell of Stackpole Court.   Thomas 32-130 1974 £25

A LETTER from A Gentleman in Yorkshire.   1695. Small 4to., new half morocco.   Quaritch 939-591 1974 £30

A LETTER from Toby of Totness to Caleb d'Anvers Esqr.   (London, 1732?). Plates, folio, frayed.   Ximenes 35-21 1974 $250

A LETTER to a Member of Parliament Concerning the Present State of Affairs at Home and Abroad.   London, 1740. 8vo., modern quarter calf, gilt.   Dawsons PM 247-178 1974 £20

A LETTER To a Member of Parliament, On the Settling a Trade To the South-Sea of America.   (London), n.d. 8vo., quarter calf, scarce, first edition.   Ximenes 35-252 1974 $70

A LETTER to a Member of Parliament Relating to the Bill for the Opening of a Trade.   London, 1741. 8vo., modern boards, first edition.   Dawsons PM 247-179 1974 £38

A LETTER to Lord George Germaine, Giving an Account of the Origin of the Dispute Between Great Britain and the Colonies.   London, 1778. 8vo., modern boards.   Dawsons PM 247-176 1974 £15

A LETTER To the Right Honourable The Earl of Buckinghamshire, President of the Board of Commissioners for the Affairs of India, on the Subject of an Open Trade to India.   1813. 8vo., marbled paper wrappers, first edition.   Bow Windows 66-423 1974 £7.50

LETTERS from a Celebrated Nobleman to his Heir.   1783. Small 8vo., old wrappers, rare, first edition.   Hill 126-48 1974 £65

LETTERS OF Distinguished Musicians.   1867. 8vo., contemporary calf, gilt.   Hill 126-181 1974 £12.50

THE LETTERS of Junius.   1770. Small 8vo., contemporary half sheep.   Hill 126-146 1974 £18

LETTERS of Mrs. Riversdale.   London, 1803. 3 vols., 12mo., orig. blue boards, first edition, excellent copy.   Ximenes 36-84 1974 $125

LETTSOM, JOHN COAKLEY   The Naturalist's and Traveller's Companion.   London, 1774. 8vo., old half calf, rubbed, second edition, scarce.   Ximenes 36-138 1974 $75

LEUPOLD, JACOB   Theatrum Machinarum Hydrotechnicarum.   Leipzig, 1724. Folio, contemporary half vellum, plates, first edition.   Dawsons PM 245-473 1974 £90

LEUPOLD, JACOB   Theatri Machinarum Hydraulicarum.   Leipzig, 1724-5. Folio, 2 vols., contemporary half vellum, fine, plates, first edition.   Dawsons PM 245-471 1974 £265

LEUPOLD, JACOB   Theatrum Machinarum Generale.   Leipzig, 1724. Folio, contemporary half vellum, plates, first edition.   Dawsons PM 245-472 1974 £195

LEVANT, OSCAR   The Memoirs of an Amnesiac. Putnam, 1965. Austin 51-557. 1973 $6

LEVANT, OSCAR   The Unimportance of Being Oscar. Putnam, 1968. 255p., illus. Austin 51-558 1973 $6.50

LE VASSEUR, LEON   Ephemerides Ordinis Cartusiensis. 1890-93. 5 vols., 4to., half morocco, rubbedl Howes 185-1369 1974 £60

LE VAYER DE BOUTIGNY, ROLAND   The Famous Romance of Tarsis and Zelie. London, 1685. Folio, contemporary calf, first English edition. Dawsons PM 252-656 1974 £145

LEVER, CHARLES   Barrington. 1863. 8vo., plates, half calf gilt, first edition. Quaritch 939-620 1974 £10

LEVER, CHARLES   Charles O'Malley, the Irish Dragoon. (1841). 2 vols., half morocco, worn, plates, illus. by Phiz, first edition in book form. Allen 216-870 1974 $15

LEVER, CHARLES   Charles O'Malley, the Irish Dragoon. Dublin, 1842. 2 vols., 8vo., orig. cloth, illus. Emerald 50-538 1974 £7

LEVER, CHARLES   Confessions of Con. Cregan. (1860). 2 vols., 8vo., illus., half calf. Quaritch 939-621 1974 £10

LEVER, CHARLES   Cornelius O'Dowd Upon Men and Women. Edinburgh, & London, 1864-65. 3 vols., 8vo., orig. cloth gilt, fine, first edition. Quaritch 939-622 1974 £20

LEVER, CHARLES   The Daltons. London, 1852. 2 vols., 8vo., illus., full green leather. Emerald 50-539 1974 £7.50

LEVER, CHARLES   The Daltons or Three Roads in Life. London, 1852. 2 vols. in 1, first edition bound from parts, 8vo., plates nearly all clear, binding bit rubbed, illus. by Phiz. Current BW9-245 1974 $32.50

LEVER, CHARLES   The Knight of Gwynne. London, 1872. 8vo., illus., half green roan. Emerald 50-540 1974 £7.50

LEVER, CHARLES   Luttrell of Arran. London, 1865. 8vo., plates, orig. cloth, first edition. Dawsons PM 252-657 1974 £15

LEVER, CHARLES   Maurice Tiernay. n.d. Tall 8vo., rubbed, half contemporary calf gilt. Smith 194-486 1974 £5

LEVER, CHARLES   Maurice Tiernay, The Soldier of Fortune. London, n.d. 8vo., contemporary half morocco, very good copy, first edition. Ximenes 37-128 1974 $27.50

LEVER, CHARLES   Roland Cashel. London, 1850. 8vo., dark green half morocco, gilt, first edition. Dawsons PM 252-658 1974 £16

LEVER, CHARLES   Tales of Trains. London, 1845. 8vo., later half morocco, spine gilt, very good copy, first edition. Ximenes 37-129 1974 £30

LEVEY   Bob Norberry. Dublin, 1844. 8vo., plates, half calf, morocco label, first edition. Dawsons PM 252-659 1974 £15

LEVIN, MEYER   The Golden Mountain. 1932. 357 pages, illus. Austin 57-376 1974 $10

LEVINGTON, JOHN   Scripture Baptism Defended. Chicago, 1867. Cloth, third edition. Hayman 57-317 1974 $10

LEVINSON, ANDRE   La Danse d'Aujourd Hui. Paris, 1929. 4to., illus., rebound, English first edition. Covent 56-295 1974 £52.50

LEVITT, SAUL   The Andersonville Trial. Random, 1960. 120p., illus. Austin 51-559 1973 $6.50

LEVRET, ANDRE   Essai sur l'abus des Regles. Paris, 1766. 8vo., quarter calf, first edition. Gumey 64-129 1974 £20

LEVRET, ANDRE   Observations sur la Cure Radicale de Plusiers. Paris, 1749. 8vo., contemporary mottled calf, first edition. Dawsons PM 249-341 1974 £80

LEVRET, ANDRE   Observations sur les Causes et les Accidens de Plusieurs Accouchemens Laborieux. Paris, 1747. 8vo., marbled calf, rubbed, first edition. Schuman 37-152 1974 $160

LEVRING, T.   Six Taxonomic Papers on Marine Algae. Sweden, 1937-59. Large 8vo., wrappers. Wheldon 131-1433 1974 £10

LEVY, MELVIN   Gold Eagle Guy. Random, 1935. 188p. Austin 51-560 1973 $8.50

LEVYNS, M. R.   A Guide to the Flora of the Cape Peninsula. Cape Town, (1929). 8vo., cloth, illus. Wheldon 131-1325 1974 £5

LEWES, GEORGE HENRY   The Physiology of Common Life. Edinburgh & London, 1859-60. 2 vols., small 8vo., contemporary half calf, first edition. Schuman 37-153 1974 $85

LEWES, GEORGE HENRY   Sea-Side Studies at Ilfracombe. 1858. 8vo., orig. cloth, plates. Wheldon 129-222 1974 £10

LEWIN, JOHN WILLIAM   A Natural History of the Birds of New South Wales. 1822. Imp. 4to., modern half levant morocco gilt, plates. Wheldon 131-73 1974 £1,250

LEWIN, JOHN WILLIAM   A Natural History of the Birds of New South Wales, Collected, Engraved, and Faithfully Painted after Nature. 1822. Folio, dark brown levant morocco by Bayntun, panelled back, marbled boards, very fine copy, hand coloured etched plates entirely free from foxing. Broadhurst 24-1124 1974 £1,000

LEWIN, PHILIP   The Foot and Ankle, Their Injuries, Diseases, Deformities and Disabilities. Philadelphia, 1940. Rittenhouse 46-412 1974 $15

LEWINE, J.   Bibliography of 18th Century Art and Illustrated Books. London, 1898. Large 8vo., plates, cloth, limited, first edition. Dawsons PM 10-359 1974 £27

LEWINE, J.   Bibliography of Eighteenth Century Art and Illustrated Books. 1898. Thick imp. 8vo., half morocco, plates, limited, orig. edition. Howes 185-738 1974 £30

LEWIS, ALFRED HENRY   Wolfville. New York, (1897). Orig. red cloth, first edition, first issue. Bradley 35-311 1974 $40

LEWIS, ALFRED HENRY   Wolfville Days. New York, (1902). Fine, pictorial red cloth, frontispiece, first edition. Bradley 35-312 1974 $40

LEWIS, ALFRED HENRY   Wolfville Foulks. New York, 1908. Pictorial brick colored cloth, first edition. Bradley 35-219 1974 $20

LEWIS, B. PALMER   John Hardie of Thornhill his Life, Letters and Times. New York, (1928). 8vo., orig. bindings, inscribed. Butterfield 8-6 1974 $15

LEWIS, CECIL DAY
Please turn to
DAY-LEWIS, CECIL

Caution: There is a Lewis, Cecil

LEWIS, CLIVE STAPLES   The Allegory of Love. 1938. English first edition. Covent 56-1870 1974 £10.50

LEWIS, CLIVE STAPLES   Hamlet: The Prince or the Poem? 1942. Fine, presentation copy, inscribed by author, wrappers, first edition. Covent 51-1124 1973 £6.30

LEWIS, CLIVE STAPLES   The Screwtape Letters. London, 1942. First edition, very good copy, scarce, orig. cloth. Crane 7-176 1974 £5

LEWIS, CLIVE STAPLES   Spirits in Bondage, a Cycle of Lyrics. London, 1919. First edition, very nice copy, rare, orig. cloth. Crane 7-175 1974 £20

LEWIS, CLIVE STAPLES   The Voyage of the Dawn Treader. London, n.d., 1st ed. Biblo & Tannen 210-749 1973 $15

LEWIS, CLIVE STAPLES   The Weight of Glory. 1942. Wrappers, English first edition. Covent 56-826 1974 £12.50

LEWIS, C. T. COURTNEY   The Picture Printer of the Nineteenth Century. London, 1911. Orig. pictorial cloth, gilt, plates. Dawson's 424-133 1974 $85

LEWIS, DAVID   Miscellaneous Poems by Several Hands. 1726. 8vo., contemporary calf, gilt. Quaritch 936-134 1974 £42

LEWIS, FLORENCE   Cours de Peinture sur Procelaine. Paris, 1883. Brown cloth, plates. Dawson's 424-112 1974 $30

LEWIS, G. B.   The Life and Troubles of Mr. Bower. Jamieson, Higgins, 1902. 441p., illus. Austin 54-642 1973 $12.50

LEWIS, GEORGE GRIFFIN   The Practical Book of Oriental Rugs. 1920. Small thick 4to., dec. cloth, faded, plates, fifth edition. Quaritch 940-408 1974 £35

LEWIS, GRACE H.   With Love From Gracie. Harcourt, 1955. 335p. Austin 54-627 1973 $8.50

LEWIS, HARRISON   Lewis Technique of Acting. 1942. Austin 51-561 1973 $7.50

LEWIS, HENRY CARVILL   Papers and Notes on the Glacial Geology of Great Britain and Ireland. 1894. 8vo., cloth, illus. Hammond 201-372 1974 £10

LEWIS, J.   The History and Antiquities. 1736. 4to., plates, illus., contemporary calf, second edition. Quaritch 939-410 1974 £90

LEWIS, J. SYDNEY   Old Glass and How to Collect it. n.d. Illus., worn. Covent 55-462 1974 £7.50

LEWIS, J. VANCE   Out of the Ditch. Houston, 1910. Cloth. Hayman 57-446 1974 $20

LEWIS, JOHN   The History and Antiquities Ecclesiastical and Civil of the Isle of Tenet in Kent. London, 1723. 4to., old half calf, first edition. Dawsons PM 251-45 1974 £70

LEWIS, JOHN FREDERICK   History of the Apprentices' Library. Philadelphia, 1924. 8vo., boards, illus., inscribed. Rich Summer-82 1974 $10

LEWIS, LLOYD   It Takes All Kinds. Harcourt, 1947. 276p. Austin 54-626 1973 $7.50

LEWIS, MATTHEW GREGORY   The Isle of Devils. 1912. One of 20 numbered copies on large paper, half cloth, covers somewhat warped & rubbed at edges, else very good, first edition. Covent 51-1126 1973 £25

LEWIS, MATTHEW GREGORY   The Monk. London, n.d. 2 vols., limited to 300 copies, uncut. Biblo & Tannen 210-756 1973 $18.50

LEWIS, MATTHEW GREGORY   The Monk. c. 1880. 2 vols., rebacked, limited edition. Allen 216-1014 1974 $12.50

LEWIS, MATTHEW GREGORY   Tales of Terror and Wonder. 1887. Printed label, worn, English first edition. Covent 56-828 1974 £5.25

LEWIS, MATTHEW GREGORY   Tales of Wonder. London, 1801. 2 vols., tall 8vo., contemporary tree calf, first edition. Dawsons PM 252-660 1974 £75

LEWIS, OSCAR   The Lost Years. Knopf, 1951. 121p. Austin 54-628 1973 $6.50

LEWIS, PERCY WYNDHAM
Please turn to
LEWIS, WYNDHAM

LEWIS, SAMUEL   Lewis's Atlas. London, 1846. 4to., orig. cloth, gilt, scarce. Emerald 50-546 1974 £25

LEWIS, SAMUEL   A Topographical Dictionary of England. 1831-35. 2 vols., 4to., orig. cloth. Smith 193-236 1973 £5

LEWIS, SAMUEL   A Topographical Dictionary of England. 1840. 4 vols., 4to., buckram, fourth edition. Quaritch 939-161 1974 £15

LEWIS, SAMUEL   A Topographical Dictionary of England. 1842. 5 vols., 4to., orig. cloth, fifth edition. Howes 186-2081 1974 £38

LEWIS, SAMUEL   A Topographical Dictionary of England. 1845. 4 vols., 4to., orig. cloth gilt, fifth edition. Smith 194-299 1974 £30

LEWIS, SAMUEL   A Topographical Dictionary of England, Wales, Scotland and Ireland. 1849-51. 13 vols., 4to., orig. cloth, fine. Quaritch 939-160 1974 £110

LEWIS, SINCLAIR   Ann Vickers. Garden City, 1933. First edition, limited to 2,350 copies on rag paper, d.w. worn, some foxing, else fine. Ross 87-355 1974 $17.50

LEWIS, SINCLAIR   Babbitt. New York, (1922). First edition, first state, lacks d.j., orig. binding. Butterfield 10-339 1974 $15

LEWIS, SINCLAIR   Bethel Merriday. Doubleday, 1940. 390p. Austin 54-628 1973 $6

LEWIS, SINCLAIR   Bethel Merriday. New York, 1940. Early printing, good d.j., orig. binding. Butterfield 10-340 1974 $8

LEWIS, SINCLAIR   Cass Timberlaine. Random, 1945. 390p., orig. ed. Austin 54-629 1973 $4.50

LEWIS, SINCLAIR   Cass Timberlane. New York, 1945. Orig. binding, lacking d.w., first edition, fine. Ross 87-357 1974 $10

LEWIS, SINCLAIR   Elmer Gantry. New York, (1927). First edition, first state, orig. binding. Butterfield 10-341 1974 $10

LEWIS, SINCLAIR   Elmer Gantry. 1927. Fresh copy, first issue with "Cantry" on spine. Allen 216-1270 1974 $20

LEWIS, SINCLAIR   Elmer Gantry. New York, (1927). First edition, 8vo., fine, card with author's signature laid in. Current BW9-246 1974 $22.50

LEWIS, SINCLAIR   Elmer Gantry. New York, 1927. First edition, first binding, with uncorrected "G", some browning, name & date in ink on fly leaf, nice. Ross 87-358 1974 $30

LEWIS, SINCLAIR   Free Air. New York, 1919. First edition. Butterfield 10-342 1974 $25

LEWIS, SINCLAIR   From Main Street to Stockholm. Harcourt, 1952. 307p. Austin 54-641 1973 $12.50

LEWIS, SINCLAIR   Gideon Planish. Random, 1943. 439p. Austin 54-630 1973 $6.50

LEWIS, SINCLAIR   Gideon Planish. New York, (1943). First printing in d.j., orig. binding. Butterfield 10-343 1974 $10

LEWIS, SINCLAIR   The God Seeker. Random, 1949. 422p. Austin 54-631 1973 $6

LEWIS, SINCLAIR   The Innocents. New York & London, (1917). First edition, orig. binding. Butterfield 10-345 1974 $17.50

LEWIS, SINCLAIR   It Can't Happen Here. Collier, 1935. 458p. Austin 54-633 1973 $5

LEWIS, SINCLAIR   It Can't Happen Here. Doubleday, Doran, 1935. 458p. Austin 54-632 1973 $6

LEWIS, SINCLAIR   It Can't Happen Here. New York, 1935. 1st ed. Biblo & Tannen 214-748 1974 $10

LEWIS, SINCLAIR   It Can't Happen Here. New York, 1935. First edition, orig. binding, name in ink on free fly leaf, lacking d.w., nice. Ross 87-359 1974 $10

LEWIS, SINCLAIR It Can't Happen Here. New York, 1935.
1st ed. Biblo & Tannen 210-757 1973 $12.50

LEWIS, SINCLAIR John Dos Passos' Manhattan Transfer. New
York & London, 1926. Limited to 975 copies, orig. binding. Butterfield 10-347
1974 $12.50

LEWIS, SINCLAIR Kingsblood Royal. Random, 1947. 348p.
Austin 54-634 1973 $5

LEWIS, SINCLAIR Main Street. New York, 1920. First edition,
first issue, with perfect type lower right hand corner of p. 387 and perfect folio
at p. 54, blue cloth, name in ink on free fly leaf, lacking d.w., near fine. Ross
87-360 1974 $35

LEWIS, SINCLAIR The Man Who Knew Coolidge. New York,
1928. 1st ed. Jacobs 24-103 1974 $20

LEWIS, SINCLAIR Mantrap. 1926. First edition. Allen
216-1272 1974 $10

LEWIS, SINCLAIR Our Mr. Wrenn. New York & London, 1914.
First edition, small white spot on backstrip, orig. binding. Butterfield 10-348
1974 $35

LEWIS, SINCLAIR Prodigal Parents. Collier, 1938. 30lp.
Austin 54-635 1973 $5

LEWIS, SINCLAIR Prodigal Parents. Doubleday, Doran, 1938.
30lp. Austin 54-636 1973 $6.50

LEWIS, SINCLAIR Selected Short Stories. Garden City, 1935.
First edition, orig. binding. Butterfield 10-350 1974 $8.50

LEWIS, SINCLAIR Storm in the West. Stein and Day, 1963.
192p., illus. Austin 54-640 1973 $8.50

LEWIS, SINCLAIR The Trail of the Hawk. New York & London,
(1915). First edition, orig. binding. Butterfield 10-351 1974 $75

LEWIS, SINCLAIR Work of Art. Collier, 1934. 452p. Austin
54-638 1973 $5

LEWIS, SINCLAIR Work of Art. Doubleday, 1934. 452p.
Austin 54-637 1973 $6

LEWIS, SINCLAIR Work of Art. Garden City, 1934. First edition,
good d.j., orig. binding. Butterfield 10-352 1974 $12.50

LEWIS, SINCLAIR Work of Art. Garden City, 1934. Purple
cloth, slight foxing on foredge, else fine, unusually well preserved d.w. Ross
87-361 1974 $15

LEWIS, SINCLAIR World So Wide. Random, 1951. 250p.
Austin 54-639 1973 $6.50

LEWIS, SYNDHAM The Wild Body. London, 1927. 1st ed.
Biblo & Tannen 210-758 1973 $15

LEWIS, T. A Welsh Leech Book, or, Llyfr o Feddyginiaeth.
Liverpool, 1914. Plates, crown 8vo., orig. cloth, binding little faded,
presentation inscription. Broadhurst 24-1550 1974 £10

LEWIS, THOMAS Lectures on the Heart. New York, 1915.
Jacobs 24-154 1974 $18

LEWIS, W. The Apes of God. 1930. 4to., cloth, orig. dust-
wrapper, limited, signed, first edition. Quaritch 936-472 1974 £40

LEWIS, W. Commercium Philosophico-Technicum. London,
1763-5. 4to., 2 vols., old half calf, repaired, large folding frontis., plates.
Gurney 66-104 1974 £75

LEWIS, WILLIAM An Experimental History of the Materia Medica.
1761. Coloured frontispiece, 4to., modern calf, sound if slightly amateur
binding. Thomas 32-319 1974 £28

LEWIS, WILLIAM An Experimental History of the Materia Medica.
1761. 4to., modern calf. Thomas 28-265 1972 £28

LEWIS, WILLIAM An Experimental History of the Materia Medica.
London, 1768. Large 4to., contemporary calf, worn. Schuman 37-154 1974
$115

LEWIS, WILLIAM An Experimental History of the Materia Medica.
London, 1768. Large 4to., contemporary calf, second edition. Schumann 35-
277 1974 $135

LEWIS, WYNDHAM Blasting and Bombardiering. 1937. Plates,
first edition. Howes 186-304 1974 £12.50

LEWIS, WYNDHAM The Caliph's Design. 1919. Orig. stiff marbled wrappers, English first edition. Covent 56-830 1974 £22.50

LEWIS, WYNDHAM The Caliph's Design. 1919. Stiff wrappers,
English first edition. Covent 56-829 1974 £25

LEWIS, WYNDHAM The Diabolical Principle and the Dithyrambic
Spectator. 1931. Crown 8vo., orig. cloth, faded, first edition. Howes 186-
305 1974 £10.50

LEWIS, WYNDHAM The Diabolical Principle and the Dithyrambic
Spectator. 1931. First edition, crown 8vo., d.w., orig. cloth, fine.
Broadhurst 24-774 1974 £12

LEWIS, WYNDHAM Doom of Youth. 1932. Bookplate, name on
fly, else nice copy, scarce. Covent 51-2423 1973 £17.50

LEWIS, WYNDHAM Filibusters in Barbary. New York, 1932. First
U. S. edition, plates, fine, worn d.w. Covent 51-2424 1973 £7.50

LEWIS, WYNDHAM The Ideal Giant: The Code of a Herdsman:
Cantleman's Spring-Mate. (1917). Wire-stitched & strung on silk thread into
portfolio, as issued, boards little soiled, fresh clean copy internally, very scarce.
Ross 86-318 1974 $225

LEWIS, WYNDHAM The Jews: Are They Human? 1939. Scarce,
very good copy, first edition. Covent 51-1128 1973 £12.50

LEWIS, WYNDHAM Men Without Art. London, 1934. Lacking
d.w., some dust staining, nice copy. Ross 86-319 1974 $30

LEWIS, WYNDHAM The Mysterious Mr. Bull. 1938. English first
edition. Covent 56-1872 1974 £6.50

LEWIS, WYNDHAM The Mysterious Mr. Bull. 1938. Very good
copy, slightly frayed d.w., first edition, fore edges marked. Covent 51-1130
1973 £12.50

LEWIS, WYNDHAM Satire and Fiction. n.d. Small 4to., orig.
wrappers, English first edition. Covent 56-833 1974 £17.50

LEWIS, WYNDHAM Satire and Fiction. 1930. 4to., wrappers,
first edition. Rota 189-568 1974 £5

LEWIS, WYNDHAM Tarr. New York, 1918. Orig. binding, first
edition, has signature of Edward J. O'Brien on the end paper with Latin quotation
in his hand, small nick in faded spine, nice copy, scarce. Ross 87-363 1974
$140

LEWIS, WYNDHAM Tarr. New York, 1918. First edition, small
nic in faded spine, nice copy, rare, signature of Edward J. O'Brien. Ross 86-320
1974 $160

LEWIS, WYNDHAM Time and Western Man. London, 1927. First
edition, lacking d.w., glassine wrapper, fine, tight copy. Ross 87-364 1974
$27.50

LEWIS, WYNDHAM The Wild Body, A Soldier of Humor and Other
Stories. London, 1927. Orig. binding, first edition, d.w. somewhat darkened,
else fine. Ross 87-365 1974 $75

LEWIS, WYNDHAM Wyndham Lewis the Artist from 'Blast' to
Burlington House. 1939. Orig. cloth, illus. Marsden 37-293 1974 £10

LEWISOHN, LUDWIG   Adam. Harper, 1929. Austin 62-356 1974
$12.50

LEWISOHN, LUDWIG   The Answer. Liveright, 1939. Austin 62-357
1974 $8.50

LEWISOHN, LUDWIG   Breathe Upon These. Bobbs, Merrill, 1944.
Austin 62-358 1974 $7.50

LEWISOHN, LUDWIG   The Broken Snare. Dodge, 1908. 289p.
Austin 62-359 1974 $17.50

LEWISOHN, LUDWIG   The Case of Mr. Crump. Paris, 1926. 4to.,
orig. printed wrappers (somewhat soiled & worn), first edition, limited to 500
numbered copies for America, signed by author, very good copy. MacManus
224-276 1974 $40

LEWISOHN, LUDWIG   Case of Mr. Crump. 1930. 318 pages.
Austin 57-388 1974 $10

LEWISOHN, LUDWIG   Creative America. 1933. 749 pages.
Austin 57-390 1974 $12.50

LEWISOHN, LUDWIG   The Creative Life. Boni, Liveright, 1924.
Austin 62-360 1974 $10

LEWISOHN, LUDWIG   The Creative Life. 1924. 211 pages.
Austin 57-391 1974 $10

LEWISOHN, LUDWIG   Expression in America. Harper, 1932.
Austin 62-361 1974 $10

LEWISOHN, LUDWIG   Expression in America. 1932. 624 pages.
Austin 57-392 1974 $10

LEWISOHN, LUDWIG   For Ever Wilt Thou Love. Dial, 1939.
Austin 62-362 1974 $12.50

LEWISOHN, LUDWIG   Haven. 1940. 340 pages. Austin 57-393
1974 $10

LEWISOHN, LUDWIG   The Island Within. Harper, 1928. 350p.
Austin 62-364 1974 $6.50

LEWISOHN, LUDWIG   Israel. Boni, Liveright, 1925. 280p., orig.
ed. Austin 62-363 1974 $6

LEWISOHN, LUDWIG   A Jew Speaks. Harper, 1931. Austin 62-365
1974 $12.50

LEWISOHN, LUDWIG   The Last Days of Shylock. Harper, 1939.
Austin 62-366 1974 $6

LEWISOHN, LUDWIG   The Magic Word. Farrar, 1950. Austin
62-367 1974 $10

LEWISOHN, LUDWIG   Mid-Channel. Harper, 1929. Austin 62-368
1974 $6

LEWISOHN, LUDWIG   The Modern Drama. Huebsch, 1916. 340p.
Austin 62-369 1974 $12.50

LEWISOHN, LUDWIG   The Permanent Horizon. Harper, n.d. 223p.,
orig. ed. Austin 62-370 1974 $10

LEWISOHN, LUDWIG   This People. Harper, 1933. Austin 62-371
1974 $12.50

LEWISOHN, LUDWIG   Up Stream. Boni, Liveright, 1922. 248p.,
orig. ed. Austin 62-372 1974 $5

LEWISOHN, SAM A.   Painters and Personality. New York, 1948.
Biblo & Tannen 210-236 1973 $12.50

LEWORTHY, W.   The Trial Between William Leworthy and the
Globe Insurance Company. 1810. 8vo., calf. Quaritch 939-540 1974 £20

LEWYS, GEORGES   Temple of Pallas-Athenae. 1924. Boxed,
signed, limited edition. Allen 216-1020 1974 $10

LEYBOURN, WILLIAM   Arithmetick. London, 1657. 8vo., contemporary calf, rebacked, fine, first edition. Dawsons PM 245-474 1974 £125

LEYBOURN, WILLIAM   Cursus Mathematicus. London, 1690. Folio,
contemporary calf, fine, plates, first edition. Dawsons PM 245-475 1974 £115

LEYBOURN, WILLIAM   Pleasure with Profit. London, 1694. Folio, contemporary calf, plates, first edition. Dawsons PM 245-476 1974 £150

LEYDEN, ERNST VON   Klinik der Ruckenmarks-Krankheiten. Berlin,
1874-75-76. Thick 8vo., contemporary half calf, plates, first edition. Schumann
35-278 1974 $165

LEYDEN, JOHN   A Historical and Philosophical Sketch of the
Discoveries and Settlements of the Europeans in Northern and Western Africa at the
Close of the 18th Century. Edinburgh, 1799. First edition, presentation
inscription from author, post 8vo., half calf, good copy, scarce. Sawyer 293-10
1974 £42

LEYDIG, F.   Tafeln zur Vergleichenden Anatomie, Heft 1
Zur Nervensystem und den Sinnesorganen der Wurmer und Gliederfussler.
Tubingen, 1864. Folio, half calf, plates, worn. Wheldon 128-911 1973 £7.50

LEYEL, C. F.   The Magic of Herbs. 1920. 8vo., orig. cloth,
dust jacket, uncut edges, very nice copy, scarce first issue. Wheldon
131-1810 1974 £10

LEYLAND, JOHN   The British Tar in Fact and Fiction. 1911. 8vo.,
orig. cloth. Broadhurst 23-1668 1974 £10

L'HERITIER DE BRUTELLE, C. L.   Sertum Anglicum. Paris, 1788(-1790).
Folio, new quarter morocco, plates, uncut, rare. Wheldon 130-1426 1974
£50

L'HERITIER DE BRUTELLE, C. L.   Stirpes Novae aut Minus Cognitae. Paris,
1784-85. Folio, modern boards, uncut, plates. Wheldon 130-1425 1974 £75

L'HERITIER DE BRUTELLE, C. L.   Stirpes Novae aut Minus Cognitae. Paris,
1784-85. Folio, modern boards, morocco back, plates. Wheldon 129-1493
1974 £120

L'HERITIER DE BRUTELLE, C. L.   Stirpes Novae aut Minus Cognitae. Paris,
1784-85 (-1791). Folio, contemporary tree calf gilt, engraved plates, complete
copy, rare. Wheldon 128-1492 1973 £600

L'HOPITAL, WINEFRIDE DE   Westminster Cathedral & Its Architect. 1919.
2 vols., 4to., plates. Allen 213-1865 1973 $25

L'HOSPITAL, GUILLAUME FRANCOIS ANTOINE DE   Marquis de St. Mesme.
Paris, 1720. 4to., half contemporary vellum, plates. Zeitlin 235-140 1974
$67.50

L'HOSPITAL, GUILLAUME FRANCOIS ANTOINE DE   An Analytick Treatise
of Conick Sections, and Their Use for Resolving of Equations in Determinate and
Intermediate Problems. London, 1723. 4to., calf, rebacked, first edition in
English. Goodspeed's 578-190 1974 $100

L'HOSPITAL, GUILLAUME FRANCOIS ANTOINE DE   Traite Analytique des
Sections Coniques et de leur Usage. Paris, 1707. 4to., calf, first edition.
Goodspeed's 578-189 1974 $100

LIAIS, E.   Climats, Geologie, Faune et Geographie
Botanique de Bresil. Paris, 1872. Roy. 8vo., cloth, maps, scarce. Wheldon
131-372 1974 £20

LIBAVIUS, ANDREAS   Praxis Alchymiae. 1604. 8vo., contemporary
vellum, illus., first edition in Latin. Dawsons PM 245-477 1974 £95

LIBELLUS Lapidum. Sussex, 1924. Orig. pictorial wrappers, wood-engravings.
Smith 194-517 1974 £8

LIBER DE Analemmate. Rome, 1562. 4to., vellum, first edition. Gurney 64-
182 1974 £90

LIBER Facetiarum. Boston, 1811. 12mo., contemporary sheep, scarce, first
edition. Ximenes 33-393 1974 $50

LIBERTY and Patriotism; a Miscellaneous Ode, With Explanatory Notes and
Anecdotes. London, 1778. 4to., old half calf worn, first edition, ex-library,
rare. Ximenes 36-161 1974 $125

LIBRARY Of Anglo-Catholic Theology. Oxford, 1841-60. 88 vols., orig. cloth, faded. Howes 185-1371 1974 £435

LIBRARY of Congress, Washington. Washington, c. 1915. Pict. wrapper, color illus. Jenkins 61-783 1974 $12.50

LIBRARY of Old Authors. 1855-1890. 54 vols., buckram, ex-library. Allen 216-N 1974 $300

LIBRI, G.   Monuments Inedits ou Peu Connus. London, 1864. Folio, half morocco, rubbed, lithographic illus., second edition. Goodspeed's 578-488 1974 $100

LIBRI DVO de Semine. 1533. Small 8vo., boards, label. Dawsons PM 249-195 1974 £90

LICHTENBERGER, JOHANN   Prognosticatio...Quam Olim Scripsit Super Magna illa Saturni oc Iovis Coniunctione. (Cologne), 1526. Full length woodcut portrait, woodcut illus., small 4to., modern binding. Thomas 32-133 1974 £600

LICHTENSTEGER, GEORG   Vorstellung der Gebeine und Muskeln des Menschlichen Korpers. (Numberg), 1774. Plates, folio, contemporary boards, first edition. Schumann 35-279 1974 $150

LIDA, RAIMUNDO   Belleza, Arte y Poesia en la Estetica de Santayana. Tucuman, 1943. Biblo & Tannen 210-912 1973 $7.50

LIDDEL, DUNCAN   Operum Omnium Iatro-Galenicorum, ex Intimis Artis Medicae Adytis, & Penetralibus Erutorum Tomus Unicus. Lyons, 1624. 2 works in 1 vol., 4to., old calf, first combined edition. Schuman 37-155 1974 $135

LIDDELL, H. G.   A Greek-English Lexicon. Oxford, 1897. Thick 4to., buckram, rubbed, eighth edition. Smith 194-561 1974 £5

LIDDELL-HART, BASIL HENRY   Colonel Lawrence: The Man Behind the Legend. 1934. Austin 61-567 1974 $12.50

LIDDELL-HART, BASIL HENRY   La Vie du Colonel Lawrence. 1935. Fine, wrappers. Covent 51-2417 1973 £5.25

LIEBEIG, JUSTUS VON   Handbuch der Chemie. Heidelberg, 1843. 2 vols., 8vo., half cloth, first edition. Schuman 37-156 1974 $145

LIEBER, FRANCIS   Constitution and Plan of Education for Girard College for Orphans. 1834. Boards, ex-library, text crinkled by damp. Allen 216-514 1974 $10

LIEBIG, JUSTUS VON   Animal Chemistry. London, 1842. 8vo., orig. cloth, first edition in English. Dawsons PM 245-478 1974 £25

LIEBIG, JUSTUS VON   Chemische Briefe. Leipzig and Heidelberg, 1865. 8vo., orig. half blue buckram, ex-library. Zeitlin 235-284 1974 $22.50

LIEBIG, JUSTUS VON   Familiar Letters on Chemistry. London, 1844. Small 8vo., orig. red cloth, rebacked, first separate edition in English. Dawsons PM 245-480 1974 £10

LIEBIG, JUSTUS VON   Familiar Letters on Chemistry. London, 1851. 8vo., orig. red cloth, worn. Dawsons PM 245-479 1974 £8

LIEBIG, JUSTUS VON   The Natural Laws of Husbandry. London, 1863. 8vo., orig. cloth, old inscriptions, first English edition, top of spine slightly torn. Gurney 66-105 1974 £20

LIEBLING, A. J.   Between Heals. S & S, 1962. 191p. Austin 54-644 1973 $4

LIEBLING, A. J.   The Road Back to Paris. Doubleday, 1944. 300p. Austin 54-645 1973 $6

LIEUTAUD, JOSEPH   Historia Anatomico-Medicae, Sistens. Paris, 1767. 2 vols. Rittenhouse 46-414 1974 $150

LIEUTAUD, JOSEPH   Synopsis Universae Praxeos-Medicae. 1765. 4to., contemporary calf, rebacked, first edition. Dawsons PM 249-342 1974 £25

LIEVRE, EDOUARD   Les Collections Celebres D'Oeuvres D'Art. Paris, 1866-69. 2 vols., folio, plates, morocco backed boards. Bow Windows 62-569 1974 £21

LIEVRE, EDOUARD   Works of Art in the Collections of England. (1871). Imp. folio, plates, morocco. Quaritch 940-462 1974 £35

LIFE, Adventures & Anecdotes of "Beau" Hickman. Potomac, 1879. 60p., illus., paper. Austin 54-44 1973 $12.50

LIFE and Adventures of Lady Anne, the Little Pedlar. 1823. Engraved frontis., slight soiling, 12mo., full calf, ads at end. George's 610-470 1973 £5.25

LIFE And Characteristics of Right Reverand Alfred A. Curtis D. D. Kennedy, 1913. Austin 62-748 1974 $15

THE LIFE of General Tom Thumb. New York, n.d. Orig. brown cloth, 2 1/8 X 1 1/2. Gregory 44-404A 1974 $35

LIFE of John Charles Fremont. New York, 1856. Pict. wrappers. Hayman 59-551 1974 $10

THE LIFE OF John Dolland. London, 1808. 4to., old half-calf, rebacked. Gurney 64-75 1974 £60

LIFE of Philip, the Indian Chief. Salem, 1827. 16mo., orig. wrappers frayed, spine chipped, first edition. Frohnsdorff 16-503 1974 $27.50

LIFE of Rolla: a Peruvian Tale. 1800. With half title, copperplate frontispiece, 12mo., orig. boards, parchment spine, little rubbed, lacks label, good copy. George's 610-474 1973 £10

THE LIFE of Saint David. 1927. 4to., limp vellum, slip-case, fine. Hammond 201-756 1974 £65

THE LIFE of St. Edward the Confessor. 1920. Large 4to., quarter roan. Thomas 32-294 1974 £85

THE LIFE of the Archpriest Avvakum. 1924. Orig. cloth, dust wrapper, scarce, faded, first edition. Rota 188-428 1974 £8

THE LIFE Of the Holy Mother St. Teresa. 1757. Contemporary calf, rebacked. Howes 185-1704 1974 £20

THE LIFE of the Learned Antiquary, Sir William Dugdale. London, 1713. 8vo., disbound, some foxing, first edition. Ximenes 37-56 1974 $30

THE LIFE of William III. 1703. 8vo., plates, contemporary calf, first edition. Quaritch 936-263 1974 £10

LIFE'S Book of Animals. New York, 1898. Oblong 4to., pictorial cloth, full page illus., very good copy. Frohnsdorff 16-504 1974 $15

LIGHT, MAJOR   Sicilian Scenery from Drawings by P. de Wint. 1823. Engraved plates, first edition, med. 4to., half antique calf by Bayntun, panelled back, raised bands, marbled boards, uncut, exceptionally fine copy. Broadhurst 24-1637 1974 £75

LIGHTHALL, W. D.   Canadian Poems and Lays. London & New York, n.d. Hood's 104-762 1974 $10

LIGHTHALL, W. D.   Old Measures. Montreal, 1922. Inscribed. Hood's 103-737 1974 $22.50

LIGNE, PRINCE DE   Fragments de l'Histoire de Ma Vie. Paris, 1938. 2 vols., 4to., three quarter black hard grain morocco, gilt, uncut. L. Goldschmidt 42-283 1974 $12.50

LIISBERG, J.   Danmarks Spiselige Svampe. Copenhagen, (1876). 8vo., orig. wrappers, plates. Wheldon 129-1261 1974 £5

LILFORD, THOMAS L. POWYS, LORD   Lord Lilford on Birds. 1903. Crown 4to., cloth, plates. Wheldon 128-506 1973 £5

LILFORD, THOMAS L. POWYS, LORD   Lord Lilford on Birds. 1903. Crown 4to., orig. cloth, plates. Wheldon 129-494 1974 £15

LILFORD, THOMAS L. POWYS, LORD   Lord Lilford on Birds. 1903. Crown 4to., cloth, plates. Wheldon 131-643 1974 £7.50

LILFORD, THOMAS L. POWYS, LORD   Notes on the Birds of Northamptonshire and Neighbourhood. 1895. 2 vols., 4to., contemporary half morocco, weak joints, photogravure plates, large paper edition, limited. Wheldon 128-505 1973 £20

LILLO, GEORGE   The London Merchant. Grove, 1952. 121p. Austin 51-562 1973 $5

LILLY, JOHN   Dramatic Works. 1858. 2 vols., 16mo., ex-library. Allen 216-1823 1974 $15

LILLY, JOHN   The Dramatic Works of. London, 1858. 2 vols., small 8vo., contemporary half morocco, faded. Bow Windows 62-570 1974 £15

LILLY, JOHN   The Dramatic Works Of. 1892. 8vo., 2 vols., orig. cloth. Bow Windows 64-592 1974 £10.50

LIMBORCH, PHILIP A.   Theologia Christiana. Amsterdam, 1695. Folio, contemporary speckled calf, rubbed. Smith 194-171 1974 £9.50

LIMEBEER, ENA   To A Proud Phantom. 1923. Marbled boards, English first edition. Covent 56-634 1974 £17.50

LIMNER, LUKE   London Out of Town. n.d. (c. 1860). Orig. pict. wrappers, covers soiled, spine defective, text spotted, illus. Covent 51-1894 1973 £10

LIN YUTANG   Chinatown Family. Day, 1948. Austin 62-374 1974 $7.50

LINAND, BARTHELEMI   Nouveau Traite des Eaux Minerales de Forges. Paris & Forges, 1697. 8vo., contemporary calf, large folding plate, first edition. Gurney 66-106 1974 £20

LINCK, JOH W.   De Raia Torpedine. Leipzig, 1788. 8vo., blue half morocco. Gurney 64-130 1974 £16

LINCOLN, ABRAHAM   Gems from. New York, (1865). Printed wrappers. Hayman 59-356 1974 $20

LINCOLN, ABRAHAM   Lincoln's Last Speech in Springfield in the Campaign of 1858. 1925. 4to., frontis., first printing. Butterfield 10-353 1974 $25

LINCOLN, ABRAHAM   The Martyr's Monument. New York, (1865). Cloth. Hayman 59-358 1974 $17.50

LINCOLN, ABRAHAM   Message from the President . . . Respecting the Cause of the Recent Outbreaks of the Indian Tribes in the Northwest. Washington, 1863. Butterfield 10-315 1974 $15

LINCOLN, ABRAHAM   Message of the President . . . to the Two Houses of Congresses at the Commencement of the Second Session of the 38th Congress. Washington, 1864. Jenkins 48-380 1973 $20

LINCOLN, ABRAHAM   Political Debates Between Hon. Abraham Lincoln and Hon. Stephen A. Douglas. Columbus, 1860. First edition, first state, with all issue points in first state, very rare thus. Jenkins 61-1380 1974 $125

LINCOLN, JOSEPH C.   Cape Cod Ballads and Other Verse. Trenton, 1902. Orig. dec. cloth, first edition, with author's signature tipped-in, illus. MacManus 224-277 1974 $27.50

LINCOLN, JOSEPH C.   Mr. Pratt. New York, 1906. First edition, first state with page numbers lacking from table of contents, cloth, slightly stained. Wilson 63-540 1974 $22.75

LINCOLN COUNTY MUNICIPAL COUNCIL   Proceedings, May 18, 1857 to Oct. 29, 1868. Niagara. Orig. mottled board covers, spine rebacked in leather. Hood's 102-617 1974 £60

LIND, JAMES   Three Letters. London, 1757. 8vo., modern boards. Dawsons PM 247-180 1974 £30

LINDAU, G.   Kryptogamenflora fur Anfanger. Berlin, 1917. 8vo., orig. boards. Wheldon 129-1262 1974 £5

LINDAU, G.   Krptogamenflora fur Anfanger. Berlin, 1922. 8vo., buckram. Wheldon 129-1263 1974 £15

LINDAU, G.   Kryptogamenflora fur Anfanger, Vol. 2, Die Mikroskopischen Pilze. Berlin, 1922. 2 vols., 8vo., orig. boards, very scarce, revised second edition. Wheldon 131-1435 1974 £15

LINDAU, G.   Kryptogamenflora fur Anfanger, Vol. 2 Die Mikroskopischen Pilze. Berlin, 1922. 2 vols., 8vo., orig. boards, text-figures, very scarce, orig. printing, revised second edition. Wheldon 128-1390 1973 £15

LINDAU, G.   Kryptogamenflora fur Anfanger, Bd 1, Die Hoheren Pilze, Basidiomycetes. Berlin, 1928. 8vo., cloth, plates, third edition. Wheldon 131-1434 1974 £7.50

LINDBERG, JOHN S.   The Background of Swedish Emigration to the U. S. 1930. Cloth, orig. edition. Austin 57-404 1974 $10

LINDBERGH, ANNE MORROW   Listen! New York, 1938. First edition. Biblo & Tannen 213-566 1973 $7.50

LINDBERGH, ANNE MORROW   Listen! The Wind. New York, 1938. 1st ed. Biblo & Tannen 210-764 1973 $6.50

LINDBERGH, ANNE MORROW   North to the Orient. New York, 1935. First edition. Biblo & Tannen 213-567 1973 $10

LINDEN, DIEDERICK WESSEL   An Experimental Dissertation. London, 1751. 8vo., disbound, uncut. Gurney 64-131 1974 £15

LINDEN, J.   Iconographie des Orchidees. Brussels, 1860. Folio, half green morocco, plates, rare. Wheldon 130-38 1974 £450

LINDEN, J.   Lindenia. Ghent, 1886-97. 12 vols., large 4to., contemporary half leather, worn. Traylen 79-33 1973 £525

LINDEN, J.   Pescatorea, Iconographie des Orchidees. Brussels, 1860. Folio, half green morocco, coloured plates, very rare, nice copy. Wheldon 128-1560 1973 £450

LINDEN, J. A. VAN DER   De Scriptis Medicis Libri Duo. Amsterdam, 1662. 8vo., old vellum. Gurney 66-107 1974 £60

LINDER, D. H.   A Monograph of the Helicosporous Fungi. 1929. Roy 8vo., buckram, plates. Wheldon 129-1264 1974 £7.50

LINDER, USHER   Reminiscences of the Early Bench and Bar of Illinois. Chicago, 1879. 8vo., orig. bindings. Butterfield 8-151 1974 $15

LINDLEY, GEORGE   A Guide to the Orchard and Kitchen Garden. London, 1831. 8vo., orig. cloth-backed boards. Hammond 201-26 1974 £6

LINDLEY, JOHN   Digitalium Monographia. 1821. Roy folio, orig. cloth, plates. Wheldon 129-933 1974 £175

LINDLEY, JOHN   The Fossil Flora of Great Britain. 1831-37. 3 vols., 8vo., orig. cloth, plates, somewhat foxed. Wheldon 128-1009 1973 £45

LINDLEY, JOHN   The Fossil Flora of Great Britain. 1831-37. 8vo., 3 vols., contemporary half calf. Wheldon 129-834 1974 £40

LINDLEY, JOHN   The Fossil Flora of Great Britain. 1831-37. 8vo., 3 vols., half calf, plates. Wheldon 130-946 1974 £60

LINDLEY, JOHN   Ladies' Botany. London, 1837. 8vo., 2 vols., contemporary half calf, gilt, plates, third edition. Hammond 201-658 1974 £50

LINDLEY, JOHN   A Natural System of Botany. 1836. 8vo., orig. cloth, third edition. Wheldon 128-1127 1973 £15

LINDLEY, JOHN   A Natural System of Botany. 1836. 8vo., orig. cloth, second edition. Wheldon 130-1034 1974 £15

LINDLEY, JOHN   Pomologia Britannica. 1841. 3 vols., roy. 8vo., contemporary half morocco, fully gilt backs, gilt edges, hand-coloured engraved plates. Wheldon 128-1701 1973 £600

LINDLEY, JOHN   Pomologia Britannica. 1841. Roy 8vo., 3 vols., contemporary half morocco, gilt, plates. Wheldon 129-27 1974 £600

LINDLEY, JOHN   A Synopsis of the British Flora. 1829. Post 8vo., contemporary half morocco, scarce, first edition. Wheldon 130-1099 1974 £10

LINDLEY, JOHN   The Theory and Practice of Horticulture. 1855. 8vo., orig. cloth, second edition. Wheldon 128-1494 1973 £7.50

LINDLEY, JOHN   The Treasury of Botany. 1874 or 1899. 2 vols., small 8vo., cloth, plates, new edition. Wheldon 128-1129 1973 £5

LINDLEY, JOHN   The Vegetable Kingdom. 1853. 8vo., cloth, text-figures, third edition. Wheldon 128-1126 1973 £12

LINDMAN, C. A. M.   Svensk Fanerogamflora. Stockholm, 1926. 8vo., cloth, second edition. Wheldon 130-1177 1974 £5

LINDSAY, ALEXANDER WILLIAM CRAWFORD
Please turn to
CRAWFORD, ALEXANDER WILLIAM CRAWFORD LINDSAY

LINDSAY, COLIN   De Ecclesia et Cathedra. 1877. 2 vols., thick 8vo., damp-stained. Howes 185-1373 1974 £5.50

LINDSAY, F.   Panama and the Canal Today. Boston, (1913). 8vo., illus., orig. cloth, faded. Bow Windows 62-571 1974 £5

LINDSAY, HOWARD   Happy Hunting. Random, 1957. Austin 51-563 1973 $7.50

LINDSAY, HOWARD   Remains To Be Seen. Random House, 1951. 185p., illus. Austin 51-564 1973 $7.50

LINDSAY, JACK   A Handbook of Freedom. 1939. Wrappers, book-label, advance proof copy. Covent 55-727 1974 £12.50

LINDSAY, JACK   Marc Antony: His World and His Contemporaries. 1936. 8vo., contemporary brown half morocco, cloth sides, copper plate presentation inscription, illus., first edition. Bow Windows 66-425 1974 £6.50

LINDSAY, JACK   William Blake. 1927. Cloth-backed boards, bookplate, English first edition. Covent 56-153 1974 £25

LINDSAY, JACK   William Blake: Creative Will and the Poetic Image. 1927. Cloth backed boards, fine. Covent 51-666 1973 £15

LINDSAY, LORD   Sketches of the History of Christian Art. 1847. 3 vols., calf, some covers detached. Eaton Music-629 1973 £15

LINDSAY, PHILIP   King Henry V, a Chronicle. 1934. Plates, first edition. Covent 55-1008 1974 £5.25

LINDSAY, PHILIP   King Richard III, a Chronicle. 1933. Plates, booklabel. Covent 55-1009 1974 £5.25

LINDSAY, PHILIP   Kings of Merry England. 1936. Presentation inscription, illus. Covent 55-1010 1974 £8.50

LINDSAY, PHILIP   The Little Wench. 1935. Presentation inscription, faded. Covent 55-1011 1974 £7.50

LINDSAY, VACHEL   Collected Poems. New York, 1930. Revised edition, illus. by author, signed by author, orig. binding. Butterfield 10-355 1974 $20

LINDSAY, VACHEL   The Congo and Other Poems. New York, 1922. Inscribed by author, orig. binding. Butterfield 10-356 1974 $10

LINDSAY, W. L.   A Popular History of British Lichens. 1856. Post 8vo., cloth, plates, scarce. Wheldon 130-1312 1974 £5

LINDSAY, W. L.   A Popular History of British Lichens. 1856. 8vo., cloth, plates, scarce. Wheldon 131-1436 1974 £7.50

LINDSEY, COLIN   De Ecclesia et Cathedra. 1877. 2 vols., thick 8vo., orig. cloth. Howes 185-1374 1974 £5.50

LINE, FRANCIS   Explicatio Horologii in Hort Regio Londini in Anglia an. 1669. Small 4to., old half vellum, plate, first edition. Zeitlin 235-141 1974 $275

LINE-UP: A Collection of Crime Stories by Famous Mystery Writers. New York, 1940. 1st ed. Biblo & Tannen 210-513 1973 $8.50

LINEN, JAMES   The Poetical and Prose Writings. New York, 1864. Austin 62-375 1974 $17.50

LINEN, JAMES   The Poetical and Prose Writings. 1864. Austin 57-406 1974 $17.50

LING, NICHOLAS   Politeuphuia. London, n.d. 12mo., old calf, gilt, bit worn, tenth edition. Ximenes 37-131 1974 $175

LINGARD, JOHN   A History of England from the First Invasion By the Romans. 1837-83. 13 vols., 8vo., orig. cloth, fourth edition. Smith 194-704 1974 £8

LINN, JOHN BLAIR   Annals of Buffalo Valley, Pennsylvania. Harrisburg, 1877. 8vo., quarter leather. Saddleback 14-678 1974 $75

LINN, JOHN BLAIR   Valerian. Philadelphia, 1805. 4to., orig. boards, worn, first edition, browned & foxed. MacManus 224-278 1974 $75

LINN, TICHARD   A History of Banbridge. Banbridge, 1935. 8vo., map, illus., cloth boards. Emerald 50-551 1974 £8.50

LINNAEUS   A Catalogue of the Works of. London, 1933-36. 2 vols., 4to., orig. green buckram, plates, fine, second edition. Dawsons PM 10-364 1974 £10

LINNE, CARL VON   Bibliographia Linnaeana. Uppsala, 1907. Roy. 8vo., orig. wrapper, plates. Wheldon 129-168 1974 £15

LINNE, CARL VON   Bref Och Skrifvelser af Och Till Carl Van Linne. Uppsala & Stockholm, 1907-43. 9 vols. (of 10), roy. 8vo., orig. wrappers. Wheldon 128-116 1973 £25

LINNE, CARL VON   Carl von Linne. Stockholm, 1907. 8vo., modern full brown niger morocco, scarce. Wheldon 130-217 1974 £5

LINNE, CARL VON   A Collection of 24 Papers. Stockholm, 1739-59. 8vo., plates, enclosed in modern folder. Wheldon 128-46 1973 £70

LINNE, CARL VON   The Elements of Botany. London, 1775. 8vo., contemporary calf, plates. Gurney 64-132 1974 £20

LINNE, CARL VON   The Families of Plants. Lichfield, 1787. 8vo., contemporary calf. Wheldon 129-938 1974 £40

LINNE, CARL VON   The Families of Plants. Lichfield, 1787. 8vo., 2 vols., contemporary calf. Wheldon 131-263 1974 £40

LINNE, CARL VON   Fauna Suecicae. Leipzig, 1800. 8vo., half calf, plate, scarce. Wheldon 130-206 1974 £35

LINNE, CARL VON   Fauna Svecica. Leyden, 1746. 8vo., old half calf, plates. Wheldon 130-205 1974 £150

LINNE, CARL VON   Fauna Svecica, Sistens Animalia Sveciciae Regni. Leyden, 1746. 8vo., old half calf, folding plates, frontispiece. Wheldon 128-210 1973 £150

LINNE, CARL VON   Fauna Svecica. Stockholm, 1746. 8vo., contemporary calf, plates. Wheldon 129-282 1974 £180

LINNE, CARL VON   Flora Lapponica. Amsterdam, 1737. 8vo., contemporary calf, plates. Wheldon 129-1098 1974 £75

LINNE, CARL VON   Flora Lapponica. Amsterdam, 1737. 8vo., contemporary calf, rare first edition. Wheldon 131-266 1974 £100

LINNE, CARL VON   Flora Lapponica. 1792. 8vo., new half calf, plates, second edition. Wheldon 130-210 1974 £50

LINNE, CARL VON   Flora Lapponica. 1792. 8vo., new half calf, plates, frontispiece, second edition. Wheldon 128-1281 1973 £30

LINNE, CARL VON   Flora Suecica. Stockholm, 1755. 8vo., contemporary calf, folding plate, rare, second edition. Wheldon 128-1280 1973 £50

LINNE, CARL VON   Flora Zeylanica. Stockholm, 1747. 8vo., modern half calf, plates, nice copy, rare first edition. Wheldon 131-265 1974 £180

LINNE, CARL VON   Genera Plantarum. Leyden, 1742. 8vo., contemporary vellum. Wheldon 130-211 1974 £90

LINNE, CARL VON   Genera Plantarum. Paris, 1743. 8vo., contemporary calf, plates. Wheldon 130-212 1974 £50

LINNE, CARL VON   Genera Plantarum. Paris, 1743. 8vo., plates, contemporary calf, folding table. Wheldon 128-1131 1973 £50

LINNE, CARL VON   Genera Plantarum. Stockholm, 1754. 8vo., contemporary calf gilt, fifth edition. Wheldon 129-936 1974 £100

LINNE, CARL VON   Genera Plantarum. Stockholm, 1754. 8vo., contemporary half calf, extremely scarce orig. issue, fifth edition. Wheldon 128-1132 1973 £100

LINNE, CARL VON   Genera Plantarum. Stockholm, 1754. 8vo., contemporary half calf, fifth edition. Wheldon 130-213 1974 £100

LINNE, CARL VON   Genera Plantarum. Vienna, 1767. 8vo., contemporary vellum. Wheldon 131-261 1974 £30

LINNE, CARL VON   Genera Plantarum. Vienna, 1767. 8vo., contemporary vellum. Wheldon 129-937 1974 £30

LINNE, CARL VON   Genera Plantarum Eorumque Characters Naturales. With Supplements: a) Corollarium Generum Plantarum. b) Methodus Sexualis Sistens Genera Plantarum. Leyden, 1737. 8vo., half calf, folding plate, fine, first edition. Kraus 137-60 1974 £1,850

LINNE, CARL VON   Linne Lefnadsteckning. Stockholm, 1903. Roy. 8vo., cloth, 2 vols. Wheldon 129-169 1974 £12

LINNE, CARL VON   Linne Portrait. Stockholm, 1907. 4to., linson, plates. Wheldon 130-218 1974 £15

LINNE, CARL VON   Materia Medica, Liber I. de Plantis. Stockholm, 1749. 8vo., contemporary calf, first edition. Schumann 35-280 1974 $165

LINNE, CARL VON   Philosophia Botanica. Stockholm, 1751. 8vo., old boards, plates. Wheldon 129-935 1974 £75

LINNE, CARL VON   Philosophia Botanica. Stockholm, 1751. 8vo., nineteenth century half cloth, plates, rare, first edition. Wheldon 130-208 1974 £100

LINNE, CARL VON   Philosophia Botanica. Stockholm, 1751. 8vo., old boards, rare first edition. Wheldon 131-264 1974 £75

LINNE, CARL VON   Philosophia Botanica. Berlin, 1790. 8vo., half parchment, plates. Gurney 64-134 1974 £20

LINNE, CARL VON   Philosophia Botanica. Berlin, 1790. 8vo., half parchment, portrait, plates. Gurney 66-108 1974 £20

LINNE, CARL VON   Philosophia Botanica in Qua Explicantur Fundamenta Botanica. Stockholm, 1751. 8vo., 19th century half cloth, plates, very rare first edition. Wheldon 128-1133 1973 £100

LINNE, CARL VON   Species Plantarum. Vienna, 1764. 2 vols., 8vo., contemporary calf, nice copy, third edition. Wheldon 128-1135 1973 £35

LINNE, CARL VON   Species Plantarum. Vienna, 1764. 8vo., 2 vols., contemporary vellum, third edition. Wheldon 129-934 1974 £50

LINNE, CARL VON   Species Plantarum. Vienna, 1764. 8vo., third edition, 2 vols., contemporary calf. Wheldon 130-207 1974 £25

LINNE, CARL VON   Species Plantarum. Vienna, 1764. 2 vols., 8vo., contemporary vellum, rare, third edition. Wheldon 131-260 1974 £50

LINNE, CARL VON   The Story of His Life. 1923. 8vo., cloth. Wheldon 129-170 1974 £15

LINNE, CARL VON   Supplementum Plantarum. Tokyo, 1930. 8vo., half calf. Wheldon 130-1035 1974 £15

LINNE, CARL VON   Systema Natura. Stockholm, 1758. 2 vols., 8vo., contemporary calf, vol. 2 same style modern binding, tenth edition, Carl Von Linne the Younger's copy with his signature. Kraus 137-59 1974 $750

LINNE, CARL VON   Systema Naturae per Regna Tria Naturae. Stockholm, 1766-68. 3 vols. in 4, 8vo., contemporary half calf, plates, rare, complete copy, twelfth edition. Wheldon 128-44 1973 £250

LINNE, CARL VON   Systema Naturae per Regna Tria Naturae. Coimbra, 1793-94. 9 vols., small 8vo., sewed, uncut. Wheldon 128-45 1973 £60

LINNE, CARL VON   Systema Naturae, Sive Regna Tria Naturae Systematice Proposita per Classes, Ordina, Genera, & Species. Leyden, 1735. Folio, 19th century leather backed boards by J. Edmond, cloth case, first edition, some damp and dust discoloring, engraved exlibris of Sir Charles W. Thompson. Kraus 137-58 1974 $38,500

LINNE, CARL VON   Systeme Sexuel des Vegetaux. Paris, (1798). 8vo., boards. Wheldon 128-1137 1973 £12

LINNE, CARL VON   Systema Naturae. 1793-94. Small 8vo., 9 vols., sewed, uncut. Wheldon 130-203 1974 £60

LINNE, CARL VON   Systema Vegetabilium. Gottingen, 1825-28. 5 vols., 8vo., new cloth, scarce, sixteenth edition. Wheldon 128-1134 1973 £32

LINNE, CARL VON   Systema Vegetabilium. Gottingen, 1825-28. 5 vols., 8vo., new cloth, sixteenth edition. Wheldon 131-262 1974 £32

LINNE, CARL VON   Voyages and Travels in the Levant. 1766. 8vo., contemporary calf, rebacked, first edition in English. Wheldon 130-204 1974 £120

LINTON, E. LYNN   Witch Stories. London, 1861. Worn spine, detached cover. Rittenhouse 46-415 1974 $15

LINTON, EDWARD F.   The Hortons of Howroyde and Some Allied Families. 1911. 3 parts in 1 vol., roy. 8vo., orig. cloth. Howes 186-1641 1974 £12.50

LIONARDI, ALESSANDRO   Dialogi Della Inventione Poetica. Venice, 1554. Small 4to., old vellum, stained. Thomas 28-260 1972 £30

LIPPARD, GEORGE   Legends of the American Revolution. 1876. Allen 216-1025 1974 $12.50

LIPPARD, GEORGE   New York: Its Upper Ten and Lower Million. Cincinnati, 1853. Orig. cloth, ends of spine chipped away, first edition, printed in double columns. MacManus 224-279 1974 $50

LIPPARD, GEORGE   Quaker City, or, Monks of Monk Hall. 1876. Allen 216-1024 1974 $10

LIPPMANN, WALTER   A Preface to Morals. New York, 1929. First printing, orig. binding, d.j. Butterfield 10-357 1974 $12.50

LIPS, EVA   Rebirth of Liberty. 1942. Austin 62-377
1974 $10

LIPSCOMB, GEORGE   An Essay. Warwick, 1799. 8vo., half calf.
Gurney 64-135 1974 £15

LIPSCOMB, GEORGE   History and Antiquities of the County of
Buckingham. 1847. 4 vols., roy. 4to., half calf, plates. Quaritch 939-309
1974 £200

LIPSCOMBE, GEORGE   The History and Antiquities of the County of
Buckingham. London, 1847. 4 vols., 4to., half green morocco gilt, plates, maps.
Traylen 79-313 1973 £220

LIPSCOMB, GEORGE   Journey into South Wales. London, 1802.
8vo., half calf, spine gilt, very good copy, tinted frontispiece, first edition.
Ximenes 37-133 1974 $45

LIPSIUS, DAVID   Tractatus de Hydropisis. 1624. Small 4to.,
full morocco, rare. Broadhurst 23-1242 1974 £200

LIPSIUS, DAVID   Tractatus de Hydropisis. 1624. Small 4to.,
full brown levant morocco by Sangorski & Sutcliffe, very rare, fine. Broadhurst
24-1251 1974 £225

LIPSIUS, JUSTUS   De Militia Romana Libri Quinque. Antwerp,
1598-1610. 4to., orig. blind-stamped pigskin. Traylen 79-145 1973 £45

LIPSIUS, JUSTUS   De Militia Romana Libri V. Commentarius ad
Polybium. Antwerp, 1614. 4to., old stamped calf, torn spine. Allen 213-630
1973 $30

LIPSIUS, JUSTUS   Monita et Exempla Politica Libri Duo.
Antwerp, 1606. Vellum. Allen 213-631 1973 $27.50

LIPSIUS, JUSTUS   Saturnalium Sermonum Libri Duo. Antwerp,
1585. 4to., 19th century half calf, some stains, folding plates. Thomas 32-240
1974 £60

LIPSKY, LOUIS   Shields of Honor. Nesher, 1927. 247p.
Austin 62-380 1974 $12.50

LIPSKY, LOUIS   Shields of Honor. 1927. 247 pages.
Austin 57-408 1974 $12.50

LIPSKY, LOUIS   Stories of Jewish Life. Nesher, 1927.
Austin 62-379 1974 $12.50

LIPSKY, LOUIS   Thirty Years of American Zionism. Nesher,
1927. Austin 62-378 1974 $12.50

LIPTON, JULIUS   Poems of Strife. 1935. Wrappers, English first
edition. Covent 56-298 1974 £5.25

LIPTON, LAWRENCE   The Holy Barbarians. Messner, 1959. 318p.,
illus. Austin 54-646 1973 $7.50

LIPTZIN, SOL   Germany's Stepchildren. 1944. 298p., orig.
ed. Austin 62-383 1974 $10

THE LIQUOR Prohibition Appeal, 1895. London, 1895. Hood's 104-652
1974 $10

LISFRANC, JACQUES   Des Diverses Methodes et Differens Procedes pour
l'Obliteration des Arteres. Paris, 1834. 4to., modern boards, first edition. Schumann 35-281 1974 $210

LISLE, FRANCOIS DE   La Legende de Charles. Reims, 1576. Small
8vo., full jansenist crimson levant morocco, gilt, first edition. L. Goldschmidt
42-69 1974 $425

LIST of Members of the Hiberman Society. Philadelphia, 1884. 42 pages.
Austin 57-327 1974 $12.50

LIST of the Vertebrated Animals Now or Lately Living in the Gardens of the
Zoological Society of London. 1883. 8vo., cloth, eighth edition. Wheldon
131-441 1974 £5

LIST of the Vertebrated Animals Now or Lately Living in the Gardens of the
Zoological Society of London. 1896. 8vo., cloth, ninth edition. Wheldon
131-442 1974 £5

LISTER, A.   A Monograph of the Mycetozoa. 1894. 8vo.,
cloth, plates. Wheldon 129-1265 1974 £5

LISTER, A.   A Monograph of the Mycetozoa. 1894. 8vo.,
cloth, plates, ex-library, first edition. Wheldon 130-1314 1974 £5

LISTER, A.   A Monograph of the Mycetozoa. 1911. 8vo.,
cloth, plates, scarce, second edition. Wheldon 129-1266 1974 £15

LISTER, H.   Hamilton, Canada; Its History, Commerce,
Industries, Resources. Hamilton, 1913. Illus. Hood's 102-621 1974 $30

LISTER, JOSEPH   An Address on the Treatment of Wounds Delivered
in the Surgical Section of the International Medical Congress, Aug. 8, 1881.
London, 1881. 8vo., half morocco. Gurney 66-111 1974 £50

LISTER, JOSEPH   The Collected Papers Of. Oxford, 1909. 4to.,
orig. blue buckram, gilt, uncut, first edition. Dawsons PM 249-344 1974 £105

LISTER, JOSEPH   Observation on the Contractile Tissue of the Iris.
(1853). 8vo., calf, rebacked. Schumann 35-282 1974 $125

LISTER, JOSEPH   Observations on Ligature of the Arteries on the
Antiseptic System. Edinburgh, 1869, corrected 1870. 8vo., half morocco,
plates, second issue with slip with new date pasted on title, presentation inscription.
Gurney 66-112 1974 £125

LISTER, JOSEPH   On the Effects of the Antiseptic System of Treatment Upon the Salubrity of a Surgical Hospital. Edinburgh, 1870. 8vo., half
morocco, presentation copy inscribed by author, first separate edition. Gurney
66-113 1974 £125

LISTER, JOSEPH   Remarks on a Case of Compound Dislocation of
the Ankle With Other Injuries. Edinburgh, 1870. 8vo., half morocco,
presentation copy inscribed by author. Gurney 66-110 1974 £125

LISTER, JOSEPH   The Third Huxley Lecture Delivered Before the
Medical School of Charing Cross Hospital. London, 1907. 8vo., orig. cloth,
first separate publication. Schuman 37-157 1974 $65

LISTER, MARTIN   Hippocratis Aphorismi, cum Commentariolo.
London, 1703. Rittenhouse 46-416 1974 $35

LISTER, MARTIN   Octo Exercitationes Medicinales. 1697. 12mo.,
old panelled calf. Dawsons PM 249-345 1974 £90

LISTER, MARTIN   Octo Exercitationes Medicinales. London,
1697. Small 8vo., contemporary panelled calf, rebacked, first edition printed
in England. Schuman 37-158 1974 $215

LISTER, THOMAS HENRY   Arlington. London, 1832. 3 vols., 12mo.,
contemporary half morocco, first edition. Dawsons PM 252-661 1974 £35

LITCHFIELD, FREDERICK   Antiques, Genuine & Spurious. 1924. Illus.,
plates. Covent 55-463 1974 £10.50

LITCHFIELD, FREDERICK   Illustrated History of Furniture. 1922. Imp.
4to., plates, illus., coloured frontispiece, very good copy, orig. cloth.
Broadhurst 24-136 1974 £6

LITCHFIELD, FREDERICK   Pottery and Porcelain. 1912. 8vo., orig. cloth,
coloured frontis., plates, illus. Bow Windows 66-426 1974 £7

LITCHFIELD, FREDERICK   Pottery and Porcelain. London, 1912. Small
4to., color plates. Biblo & Tannen 210-76 1973 $25

LITCHFIELD, R. B.   Tom Wedgwood. 1904. 8vo., orig. cloth,
scarce. Broadhurst 23-135 1974 £15

LITERARY Anecdotes of the Nineteenth Century. 1895. One of 1000 copies,
plates, buckram, spine faded, bookplate, very nice copy, first edition. Covent
51-2025 1973 £7.50

LITT, W. Wrestliana: or, An Historical Account of Ancient and Modern Wrestling. Whitehaven, 1823. First edition, crown 8vo., orig. paper printed wrapper, uncut, wrapper frayed, rare. Broadhurst 24-1457 1974 £20

LITTLE, C. E. Cyclopedia of Classified Dates. 1900. 4to., binding badly scratched. Allen 216-1028 1974 $15

LITTLE, JOHN B. The History of Butler County, Alabama. Cincinnati, 1885. 12mo., cloth, map. Saddleback 14-1 1974 $35

LITTLE, O. H. The Geography and Geology of Makalla. Cairo, 1925. Roy. 8vo., buckram, plates, maps, frontispiece, library stamp, scarce. Wheldon 128-1010 1973 £7.50

LITTLE, WILLIAM The Shorter Oxford English Dictionary on Historical Principles. Oxford, 1947. 2 vols. Biblo & Tannen 213-761 1973 $32.50

LITTLE Bo Peep. New York, n.d. (c. 1850's). Narrow 4to., colored pictorial wrappers, hand colored engravings, mint copy. Frohnsdorff 16-506 1974 $40

LITTLE BROTHER and Little Sister and Other Tales. 4to., cloth, illus., signed, limited edition. Broadhurst 23-164 1974 £60

THE LITTLE Forget-Me-Not. London. Color plates, front hinge cracked, orig. cloth, 2 1/2 X 2. Gregory 44-406 1974 $85

A LITTLE Garland of Celtic Verse. Portland, 1907. Boards, unopened, fine, second edition. Covent 55-42 1974 £5.25

THE LITTLE Lexicon, or, The Multum in Parvo. London, (1843). Full red morocco, wallet flap, 3 1/8 X 2. Gregory 44-405 1974 $12.50

LITTLE Lucy: or, The Pleasant Day. New Haven, n.d. (c. 1830). Woodcuts, orig. pictorial wrappers, fine, 2 3/4 X 4 1/4 inches. Frohnsdorff 16-507 1974 $15

THE LITTLE Man: and The Little Maid. Providence, 1849. 12mo., orig. pictorial wrappers, all edges gilt, engravings, small piece missing from one margin, else mint. Frohnsdorff 16-508 1974 $45

THE LITTLE Post-Office; or, My Brothers and Sisters. New Haven, 1835. 16mo., pictorial wrappers, woodcuts. Frohnsdorff 16-515 1974 $15

LITTLE Red Riding Hood. Watertown, NY, ca. 1886. Biblo & Tannen 210-750 1973 $25

THE LITTLE Review. San Francisco, 1916. Wrappers, fine. Rota 188-529 1974 £8

THE LITTLE Review. New York, 1922. 4to., wrappers, fine. Rota 188-530 1974 £10

THE LITTLE Review. New York, 1926. 4to., wrappers. Rota 188-531 1974 £10

THE LITTLE Robinson Crusoe. Philadelphia, n.d. (c. 1840). Square 16mo., embossed cloth, spine ends chipped, woodcut illus. Frohnsdorff 16-516 1974 $15

THE LITTLE Warbler; Scottish Songs; English and Irish Songs. 1806 and n.d. 2 vols. in 1, woodcut frontis., full calf, joints cracked, ex-libris copies, 68 X 45 mm. in size. George's 610-530 1973 £12.50

LITTLER, F. M. A Handbook of the Birds of Tasmania and Its Dependencies. 1910. 8vo., illus., rebound, scarce, rexine. Wheldon 128-507 1973 £12

LITTRE, EMILE Dictionnaire de la Langue Francaise. Paris, 1875-83. 4 vols., large 4to., orig. half leather, fine. L. Goldschmidt 42-284 1974 $120

LITURGIA: Seu Liber Precum Communium et Administrationis Sacramentorum Aliorumque Rituum et Ceremoniarum in Ecclesia Anglicana Receptus. 1759. 12mo., contemporary calf, engraved frontispiece, corners worn. Bow Windows 66-427 1974 £8.50

LITURGIE, Seu Liber Precum Communium, et Administrationis Sacramentorum, Aliorumque Rituum Atque Ceremoniarum Ecclesiae. London, 1696. Small 8vo., old calf. Traylen 79-181 1973 £8

LITZMANN, CARL CONRAD THEODOR Die Formen des Beckens Insbesondere des Engen weiblichen Beckens. Berlin, 1861. Large 4to., boards, plates, first edition. Schumann 35-283 1974 $145

LIVELY, EDWARD A True Chronologie of the Times of the Persian Monarchie. London, 1597. Small 8vo., contemporary vellum gilt, first edition. Dawsons PM 251-270 1974 £140

LIVERMORE, A. A. The War With Mexico Reviewed. Boston, 1850. First edition. Jenkins 61-1597 1974 $17.50

LIVERPOOL: Album of Liverpool and New Brighton Views. Germany, (n.d.). Small 4to., orig. quarter cloth, covers marked, corners worn, illus., map. Bow Windows 66-428 1974 £5

THE LIVING Animals of the World. n.d. 2 vols., 4to., illus, plates, orig. buckram. Smith 193-757 1973 £6

LIVINGSTON, FLORA V. Bibliography of the Works of Rudyard Kipling, and Supplement to the Bibliography. New York & Cambridge, 1927-38. 2 vols., 8vo., cloth, autographed by author. Goodspeed's 578-490 1974 $50

LIVINGSTON, FLORA V. Bibliography of the Works of Rudyard Kipling. New York, 1927. Orig. edition, scarce. Howes 185-728 1974 £15

LIVINGSTON, W. K. Pain Mechanisms. New York, 1943. Rittenhouse 46-417 1974 $10

LIVINGSTONE, DAVID Missionary Travels and Researches in South Africa. London, 1857. 8vo., orig. embossed cloth, gilt, illus., fine, first edition. Dawsons PM 250-53 1974 £60

LIVINGSTONE, DAVID Narrative of an Expedition to the Zambesi and Its Tributaries. New York, 1866. 1st Amer. ed., illus. Jacobs 24-136 1974 $50

LIVINGSTONE, DAVID Narrative of an Expedition to the Zambesi and Its Tributaries; and of the Discovery of the Lakes Shirwa and Nyassa. 1865. Demy 8vo., fine, contemporary inscription, illus., folding map, first edition, orig. cloth. Broadhurst 24-1641 1974 £65

LIVINGSTON, SIGMUND Must Men Hate? Harper, 1944. 344p. Austin 62-385 1974 $8.50

LIVIUS, BARHAM Considerations on the Advantages of Steam Navigation on Canals. London, 1841. 8vo., boards, first edition. Hammond 201-863 1974 £36

LIVOIS, E. Recherches sur les Echinocoques Chez l'Homme et Chez les Animaux. Paris, 1843. 4to., orig. wrappers, uncut, plate, library stamp, presentation copy, rare. Wheldon 128-282 1973 £7.50

LES LIVRES de L'Enfance du XVe AU XIXe Siecle. Paris, (1931?). 2 vols., 4to., plates, orig. wrappers, uncut, limited. Dawsons PM 10-258 1974 £80

LIZARS, JOHN Observations on Extraction of Diseased Ovaria. Edinburgh, 1825. Folio, contemporary half calf, first edition. Dawsons PM 249-346 1974 £385

LIZARS, R. Humours of '37, Grave, Gay and Grim. Toronto, 1897. First edition. Hood's 102-618 1974 $45

LIZARS, R. In the Days of the Canada Company. Toronto, 1896. First edition, portraits, illus. Hood's 102-619 1974 $65

LLANDAFF, BISHOP OF Some Account of the Condition of the Fabric of Llandaff Cathedral. 1860. 4to., orig. cloth, plates, second edition. Smith 194-289 1974 £5

LLEWELLYN, OWEN The South Bound Car. 1907. Plates, text illus., map, orig. dec. cloth gilt, fine. Covent 51-2475 1973 £7.50

LLOYD, C. G. Mycological Writings. Cincinnati, 1898-1925. 8vo., 4to., half calf. Wheldon 129-1267 1974 $75

LLOYD, E.   Archaeologia Britannica. Oxford, 1707.
Folio, half calf. Quaritch 939-162 1974 £30

LLOYD, EUSEBIUS ARTHUR   A Treatise on the Nature and Treatment of Scro-
phula. London, 1821. 8vo., new boards, first edition. Dawsons PM 249-347
1974 £18

LLOYD, HUGONE   Phrases Elegantiores Ex Caesaris Commentariis
Cicerone. 1654. Small 8vo., contemporary calf. Bow Windows 62-576
1974 £7.75

LLOYD, J.   Flore de la Loire-Inferieure. 1844. 12mo.,
half calf. Wheldon 130-1178 1974 £5

LLOYD, J.   Flore de l'Quest de la France. 1854. 12mo.,
vellum. Wheldon 130-1179 1974 £6

LLOYD, J.   Flore de l'Quest de la France. Rochefort, 1886.
Post 8vo., morocco, scarce, fourth edition. Wheldon 129-1099 1974 £10

LLOYD, J. E.   A History of Carmarthenshire. Cardiff, 1935
and 39. 4to., 2 vols., orig. cloth. Broadhurst 23-1448 1974 £25

LLOYD, J. E.   A History of Carmartheshire. Cardiff, 1935 and
1939. Plates, text illus., maps, 2 vols., med. 4to., orig. cloth, bindings
faded. Broadhurst 24-1460 1974 £25

LLOYD, JOHN   The Great Forest of Brecknock. 1905. 4to.,
contemporary half morocco, boards. Broadhurst 23-1449 1974 £30

LLOYD, JOHN URI   Etidorhpa, or, the End of Earth. Cincinnati,
c. 1895. First edition, limited, illus., cloth measurably worn, signatures sprung.
Wilson 63-546 1974 $25

LLOYD, L.   Field Sports of the North of Europe. 1831.
2 vols., 8vo., half calf, maps, plates, scarce, second edition. Wheldon
128-211 1973 £12

LLOYD, N.   Garden Craftsmanship in Yew and Box. 1925.
Small 4to., plates. Wheldon 129-1611 1974 £7.50

LLOYD, R.   The Capricious Lovers. 1764. 8vo., cloth, first
edition. Quaritch 936-135 1974 £6

LLOYD, ROBERT   The Actor A Poem. London, 1924. 8vo.,
orig. vellum-backed dec. boards, limited. Dawsons PM 252-662 1974 £16

LLOYD, ROBERT   Poems. London, 1762. 4to., contemporary
calf, spine gilt, worn, first edition. Ximenes 37-134 1974 £100

LLOYD, SUSETTE HARRIET   Sketches of Bermuda. London, 1835. First
edition, 12mo, full page plates, map, some age browning, orig. binding, calf
spine, marbled boards. Current BW9-561 1974 $65

LLOYD, T.   Trail of Thomas O. Selfridge. Boston, (1806).
12mo., calf. Putman 126-77 1974 $12

LLOYD, W. V.   The Sheriffs of Montgomeryshire. 1876. 8vo.,
orig. cloth, scarce. Broadhurst 23-1450 1974 £10

LLOY.D GEORGE, DAVID   Better Times. 1910. 8vo., orig. cloth, first
edition. Rota 190-629 1974 £10

LLOYD'S   Treatise on Hats. London, 1821. 8vo., half
contemporary calf, folding frontis. Gregory 44-191 1974 $50

LLUECA, F. G.   Los Numulitidos de Espana. Madrid, 1929.
Roy. 8vo., cloth, plates, text-figures. Wheldon 128-912 1973 £12

LLUECA, F. G.   Los Numulitidos de Espana. Madrid, 1929.
Roy 8vo., cloth, plates. Wheldon 130-947 1974 £12

LLWYD, H.   Commentarioli Britannicae Descriptionis
Fragmentum. Cologne, 1572. Small 8vo., old calf, first edition. Quaritch
939-163 1974 £160

LLWYD, RICHARD   Poetical Works Of. 1837. 8vo., orig. cloth.
Broadhurst 23-1452 1974 £6

LLYFR Y PREGETH-WR. 1927. Crown 4to., limp blue buckram, uncut, limited
edition. Broadhurst 23-1035 1974 £55

LLYWARC HEN   Heroic Elegies and Other Pieces of. 1792.
Amateurishly rebound. Allen 216-1826 1974 $25

LOBB, THEOPHILUS   National Methods of Curing Fevers. London,
1734. 8vo., contemporary panelled calf, rebacked, plates, first edition. Schumann 35-284 1974 $145

LOBENSTINE, WILLIAM C.   Extracts from the Diary of. N.P., 1920.
Cloth, boards, label, fine, first edition. Bradley 35-44 1974 $50

LOCARD, A.   Histoire des Mollusques dans l'Antiquite.
Lyons, 1884. Roy. 8vo., wrappers, plate. Wheldon 128-844 1973 £5

LOCATELLI-MILESI, ACHILLE   L'Opera di Gaetano Previati. Milan, 1906.
4to., wrappers, plates. Minters 37-201 1973 $14

LOCHE, VICTOR   Exploration Scientifique de l'Algerie. Paris,
1867. 4to., new half red morocco, plates. Wheldon 131-75 1974 £120

LOCHER, JACOB   Libri Philomusi. Strassburg, 1497. Small 4to.,
very fine woodcuts, old boards, first edition, very fine, wide margins. Schafer
10-89 1974 sFr 8,000

LOCHNER VON HUMMELSTEIN, J. H.   Rariora Musei Besleriani.
Nuremberg, 1716. Folio, newly rebound in half calf antique style, engraved
double plates, rare. Wheldon 128-47 1973 £50

LOCHNER VON HUMMELSTEIN, J. H.   Rariora Musei Besleriani.
Nuremberg, 1716. Folio, rebound in half calf antique, plates, rare. Wheldon
131-170 1974 £50

LOCKE, ALAIN   When Peoples Meet. 1946. 825p., rev. ed.
Austin 62-386 1974 $17.50

LOCKE, DAVID ROSS   The Nasby Letters. Toledo, (1893). Rare,
orig. binding. Butterfield 10-22 1974 $50

LOCKE, G. H.   Builders of the Canadian Commonwealth.
Toronto, 1923. Hood's 102-30 1974 $10

LOCKE, G. H.   Builders of the Canadian Commonwealth.
Toronto, 1923. Hood's 104-35 1974 $10

LOCKE, JOHN   Directions Concerning Education. 1933.
4to., half morocco. Quaritch 939-164 1974 £35

LOCKE, JOHN   An Essay Concerning Humane Understanding.
1706. Folio, half calf, fifth edition. Howes 185-1920 1974 £50

LOCKE, JOHN   Further Considerations Concerning Raising the
Value of Money. London, 1695-96. 4 works in 1, 8vo., 18th century
sprinkled calf, first edition. Dawsons PM 247-181 1974 £600

LOCKE, JOHN   Two Treatises of Government. London, 1698.
8vo., contemporary panelled calf, third edition. Dawsons PM 247-182
1974 £75

LOCKE, JOHN   The Works of. 1722. 3 vols., folio,
engraved portrait, contemporary calf, bookplate, second edition. Bow Windows
66-431 1974 £115

LOCKE, WILLIAM J.   A Christmas Mystery. London, 1922. First
edition, square 8vo., full color illus., fine. Current BW9-54 1974 $22.50

LOCKER-LAMPSON, FREDERICK   The Rowfant Library. London, 1886.
2 vols., tall 8vo., orig. boards, uncut, fine, limited. Dawsons PM 10-366
1974 £75

LOCKER-LAMPSON, FREDERICK   The Rowfant Library. London, 1886-1900.
2 vols., tall 8vo., orig. boards, uncut. Dawsons PM 252-663 1974 £80

LOCKHART, GEORGE 1673-1731   Memoirs Concerning the Affairs of Scotland.
1714. 8vo., contemporary panelled calf. Quaritch 936-136 1974 £18

LOCKHART, JOHN GIBSON   Ancient Spanish Ballads; Historical and Romantic. London, 1841. 4to., contemporary morocco, richly gilt, joints and corners rubbed, chromolithographic title-pages, new edition, vignettes, fine, bookplate. MacManus 224-280 1974 $60

LOCKHART, JOHN GIBSON   The Life of Robert Burns. Liverpool, 1914. 2 vols., quarter vellum, gilt, fine, English first edition. Covent 56-201 1974 £15

LOCKHART, JOHN GIBSON   The Life of Sir Walter Scott. Edinburgh, 1902. 10 vols., orig. buckram, leather labels. Howes 185-427 1974 £28

LOCKHART, JOHN GIBSON   Memoirs of the Life of Sir Walter Scott. Edinburgh, 1837-38. 7 vols., 8vo., orig. cloth, rubbed, first edition. Howes 186-401 1974 £21

LOCKHART, JOHN GIBSON   Memoirs of the Life of Sir Walter Scott. 1902. 5 vols., illus., excellent edition. Austin 61-615 1974 $47.50

LOCKHART, JOHN GIBSON   Valerius. Edinburgh, 1821. 3 vols., 12mo., contemporary half calf, first edition. Dawsons PM 252-664 1974 £55

LOCKLEY, FRED   Oregon's Yesterdays. New York, 1928. Green cloth, inscription, fine, first edition. Bradley 35-289 1974 $25

LOCKRIDGE, ROSS, JR.   Raintree County. Boston, 1948. 1st ed. Biblo & Tannen 210-764 1973 $10

LOCKWOOD, FRANK C.   Pioneer Days in Arizona from the Spanish Occupation to Statehood. New York, 1932. Illus., first edition, scarce, nearly mint. Jenkins 61-142 1974 $32.50

LOCKWOOD, HENRY   Masaniello and Other Poems. 1883. Cloth gilt, presentation copy, inscribed, English first edition. Covent 56-871 1974 £6.30

LOCKWOOD, LUKE VINCENT   Gardens of Colony and State. (New York), 1931. Vol. 1, folio, illus., fine, orig. cloth. Gregory 44-192 1974 $70

LOCKWOOD, LUKE VINCENT   The Walpole Society. The Furniture Collectors' Glossary. New York, 1913. 8vo., boards, cloth back, paper labels, presentation copy inscribed by author. Goodspeed's 578-214 1974 $25

LODDER, J.   Die Hefesammlung des Centraalbureau. Amsterdam, 1934. Roy 8vo., buckram. Wheldon 129-1269 1974 £7.50

LODDIGES, CONRAD   The Botanical Cabinet. London, 1818-33. 20 vols., 4to., calf, rebacked worn, plates. Traylen 79-34 1973 £750

LODDIGES, CONRAD   Catalogue of Plants. 1818. Small 4to., modern boards, eleventh edition. Wheldon 129-1496 1974 £10

LODGE, HENRY CABOT   George Washington. Boston, c. 1898. 2 vols., top edge gilt, illus., green cloth, Standard Library Edition, tissue guards. Wilson 63-278 1974 $10

LODGE, HENRY CABOT   A Short History of the English Colonies in America. New York, 1881. rev. ed., inner hinge split. Biblo & Tannen 213-58 1973 $12.50

LODGE, OLIVER   Modern Views of Electricity. London, 1907. 8vo., red cloth. Dawsons PM 245-481 1974 £5

LODGE, OLIVER W. F.   Poems. Birmingham, 1915. Orig. buckram, presentation, inscribed, first edition. Howes 185-304 1974 £5

LODGE, R. B.   Bird Hunting Through Wild Europe. (1908). 8vo., cloth, illus. Wheldon 130-571 1974 £5

LODGE, RUPERT   The Great Thinkers. London, 1949. Author's sgd. pres. Biblo & Tannen 213-980 1973 $15

LOEB, JACQUES   Untersuchungen zur Physiologischen. 1891-2. 8vo., 2 vols., orig. wrappers, first edition. Gurney 64-136 1974 $15

LOEB, JACQUES   Untersuchungen zur Physiologischen Morphologie der Thiere. Wurzburg, 1891-92. 8vo., 2 vols., orig. wrappers, plates, first edition. Gurney 66-114 1974 £15

LOEB, JAMES   Die Bronzen der Sammlung. 1913. 4to., inscribed, plates. Allen 213-640 1973 $30

LOEB, LEO   The Biological Basis of Individuality. Springfield, 1945. First edition, orig. binding. Wilson 63-380 1974 $10

LOEBENSTEIN-LOEBEL, EDUARD LUDWIG   Wesen und Heilung der Epilepsie. Leipzig, 1818. 8vo., orig. boards, fine, first edition. Schumann 35-285 1974 $95

LOEDERER, R. A.   Voodoo Fire in Haiti. London, 1935. 8vo., illus., map, orig. cloth. Bow Windows 62-577 1974 £8.50

LOENING, GROVER C.   Military Aeroplanes. Boston, 1916. 8vo., cloth, illus., third edition. Hammond 201-874 1974 £6

LOEPELMANN, M.   Die Liederhandschrift des Cardinals de Rohan. Goettingen, 1923. 8vo., half leather. Kraus B8-145 1974 $20

LOFLING, P.   Reise nach den Spanischen Landern in Europe und America. 1766. 8vo., contemporary boards. Wheldon 129-1566 1974 £100

LOFLING, P.   Reise Nach den Spanischen Landern in Europa und America. Berlin & Stralsund, 1766. 8vo., contemporary boards, plates. Wheldon 131-1605 1974 £100

LOFT, CAPEL   Remarks on the Letter of the Rt. Hon. Edmund Burke. London, 1790. 8vo., modern boards. Dawsons PM 247-183 1974 £15

LOFTIE, W. J.   A History of London. 1883. 2 vols., plates, maps, half morocco gilt, rubbed. Smith 194-265 1974 £9.50

LOFTIE, W. J.   Landseer and Animal Painting in England. n.d. Plates, pictorial cloth, rubbed, scarce. Marsden 39-266 1974 £12

LOFTIE, W. J.   Lessons in the Art of Illuminating. London, n.d. Green cloth, gilt, plates. Dawson's 424-134 1974 $35

LOFTING, HUGH   Doctor Dolittle in the Moon. New York, (1928). 8vo., pictorial cloth, color frontispiece, illus., first edition. Frohnsdorff 16-520 1974 $15

LOFTING, HUGH   Doctor Dolittle's Garden. New York, 8vo., pictorial cloth, color frontispiece, illus., first edition. Frohnsdorff 16-519 1974 $10

LOFTING, HUGH   Doctor Dolittle's Return. Very good copy, first edition. Frohnsdorff 16-523 1974 $10

LOFTING, HUGH   Doctor Dolittle's Return. New York, 1933. 8vo., cloth with pict. label, illus. by author, bookplate, first edition, autographed by author. Frohnsdorff 15-93 1974 $17.50

LOFTING, HUGH   Doctor Dolittle's Return. New York, 1933. 8vo., pictorial cloth, color frontis., illus., fine, orig. d.j., first edition. Frohnsdorff 16-522 1974 $20

LOFTING, HUGH   The Twilight of Magic. New York, 1930. 8vo., cloth, color frontispiece, illus. by L. Lenski, first edition. Frohnsdorff 16-524 1974 $17.50

LOGAN, J. D.   Preludes, Sonnets and Other Verses. Toronto, 1906. Hood's 103-738 1974 $10

LOGAN, MARIA   Poems on Several Occasions. 1793. 4to., contemporary calf, rebacked, first edition. Quaritch 936-137 1974 £35

LOGGAN, D.   Oxonia Illustrata. Oxford, 1675. Folio, plates, old calf, rebacked. Quaritch 939-519 1974 £675

LOHWAG, H.   Anatomie der Asco-und Basidiomyceten. Berlin, 1941. Roy. 8vo., wrappers, text-figures, scarce orig. issue. Wheldon 128-1393 1973 £12

LOMAX, JOHN A.   Adventures of a Ballad Hunter. Macmillan, 1947. Austin 51-565 1973 $8.50

LOMBROSO, C.　　　　La Donna Delinquente, la Prostituta e la Donna Normale. Turin, 1893. 8vo., quarter calf, rubbed, folding plates, first edition. Gurney 66-115 1974 £20

LOMMIUS, JODOCUS　　　　Observationum Medicinalium. 1726. Small 8vo., contemporary calf, worn, gilt. Dawsons PM 249-348 1974 £12

LONCHAMP, F. C.　　　　L'Estampe et le Livre a Gravures. Lausanne, (1920). Large 8vo., cloth, illus., limited. Dawsons PM 10-368 1974 £36

LONCHAMPS, CHARLES DE　　　　Poesies Fugitives. Paris, 1821. 2 vols., small 12mo., contemporary red straight grain morocco, gilt. L. Goldschmidt 42-285 1974 $25

LONDE, CHARLES　　　　Nouveaux Elemens d'Hygiene. Paris, 1827. 8vo., 2 vols., contemporary half calf, first edition. Dawsons PM 249-349 1974 £28

LONDON, HANNAH　　　　Shades of My Forefathers. Springfield, Mass., 1941. 199p., illus., limited to 500 copies, signed by author. Austin 62-387 1974 $27.50

LONDON, HANNAH　　　　Shades of My Forefathers. 1941. Illus., signed, limited. Austin 57-412 1974 $27.50

LONDON, JACK　　　　The Abysmal Brute. New York, 1913. Ballinger 1-167 1974 $35

LONDON, JACK　　　　The Abysmal Brute. New York, 1913. Orig. cloth, some rubbing, first edition. MacManus 224-281 1974 $35

LONDON, JACK　　　　The Apostate. Chicago, n.d. Very good copy, little soiled wrappers. Covent 51-2440 1973 £12.50

LONDON, JACK　　　　Before Adam. New York, 1907. Plates, illus., faded, book-label. Covent 55-1036 1974 £15

LONDON, JACK　　　　Before Adam. 1913. 242p., illus. Austin 54-647 1973 $6.50

LONDON, JACK　　　　Burning Daylight. Macmillan, 1910. 361p., orig. illus. ed. Austin 54-648 1973 $7.50

LONDON, JACK　　　　Burning Daylight. Arco, Lond., 1968. 304p. Austin 54-649 1973 $4.50

LONDON, JACK　　　　The Call of the Wild. Grosset, Dunlap, 1903. 211p., illus. Austin 54-650 1973 $5

LONDON, JACK　　　　The Call of the Wild. New York, 1903. 12mo., cloth, first edition. Goodspeed's 578-215 1974 $15

LONDON, JACK　　　　The Call of the Wild. New York, 1903. Orig. dec. cloth, little rubbed, first edition, very good copy. MacManus 224-282 1974 $45

LONDON, JACK　　　　The Call of the Wild. New York, 1903. First edition, first issue, green cloth not vertically ribbed, lacking d.w., owner's name in ink on free fly leaf, unusually bright, tight copy, gilt on front cover & spine near pristine. Ross 87-367 1974 $90

LONDON, JACK　　　　The Faith of Men. Regent, 1904. 286p. Austin 54-652 1973 $6.50

LONDON, JACK　　　　The Faith of Men. Macmillan, 1904. 286p., orig. ed. Austin 54-651 1973 $7.50

LONDON, JACK　　　　The Game. Grosset, Dunlap. 1905. 182p., illus. Austin 54-654 1973 $6.50

LONDON, JACK　　　　The Game. Macmillan, 1905. 182p., orig. ed., illus. Austin 54-653 1973 $8.50

LONDON, JACK　　　　The Game. 1905. Orig. pictorial cloth, illus., plates. Covent 55-1038 1974 £10.50

LONDON, JACK　　　　The Game and the Abysmal Brute. London, Arco, 1967. 142p. Austin 54-655 1973 $4

LONDON, JACK　　　　The Iron Heel. Macmillan, 1907. 354p. Austin 54-656 1973 $7.50

LONDON, JACK　　　　The Iron Heel. Grossett, Dunlap, 1934. 354p., hard cover ed. Austin 54-657 1973 $6

LONDON, JACK　　　　Jack London; American Rebel. Citadel, 1947. 533p. Austin 54-672 1973 $10

LONDON, JACK　　　　John Barleycorn. Grosset, Dunlap, 1913. 343p., illus. Austin 54-658 1973 $7.50

LONDON, JACK　　　　John Barleycorn. New York, 1913. Orig. cloth, lettering of spine rubbed off, illus., first edition, second printing. MacManus 224-283 1974 $40

LONDON, JACK　　　　John Finkelman. Stockholm, 1914. Orig. front wrapper, half-leather, first Swedish edition. Ballinger 1-168 1974 $15

LONDON, JACK　　　　The Letters of Western Authors. 1935. Wrappers, English first edition. Covent 56-872 1974 £25

LONDON, JACK　　　　Love of Life. Regent, 1906. 265p. Austin 54-660 1973 $7.50

LONDON, JACK　　　　Love of Life. Review of Reviews, 1911. 265p. Austin 54-659 1973 $8.50

LONDON, JACK　　　　Martin Eden. Macmillan, 1908. 411p. Austin 54-662 1973 $6.50

LONDON, JACK　　　　Martin Eden. Macmillan, 1908. 411p., orig. ed. Austin 54-661 1973 $10

LONDON, JACK　　　　Martin Eden. New York, 1909. Cloth, frontispiece, first edition. Dawson's 424-291 1974 $20

LONDON, JACK　　　　Martin Eden. Macmillan, ca. 1956. 381p. Austin 54-663 1973 $6

LONDON, JACK　　　　The Mutiny of the Elsinore. 1915. Worn covers, frontispiece. Covent 55-1040 1974 £7.50

LONDON, JACK　　　　The Night Born. Grosset, Dunlap, 1913. 290p. Austin 54-664 1973 $7.50

LONDON, JACK　　　　The Road. Ondon, Arco, 1967. 150p. Austin 54-665 1973 $8.50

LONDON, JACK　　　　The Scarlet Plague and Before Adam. London, Arco, 1968. 173p. Austin 54-666 1973 $7.50

LONDON, JACK　　　　The Sea Wolf. Macmillan, 1904. 366p., illus. Austin 54-667 1973 $7.50

LONDON, JACK　　　　The Sea-Wolf. London, 1904. First English edition, illus., near fine, light glassine wrapper. Ross 87-369 1974 $15

LONDON, JACK　　　　The Sea-Wolf. New York, 1904. First edition, second issue, with copyright notices dated 1903 & 1904 and lettering on spine in white, illus., orig. binding, penciled name inside front cover, lacking d.w., very nice. Ross 87-368 1974 $25

LONDON, JACK　　　　Smoke Bellew. New York, 1912. Cloth, first edition. Dawson's 424-292 1974 $35

LONDON, JACK　　　　The Son of the Wolf. Boston & New York, 1900. Orig. cloth, stamped in silver, first edition, third printing, about fine copy. MacManus 224-284 1974 $110

LONDON, JACK　　　　The Son of the Wolf. Boston & New York, 1900. Orig. dec. cloth, frontispiece, first American edition. Covent 55-1041 1974 £75

LONDON, JACK　　　　South Sea Tales. Macmillan, ca. 1956. Austin 54-668 1973 $6

LONDON, JACK　　　　The Valley of the Moon. Macmillan, 1913. 530p., orig. ed. Austin 54-669 1973 $8.50

LONDON, JACK   The Valley of the Moon. 1914. English first edition. Covent 56-873 1974 £5.25

LONDON, JACK   When God Laughs. International Fiction Library, 1911. 319p. Austin 54-670 1973 $6

LONDON, JACK   When God Laughs and Other Stories. Leipzig, 1912. Wrappers, English first edition. Covent 56-1892 1974 £6.30

LONDON, JACK   White Fang. New York, 1906. 8vo., pictorial cloth, illus., spine ends worn, endpapers cracked at hinges, first edition. Frohnsdorff 16-525 1974 $10

LONDON, JACK   White Fang. Macmillan, 1956. 329p. Austin 54-671 1973 $6

LONDON   Early Drawings and Pictures of London, With Some Contemporary Furniture. 1920. 4to., plates, buckram. Quaritch 940-171 1974 £25

LONDON - GUILDHALL LIBRARY   Cat. of the Library...Instituted in the Year 1824. London, 1859. Demy 8vo., half morocco, slightly rubbed. Forster 97-235 1974 £7.50

LONDON - UNIVERSITY - LIBRARY   Catalogue of Books on Archaeology. London, 1935-40. 6 parts in 1 vol., folio, quarter tan morocco, fine. Dawsons PM 10-617 1974 £20

LONDON Almanack for the Year of Christ 1753. Orig. red morocco, gilt, edges worn & rounded, 2 1/4 X 1 1/4. Gregory 44-407 1974 $45

LONDON Almanack, 1779. Black and gold with red overlay, portrait, 2 1/4 X 1 5/16. Gregory 44-408 1974 $100

THE LONDON Almanack, 1780. Full plain red morocco, matching case, fine, 2 1/4 X 1 5/16. Gregory 44-409 1974 $110

THE LONDON Almanack, 1783. Red, green and cream inlaid binding, matching case, 2 3/8 X 1 3/8. Gregory 44-410 1974 $95

THE LONDON Almanack. 1790. Full red morocco, fine, matching case little worn, 2 1/4 X 1 3/8. Gregory 44-411 1974 $85

THE LONDON Almanack, 1794. Dark Green and cream morocco, matching case, 2 1/4 X 1 3/8. Gregory 44-412 1974 $95

THE LONDON Almanack. 1795. Red, black and gold morocco, lacks backstrip, matching case rubbed, 2 1/4 X 1 5/8. Gregory 44-413 1974 $65

THE LONDON Almanack. 1797. Full red straight grain morocco, loose in binding, 1 1/4 X 1 1/4. Gregory 44-414 1974 $50

THE LONDON Almanack. 1806. Full red morocco, silver clasp, fine, 2 1/4 X 1 1/2. Gregory 44-415 1974 $95

LONDON Almanack for the Year of Christ 1807. Red morocco, top edge of front cover & spine worn, 2 3/8 X 1 3/8. Gregory 44-416 1974 $45

LONDON Almanack for the Year of Christ, 1808. 1808. Folded engraved view, size 2 1/4 by 1 1/3 inches, orig. red morocco gilt inlaid in brown, beige and black leathers, gilt edges, slip case, good copy, scarce. Sawyer 293-223 1974 £65

THE LONDON Almanack, 1809. Red, black and gold onlays, 2 1/4 X 1 3/8. Gregory 44-417 1974 $40

THE LONDON Almanack, 1809. Full red straight grain morocco, 1 1/4 X 1 1/4. Gregory 44-418 1974 $65

THE LONDON Almanack, 1821. Full black morocco, wallet flap, fine, 2 1/4 X 1 3/8. Gregory 44-419 1974 $75

THE LONDON Almanack. 1821. Orig. brown morocco richly gold tooled, unusually fine, 2 1/4 X 1 3/8. Gregory 44-420 1974 $110

LONDON Almanack for the Year of Christ, 1826. Full brown morocco, gilt clasp, 1 1/4 X 1 1/4. Gregory 44-421 1974 $65

THE LONDON Almanack. 1833. Orig. diced calf, wallet flap, 2 1/4 X 1 1/2. Gregory 44-422 1974 $85

THE LONDON Almanack. 1838. Full bright red straight grain morocco, wallet flap, fine. Gregory 44-423 1974 $85

LONDON Almanack for the Year of Christ 1847. Full red morocco, wallet flap, 1 1/4 X 1 1/4. Gregory 44-424 1974 $45

THE LONDON Almanack. 1851. Orig. black morocco, matching slip case, 2 3/8 X 1 1/4. Gregory 44-425 1974 $60

THE LONDON Almanack. 1874. Full red morocco, matching case, 2 3/8 X 3/4. Gregory 44-426 1974 $40

LONDON AND MIDDLESEX HISTORICAL SOCIETY   Transactions and Programs from 1902-1917. Bound in 1 vol. Hood's 102-849 1974 $75

LONDON and North Western Railway Company, The Llanelly Railway Company and the Great Western Railway Company. Agreement No. 301. F'cap folio, binder's boards, linen spine, mint. Broadhurst 24-1286 1974 £16

LONDON and North Western Railway Company and the Great Western Railway Company, Agreement No. 296. 1888. F'cap folio, binder's boards, linen spine, mint. Broadhurst 24-1285 1974 £16

LONDON and North Western Railway Report of Directors. 1896. Folio, morocco. Quaritch 939-82 1974 £30

LONDON and North Western Railway Rules and Regulations for the Conduct of the Traffic. 1880. Small 8vo., limp leather. Quaritch 939-83 1974 £12

LONDON and North Western Railway Rules and Regulations for the Conduct of the Traffic. 1904. 12mo., cloth, stained. Quaritch 939-84 1974 £9.50

LONDON and North Western Railway Rules and Regulations for the Conduct of Traffic. (1916). 12mo., cloth. Quaritch 939-85 1974 £8.75

LONDON Catalogue of Books With Their Sizes, Prices and Publishers. London, 1827. Demy 8vo., cloth faded. Forster 97-260 1974 £6

LONDON SCHOOL OF ECONOMICS   Cat. of a Collection of Works on Publishing and Bookselling. London, 1936. Limited to 250 copies on special paper for presentation, roy. 8vo., orig. wrappers. Forster 97-263 1974 £6

LONDON Stage. Collection of Most Reputed Tragedies, Comedies, Operas, etc. Performed at Theatres Roayl. c.1825. 4 vols., half calf, rubbed. Allen 216-2132 1974 £30

LONDON Vanished & Vanishing. London, (1905). Edition de Luxe, limited to 250 copies, signed by P. Norman, cold. plates, post 4to., orig. white cloth soiled. Forster 97-267 1974 £5

LONDONDERRY, ROBERT STEWART, 2ND MARQUIS OF, 1769-1822   Memoirs and Correspondence of. London, 1849-51. 9 vols., 8vo., cloth boards, rare. Emerald 50-128 1974 £30

LONDONDERRY, ROBERT STEWART, 2ND MARQUIS OF, 1769-1822   Memoirs and Correspondence. 1848-49. 4 vols., orig. cloth, frayed. Howes 186-692 1974 £10

LONE, E. MIRIAM   Some Noteworthy Firsts in Europe During the 15th Century. New York, 1930. 8vo., orig. cloth, plates. Dawsons PM 10-371 1974 £8

LONELICH, HERRY   The History of the Holy Grail. London, 1824-25. 2 vols., 4to., orig. wrappers. Dawsons PM 252-665 1974 £7.50

LONG, A. L.   Memoirs of Robert E. Lee. 1866. Large 8vo., orig. binding. Butterfield 10-165 1974 $15

LONG, CHARLES EDWARD   Royal Descent. London, 1845. 4to., red morocco, gilt, first edition. Dawsons PM 251-127 1974 £50

LONG, EDWARD   English Humanity. London, 1778. 8vo., disbound. Dawsons PM 247-184 1974 £20

LONG, ESMOND R.   Selected Readings In Pathology.   Springfield, 1929. Tall 8vo., cloth, library stamps, illus.   Rittenhouse 46-419 1974 $25

LONG, G.   English Inns and Road-Houses.   (1937). 8vo., orig. cloth, photos., plates, coloured frontispiece, first edition.   Bow Windows 66-436 1974 £6.50

LONG, JOHN   John Long's Voyages and Travels in the Years 1768-88.   1922. Dec. cloth, gilt top, folding map, very good copy.   Dykes 22-132 1973 $10

LONG, JOHN   Voyages and Travels Of an Indian Interpreter and Trader.   London, 1791. Mottled cover, leather spine.   Hood's 103-546 1974 $375

LONG, JOHN   Voyages and Travels Of an Indian Interpreter and Trader.   London, 1791. 4to., full polished calf, leather label, rubbed, first edition.   Traylen 79-489 1973 £240

LONGBRIDGE, FREDERICK   The Holiday Train, a Song of "Dulce Domum".   New York & London, (c. 1870). 12mo., colored pictorial wrappers, illus., very fine.   Current BW9-114 1974 $22.50

LONGFELLOW, HENRY WADSWORTH   Coplas de Don Jorge Manrique.   Boston, 1833. 12mo., orig. blue cloth, nice, first edition.   Ximenes 36-140 1974 $65

LONGFELLOW, HENRY WADSWORTH   Courtship of Miles Standish.   1858. Binding spotted, spine worn, first edition, first issue.   Allen 216-1035 1974 $20

LONGFELLOW, HENRY WADSWORTH   The Courtship of Miles Standish and Other Poems.   Boston, 1858. First American edition, first state, book ad. insert, orig. binding.   Wilson 63-547 1974 $38.75

LONGFELLOW, HENRY WADSWORTH   The Courtship of Miles Standish.   Boston, 1858. First American edition, first issue, with "treacherous" for "ruddy", brown cloth, publisher's ad for Waverley Novels tipped in, one corner slightly rubbed, unusually fine, tight copy, rare in such condition.   Ross 87-370 1974 $200

LONGFELLOW, HENRY WADSWORTH   The Courtship of Miles Standish and Other Poems.   Boston, 1858. Orig. cloth, ends of spine and corners rubbed, first American printing, fine.   MacManus 224-285 1974 $75

LONGFELLOW, HENRY WADSWORTH   The Golden Legend.   Boston, 1851. Orig. cloth, few stains, corners little rubbed, first printing, fine, bright & tight copy.   MacManus 224-286 1974 $32.50

LONGFELLOW, HENRY WADSWORTH   Hyperion, a Romance.   New York, 1839. 2 vols., orig. boards, some rubbing & waterstaining, first edition, some foxing.   MacManus 224-287 1974 $50

LONGFELLOW, HENRY WADSWORTH   Poems.   Boston, 1884. Revised edition, 8vo., brown tree calf, excellent condition, contents mint, illus.   Current BW9-247 1974 $35

LONGFELLOW, HENRY WADSWORTH   Poems of Places.   Boston, 1876. 8vo., orig. cloth, inscribed, first edition.   Rota 189-573 1974 £25

LONGFELLOW, HENRY WADSWORTH   Poetical Works.   1881. 2 vols., folio, morocco, plates.   Allen 216-O 1974 $25

LONGFELLOW, HENRY WADSWORTH   Prose Works.   Boston, 1857. First edition, 2 vols., 24mo., first state, orig. binding.   Wilson 63-549 1974 $20

LONGFELLOW, HENRY WADSWORTH   The Seaside and the Fireside.   Boston, 1850. First edition, 12mo., brown cloth, top of spine worn with minor repair, else near fine.   Current BW9-248 1974 $20

LONGFELLOW, HENRY WADSWORTH   The Seaside and Fireside.   Boston, 1850. Orig. cloth, ends of spine worn, some staining, first edition, light foxing.   MacManus 224-288 1974 $27.50

LONGFELLOW, HENRY WADSWORTH   Song of Hiawatha.   1855. Modern half calf, first edition.   Allen 216-1037 1974 $20

LONGFELLOW, HENRY WADSWORTH   The Song of Hiawatha.   Boston, 1855. This copy has all first edition points with letter "n" on page 279, orig. brown cloth.   Wilson 63-550 1974 $67.50

LONGFELLOW, HENRY WADSWORTH   The Song of Hiawatha.   Boston, 1855. Orig. cloth, first American printing, very fresh copy.   MacManus 224-289 1974 $85

LONGFELLOW, HENRY WADSWORTH   The Song of Hiawatha.   Boston, 1855. 12mo., contemporary green calf, back faded, marbled edges, presentation copy, first American edition.   Goodspeed's 578-216 1974 $250

LONGFELLOW, HENRY WADSWORTH   The Song of Hiawatha.   London, 1855. 8vo., orig. cloth, fine, first edition.   Dawsons PM 252-666 1974 £250

LONGFELLOW, HENRY WADSWORTH   The Song of Hiawatha.   Boston, 1898. Illus. by Remington, orig. red dec. cloth, faded spine, interior very good.   Current BW9-249 1974 $27.50

LONGFELLOW, HENRY WADSWORTH.   The Song of Hiawatha.   New York, 1910.   Biblo & Tannen 213-568 1973 $15

LONGFELLOW, HENRY WADSWORTH   The Song of Hiawatha.   Boston & New York, 1911. Small 4to., cloth with pictorial overlay by Maxfield Parrish, illus. by Frederick Remington, fine copy, first edition.   Frohnsdorff 15-129 1974 $35

LONGFELLOW, HENRY WADSWORTH   The Song of Hiawatha.   Boston, 1855. First American edition, first printing, with ads dated November and "dove" for "dived", brown cloth, unusually fine, tight copy, tight hinges, very rare in such condition.   Ross 87-371 1974 $125

LONGFELLOW, HENRY WADSWORTH   Tales of a Wayside Inn.   1863. First edition.   Allen 216-1038 1974 $15

LONGFELLOW, HENRY WADSWORTH   Tales of a Wayside Inn.   Boston, 1863. Orig. cloth, vignette title-page, ends of spine rubbed, first American edition, very good copy.   MacManus 224-290 1974 $37.50

LONGLEY, J. W.   Love.   Toronto, 1898.   Hood's 103-416 1974 $10

LONGMAN & LOCH   Pins and Pincushions.   London, 1911. Illus., 8vo., orig. cloth.   Gregory 44-193 1974 $22.50

LONGMORE, T.   Richard Wiseman, Surgeon and Sergeant-Surgeon to Charles II.   London, 1891. 8vo., orig. cloth, portrait, first edition.   Gurney 66-116 1974 £15

LONGSTREET, AUGUSTUS B.   Georgia Scenes.   New York, 1851. Orig. illus., foxing, second edition.   Rinsland 58-901 1974 $32

LONGSTREET, JAMES   From Manassas to Appomattox.   Philadelphia, 1896. Plates, maps, portraits, front hinge cracked, orig. binding.   Butterfield 10-166 1974 $50

LONGUEVILLE, PETER   The English Hermit.   (c. 1800). Woodcuts, 16mo., orig. ptd. boards, lacks most of spine, stitching loose.   George's 610-482 1973 £10

LONGUEVILLE, PETER   The English Hermit.   (c. 1800). Woodcut frontis., full page woodcuts, incomplete copy, 12mo., orig. Dutch floral boards, sides virtually detached.   George's 610-483 1973 £7.50

LONGUS   Les Amours Pastorales de Daphnis et Chloe.   1933. 4to., illus., half vellum, uncut, slip case, limited.   Bow Windows 62-36 1974 £160

LONGUS   Daphnis and Chloe.   New York, 1926. Sm. 4to., orig. cl., gilt, ltd. to 250 copies.   Jacobs 24-104 1974 $25

LONGUS   The Pastoral Loves of Daphnis and Chloe.   1924. Orig. cloth, signed, first edition.   Rota 188-692 1974 £5

LONGYEAR, B. O.   Trees and Shrubs of the Rocky Mountain Region.   New York, 1927. Post 8vo., cloth, plates, drawings.   Wheldon 131-1742 1974 £5

LONICER, PHILIP   Icones Livianae. Frankfurt, 1572. Small oblong 4to., portrait, large woodcuts by Jost Amman, contemporary limp vellum, fine. Schafer 10-84 1974 sFr 2,200

LOOMIS, CHARLES B.   Cheerful Americans. Holt, 1903. 299p., illus. Austin 54-673 1973 $7.50

LOOS, ANITA   Gigi. Random, 1952. 169p., illus. Austin 51-567 1973 $7.50

LOOS, ANITA   A Girl Like I. Viking, 1966. 275p., illus. Austin 51-568 1973 $6

LOOSJES, VINCENT   Gedenkschriften Wegens het 4e Eeuwgetijde van de Uitvinding der Boekdrukkunst door Lourens Janszoon Koster. Haarlem, 1824. 8vo., plates, engraved portrait, polished half calf. Kraus B8-348 1974 $65

LOPEZ-REY, JOSE   Francisco de Goya. New York, 1950. Sm. 4to., illus. Biblo & Tannen 214-269 1974 $8.50

LORCH, FRED W.   The Trouble Begins At Eight. 1968. 375p., illus. Austin 51-569 1973 $10

LORD, ELIOT   Comstock Mining and Miners. Washington, 1883. Thick 4to., orig. bindings. Butterfield 8-333 1974 $35

LORD, ELIOT   The Italian In America. Buck, 1905. 268p., illus., orig. ed. Austin 62-388 1974 $10

LORD, W. B.   Shifts and Expedients of Camp Life, Travel and Explorations. 1876. 8vo., orig. cloth. Broadhurst 23-1671 1974 £30

THE LORD'S Prayer With Hymns and Illustrations for Little Children. (London), (c. 1890). 8vo., full color illus., very fine. Current BW9-119 1974 $18

LORENTZ, HENDRIK ANTOON   The Theory of Electrons. Leipzig, 1909. 8vo., orig. cloth, first edition. Schumann 35-286 1974 $165

LORENTZ, HENDRIK ANTOON   Zichtbare en Onzichtbare Bewegingen. 1901. 8vo., orig. three quarter pebbled cloth, boards. Zeitlin 235-142 1974 $45

LORENTZ, T.   Beitrag zur Kenntniss der Ornithologischen Fauna an der Nordseite des Kaukasus. Moscow, 1887. 4to., half roan, hand-coloured photogravures. Wheldon 128-508 1973 £10

LORIMER, JOHN   A Concise Essay on Magnetism. London, 1795. 4to., half calf, plates, first edition. Schumann 35-287 1974 $135

LORINI, BONAINTO   Le Fortificationi. Venice, 1609. Folio, old boards, illus., library stamp, uncut, second edition. Traylen 79-147 1973 £140

LORIOT, ANTOINE JOSEPH   Extrait en Abrege. (1774). 4to., disbound. Zeitlin 235-286 1974 $27.50

LORIOT, ANTOINE JOSEPH   A Practical Essay on a Cement. London, 1777. 8vo., modern boards. Zeitlin 235-285 1974 $75

LORITI, HEINRICH GLAREANUS
Please turn to
GLAREANUS, HENRICUS

LORMOIS DE   Le Vernisseur Parfait ou Manuel du Vernisseur. 1771. Small 8vo., boards, cloth spine, rare. Quaritch 940-173 1974 £65

LORNE, MARQUIS OF   Canadian Pictures Drawn With Pen and Pencil. London, 1892. Engraved illus., folding tinted map. Hood's 102-156 1974 $17.50

LORRAIN, ALFRED M.   The Helm, the Sword, and the Cross. Cincinnati, 1862. Cloth, worn. Hayman 57-389 1974 $15

LORRY, ANNE CHARLES DE   De Melancholia et Morbis Melancholicis. Paris, 1765. 2 vols., 8vo., contemporary mottled calf, rubbed, first edition. Schuman 37-159 1974 $115

LORRY, PAUL CHARLES   Essai de Dissertation, ou Recherches sur le Mariage en sa Qualite de Contrat et de Sacrement. Paris, 1760. 12mo., fine copy, contemporary leather. Schumann 499-61 1974 sFr 75

LOS ANGELES: A Guide to the City and Its Environs. New York, 1941. Red-stamped green cloth, illus., first edition. Bradley 35-45 1974 $10

LOS Angeles: A Guide to the City and Its Environs. New York, 1941. Orig. green cloth, mint, dust jacket, first edition. Bradley 35-233 1974 $15

LOSSING, BENSON J.   The Pictorial Field-Book of the War of 1812. New York, 1868. Cover mended, new end papers, engravings on wood, frontis. stained. Hood's 102-110 1974 $60

LOSSING, BENSON J.   Seventeen Hundred and Seventy Six. New York, 1847. 1st ed. Biblo & Tannen 213-59 1973 $42.50

LOTH, OTTO   A Catalogue of the Arabic Manuscripts in the Library of the India Office. London, 1877. 4to., orig. cloth, uncut. Dawsons PM 10-373 1974 £11

THE LOTTERY Ticket; or, The Evils of Gaming. Edinburgh, 1825. 16mo., boards, cloth spine, engraved frontispiece, engraved title vignette, very good copy. Frohnsdorff 15-95 1974 $20

THE LOTTERY Ticket; or, The Evils of Gaming. Edinburgh, 1825. 16mo., boards, cloth spine, engraved frontispiece. Frohnsdorff 16-527 1974 $20

LOTZE, H.   Mikrocosmus. Leipzig, 1856. Crown 8vo., contemporary straight grained green morocco, presentation inscription from author. Forster 97-305 1974 £3

LOTZE, RUDOLPH H.   Medicinische Psychologie. Leipzig, 1852. 8vo., orig. boards, slipcase, uncut, first edition. Gurney 64-137 1974 £90

LOTZE, RUDOLPH H.   Medicinische Psychologie Oder Physiologie der Selle. Leipzig, 1852. 8vo., orig. boards, joint weak, slipcase, uncut. Gurney 66-117 1974 £75

LOUBAT, ALPHONSE   The American Vine Dressers Guide. New York, 1827. Scarce, orig. cover, first edition. Ballinger 1-288 1974 $35

LOUBAT, J. F.   The Medallic History of the United States of America, 1776-1876. New York, 1878. Folio, 2 vols., vol. 1 text, vol. 2 numbered plates, fine. Butterfield 10-385 1974 $125

LOUBIER, J.   Der Bucheinband in Alter und Neuer Zeit. Berlin & Leipzig, (1904). Small 4to., illus., cloth. Quaritch 940-605 1974 £7.50

LOUDON, J.   De Indische Archipel. The Hague, 1865. Large folio, contemporary half red morocco gilt, very rare. Traylen 79-524 1973 £300

LOUDON, JANE   Instructions in Gardening for Ladies. 1840. 12mo., orig. cloth, illus., very scarce first edition. Wheldon 131-1539 1974 £12

LOUDON, JANE   The Ladies' Flower-Garden of Ornamental Annuals. London, 1840. 4to., half green morocco, gilt, plates, first & best edition. Traylen 79-35 1973 £125

LOUDON, JANE   The Ladies' Flower Garden of Ornamental Annuals. 1840. 4to., contemporary half green morocco gilt, hand coloured plates, trifle rubbed. Wheldon 128-1496 1973 £170

LOUDON, JANE   The Ladies' Flower Garden of Ornamental Annuals. London, 1840. 4to., cloth, worn. Traylen 79-36 1973 £110

LOUDON, JANE   The Ladies' Flower Garden of Ornamental Bulbous Plants. 1841. 4to., contemporary half green morocco gilt, hand coloured plates, first and best issue. Wheldon 128-1497 1973 £220

LOUDON, JOHN CLAUDIUS   Arboretum et Fruticetum Britannicum. 1844. or 1854. 8 vols., 8vo., orig. cloth, plates, text figures, second edition. Wheldon 128-1607 1973 £30

LOUDON, JOHN CLAUDIUS   Arboretum et Fruticetum Britannicum. 1844.
8vo., new cloth, 8 vols., second edition. Wheldon 129-1612 1974 £40

LOUDON, JOHN CLAUDIUS   Arboretum et Fruticetum Britannicum. 1844.
8 vols., 8vo., orig. cloth, plates, nice copy. Wheldon 131-1743 1974 £60

LOUDON, JOHN CLAUDIUS   An Encyclopaedia of Gardening. 1824. Thick
8vo., contemporary half calf, gilt, illus., second edition. Hammond 201-657
1974 £22

LOUDON, JOHN CLAUDIUS   Encyclopaedia of Plants. 1855. 8vo., modern
full calf, gilt, text fiugres, new edition. Wheldon 128-1138 1973 £15

LOUDON, JOHN CLAUDIUS   An Encyclopaedia of Plants. 1829. 8vo.,
contemporary half calf. Wheldon 129-1498 1974 £15

LOUDON, JOHN CLAUDIUS   An Encyclopaedia of Plants. 1829. 8vo.,
contemporary half calf, scarce first edition. Wheldon 131-1540 1974 £15

LOUDON, JOHN CLAUDIUS   An Encyclopaedia of Plants. 1855. 8vo.,
contemporary half morocco. Wheldon 129-1499 1974 £15

LOUDON, JOHN CLAUDIUS   Loudon's Hortus Britannicus. 1850. 8vo., half
calf. Wheldon 128-1495 1973 £10

LOUDON, JOHN CLAUDIUS   The Magazine of Natural History. London,
1829-33. 6 vols., 8vo., old half calf, rubbed, illus. Traylen 79-96 1973 £10

LOUDON, JOHN CLAUDIUS   The Suburban Horticulturist. 1842. 8vo.,
cloth. Wheldon 131-1541 1974 £7.50

LOUDON, JOHN CLAUDIUS   A Treatise on Forming, Improving and Managing
Country Residences. London, 1806. 4to., 2 vols., contemporary calf, gilt,
plates, first edition. Hammond 201-659 1974 £165

LOUDON, JOHN CLAUDIUS   Trees and Shrubs, an Abridgement of the Arboretum
and Fruticetum Britannicum. 1875. 8vo., binders' cloth. Wheldon 131-1744
1974 £10

LOUDON, JOHN CLAUDIUS   Trees and Shrubs. 1883. 8vo., half leather.
Wheldon 129-1613 1974 £15

LOUDON, W. J.   Sir William Mulock. Toronto, 1932. Faded
cover. Hood's 104-272 1974 $10

LOUIS, ANTOINE   Memoire Contre la Legitimite des Naissances Pre-
tendres Tardives. Paris, 1764. 8vo., contemporary speckled calf, first editions.
Schumann 35-288 1974 $95

LOUIS, PIERRE CHARLES ALEXANDRE   Recherches Anatomico Pathologiques.
Paris, 1825. 8vo., 19th century calf, first edition. Dawsons PM 249-350
1974 £90

LOUIS, PIERRE CHARLES ALEXANDRE   Recherches Anatomiques. Paris, 1829.
8vo., 2 vols., 19th century blue cloth, first edition. Dawsons PM 249-353
1974 £95

LOUIS, PIERRE CHARLES ALEXANDRE   Researches on Phthisis. London, 1844.
8vo., orig. cloth, gilt, rebacked. Dawsons PM 249-352 1974 £15

LOUIS-MARIE, P.   Flore-Manuel de la Province de Quebec,
Canada. Montreal, (1931). Roy. 8vo., cloth, coloured plates. Wheldon
128-1282 1973 £5

LOUIS-PHILIPPE, KING OF FRANCE   Catalogue de Livres Provenant des
Bibliotheques du feu Roi Louis-Philippe. Paris, 1852. 2 vols., 8vo., half calf
and half cloth. Kraus B8-146 1974 $45

LOUNSBURY, T. R.   History of the English Language. 1894.
Revised & enlarged edition. Austin 61-617 1974 $10

LOUP, MICHEL   Solution du Probleme Aerienne. Paris, 1853.
Small 8vo., orig. yellow printed wrappers, fine, first and only edition. Dawsons
PM 245-482 1974 £25

LOUREIRO, J. DE   Flora Cochinchinensis. Lisbon, 1790. 4to.,
new buckram, uncut. Wheldon 129-1102 1974 £60

LOURIE, ARTHUR   Sergei Koussevitzky and his Epoch. New
York, 1931. 1st ed., illus. Biblo & Tannen 214-870 1974 $7.50

LOUTHERBOURG, P. J. DE   The Romantic and Picturesque Scenery of
England and Wales. 1805. Roy. folio, contemporary half red morocco, plates,
fine. Quaritch 939-165 1974 £750

LOUVET DE COUVRAY, JEAN BAPTISTE   Les Amours du Chevalier de Faublas.
Paris, 1884. 5 vols., 12mo., three quarter black morocco, gilt, illus., orig.
wrapper. L. Goldschmidt 42-70 1974 $32.50

LOUYER-VILLERMAY, JEAN BAPTISTE   Recherches Historiques et Medicales sur
l'Hypocondrie. Paris, 1802. Small 8vo., boards, first edition. Schumann 35-
289 1974 $65

LOUYS, PIERRE   Les Adventures du Roi Pausole. Paris, n.d.
Illus., one of 1000 numbered copies. Jacobs 24-105 1974 $25

LOUYS, PIERRE   Aphrodite. N.p., n.d. Ltd. ed., unopened
copy. Biblo & Tannen 213-569 1973 $10

LOUYS, PIERRE   Aphrodite. Paris, 1896. Ltd. ed. Biblo &
Tannen 213-570 1973 $15

LOUYS, PIERRE   Aphrodite. Paris, (c.1900). 8vo., cloth,
orig. wrapper, illus. L. Goldschmidt 42-286 1974 $15

LOUYS, PIERRE   Aphrodite. Paris, 1900. Narrow crown 8vo.,
full morocco, gilt, orig. wrappers, illus., first English edition. Howes
186-311 1974 £25

LOUYS, PIERRE   Aphrodite. Paris, 1906. 8vo., rebound, half
green morocco, gilt, first English edition. Rota 190-635 1974 £5

LOUYS, PIERRE   Archipel. Paris, 1906. 12mo., olive green
cloth, gilt, uncut, first edition. L. Goldschmidt 42-287 1974 $15

LOUYS, PIERRE   Les Poesies de Meleagre. Paris, 1893.
18mo., full green morocco, gilt, uncut, first edition. L. Goldschmidt 42-288
1974 $35

LOUYS, PIERRE   Woman and Puppet. N. P., 1930. Boards,
vellum backstrip, illus., limited to 2,500 copies, very good. Wilson 63-551
1974 $16.75

LOUYS, PIERRE   Woman and Puppet. 1930. Ltd. ed. Biblo &
Tannen 213-571 1973 $15

LOVAT, SIMON FRASER   Memoires de la Vie Du Lord Lovat.
Amsterdam, 1747. 8vo., wrappers. Bow Windows 62-584 1974 £7.50

LOVE, JOHN   Geodaesia. 1786. 8vo., contemporary polished
calf, gilt. Zeitlin 235-143 1974 $135

LOVE, JR., W. DE LOSS   The Fast and Thanksgiving Days of New England.
1895. 8vo., orig. bindings. Butterfield 8-345 1974 $20

THE LOVE Gift and Token of Regard. Liverpool, 1848. Orig. gold stamped red
cloth, full page engravings, 2 1/8 X 2. Gregory 44-427 1974 $55

THE LOVE of an Unkown Solider, Found in a Dug-Out. Toronto, 1918. Hood's
104-121 1974 $15

LOVE Songs of English Poets; 1500-1800. 1892. Large paper edition, limited to
100 numbered copies, inscribed from publisher, buckram, bevelled edges, gilt
top. Covent 51-68 1973 £5.25

LOVECHILD, MRS.   Easy Reading. London, 1814. 12mo., illus.,
contemporary sheep. Dawsons PM 252-667 1974 £7

LOVELACE, RICHARD   Lucasta. 1864. Illus., first edition. Austin
61-618 1974 $17.50

LOVELL, ROBERT   Enchiridion Botanicum. Oxford, 1665.
Small 8vo., contemporary calf, rebacked. Thomas 28-266 1972 £50

LOVELL, ROBERT   Pambotanologia. Oxford, 1665. 12mo.,
contemporary calf, second edition. Schuman 37-160 1974 $250

LOVER, SAMUEL　　　　Legends and Stories of Ireland.　Dublin,
1832.　8vo., half roan, label, second edition.　Emerald 50-556　1974　£5

LOVER, SAMUEL　　　　Songs and Ballads.　1839.　First edition, 8vo.,
half green polished calf gilt, spine with floral tools gilt, top edges gilt, fine copy,
scarce.　Sawyer 293-207　1974　£8

LOVETT, H. A.　　　　Canada and the Grand Trunk, 1829-1924.
(Toronto, 1924).　Inscribed, signed.　Hood's 103-293　1974　$35

LOVETT, R. M.　　　　History of the Novel in England.　1932.
Allen 216-1224　1974　$10

LOVEWELL, BERTHA ELLEN　　The Life of St. Cecilia.　1898.　Ex-library,
library binding.　Austin 61-619　1974　$22.50

LOW, DAVID　　　　Low's Political Parade.　(1936)　Oblong 4to.,
cloth-backed boards, English first edition.　Covent 56-874　1974　£12.50

LOW, DAVID　　　　On the Domesticated Animals of the British
Islands.　1845.　8vo., orig. cloth repaired.　Wheldon 129-387　1974　£12

LOW, DAVID　　　　Years of Wrath.　New York, 1946.　4to.,
1st ed.　Biblo & Tannen 210-68　1973　$12.50

LOW, FRANCES H.　　　　Queen Victoria's Dolls.　1894.　4to., orig.
dec cloth, illus., English first edition.　Covent 56-1651　1974　£15

LOW, FRANCES H.　　　　Queen Victoria's Dolls.　London, 1894.
4to., illus., orig. cloth.　Bow Windows 62-585　1974　£28

LOW, G. C.　　　　The Literature of the Charadriiformes.　1931.
8vo., cloth, scarce, second edition.　Wheldon 130-177　1974　£10

LOWE, A.　　　　General View of the Agriculture of the County
of Berwick.　1794.　4to., modern boards, plates, coloured map, folding table.
Wheldon 128-1658　1973　£12

LOWE, A.　　　　General View of the Agriculture of the County
of Berwick.　1794.　4to., modern boards, plates.　Wheldon 131-1788　1974
£12

LOWE, EDWARD JOSEPH　　Beautiful Leaved Plants.　1861.　Coloured
plates, roy. 8vo., spine faded, contemporary name on fly, very fine copy, orig.
cloth.　Broadhurst 24-1127　1974　£25

LOWE, EDWARD JOSEPH　　Beautiful Leaved Plants.　1872.　Roy. 8vo.,
orig. cloth, gilt, plates.　Wheldon 131-1542　1974　£30

LOWE, EDWARD JOSEPH　　Beautiful Leaved Plants.　1891.　Roy. 8vo.,
cloth, plates, third edition.　Wheldon 129-1500　1974　£15

LOWE, EDWARD JOSEPH　　Ferns: British and Exotic.　1856-60.　8 vols.,
roy. 8vo., contemporary full green morocco gilt, plates.　Wheldon 131-1437
1974　£60

LOWE, EDWARD JOSEPH　　Ferns: British and Exotic.　1872.　8 vols., roy.
8vo., orig. cloth, coloured plates, new edition.　Wheldon 128-1394　1973　£25

LOWE, EDWARD JOSEPH　　Ferns: British and Exotic.　1872.　8 vols., roy.
8vo., orig. cloth, plates, new edition.　Wheldon 131-1438　1974　£50

LOWE, EDWARD JOSEPH　　A Natural History of British Grasses.　(1858).
Roy. 8vo., cloth, plates.　Wheldon 131-1234　1974　£12

LOWE, EDWARD JOSEPH　　A Natural History of British Grasses.　1858.
Roy. 8vo., full green morocco gilt, plates, first edition.　Wheldon 130-1101
1974　£15

LOWE, EDWARD JOSEPH　　A Natural History of British Grasses.　London,
1864.　Roy. 8vo., orig. cloth, gilt, plates, first edition.　Hammond 201-660
1974　£10

LOWE, EDWARD JOSEPH　　A Natural History of New and Rare Ferns.　1862.
Roy. 8vo., orig. cloth, plates.　Wheldon 129-1408　1974　£10

LOWE, EDWARD JOSEPH　　A Natural History of New and Rare Ferns.
1871.　Roy. 8vo., orig. cloth, plates.　Wheldon 129-1409　1974　£7.50

LOWE, EDWARD JOSEPH　　A Natural History of New and Rare Ferns.
1871.　Roy. 8vo., orig. cloth, plates.　Wheldon 131-1439　1974　£10

LOWE, EDWARD JOSEPH　　Our Native Ferns.　1865-67.　Orig. cloth,
2 vols., plates, woodcuts.　Wheldon 129-1410　1974　£12

LOWE, EDWARD JOSEPH　　Our Native Ferns.　1874-80.　2 vols., roy.
8vo., orig. cloth, coloured plates, nice clean copy.　Wheldon 128-1395　1973
£10

LOWE, EDWARD JOSEPH　　Our Native Ferns.　1874-80.　Roy. 8vo., orig.
cloth, 2 vols., plates, ex-library.　Wheldon 130-1315　1974　£10

LOWE, JOSEPH　　　　The Present State of England in Regard to
Agriculture.　1823.　Half calf, second edition.　Howes 186-1497　1974　£18

LOWE, P. R.　　　　Our Common Sea Birds.　(1913).　4to., cloth.
Wheldon 131-647　1974　£5

LOWE, ROBERT　　　　General View of the Agriculture of the County
of Nottingham.　London, 1798.　8vo., contemporary half morocco, second
edition.　Dawsons PM 247-185　1974　£35

LOWE, W. P.　　　　The Trail that is Always New.　1932.　8vo.,
orig. cloth, illus.　Wheldon 130-178　1974　£7.50

LOWE, W. BEZANT　　　　The Heart of Northern Wales.　1912 and 27.
8vo., 2 vols., orig. cloth.　Broadhurst 23-1456　1974　£12

LOWE, W. BEZANT　　　　The Heart of Northern Wales, As It Was and As
It Is.　Llanfairfechan, 1912 and 1927.　Profusely illus., 2 vols., demy 8vo.,
good copy, orig. cloth, fine.　Broadhurst 24-1464　1974　£12

LOWELL, AMY　　　　John Keats.　1925.　Plates.　Allen 216-960
1974　$10

LOWELL, JAMES RUSSELL　　Among My Books.　Boston, 1876.　Second series,
first edition, 12mo., rare first issue.　Current BW9-250　1974　$30

LOWELL, JAMES RUSSELL　　Conversations on Some of the Old Poets.　Cambridge, 1845.　First edition, 12mo., spine faded and worn, gilt dec. boards, fair,
text very good, author's signature laid in.　Current BW9-251　1974　$30

LOWELL, JAMES RUSSELL　　Conversations on Sone of the Old Poets.
Cambridge, 1846.　12mo., cloth, very fine copy, second edition.　Goodspeed's
578-219　1974　$35

LOWELL, JAMES RUSSELL　　Conversations on Old Poets.　New York,
1901.　12mo.　Biblo & Tannen 213-789　1973　$7.50

LOWELL, JAMES RUSSELL　　Heartease and Rue.　Boston and New York, 1888.
First edition, 16mo., green paper boards, white cloth shelf back, spine soiled, good
copy, scarce.　Current BW9-252　1974　$32

LOWELL, JAMES RUSSELL　　The Works of.　Boston, n.d.　11 vols., orig.
binding, Standard Library edition.　Wilson 63-552　1974　$25

LOWELL, JAMES RUSSELL　　The Writings of.　Houghton, Mifflin, 1891.
10 vols.　Austin 54-674　1973　$72.50

LOWELL, JAMES RUSSELL　　A Year's Life.　Boston, 1841.　16mo.,
contemporary half morocco, fine copy.　Goodspeed's 578-218　1974　$50

LOWELL, MAURICE　　　　Listen In.　Dodge, 1937.　114p.　Austin
51-570　1973　$8.50

LOWENFELS, WALTER　　　　Apollinaire.　Paris, 1930.　Imp. 8vo.,
quarter morocco, rubbed.　Rota 188-542　1974　£12

LOWENFELS, WALTER　　　　Apollinaire.　Paris, 1930.　Large 4to., roan
spine, dec. board, uncut, scarce, first edition.　Minters 37-261　1973　$75

LOWENFELS, WALTER　　　　U. S. A. with Music.　Paris, 1930.　8vo.,
wrappers, fine, inscribed, first edition.　Rota 190-636　1974　£12.50

LOWENTHAL, MARVIN　　　　H. Szold: Life and Letters.　New York, 1942.
Orig. ed.　Biblo & Tannen 214-804　1974　$8.50

LOWENTHAL, MARVIN   Henrietta Szold. 1942. 350 pages, illus.
Austin 57-414 1974 $10

LOWENTHAL, MARVIN   The Jews of Germany. Longmans, 1936.
Austin 62-390 1974 $8.50

LOWER, MARK ANTHONY   The Curiosities. London, 1845. 8vo., orig.
cloth, gilt, illus., first edition.   Hammond 201-432 1974 £10

LOWER, MARK ANTHONY   Patronymica Britannica. London and Lewes,
1860. 4to., orig. cloth, worn, rebacked.   Bow Windows 62-586 1974 £6.75

LOWER, MARK ANTHONY   Patronymica Britannica. London, 1860. Roy
8vo., contemporary blind-stamped calf, gilt.   Hammond 201-433 1974 £12

LOWER, MARK ANTONY   The Worthies of Sussex. 1865. 4to., illus.,
half brown levant morocco, plates.   Howes 186-2206 1974 £30

LOWER, MARK ANTHONY   The Worthies of Sussex. Lewes, 1865. 4to.,
half morocco, plates.   Quaritch 939-565 1974 £45

LOWER, RICHARD   Tractatus de Corde. London, 1680. 8vo.,
contemporary calf, plates.   Gurney 64-138 1974 £145

LOWNDES, WILLIAM   A Report Containing an Essay for the Amendment
of the Silver Coins. London, 1695. 8vo., contemporary panelled calf, first
edition.   Dawsons PM 247-186 1974 £85

LOWNDES, WILLIAM THOMAS   The Bibliographer's Manual of English
Literature. London, 1871. 11 parts in 4 vols., 8vo., orig. cloth.   Dawsons PM
10-377 1974 £35

LOWRIE, SARAH DICKSON   Strawberry Mansion First Known as Somerton,
The House of Many Masters. New York, 1941. First edition, 8vo., d.j., boxed,
illus., uncut, mint.   Current BW9-413 1974 $35

LOWRY, ANNA M.   Rome's Awful Persecutions. 1914.
128 pages. Austin 57-415 1974 $10

LOWRY, ANNA M.   Rome's Awful Persecutions. 1914. Austin
62-391 1974 $10

LOWRY, MALCOLM   Under the Volcano. New York, 1947. 1st ed.
Jacobs 24-106 1974 $15

LOWRY, THOMAS MARTIN   Historical Introduction to Chemistry. London,
1915. 8vo., orig. cloth, gilt, illus., first edition.   Dawsons PM 245-483 1974
£7

LOWSLEY, OSWALD SWINNERY   Clinical Urology. Baltimore, 1944.
2 vols., second edition.   Rittenhouse 46-422 1974 $15

LOYD, L. W. R.   Lundy, Its History and Natural History. 1925.
8vo., cloth, illus., scarce.   Wheldon 131-373 1974 £7.50

LOZANO, P.   A True and Particular Relation of the Dreadful
Earthquake Which Happened at Lima . . . the 28th of October, 1746. 1748.
8vo., contemporary calf, joints cracked, plates, maps.   Wheldon 128-1011
1973 £35

LUARD, JOHN   Views In India, Saint Helena and Car Nicobar.
N.P., n.d. Folio, old half blue morocco, gilt, plates.   Traylen 79-525
1973 £40

LUBBOCK, BASIL   Adventures by Sea from Art of Old Time.
1925. 4to., orig. bevelled buckram gilt, plates, limited, first edition.   Howes
186-1735 1974 £30

LUBBOCK, JOHN
Please turn to
AVEBURY, JOHN LUBBOCK

LUBBOCK, R.   Observations on the Fauna of Norfolk.
Norwich, 1848. 8vo., cloth, plates, map.   Wheldon 128-212 1973 £5

LUBBOCK, R.   Observations on the Fauna of Norfolk.
Norwich, 1879. 8vo., cloth, plates, folding map, new edition.   Wheldon
128-213 1973 £5

LUBBOCK, R.   Observations on the Fauna of Norfolk,
Particularly on the District of the Broads. Norwich, 1845. 8vo., cloth, plates.
Wheldon 131-374 1974 £7.50

LUBIENICZKI, STANISLAS   Theatrum Cometicum. Amsterdam, 1668, 1667,
1668. Folio, 2 vols., contemporary calf, fine, first edition.   Dawsons PM 245-
484 1974 £525

LUBKE, W.   Outlines of the History of Art. 1903. 4to.,
2 vols., orig. cloth, illus.   Broadhurst 23-136 1974 £6

LUBKE, W.   Outlines of the History of Art. 1904. 2 vols.,
globe 4to., illus., orig. cloth, fine.   Broadhurst 24-138 1974 £5

LUBRANI, IACOBI   Suaviludia Musarum ad Sebethi Ripam. 1690.
Small 4to., contemporary vellum, rebacked, engraved frontispiece.   Bow
Windows 66-437 1974 £18

LUC, J. A. DE   Letters on the Physical History of the Earth.
1831. 8vo., new cloth.   Wheldon 129-835 1974 £15

LUCANUS, MARCUS ANNAEUS   De Bello Civili Apud Pharsaliam Libri X.
Lyons, 1533. Small 8vo., early polished calf gilt, raised bands.   Thomas 28-291
1972 £31.50

LUCANUS, MARCUS ANNAEUS   Civilis Belli Libri X. Paris, 1543. 16mo.,
19th century French crimson crushed levant morocco gilt, pretty copy.   Thomas
32-243 1974 £50

LUCANUS, MARCUS ANNAEUS   De Bello Civili Apud Pharsaliam Libri X.
Doctissimis Argumetis and Schiliis Ornati. Lyons, 1533. Small 8vo., early
polished calf gilt, raised bands.   Thomas 32-242 1974 £31.50

LUCANUS, MARCUS ANNAEUS   Pharsalia. 1502. Early 19th century
calf, gilt, new label, first Aldine edition.   Thomas 30-8 1973 £100

LUCANUS, MARCUS ANNAEUS   The Pharsalia of Lucan. London, 1903. Biblo
& Tannen 214-633 1974 $10

LUCAS, A. H. S.   The Animals of Australia. 1909. 8vo., orig.
cloth.   Broadhurst 23-1159 1974 £6

LUCAS, A. H. S.   The Birds of Australia. 1911. 8vo., orig.
cloth.   Broadhurst 23-1160 1974 £6

LUCAS, EDWARD   Auswahl Werthvoller Obstsorten. Ravensburg,
1871-1872. 8vo., 4 vols., contemporary half shagreen, first edition.   Schumann
35-290 1974 $110

LUCAS, EDWARD VERRALL 1868-   John Constable the Painter. 1924. Roy.
4to., plates, cloth, gilt.   Quaritch 940-63 1974 £15

LUCAS, EDWARD VERRALL 1868-   Playtime and Company. 1925. Illus., very
good, cloth backed pictorial boards, first edition.   Covent 51-1693 1973 £10

LUCAS, EDWARD VERRALL 1868-   Playtime and Company. 1925. Cloth backed
boards, faded, drawings.   Covent 55-2670 1973 £10

LUCAS, EDWARD VERRALL 1868-   Playtime and Company. 1925. Small 4to.,
boards, buckram back, uncut, d.w., fine, limited edition.   Sawyer 292-321
1974 £105

LUCAS, ELIJAH   Shall Liberty Die or Patriots to the Front.
1897. 540 pages. Austin 57-416 1974 $12.50

LUCAS, ELIJAH   Shall Liberty Die or Patriots to the Front.
Lucas, 1897. Austin 62-392 1974 $12.50

LUCAS, F. C.   An Historical Souvenir Diary of the City of
Winnipeg, Canada. Winnipeg, 1923. Photographs.   Hood's 104-862 1974
$12.50

LUCAS, F. L.   The Golden Cockerel Greek Anthology.
Golden Cockerel Press, 1937. F'cap. folio, bound by Sangorski & Sutcliffe in
quarter morocco, uncut, limited to 206 copies, illus., fine.   Broadhurst 24-984
1974 £60

LUCAS, FRED W.   The Annals of the Voyages of the Brothers Nicolo
and Antonio Zeno in the North Atlantic. . .   London, 1898. Folio, maps, gilt
stamped maroon cloth and leather, boxed.   Butterfield 10-360 1974 $75

LUCAS, H.   Exploration Scientifique de l'Algerie 1840-
42. Histoire Naturelle des Animaux Articules.   Paris, (1846-)49. 4 vols.,
4to., new buckram, plates.   Wheldon 131-827 1974 £120

LUCAS, PROSPER   Traite Philosophique et Physiologique de l'Here-
dite. Paris, 1847-1850. 8vo., 2 vols., contemporary morocco-backed boards,
first edition. Schumann 35-291 1974 $110

LUCAS, ROBERT   Message of the Governor of Ohio, at the Second
Session of the Thirty-Third General Assembly, June 8, 1835. Columbus, 1835.
Disbound, some stains on title. Hayman 59-480 1974 $12.50

LUCAS, W. J.   British Dragonflies. 1900. 8vo., orig. buckram, plates. Wheldon 129-657 1974 £12

LUCAS, W. J.   British Dragonflies. 1900. 8vo., orig.
buckram, plates, scarce. Wheldon 131-828 1974 £12

LUCAS, W. J.   A Monograph of the British Orthoptera. 1920.
8vo., cloth, plates, scarce. Wheldon 129-658 1974 £10

LUCCA   L'Instituto de'Pubblici Studj de S. Frediano.
1796. Rare, unbound. Covent 55-1315 1974 £20

LUCHAIRE, ACHILLE   Histoire des Institutions Monarchiques de la
France sous les Premiers Capetiens. Paris, 1891. 2 vols. in 1, roy. 8vo.,
buckram, scarce, orig. & best edition. Howes 186-1023 1974 £14

LUCHET, JEAN PIERRE DE   Paris en Miniature. Amsterdam, 1784. 12mo.,
full marbled sheep, uncut. L. Goldschmidt 42-71 1974 $25

LUCIANI, LUIGI   Human Physiology. London, 1911-21. 8vo.,
5 vols., orig. cloth, illus., first edition. Schumann 35-292 1974 $135

LUCIDI, ANGELUS   De Visitatione Sacrorum Liminum Instructio
S. C. Concilii. Rome, 1883. 3 vols., roy. 8vo., half roan, rubbed. Howes
185-1379 1974 £10

LUCILIUS   Carminum Reliquiae. 1904-05. 2 vols.,
half calf. Allen 213-651 1973 $15

LUCKOMBE, PHILIP   A Concise History of the Origin and Progress of
Printing. London, 1770. 8vo., modern half calf, first edition. Dawsons PM
10-379 1974 £140

LUCRETIUS CARUS, TITUS   Lucretius Carus the Epicurean Philosopher.
Oxford, 1682. 8vo., contemporary sprinkled calf, first English edition. Dawsons
PM 252-668 1974 £105

LUCRETIUS CARUS, TITUS   Titi Lucretii Cari de Rerum Natura Libros Sex.
Parisiis, 1680. 4to., contemporary calf, rebacked. Bow Windows 66-438 1974
£18

LUCY, HENRY W.   A Diary of Two Parliaments. London, 1892.
2 vols., 8vo., cloth boards, illus. Emerald 50-559 1974 £5

LUCY and Arthur. Philadelphia, 1844. Small 8vo., illus., inscription, orig.
cloth. Bow Windows 62-172 1974 £5

LUDICROUS Exhibition in the Open Air. (Sheffield), 1794. 4to., worn, rare.
Ximenes 35-177 1974 $65

LUDLOW, EDMUND   Memoirs of. London, 1751. Small folio,
full speckled calf, complete folio edition. Emerald 50-560 1974 £22

LUDLOW, FITZ HUGH   The Heart of the Continent. New York, 1871.
8vo., orig. bindings, illus. Butterfield 8-708 1974 $12.50

LUDLOW, JAMES F.   Heart of the Continent. New York, 1870. New
cloth, first edition. Putnam 126-313 1974 $15

LUDOLF OF SAXONY   Vita Jesu Christi e Quatuor Evangelis. Paris
& Rome, 1865. Folio, half calf, best edition. Howes 185-1380 1974 £25

LUDWIG, EMIL   Bismark. Putnam, 1927. 405p., illus.
Austin 51-571 1973 $12.50

LUDWIG, M. CHRISTIAN   A Dictionary English German & French.
Leipzig, 1706. 4to., contemporary calf. Smith 194-172 1974 £7.50

LUFF, JOHN N.   The Postage Stamps of the United States, 19th
Century Issues; Part One Postmasters' Provisionals. New York, 1937. Portrait
frontispiece, plates, 4to., orig. cloth. Sawyer 293-246 1974 £18

LUGLI, G.   I Monumenti Antichi di Roma e Suburbio.
1934-38. Vols. 2 & 3 only. Allen 213-661 1973 $12.50

LUGO, JUAN DE   Opera Omnia. Venice, 1751. 7 vols. in 3,
folio, rebound, cloth. Howes 185-1381 1974 £21

LUGRIN, N. DE B.   The Pioneer Women of Vancouver Island,
1843-1866. Victoria, 1928. Hood's 103-23 1974 $22.50

LUHAN, MABEL DODGE   Intimate Memories. New York, (1933). Cloth,
dust wrapper, frontispiece, first edition. Dawson's 424-293 1974 $25

LUHAN, MABEL DODGE   Intimate Memories. 1933. Dust wrapper, fine,
unopened, English first edition. Covent 56-878 1974 £21

LULLIN DE CHATEAUVIEUX, JACOB FREDERIC   Lettres sur l'Italie. Paris,
1834. 8vo., contemporary dark half green sheep. L. Goldschmidt 42-289
1974 $20

LUMLEY, FREDERICK E.   Ourselves and the World. 1931. 591 pages.
Austin 57-417 1974 $10

LUNAN, J.   Hortus Jamaicensis. Jamaica, 1814. 2 vols.,
4to., orig. cloth, modern rebacking, very rare. Wheldon 128-1283 1973 £225

LUNAN, J.   Hortus Jamaicensis. Jamaica, 1814. 4to.,
2 vols., orig. cloth, rare. Wheldon 130-1181 1974 £225

LUND, P. W.   E Museo Lundii. Copenhagen, 1888-1915.
4to., orig. boards, plates. Wheldon 129-836 1974 £35

LUND, P. W.   E Museo Lundii. Copenhagen, 1888-1915.
3 vols. in 5, 4to., orig. boards, plates. Wheldon 131-1038 1974 £35

LUNDKVIST, ARTUR   Ikarus' Flykt. Stockholm, 1939. Wrappers,
fine, unopened copy. Covent 51-1279 1973 £7.50

LUPUS   Divinum ac Immobile S. Petri. 1681. Thick
samll 4to., contemporary calf, rebacked, first edition. Howes 185-1382 1974
£18

LUSSAC, JOSEPH LOUIS GAY
Please turn to
GAY-LUSSAC, JOSEPH LOUIS

LUTHER, MARTIN   Acta. F. Martini Luther August. (Wittenberg,
1518). Small 4to., marbled boards, red morocco back, light stains, very scarce,
fine, first edition. Harper 213-180 1973 $550

LUTHER, MARTIN   Ain Gute Trostliche Predig. Augsburg, 1520.
Small 4to., marbled boards, red morocco back, fine. Harper 213-182 1973
$475

LUTHER, MARTIN   Ain Sermon von der Beraytung Zum Sterben.
(Augsburg, 1519). 4to., marbled boards, red morocco back, fine, very rare.
Harper 213-181 1973 $650

LUTHER, MARTIN   An Die Radherrn. (Augsburg), 1524. Small
4to., marbled boards, red morocco back. Harper 213-193 1973 $525

LUTHER, MARTIN   An die Radherrn aller Stedte Deutsches Lands.
Wittenberg, 1524. Small 4to., boards, woodcut border, fine, first edition.
Harper 213-192 1973 $1000

LUTHER, MARTIN   Antwortt Deutsch auff Konig Heinrichs von Engelland Buch. Wittenberg, 1522. Small 4to., marbled boards, red morocco back, woodcut border, fine, first edition in German. Harper 213-189 1973 $1100

LUTHER, MARTIN   Assertio Omnium Articulorum M. Lutheri. Wittenberg, 1520. Small 4to., marbled boards, red morocco back, rare, very fine, first edition. Harper 213-185 1973 $1100

LUTHER, MARTIN   Auff das Uberchristenlich. (Augsburg), 1521. 4to., marbled boards, red morocco back, fine. Harper 213-186 1973 $500

LUTHER, MARTIN   A Catechism for the People. 1892. Soiled. Covent 55-2607 1973 £7.50

LUTHER, MARTIN   Christiana, & Inconsternata Responsio, Caesaree Maiestati, Principibus & Dominis Wormatie Facta Anno. (Strassburg, 1521). Small 4to., marbled boards, red morocco back. Harper 213-187 1973 $800

LUTHER, MARTIN   Colloquia Oder Tischreden Doctor Martini Lutheri. Frankfurt, 1567. Thick folio, contemporary pigskin, wooden boards, portraits, rare, excellent copy. Harper 213-177 1973 $750

LUTHER, MARTIN   A Commentarie Vpon the Epistle . . . to the Galathians. 1575. Small 4to., old calf, worn but sound, strip cut from top margin of title, else clean and sound. Thomas 32-45 1974 £130

LUTHER, MARTIN   Das Eyn Christliche Versamlung Odder Gemeyne. Wittenberg, 1523. 4to., marbled boards, red morocco back, woodcut border, very fine, first edition. Harper 213-190 1973 $600

LUTHER, MARTIN   Das Gebet Mose, des Mans Gottes. Wittenberg, 1546. 4to., boards, portrait, browned, second edition in German. Harper 213-200 1973 $300

LUTHER, MARTIN   De Captivitate Babylonica Ecclesiae Praeludium. Wittenberg, (1520). Small 4to., modern half vellum, very fine, orig. edition. Schafer 8-125 1973 sFr. 3,000

LUTHER, MARTIN   De Votis Monasticis. Wittenberg, (1521). 4to., vellum, rare, fine, large copy, first edition. Harper 213-188 1973 $450

LUTHER, MARTIN   Ein Mercklich Nutz Predig Wie Man on Verschuldung mit Zytlichen gut Umbgan sol. Basel, 1520. Small 4to., red morocco back, marbled boards, very fine, rare edition. Harper 213-184 1973 $725

LUTHER, MARTIN   Ein Sermon von dem Hochwirdigen Sacrament des Heyligen Waren Leichnams Christi. (Nurnberg, 1520). Small 4to., marbled boards, red morocco back, fine. Harper 213-183 1973 $475

LUTHER, MARTIN   Enchiridion. Dresden, 1615. Small 8vo., illus., woodcuts, contemporary gilt brown calf. Harper 213-202 1973 $3250

LUTHER, MARTIN   Epistolarum . . . Tomus Primus. Jena & Eisleben, 1556, 1565. 2 vols. in 1, thick 4to., contemporary blind-stamped pigskin, wooden boards, raised bands, rare, first editions. Harper 213-178 1973 $850

LUTHER, MARTIN   Ermanunge Zum Frid, Auff die Zwolff Bawrschafft in Schwaben. Nurnberg, 1525. Small 4to., marbled boards, red morocco back. Harper 213-195 1973 $750

LUTHER, MARTIN   Der Hundert vnnd Eylfft Psalm Aussgelegt. (Augsburg), 1530. Small 4to., marbled boards, red morocco back, fine. Harper 213-196 1973 $400

LUTHER, MARTIN   Resolutiones Disputationum de Indulgentiarum Virtute. (Wittenberg), 1518. Small 4to., modern half vellum, very fine, orig. edition. Schafer 8-126 1973 sFr. 1,800

LUTHER, MARTIN   Sermo de Virtute Excommunicationis a Linguis Tertiis Tandem Everberatus. Leipzig, 1518. 4to., marbled boards, red morocco spine, fine, rare. Harper 213-179 1973 $525

LUTHER, MARTIN   Tomus Primus et Iden Ultimus Omnium Operum Reuerendi Patris. Jena, 1556-58. 4 vols., folio, woodcut borders, full page woodcuts, contemporary blind stamped pig skin over wooden boards, clasps missing, fine, very rare edition. Schumann 499-63 1974 sFr 4,100

LUTHER, MARTIN   Vier Predigten des Ehwirdigen Herrn D. Martini Luthers. Wittenberg, 1546. 4to., boards, woodcut, waterstained, first edition. Harper 213-201 1973 $100

LUTHER, MARTIN   Vom Reyche Gottes Was es Sey vnd Wie. (Augsburg, 1524). Small 4to., marbled boards, red morocco back, woodcut border. Harper 213-194 1973 $650

LUTHER, MARTIN   Vom Schem Hamphoras. Wittenberg, 1543. Small 4to., boards, fine, very rare, first edition, first issue. Harper 213-199 1973 $555

LUTHER, MARTIN   Von Anbeten des Sacraments, des Hailigen Leichnams Christi. (Augsburg), 1523. Small 4to., marbled boards, red morocco back, woodcut. Harper 213-191 1973 $450

LUTHER, MARTIN   Von den Juden vnd Iren Lugen. Wittenberg, 1543. Small 4to., full red morocco, rare, first edition. Harper 213-198 1973 $750

LUTHER, MARTIN   Von Denn Geystlichen vnd Kloster Gelubden. Wittenberg, 1522. Small 4to., modern half vellum, very fine, first German edition. Schafer 8-127 1973 sFr. 2,300

LUTHER, MARTIN   Warnunge . . . An Seine Lieben Deudschen. (Strassburg), 1531. Small 4to., marbled boards, red morocco back, fine, portraits. Harper 213-197 1973 $475

LUTYENS, EDWIN   Houses and Gardens Described & Criticised by Sir Lawrence Weaver. 1925. Eaton Music-631 1973 £7.50

LUTZKI, JOSEPH   Mordecai Kazaz. 1828-41. 4to., old quarter green morocco, worn. Dawsons PM 251-272 1974 £250

LUX, JOSEF AUGUST   Otto Wagner, Eine Monographie. Munich, 1914. 4to., boards, foxed, illus., rare. Minters 37-577 1973 $90

LUXAN, DIEGO PEREZ DE
Please turn to
PEREZ DE LUXAN, DIEGO

LUXMOORE, C. F. C.   English Saltglazed Earthenware. Exeter, 1924. Roy. 4to., plates, cloth. Quaritch 940-649 1974 £72

LUZERNE, FRANK   The Lost City. New York, 1872. 8vo., orig. bindings, illus. Butterfield 8-63 1974 $12.50

LUZERNE, FRANK   The Lost City! Drama of the Fire-Fiend! or, Chicago, As it Was, and As it Is. New York, 1872. Maps, engravings, photos, purple gilt cloth, back faded, unusually clean. Butterfield 10-143 1974 $20

LYCOSTHENES, CONRADUS   Prodigiorum ac Ostentorum Chronicon. Basel, 1557. Folio, contemporary limp vellum, woodcuts, very good, first edition. Schafer 8-96 1973 sFr. 3,400

LYDEKKER, RICHARD   Animal Portraiture. (1912). Imp. 4to., orig. cloth, plates. Wheldon 131-443 1974 £50

LYDEKKER, RICHARD   Catalogue of Fossil Birds. 1891. 8vo., cloth, woodcuts, scarce. Wheldon 129-837 1974 £10

LYDEKKER, RICHARD   Catalogue of Fossil Mammalia in the British Museum. 1885-87. 5 vols., 8vo., orig. cloth, text-figures, scarce. Wheldon 128-1012 1973 £15

LYDEKKER, RICHARD   The Game Animals of Africa. 1926. Roy. 8vo., cloth, plates, very scarce, second edition. Wheldon 131-504 1974 £40

LYDEKKER, RICHARD   A Geographical History of Mammals.   Cambridge, 1896. 8vo., cloth.   Wheldon 130-410 1974 £7.50

LYDEKKER, RICHARD   A Handbook to the Carnivora. 1896. Crown 8vo., cloth, plates. Wheldon 129-388 1974 £7.50

LYDEKKER, RICHARD   A Hand-Book to the Carnivora Pt. 1, Cats, Civets and Mungooses. 1895. 8vo., cloth-backed boards, plates. Wheldon 131-507 1974 £6

LYDEKKER, RICHARD   Handbook to the Marsupialia and Monotremata. 1894. 8vo., cloth, plates. Wheldon 130-408 1974 £7.50

LYDEKKER, RICHARD   A Hand-Book to the Marsupialia and Monotremata. 1894. Crown 8vo., modern half morocco, plates. Wheldon 131-505 1974 £10

LYDEKKER, RICHARD   A Handbook to the Marsupialia and Monotremata. 1896. Crown 8vo., cloth, plates. Wheldon 130-409 1974 £10

LYDEKKER, RICHARD   A Hand-Book to the Marsupialia and Monotremata. 1896. Crown 8vo., cloth, plates. Wheldon 131-506 1974 £10

LYDEKKER, RICHARD   The Horse and Its Relatives. 1912. 8vo., cloth, plates, figures. Wheldon 128-334 1973 £7.50

LYDEKKER, RICHARD   Reptiles, Amphibia, Fishes and Lower Chordates. 1912. 8vo., cloth, scarce, text-figures, map, coloured and plain plates. Wheldon 128-649 1973 £6

LYDEKKER, RICHARD   The Royal National History, 1893-1896. 6 vols., 4to., plates, engravings, half morocco. Smith 194-814 1974 £18

LYDEKKER, RICHARD   The Royal Natural History. 1893-96. 6 vols. in 12, imp. 8vo., orig. cloth, text-figures, coloured plates. Wheldon 128-285 1973 £18

LYDEKKER, RICHARD   The Royal Natural History. 1893-96. 6 vols., imp. 8vo., half morocco, trifle rubbed, coloured plates, text-figures. Wheldon 128-286 1973 £18

LYDEKKER, RICHARD   The Royal Natural History. 1893-96. 6 vols., roy. 8vo., half calf gilt, marbled edges, engravings, coloured plates. Wheldon 128-284 1973 £25

LYDEKKER, RICHARD   Wildlife of the World. 1916. 3 vols., plates, orig. pictorial cloth. Smith 193-759 1973 £15

LYDENBERG, HARRY MILLER   Paper or Sawdust. New York, 1924. Green cloth. Dawson's 424-188 1974 $10

LYDIS, MARIETTE   Mariette Lydis. Buenos Aires, 1945. 4to., wrapper, plates, limited edition. Minters 37-858 1973 $10

LYELL, CHARLES   Elements of Geology. 1838. Crown 8vo., orig. boards, cloth back, uncut, nice copy, rare first edition. Wheldon 131-1041 1974 £60

LYELL, CHARLES   Elements of Geology. 1865. 8vo., cloth, sixth edition. Wheldon 129-839 1974 £12

LYELL, CHARLES   Elements of Geology. 1865. 8vo., cloth, sixth edition. Wheldon 131-1042 1974 £12

LYELL, CHARLES   The Geological Evidences of the Antiquity of Man. 1863. Plates, illus., first edition, demy 8vo., contemporary half calf, marbled boards, little light scoring, else fine. Broadhurst 24-1128 1974 £15

LYELL, CHARLES   The Geological Evidences of the Antiquity of Man with Remarks on Theories of the Origin of Species by Variation. 1863. 8vo., orig. cloth, text figures, second edition. Wheldon 128-1015 1973 £10

LYELL, CHARLES   The Geological Evidences of the Antiquity of Man With Remarks on Theories of the Origin of Species by Variation. 1863. 8vo., half morocco, frontis., revised third edition. Wheldon 128-1016 1973 £7.50

LYELL, CHARLES   The Geological Evidences of the Antiquity of Man. 1863. 8vo., orig. cloth, second edition. Wheldon 129-841 1974 £10

LYELL, CHARLES   The Geological Evidences of the Antiquity of Man With Remarks on Theories of the Origin of Species by Variation. 1863. 8vo., orig. cloth, second edition. Wheldon 131-1043 1974 £12

LYELL, CHARLES   A Manual of Elementary Geology. 1855. 8vo., orig. cloth, rebacked, illus., fifth edition. Hammond 201-375 1974 £12.50

LYELL, CHARLES   A Manual of Elementary Geology. 1855. 8vo., contemporary calf, rebacked, fifth edition. Wheldon 130-951 1974 £10

LYELL, CHARLES   The Principles of Geology. London, 1830-33. 3 vols., 8vo., illus., plates, half calf, fine, first edition. Gilhofer 61-36 1974 sFr. 2,500

LYELL, CHARLES   Principles of Geology. 1830-33. 3 vols., 8vo., orig. cloth and orig. boards, coloured map, plates, (some coloured). Wheldon 128-1013 1973 £200

LYELL, CHARLES   Principles of Geology. 1830-33. 8vo., 3 vols., modern cloth, plates. Wheldon 129-838 1974 £150

LYELL, CHARLES   Principles of Geology. 1830-33. 3 vols., 8vo., modern cloth, plates, rare first edition. Wheldon 131-1039 1974 £150

LYELL, CHARLES   Principles of Geology, Being an Attemp to Explain the Former Changes of the Earth's Surface, By Reference to Causes Now in Operation. London, 1832-32-33. 3 vols, 8vo., plates, contemporary blue boards, title labels, plates for the most part finely colored by hand, uncut margins, vol. 1 second edition, vols. 2 & 3 first editions, good. Schafer 10-132 1974 SFr 1,300

LYELL, CHARLES   Principles of Geology. 1835. 12mo., 4 vols., contemporary half calf, gilt, plates, fourth edition. Hammond 201-376 1974 £20

LYELL, CHARLES   Principles of Geology. 1853. 8vo., orig. cloth, plates, scarce, ninth edition. Wheldon 130-949 1974 £15

LYLY, JOHN   Euphues. Birmingham, 1868. Biblo & Tannen 213-790 1973 $15

LYELL, CHARLES   Principles of Geology. 1853. 8vo., plates, contemporary calf, ninth revised edition. Wheldon 131-1040 1974 £15

LYELL, CHARLES   Principles of Geology. 1867-68. 8vo., 2 vols., orig. cloth, tenth edition. Hammond 201-377 1974 £16

LYELL, CHARLES   Principles of Geology. 1872. 2 vols., thick demy 8vo., plates, orig. cloth gilt, revised eleventh edition. Smith 193-860 1973 £14.50

LYELL, CHARLES   Principles of Geology. 1875. 2 vols., 8vo., orig. cloth, maps, plates, nice copy, scarce, twelfth edition. Wheldon 128-1014 1973 £20

LYELL, CHARLES   Principles of Geology. 1875. 8vo., 2 vols., orig. cloth, plates, scarce, twelfth edition. Wheldon 130-950 1974 £20

LYELL, CHARLES   The Student's Elements of Geology. 1878. 8vo., cloth, third edition. Wheldon 129-840 1974 £5

LYELL, CHARLES   Travels in North America, Canada, and Nova Scotia; With Geological Observations. 1855. Second edition, 2 vols., crown 8vo., contemporary calf, lacking one leather label on vol. 2, engraved plates, fine. Broadhurst 24-1644 1974 £45

LYELL, JAMES P. R.   Early Book Illustration in Spain. London, 1926. 4to., orig. cloth, fine, limited. Dawsons PM 10-381 1974 £72

LYELL, K. M.   A Geographical Handbook of all the Known Ferns. 1870. Crown 8vo., orig. cloth, scarce. Wheldon 130-1317 1974 £5

LYFORD, JAMES O.   History of Concord, New Hampshire. (Concord, 1903). 2 vols., 8vo., cloth. Saddleback 14-549 1974 $45

LYMAN, CHESTER S.   Around the Horn to the Sandwich Islands and California. New Haven, 1924. Cloth, first edition. Hayman 57-462 1974 $17.50

LYMAN, GEORGE D.   John Marsh, Pioneer. New York, 1930. Orig. blue cloth, illus., first edition. Bradley 35-236 1974 $20

LYNCH, BOHUN   The Prize Ring. London, 1925. 4to., illus., Ltd. to 750 copies, vellum back, bds. Biblo & Tannen 214-445 1974 $50

LYNDE, HUMPHREY   A Case for the Spectacles. London, 1638. Thick small 4to., contemporary calf, nice crisp copy, first edition. Ximenes 37-135 1974 $75

LYNDEWODE, WILLIAM   Provinciale. Oxford, 1689. Folio, rebacked, contemporary calf, best edition. Howes 185-1386 1974 £35

LYNDORADI   Ein Vnuorgreifflicher Politischer Brieff. 1619. Small 4to., unbound. Schumann 499-64 1974 sFr 520

LYON, B. B. VINCENT   Non-Surgical Drainage of the Gall Tract. Philadelphia, 1923. Rittenhouse 46-423 1974 $15

LYON, CALEB   Narrative and Recollections of Van Dieman's Land During a Three Years' Captivity of Stephen S. Wright; Together With an Account of the Battle of Prescott In Which He Was Taken Prisoner. New York, 1844. Black cloth, excellent condition. Hood's 102-569 1974 $325

LYON, D. M.   History of the Lodge of Edinburgh. Edinburgh, 1873. 4to., portraits, foxing, orig. cloth. Bow Windows 62-346 1974 £7.50

LYON, GEORGE FRANCIS   A Brief Narrative of an Unsuccessful Attempt to Reach Repulse Bay Through Sir Thomas Rowe's "Welcome", in His Majesty's Ship Griper in the Year 1824. London, 1825. Chart, engravings, three quarter leather, inscribed and signed. Hood's 102-62 1974 $80

LYON, GEORGE FRANCIS   A Brief Narrative of an Unsuccessful Attempt to Reach Repulse Bay. London, 1825. 8vo., half calf, gilt, foxed, plates. Traylen 79-509 1973 £18

LYON, GEORGE FRANCIS   The Private Journal of . . . of H. M. S. Hecla, During the Recent Voyage of Discovery Under Captain Parry. 1824. Engraved plates, folding map, first edition, demy 8vo., contemporary half calf, marbled boards, rubbed, presentation copy inscribed by author. Broadhurst 24-1645 1974 £35

LYON, JOHN   The History of the Town and Port of Dover. 1813. 2 vols., 4to., orig. boards, plates. Howes 186-2054 1974 £38

LYON, JOHN   The History of the Town and Port of Dover. 1813. 2 vols., 4to., plates, modern boards. Quaritch 939-411 1974 £25

LYON, JOHN   The History of the Town and Port of Dover. London and Dover, 1813-14. 4to., 2 vols., contemporary elaborately bline-stamped calf, first edition. Dawsons PM 251-47 1974 £100

LYON, P.   Observations on the Barrenness of Fruit Trees. Edinburgh, 1813. 8vo., orig. boards, plate, rare. Wheldon 130-1483 1974 £35

LYON, WILLIAM   Chronicles of Finchampstead in the County of Berkshire. 1895. 4to., illus., orig. quarter morocco, frontispiece. Howes 186-1974 1974 £8.50

LYONS, D.   Magna Britannia. 1806. Vol. 1, 4to., plates, lacks binding. Smith 193-171 1973 £12

LYONS, RICHARD B. P.   A Record of British Diplomacy. 1913. 2 vols., thick 8vo., orig. cloth gilt, label. Howes 186-1029 1974 £6.50

LYRA, NICOLAS DE
Please turn to
NICOLAS DE LYRA

LYSER, MICHAEL   Culter Anatomicus. Copenhagen, 1665. 12mo., half calf, woodcuts. Schumann 35-294 1974 $110

LYSONS, DANIEL   The Environs of London. (1791)-1800. 5 vols., 4to., plates, contemporary holf morocco. Quaritch 939-460 1974 £85

LYSONS, DANIEL   The Environs of London. London, 1792-1800. 4to., 5 vols., contemporary diced calf, gilt, plates, first edition. Dawsons PM 251-48 1974 £145

LYSONS, DANIEL   The Environs of London. 1811. 2 vols. in 4, roy. 4to., plates, fine, contemporary russia, second & best edition. Quaritch 939-461 1974 £90

LYSONS, DANIEL   Magna Britannia. Cumberland, 1816. Vol. the fourth, folding map, engraved plates, demy 4to., newly bound half light brown calf, leather labels, mint, no foxing. Broadhurst 24-1465 1974 £65

LYSONS, SAMUEL   A Collection of Gloucestershire Antiquities. 1803. Folio, plates, half calf. Quaritch 939-361 1974 £50

LYSONS, SAMUEL   A Collection of Gloucestershire Antiquities. London, 1804. Folio, half morocco, plates. Dawsons PM 251-49 1974 £75

LYTE, H. C. MAXWELL   A History of Eton College. 1875. 8vo., plates, cloth, gilt, engravings. Quaritch 939-310 1974 £5

LYTTELTON, GEORGE, 1ST BARON, 1709-1773   Considerations Upon the Present State of Our Affairs. London, 1739. 8vo., disbound, second edition. Dawsons PM 247-187 1974 £15

LYTTELTON, GEORGE, 1ST BARON, 1709-1773   Dialogues of the Dead. 1760. 8vo., contemporary calf gilt, second edition. Hill 125-278 1974 £21

LYTTELTON, GEORGE, 1ST BARON, 1709-1773   Dialogues of the Dead. London, 1765. 8vo., contemporary tree calf, fine, fourth edition. Dawsons PM 252-670 1974 £20

LYTTELTON, GEORGE LYTTELTON, 1ST BARON 1709-1773   A Few Thoughts About Shakespeare. Stourbridge, n.d. Cloth, label, scarce, slipcase. Covent 55-1348 1974 £20

LYTTELTON, GEORGE, 1ST BARON, 1709-1773   The History and Life of King Henry II. 1767-71. 4 vols., 4to., contemporary polished tree calf, gilt, second edition. Howes 186-908 1974 £22.50

LYTTELTON, GEORGE, 1ST BARON, 1709-1773   Letters. London, 1735. 12mo., later calf, rebacked, waterstaining, first edition. Grinke 8-250 1973 £25

LYTTELTON, GEORGE, 1ST BARON, 1709-1773   Letters of. 1780. Small 8vo., contemporary calf backed boards, first edition. Fenning 17-171 1973 £28

LYTTELTON, GEORGE, 1ST BARON, 1709-1773   Letters from a Persian in England to his Friend at Ispahan. 1735. Small 8vo., contemporary calf, third edition. Howes 184-263 1973 £10.50

LYTTELTON, GEORGE, 1ST BARON, 1709-1773   Observations on the Conversion and Apostleship of St. Paul. 1747. 8vo., contemporary calf, first edition. Hill 125-279 1974 £15

LYTTELTON, GEORGE, 1ST BARON, 1709-1773   Poetical Works. Glasgow, 1787. Folio, full mottled calf, rebacked, gilt, rubbed, foxing. Heffer 38-42 1973 £19

LYTTELTON, GEORGE, 1ST BARON, 1709-1773   The Works of. London, 1774. 4to., frontis., morocco label, misbound, first collected edition. Dawsons PM 243-262 1973 £24

LYTTON, CONSTANCE   Prisons and Prisoners. 1914. Portraits, book-label, faded, English first edition. Covent 56-1351 1974 £6.30

LYTTON, EDWARD GEORGE EARLE LYTTON BULWER-LYTTON, 1ST BARON, 1803-1873.   The Caxtons. Edinburgh & London, 1849. 3 vols., 8vo., orig. cloth, uncut, first edition. Dawsons PM 252-671 1974 £25

LYTTON, EDWARD GEORGE EARLE LYTTON BULWER-LYTTON, 1ST BARON. 1803-1873.   The Duchess de la Valliere. London, 1836. 8vo., modern boards, first edition. Dawsons PM 252-672 1974 £14

LYTTON, EDWARD GEORGE EARLE LYTTON BULWER-LYTTON, 1ST BARON. 1803-1873. Eugene Aram. London, 1832. 3 vols., 8vo., contemporary half calf, fine, first edition. Dawsons PM 252-673 1974 £25

LYTTON, EDWARD GEORGE EARLE LYTTON BULWER-LYTTON, 1ST BARON. 1803-1873. The Last Days of Pompeii. London, 1834. 3 vols., 12mo., orig. boards, first edition. Dawsons PM 252-674 1974 £80

LYTTON, EDWARD GEORGE EARLE LYTTON BULWER-LYTTON, 1ST BARON 1803-1873 The Last Days of Pompeii. 1834. 8vo., 3 vols., contemporary drab boards, first edition. Quaritch 936-475 1974 £60

LYTTON, EDWARD GEORGE EARLE LYTTON BULWER-LYTTON, 1ST BARON 1803-1873 The Last Days of Pompeii. New York, 1926. Bilbo & Tannen 210-172 1973 $7.50

LYTTON, EDWARD GEORGE EARLE LYTTON BULWER-LYTTON, 1ST BARON 1803-1873 Novels. n.d. Small 8vo., 20 vols., green cloth, Knebworth edition. Quaritch 936-474 1974 £10

LYTTON, EDWARD ROBERT BULWER-LYTTON, 1ST EARL OF, 1831-1891 Clytemnestra. 1855. 8vo., orig. patterned cloth, worn, bookplate. Covent 55-1100 1974 £10.50

LYTTON, EDWARD ROBERT BULWER-LYTTON, 1ST EARL OF, 1831-1891 Marah. 1892. Bookplate, English first edition. Covent 56-560 1974 £25

LYTTON, GRACE   Scenario Writing Today. Houghton, Mifflin, 1921. Austin 51-572 1973 $7.50

M

M'ADAM, JOHN LOUDON   Remarks on the Present State of Road Making. Bristol, 1816. 8vo., quarter calf, first edition. Gurney 66-118 1974 £120

M'ADAM, JOHN LOUDON   Remarks on the Present System of Road Making. London, 1820. 8vo., old boards, new cloth back. Schuman 37-161 1974 $85

M'ADAM, JOHN LOUDON   Remarks on the Present System of Road Making. London, 1820. 8vo., boards, third edition. Hammond 201-876 1974 £18

M'ADAM, JOHN LOUNDON   Remarks on the Present System of Road Making. London, 1820. 8vo., orig. boards, rebacked, third edition. Hammond 201-940 1974 £20

MC ADIE, ALEXANDER   The Clouds and Fogs of San Francisco. San Francisco, 1912. 8vo., uncut, printed boards, dust jacket, illus. Butterfield 8-578 1974 $22.50

MAC ALISTER, R. A. S.   The Book of the Taking of Ireland. Dublin, 1938-40. 3 vols., 8vo., green cloth, gilt. Emerald 50-569 1974 £7.50

MAC ALISTER, R. A. S.   Ireland in Pre-Celtic Times. Dublin, 1921. 8vo., cloth boards, new cloth. Emerald 50-566 1974 £12

MAC ALISTER, R. A. S.   Lebor Gabala Erenn. Dublin, 1938-39. 8vo., cloth boards. Emerald 50-570 1974 £5

MAC ALISTER, R. A. S.   Tara, a Pagan Sanctuary of Ancient Ireland. New York, 1931. 8vo., cloth boards. Emerald 50-567 1974 £8

MC ALLISTER, R. E.   Newfoundland and Labrador. St. John's, n.d. Plates, charts, maps. Hood's 104-217 1974 $12.50

M'ALPINE, A. N.   How to Know Grasses. 1890. Small 8vo., cloth, plates, scarce. Wheldon 129-939 1974 £5

MAC ALPINE, D.   The Botanical Atlas. Edinburgh, 1883. Small folio, 2 vols., cloth, plates, scarce. Wheldon 131-1171 1974 £10

MC ALPINE, D.   Fungus Diseases of Citrus Trees in Australia. Melbourne, 1899. 8vo., new cloth, scarce. Wheldon 129-1270 1974 £5

MC ALPINE, D.   The Rusts of Australia. Melbourne, 1906. Large 8vo., cloth, plates, very scarce. Wheldon 131-1440 1974 £7.50

MC ALPINE, D.   The Smuts of Australia. Melbourne, 1910. 8vo., cloth, scarce. Wheldon 130-1318 1974 £7.50

MAC ALPINE, D.   Zoological Atlas, Including Comparative Anatomy, Invertebrate and Vertebrata. Edinburgh, 1881. 2 vols. in 1, oblong 4to., orig. boards, coloured plates. Wheldon 128-287 1973 £10

MAC ARTHUR, JOHN ROBERTSON   Ancient Greece in Modern America. 1943. Illus. Austin 57-420 1974 $10

MC ARTHUR, P.   Around Home. Toronto, 1925. Hood's 104-560 1974 $10

MC ATEE, W. L.   The Ring-Necked Pheasant. Washington, D.C., 1945. 8vo., cloth, plates. Wheldon 130-573 1974 £7.50

M'BAIN, J. M.   Bibliography of Arbroath Periodical Literature and Political Broadsides. Arbroath, 1889. F'cap. 4to., orig. cloth, fine. Broadhurst 24-382 1974 £5

MAC BETH, R. G.   The Making of the Canadian West. Toronto, 1905. Portraits, illus. Hood's 102-813 1974 $20

MAC BRIDE, T. H.   The Myxomycetes. New York, 1934. Roy 8vo., cloth, plates. Wheldon 129-1271 1974 £7.50

MAC BRIDE, T. H.   The North American Slime-Moulds. New York, 1899. 8vo., cloth, plates. Wheldon 131-1441 1974 £10

MC BRYDE, JAMES   Epistolae. 1898. 4to., full vellum. Broadhurst 23-1462 1974 £5

MC BRYDE, JAMES   Epistolae. 1898. Plates, f'cap 4to., full vellum, fine. Broadhurst 24-1467 1974 £5

MC CABE, JOSEPH   George Bernard Shaw: A Critical Study. 1914. Portrait, covers faded & stained, very good copy, scarce, first edition. Covent 51-1685 1973 £10.50

MC CABE, JOSEPH   Life and Letters of George Jacob Holyoake. London, 1908. 2 vols., 8vo., orig. cloth. Dawsons PM 247-152 1974 £15

MC CAIG, NORMAN   Far Cry. London, 1943. First edition, very nice copy, scarce, wrappers. Crane 7-186 1974 £10

MC CALL, SAMUEL W.   Patriotism of the American Jew. 1924. 288 pages. Austin 57-419 1974 $10

MC CALLUM, JOHN   That Kelly Family. Barnes, 1957. 229p., illus. Austin 51-573 1973 $7.50

MC CARDELL, RAY L.   The Show Girl and Her Friends. Street, Smith, 1904. Austin 51-574 1973 $10

MC CARTHY, JUSTIN   Camiola, a Girl With a Fortune. 1885. First edition, 3 vols., half title in each vol., catalogue at end vol. 1, orig. blue illus. cloth, very good copy, scarce. Sawyer 293-208 1974 £68

MC CARTHY, JUSTIN   A History of Our Own Times. 1899-98. 4 vols., crown 8vo., full prize calf gilt. Howes 186-1033 1974 £15

MC CARTHY, JUSTIN   A History of Our Own Times from the Accession of Queen Victoria to the Accession of Edward VII. 1880-1905. 7 vols., 8vo., green half morocco, gilt panelled backs. Bow Windows 66-460 1974 £19

MC CARTHY, JUSTIN   A History of Our Own Times. London, 1892. 8vo., 2 vols., contemporary tree calf, gilt, new edition. Dawsons PM 251-285 1974 £10

MC CARTHY, M. J. F.   Priests and People in Ireland. Dublin, 1902. 8vo., orig. cloth, illus., some spotting, covers faded. Bow Windows 66-461 1974 £5

MC CARTHY, MARY   Sights & Spectacles. 1956. Austin 51-575 1973 $7.50

MAC CARTHY-REAGH, JUSTIN   Catalogue des Livres Rares et Precieux de la Bibliotheque de feu M. le Comte de Mac-Carthy Reagh. Paris, 1815. 2 vols., in 3, large 8vo., boards, cloth backs, uncut, large paper copy, very fine. Kraus B8-148 1974 $180

MC CARTY, D. G.   History of Palo Alto County. Cedar Rapids, 1910. Cloth, illus., frayed, worn. Putnam 126-190 1974 $22.50

MC CARTY, WILLIAM   Songs, Odes, and Other Poems. . . . Naval. Philadelphia, 1842. Rubbed. Rinsland 58-68 1974 $15

MC CAUSLAND, ELIZABETH   George Inness. Springfield, 1946. 4to. Biblo & Tannen 214-172 1974 $18.50

MC CLELLAN, R. GUY   The Golden State: A History of the Region West of the Rocky Mountains . . . With a History of Mormonism and the Mormons. Chicago, (c. 1890). Thick 8vo., illus., maps, rebound in quarter leather, marbled boards, good. Current BW9-441 1974 $35

MC CLELLAND, NANCY   Historic Wall-papers. Philadelphia and London, 1924. Grey buckram, illus., plates. Dawson's 424-233 1974 $100

MC CLELLAND, NANCY   The Practical Book of Decorative Wall Treatments. 1926. Dec. cloth, illus. Covent 55-910 1974 £12.50

MC CLINTIC, GUTHRIE   Me and Kit. Little, Brown, 1955. 341p., illus. Austin 51-576 1973 $6.50

MC CLINTOCK, FRANCIS LEOPOLD   A Narrative of the Late Sir Franklin. 1859. 8vo., orig. cloth, first edition. Broadhurst 23-1674 1974 £25

MC CLINTOCK, FRANCIS LEOPOLD   The Voyage of the "Fox" In the Arctic Seas. London, 1859. 8vo., half calf, plates, leather label, first edition. Traylen 79-510 1973 £16

MC CLINTOCK, FRANCIS LEOPOLD   The Voyage of the "Fox" in the Arctic Seas. 1859. 8vo., orig. cloth, plates, maps. Wheldon 129-283 1974 £25

MC CLINTOCK, FRANCIS LEOPOLD   The Voyage of the "Fox" in the Arctic Seas. 1859. 8vo., orig. cloth, maps, plates, very scarce. Wheldon 128-214 1973 £25

MC CLINTOCK, FRANCIS LEOPOLD   The Voyage of the "Fox" in the Arctic Seas. Boston, 1860. 8vo., orig. cloth, plates, maps, scarce, first American edition. Wheldon 130-293 1974 £15

MC CLINTOCK, FRANCIS LEOPOLD   The Voyage of the "Fox" in the Arctic Seas. London, 1859. Three quarter leather, spine tooled and stamped in gold, fold-out map, bookplate, illus. Hood's 102-63 1974 $40

MC CLINTOCK, JAMES H.   Arizona; Prehistoric, Aboriginal, Pioneer, Modern. Chicago, 1916. 3 vols., 4to., three quarter leather. Saddleback 14-6 1974 $150

MC CLINTOCK, JOHN S.   Pioneer Days in the Black Hills. Deadwood, (1939). Orig. cloth, fine, scarce, first edition. Bradley 35-423 1974 $94

MAC CLINTOCK, LANDER   The Contemporary Drama of Italy. Boston, 1920. Biblo & Tannen 213-900 1973 $6.50

M'CLUNE, JAMES   History of the Presbyterian Church in the Forks of Brandywine. Philadelphia, 1885. 8vo., orig. bindings. Butterfield 8-490 1974 $15

MC CLUNG, J. W.   Minnesota As It is in 1870. St. Paul, 1870. 12mo., wrappers. Saddleback 14-518 1974 $20

MC CLUNG, NELLIE L.   In Times Life These. Toronto, 1915. Hood's 102-528 1974 $7.50

MC CLURE, A. K.   Old Time Notes of Pennsylvania. Philadelphia, 1905. 2 vols., Autograph edition, limited to 1,000 numbered copies, signed by author, top edges gilt, others uncut, illus., orig. bindings, tissue guards. Wilson 63-77 1974 $45

MC CLURE, DAVID   System of Education for the Girard College for Orphans. 1838. New buckram, rubber stamp. Allen 216-516 1974 $10

MC CLURE, MICHAEL   The Beard. n.d. Orig. white wrappers lettered in blue. Covent 51-1205 1973 £15

MAC COLL, D. S.   Nineteenth Century Art. Glasgow, 1902. Plates, orig. cloth, worn. Marsden 39-288 1974 £12

MC COLLUM, RANDALL   Sketches of the Highlands of Cavan. Belfast, 1856. 8vo., cloth boards, faded. Emerald 50-643 1974 £6.50

MC CONNOCHIE, JOHN   The Bute Docks, Cardiff, and the Mechanical Appliances for Shipping Coal. 1876. 8vo., boards, plates, first separate edition. Hammond 201-880 1974 £20

MC CORD, DAVID   Oddly Enough. Cambridge, 1926. 12mo., boards, cloth back, corners trifle worn, autographed by author, first edition. Goodspeed's 578-263 1974 $10

MC CORD, F. A.   Handbook of Canadian Dates. Montreal, 1888. Bookplate. Hood's 102-31 1974 $20

MC CORD, F. A.   Handbook of Canadian Dates. Montreal, 1888. Book-plate. Hood's 104-39 1974 $20

MC CORD, WILLIAM B.   Souvenir History of Ye Old Town of Salem, Ohio. Salem, 1906. 16mo., cloth. Saddleback 14-620 1974 $10

MACCORMAC, HENRY   Metanoia, a Plea for the Insane. London, 1861. 8vo., half calf, first edition. Schuman 37-162 1974 $45

MC CORMICK, HARRIET HAMMOND   Landscape Art, Past and Present. New York, 1923. Illus., cloth, boards, fine, first edition. Bradley 35-244 1974 $38

MC CORMICK, W. T.   A Ride Across Iceland in the Summer of 1891. 1892. Frontispiece, first edition, crown 8vo., orig. cloth, fine. Broadhurst 24-1646 1974 £5

MC COSH, JAMES   The Scottish Philosophy. 1875. Orig. cloth, frayed, ex-library. Howes 185-1923 1974 £5

MAC COUN, TOWNSEND   The Holy Land in Geography and History. Chicago, 1897. 2v., 12mo. Biblo & Tannen 210-1005 1973 $8.50

MC COY, F.   Natural History of Victoria. Melbourne, 1878-90. 2 vols. in 20 parts, roy. 8vo., orig. wrappers, half red morocco book boxes, complete copies, very rare, coloured plates. Wheldon 128-215 1973 £250

MC COY, F.   Natural History of Victoria. Melbourne, 1878-90. Roy 8vo., 2 vols., orig. wrappers, rare. Wheldon 130-41 1974 £250

MC COY, HORACE   They Shoot Horses Don't They. 8vo., orig. cloth, scarce, first English edition. Rota 189-581 1974 £6

MC COY, JOSEPH G.   Historic Sketches of the Cattle Trade of the West and Southwest. Kansas City, 1874. Illus. Jenkins 61-1559 1974 $300

MC COY, JOSEPH G.   Historic Sketches of the Cattle Trade of the West and Southwest. Washington, 1932. Scarce reprint. Jenkins 61-1558 1974 $27.50

MC CRAE, J.   In Flanders Fields. Toronto, 1919. Illus. Hood's 103-739 1974 $17.50

MC CROREY, J. G.   Wheeling. Portland, c.1905. Oblong 8vo., wrapper, boards. Saddleback 14-754 1974 $15

MC CULLERS, CARSON   Reflections in a Golden Eye. 1941. Inner hinge foxed, first edition. Allen 216-1062 1974 $10

MAC CULLOCH, J. A.   Medieval Faith and Fable. 1932. Faded. Howes 186-1876 1974 £5

MC CULLOCH, JOHN RAMSAY   Discours sur l'Origine, le Progres. Geneve, 1825. 8vo., 2 works in 1, quarter roan, first French edition. Dawsons PM 247-189 1974 £35

MC CULLOCH, JOHN RAMSAY   The Literature of Political Economy. London, 1845. 8vo., orig. blind-stamped cloth, first edition. Dawsons PM 247-192 1974 £55

MC CULLOCH, JOHN RAMSEY   The Principles of Political Economy. London, 1830. 8vo., contemporary calf, second edition. Dawsons PM 247-190 1974 £45

MC CULLOCH, JOHN RAMSAY   A Treatise on Metallic and Paper Money and Banks. Edinburgh, 1858. 4to., half calf, first separately published edition. Quaritch 939-167 1974 £20

MC CULLOCH, JOHN RAMSEY   A Treatise on the Principles and Practical Influence of Taxation and the Funding System. London, 1845. 8vo., orig. blind stamped cloth, first edition. Dawsons PM 247-191 1974 £65

MC CUTCHEON, GEORGE BARR   Beverly of Graustark. Dodd, Mead, 1904. 357p., illus. Austin 54-675 1973 $6

MC CUTCHEON, GEORGE BARR   Blades. Dodd, 1928. 344p. Austin 54-676 1973 $6.50

MC CUTCHEON, GEORGE BARR   Castle Craney Crow. Stone, 1902. 391p. Austin 54-677 1973 $7.50

MC CUTCHEON, GEORGE BARR   Cowardice Court. Dodd, Mead, 1906. 140p., illus. Austin 54-678 1973 $6.50

MC CUTCHEON, GEORGE BARR   The Day of the Dog. Dodd, 1905. 137p., illus. Austin 54-679 1973 $7.50

MC CUTCHEON, GEORGE BARR   Graustark. American News Co., 1901. 459p., "Special Limited ed." Austin 54-680 1973 $6.50

MC CUTCHEON, GEORGE BARR   Graustark. Chicago, 1901. Orig. illus. cloth, some rubbing, first printing. MacManus 224-294 1974 $55

MC CUTCHEON, GEORGE BARR   The Inn of the Hawk and Raven. Dodd, 1927. 360p. Austin 54-681 1973 $6

MC CUTCHEON, GEORGE BARR   The Man From Brodney's. Dodd, Mead, 1908. 355p., illus. Austin 54-682 1973 $6

MC D., M.   Dora Myrl the Lady Detective. 1900. 8vo., orig. blue pictorial cloth, first edition. Rota 190-184 1974 £12.50

MC DERMOT, E. T.   History of the Great Western Railway. 1927-31. 8vo., orig. cloth, gilt, plates. Hammond 201-927 1974 £20

MC DERMOTT, FREDERICK   The Life and Work of. London, 1887. 8vo., orig. cloth, gilt, plates, illus., first edition. Hammond 201-909 1974 £10.50

MAC DIARMID, HUGH, PSEUD.
Please turn to
GRIEVE, CHRISTOPHER MURRAY

MAC DONAGH, DONAGH   Veterans and Other Poems. Dublin, 1941. Orig. wrapper, fine, first edition. Rota 188-563 1974 £21

MAC DONAGH, M.   Daniel O'Connell and the Story of Catholic Emancipation. Dublin, 1929. 8vo., cloth boards, faded. Emerald 50-652 1974 £5

MAC DONAGH, MICHAEL   The Life of William O'Brien. 1928. Plates, buckram, English first edition. Covent 56-888 1974 £5

MAC DONAGH, THOMAS   Lyrical Poems. Dublin, 1913. Fine, slightly soiled covers, limited to 500 copies. Covent 51-2386 1973 £10

MAC DONAGH, THOMAS   Poetical Works. Dublin, 1917. 8vo., cloth-backed boards, first edition. Quaritch 936-480 1974 £9

MC DONALD, A.   A Complete Dictionary of Practical Gardening. 1807. 4to., 2 vols., contemporary half calf, gilt. Wheldon 129-28 1974 £300

MAC DONALD, AUGUSTIN S. A Collection of Verse by California Poets. San Francisco, 1914. 8vo., orig. bindings. Butterfield 8-44 1974 $15

MC DONALD, D.   Sweet-Scented Flowers and Fragrant Leaves. (1895). Crown 8vo., cloth, coloured plates, scarce. Wheldon 128-1498 1973 £5

MAC DONALD, D. G. F.   Cattle, Sheep and Deer. 1872. 8vo., cloth, portrait. Wheldon 129-389 1974 £7.50

MAC DONALD, E. M.   Golden Jubilee, 1869-1919. Toronto, 1919. Hood's 103-296 1974 $15

MC DONALD, EDWARD   The Posthumous Papers of D. H. Lawrence. London, 1936. Fine, orig. binding, first edition. Ross 87-343 1974 $45

MAC DONALD, F.   Jean Jacques Rousseau; A New Criticism. 1906. 2 vols., 8vo., orig. cloth, plates, spines faded. Bow Windows 66-590 1974 £8

MAC DONALD, G.   Dealings with the Fairies. 1868. 8vo., orig. cloth, illus. Bow Windows 64-598 1974 £5

MAC DONALD, GEORGE   Adela Cathcart. n.d. 423 pages. Austin 61-627 1974 $10

MAC DONALD, GEORGE   A Dish of Orts. 1895. Dec. cloth gilt, faded, enlarged edition. Covent 55-1057 1974 £7.50

MAC DONALD, GEORGE   The Portent. 1864. Parchment-vellum spine, English first edition. Covent 56-889 1974 £10.50

MAC DONALD, GEORGE   Robert Falconer. n.d. Frontispiece, English first edition. Covent 56-890 1974 £10.50

MAC DONALD, GEORGE   What's Mine's Mine. 1886. 531 pages. Austin 61-630 1974 $10

MAC DONALD, GEORGE   Within and Without. 1855. Orig. cloth, scarce, worn, first edition. Rota 188-564 1974 £35

MAC DONALD, HECTOR MUNRO   Electric Waves. Cambridge, 1902. 8vo., orig. red cloth, first edition. Dawsons PM 245-486 1974 £8

MAC DONALD, HUGH   John Dryden, A Bibliography of Early Editions and of Drydeniana. Oxford, 1939. Portrait, roy. 8vo., orig. cloth, d.w. Forster 98-105 1974 £21

MAC DONALD, J. A.   Troublous Times in Canada: A History of the Fenian Raids of 1866 and 1870. Toronto, 1910. Hood's 102-622 1974 $25

MAC DONALD, JAMES   History of Hereford Cattle. 1909. 8vo., new buckram, gilt. Wheldon 129-391 1974 £20

MAC DONALD, JAMES   History of Hereford Cattle. 1909. Herefords, 1909. 8vo., new half calf, illus., scarce, nice copy, revised second edition. Wheldon 131-510 1974 £20

MAC DONALD, JAMES   History of Polled Aberdeen. Edinburgh, 1882. Cloth. Hayman 57-463 1974 $10

MAC DONALD, JAMES   History of Polled Aberdeen or Angus Cattle. 1882. 8vo., cloth, plates, very scarce. Wheldon 131-509 1974 £15

MAC DONALD, JAMES   Sinclair, History of Polled Aberdeen. 1882. 8vo., cloth, plates, scarce. Wheldon 129-390 1974 £15

MAC DONALD, JOHN   The Moving Target. New York, 1949. 1st ed., scarce. Biblo & Tannen 210-490 1973 $25

MC DONALD, JOHN   Secrets of the Great Whiskey Ring. St. Louis, 1880. Cloth, inscribed. Hayman 57-473 1974 $10

MC DONALD, JOHN   Secrets of the Great Whiskey Ring: and Eighteen Months in the Penitentiary. St. Louis, 1880. Autographed. Jenkins 61-1561 1974 $12.50

MAC DONALD, M. C.   Down North. London, 1943. Illus. Hood's 102-64 1974 $7.50

MAC DONALD, R. M.   Opals and Gold. 1928. 8vo., orig. cloth, plates. Broadhurst 23-1673 1974 £6

MAC DONALD, THOMAS W.   About Collecting Bookplates. 1941. Cloth, illus., boards. Dawson's 424-77 1974 $35

MAC DONALD, W.   Greater Poems of the Bible. Toronto, 1943. Signed, limited edition. Hood's 103-740 1974 $12.50

MAC DOUGAL, D. T.   Tree Growth. Leyden, 1938. Orig. boards. Wheldon 129-1615 1974 £5

MAC DOUGALL, G. L.   A Short History of the 29 CDN ARMD RECCE REGT. Amsterdam, (1945). Card cover, signed by author. Hood's 102-111 1974 $17.50

MC DOUGALL, J. E.   If You Know What I Mean. Toronto, 1929. Hood's 102-662 1974 $7.50

MC DOUGALL, JOHN   Saddle, Sled and Snowshoe. Toronto, 1896. Illus. Hood's 102-814 1974 $20

MC DOUGALL, JOHN   Saddle, Sled and Snowshoe. Toronto, (1896). Mended spine, illus. Hood's 103-807 1974 $17.50

MC DOUGALL, W. B.   Plant Ecology. 1927. 8vo., cloth, frontispiece. Wheldon 129-940 1974 £4.50

MC DOWALL, R. J. S.   The Control of the Circulation of the Blood. London, 1938. 8vo., blue cloth, dust wrapper, first edition. Dawsons PM 249-356 1974 £9

MC DOWELL, EPHRAIM   Biography of. New York, 1897. Thick 8vo., disbound, plates, revised edition. Rittenhouse 46-436 1974 $22.50

MC DOWELL, F. D.   The Champlain Road. Toronto, 1940. Hood's 103-655 1974 $10

MC ELROY, ROBERT   Jefferson Davis, the Unreal and Real. New York & London, 1937. 2 vols., first edition, backstrips faded, orig. binding. Butterfield 10-167 1974 $12.50

MAC EWEN, WILLIAM   Pyogenic Infective Diseases of the Brain and
Spinal Cord, Meningitis, Abscess of Brain, Infective Sinus Thrombosis. Glasgow,
1893. 8vo., orig. cloth, plates. Gurney 66-119 1974 £55

MAC EWEN, WILLIAM   Pyogenic Infective Diseases of the Brain and Spinal Cord. Glasgow, 1893. 8vo., orig. cloth, illus., plates, first edition. Schumann 35-295 1974 $185

MAC FALL, HALDANE   Beautiful Children...Immortalized by the Masters.
London, n.d. Fine tipped in color plates, 4to., orig. binding. Wilson 63-299
1974 $28.50

MAC FALL, HALDANE   Ibsen. New York, 1907. Biblo & Tannen
210-884 1973 $7.50

MAC FALL, HALDANE   The Splendid Wayfaring. 1913. First edition,
crown 4to., illus., orig. cloth, fine. Broadhurst 24-775 1974 £30

MAC FAREN, WALTER   Memories. 1905. Illus., English first edition.
Covent 56-972 1974 £10.50

MAC FARLANE, CHARLES   Romance of History. 1832. 2 vols. in 1,
new buckram. Allen 213-1624 1973 $12.50

MAC FARLANE, CHARLES   The Romance of History. London, 1832. 12mo.,
3 vols., half calf, first edition. Dawsons PM 251-275 1974 £36

MAC FARLANE, CHARLES   The Romance of History. London, 1832. 8vo.,
3 vols., contemporary half calf, plates. Dawsons PM 252-675 1974 £36

MAC GEOGHEGAN, J.   History of Ireland. Dublin, 1831-32. 3 vols.,
8vo., half green morocco gilt. Quaritch 939-623 1974 £25

MAC GEORGE, ANDREW   Old Glasgow. Glasgow, 1880. 4to., orig.
cloth, gilt, illus., plates. Howes 186-2179 1974 £8.50

MAC GIBBON, DAVID   The Architecture of Provence and the Riviera.
Edinburgh, 1888. 8vo., illus., cloth. Quaritch 940-530 1974 £5

MAC GIBBON, DAVID   The Castellated and Domestic Architecture of
Scotland. Edinburgh, 1887-92. 5 vols., roy. 8vo., buckram, illus. Quarich
939-661 1974 £85

MAC GIBBON, DAVID   The Ecclesiastical Architecture of Scotland.
Edinburgh, 1896-7. Roy 8vo., 3 vols., orig. cloth. Broadhurst 23-1463 1974
£42

M'GILL, WILLIAM   A Practical Essay on the Death of Jesus Christ.
Edinburgh, 1786. 8vo., contemporary calf. Hill 126-163 1974 £15

MAC GILLIVRAY, W.   A History of British Quadrupeds. Edinburgh,
1838. Post 8vo., orig. cloth, plates, vignette. Wheldon 129-392 1974 £7.50

MAC GILLIVRAY, W.   Lives of Eminent Zoologists from Aristole to
Linnaeus. Edinburgh, 1834. 12mo., orig. cloth gilt, second edition. Wheldon
131-235 1974 £15

MC GIVERN, ED   Ed McGivern's Book on Fast and Francy Revolver
Shooting and Police Training. Boston, 1945. D.j., orig. binding. Butterfield
10-279 1974 $25

MC GOLRICK, EDWARD   The Unchangeable Church. 1908. 8 books
in 2 vols., illus. Austin 57-424 1974 $15

MC GONAGALL, WILLIAM   Poetic Gems, Selected from the Works of. 1855.
Portrait, boards, upper joint split, spine worn, edges little rubbed, Allen
Ginsberg's copy signed by him with a design in pen in his hand. Covent 51-775
1973 £21

MC GOODWIN, HENRY   Architectural Shades and Shadows. Boston,
1904. 4to., illus., orig. cloth, second edition. Bow Windows 62-612 1974
£5.50

MAC GOWAN, KENNETH   The Theatre of Tomorrow. Boni, Liveright,
1921. 302p., illus. Austin 51-577 1973 $17.50

MC GRATH, RAYMOND   Glass in Architecture and Decoration. 1937.
Roy. 4to., illus., cloth, orig. & best edition. Quaritch 940-618 1974 £25

MAC GREGOR, GEORGE   The History of Burke and Hare and of the
Resurrectionist Times. Glasgow, 1884. 8vo., contemporary half calf, rebacked,
plates, library stamps. Bow Windows 66-442 1974 £12.50

MAC GREGOR, JESSIE   Gardens of Celebrities and Celebrated
Gardens In and Around London. London, 1918. Plates, drawings, dust jacket.
Ballinger 1-289 1974 $12.50

MAC GREGOR, JESSIE   Gardens of Celebrities and Celebrated Gardens
in and Around London. 1918. Crown 4to., cloth, plates, scarce. Wheldon
130-1434 1974 £7.50

MC GREGOR, R. C.   A Manual of Philippine Birds. Manila, 1909.
8vo., half morocco, scarce. Wheldon 130-575 1974 £25

MC GROARTY, JOHN S.   California: Its History and Romance. Los
Angeles, 1911. First edition, foxed. Jenkins 61-361 1974 $10

MC GROARTY, JOHN S.   California of the South. Chicago, 1933.
5 vols., 4to., cloth. Saddleback 14-177 1974 $45

MC GROARTY, JOHN S.   History of Los Angeles County. Chicago,
1923. 3 vols., 4to., cloth, illus. Saddleback 14-178 1974 $25

MC GROARTY, JOHN S.   Los Angeles from the Mountains to the Sea.
Chicago, (1921). 2 vols., 4to., three quarter leather, special limited edition.
Saddleback 14-179 1974 $25

MC GROARTY, JOHN S.   Southern California. San Diego, 1915. 8vo.,
wrapper. Saddleback 14-180 1974 $10

MC GUINNESS, NORAH   A Sentimental Journey through France and Italy.
1926. Square 8vo., cloth-backed pictorial boards, English first edition. Covent
56-703 1974 £8.50

M'GUIRE, E. C.   The Religious Opinions and Character of
Washington. New York, 1936. Jenkins 61-2600 1974 $10

MC HENRY, JAMES   The Insurgent Chief. Glasgow, n.d. 8vo.,
cloth boards. Emerald 50-656 1974 £6

MAC HUGH, HUGH   Get Next. Dillingham, 1905. 111p., illus.
Austin 54-683 1973 $6

MAC HUGH, HUGH   I'm From Missouri. Dillingham, 1904. 107p.,
illus. Austin 54-684 1973 $6

MAC HUGH, HUGH   Out For the Coin. Dillingham, 1903. 107p.,
illus. Austin 54-685 1973 $6

MAC HUGH, HUGH   You Can Search Me. Dillingham, 1905.
119p., illus. Austin 54-686 1973 $6.50

MC HUGH, VINCENT   The Blue Hen's Chickens. New York, 1947.
1st ed. Biblo & Tannen 210-766 1973 $7.50

MC IAN, R. R.   The Clans of the Scottish Highlands. 1857.
2 vols., small folio, orig. morocco gilt, plates. Quaritch 939-663 1974 £800

MC IAN, R. R.   Gaelic Gatherings. 1848. Folio, plates,
half red morocco. Quaritch 939-662 1974 £400

MAC INNES, C. M.   In the Shadow of the Rockies. London, 1930.
Maps, illus. Hood's 103-808 1974 $45

MC INTOSH, CHARLES   The Book of the Garden. 1853-55. Roy. 8vo.,
2 vols., orig. cloth. Wheldon 129-1501 1974 £15

MC INTOSH, CHARLES   The Flower Garden. 1845. 12mo., orig. cloth
gilt, coloured plates. Wheldon 128-1499 1973 £12

MC INTOSH, CHARLES   The Greenhouse. 1838. Crown 8vo., half
morocco, plates. Wheldon 131-1543 1974 £15

MC INTOSH, CHARLES   The New and Improved Practical Gardener.
London, 1862. 1 vol. in 2, 8vo., plates, cloth, portrait. Bow Windows
62-628 1974 £65

MC INTOSH, CHARLES   The New and Improved Practical Gardener. 1862. 8vo., orig. cloth, plates. Bow Windows 64-780 1974 £65

MC INTOSH, D.   Diseases of Horses and Cattle. Chicago, (1895). 8vo., cloth, fine. Putman 126-16 1974 $5

MAC INTOSH, GEORGE   Biographical Memoir of. Glasgow, 1847. 8vo., orig. green cloth, plates, first edition. Dawsons PM 245-487 1974 £10

MC INTOSH, MARIA JANE   The Lofty and the Lowly. New York, 1853. 2 vols., orig. cloth, some rubbing, first edition. MacManus 224-295 1974 $30

MC INTOSH, W. C.   The Resources of the Sea. 1899. 8vo., cloth, illus. Wheldon 129-224 1974 £5

MC INTOSH, W. D.   One Hundred Years In the Zorra Church. Toronto, 1930. Photographs. Hood's 103-251 1974 $10

MC INTYRE, J. LEWIS   Giordano Bruno. 1903. Portrait, scarce. Howes 185-1825 1974 £8.50

MC INTYRE, JOHN T.   Ashton-Kirk Criminologist. Philadelphia, 1918. 8vo., orig. cloth, illus., first edition. Rota 190-325 1974 £9

MC INTYRE, JOHN T.   Ashton-Kirk Secret Agent. Philadelphia, 1912. 8vo., orig. red pictorial cloth, first edition. Rota 190-324 1974 £10

MAC KAIL, J. W.   Biblia Innocentium. Hammersmith, 1892. Small 4to., orig. limp vellum, fine. Dawsons PM 252-1096 1974 £150

MAC KAIL, J. W.   William Morris. Portland, 1942. 12mo., wrappers, book-plate, fine. Covent 55-1122 1974 £20

MAC KAY, C.   Memoirs of Extraordinary Popular Delusions and the Madness of Crowds. London, 1869. 2 vols., 8vo., illus., orig. cloth. Bow Windows 62-592 1974 £6.50

MAC KAY, CHARLES   A Tour In the United States and Canada. London, n.d. 2 vols. in 1, illus., plates, second edition. Hood's 103-547 1974 $60

MAC KAY, D.   The Honourable Company. Toronto, 1936. Maps, first edition. Hood's 103-809 1974 $22.50

MC KAY, W.   John Hoppner. 1909. Orig. cloth, plates. Marsden 39-237 1974 £30

MAC KAYE, PERCY   Caliban. Doubleday, Page, 1916. 223p., illus. Austin 51-578 1973 $12.50

MAC KAYE, PERCY   The Canterbury Pilgrims. Macmillan, 1903. Austin 51-579 1973 $7.50

MAC KAYE, PERCY   To-Morrow. Stokes, 1912. Austin 51-580 1973 $7.50

MC KEEN, SILAS   A History of Bradford. Montpelier, 1875. 8vo., orig. bindings, frontispiece, fine. Butterfield 8-647 1974 $10

MC KEEVOR, THOMAS   A Voyage to Hudson's Bay, During the Summer of 1812. London, 1819. 8vo., quarter cloth and boards, very good copy, plates, frontispiece, first edition. Ximenes 37-136 1974 $75

MC KELVEY, S. D.   The Lilac. New York, 1928. 4to., cloth, illus. Wheldon 130-1559 1974 £35

MC KELVIE, B. A.   Early History of the Province of British Columbia. Toronto, 1926. Illus. Hood's 103-810 1974 $25

MC KENNA LAMBERT   Aitdiogluim Dana. Dublin, 1939-40. 2 vols., 8vo., cloth boards. Emerald 50-662 1974 £5

MC KENNEY, RUTH   All About Eileen. Harcourt, Brace, 1947. Illus. Austin 54-687 1973 $5

MC KENNEY, RUTH   Far, Far, From Home. Harper, 1954. 210p., illus. Austin 54-688 1973 $6.50

MC KENNEY, RUTH   Industrial Valley. Harcourt, Brace, 1939. 379p., orig. ed. Austin 54-689 1973 $10

MC KENNEY, RUTH   Jake Home. Harcourt, Brace, 1943. 503p. Austin 54-690 1973 $7.50

MC KENNEY, RUTH   The Loud Red Patrick. Harcourt, Brace, 1947. 161p. Austin 54-691 1973 $6

MC KENNEY, RUTH   Love Story. Harcourt, Brace, 1950. 303p. Austin 54-692 1973 $6.50

MC KENNEY, RUTH   The McKenney's Carry On. Harcourt, Brace, 1939. 219p. Austin 54-693 1973 $6.50

MC KENNEY, THOMAS L.   The Indian Tribes of North America With Biographical Sketches and Anecdotes of the Principal Chiefs. Edinburgh, 1933-34. 3 vols., small 4to., new edition, full page plates, immaculate set. Butterfield 10-316 1974 $300

MC KENNY, THOMAS L.   The Indian Tribes of North America. Edinburgh, 1933-4. Plates in colour, photogravure portraits, maps, 3 vols., extra med. 8vo., top edges gilt, others uncut, very fine copy, many pages unopened. Broadhurst 24-1649 1974 £85

MAC KENZIE, A.   History of the MacDonalds and Lords of the Isles. Inverness, 1881. 8vo., quarter roan, worn, first edition. Bow Windows 62-594 1974 £12.50

MAC KENZIE, ALEX   The Life and Speeches of Hon. George Brown. Toronto, 1882. Hood's 103-218 1974 $12.50

MAC KENZIE, ALEXANDER   Voyages from Montreal Through the Continent of North America. Toronto, n.d. 2 vols., boards, paper labels, uncut. Bradley 35-238 1974 $35

MAC KENZIE, ALEXANDER   Voyages From Montreal, 1789-1793. New York, 1802. Full leather, first American edition. Hood's 103-548 1974 $425

MAC KENZIE, COLIN   Five Thousand Receipts in all the Useful and Domestic Arts. 1823. First edition, 12mo., newly bound half calf by Bayntun, marbled boards, fine. Broadhurst 24-1255 1974 £40

MAC KENZIE, COLIN   One Thousand Experiments in Chemistry. London, 1821. 8vo., old half green morocco, rare, first edition. Zeitlin 235-288 1974 $150

MAC KENZIE, COLIN   One Thousand Experiments in Chemistry. London, 1822. 8vo., modern blue paper, boards, uncut. Zeitlin 235-289 1974 $120

MAC KENZIE, COMPTON   The Darkening Green. 1934. Presentation copy, inscribed by author, cover stained, first edition. Covent 51-1220 1973 £5

MAC KENZIE, COMPTON   Extraordinary Women. 1928. Dust wrapper, fine, unopened, English first edition. Covent 56-898 1974 £5

MAC KENZIE, COMPTON   Extraordinary Women. London, 1928. No. 70 of edition limited to 2,000 copies (100 signed), orig. binding, d.w. tattered, else fine, signed. Ross 87-372 1974 £22.50

MAC KENZIE, COMPTON   First Athenian Memories. London, 1931. Orig. binding, bookplate, name in ink on fly leaf, slight crease in spine, nice. Ross 87-373 1974 £15

MAC KENZIE, COMPTON   From Theatre to Convent. 1936. Dust wrapper, plates, English first edition. Covent 56-899 1974 £10.50

MAC KENZIE, COMPTON   Gallipoli Memories. London, 1929. Orig. binding, first edition, fine. Ross 87-374 1974 £15

MAC KENZIE, COMPTON   Greek Memories. London, 1932. Orig. binding, bookplate, first edition, creased spine, nice. Ross 87-375 1974 £20

MAC KENZIE, COMPTON   Guy and Pauline. 1915. Author's signed presentation, spine rubbed & marked, damp marks on front cover, else very good copy, first edition. Covent 51-1221 1973 £6.50

MAC KENZIE, COMPTON   Marathon and Salamis. 1934. Presentation copy, inscribed from author, illus., cover somewhat dust soiled, very good copy, first edition. Covent 51-1222 1973 £6.30

MAC KENZIE, COMPTON   Poems. Oxford, 1907. 8vo., orig. grey wrappers, uncut, fine, first edition. Quaritch 936-481 1974 £25

MAC KENZIE, COMPTON   Poems. Oxford and London, 1907. Orig. cloth, wrappers, scarce, first edition. Rota 188-572 1974 £28

MAC KENZIE, COMPTON   Poems. Oxford & London, 1907. Wrappers, covers somewhat browned & frayed, presentation copy inscribed from author, nice copy, very scarce. Covent 51-2447 1973 £40

MAC KENZIE, COMPTON   Santa Claus in Summer. London, 1924. First edition, drawings, some foxing & grubby margins, good ex-library copy, orig. pictorial cloth. Crane 7-184 1974 £6

MAC KENZIE, COMPTON   Sinister Street. 1913-14. 2 vols., faded, orig. cloth, first edition. Rota 188-573 1974 £10

MAC KENZIE, COMPTON   Sylvia & Michael. London, 1919. Orig. binding, first edition, nice. Ross 87-376 1974 $12.50

MAC KENZIE, F.   The Architectural Antiquities of the Collegiate Chapel of St. Stephen. 1844. Atlas folio, plates. Quaritch 939-483 1974 £35

MC KENZIE, F. A.   Canada's Day of Glory. Toronto, 1918. Autographed. Hood's 103-116 1974 $10

MAC KENZIE, HENRY   The Lounger. Edinburgh, 1785-86. Small folio, boards, morocco label, first edition. Dawsons PM 252-676 1974 £200

MAC KENZIE, HENRY   The Lounger. London, 1787. Small 8vo., 3 vols., contemporary tree calf, third edition. Hammond 201-314 1974 £9.50

MAC KENZIE, HENRY   The Man of Feeling. 1773. 12mo., contemporary calf, corners worn, rebacked, frontispiece, new edition. Bow Windows 66-443 1974 £9.50

MAC KENZIE, HENRY   The Man of Feeling. 1928. One of 1475 copies, presentation copy inscribed from editor, cloth backed boards, near fine, first edition. Covent 51-1652 1973 £5.25

MAC KENZIE, JAMES   Angina Pectoris. London, 1923. Large 8vo., orig. cloth, illus., first edition. Gurney 64-140 1974 £20

MACKENZIE, JAMES   Diseases of the Heart. London, 1908. 1st ed., illus. Jacobs 24-155 1974 $65

MAC KENZIE, JAMES   Diseases of the Heart. London, 1918. 4to., orig. red cloth, third edition. Dawsons PM 249-358 1974 £8

MAC KENZIE, JAMES   The History of Health, and the Art of Preserving It. Edinburgh, 1758. 8vo., contemporary calf, first edition. Schumann 35-296 1974 $145

MC KENZIE, KENNETH   Concordanza Delle Rime di Francesco Petrarca. Oxford, 1912. Jacobs 24-119 1974 $35

MAC KENZIE, KENNETH R. H.   The Marvellous Adventures and Rare Conceits of Master Tyll Owlglass. Boston, 1860. 8vo., blue cloth pictorially stamped in gold, bevelled edges, all edges gilt, color plates, illus., spine ends and corners worn. Frohnsdorff 15-99 1974 $10

MAC KIE, CHARLES   Itinerary of the Great Northern Railway from London to York. London, 1854. 8vo., orig. engraved wrapper, illus., new edition. Hammond 201-925 1974 £12

MAC KINDER, H. J.   The Rhine: Its Valley and History. 1908. Med. 8vo., text illus., folding maps, water colour drawings, coloured plates, orig. cloth, fine. Broadhurst 24-1650 1974 £5

MAC KINLAY, J. M.   Ancient Church Dedications In Scotland. 1910-14. 2 vols. Allen 213-1626 1973 $12.50

MC KINLEY, CHARLES, JR.   Harriett. New York, 1946. 8vo., cloth, 1st ed., illus. Frohnsdorff 16-301 1974 $8.50

MAC KINNEY, LOREN CAREY   The Medieval World. New York, 1947. Illus. Biblo & Tannen 214-634 1974 $9.50

MAC KINNON, JAMES   The Growth and Decline of the French Monarchy. 1902. Thick 8vo. Howes 186-1038 1974 £5.50

MACKINSTRY, ELIZABETH   The Fairy Alphabet: As Used by Merlin. New York, 1933. Small 4to., pict. boards, cloth spine, illus., fine copy, dust jacket, first edition. Frohnsdorff 15-96 1974 $17.50

MACKINSTRY, ELIZABETH   Puck in Pasture. New York, 1925. 8vo., dec. boards, cloth spine, paper label, illus., corners worn, first edition. Frohnsdorff 15-97 1974 $10

MAC KINSTRY, ELIZABETH   Puck in Pasture. New York, 1925. Dec. boards, cloth spine, edges of boards and spine ends worn, first edition. Frohnsdorff 16-529 1974 $12.50

MAC KINTOSH, HAROLD   Early English Figure Pottery. London, (1938). Imp. 8vo., plates, fine, orig. cloth. Bow Windows 62-596 1974 £22.50

MAC KINTOSH, J.   The Discovery of America By Christopher Columbus. Toronto, 1836. Leather, worn. Hood's 104-525 1974 $95

MAC KINTOSH, J.   The Discovery of America by Christopher Columbus; and The Origin of the North American Indians. Toronto, 1836. Stiff card cover, leather spine, some pages waterstained, cover worn. Hood's 102-467 1974 $95

MAC KINTOSH, JAMES   Memoirs of the Life Of. 1835. 8vo., 2 vols., contemporary half calf. Hill 126-164 1974 £12.50

MAC KINTOSH, WILLIAM   Substance of the Speech of. London, 1824. 8vo., modern brown morocco, uncut, presentation copy, first edition. Dawsons PM 241-457 1974 £60

MAC KINTOSH, WILLIAM   Vindiciae Gallicae. London, 1791. 8vo., contemporary calf, gilt. Dawsons PM 251-278 1974 £18

MC KNIGHT, CHARLES   Captain Jack, The Scout. Philadelphia, (1873). Orig. cloth, extremities worn, another edition published in the same year as the first, but with different title and imprint. MacManus 224-296 1974 $25

MAC KNIGHT, JAMES   A Harmony of the Four Gospels in Which the Natural Order of Each is Preserved. 1763. 2 vols., 4to., contemporary calf, rebacked, second edition. Howes 185-1391 1974 £7.50

MC LAUGHLIN, S. B.   The Canadian Educator for Home and School Use. Toronto, 1922. 2 vols., illus. Hood's 103-337 1974 $20

MAC LAURIN, COLIN   An Account of Sir Isaac Newton's Philosophical Discoveries. London, 1748. 4to., old calf, rebacked, leather label, diagrams. Traylen 79-254 1973 £21

MC LAURIN, JOHN J.   Sketches in Crude-Oil. Harrisburg, 1896. 8vo., orig. bindings. Butterfield 8-492 1974 $20

MACLAY, EDGAR S.   Reminiscences of the Old Navy from the Journals and Private Papers of Captain Edward Trenchard and Rear-Admiral Stephen Decatur Trenchard. New York & London, 1898. Limited to 750 copies. Hayman 59-364 1974 $10

MACLAY, WILLIAM   The Journal of . . . United States Senator from Pennsylvania, 1789-91. New York, 1927. D.j., orig. binding. Butterfield 10-361 1974 $7.50

MAC LEAN, ANNIE MARION   Modern Immigration. 1925. Ex-library. Austin 57-426 1974 $12.50

MAC LEAN, J. P.   The Mound Builders. Cincinnati, 1885. Cloth. Hayman 59-481 1974 $20

MC LEAN, JOHN   The Indians of Canada: Their Manners and Customs. Toronto, 1889. Worn, full page illus. Hood's 102-468 1974 $7.50

M'LEAN, JOHN   Notes of Twenty-Five Years Service in the Hudsons Bay Territory. London, 1849. 2 vols., three quarter morocco, first edition. Jenkins 61-1420 1974 $185

MAC LEAY, K.   The Highlanders of Scotland. London, 1870. 2 vols., large folio, hand colored lithographs, scarce, orig. cloth, some stains and repairs to spine. Gregory 44-196 1974 $700

MAC LEISH, ARCHIBALD   The Fall of the City. New York, (1937). Orig. printed boards, somewhat soiled & rubbed, first edition, signed by author. MacManus 224-297 1974 $30

MAC LEISH, ARCHIBALD   Frescoes for Mr. Rockefeller's City. New York, (1933). Orig. printed wrappers, first edition, presentation copy from the author, signed, fine. MacManus 224-298 1974 $25

MAC LEISH, ARCHIBALD   The Hamlet of. 1928. First American edition, very good copy, largely unopened, slightly worn d.w., first edition. Covent 51-1224 1973 £5

MAC LEISH, ARCHIBALD   The Happy Marriage and Other Poems. Boston, 1924. Orig. boards, paper label, spine faded, first edition, removed bookplate, fine. MacManus 224-299 1974 $30

MAC LEISH, ARCHIBALD   New Found Land. Boston & New York, 1930. Orig. cloth, first edition, one of 500 copies, fine, bookplate removed. MacManus 224-301 1974 $25

MAC LEISH, ARCHIBALD   The Pot of Earth. Boston, 1925. Orig. cloth backed pictorial boards, first trade edition, bookplate removed, fine copy. MacManus 224-302 1974 $25

MAC LEISH, ARCHIBALD   Streets in the Moon. Boston & New York, 1926. Orig. cloth, slight fading, first edition, limited to 540 copies, very good. MacManus 224-305 1974 $27.50

MAC LEISH, ARCHIBALD   Tower of Ivory. New Haven, 1917. Boards, paper labels, first edition, bookplate removed, very fine copy. MacManus 224-306 1974 $50

MC LENNAN, J. S.   Louisbourg from Its Foundation to Its Fall. London, 1918. Illus., maps, first edition. Hood's 104-219 1974 $85

MC LENNAN, J. S.   Louisbourg From Its Foundation to Its Fall, 1713-1758. London, 1918. Illus., first edition, coloured folding map, pocket of maps. Hood's 102-197 1974 $85

MC LENNAN, WILLIAM   The Span o' Life. New York & Toronto, 1899. Signed picture of McLennan tipped in. Hood's 102-530 1974 $17.50

MC LEOD, ALEXANDER   The Trial of...for the Murder of Amos Durfee at the Burning and Destruction of the Steamboat Caroline. New York & Albany, 1841. Orig. heavy card covers, cloth spine, some foxing. Hood's 102-580 1974 $150

MC LEOD, ALEXANDER   The Trial of...for the Murder of Amos Durfee at the Burning and Destruction of the Steamboat Caroline. New York, 1841. Orig. covers, cloth spine, foxing. Hood's 104-665 1974 $150

MC LEOD, R. R.   Further Studies in Nature. Halifax, 1910. Hood's 104-443 1974 $10

M'MAHON, B.   The American Gardener's Calendar. Philadelphia, 1806. 8vo., contemporary sheep, rebacked in calf gilt, scarce. Wheldon 131-1544 1974 £75

MAC MANUS, SEUMAS   In Chimney Corners. 1904. 281 pages. Austin 61-633 1974 $10

MAC MANUS, SEUMAS   The Story of the Irish Race. 1944. Signed, revised fourth edition. Austin 61-636 1974 $10

MC MASTER, E. D.   The True Life of a Nation. New Albany, 1856. 8vo., orig. bindings. Butterfield 8-165 1974 $10

MAC MICHAEL, J. HOLDEN   The Story of Charing Cross. 1906. 360 pages, frontispiece. Howes 186-2128 1974 £5

MAC MICHAEL, WILLIAM   The Gold-Headed Cane. London, 1827. 8vo., orig. boards, uncut, first edition. Dawsons PM 249-359 1974 £70

MAC MICHAEL, WILLIAM   The Gold-Headed Cane. London, 1828. 8vo., old calf, gilt, second edition. Gurney 64-141 1974 £25

MAC MICHAEL, WILLIAM   The Gold-Headed Cane. 1915. Illus. Austin 61-637 1974 $12.50

MAC MICHAEL, WILLIAM   Gold-Headed Cane. New York, 1926. Reprint. Rittenhouse 46-427 1974 $17.50

MAC MILLAN, CYRUS   McGill and Its Story. London, 1921. Hood's 102-419 1974 $10

MAC MILLAN, DOUGALD   Plays of the Restoration and Eighteenth Century As They Were Enacted At the Theatres. 1931. Orig. edition. Austin 61-638 1974 $12.50

MAC MILLAN, H.   Holidays on High Lands. 1873. Small 8vo., cloth, second edition. Wheldon 130-1513 1974 £5

MAC MILLAN, H. F.   Tropical Gardening and Planting. 1925. 8vo., cloth, illus., third edition. Wheldon 129-1502 1974 £5

MC MILLAN, WILLIAM   The Worship of the Scottish Reformed Church, 1550-1638. 1931. Howes 185-1393 1974 £6

MC MULLEN, J.   The History of Canada, From Its First Discovery to the Present Time. Brockville, 1855. Hood's 102-570 1974 $40

MAC MUNN, G. F.   The Armies of India. London, 1911. Small 4to., plates. Traylen 79-149 1973 £6

MAC MURCHY, A.   The Canadian Railway Act, 1906-1910. Toronto, 1911. Second edition. Hood's 104-832 1974 $22.50

MC NAB, G. G.   The Development of Higher Education in Ontario. Toronto, 1925. Ex-library. Hood's 103-339 1974 $15

MAC NAIR, P.   The Geology and Scenery of the Grampians and the Valley of Strathmore. Glasgow, 1908. Plates, diagrams, maps, 2 vols., demy 4to., orig. cloth, fine. Broadhurst 24-1468 1974 £12

MAC NALLY, L.   Retaliation. 1782. 8vo., cloth, first edition. Quaritch 936-139 1974 £5

MAC NALLY, LEONARD   Fashionable Levities. London, 1785. 8vo., modern boards, second edition. Dawsons PM 252-678 1974 £12

MAC NALLY, LEONARD   Fashionable Levities. London, 1785. 8vo., modern boards, first edition. Dawsons PM 252-677 1974 £14

MAC NAMARA, FRANCIS   Miscellaneous Writings of Henry the Eighth. Golden Cockerel Press, (Waltham St. Lawrence, 1924). Orig. vellum backed boards, spine somewhat soiled, one of 365 copies, frontispiece portrait, fine. MacManus 224-186 1974 $60

MC NAMEE, GRAHAM   You're On the Air. Harper, 1926. 207p., illus. Austin 51-582 1973 $10

MC NAUGHER, JOHN   The Psalms in Worship. Pittsburgh, 1907. Biblo & Tannen 214-878 1974 $15

MAC NEICE, LOUIS   The Agamemnon of Aeschylus. 1936. Dust wrapper, fine. Covent 55-1062 1974 £7.50

MAC NEICE, LOUIS   Autumn Journal. London, 1939. 8vo., orig. cloth, fine, uncut, first edition. Dawsons PM 252-679 1974 £16

MAC NEICE, LOUIS   Geothe's Faust. 8vo., orig. orange cloth, fine, inscribed, first edition. Quaritch 936-482 1974 £75

MAC NEICE, LOUIS   I Crossed the Minch. 1938. 8vo., cloth, illus., first edition. Quaritch 936-483 1974 £35

MAC NEICE, LOUIS   The Last Ditch. Dublin, 1940. Orig. linen backed boards, fine, limited, first edition. Howes 185-93 1974 £21

MAC NEICE, LOUIS   Modern Poetry: A Personal Essay. 1938. Nice copy, scarce, covers faded, first edition. Covent 51-1225 1973 £10

MAC NEICE, LOUIS   Poems. 1935. Dust wrapper, English first edition. Covent 56-900 1974 £10

MAC NEICE, LOUIS   Poems. London, 1935. Lacking d.w., near mint, orig. binding. Ross 86-330 1974 $25

MAC NEICE, LOUIS   Poems. 1935. Dust wrapper, fine, first edition. Howes 185-311 1974 £15

MAC NEICE, LOUIS   The Poetry of W. B. Yeats. London, 1941. Second printing, bookplate, spine faded, nice copy, orig. binding. Ross 86-331 1974 $7.50

MC NEILL, RONALD   Ulster's Stand for Union. London, 1922. 8vo., cloth boards. Emerald 50-673 1974 £6.50

MAC NEVIN, THOMAS   The Confiscation of Ulster. Dublin, 1846. 2 vols. in 1, full leather, soiled. Emerald 50-674 1974 £6.50

MC NICOL, DONALD   Remarks on Dr. Samuel Johnson's Journey to the Hebrides. London, 1779. 8vo., contemporary half calf, first edition. Dawsons PM 252-578 1974 £14

MC NULTY, JOHN   A Man Gets Around. Little, Brown, 1951. 180p. Austin 54-695 1973 $6.50

MC NULTY, JOHN   The World of John McNulty. Doubleday, 1957. 357p. Austin 54-694 1973 $7.50

MAC PHAIL, ANDREW   Three Persons. 1929. Plates, very good copy, first edition. Covent 51-1108 1973 £5.25

MC PHERSON, AIMEE SEMPLE   This is That Personal Experiences Sermons and Writings. Los Angeles, (1921). Large 8vo., photo illus., orig. binding. Butterfield 10-362 1974 $20

MAC PHERSON, D.   Cartoons. Toronto, n.d. Hood's 104-172 1974 $10

MC PHERSON, EDWARD   The Political History of the United States During the Great Rebellion. Washington, 1865. Jenkins 61-1565 1974 $10

MAC PHERSON, H. A.   The Birds of Cumberland. Carlisle, 1886. 8vo., orig. cloth. Wheldon 130-576 1974 £7.50

MAC PHERSON, H. B.   The Home-Life of a Golden Eagle. 1910. Roy. 8vo., cloth, plates, second edition. Wheldon 131-651 1974 £5

MAC PHERSON, JAMES   Morison's Edition of the Poems of Ossian. Perth, 1795. Contemporary calf, gilt. Dawson's 424-195 1974 $50

MAC PHERSON, JAMES   Temora. London, 1763. 4to., contemporary calf, rebacked, label, first edition. Dawsons PM 252-680 1974 £25

MAC PHERSON, STEWART   Practical Harmony. London, 1907. Biblo & Tannen 214-751 1974 $7.50

MC QUEEN, JAMES   A Geographical Survey of Africa. London, 1840. Bdg. soiled and worn, top of spine torn. Biblo & Tannen 210-1006 1973 $37.50

MAC QUEEN, M. A.   Skye Pioneers and "The Island". Winnipeg, 1929. Portraits, illus. Hood's 104-221 1974 $30

MAC QUER, PIERRE JOSEPH   Elements of the Theory and Practice of Chymistry. London, 1764. 8vo., 2 vols., contemporary calf, plates, second edition. Schumann 35-297 1974 $110

MAC QUOID, KATHARINE S.   The Evil Eye and Other Stories. London, 1876. 1st ed., scarce. Biblo & Tannen 210-633 1973 $32.50

MAC QUOID, PERCY   The Dictionary of English Furniture. 1924-27. 3 vols., folio, plates, cloth, first edition. Quaritch 940-581 1974 £160

MACQUOID, PERCY   The Dictionary of English Furniture from the Middle Ages to the Late Georgian Period. London, 1924-27. Folio, 3 vols., colored plates, illus., first edition, lacking d.w.'s, rare, fine to near mint. Ross 87-196 1974 $400

MAC QUOID, PERCY   The Dictionary of English Furniture from the Middle Ages to the Late Georgian Period. 1924-27. 3 vols., folio, coloured plates, illus. Bow Windows 66-447 1974 £95

MAC QUOID, PERCY   Four Hundred Years of Children's Costumes from the Great Masters, 1400-1800. London, (1923). First edition, 8vo., full color laid on plates, minor page & cover spotting, else very good. Current BW9-108 1974 $35

MAC QUOID, PERCY   A History of English Furniture. 1904-08. 4 vols., folio, plates, buckram, gilt. Quaritch 940-580 1974 £75

MACRAY, W. D.   Notes Which Passed Between Charles II and the Earl of Clarendon, at Meetings of the Privy Council, 1660-67, Together With a Few Letters. 4to., quarter roan, top edges gilt. Thomas 32-287 1974 £55

MAC READY, NEVIL   Annals of an Active Life. (1924). 2 vols., plates, faded. Howes 186-1736 1974 £5

MAC READY, WILLIAM CHARLES   Diaries, 1833-51. 1912. 2 vols., plates, spines slightly faded. Allen 216-2133 1974 $17.50

MC SHERRY, JAMES   Father Laval. Baltimore, 1860. Cloth, bookplate. Hayman 57-208 1974 $20

MC SHERRY, JAMES   History of Maryland. Baltimore, 1849. 8vo., cloth, 405 pages. Saddleback 14-466 1974 $45

MC SKIMIN, SAMUEL   The History and Antiquities of Carrickfergus. Belfast, 1823. 8vo., plates, half roan, second edition. Emerald 50-675 1974 £15

MC SKIMIN, SAMUEL   The History and Antiquities of Carrickfergus. Belfast, 1829. 8vo., half calf, plates, third edition. Emerald 50-676 1974 £18

MC SKIMIN, SAMUEL   The History and Antiquities of Carrickfergus. Belfast, 1909. 8vo., cloth boards, new edition. Emerald 50-678 1974 £15

MC SORLEY, EDWARD   The Young McDermott. Harper, 1949. Austin 62-396 1974 $8.50

M'URE, JOHN   A View of the City of Glasgow. Glasgow, 1736. Small 8vo., 19th century morocco, gilt, first edition. Dawsons PM 251-58 1974 £65

MAC WATT, J.   The Primulas of Europe. 1923. Crown 8vo., cloth, illus., scarce. Wheldon 129-1503 1974 £5

MC WILLIAM R.   An Essay on the Origin and Operation of the Dry Rot. 1818. 4to., orig. boards, buckram, uncut. Wheldon 129-1273 1974 £30

MC WILLIAM, R.   An Essay on the Origin and Operation of the Dry Rot. 1818. 4to., orig. boards, rebacked in buckram, uncut, plates, very scarce. Wheldon 131-1442 1974 £30

MC WILLIAMS, CAREY   Prejudice. Little, Brown, 1944. 337p., orig. ed. Austin 62-397 1974 $7.50

MC WILLIAMS, MRS. R. F.   All Along the River. Winnipeg, 1930. Illus., inscribed. Hood's 104-863 1974 $12.50

MC WILLIAMS, VERA   Lafcadio Hearn. Boston, 1946. Biblo & Tannen 210-874 1973 $7.50

M. G. Les Enfans Spirituels, ou Les Savants du 1er Age. Paris, (c. 1815). Full diced calf, full page engravings, 2 1/2 X 2. Gregory 44-428 1974 $75

M., W.   The Queens Closet Opened. London, 1671. 3 parts in 1 vol., 12mo., 19th century calf. Quaritch 939-166 1974 £275

MAAK, R. K.   Album Risunkov K Puteshestvia na Amur.
(St. Petersburg, 1859). Folio, orig. cloth, plates, rare. Wheldon 131-375
1974 £100

MABERLY, CATHERINE   Emily. London, 1840. 3 vols., 12mo., first
edition, contemporary half calf, spines gilt, nice. Ximenes 36-141 1974 $70

MABERLY, J.   The Print Collector. New York, 1880. Med.
8vo., very good copy, plates, first edition, orig. cloth. Broadhurst 24-139
1974 £10

THE MABINOGION. 1849. 3 vols., half dark green morocco, boards, gilt,
uncut, foxing, fine. Broadhurst 23-1459 1974 £75

MABLY, GABRIEL BONNOT DE   Parallele des Romains et des Francois.
Paris, 1740. 2 vols., 12mo., contemporary tan calf, morocco labels, fine, first
edition. L. Goldschmidt 42-72 1974 $150

MABLY, GABRIEL BONNOT DE   Remarks Concerning the Government and the
Laws of the United States of America. Dublin, 1785. 8vo., cloth boards. Dawsons PM 251-273 1974 £28

MACARIUS, S. AEGYPTIUS   Opera Opuscula Nonnulla Apophthegmata.
Lipsiae, 1714. 8vo., vellum, rubbed. Schumann 499-65 1974 sFr 75

MAC AULAY, ROSE   A Casual Commentary. 1925. Orig. cloth,
dust wrapper, first edition. Rota 188-560 1974 £5

MACAULAY, ROSE   Cathwords and Claptrap. 1926. Orig. boards,
English first edition. Covent 56-882 1974 £7.50

MACAULAY, ROSE   Crewe Train. 1926. 8vo., cloth, dust-wrapper,
first edition. Quaritch 936-478 1974 £10

MACAULAY, ROSE   Crewe Train. London, 1926. First edition,
immaculate copy, orig. blue and brick red Collins binding, pictorial d.w. is
chipped, scarce. Crane 7-182 1974 £10

MACAULAY, ROSE   Going Abroad. 1934. 8vo., cloth, dust-wrapper, first edition. Quaritch 936-479 1974 £12

MACAULAY, ROSE   Keeping Up Appearances. 1928. Dust wrapper,
English first edition. Covent 56-883 1974 £10

MACAULAY, ROSE   The Lee Shore. n.d. (1912). Scarce, very nice
copy, spine slightly dusty, first edition. Covent 51-1201 1973 £10.50

MAC AULAY, ROSE   Personal Pleasures. 1936. 395 pages.
Austin 61-622 1974 $10

MACAULAY, ROSE   The Two Blind Countries. 1914. English first
edition. Covent 56-884 1974 £21

MACAULAY, ROSE   The Writings of E. M. Forster. 1938. Spine
slightly faded, fine, first edition. Covent 51-717 1973 £5.25

MAC AULAY, THOMAS BABINGTON   Critical and Historical Essays. 1843.
3 vols., contemporary half calf, second edition. Howes 186-312 1974 £12.50

MACAULAY, THOMAS BABINGTON   Critical and Historical Essays. 1850.
8vo., contemporary calf, gilt spine, portrait, engraved vignette title, new
edition. Bow Windows 66-439 1974 £6

MAC AULAY, THOMAS BABINGTON   The History of England. 1849-76.
8vo., polished calf, gilt. Quaritch 936-476 1974 £120

MAC AULAY, THOMAS BABINGTON   The History of England from the
Accession of James the Second. 1861. 5 vols., full polished tree calf gilt,
labels. Howes 186-1030 1974 £30

MAC AULAY, THOMAS BABINGTON   History of England. 1899. 10 vols.,
illus., very good edition. Austin 61-626 1974 $75

MAC AULAY, THOMAS BABINGTON   The History of England from the
Accession of James II. 1913-15. 6 vols., roy. 8vo., gilt, plates, best illus.
library edition. Howes 186-1031 1974 £24

MAC AULAY, THOMAS BABINGTON   The History of England. London, 1913-
15. 6 vols., large 8vo., illus., orig. cloth, presentation copy. Bow Windows
62-591 1974 £14

MAC AULAY, THOMAS BABINGTON   Lays of Ancient Rome. 1926. Plates,
fine, first edition. Covent 55-893 1974 £7.50

MAC CAULAY, THOMAS BABINGTON   Miscellaneous Writings. 1860. 8vo.,
gilt, red leather, frontis. Quaritch 936-477 1974 £10

MAC AULAY, THOMAS BABINGTON   The Miscellaneous Writings. 1860.
Large 8vo., 2 vols., orig. brown cloth, uncut, fine, first edition. Hill 126-162
1974 £18

MACAULAY, THOMAS BABINGTON   Two Essays on the Earl of Chatham. London, 1901. 4to., contemporary half brown morocco, uncut. Dawsons PM 251-
128 1974 £10

MACAULEY, THOMAS BABINGTON   The Works. London, 1865. 8vo., 12
vols., contemporary half calf, boards, new edition. Dawsons PM 251-274 1974
£180

MAC AULAY-GRAHAM, CATHERINE   Observations on the Reflections of the
Rt. Hon. Edmund Burke on the Revolution in France. London, 1790. 8vo.,
modern boards. Dawsons PM 247-188 1974 £15

MACE, T.   Musick's Monument. 1676. Small folio,
early 18th century calf, fine, scarce. Quaritch 940-814 1974 £450

MACEWEN, WILLIAM   Pyogenic Infective Diseases of the Brain and
Spinal Cord. Glasgow, 1893. 8vo., orig. cloth, first edition. Gurney 64-
139 1974 £55

MACH, ERNST   Optisch-Akustische Versuche. Prague,
1873. 8vo., half cloth, good copy, first edition. Schafer 8-167 1973 sFr. 900

MACHAR, AGNES M.   For King and Coutry: A Story of 1812. Toronto,
1874. Spine faded. Hood's 102-529 1974 $20

MACHAR, A. M.   Lays of the True North. London, 1902. Card
cover, enlarged edition. Hood's 103-741 1974 $10

MACHAR, A. M.   The Story of Old Kingston. Toronto, 1908.
Hood's 103-656 1974 $35

MACHAULT, J. B. DE   Eloges et Discours sur la Triomphante
Reception du Roy en sa Ville de Paris. Paris, 1629. Folio, full blue levant
morocco, gilt, illus. L. Goldschmidt 42-73 1974 $1,100

MACHEN, ARTHUR   The Anatomy of Tobacco. 1884. Full
parchment, first edition. Rota 188-568 1974 £35

MACHEN, ARTHUR   The Chronicle of Clemendy. (London), 1888.
One of 250 numbered copies, plates, vignettes, quarter vellum gilt, raised bands,
some foxing, nice copy, Herbert Jones' copy with his bookplate & signature,
A.L.s. from author to Jones. Covent 51-2442 1973 £35

MACHEN, ARTHUR   Dreads and Drolls. London, 1926. 1st ed.
Biblo & Tannen 210-634 1973 $12.50

MACHEN, ARTHUR   Far Off Things. London, 1922. 1st ed.
Biblo & Tannen 210-767 1973 $12.50

MACHEN, ARTHUR   The Heptameron. 1886. Boards, portrait, English first edition. Covent 56-895 1974 £21

MACHEN, ARTHUR   The Hill of Dreams. London, 1907. Orig.
cloth, somewhat rubbed, first edition, second issue. MacManus 224-308
1974 $32.50

MACHEN, ARTHUR   The London Adventure. 1924. Boards, signed,
English first edition. Covent 56-896 1974 £12.50

MACHEN, ARTHUR   Notes and Queries. 1926. One of 265 copies,
signed by author, fine, first edition. Covent 51-1218 1973 £15

MACHEN, ARTHUR   Ornaments in Jade. New York, 1924. Orig.
cloth, first edition, one of 1000 copies, signed by author, boxed, fine. MacManus
224-309 1974 $25

MACHEN, ARTHUR   Precious Balms. 1924. One of 265 copies, numbered & signed by author, buckram, printed label, fine. Covent 51-2443 1973 £10.50

MACHEN, ARTHUR   Things Near and Far. 1923. Presentation copy inscribed by author, d.w. Covent 51-2445 1973 £10.50

MACHEN, ARTHUR   Things Near and Far. London, 1923. Orig. paper covered boards, paper label, first edition, one of 100 numbered copies, signed by author, fine, boxed. MacManus 224-310 1974 $37.50

MACHIAVELLI, NICCOLO   The Florentine History in VIII Books. 1674. Small 8vo., half calf, stained, first edition. Howes 186-1036 1974 £42

MACHIAVELLI, NICCOLO   Il Principe di Niccolo Machiavelli. Florence, 1532. Small 4to., 18th century English red morocco gilt, rebacked, first Florence edition. Dawsons PM 250-54 1974 £1600

MACHIAVELLI, NICCOLO   The Works of. 1680. Folio, 19th century polished calf, gilt, rebacked with orig. strip, large armorial bookplate of Sir William Augustus Fraser. Thomas 32-121 1974 £75

MACHIAVELLI, NICCOLO   Works. 1905. 2 vols., orig. buckram backed boards. Howes 185-537 1974 £12.50

MACHINE NOUVELLE pour la Conduite des Eaux. Paris, n.d. 12mo., wrappers. Gurney 64-213 1974 £12

MACHINE Nouvelle Pour la Conduite des Eaux, pour les Batimens, pour la Navigation, et pour la Plupart des autres Arts. Paris, n.d. (late 17th c.). 12mo., wrappers. Gurney 66-184 1974 £12

MACK, GERSTLE   Toulouse-Lautrec. New York, 1938. lst ed. Biblo & Tannen 214-534 1974 $12.50

MACKAIL, J. W.   Biblia Innocentium. 1892. 8vo., limp vellum with ties. Hammond 201-727 1974 £155

MACKAIL, J. W.   Five Essays and Addresses. 1902-05. Quarter vellum, 5 vols., English first edition. Covent 56-964 1974 £35

MACKAIL, J. W.   The Life of William Morris. 1920. 2 vols., large 8vo., orig. linen backed boards, scarce. Howes 185-341 1974 £12.50

MACKAIL, J. W.   William Morris. 1901. 8vo., limp vellum. Hammond 201-743 1974 £65

MACKAIL, J. W.   William Morris: An Address Delivered . . . at Kelmscott House. 1902. Booklabel, vellum backed boards, fine, first edition. Covent 51-1324 1973 £5

MACKAY, JOHN W.   Mark! New York, (1936). Photos, line drawings, 8vo., illus., mint. Current BW9-188 1974 $18.50

MACKEN, WALTER   Home Is the Hero. Macmillan, 1953. 114p. Austin 51-581 1973 $8.50

MACKIE, S. J.   A Handbook of Folkestone. Folkestone, 1862. 8vo., orig. paper wrappers, neatly rebacked, portrait, plates, folding plans, third edition. Bow Windows 66-444 1974 £5.85

MACLISE, DONALD   The Story of the Norman Conquest. 1866. Oblong folio, orig. cloth, plates. Marsden 37-302 1974 £12

MACLISE, JOSEPH   Surgical Anatomy. Philadelphia, 1859. Folio, cloth gilt, coloured plates, name on title somewhat shabby, but sound. Thomas 32-323 1974 £25

MACOUN, JOHN   Catalogue of Canadian Birds. Ottawa, 1903-1904. 8vo., cloth bound. Bow Windows 64-173 1974 £5

MACQUER, PIERRE J.   A Dictionary of Chemistry. London, 1771. 2 vols., 4to., contemporary calf, leather labels, plates. Traylen 79-245 1973 £75

MACVICAR, S. M.   The Distribution of Hepaticae in Scotland. Edinburgh, 1910. 8vo., cloth. Wheldon 128-1396 1973 £5

MACVICAR, S. M.   The Students Handbook of British Hepatics. Eastbourne, 1926. 8vo., cloth, illus., second edition. Wheldon 128-1397 1973 £5

MADACH, IMRE   The Tragedy of Man. Macmillan, 1935. Austin 51-583 1973 $8.50

MADAN, FALCONER   A Chart of Oxford Printing. (London), 1904. 4to., contemporary half morocco, limited, first book form edition, second issue. Dawsons PM 10-386 1974 £26

MADAN, FALCONER   Oxford Books. Oxford, 1895-1931. 3 vols., 8vo., orig. cloth, fine. Dawsons PM 10-387 1974 £35

MADAN, FALCONER   Records of the Club at Oxford. Oxford, 1917. 8vo., cloth, faded, limited. Quaritch 939-770 1974 £6

MADAN, SPENCER   Hugo Grotius on the Truth of Christianity. 1782. 8vo., contemporary tree calf, gilt. Hill 126-122 1974 £18

MADARIAGA, SALVADORE DE   Don Quixote. 1934. Large 8vo., orig. canvas backed boards, uncut, hand made paper, limited. Bow Windows 62-399 1974 £68

MADARIAGA, SALVADOR DE   Don Quixote: In Introductory Essay in Psychology. 1934. Med. 8vo., boards, linen spine, uncut, printed in blue and black, limited to 235 copies, orig. prospectus, fine. Broadhurst 24-1010 1974 £50

MADARIAGA, SALVADORE DE   Shaw Gives Himself Away. 1939. 8vo., frontispiece, orig. morocco, engraved. Bow Windows 62-400 1974 £135

MADDEN, J. P. A.   Notes et Notices. Versailles, 1864. Wrappers. Rittenhouse 46-429 1974 $10

MADDEN, SAMUEL   Themistocles, the Lover of his Country. 1729. Small 8vo., cloth, first edition. Quaritch 936-140 1974 £6

MADDOCK, A. B.   Practical Observations on Mental and Nervous Disorders. London, 1854. 8vo., old half calf, rubbed, first edition. Gurney 66-120 1974 £15

MADDOCK, JAMES   The Florist's Directory. London, 1810. Orig. grey boards, color plates, 8vo. Gregory 44-197 1974 $165

MADDOX, ISAAC   A Sermon Preached Before His Grace Charles Duke of Malborough. (1752). Small 4to., calf back, modern boards. Quaritch 939-462 1974 £8

MADDOX, ISAAC   A Sermon Preached Before the Incorporated Society for the Propagation of the Gospel In Foreign Parts . . . St. Mary-le-Bow 15 Feb., 1733. 1734. Small 4to., modern sheep. Thomas 28-29 1972 £18

MADDOX, WILLES   Views of Lansdown Tower, Bath. Bath & London, 1844. Large folio, orig. quarter morocco, plates. Traylen 79-386 1973 £105

MADELIN, LOUIS   Fouche. Paris, 1930. 2 vols., buckram, portrait. Howes 186-823 1974 £7.50

MADGE, S. J.   Domesday of Crown Lands. 1938. Plates. Allen 213-1629 1973 $10

MADOX, THOMAS   Baronia Anglica. 1736. Folio, contemporary calf, first edition. Quaritch 939-737 1974 £35

MADOX, THOMAS   Firma Burgi. 1726. Folio, half calf. Quartich 939-168 1974 £38

MADOX, THOMAS   The History and Antiquities of the Exchequer of the Kings of England. 1711. Folio, contemporary panelled calf, plates, first edition. Quaritch 939-169 1974 £45

MADOX, THOMAS   The History and Antiquities of the Exchequer of the Kings of England. 1769. 2 vols., 4to., contemporary tree calf gilt, second edition. Quaritch 939-170 1974 £60

MADOX, THOMAS   The History and Antiquities of the Exchequer of the Kings of England in Two Periods. London, 1769. 4to., 2 vols., buckram, gilt, second edition. Hammond 201-249 1974 £50

MADRAS Exhibition of 1859 of the Raw Products of Southern India. Madras, 1858. 8vo., orig. wrappers. Wheldon 131-1789 1974 £10

MADRAY, MRS. I. C.   A History of Bee County With Some Brief Sketches About Men and Events in Adjoining Counties. Beeville, 1931. 8vo., cloth. Saddleback 14-712 1974 $60

MADRIGAL TOSTADO DE RIVERA, ALFONSON DE   Libro Delas Quatro Questiones. Salamanca, 1507. 2 works in 1 vol., folio, old half leather, fine, rare, first editions. Harper 213-106 1973 $475

MADVIG, J. N.   Den Romerske Stats Forfatning og Forvaltning. 1881. 2 vols., half calf, worn spine, first edition. Allen 213-671 1973 $12.50

MAETERLINK, MAURICE   Aglavaine and Selysette. Dodd, 1915. Austin 51-584 1973 $6

MAETERLINCK, MAURICE   Alladine et Palomides. Brussels, 1894. 12mo., contemporary half vellum, orig. wrapper, uncut, first edition. L. Goldschmidt 42-290 1974 $40

MAETERLINK, MAURICE   The Betrothal. Dodd, 1918. 222p. Austin 51-585 1973 $6.50

MAETERLINCK, MAURICE   The Buried Temple. London, 1902. 8vo., cloth, frontispiece. Minters 37-253 1973 $24

MAETERLINK, MAURICE   Joyzelle and Monna Vanna. Dodd, Mead, 1907. Austin 51-586 1973 $6.50

MAETERLINK, MAURICE   Mary Magdalene. Dodd, 1910. Austin 51-587 1973 $6.50

MAETERLINK, MAURICE   Monna Vanna. Harper, 1903. Austin 51-588 1973 $6.50

MAETERLINK, MAURICE   Princess Maleine. Dodd, Mead, 1911. 208p. Austin 51-589 1973 $6.50

MAETERLINK, MAURICE   Sister Beatrice and Adriane & Barbe Bleue. Dodd, 1908. Austin 51-590 1973 $6

MAETERLINCK, MAURICE   Theatre. Brussels, 1901-02. 3 vols., large 8vo., contemporary tobacco brown three quarter levant morocco, first collected edition. L. Goldschmidt 42-291 1974 $150

MAETERLINCK, MAURICE   La Vie des Abeilles. Lyons, 1924. 8vo., contemporary half vellum, gilt, limited edition. L. Goldschmidt 42-292 1974 $12.50

MAETERLINCK, MAURICE   Wisdom and Destiny. 1898. Dec. cloth, English first edition. Covent 56-905 1974 £10.50

MAFFEI, F. SCIPIONE   Delia Formazione De'Fulmini Trattato. 1747. 4to., contemporary vellum, fine, first edition. Dawsons PM 245-489 1974 £35

MAFFEI, F. SCIPIONE   Istoria Diplomatica che Serve d'Introduzione all Arte Critica in tal Materia. Mantova, 1727. 4to., boards, plates, red morocco back, gilt, first and only edition. Harper 213-107 1973 $275

MAFFITT, JOHN NEWLAND   Poems. Louisville, 1839. 8vo., orig. bindings, boards. Butterfield 8-190 1974 $10

MAGALOTTI, LORENZO
Please see also
ACCADEMIA DEL CIMENTO

Caution: His own works are entered under his name

MAGGARD, J. H.   Rough and Tumble Engineering. Iowa City, (c.1900). Plates, illus., pictorial cloth, fourth edition. Bradley 35-239 1974 $22.50

MAGGS BROTHERS   Catalogue No. 45, Bibliotheca Americana et Philippina. London, 1925. Part IV, illus., small 4to., wrappers. Kraus B8-149 1974 $18

MAGGS BROTHERS   Catalogue No. 484, London. London, 1926. Small 4to., orig. wrapper, illus. L. Goldschmidt 42-19 1974 $12.50

MAGGS BROTHERS   Catalogue No. 502, Bibliotheca Americana. London, 1928. Part VII, wrappers, illlus., 4to. Kraus B8-150 1974 $10

MAGINI, GIOVANNI ANTONIO   Tabvlae Primi Mobilis. 1604. Folio, contemporary limp vellum. Zeitlin 235-144 1974 $450

MAGIRUS, JOANN   Physiologiae Peripateticae. London, 1619. Contemporary calf, worn. Thomas 28-267 1972 £125

MAGIRUS, JOHANN   Physiologiae Peripateticae Libri. (Cambridge,) 1642. 4to., contemporary calf, second English edition. Dawsons PM 249-360 1974 £55

MAGNA Charta, Cum Statutis, tum Antiquis, tum Recentibus. 1608. Small 8vo., contemporary sheep. Thomas 28-194 1972 £35

MAGNA Charta, cum Statutis, tum Antiquis, tum Recentibus . . . Cui Adjecta Sunt Nonnulla Statua, Nunc Demum Tipis Adita. 1608. Partly in black letter, small 8vo., contemporary sheep, spine and corners repaired, generally in good condition. Thomas 32-122 1974 £35

MAGNI, JACOBUS   Sophologium. (Strasburg, 1475). Folio, contemporary blind-stamped calf, fine, early edition. Gilhofer 61-1 1974 sFr. 11,000

MAGNI, JACOBUS   Sophologium. (Strassburg, c.1476). Folio, modern calf over old wooden boards, raised bands. Schafer 8-168 1973 sFr. 2,900

MAGNI, PIETRO PAOLO   Discorso Sopra il Modo di Fare i Cauterii. Brescia, 1618. 4to., boards, illus. Schumann 35-298 1974 $190

MAGNOL, PIERRE   Botanicum Monspeliense. Montpellier, 1686. 8vo., calf, plates, second edition. Wheldon 129-1103 1974 £50

MAGNOL, PIERRE   Botanicum Monspeliense. Montpellier, 1686. 8vo., calf, plates. Wheldon 131-1327 1974 £50

MAGNOL, PIERRE   Hortus Regius Monspeliensis. Montpellier, 1697. 8vo., sheep, plates. Gurney 64-142 1974 £90

MAGNOL, PIERRE   Hortus Regius Monspeliensis, Sive Catalogus Plantarum que in Horto Regio Monspeliensi Demonstrantur. Montpellier, 1697. 8vo., sheep, plates, orig. probably only edition, rare. Gurney 66-121 1974 £90

MAGNUS, LAURIE   A Dictionary of European Literature. 1926. Thick roy. 8vo., orig. buckram, scarce, orig. edition. Howes 185-313 1974 £7.50

MAGNY, C. D.   Archeologique Heraldique. 1867. Folio, buckram. Allen 213-1630 1973 $25

MAGRATH, JOHN R.   The Obituary Book of Queen's College, Oxford. Oxford, 1910. Orig. limp vellum. Smith 194-273 1974 £5

MAGRATH, JOHN R.   The Queen's College. 1921. 2 vols., imp. 8vo., orig. buckram, plates. Howes 186-2164 1974 £10.50

MAGUIRE, JOHN FRANCIS   The Irish in America. London, 1868. 1st ed., orig. cl. Jacobs 24-20 1974 $80

MAGYAR Poetry: Selections from Hungarian Poets. New York, 1899. 12mo. Biblo & Tannen 213-788 1973 $10

MAHAN, ALFRED THAYER   The Influence of Sea Power Upon History. Boston, 1890. Orig. cloth, first edition. Jenkins 61-1423 1974 $85

MAHAN, ALFRED THAYER   The Influence of Sea Power Upon History. 1892. Roy. 8vo., maps, first English edition. Howes 186-1737 1974 £6.50

MAHAN, ALFRED THAYER   The Influence of Sea Power. London, 1892.
2 vols., maps. contemporary dark green calf gilt, first edition. Smith 194-767
1974 £15

MAHAN, ALFRED THAYER   The Influence of Sea Power Upon History,
1660-1783. London, 1890. Contemporary dark green calf, maps. Smith
194-768 1974 £7.50

MAHAN, ALFRED THAYER   The Life of Nelson. 1897. 8vo., 2 vols., orig.
cloth. Broadhurst 23-1676 1974 £6

MAHAN, ALFRED THAYER   The Life of Nelson: The Embodiment of the Sea
Poer of Great Britain. 1897. 2 vols., demy 8vo., good copy, maps, orig. cloth,
fine. Broadhurst 24-1651 1974 £6

MAHAN, ALFRED THAYER   The Life of Nelson. Boston, 1918. 2 vols.,
illus. Jacobs 24-107 1974 $25

MAHAN, DENNIS HART   Summary of the Course of Permanent Fortification.
1860. 4to., contemporary half grained leather, gilt. Zeitlin 235-145 1974
$125

THE MAHAVANSI, the Raja-Ratnacari, and the Raja-Vali. London, 1833.
3 vols. in 1, thick 8vo., half blue calf, rubbed. Traylen 79-536 1973 £25

MAHON, CHARLES STANHOPE   Considerations on the Means of Preventing
Fraudulent Practices on the Gold Coin. London, 1775. 4to., fine, uncut,
first edition. Dawsons PM 247-193 1974 £45

MAHON, PHILIP HENRY   History of the War of the Succession in Spain.
1836. Contemporary calf, label, second edition. Howes 186-1738 1974 £7.50

MAIDEN, J. H.   A Critical Revision of the Genus Eucalyptus.
Sydney, 1909-21. Vols. 1-4 and Vol. 5 parts 1-5, 4to., cloth, plates.
Wheldon 128-1609 1973 £35

MAIDEN, J. H.   A Critical Revision of the Genus Eucalyptus.
Sydney, 1909-21. 4to., 5 vols., cloth, plates. Wheldon 130-1560 1974 £35

MAIDEN, J. H.   The Forest Flora of New South Wales. Sydney,
1904-23. 8 vols., 4to., new cloth, plates, rare. Wheldon 128-1610 1973 £90

MAIDEN, J. H.   The Forest Flora of New South Wales. Sydney,
1904-23. 4to., 8 vols., new cloth, plates, rare. Wheldon 130-1561 1974 £90

MAIDMENT, JAMES   Liber Conventus S. Katherine Senensis Prope
Edinburgum. Edinburgi, 1841. Small 4to., contemporary half morocco, little
rubbed, some spotting, bookplate. Bow Windows 66-448 1974 £14

MAIGNAN, EMANUEL   Perspectiva Horaria Sive de Horographia Gnomo-
nica Tum Theoretica. Rome, 1648. Thick folio, contemporary vellum, plates,
first edition. Schumann 35-299 1974 $875

MAILLARD, N. DORAN   The History of the Republic of Texas. London,
1842. Orig. cloth, Dr. Joe B. Frantz's copy inscribed by him. Jenkins
61-1424 1974 $275

MAILLE, JEAN   Exposition des Proprietes du Spalme, Considere
Comme Courroi, Pour la Conservation des Batimens de Mer. Paris, 1763. 8vo.,
boards. Gurney 66-122 1974 £20

MAILLET, BENOIT DE   Telliamed ou Entretiens d'un Philosophe. Amsterdam, 1748. 8vo., 2 vols., contemporary calf, first edition. Gurney 64-143
1974 £35

MAILLOT, E.   Lecons sur le Ver a Sole du Murier. Paris and
Montpellier, 1885. 8vo., new cloth, plates. Wheldon 129-659 1974 £7.50

MAILLOT, E.   Lecons sur le Ver a Soie du Murier. Paris
& Montpellier, 1885. 8vo., new cloth, plates, scarce. Wheldon 131-829
1974 £7.50

MAILS, THOMAS E.   The Mystic Warriors of the Plains. New York,
1922. 4to., illus. Biblo & Tannen 210-178 1973 $20

MAIMONIDES
Please turn to
MOSES BEN MAIMOIN, 1135-1204

MAINWARING, THOMAS   A Defence of Amicia. London, 1673. Small
8vo., half calf. Quaritch 939-331 1974 £25

MAIRE, ALBERT   Pascal Pamphletaire, Les Lettres Provinciales.
Paris, 1925-26. 2 vols., 8vo., orig. printed wrappers, second edition. Dawsons
PM 10-472 1974 £26

MAIRE, ALBERT   Pascal Philosophie, les Pensees. Paris, 1926.
8vo., orig. wrappers, uncut. Dawsons PM 10-473 1974 £14

MAISTRE, JOSEPH DE   De l'Eglise Gallicane dans Son Rapport Avec
le Souverain Pontife. Lyons, 1821. 8vo., orig. wrapper, uncut, first edition.
L. Goldschmidt 42-293 1974 $30

MAISTRE, JOSEPH DE   Sur les Delais de la Justice Divine. Lyons,
Paris, 1856, 1857. 2 vols. in 1, 8vo., contemporary half sheep, gilt.
L. Goldschmidt 42-294 1974 $17.50

MAISTRE, XAVIER DE   Voyage Autour de ma Chambre. Boston & New
York, 1901. Parchment back, rubbed, foxing. Ballinger 1-31 1974 $15

MAITLAND, CHARLES   The Church in the Catacombs. London, 1847.
3/4 calf. Jacobs 24-158 1974 $15

MAITLAND, EDWARD   Clothed With the Sun. London, 1889.
Rittenhouse 46-431 1974 $15

MAITLAND, F. L.   Narrative of the Surrender of Buonaparte.
London, 1826. 2nd ed., 1/2 calf and marbled bds. Jacobs 24-163 1974 $15

MAITLAND, F. W.   Domesday Book and Beyond. 1907. Orig.
buckram, soiled, first edition. Howes 186-1046 1974 £7.50

MAITLAND, F. W.   Domesday Book and Beyond. Cambridge, 1921.
Med. 8vo., orig. cloth, fine. Broadhurst 24-1257 1974 £10

MAITLAND, F. W.   Roman Canon Law in the Church of England.
1898. Orig. buckram, first edition. Howes 185-1400 1974 £7.50

MAITLAND, JAMES A.   The Three Cousins. Philadelphia, 1860.
Orig. cloth, ends of spine little torn. MacManus 224-311 1974 $27.50

MAITLAND, S. R.   The Dark Ages. 1890. Worn, fifth & best
edition. Howes 186-1047 1974 £5

MAITLAND, W.   The History and Antiquities of Scotland. 1757.
2 vols., folio, contemporary calf, rebacked. Quaritch 939-664 1974 £20

MAITTAIRE, MICHAEL   Annales Typographici. The Hague, 1719-22.
Thick 4to., contemporary sprinkled calf gilt, raised bands. Thomas 28-118
1972 £40

MAJOR, CLARE TREE   Playing Theatre. Oxford, 1930. 269p., illus.
Austin 51-591 1973 $8.50

MAJOR, HOWARD   The Domestic Architecture of the Early American
Republic. Philadelphia and London, 1926. Cloth, dust wrapper, illus. Dawson's
424-234 1974 $50

MAJOR, JOSHUA   The Theory and Practice of Landscape Gardening.
1852. 4to., portrait, plates, orig. cloth, first edition. Bow Windows 64-174
1974 £58

MAJOR, R. H.   The Life of Prince Henry of Portugal. London,
1868. 8vo., portraits, maps. Traylen 79-490 1973 £7

MAJORS, ALEXANDER   Seventy Years on the Frontier. Chicago – New
York, 1893. 8vo., orig. bindings. Butterfield 8-709 1974 $25

MAKERS of Canada. Toronto, 1912. 11 vols., cloth, leather spine, gilt.
Hood's 104-901 1974 $110

MALACARNE, MICHELE VINCENZO GIACINTO   Encefalotomia nuova Universale. Turin, 1780. 12mo., contemporary half calf, first edition. Schumann 35-
301 1974 $325

MALAPERTIUS, CAROLUS   Evclidis Elementorvm Libri Sex Priores. 1620.
Small 8vo., contemporary vellum. Zeitlin 235-72 1974 $250

MALCOLM, ALEXANDER   A New System of Arithmetick. London, 1730. 4to., contemporary polished calf, first edition. Schumann 35-302 1974 $285

MALCOLM, ALEXANDER   A Treatise on Musick. Edinburgh, 1721. 8vo., plates, contemporary calf, fine. Quaritch 940-815 1974 £80

MALCOM, HOWARD   Theological Index. Boston, 1868. 8vo., cloth. Kraus B8-151 1974 $18

MALCOLM, JAMES PELLER   Anecdotes of the Manners and Customs of London. London, 1811. 4to., orig. boards rebacked, uncut, third edition. Dawsons PM 251-50 1974 £30

MALCOLM, M. VARTON   The Armenians in America. Pilgrim, 1919. 142p., illus. Austin 62-398 1974 $12.50

MALCOLM, W.   Gold Fields of Nova Scotia. Ottawa, 1912. Roy. 8vo., buckram, plates, illus. Wheldon 131-1044 1974 £5

MALCOLMSON, JOHN GRANT   Observations on Some Forms of Rheumatism Prevailing in India. Madras, 1835. 8vo., orig. wrappers. Schumann 35-404 1974 $65

MALCOUIN, P. G.   Chimie Medicinale, Contenant la Maniere de Preporer les Remedes les Plus Usites. Paris, 1755. 12mo., 2 vols., contemporary calf. Gurney 66-123 1974 £20

MALDCLEWITH, RONSBY   The Professor's Love-life. New York, 1919. Ltd. to 200 numbered copies. Biblo & Tannen 214-752 1974 $10

MALDONADO, JUAN   A Commentary on S. Matthew's Gospel. 1888. 2 vols., thick 8vo., faded, scarce. Howes 185-1402 1974 £5.75

MALE, ROY R.   Hawthorne's Tragic Vision. Univ. of Texas, 1957. 187p., hard cover ed. Austin 54-696 1973 $7.50

MALET, CAPTAIN   Annals of the Road. London, 1876. Orig. red cloth, gilt. Dawson's 424-113 1974 $85

MALEVINSKY, MOSES L.   The Science of Playwriting. Brentano, 1925. 356p. Austin 51-592 1973 $15

MALHERBE, FRANCOIS DE   Lettres. Paris, 1822. 2 vols., 8vo., gilt, contemporary half dark green polished calf. L. Goldschmidt 42-74 1974 $35

MALHERBE, FRANCOIS DE   Oeuvres. Paris, 1862. 4 vols., three quarter morocco, gilt, uncut. L. Goldschmidt 42-75 1974 $60

MALLARME, STEPHANE   Vers de Circonstance. Paris, 1920. One of 1030 numbered copies, wrappers, covers little split at joints, very good copy. Covent 51-1229 1973 $5.25

MALLES DE BEAULIEU, MME.   Le la Bruyere des Jeunes Demoiselles, ou Principaux Caracteres des Jeunes Personnes. Paris, 1830. 12mo., contemporary sheep, spine gilt, good fresh copy, with half title, engraves plates & frontis. George's 610-496 1973 £7.50

MALLESON, G. B.   History of the Indian Mutiny. 1878-80. 4 vols., thick 8vo., orig. cloth, faded. Howes 186-1739 1974 £30

MALLET, DAVID   Elvira. 1763. 8vo., cloth, first edition. Quaritch 936-141 1974 £8

MALLET, DAVID   Mustapha. 1739. 8vo., cloth, fine, first edition. Quaritch 936-142 1974 £8

MALLET, T.   Glimpses of the Barren Lands. New York, 1930. Illus. Hood's 103-72 1974 $20

MALLET, T.   Plain Tales of the North. New York, 1925. Sketches, illus. Hood's 103-73 1974 $25

MALLETT, W. E.   In Introduction to Old English Furniture. n.d. (c. 1920). Demy 4to., boards, cloth spine, binding fair, plates fine, illus. Broadhurst 24-141 1974 £5

MALLEUS Maleficarum. 1620. 2 vols. in 1, small 8vo., 19th century cloth backed boards, browning. Howes 186-1879 1974 £32

MALLEUS Maleficarum. 1928. Folio, orig. buckram, parchment back, frontispiece. Howes 186-1880 1974 £28

MALLEUS Maleficarum. (London), 1928. Small folio, orig. cloth, portrait. Dawsons PM 252-1072 1974 £42

MALLORY, DANIEL   Short Stories and Reminiscences of the Last Fifty Years. New York, 1842. 12mo., 2 vols. in 1, contemporary stamped calf, rubbed, first edition. MacManus 224-312 1974 $45

MALLORY, HENRY   Gems of Thought and Character Sketches. Hamilton, 1895. 8vo., cloth. Putnam 126-209 1974 $25

MALLOY, WILLIAM M.   Treaties, Conventions, International Acts, Protocols and Agreements. Washington, 1910. 2 vols., thick 8vo., cloth, ex-library. Howes 186-1051 1974 £15

MALMESTROM, E.   Ur Linnes Tankervarld och Religiosa Liv. Stockholm, 1932. 8vo., cloth. Wheldon 131-257 1974 £5

MALMIN, RASMUS   Who's Who Among Pastors in All the Norwegian Lutheran Synods of America. 1928. Illus., photographs, third edition. Austin 57-432 1974 $37.50

MALO, CHARLES   Les Papillons. Paris, (n.d., circa 1817). 12mo., 19th century polished calf, gilt, plates. Bow Windows 64-175 1974 £60.50

MALO, CHARLES   La Voliere des Dames. Paris, (1816). 16mo., contemporary calf, gilt, plates. Wheldon 131-76 1974 £70

MALORY, THOMAS   The Boy's King Arthur. New York, 1917. lst ed. Biblo & Tannen 210-170 1973 $12.50

MALORY, THOMAS   Le Morte Darthur. 1920. 2 vols., ex-library. Austin 61-639 1974 $17.50

MALORY, THOMAS   Le Morte d'Arthur. 1923. 2 vols., small crown 4to., plates, orig. dec. cloth. Smith 194-725 1974 £9.50

MALORY, THOMAS   Le Morte D'Arthur. London, 1925. 2 vols. Biblo & Tannen 214-635 1974 $15

MALORY, THOMAS   Le Morte Darthur. 1933. 4to., 2 vols., full red morocco, uncut, limited edition. Broadhurst 23-1085 1974 £95

MALORY, THOMAS   Le Morte Darthur. Shakespeare Head Press, 1933. Printed in red & black, 2 vols., 4to., full red morocco, top edges gilt, others uncut, limited to 370 copies, fine. Broadhurst 24-1043 1974 £95

MALORY, THOMAS   The Noble and Joyous Book Entytled le Morte Darthur. Chelsea, 1913. Folio, illus., orig. cowhide, fine. Dawsons PM 252-681 1974 £25

MALORY, THOMAS   The Noble and Joyous Book Entytled le Morte Darthur. Chelsea, (1913). Folio, illus., orig. brown hide, limited. Bow Windows 62-37 1974 £950

MALORY, THOMAS   The Noble and Joyous Boke Entytled Le Morte D'Arthur. Oxford, 1933. 4to., full morocco gilt, 2 vols., English first edition. Covent 56-1164 1974 £165

MALORY, THOMAS   The Romance of King Arthur and His Knights. 1917. Small 4to., illus., half crushed levant morocco, fine, first edition. Howes 185-391 1974 £32

MALOT, HECTOR   Sans Famille. Paris, c. 1880. Full page woodcuts, highly gilt dec. covers on red cloth, spine ends rubbed. Current BW9-253 1974 $18

MALOUIN, P. J.   Chimie Medicinale. Paris, 1755. 12mo., 2 vols., contemporary calf, second edition. Gurney 64-144 1974 £20

MALPIGHI, MARCELLO   Consultationes Medicae. Venice, 1747. 2 works in 1 vol., 8vo., contemporary vellum. Schuman 37-163 1974 $165

MALPIGHI, MARCELLO   Consultationum Medicinalium. Padua, 1713. 4to., contemporary calf, first edition. Schumann 35-303 1974 $325

MALPIGHI, MARCELLO   Opera Omnia. 1686. Folio, contemporary vellum, plates, first edition. Dawsons PM 249-361 1974 £400

MALRAUX, ANDRE   Days of Wrath. New York, 1936. Small 8vo., cloth, shaken. Minters 37-104 1973 $10

MALTBY, ISAAC   The Elements of War. Boston, 1813. 8vo., orig. bindings, plates, second edition. Butterfield 8-255 1974 $17.50

MALTE-BRUN, M.   Universal Geography. Edinburgh & London, 1822-33. 9 vols., contemporary polished calf gilt, leather labels, diagrams. Smith 194-628 1974 £25

MALTHUS, THOMAS ROBERT   An Essay on the Principle of Population. 1806. 8vo., full contemporary calf, third edition. Broadhurst 23-1247 1974 £45

MALTHUS, THOMAS ROBERT   An Essay on the Principle of Population. 1826. 2 vols., demy 8vo., contemporary half light brown calf, marbled boards, exceptionally fine copy. Broadhurst 24-1260 1974 £40

MALTHUS, THOMAS ROBERT   A Letter to Samuel Whitbread. London, 1807. 8vo., wrappers, second edition. Dawsons PM 247-194 1974 £30

MALTHUS, THOMAS ROBERT   Principles of Political Economy. 1836. Orig. cloth, paper label, second edition. Smith 193-595 1973 £20

MALTHUS, THOMAS ROBERT   Principles of Political Economy. London, 1836. 8vo., orig. maroon cloth, second edition. Dawsons PM 247-195 1974 £70

MALTHUS, THOMAS ROBERT   Principles of Political Economy Considered With a View to Their Practical Application. London, 1820. 8vo., contemporary calf, John Mitford's copy with his signature, first edition. Ximenes 37-137 1974 $250

MALVEZZI, VIRGILO   Discourses upon Cornelius Tacitus. London, 1642. Folio, modern half calf, first edition in English. Dawsons PM 251-280 1974 £75

MALVEZZI, VIRGILIO   Romvlvs and Tarqvin. London, 1637. 12mo., modern vellum, morroco label, first English edition. Dawsons PM 252-683 1974 £75

MAMMATT, EDWARD   A Collection of Geological Facts and Practical Observations. London, 1834. Thick 4to., orig. cloth boards, uncut, plates. Traylen 79-88 1973 £60

MAN, J.   The History and Antiquities . . . . of Reading. Reading, 1816. 4to., buckram, plates. Quaritch 939-302 1974 £25

MAN, J.   The History and Antiquities Ancient & Modern of the Borough of Reading In the County of Berks. Reading, 1816. 4to., plates, half contemporary leather, illus., first edition. Smith 194-248 1974 £15

MAN Into Beast, Strange Tales of Transformation. New York, 1947. 1st ed. Biblo & Tannen 210-671 1973 $12.50

MANCHEE, T. J.   The Bristol Charities. Bristol, 1831. 2 vols., 4to., plate, cloth backs, orig. boards. Quaritch 939-843 1974 £50

THE MANCHESTER Songster. Manchester, 1792. 8vo., full morocco, uncut, scarce. Broadhurst 23-1468 1974 £20

MANCINI - NIVERNOIS   Fables. Paris, 1796. 2 vols., 8vo., half leather. Schumann 499-66 1974 sFr 150

MANCO-CAPAC PSEUD.
Please turn to
MAURY, MATTHEW FONTAINE

MANDEVILLE, JOHN   The Buke. 1889. Folio, contemporary half dark red morocco, uncut, worn, fine. Dawsons PM 251-281 1974 £250

MANDEVILLE, JOHN   The Travels of. London, 1905. 8vo., browned, orig. cloth. Bow Windows 62-600 1974 £6

MANDEVILLE, JOHN   The Travels of. London, 1923. Full blue calf, gilt, illus. Bradley 35-420 1974 $25

MANDEVILE, JOHN   The Voyages & Travels. 1684. Small 4to., 19th century blind stamped calf, rebacked, rare. Thomas 28-195 1972 £75

MANDEVILLE, JOHN   Voiage & Travayle of Sir John Maundeville. 1887. Half vellum, illus., limited edition. Allen 213-1633 1973 $10

MANDINI, DOMENICO ANTONIO   La Vecchiezza. Bologna, 1800. 8vo., vellum, first edition. Schumann 35-304 1974 $145

MANDL, L.   Traite Pratique du Microscope. Paris, 1839. 8vo., modern boards, rare. Wheldon 130-878 1974 £25

MANDRUZZATO, SALVADORE   Notizie sulle Fonti Marziali di Sacile. 1827. 8vo., plain beige wrappers, fine, unopened, uncut. Zeitlin 235-290 1974 $45

MANELPHUS, JOHANNES   Tractus de Fletu et Lacrymis. Rome, 1618. 16mo., full contemp. calf, gilt and panelled spine. Jacobs 24-156 1974 $55

MANELPHUS, JOHANNES   Tractatus de Fletu, and Lacrymis. Rome, 1618. Small 8vo., disbound, clean and sound. Thomas 32-330 1974 £40

MANET, EDOUARD   Histoire de Edouard Manet et de son Oeuvre. Paris, 1906. 8vo., illus., half morocco, rubbed. Quaritch 940-174 1974 £7

MANEY, RICHARD   Fanfare. Harper, 1957. 374p., illus. Austin 51-593 1973 $7.50

MANGAN, JAMES CLARENCE   Selected Poems. Boston, 1897. First U. S. edition, fine copy. Covent 51-1232 1973 £5.25

MANGANO, ANTONIO   Sons of Italy. 1917. 234 pages, illus. Austin 57-433 1974 $17.50

MANGANO, ANTONIO   Sons of Italy. 1917. 234p. Austin 62-400 1974 $17.50

MANGET, JEAN JACQUES   Bibliotheca Pharmaceutico-Medica. (Geneva), 1730. Folio, 2 vols., contemporary calf, plates. Schumann 35-305 1974 $265

MANGIN, L.   Sur la Flore Planctonique de la Rade de Saint-Vaast-la-Haigue 1908-12. Paris, 1913. Wheldon 131-1443 1974 £5

MANGIN, L.   Travaux Cryptogamiques Dedies a Louis Mangin. Paris, 1931. 4to., wrappers, plates. Wheldon 128-1398 1973 £7.50

MANGIN, M. L.   Phytoplancton de la Croisiere. Paris, 1912. 4to., plates, tables. Wheldon 130-262 1974 £5

MANIFOLD-CRAIG, R.   The Weird of "The Silken Thomas". Aberdeen, 1900. 8vo., cloth boards, scarce. Emerald 50-582 1974 £5

MANILIUS, MARCUS   Astronomicon ad Caesarem Agustum Noviter ac Diligentissime Ememdatum. Rome, 1510. Small 4to., old vellum, clean and sound. Thomas 32-320 1974 £60

MANILIUS, MARCUS   Astronomicon ad Casarem Augustum. Lyons, 1566. 16mo., 19th century half leather. Schuman 37-164 1974 $115

MANILIUS, MARCUS   The Five Books of. 1700. Frontispiece, engraved diagrams, modern sheep. Thomas 32-321 1974 £45

MANKATO· Its First Fifty Years. Mankato, 1903. 8vo., cloth, 345 pages. Saddleback 14-519 1974 $25

MANLEY, MARY DE LA RIVIERE   Lucius. London, 1717. 4to., modern calf gilt, morocco labels, fine, first edition. Dawsons PM 252-684 1974 £160

MANLEY, MARY DE LA RIVIERE   A Modest Enquiry into the Reasons of the Joy Expressed by a Certain Sett of People. 1714. Small 8vo., cloth, uncut, fine, first edition, second issue. Quaritch 936-144 1974 £45

MANLEY, MARY DE LA RIVIERE   A Modest Enquiry into the Reasons of the Joy Expressed by a Certain Sett of People. 1714. 8vo., cloth, uncut, first edition, first issue. Quaritch 936-143 1974 £60

MANLEY, MARY DE LA RIVIERE   Secret Memoirs and Manners of Several Persons of Quality, of both Sexes. 1709. 8vo., 2 vols., contemporary panelled calf, gilt, first edition. Quaritch 936-145 1974 £50

MANLEY, MARY DE LA RIVIERE   A Stage Coach Journey to Exeter.   London, 1725.   8vo., modern boards, second edition.   Dawsons PM 252-685 1974 £50

MANLY, WILLIAM LEWIS   Death Valley in '49.   1927.   Dec. cloth, gilt top, frontis., map, fine copy.   Dykes 22-137 1973 $10

MANLY, WILLIAM LEWIS   Death Valley in '49.   Chicago, 1927.   Map, frontis., inscribed & signed by M. M. Quaife.   Hood's 102-827 1974 $22.50

MANLY, WILLIAM LEWIS   Death Valley in '49.   New York, 1929.   Illus.   Jacobs 24-21 1974 $18

MANN, ALBERT W.   History of the Forty-Fifth Regiment Massachusetts Volunteer Militia, "The Cadet Regiment".   (Boston, 1908).   Orig. binding.   Butterfield 10-168 1974 $17.50

MANN, CHARLES E.   The Story of Dogtown.   Gloucester, 1896.   Illus., scarce.   Ballinger 1-290 1974 $13

MANN, HORACE K.   The Lives of the Popes In the Early Middle Ages.   1902-10.   8 vols. in 9, library stamp.   Howes 185-1403 1974 £30

MANN, KLAUS   Andre Gide.   New York, 1943.   Biblo & Tannen 210-861 1973 $8.50

MANN, S. S.   The Settlement and Early Settlers of Coos Bay.   Marshfield, 1879.   8vo., wrapper, boards.   Saddleback 14-653 1974 $125

MANN, THOMAS   An Exchange of Letters.   New York, 1937.   Portrait, wrappers, fine, first American edition.   Covent 55-1067 1974 £6

MANN, THOMAS   The Magic Mountain.   1927.   2 vols., spines slightly faded, fine, slightly soiled & frayed d.w., first edition.   Covent 51-1236 1973 £8.40

MANN, THOMAS   Nocturnes.   New York, 1934.   Autographed, limited, first edition.   Jenkins 48-311 1973 $35

MANN, THOMAS   Nocturnes.   New York, 1934.   Orig. cloth, lithographs, label on spine, first edition in English, one of 1000 copies, signed by author.   MacManus 224-313 1974 $40

MANN, THOMAS   A Sketch of My Life.   Paris, 1930.   8vo., orig. cloth, first edition in English.   Rota 189-591 1974 £7.50

MANNERING, GUY   Rosalvo Delmonmort.   Boston, 1818.   12mo., contemporary quarter calf rather worn, first edition, uncut copy.   Ximenes 36-90 1974 $175

MANNERS, JOHN   Some Account of the Military, Political and Social Life of.   1899.   Frontispiece, illus.   Howes 186-1052 1974 £6

MANNERS, JOHN HENRY   Journal of a Trip to Paris.   1814.   4to., full contemporary calf, rebacked.   Broadhurst 23-1677 1974 £30

MANNERS, JOHN HENRY   A Tour Through Part of Belgium and the Rhenish Provinces.   London, 1822.   4to., contemporary half morocco.   Traylen 79-560 1973 £25

MANNING, ANNE   The Colloquies of Edward Osborne.   1860.   Small 8vo., contemporary calf, gilt, third edition.   Hill 126-196 1974 £7.50

MANNING, HUGO   Buenos Aires.   Buenos Aires, 1942.   Small stain on upper cover, very good copy, wrappers, only 200 copies of this first edition printed, signed holograph note by author in text.   Covent 51-1237 1973 £10

MANNING, JAMES   A New Booke, Intituled, I am for You all, Complexions Castle.   Cambridge, 1604.   Small 4to., light brown half leather boxcase, orig. edition.   Kraus 137-62 1974 $1,600

MANNING, OWEN   The History and Antiquities of the County of Surrey.   London, 1804.   Folio, 3 vols., contemporary beige morocco, first edition.   Dawsons PM 251-51 1974 £420

MANNING, OWEN   The History and Antiquities of the County of Surrey.   London, 1804-14.   3 vols., large folio, contemporary half calf, plates.   Traylen 79-390 1973 £95

MANNINGHAM, RICHARD   Artis Obstetricariae Compendium.   Halle, 1746.   4to., boards, first edition published in Germany.   Schuman 37-165 1974 $175

MANNIX, EDWARD J.   The American Convert Movement.   1923.   Austin 62-401 1974 $10

MANNIX, MARY   The Fortunes of a Little Emigrant.   Notre Dame, n.d. 266 pages.   Austin 57-435 1974 $10

MANNIX, MARY   The Fortunes of a Little Emigrant.   Notre Dame, Ind., ca. 1925.   Austin 62-402 1974 $10

MANSEL-PLEYDELL, J. C.   The Birds of Dorsetshire.   n.d. (1887).   Demy 8vo., uncut, unopened, orig. cloth, fine, presentation copy inscribed by author.   Broadhurst 24-1133 1974 £6

MANSEL-PLEYDELL, J. C.   Flora of Dorsetshire.   Dorchester, 1895.   8vo., cloth, maps, scarce, second edition.   Wheldon 128-1203 1973 £7.50

MANSEL-PLEYDELL, J. C.   Flora of Dorsetshire.   Dorchester, 1895.   8vo., cloth, maps, scarce, second edition.   Wheldon 131-1235 1974 £7.50

MANSFIELD, EDWARD D.   The Mexican War.   New York, 1849.   Charts.   Jenkins 61-1599 1974 $15

MANSFIELD, EDWARD D.   Popular and Authentic Lives of Ulysses S. Grant and Schuyler Colfax.   Cincinnati, 1868.   Orig. binding, frontispiece portrait, maps, dull, edge wear, lacks front free bland endpaper.   Wilson 63-186 1974 $10

MANSFIELD, KATHERINE   The Dove's Nest.   London, 1923.   1st ed., 2nd binding.   Jacobs 24-108 1974 $25

MANSFIELD, KATHERINE   The Garden Party.   London, 1922.   1st ed., 2nd binding, orig. cl., ochre lettering.   Jacobs 24-109 1974 $35

MANSFIELD, KATHERINE   The Garden Party and Other Stories.   London, 1922.   First edition, with "sposition" for "position", orange lettering on cover, owner's name in ink on free fly, lacking d.w., heavy dec. paper wrappers, near fine, scarce.   Ross 87-377 1974 $40

MANSFIELD, KATHERINE   The Garden Party and Other Stories.   London, 1922.   8vo., orig. cloth, uncut, first edition.   Dawsons PM 252-686 1974 £20

MANSFIELD, KATHERINE   The Garden Party and Other Stories.   1939.   Roy 8vo., orig. cloth, uncut.   Broadhurst 23-796 1974 £65

MANSFIELD, KATHERINE   Letters.   1928.   2 vols., first edition.   Allen 216-1081 1974 $10

MANSFIELD, KATHERINE   Letters.   (1929).   518 pages.   Austin 61-641 1974 $12.50

MANSFIELD, KATHERINE   The Little Girl and Other Stories.   New York, 1924.   Orig. binding, lacking d.w., spine & label slightly rubbed, else fine.   Ross 87-378 1974 $10

MANSFIELD, KATHERINE   Poems.   London, 1923.   First English edition, spine faded, label missing, d.w. severed & laid in 2 parts, good working copy of scarce title.   Ross 87-379 1974 $25

MANSFIELD, KATHERINE   Prelude.   Richmond, (1918).   Orig. cloth, worn, rare, first edition.   Rota 188-598 1974 £65

MANSFIELD, KATHERINE   Something Childish.   1924.   Crown 8vo., first edition.   Howes 185-314 1974 £7.50

MANSFIELD, T. C.   Alpines in Colour and Cultivation.   (1942).   8vo., cloth, plates.   Wheldon 130-1435 1974 £5

MANSFORD, JOHN G.   Researches into the Nature and Causes of Epilepsy.   Bath, 1819.   8vo., orig. boards, first edition.   Schumann 35-306 1974 $95

MANSHIP, H.   The History of Great Yarmouth.   1854-56.   2 vols., 4to., cloth.   Quaritch 939-498 1974 £20

MANSON, J. B.   The Life and Work of Edgar Degas. 1927.
Boards, vellum spine, plates. Eaton Music–570 1973 £8

MANT, RICHARD   An Essay on Commerce. (N.P., 1799). 4to.,
disbound. Dawsons PM 247-196 1974 £30

MANTELL, GIDEON ALGERNON   The Fossils of the South Downs. 1822. 4to.,
contemporary half calf, neatly rebacked, coloured map, plates (some coloured),
scarce. Wheldon 128-1018 1973 £50

MANTELL, GIDEON ALGERNON   The Fossils of the South Downs. 1822. 4to.,
contemporary half calf, rebacked, plates, scarce. Wheldon 130-952 1974 £50

MANTELL, GIDEON ALGERNON   The Fossils of the South Downs. 1822. 4to.,
contemporary half calf, plates. Wheldon 131-1045 1974 £50

MANTELL, GIDEON ALGERNON   The Fossils of the South Downs. 1822-29.
3 vols. in 1, 4to., plates, half calf, rebound. Quaritch 939-566 1974 £70

MANTELL, GIDEON ALGERNON   Geological Excursions Round the Isle of
Wight. London, 1847. 8vo., orig. cloth, gilt, illus., plates, first edition.
Hammond 201-379 1974 £30

MANTELL, GIDEON ALGERNON   The Geology of the South-East of England.
London, 1833. 8vo., orig. boards, fine, illus., plates, first edition. Hammond
201-378 1974 £25

MANTELL, GIDEON ALGERNON   The Invisible World Revealed by the
Microscope. 1850. 8vo., orig. cloth, plates, new edition. Bow Windows 64-
176 1974 £6.75

MANTELL, GIDEON ALGERNON   Petrifactions and Their Teachings. 1851.
Crown 8vo., orig. cloth, plates. Wheldon 131-1046 1974 £10

MANTELL, GIDEON ALGERNON   Pictorial Atlas of Fossil Remains. 1850.
4to., orig. cloth, coloured frontis., plain plates, scarce. Wheldon 128-1019
1973 £25

MANTELL, GIDEON ALGERNON   Pictorial Atlas of Fossil Remains. 1850.
4to., orig. cloth, plates, scarce. Wheldon 130-953 1974 £25

MANTELL, GIDEON ALGERNON   A Pictorial Atlas of Fossil Remains. 1850.
Demy 4to., full contemporary calf, panelled back, tooled gilt, all edges gilt,
slight weakness top of front hinge, else fine, coloured plates. Broadhurst 24-1134
1974 £75

MANTELL, GIDEON ALGERNON   Thoughts on Animalcules. London, 1846.
8vo., orig. cloth, plates, foded, first edition. Bow Windows 62-602 1974 £15

MANTELL, GIDEON ALGERNON   The Wonders of Geology. 1840. 8vo.,
2 vols., orig. cloth, fourth edition. Bow Windows 64-177 1974 £14

MANTLE, BURNS   Contemporary American Playwrights. Dodd,
1938. 357p. Austin 51-594 1973 $10

A MANUAL of Lithography. London, 1820. 8vo., grey boards, frontispiece,
uncut, plates, first English edition. Dawsons PM 10-508 1974 £90

MANUEL, M.   The Authentic History of Captain Castagnette.
n.d. 4to., orig. cloth, illus., rare. Covent 55-883 1974 £65

MANUEL, M.   Authentic History of Captain Castagnette,
Nephew of the 'Man with the Wooden Head'. (c. 1865). Engravings, 4to., orig.
pictorial boards, rubbed, stitching weak. George's 610-498 1973 £5

MANUFACTURING and Business Opportunities in Western Canada Along the Lines
of the Canadian Pacific Railway. 1911. Second edition, card cover. Hood's
102-819 1974 $15

MANUTIUS, ALDUS   Le Attioni di Castruccio Castracane. Rome,
1590. Small 4to., old vellum, morocco label. Thomas 30-130 1973 £35

MANUTIUS, ALDUS   Eleganze. 1563. Vellum backed boards.
Thomas 30-117 1973 £18

MANUTIUS, ALDUS   Grammaticae Institutiones Graecae. 1515.
Small 4to., old vellum, very rare. Thomas 30-32 1973 £30

MANUTIUS, ALDUS   Orthographiae Ratio. 1591. Contemporary
vellum. Thomas 30-125 1973 £21

MANUTIUS PAULUS   Antiquitatum Romanarum. Paris, 1557. 18th
century sheep, rubbed. Thomas 30-128 1973 £30

MANUTIUS, PAULUS   Antiquitatum Romanarum. 1557. Tall 4to.,
18th century mottled calf, rubbed. Thomas 30-109 1973 £30

MANUTIUS, PAULUS   Antiquitatum Romanarum. 1559. Vellum,
browned. Thomas 30-112 1973 £30

MANUTIUS, PAULUS   Epistolarum Libri X. Lausannae, 1574. Vellum.
Thomas 30-129 1973 £35

MANUTIUS, PAULUS   Tre Libri di Lettere Volgari. 1556. Old
vellum gilt, morocco labels, first edition in Italian. Thomas 30-106 1973 £30

MANY a Little Makes a Nickle. Boston, 1860. 8vo., orig. blue cloth, plates.
Ximenes 33-423A 1974 $12.50

MANZINI, D. LUIGI   Applausi Festivi Fatti in Roma per l'Elezzione
di Ferdinando III al Regno de Romani. Rome, 1637. Small 4to., calf, generally
worn and soiled, engraved folding plates. Thomas 32-342 1974 £12

MAPLESON, THOMAS   A Treatise on the Art of Cupping. London, 1813.
12mo., contemporary calf-backed boards. Schumann 35-307 1974 $95

MAPS and Descriptions of Routes of Exploration in Alaska in 1898. Washington,
1899. Wrapper. Jenkins 61-87 1974 $15

MARAIS, PAUL   Catalogue des Incunables de la Bibliotheque
Mazarine. Paris, 1893. Wrappers. Kraus B8-153 1974 $45

MARAIS, PAUL   Catalogue des Incunables de la Bibliotheque
Mazarine. Paris, 1893-98. 2 vols., orig. printed wrappers, uncut, scarce.
Dawsons PM 10-298 1974 £34

MARANA, G. P.   The Eight Volumes of Letters Writ by a Turkish
Spy. Dublin, 1736. Small 8vo., 8 vols., contemporary calf, gilt, frontispiece.
Quaritch 936-146 1974 £25

MARANON, GREGORIO   Tiberio. Buenos Aires, 1939. Biblo & Tannen
213-467 1973 $9.50

MARBOT, ANTOINE A. MARCELLIN   Memoires. Paris, c.1895. 3 vols.,
half crimson morocco, gilt. Howes 186-1740 1974 £12

MARBURY, ELIZABETH   My Crystal Ball. Boni, Liveright, 1923.
355p., illus. Austin 51-596 1973 $10

MARC, FRANZ   Briefe aus Dem Feld. Berlin, 1941. 8vo.,
boards, cloth spine, plates. Minters 37-468 1973 $16

MARCANTONIO, VITO   I Vote My Conscience. 1956. Austin 62-403
1974 $10

MARCET, JANE   Conversations on Chemistry. London, 1825.
12mo., 2 vols., contemporary calf. Zeitlin 235-291 1974 $45

MARCH, FRANCIS A.   An Anglo-Saxon Reader. 1878. 166 pages.
Austin 61-643 1974 $17.50

MARCH, FRANCIS A.   A Comparative Grammar of the Anglo-Saxon
Language. 1880. 253 pages. Austin 61-642 1974 $27.50

MARCH, T. C.   Flower and Fruit Decoration. 1862. 8vo.,
orig. picture boards, scarce. Wheldon 131-1545 1974 £5

MARCH, WILLIAM   Come In At the Door. Smith, Haas, 1934.
349p. Austin 54-698 1973 $10

MARCH, WILLIAM   Company K. Smith, Haas, 1933. 260p.,
orig. hard cover ed. Austin 54-697 1973 $8.50

MARCH, WILLIAM   The Looking Glass. Little, Brown, 1943. 346p.
Austin 54-699 1973 $10

MARCH, WILLIAM   October Island. Little, Brown, 1952. 246p.
Austin 54-700 1973 $10

MARCH, WILLIAM   Trial Balance. Harcourt, Brace, 1945. 506p.
Austin 54-701 1973 $12.50

MARCHAND, JEAN HENRI   Les Vues Simples d'un Bon-Homme. Paris,
1776. 8vo., modern boards, morocco label. L. Goldschmidt 42-76 1974 $25

MARCHAND, L.   Enumeration Methodique et Raisonnee. Paris,
1896. Roy 8vo., buckram. Wheldon 129-1274 1974 £7.50

MARCHAND, L.   Recherches Organographiques et Organogeniques sur le Coffea Arabica. Paris, 1864. 8vo., plates, scarce. Wheldon 130-
1593 1974 £5

MARCHESINUS, JOHANNES   Mammotrectus Super Bibliam. Mainz, 1470.
Folio, modern calf, rare. Thomas 28-339 1972 £1000

MARCHIAFAVA, E.   On Summer-Autumn Malarial Fevers. 1894.
Large 8vo., orig. cloth, plates. Dawsons PM 249-364 1974 £6

MARCHMONT, A. W.   The Old Mill Mystery. New York, (1892).
Orig. wrappers, English first edition. Covent 56-1716 1974 £5

MARCO POLO
Please turn to
POLO, MARCO, 1254-1323

MARCOSSON, ISAAC F.   Charles Frohman. 1916. 439p., illus.
Austin 51-597 1973 $12.50

MARCUS, JACOB RADER   The Rise and Destiny of the German Jew.
1934. 365p., orig. ed. Austin 62-406 1974 $10

MARCUS Aurelius Year Book. London, 1906. Orig. grey cloth, 2 3/4 X 2.
Gregory 44-429 1974 $15

MARCUS Ward's Japanese Picture Stories. London & Belfast, n.d. (c. 1870).
4to., full color illus., leaves are accordian-fold and loose in pictorial cloth
covers, scarce. Frohnsdorff 15-98 1974 $20

MARCY, RANDOLPH B.   Exploration of the Red River of Louisiana in the
Year 1852. Washington, 1854. Plates, large folding maps in separate folder,
foxed. Jenkins 61-1442 1974 $25

MARE, MARGARET   The World of Charlotte Yonge. London, 1947.
Inner hinges split. Biblo & Tannen 210-942 1973 $7.50

MARECHAL, SYLVAIN   Histoire Universelle en Style Lapidaire.
Paris, 1800. Large 8vo., contemporary tree sheep, gilt, first edition.
L. Goldschmidt 42-77 1974 $25

MAREY, ETIENNE-JULES   Animal Mechanism. 1874. Crown 8vo., cloth,
second edition. Wheldon 131-444 1974 £5

MAREY, ETIENNE-JULES   Le Mouvement. Paris, 1894. 8vo., half morocco, plates, illus., first edition. Schumann 35-309 1974 $110

MAREY, ETIENNE-JULES   Le Vol des Oiseaux. Paris, 1890. 8vo., first
edition, quarter morocco. Gurney 64-145 1974 £35

MAREY, J.   La Chronophotographie. Paris, 1899. 8vo.,
wrappers, very rare, illus. Gurney 66-124 1974 £45

MARGUERITTE, PAUL   Ma Grande. Paris, 1893. Illus., spine ends
worn, else very good, 8vo. Current BW9-254 1974 $27.50

MARIANA, JUAN   The General History of Spain. London, 1699.
Folio, calf, first English edition. Export 714-214 1973 £14

MARIANO, JOHN HORACE   The Italian Contribution to American
Democracy. 1921. 317 pages. Austin 57-440 1974 $15

MARIANUS, SCOTUS   Chronica . . . Adiecimus Martini Poloni . . .
Eiusdem Argumenti Historiam. 1559. 2 parts in 1 vol., first edition, folio, late
17th century sprinkled calf, rebacked and recornered, rare, Astle Library stamp
and 2 pages of MS. notes. Thomas 32-123 1974 £300

MARIE, GRAND DUCHESS OF RUSSIA   Education of a Princess. New York,
1932. Sgd. Biblo & Tannen 213-689 1973 $12.50

MARIE-VICTORIN, FRERE   Flore Laurentienne. Montreal, 1935. 4to.,
cloth, map. Wheldon 129-1105 1974 £12

MARIE-VICTORIN, FRERE   Flore Laurentienne. Montreal, 1935. Demy
4to., cloth. Wheldon 131-1328 1974 £12

MARIN, MICHEL-ANGE   Vies des Peres de Deserts d'Orient. Lyons &
Paris, 1824. 9 vols., thick 8vo., half roan, worn. Howes 185-1412 1974
£15

THE MARINE Room of the Peabody Museum of Salem. Salem, 1921. First edition.
Jenkins 61-1514 1974 $10

MARINETTI, F. T.   Notari Scrittore Nuovo. Milan & Villasanta,
n.d. 16mo., wrappers, illus. Minters 37-405 1973 $25

MARIS, M.   Relations d'un Voyage au Texas et en Haiti.
Bruxelles, 1863. Orig. yellow printed wrappers, fine, exceptionally rare.
Jenkins 61-1444 1974 $350

THE MARITIME Provinces: A Handbook for Travellers. Boston, 1887. Maps,
fifth edition. Hood's 104-40 1974 $50

MARIVAUX, PIERRE CARLET DE CHAMBLAIN DE   La Vie de Marianne. Paris,
1734-36. 6 tomes in 1 vol., small 8vo., full crimson jansenist morocco, gilt,
first edition. L. Goldschmidt 42-78 1974 $150

MARJORAM, J., PSEUD.
Please turn to
MOTTRAM, RALPH HALE

MARJORIBANKS, EDWARD   The Life of Lord Carson. London, 1932-34.
2 vols., 8vo., cloth boards. Emerald 50-584 1974 £5

MARK, E. L.   Maturation, Fecundation and Segmentation of
Limax Campestris. 1881. 8vo., boards, plates. Wheldon 128-846 1973 £7.50

MARKEY, GENE   Literary Lights. New York, 1923. 1st ed.
Biblo & Tannen 210-69 1973 $7.50

MARKHAM, A. H.   The Life of C. R. Markham. 1917. 8vo.,
cloth, plates, portraits. Wheldon 129-175 1974 £5

MARKHAM, EDWIN   The Man With the Hoe. New York, 1899.
Orig. cloth, second edition, first state, presentation copy from author, signed,
bit rubbed. MacManus 224-314 1974 $35

MARKHAM, F.   The Booke of Honour. London, 1625. Folio,
mottled calf gilt. Quaritch 939-738 1974 £70

MARKHAM, GERVASE   Hungers Prevention. London, 1621. 8vo.,
contemporary sheep, first edition. Dawsons PM 247-197 1974 £450

MARKHAM, GERVASE   Hungers Prevention. London, 1655. Small
8vo., antique style sheep, second edition. Quaritch 939-171 1974 £220

MARKHAM, GERVASE   The Young Sportsmen's Instructor. 1820.
Limited edition printed on vellum, engraved frontispiece, size 2 1/2 by 1 7/10
inches, contemporary brown calf gilt, binding rubbed at joints and corners, good
copy, rare. Sawyer 293-224 1974 £525

MARKHAM, V. R.   Paxton and The Bachelor Duke. 1935. 8vo.,
cloth, plates, scarce. Wheldon 129-176 1974 £7.50

MARKLE, GLADYS JONES   The Presbyterian Congregation at Hazleton.
Hazleton, 1938. 8vo., orig. bindings, illus., signed, limited edition. Butterfield 8-493 1974 $20

MARKS, MORRIS   The Rise and Fall of Rogoff. 1928. 320p.
Austin 62-409 1974 $7.50

MARKS, PERCY L.   The Principles of Architectural Design. 1907.
Illus. Covent 55-67 1974 £8.50

MARLOR, JOSEPH   Coal Mining. London, 1854. 8vo., orig. cloth, gilt, plates, first edition. Hammond 201-809 1974 £11

MARLOWE, CHRISTOPHER   The Tragical History of Doctor Faustus. 1903. Orig. blind stamped green cloth, uncut. Howes 186-13 1974 £12.50

MARLOWE, CHRISTOPHER   The Works Of. 1885. 3 vols., contemporary green calf gilt, limited edition. Smith 194-224 1974 £5

MARLOWE, GEORGE FRANCIS   Coaching Roads of Old New England. New York, 1945. Biblo & Tannen 213-69 1973 $6

MARMADUKE Multiply's Merry Method of Making Minor Mathematicians. (1818). Lacks the title, damp stained throughout, 12mo., orig. boards, roan spine, soiled and rubbed, copperplate illus. George's 610-500 1973 £25

MARMER, H. A.   The Tide. New York, 1926. 8vo., cloth, illus. Wheldon 131-316 1974 £7.50

MARMONTEL, JEAN FRANCOIS   Belisaire. Amsterdam, 1767. 8vo., uncut copy, contemporary half calf, two corners torn off without loss of text. Schumann 499-68 1974 sFr 90

MARMONTEL, JEAN FRANCOIS   Oeuvres. Paris, 1819. 12 parts in 6 vols., 8vo., contemporary marbled tan calf, gilt, fine. L. Goldschmidt 42-79 1974 $75

MARNOCK, R.   The Plantation, Leighton Buzzard. 1872. Small 8vo., calf, rare. Wheldon 131-1747 1974 £5

MAROLOIS, SAMUEL   Opera Mathematica. 1638. Small folio, contemporary mottled calf, gilt, plates. Zeitlin 235-146 1974 $950

MAROUZEAU, J.   Dix Annees de Bibliographie Classique, 1914-1924. 2 vols. Bound; bdgs. stained, text very good cond. Biblo & Tannen 214-636 1974 $27.50

MARPLES, G.   Sea Terns. 1934. Small 4to., cloth, plates. Wheldon 129-499 1974 £7.50

MARPLES, G.   Sea Terns. 1934. Small 4to., cloth, plates. Wheldon 131-653 1974 £10

MARQUAND, ALLAN   Benedetto & Santi Buglioni. 1921. 4to., illus. Allen 213-1313 1973 $15

MARQUAND, ALLAN   Brothers of Giovanni Della Robbia, Fra Mattia, Luca, Girolamo, Fra Ambrogio. 1928. New buckram. Allen 213-1743 1973 $17.50

MARQUAND, ALLAN   Della Robbias In America. 1912. 4to., plates. Allen 213-1744 1973 $12.50

MARQUAND, JOHN P.   B. F.'s Daughter. Little, Brown, 1946. 439p. Austin 54-702 1973 $5

MARQUAND, JOHN P.   H. M. Pulham Esquire. Little, Brown, 1941. 431p. Austin 54-703 1973 $6.50

MARQUAND, JOHN P.   H. M. Pulham, Esquire. Boston, 1941. 1st ed. Biblo & Tannen 214-753 1974 $7.50

MARQUAND, JOHN P.   H. M. Pulham, Esquire. Boston, (1941). 8vo., cloth, dust jacket, first edition. Goodspeed's 578-225 1974 $10

MARQUAND, JOHN P.   The Late George Apley. Little, Brown, 1937. 354p. Austin 54-704 1973 $6

MARQUAND, JOHN P.   Melville Goodwin U.S.A. Little, Brown, 1951. 596p. Austin 54-705 1973 $6.50

MARQUAND, JOHN P.   Sincerely, Willis Wayde. Little, Brown, 1955. 416p. Austin 54-706 1973 $5

MARQUAND, JOHN P.   So Little Time. Little, Brown, 1943. 594p. Austin 54-707 1973 $6.50

MARQUAND, JOHN P.   Stopover: Tokyo. Little, Brown, 1957. 313p. Austin 54-708 1973 $6.50

MARQUAND, JOHN P.   Thirty Years. Little, Brown, 1954. 466p. Austin 54-709 1973 $6

MARQUAND, JOHN P.   Wickford Point. Sun Dial, 1940. 458p. Austin 54-710 1973 $6

MARQUAND, JOHN P.   Women and Thomas Harrow. Little, Brown, 1958. 403p. Austin 54-711 1973 $5

MARQUIS, DON   Archy's Life of Mehitabel. 1933. 182p., hard cover ed. Austin 54-712 1973 $6.50

MARQUIS, DON   The Awakening & Other Poems. 1924. Cloth backed boards, very good copy, spare title label tipped in, first edition. Covent 51-1248 1973 £5.25

MARQUIS, DON   The Awakening and Other Poems. Doubleday, Page, 1925. 104p. Austin 54-713 1973 $10

MARQUIS, DON   The Dark Hours. Doubleday, 1924. 155p. Austin 51-598 1973 $8.50

MARQUIS, DON   The Dark Hours. Cape, Lond., 1926. 158p. Austin 51-599 1973 $10

MARQUIS, DON   Noah, Jonah and Cap'n John Smith. Appleton, 1921. 158p. Austin 54-714 1973 $6.50

MARQUIS, DON   The Old Soak and Hail and Farewell. Doubleday, 1921. 141p., illus. Austin 54-715 1973 $6

MARQUIS, DON   The Old Soak. Sun Dial, 1937. 32p. + 170p., 2 vols. in one. Austin 54-716 1973 $8.50

MARQUIS, DON   Old Soak's History of the World. Doubleday, 1925. 170p. Austin 54-717 1973 $6

MARQUIS, DON   Pandora Lifts the Lid. Doran, 1924. 299p. Austin 54-718 1973 $6

MARQUIS, DON   Sun Dial Time. Garden City, 1936. First edition, portion of d.w. flap mounted front free endpaper, orig. binding. Wilson 63-554 1974 $10

MARRET, L.   Icones Florae Alpinae Plantarum. Paris, 1911. Imperial 8vo., orig. covers, plates. Wheldon 129-1106 1974 £5

MARRINER, G. R.   The Kea. Christchurch, 1908. 8vo., cloth, illus., frontispiece. Wheldon 128-512 1973 £7.50

MARRIOTT, J. A. R.   A Short History of France. New York, 1944. Biblo & Tannen 213-690 1973 $7.50

MARRIOTT, JAMES   Plan of a Code of Laws for the Province of Quebec. London, 1774. Crown 8vo., card cover. Hood's 103-778 1974 $275

MARRIOTT, WILLIAM   A Collection of English Miracle-Plays or Mysteries. Paris, 1838. 8vo., orig. boards, paper label, slightly rubbed, foxed, uncut, first edition. Bow Windows 66-451 1974 £14

MARRONI, S.   Raccolta dei Principali Costumi Religiosi e Militari della Corte Pontificia. (c. 1830). Folio, engravings, plates. Quaritch 940-727 1974 £20

MARROT, H. V.   Life and Letters of John Galsworthy. 1936. Plates. Allen 216-629 1974 $10

MARRYAT, FLORENCE   A Broken Blossom. 1879. First edition, 3 vols., half title in vol. 1, catalogue at end of vol. 1, orig. green cloth, uncut, inscribed by author on fly leaf of each vol., scarce. Sawyer 293-209 1974 £115

MARRYAT, FRANK   Mountains and Molehills. London, 1855. Orig. cloth, first edition. Dawson's 424-294 1974 $150

MARRYAT, FREDERICK   A Diary In America. Philadelphia, 1839. 2 vols., linen. Hood's 103-549 1974 $75

MARRYAT, FREDERICK   Masterman Ready. London, 1841-42. 3 vols., 8vo., orig. blind-stamped cloth, presentation inscription, first edition. Dawsons PM 252-687 1974 £135

MARRYAT, FREDERICK   Newton Forster. London, 1832. 3 vols.,
8vo., orig. boards, first edition. Dawsons PM 252-688 1974 £130

MARRYAT, FREDERICK   The Settlers in Canada. London, 1844.
2 vols., browning, first edition. Hood's 104-566 1974 $65

MARRYAT, FREDERICK   The Settlers in Canada. London, 1844. First
edition, 2 vols., spine mended vol. 1. Hood's 102-531 1974 $65

MARRYAT, FREDERICK   Works. London, n.d. 8vo., 13 vols., half blue
polished calf, gilt. Hammond 201-316 1974 £45

MARS, AMAURY   Reminiscences of Santa Clara Valley and San
Jose. (San Francisco, 1901). 8vo., cloth. Saddleback 14-185 1974 $40

MARSANO, E. B.   The Strange Land. 1935. 249 pages. Austin
57-442 1974 $10

MARSDEN, J. B.   The History of the Later Puritans. 1852.
Orig. cloth, worn, inscribed. Howes 185-1415 1974 £5

MARSDEN, JOSHUA   Leisure Hours. New York, 1812. Rebound,
lacking portrait. Butterfield 10-28 1974 $15

MARSDEN, VICTOR   King of the Jews. Funk, Wagnall, 1914.
Austin 51-601 1973 $10

MARSDEN, WILLIAM   The History of Sumatra. London, 1784. 4to.,
old tree calf, rebacked, leather label, second edition. Traylen 79-526 1973
£50

MARSDEN, WILLIAM   The History of Sumatra. London, 1811.
4to., contemporary calf, fine, third edition. Traylen 79-527 1973 £120

MARSH, EDWARD   Georgian Poetry, 1911-1912. London, 1913.
Eighth edition, boards beginning to wear at hinges, lacking d.w., very nice copy.
Ross 86-191 1974 $10

MARSH, EDWARD   Georgian Poetry, 1913-1915. London, first
edition, very light foxing, tear in spine at top & bootom of hinges, lacking d.w.,
nice copy. Ross 86-192 1974 $10

MARSH, EDWARD   Georgian Poetry, 1913-1915. London, 1915.
Owner's name in ink on free fly, orig. blue boards, lacking d.w., internally
unusually bright, nearly pristine copy. Ross 86-193 1974 $12.50

MARSH, EDWARD   Georgian Poetry, 1916-1917. London, 1918.
D.w. somewhat chipped, 1-inch tear at top, near fine, orig. binding. Ross
86-194 1974 $10

MARSH, EDWARD   Georgian Poetry, 1920-22. London, 1922.
First edition, orig. binding, very nice copy. Ross 86-195 1974 $12.50

MARSH, GEORGE P.   Lectures On the English Language. 1859.
697 pages. Austin 61-645 1974 $27.50

MARSH, HARRIET A.   History of Detroit for Young People. Chicago,
1935. 8vo., cloth. Saddleback 14-506 1974 $10

MARSH, HENRY   A New Survey of the Turkish Empire and Government. London, 1663. 12mo., contemporary calf, fine, first edition. Dawsons
PM 251-283 1974 £115

MARSH, O. C.   Odontomithes. Washington, 1880. 4to.,
plates, woodcuts, orig. cloth. Bow Windows 64-178 1974 £8.50

MARSH, RICHARD   The Bettle. 1897. First edition, crown 8vo.,
illus., fine, scarce, orig. cloth. Broadhurst 24-776 1974 £55

MARSH, RICHARD   Curios. London, 1898. 1st ed. Biblo &
Tannen 210-635 1973 $20

MARSH, RICHARD   The Seen and the Unseen. New York, 1900.
Biblo & Tannen 210-636 1973 $20

MARSH, W. LOCKWOOD   Aeronautical Prints and Drawings. London, 1924.
4to., blue cloth, gilt, fine, plates, first edition. Dawsons PM 245-491 1974
£45

MARSHALL, A. M.   Lectures on the Darwinian Theory. 1894. 8vo.,
cloth, illus. Wheldon 128-50 1973 £5

MARSHALL, ARTHUR   Explosives. 1917. 2 vols., illus., first
edition. Covent 55-1316 1974 £20

MARSHALL, ARTHUR   Explosives. London, 1917-32. Roy 8vo., 3
vols., cloth, illus., second edition. Hammond 201-877 1974 £38

MARSHALL, C. H. T.   A Monograph of the Capitonidae. 1870-71.
Roy 4to., contemporary half calf, plates. Wheldon 129-29 1974 £725

MARSHALL, C. H. T.   A Monograph of the Capitonidae. London,
1871. 4to., full green morocco, plates. Traylen 79-109 1973 £680

MARSHALL, CHARLES   A Plain and Easy Introduction to the Knowledge
and Practice of Gardening. London, 1800. 12mo., contemporary half calf, gilt,
third edition. Hammond 201-28 1974 £7.50

MARSHALL, DAVID   Grand Central. New York, 1946. Illus.
Biblo & Tannen 213-85 1973 $6

MARSHALL, F.   Old English Embroidery. 1894. Large 8vo.,
plates, illus., cloth. Quaritch 940-764 1974 £12

MARSHALL, GEORGE W.   The Genealogist's Guide to Printed Pedigrees.
London, 1879. Roy 8vo., orig. cloth, first edition. Hammond 201-434 1974 £6

MARSHALL, HERMAN W.   Foot Knowledge. Boston, 1923. First edition.
Rittenhouse 46-727 1974 $10

MARSHALL, JOHN   The Life of George Washington.
Fredericksburg, 1926. 5 vols., illus., orig. binding. Wilson 63-279 1974
$28.50

MARSHALL, JOHN FREDERICK   The British Mosquitoes. 1938. Roy. 8vo.,
orig. cloth, illus. Broadhurst 23-1164 1974 £8

MARSHALL, JOHN FREDERICK   The British Mosquitoes. 1938. Roy. 8vo.,
plates, illus., orig. cloth, fine. Broadhurst 24-1135 1974 £8

MARSHALL, R. C.   Silviculture of the Trees of Trinidad and Tobago,
British West Indies. 1939. 8vo., cloth, plates. Wheldon 128-1612 1973 £10

MARSHALL, W. F.   Ulster Sails West. (1943). 79 pages.
Austin 57-445 1974 $10

MARSHALL, W. G.   Through America. London, 1881. Illus.,
gilt-stamped pictorial cloth, first edition. Bradley 35-240 1974 $27.50

MARSHALL, WILLIAM   History Versus the Whitman Saved Oregon Story.
Chicago, 1904. Jenkins 61-2074 1974 $10

MARSHALL, WILLIAM   Minutes, Experiments, Observations, and General
Remarks on Agriculture. London, 1799. 8vo., 2 vols., contemporary half calf,
gilt, new edition. Hammond 201-29 1974 £30

MARSHALL, WILLIAM   Planting and Ornamental Gardening. 1785.
8vo., contemporary calf gilt. Wheldon 130-1437 1974 £25

MARSHALL, WILLIAM   Planting and Ornamental Gardening. London,
1785. 8vo., contemporary calf, first edition. Hammond 201-30 1974 £38

MARSHALL WILLIAM   Planting and Ornamental Gardening. 1785.
Thick 8vo., contemporary calf, first edition. Howes 186-1506 1974 £55

MARSHALL, WILLIAM   Planting and Rural Ornament. London, 1796.
2 vols., 8vo., contemporary calf, labels. Dawsons PM 247-198 1974 £35

MARSHALL, WILLIAM   Planting and Rural Ornament. London, 1796.
8vo., 2 vols., contemporary tree calf, gilt, fine, second edition. Hammond 201-
31 1974 £40

MARSHALL, WILLIAM   Planting and Rural Ornament Being a Second
Edition With Large Additions of Planting and Ornamental Gardening. 1796.
8vo., 2 vols., contemporary calf. Wheldon 128-1504 1973 £25

MARSHALL, WILLIAM   The Rural Economy of Glocestershire. London, 1796. 8vo., 2 vols., half calf, gilt, second edition. Hammond 201-32 1974 £30

MARSHALL, WILLIAM   The Rural Economy of Norfolk. 1787. 8vo., 2 vols., half calf, boards, uncut, first edition. Broadhurst 23-1165 1974 £50

MARSHALL, WILLIAM   The Rural Economy of Norfolk. 1787. Med. 8vo., half calf, marbled boards, 2 vols., first edition, uncut, fine. Broadhurst 24-1136 1974 £55

MARSHALL, WILLIAM   The Rural Economy of Norfolk. London, 1795. 8vo., 2 vols., contemporary half calf, gilt, second edition. Hammond 201-34 1974 £35

MARSHALL, WILLIAM   The Rural Economy of the Midland Counties. London, 1796. 8vo., 2 vols., contemporary half calf, gilt, second edition. Hammond 201-33 1974 £30

MARSHALL, WILLIAM   The Rural Economy of the Southern Counties. London, 1798. 8vo., 2 vols., contemporary half calf, gilt, first edition. Hammond 201-35 1974 £35

MARSHALL, WILLIAM   The Rural Economy of the Southern Counties. 1798. 8vo., 2 vols., half calf, first edition. Broadhurst 23-1166 1974 £45

MARSHALL, WILLIAM   The Rural Economy of the West of England. London, 1796. 8vo., 2 vols., contemporary half calf, gilt, first edition. Hammond 201-36 1974 £32

MARSHALL, WILLIAM   The Rural Economy of Yorkshire. 1788. 2 vols., 8vo., contemporary calf. Quaritch 939-601 1974 £30

MARSHALL, WILLIAM   The Rural Economy of Yorkshire. London, 1796. 8vo., 2 vols., contemporary half calf, gilt, second edition. Hammond 201-37 1974 £32

MARSILLAC, J.   La Vie de Guillaume Penn. . . Contenant L'Histoire des Premiers Fondemens de Philadelphie . . . Paris, 1791. 2 vols. bound in one full leather binding. Jenkins 61-2153 1974 £17.50

MARSOLLIER, JACQUES   Histoire du Ministere du Cardinal Ximenes. Toulouse, 1694. 2 vols., 12mo., contemporary mottled calf, fine, second edition. Ximenes 35-608 1974 $40

MARSOLLIER, JACQUES   Histoire du Ministere du Cardinal Ximenes. Paris, 1739. 2 vols. in 1, 12mo., contemporary red morocco, fine. Ximenes 35-609 1974 $30

MARSTON, JOHN   The Plays. 1934-39. 3 vols., fine, first edition. Covent 55-1079 1974 £22.50

MARSTON, JOHN   Works. 1856. 3 vols., 16mo., half morocco. Allen 216-1926 1974 $17.50

MARSTON, JOHN   Works. 1887. 8vo., 3 vols., cloth. Quaritch 936-484 1974 £35

MARSTON, JOHN   Works. 1887. 3 vols. Allen 216-1927 1974 $15

MARSTON, JOHN   Works. 1887. 3 vols., ex-library. Allen 216-2252 1974 $25

MARTENS, CONRAD   Conrad Martens, The Man and His Art. Sydney, 1920. 4to., plates, cloth, illus., dust jacket. Quaritch 940-175 1974 £50

MARTENS, E. VON   Land and Freshwater Mollusca. 1890-1901. Roy. 4to., new buckram, coloured and plain plates, rare. Wheldon 128-832 1973 £45

MARTENS, F. H.   A Thousand and One Nights of Opera. New York, 1927. Biblo & Tannen 214-882 1974 $12.50

MARTIN, LOUIS-AIME   Le Langage des Fleurs. Bruxelles, 1830. Coloured engraved plates, 12mo., half calf, board sides. George's 610-503 1973 £7.50

MARTIN, ROBERT MONTGOMERY   The British Colonies. London & New York, (1851-57?). 6 vols. in 3, three quarter leather, frontis., plates. Hood's 104-653 1974 $375

MARTIN, ROBERT MONTGOMERY   The History, Antiquities, Topography, and Statistics of Eastern India. London, 1838. 8vo., 3 vols., orig. cloth, first edition. Dawsons PM 251-53 1974 £60

MARTIN, ROBERT MONTGOMERY   History of the British Colonies. London, 1834. 8vo., 5 vols., orig. brown cloth, gilt. Dawsons PM 251-282 1974 £145

MARTIN, ROBERT MONTGOMERY   The Hudson's Bay Territories and Vancouver's Island, With on Exposition of the Chartered Rights, Conduct and Policy of the Honble. London, 1849. Orig. boards, inscription by author. Hood's 102-820 1974 $150

MARTIN, ROBERT MONTGOMERY   The Hudson's Bay Territories and Vancouver's Island. London, 1849. Orig. boards. Hood's 104-865 1974 $150

MARTIN-DONOS, V. DE   Florule du Tam. 1864-67. 8vo., half calf. Wheldon 130-1182 1974 £7.50

MARTIN-SAINT-ANGE, GASPARD-JOSEPH   Recherches Anatomiques et Physiologiques sur le Developpement du Foetus. Paris, 1850. Large 4to., half morocco, first edition. Schumann 35-310 1974 $75

MARTIN-SANS, E.   L'Empoisonnement par les Champignons. Paris, 1929. 8vo., buckram, scarce. Wheldon 129-1277 1974 £10

MARTINEAU, HARRIET   Autobiography. 1877. 2 vols., buckram, ex-library. Allen 216-1085 1974 $15

MARTINEAU, HARRIET   The History of England During the Thirty Years' Peace. 1849-50. 2 vols., roy. 8vo., orig. cloth, first edition. Howes 186-1059 1974 £8.50

MARTINEAU, HARRIET   Mary Campbell. Wellington, 1828. First edition, engraved frontis., half calf, clean ex-libris. George's 610-513 1973 £5

MARTINEAU, HENRI   L'Oeuvre de Stendhal. Paris, 1945. Square 8vo., full cloth, orig. wrapper, uncut. L. Goldschmidt 42-383 1974 $12.50

MARTINEAU, P.   Gardening in Sunny Lands. 1924. 8vo., cloth, plates, scarce. Wheldon 130-1438 1974 £5

MARTINEZ, MARTIN   Anatomia Completa del Hombre. Madrid, 1775. 4to., contemporary calf, plates. Schumann 35-312 1974 $110

MARTINI, JOSEPH   Bibliotheque Joseph Martini. Milan, 1934-35. 2 parts, 4to., orig. wrappers. Dawsons PM 10-395 1974 £8

MARTIN, BENJAMIN   Biographia Philosophica. London, 1764. 8vo., old calf. Traylen 79-246 1973 £25

MARTIN, BENJAMIN   Gramatica Delle Scienze Filosofiche. 1778. 8vo., orig. boards, uncut. Zeitlin 235-147 1974 $45

MARTIN, BENJAMIN   A Plain and Familiar Introduction to the Newtonian Philosophy. 1754. 8vo., half calf antique, copper plates, some damp stains and spotting, first edition. Bow Windows 66-452 1974 £44

MARTIN, BENJAMIN   The Young Gentleman and Lady's Philosophy in a Continued Survey of the Works of Nature and Art. 1759 and 1763. 2 vols., demy 8vo., contemporary vellum, leather labels, little browning of text, first edition, engraved plates. Broadhurst 24-1261 1974 £30

MARTIN, BENJAMIN ELLIS   The Stones of Paris in History and Letters. New York, 1899. First edition, orig. binding, 2 vols., illus., top edges gilt. Wilson 63-600C 1974 $12.50

MARTIN, C. T.   Theodor Krieger's Leben. Cleveland, 1907. 243 pages. Austin 57-443 1974 $12.50

MARTIN, CECIL P.   Prehistoric Man in Ireland. London, 1935. Large 8vo., illus., dust jacket. Emerald 50-590 1974 £12

MARTIN, CHARLES   Le Boletus Subtomentosus. Berne, 1903. Roy 8vo., half buckram, plates. Wheldon 129-1276 1974 £5

MARTIN, EDWARD S.   The Life of Joseph Hodges Choate. 1920.
2 vols., portraits. Howes 186-707 1974 £5.50

MARTIN, FREDERICK   The Life of John Clare. 1865. Presentation
copy, inscribed from author, covers stained, first edition, very good copy.
Covent 51-2262 1973 £8.50

MARTIN, G. C.   The Adult School Movement. 1924. 8vo.,
orig. cloth, illus. Bow Windows 64-602 1974 £6.50

MARTIN, GEORGE M.   Emmy Lou. McClure, 1902. 279p., illus.
Austin 54-719 1973 $7.50

MARTIN, H. N.   Physiological Papers. Baltimore, 1895. 4to.,
orig. cloth, trifle stained. Wheldon 128-288 1973 £10

MARTIN, HENRI   Histoire de France. Paris, c.1870. 17 vols.,
contemporary half calf, rubbed. Howes 186-1058 1974 £25

MARTIN, JAMES   Memorandoms. Cambridge, 1937. Bookplate,
English first edition. Covent 56-1080 1974 £12.50

MARTIN, JOHN   An Account of the Tonga Islands in the South Pacific Ocean. Edinburgh, 1827. 16mo., 2 vols., cloth, third edition. Putman
126-47 1974 $22

MARTIN, JOHN   The Dance. New York, 1946. 4to. Biblo &
Tannen 210-951 1973 $7.50

MARTIN, JOHN   Illustrations of the Bible. London, 1839. Folio,
plates, contemporary half morocco. Marlborough 70-41 1974 £150

MARTIN, L. A.   North to Nome. Chicago, 1939. Photographs.
Hood's 102-65 1974 $10

MARTIN, LOUIS   Plan d'une Bibliotheque Universelle. Paris,
1837. 8vo., boards. Kraus B8-155 1974 $25

MARTIN, MARCUS J.   Wireless Transmission of Photographs. 1916.
Scarce, illus. Covent 55-1236 1974 £15

MARTIN, MATHEW   Letter to the Right Hon. Lord Pelham. c., 1803.
8vo., boards, inscribed. Hammond 201-250 1974 £16

MARTIN, OLGA J.   Hollywoods Movie Commandments. Wilson,
1937. Austin 51-602 1973 $12.50

MARTIN, P. I.   A Geological Memoir On a Part of Western
Sussex. 1828. 4to., orig. cloth, coloured plates, scarce. Wheldon 128-1021
1973 £10

MARTIN, P. I.   A Geological Memoir on a Part of Western
Sussex. 1828. 4to., orig. cloth, plates, scarce. Wheldon 131-1047 1974
£10

MARTIN, P. I.   A Geological Memoir on a Part of Western Sussex.
London, 1828. 4to., orig. cloth-backed boards, plates, first edition. Hammond
201-380 1974 £25

MARTIN, PETE   Hollywood Without Make-Up. Lippincott,
1949. 255p. Austin 51-603 1973 $6.50

MARTIN, ROBERT MONTGOMERY   History of the British Colonies. London,
1835. 5 vols., 8vo., contemporary mauve calf, gilt. Traylen 79-433 1973
£75

MARTIN, SUCCESS   Specimen des Principaux Articles Fabriques et
Vendus par les Maisons H. Fromont et Journet Reunies. Paris, 1879. Large
4to., orig. printed wrappers, illus. Kraus B8-328 1974 $85

MARTIN, T.   The History of the Town of Thetford. 1779.
4to., plates, modern boards. Quaritch 939-172 1974 £15

MARTIUS, K. F. P. VON   Beschreibung Einiger Neuen Nopaleen.
Breslau, 1832. 4to., modern boards, plates, rare. Wheldon 131-1675 1974 £20

MARTIUS, K. F. P. VON   Historia Naturalis Palmarum, Vol. 1 de Palmis
Generatim. Munich, 1831-50. Folio, unbound, uncut, coloured plates,
complete copy, very rare. Wheldon 128-1613 1973 £120

MARTIUS, K. F. P. VON   Historia Naturalis Palmarum, Vol. 3 Expositio
Palmarum Systematica. Munich, (1837-53). Folio, unbound, uncut, coloured
plates. Wheldon 128-1614 1973 £120

MARTIUS, K. F. P. VON   The Natural History, the Diseases ... of Brazil.
Calcutta, 1845. 8vo., boards. Gurney 64-146 1974 £40

MARTYN, BENJAMIN   An Impartial Enquiry into the State and Utility
of the Province of Georgia. London, 1741. 8vo., mottled calf, first edition.
Dawsons PM 247-199 1974 £105

MARTYN, CHARLES   The William Ward Genealogy. New York,
1925. 8vo., cloth. Saddleback 14-794 1974 $65

MARTYN, THOMAS   Aranei. 1793. Roy. 4to., contemporary calf
neatly rebacked, hand-coloured plates, nice complete copy, rare. Wheldon
128-913 1973 £325

MARTYN, THOMAS   Aranei. 1793. Roy. 4to., modern half
morocco, gilt, plates, rare. Wheldon 131-78 1974 £500

MARTYN, THOMAS   Aranei. 1793. Roy 4to., modern half morocco,
gilt, plates. Wheldon 129-30 1974 £500

MARTYN, THOMAS   The English Entomologist. 1792. Roy. 4to.,
full morocco gilt, plates. Wheldon 131-79 1974 £250

MARTYN, THOMAS   The English Entomologist. 1792. Roy 4to.,
new half morocco, gilt, uncut. Wheldon 129-31 1974 £150

MARTYN, THOMAS   The English Entomologist Exhibiting all the
Coleopterous Insects Found in England. 1792. Roy. 4to., newly bound in full
brown morocco gilt, gilt edges, hand coloured stipple engraved plates. Wheldon
128-765 1973 £250

MARTYN, THOMAS   Entomologist Anglois. 1792. Roy. 4to., newly
bound in full morocco gilt, gilt edges, hand-coloured stipple-engraved plates.
Wheldon 128-766 1973 £250

MARTYN, THOMAS   The Language of Botany. 1807. 8vo., new
cloth. Wheldon 131-1172 1974 £10

MARTYN, THOMAS   Linnaeus's System of Vegetables. 1788. 8vo.,
orig. cloth, plates, worn, first edition. Bow Windows 64-179 1974 £28

MARTYN, THOMAS   Thirty-Eight Plates With Explanations: Intended
to Illustrate Linnaeus's System of Vegetables. 1799. 8vo., modern boards,
plates. Wheldon 131-268 1974 £35

MARTYN, THOMAS   Thirty-Eight Plates With Explanations Intended
to Illustrate Linnaeus's System of Vegetables and Particularly Adapted to the
Letters on the Elements of Botany. 1799. 8vo., half morocco, uncut, hand
coloured plates. Wheldon 128-1140 1973 £25

MARTYN, THOMAS   The Universal Conchologist. 1789. 4to., 2
vols., half brown morocco, plates, rare. Wheldon 130-43 1974 £350

MARTYR, PETER
Please turn to
ANGHIERA, PIETRO MATIRE D'

MARTYROLOGE Romain. Paris, 1931. Orig. wrappers, 688 pages. Howes
185-1421 1974 £5

THE MARTYRS Who, For Our Country, Gave Up Their Lives in the Prison Pens in
Andersonville, Georgia. Washington, 1866. Wrapper. Jenkins 61-1451 1974
$22.50

MARVELL, ANDREW   A Collection of Poems on Affairs of State.
London, 1689. 4to., paper wrappers, first edition. Dawsons PM 252-689
1974 £85

MARVELL, ANDREW   Mrs. Craddock. 1903. Small wrinkle in spine,
else very good, first edition. Covent 51-1257 1973 £10.50

MARVELL, ANDREW   Poems and Satires. 1892. 2 vols., boards,
cloth sides, gilt tops, very nice copy, one of 200 numbered copies on large paper,
portrait, first edition. Covent 51-1251 1973 £15

MARVELL, ANDREW   Works. 1776. Roy 4to., 3 vols., half calf,
portrait. Quaritch 936-150 1974 £30

MARWICK, THOMAS PURVES The History and Construction of Staircases. Edinburgh, 1888. 8vo., cloth, plates, first edition. Hammond 201-879 1974 £6

MARX, ARTHUR   Life With Groucho. Simon, Schuster, 1954.
Austin 51-605 1973 $6

MARX, GROUCHO   Groucho and Me. Geis, 1959. 344p., illus.
Austin 51-604 1973 $6

MARX, KARL   Das Kapital. 1883-85-94. 3 vols., 8vo.,
contemporary half russia, labels, first & third editions. Dawsons PM 247-200
1974 £750

MARX, KARL   Das Kapital. 1883-85-94. 3 vols., 8vo.,
contemporary half russia, first & third editions. Dawsons PM 250-55 1974
£750

MARY and Her Cat. 1804. Engravings, 12mo., orig. wrappers. George's
610-514 1973 £5

MARY Schweidler, the Amber Witch. London, 1846 and 1844. Marbled boards,
calf. Dawson's 424-342 1974 $30

MARYLAND: Its Resources, Industries and Institutions. Balitmore, 1893. Fine
large folding maps in color, illus. Jenkins 61-1456 1974 $27.50

MARYON, HERBERT   Modern Sculpture: Its Methods and Ideals.
1933. First edition, illus., spine & covers little rubbed, else fine. Covent
51-128 1973 £6

MAS, A.   Le Verger. Paris, (1865-72). Roy 8vo., 8
vols., half brown morocco, plates, rare. Wheldon 130-1484 1974 £186

MASAYOSHI, KEISAI   Ryakuga-Shiki: "Drawings in the Abbreviated
Style". n.d. 1 vol., new covers. Quaritch 940-410 1974 £95

MASCIOTTA, MICHELANGELO Ottone Rosai. Florence, 1940. 4to.,
plates, wrapper. Minters 37-433 1973 $20

MASEFIELD, JOHN   Ballads and Poems. 1910. English first edition.
Covent 56-916 1974 £10

MASEFIELD, JOHN   The Collected Poems of. (1923). 784 pages.
Austin 61-647 1974 $10

MASEFIELD, JOHN   The Collected Poems Of. London, 1923.
Orig. cloth, leather label, fine, autographed, special limited edition. Jenkins
48-316 1973 $50

MASEFIELD, JOHN   The Coming of Christ. 1928. Uncut, fine,
orig. parchment backed boards, first edition. Howes 185-319 1974 £6.50

MASEFIELD, JOHN   Easter, a Play for Singers. (1929). Fine, orig.
buckram, uncut, limited, first edition. Howes 185-320 1974 £5.50

MASEFIELD, JOHN   John M. Synge: A Few Personal Recollections
With Biographical Notes. Letchworth, 1916. One of 200 copies, wrappers, very
good copy. Covent 51-1801 1973 £9.50

MASEFIELD, JOHN   A Letter From Pontus and Other Verse. 1936.
First American edition. Austin 61-656 1974 $10

MASEFIELD, JOHN   Lines Spoken By . . . at the Tercentenary of
Harvard University 18 September, 1936. (1937). 8vo., orig. cloth, signed
by Masefield, limited, first edition. Bow Windows 66-454 1974 £10

MASEFIELD, JOHN   Melloney Holtspur. London, 1922. Signed,
limited edition. Jenkins 48-317 1973 $15

MASEFIELD, JOHN   Melloney Holtspur. Macmillan, 1923.
Austin 51-607 1973 $7.50

MASEFIELD, JOHN   Melloney Holtspur or the Pangs of Love. New
York, 1922. Limited to 1,000 numbered copies, signed by author, orig. binding.
Wilson 63-555 1974 $25

MASEFIELD, JOHN   Recent Prose. 1933. Ex-library. Austin
61-665 1974 $10

MASEFIELD, JOHN   Reynard the Fox. 1919. Orig. parchment
backed boards, first edition. Howes 185-322 1974 £8.50

MASEFIELD, JOHN   Reynard the Fox. New York, 1919. Cloth,
fine, first edition. Rinsland 58-976 1974 $35

MASEFIELD, JOHN   Selected Poems. 1922. Orig. parchment
backed boards, limited, first edition. Howes 185-323 1974 £7.50

MASEFIELD, JOHN   South and East. London, 1929. Folio, orig.
cloth backed boards, first illus. edition, one of 400 numbered copies, signed by
author, fine, boxed. MacManus 224-315 1974 $30

MASEFIELD, JOHN   The Taking of Helen. 1923. Signed, quarter
parchment-vellum, English first edition. Covent 56-917 1974 £6.30

MASEFIELD, JOHN   The Taking of the Gry. 1934. Orig. blue
buckram, gilt, limited, first edition. Howes 185-324 1974 £5.50

MASEFIELD, JOHN   The Tragedy of Nan. Kennerley, 1909.
Austin 51-608 1973 $7.50

MASEFIELD, JOHN   Tragedy of Pompey the Great. Macmillan,
1914. 137p., rev. ed. Austin 51-609 1973 $7.50

MASEFIELD, JOHN   Tristan and Isolt. 1927. Signed, quarter parchment vellum, English first edition. Covent 56-919 1974 £6.30

MASEFIELD, JOHN   The Wanderer, of Liverpool. 1930. 4to., buckram, fine, illus., limited edition. Quaritch 936-485 1974 £18

MASEFIELD, JOHN   The Wanderer of Liverpool. New York, 1930.
Limited to 350 numbered copies, roy. 8vo., signed & numbered, colored frontis.,
full page plates, orig. green paper covers, black cloth spine, some fading top of
covers, else very fine. Current BW9-256 1974 $35

MASEREEL, FRANS   Du Noir au Blanc/Von Schwarz zu Weiss.
Zurich, 1939. Large 4to., boards, woodcuts, limited edition. Minters 37-470
1973 $26

MASEREEL, FRANS   Die Passion Eines Menschen. Munich, 1921.
Limited to 750 copies, woodcuts, 4to., half calf, top edges gilt, dust wrappers,
slip case, fine. Sawyer 293-210 1974 £42

MASEREEL, FRANS   Die Passion Eines Menschen. Munich, 1924.
Large 4to., boards, woodcuts, limited edition. Minters 37-469 1973 $20

MASKELL, ALFRED   Ivories. 1905. Roy. 8vo., plates, half
orange red morocco, gilt, plates, bookplate. Quaritch 940-464 1974 £20

MASKELL, W. M.   An Account of the Insects Noxious. Wellington,
1887. 8vo., cloth, plates. Wheldon 129-660 1974 £7.50

MASKELL, W. M.   An Account of the Insects Noxioux to
Agriculture and Plants In New Zealand. Wheldon 131-830 1974 £7.50

MASKELL, WILLIAM   Holy Baptism. 1848. Orig. cloth, printed
label, rubbed, second edition. Howes 185-1423 1974 £5

MASON, A. E. W.   Lawrence Clavering. 1897. 8vo., orig. cloth,
scarce, first edition. Rota 190-660 1974 £5

MASON, CHARLOTTE   The Lady's Assistant for Regulatins and
Supplying Her Table. 1775. 8vo., contemporary sheep, second edition.
Quaritch 939-173 1974 £70

MASON, GEORGE CHAMPLIN Newport Illustrated. New York, 1854. 8vo.,
orig. cloth, woodcuts. Butterfield 8-569 1974 $25

MASON, J. A.   A Treatise on the Climate and Meteorology of
Madeira. 1850. 8vo., orig. cloth gilt, plates. Wheldon 130-295 1974 £5

MASON, J. MONCK   Comments on the Plays of Beaumont & Fletcher.
Quarter old-style mottled calf, marbled boards, rebound. Covent 55-163
1974 £21

MASON, J. MONCK   Comments on the Plays of Beaumont and Fletcher. 1798. New buckram. Allen 216-2094 1974 $12.50

MASON, LAWRENCE   Genesis A, Translated From the Old English By. 1915. Ex-library, sturdy library binding. Austin 61-674 1974 $17.50

MASON, STUART   Bibliography of Oscar Wilde. n.d. Cloth gilt, plates, English first edition. Covent 56-1330 1974 £15

MASON, WILLIAM   Caractacus. London, 1759. 8vo., modern boards, second edition. Dawsons PM 252-690 1974 £14

MASON, WILLIAM   Poems. York, 1773. Small 8vo., rebacked, contemporary calf, third edition. Bow Windows 62-609 1974 £15.50

MASON-MANHEIM, MADELINE   Hill Fragments. 1925. Drawings. Austin 61-675 1974 $10

MASPERO. M.   Un Manuel de Hierarchiè Egyptienne. Paris, 1890. Two plates. Biblo & Tannen 210-1009 1973 $27.50

MASSA, NICOLA   Liber De Febre Pestilentiali. 1556. 8vo., modern vellum. Dawsons PM 249-365 1974 £90

MASSACHUSETTS   The Andros Tracts. Boston, 1868. 3 vols., Frontis. port. in ea. vol. 3/4 lea. and marbled bds; covers chipped and worn but very good copies. One of 150 copies. Jacobs 24-4 1974 $125

MASSACHUSETTS   A Guide to Its Places and People. Boston, 1937. 8vo., orig. bindings, dust jacket. Butterfield 8-256 1974 $25

MASSALONGO, D. A.   Prodromus Florae Fossilis Senogalliensis. Milan, 1854. 4to., chromolithograph plates. Wheldon 128-1022 1973 £5

MASSART, J.   Esquisse de la Geographie Botanique de la Belgique. Brussels, 1910. 2 vols., roy. 8vo., cloth, photographs, maps, diagrams. Wheldon 128-1285 1973 £7.50

MASSART, J.   Esquisse de la Geographie Botanique de la Belgique. Brussels, 1910. 2 vols., roy. 8vo., half brown morocco neat, maps, photographs, diagrams. Wheldon 128-1286 1973 £10

MASSART, J.   Esquisse de la Geographie Botanique de la Belgique. Brussels, 1910. 2 vols., roy. 8vo., half brown morocco, maps. Wheldon 131-1331 1974 £10

MASSART, J.   Une Mission Biologique Belge au Bresil. Brussels, 1929-30. 2 vols. in 1, roy. 8vo., half morocco, plates, maps. Wheldon 131-378 1974 £15

MASSE, G. C. E.   A Bibliography of First Editions of Books Illustrated By Walter Crane. 1923. Frontispiece, cloth back, boards, scarce. Marsden 39-103 1974 £12

MASSEE, G.   British Fungi. 1891. 8vo., cloth, plates. Wheldon 129-1279 1974 £3.50

MASSEE, G.   British Fungus-Flora. 1892-95. 8vo., 4 vols., cloth. Wheldon 129-1280 1974 £10

MASSEE, G.   British Fungus-Flora. 1892-95. 8vo., 4 vols., cloth. Wheldon 130-1321 1974 £15

MASSEE, G.   British Fungus-Flora. 1892-95. 4 vols., 8vo., cloth, scarce. Wheldon 131-1444 1974 £15

MASSEE, G.   Mildews, Rusts and Smuts. 1913. 8vo., cloth, scarce, plates. Wheldon 129-1281 1974 £3

MASSEE, G.   A Monograph of the Myxogastres. 1892. Roy 8vo., cloth, scarce, plates. Wheldon 129-1278 1974 £10

MASSEE, G.   A Monograph of the Thelephoreae. 1888-89. 8vo., cloth. Wheldon 130-1323 1974 £5

MASSERMAN, PAUL   The Jews Come to America. 1932. 477 pages. Austin 57-447 1974 $15

MASSEY, EDWARD   Plots and Playwrights. Little, Brown, 1917. Austin 51-610 1973 $7.50

MASSEY, GERALD   Ancient Egypt. London, 1907. 4to., 4 vols., orig. brown cloth, fine, first edition. Dawsons PM 251-54 1974 £40

MASSINGER, PHILIP   Plays, With Notes. 1805. 4 vols., buckram. Allen 216-1929 1974 $25

MASSINGER, PHILIP   The Unnatvrall Combat. London, 1639. Small 4to., full red morocco gilt, first edition. Dawsons PM 252-691 1974 £475

MASSINGHAM, DOROTHY   The Lake. Doubleday, 1934. Austin 51-612 1973 $7.50

MASSON, GEORGES   Les Arts Graphiques a l'Exposition de Vienne. Paris, 1875. 8vo., orig. printed wrappers. Kraus B8-350 1974 $35

MASSON, MICHEL   Vierge et Martyre. Paris, 1836. 2 vols., 8vo., contemporary half cloth, first edition. L. Goldschmidt 42-296 1974 $15

MASSON, ROSALINE   I Can Remember Robert Louis Stevenson. 1922. Orig. edition. Austin 61-676 1974 $10

MASTERS, EDGAR LEE   Children of the Market Place. New York, 1922. First edition, orig. binding. Butterfield 10-382 1974 $8.50

MASTERS, EDGAR LEE   Children of the Market Place. Macmillan, 1922. 469p. Austin 54-720 1973 $10

MASTERS, EDGAR LEE   The Golden Fleece of California. Weston, n.d. (1936). Edition limited to 550 copies, signed by author & artist, light glassine wrapper, near mint, badly torn box. Ross 87-380 1974 $45

MASTERS, EDGAR LEE   Great Valley. 1916. First edition. Allen 216-1090 1974 $12.50

MASTERS, EDGAR LEE   Mitch Miller. Macmillan, 1920. 262p., illus. Austin 54-721 1973 $6

MASTERS, EDGAR LEE   Mitch Miller. New York, 1920. First edition, first state, d.w. somewhat soiled & chipped, else fine, orig. binding, scarce in d.w. Ross 87-381 1974 $25

MASTERS, EDGAR LEE   Skeeters Kirby. Macmillan, 1923. 394p. Austin 54-722 1973 $6

MASTERS, EDGAR LEE   Skeeters Kirby. New York, 1923. Orig. binding, first edition, small chip in d.w., else fine. Ross 87-382 1974 $15

MASTERS, EDGAR LEE   Songs and Satires. New York, 1916. Orig. binding, first edition, bookplate, covers lightly spotted & rubbed, nice. Ross 87-383 1974 $10

MASTERS, EDGAR LEE   Spoon River Anthology. New York, 1915. First edition, sixth impression, blue cloth, gilt lettering on cover & spine, name in ink on free fly, nice, lacking d.w. Ross 87-384 1974 $15

MASTERS, EDGAR LEE   Spoon River Anthology. New York, 1915. First edition, first issue, very fine, slipcased. Jenkins 61-1553 1974 $125

MASTERS, EDGAR LEE   Starved Rock. Macmillan, 1919. 171p. Austin 54-723 1973 $10

MASTERS, EDGAR LEE   The Tale of Chicago. New York, 1933. First U.S. edition. Covent 56-920 1974 £10.50

MASTERSON, THOMAS   Mastersons Arithmetick. London, 1634. 8vo., orig. sheep, rebacked, second edition. Dawsons PM 245-495 1974 £125

MATCHAM, MARY EYRE   The Nelsons of Burnham Thorpe. 1911. Frontispiece, plates. Howes 186-1100 1974 £5.25

MATHER, COTTON   Magnolia Christi Americana. Hartford, 1853. 2 vols., bindings torn. Biblo & Tannen 213-70 1973 $42.50

MATHER, EDWARD   Nathaniel Hawthorne. Crowell, 1940. 356p., illus. Austin 54-724 1973 $12.50

MATHER, F. A.   Isaac Master, Reconstruction of the Work of Gaddo Gaddi. 1932. 4to., plates, new buckram. Allen 213-1489 1973 $15

MATHER, SAMUEL   The Figures or Types of the Old Testament. Dublin, 1685. Second edition, 4to., modern half brown hardgrain morocco, upper joint a bit weak. Thomas 32-47 1974 £50

MATHER, SAMUEL   The Figures of Types of the Old Testament . . . Explain'd and Improv'd in Sundry Sermons. London, 1705. Old calf, worn, second edition, plus table and errata. Jenkins 61-1554 1974 $27.50

MATHERS, J.   The History of Mr. John Decastro and His Brother Bat. Pittsburg, 1902. 2 vols., 8vo., contemporary half morocco, frontispiece. Bow Windows 66-457 1974 £8.50

MATHESON, ANNIE   Happy Childhood. London, n.d. (c. 1880). Square 24mo., pictorial wrappers, illus., fine. Frohnsdorff 16-539 1974 $10

MATHEWS,   Some Sources of Southernisms. Univ. of Alabama, 1948. 154p. Austin 54-725 1973 $7.50

MATHEWS, CORNELIUS   The Motley Book: A Series of Tales and Sketches of American Life. New York, 1840. Orig. cloth, extremities worn, third edition. MacManus 224-316 1974 $37.50

MATHEWS, E. R. NORRIS   Bristol Bibliography. Bristol, 1916. 4to., half cloth. Kraus B8-22 1974 $15

MATHEWS, E. R. NORRIS   Early Printed Books and Manuscripts in the City Reference Library, Bristol. Bristol, 1899. 4to., plates, orig. half imitation vellum. Dawsons PM 10-397 1974 £7

MATHEWS, G. M.   The Birds of Australia. 1910-27. Roy 4to., 13 vols., half morocco. Wheldon 129-32 1974 £4,800

MATHEWS, G. M.   Manual of the Birds of Australia. 1921. Crown 4to., cloth, plates. Wheldon 129-500 1974 £20

MATHEWS, JOHN J.   Wah'Kon Tah: The Osage and the White Man's Road. Norman, 1932. Dust jacket, first edition. Jenkins 61-1555 1974 $10

MATHEWS, JOHN JOSEPH   Talking to the Moon. Chicago, 1945. Tan cloth, illus., dust jacket, mint, first edition. Bradley 35-243 1974 $10

MATHIAS, THOMAS JAMES   The Pursuits of Literature. London, 1808. Biblo & Tannen 213-793 1973 $10

MATHIEU, C.   Flore Generale de Belgique. 1853-55. 8vo., half morocco, 2 vols. Wheldon 129-1108 1974 £15

MATORA-OISHI   Geishu Itsukushima Zue. (1842). 10 vols., illus., orig. dark blue covers, complete set. Quaritch 940-411 1974 £300

MATSCHAT, CECILE H.   American Wild Flowers. New York, 1940. 4to., pictorial covers and endpapers, full color pictures, very good. Current BW9-573 1974 $13.50

MATSON, N.   Reminiscences of Bureau County. Princeton, 1872. Orig. cloth, plates, frontispiece, first edition. Bradley 35-181 1974 $60

MATSUMOTO, TORU   A Brother Is a Stranger. Day, 1946. 318p. Austin 62-412 1974 $12.50

MATSUMURA, J.   Tentamen Florae Lutchuensis. Tokyo, 1899. 4to., sewed, scarce. Wheldon 128-1274 1973 $7.50

MATSUURA, H.   A Bibliographical Monograph on Plant Genetics. Tokyo, 1929. Roy 8vo., scarce. Wheldon 129-177 1974 £7.50

MATTHEW OF PARIS
Please turn to
PARIS, MATTHEW

MATTHEW, G. F.   Report on the Cambrian Rocks of Cape Breton. Ottawa, 1903. Plates. Hood's 104-447 1974 $20

MATTHEW, P.   On Naval Timber and Arboriculture. Edinburgh, 1831. 8vo., orig. boards, rebacked, rare, first edition. Wheldon 130-245 1974 £300

MATTHEWS, A. G.   Calamy Revised: Being a Revision of Edmund Calamy's Account of the Ministers and Others Ejected & Silences. Howes 185-1027 1974 £10

MATTHEWS, BRANDER   The Development of the Drama. Scribner, 1926. 351p. Austin 51-613 1973 $7.50

MATTHEWS, BRANDER   Moliere. Scribner, 1910. 385p., illus. Austin 51-614 1973 $17.50

MATTHEWS, BRANDER   Playwrights on Playmaking and other Studies of the Stage. New York, 1923. 1st ed. Biblo & Tannen 210-966 1973 $7.50

MATTHEWS, BRANDER   Poems of American Patriotism. New York, 1922. Illus. by N. C. Wyeth, first edition so collected, 8vo., full color illus., spine faded, else fine. Current BW9-394 1974 $22.50

MATTHEWS, BRANDER   Shakespeare As a Playwright. Scribner, 1913. 399p., orig. ed. Austin 51-615 1973 $12.50

MATTHEWS, BRANDER   A Study of the Drama. Houghton, Mifflin, 1910. 320p., illus. Austin 51-616 1973 $10

MATTHEWS, BRANDER   Tales of Fantasy and Fact. New York, 1896. 8vo., orig. cloth, first edition. Rota 190-851 1974 £8

MATTHEWS, CORNELIUS   The Motley Book . . . Tales and Sketches of American Life. New York & Boston, 1840. Illus., third edition, revised, orig. binding, fine full page engravings. Butterfield 10-16 1974 $45

MATTHEWS, HENRY   The Diary of an Invalid. London, 1820. 8vo., binder's cloth, foxed, second edition. Traylen 79-561 1973 £5

MATTHIESSEN, F. O.   The Achievement of T. S. Eliot. 1935. Ex-library, orig. unrevised edition. Austin 61-677 1974 $10

MATTINGLY, HAROLD   Outlines of Ancient History. Cambridge, 1914. Illus. Biblo & Tannen 214-637 1974 $15

MATTINGLY, HAROLD   Roman Coins. New York, 1928. Plates. Biblo & Tannen 214-638 1974 $8.50

MATTIOLI, PIERANDREA   Herbarz: Ginak Bylinar. Prague, 1562. Folio, brown leather, first edition with large woodcuts, portrait. Kraus 137-63 1974 $2,600

MATTISON, H.   Spirit-Rapping Unveiled! New York, 1855. New edition with appendix, orig. binding. Butterfield 10-383 1974 $25

MATTSON, HANS   Reminiscences. St. Paul, 1891. Illus. Austin 57-449 1974 $12.50

MATTSON, HANS   Reminiscences. St. Paul, MN, 1891. 314p., illus. Austin 62-413 1974 $12.50

MATURIN, CHARLES ROBERT   Melmoth the Wanderer. 1892. 3 vols., crown 8vo., orig. smooth cloth, uncut, new edition. Howes 185-327 1974 £60

MAUBRAY, JOHN   The Female Physician. London, 1724. 8vo., contemporary panelled calf, first edition. Schumann 35-313 1974 $150

MAUCH Chunk, Pennsylvania: The Switchback Railroad. Brooklyn, 1898. Wrappers, photos. Jenkins 61-2154 1974 $27.50

MAUCLAIR, C.   Les Miniatures de l'Empire et de la Restauration. 1913. 4to., vellum paper, plates, half morocco, orig. wrapper, numbered, limited edition. Quaritch 940-178 1974 £25

MAUCLAIR, CAMILLE   Turner. New York, 1939. Folio, color plates. Biblo & Tannen 210-392 1973 $22.50

MAUDE, JOHN   Visit To the Falls of Niagara in 1800. London, 1826. Plates, Cambridge calf, presentation, raised bands. Hood's 104-707 1974 $550

MAUDUIT, ISRAEL   Considerations on the Present German War. London, 1761. 8vo., contemporary calf, gilt, fourth edition. Hammond 201-613 1974 £8.50

MAUDUIT, ISRAEL   The Parallel. London, 1742. 8vo., modern boards, first edition. Dawsons PM 251-458 1974 £10

MAUGHAM, WILLIAM SOMERSET   Ah King: Six Stories. (1933). 8vo., orig. cloth, first edition. Bow Windows 66-458 1974 £7.75

MAUGHAM, WILLIAM SOMERSET   L'Archipel anx Sirenes. Paris, n.d. Illus., numbered, worn, first French edition. Covent 55-1081 1974 £15

MAUGHAM, WILLIAM SOMERSET   Books and You. 1940. Ex-library, first American edition. Austin 61-680 1974 $12.50

MAUGHAM, WILLIAM SOMERSET   Cakes and Ale. n.d. Orig. lithograph, one of 1000 copies, numbered & signed by author & artist, full leather, d.w., glassine wrapper, slip case, immaculate copy. Covent 51-2453 1973 £25

MAUGHAM, WILLIAM SOMERSET   Cakes and Ale. 1930. Frayed, English first edition. Covent 56-922 1974 £7.50

MAUGHAM, WILLIAM SOMERSET   Cakes and Ale. 1930. Fine, crisp copy, browned d.w. Covent 51-2454 1973 £6.30

MAUGHAM, WILLIAM SOMERSET   Christmas Holiday. New York, 1939. First edition, 8vo., inner hinge slightly cracked, very good copy. Current BW9-56 1974 $12.50

MAUGHAM, WILLIAM SOMERSET   The Circle. 1921. 8vo., orig. cloth, wrappers, first edition. Rota 189-608 1974 £5

MAUGHAM, WILLIAM SOMERSET   The Constant Wife. New York & Los Angeles, 1926. Wrappers. Covent 55-1082 1974 £7.50

MAUGHAM, WILLIAM SOMERSET   The Constant Wife. 1929. 8vo., cloth, signed. Quaritch 936-489 1974 £20

MAUGHAM, WILLIAM SOMERSET   Don Fernando. 1935. First American edition. Austin 61-685 1974 $10

MAUGHAM, WILLIAM SOMERSET   Don Fernando. 1935. Orig. dec. cloth gilt, fine bright copy, excellent d.w. Covent 51-2457 1973 £7.50

MAUGHAM, WILLIAM SOMERSET   Encore. Doubleday, 1952. Austin 51-617 1973 $10

MAUGHAM, WILLIAM SOMERSET   The Gentleman in the Parlour. 1930. Orig. dec. cloth gilt, fine, d.w. Covent 51-2458 1973 £7.50

MAUGHAM, WILLIAM SOMERSET   The Hour Before Dawn. New York, 1942. 8vo., cloth, presentation inscription. Quaritch 936-488 1974 £35

MAUGHAM, WILLIAM SOMERSET   The Judgement Seat. 1934. Frontis., woodcut, one of 150 copies, numbered & signed by author & artist, fine. Covent 51-2459 1973 £25

MAUGHAM, WILLIAM SOMERSET   The Magician. 1908. Rebound, cloth. Covent 55-1085 1974 £6

MAUGHAM, WILLIAM SOMERSET   The Magician. 1908. Worn covers, book-plate. Covent 55-1084 1974 £15.75

MAUGHAM, WILLIAM SOMERSET   The Makings of a Saint. 1898. Orig. cloth, colonial edition. Rota 188-626 1974 £25

MAUGHAM, WILLIAM SOMERSET   The Merry-Go-Round. 1904. Covers somewhat worn, scarce. Covent 51-2460 1973 £15

MAUGHAM, WILLIAM SOMERSET   The Moon and Sixpence. 1919. Small 8vo., orig. cloth, first edition. Quaritch 936-487 1974 £45

MAUGHAM, WILLIAM SOMERSET   The Moon and Sixpence. 1919. Orig. cloth, first edition, second issue. Rota 188-627 1974 £7.50

MAUGHAM, WILLIAM SOMERSET   The Moon and Sixpence. 1919. Orig. cloth, first edition, third issue. Rota 188-628 1974 £6.50

MAUGHAM, WILLIAM SOMERSET   The Moon and Sixpence. London, 1919. 8vo., orig. cloth, first edition, first issue. Dawsons PM 252-692 1974 £35

MAUGHAM, WILLIAM SOMERSET   Of Human Bondage. London, (1915). Orig. cloth, first English edition, first issue with ads at rear, fine, plush-lined box. MacManus 224-317 1974 $100

MAUGHAM, WILLIAM SOMERSET   On a Chinese Screen. 1922. 8vo., orig. cloth, fine, d.w., first edition. Rota 189-609 1974 £5

MAUGHAM, WILLIAM SOMERSET   Plays. Doubleday, Doran. Austin 51-618 1973 $10

MAUGHAM, WILLIAM SOMERSET   Portrait of. Fine, orig., signed. Bow Windows 64-759 1974 £74

MAUGHAM, WILLIAM SOMERSET   The Sacred Flame. 1928. Ex-library, first American edition. Austin 61-693 1974 $12.50

MAUGHAM, WILLIAM SOMERSET   Six Stories Written in the First Person Singular. New York, 1931. 8vo., orig. cloth, first edition. Rota 189-611 1974 £6

MAUGHAM, WILLIAM SOMERSET   Strictly Personal. New York, 1941. Orig. cloth, label on spine, first edition, one of 515 numbered copies, signed by author, fine. MacManus 224-318 1974 $35

MAUGHAM, WILLIAM SOMERSET   Theatre. Doubleday, 1937. 292p. Austin 51-619 1973 $7.50

MAUGHAM, WILLIAM SOMERSET   The Unconquered. New York, 1944. 12mo., 1st ed., one of 300 numbered copies, signed, with additional penned pres. initialed by Maugham. Biblo & Tannen 214-754 1974 $100

MAUGHAM, WILLIAM SOMERSET   The Unconquered. New York, 1944. First edition, limited to 300 numbered copies, signed by author, crown 8vo., mint, orig. cloth. Broadhurst 24-792 1974 £50

MAULSBY, F. R.   Rucson, Arizona. Tucson, (1913). 12mo., wrapper. Saddleback 14-7 1974 $12.50

MAUN-GWU-DAUS   An Account of the North American Indians. Leicester, 1848. 8vo., orig. printed front wrapper, back wrapper missing, first edition, very good copy. Ximenes 36-142 1974 $175

MAUND, BENJAMIN   The Botanic Garden. (1825-50). 18 vols., small 4to., full green morocco gilt, plates, very rare. Wheldon 131-81 1974 £1,200

MAUND, BENJAMIN   The Botanic Garden. 1825 (-1850). 16 vols. in 9, small 4to., contemporary half morocco, hand-coloured plates, complete set, large paper edition, nice copy. Wheldon 128-1702 1973 £450

MAUND, BENJAMIN   The Botanic Garden. 1825-(1850). Small 4to., contemporary half morocco. Wheldon 129-34 1974 £600

MAUND, BENJAMIN   The Botanic Garden. London, 1825-(1851). 13 vols., small 4to., contemporary half green morocco gilt, plates, complete set. Traylen 79-38 1973 £500

MAUNDER, SAMUEL   The Treasury of Natural History. 1862. Small 8vo., red calf gilt, sixth edition. Wheldon 131-171 1974 £7.50

MAUNOIR, JEAN PIERRE   Memoires. Geneva, (1802). 8vo., orig. wrappers, unopened, plates, first edition. Schumann 35-314 1974 $75

MAUNOIR, THEODORE   Essai sur Quelques Points de l'Histoire de la Cataracte. Paris, 1833. 4to., contemporary half morocco, first editions. Schumann 35-315 1974 $95

MAUPASSANT, GUY. DE   Le Horla. Paris, 1887. 12mo., three quarter levant morocco, gilt, first edition. L. Goldschmidt 42-297 1974 $45

MAUPASSANT, GUY DE   Monsieur Parent. Paris, 1886. 12mo.,
contemporary three quarter pink cloth, orig. wrapper, uncut, first edition.
L. Goldschmidt 42-298 1974 $45

MAUPASSANT, GUY DE   Works. New York, 1925. 17 vols., 8vo.,
illus., blue cloth, leather labels, fine. Ballinger 1-172 1974 $50

MAUPERTUIS, PIERRE LOUIS MOREAU DE   Dissertation Physique a l'Occasion
du Negre Blanc. Leide, 1744. 12mo., old worn calf, rebacked. Gurney
66-126 1974 £90

MAUPERTUIS, PIERRE LOUIS MOREAU DE   La Figure de la Terre. Paris,
1738. 8vo., contemporary calf, plates, first edition. Schuman 37-186 1974
$250

MAUPERTUIS, PIERRE LOUIS MOREAU DE   The Figure of the Earth. London,
1738. 8vo., contemporary calf, plates, first edition in English. Schuman
37-187 1974 $165

MAUPERTUIS, PIERRE LOUIS MOREAU DE   Venus Physique. N.P., 1745.
2 parts in 1 vol., 12mo., boards, first edition. Schuman 37-167 1974 $275

MAURAULT, O.   Marges d'Histoire. Montreal, 1929. Card
cover. Hood's 103-155 1974 $12.50

MAURAULT, O.   Propos et Portraits. Montreal, (1940).
Unopened. Hood's 104-489 1974 $12.50

MAURIAC, CLAUDE   Jean Cocteau, ou la Verite du Mensonge.
Paris, 1945. 16mo., wrappers. Minters 37-326 1973 $12.50

MAURICE, THOMAS   Indian Antiquities. London, 1794-1806. 8vo.,
contemporary calf, gilt, second edition. Dawsons PM 251-55 1974 £60

MAURICE, THOMAS   Observations Connected with Astronomy and
Ancient History. London, 1816. 4to., orig. boards, uncut, unopened, first
edition. Gurney 64-147 1974 £16

MAURICE, THOMAS   Observations Connected With Astronomy and
Ancient History. London, 1816. 4to., orig. boards, uncut, unopened, plates,
first edition, fine. Gurney 66-127 1974 £16

MAURICEAU, FRANCOIS   De Mulierum Praegnantium Parturientium. Paris,
1681. 4to., contemporary calf, rebacked, first Latin edition. Dawsons PM 249-
366 1974 £110

MAURO, MARCO   Annotationi Sopra la Lettione della Spera del
Sacrobosto Dove si Sichiarano Tutti e Principii Mathematici & Naturali. Florence,
1550. 4to., quarter calf, woodcuts, altered & enlarged second edition. Gurney
66-128 1974 £105

MAUROIS, ANDRE   Ariel ou la Vie de Shelley. Paris, 1924.
8vo., orig. wrapper, illus., limited edition. L. Goldschmidt 42-300 1974 $10

MAUROIS, ANDRE   Ariel ou la Vie de Shelley. Paris, 1929.
Roy. 8vo., orig. wrapper, uncut, illus., limited edition. L. Goldschmidt
42-301 1974 $12.50

MAUROIS, ANDRE   Aspects de la Biographie. Paris, 1928. 8vo.,
wrappers, limited edition. Minters 37-109 1973 $15

MAUROIS, ANDRE   Dialogues dur le Commandement. Paris,
1924. 12mo., orig. wrapper, first edition. L. Goldschmidt 42-302 1974 $15

MAUROIS, ANDRE   Meipe ou la Delivrance. Paris, 1926. 12mo.,
orig. wrapper, uncut, first edition. L. Goldschmidt 42-303 1974 $20

MAUROLYCUS, FRANCISCUS Cosmographia. Venice, 1543. 4to., vellum,
fine, first edition. Dawsons PM 245-496 1974 £750

MAURY, MATTHEW FONTAINE The Physical Geography of the Sea. London,
1856. Roy. 8vo., orig. cloth, plates, second edition. Wheldon 130-263 1974
£12

MAURY, MATTHEW FONTAINE The Physical Geography of the Sea and Its
Meteorology. 1860. 8vo., orig. cloth, plates, maps. Wheldon 131-317
1974 £15

MAURY, MATTHEW FONTAINE The Physical Geography of the Sea. 1860.
8vo., orig. cloth, plates, new edition. Wheldon 130-264 1974 £10

MAURY, MATTHEW FONTAINE The Physical Geography of the Sea. 1863.
8vo., full calf, plates. Wheldon 129-225 1974 £10

MAURY, MATTHEW FONTAINE The Physical Geography of the Sea and Its
Meteorology. 1863. 8vo., full calf, plates. Wheldon 131-318 1974 £10

MAURY, SARAH MYTTON   An Englishwoman in America. London, 1848.
lst ed. Jacobs 24-22 1974 $25

MAUVILLON, JACOB   Essai sur l'Influence de la Poudre a Canon. 1782.
8vo., contemporary speckled calf, gilt, plates, first edition. Dawsons PM 245-
497 1974 £11

MAVOR, WILLIAM   The British Nepos. 1798. First edition, 12mo.,
contemporary sheep, joints cracked, engraved frontis., woodcuts. George's
610-517 1973 £7.50

MAVROGORDATO, JOHN   Cassandra in Troy. 1914. Buckram, gilt top,
cover little marked, very good copy, first edition. Covent 51-1259 1973 £5.25

MAW, GEORGE   A Monograph of the Genus Crocus. 1886.
4to., orig. cloth, plates. Wheldon 129-35 1974 £320

MAXIMILIAM I.   Freydal. Vienna, 1880-82. Folio, 2 vols.,
orig. boards, fine, first edition. Dawsons PM 251-284 1974 £100

MAXIMUS TYRIUS   Sermones Sive Disputationes XLI. Geneva,
1557. 2 vols., vellum, first edition. Thomas 28-293 1972 £60

MAXWELL, H.   Memories of the Months. 1897-1922. 8vo.,
orig. cloth. Wheldon 129-286 1974 £12

MAXWELL, HERBERT   The Story of the Tweed. 1905. Large 4to.,
orig. buckram, plates, limited edition. Howes 186-2181 1974 £15

MAXWELL, JAMES CLERK   An Elementary Treatise on Electricity. Oxford,
1888. 8vo., brown cloth, plates, second edition. Dawsons PM 245-500 1974
£5

MAXWELL, JAMES CLERK   An Elementary Treatise on Electricity. Oxford,
1881. 8vo., brown cloth, plates, first edition. Dawsons PM 245-499 1974 £8

MAXWELL, JAMES CLERK   The Scientific Papers of James Clerk Maxwell.
1890. Roy 4to., orig. red cloth, gilt. Zeitlin 235-148 1974 $300

MAXWELL, JAMES CLERK   A Treatise on Electricity and Magnetism. Oxford,
1873. 8vo., 2 vols., orig. maroon cloth, fine, uncut, gilt, first edition. Dawsons
PM 245-498 1974 £130

MAXWELL, JAMES CLERK   A Treatise on Electricity and Magnetism. Oxford, 1881. 8vo., 2 vols., cloth, plates, second edition. Schumann 35-316
1974 $145

MAXWELL, JOHN BART   Letters from Lord Pollock to the Rev. Robert Wodrow. Edinburgh, 1835. Small 8vo., half roan, uncut, rare. Hill 126-165
1974 £35

MAXWELL, MARIUS   Elephants and Other Big Game Studies. 1930.
Oblong 4to., cloth. Wheldon 130-411 1974 £5

MAXWELL, MARIUS   Stalking Big Game With a Camera in Equatorial
Africa. 1925. 4to., orig. cloth, plates, covers faded, second edition. Bow
Windows 66-459 1974 £8.50

MAXWELL, MARIUS   Stalking Big Game With a Camera in Equatorial
Africa, With a Monograph on the African Elephant. 1925. Roy. 4to., binding
little faded, plates after photos, orig. cloth, fine. Broadhurst 24-1654 1974 £12

MAXWELL, MARIUS   Stalking Big Game With a Camera In
Equatorial Africa. 1925. Roy. 4to., cloth. Wheldon 131-512 1974 £15

MAXWELL, MARIUS   Stalking Big Game With a Camera in Equatorial
Africa. 1925. Roy. 4to., cloth, plates. Wheldon 128-336 1973 £7.50

MAXWELL, MARIUS   Stalking Big Game with a Camera. 1925. Roy 4to., orig. cloth. Broadhurst 23-1679 1974 £12

MAXWELL, MARY ELIZABETH (BRADDON)   The Captain of the Vulture. London, 1867. 8vo., orig. blue cloth, revised second edition, frontis., very good copy. Ximenes 36-28 1974 $25

MAXWELL, WILLIAM HAMILTON 1792-1850   The Bivouac. 1837. 3 vols., small 8vo., half calf, rebacked, first edition. Howes 186-319 1974 £25

MAXWELL, WILLIAM HAMILTON 1792-1850   The Fortunes of Hector O'Halloran. n.d. Full green morocco, plates. Covent 55-2826 1973 £32.50

MAXWELL, WILLIAM HAMILTON 1792-1850   The Fortunes of Hector O'Halloran, and His Man Mark Anthony O'Toole. 1843. Quarter calf, engravings, few foxed. Eaton Music-624 1973 £5

MAW, GEORGE   A Monograph of the Genus Crocus. London, 1886. 4to., cloth, plates, scarce. Traylen 79-39 1973 £350

MAW, GEORGE   A Monograph of the Genus Crocus. 1886. 4to, orig. cloth, plates, illus. Bow Windows 64-180 1974 £450

MAWE, J.   The Voyager's Companion. 1825. 12mo., orig. boards, plates, frontispiece, fourth edition. Bow Windows 64-182 1974 £7.50

MAWE, T.   The Universal Gardener and Botanist. 1797. 4to., contemporary calf, engraved plates, very scarce, revised second edition. Wheldon 128-1505 1973 £20

MAWE, T.   The Universal Gardener and Botanist. 1797. 4to., contemporary calf, plates, scarce, second edition. Wheldon 130-1439 1974 £20

MAWSON, T. H.   The Art and Craft of Garden Making. 1900. 4to., orig. dec. cloth, illus. Wheldon 130-1440 1974 £5

MAWSON, T. H.   The Art and Craft of Garden Making. 1907. Roy. 4to., orig. cloth, illus., third edition. Wheldon 128-1506 1973 £6

MAWSON, T. H.   The Art and Craft of Garden Making. 1926. Folio, orig. cloth, coloured plates, illus, fifth edition. Wheldon 128-1507 1973 £10

MAY, BETTY   Tiger-Woman. 1929. Plates, English first edition. Covent 56-280 1974 £15

MAY, JOHN B.   The Hawks of North America. New York, 1935. Roy. 8vo., cloth, coloured and plain plates, maps, very scarce. Wheldon 128-514 1973 £20

MAY, JOHN B.   The Hawks of North America. New York, 1935. 4to., cloth, plates, scarce, first edition. Putman 126-32 1974 $14

MAY, JOHN B.   The Hawks of North America. New York, 1935. Roy. 8vo., cloth, illus., very scarce. Wheldon 131-656 1974 £20

MAY, PHIL   Fun, Frolic, and Fancy. 1894. Wrappers, English first edition. Covent 56-1924 1974 £7.50

MAY, PHIL   The Phil May Album. 1900. Spine dull, else very good copy, first edition. Covent 51-1261 1973 £10.50

MAY, PHIL   A Phil May Medley. London, (1903). Oblong 4to., pictorial wrappers, very good copy. Frohnsdorff 16-540 1974 $20

MAY, PHIL   Phil May's "Graphic" Pictures. London, (1897). Oblong 4to., pictorial boards, cloth spine, color illus., very good copy. Forhnsdorff 16-541 1974 $25

MAY, SOPHIE   Christmas Fairies. Memphis, 1861. First edition, small 12mo., gilt dec. blue cloth, near fine. Current BW9-57 1974 $85

MAY, THOMAS   The Constitutional History of England. 1912. 3 vols., best edition. Howes 186-1068 1974 £18

MAY, THOMAS   A Discourse Concerning the Successe of Former Parliaments. 1642. 4to., disbound, first edition. Dawsons PM 251-459 1974 £18

MAY, THOMAS   The History of the Parliament of England. 1647. 1 vol., folio, contemporary calf, rebacked, first edition. Howes 186-1067 1974 £45

MAY, THOMAS   The Tragedie of Cleopatra Queen of Aegypt. London, 1639. 12mo., contemporary sheep, rare, first edition. Dawsons PM 252-693 1974 £750

THE MAY BOOK. 1901. 4to., orig. dec. cloth, fine, English first edition. Covent 56-1418 1974 £15.75

MAYBECK, BERNARD R.   Palace of Fine Arts and Lagoon. San Francisco, 1915. 8vo., stiff wrappers, plates. Minters 37-20 1973 $14

MAYCOCK, J. D.   Flora Barbadensis. 1830. 8vo., orig. cloth, paper label, coloured map. Wheldon 128-1287 1973 £50

MAYDMAN, HENRY   Naval Speculations, and Maritime Politicks. London, 1691. Small 8vo., old calf, rebacked, inscribed, presentation. Traylen 79-150 1973 £105

MAYER, A. L.   Mittelalterliche Plastik in Spanien. 1922. Folio, plates. Allen 213-1644 1973 $10

MAYER, ARTHUR   Merely Colossal. S & S, 1953. 264p., illus. Austin 51-620 1973 $7.50

MAYER, JULIUS ROBERT   Die Mechanik der Warme. Stuttgart, 1867. 8vo., modern boards, fine, first edition. Dawsons PM 245-502 1974 £75

MAYER, LUIGI   Views In Egypt. London, 1805. Folio, dark blue straight-grained morocco, gilt, fine, plates. Traylen 79-456 1973 £95

MAYERNE, THEODORE TURQUET DE   Praxeos Mayernianae. 1690. 8vo., contemporary calf, first edition. Dawsons PM 249-367 1974 £90

MAYHEW, HENRY   London Labour and the London Poor. London, (1861). 79 parts in 3 vols., 8vo., contemporary half morocco, plates, fine, first edition. Dawsons PM 247-201 1974 £160

MAYHEW, HENRY   London Labour and the London Poor. (1864). 3 vols., 8vo., illus., orig. cloth gilt, fine. Quaritch 939-463 1974 £45

MAYHOW, JOHN   Tractatus Quinque Medico-Physici. Oxford, 1674. 8vo., modern calf antique, plates, first edition. Traylen 79-247 1973 £750

MAYNADIER, HOWARD   The Arthur of the English Poets. Boston, 1907. Biblo & Tannen 214-639 1974 $8.50

MAYNARD, FRANCOIS DE   Les Oeuvres. Paris, 1646. 4to., red levant morocco, gilt, fine, first edition. L. Goldschmidt 42-80 1974 $700

MAYNARD, THEODORE   Poems. 1919. 169 pages. Austin 61-694 1974 $10

MAYNARD, U.   La Sainte Vierge. Paris, 1877. Thick imp. 8vo., orig. cloth gilt, illus., plates. Howes 185-1427 1974 £5

MAYNWARING, EVERARD   Morbus Polyrhizos and Polymorphaeus. London, 1672. Small 8vo., contemporary calf, rebacked. Schumann 35-317 1974 $245

MAYO, EARL OF   A History of the Kildare Hunt. London, 1913. 8vo., cloth boards, illus. Emerald 50-597 1974 £8.50

MAYO, BERNARD   Henry Clay Spokesman of the New West. 1937. Large 8vo., scarce, orig. binding. Butterfield 10-191 1974 $20

MAYO, CHARLES HERBERT   Bibliotheca Dorsetiensis. London, 1885. 4to., orig. cloth gilt, limited. Dawsons PM 10-401 1974 £48

MAYO, CHARLES HERBERT   A Genealogical Account of the Mayo and Elton Families. London, 1908. 4to., green buckram gilt, uncut. Dawsons PM 251-129 1974 £15

MAYO, HERBERT   Letters on the Truths Contained in Popular Superstitions. Frankfort & Edinburgh, 1849. Contemporary half calf, label, nice copy. Covent 51-2505 1973 £6.30

MAYO, JOHN HORSLEY   Medals & Decorations of the British Army & Navy. 1897. 2 vols., roy. 8vo., plates, orig. cloth gilt. Smith 193-80 1973 £20

MAYO-SMITH, RICHMOND   Emigration and Immigration. 1890. Ex-library, orig. edition. Austin 57-451 1974 $12.50

MAYO-SMITH, RICHMOND   Emigration and Immigration. Scribner, 1890. 316p., orig. ed. Austin 62-414 1974 $12.50

MAYOW, JOHN   Tractatus Quinque Medico-Physici, Quorum Primus Agit de Sal-Nitro, et Spiritu Nitro-Aereo. Oxford, 1674. First edition, 8vo., contemporary vellum, engraved folding plates. Kraus 137-64 1974 $2,850

MAYR, E.   Birds of the Southwest Pacific. New York, 1945. Crown 8vo., cloth, plates, scarce. Wheldon 130-577 1974 £7.50

MAZAS, ALEXANDRE   Les Hommes Illustres de l'Orient. Pairs, 1847. 2 vols., contemporary cloth-backed boards. Howes 186-1069 1974 £7.50

MAZE, A.   Notes d'un Collectionneur. 1870. Imp. 4to., plates, buckram, rare. Quaritch 940-650 1974 £25

MAZONN, JULIUS FERDINAND   Zur Pathologie der Bright'schen Krankheit. Kiev, 1851. 8vo., contemporary boards. Schumann 35-318 1974 $65

MAZZINI, JOSEPH   Life and Writings. 1890-91. 6 vols., small 8vo., damp-stained, scarce, new edition. Howes 186-320 1974 £20

MEAD, G. R. S.   Pistis Sophia. London, 1947. Biblo & Tannen 210-981 1973 $9.50

MEAD, G. R. S.   Thrice Greatest Hermes. London, 1949. 3 vols., very good set. Biblo & Tannen 210-980 1973 $40

MEASON, GILBERT LAING   A Letter to William Joseph Denison. London, 1823. 8vo., boards, first London edition. Hammond 201-251 1974 £5

MEAD, HENRY   The Sepoy Revolt. London, 1857. 8vo. Traylen 79-528 1973 £10

MEAD, MARGARET   The Maoris and Their Arts. New York, 1945. 1st ed., illus. Biblo & Tannen 210-179 1973 $9.50

MEAD, MARTHA N.   Asheville: In the Land of the Sky. Richmond, 1942. 8vo., cloth. Saddleback 14-604 1974 $10

MEAD, MATHEW   Der Beynahe Ein Christ Endeckt. Selins-Grove, 1830. Leather backed boards. Hayman 59-371 1974 $10

MEAD, RICHARD   Bibliotheca Meadiana. (London, 1755). 8vo., contemporary half vellum. Schuman 37-168 1974 $110

MEAD, RICHARD   A Discourse on the Small Pox and Measles. London, 1748. 8vo., half calf. Gurney 64-148 1974 £36

MEAD, RICHARD   The Medical Works. Edinburgh, 1775. 8vo., calf, new edition. Schumann 35-319 1974 $125

MEAD, RICHARD   Monita et Praecepta Medica. Leiden, 1773. 8vo., contemporary stiff vellum, fine. Dawsons PM 249-368 1974 £35

MEAD, RICHARD   A Short Discourse Concerning Pestilential Contagion. London, 1720. 8vo., quarter calf, uncut, first edition. Gurney 64-149 1974 £55

MEAD, RICHARD   A Treatise Concerning the Influence of the Sun and Moon Upon Human Bodies, and Diseases Thereby Produced. London, 1748. 8vo., contemporary calf, fine. Gurney 66-129 1974 £40

MEAD, RICHARD   A Treatise Concerning the Influence of the Sun and Moon upon Human Bodies. London, 1748. 8vo., contemporary calf. Gurney 64-150 1974 £40

MEAD, SHEPHERD   The Big Ball of Wax. Simon, Schuster, 1954. 246p. Austin 54-726 1973 $6.50

MEAD, SHEPHERD   The Carefully Considered Rape of the World. S & S, 1965. 245p. Austin 54-727 1973 $4

MEAD, SHEPHERD   "Dudley, There Is No Tomorrow" Then How About This Afternoon. S & S, 1963. 288p. Austin 54-728 1973 $6.50

MEAD, SHEPHERD   Er, or The Brassbound Beauty. S & S, 1969. 250p. Austin 54-730 1973 $6

MEAD, SHEPHERD   How To Get Rich in T. V. Without Really Trying. Simon, Schuster, 1956. 180p., illus. Austin 54-730 1973 $6

MEAD, SHEPHERD   How to Live Like a Lord Without Really Trying. S & S, 1964. 253p., illus. Austin 54-731 1973 $6.50

MEAD, SHEPHERD   How to Succeed in Business Without Really Trying. Simon, Schuster, 1952. 148p., illus. Austin 54-732 1973 $3.50

MEAD, SHEPHERD   How to Succeed With Women Without Really Trying. Ballatine, 1957. 154p., illus., hard cover ed. Austin 54-734 1973 $6.50

MEAD, SHEPHERD   The Magnificent Macinnes. Farrar, Straus, 1949. 255p. Austin 54-734 1973 $7.50

MEADE, GEORGE   The Life and Letters of George Gordon Meade Major-General United States Army. New York, 1913. Large 8vo., 2 vols., nice set, foldout maps, orig. binding. Butterfield 10-169 1974 $35

MEADE, WILLIAM   Sermon on Confirmation . . . Preached in Winchester, on Sunday, December 12, 1830. Georgetown, 1831. Disbound. Hayman 59-645 1974 $10

MEADOWS, KENNY   Heads of the People. 1841. 2 vols., plates. Allen 216-1097 1974 $15

MEADOWS, MARY JANE   The Life, Voyages, and Surprising Adventures of. London, n.d. (c. 1802). 12mo., disbound, first edition. Ximenes 36-85 1974 $35

MEANS, PHILIP AINSWORTH   Ancient Civilizations of the Andes. New York, 1931. 1st ed., col. frontis., illus. Jacobs 24-23 1974 $15

MEARS, ELIOT GUNNELL   Resident Orientals on the American Pacific Coast. 1928. 545 pages. Austin 57-452 1974 $17.50

MEASON, GILBERT LAING   On the Landscape Architecture of the Great Painters of Italy. 1828. 4to., contemporary blind tooled russia, rebacked, plates. Quaritch 940-532 1974 £78

MECKEL, JOHANN FRIEDRICH   Physiologische und Anatomische. Berlin, 1755. 4to., contemporary boards, plates. Schumann 35-320 1974 $135

MEDAILLES Sur les Principaux Evenements du Regne de Louis le Grand, Avec des Explications Historiques. Paris, 1702. Folio, contemporary mottled calf gilt, worn, first edition. Harper 213-108 1973 $250

MEDIAEVAL hymns. New York, 1868. 12mo., 7th ed. Biblo & Tannen 213-468 1973 $5

MEDICAL Botany: Or History of Plants in the Materia Medica of the London, Edinburgh and Dublin Pharmacopoeias. 1821. 2 vols., 8vo., binders cloth, plates. Wheldon 131-1812 1974 £70

THE MEDICAL Bulletin (War Medicine). Paris, 1917-19. Vols. 1 & 2, 8vo., quarter shagreen, not uniform. Gurney 66-130 1974 £25

MEDINA, JOSE TORIBIO   Algunas Noticias de Leon Pancaldo, 1537-38. Santiago, 1908. Cloth. Kraus B8-158 1974 $25

MEDINA, JOSE TORIBIO   Biblioteca Hispano-Chilena, 1523-1817. Santiago, 1897-99. 3 vols., 4to., cloth. Kraus B8-160 1974 $120

MEDINA, JOSE TORIBIO   Historia del Tribunal del Santo Oficio de la Inquisicion de Lima, 1569-1820. Santiago, 1887. 2 vols. in 1, buckram. Kraus B8-161 1974 $45

MEDINA, JOSE TORIBIO   La Imprenta in Mexico, 1539-1821. Santiago, 1908-12. 8 vols., large 8vo., cloth. Kraus B8-163 1974 $250

MEDINA, JOSE TORIBIO   La Primitiva Inquisicion American, 1493-1569. Santiago, 1914. 2 vols. in 1, thick 8vo., cloth, orig. edition. Kraus B8-164 1974 $45

MEDINA, PEDRO DE   L'Art del Navegar. Venice, 1554. Small 4to., woodcut illus., old vellum. Traylen 79-151 1973 £360

MEDINACELI, DUQUE DE   Aves de Rapina y su Caza. Madrid, n.d. Roy. 8vo., orig. cloth, plates, second edition. Wheldon 131-657 1974 £30

MEDIOLANO, JOANNE DE   Schola Salernitana. Boterodami, 1649. 24mo., full calf, signature. Rittenhouse 46-448 1974 $75

THE MEDITERRANEAN. n.d. 4to., contemporary half morocco, foxed, plates. Broadhurst 23-1680 1974 £60

MEDULLA Medicinae Universae: Or, A . . . Dispensatory. 1749. Disbound, corrected and revised third edition. Thomas 32-324 1974 £12.50

MEDWIN, T.   The Angler in Wales. 1834. 2 vols., 8vo., illus., modern boards, foxed. Quaritch 939-688 1974 £22.50

MEE, ARTHUR   The Children's Encyclopaedia. n.d. 10 vols., roy. 8vo., illus., half morocco gilt. Smith 193-292 1973 £15

MEE, ARTHUR   The King's England. London, 1939. 39 vols., 8vo., faded, illus. Traylen 79-305 1973 £40

MEE, CORNELIA   A Manual of Knitting, Netting and Crochet Work. 1842. Small oblong 8vo., plates, contemporary calf, scarce, first edition. Quaritch 940-763 1974 £35

MEEHAN, T.   The Native Flowers and Ferns of the United States. Boston, 1878-79. Roy 8vo., new cloth, plates. Wheldon 130-1184 1974 £15

MEEK, A.   The Migrations of Fish. 1916. 8vo., cloth, plates. Wheldon 130-705 1974 £10

MEEK, A. S.   A Naturalist in Cannibal Land. 1912. 8vo., orig. cloth, illus. Broadhurst 23-1681 1974 £5

MEEHAN, THOMAS   The Native Flowers and Ferns of the United States. Philadelphia, 1880. 2 vols. in 1, roy. 8vo., new cloth. Wheldon 131-1332 1974 £15

MEEKER, EZRA   The Busy Life of Eighty Five Years. Seattle, 1916. Jenkins 61-2076 1974 $15

MEEKER, EZRA   Pioneer Reminiscences of Puget Sound, the Tragedy of Leschi. Seattle, 1905. Illus., first edition, inscribed & signed by author. Jenkins 61-2577 1974 $47.50

MEEKER, N. C.   Life in the West. New York, 1868. 8vo., orig. bindings, inscribed. Butterfield 8-312 1974 $15

MEERSCH, P. G. VAN DER   Recherches sur la Vie et les Travaux des Imprimeurs Belges et Neerlandais, Etablis a l'Etranger et sur la Part Qu'Ils ont Prise a la Regeneration Litteraire de l'Europe au 15e Siecle. Ghent, 1856. Vol. 1, illus., 8vo., orig. printed wrappers, uncut, unopened. Kraus B8-351 1974 $67.50

MEERWEIN, KARL FRIEDRICH   L'Art de Voler a la Maniere des Oiseaux. Basle, 1785. 8vo., cloth, gilt, fine, uncut, second edition in French. Dawsons PM 245-504 1974 £235

MEERWEIN, KARL FRIEDRICH   A Arte de Voar a Maneira dos Pasaros. 1812. Small 8vo., mottled calf, gilt, fine, first portugese edition. Dawsons PM 245-505 1974 £75

MEGINNESS, J. F.   Otzinachson. Philadelphia, 1857. 8vo., orig. bindings, first edition. Butterfield 8-494 1974 $20

MEGROZ, R. L.   Dante Gabriel Rossetti. 1928. Blue cloth, rebound, illus., scarce. Marsden 37-407 1974 £7

MEGROZ, R. L.   Walter de la Mare. 1924. Fine, English first edition. Covent 56-1709 1974 £5.25

MEHEE DE LA TOUCHE, JEAN CLAUDE HIPPOLYTE   Traite des Lesions de la Tete. Avignon, 1774. Small 8vo., contemporary calf. Schumann 35-323 1974 $110

MEHERIN, ELENORE   Chickie. Grosset, Dunlap, 1923. 529p., illus. Austin 51-621 1973 $8.50

MEHTA, NANALAL CHAMANIAL   Studies in Indian Painting. Bombay, 1926. First edition, 8vo., fine tipped in color plates, half tone plates, orig. green cloth, very good, unique. Current BW9-549 1974 $38.50

MEIGHAN, CHRISTOPHER   A Treatise of the Nature and Powers of the Baths and Waters of Bareges. London, 1764. 8vo., contemporary mottled calf, new edition. Schumann 35-324 1974 $65

MEIGNAN, GUILLAUME-RENE   Les Propheties Messianiques de l'Ancien Testament ou la Divinite du Christianisme Demonstree par la Bible. Paris, 1859. Cloth, first edition. Howes 185-1428 1974 £5.75

MEIGS, CORNELIA L.   The Steadfast Princess. Macmillan, 1928. 87p., paper. Austin 51-622 1973 $8.50

MEIJER, CORNELIS   L'Arte di Restituire a Roma la Tralasciata Nauigatione del suo Teuere. Roma, 1685-89. Folio, old half calf, rebacked, illus. Traylen 79-565 1973 £200

MEINECKE, FRIEDRICH   Die Deutsche Katastrophe. Zurich, 1946. Biblo & Tannen 213-691 1973 $8.50

MEINEKE, A.   Analecta Alexandrina. 1843. Half cloth, worn spine. Allen 213-689 1973 $12.50

MEINERTZHAGEN, R.   Nicoll's Birds of Egypt. 1930. Roy 4to., orig. cloth, plates. Broadhurst 23-1167 1974 £70

MEINHOLD, WILLIAM   Sidonia the Sorceress. London, 1894. 2 vols. Rittenhouse 46-449 1974 $20

MEINRAT, SAINT   Histori vom Leben unnd Sterben dess H. Einsidels und Martyrers S. Meinradis. Freiburg, 1587. 2 parts in 1 vol., 4to., contemporary limp vellum, fine, rare, complete copy. Harper 213-109 1973 $1450

MEIR ARAMA   Urim Ve'tumin. Venice, 1603. First edition, small 4to., cloth backed boards. Thomas 32-56 1974 £75

MEISTER, HANS-PETER   Das Recht des Architekten. Berlin, 1939. 8vo., cloth. Minters 37-556 1973 $10

MEISTER der Schreibkunst aus Drei Jahr hunderten. Stuttgart, 1923. 4to. Biblo & Tannen 210-62 1973 $15

MELA, POMPONIUS   De Situ Orbis. 1518. Vellum, stain, old Aldine edition. Thomas 30-41 1973 £50

MELA, POMPONIUS   Iulius Solinus. Venice, 1518. Small 8vo., parchment backed boards, good copy, only Aldine edition. Thomas 32-212 1974 £45

MELANCHTHON, PHILIP   Didymi Faventini Adversus Thomam Placentinum. (Basel), 1521. Small 4to., woodcut title border, modern boards, waterstains, rare Basle edition. Schafer 8-128 1973 sFr. 1,200

MELANCHTHON, PHILIP   Liber Continens Continua Series Epistolas. Leipzig, 1569. Large 8vo., contemporary vellum, fine, book-plate, first edition. Schafer 8-131 1973 sFr. 700

MELANCHTHON, PHILIP   Loci Praecipui Theologici. Wittenberg, 1569. 8vo., contemporary calf over wooden boards, waterstains, portrait. Schafer 8-130 1973 sFr. 450

MELANCHTHON, PHILIP   Oratio Uber der Leich des Ehrwirdigen Herrn D. Martini Luthers. Wittenberg, 1546. 4to., boards, first edition in German. Harper 213-207 1973 $450

MELANCHTHON, PHILIP   Verzaichnug vnd Kurtzliche Antzaigung in dz Euangeliu Joan. (Augsburg), 1524. Small 4to., modern half vellum, very fine, first (only?) German edition.   Schafer 8-129 1973 sFr. 1,400

MELCHIORRI, G.   L'Ape Italiana delle Belle Arti, Giornale, Dedicato ai Loro Cultori ed Amatori. Rome, 1835-37. 3 vols., folio, plates, calf gilt.   Quaritch 940-179 1974 £30

MELESE, PIERRE   Le Theatre et le Public. A Paris Sous Louis XIV, 1659-1715. Paris, 1934. Wrappers, unopened, illus. Eaton Music-520 1973 £5

MELIA, PIUS   The Origin, Persecutions and Doctrines of the Waldenses. 1870. Imp. 8vo., orig. cloth, plates. Howes 185-1429 1974 £8.50

MELIA, RAPHAEL   The Woman Blessed by All Generations. 1868. Orig. cloth, illus., scarce. Howes 185-1430 1974 £5.75

MELIN, E.   Researches into the Blueing of Ground Woodpulp. 1934. 8vo., cloth. Wheldon 129-1288 1974 £5

MELIN, E.   Untersuchungen uber die Bedeutung. Jena, 1925. Roy 8vo., half leather, scarce. Wheldon 129-1287 1974 £5

MELLAND, F.   Elephants in Africa. 1938. 8vo., cloth, illus., scarce. Wheldon 128-337 1973 £5

MELLEN, IDA M.   The Science and Mystery of the Cat. New York, 1949. Illus. Biblo & Tannen 214-578 1974 $7.50

MELLER, SIDNEY   Roots in the Sky. Macmillan, 1938. Austin 62-416 1974 $10

MELLERSH, W. L.   A Treatise on the Birds of Gloucestershire. Gloucester & London, 1902. Roy. 8vo., half blue morocco gilt, map, plates. Wheldon 128-515 1973 £7.50

MELLET, F. N.   L'Art du Menuisier en Meubles et de l'Ebeniste. 1825. 8vo., plates, orig. green boards, uncut, worn spine, very scarce. Quaritch 940-583 1974 £85

MELLONE, S. H.   Western Christian Thought in the Middle Ages. Edinburgh, 1935. Biblo & Tannen 214-640 1974 $12.50

MELLONI, MACEDONIO   La Thermochrose ou la Coloration Calorifique. Paris, 1850. 8vo., illus., black pebbled cloth, first edition. Zeitlin 235-150 1974 $225

MELMOTH, WILLIAM   Letters on Several Subjects. 1795. 8vo., contemporary sprinkled calf gilt, fine, tenth edition. Quaritch 936-151 1974 £6

MELVILLE, HENRY   The Rise and Progress of Trinity College. Toronto, 1852. Orig. boards, uncut, second edition. Hood's 104-402 1974 $65

MELVILLE, HENRY   The Rise and Progress of Trinity College, Toronto; With a Sketch of the Life of the Lord Bishop of Toronto as Connected With Church Education in Canada. Toronto, 1852. Second edition, orig. boards, uncut. Hood's 102-420 1974 $65

MELVILLE, HERMAN   The Apple-Tree Table and Other Sketches. Princeton, 1922. Orig. cloth backed boards, extremities rubbed, first trade edition, limited. MacManus 224-319 1974 $27.50

MELVILLE, HERMAN   Benito Cereno. 1926. 4to., binding spotted, bookplate. Allen 216-1100 1974 $10

MELVILLE, HERMAN   Benito Cereno. 1926. Folio, orig. buckram, gilt, uncut, unopened, dust-wrapper, illus. Hammond 201-775 1974 £15

MELVILLE, HERMAN   Benito Cereno. London, 1926. Orig. cloth, pictures, one of 1,650 copies, fine, tattered dust jacket. MacManus 224-347 1974 $30

MELVILLE, HERMAN   Israel Potter. 30lp., illus. Austin 54-736 1973 $8.50

MELVILLE, HERMAN   Israel Potter: His Fifty Years in Exile. New York, 1855. 8vo., orig. purple cloth, first edition. Ximenes 37-139 1974 $45

MELVILLE, HERMAN   Israel Potter: His Fifty Years of Exile. London, 1855. Small 8vo., half calf, first English edition, very scarce, sound copy. Ximenes 36-144 1974 $100

MELVILLE, HERMAN   Israel Potter: His Fifty Years of Exile. New York, 1855. Orig. cloth, ends of spine worn, some rubbing, first edition, good copy, second printing. MacManus 224-320 1974 $110

MELVILLE, HERMAN   John Marr and Other Poems. Princeton, 1922. Orig. cloth backed boards, limited edition, fine. MacManus 224-321 1974 $37.50

MELVILLE, HERMAN   Journal of a Visit to London and the Continent. Harvard Univ., 1948. 189p. Austin 54-738 1973 $12.50

MELVILLE, HERMAN   Journal of a Visit to Europe and the Levant. Princeton Univ., 1955. 299p. Austin 54-737 1973 $17.50

MELVILLE, HERMAN   Journal Up the Straits, October 11, 1856 to May 5, 1857. New York, 1935. Orig. cloth, leather label, first edition, very fine copy. MacManus 224-322 1974 $60

MELVILLE, HERMAN   Mardi. Boni, 1925. 546p. Austin 54-739 1973 $10

MELVILLE, HERMAN   Moby Dick. New York, 1930. Biblo & Tannen 213-573 1973 $20

MELVILLE, HERMAN   Moby Dick. Garden City, 1937. Rubbed, illus. edition. Rinsland 58-52 1974 $10

MELVILLE, HERMAN   Moby Dick or The Whale. New York, 1930. Illus. by Rockwell Kent, orig. illus. cloth, spine little rubbed, first trade edition, bookplate removed, fine. MacManus 224-323 1974 $25

MELVILLE, HERMAN   Omoo. Estes, 1892. 365p., illus. Austin 54-740 1973 $8.50

MELVILLE, HERMAN   Redburn: His First Voyage. New York, 1849. Orig. cloth, stained, spine rather chipped, foxed, first American edition, second printing, fair copy. MacManus 224-323A 1974 $100

MELVILLE, HERMAN   Typee. London, 1861. 8vo., orig. purple cloth, faded spine, very nice copy, new edition. Ximenes 37-140 1974 $50

MELVILLE, HERMAN   Typee. Estes, 1892. 389p. Austin 54-741 1973 $10

MELVILLE, HERMAN   Typee. Aventino, 1931. 360p., illus. Austin 54-742 1973 $7.50

MELVILLE, HERMAN   The Works. London, 1922-24. 16 vols., 8vo., blind-stamped cloth boards, gilt, collected edition. Dawsons PM 252-694 1974 £325

MELVILLE, JAMES   The Memoirs of Sir James Melvil of Hal-Hill. 1683. Folio, contemporary sheep, first edition. Howes 186-1072 1974 £42

MELVILLE, LEWIS   An Injured Queen. 1912. 2 vols., thick 8vo., plates. Howes 186-689 1974 £5

MELVILLE, LEWIS   The Windsor Beauties. Boston, 1928. Illus. Biblo & Tannen 213-692 1973 $8.50

THE MELVILLE Book of Roundels. 1916. Large 4to., illus., quarter pigskin, top edges gilt. Thomas 32-292 1974 £80

MEMBERS of the Legislature of the State of Texas from 1846-1939. (Austin), 1939. Stiff wrappers. Jenkins 61-1568 1974 $15

MEMOIRES pou Servir A l'Histoire de Brandebourg. 1750. 12mo., contemporary calf. Dawsons PM 251-224 1974 £10

MEMOIRE sur l'Huile de Petrole en Generale, et Particulierement sur Celle de Gabian. Besiers, 1752. 4to., preserved in cloth box, rare. Schafer 10-134 1974 sFr 480

MEMOIR OF THE Life and Trial of James Mackcoull. Edinburgh, 1822. 8vo., half calf, first edition. Dawsons PM 251-286 1974 £30

MEMOIRS and Secret Chronicles of the Courts of Europe. New York & Akron, 1901. 11 vols., illus., Jap. vellum. Ballinger 1-291 1974 $35

MEMOIRS of a London Doll. New York, 1922. 12mo., cloth, illus., first edition autographed by illus. Frohnsdorff 16-542 1974 $15

MEMOIRS of a Man of Fashion. London, 1821. 3 vols., 12mo., orig. blue boards, spines quite worn, first edition, very rare. Ximenes 36-86 1974 $90

MEMOIRS of Sir Simeon Supple, Member for Rotborough. London, 1785. 8vo., disbound, first edition. Ximenes 36-162 1974 $50

MEMOIRS of the Life of Stephen Fox. London, 1717. 8vo., brown morocco, rubbed, gilt, portrait. Ximenes 35-219 1974 $17.50

MEMOIRS of the Literary and Philosophical Society of Manchester. 1824. Vol. IV, 8vo., publisher's cloth, folding plates. Bow Windows 66-462 1974 £36

MEMORANDUMS, Tables and Schedule of Articles Comprising the Outfit for a Whaling Voyage. New Bedford, n.d. 12mo., orig. wrappers, spine chipped, Ximenes 37-220 1974 $30

A MEMORIAL and Biographical History of Northern California. Chicago, 1891. 4to., leather, illus. Saddleback 14-205 1974 $75

A MEMORIAL and Biographical History of Northern California. Chicago, 1891. 4to., illus., leather. Saddleback 14-206 1974 $65

A MEMORIAL and Biographical History of Northern California. Chicago, 1891. 4to., leather, illus., dampstained. Saddleback 14-207 1974 $50

MEMORIAL Des Allies. N. P., 1926. Large folio-size sheets loose in gilt dec. board portfolio with string tie, profusely illus., lacks single sheet, scarce, very good copy. Wilson 63-468 1974 $50

A MEMORIAL OF God's Last Twenty Nine Years Wonders in England. London, 1689. Marbled boards, calf. Dawson's 424-196 1974 $50

MENCKEN, AUGUST   By the Neck. New York, (1942). Orig. binding, d.j., T.L.s. by author laid in. Butterfield 10-386 1974 $17.50

MENCKEN, HENRY LOUIS   The American Language. New York, 1919. First edition, no. 645 of 1500 copies, front hinge slightly weakened, lacking d.w., nice copy, orig. binding. Ross 86-332 1974 $40

MENCKEN, HENRY LOUIS   The Artist. Boston, 1912. 16mo., first edition, first issue, backstrip chipped, orig. binding. Butterfield 10-388 1974 $17.50

MENCKEN, HENRY LOUIS   Book of Burlesques. 1916. Clippings pasted on flyleaves and title, first edition. Allen 216-1104 1974 $10

MENCKEN, HENRY LOUIS   A Book of Prefaces. Knopf, 1922. 288 pages. Austin 54-743 1973 $7.50

MENCKEN, HENRY LOUIS   Damn! New York, 1918. Second printing, covers dull, orig. binding. Butterfield 10-391 1974 $12.50

MENCKEN, HENRY LOUIS   Europe After 8:15. Lane, 1914. First edition, 222 pages. Austin 54-745 1973 $17.50

MENCKEN, HENRY LOUIS   Europe After 8:15. New York and Toronto, 1914. Front hinge cracked, second issue, orig. binding. Butterfield 10-404 1974 $12.50

MENCKEN, HENRY LOUIS   George Bernard Shaw, His Plays. Boston & London, 1905. First edition, scarce, ink blobs on cover label and endpapers. Butterfield 10-392 1974 $15

MENCKEN, HENRY LOUIS   Heliogabalus. New York, 1920. First edition, orig. binding, shaken. Butterfield 10-403 1974 $12.50

MENCKEN, HENRY LOUIS   In Defense of Women. New York, 1918. Orig. cloth, first edition, very fine, bright copy. MacManus 224-325 1974 $40

MENCKEN, HENRY LOUIS   In Defense of Women. Knopf, 1924. 210 pages. Austin 54-744 1973 $7.50

MENCKEN, HENRY LOUIS   In Defense of Women. New York, (1928). 12mo., cloth, presentation copy, inscription in author's hand, eleventh printing. Goodspeed's 578-232 1974 $30

MENCKEN, HENRY LOUIS   A Little Book in C Major. New York, 1916. Orig. cloth, joints bit rubbed, first edition, presentation copy to Mrs. B. G. Murray, fine. MacManus 224-326 1974 $75

MENCKEN, HENRY LOUIS   A Little Book in C Major. New York, 1916. First edition, name stamp of owner on endpapers & several text pages, orig. binding. Butterfield 10-393 1974 $35

MENCKEN, HENRY LOUIS   Men Versus the Man. New York, 1910. Orig. cloth vertically ribbed, first edition, fine. MacManus 224-327 1974 $35

MENCKEN, HENRY LOUIS   Notes on Democracy. New York, (1926). 12mo., cloth, inscription in author's hand, presentation copy, second printing. Goodspeed's 578-231 1974 $25

MENCKEN, HENRY LOUIS   Notes on Democracy. New York, (1926). Orig. cloth backed boards, paper label, first edition, one of 235 numbered copies, signed by author, boxed, about fine. MacManus 224-328 1974 $100

MENCKEN, HENRY LOUIS   Notes on Democracy. New York, (1926). First printing, covers dull, orig. binding. Butterfield 10-396 1974 $15

MENCKEN, HENRY LOUIS   Prejudices. New York, (1919-21-23-24-26-27). First - Sixth series in 6 vols., series 1, 4, 5, and 6 are first editions, sixth series signed by Mencken, orig. bindings. Butterfield 10-397 1974 $75

MENCKEN, HENRY LOUIS   Prejudices. 1924-1927. Allen 216-1108 1974 $50

MENCKEN, HENRY LOUIS   Prejudices. Fifth Series. New York, (1926). Orig. cloth backed boards, paper label, first edition, one of 200 numbered copies, signed by author, fine. MacManus 224-329 1974 $125

MENCKEN, HENRY LOUIS   Selected Prejudices. New York, 1927. First issue, d.j., orig. binding. Butterfield 10-398 1974 $7.50

MENCKEN, HENRY LOUIS   Treatise on the Gods. New York, 1930. Orig. blue vellum, gilt, first edition, one of 375 numbered copies, signed by author, boxed, fine. MacManus 224-330 1974 $95

MENDEL, EMANUEL   Die Manie. 1881. 8vo., orig. green printed wrappers, first edition. Dawsons PM 249-369 1974 £24

MENDELEEF, DIMITRI IVANOVICH   The Principles of Chemistry. London, 1897. 8vo., 2 vols., orig. cloth, backs faded, illus. Gurney 66-131 1974 £20

MENDELSOHN, S.   The Polish Jews Behind the Nazi Ghetto Walls. 1942. 31p., illus. Austin 62-752 1974 $12.50

MENDELSSOHN, SIDNEY   Mendelssohn's South African Bibliography. London, 1910. 2 vols., 4to., illus., cloth. Dawsons PM 11-528 1974 £22.05

MENDELSSOHN-BARTHOLDY, F.   Letters from Italy & Switzerland. 1862-63. 2 vols., half contemporary calf gilt. Smith 193-146 1973 £6

MENDL, R. W. S.   The Appeal of Jazz. (1927). Worn dust wrapper, fine. Covent 55-1131 1974 £25

MENJOU, ADOLPHE   It Took Nine Tailors. McGraw Hill, 1948. 238p., illus. Austin 51-623 1973 $7.50

MENNIS, JOHN   Facetiae. London, (1874). 2 vols., 8vo., orig. boards, illus., worn, portrait. Bow Windows 62-615 1974 £15

MENNIS, JOHN   Facetiae. Musarum Deliciae. (1874). 2 vols., 8vo., old half morocco, marbled sides, plates, orig. woodcuts. Bow Windows 66-463 1974 £18.50

MENOCCHIO, GIOVANNI STEFANO   Commentarii Totius S. Scripturae. Avignon, 1768. 4to., 4 vols., contemporary mottled calf, gilt, worn. Bow Windows 61-607 1973 £14.50

MENOCCHIO, GIOVANNI STEFANO   De Republica Hebraeorum Libri Octo. Paris, 1648. Folio, old vellum, lacking label, woodcut initials, first edition. Howes 184-283 1973 £18

MENON, LE SIEUR   La Cuisiniere Bourgeoise Suivie de l'Office. Bruxelles, 1759. 12mo., orig. wrappers, uncut, rubbed & heavily worn. Schumann 499-70 1974 sFr 550

MENSHIKOV, ALEXANDR DANILOVICH   Memoirs Of. 1819. Small 8vo., half calf. Hill 126-167 1974 £7.50

MENZBIER, M. A.   Ptitsy Rossii. Moscow, 1918. Roy 8vo., orig. wrappers. Wheldon 129-502 1974 £5

MENZEL, K.   Die Trierer Ada-Handschrift. Leipzig, 1889. Folio, orig. half cloth, illus. Kraus B8-167 1974 $175

MENZEL, W.   History of Germany. 1852-69. 3 vols., half contemporary calf gilt, portraits. Smith 193-616 1973 £6

MERARD DE SAINT-JUST, SIMON PIERRE   Fables et Contes mis en Vers. Paris, (1794). Printed on vellum, engraved portrait inserted, 8vo., 2 parts in 1 vol., citron levant morocco, top edges gilt, others uncut, half morocco sleeve and slip-in-case, fine, Robert Hoe's copy with his bookplate. Sawyer 293-69 1974 £850

MERAT, ALBERT   Petit Poeme. Paris, 1903. Square 12mo., half cloth, orig. wrapper, uncut, first edition. L. Goldschmidt 42-305 1974 $15

MERAT, F. V.   Nouvelle Flore des Environs de Paris. Paris, 1821. 12mo., calf, second edition. Wheldon 130-1185 1974 £5

MERCATOR, G.   Cornubia, Devonia, Somersetus, Dorcestria. . . (Amsterdam, 1638). Map. Quaritch 939-174 1974 £35

MERCATOR, G.   Eboracum, Lincolnia, Derbia, Staffordia . . . . (Amsterdam, 1638). Map. Quaritch 939-175 1974 £30

MERCATOR, G.   Northumbria, Cumberlandia, et Dinelmensis Episcopatus. (Amsterdam, 1638). Map. Quaritch 939-176 1974 £35

MERCATOR, G.   Warwicum, Northamtonia, Huntingdonia, Cantabrigia . . . . (Amsterdam, 1638). Map. Quaritch 939-177 1974 £35

MERCATOR, NICOLAUS   Institutionum Astronomicarum Libri Duo. 1676. 8vo., contemporary calf, gilt, first edition. Dawsons PM 245-508 1974 £130

MERCER, DAVID   After Haggerty. n.d. Very good copy in stapled wrappers, first edition. Covent 51-1263 1973 £10

MERCER, SAMUEL A. B.   The Tell El-Amarna Tablets. Toronto, 1939. 2 vols., ltd. ed., bdgs. faded. Biblo & Tannen 210-1010 1973 $57.50

MERCHANT, WILLIAM   The Desk Set. French, 1956. 84p., paper. Austin 51-624 1973 $6.50

MERCIER, DESIRE J.   Memorial Jubilaire du Cardinal Mercier. c.1925. 4to., half morocco gilt, illus. Howes 185-1432 1974 £6.50

MERCIER, LOUIS J. A.   Le Mouvement Humaniste aux Etats-Unis. Paris, 1928. Inscribed by author, wrapper, front loose. Butterfield 10-407 1974 $10

MERCIER, LOUIS SEBASTIEN   Le Nouveau Paris. Paris, 1797. 6 vols., 8vo., contemporary mottled tan calf, gilt, rare, first edition. L. Goldschmidt 42-81 1974 $250

MERCURE de France. Paris, 1786. 7 vols., 12mo., contemporary half leather, gilt spines. Schumann 499-72 1974 sFr 180

MERCURIO, G. S.   La Commare o Riccoglitrice. Milan, 1618. 8vo., orig. paper boards. Dawsons PM 249-370 1974 £120

MERCX, LOUIS F.   Fleurs et Fleurettes. Moulins, (1846). 8vo., contemporary boards, illus., gilt. L. Goldschmidt 42-306 1974 $150

MEREDITH, GEORGE   The Amazing Marriage. 1895. Small 8vo., 2 vols., orig. cloth, signature, first edition. Quaritch 936-490 1974 £35

MEREDITH, GEORGE   The Amazing Marriage. 1895. Orig. cloth, 2 vols., English first edition. Covent 56-931 1974 £12.50

MEREDITH, GEORGE   The Amazing Marriage. Westminster, 1895. 2 vols., 8vo., orig. cloth, faded, uncut, first edition. Bow Windows 62-617 1974 £18

MEREDITH, GEORGE   The Amazing Marriage. Westminster, 1895. 2 vols., 8vo., orig. cloth, first edition. Dawsons PM 252-695 1974 £20

MEREDITH, GEORGE   As Essay On Comedy and the Uses of the Comic Spirit. (1897). Ex-library. Austin 61-696 1974 $10

MEREDITH, GEORGE   Bibliography and Various Readings. 1911. Orig. cloth, first edition. Rota 188-650 1974 £5

MEREDITH, GEORGE   Diana of the Crossways. 1885. 8vo., 3 vols., orig. cloth, first edition. Rota 189-621 1974 £30

MEREDITH, GEORGE   Evan Harrington. New York, 1860. 8vo., orig. cloth, worn, first American edition. Rota 189-620 1974 £5

MEREDITH, GEORGE   Jump to Glory Jane. 1892. Orig. dec. boards, dust soiled, limited edition. Smith 194-491 1974 £6

MEREDITH, GEORGE   Letters to Algernon Charles Swinburne and Theodore Watts-Dunton. Pretoria, 1922. First limited edition, 8vo., orig. wrappers, presentation copy by the publisher to Meredith's son, scarce, limited to 30 copies. Sawyer 293-212 1974 £120

MEREDITH, GEORGE   Letters to Various Correspondents. Pretoria, 1924. Limited to 30 copies, 8vo., orig. blue wrappers, fine, inscribed by the publisher. Sawyer 293-213 1974 £120

MEREDITH, GEORGE   Lord Ormont and His Aminta. 1894. 3 vols., first edition, crown 8vo., orig. cloth, fine, scarce, only 1500 copies issued. Broadhurst 24-809 1974 £35

MEREDITH, GEORGE   Lord Ormont and his Aminta. 1894. Crown 8vo., 3 vols., orig. cloth, fine, scarce, first edition. Broadhurst 23-807 1974 £35

MEREDITH, GEORGE   One of Our Conquerors. 1891. 3 vols., covers very slightly rubbed, first edition. Allen 216-1112 1974 $50

MEREDITH, GEORGE   Poems. London, n.d. (1851). 8vo., orig. dark green cloth, first edition, with errata slip, tipped in at end, very good copy. Ximenes 36-146 1974 $175

MEREDITH, GEORGE   The Shaving of Shagpat. London, 1856. First edition, first issue, label neatly removed, nice copy, orig. red cloth gilt, leather backed cloth box. Covent 51-1265 1973 £40

MEREDITH, GEORGE   Works. 1912. 24 vols., 8vo., half crimson calf, gilt, faded, frontispieces. Howes 186-321 1974 £90

MEREDITH, GRACE   Girl Captives of the Cheyennes. Los Angeles, 1927. Orig. cloth, illus., fine, first edition. Putnam 126-315 1974 $20

MEREDITH, OWEN PSEUD.
Please turn to
LYTTON, EDWARD ROBERT BULWER-LYTTON, 1ST EARL OF 1831-1891

MERIAN, M. S.   Dissertatio de Generatione et Metamorphosibus Insectorum Surinamensium - Dissertation sur la Generation et les Transformations des Insectes de Surinam. The Hague, 1726. Roy. folio, contemporary red French morocco, fully gilt back, hand coloured engraved plates, nice copy. Wheldon 128-1703 1973 £5,000

MERILLAT, L. A.   Veterinary Military History of the U.S. Kansas City, 1935. Orig. cloth, 2 vols., fine, inscribed, first edition. Putman 126-29 1974 $50

MERIMEE, PROSPER   Carmen. (1916). 4to., orig. red buckram
gilt, illus., plates, first edition.   Howes 185-45 1974 £12.50

MERIMEE, PROSPER   La Jaquerie. Paris, 1828. 8vo., full
tobacco brown morocco, gilt, first edition. L. Goldschmidt 42-307 1974 $225

MERIMEE, PROSPER   Notice sur les Peintures de l'Eglise de
Saint-Savin. 1845. Roy. folio, half leather, plates. Quaritch 940-180 1974
£21

MERINO DE JESU-CHRISTO, PADRE ANDRES   Escuela Paleographica.
Madrid, 1780. Folio, mottled calf, stains. Thomas 28-119 1972 £100

MERITON, GEORGE   The Praise of York-Shire Ale. York, 1697.
Small 8vo., full morocco gilt, rare, third edition. Dawsons PM 252-696
1974 £110

MERIVALE, CHARLES   History of the Romans Under the Empire.
1850. 7 vols., second edition. Allen 213-696 1973 $15

MERIVALE, JOHN HERMAN   Orlando in Roncesvalles. London, 1814. 8vo.,
orig. pink boards, spine chipped, first edition. Ximenes 36-147 1974 $27.50

MERKEL, A.   Tallahassee, a Ballad of Nova Scotia In the
Sixities. Halifax, 1945. Drawings. Hood's 103-744 1974 $12.50

MERMAN, ETHEL   Who Could Ask For Anything More. Doubleday,
1955. Austin 51-625 1973 $6.50

MERRETT, CHRISTOPHER   Pinax Rerum Naturalium Britannicarum. London, 1667. 8vo., contemporary calf, second edition. Gurney 64-152 1974
£85

MERRICK, LEONARD   The Actor-Manager. Dutton, 1919. 332p.
Austin 51-626 1973 $12.50

MERRICK, LEONARD   Mr. Bazalgette's Agent. 1888. Orig. wrappers, scarce, English first edition. Covent 56-1718 1974 £52.50

MERRIFIELD, EDWARD   The Story of the Captivity and Rescue from the
Indians of Luke Swetland. Scranton, 1915. 8vo., orig. bindings, inscribed.
Butterfield 8-495 1974 $15

MERRILL, ELMER TRUESDELL   Essays in Early Christian History. London,
1924. Biblo & Tannen 214-641 1974 $15

MERRILL, G. P.   A Treatise on Rocks. New York, 1897. 8vo.,
orig. cloth, plates. Bow Windows 64-184 1974 £6.50

MERRIMAN, H. G.   Northwest Verse. Caldwell, (1931). Cloth,
fine copy, dust wrapper, scarce, first edition. Dykes 22-116 1974 $12.50

MERRIMAN, HENRY SETON   The Slave of the Lamp. 1892. First edition,
2 vols., half title in each preceded by blank leaf, orig. light blue copy, fine.
Sawyer 293-214 1974 £63

MERRIMAN, N. J.   The Kafir, the Hottentot and the Frontier
Farmer. 1853. First edition, map, hand coloured plates, illus., 16mo., orig.
cloth, faded, good copy. Sawyer 293-11 1974 £55

MERRITT, A.   The Moon Pool. New York, 1919. First U. S.
edition, very nice copy. Covent 51-1266 1973 £5

MERRITT, WILLIAM HAMILTON   A Brief Review of the Revenue, Resources and
Expenditures of Canada, Compared With Those of the Neighboring State of New
York. St. Catharines, 1845. Orig. wrappers, with appendix. Hood's 102-
571 1974 $100

MERRITT, WILLIAM HAMILTON   A Brief Review of the Revenue Resources and
Expenditures of Canada. St. Catharines, 1845. Orig. wrappers. Hood's 104-
654 1974 $100

MERRITT, WILLIAM HAMILTON   Canada and National Service. Toronto, 1927.
Hood's 103-299 1974 $10

MERRITT, W. W.   A History of the County of Montgomery From
the Earliest Days to 1906. Red Oak, 1906. 8vo., cloth. Saddleback 14-412
1974 $20

MERRY, ROBERT   Lorenzo. 1791. 8vo., cloth, first edition.
Quaritch 936-152 1974 £6

MERRY, ROBERT   Lorenzo. London, 1791. 8vo., modern
boards, fine, first edition. Dawsons PM 252-697 1974 £15

THE MERRY Devil of Edmonton. 1897. Austin 51-1007 1973 $6.50

MERRY Little People. New York, 1885. First edition, 8vo., illus., orig.
boards with some soiling and a nick here & there, in general very nice. Current
BW9-122 1974 $35

THE MERRY Widow. Burt, 1909. 331p. Austin 51-627 1973 $7.50

MERSENNE, MARIN   Cogitata Physico Mathematica. 1644. 4to.,
woodcuts, contemporary calf, gilt, label. Zeitlin 235-152 1974 $650

MERSENNE, MARIN   Les Preludes de l'Harmonie Universelle. Paris,
1634. First edition, small 8vo., vellum. Schumann 500-28 1974 sFr 1,500

MERSENNE, MARIN   Les Preludes de l'Harmonie Universelle. Paris,
1634. First edition, small 8vo., vellum. Schumann 499-71 1974 sFr 1500

MERSENNE, MARIN   Les Questions Theologiques, Physiques, Morales,
et Mathematiques. Paris, 1634. Small 8vo., vellum, first edition. Schumann
500-27 1974 sFr 4,500

MERWIN, HENRY C.   The Life of Bret Harte. Houghton, 1911.
362p., illus., orig. ed. Austin 54-746 1973 $12.50

MERYON, CHARLES   The Etchings Of. 1921. Plates, boards,
vellum spine. Eaton Music-639 1973 £10

MERYON, CHARLES   The Etchings of Charles Meryon. 1921. 4to.,
plates, half vellum. Quaritch 940-181 1974 £15

MESICK, JANE LOUISE   The English Traveller in America, 1785-1835.
1922. Partly unopened, orig. binding. Butterfield 10-408 1974 $10

MESSAGES and Papers of the Presidents. New York, 1897. 20 vols., 8vo.,
black leather, gilt, illus, mint. Rinsland 58-926 1974 $100

MESSEL, OLIVER   Romeo and Juliet. 1936. Roy 8vo., plates,
English first edition. Covent 56-704 1974 £12.50

LES METAMORPHOSES de Lucile. Paris, 1821. Square 16mo., orig. blue
boards. Gregory 44-52 1974 $275

METAMORPHOSIS, or A Transformation of Pictures . . . for the Amusement of
Young Persons. New York, 1816. 8vo., orig. cloth, woodcuts, rare. Gregory
44-53 1974 $250

METCALF, M. M.   The Opalinid Ciliate Infusorians. 1923.
8vo., wrappers, maps. Wheldon 131-939 1974 £10

METCALF, M. M.   The Opalinid Ciliate Infusorians. 1923. 8vo.,
wrappers, maps. Wheldon 129-788 1974 £10

METCALF, R. L.   The Great Fight for Free Silver. N. P.,
1897. Illus. Jenkins 61-252 1974 $15

METCALFE, JOHN   The Smoking Leg and Other Stories. 1925.
Cloth-backed boards, English first edition. Covent 56-933 1974 £3.50

METMAN, L.   Palais de Louvre: Le Bois. Paris, n.d.
(c. 1900). Plates loose in 2 folders, crown folio, boards, cloth spines, ties, fine.
Broadhurst 24-147 1974 £10

METSCHL, JOHN   The Rudolph J. Nunnemacher Collection of
Projectile Arms. Milwaukee, 1928. 2 vols., red buckram and 1/2 black lea.
Jacobs 24-159 1974 $250

METSCHNIKOFF, ELIAS   Embryologie des Scorpions. Leipzig, 1870.
8vo., contemporary three quarter morocco, plates, first edition. Schuman
37-169 1974 $135

METSCHNIKOFF, ELIAS   Immunitat bei Infektionskrankheiten. Jena,
1902. 8vo., orig. wrappers, coloured illus. Gurney 66-132 1974 $20

METYARD, ELIZA   The Hallowed Spots of Ancient London. 1870.
8vo., orig. cloth, engravings, prize label, corners worn. Bow Windows 66-464
1974 £7.50

MEUDER, E. P.   Analysis Antimonii Physico-Chymico-Rationalis.
Dresden and Leipzig, 1738. Small 8vo., contemporary half vellum.   Schumann
35-329 1974 $85

MEURGEY, JACQUES   Les Principaux Manuscits et Peintures du
Musee Conde a Chantilly.   Paris, 1930. Folio, plates, cloth. Kraus B8-36
1974 $95

MEW, CHARLOTTE   The Farmer's Bride. 1916. Orig. cloth,
scarce, wrappers, first edition. Rota 188-652 1974 £20

MEW, CHARLOTTE   The Rambling Sailor. 1929. Orig. boards,
portrait, dust wrapper, fine, first edition. Howes 186-323 1974 £7.50

MEXIA, PEDRO   The Historie of All the Roman Emperors.
London, 1604. Folio, engraved title, old calf, rebacked; prelim. leaves missing.
Jacobs 24-160 1974 $20

MEYEN, FRANZ JULIUS FERDINAND   Neues System der Pflanzen-Physiologie.
Berlin, 1837-1839. 8vo., 3 vols., contemporary half calf, plates, illus., first
edition. Schumann 35-330 1974 $125

MEYEN, FRANZ JULIUS FERDINAND Outlines of the Geography of Plants. 1846.
8vo., new cloth, folding plate. Wheldon 128-1141 1973 £5

MEYER, CORNELIS
Please turn to
MEIJER, CORNELIS

MEYER, EDUARD   Caesars Monarchie und das Principat des
Pompejus. Stuttgart, 1922. Biblo & Tannen 214-642 1974 $20

MEYER, EDUARD   Histoire de l'Antiquite. Paris, 1914-1926.
2 bound vols. Biblo & Tannen 214-943 1974 $20

MEYER, ERNEST L.   Bucket Boy. Hastings House, 1947. 236p.
Austin 62-417 1974 $10

MEYER, ERNST VON   A History of Chemistry, From Earliest Times to
the Present Day. London, 1891. Rittenhouse 46-452 1974 $10

MEYER, ERNST VON   A History of Chemistry, From Earliest Times to
the Present Day. London, 1906. Third English edition. Rittenhouse 46-451
1974 $15

MEYER, F. W.   The Best Hardy Perennials. Liverpool, 1901.
Imperial 8vo., cloth, plates. Wheldon 129-1505 1974 £10

MEYER, FRED   Sculpture in Ceramic. New York, n.d.
4to., illus. Biblo & Tannen 213-401 1973 $8

MEYER, G. F. W.   Beitrage zur Chorographischen Kenntniss des
Flussgebiets der Innerste in den Furstenthumern Grubenhagen und Hildesheim.
Gottingen, 1822. 2 vols., 8vo., orig. limp boards, rare, plates. Wheldon
131-1333 1974 £20

MEYER, G. F. W.   Beitrage zur Chorographischen Kenntniss das
Flussgebiets der Innerste in den Furstenthumern Grubenhagen und Hildesheim.
Gottingen, 1822. 2 vols., 8vo., orig. limp boards, folding plates, rare.
Wheldon 128-1288 1973 £20

MEYER, G. F. W.   Chloris Hanoverana. 1836. 4to., old half
leather, scarce. Wheldon 130-1186 1974 £25

MEYER, H. A.   Fauna der Kieler Bucht. Leipzig, 1865-72.
2 vols., 4to., orig. boards, plates, scarce. Wheldon 131-901 1974 £45

MEYER, H. L.   Coloured Illustrations of British Birds and Their
Eggs. 1842-50. 7 vols., 8vo., contemporary half green morocco, nice copy,
hand-coloured plates, first octavo edition. Wheldon 128-520 1973 £200

MEYER, H. L.   Coloured Illustrations of British Birds and their
Eggs. London, 1842-1850. 8vo., 7 vols., contemporary green half morocco,
gilt, plates, first edition, first issue. Hammond 201-661 1974 £285

MEYER, HANS H.   Experimental Pharmacology. Philadelphia,
1926. Second English edition. Rittenhouse 46-453 1974 $10

MEYER, OSKAR EMIL   Die Kinetische Theorie der Gase. Breslau, 1877.
8vo., half morocco, gilt, ex-library. Zeitlin 235-153 1974 $57.50

MEYER, ROBERT   Autobiography. 1949. Austin 62-418 1974
$10

MEYERHOF, OTTO   Chemical Dynamics of Life Phaenomena.
Philadelphia, 1924. Rittenhouse 46-455 1974 $10

MEYERSTEIN, E. H. W.   In Time of War. 1942. 8vo., orig. cloth,
wrappers, inscription, first edition. Rota 189-624 1974 £5

MEYERSTEIN, E. H. W.   The Trireme. Oxford, (1921). Orig. boards,
English first edition. Covent 56-1934 1974 £12.50

MEYERSTEIN, E. H. W.   The Visionary and Other Poems. 1941. Wrappers, English first edition. Covent 56-1936 1974 £5.25

MEYLAN, C.   Les Hepatiques de la Suisse. Zurich, 1924.
4to., new buckram. Wheldon 130-1326 1974 £5

MEYNELL, ALICE   Ceres' Runaway and Other Essays. (n.d.). 8vo.,
orig. cloth, signed, rubbed. Bow Windows 64-605 1974 £5

MEYNELL, ALICE   The Children. New York, 1897. Dec. linen,
first U.S. edition. Covent 56-937 1974 £6.30

MEYNELL, ALICE   Collected Poems. 1913. Buckram, presentation copy, inscribed, English first edition. Covent 56-938 1974 £10

MEYNELL, ALICE   Essays. 1914. First edition, demy 8vo.,
boards, linen spine, paper printed label, uncut, limited to 250 copies on hand
made paper, presentation copy inscribed by author, fine. Broadhurst 24-810
1974 £12

MEYNELL, ALICE   A Father of Women and Other Poems. 1917.
Small 8vo., orig. grey wrappers, sewn, first edition. Quaritch 936-491 1974 £6

MEYNELL, ALICE   The Last Poems of. London, 1923. Orig.
binding, first edition, lacking d.w., unopened, near fine. Ross 87-386 1974
$10

MEYNELL, ALICE   Later Poems. London, 1902. 16mo., cloth,
first edition. Goodspeed's 578-233 1974 $10

MEYNELL, ALICE   Poems. London, 1913. Third impression, orig.
binding, covers somewhat worn, spine faded, internally fine. Ross 87-387 1974
$15

MEYNELL, ALICE   The Rhythm of Life and Other Essays. London,
1896. Third edition, bookplate, spine somewhat faded, slight staining inside
covers, orig. binding, nice. Ross 87-388 1974 $10

MEYNELL, ALICE   Selected Poems. London, 1930. Orig. binding,
lacking d.w., unopened, fine. Ross 87-389 1974 $30

MEYNELL, FRANCIS   Typography. London, 1923. Orig. blue boards,
complimentary copy. Dawson's 424-165 1974 $30

MEYNELL, GERARD P.   Pages from Books. London, 1927. 4to.,
buckram. Goodspeed's 578-496 1974 $15

MEYNELL, H.   The Meynellian Science. 1848. Small 8vo.,
orig. red morocco gilt, rare. Quaritch 939-178 1974 £30

MEYNELL, WILFRID   A Dickens Friendship. (N.P., 1931).
8vo., wrappers, trifle chipped, paper label, presentation copy, first edition.
Goodspeed's 578-234 1974 $50

MEYNIS, D.   La Montagne Sainte Lyon. Lyons, 1880.
Plates, illus., full hard grain morocco gilt. Howes 185-1435 1974 £5

MEYRICK, E.   Fauna Hawaiiensis - Macrolepidoptera.
Cambridge, 1899. 4to., unbound, plates. Wheldon 131-831 1974 £5

MEYRICK, E.   Fauna Hawaiiensis – Macrolepidoptera. 1899. 4to., half morocco. Wheldon 131-831A 1974 £7.50

MEYRICK, GORDON   The Ghost Hunters. London, 1947. 1st ed. Biblo & Tannen 210-638 1973 $10

MEYRICK, SAMUEL RUSH   The Costume of Original Inhabitants of the British Islands. (c. 1830). Folio, plates, orig. boards, morocco back, uncut. Quaritch 940-728 1974 £95

MEYRICK, SAMUEL RUSH   The Costume of the Original Inhabitants of the British Isles from the Earliest Periods to the Sixth Century; to Which is Added, That of the Gothic Nations on the Western Coasts of the Baltic. 1815. Coloured frontispiece & plates, crown folio, contemporary half morocco rubbed, first issue. Broadhurst 24-811 1974 £175

MEYRICK, SAMUEL RUSH   A Critical Enquiry Into Antient Armour. 1824. 3 vols., folio, plates, full dark blue levant morocco, gilt, fine set, first edition. Quaritch 940-699 1974 £400

MEYRICK, SAMUEL RUSH   A Critical Inquiry into Antient Armour. London, 1842. Folio, 3 vols., blue cloth gilt, fine, second edition. Dawsons PM 251-395 1974 £250

MEYRICK, SAMUEL RUSH   The Costume of Original Inhabitants of the British Islands. 1815. Folio, orig. calf. Quaritch 939-179 1974 £200

MEYRICK, SAMUEL RUSH   Engraved Illustrations of Antient Arms and Armour, from the Collection at Goodrich, Herefordshire. 1830. 2 vols., folio, plates, half red morocco, rubbed. Quaritch 940-701 1974 £65

MEYRICK, SAMUEL RUSH   Engraved Illustrations of Antient Arms and Armour. London, 1830. 2 vols., folio, frontispiece, foxed, half roan, worn. Bow Windows 62-619 1974 £65

MEYRICK, SAMUEL RUSH   The History and Antiquities of the County of Cardigan. 1810. 4to., full contemporary russia, gilt, first edition. Broadhurst 23-1473 1974 £35

MEYRICK, SAMUEL RUSH   The History and Antiquities of the County of Cardigan . . . To Which is Added a Parliamentary History, List of High Sheriffs. Brecon, 1907. Roy. 4to., publisher's half morocco, top edges gilt, illus., fine. Broadhurst 24-1472 1974 £24

MEYRICK, SAMUEL RUSH   The History and Antiquities of the County of Cardigan. 1810. First edition, demy 4to., full contemporary russia, panelled back, engraved plates, edges gilt, slight foxing of few plates, with list of subscribers, fine. Broadhurst 24-1471 1974 £35

MEYRICK, SAMUEL RUSH   Observations Upon the History of Hand Firearms and Their Apputenances. 1828. Roy. 4to., printed wrappers, scarce. Quaritch 940-700 1974 £6

MICALI, GIUSEPPE   Antichi Monementi Per Servire All. 1810. Large folio, map, plates, disbound. Bow Windows 62-620 1974 £10.50

MICALI, GIUSEPPE   Antichi Monumenti Per Servire all'Opera Intitolarta l'Italia Avanti il Dominio dei Romani. Florence, 1810. Roy. folio, plates, half rough calf. Quaritch 940-335 1974 £35

MICALORI, GIACOMO   Della Sfera Mondiale . . . Libri Quattro. 1626. 4to., old half vellum, gilt, first edition. Dawsons PM 245-510 1974 £35

MICHAEL, A. D.   British Oribatidae. 1884-88. 2 vols., 8vo., orig. cloth, plates. Wheldon 131-940 1974 £25

MICHAEL, A. D.   British Tyroglyphidae. 1901-03. 2 vols., 8vo., cloth, coloured plates, scarce. Wheldon 128-915 1973 £12

MICHAEL, A. D.   British Tyroglyphidae. 1901-03. 8vo., 2 vols., cloth, plates, scarce. Wheldon 130-880 1974 £15

MICHAEL, E.   Fuhrer fur Pilzfreunde. 1918-19. 8vo., orig. picture boards, 3 vols., illus. Wheldon 129-1289 1974 £7.50

MICHAEL, WOLFGANG   England Under George I. 1936-39. 2 vols., orig. edition. Howes 186-1074 1974 £12.50

MICHAEL SCOTUS   Please turn to SCOTT, MICHAEL

MICHAEL VRATISLAVIENSIS   Introductorium Astronomie Cracoviense Elucidans Almanach. Cracow, 1507. 4to., boards, leather spine, large woodcut diagrams, Georg Tannstetter's copy. Kraus 137-65 1974 $1,500

MICHAELSEN, W.   Die Fauna Sudwest-Australiens. Jena, 1907-30. 5 vols., 70 parts in 22, imp. 8vo., wrappers, plates, maps, complete set. Wheldon 128-219 1973 £35

MICHAUD, REGIS   Panorama de la Litterature Americaine Contemporaine. Paris, 1926. One of 200 numbered copies on velin, quarter leather, front wrapper preserved, very nice copy, scarce. Covent 51-2097 1973 £17.50

MICHAUX, F. A.   The North American Sylva. Philadelphia, 1857. Imperial 8vo., orig. blind-stamped brown morocco. Wheldon 130-45 1974 £475

MICHAUX, HENRY   Ecuador, Journal de Voyage. Paris, 1929. 12mo., orig. wrapper, uncut, first edition. L. Goldschmidt 42-308 1974 $15

MICHEL, HENRI   L'Imprimeur Colard Mansion et le 'Boccace' de la Bibliotheque d'Amiens. Paris, 1925. 4to., plates, stiff paper wrappers, spine slightly torn. Kraus B8-354 1974 $45

MICHEL, MARIUS   La Reliure Francaise Deupis l'Invention de l'Imprimerie Jusqu'a la fin du XVIIIe Siecle. Paris, 1880. Boards, orig. wrappers bound in, uncut. Kraus B8-171 1974 $75

MICHEL, MARIUS   La Reliure Francaise Depuis l'Invention de l'Imprimerie Jusqu'a la fin du XVIIIe Siecle. Paris, 1880. Large 4to., green half calf, top edges gilt, wrappers bound in, engraved frontispiece, plates. Kraus B8-170 1974 $150

MICHELET, JULES   The Bird. 1868. Cloth, illus. by Giacomelli. Eaton Music-599 1973 $5

MICHELI, PIERANTONIO   I Cinque Libri di Plante Codex Marciano. Venice, 1940. 4to., cloth, plates. Wheldon 130-1617 1974 £25

MICHELI, PIERANTONIO   I Cinque Libri di Piante Codex Marciano. Venice, 1940. 4to., cloth, coloured and plain plates. Wheldon 128-1685 1973 £25

MICHELI, PIERANTONIO   Nova Plantarum Genera. 1729. 4to., plates, modern buckram. Wheldon 129-1291 1974 £120

MICHELI, PIERANTONIO   Nova Plantarum Genera Juxta Tourneforti Methodum Disposita. Florence, 1729. 4to., contemporary calf, plates. Wheldon 131-1175 1974 £150

MICHELI, PIERANTONIO   Nova Plantarum Genera. Florence, 1729. 4to., contemporary calf, plates. Wheldon 129-942 1974 £120

MICHELINI, FAMIANO   Trattato della Direzione De Fivmi. 1700. Small 4to., contemporary vellum, boards, gilt. Zeitlin 235-154 1974 $150

MICHIGAN   Appeal, by the Convention of Michigan, to the People of the United States; With Other Documents, In Relation to the Boundary Question, Between Michigan and Ohio. Detroit, 1835. 8vo., disbound, very good copy, rare, first edition. Ximenes 37-141 1974 $275

MICHLER, N. H.   Routes from the Western Boundary of Arkansas to Santa Fe and the Valley of the Rio Grande. Washington, 1850. First edition. Jenkins 61-1649 1974 $15

MICHOTTE, E.   L'Agave, Culture et Exploitation. Paris, 1914. Roy. 8vo., wrappers, illus. Wheldon 131-1676 1974 £7.50

MICHOTTE, E.   Agaves et Fourcroyas Culture et Exploitation. Paris, 1931. Roy. 8vo., wrappers, illus., revised third edition. Wheldon 131-1677 1974 £7.50

A MID-NINETEENTH Century Italian Architects Pattern Book. c. 1860. Oblong folio, quarter roan, cloth boards, waterstained, worn. Quaritch 940-492 1974 £500

MIDDLEBROOK, LOUIS F.   History of Maritime Connecticut During the American Revolution, 1775-1783. Salem, 1925. 2 vols., partly uncut, first edition, fine. Butterfield 10-43 1974 $25

MIDDLETON, ALICIA   Life in Carolina and New England During the 19th Century. Bristol, 1929. First edition, 8vo., limited to 500 copies, portraits, mint, uncut, with the errata slip. Current BW9-395 1974 $38.50

MIDDLETON, CHRISTOPHER   A Vindication of the Conduct of Captain Christoper Middleton. London, 1743. Three quarter leather, mottled boards, foxed. Hood's 103-74 1974 $450

MIDDLETON, CONYERS   Germana Quaedum Antiquitatis Eruditae Monumenta Quibus Romanorum Veterum Ritus Varii Tam Sacri Quam Profani. 1745. Contemporary calf, engravings (some folding). Eaton Music-642 1973 £30

MIDDLETON, CONYERS   Miscellaneous Works. 1755. 5 vols., new buckram, rubber stamp, second edition. Allen 213-698 1973 $25

MIDDLETON, GEORGE   Embers. Austin 51-628 1973 $8.50

MIDDLETON, GEORGE   Tradition. Holt, 1913. 173p. Austin 51-629 1973 $8.50

MIDDLETON, J. E.   Sea Dogs and Men at Arms. New York, 1918. Autographed. Hood's 103-745 1974 $10

MIDDLETON, J. E.   Toronto's 100 Years. Toronto, 1934. Illus., bound. Hood's 103-659 1974 $20

MIDDLETON, J. J.   Grecian Remains in Italy. 1812. Folio, plates, half morocco, gilt. Quaritch 940-336 1974 £420

MIDDLETON, JESSE A.   Another Grey Ghost Book. London, 1914. 1st ed. Biblo & Tannen 210-639 1973 $15

MIDDLETON, JESSE A.   The White Ghost Book. London, 1916. Biblo & Tannen 210-640 1973 $15

MIDDLETON, RICHARD   The Day Before Yesterday. 1913. 246 pages. Austin 61-702 1974 $10

MIDDLETON, RICHARD   The Ghost Ship, and Other Stories. 1912. First edition, crown 8vo., scarce, orig. cloth, fine. Broadhurst 24-812 1974 £6

MIDDLETON, RICHARD   New Tales of Horror. London, n.d. Biblo & Tannen 210-641 1973 $12.50

MIDDLETON, T.   History of Hyde and Its Neighbourhood. Hyde, 1932. Med. 8vo., orig. cloth, illus., fine. Broadhurst 24-1473 1974 £6

MIDDLETON, THOMAS   A Tragi-Coomodie. 1778-89. 8vo., half calf. Quaritch 936-154 1974 £10

MIDDLETON, THOMAS   A Tragi-Coomodie. London, 1778. 8vo., calf, gilt, first edition. Ximenes 37-142 1974 $85

MIDDLETON, THOMAS   Works. 1885. 8 vols., buckram, ex-library, not quite uniform. Allen 216-1931 1974 $50

MIDGLEY, HARRY   Thoughts from Flanders. Belfast, 1924. 12mo., wrappers, English first edition. Covent 56-2145 1974 £5.25

MIERS, J.   Contributions to Botany. 1860-69. 4to., cloth, plates. Wheldon 129-943 1974 £20

MIERS, J.   Contributions to Botany. 1864-71. 4to., cloth. Wheldon 129-944 1974 £15

MIERS, J.   Contributions to Botany. 1864-71. Vol. 3, 4to., cloth, plates, rare. Wheldon 131-1176 1974 £15

MIERS, J.   Contributions to Botany, Vol. 3, Containing a Complete Monograph of the Menispermaceae. 1864-71. 4to., cloth, plates by author, rare. Wheldon 128-1142 1973 £12

MIERS, J.   On the Lecythidaceae. 1874. Plates. Wheldon 128-1289 1973 £5

MIFFLIN, LLOYD   At the Gates of Song. 1901. Square 8vo., orig. cloth, gilt, first English edition. Howes 185-328 1974 £5

MIGNE, J-P.   Appendix ad Saeculum X. Paris, 1853. Roy. 8vo., half vellum, labels. Howes 185-1437 1974 £6

MIGNE, J-P.   Dictionnaire des Apocryphes. Paris, 1856-58. 2 vols., thick roy. 8vo., half buckram. Howes 185-1438 1974 £7.50

MIGNE, J-P.   Scripturae Sacrae Cursus Completus. Paris, 1866-67. 21 vols., roy. 8vo., cloth. Howes 185-1441 1974 £55

MIGNE, J-P.   Theologiae Cursus Completus. Paris, 1837-45. 26 vols. in 14, thick roy. 8vo., half veluum, morocco labels. Howes 185-1442 1974 £55

MIGNET, FRANCOIS   Notices et Memoires Historiques. Paris, 1843. 2 vols., 8vo., contemporary three quarter hard grain morocco, gilt, first edition. L. Goldschmidt 42-309 1974 $27.50

MIGULA, W.   Kryptogamen-Flora von Deutschland. 1904. 8vo., half morocco, plates. Wheldon 129-2192 1974 £12

MIGULA, W.   Kryptogamen-Flora von Deutschland. (1911-12). 8vo., 2 vols., plates, orig. half morocco. Wheldon 129-1293 1974 £25

MIGULA, W.   Kryptogamen-Flora von Deutschland, Deutsch-Osterreich und der Schweiz, Band 1 Moose. Gera, 1904. 8vo., half morocco, plates, rubbed. Wheldon 131-1445 1974 £12

MIGULA, W.   Kryptogamen-Flora von Deutschland, Deutsch-Osterreich und der Schweiz, Band 3 Pilze, Teil 2 Basidiomycetes. Gera, (1911-12). 2 vols., 8vo., orig. half morocco, plates. Wheldon 131-1446 1974 £25

MILANI, MARIO   Alberto Martini. Milan, 1944. Folio, boards, illus., plates. Minters 37-194 1973 $30

MILBANKE, RALPH   Astarte: A Fragment of Truth Concerning George Gordon Byron, Sixth Lord Byron, Recorded by His Grandson. 1921. Med. 8vo., boards, linen spine, paper printed labels, uncut, good copy, one of 125 copies, engraved portraits. Broadhurst 24-267 1974 £8

MILBURN, WILLIAM HENRY   The Pioneers, Preachers and People of the Mississippi Valley. New York, 1860. 8vo., orig. bindings, first edition. Butterfield 8-314 1974 $15

MILES, ALFRED H.   The Poets and the Poetry of the Century. n.d. Faded, English first edition. Covent 56-1383 1974 £10

MILES, H. H.   The History of Canada Under French Regime, 1535-1763. Montreal, 1872. Map, browning. Hood's 103-550 1974 $22.50

MILES, W. A.   The Artifice. 1780. 8vo., cloth, first edition. Quaritch 936-155 1974 £7

MILES, W. J.   Modern Practical Farriery. (c., 1891). 4to., half calf, morocco label, plates. Bow Windows 64-186 1974 £5.50

MILEY, JOHN   The History of the Papal States. 1850. 3 vols., orig. cloth, worn, first edition. Howes 186-1075 1974 £12.50

MILEY, JOHN   Rome As It Was Under Paganism and As It Became Under the Popes. 1843. 2 vols., orig. cloth, faded, first edition. Howes 185-1448 1974 £6

MILHOUS, KATHERINE   Snow Over Bethlehem. New York, 1945. 8vo., cloth, illus. by author, fine, dust jacket, first edition. Frohnsdorff 16-546 1974 $10

THE MILITARY Costume of Turkey . . . Dedicated by Permission to His Excellency the Minister of the Ottoman Porte to His Britannic Majesty. (1818). Folio, plates, contemporary green straight grain morocco gilt. Quaritch 940-729 1974 £60

MILITARY Dictionary: English-French, French-English. Ottawa, 1945. Hood's 104-123 1974 $20

MILITARY Report on Somaliland. 1907. Small 8vo., orig. leather-backed boards, plates, maps. Howes 186-1760 1974 £5

MILITARY Society of Ireland Pamphlets. Dublin, 1892-94. 8vo., orig. wrappers. Emerald 50-598 1974 £15

MILL, H. R.   The Record of the Royal Geographical Society. London, 1930. 8vo., illus., orig. cloth, portrait. Bow Windows 62-621 1974 £5.75

MILL, JOHN STUART   A.L.S. 1869. 8vo., 3 pages. Dawsons PM 252-698 1974 £200

MILL, JOHN STUART   Auguste Comte and Positivism. 1866. 8vo., orig. cloth, second edition. Broadhurst 23-1248 1974 £8

MILL, JOHN STUART   An Examination of Sir William Hamilton's Philosophy. 1878. Orig. cloth, fifth edition. Smith 194-891 1974 £5

MILL, JOHN STUART   Nature. 1874. Large 8vo., orig. green cloth, uncut, fine, first edition. Hill 126-170 1974 £20

MILL, JOHN STUART   Nature, the Utility of Religion, and Theism. 8vo., orig. cloth, first edition. Broadhurst 23-1249 1974 £8

MILL, JOHN STUART   On Liberty. London, 1859. Orig. cloth, first edition. Gilhofer 61-49 1974 sFr. 850

MILL, JOHN STUART   The Subjection of Women. Philadelphia, 1869. Orig. cloth, signed by Dr. Mary M. Crawford. Jenkins 61-1652 1974 $45

MILL, JOHN STUART   The Subjection of Women. London, 1869. 8vo., orig. cloth, first edition. Schuman 37-170 1974 $150

MILLAIS, JOHN EVERETT   The Life and Letters of. 1900. 2 vols., dec. cloth gilt, illus., second edition. Marsden 37-307 1974 £14

MILLAIS, JOHN GUILLE   British Deer and Their Horns. 1897. Folio, orig. half morocco, illus., special limited edition. Wheldon 131-513 1974 £160

MILLAIS, JOHN GUILLE   Far Away up the Nile. 1924. Roy 8vo., cloth, plates, scarce. Wheldon 130-296 1974 £15

MILLAIS, JOHN GUILLE   Game Birds and Shooting Sketches. 1892. Folio, orig. half morocco, plates, fine. Wheldon 130-48 1974 £140

MILLAIS, JOHN GUILLE   Life and Letters of John Everett Millais. 1899. 2 vols., illus. Austin 61-703 1974 £27.50

MILLAIS, JOHN GUILLE   Magnolias. 1927. Roy. 8vo., cloth: Wheldon 129-1616 1974 £10

MILLAIS, JOHN GUILLE   The Mammals of Great Britain and N. Ireland. 1904-06. Imperial 4to., 3 vols., orig. half buckram, plates. Wheldon 130-414 1974 £150

MILLAIS, JOHN GUILLE   The Natural History of British Game Birds. 1909. Folio, orig. buckram, illus., limited edition. Wheldon 130-46 1974 £200

MILLAIS, JOHN GUILLE   The Natural History of British Game Birds. London, 1909. Folio, orig. cloth, gilt, illus., plates, first edition. Hammond 201-662 1974 £225

MILLAIS, JOHN GUILLE   The Natural History of the British Surface-Feeding Ducks. 1902. Roy 4to., orig. cloth, illus., plates, rare, limited edition. Wheldon 130-47 1974 £200

MILLAIS, JOHN GUILLE   Rhododendrons. 1917. Folio, plates, orig. buckram, limited edition. Smith 193-16 1973 £75

MILLAIS, JOHN GUILLE   Rhododendrons. 1917 & 1924. Folio, 2 vols., plates, orig. cloth, illus. Bow Windows 64-187 1974 £260

MILLAIS, JOHN GUILLE   Rhododendrons. London, 1917-24. 2 vols., folio, plates, limited edition. Traylen 79-40 1973 £195

MILLAIS, JOHN GUILLE   Rhododendrons. 1917-24. 2 vols., folio, orig. cloth, plates, very scarce. Wheldon 131-85 1974 £230

MILLAIS, JOHN GUILLE   Rhododendrons. 1917-24. 2 vols., folio, newly bound in half green morocco, gilt, coloured and collotype plates, very scarce. Wheldon 128-1615 1973 £200

MILLARD, BAILEY   History of the San Francisco Bay Region. Chicago, 1924. 3 vols., 4to., cloth, illus. Saddleback 14-193 1974 $65

MILLARD, BAILEY   History of the San Francisco Bay Region. Chicago, 1924. 3 vols., 4to., cloth, illus. Saddleback 14-194 1974 $50

MILLAY, EDNA ST. VINCENT   Aria da Capo. New York & London, (1920). Stains on edges of free endpapers, first book printing, orig. binding. Butterfield 10-410 1974 $10

MILLAY, EDNA ST. VINCENT   The Buck in the Snow and Other Poems. New York and London, 1928. First edition, front hinge cracked, orig. binding. Butterfield 10-411 1974 $7.50

MILLAY, EDNA ST. VINCENT   The Buck in the Snow and Other Poems. New York & London, 1928. Orig. cloth backed boards, first edition, one of 479 numbered copies, signed by author, very fine, boxed (defective). MacManus 224-331 1974 $60

MILLAY, EDNA SAINT VINCENT   Fatal Interview. New York, 1931. 1st ed. Biblo & Tannen 210-770 1973 $8.50

MILLAY, EDNA ST. VINCENT   Fatal Interview. New York and London, 1931. 8vo., linen-backed boards, signed, first edition. Rich Summer-83 1974 $80

MILLAY, EDNA SAINT VINCENT   Huntsman, What Quarry? New York, 1939. 1st ed. Biblo & Tannen 210-771 1973 $8.50

MILLAY, EDNA SAINT VINCENT   Huntsman, What Quarry? New York, 1939. 1st ed. Biblo & Tannen 214-757 1974 $9.50

MILLAY, EDNA ST. VINCENT   The Murder of Lidice. New York & London, 1942. First edition, wrapper. Butterfield 10-414 1974 $7.50

MILLAY, EDNA ST. VINCENT   The Murder of Lidice. New York & London, 1942. Orig. wrappers, first edition, fine. MacManus 224-332 1974 $25

MILLAY, EDNA ST. VINCENT   Poems Selected for Young People. New York & London, 1929. Orig. cloth backed boards, first edition, limited, fine, in worn box. MacManus 224-333 1974 $25

MILLAY, EDNA ST. VINCENT   The Princess Marries the Page. New York & London, 1932. Tall 8vo., type set by hand at the Golden Hind Press, ink stains on back cover, orig. binding. Butterfield 10-415 1974 $12.50

MILLAY, EDNA ST. VINCENT   Renascence and Other Poems. New York, 1917. First edition, cloth covers stained. Butterfield 10-416 1974 $10

MILLAY, EDNA ST. VINCENT   Two Slatterns and a King. 1921. Sewn, black spot on half-title. Allen 216-1512 1974 $20

MILLAY, EDNA ST. VINCENT   Wine From These Grapes, and, Epitaph for the Race of Man. New York & London, 1934. 2 separate vols. issued together, fine, limited, large paper, first edition, orig. binding. Butterfield 10-418 1974 $40

MILLER, ARTHUR   Death of a Salesman. 1952. Austin 51-630 1973 $6.50

MILLER, ARTHUR   Focus. Reynal, 1945. Austin 62-419 1974 $6.50

MILLER, C. O.   The History and Antiquities of the Doric Race. Oxford, 1830. 8vo., 2 vols., polished calf, fine, first English edition. Dawsons PM 251-57 1974 ·£15

MILLER, E.   Scripture History, With the Lives of the Most Celebrated Apostles. 1819. Third edition, engraved frontis., engraved plates, 3 vols. in 1, small 8vo., calf, rebacked with buckram, portion of old spine laid down. George's 610-519 1973 £5

MILLER, E. C.   Plant Physiology. New York, 1938. 8vo., cloth, second edition. Wheldon 131-1177 1974 $7.50

MILLER, EMILY HUNTINGTON   What Happened on a Christmas Eve.   New York, 1888. First edition, 12mo., presentation copy, orig. green cloth.   Current BW9-59 1974 $14.50

MILLER, FRANCIS TREVELYAN   Byrd's Great Adventure.   London, (1930). 8vo., maps, frontis., illus., orig. cloth.   Bow Windows 62-145 1974 £6.50

MILLER, FRANCIS TREVELYAN   Lindbergh, His Story in Pictures.   New York & London, 1929. Collector's edition, limited to 250 copies, signed by author, scarce postal item with 5 cancelled airmail stamps laid down on front endpapers.   Butterfield 10-79 1974 $75

MILLER, FRANCIS W.   Cincinnati's Beginnings.   Cincinnati, 1880. 8vo., orig. bindings.   Butterfield 8-74 1974 $17.50

MILLER, H.   The Cruise of the Betsey.   Edinburgh, 1858. Post 8vo., new cloth, first edition.   Wheldon 130-954 1974 £12

MILLER, H.   A New Selection of Psalms, Hymns, and Spiritual Songs.   Cincinnati, 1836. Leather.   Hayman 57-500 1974 $10

MILLER, H.   Northwest Water Boundary.   Seattle, 1942. Card cover.   Hood's 102-767 1974 $7.50

MILLER, H.   Sketch-book of Popular Geology.   Edinburgh, 1859. 8vo., orig. cloth.   Wheldon 129-844 1974 £5

MILLER, HENRY   The Air-Conditioned Nightmare.   (New York), 1945. Orig. cloth, first edition.   Rota 188-660 1974 £6.50

MILLER, HENRY   Black Spring.   Paris, 1936. Orig. cloth, rare, first edition.   Rota 188-657 1974 £125

MILLER, HENRY   Black Spring.   Paris, 1936. First edition, pictorial printed wrappers, with the cog design on the upper wrapper, very small inked name on free fly, wrappers lightly rubbed & chipped, else fine, very rare.   Ross 87-391 1974 $350

MILLER, HENRY   Black Spring.   Paris, 1936. First edition, picatorial printed wrappers, with cog design on upper wrapper, very small inked named on free fly, wrappers lightly rubbed & chipped, fine, very rare.   Ross 86-334 1974 $375

MILLER, HENRY   The Colossus of Maroussi.   Norfolk, 1941. First U. S. edition, cover dull, very good copy.   Covent 51-1270 1973 £6.30

MILLER, HENRY   The Cosmological Eye.   Norfolk, Conn., 1939. 1st ed.   Biblo & Tannen 210-772 1973 $10

MILLER, HENRY   The Cosmological Eye.   Norfolk, 1939. Orig. cloth, first edition.   Rota 188-658 1974 £6.50

MILLER, HENRY   The Cosmological Eye.   Norfolk, 1939. Fine, orig. binding, lacking d.w.   Ross 86-336 1974 $22.50

MILLER, HENRY   The Cosmological Eye.   Norfolk, (1939). Orig. cloth, first edition, fine, somewhat worn dust jacket.   MacManus 224-334 1974 $25

MILLER, HENRY   The Cosmological Eve.   London, 1945. First English edition, fine, d.w., orig. binding.   Ross 86-335 1974 $15

MILLER, HENRY   Max and the White Phagocytes.   Paris, 1938. Thick tan wrappers, unopened, near fine, thus rare.   Ross 87-394 1974 $160

MILLER, HENRY   Money and How It Gets that Way.   Paris, (1937). Small 4to., orig. black wrappers, gilt, first edition.   Quaritch 936-492 1974 £35

MILLER, HENRY   Money and How It Gets That Way.   Paris, (1938). Limited to 495 copies, fine, largely unopened, orig. wrappers, very scarce.   Covent 51-1274 1973 £80

MILLER, HENRY   Obscenity and the Law of Reflection.   Yonkers, 1945. Wrappers, orig. cloth.   Rota 188-661 1974 £6

MILLER, HENRY   Sunday After the War.   Norfolk, Conn., 1944. 1st ed.   Biblo & Tannen 213-575 1973 $8.50

MILLER, HENRY   Sunday After the War.   Norfolk, (1944). 8vo., orig. cloth, first edition.   Rota 189-630 1974 £5.50

MILLER, HENRY   Sunday After the War.   Norfolk, (1944). Orig. cloth, first edition, fine, dust jacket.   MacManus 224-336 1974 $30

MILLER, HENRY   Tropic of Cancer.   Paris, 1934. Small 8vo., orig. stiff paper wrappers, fine, signature, first edition.   Quaritch 936-493 1974 £500

MILLER, HENRY   Tropic of Capricorn.   Paris, 1939. 8vo., orig. wrappers, inscribed, first edition.   Dawsons PM 252-699 1974 £185

MILLER, HENRY   What Are You Going to do About Alf?   1938. 12mo., orig. cloth, wrappers, new edition.   Rota 189-629 1974 £5

MILLER, HENRY   The Wisdom of the Heart.   Norfolk, (1941). Orig. cloth, first edition, fine, dust jacket.   MacManus 224-337 1974 $25

MILLER, HENRY   The World of Sex.   N.P., (1940). Limited to 1000 copies, 8vo., very fine, laid in is small piece of paper in author's hand.   Current BW9-261 1974 $32

MILLER, HERBERT   Races, Nations and Classes.   Lippincott, 1924.   Austin 62-420 1974 $12.50

MILLER, HERBERT   The School and the Immigrant.   1916. 102p.   Austin 62-421 1974 $10

MILLER, HUGH   The Cruise of the Betsey.   Edinburgh and London, 1858. 8vo., orig. cloth, rebacked, gilt, first edition.   Hammond 201-381 1974 £12

MILLER, J. O.   Year Book of the University of Toronto, 1886-87.   Toronto, 1887. Fly leaf torn.   Hood's 102-34 1974 $30

MILLER, J. O.   Year Book of the University of Toronto.   Toronto, 1887. Torn flyleaf.   Hood's 104-42 1974 $30

MILLER, J. S.   An Illustration of the Sexual System of Linnaeus.   1779. Roy 8vo., orig. boards, plates, uncut.   Wheldon 130-1038 1974 £72

MILLER, J. S.   A Natural History of the Crinoidera.   Bristol, 1821. 4to., old half calf, worn, tinted lithographic plates.   Wheldon 128-916 1973 £50

MILLER, J. S.   A Natural History of the Crinoidea.   Bristol, 1821. 4to., contemporary half calf, plates.   Wheldon 129-789 1974 £50

MILLER, J. S.   A Natural History of the Crinoidea.   Bristol, 1821. 4to., old half calf, worn, plates.   Wheldon 131-941 1974 £50

MILLER, JAMES   Are These Things So?   London, 1740. Disbound, leaves shaved.   Dawsons PM 252-700 1974 £30

MILLER, JAMES   Harlequin-Horace.   London, 1731. 8vo., quarter morocco, frontispiece, first edition.   Dawsons PM 252-701 1974 £35

MILLER, JAMES   The Universal Passion.   London, 1737. 8vo., modern boards, first edition.   Dawsons PM 252-702 1974 £12

MILLER, KENNETH D.   The Czecho-Slovaks in America.   Doran, 1922.   Austin 62-423 1974 $12.50

MILLER, KENNETH D.   Peasant Pioneers.   1925. 200 pages, illus.   Austin 57-457 1974 $10

MILLER, KENNETH D.   Peasant Pioneers.   1925. 220p., illus.   Austin 62-424 1974 $10

MILLER, MAX   I Cover the Waterfront.   New York, 1936. Author's sgd. pres.   Biblo & Tannen 214-758 1974 $7.50

MILLER, MERLE   The Judges and the Judged.   Doubleday, 1952.   Austin 51-63- 1973 $6

MILLER, MERLE   Only You, Dick Daring.   Sloane, 1964. 350p.   Austin 54-747 1973 $7.50

MILLER, PHILIP   Figures of Beautiful, Useful and Uncommon
Plants. 1809. Folio, modern half calf. Wheldon 129-36 1974 £750

MILLER, PHILIP   Figures of the Most Beautiful, Useful and
Uncommon Plants Described in the Gardener's Dictionary. 1760. 2 vols., folio,
contemporary calf, neatly rebacked, hand coloured engraved plates. Wheldon
128-1704 1973 £850

MILLER, PHILIP   The Gardener's and Botanist's Dictionary. 1807.
Folio, contemporary half russia, plates, ninth edition. Wheldon 129-1508 1974
£60

MILLER, PHILIP   The Gardener's Dictionary. 1759. Folio,
old reversed calf, engraved plates, frontis., scarce, revised seventh edition.
Wheldon 128-1508 1973 £50

MILLER, PHILIP   Dictionnaire des Jardiniers. 1785-90. 4to.,
contemporary calf gilt. Wheldon 129-1509 1974 £100

MILLER, PHILIP   Figures of Beautiful, Useful and Uncommon
Plants Described In the Gardener's Dictionary. 1809. 2 vols. in 1, folio,
modern half calf antique, plates. Wheldon 131-86 1974 £750

MILLER, PHILIP   The Gardeners Dictionary. 1741. 2 vols.,
8vo., contemporary calf, scarce, second edition. Wheldon 131-1546 1974
£15

MILLER, PHILIP   The Gardeners Dictionary. 1752. Thick folio,
contemporary calf, plates, sixth edition. Bow Windows 64-188 1974 £42

MILLER, PHILIP   The Gardener's Dictionary. 1752. Folio, full
calf, plates, scarce, sixth edition. Wheldon 130-1442 1974 £75

MILLER, PHILIP   The Gardener's Dictionary. 1759. Folio, old
reversed calf, plates, scarce, seventh edition. Wheldon 130-1443 1974 £50

MILLER, PHILIP   The Gardener's Dictionary. 1768. Folio,
contemporary calf, plates, frontis. Wheldon 129-1507 1974 £85

MILLER, W.   Catalogue of a Pickwick Exhibition Held at the
Dickens House, 48 Doughty St., London, W.C.1. March-April, 1936. illus.,
demy 8vo., half vellum, orig. wrappers bound in, newspaper clippings inserted.
Forster 98-59 1974 £3.50

MILLER, W.   A Dictionary of English Names of Plants. 1884.
8vo., cloth. Wheldon 130-1445 1974 £7.50

MILLER, W.   What England Can Teach Us About Gardening.
New York, 1911. Crown 4to., cloth, plates. Wheldon 131-1547 1974 £5

MILLER, W. G.   Thirty Years in the Itinerancy. Milwaukee,
1875. Cloth. Hayman 57-390 1974 $12.50

MILLER, W. J. C.   Essays and Nature Studies. 1899. Roy 8vo.,
cloth, limited edition. Wheldon 130-297 1974 £5

MILLER, W. S.   The School of Musketry at Hythe. 1892.
Oblong 4to., illus., orig. cloth gilt. Quaritch 939-412 1974 £22.50

MILLER, WILLIAM   Evidence from Scripture. and History of the Second
Coming of Christ, About the Year 1843. Troy, 1836. Cloth, paper label,
inserted errata slip, backstrip needs tightening. Butterfield 10-419 1974 $45

MILLES, THOMAS   The Catalogue of Honor. 1610. Thick folio,
full sprinkled calf, rebacked, label, stained. Howes 186-1642 1974 £90

MILLET, J. F.   Millet, Raconte par lui-meme. 1921.
3 vols., 4to., plates, half morocco, orig. wrappers, limited edition. Quaritch
940-183 1974 £150

MILLIKIN, JAMES   The Life Story of. Decatur, 1926. 8vo., cloth.
Putman 126-144 1974 $10

MILLINGEN, JOHN GIDEON   Curiosities of Medical Experience.
Philadelphia, 1838. Rittenhouse 46-458 1974 $10

MILLINGTON, JOHN   An Epitome of the Elementary Principles of Natural and Experimental Philosophy. London, 1823. 8vo., orig. boards, rebacked,
plates. Dawsons PM 245-513 1974 £17

MILLIS, H. A.   The Japanese Problem in the U. S. Macmillan,
1915. Austin 62-426 1974 $22.50

MILLS, CHARLES   The History of Chivalry. London, 1826.
2 vols., contemp. calf and marbled bds. Jacobs 24-161 1974 $30

MILLS, JOHN   The Old English Gentleman. London, 1841.
3 vols., 12mo., half morocco, first edition. Dawsons PM 252-703 1974 $45

MILLS, JOHN   Stable Secrets. London, 1863. Crown 8vo.,
orig. cloth, gilt, first edition. Hammond 201-626 1974 £7.50

MILLS, S.   Lake Medad and Waterdown. Hamilton, 1937.
Card cover, illus. Hood's 103-660 1974 $25

MILLS, THOMAS   An Essay on the Utility of Blood-Letting in Fever.
Dublin, 1813. 8vo., orig. boards, rebacked, first edition. Dawsons PM 249-
371 1974 £16

MILLS, W. JOY   Historic Houses of New York. Philadelphia,
1903. Biblo & Tannen 214-29 1974 $67.50

MILLS, WILLIAM   Centennial Historical Address, Greene County
Ohio, Delivered at Xenia, July 4, 1876. 1876. Printed wrappers, worn,
chipped, some stains, very rare. Hayman 59-462 1974 $10

MILLS, WILLIAM C.   Certain Mound and Village Sites in Ohio.
Columbus, 1926. Vol. 4, cloth. Hayman 59-489 1974 $15

MILLSPAUGH, C. F.   Flora of Santa Catalina Island. 1923. 8vo.,
plates. Wheldon 130-1187 1974 £5

MILMAN, HENRY HART   History of Latin Christianity Including that of
the Popes to the Pontificate of Nicholas V. New York, 1881. 8 vols. in 4,
measurable backstrip edge and corner wear, orig. binding. Wilson 63-600D
1974 $20

MILMAN, HENRY HART   The Poetical Works. London, 1839. 3 vols.,
8vo., orig. rose cloth, fine copy, engraved frontispiece, first collected edition.
Ximenes 37-143 1974 $25

MILN, J.   Official Automobile Road Guide of Canada.
Toronto, 1930. Leather. Hood's 104-831 1974 $17.50

MILNE, ALAN ALEXANDER   By Way of Introduction. (1929). 8vo., orig.
cloth, first edition. Bow Windows 66-467 1974 £9.50

MILNE, ALAN ALEXANDER   The Christopher Robin Birthday Book. London,
(1930). 12mo., red cloth, gilt, illus., few lightly pencilled entries, very good
copy, first edition. Frohnsdorff 15-103 1974 $12.50

MILNE, ALAN ALEXANDER   The Christopher Robin Reader. New York,
(1929). 8vo., gilt, pictorial cloth, spine ends & corners worn, illus., first
edition. Frohnsdorff 16-549 1974 $10

MILNE, ALAN ALEXANDER   The Christopher Robin Story Book. New York,
(1929). 8vo., blue cloth gilt, illus., fine, orig. dust jacket, first American
edition. Frohnsdorff 15-106 1974 $15

MILNE, ALAN ALEXANDER   The Christopher Robin Story Book. London,
(1929). 8vo., blue cloth, gilt, illus., first edition. Frohnsdorff 15-105 1974
$20

MILNE, ALAN ALEXANDER   First Plays. Knopf, 1922. Austin 51-632
1973 $6.50

MILNE, ALAN ALEXANDER   Fourteen Songs from "When We Were Very
Young". London, (1936). Large 4to., boards, paper label, cloth spine, d.j.,
very good copy. Frohnsdorff 16-550 1974 $15

MILNE, ALAN ALEXANDER   A Gallery of Children. London, (1925). 4to.,
blue cloth, gilt lettering, pictorial paste label, full page color plates, very good
copy, orig. d.j., first edition. Frohnsdorff 15-102 1974 $30

MILNE, ALAN ALEXANDER   The House at Pooh Corner. London, (1928).
First edition, very good copy, slightly worn d.j., gilt pictorial cloth, top edge
gilt. Frohnsdorff 16-552 1974 $65

MILNE, ALAN ALEXANDER   The House at Pooh Corner. 1928. Limited first edition, illus. by E. H. Shepard, small 4to., buckram backed boards, uncut, unopened, dust wrappers, fine, limited to 350 copies on hand made paper, signed by author and artist. Sawyer 293-216 1974 £110

MILNE, ALAN ALEXANDER   The House at Pooh Corner. London, (1929). 8vo., full blue crushed morocco, third edition, spine ends & corners rubbed. Frohnsdorff 16-553 1974 $20

MILNE, ALAN ALEXANDER   The King's Breakfast. London, (1925). Small 4to., pictorial boards, cloth spine, first edition. Frohnsdorff 16-554 1974 $17.50

MILNE, ALAN ALEXANDER   More "Very Young" Songs. London, (1928). Large 4to., boards, paper label, cloth spine, first edition. Frohnsdorff 16-555 1974 $25

MILNE, ALAN ALEXANDER   Now We Are Six. Toronto, (1925). 8vo., orig. boards, illus., very good copy, first Canadian edition, scarce. Frohnsdorff 15-109 1974 $25

MILNE, ALAN ALEXANDER   Now We Are Six. New York, (1927). 8vo., cloth, illus., very good copy, first American edition. Frohnsdorff 15-108 1974 $15

MILNE, ALAN ALEXANDER   Now We are Six. Toronto, (1925). 8vo., pictorial boards, very good copy, first Canadian edition. Frohnsdorff 16-558 1974 $25

MILNE, ALAN ALEXANDER   Now We are Six. New York, (1927). 8vo., pictorial gilt cloth, very good copy, first American edition. Frohnsdorff 16-557 1974 $15

MILNE, ALAN ALEXANDER   Now We Are Six. London, (1927). 8vo., red cloth pictorially gilt, top edge gilt, illus., very good copy, first edition. Frohnsdorff 15-107 1974 $37.50

MILNE, ALAN ALEXANDER   Now We are Six. London, (1927). 8vo., pictorial gilt cloth, top edge gilt, very good copy, first edition. Frohnsdorff 16-556 1974 $40

MILNE, ALAN ALEXANDER   Now We Are Six. London, (1927). 12mo., cloth, dust jacket, fine, first edition. Goodspeed's 578-240 1974 $60

MILNE, ALAN ALEXANDER   A Play in 3 Acts. Putnam, 1926. 219p. Austin 51-634 1973 $7.50

MILNE, ALAN ALEXANDER   Second Plays. Knopf, 1922. Austin 51-633 1973 $7.50

MILNE, ALAN ALEXANDER   Songs from "Now We Are Six". 1927. 4to., cloth backed boards, spine little cockled, very nice copy. Covent 51-1288 1973 £6.30

MILNE, ALAN ALEXANDER   Toad of Toad Hall. New York, 1929. 8vo., pictorial boards, mint, d.j., first American edition. Frohnsdorff 16-560 1974 $15

MILNE, ALAN ALEXANDER   Toad of Toad Hall. London, (1929). 8vo., pictorial gilt cloth, top edge gilt, very fine, d.j., first edition. Frohnsdorff 16-559 1974 $25

MILNE, ALAN ALEXANDER   Two People. New York, 1931. First edition, 8vo., spine faded, else very good, with author's signature laid in. Current BW9-262 1974 $15

MILNE, ALAN ALEXANDER   Very Young Verses. London, (1929). 8vo., cloth, first edition, illus. Frohnsdorff 16-561 1974 $10

MILNE, ALAN ALEXANDER   When I Was Very Young. New York, 1930. Orig. cloth, paper label, illus., first edition, one of 842 numbered copies, signed by author, very fine. MacManus 224-338 1974 $50

MILNE, ALAN ALEXANDER   When We Were Very Young. London, (1924). 8vo., blue cloth pictorially gilt, top edge gilt, illus., third edition. Frohnsdorff 15-111 1974 $12.50

MILNE, ALAN ALEXANDER   When We Were Very Young. London, (1924). 8vo., pictorial gilt cloth, top edge gilt, very good copy, third edition. Frohnsdorff 16-562 1974 $15

MILNE, ALAN ALEXANDER   Winnie-the-Pooh. 1926. Orig. full lambskin, gilt, inscription, English first edition. Covent 56-950 1974 £35

MILNE, ALAN ALEXANDER   Winnie the Pooh. 1926. Orig. pictorial cloth gilt, illus. Smith 193-391 1973 £10

MILNE, ALAN ALEXANDER   Winnie-The-Pooh. London, (1926). 8vo., green cloth, pictorial design in gold, top edge gilt, illus., spine ends & corners rubbed, first edition. Frohnsdorff 15-112 1974 $35

MILNE EDWARDS, HENRI   A Monograph of the British Fossil Corals. 1850-72. 2 vols., 4to., half calf, plates, complete work. Wheldon 131-1048 1974 £50

MILNER, ALFRED   The Milner Papers. 1931. Large 8vo., plates, buckram, scarce. Howes 186-1077 1974 £7.50

MILNER, J.   The History . . . . of Winchester. (1798). 2 vols., 4to., half calf, plates. Quaritch 939-376 1974 £20

MILNER, T.   A Descriptive Atlas of Astronomy. (c. 1860). 4to., contemporary half morocco, rubbed, coloured plates. Bow Windows 66-468 1974 £60

MILNES, JACOB   Sectionum Conicarum Elementa Nova Methodo Demonstrata. 1712. 8vo., contemporary calf, plates, second edition. Hammond 201-882 1974 £12

MILNES, JAMES   Sectionum Conicarum Elementa Nova Methodo Demonstrata. Oxford, 1702. 8vo., contemporary mottled boards, half calf, re-backed, first edition. Dawsons PM 245-512 1974 £25

MILNES, RICHARD MONCKTON   Palm Leaves. 1844. Small 8vo., orig. plain cloth, presentation, first edition. Howes 185-330 1974 £35

MILNES, RICHARD MONCKTON   The Poems. 1838. 2 vols., contemporary half vellum gilt, first edition. Howes 185-331 1974 £35

MILTON, JOHN   A'Allegro & Il Penseroso. 1858. Roy. 8vo., vignettes, orig. cloth gilt. Smith 193-660 1973 £5

MILTON, JOHN   Areopagitica. 1907. 4to., limp vellum. Hammond 201-745 1974 £120

MILTON, JOHN   Areopagitica. 1927. 8vo., orig. parchment boards, book plate. Bow Windows 64-608 1974 £4.50

MILTON, JOHN   Comus. 1858. Engraved illus., 918 pages. Austin 61-705 1974 $10

MILTON, JOHN   Comus. (1921). 4to., dec. boards, signed. Broadhurst 23-165 1974 £75

MILTON, JOHN   Comus, A Mask. 1931. Small folio, quarter buckram over boards, gilt, illus. Hammond 201-765 1974 £75

MILTON, JOHN   Four Poems. 1933. Roy 8vo., embossed reversed calf, illus., fine. Hammond 201-768 1974 £50

MILTON, JOHN   Four Poems. 1933. Super roy 8vo., full calf, uncut, mint, limited edition. Broadhurst 23-1047 1974 £60

MILTON, JOHN   The History of Britain. London, 1695. 8vo., contemporary calf, worn. Dawsons PM 252-706 1974 £110

MILTON, JOHN   Hymn on the Morning of Christ's Nativity. 1928. Woodcut illus., initials in red supplied by hand, folio, orig. printed wrappers, fine, scarce. Sawyer 293-46 1974 £135

MILTON, JOHN   In Answer to a Book. London, 1649. 4to., calf antique, fine, rare, first edition. Dawsons PM 252-705 1974 £250

MILTON, JOHN   Letters of State. London, 1694. 12mo., contemporary calf, first edition. Dawsons PM 252-707 1974 £300

MILTON, JOHN   Literae Pseudo-Senatus Anglicani.   (London),
1676. 12mo., first? or second edition. Dawsons PM 252-708 1974 £65

MILTON, JOHN   Literare Pseudo-Senatus Anglicani. 1676.
12mo., contemporary vellum, first edition. Bow Windows 62-623 1974 £65

MILTON, JOHN   The Mask of Comus. 1937. Crown folio, parchment boards, uncut, limited edition. Broadhurst 23-1078 1974 £45

MILTON, JOHN   Masque of Comus. n.d. Illus., boxed, fine.
Austin 61-706 1974 $12.50

MILTON, JOHN   The Masque of Comus. Cambridge, n.d. Orig.
binding, illus. with water-colors, mint, orig. box, first edition. Ross 87-280
1974 $20

MILTON, JOHN   Of Reformation Touching Church Discipline In
English. 1916. Ex-library, sturdy library binding. Austin 61-707 1974 $37.50

MILTON, JOHN   Paradise Lost. London, 1688. Folio, contemporary calf, gilt. Marlborough 70-15 1974 £195

MILTON, JOHN   Paradise Lost. Birmingham, 1758. 2 vols.,
large 8vo., contemporary morocco gilt, first Baskerville edition. Dawsons PM
252-709 1974 £150

MILTON, JOHN   Paradise Lost. 1795. 3 vols., contemporary
mottled calf gilt, rubbed. Smith 194-173 1974 £6

MILTON, JOHN   Paradise Lost. London, 1817. 4 vols.,
12mo., contemporary gilt framed calf, foxing. Bow Windows 62-624 1974
£12.50

MILTON, JOHN   Paradise Lost. Boston, 1820. 16mo., full
calf, front outer hinge cracked, base of spine chipped, engraved half title.
Frohnsdorff 15-113 1974 $12.50

MILTON, JOHN   Paradise Lost. c.1870. Large 4to., plates,
contemporary half crimson morocco gilt. Howes 186-158 1974 £18

MILTON, JOHN   Paradise Lost. 1905. 4to., orig. red cloth,
plates. Smith 194-723 1974 £9

MILTON, JOHN   Paradise Lost. Liverpool, 1906. Crown 4to.,
orig. holland-backed boards, label, plates. Howes 186-35 1974 £12.50

MILTON, JOHN   Paradise Lost. 1937. Folio, half black pigskin,
uncut. Broadhurst 23-1001 1974 £150

MILTON, JOHN   Paradise Lost. Golden Cockerel Press, 1937.
F'cap folio, half black pigskin by Zaehnsdorf, top edges gilt, others uncut, one
of 200 copies, wood engravings, fine. Broadhurst 24-983 1974 £150

MILTON, JOHN   Paradise Lost. New York, 1940. Sm. 4to.,
illus. Biblo & Tannen 214-731 1974 $10

MILTON, JOHN   Paradise Lost, A Poem, In Twelve Books.
Boston, 1820. 16mo., full leather, upper joint cracked, engraved half title.
Frohnsdorff 16-565 1974 $12.50

MILTON, JOHN   Paradise Lost and Paradise Regain'd. San
Francisco, 1936. Limited Editions Club. Folio, orig. cloth backed dec. boards,
paper label, one of 1500 numbered copies, signed by illus., very fine, boxed,
illus. MacManus 224-345 1974 $35

MILTON, JOHN   Poems in English. 1926. Roy 8vo., dec. boards,
parchment spines, uncut, limited edition. Broadhurst 23-1061 1974 £50

MILTON, JOHN   Poems in English with Illustrations by William
Blake. London, 1926. 2 vols., 8vo., illus., orig. vellum backed boards,
limited. Bow Windows 62-682 1974 £60

MILTON, JOHN   Poetical Works. 1874. 3 vols., new buckram.
Allen 216-1933 1974 $30

MILTON, JOHN   Poetical Works. 1894. Demy 8vo., orig.
cloth, fine. Broadhurst 24-297 1974 £8

MILTON, JOHN   The Poetical Works Of. n.d. Thick 8vo.,
plates, contemporary morocco, gilt. Smith 193-253 1973 £5

MILTON, JOHN   Poetical Works of. 1853. 3 vols. Austin
61-708 1974 $17.50

MILTON, JOHN   Poetical Works of. 1892. 2 vols., illus.
Austin 61-709 1974 $12.50

MILTON, JOHN   Pro Popvlo Anglicano Defensio. Londini, 1651.
12mo., mottled calf, well rebacked. Thomas 32-179 1974 £60

MILTON, JOHN   The Prose Works Of. 1835. Roy. 8vo.,
contemporary tree calf, gilt, rubbed. Smith 194-360 1974 £6.50

MILTON, JOHN   The Prose Works of John Milton. London,
1848. 3 vols. Biblo & Tannen 213-795 1973 $13.50

MILTON, JOHN   The Ready and Easy Way to Estabish A Free
Commonwealth. 1915. Ex-library, sturdy library binding. Austin 61-710 1974
$37.50

MILTON, JOHN   The Tenure of Kings and Magistrates. 1911.
Ex-library, sturdy library binding, water stains. Austin 61-711 1974 $37.50

MILTON, JOHN   Works. 1863. 8 vols., buckram, ex-library.
Allen 216-1932 1974 $35

MILTON, W. W. F.   The Northwest Passage by Land, Being the
Narrative of an Expedition from the Atlantic to the Pacific. London, 1865.
Plates, color folding maps, orig. three quarter calf, fine, Charles Clifford's copy,
signed. Jenkins 61-1654 1974 $45

MILWARD, THOMAS   Peleia. London, 1763. 4to., modern wrappers,
first edition. Ximenes 37-144 1974 $45

MINCHIN, E. A.   An Introduction to the Study of the Protozoa.
(1912). 8vo., cloth, scarce. Wheldon 130-881 1974 £7.50

MINCHIN, E. A.   An Introduction to the Study of the Protozoa With
Special Reference to the Parasitic Forms. 1922. 8vo., cloth, text-figures,
scarce. Wheldon 128-917 1973 £7.50

MINER, HARRIET STEWART   Orchids, the Royal Family of Plants. Boston,
1885. Large 4to., plates. Traylen 79-41 1973 £45

MINER, J.   Jack Miner and The Birds. Chicago, 1923.
Illus. Hood's 103-370 1974 $10

MINIATURE Almanack for 1824. Boston. Old Marbled wrappers, fine, 2 3/4 X
1 7/8. Gregory 44-432 1974 $55

MINIATURES and Borders from a Flemish Horae. 1911. Small 4to., morocco
backed cloth boards, plates, portrait. Bow Windows 62-627 1974 £6

MINKMAN, J.   L'Harmonie dans l'Imprimerie Demontree par
la Pratique Decrite et Jugee en Theorie. Arnheim, 1885. Second edition, 4to.,
orig. printed wrappers, uncut. Kraus B8-355 1974 $37.50

MINKOWSKI, HERMANN   Raum und Zeit. Leipzig und Berlin, 1909. 8vo.,
orig. wrappers, frontispiece, first separate edition. Dawsons PM 245-515 1974
£265

MINNESOTA   The Debates and Proceedings of the Minnesota
Constitutional Convention. St. Paul, 1857. Three quarter brown calf, marbled
boards, leather labels. Bradley 35-248 1974 $80

MINNESOTA History. 1925. 221 pages, paper. Austin 57-459 1974
$10

MINNESOTA-Korets Norgesfaerd 1923. Minneapolis, n.d., ca. 1924. Austin
62-452 1974 $12.50

THE MINOR Jockey Club. London, n.d. 8vo., disbound, first edition.
Ximenes 35-115 1974 $50

MINOT, GEORGE RICHARDS   The History of the Insurrections in Massachusetts. Boston, 1810. 8vo., nineteenth century half calf, gilt, second edition. Hammond 201-627 1974 £16

MINSHEU, JOHN   Guide to the Tongues. 1617. Old calf, rebacked, royal copy, autograph of Sir James Edward Smith. Allen 216-463 1974 $150

MINTO, WALTER   An Inaugural Oration, On the Progress and Importance of the Mathematical Sciences. Trenton, 1787. 8vo., modern cloth, first edition. Schuman 37-171 1974 $200

MINTO, WILLIAM   Characteristics of English Poets. 1897. Austin 61-712 1974 $10

MINTORN, JOHN   The Hand-Book for Modelling Wax Flowers. London, 1844. 12mo., orig. cloth, gilt. Hammond 201-714 1974 £6

MIQUEL, F. A. G.   Monographia Generis Melocacti. Bratislava & Bonn, 1840. 4to., boards, plates. Wheldon 131-1678 1974 £25

MIRABAUD   Systeme de la Nature, ou des Loix Du Monde Physique et du Monde Moral. London, 1774. 2 vols., leather, excellent condition. Rittenhouse 46-459 1974 $60

MIRABEAU, HONORE GABRIEL RIQUETTI DE   Errotika Biblion. Paris, 1792. 8vo., half sheep, gilt, fine, second edition. L. Goldschmidt 42-82 1974 $40

MIRABEAU, HONORE GABRIEL RIQUETTI DE   Histoire Secrete. (Alencon), 1789. 2 vols., 8vo., half hard grain morocco, first edition. L. Goldschmidt 42-84 1974 $60

MIRABEAU, HONORE GABRIEL RIQUETTI DE   Histoire Secrete de la Cour de Berlin. (N.P.), 1789. 2 vols., 8vo., contemporary speckled calf, morocco labels, rare, first edition. Bow Windows 66-469 1974 £32

MIRABEAU, HONORE GABRIEL RIQUETTI DE   Histoire Secrette de la Cour de Berlin. London, 1789. 3 vols., 8vo., orig. wrapper, uncut, leather cases. L. Goldschmidt 42-83 1974 $65

MIRABEAU, HONORE GABRIEL RIQUETTI DE   Des Lettres de Cachet et des Prisons d'Etat. Hamburg, 1782. 2 vols. in 1, 8vo., contemporary half sheep, gilt, very clean copy, first edition. L. Goldschmidt 42-85 1974 $50

MIRABEAU, HONORE GABRIEL RIQUETTI DE   The Secret History of Court of Berlin. Dublin, 1789. 8vo., contemporary calf, gilt, first Dublin edition. Hammond 201-459 1974 £8.50

MIRBEAU, OCTAVE   Dingo. Paris, 1913. Roy. 8vo., half hard grain morocco, gilt, orig. wrapper, uncut, first edition. L. Goldschmidt 42-310 1974 $75

MIRBEAU, OCTAVE   Le Jardin des Supplices. Paris, 1923. Square 8vo., orig. pictorial wrapper, illus. L. Goldschmidt 42-311 1974 $25

MIRBEAU, OCTAVE   Le Journal d'une Femme de Chambre. Paris, 1900. Roy. 8vo., full cloth, uncut, orig. wrapper, first edition. L. Goldschmidt 42-312 1974 $150

MIRBEL, C. F. B. DE   Nouvelles notes sur le Cambium. Paris, 1842. 4to., old cloth, plates. Wheldon 130-1039 1974 £7.50

MIRRLEES, HOPE   Lud-in-the-Mist. 1926. Foxing, English first edition. Covent 56-1751 1974 £8.50

A MIRROR FOR the Female Sex. London, 1799. Full contemporary calf, engravings, rebacked, second edition. Dawson's 424-48 1974 $60

MISCELLANEA Curiosa. London, 1708-23-07. 3 vols., 8vo., contemporary calf, rubbed, plates, scarce, first & second editions. Traylen 79-248 1973 £75

MISSALE Romanum ex Decreto Sacrosancti Concilii Tridentini Restitutum, Pii Quinti. Rome, 1609. Thick folio, contemporary full red morocco, gilt, fine. Harper 213-111 1973 $485

MISSALE Salzburgense. Basel, 1510. Folio, orig. blind-stamped brown calf, wooden boards, woodcuts, rare, cloth box, complete copy. Harper 213-110 1973 $6500

MISSISSIPPI   Constitution and Ordinanaces of the State of... Washington, 1869. Jenkins 61-1682 1974 $12.50

MISSISSIPPI RIVER COMMISSION   Annual Report, 1882. Washington, 1883. Folding plates. Jenkins 61-1700 1974 $10

MISSISSIPPI RIVER COMMISSION   Annual Report, 1883. Washington, 1884. Folding plates. Jenkins 61-1701 1974 $12.50

MISTER, MARY   Mungo. 1818. Full page woodcuts, 12mo., orig. boards, roan spine. George's 610-535 1973 £6

MISTRAL, FREDERIC   Le Poeme du Rhone en XII Chants. Paris, 1897. 12mo., contemporary cloth, uncut, first edition. L. Goldschmidt 42-313 1974 $50

MITCHELL, DONALD G.   Avant-Propos. (1884). 12mo., broadside, inscribed by author. Goodspeed's 578-244 1974 $15

MITCHELL, DONALD G.   Dream Life. New York, 1851. 12mo., cloth, first edition. Goodspeed's 578-241 1974 $10

MITCHELL, DONALD G.   Fudge Doings. New York, 1855. 12mo., 2 vols., cloth, some foxing, first edition. Goodspeed's 578-243 1974 $10

MITCHELL, F. S.   The Birds of Lancashire. 1892. 8vo., cloth, plates, second edition. Wheldon 130-582 1974 £5

MITCHELL, JAMES M.   Detroit in History and Commerce. Detroit, 1891. Cloth. Hayman 57-491 1974 $12.50

MITCHELL, JOSEPH   McSorley's Wonderful Saloon. Duell, Sloan, Pearce, 1943. 253p. Austin 54-748 1973 $6.50

MITCHELL, MARGARET   Gone With the Wind. New York, 1936. Orig. cloth, first issue, fine, dust jacket with frayed extremities. MacManus 224-341 1974 $70

MITCHELL, ORMSBY MACKNIGHT   The Orbs of Heaven. London, (c., 1852). 8vo., orig. blue cloth, plates, illus., third edition. Dawsons PM 245-516 1974 £6

MITCHELL, SAMUEL LATHAM
Please turn to
MITCHILL, SAMUEL LATHAM

MITCHELL, SILAS WEIR   The Adventures of Francois. Century, 1898. 321 pages, first edition. Austin 54-749 1973 $10

MITCHELL, SILAS WEIR   The Adventures of Francois. Century, 1909. 32lp. Austin 54-750 1973 $6.50

MITCHELL, SILAS WEIR   The Autobiography of a Quack. Century, 1915. 31lp. Austin 54-751 1973 $6.50

MITCHELL, SILAS WEIR   Characteristics. Century, 1905. 307p. Austin 54-752 1973 $6.50

MITCHELL, SILAS WEIR   Circumstance. Century, 1902. 495p., orig. ed. Austin 54-753 1973 $7.50

MITCHELL, SILAS WEIR   Circumstance. Century, 1909. 495p. Austin 54-754 1973 $6.50

MITCHELL, SILAS WEIR   A Comedy of Conscience. Century, 1903. 129p., illus. Austin 54-755 1973 $10

MITCHELL, SILAS WEIR   Complete Poems. Century, 1914. 447p. Austin 54-756 1973 $12.50

MITCHELL, SILAS WEIR   Constance Trescot. Grosset, Dunlap, 1905. 384p. Austin 54-758 1973 $6.50

MITCHELL, SILAS WEIR   Constance Trescot. Century, 1905. 384p.
Austin 54-759 1973 $7.50

MITCHELL, SILAS WEIR   Constance Trescott. Century, 1905. 384p.,
1st ed. Austin 54-757 1973 $10

MITCHELL, SILAS WEIR   Doctor and Patient. Philadelphia, 1888.
Rittenhouse 46-464 1974 $15

MITCHELL, SILAS WEIR   Dr. North and His Friends. Century, 1900.
499p., 1st ed. Austin 54-760 1973 $7.50

MITCHELL, SILAS WEIR   Dr. North and His Friends. Century, 1915.
499p. Austin 54-761 1973 $6.50

MITCHELL, SILAS WEIR   Far in the Forest. Century, 1905. Austin 54-
762 1973 $6.50

MITCHELL, SILAS WEIR   The Guillotine Club. Century, 1910. 285p.,
illus. Austin 54-763 1973 $10

MITCHELL, SILAS WEIR   Hugh Wynne. Century, 1897. 2 vols., 306p.,
261p., orig. ed. Austin 54-764 1973 $10

MITCHELL, SILAS WEIR   Hugh Wynne. New York, 1899. Continental
edition, illus., 2 vols., orig. binding. Butterfield 10-422 1974 $8.50

MITCHELL, SILAS WEIR   Hugh Wynne. Century, 1900. 567p., illus.
Austin 54-765 1973 $6.50

MITCHELL, SILAS WEIR   Hugh Wynne. Century, 1908. 565p., illus.
Austin 54-766 1973 $7.50

MITCHELL, SILAS WEIR   Hugh Wynne. Century, 1915. 567p., illus.
Austin 54-767 1973 $6

MITCHELL, SILAS WEIR   In War Time. Century, 1905. 423 pages.
Austin 54-769 1973 $6.50

MITCHELL, SILAS WEIR   In War Time. Century, 1912. 423p., orig. ed.
Austin 54-768 1973 $7.50

MITCHELL, SILAS WEIR   John Sherwood Ironmaster. Century, 1911.
316p., orig. ed. Austin 54-770 1973 $7.50

MITCHELL, SILAS WEIR   John Sherwood Ironmaster. Century, 1911.
316p. Austin 54-771 1973 $6.50

MITCHELL, SILAS WEIR   The Red City. Century, 1908. 421p., illus.,
1st ed. Austin 54-772 1973 $10

MITCHELL, SILAS WEIR   The Red City. Century, 1909. 421p., illus.
Austin 54-773 1973 $6.50

MITCHELL, SILAS WEIR   Roland Blake. Century, 1905. 379p. Austin
54-774 1973 $6.50

MITCHELL, SILAS WEIR   Wear and Tear. Philadelphia, 1871. Fourth
edition. Rittenhouse 46-689 1974 $10

MITCHELL, SILAS WEIR   Westways. Century, 1913. 510p. Austin
54-776 1973 $6.50

MITCHELL, SILAS WEIR   Westways. Century, 1913. 510p., 1st ed.
Austin 54-775 1973 $7.50

MITCHELL, SILAS WEIR   When All the Woods Are Green. Century,
1901. 419p., orig. ed. Austin 54-777 1973 $7.50

MITCHELL, SILAS WEIR   When All the Woods are Green. Century,
1905. 419p. Austin 54-778 1973 $6.50

MITCHELL, SILAS WEIR   The Youth of Washington. Century, 1904.
290p., 1st ed. Austin 54-779 1973 $10

MITCHELL, SILAS WEIR   The Youth of Washington. Century, 1909.
292p. Austin 54-780 1973 $6.50

MITCHILL, SAMUEL LATHAM   An Oration. New York, 1793. 8vo., disbound,
first edition. Ximenes 34-194 1974 $45

MITCHILL, SAMUEL LATHAM   The Picture of New York. 1807. Orig. calf.
Austin 55-200 1973 $95

THE MITE. Grimsby, 1891. Orig. calf, gold stamped, fine, scarce, 7/8 X 3/4.
Gregory 44-433 1974 $110

MITFORD, MARY RUSSELL   Findens' Tableaux. 1841. 4to., plates,
lacks binding. Smith 193-392 1973 £5

MITFORD, MARY RUSSELL   Our Village. 1893. Crown 8vo., illus., orig.
pictorial cloth gilt, first edition. Howes 186-476 1974 £5

MITFORD, MARY RUSSELL   Our Village. 1893. Crown 8vo., orig. plain
cloth, illus., first edition. Howes 185-527 1974 £5

MITFORD, MARY RUSSELL   Our Village. London, 1893. Second edition,
12mo., pen & ink drawings, spine spoiled, top chipped, gilt dec. front cover bright
& clean, interior very fine. Current BW9-263 1974 £12.50

MITFORD, MARY RUSSELL   Our Village. 1910. 8vo., polished green calf,
foxing. Bow Windows 64-611 1974 £10.50

MITFORD, MARY RUSSELL   Recollections of a Literary Life. 1852. First
editions, 3 vols., 8vo., orig. blue cloth gilt, library labels removed from upper
covers, damp stains, very scarce. Sawyer 293-228 1974 £15.75

MITFORD, NANCY   Wigs on the Green. 1935. Inscribed, English
first edition. Covent 56-952 1974 £10

MITFORD, WILLIAM   The History of Greece. London, 1835.
12mo., 8 vols., 3/4 lea. Biblo & Tannen 213-473 1973 $57.50

MITHOBIUS, BURCHARD   Stereometria. (1544). Small 8vo., woodcuts.
Zeitlin 235-155 1974 $150

MITSUOKA, TADANARI   Ceramic Art of Japan. Japan, 1949. 12mo.,
illus., color plates. Biblo & Tannen 214-388 1974 $12.50

MITTON, G. E.   The Lost Cities of Ceylon. 1917. 8vo., orig.
cloth, maps, illus., pencilled inscription. Bow Windows 66-472 1974 $7.50

MIVART, ST. GEORGE   The Cat. New York, 1900. 8vo., cloth.
Wheldon 130-416 1974 £15

MIVART, ST. GEORGE   A Monograph of the Lories. 1896. Roy 4to.,
orig. cloth, plates. Broadhurst 23-1168 1974 £750

MIYOSHI, M.   Japanische Bergkirschen ihre Wildformen. Tokyo, 1916. Roy 8vo., cloth, plates. Wheldon 129-1617 1974 £15

MIZALDUS, ANTONIUS   Cometographia. 1549. Small 4to., old half calf,
rebacked, first edition. Dawsons PM 245-517 1974 £120

MIZALDUS, ANTONIUS   Ephemerides Aeris Perpetvae. Paris, 1554.
16mo., 19th century half calf, red edges, signature of Patrik Lord Drumond on title.
Thomas 32-325 1974 £40

MIZALDUS, ANTONIUS   Opusculorum Pars Prima. Paris, 1607. Small
8vo., modern half cloth. Schuman 37-172 1974 $85

MIZENER, ARTHUR   The Far Side of Paradise. Boston, 1951.
1st ed. Biblo & Tannen 214-707 1974 $8.50

MIZENER, ARTHUR   A Catalogue of the First Editions of Archibald
MacLeish. 1938. Wrappers. Covent 55-1061 1974 £10.50

MLLE. New York. Vols. 1-10, 1895. Austin 54-782 1973 $37.50

MOAT, LOUIS S.   Frank Leslie's Illustrated Famous Leaders. New
York, (1896). Cloth. Hayman 57-95 1974 $12.50

MOBIUS, MARTIN RICHARD   Moritz Ernst Lesser in Arbeitsgemeinschaft
mit Leopold Stelten. Berlin, Leipzig, Vienna, 1929. 4to., cloth, soiled,
plates, foxing. Minters 37-552 1973 $24

MOCATTA, FREDERIC DAVID   Catalogue of the Printed Books and Manuscripts
Forming the Library of. London, 1904. 4to., orig. boards, uncut. Dawsons
PM 10-411 1974 £10

MOCHI, UGO   African Shadows. New York, 1933. Illus.
Biblo & Tannen 214-505 1974 $10

MOCKET, RICHARD   God and the King. London, 1663. Small 4to.,
quarter calf, boards. Dawsons PM 251-287 1974 £10.50

MOCQUEREAU, ANDRE   Monographies Gregoriennes. Rome, 1910-24.
4 parts in 1 vol., buckram. Howes 185-1481 1974 £5

MOCQUEREAU, ANDRE   Le Nombre Musical Gregorien ou Rythmique
Gregorienne, Theorie et Pratique. Paris, 1908-27. 2 vols., roy. 8vo., half
morocco, buckram, scarce. Howes 185-1480 1974 £12.50

MODELES des Enfans. Paris, 1815. 16mo., orig. cloth, leather label, plates,
frontis. Gregory 44-54 1974 $27.50

MODERN American Plays. Harcourt-Brace, 1920. 544p. Austin 51-41 1973
$10

MODERN Commerce, Transport, Motoring & Aviation. c. 1935. 4to., illus.,
plates, contemporary red morocco, limited edition. Smith 193-889 1973 £5

MODERWELL, H. K.   The Theatre of Today. Lane, 1914. Illus.
Austin 51-635 1973 $10

A MODEST Enquiry Concerning the Election of the Sheriffs of London. London,
1682. Small 4to., unbound. Traylen 79-363 1973 £10

MOE, LOUIS   The Forest Party. New York, 1930. Oblong
4to., pictorial boards, cloth spine, full page color plates, first edition.
Frohnsdorff 16-567 1974 $25

MOEHLER, JOHANN-ADAM   L'Eglise est Une. Paris, 1939. Roy. 8vo.,
portrait. Howes 185-1454 1974 £5.50

MOEHLER, JOHANN-ADAM   Histoire de l'Eglise. Paris, 1868-69. 3 vols.,
half calf, morocco labels. Howes 185-1453 1974 £6.50

MOEHLMAN, CONRAD HENRY   The Catholic - Protestant Mind. 1929.
211 pages. Austin 57-462 1974 $12.50

MOET   Traite de la Culture des Renoncules, des
Oeillets, des Auricules, et des Tulips. Paris, 1754. Contemporary calf,
rubbed, second edition. Wheldon 131-1548 1974 £25

MOFFAT, JOHN S.   The Lives of Robert and Mary Moffat. 1885.
Orig. photo portraits, illus., third edition, demy 8vo., orig. cloth, frontispiece
& title browned, loosely inserted A.L.s. written by Robert Moffat. Broadhurst
24-1655 1974 £10

MOFFATT, HAROLD CHARLES   Old Oxford Plate. 1906. 4to., full morocco,
plates, English first edition. Covent 56-1653 1974 £35

MOFFATT, JAMES   The First Five Centuries of the Church.
Nashville, 1938. Biblo & Tannen 214-644 1974 $7.50

MOFFET, T.   Insectorum Sive Minimorum Animalium
Theatrum. 1634. Folio, contemporary calf, woodcuts, neatly rebacked, first
edition. Wheldon 128-770 1973 £150

MOFFET, T.   Insectorum Sive Minimorum Animalium
Theatrum. Londini, 1634. Folio, contemporary calf, woodcuts, rare first
edition. Wheldon 131-833 1974 £300

MOFFETT, MARJORIE   The One-Woman Show. French, 1935.
Austin 51-636 1973 $8.50

MOIR, D. M.   Outlines of the Ancient History of Medicine.
Edinburgh, 1831. Rebacked. Rittenhouse 46-474 1974 $50

MOISSENET, L.   Observations on the Rich Parts of the Lodes of
Cornwall. 1877. Fine. Covent 55-1317 1974 £17.50

MOIVRE, ABRAHAM DE   The Doctirne of Chances. London, 1756.
Large 4to., contemporary half calf, third edition. Schuman 37-173 1974 $175

MOLESWORTH, MRS. MARY LOUISA STEWART 1842-   Hathercourt Rectory.
London, 1878. 3 vols., library labels, rubber stamps, very good copy, somewhat
worn half calf, first edition. Covent 51-1294 1973 £15.75

MOLESWORTH, MRS. MARY LOUISA STEWART 1842-   The House that Grew.
1900. Orig. dec. cloth, plates, English first edition. Covent 56-953 1974
£10.50

MOLESWORTH, MRS. MARY LOUISA STEWART 1842-   Miss Mouse and Her
Boys. London, 1897. 8vo., pict. cloth cover, illus. Frohnsdorff 15-9 1974 $15

MOLESWORTH, MRS. MARY LOUISA STEWART 1842-   This and That. 1899.
Orig. dec. cloth, plates, English first edition. Covent 56-955 1974 £10.50

MOLESWORTH, MRS. MARY LOUISA STEWART 1842-   Uncanny Tales.
London, c. 1896. First edition. Biblo & Tannen 210-642 1973 $25

MOLEVILLE, BERTRAND DE   Private Memoirs Relative to the Last Year.
London, 1797. 3 vols., 8vo., portraits, foxing, contemporary calf. Bow
Windows 62-629 1974 £10.50

MOLEY, RAYMOND   The Hays Office. Bobbs, Merrill, 1945.
266p., illus. Austin 51-637 1973 $10

MOLIERE, JEAN BAPTISTE POQUELIN   La Comtesse D'Escarbagnas.
Amsterdam, 1689. Small 12mo., full green morocco, gilt. L. Goldschmidt
42-86 1974 $55

MOLIERE, JEAN BAPTISTE POQUELIN   Dom Garcie de Navarre. Amsterdam,
1689. Small 12mo., full green morocco, gilt. L. Goldschmidt 42-87 1974
$55

MOLIERE, JEAN BAPTISTE POQUELIN   Les Fourberies de Scapin. Amsterdam,
1693. Small 12mo., full green morocco, gilt. L. Goldschmidt 42-88 1974 $60

MOLIERE, JEAN BAPTISTE POQUELIN   Oeuvres. Paris, 1873-1900.
13 vols., 8vo., and 4to., three quarter morocco, gilt, uncut. L. Goldschmidt
42-89 1974 $260

MOLIERE, JEAN BAPTISTE POQUELIN   Oeuvres Completes de Moliere.
Paris, 1858. 3 vols., half morocco, edition Variorum, raised bands, French text.
Wilson 63-558 1974 $18.75

MOLIERE, JEAN BAPTISTE POQUELIN   The Plays of Moliere in French. Edinburgh, 1907. 8vo., orig. cloth. Bow Windows 64-612 1974 £10.50

MOLIERE, JEAN BAPTISTE POQUELIN   The Plays of. Edinburgh, 1926. Crown
8vo., 8 vols., orig. cloth, uncut. Broadhurst 23-423 1974 £15

MOLIERE, JEAN BAPTISTE POQUELIN   The Plays of . . . In French With an
English Translation. Edinburgh, 1926. 8 vols., crown 8vo., top edges gilt,
others uncut, etchings. Broadhurst 24-398 1974 £15

MOLIERE, JEAN BAPTISTE POQUELIN   Ouvres Completes de. Paris, 1868. 4to.,
contemporary quarter morocco, foxing, plates. Bow Windows 64-613 1974 £20

MOLINARUS, JOHANNES BAPTISTA   De Apoplexia Specimen. Vienna, 1753.
4to., contemporary limp boards, first edition. Schuman 35-333 1974 $85

MOLINIER, EMILE   Les Ivoires. Paris, (1896?). Folio, plates,
orig. wrapper, white buckram. Quaritch 940-465 1974 £35

MOLINIER, EMILE   Royal Interiors and Decorations of the XVIIth and
XVIIIth Centuries. Paris, London, 1902. 3 vols., plates colored by hand, thick
folio, full red morocco, top edges gilt, uncut, no. 8 of 10 copies of an "aquarelle
edition", printed for Mrs. Otto Kahn with her bookplate. Kraus B8-420 1974
$385

MOLISCH, H.   Leuchtende Pflanzen. Jena, 1912. 8vo.,
cloth, plates. Wheldon 129-945 1974 £7.50

MOLISCH, H.   Mikrochemie der Pflanze. Jena, 1923. Roy.
8vo., boards, third edition. Wheldon 131-1178 1974 £5

MOLL, HERMAN   Atlas Minor. London, n.d. 4to., contemporary
panelled calf, scarce. Traylen 79-418 1973 £200

MOLL, HERMAN   A System of Geography. London, 1701.
Folio, contemporary panelled calf. Traylen 79-434 1973 £165

MOLL, J. W.   Botanical Pen-Portraits. The Hague, 1923.
Roy. 8vo., cloth, text-figures. Wheldon 128-1686 1973 £5

MOLLER, A.   Phycomyceten und Ascomyceten. Jena, 1901.
Roy 8vo., new buckram, plates. Wheldon 129-1294 1974 £7.50

MOLLER, A.   Protobasidiomyceten. Jena, 1895-1901. 8vo.,
cloth, plates. Wheldon 129-1295 1974 £12

MOLLER, F. H.   Fungi of the Faeroes. Part 1 Basidiomycetes.
Copenhagen, 1945. Roy. 8vo., wrappers, plates. Wheldon 131-1447 1974
£7.50

MOLLOY, J. FITZGERALD   The Romance of the Irish Stage. Dodd, Mead,
1897. Austin 51-638 1973 $15

MOLNAR, FERENC   Plays. Vanguard Press, 1929. 823p. Austin
51-639 1973 $17.50

MOLTHEIN, A. W. RITTER VON   Bunte Hafnerkeramik der Renaissance.
Wien, 1906. 4to. plates, orig. cloth, limited. Bow Windows 62-630 1974
£75

MOLYNEAUX, WILLIAM   The Case of Ireland. Dublin, 1773. 8vo.,
old calf, rebacked. Quaritch 939-624 1974 £20

MOLYNEUX, WILLIAM   The Case of Ireland's Being Bound by Acts of
Parliament in England. Dublin, 1725. 2 parts in 1 vol., 12mo., half calf,
best edition. Howes 186-1079 1974 £25

MOMMSEN, T.   History of Rome. 1895. 5 vols. Allen
213-733 1973 $20

MOMMSEN, T.   The History of Rome. 1901. 5 vols.,
contemporary tree calf gilt, raised bands, revised new edition. Smith 194-35
1974 £15

MOMMSEN, T.   Roemische Geschichte. 1923-27. Vols. 1,
2, 3, & 5 only. Allen 213-734 1973 $17.50

MONACELLI, FRANCISCO   Formularium Legale Practicum Fori
Ecclesiastici. Rome, 1844. 4 parts in 3 vols., folio, vellum, labels, last &
best edition. Howes 185-1456 1974 £35

MONAGHAN, FRANK   This Was New York. New York, 1943.
Biblo & Tannen 213-76 1973 $7.50

MONAGHAN, JAY   Lincoln Bibliography: 1839-1939. Springfield,
1943. 2 vols., almost 4,000 entries. Jenkins 61-1374 1974 $15

MONAHAN, MICHAEL   Palms of Papyrus. East Orange, 1909. Orig.
silken cloth gilt, fine, revised second edition. Covent 55-1545 1974 £6.30

MONARDES, NICOLAS   Delle Cose che Vengono Portate dall'India. Venice, 1575. 8vo., contemporary limp vellum, first edition in Italian. Schumann
35-334 1974 $485

MONCEAU, HENRI LOUIS DUHAMEL DU
Please turn to
DUHAMEL DU MONCEAU, HENRI LOUIS

MONCK, GEORGE   Musarum Cantabrigiensium Threnodia.
Cantabrigiae, 1670. 4to., contemporary boards, first edition. Dawsons PM
252-711 1974 £50

MONCKTON, H. W.   Geology in the Field. 1909-10. 8vo., cloth,
plates, scarce. Wheldon 128-976 1973 £5

MONCONYS, BALTHASAR DE   Journal des Voyages. Lyon, 1665-6. 4to.,
3 vols., contemporary calf, plates, first edition. Gurney 64-154 1974 £145

MONCRIEFF, A. R. HOPE   Bonnie Scotland. 1904. 4to., orig. cloth,
plates, uncut. Bow Windows 64-614 1974 £10.50

MONCRIEFF, A. R. HOPE   The New World of Today. 1920-22. 8 vols.,
4to., illus., maps, orig. cloth. Smith 193-537 1973 £5

MONCRIEFF, A. R. HOPE   Surrey. London, 1906. 8vo., plates, map, full
polished calf, gilt, raised bands. Bow Windows 62-631 1974 £7.50

MONCRIEFF, THOMAS   Memoirs. Glasgow, 1819. 12mo., old quarter
roan. Hill 126-171 1974 £8.50

MONDELET, D.   Report of the Commissioners Appointed Under
the Lower Canada Act 4th William IV. Quebec, 1835. Orig. wrappers.
Hood's 103-780 1974 $40

MONFALCON, JEAN BAPTISTE   Histoire des Marais. Paris, 1824. 8vo.,
contemporary half calf, first edition. Schuman 37-174 1974 $80

MONGE, GASPARD   Geometrie Descriptive. Paris, (1798-99). 4to.,
half vellum, plates, first edition. Schumann 35-335 1974 $350

MONGE, GASPARD   Geometrie Descriptive. Paris, (1799). 4to.,
marbled boards, gilt, plates, first edition. Dawsons PM 245-518 1974 £55

MONIER, PIERRE   The History of Painting. 1699. 8vo., old
calf, engraved frontispiece, first edition in English. Bow Windows 64-615
1974 £140

MONIER, PIERRE   The History of Painting. London, 1699. 8vo.,
contemporary calf, rebacked, first English edition. Quaritch 940-794 1974 £60

MONK, MARIA   Awful Disclosures By . . . of the Hotel Dieu
Nunnery of Montreal. New York, c. 1855. Some internal staining, foxing,
measurably worn. Wilson 63-2 1974 $12.50

MONKHOUSE, W. COSMO   The Earlier English Water-Colour Painters.
1890. 8vo., copper plates, some dust and finger marks, slight spotting. Bow
Windows 66-473 1974 £16.75

MONKHOUSE, W. COSMO   The Earlier English Water-Colour Painters.
1890. Folio, orig. quarter morocco, illus., plates. Covent 55-111 1974 £45

MONKHOUSE, W. COSMO   The Earlier English Water-Colour Painters. 1897.
Orig. cloth, rubbed, scarce, second edition. Marsden 39-306 1974 £5

MONKHOUSE, W. COSMO   Masterpieces of English Art. 1870. Dec.
cloth gilt, illus. Covent 55-112 1974 £10.50

MONKHOUSE, W. COSMO   The Works of Sir Edwin Landseer. London,
(n.d.). 4to., illus., plates, foxing, old half morocco. Bow Windows 62-553
1974 £12

MONKSHOOD, G. F.   My Lady Ruby and John Basileon. 1899. Half
vellum, presentation copy, inscribed, English first edition. Covent 56-1719
1974 £55

MONNAIES D'Or Romaines & Byzantines. Paris, 1896. 4to., plates, orig.
wrappers. Bow Windows 62-687 1974 £6

MONOGRAPHIE de la Cathedrale D'Orvieto par N. Benois, A. Resanoff et
A. Krakau. Paris, 1877. Large folio, quarter leather, plates, foxing.
Ballinger 1-293 1974 $35

MONRAVA, ANTONIO   Desterro Critico das Falsas Anatomias. Lisbon,
1739. 4to., contemporary calf, first editions. Schumann 35-336 1974 $120

MONRO, ALEXANDER   The Anatomy of the Human Bones and Nerves.
Edinburgh, 1750. 12mo., contemporary calf. Schumann 35-337 1974 $95

MONRO, DONALD   A Treatise on Medical and Pharmaceutical Chymistry. London, 1788-90. 8vo., 4 vols., contemporary calf, labels, first edition.
Dawsons PM 245-519 1974 £65

MONRO, HAROLD   Before Dawn. 1911. 8vo., orig. cloth, first
edition. Rota 189-639 1974 £8

MONRO, HAROLD   Children of Love. 1914. Orig. cloth,
wrappers, third edition. Rota 188-679 1974 £5

MONRO, HAROLD   Real Property. London, 1922. No. 61 of edition limited to 100 copies, specially printed on linen rag paper, signed, orig. wrappers, fine, glassine jacket. Ross 86-197 1974 $70

MONRO, HAROLD   Strange Meetings. 1917. Orig. cloth, wrappers, foxed, first edition. Rota 188-680 1974 £5

MONRO, HAROLD   Strange Meetings. London, 1917. Orig. dec. grey paper covers, signed, very nice tight copy, backstrip intact, rare thus. Ross 86-198 1974 $55

MONRO, HAROLD   The Winter Solstice. London, 1928. Drawings, large paper edition, no. 205 of 500 copies, hand made paper, near mint, signed. Ross 86-199 1974 $20

MONRO, ROBERT   His Expedition. London, 1637. Small folio, contemporary calf, first edition. Dawsons PM 251-288 1974 £120

MONROE, JAMES   Message from the President Transmitting a Copy of a Convention of Navigation and Commerce Between the United States and France, Concluded and Signed at Washington, 24th June, 1822. Washington, 1823. Half Morocco, signature of Monroe pasted down. Jenkins 61-1739 1974 $55

MONROE, JOEL H.   Historical Records of a Hundred and Twenty Years, Auburn, New York. (Geneva), 1913. 12mo., cloth. Saddleback 14-583 1974 $12.50

MONROE, N. ELIZABETH   The Novel and Society. Univ. of N. Carolina, 1941. 282p. Austin 54-783 1973 $15

MONSELET, CHARLES   Oublies et Dedaignes. Paris, 1885. Roy. 8vo., orig. wrapper, uncut. L. Goldschmidt 42-314 1974 $15

MONSELET, CHARLES   Panier Fleuri. Paris, 1873. 12mo., half cloth a la Bradel, orig. wrapper, uncut, first edition. L. Goldschmidt 42-315 1974 $15

MONSELET, CHARLES   Les Poesies Completes. Paris, 1880. 12mo., full Jansenist morocco, gilt, uncut, orig. wrapper. L. Goldschmidt 42-316 1974 $45

MONSON-FITZJOHN, G. J.   Drinking Vessels of Bygone Days. (1927). 8vo., orig. cloth, first edition. Bow Windows 64-617 1974 £6.50

MONSON-FITZJOHN, G. J.   Quaint Signs of Olde Inns. 1926. 8vo., orig. cloth, uncut, illus., frontispiece. Bow Windows 66-474 1974 £5.15

MONSTRELET, ENGUERRAN DE   Volume Premier. Paris, 1572. 2 vols., early 19th century dark blue straight grain morocco, gilt. L. Goldschmidt 42-90 1974 $400

MONTAGNE, C.   Sylloge Generum Specierumque Cryptogamarum. Paris, 1856. 8vo., half calf. Wheldon 129-1411 1974 £30

MONTAGU, E. W.   Reflections On Rise & Fall of Antient Republicks. 1760. Revised second edition. Allen 213-735 1973 $10

MONTAGU, ELEANORA LOUISA   Edith of Graystock. London, 1833. 8vo., orig. stiff printed wrappers, rebacked, first edition. Ximenes 37-145 1974 $25

MONTAGU, ELIZABETH   An Essay on the Writings and Genius of Shakespeare. London, 1769. 8vo., contemporary calf, fine, first edition. Dawsons PM 252-712 1974 £60

MONTAGU, ELIZABETH   An Essay on the Writings and Genius of Shakespeare. London, 1777. Austin 51-641 1973 $25

MONTAGU, ELIZABETH   The Letters. 1809-13. 4 vols., small 8vo., contemporary calf, first edition. Howes 186-326 1974 £7.50

MONTAGU, ELIZABETH   Queen of Bluestockings. 1906. 2 vols., plates, spines slightly worn. Allen 216-2043 1974 $10

MONTAGU, G.   Ornithological Dictionary of British Birds. 1833. 8vo., cloth, second edition. Wheldon 131-662 1974 £5

MONTAGU, MARY WORTLEY   The Letters and Works. 1837. 3 vols., contemporary full calf gilt, first edition. Howes 185-335 1974 £15.50

MONTAGU, MARY WORTLEY   Letters . . . during her Travels in Europe, Asia and Africa. 1775. 12mo., contemporary sheep. Hill 126-172 1974 £6.50

MONTAGUE, CHARLES EDWARD 1867-1928   Fiery Particles. London, 1923. Orig. binding, first edition, fly leaves browned, lacking d.w., fine. Ross 87-400 1974 $15

MONTAGUE, CHARLES EDWARD 1867-1928   A Hind Let Loose. 1910. Crown 8vo., orig. cloth, presentation stamp, first edition. Howes 186-327 1974 £5

MONTAGUE, CHARLES EDWARD 1867-1928   The Right Place, a Book of Pleasures. London, 1924. Orig. binding, first edition, lacking d.w., near fine. Ross 87-401 1974 $12.50

MONTAGUE, CHARLES EDWARD 1867-1928   Rough Justice. 1926. 8vo., orig. cloth, presentation inscription, first edition. Rota 190-681 1974 £6

MONTAGUE, CHARLES EDWARD 1867-1928   Rough Justice. London, 1926. First edition, orig. binding, very nice, slightly torn and chipped d.w. Ross 87-402 1974 $12.50

MONTAGUE, CHARLES EDWARD 1867-1928   A Writer's Notes on His Trade. London, 1930. No. 360 of edition limited to 750 copies, signed by H. M. Tomlinson, owner's name in ink on fly, fine, orig. binding. Ross 87-403 1974 $20

MONTAGUE, CHARLES EDWARD 1867-1928   A Writer's Notes on His Trade. 1930. One of 750 copies, numbered & signed, quarter buckram, spine little faded, fine copy. Covent 51-2470 1973 £5.25

MONTAIGNE, MICHEL DE   The Autobiography of Michel de Montaigne. Boston, 1935. Editor's sgd. pres. Biblo & Tannen 213-796 1973 $9.50

MONTAIGNE, MICHEL DE   Les Essais. Paris, 1652. Folio, full vellum. L. Goldschmidt 42-91 1974 $250

MONTAIGNE, MICHEL DE   Essais. Paris, 1865. 4 vols., roy. 8vo., half French morocco, gilt. Howes 185-336 1974 £20

MONTAIGNE, MICHEL DE   Essais . . . Livre Premier. Bordeaux, 1580. 2 vols., small 8vo., 19th century calf, gilt back, rare first edition, with the second title in an apparently unique first state. Kraus 137-66 1974 $18,000

MONTAIGNE, MICHEL DE   The Essayes. London, 1632. Small folio, contemporary calf, third English edition. Dawsons PM 252-1097 1974 £110

MONTAIGNE, MICHEL DE   Essays. 1800. 12mo., new boards, uncut. Hill 126-173 1974 £15

MONTAIGNE, MICHEL DE   The Essays. 1902. 4 vols., portraits, orig. green buckram gilt, plates, new edition. Howes 186-328 1974 £12

MONTAIGNE, MICHEL DE   Essays. 1931. 8vo., 2 vols., brown pigskin with green morocco labels and onlays. Hammond 201-777 1974 £45

MONTALEMBERT, CHARLES   Les Moines d'Occident. Paris, 1863-77. 7 vols., full plain brown morocco, gilt. Howes 185-1457 1974 £45

MONTALEMBERT, CHARLES   The Monks of the West from St. Benedict to St. Bernard. Edinburgh, 1861-79. 7 vols., 8vo., orig. cloth, slight spotting, very good set. Bow Windows 66-475 1974 £36

MONTALEMBERT, CHARLES   The Monks of the West From St. Benedict to St. Bernard. 1896. 6 vols., orig. cloth, scarce. Howes 185-1459 1974 £25

MONTALEMBERT, CHARLES   The Monks of the West From St. Benedict to St. Bernard. 1896. 6 vols., half light brown levant morocco, fine, best English edition. Howes 185-1458 1974 £45

MONTANUS, JOANNIS BAPTISTA   Consultationum Medicarum. Basel, 1565. Folio, old calf. Schumann 35-338 1974 $135

MONTE, GUIDO UBALDI   Planisphaeriorvm Vinversalivm Theorica. 1579. 4to., contemporary limp vellum, rare, first edition. Zeitlin 235-156 1974 $250

MONTEATH, ROBERT   The Forester's Guide and Profitable Planter.
Edinburgh, 1824. 8vo., contemporary calf, plates, second edition.   Wheldon
130-1565 1974 £5

MONTEATH, ROBERT   Miscellaneous Reports on Woods and Plantations.
Dundee, 1827. 8vo., orig. boards, first edition.   Hammond 201-39 1974 £7.50

MONTEFIORE, C. G.   Rabbinic Literature and Gospel Teachings.
London, 1930.   Biblo & Tannen 214-798 1974 $10

MONTEIRO, J. J.   Angola and the River Congo. 1875. Crown
8vo., orig. cloth. Broadhurst 23-1684 1974 £25

MONTESQUIEU, CHARLES LOUIS DE SECONDAT 1689-1755   The Spirit of the
Laws. Appleton, 1900. 2 vols. Austin 54-518 1973 $17.50

MONTESQUIEU, CHALRES LOUIS DE SECONDAT   Le Temple de Gnide.
Paris, 1725. 12mo., contemporary calf, gilt, first separate edition.
L. Goldschmidt 42-92 1974 $20

MONTESQUIEU, CHARLES LOUIS DE SECONDAT 1689-1755   Oeuvres de.
1758. 3 vols., 4to., maps, contemporary speckled calf. Bow Windows 66-476
1974 £18

MONTESQUIOU, ROBERT DE   Pays des Aromates. Paris, 1900. Portrait,
illus., 4to., orig. wrappers, limited to 150 copies, presentation copy with an
autograph poem signed by author. Thomas 32-180 1974 £30

MONTESSORI, MARIA   Manuale di Pedagogia Scientifica. Naples,
1921. 8vo., illus., orig. printed wrappers, fine, unopened, first edition.
Gilhofer 61-88 1974 sFr. 200

MONTFAUCON, D. BERNARDI DE   Palaeographia Graeca. Paris, 1708.
Folio, contemporary vellum covered boards, first edition. Dawsons PM 251-
152 1974 £75

MONTGOMERY, D.   The Gaspe Coast In Focus. New York, 1940.
Photographs. Hood's 103-182 1974 $12.50

MONTGOMERY, ELIZABETH   Reminiscences of Wilmington, In Familiar
Village Tales. Philadelphia, 1851. 8vo., plates, cloth, scarce. Saddleback
14-342 1974 $35

MONTGOMERY, ELIZABETH   Reminiscences of Wilmington, In Familiar
Village Tales. Wilmington, 1872. 8vo., plates, cloth, second edition.
Saddleback 14-343 1974 $15

MONTGOMERY, FRANCES TREGO   Billy Whiskers' Adventures. 4to.,
color plates, frayed dust jacket, very good copy. Frohnsdorff 15-114A 1974
$10

MONTGOMERY, FRANCES TREGO   Billy Whiskers and the Radio. 4to.,
color plates, worn dust jacket, very good copy, first edition. Forhnsdorff
15-114B 1974 $15

MONTGOMERY, FRANCES TREGO   Billy Whiskers at Home. 4to., color
plates, repaired dust jacket, very good copy. Frohnsdorff 15-114C 1974 $10

MONTGOMERY, FRANCES TREGO   Billy Whiskers at the Fair. 4to., color
plates, frayed dust jacket, very good copy. Frohnsdorff 15-114D 1974 $10

MONTGOMERY, FRANCES TREGO   Billy Whiskers' Friends. 4to., pictorial
boards, cloth spine, color plates, edges rubbed, very good copy. Frohnsdorff
15-114E 1974 $10

MONTGOMERY, FRANCES TREGO   Billy Whiskers in an Aeroplane. (1912).
4to., pictorial boards, cloth spine, color plates, edges rubbed. Frohnsdorff
15-114F 1974 $12.50

MONTGOMERY, FRANCES TREGO   Billy Whiskers in France. (1919). 4to.,
color plates, pictorial boards, cloth spine, edges rubbed. Frohnsdorff 15-114G
1974 $10

MONTGOMERY, FRANCES TREGO   Billy Whiskers in the Movies. (1921).
4to., color plates, fine copy, orig. dust jacket. Frohnsdorff 15-114H 1974 $15

MONTGOMERY, FRANCES TREGO   Billy Whiskers Kidnaped. (1910). 4to.,
pictorial boards, cloth spine, color plates, very good copy, dust jacket.
Frohnsdorff 15-114J 1974 $10

MONTGOMERY, FRANCES TREGO   Billy Whiskers' Twins. (1911). 4to.,
pictorial boards, cloth spine, color plates, very good copy. Frohnsdorff
15-114L 1974 $10

MONTGOMERY, JAMES   Greenland and Other Poems. 1819. First
edition, demy 8vo., orig. boards, uncut, binding trifle worn, presentation copy,
inscribed by author, inserted is orig. poem 'The Dying Girls' Request' written
in author's hand. Broadhurst 24-816 1974 £75

MONTGOMERY, JAMES   Poems on the Abolition of the Slave Trade.
London, 1809. 4to., plates, German half roan. Dawsons PM 247-202
1974 £60

MONTGOMERY, JAMES   Poems on the Abolition of the Slave Trade.
London, 1809. 4to., plates, half roan. Dawsons PM 252-1098 1974 £60

MONTGOMERY, JAMES   The Poetical Works of. London, 1820.
3 vols., 12mo., contemporary straight grained calf, rebacked, morocco labels.
Bow Windows 62-636 1974 £20

MONTGOMERY, JAMES   The World Before the Flood. 1826-25. 12mo.,
contemporary half calf, rebacked, presentation copy, inscribed, seventh edition.
Covent 56-957 1974 £35

MONTGOMERY, L. M.   Anne of Avonlea. Boston, 1909. 8vo.,
gilt lettered cloth, very good copy, first edition, frontispiece. Frohnsdorff
16-580 1974 $15

MONTGOMERY, L. M.   The Golden Road. London, 1929. Third
reprint. Hood's 104-567 1974 $10

MONTGOMERY, L. M.   The Story Girl. Boston, 1911. 8vo., gilt
lettered cloth, very good copy, first edition. Frohnsdorff 16-581 1974 $10

MONTGOMERY, L. M.   The Story Girl. Boston, 1911. 1st ed.
Biblo & Tannen 210-773 1973 $12.50

MONTGOMERY, M. W.   History of Jay County. Chicago, (1864). 12mo.,
orig. cloth, scarce. Putnam 126-165 1974 $62

MONTGOMERY, RUTHERFORD   High Country. New York, The Derrydale
Press, 1938. Photos, faded red cloth covers, red leather labels, front inner
hinge loose, very good, limited to 950 copies. Current BW9-167 1974 $30

THE Months. Boston, 1878. Printed wrappers, chromolithograph illus., very
good copy, 5 3/4" X 3" when folded, extending to long strip of twelve panels.
Frohnsdorff 15-181 1974 $12

MONTI, ACHILLE   The Fundamental Data of Modern Pathology.
1900. 8vo., orig. cloth. Dawsons PM 249-375 1974 £4.50

MONTESQUIEU, CHARLES LOUIS DE SECONDAT   Considerations. Paris, 1735.
8vo., contemporary mottled calf. Dawsons PM 251-335 1974 £15

MONTORGUEIL, GEORGES   France, son Histoire. Paris, (1896-99).
3 vols., 4to., contemporary three quarter hard grain morocco, gilt, uncut, illus.
L. Goldschmidt 42-318 1974 $115

MONTREAL STAR   Wild Flowers of Canada. Montreal, 1893.
Plates, scuffed. Hood's 104-173 1974 $55

MONTREUX, NICOLAS DE   Honours Academie. 1610. Small folio, old
calf, worn but sound. Thomas 32-181 1974 £150

MONTREUX, NICOLAS DE   Honovrs Academie. London, 1610. 5 parts
in 1 vol., folio, half russia, first English edition. Dawsons PM 252-713 1974
£320

MONTUCLA, JEAN ETIENNE   Histoire des Mathematiques. Paris, 1758. Large
4to., 2 vols., contemporary calf, rebacked, plates, first edition. Schumann 35-
339 1974 $310

MONTUCLA, JEAN ETIENNE   Histoire des Mathematiques. Paris, (1799-1802).
4to., 4 vols., plates, green polished calf, fine. Zeitlin 235-157 1974 $385

MONUMENTA Historic Britannica. 1848. Thick folio, map, plates, orig.
half roan, rubbed. Howes 186-1158 1974 £35

MONYPENNY, W. F.　　　　The Life of Benjamin Disraeli.　1910-20.　8vo., 6 vols., portraits, illus., cloth.　Quaritch 936-370　1974　£16

MONYPENNY, W. F.　　　　The Life of Benjamin Disraeli.　1929. 2 vols., thick 8vo., illus., new revised edition.　Howes 186-777　1974　£15

MOODY, EDWARD C.　　　　Handbook History of the Town of York. Augusta, 1914.　8vo., cloth.　Saddleback 14-458　1974　$12.50

MOODY, GRANVILLE　　　　A Life's Retrospect.　Cincinnati, (1890).　Cloth. Hayman 57-391　1974　$10

MOODY, T. W.　　　　The Londonderry Plantation.　Belfast, 1939. 8vo., cloth boards, map.　Emerald 50-610　1974　£25

MOODY, WILLIAM V.　　　　The Faith Healer.　Macmillan, 1910.　164p. Austin 51-642　1973　$6.50

MOON, GRACE PURDIE　　　　Indian Legends in Rhyme.　New York, (1917). 4to., gilt lettered cloth, pictorial cover label, full color plates, illus. by Karl Moon, fine, orig. d.j., first edition.　Frohnsdorff 16-566　1974　$35

MOOR, JAMES　　　　On the End of Tragedy, According to Aristotle. Glasgow, 1763.　8vo., disbound, first edition.　Ximenes 37-146　1974　$75

MOORE, C. H.　　　　Character of Renaissance Architecture.　1905. Recased, blind stamp.　Allen 213-1656　1973　$12.50

MOORE, CLEMENT CLARKE　　Denslow's Night Before Christmas.　Chicago, (1902).　4to., cloth, pictorial paste label, illus. in full color by Denslow, worn, inner hinges cracked, some pencil scribbling.　Frohnsdorff 15-116　1974　$17.50

MOORE, CLEMENT CLARKE　　The Night Before Christmas.　New York, n.d. 16mo., pictorial boards, woodcuts, cloth spine, fine.　Frohnsdorff 16-569 1974　$15

MOORE, CLEMENT CLARKE　　The Night Before Christmas, or, A Visit of St. Nicholas.　New York, 1888.　4to., color plates, covers detached. Frohnsdorff 16-572　1974　$10

MOORE, CLEMENT CLARKE　　The Night Before Christmas, or, A Visit of St. Nicholas.　New York, 1888.　4to., pictorial wrappers, overstitched, colour plates.　Frohnsdorff 16-571　1974　$20

MOORE, CLEMENT CLARKE　　The Night Before Christmas.　New York, 1928. 4to., pictorial boards, cloth spine, corners rubbed, first edition thus.　Frohnsdorff 15-117　1974　$17.50

MOORE, CLEMENT CLARKE　　The Night Before Christmas.　New York, 1944. 8vo., pictorial boards, spiral bound, spine ends chipped, very good copy, with animated pictures.　Frohnsdorff 16-570　1974　$15

MOORE, CLEMENT CLARKE　　A Visit from Santa Claus.　Boston, n.d. (c. 1860).　Small 4to., wrappers, illus., spine crudley overstitched, good copy. Frohnsdorff 15-115　1974　$30

MOORE, CLEMENT CLARKE　　A Visit from St. Nicholas.　Cliffdale, 1930. 8vo., limited to 500 copies, frontis., dec. colored paper boards, very fine. Current BW9-61　1974　$18.75

MOORE, EVA　　　　Exits and Entrances.　Stokes, 1923.　259p., illus.　Austin 51-643　1973　$7.50

MOORE, E. S.　　　　Canada's Mineral Resources.　Toronto, 1929. Maps.　Hood's 103-371　1974　$10

MOORE, EDWARD　　　　Liverpool in King Charles the Second's Time. Liverpool, 1899.　Plates, map, limited to 250 copies, crown 4to., good copy, orig. cloth.　Broadhurst 24-1477　1974　£6

MOORE, EDWARD　　　　Liverpool in King Charles the Second's Time. Liverpool, 1899.　Crown 4to., orig. cloth, limited edition.　Broadhurst 23- 1475　1974　£10

MOORE, EDWARD　　　　Moores Fables for the Female Sex.　London, 1799.　12mo., contemporary calf, plates.　Dawsons PM 252-714　1974　£8

MOORE, EDWARD　　　　The World.　London, 1774.　12mo., 4 vols., contemporary calf, new edition.　Hammond 201-318　1974　£10.50

MOORE, EDWARD　　　　The World.　London, 1794.　12mo., 4 vols., contemporary tree calf, gilt, plates.　Hammond 201-319　1974　£10

MOORE, F.　　　　The Lepidoptera of Ceylon.　London, 1880-87. 3 vols., 4to., full red morocco gilt, plates.　Traylen 79-73　1973　£750

MOORE, F. A.　　　　Gems for You.　Manchester, 1850.　8vo., orig. bindings.　Butterfield 8-354　1974　$35

MOORE, F. F.　　　　The Keeper of the Robes.　(n.d.).　8vo., orig. cloth, plates.　Bow Windows 64-618　1974　£8.50

MOORE, FRANK　　　　Memorial Ceremonies at the Graves of Our Soldiers, Saturday, May 30, 1868.　Washington, 1869.　Thick 8vo., orig. binding.　Butterfield 10-170　1974　$25

MOORE, FRANK　　　　The Rebellion Record: A Diary of American Events.　New York, 1862-68.　11 vols., orig. green gilt coth.　Butterfield 10-171　1974　$110

MOORE, G.　　　　Esther Waters.　London, 1894.　8vo., faded, coloured patterned cloth, first edition.　Bow Windows 62-638　1974　£5.50

MOORE, G.　　　　In Single Strictness.　London, 1922.　8vo., orig. parchment backed boards, limited.　Bow Windows 62-639　1974　£8.50

MOORE, GEORGE　　　　Aphrodite in Aulis.　London, 1930.　No. 1749 of edition limited to 1825 copies, printed from hand set type on English hand made paper, signed, parchment boards, small dent in spine, glassine wrapper, box somewhat worn, but intact, unopened, near fine.　Ross 86-340　1974　$35

MOORE, GEORGE　　　　Aphrodite in Aulis.　London, (1930).　8vo., bookplate, vellum, limited, first edition.　Bow Windows 62-637　1974　£25

MOORE, GEORGE　　　　Aphrodite in Aulis.　1931.　Orig. cloth backed boards, label, presentation, inscription, revised edition.　Howes 186-329 1974　£10

MOORE, GEORGE　　　　Avowals.　1919.　No. 312 of edition limited to 1000 numbered copies, signed by author, vellum backed boards, fine copy. Covent 51-1296　1973　£5.25

MOORE, GEORGE　　　　Avowals.　London, 1919.　Orig. parchment backed boards, paper label, first edition, one of 1000 numbered copies, signed by author, fine, worn dust jacket.　MacManus 224-341A　1974　$25

MOORE, GEORGE　　　　The Bending of the Bough.　1900.　8vo., orig. cloth, first edition.　Rota 189-641　1974　£6

MOORE, GEORGE　　　　The Brook Kerith.　New York, 1929.　Orig. 1/2 vel. bds., 12 engravings, ltd. to 500 sgd. copies.　Jacobs 24-115　1974　$30

MOORE, GEORGE　　　　The Brook Kerith.　1929.　Roy 8vo., full vellum, uncut, signed, limited edition.　Broadhurst 23-733　1974　£25

MOORE, GEORGE　　　　The Brook Kerith.　1929.　Roy. 8vo., full vellum, uncut, orig. broad slip in case, limited to 375 copies, engravings by Stephen Gooden, signed by author & artist.　Broadhurst 24-689　1974　£25

MOORE, GEORGE　　　　The Brook Kerith.　London, 1929.　Engravings by Stephen Gooden, no. 301 of edition limited to 375 copies, printed on hand made paer from hand set type, signed by author & artist, vellum covers foxed, torn box, internally fine.　Ross 86-208　1974　$50

MOORE, GEORGE　　　　The Coming of Gabrielle.　London, 1920. Orig. 1/2 vel. bds., soiled, ltd. to 1000 copies, sgd. by author.　Jacobs 24-112 1974　$10

MOORE, GEORGE　　　　The Coming of Gabrielle.　London, 1920.　No. 303 of edition limited to 1000 copies, signed, quarter vellum, unopened, d.w. somewhat faded, fine.　Ross 86-341　1974　$35

MOORE, GEORGE　　　　A Communication to My Friends.　1933.　One of 1000 numbered copies, quarter morocco, very good copy, first edition.　Covent 51-1298　1973　£5.25

MOORE, GEORGE   A Communication to My Friends. London, 1933.
No. 574 of edition limited to 1000 copies, quarter morocco, d.w. slightly soiled &
chipped, near mint. Ross 86-209 1974 $35

MOORE, GEORGE   Elick and Soracha. New York, 1926. 8vo.,
signed, limited edition. Emerald 50-618 1974 £6.50

MOORE, GEORGE   Fragments from Heloise & Abelard. 1921.
Wrappers, very good copy, with errata. Covent 51-1301 1973 £5.25

MOORE, GEORGE   Hail and Farewell. London, 1911. 3 vols.,
1st ed. Jacobs 24-111 1974 $35

MOORE, GEORGE   Hail and Farewell. New York, 1925.
2 vols., 8vo., cloth boards. Emerald 50-616 1974 £8.50

MOORE, GEORGE   Hail and Farewell. I Ave - II Salve - III Vale.
London, 1911-12-(14). 3 vols., 12mo., cloth, first edition. Goodspeed's
578-257 1974 $15

MOORE, GEORGE   Heloise and Abelard. New York, 1921. Orig.
1/2 vel. bds., 2 vols., ltd. to 1250 sets. Jacobs 24-113 1974 $20

MOORE, GEORGE   Impressions and Opinions. London, 1891.
12mo., cloth, first edition, first issue. Goodspeed's 578-249 1974 $15

MOORE, GEORGE   Impressions and Opinions. 1891. Orig.
blue cloth, ex-library. Rota 188-687 1974 £8.50

MOORE, GEORGE   Letters from. New York, 1929. Signed,
numbered, cloth backed boards, mint. Covent 55-1109 1974 £15.75

MOORE, GEORGE   The Making of an Immortal. New York, 1927.
No. 407 of edition limited to 1240 copies, signed, protected by tissue wrapper,
orig. binding, unopened, fine. Ross 86-342 1974 $17.50

MOORE, GEORGE   Memoirs of My Dead Life. 1921. Half
parchment, signed, dust wrapper. Rota 188-689 1974 £5

MOORE, GEORGE   Memoirs of My Dead Life. London, 1921. No.
204 of edition limited to 1030 copies, printed on hand made paper from hand set
type, signed, parchment covers slightly faded, bookplate, fine. Ross 86-343
1974 $30

MOORE, GEORGE   Modern Painting. 1893. 8vo., orig. cloth,
first edition. Rota 190-682 1974 £10

MOORE, GEORGE   Moore Versus Harris. Chicago, 1925. Square
12mo., wrappers, first American edition. Covent 55-1110 1974 £8.50

MOORE, GEORGE   The Passing of the Essenes. 1930. Full
parchment, signed, fine, slipcase. Rota 188-691 1974 £5

MOORE, GEORGE   Peronnik the Fool. 1933. 4to., full vellum,
uncut, signed, limited edition. Broadhurst 23-736 1974 £25

MOORE, GEORGE   Peronnik the Fool. 1933. Engravings, globe
4to., full vellum, uncut, limited to 525 copies, signed by author & artist, illus.
by Stephen Gooden, fine. Broadhurst 24-692 1974 £25

MOORE, GEORGE   Pure Poetry. 1924. One of 1250 numbered
copies, vellum backed boards, fine, d.w., first edition. Covent 51-1304 1973
£6.30

MOORE, GEORGE   Spring Days. 1888. 371 pages. Austin
61-720 1974 $12.50

MOORE, GEORGE   A Story-Teller's Holiday. 1918. 8vo., orig.
parchment backed boards, fine. Bow Windows 64-619 1974 £18

MOORE, GEORGE   A Story Teller's Holiday. 1928. 2 vols., med.
8vo., marbled boards, cloth spine, very fine, frayed dust wrappers, first ordinary
edition. Broadhurst 24-400 1974 £5

MOORE, GEORGE   The Talking Pine. Paris, 1931. Tall 8vo.,
orig. cloth, first edition. Rota 189-644 1974 £6

MOORE, GEORGE   Ulick and Soracha. New York, 1926. Orig.
1/2 vel. bds., ltd. to 1250 numbered and signed copies. Jacobs 24-114 1974 $10

MOORE, GEORGE   Ulick and Soracha. London, 1926. No. 153
of edition limited to 1250 copies, japon vellum, signed, near mint, d.w., orig.
binding. Ross 86-210 1974 $25

MOORE, GEORGE   The Untilled Field. 1903. Crown 8vo.,
orig. scarlet cloth, gilt, first edition. Howes 186-331 1974 £7.50

MOORE, GEORGE   The Untilled Field. London, 1903. Orig. cl.,
1st ed. Jacobs 24-110 1974 $25

MOORE, GEORGE   The Use of the Body in Relation to the Mind.
New York, 1849. Small 8vo., half leather, first American edition. Schuman
37-175 1974 $50

MOORE, GEORGE H.   Washington as an Angler. New York, 1887.
12mo., orig. bds. Jacobs 24-24 1974 $30

MOORE, HANNAH W.   Ellen Ramsay. 1824. 12mo., 3 vols., contemporary half calf, fine. Hill 126-197 1974 £50

MOORE, HENRY   Shelter Sketch Book. (1945). 8vo., orig.
cloth, first edition. Rota 190-683 1974 £6.50

MOORE, JACOB BAILEY   Astounding Facts in the Life of a Clergyman.
Manchester, 1863. 8vo., printed wrapper. Butterfield 8-355 1974 $15

MOORE, JACOB BAILEY   Lives of the Governors of New Plymouth and
Massachusetts Bay. Boston, 1851. Orig. binding, ornate gilt backstrip. Butterfield 10-374 1974 $12.50

MOORE, JAMES   History of the Cooper Shop Volunteer Refreshment
Saloon. Philadelphia, 1866. Jenkins 61-2156 1974 $10

MOORE, JAMES   Kilpatrick and Our Cavalry. New York,
1865. Inscribed, orig. binding. Butterfield 10-172 1974 $27.50

MOORE, JAMES   A Narrative of the Campaign of the British Army
in Spain. 1809. 8vo., contemporary half calf, corners worn, folding plans,
third edition. Bow Windows 66-479 1974 £15

MOORE, JAMES   A Narrative of the Campaign of the British Army
in Spain. London, 1809. 4to., contemporary calf, gilt, second edition. Hammond 201-614 1974 £20

MOORE, JONAS   A Mathematical Compendium. 1681. 12mo.,
contemporary calf, worn. Zeitlin 235-158 1974 $225

MOORE, JOSEPH   Birman Empire. London, 1825-26. 4 parts,
folio, orig. wrappers, plates. Traylen 79-530 1973 £220

MOORE, JULIA A.   The Sentimental Song Book. Cleveland, 1877.
16mo., orig. bindings, portrait. Butterfield 8-291 1974 $25

MOORE, MARIANNE   The Pangolin and Other Verse. London, 1936.
Edition limited to 120 copies, contains inscription on fly, dec. paper covered bds.,
pristine condition, drawings, heavy dec. paper wrapper, rare. Ross 87-407
1974 $400

MOORE, MARIANNE   Poems. London, 1921. Orig. sewn dec. paper
wrappers, mint, scarce, additional heavy paper wrapper, first edition. Ross
87-409 1974 $300

MOORE, MARIANNE   Poems. London, 1921. Orig. sewn dec. paper
wrappers, inscription by author, corrections in author's hand, mint, protected by
Manila envelope. Ross 86-345 1974 $750

MOORE, MARIANNE   Poems. London, 1921. Orig. sewn dec. paper
wrappers, inscription written by author on fly, corrections in author's hand, mint,
protected by Manila envelope with author's name & address. Ross 87-408 1974
$750

MOORE, MARIANNE   Selected Poems. London, 1935. Inscribed
in author's hand, small autobiographical articles by author laid in, pristine
condition, yellow d.w., additional outer wrapper of heavy dec. paper. Ross
87-410 1974 $150

MOORE, MARIANNE   Selected Poems. London, 1935. Inscription in author's hand, small news article by author laid in, pristine condition, yellow d.w., additional outer wrapper of heavy dec. paper. Ross 86-346 1974 $200

MOORE, MARIANNE   What Are Years. New York, 1941. Orig. cloth, first edition. Rota 188-693 1974 £10

MOORE, NICHOLAS   The Glass Tower. (1945). 8vo., black dec. boards, dust-wrapper, presentation inscription, first edition. Quaritch 936-496 1974 £28

MOORE, NORMAN   The History of St. Bartholomew's Hospital. London, 1918. 2 vols., thick 4to., illus., orig. cloth, faded. Bow Windows 62-640 1974 £16.50

MOORE, OLIVE   Repentance at Leisure. New York, 1930. 8vo., orig. cloth, dust wrapper, first edition. Rota 189-645 1974 £5

MOORE, S.   The Proceeding to the Coronation of their Majesties King William and Queen Mary. 1689. Morocco case. Quaritch 939-492 1974 £180

MOORE, TEX   The West. (Wichita Falls), 1935. Wrapper, from Ramon Adams' Library, scarce. Jenkins 61-1762 1974 $20

MOORE, THOMAS   A Bibliographical Hand-List of the First Editions Of. Dublin, 1934. 8vo., wrappers. Quaritch 936-497 1974 £5

MOORE, THOMAS   The Clematis as a Garden Flower. 1872. 8vo., orig. cloth, plates. Wheldon 131-1549 1974 £12

MOORE, THOMAS   The History of Ireland from the Earliest Kings of the Realm Down to Its Last Chief. (n.d.). 4 vols., 8vo., orig. cloth, vignette titles, slight spotting. Bow Windows 66-481 1974 £5

MOORE, THOMAS   Illustrations of Orchidaceous Plants. 1857. Large 8vo., half dark green morocco, hand-coloured plates. Wheldon 128-1705 1973 £250

MOORE, THOMAS   Intercepted Letters. London, 1813. 8vo., contemporary calf, rebacked, fourth edition. Dawsons PM 252-715 1974 £10

MOORE, THOMAS   The Life and Death of Lord Edward Fitzgerald. Paris, 1831. Crown 8vo., contemporary half French morocco. Howes 186-190 1974 £5.50

MOORE, THOMAS   Life, Letters and Journals of Lord Byron. 1838. Roy. 8vo., contemporary diced calf gilt. Howes 186-66 1974 £6.50

MOORE, THOMAS   Love of the Angels. 1823. New buckram. Allen 216-885 1974 $10

MOORE, THOMAS   The Loves of the Angels. London, 1823. 8vo., orig. boards, label, first edition. Dawsons PM 252-716 1974 £23

MOORE, THOMAS   The Loves of the Angels. London, 1823. 8vo., orig. boards, rebacked, first edition. Hammond 201-320 1974 £25

MOORE, THOMAS   Memoirs of the Life of the Right Honourable Richard Brinsley Sheridan. 1825. 4to., contemporary blue morocco, gilt, first edition. Quaritch 936-577 1974 £30

MOORE, THOMAS   Memoirs of a Life of Rt. Hon. Richard Brinsely Sheridan. 1853. 2 vols., half morocco. Allen 216-2286 1974 $15

MOORE, THOMAS   Moore's Irish Melodies. London, n.d. 4to., illus., gilt. Emerald 50-622 1974 £7.50

MOORE, THOMAS   Nature-Printed British Ferns. 1863. 2 vols., 8vo., orig. cloth, gilt, plates. Wheldon 131-1448 1974 £50

MOORE, THOMAS   The Octavo Nature-Printed British Ferns. 1859. 2 vols., orig. red cloth, Vol. 1 unstitched, Vol. 2 some pages unstitched. Eaton Music-646 1973 £30

MOORE, THOMAS   Poetical Works, Collected By Himself. 1854. 10 vols., crown 8vo., orig. cloth. Howes 185-339 1974 £16

MOORE, THOMAS   The Poetical Works of the Late Thomas Little, Esq. London, 1801. 8vo., modern calf, first edition, very good clean copy, scarce. Ximenes 36-151 1974 $100

MOORE, THOMAS   A Popular History of the British Ferns. 1862. Crown 8vo., orig. cloth, plates, new edition. Wheldon 131-1449 1974 £5

MOORE, THOMAS   A Selection of Irish Melodies. Dublin, n.d. 2 vols., small folio, half green leather. Emerald 50-620 1974 £8

MOORE, THOMAS   A Selections of Popular National Airs. Dublin, 1889. Ex-library. Austin 61-721 1974 $37.50

MOORE, THOMAS STURGE 1870-   Altdorfer. 1900. Cloth backed boards, dust soiled, plates. Covent 55-1112 1974 £5.25

MOORE, THOMAS STURGE 1870-   Correggio. 1906. Plates, orig. cloth gilt, top edges gilt, spine faded, bookplate, very good, first edition. Covent 51-1309 1973 £5.25

MOORE, THOMAS STURGE 1870-   Judas. Chicago, 1924. Austin 61-723 1974 $12.50

MOORE, THOMAS STURGE 1870-   Some Soldier Poets. 1919. Covent 53-292 1974 £7.50

MOORE, THOMAS STURGE 1870-   Some Soldier Poets. 1919. Near fine, first edition. Covent 51-1312 1973 £5.25

MOORE, THOMAS STURGE 1870-   The Vinedresser and Other Poems. 1899. First edition, very good copy. Covent 51-1314 1973 £5.25

MOORE, VIRGINIA   Homer's Golden Chain. New York, 1936. 1st ed. Biblo & Tannen 210-775 1973 $7.50

MOORE, W. H.   Railway Nationalisation and the Average Citizen. Toronto, 1917. Hood's 102-768 1974 $7.50

MOORHOUSE, H.   Deep Furrows. Toronto & Winnipeg, 1918. Hood's 104-866 1974 $12.50

MOR, A.   Antonio Moro: Son Oeuvre et son Temps. Brussels, 1910. 4to., plates, half morocco, gilt. Quaritch 940-186 1974 £45

MORAND, PAUL   Closed all Night. 1924. Small 4to., orig. buckram gilt, first edition. Howes 186-332 1974 £6

MORANT, G. S. DE   A History of Chinese Art. 1931. Roy. 8vo., plates, illus., cloth. Quaritch 940-412 1974 £5

MORANT, PHILIP   The History and Antiquities of the County of Essex. 1768. 2 vols., folio, half red morocco, plates, rebacked, first edition. Howes 186-2006 1974 £150

MORANT, PHILIP   The History and Antiquities of the County of Essex. Chelmsford, 1816. 2 vols., folio, early 19th century cloth. Quaritch 939-353 1974 £55

MORAZZONI, G.   Il Libro Illustrato Veneziano del Settecento. Milan, 1943. 4to., plates, orig. boards. Dawsons PM 10-416 1974 £35

MORAZZONI, G.   Le Porcellane Italiane. Milan, 1935. Large crown 4to., orig. quarter morocco, covers and edges worn, illus. Bow Windows 66-482 1974 £68

MORDAUNT, ELINOR   Full Circle. 1931. 8vo., orig. cloth, first edition. Rota 189-617 1974 £5

MORDEN, J. C.   Historic Niagara Falls. Niagara Falls, 1932. Portraits, illus. Hood's 103-661 1974 $25

MORDEN, WILLIAM J.   Across Asia's Snows and Deserts. New York, 1927. Sgd., bdg. spotted. Biblo & Tannen 213-693 1973 $10

MORE, ALEXANDER GOODMAN   Contributions Towards Cybele Hibernica. Dublin, 1898. 8vo., map, fine. Emerald 50-624 1974 £7

MORE, ALEXANDER GOODMAN   Life and Letters of. Dublin, 1898. 8vo., orig. cloth, map, inscription, first edition. Bow Windows 62-642 1974 £9.50

MORE, HANNAH   A.L.S. (1776). 4to., 8 full pages, cloth folder. Dawsons PM 252-717 1974 £250

MORE, HANNAH   Florio. 1786. 4to., contemporary boards, first edition. Quaritch 936-158 1974 £25

MORE, HANNAH   Florio. London, 1786. 4to., disbound, very good copy, first edition. Ximenes 37-147 1974 $60

MORE, HANNAH   Florio. 1787. 4to., modern blue paper wrappers, fine, second edition. Quaritch 936-159 1974 £10

MORE, HANNAH   The Happy Waterman; and, The Portfolio. New York, n.d. (c. 1830). 16mo., pictorial wrappers, woodcuts, very good copy. Frohnsdorff 16-575 1974 $20

MORE, HANNAH   The Inflexible Captive. 1774. 8vo., calf, first edition. Quaritch 936-160 1974 £50

MORE, HANNAH   Moral Sketches or Prevailing Opinions and Manners, Foreign and Domestic. 1819. Large 12mo., orig. boards, printed paper title label, uncut, fourth edition. Bow Windows 66-484 1974 £7.50

MORE, HANNAH   Percy. London, 1778. 8vo., modern boards, first edition. Dawsons PM 252-718 1974 £15

MORE, HANNAH   Practical Piety. 1812. 2 vols., full diced calf. Allen 216-1140 1974 $15

MORE, HANNAH   Sacred Dramas. 1791. Buckram, ex-library seventh edition. Allen 216-1141 1974 $10

MORE, HANNAH   A Search After Happiness. (1773). 4to., modern brown wrappers, first edition. Quaritch 936-161 1974 £40

MORE, HANNAH   Tales for the Common People. 1834. Small 8vo., cloth. Hammond 201-133 1974 £6

MORE, HANNAH   Village Politics. London, 1792. 8vo., modern boards, first edition. Dawsons PM 247-203 1974 £30

MORE, HANNAH   The Works Of. 1801 and 1805. 8vo., 10 vols., orig. cloth, first editions. Bow Windows 64-620 1974 £80

MORE, HENRY   Discourses on Several Texts of Scripture. 1692. Contemporary panelled calf, first edition. Howes 185-1464 1974 £35

MORE, HENRY   A Modest Enquiry Into the Mystery of Iniquity. 1664. Folio, contemporary sheep, first edition. Howes 185-1465 1974 £65

MORE, SARAH   The Two Soldiers. Bath, n.d. (1795). 16mo., woodcuts, very good copy. Frohnsdorff 16-576 1974 $35

MORE, THOMAS   A Fruteful, Pleasaunt & Wittie Worke, of the Beste State of a Publique Weale, and of the Newe Yle, Called Utopia. London, (1556). Small 8vo., calf spine, marbled boards, black letter, generally clean and sound, second edition, first state. Thomas 32-182 1974 £1,250

MORE, THOMAS   The Life of Sir Thomas More. London, 1726. 8vo., contemporary calf, rubbed, spine gilt, frontispiece, portrait, second edition. Ximenes 37-148 1974 $45

MORE, THOMAS   Thomae Mori. 1563. Small 4to., rebacked, calf antique, gilt, woodcut, first collected edition. Bow Windows 62-643 1974 £120

MORE, THOMAS   Utopia. Hammersmith, 1893. Small 4to., orig. limp vellum, uncut. Dawsons PM 252-1099 1974 £380

MORE, THOMAS   Utopia. 1895. 450 pages. Howes 186-334 1974 £7.50

MORE, THOMAS   Utopia. 1906. Printed in black and red, roy. 8vo., Holland backed boards, corners slightly buckled, very good copy, scarce, limited to 100 copies. Sawyer 293-47 1974 £450

MORE, THOMAS   The Utopia of Thomas More. Oxford, 1895. Spine rubbed. Biblo & Tannen 213-797 1973 $15

MORE, THOMAS   The Workes Of. 1557. Thick Small folio, 18th century calf, rebacked, first collected edition. Thomas 28-249 1972 £600

MORE Miseries!! London, 1806. 12mo., modern cloth, frontispiece, uncut, first edition. Ximenes 33-303 1974 $30

MOREAS, JEAN   Les Cantilenes. Paris, 1886. 12mo., uncut, contemporary half vellum, first edition. L. Goldschmidt 42-319 1974 $40

MOREAU, PIERRE   Les Sainctes Prieres. Paris, 1632. Small 8vo., contemporary red morocco, fine, rare, first edition. Marlborough 70-11 1974 £250

MOREHOUSE, WARD   Just the Other Day. McGraw Hill, 1953. Austin 51-644 1973 $7.50

MOREHOUSE, WARD   Matinee Tomorrow. Whittlesey, 1949. Austin 51-645 1973 $10

MOREL, BENOIT AUGUSTIN   Traite des Degenerescences Physiques. Paris, 1857. Large 4to., contemporary half calf, plates, first edition. Schumann 35-340 1974 $75

MOREL, J. M.   Theorie des Jardins. Paris, 1776. 8vo., half calf, rare. Wheldon 131-1550 1974 £25

MORELL, J. D.   An Introduction to Mental Philosophy On the Inductive Method. London, 1862. 8vo., contemporary calf, first edition. Traylen 79-182 1973 £5

MORELL, THOMAS   Judas Maccabaeus. N. P., n.d. Very scarce, first edition. Ximenes 37-149 1974 $30

MORELLY, ABBE   Code de la Nature. Par-Tout, 1755. Small 8vo., contemporary marbled calf, gilt, worn, rare first edition. Gilhofer 61-20 1974 sFr. 1,200

MORELY, HENRY   A First Sketch of English Literature. 1890. Orig. edition. Austin 61-725 1974 $12.50

MORES, EDWARD ROWE   A Dissertation upon English Typographical Founders and Founderies. New York, 1924. Boards, unopened. Dawson's 424-166 1974 $40

MORET, ALEXANDRE   The Nile and Egyptian Civilization. London, 1927. 8vo., maps, plates, orig. cloth. Bow Windows 62-644 1974 £6.50

MOREWOOD, SAMUEL   A Philosophical and Statistical History of the Inventions and Customs of Ancient and Modern Nations. Dublin, 1838. Thick 8vo., half morocco, gilt, illus. Hammond 201-252 1974 £24

MOREY, F.   A Guide to the Natural History of the Isle of Wight. 1909. 8vo., cloth, plates, map. Wheldon 128-220 1973 £10

MOREY, F.   A Guide to the Natural History of the Isle of Wight. 1909. 8vo., cloth, plates. Wheldon 130-298 1974 £10

MORFI, FRAY JUAN AGUSTIN   History of Texas, 1673-1779. Albuquerque, 1935. 2 vols., limited to 500 sets. Jenkins 61-1765 1974 $175

MORGAGNI, GIOVANNI BATTISTA   De Sedibus et Causis Morborum per Anatomen Indagatis Libri Quinque. Venice, 1761. 2 vols., folio, very fine, half vellum, first edition. Gilhofer 61-22 1974 sFr. 4,800

MORGAGNI, GIOVANNI BATTISTA   The Seats and Causes of Diseases. London, 1769. 4to., 3 vols., modern half calf, fine, first edition in English. Dawsons PM 249-376 1974 £400

MORGAGNI, GIOVANNI BATTISTA   The Seats and Causes of Diseases. London, 1822. 8vo., 2 vols., contemporary half calf. Dawsons PM 249-377 1974 £120

MORGAN, A. P.   North American Fungi. 1889-92. 8vo., plates, buckram. Wheldon 129-1298 1974 £5

MORGAN, AUGUSTUS DE   A Budget of Paradoxes. London, 1872. 8vo., orig. blue cloth, uncut, first edition. Dawsons PM 245-523 1974 £20

MORGAN, AUGUSTUS DE   The Differential and Integral Calculus.   London, (1842). 8vo., orig. blind-stamped, cloth, uncut, first edition.   Dawsons PM 245-522 1974 £15

MORGAN, C. L.   Emergent Evolution. 1923. 8vo., cloth. Wheldon 130-122 1974 £5

MORGAN, C. L.   Habit and Instinct. 1896. 8vo., cloth, frontispiece. Wheldon 131-446 1974 £10

MORGAN, CHARLES   The Gunroom. 1919. Endpapers foxed, fine copy, scarce, first edition. Covent 51-1317 1973 £21

MORGAN, GEORGE   Annals, Comprising Memoirs, Incidents and Statistics of Harrisburg from the Period of Its First Settlement. Harrisburg, 1858. First edition, illus., clipping mounted rear inside cover, very light foxing, orig. binding. Wilson 63-72 1974 $22.50

MORGAN, H. J.   The Dominion Annual Gersiter ond Review. Toronto, 1884. Hood's 104-43 1974 $12.50

MORGAN, HARRY T.   Chinese Symbols and Superstitions. South Pasadena, Ca., 1942. 1st ed., illus. Biblo & Tannen 214-389 1974 $15

MORGAN, J. DE   Fouilles a Dahchour Mars-Juin 1894. Fouilles a Cahchour en 1894-95. Vienna, 1895-1903. 2 vols. in 1, 4to., half morocco, plates. Quaritch 940-337 1974 £30

MORGAN, JAMES MORRIS   Recollections of a Rebel Reefer. Boston, 1917. Half morocco, inscribed. Jenkins 48-96 1973 $27.50

MORGAN, JOHN   A Compleat History of the Piratical States of Barbary, viz. Algiers, Tunis, Tripoli, and Morocco. London, 1750. 8vo., old panelled calf, gilt, rubbed. Traylen 79-458 1973 £45

MORGAN, JOHN PIERPONT   Catalogue des Porcelaines Francaises. 1910. Folio, plates, full polished calf, gilt, uncut, limited edition. Quaritch 940-651 1974 £175

MORGAN, LADY SYDNEY   O'Donnel. Dublin, 1814. 12mo., 3 vols., oria. boards, uncut, first edition. Quaritch 936-498 1974 £60

MORGAN, LEWIS H.   The American Beaver and His Works. Philadelphia, 1868. Large 8vo., green gilt cloth, fine, first edition. Butterfield 10-83 1974 $75

MORGAN, LEWIS H.   Houses and House-Life of the American Aborigines. Washington, 1881. 4to., three quarter morocco, plates. Butterfield 8-607 1974 $100

MORGAN, MC NAMARA   Philoclea. 1754. 8vo., cloth, signature, first edition. Quaritch 936-163 1974 £10

MORGAN, NATHANIEL S.   Morgan Genealogy, a History of James Morgan, of New London, Conn. and His Descendants. Hartford, 1869. Orig. binding, lithograph portraits. Butterfield 10-271 1974 $20

MORGAN, NEE OWENSON   The Life and Times of Salvator Rosa. 1824. 8vo., 2 vols., cloth, uncut, frontispiece. Hill 126-175 1974 £28

MORGAN, S.   The Life and Times of Salvator Rosa. London, 1855. 8vo., presentation, cloth boards. Emerald 50-625 1974 £7.50

MORGAN, T. C.   Book Without. 1841. 2 vols., new buckram. Allen 216-1336 1974 $10

MORGAN, T. H.   Experimentelle Zoologie. Leipzig, 1909. 8vo., cloth. Wheldon 130-362 1974 £5

MORGAN, THOMAS   Philosophical Principles of Medicine. London, 1725. 8vo., contemporary panelled calf, first edition. Schumann 35-341 1974 $95

MORGAN, WALLACE M.   History of Kern County, California. Los Angeles, 1914. 4to., three quarter leather, illus. Saddleback 14-196 1974 $75

MORGAN, WILLIAM   Psalmau Dafydd gan. 1929. 4to., quarter niger morocco, dec. boards, uncut, limited edition. Broadhurst 23-1040 1974 £75

MORGAN, WILLIAM THOMAS   A Bibliography of British History. Bloomington, 1934. Large 8vo., orig. cloth. Dawsons PM 10-419 1974 £12

MORGAN-POWELL, S.   Memories That Live. Toronto, 1929. Hood's 102-339 1974 $7.50

MORGAN LIBRARY   A Check-List of Coptic Manuscripts in the Pierpont Morgan Library. New York, 1919. 4to., boards, buckram back. Goodspeed's 578-498 1974 $20

MORGAND, DAMASCENE   Livres dans de Riches Reliures des 16me, 17me, 18me et 19me Siecles. Paris, 1910. Small folio, plates, three quarter brown morocco, top edges gilt, foredge uncut, marbled endpapers, orig. wrappers bound in. Kraus B8-178 1974 $175

MORGENSTERN, G.   Sermones Contra Omnem Mudi Puersum Statu. Strasburg, 1508. Small 4to., modern calf. Thomas 28-295 1972 £60

MORGENTHAU, HENRY   Ambassador Morgenthau's Story. Doubleday, 1918. Austin 62-429 1974 $6.50

MORGOLIN, ARNOLD D.   The Jews of Eastern Europe. Seltzer, 1926. Austin 62-408 1974 $12.50

MORIARTY, G. P.   Dean Swift and His Writings. 1893. Portraits, orig. cloth gilt, spine faded, very good copy, first edition. Covent 51-1781 1973 £6.30

MORIARTY, HENRIETTA MARIA   Viridarium. 1806. 8vo., contemporary calf, rubbed, plates, very rare. Wheldon 131-87 1974 £100

MORICE, A. G.   Fifty Years in Western Canada. Toronto, 1930. Ex-library. Hood's 102-252 1974 $12.50

MORIER, JAMES   The Adventures of Hajji Baba. London, 1824. 3 vols., 8vo., orig. boards, fine, uncut, first edition. Dawsons PM 252-719 1974 £45

MORIER, JAMES   Ayesha. London, 1834. 3 vols., 12mo., contemporary half calf, first edition. Dawsons PM 252-720 1974 £30

MORIER, JAMES   A Journey Through Persia, Armenia, and Asia Minor, to Constantinople. London, 1812-18. 2 vols., 4to., half calf, foxing. Traylen 79-531 1973 £135

MORIN, JACQUES   Les Armes & Blasons des Chevaliers de l'Ordre du Saint Esprit. 1623. Folio, vellum, plates. Allen 213-1657 1973 $75

MORIN, JEAN BAPTISTE   Trigonometriae Canonicae Libri Tres. 1633. 4to., contemporary calf, gilt, inscription. Zeitlin 235-159 1974 $475

MORIN, L. P.   Papiers du Musique. Montreal, 1930. Cloth. Hood's 102-36 1974 $15

MORIN, P.   Remarques Necessaires Pour la Culture des Fleurs. Paris, 1678. Small 8vo., contemporary calf, weak joint, frontispiece, rare. Wheldon 128-1509 1973 £15

MORIN, VICTOR   The Historical Records of Old Montreal. Montreal, 1944. Card cover, bilingual. Hood's 103-783 1974 $12.50

MORISON, JAMES C.   The Life and Times of St. Bernard. 1863. Half calf gilt. Howes 185-961 1974 £5

MORISON, R.   An Account of the Morisonian Herbarium. Oxford, 1914. 8vo., cloth, plates, scarce. Wheldon 129-178 1974 £10

MORISON, R.   Plantarum Historiae Universalis Oxoniensis. Oxford, 1680-99. Folio, 2 vols., contemporary diced calf gilt, plates, portrait. Wheldon 129-946 1974 £265

MORISON, S.   A Review of Recent Typography in England. 1927. 8vo., orig. cloth, illus. Broadhurst 23-424 1974 £12

MORISON, S.   A Review of Recent Typography in England, the United States, France and Germany. 1927. Demy 8vo., illus., orig. cloth, fine. Broadhurst 24-401 1974 £12

MORISON, SAMUEL E.   Builders of the Bay Colony. (1930). Large 8vo., plates, scarce. Howes 186-1085 1974 £6.50

MORISON, SAMUEL ELIOT   Admiral of the Ocean Sea. Boston, 1942. 1st ed., 2 vols., illus. Jacobs 24-13 1974 $75

MORISON, STANLEY   The Art of the Printer. 1925. 4to., orig. cloth, first edition. Rota 190-690 1974 £18

MORISON, STANLEY   The Art of the Printer. London, 1925. 4to., plates, orig. cloth. Dawsons PM 10-427 1974 £40

MORISON, STANLEY   The Fleuron. London & Cambridge, 1923-30. 7 vols., 4to., illus., cloth-backed boards, orig. cloth. Dawsons PM 10-432 1974 £380

MORISON, STANLEY   German Incunabula in the British Museum. London, 1928. Folio, illus., orig. buckram gilt, limited. Dawsons PM 10-422 1974 £100

MORISON, STANLEY   Handbuch der Druckerkunst. Berlin, 1925. 4to., illus., green cloth. Kraus B8-356 1974 $85

MORISON, STANLEY   On Type Faces. London, 1923. 4to., orig. cloth-backed marbled boards. Dawsons PM 10-423 1974 £50

MORISON, STANLEY   A Reveiw of Recent Typography in England. London, 1927. 8vo., orig. blue cloth. Dawsons PM 10-420 1974 £12

MORISON, STANLEY   Type Designs of the Past and Present. London, 1926. 8vo., illus., orig. buckram, first book form edition. Dawsons PM 10-428 1974 £12

MORISON, STANLEY   Typenformen der Vergangenheit und Neuzeit. Hellerau, 1928. 4to., orig. parchment-backed boards, first German edition. Dawsons PM 10-429 1974 £8

MORLAND, GEORGE   Memoirs of the Life of the Late George Morland. 1806. Roy. 4to., plates, contemporary calf. Quaritch 940-187 1974 £35

MORLAND, GILBEY W.   George Morland, His Life and Works. 1907. 4to., dec. cloth, gilt, plates. Marsden 37-316 1974 £5

MORLAND, JOHN   A Rational Account of the Causes of Chronic Diseases . . . To Which is Annexed, New Strictures on the Theory of Fevers, with an Appendix on Diet and Excercise. London, n.d. (c. 1780). Second edition, 8vo., boards. Gurney 66-133 1974 £15

MORLAND, SAMUEL   The Count of Pagan's Method of Delineating. London, 1667. Folio, stitched. Gurney 64-155 1974 £80

MORLEY, C.   Plum Pudding of Divers Ingredients. New York, 1921. First edition, 8vo., drease in back cover, included is a letter from the publisher to Mr. Henry Hazlett, fine. Current BW9-264 1974 $20

MORLEY, CHRISTOPHER   Chimneysmoke. New York, 1921. First U.S. edition. Covent 56-1839 1974 £6.30

MORLEY, CHRISTOPHER   The Goldfish Under the Ice. London, 1929. No. 14 of the Woburn Books, no. 563 of edition limited to 530 copies, signed, mint, orig. binding, first edition. Ross 87-415 1974 $20

MORLEY, CHRISTOPHER   The Haunted Bookshop. New York, 1919. 1st ed., spine torn. Biblo & Tannen 210-643 1973 $15

MORLEY, CHRISTOPHER   Letters of Askance. Philadelphia, 1939. 1st ed. Biblo & Tannen 210-776 1973 $7.50

MORLEY, CHRISTOPHER   Letters of Askance. Philadelphia & New York, 1939. Dust jacket, signed, first edition. Ballinger 1-185 1974 $12.50

MORLEY, CHRISTOPHER   Poems. Garden City, 1929. First edition, tissue wrapper torn at bottom, else mint. Ross 87-416 1974 $17.50

MORLEY, CHRISTOPHER   "Rare" Books. New York, 1935. Orig. wrappers, sewn as issued, first & only edition, one of 75 numbered copies, fine. MacManus 224-343 1974 $50

MORLEY, CHRISTOPHER   Seacoast of Bohemia. Doubleday, Doran, 1929. 68p., illus. Austin 51-647 1973 $7.50

MORLEY, CHRISTOPHER   Seacoast of Bohemia. Doubleday, Doran, 1929. 68p., illus., 1st ed. Austin 51-646 1973 $10

MORLEY, CHRISTOPHER   Thorofare. Harcourt, Brace, 1942. Austin 62-430 1974 $7.50

MORLEY, CHRISTOPHER   Thunder on the Left. Garden City, 1925. First edition, orig. binding, nice, repaired & darkened d.w. Ross 87-417 1974 $12.50

MORLEY, CHRISTOPHER   The Trojan Horse. Random House, 1941. 199p., 1st ed. Austin 51-648 1973 $7.50

MORLEY, CHRISTOPHER   Where the Blue Begins. New York, 1922. 12mo., first edition, author's signed presentation. Biblo & Tannen 213-577 1973 $17.50

MORLEY, CHRISTOPHER   Works. New York, 1927. 12 vols., signed, Haverford edition. Ballinger 1-186 1974 $125

MORLEY, EDITH   The Life and Times of Henry Crabb Robinson. 1935. Orig. edition. Austin 61-726 1974 $10

MORLEY, HENRY   The Life of Bernard Palissy. 1852. 2 vols., 8vo., cloth, library labels. Quaritch 940-654 1974 £20

MORLEY, HENRY   Of English Literature in the Reign of Queen Victoria. Leipzig, 1881. Cloth gilt, rubbed. Covent 55-1016 1974 £5.25

MORLEY, HENRY   Palissy the Potter, the Life of Bernard Palissy of Saintes. 1852. 2 vols. Eaton Music-656 1973 £5

MORLEY, JOHN   The Life of William Ewart Gladstone. 1903. 8vo., 3 vols., plates, orig. cloth, illus., first edition. Quaritch 936-394 1974 £6

MORLEY, JOHN   The Life of William Ewart Gladstone. 1905-06. 2 vols., contemporary dark blue polished calf, gilt, rubbed. Smith 194-661 1974 £8

MORLEY, JOHN   Life of William Ewart Gladstone. 1903. 3 vols., orig. edition. Austin 61-728 1974 $22.50

MORLEY, JOHN   Recollections. 1917. 2 vols. Allen 216-1153 1974 $12.50

MORLEY, JOHN   Recollections. 1917. 2 vols., ex-library. Austin 61-729 1974 $15

MORLEY, JOHN   Works. 1921. 8vo., 15 vols., cloth, faded. Quaritch 936-499 1974 £30

MORLEY, THOMAS   Madrigals to Foure Voices. 1600. Small 4to., disbound in cloth folder. Quaritch 940-816 1974 £120

MORLEY, WILLIAM H.   A Descriptive Catalogue of the Historical Manuscripts in the Arabic and Persian Languages. London, 1854. 8vo., cloth, presentation inscription. Dawsons PM 10-435 1974 £7

MORNAY, PHILIPPE DE   Memoires. 4to., 17th century calf, gilt, first edition. Dawsons PM 251-112 1974 £18

MORNING & Evening Amusements, at Merlin's Mechanical Museum, No. 11, Princes Street, Hanover Square. (London, c. 1780). 32mo., orig. marbled wrappers, fine. Ximenes 36-143 1974 $85

MORNING GLORY, MISS   The American Diary. New York, 1902. 8vo., boards stamped in gold, illus; lst ed. Frohnsdorff 16-39 1974 $12.50

MOROSINI, ANDREA   Storia Della Republica Veneziana Scritta per Pubblico Decreto. Venezia, 1782-87. 5 vols., 4to., old half calf, marbled sides. Bow Windows 66-486 1974 £45

MORPURGO, IDA BOHATTA   The Gnome's Almanack. New York, 1942. 16mo., pictorial boards, color illus., very good copy. Frohnsdorff 16-578 1974 $10

MORRES, HERVEY REDMOND   Impartial Reflections Upon the Question for Equalizing the Duties. London, 1785. 8vo., modern boards. Dawsons PM 247-204 1974 £15

MORRIS, ALEXANDER   Canada and Her Resources. Montreal, 1855. Gift plate signed by Morris, handwritten letter from Morris tipped in. Hood's 102-572 1974 $50

MORRIS, ALEXANDER   The Treaties of Canada With the Indians of Manitoba and the North-West Territories, Including the Negotiations on Which They are Based. Toronto. Hood's 102-821 1974 $40

MORRIS, ALEXANDER   The Treaties of Canada With the Indians of Manitoba and the North-West Territories. Toronto, 1880. Scuffed. Hood's 104-867 1974 $40

MORRIS, BEVERLEY R.   British Game Birds & Wildfowl. n.d. 4to., plates, binders cloth. Smith 193-738 1973 £75

MORRIS, BEVERLEY R.   British Game Birds and Wildfowl. (n.d., 1855). 4to., orig. cloth, plates, first edition. Bow Windows 64-189 1974 £150

MORRIS, BEVERLEY R.   British Game Birds and Wildfowl. (1864). 4to., new half red levant morocco, gilt, plates. Wheldon 130-51 1974 £220

MORRIS, BEVERLEY R.   British Game Birds and Wildfowl. 1891. 4to., modern half green polished levant morocco, gilt, fine, third edition. Wheldon 131-88 1974 £240

MORRIS, CLARA   The Life of a Star. New York, 1906. lst ed. Biblo & Tannen 210-967 1973 $8.50

MORRIS, CLARA   Life On the Stage. McClure, Philips, 1901. Austin 51-649 1973 $7.50

MORRIS, CLARA   A Pasteboard Crown. Scribner, 1902. 370p. Austin 51-650 1973 $10

MORRIS, CLARA   Stage Confidences. Lothrop, 1902. 316p., illus. Austin 51-651 1973 $10

MORRIS, CORBYN   An Essay Towards Fixing the True Standards of Wit, Humour, Raillery, Satire and Ridicule. London, 1744. 8vo., half morocco, gilt, very scarce, first edition. Ximenes 37-150 1974 $100

MORRIS, EDWARD   False Colours. 1793. 8vo., cloth, first edition. Quaritch 936-164 1974 £7

MORRIS, EDWARD   The Secret. London, 1799. 8vo., modern boards, first edition. Dawsons PM 252-721 1974 £15

MORRIS, EDWARD   A Short Enquiry into the Nature and Monopoly and Forestalling. London, 1800. 8vo., modern boards, third edition. Dawsons PM 247-205 1974 £18

MORRIS, FRANCIS ORPEN   A History of British Birds. London, n.d. Cloth, 8 vols., plates. Dawsons 424-318 1974 $75

MORRIS, FRANCIS ORPEN   A History of British Birds. n.d. 8vols., plates, half contemporary red levant morocco, gilt. Smith 193-739 1973 £40

MORRIS, FRANCIS ORPEN   A History of British Birds. 1851-57. 6 vols., roy. 8vo., orig. cloth, plates. Wheldon 131-89 1974 £180

MORRIS, FRANCIS ORPEN   A History of British Birds. 1857-63. Roy. 8vo., orig. cloth, 6 vols., plates. Wheldon 130-52 1974 £140

MORRIS, FRANCIS ORPEN   A History of British Birds. (1863-67). Crown 8vo., orig. red cloth, 8 vols., plates. Wheldon 130- 584 1974 £70

MORRIS, FRANCIS ORPEN   A History of British Birds. 1870. 8vo., orig. cloth, 6 vols., plates, second edition. Bow Windows 64-190 1974 £120

MORRIS, FRANCIS ORPEN   A History of British Birds. 1870. Roy. 8vo., 6 vols., new half polished brown morocco, gilt, plates, fine. Wheldon 130-53 1974 £225

MORRIS, FRANCIS ORPEN   A History of British Birds. 1895-97. 6 vols., roy. 8vo., cloth, plates, revised fourth edition. Wheldon 131-90 1974 £150

MORRIS, FRANCIS ORPEN   A History of British Birds. London, 1895-7. Roy. 8vo., orig. cloth, gilt, 6 vols., plates, fourth edition. Hammond 201-663 1974 £180

MORRIS, FRANCIS ORPEN   A History of British Birds. London, 1895-7. Roy. 8vo., 6 vols., orig. blue half morocco, gilt. Hammond 201-664 1974 £185

MORRIS, FRANCIS ORPEN   A History of British Birds. 1895-97. Roy. 8vo., orig. paper printed wrappers, hand coloured plates, 36 monthly parts, very scarce, exceptionally fine set, revised fourth edition. Broadhurst 24-1137 1974 £225

MORRIS, FRANCIS ORPEN   A History of British Butterflies. 1891. 4to., orig. cloth, plates, sixth edition. Bow Windows 64-781 1974 £10

MORRIS, FRANCIS ORPEN   A History of British Butterflies. 1891. Roy. 8vo., orig. cloth, plates, sixth edition. Wheldon 130-774 1974 £20

MORRIS, FRANCIS ORPEN   A History of British Butterflies. 1895. Small 4to., cloth, plates, eighth edition. Wheldon 131-835 1974 £20

MORRIS, FRANCIS ORPEN   A History of British Butterflies. 1904. Roy. 8vo., orig. dec. cloth, plates, ninth edition. Wheldon 130-775 1974 £20

MORRIS, FRANCIS ORPEN   A Natural History of British Moths. 1872. 4 vols., roy. 8vo., cloth, coloured plates, nice clean copy, first edition. Wheldon 128-773 1973 £18

MORRIS, FRANCIS ORPEN   A Natural History of British Moths. 1891. 4 vols., roy. 8vo., orig. cloth, plates, third edition. Wheldon 131-836 1974 £25

MORRIS, FRANCES ORPEN   A Natural History of British Moths. 1891. 8vo., orig. cloth, 4 vols., third edition. Bow Windows 64-782 1974 £36

MORRIS, FRANCIS ORPEN   A Natural History of the Nests and Eggs of British Birds. 1859-63. 3 vols., roy. 8vo., contemporary half green morocco, panelled backs, gilt edges, coloured plates. Wheldon 128-524 1973 £15

MORRIS, FRANCIS ORPEN   A Natural History of the Nests and Eggs of British Birds. 1864, 1863, 1863. 3 vols., roy. 8vo., half morocco, plates. Wheldon 131-664 1974 £25

MORRIS, FRANCIS ORPEN   A Natural History of the Nests and Eggs of British Birds. 1870-71. 3 vols., roy. 8vo., orig. cloth, second edition. Wheldon 128-525 1973 £12

MORRIS, FRANCIS ORPEN   A Natural History of the Nests and Eggs of British Birds. 1875. Roy. 8vo., 3 vols., orig. cloth, plates. Wheldon 130-585 1974 £20

MORRIS, FRANCIS ORPEN   A Natural History of the Nests and Eggs of British Birds. 1879. Roy. 8vo., 3 vols., orig. cloth. Wheldon 129-505 1974 £10

MORRIS, FRANCES ORPEN   A Series of Picturesque Seats. n.d. 6 vols., crown 4to., dec. cloth, plates. Marsden 37-317 1974 £25

MORRIS, FRANCIS ORPEN   A Series of Picturesque Views of Seats of the Noblemen and Gentlemen of Great Britain and Ireland. (1860-80). 7 vols., 4to., plates, orig. dec. cloth gilt, worn. Quaritch 940-533 1974 £85

MORRIS, FRANCIS ORPEN   A Series of Picturesque Views. London, (c. 1890). 5 vols., 4to., orig. cloth, gilt. Bow Windows 62-645 1974 £15

MORRIS, GLADYS E.   Tales From Bernard Shaw. 1929. Austin
51-878 1973 $10

MORRIS, GOUVERNEUR   An Answer to War in Disguise. New York,
1806. 8vo., orig. marbled wrappers, printed paper side label, very good copy,
first edition. Ximenes 37-151 1974 $50

MORRIS, HARRISON S.   Walt Whitman: A Brief Biography. Cambridge,
1929. Cloth, dust wrapper. Dawson's 424-311 1974 $30

MORRIS, JOHN   The Life of Father John Gerard of the Society
of Jesus. 1881. Orig. cloth, rebacked, plates, third & best edition. Howes
185-1210 1974 £6.50

MORRIS, JOHN   The Troubles of Our Catholic Forefathers.
1872-77. 3 vols., orig. cloth, scarce, orig. edition. Howes 185-1469 1974
£22.50

MORRIS, KENNETH   The Secret Mountain and Other Tales. 1926.
Small 4to., cloth gilt, fine, English first edition. Covent 56-1752 1974 £10.50

MORRIS, MAY   William Morris. Oxford, 1936. Orig. linen-
backed boards, 2 vols., illus., English first edition. Covent 56-965 1974 £175

MORRIS, R.   Flora Conspicua. 1826. Roy. 8vo., hand
coloured plates, contemporary full green morocco gilt, scarce. Wheldon 128-1511
1973 £170

MORRIS, R. H.   Chester in the Plantagenet and Tudor Reigns.
n.d. Roy 8vo., buckram. Broadhurst 23-1478 1974 £10

MORRIS, WILLIAM   An Address Delivered. 1898. 8vo., uncut,
orig. boards, cloth back, first edition. Dawsons PM 252-722 1974 £24

MORRIS, WILLIAM   An Address Delivered. 1902. 8vo., Chinese
vellum-backed boards, first edition. Dawsons PM 252-723 1974 £10

MORRIS, WILLIAM   An Address Delivered at the Distribution of
Prizes to Students of the Birmingham Municipal School of Art, 1894. 1898.
Cloth backed boards, fine copy, first edition. Covent 51-1320 1973 £5.25

MORRIS, WILLIAM   Architecture and History, and Westminster
Abbey. London, (1900). 8vo., orig. paper boards, stained. Bow Windows
62-647 1974 £7.50

MORRIS, WILLIAM   Architecture and History and Westminster
Abbey. 1900. Orig. boards, fine. Covent 55-68 1974 £12.50

MORRIS, WILLIAM   The Art of, a Record. 1897. Folio, blue
buckram sides, excellent condition, limited edition de luxe. Thomas 28-40
1972 £125

MORRIS, WILLIAM   Child Christopher and Goldiland and the Fair.
1895. 16mo., 2 vols., holland-backed boards. Hammond 201-736 1974 £85

MORRIS, WILLIAM   Child Christopher and Goldilind the Fair.
Kelmscott Press, 1895. Woodcut title page, borders and initials, printed in red
and black, 2 vols., 16mo., orig. Holland backed boards, paper labels, fine copy,
limited to 600 copies, with rare errata slip in vol. 1. Sawyer 293-182 1974 £75

MORRIS, WILLIAM   Communism. London, 1903. 8vo., modern
boards, first edition. Dawsons PM 252-724 1974 £12

MORRIS, WILLIAM   The Defence of Guenevere and Other Poems.
1858. 8vo., orig. cloth, fine, first edition. Broadhurst 23-808 1974 £30

MORRIS, WILLIAM   The Defence of Guenivere and Other Poems. 18-
92. 8vo., limp vellum with ties. Hammond 201-724 1974 £110

MORRIS, WILLIAM   The Defence of Guenevere and Other Poems.
London & New York, 1904. 8vo., full page plates, very milde fading of spine,
red cloth gilt dec. cover, fine. Current BW9-265 1974 $27.50

MORRIS, WILLIAM   A Dream of John Ball and A King's Lesson.
Kelmscott Press, 1892. Small 4to., golden type in black & red, woodcut, limp
vellum, silk ties, uncut, fine, limited to 300 copies. Broadhurst 24-1016 1974
£145

MORRIS, WILLIAM   The Dream of John Ball and a King's Lesson. 18-
92. 8vo., limp vellum with ties. Hammond 201-725 1974 £165

MORRIS, WILLIAM   Earthly Paradise. 1871. 3 vols., ex-library.
Allen 216-1159 1974 $10

MORRIS, WILLIAM   Earthly Paradise. 1896. 4 vols. Allen
216-2258 1974 $15

MORRIS, WILLIAM   The Earthly Paradise. Kelmscott Press, 1896-
97. Printed in golden type in black & red, 8 vols., 4to., full limp vellum, silk
ties, uncut, limited to 235 copies, fine. Broadhurst 24-1019 1974 £300

MORRIS, WILLIAM   The Earthly Paradise. Kelmscott Press, 1896-
97. Woodcut title, fine woodcut borders, 8 vols., 8vo., orig. limp vellum, uncut,
blue silk ties, fine set, limited to 225 copies. Sawyer 293-183 1974 £315

MORRIS, WILLIAM   The Earthly Paradise. 1896-7. 8vo., 8 vols.,
limp vellum with ties. Hammond 201-739 1974 £325

MORRIS, WILLIAM   The Earthly Paradise. 1905. Cloth gilt, fine,
4 vols., English first edition. Covent 56-1944 1974 £10

MORRIS, WILLIAM   Gertha's Lovers. Portland, 1902. 16mo.,
wrappers, fine, first American edition. Covent 55-1114 1974 £12.50

MORRIS, WILLIAM   Gothic Architecture. Kelmscott Press, 1893.
Printed in red and black on vellum, 16mo., orig. boards, one of 45 copies, fine,
presentation copy inscribed. Broadhurst 24-1017 1974 £275

MORRIS, WILLIAM   Gothic Architecture. 1893. 12mo., holland-
backed boards. Hammond 201-729 1974 £60

MORRIS, WILLIAM   Gothic Architecture. 1893. Linen back, grey
boards, fine. Marsden 39-262 1974 £40

MORRIS, WILLIAM   The History of Over the Sea. Portland, 1909.
16mo., wrappers, slip-case, fine, first American edition. Covent 55-1115
1974 £12.50

MORRIS, WILLIAM   The History of Pattern Designing & The Lesser
Arts of Life; in Lectures on Art, Delivered in Support of the Society for the
Protection of Ancient Buildings. 1882. Covers dampstained, very good copy,
partly unopened. Covent 51-2472 1973 £8.50

MORRIS, WILLIAM   Lectures on Art. 1882. English first edition.
Covent 56-961 1974 £10

MORRIS, WILLIAM   A Letter on the Subject of the Clergy Reserves
and Rectories Addressed to the Very Rev. Principal MacFarlan, and the Rev. R.
Burns D.D. Toronto, 1838. With appendix, marbled boards, leather spine.
Hood's 102-624 1974 $85

MORRIS, WILLIAM   The Life and Death of Jason. 1867. 8vo.,
orig. cloth, first edition. Rota 189-650 1974 £25

MORRIS, WILLIAM   Love is Enough. 1897. 4to., limp vellum with
ties, illus. Hammond 201-741 1974 £200

MORRIS, WILLIAM   Love is Enough. 1898. Limp vellum, uncut,
limited edition. Broadhurst 23-1059 1974 £200

MORRIS, WILLIAM   Love is Enough, or the Freeing of Pharamond.
Kelmscott Press, 1898. Woodcut frontispiece, limp vellum, silk ties, uncut,
limited to 300 copies, fine. Broadhurst 24-1020 1974 £200

MORRIS, WILLIAM   The Odyssey of Homer. 1887. 2 vols.,
crown 4to., half morocco, gilt uncut. Howes 186-335 1974 £35

MORRIS, WILLIAM   Pilgrims of Hope. 1901. Top of spine slightly
torn. Allen 216-1161 1974 $10

MORRIS, WILLIAM   Poems by the Way. 1891. Small 4to., buckram,
first general edition. Quaritch 936-500 1974 £4

MORRIS, WILLIAM G.   Report Upon the Customs District, Public Service,
and Resources of Alaska Territory. Washington, 1879. Fine contemporary three
quarter morocco, scarce, very fine. Jenkins 61-88 1974 $22.50

MORRIS, WILLIAM   The Sage Library. 1891-1905. 6 vols., crown
8vo., publisher's half green morocco binding, fine. Broadhurst 24-818 1974 £30

MORRIS, WILLIAM   Sir Galahad, a Christmas Mystery. Chicago,
1904. 12mo., limited to 525 copies, frontis., very fine. Current BW9-63 1974
$35

MORRIS, WILLIAM   The Story of Amis & Amile. Portland, 1896.
12mo., wrappers, vellum, fine. Covent 55-1117 1974 £12.50

MORRIS, WILLIAM   The Story of Child Christopher and Goldilind
the Fair. 1895. 2 vols., 16mo., orig. linen backed boards. Howes 185-269
1974 £48

MORRIS, WILLIAM   The Story of the Glittering Plain. 1891. 8vo.,
stiff vellum with ties. Hammond 201-723 1974 £165

MORRIS, WILLIAM   The Story of the Glittering Plain. 1894. 4to.,
limp vellum with ties, illus. Hammond 201-730 1974 £160

MORRIS, WILLIAM   The Sundering Flood. Kelmscott Press, 1898.
Woodcut title page, initials and frames, map, printed in red and black, 8vo.,
orig. Holland backed boards, uncut, fine, limited to 300 copies. Sawyer
293-184 1974 £160

MORRIS, WILLIAM   The Tale of King Coustains the Emperor.
Portland, 1912. 12mo., wrappers, fine, slip-case. Covent 55-1119 1974
£12.50

MORRIS, WILLIAM   A Tale of the House of the Wolfings. 1889.
4to., cloth, rebound, label, inscribed, fine. Covent 55-1118 1974 £125

MORRIS, WILLIAM   Under an Elm-Tree. 1891. 16mo., orig.
cloth, scarce, unopened, first edition. Rota 188-702 1974 £5

MORRIS, WILLIAM   The Well at the World's End. 1896. 4to., limp
vellum with ties, illus. Hammond 201-737 1974 £225

MORRIS, WILLIAM   The Wood Beyond the World. 1894. 8vo., limp
vellum with ties. Hammond 201-733 1974 £175

MORRIS, WILLIAM   The Collected Works. London, 1910.
24 vols., orig. boards, plates, fine, collected edition. Dawsons PM 252-725
1974 £220

MORRISON, ALFRED   The Collection of Autograph Letters and
Historical Documents Formed By. 1893-96. 4 vols., imp. 8vo., orig. holland
backed boards, printed labels. Howes 185-765 1974 £10

MORRISON, AMES   Pigs. French, 1923. Austin 51-652 1973
$7.50

MORRISON, ANNIE L.   History of San Luis Obispo County, California.
Los Angeles, 1917. 4to., three quarter leather, rebacked, illus. Saddleback
14-197 1974 $135

MORRISON, ARTHUR   Chronicles of Martin Hewitt. 1895. 8vo.,
orig. cloth, illus., first edition. Rota 190-329 1974 £18

MORRISON, ARTHUR   Zig-Zags at the Zoo. 1894. Drawings, nice
copy, inscription, first edition. Covent 51-1327 1973 £12.50

MORRIX, WILLIAM   Poems By the Way. 1891. Buckram, worn,
inscribed. Covent 55-1116 1974 £6.30

MORSE, H.   Back to Shakespeare. 1915. Small 8vo., calf,
gilt. Quaritch 936-562 1974 £8

MORSE, H. N.   The Country Church in Industrial Zones. New
York, c.1922. 8vo., cloth, maps. Saddleback 14-671 1974 $15

MORSE, JEDIDIAH   The American Universal Geography. Charlestown, 1819. 2 vols., old calf, worn, red labels, seventh edition. Butterfield
10-423 1974 $75

MORSE, JEDIDIAH   Geography Made Easy. 1790. 12mo., contemporary calf, plates. Zeitlin 235-160 1974 $250

MORSE, JEDIDIAH   Geography Made Easy. Boston, 1816.
Leather, maps, foxed. Rinsland 58-910 1974 $35

MORSE, SAMUEL F. B.   Examination of the Telegraphic Apparatus and
the Processes in Telegraphy. Washington, 1869. Wrapper. Jenkins 61-1770
1974 $10

MORSE, W. I.   The Land of New Adventure. London, 1932.
Photographs, hand made paper, numbered, limited edition. Hood's 103-184
1974 $50

MORTILLET, GABRIEL DE   Le Signe de la Croix Avant le Christianisme.
Paris, 1866. New grey cloth binding. Eaton Music-647 1973 £6

MORTIMER, JOHN   The Whole Art of Husbandry. London, 1708.
8vo., contemporary panelled calf, second edition. Hammond 201-40 1974 £21

MORTIMER, W. W.   The History of the Hundred of Wirral. Birkenhead, 1847. Boards, foxing. Broadhurst 23-1479 1974 £6

MORTON, G. H.   The Geology of the Country Around Liverpool
Including the North of Flintshire. 1897. 8vo., cloth, plates, new edition.
Wheldon 131-1049 1974 £5

MORTON, HENRY H.   Genito-Urinary Diseases and Syphilis.
Philadelphia, 1906. Revised, enlarged second edition. Rittenhouse 46-480
1974 $10

MORTON, J.   The Natural History of Northamptonshire.
1712. Folio, half calf. Quaritch 939-504 1974 £65

MORTON, J. S.   Reminiscences of the Lower St. Joseph River
Valley. Benton Harbor, n.d. 12mo., cloth. Saddleback 14-507 1974 $15

MORTON, JAMES   The Monastic Annals of Teviotdale.
Edinburgh, 1832. 4to., cloth, plates, foxed. Howes 186-2182 1974 £8.50

MORTON, JOHN M.   Box and Cox. Taylor, 1847. Austin 51-653
1973 $6.50

MORTON, JOHN M.   Grimshaw, Bagshaw and Bradshaw. Taylor,
1851. Austin 51-654 1973 $6.50

MORTON, JOHN M.   The Irish Tiger. French, n.d. Austin 51-655
1973 $6.50

MORTON, JOHN M.   Slasher and Crasher. Taylor, 1849. Austin
51-656 1973 $6.50

MORTON, JOHN M.   A Thumping Legacy. French. Austin 51-657
1973 $6.50

MORTON, JOHN M.   To Paris and Back for Five Pounds. n.d.
Austin 51-658 1973 $6.50

MORTON, JOHN M.   The Two Bonnycastles. Taylor, 1851. 32p.
Austin 51-659 1973 $6.50

MORTON, LESLIE T.   A Medical Bibliography. London, 1943. 8vo.,
brown cloth, first edition. Dawsons PM 249-60 1974 £5.50

MORTON, RICHARD   Opera Medica. Lyons, 1697. 9 works in
1 vol., thick 4to., contemporary vellum. Schuman 37-176 1974 $145

MORTON, RICHARD   Phthisiologia. 1689. 8vo., contemporary speckled calf, worn, first edition. Dawsons PM 249-378 1974 £485

MORTON, RICHARD   Phthisiologia. London, 1694. 8vo., contemporary panelled calf, rebacked, first edition in English. Dawsons PM 249-379
1974 £110

MORTON, THOMAS   All That Glitters Is Not Gold. Taylor, 1860.
Austin 51-660 1973 $8.50

MORTON, THOMAS   Children In the Wood. French, 1793.
Austin 51-661 1973 $7.50

MORTON, THOMAS   Columbus. London, 1792. 8vo., modern
boards, fine, first edition. Dawsons PM 252-726 1974 £15

MORTON, THOMAS   A Cure for the Heart-Ache. London, 1797.
8vo., modern boards, first edition. Dawsons PM 252-727 1974 £15

MORTON, THOMAS   Go To Bed Tom. Taylor, 1854. Austin
51-662 1973 $6.50

MORTON, THOMAS   Of the Institution of the Sacrament of the
Blessed Bodie and Blood of Christ. 1635. Folio, 18th century panelled calf,
enlarged second edition. Howes 185-1471 1974 £28

MORTON, THOMAS   Pretty Piece of Business. French. Austin
51-663 1973 $6.50

MORTON, THOMAS   Secrets Worth Knowing. London, 1798.
8vo., modern boards, first edition. Dawsons PM 252-728 1974 £15

MORTON, THOMAS   The Surgical Anatomy of the Groin, the Femoral,
and Popliteal Regions. London, 1839. Large 8vo., orig. cloth, illus., first edition. Schumann 35-342 1974 $135

MORTON, THOMAS   Town and Country. London, 1807. 8vo.,
modern boards, first edition. Dawsons PM 252-729 1974 £15

MORTON, THOMAS   The Way to Get Married. London, 1796.
8vo., modern boards, first edition. Dawsons PM 252-730 1974 £15

MOSCARDELLI, NICOLA   L'Aria di Roma. Turin, 1930. 16mo.,
wrappers. Minters 37-196 1973 $10

MOSEL, TAD   Other Peoples Houses. Simon and Schuster,
1956. Austin 51-665 1973 $7.50

MOSELEY, H. N.   Notes By a Naturalist On the "Challenger".
1879. 8vo., cloth, plates, map, nice clean copy. Wheldon 131-321 1974
£12

MOSELEY, H. N.   Notes By a Naturalist on the "Challenger"
Being an Account of Various Observations Made During the Voyage of H. M. S.
Challenger, 1872-76. 1879. 8vo., cloth, map, coloured plates. Wheldon
128-221 1973 £7.50

MOSELEY, HENRY   A Treatise On Hydrostatics and Hydrodynamics.
Cambridge, 1830. 8vo., orig. cloth, paper label, plates, first edition.
Schuman 37-177 1974 $85

MOSELEY, HENRY   A Treatise on Mechanics. 1839. Improved
second edition. Covent 55-1318 1974 £6.50

MOSELEY, W. M.   An Essay on Archery. (Worcester), 1792.
8vo., frontispiece, plates, old mottled calf, morocco label, first edition. Bow
Windows 62-651 1974 £90

MOSELLANUS, PETRUS   Pedologia . . . in Puerorum Usum Conscripta.
Cracow, 1521. Small 4to., modern half morocco, good copy, interesting
contemporary annotations, very rare, early edition. Schafer 10-106 1974
sFr 2,300

MOSELY, EPHRAIM   Teeth, their Natural History. London, 1862.
8vo., orig. cloth, gilt, first edition. Hammond 201-536 1974 £7

MOSER-CHARLOTTENFELS   Collection Henri Moser-Charlottenfels: Armes
et Armures Orientales. Leipzig, 1912. Roy. folio, plates, half calf, slipcase,
limited edition. Quaritch 940-702 1974 £150

MOSES, ANNA MARY (ROBERTSON) 1860-   American Primitive. New York,
1946. 4to., first edition, color plates. Biblo & Tannen 213-277 1973 $22.50

MOSES, HENRY   A Collection of Antique Vases. (1814). 4to.,
contemporary cloth, plates, engravings. Covent 55-113 1974 £25

MOSES, HENRY   A Collection of Vases, Altars, Paterae, Tripods,
Candelabra, Sarcophagi, etc. (1814). Small 4to., engravings, half roan,
bookplate. Quaritch 940-338 1974 £30

MOSES BEN MAIMON, 1135-1204   Liber Doctor Perplexarum. Basle,
1629. Small 4to., contemporary calf, worn. Smith 193-117 1973 $15

MOSHE Almosnino Moshe. Saloniki, 1572. First edition, bad wormhole, some
stains, small 4to., old calf, rebacked, rare. Thomas 32-60 1974 £220

MOSHE CORDOVERO TOMER DEVORAH   Or Ne'erav. Venice, 1587. Small
8vo., shagreen, woodcut border. Thomas 32-58 1974 £100

MOSHEIM, JOHN L.   An Ecclesiastical History. 1838. 2 vols.,
thick 8vo., contemporary full calf gilt. Howes 185-1472 1974 £6.50

MOSHEMIUS, J. LAURENT   De Rebus Christianorum Ante Constantinum
Magnum Commentarii. Helmstadii, 1753. 4to., full calf, gilt stamp, slight
spotting, very good copy. Bow Windows 66-488 1974 £15

MOSKOWITZ, HENRY   Alfred E. Smith. Seltzer, 1924. Austin
62-433 1974 $8.50

MOSLY, EPHRAIM   Teeth, Their Natural History. London, 1862.
Cover neatly detached. Rittenhouse 46-483 1974 $25

MOSS, ARTHUR   The Legend of the Latin Quarter. New York,
1946. Biblo & Tannen 213-798 1973 $6.50

MOSS, C. E.   Vegetation of the Peak District. Cambridge,
1913. 8vo., cloth, maps, illus., scarce. Wheldon 129-1006 1974 £7.50

MOSS, FLETCHER   Pilgrimages. 1901-20. Roy 8vo., orig. cloth.
Broadhurst 23-1480 1974 £70

MOSS, FLETCHER   Pilgrimages. 1903-30. Orig. cloth. Broadhurst 23-1481 1974 £30

MOSS, FLETCHER   Pilgrimages. 1903-30. Vols. 2 - 7, illus.,
roy. 8vo., orig. cloth, fine. Broadhurst 24-1480 1974 £30

MOSS, FLETCHER   Pilgrimages to Old Homes. 1901-20. 7 vols.,
roy. 8vo., illus., buckram. Quaritch 939-180 1974 £35

MOSS, THOMAS   A Treatise of Gauging. London, 1779. 8vo.,
contemporary calf. Hammond 201-885 1974 £9.50

MOSS, W. G.   The History and Antiquities of the Town and
Port of Hastings. 1824. Roy. 8vo., contemporary half black calf, plates,
foxing, first edition. Howes 186-2200 1974 £30

MOSSMAN, S.   New Japan. 1873. Contemporary half calf.
Broadhurst 23-1686 1974 £5

MOSSO, ANGELO   Der Mensch auf den Hochalpen. Leipzig, 1899.
8vo., boards, illus. Gurney 64-156 1974 £12

MOSSO, ANGELO   Der Mensch auf den Hochalpen. Leipzig, 1899.
8vo., boards, illus. Gurney 66-134 1974 £12

MOSZKOWSKI, A.   Einstein the Searcher. 1921. First edition.
Covent 55-1319 1974 £6.50

MOTHER Goose. 1913. 4to., dec. white buckram, plates, illus., fine, signed.
Broadhurst 23-163 1974 £80

MOTHER GOOSE   Denslow's Mother Goose, Being the Old Familiar
Rhymes and Jingles. New York, 1901. 4to., pictorial boards, rebacked,
rehinged, some marginal tears, first edition. Frohnsdorff 16-582 1974 $40

MOTHER GOOSE   Mother Goose as Told by Kellogg's Singing
Lady. Battle Creek, 1933. Small 4to., pictorial wrappers, color illus., fine
copy. Frohnsdorff 15-119 1974 $10

MOTHER GOOSE   Mother Goose Magic Window. New York,
(1943). 4to., pictorial boards, spiral bound, color illus, very good copy.
Frohnsdorff 16-585 1974 $15

MOTHER GOOSE   Old Nurse's Book of Rhymes, Jingles and
Ditties. Philadelphia, n.d. (c. 1860). 12mo., orig. pictorial wrappers (edges
frayed), hand colored engravings, very good copy. Frohnsdorff 16-586 1974
$65

MOTHERBY, GEORGE   A New Medical Dictionary. 1775. Folio,
old calf, rebacked, plates, rubbed. Thomas 28-268 1972 £25

MOTLEY, JOHN LOTHROP   The Rise of the Dutch Republic. London, 1889. 8vo., 3 vols., blue morocco, gilt, new edition. Dawsons PM 251-289 1974 £15

MOTOGRAPH Moving Picture Book. 1898. Coloured illus., 4to., orig. cloth backed boards, little soiled. George's 610-544 1973 £25

MOTT, DAVID WALLACE   The Story of the Pioneer Days of a Masonic Lodge in the Far West. (Santa Paula, 1928). 12mo., cloth, presentation. Saddleback 14-198 1974 $15

MOTT, F. T.   The Flora of Leicestershire. 1886. 8vo., cloth, coloured maps. Wheldon 128-1204 1973 £10

MOTT, FRANK LUTHER   Golden Multitudes. New York, 1947. lst ed. Biblo & Tannen 213-799 1973 $7.50

MOTT, J. T.   The Last Days of Francis the First and Other Poems. 1843. 8vo., cloth, first edition. Quaritch 936-502 1974 £10

MOTTELEY, C.   Apercu sur les Erreurs de la Bibliographie Speciale des Elzevirs & de Leurs Annexes, Avec Quelques Decouvertes Curieuses sur la Typographie Hollandaise & Belge du XVIIe Siecle. Brussels, 1848. Orig. printed wrappers, 16mo. Kraus B8-61 1974 $27.50

MOTTEUX, PETER ANTHONY   Love's a Jest. London, 1696. 4to., modern cloth, book-plate, first edition. Dawsons PM 252-731 1974 £100

MOTTLEY, JOHN   Joe Miller's Jests. London, 1739. 8vo., modern half calf, third edition. Dawsons PM 252-732 1974 £35

MOTTRAM, RALPH HALE   The Spanish Farm. 1924-26. 3 vols., orig. cloth, first edition. Rota 188-711 1974 £10

MOULE, THOMAS   Bibliotheca Heraldica Magnae Britanniae. 1822. Roy. 8vo., full morocco, illus., scarce, first edition. Howes 186-1644 1974 £28

MOULIN, ETINNE   Traite de l'Apoplexie. Paris, 1819. 8vo., contemporary marbled calf, first edition. Schumann 35-344 1974 $85

MOULIN-ECKART, RICHARD COUNT DU   Cosima Wagner. New York, 1930. Illus., 2 vols. Biblo & Tannen 214-930 1974 $15

MOULT, THOMAS   Down Here the Hawthorn. 1921. 61 pages. Austin 61-731 1974 $10

MOULTON, RICHARD G.   Shakespeare as a Dramatic Artist. Oxford, 1888. Austin 51-667 1973 $10

MOUNTAIN, G. J.   Visit to the Gaspe Coast. Quebec, 1943. Quebec, 1943. Card cover. Hood's 102-302 1974 $12.50

MOUNTAIN, G. J.   Visit to the Gaspe Coast. Quebec, 1943. Limited edition. Hood's 104-319 1974 $12.50

MOUNTAINE, WILLIAM   An Account of the Methods used to Discribe Lines. 1758. Small 4to., disbound. Zeitlin 235-105 1974 $127.50

MOUNTENEY-JEPHSON, A. J.   Emin Pasha and the Rebellion at the Equator. 1890. Thick demy 8vo., plates, orig. pictorial buckram gilt, second edition. Smith 194-586 1974 £8.50

MOUREY, G.   La Peinture Anglaise du XVIIIe Siecle. Paris & Brussels, 1928. 4to., plates, sewed. Quaritch 940-188 1974 £10

MOURLON, M.   Geologie de la Belgique. Brussels, 1880-81. 2 vols. in 1, 8vo., half calf. Wheldon 131-1050 1974 £7.50

MOURRAILLE, J. R.   Traite de la Resolution des Equations Invariables. Paris, 1770. 4to., contemporary mottled calf, gilt, plates. Dawsons PM 245-524 1974 £20

MOUTON, EUGENE   L'Art d'Ecrire un Livre, de l'Imprimer et de le Publier. Paris, 1896. 4to., orig. printed wrappers, three quarter leather, gilt back, uncut. Kraus B8-357 1974 $65

MOUTON-FONTENILLE, J. P.   Tableau des Systemes de Botanique. Lyons, 1801. 8vo., contemporary calf, tables. Wheldon 128-1143 1973 £10

MOVIE Lot to Beachhead. Doubleday, 1945. 291p., illus. Austin 51-566 1973 $8.50

MOWRY, W. A.   Marcus Whitman and the Early Days of Oregon. New York, 1901. Fine copy. Jenkins 61-2084 1974 $25

MOXON, JOSEPH   Mechanick Exercises. 1677-1680. 4to., eighteenth century tree calf, rebacked, first edition. Dawsons PM 245-525 1974 £340

MOYES, HENRY   Heads of a Course of Lectures on the Natural History of the Celestial Bodies. N.P. (Boston?), n.d. (1784?). 8vo., sewn, first edition, very scarce. Ximenes 37-152 1974 $75

MOYNIHAN, BERKELEY   Abdominal Operations. Philadelphia, 1914. 2 vols., revised third edition. Rittenhouse 46-484 1974 $10

MOYNIHAN, BERKELEY   Abdominal Operations. Philadelphia, 1926. 2 vols., fourth edition. Rittenhouse 46-485 1974 $10

MOYNIHAN, BERKELEY   The Spleen, and Some of Its Diseases. Philadelphia, 1921. Rittenhouse 46-488 1974 $15

MOZART, WOLFGANG AMADEUS   Cosi Fan Tutte o Sia la Fouola Degli Emanti. Bonn, c. 1790. Quarter morocco, rebound. Eaton Music-521 1973 £25

MOZART, WOLFGANG AMADEUS   Dans Bandchen. Leipzig, (1795). Oblong folio, unbounc, uncut, first edition. Quaritch 940-817 1974 £75

MUDD, W.   A Manual of British Lichens. Darlington, 1861. Roy 8vo., orig. cloth, plates. Wheldon 129-1412 1974 £16

MUDDIMAN, BERNARD   The Men of the Nineties. 1920. One of 250 copies, quarter parchment vellum, very nice copy. Covent 51-2488 1973 £6.50

MUDFORD, WILLIAM   An Historical Account of the Campaign In the Netherlands. London, 1817. 4to., plates, contemporary red straight grained morocco gilt. Traylen 79-154 1973 £180

MUDGE, ZACHARIAH ATWELL   The Forest Boy: A Sketch of the Life of Abraham Lincoln. New York, (1867). Cloth, spine faded, minor spotting. Hayman 59-360 1974 $10

MUDIE, ROBERT   The Feathered Tribes of British Islands. 1835. 2 vols., 8vo., orig. brown cloth, plates, second edition. Wheldon 131-665 1974 £25

MUDIE, ROBERT   The Feathered Tribes of the British Islands. 1835. 8vo., 2 vols., orig. cloth, second edition. Wheldon 130-587 1974 £22

MUDIE, ROBERT   The Feathered Tribes of the British Islands. 1835. 8vo., 2 vols., orig. brown cloth, plates. Wheldon 129-507 1974 £22

MUDIE, ROBERT   The Feathered Tribes of the British Islands. 1835. 2 vols., 8vo., contemporary full green calf gilt, plates, second edition. Wheldon 131-91 1974 £35

MUDIE, ROBERT   The Feathered Tribes of the British Islands. 1841. Crown 8vo., 2 vols., orig. cloth, third edition. Wheldon 129-508 1974 £15

MUDIE, ROBERT   The Picture of Australia. London, 1829. 8vo., half dark red calf, gilt, browning. Traylen 79-553 1973 £60

MUDIE-SMITH, R.   The Religious Life of London. 1904. 8vo., orig. cloth, folding maps, charts, some spotting, covers faded. Bow Windows 66-491 1974 £10

MUELLER, DAN   Chico of the Cross U P Ranch. Chicago, 1938. Decor. cloth, illus. Dykes 24-107 1974 $10

MUELLER, DAN   My Life with Buffalo Bill. Chicago, 1948. Cloth, illus., lst ed. Dykes 24-108 1974 $12.50

MUELLER, F. VON   Eucalyptographia. Melbourne, 1879-84. 4to., new buckram, plates. Wheldon 129-1618 1974 £90

MUELLER, F. VON   Iconography of Australian Species of Acacia. Melbourne, 1887-88. 13 parts in 2 vols., 4to., cloth, plates, complete copy, rare. Wheldon 128-1618 1973 £65

MUELLER, F. VON   Index Perfectus ad Caroli Linnaei Species Plantarum, Nempe Earum Primam Editionem. Melbourne, 1880. 8vo., orig. wrappers, very scarce. Wheldon 128-1136 1973 £7.50

MUELLER, F. VON   Select Extra-Tropical Plants. Sydney, 1881. 8vo., orig. cloth. Wheldon 129-1662 1974 £10

MUELLER, F. VON   Select Extra-Tropical Plants Readily Eligible for Industrial Culture or Naturalisation. Calcutta, 1880. 8vo., cloth, inscribed. Wheldon 131-1791 1974 £10

MUELLER, F. VON   Select Plants Readily Eligible for Industrial Culture or Naturalisation in Victoria. Melbourne, 1876. 8vo., orig. wrappers, presentation copy, inscription. Wheldon 128-1659 1973 £10

MUELLER, F. VON   Select Plants Readily Eligible for Industrial Culture or Naturalisation in Victoria. Melbourne, 1876. 8vo., orig. wrappers, presentation copy. Wheldon 130-1595 1974 £10

MUELLER, JOHANNES, REGIOMONTANUS 1436-1476   Calendarium. (Venice, 1483). Small 4to., boards, leather spine, woodcut diagrams, Georg Tannstetter's copy. Kraus 137-71 1974 $375

MUENSTER, SEBASTIAN   Organum Uranicum. 1536. 4to., modern half calf, gilt. Zeitlin 235-161 1974 $350

MUENSTER, SEBASTIAN   Rudimenta Mathematica. 1551. Folio, half calf, worn, illus., first edition. Dawsons PM 245-528 1974 £120

MUGO, THOMAS   The Bewick Collector. 1866-68. 8vo and 4to., orig. cloth, illus. Hammond 201-471 1974 £75

MUIR, EDWIN   John Knox: Portrait of a Calvinist. 1929. Illus., upper board very lightly spotted, nice copy, worn d.w., first edition. Covent 51-1330 1973 £12.50

MUIR, EDWIN   The Three Brothers. 1931. English first edition. Covent 56-1947 1974 £45

MUIR, EDWIN   Variations on a Time Theme. 1934. Boards, very good copy, first edition. Covent 51-1332 1973 £5.25

MUIR, PERCY H.   Points. London, 1931. 8vo., plates, orig. parchment-backed boards, limited. Dawsons PM 10-438 1974 £80

MUIR, PERCY H.   Points. London, 1931. 8vo., plates, orig. parchment-backed boards, limited. Dawsons PM 252-733 1974 £80

MUIR, RAMSAY   Bygone Liverpool. Liverpool, 1913. 4to., orig. cloth gilt, plates, first edition. Dawsons PM 251-56 1974 £35

MUIR, RAMSAY   A History of Liverpool. 1907. Extra Crown 8vo., orig. cloth, illus. Broadhurst 23-1483 1974 £6

MUIR, WILLIAM   The Caliphate. Edinburgh, 1924. Large 8vo., maps, new revised & best edition. Howes 186-1090 1974 £6.50

MUIRHEAD, G.   The Birds of Berwickshire. Edinburgh, 1889-95. 8vo., 2 vols., orig. blue cloth, scarce. Wheldon 130-588 1974 £12

MUIRHEAD, JAMES PATRICK   Correspondence of the Late James Watt. London, 1846. Roy 4to., orig. half cloth, gilt, uncut. Zeitlin 235-301 1974 $125

MUKERJI, DHAN GOPAL   Fierce-Face. New York, 1936. 8vo., cloth, illus. by Dorothy P. Lathrop, fine copy, slightly worn d.j., first edition. Frohnsdorff 16-481 1974 $10

MULFORD, CLARENCE E.   The Bar-20 Rides Again. n.d. Dust wrapper, rubbed. Covent 55-1522 1974 £5

DE MULIERUM PASSIONIBUS Liber. 1793. 8vo., quarter morocco, marbled boards, first edition. Dawsons PM 249-380 1974 £145

MULLENS, WILLIAM HERBERT   A Bibliography of British Ornithology. (1916)-1917. 8vo., half morocco gilt, very scarce, limited. Wheldon 128-124 1973 £75

MULLENS, WILLIAM HERBERT   A Geographical Bibliography of British Ornithology to 1918 Arranged Under Counties. 1920. 8vo., cloth. Wheldon 128-125 1973 £7.50

MULLENS, WILLIAM HERBERT   A Geographical Bibliography of British Ornithology to 1918. 1920. 8vo., cloth. Wheldon 131-236 1974 £10

MULLER, C. O.   The History and Antiquities of the Doric Race. London, 1839. 2 vols., 8vo., maps, orig. cloth-backed boards, worn, second edition. Bow Windows 62-653 1974 £8.75

MULLER, DAN   Chico of the Cross UP Ranch. Chicago, (1938). Dec. cloth, drawings by author, fine, first edition. Dykes 22-16 1973 $10

MULLER, F. M.   Science of Thought. 1887. Allen 216-1401 1974 $10

MULLER, GERHARD FRIEDRICH   Voyages from Asia to America. London, 1761. 4to., unbound, maps, first edition. Traylen 79-492 1973 £325

MULLER, H.   The Fertilisation of Flowers. 1883. 8vo., orig. cloth, text-figures, very scarce, nice copy. Wheldon 128-1144 1973 £20

MULLER, JOHANN AUGUST   Versuch eines Huttenmannischen Berights. Leipzig, 1825. 8vo., orig. marbled boards, fine, first edition. Dawsons PM 245-526 1974 £8.50

MULLER, JOHANN WOLFGANG   Repertorium der Mathematischen Literatur. Augsburg und Leipzig, (1822). 8vo., quarter calf, gilt, first edition. Dawsons PM 245-527 1974 £15

MULLER, JOHANNES   Handbuch der Physiologie des Menschen. 1837-1840. 8vo., 2 vols., contemporary boards, first edition. Schumann 35-346 1974 $135

MULLER, JOHANNES   Uber den Feinern bau und die Formen der Krankhaften Geschwulste. Berlin, 1838. 4to., unbound, uncut, fine, rare, first edition. Dawsons PM 249-381 1974 £375

MULLER, MARGARETHE   Carla Wenckebach. Ginn, 1908. Austin 62-435 1974 $8.50

MULLER, MAX   The Collected Works of. 1901-06. 19 vols. of 20, 8vo., orig. cloth, plates, illus. Bow Windows 66-492 1974 £48

MULLER, O.   Cryptogamen Flora. Gera, 1876-77. Folio, orig. cloth, coloured plates, scarce. Wheldon 128-1402 1973 £25

MULLINER, H. H.   The Decorative Arts in England 1660-1780. (1923). Folio, illus., half vellum. Quaritch 940-466 1974 £15

MULLINGER, JAMES B.   The University of Cambridge from the Earliest Times to the Royal Injunctions of 1535. Cambridge, 1873. 3 vols., thick 8vo., half morocco, fine. Traylen 79-316 1973 £20

MULROONEY, P. J.   St. Brigid's Parish, Toronto, 1920-1945. Toronto, (1945?). Illus. Hood's 104-320 1974 $10

MULSANT, E.   Histoire Naturelle des Oiseaux-Mouches. Lyons, (1873-) 1876-77. 4 vols., 4to., half red calf, rare. Wheldon 131-666 1974 £75

MULSANT, E.   Histoire Naturelle des Oiseaux-Mouches. Lyons, (1873)-1876-77. 4 vols., 4to., half red morocco, plates, very rare. Wheldon 131-92 1974 £1,250

MULVANEY, CHARLES P.   The History of the Northwest Rebellion of 1885. . . . Including a History of the Indian Tribes of North-West Canada. Toronto, 1885. First edition, thick 12mo., maps, spine and hinges repaired, covers worn, interior fine. Current BW9-397 1974 $18.75

MULVANEY, CHARLES P.   The History of the North-West Rebellion of 1885. Toronto, 1885. Hood's 104-869 1974 $40

MULVANEY, CHARLES P.   The History of the North-West Rebellion of 1885 ...Including a History of the Indian Tribes of North-Western Canada. Toronto, 1885. Illus., portraits, maps, engravings, cover scuffed. Hood's 102-822 1974 $35

MUMBY, FRANK ARTHUR   Publishing and Bookselling. 1930. 8vo., orig. cloth. Broadhurst 23-430 1974 £6

MUMBY, FRANK ARTHUR   Publishing and Bookselling. London, 1934. 8vo., plates, illus., orig. cloth, first edition. Dawsons PM 10-439 1974 £5

MUMEY, NOLIE   A Study of Rare Books. Denver, 1930. Boards, buckram, signed, illus. Dawson's 424-209 1974 $50

MUMFORD, JOHN KIMBERLY   Oriental Rugs. New York, 1905. Imp. 8vo., plates, illus., cloth, third edition. Quaritch 940-413 1974 £75

MUMFORD, JOHN KIMBERLY   Oriental Rugs. New York, 1927. Pict. cloth, 4to., color plates, text illus., folding maps. Wilson 63-283 1974 $10

MUMFORD, LEWIS   The Culture of Cities. New York, c. 1938. First edition, illus. Wilson 63-36 1974 $10

MUNCHENER Porte-Monnaie Kalender fur das Schaftjahr 1876. Munich. Gilt metal cover, 1 3/4 X 1 1/4, fine. Gregory 44-399 1974 $30

MUNDAY, ANTHONY   A Briefe Chronicle of the Successe of Times, From the Creation of the World, to This Instant. London, 1611. 8vo., early sheep, rubbed, hinges tender, first edition, good sound copy. Ximenes 36-153 1974 $125

MUNIMENTA Gildhallae Londoniensis. 1859-62. 3 vols. in 4, orig. half roan, rubbed. Howes 186-1181 1974 £35

MUNNINGS, ALFRED JAMES   Pictures of Horses and English Life. London, 1927. 4to., illus., scarce, orig. edition. Traylen 79-290 1973 £85

MUNNINGS, ALFRED JAMES   Pictures of Horses and English Life. 1927. 4to., full vellum gilt, fine, English first edition. Covent 56-1485 1974 £250

MUNOZ Y MANZANO DE LA VINAZA, CIPRIANO   Bibliografia Espanola de Lenguas. Madrid, 1892. 4to., cloth. Dawsons PM 11-549 1974 £14.75

MUNRO, ALEXANDER   An Enquiry into the New Opinions. London, 1696. 8vo., contemporary calf, rebacked, first edition. Dawsons PM 251-510 1974 £15

MUNRO, C. K.   At Mrs. Beam's. Knopf, 1923. Austin 51-668 1973 $8.50

MUNROE, JAMES PHINNEY   The New England Conscience. Boston, 1915. Biblo & Tannen 213-71 1973 $7.50

MUNROE, K.   At War With Pontiac. London, 1896. 8vo., illus., orig. pictorial cloth. Bow Windows 62-654 1974 £6

MUNROE, K.   Through Swamp and Glade. London, 1897. 8vo., illus., orig. pictorial cloth. Bow Windows 62-655 1974 £5

MUNROE, K.   With Crockett and Bowie. London, 1898. 8vo., plates, orig. pictorial cloth. Bow Windows 62-656 1974 £6

MUNSELL, A. H.   Atlas of the Munsell Color System. N.P., n.d. Cloth, charts. Dawson's 424-167 1974 $35

MUNSON, LAURA GORDON   Flowers From My Garden. New York, 1864. 4to., plates, worn. Traylen 79-42 1973 £38

MUNSTER, SEBASTIAN
Please turn to
MUENSTER, SEBASTIAN

MUNSTERBERG, HUGO   American Traits. Houghton, Mifflin, 1901. Austin 62-437 1974 $7.50

MUNSTERBERG, HUGO   The Americans. 1904. 619 pages. Austin 57-468 1974 $10

MUNSTERBERG, HUGO   The Americans. McChire, 1904. Austin 62-438 1974 $10

MUNSTERBERG, HUGO   The Eternal Life. Houghton, 1905. Austin 62-439 1974 $7.50

MUNSTERBERG, HUGO   The War and America. Appleton, 1914. Austin 62-440 1974 $10

MUNTHE, AXEL   Letters from a Mourning City. London, 1899. Orig. binding, second edition, presentation inscription, nice. Ross 87-419 1974 $12.50

MUNTHE, AXEL   Vagaries. London, 1898. Orig. binding, first edition, very nice copy. Ross 87-421 1974 $12.50

MUNTING, A.   Naauwkeurige Beschryving der Aardgewassen. Leyden, 1696. Folio, contemporary calf gilt, plates, rare. Wheldon 130-54 1974 £525

MUNTING, A.   Waare Oeffening de Planten. Amsterdam, 1672. 4to., contemporary vellum, plates, rare first edition. Wheldon 131-1552 1974 £100

MUNTZ, EARL EDWARD   Race Contact. Appleton-Century, 1927. Austin 62-441 1974 $17.50

MUNTZ, J. H.   Encaustic: Or, Count Caylus's Method of Painting in the Manner of the Ancients. 1760. Small 8vo., contemporary calf. Quaritch 940-189 1974 £45

MURATORI, LODOVICO ANTONIO   Relation des Missions du Paraguai. Paris, 1754. 8vo., contemporary mottled calf, spine gilt, first edition, fine, folding map. Ximenes 36-154 1974 $100

MURCH, HERBERT S.   The Knight of the Burning Pestle by Beaumont and Fletcher. 1908. Ex-library, sturdy library binding. Austin 61-30 1974 $37.50

MURCHISON, CHARLES   A Treatise on the Continued Fevers of Great Britain. London, 1862. 8vo., half calf, diagrams, coloured plates, dampstained plates. Gurney 66-135 1974 £20

MURCHISON, RODERICK I.   Outline of the Geology of the Neighbourhood of Cheltenham. Cheltenham, 1844. 8vo., plates, orig. cloth, new edition. Quaritch 939-362 1974 £20

MURCHISON, RODERICK I.   Siluria. 1859. 8vo., contemporary half calf, worn, plates. Wheldon 129-846 1974 £25

MURCHISON, RODERICK I.   Siluria, the History of the Oldest Fossiliferous Rocks and Their Foundations. 1859. 8vo., orig. cloth, plates, coloured frontispiece, folding coloured map, revised third edition. Wheldon 128-1024 1973 £20

MURCHISON, RODERICK I.   The Silurian System. 1839. 4to., 2 vols., contemporary russia, woodcuts, plates. Wheldon 129-845 1974 £275

MURCHISON, RODERICK I.   The Silurian System. 1839. 4to., contemporary full calf, gilt, woodcuts. Wheldon 130-55 1974 £275

MURET, MARC-ANTOINE   Variarum Lectionum Libri XV. Antwerp, 1580. 8vo., contemporary pigskin over wooden boards, covers richly blind tooled, very fine copy, important enlarged edition. Schafer 10-105 1974 sFr 750

MURET, MARC-ANTOINE   Variarum Lectionum Libri XVIIII. 1791-1828. 2 vols. Allen 213-1664 1973 $10

MURIE, J.   On the Habits, Structure and Relations of the Three-banded Armadillo. 1872. 4to., plates. Wheldon 131-514 1974 £7.50

MURNER, THOMAS   Die Schelmenzunft. Berlin, 1925. 4to., illus., wrappers. Kraus B8-180 1974 $15

MURPHY, ARTHUR   All in the Wrong. 1761. 8vo., boards, first edition. Quaritch 936-165 1974 £8

MURPHY, ARTHUR   Alzuma. 1773. 8vo., cloth, first edition. Quaritch 936-166 1974 £9

MURPHY, ARTHUR   The Apprentice. 1756. 8vo., cloth, first edition. Quaritch 936-167 1974 £8

MURPHY, ARTHUR   The Desert Island. 1760. 8vo., cloth, frontispiece, first edition. Quaritch 936-168 1974 £8

MURPHY, ARTHUR   The Life of David Garrick. 1801. 8vo., 2 vols., contemporary calf, gilt, first edition. Hill 126-110 1974 £25

MURPHY, ARTHUR   The Old Maid. 8vo., cloth, uncut, first edition. Quaritch 936-170 1974 £10

MURPHY, ARTHUR   The Orphan of China. 1759. 8vo., cloth, second edition. Quaritch 936-172 1974 £5

MURPHY, ARTHUR   The Orphan of China. 1759. 8vo., cloth, first edition. Quaritch 936-171 1974 £12

MURPHY, ARTHUR   The School for Guardians. London, 1767. 8vo., modern boards, first edition. Dawsons PM 252-736 1974 £14

MURPHY, ARTHUR   Zenobia. London, 1768. 8vo., modern boards, first edition. Dawsons PM 252-737 1974 £15

MURPHY, FRANCIS   Memories of Francis Murphy. Long Beach, Cal., n.d., ca. 1907. 196p., illus. Austin 62-442 1974 $17.50

MURPHY, GWENDOLEN   A Bibliography of English Character Books. London, 1925. Small 4to., orig. wrappers, uncut, unopened. Dawsons PM 10-442 1974 £8

MURPHY, GWENDOLYN   A Select Bibliography of the Writings of Alfred W. Pollard. Oxford, 1938. 8vo., orig. boards, fine, limited. Dawsons PM 10-493 1974 £15

MURPHY, JOHN M.   American Game Bird Shooting. New York, 1882. First edition, 8vo., woodcut illus., orig. green cloth, some spotting on binding, interior mint. Current BW9-190 1974 $40

MURPHY, JOHN NICHOLAS   Terra Incognita. 1873. Thick large 8vo., bookplate, scarce. Howes 185-1476 1974 £7.50

MURPHY, PATRICK   Rudiments of the Primary Forces of Gravity, Magnetism, and Electricity. London, 1830. 8vo., old-style boards, first edition. Schumann 35-347 1974 $95

MURPHY, ROBERT E.   Progressive West Virginians. (1905). Orig. cloth, illus. Putnam 126-259 1974 $22.50

MURPHY, ROBERT E.   Progressive West Virginians. Wheeling, 1905. 4to., leather. Saddleback 14-755 1974 $40

MURPHY, T. W.   Dublin After the Six Days Insurrection. Dublin, (1916). 8vo., cloth boards. Emerald 50-635 1974 £5

MURPHY, THOMAS   The Presbytery of the Log College. Philadelphia, (1889). 8vo., orig. bindings, plates. Butterfield 8-497 1974 $20

MURPHY, THOMAS D.   The Wonderlands of the American West. Boston, 1913. 8vo., orig. bindings. Butterfield 8-710 1974 $15

MURPHY, WILLIAM S.   The Textile Industries. 1910. 8 vols., illus., fine. Covent 55-1320 1974 £30

MURR, J.   Neue Uebersicht Uber die Farn und Blutenpflanzen Van Vorarlberg und Liechtenstein. Bregenz, 1923-26. 8vo., cloth, plates, scarce. Wheldon 131-1335 1974 £10

MURRAY, A.   The Northern Flora. Edinburgh, 1836. 8vo., orig. printed boards, cloth back, plates, rare. Wheldon 128-1205 1973 £7.50

MURRAY, A. G.   "Going Back". Princeton, 1934. First edition, 4to., photos, orig. orange cloth, bit soiled, one illus. loose, else perfect. Current BW9-414 1974 $28.50

MURRAY, ALICE EFFIE   A History of the Commercial and Financial Relations Between England and Ireland. London, 1903. 8vo., cloth boards. Emerald 50-636 1974 £6

MURRAY, ANDREW   Ship-Building in Iron and Wood. Edinburgh, 1863. 4to., cloth, gilt, plates, second edition. Hammond 201-703 1974 £24.50

MURRAY, CHARLES A.   Travels in North America During the Years 1834, 1835, and 1836, Including a Summer Residence With the Pawnee Tribe of Indians. London, 1839. 2 vols., first edition. Jenkins 61-1773 1974 $85

MURRAY, FRANCIS EDWIN   A Bibliography of Austin Dobson. Derby, 1900. Oblong 4to., orig. jap-vellum-backed boards, uncut. Dawsons PM 10-191 1974 £22

MURRAY, GILBERT   Aeschylus. 1939. Paper printed wrapper, inscribed, first edition. Broadhurst 23-857 1974 £5

MURRAY, GILBERT   Aeschylus. Oxford, 1940. 8vo., orig. cloth, inscribed, first edition. Broadhurst 23-858 1974 £5

MURRAY, GILBERT   Aristophanes. Oxford, 1933. 8vo., orig. cloth, inscribed, first edition. Broadhurst 23-852 1974 £5

MURRAY, GILBERT   Aristophanes. Oxford, 1933. Orig. cloth, inscribed, first edition. Broadhurst 23-853 1974 £6

MURRAY, GILBERT   The Electra of Euripides. 1905. Crown 8vo., half vellum, gilt, first edition. Broadhurst 23-826 1974 £10

MURRAY, GILBERT   The Classical Tradition in Poetry. Oxford, 1927. Crown 8vo., orig. cloth, first edition. Broadhurst 23-846 1974 £6

MURRAY, GILBERT   Essays and Addresses. 1921. 8vo., orig. cloth, inscribed, first edition. Broadhurst 23-843 1974 £5

MURRAY, GILBERT   The Eumenides of Aeschylus. 1925. Crown 8vo., orig. cloth, inscribed, first edition. Broadhurst 23-845 1974 £5

MURRAY, GILBERT   Four Stages of Greek Religion. New York, 1912. 8vo., orig. cloth, inscribed, first edition. Broadhurst 23-834 1974 £6

MURRAY, GILBERT   Gobi. 1890. Crown 8vo., orig. cloth, inscribed, third edition. Broadhurst 23-822 1974 £6

MURRAY, GILBERT   Gobi. 1890. Orig. cloth, mint, third edition. Broadhurst 23-823 1974 £6

MURRAY, GILBERT   The Iphigenia on Tauris of Euripides. New York, 1915. Crown 8vo., full morocco, limited edition. Broadhurst 23-837 1974 £20

MURRAY, GILBERT   Liberality and Civilization. 1938. Post 8vo., orig. cloth, inscribed, first edition. Broadhurst 23-855 1974 £5

MURRAY, GILBERT   The Oresteia. 1928. Crown 8vo., orig. cloth, inscribed, first edition. Broadhurst 23-847 1974 £6

MURRAY, GILBERT   Oxford Poetry. Oxford, 1913. Crown 8vo., boards, uncut, first edition. Broadhurst 23-835 1974 £5

MURRAY, GILBERT   The Story of Nefrekepta from a Demotic Papyrus. Oxford, 1911. Crown 4to., boards, uncut, inscribed, first edition. Broadhurst 23-833 1974 £5

MURRAY, GILBERT   The Trojan Women of Euripides. 1905. Crown 8vo., orig. cloth, inscribed, first edition. Broadhurst 23-828 1974 £5

MURRAY, GILBERT   The Trojan Women of Euripides. Philadelphia, 1915. Small 4to., full morocco, gilt, uncut, inscribed. Broadhurst 23-836 1974 £50

MURRAY, HUGH   An Historical and Descriptive Account of British America. Edinburgh, 1839. 3 vols., engravings, second edition. Hood's 104-655 1974 $150

MURRAY, JOHN   Bathymetrical Survey. Edinburgh, 1910. 8vo., 6 vols., plates, contemporary half pig skin. Bow Windows 64-193 1974 £150

MURRAY, J. A.   Opuscula in Quibus Commentationes Varias tam Medicas Quam ad Rem Naturalem Spectantes Retractavit Emendavit Auxit. Gottingen, 1785-86. 2 vols. in 1, 8vo., boards, plates. Wheldon 128-1145 1973 £5

MURRAY, J. F.   A Picturesque Tour of the River Thames On Its Western Course. 1849. 8vo., cloth, maps, first edition. Quaritch 939-260 1974 £15

MURRAY, JOHN   Bathymetrical Survey of the Scottish Fresh Water Lochs During the Years 1897-1909. Edinburgh, 1910. Roy. 8vo., plates, half contemporary pigskin gilt. Smith 193-217 1973 £5.50

MURRAY, JOHN   Bathymetrical Survey of the Scottish Fresh Water Lochs. Edinburgh, 1910. Roy. 8vo., half morocco, plates, maps. Wheldon 131-322 1974 £7.50

MURRAY, JOHN   Bathymetrical Survey of the Scottish Fresh Water Lochs, Report on the Scientific Results. Edinburgh, 1910. 6 vols., roy. 8vo., orig. half pigskin, coloured maps, plates, very scarce set. Wheldon 128-158 1973 £100

MURRAY, JOHN   A Comparative View of the Huttonian and Nep-tunian Systems of Geology. Edinburgh, 1802. 8vo., old half calf, rebacked. Gurney 64-157 1974 £45

MURRAY, JOHN   The Physiology of Plants. London, 1833. 8vo., orig. cloth, illus., first edition. Hammond 201-665 1974 £5

MURRAY, JOHN WILSON   Memoirs of a Great Detective. New York, 1905. Biblo & Tannen 210-495 1973 $15

MURRAY, K. M. E.   The Constitutional History of the Cinque Ports. 1935. Frontispiece. Howes 186-2055 1974 £6

MURRAY, LINDLEY   English Exercises Adapted to Murray's English Grammar. 1822. Old calf, worn. Austin 61-736 1974 $10

MURRAY, LINDLEY   English Grammar. London, 1866. Cloth. Austin 61-737 1974 $10

MURRAY, LINDLEY   The English Reader. Newark, 1837. Orig. calf, good condition. Austin 61-738 1974 $12.50

MURRAY, LINDLEY   Memoirs of the Life and Writings of. York, 1826. 8vo., contemporary half calf, gilt, first edition. Hammond 201-283 1974 £8

MURRAY, LINDLEY   Murray's English Reader. Albany, 1829. Lea-ther. Hayman 57-513 1974 $12.50

MURRAY, LINDLEY   Sequel to the English Reader. 1839. Old calf, worn. Austin 61-739 1974 $10

MURRAY, LINDLEY   The Young Man's Best Companion and Book of General Knowledge. 1828. Plates, 8vo., calf, head of spine defective. George's 610-549 1973 £5

MURRAY, MARGARET ALICE   The God of the Witches. London, n.d. Signed. Rittenhouse 46-496 1974 $15

MURRAY, MARGARET ALICE   The Witch-Cult In Western Europe. Oxford, 1921. Rittenhouse 46-497 1974 $15

MURRAY, MUNGO   A Treatise on Ship-Building and Navigation. London, 1754. 4to., contemporary calf, plates, fine, first edition. Dawsons PM 245-529 1974 £170

MURRAY, R.   A Proposal for a National Bank. London, 1696. 4to., half speckled calf gilt. Quaritch 939-181 1974 £75

MURRAY, ROSALIND   The Good Pagan's Failure. 1943. Demy 8vo., author's proof copy, corrections in margins and 8 pages of typed MS. of additional matter by author. Broadhurst 24-416 1974 £10

MURRAY, ROSALIND   Hard Liberty. 1929. 3 parts, crown 8vo., paper wrappers, author's proof copy, with corrections in margins by author. Broadhurst 24-413 1974 £10

MURRAY, ROSALIND   Time and the Timeless. 1942. Crown 8vo., paper printed wrapper, first edition, author's proof copy, corrections and additional matter by author. Broadhurst 24-415 1974 £5

MURRAY, ROSALIND   Unstable Ways. 1914. First edition, crown 8vo., disbound, author's proof copy, with MS marginal corrections in author's hand. Broadhurst 24-412 1974 £5

MURRAY, THOMAS   The Story of the Irish in Argentina. 1919. Ex-library. Austin 57-469 1974 $17.50

MURRAY, W. H. H.   Daylight Land. Boston, 1888. Illus. Hood's 104-870 1974 $27.50

MURRAY, W. W.   The Epic of Vimy. Ottawa, 1936. Photographs, first edition. Hood's 103-118 1974 $17.50

MURRY, JOHN MIDDLETON   Autobiography: Between Two Worlds. 1936. Austin 61-740 1974 $12.50

MURRY, JOHN MIDDLETON   Reminiscences of D. H. Lawrence. London, 1933. D.w. soiled & slightly torn, nice, orig. binding. Ross 86-305 1974 $15

MURRY, JOHN MIDDLETON   Son of Woman: The Story of D. H. Lawrence. 1931. Plates, fine, first edition. Covent 51-1105 1973 £5.25

MUSAEUS   Opusculum de Herone & Leandro. 1517. Vellum, worn, woodcuts. Thomas 30-38 1973 £25

MUSCHENBROEK, PETER VON   Grundlehren der Naturwissenschaft. Leipzig, 1747. 8vo., contemporary half calf. Dawsons PM 245-530 1974 £15

MUSCULUS, WOLFGANG   Commonplaces of Christian Religion. 1563. Folio, old calf, well rebacked, first edition, black letter, large device on title, scattered wormholes, some untrimmed leaves, else clean and sound. Thomas 32-48 1974 £125

MUSEUM of Diversion, and Horrible Tales, Among Which is the Heart-Rending Account of the Burial of a Living Girl. Palmer, 1843. 8vo., early plain wrappers, first edition, rare. Ximenes 36-107 1974 $60

MUSEUM for Young Gentlemen and Ladies. Salisbury, 1778. Ninth edition, woodcuts, small 12mo., contemporary quarter calf, very rare. George's 610-551 1973 £45

MUSGRAVE, RICHARD   Memoirs. London and Dublin, 1801. 4to., contemporary half speckled calf, first edition. Dawsons PM 251-290 1974 £20

MUSGRAVE, RICHARD   Memoirs of the Different Rebellions in Ireland. Dublin, 1802. 2 vols., 8vo., orig. boards, uncut, plates, maps, third edition. Bow Windows 66-493 1974 £18.50

MUSGRAVE, SAMUEL   An Essay on the Nature and Cure of the Worm-Fever. London, 1776. 8vo., boards, few small round wormholes. Gurney 66-136 1974 £10

MUSGRAVE, SAMUEL   Two Dissertations. London, 1782. 8vo., orig. marbled boards, uncut, first edition. Dawsons PM 245-569 1974 £20

MUSGRAVE, WILLIAM   Iulii Vitalis Epitaphium Cum Notis Criticis Ex-plicationeq. 1711. 8vo., contemporary calf, first edition. Dawsons PM 251-59 1974 £12.50

THE MUSIC of Poets, a Musicians' Birthday Book. 1889. 8vo., marbled boards, morocco spine. Eaton Music-526 1973 £10

MUSIC TEACHERS' NATIONAL ASSOCIATION   Volume of Proceedings for 1938 through 1948. Oberlin, Ohio and Pittsburgh, 1939-1950. 10 vols., bound. Biblo & Tannen 214-888 1974 $75

MUSSCHENBROEK, JOHANN VAN   Beschreilbung der Doppelten. 1765. 8vo., wrappers, plates. Gurney 64-158 1974 £35

MUSSCHENBROEK, JOHANN VAN   Beschreibung der Doppelten und Einfachen Luftpumpe Nebst Einer Sammlung von Verschiedenen Nutzlichen und Lehrreichen Versuchen. Augsburg, 1765. 8vo., wrappers, folding plates. Gurney 66-137 1974 £35

MUSSCHENBROEK, PIETER VAN   Compendium Physicae Experimentalis. Leyden, 1762. 8vo., contemporary calf, worn, plates, new edition.   Schuman 37-178 1974 $175

MUSSCHENBROEK, PIETER VAN   Course de Physique Experimentale et Mathematique. Paris, 1769. 4to., 3 vols., contemporary mottled calf, labels, gilt. Zeitlin 235-163 1974 $225

MUSSET, ALFRED DE   La Confession d'un Enfant du Siecle. Paris, 1891. Limited to 50 copies on Japanese vellum, engraved plates, roy. 8vo., blue levant morocco, gilt border, gilt edges, orig. wrapper preserved, fine copy, scarce. Sawyer 293-234 1974 £145

MUSSET, ALFRED DE   Oeuvres Completes. Paris, 1865-66. 10 vols., 8vo., contemporary full levant morocco, gilt, superb copy, first edition. L. Goldschmidt 42-320 1974 $900

MUYBRIDGE, E.   Descriptive Zoopraxography. Philadelphia, 1893. 8vo., orig. wrappers, illus., scarce. Wheldon 129-341 1974 £7.50

MY GRANDFATHER's Farm. Edinburgh, 1829. 12mo., orig. boards, uncut. Hill 126-183 1974 £12.50

MY Young Days. London, 1872. Illus., fine, orig. cloth, 8vo. Gregory 44-277 1974 $22.50

MYERS, IRENE T.   A Study In Epic Development. 1901. Ex-library, sturdy library binding. Austin 61-742 1974 $17.50

MYERS, L. H.   The Orissers. 1922. Roy. 8vo., orig. dec. boards, gilt, limited, first edition. Howes 185-346 1974 £10

MYERSCOUGH-WALKER, R.   Stage and Film Decor. London, 1940. 4to., mounted plates in color. Biblo & Tannen 213-902 1973 $27.50

MYLIUS, G.   Das Polyderm. Stuttgart, 1913. 4to., plates, wrappers. Wheldon 131-1179 1974 £5

MYLNE, ROBERT SCOTT   The Master Masons. Edinburgh, 1893. Folio, orig. cloth, plates, illus. Bow Windows 64-624 1974 £24.50

MYLNE, ROBERT SCOTT   The Master Masons to the Crown of Scotland. Edinburgh, 1893. Folio, cloth, illus. Quaritch 939-665 1974 £15

MYLNE, ROBERT SCOTT   The Master Masons to the Crown of Scotland and Their Works. Edinburgh, 1893. Blue cloth, gilt design on cover, illus., Eaton Music-650 1973 £7.50

MYLONAS, GEORGE E.   The Balkan States. St. Louis, 1946. Biblo & Tannen 213-694 1973 $12.50

MYNSICHT, ADRIAN VON   Thesaurus and Armamentarium Medico-Chymicum. London, 1682. Small 8vo., half calf, first edition in English. Schumann 35-349 1974 $175

MYRTLE, ANDREW SCOTT   Practical Observations on the Harrogate Mineral Waters. London, 1867. 8vo., orig. cloth, gilt, first edition. Hammond 201-585 1974 £9.50

MYRTLE, HARRIET   A Story Book of Country Scenes. London, 1846. 12mo., blind stamped cloth, gilt dec. spine, plates, illus. Frohnsdorff 16-600 1974 $15

THE MYSTERIES of Wall Street. Schenectady, (1884). Orig. binding, with errata. Butterfield 10-500 1974 $7.50

MYSTERY WRITERS OF AMERICA.   The Mystery Writer's Handbook. Harper, 1956. 268p. Austin 54-784 1973 $10

N

NABBES, THOMAS   The Bride. London, 1640. 4to., calf antique, woodcut, first edition. Dawsons PM 252-738 1974 £250

NABBES, THOMAS   The Vnfortunate Mother. London, 1640. 4to., half calf, first edition. Dawsons PM 252-739 1974 £210

NABOKOV, VLADIMIR   Ada, or Ardor. n.d. Pirated edition, covers little marked, very good copy, d.w. Covent 51-1344 1973 £8.50

NABOKOV, VLADIMIR   The Real Life of Sebastian Knight. London, 1945. First English edition, very good copy, orig. cloth. Crane 7-190 1974 £5

NABOKOV, VLADIMIR   The Real Life of Sebastian Knight. London, 1945. First edition. Covent 55-1134 1974 £6.30

NAEGELI, C.   The Microscope. 1892. 8vo., cloth, second edition. Wheldon 130-123 1974 £7.50

NALSON, JOHN   The Character of a Rebellion. London, 1681. Folio, disbound, first edition. Dawsons PM 251-291 1974 £18

NALSON, JOHN   Foxes and Firebrands. Dublin and London, 1682. 8vo., contemporary calf, rebacked, fine, second edition. Dawsons PM 251-511 1974 £20

NAMMERS, ERWIN ESSER   Twenty Centuries of Catholic Church Music. Milwaukee, 1949. Biblo & Tannen 214-891 1974 $7.50

NANCE, ALBINIUS   Botschaft des Gouverneurs Albinius Nance an Die Legislatur von Nebraska. Lincoln, 1883. Wrapper. Jenkins 61-1787 1974 $10

NANNFELDT, J. A.   Studien uber die Morphologie und Systematik. 1932. 4to., buckram, plates, scarce. Wheldon 129-1300 1974 £12

NANSEN, FRIDTJOF   "Farthest North". London, 1898. 2 vols., 8vo., maps, plates, illus., orig. cloth, gilt. Bow Windows 62-660 1974 £14

NANSEN, FRIDTJOF   Farthest North. 1904. 8vo., cloth, plates. Wheldon 130-299 1974 £7.50

NANSEN, FRIDTJOF   Fram Over Polhavet. 1897. 2 vols., 8vo., plates, orig. cloth, fine, rare, first edition. Dawsons PM 250-56 1974 £65

NANSEN, FRIDTJOF   In Northern Mists, Arctic Exploration in Early Times. New York, 1911. Illus., 2 vols., handsomely bound, fine set. Hood's 102-68 1974 $50

NANSEN, ODD   From Day to Day. New York, 1949. Illus. Biblo & Tannen 213-695 1973 $8.50

NANTUCKET, 'Sconset and Along Shore. Nantucket, 1892. Boards, photos. Jenkins 61-1519 1974 $12.50

NAPIER, MRS. ALEXANDER   A Noble Bake Off Cookry. 1882. Patterned parchment boards. Covent 55-694 1974 £35

NAPIER, F. P.   History of the War in the Peninsula. London, 1892. 6 vols., 8vo., maps, orig. cloth. Bow Windows 62-661 1974 £7.50

NAPIER, JOHN   The Construction of the Wonderful Canon of Logarithms. 1889. 4to., cloth, leather label, uncut, first English edition. Traylen 79-250 1973 £15

NAPIER, JOHN   The Construction of the Wonderful Canon of Logarithms. Edinburgh & London, 1889. 4to., buckram boards, morocco labels, fine. Dawsons PM 10-445 1974 £25

NAPIER, JOHN   A Description of the Admirable Table of Logarithmes. London, 1618. 12mo., old calf, gilt, first edition, second issue. Dawsons PM 245-532 1974 £850

NAPIER, JOHN   A Description of the Admirable Table of Logarithmes. London, 1618. 12mo., old calf, first English edition, second issue. Dawsons PM 250-57 1974 £850

NAPIER, JOHN   Logarithmorum Canonis Descriptio. Lyons, 1620. 3 parts in 1 vol., 8vo., contemporary vellum, fine. Traylen 79-249 1973 £200

NAPIER, JOHN   Mirifici Logarithmorvm Canonis Constrvctio. 16-19. Small 4to., calf antique, first edition. Dawsons PM 245-533 1974 £250

NAPIER, JOHN   Tercentary Memorial Colume. London, 1915. 4to., cloth, uncut. Traylen 79-252 1973 £10

NAPIER, MARK   History Rescued. Edinburgh, 1870-63. 2 works in 1 vol., orig. cloth. Howes 186-1094 1974 £6.50

NAPIER, MARK   Memoirs of the Marquis of Montrose. Edinburgh, 1856. 2 vols., thick 8vo., orig. blue cloth, plates. Howes 186-1082 1974 £8.50

NAPIER, MARK   Memorials and Letters Illustrative of the Life and Times of John Graham of Claverhouse. Edinburgh, 1859-62. 3 vols., orig. blue cloth, plates. Howes 186-788A 1974 £15

NAPIER, WILLIAM FRANCIS PATRICK   History of the War in the Peninsular. London, 1828-49. 8vo., 6 vols., modern red half morocco, fine, first edition. Dawsons PM 251-292 1974 £115

NAPOLI, Dalla Stamperia Reale. 12 vols., 4to., plates, engravings, worn, contemporary roan backed boards. Bow Windows 62-757 1974 £50

NARES, EDWARD   Heraldic Anomalies. 1823. Small 8vo., 2 vols., contemporary half calf. Hill 126-184 1974 £28

NARES, EDWARD   Heraldic Anomalies. London, 1824. 8vo., 2 vols., orig. cloth-backed boards, second edition. Hammond 201-435 1974 £16

NARES, EDWARD   Think's-I-To-Myself. London, 1811. 2 vols., 12mo., contemporary diced calf gilt, rare first edition. Dawsons PM 252-740 1974 £60

NARES, ROBERT   Remarks on the Nature of Pantomime. London, 1789. 8vo., disbound, rare, first edition. Ximenes 37-154 1974 $150

NARES, ROBERT 1753-1829   Glossary. 1901. 2 vols. Allen 216-1403 1974 $12.50

NARES, ROBERT 1753-1829   Principles of Government. London, 1792. 8vo., modern boards. Dawsons PM 247-206 1974 £30

NARODNI Adresar. New York, 1937. Austin 62-116 1974 $47.50

NARRATIVES for the Young. n.d. Small 8vo., half contemporary roan, wood engravings, rubbed. Smith 194-760 1974 £5

NARRATIVES for the Young. n.d. Small 8vo., half contemporary roan, wood engravings, rubbed. Smith 194-761 1974 £7.50

NASH, C. W.   Vertebrates of Ontario. Toronto, 1908. Illus. Hood's 103-372 1974 $10

NASH, JOHN   Ovid's Elegies. 1925. Cloth back, boards, illus., fine, limited edition. Marsden 37-328 1974 £15

NASH, JOHN HENRY   The Library of William Andrews Clark, Jr. San Francisco, 1921. Boards, linen back, slipcase. Dawson's 424-79 1974 $85

NASH, JOSEPH   British Song Birds. 1872. Small 8vo., orig. cloth, plates. Wheldon 131-667 1974 £15

NASH, JOSEPH   The Mansions of England in the Olden Time. 1874. Folio, full green morocco, plates, bookplates. Quaritch 940-534 1974 £55

NASH, JOSEPH   A Practical Treatise on British Song Birds. London, 1824. 12mo., orig. printed boards, rebacked, plates, first edition. Hammond 201-666 1974 £32

NASH, OGDEN   Good Intentions. Little, Brown, 1942. 179p. Austin 54-785 1973 $7.50

NASH, OGDEN   Good Intentions. Boston, 1942. Orig. binding, first edition, d.w. lightly soiled, faded spine, else fine. Ross 87-422 1974 $15

NASH, OGDEN   Hard Lines and Others. 1932. Illus., very good copy, pictorial cloth backed boards, inscription. Covent 51-2485 1973 £8.50

NASH, OGDEN   Hard Lines and Others. 1932. Cloth-backed boards, fine, English first edition. Covent 56-981 1974 £10

NASH, OGDEN   The Private Dining Room. Little, Brown, 1952. 169p., 1st ed. Austin 54-786 1973 $7.50

NASON, ELIAS   The Life and Times of Charles Sumner. Boston, 1874. First edition, orig. binding. Wilson 63-250 1974 $10

THE NASSAU Herald. Class of 1917, Princeton University. (F. Scott Fitzgerald's College Yearbook). Princeton, 1917. 1st ed., bound. Biblo & Tannen 214-704 1974 $125

NATALIBUS, PETRUS DE   Catalogus Sanctorum. Strassburg, 1521. Small folio, contemporary calf, rebacked. Thomas 28-296 1972 £22

NATALIBUS, PETRUS DE   Catalogus Sanctorum et Gestorum Eorum ex Diversis Voluminibus Collectus. Lyons, 1514. Folio, fine woodcuts, splendid copy, pristine condition, contemporary blind stamped pigskin over wooden boards, two clasps, first Sacon edition. Schafer 10-90 1974 sFr 3,400

NATALIS, ALEXANDER   Historia Ecclesiastica Veteris Novique Testamenti. Venice, 1776-77. 10 vols., folio, portrait, contemporary half vellum. Howes 185-1486 1974 £40

NATHAN, GEORGE J.   The Bachelor Life. Reynal, Hitchcock, 1941. 262p., illus. Austin 54-787 1973 $8.50

NATHAN, GEORGE J.   Critics' Prize Plays. World, 1945. 377p. Austin 51-669 1973 $8.50

NATHAN, GEORGE J.   The Intimate Notebooks of George Jean Nathan. Knopf, 1932. 326p. Austin 54-788 1973 $8.50

NATHAN, GEORGE J.   Materia Critica. Knopf, 1924. 242p. Austin 54-789 1973 $10

NATHAN, GEORGE J.   Monks Are Monks. Knopf, 1929. 300p. Austin 54-790 1973 $8.50

NATHAN, GEORGE J.   The Theatre Book of the Year 1944-45. Knopf, 1945. Austin 51-670 1973 $8.50

NATHAN, GEORGE J.   Theatre Book of the Year 1946-47. Knopf, 1948. Austin 51-671 1973 $8.50

NATHAN, GEORGE J.   The World of George Jean Nathan. Knopf, 1952. Austin 51-672 1973 $8.50

NATIONAL COMMISSION ON LAW OBSERVANCE & ENFORCEMENT Report on Crime and the Foreign Born. 1931. Austin 62-443 1974 $27.50

NATIONAL Gallery Illustrations, Italian Schools. London, 1937. Biblo & Tannen 210-249 1973 $8.50

NATIONAL GALLERY OF ART   Book of Illustrations. Washington, 1941. 1st ed., 4to. Biblo & Tannen 210-250 1973 $12.50

THE NATIONAL History of France. 1927-38. 10 vols. in 11, orig. edition. Howes 186-1099 1974 £55

NATIONAL Home for Disabled Volunteer Soldiers, Northwestern Branch, Milwaukee County, Wisconsin. New York, 1894. Boards, photos. Jenkins 61-2669 1974 $20

NATIONAL LIBERAL IMMIGRATION LEAGUE   The Press on the League. New York, 1907. Austin 62-444 1974 $10

NATIONAL Manuscripts of Scotland. Southampton, 1867-(73). 3 vols., imp. folio, half roan, foxing. Quaritch 939-666 1974 £70

NATIONAL Military Home, Dayton. Dayton, c. 1900. Small folio, pict. wrappers, photos. Jenkins 61-2004 1974 $12.50

THE NATIONAL Portrait Gallery of Distinguished Americans. Philadelphia, 1834. 1st ed., bdgs. worn, 3 vols. Biblo & Tannen 213-322 1973 $52.50

THE NATIONAL Portrait Gallery of Distinguished Americans. Philadelphia, 1852. 4to., 4 vols., fine steel engraved portraits, backstrips faded, else almost new. Butterfield 10-430 1974 $85

NATIONAL RESOURCES BOARD   A Report on National Planning and Public Works. Washington, 1934. 4to., orig. binding, illus., charts, maps. Wilson 63-28 1974 $15

NATIONAL VAUDEVILLE ARTISTS   National Vaudeville Artists. 1924, n.p. Austin 51-673 1973 $37.50

NATTES, J. C.   Scotia Depicta. 1804. Oblong folio, engravings, orig. cloth. Marsden 37-335 1974 £60

NATTES, J. C.   Scotia Depicta. 1804. Folio, etchings, contemporary calf, foxing, frontispiece. Quaritch 939-667 1974 £125

NATURAL History of Birds . . . for the Amusement and Instruction of Children. London, 1791. 6 parts in 2 vols., full mottled calf, hand colored plates, labels, 8vo., complete. Gregory 44-55 1974 $185

NATURAL History of Remarkable Trees, Shrubs and Plants. Dublin, 1821. 12mo., contemporary sheep, full page woodcuts. George's 610-559 1973 £5.25

NATURAL HISTORY of Waterbirds. (c., 1810). 12mo., orig. paper wrappers, fine, engravings. Quaritch 936-334 1974 £25

THE NATURE of Contracts Consider'd, As They Relate to the Subscriptions, Taken In By the South Sea Company. London, 1720. 8vo., half calf, scarce, first edition. Ximenes 35-251 1974 $60

NATURE-Printing, a Collection of 105 Nature-Printed Plates. Late 18th century. 1 vol., small folio, boards. Wheldon 128-1146 1973 £30

NAUDIN, C.   Nouvelles Recherches sur L'Hybridite dans les Vegetaux. Paris, (1865). 4to., orig. wrappers, plates. Wheldon 130-1040 1974 £75

NAUDIN, C.   Les Plantes a Feuillage Colore. Paris, 1867. 4to., orig. wrappers, uncut, second edition. Wheldon 129-1510 1974 £10

NAUMANN, J. A.   Naturgeschichte der Vogel Deutschlands. Gera, 1897-1905. 12 vols., folio, orig. cloth, coloured plates, plain plates, complete copy. Wheldon 128-526 1973 £220

NAUMANN, J. F.   Iconographie d'Oiseaux d'Europe et de leurs Oeufs. Paris, 1910. 4 vols., orig. wrappers, plates, rare French edition. Wheldon 131-94 1974 £175

NAUMBURG, E. M. B.   The Birds of Matto Grosso. New York, 1630. 8vo., plates. Wheldon 130-589 1974 £15

NAUNTON, G. H.   Japanese Sword Fittings. 1912. 4to., cloth, faded, scarce, plates. Quaritch 940-414 1974 £120

NAUNTON, ROBERT   The Court of Queen Elizabeth. London, 1814. 4to., illus., dark brown levant morocco, blind tooled; doublures of green levant, gilt tooled; brown silk end-leaves; all edges gilt; 21 plates. Jacobs 24-62 1974 $650

NAUSEA, FRIEDRICH   Contra Universos Catholicae Fidei Adversarios in Symbolum Apostolorum Catholica. Mayence, 1529. 4to., contemporary blind-stamped half calf over wooden boards, very fine, first edition. Schafer 8-133 1973 sFr. 1,800

THE NAVAL Review. 1920-25. 6 vols., 8vo., maps, diagrams, cloth, half morocco, rubbed, stains. Bow Windows 62-665 1974 £12.50

NAVARRETE, MARTIN FERNANDEZ DE   Coleccion de Los Viajes, Y Descubrimientos Que Hicieron Por Mar Los Espanoles Desde Fines Del Siglo XV, Con Varios Documentos. Madrid, 1829-1859. 5 vols., full mottled calf, folded map. Jenkins 61-1776 1974 $150

NAVARRO, A. DE   Causeries on English Pewter. (1911). Roy. 8vo., plates, cloth. Quaritch 940-681 1974 £6

NAVILLE, ARNOLD   Notes Bibliographiques sur l'Oeuvre de Andre Gide. Paris, 1930. 4to., orig. wrapper, uncut, inscribed, limited edition. L. Goldschmidt 42-232 1974 $25

NAYLER, GEORGE   A Collection of Coats of Arms Borne by the Nobility and Gentry of the County of Glocester. 1792. 4to., half calf, engraved plates, some foxing. Bow Windows 66-496 1974 £45

NEAGOE, PETER   Storm. Paris, 1932. 8vo., orig. cloth, wrappers, first edition. Rota 190-704 1974 £8.50

NEAL, JOHN   Portland, Illustrated. Portland, 1874. 12mo., cloth, 160 pages. Saddleback 14-459 1974 $12.50

NEALE, J. P.   Design Books. 1795. Small oblong 8vo., plates, paper wrappers, cloth case. Bow Windows 62-666 1974 £420

NEALE, J. P.   The History and Antiquities of the Abbey Church of St. Peter. 1818-23. 2 vols., folio, contemporary half morocco gilt, plates, fine. Quaritch 939-484 1974 £110

NEALE, J. P.   Views of the Seats of Noblemen and Gentlemen. 1818-29. Full purple calf, plates, faded. Marsden 37-336 1974 £120

NEALE, JOHN MASON   A Commentary On the Psalms. 1874. 4 vols., thick crown 8vo., best edition. Howes 185-1488 1974 £21

NEALE, JOHN MASON   A History of the Holy Eastern Church. 1850. 2 vols., orig. cloth, illus., plates. Howes 185-1487 1974 £15

NEALE, WILLIAM JOHNSON   The Priors of Prague. London, 1836. 3 vols., 12mo., orig. quarter cloth and boards, printed paper labels, first edition. Ximenes 37-155 1974 $40

NEANDER, JOHANN AUGUST   General History of the Christian Religion and Church. Edinburgh, 1847-50. 6 vols., orig. cloth, frayed. Howes 185-1489 1974 £20

NEANDER, JOHANNES   Tabacologia. 1622. 4to., contemporary limp vellum, first edition. Dawsons PM 249-382 1974 £95

NEBBIA, UGO   Un Inverno a Rovetta di Arturo Tosi. Milan, 1944. Folio, plates, wrapper. Minters 37-211 1973 $14

NEBRASKA ASSOCIATION OF TROTTING HORSE BREEDERS   Constitution, By-Laws and Trotting Rules of. Syracuse, 1890. Wrapper. Jenkins 61-1779 1974 $22.50

NEBRASKANS, 1854-1904. Omaha, 1904. 8vo., leather, 305 pages, rebacked. Saddleback 14-534 1974 $17.50

NECKER, JACQUES   Du Pouvoir Executif Dans les Grands Etats. 1792. 2 vols., 8vo., contemporary sprinkled calf, fine, first edition. Dawsons PM 247-207 1974 £55

NEDHAM, MARCHAMONT   Digitud Dei. London, 1649. 4to., modern half roan, first edition. Dawsons PM 252-741 1974 £20

NEDHAM, MARCHAMONT   A Pacquet of Advices and Animadversions. London, 1676. 4to., modern boards, first edition. Dawsons PM 251-293 1974 £25

NEEDHAM, J. G.   The Life of Inland Waters. Ithaca, 1937. 8vo., cloth, illus., third edition. Wheldon 128-160 1973 £5

NEEDHAM, JOHN TURBERVILLE   A Letter from Paris. London, 1746. 4to., stitched as issued, signed. Dawsons PM 245-534 1974 £30

NEEDLER, G. H.   The Battleford Column. Montreal & Toronto, n.d. Hood's 104-769 1974 $10

NEES VON ESENBECK, C. G.   Flora Africae Australioris. Glogau, 1841. 8vo., roan. Wheldon 129-1109 1974 £20

NEES VON ESENBECK, C. G.   Hymenopterorum Ichneumonibus Affinium Monographiae. Stuttgart and Tubingen, 1834. 2 vols. in 1, 8vo., new cloth. Wheldon 128-777 1973 £12

NEGRETTI, HENRY   A Treatise On Meteorological Instruments. London, 1864. 8vo., orig. cloth, illus., first edition. Schuman 37-179 1974 $85

NEGRI, G.   Erbario Figurato, Illustrazione e Descrizione Delle Pianti Usuali con Speciale Riguardo Alle Piante Medicinali. Milan, 1904. Roy. 8vo., orig. cloth, coloured plates. Wheldon 128-1688 1973 £15

NEGRI, G.   Erbario Figurato, Illustrazione e Descrizione Delle Pianti Usuali con Speciale Riguardo Alle Piante Medicinali. Milan, 1904. Roy. 8vo., orig. cloth, plates. Wheldon 131-1813 1974 £15

NEIFELD, ERNST JEREMIAS   Ratio Medendi Morbis Circuli Sanguinei. Breslau, 1773. 8vo., wrappers, first edition. Schuman 37-180 1974 $45

NEIGHBORS: Studies in Immigration from the Standpoint of the Episcopal Church. 1919. 246p., illus. Austin 62-150 1974 $15

NEIHARDT, JOHN G.   The River and I. New York - London, 1910. 8vo., orig. bindings, plates. Butterfield 8-322 1974 $15

NEIHARDT, JOHN G.   The Song of Hugh Glass. New York, 1915. Green cloth, gilt, first edition. Bradley 35-261 1974 $20

NEIHARDT, JOHN G.   The Song of Jed Smith. New York, 1941. Cloth, dust jacket, gilt, fine, first edition. Bradley 35-263 1974 $24

NEIHARDT, JOHN G.   The Song of the Indian Wars. New York, 1925. Pictorial red cloth, first trade edition. Bradley 35-262 1974 $16

NEIHARDT, JOHN G.   The Splendid Wayfaring. New York, 1920. Green cloth, illus., gilt, first edition. Bradley 35-264 1974 $26

NEILD, J.   State of the Prisons in England, Scotland and Wales. 1812. 4to., half calf, frontispiece. Quaritch 939-185 1974 £60

NEILHARDT, JOHN G.   A Cycle of the West. Macmillan, 1949. 5 vols. in one. Austin 54-791 1973 $17.50

NEILSON, HARRY B.   Droll Doings. London, n.d. (c. 1909). Folio, pictorial boards, cloth spine, spine ends and corners worn, very good copy, color plates. Frohnsdorff 16-604 1974 $20

NEILSON, HARRY B.   Droll Doings, With Verses by the Cockiolly Bird. London, n.d. (c. 1900). Folio, pictorial boards, cloth spine, spine ends and corners rubbed, worn spot on front cover, fine color illus. by Neilson. Frohnsdorff 15-124 1974 $20

NEILSON, W. A.   The Facts About Shakespeare. Macmillan, 1913. Austin 51-674 1973 $6.50

NELL In Bridewell. 1932. 8vo., illus., fine woodcuts, 326 pages. Rinsland 58-972 1974 $25

NELSON, E. W.   Wild Animals of North America. Washington, 1930. Illus., red cloth, gilt, revised edition. Bradley 35-265 1974 $12.50

NELSON, JAMES   An Essay on the Government of Children. London, 1753. 8vo., contemporary calf, first edition. Schumann 35-350 1974 $110

NELSON, O. N.   History of the Scandinavians and Successful Scandinavians in the U. S. 1899. Illus., second revised edition. Austin 57-473 1974 $27.50

NELSON, ROBERT   An Address to Persons of Quality and Estate. London, 1715. 8vo., contemporary calf, rebacked, gilt, first edition. Hammond 201-254 1974 £12.50

NELSON, T.   The Isle of Wight in a Series of Views. (c.1870) Oblong 8vo., plates, cloth, worn. Quaritch 939-844 1974 £45

NELSON, T.   Salt Lake City, With a Sketch of the Route of the Central Pacific Railroad from Omaha to Salt Lake City, and Thence to San Francisco. Salt Lake City, c. 1890. 8vo., cloth, illus., foxed. Jenkins 61-2474 1974 $12.50

NELSON, T. H.   The Birds of Yorkshire. 1907. 2 vols., 4to., cloth, coloured frontispieces, plates, large paper issue, scarce. Wheldon 129-527 1973 £15

NELSON, WILLIAM   The Rights of the Clergy of Great Britain. 1709. Thick 8vo., contemporary calf. Howes 185-1490 1974 £7.50

NEMIROVITCH-DANTCHENKO, VLADIMIR   My Life in the Russian Theatre. 1937. Plates, dust wrapper, English first edition. Covent 56-2074 1974 £5.25

NENNO, FAUSTINA   Placentia Round Table Club. Placentia, c.1938. 8vo., cloth, limited. Saddleback 14-201 1974 $25

NERSES IV, PATRIARCH OF ARMENIA 100-1173   Preces Sancti Nerestis Clajensis Armeniorum Patriarchae. Venice, 1837. 8vo., half morocco, engraved portrait and vignette. Kraus B8-358 1974 $150

NERVAL, GERARD DE
Please turn to
GERARD DE NERVAL

NESBIT, EDITH   Miss Mischief. London, n.d. (c. 1890's). 12mo., glazed pictorial boards, cloth spine, color plates, sepia illus., very good copy. Frohnsdorff 16-606 1974 $17.50

NESBIT, WILBUR DICK   The Land of Make-Believe and Other Christmas Poems. New York & London, 1907. First edition, 8vo., illus., colored frontis., mint. Current BW9-65 1974 $11.50

NESBIT, WILBUR DICK   The Paths of Long Ago. Chicago, 1926. First edition. Biblo & Tannen 214-760 1974 $7.50

NESBIT, WILLIAM 1876-   How to Hunt With the Camera. (1931). 4to., cloth, illus. Wheldon 130-127 1974 £5

NESBITT, FRANCES E.   Algeria & Tunis, Painted and Described. London, 1906. 8vo., full page full color illus., very nice, dec. front cover and spine. Current BW9-577 1974 $35

NESBITT, ROBERT   Human Osteogeny Explained in Two Lectures, Read In the Anatomical Theatre of the Surgones of London, July 1 & 2, 1731. London, 1736. 8vo., contemporary calf, plates, first edition. Schuman 37-181 1974 $95

NESTORE   Lettre de Nestore, Escrite a Polidor. N. P., 1659. Small 4to., new boards. Quaritch 940-190 1974 £25

NETHERCLIFT, F. G.   The Autograph Souvenir. n.d. Rebacked. Covent 55-145 1974 £21

NETHERLANDISH SCHOOL   Exhibitions of Pictures by Masters of the Netherlandish and Allied Schools of the XVth Centuries. 1892. Roy. 4to., plates, buckram. Quaritch 940-191 1974 £20

NETTLE, R.   The Salmon Fisheries of the St. Lawrence and Its Tributaries. Montreal, 1857. Hood's 103-373 1974 $45

NETTLEFOLD, J. S.   Practical Housing. 1908. 8vo., orig. cloth, gilt, plates, illus., first edition. Hammond 201-966 1974 £6

NETTLEFORD, FREDERICK JOHN   Catalogue of the Pictures and Drawings in the Collection of. Vol. 4, 4to., navy blue morocco, gold panelled. Eaton Music-651 1973 $10

NETTLEFOLD, FREDERICK JOHN   A Catalogue of the Pictures and Drawings in the Collection of. 1933-38. 4 vols., 4to., green morocco, uncut, cloth boxes, fine clean copy, rare de luxe edition. Quaritch 940-192 1974 £375

NETTLEFOLD, FREDERICK JOHN   The Collection of Bronzes and Castings in Brass and Ormolu Formed by. 1934. Folio, plates, cloth, gilt. Quaritch 940-682 1974 £30

NETTLESHIP, J. T.   George Morland and the Evolution from Him of Some Later Painters. 1898. Plates, copper plate engravings, crown 4to., very good copy, little foxing, orig. cloth. Broadhurst 24-153 1974 £5

NETTO & SELMAN   Die Kunst zu Stricken. Leipzig, 1800. Oblong folio, orig. grey wrappers, full page illus. plain & color, scarce. Gregory 44-213 1974 $350

NEUBERGER, R. L.   Our Promised Land. New York, 1938. Hood's 103-817 1974 $10

NEUBURG, VICTOR   Songs of the Groves. 1921. Cloth-backed boards, presentation copy, inscribed, English first edition. Covent 56-986 1974 £15.75

NEUMAN, FRED G.   The Story of Paducah, Kentucky. Paducah, 1927. 8vo., cloth. Saddleback 14-448 1974 $50

NEUMANN, CASPAR   The Chemical Works of. London, 1759. 4to., contemporary calf, gilt, first edition in English. Dawsons PM 245-536 1974 £95

NEUMANN, J. B.   Max Beckmann. New York & Munich, n.d. 4to., stiff wrappers, plates. Minters 37-449 1973 $12.50

NEUMANN, W. A.   Der Reliquienschatz des Hauses Braunschweig-Luneburg. Vienna, 1891. Folio, engravings, three quarter black morocco, rubbed, limited to 300 copies. Kraus B8-421 1974 $250

NEURDENBURG, ELIZABETH   Old Dutch Pottery and Tiles. 1923. 4to., illus., buckram. Quaritch 940-652 1974 £36

NEURDENBURG, ELIZABETH   Old Dutch Pottery and Tiles. 1923. Illus., pigskin, signed, fine. Covent 55-471 1974 £45

NEVADA. San Francisco, 1915. 12mo., wrapper, 64 pages. Saddleback 14-540 1974 $12.50

NEVE, PHILIP   Cursory Remarks on Some of the Ancient English Poets. London, 1789. 8vo., cloth, uncut, first edition. Dawsons PM 252-742 1974 £120

NEVE, R.   The City and Country Purchaser's and Builders Dictionary. 1736. 8vo., plates, orig. sheep, third edition. Quaritch 940-535 1974 £50

NEVILL, RALPH   British Military Prints. 1909. 4to., orig. cloth, coloured plates, illus., slight foxing, covers faded. Bow Windows 66-498 1974 £18

NEVILL, RALPH   British Military Prints. London, 1909. 4to., cloth, gilt. Hammond 201-615 1974 £12.50

NEVILL, RALPH   British Military Prints. London, 1909. 4to., plates, orig. cloth, fine. Dawsons PM 10-449 1974 £25

NEVILL, RALPH   Old English Sporting Books. 1924. Plates, limited to 1500 numbered copies, spine faded, some plates dust stained, nice copy, buckram. Covent 51-2196 1973 £35

NEVILL, RALPH   Old English Sporting Books. London, 1924.
Large 4to., plates, orig. buckram gilt. Dawsons PM 10-450 1974 £40

NEVILL, RALPH   Old English Sporting Books. 1924. Plates,
some mounted and in colour, roy. 4to., top edges gilt, others uncut, fine unfaded
copy, dust wrapper, limited to 1500 copies, orig. cloth. Broadhurst 24-421
1974 £55

NEVILL, RALPH   Old French Line Engravings. 1924. 4to., full
padded calf, gilt, rubbed, uncut, limited, edition-de-luxe. Quaritch
940-193 1974 £50

NEVILLE, ALEXANDER   De Furoribus Norfolciensium Ketto Duce.
1575. Small 4to., calf, bit worn, joints cracked but reasonably sound, woodcut
borders, has both dedications. Thomas 32-124 1974 £60

NEVILLE, JOHN   Hydraulic Tables, Coefficients, and Formulae
for Finding the Discharge of Water from Orifices. 1853. Worn. Covent
55-1322 1974 £10.50

NEVILLE, R. C.   Saxon Obsequies. 1852. Folio, orig. cloth,
plates, scarce. Quaritch 939-324 1974 £45

NEVILLE, RALPH   Old English Sporting Books. 1924. 4to.,
half red morocco gilt, limited. Quaritch 939-186 1974 £65

NEVIN, ALFRED   Centennial Biography: Men of Mark of
Cumberland Valley, Pennsylvania. Philadelphia, 1876. 4to., cloth.
Saddleback 14-673 1974 $25

NEVIN, ALFRED   History of the Presbytery of Philadelphia. Philadelphia, 1888. 8vo., orig. bindings. Butterfield 8-551 1974 $12.50

NEVINSON, C. R. W.   Modern War. 1917. 4to., orig. cloth,
signature, first edition. Rota 188-722 1974 £10

NEW and Complete Instructions for the Hautboy Containing the Easiest and Most
Improved Rules for Learners to Play. Preston, (c. 1780). Oblong 4to., orig.
paper wrappers, soiled, frontispiece. Quaritch 940-818 1974 £85

THE NEW Annual Register, or General Repository of History, Politics and
Literatrue for 1798. London, 1799. Half calf. Emerald 50-808 1974 £5

NEW Actor Jokes--No. 25. Ottenheimer, 1914. 64p., paper. Austin 54-805
1973 $6.50

THE NEW Book of Nonsense. Philadelphia, 1864. Austin 54-246 1973 $15

THE NEW Capitol at Harrisburg, Pennsylvania. Harrisburg, c. 1900. Small
folio, pict. wrapper, photos. Jenkins 61-2159 1974 $12.50

A NEW Catechism, With Dr. Hickes's Thirty Nine Articles. London, 1710.
8vo., disbound, third edition. Ximenes 35-27 1974 $15

THE NEW Cries of London. London, 1823. 12mo., 11 engraved plates. orig. or
contemp. boards, roan spine with gilt lettering. Frohnsdorff 16-245 1974 $200

NEW Cyclopaedia of Botany & Complete Book of Herbs. London, n.d. 2 vols.,
full dark calf, color plates, 8vo. Gregory 44-214 1974 $135

NEW Directions in Prose and Poetry. 1941. Dust wrapper, fine. Covent 55-43
1974 £17.50

THE NEW Dressmaker. 1921. Illus., fine, third edition. Covent 56-1236
1974 £5.25

NEW English Theatre. London, 1776-77. 12 vols., 8vo., plates, vignettes,
contemporary red straight-grained morocco. Dawsons PM 252-743 1974 £125

THE NEW Europe. 1916-20. 17 vols. in 16, roy. 8vo., map, cloth, orig.
wrappers. Howes 186-1103 1974 £65

THE NEW Festival of Wit, or Cabinet of Humour. London, 1814. 12mo., uncut,
contemporary half calf, first edition. Ximenes 33-392 1974 £65

NEW Flora and Sylva. 1928-40. 12 vols., 8vo., orig. buckram, very scarce.
Wheldon 131-1554 1974 £60

NEW Flora and Sylva. 1929-40. Vols. 1 - 12, roy. 8vo., in parts as issued.
Wheldon 131-1555 1974 £40

NEW HAMPSHIRE   Report of the Adjutant General of the State of
New Hampshire for 1865. Concord, 1865. 2 vols., foxed. Jenkins 61-1820
1974 $12.50

THE NEW London Cookery and Complete Domestic Guide. n.d. Frontispiece,
plates, full calf, worn, rubbed. Covent 55-685 1974 £12.50

NEW MEXICO   A Guide to the Colorful State. New York, 1940.
8vo., orig. bindings, dust jacket. Butterfield 8-391 1974 $12.50

NEW ORLEANS BOARD OF HEALTH   Annual Report, 1849. New Orleans,
1850. Large folding chart, disbound. Jenkins 61-1396 1974 $12.50

NEW ORLEANS BOARD OF HEALTH   By-Laws and Ordinances. New Orleans,
1849. Large folding charts. Jenkins 61-1397 1974 $12.50

NEW Paths. 1918. Fin, boards, scarce, first edition. Covent 55-45 1974
£25

NEW Poems: 1940. New York, 1941. 1st ed. Biblo & Tannen 213-613 1973
$7.50

A NEW Royal and Universal Dictionary of Arts and Sciences. 1770. 2 vols. in
1, folio, contemporary calf, worn, joints cracked, frontispiece, plates, maps.
Bow Windows 66-178 1974 £78

NEW Series Toy Books. Little Paul's Christmas. London, (c. 1890). 8vo., very
good condition, full color full page illus., dec. front cvoer. Current BW9-89
1974 $18.50

NEW Stage Jokes. Wehman Bros., 1910. 58p., paper. Austin 54-1027 1973
$7.50

A NEW System of Domestic Cookery. 1860. Frontispice, plates, foxing, new
edition. Covent 55-686 1974 £8.50

A NEW Theatrical Dictionary. 1792-93. 12mo., newly bound half calf, marbled
boards, contrasting title label, marginal notes, scarce. Broadhurst 24-489 1974
£45

NEW York. Brooklyn, c. 1910. Small folio, wrappers, illus. Jenkins 61-1899
1974 $10

NEW YORK   First Annual Report of the Bureau of Industries
and Immigration. Albany, 1912. Austin 62-446 1974 $27.50

NEW YORK HISTORICAL SOCIETY - LIBRARY   Catalogue of the Books, Tracts,
Newspapers, Maps, Charts, Views, Portraits, and Manuscripts in the. New York,
1813. Wrapper, uncut. Jenkins 61-1868 1974 $15

NEW YORK METROPOLITAN MUSEUM OF ART   Catalogue, Memorial
Exhibition of the Work of George Bellows. 1925. 4to., faded wrappers,
plates. Minters 37-2 1973 $25

NEW YORK MUSEUM OF MODERN ART   Catalogue, Edward Hopper,
Retrospective Exhibition, Nov. 1 - Dec. 7, 1933. 4to., worn wrappers, plates,
scarce. Minters 37-15 1973 $18.50

NEW YORK MUSEUM OF MODERN ART   First Loan Exhibition, November,
1929, Cezanne, Gauguin, Seurat, Van Gogh. Large 4to., wrappers, plates,
scarce, very good copy, second edition. Minters 37-116 1973 $32.50

NEW YORK STATE: OTSEGO ELECTIONS   An Impartial Statement of the
Controversy, Respecting the Decision of the Late Committee of Canvassers. New
York, 1792. 8vo., disbound, very scarce, first edition. Ximenes 37-156 1974
$45

NEW York and the War With Spain: and, Col. Burt's Civil War Reminiscences. Albany, 1903. Jenkins 61-1900 1974 $15

NEW York at the Jamestown Exposition, Norfolk, Virginia, 1907. Albany, 1909. Illus., several folding photos. Jenkins 61-2538 1974 $10

THE NEW York Book of Poetry. New York, 1837. Gilt stamp cloth, worn. Butterfield 10-438 1974 $25

THE NEW ZEALAND Official Year-Book, 1912. Wellington, 1912. 8vo., orig. quarter cloth, printed boards, frontispiece, graphs, maps. Bow Windows 66-506 1974 £19.50

NEWBERRY, CLARE TURLAY   Barkis. New York, 1938. Oblong 4to., very good copy, d.j., first edition, pictorial boards. Frohnsdorff 16-607 1974 $15

NEWBERRY, CLARE TURLAY   Marshmallow. New York, (1942). Oblong 4to., pictorial boards, illus., fine, d.j., first edition, extra illus. tipped in at back still intact. Frohnsdorff 16-608 1974 $17.50

NEWBERRY LIBRARY, CHICAGO   Check List of 15th Century Books In Newberry Library & Other Libraries of Chicago. 1933. Allen 213-1668 1973 $10

NEWBIGIN, M. I.   Canada. London, (c.1926). 8vo., maps, illus., orig. cloth. Bow Windows 62-668 1974 £5.50

NEWBOLT, FRANCIS   The History of the Royal Society of Painter-Etchers and Engravers. 1930. Small 4to., cloth gilt, English first edition. Covent 56-1487 1974 £7.50

NEWBOLT, HENRY   Drake's Drum and Other Songs of the Sea. (N. P., n.d.). Crown 4to., orig. cloth, coloured and mounted illus., slight spotting. Bow Windows 66-499 1974 £9.50

NEWBOLT, HENRY   Poems: New and Old. 1921. 268 pages. Austin 61-746 1974 $10

NEWCASTLE, WILLIAM CAVENDISH DE   A General System of Horsemanship. London, 1743. Large folio, orig. mottled calf. Marlborough 70-19 1974 £750

NEWCASTLE, WILLIAM CAVENDISH   A General System of Horsemanship in All Its Branches. 1743. 2 vols., roy. folio, plates, old calf. Quaritch 939-845 1974 £2000

NEWCOMB, REXFORD, JR.   Ceramic Whitewares. New York, 1947. Biblo & Tannen 214-66 1974 $15

NEWCOMB, REXFORD   In the Lincoln Country. Philadelphia, 1928. Green cloth, illus., fine, first edition. Bradley 35-230 1974 $15

NEWCOMB, REXFORD   The Old Mission Churches and Historic Homes of California. Philadelphia, 1925. First edition, small 4to., illus, fine, orig. dust wrapper, orig. binding, bookplate. Wilson 63-123 1974 $47.50

NEWCOMB, SIMON   Researches On the Motion of the Moon. Washington, 1878. Large 4to., orig. pictured wrappers, first edition. Schuman 37-182 1974 $110

NEWCOMBE, P.   The History of the Ancient and Royal Foundation. 1795. 4to., half morocco. Quaritch 939-388 1974 £10

NEWCOME, WILLIAM   An Historical View of the English Biblical Translations. Dublin, 1792. 8vo., new half calf. Hill 126-186 1974 £21

NEWELL, C.   History of the Revolution in Texas . . . Together With the Latest Geographical, Topographical and Statistical Accounts of the Country. New York, 1838. Orig. cloth, foxed, fine folding map, first edition, first issue, rare. Jenkins 61-1951 1974 $325

NEWELL, PETER   Their First Formal Call. New York, 1906. 8vo., cloth, pictorial label, plates, bookplate removed, clean and tight copy, first edition. Frohnsdorff 16-609 1974 $10

NEWELL, PETER   Topsys & Turvys. New York, 1893. Oblong 4to., pictorial boards, edges worn, paper chipped off spine, color illus., first edition. Frohnsdorff 16-610 1974 $60

NEWHALL, BEAUMONT   The History of Photography. New York, 1949. Col. frontis., illus., inscribed by author. Jacobs 24-52 1974 $18

NEWHALL, C. S.   The Trees of Northeastern America. New York, 1890 or 1894. 8vo., cloth. Wheldon 130-1566 1974 £5

NEWHAM, WILLIAM   Essay on Superstition. London, 1830. 8vo., three quarter morocco, first edition. Schumann 35-351 1974 $85

NEWLANDS, JAMES   The Carpenter's and Joiner's Assistant. n.d. Folio, plates, illus., half morocco. Quaritch 940-536 1974 £30

NEWMAN, E.   A History of British Ferns. 1854. 8vo., cloth, gilt, illus., third edition. Wheldon 131-1452 1974 £5

NEWMAN, E.   A History of British Ferns and Allied Plants. 1844. 8vo., cloth, illus. Wheldon 129-1413 1974 £5

NEWMAN, E.   An Illustrated Natural History of British Butterflies and Moths. n.d. Roy. 8vo., orig. cloth, gilt. Wheldon 131-838 1974 £5

NEWMAN, ERNEST   Gluck and the Opera. 1895. English first edition. Covent 56-1953 1974 £6.50

NEWMAN, HORATIO HACKETT   The Biology of Twins (Mammals). Chicago, 1917. Rittenhouse 46-501 1974 $15

NEWMAN, HORATIO HACKETT   Multiple Human Births. New York, 1940. Rittenhouse 46-502 1974 $15

NEWMAN, JOHN HENRY   An Essay On the Development of Christian Doctrine. 1845. Contemporary half calf, rubbed, first edition. Howes 185-1494 1974 £7.50

NEWMAN, JOHN HENRY   Letters and Correspondence of. 1891. 2 vols., portraits, first edition. Howes 185-1495 1974 £6.50

NEWMAN, JOHN HENRY   Verses on Various Occasions. London, 1868. 8vo., orig. cloth, inscribed, first edition. Dawsons PM 252-744 1974 £30

NEWMAN, SAMUEL   A Concordance to the Holy Scriptures. Cambridge, 1672. Thick folio, contemporary calf, second edition. Howes 185-1499 1974 £21

NEWMAN, SAMUEL   A Large and Complete Concordance to the Bible. 1650. Thick folio, old calf, rebacked. Thomas 28-30 1972 £25

NEWMAN, SYLVANUS CHACE   Rehoboth in the Past. Pawtucket, 1860. 8vo., orig. bindings. Butterfield 8-570 1974 $17.50

NEWMARK, HARRIS   Sixty Years in Southern California. 1930. Red cloth, scarce, third edition. Putnam 126-275 1974 $38

NEWPORT Illustrated. New York, 1897. Boards, binding stained, photographs. Jenkins 61-2267 1974 $20

NEWSHOLME, ARTHUR   Epidemic Diphtheria. London, 1898. Inscribed. Rittenhouse 46-504 1974 $15

NEWSPAPER GUILD OF AMERICA   Heywood Broun As He Seemed to U.S. Random, 1940. 48p. Austin 54-174 1973 $7.50

NEWTE, T.   Prospects and Observations. 1791. 4to., plates, contemporary calf, gilt. Quaritch 939-187 1974 £85

NEWTON, ALFRED EDWARD   The A. Edward Newton Collection of Books and Manuscripts. New York, 1941. 3 vols., worn. Ballinger 1-295 1974 $45

NEWTON, ALFRED 1829-1907   A Dictionary of Birds. London, 1899. 8vo., contemporary half morocco, gilt, illus. Hammond 201-667 1974 £5.50

NEWTON, ALFRED 1829-1907   A Dictionary of Birds. 1893-96. 8vo., cloth, text figures, cheap issue. Wheldon 128-529 1973 £5

NEWTON, ALFRED 1829-1907   A Dictionary of Birds. 1893-96. 8vo., cloth. Wheldon 130-591 1974 £7.50

NEWTON, ALFRED EDWARD   The Amenities of Book-Collecting and Kindred Affections. Boston, 1918. Boards, cloth backstrip, illus. Wilson 63-354 1974 $12.50

NEWTON, ALFRED EDWARD   The Amenities of Book Collecting and Kindred Affections. 1920. Coloured frontis., illus., linen backed boards, fine, first edition. Covent 51-279 1973 £6.50

NEWTON, ALFRED EDWARD   The Amenities of Book-Collecting and Kindred Affections. New York, (1935). 16mo., cloth, dust jacket, very scarce, first Modern Library edition. Goodspeed's 578-507 1974 $37.50

NEWTON, ALFRED EDWARD   Derby Day. Boston, 1934. 8vo., boards, buckram back, autographed, large paper, fine, publisher's box, first edition. Goodspeed's 578-506 1974 $25

NEWTON, ALFRED EDWARD   Derby Day and Other Adventures. 1934. Plates, signed, limited. Allen 216-1197 1974 $10

NEWTON, ALFRED EDWARD   Doctor Johnson. Boston, 1923. Numbered, hand made paper, rubbed, signed. Ballinger 1-187 1974 $25

NEWTON, ALFRED EDWARD   End Papers. Boston, 1933. 8vo., cloth, d.w., frontis., signed, first edition. Quaritch 936-504 1974 £25

NEWTON, ALFRED EDWARD   The Greatest Book in the World and Other Papers. Boston, (1925). 12mo., boards, cloth back, paper label, fine clean copy, first edition. Goodspeed's 578-503 1974 $15

NEWTON, ALFRED EDWARD   Newton on Blackstone. Philadelphia, 1937. Small 4to., cloth, dw., fine, presentation copy, inscribed, first edition. Quaritch 936-505 1974 £20

NEWTON, ALFRED EDWARD   A Thomas Hardy Memorial. 1931. Wrappers, fine, illus., inscribed. Covent 55-809 1974 £7.50

NEWTON, ALFRED EDWARD   A Tourist In Spite of Himself in Egypt. Boston, 1929. 12mo., boards, first edition. Goodspeed's 478-270 1974 $15

NEWTON, ALFRED EDWARD   A Tourist in Spite of Himself. Boston, 1930. 8vo., illus., boards, first edition. Quaritch 936-506 1974 £20

NEWTON, ALFRED EDWARD   A Tourist in Spite of Himself. Boston, 1930. Fifth impression, inscribed & signed by author, orig. binding, ex-library, very good copy. Wilson 63-559 1974 $10

NEWTON, CHARLOTTE   The Constant Flame. Madison, NJ, 1937. 1st ed., author's sgd. pres. Biblo & Tannen 214-761 1974 $7.50

NEWTON, ERIC   Christopher Wood, His Life and Work. 1938. Cloth back, plates. Marsden 37-536 1974 £8

NEWTON, HARRY   Your Books, My Son. 1934. Roy. 8vo., orig. buckram, morocco label. Howes 185-781 1974 £12.50

NEWTON, ISAAC   Bernhardi Med. D. Geographia Generalis. Cambridge, 1681. 8vo., contemporary calf, second English edition. Dawsons PM 245-538 1974 £45

NEWTON, ISAAC   Bernhardi Vareni Med. D. Geographia Generalis. Cambridge, 1672. 8vo., contemporary calf, plates, first English edition. Dawsons PM 245-537 1974 £95

NEWTON, ISAAC   The Chronology of Ancient Kingdoms Amended. London, 1728. Large and thick paper, contemporary calf, worn, plates, first edition. Dawsons PM 245-551 1974 £45

NEWTON, ISAAC   Correspondence of Sir Isaac Newton and Professor Cotes. London, 1850. 8vo., orig. cloth, first edition. Dawsons PM 245-559 1974 £15

NEWTON, ISAAC   Excerpta Quaedam e Newtoni Principiis Philosophiae Naturalis. Cambridge, 1765. Large 4to., half calf, plates, first edition. Schuman 37-184 1974 $345

NEWTON, ISAAC   Lectiones Opticae. London, 1729. 4to., contemporary calf, rebacked, plates, fine, first edition. Dawsons PM 245-554 1974 £190

NEWTON, ISAAC   The Method of Fluxions. London, 1736. 4to., old calf, gilt, first edition. Dawsons PM 245-555 1974 £210

NEWTON, ISAAC   La Methode des Fluxions. Paris, 1740. 4to., contemporary French calf, gilt, first edition in French. Dawsons PM 245-556 1974 £65

NEWTON, ISAAC   La Methode des Fluxions. Paris, 1740. 4to., contemporary calf. Gurney 64-160 1974 £75

NEWTON, ISAAC   Observations upon the Prophecies of Daniel. London, 1733. 4to., contemporary sprinkled calf, gilt, first edition. Hammond 201-888 1974 £40

NEWTON, ISAAC   Opera Quae Extant Omnia. 1779-1785. 4to., 5 vols., contemporary polished calf, gilt, first and only collected edition. Dawsons PM 245-558 1974 £480

NEWTON, ISAAC   Optice. London, 1706. 4to., modern marbled boards, plates, first Latin edition. Dawsons PM 245-549 1974 £165

NEWTON, ISAAC   Optice: Sive de Reflexionibus, Refractionibus, Inflexionibus & Coloribus Lucis Libri Tres. London, 1706. Large 4to., contemporary calf, first edition in Latin. Schuman 37-183 1974 $750

NEWTON, ISAAC   Opticks. London, 1718. 8vo., contemporary panelled calf, plates, second edition. Dawsons PM 245-550 1974 £95

NEWTON, ISAAC   Opticks. London, 1904. 4to., contemporary calf, plates, rebacked, first edition. Dawsons PM 250-59 1974 £850

NEWTON, ISAAC   Opuscula Mathematica. 1744. 4to., 3 vols., contemporary vellum, plates. Dawsons PM 245-557 1974 £110

NEWTON, ISAAC   Philosophiae Naturalis Principia Mathematica. 1713. 4to., contemporary speckled calf, fine, second edition. Dawsons PM 245-541 1974 £185

NEWTON, ISAAC   Philosophiae Naturalis Principia Mathematica. Cantabrigiae, 1713. 4to., full morocco, morocco label, unusually crisp and clean copy, second edition. Bow Windows 66-504 1974 £230

NEWTON, ISAAC   Philosophiae Naturalis Principia Mathematica. Cantabrigiae, 1713. 4to., contemporary panelled calf, second edition. Dawsons PM 250-58 1974 £280

NEWTON, ISAAC   Philosophiae Naturalis Principia Mathematica. Cambridge, 1713. Second edition, folding engraved plates, text diagrams, excellent condition within, 4to., contemporary panelled calf, rebacked, two corners trifle worn. Thomas 32-326 1974 £350

NEWTON, ISAAC   Philosophiae Naturalis Principia Mathematica. Amsterdam, 1714. 4to., contemporary calf, rebacked. Broadhurst 23-1251 1974 £60

NEWTON, ISAAC   Philosophiae Naturalis Principia Mathematica. 1714. 4to., half calf, gilt, first Amsterdam edition. Hammond 201-889 1974 £165

NEWTON, ISAAC   Philosophiae Naturalis Principia Mathematica. London, 1726. 4to., contemporary panelled calf, rebacked, gilt, third edition. Hammond 201-890 1974 £85

NEWTON, ISAAC   Philosophiae Naturalis Principia Mathematica. London, 1726. 4to., modern full brown morocco, inscription, uncut, fine. Traylen 79-253 1973 £95

NEWTON, ISAAC   Philosophiae Naturalis Principia Mathematica. 1726. 4to., contemporary calf, third edition. Dawsons PM 245-542 1974 £115

NEWTON, ISAAC   Philosophiae Naturalis Principia Mathematica. London, 1726. Large 4to., contemporary calf, worn, rebacked, third edition, third issue. Schumann 35-352 1974 $1,500

NEWTON, ISAAC   Philosophiae Naturalis Principa Mathematica. 1739(-1740-1742). 4to., 3 vols., old half calf, uncut, first Jesuit edition. Dawsons PM 245-543 1974 £95

NEWTON, ISAAC   Philosophiae Naturalis Principia Mathematica. 1760. 4to., 3 vols., contemporary calf, rebacked, gilt, second Jesuit edition. Dawsons PM 245-544 1974 £65

NEWTON, ISAAC   Sir Isaac Newton's Mathematische Principien der Naturlehre. Berlin, 1872. 8vo., half cloth, gilt, fine, first edition in German. Dawsons PM 245-548 1974 £55

NEWTON, ISAAC   A Treatise of the System of the World. London, 1728. 8vo., modem calf, gilt, first edition in English. Dawsons PM 245-552 1974 £120

NEWTON, JOHN   Cosmographia. London, 1679. 8vo., eighteenth century calf, plates, first edition. Dawsons PM 245-572 1974 £52

NEWTON, JOHN   Olney Hymns. 1807. 12mo., old morocco backed calf, wom, new edition. Bow Windows 64-626 1974 £6

NEWTON, RICHARD   The Jewish Tabernacle. Carter, 1864. Austin 62-752 1974 $12.50

NEWTON, THOMAS   Seneca: His Tenne Tragedies. London, 1927. 2 vols., edition limited to 1,025 copies, edges slightly bumped, orig. binding, fine copy, scarce. Ross 87-175 1974 $150

NEY, F. J.   Britishers in Britain. London, 1911. Illus. Hood's 104-403 1974 $10

NICERON, J. P.   Memoires Pour Servir a l'Historie des Hommes Illustres dans la Republique des Lettres, Avec Une Catalogue Raisonne de Leurs Ouvrages. Paris, 1733. 12mo., calf, vol. 21 only. Kraus B8-183 1974 $20

NICETAS Acominatus Choniates. Paris, 1647. Folio, contemporary half calf, label. Howes 186-662 1974 £40

NICHOLAS, THOMAS   Annals and Antiquities of the Counties and County Families of Wales. 1872. Roy 8vo., orig. cloth. Broadhurst 23-1486 1974 £20

NICHOLAS, THOMAS   The Pedigree of the English People. London, 18-78. 8vo., orig. cloth, gilt, fifth edition. Hammond 201-436 1974 £6

NICHOLLS, GEORGE   A History of the English Poor Law. 1854. 2 vols., 8vo., half red morocco, gilt. Quaritch 939-188 1974 £20

NICHOLLS, GEORGE   A History of the English Poor Law. 1904-1898-99. 3 vols., best edition. Howes 186-1523 1974 £21

NICHOLLS, WILLIAM   A Comment on the Book of Common-Prayer. London, 1710. Folio, portrait, contemporary calf, rebacked, first edition. Bow Windows 62-672 1974 £28

NICHOLS, BEVERLEY   Are They the Same At Home? 1927. 301 pages. Austin 61-747 1974 $10

NICHOLS, BEVERLEY   A Book of Old Ballads. n.d. Illus., worn covers, ex-library, plates. Austin 61-748 1974 $12.50

NICHOLS, BOWYER   Words and Days. 1895. Small 8vo., gilt, contemporary full brown crushed morocco. Howes 185-24 1974 £20

NICHOLS, J. G.   Collectanea Topographica et Genealogica. 1834-43. 8 vols., roy. 8vo., plates, half blue morocco gilt. Quaritch 939-739 1974 £52.50

NICHOLS, J. G.   Literary Remains of King Edward the Sixth. London, 1857. 2 vols., 4to., orig. quarter roan, worn. Bow Windows 62-670 1974 £62

NICHOLS, J. L.   The Business Guide. Naperville, 1895. Orig. binding, fiftieth edition. Butterfield 10-439 1974 $7.50

NICHOLS, J. T.   The Fresh Water Fishes of China. New York, 1943. 4to., orig. cloth, plates. Wheldon 129-584 1974 £25

NICHOLS, GEORGE WARD   The Sanctuary. New York, 1866. Cloth. Hayman 57-211 1974 $10

NICHOLS, GEORGE WARD   The Story of the Great March from the Diary of a Staff Officer... New York, 1865. First American edition, 8vo., full page woodcut illus., fine fold out maps, very fine. Current BW9-402 1974 $27.50

NICHOLS, JOHN   Biographical and Literary Anecdotes of William Bowyer. London, 1782. 4to., contemporary half red morocco gilt, fine. Dawsons PM 10-453 1974 £50

NICHOLS, JOHN   Biographical and Literary Anecdotes of William Bowyer. London, 1782. Full calf, frontis. Dawson's 424-168 1974 $60

NICHOLS, JOHN   Collection Of All the Wills, Now Known to be Extant, of Kings and Queens of England, Princes & Princesses of Wales, et al. 1780. New buckram. Allen 213-1671 1973 $25

NICHOLS, JOHN   Illustrations of Literary History of the 18th Century. 1807-58. 8 vols., new buckram. Allen 216-P 1974 $125

NICHOLS, JOHN 1745-1826   The History and Antiquities of the County of Leicester. 1795-1811. 4 vols. in 8, folio, plates, half russia, orig. edition. Quaritch 939-428 1974 £650

NICHOLS, JOHN 1745-1826   The History and Antiquities of the County of Leicester. 1795-1811. 4 vols. in 8, folio, plates, fine, morocco gilt, orig. edition. Quaritch 939-429 1974 £800

NICHOLS, ROBERT   The Budded Branch. (1918). Cloth-backed dec. boards, fine, book-plate. Covent 55-164 1974 £15

NICHOLS, ROBERT   The Smile of the Sphinx. 1920. Orig. buckram backed boards, uncut, limited edition. Howes 185-348 1974 £7.50

NICHOLS, ROSE STANDISH   English Pleasure Gardens. New York, 1902. First edition, plans, reproductions of orig. photos and drawings by author, orig. binding, bookplate. Wilson 63-322 1974 $12.50

NICHOLS, ROSE STANDISH   Spanish and Portugese Gardens. Boston, 1924. First edition, illus., orig. binding. Wilson 63-323 1974 $15

NICHOLS, WALLACE BERTRAM   The Song of Sharruk. 1916. Presentation copy, inscribed, English first edition. Covent 56-1965 1974 £7.50

NICHOLS, WILLIAM FORD   Days of My Age. San Francisco, 1923. 8vo., orig. bindings, inscribed, limited edition. Butterfield 8-48 1974 $10

NICHOLS DE LYON, C. W.   The Decadents. Ogilvie, 1899. 172p. Austin 54-794 1973 $12.50

NICHOLSON, CLAUD   Ugly Idol. 1896. Orig. pictorial cloth, English first edition. Covent 56-768 1974 £25

NICHOLSON, E.   Indian Snakes. Madras, (1874). 8vo., cloth, plates, very scarce. Wheldon 131-764 1974 £15

NICHOLSON, E. M.   Birds In England. 1926. 8vo., cloth, wood engravings, scarce. Wheldon 131-671 1974 £5

NICHOLSON, G.   The Illustrated Dictionary of Gardening. (1884-88, 1901). 4to., 12 vols., orig. dec. cloth, illus. Wheldon 130-1447 1974 £12

NICHOLSON, G.   The Illustrated Dictionary of Gardening. 1884-88, 1901. 4to., 5 vols., orig. half morocco. Wheldon 130-1448 1974 £15

NICHOLSON, G.   The Illustrated Dictionary of Gardening. 1885-89. 4 vols. in 9, 4to., orig. cloth, illus., coloured plates. Wheldon 128-1514 1973 £7.50

NICHOLSON, G.   The Illustrated Dictionary of Gardening. (1886)-1888. 4to., contemporary cloth, 4 vols. in 2, plates. Bow Windows 64-196 1974 £10

NICHOLSON, H. A.   On the Structure and Affinities of the "Tabulate Corals". 1879. Roy 8vo., cloth, scarce. Wheldon 130-958 1974 £10

NICHOLSON, JOSEPH   The History and Antiquities of the Counties of Westmorland and Cumberland. London, 1777. 4to., 2 vols., contemporary calf, gilt, labels, first edition. Dawsons PM 251-60 1974 £95

NICHOLSON, KENYON   The Barker. French, 1927. 150p., illus. Austin 51-675 1973 $7.50

NICHOLSON, KENYON   Sailor Beware! Farrar & Rinehart, 1933. Austin 51-677 1973 $7.50

NICHOLSON, KENYON   Torch Song. French, 1930. Austin 51-676 1973 $7.50

NICHOLSON, MEREDITH   A Reversible Santa Claus. Boston, 1917. First edition, 8vo., colored illus., very minor cover soiling, interior fine. Current BW9-66 1974 $15

NICHOLSON, PETER   New Carpenter's Guide. n.d. 4to., half calf, plates, enlarged & improved edition. Marsden 37-339 1974 £8

NICHOLSON, W. A.   A Flora of Norfolk. 1914. 8vo., cloth, maps, scarce. Wheldon 129-1007 1974 £5

NICHOLSON, WILLIAM   An Almanac of Twelve Sports. 1898. Pictorial boards, rubbed, soiled. Marsden 39-332 1974 £15

NICHOLSON, WILLIAM   The First Principles of Chemistry. 1792. 8vo., contemporary half calf, second edition. Zeitlin 235-293 1974 $100

NICHOLSON, WILLIAM   An Introduction to Natural Philosophy. London, 1787. 8vo., 2 vols., contemporary calf. Zeitlin 235-292 1974 $150

NICHOLSON, WILLIAM   An Introduction to Natural Philosophy. London, 1790. 8vo., 2 vols., contemporary calf, gilt, plates, third edition. Dawsons PM 245-573 1974 £12

NICHOLSON, WILLIAM   A Journal of Natural Philosophy, Chemistry, and the Arts. London, 1812. 8vo., contemporary half calf. Dawsons PM 245-574 1974 £6

NICHOLSON, WILLIAM   A Journal of Natural Philosophy, Chemistry, and the Arts. London, 1813. 8vo., half calf, plates. Dawsons PM 245-576 1974 £5

NICHOLSON, WILLIAM   A Journal of Natural Philosophy, Chemistry, and the Arts. London, 1813. 8vo., contemporary half calf, plates. Dawsons PM 245-575 1974 £6

NICHTENHAUSER, ADOLF   Films in Psychiatry, Psychology and Mental Health. 1953. Austin 51-678 1973 $12.50

NICKSON, C.   History of Runcom. 1887. 4to., orig. cloth. Broadhurst 23-1490 1974 £10

NICOL, W.   The Planter's Kalendar. Edinburgh, 1812. 8vo., contemporary calf, plates. Wheldon 131-1556 1974 £12

NICOLAI, J. C.   Das Merkwurdigste aus der Geschichte. 1808. 8vo., orig. wrappers, uncut. Gumey 64-161 1974 £18

NICOLAS DE LYRA   Postilla. 1515. Small 4to., nineteenth century vellum, gilt, soiled. Thomas 31-307 1973 £75

NICOLAS, NICHOLAS H.   A Roll of Arms of the Reign of Edward II. 1829. 8vo., plate, contemporary calf. Quaritch 939-740 1974 £20

NICOLAY, JOHN   The Army in the Civil War. (1885). 16 vols., blue cloth, fine. Putman 126-65 1974 $44

NICOLE, PIERRE   Moral Essays. London, 1677-78. 2 vols. in 1, 12mo., contemporary calf, first English edition. Dawsons PM 252-745 1974 £185

NICOLL, ALLARDYCE   The Development of the Theatre. 1927. 4to., illus., rubbed. Covent 55-1440 1974 £10.50

NICOLL, ALLARDYCE   Film and the Theatre. c. 1936. First edition, spine faded, upper cover little spotted, very good copy. Covent 51-404 1973 £5.25

NICOLL, ALLARDYCE   A History of Late Nineteenth Century Drama, 1850-1900. 2 vols., presentation copy from author, very good, dust wrappers. Covent 51-589 1973 £5.25

NICOLL, ALLARDYCE   Stuart Masques and the Renaissance Stage. London, 1937. 4to., illus., front inner hinge cracked, orig. cloth. Gregory 44-215 1974 £32.50

NICOLL, H. C.   The Story of Christ Church St. Leonards on Sea. St. Leonards-on-Sea, 1909. 4to., plates, illus. Howes 186-2201 1974 £5

NICOLL, M.   Nicoll's Birds of Egypt. 1930. 2 vols., 4to., orig. cloth, plates, very scarce. Wheldon 131-95 1974 £130

NICOLL, W. ROBERTSON   A Bookman's Letters. London, 1913. 8vo., orig. buckram gilt, fine, first edition. Dawsons PM 10-454 1974 £6

NICOLSON, HAROLD   Some People. London, 1927. First edition, very nice copy, orig. cloth. Crane 7-202 1974 £5

NICOLSON, JOSEPH   The History and Antiquities of the Counties of Westmorland and Cumberland. London, 1777. 2 vols., 4to., half green morocco, maps. Traylen 79-404 1973 £30

NICOLSON, W.   The English, Scotch, and Irish Historical Libraries. 1736. Folio, old calf, third edition. Quaritch 939-189 1974 £30

NICOLSON, W.   The English, Scotch and Irish Historical Libraries. London, 1776. 3 parts in 1 vol., 4to., contemporary full speckled calf. Dawsons PM 10-455 1974 £65

NICOLSON, W.   The Irish Historical Library. Dublin, 1724. 8vo., contemporary calf gilt, first edition. Quaritch 939-625 1974 £60

NIEBUHR, BARTHOLD GEORG   Roemische Geschichte. 1828-32. 3 vols., half calf, worn spine. Allen 213-759 1973 $12.50

NIEDECKER, LORINE   North Central. 4to., buckram, fine, dust wrapper, signed, first edition. Rota 188-725 1974 £5.25

NIELSEN, KAY   East of the Sun and West of the Moon. New York, n.d. Orig. pictorial cloth, first U.S. edition. Covent 56-705 1974 £65

NIELSEN, T. M.   How a Dane Became an American. Cedar Rapids, Iowa, 1935. Austin 62-449 1974 $12.50

NIEREMBERG, JOHANNES EUSEBIUS   Historia Naturae, Maxime Peregrinae, Libris XVI Distincta. Antwerp, 1635. Folio, splendid woodcuts, contemporary vellum over boards, first edition, very fine copy. Schafer 10-133 1974 sFr 3,600

NIESE, BENEDICTUS   Grundriss der Romischen Geschichte. Munich, 1923. Biblo & Tannen 214-646 1974 $12.50

NIETHAMMER, G.   Handbuch der Deutschen Vogelkunde. Leipzig, 1937-42. 3 vols., 8vo., cloth, plates, rare. Wheldon 131-672 1974 £30

NIETZSCHE, FRIEDRICH   The Complete Works of. Edinburgh, 1909-13. 18 vols., 8vo., orig. cloth, portrait frontispieces, limited editions. Bow Windows 66-508 1974 £110

NIETZSCHE, FRIEDRICH   Die Geburt der Tragodie aus dem Geiste der Musik. Leipzig, 1872. 8vo., half cloth, orig. printed wrappers, first edition. Gilhofer 61-58 1974 sFr 550

T'NIEUW Hoorns Lied-Boekje. Beukelman, n.d. (18th c.). Full old calf, rubbed, top little worn, 3 X 2. Gregory 44-436 1974 $135

T'NIEUWE Groot Lied Bookje te Hoorn. Beukelman, (c. 1750). Full old green vellum, 2 7/8 X 1 3/4. Gregory 44-435 1974 $135

NIEUWENTYT, BERNARD   The Religious Philosopher. London, 1724. 8vo., contemporary calf, rebacked, third edition in English. Dawsons PM 245-577 1974 £30

NIGGLI, P.   Gesteins-und Mineralprovinzen, Band 1, Einfuhrung, Zielsetzung. Berlin, 1923. Roy. 8vo., cloth, text-figures, tables. Wheldon 128-1025 1973 £7.50

NIGHTINGALE, FLORENCE   Army Sanitary Administration. London, (n.d.) 8vo., orig. wrappers. Dawsons PM 249-387 1974 £5

NIGHTINGALE, FLORENCE   Mortality of the British Army. London, 1858. Folio, orig. wrappers, worn, plates. Dawsons PM 249-385 1974 £50

NIGHTINGALE, FLORENCE   Notes on Nursing. London, n.d. 8vo., orig. cloth, gilt, fine, first edition, third issue. Dawsons PM 249-386 1974 £28

NIGHTINGALE, FLORENCE   Notes On Nursing. London, (1859). 8vo., orig. cloth boards, gilt, first edition. Gilhofer 61-50 1974 sFr 800

NIGHTINGALE, FLORENCE   Notes on Nursing. New York, 1860. 12mo., orig. cloth, some foxing. Bow Windows 66-509 1974 £12.50

NIGHTINGALE, J. E.   Contributions Towards the History of Early English Porcelain, from Contemporary Sources. Salisbury, 1881. Roy. 8vo., half morocco, gilt, worn, scarce. Quaritch 940-653 1974 £30

THE NIGHTINGALE of Ladies' Vocal Companion. Albany, 1807. 12mo., contemporary quarter calf, foxing. Ximenes 35-246 1974 $22.50

NIHELL, MRS. ELIZABETH   A Treatise on the Art of Midwifery. London, 1760. 8vo., contemporary calf, rebacked, first edition. Schumann 35-358 1974 $135

NIHELL, JAMES   New and Extraordinary Observations Concerning the Prediction of Various Crises By the Pulse. London, 1741. 8vo., old vellum, first edition. Schuman 37-190 1974 $165

NIJINSKY, ROMOLA   Nijinsky. S & S, 1934. Austin 51-679 1973 $7.50

NIJINSKY, VASLAV   The Diary of Vaslav Nijinsky. New York, 1936. Biblo & Tannen 210-952 1973 $12.50

NIKLASON, C. R.   Commercial Survey of the Pacific Southwest. Washington, 1930. Charts, large colored folding maps. Jenkins 61-1957 1974 $10

NIKLITSCHEK, A.   Water Lilies and Water Plants. 1932. Roy. 8vo., cloth, plates, drawings. Wheldon 131-1557 1974 £5

NIKLITSCHEK, A.   Water Lilies and Water Plants. 1932. 4to., orig. cloth, illus. Bow Windows 64-197 1974 £6

NILES, GRACE GREYLOCK   The Hoosac Valley Its Legends and Its History. New York - London, 1912. 8vo., orig. bindings. Butterfield 8-260 1974 $25

NILSSON, M. P.   The Minoan-Mycenaean Religion and Its Survival In Greek Religion. Lund, 1927. Roy. 8vo., plates, illus., orig. buckram. Smith 193-833 1973 £7.50

NIMMO, W.   The History of Stirlingshire. 1880. 8vo., 2 vols., orig. cloth, third edition. Bow Windows 64-629 1974 £15

"NIMROD" PSEUD.
Please turn to
APPERLY, CHARLES JAMES

NIN, A.   Ladders to Fire. New York, 1946. 1st ed., engravings. Biblo & Tannen 210-779 1973 $10

NIN, ANAIS   D. H. Lawrence. Paris, 1932. No. 41 of edition limited to 550 copies, orig. binding, fine, name in ink on fly. Ross 87-444 1974 $80

THE 1951 Film Daily Yearbook of Motion Pictures. 1951. 1152p. Austin 51-307 1973 $17.50

1937-38 ANTHOLOGY. Contemporary Play, 1938. Austin 51-524 1973 $12.50

NISARD, CHARLES   Histoire des Livres Populaires ou de la Colportage. Paris, 1864. 2 vols., contemporary blue half calf. Dawsons PM 10-457 1974 £50

NISBET, HUME   The Haunted Station and Other Stories. 1894. Orig. pictorial cloth, English first edition. Covent 56-440 1974 £8.50

NISBET, J.   The Forester. 1905. 8vo., 2 vols., cloth, illus., scarce. Wheldon 130-1568 1974 £5

NISBET, J.   The Forester. 1925. 8vo., 2 vols., cloth, illus. Wheldon 129-1629 1974 £5

NITSCHKE, T. R. J.   Pyrenomycetes Germanici. Breslau, 1867-70. 8vo., new cloth. Wheldon 129-1304 1974 £20

NITZCH'S Pterylography. 1867. Folio, boards, worn, plates. Wheldon 131-673 1974 £10

NIVEN, FREDERICK   Colour in the Canadian Rockies. Toronto, 1937. Illus. in full colour, woodcuts. Hood's 102-159 1974 $17.50

NIVERNOIS, LOUIS JULES, DUC DE MANCINI   Fables. Paris, 1796. 2 vols., engraved frontis., 8vo., contemporary half leather. Schumann 499-75 1974 sFr 110

NIWA, T.   Chrysanthemums of Japan. London, (1937). Color plates, fine, orig. cloth, 8vo. Gregory 44-217 1974 $27.50

NIWA, T.   Chrysanthemums of Japan. 1937. Large demy 8vo., plates, orig. buckram, first English edition. Smith 194-17 1974 £5

NIX, EVETT DUMAS   Oklahombres. (St. Louis, 1929). 8vo., orig. bindings. Butterfield 8-447 1974 $25

NIX, EVETT DUMAS   Oklahombres: Particularly the Wilder Ones. St. Louis, 1929. Jenkins 61-2033 1974 $28.50

NIXON, ANTHONY   The Three English Brothers. 1607. Small 4to., woodcut frontispiece, first edition. Bow Windows 64-630 1974 £850

NIXON, PAT I.   A Century of Medicine In San Antonio. San Antonio, 1936. Boxed, mint, limited, special edition. Jenkins 48-488 1973 $60

NIXON, F. H.   Population. Melbourne, 1862. 8vo., orig. wrappers, rare. Wheldon 131-383 1974 £5

NOAILLES, MARQUIS DE   Henri de Valois et la Pologne en 1572. Paris, 1878. 2 vols., 8vo., half cloth. L. Goldschmidt 42-324 1974 $15

NIZET, F.   Notice sur les Catalogues de Bibliotheques
Publiques. Brussels, 1888. 8vo., orig. wrappers, third edition. Kraus B8-184
1974 $18

NOBILI, FLAMINIO   Trattato Dell'amore Humano. Lucca, 1567.
First edition, little foxed, else sound, small 4to., contemporary limp vellum,
ownership inscription of Pompeio Arnolfini. Thomas 32-149 1974 £75

NOBILI, RICCARDO   The Gentle Art of Faking. 1922. 4to.,
illus., first edition. Covent 55-472 1974 £12.50

NOBLE, MARK   Memoirs. Birmingham and London, 1784. 8vo.,
2 vols., half cloth, uncut, first edition. Dawsons PM 251-294 1974 £10

NOBLE, MARK   Memoirs of the Protectorate-House of
Cromwell. Birmingham, 1784. 2 vols., contemporary calf, rebacked, plate.
Howes 186-750 1974 £15

NOBLE, PETER   Ivor Novello. Falcon, 1951. 307p., illus.
Austin 51-680 1973 $10

NOBLE, PETER   The Negro in Films. n.d. Dust wrapper,
illus., fine. Covent 55-410 1974 £8.50

NOBLE, PETER   The Negro In Films. 1937. 288p., illus.,
orig. ed. Austin 51-681 1973 $10

NOBLE, W. B.   A Guide to the Watering Places. Teignmouth,
1823. 8vo., plates, half green morocco gilt, fine. Traylen 79-322 1973 £90

NOCK, A. D.   Conversion. Oxford, 1933. Biblo & Tannen
213-126 1973 $7.50

NOCK, ALBERT JAY   Francois Rabelais. New York, 1929. 1st ed.
Biblo & Tannen 210-909 1973 $7.50

NODIER, CHARLES   Journal de l'Expedition des Portes de Fer.
Paris, 1844. Roy. 8vo., boards, uncut, mint, first edition. L. Goldschmidt
42-325 1974 $130

NOEL, MARY   Villains Galore. Macmillan, 1954. 320p.
Austin 54-795 1973 $10

NOEL, THEOPHILUS   Autobiography and Reminiscences Of. Chicago,
1904. Cloth, fine, signed. Hayman 57-527 1974 $50

NOEL, THEOPHILUS   Autobiography and Reminiscences of. Chicago,
1904. Very fine bright copy. Jenkins 61-1958 1974 $85

NOLAN, E. H.   The Illustrated History of the British Empire in
India. London, (c.1860). 2 vols. in 8, 8vo., plates, orig. cloth, gilt, worn.
Bow Windows 62-678 1974 $12.50

NOLAN, E. H.   The Illustrated History of the Crimean War.
c.1860. 2 vols., thick 8vo., plates. Howes 186-1751 1974 £8.50

NOLAN, J. BENNETT   The Foundation of the Town of Reading in
Pennsylvania. Reading, 1929. 2 letters signed by author laid in, with author's
bookplate. Jenkins 61-2160 1974 $15

NOLL, ARTHUR H.   A Short History of Mexico. Chicago, 1890.
Jenkins 61-1960 1974 $17.50

NOLLET, JEAN ANTOINE   L'Art des Experiences ou Avis aux Amateurs de
la Physique. Paris, 1770. 12mo., 3 vols., orig. soft boards, plates, first edition.
Dawsons PM 245-581 1974 £42

NOLLET, JEAN ANTOINE   Lecons de Physique Experimentale. Paris, 1771-
69-68-71. 12mo., 6 vols., contemporary calf, plates. Gurney 64-163 1974
£40

NOLLET, JEAN ANTOINE   Lettres sur l'Electricite. Paris, 1760. 12mo.,
2 vols., contemporary mottled calf, gilt, plates. Dawsons PM 245-580 1974
£35

NOLLET, JEAN ANTOINE   Saggio Intorno all' Electricita de' Corpi. 1747.
8vo., contemporary mottled sheep, first edition in Italian. Dawsons PM 245-579
1974 £10

NOLTE, FREDERICK   L'Europe Militaire et Diplomatique au Dix-
Neuvieme Siecle. Paris, 1884. 4 vols., contemporary half calf. Howes
186-1105 1974 £17.50

NONNUS PANOPOLITA   Dionysiacorum Libri XLVIII. 1819-26.
2 vols., boards, worn. Allen 213-764 1973 $12.50

NONNUS PANOPOLITA   Graeca Paraphrasis Sancti Evangelii Secundum
Joannem. 1589. Vellum. Allen 213-765 1973 $22.50

A NONSENSE Anthology. Scribners, 1903. 289p. Austin 54-1028 1973 $7.50

NONSENSORSHIP. Putnam, 1922. 181p., illus. Austin 51-760 1973 $12.50

NOORTWYK, WILLEM   Uteri Humani Gravidi Anatome et Historia. Leyden, 1743. 4to., contemporary calf-backed boards, first edition. Schumann 35-
362 1974 $350

NORDEN, FREDERICK LUDVIG   Travels in Egypt and Nubia. 1757. 2 vols.,
engraved extending plates, contemporary calf, rebacked. Bow Windows
66-512 1974 £80

NORDEN, JOHN   Speculum Britanniae. N.P., 1593. Small
4to., 19th century calf gilt, maps, first edition. Traylen 79-364 1973 £300

NORDHOFF, CHARLES   Northern California, Oregon, and the Sandwich
Islands. New York, 1874. Large 8vo., orig. bindings. Butterfield 8-457 1974
$22.50

NORE, ALFRED DE   Les Animaux Raisonnent. Paris, (c., 1870).
8vo., 19th century morocco backed boards. Bow Windows 64-199 1974 £5.50

NORGATE, KATE   England Under the Angevin Kings. 1887.
2 vols., scarce, orig. edition. Howes 186-1106 1974 £12

NORLIE, OLAF MORGAN   Eielsen Was First. 1942. 118 pages. Austin
57-476 1974 $27.50

NORLIE, OLAF MORGAN   History of the Norwegian People in America.
Minneapolis, 1925. 602p., illus., orig. ed. Austin 62-450 1974 $20

NORLIE, OLAF MORGAN   The United Church Home Missions. Minneapolis,
1909. 200p., illus. Austin 62-451 1974 $17.50

NORMAN, J. B.   A Systematic Monograph of the Flat Fishes,
Vol. 1, Psettodidae, Bothidae, Pieuronectidae. 1934. 4to., orig. cloth, text
figures, scarce orig. printing. Wheldon 128-650 1973 £10

NORMAN, SYLVA   Nature Has no Tune. 1929. English first edition. Covent 56-635 1974 £8.50

NORMANBY, CONSTANTIN HENRY PHIPPS, MARQUIS OF   The Contrast.
London, 1832. 3 vols., 12mo., contemporary half calf, first edition. Dawsons
PM 252-785 1974 £15

NORMANBY, CONSTANTIN HENRY PHIPPS, MARQUIS OF   A Year of
Revolution. 1857. 2 vols., full polished calf, gilt. Howes 186-1107 1974
£8.50

NORMINGTON, THOMAS   The Lancashire and Yorkshire Railway. Manchester, 1898. Roy 8vo., orig. cloth, gilt, plates, first edition. Hammond 201-
930 1974 £25

NORRIS, J. W.   Norris's Business Directory and Statistics of
Chicago, for 1846. Chicago, 1883. Uncut, printed yellow wrappers. Bradley
35-75 1974 $12

NORRIS, JOHN   An Account of Reason & Faith. 1697.
Contemporary calf, first edition. Howes 185-1502 1974 £35

NORRIS, JOHN A Practical Treatise Concerning Humility. London, 1707. Contemporary panelled calf, rubbed. Smith 194-174 1974 £7.50

NORRIS, RICHARD The Physiology and Pathology of the Blood. London, 1882. 8vo., orig. cloth, gilt, plates, first edition. Hammond 201-550 1974 £5

NORRIS, SAMUEL An Antidote or Soveraigne Remedie Against the Pestiferous Writings of all English Sectaries. 1619. Small 4to., contemporary limp vellum. Howes 185-1503 1974 £25

NORSKE NORDHAVS-EXPEDITION Norwegian North Atlantic Expedition, 1876-78. Christiania, 1880-1901. 28 parts, large 4to., orig. wrappers, maps, coloured plates, complete set. Wheldon 128-162 1973 £75

NORTH, A. Carmichael. Toronto, 1919. Illus., marginal dec. Hood's 102-532 1974 $10

NORTH, ARTHUR TAPPAN Ely Jacques Kahn. New York, London, 1931. 4to., boards, soiled, plates. Minters 37-542 1973 $24

NORTH, ARTHUR TAPPAN Ralph Adams Cram: Cram and Ferguson. New York & London, 1931. 4to., boards, plates. Minters 37-521 1973 $22.50

NORTH, ARTHUR TAPPAN Raymond M. Hood. New York & London, 1931. 4to., boards, plates. Minters 37-540 1973 $22.50

NORTH, MAJOR Journal of an English Officer In India. London, 1858. 8vo., portrait. Traylen 79-532 1973 £7.50

NORTH, MARIANNE Recollections of a Happy Life. 1892. 8vo., 2 vols., cloth, portraits, second edition. Wheldon 129-180 1974 £6

NORTH, MARIANNE Recollections of a Happy Life. 1897. Demy 8vo., 2 vols., portraits, map, orig. cloth, fine. Broadhurst 24-1138 1974 £6

NORTH Carolina and Louisiana: Documents and Papers and Constitutions of Those States. Washington, 1868. Jenkins 61-1404 1974 $12.50

NORTH Carolina and Louisiana: Documents and Papers and Consititutions. Washington, 1868. Jenkins 61-1978 1974 $12.50

NORTH Pacific Ports: A Compliation of Useful Marine, Exporting and Importing Information for Alaska and the Western Coast of Canada and the United States. Seattle, 1915. Second edition, worn. Hood's 102-824 1974 $12.50

NORTH Western Ontario: Its Boundaries, Resources and Communications. Toronto, 1879. Hood's 102-625 1974 $20

NORTHALL, G. F. English Folk-Rhymes. 1892. New buckram. Allen 216-1404 1974 $10

NORTHCOTE, JAMES One Hundred Fables. 1828. 8vo., half calf. Hill 126-100 1974 £10.50

NORTHCOTE, WILLIAM A Concise History of Anatomy. London, 1772. 8vo., half calf, first edition. Schumann 35-363 1974 £115

NORTHEND, MARY H. American Glass. New York, 1936. Illus., frontispiece. Covent 55-473 1974 £5.50

NORTHUP, SOLOMON Twelve Years a Slave. Auburn, 1853. Orig. binding. Butterfield 10-117 1974 $20

NORTON, CHARLES ELIOT Letters. 1913. 2 vols., plates. Allen 216-1207 1974 $10

NORTON, H. Brazilian Flowers. 1893. Folio, orig. half roan folio, plates, rare. Wheldon 130-56 1974 £1,200

NORTON, E. H. Brazilian Flowers Drawn from Nature in the Years 1880-1882 In the Neighbourhood of Rio de Janeiro. 1893. Elephant folio, orig. half roan folio, hand-coloured plates, excessively rare. Wheldon 128-1291 1973 £1,000

NORTON, JOHN N. The Life of George Washington. New York, 1860. Cloth, spine faded. Hayman 59-416 1974 $10

NORTON, R. A History of Gold Snuff Boxes. 1938. 8vo., plates, full leather gilt, rubbed, frontispiece. Quaritch 940-683 1974 £12

NORWEGIAN - American Studies and Records. 1940. 183 pages. Austin 57-478 1974 $10

NORWOOD, HAYDEN The Marble Man's Wife. Scribner, 1947. 200p. Austin 54-796 1973 $12.50

NORWOOD, SETH W. Sketches of Brooks History. Dover, (1935). 8vo., orig. bindings. Butterfield 8-208 1974 $10

NOTABLE British Trials. 1920-30. 33 vols., orig. cloth. Howes 185-354 1974 £52.50

NOTES OF Mr. Jamesons Lectures on Natural History. (Edinburgh), 1822-3. 8vo., quarter parchment, uncut, inscription. Gurney 64-118 1974 £20

NOTES of Mr. Jamesons' Lectures on Natural History. (Edinburgh), 1822-23. 8vo., quarter parchment, uncut, bookplate. Gurney 66-92 1974 £20

NOTES on the Cape of Good Hope, Made During an Excursion in That Colony in the Year 1820. 8vo., orig. boards, rebacked, good copy, rare. Sawyer 293-3 1974 £140

NOTHING to Wear. London, 1858. Square 12mo., orig. orange boards, cloth back, color plates. Gregory 44-218 1974 $47.50

NOTICES of the Modern Samaritans, Illustrated by Incidents in the Life of Jacob Esh Shelaby. London, 1855. 4to., orig. red cloth, fine, first edition. Ximenes 33-420 1974 $20

NOTRE Nord-Ouest Provincial: Etude sur la Vallee de l'Ottawa. Montreal, 1887. Paper cover. Hood's 104-714 1974 $17.50

NOTT, JOHN Petrarch Translated. London, 1808. 8vo., orig. blue boards, drab paper backstrip printed paper label, very good copy, second edition. Ximenes 37-158 1974 $20

NOTT, KATHLEEN Mile End. 1938. Spine faded, English first edition. Covent 56-636 1974 £6.30

NOTT, STANLEY CHARLES Chinese Jade in the Stanley Charles Nott Collection. West Palm Beach, 1942. 4to., half tone plates, line engravings, limited to 1000 copies. Biblo & Tannen 213-357 1973 $87.50

NOTZ, CORNELIA The Tariff, a Bibliography. Washington, 1934. Jenkins 61-2420 1974 $25

NOTZING, BARON VON SCHRENCK Phenomena of Materialisation. London, 1920. Biblo & Tannen 210-982 1973 $18.50

NOURRISSON, JEAN FELIX J. J. et le Rousseauisme. Paris, 1903. 8vo., orig. wrapper. L. Goldschmidt 42-113 1974 $12.50

NOURSE, J. E. Narrative of the Second Arctic Expedition Made by Charles F. Hall. Washington, 1879. Illus., maps. Hood's 104-88 1974 $80

NOUVA Raccolta de Cento Principali Vedute Antiche e Moderne dell'Alma Citta' di Roma. Rome, 1796. Oblong small folio, 19th century French quarter roan, engraved title, plates. Thomas 32-344 1974 £200

NOUVEAU Recueil de Cantiques ou Chansonnier Maconnique. Paris, (1820). 12mo., contemporary French morocco gilt. Howes 186-1833 1974 £12.50

NOUVEAUX Voyages de Mr. Le Baron de Lahontan. (1703). 2 vols., orig. full leather. Hood's 103-544 1974 $500

NOVITATES Zoologicae. 1894-1933. Vols. 1 - 38, 4to., half calf. Wheldon 131-449 1974 £260

NOWELL, W.   Diseases of Crop-Plants in the Lesser Antilles.
(1923). 8vo., cloth, scarce. Wheldon 129-1663 1974 £5

NOWLAND, JOHN   Early Reminiscences of Indianapolis. 1870.
Cloth, first edition. Putnam 126-168 1974 $20

NOYES, AL J.   In the Land of Chinook. Helena, (1917).
Plates, cloth, gilt, fine, first edition. Bradley 35-254 1974 $80

NOYES, AL J.   In the Land of the Chinook or the Story of
Blaine County. Helena, (c.1917). 8vo., cloth. Saddleback 14-540 1974
$35

NOYES, ALFRED   The Elfin Artist and Other Poems. Edinburgh,
1920. 1st ed. Biblo & Tannen 214-762 1974 $8.50

NOYES, ALFRED   The Elfin Artist and Other Poems. 1920.
Austin 61-753 1974 $10

NOYES, ALFRED   Forty Singing Seamen and Other Poems. New
York, (1930). 8vo., pictorial boards, cloth spine, color plates, illus. by
Mac Kinstry, first edition. Frohnsdorff 16-528 1974 $15

NOYES, ALFRED   No Other Man. 1940. Illus., first American
edition. Austin 61-754 1974 $12.50

NOYES, ALFRED   The Opalescent Parrot. 1929. First edition.
Austin 61-755 1974 $12.50

NOYES, ALFRED   Rada: A Belgian Christmas Eve. 1915. Illus.,
first edition. Austin 61-757 1974 $12.50

NOYES, ALFRED   The Wine Press: A Tale of War. 1913. First
edition. Austin 61-760 1974 $12.50

NUESCH, E.   Die Hausbewohnenden Hymenomyceten. 1919.
8vo., plate, buckram. Wheldon 129-1307 1974 £5

NUGENT   A New Method of Learning with Facility the
Greek Tongue. London, 1759. 8vo., contemporary calf, second edition.
Bow Windows 62-685 1974 £7.50

NUGENT, THOMAS   The Grand Tour. London, 1749. 4 vols.,
12mo., contemporary half calf, rather worn, ex-library, first edition. Ximenes
37-159 1974 $75

NUOVA Collezione di Vedute di Roma, Antiche, e Moderne. Rome, n.d.
Oblong 4to., old diced calf, gilt, leather label. Traylen 79-566 1973 £65

NURSERY Melodies, or Pretty Rhymes in Easy Verse. New York, n.d. (c. 1850).
12mo., hand colored pictorial wrappers, engravings. Frohnsdorff 16-612 1974
$15

NURSEY, W. R.   The Story of Isaac Brock. Toronto, 1909.
Boards, illus., mended spine, second edition. Hood's 103-220 1974 $10

NUSSEY, HELEN G.   London Gardens of the Past. London, 1939.
Biblo & Tannen 210-203 1973 $12.50

NUTTALL, G. C.   Wild Flowers as They Grow. 1911-14.
7 vols., orig. pictorial cloth gilt, plates. Smith 193-17 1973 £5

NUTTALL, JEFF   Love Poems. Brighton, n.d. Small 4to., presentation copy, inscribed, wrappers., English first edition. Covent 56-995 1974
£10

NUTTALL, THOMAS   A Journal of Travels Into the Arkansas
Territory. Philadelphia, 1821. Folding map, engraved plates, full orig. mottled
calf, gilt. Jenkins 61-1985 1974 $375

NUTTING, WALLACE   Maine Beautiful. Framingham, (1924). First
edition, 8vo., illus., full page sepia plates, fine. Current BW9-403 1974 $18

NUTTING, WALLACE   Massachusetts Beautiful. Framingham, (1923).
4to., orig. bindings, dust jacket, illus., first edition. Butterfield 8-261 1974
$10

NYE, BILL   Bill Nye's Comic History of the U.S.
Thompson, Chicago, 1894. 329p., illus. Austin 54-798 1973 $10

NYE, BILL   Bill Nye's Remarks. Thompson, Thomas, Chicago
1891. Illus. Austin 54-799 1973 $8.50

NYE, BILL   A Guest At the Ludlow. Bowen, Merrill, 1896.
272p., illus. Austin 54-797 1973 $6

NYE, BILL   Nye and Riley's Wit and Humor. Homewood,
1902. 544p., illus. Austin 54-800 1973 $12.50

NYE-STARR, KATE   A Self Sustaining Woman. Chicago, 1888.
Cloth, fine, rare. Hayman 57-530 1974 $1,250

NYLANDER, W.   Synopsis Methodica Lichenum Omnium Hucusque
Cognitorum. Paris, (1858-60). Vol. 1 and Vol. 2 part 1, 8vo., wrappers,
coloured plates, rare. Wheldon 128-1406 1973 £10

NYS, D.   Cosmologie. Louvain, 1925-29. 4 vols.,
cloth. Howes 185-1938 1974 £7.50

O

O LE Tala Saasaa I Le Ekalesia a le Mesia. London, 1860. Contemporary roan backed boards. Thomas 28-84 1972 £15.75

OAKLEIGH, T.   The Oakleigh Shooting Code. 1836. Small 8vo., orig. boards. Wheldon 128-531 1973 £10

OAKLEY, VIOLET   The Holy Experiment. Philadelphia, 1922. Roy. folio, plates, golden brown goat skin, signed, numbered, limited edition. Quaritch 940-194 1974 £30

O'BEIRNE, THOMAS LEWIS   The Generous Imposter. 1781. 8vo., cloth, first edition. Quaritch 936-173 1974 £5

OBERBECK, GRACE J.   History of La Crescenta-La Canada Valleys. Montrose, 1938. 12mo., cloth, presentation, limited. Saddleback 14-211 1974 $12.50

OBERBECK, GRACE J.   History of La Crescenta-La Canada Valleys. Montrose, 1938. 12mo., cloth, second printing. Saddleback 14-212 1974 $10

OBERHOLSER, HARRY C.   The Bird Life of Louisiana. New Orleans, 1938. 8vo., new cloth, plates. Wheldon 131-675 1974 £20

OBERHOLSER, HARRY C.   A Preliminary List of the Birds of Wayne County. Columbus, 1896. 8vo., marbled boards. Butterfield 8-420 1974 $10

OBERHOLTZER, ELLIS PAXTON   Philadelphia: A History of the City and Its People. Philadelphia, (1912). 4 vols., 4to., three quarter cloth, rebacked, illus. Saddleback 14-675 1974 $60

OBERHOLTZER, MRS. S. L.   Hope's Heart Bells. Philadelphia, 1884. Orig. cloth, rubbed, first edition. MacManus 224-348 1974 $25

OBERTHUR, C.   Etudes d'Entomologie. Rennes, 1884. Roy. 8vo., half morocco, plates, foxing. Wheldon 131-840 1974 £5

OBERTHUR C.   Etudes de Lepidopterologie Comparee. Rennes, 1904-22. 23 vols. in 17, 8vo. & 4to., new buckram, illus. Wheldon 131-839 1974 £500

OBOLER, ARCH   Oboler Omnibus. 1945. Austin 51-682 1973 $10

O'BRIEN, EDWARD   Best British Short Stories of 1935. 252 pages. Austin 61-105 1974 $10

O'BRIEN, EDWARD   Best British Short Stories of 1939. 295 pages. Austin 61-109 1974 $12.50

O'BRIEN, EDWARD   Best British Short Stories of 1940. 294 pages. Austin 61-110 1974 $12.50

O'BRIEN, EDWARD J.   The Short Story Case Book. Farrar, Rinehart, 1935. 635p. Austin 54-801 1973 $12.50

O'BRIEN, EDWARD J.   The Best Short Stories of 1927. New York, 1927. Spine somewhat faded, lacking d.w., name in ink on free fly, nice copy, orig. binding. Ross 86-257 1974 $15

O'BRIEN, FRANK G.   Minnesota Pioneer Sketches from the Personal Recollections and Observations of a Pioneer Resident. Minneapolis, 1904. 8vo., cloth. Saddleback 14-520 1974 $25

O'BRIEN, JOHN S.   By Dog Sled for Byrd. Chicago, 1931. Blue cloth, illus., first edition. Bradley 35-418 1974 $10

O'BRIEN, MICHAEL J.   George Washington's Associations with the Irish. Kennedy, 1937. Austin 62-456 1974 $8.50

O'BRIEN, MICHAEL J.   A Hidden Phase of American History. 1919. Portraits, illus., orig. edition. Austin 57-482 1974 $11.25

O'BRIEN, MICHAEL J.   A Hidden Phase of American History. Dodd, Mead, 1919. 533p., illus., orig. ed. Austin 62-457 1974 $11.25

O'BRIEN, MILDRED   The Rug and Carpet Book. New York, 1946. First edition. Biblo & Tannen 210-196 1973 $8.50

O'BRIEN, R. BARRY   The Autobiography of Theobald Wolfe Tone. Dublin, (1893). 2 vols. in 1, 8vo. Emerald 50-689 1974 £10.50

O'BRIEN, R. BARRY   The Life of Charles Stewart Parnell. London, 1899. 2 vols., 8vo., cloth boards. Emerald 50-690 1974 £6.50

O'BRIEN, R. J.   Will Rogers. Winston, 1935. 288p., illus. Austin 54-875 1973 $6

O'BRIEN, WILLIAM   Cross Purposes. London, (n.d.). 8vo., modern boards, first edition. Dawsons PM 252-747 1974 £15

O'BRIEN, WILLIAM   The Duel. London, 1772. 8vo., modern boards, fine, first edition. Dawsons PM 252-748 1974 £15

O'BRIEN, WILLIAM   The Irish Revolution and How It Came About. Dublin, n.d. 8vo., cloth boards. Emerald 50-693 1974 £5.50

O BRUADAIR, DAVID   The Poems of. London, 1910. 2 vols., 8vo., cloth boards. Emerald 50-695 1974 £6.50

OBSERVATIONS Arising from the Declaration of War Against Spain. London, 1739. 8vo., modern quarter calf, gilt, first edition. Dawsons PM 247-208 1974 £24

OBSERVATIONS on the Conduct of Great Britain. London, 1729. 8vo., fine, modern boards, first edition. Dawsons PM 247-209 1974 £30

OBSERVATIONS On the Conduct of Great Britain With Regard to the Negociations and Other Transactions Abroad. London, 1729. 8vo., disbound, first edition. Ximenes 35-506 1974 $40

OBSERVATIONS on the Present Difficulties of the Country, Contained in Strictures on Two Pamphlets. London, 1816. 8vo., sewn as issued, first edition. Ximenes 37-69 1974 $22.50

OBSERVATIONS on the Woollen Manufacture, in the West-Riding of the County of York. Leeds, 1808. 8vo., disbound, rare, first edition. Ximenes 37-224 1974 $45

OBSERVATIONS sur les Domaines du Roi. 1787. 8vo., modern half cloth. Dawsons PM 251-295 1974 £18

OBSERVATIONS Upon the Laws of Excise. London, (n.d.). 8vo., disbound, uncut, first edition. Dawsons PM 247-210 1974 £15

OBSERVATIONS Upon the Present Controversy About the Mode of Assessment for the Poor's Rates in the City of Norwich. Norwich, 1785. 8vo., fine, old marbled paper wrappers, first edition. Dawsons PM 247-211 1974 £25

THE OBSERVER. 1791-95. 5 vols., contemporary tree calf. Howes 186-341 1974 £15

O'CALLAGHAN, JEREMIAH   The Holy Bible Authenticated. 1858. 244 pages. Austin 57-483 1974 $10

O'CALLAGHAN, P. P.   The Married Bachelor. French, ca. 1829. Austin 51-683 1973 $6.50

O'CASEY, SEAN   Collected Plays. Macmillan, 1950. 314p. Austin 51-684 1973 $5

O'CASEY, SEAN   Five Irish Plays. 1935. Crown 8vo., orig. cloth, first edition. Broadhurst 23-889 1974 £5

O'CASEY, SEAN   I Knock At the Door. Macmillan, 1949. Austin 51-685 1973 $6.50

O'CASEY, SEAN   Oak Leaves and Lavendar. Macmillan, 1947. Austin 51-686 1973 $8.50

O'CASEY, SEAN   The Plough and the Stars. Macmillan, 1926. Austin 51-687 1973 $7.50

O'CASEY, SEAN   Rose and Crown. Macmillan, 1952. 323p.
Austin 51-688 1973 $6.50

O'CASEY, SEAN   The Shadow of a Gunman. French, 1932.
Austin 51-689 1973 $8.50

O'CASEY, SEAN   The Silver Tassie. 1928. Orig. cloth,
fine, dust wrapper, first edition. Rota 188-730 1974 £5

O'CASEY, SEAN   The Silver Tassie. 1928. First edition, crown
8vo., boards, cloth spine, paper printed labels, fine. Broadhurst 24-819 1974 £6

O'CASEY, SEAN   The Story of the Irish Citizen Army. Dublin,
and London, 1919. Wrappers, scarce. Rota 188-729 1974 £21

O'CASEY, SEAN   Sunset and Evening Star. Macmillan, 1954.
Austin 51-690 1973 $6

O'CASEY, SEAN   Windfalls. 1934. Orig. cloth, faded,
first edition. Rota 188-731 1974 £5

O'CATHASAIGH, P.   The Story of the Irish Citizen Army. Dublin,
1919. 8vo., orig. wrappers, first edition. Dawsons PM 252-749 1974 £20

OCHSNER, ALBERT J.   A New Clinical Surgery. Chicago, 1911.
Revised third edition. Rittenhouse 46-505 1974 $10

O'CONNELL, CHARLES   The Other Side of the Record. Knopf, 1947.
Austin 51-691 1973 $7.50

O'CONNELL, DANIEL   Life and Speeches of. Dublin, 1846. 2 vols.,
8vo., red cloth, worn, library stamp. Emerald 50-701 1974 £7.50

O'CONNELL, J. J.   Catholicity in the Carolinas and Georgia.
1879. Orig. ed. Austin 62-459 1974 $17.50

O'CONNELL, J. J.   Catholicity in the Carolinas and Georgia.
1879. Ex-library. Austin 57-484 1974 $27.50

O'CONNELL, MORGAN JOHN   The Last Colonel of the Irish Brigade.
London, 1892. 2 vols., 8vo., cloth boards. Emerald 50-702 1974 £9

O'CONNELL, WILLIAM CARDINAL   Recollections of Seventy Years. Houghton,
Mifflin, 1934. 395p., illus. Austin 62-458 1974 $12.50

O'CONNOR, FRANK   Bones of Contention and Other Stories. 1936.
Austin 61-761 1974 $12.50

O'CONNOR, FRANK   Death in Dublin. 1937. 270 pages. Austin
61-762 1974 $10

O'CONNOR, FRANK   A Picture Book. Dublin, 1943. Linen-backed
boards, browned, drawings. Covent 55-554 1974 £35

O'CONNOR, FRANK   The Saint and Mary Kate. 1932. Spine faded,
Roger Senhouse's copy with his signature in pencil, first edition. Covent
51-1375 1973 £8.40

O'CONNOR, HARVEY   The Guggenheim's. Covici, 1937. 496p.,
illus. Austin 62-461 1974 $10

O'CONNOR, JAMES   History of Ireland. New York, n.d. 2 vols.,
8vo., ex-library. Emerald 50-704 1974 £6

O'CONNOR, JAMES   History of Ireland, 1798-1924. London, 1926.
2 vols., 8vo., scarce. Traylen 79-338 1973 £8

O'CONNOR, RICHARD   Ambrose Bierce. Little, Brown, 1967. 333p.
Austin 54-802 1973 $6

O'CONNOR, THOMAS   An Impartial and Correct History of the War
Between the United States and Great Britain, 1812. New York, 1815. Worn,
leather, browned. Hood's 104-130 1974 $85

O'CONNOR, THOMAS   An Impartial and Correct History of the War
Between the United States of America, and Great Britain. New York, 1815.
Worn leather binding, pages browned & stained but readable, new leather spine.
Hood's 102-112 1974 $85

O'CONOR, C.   Rerum Hibernicarum Scriptores Veteres.
Buckingham, 1814-26. 4 vols., 4to., cloth. Quaritch 939-626 1974 £40

ODART, COUNT   Ampelographie Universelle ou Traite des
Cepages les Plus Estimes dans Tous les Vignobles de Quelque Renom. Paris,
1862. 8vo., half red morocco, gilt, scarce, fifth edition. Wheldon 131-1792
1974 £10

O'DAY, EDWARD F.   Bel-Air Bay. Los Angeles, 1927. 4to.,
leather. Saddleback 14-213 1974 $20

ODDI, MUZIO   Fabrica et uso del Compasso Polimetro. 1633.
4to., contemporary vellum, first edition. Dawsons PM 245-582 1974 £75

AN ODE to the Right Honourable Sir Peter Warren, Knight of the Bath. London,
1747. 4to., old half calf, spine worn, first edition, ex-library, very scarce.
Ximenes 36-163 1974 $75

ODELL, MARY THERESA   The Old Theatre, Worthing. Aylesbury, 1938.
4to., orig. cloth, coloured frontispiece, illus., inscribed and signed by author.
Bow Windows 66-681 1974 £8.75

ODETS, CLIFFORD   Clash by Night. New York, 1942. 1st ed.
Biblo & Tannen 213-581 1973 $10

O'DONOGHUE, FREEMAN   Catalogue of Engraved British Portraits.
1908-25. 6 vols., roy. 8vo., orig. cloth. Marsden 37-345 1974 £25

O'DONOVAN, EDMOND   The Merv Oasis: Travels and Adventures East of
the Caspian During the Years 1879-80-81 Including Five Months Residence Among
the Tekkes of Merv. 1882. Folding map, first edition, 2 vols., very fine copy,
scarce, orig. cloth. Broadhurst 24-1659 1974 £45

O'DUFFY, EIMAR   Printer's Errors. Dublin & London, n.d. Spine
faded, head band torn, very good copy. Covent 51-1380 1973 £5.25

OERSTED, A. S.   L'Amerique Centrale, Recherches sur sa Flore et
sa Geographie Physique. Copenhagen, 1863. Folio, orig. boards, plates.
Wheldon 130-1191 1974 £120

L'OEUVRE Priapique des Anciens et des Modernes. Paris, 1914. Half maroon
morocco, plates. Howes 186-1905 1974 £6

OF THE FRIENDSHIP of Amis and Amile. 1894. 12mo., holland-backed boards.
Hammond 201-731 1974 £75

THE OFFICIAL Guide to the Klondyke Country and the Gold Fields of Alaska
With the Official Maps. Chicago, 1897. Cloth, profusely illus. Hayman 59-6
1974 $15

THE OFFICIAL Records of Robert Dinwiddie, Lieutenant-Governor of the Colony
of Virginia, 1751-58. Richmond, 1883. Jenkins 61-2539 1974 $20

OFFICIUM Beatae Mariae-Virginis. Antwerp, 1700. 8vo., contemporary black
morocco, gilt back, fine, full page engravings. Schumann 499-76 1974 sFr
420

O'FLAHERTY, KATHERINE   The Awakening. Chicago and New York, 1899.
Orig. binding. Butterfield 10-11 1974 $12.50

O'FLAHERTY, LIAM   Civil War. (1925). Orig. cloth, first edition.
Rota 188-736 1974 £6

O'FLAHERTY, LIAM   Civil War. London, 1925-26. 3 works, orig.
wrappers, fine, limited, first editions. Dawsons PM 252-750 1974 £95

O'FLAHERTY, LIAM   A Cure for Unemployment. 1931. Wrappers,
frontispiece, English first edition. Covent 56-1971 1974 £6.30

O'FLAHERTY, LIAM   A Cure for Unemployment. 1931. Wrappers,
signed, English first edition. Covent 56-1970 1974 £12.50

O'FLAHERTY, LIAM   Darkness, a Tragedy. London, 1926. First
edition, proof copy, frontispiece portrait, orig. drab wrappers. Crane 7-204
1974 £25

O'FLAHERTY, LIAM   The Extasy of Angus.   London, 1931.   First edition, limited to 350 numbered copies, signed by author, 4to., green buckram, very nice copy, extremely scarce.   Crane 7-209 1974 £30

O'FLAHERTY, LIAM   The Fairy Goose and Two Other Stories.   New York, 1927.   First edition, limited to 1190 copies, numbered, signed by author, 12mo., patterned boards, very nice copy.   Crane 7-206 1974 £20

O'FLAHERTY, LIAM   The House of Gold.   London, (1929).   8vo., signed, dust jacket, first edition.   Emerald 50-718 1974 £9

O'FLAHERTY, LIAM   The Life of Tim Healy.   1927.   First edition, demy 8vo., portrait, fine, orig. cloth.   Broadhurst 24-822 1974 £6

O'FLAHERTY, LIAM   The Life of Tim Healy.   London, 1927.   First edition, spine slightly faded, nice copy, orig. cloth, scarce.   Crane 7-205 1974 £8.50

O'FLAHERTY, LIAM   The Martyr.   London, 1933.   Fine, orig. cloth, first edition, dust wrapper.   Crane 7-211 1974 £5

O'FLAHERTY, LIAM   The Mountain Tavern.   1929.   Faded covers, worn dust wrapper.   Covent 55-1148 1974 £10

O'FLAHERTY, LIAM   The Puritan.   London, 1932.   First edition, orig. cloth, d.w., extremely fine copy.   Crane 7-210 1974 £6

O'FLAHERTY, LIAM   Red Barbara and Other Stories.   New York, 1928.   Cloth-backed boards, signed, English first edition.   Covent 56-997 1974 £17.50

O'FLAHERTY, LIAM   Red Barbara and Other Stories.   New York, 1928.   First edition, limited to 600 copies, signed by author, fine, orig. cloth.   Crane 7-207 1974 £18

O'FLAHERTY, LIAM   Shame the Devil.   1934.   First edition, med. 8vo., uncut, fine, faded d.w., special edition of 105 copies signed by author, loosely inserted is page of the orig. typescript lightly corrected.   Broadhurst 24-823 1974 £21

O'FLAHERTY, LIAM   Skerrett.   London, 1932.   8vo., signed, dust jacket, first edition.   Emerald 50-719 1974 £9

O'FLAHERTY, LIAM   Spring Sowing.   1924.   Crown 8vo., boards, cloth, first edition.   Broadhurst 23-893 1974 £5

O'FLAHERTY, LIAM   The Tent.   1926.   First edition, crown 8vo., orig. cloth, fine.   Broadhurst 24-821 1974 £5

O'FLAHERTY, LIAM   The Tent.   1926.   Frayed dust wrapper, fine.   Covent 55-1149 1974 £8.50

O'FLAHERTY, LIAM   A Tourist's Guide to Ireland.   n.d. 8vo., dec. boards, first edition.   Broadhurst 23-892 1974 £5

O'FLAHERTY, LIAM   Two Years.   London, 1930.   First edition, very nice copy, chipped d.w., orig. cloth.   Crane 7-208 1974 £5

O'FLAHERTY, LIAM   The Wild Swan and Other Stories.   1932.   Buckram, signed, English first edition.   Covent 56-998 1974 £6.30

O'FLAHERTY, TOM   Aranmen All.   1934.   Plates, dust wrapper, fine, English first edition.   Covent 56-1972 1974 £6.50

OGDEN, C. K.   The History of Civilisation.   London, 1936.   Tall 8vo., orig. blue cloth gilt, fine, first edition.   Dawsons PM 251-296 1974 £80

OGDEN, E. D.   Tariff, or Rates of Duties Pyable on Goods.   New York, 1867.   8vo., contemporary quarter roan gilt.   Dawsons PM 247-212 1974 £10

OGG, FREDERIC AUSTIN   The Opening of the Mississippi.   New York, 1904.   Cloth, maps, gilt, inscription, first edition.   Bradley 35-281 1974 $35

OGG, FREDERIC AUSTIN   The Opening of the Mississippi.   1904.   Orig. cloth, first edition.   Putnam 126-331 1974 $12.75

OGIER GHISLAIN DE BUSBECQ
Please turn to
BUSBECQ, OGIER GHISLAIN DE

OGILBY, JOHN   Britannia Depicta.   London, 1724.   Small 4to., old calf, rebacked, maps.   Traylen 79-306 1973 £135

OGILVIE, F. M.   Field Observations on British Birds.   (1920).   Roy. 8vo., boards, cloth back, maps, plates, new edition.   Wheldon 131-676 1974 £5

OGLE, GEORGE A.   Standard Atlas of Paulding County, Ohio.   Chicago, 1917.   New cloth.   Hayman 59-495 1974 $50

OGLE, OCTAVIUS   Royal Letters Addressed to Oxford.   1892.   Roy. 8vo., orig. half roan.   Howes 186-1119 1974 £7.75

OGLE, T. ACRES   The Irish Militia Officer.   Dublin, 1873.   8vo., cloth boards.   Emerald 50-721 1974 £5.50

O'GORMAN, EDITH   Trials and Tribulations of Miss Edith O'Gorman.   1871.   264p.   Austin 62-462 1974 $10

O'GRADY, STANDISH   In the Wake of King James.   London, 1897.   8vo., cloth boards, scarce, second edition.   Emerald 50-723 1974 £5

O'HANLON, JOHN   Irish - American History of the U. S.   1907.   2 vols., 677 pages.   Austin 57-486 1974 $37.50

O'HARA, JOHN   Appointment in Samarra.   New York, 1934.   lst ed.   Jacobs 24-117 1974 $100

O'HARA, KANE   Midas.   London, 1764.   8vo., modern boards, first edition.   Dawsons PM 252-751 1974 £15

O'HARA, KANE   Tom Thunb.   1830.   12mo., half morocco, illus.   Covent 55-553 1974 £25

O'HARA, KANE   The Two Misers.   1775.   8vo., cloth, first edition.   Quaritch 936-174 1974 £5

O'HARRA, CLEOPHAS C.   A Bibliography of the Geology and Mining Interests of the Black Hills Region.   Rapid City, 1917.   8vo., wrapper.   Butterfield 8-597 1974 $12.50

O'HARRA, CLEOPHAS C.   The White River Badlands.   Rapid City, 1920.   8vo., wrapper, plates.   Butterfield 8-598 1974 $20

O'HEYNE, JOHN   The Irish Dominicans of the Seventeenth Century.   Dundalk, 1902.   8vo., cloth boards.   Emerald 50-725 1974 £6.50

OHIO   Official Roster of the Soldiers of the State of Ohio in the War of the Rebellion, 1861-66, and in the War With Mexico, 1846-48.   Norwalk, 1895.   Vol. XII, half leather.   Hayman 59-122 1974 $15

OISEAU, L.   Revue d'Histoire Naturelle.   Paris, 1620-58.   8vo., cloth, scarce.   Wheldon 130-592 1974 £200

OJETTI, BENEDICTO   Synopsis Rerum Moralium et Juris Pontifici.   Rome, 1909-12.   3 vols., thick roy. 8vo., half vellum.   Howes 185-1507 1974 £15

O'KEEFE, ADELAIDE   National Characters Exhibited in Forty Geographical Poems, With Plates.   Lymington, 1818.   12mo., contemporary half calf, marbled boards, first edition.   MacManus 224-349 1974 $40

O'KEEFE, JOHN   The Prisoner at Large.   1788.   8vo., cloth, first edition.   Quaritch 936-175 1974 £8

O'KEEFE, JOHN   Wild Oats.   London, 1794.   8vo., modern boards, first authorised edition.   Dawsons PM 252-752 1974 £15

O'KEEFE, JOHN   The World in a Village. London, (n.d.).
8vo., modern boards, first edition.   Dawsons PM 252-753 1974 £15

OKEY, THOMAS   The Story of Paris. London, 1919. 12mo.,
illus. Biblo & Tannen 213-470 1973 $9.50

OKIE, HOWARD PITCHER   Old Silver and Old Sheffield Plate. Garden
City, 1945. Illus., orig. binding. Wilson 63-284 1974 $18.50

OKUBO, MINE   Citizen 13660. Columbia Univ., 1946.
Orig. ed. Austin 62-463 1974 $10

OLCOTT, RITA   Song In His Heart. 1939. 304p., illus.
Austin 51-692 1973 $8.50

OLD and New Views of Niagara Falls. Niagara Falls, 1899. Photographs.
Hood's 103-664 1974 $20

OLD California Missions. San Francisco, 1889. Photographs, wrapper, spine
loose. Jenkins 61-374 1974 $12.50

OLD English Drama. Oxford, 1878. Austin 51-1009 1973 $7.50

OLD Nursery Stories. New York, (1892). 8vo., full page full color pictures,
orig. pictorial boards, rebacked, edges & corners worn, some soiling on pages.
Current BW9-124 1974 $18.75

OLD Providence, A Collection of Facts and Traditions Relating to Various Buildings
and Sites of Historic Interest in Providence. Providence, 1918. 8vo., illus.,
orig. wrappers, fine. Current BW9-425 1974 $12

OLD Santa Fe: Twelve Hand-Colored Views. Kansas City, c. 1900. Oblong
folio, mint. Jenkins 61-1852 1974 $15

THE OLD West: Pioneer Tales of San Bernardino County. San Bernardino,
(1940). 8vo., wrapper. Saddleback 14-326 1974 $17.50

OLDENBURG, HENRY   A Farther Brief and True Narration of the Late
Wars Risen in New-England. (London, 1676). 8vo., orig. bindings, blue boards,
limited edition. Butterfield 8-571 1974 $10

OLDER, FREMONT   My Own Story. San Francisco, 1919.
Jenkins 61-376 1974 $10

OLDFIELD, CLAUDE HOUGHTON   The Beast. Belfast, 1936. Signed, illus.,
d.j. Ballinger 1-145 1974 $12.50

OLDFIELD, CLAUDE HOUGHTON   The Beast. Belfast, 1936. One of 250
copies, signed by author and artist, presentation copy inscribed from author, 4to.,
gilt top, buckram, cover faded, else fine. Covent 51-939 1973 $5.25

OLDFIELD, CLAUDE HOUGHTON   The Phantom Host. 1917. Wrapppers, fine,
first edition. Covent 55-851 1974 $10.50

OLDFIELD, CLAUDE HOUGHTON   The Phantom Host and Other Verses. 1917.
First edition, f'cap. 8vo., paper printed wrapper, exceptionally fine, presentation
inscription by author. Broadhurst 24-725 1974 £10

OLDFIELD, CLAUDE HOUGHTON   This Was Ivor Trent. 1935. First edition,
crown 8vo., mint, d.w., orig. cloth, presentation copy inscribed by author.
Broadhurst 24-730 1974 £6

OLDFIELD, CLAUDE HOUGHTON   Three Fantastic Tales. 1934. One of 275
copies (this copy one of 25 out of series), with author's presentation inscription,
frontis., buckram, gilt top, fine, first edition. Covent 51-945 1973 £5.25

OLDHAM, HENRY   The Man from Texas. Philadelphia, (1884).
Orig. cloth, first edition. MacManus 224-350 1974 $75

OLDHAM, R. D.   Manual of the Geology of India. Calcutta,
1893. Roy. 8vo., half morocco, plates. Wheldon 131-1054 1974 £12

OLDMIXON, JOHN   The British Empire in America, Containing the
History of the Discovery, Settlement, Progress and State of the British Colonies on
the Continent. London, 1741. Corrected & amended second edition, 2 vols.,
cloth boards, leather spine, maps, leather corners, no foxing. Hood's 102-573
1974 $550

OLDYS, WILLIAM   A Critical and Historical Account Of All the
Celebrated Libraries in Foreign Countires. London, 1739. 12mo., contemporary
sheep gilt, first edition. Dawsons PM 10-461 1974 £80

O'LEARY, JEREMIAH   My Political Trial and Experiences. 1919.
546 pages. Austin 57-488 1974 $12.50

O'LEARY, JEREMIAH   My Political Trial and Experiences. 1919.
Austin 62-464 1974 $12.50

OLIN, STEPHEN   Greece and the Golden Horn. New York,
1854. Orig. binding. Butterfield 10-50 1974 $10

OLIPHANT, MARGARET O.   The Literary History of England, 1790-1825.
1882. 3 vols., orig. edition. Howes 185-357 1974 £8.50

OLIPHANT, MARGARET O.   Literary History of England in End of 18th and
Beginning of 19th Century. 1882. 3 vols., half morocco, slightly rubbed.
Allen 216-1349 1974 $17.50

OLIPHANT, T.   Catalogue of the Manuscript Music In the
British Museum. London, 1842. Tall 8vo., orig. boards, paper label. Dawsons
PM 10-462 1974 £8

OLIPHANT, T. L. KINGTON   Rome and Reform. 1902. 2 vols., buckram,
scarce. Howes 185-1509 1974 £8.50

THE OLIVE Branch. 1844. Pamphlet, 47 pages. Austin 57-41 1974
$17.50

OLIVER, D.   Flora of Tropical Africa. 1868-1902. 8vo.,
cloth. Wheldon 130-1192 1974 £70

OLIVER, D.   Illustrations of the Principal Natural Orders of
the Vegetable Kingdom. 1874. Oblong 4to., cloth, scarce, first edition.
Wheldon 130-1041 1974 £10

OLIVER, E. H.   The Winning of the Frontier. Toronto, 1930.
Spine mended. Hood's 102-303 1974 $17.50

OLIVER, F. W.   The Natural History of Plants, Their Forms,
Growth, Reproduction and Distribution. 1894. 2 vols., imp 8vo., half morocco,
edges gilt, illus., plates in colour, fine. Broadhurst 24-1139 1974 £20

OLIVER, F. W.   The Natural History of Plants. 1894. Imperial
8vo., 2 vols., half morocco, gilt. Broadhurst 23-1169 1974 £20

OLIVER, GEORGE   Collections Towards Illustrating the Biography
of the . . . . Members of the Society of Jesus. 1845. Orig. cloth, rebacked,
scarce, second edition. Howes 185-1510 1974 £8.50

OLIVER, GEORGE   Historic Collections, Relating to Monasteries
in Devon. Exeter, 1820. 8vo., half morocco. Howes 185-1511 1974 £7.50

OLIVER, JOHN   A Present to be Given to Teeming Women.
London, 1669. 8vo., contemporary mottled calf, joints a bit worn, very good
copy, second edition. Ximenes 37-160 1974 $125

OLIVER, STEPHEN   Scenes and Recollections of Fly-Fishing, in
Northumberland, Cumberland and Westmorland. 1834. 8vo., half calf, gilt,
vignettes. Bow Windows 66-515 1974 £12.50

OLIVER, WILLIAM   Eight Months in Illinois. Chicago, 1924.
Cloth, gilt, fine, dust jacket, uncut, unopened. Bradley 35-182 1974 $28

OLIVER And Boyd's Little Warbler. Edinburgh, (c. 1820). Vols. 1 & 2 only
in 1 vol., full calf, joints rubbed, ex-libris. George's 610-531 1973 £7.50

OLIVERS, THOMAS   An Answer to Mr. Mark Davis's Thoughts on Dancing. 1792. Small 8vo., unbound. Hill 126-66 1974 £5.50

OLIVIER, G.   Monographie des Pies-Grieches du Genre Lanius. Rouen, 1944. Roy 8vo., wrappers, plates. Wheldon 130-594 1974 £5

OLLIVER, C. W.   An Analysis of Magic and Witchcraft. London, 1928. Rittenhouse 46-508 1974 $10

OLMSTEAD, A. T.   History of Palestine & Syria to the Macedonian Conquest. New York & London, 1931. Crown 4to., frontispiece, illus., orig. pictorial buckram. Smith 194-34 1974 £5

OLMSTED, FREDERICK LAW   Preliminary Report in Regard to a Plan of Public Pleasure Grounds for the City of San Francisco. New York, 1866. 8vo., orig. grey printed wrappers, worn spine, rare, good copy, first edition. Ximenes 37-161 1974 $300

OLNEY, J.   A Practical System of Modern Geography. New York, 1845. Pictorial boards, woodcuts, fifty-eighth edition. Hayman 57-612 1974 £10

OLPHE-GALLIARD, L.   Faune Ornithologique de l'Europe. Bayonne and Paris, 1884-96. 8vo., 4 vols., wrappers. Wheldon 129-512 1974 £20

OLSCHKI, LEO S.   Manuscrits sur Velin Avec Miniatures du Xe au SVIe Siecle. Florence, 1910. Folding color plates, illus., 4to., cloth, spine repaired, presentation copy, inscribed by Olschki. Kraus B8-187 1974 $50

OLSON, CHARLES   Maximus Poems IV, V, VI. n.d. English first edition. Covent 56-1973 1974 £45

OLSON, ERNEST W.   History of the Swedes of Illinois. 1908. Illus., 933 pages. Austin 57-489 1974 $47.50

OLTMANNS, F.   Morphologie und Biologie der Algen. Jena, 1922-23. Roy 8vo., orig. cloth, 3 vols., second edition. Wheldon 129-1414 1974 £35

OMALIUS, D'HALLOY, J. B. J. D'   Memoires Pour Servir a la Description Geologique des Pays-Bas, de la France et de Quelques Contrees Voisines. Namur, 1828. 8vo., modern boards, folding coloured map, plates. Wheldon 128-1026 1973 £20

OMAN, CHARLES   A History of England. 1913-41. 8vo., 8 vols., maps, cloth. Quaritch 936-508 1974 £8

OMAR KHAYYAM   Bish Ta Dui Gilia. 1902. Small 4to., vellum, wrappers. Bow Windows 62-696 1974 £16

OMAR KHAYYAM   Rubaiyat of. London, 1906. 8vo., contemporary parchment. Bow Windows 62-697 1974 £6

OMAR KHAYYAM   The Ruba'iyat. 1913. Presentation, inscribed, foxing. Covent 55-1156 1974 £15

OMAR KHAYYAM   Rubaiyat. Boston & London, 1898. 2 vols., orig. dec. cloth gilt, gilt tops, nice copy, damp-stained cloth dust wrappers. Covent 51-1050 1973 £7.50

OMAR KHAYYAM   The Ruba'iyat. 1889. 12mo., full vellum gilt, fine, inscribed, presentation. Covent 55-1154 1974 £32.50

OMAR KHAYYAM   Rubaiyat. (1909). 4to., orig. white buckram, illus., fine. Howes 185-141 1974 £25

O'MEARA, CARROLL   Television Program Production. Ronald Press, 1955. 361p., illus. Austin 51-693 1973 $8.50

THE OMNIBUS of Crime. New York, 1929. 1st ed. Biblo & Tannen 213-528 1973 $20

OMWAKE, JOHN   The Conestoga Six Horse Bell Teams of Eastern Pennsylvania. Cincinnati, 1930. Lavishly illus., orig. binding. Butterfield 10-444 1974 $65

ONE Act Plays for Stage and Study. New York, 1924. Spine faded. Covent 51-81 1973 £5.25

100 Views of Toronto, the Queen City of Canada. Toronto, n.d. Photographs. Hood's 104-715 1974 $17.50

ONEBY, JOHN   A True and Faithful Narrative of. (1726). 8vo., cloth, uncut. Quaritch 936-177 1974 £20

ONEIDA HISTORICAL SOCIETY   Transactions of . . ., at Utica, With the Annual Addresses and Reports for 1881, the Paris Reinterment and Papers Read Before the Society. New York, 1881. Wrapper. Jenkins 61-1931 1974 $15

O'NEILL, EUGENE   Ah, Wilderness! French, 1933. Austin 51-694 1973 $7.50

O'NEILL, EUGENE   Ah, Wilderness! Random, 1933. Orig. ed. Austin 51-695 1973 $7.50

O'NEILL, EUGENE   Beyond the Horizon. Boni & Liveright, 1920. Orig. ed. Austin 51-696 1973 $6.50

O'NEILL, EUGENE   Days Without End. New York, (1934). Orig. leather, label, first edition, one of 325 numbered copies, signed by author, fine, in defective box. MacManus 224-351 1974 $85

O'NEILL, EUGENE   The Emperor Jones. New York, 1928. Orig. cloth backed boards, illus. by Alexander King, first illus. edition, one of 775 numbered copies, signed by author, dust jacket, in defective box. MacManus 224-352 1974 $100

O'NEILL, EUGENE   The Emperor Jones, Diff'rent, The Straw. Boni & Liveright, 1921. 285p., orig. ed. Austin 51-697 1973 $7.50

O'NEILL, EUGENE   Gold. New York, 1920. Orig. cloth, first edition. Rota 188-750 1974 £10

O'NEILL, EUGENE   The Hairy Ape. New York, 1929. 4to., orig. dec. boards, illus. by Alexander King, first separate & illus. edition, one of 775 numbered copies, signed by author, spine sun-darkened dust jacket, fine, in defective box. MacManus 224-353 1974 $100

O'NEILL, EUGENE   Lazarus Laughed. New York, 1927. First edition, backstrip faded, orig. binding. Butterfield 10-445 1974 $7.50

O'NEILL, EUGENE   Long Day's Journey Into Night. Yale Univ., 1956. 176p., orig. ed. Austin 51-698 1973 $5

O'NEILL, EUGENE   Lost Plays of Eugene O'Neill. Citadel, n.d. Austin 51-699 1973 $12.50

O'NEILL, EUGENE   Marco Millions. New York, 1927. First edition, orig. binding. Butterfield 10-446 1974 $10

O'NEILL, EUGENE   Mourning Becomes Electra. Liveright, 1931. 256p., orig. ed. Austin 51-700 1973 $6.50

O'NEILL, EUGENE   Strange Interlude. Liveright, 1928. 352p., orig. ed. Austin 51-701 1973 $6

O'NEILL, EUGENE   Strange Interlude. New York, 1928. 4to., orig. vellum, leather label, first edition, one of 750 numbered copies, signed by author, fine, in defective box. MacManus 224-354 1974 $125

O'NEILL, EUGENE   Strange Interlude. New York, 1928. Signed, numbered, boxed. Ballinger 1-190 1974 $65

O'NEILL, EUGENE   Strange Interlude. New York, 1928. First U.S. edition. Covent 56-1001 1974 £10

O'NEILL, EUGENE   Thirst and Other One-Act Plays. Boston, 1914. First American edition, cloth backed boards, lower cover little marked, very nice copy, scarce. Covent 51-1389 1973 £55

ONFROY, HENRI   Historie des Papeteries a la Cuve d'Arches et d'Archettes. 1912. 4to., red grained cloth, marbled boards, revised third edition. Covent 55-1172 1974 £15

ONGLEY, ROBERT HENRY   An Essay on the Nature and Use of the Militia. London, 1757. 8vo., half polished calf, gilt. Hammond 201-616 1974 £8.50

ONIONS, OLIVER   Admiral Eddy. London, 1907. 1st ed. Biblo & Tannen 210-647 1973 $22.50

ONIONS, OLIVER   Collected Ghost Stories. London, 1935. 1st ed. Biblo & Tannen 210-648 1973 $15

ONIONS, OLIVER   The Compleat Bachelor. 1900. Dec. cloth, gilt top, covers little dull, very good copy, first edition. Covent 51-1390 1973 £7.50

ONIONS, OLIVER   The Drakestone. 1906. Orig. cloth, first edition. Howes 185-361 1974 £5

ONIONS, OLIVER   Ghosts in Daylight. London, 1924. 1st ed. Biblo & Tannen 210-649 1973 $15

ONIONS, OLIVER   Tales from a Far Riding. 1902. Orig. cloth, first edition. Howes 185-362 1974 £6

ONOFRI, ARTURO   Vincere il Drago! Turin, 1928. 8vo., wrapper, unopened. Minters 37-197 1973 $15

ONOFRI, ARTURO   Zolla Ritorna Cosmo. Turin, 1930. 8vo., wrapper, unopened. Minters 37-198 1973 $14

ONOSANDER   Del 'Ottimo Capitano Generale. 1556. Calf, first Italian translation. Allen 213-782 1973 $20

ONTARIO Archaeological Reports, 1894-1928. Unbound. Hood's 104-902 1974 $225

ONTARIO - DEPT. OF AGRICULTURE   Report of the Provincial Instructor in Road-Making. Toronto, 1897. Illus. Hood's 102-769 1974 $7.50

ONTARIO DEPARTMENT OF EDUCATION   Catalogue of Books Recommended for Public and Separate School Libraries. Toronto, 1915. Clothbound. Hood's 104-49 1974 $10

ONTARIO - DEPT. OF PUBLIC WORKS   Seventh Annual Report of the Commissioner of Highways, Ontario, 1902. Toronto, 1903. Card covers, illus., some staining. Hood's 102-771 1974 $7.50

ONTARIO HISTORICAL SOCIETY   Annual Reports for 1898 to 1923. Bound in 5 vols., marbled boards, cloth spines and corners, excellent condition. Hood's 102-851 1974 $125

ONTARIO - LEGISLATIVE ASSEMBLY   Rules, Orders, and Forms of Proceeding of. Ottawa, 1868. Bound in with index, orig. hard cover, excellent condition. Hood's 102-626 1974 $45

ONWHYN, THOMAS   Tourists in Wales & Pencillings in the Principalities by a Pedestrian Artist. London, n.d. Oblong 8vo., half morocco, plates foxed, orig. printed wrappers, first edition. Ximenes 37-162 1974 $60

THE OPAL: A Pure Gift for the Holidays. New York, 1847. 8vo., illus., publisher's morocco, gilt, first edition. Goodspeed's 578-274 1974 $15

OPIE, A.   Tales of Real Life. 1816. Third edition, 3 vols., 12mo., contemporary tree calf, trifle rubbed. George's 610-564 1973 £8.50

OPINION of the Supreme Court of the United States in the Minnesota Rate Cases. Washington, 1913. Jenkins 61-1667 1974 $12.50

OPINION of the Supreme Court of the United States in the Minnesota Rate Cases. Washington, 1913. Jenkins 61-2052 1974 $12.50

OPINIONS Of Counsel, On the Rights Vested In the Delaware and Raritan Canal and Camden and Amboy Rail Road. Princeton, 1835. 8vo., disbound. Ximenes 35-8 1974 $40

OPPENHEIM, SAMUEL   The Early History of the Jews in New York 1654-1664. Oppenheim, 1909. Austin 62-466 1974 $37.50

OPPENHEIM, SAMUEL   The Early History of the Jews in New York. 1909. 96 pages. Austin 57-492 1974 $37.50

OPPENHEIMER, H. R.   Florula Transiordanica. Geneva, 1931. 8vo., map, sewed. Wheldon 128-1292 1973 £5

OPPERMANN AND DE JANZE   Choix de Bronzes et de Terres Cuites des Collections Oppermann et de Janze. Paris & Brussels, 1929. 4to., plates, sewed, very scarce. Quaritch 940-467 1974 £25

ORAGE, A. R.   Friedrich Nietzsche. 1906. Orig. paper boards, orig. cloth, first edition. Rota 188-751 1974 £7

ORBELIANI, SULKHAN-SABA   The Book of Wisdom and Lies. Kelmscott Press, 1894. Woodcut title page, borders and initials, printed in black and red, 8vo., orig. limp vellum with ties, fine, limited to 250 copies. Sawyer 293-185 1974 £160

ORBIGNY, ALCIDE DESSALINES D'   Galerie Ornithologique ou Collection D' Oiseaux D' Europe. Paris, (1836-39). 4to., contemporary leather backed boards, plates, rare. Wheldon 131-96 1974 £780

ORCHID Album, Comprising Coloured Figures and Descriptions of New, Rare and Beautiful Orchidaceous Plants. 1882-97. 11 vols., 4to., orig. brown cloth, gilt, coloured plates, complete set, rare. Wheldon 128-1565 1973 £1,250

ORCHIDOLOGIA Zeylanica. Colombo, 1936-41. Vols. 3-8 bound in 3 vols., crown 4to., cloth. Wheldon 128-1566 1973 £15

ORCUTT, WILLIAM DANA   In Quest of the Perfect Book. London, 1926. 4to., orig. cloth, illus., plates. Dawsons PM 10-463 1974 £8

ORCUTT, WILLIAM DANA   In Quest of the Perfect Book. 1926. Orig. cloth gilt, plates, first trade edition. Howes 185-786 1974 £6.50

ORCUTT, WILLIAM DANA   The Madonna of Sacrifice. Chicago, 1913. Presentation copy. Ballinger 1-192 1974 $15

ORCZY, BARONESS   Castles in the Air. 1921. Bookplate, English first edition. Covent 56-1974 1974 £7.50

ORCZY, BARONESS   Leatherface. 1919. 8vo., orig. cloth, inscribed, first edition. Rota 190-725 1974 £12.50

ORCZY, BARONESS   The Scarlet Pimpernel. New York, 1927. 1st Amer. Ed. Biblo & Tannen 210-782 1973 $10

THE ORDER of Exercises in the Chapel of Transylvania University. Lexington, 1825. 8vo., modern cloth, rare, first edition. Ximenes 33-448 1974 $165

ORDERS and Directions. London, 1630. Small 4to., paper wrappers, fine, first edition. Dawsons PM 251-217 1974 £25

ORDERS In Council of the Imperial Government. Ottawa, 1900. Mended spine. Hood's 104-601 1974 $45

THE OREGONIAN Souvenir, 1850-1892. Portland, 1892. Folio, rebacked, leather. Saddleback 14-657 1974 $50

O'REILLY, BERNARD   Greenland. London, 1818. Plates, maps, orig. heavy card, unfoxed. Hood's 103-77 1974 $150

O'REILLY, E.   A Chronological Account of Nearly Four Hundred Irish Writers. Dublin, 1820. 4to., cloth. Dawsons PM 11-574 1974 £7.35

O'REILLY, EDMUND J.   The Relations of the Church to Society. 1892. 8vo., orig. cloth. Howes 185-1515 1974 £5

O'REILLY, HENRY   Memorial of . . . Proposing a System of Intercommunication . . . Between the Atlantic and Pacific States. Washington, 1852. Jenkins 61-1988 1974 $15

O'REILLY, JOHN BOYLE   Moondyne Joe. n.d. 315 pages, illus.
Austin 57-493 1974 $12.50

ORELLANA-PIZARRO, ANTONIO DE   Francisco Pizarro. Trujillo, 1928. First
edition, 16mo., woodcuts, hand made paper, orig. pictorial orange and black
front wrapper, fine. Current BW9-584 1974 $22.50

ORIBASIUS, SARDINIANUS   Synopseos ad Eustathium Filium Libri Novem.
1554. Vellum gilt, morocco labels. Thomas 30-100 1973 £50

ORIGINAL Account of the Desperate Engagement and Capture of the General
Washington, Alexander Boyle, Commander, Which Was Attacked by Two Barbary
Corsairs, Up the Mediterranean. London, n.d. 12mo., half morocco, folding
hand-coloured frontispiece. Ximenes 37-173 1974 $40

ORIGINAL Poems for Infant Minds. London, n.d. (c. 1857). Vols. 1 & 2,
16mo., orig. cloth, gilt lettered spine, engraved frontispieces. Frohnsdorff
15-163 1974 $25

ORIGINAL Letters Relating to the Ecclesiastical Affairs of Scotland. Edinburgh,
1851. 2 vols., 4to., cloth, orig. edition. Quaritch 939-643 1974 £20

ORIGINAL Poems For Infant Minds. Exeter, 1808. 16mo., 2 vols. in 1, full
calf, worn, lacking front free endpaper. Frohnsdorff 15-164 1974 $50

ORIGO, IRIS   The Last Attachment. New York, 1949.
Biblo & Tannen 213-739 1973 $9.50

O'RIORDAN, CONAL   Married Life. 1924. Presentation copy,
initialled by author, very good copy, first edition. Covent 51-1391 1973 £5.25

O'RIORDAN, M.   Catholicity and Progress in Ireland. London,
1906. 8vo., cloth boards, third edition. Emerald 50-739 1974 £5.50

ORLIK, EMIL   Kleine Holzschnitte. Berlin, 1920. 4to.,
orig. fitted case, woodcuts. Marlborough 70-47 1974 £150

ORLOW, ABRAM   Manual on the Immigration Laws of the United
States. Philadelphia, 1938. Austin 62-467 1974 $10

ORLOWSKI, ALEXANDER   A Collection of His Original Lithographs. St.
Petersburg, 1816-1820. Orig. printed wrappers, fine. Marlborough 70-32 1974
£600

ORME, E.   An Essay on Transparent Prints, and on
Transparencies in General. 1807. 4to., contemporary russia gilt, engraved
vignettes, plates. Quaritch 940-195 1974 £500

ORME, EDWARD   Historic, Military, and Naval Anecdotes. London, 1819. 4to., brown half morocco gilt. Dawsons PM 251-397 1974 £400

ORME, W.   Rudiments of Landscape Drawing, and
Perspective. (1801-02). Oblong folio, plates, old calf, rebacked, rare.
Quaritch 940-196 1974 £75

ORMEROD, GEORGE   The History of the County Palatine and City of
Chester. London, 1882. 3 vols., folio, orig. cloth-backed boards, worn,
uncut, revised second edition. Traylen 79-320 1973 £115

ORMEROD, GEORGE   History of the County Palatine and City of
Chester. 1882. 3 vols., folio, illus., cloth backs, revised second edition.
Quaritch 939-332 1974 £185

ORMEROD, HANSON   The Pedigree of Hanson of Woodhouse and Hoyle
of Swift Place, co. York, and, A Supplement to the Pedigree of Hanson and
Hoyle. Oxford, 1916-18. 2 vols., roy. 8vo., boards, paper printed lables,
uncut, limited to 30 copies, hand made paper, fine. Broadhurst 24-1429 1974
£12

ORMSBEE, HELEN   Back Stage With Actors. Crowell, 1938.
343p., illus., orig. ed. Austin 51-702 1973 $10

ORNER, B. C.   Annual Report of the Acting Adjutant General of
the Territory of Oklahoma for the Year 1898. Guthrie, 1898. Yellow ptd.
wrapper, tipped in T.L.s. from Adj. Gen. F. M. Bantan. Jenkins 61-2037
1974 $17.50

ORNITHOLOGISCHE Monatsberichte. Berlin, 1893-1939. Vols. 1 - 45 in 35
vols., 8vo., uniform half calf. Wheldon 131-677 1974 £200

ORNITZ, SAMUEL   Haunch, Paunch and Jowl. Boni, Liveright,
1923. Austin 62-469 1974 $6.50

ORNITZ, SAMUEL   A Yankee Passional. Boni, Liveright, 1927.
Austin 62-470 1974 $8.50

O'ROURKE, JOHN F.   The Construction of the Poughkeepsie Bridge.
New York, 1888. First edition, 8vo., fold out photos, drawings, orig. gray paper
covers bit worn and chipped, interior and all plates and drawings excellent.
Current BW9-400 1974 $22.50

OROZCO, JOSE CLEMENTE   Jose C. Orozco: 10 Reproductions of his
Mural Paintings. Mexico, 1944. Color plates, matted and suitable for framing.
Biblo & Tannen 214-321 1974 $15

ORPHEUS, C. KERR   Orpheus C. Kerr Papers. Carleton, 1865.
Vol. I, 382p. Austin 54-792 1973 $10

ORRERY, CHARLES BOYLE, 4TH EARL OF   Memoirs of the Life and Character of.
1732. 8vo., old calf, first edition. Quaritch 939-824 1974 £35

ORRERY, JOHN BOYLE, 5TH EARL OF
Please turn to
CORK AND ORRERY, JOHN BOYLE, 5TH EARL OF

ORSINI, FELICE   The Austrian Dungeons in Italy. 1856. Pictorial boards, presentation copy inscribed, English first edition. Covent 56-1004
1974 £25

ORTEGA, LUIS B.   California Haekamore. 1948. Illus., 1st ed.
Dykes 24-111 1974 $20

ORTEGA, LUIS B.   California Stock Horse. 1949. Illus., autographed by author. Dykes 24-110 1974 $20

ORTH, SAMUEL P.   Our Foreigners. Yale Univ., 1920. 255p.,
illus. Austin 62-471 1974 $7.50

ORTON, J.   Turf Annals of York and Doncaster. York,
1844. 8vo., half green crushed levant morocco gilt. Quaritch 939-190
1974 £15

ORTROY, F. VAN   Bio-Bibliographie de Gemma Frisius, Fondateur
de l'Ecole Belge de Geographie. Bruxelles, 1920. Plates, illus., roy. 8vo.,
orig. wrappers. Forster 98-265 1974 £6

ORWELL, GEORGE   Animal Farm. 1945. Crown 8vo., orig. cloth,
scarce, first edition. Broadhurst 23-899 1974 £30

ORWELL, GEORGE   Animal Farm. 1945. Crown 8vo., fine, d.w.,
name neatly erased from blank leaf, orig. cloth, scarce. Broadhurst 24-825
1974 £35

ORWELL, GEORGE   Animal Farm. London, 1945. 8vo., orig.
green cloth, first edition. Dawsons PM 252-755 1974 £55

ORWELL, GEORGE   The Lion and the Unicorn. 1941. Crown 8vo.,
orig. cloth, first edition. Broadhurst 23-898 1974 £10

ORWELL, GEORGE   The Lion and the Unicorn. 1941. First edition,
crown 8vo., orig. cloth, fine. Broadhurst 24-824 1974 £10

ORWELL, GEORGE   The Lion and the Unicorn. London, 1941.
8vo., orig. cloth, fine, first edition. Dawsons PM 252-756 1974 £22

ORWELL, GEORGE   The Road to Wigan Pier. 1937. Cloth-boards,
English first edition. Covent 56-1976 1974 £7.50

ORWELL, GEORGE   The Road to Wigan Pier. 1937. Plates, orig.
yellow cloth wrappers, English first edition. Covent 56-1977 1974 £7.50

ORWELL, GEORGE   The Road to Wigan Pier. London, 1937. 8vo.,
orig. cloth, plates, first edition. Dawsons PM 252-758 1974 £20

ORWELL, GEORGE   The Road to Wigan Pier. 1937. Plates, orig. orange limp cloth, first edition. Howes 186-348 1974 £12.50

OSBORN, FRANCIS   Advice to a Son. Oxford, 1658. Both parts in 1 vol., 12mo., contemporary sheep, slight repairs. Thomas 32-184 1974 £50

OSBORN, H. F.   The Age of Mammals In Europe, Asia & North America. New York, 1910. Roy. 8vo., illus., orig. cloth. Smith 193-760 1973 £9.50

OSBORN, H. F.   The Age of Mammals in Europe, Asia and North America. New York, 1910. 8vo., cloth, illus. Wheldon 128-342 1973 £12

OSBORN, H. F.   The Titanotheres of Ancient Wyoming, Dakota and Nebraska. Washington, 1929. 2 vols., 4to., cloth, plates, text-figures. Wheldon 128-1028 1973 £20

OSBORN, M.   Die Kunst des Rokoko. Berlin, 1929. 4to., plates, half cloth, fine. Quaritch 940-795 1974 £12

OSBORN, MAX   Max Pechstein. Berlin, 1922. 4to., cloth spine, boards, illus. Minters 37-483 1973 $36.50

OSBORN, WILLIAM   Essays on the Practice of Midwifery. London, 1792. 8vo., contemporary tree calf, first edition. Schumann 35-365 1974 £95

OSBORNE, A. C.   The Migration of Voyageurs from Drummond Island to Penetanguishene in 1828. 1899. Hood's 104-718 1974 $15

OSBORNE, CHARLES CHURCHILL   Philip Bourke Marston. 1926. Boards, first edition. Covent 55-1080 1974 £5.25

OSBORNE, E. A.   The Facts About a Christmas Carol. London, 1937. Limited to 55 copies on Noggin hand made paper, med. 8vo., orig. buckram, Forster 98-68 1974 £5

OSBORNE, E. C.   Osborne's London and Birmingham Railway Guide. Birmingham, (1840). Small 8vo., illus., half calf. Quaritch 939-87 1974 £50

OSBORNE, FRANCIS   Political Reflections upon the Government of the Turks. London, 1656. 12mo., contemporary sheep. Dawsons PM 251-298 1974 £85

OSBORNE Collection of Early Children's Books. Otley, ca., 1840. Wrappers, fine. Dawson's 424-219 1974 $75

OSBURN, WILLIAM   The Antiquities of Egypt. 1841. 8vo., orig. cloth, rebacked, engravings. Covent 55-626 1974 £12.50

OSGOOD, CHARLES GROSVENOR   The Classical Mythology of Milton's English Poems. 1900. Ex-library, sturdy library binding, orig. edition. Austin 61-772 1974 $10

OSGOOD, FRANCES S.   Poems. Clark, Austin, 1845. 252p. Austin 54-804 1973 $12.50

OSGOOD, FRANCIS S.   Puss in Boots and the Marquis of Carabas. New York, 1844. First edition, illus., small 8vo. Current BW9-138 1974 $27.50

OSGOOD, HENRY O.   So This Is Jazz. Little, Brown, 1926. 258p., illus., orig. ed. Austin 51-703 1973 $10

OSGOOD, HERBERT L.   The American Colonies in the Eighteenth Century. New York, (1930). 2 vols., cloth, fine. Bradley 35-292 1974 $28

O'SHAUGHNESSY, ARTHUR   An Epic of Women. 1870. 8vo., orig. purple cloth, gilt, rare. Covent 55-1170 1974 £95

O'SHIEL, K. R.   Handbook of the Ulster Question. Dublin, 1923. 8vo., cloth boards, maps. Emerald 50-743 1974 £6.50

OSLER, WILLIAM   An Alabama Student and Other Biographical Essays. London, 1908. Bookplates, very good copy. Rittenhouse 46-513 1974 $37.50

OSLER, WILLIAM   Case of Aneurism of the Hepatic Artery With Multiple Abcesses of the Liver. Montreal, 1877. 8vo., disbound, plate. Rittenhouse 46-516 1974 $50

OSLER, WILLIAM   Memorial Number, Appreciations and Reminiscences. Montreal, 1926. Numbered, worn. Rittenhouse 46-515 1974 $60

OSLER, WILLIAM   The Old Humanities and the New Science. Boston, 1920. Hood's 102-341 1974 $12.50

OSLER, WILLIAM   The Principles and Practice of Medicine. Edinburgh and London, 1892. 8vo., orig. cloth, first English edition. Dawsons PM 249-389 1974 £55

OSLER, WILLIAM   Studies in Typhoid Fever. Baltimore, (n.d.) Large 8vo., red cloth. Dawsons PM 249-390 1974 £22

OSLER, WILLIAM   A Way Of Life. New York, 1937. Hood's 103-424 1974 $10

OSMONT, J. B. L.   Dictionnaire Typographique, Historique et Critique Des Livres Rares. Paris, 1768. 2 vols., contemporary mottled calf, first edition. Dawsons PM 10-465 1974 £40

OSORIO, JERONIMO   De Rebus Emmanuelis Lusitaniae Regis. Cologne, 1586. Thick 8vo., contemporary limp red vellum, fine. Schafer 8-134 1973 sFr. 800

LE OSSERVATIONI Della Lingua Volgare de Diversi Hvomini Illvstri. Venice, 1565. Small 8vo., vellum. Thomas 28-259 1972 £25

OSSIAN   The Poems of. London, 1807. 3 vols., 8vo., orig. boards, uncut, first edition. Dawsons PM 252-759 1974 £55

OSTENSO, MARTHA   The Dark Dawn. Dodd, Mead, 1926. 294p. Austin 62-472 1974 $6.50

OSTENSO, MARTHA   The Mad Carews. Dodd, Mead, 1927. 346p. Austin 62-473 1974 $6.50

OSTENSO, MARTHA   O, River Remember. Dodd, Mead, 1943. Austin 62-474 1974 $7.50

OSTENSO, MARTHA   The Stone Field. Dodd, Mead, 1937. Austin 62-475 1974 $7.50

OSTENSO, MARTHA   The Sunset Tree. Dodd, Mead, 1949. Austin 62-476 1974 $7.50

OSTENSO, MARTHA   The Waters Under the Earth. Dodd, Mead, 1930. Austin 62-478 1974 $7.50

OSTENSO, MARTHA   Wild Geese. Dodd, Mead, 1925. Austin 62-477 1974 $6.50

OSTENSO, MARTHA   The Young May Moon. Mead, Dodd, 1929. Austin 62-479 1974 $7.50

OSTERMAN, MARJORIE K.   Damned If You Do--Damned If You Don't. Chilton, 1962. Austin 62-480 1974 $7.50

O'SULLIVAN, M. D.   Old Galway. Cambridge, 1942. 8vo., dust jacket, illus., first edition. Emerald 50-745 1974 £15

O'SULLIVAN, SEUMAS PSEUD.
Please turn to
STARKEY, JAMES

O'SULLIVAN, VINCENT   A Sextet of Singers. n.d. Oblong 8vo., orig. buckram, English first edition. Covent 56-1980 1974 £5.25

THE OTHER Side of the Moon. New York, 1949. 1st ed. Biblo & Tannen 210-589 1973 $10

OTTEN, BERNARD J.   A Manual Of the History Of Dogmas. 1917-18. 2 vols., 8vo., orig. cloth. Howes 185-1516 1974 £6

OTTLEY, HENRY   A Biographical and Critical Dictionary of Recent and Living Painters and Engravers. London, 1875. 8vo., gilt-framed tree calf, morocco label. Dawsons PM 10-466 1974 £9

OTTO, ANDREAS   Anthroposcopia seu Judicium Hominis de Homine. Konigsberg, 1647. 12mo., half calf, first edition. Schuman 37-191 1974 $95

OTTO, BISHOP OF FREISING   Rerum ab Origine Mundi ad Ipsius Usque Tempora Gestarum, Libri Octo. Strassburg, 1515. Folio, woodcut border, modern half vellum, very fine, first edition. Schafer 8-135 1973 sFr. 1,200

OTTOLENGUI, RODRIGUES   The Crime of the Century. New York, 1896. First U.S. edition. Covent 56-340 1974 £25

OTWAY, THOMAS   Windsor Castle. London, 1685. 4to., modern quarter morocco, first edition. Dawsons PM 252-760 1974 £190

OTWAY, THOMAS   Works. 1813. 8vo., 3 vols., calf, gilt. Quaritch 936-509 1974 £50

OTWAY, THOMAS   The Works of. Nonesuch Press, 1926. 3 vols., crown 4to., dec. boards, vellum spines, uncut, one of 90 sets, hand made paper, fine. Broadhurst 24-1023 1974 £75

OTWAY, THOMAS   The Works Of. 1926. Crown 4to., 3 vols., dec boards, vellum, uncut. Broadhurst 23-1062 1974 £75

OTWAY, THOMAS   The Complete Works. 1926. 3 vols., 4to., uncut, orig. boards, limited edition. Dawsons PM 252-761 1974 £45

OTWAY, THOMAS   The Complete Works Of. Bloomsbury, 1926. 4to., orig. quarter buckram, 3 vols., worn. Bown Windows 64-631 1974 £35

OUDEMANS, C. A. J. A.   Aanteekeningen op Het Systematisch en Pharmacognostisch Botanische Gedeelte der Pharmacopoea Neerlandica. Rotterdam, 1854-56. 8vo., boards, plates. Wheldon 131-1814 1974 £7

OUGHTRED, WILLIAM   The Circles of Proportion and the Horizontal Instrument. London, 1633. 4to., calf antique, plates. Dawsons PM 245-583 1974 £600

OUGHTRED, WILLIAM   Key of the Mathematicks. London, 1694. Small 8vo., contemporary calf, rebacked. Schumann 35-366 1974 $375

OUGHTRED, WILLIAM   Trigonometria. London, 1657. Small 4to., contemporary calf, fine, rebacked, first edition. Dawsons PM 245-584 1974 £185

OULTON, W. C.   Picture of Margate, and Its Vicinity. 1820. 8vo., plates, orig. printed boards. Quaritch 939-413 1974 £35

OUR ISLANDS and Their People 1899. 2 vols., 784p., illus. Austin 62-730 1974 $95

OUR Old Nursery Rhymes. Philadelphia, (1911). First American edition, square 8vo., d.j., full page full clor illus., entirely mint. Current BW9-125 1974 $32.50

OUR Own Country, Descriptive, Historical, Pictorial. n.d. 6 vols., 4to., woodcut plates, orig. dec. cloth gilt. Smith 193-239 1973 £6

OURSLER, FULTON   The Spider. French, 1932. Austin 51-704 1973 $7.50

OUTCAULT, R. F.   The Buster Brown Drawing Book. N.p., 1903. Illus. Frohnsdorff 16-155 1974 $20

OUTRAM, WILLIAM   De Sacrificiis Libri Duo. 1677. Small 4to., contemporary calf, rebacked, first edition. Howes 185-1517 1974 £21

OVERACKER, LOUISE   Money in Elections. New York, 1932. First edition, orig. binding. Wilson 63-220 1974 $10

OVER the Sierras. Oakland Pier, 1904. Photogravures, boards, spine weak. Jenkins 61-377 1974 $13

OVERALL, JOHN   The Convocation Book of MDCVI. Oxford, 1844. Orig. cloth, portrait, best edition. Howes 185-1518 1974 £5.50

OVERBEKE, BONAVENTURA VAN   Reliquiae Antiquae Urbis Romae. Amsterdam, 1708. Large folio, contemporary Dutch red morocco, gilt. Marlborough 70-16 1974 £220

OVERBEKE, B. D   Les Restes de l'Ancienne Rome. The Hague, 1763. 3 vols., roy. folio, half calf, plates, worn, clean copy. Quaritch 940-339 1974 £250

OVERTON, RICHARD   Lambeth Faire. 1641. Small 4to., modern quarter morocco, first edition. Dawsons PM 252-762 1974 £180

OVIDIUS NASO, PUBLIUS   Annotationes In Omnia Ouidij Opera. 1516. Old vellum. Thomas 30-35 1973 £25

OVIDIUS NASO, PUBLIUS   Fastorum Libri. Venice, 1508. Woodcut border, small folio, half calf, marbled boards, rubbed and damaged at corners, wormholes. Thomas 32-246 1974 £75

OVIDIUS NASO, PUBLIUS   Fastorum Libri. Venice, 1508. Small folio, half calf, marbled boards, rubbed. Thomas 28-297 1972 £75

OVIDIUS NASO, PUBLIUS   The Love Books of. London, 1925. 8vo., orig. blue cloth, gilt, uncut, bookplate, limited. Dawsons PM 252-764 1974 £9

OVIDIUS NASO, PUBLIUS   Metamorphoseon Libri X. Philadelphia, 1790. Half calf, worn, first American edition. Allen 213-790 1973 $20

OVIDIUS NASO, PUBLIUS   Metamorphosis. 1697. Vol. 1 only, old calf, plates. Allen 213-791 1973 $10

OVIDIUS NASO, PUBLIUS   Metamorphoses. 1505. Folio, contemporary half blind-stamped pigskin, wooden boards. Marlborough 70-2 1974 £600

OVIDIUS NASO, PUBLIUS   Opera. 1533-34. 18th century red morocco gilt, old vellum. Thomas 30-69 1973 £21

OVIDIUS NASO, PUBLIUS   Translation of First Book of Ovid's Tristia. 1821. New buckram. Allen 213-794 1973 $12.50

OWEN, DAVID DALE   Report of a Geological Survey of Wisconsin, Iowa and Minnesota. Philadelphia, 1852. 2 vols., 4to., orig. cloth, maps. Wheldon 131-1055 1974 £15

OWEN, D. J.   History of Belfast. Belfast, 1921. 8vo., illus., cloth boards. Emerald 50-749 1974 £7.50

OWEN, DAVID DALE   Report of a Geological Survey of Wisconsin, Iowa and Minnesota. Philadelphia, 1852. 2 vols., 4to., orig. cloth, folding coloured map, plates. Wheldon 128-1029 1973 £15

OWEN, E.   Observations on the Earths, Rocks, Stones and Minerals. 1754. 8vo., plates, contemporary boards, new calf back. Quaritch 939-363 1974 £18

OWEN, ELIAS   Old Stone Crosses of the Vale of Clwyd and Neighbouring Parishes, together with, Some Account of Ancient Manners and Customs. 1886. Plates, text illus., roy. 4to., quarter roan, large paper copy, with list of subscribers, fine. Broadhurst 24-1485 1974 £12

OWEN, ELIAS   Old Stone Crosses. 1886. Roy 4to., quarter roan. Broadhurst 23-1496 1974 £12

OWEN, GEORGE   The Taylors Cussion. 1906. Folio, limited issue, orig. cloth. Broadhurst 23-1497 1974 £8

OWEN, GEORGE   The Taylors Cussion. 1906. Folio, limited issue, with list of subscribers. Broadhurst 24-1486 1974 £8

OWEN, GEORGE   The Taylors Cussion. 1906. Folio, orig. cloth, faded. Howes 186-2218 1974 £10

OWEN, GEORGE LEADER   Notes on the History and Text of Our Early English Bible, and of Its Translation into Welsh. 1901. Crown 4to., good copy, orig. cloth. Broadhurst 24-426 1974 £6

OWEN, GEORGE LEADER   Notes on the History and Text of our Early English Bible. 1901. Crown 4to., orig. cloth. Broadhurst 23-439 1974 £6

OWEN, H.   A History of Shrewsbury. 1825. 2 vols., 4to., illus., calf gilt, plates, rebacked. Quaritch 939-533 1974 £35

OWEN, HENRY   Old Pembroke Families. 1902. Crown 4to., orig. cloth, uncut, scarce. Broadhurst 23-1498 1974 £10

OWEN, J.   Exercitations on the Epistle to the Hebrews. 1668. Folio, contemporary calf, upper joint a bit cracked, rubbed, light water staining, not unreasonable copy. Thomas 32-49 1974 £45

OWEN, JOHN   The Doctrine of Justification By Faith. London, 1677. Small 4to., contemporary calf, rebacked. Smith 194-175 1974 £35

OWEN, JOHN   The Journals and Letters of. New York, 1927. 2 vols., limited to 550 copies, mint, maps, plates. Jenkins 61-2108 1974 $55

OWEN, JOHN   The Works. Edinburgh, 1850-53. 16 vols., orig. cloth, best edition. Howes 185-1520 1974 £40

OWEN, P. A.   Pioneer Sketches of Long Point Settlement, or Norfolk's Foundation Builders and Their Family Genealogies. Toronto, 1898. First edition. Hood's 102-627 1974 $85

OWEN, R.   Description of the Fossil Reptilia of South Africa in the Collection of the British Museum. 1876. 4to., orig. cloth, plates (many folding). Wheldon 128-1031 1973 £100

OWEN, R.   A History of British Fossil Mammals and Birds. 1846. 8vo., new cloth, woodcuts, folding table, scarce. Wheldon 128-1032 1973 £10

OWEN, R.   A History of British Fossil Reptiles. 1849-84. Roy 4to., 4 vols., buckram. Wheldon 129-848 1974 £80

OWEN, R.   A History of British Fossil Reptiles. 1849-84. 4 vols., roy. 4to., buckram, extremely scarce. Wheldon 131-1056 1974 £80

OWEN, R.   Odontography. 1840-45. 2 vols., roy. 8vo., contemporary half russia, plates, very scarce. Wheldon 131-515 1974 £70

OWEN, R.   On the Classification and Geographical Distribution of the Mammalia. 1859. 8vo., orig. cloth. Wheldon 131-516 1974 £15

OWEN, R.   On the Classification and Geographical Distribution of the Mammalia. 1859. 8vo., orig. cloth. Wheldon 128-343 1973 £20

OWEN, R.   Oxford. Inventory of the Historical Monuments in the City of Oxford. 1939. Demy 4to., illus., orig. cloth, fine. Broadhurst 24-1488 1974 £6

OWEN, R.   Oxford. 1939. 4to., orig. cloth. Broadhurst 23-1500 1974 £6

OWEN, R.   Palaeontology or a Systematic Summary of Extinct Animals and Their Geological Relations. 1861. 8vo., orig. cloth, second edition. Wheldon 128-1033 1973 £10

OWEN, R.   Palaeontology. 1680. 8vo., orig. cloth, scarce. Wheldon 130-959 1974 £6

OWEN, R.   Palaeontology. 1860. 8vo., orig. cloth, nice copy, very scarce first edition. Wheldon 131-1057 1974 £25

OWEN, R.   Report to the County of Lanark. Glasgow, 1821. 4to., orig. wrappers. Quaritch 939-668 1974 £85

OWEN, R.   Researches on the Fossil Remains of the Extinct Mammals of Australia. 1877. 2 vols., 4to., orig. blue cloth, large folding frontispiece, plates, very rare. Wheldon 128-1030 1973 £250

OWEN, RICHARD   Description of the Skeleton of an Extinct Gigantic Sloth. 1842. 4to., cloth bound, plates. Bow Windows 64-201 1974 £46

OWEN, ROBERT   An Address Delivered to the Inhabitants of New Lanark. London, 1817. 8vo., blue paper wrappers, third edition. Dawsons PM 247-213 1974 £25

OWEN, ROBERT   Debate on the Evidences of Christianity. Cincinnati, 1829. 2 vols. in 1, 12mo., contemporary calf, rubbed, spine gilt, second edition. Ximenes 36-156 1974 $125

OWEN, ROBERT   Examen Impartial des Nouvelles Vues de. Paris, 1821. 8vo., full morocco gilt, plates, first French edition. Dawsons PM 247-214 1974 £175

OWEN, WALTER   More Things in Heaven. London, 1947. 1st ed. Biblo & Tannen 210-650 1973 $10

OWEN, WILFRED   Poems. London, 1920. First edition, red boards, name in ink on free fly, internally fine, scarce. Ross 86-366 1974 $170

OWEN, WILFRED   Poems. London, 1920. First edition, newly rebound in full red levant morocco. Crane 7-215 1974 £60

OWEN, WILFRED   Poems. London, 1920. First edition, red boards, covers somewhat stained & slightly bubbled, spine label darkened but intact, usual browning of fly leaves, good scarce. Ross 87-449 1974 $85

OWEN, WILFRED   The Poems of. London, 1931. New edition, orig. binding, mint, d.w. Ross 86-367 1974 $17.50

OWENS, WILLIAM A.   Swing and Turn: Texas Play Party Games. Austin, 1937. Jenkins 61-831 1974 $20

OWST, G. R.   Preaching In Medieval England. 1926. Illus., plates, scarce, orig. edition. Howes 185-1521 1974 £7.50

OXFORD, HORACE WALPOLE, EARL OF
Please turn to
WALPOLE, HORACE, EARL OF OXFORD, 1717-1797

OXFORD Book of English Prose. 1925. Small 8vo., full polished crimson calf, gilt, morocco labels, paper edition. Howes 186-353 1974 £8.50

OXFORD - UNIVERSITY - QUEEN'S COLLEGE   The Obituary Book of Queen's College, Oxford, an Ancient Sarum Kalendar. 1910. Small folio, orig. stiff parchment wrappers. Howes 185-1626 1974 £7.50

OXFORD Delineated: Or a Sketch of the History and Antiquities and a General Topographical Description of That Celebrated University and City. Oxford, 1831. 4to., contemporary half red morocco, plates, foxing. Traylen 79-377 1973 £20

OXLEY, JOHN   Journals of Two Expeditions Into the Interior of New South Wales. London, 1820. 4to., half red morocco, worn, plates, library stamp. Traylen 79-554 1973 £265

OZANAM, JACQUES   Cours de Mathematique. Paris, 1697. 5 vols. in 2, thick 8vo., contemporary vellum, frontispiece, plates. Schuman 37-192 1974 $175

OZANAM, JACQUES   Recreations in Mathematics and Natural Philosophy. 1803. 8vo., 4 vols., plates, contemporary three quarter straight-grained red morocco, gilt. Zeitlin 235-167 1974 $145

OZANAM, JACQUES   Recreations Mathematical and Physical. 1708. 8vo., contemporary calf, corners worn, complete copy, engraved plates. Bow Windows 66-522 1974 £36

OZANAM, JACQUES   Recreations in Mathematics and Natural Philosophy. 1814. 4 vols., demy 8vo., contemporary full brown calf, panelled backs, copperplates, binding little rubbed. Broadhurst 24-1274 1974 £50

OZANAM, JACQUES   Tabulae Sinuum Tangentium. 1697. 8vo., contemporary panelled calf, fine. Zeitlin 235-168 1974 $75

P

P., W.   The Use of a Mathematical Instrument, called a Quadrant. London, 1655. 8vo., orig. marbled wrappers, first and only edition. Dawsons PM 245-585 1974 £250

P., W.   Notae Breves in Dissertationem Nuper Editam de Medicorum Apud Veteres Romanos. London, 1726. Rittenhouse 46-518 1974 $25

PAASCH, H.   Illustrated Marine Encyclopedia. Antwerp, 1890. Med. 8vo., full contemporary red morocco, panelled back, portrait, plates, edges gilt, fine. Broadhurst 24-1660 1974 £20

PAASCH, H.   Illustrated Marine Encyclopedia. 1890. 8vo., full contemporary morocco, gilt. Broadhurst 23-1691 1974 £20

PABST, G.   Cryptogamen-Flora Enthaltend die Abbildung und Beschreibung der Votzuglichsten Cryptogamen Deutschlands und der Angrenzenden Lander. Gera, 1875. 4to., orig. boards, plates. Wheldon 131-1455 1974 £45

PACH, WALTER   Vincent Van Gogh. New York, 1936. 1st ed., color plates. Biblo & Tannen 214-547 1974 $8

PACHUMERES, GEORGE   Paraphrasis In Omnia Dionysii Areopagitae. Paris, 1561. Small 8vo., full black levant morocco gilt, excellent condition, very rare. Thomas 28-298 1972 £30

PACIFIC Railroad Explorations. Washington, 1855-60. 13 vols., new cloth, plates, charts, color lithographs, folding maps. Jenkins 61-2113 1974 $475

PACK, GEORGE T.   Tumors of the Hands and Feet. St. Louis, 1939. Rittenhouse 46-519 1974 $15

PACK, RICHARDSON   Miscellanies in Verse and Prose. London, 1719. 8vo., contemporary calf, rebacked, second edition. Dawsons PM 252-767 1974 £60

PACK, RICHARDSON   A New Collection of Miscellanies in Prose and Verse. London, 1725. 8vo., contemporary calf, first edition. Dawsons PM 252-768 1974 £85

PACKARD, A. S.   Monograph of the Bombycine Moths of North America. Washington, 1914. 4to., orig. cloth, plates. Bow Windows 64-203 1974 £6.50

PACKARD, A. S.   A Monograph of the Geometrid Moths. Washington, 1876. Roy 4to., cloth, plates. Wheldon 129-666 1974 £7.50

PACKARD, F. R.   Life & Times of Ambroise Pare, 1510-90. 1921. Plates. Allen 213-1692 1973 $15

PACKARD, FRANCIS R.   Some Account of the Pennsylvania Hospital of Philadelphia. Philadelphia, 1938. Signed. Rittenhouse 46-531 1974 $25

PADDOCK, B. B.   A Twentieth Century History and Biographical Record of North and West Texas. Chicago, 1906. 2 vols., 4to., half leather, illus. Saddleback 14-714 1974 $125

PADDOCK, JOHN D.   A Brief History of Malvern. Malvern, 1917. 8vo., cloth. Saddleback 14-413 1974 $25

PADELFORD, FREDERICK MORGAN   Essays On the Study and Use Of Poetry By Plutarch and Basil the Great. 1902. Ex-library, sturdy library binding, orig. edition. Austin 61-773 1974 $10

PADELFORD, FREDERICK MORGAN   Selected Translations From Scaliger's Poetics. 1905. Ex-library, sturdy library binding. Austin 61-774 1974 $27.50

PADELLARO, NAZARENO   Libro di Lettura Per la Quinta Clase. ca. 1935. Austin 62-481 1974 $12.50

PADGETT, EARL CALVIN   Skin Grafting from a Personal and Experimental Viewpoint. Springfield, 1942. Rittenhouse 46-520 1974 $12.50

PADUANIUS, JOANNES
Please turn to
PADOVANI, GIOVANNI

PAEILE, CHARLES   Essai Historique et Critique sur l'Invention de l'Imprimerie. Lille, 1859. 8vo., blue half morocco, gilt back. Kraus B8-361 1974 $45

PAGANO, GIUSEPPE   Tecnica dell 'Abitazione. Milan, 1936. Square 8vo., wrapper, plates, illus. Minters 37-560 1973 $25

PAGE, CHARLES G.   Psychomancy. New York, 1853. Wrapper. Butterfield 10-441 1974 $10

PAGE, D.   Handbook of Geological Terms. 1865. Crown 8vo., cloth, second edition. Wheldon 129-849 1974 £7.50

PAGE, F. E.   The Story of Smithville. Welland, 1923. Hood's 102-628 1974 $35

PAGE, F. E.   The Story of Smithville. Welland, 1923. Hood's 104-720 1974 $35

PAGE, PHILIP   Cumberland Hotel. n.d. Illus., sheepskin, signed, numbered, handmade paper, limited edition. Covent 55-762 1974 £6.30

PAGE, THOMAS   A Narrative of the Loss of the Ship Fanny. London, 1805. 8vo., half morocco, very scarce, first edition. Ximenes 37-163 1974 $40

PAGE, THOMAS NELSON   In Ole Virginia of Marse Chan and Other Stories. New York, 1887. 12mo., cloth, very good copy, first edition. Goodspeed's 578-276 1974 $15

PAGE, THOMAS NELSON   Santa Claus's Partner. New York, 1899. First edition, 12mo., full color illus., orig. red cloth, very good. Current BW9-68 1974 $17.50

PAGE, THOMAS NELSON   Santa Claus's Partner. New York, 1899. Gilt top, illus., 1st ed. Dykes 24-68 1974 $10

PAGE, WILL A.   Behind the Curtain of Broadway Beauty Trust. Miller, 1926. 227p., illus. Austin 51-705 1973 $7.50

PAGET, ARTHUR   The Paget Papers. 1896. 2 vols., plates, orig. cloth. Howes 186-1122 1974 £6.50

PAGET, FRANCIS EDWARD   The Owlet of Owlstone Edge. 1861. Orig. cloth, gilt, inscription, second edition. Covent 56-1009 1974 £5

PAGET, JAMES   An A.L.s. by Sir James Paget. (1814-1899). Small 8vo., orig. cloth. Bow Windows 64-641 1974 £20

PAGET, JAMES   Lectures on Surgical Pathology. London, 1853. 8vo., 2 vols., orig. cloth, illus., first edition, library stamps. Gurney 66-139 1974 £20

PAGET, JAMES   Lectures on Surgical Pathology. London, 1853. 8vo., 2 vols., orig. cloth, first edition. Gurney 64-167 1974 £20

PAGET, THOMAS CATESBY   An Essay on Human Life. London, 1734. 4to., modern boards, first edition. Dawsons PM 252-769 1974 £11

PAGET, THOMAS CATESBY   Some Reflections upon the Administration of Government. London, 1740. 8vo., modern blue paper wrappers, first edition. Dawsons PM 251-468 1974 £10

PAGET, VIOLET   For Maurice. London, 1927. Biblo & Tannen 210-630 1973 $15

PAGI, ANTOINE   Critica Historico-Chronologica in Universos Annales Ecclesiasticos Caesaris Cardinalis Baronii. Antwerp, 1727. 4 vols., folio, contemporary vellum, best edition. Howes 185-1524 1974 £30

PAGNINI, GIOVANNI   Costruzione ed uso del Compasso. 1753. Small 4to., contemporary vellum. Zeitlin 235-169 1974 $97.50

PAIGE, LUCIUS R.   History of Cambridge, Massachusetts, 1630-1877. Boston, 1877. Large 8vo., inside hinges cracked, clippings relating to author pasted in. Butterfield 10-375 1974 $15

PAIN, WILLIAM   The Practical Builder. 1799. Engraved plates, folding leaves of ads inserted at end, 4to., sprinkled calf, rebacked. Thomas 32-12 1974 £70

PAINE, ALBERT BIGELOW   Captain Bill McDonald: Texas Ranger. New York, 1909. First edition, purple cloth. Jenkins 61-1560 1974 $25

PAINE, ALBERT BIGELOW   Mark Twain's Notebook. New York, 1935. Cloth, illus., first edition. Dawson's 424-297 1974 $17.50

PAINE, NATHANIEL   Early American Imprints, 1640-1700, Belonging to the Library of the American Antiquarian Society. Worcester, 1896. Wrapper. Jenkins 61-2114 1974 $27.50

PAINE, THOMAS   Common Sense; to which is Added an Appendix. London, 1792. New edition, tan paper boards, brown cloth spine, fine, 8vo. Current BW9-403A 1974 $30

PAINE, THOMAS   Common Sense. Newburyport, (1776). Plain white wrappers, new edition. Bradley 35-294 1974 $100

PAINE, THOMAS   A Letter Addressed to the Abbe Raynal on the Affairs of North-America in Which the Mistakes in the Abbe's Account of the Revolution of America are Corrected and Cleared Up. London, 1792. 8vo., moderate foxing, rebound. Current BW9-404 1974 $28.50

PAINE, THOMAS   Letter Addressed to the Abbe Raynal on the Affairs of North America. Philadelphia, 1783. 8vo., unbound. Hill 126-205 1974 £12.50

PAINE, THOMAS   Letter Addressed to the Addressers on the Late Proclamation. London, 1792. 8vo., modern boards. Dawsons PM 247-215 1974 £15

PAINE, THOMAS   Letters Addressed to the Addressers, on the Late Proclamation. London, 1792. First edition, 8vo., mild foxing. Current BW9-405 1974 $28.50

PAINE, THOMAS   Plain Truth. Philadelphia, 1776. Disbound, fine, foxing, first edition. Bradley 35-296 1974 $250

PAINE, THOMAS   Rights of Man. New York, n.d. 3 vols., three quarter dark red morocco gilt. Bradley 35-295 1974 $85

PAINE, THOMAS   Rights of Man. London, 1791. 8vo., modern boards, second edition. Dawsons PM 247-216 1974 £15

PAINE, THOMAS   The Rights of Man. 1826. Unbound. Hill 126-206 1974 £5.50

PAINE, THOMAS   Two Letters to Lord Onslow. London, 1792. 8vo., modern boards, fourth edition. Dawsons PM 247-217 1974 £15

PAINE, THOMAS   The Working Man's Political Companion. 1832. 8vo., orig. cloth. Bow Windows 64-642 1974 £10.50

THE PAINTER'S, Gilder's and Varnishers Manual. (c.1830). 12mo., orig. printed boards, very worn, new cloth spine, woodcuts, rare. Quaritch 940-197 1974 £45

THE PAINTER'S, Gilder's, and Varnisher's Manual. London & New York, 1836. 12mo., orig. violet patterned cloth, faded, foxing, nice copy, corrected new edition. Ximenes 37-53 1974 $45

PAINTING and Sculpture in the Museum of Modern Art. New York, 1948. 4to., illus. Biblo & Tannen 213-205 1973 $12.50

PALACIOS, FELIX   Palestra Farmaceutica, Chimico-Galenica. Madrid, 1792. Folio, contemporary vellum, plates. Schumann 35-366A 1974 $95

PALACIOS, FELIX   Palestra Pharmaceutica. Madrid, 1763. Folio, unbound. Zeitlin 235-294 1974 $175

THE PALAEOGRAPHICAL SOCIETY   Facsimiles of Manuscripts and Inscriptions. 1873-94. 6 vols., large folio, half purple morocco, scarce. Howes 185-790 1974 £485

PALAEOGRAPHY: Genealogy and Topography. 1930. Demy 4to., paper printed wrapper, fine. Broadhurst 24-1389 1974 £6

PALAEPHATUS   De Historiis Incredibilibus. Pesaro, 1511. 4to., dec. boards, first separate & first Latin edition. Harper 213-113 1973 $785

PALAEPHATUS   De non Credendis Fabulosis Narrationibus. Bologna, 1515. 4to., half vellum, excellent copy, rare edition. Harper 213-114 1973 $525

PALAEOPHILUS, ANGLICANUS   The Conduct of Queen Elizabeth. London, 1729. 8vo., modern boards. Dawsons PM 247-218 1974 £20

PALATINO, G.   Libro Di M. Giovanbattista Palatino Cittadino Romano. Rome, 1548. Small 4to., excellent copy, modern vellum. Quaritch 940-468 1974 £600

PALAZZESCHI, ALDO   Due Imperi . . . Mancati. Florence, 1920. 8vo., wrapper. Minters 37-406 1973 $20

PALAZZESCHI, ALDO   La Piramide. Florence, 1926. 8vo., covers soiled, wrapper. Minters 37-407 1973 $25

PALENCIA, ISABEL   Smoldering Freedom. Longmans, 1945. Austin 62-482 1974 $10

PALERMO, FRANCESCO   Classazione dei Libri a Stampa dell' I. e R. Palatina. Florence, 1854. Roy. 8vo., three quarter polished calf. Kraus B8-189 1974 $16

PALEY, F. A.   Illustrations of Baptismal Fonts. 1844. Illus. Covent 55-474 1974 £12

PALEY, F. A.   Manual of Gothic Mouldings. 1877. Cloth, plates, fourth edition. Eaton Music-655 1973 £5

PALEY, WILLIAM   An Essay. London, 1792. 8vo., modern boards, fine, first separate edition. Dawsons PM 251-302 1974 £12

PALEY, WILLIAM   The Principles of Moral and Political Philosophy. London, 1785. 4to., contemporary tree calf, gilt, first edition. Dawsons PM 250-60 1974 £100

PALEY, WILLIAM   The Principles of Moral and Political Philosophy. 1788. 2 vols., contemporary tree calf, gilt, fine. Howes 185-1942 1974 £14.50

PALGRAVE, F.   The Rise and Progress of the English Commonwealth. 1832. 2 vols., 4to., orig. cloth, uncut. Quaritch 939-191 1974 £12

PALGRAVE, F. T.   A Golden Treasury of Songs and Lyrics. New York, 1911. 4to., colour plates, pictorial cloth, covers little marked. Covent 51-1404 1973 £8.50

PALGRAVE, F. T.   The Treasury of Sacred Song. Oxford, 1889. Fine, quarter vellum. Covent 55-50 1974 £7.50

PALGRAVE, ROBERT HARRY INGLIS   Notes on Banking. London, 1873. 8vo., maroon cloth, faded. Dawsons PM 247-219 1974 £10

PALGRAVE, ROBERT HARRY INGLIS   Palgrave's Dictionary of Political Economy. 1926. 3 vols., thick 8vo., orig. buckram. Smith 194-683 1974 £10

PALGRAVE, W. GIFFORD   Narrative of a Year's Journey Through Central and Eastern Arabia, (1862-63). 1865. 2 vols., 8vo., contemporary half calf, rebacked, library stamp, large coloured folding map, first edition.   Bow Windows 66-523 1974 £24

PALISSOT, CHARLES   La Dunciade. London, 1771. 2 vols., small 8vo., contemporary boards, gilt. L. Goldschmidt 42-94 1974 $20

PALISSOT, CHARLES   Oeuvres. Liege, 1777. vols. 1 - 6, 8vo., contemporary full marbled calf, gilt, plates. L. Goldschmidt 42-93 1974 $120

PALLADIO, ANDREA   The Architecture of A. Palladio. 1721. 2 vols., folio, plates, contemporary panelled calf, rubbed. Quaritch 940-538 1974 £250

PALLADIO, ANDREA   The Four Books of Architecture. London, n.d. Folio, modern brown morocco, plates, fine. Dawsons PM 251-93 1974 £150

PALLADIO, ANDREA   I Quattro Libri Dell'Architettura. Venice, 1570. Folio, illus., 18th century half calf, woodcuts, fine, first edition. Dawsons PM 250-61 1974 £1200

PALLADIO, ANDREA   IQuattro Libri Dell' Architettura Di Andrea Palladio. Venice, 1581. Small folio, woodcuts, old vellum, good copy, second edition. Quaritch 940-537 1974 £380

PALLADIO, ANDREA   Le Fabbriche e Disegni di Andrea Palladio Raccolti ed Illustrati da Ottavio Bertotti Scamozzi. 1796-97. 5 vols., small 4to., contemporary boards, gilt, calf spines, morocco labels. Quaritch 940-539 1974 £150

PALLADIUS, RUTILIUS TAURUS AEMILIANUS   De Re Rustica. Paris, 1543. Small 8vo., contemporary English calf. Thomas 28-299 1972 £30

PALLAS, P. S.   Lyst der Plant-Dieren. Utrecht, 1768. 8vo., half calf, uncut, plates. Wheldon 129-791 1974 £15

PALLAS, Z.   Zoographia Rosso-Asiatica. St. Petersburg, (1811-14), 1831. Vols. 1 & 2, 4to., half calf, weak joints, hand coloured plates, very rare. Wheldon 128-535 1973 £200

PALLAVICINO, PIETRO SFORZIA   Vera Decumenici Concilii Tridenti . . . . Historia. 1775. 3 vols. in 1, thick folio, half calf. Howes 185-1085 1974 £10.50

PALLETTA, GIOVANNI BATTISTA   Adversaria Chirurgica Prima. N.P., n.d. 4to., contemporary boards, plates, first edition. Schuman 37-194 1974 $125

PALLISER, MRS. BURY
Please turn to
PALLISER, FANNY MARRYAT

PALLISER, FANNY (MARRYAT)   Historic Devices, Badges and War-Cries. 1870. Allen 213-1690 1973 $12.50

PALLISER, FANNY (MARRYAT)   History of Lace. 1865. 8vo., illus., orig. dec. cloth, recased, first edition. Quaritch 940-767 1974 £30

PALLISER, FANNY (MARRYAT)   Histoire de la Dentelle Traduit par la Comptesse Gedeon de Clermont-Tonnerre. Paris, 1892. Imp. 8vo., wood engravings, dec. cloth, gilt, plates. Quaritch 940-768 1974 £20

PALLISER, FANNY (MARRYAT)   A History of Lace. London, 1902. Buckram, plates. Dawson's 424-235 1974 $75

PALLISER, JOHN   Solitary Rambles and Adventures of a Hunter in the Prairies. London, 1853. First edition, illus., three quarter calf. Jenkins 61-2116 1974 $85

PALLISER, JOHN   Solitary Rambles and Adventures of a Hunter in the Prairies. London, 1853. Illus., first edition, orig. cloth, spine repaired. Jenkins 61-2115 1974 $85

PALLUCCHINI, RODOLFO   Le Acqueforti Del Canaletto. Venice, 1945. Lg. oblong fol., illus., orig. dec. bds., ltd. to 1000 copies. Jacobs 24-51 1974 $50

PALMEDO, ROLAND   Skiing the International Sport. New York, The Derrydale Press, (1937). Illus., limited to 950 copies, scarce, 4to., bright clean copy, near mint, publisher's review copy. Current BW9-172 1974 $275

PALMER, A. S.   Folk-Etymology. 1882. New buckram. Allen 216-1405 1974 $12

PALMER, ALBERT W.   Orientals in American Life. Friendship, 1934. Austin 62-483 1974 $8.50

PALMER, C. H.   The Salmon Rivers of Newfoundland. Boston, 1928. Illus., maps. Hood's 104-226 1974 $30

PALMER, CLARA S.   Annals of Chicopee Street. Chicopee, 1898. 12mo., cloth. Saddleback 14-492 1974 $10

PALMER, EDWIN O.   History of Hollywood. Hollywood, 1938. 8vo., cloth, revised edition. Saddleback 14-222 1974 $45

PALMER, F.   Proposals Humbly Offered to the Honourable House of Commons. (1714). Folio, disbound. Quaritch 939-286 1974 £15

PALMER, F. P.   The Death and Burial of Cock Robin. New York, ca. 1850. 12mo., hand-colored wrappers. Frohnsdorff 16-225 1974 $15

PALMER, FRIEND   Early Days in Detroit. Detroit, (1906). 8vo., orig. bindings. Butterfield 8-113 1974 $35

PALMER, HERBERT EDWARD   The Judgement of Francois Villon. 1927. Orig. vellum-backed boards, gilt, fine, limited, first edition. Howes 185-369 1974 £5.25

PALMER, J.   The History of the Siege of Manchester. Manchester, 1822. 8vo., disbound, scarce. Broadhurst 23-1502 1974 £15

PALMER, JOHN   Awful Shipwreck. Boston, 1836. 8vo., contemporary plain wrappers, woodcut frontispiece, first edition. Ximenes 37-164 1974 $200

PALMER, JOHN   The Censor and the Theatres. 1913. 307p., orig. ed. Austin 51-706 1973 $10

PALMER, PETER   History of Lake Champlain. New York, ca., 1890. Orig. cloth, plates. Putman 126-89 1974 $16

PALMER, THOMAS   An Essay of the Meanes Hovv to Make Our Trauailes. London, 1606. 4to., disbound, half morocco slipcase, scarce, first edition. Rich Summer-86 1974 $375

PALMER, W. J.   Report of Surveys Across the Continent in 1867-68. Philadelphia, 1869. 8vo., orig. wrappers, map. Wheldon 128-224 1973 £20

PALMER, WILLIAM   Egyptian Chronicles. London, 1861. 2 vols., spines faded. Biblo & Tannen 210-1012 1973 $52.50

PALMER, WILLIAM   Origines Liturgicae. Oxford, 1832. 2 vols., orig. cloth backed boards, uncut. Howes 185-1526 1974 £12.50

PALMER, WINTHROP   Dance News Annual 1953. 211p., illus. Austin 51-707 1973 $10

PALMERIN OF ENGLAND   The First Part of the No Lesse Rare. London, 1639. 2 parts in 1 vol., 4to., 18th century calf-backed boards, damp-stains. Dawsons PM 252-770 1974 £265

PALMERINI, TOMMASO   Considerazioni Sopra il Discorso del Sig. Galilei Galilei Intorno Alle Cose, Che Stanno in su l'Acqua. Pisa, 1612. Small 4to., vellum, first edition, with added unrecorded leaf. Schumann 500-12 1974 sFr 5,500

PAMBOUR, FRANCOIS MARIE, COMTE GUYONNEAU DE
Please turn to
GUYONNEAU DE PAMBOUR, FRANCOIS MARIE COMTE

PANAMA-CALIFORNIA INTERNATIONAL EXPOSITION   Official Publication, San Diego, 1916. Brooklyn, 1916. Wrapper, small folio, hand colored photos. Jenkins 61-373 1974 $10

PANASSIE, HUGUES   Guide to Jazz. Houghton, 1956. 312p., illus. Austin 51-708 1973 $12.50

PANCIROLLUS, G.   The History of Many Memorable Things Lost. 1715. 2 vols., 8vo., contemporary panelled calf, rare. Wheldon 128-53 1973 £30

PANCOAST, CHARLES EDWARD   A Quaker Forty-Niner. Philadelphia, 1930. Cloth, scarce, first edition. Bradley 35-47 1974 $15

PANCOAST, JOSEPH   A Treatise on Operative Surgery. Philadelphia, 1844. Large 4to., cloth, plates, first edition. Schumann 35-367 1974 $245

PANERAJ, VINCENZIO   Principi di Musica Teorico-Pratici. Florence, (c. 1780). Small folio, modern wrappers, first edition. Quaritch 940-819 1974 £150

PANKHURST, SYLVIA   Writ on Cold Slate. n.d. Wrappers, very good copy, scarce, first edition. Covent 51-1777 1973 £6.30

PANORAMA of the Hudson, Showing Both Sides of the River from New York to Poughkeepsie. (New York, 1906). Blue printed wrappers, new edition. Bradley 35-276 1974 $12.50

PANORMITANUS, NICHOLAUS TEDESCUS
Please turn to
TEDESCHI, NICCOLO, ABP. OF PALERMO

PANTALEON, HEINRICUS   Prosopographiae Heroum Atque Illustrium Virorum Totius Germaniae pars Tertia Equeprimaria. Basle, 1566. Part 3 only of 3, folio, contemporary French panelled calf, gilt and blind tooled. Thomas 32-248 1974 £35

PANUNZIO, CONSTANTINE   Immigration Crossroads. 1927. 307 pages. Austin 57-511 1974 $10

PANUNZIO, CONSTANTINE   Immigration Crossroads. Macmillan, 1927. Austin 62-485 1974 $10

PANUNZIO, CONSTANTINE   The Soul of an Immigrant. Macmillan, 1921. Orig. ed. Austin 62-486 1974 $7.50

PAOLE, JOHN   Twould Puzzle a Conjurer. Taylor, 1824. Austin 51-750 1973 $6.50

PAOLI, DOMENICO   Ricerche sul Moto Molecolare de Solidi. 1825. 8vo., orig. blue wrappers, fine, unopened, uncut. Zeitlin 235-170 1974 $165

PAPACINO D'ANTONI, ALESSANDRO VITTORIO   A Treatise on GunPowder. London, 1789. 8vo., contemporary calf, plates, gilt. Dawsons PM 245-587 1974 £150

PAPAZOFF, GEORGES   Pascin . . . Pascin . . . C'est Moi! Paris, 1932. 8vo., wrapper, unopened. Minters 37-118 1973 $30

PAPINI, GIOVANNI   Testimonianze. Milan, 1918. Small 8vo., wrapper. Minters 37-422 1973 $22.50

PAPINI, GIOVANNI   Testimonianze. Milan, 1919. 16mo., wrappers, second edition. Minters 37-423 1973 $20

PAPINI, GIOVANNI   24 Cervelli. Saggi non Critici. Milan, 1917. 8vo., half vellum, boards, revised second edition. Minters 37-424 1973 $20

PAPINI, GIOVANNI   24 Cervelli. Saggi non Critici. Milan, 1918. 8vo., wrappers, fourth edition. Minters 37-425 1973 $18

PAPINI, GIOVANNI   Un Uomo Finito. Florence, 1925. 8vo., orig. dec. baords, twelfth edition. Minters 37-426 1973 $14.50

PAPINI, GIOVANNI   Cento Pagine di Poesia. Florence, 1920. Wrapper, third edition. Minters 37-408 1973 $30

PAPINI, GIOVANNI   Crepuscolo dei Filosofi. Florence, 1914. 16mo., wrappers, second edition. Minters 37-409 1973 $22

PAPINI, GIOVANNI   Crepuscolo dei Filosofi. 1921. Fourth edition. Minters 37-409A 1973 $18.50

PAPINI, GIOVANNI   Dante Vivo. London, 1934. 4to., cloth, soiled, plates. Minters 37-410 1973 $16

PAPINI, GIOVANNI   Giorni di Festa. Florence, 1920. 8vo., wrapper, second edition. Minters 37-411 1973 $25

PAPINI, GIOVANNI   Gog. Florence, 1931. 8vo., wrappers. Minters 37-412 1973 $20

PAPINI, GIOVANNI   Gog. Florence, 1931. 8vo., wrappers. Minters 37-413 1973 $18

PAPINI, GIOVANNI   Il Tragico Quotidiano e il Pilota Cieco. Florence, 1920. 8vo., wrapper, fourth edition. Minters 37-414 1973 $16

PAPINI, GIOVANNI   Guido Mazzoni. Florence, 1913. 8vo., wrappers, worn. Minters 37-415 1973 $16

PAPINI, GIOVANNI   L'Altra Meta. Saggio di Filosofia Mefistofelica. Milan, 1916. 8vo., wrapper, second edition. Minters 37-416 1973 $20

PAPINI, GIOVANNI   La Corona d'Argento. Milan, 1944. 8vo., wrapper, unopened, fourth edition. Minters 37-417 1973 $15

PAPINI, GIOVANNI   Le Memorie d'Iddio. Florence, 1911. 8vo., wrappers, first edition. Minters 37-418 1973 $18

PAPINI, GIOVANNI   Opera Prima. Florence, 1921. 8vo., wrapper, third edition. Minters 37-419 1973 $15

PAPINI, GIOVANNI   Sant' Agostino. Florence, 1930. 16mo., cloth. Minters 37-420 1973 $16.50

PAPINI, GIOVANNI   Stroncatura. Florence, 1918. 8vo., wrappers, third edition. Minters 37-421 1973 $18

PAPWORTH, J. B.   Select Views of London. 1816. Imp. 8vo., contemporary half calf, plates, fine. Quaritch 939-464 1974 £1650

PAQUET, L. A.   Droit Public de l'Eglise. Mended paper covers. Hood's 103-258 1974 $12.50

PAQUET, L. A.   Etudes et Appreciations; Fragments Apologetiques. Quebec, 1917. Wrappers. Hood's 102-729 1974 $7.50

PAQUIN, JACQUES   Journal Historiques des Evenemens Arrives a Saint Eustache, Pendant la Rebellion du Comte du Lac des Deux Montagnes. Montreal, 1838. Very rare, orig. paper covers, three quarter leather, marbled boards. Hood's 102-730 1974 $400

PARA DU PHANJAS, FRANCOIS   Theorie des Nouvelles Decouvertes. Paris, 1786. 8vo., calf, gilt, plates, first edition. Gurney 64-168 1974 £35

THE PARABLE of the Bear-Baiting. London, 1691. Small 4to., disbound, first edition. Ximenes 35-116 1974 $80

THE PARABLE of the Magpies. London, 1691. Small 4to., uncut, unopened, rare, first edition. Ximenes 35-117 1974 $150

THE PARABLE of the Magpies. London, 1691. Small 4to., disbound. Ximenes 35-118 1974 $125

PARACELSUS   Spittal Buch. Muelhausen, 1562. Small 4to., full morocco, first edition, fine. Kraus 137-70 1974 $975

PARADIN, CLAUDE   Quadrins Historiques de la Bible. Lyon, 1553. Small 4to., full brown morocco, woodcuts, rare, first edition, first impression. Harper 213-116 1973 $1950

PARADIN, GUILLAUME   Histoire de Nostre Temps. Lyons, 1552.
16mo., full polished calf, gilt. L. Goldschmidt 42-95 1974 $160

PARADIN, GUILLAUME   Historiarum Memorabilium Ex Genesi Descriptio.
Ex Exodo, Sequentibusq; Libris Descriptio. Lyons, 1558. Small 8vo., modern calf,
old style, woodcuts by Bernard Salomon. Thomas 32-249 1974 £250

THE PARADISE or Garden of the Holy Fathers. 1907. 2 vols., very good copy.
Covent 51-2508 1973 £12

PARBONI, P.   Nuova Raccolta Delle Principali Vedute
Antiche. 1826. Oblong atlas folio, plates, old half roan, worn. Bow
Windows 62-702 1974 £75

PARCHAPPE, MAX   Traite Theorique et Pratique de la Folie. Paris,
1841. 8vo., contemporary half calf. Dawsons PM 249-394 1974 £8

PARDE, L.   Arboretum National des Barres. Paris, 1906.
Imperial 8vo., 2 vols., orig. wrappers and portfolio. Wheldon 129-1621 1974
£10

PARDOE, JULIA   Louis the Fourteenth. London, 1847. 8vo.,
3 vols., contemporary calf, fine, first edition. Dawsons PM 251-303 1974 £28

PARE, AMBROISE   Les Oevvres d'Ambroise Pare. 1664. Folio,
modern quarter calf. Dawsons PM 249-395 1974 £495

PARECBOLAE Sive Excerpta e Corpore Statutorum Universitatis Oxoniensis.
Oxford, 1674. Small 8vo., old sheep, second edition. Quaritch 939-520
1974 £15

PARECBOLAE Sive Excerpta e Corpore Statutorum Universitatis Oxoniensis.
Oxford, 1710. Small 8vo., cloth, calf back. Quaritch 939-521 1974 £20

PARENT, O.   Dipteres Dolichopodides Exotiques. Saint-Lo,
1930. Roy. 8vo., plates. Wheldon 131-841 1974 £5

PARENT-DUCHATELET, ALEXANDRE JEAN BAPTISTE   De la Prostitution. Paris, 1857. 8vo., 2 vols., contemporary quarter morocco. Dawsons PM 249-396
1974 £30

PARE, AMBROISE   Deux Livres de Chirurgie. Paris, 1573.
Small 8vo., woodcut border, red morocco, gilt, excellent copy, rare first
edition. Gilhofer 61-6 1974 sFr. 12,000

PARIS GALERIE BERNHEIM-JEUNE   Catalogue Exposition Vlaminck. 1921.
16mo., wrapper, plates. Minters 37-143 1973 $12

PARIS GALERIE DIETRICH   Invitation to the Exposition Raoul Ubac.
1941. 16mo., wrappers, plates. Minters 37-374 1973 $12.50

PARIS HOTEL DROUOT   Atelier Eugen Carriere Catalogue de Quatre-
Vingt-Dix-Neuf Oeuvres. 1906. Folio, wrapper, plates. Minters 37-241
1973 $30

PARIS, J.   Philosophy in Sport Made Science in Earnest.
London, 1827. 3 vols., orig. boards, vol. 3 rebacked, scarce. Gregory 44-57
1974 $175

PARIS, JOHN AYTON   A Guide to the Mount's Bay and the Land's
End. 1824. Orig. cloth backed boards, label, uncut, worn, second enlarged
edition. Howes 186-1993 1974 £12.50

PARIS, JOHN AYRTON   Pharmacologia. London, 1822. 2 vols.,
8vo., quarter sheep, enlarged fifth edition. Rittenhouse 46-523 1974 £55

PARIS, JOHN AYRTON   Philosophy in Sport Made Science in Earnest.
1827. Tall 12mo., 3 vols., orig. boards, uncut, fine. Zeitlin 235-171 1974
$175

PARIS DE MEYZIEU, JEAN BAPTISTE   Bibliotheca Parisiana. London, 1791.
Small 8vo., paper wrappers, cloth case. Kraus B8-191 1974 $50

PARIS Chez Bernheim Jeune, Cat. Oeuvres Nouvelles de Van Dongen. 1911.
12mo., wrappers, plates. Minters 37-139 1973 $18

PARIS, MATTHEW   Historia Major. 1640-39. Folio, contemporary
calf, rebacked, gilt crest of George Thornhill with his armorial bookplate within,
full page portrait, light stain at foot of lower outer margin, else excellent, 2 parts
in 1 vol. Thomas 32-125 1974 £45

PARIS CHIT-CHAT: Or a View of the Society, Manners, Customs, Literature, and
Amusements of the Parisians. 1816. 3 vols., 12mo., orig. boards, uncut, tiny
worm holes through vol. 2, second edition. Bow Windows 66-525 1974 £12.50

PARIS ou le Livre des Cent-et-un. Paris, 1831-34. 15 vols., 8vo.,
contemporary half leather, first edition. L. Goldschmidt 42-326 1974 $150

PARISE, MASANIELLO   Trattato Teorico. Rome, 1889. 8vo., quarter
morocco, spine rubbed, signed. Bow Windows 64-333 1974 £10.50

PARISET, ERNEST   Histoire de la Soie. Paris, 1862. 8vo., modern
boards, first edition. Dawsons PM 245-590 1974 £13

PARISH, W. D.   Domesday Book in Relation to the County of
Sussex. Sussex, 1886. Folio, map, orig. cloth. Bow Windows 62-892
1974 £15

PARISH, W. D.   Domesday Book in Relation to the County of
Sussex. Lewes, 1886. Folio, very fine, orig. cloth, map, plates. Broadhurst
24-1536 1974 £15

THE PARISH Register of Putney, In the County of Surrey. 1913-16. 3 vols.,
red crushed levant morocco, superb copy. Smith 193-219 1973 £20

PARK, J. RICHARDSON   Human Sexuality. Philadelphia, 1906.
Rittenhouse 46-526 1974 $10

PARK, MUNGO   Travels in the Interior Districts of Africa.
London, 1799 & 1815. 4to., 2 vols., contemporary calf, morocco label, first
edition. Dawsons PM 250-62 1974 £160

PARK, ROBERT E.   Old World Traits Transplanted. Harper, 1921.
Orig. ed. Austin 62-487 1974 $10

PARK, ROSWELL   An Epitome of the History of Medicine.
Philadelphia, 1897. Rittenhouse 46-524 1974 $15

PARK, ROSWELL   An Epitome of the History of Medicine.
Philadelphia, 1903. Illus., second edition. Rittenhouse 46-525 1974 $15

PARKER, AGNES MILLER   Down the River. 1937. 4to., half morocco,
boards, English first edition. Covent 56-706 1974 £17.50

PARKER, B.   Out In the Wood. C., 1900. Oblong 4to.,
orig. coloured pictorial boards, illus., plates. Hammond 201-134 1974 £10

PARKER, DOROTHY   After Such Pleasures. Viking, 1935. 232p.
Austin 54-806 1973 $7.50

PARKER, DOROTHY   After Such Pleasures. New York, 1933. One
of 250 copies, numbered & signed by author, buckram, fine, slipcase. Covent
51-2524 1973 £21

PARKER, DOROTHY   Enough Rope. Liveright, 1926. 110p.
Austin 54-807 1973 $6

PARKER, DOROTHY   Here Lies. Literary Guild, 1939. 362p.
Austin 54-808 1973 $6.50

PARKER, DOROTHY   The Ladies of the Corridor. Viking, 1954.
Austin 51-709 1973 $7.50

PARKER, DOROTHY   The Ladies of the Corridor. French, 1953.
Austin 51-710 1973 $6.50

PARKER, DOROTHY   Laments for the Living. New York, 1930. First
U. S. edition, fine, slightly torn & frayed d.w. Covent 51-1399 1973 £7.50

PARKER, DOROTHY   Laments for the Living. New York, 1930.
Dust wrapper, first U.S. edition. Covent 56-1011 1974 £7.50

PARKER, DOROTHY   Not So Deep As a Well. New York, 1936.
Boxed, autographed, numbered, limited special edition. Jenkins 48-355
1973 $25

PARKER, DOROTHY   Viking Portable Library. Viking, 1944.
544p., orig. unrev. ed. Austin 54-809 1973 $6.50

PARKER, E.   Proposals Humbly Offered to the Consideration
of the Honourable House of Commons. (1714). Folio, disbound. Quaritch
939-287 1974 £16

PARKER, EMMA   The Guerilla Chief. 1815. 12mo., 3 vols.,
contemporary half calf, fine, rare. Hill 126-198 1974 £75

PARKER, GILBERT   An Adventurer of the North. New York, 1896.
Title page clipped. Hood's 102-535 1974 £12.50

PARKER, GILBERT   An Adventurer of the North. New York, 1896.
Hood's 104-569 1974 £12.50

PARKER, GILBERT   The Money Master, Being the Curious History of
Jean Jacques Barbille. Toronto, 1915. Illus. Hood's 102-536 1974 $10

PARKER, GILBERT   Old Quebec. New York, 1903. 1st ed.,
illus. Biblo & Tannen 213-19 1973 $15

PARKER, HENRY   The Case of Shipmony. 1640. Small 4to.,
disbound, first edition. Dawsons PM 247-220 1974 £40

PARKER, HENRY   Dives and Pauper. London, 1493. 4to.,
18th century red morocco, gilt, morocco labels, rare first edition. Dawsons PM
252-771 1974 £14,750

PARKER, HENRY   The Vintners Answer. London, 1642. Small
4to., brown paper wrappers, first edition. Dawsons PM 251-304 1974 £115

PARKER, JOHN L.   Henry Wilson's Regiment. Boston, 1887.
Shaken, covers dampstained. Butterfield 10-173 1974 $10

PARKER, LOUIS N.   Ma Vourneen. Dodd, Mead, 1916. 208p.
Austin 51-711 1973 $7.50

PARKER, MARY ANN   A Voyage Round the World, In the Gorgon Man
of War. London, 1795. 8vo., quarter calf, rubbed, scarce. Traylen 79-435
1973 £125

PARKER, S. C.   The Book of St. Andrew's. Toronto, 1930.
Illus. Hood's 103-259 1974 $10

PARKER, T. N.   Description of a New Quart and Bushel Measure.
Shrewsbury, 1839. 3 works in 1 vol., 8vo., contemporary cloth. Dawsons PM
247-221 1974 £15

PARKER, THOMAS N.   An Essay, or Practical Inquiry Concerning the
Hanging & Fastening of Gates and Wickets. 1801. 8vo., marbled paper
wrappers, scarce. Quaritch 940-540 1974 £18

PARKES, E. A.   A Manual of Practical Hygiene. 1883.
Thick demy 8vo., plates, contemporary calf gilt, sixth edition. Smith 194-772
1974 £6

PARKHURST, FREDERICK S.   History of Kenmore, Erie County, New York.
(Kenmore, 1926). 8vo., cloth. Saddleback 14-587 1974 $15

PARKHURST, FREDERICK S.   History of the Town of Tonawanda, Erie County,
New York, 1805-1930. (Kenmore, 1930). 8vo., cloth. Saddleback 14-588
1974 $15

PARKINSON, JAMES   Old Cottages, Farm Houses and Other Half
Timber Buildings in Shropshire, Herefordshire, and Cheshire. 1904. Plates.
Marsden 39-343 1974 £5

PARKINSON, JAMES   Organic Remains of a Former World. London,
1802-1808-1811. 4to., 3 vols., orig. boards, plates, first edition. Schumann
35-368 1974 $250

PARKINSON, JAMES   Organic Remains of a Former World. 1820,
1811. 4to., 3 vols., orig. cloth, plates. Wheldon 129-850 1974 £55

PARKINSON, JAMES   Organic Remains of a Former World. 1820, 1811.
3 vols., 4to., orig. cloth, plates. Wheldon 131-1059 1974 £55

PARKINSON, JAMES   Organic Remains of a Former World. 1833.
3 vols. in 2, 4to., new buckram, hand-coloured plates, rare, second edition.
Wheldon 128-1034 1973 £50

PARKINSON, JAMES   Organic Remains of a Former World. 1833.
4to., new buckram, plates, rare, second edition. Wheldon 130-961 1974 £50

PARKINSON, JOHN   Paradisi in Sole Paradisus Terrestris. 1629.
Small folio, contemporary calf, rebacked, woodcuts, first edition. Wheldon
131-1558 1974 £400

PARKINSON, JOHN   Paradisi in Sole Paradisus Terrestris. 1629.
Small folio, contemporary calf, neatly rebacked, woodcuts, first edition. Wheldon
128-1517 1973 £275

PARKINSON, JOHN   Paradisi in Sole Paradisus Terrestris. 1656.
Folio, nineteenth century tree calf gilt, woodcuts, second edition. Wheldon
130-57 1974 £350

PARKINSON, JOHN   Paradisi in Sole Paradisus Terrestris. Methuen,
1904. Folio, buckram backed boards, fine, facsimile reprint of first edition.
Gregory 44-226 1974 $125

PARKINSON, JOHN   Paradisi in Sole Paradisus Terrestris. 1904.
Folio, orig. boards, holland backed, uncut. Bow Windows 64-204 1974 £48

PARKINSON, JOHN   Paradisi in Sole Paradisus Terrestris. London,
1904. Folio, orig. boards, uncut. Rich Summer-87 1974 £65

PARKINSON, JOHN   Theatrum Botanicum. 1640. Folio, contemporary calf. Wheldon 129-1690 1974 £250

PARKINSON, JOHN   Theatrum Botanicum. 1640. Folio, newly
bound in half calf, woodcuts, good condition. Wheldon 128-1689 1973 £225

PARKINSON, JOHN   Theatrum Botanicum. 1640. Folio, half calf,
woodcuts. Wheldon 130-1619 1974 £225

PARKINSON, JOHN   Theatrum Botanicum. London, 1640. Thick
folio, old-style calf, rebacked, first edition. Schumann 35-369 1974 $685

PARKINSON, JOHN   Theatrum Botanicum, The Theater of Plantes.
1640. Folio, contemporary calf, woodcuts, rebacked. Wheldon 131-1815
1974 £575

PARKINSON, R.   The Old-Church Clock. 1880. Fifth edition,
illus., large paper copy, crown 4to., good copy, with list of subscribers.
Broadhurst 24-1492 1974 £5

PARKINSON'S Physician Based on Culpeper. London, 1821. 8vo., half calf,
color plates. Gregory 44-78 1974 $57.50

PARKMAN, FRANCIS   The Conspiracy of Pontiac and the Indian War
After the Conquest of Canada. Boston, 1877. 2 vols. Jenkins 61-2208 1974
$11.50

PARKMAN, FRANCIS   A Half-Century of Conflict. Boston, 1892.
1st ed., 2 vols., ltd. to 75 copies. Jacobs 24-26 1974 $50

PARKMAN, FRANCIS   Historic Handbook of the Northern Tour.
Boston, 1885. Dec. cover, cloth, illus. Hood's 103-784 1974 $12.50

PARKMAN, FRANCIS   The Old Regime in Canada. Boston, 1874. 1st ed., ltd. to 75 copies. Jacobs 24-25 1974 $45

PARKMAN, FRANCIS   Works. Boston, 1910. 17 vols., blue cloth, excellent. Hood's 103-841 1974 $125

PARKYNS, G. J.   Monastic and Baronial Remains. 1816. 2 vols., 8vo., contemporary red straight-grained morocco. Quaritch 939-192 1974 £75

PARKYNS, THOMAS   The Inn-Play. 1727. Small 4to., full calf, English first edition. Covent 56-2050 1974 £52.50

PARLATORE, P.   Les Collections Botaniques du Musee Royal de Physique et d'Histoire Naturelle de Florence au Printemps de MDCCCLXXIV. Florence, 1874. 8vo., cloth, plates. Wheldon 128-1147 1973 £7.50

PARLIAMENT   The History and Proceedings of the House of Lords. London, 1742. 8 vols., 8vo., contemporary quarter sheep, fine, first edition. Dawsons PM 247-138 1974 £65

PARLIAMENT   The History and Proceedings of the House of Commons. London, 1742. 14 vols., 8vo., uncut, contemporary quarter sheep, first edition. Dawsons PM 247-137 1974 £75

PARLIAMENTARY Select Committee on National Expenditure. 1941-45. 5 vols., cloth. Howes 186-1519 1974 £6.50

PARMENTIER, A.   Instructions sur les Moyens de Suppleer le Sucre dans les Principaux Usages qu'on Fait pour la Medecine et l'Economie Domestique. Paris, 1808. 8vo., old marbled wrappers, first edition. Gurney 66-140 1974 £28

PARMENTIER, A.   Precis d'Experiences et Observations sur les Differentes Especes de Lait, Considerees dans Leurs Rapports avec la Chimie, la Medecine et l'Economie Rurale. Strasburg, 1799. 8vo., old quarter calf, back worn, first edition. Gurney 66-141 1974 £28

PARMENTIER, A.   Traite sur la Culture et les Usages des Pommes de Terre, de la Patate, et du Topinambour. Paris, 1789. 8vo., quarter calf, uncut, first edition. Gurney 66-142 1974 £28

PARNASSE Satyrique. Brussels, 1881. 3 vols., 12mo., contemporary three quarter red morocco, gilt, uncut. L. Goldschmidt 42-327 1974 $70

PARNELL, HENRY   A History of the Penal Laws Against the Irish Catholics. London, 1825. 8vo., quarter cloth, rebound, fourth edition. Emerald 50-752 1974 £6

PARNELL, HENRY   A Treatise on Roads. London, 1833. 8vo., cloth boards, scarce, first edition. Emerald 50-753 1974 £15

PARNELL, HENRY   A Treatise on Roads. London, 1833. 8vo., contemporary cloth, rebacked, plates, first edition. Hammond 201-893 1974 £36

PARNELL, R.   The Grasses of Britain. Edinburgh, (1842-) 45. Roy. 8vo., cloth, plates, scarce. Wheldon 128-1208 1973 £10

PARNELL, R.   The Grasses of Britain. Edinburgh, (1842-) 1845. Roy. 8vo., orig. cloth, plates, rare. Wheldon 131-1237 1974 £17

PARNELL, R.   The Grasses of Scotland. Edinburgh, 1842. 8vo., orig. cloth, plates, scarce. Wheldon 131-1236 1974 £7.50

PARNELL, R.   The Grasses of Scotland. Edinburgh, 1842. Roy. 8vo., orig. cloth, worn, plates, scarce. Wheldon 128-1207 1973 £5

PARNELL, THOMAS   Poems. Dublin, 1927. First edition, woodcut, demy 8vo., boards, linen spine, uncut, fine. Broadhurst 24-831 1974 £20

PARNELL, THOMAS   The Poetical Works of. Edinburgh, 1778. 2 vols., 12mo., full green calf, gilt. Emerald 50-754 1974 £5

PARNY, EVARISTE   La Guerre des Dieux Anciens et Modernes. (1888). 8vo., half calf, gilt spine, top edges gilt, most others uncut, orig. wrappers bound in, frontispiece, rare. Bow Windows 66-527 1974 £5.50

LE PAROISSIEN des Tout Petits. Limoges, c. 1840. Orig. brown morocco, frontis., 2 1/16 X 1 1/2. Gregory 44-438 1974 $35

PAROLETTI, MODESTO   Libro Secondo Dei Secoli Della R. C. Di Savoia Ovvero Delle Istorie Piemontesi. Turin, c. 1800. 8vo., contemporary Italian red morocco gilt. Thomas 32-81 1974 £30

PARR, ELNATHAN   The Workes Of. 1632. Small folio, full modern brown crushed levant morocco. Thomas 28-101 1972 £35

PARR, SAMUEL   Bibliotheca Parriana. London, 1827. Large 8vo., contemporary cloth, rebacked. Dawsons PM 10-470 1974 £45

PARRISH, MORRIS LONGSTRETH   Charles Kingsley & Thomas Hughes. 1936. 4to., plates, limited, orig. edition. Allen 216-196 1974 $75

PARRISH, MORRIS LONGSTRETH   Charles Kingsley and Thomas Hughes. London, 1936. 4to., orig. cloth, uncut. Dawsons PM 10-471 1974 £80

PARRISH, MORRIS LONGSTRETH   Victorian Lady Novelists. 1933. 4to., plates. Thomas 32-69 1974 £30

PARRISH, MORRIS LONGSTRETH   Victorian Lady Novelists. 1933. 4to., plates, limited edition. Allen 216-195 1974 $15

PARROT, JOSEPH   Clinique des Nouveau-Nes - L'Anthrepsie. Paris, 1877. 8vo., half morocco, first edition. Schumann 35-370 1974 $85

PARRY, ALBERT   Garrets and Pretenders. 1932. 383p., orig. ed. Austin 51-712 1973 $10

PARRY, C. HUBERT H.   The Evolution of the Art of Music. New York, 1930. Orig. ed. Biblo & Tannen 214-896 1974 $8.50

PARRY, JOHN S.   Observations on Relapsing Fever. 1870. 8vo., contemporary half calf. Dawsons PM 249-397 1974 £15

PARRY, TOM   P.P. or The Man and the Tiger. French, n.d. Austin 51-713 1973 $6.50

PARSEVAL-GRANDMAISON, F. A.   Les Amours Epiques. Paris, 1806. 8vo., contemporary boards, uncut, second enlarged edition. L. Goldschmidt 42-328 1974 $15

PARSON, W.   Staffordshire General and Commercial Directory. (1818). 12mo., contemporary sheep, worn, some stains, lacking the map. Bow Windows 66-529 1974 £25

PARSONS, FRANCIS   The Hartford Wits. 1936. 29p. Austin 54-810 1973 $10

PARSONS, FRANK ALVAH   Interior Decoration. New York, 1918. 8vo., cloth, plates. Minters 37-562 1973 $16.50

PARSONS, KATHERINE B.   History of Fifty Years: Ladies Literary Club, Salt Lake City, Utah. Salt Lake City, 1927. 12mo., presentation, cloth. Saddleback 14-730 1974 $12.50

PARSONS, MARY ELIZABETH   The Wild Flowers of California. San Francisco. 1897. 8vo., cloth, plates, scarce. Wheldon 130-1194 1974 £5

PARSONS, MARY ELIZABETH   The Wild Flowers of California. San Francisco, 1912. Illus., orig. binding. Butterfield 10-134 1974 $15

PARSONS, T. W.   The First Canticle Inferno of the Divine Comedy of Dante Alighierie. New York, 1867. Small 4to., cloth, worn, presentation copy with signed inscription. Goodspeed's 578-279 1974 $15

PARTINGTON, CHARLES F.   The British Cyclopaedia of Natural History. 1835-1837. 8vo., 3 vols., orig. cloth, first edition. Bow Windows 64-205 1974 $18

PARTINGTON, RUTH   Knitting Work. Brown, Taggard, Chase, 1859. 408p., illus. Austin 54-916 1973 $15

PARTINGTON, WILFRED GEORGE   Thomas J. Wise In the Original Cloth. 1946. Orig. buckram gilt, dust wrapper, plates. Smith 193-423 1973 £11

PARTON, JAMES   Caricature . . . and Other Comic Art . . . In All Times and Many Lands. New York, 1877. Orig. binding, illus., corner wear, marked edge, backstrip darkened. Wilson 63-300 1974 $25

PARTON, JAMES   History of the Sewing Machine. Lancaster, n.d. 8vo., orig. wrappers, fine. Ximenes 35-368 1974 $35

PARTON, JAMES   Life of Voltaire. 1881. 2 vols., thick 8vo., orig. cloth gilt, frontispiece. Howes 185-540 1974 £5

PARTON, S. P.   Fern Leaves from Fanny's Portfolio. 1853. Orig. cloth, illus. by Birket Foster. Eaton Music-585 1973 £5

PARTRIDGE, C. H.   The Progress of Man. Lindsay, 1943. Hood's 104-492 1974 $10

PARTRIDGE, C. H.   The Progrees of Man. Lindsay, 1943. Hood's 102-342 1974 $10

PARTRIDGE, DAVID   Crimes of Passion. New York, 1947. 1st ed. Biblo & Tannen 210-496 1973 $8.50

PARTRIDGE, HELEN   A Lady Goes to Hollywood. Macmillan, 1941. Austin 51-714 1973 $7.50

PARTRIDGE, SETH   The Description and Use of an Instrument called the Double Scale of Proportion. London, 1661. 8vo., contemporary calf, rare, first edition. Dawsons PM 245-591 1974 £500

PARTY Spirit and Popery. 1847. 126 pages. Austin 57-27 1974 $17.50

PASADENA, the Land of Flowers. New York, 1894. Photogravures, wrapper. Jenkins 61-380 1974 $19.50

PASADENA BOARD OF TRADE   Illustrated Souvenir Book Showing a Few Pasadena Homes, Schools, Churches, Etc. Pasadena, 1903. Oblong 12mo., wrapper. Saddleback 14-225 1974 $12.50

PASCAL, BLAISE   Les Provinciales. Paris, 1886-95. 2 vols., 8vo., three quarter hardgrain morocco, gilt. L. Goldschmidt 42-96 1974 $25

PASCAL, BLAISE   Les Provinciales ou Lettres Ecrites par Louis de Montalte a une Provincial de ses Amis. Leyden, 1761. 4 vols., 12mo., contemporary wrappers, inscription, uncut, very well preserved copy. Schumann 499-77 1974 sFr 180

PASCAL, BLAISE   Pensees sur la Religion et sur Quelques Autres Sujets. Paris, 1670. Small 8vo., 19th century crimson levant morocco, gilt, excellent copy, first counterfeit edition. L. Goldschmidt 42-97 1974 $275

PASCAL, BLAISE   The Provincial Letters of. 1847. 8vo., orig. cloth, portrait, covers faded. Bow Windows 66-530 1974 £6.50

PASCAL, BLAISE   Traitez de l'Equilibre des Liqueurs, et de la Pesanteur de la Masse de l'Air. Paris, 1698. 12mo., contemporary calf, plates, third edition. Schuman 37-195 1974 $245

PASCAL, JEAN B. E.   Origines et Raison de la Liturgie Catholique en Forme de Dictionnaire. Paris, 1863. Imp. 8vo., half cloth. Howes 185-1538 1974 £7.50

PASCOLI, ALLESSANDRO   Il Corpo-Umano. Venice, 1750. 4to., old limp boards, worn, plates, first edition. Schuman 37-196 1974 $110

PASCOLI, L.   Vite de' Pittori, Scultori, ed Architetti Perugini. Rome, 1732. 4to., contemporary vellum, worn, scarce, first edition. Quaritch 940-198 1974 £65

PASLEY, FRED D.   Al Capone. Garden City, 1930. 355p., illus. Austin 62-488 1974 $7.50

PASQUALI, FILIPPO   Tractatus Amplissimus de Viribus Patriae Potestatis. 1619. Vellum. Allen 213-1696 1973 $15

PASQUALI, NICOLO   Thorough Bass Made Easy. n.d. Oblong folio, uncut, sewed in orig. wrappers. Quaritch 940-820 1974 £40

PASQUIER, ESTIENNE   Les Recherches de la France. Paris, 1596. Folio, full contemporary limp vellum, gilt, fine, first edition. L. Goldschmidt 42-98 1974 $400

PASS, CRISPIN VAN DER   Hortus Floridus. London, 1928-29. Oblong 4to., 2 vols., vellum, plates, one of 30 copies on Arnold hand made paper, fine. Gregory 44-227 1974 $165

PASS, CRISPIN VAN DER   Hortus Floridus, the Second Book. 1929. Oblong 4to., orig. half green morocco, plates, frontispieces, numbered, limited edition. Wheldon 128-1518 1973 £12

PASSANO, G.   I Novellieri Italiani in Prosa. Milano, 1864. Half calf. Kraus B8-193 1974 $20

THE PASSIONATE Pilgrim. 1896. Small 8vo., orig. boards, printed labels, uncut, limited edition. Howes 185-538 1974 £40

PASTERNAK, JOE   Easy the Hard Way. Putnam, 1956. 301p., illus. Austin 51-715 1973 $6.50

PASTEUR, LOUIS   Etudes sur le Vin. Paris, 1866. 8vo., half morocco, wrappers, uncut, first edition. Gurney 64-169 1974 £65

PASTEUR, LOUIS   Etudes sur le Vin. Paris, 1873. 8vo., old quarter leather, worn, plates. Gurney 64-170 1974 £25

PASTEUR, LOUIS   Examen Critique d'un Ecrit Posthume. Paris, 1879. 8vo., full green shagreen, gilt, plates. Gurney 64-171 1974 £105

PASTONCHI: A Specimen of a New Letter for Use On the Monotype. 1928. 4to., orig. cloth, fine, ordinary edition. Howes 185-792 1974 £5

PASTONCHI: A Specimen of a New Letter for Use On the Monotype. 1928. 4to., orig. vellum backed boards, fine, special edition. Howes 185-791 1974 £16.50

PASTONCHI: A Specimen of a New Letter for Use on the "Monotype". (1928). 4to., orig. cloth, illus., some spotting, printed by hand on Fabriano paper, limited edition. Bow Windows 66-531 1974 £20

PASTONCHI: A Specimen of a New Letter for Use on the "Monotype". London, 1928. Small folio, orig. cloth, illus. Dawsons PM 10-66 1974 £23

PASTOR, LUDWIG   The History of the Popes, From the Close Of the Middle Ages. 1906-30. 19 vols., orig. cloth. Howes 185-1539 1974 £65

THE PASTOR, a Poem. New York, 1821. 12mo., orig. grey-green printed wrappers, very good copy, first edition. Ximenes 37-179 1974 $40

PATCHEN, KENNETH   The Memoirs of a Shy Pornographer. New York, 1945. 8vo., orig. cloth, first edition. Rota 190-737 1974 £6

PATCHEN, KENNETH   The Teeth of the Lion. 1942. Wrappers, damp-stained, first American edition. Covent 55-1179 1974 $7.50

PATER, WALTER   Marius the Epicurean. 1903. 2 vols., half morocco, fine. Covent 55-1180 1974 £5.25

PATER, WALTER   Studies in the History of Renaissance. 1873. Bookplate, very good copy. Covent 51-2525 1973 £20

PATER, WALTER   Works. 1900-1901. 9 vols., buckram, ex-library. Allen 216-Q 1974 $45

PATER, WALTER   Works. 1900-01. 9 vols., orig. silk cloth, uncut, foxing, limited, de Luxe edition. Howes 186-359 1974 £42

PATERSON, D.   British Itinerary Being a New and Accurate Delineation. 1785. 2 vols. in 1, 8vo., contemporary calf, worn, first edition. Quaritch 939-219 1974 £60

PATERSON, JAMES   Pietas Londinensis. London, 1714. Small 8vo., old calf, rebacked. Traylen 79-365 1973 £6

PATERSON, R. A.   A History of the 10th Canadian Infantry Brigade. Hilversum, 1945. Card cover, maps. Hood's 102-114 1974 $12.50

PATERSON, WILLIAM   An Inquiry into the Reasonableness and Consequences of an Union With Scotland. London, 1706. 8vo., contemporary calf gilt, first edition. Dawsons PM 247-222 1974 £75

DE PATIENTIA Aurei Libri Tres. 1497. 4to., browned, old boards, first edition. Bow Windows 62-61 1974 £550

PATIN, CHARLES   Traite des Tourbes Combustibles. Paris, 1663. 4to., contemporary calf, gilt, first edition. Dawsons PM 245-593 1974 £75

PATMORE, COVENTRY·   The Angel in the House. 1854. 8vo., orig. cloth, first edition. Bow Windows 64-647 1974 £22.50

PATMORE, COVENTRY   The Angel in the House. Boston, 1856. 8vo., orig. cloth, first American edition. Rota 189-687 1974 £5

PATMORE, COVENTRY   Faithful for Ever. London, 1860. Orig. cloth, nice copy, first edition. Covent 51-1409 1973 £10

PATMORE, COVENTRY   Florilegium Amantis. (1879). 8vo., orig. cloth, first edition. Rota 189-688 1974 £5

PATMORE, COVENTRY   Poems. 1890. 2 vols., small 8vo., full crushed green levant morocco, fourth collective edition. Howes 185-372 1974 £27.50

PATON, JAMES   The Fine Art Collection of Glasgow. Glasgow, 1906. Crown 4to., plates, foxing, orig. cloth. Bow Windows 62-706 1974 £5.50

PATON, JAMES   Scottish History and Life. Glasgow, 1902. Roy. 4to., orig. silken cloth, illus. Howes 186-2183 1974 £12.50

PATOUILLARD, N.   Essai Taxonomique sur les Familles. 1900. 8vo., cloth. Wheldon 129-1310 1974 £10

PATOUILLARD, N.   Les Hymenomycetes d'Europe. Paris, 1887. 8vo., cloth, plates. Wheldon 129-1309 1974 £5

PATRI, ANGELO   Child Training. Appleton, 1922. 434p. Austin 62-489 1974 $7.50

PATRICK, JOHN   A New Improvement of the Quick-Silver Barometer. London, (n.d.). 4to., half green calf, gilt, ex-library. Zeitlin 235-172 1974 $365

PATRICK, JOHN   The Teahouse of the August Moon. Putnam, 1941. Austin 51-716 1973 $6.50

PATRICK, SIMON   The Hearts Ease. London, 1671. Small 8vo., 19th century ripple cloth, rebound, third edition. Smith 194-178 1974 £18

PATRICK, SYMON   A Commentary Upon the Fifth Books of Moses, Called Deuteronomy. 1700. Thick small 4to., half vellum, first edition. Howes 185-1540 1974 £12.50

PATRICK, SYMON   A Commentary Upon the Two Books of Chronicles. 1706. Thick small 4to., old calf, rebacked, first edition. Howes 185-1541 1974 £15

PATRICK, SYMON   A Treatise of the Necessity and Frequency of Receiving the Holy Communion. 1685. 12mo., contemporary calf, rebacked, first edition. Howes 185-1542 1974 £25

PATRITIUS, FRANCESCO   Oratio ad Innocentium VIII. (Rome, 1484). Small 4to., marbled wrappers, fine, rare. Harper 213-117 1973 $255

PATRIZI, FRANCESCO   Il Sacro Regno. 1553. Vellum gilt, morocco labels, dampstaining. Thomas 30-99 1973 £30

PATTERSON, A. H.   Wild Life on a Norfolk Estuary. 1907. 8vo., cloth, illus., scarce. Wheldon 130-301 1974 £7.50

PATTISON, EMILIA F. S.   Sir Frederick Leighton. (1821). Drawings, illus., orig. cloth, disbound. Marsden 37-288 1974 £12

PATTON, PHILIP   The Natural Defence of an Insular Empire. Southampton, 1810. 4to., half calf, first edition. Hammond 201-705 1974 £8.50

PAUL, ELLIOT   All the Brave. Modern Age, 1939. 29p., illus., paper. Austin 54-831 1973 $12.50

PAUL, ELLIOT   The Black Gardenia. Random, 1958. 305p. Austin 54-811 1973 $6.50

PAUL, ELLIOT   Concert Pitch. Random House, 1938. 413p. Austin 54-812 1973 $7.50

PAUL, ELLIOT   Desperate Scenery. Random, 1954. 302p. Austin 54-813 1973 $6.50

PAUL, ELLIOT   Fracas in the Foothills. Random, 1940. 431p. Austin 54-814 1973 $7.50

PAUL, ELLIOT   A Ghost Town On the Yellowstone. Random, 1948. 341p. Austin 54-815 1973 $6.50

PAUL, ELLIOT   Hugger-Mugger In the Louvre. Random, 1940. 326p. Austin 54-816 1973 $7.50

PAUL, ELLIOT   I'll Hate Myself in the Morning and Summer in December. Random, 1945. 315p. Austin 54-817 1973 $7.50

PAUL, ELLIOT   Intoxication Made Easy. Modern Age, 1941. 146p. Austin 54-830 1973 $7.50

PAUL, ELLIOT   The Last Time I Saw Paris. Random, 1942. 421p. Austin 54-818 1973 $6

PAUL, ELLIOT   The Life and Death of a Spanish Town. Random, 1937. 427p. Austin 54-819 1973 $5

PAUL, ELLIOT   The Life and Death of a Spanish Town. New York, 1937. Sgd. by author. Jacobs 24-118 1974 $15

PAUL, ELLIOT   Linden on the Saugus Branch. Random, 1947. 401p. Austin 54-820 1973 $6.50

PAUL, ELLIOT   Mayhem in B-Flat. Random, 1940. 304p. Austin 54-821 1973 $7.50

PAUL, ELLIOT   Murder On the Left Bank. Random, 1951. 314p. Austin 54-822 1973 $6.50

PAUL, ELLIOT   My Old Kentucky Home. Random, 1949. 438p. Austin 54-823 1973 $6.50

PAUL, ELLIOT   The Mysterious Mickey Finn or Murder At the Cafe du Dome. Modern Age., 1939. 243p., paper. Austin 54-824 1973 $8.50

PAUL, E.   The Romance of Tristram of Lyones & La Beale Isoude. (c.1926). Crown 4to., plates, inscription, uncut, orig. dec. cloth. Bow Windows 62-707 1974 £7.50

PAUL, ELLIOT   Springtime in Paris. Random, 1950. 364p. Austin 54-825 1973 $6.50

PAUL, ELLIOT   The Stars and Stripes Forever. Random, 1939. 393p. Austin 54-826 1973 $6.50

PAUL, ELLIOT   That Crazy American Music. Bobb, Merril, 1957. 317p. Austin 54-827 1973 $10

PAUL, ELLIOT   Understanding the French. Random, 1955. 186p. Austin 54-828 1973 $8.50

PAUL, ELLIOT   Waylaid in Boston. Random, 1953. 274p. Austin 54-829 1973 $6.50

PAUL, ELLIOT   With a Hays Nonny Nonny. Random, 1942. 188p., illus. Austin 51-717 1973 $10

PAUL, FORD   Peak's Island. Portland, 1892. 12mo., half morocco, orig. wrappers bound in, first edition. Goodspeed's 578-280 1974 $15

PAUL, WILLIAM   The Rose Annual. 1861-81. 6 parts, roy. 8vo., orig. wrappers, coloured plates. Wheldon 128-1519 1973 £40

PAUL, WILLIAM   The Rose Garden. 1881. Roy. 8vo., orig. red cloth, colour-printed plates, scarce, eighth edition. Wheldon 128-1520 1973 £40

PAUL, WILLIAM   The Rose Garden. 1848. Roy 8vo., plates, orig. cloth, rare, first edition. Wheldon 130-58 1974 £115

PAUL, WILLIAM   The Rose Garden. 1888-98. 8vo., orig. cloth, plates, ninth edition. Bow Windows 64-206 1974 £8

PAUL, WILLIAM   The Rose Garden. (1889). 4to., orig. cloth, plates, very scarce. Wheldon 131-1559 1974 £40

PAUL-LOUIS   Ancient Rome at Work. New York, 1927. Illus. Biblo & Tannen 214-648 1974 $7.50

PAUL et Virginie. Paris, c. 1825. Orig. rose moire boards, black leather label, color plates, 2 3/4 X 1 7/8. Gregory 44-439 1974 $165

PAULDING, JAMES KIRKE   Westward Ho! New York, 1832. 2 vols., orig. cloth, first edition, foxed, vol. 2 is somewhat stained. MacManus 224-355 1974 $45

PAULHAN, JEAN   Les Hain-Tenys. Paris, 1938. 12mo., orig. wrapper, uncut. L. Goldschmidt 42-329 1974 $15

PAULI, GUSTAV   Paula Modersohn-Becker. Leipzig, 1919. Large 4to., boards, plates, worn. Minters 37-477 1973 $28

PAULIAN, AIME HENRI   Dictionnaire de Physique. 1787. 8vo., 5 vols., plates, contemporary mottled calf, labels, gilt. Zeitlin 235-174 1974 $145

PAULIAN, AIME HENRI   Dictionnaire de Physique Portatif. 1758. 8vo., contemporary calf, gilt, ex-library. Zeitlin 235-173 1974 $95

PAULIAN, AIME-HENRI   L'Electricite Soumise a un Nouvel Examen. 1768. 8vo., contemporary calf, gilt, plates, first edition. Dawsons PM 245-595 1974 £65

PAULUS   Magicon. New York, 1868. Austin 62-490 1974 $17.50

PAULUS   Magicon. Reed, 1868. 152 pages. Austin 57-514 1974 $15

PAULUS DE SANCTA MARIA   Dyalogus Qui Vocatur Scrutinium Scripturarum. (Strassburg, c. 1474). Folio, full brown levant morocco, gilt, fine. Harper 213-118 1973 $1750

PAULUS DE SANCTA MARIA   Scrutinium Scripturarum. Rome, 1471. Small folio, 17th century calf, raised bands, gilt, second edition. Thomas 28-300 1972 £850

PAUQUET FRERES   Modes et Costumes Historiques. (c. 1870). Roy. 4to., plates, boards, morocco back, rubbed. Quaritch 940-731 1974 £150

PAUSANIAS   Graeciae Descriptio. 1896-1907. Vols. 1-3 part 1 only, sewn. Allen 213-809 1973 $50

PAUSANIUS   Veteris Graeciae Descriptio. Florence, 1551. Folio, dull 19th century quarter roan, first edition. Thomas 28-301 1972 £25

PAVLOV, IVAN PETROVITCH   Die Arbeit der Verdauungsdrusen. 1898. 8vo., illus., half morocco, fine, first German edition. Dawsons PM 250-63 1974 £500

PAVLOV, IVAN PETROVITCH   Lectures on Conditioned Reflexes. (1928). 8vo., cloth. Wheldon 130-363 1974 £18

PAVLOV, IVAN PETROVITCH   Lectures on Conditoned Reflexes. New York, (1941). 2 vols., 8vo., orig. cloth, illus., portrait. Bow Windows 66-533 1974 £25

PAX, F.   Monograph der Gattung Primula. (1889). 8vo., wrappers. Wheldon 131-1560 1974 £5

PAYER, J.   Botanique Cryptogamique ou Histoire des Familles Naturelles des Plantes. Paris, 1850. Roy 8vo., orig. wrappers. Wheldon 130-1330 1974 £7.50

PAYN, JAMES   A Stumble on the Threshold. 1892. 2 vols., orig. cloth, fine. Covent 55-1181 1974 £25

PAYNE, EDWARD F.   The Charity of Charles Dickens, His Interest in the Home for Fallen Women and a History of the Strange Case of Caroline Maynard Thompson. Boston, 1929. First U. S. edition, one of 100 copies, fine, card slip case, fine. Covent 51-551 1973 $21

PAYNE, G. E.   Upper Canada College. N.P., n.d. Sketches. Hood's 104-175 1974 $35

PAYNE, JOHN   Flowers of France. 1906-07. 3 vols., orig. vellum gilt, limited numbered edition. Howes 186-552 1974 £12

PAYNE, JOHN HOWARD   Ali Pacha. 1823. 16mo., sewn as issued. Allen 216-2147 1974 $10

PAYNE, JOHN HOWARD   Ali Pacha. New York, 1823. 12mo., sewn as issued, first edition. Ximenes 37-165 1974 $75

PAYNE, JOSEPH FRANK   The Fitz-Patrick Lectures for 1903. Oxford, 1904. Rittenhouse 46-530 1974 $20

PAYNE, WILLIAM   An Introduction to the Game of Draughts. London, 1756. 8vo., 19th century half calf, first edition. Dawsons PM 252-553 1974 £90

PAYNE-GALLWEY, R.   High Pheasants in Theory and Practice. 1913. Small 4to., orig. boards. Wheldon 129-537 1973 £5

PAYNE, WYNDHAM   Town and Country. n.d. Plates, buckram back, dec. boards, limited edition. Marsden 30-346 1974 £6

PAYNE-GALLWEY, RALPH   A Summary of the History, Construction and Effects in Warfare. 1907. 4to., illus., scarce. Howes 186-1675 1974 £18

PAYNE-GALLWEY, RALPH   A Summary of the History, Construction & Effects In Warfare of the Projetile-Throwing Engines of the Ancients. 1907. 4to., illus., orig. cloth, signed, first edition. Smith 194-773 1974 £22

PAYNE'S Universum. London, n.d. 4to., contemporary morocco gilt, plates, foxed. Smith 193-90 1973 £7.50

PAYNTER, JOHN H.   Horse and Buggy Days with Uncle Sam.   New York, 1943. Orig. binding, d.j. Butterfield 10-112 1974 $10

PEABODY, JOSEPHINE P.   Marlowe. Houghton, 1901. 156p. Austin 51-718 1973 $6.50

PEABODY, JOSEPHINE P.   The Piper. Houghton, 1911. Austin 51-719 1973 $6.50

PEABODY, JOSEPHINE P.   Portrait of Mrs. W. Houghton, 1922. 150p. Austin 51-720 1973 $7.50

PEABODY, JOSEPHINE P.   The Wolf of Gubbio. Houghton, 1913. Austin 51-721 1973 $6.50

PEACH, B. N.   Geology of the Neighbourhood of Edinburgh. 1910. 8vo., cloth, plates, scarce, second edition. Wheldon 130-962 1974 £12

PEACHAM, H.   Coach and Sedan. 1925. 4to., boards, limited. Quaritch 939-220 1974 £5

PEACHEY, EMMA   The Royal Guide to Wax Flower Modelling. 1851. 8vo., orig. blue cloth, plates, scarce. Quaritch 940-469 1974 £35

PEACHEY, EMMA   The Royal Guide to Wax Flower Modelling. 1851. 8vo., orig. brown cloth, plates, very scarce. Wheldon 131-1561 1974 £25

PEACOCK, R. B.   Glossary of the Dialect of the Undred of Lonsdale, North and South of the Sands. 1869. Demy 8vo., orig. cloth, fine. Broadhurst 24-1496 1974 £10

PEACOCK, RONALD   The Poet In the Theatre. Harcourt, Brace, 1946. Austin 51-722 1973 $7.50

PEACOCK, THOMAS LOVE   The Genius of the Thames. London, 1810. 8vo., contemporary morocco gilt, first edition. Dawsons PM 252-772 1974 £75

PEACOCK, THOMAS LOVE   Gryll Grange. London, 1861. 8vo., modern quarter calf, gilt, first edition. Dawsons PM 252-773 1974 £50

PEACOCK, THOMAS LOVE   The Misfortunes of Elphin. 1928. 8vo., dec. cloth, uncut, limited edition. Broadhurst 23-1038 1974 £35

PEACOCK, THOMAS LOVE   The Misfortunes of Elphin. 1928. 8vo., buck-ram-backed cloth. Hammond 201-762 1974 £55

PEACOCK, THOMAS LOVE   Rhododaphne. 1818. 8vo., contemporary morocco, inscription, first edition. Bow Windows 64-649 1974 £60

PEAKE, G. A.   Notes on Dental Anatomy. 1915. 8vo., limp boards, scarce, third edition. Wheldon 131-450 1974 £5

PEAKE, MERVYN   The Hunting of the Snark. 1942. 8vo., orig. illus. paper boards, illus. Bow Windows 64-650 1974 £7.50

PEAKE, MERVYN   Rhymes Without Reason. 1944. Plates, soiled covers. Covent 55-1182 1974 £12.50

PEAKE, ORA BROOKS   The Colorado Range Cattle Industry. Glendale, 1937. First edition, 8vo., illus., uncut, pristine copy. Current BW9-357 1974 $38.50

PEAKE, ORA BROOKS   The Colorado Range Cattle Industry. Glendale, 1937. Uncut, illus., top edge gilt. Jenkins 61-529 1974 $35

PEAKE, R. B.   The Characteristic Costume of France. 1819. 4to., plates, modern half morocco. Quaritch 940-732 1974 £70

PEAKE, RICHARD B.   Amateurs and Actors. French, 1818. 25p. Austin 51-723 1973 $7.50

PEARCE, ZACHARY   A Sermon On Self-Murder. London, 1773. 8vo., modern half calf, third edition. Schuman 37-197 1974 $65

PEARSE   The Conformists Plea for the Non-Conformists. London, 1681. Small 4to., unbound. Traylen 79-184 1973 £6

PEARSE, PADRAIC H.   The Collected Works of. n.d. 4 vols., 8vo., cloth boards. Emerald 50-761 1974 £12

PEARSON, ALEXANDER   Annals of Kirby Lonsdale and Lunesdale in Bygone Days. 1930. Demy 4to., uncut, plates, orig. cloth, fine. Broadhurst 24-1497 1974 £20

PEARSON, EDMUND LESTER   Books in Black or Red. New York, 1923. First edition, orig. binding. Butterfield 10-450 1974 $15

PEARSON, EDMUND LESTER   Instigation of the Devil. New York, 1930. 1st ed. Biblo & Tannen 210-497 1973 $10

PEARSON, EDMUND LESTER   Studies in Murder. New York, 1924. Illus., black cloth, first edition. Bradley 35-387 1974 $15

PEARSON, EDWIN   Banbury Chap Books and Nursery Toy Book. London, 1890. 4to., cloth. Rich Summer-26 1974 $25

PEARSON, EDWIN   Banbury Chap Books and Nursery Toy Book Literature. London, 1890. Orig. boards, cloth. Dawson's 424-46 1974 $60

PEARSON, H. G.   Beyond Petsora Eastward. 1899. Roy. 8vo., cloth, illus., coloured plate. Wheldon 128-538 1973 £8

PEARSON, H. G.   Beyond Petsora Eastward. 1899. Roy 8vo., cloth, illus. Wheldon 130-302 1974 £10

PEARSON, H. G.   Three Summers Among the Birds of Russian Lapland. 1904. 8vo., cloth, map, plates, scarce. Wheldon 128-539 1973 £10

PEARSON, H. H. W.   Gnetales. Cambridge, 1929. Roy. 8vo., cloth, plates, orig. printing. Wheldon 128-1148 1973 £7.50

PEARSON, H. J.   Three Summers Among the Birds of Russian Lapland. 1904. 8vo., cloth, scarce, plates. Wheldon 131-679 1974 £10

PEARSON, HESKETH   G. B. S. Harper, 1942. Austin 51-724 1973 $7.50

PEARSON, HESKETH   G. B. S. Collins, 1951. Austin 51-725 1973 $6

PEARSON, JOHN   An Exposition of the Creed. London, 1676. Folio, contemporary calf, rubbed, revised fourth edition. Smith 194-179 1974 £12

PEARSON, JOHN   An Exposition of the Creed. 1683. Folio, contemporary calf, revised fifth edition. Howes 185-1547 1974 £6.50

PEARSON, JOHN   An Exposition of the Creed. 1741. Folio, full tree calf, raised bands, morocco label, engraved portrait, very good copy. Bow Windows 66-534 1974 £15

PEARSON, JOHN   An Exposition of the Creed. 1833. 2 vols., contemporary calf gilt, revised new edition. Howes 185-1548 1974 £6.50

PEARSON, JOHN SIDNEY   Some Considerations on Zymotic Enteritis. 4to., orig. cloth. Bow Windows 64-651 1974 £25

PEARSON, T. GILBERT   Birds of America. New York, 1936. 4to., cloth, plates. Wheldon 131-680 1974 £5

PEARSON, T. GILBERT   Portraits and Habits of Our Birds. New York, 1920. Small 8vo., 2 vols., full page full color plates, photos, drawings, very good condition, interior mint. Current BW9-578 1974 $22.50

PEARSON, TALBOT   Encores On Main Street. 1948. 175p., illus. Austin 51-726 1973 $10

PEARSON, W.   Select Views of the Antiquities of Shropshire.
(1807). Oblong, folio, half morocco. Quaritch 939-534 1974 £30

PEARSON, W. H.   Recollections and Records of Toronto of Old.
Toronto, 1914. Mended, illus. Hood's 103-665 1974 $17.50

PEARSON'S Irish Reciter and Reader. 1904. Name & bookplate on d.w., else
fine. Covent 51-83 1973 £5

PEARY, R. E.   The North Pole. 1910. Crown 4to., orig.
cloth. Broadhurst 23-1692 1974 £6

PEASE, HOWARD   Border Ghost Stories. London, 1919. Ist ed.
Biblo & Tannen 210-651 1973 $20

PEASE, HOWARD   Border Ghost Stories. 1919. 8vo., orig. cloth,
first edition. Rota 190-854 1974 £5

PEASE, ZEPHANIAH W.   The Centenary of the Merchants National Bank.
New Bedford, 1925. First edition, 8vo., illus., fine. Current BW9-579 1974
$7.50

PEATTIE, ELIA W.   A Mountain Woman. Chicago, 1896. Scarce,
first edition. Ballinger 1-34 1974 $70

PEATTIE, RODERICK   The Great Smokies and The Blue Ridge. New
York, c. 1943. Illus., orig. binding. Wilson 63-112 1974 $12.75

PECHEY, JOHN   A Plain Introduction to the Art of Physick. London, 1697. 8vo., contemporary sheep, rebacked, first edition. Dawsons PM
249-399 1974 £140

PECHLIN, JOHANNES NICOLAS   Observationum Physico-Medicarum Libri Tres.
Hamburg, 1691. 4to., contemporary vellum, first edition. Schumann 35-372
1974 $110

PECK, F.   Academia Tertia Anglicana. London, 1727.
Folio, contemporary calf gilt, rebacked. Smith 193-126 1973 £55

PECK, GEORGE   Wyoming. New York, 1858. 8vo., orig. bindings. Butterfield 8-501 1974 $35

PECK, GEORGE W.   Peck's Bad Boy and His Pa. Chicago, 1883.
12mo., orig. printed wrappers, first edition. Goodspeed's 578-281 1974 $35

PECK, GEORGE W.   Peck's Bad Boy with the Circus. Stanton,
Van Vliet, 1905. 3l9p., illus., orig. ed. Austin 54-832 1973 $10

PECK, WALTER EDWIN   Shelley, His life and Work. 1927. Frontispiece,
plates, 2 vols., English first edition. Covent 56-1174 1974 £7.50

PECLET, JEAN CLAUDE EUGENE   Traite de l'Eclairage. Paris, 1827. 8vo.,
contemporary boards, plates, fine, first edition. Dawsons PM 245-597 1974 £48

PEDDIE, ALEXANDER   The Necessity for Some Legalised Arrangements
for the Treatment of Dipsomania. Edinburgh, 1858. 8vo., orig. cloth. Gurney
64-174 1974 £20

THE PEDIGREE of Hanson of Woodhouse and Hoyle of Swift Place. 1916, 18, and
19. 8vo., full morocco, gilt. Broadhurst 23-1400 1974 £35

PEDIGREES Recorded at the Visitations of the County Palatine of Durham.
1887. 8vo., cloth. Quaritch 939-761 1974 £10

PEDRICK, GALE   Borough Seals of the Gothic Period. 1904.
8vo., orig. parchment backed boards, covers soiled, library stamps, plates. Bow
Windows 66-537 1974 £12.50

PEEBLES, WILLIAM   The Crisis. Edinburgh, 1804. 8vo.,
contemporary half straight-grained morocco, gilt, second edition. Ximenes
37-166 1974 $25

PEELE, GEORGE   Works. 1829. Small 8vo., 3 vols., calf, gilt,
second edition. Quaritch 936-512 1974 £50

PEELE, GEORGE   Works. 1888. 2 vols., ex-library, spine
frayed. Allen 216-2262 1974 $12.50

PEELE, GEORGE   Works. 1888. 2 vols., new buckram, blind
stamp. Allen 216-1836 1974 $19.50

PEELE, GEORGE   Works. 1888. 2 vols., new buckram, blind
stamp. Allen 216-1836 1974 $19.50

PEEPS into Fairyland. London, n.d. (c. 1890). Oblong 4to., glazed pictorial
boards, cloth spine, stand up three dimensional plates. Frohnsdorff 16-593
1974 $100

PEERY, PAUL D.   Chimes and Electronic Carillons. New York,
1948. Illus. Biblo & Tannen 214-897 1974 $10

PEGGE, SAMUEL   A Series of Dissertations on Some Elegant and Very
Valuable Anglo-Saxon Remains. London, 1756. 4to., boards, first edition.
Hammond 201-718 1974 £12

PEGGE, SAMUEL   A Series of Dissertations on Some Elegant and
very Valuable Anglo-Saxon Remains. 1757. 4to., contemporary frontispiece,
plates. Hill 126-208 1974 £28

PEGUY, CHARLES   Le Mystere de la Charite de Jeanne d'Arc.
Paris, (1910). 3 vols., 12mo., contemporary brown morocco, gilt, uncut, first
editions. L. Goldschmidt 42-331 1974 $20

PEGUY, CHARLES   Le Mystere de la Charite de Jeanne d'Arc.
New York, 1943. 8vo., cloth, uncut, dust wrapper. L. Goldschmidt 42-330
1974 $25

PEIGNOT, GABRIEL   Dictionnaire Critique, Litteraire et
Bibliographique des Principaux Livres. Paris, 1806. 2 vols. in 1, 8vo., uncut,
contemporary red half calf. Dawsons PM 10-475 1974 £11

PEIGNOT, GABRIEL   Dictionnaire Critique, Litteraire et
Bibliographique. 1806. 2 vols., thick 8vo., orig. wrappers, uncut. Thomas
28-121 1972 £20

PEIGNOT, GABRIEL   Repertoire Bibliographique Universel. 1812.
8vo., orig. wrappers, uncut, worn. Thomas 28-120 1972 £12.50

PEIGNOT, GABRIEL   Repertoire de Bibliographies Speciales,
Curieuses et Instructives. Paris, 1810. Boards. Kraus B8-194 1974 $35

PEILE, H. D.   The Butterflies of Mesopotamia. Bombay,
1922. 8vo., half morocco, plate. Wheldon 131-843 1974 £5

PEILE, H. D.   A Guide to Collecting Butterflies of India.
1937. 8vo., cloth, plates. Wheldon 131-842 1974 £10

PEIRCE, CHARLES   The Portsmouth Miscellany. Portsmouth, 1804.
16mo., old calf, rubbed. Butterfield 10-451 1974 $25

PEIRCE, JAMES   A Vindication of the Dissenters. 1718. 8vo.,
contemporary calf, second edition. Hill 126-209 1974 £15

PELETIER, JACQUES   L'Algebre Departie an Deus Livres. Lyons,
1554. Small 8vo., contemporary limp vellum, first edition. Schuman 37-198
1974 $850

PELHAM, H. F.   Outlines of Roman History. New York, 1905.
Biblo & Tannen 214-649 1974 $7.50

PELLAND, ALFRED   La Gaspesie, Esquisse Historique; ses Ressources
ses Progres et son Avenir. Quebec, 1914. Card cover, photos. Hood's 102-
731 1974 $7.50

PELLECHET, M.   Catalogue des Incunables des Bibliotheques
Publiques de Lyon. Lyon, 1893. 8vo., orig. wrappers, cloth, uncut, plates.
Dawsons PM 10-476 1974 £40

PELLETIER, BERTRAND   Observations sur la Strontiane. (Paris, 1797).
8vo., boards, some stains. Gurney 66-143 1974 £18

PELLETIER, LEON   La Typographie, Poeme. Geneva, 1832.
Three quarter morocco, wrappers bound in. Kraus B8-363 1974 $58.50

PELLION, P. GUY   Catalogue des Livres Rares et Precieux. Paris,
1882. 8vo., half cloth, orig. wrappers bound in, uncut, illus. Kraus B8-195
1974 $25

PELLISSON FONTANIER, PAUL   Relation Contenant l'Histoire de l'Academie
Francoise. Paris, 1672. 12mo., contemporary mottled calf, gilt.
L. Goldschmidt 42-99 1974 $70

PELOUZE, EDMOND   Traite de l'Eclairage. Paris, 1839. 8vo., 2
vols., orig. printed wrappers, first edition. Zeitlin 235-295 1974 $140

PELTIER, JEAN CHARLES ATHANASE   Meteorologie. Paris, 1840. 8vo., orig.
printed wrappers, plates, uncut. Zeitlin 235-175 1974 $87.50

PELZER, LOUIS   The Cattlemen's Frontier. Glendale, 1936.
First edition, fine, uncut. Jenkins 61-2130 1974 $35

PEMBER, EDWARD HENRY   The Finding of Pheidippides and Other Poems.
1901. Orig. calf backed green cloth, limited, first edition. Howes 185-376
1974 £6

PEMBERTON, HENRY   A View of Sir Isaac Newton's Philosophy. London, 1728. Roy 4to., plates, modern blue buckram, gilt, uncut. Zeitlin 235-
165 1974 $125

PEMBERTON, MAX   Jewel Mysteries I Have Known. 1894. 8vo.,
orig. blue pictorial cloth, illus., first edition. Rota 190-333 1974 £15

PEMBERTON, RALPH   The Medical and Orthopaedic Management of
Chronic Arthritis. New York, 1934. Rittenhouse 46-532 1974 $10

PEMBLE, WILLIAM   A Brief Introduction to Geography. Oxford,
1675. Small 4to., unbound, woodcuts, fifth edition. Traylen 79-255 1973
£20

PENILLION OMAR Khayyam. 1928. Crown 4to., buckram, uncut, limited
edition. Broadhurst 23-1039 1974 £35

PENILLION Omar Khayyam. 1928. Engravings, buckram, unopened, numbered.
Covent 55-785 1974 £45

PENLEY, AARON   Sketching from Nature in Water-Colours.
London, (n.d.). 4to., orig. cloth, worn. Bow Windows 62-708 1974 £10

PENN, G.   A Comparative Estimate of the Mineral and
Mosaical Geologies. 1822. 8vo., contemporary half calf, rare. Wheldon
131-1060 1974 £15

PENN, WILLIAM   A Letter from William Penn, To His Wife and
Children, Written a Short Time Before His First Voyage to America. Lancaster,
1785. 8vo., modern cloth. Ximenes 37-167 1974 $27.50

PENN, WILLIAM   No Cross, No Crown. 1702. 12mo., contemporary panelled sheep, sixth edition. Hill 126-210 1974 £10.50

PENN, WILLIAM   No Cross, No Crown. 1750. 2 parts in 1 vol.,
new buckram, ninth edition. Allen 216-1941 1974 $12.50

PENN, WILLIAM   Some Fruits of Solitude in Reflections and
Maxims, Relating to the Conduct of Human Life. 1901. One of 250 numbered
copies, full vellum, fine copy, first edition. Covent 51-657 1973 £25

PENN, WILLIAM   Welshmen as Factors. Utica, 1899. Illus.
Austin 57-517 1974 $25

PENN, WILLIAM   Welshman as Factors. New York, 1899.
429p., illus. Austin 62-493 1974 $27.50

PENNANT, THOMAS   Arctic Zoology. London, 1784-87. 3 vols.,
4to., contemporary calf, rebacked, leather labels, rare first edition. Traylen
79-118 1973 £160

PENNANT, THOMAS   British Zoology. 1812. 4 vols., 8vo.,
contemporary calf gilt, engraved frontispieces, engraved plates, fifth edition.
Wheldon 128-226 1973 £25

PENNANT, THOMAS   British Zoology. 1812. 8vo., 4 vols., orig.
cloth, uncut, plates, worn. Wheldon 129-291 1974 £25

PENNANT, THOMAS   An Extensive Collection of 17 Works. London,
Chester and Warrington, 1774-1804. 4to., and large 4to., contemporary diced
calf, rebacked, gilt, 28 vols., plates. Hammond 201-720 1974 £845

PENNANT, THOMAS   Genera of Birds. 1781-86. 2 works in 1 vol.,
4to., contemporary calf gilt, plates, second edition. Wheldon 131-681 1974
£15

PENNANT, THOMAS   The Literary Life of. 1793. Crown 4to., contemporary half calf, boards. Broadhurst 23-1509 1974 £25

PENNANT, THOMAS   The Literary Life of. London, 1793. 4to.,
orig. boards, frontispiece, first edition. Dawsons PM 252-774 1974 £55

PENNANT, THOMAS   Of London. London, 1790. 4to., half morocco, boards, gilt, first edition. Dawsons PM 251-62 1974 £85

PENNANT, THOMAS   Some Account of London. London, 1793. 4to.,
contemporary blue straight-grained half calf, gilt, third edition. Dawsons PM
251-63 1974 £170

PENNANT, THOMAS   Synopsis of Quadrupeds. Chester, 1771. 8vo.,
modern full calf, plates, rare, first edition. Wheldon 130-417 1974 £38

PENNANT, THOMAS   A Tour In Scotland, and Voyage to the Hebrides,
1772. London, 1790. 2 vols., 4to., old marbled calf gilt, leather labels,
plates, foxing. Traylen 79-383 1973 £35

PENNECUIK, A.   An Historical Account of the Blue Blanket.
Edinburgh, 1722. 8vo., old calf, first edition. Quaritch 939-670 1974 £90

PENNELL, ELIZABETH ROBINS   Charles Godfrey Leland. Houghton, 1906.
2 vols. Austin 54-833 1973 $12.50

PENNELL, ELIZABETH ROBINS   The Life and Letters of. 1929. 2 vols., plates,
fine. Marsden 39-347 1974 £10

PENNELL, ELIZABETH ROBINS   The Life and Letters of Joseph Pennell. 1930.
2 vols., large 8vo., illus., fine, scarce. Howes 185-794 1974 £8.50

PENNELL, ELIZABETH ROBINS   The Life of James McNeill Whistler. 1908.
2 vols., cloth backed boards, plates, edges untrimmed, exceptionally fine set.
dust wrappers, first edition. Covent 51-1959 1973 £30

PENNELL, ELIZABETH ROBINS   Whistler the Friend. Philadelphia, 1930.
Plates, English first edition. Covent 56-71 1974 £10

PENNELL, JOSEPH   The Adventures of an Illustrator. Boston, 1925.
First edition, 4to., colored frontis., very fine. Current BW9-580 1974 $20

PENNELL, JOSEPH   The Life and Letters of. 1930. 2 vols., 8vo.,
orig. cloth, illus., small portrait. Bow Windows 66-538 1974 £8.50

PENNELL, JOSEPH   A London Reverie. 1928. 4to., orig.
buckram gilt, plates, first edition. Howes 186-2133 1974 £5

PENNELL, JOSEPH   A London Reverie. New York, 1937. 4to.
Biblo & Tannen 210-277 1973 $12.50

PENNELL, JOSEPH   Memorial Exhibition of the Works of . . . Held
Under the Auspices of the Philadelphia Print Club. (Philadelphia), 1926. First
edition, 8vo., illus., mint. Current BW9-581 1974 $25

PENNELL, JOSEPH   Pen Drawing and Pen Draughtsmen. 1897.
Thick 4to., orig. buckram gilt, illus., fine. Howes 185-793 1974 £22.50

PENNETI, ANTONIO   Officium cum Missa Sancte Syndonis Sudarium
Christi Vulgariter Nuncupate. Lyons, n.d. (c. 1515). Small 4to., old marbled
wrappers, loose in vellum wrappers. Schumann 499-78 1974 sFr 1,600

PENNINGTON, A.   British Zoophytes. 1885. 8vo., cloth, plates,
scarce. Wheldon 128-919 1973 £5

PENNINGTON, M.   Railways and Other Ways: Being Reminiscences
of Canal and Railway Life During a Period of Sixty-Seven Years. Toronto, 1894.
Hood's 102-772 1974 $20

PENNSYLVANIA   Annaul Report of the Adjutant General of...
Harrisburg, 1867. Foxed. Jenkins 61-2135 1974 $13.50

PENNSYLVANIA   First Annual Report of the Commissioner of
Labor and Industry 1913. Harrisburg, 1915. Austin 62-494 1974 $27.50

PENNSYLVANIA   Names of Foreigners Who Took the Oath of
Allegiance to the Province and State of Pennsylvania. Harrisburg, 1892. 8vo.,
rebound. MacManus 221-733 1973 $17.50

PENNSYLVANIA   Names of Foreigners Who Took the Oath of
Allegiance to the Province and State of Pennsylvania. Harrisburg, 1892. 8vo.,
rebound. MacManus 223-778 1974 $17.50

PENNSYLVANIA   Names of Persons for Whom Marriage Licences
Were Issued Previous to 1784. 1860. New buckram, rubber stamp. Allen 215-
1586 1973 $25

PENNSYLVANIA   Names of Persons for Whom Marriage Licenses
Were Issued in the Province of Pennsylvania Previous to 1790. Harrisburg, 1890.
Half morocco, marbled boards. Wilson 60-89 1973 $15

PENNSYLVANIA   Two-Hundredth Anniversary, London Grove
Meeting 1714-1914. Very good condition. Ballinger 1-306 1974 $20

PENNSYLVANIA SOCIETY FOR THE ENCOURAGEMENT OF AMERICAN
MANUFACTURES   Memorial of. Washington, 1822. Jenkins 61-2155 1974
$15

PENNSYLVANIA Soldiers' and Sailors' Home, Erie, Pennsylvania. Erie, c. 1892.
Wrappers, photos. Jenkins 61-2164 1974 $10

PENNSYLVANIA, STATE LIBRARY   Catalog of the . . . Jan., 1878. Harris,
1878. 2 parts, orig. binding, marbled edges. Wilson 63-83 1974 $16.75

PENNY, A. J.   An Introduction to the Study of Jacob Boehme's
Writings. New York, 1901. First edition. Covent 55-1018 1974 £6.50

PENNY Pictorial Library. (c. 1840). Orig. printed wrappers, colored frontis.,
8 vols., 8vo., fine. Gregory 44-58 1974 $95

PENROSE, CHARLES B.   A Text-Book of Diseases of Women.
Philadelphia, 1898. Underlining, second edition. Rittenhouse 46-534 1974
$10

PENROSE, FRANCIS CRANMER   An Investigation of the Principles of Athenian
Architecture. 1888. Roy. folio, plates, morocco spine, worn, cloth sides, soiled.
Quaritch 940-541 1974 £65

PENROSE, MATT R.   Pots 'o Gold. Reno, (1935). 8vo., orig. bindings. Butterfield 8-334 1974 $12.50

PENROSE, ROLAND   The Road is Wider Than Long. 1939. Photos,
one of 500 numbered copies on art paper, nice copy, first edition. Covent
51-1420 1973 £10

PENTON, STEPHEN   The Guardian's Instruction. London, 1688.
12mo., contemporary calf, first edition. Dawsons PM 252-775 1974 £140

PENZER, N. M.   The Tin Resources of the British Empire.
London, 1921. 8vo., illus., inscribed, orig. cloth, first edition. Bow Windows
62-711 1974 £7.50

PEPE, WILLIAM   A Narrative of the Political and Military
Events Which Took Place at Naples, 1820-21. London, 1821. Orig. stiff
wrappers, first edition. Smith 193-620 1973 £7.50

PEPLE, EDWARD   The Littlest Rebel. Random, 1939. 214p.,
illus. Austin 51-959 1973 $10

PEPLER, H. D. C.   The Four Minstrels of Bremen. Sussex, n.d.
Marbled wrappers, English first edition. Covent 56-1139 1974 £6.30

PEPLER, H. D. C.   The Ox and the Ass. London, (1932). 8vo.,
orig. patterned paper wrappers. Bow Windows 62-795 1974 £6

PEPOON, H. S.   An Annotated Flora of the Chicago Area. Chicago, 1927. 8vo., wrapper, illus., maps. Butterfield 8-153 1974 $10

PEPPER, WILLIAM   Progressive Pernicious Anaemia. 1875. 8vo.,
contemporary half calf. Dawsons PM 249-401 1974 £9

PEPYS, SAMUEL   Diary and Correspondence from his MS. 1875-
79. 8vo., 6 vols., plates, cloth. Quaritch 936-514 1974 £15

PEPYS, SAMUEL   Diary and Correspondence Of. 1848. 5 vols.,
new library binding, enlarged third edition. Austin 61-780 1974 $67.50

PEPYS, SAMUEL   Diary and Correspondence of. London, 1890.
4 vols., 8vo., orig. cloth, rubbed. Bow Windows 62-712 1974 £10

PEPYS, SAMUEL   The Diary Of. London and Cambridge, 1897.
8vo., 10 vols., contemporary tree calf, gilt. Dawsons PM 251-307 1974 £110

PEPYS, SAMUEL   The Diary of. 1926. Plates, signed, buckram,
gilt, English first edition. Covent 56-717 1974 £15

PEPYS, SAMUEL   Memoires. London, 1690. 8vo., contemporary
calf, fine, first edition. Dawsons PM 251-398 1974 £285

PEPYS, SAMUEL   Memoirs. 1825. 4to., 2 vols., orig. boards,
uncut, portraits, first edition. Quaritch 936-513 1974 £200

PERCIVAL, J.   The Wheat Plant. 1921. Roy. 8vo., cloth,
illus. Wheldon 128-1149 1973 £20

PERCIVAL, ROBERT   An Account of the Island of Ceylon. London,
1803. 4to., quarter sheep, map, foxing, first edition. Bow Windows 62-714
1974 £80

PERCIVAL, THOMAS   Medical Ethics. London, 1803. 8vo., contemporary calf, rebacked, first edition. Schumann 35-373 1974 $165

PERCY, ADRIAN   Twice Outlawed. Chicago, n.d. Cloth. Putnam 126-148 1974 $50

PERCY, PIERRE-FRANCOIS   Manuel du Chirurgien-d'Armee. Paris, 1792.
Small 8vo., contemporary calf, first edition. Schumann 35-374 1974 $115

PERCY, THOMAS   The Beggar's Daughter of Bednall Green. 1832.
Title vignette, wood engravings, small 8vo., green boards, upper joint worn,
good copy. Sawyer 293-244 1974 £8

PERCY, THOMAS   Five Pieces of Runic Poetry. London, 1763.
8vo., brown russia, first edition. Dawsons PM 252-777 1974 £52

PERCY, THOMAS   The Hermit of Warkworth. London, 1771.
4to., contemporary calf, first edition. Dawsons PM 252-778 1974 £35

PERCY, THOMAS   The Hermit of Warkworth. Alnwick, 1807.
Full calf, gilt, woodcuts, second edition. Dawson's 424-47 1974 $100

PERCY, THOMAS   Reliques of Ancient English Poetry. London, 1765. 3 vols., 8vo., contemporary calf, gilt, first edition. Dawsons PM 252-1100 1974 £75

PERCY, THOMAS   Reliques of Ancient English Poetry. 1765. 8vo., 3 vols., full contemporary calf, first edition. Broadhurst 23-902 1974 £120

PERCY, THOMAS   Reliques of Ancient English Poetry. 1765. 3 vols., first edition, 8vo., full contemporary calf, fine, complete with blank leaf with Sonnet on recto in vol. 1, half titles to vols. 2 & 3, errata and ads at end of vol. 3. Broadhurst 24-837 1974 £125

PERCY, THOMAS   Reliques of Ancient English Poetry. London, 1765. 3 vols., 8vo., early 19th century russia, fine, first edition. Dawsons PM 252-554 1974 £400

PERCY, THOMAS   Reliques of Ancient English Poetry. Philadelphia, 1823. 3 vols., 8vo., orig. light blue boards, printed paper labels, first American edition, superb copy. Ximenes 36-157 1974 $100

PERCY, THOMAS   Reliques of Ancient English Poetry. 1844. 3 vols., small 8vo., full contemporary morocco. Howes 185-377 1974 £35

PERCY SLADEN TRUST EXPEDITION   Reports of the . . . to the Indian Ocean in 1905. 1907-36. 8 vols., 4to., in parts as issued, plates, maps. Wheldon 128-147 1973 £95

PERELMAN, S. J.   Acres and Pains. Reynal, Hitchcock, 1947. 126p., illus. Austin 54-834 1973 $6

PERELMAN, S. J.   Baby, Its Cold Inside. Simon, Schuster, 1970. 253p. Austin 54-835 1973 $6.50

PERELMAN, S. J.   Crazy Like a Fox. Random, 1944. 269p. Austin 54-836 1973 $6

PERELMAN, S. J.   The Dream Department. Random, 1943. 209p. Austin 54-837 1973 $8.50

PERELMAN, S. J.   The Ill Tempered Clavichord. Simon, Schuster, 1952. 244p. Austin 54-838 1973 $7.50

PERELMAN, S. J.   Keep It Crisp. Random, 1946. 257p. Austin 54-839 1973 $6.50

PERELMAN, S. J.   Listen to the Mocking Bird. Simon, Schuster, 1949. 153p., illus. Austin 54-840 1973 $6.50

PERELMAN, S. J.   The Most of S. J. Perelman. Simon, Schuster, 1958. 650p., hard cover ed. Austin 54-841 1973 $7.50

PERELMAN, S. J.   The Rising Gorge. Simon, Schuster, 1961. 287p. Austin 54-842 1973 $6

PERELMAN, S. J.   Swiss Family Perelman. Simon, Schuster, 1950. Illus. Austin 54-843 1973 $6.50

PERELMAN, S. J.   Westward Ho! Simon, Schuster, n.d. 159p., illus. Austin 54-844 1973 $6.50

PEREZ DE LUXAN, DIEGO   Expedition Into New Mexico Made by Antonio de Espejo, 1582-83. Los Angeles, 1929. Limted to 500 copies, first publication of the Quivira Society. Jenkins 61-1849 1974 $85

PERIPLUS OF THE ERYTHRAEAN   Travel & Trade In the Indian Ocean. 1912. New buckram. Allen 213-1930 1973 $15

PERKINS, C. C.   Tuscan Sculptors: Their Lives, Works & Times. 1864. 2 vols., 4to., cloth, illus. from orig. drawings and photos. Eaton Music-658 1973 £15

PERKINS, FRANCES   The Roosevelt I Knew. New York, 1946. 1st ed., illus. Biblo & Tannen 213-90 1973 $8.50

PERKINS, HENRY   The Perkins Library. London, 1873. Large 4to., morocco. Kraus B8-196 1974 $37.50

PERKINS, JAMES H.   Annals of the West. Cincinnati, 1847. Three quarters leather, marbled boards. Bradley 35-300 1974 $28

PERKS, SYDNEY   Essays on Old London. 1927. 4to., illus., orig. buckram backed boards. Howes 186-2134 1974 £5

PERNETY, ANTOINE-JOSEPH   Dictionnaire Mytho-Hermetique. Paris, 1758. 8vo., contemporary calf, first edition. Gurney 64-175 1974 £50

PERNIN, P.   The Finger of God is There. Montreal, 1874. 18mo., orig. bindings, portrait. Butterfield 8-735 1974 $20

PEROCHON, ERNEST   Nene. Paris, 1920. 12mo., three quarter levant morocco, gilt, first edition. L. Goldschmidt 42-333 1974 $10

PEROLD, A. I.   A Treatise on Viticulture. 1927. 8vo., cloth, very scarce. Wheldon 131-1793 1974 £10

PEROTTUS, NICOLAUS   Cornucopiae. 1513. Folio, 18th century quarter calf, marbled boards, rubbed. Thomas 30-24 1973 £80

PERRAULT, CHARLES   Contes De. Paris, 1836. 8vo., orig. printed boards, worn, foxing. Bow Windows 64-654 1974 £8.50

PERRAULT, CHARLES   Histories or Tales of Past Times. London, (n.d.) 8vo., buckram-backed boards, fine, limited edition. Dawsons PM 252-779 1974 £20

PERRAULT, CHARLES   Memoires Pour Servir a l'Histoire Naturelle des Animaux et des Plantes. Amsterdam, 1736. 4to., half calf, engraved plates, frontis. Wheldon 128-289 1973 £40

PERRAULT, CHARLES   Tales of Passed Times Written for Children. 1922. Coloured illus., small 4to., orig. parchment, one of 200 numbered copies, signed by artist, nice copy. Covent 51-3242 1973 £15

PERRIER, E.   Les Colonies Animales et la Formation des Organismes. Paris, 1881. Roy. 8vo., half calf, plates. Wheldon 131-943 1974 £7.50

PERRIER, F.   Icones et Segmenta Illustrium e Marmore Tabularum Quae Romae Adhuc Extant a Francisco Perrier . . . . Paris, 1645. Folio, plates, contemporary calf. Quaritch 940-342 1974 £50

PERRIN, JEAN   Traite de Chimie Physique. Paris, 1903. 8vo., orig. printed paper wrappers, first edition. Dawsons PM 245-600 1974 £15

PERRIN, M.   Traite d'Anesthesie Chirurgicale. Paris, 1863. 8vo., quarter sheep, first edition. Gurney 64-176 1974 £15

PERRIN, WILLIAM HENRY   History of Effingham County, Illinois. Chicago, 1883. 8vo., quarter leather, illus. Saddleback 14-393 1974 $50

PERRIN, WILLIAM HENRY   History of Morrow County and Ohio. Chicago, 1880. 8vo., cloth, rebound, illus. Saddleback 14-623 1974 $60

PERRIN DU LAC, FRANCOIS MARIE   Reise in Die Beyden Louisianen. Vienna, 1807. Half morocco, fine folding map. Jenkins 61-2191 1974 $125

PERRIN DU LAC, FRANCOIS MARIE   Travels Through the Two Louisianas, and Among the Savage Nations of the Missouri. London, 1807. First edition in English. Jenkins 61-2192 1974 $125

PERROT, GEORGES   A History of Art in Chaldaea and Assyria. London, 1834. 2 vols., 4to., engravings and color plates. Biblo & Tannen 210-267 1973 $24.50

PERROT, GEORGES   History of Art in Sardinia, Judaea, Syria and
Asia Minor. London, 1890. 2 vols. Biblo & Tannen 210-268 1973 $37.50

PERROT, JOHN   A Sea of the Seed's Sufferings. London, 1661.
Small 4to., half calf, worn covers detached, first edition. Ximenes 37-170
1974 $250

PERROUD, B. P.   Melanges Entomologiques. 1846-55. 3 parts
in 1, 8vo., half cloth. Wheldon 128-782 1973 £5

PERROUT, RENE   Les Images d'Epinal. Paris, (1914). 4to.,
orig. wrappers, plates, illus. Gregory 44-234 1974 $62.50

PERRY, ARTHUR LATHAM   Williamstown and Williams College. N.P., 1899.
Large 8vo., orig. bindings. Butterfield 8-263 1974 $25

PERRY, BLISS   The Heart of Emerson's Journals. Boston & New
York, (1926). 8vo., spine bit faded, else perfect, A.L.s. from author loosely
laid in. Current BW9-266 1974 $22.50

PERRY, CHARLES   An Enquiry into the Nature and Principles of the
Spaw Waters. London, 1734. 8vo., contemporary calf, rebacked, gilt, first edition. Hammond 201-586 1974 £21

PERRY, GEORGE   Conchology. 1811. Folio, contemporary olive
straight-grain morocco, plates, gilt. Wheldon 130-59 1974 £400

PERRY, GEORGE   Conchology. 1811. Folio, contemporary green
straight grained morocco, plates. Bow Windows 64-208 1974 £180

PERRY, GEORGE   Conchology. 1811. Folio, half morocco,
boards, gilt, fine. Broadhurst 23-1171 1974 £350

PERRY, HENRY F.   History of the Thirty-Eighth Regiment Indiana
Volunteer Infantry. Palo Alto, 1906. Cloth, signed. Hayman 57-92 1974 $35

PERRY, J. T.   Dinanderie. 1910. 4to., plates, cloth, illus.
Quaritch 940-684 1974 £20

PERRY, JAMES   The Electrical Eel. London, 1777. 4to.,
modern calf, fine, scarce, first edition. Dawsons PM 252-780 1974 £175

PERRY, JOHN   An Account of the Stopping of Daggenham Breach.
London, 1721. 8vo., contemporary calf, rebacked, gilt, first edition. Hammond
201-858 1974 £48

PERRY, WILLIAM   The Royal Standard English Dictionary. Boston,
1802. Sixth American edition, leather, little worn, lower joints tender. Hayman
59-542 1974 $15

PERSE, ST. JOHN   Anabasis. London, 1930. First edition, orig.
binding, ordinary issue, spine & top of covers sun faded, nice. Ross 87-176
1974 $25

PERSHING, JOHN J.   My Experiences in the World War. New York,
1931. First edition, 2 vols., orig. binding, illus., top edges gilt, slipcase, dust
wrappers. Wilson 63-470 1974 $14.50

PERSHING, JOHN J.   My Experiences in the World War. New York,
1931. Cloth, first edition. Hayman 57-632 1974 $10

PERSIUS FLACCUS, AULUS   Satirae. Venice, 1516. Small folio, old
Italian vellum, small woodcuts, good sound copy. Thomas 32-250 1974 £40

PERSSON, P.   Strena Philologica Upsaliensis. 1922. Sewn.
Allen 213-819 1973 $10

PERZYNSKI, T.   Japanische Masken. Berlin & Leipzig, 1925.
4to., cloth. Quaritch 940-416 1974 £10

PESATURO, UBALDO   Italo-Americans of Rhode Island. 1940.
193p., illus. Austin 62-496 1974 $27.50

PESCOTT, E. E.   The Native Flowers of Victoria. Melbourne,
n.d. 8vo., cloth, plates. Wheldon 131-1341 1974 £7.50

PESTALOZZI, JOHANN HEINRICH   Elementarbucher. Zurich & Bern, 1803-
04. 6 vols., 8vo., half calf, gilt back, first edition. Schumann 499-79 1974
sFr 1,400

PETAVIUS, DIONYSIUS   Dogmata Theologica. Paris, 1865-67. 8vols.,
thick roy. 8vo., half straight grained morocco. Howes 185-1551 1974 £38

PETCH, T.   The Diseases of the Tea Bush. 1923. 8vo.,
cloth, scarce. Wheldon 129-1664 1974 £5

PETER, CHARLES   New Observations On the Venereal Disease.
London, 1695. 12mo., modern calf antique, second edition. Traylen 79-256
1973 £120

PETER Piper's Practical Principals of Plain and Perfect Pronunciations. Brooklyn,
1936. Paper wrappers, fine. Ballinger 1-35 1974 $40

PETER Prim's Proverbs, to Please Little People. New York, n.d. (c. 1850).
8vo., hand colored wrappers, frayed, hand colored engravings. Frohnsdorff
15-131 1974 $17.50

PETERBOROUGH Psalter and Bestiary of the Fourteenth Century. 1921. Folio,
orig. half morocco gilt. Bow Windows 62-779 1974 £120

PETERMAN, THOMAS DRAPER   Historical Sketches of Fayette County Iowa.
N.P., n.d. 12mo., cloth. Saddleback 14-414 1974 $35

PETERMANN, W. L.   Das Pflanzenreich. Leipzig, 1838-(1845).
2 vols., 4to., contemporary half calf, plates. Wheldon 131-97 1974 £120

PETERMANN: Vereinigte Staaten von Nord Amerkika . . . Gotha, 1874.
Map linen-mounted and folding, cloth covers stained. Wilson 63-48 1974
$12.50

PETERS, DE WITT C.   The Life and Adventures of Kit Carson. New
York - Providence, 1859. Large 8vo., orig. bindings, plates. Butterfield 8-
712 1974 $10

PETERS, HARRY T.   Currier & Ives Printmakers to the American
People. New York, 1929-31. 2 vols., 4to., buckram, very fine copy, first
edition. Goodspeed's 578-513 1974 $450

PETERS, HERMANN   Aus Pharmazeutischer Vorzeit. Berlin, 1891,
1899. 2 vols., 8vo., contemporary half morocco, worn, illus. Schuman
37-199 1974 $45

PETERS, HERMANN   Pictorial History of Ancient Pharmacy.
Chicago, 1902. Rittenhouse 46-538 1974 $15

PETERS, J. L.   Check List of the Birds of the World, Vol. 5.
Cambridge, 1945. 8vo., cloth. Wheldon 131-682 1974 £6

PETERS, JOHN C.   A Treatise on Apoplexy. New York, 1853.
8vo., orig. cloth, first edition. Dawsons PM 249-402 1974 £22

PETERS, MADISON C.   American for America. 1916. Austin 62-497
1974 $8.50

PETERS, MADISON C.   The Jews in America. Winston, 1905.
Austin 62-498 1974 $10

PETERS, MADISON C.   Justice to the Jew. Neily, 1899. 359p.
Austin 62-499 1974 $10

PETERS, W. C. H.   Naturwissenschaftliche Reise Nach
Mossambique. Berlin, 1882. 4to., orig. boards, cloth back, plates, very
scarce. Wheldon 131-765 1974 £75

PETERSEN, A. C.   Catalogue de Livres Astronomiques,
Mathematiques, et Physiques. Berlin, 1855. 8vo., orig. wrappers. Kraus
B8-197 1974 $50

PETERSEN, CARL   Kort Afhandling Calcinationer. Stockholm,
1761. 4to., unbound. Gurney 64-226 1974 £8

PETERSEN, E.   Taschenbuch fur den Kakteenfreund.
Esslingen, 1927. Crown 8vo., boards, plates, second edition. Wheldon
131-1682 1974 £5

PETERSEN, WILLIAM J.   Steamboating on the Upper Mississippi.
Iowa City, 1937. Fine, cloth, gilt, first edition. Bradley 35-301 1974 $80

PETERSHAM, MAUD   The Ark of Father Noah and Mother Noah.
New York, 1934. 1st ed., illus. Biblo & Tannen 214-741 1974 $7.50

PETERSON, ARTHUR   The Homes of Tennyson. 1905. Illus. Austin
61-778 1974 $17.50

PETERSON, EDWARD   History of Rhode Island. New York, 1853.
Engraved title, engravings. Jenkins 61-2268 1974 $22.50

PETERSON, H. C.   Propaganda for War. Norman, 1939. Orig.
binding, illus. Wilson 63-471 1974 $10

PETHERICK, EDWARD A.   Catalogue of the York Gate Library fromed by
S. William Silver. London, 1886. Large thick 8vo., second enlarged edition,
vellum. Kraus B8-240 1974 $35

PETHERICK, JOHN   Egypt, The Soudan and Central Africa: With
Explorations from Khartoum on the White Nile to the Regions to the Equator, Being
Sketches from Sixteen Year's Travel. 1861. First edition, folding map, demy
8vo., orig. cloth, fine. Broadhurst 24-1662 1974 £20

PETIT, PIERRE   Dissertation sur la Nature des Cometes.
Paris, 1665. 4to., contemporary calf, worn, first edition. Schuman 37-200
1974 $95

PETIT, PIERRE   In Tres Priores Aretaei Cappadocis Libros
Commentarii. London, 1726. Large 4to., contemporary wrappers, rebacked,
first edition. Schuman 37-6 1974 $110

PETIT DE JULLEVILLE, LOUIS   Histoire de la Langue et de la Litterature
Francaise des Origines a 1900. Paris, 1896-99. 8 vols., 4to., blue cloth, gilt.
Kraus B8-198 1974 $145

PETIT Almanach des Dames: Cinquieme Annee 1815. Paris. 12mo., little
rubbed, contemporary green half calf, engraved illus. Bow Windows 66-539
1974 £5

PETIT Bijou des Enfans, le. Annee 1816. Paris. Full red morocco, gold stamped,
light blue cloth case, 7/8 X 5/8. Gregory 44-440 1974 $175

LE PETIT Fabuliste. Paris, (c. 1830). Orig. boards, fine, 3 X 2. Gregory
44-441 1974 $65

PETIT Fabuliste. Paris, (c. 1850). Engraved plates, size 1 by 2/3 inches, orig.
red morocco gilt, gilt edges, good copy, scarce. Sawyer 293-225 1974 £65

LE PETIT la Fontaine. Paris, (c. 1825). Pictorial title, full page plates, full
red morocco, gilt, 1 3/4 X 2 5/8. Gregory 44-442 1974 $100

LE PETIT Momus. Paris, 1832. Full gold stamped red morocco, full page
engravings, 1 1/32 X 3/4. Gregory 44-443 1974 $110

LE PETIT Paroissien de la Jeunesse. Paris, (c. 1825). Orig. red glazed boards,
matching slip case lacking bottom, 1 3/4 X 1 1/8. Gregory 44-445 1974 $55

LE PETIT Paroissien l'Enfance. Paris, c. 1830. Orig. red morocco, fine, 1 1/16
X 3/4. Gregory 44-444 1974 $87.50

LE PETIT Poucet, Annee 1818. Dedie a l'Enfance. Paris. Full red morocco, gold
stamped, 1 X 5/8. Gregory 44-446 1974 $115

PETITION of Cato West, and Others, in Behalf of Themselves and the Other
Inhabitants of the Mississippi Territory. (Washington, 1800). 8vo., disbound,
first edition, rare. Ximenes 36-150 1974 $175

PETITOT, J.   Les Emaux de Petitot du Musee du Louvre.
1862-64. 2 vols., 4to., plates, half green morocco, gilt. Quaritch 940-199
1974 £24

PETRAK, F.   Die Gattungen der Pyrenomyzeten. 1926-27.
Roy 8vo., new cloth. Wheldon 130-1331 1974 £20

PETRARCA, FRANCESCO   Le Cose Volgari. 1501. Early 19th century
morocco, raised gilt bands, first aldine edition. Thomas 30-6 1973 £400

PETRARCA, FRANCESCO   Love Rimes of Petrarch. Ithaca, 1932. First
edition. Biblo & Tannen 213-475 1973 $15

PETRARCA, FRANCESCO   Opera Latina. Basel, 1496. Folio, fine,
contemporary blind-tooled calf over wooden boards, first collective edition.
Schafer 8-136 1973 sFr. 4,800

PETRARCA, FRANCESCO   Il Petrarcha. 1514. Early 19th century
morocco gilt, raised bands. Thomas 30-27 1973 £100

PETRARCA, FRANCESCO   Il Petrarcha con l'Espositione di M. Giovanni
Andrea Gesualdo. Venice, 1553. 2 parts in 1 vol., 4to., red morocco gilt,
cloth case. Thomas 32-83 1974 £150

PETRARCA, FRANCESCO   De Remediis Utriusque Fortunae. 1492. Folio,
18th century calf, gilt, plates. Bow Windows 64-656 1974 £550

PETRARCA, FRANCESCO   De Remediis Utriusque Fortunae. 1649. 12mo.,
contemporary vellum, fine, rare. Zeitlin 235-176 1974 $125

PETRARCA, FRANCESCO   Rime. Florence, 1880. Full vellum, gilt.
Broadhurst 23-881 1974 £10

PETRARCA, FRANCESCO   Le Rime di Petrarca. Florence, 1900. Orig.
brown calf, gilt, very nice, 2 1/2 X 1 3/4. Gregory 44-447 1974 $22.50

PETRARCA, FRANCESCO   Sonetti, Canzoni, E. Triomphi. Venice, 1541.
Small 4to., Italian dark brown morocco sides set into modern dark brown hardgrain
morocco, lacks last 4 leaves. Thomas 32-251 1974 £50

PETRI, B.   Die Wartung. Leipzig, 1831. 8vo., half
leather. Wheldon 129-394 1974 £5

PETRI, GIROLAMO   L'Orbe Cattolico Ossia Atlante Geografico
Storico Ecclesiastico. Rome, 1858-59. 3 vols., contemporary half morocco.
Howes 185-1552 1974 £6

PETRIE, S.   Trial of an Action for Thirty Seven Thousand
Pounds. 1782. 8vo., half calf. Quaritch 939-578 1974 £7.50

PETRIE, W. M. FLINDERS   Abydos. 1902-03. 2 vols., parts 1 & 2,
loose in binding. Bow Windows 66-204 1974 £7.50

PETRIE, W. M. FLINDERS   Abydos. 1902-04. 3 vols., parts 1, 2 & 3,
1 joint torn. Bow Windows 66-205 1974 £12

PETRIE, W. M. FLINDERS   Egyptian Tales. London, 1913. Biblo & Tannen
210-1013 1973 $8.50

PETROFF, IVAN   A Preliminary Report Upon the Population,
Industry, and Resources of Alaska. Washington, 1881. Foxed, fine large folding
map. Jenkins 61-93 1974 $22.50

PETRONIUS, GAIUS   The Complete Works of. New York, 1932.
Illus., orig. binding. Wilson 63-600F 1974 $10

PETRONIUS ARBITER   The Satyricon. Chicago, 1927. 2 vols., orig.
cl., ltd. to 960 numbered copies. Jacobs 24-120 1974 $25

PETROVITCH, WOISLAV M.   Hero Tales and Legends of the Serbians. 1917.
Large 8vo., orig. pictorial cloth, first edition. Howes 186-1902 1974 £5

PETRUNKEVITCH, A.   A Study of Amber Spiders. 1942. 8vo., plates,
344 pp. Wheldon 129-853 1974 £7.50

PETRUS, HISPANUS
Please turn to
JOHANNES XXI, POPE

PETTENKOFER, MAX JOSEF VON   Boden Und Grundwasser in ihren
Beziehungen zu Cholera und Typhus.   Munich, 1869. 8vo., orig. pictured
wrappers, first separate edition.   Schuman 37-201 1974 $110

PETTIGREW, THOMAS   On Superstitions Connected With the History
and Practice of Medicine and Surgery.   London, 1844.   Rittenhouse 46-536
1974 $55

PETTIGREW, THOMAS J.   Chronicles of the Tombs.   1857.   Orig. edition.
Austin 61-785 1974 $10

PETTUS, JOHN   Fleta Minor.   London, 1686.   Folio, old
panelled calf, rebacked, leather label.   Traylen 79-257 1973 £160

PETTUS, JOHN   Fodinae Regales.   London, 1670.   Folio,
plates, contemporary calf, leather label, first edition.   Traylen 79-258 1973
£135

PETTY, MARY   This Petty Pace.   New York, 1945.   4to.,
1st ed.   Biblo & Tannen 210-70 1973 $7.50

PETTY, WILLIAM   The Political Anatomy of Ireland.   London,
1691.   Small 8vo., calf, first edition.   Quaritch 939-627 1974 £95

PETTY, WILLIAM   Tracts.   Dublin, 1769.   8vo., contemporary
tree calf, gilt, worn, fine, scarce, first collected edition.   Bow Windows
62-717 1974 £68

PEUCER, GASPARD   Commentarius de Praecipuis Generibus
Divinationum.   Wittenberg, 1560.   Orig. sheep, stain, good firm condition.
Rittenhouse 46-537 1974 $150

PEYSONNEL, JEAN   De Temporibus Humani Partus.   1666.   Small
8vo., contemporary sheep, worn.   Dawsons PM 249-403 1974 £25

PEYTON, J. LEWIS   History of Augusta County.   Staunton, 1882.
Modern cloth.   Hayman 57-725 1974 $32.50

PFEIFFER, BERTOLD   Album Der Erzeugnisse der Ehemaligen
Wurttembergischen Manufaktur Alt-Ludwigsburg.   Stuttgart, (1906).   Oblong
4to., illus., plates, covers little soiled, orig. cloth.   Bow Windows 66-540
1974 £65

PFEIFFER, C.   Naturgeschichte Deutscher Land und Susswasser
Mollusken.   Weimar, 1821-28.   3 vols. in 1, 4to., half calf, hand-coloured
plates, rare.   Wheldon 128-848 1973 £60

PFEIFFER, IDA   A Visit to Iceland and the Scandinavian North.
1852.   First edition, crown 8vo., orig. cloth, very good copy, tinted lithographs.
Broadhurst 24-1663 1974 £25

PFEIFFER, L.   Abbildung und Beschreibung Bluhendes
Cacteen. Figures des Cactees en Fleur.   Cassel, 1843-50.   2 vols., small
folio, modern cloth, rare, plates.   Wheldon 131-1683 1974 £180

PFEILSCHMIDT, ANDREAS   Ein Huebsch unnd Christlich Spiel des Gantzen
Buchs Esther.   Frankfurt, 1555.   Small 8vo., old vellum, first edition.   Schumann
499-80 1974 sFr 820

PFLUGER, EDUARD F. W.   Disquisitiones de Sensu Electrico.   Bonn, 1860.
Large 4to., cloth-backed boards, unopened, first edition.   Schumann 35-375
1974 $75

PFORDTEN, H. VON DER   Deutsche Musik.   Leipzig, 1920.   Biblo &
Tannen 213-884 1973 $9.50

PHAEDRUS   Fabularum Aesopiarum Libri Quinque.   Leyden,
1727.   4to., vellum, engraved frontis., rare edition.   Schumann 499-81 1974
sFr 750

PHAEDRUS   The Fables of...Translated into English Prose.
1753. 8vo., contemporary calf, worn, second edition.   Broadhurst 23-1254 1974
£5

PHARE, E. E.   The Poetry of Gerard Manley Hopkins: A
Survey and Commentary.   1933.   Spine faded, else very good, first edition.
Covent 51-936 1973 £5.25

PHARMACOPOEA Hispana.   Madrid, 1794.   4to., contemporary calf, first
edition.   Gurney 66-144 1974 £90

PHARMACOPOEIA Collegii Regalis Medicorum Londinensis.   London, 1746.
4to., modern half brown morocco, frontispiece.   Traylen 79-259 1973 £38

PHELPS, MRS. ALMIRA H. LINCOLN   Lectures to Young Ladies.   Boston,
1833.   Orig. cloth.   Dawson's 424-343 1974 $25

PHELPS, ELIZABETH STUART
Please turn to
WARD, ELIZABETH STUART PHELPS, 1844-1911

PHELPS, HENRY P.   The King Memorial.   Albany, 1893.   Fine.
Ballinger 1-308 1974 $17

PHELPS and Ensign--Traveller's Guide Through the United States.   New York,
1844.   16mo.   Biblo & Tannen 213-83 1973 $37.50

PHILADELPHIA PRINT CLUB   A History Of.   Philadelphia, 1929.   Illus.
Ballinger 1-309 1974 $10

PHILAENUS, JUNIUS   A Letter to Thomas Jefferson.   New York, 1802.
8vo., disbound, very scarce, first edition.   Ximenes 37-120 1974 $75

THE PHILANTROPIST, or, Repository for Hints and Suggestions Calculated to
Promote the Comfort and Happiness of Man.   1811-19.   7 vols., demy 8vo.,
contemporary half calf, marbled boards, scarce, fine.   Broadhurst 24-1276 1974
£120

THE PHILANTROPIST.   1811-19.   8vo., 7 vols., contemporary half calf, boards.
Broadhurst 23-1255 1974 £110

PHILBY, HARRY ST. JOHN BRIDGER   A Pilgrim in Arabia.   Golden Cockerel
Press, 1943.   Limited to 350 copies, portrait frontispiece, roy. 8vo., niger
backed buckram boards, uncut, top edges gilt, as issued, good copy.   Sawyer
293-151 1974 £92

PHILIP, A. P. W.   A Treatise on Indigestion.   London, 1822.
8vo., contemporary calf, rebacked.   Dawsons PM 249-404 1974 £25

PHILIP, ROBERT   The Life and Times of the Reverend George
Whitefield.   1837.   Orig. cloth, portrait.   Howes 185-1777 1974 £7.50

PHILIPOT, J.   A Perfect Collection or Catalogue of all
Knights Batchelours.   1660.   Small 8vo., half calf.   Quaritch 939-741 1974
£40

PHILIPOT, T.   Villare Cantianum.   Lynn, 1776.   Folio, half
calf, second edition.   Quaritch 939-414 1974 £30

PHILIPPE, CHARLES-LOUIS   Bubu of Montparnasse.   Paris, 1932.   First
edition, small 8vo., paper printed wrapper, wrapper slightly dust stained.
Broadhurst 24-658 1974 £10

PHILIPPE, JULES   Origine de l'Imprimerie a Paris, d'Apres des
Documents Inedits.   Paris, 1885.   4to., orig. printed wrappers, uncut, plates.
Kraus B8-364 1974 $65

PHILIPPI, R. A.   Enumeratio Molluscorum Siciliae cum Viventium
tum in Tellure Tertiaria Fossilium.   Halle, 1844.   Vol. 2 only, 4to., orig.
boards, plates, rare.   Wheldon 128-849 1973 £25

PHILIPPS, H.   The Grandeur of the Law.   London, 1684.
8vo., old calf, bookplate.   Smith 193-119 1973 £12

PHILIPS, AMBROSE   Humfrey.   London, 1723.   8vo., modern
boards, first edition.   Dawsons PM 252-782 1974 £15

PHILIPS, AMBROSE   Humfrey, Duke of Gloucester. 1723. 8vo., cloth, first edition. Quaritch 936-181 1974 £12

PHILIPS, KATHERINE   Poems. London, 1664. 8vo., contemporary sheep, first unathorised edition. Dawsons PM 252-784 1974 £120

PHILIPS, JOHN   Cyder. London, 1708. 8vo., contemporary speckled sheep, first edition, first issue. Dawsons PM 252-783 1974 £45

PHILIPS, JOHN   Poems. London, 1744. 2 vols. in 1, 8vo., frontispiece, fourth & tenth editions. Smith 193-120 1973 £7.50

PHILIPS, STEPHEN   Herod. Lane, 1905. Austin 51-727 1973 $6.50

PHILIPS, STEPHEN   Paolo & Francesca. Lane, 1905. 120p. Austin 51-728 1973 $6.50

PHILLIP, ARTHUR   The Voyage of Governor Phillip to Botany Bay. Dublin, 1790. 8vo., contemporary calf, library bookplate, very nice copy, frontispiece, plates, first Irish edition. Ximenes 37-171 1974 $125

PHILLIPPES, HENRY   A Mathematical Manual. London, 1684. 12mo., orig. sheep, plates. Dawsons PM 245-601 1974 £75

PHILLIPPS, CHARLES   The Speeches of. Saratoga Springs, 1820. Orig. boards, uncut, paper label on spine, little browned owing to quality of paper, probably unopened. Thomas 32-8 1974 £12

PHILLIPPS, S. M.   State Trials; or, A Collection of the Most Interesting Trials, Prior to the Revolution of 1688. 1826. 2 vols., 8vo., corners worn, contemporary calf, neatly rebacked. Bow Windows 66-541 1974 £14.50

PHILLIPPS, THOMAS   Collections for Wiltshire. c. 1822. Contemporary diced russia. Thomas 28-324 1972 £60

PHILLIPPS, THOMAS   The Romance of Sowdone of Babyloyne and of Ferumbras his Sone. 1854. 4to., roan spine, unopened copy. Thomas 32-285 1974 £35

PHILLIPPS LIBRARY   Catalogue of Printed Books at Middle Hill. (Middle Hill, 1827-71). Folio, tan half morocco, uncut, top edges gilt. Kraus B8-199 1974 $175

PHILLIPS, DAVID GRAHAM   Fashionable Adventures of Joshua Craig. 1909. Allen 216-1299 1974 $10

PHILLIPS, ELIZABETH   A History of the Pioneers of the Welsh Coalfield. 1925. Illus. Covent 55-1323 1974 £12.50

PHILLIPS, EMMETT   Sacramento Valley and Foothill Counties of California. (Sacramento), 1915. 8vo., wrapper, illus. Saddleback 14-232 1974 $10

PHILLIPS, G. E.   The Extinction of the Ancient Hierarchy. London & Edinburgh, 1905. Plates, library label, scarce. Howes 185-1556 1974 £7.50

PHILLIPS, G. F.   Principles of Effect and Colour. (1849). 4to., orig. blind stamped cloth, rebacked, plates. Quaritch 940-200 1974 £40

PHILLIPS, GEORGES   Du Droit Ecclesiastique Dans ses Principes Generaux. Paris, 1850-51. 3 vols., half morocco, foxing. Howes 185-1557 1974 £15

PHILLIPS, HENRY   Floral Emblems. London, 1825. 8vo., orig. linen boards, plates, illus., first edition. Hammond 201-642 1974 £28

PHILLIPS, J.   Geology of Oxford and the Valley of the Thames. Oxford, 1871. 8vo., cloth, scarce, plates. Wheldon 131-1061 1974 £10

PHILLIPS, J.   Illustrations of the Geology of Yorkshire. 1875. 4to., cloth, plates, third edition. Wheldon 131-1062 1974 £16

PHILLIPS, J.   A Monograph of British Belemnitidae: Jurassic. 1865-70, 1909. 5 parts & index, cloth binder, plates. Wheldon 131-1063 1974 £10

PHILLIPS, J. D.   American Waterfowl. Boston & New York, 1930. First edition, 8vo., illus., maps, near fine. Current BW9-191 1974 $25

PHILLIPS, J. R.   Memoirs of the Ancient Family of Owen. 1886. 8vo., orig. cloth. Broadhurst 23-1510 1974 £5

PHILLIPS, JAMES DUNCAN   Salem in the Seventeenth Century. 1933. 8vo., orig. bindings, first edition. Butterfield 8-264 1974 $10

PHILLIPS, JOHN   The Character of a Popish Successor. London, 1681. Small folio, disbound, first edition. Dawsons PM 251-513 1974 £30

PHILLIPS, JOHN ARTHUR   Elements of Metallurgy. London, 1874. 8vo., orig. cloth, fine, first edition. Dawsons PM 245-602 1974 £6

PHILLIPS, LE ROY   A Bibliography of the Writings of Henry James. Boston & New York, 1906. 8vo., orig. marbled boards, first edition. Dawsons PM 10-314 1974 £12

PHILLIPS, LE ROY   A Bibliography of the Writings of Henry James. Boston & New York, 1906. 8vo., orig. marbled boards, inscribed presentation, first edition. Dawsons PM 252-495 1974 £12

PHILLIPS, N.   Holland and the Canadians. Amsterdam, n.d. Photographs. Hood's 103-120 1974 $27.50

PHILLIPS, P. LEE   Alaska and the Northwest Part of North America, 1588-1898. Washington, 1898. Wrapper, foxed. Jenkins 61-94 1974 $12.50

PHILLIPS, R.   An Easy Grammar of Natural and Experimental Philosophy. 1807. First edition, engraved plates, 12mo., contemporary morocco. George's 610-586 1973 £7.50

PHILLIPS, R.   Geography, on a Popular Plan, Designed for the Use of Schools, and Young Persons. 1808. Fifth edition, maps, diagrams, 1 vol. in 2, 12mo., contemporary sheep, worn, one cover detached, other joints weak, ads at end. George's 610-587 1973 £5

PHILLIPS, RICHARD   A Popular Dictionary of Facts and Knowledge. 1829. 12mo., contemporary cloth, second edition. Hill 126-211 1974 £18

PHILLIPS, SAMUEL   A Word in Season. Boston, 1727. 12mo., contemporary calf over wooden boards, worn, first edition, text browned, ads at end. Thomas 32-4 1974 £45

PHILLIPS, W. A.   Manual of the Mammals of Ceylon. Colombo, 1935. Roy. 8vo., cloth, plates, presentation copy. Wheldon 131-517 1974 £25

PHILLIPS, WALTER ALISON   History of the Church of Ireland. 1934. 8vo., orig. cloth. Howes 185-1558 1974 £7.50

PHILLIPS, WALTER ALISON   The Revolution in Ireland. New York, 1923. 8vo., cloth boards. Emerald 50-779 1974 £6.50

PHILLIPS, WILLIAM   An Elementary Introduction to the Knowledge of Mineralogy. 1816. First edition, crown 8vo., orig. boards, uncut, very fine copy, ads at end. Broadhurst 24-1277 1974 £20

PHILLIPS, WILLIAM   An Elementary Introduction to the Knowledge of Mineralogy. 1816. Crown 8vo., orig. boards, uncut, first edition. Broadhurst 23-1256 1974 £20

PHILLIPS, WILLIAM   An Elementary Introduction to the Knowledge of Mineralogy. 1823. 8vo., half calf, third edition. Wheldon 130-963 1974 £12

PHILLIPS, WILLIAM   A Manual of the British Discomycetes. 1893. Crown 8vo., cloth, plates, second edition. Wheldon 130-1332 1974 £5

PHILLIPS, WILLIAM   A Selection of Facts from the Best Authorities.
1818. 8vo., half calf.   Wheldon 131-1064 1974 £10

PHILLIPS, WILLIAM ADDISON   The Conquest of Kansas. Boston, 1856. 8vo.,
orig. bindings, first edition.   Butterfield 8-179 1974 $17.50

PHILLIPS COLLECTION   A Museum of Modern Art and Its Sources.
Washington, 1932. 10 color plates and over 300 reproductions. Biblo & Tannen
214-341 1974 $32.50

PHILLOTT, D. C.   The Bag-Nama-yi Nasiri. 1908. Roy. 8vo.,
cloth gilt, frontispiece, text-figures, scarce, limited edition. Wheldon 128-543
1973 £15

PHILLPOTTS, EDEN   Becoming. 1932. 8vo., cloth, limited, signed,
first edition.   Quaritch 936-515 1974 £8

PHILLPOTTS, EDEN   Children of the Mist. 1898. Small 8vo., orig.
cloth, frontispiece, first edition.   Quaritch 936-516 1974 £8

PHILLPOTTS, EDEN   A Comedy Royal in Four Acts. London, 1925.
8vo., orig. parchment backed boards, uncut, limited, first edition. Bow
Windows 62-719 1974 £8.50

PHILLPOTTS, EDEN   Folly and Fresh Air. 1891. 8vo., orig. cloth,
scarce, first edition.   Rota 189-694 1974 £6

PHILLPOTTS, EDEN   A Hundred Lyrics. 1930. Limited to 160
numbered copies, signed by author, half vellum, fine copy. Covent 51-1435
1973 £5.25

PHILLPOTTS, EDEN   My Shrubs. 1915. 4to., cloth, plates, scarce.
Wheldon 130-1569 1974 £5

PHILLPOTTS, EDEN   Up Hill, Down Dale. London, n.d. Biblo &
Tannen 210-652 1973 $10

PHILLPOTTS, HENRY   Collection of 3 Controversial Works On the
Roman Catholic Question. 1827-28. Contemporary calf, gilt. Howes
185-1559 1974 £7.50

PHILO-LEXIKON   Handbuch des Judischen Wissens. Berlin,
1935.   Biblo & Tannen 213-633 1973 $9.50

PHILOLOGICAL Museum. 1823-1833. Vols. 1 & 2 only. Allen 213-827
1973 $15

PHILOSTRATUS LES Images. 1614. Folio, contemporary French red morocco,
gilt.   Marlborough 70-9 1974 £600

PHINNEY, ELIAS   History of the Battle of Lexington. Boston,
(1875). Printed gray wrappers, frontispiece. Bradley 35-10 1974 $10

PHIPPS, CONSTANTIN HENRY, MARQUIS OF NORMANBY
Please turn to
NORMANBY, CONSTANTIN HENRY PHIPPS, MARQUIS OF

PHIPPS, CONSTANTIN-JEAN   Voyage au Pole Boreal, Fait en 1773 . . .
Paris, 1775. Folding maps, plates, full leather, tooled & stamped in gold, mottled
end papers, beautiful condition. Hood's 102-70 1974 $225

PHIPPS, CONSTANTIN-JEAN   Voyage au Pole Boreal, Fait en 1773. Paris,
1775. Full leather, plates, maps. Hood's 104-89 1974 $225

PHIPPS, JOSEPH   Observations on a Late Anonymous Publication,
Intituled, a Letter to the Author of a Letter to Dr. Formery, in Vindication of
Robert Barclay, and the Principles of the People called Quakers. London, 1767.
Plain wrappers, presumably first edition. Hayman 59-579 1974 $15

PHIPSON, E.   The Animal-Lore of Shakspeare's Time. 1883.
8vo., cloth, frontispiece, scarce.   Wheldon 128-126 1973 £10

PHIPSON, THOMAS LAMBE   Le Preparateur-Photographe. Paris, 1864.
8vo., orig. pictured wrappers, illus., first edition. Schuman 37-202 1974 $195

PHOTOGRAPHIE, 1939. Paris, 1938. 4to., plates. Biblo & Tannen 210-291
1973 $8.50

PHOTOS of Northeast Harbor, Mount Desert Island. Northeast Harbor, 1904.
Pict. wrapper.   Jenkins 61-2197 1974 $12.50

PHYTHIAN, J. E.   Fifty Years of Modern Painting. 1910. Crown
8vo., illus., orig. cloth.   Marsden 39-350 1974 £5

PIA Fraus, Oder Spannisch Natur Welche Durch die Geschworne Spanische Diener,
die Jesuiten, in Alle Deutsche Gemuther zu Plantzen Begert und Unterstanden
Wird. N.P., 1620. 4to., wrappers.   Schumann 499-82 1974 sFr 500

PIACENTINI, MARCELLO   Francesco Fichera. Geneva, 1931. 4to.,
cloth, plates.   Minters 37-530 1973 $25

PICARD, JEAN   Degre du Meridien entre Paris et Amiens. Paris,
1740. 8vo., contemporary tree calf, gilt, plates. Dawsons PM 245-603 1974
£25

PICART, BERNARD   Figures de la Bible. The Hague, 1728. Folio,
contemporary (probably orig.) calf, engravings, gilt borders. Schumann 499-83
1974 sFr 1,600

PICARD, MAX   Expressionistische Bauernmalerei. Munich,
1922. 4to., cloth spine, plates, third edition. Minters 37-484 1973 $22

PICASSO, PABLO   Le Desir Attrape par la Queue. Paris, 1945.
12mo., orig. wrapper, uncut, first edition. L. Goldschmidt 42-334 1974 $20

PICCOLOMINI, ENEA SILVIO
Please turn to
PIUS II, POPE

PICCOLPASSI, CYPRIAN   Les Troys Libvres de l'Art du Potier Esquels se
Traicte non Seulement de la Practique. 1860. Folio, plates, contemporary half
morocco gilt, scarce.   Quaritch 940-655 1974 £50

PICKARD, SAMUEL T.   Whittier-Land, A Handbook of North Essex.
Boston, 1904. First edition, 12mo., illus., ex-library, good. Current Bw9-293
1974 $9.50

PICKERING, A. J.   The Cradle and Home of the Hosiery Trade.
1940. 4to., boards, cloth.   Broadhurst 23-1257 1974 £5

PICKERING, A. J.   The Cradle and Home of the Hosiery Trade.
1940. Demy 4to., boards, cloth spine, illus., inscribed presentation copy from
author.   Broadhurst 24-1278 1974 £5

PICKERING & CHATTO   An Illustrated Catalogue of Old and Rare Books.
London, 1902. 4to., orig. cloth, plates, illus. Dawsons PM 10-482 1974
£5

PICKETT, MONTGOMERY   The Fourth Physician. Chicago, 1911. First
edition, 12mo., illus., very good.   Current BW9-70 1974 $7.50

PICKFORD, MARY   Sunshine and Shadow. Doubleday, 1955.
224p., illus.   Austin 51-729 1973 $6.50

PICKTHALL, M. L. C.   The Lamp of Poor Souls, and Other Poems.
Toronto, 1916. Hood's 104-775 1974 $12.50

PICKTHALL, M. L. C.   Little Songs: A Book of Poems. Toronto, 1925.
Boxed. Hood's 104-776 1974 $17.50

PICTET, F. J.   Histoire Naturelle Generale et Particuliere.
Paris, 1845. Roy 8vo., contemporary half calf, boards, scarce. Broadhurst
23-1172 1974 £50

PICTET, F. J.   Histoire Naturelle Generale et Particuliere des
Insectes Nevropteres. Paris, 1845. Coloured plates, roy. 8vo., contemporary
half green calf, marbled boards, scarce, fine. Broadhurst 24-1144 1974 £55

PICTON, JAMES A.   Miscellaneous Essays and Papers. Liverpool,
1857-86. 8vo., contemporary half morocco. Broadhurst 23-1511 1974 £30

PICTON, JAMES A.   Miscellaneous Essays and Papers. Liverpool,
1857-86. Demy 8vo., contemporary half morocco, binding rubbed. Broadhurst
24-1500 1974 £35

PICTON'S 100 Years: A Historical Record of Achievement. Picton, 1937.
Illus. Hood's 104-724 1974 $20

PICTON'S 100 Years: A Historical Record of Achievement. Picton, 1937. Card
covers, illus. Hood's 102-629 1974 $20

A PICTORIAL Museum of Regal. London, 1845. 2 vols., 4to., contemporary
half roan, rubbed, plates, engravings. Bow Windows 62-691 1974 £8.50

PICTORIUS, GEORG   Zootropheion, seu Leporarium, Quorundam
Animalium Quadrupedum & Avicularum. Basel, (1560). Small 8vo., old calf,
worn, rare, fine copy. Harper 213-119 1973 $450

A PICTURE of St. Petersburgh. London, 1815. Folio, plates, new boards.
Marlborough 70-30 1974 £300

PICTURES and Portraits of the Life & Land of Burns. n.d. 2 vols., 4to.,
half contemporary calf gilt. Smith 193-218 1973 £15

PICTURES From Punch. 1894-96. 6 vols., portraits, illus., cloth, gilt, fine.
Marsden 39-358 1974 £12

PICTURESQUE Alaska. New York, c. 1892. Photographs, stained. Jenkins
61-95 1974 $20

PICTURESQUE Chicago. Chicago, 1883. Foldout, boards. Jenkins 61-1123
1974 $27.50

PICTURESQUE Lowell: Photogravures. Lowell, 1896. Wrapper, 12mo. Jenkins
61-1521 1974 $15

PICTURESQUE Mackinac, Michigan. Mackinac, c. 1899. Loose wrappers,
photos. Jenkins 61-1631 1974 $12.50

PICTURESQUE Middlesboro· The Magic City. (Middlesboro, c.1907). Oblong
16mo., wrapper. Saddleback 14-447 1974 $10

PICTURESQUE Representations of the Dress and Manners of the Turks. n.d.
Full grained morocco, gilt, plates, illus. Covent 55-530 1974 £75

PICTURESQUE Springfield, Massachusetts. New York, 1895. Pict. wrappers,
photos. Jenkins 61-1522 1974 $17.50

PIDDINGTON, HENRY   The Sailor's Horn-Book for the Law of Storms.
1848. Orig. cloth, rebacked. Howes 186-1753 1974 £5.50

PIEDMONT, ALEXIS OF PSEUD.
Please turn to
RUSCELLI, GIROLAMO

PIEMONTESE, ALESSIO PSEUD.
Please turn to
RUSCELLI, GIROLAMO

PIEPERS, M. C.   The Rhopalocera of Java. The Hague and
London, 1909-13. Parts 1 - 3, roy. 4to., orig. wrappers, coloured plates,
very scarce. Wheldon 128-785 1973 £20

PIERCE, F. N.   The Genitalia of the Group Geometridae of the
Lepidoptera of the British Islands. Liverpool, 1914. Roy. 8vo., half calf gilt,
plates. Wheldon 131-845 1974 £7.50

PIERCE, F. N.   The Genitalia of the Group Noctuidae of the
Lepidopteria of the British Islands. Liverpool, 1909. 8vo., orig. cloth. Broadhurst 23-1175 1974 £5

PIERCE, F. N.   The Genitalia of the Group Noctuidae of the
Lepidopteria of the British Islands. Liverpool, 1909. Med. 8vo., plates, orig.
cloth, fine. Broadhurst 24-1146 1974 £5

PIERCE, F. N.   The Genitalia of the Group Noctuidae of the
Lepidoptera of the British Islands. Liverpool, 1909. Roy. 8vo., half calf,
plates. Wheldon 131-844 1974 £7.50

PIERCE, FREDERICK ERASTUS   The Collaboration of Webster and Dekker.
1909. Ex-library, sturdy library binding, orig. edition. Austin 61-787 1974
$10

PIERCE, G. A.   The Dickens Dictionary. 1914. Cloth, revised
edition. Dawsons PM 11-620 1974 £11

PIERCE, LORNE   Albert Durrant Watson, An Appraisal. Toronto,
1923. Card cover, signed, special limited edition. Hood's 103-222 1974 $10

PIERCE, LORNE   Marjorie Pickthall, A Book of Remembrance.
Toronto, 1925. Hood's 104-777 1974 $17.50

PIERCE, LORNE   William Kirby, Portrait of a Tory Loyalist.
Toronto, 1929. Illus. Hood's 103-223 1974 $10

PIERCE, THOMAS   A Sermon. London, 1661. 4to., modern boards,
first edition. Dawsons PM 251-514 1974 £20

PIERPONT MORGAN, JOHN
Please turn to
MORGAN, JOHN PIERPONT

PIERSIG, R.   Deutschlands Hydrachniden. Stuttgart, 1897-
1900. 6 parts in 1 vol., 4to., new buckram, plain and partly coloured plates, very
scarce. Wheldon 128-920 1973 £35

PIERSOL, GEORGE A.   Human Anatomy. Philadelphia, 1923.
Eighth edition. Rittenhouse 46-539 1974 $15

PIERSON, EMILY CATHERINE   Jamie Parker, the Fugitive. Hartford, 1851.
12mo., orig. dark brown cloth, very good copy, first edition. Ximenes 37-172
1974 $75

PIERSON, ERNEST D.   Society Verse by American Writers. Benjamin,
Bells, 1880. 145p. Austin 54-845 1973 $10

PIERSON, J. L.   10,000 Chinese-Japanese Characters. 1926.
4to., 760 pages. Howes 186-1903 1974 £16

PIGAL, E. J.   Proverbes et Bons Mots Mis en Action d'Apres
les Moeurs Populaires. (Paris, 1822-24). Folio, contemporary green half calf,
gilt, extremely scarce. Quaritch 940-733 1974 £650

PIGGOTT, SOLOMON   Suicide and Its Antidotes. London, 1824.
8vo., modern half morocco, frontispiece, first edition. Schuman 37-203 1974
$85

PIGNANIOL. ANDRE   La Conquete Romaine. Paris, 1927. Rebound.
Biblo & Tannen 214-651 1974 $10

PIGNATA, GUISEPPE   The Adventures of. New York, n.d. Limited
to 520 copies of which 1 - 495 were numbered, this un-numbered copy
apparently one of the remaining 25, signed by Arthur Symons. Wilson 63-572
1974 $15

PIGNORIA, LORENZO   Le Origini di Padova. Padua, 1625. 4to.,
contemporary vellum, woodcuts, scarce, fine, orig. edition. Harper 213-112
1973 $400

PIGOT, I. M. B.   History of the City of Chester. Chester, 1815.
8vo., contemporary half calf, boards. Broadhurst 23-1512 1974 £10

PIJOAN Y SOTERAS, JOSE   History of Art. 1933. 3 vols., 8vo., orig.
cloth, coloured plates, illus., second edition. Bow Windows 66-543 1974 £24

PIJOAN Y SOTERAS, JOSE   History of Art. 1933. Crown 4to., 3 vols.,
orig. cloth, plates. Broadhurst 23-158 1974 £20

PIJOAN Y SOTERAS, JOSE   History of Art. 1933. Coloured plates, 3 vols., crown 4to., orig. cloth, fine, d.w., monochrome plates. Broadhurst 24-163 1974 £25

PIJOAN Y SOTERAS, JOSE   History of Art. 1933. 3 vols., roy. 8vo., cloth, plates, dust wrappers. Quaritch 940-796 1974 £27

PIJOAN Y SOTERAS, JOSE   Summa Artis. Madrid, 1931-45. Thick roy. 8vo., cloth, plates. Howes 184-1634 1973 £18.50

PIKE, ZEBULON MONTGOMERY   Exploratory Travels Through the Western Territories of North America. London, 1811. Leather spine & corners, marbled edges, folding map, very fine. Hood's 102-825 1974 $400

PIKE, ZEBULON MONTGOMERY   Exploratory Travels Through the Western Territories of North America...and the North-Eastern Provinces of New Spain, 1805-07. London, 1811. Fine maps, first English edition. Jenkins 61-2201 1974 $425

PIKE, ZEBULON MONTGOMERY   Exploratory Travels Through the Western Territories of North America. London, 1811. Leather spine, map, fine. Hood's 104-875 1974 $400

PIKE, ZEBULON MONTGOMERY   The Southwestern Expedition of. 1925. Dec. cloth, gilt top, frontis. portrait, map, fine copy. Dykes 22-135 1973 $10

PILAT, A.   A Handbook of Mushrooms. n.d. 8vo., cloth, plates. Wheldon 131-1458 1974 £5

PILCHER, VERONICA   The Searcher. 1929. Crown 4to., orig. cloth backed boards, limited, first edition. Howes 185-232 1974 £7.50

THE PILGRIM Children. (London, c. 1890). Full color pictures, dec. front cover, rebacked, very fine. Current BW9-127 1974 $17.50

PILGRIM Songs. Ditchling, n.d. (c. 1925). Quarter morocco, spine faded, bookplate, nice copy. Covent 51-2558 1973 £8.50

A PILGRIMAGE to Salem in 1838 by a Southern Admirer of Nathaniel Hawthorne. Salem, 1916. 8vo., printed wrappers, first edition. Goodspeed's 578-126 1974 $25

PILKINGTON, M.   A Dictionary of Painters from the Revival of the Art to the Present Period. 1810. Full contemporary calf, gilt, new edition. Marsden 39-351 1974 £10

PILKINGTON, MARY   The Asiatic Princess. 1800. First edition, with half titles, engraved frontis., 2 vols. in 1, 12mo., contemporary boards, rubbed, roan spine defective, fine internally. George's 610-593 1973 £12.50

PILKINGTON, MATTHEW   Poems on Several Occasions. London, 1731. 8vo., frontispiece, speckled calf, rebacked. Bow Windows 62-720 1974 £8.50

PILLEAU, H.   Sketches in Egypt. 1845. Folio, plates, half morocco, worn. Quaritch 940-201 1974 £65

PILLER, M.   Iter per Poseganam Sclavoniae Provinciam. Budapest, 1783. 4to., contemporary boards, plates. Wheldon 129-294 1974 £85

PILLER, M.   Iter Per Poseganam Sclavoniae Provinciam. Budapest, 1783. 4to., contemporary boards, plates, very rare. Wheldon 131-385 1974 £85

PILLING, JAMES C.   Bibliography of the Eskimo Language. Washington, 1887. Loose wrapper. Jenkins 61-96 1974 $10

PILLSBURY, HOBART   New Hampshire, Resources, Attractions, and Its People. New York, 1927. 5 vols., 4to., cloth. Saddleback 14-550 1974 $40

PILON, FREDERICK   The Deaf Lover. 1780. 8vo., cloth, first edition. Quaritch 936-182 1974 £8

PILON, FREDERICK   He Would be a Soldier. London, 1786. 8vo., modern boards, first edition. Dawsons PM 252-786 1974 £15

PILON, FREDERICK   He Would be a Soldier. 1786. 8vo., boards, first edition. Quaritch 936-183 1974 £8

PINAEUS, SEVERINUS I.   De Integritatis et Corruptionies Virinum Notis. Leyden, 1641. 5 works in 1 vol., 12mo., half calf, plates. Schuman 37-204 1974 $135

PINCHARD, MRS.   The Two Cousins, a Moral Story. 1798. 12mo., contemporary sheep, joints cracked, good internally, copperplate frontis., with half title. George's 610-594 1973 £10

PINCKARD, GEORGE   Notes On the West Indies. London, 1806. 3 vols., 8vo., half calf gilt, new labels, first edition. Traylen 79-493 1973 £120

PINCKNEY, PAULINE A.   American Figureheads and Their Carvers. New York, 1940. 4to., lst ed. Biblo & Tannen 210-183 1973 $22.50

PINDAR, PETER PSEUD.
Please turn to
WOLCOT, JOHN 1738-1819

PINDARUS   Olympia. Pythia. Nemea. Isthmia. Rome, (1515). 4to., 18th century calf, gilt, second edition. Harper 213-120 1973 $825

PINDARUS   Olympia, Pythia, Nemea, Isthmia. Ebroduni, 1624. 12mo., vellum. Schumann 499-84 1974 sFr 75

PINDARUS   Olympia, Pythia, Nemea, Isthmia. Glasguae, 1754-58. 3 vols., 32mo., full leather, very fine. Schumann 499-85 1974 sFr 620

PINEL, PHILIPPE   La Medecine Clinique. Paris, (1802). 8vo., contemporary marbled calf, first edition. Schumann 35-378 1974 $135

PINEL, PHILIPPE   A Treatise on Insanity. 1806. 8vo., half morocco, uncut, first edition. Gurney 64-178 1974 £135

PINEL, PHILIPPE   A Treatise on Insanity. Sheffield, 1806. 8vo., half morocco, uncut, first edition, plates foxed, very rare. Gurney 66-145 1974 £135

PINELLI, BARTOLOMEO   Nuova Raccolta di Cinquanta Costumi Pittoreschi. Rome, 1816. 2 vols. in 1, oblong folio, plates, old calf backed marbled boards. Smith 193-504 1973 £50

PINELLI, MAFFEI   Bibliotheca Pinelliana. London, 1789. 8vo., contemporary half calf. Dawsons PM 10-484 1974 £64

PINERO, A. W.   The Gay Lord Quex. Russell, 1900. 186p. Austin 51-730 1973 $10

PINERO, A. W.   The Weaker Sex. Baker, 1894. 133p., paper. Austin 51-731 1973 $7.50

PINK, M. ALDERTON   A Realist Looks at Democracy. 1930. First edition. Covent 55-872 1974 £7.50

PINKERTON, ALLAN   The Detective and the Somnambulist. Chicago, 1875. First U. S. edition, illus., orig. dec. cloth gilt, covers little marked, bookseller's stamp, nice copy, illus. ads at end. Covent 51-540 1973 £21

PINKERTON, ALLAN   The Gypsies and the Detectives. New York, 1882. Plates, dec. cloth gilt. Covent 55-589 1974 £21

PINKERTON, JOHN   The History of Scotland from the Accession of the House of Stuart. 1797. 2 vols., 4to., buckram. Quaritch 939-671 1974 £10

PINKERTON, JOHN   Lives of the Scottish Saints. 1889. 2 vols., roy. 8vo., orig. buckram, labels, scarce, limited. Howes 185-1562 1974 £12.50

PINKERTON, JOHN   Vitae Antiquae Sanctorum. London, 1789. 8vo., full speckled calf, gilt, label, rare. Emerald 50-781 1974 £35

PINKERTON, K.   Wilderness Wife. New York, 1939. Profusely illus. Hood's 102-71 1974 $10

PINKERTON, THOMAS A.   The Last Master of Carnandro. n.d. Orig. dec. cloth. Covent 55-1192 1974 £10.50

PINKERTON, WILLIAM A.   "Forgery". N. P., 1905. Orig. printed wrappers, portraits. Wilson 63-39 1974 $10

PINNEY, JOEL   An Exposure of the Causes of the Present Deteriorated Condition of Health. 1830. Orig. boards. Covent 55-1324 1974 £25

PINNEY, N. A.   History of the 104th Regiment Ohio Volunteer Infantry from 1862 to 1865. Akron, 1886. Wrappers, little dust soiled. Hayman 59-116 1974 $35

PINOT, VIRGILE   La Chine et la Formation de l'Esprit Philosophique en France. Paris, 1932. Roy. 8vo., orig. wrappers, scarce. Howes 185-1954 1974 £5.50

PINTO, SERPA   How I Crossed Africa. London, 1881. lst ed., illus. Biblo & Tannen 213-699 1973 $35

PINTO, V. DE SOLA   Sir Charles Sedley. 1927. Plates, orig. edition. Howes 186-402 1974 £5.50

PINZA, EZIO   Ezio Pinza. Rinehart, 1946. 307p., illus. Austin 62-504 1974 $8.50

A PIONEER Quaker Doctor Comes to San Francisco. 1931. Illus. Dawson's 424-66 1974 $12.50

PIORRY, PIERRE ADOLPHE   De la Percussion Mediate. Paris, 1828. 8vo., orig. grey printed wrappers, uncut, fine, first edition. Dawsons PM 249-405 1974 £95

PIOTROWSKA, IRENA   The Art of Poland. New York, 1947. 4to., illus. Biblo & Tannen 214-427 1974 $25

PIOZZI, HESTER LYNCH   Anecodotes of the Late Samuel Johnson. London, 1786. 8vo., contemporary marbled boards, first edition. Dawsons PM 252-579 1974 £80

PIOZZI, HESTER LYNCH   British Synonymy. 1794. 8vo., 2 vols., orig. boards, uncut, first edition. Quaritch 936-184 1974 £30

PIOZZI, HESTER LYNCH   British Synonymy. London, 1794. 2 vols., contemporary tree calf, first edition. Dawsons PM 252-580 1974 £70

PIOZZI, HESTER LYNCH   550 Signed Autograph Letters to the Williams Family of Bodylwddan. 1796-1821. 4to., signed, half calf gilt. Dawsons PM 252-583 1974 £32,000

PIOZZI, HESTER LYNCH   The Florence Miscellany. Florence, 1785. 8vo., contemporary tree calf gilt, fine, first edition. Dawsons PM 252-581 1974 £250

PIOZZI, HESTER LYNCH   The Intimate Letters. London, 1914. 8vo., plates, orig. cloth backed boards. Dawsons PM 252-582 1974 £6

PIOZZI, HESTER LYNCH THRALE   Letters to . . . Johnson Please turn to JOHNSON, SAMUEL

PIOZZI, HESTER LYNCH   Observations and Reflections. London, 1789. 2 vols. in 1, contemporary half sheep, first edition. Dawsons PM 252-584 1974 £80

PIOZZI, HESTER LYNCH   Observations and Reflections made in the Course of a Journey through France, Italy, and Germany. 1789. 8vo., 2 vols., contemporary tree calf, first edition. Quaritch 936-185 1974 £70

PIPER, CHARLES V.   Flora of the State of Washington. Washington, 1906. Wrapper. Jenkins 61-2578 1974 $15

PIRANDELLO, LUIGI   Each In His Own Way. Dutton, 1923. Austin 51-732 1973 $10

PIRANDELLO, LUIGI   Shoot. Dutton, 1926. Austin 51-733 1973 $12.50

PIRANESI, G. B.   Antichita Romane. Rome, 1756. 4 vols., imp. folio, plates, half crimson morocco gilt, fine. Quaritch 940-542 1974 £3,000

PIRKIS, C. L.   The Experiences of Loveday Brooke. 1894. 8vo., orig. cloth, frontispiece, first edition. Rota 190-338 1974 £20

PIRRIE, WILLIAM   Acupressure. London, 1867. 8vo., orig. cloth, first edition. Schumann 35-380 1974 $145

PISANELLI, BALDASSARE   Trattato della Natura de Cibi et del Bere. Venice, 1587. 4to., vellum. Traylen 79-260 1973 £45

PISANELLI, BALDASSARE   Trattato della Natura de' Cibi et del Bere. Venice, 1629. 16mo., modern boards. Thomas 32-339 1974 £18

PISANI, M. F.   Traite Elementaire de Mineralogie. Paris, 1883. 8vo., red quarter calf, second edition. Dawsons PM 245-604 1974 £10

PISO, G.   Gulielmi Pisonis. 1658. Folio, orig. cloth, illus., first edition. Bow Windows 64-211 1974 £370

PISTORIUS, WILHELM FRIEDRICH VON   Lebens-Beschreibung Herrn Goetzens von Berlichingen. Nuremberg, 1775. Engraved folding frontis., small 8vo., contemporary vellum. Schumann 499-86 1974 sFr 775

PITARO, A.   La Science de la Setifere. Perpignan, 1828. 8vo., plates, contemporary half calf, gilt. Quaritch 940-769 1974 £30

PITCAIRN, ARCHIBALD   Dissertationes Medicae. Rotterdam, 1701. 4to., half calf, first edition. Schumann 35-381 1974 $145

PITCAIRN, ARCHIBALD   The Whole Works. London, 1727. 8vo., contemporary panelled calf, rebacked. Gurney 66-146 1974 £42

PITISCUS, BARTHOLOMEW   Trigonometry. London, (c., 1634). Small 4to., modern polished calf. Dawsons PM 245-605 1974 £175

PITKIN, WALTER B.   Must We Fight Japan. Century, 1921. Austin 62-505 1974 $10

PITMAN, C. R. S.   A Game Warden Takes Stock. 1942. 8vo., cloth, illus. Wheldon 131-386 1974 £10

PITMAN, JOSEPH S.   Report on the Trial of Thomas Wilson Dorr, for Treason Against the State of Rhode Island... Boston, 1844. First edition, 8vo., orig. stitching, some soiling to covers, top right corner of back cover missing. Current BW9-426 1974 $25

PITMAN, ROBERT   A Question of Obscenity. Scorpion, 1960. Austin 51-734 1973 $8.50

PITRAT, JOHN CLAUDIUS   Paul and Julia. 1855. 319p., illus. Austin 62-506 1974 $17.50

PITT, CHRISTOPHER   Vida's Art of Poetry. London, 1725. 12mo., modern cloth, good copy, first edition. Ximenes 37-174 1974 $45

PITT, ROBERT   The Craft and Frauds of Physick Expos'd. London, 1703. Small 8vo., nineteenth century half morocco. Schumann 35-382 1974 $135

PITT, WILLIAM, 1ST EARL OF CHATHAM 1708-1778   Correspondence. 1838-40. 8vo., 4 vols., half calf, gilt. Quaritch 936-518 1974 £32

PITTARD, EUGENE   Race and History. New York, 1926. Biblo & Tannen 214-581 1974 $15

PITTENGER, WILLIAM   Daring and Suffering. New York, 1887. Cloth. Hayman 57-100 1974 $12.50

PITTON DE TOURNEFORT, JOSEPH
Please turn to
TOURNEFORT, JOSEPH PITTON DE

PITTS, JOHN   The Character of a Primitive Bishop. 1714. 8vo., contemporary sheep, second edition. Hill 126-212 1974 £8.50

PITTS, JOSEPH   A True and Faithful Account of the Religion and Manners of the Mohammetans. Exon, 1704. 8vo., contemporary calf, rebacked. Traylen 79-533 1973 £45

PITTSBURGH. Pittsburgh, c. 1903. Wrappers, photographs. Jenkins 61-2166 1974 $12.50

PITTSBURGH and Alleghany. New York, 1882. Foldout, boards, repaired, 12mo. Jenkins 61-2167 1974 $18.50

PITTSBURGH and Allegheny. Brooklyn, 1898. Wrappers, illus. Jenkins 61-2168 1974 $10

PIUS II, POPE   Commentariorum . . . de Concilio Basileae Celebrato Libri Duo. (Basel, c. 1525). Folio, modern boards, very fine, very rare first edition. Schafer 8-137 1973 sFr. 3,200

PIUS II, POPE   Commentariorum . . . de Concilio Basileae Celebrato Libri duo, Olim Quidem Scripti. (Basel, c. 1525). Folio, modern boards, very fine, contemporary manuscript annotations, very rare first edition. Schafer 10-107 1974 sFr 3,200

PLA, JOSE   Sixe Sonatas for Two German Flutes or Two Violins and a Bass. Welcker, (c. 1770). 3 parts, small folio, disbound, marbled boards folder, first edition. Quaritch 940-821 1974 £45

A PLAIN Plantain. Ditchling, 1922. Small 8vo., canvas boards. Traylen 79-215 1973 £6

PLAISTED, BARTHOLOMEW   A Journal from Calcutta in Bengal, by Sea to Busserah; to which is added, Directions by Capt. Eliot Eliot, for Passing Over the Little Desert from Busserah. London, 1757. 12mo., contemporary calf, rebacked, first edition. Ximenes 36-158 1974 $125

PLANCHE, JAMES ROBINSON   Beauty and the Beast. Taylor, 1841. Austin 51-735 1973 $7.50

PLANCHE, JAMES ROBINSON   Captain of the Watch. Taylor, 1841. 33p. Austin 51-736 1973 $6.50

PLANCHE, JAMES ROBINSON   A Cyclopaedia of Costume. 1876-79. 2 vols., thick 4to., plates, contemporary vellum gilt. Smith 193-76 1973 £35

PLANCHE, JAMES ROBINSON   High, Low Jack and the Game. French, 1838. Austin 51-737 1973 $6.50

PLANCHE, JAMES ROBINSON   History of British Costume. 1881. Small 8vo., illus., cloth, third edition. Quaritch 940-734 1974 £5

PLANCHE, JAMES ROBINSON   The Invisible Prince. Taylor, 1846. 35p. Austin 51-738 1973 $7.50

PLANCHE, JAMES ROBINSON   The Jacobite. Taylor, 1847. 35p. Austin 51-739 1973 $7.50

PLANCHE, JAMES ROBINSON   King Charming. French, n.d. Austin 51-740 1973 $8.50

PLANCHE, JAMES ROBINSON   The Loan of a Lover. Taylor. Austin 51-741 1973 $6.50

PLANCHE, JAMES ROBINSON   The Pride of the Market. Taylor, 1847. Austin 51-742 1973 $8.50

PLANCHE, JAMES ROBINSON   Promotion. French, n.d. Austin 51-743 1973 $6.50

PLANCHE, JAMES ROBINSON   Secret Service. Taylor, n.d. Austin 51-744 1973 $6.50

PLANCHON, L.   Influence de Divers Milieux Chimiques. 1900. Roy 8vo., plates. Wheldon 129-1319 1974 £5

PLANCK, MAX   Acht Vorlesungen uber Theoretische Physik. Leipzig, 1910. 8vo., orig. green cloth, gilt, fine, first edition. Dawsons PM 245-606 1974 £25

PLANCK, MAX   Das Wesen des Lichts. Berlin, 1920. 8vo., orig. wrappers, first edition. Gurney 64-180 1974 £9.50

PLANCK, MAX   Einfhuring in die Mechanik Deformierbarer Korper. Leipzig, 1919. 8vo., orig. printed grey boards, first edition. Dawsons PM 245-607 1974 £24

PLANCK, MAX   Einfuhrung in die Mechanik Deformierbarer Korper. Leipzig, 1919. 8vo., orig. half cloth, pictured boards, illus., first edition. Schuman 37-205 1974 $85

PLANCK, MAX   Treatise on Thermodynamics. 1903. 8vo., orig. cloth, slight spotting, first English edition. Bow Windows 66-544 1974 £16

PLANTA, R. VON   Grammatik der Oskischumbrischen Dialekte. 1897. Vol. 2 only, new buckram. Allen 213-833 1973 $15

PLANTAGENET Roll of the Blood Royal. London, 1908. 4to., inscription, orig. cloth. Bow Windows 62-721 1974 £12.50

PLANTE, GASTON   The Storage of Electrical Energy. London, 1887. 8vo., orig. blue cloth, faded, first English edition. Dawsons PM 245-608 1974 £8.50

PLANTIN, FONDERIE TYPOGRAPHIQUE, S. A.   Caractéres de Texte Modernes et Classiques, Ornements, Filets en Cuivre, Initiales et Vignettes. Brussels, n.d. (1937). 4to., publisher's printed cloth. Kraus B8-368 1974 $45

PLASKITT, F. J. W.   Microscopic Fresh Water Life. 1926. 8vo., cloth, illus. Wheldon 129-226 1974 £3.50

PLATE, L.   Fauna et Anatomica Ceylonica. Jena, 1922-31. 4 vols., roy. 8vo., plates, sewed. Wheldon 131-387 1974 £45

PLATINA, B.
Please turn to
PLATINA, BARTOLOMEO DE SACCHI

PLATINA, BARTOLOMEO DE'SACCHI   Les Genealogies Faitz et Gestes des Sainctz. Paris, 1519. Folio, full white pigskin, gilt, slipcase. L. Goldschmidt 42-100 1974 $550

PLATO   Chalcidii Luculenta Timaei Platonis Traductio. Paris, 1520. Small folio, modern half sprinkled calf, marbled boards, diagrams. Thomas 32-252 1974 £50

PLATO   Dialogi Sec. Thrasylli Tetralogias Dispositi. 1890-93. 6 vols. Allen 213-1080 1973 $15

PLATO   Hipparchus. Paris, 1553. 4to., early 17th century Italian brown morocco. Thomas 28-141 1972 £60

PLATO   Lysis. Florence, 1551. 8vo., contemporary limp vellum, rare, fine, first separate edition. Harper 213-121 1973 $950

PLATO   Opera Omnia. 1513. 2 parts in 1 vol., small folio, early 19th century English blind-tooled russia, rebacked, first edition in Greek. Thomas 30-22 1973 £900

PLATO   Opera Quae Feruntur Omnia. Turin, 1839. Thick 4to., 3/4 vellum and cl. Jacobs 24-172 1974 $25

PLATO   Operum a Marsilio Ficino Tralatorum. Lyon, 1550. 5 vols., 16mo., 18th century calf gilt, morocco labels, worn. Thomas 28-302 1972 £12

PLATO   Works. 1772. 2 vols., new buckram, illus., rubber stamp, third edition. Allen 213-834 1973 $15

PLATT, HUGH   A Discoverie of Certaine English Wants. London, 1595. 4to., half morocco, fine, first edition. Dawsons PM 247-225 1974 £550

PLATT, HUGH JEWEL   The Jewel House of Art and Nature. London, 1653. 4to., contemporary calf, rebacked, second edition, good copy. Gurney 66-147 1974 £125

PLATT, HUGH JEWEL   The Jewel House of Art and Nature. London, 1653. 4to., calf-backed boards, woodcuts, second edition. Schumann 35-384 1974 $265

PLATT, RUTHERFORD   Our Flowering World. New York, 1947. Biblo & Tannen 213-853 1973 $12.50

PLATTER, FELIX   Observationum in Hominis Affectibus Plerisque, Corpori & Animo, Functionum Laesione. Basle, 1614. 8vo., contemporary vellum over thin boards, first edition, good copy. Schafer 10-135 1974 sFr 750

PLATTNER, CARL FRIEDRICH   Die Probirkunst mit dem Lothrohre. Leipzig, 1907. 8vo., calf-backed boards, illus. Schuman 37-206 1974 $75

PLAUTUS, TITUS MACCIUS   Comedies of Plautus. 1852. 2 vols. Austin 51-745 1973 $12.50

PLAUTUS, TITUS MACCIUS   Comoediae Superstites Viginti. 1779-80. 2 vols. in 4. Allen 213-857 1973 $12.50

PLAUTUS, TITIUS MACCIUS   Comoediae XX. 1522. Vellum, stains. Thomas 30-60 1973 £40

PLAUTUS, TITIUS MACCIUS   Comoediae XX. Venice, 1522. Vellum, morocco label, slightly rubbed, erasure of names has caused stain on first ten leaves affecting headlines but not text. Thomas 32-213 1974 £40

PLAUTUS, TITIUS MACCIUS   Comoediae XX. 1522. 18th century vellum gilt, morocco labels. Thomas 30-59 1973 £45

PLAW, JOHN   Ferme Ornee. 1803. 4to., plates, half leather, worn, uncut, new edition. Quaritch 940-543 1974 £55

PLAYFAIR, J.   Explication de Playfair sur la Theorie. Paris and London, 1815. 8vo., plates. Wheldon 129-855 1974 £40

PLAYFAIR, J.   Explication de Playfair sur la Theorie de la Terre par Hutton. Paris & London, 1815. 2 parts in 1 vol., 8vo., cloth, plates. Wheldon 131-1067 1974 £40

PLAYFELLOWS. London, (c. 1910). Square 8vo., softly colored illus., pictorial front cover, interior very good. Current BW9-128 1974 $18

PLAYS For Our American Holidays. Dodd, Mead, 1928. Austin 51-826 1973 $8.50

PLEASANTS, ADELINA   History of Orange County, California. Los Angeles, 1931. 3 vols., 8vo., cloth. Saddleback 14-235 1974 $100

PLEASONTON, AUGUSTUS J.   The Influence of the Blue Ray of the Sunlight and of the Sky. Philadelphia, 1876. Biblo & Tannen 210-983 1973 $15

PLEASONTON, AUGUSTUS J.   The Influence of the Blue Ray of the Sunlight and of the Blue Colour of the Sky, In Developing Animal and Vegetable Life. Philadelphia, 1876. Blue gilt cloth, frontis. Butterfield 10-455 1974 $35

PLEMPIUS, VOPISCUS FORTUNATUS   De Fundamentis Medicinae Libri Sex. 1638. 4to., contemporary stiff vellum, first edition. Dawsons PM 249-406 1974 £265

PLENK, JOSEPH JACOB   Selectus Materiae Chirurgicae. Vienna, 1775. 8vo., orig. wrappers, uncut, first edition. Traylen 79-261 1973 £18

PLENCK, JOSEPH JACOB, RITTER VON
Please turn to
PLENK, JOSEPH JACOB

PLESKE, T.   Birds of the Eurasian Tundra. Boston, 1928. 4to., new cloth. Wheldon 131-684 1974 £40

THE PLIGHT of the Jew. n.d., ca. 1945. Austin 62-622 1974 $12.50

PLIMSOLL, SAMUEL   Our Seamen. 1873. 4to., orig. cloth, first edition. Broadhurst 23-1694 1974 £30

PLINIUS CAECILIUS SECUNDUS, CAIUS   Epistolarum Libri X. 1518. 18th century russia, gilt, rubbed. Thomas 30-39 1973 £50

PLINIUS CAECILIUS SECUNDUS, C.   The Letters of Pliny the Younger. London, 1751. 2 vols., 4to., full calf. Emerald 50-740 1974 £18

PLINIUS SECUNDUS, GAIUS   Epistolarum Libri X. Paris, 1533. Folio, old red brown morocco, stained in upper corner. Thomas 32-255 1974 £35

PLINIUS SECUNDUS, GAIUS   Historia Naturalis. (Venice, 1472). Folio, 18th century mottled calf, gilt, morocco labels, fine, third edition. Dawsons PM 250-64 1974 £4500

PLINIUS SECUNDUS, GAIUS   Historia Naturale. Venice, 1516. Small folio, old limp vellum. Thomas 30-144 1973 £75

PLINIUS SECUNDUS, GAIUS   De Naturalis Historie Libri XXVII. Venice, 1525. Woodcut borders and maps, small folio, vellum backed boards. Thomas 32-254 1974 £65

PLINIUS SECUNDUS, GAIUS   Naturalis Historiae. 1536-35-35. 3 vols., old calf, rubbed, worn, bookplates. Thomas 30-74 1973 £35

PLINIUS SECUNDUS, GAIUS   Pliny, Caii Plinii Historiae Naturalis Libri XXXVII. Paris, 1723. 2 vols., folio, contemporary calf, rebacked, plates. Wheldon 131-172 1974 £50

PLINY THE ELDER
Please turn to
PLINIUS SECUNDUS, GAIUS

PLINY THE YOUNGER
Please turn to
PLINIUS CAECILIUS SECUNDUS, GAIUS

PLOMER, HENRY R.   A Dictionary of the Printers and Booksellers Who Were at Work in England, Scotland and Ireland from 1726-75. London, 1932. F'scap 4to., orig. boards, linen back, fine. Forster 98-80 1974 £15

PLOMER, HENRY R.   A Short History of English Printing. London, 1900. 4to., orig. buckram gilt, first edition. Dawsons PM 10-487 1974 £16

PLOMER, WILLIAM   The Fivefold Screen. 1932. Roy. 8vo., foxing, limited, first edition. Howes 185-381 1974 £15

PLOMER, WILLIAM   The Fivefold Screen. London, 1932. 4to.,
orig. cloth, first edition. Dawsons PM 252-787 1974 £22

PLOMER, WILLIAM   I Speak of Africa. 1927. Faded, frayed dust
wrapper. Covent 55-1196 1974 £35

PLOMER, WILLIAM   Sado. 1931. 8vo., orig. cloth, first edition.
Rota 189-700 1974 £5

PLOMER, WILLIAM   Sado. 1931. Fine, dust wrapper, scarce.
Covent 55-1197 1974 £25

PLOOS VAN AMSTEL, CORNELIS   Collections d'Imitations de Dessins. 1821.
2 vols., atlas folio, plates, contemporary diced calf, gilt, rebacked, leather
labels, rubbed, limited. Quaritch 940-202 1974 £3,000

PLOOS VAN AMSTEL, CORNELIS   Epreuves de Plusieurs Sortes de Caracteres.
Amsterdam, (1770?). 8vo., orig. printed boards, very fine. Harper 213-122
1973 $450

PLOT, ROBERT   The Natural History of Oxfordshire. Oxford,
1705. Folio, contemporary panelled calf, plates. Quaritch 939-522 1974 £150

PLOT, ROBERT   The Natural History of Stafford-shire. Oxford,
1686. Folio, green morocco gilt, plates, worn. Traylen 79-387 1973 £125

PLOT, ROBERT   The Natural History of Stafford-shire. Oxford,
1686. Folio, contemporary calf, plates. Quaritch 939-550 1974 £175

PLOT, ROBERT   De Origine Fontium. Oxford, 1685. 8vo., contemporary calf, second edition. Dawsons PM 245-610 1974 £40

PLOTINUS   The Philosophy of the Gifford Lectures at St.
Andrews, 1917-1918. London, 1923. 2 vols., orig. cloth, second edition.
Smith 194-893 1974 £6

PLOTINUS   Plotin. Paris, 1924-26. 3 vols., 1/2 lea.,
bdgs. rubbed. Biblo & Tannen 213-476 1973 $52.50

PLOTINUS   Select Works. London, 1817. Full contemporary
calf, inscribed copy from author. Jacobs 24-174 1974 $20

PLOUGHE, SHERIDAN   History of Reno County, Kansas. Indianapolis,
1917. 4to., cloth. Saddleback 14-430 1974 $35

PLOW, CARL   Dania. San Francisco, 1933. 185p., illus.
Austin 62-507 1974 $37.50

PLOWDEN, E.   An Historical Review of Ireland. 1803.
2 vols. in 3, 4to., half calf, foxing. Quaritch 939-628 1974 £20

PLOWMAN, MAX   An Introduction to the Study of Blake. 1927.
Illus. Bow Windows 66-57 1974 £5

PLOWRIGHT, C. B.   A Monograph of the British Uredineae and
Ustilagineae. 1889. 8vo., cloth, plates, text-figures. Wheldon 128-1409
1973 £5

PLOWRIGHT, C. B.   A Monograph of the British Uredineae and Ustilagineae. 1889. 8vo., cloth, plates. Wheldon 130-1334 1974 £5

PLUCHE, NOEL ANTOINE   Spectacle de la Nature. 1736-37. 3 vols.,
8vo., contemporary calf, plates, second & third editions. Wheldon 131-174
1974 £20

PLUCHE, NOEL ANTOINE   La Spectacle de la Nature. Utrecht and Paris,
1733-39. 12mo., 4 vols., half calf. Wheldon 129-95 1974 £12

PLUCHE, NOEL ANTOINE   Le Spectacle de la Nature, ou Entretiens sur
les Particularites de l'Histoire Naturelle. Utrecht & Paris, 1733-39. 4 vols.,
12mo., half calf, worn, plates. Wheldon 131-173 1974 £20

PLUCHE, NOEL ANTOINE   Spectacle de la Nature. 1736-37. 8vo., 3
vols., contemporary calf. Wheldon 129-94 1974 £20

PLUES, M.   Rambles in Search of Flowerless Plants. 1865.
Roy. 8vo., cloth, plates, second edition. Wheldon 131-1459 1974 £5

PLUKENET, L.   Index Linnaeanus in Leonhardi Plukenetii Opera
Botanica. Hamburg, 1779. 4to., modern boards. Wheldon 131-1183 1974
£7.50

PLUKENET, L.   Opera Omnia Botanica in Sex Tomos Divisa.
1720, (1691-1705). Vols. 1-3 in 2 vols., 4to., contemporary calf, plates.
Wheldon 131-1182 1974 £65

PLUMARD DE DANGEUL   Remarques sur les Avantages et les
Desavantages de la France et de la Grande-Bretagne. 1754. 12mo., rubbed,
morocco label, contemporary sheep, waterstained. Bow Windows 66-545 1974
£36

PLUMIER, C.   Description des Plantes de l'Amerique. Paris,
1693. Folio, modern full brown morocco, uncut, plates, fine, rare. Wheldon
130-1196 1974 £500

PLUMIER, C.   Description des Plantes de l'Amerique. Paris,
1693. Folio, modern full brown morocco, uncut, engraved plates, fine large
copy, very rare. Wheldon 128-1296 1973 £500

PLUMPTRE, E. H.   The Life of Thomas Ken. London, 1889.
2 vols., 8vo., illus., foxing, orig. cloth. Bow Windows 62-532 1974 £8.50

PLUNKET, WILLIAM C.   A Book for Tourists in Ireland. London, 1863.
8vo., new cloth boards. Emerald 50-783 1974 £5

PLUNKETT, JOS. MARY   The Poems of J. Mary Plunkett. Dublin, 1916.
1st ed. Biblo & Tannen 214-765 1974 $10

PLUQUET, L'ABBE   Memoires Pour Servir a l'Histoire des
Egaremens de l'Esprit Humain par Rapport a la Religion Chretienne. Paris, 1762.
2 vols. Rittenhouse 46-540 1974 $35

PLUTARCHUS   A Consolatorie Letter or Discourse. Boston and
New York, 1905. Rubbed. Ballinger 1-36 1974 $15

PLUTARCHUS   Lives of the Noble Grecians and Romans.
Shakespeare Head Press, 1928. 8 vols., med. 8vo., top edges gilt, others uncut,
mint, dust wrappers, limited to 500 copies, orig. cloth. Broadhurst 24-1041 1974
£85

PLUTARCHUS   The Lives of the Noble Grecians and Romanes.
Oxford, 1928. 8 vols., 8vo., orig. black cloth, limited edition. Dawsons PM
252-788 1974 £70

PLUTARCHUS   Plutarch's Lives of the Noble Grecians and Romans.
1928. 8vo., 8 vols., orig. cloth, uncut, limited. Broadhurst 23-1083 1974 £85

PLUTARCHUS   The Lives of the Noble Grecians and Romanes.
Boston, 1928. 8 vols., orig. cloth backed boards, limited to 500 copies. Jacobs
24-121 1974 $125

PLUTARCHUS   The Lives of the Noble Grecians and Romanes.
1929-30. 5 vols., 4to., buckram, uncut, limited. Howes 186-339 1974 £65

PLUTARCHUS   Quae Extant Opera. Geneva, 1572. Red
straight grain morocco, gilt, bookplate. Thomas 28-304 1972 £12

PLUTARCHUS   Sapientissimi Plutarchi Paralellum Vitae
Romanorum et Graecorum. Florence, 1517. First edition, in Greek, folio, 16th
century English calf over wooden boards, well rebacked, some marginal stains.
Thomas 32-256 1974 £250

PLUTARCHUS   Sapientissimi Plutarchi Paralellum Vitae
Romanorum et Graecorum. Florence, 1517. First edition in Greek, folio, vellum,
morocco labels, uncut, unpressed, tall copy, some untrimmed leaves, lacks title.
Thomas 32-257 1974 £100

PLUTARCHUS　　　　　Uber Jsis und Osiris.　Berlin, 1850.　Binding worn.　Biblo & Tannen 213-477 1973 $15

PLUTARCHUS　　　　　Vite Degli Huomini Greci et Romani.　Venetia, 1607.　4to., vellum.　Schumann 499-87 1974 sFr 100

POCAHONTAS.　New York, c. 1875.　Full color illus., 8vo., pictorial front wrapper, fine, rebacked.　Current BW9-129 1974 $22.50

POCOCK, NICHOLAS　　　　Records of the Reformation.　1880.　2 vols., thick 8vo., orig. cloth, damp-stained, scarce.　Howes 186-1137 1974 £18

POCOCK, R.　　　　　A Man in the Open.　Indianapolis, 1912. Hood's 102-537 1974 $10

POCOCK, R. I.　　　　　The Carboniferous Arachnida.　1911.　4to., plates.　Wheldon 131-1068 1974 £5

POE, EDGAR ALLAN　　　　The Bells.　Philadelphia, 1881.　Square 8vo., orig. dec. cloth, illus.　Covent 55-1198 1974 £5.25

POE, EDGAR ALLAN　　　　Gedichte.　Munchen & Leipzig, 1909.　One of 1000 numbered copies, quarter vellum gilt, boards rubbed at corners, nice copy.　Covent 51-2529 1973 £10.50

POE, EDGAR ALLAN　　　　Letters Till Now Unpublished.　Philadelphia, 1925.　Roy 8vo., cloth-backed boards, English first edition.　Covent 56-1037 1974 £22.50

POE, EDGAR ALLEN　　　　The Literate.　New York, 1850.　1st ed., hinges split.　Biblo & Tannen 210-790 1973 $18.50

POE, EDGAR ALLAN　　　　The Murders in the Rue Morgue.　Philadelphia, (1895).　Tall folio, cloth covers dusty and spotted, printed paper label.　Butterfield 10-456 1974 $20

POE, EDGAR ALLAN　　　　Poems.　New York, 1872.　Portrait, first edition.　Covent 55-1199 1974 £7.50

POE, EDGAR ALLAN　　　　Poems of.　New York, 1929.　Numbered, limited edition.　Rinsland 58-77A 1974 $85

POE, EDGAR ALLAN　　　　Poetical Works.　n.d.　Orig. dec. cloth, gilt, plates, English first edition.　Covent 56-1039 1974 £10

POE, EDGAR ALLAN　　　　Poetical Works.　n.d.　Full contemporary morocco, rebacked, English first edition.　Covent 56-1038 1974 £20

POE, EDGAR ALLAN　　　　Selected Tales of Mystery.　1909.　Small 4to., orig. dec. cloth gilt, English first edition.　Covent 56-716 1974 £17.50

POE, EDGAR ALLAN　　　　Some Edgar Allan Poe Letters.　St. Louis, 1915.　Small 4to., boards, first edition.　Goodspeed's 578-285 1974 $10

POE, EDGAR ALLAN　　　　Tales and Sketches.　1852.　12mo., contemporary half calf, bookplate, English first edition.　Covent 56-1995 1974 £21

POE, EDGAR ALLAN　　　　Tales of Mystery and Imagination.　1935. 4to., orig. full blue leather, gilt, plates.　Howes 185-392 1974 £32

POE, EDGAR ALLAN　　　　Tales of Mystery and Imagination.　London, 1935.　No. 300 of limited edtion of 460 copies, signed, box loosening but not split, book is pristine, light glassine wrapper, illus. by Arthur Rackham.　Ross 87-472 1974 $250

POE, EDGAR ALLAN　　　　The Works of.　London, (n.d.).　8vo., full green claf, plates, collected edition.　Dawsons PM 252-789 1974 £10

POE, EDGAR ALLAN　　　　The Complete Works.　New York, 1902.　Half vellum, 10 vols., plates, English first edition.　Covent 56-1036 1974 £47.50

POE, EDGAR ALLAN　　　　The Works of.　New York & Pittsburg, 1903. 10 vols., orig. cloth, paper labels, one of 1000 numbered sets, fine set. MacManus 224-359 1974 $100

POE, JOHN W.　　　　　The Death of Billy the Kid.　Boston, 1933. Cloth, dust jacket, fine, scarce.　Jenkins 61-217 1974 $22.50

POEMS for Spain.　1939.　Faded spine, first edition.　Covent 55-51 1974 £7.50

POEMS on Various Subjects; to which are added, Latin Essays.　London, 1772. 4to., old half calf, first edition, very scarce, ex-library.　Ximenes 36-164 1974 $40

POETICA Erotica.　New York, 1921.　2 vols., orig. 1/2 vel. bds., ltd. to 1550 sets.　Jacobs 24-122 1974 $15

POETRY: A Magazine of Verse.　1937.　Wrappers, fine.　Covent 55-137 1974 £35

THE POETRY Bookshop.　London, 1915-22.　5 vols., 8vo., inscription, orig. boards, foxing, worn, faded.　Bow Windows 62-365 1974 £21

POETRY of the College Magazine.　Windsor, 1819.　8vo., orig. drab boards, first edition, very scarce.　Ximenes 36-159 1974 $100

POETS and Poetry of Kansas.　Chicago, 1894.　8vo., orig. bindings.　Butterfield 8-180 1974 $10

POET'S CLUB　　　　　The Third Book of.　1913.　Boards, spine slightly faded, very good copy, first edition.　Covent 51-103 1973 £6.30

POGANY, WILLY　　　　The Kasidah of Haji Abdu El-Yezdi.　Philadelphia, 1931.　4to., pictorial cloth, English first edition.　Covent 56-708 1974 £27.50

POGANY, WILLY　　　　Parsifal.　1912.　4to., orig. suede calf gilt, illus., plates, frayed, first edition.　Howes 186-366 1974 £10

POGGIO　　　　　The Facetiae of Poggio and other Medieval Story-Tellers.　London, n.d.　Biblo & Tannen 213-478 1973 $6.50

POINCARE, JULES HENRI　　　Electricite et Optique.　Paris, 1890.　8vo., blue cloth, first edition.　Dawsons PM 245-611 1974 £8

POINCARE, JULES HENRI　　　Elektricitat und Optik.　1892.　8vo., orig. printed wrappers, unopened, uncut.　Zeitlin 235-177 1974 $45

POINSETT, J. R.　　　　Hostile Disposition Upon the Part of the Indians on the Western Frontier.　Washington, 1838.　Jenkins 61-2202 1974 $22.50

POINTER, JOHN　　　　Miscellanea In Usum Juventutis Academicae. 1718.　New buckram, rubber stamp.　Allen 213-879 1973 $12.50

POLAIN, M. LOUIS　　　　Catalogue des Livres Imprimes au Quinzieme Siecle des Bibliotheques de Belgique.　Brussels, 1932.　4 vols., large 8vo., illus., cloth.　Dawsons PM 10-299 1974 £120

POLE, REGINALD　　　　Ad Henricu Octauum Britanniae Regem, Pro Ecclesiasticae Unitatis Defensione, Libri Quatuor.　Rome, (1536).　First edition, lacks second blank leaf, three names cut from blank portions of title, very skifully repaired, very fine copy, folio, 19th century old style blind tooled dark brown morocco, fully panelled sides, book label of Henry Huth, etched bookplate of O. F. Grazebrook of Stourton Castle.　Thomas 32-127 1974 £450

POLE, REGINALD　　　　Liber de Concilio.　Venice, 1562.　2 vols. in 1, small 8vo., 19th century calf, rubbed.　Thomas 30-145 1973 £45

POLE, THOMAS　　　　The Anatomical Instructor.　London, 1790.　8vo., contemporary boards, plates, first edition.　Schumann 35-385 1974 $135

POLE, THOMAS　　　　The Anatomical Instructor.　London, 1790. 8vo., contemporary calf, plates, first edition.　Schuman 37-207 1974 $95

POLEHAMPTON, E.　　　　The Gallery of Nature and Art.　1819.　6 vols., 8vo., contemporary half calf, worn, plates, second edition.　Wheldon 131-175 1974 £20

POLEY, A. F. E.　　　　St Paul's Cathedral.　1927.　Roy. folio, plates, half morocco, rubbed.　Quaritch 939-465 1974 £10

POLHILL, EDWARD   Speculum Theologiae in Christo.   1678.   Small 4to., 19th century calf, rebacked.   Howes 185-1571 1974 £30

POLITIANUS, ANGELUS
Please turn to
POLIZIANO, ANGELO

POLITICAL History of England.   1905-10.   12 vols., 8vo., orig. cloth, dust soiling, library stamp.   Bow Windows 66-546 1974 £35

THE POLITICAL History of England.   1906-10.   8vo., 12 vols., full contemporary polished calf, gilt, labels.   Broadhurst 23-1260 1974 £70

THE POLITICAL History of England.   1906-10.   12 vols., red cloth binding. Broadhurst 23-1261 1974 £35

POLITZER, ADAM   The Membrana Tympani in Health and Disease. New York, 1869.   Color illus.   Rittenhouse 46-541 1974 $20

POLIZIANO, ANGELO   Opera.   1498.   Folio, contemporary German blind stamped calf, wooden boards, first edition.   Thomas 30-2 1973 £650

POLK, JAMES K.   Message . . . Calling for Information Relative to the Mode of Raising Funds for Carrying on the War With Mexico.   Washington, 1846.   Jenkins 61-1603 1974 $12.50

POLK, JAMES K.   Message from the President at the Commencement of the First Session of the 29th Congress.   Washington, 1845.   Rare.   Jenkins 61-2204 1974 $85

POLK, R. L.   Men of Minnesota.   St. Paul, 1915.   8vo., leather, 520 pages.   Saddleback 14-521 1974 $17.50

POLK, R. L.   Polk's Vallejo (California) City Directory. San Francisco, c.1937.   8vo., cloth, 488 pages.   Saddleback 14-237 1974 $12.50

POLLACK, QUEENA   Peggy Eaton, Democracy's Mistress.   New York, 1931.   Virtually new copy in frayed d.j.   Butterfield 10-463 1974 $10

POLLAK, JAMES S.   The Golden Egg.   Holt, 1946.   Austin 62-508 1974 $8.50

POLLARD, ALFRED W.   Early English Books, A History of the Decoration and Illustration of Books in the 15th & 16th Centuries.   London, 1893.   8vo., illus., orig. cloth gilt, first edition.   Dawsons PM 10-488 1974 £6

POLLARD, ALFRED W.   Fine Books.   London, 1912.   Large 8vo., plates, orig. gilt stamped buckram, first edition.   Dawsons PM 10-490 1974 £40

POLLARD, ALFRED W.   Italian Book Illustrations: Chiefly of the 15th Century.   1894.   Illus., nice copy, first edition.   Covent 51-2193 1973 £10

POLLARD, EDWARD A.   Black Diamonds.   New York, 1860.   Biblo & Tannen 213-65 1973 $37.50

POLLARD, EDWARD A.   The Lost Cause.   New York, 1867.   8vo., contemporary sheep, rebacked, first edition.   Dawsons PM 251-311 1974 £28

POLLARD, EDWARD A.   Southern History of the War. The First Year. New York, 1864.   Fine, orig. binding.   Butterfield 10-175 1974 $15

POLLARD, EDWARD A.   Southern History of the War. The Second Year. New York, 1864.   Fine, orig. binding.   Butterfield 10-176 1974 $15

POLLARD, EDWARD A.   Southern History of the War. The Third Year. New York, 1865.   Fine, first edition, orig. binding.   Butterfield 10-177 1974 $25

POLLARD, H. B.   A History of Firearms.   1930.   Crown 4to., orig. cloth, plates.   Broadhurst 23-159 1974 £20

POLLARD, H. B. C.   British and American Game Birds.   1945. 4to., cloth, coloured plates.   Wheldon 128-545 1973 £7.50

POLLARD, JOSEPHINE   The Decorative Sisters.   New York, 1881. 4to., pict. boards, cloth spine, lithographs.   Frohnsdorff 16-277 1974 $15

POLLEN, F. P. L.   Recherches sur la Faune de Madagascar.   Leyden, (1869-)77.   4to., half calf, plates.   Wheldon 131-944 1974 £30

POLLINI, GIROLAMO   L'Historia Ecclesiastica Della Rivolvzion D'Inghilterra.   Rome, 1594.   Small 4to., old vellum, browned.   Thomas 30-131 1973 £30

POLLITT, CHARLES   De Quincey's Editorship of the Westmorland Gazette, 1818-19.   Kendal, 1890.   First edition, demy 8vo., printed paper wrapper, cover title little foxed, else fine, inscribed presentation copy from author.   Broadhurst 24-636 1974 £5

POLLOCK, CHANNING   The Enemy.   Brentano, 1925.   Austin 51-746 1973 $7.50

POLLOCK, CHANNING   Guide Posts in Chaos.   Crowell, 1942. Austin 51-747 1973 $8.50

POLLOCK, CHANNING   Harvest of my Years.   Bobbs, 1943.   395p. Austin 51-748 1973 $6.50

POLLOCK, FREDERICK   The History of English Law Before the Time of Edward I.   Cambridge, 1911.   Second edition, small 4to., 2 vols., presentation copy.   Butterfield 10-462 1974 $35

POLLOK, R.   The Course of Time.   Portland, 1841.   Orig. cloth, 3 1/2 X 2 1/2.   Gregory 44-450 1974 $8.50

POLLUS, JULIUS   Vocabularii Index In Latinum Tralatus.   1502. Small folio, calf, first edition.   Thomas 30-7 1973 £150

POLO, MARCO   Book of Ser Marco Polo.   1903.   2 vols. Allen 213-1714 1973 $35

POLO, MARCO   The Book of Ser Marco Polo.   1903.   2 vols., thick roy. 8vo., plates, orig. buckram gilt, maps, revised third edition.   Smith 193-625 1973 £20

POLO, MARCO   Most Noble & Famous Travels.   1929. Crown 4to., maps, illus., orig. vellum backed buckram, gilt, limited edition. Smith 193-307 1973 £23

POLYBIUS   Historiarum Libri Qui Supersunt.   Paris, 1609. Folio, contemporary calf, gilt armorial stamp of Christopher Hatton, raised bands, Latin and Greek text in parallel columns.   Thomas 32-84 1974 £80

POMERANZ, HERMAN   Medicine in the Shakespearean Plays and Dickens Doctors.   Powell, 1936.   Austin 51-749 1973 $15

POMIANE, EDOUARD DE   Good Fare.   London, 1932.   Biblo & Tannen 214-785 1974 $7.50

POMME, PIERRE   Traite des Affections Vaporeuses des Deux Sexes. Paris, 1782.   4to., contemporary mottled sheep.   Dawsons PM 249-407 1974 £60

POMODORO, GIOVANNI   La Geometria Prattica.   (1667).   Small folio, old boards, plates.   Zeitlin 235-179 1974 $85

POMODORO, GIOVANNI   La Geometria Prattica.   (1667).   Folio, plates, old boards, rare.   Zeitlin 235-178 1974 $150

POMPEN, AURELIUS   The English Versions of the Ship of Fools. London, 1925.   8vo., plates, foxing, inscribed, orig. cloth.   Bow Windows 62-725 1974 $8.50

POMPONIUS MELAE   De Situ Orbis Libri tres, ad Omnium Angliae & Hiberniae Codicum. Eton, 1761. Small 4to., old boards, new calf spine, maps. Traylen 79-437 1973 £10

PONCELET, JEAN VICTOR   Cours de Mecanique. Paris, 1874. 8vo., half calf, plates. Dawsons PM 245-612 1974 £12

POND, J. B.   Eccentricities of Genius. 1901. Portraits, dec. cloth gilt. Covent 55-1202 1974 £12.50

PONNELLE, LOUIS   St. Philip Neri and the Roman Society of His Times. 1932. Portraits, scarce. Howes 185-1554 1974 £6

PONOMAREV, SERGEJ I.   Materialy Dija Bibliografii Literatury. Sanktpeterburg, 1883. 8vo., cloth. Dawsons PM 11-627 1974 £6.50

PONTANUS, JOANNES JOVIANUS   Amorum Libri II. 1533. 2 vols., 18th century vellum gilt, morocco labels. Thomas 30-45 1973 £75

PONTANUS, JOANNES JOVIANUS   Opera. 1518. Vol. 1 only of 3, contemporary calf, gilt, stains, rebacked. Thomas 30-40 1973 £25

PONTANUS, JOANNES JOVIANUS   Opera. 1513. Vellum, gilt, morocco labels. Thomas 30-25 1973 £25

PONTEDERA, J.   Compendium Tabularum Botanicarum in Quo Plantae CCLXXII ab eo in Italia Nuper Detectae Recensentur. Padua, 1718. 4to., contemporary vellum. Wheldon 128-1150 1973 £25

PONTEDERA, J.   Compendium Tabularum Botanicarum in Quo Plantae . Padua, 1718. 4to., contemporary vellum. Wheldon 131-1184 1974 £25

PONTEY, WILLIAM   The Forest Pruner. London, 1810. 8vo., orig. cloth-backed boards, uncut, plates, third edition. Hammond 201-42 1974 £14

PONTEY, WILLIAM   The Profitable Planter. 1809. 8vo., orig. boards, uncut, plate, third edition. Wheldon 129-1623 1974 £10

PONTEY, WILLIAM   The Profitable Planter. 1809-10. 8vo., contemporary calf, gilt, plates, third edition. Hammond 201-43 1974 £30

PONTEY, WILLIAM   The Rural Improver. London, 1822. 4to., contemporary calf, rebacked, plates, first edition. Hammond 201-44 1974 £36

PONTIFICALE Romanum. Venice, 1561. Folio, contemporary goatskin over wooden boards, later label, worn. Thomas 28-306 1972 £50

PONTIFICALE Romanum. Antwerp, 1627. Folio, mid 17th century Roman brown morocco, bookplate. Thomas 28-142 1972 £125

PONTOPPIDAN, E.   The Natural History of Norway. 1755. Folio, contemporary calf, plates, scarce. Wheldon 130-303 1974 £175

PONZI, ANDREW   The Fabulous Ponzi. Alpina. 1948. Austin 62-509 1974 $10

POOL, E. H.   "Don't Give Up the Ship"; A Catalogue of the Eugene H. Pool Collection of Captain James Lawrence. Salem, 1942. Limited edition, illus., inscribed & signed by Pool. Hood's 102-38 1974 $25

POOL, E. H.   "Don't Give Up the Ship". Salem, 1942. Illus., inscribed, limited edition. Hood's 104-51 1974 $25

POOL, MATTHEW   Synopsis Criticorum Aliorumque Sacrae Scripturae Interpretum et Commentatorum. Francofurt, 1679. 5 vols., folio, old vellum, rall crisp set. Smith 194-181 1974 £25

POOL, WILLIAM   Landmarks of Niagara County, New York. 1897. 3 parts. Hood's 102-630 1974 $25

POOL, WILLIAM   Landmarks of Niagara County, New York. 1897. Hood's 104-725 1974 $25

POOLE, C. H.   Staffordshire Poets. Lytham, 1928. 8vo., portraits, orig. cloth. Bow Windows 62-726 1974 £6.75

POOR, H. V.   Manual of the Railroads of the United States. New York, 1883. 8vo., orig. cloth. Broadhurst 23-1696 1974 £10

POOR LAW BOARD   Eighteenth Annual Report. 1866. Orig. wrappers, cloth back. Howes 186-1538 1974 £6.50

POOR LAW BOARD   Nineteenth Annual Report. 1867. Orig. wrappers, cloth back. Howes 186-1539 1974 £6.50

POOR LAW COMMISSION   Fifth Annual Report. 1839. Folio, orig. wrappers, cloth back. Howes 186-1540 1974 £10

POOR Law Schools Committee Minutes of Evidence. 1896. 2 vols., orig. wrappers, folio, cloth backs. Howes 186-1541 1974 £15

POORTENAAR, J.   Art of the Book and Its Illustration. 1935. 4to., plates. Allen 216-202 1974 $17.50

THE "POP-UP" Puss in-Boots. New York, (1934). 4to., pictorial boards, "pop-up" illus. in excellent condition. Frohnsdorff 16-594 1974 $25

POPE, ALEXANDER   An Epistle from Mr. Pope. London, 1734. Folio, modern boards, first edition. Dawsons PM 252-790 1974 £110

POPE, ALEXANDER   An Essay on Man. London, 1733. 8vo., modern half calf, woodcut. Dawsons PM 252-791 1974 £80

POPE, ALEXANDER   An Essay on Man. (1733). Folio, sewed, uncut, first edition. Quaritch 936-191 1974 £36

POPE, ALEXANDER   The First Satire of the Second Book of Horace. 1733. Folio, sewed, uncut, first edition. Quaritch 936-192 1974 £45

POPE, ALEXANDER   Horace his Ode to Venus. 1737. Folio, red levant morocco, gilt, first edition. Quaritch 936-193 1974 £70

POPE, ALEXANDER   Letters of. London, 1737. 4to., worn, contemporary calf. Bow Windows 62-727 1974 £14.50

POPE, ALEXANDER   Of Taste. 1732. 8vo., modern boards, first octavo edition. Dawsons PM 252-792 1974 £35

POPE, ALEXANDER   Of the Characters of Women. 1735. Folio, stiff marbled wrappers, first edition. Quaritch 936-195 1974 £35

POPE, ALEXANDER   Of the Use of Riches. London, 1732-33. 8vo., contemporary calf, rebacked. Dawsons PM 252-793 1974 £50

POPE, ALEXANDER   One Thousand Seven Hundred and Thirty Eight. 1738. Folio, 2 vols., sewed, uncut, first editions. Quaritch 936-196 1974 £70

POPE, ALEXANDER   Poetical Works . . . to Which is Prefixed the Life of the Author. 1821. One of 100 copies on large paper, 2 vols., full contemporary straight grained morocco, sides & backs panelled in gilt, very nice set, first edition. Covent 51-1451 1973 £35

POPE, ALEXANDER   A Pope Library, A Catalogue of Plays, Poems, and Prose by Alexander Pope. London, 1931. 4to., orig. red cloth gilt, uncut, first edition. Dawsons PM 10-494 1974 £40

POPE, ALEXANDER   Pope's Own Miscellany. 1935. Roy 8vo., orig. cloth, uncut, limited edition. Broadhurst 23-1077 1974 £25

POPE, ALEXANDER   Pope's Own Miscellany. Nonesuch Press, 1935. Roy. 8vo., uncut, limited to 750 copies, orig. cloth, fine. Broadhurst 24-1038 1974 £25

POPE, ALEXANDER   The Rape of the Lock. London, 1798. 8vo., foxing, frontispiece, plates, straight grained morocco, gilt. Bow Windows 62-728 1974 £10.50

POPE, ALEXANDER   The Rape of the Lock. 1896. Drawings,
gilt, cloth, fine. Rinsland 58-975 1974 $22.50

POPE, ALEXANDER   The Works of. London, n.d. Thick 8vo.,
contemporary morocco, steel engravings. Smith 193-255 1973 £6.50

POPE, ALEXANDER   Works. 1764. 6 vols., small 8vo., plates,
contemporary calf. Howes 186-367 1974 £21

POPE, ALEXANDER   The Works of. London, 1776. 6 vols.,
12mo., plates, foxing, contemporary calf, rebacked, morocco labels, rubbed.
Bow Windows 62-729 1974 £27

POPE, ALEXANDER   The Works. 1777. 12mo., 8 vols., contemporary polished calf. Quaritch 936-190 1974 £36

POPE, ALEXANDER   The Works Of. 1806. 8vo., contemporary tree
calf, 10 vols., worn. Bow Windows 64-658 1974 £16

POPE, ALEXANDER   Works. 1847. 8 vols., demy 8vo., full
length brown calf by Oldfield, panelled backs, raised bands, attractive set.
Broadhurst 24-1714 1974 £60

POPE, ALEXANDER   Works. 1875. Med. 8vo., orig. cloth, good
copy. Broadhurst 24-298 1974 £10

POPE, J.   Memoirs of the Right Honourable Sir John
Alexander Mac Donald. Toronto, (1930). Hood's 103-224 1974 $35

POPE, JOHN   Report of an Exploration of the Territory of
Minnesota. Washington, 1850. Large folding map. Jenkins 61-1668 1974 $15

POPE'S Own Miscellany. 1935. Buckram, gilt, faded, numbered. Covent
55-1143 1974 £25

POPHAM, JOHN   Reports and Cases Collected by the Learned . . .
1656. Small folio, contemporary sheep, covers worn, some marginal worming,
first edition. Bow Windows 66-548 1974 £18.50

POPP, JOSEPH   Bruno Paul. Munich, n.d. Large 4to., cloth
spine, faded boards, plates. Minters 37-563 1973 $40

POPPEN, S.   Amerikanische Amtstatigkeit Eines Lutherischen
Pfarrers. 1914. Illus., 248 pages. Austin 57-531 1974 $15

POPULAR County Histories. 1886-1900. 15 vols., 8vo., cloth. Quaritch
939-196 1974 £35

POPULUS, B.   Claude Gillot, 1673-1722, Catalogue de l'Oeuvre
Grave. Paris, 1930. Plates, illus., demy 4to., buckram, orig. wrappers bound
in, fine. Forster 98-313 1974 £10

PORCHE, FRANCOIS   Charles Baudelaire. 1928. Plates, faded,
English first edition. Covent 56-105 1974 £5.25

PORCIUS, PUBLIUS   Pugna Porcorum. Paris, 1539. 8vo., modern
boards, very fine copy. Schafer 10-108 1974 sFr 1,200

PORNY, MARK ANTHONY   The Elements of Heraldry. London, 1765. 8vo.,
half calf, gilt, plates. Hammond 201-438 1974 £14

PORNY, MARK ANTHONY   The Elements of Heraldry. London, 1787. 8vo.,
contemporary calf, gilt, plates, fourth edition. Hammond 201-439 1974 £12

PORNY, MARC ANTHONY   Nouveau Dictionnaire Francois & Anglois . . .
Extrait des Meilleurs Auteurs. London, 1763. Small 8vo., contemporary gilt
lined morocco, richly gilt back, green label. Kraus B8-224 1974 $37.50

PORRITT, EDWARD   Sixty Years of Protection in Canada, 1846-1907.
London, 1908. Hood's 102-393 1974 $17.50

PORRITT, EDWARD   The Unreformed House of Commons. 1903.
2 vols., thick 8vo., orig. buckram gilt, scarce, inscribed presentation, orig.
& best edition. Howes 186-1139 1974 £18

THE PORT of New York: General Report, Piers, Wharves and Docks, and Atlas of
Port Facilities Maps. Washington, 1932. 3 vols., wrappers, illus., charts,
folding maps. Jenkins 61-1910 1974 $20

PORTA, GIOVANNI BATTISTA   Physiognomoniae Coelestis. 1606. 8vo.,
contemporary vellum, bookplate. Bow Windows 61-680 1973 £68

PORTALEONE, ABRAHAM   De Auro Dialogi Tres. Venice, 1584. 4to., old
style vellum, first edition. Schumann 35-388 1974 $210

PORTALIS, ROGER   Les Dessinateurs d'Illustrations au 18me Siecle.
Paris, 1877. 2 vols., wrappers, uncut copy. Kraus B8-225 1974 $65

PORTER, ARTHUR KINGSLEY   Medieval Architecture. 1912. 2 vols., plates.
Allen 213-1718 1973 $50

PORTER, ENDYMION   A. L. S. n.d. Folio, 1 page. Dawsons PM
252-796 1974 £175

PORTER, G. R.   The Nature and Properties of the Sugar Cane.
1830. 8vo., new cloth, plates, scarce. Wheldon 129-1665 1974 £15

PORTER, G. R.   A Treatise on the Origin, Progressive
Improvement and Present State of the Manufacture of Porcelain and Glass.
(c. 1845). 8vo., orig. cloth. Quaritch 940-656 1974 £15

PORTER, J. L.   The Giant Cities of Bashan. 1866. 8vo.,
orig. cloth gilt, plates. Quaritch 940-343 1974 £10

PORTER, JANE   The Pastor's Fireside. 1817. 12mo., 4 vols.,
orig. boards, labels, first edition. Broadhurst 23-904 1974 £45

PORTER, JANE   The Pastor's Fireside. 1817. First edition,
4 vols., 12mo., orig. boards, paper labels, uncut, spines defective, good copy,
complete with half titles. Broadhurst 24-838 1974 £45

PORTER, JANE   The Scottish Chiefs. New York, 1926. Full
page full color pictures, pictorial front cover, 8vo., fine. Current BW9-589
1974 $20

PORTER, JANE   Sir Edward Seaward's Narrative of His
Shipwreck and Consequent Discovery of Certain Caribbean Islands. 1841.
3 vols., half calf, rubbed. Allen 216-1338 1974 $12.50

PORTER, JANE   Sir Edward Seaward's Narrative of His Shipwreck.
London, 1832. 3 vols., 12mo.; contemporary half calf, gilt, second edition.
Dawsons PM 252-797 1974 £28

PORTER, JANE   Tales Round a Winter Hearth. 1826. 12mo., 2
vols., early half calf, first edition. Quaritch 936-520 1974 £25

PORTER, JENNIE HENDERSON   Hannah Johnson and Polly Palmer With Some
of Their Kinsfolk. (Kansas City), 1930. 8vo., cloth. Saddleback 14-786
1974 $12.50

PORTER, KATHERINE ANNE   Hacienda. New York, 1934. 8vo., orig.
cloth, first edition. Rota 190-750 1974 £6

PORTER, KATHERINE ANN   The Leaning Tower and Other Stories. New
York, 1944. Orig. binding, first edition, lacking d.w., small spots on spine,
very nice. Ross 87-460 1974 $17.50

PORTER, MILLIE JONES   Memory Cups of Panhandle Pioneers. Clarendon,
Texas, 1945. Cloth, illus., lst ed. Dykes 24-149 1974 $40

PORTER, P. A.   A Brief History of Old Fort Niagara. Niagara
Falls, 1896. Photographs, wrappers. Hood's 103-666 1974 $30

PORTER, R. K.   Travelling Sketches in Russia and Sweden, 1805-
08. 1809. 2 vols. in 1, roy. 4to., plates, contemporary calf, gilt. Quaritch
940-735 1974 £350

PORTER, THOMAS CONRAD   Flora of Pennsylvania. Boston, 1903.
Rittenhouse 46-549 1974 $10

PORTER, WILLIAM HENRY   Observations on the Surgical Pathology of the Larynx and Trachea. London, 1837. 8vo., contemporary boards, cloth. Dawsons PM 249-408 1974 £50

PORTER, WILLIAM SYDNEY   Cabbages and Kings. New York, 1904. Orig. cloth, hinges tender, first edition, about fine. MacManus 224-361 1974 $50

PORTER, WILLIAM SYDNEY   The Gift of the Magi. London, 1939. Illus. by Stephen Gooden, d.w. with few small spots, near mint copy, orig. binding. Ross 86-207 1974 $10

PORTER, WILLIAM SYDNEY   Letters to Litholpolis. 1922. Gilt boards, English first edition. Covent 56-625 1974 £10.50

PORTER, WILLIAM SYDNEY   Letters to Litholpolis from O. Henry to Mabel Wagnalls. New York, 1922. 12mo., boards, first edition. Goodspeed's 578-288 1974 $10

PORTER, WILLIAM SYDNEY   Options. New York, 1909. 8vo., orig. cloth, first edition. Rota 189-451 1974 £8.50

PORTER, WILLIAM SYDNEY   Postscripts. New York and London, 1923. First edition, later binding. Butterfield 10-464 1974 $10

PORTER, WILLIAM SYDNEY   Roads of Destiny. New York, 1909. 8vo., orig. cloth, first edition. Rota 189-452 1974 £10

PORTER, WILLIAM SYDNEY   Sixes and Sevens. New York, 1911. 8vo., orig. cloth, first edition. Rota 189-453 1974 £10

PORTER, WILLIAM SYDNEY   The Trimmed Lamp and Other Stories. New York, 1907. 8vo., orig. cloth, first edition. Rota 189-449 1974 £12

PORTER, WILLIAM SYDNEY   The Voice of the City. New York, 1908. 8vo., orig. cloth, first edition. Rota 189-450 1974 £7.50

PORTER, WILLIAM SYDNEY   The Voice of the City and Other Stories. New York, Limited Editions Club, 1935. Limited edition, signed by artist, coloured plates, illus., 4to., orig. cloth, fine. Sawyer 293-203 1974 £75

PORTIUS, SIMON
Please turn to
PORZIO, SIMONE

PORTLAND and the Columbia River. Portland, c. 1900. Small folio, wrapper, photographs. Jenkins 61-2086 1974 $10

THE PORTLAND Suburban Directory. Portland, c.1922. 8vo., 503 pages, cloth. Saddleback 14-460 1974 $15

PORTLOCK, JOSEPH ELLISON   Report on the Geology of the County of Londonderry. Dublin, 1843. 8vo., plates, map. Emerald 50-789 1974 £8

PORTLOCK, JOSEPH ELLISON   Report on the Geology of the County of Londonderry. Dublin, 1843. Thick 8vo., orig. cloth, rebacked, gilt, plates, first edition. Hammond 201-387 1974 £42

PORTLOCK, MRS. R.   Twenty-Five Years of Canadian Life. Toronto, 1901. Hood's 103-261 1974 $17.50

PORTLOCK, NATHANIEL   A Voyage Round the World; But More Particularly to the Northwest Coast of America, 1785-88. London, 1789. Folio, old calf, rebacked, gilt, leather label, nice, first edition, copperplates. Butterfield 10-465 1974 $400

PORTRAIT and Biographical Album of Jo Daviess County, Illinois. Chicago, 1889. 4to., leather, stained. Saddleback 14-385 1974 $45

PORTRAIT and Biographical Record of Denver and Vicinity. Chicago, 1898. 4to., cloth, rebound. Saddleback 14-329 1974 $65

PORTRAIT and Biographical Record of Dubuque, Jones and Clayton Counties, Iowa. Chicago, 1894. 4to., leather. Saddleback 14-409 1974 $35

PORTRAIT and Biographical Record of Lehigh, Northampton and Carbon Counties, Pennsylvania. Chicago, 1894. 4to., cloth, rebound. Saddleback 14-677 1974 $50

PORTRAIT And Biographical Record, of Lehigh, Northampton and Carbon Counties, Pennsylvania. Chicago, 1894. Portraits, illus. Rinsland 58-77B 1974 $100

PORTRAIT and Biographical Record of Western Oregon. Chicago, 1904. 4to., leather, illus. Saddleback 14-656 1974 $75

PORTRAIT Medals of Italian Artists of the Renaissance. 1912. One of 750 copies, coloured frontis., plates, 4to., very good copy, first edition. Covent 51-2127 1973 £10.50

PORTRAITS of the British Poets. London, 1824. Large 8vo., engraved portraits, red morocco. Dawsons PM 252-798 1974 £35

PORTRAITS Photographies des Heimathloses. 1853-58. 4to., 2 vols., old boards, lithograph portraits. Gurney 66-148 1974 £70

THE PORTS of Baltimore, Maryland, Washington, D. C. and Alexandria, Virginia. Washington, 1926. Wrapper, illus., charts, folding maps. Jenkins 61-787 1974 $10

THE PORTS of Baltimore, Maryland, Washington, D. C. and Alexandria, Virginia. Washington, 1926. Wrapper, illus., charts, fine folding maps. Jenkins 61-1460 1974 $10

THE PORTS of Baltimore, Maryldn, Washington, D. C. and Alexandria, Virginia. Washington, 1926. Wrapper, illus., charts, fine folding maps. Jenkins 61-2545 1974 $10

THE PORTS of Philadelphia, Penn., Camden and Gloucester, N. J. Washington, 1939. Wrapper, illus., charts, fine folding maps. Jenkins 61-1827 1974 $10

THE PORTS of Philadelphia, Pa., Camden and Gloucester, N. J. Washington, 1939. Wrappers, illus., charts, fine folding maps. Jenkins 61-2169 1974 $10

THE PORTS of San Francisco, Oakland, Berkeley, Richmond, Upper San Francisco Bay, Santa Cruz, and Monterey, California. Washington, 1933. Wrapper, illus., charts, fine folding maps. Jenkins 61-384 1974 $10

PORZIO, SIMONE   De Humana Mente Disputatio. Florence, 1551. Small 4to., contemporary vellum over boards, very fine copy, first edition, very rare. Schafer 10-136 1974 sFr 1,200

POSADA, EDUARDO   Bibliografia Bogotana. Bogota, 1917-25. 2 vols., half morocco. Kraus B8-226 1974 $35

POSEPNY, F.   The Genesis of Ore-Deposits. New York, 1902. 8vo., cloth, second edition. Wheldon 130-965 1974 £7.50

POST, C. C.   Ten Years a Cowboy. Chicago, 1905. New blue cloth, gilt, illus. Bradley 35-305 1974 $10

POST, GEORGE W.   The Cottage Physician. Springfield, 1900. Illus. Rittenhouse 46-543 1974 $10

POST, LOUIS F.   The Deportations Delirium of Nineteen-Twenty. Kerr. 338p., orig. ed. Austin 62-510 1974 $10

POST, MELVILLE DAVISSON   The Bradmoor Murder. New York, (1929). 8vo., orig. cloth, fine, first edition. Rota 190-339 1974 £8

POST, MELVILLE DAVISSON   Monsieur Jonquelle. New York, 1923. 1st ed. Biblo & Tannen 210-499 1973 $17.50

POST, MELVILLE DAVISSON   The Silent Witness. New York, (1930). 8vo., orig. cloth, first edition. Rota 190-340 1974 £5

POST, MELVILLE DAVISSON   The Sleuth of St. James Square. New York, 1920. 1st ed. Biblo & Tannen 210-500 1973 $35

POST, MELVILLE DAVISSON   Walker of the Secret Service. New York, 1924. 1st ed. Biblo & Tannen 210-501 1973 $20

POSTE, B.   The History of the College of All Saints. 1847. 4to., orig. leather cloth, illus., portraits. Bow Windows 64-660 1974 £6.50

POSTLETHWAYT, MALACHY   A Short State of the Progress of the French Trade and Navigation. London, 1756. 8vo., modern boards, first edition. Dawsons PM 247-226 1974 £25

POSTNIKOV, NIKOLAI MIKHAILOVICH   Catalogue of Christian Antiquities Belonging to. (Moscow, ?1870). 8vo., half morocco, worn, library stamps. Quaritch 940-344 1974 £15

POTAIN   Details des Ouvrages de Menuiserie Pour les Batimens. 1749. 8vo., contemporary mottled calf, gilt, fine copy, rare. Quaritch 940-544 1974 £50

POTE, J.   The History and Antiquities of Windsor Castle. 1749. 4to., plates, old calf. Quaritch 939-303 1974 £30

POTE, J.   Les Delices de Windsore. Eton, 1755. Small 8vo., plates, modern boards. Quaritch 939-204 1974 £30

POTOCKI, GEOFFREY   Surprising Songs. 1930. Signed by author, sewing little strained, very good unopened copy, orig. wrappers are dusty, first edition. Covent 51-1453 1973 £5.25

POTOCKI, J.   Voyage dans Quelques Parties de la Basse-Saxe pour la Recherche des Antiquites Slaves ou Vendes. Hamburg, 1795. Large 4to., orig. boards, uncut, illus., fine, rare. Harper 213-124 1973 $450

POTT, JAMES   Synonymes of. 1808. Small 8vo., 2 vols., contemporary half calf. Hammond 201-285 1974 £8.50

POTTER, BEATRIX   Ginger and Pickles. London, 1909. Orig. boards, lacking lower third of backstrip, first edition, 5 5/8" X 7". Frohnsdorff 15-133 1974 £30

POTTER, BEATRIX   Ginger & Pickles. New York & London, (1937). Square 32mo., d.j. little soiled, full page colored illus. by author, near mint. Current BW9-130 1974 $14.50

POTTER, BEATRIX   Histoire de Paupette-a-L'Epingle. London, n.d. Square 32mo., d.j. bit soiled, full page colored illus. by author, near mint. Current BW9-131 1974 $37.50

POTTER, BEATRIX   The Pie and the Patty-Pan. 1905. First edition, coloured plates, illus., crown 8vo., orig. blue grey boards, almost loose in case. George's 610-598 1973 £12

POTTER, BEATRIX   The Pie and The Patty Pan. New York, (1933). Square 32mo., d.j. bit soiled, full page colored illus. by author, near mint. Current BW9-132 1974 $12

POTTER, BEATRIX   The Story of Miss Moppet. 1906. Square 12mo., plates, orig. cloth, rare first issue, first edition. Howes 186-369 1974 £65

POTTER, BEATRIX   The Tailor of Gloucester. New York, (1903). Square 32mo., d.j. soiled & torn, full page colored illus. by author, near mint. Current BW9-133 1974 $20

POTTER, BEATRIX   The Tailor of Gloucester. 1903. 16mo., orig. dark green boards, coloured illus., good clean copy, first published edition. George's 610-600 1973 £15

POTTER, BEATRIX   The Tale of Benjamin Bunny. 1904. First edition, coloured illus., 16mo., orig. tan boards. George's 610-601 1973 £10

POTTER, BEATRIX   The Tale of Jemima Puddle-Duck. London, 1908. 16mo., green boards, small armorial bookplate, fine copy, first edition. Frohnsdorff 15-135 1974 $65

POTTER, BEATRIX   The Tale of Jeremy Fisher. London, (1906). 16mo., green boards, spine cracked along outer edges, early edition. Frohnsdorff 15-136 1974 $10

POTTER, BEATRIX   The Tale of Peter Rabbit. 1902. Small 8vo., orig. olive green boards, good copy, rare, coloured frontis., second printing, one of 200 copies. George's 610-603 1973 £45

POTTER, BEATRIX   The Tale of Pigling Bland. London, 1913. 16mo., green boards, lacks frontispiece, nice copy, first edition. Frohnsdorff 15-137 1974 $20

POTTER, BEATRIX   The Tale of Pigling Bland. 1913. Square 12mo., plates, orig. boards, first edition, first issue. Howes 186-370 1974 £28

POTTER, BEATRIX   The Tale of the Flopsy Bunnies. New York, (1909). 16mo., boards, portion of backstrip missing, first American edition. Frohnsdorff 15-134 1974 $15

POTTER, BEATRIX   The Tale of Timmy Tiptoes. New York, (1939). 32mo., full page illus. in color by author, near mint, d.j. little soiled. Current BW9-134 1974 $17.50

POTTER, BEATRIX   The Tale of Timmy Tiptoes. London, 1911. 16mo., boards, nice copy, first edition, child's name inscribed verso frontispiece. Frohnsdorff 15-140 1974 $45

POTTER, BEATRIX   The Tale of Timmy Tiptoes. London, 1911. 16mo., boards, very good copy, first edition. Frohnsdorff 15-138 1974 $50

POTTER, BEATRIX   The Tale of Timmy Tiptoes. London, 1911. 16mo., boards, bookplate of the Marquess of Bath, presentation inscription, nice copy, first edition. Frohnsdorff 15-139 1974 $60

POTTER, BEATRIX   Tale of Timmy Tiptoes. 1911. First edition, coloured plates by author, 16mo., orig. brown boards. George's 610-604 1973 £7.50

POTTER, BEATRIX   The Tale of Tom Kitten. New York, (1935). Square 32mo., full page colored illus. by author, near mint, d.j. little soiled. Current BW9-135 1974 $17.50

POTTER, BEATRIX   The Tale of Tom Kitten. New York, n.d. (c. 1918). Faded red boards, nice early edition. Frohnsdorff 15-141 1974 $13.50

POTTER, BEATRIX   The Tale of Two Bad Mice. New York, (1904). Square 32mo., d.j. little soiled, near mint, full page colored illus. by author. Current BW9-136 1974 $20

POTTER, BEATRIX   Wag-By-Wall. Boston, 1944. 16mo., cloth, pictorial label, woodcut dec. by J. J. Lankes, first edition. Frohnsdorff 15-143 1974 $20

POTTER, ELISHA R.   An Address to the Freemen of the State of Rhode Island. Newport, (1810). First edition, 12mo., fine, orig. stitching. Current BW9-416 1974 $38.75

POTTER, ELISHA R.   Report upon Public Schools and Education in Rhode Island. Providence, 1855. 8vo., orig. bindings, fine. Butterfield 8-572 1974 $20

POTTER, WILLIAM   The Roman or Turkish Bath. Manchester and London, 1859. 8vo., boards, first edition. Hammond 201-587 1974 £9

POTTER'S Cyclopaedia of Botanical Drugs and Preparations. 1932. Crown 8vo., cloth, plates, fourth edition. Wheldon 131-1816 1974 £5

POUCHER, W. A.   Lakeland Through the Lens. 1940. Demy 4to., orig. cloth, profusely illus., orig. cloth, first edition, fine. Broadhurst 24-1503A 1974 £5

POUCHET, FELIX ARCHIMEDE   Theorie Positive de l'Ovulation Spontanee. Paris, 1847. 8vo., orig. wrappers, second edition. Schumann 35-390 1974 $110

POUCHOT, PIERRE   Memoir Upon the Late War in North America, Between the French and English, 1755-60. Roxbury, 1866. 2 vols., three quarter leather, mottled covers & endpapers, spine tooled, 4to., illus., no. 1 of 7 copies done on Whatman's drawing paper. Hood's 102-115 1974 $1,500

POULIOT, J. C.   Historical Reminder. Quebec, 1927. Card cover, unopened. Hood's 103-785 1974 $15

POULSON, GEORGE   The History and Antiquities of the Seigniory of Holderness, in the East Riding of the County of York, Including the Abbies of Meaux and Swine, With the Priories of Nunkeeling and Burstall. Hull, 1840-1. 2 vols., roy. 4to., contemporary half brown morocco, panelled backs, very fine. Broadhurst 24-1505 1974 £66

POULTON, E. B.   The Colours of Animals. 1890. Crown 8vo., cloth. Wheldon 130-365 1974 £5

POULTON, E. B.   Essays on Evolution, 1889-1907. 1908. 8vo., cloth. Wheldon 128-54 1973 £5

POUND, ARTHUR   The Golden Earth. New York, 1935. First edition, orig. binding, portion d. w. flap mounted inside front cover. Wilson 63-64 1974 $12.75

POUND, EZRA   ABC of Reading. 1934. Exceptionally fine bright copy, unfaded cloth, first edition. Covent 51-1456 1973 £12.50

POUND, EZRA   ABC of Reading. London, 1934. 8vo., orig. cloth, first edition. Dawsons PM 252-799 1974 £25

POUND, EZRA   A B C of Reading. London, 1934. First edition, red cloth, lacking d.w., bright sound copy. Ross 86-377 1974 $60

POUND, EZRA   ABC of Reading. 1934. Orig. cloth, dust wrapper, first edition. Rota 188-766 1974 £10

POUND, EZRA   Cathay. 1915. First edition, crown 8vo., paper printed wrapper, uncut, mint, scarce. Broadhurst 24-839 1974 £50

POUND, EZRA   Cathay. 1915. Small 8vo., stiff paper wrappers, signature, first edition. Quaritch 936-521 1974 £35

POUND, EZRA   A Draft of XXX Cantos. 1933. Orig. cloth, scarce, first English edition. Rota 188-765 1974 £10

POUND, EZRA   Exultations. London, 1909. Dark red boards, fine. Dawson's 424-298 1974 $85

POUND, EZRA   Exultations Of. 1909. 8vo., orig. cloth, gilt, first edition. Rota 189-704 1974 £40

POUND, EZRA   Imaginary Letters. Paris, 1930. First edition, one of 300 numbered copies on Navarre Paper, very fine, unopened. Covent 51-1468 1973 £37.50

POUND, EZRA   Imaginary Letters. Paris, 1930. Small 4to., orig. stiff wrappers, fine, first edition. Quaritch 936-522 1974 £45

POUND, EZRA   An Immorality. (1923). Illus., English first edition. Covent 56-1048 1974 £12

POUND, EZRA   Make It New. London, 1934. First edition, lacking d.w., spine somewhat faded, nice, orig. binding. Ross 86-380 1974 $60

POUND, EZRA   'Noh', or Accomplishment. London, 1916. First edition, spine faded, very good copy, scarce 1250 copies printed, orig. cloth. Crane 7-233 1974 £40

POUND, EZRA   Personae. London, 1909. Booklabel of Bache Mathews, nice copy, first edition. Covent 51-1475 1973 £35

POUND, EZRA   Personae. London, 1909. Small 8vo., fine, orig. boards, first edition. Dawsons PM 252-800 1974 £60

POUND, EZRA   Personae. London, 1909. First edition, light brown boards, bookplate, spine shelf worn top & bottom, nice copy. Ross 86-381 1974 $85

POUND, EZRA   Poems, 1918-21. New York, 1921. First U. S. edition, parchment vellum spine trifle yellowed, exceptionally fine copy. Covent 51-2531 1973 £45

POUND, EZRA   Polite Essays. London, 1937. First edition, lacking d.w., fine, orig. binding. Ross 86-382 1974 $65

POUND, EZRA   Provenca. Boston, (1910). 8vo., orig. cloth, scarce, first edition. Rota 189-705 1974 £30

POUND, EZRA   Ra Hio: The Great Learning, Newly Rendered into the American Language. 1936. Nice copy, first edition. Covent 51-1480 1973 £12.50

POUND, EZRA   Selected Poems. 1928. Spine faded, nice copy, first edition. Covent 51-1478 1973 £8.50

POUND, EZRA   Selected Poems. London, 1928. Orig. cloth, first edition, fine copy. MacManus 224-362 1974 $40

POUND, EZRA   The Spirit of Romance. London, (n.d.). 8vo., orig. cloth, fine, first edition. Dawsons PM 252-801 1974 £50

POUND, EZRA   Ta Hio. 1936. Orig. cloth, scarce, d.w., first English edition. Rota 188-767 1974 £20

POUND, EZRA   Umbra. London, 1920. Inscription, cloth backed boards, first edition. Covent 51-1482 1973 £40

LA POUPEE Bien Elevee, Suivi de la Lanterne Magique. Paris, (c. 1845). Half green morocco, some of marbled paper on back cover missing, plates. Gregory 44-107 1974 $32.50

POURRAT, P.   Christian Spirituality. 1922-27. 3 vols., scarce. Howes 185-1573 1974 £16

POUSSIN, J. C.   Dictionnaire de la Tradition Pontificale. Paris, 1855. 2 vols., imp. 8vo., cloth backed boards. Howes 185-1574 1974 £6.50

POUSSIN, NICOLAS   Nicolas Poussin, Premier Peintre du Roi, 1594-1665. 1914. Folio, plates, half morocco, orig. wrapper, limited. Quaritch 940-205 1974 £80

POUZOLZ, P. C. M.   Flore du Department du Gard. Montpellier, 1862. 2 vols. in 1, 8vo., half morocco, plates, scarce. Wheldon 128-1299 1973 £10

POVAH, ALFRED   The Annals of the Parishes of St. Olave Hart Street. 1894. Thick 4to., illus., orig. half morocco, plates, de Luxe edition. Howes 186-2136 1974 £21

THE POW-WOW. 1914-1915. 2 vols. bound in 1, folio, cloth, illus. Howes 186-1754 1974 £8.50

POWDERLY, T. V.   Thirty Years of Labor. Columbus, 1890. Cloth. Hayman 57-636 1974 $15

POWDERMAKER, HORTENSE   Hollywood. Little, 1950. 342p., orig. ed. Austin 51-751 1973 $7.50

POWELL, DAWN   The Golden Spur. Viking, 1962. 247p. Austin 54-846 1973 $6.50

POWELL, DAWN   The Locusts Have No Kings. Scribner, 1948. 286p. Austin 54-847 1973 $6

POWELL, DAWN   My Home is Far Away. Scribner, 1944. 313p. Austin 54-848 1973 $6.50

POWELL, DAWN   Sunday, Monday and Always. Houghton, Mifflin, 1952. 213p. Austin 54-849 1973 $6.50

POWELL, DAWN   A Time to be Born. Scribner, 1942. 344p. Austin 54-850 1973 $6

POWELL, DAWN   The Wicked Pavilion. Houghton, Mifflin, 1954. 306p. Austin 54-851 1973 $6.50

POWELL, DILYS   Descent from Parnassus. 1934. 8vo., cloth,
first edition. Quaritch 936-523 1974 £7

POWELL, WILLIAM H.   The Fifth Army Corps During the Civil War.
New York & London, 1896. Maps, illus., large 8vo., limited to 750 copies, orig.
binding. Butterfield 10-179 1974 $27.50

POWELL-COTTON, P. H. G.   A Sporting Trip Through Abyssinia. London,
1902. Crown 4to., plates, orig. buckram. Smith 194-577 1974 £10

POWER, D'ARCY   William Harvey. London, 1897. Rittenhouse
46-544 1974 $10

POWER, HENRY   Experimental Philosophy. London, 1664. 4to.,
contemporary calf, rebacked, first edition. Schumann 35-391 1974 $1,650

POWER, MARGUERITE COUNTESS OF BLESSINGTON
Please turn to
BLESSINGTON, MARGUERITE (POWER) FARMER GARDINER, COUNTESS OF

POWER, MAURA   An Irish Astronomical Tract. London, 1914.
8vo., green cloth, gilt. Emerald 50-791 1974 £5.50

POWER, TYRONE   Born To Good Luck. 1832. Austin 51-752
1973 $8.50

POWER, TYRONE   How To Pay the Rent. Taylor, 1840. Austin
51-753 1973 $8.50

POWER, TYRONE   Paddy Carey. French, n.d. Austin 51-754
1973 $8.50

POWER, TYRONE   St. Patrick's Eve. Taylor, 1837. 50p.
Austin 51-755 1973 $10

POWER, VICTOR O'D.   A Secret of the Past. 1893. 3 vols., orig.
dec. blue cloth gilt. Covent 55-1490 1974 £12.50

POWERS, LAURA B.   Historic Tales of the Old Missions for Boys and
Girls. San Francisco, (1902). Cloth, fine. Hayman 57-70 1974 $7.50

POWERS, WILLIAM DUDLEY   Uncle Isaac: or, Old Days in the South.
Richmond, 1899. Cloth. Hayman 59-545 1974 $12.50

POWLEY, EDWARD B.   The House of De la Pomerai. Liverpool,
1944. 4to., orig. buckram-backed boards. Howes 186-1647 1974 £8.50

POWYS, JOHN COWPER   The Art of Forgetting the Unpleasant. n.d.
16mo., fine, wrappers, English first edition. Covent 56-2001 1974 £5.25

POWYS, JOHN COWPER   The Art of Happiness. n.d. 16mo., fine, wrappers, English first edition. Covent 56-2002 1974 £5.25

POWYS, JOHN COWPER   The Art of Happiness. 1935. Dust wrapper,
fine. Covent 55-1208 1974 £8.50

POWYS, JOHN COWPER   The Art of Happiness. 1935. Dust wrapper,
fine, English first edition. Covent 56-1053 1974 £8.50

POWYS, JOHN COWPER   Confessions of Two Brothers. New York, 1916.
Fine, first American edition. Covent 55-1213 1974 £20

POWYS, JOHN COWPER   Enjoyment of Literature. 1938. Illus. Austin
61-795 1974 $12.50

POWYS, JOHN COWPER   In Defence of Sensuality. New York, 1930.
First U.S. edition. Covent 56-1054 1974 £25

POWYS, JOHN COWPER   Maiden Castle. 1936. 539 pages. Austin
61-796 1974 $12.50

POWYS, JOHN COWPER   The Meaning of Culture. 1930. Book-plate,
dust wrapper, fine. Covent 55-1211 1974 £12.50

POWYS, JOHN COWPER   Mortal Strife. London, 1942. Lacking d.w.,
very nice copy, orig. binding. Ross 86-390 1974 $20

POWYS, JOHN COWPER   Visions and Revisions. 1915. 298 pages.
Austin 61-798 1974 $17.50

POWYS, JOHN COWPER   Wolf Solent. 1929. 2 vols., orig. edition.
Austin 61-799 1974 $12

POWYS, LITTLETON A.   Ode to the West Wind. n.d. Fine, wrappers,
English first edition. Covent 56-2005 1974 £5.25

POWYS, LLEWELYN   A Baker's Dozen. 1941. Portrait, drawings,
fine, d.w. Covent 51-2534 1973 £5.25

POWYS, LLEWELYN   Black Laughter. New York, 1924. First
edition, lacking d.w., covers lightly worn, very nice, orig. binding. Ross
86-391 1974 $35

POWYS, LLEWELYN   Black Laughter. London, 1925. First English
edition, very good copy, name on fly, orig. cloth. Crane 7-238 1974 £6.50

POWYS, LLEWELYN   Ebony and Ivory. 1923. Fine, faded & slightly
frayed d.w. Covent 51-2536 1973 £7.50

POWYS, LLEWELYN   Henry Hudson. 1927. Frontispiece, maps,
first edition. Covent 55-1216 1974 £7.50

POWYS, LLEWELYN   Skin for Skin. 1926. One of 900 numbered
copies, fine, cloth backed boards, worn d.w., first edition. Covent 51-1494
1973 £10

POWYS, LLEWELYN   Skin for Skin. 1926. Limited, first English
edition. Howes 185-384 1974 £12.50

POWYS, LLEWELYN   Skin for Skin. London, 1926. No. 690 of
edition limited to 900 copies, hinge starting to loosen at bottom, nice, scarce,
orig. binding. Ross 86-392 1974 $35

POWYS, LLEWELYN   Thirteen Worthies. 1923. First American
edition. Austin 61-803 1974 $12.50

POWYS, LLEWELYN   The Verdict of Bridlegoose. 1927. One of
900 numbered copies, cloth backed boards, fine, first edition. Covent 51-1496
1973 £6.50

POWYS, LLEWELYN   The Verdict of Bridlegoose. 1927. One of
900 numbered copies, fine, d.w., first edition. Covent 51-1495 1973 £10

POWYS, THEODORE FRANCIS   Black Bryony. London, 1923. First edition,
fine, d.w., orig. cloth, inscribed by author, removal of bookplate has marked
fly leaf. Crane 7-242 1974 £17

POWYS, THEODORE FRANCIS   Brief Diversions. Cambridge, 1922. Cloth
backed boards, very good copy, first edition. Covent 51-1511 1973 £7.50

POWYS, THEODORE FRANCIS   Captain Patch. London, 1935. First edition,
very nice copy, bookplate, orig. cloth, scarce. Crane 7-265 1974 £6.50

POWYS, THEODORE FRANCIS   Christ in the Cupboard. London, 1930. First
edition, limited to 500 numbered copies, signed by author, wrappers, very nice
copy. Crane 7-255 1974 £15

POWYS, THEODORE FRANCIS   Christ in the Cupboard. London, 1930. Paper
covers, no. 244 of edition limited to 500 copies, signed, faded covers, fine.
Ross 86-393 1974 $15

POWYS, THEODORE FRANCIS   The Dewpond. 1928. Orig. cloth, fine, d.w.,
first edition. Rota 188-768 1974 £9

POWYS, THEODORE FRANCIS   The Dewpond. London, 1928. First edition,
limited to 530 numbered copies, signed by author, fine, d.w., orig. cloth.
Crane 7-249 1974 £15

POWYS, THEODORE FRANCIS   Fables. London, 1929. First edition, orig. cloth, drawings, limited to 750 numbered copies, signed by author, a very fine copy, d.w. Crane 7-252 1974 £25

POWYS, THEODORE FRANCIS   Fables. London, 1929. Drawings, no. 79 of edition limited to 750 copies, first edition, signed, very near mint, orig. binding. Ross 86-394 1974 $35

POWYS, THEODORE FRANCIS   The House With the Echo. London, 1928. First edition, limited to 200 numbered copies, signed by author, patterned boards, very nice copy. Crane 7-250 1974 £7.50

POWYS, THEODORE FRANCIS   The House With the Echo. London, 1928. First edition, limited to 200 numbered copies, signed by author, patterned boards, very nice copy. Crane 7-251 1974 £18

POWYS, THEODORE FRANCIS   I for One. 1923. Cloth backed boards, very good copy, first edition. Covent 51-1513 1973 £5.25

POWYS, THEODORE FRANCIS   Innocent Birds. London, 1926. First edition, slight foxing, fine, d.w., orig. cloth. Crane 7-247 1974 £6

POWYS, THEODORE FRANCIS   An Interpretation of Genesis. London, 1929. New edition, limited to 490 copies, signed by author, patterned boards, fine, d.w. Crane 7-253 1974 £20

POWYS, THEODORE FRANCIS   The Key of the Field. 1930. Woodcut, one of 550 copies numbered & signed by author, fine, buckram, Furnival Book No. 1, first edition. Covent 51-1499 1973 £7.50

POWYS, THEODORE FRANCIS   The Key to the Field. London, 1930. First edition, limited to 550 numbered copies, signed by author, tall 8vo., fine, orig. cloth. Crane 7-260 1974 £15

POWYS, THEODORE FRANCIS   The Key of the Field. London, 1930. No. 1 of Furnival Books, no. 137 of edition limited to 550 copies, woodcut, signed, light paper & glassine wrappers, very near mint. Ross 86-395 1974 $25

POWYS, THEODORE FRANCIS   Kindness in a Corner. 1930. Crown 8vo., d.w., fine, first edition. Howes 186-373 1974 £18

POWYS, THEODORE FRANCIS   Kindness in a Corner. 1930. Fine, d.w., drawing in title page, first edition. Covent 51-1500 1973 £5.25

POWYS, THEODORE FRANCIS   Kindness in a Corner. London, 1930. First edition, fine, d.w., orig. cloth. Crane 7-257 1974 £6

POWYS, THEODORE FRANCIS   Kindness in a Corner. London, 1930. First edition, limited to 200 numbered copies, signed by author, patterned boards, very fine copy. Crane 7-258 1974 £25

POWYS, THEODORE FRANCIS   The Left Leg. London, 1923. First edition, slight foxing, fine copy, d.w., scarce, orig. cloth. Crane 7-243 1974 £10

POWYS, THEODORE FRANCIS   The Life and Letters of Walter H. Page. 1923. Plates, 2 vols., presentation inscription, English first edition. Covent 56-1058 1974 £10.50

POWYS, THEODORE FRANCIS   Mark Only. London, 1924. First edition, fine copy, d.w., scarce, orig. cloth. Crane 7-244 1974 £10

POWYS, THEODORE FRANCIS   Mr. Tasker's Gods. London, 1925. First edition, fine, d.w., orig. cloth. Crane 7-245 1974 £7.50

POWYS, THEODORE FRANCIS   Mr. Weston's Good Wine. London, 1927. First edition, drawings, limited to 660 numbered copies, signed by author, very nice copy, inscribed by author, orig. cloth. Crane 7-248 1974 £50

POWYS, THEODORE FRANCIS   Mr. Weston's Good Wine. London, 1927. Drawings, no. 348 of edition limited to 660 copies, lacking d.w., very fine, orig. binding. Ross 86-400 1974 $50

POWYS, THEODORE FRANCIS   Mr. Weston's Good Wine. New York, 1928. Half black buckram, first U.S. edition. Covent 56-2007 1974 £21

POWYS, THEODORE FRANCIS   Mockery Gap. London, 1925. First edition, fine, d.w., orig. cloth. Crane 7-246 1974 £7.50

POWYS, THEODORE FRANCIS   Soliloquies of a Hermit. 1926. Near fine, first edition. Covent 51-1502 1973 £10

POWYS, THEODORE FRANCIS   Soliloquies of a Hermit. London, 1918. First English edition, boards worn at corners, nice copy, bookplate. Crane 7-241 1974 £15

POWYS, THEODORE FRANCIS   Soliloquies of a Hermit. London, 1918. First English edition, signed, orig. somewhat rubbed d.w., fine, orig. binding. Ross 86-397 1974 $50

POWYS, THEODORE FRANCIS   The Soliloquy of a Hermit. New York, 1916. Cloth gilt, portrait, dust wrapper. Covent 55-1223 1974 £45

POWYS, THEODORE FRANCIS   Talking: One of a Series of Essays Entitled: These Diversions. 1926. Signed by author, portrait, fine, largely unopened copy, d.w., first edition. Covent 51-1518 1973 £6.30

POWYS, THEODORE FRANCIS   The Tithe Barn and The Dove & the Eagle. 1932. First edition, limited to 350 numbered copies, signed by author, very fine copy, bookplate, orig. cloth. Crane 7-263 1974 £30

POWYS, THEODORE FRANCIS   The Two Thieves. 1932. Small 8vo., boards, gilt, fine, unopened, first edition. Quaritch 936-525 1974 £18

POWYS, THEODORE FRANCIS   The Two Thieves. London, 1932. First edition, limited to 85 numbered copies, signed by author, patterned boards, very fine copy. Crane 7-264 1974 £30

POWYS, THEODORE FRANCIS   Unclay. London, 1931. First edition, limited to 160 numbered copies, signed by author, rebound half brown calf, gilt, fine state, inscribed by author. Crane 7-261 1974 £45

POZZO, ANDREA   Rules and Examples of Perspective Proper for Painters and Architects. London, 1707. Large folio, old calf, rebacked, plates, good crisp copy. Quaritch 940-545 1974 £350

POWYS, THEODORE FRANCIS   Uncle Dottery, a Christmas Story. Bristol, 1930. Wood engravings, first edition, limited to 300 numbered copies, signed by author, patterned boards, very fine, rare. Crane 7-254 1974 £50

POWYS, THEODORE FRANCIS   Uriah on the Hill. Cambridge, 1930. First edition, limited to 85 numbered copies, hand made paper, signed by author, tall 8vo., buckram, very fine, rare. Crane 7-259 1974 £40

POWYS, THEODORE FRANCIS   What Lack I Yet? San Francisco, 1927. No. 2 of 10 copies, signed by author, covers faded at edges, very good copy, wrappers. Covent 51-1504 1973 £75

POWYS, THEODORE FRANCIS   When Thou Wast Naked. Waltham St. Lawrence, Golden Cockerel Press, 1931. First edition, wood engravings, limited to 500 copies, numbered, signed by author, patterned boards, very fine. Crane 7-262 1974 £35

POWYS, THEODORE FRANCIS   The White Paternoster and Other Stories. London, 1930. First edition, limited to 310 numbered copies, signed by author, patterned boards, very nice copy, neat name on fly. Crane 7-256 1974 £20

POWYS, THEODORE FRANCIS   The White Paternoster and Other Stories. 1930. Exceptionally fine copy, slightly worn d.w., first edition. Covent 51-1506 1973 £10.50

POWYS, THEODORE FRANCIS   Wonder Hero. 1933. One of 6 copies specially bound, numbered & signed by author, fine copy, full red morocco, raised panelled spine, first edition. Covent 51-1519 1973 £40

POWYS, THOMAS L., LORD LILFORD
Please turn to
LILFORD, THOMAS L. POWYS, LORD

POZZI, GIOVANNI   Elementi di Fisiologia Patologica, Igiene e
Terapia Generale. Milan, 1828. 3 vols., 8vo., contemporary leather-backed
boards, frontispiece, rubbed, first edition. Schuman 37-209 1974 $65

POZZI, S.   A Treatise on Gynaecology. 1892. 8vo., 3
vols., orig. cloth, fine, illus. Dawsons PM 249-410 1974 £8

PRACTICAL Carpentry, Joinery and Cabinet Making. 1835. Illus., damp
stained. Covent 55-1433 1974 £35

PRAEGER, ROBERT LLOYD   An Account of the Genus Sedum as Found in
Cultivation. 1921. 8vo., buckram, scarce. Wheldon 130-1450 1974 £7.50

PRAEGER, ROBERT LLOYD   The Way that I Went. Dublin, 1937. Roy.
8vo., illus., blue cloth, first edition. Emerald 50-794 1974 £7.50

PRAIN, D.   Botanical Notes and Papers. Calcutta, 1901.
8vo., half morocco, plates. Wheldon 130-1045 1974 £10

PRAIN, D.   Botanical Notes and Papers. Calcutta, 1901.
8vo., orig. cloth, plates, maps. Wheldon 129-1112 1974 £10

PRAIN, D.   Memoirs and Memoranda. Calcutta, 1894.
8vo., new cloth, plates. Wheldon 130-1046 1974 £10

PRAIN, D.   Memoirs and Memoranda. Calcutta, 1894.
8vo., half morocco, plates. Wheldon 129-1111 1974 £10

THE PRAISE and Happiness of the Countrie-life. 1938. Crown 8vo., quarter
morocco, limited edition. Broadhurst 23-1055 1974 £65

PRANG'S NATURAL History Series for Children. Boston, 1878. Wrappers, illus.,
inscription. Dawson's 424-213 1974 $30

PRASAD, RAMA   Nature's Finer Forces. Madras, 1947. Biblo
& Tannen 210-984 1973 $7.50

PRATENSIS, JASON   De Uteris Libri Duo. Amsterdam, 1657.
3 works in 1 vol., thick 12mo., contemporary vellum, second editions.
Schuman 37-210 1974 $195

PRATT, ANNE   The British Grasses and Sedges. (1861). 8vo.,
orig. cloth, coloured plates. Wheldon 128-1210 1973 £5

PRATT, ANNE   The British Grasses and Sedges. (1871). 8vo.,
orig. cloth, plates. Wheldon 131-1239 1974 £6

PRATT, ANNE   The Ferns of Great Britain and Their Allies.
(1861). 8vo., orig. cloth, plates. Wheldon 131-1460 1974 £7.50

PRATT, ANNE   The Flowering Plants and Ferns of Great Britain.
(1850-70). 8vo., 7 vols., orig. green cloth. Wheldon 129-1011 1974 £30

PRATT, ANNE   Poisonous, Noxious and Suspected Plants.
London, n.d. Roy. 8vo., orig. printed wrappers, worn, plates, orig. edition.
Traylen 79-44 1973 £5

PRATT, ANNE   Poisonous, Noxious, and Suspected Plants of
Our Fields and Woods. (1857). 12mo., orig. cloth, coloured plates, very
scarce. Wheldon 128-1211 1973 £5

PRATT, ANNE   Poisonous, noxious and Suspected Plants of our
Fields and Woods. 1857. 4to., half leather. Wheldon 129-1691 1974 £5

PRATT, ANNE   Poisonous, Noxious, and Suspected Plants of
Our Fields and Woods. (1857). 4to., orig. printed wrappers, plates, scarce.
Wheldon 130-1620 1974 £10

PRATT, A. E.   Two Years Among New Guinea Cannibals. 1906.
8vo., cloth, illus., second edition. Wheldon 129-295 1974 £10

PRATT, EDWIN A.   British Canals. London, 1906. 8vo., orig.
cloth, gilt, plates, first edition. Hammond 201-859 1974 £6.50

PRATT, E. J.   Dunkirk. Toronto, 1941. Wrappers. Hood's
104-780 1974 $15

PRATT, E. J.   The Iron Door. Toronto, 1927. Illus., limited
edition. Hood's 104-781 1974 $17.50

PRATT, E. J.   The Roosevelt and the Antinoe. New York,
1930. Signed, limited edition. Hood's 104-782 1974 $25

PRATT, S. J.   The Fair Circassian. 1781. 8vo., cloth, first
edition. Quaritch 936-197 1974 £8

PRATT, WALDO S.   St. Nicholas Songs with Illustrations. New York,
(1885). First edition, 4to., leather spine, very good. Current BW9-73 1974
$18

PRATT, WALDO S.   St. Nicholas Songs With Illustrations. New
York, (1885). First edition, 4to., orig. green pictorial boards, rebacked, fine.
Current BW9-82 1974 $18

PRATT, WALTER MERRIAM   Seven Generations. N.P., 1930. Large 8vo.,
orig. bindings. Butterfield 8-268 1974 $15

PRAUN, S. VON   Abbildung und Beschreilbung. 1859-75. 4to.,
2 vols., half morocco. Wheldon 129-672 1974 £60

THE PRAYER BOOK of King Edward VII. London, 1903. Brown leather, boards.
Dawson's 424-65 1974 $225

PRAYERS for Every Day in the Week. London, n.d. Orig. brown cloth, 2 5/8 X
2, inscription. Gregory 44-451 1974 $14.50

PRAYERS for Sundays, Holy-Days, and Other Festivals. 1705. Thick 12mo.,
contemporary calf, worn. Howes 185-1575 1974 £7.50

PREININGER, MARGARET   Japanese Flower Arrangement for the Modern
Home. Boston, 1936. 4to., plates, drawings, fine, orig. cloth. Gregory
44-252 1974 $13.50

PRELLER, LUDWIG   Griechische Mythologie. 1884. 2 vols. in
1, half calf. Allen 213-886 1973 $10

PRENTISS, CHARLES   New England Freedom: A Poem Delivered Before
the Washington Benevolent Society, in Brimfield, Feb. 22, 1813. Brookfield,
1813. 8vo., quarter cloth, ex-library, first edition, very scarce. Ximenes
36-168 1974 $50

PRENTISS, HENRY MELLON   The Great Polar Current. New York, 1897.
12mo., fine, glassine wrappers. Ballinger 1-37 1974 $10

PRESBREY, FRANK   The Empire of the South. (Washington, 1898).
4to., map, index, pictorial wrapper, photo illus. Butterfield 10-491 1974 $10

PRESBYTERY OF HUNTINGTON   The Historical Memorial of the Centennial
Anniversary of the . . . Held in Huntington, Pa., April 9, 1895. Philadelphia,
1895. Orig. binding, 4to., illus. Wilson 63-100 1974 $14.50

PRESCOTT, FREDERICK C.   The Poetic Mind. 1922. Hard cover edition.
Austin 61-804 1974 $10

PRESCOTT, HARRIETT ELIZABETH
Please turn to
SPOFFORD, HARRIET ELIZABETH PRESCOTT

PRESCOTT, WILLIAM H.   History of the Conquest of Mexico. London,
1844. 8vo., new calf, gilt, labels, 5 vols. Dawsons PM 251-312 1974 £75

PRESCOTT, WILLIAM H.   History of the Conquest of Peru. 1855. 2 vols.,
illus., fine, calf, seventh edition. Covent 56-630 1974 £45

PRESCOTT, WILLIAM H.   History of the Conquest of Peru. New York,
1847. 1st ed., 2 vols., port. frontis. Jacobs 24-27 1974 $75

PRESCOTT, WILLIAM H.   History of the Reign of Ferdinand & Isabella.
1854. 3 vols., contemporary calf gilt, portraits.   Smith 193-631 1973 £7.50

PRESCOTT, WILLIAM H.   Works. Philadelphia, 1882-83. 16 vols.,
crown 8vo., half maroon morocco gilt.   Howes 186-1147 1974 £30

THE PRESENT Interest of Tangier.   N.P., n.d. Folio, first edition.   Ximenes
35-321 1974 $60

PRESLAND, JOHN   Satni: A Tragedy. (1929). Small 4to., orig.
cloth, uncut, numbered, signed by author, limited, first edition.   Bow Windows
66-551 1974 £6.50

THE PRESS on the League.   New York, 1907. Pamphlet, 16 pages.   Austin
57-471 1974 $10

PRESSAVIN, JEAN BAPTISTE   Nouveau Traite des Vapeurs. Lyon, 1771.
Second edition.   Rittenhouse 46-546 1974 $35

PRESTET, JEAN   Elemens des Mathematiques. Paris, 1675. 4to.,
contemporary calf, rebacked, first edition.   Dawsons PM 245-613 1974 £35

PRESTON, A. E.   The Church & Parish of St. Nicholas,
Abingdon. Oxford, 1929. Thick demy 8vo., plates, orig. cloth.   Smith
193-175 1973 £6

PRESTON, HAYTER   The House of Vanities. London, 1922. 12mo.,
1st ed., illus.   Frohnsdorff 16-339 1974 $10

PRESTON, T. A.   The Flowering Plants of Wilts. 1888. 8vo.,
cloth, maps, scarce.   Wheldon 128-1212 1973 £6

PRESTON, T. A.   The Flowering Plants of Wilts. 1888. 8vo.,
cloth, maps, scarce.   Wheldon 131-1240 1974 £10

PRESTON, W. T. R.   The Life and Times of Lord Strathcona.
Toronto, n.d.   Hood's 104-278 1974 $15

PRESTWICH, GRACE ANNE   Life and Letters of Sir Joseph Prestwich. Edinburgh and London, 1899. 8vo., orig. cloth, gilt, plates, first edition.   Hammond
201-388 1974 £10

PRESTWICH, J.   Collected Papers on Some Controverted Questions
of Geology. New York, 1895. 8vo., cloth, tables, plates, frontispiece.
Wheldon 128-1035 1973 £5

PRESTWICH, J.   On Certain Phenomena Belonging to the Close
of the Last Geological Period and Their Bearing Upon the Tradition of the Flood.
1895. 8vo., orig. cloth, text-figures.   Wheldon 128-1037 1973 £5

PRETYMAN, HERBERT EDWARD Journal, Written During His Expedition to the
Kittar Mountains, Between Kenneh and the Red Sea, 1891. 1892. First edition,
portrait frontispiece, map, illus., square 8vo., orig. pict. cloth gilt, scarce.
Sawyer 293-231 1974 £95

PREVIATI, GAETANO   I Principii Scientifici del Divisionismo.
Turin, 1929. 8vo., wrapper, foxed, illus., second edition.   Minters 37-200
1973 $27.50

PREVOST, A. F.   Histoire Generale des Voyages ou Nouvelle
Collection. Paris, 1746-61. 17 vols., 4to., contemporary calf, leather
labels, gilt, rubbed, scarce.   Traylen 79-438 1973 £150

PREVOST, ABBE   Manon Lescaut. London & New York, 1928.
Small folio, cloth, illus., limited edition.   Minters 37-233 1973 $38

PREVOST, C.   L'escrime et le Duel. Paris, 1891. 8vo.,
contemporary half morocco, rebacked.   Bow Windows 64-334 1974 £8.50

PREVOST, PIERRE   Du Calorique Rayonnant. Paris, 1809. 8vo.,
contemporary morocco-backed boards, first edition.   Schumann 35-392 1974 $95

PREZZOLINI, GIUSEPPE   Discorso su Giovanni Papini. Florence, 1915.
8vo., wrapper.   Minters 37-427 1973 $20

PREZZOLINI, GIUSEPPE   Giovanni Papini. Turin, 1925. 8vo.,
wrapper, scarce.   Minters 37-428 1973 $27

PREZZOLINI, GIUSEPPE   Mi Pare. Milan & Turin, 1925. 8vo., uncut,
wrappers.   Minters 37-432 1973 $27.50

PREZZOLINI, GIUSEPPE   Il Sarto Spirituale. Florence, 1907. 8vo.,
wrapper.   Minters 37-204 1973 $30

PRICE, CON.   Memories of Old Montana. Hollywood,
c.1945. 8vo., cloth.   Saddleback 14-531 1974 $15

PRICE, HARRY   Fifty Years of Psychical Research. 1939.
Illus., presentation inscription, first edition.   Howes 186-1908 1974 £7.50

PRICE, HARRY   The Most Haunted House in England. 1940.
Illus., presentation, inscribed, first edition.   Howes 186-1909 1974 £7.50

PRICE, HARRY   Poltergeist Over England. 1945. Plates,
illus., presentation, inscribed, first edition.   Howes 186-1910 1974 £7

PRICE, HARRY   Poltegeist Over England. London, 1945.
Rittenhouse 46-548 1974 $15

PRICE, HARRY   Search for Truth. 1942. Plates, inscribed,
presentation, first edition.   Howes 186-1911 1974 £7.50

PRICE, JOHN EDWARD   A Descriptive Account of the Guildhall of the
City of London. London, 1886. Folio, orig. red cloth gilt, first edition.   Dawsons PM 251-96 1974 £15

PRICE, RICHARD   Observations on Reversionary Payments. 1772.
2 vols. in 1, 8vo., contemporary calf, fine.   Quaritch 939-201 1974 £65

PRICE, RICHARD   Observations on the Importance of the American
Revolution. Boston, 1784. Three quarter leather.   Jenkins 61-2217 1974 $37.50

PRICE, S.   Illustrations of Fungi of Our Fields and Woods.
London, 1864. 4to., orig. cloth, color plates, vol. 1 only.   Gregory 44-211
1974 $95

PRICE, S.   Illustrations of the Fungi of Our Fields and
Woods. 1864-65. Roy 4to., new half morocco, plates.   Wheldon 130-60
1974 £90

PRICE, UVEDALE   Dialogue on the Distinct Characters of the
Picturesque and the Beautiful. 1801. Quarter calf.   Eaton Music-664 1973
£8

PRICE, UVEDALE   An Essay on the Picturesque. London and Hereford, 1796 and 1798. 8vo., 2 vols., contemporary calf, scarce.   Broadhurst 23-
161 1974 £45

PRICE, UVEDALE   Essays on the Picturesque. 1810. 3 vols.,
8vo., contemporary diced calf gilt.   Quaritch 940-546 1974 £50

PRICE-BROWN, J.   The Mac's of '37, A Story of the Canadian
Rebellion. Toronto, 1910. Worn.   Hood's 104-570 1974 $15

PRICHARD, A. M.   Allied Families of Read, Corgin, Luttrell,
Bywaters: Starting from Culpepper County, Virginia. Staunton, 1930. 8vo.,
cloth.   Saddleback 14-789 1974 $30

PRICHARD, HESKETH   Hunting Camps in Wood and Wilderness. New
York, 1910. 4to., orig. cl., illus.   Jacobs 24-165 1974 $15

PRICHARD, H. H.   Through Trackless Labrador. London, 1911.
Photographs, illus., map.   Hood's 103-186 1974 $60

PRICHARD, JAMES COWLES The Natural History of Man. 1848. 8vo.,
contemporary half russia, plates, third edition.   Wheldon 130-366 1974 £40

PRICHARD, JAMES COWLES   The Natural History of Man. London, 1855. 2 vols., 8vo., plates, orig. cloth, rubbed, enlarged fourth edition. Bow Windows 62-734 1974 £20

PRICHARD, JAMES COWLES   The Natural History of Man. 1855. 2 vols., 8vo., orig. cloth, plates. Wheldon 131-451 1974 £40

PRICHARD, JAMES COWLES   Researches into the Physical History of Mankind. 1841-37-47. 8vo., orig. cloth, plates, 5 vols. Bow Windows 64-214 1974 £62

PRICHARD, JAMES COWLES   A Treatise on Diseases of the Nervous System. London, 1822. 8vo., contemporary mauve cloth, fine, first edition. Dawsons PM 249-411 1974 £90

PRICHARD, JAMES COWLES   A Treatise on Insanity. London, 1835. 8vo., orig. cloth, first edition. Schumann 35-393 1974 $235

PRICHARD, JAMES COWLES   A Treatise On Insanity and Other Orders Affecting the Mind. London, 1835. 8vo., old calf, rebacked, library stamp, first edition. Traylen 79-262 1973 £95

PRICKETT, M.   An Historical and Architectural Description of the Priory Church. Cambridge, 1831. 8vo., plates, modern boards. Quaritch 939-603 1974 £6.50

PRIDEAUX, H.   The True Nature of Imposture Fully Display'd in the Life of Mahomet. 1723. 8vo., crimson morocco, gilt, eighth edition. Quaritch 936-198 1974 £20

PRIDEAUX, MATHIAS   An Easy and Compendious Introdvction for Reading all Sorts of Histories. 1682. 4to., contemporary calf, sixth edition. Dawsons PM 251-313 1974 £175

PRIDEAUX, MATHIAS   An Easy and Compendious Introduction for Reading all Sorts of Histories. Oxford, 1682. Small 4to., contemporary panelled calf, fine. Goodspeed's 578-289 1974 £50

PRIERES Ordinaires des Soldatz de l'Armee, Conduite par Monsieur le Prince de Conde. (N.P.), 1562. 4to., boards, fine, scarce. Harper 213-125 1973 $225

PRIEST, C. D.   The Birds of Southern Rhodesia. 1933-36. Roy 8vo., orig. cloth, 4 vols., plates. Wheldon 130-602 1974 £120

PRIEST, C. D.   The Birds of Southern Rhodesia. 1933-36. 4 vols., roy. 8vo., orig. cloth, text-figures, map, coloured plates, nice copy. Wheldon 128-547 1973 £120

PRIEST, JOSIAH   American Antiquities, and Discoveries in the West. Albany, 1833. Contemporary calf, red label, fine. Butterfield 10-469 1974 $20

PRIEST, JOSIAH   American Antiquities and Discoveries in the West. Albany, 1834. Map, frontispiece, damaged, full leather. Jenkins 61-2218 1974 $10

PRIESTLEY, JOHN BOYNTON   Angel Pavement. 1930. Brilliant copy, near perfect d.w. Covent 51-2538 1973 £5

PRIESTLEY, JOHN BOYNTON   Angel Pavement. 1930. 8vo., buckram, first edition, signed. Quaritch 936-526 1974 £9

PRIESTLEY, JOHN BOYNTON   Angel Pavement. London, 1930. First edition. Biblo and Tannen 210-792 1973 $15

PRIESTLEY, JOHN BOYNTON   Angel Pavement. London, 1930. 8vo., orig. buckram, frontis., first limited edition. Bow Windows 62-735 1974 £8.50

PRIESTLEY, JOHN BOYNTON   Dangerous Corner. 1932. 273 pages. Austin 61-808 1974 $10

PRIESTLEY, JOHN BOYNTON   Faraway. 1932. Fine, d.w., English first edition. Covent 56-1064 1974 £5

PRIESTLEY, JOHN BOYNTON   Faraway. 1932. Blue buckram, English first edition. Covent 56-1063 1974 £7.50

PRIESTLEY, JOHN BOYNTON   George Meredith. New York, 1926. Inscribed and signed by Calvin Coolidge. Jenkins 61-715 1974 $37.50

PRIESTLEY, JOHN BOYNTON   Johnson Over Jordan. Harper, 1939. 144p., illus. Austin 51-756 1973 $10

PRIESTLEY, JOHN BOYNTON   Theatre Outlook. 1947. Austin 51-757 1973 $8.50

PRIESTLEY, JOHN BOYNTON   Theatre Outlook. London, 1947. First edition, Biblo & Tannen 213-904 1973 $9.50

PRIESTLEY, JOHN BOYNTON   Time and the Conways. French, 1937. Austin 51-758 1973 $8.50

PRIESTLEY, JOHN BOYTON   The Town Major of Miraucourt. 1930. Orig. vellum gilt, limited edition. Smith 193-398 1973 £5.50

PRIESTLEY, JOSEPH   A Comparison of the Institutions of Moses with those of the Hindoos and other Ancient Nations. Northumberland, 1799. 8vo., orig. boards, rebacked, uncut, unopened, first edition. Hammond 201-504 1974 £55

PRIESTLEY, JOSEPH   A Course of Lectures on Oratory and Criticism. London, 1777. 4to., contemporary calf, gilt, rebacked, first edition. Hammond 201-505 1974 £42

PRIESTLEY, JOSEPH   A Discourse on Occasion of the Death of Dr. Price. London, 1791. 8vo., boards, first edition. Hammond 201-506 1974 £17.50

PRIESTLEY, JOSEPH   Disquisitions Relating to Matter and Spirit. Birmingham, 1782. 8vo., contemporary half mottled calf, gilt. Hammond 201-508 1974 £36

PRIESTLEY, JOSEPH   Disquisitions Relating to Matter and Spirit. Birmingham, 1782. 8vo., orig. boards, rebacked, second editions. Hammond 201-507 1974 £40

PRIESTLEY, JOSEPH   Dr. Priestley's Letter to the Inhabitants of Birmingham. London, 1791. 8vo., boards, first edition. Hammond 201-509 1974 £12

PRIESTLEY, JOSEPH   The Evidence of the Resurrection of Jesus Considered in a Discourse. Birmingham, 1791. Unbound in cardboard wraps, text complete. Biblo & Tannen 213-986 1973 $37.50

PRIESTLEY, JOSEPH   The Evidence of the Resurrection of Jesus Considered. Birmingham, 1791. 8vo., boards, first edition. Hammond 201-510 1974 £18

PRIESTLEY, JOSEPH   An Examination of Dr. Reid's Inquiry into the Human Mind on the Principles of Common Sense. London, 1775. 8vo., contemporary half calf, gilt, second edition. Hammond 201-511 1974 £28

PRIESTLEY, JOSEPH   Experiments and Observations. 1790. 8vo., 3 vols., contemporary calf. Zeitlin 235-297 1974 $385

PRIESTLEY, JOSEPH   Experiments and Observations. 1781. 8vo., 2 vols., orig. boards, uncut. Zeitlin 235-296 1974 $475

PRIESTLEY, JOSEPH   Experiments and Observatons On Different Kinds of Air. London, 1781-84-77-79. 4 vols., 8vo., orig. boards, uncut, plates, early editions. Traylen 79-263 1973 £80

PRIESTLEY, JOSEPH   Historical Account of the Navigable Rivers, Canals, and Railways, of Great Britain. London, 1831. 8vo., contemporary publisher's morocco, gilt, first edition. Hammond 201-860 1974 £85

PRIESTLEY, JOSEPH   Historical Account of the Navigable Rivers, Canals, and Railways. 1831. 4to., library cloth. Quaritch 939-88 1974 £120

PRIESTLEY, JOSEPH   The History and Present State of Electricity.   London, 1769. 4to., contemporary calf, rebacked, second edition.   Dawsons PM 245-614 1974 £48

PRIESTLEY, JOSEPH   An History of the Corruptions of Christianity. Birmingham, 1782. 8vo., 2 vols., orig. wrappers, uncut, first edition.   Hill 126-219 1974 £35

PRIESTLEY, JOSEPH   An History of the Early Opinions Concerning Jesus Christ.   Birmingham, 1786. 8vo., 4 vols., orig. boards, rebacked, uncut, unopened, first edition.   Hammond 201-512 1974 £45

PRIESTLEY, JOSEPH   An Inquiry into the Knowledge of the Antient Hebrews concerning a Future State.   London, 1801. 8vo., boards, first edition. Hammond 201-513 1974 £20

PRIESTLEY, JOSEPH   Lectures on History and General Policy.   Dublin, 1788. 8vo., contemporary half calf, gilt, first Dublin edition.   Hammond 201-515 1974 £30

PRIESTLEY, JOSEPH   Lectures on History and General Policy.   Birmingham, 1788. 4to., contemporary calf, gilt, rebacked, plates, first edition.   Hammond 201-514 1974 £55

PRIESTLEY, JOSEPH   Letters to a Young Man.   London, 1792. 8vo., boards, first edition.   Hammond 201-518 1974 £16

PRIESTLEY, JOSEPH   A Letter to Jacob Bryant.   London, 1780. 8vo., boards, first edition.   Hammond 201-516 1974 £22

PRIESTLEY, JOSEPH   A Letter to the Rev. Mr. John Palmer.   Bath, 1779. 8vo., boards, first edition.   Hammond 201-517 1974 £24

PRIESTLEY, JOSEPH   Letters to the Right Honourable Edmund Burke. Birmingham, 1791. 8vo., modern boards, second edition.   Dawsons PM 247-228 1974 £15

PRIESTLEY, JOSEPH   Philosophical Empiricism.   London, 1775. 8vo., sewn, uncut.   Zeitlin 235-298 1974 $350

PRIESTLEY, JOSEPH   The Proper Objects of Education in the Present State of the World.   London, 1791.   Unbound in cardboard wraps.   Biblo & Tannen 213-987 1973 $22.50

PRIESTLEY, JOSEPH   A Reply to the Animadversions on the History of the Corruptions of Christianity.   Birmingham, 1783. 8vo., boards, first edition. Hammond 201-520 1974 £17.50

PRIESTLEY, JOSEPH   A Sermon Preached at the Gravel Pit Meeting. London, 1793. 8vo., boards, first edition.   Hammond 201-521 1974 £15

PRIESTLEY, JOSEPH   A Third Letter to Dr. Newcome.   Birmingham, 1781. 8vo., boards, first edition.   Hammond 201-522 1974 £12.50

PRIESTLEY, JOSEPH   Two Letters to Dr. Newcome.   Birmingham, 17-80. 8vo., boards, first edition.   Hammond 201-523 1974 £16

PRIME, ALFRED COXE   Three Centuries of Historic Silver. Philadelphia, 1938. Orig. binding, illus., limited to 1,000 numbered copies. Wilson 63-285 1974 $50

PRIMROSE, JAMES   De Vulgi Erroribus in Medicina Libri IV. Rotterdam, 1658. 12mo., half calf.   Schuman 37-208 1974 $110

PRINCE, EZRA M.   Transactions of the McLean County Historical Society.   Bloomington, 1900. Orig. cloth, gilt, portraits, mint, rare, first edition.   Bradley 35-231 1974 $15

PRINCE, JOHN 1643-1723   Danomnii Orientales Illustres.   Exeter, 1701. Folio, old bind-stamped calf.   Traylen 79-323 1973 £16

PRINCE, JOHN CRITCHLEY   The Life of John C. Prince.   Manchester, 1880. 1st ed.   Biblo & Tannen 213-584 1973 $15

PRINCE, JOHN CRITCHLEY   The Poetical Works of John Critchley Prince. Manchester, 1880. 1st ed., 2 vols.   Biblo & Tannen 213-583 1973 $20

PRINCE, WILLIAM ROBERT   The Pomological Manual.   New York, 1831. 8vo., orig. quarter cloth and blue boards, printed paper label, fine unopened copy, first edition.   Ximenes 37-182 1974 $200

PRINCESS Mary's Gift Book.   London, (1914). 4to., cloth, mounted color plate, illus.   Frohnsdorff 15-151 1974 $10

THE PRINCETON Bric-a-Brac.   Vol. 41--Class of 1917. (F. Scott Fitzgerald) Princeton, 1917. 1st ed., oblong 4to.   Biblo & Tannen 214-705 1974 $200

PRINCETON in the World War with a Sketch on page 381 of the War Record of Francis Scott Fitzgerald.   Princeton U., 1932. 1st ed.   Biblo & Tannen 214-706 1974 $75

PRINGLE, J. F.   Lunenburgh.   Cornwall, 1890. First edition. Hood's 104-229 1974 $60

PRINGLE, J. F.   Lunenburgh.   Cornwall, 1890. First edition. Hood's 102-207 1974 $60

PRINGLE, JOHN   Observations on the Diseases of the Army.   London, 1752. 8vo., speckled calf, first edition.   Dawsons PM 249-412 1974 £200

PRINSEP, J.   Musae Etonenses.   1755. 2 vols., 8vo., old calf, gilt.   Quaritch 939-311 1974 £6

PRINTING-OFFICE Characters; or, "Types" of Printing-Office Life.   London, 1881. Small 8vo., orig. printed wrappers.   Kraus B8-360 1974 $25

PRINZHORN, HANS   Bildnerei der Geisteskranken.   Berlin, 1922. 4to., plates, illus., printed boards.   Quaritch 940-206 1974 £15

PRIOR, MATTHEW   The History of His Own Time.   London, 1740. 2 vols., 8vo., contemporary panelled calf, second edition.   Dawsons PM 252-802 1974 £20

PRIOR, MATTHEW   An Ode Humbly Inscrib'd to the Queen.   1706. Folio, disbound, first edition.   Quaritch 936-199 1974 £12

PRIOR, MATTHEW   Poems on Several Occasions.   1754. 2 vols., calf, 2 covers detached.   Allen 216-2052 1974 $12.50

PRIOR, MATTHEW   Poems on Several Occasions.   1718. Folio, large paper copy, engraved frontispiece, contemporary red morocco gilt, rebacked, preserving orig. spine.   Bow Windows 66-554 1974 £145

PRIOR, MATTHEW   Poems on Several Occasions.   1718. Folio, contemporary calf, rebacked, frontispiece.   Quaritch 936-200 1974 £30

PRIOR, MATTHEW   Solomon de Mundi Vanitate.   Oxford, 1734. 4to., modern boards, first edition.   Dawsons PM 252-805 1974 £12

PRIOR, MATTHEW   Poems on Several Occasions.   London, 1718. Folio, contemporary panelled calf, gilt.   Dawsons PM 252-804 1974 £85

PRIOR, MATTHEW   Poems On Several Occasions.   London, 1709. 8vo., contemporary panelled calf, second edition.   Dawsons PM 252-803 1974 £65

PRIOR, R. C. A.   On the Popular Names of British Plants.   1879. Crown 8vo., cloth, scarce, third edition.   Wheldon 130-1104 1974 £6

PRIOR, SAMUEL   All the Voyages Round the World.   London, n.d. Thick tall 8vo., engravings, contemporary sheep gilt.   Smith 193-538 1973 £12

PRISCIANUS   Grammatica.   1527. 19th century calf gilt. Thomas 30-67 1973 £36

PRITCHARD, ANDREW   A History of Infusorial Animalcules.   1852. 8vo., orig. cloth, plates, new enlarged edition.   Bow Windows 64-215 1974 £6

PRITCHARD, ANDREW   A History of Infusoria.   1861. 8vo., orig. cloth, plates, scarce, fourth edition.   Wheldon 130-885 1974 £20

PRITCHARD, ANDREW   A History of Infusoria. 1861. 8vo., orig.
cloth, plates, fourth edition. Wheldon 131-945 1974 £18

PRITCHARD, ANDREW   A History of Infusoria. 1861. 8vo., orig.
cloth, plates, scarce, revised fourth edition. Wheldon 128-55 1973 £12

PRITZEL, G. A.   Thesaurus Literaturae Botanicae. Leipzig, 1872.
4to., half morocco, second edition. Wheldon 129-181 1974 £25

PROBUS, M. VALERIUS   De notis Romanorum. Venice, 1525. 4to.,
colored wrappers, fine, woodcut. Harper 213-126 1973 $575

PROCEEDINGS in the French Chambers. 1847. 4to., cloth, orig. wrappers.
Howes 186-1229 1974 £12.50

PROCEEDINGS of the Association for Promoting the Discovery of the Interior
Parts of Africa. London, 1790. 4to., old half calf, first edition, very good copy,
fine large folding map. Ximenes 36-2 1974 $275

PROCEEDINGS of the Celebration of the Three Hundredth Anniversary of the
First Recognized Use of Cinchona Held at the Missouri Botanical Gardens, St.
Louis, October 31-November 1, 1930. St. Louis, 1931. 4to., orig. printed
wrappers faded and marked, plates, slight foxing. Bow Windows 66-555 1974 £6

PROCEEDINGS of the Grand Lodge of Ancient Free and Accepted Masons of
Montana. Helena, 1891. 12mo., wrapper. Saddleback 14-536 1974 £10

PROCEEDINGS of the Special Committee Appointed for the Purpose of Inquiring
. . . Rates of Profit Made Thereon By Dealers. Ottawa, 1920. Wrappers.
Hood's 104-592 1974 $12.50

PROCESSION of Pope Clement VII and the Emperor Charles V. Edinburgh,
1875. Folio, orig. dec. cloth, illus., limited. Howes 186-1150 1974 £21

PROCESSIONARIUM Iuxta Ritum Sacri Ordinis Praedicatorum S. P. N. Dominici.
Rome, 1610. Small 8vo., Italian black morocco gilt, worn. Thomas 28-143
1972 £50

PROCLAMATIONS for Thanksgiving Issued by the Continental Congress, President
Washington, By the National and State Governments on the Peace of 1815, and by
the Governors of New York Since the Introduction of the Custom. Albany, 1858.
Small 4to., orig. binding. Butterfield 10-510 1974 $25

PROCLUS, DIADOCHUS   La Sfera di Proclo Liceo Tradotta. 1573. 4to.,
modern boards, first edition. Dawsons PM 245-617 1974 £35

PROCTER, BRYAN W.   Dramatic Scenes. 1857. 368 pages. Austin
61-823 1974 $12.50

PROCTOR, JOHN   Short Lives of the Dominican Saints. 1901.
8vo., orig. cloth, label. Howes 185-1578 1974 £6

PROCTOR, R. A.   A Star Atlas. London, 1874. Folio, plates,
orig. cloth, rubbed, third edition. Bow Windows 62-738 1974 £7.50

PROCTOR, ROBERT   Jan Van Doesborgh, Printer at Antwerp.
London, 1894. 4to., contemporary half morocco gilt, plates. Dawsons PM
10-500 1974 £25

PROFESSIONISTI Italiani. 1935. 155p., illus. Austin 62-291 1974 $37.50

PROFILES From the New Yorker. Knopf, 1938. 400p. Austin 54-793 1973 $8.50

THE PROGRESS of a Society. New York, 1817. 3 parts, small 8vo., orig.
boards, top of spine chipped, first edition, very good unopened copy. Ximenes
36-167 1974 $85

PROKOSCH, FREDERIC   Chosen Poems. New York, 1947. 1st ed.
Biblo & Tannen 210-793 1973 $10

PROKSCH, JOHANN KARL   Die Litteratur Uber die Venerischen. Bonn,
1889-1900. 8vo., grey cloth, 5 vols., fine. Dawsons PM 249-63 1974 £65

PROLETARIAN Literature in the United States. n.d. First edition, covers little
stained, back discoloured. Covent 51-91 1973 £5.25

PROLETARIAN Literature in the United States. n.d. Faded covers. Covent
55-23 1974 £6.30

PROMINENT Americans of Swiss Origin. 1932. Photographs, 266 pages.
Austin 57-661 1974 $17.50

PRONOSTICATIO Queda Mirabilis Divinitus Partim Revelata Partim Celesti
Costellatione Premonstrata. Lyons, 1515. Small 8vo., modern blind stamped
pigskin, slip case. Thomas 32-132 1974 £150

PRONTI, D.   Nuova Raccolta di 100 Vedutine Antiche Della
Citta di Roma e Sue Vicinanze. 1795. Vol. 1 only, half calf, illus. Allen
213-890 1973 $12.50

PROPERT, W. A.   The Russian Ballet, 1921-29. London, 1931.
Folio, plates, inscription by author to Marie Rambert, orig. cloth. Gregory 44-15
1974 $125

PROPERTIUS   Elegies. 1933. New buckram. Allen
213-891 1973 $15

PROPHETT, A.   The Twilight Age. 1933. Fine, slightly frayed
d.w., first edition, scarce. Covent 51-924 1973 £8.50

PROPHETT, A.   The Twilight Age. 1933. Spine discoloured,
else very good, scarce, first edition. Covent 51-925 1973 £6.30

THE PROPOSAL Commonly Called Sir Matthew Decker's Scheme for One General
Tax Upon Houses Laid Open. London, 1757. 8vo., modern boards, fine, first
edition. Dawsons PM 247-230 1974 £30

A PROPOSAL for Raising Sixty Thousand Pound per Annum. (1714). Folio,
disbound. Quaritch 939-288 1974 £15

PROPOSALS for Raising a Loan of 260,000 1. Yearly for the Use of the Publick.
(1711). Folio, disbound. Quaritch 939-145 1974 £20

PROROK, BYRON DE   In Quest of Lost Worlds. New York, 1936.
Biblo & Tannen 213-127 1973 $7.50

PROSKE, BEATRICE GILMAN   Brookgreen Gardens. Brookgreen, S.C., 1943.
Illus. Biblo & Tannen 214-489 1974 $12.50

PROSPECTUS of the South Baltimore Company. Baltimore, 1833. 12mo.,
wrappers, map. Ximenes 35-9 1974 $30

PROUST, MARCEL   47 Lettres Inedites de Marcel Proust a Walter
Barry. Paris, 1930. No. 39 of edition limited to 250 copies, heavy white
paper covers, piece of orig. tissue wrapper missing, box badly split, back and
bottom missing, book itself fine. Ross 87-463 1974 $65

PROUST, MARCEL   47 Unpublished Letters from Marcel Proust to
Walter Berry. Paris, 1930. 4to., orig. wrappers, first edition, one of 200
numbered copies on Arches paper, fine, orig. publisher's box. MacManus
224-363 1974 $75

PROUST, MARCEL   Quelques Lettres de Marcel Proust a Simone de
Caillavet. Paris, 1928. One of 1000 numbered copies on velin, portraits,
wrappers, sewing little weak, nice copy. Covent 51-2539 1973 £5.25

PROUST, MARCEL   Six Lettres de Marcel Proust. Paris, 1929.
Fine, unopened copy, wrappers. Covent 51-1527 1973 £20

PROUT, J. S.   Picturesque Antiquities of Bristol. Bristol,
n.d. Folio, half green morocco gilt, plates. Traylen 79-331 1973 £105

PROUT, SAMUEL   Hints on Light and Shadow. 1838. Folio,
plates, orig. cloth. Quaritch 940-207 1974 £30

PROUT, SAMUEL   Sketches by. 1915. Half red morocco,
plates, rebound. Marsden 39-356 1974 £7

PROUT, WILLIAM   Chemistry Meteorology and the Function of Digestion. London, 1834. 8vo., half calf, rebacked, first edition. Dawsons PM
245-619 1974 £10

PROUTY, OLIVE HIGGINS   Stella Dallas. 304p., illus. Austin 51-759 1973 $7.50

PROVIDENCE, Rhode Island. New York, 1893. Boards, photos. Jenkins 61-2272 1974 $12.50

PROWSE, DANIEL WOODLEY   A History of Newfoundland From the English Colonial and Foreign Records. London, 1896. Second edition, revised and corrected. Hood's 102-208 1974 $85

PROZIO, SIMONE   De Coloribus Libellus. Florence, 1548. 8vo., old style vellum, first edition, first issue. Schumann 35-389 1974 $165

PRUDENTIUS CLEMENS, AURELIUS   Opera. 1501. Small 4to., old vellum, bookplate. Thomas 30-5 1973 £40

PRUDHOMME, LOUIS   Voyage a la Guiane et a Cayenne. Paris, (1797). 8vo., contemporary sheep-backed boards, maps, first edition. Harper 213-127 1973 $175

PRUNAIRE, ALFRED   Les Plus Beaux Types de Lettres d'Apres les Maitres de cet Art. Paris, n.d. (1895). 4to., text uncut & unopened, plates, orig. publisher's half cloth portfolio. Kraus B8-372 1974 $85

PRUVOST, R.   Robert Greene et ses Romans, 1558-02. 1938. Sewn. Allen 216-1805 1974 $15

PRYCE, WILLIAM   Mineralogia Cornubiensis. London, 1778. Folio, half calf, gilt, plates, first edition. Hammond 201-897 1974 £150

PRYCE, WILLIAM   Mineralogia Comubiensis. 1778. Folio, half brown morocco, gilt, uncut. Zeitlin 235-180 1974 $575

PRYER, H.   Rhopolocera Nihonica. Tokyo, 1935. 4to., half leather, plates. Wheldon 130-779 1974 £25

PRYNNE, WILLIAM   The Fourth Part of a Brief Register, Kalender and Survey of the Several Kinds, Forms of Parliamentary Writs. 1664. Partly in black letter, thick small 4to., contemporary calf, binding springing at one point, else excellent state. Thomas 32-134 1974 £21

PRYNNE, WILLIAM   The Fourth Part of a Brief Register, Kalender and Survey. London, 1664. Small 4to., old calf. Quaritch 939-202 1974 £75

PRYNNE, WILLIAM   The Fourth Part of a Brief Register. 1664. Thick small 4to., contemporary calf. Thomas 28-199 1972 £21

PRYNNE, WILLIAM   An Humble Remonstrance to His Maiesty, Against the Tax of Ship-Money. 1641. Small 4to., disbound, first edition. Dawsons PM 247-231 1974 £55

PRYNNE, WILLIAM   A Quench-Coale. N.P. (Amsterdam), 1637. Small 4to., contemporary calf, rubbed, spine worn, first edition, crisp copy. Ximenes 36-171 1974 $75

PTOLEMAEUS, CLAUDIUS   Geographie Opus Novissima Traductione e Grecorum. Strassburg, 1513. 2 vols., folio, blind stamped pigskin, fine. Dawsons PM 250-65 1974 £7500

PTOLEMAEUS, CLAUDIUS   Handbuch der Astronomie. 1912-13. 2 vols. Allen 213-893 1973 $18.25

PTOLEMAEUS, CLAUDIUS   Trattato Della Descrittione Della Sfera Celeste in Piano. Bologna, 1572. 4to., modern boards, first edition in Italian. Dawsons PM 245-620 1974 £65

PUBLIC and Parlor Readings. Lee, Shepard, 1871. Austin 51-640 1973 $10

PUCKLE, JOHN   The Church and Fortress of Dover Castle. Oxford, 1864. 8vo., orig. cloth, folding plans, coloured and other plates. Bow Windows 66-556 1974 $9.50

PUDOVKIN, V. I.   Film Technique. Newnes, 1935. 204p. Austin 51-761 1973 $6.50

PUGET, L. DE   Observations sur la Structure des Yeux de Divers Insectes. Lyons, 1706. 8vo., calf, gilt, plates, rare. Wheldon 130-780 1974 £20

PUGH, E.   Cambria Depicta. 1816. Roy. 4to., plates, half red morocco gilt, illus. Quaritch 939-689 1974 £700

PUGH, JOHN   A Treatise on the Science of Muscular Action. London, 1794. Large 4to., contemporary marbled calf. Schumann 35-395 1974 $110

PUGIN, AUGUSTUS CHARLES 1762-1832   Paris and Its Environs. 1829-31. 4to., orig. wrappers. Smith 194-606 1974 £18

PUGIN, AUGUSTUS CHARLES 1762-1832   Specimens of Gothic Architecture. 1822. 2 vols., plates, quarter red morocco, gilt, first edition. Marsden 39-357 1974 £21

PUGIN, AUGUSTUS CHARLES 1762-1832   A Series of Ornamental Timber Gables. 1854. Crown 4to., quarter morocco, second edition. Covent 55-71 1974 £30

PUGIN, AUGUSTUS WELBY NORTHMORE 1812-1852   Fifteenth and Sixteenth Century Ornaments. Edinburgh, 1904. 4to., blue cloth, stained, plates, frontis. in colour. Eaton Music-665 1973 £10

PUGIN, AUGUSTUS WELBY NORTHMORE 1812-1852   Glossary of Ecclesiastical Ornament and Costume. 1868. Imp. 4to., plates, orig. quarter morocco, gilt, revised and enlarged third edition. Quaritch 940-471 1974 £50

PUISSANT, LOUIS   Traite de Geodesie. Paris, 1805. 4to., orig. boards, plates. Zeitlin 235-184 1974 $75

PULINGS, GASTON   Arrets Facultatifs. Paris, 1925. Small 8vo., wrappers, signed, plates. Minters 37-246 1973 $25

PULLAN, MRS.   The Lady's Manual of Fancy-Work. New York, 1859. 8vo., plates, cloth gilt, clean copy. Quaritch 940-770 1974 £20

PULTENEY, RICHARD   A General View of the Writings of Linnaeus. 1781. 8vo., contemporary calf, rare first edition. Wheldon 128-117 1973 £36

PULTENEY, RICHARD   A General View of the Writings of Linnaeus. 1805. 4to., contemporary calf, plates, second edition. Wheldon 129-172 1974 £35

PULTENEY, RICHARD   Historical and Biographical Sketches. 1790. 8vo., modern buckram, 2 vols. Wheldon 129-182 1974 £30

PULTENEY, WILLIAM EARL OF BATH
Please turn to
BATH, WILLIAM PULTENEY, EARL OF

PUMPELLY, RAPHAEL   Across America and Asia. New York, 1870. Revised second edition, map. Butterfield 10-471 1974 $15

PUMPELLY, RAPHAEL   Across America and Asia. New York, 1870. Gilt stamped cloth, edges rubbed, map, photo views. Butterfield 10-470 1974 $20

PUMPELLY, RAPHAEL   Across America and Asia. New York, 1870. 8vo., orig. bindings, first edition. Butterfield 8-19 1974 $25

PUNCH Library of Humour. n.d. 25 vols., illus., orig. cloth gilt. Smith 193-678 1973 £8

PURCELL, EDWARD S.   Life of Cardinal Manning. 1896. 2 vols., thick 8vo., contemporary half calf. Howes 185-1406 1974 £5.50

PURCELL, MAE F.   History of Contra Costa County. Berkeley, 1940. 8vo., cloth, illus. Saddleback 14-239 1974 $40

PURCHAS, SAMUEL   Purchas, His Pilgrimage Or Relations of the
World and the Religions Observed. London, 1617. Full leather, raised bands,
enlarged third edition. Hood's 103-551 1974 $1250

PURCHASE, S.   A Theatre of Politicall Flying-Insects. 1657.
4to., modern full calf, rare. Wheldon 130-781 1974 £130

PURDUE University. Lafayette, c. 1910. Hand colored illus. Jenkins 61-1134
1974 $10

PURKINJE, JOHANN EVANGELISTA   De Cellulus Antherarum Fibrosis. Breslau, 1830. 4to., orig. boards, first edition. Schumann 35-396 1974 $275

PURTON, T.   A Botanical Description of British Plants in the
Midland Counties. Stratford, 1817-21. 8vo., 3 vols., modern boards, plates,
rare. Wheldon 130-1105 1974 £55

PURTON, T.   A Botanical Description of British Plants in the
Midland Counties. Stratford-Upon-Avon, 1817-21. 3 vols., 8vo., modern
boards, coloured plates, rare. Wheldon 128-1213 1973 £55

PURUCKER, G. DE   The Esoteric Tradition. 1935. 8vo., 2 vols.,
orig. cloth. Broadhurst 23-1759 1974 £6

PURVES-STEWART, JAMES   The Diagnosis of Nervous Diseases. New
York, 1924. Revised sixth edition. Rittenhouse 46-550 1974 $10

PUSCHMANN, THEODOR   Handbuch der Geschichte der Medezin.
Jena, 1902-05. 3 vols., 8vo., half leather, first edition. Schuman 37-211
1974 $135

PUSHKIN, ALEKSANDR SERGIEEVICH 1799-1837   Boris Godounov. Paris,
(1927). 8vo., full red calf, plates, drawings, slipcases. Bow Windows 62-739
1974 £295

PUSHKIN, ALEKSANDR SERGIEEVICH 1799-1837   The Captain's Daughter.
London, 1859. Contents little loose, good copy, first edition. Covent 51-1627
1973 £12.50

PUSHKIN, ALEKSANDR SERGIEEVICH 1799-1837   The Queen of Spades.
1928. One of 250 numbered copies on Rives vellum, coloured frontis., engravings,
small 4to., orig. quarter vellum, fine, first edition. Covent 51-2184 1973 £12

PUSS In Boots. (London, c. 1890). 8vo., colored pictures, dec. front cover,
rebacked, nice despite pencil scratches on blank page. Current BW9-137 1974
$18.50

PUTEO, PARIS DE   Trac. de re Mili. & Duel. 1543. 8vo.,
woodcut, contemporary vellum, scarce. Bow Windows 62-740 1974 £60

PUTNAM, G. H.   Censorship of the Church of Rome and Its
Influence Upon Production and Distribution of Literature. 1906. 2 vols. Allen
216-203 1974 $15

PUTNAM, GEORGE H.   A Prisoner of War in Virginia 1864-65. New
York, 1912. Cloth. Hayman 59-118 1974 $10

PUTMAN, GEORGE PALMER   Wide Margins. New York, 1942. 1st ed.
Biblo & Tannen 210-905 1973 $10

PUTNAM, BRENDA   The Sculptor's Way. New York, 1948. 4to.,
illus. Biblo & Tannen 214-490 1974 $15

PUTNAM, SAMUEL   The World of Jean de Bosschere. 1931. Full
buckram, illus., dust wrapper, fine. Covent 55-247 1974 £21

PUTNAM, SAMUEL   The World of Jean de Bosschere. n.d. Orig.
buckram, fine, illus., English first edition. Covent 56-1825 1974 £21

PUTNAM, SAMUEL   The World of Jean de Bosschere. With a Letter
of Paul Valery. N. P., n.d. Orig. vellum backed boards, somewhat soiled,
first edition, one of 100 numbered copies, signed etching by Bosschere bound in,
internally very fine. MacManus 224-364 1974 $85

PUTTENHAM, GEORGE   The Arte of English Poesie. London, 1589.
Small 4to., levant morocco, gilt, fine, rare first edition. Dawsons PM 252-807
1974 £6000

A PUZZLE for a Curious Girl. 1819. New edition revised, engraved plates,
12mo., orig. boards, roan spine, corners trifle rubbed. George's 610-612 1973
£6

PYCRAFT, W. P.   A History of Birds. 1910. 8vo., cloth,
plates. Wheldon 131-687 1974 £7.50

PYCRAFT, W. P.   The Standard Natural History from Amoeba to
Man. (1931). Roy. 8vo., cloth, plates. Wheldon 131-452 1974 £5

PYE, HENRY JAMES   The Siege of Meaux. London, 1794. 8vo.,
modern boards, first edition. Dawsons PM 252-808 1974 £15

PYLE, HOWARD   The Merry Adventures of Robin Hood. New
York, 1925. 8vo., d.j., illus., very fine. Current BW9-121 1974 $32.50

PYLE, HOWARD   Price of Blood. 1899. Coloured plates.
Allen 216-185 1974 $10

PYLE, HOWARD   The Price of Blood. Boston, 1899. First edition,
frontis. loose. Butterfield 10-472 1974 $25

PYLE, HOWARD   The Story of King Arthur and His Knights. New
York, 1903. Orig. pictorial cloth, slightly soiled, hinges cracked, first edition,
illus., bookplate, fine copy. MacManus 224-365 1974 $42.50

PYLE, HOWARD   Wonder Clock Plays. New York and London,
1925. Orig. dec. cloth, trifle soiled, illus. with photos and drawings, first
edition of this version, fine copy. MacManus 224-366 1974 $60

PYM, HORACE N.   Odds and Ends At Foxwold. 1887. Large 8vo.,
orig. cloth, uncut, plates. Dawsons PM 10-501 1974 £9

PYNE, J. B.   Lake Scenery of England. (1859). Small
folio, plates, cloth gilt. Quaritch 939-204 1974 £35

PYNE, WILLIAM HENRY   The History of the Royal Residences of Windsor
Castle. 1819. 3 vols., imp. 4to., half calf. Quaritch 939-205 1974 £500

PYNE, WILLIAM HENRY   The History of the Royal Residences of Windsor
Castle. 1819. 3 vols., imp. 4to., drawings, contemporary calf, rebacked.
Quaritch 940-208 1974 £550

PYRE, J. F. A.   Century Outlines For a Course In English
Literature. 1910. Austin 61-825 1974 $10

PYNE, WILLIAM HENRY   The History of the Royal Residences of Windsor
Castle. London, 1819. 3 vols., roy. 4to., contemporary calf gilt, plates,
rebacked. Traylen 79-307 1973 £380

Q

QUAGLIO, DOMINICUS   Merkwurdige Gebaeude des Teutschen Mittelalters. n.d. Large folio, plates, contemporary cloth. Marlborough 70-33 1974 £480

QUAIFE, M. M.   The John Askin Papers. Detroit, 1928. Vol. 1 only. Hood's 102-574 1974 $40

QUAIFE, M. M.   The Southwestern Expedition of Zebulon M. Pike. Chicago, 1925. Inscribed & signed by Quaife, frontis., map. Hood's 102-828 1974 $22.50

QUAIFE, MILO M.   Chicago's Highways Old and New. Chicago, 1923. Orig. brown cloth, illus., first edition. Bradley 35-81 1974 $16

QUAIFE, MILO M.   Chicago's Highways Old and New, From Indian Trail to Motor Road. Chicago, 1923. Jenkins 61-1125 1974 $12

QUAIFE, MILO MILTON   Pictures of Gold Rush California. 1949. Gilt decor. cloth., gilt top, illus., 1st ed. Dykes 24-78 1974 $10

QUAIN, JONES   Elements of Anatomy. 1896-93-94. 3 vols. in 8 parts, roy. 8vo., illus., orig. cloth, tenth edition. Smith 193-872 1973 £5

QUAIN, JONES   Elements of Descriptive and Practical Anatomy. London, 1828. 8vo., modern quarter calf, uncut, first edition. Dawsons PM 249-414 1974 £65

QUAIN, JONES   Human Anatomy. Philadelphia, 1849. 2 vols., illus., first American edition. Rittenhouse 46-725 1974 $17

QUANTIN, A.   Les Origines de l'Imprimerie et son Introduction en Angleterre . . . d'Apres de Recentes Publications Anglaises. Paris, 1877. 4to., half leather, no. 235 of 275 copies, on papier d'Hollande, printed in red and black. Kraus B8-373 1974 $65

QUANTZ, JOHANN JOACHIM   Grondig Onderwys Van den Aardt en de Regte Behandeling der Dwarsfluit. Amsterdam, (?1752). 4to., plates, leather back, contemporary boards, uncut. Quaritch 940-822 1974 £185

QUARITCH, BERNARD   A Catalogue of Books in English History and Literature. 1930. 2 parts in 1 vol., 4to., plates, buckram. Quaritch 939-206 1974 £20

QUARITCH, BERNARD   A Catalogue of English and Foreign Bookbindings Offered for Sale by Bernard Quaritch Ltd. 1921. 4to., plates, half morocco. Quaritch 940-607 1974 £50

QUARITCH, BERNARD   A Catalogue of Illuminated and Other Manuscripts, Together With Some Works on Palaeography. London, 1931. Folio, orig. boards, plates. Kraus B8-227 1974 $45

QUARITCH, BERNARD   Catalogue of the Literature and History of the British Islands. 1899-1900. 6 parts in 1 vol., cloth, orig. wrappers. Howes 185-812 1974 £6

QUARLES, FRANCIS   Divine Poems. 1669. 12mo., 19th century blind tooled calf, plates. Thomas 28-251 1972 £30

QUARLES, FRANCIS   Divine Poemes. 1669. Small 8vo., 19th century sprinkled calf gilt, rebacked, engraved title. Thomas 32-186 1974 £40

QUARLES, FRANCIS   Emblems, Divine and Moral. 1839. Small 8vo., contemporary half calf, worn, plates. Howes 185-160 1974 £7.50

QUARLES, FRANCIS   Job Militant. London, 1624. 4to., calf antique, first edition. Dawsons PM 252-809 1974 £285

THE QUARTERLY Journal of the Royal Economic Society. 1929-36. Orig. wrappers, frayed. Howes 186-1406 1974 £30

THE QUATRAINS of Omar Khayyam. 1883. Contemporary half calf, gilt, label, rubbed. Covent 55-1151 1974 £10.50

THE QUATRAINS of Omar Khayyam. Worcester, 1906. Signed, frontispiece, faded. Covent 55-1152 1974 £25

QUATREFAGES DE BREAU, ARMAND DE   Unite de l'Espece Humaine. Paris, 1861. 8vo., orig. printed wrappers, fine, uncut, first edition. Gilhofer 61-51 1974 sFr 300

QUATTROCIOCCHI, NICCOLO   Love and Dishes. Bobbs, Merrill. 416p., illus. Austin 62-520 1974 $8.50

QUAYLE, WILLIAM A.   The Poet's Poet and Other Essays. Cincinnati, 1897. Biblo & Tannen 210-906 1973 $6.50

QUEBEC LITERARY AND HISTORICAL SOCIETY   Transactions, Sessions of 1873-74. Quebec, 1927. Hood's 104-904 1974 $12.50

QUEEN, ELLERY   The New Adventures Of. New York, 1940. 8vo., orig. cloth, first edition. Rota 190-341 1974 £6

QUEEN, ELLERY   Rogue's Gallery. Boston, 1945. 1st ed. Biblo & Tannen 214-690 1974 $10

QUEEN, ELLERY   The Roman Hat Mystery. 1929. Very good copy, first edition. Covent 51-2305 1973 £15

QUEEN, ELLERY   To the Queen's Taste. Boston, 1946. 1st ed. Biblo & Tannen 210-506 1973 $15

THE QUEEN'S Christmas Carol. London, 1905. First edition, small 4to., illus., white cloth covers little soiled, slightly warped, interior fine. Current BW9-14 1974 $10

QUEEN'S Own Cameron Highlanders, Historical Records of. 1909. 2 vols., 4to., plates, maps, orig. cloth gilt. Smith 193-718 1973 £14.50

QUEKETT, J.   Lectures on Histology. 1852-54. 8vo., 2 vols. in one, cloth. Wheldon 129-96 1974 £15

QUEKETT, J.   Lectures On Histology Delivered at the Royal College of Surgeons of England, 1850-51, 1851-52. 1852-54. 2 vols. in 1, 8vo., cloth, woodcuts. Wheldon 131-176 1974 £15

QUELET, L.   Flore Mycologique de la France. Paris, 1888. 8vo., cloth. Wheldon 129-1321 1974 £10

QUENNELL, M.   A History of Everyday Things in England. New York, n.d. Biblo & Tannen 213-701 1973 $15

QUENNELL, PETER   Hogarth's Progress. New York, 1955. Biblo & Tannen 210-157 1973 $8

QUENSTEDT, FRIEDRICH AUGUST VON   Methode der Krystallographie. 1840. 8vo., orig. marbled boards. Zeitlin 235-299 1974 $85

QUERCETANUS, JOSEPH   Tetras Gravissimorum Totius Capitis Affectuum. 1606. 8vo., contemporary vellum, first edition. Dawsons PM 249-415 1974 £85

QUESTED, JOHN   A Treatise on Railway Surveying and Levelling. London, 1846. 8vo., orig. cloth, rebacked, plates, illus., first edition. Hammond 201-912 1974 £15

QUETELET, LAMBERT ADOLPHE JACQUES   Anthropometrie ou Mesure des Differentes Facultes de l'Homme. Bruxelles, 1871. 8vo., orig. printed wrappers, fine, unopened, first edition, first issue. Gilhofer 61-57 1974 sFr. 700

QUEUEDO Y VILLEGAS, DOM FRANCISCO GOMEZ DE   The Visions Of. London, 1673. Contemporary calf rebacked with modern calf antique, corrected fifth edition. Smith 193-121 1973 £25

QUEVEDO Y VILLEGAS, FRANCISCO GOMEZ DE   Fortune in Her Wits.
London, 1697. 8vo., contemporary calf, gilt, fine, first English edition.
Dawsons PM 252-810 1974 £215

QUIGLEY, HUGH   The Irish Race in California, and on the
Pacific Coast. San Francisco, 1878. Illus., ex-library. Austin 57-537
1974 $47.50

QUIGLEY, MARTIN   Decency In Motion Pictures. Macmillan, 1937.
Austin 51-762 1973 $8.50

QUILICI, NELLO   Il Mito Ferrara Negli Affreschi del Palazzo
Comunale di Achille Funi. Milan, 1939. 4to., cloth, plates. Minters
37-186 1973 $18

QUILLER-COUCH, A. T.   The Adventures of Harry Revel. New York,
1903. Biblo & Tannen 210-794 1973 $7.50

QUILLER-COUCH, A. T.   I Saw Three Ships and Other Winter Tales.
London, 1893. 1st ed. Biblo & Tannen 210-654 1973 $18.50

QUILLER-COUCH, A. T.   Old Fires and Profitable Ghosts. London,
1900. 1st ed. Biblo & Tannen 210-653 1973 $15

QUILLER-COUCH, ARTHUR   On the Art of Reading. New York, 1920.
Biblo & Tannen 210-907 1973 $7.50

QUILLER-COUCH, A. T.   Shakespeare's Christmas and Other Stories.
London, 1905. First edition, 8vo., illus., very good. Current BW9-74 1974
$12

QUILLER-COUCH, ARTHUR   The Golden Pomp. 1895. 382 pages. Austin
61-827 1974 $12.50

QUILLER-COUCH, ARTHUR   Memoirs and Opinions. 1945. First edition.
Austin 61-829 1974 $12.50

QUILLER-COUCH, ARTHUR   On the Art of Reading. 1920. 250 pages.
Austin 61-830 1974 $10

QUILLER-COUCH, ARTHUR   Shakespeare's Workmanship. Cambridge,
1913. Pocket edition. Austin 61-833 1974 $10

QUILLER-COUCH, ARTHUR   The Ship of Stars. 1899. First American
edition. Austin 61-834 1974 $12.50

QUILLER-COUCH, ARTHUR   Studies In Literature. 1930. 261 pages.
Austin 61-835 1974 $12.50

QUILLER-COUCH, ARTHUR   True Tilda. 1909. First American edition.
Austin 61-836 1974 $10

QUILLER-COUCH, ARTHUR   The Twelve Dancing Princesses. n.d. Illus.,
ex-library, rubbed. Austin 61-837 1974 $12.50

QUILLER-COUCH, ARTHUR   The Twelve Dancing Princesses and Other Fairy
Tales. New York, n.d. Illus. by Kay Nielsen, 8vo., blue pictorially gilt
cloth, very good copy, mounted color plates. Frohnsdorff 16-605 1974 $30

QUILLER-COUCH, ARTHUR T.   Q's Mystery Stories. London, 1937. 1st ed.
Biblo & Tannen 210-510 1973 $12.50

QUILTER, H.   Giotto. London, 1880. Small 4to., orig.
cloth, plates, frontispiece. Bow Windows 62-379 1974 £5.75

QUILTER, HARRY   Opinions on Men, Women, & Things. London,
1909. 8vo., inscription, orig. cloth, first edition. Bow Windows 62-741
1974 £5

QUILTER, HARRY   Opinions on Men, Women and Things. 1909.
Buckram gilt, English first edition. Covent 56-1079 1974 £6.50

QUILTER, HARRY   Preferences in Art, Life, and Literature.
1892. 4to., orig. dec. vellum gilt, plates. Covent 55-118 1974 £35

QUIN, CHARLES WILLIAM   A Treatise on the Dropsy of the Brain. London,
1790. 8vo., contemporary mottled calf, first edition. Schumann 35-397 1974
$135

QUIN, M. J.   A Steam Voyage Down the Danube. 1835.
2 vols. in 1, large 12mo., half calf, map, plates, some foxing and stains,
second edition. Bow Windows 66-559 1974 £18

QUIN, THEOPHILUS   Biographical Exemplar. 1814. 12mo., orig.
boards, edges uncut, with half title, ads at end. George's 610-615 1973 £5

QUINBY, G. W.   The Gallows. Cincinnati, 1856. 8vo.,
blind-stamped cloth, worn, faded. Dawsons PM 247-236 1974 £15

QUINCY, JOHN   Lexicon Physico-Medicum. London, 1719.
8vo., contemporary panelled calf, first edition. Gurney 64-183 1974 £20

QUINCY, JOHN   Lexicon Physico-Medicum. London, 1719.
8vo., contemporary panelled calf, spine slightly worn, first edition, few minor
stains. Gurney 66-149 1974 £20

QUINCY, JOHN   Lexicon Physico-Medicum. London, 1730. 8vo.,
contemporary panelled calf, rebacked, gilt, illus., fourth edition. Hammond
201-551 1974 £15

QUINCY, JOHN   Santorio, Santorio. London, 1728. 8vo.,
frontispiece, plate, dampstains, fourth edition. Rittenhouse 46-551 1974 $60

QUINN, ARTHUR H.   Representative American Plays. Century,
1917. Austin 51-763 1973 $10

QUINN, JOHN   The Library of. New York, 1923-24. 5 vols.,
8vo., wrappers, one torn. Goodspeed's 578-520 1974 $15

QUINTANILHA, A.   Le Probleme de la Sexualite Chez les Champignons. 1933. Roy 8vo., orig. wrappers. Wheldon 130-1337 1974 £7.50

QUINTANILLA   All the Brave. New York, n.d. 4to., orig.
printed wrappers, plates, first trade edition. Ximenes 33-207 1974 $40

QUINTI, GIUSEPPE   Maravigliosi Secreti Medicinali Chimici. 1711.
12mo., contemporary calf, gilt. Dawsons PM 245-623 1974 £60

QUIRINI, ANGELO MARIA   Liber Singularis de Oprimorum Scriptorum
Editionibus Quae Romae Primum Prodierunt Post Divinum Typographiae Inventum.
Lindau, 1761. 4to., engraved plates, contemporary boards. Kraus B8-228
1974 $65

THE QUIZZICAL Valentine Writer. London, (c. 1835). Orig. pict. wrappers,
8vo., colored frontis. Gregory 44-305 1974 $12.50

R

R., J. Contraband Christmas. New York, 1864. First edition, 16mo., illus., spine ends worn away, covers dull, some interior foxing, else good. Current BW9-49 1974 $38.50

RABELAIS, FRANCOIS Affentheurliche, Naupengeheurliche Geschichtklitterung. (Strassburg), 1631. Small 8vo., contemporary vellum over boards, woodcuts, good copy. Schuman 499-90 1974 sFr 2,500

RABELAIS, FRANCOIS Five Books of the Lives, Heroic Deeds and Sayings of Gargantua and His Son Pantagruel. 1892. 2 vols., 4to., orig. cloth, printed on japon paper, portrait, plates, covers marked, spotted, uncut, limited. Bow Windows 66-560 1974 £18

RABELAIS, FRANCOIS Tout ce Qui Existe de ses Oeuvres. Paris, n.d. 12mo., 1/2 calf, bdg. rubbed. Biblo & Tannen 210-908 1973 $9.50

RABELAIS, FRANCOIS Les Oeuvres de M. Francois Rabelais. N.P., 1553. 16mo., full tobacco brown levant morocco, gilt, first collected edition. L. Goldschmidt 42-101 1974 $900

RABELAIS, FRANCOIS Oeuvres. Paris, 1913-22. 4 vols., 4to., orig. wrapper, frontispiece. L. Goldschmidt 42-102 1974 $45

RABELAIS, FRANCOIS The Works. c. 1920. 2 vols., orig. cloth, gilt, illus. Howes 186-376 1974 £7.50

RABELAIS, FRANCOIS The Complete Works. London, 1927. 2 vols., ltd. to 4300 sets. Jacobs 24-123 1974 $25

RABELAIS, FRANCOIS The Complete Works. London, 1927. 2 vols., 8vo., illus., orig. cloth, gilt, uncut. Dawsons PM 252-811 1974 £20

RABELAIS, FRANCOIS All the Extant Works of Rabelais. New York, 1929. 4to., orig. buckram backed bds., 3 vols., ltd. to 200 numbered copies. Jacobs 24-124 1974 $125

RABENHORST, G. L. Flora Europeae Algarum. Leipzig, 1864-68. 8vo., half cloth, scarce. Wheldon 130-1338 1974 £20

RABENHORST, G. L. Flora Europeae Algarum Aquae Dulcis et Submarinae. Leipzig, 1864-68. 3 vols. in 2, 8vo., half cloth, scarce. Wheldon 128-1412 1973 £20

RABENHORST, G. L. Fungi Europaei Exsiccati. Dresden, 1859-76. 3 vols., 4to., half cloth, extremely rare. Wheldon 128-1411 1973 £75

RABIQUEAU, CHARLES Le Spectacle du Feu Elementaire. Paris, 1753. 8vo., contemporary calf, plates, first edition. Schuman 37-213 1974 $110

RACINE, JEAN Relation de ce Qui s'Est Passe au Siege de Namur. Paris, 1692. Folio, contemporary calf, gilt, rare, first edition. L. Goldschmidt 42-103 1974 $365

RACINE, LOUIS La Religion, Poeme. Paris, 1785. 12mo., contemporary mottled sheep, gilt, ninth edition. Bow Windows 62-743 1974 £5.50

RACINET, AUGUSTE Le Costume Historique. Paris, 1888. Plates, folio, text volume boards, cloth portfolios with ties, large edition in parts as issued. Schumann 499-91 1974 sFr 1,700

RACINET, AUGUSTE Le Costume Historique. Paris, 1888. 1 vol. text and 20 parts containing 500 plates (color & tinted), text vol. boards, plates in 20 cloth portfolios with ties, large edition in parts as issued. Kraus B8-422 1974 $495

RACKHAM, ARTHUR The Arthur Rackham Fairy Book. 1933. Large 8vo., orig. full vellum gilt, illus., limited, first edition. Howes 185-390 1974 £100

RACKHAM, ARTHUR The Arthur Rackham Fairy Book. London, 1933. No. 141 of limited edition of 460 copies, signed, very slight darkening of spine, mint, unopened, orig. box, glassine wrapper immaculately preserved. Ross 87-467 1974 $250

RACKHAM, ARTHUR Cinderella. 1919. Roy. 8vo., cloth backed boards, very fine, scarce, separately mounted coloured frontis., illus. Covent 51-2541 1973 £27.50

RACKHAM, ARTHUR Cinderella. 1919. 4to., orig. buckram backed boards, gilt, illu. Howes 185-389 1974 £75

RACKHAM, ARTHUR The Legend of Sleepy Hollow. London, (1928). Crown 4to., orig. morocco, illus., gilt, plates. Bow Windows 62-744 1974 £55

RACKHAM, ARTHUR Peter Pan in Kensington Gardens. 1906. Orig. cloth, plates, rubbed, second edition. Marsden 37-381 1974 £35

RACKHAM, ARTHUR The Ring of the Niblung. (1911). Full morocco gilt, 2 vols., English first edition. Covent 56-711 1974 £60

RACKHAM, ARTHUR Rip Van Winkle. London, 1908. Crown 4to., plates, foxing, orig. green cloth, illus. Bow Windows 62-745 1974 £30

RACKHAM, ARTHUR The Sleeping Beauty. 1920. Orig. cloth, plates, illus., dust wrapper, fine. Rota 188-786 1974 £20

RACKHAM, ARTHUR Some British Ballads. (1919). Limited to 575 copies signed by artist, coloured plates and other illus. by Rackham, 4to., orig. parchment sides, vellum back gilt, top edges gilt, fine. Sawyer 293-253 1974 £150

RACKHAM, B. Catalogue of English Porcelain, Earthenware, Enamels. London, 1915. Small 4to., plates, orig. paper boards, worn. Bow Windows 62-746 1974 £5

RACKHAM, B. Catalogue of the Herbert Allen Collection of English Porcelain. London, 1923. Large 8vo., plates, label, orig. cloth, faded, second edition. Bow Windows 62-747 1974 £18

RACKHAM, B. Catalogue of the Le Blond Collection of Corean Pottery. London, 1918. 8vo., frontispiece, plates, orig. cloth. Bow Windows 62-748 1974 £5

RACKHAM, B. English Pottery. 1924. Roy. 4to., plates, pigskin, gilt, scarce, limited. Quaritch 940-658 1974 £65

RADA, JUAN DE Controversiarum Theologicarum Inter S. Thomam. 1586. 4to., new buckram. Allen 213-1730 1973 $35

RADCLIFFE, ANNE Gaston de Blondeville. London, 1826. 4 vols., 12mo., orig. boards, fine, first edition. Dawsons PM 252-812 1974 £80

RADCLIFFE, ANN A Journey Made in the Summer of 1794. London, 1794. 4to., contemporary tree calf, first edition. Ximenes 35-1 1974 $125

RADCLIFFE, ANN A Journey Made in the Summer of 1794. Dublin, 1795. 8vo., contemporary tree calf, first Irish edition. Ximenes 35-2 1974 $75

RADCLIFFE, ANN The Mysteries of Udolpho. 1794. 12mo., 4 vols., contemporary full calf, first edition. Broadhurst 23-913 1974 £130

RADCLIFFE, ANN The Mysteries of Udolpho. 1794. 4 vols., 12mo., contemporary sheep, rubbed, newly rebacked, first edition. Bow Windows 66-561 1974 £140

RADCLIFFE, ANN The Mysteries of Udolpho. 1794. First edition, 4 vols., 12mo., contemporary full calf, hinges trifle weak, fine, tall copy, complete with half titles. Broadhurst 24-845 1974 £140

RADCLIFFE, ANNE The Mysteries of Udolpho. Dublin, 1800. 3 vols., 8vo., half calf, worn, boxed. Emerald 50-804 1974 £35

RADCLIFFE, ANNE A Sicilian Romance. Philadelphia, 1795. 12mo., contemporary sheep, first American edition. Ximenes 35-3 1974 $30

RADCLIFFE, ANNE A Sicilian Romance. 1798. 12mo., 2 vols., contemporary calf, gilt, fine. Hill 126-199 1974 £32

RADCLIFFE, CHARLES BLAND   Epilepsy and Other Affections of the Nervous System. London, 1854. 8vo., orig. cloth, first edition.   Schuman 37-214 1974 $85

RADCLYFFE, C. W.   Memorials of Westminster School. (c.1844). Roy. 8vo., half morocco, plates.   Quaritch 939-487 1974 £65

RADCLYFFE, CHARLES W.   Memorials of Rugby. Rugby, 1843. Folio, half maroon morocco, rebacked, plates, scarce. Traylen 79-403 1973 £75

RADDE, G.   Die Sammlungen des Kaukasischen Museums. 1899-1901. 4to., 3 vols., orig. cloth backed boards. Wheldon 129-97 1974 £20

RADDE, G.   Omis Caucasica. Kassel, 1884. 4to., orig. cloth, plates, scarce. Wheldon 130-61 1974 £120

RADDE, G.   Reisen im Suden von Ost-Sibirien in den Jahren 1855-59. St. Petersburg, 1862. Roy. 4to., cloth, plates. Wheldon 131-518 1974 £70

RADEMAKER, A.   L'Arcadie Hollandaise. Amsterdam, 1730. Large folio, engravings, half calf, uncut. Quaritch 940-209 1974 £200

RADIGUET, RAYMOND   Le Bal du Comte d'Orgel. Paris, 1924. 12mo., three quarter red morocco, gilt, uncut, orig. wrapper, first edition. L. Goldschmidt 42-341 1974 $300

RADIO Annual and Television Yearbook. 25th ed. 1952. Austin 51-764 1973 $27.50

RADIO Censorship. Wilson, 1939. 297p. Austin 51-936 1973 $10

RADIR, RUTH ANDERSON   Modern Dance for the Youth of America. New York, 1944. Illus. Biblo & Tannen 214-900 1974 $8.50

RAEMAEKERS, LOUIS   American in the War. New York, 1918. 4to., 1st ed. Biblo & Tannen 214-57 1974 $17.50

RAEMAEKERS, LOUIS   The Great War. 1916-19. 3 vols., roy. folio, half buckram, rubbed, drawings, limited, edition de luxe. Quaritch 940-210 1974 £35

RAEMDONCK, J. VAN   Gerard Mercator sa Vie et ses Oeuvres. St. Nicolas, 1869. Frontispiece, folding plate, 4to., half cloth. Kraus B8-168 1974 $85

RAFFALD, ELIZABETH   The Experienced English Housekeeper. London, 1805. 8vo., portrait, plates, stains, old calf, rebacked. Bow Windows 62-750 1974 £36

RAFFALOVICH, GEORGE   The History of a Soul. London, 1910. One of 1000 numbered copies, very good copy, first edition. Covent 51-1549 1973 £20

RAFFETY, CHARLES W.   Poems. (N.P., n.d.). 6 vols., 8vo., limp calf, inscription, second edition. Bow Windows 62-751 1974 £15

RAFINESQUE, CONSTANTINE SAMUEL 1783-1840   Florula Ludoviciana. New York, 1817. Small 8vo., contemporary half morocco, very rare. Wheldon 131-1346 1974 £250

RAFINESQUE, CONSTANTINE SAMUEL 1783-1840   Medical Flora. Philadelphia, 1828-30. 2 vols., 12mo., orig. printed boards and contemporary sheep, plates. Wheldon 128-1690 1973 £175

RAFINESQUE, CONSTANTINE SAMUEL 1783-1840   Medical Flora. Philadelphia, 1828-30. 12mo., modern half calf, 2 vols., plates. Wheldon 129-1692 1974 £300

RAFINESQUE, CONSTANTINE SAMUEL 1783-1840   Medical Flora. Philadelphia, 1828-30. 2 vols., 12mo., modern half calf. Wheldon 131-1817 1974 £300

RAFINESQUE, CONSTANTINE SAMUEL 1783-1840   The Pleasures and Duties of Wealth. Philadelphia, 1840. 8vo., sewn, very scarce, foxed, first edition. Ximenes 37-183 1974 $80

RAFOLS, J. F.   Ramon Casas. Barcelona, n.d. 4to., boards, cloth spine. Minters 37-230 1973 $12

RAGGEDY Ann and Andy. Akron, 1944. 8vo., pictorial boards, spiral bound, animated. Frohnsdorff 16-595 1974 $20

RAGUET, CONDY   The Examiner, and Journal of Political Economy Devoted to the Advancement of the Cause of State Rights and Free Trade. Philadelphia, 1833-34. Vols. 1 complete in 26 issues bound in new cloth, leather label. Jenkins 61-2226 1974 $35

RAHIR, EDOUARD   La Bibliotheque de Feu Edouard Rahir. Paris, 1930-35. 3 parts, 4to., plates, orig. wrappers. Dawsons PM 10-503 1974 £15

RAHIR, EDOUARD   La Bibliotheque de l'Amateur. Paris, 1907. Large 8vo., contemporary red half morocco. Dawsons PM 10-504 1974 £40

RAHN, JOHANN HEINRICH   An Introduction to Algebra. London, 1668. 4to., contemporary calf, rebacked, fine, first edition. Dawsons PM 245-624 1974 £95

THE RAILWAY Bell and Illustrated London Advertiser Map. 1845. Map, illus., portraits. Bow Windows 62-578 1974 £6.50

RAILWAY Centenary 1825-1925. (1925). 4to., plates, illus., cloth. Quaritch 939-89 1974 £6

RAIMONDI, A.   Minerales del Peru. Lima, 1878. Roy 8vo., orig. wrappers, scarce. Wheldon 130-966 1974 £5

RAINAUDO, TEOFILO
Please turn to RAYNAUD, THEOPHILE

RAINE, J.   A Brief Historical Account of the Episcopal Castle. Durham, 1852. 4to., cloth, plates. Quaritch 939-348 1974 £12

RAINE, WILLIAM MAC LEOD   Famous Sheriffs and Western Outlaws. Garden City, 1929. Dec. cloth, fine, first edition. Bradley 35-309 1974 $26

RAINEY, GEORGE   On the Formation of the Skeletons of Animals. 1857. 8vo., contemporary half calf. Dawsons PM 249-416 1974 £9

RAINIER National Park, Moutain Glacier Wonderland. Tacoma, c. 1900. Small folio, wrappers, hand colored. Jenkins 61-2584 1974 $12.50

RAINSFORD, MARCUS   An Historical Account of the Black Empire of Hayti. London, 1805. 4to., contemporary tree calf gilt, leather label, plates, foxing. Traylen 79-494 1973 £80

RAITHBY, J.   An Index to the Statutes at Large from Magna Carta. 1814. 3 vols., 8vo., contemporary russia. Quaritch 939-254 1974 £20

RALEIGH, WALTER   The Discoverie of the Large and Bewtiful Empire of Guiana. London, 1928. 4to., buckram, uncut, maps. Traylen 79-495 1973 £25

RALEIGH, WALTER   The Discoverie of the Large and Bewtiful Empire of Guiana By. 1928. 4to., orig. quarter vellum, maps, frontispiece portrait, uncut, on jap vellum, limited edition. Bow Windows 66-562 1974 £22.50

RALEIGH, WALTER   The English Voyages of the Sixteenth Century. Glasgow, 1906. 8vo., orig. cloth, portrait, signature of Sydney Jeffery. Bow Windows 66-563 1974 £6.50

RALEIGH, WALTER   The History of the World. London, 1614. Full calf, rebound, first edition. Dawson's 424-333 1974 $675

RALEIGH, WALTER   An Introduction to a Breviary of the History of England, With the Reign of King William the I. 1693. First edition, lacks portrait, title bit soiled, small 8vo., half calf, rubbed and rebacked. Thomas 32-135 1974 £45

RALEIGH, WALTER   The Poems of Sir Walter Raleigh. London, 1892. 12mo. Biblo & Tannen 210-910 1973 $8.50

RALEIGH, WALTER   Romance: Two Lectures Delivered at Princeton University, May 4 & 5, 1915. 1916. Ex-library. Austin 61-839 1974 $10

RALEIGH, WALTER   Shakespeare. Macmillan, 1907. 232p., orig. ed. Austin 51-765 1973 $6.50

RALPH, J.   A Critical Reveiw of the Publick Buildings. 1734. 8vo., old calf, first edition. Quaritch 939-467 1974 £50

RALPH, JAMES   The Case of Our Present Theatrical Disputes, Fairly Stated. London, 1743. 8vo., disbound, good copy, very rare, first edition. Ximenes 37-184 1974 $250

RALPH, JAMES   The Taste of the Town. London, 1731. 12mo., contemporary calf, first edition, second issue. Ximenes 35-12 1974 $175

RALSTON, JAMES   Old Manchester. Manchester, 1875. 4to., plates, orig. quarter roan, limited edition. Howes 186-2076 1974 £10

RAMANUJAN, SRINIVASA   Collected Papers of. (Cambridge, 1927. 8vo., orig. cloth. Bow Windows 66-564 1974 £10.15

RAMAZZINI, BERNARDINO   Ephemerides Barometricae Mutinenses. 1695. Small 8vo., contemporary vellum, fine, first edition. Dawsons PM 245-625 1974 £75

RAMAZZINI, BERNARDINO   De Fontium Mutinensium Admiranda Scaturigine. 1713. 8vo., half calf, plate. Dawsons PM 245-626 1974 £55

RAMAZZINI, BERNARDINO   De Morbis Artificium Diatriba. 1713. Small 8vo., orig. boards, uncut. Dawsons PM 249-417 1974 £65

RAMAZZINI, BERNARDINO   Opera Omnia Medica et Physiologica. 1739. 4to., half calf, gilt. Dawsons PM 249-418 1974 £45

RAMBLES Among the Channel Islands, By a Naturalist. (c. 1855). 12mo., orig. cloth, nice clean copy. Wheldon 131-380 1974 £10

RAMBOSSON, JEAN   Histoire des Astres. Paris, 1874. 8vo., quarter crimson morocco, gilt, plates, illus., fine, first edition. Dawsons PM 245-627 1974 £14

RAMELLI, AGOSTINO   Le Diverse et Artificiose Machine. Paris, 1588. Folio, modern vellum, first edition. Marlborough 70-8 1974 £1,500

RAMIE, SUZANNE   Ceramiques de Picasso. Geneva, 1948. Folio, color plates. Biblo & Tannen 214-420 1974 $20

RAMIREZ, JOSE FERNANDO   Bibliotheca Mexicana. London, 1880. 8vo., half cloth. Kraus B8-230 1974 $35

RAMIRO, ERASTENE   Felicien Rops. 1905. Small 4to., orig. wrappers, plates, English first edition. Covent 56-1499 1974 £65

RAMSAY, ALLAN   The Gentle Shepherd. Edinburgh, 1776. 12mo., contemporary calf, worn, plates. Quaritch 936-201 1974 £15

RAMSAY, ALLAN   The Gentle Shepherd. Edinburgh, 1808. 4to., full polished calf, gilt. Quaritch 936-529 1974 £35

RAMSAY, ALLAN   The Gentle Shepherd; A Scots Pastoral Comedy. Falkirk, 1776. 12mo., modern calf gilt, slight staining. MacManus 224-367 1974 $35

RAMSAY, ALLAN   The Tea-Table Miscellany. Edinburgh, 1760. Small 8vo., calf, gilt, frontispiece. Quaritch 936-202 1974 £35

RAMSAY, ANDREW MICHAEL   The Travels of Cyrus. 1736. 12mo., contemporary calf, fifth edition. Hill 126-223 1974 £5.50

RAMSAY, J. R.   Win-On-Ah. Toronto, 1869. Hood's 104-783 1974 $30

RAMSAY, JOHN   American Potters and Pottery. Boston, 1939. Top of spine nicked. Biblo & Tannen 214-67 1974 $15

RAMSAY, T. W.   Costumes On the Western Coast of Africa. London, 1833. 4to., orig. printed wrappers, uncut, plates. Traylen 79-460 1973 £250

RAMSAY, W. M.   The Church in the Roman Empire Before A.D. 170. New York, 1893. Illus; front inner hinge split. Biblo & Tannen 214-653 1974 $15

RAMSDELL, CHARLES W.   Reconstruction in Texas. New York, 1910. Jenkins 61-2229 1974 $75

RAMSDEN, H. A.   Siamese Porcelain and Other Tokens. Yoyohama, 1911. First edition, 12mo., full page colored plates brilliant, clear and perfect, some cracking at spine, else very fine. Current BW9-603 1974 $20

RAMSDEN, JESSE   An Account of Experiments. London, 1792. 4to., old wrappers, rare, first edition. Zeitlin 235-185 1974 $75

RAMSEY, ALEXANDER   Address Delivered. St. Paul, 1857. 8vo., orig. printed wrappers, first edition. Ximenes 35-13 1974 $45

RAMSEY, FRED, JR.   Jazzmen. Harcourt, 1939. Austin 51-767 1973 $7.50

RAMUS, PETRUS
Please turn to
LA RAMEE, PIERRE DE

RANBECK, AEGIDIUS   Saints of the Order of S. Benedict. 1896. Plates, buckram, scarce. Howes 185-1582 1974 £7.50

RANDALL, EMILIUS O.   History of Ohio. New York, 1912. 8vo., 5 vols., orig. bindings, gilt. Butterfield 8-421 1974 $85

RANDALL, JAMES RYDER   Maryland, My Maryland and Other Poems. Baltimore, 1908. First edition, 12mo., frontis., very good. Current BW9-268 1974 $15

RANDOLPH, EDMUND JENNINGS   A Vindication of Mr. Randolph's Resignation. Philadelphia, 1795. 8vo., half cloth, first edition, third issue. Ximenes 35-14 1974 $27.50

RANDOLPH, P. B.   Eulis! London, 1896. 8vo., orig. cloth, label. Bow Windows 62-752 1974 £6.50

RANDOLPH, THOMAS   The Poems and Amyntas of. 1917. Plates, very good copy, presentation copy inscribed from editor, first edition. Covent 51-1553 1973 £5.25

RANG, P. K. S. L.   Histoire Naturelle des Aplysiens. Paris, 1828. 4to., half calf, plates, very scarce. Wheldon 131-903 1974 £25

RANGER'S Progress. London, 1760. 8vo., contemporary sheep, fine, first edition. Dawsons PM 252-813 1974 £140

RANKE, HERMANN   The Art of Ancient Egypt. 1936. 4to., orig. buckram gilt, plates, dust soiling. Smith 194-92 1974 £5.50

RANKE, HERMANN   Meisterwerke der Aegyptischen Kunst. Basel, 1948. 4to., 64 plates. Biblo & Tannen 214-392 1974 $15

RANKE, JOHANNES   Das Blut. Munich, 1878. Small 8vo., illus., contemporary half cloth, first edition. Schuman 37-215 1974 $65

RANKE, LEOPOLD VON   A History of England. Oxford, 1875. 6 vols., orig. cloth, stain, orig. edition. Howes 186-1152 1974 £35

RANKING, JOHN   Historical Researches. London, 1826. 4to., contemporary diced calf. Dawsons PM 251-319 1974 £75

RANNIE, DAVID WATSON   Wordsworth and His Circle. 1907. Plates, fine, d.w., first edition. Covent 51-2045 1973 £5.25

RANSOM, JOHN CROWE   The World's Body. New York, 1938. First U.S. edition. Covent 56-1081 1974 £9.50

RANSOME, ARTHUR   Oscar Wilde. Mitchell, Kennerley, 1913. Austin 51-768 1973 $6.50

RANSOME, ARTHUR   Oscar Wilde, a Critical Study. 1912. Portrait, cloth gilt, English first edition. Covent 56-1332 1974 £5.25

RANSOME, H. M.   The Sacred Bee in Ancient Times. 1937. 8vo.,
cloth, plates. Wheldon 129-721 1974 £5

RANSON, WYLLYS C.   Historical Outline of the Ransom Family of
America. Ann Arbor, 1903. 8vo., cloth. Saddleback 14-788 1974 $65

RAOUL-ROCHETTE, D.   Peintures Antiques Inedites Precedees de
Recherches sur l'Emploi de la Peinture dans la Decoration des Edifices Sacres et
Publics. Paris, 1836. 4to., plates, half red morocco, fine, gilt. Quaritch
940-345 1974 £38

RAPHAEL   Parerga atq. Ornamenta, ex Raphaelis Sanctii
Prototypis. Rome, (c. 1700?). Folio, 18th century panelled calf. Quaritch
940-211 1974 £17.50

RAPHAELSON, SAMSON   Jason. Random, 1942. Austin 51-766 1973
$7.50

RAPHSON, JOSEPH   Analysis Aequationum Universalis. London, 16-
97. 4to., contemporary panelled calf, second edition. Dawsons PM 245-630
1974 £80

RAPIN, RENE   A Comparison Between the Eloquence of
Demosthenes and Cicero. Oxford, 1672. 8vo., contemporary calf, first English
edition. Dawsons PM 252-814 1974 £55

RAPIN, RENE   Reflections Upon the Eloquence of These Times.
London, 1672. 8vo., contemporary rough calf, first edition. Ximenes 35-15
1974 $125

RAPIN DE THOYRAS, P.   The History of England. 1732-33. 2 vols.,
thick folio, contemporary calf, second edition. Howes 186-1153 1974 £25

RAPIN DE THOYRAS, PAUL   The History of England. London, 1732-47.
Folio, contemporary calf, second edition. Dawsons PM 251-320 1974 £50

RASCOE, BURTON   Belle Starr, "The Bandit Queen". New York,
1941. Cloth, illus., fine, dust wrapper. Dykes 22-157 1973 $22.50

RASCOE, BURTON   Fanfare. New York, 1920. Wrappers, fine,
first American edition. Covent 55-1098 1974 £10

RASHDALL, H.   The Universities of Europe in the Middle Ages.
Oxford, 1936. 3 vols., 8vo., cloth, second edition. Dawsons PM 11-642
1974 £8.40

RASMUSSEN, K.   Across Arctic America. New York & London,
1927. Maps, illus. Hood's 104-79 1974 $35

RASPAIL, FRANCOIS VINCENT   Nouveau Systeme de Physiologie Vegetale et
de Botanique. Brussels, 1837. 2 vols., roy. 8vo., orig. wrappers and boards,
second edition. Wheldon 128-1152 1973 £15

RASPAIL, FRANCOIS VINCENT   Nouveau Systeme de Physiologie Vegetable.
Paris, 1837. 8vo. and roy. 8vo., half calf. Wheldon 129-950 1974 £20

RASPE, M.   The Adventures of Baron Munchausen. London,
n.d. 4to., orig. cloth, gilt, illus., third edition. Hammond 201-482 1974 £5

RASTALL, W. D.   A History of the Antiquities of the Town and
Church of Southwell. London, 1787. 4to., dark green cloth, gilt, plates.
Bow Windows 62-753 1974 £28

RASTELL, JOHN   The Pastime of People. London, 1811. 4to.,
contemporary calf, rebacked, woodcuts. Bow Windows 62-754 1974 £22.50

RASTELL, WILLIAM   A Collection of Entries of Declarations, Barres,
Replications, Rejoynders, Issues, Verdicts. 1670. Folio, contemporary reversed
calf worn, little damp marked, inscription and signature on title. Bow Windows
66-566 1974 £45

RATCHFORD, FANNIE ELIZABETH   The Brontes Web of Childhood. 1941.
Illus., orig. edition. Austin 61-842 1974 $10

RATCLIFFE, DOROTHY UNA   Equatorial Dawn. 1936. Half morocco, fine,
English first edition. Covent 56-1266 1974 £7.50

RATCLIFFE, F.   Flying Fox and Drifting Sand. 1938. 8vo.,
cloth, plates, maps. Wheldon 128-228 1973 £5

RATHBONE, MRS. H. M.   The Poetry of Birds. Liverpool and London,
1833. 4to., full red levant morocco, gilt, plates, rare. Wheldon 130-62 1974
£75

RATHBORNE, ST. GEORGE   Miss Fairfax of Virginia. New York, (1889).
Cloth. Hayman 57-216 1974 $12.50

RATHBUN, M. J.   The Cancroid Crabs of America. Washington,
1930. 8vo., new cloth, plates. Wheldon 129-792 1974 £25

RATHBUN, M. J.   The Cancroid Crabs of America. Washington,
1930. 8vo., new cloth, plates, scarce. Wheldon 130-886 1974 £25

RATISBONNE, MARIE THEODORE   Conferences aux Religieuses Professes de
Paris et de Grandbourg. Paris, 1908. Roy. 8vo., cloth. Howes 185-1583
1974 £5

RATTIGAN, TERENCE   The Deep Blue Sea. Random, 1952. 175p.
Austin 51-769 1973 $8.50

RATTO, MARIO ORSINI   L'Avvenire Degli Italo-Americani. Milano,
1933. Austin 62-525 1974 $27.50

RATTO, MARIO ORSINI   Gli Stati Uniti de Domani. Milano, 1930.
Austin 62-524 1974 $27.50

RATZEL, FRIEDRICH   The History of Mankind. London, 1896-8. 8vo.,
polished green calf, gilt, fine. Dawsons PM 251-321 1974 £9

RAUCHDORN, HEINRICH   Practica und Process Peinlicher Halszgerichts
Ordnung aus Keyserlichen, Geistlichen, Weltlichen und Sechsischen Rechten.
Bautzen, 1564. 4 parts in 1 vol., folio. Schumann 499-92 1974 sFr 1,100

RAUCOURT DE CHARLEVILLE   Memoire sur les Experiences Lithographiques Faites
a l'Ecole Royale des Ponts et Chaussees de France. Toulon, 1819. 8vo., half
leather, lacking the two plates. Kraus B8-231 1974 $85

RAUM, JOHN O.   The History of New Jersey. Philadelphia, (1877).
8vo., 2 vols., three quarter morocco, boards. Butterfield 8-376 1974 $45

RAVAGE, M. E.   An American in the Making. Harper, 1917.
Orig. ed. Austin 62-526 1974 $7.50

RAVAGE, M. E.   The Jew Pays. 1919. 152 pages. Austin
57-541 1974 $10

RAVATON, HUGUES   Chirurgie d'Armee, ou Traite des Plaies d'Armes
a Feu, et d'Armes Blanches. Paris, 1768. 8vo., contemporary calf, plates,
first edition, few minor stains. Gurney 66-150 1974 £80

RAVELET, ARMAND   Blessed J. B. De La Salle. Paris & Tours,
1888. Thick imp. 8vo., orig. morocco backed cloth, gilt, fine. Howes
185-1108 1974 £8.50

RAVEN, C. E.   Life and Works of John Ray. Cambridge, 1942.
8vo., cloth, portrait. Wheldon 129-183 1974 £7.50

THE RAVEN Club Papers. London, 1871. 8vo., orig. blue cloth, worn, first
edition. Ximenes 33-21 1974 $10

RAVENSCROFT, E.   The Anatomist. (1771). 8vo., cloth. Quaritch
936-204 1974 £5

RAVER, PIERRE   Sommaire d'Une Histoire Abrege de l'Anatomie
Pathologique. Paris, 1818. 8vo., quarter vellum. Gurney 66-151 1974 £35

RAVERAT, GWEN   Four Tales from Hans Andersen. 1935. Orig.
cloth, illus., frontispiece, woodcuts. Marsden 37-386 1974 £6

RAVIGNAN, J. DE   Conferences Prechees a Notre-Dame de Paris
de 1847 a 1846. Paris, 1860. 4 vols., thick 8vo., half calf, rubbed. Howes
185-1584 1974 £7.50

RAVINDRANATHA, THAKURA   Gitanjali. London, 1914. First trade edition, late impression, lacking d.w., orig. binding, spine somewhat foxed, nice. Ross 87-606 1974 $10

RAVINDRANATHA, THAKURA   The King of the Dark Chamber. MacMillan, 1914. Austin 51-941 1973 $7.50

RAVINDRANATHA, THAKURA   The Post Office. Churchtown, 1914. Orig. cloth backed boards, bit rubbed and soiled, first English Lanugage edition, one of 400 numbered copies, about fine. MacManus 224-419 1974 $40

RAVINDRANATHA, THAKURA   Sacrifice and Other Plays. 1917. Austin 51-942 1973 $7.50

RAWLINSON, E.   Designs for Factory Furnace and Other Tall Chimney Shafts. 1858. Imp. folio, plates, orig. cloth, rebacked, rare. Quaritch 940-547 1974 £300

RAWLINSON, G.   Herodotus History. Nonesuch Press, 1935. Folio, half blue parchment, uncut, maps, limited to 675 copies, fine, unfaded. Broadhurst 24-1036 1974 £100

RAWNSLEY, H. D.   Literary Associations of the English Lakes. Glasgow, 1901. Second edition, plates, 2 vols., very good copy, booklabels, endpapers browned. Covent 51-1166 1973 £5.25

RAWSTORNE, LAWRENCE   Gamonia. 1837. 8vo., plates, orig. green morocco, gilt, rare first edition. Quaritch 939-847 1974 £175

RAWSTORNE, LAWRENCE   Gamonia. 1837. Roy 8vo., orig. green roan, gilt, plates, rare, first edition. Wheldon 130-63 1974 £100

RAWSTORNE, LAWRENCE   Gamonia. 1929. Roy. 8vo., plates, orig. buckram gilt. Howes 185-397 1974 £12.50

RAY, F. M.   The Christmas Tree and Other Poems. Portland, 1874. 12mo., cloth, presentation copy, first edition. Goodspeed's 578-291 1974 $10

RAY, J. H. RANDOLPH   My Little Church Around the Corner. S & S, 1957. 365p., illus. Austin 51-770 1973 $8.50

RAY, JOHN   Catalogus Plantarum Angliae, et Insularum Adjacentium. London, 1670. Small 8vo., contemporary calf, first edition. Schuman 37-216 1974 $175

RAY, JOHN   Catalogus Plantarum Angliae et Insularum Adjacentium. 1677. 8vo., contemporary calf, engraved plates, second edition. Wheldon 128-1214 1973 £65

RAY, JOHN   Catalogus Plantarum Circa. 1660. 8vo., old panelled calf, first edition. Bow Windows 64-219 1974 £425

RAY, JOHN   A Collection of Curious Travels and Voyages. 1738. 2 vols., 8vo., new half calf, engraved plates, second (third) edition. Wheldon 128-229 1973 £40

RAY, JOHN   A Collection of English Words Not Generally Used. 1674. 8vo., 19th century calf, rare first edition. Wheldon 131-389 1974 £120

RAY, JOHN   A Collection of English Proverbs. Cambridge, 1678. 8vo., contemporary calf, rebacked, rubbed, second edition. Bow Windows 66-567 1974 £27.50

RAY, JOHN   A Compleat Collection of English Proverbs. 17-68. 8vo., contemporary calf, fourth edition. Hill 126-224 1974 £21

RAY, JOHN   A Compleat Collection of English Proverbs. London, 1768. 8vo., old half calf. Dawsons PM 251-155 1974 £25

RAY, JOHN   Further Correspondence. 1928. 8vo., cloth, plates, portraits. Wheldon 130-187 1974 £7.50

RAY, JOHN   De Historia Piscium Libri Quatuor. Oxford, 1686. Folio, contemporary calf, neatly rebacked, engraved plates, engraved frontispiece, nice copy. Wheldon 128-655 1973 £265

RAY, JOHN   De Historia Piscium Libri Quatuor. Oxford, 1686. Folio, contemporary calf, rebacked, plates. Wheldon 130-708 1974 £265

RAY, JOHN   L'Histoire Naturelle Eclaircie dans une de ses Parties Principales, l'Ornithologie. Paris, 1767. 4to., modern half calf antique, engraved plates, scarce. Wheldon 128-550 1973 £50

RAY, JOHN   Historia Plantarum Generalis. 1686-88, 1704. 3 vols., folio, contemporary calf, rebacked, first edition. Wheldon 128-1154 1973 £350

RAY, JOHN   Historia Plantarum Generalis. (1686-88). Folio, contemporary calf, 3 vols. Wheldon 129-951 1974 £350

RAY, JOHN   Historia Plantarum Generalis. 1686-88, 1704. Folio, 3 vols., contemporary calf, rebacked, first edition. Wheldon 130-1047 1974 £350

RAY, JOHN   Historia Plantarum. Londini, 1686-1704. 3 vols., folio, contemporary spotted calf, morocco labels, first edition. Dawsons PM 250-66 1974 £650

RAY, JOHN   Historia Plantarum Generalis. 1693-1704. 3 vols., folio, contemporary calf, rebacked. Wheldon 131-1188 1974 £350

RAY, JOHN   Miscellaneous Discourses. 1850. Roy 8vo., new cloth. Wheldon 130-131 1974 £10

RAY, JOHN   Observations Topographical, Moral and Physiological: Made In a Journey Through Part of the Low Countries. London, 1673. Modern morocco gilt, plates, rebound. Smith 193-122 1973 £10

RAY, JOHN   Philosophical Letters. 1718. 8vo., contemporary calf, scarce, first edition. Wheldon 130-130 1974 £70

RAY, JOHN   Stirpium Europaearum Extra Britannias Nascentium Sylloge. 1694. 8vo., contemporary calf, portrait. Wheldon 128-1302 1973 £80

RAY, JOHN   Stirpium Europaearum extra Britannias. 1694. 8vo., contemporary vellum. Wheldon 129-1114 1974 £80

RAY, JOHN   Stirpium Europearum Extra Britannias Nascentium Sylloge. 1694. 8vo., contemporary vellum, rare. Wheldon 131-1347 1974 £80

RAY, JOHN   Stirpium Europaearum Extra Britannias Nascentium Sylloge. 1694. 8vo., modern half calf. Wheldon 130-1198 1974 £35

RAY, JOHN   Synopsis Methodica Stirpium Britannicarum. 1690. 8vo., modern half calf, plates. Wheldon 129-1012 1974 £40

RAY, JOHN   Synopsis Methodica Stirpium Britannicarum. 1724. 2 vols., 8vo., contemporary calf, rebacked, plates, third edition. Wheldon 128-1215 1973 £25

RAY, JOHN   Synopsis Methodica Stirpium Britannicarum. 1724. 8vo., modern red morocco, third edition. Wheldon 129-1013 1974 £25

RAY, JOHN   Synopsis Methodica Stirpium Britannicarum. 1724. 8vo., contemporary panelled vellum, gilt, plates. Wheldon 130-1106 1974 £35

RAY, JOHN   Three Physico-Theological Discourses. 1713. 8vo., contemporary panelled calf, plates, third edition. Wheldon 131-177 1974 £70

RAY, JOHN   Travels Through the Low-Countries. London, 1738. 2 vols., 8vo., contemporary calf, leather labels, plates. Traylen 79-563 1973 £65

RAY, MARCEL   George Grosz. Paris, 1927. Small 8vo., plates, wrappers. Minters 37-345 1973 $25

RAY, WILLIAM   Poems. New York, 1826. 12mo., contemporary quarter calf, second edition. Ximenes 35-16 1974 $20

RAY SOCIETY   Botanical and Physiological Memoirs. 1853.
8vo., cloth, plates. Wheldon 131-1189 1974 £7.50

RAY SOCIETY   Reports and Papers on Botany. 1846-49.
2 vols., 8vo., cloth, plates. Wheldon 128-1155 1973 £10

RAY SOCIETY   Reports on the Progress of Zoology and Botany,
1841-44. 1845-47. 2 vols., 8vo., cloth. Wheldon 128-290 1973 £6

RAYE, C.   A Picturesque Tour Through the Isle of Wight.
1825. Oblong 8vo., orig. half roan, plates. Quaritch 939-377 1974 £250

RAYES, PROSPER, E.   Las Estepas de Espana y su Vegetacion. Madrid,
1915. Roy 8vo., new cloth, illus. Wheldon 129-1115 1974 £10

RAYET, O.   Histoire de la Ceramique Grecque. Paris,
1888. Imp. 8vo., plates, half polished calf, gilt, scarce. Quaritch 940-659
1974 £20

RAYLEIGH, JOHN WILLIAM STRUTT   Argon. Washington, 1896. Large 4to.,
orig. cloth, gilt, fine, first edition. Dawsons PM 245-632 1974 £65

RAYLEIGH, JOHN WILLIAM STRUTT   Argon, a New Constituent of the
Atmosphere. London, 1895. 4to., cloth folder, orig. printed wrappers, rare
first edition. Gilhofer 61-68 1974 sFr. 1,800

RAYLEIGH, JOHN WILLIAM STRUTT   Scientific Papers. Cambridge, 1899-1920.
Large 8vo., 6 vols., orig. cloth, fine, first edition. Dawsons PM 245-633 1974
£110

RAYMOND, DORA NEILL   Oliver's Secretary. 1932. Illus., 341 pages.
Austin 61-843 1974 $10

RAYMOND, E. T.   Portraits of the Nineties. 1921. 8vo., illus.,
orig. cloth, scarce, first edition. Rota 189-728 1974 £5

RAYMOND, GEORGE LANSING   A Collection of This Author's Works on Art
and Aesthetics. New York, 1908-21. 8 vols., 8vo., plates, orig. blue cloth.
Quaritch 940-212 1974 £25

RAYMOND, JAMES GRANT   The Life of Thomas Dermody. London, 1806.
2 vols., 8vo., later mottled calf, first edition. Ximenes 35-17 1974 $45

RAYMOND, THOMAS L.   Stephen Crane. Newark, 1923. Orig. cloth
backed boards, label, first edition, one of 250 numbered copies, fine.
MacManus 224-111 1974 $25

RAYMOND, THOMAS L.   Stephen Crane. Newark, 1923. First U. S.
edition, cloth backed marbled boards, fine. Covent 51-2283 1973 £17.50

RAYMOND, W. O.   The River St. John. Sackville, 1943. Maps,
illus. Hood's 104-231 1974 $35

RAYMOND, W. O.   The River St. John, Its Physical Features,
Legends and History from 1604 to 1784. Sackville, 1943. Hood's 102-210 1974
$35

RAYMUNDO da Silva, B.   Contribuicae Para a Historia Natural des Lepid-
opteros do Brasil. Rio de Janeiro, 1907. 4to., half calf, plates, rare. Wheldon 130-783 1974 £15

RAYNAL, GUILLAUME THOMAS FRANCOIS   Histoire Philosophique et Politique
des Etablissemens et du Commerce des Europeens dans les Deux Indies. Geneva,
1780. 10 vols. 8vo., and 1 atlas 4to., contemporary calf, plates, maps, fine.
Schumann 499-93 1974 sFr 1,300

RAYNAL, MAURICE   Juan Gris. Paris, 1920. Large 4to., boards,
uncut, plates, limited edition. Minters 37-281 1973 $185

RAYNAL, MAURICE   Modern French Painters. 1929. 4to., plates,
buckram, English first edition. Covent 56-1495 1974 £10.50

RAYNAL, PAUL   The Unknown Warrior. 1928. Austin 51-771
1973 $10

RAYNALDUS, ODORICO   Annales Ecclesiastici ab Anno Quo Desinit
Card. Caes. Baronius MCXCVIII. Cologne, 1693-94-90. 8 vols., folio,
contemporary sheep. Howes 185-1585 1974 £60

RAYNAUD, THEOPHILUS   De Ortu Infantium Contra Naturam, per
Sectionem Caesaream, Tractatio. Lyons, 1637. Small 8vo., polished calf,
rare. Schuman 37-217 1974 $110

REA, C.   British Basidiomycetae. Cambridge, 1922.
8vo., 2 vols., buckram. Wheldon 129-1324 1974 £8

REA, C.   British Basidiomycetae. Cambridge, 1922.
8vo., cloth, scarce. Wheldon 130-1342 1974 £8

REA, C.   British Basidiomycetae. Cambridge, 1922.
8vo., cloth, 2 vols. Wheldon 129-1325 1974 £10

REA, JOHN   Flora. London, 1665. Folio, contemporary
panelled calf, rebacked, plates, fine, first edition. Traylen 79-46 1973 £98

REA, JOHN   Flora. London, 1676. Folio, contemporary
calf, rebacked, fine, plates. Traylen 79-47 1973 £75

READ, D. B.   The Canadian Rebellion of 1837. Toronto,
1896. Hood's 102-631 1974 $17.50

READ, D. B.   The Lieutenant-Governors of Upper Canada and
Ontario, 1792-1899. Toronto, 1900. Hood's 103-33 1974 $10

READ, D. B.   Life and Times of Gen. John Graves Simcoe.
Toronto, 1890. Hood's 103-226 1974 $17.50

READ, D. B.   Life and Times of Major-General Sir Isaac Brock.
Toronto, 1894. Hood's 102-256 1974 $20

READ, DANEIL   An Address Delivered. Madison, 1856. 8vo.,
disbound, first edition. Ximenes 35-18 1974 $20

READ, HERBERT   Ecologues. 1919. Buckram-backed dec.
boards, fine, vignettes. Covent 55-1243 1974 £35

READ, HERBERT   The End of a War. 1933. Boards, faded, English first edition. Covent 56-1082 1974 £5.25

READ, HERBERT   English Stained Glass. 1926. 4to., illus.,
plates, buckram. Covent 55-119 1974 £35

READ, HERBERT   Red Indians. 1844. Maps, orig. patterned cloth,
fine. Covent 53-215 1974 £42.50

READ, JOHN   A Summary View of the Spontaneous Electricity of
the Earth and Atmosphere. London, 1793. 8vo., modern half calf, first edition.
Dawsons PM 245-635 1974 £70

READ, THOMAS BUCHANAN   Female Poets of America. 1857. Spine worn,
seventh edition. Allen 216-1518 1974 $10

READ, THOMAS BUCHANAN   A Summer Story. Philadelphia, 1865. 12mo.,
orig. green cloth, first edition. Ximenes 35-19 1974 $15

READE, CHARLES   Foul Play. 1868. Half morocco gilt, English
first edition. Covent 56-1085 1974 £5.25

READE, CHARLES   Foul Play. (New York, c. 1872). 12mo.,
wrappers, first edition. Goodspeed's 578-292 1974 $10

READE, CHARLES   A Woman-Hater. Edinburgh, 1877. 3 vols.,
8vo., orig. blue cloth, first edition. Ximenes 35-20 1974 $80

READING, Pennsylvania: Indelible Photographs. New York, 1891. Wrappers,
illus. Jenkins 61-2171 1974 $12.50

REASONS for a War Against Spain, In a Letter from a Merchant of London, to a
Member of the House of Commons. London, 1737. 8vo., modern quarter calf,
gilt. Dawsons PM 247-237 1974 £42

REASONS for Improving the Fisheries and Linnen Manufacture of Scotland.
London, 1727. 8vo., modern boards, first edition. Dawsons PM 247-238 1974
£35

REASONS for Obtaining a Seal to Mark all Plain Black Silks. (1713). Folio, disbound. Quaritch 939-244 1974 £12

REASONS Humbly Offer'd Against Laying a Further Duty on Yarn Imported from Ireland. (1711). Folio, disbound. Quaritch 939-289 1974 £12

REASONS Humbly Offered by the Leather-Sellers of the Cities of London and Westminster. (1711). Folio, disbound. Quaritch 939-158 1974 £12

REASONS Humbly Offer'd to the Honourable House of Commons. (1714). Folio, disbound. Quaritch 939-70 1974 £14

REAUMUR, RENE ANTOINE FERCHAULT DE   Memoires Pour Servir a l'Histoire des Insectes. Paris, 1734-42. 6 vols., 4to., contemporary calf gilt, rare, plates, complete copy. Wheldon 131-848 1974 £250

REAVEY, GEORGE   Nostradam: A Sequence of Poems. Paris, 1935. Limited to 250 copies, very good, wrappers, presentation copy from author. Covent 51-1563 1973 £10.50

REBAY, HILLA   In Memory of Wassily Kandinsky.   New York, 1945. 4to., boards, illus. Minters 37-587 1973 $37.50

REBAY, HILLA   Kandinsky. 1945. 4to., boards, illus., plates. Minters 37-588 1973 $30

REBELLIAU, ALFRED   Bossuet, Historien du Protestantisme. Paris, 1909. Contemporary half morocco. Howes 185-991 1974 £5.50

REBOUL, GUILLAUME   Le Nouveau Panurge. Lyons, 1615. 16mo., contemporary light brown calf, gilt, morocco label. L. Goldschmidt 42-104 1974 $150

DEN RECHTEN Ommegonck Vande Gevioleerde Stadt van Amsterdam. (Amsterdam, 1650). Small 4to., modern paper wrappers, good copy. Sawyer 293-18 1974 £14

RECORDE, ROBERT   Arithmetick. London, 1699. 4to., contemporary calf. Dawsons PM 245-636 1974 £95

RECUEIL de Costumes Suisses. Paris, n.d. (c. 1810-15). Orig. etchings, in contemporary hand coloring, numbered, 8vo., three quarter green morocco. Schumann 499-94 1974 sFr 6,000

RECUEIL des Traitez de Prix, de Commerce, Navigation et Marine.   Lyon, n.d. 7 parts in 1 vol., 12mo., contemporary sheep gilt. Smith 193-123 1973 £20

REDDING, C.   The Pictorial History of the County of Lancaster. 1844. Roy. 8vo., contemporary half red morocco, illus., frayed. Howes 186-2077 1974 £5

REDE, WILLIAM LEMAN   The Royal Rake. London, 1842. Large 4to., orig. cloth, first edition. Ximenes 35-22 1974 $40

REDFIELD, JOHN   Music, a Science and an Art. New York, 1935. Illus. Biblo & Tannen 214-901 1974 $8.50

REDGRAVE, S.   Dictionary of Artists of the English School. 1878. Cloth, new revised edition. Eaton Music-667 1973 £5

REDI, FORREST   Young Tom. 1944. 8vo., orig. cloth, first edition. Rota 189-734 1974 £5

REDI, FRANCESCO   Bibliografia delle Opere di Francesco Redi. 1941. Kraus B8-232 1974 $10

REDI, FRANCESCO   Osservazioni di Francesco Redi. Florence, 1684. 4to., old vellum, plates, rare, first edition. Wheldon 130-367 1974 £120

REDI, FRANCESCO   Osservazioni . . . Intorno Agli Animali Viventi Che Si Trovano Negli Animali Viventi. Florence, 1684. 4to., old vellum, engraved plates, rare, first edition. Wheldon 128-291 1973 £120

REDI, FRANCESCO   Osservazioni Intorno alle Vipere. Florence, 1685-86. 4to., contemporary vellum. Wheldon 131-766 1974 £40

REDMOND, JOHN   The Home Rule Bill. London, 1912. 8vo., cloth backed boards. Emerald 50-809 1974 £5.50

REDWOOD, B.   Petroleum. 1906. 8vo., cloth, plates. Wheldon 129-857 1974 £10

REECH, F.   Cours de Mecanique. Paris, 1852. 4to., contemporary leather-backed boards, first edition. Schuman 37-188 1974 $110

REED, CHARLES BERT   The First Great Canadian, The Story of Pierre Le Moyne. Chicago, 1910. Hood's 103-227 1974 $17.50

REED, CHARLES BERT   Masters of the Wilderness. Chicago, (1914). Frontispiece, olive cloth, gilt, first edition. Bradley 35-146 1974 $10

REED, F. R. C.   The Lower Palaeozoic Trilobites of the Girvan District, Ayrshire. 1903-35. 4to., half calf, orig. wrappers, plates. Wheldon 131-1070 1974 £10

REED, F. W.   A Bibliography of Alexandre Dumas Pere. Middlesex, 1933. Limited to 300 copies, crown 4to., orig. buckram, fine. Forster 98-115 1974 £21

REED, G. WALTER   History of Sacramento County, California. Los Angeles, 1923. 4to., three quarter leather, illus. Saddleback 14-245 1974 $100

REED, H. S.   A Short History of the Plant Sciences. 1942. Roy 8vo., cloth, illus. Wheldon 129-184 1984 £7.50

REED, J. EUGENE   The Masterpieces of German Art. Philadelphia, ca. 1900. 2 vols., folio, full. publisher's leather. Jacobs 24-53 1974 $25

REED, JOSEPH   Tom Jones. London, 1769. 8vo., modern boards, first edition. Dawsons PM 252-815 1974 £15

REED, MARK   Petticoat Fever. French, 1935. 125p. Austin 51-772 1973 $7.50

REED, T. A.   The Scaddings, A Pioneer Family In York. 1944. Portraits, illus., inscribed. Hood's 103-34 1974 $15

REED, VERNER Z.   Lo-To-Kah. New York, 1897. Cloth, illus. Hayman 57-654 1974 $12.50

REED, WILLIAM B.   Reprint of the Original Letters from Washington to Joseph Reed, During the American Revolution. Philadelphia, 1852. Jenkins 61-2260 1974 $17.50

REES, GEORGE   Practical Observations on Disorders of the Stomach. London, 1811. 8vo., orig. boards, uncut, second edition. Dawsons PM 249-419 1974 £16

REES, JAMES   The Dramatic Authors of America. Philadelphia, 1845. 12mo., orig. wrappers, scarce, first edition. Ximenes 35-23 1974 $45

REES, W. J.   Lives of the Cambro British Saints of the Fifth and Immediate Succeeding Centuries. 1853. Thick roy. 8vo., orig. cloth. Howes 185-1589 1974 £12.50

REEVE, ARTHUR B.   The Ear in the Wall. New York, 1916. First U. S. edition, near mint, frontis. Covent 51-543 1973 £15

REEVE, ARTHUR B.   The Panama Plot. New York, 1918. 8vo., orig. black pictorial cloth, first edition. Rota 190-344 1974 £10

REEVE, ARTHUR B.   The Poisoned Pen. New York, 1913. 8vo., orig. cloth, scarce, first edition. Rota 190-342 1974 £15

REEVE, ARTHUR B.   The Social Gangster. New York, 1916. 8vo., orig. cloth, first edition. Rota 190-343 1974 £10

REEVE, J. STANLEY   Further Fox-Hunting Recollections. New York, 1935. Cloth, leather labels, first edition. Bradley 35-310 1974 $16

REEVE, J. STANLEY   Radnor Reminiscences. 1921. Photographs, silhouettes, orig. binding. Butterfield 10-300 1974 $35

REEVE, L.   Conchologia Systematica. 1841. Vol. 1 only, 4to., new buckram, plates, folding table, rare.   Wheldon 128-850 1973 £15

REEVE, W.   Suuny-San. Toronto, 1922. Hood's 104-571 1974 $10

REEVES, WILLIAM   Ecclesiastical Antiquities of Down. Dublin, 1847. 4to., cloth boards, bookplate. Emerald 50-813 1974 £25

REFLECTIONS On a Late Speech By the Lord Haversham In So Far as It Relates to the Affairs of Scotland. London, 1704. 4to., fine, cloth box, uncut, first edition. Dawsons PM 247-239 1974 £30

REFLEXIONS sur le Seul Moyen de Terminer la Guerre. 1796. 8vo., orig. drab blue paper wrappers, uncut, unopened, first edition. Dawsons PM 251-323 1974 £10

REFORM of the University of Glasgow. Glasgow, 1835. 8vo., unbound. Hill 126-88 1974 £6.50

REFUGEE. Prentice-Hall, 1940. Austin 62-346 1974 $10

REFUGEE ECONOMIC CORPORATION   Quest for Settlement. New York, 1948. Austin 62-528 1974 $10

REFUGEES In America. Harper, 1947. Austin 62-124 1974 $17.50

REGEL, E.   Florula Ajanensis. 1859. Modern cloth, rare. Wheldon 128-1304 1973 £18

REGENER, EDGAR ALFRED   E. M. Lilien. Goslar, 1905. 4to., orig. dec. cloth, illu., plates. Minters 37-251 1973 $30

REGER, P. AMBROSIUS   Die Benediktiner in Alabama und Geschichte der Grundung Von St. Bernard. Baltimore, 1898. 12mo., cloth. Saddleback 14-2 1974 $15

REGGIO, PIETRO   Songs Set by. (N.P., n.d.). 2 parts in 1 vol., folio, contemporary panelled calf, fine, first edition. Dawsons PM 252-816 1974 £485

REGIMEN Sanitatis cum Expositione Magistri Arnaldi de Villa Nova Cathellano. Venice, n.d. 4to., boards, woodcut portrait. Schuman 37-227 1974 $950

REGIOMONTANUS
Please turn to
MUELLER, JOHANNES

REGISTRUM Magni Sigilli Regum Scotorum. Edinburgh, 1882-86. 3 vols., thick roy. 8vo., orig. cloth. Howes 186-1160 1974 £21

REGNARD, JEAN FRANCOIS   Oeuvres. Paris, 1820. 6 vols., 8vo., contemporary mottled tree sheep, gilt. L. Goldschmidt 42-105 1974 $60

REGNAULT, HENRI VICTOR   Relation des Experiences. (Paris, 1847). Thick 4to., contemporary boards, uncut. Zeitlin 235-188 1974 $75

REGNIER, HENRI DE   Le Bon Plaisir. Paris, 1902. 12mo., three quarter cloth, orig. wrapper, uncut, first edition. L. Goldschmidt 42-343 1974 $12.50

REGOOR, M.   De Schermkunst Voor Het Volksonderwus. 1866. 8vo., orig. cloth. Bow Windows 64-335 1974 £5

REGULATIONS For the Order and Discipline of the Troops of the U. S. Hartford, 1779. Plates, leather, worn. Rinsland 58-962 1974 $100

REHM, H.   Zur Kenntnis der Discomyceten Deutschlands. Munich, 1912-15. Roy 8vo., boards. Wheldon 129-1326 1974 £5

REICHEL, WILLIAM C.   A History of the Rise, Progress, and Present Condition of the Bethlehem Female Seminary. Philadelphia, 1858. 8vo., orig. bindings. Butterfield 8-504 1974 $17.50

REICHENBACH, CHARLES VON   Physico-Physiological Researches. London, 1850. 8vo., half calf, first edition in English. Schumann 35-328 1974 $145

REICHENBACH, CHARLES VON   Researches on Magnetism, Electricity, Heat, Light, Crystallization, and Chemical Attraction. Edinburgh, 1850. 8vo., orig. cloth, gilt, plates, first edition in English. Dawsons PM 245-637 1974 £14

REICHENBACH, H. G.   Beitrage zu Einer Orchideenkunde Central Amerika's. Hamburg, 1866. 4to., plates, rare. Wheldon 128-1570 1973 £7.50

REICHENBACH, H. G.   Beitrage zu Einer Orchideenkunde Central-Amerika's. Hamburg, 1866. 4to., plates, rare. Wheldon 130-1530 1974 £7.50

REICHENBACH, H. G.   Otia Botanica Hamburgensia. Hamburg, 1878-81. 4to., very scarce. Wheldon 128-1571 1973 £7.50

REICHENBACH, H. G.   Otia Botanica Hamburgensia. Hamburg, 1878-81. 4to., scarce. Wheldon 130-1531 1974 £7.50

REICHENBACH, H. G. L.   Icones Florae Germanicae. Leipzig and Gera, 1837-1909. Vols. 1-24, 4to., modern green half morocco, hand-coloured plates, rare. Wheldon 128-1305 1973 £1,000

REICHENOW, A.   Vogebilder aus Fernen Zonen. Kassel, 1878-83. Folio, plates, foxing. Traylen 79-110 1973 £150

REICHERT, C. B.   Beschreibung Einer Fruhzeitigen Menschlichen Frucht im Blaschenformigen Bildungszustande. Berlin, 1873. 4to., orig. boards, plates, somewhat foxed. Wheldon 128-292 1973 £7.50

REID, C.   The Pliocene Floras of the Dutch-Prussian Border. The Hague, 1915. 4to., limp boards, plates. Wheldon 128-1039 1973 £7.50

REID, EDITH G.   The Great Physician. London, 1936. Hood's 103-608 1974 $12.50

REID, FORREST   Apostate. London, (1926). Cloth, first edition. Dawson's 424-122 1974 $17.50

REID, FORREST   Apostate. 1926. One of 50 copies, numbered & signed by author, orig. white buckram, gilt top, fine copy. Covent 51-2546 1973 £25

REID, FORREST   At the Door of the Gate. London, 1915. 8vo., scarce, worn, first edition. Emerald 50-815 1974 £5

REID, FORREST   Illustrators of the Sixties. 1928. Orig. cloth, plates, dust wrapper, scarce. Marsden 39-371 1974 £55

REID, FORREST   The Kingdom of Twilight. London, 1904. 8vo., rare, first edition. Emerald 50-814 1974 £25

REID, FORREST   Peter Waring. 1937. 8vo., orig. cloth, wrappers, first edition. Rota 189-732 1974 £8.50

REID, FORREST   Retrospective Adventures. 1941. Dust wrapper, worn, English first edition. Covent 56-1087 1974 £15.75

REID, G. H.   An Essay on the New South Wales. Sydney, 1876. 8vo., orig. wrappers, map, first edition. Ximenes 35-26 1974 $40

REID, H. A.   History of Pasadena. Pasadena, 1895. Large 8vo., orig. cloth, illus., scarce, first edition. Putnam 126-277 1974 $110

REID, H. J.   The History of Wargrave, Berks. Reading, 1885. Orig. cloth, plates, very scarce, first edition. Smith 193-178 1973 £9.50

REID, HARVEY   Biographical Sketch of Enoch Long. Chicago, 1884. 8vo., orig. bindings. Butterfield 8-155 1974 $10

REID, J. B.   Complete Word and Phrase Concordance to Poems and Songs of Burns. 1889. Buckram, slightly browned. Allen 216-1991 1974 $15

REID, J. G.   At the Sign of the Brush and Pen. 1898. Sq. 8vo., buckram, illus., English first edition. Covent 56-65 1974 £15

REID, J. T.   It Happened in Taos. New Mexico, 1946.
118p., illus. Austin 62-529 1974 $12.50

REID, JAMES SEATON   History of the Presbyterian Church in Ireland.
Belfast, 1867. 3 vols., new cloth, new edition. Emerald 50-822 1974 £7.50

REID, JOHN C.   Reid's Tramp: or, A Journal of Incidents of Ten
Months Travel Through Texas, New Mexico, Arizona, Sonora and California.
Austin, 1935. Jenkins 61-2243 1974 $22.50

REID, MAYNE   Bruin: The Grand Bear Hunt. Boston, 1861.
12mo., embossed cloth, spine stamped in gold, engraved illus., spine ends
rubbed, first American edition, early issue with inscription. Frohnsdorff 15-152
1974 $20

REID, MAYNE   The Headless Horseman. London, (n.d.). 2 vols.,
8vo., plates, orig. cloth gilt, first edition. Dawsons PM 252-817 1974 £175

REID, MAYNE   The White Chief. London, 1855. 3 vols., 8vo.,
orig. cloth, faded, uncut, first edition. Dawsons PM 252-818 1974 £70

REID, MAYNE   The Young Voyageurs. London, n.d. Illus.,
new edition. Hood's 103-501 1974 $12.50

REID, THOMAS   Travels in Ireland in the Year 1822. 1823.
First edition, demy 8vo., orig. boards, paper printed label, uncut, scarce, fine.
Broadhurst 24-1512 1974 £30

REID, THOMAS   Travels in Ireland. 1823. 8vo., orig. boards,
uncut, scarce. Broadhurst 23-1525 1974 £30

REID, THOMAS MAYNE
Please turn to
REID, MAYNE

REID, WILLIAM   An Attempt to Develop the Law of Storms.
London, 1838. 8vo., half calf, first edition. Schuman 37-218 1974 $125

REIDEMEISTER, L.   Ming-Porzellane in Schwedischen Sammlungen.
Berlin & Leipzig, 1935. 4to., plates, canvas, scarce. Quaritch 940-417 1974
£12

REIFENBERG, A.   Ancient Hebrew Arts. New York, 1950.
Biblo & Tannen 214-91 1974 $15

REIFFENSTUEL, JOHANN GEORG   Jus Canonicum Universum Clara Methodo
Juxta Titulus Quinque Librorum Decretalium. Venice, 1742. 6 vols. in 3,
folio, contemporary vellum. Howes 185-1590 1974 £45

REIMANN, MAX   Wilhelm Haller. Berlin, Leipzig & Vienna,
1930. 4to., boards, cloth spine, foxing, plates. Minters 37-537 1973 $25

REINES, BERNARD J.   For Country and Nankind. 1944. 241p.
Austin 51-773 1973 $7.50

REIS, JOHANN PHILIPP   Ueber Telephonie Durch den Galvanischen
Strom. (Frankfurt, 1861). 8vo., cloth folder, rare first edition. Gilhofer
61-52 1974 sFr. 2,300

REISCH, GREGOR   Margarita Philosophica Totius Philosophiae
Rationalis, Naturalis & Moralis Principia. Freiburg, 1503. 4to., large folding
woodcut map, woodcuts, brown calf, both covers tooled in gold, raised bands,
very fine, extremely rare first edition. Schafer 10-138 1974 sFr 12,000

REISNER, GEORGE ANDREW   Mycerinus. Cambridge, 1931. Roy. 4to.,
plates, illus., cloth. Quaritch 940-346 1974 £35

REISS, LIONEL S.   My Models Were Jews. 1938. Drawings,
etchings, limited. Austin 57-545 1974 $37.50

REITH, J. C. W.   Broadcast Over Britain. c. 1925. Spine faded,
very good copy, first edition. Covent 51-292 1973 £7.50

REITTER, E.   Fauna Germanica. Stuttgart, 1908-16. 8vo.,
5 vols., orig. cloth, plates, scarce. Wheldon 130-784 1974 £35

REKO, V. A.   Magische Gifte, Rausch und Betaubungsmittel der
Neuen Welt. Leipzig, 1936. 8vo., wrappers, scarce. Wheldon 131-1818
1974 £5

RELATION de ce Qui s'Est Passe au Siege de Quebec, et de la Prise du Canada.
(Quebec), 1855. Plate, cover torn at corner. Hood's 102-737 1974 $35

RELATION de ce Qui s'Est Passe au Siege de Quebec. (Quebec), 1855. Plate,
paper cover. Hood's 104-656 1974 $35

A RELATION of the Siege of Candia. London, 1670. 8vo., contemporary sheep,
fine. Dawsons PM 251-324 1974 £135

RELHAN, R.   Flora Cantabrigiensis. Cambridge, 1820.
8vo., half calf, plates, scarce, third edition. Wheldon 128-1216 1973 £5

RELHAN, R.   Flora Cantabrigiensis. Cambridge, 1820.
8vo., half calf, plates, scarce. Wheldon 131-1241 1974 £5

RELPH, JOSIAH   A Miscellany of Poems. Glasgow, 1747.
8vo., contemporary calf, first edition. Dawsons PM 252-819 1974 £70

REMAK, ROBERT   Galvanotherapie. Paris, 1860. 8vo., cloth-
backed boards, first edition in French. Schumann 35-401 1974 $85

REMBRANDT   The Complete Work Of. Paris, 1897-1906.
8 vols., folio, half brown levant morocco gilt. Quaritch 940-214 1974 £750

REMINGTON, FREDERIC   Pony Tracks. New York, 1895. Pictorial
cloth, attractive copy, first edition. Butterfield 10-475 1974 $90

REMINGTON, FREDERIC   Pony Tracks. New York, 1895. Tall 8vo., pictorial cloth, scarce. Butterfield 8-716 1974 $175

REMINISCENCES of Oregon Pioneers. Pendleton, 1937. 8vo., 257 pages,
cloth. Saddleback 14-659 1974 $15

REMINISCENCES of the Monks of St. Giles. Edinburgh, 1883-99. Bound up
from the orig. parts into 2 vols., square 8vo., contemporary full levant morocco,
panelled backs, top edges gilt, others uncut, very rare, fine. Broadhurst 24-1413
1974 £40

REMINISCENCES of the Monks of St. Giles. Edinburgh, 1883-99. Square 8vo.,
contemporary full levant morocco, gilt. Broadhurst 23-1373 1974 £35

REMY, NICOLAS   Demonolatry. 1930. One of 1275 numbered
copies, this copy unnumbered, small 4to., back hinge cracked, very good copy.
Covent 51-2514 1973 £12.50

RENAN, ERNEST   Collection of Works. Paris, 1922-24. 8 vols.,
orig. wrappers, frayed. Howes 185-1592 1974 £20

RENAN, ERNEST   Histoire des Origines du Christianisme. Paris,
1895. 7 vols., demy 8vo., contemporary half calf, rubbed. Howes 185-1596
1974 £18

RENAN, ERNEST   Vie de Jesus. Paris, 1863. 8vo., late 19th
century red half morocco, gilt top, orig. printed wrappers bound in, first edition,
very fine copy. Schafer 10-147 1974 sFr 800

RENARD, JULES   Correspondance. Paris, 1927-28. 5 vols.,
8vo., three quarter light brown levant morocco, gilt, limited, first edition.
L. Goldschmidt 42-344 1974 $45

RENAUDOT, EUSEBE   L'Antimoine Iustifie et l'Antimoine Triomphant.
Paris, n.d. 4to., contemporary limp vellum, first edition. Schumann 35-403
1974 $175

RENDER, WILHELM   A Tour through Germany. London, 1801.
2 vols., 8vo., contemporary half calf, plates, first edition. Ximenes 35-29
1974 $40

RENIER, G. J.   Oscar Wilde. 1933. One of 500 numbered
copies, signed by author, portrait, gilt top, very good copy, first edition. Covent
51-2002 1973 £5.25

RENIER, G. J.   Oscar Wilde. 1933. Orig. wrapper, buckram, portrait, English first edition. Covent 56-1334 1974 £21

RENNEVILLE, M. DE   Contes a ma Petite Fille et a Mon Petit Garcon. Paris, 1823. 12mo., engravings, contemporary half calf, rubbed, fifth edition. Bow Windows 62-761 1974 £8.50

RENNIE, JAMES   Alphabet of Scientific Angling. London, 1833. 8vo., orig. rose cloth, printed paper side label, first edition. Ximenes 37-186 1974 $40

RENNIE, JOHN   Report and Estimate on the Improvement of the Drainage and Navigation of the South and Middle Level of the Fens. London, 18-10. 4to., disbound, gilt. Hammond 201-861 1974 £95

RENOUARD, P.   Bibliographie des Editions de Simon de Colines 1520-1546. Paris, 1894. 8vo., wrappers, uncut, orig. edition. Goodspeed's 578-441 1974 $50

THE RENOWNED History of Dame Trot and Her Cat. Banbury, ca. 1830. 24mo., 11 woodcuts, mint copy, uncut. Frohnsdorff 16-262 1974 $25

RENSSELAER, J. VAN   Lectures on Geology. New York, 1825. 8vo., orig. boards, uncut. Hill 126-112 1974 £28

RENWICK, JAMES   Report on the Water Power, at Kingsbridge, Near the City of New York. New York, 1827. 8vo., orig. printed wrappers, worn spine, unopened copy, folding maps, very scarce, first edition. Ximenes 37-187 1974 $90

REPORT Accepted by the Charlestown Wharf Company, June 5, 1838. Boston, 1838. Large folded map, lacks wrapper, maps fine. Butterfield 10-376 1974 $35

REPORT from the Committe, to Who the Petition of the Proprietors of the Stock of the Governor and Company for Raising the Thames Water in York-Building is Referred. 1733. Folio, disbound, dust staining. Broadhurst 24-1293 1974 £5

REPORT from the Parliamentary Select Committee on War Office Contracts. 1900. Folio, orig. wrappers. Howes 186-1295 1974 £7.50

REPORT from the Select Committee of the House of Commons on Petitions Relating to the Corn Laws. 1814. 8vo., half calf. Quaritch 939-479 1974 £40

REPORT from the Select Committee on the British Museum. 1836. 4to., plate, cloth back, boards. Quaritch 939-438 1974 £10

REPORT of the Commission of Inquiry into the Supplies for the British Army in the Crima. 1855. 2 vols., folio, cloth backs, orig. blue wrappers. Howes 186-1709 1974 £21

REPORT of the Commissioners Appointed to Inquire into the Constitution and Government of the British Museum. 1850. 4to., cloth back, boards. Quaritch 939-439 1974 £10

REPORT of the Commissioners Appointed to Inquire into the Constitution and Government of the British Museum. 1850. 2 vols., folio, half calf, scarce. Howes 185-604 1974 £40

REPORT of the Commissioners of the Sinking Fund: 1818-1829. Washington, 1818-29. Contemporary three quarter leather, lacking report for 1819. Jenkins 61-2249 1974 $27.50

REPORTS of the Committee of Investigation Sent in 1873 By the Mexican Government to the Frontier of Texas. New York, 1875. Superb color folding maps, rare. Jenkins 61-2253 1974 $185

REPORT Of the Committee Of the Board Of Agriculture. London, 1795. 4to., contemporary calf, morocco gilt label. Dawsons PM 247-241 1974 £85

REPORT of the Committee on Puerto Ricans in New York City. 1948. Austin 62-517 1974 $12.50

REPORT of the Directors of the Boston and Worcester Rail-Road Corporation. Boston, 1832. 8vo., quarter morocco slipcase. Ximenes 35-11 1974 $50

REPORT of the Directors to the Stockholders of the Illinois Central Rail-Road Company. New York, 1853. Printed wrappers, rare. Bradley 35-183 1974 $100

REPORT of the Governor of Oklahoma Territory. Washington, 1893. Ptd. wrapper, fine content. Jenkins 61-2040 1974 $12.50

REPORT OF the Great Conspiracy Case. Detroit, 1851. Leather, rebacked. Hayman 57-495 1974 $75

REPORT of the Institution for the Education of Deaf and Dumb Children. Edinburgh, 1816. 8vo., unbound. Hill 126-89 1974 £10.50

REPORT of the Inter-Departmental Committee on Medical Inspection and Feeding of Children. 1905. 2 vols., folio, orig. wrappers, cloth backs. Howes 186-1412 1974 £15

REPORT of the Joint Committee Appointed to Investigate the Condition and Treatment of Prisoners of War. Richmond, 1865. Sewn, fine, uncut, rare. Jenkins 61-662 1974 $27.50

REPORT of the Joint Special Committee to Investigate Chinese Immigration. 1877. 1281 pages. Austin 57-126 1974 $47.50

REPORT of the Military Governor of Puerto Rico on Civil Affairs. 1902. Austin 62-519 1974 $47.50

REPORT of the Municipal Commissioners Appointed to Enquire Into the State of Corporations In England & Wales, Oct. 24th, 1833. Reading, 1833. Thick demy 8vo., contemporary roan gilt. Smith 193-179 1973 £5

THE REPORT of the Municipal Commissioners on the City and County of the City of Coventry. Coventry, 1835. Old half vellum. Howes 186-2219 1974 £5

REPORT of the Parliamentary Committee on the Signet and Privy Seal Offices. 1849. Folio, cloth. Howes 186-1215 1974 £6

REPORT of the Royal Commission Upon the Duties of the Metropolitan Police. 1908. 2 vols., folio, buckram. Howes 186-993 1974 £25

REPORT of the Secretary of the Interior Transmitting Certain Papers Relating to Private Land Claims in Arizona Known as El Sopori. Washington, 1882. Jenkins 61-147 1974 $17.50

REPORT of the Secretary of the Treasury of the Commerce and Navigation of the United States. Washington, 1862. 2 vols. in 1, full calf. Jenkins 61-2250 1974 $12.50

REPORT of the Select Committee on the Formation of an Ice Bridge Over the St. Lawrence at Quebec. Quebec, 1853. Hood's 104-600 1974 $15

REPORT of the Select Committee to whom was referred the subject of the practibility of preventing the intro. of Foreign Paupers into the state. Massachusetts, 1835. Austin 62-177 1974 $37.50

REPORT of the Subcommittee of the Comm. On Judiciary Appointed to Investigate the Administration of the Civil Service Laws of the State of New York. Albany, 1895. Orig. binding, hinges cracked internally. Wilson 63-65 1974 $12.50

REPORT of the Trail of the Hon. Samuel Chase . . . . for High Crimes and Misdemeanors. Baltimore, 1805. Orig. boards, uncut, first edition. Bradley 35-388 1974 $60

REPORT of the Trial of Prof. John W. Webster, Indicted for the Murder of Dr. George Parkman. Boston, 1850. Dec. boards, new half morocco, first edition. Bradley 35-389 1974 $60

REPORT on the Canadian Gold Fields and the Best Means of Their Development. Quebec, 1865. Folding maps, paper cover. Hood's 102-735 1974 $10

REPORT On the Canadian Gold Fields and the Best Means of Their Development. Quebec, 1865. Maps, paper cover. Hood's 104-622 1974 $10

REPORT on the Surrender and Destruction of Navy Yeards: Pensacola, Norfolk, and Harpers Ferry. Washington, 1862. Jenkins 61-2252 1974 $15

THE REPORT, Ordinance, and Addresses of the Convention of the People of South Carolina. Columbia, 1832. 8vo., disbound, uncut, first edition. Ximenes 35-249 1974 $45

REPORTS Of the Military Operations During the Rebellion, 1861-65. 2 vols. Rinsland 58-949 1974 $32

REPPLIER, A.   Mere Marie of the Ursulines, a Study in
Adventure. Garden City, 1931. Hood's 102-257 1974 $7.50

REPPLIER, AGNES   The Fireside Sphinx. Boston, 1901. 1st ed.
Biblo & Tannen 213-590 1973 $15

REPRESENTATIVE Men of North Dakota. Fargo, 1913. 4to., leather 163 pages.
Saddleback 14-610 1974 $50

REPRESENTATIVE POEMS of Living Poets. 1886. English first edition. Covent
56-1422 1974 £8.50

REPTON, HUMPHRY   Designs for the Pavillon at Brighton. 1808.
Folio, plates, orig. boards. Quaritch 939-567 1974 £550

REPTON, HUMPHRY   Fragments On the Theory and Practice of
Landscape Gardening. London, 1816. Large 4to., diced russia gilt, fine,
plates. Traylen 79-49 1973 £450

REPTON, HUMPHRY   Fragments On the Theory and Practice of
Landscape Gardening. London, 1816. 4to., full green levant morocco, plates,
raised bands, uncut, rare, magnificent copy. Traylen 79-50 1973 £1,050

REPTON, HUMPHRY   Observations on the Theory and Practice of
Landscape Gardening. 1803. Imp. 4to., orig. printed boards, neatly rebacked
in red morocco, morocco-backed slip case, hand-coloured plates, illus., nice
copy. Wheldon 128-1525 1973 £800

REPTON, HUMPHRY   Observations on the Theory and Practice of
Landscape Gardening. 1803. Imperial 4to., orig. printed boards, rebacked,
plates. Wheldon 130-64 1974 £800

REPTON, HUMPHRY   Observations on the Theory and Practice of
Landscape Gardening. 1803. Imperial 4to., new half brown morocco gilt, illus.,
plates. Wheldon 130-65 1974 £700

REPTON, HUMPHRY   Observations On the Theory and Practice of
Landscape Gardening. 1803. Imp. 4to., new half brown morocco gilt, hand
coloured and other plates, illus., complete copy, first edition. Wheldon
128-1526 1973 £700

REPTON, HUMPHRY   Observations On the Theory and Practice of
Landscape Gardening. London, 1803. Folio, full green morocco, gilt, uncut,
plates, superb copy. Traylen 79-51 1973 £900

REPUBLICAN NATIONAL COVENTION   Official Report of the Proceedings of
the Twentieth . . . Held in Chicago, Illinois, June, 14, 15 and 16, 1932,
Resulting in Renomination of Herbert Hoover and Charles Curtis. New York,
(1932). Cloth. Hayman 59-574 1974 $10

RERESBY, JOHN   Memoirs. 1734. Contemporary panelled
calf, first edition. Howes 186-1163 1974 £18

RERESBY, TAMWORTH   A Miscellany of Ingenious Thoughts and
Reflections. London, 1721. 4to., contemporary calf, first edition. Ximenes
35-30 1974 $95

RESTIF DE LA BRETONNE, NICOLAS EDME   Les Contemporaines. Paris, 1780-
87. 21 vols., 12mo., half red hard grain morocco, gilt, illus. L. Goldschmidt
42-106 1974 $425

RESTIF DE LA BRETONNE, NICOLAS EDME   Monsieur Nicolas. London,
1930-31. 6 vols., 4to., orig. buckram, plates, uncut, limited edition. Dawsons
PM 252-820 1974 £48

RESTORATION OF THE Earth's Lost History. San Francisco, 1868. Cloth.
Dawson's 424-197 1974 $20

RESTORATION of the White House. Washington, 1903. Large 8vo., first edition,
full page drawings, plates, covers spotted, else fine. Current BW9-443 1974
$25

RESTORATION Verse, 1660-1715. London, 1930. Biblo & Tannen 210-890
1973 $8.50

RESTRICTION of Immigration. Wilson, 1924. Austin 62-501 1974 $12.50

RETERA, W.   P. Kramer. Amsterdam, n.d. 8vo., plates,
wrappers. Minters 37-548 1973 $18

RETROSPECTUS and Prospectus the Nonesuch Dickens. Bloomsbury, 1937.
8vo., illus., orig. cloth gilt, orig. wrappers. Dawsons PM 10-459 1974 £16

RETZ, CARDINAL DE   Oeuvres. Paris, 1870-96. 10 vols., 8vo.,
three quarter levant morocco, gilt, uncut. L. Goldschmidt 42-108 1974 $170

RETZCH, F. A. MORITZ   Outlines to Shakespeare. Leipzig & London,
1838-42. 6 parts in 2 vols., 4to., contemporary half morocco, plates, rubbed.
Howes 186-410 1974 £8.50

REUME, A. DE   Recherches Historiques. Brussels, 1847. 8vo.,
orig. printed paper wrappers, first edition. Dawsons PM 251-131 1974 £50

REVALUATIONS: Studies in Biography. 1931. Fine, partly unopened, dust
wrapper, first edition. Covent 51-1167 1973 £7.50

REVERDY, PIERRE   Flaques de Verre. Paris, 1929. 12mo., orig.
wrapper, uncut, first edition. L. Goldschmidt 42-346 1974 $12.50

REVERDY, PIERRE   Pierres Blanches. (1930). 8vo., unopened,
uncut, limited edition. Minters 37-78 1973 $100

REVERE, PAUL   An Outline of the Life and Works of . . . With
a Partial Catalogue of Silverware Bearing His Name. Newburyport, (1901).
Illus., tall 8vo., very good. Current BW9-415 1974 $18

A REVIEW Of the Excise-Scheme. London, 1733. 8vo., modern boards, first
edition. Dawsons PM 247-242 1974 £20

THE REVIVAL of Printing: A Bibliographical Catalogue of Works Issued by the
Chief Modern English Presses. 1912. One of 350 numbered copies, collotype
plates, linen backed boards, gilt top, bookplate, spare printed label tipped in at
end, first edition. Covent 51-242 1973 £37.50

REVUE Entomologique. Strasburg, 1833-35. Vols. 1 - 3, 8vo., half morocco
and orig. wrappers, coloured plates, extremely rare. Wheldon 128-788 1973
£20

REVY, J. J.   Hydraulics of Great Rivers. London, 1874.
Folio, orig. cloth, rebacked, plates. Dawsons PM 245-638 1974 £18

REXFORD, ORCELLA   101 Useful Weeds and Wildings. San Francisco,
1941. Sgd., illus. Biblo & Tannen 214-786 1974 $10

REY, CAPTAIN   Voyage from France to Cochin--China, in the
Years 1819 and 1820. London, 1821. 3/4 lea. and bds. Biblo & Tannen 210-1014
1973 $17.50

REY, G.   Etude sur les Monuments de l'Architecture
Militaire des Croises en Syrie. 1871. 4to., plates. Allen 213-1736 1973
$35

REYES, ALFONSO   Mexican Heritage. New York, 1946. 4to.
Biblo & Tannen 210-292 1973 $15

REYHER, SAMUEL   Dissertatio de Nummis quibusdam ex Chymico Me-
tallo Factis. 1692. 4to., half vellum. Dawsons PM 245-639 1974 £55

REYMOND, ARNOLD   History of the Sciences in Greco-Roman
Antiquity. London, 1927. Diagrams. Rittenhouse 46-557 1974 $16

REYMOND, MARCEL   La Sculpture Florentine. 1900. Large thick
folio, illus., plates, embossed calf, gilt, foxing. Rich Summer-89 1974 $40

REYMONT, WLADYSLAW STANISLAW   The Peasants. 1925. 4 vols. Austin
57-546 1974 $17.50

REYMONT, WLADYSLAW STANISLAW   The Peasants. 1925. Austin 62-531
1974 $17.50

REYNARD the Fox in South Africa; or, Hottentot Fables and Tales. London, 1864.
1st ed. Biblo & Tannen 213-729 1973 $27.50

REYNARDSON, C. T. S. BIRCH   Sports & Anecdotes of Bygone Days in England,
Scotland, Ireland, Italy and the Sunny South. London, 1887. 8vo., full page
full color prints, very good. Current BW9-193 1974 $17.50

REYNER, J. H.   Cine-Photography. 1932. 180p., illus.
Austin 51-775 1973 $12.50

REYNOLDS, EDWARD   Three Treatises of the Vanity of the Creature.
1631. Small 4to., 19th century calf, first edition. Howes 185-1600 1974 £35

REYNOLDS, ELHANAN WINCHESTER   The Tangletown Letters. Buffalo,
1856. 12mo., orig. cloth, plates, first edition. Ximenes 35-31 1974 $10

REYNOLDS, FREDERICK   Beyond Dull Care. Longman, 1808. 68p.
Austin 51-776 1973 $12.50

REYNOLDS, FREDERICK   Delays and Blunders. London, 1803. 8vo.,
modern boards, first edition. Dawsons PM 252-821 1974 £15

REYNOLDS, FREDERICK   The Dramatist. Dublin, 1790. 12mo.,
disbound, scarce, first edition. Ximenes 35-32 1974 $35

REYNOLDS, FREDERICK   The Dramatist. London, 1793. 8vo., modern
boards, first authorized edition. Dawsons PM 252-822 1974 £15

REYNOLDS, FREDERICK   The Dramatist. 1793. 8vo., boards, half calf,
first edition. Quaritch 936-205 1974 £15

REYNOLDS, FREDERICK   How to Grow Rich. London, 1793. 8vo.,
modern boards, first edition. Dawsons PM 252-823 1974 £15

REYNOLDS, FREDERICK   Notoriety. London, 1793. 8vo., modern
boards, first authorized edition. Dawsons PM 252-824 1974 £15

REYNOLDS, FREDERICK   The Rage. 1795. 8vo., cloth, first edition.
Quaritch 936-206 1974 £5

REYNOLDS, FREDERICK   Speculation. 1795. 8vo., cloth, first edition.
Quaritch 936-207 1974 £8

REYNOLDS, G. W. M.   Wagner, the Wehr-Wolf. New York, n.d.
Biblo & Tannen 210-655 1973 $15

REYNOLDS, H. E.   Wells Cathedral. (Leeds), 1881. Folio, orig.
morocco backed cloth, illus., scarce. Howes 185-1601 1974 £25

REYNOLDS, HARRY   Minstrel Memories: The Story of Burnt Cork
Minstrelsy in Great Britain, 1836-1927. c. 1928. Plates, large 8vo., first
edition. Covent 51-1815 1973 £10.50

REYNOLDS, HARRY   Minstrel Memories. 1928. Roy. 8vo., orig.
cloth, illus., scarce. Broadhurst 23-171 1974 £10

REYNOLDS, HELEN WILKINSON   Dutchess County Doorways. New York,
1931. Cloth, plates. Dawson's 424-236 1974 $50

REYNOLDS, JOHN   The Pioneer History of Illinois. 1852. 12mo.,
orig. cloth, first edition. Ximenes 35-33 1974 $120

REYNOLDS, JOHN   The Triumphes of Gods Revenge Agaynst the
Cryinge, and Execrable Sinne of Willfull, and Premediated Murther. 1663.
Engraved title, slight marginal worming, small folio, old calf, joints cracking,
fourth edition. Thomas 32-136 1974 £50

REYNOLDS, JOHN HAMILTON   The Fancy. 1820. 12mo., boards, rebacked,
uncut, first edition. Quaritch 936-530 1974 £30

REYNOLDS, JOHN RUSSEL   Essays and Addresses. London, 1896. 8vo.,
orig. blue cloth, uncut, unopened, fine. Dawsons PM 249-420 1974 £10

REYNOLDS, JOSEPH   Peter Gott. Boston, 1856. 12mo., orig.
brown cloth, frontispiece, first edition. Ximenes 35-34 1974 $12

REYNOLDS, JOSHUA   Discourses Delivered to the Students of the
Royal Academy. 1905. Illus., first edition. Covent 55-746 1974 £15

REYNOLDS, JOSHUA   The Literary Works. 1892. 2 vols., full
calf gilt, presentation inscription. Marsden 39-373 1974 £10

REYNOLDS, JOSHUA   The Literary Works Of. 1819. 3 vols., 8vo.,
contemporary boards, cloth spines, worn, uncut. Quaritch 940-218 1974 £20

REYNOLDS, JOSHUA   The Literary Works Of. London, 1819. 8vo.,
3 vols., blue boards, labels, rare. Rich Summer-90 1974 $85

REYNOLDS, JOSHUA   Seven Discourses Delivered. Quarter calf,
rebound, first collected edition. Marsden 37-391 1974 £15

REYNOLDS, JOSHUA   Seven Discourses Delivered in the Royal
Academy. 1788. Contemporary calf, gilt. Marsden 39-374 1974 £35

REYNOLDS, JOSHUA   Seven Discourses Delivered in the Royal
Academy by the President. 1778. 8vo., contemporary calf, worn, scarce,
first edition. Quaritch 940-217 1974 £30

REYNOLDS, JOSHUA   Sir Joshua Reynolds, and His Works. 1856.
8vo., illus., orig. cloth, scarce. Quaritch 940-219 1974 £15

REYNOLDS, L. G.   The Control of Competition In Canada.
Cambridge, 1940. Hood's 103-308 1974 $17.50

REYNOLDS, MICHAEL   Locomotive Engine Driving. London, 1882.
8vo., orig. cloth, gilt, illus., fifth edition. Hammond 201-916 1974 £5.75

REYNOLSON, JOHN   Practical and Philosophical Principles of Making
Malt. 1809. 8vo., orig. boards, second edition. Hammond 201-45 1974 £16

REYRE, L'ABBE J.   Le Fabuliste des Enfans, ou Fables Nouvelles.
Paris, 1805. Engraved plates, 12mo., contemporary tree calf, spine gilt, joint
cracked. George's 610-624 1973 £7.50

RHAM, W. L.   The Dictionary of the Farm. 1844. Orig. cloth,
woodcut illus., first edition. Smith 193-3 1973 £7.50

RHEAD, G. W.   History of the Fan. 1910. Roy. 4to., orig.
buckram, uncut, clean copy, very scarce, limited edition. Quaritch 940-736
1974 £180

RHEAD, G. W.   Staffordshire Pots and Potters. 1906. Illus.,
rubbed, foxing, fine. Covent 55-478 1974 £15

RHEES, WILLIAM JONES   The Smithsonian Institution: Documents Relative
to Its Origin and History. Washington, 1901. 2 vols. Jenkins 61-2261 1974
$17.50

RHETORES Antiqui Graeci. 1508. Vol. 1 only of 2, folio, 19th century vellum,
gilt, morocco labels, rare. Thomas 30-18 1973 £35

RHIND, WILLIAM   A History of the Vegetable Kingdom.
Glasgow, 1857. 8vo., plates, foxing, half calf, gilt, frontispiece, portrait.
Bow Windows 62-762 1974 £8.50

RHIND, WILLIAM   A History of the Vegetable Kingdom. 1868
or 1877. Roy. 8vo., half calf, plates, scarce, revised edition. Wheldon
131-1190 1974 £10

RHINEWINE, A.   Looking Back a Century On the Centennial of
Jewish Political Equality In Canada. Toronto, 1932. Card cover, revised.
Hood's 103-552 1974 $12.50

RHIWALLON   The Physicians of Myddvai; Meddygon Myddfai.
Llandovery, 1861. 8vo., half leather, rubbed, very scarce, some ownership
stamps. Gurney 66-153 1974 £20

RHODA. London, 1816. 3 vols., 12mo., contemporary green half calf,
marbled boards, morocco labels, first edition. Dawsons PM 252-825 1974 £30

RHODE, E. C.   The Old English Herbals. 1922. 4to., orig.
buckram gilt, plates, first edition. Smith 193-21 1973 £25

RHODE, J. G.   Beitrage zur Pflanzenkunde der Vorwelt. Breslau, (1821-23). Folio, old half calf, plates. Wheldon 129-858 1974 £30

RHODE, J. G.   Beitrage zur Pflanzenkunde der Vorwelt.
Breslau, (1821-23). Folio, old half calf, plates, rare. Wheldon 131-1071
1974 £30

RHODE Island State Census. Providence, 1887. Map, new library binding.
Austin 57-549 1974 $47.50

RHODE Island Tercentenary, 1636-1936. Providence, 1937. First edition, 8vo., full page plates, mint. Current BW9-428 1974 $10

RHODE Island Tercentenary, 1636-1936. Providence, 1937. First edition, 8vo., few minor covers spots. Current BW9-428A 1974 $8

RHODES, EUGENE MANLOVE   Beyond the Desert. Boston, 1934. Orig. green cloth, mint, dust jacket, first edition. Bradley 35-313 1974 $40

RHODES, EUGENE MANLOVE   Good Men and True. New York, 1910. Orig. cloth, illus., scarce, first edition. Bradley 35-314 1974 $26

RHODES, EUGENE MANLOVE   The Proud Sheriff. Boston, n.d. Dust jacket, black-stamped orange cloth, mint, orig. edition. Bradley 35-316 1974 $12

RHODES, EUGENE MANLOVE   The Trusty Knaves. Boston, n.d. Orig. tan cloth, dust jacket, mint, orig. edition. Bradley 35-317 1974 $12

RHODES, JOHN H.   History of Battery B, First Regiment Rhode Island Light Artillery in the War to Preserve the Union. Providence, 1894. 8vo., portraits, illus., maps, fine. Current BW9-420 1974 $15

RHODES, THOMAS BARNES   Bombastes Furioso. Taylor, 1830. 18p. Austin 51-778 1973 $6.50

RHODION, EUCHARIUS
Please turn to
ROESLIN, EUCHARIUS

RHYDDERCH, JOHN   Pedigrees of the Montgomeryshire Families. 1888. 8vo., orig. cloth, scarce. Broadhurst 23-1526 1974 £10

RHYMERS CLUB   The Second Book of. London, 1894. Edition limited to 500 copies, bookplate, covers lightly worn, fine, scarce, orig. binding. Ross 86-405 1974 $150

RHYS, ERNEST   The Man at Odds. 1904. Orig. pictorial cloth, English first edition. Covent 56-1089 1974 £5.25

RHYS, GRACE   A Celtic Anthology. 1927. Fine, slightly torn d.w, spare label tipped in at end. Covent 51-48 1973 £5

RHYS, JOHN   Lectures on the Origin and Growth of Religion. London, 1898. 3rd ed. Biblo & Tannen 213-129 1973 $10

RIANCEY, HENRY DE   La Vie des Saints. Paris, 1866. Thick imp. 8vo., contemporary half morocco, gilt, plates. Howes 185-1602 1974 £8.50

RIBADENEYRA, PEDRO DE 1527-1611
Please turn to
RIVADENEIRA, PEDRO DE 1527-1611

RIBEMONT-DESSAIGNES, GEORGES   Celeste Ugolin. Paris, 1926. 12mo., orig. wrapper, uncut, first edition. L. Goldschmidt 42-347 1974 $20

RICARDO, DAVID   The High Price of Bullion. London, 1810. 8vo., contemporary wrappers, scarce, fine. Ximenes 35-35 1974 $125

RICARDO, DAVID   On the Principles of Political Economy. London, 1817. 8vo., half morocco, fine, first edition. Dawsons PM 250-67 1974 £375

RICARDO, DAVID   Reply to Mr. Bosanquet's Practical Observations on the Report of the Bullion Committee. London, 1811. 8vo., full calf antique, first edition. Dawsons PM 247-243 1974 £150

RICARDO, DAVID   The Works of. London, 1846. 8vo., orig. cloth, faded. Dawsons PM 247-244 1974 £55

RICCI, CORRADO   La Regie Gallarie di Venezia. n.d. Folio, black cloth, plates. Rich Summer-91 1974 $35

RICCI, E.   Ricami Italiani Antiche e Moderni. Florence, (1925). 4to., illus., canvas. Quaritch 940-771 1974 £12

RICCI, MARCO   XXIV Tabulas olim a Marco Ricci Bellunensi Colorib. Venice, 1743. Oblong folio, contemporary marbled boards, fine. Marlborough 70-20 1974 £600

RICCI, SEYMOUR DE   The Book Collector's Guide. Philadelphia, 1921. Limited to 1100 copies, med. 8vo., orig. cloth, bookplate. Forster 98-34 1974 £16

RICCI, SEYMOUR DE   A Catalogue of Early English Books in the Library of John L. Clawson. Buffalo, 1924. Limited to 200 copies, post 4to., orig. cloth. Forster 98-35 1974 £35

RICCI, SEYMOUR DE   Catalogue Raisonne des Premieres Impressions de Mayence, 1445-67. Mainz, 1911. Plate, demy 4to., orig. wrappers. Forster 98-33 1974 £28

RICCI, SEYMOUR DE   Census of Medieval and Renaissance Manuscripts in the United States and Canada. 1935-40. 2 vols. and index, cloth. Kraus B8-233 1974 $97.50

RICCI, SEYMOUR DE   English Collectors of Books and Manuscripts, 1530-1930, and Their Marks of Ownership. Cambridge, 1930. Plates, illus., demy 8vo., orig. buckram, d.w. Forster 98-36 1974 £15

RICCI, SEYMOUR DE   Exposition du Livre Italien Mai-Juin 1926. 1926. Post 4to., plates, orig. wrappers slightly soiled. Forster 98-37 1974 £5

RICCI, SEYMOUR DE   French Signed Bindings in the Mortimer L. Schiff Collection. British and Miscellaneous Signed Bindings in the Mortimer L. Schiff Collection. New York, 1935. 4 vols., 4to., buckram. Quaritch 940-609 1974 £190

RICCI, SEYMOUR DE   Guide de l'Amateur de Livres a Gravures du XVIIIe Siecle. Paris, 1912. 2 vols. in 1, limited to 1000 copies, plates, med. 8vo., crushed levant morocco, orig. wrappers bound in, fine. Forster 98-38 1974 £90

RICCIOLI, GIAMBATTISTA   Geographiae et Hydrographiae Reformatae. 1661. Folio, contemporary speckled calf, fine, illus., first edition. Dawsons PM 245-640 1974 £160

RICE, ELMER   American Landscape. 1939. Austin 51-779 1973 $8.50

RICE, ELMER   Cock Robin. French, 1929. Austin 51-785 1973 $8.50

RICE, ELMER   Dream Girl. 1946. Austin 51-786 1973 $8.50

RICE, ELMER   Judgment Day. 1934. Austin 51-780 1973 $8.50

RICE, ELMER   Minority Report. S & S, 1963. Austin 51-781 1973 $7.50

RICE, ELMER   Street Scene. French, 1929. 239p., illus. Austin 51-783 1973 $7.50

RICE, ELMER   A Voyage to Purilia. 1930. English first edition. Covent 56-441 1974 £5.25

RICE, ELMER   We, the People. 1933. Austin 51-784 1973 $10

RICE, HARVEY   Pioneers of the Western Reserve. New York - Boston, 1883. 8vo., orig. bindings. Butterfield 8-424 1974 $12.50

RICE, NATHAN P.   Trials of a Public Benefactor. New York, 1859. First edition. Rittenhouse 46-558 1974 $50

RICE, NATHAN P.   Trials of a Public Benefactor. New York, 1859. Orig. boards, staining. Rittenhouse 46-559 1974 $60

RICH, ARNOLD R.   The Pathogenesis of Tuberculosis. Springfield, 1944. Ex-library. Rittenhouse 46-560 1974 $10

RICH, BENJAMIN ERASTUS   Mr. Durant of Salt Lake City. Salt Lake City, 1893. 8vo., orig. cloth, fine, first edition. Ximenes 35-36 1974 $17.50

RICH, JEREMIAH   The Pen's Dexterity. (1700?). 8vo., old calf, plates, rebacked, gilt. Hammond 201-779 1974 £145

RICH, W. H.   Feathered Game of the Northeast.   New York,
1907. 8vo., orig. cloth, plates.   Wheldon 130-605 1974 £12

A RICH STOREHOUSE.   London, 1630. 8vo., contemporary calf, rebacked,
seventh edition.   Dawsons PM 249-474 1974 £265

RICHARD, ABBE JEROME   History Naturelle de l'Air et des Meteores. Paris, 1770-1771. 12mo., 10 vols., contemporary calf.   Schumann 35-405 1974
$235

RICHARD, L. C. M.   Observations on the Structure of Fruits and Seeds.
London and Norwich, 1819. 8vo., wrappers, plates.   Wheldon 129-954 1974
£7.50

RICHARD, OF CIRENCESTER   The Description of Britain. 1809. Roy. 8vo.,
maps, modern boards.   Quaritch 939-209 1974 £15

RICHARDS, ANNA M.   A New Alice in the Old Wonderland.
Philadelphia, 1896. 8vo., illus.   Frohnsdorff 16-196 1974 $15

RICHARDS, CHARLES R.   Art in History.   New York, 1922. Small 4to.,
quarter cloth, paper labels.   Covent 55-120 1974 £12.50

RICHARDS, FRED   A Persian Journey. London, 1931. Sm. 4to.,
illus.   Biblo & Tannen 214-447 1974 $15

RICHARDS, I. A.   The Foundations of Aesthetics. 1922. Plates,
presentation copy, English first edition.   Covent 56-5 1974 £12.50

RICHARDS, I. A.   How to Read a Page. 1942. Ex-library, hard
cover edition.   Austin 61-849 1974 $10

RICHARDS, J. M.   A Miniature History of the English House. 1938.
Dust wrapper, illus., fine, English first edition.   Covent 56-38 1974 £8.50

RICHARDS, LAURA E.   Five Minute Stories.   n.d. Small 4to., orig.
pictorial cloth, fine, English first edition.   Covent 56-712 1974 £7.50

RICHARDS, S. A.   Feminist Writers of the Seventeenth Century.
1914. Frontispiece, faded.   Covent 55-1020 1974 £5.25

RICHARDSON, A. E.   The English Inn, Past and Present. 1925. 4to.,
orig. cloth, plates.   Broadhurst 23-1528 1974 £5

RICHARDSON, ALBERT D.   Beyond the Mississippi. Hartford, (1869). 8vo.,
orig. bindings, new edition.   Butterfield 8-717 1974 $10

RICHARDSON, B. J.   Public School Temperance. Toronto, 1887.
Hood's 102-426 1974 $10

RICHARDSON, DOROTHY   Dawn's Left Hand. 1931. Very fine copy,
d.w., review slip laid in, first edition.   Covent 51-1573 1973 £15.75

RICHARDSON, DOROTHY   Pointed Roofs. Tokyo, n.d. Portrait, signature, English first edition.   Covent 56-1091 1974 £15

RICHARDSON, DOROTHY   Revolving Lights. 1923. Fine bright copy, first
edition.   Covent 51-1574 1973 £12.50

RICHARDSON, DOROTHY M.   Backwater. London, 1916. First edition, spine
marked, good copy, scarce, orig. cloth.   Crane 7-276 1974 £5

RICHARDSON, DOROTHY M.   John Austen and the Inseparables. 1930.
8vo., orig. cloth, first edition.   Rota 190-773 1974 £5

RICHARDSON, E.   Doors, Fantastic Adventures of a Boy Who Would
Climb. n.d. Plates, English first edition.   Covent 56-760 1974 £7.50

RICHARDSON, EDGAR PRESTON   The Way of Western Art, 1776-1914.
Cambridge, Mass., 1939. 1st ed., 4to., illus.   Biblo & Tannen 214-458 1974
$15

RICHARDSON, FREDERICK   Pinocchio. Philadelphia, 1923. Orig. pictorial cloth, plates, first U.S. edition.   Covent 56-713 1974 £25

RICHARDSON, G. F.   Geology for Beginners. 1843. Crown 8vo.,
orig. cloth, frontispiece, scarce, second edition.   Wheldon 128-1039 1973 £7.50

RICHARDSON, GEORGE   A Book of Ceilings.   New York. Folio, orig.
cloth backed boards, plates, reprinted.   Bow Windows 62-764 1974 £15

RICHARDSON, J.   The Guards in Canada. Montreal, 1848.
Inscribed from author, marbled boards, three quarter leather, fine.   Hood's
102-117 1974 $150

RICHARDSON, J.   Ichthyology of the Voyage of H. M. S. Erebus
and Terror Under the Command of Sir James Clark Ross, 1839-1843. 1844-48.
4to., new half morocco, lithographed plates, complete copy, very rare.
Wheldon 128-657 1973 £85

RICHARDSON, J.   The Museum of Natural History. (1859-62).
4 vols., 4to., orig. dec. cloth, coloured plates, scarce, gilt, nice copy.
Wheldon 128-57 1973 £30

RICHARDSON, J.   War of 1812. N. P., 1842. Marbled boards,
spine mended, ads at end.   Hood's 102-118 1974 $200

RICHARDSON, JAMES   Wonders of the Yellowstone.   New York, 1873.
Cloth, rubbed.   Hayman 57-658 1974 $10

RICHARDSON, JOHN   The Canadian Brothers.   Montreal, 1840.
Leather spine & corners, marbled boards, 2 vols.   Hood's 102-538 1974 $300

RICHARDSON, JOHN   The Museum of Natural History. London, Glasgow, Edinburgh, 1859-62. 4to., 2 vols., contemporary half calf, gilt, illus.,
plates, first edition.   Hammond 201-670 1974 £35

RICHARDSON, JOHN   Wacousta: or, The Prophecy. New York, n.d.
Pict. wrapper, foxed, uncut.   Jenkins 61-2278 1974 $15

RICHARDSON, JONATHAN   The Works. 1792. 4to., nineteenth century
half morocco, rebacked, plates, new edition.   Hill 126-225 1974 £48

RICHARDSON, JOSEPH   The Fugitive. 1792. 8vo., disbound, first edition.   Quaritch 936-208 1974 £6

RICHARDSON, JOSEPH   The Fugitive. London, 1792. 8vo., modern
boards, first edition.   Dawsons PM 252-826 1974 £15

RICHARDSON, O. W.   The Emission of Electricity from Hot Bodies. London, 1921. 8vo., blue cloth, illus., second edition.   Dawsons PM 245-641 1974
£8

RICHARDSON, R.   Extracts from the Literary and Scientific Correspondence Of. Yarmouth, 1835. 8vo., modern buckram, plates.   Wheldon 129-
186 1974 £30

RICHARDSON, ROBERT   A Briefe and Compendious Exposition Vpon the
Psalme Called Deprofundis. (1570). 4to., orig. boards, worn, small stain on
uncut fore-edges of few leaves.   Bow Windows 66-570 1974 £15

RICHARDSON, SAMUEL   Clarissa. Dublin, 1766-65. 7 vols., 12mo.,
contemporary mottled calf, gilt backs, fourth edition, fine set.   MacManus
224-371 1974 $75

RICHARDSON, SAMUEL   The Correspondence Of. 1804. 8vo., orig.
boards, 6 vols., uncut, first edition.   Bow Windows 64-666 1974 £56

RICHARDSON, SAMUEL   The History of Sir Charles Grandison. London,
1754. 7 vols., 12mo., contemporary calf, gilt, third edition.   Dawsons PM
252-827 1974 £62

RICHARDSON, SAMUEL   Letters Written to and for Practical Friends.
1741. Contemporary calf, worn, one joint cracked, first edition.   Allen 216-2053
1974 $250

RICHARDSON, SAMUEL   A New System of Short-Hand. London, 1810.
8vo., orig. boards, rebacked, plates, fourth edition.   Hammond 201-780 1974 £9

RICHARDSON, SAMUEL   Pamela. Amsterdam, 1743. 4 vols. in 2,
12mo., contemporary mottled calf, gilt.   Ximenes 35-38 1974 $65

RICHARDSON, WILLIAM   Cursory Remarks on Tragedy. London, 1774.
8vo., contemporary calf, scarce, first edition.   Ximenes 35-37 1974 $125

RICHARDSON, WILLIAM   Letter to the Right Hon. Isaac Corry, Containing an Epitome of Some of the Most Curious and Important Properties of Irish Fiorin. Belfast, 1809. 12mo., disbound, first edition.   Ximenes 37-188 1974 $27.50

RICHARDSON, WILLIAM M.   The New Hampshire Town Officer.   Concord, 1829. 8vo., orig. bindings. Butterfield 8-358 1974 $10

RICHEOME, LOUIS   Tableaux Sacrez des Figures Mystiques du Tresauguste Sacrifice et Sacrement de l'Eucharistie. Paris, 1609. 8vo., second edition, contemporary vellum, from the Prince of Liechtenstein Library. Schumann 299-96 1974 sFr 420

RICHERAND, ANTHELME   Nouveaux Elements de Physiologie. 1837. Large 8vo., marbled boards, new calf spine. Dawsons PM 249-423 1974 £9

RICHMAN, ARTHUR   Ambush. Duffield, 1922.   Austin 51-787 1973 $7.50

RICHMAN, D. C.   The Talisman. Muscatine, 1867. 8vo., orig. violet cloth, faded, first edition. Ximenes 35-39 1974 $25

RICHMAN, IRVING BERDINE   California under Spain and Mexico 1535-1847. Boston and New York, 1911. 8vo., orig. bindings, maps, plates, inscribed. Butterfield 8-51 1974 $20

RICHMAN, IRVING BERDINE   John Brown Among the Quakers and Other Sketches. Des Moines, 1904. 8vo., orig. bindings, gilt, uncut, third edition. Butterfield 8-171 1974 $15

RICHMOND, A. B.   The Nemesis of Chautauqua Lake or Circumstantial Evidence. Chicago, 1901. Orig. binding. Butterfield 10-17 1974 $17.50

RICHMOND, C. W.   List of Generic Terms Proposed for Birds 1890-1922. 1902-07. 4 parts, 8vo. Wheldon 131-688 1974 £10

RICHMOND, ELIZABETH YATES   Poems of the Western Land. Milwaukee, 1878. Square 8vo., orig. cloth, first edition. Ximenes 35-40 1974 $20

RICHMOND, GRACE   On Christmas Day in the Evening. New York, 1911. 12mo., fine, covers little soiled, illus. in color. Current BW9-75 1974 $8.75

RICHMOND, LEGH   Annals of the Poor. 1815. 16mo., old calf, foxed, top of spine torn. Allen 216-1340 1974 $12.50

RICHMOND, MABEL E.   Centennial History of Decatur and Macon County. Decatur, 1930. 8vo., cloth. Saddleback 14-394 1974 $27.50

RICHMOND, Virginia. Brooklyn, 1907. Boards, photographs. Jenkins 61-2548 1974 $12.50

RICHTER, CONRAD   The Trees. New York, 1940. 1st ed.   Biblo & Tannen 214-766 1974 $10

RICHTER, GISELA M. A.   Animals In Greek Sculpture. 1930. Plates. Allen 213-901 1973 $20

RICHTER, GISELA M. A.   Roman Portraits. New York, 1948. 4to., illus. Biblo & Tannen 213-238 1973 $9.50

RICHTER, HELENE   Geschichte der Englischen Romantik. 1911-16. Vols. 1 and vol. 2 part 1, boards, slightly shaken. Allen 216-1526 1974 $30

RICHTER, IRMA A.   Rhythmic Form in Art. 1932. 4to., illus., plates, English first edition. Covent 56-1498 1974 £10.50

RICHTER, LUDWIG   Zur Unterstuetzung der Nothleidenden im Saechsischen Erzgebirge, im Voigtlande und in den Weberdoerfern der Oberlausitz. Dresden, 1847. 8vo., contemporary binding of gilt red morocco, orig. lithographed wrapper bound in, fine, first edition. Schumann 499-97 1974 sFr 185

RICKER, ALVAN B.   Poland Centennial September 11, 1895. Portland, 8vo., cloth, illus. Saddleback 14-462 1974 $10

RICKERT, EDITH   Early English Romances in Verse. London, 1908. 12mo., illus. Biblo & Tannen 213-480 1973 $7.50

RICKETSON, SHADRACH   Means of Preserving Health. New York, 1806. 12mo., contemporary sheep, first edition. Ximenes 35-41 1974 $45

RICKETTS, CHARLES   Unrecorded Histories. 1933. Limited to 950 copies, sepia plates by author, large 8vo., orig. cream cloth, gilt design, fine. Sawyer 293-258 1974 £15

RICKETTS, CHARLES   Unrecorded Histories. 1933. Buckram, fine, English first edition. Covent 56-1094 1974 £17.50

RICKETTS, CHARLES S.   The Prado and Its Masterpieces. 1903. Folio, buckram gilt, foxed. Covent 55-121 1974 £32.50

RICKMAN, PHILIP   A Bird-Painter's Sketch Book. 1931. 4to., canvas, coloured plates, illus., first edition. Wheldon 128-551 1973 £7.50

RICKMAN, PHILIP   A Bird-Painter's Sketch Book. 1931. 4to., orig. cloth, plates. Wheldon 129-518 1974 £5

RICKMAN, PHILIP   A Bird-Painter's Sketch Book. 1931. 4to., canvas, illus., plates. Wheldon 131-689 1974 £7.50

RICKMAN, PHILIP   Bird Sketches and Some Field Observations. London, 1938. 4to., frontispiece, illus. Traylen 79-111 1973 £8

RICKMAN, THOMAS   An Attempt to Discriminate the Styles of Architecture in England. 1862. Orig. cloth, plates, illus., sixth edition. Marsden 39-379 1974 £5

RICKWORD, EDGELL   Invocations to Angels and the Happy New Year. 1928. Cloth-backed boards, inscribed, presentation copy, English first edition. Covent 56-1095 1974 £12.50

RICORD, PAUL   Le Japon ou Voyage de Paul Ricord aux Iles du Japon. Paris, 1822. 2 vols., 12mo., boards, plates. Traylen 79-534 1973 £10

RICORD, PHILIPPE   Letters On Syphilis. Philadelphia, 1854. Rittenhouse 46-561 1974 $10

RICORD, PHILIPPE   A Practical Treatise on Venereal Diseases. Philadelphia, 1845. 8vo., orig. cloth, fine, second American edition. Schumann 35-406 1974 $65

RICORD, PHILIPPE   Traite Pratique des Maladies Veneriennes ou Recherches Critiques et Experimentales sur l'Inoculation. Paris, 1838. 8vo., contemporary half calf, rubbed, rare first edition. Gilhofer 61-42 1974 sFr. 550

RIDDELL, JOHN   Comments in Refutation of Pretensions Advanced for the First Time. Edinburgh, 1860. 4to., orig. cloth, inscription on fly-leaf. Bow Windows 66-571 1974 £8.50

RIDDELL, JOHN   Comments in Refutation of Pretensions and Statements in "The Stirlings of Keir and Their Family Papers." Edinburgh, 1860. 4to., 280 pages. Howes 186-1655 1974 £8.50

RIDDELL, ROBERT   The Carpenter and Joiner. Edinburgh, (n.d.). Large 4to., frontispieces, late 19th century half morocco, worn. Bow Windows 62-765 1974 £38

RIDDELL, ROBERT   The Carpenter and Joiner, Stair Builder and Hand-Railer. Edinburgh, (c. 1865). Roy. 4to., plates, recent cloth, morocco spine. Quaritch 940-548 1974 £25

RIDDELL, W. R.   Benjamin Franklin and Canada. N.P., 1923. Card cover. Hood's 103-553 1974 $12.50

RIDDELL, W. R.   The Life of John Graves Simcoe. Toronto, 1926. Hood's 103-230 1974 $22.50

RIDDER, A. DE   Die Gemaldegalerie des A. de Ridder zu Schonberg bei Cronberg. Berlin, 1910. Roy. folio, cloth, leather back, rubbed, limited, plates. Quaritch 940-220 1974 £18

RIDDLE, ALBERT GALLATIN   Bart Ridgeley. Boston, 1873. 8vo., orig. purple cloth, scarce, first edition. Ximenes 35-43 1974 $27.50

RIDDLE, GEORGE W.   The History of Early Days in Oregon. Riddle, 1920. Wrapper. Jenkins 61-2091 1974 $27.50

RIDGEWAY, W.   The Origin and Influence of the Thoroughbred Horse. Cambridge, 1905. 8vo., cloth, text-figures. Wheldon 128-345 1973 £5

RIDING, LAURA   The Left Heresy in Literature and Life. 1939. English first edition. Covent 56-1097 1974 £8.50

RIDING, LAURA   Four Unposted Letters to Catherine. Paris, 1930. First edition, limited to 200 numbered copies, signed by author, quarter morocco, very good copy. Crane 7-278 1974 £30

RIDING, LAURA   Laura and Francisca. Majorca, 1931. 4to., orig. wrapper, signed, first edition. Rota 188-802 1974 £25

RIDING, LAURA   The Life of the Dead. (c. 1933). Limited to 200 copies, signed by author and artist, first edition, text in French and English, illus. by John Aldridge, engraved on wood, 4to., orig. boards, fine. Sawyer 293-257 1974 £72

RIDING, LAURA   Lives of Wives. 1939. English first edition. Covent 56-1096 1974 £12.50

RIDING, LAURA   A Survey of Modernist Poetry. 1927. Crown 8vo., orig. cloth-backed dec. boards, first edition. Howes 186-386 1974 £18

RIDLEY, H. N.   Spices. 1912. 8vo., cloth, illus., very scarce. Wheldon 128-1691 1973 £10

RIDLEY, H. N.   Spices. 1912. 8vo., new cloth, illus. Wheldon 129-1693 1974 £10

RIDLEY, HUMPHREY   Observationes Quaedam Medico-Practicae & Physiologicae. London, 1703. 8vo., contemporary panelled calf, plate, first edition. Schuman 37-219 1974 $165

RIDPATH, GEORGE   The Stage Condemn'd. London, 1698. 8vo., half morocco, stains, first edition. Ximenes 35-44 1974 $175

RIESE, ADAM   Rechnung Auff der Linien und Federn, Auff Allerley Handthirung Gemacht Durch Adam Riesen. Frankfurt on the Oder, 1579. 8vo., woodcut portrait, old half vellum, rare edition, very good copy. Schafer 10-139 1974 sFr 1,300

RIESENFELD, E. P.   Erdmannsdorff. Berlin, 1913. 4to., cloth, plates. Minters 37-527 1973 $25

RIESENMAN, JOSEPH   History of Northwestern Pennsylvania. New York, (1943). 3 vols., 4to., cloth. Saddleback 14-677 1974 $40

RIESENTHAL, O. VON   Die Raubvogel Deutschlands und des Angrenzenden Mitteleuropas. Cassel, 1876. 8vo., orig. cloth, plates. Wheldon 131-690 1974 £10

RIESENTHAL, O. VAN   Die Raubvogel Deutschlands Und des Angrenzenden Mittel-Europas. Cassel & Gera, 1894. Folio, orig. printed boards, rebacked in half morocco, plates, second edition. Wheldon 131-99 1974 £85

RIEZLER, WALTER VON   Beethoven. Berlin, 1936. Illus. Biblo & Tannen 214-812 1974 $9.50

RIGBY, RICHARD   An Answer to a Calumny. London, 1728. 8vo., modern boards, first edition. Dawsons PM 247-246 1974 £30

RIGG, ARTHUR   A Practical Treatise on the Steam Engine. 1888. Crown 4to., orig. cloth. Broadhurst 23-1264 1974 £10

RIGG, ARTHUR   A Practical Treatise on the Steam Engine. 1888. Plates, text illus., crown 4to., good copy, orig. cloth. Broadhurst 24-1294 1974 £10

RIGGS, DIONIS COFFIN   From Off Island. New York, 1940. Illus., 347 pages. Rinsland 58-54 1974 $20

RIGGS, LYNN   Big Lake. French, 1927. Austin 51-788 1973 $7.50

RIGGS, LYNN   Green Grow the Lilacs. French, 1931. Austin 51-789 1973 $7.50

RIGGS, LYNN   Russet Mantle and the Cherokee Night. French, 1936. Austin 51-790 1973 $7.50

RIGGS, LYNN   Sump'n Like Wing's and a Lantern to See By. French, 1928. Austin 51-791 1973 $10

RIGGS, STEPHEN RETURN   A Dakota-English Dictionary. Washington, 1910. 4to., orig. cloth, some dust marks, inner hinges cracked. Bow Windows 66-572 1974 £6.50

THE RIGHT of British Subjects to Petition and Apply to Their Representatives. 1733. 8vo., modern boards, roan back. Quaritch 939-211 1974 £12

THE RIGHTS of Parliament Vindicated On Occasion of the Late Stamp-Act. London, 1766. 8vo., half straight-grained morocco, scarce, first edition. Ximenes 35-267 1974 $125

RIHBANY, ABRAHAM MITRIE   A Far Journey. Houghton, 1914. Austin 62-532 1974 $8.50

RIIS, JACOB A.   The Battle With the Slum. 1902. Illus., orig. edition. Austin 57-552 1974 $10

RIIS, JACOB A.   The Making of an American. 1901. Illus., first edition. Austin 57-553 1974 $12.50

RIIS, JACOB A.   Neighbors. 1914. Illus., 209 pages. Austin 57-554 1974 $12.50

RIIS, JACOB A.   Neighbors. Macmillan, 1914. Austin 62-530 1974 $17.50

RIIS, JACOB A.   A Ten Year War. 1900. Illus., orig. edition. Austin 57-555 1974 $10

RILEY, CHARLES V.   Report on the Cotton Worm, Together With a Chapter on the Boll Worm. Washington, 1885. Plates, maps, some in color. Jenkins 61-2280 1974 $12.50

RILEY, ELIHU S.   A History of Anne Arundel County, In Maryland. Annapolis, 1905. 8vo., cloth. Saddleback 14-467 1974 $35

RILEY, HENRY T.   Memorials of London and London Life. London, 1868. Thick roy. 8vo., orig. cloth. Howes 186-1019 1974 £12

RILEY, J. H.   Birds from Siam and the Malay Penninsula. Washington, D.C., 1938. 8vo., orig. wrappers, scarce. Wheldon 129-519 1974 £7.50

RILEY, J. H.   Birds from Siam and the Malay Peninsula in U. S. National Museum Collected by H. M. Smith and W. L. Abbott. Washington, 1938. 8vo., orig. wrappers. Wheldon 131-691 1974 £10

RILEY, JAMES WHITCOMB   Afterwhiles. Bobb, Merrill, 1898. 196p. Austin 54-852 1973 $6

RILEY, JAMES WHITCOMB   The Boys of the Old Glee Club. Bobb, 1907. Illus. Austin 54-853 1973 $6.50

RILEY, JAMES WHITCOMB   The Flying Islands of the Night. Bobbs, Merrill, 1913. 124p., illus. Austin 54-854 1973 $15

RILEY, JAMES WHITCOMB   Green Fields and Running Brooks. Indianapolis, 1893. 1st ed. Biblo & Tannen 210-796 1973 $10

RILEY, JAMES WHITCOMB   His Pa's Romance. Bobb, Merrill, 1903. 168p., illus. Austin 54-855 1973 $7.50

RILEY, JAMES WHITCOMB   A Hoosier Romance. Bobbs, Merrill, 1912., n.p. Illus. Austin 54-856 1973 $6.50

RILEY, JAMES WHITCOMB   Love-Lyrics. Bobb, 1899. 190p., illus. Austin 54-863 1973 $6

RILEY, JAMES WHITCOMB   Nye's and Riley's Wit and Humor. Thompson and Thomas, 1900. 236p., illus. Austin 54-866 1973 $7.50

RILEY, JAMES WHITCOMB   Nye's and Riley's Wit and Humor. Thompson, Thomas, 1905. 238p. Austin 54-867 1973 $10

RILEY, JAMES WHITCOMB   An Old Sweetheart of Mine. Bobb, Merrill, 1902. n.p., illus. Austin 54-857 1973 $6

RILEY, JAMES WHITCOMB   Out to Old Aunt Mary's. (Indianapolis, n.d.). 12mo., orig. wrappers. Ximenes 35-46 1974 $25

RILEY, JAMES WHITCOMB   Out to Old Aunt Mary's. Bobb, Merrill, 1904. n.p., illus. Austin 54-858 1973 $7.50

RILEY, JAMES WHITCOMB   Pipes O' Pan at Zekesbury. Bowen, Merrill, 1891. 245p. Austin 54-859 1973 $6

RILEY, JAMES WHITCOMB   Poems and Prose Sketches. Scribner, 1910. 14 vols. Austin 54-860 1973 $47.50

RILEY, JAMES WHITCOMB   Poems Here at Home. Century, 1893. 187p., illus. Austin 54-861 1973 $6

RILEY, JAMES WHITCOMB   Rhymes of Childhood. Indianapolis, 1891. Orig. cloth, ends of spines & corners worn, first issue, with dec. of a child's head on front cover, tipped-in is a slip with Riley's signature. MacManus 224-372 1974 $50

RILEY, JAMES WHITCOMB   Riley Farm Rhymes. Bobb, 1905. 187p., illus. Austin 54-862 1973 $6

RILEY, JAMES WHITCOMB   Riley Songs O' Cheer. Bobb, Merrill, 1905. 195p. Austin 54-864 1973 $6

RILEY, JAMES WHITCOMB   Riley Songs of Home. Bobbs, Merrill, 1910. 190p., illus. Austin 54-865 1973 $6

RILKE, RAINER MARIA   Geschichten vom Lieben Gott. Leipzig, 1904. New edition, very good copy. Covent 51-1575 1973 £10.50

RILKE, RAINER MARIA   The Life of the Virgin Mary. Wurzburg, n.d. (c. 1922). Illus., very good copy. Covent 51-1576 1973 £12.50

RIMBAUD, ARTHUR   Un Coeur Sous une Soutane. Paris, 1924. 8vo., orig. wrapper, uncut, first edition. L. Goldschmidt 42-349 1974 $65

RIMBAUD, ARTHUR   A Season in Hell. n.d. Dust wrapper, faded, English first edition. Covent 56-2017 1974 £7.50

RIMBAUD, ARTHUR   Voyage en Abyssinie et au Harrar. Paris, 1928. Square 8vo., half hard grain morocco, gilt, orig. wrapper, first trade edition. L. Goldschmidt 42-350 1974 $35

RIMBAUD, ARTHUR   Oeuvres Completes. Paris, 1922. 3 vols., small 4to., orig. wrapper, uncut, limited edition. L. Goldschmidt 42-348 1974 $50

RIMBAULT, EDWARD F.   Bibliotheca Madrigaliana. 1847. 104 pages. Howes 185-818 1974 £7.50

RIME de gli Academici Occulti con le Loro Imprese e Discorsi. Brescia, 1568. 4to., vellum, plates, woodcut, excellent copy. Harper 213-128 1973 $425

RIMINGTON, CRITCHELL   Fighting Fleets. New York, 1943. Biblo & Tannen 213-696 1973 $10

RIMMEL, EUGENE   The Book of Perfumes. 1865. Orig. dec. cloth, gilt, illus., second edition. Covent 56-1985 1974 £5.50

RIMSKY-KORSAKOFF, N. A.   The Golden Cock. 1908. First edition. Eaton Music-523 1973 £10

RIMSKY-KORSAKOFF, N. A.   My Musical Life. New York, 1936. Biblo & Tannen 214-903 1974 $7.50

RINDER, FRANK   D. Y. Cameron, an Illustrated Catalogue. Glasgow, 1912. Illus. Marsden 37-112 1974 £10

RING, JOHN   A Treatise On the Cow-Pox. London, 1801-03. 2 vols., 8vo., contemporary tree calf, rebacked, plates, rare, first edition. Traylen 79-265 1973 £100

RINGELBERGH, JOACHIM STERCK VAN   Intitutiones Astronomicae Ternis Libris Contentae. 1535. Small 8vo., limp vellum. Dawsons PM 245-642 1974 £52

RINGHIERI, INNOCENTIO   Cento Giuchi Liberali. Bologna, 1551. Small 4to., French 18th century red morocco gilt. Thomas 28-307 1972 £60

RINGSTED, JOSIAH   The Farmer. London, 1790. 8vo., cloth-backed boards, new edition. Hammond 201-46 1974 £17.50

RINTOUL, L. J.   A Vertebrate Fauna of Forth. 1935. 8vo., cloth, plates, folding map. Wheldon 128-230 1973 £5

RINTOUL, L. J.   A Vertebrate Fauna of Forth. 1935. 8vo., cloth, plates. Wheldon 130-305 1974 £5

RIP Van Winkle--As played by Joseph Jefferson. Dodd, Mead. 1895. 199p., illus. Austin 54-581 1973 $12.50

RIPALDA, JUAN MARTINEZ DE   Opera Omnia. Rome, 1870-71. 4 vols., folio, cloth. Howes 185-1605 1974 £18

RIPLEY, JAMES   Select Original Letters. London, 1781. 8vo., contemporary calf, rare, first edition. Ximenes 35-47 1974 $125

RIPLEY, W. Z.   The Races of Europe. 1899. Orig. cloth, plates, maps. Smith 193-539 1973 £5.50

RISDON, TRISTRAM   The Chorographical Description .... of Devon. 1811. Half calf, rebound, uncut. Howes 186-1998 1974 £18

RISHVIN, MIKHAIL   Jen Sheng: The Root of Life. London, 1936. 12mo. Biblo & Tannen 210-985 1973 $7.50

RISLER, JEREMIAS   Leben August Gottlieb Spangenbergs. Barby, 1794. 8vo., contemporary boards, portrait. Harper 213-130 1973 $135

RISTING, SIGURD   Whales and Whale Foetuses. 1928. Charts, diagrams, wrappers. Rinsland 58-64 1974 $10

RISTORI, ADELAIDE   Memoirs and Artistic Studies of Adelaide Ristori. Doubleday, 1907. 263p., illus. Austin 51-792 1973 $7.50

RITCH, WILLIAM G.   Historical Society of New Mexico: Inaugural Address of. Santa Fe, 1881. Orig. printed wrappers, scarce. Jenkins 61-1854 1974 $40

RITCHIE, ANDREW CARNDUFF   Charles DeMuth. New York, 1950. Sm. 4to., color plates. Biblo & Tannen 210-115 1973 $9.50

RITCHIE, DAVID G.   Philosophical Studies. 1905. Plates, scarce. Howes 185-1971 1974 £6

RITCHIE, J. EWING   To Canada with Emigrants, a Record of Actual Experiences. London, 1885. Illus. Hood's 102-575 1974 £60

RITCHIE, LEITCH 1800-1865   The Romance of History. London, 1831. 12mo., 3 vols., contemporary half calf, first edition. Dawsons PM 251-326 1974 £35

RITCHIE, LEITCH 1800-1865   The Romance of History. London, 1831. 3 vols., 8vo., contemporary half calf. Dawsons PM 252-828 1974 £35

RITCHIE, LEITCH 1800-1865   Wanderings by the Seine from Havre to Roven. 1834. Roy. 8vo., plates, contemporary leather backed cloth. Smith 194-607 1974 £5

RITCHIE, LEITCH 1800-1865   Wanderings by the Seine. London, 1835. 8vo., old morocco backed cloth, rubbed, spotting. Bow Windows 61-820 1973 £8.50

RITCHIE, LEITCH 1800-1865   Wandering by the Seine, From Roven to the Source. 1835. Roy. 8vo., plates, contemporary leather backed cloth boards. Smith 194-608 1974 £6

RITSON, J.   A Digest of the Proceedings of the Court Leet of the Manor and Liberty of the Savoy. 1789. 8vo., half brown morocco gilt, uncut. Quaritch 939-212 1974 £15

RITSON, JOSEPH   Bibliographia Poetica. 1802. Contains the inserted leaves, gilt and blind tooled calf, worn at edges, rebacked but sound, excellent within. Thomas 32-187 1974 £31.50

RITSON, JOSEPH   Memoirs of the Celts or Gauls. 1827. Crown 8vo., tree calf gilt, first edition. Howes 186-1918 1974 £14.50

RITSON, JOSEPH   Pieces of Antient Popular Poetry. London, 1791. 8vo., old half morocco, first edition. Ximenes 35-49 1974 $45

RITSON, JOSEPH   Poems. London, 1795. 8vo., dark green crushed levant, gilt, first edition. Ximenes 35-50 1974 $70

RITSON, JOSEPH   The Quip Modest. London, 1788. 8vo., disbound, first edition. Ximenes 35-52 1974 $125

RITSON, JOSEPH   Remarks. London, 1783. 8vo., disbound, first edition. Ximenes 35-51 1974 $75

RITTER, D.   Lessons for the Guitar. (1782-98?). Folio, disbound in cloth folder. Quaritch 940-823 1974 £110

RITTER, JOHANN WILHELM   Das Electrische System der Korper. Leipzig, 18-05. 8vo., orig. grey boards, uncut, first edition. Dawsons PM 245-643 1974 £145

RITTI, ANT   Traite Clinique de la Folie a Double Forme. Paris, 1883. 8vo., contemporary marbled boards. Dawsons PM 249-424 1974 £15

RIVA, LUDOVICUS   Miscellanea. 1725. 4to., contemporary boards, fine, unopened, uncut. Zeitlin 235-190 1974 $65

RIVADENEIRA, PEDRO DE 1527-1611   Historia Vitae Divi Patriarchae Ignatii de Logola. Vienna, 1744. Small 4to., tree calf. Howes 185-1286 1974 £7.50

RIVAROL, ANTOINE   Oeuvres. Paris, 1857. 12mo., contemporary half cloth, foxing. L. Goldschmidt 42-109 1974 $12.50

RIVERA, DIEGO   Portrait of America. New York, 1934. 1st ed., good used copy. Biblo & Tannen 213-387 1973 $20

RIVERA, JUAN G.   The Roman Catholic Church in Porto Rico. Indianapolis, 1926. Austin 62-534 1974 $27.50

RIVERIUS, LAZARUS
Please turn to
RIVIERE, LAZARE

RIVERS, W. H. R.   Instinct and the Unconscious. Cambridge, 1924. 8vo., orig. cloth, second edition. Dawsons PM 249-425 1974 £6

RIVES, JUDITH PAGE   Tales and Souvenirs. Philadelphia, 1842. 8vo., orig. green cloth, foxed, first edition. Ximenes 35-53 1974 $25

RIVES, WILLIAM C.   Letter from the Hon. William C. Rives to a Friend, on the Important Questions of the Day. Richmond, 1860. Jenkins 61-666 1974 $13.50

RIVIERE, B. B.   A History of the Birds of Norfolk. 1930. 8vo., orig. cloth, plates. Wheldon 130-609 1974 £10

RIVIERE, JACQUES   Rimbaud. Paris, 1930. 12mo., full cloth, gilt, uncut, orig. wrapper, first edition. L. Goldschmidt 42-353 1974 $10

RIVIERE, LAZARE   Les Observations de Medecine. Lyons, 1688. 8vo., old calf. Schuman 37-220 1974 $95

RIVIERE, LAZARE   Opera Medica Universa. Lyon, 1679. Folio, contemporary blind stamped vellum. Schumann 35-407 1974 $95

RIVIERE, LAZARE   Praxis Medica. (The Hague), 1651. 8vo., contemporary vellum. Dawsons PM 249-426 1974 £20

RIVOLUZIONE E Controrivoluzione. Brooklyn, 1944. 93 pages. Austin 57-329 1974 $17.50

ROBERT, LORD BISHOP OF CLOGHER   A Journal from Grand Cairo to Mount Sinai and Back Again. 1753. 8vo., old straight-grained morocco, roughly rebacked, worn, plates, second edition. Bow Windows 66-573 1974 £19.50

ROBERT, MARIE JACQUES CLAIR   De La Vieillesse. Paris, 1777. 12mo., contemporary mottled calf, first edition. Schuman 37-221 1974 $95

ROBERT of Gloucester's Chronicle. Oxford, 1724. 2 vols., 8vo., old calf, rubbed. Quaritch 939-224 1974 £25

ROBERTON, T. B.   The Fighting Bishop, John Strachan. Ottawa, 1926. Hood's 103-231 1974 $12.50

ROBERTON, T. J.   The General Principles of Language. Montreal & Toronto, 1861. Leather, worn, second edition. Hood's 104-410 1974 $12.50

ROBERTON, THOMAS B.   A Second Helping of Newspaper Pieces. Toronto, 1937. Hood's 102-346 1974 $7.50

ROBERTON, THOMAS B.   T. B. R.: Newspaper Pieces. Toronto, 1936. Hood's 102-345 1974 $7.50

ROBERTS, B. H.   The Mormon Battalion, Its History and Achievements. Salt Lake City, 1919. Illus., folding map, fine copy. Jenkins 61-1605 1974 $50

ROBERTS, CECIL   A Man Arose. 1941. First edition, portrait, 8vo., orig. boards. Sawyer 293-103 1974 £5

ROBERTS, CHARLES G. D.   A History of Canada. Boston, 1897. Chart. Hood's 103-554 1974 $20

ROBERTS, CHARLES G. D.   In the Morning of Time. Toronto, 1922. Hood's 102-539 1974 $12.50

ROBERTS, CHARLES G. D.   The Watchers of the Trails. Boston, 1904. Illus. Hood's 102-540 1974 $10

ROBERTS, DAVID   The Holy Land. London, 1855. Brown cloth, 6 vols., morocco, gilt. Dawson's 424-116 1974 $150

ROBERTS, DAVID   Holy Land, Syria, Idumea and Arabia. Egypt and Nubia. 1849. 6 vols., atlas folio, half black morocco, gilt, raised bands, plates, fine. Quaritch 940-221 1974 £1,500

ROBERTS, EDWARD F.   Ireland in America. Putnams, 1931. 218p. Austin 62-535 1974 $12.50

ROBERTS, ELIZABETH MADOX   My Heart and My Flesh. New York, 1927. 1st ed. Biblo & Tannen 210-797 1973 $7.50

ROBERTS, ELWOOD   Biographical Annals of Montgomery County, Pennsylvania. New York, 1904. First edition, 2 vols., small 4to., half morocco, marbled end papers. Wilson 63-78 1974 $50

ROBERTS, F. J.   The Wipers Times. London, 1930. Water stained cover. Hood's 103-122 1974 $17.50

ROBERTS, G.   The Elements of Modern Geography and General History. London, (c.1820). 12mo., maps, plates, contemporary sheep, worn. Bow Windows 62-767 1974 £5.50

ROBERTS, GEORGE   The Social History of the People of the Southern Counties of England In Past Centuries. London, 1856. 8vo., illus. Traylen 79-310 1973 £5

ROBERTS, KENNETH   Captain Caution. New York, 1934. First edition, 8vo., very good, signed by author. Current BW9-269 1974 $20

ROBERTS, KENNETH   Northwest Passage. Garden City, 1937. Large paper edition, 2 vols., no. 892 of edition limited to 1050 copies, signed, orig. binding, glassine covers, mint. Ross 86-403 1974 $75

ROBERTS, KENNETH   Oliver Wiswell. New York, 1940. 2 vols., orig. cloth, first edition, one of 1,050 numbered copies, signed by author, fine. MacManus 224-374 1974 $55

ROBERTS, KENNETH   Oliver Wiswell. New York, 1940. 2 vols., large paper edition, no. 681 of edition limited to 1050 copies, signed, lacking d.w.'s, near mint, orig. binding. Ross 86-404 1974 $70

ROBERTS, KENNETH L.   Why Europe Leaves Home. Indianapolis, 1922. lst ed., illus. Biblo & Tannen 213-591 1973 $27.50

ROBERTS, L.   Along the Ottawa, a Book of Lyrics. London, 1927. Hood's 102-666 1974 $7.50

ROBERTS, L.   Canada's War in the Air. Montreal, 1943. Photos, third edition. Hood's 104-132 1974 $20

ROBERTS, LORD OF KANDAHAR   Forty-One Years in India from Subaltern to Commander-In-Chief. 1897. 2 vols., 8vo., orig. cloth, covers soiled, plates. Bow Windows 66-574 1974 £8.50

ROBERTS, M.   The Conchologist's Companion. 1824. Small 8vo., half calf, frontispiece, first edition. Wheldon 128-851 1973 £5

ROBERTS, M.   The Conchologist's Companion. 1834. Small 8vo., contemporary cloth, coloured frontispiece, second edition. Wheldon 128-852 1973 £5

ROBERTS, M.   The Conchologist's Companion. 1834. Small 8vo., contemporary morocco, frontispiece. Wheldon 129-751 1974 £5

ROBERTS, M.   Flowers of the Matin and Evensong. London, 1845. 12mo., orig. green cloth, fine, color plates. Gregory 44-261 1974 $40

ROBERTS, MICHAEL   New Signatures. 1932. Orig. blue boards, faded spine. Smith 193-402 1973 £15

ROBERTS, MORLEY   W. H. Hudson: A Portrait. 1924. Plates, very nice copy, slightly worn d.w. Covent 51-2372 1973 £5.25

ROBERTS, MORLEY   W. H. Hudson, A Portrait. London, 1924. Orig. binding, fine, first edition. Ross 87-291 1974 $15

ROBERTS, PETER   The Cambrian Popular Antiquities. 1815. Plates, contemporary calf, rebacked. Howes 186-1919 1974 £35

ROBERTS, PETER   The New Immigration. 1912. Orig. edition. Austin 57-558 1974 $10

ROBERTS, PETER   The Problem of Americanization. 1920. 246 pages. Austin 57-559 1974 $12.50

ROBERTS, T.   The English Bowman. London, 1801. 8vo., orig. cloth, first edition. Hammond 201-781 1974 £24

ROBERTS, T. G.   The Leather Bottle. Toronto, 1934. Hood's 104-784 1974 $17.50

ROBERTS, W.   The Elizabethan Grub Street. 1891. Inscribed, wrappers, near fine. Covent 55-244 1974 £10

ROBERTS, W.   Memorials of Christie's. 1897. 2 vols., plates, illus., buckram, rubbed. Marsden 37-124 1974 £10

ROBERTS, W.   Printers' Marks. London, 1893. Green cloth, illus. Dawson's 424-171 1974 $40

ROBERTS, WILLIAM   The Earlier History of English Bookselling. 1889. Presentation copy, inscribed, English first edition. Covent 56-167 1974 £20

ROBERTS, WILLIAM   Memoirs of Life and Correspondence of Mrs. Hannah More. 1834. 2 vols., new buckram. Allen 216-2045 1974 $15

ROBERTS, WILLIAM HAYWARD   Poems. London, 1774. 8vo., gilt, fine, contemporary calf, first collected edition. Ximenes 35-54 1974 $90

ROBERTSON, A. T.   Grammar of Greek New Testament In Light of Historical Research. 1923. Fourth edition. Allen 213-155 1973 $14

ROBERTSON, D.   A Tour Through the Isle of Man. 1794. Roy. 8vo., half calf. Quaritch 939-393 1974 £40

ROBERTSON, D. S.   An Englishman In America, 1785. Toronto, 1933. Hood's 103-555 1974 $30

ROBERTSON, FREDERICK W.   Sermons Preached at Trinity Chapel Brighton. London & Brighton, 1855-63. 5 vols., crown 8vo., full navy calf, gilt, labels. Howes 185-1606 1974 £15

ROBERTSON, GEORGE S.   The Kafirs of the Hindu-Kush. 1900. Med. 8vo., plates, illus., orig. cloth, fine. Broadhurst 24-1668 1974 £6

ROBERTSON, H.   A Digest of Masonic Jurisprudence, Especially Applicable to Canadian Lodges. Toronto, 1889. Second edition, revised and enlarged. Hood's 102-40 1974 $10

ROBERTSON, H. A.   Erromanga. 1902. Plates, cloth gilt, English first edition. Covent 56-1267 1974 £5.25

ROBERTSON, J. C.   Mixed Company. Toronto, 1939. Hood's 102-347 1974 $7.50

ROBERTSON, J. G.   The Life and Work of Goethe. 1932. Full prize calf gilt, plates, labels, orig. edition. Howes 186-212 1974 £5

ROBERTSON, JAMES   General View of the Agriculture in the County of Perth. Perth, 1799. 8vo., contemporary half calf, gilt, plates, second edition. Hammond 201-47 1974 £24

ROBERTSON, JOHN M.   A Short History of Freethought, Ancient and Modern. 1906. 2 vols., large 8vo., second edition. Howes 185-1973 1974 £5.75

ROBERTSON, JOHN PARISH   Four Years in Paraguay. Philadelphia, 1838. 2 vols., 12mo., contemporary half calf, first American edition. Ximenes 35-55 1974 $65

ROBERTSON, JOHN ROSS   The Diary of Mrs. John Graves Simcoe. Toronto, 1934. Illus. Hood's 104-279 1974 $55

ROBERTSON, JOHN ROSS   Sketches of Toronto Churches. Toronto, 1886. Wrappers, spine re-enforced with tape. Hood's 102-304 1974 $25

ROBERTSON, JOHN W.   Edgar Allan Poe, a Study. San Francisco, 1921. 8vo., cloth, paper labels, first edition. Goodspeed's 578-286 1974 $15

ROBERTSON, JOSEPH CLINTON   The Percy Anecdotes. London, 1820-22(23). 12mo., contemporary calf, gilt, first edition. Hammond 201-323 1974 £48

ROBERTSON, PRISCILLA   Lewis Farm, A New England Saga. Norwood, n.d. First edition, 8vo., illus., very fine. Current BW9-271 1974 $14

ROBERTSON, W.   An Index . . . of Many Records of Charters. Edinburgh, 1798. 4to., buckram. Quaritch 939-672 1974 £10

ROBERTSON, WILLIAM   An Historical Disquisition. London and Edinburgh, 1791. 4to., contemporary tree calf, gilt, first edition. Dawsons PM 251-327 1974 £30

ROBERTSON, WILLIAM   An Historical Disquisition. 1791. 4to., half calf, gilt, uncut. Broadhurst 23-1702 1974 £40

ROBERTSON, WILLIAM   An Historical Disquisition Concerning the Knowledge Which the Ancients had of India. London, 1791. 4to., contemporary tree calf, first edition. Dawsons PM 247-247 1974 £30

ROBERTSON, WILLIAM   An Historical Disquisition Concerning the Knowledge Which the Ancients had of India. 1804. 8vo., contemporary diced calf, joints cracked, worn, large folding maps, fourth edition. Bow Windows 66-575 1974 £8

ROBERTSON, WILLIAM   An Historical Disquisition Concerning the Knowledge Which the Ancients Had of India: and The Progress of Trade With That Country Prior to the Discovery of the Passage to it By the Cape of Good Hope. With Appendix. 1791. Med. 4to., half brown calf by Bayntun, folding maps, beautiful copy, with half title & errata. Broadhurst 24-1669 1974 £45

ROBERTSON, WILLIAM   Historical Works. London, 1806-9. 8vo., 12 vols., contemporary diced calf, gilt. Hammond 201-460 1974 £60

ROBERTSON, WILLIAM   The History of America. London, 1800.
4 vols., repaired, covers chipped otherwise tight and clean. Jenkins 61-2284
1974 $25

ROBERTSON, WILLIAM   The History of America. 1808. Full crimson
morocco, gilt, 2 vols., plates, English first edition. Covent 56-1400 1974 £50

ROBERTSON, WILLIAM   Phraseologia Generalis. Cambridge, 1681.
1 vol. in 2, 8vo., contemporary reversed calf, first edition. Dawsons PM
252-829 1974 £80

ROBERTSON, WILLIAM   The Works of. 1821. 10 vols., 8vo.,
contemporary calf, joints cracked, covers rubbed, folding maps, new edition.
Bow Windows 66-576 1974 £14

ROBIANO, LE COMPTE ABBE DE   Les Echecs Simplifies et Approfundis
Depuis. Bruxelles, 1847. 8vo., inscription, foxing, half calf. Bow Windows
62-769 1974 £12

ROBIN, C.   Histoire Naturelle des Vegetaux Parasites.
Paris, 1853. 8vo and roy 8vo., cloth, orig. boards, 2 vols., plates. Wheldon
129-1328 1974 £35

ROBIN, C.   Histoire Naturelle des Vegetaux Parasites Qui
Croissent sur l'Homme et sur les Animaux Vivants. Paris, 1853. 2 vols. 8vo.
& roy. 8vo., cloth & orig. boards, plates, rare. Wheldon 131-1462 1974 £35

ROBIN, C.   Memoire sur l'Evolution. Paris, 1868. 4to.,
half calf, plates. Wheldon 129-346 1974 £5

ROBIN, P. ANSELL   Animal Lore in English Literature. 1932.
Plates, text illus., fine, d.w. Covent 51-2435 1973 £8.50

ROBIN, T.   Toronto, Grey and Bruce Railway. Toronto,
1873. Hood's 102-774 1974 $40

ROBIN Hood's Garland. Wolverhampton, (c. 1800). New much improved edition,
woodcut illus., 8vo., sewn as issued. George's 610-628 1973 £6

ROBINS, BENJAMIN   An Address to the Electors and Other Free
Subjects of Great Britain. London, 1739. 8vo., modern quarter calf, gilt,
second edition. Dawsons PM 247-248 1974 £18

ROBINS, BENJAMIN   Observations on the Present Convention With
Spain. London, 1739. 8vo., modern boards, first edition. Dawsons PM
247-249 1974 £15

ROBINS, F. W.   The Story of the Lamp. Oxford, 1939. Illus.,
cloth, worn. Covent 55-479 1974 £12.50

ROBINSON, BEVERLEY   A Practical Treatise On Nasal Catarrh. New
York, 1880. Rittenhouse 46-564 1974 $15

ROBINSON, C.   Digest of Reported Cases: Superior Courts of
Ontario and Supreme Court of Canada. Toronto, 1884. Three quarter leather,
marbled boards. Hood's 104-623 1974 $30

ROBINSON, C. N.   The Transvaal War Album. (n.d.). Folio,
illus., old half roan, rubbed. Bow Windows 62-770 1974 £8.50

ROBINSON, EDWARD ARLINGTON   Cavender's House. New York, 1929.
First trade edition, orig. binding, partially unopened, mint. Ross 87-478 1974
$12.50

ROBINSON, EDWARD ARLINGTON   Cavender's House. New York, 1929.
No. 240 of edition limited to 500 copies, signed, ex-library, orig. binding, box
worn & slightly split, fine. Ross 87-477 1974 $20

ROBINSON, EDWARD ARLINGTON   Cavender's House. New York, 1929.
Orig. cloth backed boards, first edition, one of 500 numbered copies, signed by
author, boxed, fine. MacManus 224-375 1974 $25

ROBINSON, EDWARD ARLINGTON   The Glory of the Nightingales. New
York, 1930. First trade edition, orig. binding, near mint, d.w. Ross 87-479
1974 $10

ROBINSON, EDWARD ARLINGTON   The Glory of the Nightingales. New York,
1930. Orig. cloth, first edition, one of 500 numbered copies, signed by author,
boxed, fine. MacManus 224-376 1974 $25

ROBINSON, EDWARD ARLINGTON   King Jasper. New York, 1935. First
trade edition, d.w. lightly worn & chipped, small ink stamp on free fly, orig.
binding, near fine. Ross 87-480 1974 $12.50

ROBINSON, EDWIN ARLINGTON   Lancelot. New York, 1920. 12mo.,
orig. red cloth, first edition, one of 450 copies specially issued for the Lyric
Society, inscribed by author to Samuel Roth, fine. MacManus 224-377 1974
$65

ROBINSON, EDWARD ARLINGTON   Letters ... to Howard George Schmitt.
Waterville, 1943. 8vo., patterned boards, first edition. Rota 190-780 1974
£8

ROBINSON, EDWARD ARLINGTON   The Man Who Died Twice. New York,
1924. Orig. cloth backed boards, first edition, one of 500 numbered copies,
signed by author, fine, boxed (little worn). MacManus 224-378 1974 $27.50

ROBINSON, EDWARD ARLINGTON   Matthias at the Door. New York, 1931.
lst ed. Biblo & Tannen 213-592 1973 $10

ROBINSON, EDWARD ARLINGTON   Matthias at the Door. New York, 1931.
Orig. cloth, first edition, one of 500 numbered copies, signed by author, fine,
boxed. MacManus 224-379 1974 $30

ROBINSON, EDWIN ARLINGTON   Nicodemus. New York, 1932. Orig.
cloth, first edition, one of 253 numbered copies, signed by author, boxed, fine.
MacManus 224-380 1974 $30

ROBINSON, EDWARD ARLINGTON   Nicodemus: A Book of Poems. New
York, 1932. No. 235 of edition limited to 253 large paper copies, signed, lacking
d.w., backstrip somewhat faded, fine, orig. binding. Ross 87-482 1974 $25

ROBINSON, EDWIN ARLINGTON   Roman Bartholow. New York, 1923.
8vo., boards, buckram back, autographed, first edition. Goodspeed's 578-304
1974 $10

ROBINSON, EDWARD ARLINGTON   Selected Letters. New York, 1940.
8vo., orig. cloth, first edition. Rota 190-779 1974 £5

ROBINSON, EDWARD ARLINGTON   Tristram. New York, 1927. lst issue.
Biblo & Tannen 210-798 1973 $15

ROBINSON, F.   An Account of the Organization of the Army of
the U. S. Philadelphia, 1848. 12mo., cloth, 2 vols., first edition. Putman
126-28 1974 $34

ROBINSON, FREDERICK WILLIAM   A Woman's Ransom. Boston, 1864.
American edition. Austin 61-852 1974 $10

ROBINSON, H. C.   The Birds of the Malay Peninsula. 1927-39.
Imperial 8vo., 4 vols., orig. red cloth, plates. Wheldon 129-520 1974 £160

ROBINSON, H. M.   The Great Fur Land, or Sketches of the Life in
the Hudson's Bay Territory. New York, 1879. Ex-library. Hood's 102-829
1974 $25

ROBINSON, H. P.   Picture-Making by Photography. 1889. Illus.,
plates, second edition. Covent 56-1990 1974 £12.50

ROBINSON, HENRY CRABB   Books and Their Writers. 1938. Portraits,
3 vols., demy 8vo., orig. cloth, fine. Broadhurst 24-441 1974 £12

ROBINSON, HENRY CRABB   Diary, Reminiscences, and Correspondence.
1869. 8vo., 3 vols., calf, gilt, plates. Quaritch 936-531 1974 £20

ROBINSON, HENRY CRABB   Exposure of Misrepresentations. London, 1840.
12mo., orig. cloth, inscribed, scarce, first edition. Ximenes 35-56 1974
$27.50

ROBINSON, JAMES   The Whole Art of Making British Wines. 1848.
Orig. cloth, faded. Covent 55-703 1974 £15

ROBINSON, J.   A Guide to the Lakes in Cumberland. 1819.
8vo., green morocco, plates. Quaritch 939-225 1974 £50

ROBINSON, J. G.   Memoranda on Fifty Pictures. 1868. 4to.,
buckram, uncut, fine presentation copy, inscribed. Hill 126-229 1974 £16

ROBINSON, LENNOX   The Far Off Hills. French, 1941. 98p.
Austin 51-796 1973 $7.50

ROBINSON, M.   The New Family Herbal. Wakefield, n.d.
12mo., orig. cloth gilt, plates. Wheldon 130-1622 1974 £5

ROBINSON, M. F.   The Spirit of Association. London, 1913.
8vo., orig. cloth, library stamp, gilt. Bow Windows 62-771 1974 £4.75

ROBINSON, MARY   Memoirs of. London, 1803-01. 4 vols.,
8vo., contemporary half morocco, first edition. Ximenes 35-57 1974 $75

ROBINSON, MARY   Sight, Cavern of Woe, and Solitude. 1793.
4to., disbound, name torn from title. Allen 216-2054 1974 $15

ROBINSON, P.   Fishes of Fancy. 1883. 8vo., cloth.
Wheldon 129-588 1974 £5

ROBINSON, P. F.   Designs for Gate Cottages, Lodges, and Park
Entrances. London, 1837. 4to., plates, foxing, contemporary quarter roan,
third edition. Bow Windows 62-772 1974 £24

ROBINSON, P. F.   Vitruvius Britannicus. 1827. Roy. folio,
plates, orig. boards, rebacked. Quaritch 940-549 1974 £25

ROBINSON, P. J.   Montreal to Niagara In the Seventeenth
Century. (1944). Card cover. Hood's 103-556 1974 $10

ROBINSON, RALPH M.   The History of a Banking House. 1929. Dust
wrapper, fine, English first edition. Covent 56-93 1974 £10.50

ROBINSON, ROBERT   Thomas Bewick, His Life and Times. Newcastle, 1887. Orig. green cloth, illus., bookplate. Dawson's 424-38 1974 $100

ROBINSON, ROWLAND E.   Danvis Folks. Houghton, Mifflin, 1894.
349p. Austin 54-868 1973 $10

ROBINSON, ROWLAND E.   A Hero of Ticonderoga. Burlington, 1898.
16mo., buckram, first edition. Goodspeed's 578-305 1974 $10

ROBINSON, ROWLAND E.   Uncle Lisha's Shop and a Danvis Pioneer.
Tuttle, 1933. 248p., illus. Austin 54-869 1973 $12.50

ROBINSON, SARA T. L.   Kansas; Its Interior and Exterior Life. Lawrence,
1899. 8vo., orig. bindings, signed, tenth edition. Butterfield 8-182 1974 $10

ROBINSON, SOLON   Hot Corn. New York, 1854. 12mo., orig.
cloth, illus., first edition. Ximenes 35-58 1974 $15

ROBINSON, STANFORD F. H.   Celtic Illuminative Art. Dublin, 1908.
Roy. 4to., plates, buckram. Quaritch 939-629 1974 £50

ROBINSON, THOMAS   The Common Law of Kent. 1741.
Contemporary calf, first edition. Howes 186-2057 1974 £25

ROBINSON, W.   The Wild Garden. 1894. 8vo., cloth,
text-figures, plates, fourth edition. Wheldon 128-1528 1973 £5

ROBINSON, W. D.   Memoirs of the Mexican Revolution. 1821.
8vo., contemporary half calf, 2 vols. Bow Windows 64-610 1974 £48

ROBINSON, W. HEATH   Railway Ribaldry. 1935. Pictorial wrappers,
dust-soiled. Marsden 39-383 1974 £10

ROBINSON, WILLIAM H.   Catalogue 19, Early English Books. 1928.
Half morocco, presentation. Howes 185-819 1974 £7.50

ROBIOU, F.   Les Institutions de l'Ancienne Rome. Paris,
1884-88. 3 vols., 12mo., rebound. Biblo & Tannen 214-656 1974 $25

ROBLEDO, DIEGO ANTONIO DE   Compendio Cirurgico. Barcelona, 1703.
Folio, old half calf. Gumey 64-187 1974 £60

ROBO, E.   Mediaeval Farnham. Farnham, 1935. Crown
4to., orig. cloth, illus., covers faded and stained. Bow Windows 66-578 1974
£8.50

ROBSON, ALBERT H.   J. E. H. MacDonald. Toronto, 1937. Coloured illus., rebound. Hood's 102-163 1974 $12.50

ROBSON, E. W.   The Film Answers Back. Lane, 1947. 335p.,
illus. Austin 51-797 1973 $12.50

ROBSON, FRANCIS   The Life of Hyder Ally. London, 1786. 8vo.,
contemporary half calf, signed, first edition. Ximenes 35-59 1974 $30

ROBSON, GEORGE FENNELL   Scenery of the Grampian Mountains. London,
1819. Large folio, plates, modern half calf. Traylen 79-384 1973 £195

ROBSON, S. C.   The Variation of Animals In Nature. 1936.
8vo., cloth, plates, scarce. Wheldon 131-453 1974 £7.50

ROBY, JOHN   Traditions of Lancashire. London, 1867. 4to.,
2 vols., morocco, gilt, plates, fourth edition. Dawsons PM 251-64 1974 £45

ROCCHIETTI, JOSEPH   Lorenzo and Oonalaska. Winchester, 1835.
8vo., modern cloth, first edition. Ximenes 35-61 1974 $75

ROCHE, JAMES JEFFERY   Life of John Boyle O'Reilly. 1891.
Ex-library. Austin 57-561 1974 $15

ROCHE, JAMES JEFFERY   Life of John Boyle O'Reilly. Cassell, 1891.
Austin 62-537 1974 $17.50

ROCHE, REGINA MARIA   The Children of the Abbey. Philadelphia,
n.d. Illus. Austin 61-853 1974 $17.50

ROCHEFORT, CHARLES DE   Histoire Naturelle et Morale des Iles Antilles
de l'Amerique. Rotterdam, 1681. 4to., contemporary calf, illus., fourth
edition. Ximenes 35-60 1974 $325

ROCHESTER, JOHN WILMOT, EARL OF   Valentinian. London, 1685. 4to.,
maroon straight grain half morocco, first edition. Dawsons PM 252-830 1974
£120

ROCK, DANIEL   Church of Our Fathers As Seen In St. Osmund's
Rite for the Cathedral of Salisbury. 1905. 4 vols., new edition. Allen
213-1745 1973 $50

ROCK, DANIEL   The Church of Our Fathers. 1905. 4 vols.,
large 8vo., illus., new & best edition. Howes 185-1609 1974 £15

ROCK, F. L. B.   A Concise History of . . . Alexandria, Va.
Alexandria, 1883. 8vo., orig. bindings. Butterfield 8-671 1974 $20

ROCKINGHAM, CHARLES WATSON-WENTWORTH   Memoirs of. 1852.
2 vols. in 1, thick 8vo., full contemporary polished calf gilt. Howes 186-1172
1974 £15

ROCKSTRO, WILLIAM SMYTH   Abbey Lands. 1857. 8vo., contemporary half
calf, neatly rebacked, first edition. Bow Windows 66-580 1974 £21

ROCKWOOD, HARRY   Harry Sharpe, the New York Detective. New
York, (1893). Orig. wrappers, English first edition. Covent 56-342 1974 £7.50

ROCOQUE, J.   The Traveller's Companion or the Post Roads
of England and Wales. Square 12mo., orig. marbled board slip-case. Quaritch
939-221 1974 £45

ROCQUAIN, FELIX   La Cour de Rome et l'Esprit de Reforme avant
Luther. Paris, 1893-95. 2 vols., roy. 8vo., contemporary half calf, rubbed.
Howes 185-1610 1974 £10

ROCQUE, J.   A New and Accurate Survey of the Cities of
Lond and Westminster. 1747. Folio, half ledger calf. Quaritch 939-468
1974 £275

A ROD for Tunbridge Beaus. London, 1701. Folio, modern calf-backed boards,
staining, first edition. Dawsons PM 252-831 1974 £150

RODELL, FRANK H.   Pacific Coast Society of Printing House Craftmen's Clubs. San Francisco, 1926. 1st ed., morocco title label, illus. Dykes
24-269 1974 $85

RODEZ, SOUTHERN FRANCE   Statuta Synodalia Diocesis Ruthenen. Lyon,
1552. Small 4to., old limp vellum, rare first edition. Harper 213-129 1973
$1750

RODGERS, C.   New York: the World's Capital City. New York, 1848. Biblo & Tannen 213-77 1973 $10

RODGERS, SAMUEL   The Pleasures of Memory. 1801. Quarter leather, illus., new edition. Covent 56-1100 1974 £8.50

RODIN, AUGUSTE   Les Dessins de Auguste Rodin. 1897. Large folio, half brown morocco, orig. wrapper. Quaritch 940-222 1974 £300

RODIN, AUGUSTE   Rodin. A Series of 60 Photogravure Plates. 1924. Roy. folio, handmade paper, buckram, numbered, limited edition. Quaritch 940-224 1974 £75

RODIN, AUGUSTE   Rodin: Cinquante-Sept Statues. 1915. Imp. 4to., plates, half morocco, orig. wrappers, limited. Quaritch 940-223 1974 £35

RODIN, AUGUSTE   Testament. 1932. 8vo., orig. cloth, wrappers, first edition. Rota 190-781 1974 £5

RODMAN, SELDEN   The Revolutionists. 1942. Austin 51-798 1973 $12.50

RODMAN, THOMAS P.   A Poem. New Bedford, 1833. 8vo., orig. printed wrappers, first edition. Ximenes 35-62 1974 $15

RODMAN, WILLIAM L.   Diseases of the Breast, With Special Reference to Cancer. Philadelphia, 1908. Rittenhouse 46-565 1974 $10

RODRIGUES, J. BARBOSA   Sertum Palmarum Brasiliensium. Brussels, 1903. Atlas folio, 2 vols., orig. dec. cloth. Wheldon 129-1627 1974 £225

RODRIGUES, J. BARBOSA   Sertum Palmarum Brasiliensium. Brussels, 1903. 2 vols., atlas folio, orig. dec. cloth, plates, scarce. Wheldon 131-100 1974 £225

RODRIGUEZ, ALPHONSUS   The Practice of Christian Perfection. London, 1697-99. 3 vols., small 4to., 19th century half morocco. Howes 185-1611 1974 £55

RODWAY, J.   In the Guiana Forest. 1895. Crown 8vo., cloth, plates, second edition. Wheldon 129-296 1974 £5

RODWAY, J.   In the Guiana Forest. 1911. 8vo., orig. cloth, plates, new revised edition. Wheldon 131-390 1974 £5

RODWAY, L.   The Tasmanian Flora. Hobart, 1903. Roy 8vo., boards, plates. Wheldon 129-1116 1974 £15

ROE, AZEL STEVENS   James Montjoy. New York, 1850. 12mo., orig. blue cloth, first edition. Ximenes 35-63 1974 $27.50

ROE, FRED   Ancient Church Chests and Chairs in the Home Counties Round Greater London. 1929. 4to., illus., fine, dust wrapper. Covent 55-747 1974 £8.50

ROEBUCK, JOHN   An Enquiry. London, 1776. 8vo., modern boards, new edition. Dawsons PM 251-328 1974 £20

ROEDERER, JOHANN GEORG   Departu Laborioso Decades Duae. Gottingen, 1756. 4to., contemporary wrappers, worn, first edition. Schumann 35-408 1974 $95

ROEDERER, JOHANN GEORG   Icones Uteri Humani Observationibus Illustratae. Gottingen, 1759. Large folio, contemporary boards, first edition. Schumann 35-409 1974 $165

ROEMER, C. F. VON   Das Rheinische Uebergangsgebirge. Hannover, 1844. Imp. 4to., cloth, plates, scarce. Wheldon 128-1040 1973 £10

ROEPER, J.   De Organis Plantarum. Basle, 1828. 4to., old half calf. Wheldon 131-1192 1974 £5

ROETTINGER, H.   Das Alte Buch und Seine Ausstattung von XV. bis zume XIX. Jahrhundert. Vienna, n.d. Roy. 4to., boards portfolio, plates. Kraus B8-374 1974 $75

ROFFENI, GIOVANNI ANTONIO   Discorso Astrologico . . . Sopra l'Anno M. DC. XI. Bologna, 1611. Small 4to., boards, with exlibris of Prince Pietro Ginori Conti, first edition. Schumann 500-7 1974 sFr 10,000

ROGER DU NORD, COMTE   Catalogue des Livres Rares et Precieux Composant la Bibliotheque de . . . Paris, 1884. Half cloth, uncut, unopened. Kraus B8-235 1974 $20

ROGER-MARX, CLAUDE   Dunoyer de Segonzac. Paris, 1925. 4to., orig. wrappers, plates, illus., half cloth, scarce. Minters 37-89 1973 $28

ROGER MARX, CLAUDE   Vuillard et son Temps. Paris, 1945. 8vo., plates, wrappers, illus., limited edition. Minters 37-145 1973 $20

ROGER OF WENDOVER   Chronica, sive Flores Historiarum. 1841. 5 vols., orig. boards, worn. Howes 186-805 1974 £25

ROGERS, A. W.   An Introduction to the Geology of Cape Colony. 1905. Crown 8vo., cloth, plates. Wheldon 131-1072 1974 £5

ROGERS, AMMI   Memoirs of. N.P., 1824. 12mo., contemporary calf, first edition. Ximenes 35-64 1974 $15

ROGERS, AMMI   Memoirs of. Schenectady, 1826. 16mo., boards, calf backstrip, light wear, lightly foxed. Wilson 63-43 1974 $20

ROGERS, BRUCE   BR to FWG. Berkeley, 1940. 12mo., boards, parchment back, first edition. Goodspeed's 578-522 1974 $10

ROGERS, BRUCE   Instructions Concerning Erecting of a Library. Cambridge, 1903. Marbled boards, uncut. Dawson's 424-82 1974 $35

ROGERS, BRUCE   The Love Poems of John Donne. Boston, 1905. Boards, vellum, uncut, slipcase. Dawson's 424-83 1974 $30

ROGERS, BRUCE   The Psalms of David. Cambridge, 1928. Buckram, English first edition. Covent 56-1067 1974 £15

ROGERS, CAMERON   The Magnificent Idler: the Story of Walt Whitman. 1926. Portrait, fine, d.w., first edition. Covent 51-1975 1973 £5.25

ROGERS, H. D.   The Geology of Pennsylvania. Philadelphia, 1858. 4to., orig. cloth. Wheldon 130-967 1974 £45

ROGERS, HOWARD S.   History of Cass County, From 1825 to 1875. Cassopolis, 1875. 12mo., cloth. Saddleback 14-508 1974 $35

ROGERS, J. SMYTH   Syllabus of a Course of Medical Examinations and Illustrations. New York, 1823. 8vo., rare, first edition. Ximenes 35-65 1974 $35

ROGERS, JULIA ELLEN   The Tree Book. Garden City, 1922. Small 4to., color plates, bookplate, orig. binding. Wilson 63-324 1974 $17.50

ROGERS, MEYRIC R.   Carl Milles. New Haven, 1940. Plates, ltd. ed., scarce. Biblo & Tannen 210-326 1973 $57.50

ROGERS, ROBERT   A Concise Account of North America. London, 1765. Full leather. Hood's 102-576 1974 $675

ROGERS, ROBERT   A Concise Account of North America. London, 1765. Full leather. Hood's 104-658 1974 $675

ROGERS, SAMUEL   Autobiography of. Cincinnati, 1880. Cloth. Hayman 57-393 1974 $15

ROGERS, SAMUEL   An Epistle to a Friend. London, 1798. 4to., early calf, worn, first edition. Ximenes 35-66 1974 $80

ROGERS, SAMUEL   Human Life. London, 1819. 8vo., rubbed, contemporary calf, first octavo edition. Ximenes 35-68 1974 $8

ROGERS, SAMUEL   Human Life. London, 1819. 4to., orig. grey boards, worn, first edition. Ximenes 35-67 1974 $12.50

ROGERS, SAMUEL   Italy. London, 1830. 8vo., contemporary
red morocco, inscribed, first illus. edition. Ximenes 35-69 1974 $45

ROGERS, SAMUEL   Italy, a Poem. 1830-34. 2 vols., plates,
full brown morocco, gilt, presentation. Howes 185-402 1974 £50

ROGERS, SAMUEL   Italy. 1838. 4to., vignettes, contemporary
hard grained morocco gilt. Smith 193-679 1973 £18

ROGERS, SAMUEL   Poems. 1845. 2 vols., inscribed, buckram,
blind stamp. Allen 216-1532 1974 $15

ROGERS, SAMUEL   The Poems of. New York, 1851. 340 pages.
Austin 61-854 1974 $12.50

ROGERS, SAMUEL   The Poems of . . . With a Memoir. Philadelphia,
1846. Frontis., binding in poor condition, text quite clear with minor foxing.
Current BW9-272 1974 $22.50

ROGERS, SAMUEL   Recollections of the Table-Talk of . . . to Which
is Added Porsoniana. London, 1856. Second edition, 8vo., portraits, plates,
full tan calf, gilt dec. corded spine, inside fine. Current BW9-596 1974 $35

ROGERS, SAMUEL   Rogers and His Contemporaries. 1889. 2 vols.,
ex-library, tops of spines frayed. Allen 216-1534 1974 $10

ROGERS, WILL   Ether and Me. Putnam, 1937. 77p. Austin
54-870 1973 $5

ROGERS, WILL   Illiterate Digest. Boni, 1924. 351p. Austin
54-871 1973 $6

ROGERS, WILL   Letters of a Self-Made Diplomat. Boni.
263p. Austin 54-872 1973 $6.50

ROGERS, WILLIAM   La Buccomancie ou l'Art. Paris, 1851. 8vo.,
old half sheep. Gurney 64-188 1974 £25

ROGERS, WILLIAM   La Buccomancie ou l'Art de Connaitre le Passe
le Present et l'Avenir d'Une Personne, d'Apres l'Inspection de sa Bouche. Paris,
1851. 8vo., old half sheep, corners worn. Gurney 66-155 1974 £25

ROGOFF, HARRY   An East Side Epic. Vanguard, n.d. 311p.
Austin 62-538 1974 $10

ROGUES In Porcelain. 1924. Roy 8vo., cloth-backed boards, illus., plates,
English first edition. Covent 56-673 1974 £15.75

ROH, FRANZ   Aenne Biermann. Berlin, 1930. 4to., orig.
wrapper, plates. Minters 37-599 1973 $30

ROH, FRANZ   Foto-Auge/Oeil et Photo/Photo-Eye.
Stuttgart, 1929. Large 4to., orig. wrapper, photographs, rare. Minters
37-618 1973 $250

ROH, FRANZ   L. Moholy-Nagy. Berlin, 1930. 8vo.,
soiled wrappers, scarce. Minters 37-613 1973 $85

ROHAN, HENRI DUC DE   A Treatise. London, 1641. 12mo., early
mottled calf, first English edition. Ximenes 35-70 1974 $110

ROHAULT, JACQUES   Physica. London, 1710. 8vo., half calf, gilt,
plates, third edition. Hammond 201-941 1974 £28

ROHAULT, JACQUES   Traite de Physique. Paris, 1671. 2 vols. in
1, large 4to., contemporary calf, rubbed, first edition. Schuman 37-222
1974 $185

ROHDE, ELEANOUR SINCLAIR   Garden-Craft in the Bible and Other Essays.
1927. 8vo., orig. cloth backed boards, illus. Wheldon 131-1563 1974 £7.50

ROHDE, ELEANOUR SINCLAIR   A Garden of Herbs. 1926. 8vo., half
buckram, illus., revised and enlarged edition. Wheldon 131-1820 1974 £7.50

ROHDE, ELEANOUR SINCLAIR   Gardens of Delight. 1934. 8vo., orig. cloth.
Broadhurst 23-1177 1974 £5

ROHDE, ELEANOUR SINCLAIR   Gardens of Delight. 1934. Roy. 8vo., orig.
cloth, plates, fine. Broadhurst 24-1152 1974 £6

ROHDE, ELEANOUR SINCLAIR   Herbs and Herb Gardening. (1936). 8vo.,
cloth, scarce, drawings. Wheldon 131-1819 1974 £7.50

ROHDE, ELEANOUR SINCLAIR   The Old English Herbals. 1922. Crown 4to.,
orig. cloth. Broadhurst 23-1176 1974 £25

ROHDE, ELEANOUR SINCLAIR   The Old English Herbals. 1922. First edition,
crown 4to., half dark green levant morocco by Bayntun, panelled back, raised
bands, top edges gilt, coloured frontis., plain plates. Broadhurst 24-1150 1974
£35

ROHDE, ELEANOUR SINCLAIR   The Old English Herbals. 1922. Small 4to.,
plates, orig. buckram, scarce, orig. edition. Howes 185-821 1974 £25

ROHDE, ELEANOUR SINCLAIR   The Old English Herbals. London, 1922. 4to.,
orig. cloth gilt, plates, fine, first edition. Dawsons PM 10-518 1974 £45

ROHDE, ELEANOUR SINCLAIR   The Old World Pleasaunce. 1925. 8vo., cloth.
Wheldon 131-1565 1974 £5

ROHDE, ELEANOUR SINCLAIR   Oxford's College Gardens. 1932. Roy. 8vo.,
cloth, plates, scarce. Wheldon 131-1564 1974 £10

ROHDE, ELEANOUR SINCLAIR   Oxford's College Gardens. 1932. Roy. 8vo.,
cloth, plates, frontis., scarce. Wheldon 129-1523 1974 £5

ROHDE, ELEANOUR SINCLAIR   Shakespeare's Wild Flowers. (1935). 8vo.,
cloth, frontis., plates. Wheldon 130-188 1974 £7.50

ROHMER, SAX   Brood of the Witch-Queen. New York, 1924.
1st ed. Biblo & Tannen 210-657 1973 $17.50

ROHMER, SAX   Daughter of Fu Manchu. New York, 1931.
First American edition. Covent 55-652 1974 £8.50

ROHMER, SAX   The Dream Detective. New York, 1925.
Biblo & Tannen 210-658 1973 $15

ROHMER, SAX   The Romance of Sorcery. New York, n.d.
Biblo & Tannen 210-659 1973 $15

ROHMER, SAX   Tales of Chinatown. New York, 1922. 1st
ed. Biblo & Tannen 210-660 1973 $22.50

ROHMER, SAX   Tales of East and West. New York, 1933.
1st ed. Biblo & Tannen 210-661 1973 $20

ROHMER, SAX   Tales of Secret Egypt. New York, 1919.
Biblo & Tannen 210-662 1973 $18.50

ROLFE, EUSTACE NEVILLE   Naples in 1888. London, 1888. 8vo., orig.
blue cloth, illus., first edition. Ximenes 35-71 1974 $10

ROLFE, FREDERICK WILLIAM   The Bull Against the Enemy of the Anglican
Race. 1929. Crown 4to., dec. paper wrapper, mint. Broadhurst 24-598 1974
£80

ROLFE, FREDERICK WILLIAM   Chronicles of the House of Borgia. New York,
1901. 8vo., half morocco, plates, first American edition. Dawsons PM
252-832 1974 £75

ROLFE, FREDERICK WILLIAM   The Desire and Pursuit of the Whole. 1934.
Slipcase. Covent 55-525 1974 £15

ROLFE, FREDERICK WILLIAM   The Desire and Pursuit of the Whole. 1934.
8vo., orig. cloth, first edition. Broadhurst 23-656 1974 £12

ROLFE, FREDERICK WILLIAM   The Desire and Pursuit of the Whole. London,
1934. Orig. green cloth binding, gold panel on spine, near mint, slightly
chipped d.w., first edition. Ross 87-132 1974 $40

ROLFE, FREDERICK WILLIAM   Hubert's Arthur. London, 1935. Some dust
staining of spine, fine, orig. binding. Ross 86-107 1974 $30

ROLFE, FREDERICK WILLIAM   In His Own Image. London, 1901. First edition, first issue, with ad leaf, slight foxing, spine faded, near fine, scarce, orig. binding. Ross 86-108 1974 $75

ROLFE, FREDERICK WILLIAM   The Quest For. 1934. 8vo., orig. cloth, d.w., first edition. Rota 189-210 1974 £25

ROLFE, FREDERICK WILLIAM   The Rubaiyat of 'Umar Khaiyam. London, 1924. Illus., dust jacket, fine. Ballinger 1-115 1974 $25

ROLFE, FREDERICK WILLIAM   Stories Told to Me. London, 1898. Small 4to., orig. wrappers, fine, first edition. Dawsons PM 252-833 1974 £140

ROLFE, R. T.   The Romance of the Fungus World. 1925. 8vo., illus., cloth, scarce orig. printing. Wheldon 128-1418 1973 £5

ROLL Of Honor: Names of Soldiers Who Died in Defence of the American Union, Interred in New Hampshire, Mass., Conn., New Jersey, Ohio, Illinois, Wisc., Oregon, Maryland, South Carolina, Fla., Louisiana, Miss., Missouri, the Military Division of the Mississippi, the Territory of Dakota, and Texas. Washington, 1866. Wrapper, foxed. Jenkins 61-2291 1974 $22.50

ROLL Of Honor: Names of Soldiers Who Died in Defence of the American Union, Interred in New York, New Jersey, Pennsylvania, Maryland, Virginia, Illinois, Missouri, Iowa, Arkansas, Texas, Utah, and the Pacific Coast. Washington, 1867. Wrapper, foxed. Jenkins 61-2292 1974 $22.50

ROLL Of Honor: Names of Soldiers Who Died in Defence of the American Union, Interred in Arkansas, California, Indiana, Michigan, Minnesota, Nevada, and the Territories of Arizona, Colorado, Idaho, New Mexico and Washington. Washington, Wrapper, foxed. Jenkins 61-2290 1974 $22.50

ROLL Of Honor: Names of Soldiers, Victims of the Rebellion, Buried in National Cemeteries in Maine, Minnesota, Maryland, Pennsylvania, Rhode Island, Arkansas, Mississippi, Florida, Louisiana, and Colorado Territory During the Rebellion. Washington, 1866. Wrapper, foxed. Jenkins 61-2289 1974 $17.50

ROLL Of Honor XVI: Names of Soldiers Who Died in Defence of the American Union Interred in Massachusetts, New York, Gettysburg, Philadelphia, Vermont and Virginia. Washington, 1868. Wrapper, worn. Jenkins 61-2287 1974 $13.50

ROLL of Honor: Names of Soldiers Who Died in Defence of the American Union, Interred in the National Cemeteries at Fortress Monroe and Hampton, Virginia. Washington, 1866. Wrapper. Jenkins 61-2288 1974 $12.50

ROLLAND, L.   Atlas des Champignons de France. Paris, 1910. Roy 8vo., cloth portfolio. Wheldon 129-1330 1974 £25

ROLLAND, L.   Atlas des Champignons de France, Suisse, et Belgique. Paris, 1910. Large 8vo., color plates, cloth portfolio. Gregory 44-212 1974 $98

ROLLAND, ROMAIN   Beethoven the Creator. 1929. Roy. 8vo., 2 vols., orig. cloth, uncut, illus., signed, limited. Broadhurst 23-179 1974 £15

ROLLAND, ROMAIN   Colas Breugnon. Paris, (1919). 12mo., orig. wrapper, uncut, fine, first edition. L. Goldschmidt 42-354 1974 $150

ROLLE, RICHARD   The Incendium Amoris. 1915. Frontispiece, scarce. Howes 185-403 1974 £6.50

ROLT, L. T. C.   Sleep No More. 1st ed. Biblo & Tannen 210-664 1973 $7.50

ROLT, L. T. C.   Sleep No More. London, 1948. 1st ed. Biblo & Tannen 210-663 1973 $12.50

ROLVAAG, OLE EDVART   Giants in the Earth: A Saga of the Prairie. New York, 1927. Fine, first printing. Jenkins 61-2293 1974 $25

ROLVAAG, OLE EDVART   Peder Victorious. Harper, 1929. Orig. edition. Austin 62-540 1974 $7.50

ROMAINS, JULES   Donogoo Tonka ou les Miracles de la Science. Paris, 1920. 12mo., orig. wrapper, first edition. L. Goldschmidt 42-355 1974 $10

ROMAINS, JULES   Le Fauconnier. Paris, 1927. 4to., wrappers, plates. Minters 37-100 1973 $24

ROMAN, ALFRED   The Military Operations of General Beauregard in the War Between the States . . . Including a Brief Personal Sketch and Narrative of His Services in the War with Mexico, 1846-8. New York, 1884. 2 vols., orig. binding. Butterfield 10-182 1974 $20

ROMAN Vesperal of the Cistercian Order. c. 15th century. Folio, on vellum, old wooden boards, very good condition. Smith 193-124 1973 £60

THE ROMANCE of Monte Beni. Leipzig, 1860. 12mo., full vellum, gilt, fine, English first edition. Covent 56-615 1974 £110

THE ROMANCE of Sir Ysambrace. 1897. 8vo., holland-backed boards, frontispiece. Hammond 201-740 1974 £150

ROMANES, GEORGE JOHN   Animal Intelligence. (1882). Crown 8vo., cloth. Wheldon 129-348 1974 £5

ROMANES, GEORGE JOHN   Darwin and After Darwin. 1905, 1895-97. 3 vols., crown 8vo., cloth, portraits, text figures. Wheldon 128-58 1973 £6

ROMANES, GEORGE JOHN   The Life and Letters of. (1896). 8vo., cloth, plates. Wheldon 129-187 1974 £5

ROMANES, GEORGE JOHN   Mental Evolution in Animals. London, 1883. 8vo., first edition. Traylen 79-121 1973 £10

ROMANISCHE Baukunst in Frankreich Herausgegeben von Julius Baum. Stuttgart, 1910. 4to., text in German, illus., binding faded, interior fine. Current BW9-503 1974 $12.50

ROMER, A. S.   Vertebrate Paleontology. Chicago, 1933. Roy 8vo., cloth. Wheldon 129-860 1974 £5

ROMER, E.   Monographie der Molluskengattung Venus, Linne. Cassel, (1864-) 1869 (-1872). 2 vols. in 1, 4to., cloth, hand-coloured plates, rare. Wheldon 128-853 1973 £50

ROMNEY, GEORGE   Memoirs of the Life and Works Of. 1830. 4to., old calf gilt, presentation copy. Quaritch 940-225 1974 £30

RONCAGLIA, CONSTANTINO   Universa Moralis Theologia . . . ad Usum Confessariorum Explicantur. Venice, 1760. 2 vols., folio, contemporary half vellum. Howes 185-1613 1974 £12.50

RONCALLI, T.   Vetustiora Latinorum Scriptorum Chronica. Padua & Venice, 1787. 2 vols., 4to., contemporary half leather, labels. Schumann 499-99 1974 Sfr 600

LES RONDE Des Enfans. Paris, 1895. Illus., orig. printed wrappers, fine, 1 1/2 X 1 1/8. Gregory 44-456 1974 $47.50

RONDELET, GUILLAUME   Libri de Piscibus Marinis. 1554-1555. Folio, 18th century speckled calf, gilt. Marlborough 70-5 1974 £550

RONDELET, GUILLAUME   Opera Omnia Medica. (Geneva?), 1628. Small 8vo., vellum. Thomas 28-269 1972 £16

RONEHOLM, H.   Applied Art in Finland. New York, 1939. 4to., wrappers, illus. Minters 37-228 1973 $10

RONGE, J.   Practical Guide to the English Kinder-Garten. 1865. Third edition, plates, lithographs, roy. 8vo., orig. cloth. George's 610-635 1973 £10

RONNING, N. N.   Fifty Years in America. Minneapolis, 1938. 243 pages. Austin 57-563 1974 $12.50

RONSARD, PIERRE DE   La Bouquinade et Autres Gaillardises. Paris, 1921. 8vo., orig. wrapper. L. Goldschmidt 42-110 1974 $12.50

RONSARD, PIERRE DE   Oeuvres Completes. Paris, 1914-19. 8 vols., 8vo., orig. wrapper, uncut. L. Goldschmidt 42-111 1974 $50

RONTGEN, WILHELM KONRAD   Eine Neue Art von Strahlen.   1895-1896.
8vo., orig. printed paper wrappers, first edition.   Dawsons PM 245-644 1974
£1,400

RONTGEN, WILHELM KNORAD   Eine Neue Art Von Strahlen.   1895-96.
8vo., orig. printed paper wrappers, quarter morocco box, first edition.
Dawsons PM 250-68 1974 £1400

ROOS, AUDREY   Speaking of Murder.   Random, 1957.   179p.,
illus.   Austin 51-799 1973 $6.50

ROOSES, MAX   Plantijn en de Plantijnsche Drukkerif.
Brussels, 1877.   8vo., orig. printed wrappers.   Kraus B8-369 1974 $20

ROOSES, MAX   Plantin et l'Imprimerie Plantinienne.   Ghent,
1878.   8vo., buckram.   Kraus B8-370 1974 $37.50

ROOSEVELT, FRANKLIN DELANO   Nothing to Fear.   Boston, 1946.
Biblo & Tannen 213-89 1973 $10

ROOSEVELT, THEODORE   A Book-lover's Holiday in the Open.   New
York, 1923.   Biblo & Tannen 213-91 1973 $6

ROOSEVELT, THEODORE   The Free Citizen.   New York, 1956.
Biblo & Tannen 213-92 1973 $7.50

ROOSEVELT, THEODORE   Gouverneur Morris.   New York, 1888.   1st ed.
Biblo & Tannen 213-93 1973 $8.50

ROOSEVELT, THEODORE   The Life, Meaning and Messages of.   New
York, 1919.   4 vols.   Wilson 63-44 1974 $18.75

ROOSEVELT, THEODORE   Outdoor Pastimes of an American Hunter.   New
York, 1908.   New and enlarged edition, 8vo., illus., very fine.   Current BW9-
194 1974 $15

ROOSEVELT, THEODORE   Public Papers of . . ., Governor.   Albany,
1899.   First edition, 8vo., rebacked, good, signature of Roosevelt tipped-in.
Current BW9-401 1974 $37.50

ROOSEVELT, THEODORE   Ranch Life and the Hunting Trail.   New York,
1897.   Illus., fine.   Ballinger 1-311 1974 $12

ROOSEVELT, THEODORE   Ranch-Life and the Hunting Trail.   1897.   4to.,
tan linen cloth, illus., fine.   Putnam 126-336 1974 $25

ROOSEVELT, THEODORE   Thomas Hart Benton.   Boston, 1914.   12mo.
Biblo & Tannen 213-15 1973 $5

ROOSEVELT, THEODORE   The Winning of the West.   New York, 1895.
3 vols., cloth, nice set.   Jenkins 61-2296 1974 $17.50

ROOSEVELT, THEODORE   U. S. Civil Service Commission: Report of
Commissioner Roosevelt Concerning Political Assessments and the Use of Official
Influence to Control Elections.   Washington, 1891.   Wrapper.   Jenkins
61-2295 1974 $12.50

ROOT, A. I.   The ABC and XYZ of Bee Culture.   1945.
Profusely illus., demy 8vo., orig. cloth, fine.   Broadhurst 24-1153 1974 $6

ROOT, GEORGE F.   The Bugle-Call.   Chicago, (1863).   Wrappers.
Hayman 59-255 1974 $15

ROOT, OMI E.   Root's Galesburg City Directory for the Year
1861.   Galesburg, 1861.   Blind-stamped brown cloth, fine, rare, first edition.
Bradley 35-184 1974 $60

ROOT, ROBERT KILBURN   Andreas: The Legend of St. Andrew.   1899.
Ex-library, sturdy library binding.   Austin 61-855 1974 $27.50

ROOT, ROBERT KILBURN   Classical Mythology In Shakespeare.   1903.
Ex-library, sturdy library binding.   Austin 61-856 1974 $10

RORIMER, JAMES J.   Mediaeval Monuments at the Cloisters.   New
York, 1941.   Ltd. ed., folio.   Biblo & Tannen 214-93 1974 $8.50

ROS, AMANDA M.   Delina Delaney.   Belfast, (1898).   8vo., orig.
dark blue pebble-grain cloth, scarce, first edition.   Rota 190-783 1974 £25

ROS, AMANDA M.   Fumes of Formation.   Belfast, 1933.   First
edition.   Covent 55-1255 1974 £7.35

ROS, AMANDA M.   Irene Iddesleigh.   Belfast, 1897.   8vo., orig.
grey cloth, rare, first edition.   Rota 190-782 1974 £30

ROSA, GIOVANNI TITTA   Roberto Aloi.   Milan, 1940.   4to., wrapper,
plates.   Minters 37-172 1973 $12.50

ROSA, JOSE ANTONIO DA   Compendio das Minas.   Lisbon, 1794.   8vo.,
orig. wrappers, plates.   Gumey 64-189 1974 £25

ROSA, JOSE ANTONIO DA   Compendio das Minas.   Lisbon, 1794.   8vo.,
orig. wrappers, folding plates.   Gurney 66-156 1974 £25

ROSCOE, E.   Floral Illustrations of the Seasons.   1829.   4to.,
contemporary half red morocco, fully gilt back, gilt edges, hand coloured
engraved plates, nice clean copy, first edition.   Wheldon 128-1707 1973 £350

ROSCOE, E.   Floral Illustrations of the Seasons.   1829.   4to.,
half morocco gilt, plates.   Wheldon 130-66 1974 £350

ROSCOE, THOMAS   The German Novelists.   1826.   8vo., 4 vols.,
orig. boards, uncut, fine, first edition.   Quaritch 936-535 1974 £40

ROSCOE, THOMAS   The Tourist in France.   1834.   8vo., contemporary green morocco, gilt, plates.   Hammond 201-351 1974 £24

ROSCOE, THOMAS   The Tourist in Spain.   1836.   8vo., contemporary green morocco, gilt, plates.   Hammond 201-353 1974 £21

ROSCOE, THOMAS   The Tourist in Spain.   1836.   8vo., contemporary green morocco, gilt.   Hammond 201-352 1974 £24

ROSCOE, THOMAS   The Tourist in Spain.   1837.   8vo., contemporary green morocco, gilt, plates.   Hammond 201-354 1974 £22.50

ROSCOE, THOMAS   Wanderings and Excursions in North Wales.
(1835-36).   2 vols., 8vo., contemporary morocco.   Quaritch 939-690 1974 £40

ROSCOE, THOMAS   Wanderings in South Wales.   n.d.   2 vols.,
illus., English first edition.   Covent 56-1263 1974 £90

ROSCOE, WILLIAM   The Butterfly's Ball and the Grasshopper's Feast.
1883.   8vo., printed wrapper, plates.   Hammond 201-138 1974 £8

ROSCOE, WILLIAM   The Life and Pontificate of Leo the Tenth.
c.1890.   2 vols., full prize tree calf gilt, rubbed.   Howes 185-1366 1974 £7.50

ROSCOE, WILLIAM   Monandrion Plants.   Liverpool, 1828.   Folio,
plates, contemporary half roan.   Bow Windows 64-232 1974 £950

ROSCOE, WILLIAM   The Nurse.   Liverpool, 1798.   4to., modern
boards, first edition.   Ximenes 35-72 1974 $30

ROSCOE, WILLIAM   On the Origin and Vicissitudes of Literature,
Science, and Art, and Their Influence on the Present State of Society.   Liverpool,
1817.   4to., old half calf, rebacked.   Gurney 66-157 1974 £15

ROSE, GEORGE   The Proposed System of Trade With Ireland
Exploined.   London, 1785.   8vo., modern boards.   Dawsons PM 247-250
1974 £15

ROSE, JAMES ANDERSON   A Collection of Engraved Portraits.   London,
1894.   2 vols., 4to., frontispiece, plates, orig. parchment backed boards.
Bow Windows 62-775 1974 £14

ROSE, JOHN   A Quarter of an Hour Before Dinner.   London,
1788.   8vo., modern boards, second edition.   Dawsons PM 252-835 1974 £8

ROSE, PHILLIP M.   The Italian in America.   Doran, 1922.
155p., illus.   Austin 62-542 1974 $12.50

ROSE, THOMAS   The Northern Tourist.   1835.   4to., plates,
contemporary cloth, gilt.   Quaritch 939-226 1974 £50

ROSE, THOMAS   Westmorland, Cumberland, Durham and Northumberland. 1832. Plates, 2 vols., dmey 4to., binding little worn, orig. cloth, lacks page 31 of text vol. 1, with extra plate as frontispiece vols. 2. Broadhurst 24-1518 1974 £75

ROSE, THOMAS   Westmorland, Cumberland, Durham & Northumberland Illustrated. 1832. Plates, half red morocco, foxed. Marsden 39-387 1974 £45

ROSE, VICTOR M.   The Life and Services of Gen. Ben McCulloch. Philadelphia, 1888. Cloth, portraits, fine, plastic dust wrapper, slip case, first edition. Dykes 22-150 1973 $175

ROSE, VICTOR M.   Some Historical Facts in Regard to the Settlement of Victoria, Texas. Laredo, 1883. 8vo., cloth. Saddleback 14-716 1974 $20

ROSE, WILLIAM L.   A Narrative of the Celebrated Dyde Supper. New York, 1811. Plain board binding. Dawson's 424-198 1974 $35

ROSE, WILLIAM STEWART   Apology Addressed to the Traveller's Club. London, 1825. 8vo., later calf, first edition. Ximenes 35-73 1974 $22.50

ROSE, WILLIAM STEWART   Letters from the North of Italy. London, 1819. 2 vols., 8vo., orig. boards, first edition. Ximenes 35-74 1974 $35

ROSE, WILLIAM STEWART   The Orlando Furioso. London, 1823-31. 8vo., orig. cloth, unopened, first edition. Ximenes 35-75 1974 $60

ROSEBERY   Wallace, Burns, Stevenson, Appreciations. 1912. Illus., fine. Covent 55-1021 1974 £5.25

ROESLIN, EUCHARIUS   Des Divers Travaux et Enfantemens des Femmes le Moyen Pour Survenir aux Accidens Qui Peuvent Eschoir Deant et Apres Iceux Travaux. Lyon, 1584. Small 8vo., old calf, gilt, some stains, very rare, woodcuts. Gurney 66-154 1974 £200

ROESLIN, EUCHARIUS   De Divers Travaus et Enfantemenes des Femmes ...Tournez en Nostre Langue Francoyse. Paris, 1586. Small 8vo., woodcuts, orig. limp vellum, very fine. Schafer 10-141 1974 sFr 3800

ROESLIN, EUCHARIUS   De Partv Hominis. (1551). Small 8vo., modern vellum. Dawsons PM 249-422 1974 £300

ROESLIN, EUCHARIUS   De Partu Hominis, et Quae Circa Ipsum Accidunt Adeoque de Parturientum et Infantium Morbis Atque Cura. Frankfurt, 1554. Small 8vo., woodcuts, modern vellum over thin boards, rare Latin edition, good copy despite marginal repair on title. Schafer 10-140 1974 sFr 1,800

ROSENBACH, ABRAHAM SIMON WOLF   Books and Bidders. Boston, 1927. 8vo., cloth, first edition. Goodspeed's 578-523 1974 $10

ROSENBACH, ABRAHAM SIMON WOLF   Early American Children's Books. Portland, 1933. Boards, morocco, illus., signed. Dawson's 424-215 1974 $150

ROSENBACH, ABRAHAM SIMON WOLF   The Unpublishable Memoirs. 1924. Frontis., fine, English first edition. Covent 56-1101 1974 £12.50

THE ROSENBACH COMPANY   Catalogue of Rare and Important Books, Manuscripts, Autograph Letters, No. 18. Philadelphia, 1916. Wrappers. Kraus B8-236 1974 $25

ROSENBERG, L. C.   Davanzati Palace, Florence, Italy. 1922. Folio, plates. Allen 213-1748 1973 $15

ROSENBERG, LEONCE   Cubisme et Tradition. Paris, 1920. 8vo., wrapper, frayed. Minters 37-314 1973 $30

ROSENBERG, M. E.   The Museum of Flowers. 1846. Vol. 2, parts 2, 3 and 4, demy 4to., orig. wrappers, hand coloured plates. Wheldon 128-1530 1973 £7.50

ROSENFELD, MORRIS   Songs from the Ghetto. 1898. 115 pages. Austin 57-567 1974 $17.50

ROSENFELD, PAUL   Discoveries of a Music Critic. New York, 1936. Orig. ed. Biblo & Tannen 214-905 1974 $9.50

ROSENFELD, PAUL   Modern Tendencies in Music. New York, 1927. 12mo. Biblo & Tannen 214-906 1974 $6.50

ROSENFIELD, LEONORA COHEN   Portrait of a Philosopher. Harcourt, 1948. Austin 62-544 1974 $7.50

ROSENKRANTZ, ARILD   Love Lyrics from Five Centuries. 1932. 4to., full vellum, signed, plates, slipcase, fine. Covent 55-898 1974 £15

ROSENTHAL, BERTHOLD   Heimatgeschichte der Hadischen Juden. Baden, 1927. Biblo & Tannen 213-635 1973 $15

ROSENTHAL, L.   Au Jardin des Gemmes. 1924. 4to., plates, orig. wrapper. Quaritch 940-474 1974 £10

ROSENTHAL, LEONARD   Au Royaume de la Perle. Paris, 1920. 4to., half calf, gilt, English first edition. Covent 56-690 1974 £135

ROSINUS, JOANNES   Antiquitatum Romanorum Corpus Absolutissimum. 1743. 4to., old calf, worn, plates. Allen 213-937 1973 $20

ROSITER, WILLIAM S.   Days and Ways in Old Boston. Boston, 1915. Slight interior foxing, top inch of spine missing. Current BW9-385A 1974 $8

ROSITER, WILLIAM S.   Days and Ways in Old Boston. Boston, 1915. Drawings, first edition, 8vo., illus., full page drawings, photos, text illus., maps, uncut and fine on interior, binding soiled, generally very good. Current BW9-385 1974 $14.50

ROSNY, ANTOINE JOSEPH NICOLAS DE   The Child of Thirty-Six Fathers. New York, 1809. 2 vols., 12mo., contemporary half calf, scarce, first English edition. Ximenes 35-76 1974 $50

ROSS, A. H. D.   Ottawa, Past and Present. Ottawa, 1927. Illus., fading. Hood's 103-671 1974 $12.50

ROSS, ALEXANDER   Adventures of the First Settlers on the Oregon or Columbia River. 1923. Dec. cloth, gilt top, folding map, fine copy. Dykes 22-133 1973 $10

ROSS, ALEXANDER   Arcana Microcosmi. London, 1652. 8vo., polished calf gilt, second edition. Schumann 35-413 1974 $235

ROSS, ALEXANDER   The Fur Hunters of the Far West. London, 1855. 2 vols., 8vo., old polished tree calf, rebacked, gilt, first edition. Traylen 79-496 1973 £150

ROSS, ALEXANDER   The Fur Hunters of the Far West. 1924. Dec. cloth, gilt top, frontispiece, very good copy. Dykes 22-134 1973 $10

ROSS, ALEXANDER   The Fur Hunters of the Far West. Chicago, 1924. Dark green cloth, frontispiece. Bradley 35-323 1974 $16

ROSS, ALEXANDER   The Red River Settlement. 1856. First edition, lithographic frontispiece, 8vo., orig. cloth, spine faded and split at foot, covers marked, internally fine, rare. Sawyer 293-17 1974 £95

ROSS, ALEXANDER   A View of all Religions in the World. 1655. 8vo., half antique calf, second edition. Broadhurst 23-1265 1974 £30

ROSS, ALEXANDER   A View of all Religions in the World. 1658. 8vo., contemporary calf, worn, rough cloth label, some damp staining, portraits, tiny worm hole, third edition. Bow Windows 66-588 1974 £36

ROSS, ARTHUR A.   A Discourse. Providence, 1838. 12mo., orig. brown cloth, first edition. Ximenes 35-77 1974 $12.50

ROSS, ARTHUR A.   A Discourse, Embracing the Civil and Religious History of Rhode Island. Providence, 1838. 16mo., cloth, foxed, rebound. Saddleback 14-683 1974 $15

ROSS, BARNABY   Drury Lane's Last Case. New York, 1933. 1st ed. Biblo & Tannen 214-683 1974 $15

ROSS, BARNABY   The Tragedy of X. New York, 1932. 1st ed. Biblo & Tannen 214-692 1974 $7.50

ROSS, CHRISTIAN K.   The Father's Story of Charley Ross. Philadelphia, 1878. Illus., orig. binding, minimal edge wear. Wilson 63-96 1974 $12

ROSS, CHRISTIAN K.   The Father's Story of Charley Ross. Philadelphia, 1878. Cloth. Hayman 57-663 1974 $12.50

ROSS, DENMAN WALDO   On Drawing and Painting. Boston, c. 1912. Orig. binding, illus., bookplate. Wilson 63-301 1974 $10

ROSS, E. D.   The Booke of Freendeship of Marcus Tullie Cicero. (London, 1904). Orig. vellum, one of 150 numbered copies, woodcuts, bookplates, fine, printed in red & black. MacManus 224-153 1974 $75

ROSS, EDWARD A.   The Old World in the New. Century, 1914. 327p., illus., orig. ed. Austin 62-546 1974 $10

ROSS, EDWARD A.   The Old World in the New Century. Orig. edition. Austin 57-570 1974 $10

ROSS, ISHBEL   Through the Lich-Gate. Payson, 1931. Austin 51-802 1973 $7.50

ROSS, JOHN   History of Corea. n.d. 8vo., orig. cloth, plates. Broadhurst 23-1703 1974 £10

ROSS, JOHN   A Voyage of Discovery Made Under the Orders of the Admiralty in His Majesty's Ships Isabella and Alexander, for the Purpose of Exploring Baffin's Bay and Inquiring into the Probability of a North West Passage. 1819. 4to., contemporary diced calf, neatly rebacked, engraved plates, maps, charts, first edition. Bow Windows 66-589 1974 £85

ROSS, RONALD   Memoirs. London, 1923. Demy 8vo., orig. red cloth, plates. Covent 55-1095 1974 £6.50

ROSS, V.   A History of the Canadian Bank of Commerce, With an Account of the Other Banks Which Now Form Part of Its Organization. Toronto, 1920-34. 3 vols. Hood's 102-397 1974 $70

ROSS, W. A.   The Blowpipe in Chemistry, Mineralogy, and Geology. London, 1889. 8vo., cloth, gilt, illus., second edition. Hammond 201-942 1974 $8.50

ROSS, W. W.   10,000 Miles By Land and Sea. Toronto, 1876. Rebound, fabric. Hood's 103-821 1974 $17.50

ROSSELLIUS, COSMAS   Thesavrvs Artificiosae Memoria. 1579. 4to., 18th century half calf, fine. Dawsons PM 249-429 1974 £135

ROSSELLIUS, COSMAS   Thesaurus Artificiosae Memoriae. Venice, 1579. 4to., crushed purple morocco, gilt. Marlborough 70-7 1974 £195

ROSSETTI, CHRISTINA GEORGINA   The Family Letters of. 1908. Illus., orig. cloth, faded. Marsden 39-388 1974 £7

ROSSETTI, CHRISTINA GEORGINA   Goblin Market. London, 1933. No. 251 of edition limited to 410 signed copies, orig. tissue wrapper has 5 inch tear down front, very fine, illus. by Arthur Rackham. Ross 87-473 1974 $175

ROSSETTI, CHRISTINA GEORGINA   New Poems. 1900. Frontis., signed, first edition. Rota 188-808 1974 £6

ROSSETTI, CHRISTINA GEORGINA   Poems. 1930. 8vo., morocco backed marbled boards, gilt. Hammond 201-763 1974 £120

ROSSETTI, CHRISTINA GEORGINA   Poems of. 1930. 8vo., quarter calf, marbled boards, limited. Broadhurst 23-1041 1974 £75

ROSSETTI, CHRISTINA GEORGINA   Poems of. Greynog Press, 1930. Med. 8vo., quarter Hermitage calf, marbled boards, limited to 275 copies. Broadhurst 24-1008 1974 £75

ROSSETTI, CHRISTINA GEORGINA   Speaking Likenesses. London, 1874. 8vo., illus., inscription, label, orig. cloth, worn, first edition. Bow Windows 62-776 1974 £25

ROSSETTI, CHRISTINA GEORGINA   Time Flies. London, 1885. Inscription, very nice copy, first edition. Covent 51-1590 1973 £10.50

ROSSETTI, DANTE GABRIEL   Jenny. Wausau, 1899. Square 8vo., boards, English first edition. Covent 56-1104 1974 £30

ROSSETTI, DANTE GABRIEL   Poems. Leipzig, 1873. Presentation copy, inscribed from author, square 12mo., full mottled green calf, gilt panelled back, nice copy. Covent 51-3254 1973 £65

ROSSETTI, DANTE GABRIEL   Poetical Works Of. 1906. 2 vols. Austin 61-857 1974 $12.50

ROSSETTI, DANTE GABRIEL   Sonnets and Songs Towards a Work to be Called The House of Life. 1926. Wrappers, frontis. portrait, one of 200 numbered copies, very fine copy. Covent 51-1591 1973 £20

ROSSETTI, DONATO   Antignome Fisico-Matematiche. 1667. 4to., contemporary vellum, fine, first edition. Dawsons PM 245-645 1974 £52

ROSSETTI, DONATO   Cometa. (1681). 8vo., contemporary boards, fine, uncut. Zeitlin 235-192 1974 $150

ROSSETTI, DONATO   Composizione. 1671. 4to., contemporary vellum, fine, illus., first edition. Dawsons PM 245-647 1974 £80

ROSSETTI, DONATO   Insegnamenti Fisico Matematici del Dot. 1669. 4to., contemporary paper boards, rebacked, illus., first edition. Dawsons PM 245-646 1974 £55

ROSSETTI, WILLIAM MICHAEL   Dante Gabriel Rossetti. N.P., 1906. 12mo., orig. wrappers, signed, fine, first edition. Ximenes 35-78 1974 $150

ROSSETTI, WILLIAM MICHAEL   Rossetti: Preraphaelitism. 1899. Dec. cloth gilt, plates, scarce. Marsden 39-392 1974 £10.50

ROSSETTI, WILLIAM MICHAEL   Rossetti: Preraphaelitism. 1899. Plates, dec. cloth gilt, handmade paper, soiled. Marsden 39-393 1974 £30

ROSSI, GAETANO   Soluzione Esatta e Regolare del Difficilissimo Problema Della Quadratura del Circolo. 1804. 8vo., modern boards, first edition. Dawsons PM 245-648 1974 £10

ROSSINI, LUIGI   Le Antichita Romane. Rome, 1829. Large oblong folio, nineteenth century green morocco gilt, plates. Dawsons PM 251-98 1974 £1,350

ROSSINI, LUIGI   Le Antichita Romane. Rome, 1829-. Large folio, orig. half morocco, plates. Broadhurst 23-182 1974 £700

ROSSINI, LUIGI   Scenografia degl'interni delle Piu Belle Chiese e Basiliche. Rome, 1843 and 1850. Folio, orig. cloth. Broadhurst 23-183 1974 £200

ROSSLIN, EUCHARIUS   De Partu Hominis. Frankfurt, 1551. Small 8vo., 19th century half leather. Schuman 37-223 1974 $650

ROSTAFINSKI, J.   Uber Botrydium Granulatum. Leipzig, 1877. 4to., boards, plates. Wheldon 130-1344 1974 £5

ROSTAND, EDMOND   L'Aiglon. Russell, 1900. Austin 51-806 1973 $7.50

ROSTAND, EDMOND   Cyrano de Bergerac. Holt, 1928. Austin 51-805 1973 $7.50

ROSTAND, EDMOND   Cyrano de Bergerac. Mt. Vernon, 1941. Ltd. ed. Biblo & Tannen 210-788 1973 $7.50

ROSTAND, EDMOND   Le Vol de la Marseillaise. Paris, 1919. 8vo., three quarter tobacco brown levant morocco, gilt, fine, first edition. L. Goldschmidt 42-357 1974 $45

ROSTEN, LEO C.   Hollywood. Harcourt, Brace, 1941. 436p., orig. ed. Austin 51-807 1973 $10

ROSTREVOR-HAMILTON, G.   The Trumpeter of St. George. 1941. First edition, 8vo., orig. printed wrappers, engraving by Stephen Gooden, signature of Winston Churchill inside front cover, mint copy. Sawyer 293-154 1974 £35

ROSTRUP, E.   Danish Fungi. Copenhagen, 1913. Roy 8vo., buckram, portraits, plates. Wheldon 129-1332 1974 £15

ROTH, A. W.   Catalecta Botanica. Leipzig, 1797-1800.
2 vols., 8vo., contemporary wrappers, uncut, rare, engraved plates. Wheldon
128-1157 1973 £20

ROTH, ALFRED   Zwei Wohnhauser von Le Corbusier und Pierre
Jeannaret. Stuttgart, 1927. Large 4to., wrappers. Minters 37-566 1973 $60

ROTH, H. L.   A Guide to the Literature of Sugar. 1890.
8vo., cloth. Wheldon 130-190 1974 £5

ROTH, H. L.   Notes on Continental Irrigation. 1882. 8vo.,
orig. cloth, plates. Broadhurst 23-1704 1974 £5

ROTH, H. L.   Notes on Continental Irrigation. 1882. Med.
8vo., plates, orig. cloth, fine, presentation copy inscribed by author, loosely
inserted A.L.s. from author. Broadhurst 24-1670 1974 £5

ROTH, H. LING   The Yorkshire Coiners. Halifax, 1906. 4to.,
illus., cloth. Quaritch 939-604 1974 £15

ROTHA, PAUL   The Film Till Now. 1930. Plates, English first
edition. Covent 56-240 1974 £7.50

ROTHA, PAUL   Movie Parade. 1934. Austin 51-808 1973
$12.50

ROTHENSTEIN, J.   The Portrait Drawings Of. 1926. Roy 4to.,
orig. cloth, plates. Broadhurst 23-184 1974 £10

ROTHA, PAUL   Movie Parade--1888-1949. Studio, 1950.
Austin 51-809 1973 $12.50

ROTHENSTEIN, JOHN   Augustus John. London, 1945. 4to., illus.
Jacobs 24-54 1974 $10

ROTHENSTEIN, JOHN   The Life and Death of Conder. 1938. Orig.
cloth, plates. Marsden 39-86 1974 £6

ROTHENSTEIN, WILLIAM   Men and Memories, 1872-1900. 1931. Illus.
Austin 61-858 1974 $10

ROTHENSTEIN, WILLIAM   Men and Memories. 1939. 3 vols., first
editions. Marsden 37-412 1974 £15

ROTHENSTEIN, WILLIAM   A Plea for a Wider Use of Artists and Craftsmen.
c. 1917. First edition, cloth backed boards, very good copy, scarce. Covent
51-133 1973 £6.30

ROTHENSTEIN, WILLIAM   Twenty-four Portraits By William Rothenstein.
London, 1923. 4to., boards, cloth spine, plates. Minters 37-163 1973 $11

ROTHER, W. O.   Prakstischer Leitfaden fur die Anzucht und
Pflege der Kakteen mit Besonderer Berucksichtigung der Phyliokakteen. Frankfurt,
1902. 8vo., cloth. Wheldon 131-1689 1974 £5

ROTHERAM, JOHN   A Philosophical Inquiry into the Nature and Properties of Water. Newcastle, (1770). 8vo., cloth, first edition. Hammond
201-589 1974 £7.50

ROTHERT, OTTO A.   Story of a Poet: His Intimate Life. 1921.
Allen 216-321 1974 $15

ROTHFELD, OTTO   Umar Khayyam and His Age. 1922. Quarter
buckram, dust-marked. Covent 55-1160 1974 £7.50

ROTHSCHILD, FREIHERR CAR VON   Freiherrlich Carl von Rothschild'sche
Oeffentliche Bibliothek. Frankfurt a.M., 1899-1904. Vol. 2, wrappers.
Kraus B8-239 1974 $20

ROTHSCHILD, J.   Les Plantes a Feuillage Colorie. Paris, 1865.
Roy. 8vo., half morocco, coloured plates. Wheldon 128-1531 1973 £10

ROTHSCHILD, LIONEL WALTER   The Avifauna of Laysan and the Neighbouring
Islands. 1893-1900. 3 parts in 2 vols., folio, new half red morocco gilt,
plates, limited, rare. Wheldon 131-101 1974 £475

ROTHSCHILD, W.   The Avifauna of Laysan and the Neighbouring
Islands. 1893-1900. Folio, new half red morocco. Wheldon 129-39 1974
£475

ROTHSCHILD, W.   A Revision of the Lepidopterous Family
Sphingidae. Tring, 1903. 2 vols., imp. 8vo., new buckram, coloured and
plain plates, folding tables, very scarce. Wheldon 128-789 1973 £45

ROTULI Hundredorum Temp. 1812-18. 2 vols., folio, orig. boards, uncut,
rebacked, maroon leather, scarce. Howes 186-1155 1974 £65

ROTULI Parliamentorum. (1783). 6 vols., folio, half russia. Quaritch
939-13 1974 £175

ROTULI Scotiae in Turri Londinensi et in Domo Capitulari Westmonasteriensi
Asservati. 1814-19. 2 vols., folio, cloth back. Quaritch 939-20 1974 £35

ROTULORUM Patentium et Clausorum Cancellariae Hiberniae Calendarium.
1828. Folio, cloth, scarce. Howes 186-1157 1974 £20

ROUCEL, F.   Flore du Nord de la France ou Description des
Plantes Indigenes et de Celles Cultivees dans les Departments de la Lys. Paris,
1803. 2 vols., 8vo., half calf, scarce. Wheldon 128-1306 1973 £10

ROUCEL, F.   Flore du Nord de la France ou Description
des Plantes Indigenes et de Celles Cultivees dans les Departments de la Lys.
Paris, 1803. 2 vols., 8vo., half calf, scarce. Wheldon 131-1352 1974 £15

ROUGHHEAD, W.   Knave's Looking-Glass. London, 1935. 1st
ed. Biblo & Tannen 210-516 1973 $10

ROULAND, N.   Tableau Historique des Proprietes. Paris, 1784.
8vo., contemporary calf. Gurney 64-190 1974 £30

ROULE, L.   Les Poissons. Paris, 1926-37. Roy 8vo., 9
vols., wrappers, illus. Wheldon 129-589 1974 £30

ROULE, L.   Les Poissons et le Monde Vivant des Eaux.
Paris, 1926-37. 9 vols., roy. 8vo., wrappers. Wheldon 131-767 1974 £30

ROULEX, J.   Choix de Vases Peints du Musee d'Antiquites
de Leide. 1854. Folio, plates, loose in board portfolio, cloth spine.
Quaritch 940-352 1974 £20

ROUND, JOHN HORACE   Family Origins and Other Studies. 1930.
8vo., portrait, cloth. Quaritch 939-742 1974 £6.50

ROUND, JOHN HORACE   Peerage and Pedigree. London, 1910. 8vo.,
2 vols., orig. buckram, gilt, first edition. Hammond 201-443 1974 £12

ROUND, JOHN HORACE   Studies In Peerage & Family History. 1901.
Worn spine. Allen 213-1752 1973 $10

ROUND, JOHN HORACE   Studies in Peerage and Family History. Westminster, 1901. 8vo., orig. cloth, gilt, first edition. Hammond 201-444 1974 £8

ROUQUETTE, L. F.   The Great White Silence. New York, 1930.
Hood's 103-505 1974 $20

ROUS, GEORGE   A Letter to the Right Honourable Edmund Burke.
London, n.d. 8vo., modern boards, second edition. Dawsons PM 247-252
1974 £15

ROUS, GEORGE   Thoughts on Government. London, 1790.
8vo., modern boards, third edition. Dawsons PM 247-251 1974 £15

ROUS, W.   Vortrage und Aufsatze Uber
Entwickelungsmechanik der Organismen. Leipzig, 1908-20. 23 parts, 8vo.,
orig. wrappers. Wheldon 131-454 1974 £35

ROUSSEAU, JEAN-JACQUES   The Confessions of Jean Jacques Rousseau.
1901. 8vo., 2 vols., orig. cloth. Bow Windows 64-668 1974 £5.50

ROUSSEAU, JEAN-JACQUES   The Confessions. 1904. 2 vols., buckram,
unopened, English first edition. Covent 56-1108 1974 £10

ROUSSEAU, JEAN-JACQUES   Les Confessions. Paris, 1927. Ltd. ed.
Biblo & Tannen 213-594 1973 $15

ROUSSEAU, JEAN-JACQUES   The Confessions Of. 1938. Crown 8vo., full
niger morocco, 2 vols., uncut, limited edition. Broadhurst 23-1080 1974 £30

ROUSSEAU, JEAN JACQUES   Dictionnaire de Musique. Paris, 1775. 2 vols.,
8vo., plates, contemporary calf, gilt, leather labels, rubbed. Quaritch
940-824 1974 £38

ROUSSEAU, JEAN-JACQUES   Discours sur l'Origine et les Fondemens de
l'Inegalite Parmi les Hommes. Amsterdam, 1755. 8vo., contemporary calf,
gilt, frontispiece, very fine, first edition, first issue. Gilhofer 61-21 1974
sFr. 800

ROUSSEAU, JEAN JACQUES   Emile, ou de l'Education. (Paris), 1762.
4 vols., 8vo., engraved plates, contemporary mottled calf, gilt fillets, richly gilt
back, morocco title labels, very fine, complete copy, genuine first edition.
Schafer 10-148 1974 sFr 2,800

ROUSSEAU, NORBERT   L'Ecole Gregorienne de Solesmes, 1833-1910.
Rome, 1910. Quarter roan, plates. Howes 185-1482 1974 £5

ROUSSET DE MISSY, JEAN   The History of Cardinal Alberoni. London,
1719. 8vo., contemporary sheep, gilt, first edition. Dawsons PM 251-133
1974 £10

ROUTH, E. J.   A Treatise on Dynamics of a Particle. 1898.
8vo., orig. green cloth, gilt, first edition. Dawsons PM 245-649 1974 £8

ROUTHIER, A. B.   Quebec. Montreal, 1904. Illus., faded.
Hood's 103-786 1974 $22.50

ROUTLEDGE, ROBERT   A Popular History of Science. London, 1894.
Crown 8vo., orig. cloth, gilt, illus., third edition. Covent 55-1325 1974
£6.50

ROUVEYRE, EDOUARD   Comment Apprecier les Croquis, Esquisses,
Etudes, Dessins, Tableaux, Aquarelles, Pastels, Miniatures. Paris, 1911. Tall
8vo., wrapper, illus. Minters 37-254 1973 $24

ROUY, G.   Flore de France. Paris, 1893-1910. Vols.
1-12, 8vo., buckram. Wheldon 128-1307 1973 £65

ROUY, G.   Flore de France. Paris, 1893-1910. 8vo.,
buckram. Wheldon 130-1206 1974 £65

ROUY, G.   Revue de Botanique Systematique et de
Geographie Botanique. 1903-05. Vols. 1 and 2 in 1 vol., roy. 8vo., buckram,
scarce. Wheldon 128-1156 1973 £10

THE ROXBURGHE CLUB   Its History and Its Members. Oxford, 1928.
4to., quarter roan, plates. Dawsons PM 10-524 1974 £70

ROW, J.   Hebraica. Glasgow, 1644. 2 vols. in 1,
12mo., vellum, worn, soiled. Thomas 28-163 1972 £10.50

ROWE, ELIZABETH   Friendship in Death. (n.d.). 12mo., 18th
century sheep, joints cracked, some damp stains. Bow Windows 66-592 1974
£12

ROWE, ELIZABETH   Friendship in Death. 1793. 12mo., joints
cracked, contemporary sheep, worn. Bow Windows 66-591 1974 £9

ROWE, N.   The Tragedy of Jane Shore. (1714). 4to., cloth,
first edition. Quaritch 936-210 1974 £30

ROWE, NICHOLAS   A Poem. London, 1707. Folio, disbound,
foxing, inscribed, first edition. Ximenes 35-80 1974 $90

ROWE, NICHOLAS   Tamerlane. London, 1714. 12mo., modern
boards, uncut, third edition. Dawsons PM 252-838 1974 £7

ROWE, NICHOLAS   The Tragedy of Jane Shore. London, (n.d.).
4to., modern boards, first edition. Dawsons PM 252-839 1974 £60

ROWE, NICHOLAS   Ulysses. London, 1706. Small 4to.,
disbound, first edition. Ximenes 35-81 1974 $50

ROWE, RICHARD   Peter 'Possum's Portfolio. Sydney, 1858.
8vo., orig. cloth, first edition. Ximenes 35-82 1974 $45

ROWELL, HOPKINS   The Great Resources, and Superior Advantages
of the City of Joliet, Illinois. Joliet, 1871. Brown printed wrappers, fine,
scarce. Bradley 35-185 1974 $60

ROWLAND, ERON   Varina Howell, Wife of Jefferson Davis. New
York, 1927-31. 2 vols., first editions, orig. binding. Butterfield 10-183 1974
$10

ROWLAND, HELEN   Reflections of a Bachelor Girl. Dodge, 1909.
n.p. Austin 54-876 1973 $6

ROWLANDS, H.   Mona Antiqua Restaurata. Dublin, 1723.
4to., plates, contemporary mottled calf gilt, first edition. Quaritch 939-691
1974 £35

ROWLANDS, H.   Mona Antiqua Restaurata. 1766. 4to., old
calf, plates, second edition. Quaritch 939-692 1974 £40

ROWLANDS, RICHARD PSEUD.
Please turn to
VERSTEGEN, RICHARD FL. 1565-1620

ROWLANDS, SAMUEL   The Complete Works. (Glasgow), 1880.
3 vols., 4to., illus., contemporary half morocco, fine, first collected edition.
Dawsons PM 252-840 1974 £100

ROWLANDS, W.   Cambrian Bibliography. 1869. 8vo., orig.
cloth. Broadhurst 23-1536 1974 £8

ROWLANDS, W.   Cambrian Bibliography. 1869. 8vo., cloth.
Quaritch 939-693 1974 £8.75

ROWLANDSON, T.   Chesterfield Travestie. 1808. Small 8vo.,
plates, contemporary calf, worn. Quaritch 939-848 1974 £60

ROWLANDSON, T.   The Pleasures of Human Life. 1817. 8vo.,
boards, plates, second edition. Quaritch 936-536 1974 £30

ROWLANDSON, THOMAS   Hungarian and Highland Broad Sword. (London),
1799. Oblong folio, half blue morocco. Marlborough 70-27 1974 £195

ROWLANDSON, THOMAS   The Watercolor Drawings of. New York, 1947.
4to., color plates. Biblo & Tannen 214-120 1974 $27.50

ROWLEY, HUGH   Gamosagammon. London, n.d. 8vo., orig.
green cloth, worn, illus., first edition. Ximenes 35-84 1974 $10

ROWLEY, RICHARD   Workers. 1923. Roy. 8vo., orig. yellow
cloth backed boards, uncut, limited, first edition. Howes 185-407 1974 £7.50

ROWLEY, WILLIAM   A Practical Treatise on the Diseases of the Breasts.
London, 1777. 8vo., boards, second edition. Gurney 64-191 1974 £16

ROWSON, SUSANNA   Charlotte Temple. Philadelphia, 1797.
2 vols. in 1, 12mo., contemporary sheep, fine, third American edition. Ximenes
35-85 1974 $150

ROWSON, SUSANNA   Charlotte Temple. Concord, 1815. 2 vols.
in 1, 12mo., contemporary sheep. Ximenes 35-86 1974 $20

ROWSON, SUSANNA   Charlotte Temple. London, 1832. 12mo.,
later half calf, plates, frontispiece. Ximenes 35-87 1974 $15

ROWSON, SUSANNA   Sarah. Boston, 1813. 24mo., contemporary
calf, first edition. Ximenes 35-88 1974 $150

ROWZEE, LODWICK   The Qveenes Welles. London, 1632. Small
8vo., contemporary calf gilt, good copy, first edition. Traylen 79-266 1973
£95

ROY, CAMILLE   L'Universite Laval et les Fetes du Cinquantenaire.
Quebec, 1903. Wrappers neatly mended. Hood's 102-739 1974 $10

ROY. E.   Liste Alphabetique des Pretes Seculiers et
Reguliers des Seminaristes . . . . College de Levis. Levis, 1945. Hood's
104-53 1974 $10

ROY, GEORGE   Generalship. Cincinnati, 1875. Cloth. Hayman 57-218 1974 $10

ROY, J.   History of Canada for the Use of Schools and Families. Montreal, 1847. Hood's 102-428 1974 $25

ROY, P. G.   L'Ile d'Orlenas. Quebec, 1928. Coloured illus., orig. coloured card cover, English edition. Hood's 102-164 1974 $35

ROY, P. G.   Old Manors, Old Houses. Quebec, 1927. Profusely illus., card cover. Hood's 102-165 1974 $60

ROY, P. G.   Old Manors, Old Houses. Quebec, 1927. Illus., worn. Hood's 104-177 1974 $60

ROY., P. G.   La Ville de Quebec Sous le Regime Francais. Quebec, 1930. 2 vols., wrappers, illus. Hood's 103-787 1974 $50

ROY, W.   The Military Antiquities of the Romans in Britain. 1793. Folio, modern half calf. Quaritch 939-227 1974 £50

ROYAL ACADEMY   A Commemorative Catalogue of Italian Art Held in the Galleries of the Royal Academy, Burlington House. Oxford, 1931. Super roy. 4to., uncut, frontispiece in colour, plain plates, orig. cloth, fine. Broadhurst 24-35 1974 £10

ROYAL AGRICULTURAL SOCIETY OF ENGLAND   Journal. 1840-66. 27 vols., 8vo., plates, half calf, uncut. Howes 186-1564 1974 £95

ROYAL AGRICULTURAL SOCIETY OF ENGLAND   Journal Of. 1843. Contemporary half calf, rubbed, plates. Smith 194-14 1974 £10

ROYAL COLLEGE OF PHYSICIANS, LONDON   The Dispensatory of the . . . London, 1760. 8vo., contemporary calf, fourth edition. Schuman 37-224 1974 $65

ROYAL Commission on Agriculture Official Reports. 1880-82. 5 vols., thick folio, half calf, morocco labels. Howes 186-1565 1974 £95

THE ROYAL Commission on Ancient and Historical Monuments and Constructions of Scotland, Ninth Report, with Inventory of . . . in the Outer Hebrides, Skye and the Small Isles. Edinburgh, 1928. 4to., orig. cloth, maps, plates. Bow Windows 66-346 1974 £15

ROYAL Commission on Divorce and Matrimonial Causes. 1912. 5 vols., folio, cloth. Howes 186-1398 1974 £42

ROYAL Commission on Local Taxation. 1899. Folio, orig. wrappers. Howes 186-1495 1974 £5

ROYAL Commission on Poor Laws & Relief of Distress Report. 1909-10. 10 vols., folio & 8vo., orig. wrappers, cloth. Howes 186-1542 1974 £45

ROYAL ENTOMOLOGICAL SOCIETY OF LONDON, COMMITTEE ON GENERIC NOMENCLATURE   Generic Names of British Insects. 1934-49. Roy. 8vo., 9 parts, wrappers. Wheldon 131-809 1974 £5

ROYAL Historical Monuments Commission. 1925. 4to., plates, map, 215 pages. Howes 186-2117 1974 £7.50

ROYAL HORTICULTURAL SOCIETY   Conifer Conference Report, 1891. 1892. 8vo., cloth. Wheldon 131-1722 1974 £5

ROYAL HORTICULTURAL SOCIETY   Pear Conference. 1887. 8vo., cloth. Wheldon 131-1562 1974 £5

ROYAL HORTICULTURAL SOCIETY   Tree Conference: British-Grown Fruit. 1895. 8vo., cloth. Wheldon 131-1583 1974 £5

THE ROYAL Marriage, A Ballad-Opera of Three Acts. London, 1736. 8vo., modern cloth, first edition. Ximenes 37-15 1974 $125

ROYAL MEDICAL AND CHIRURGICAL SOCIETY   Catalogue of the Library. London, 1879. 3 vols., 8vo., orig. green blind-stamped cloth, plates. Dawsons PM 10-526 1974 £22

ROYAL MILITARY ACADEMY   Records. Woolwich, 1851. Imp. 4to., contemporary half red morocco, panelled back, coloured lithographs, fine. Broadhurst 24-814 1974 £60

THE ROYAL Natural History. 1893-96. 6 vols., roy. 8vo., half leather, plates, engravings. Wheldon 131-455 1974 £15

ROYAL SOCIETY   The Signatures In the First Journal-Book and the Charter-Book, Being a Facsimile of the Signatures of the Founders, Patrons and Fellows of the Society from the Year 1660. 1936. Folio, orig. half buckram, soiled. Wheldon 131-246 1974 £7.50

ROYAL SOCIETY OF EDINBURGH   Proceedings, 1890-1922. Edinburgh, 1891-1922. 25 vols., 8vo., roy. 8vo., in parts as issued. Wheldon 131-178 1974 £50

ROYAL SOCIETY OF EDINBURGH   Proceedings, a Series from 1890-1922. Edinburgh, 1891-1922. 25 vols., 8vo. and roy. 8vo., in parts as issued. Wheldon 128-61 1973 £50

ROYCE, JOSIAH   California from the Conquest. New York, 1886. Brown cloth, gilt, first edition. Bradley 35-49 1974 $30

ROYCE, JOSIAH   The Problem of Christianity. 1913. 2 vols., 8vo., orig. edition. Howes 185-1614 1974 £5

ROYCE, JOSIAH   The World and the Individual. New York, 1900. 1st ed. Author's sgd. pres. Biblo & Tannen 213-991 1973 $47.50

ROYZIUS, PETRUS   Inclyto Quiritium Regi Ferdinando in Divae Coniugis Annae Obitu. Prague, 1547. Small 4to., half vellum, rare. Schafer 8-138 1973 sFr. 600

ROZANOV, V. V.   Fallen Leaves. 1929. One of 750 numbered copies, gilt top, nice copy, first edition. Covent 51-1628 1973 £5.25

ROZEMBERGH, A.   Catalogue de l'Exposition de Ceramiques Russes Anciennes. 1929. 8vo., orig. illus. wrappers, illus. Bow Windows 66-594 1974 £6.50

ROZIER, F.   Cours Complet d'Agriculture, Theorique, Pratique, Economique, et de Medecine Rurale et Veterinaire. Paris, 1781-1805. 4to., 12 vols., old quarter calf, plates, good set. Gurney 66-158 1974 £150

RUBEL, E.   Pflanzengesellschaften der Erde. Bern-Berlin, 1930. Roy 8vo., half leather cloth. Wheldon 129-956 1974 £12.50

RUBEL, EDITH   The Merry Muse. New York, (1937). 4to., pictorial boards, cloth spine, illus., first edition, signed by author & illus. Frohnsdorff 16-543 1974 $10

RUBENS, PETER PAUL   His Life, His Work and His Time. 1899. 2 vols., 4to., plates, illus., orig. cloth. Quaritch 940-229 1974 £15

RUBENS, PETER PAUL   Rubens. (Vienna, 1938). Roy. 8vo., worn, plates, buckram. Quaritch 940-230 1974 £10

RUDD, HELEN   Catalogue of the Aldenham Library. Letchworth, 1914. 4to., orig. cloth, fine, third edition. Dawsons PM 10-530 1974 £70

RUDD, MARGARET CAROLINE   Facts. London, (n.d.). 8vo. modern boards, foxed. Dawsons PM 252-841 1974 £12

RUDDER, S.   A New History of Gloucestershire. Cirencester, 1779. Folio, plates, fine, modern levant morocco. Quaritch 939-365 1974 £190

RUDING, WALT   An Evil Motherhood. 1896. Orig. dec. cloth, English first edition. Covent 56-1548 1974 £65

RUDINGER, NICOLAUS   Topographisch-Chirurgische Anatomie des Menschen. Stuttgart, 1873-78. Thick large 8vo., contemporary half leather, first edition. Schumann 35-415 1974 $110

RUE, HARALD   Aksel Jorgensens Tegninger. Copenhagen, 1942. 4to., cloth spine, drawings. Minters 37-221 1973 $10

RUEFF, JACOB   De Conceptu et Generatione Hominis.
Frankfurt am Main, 1580. 4to., vellum, second Latin edition, very good copy.
Gurney 66-159 1974 £525

RUEL, J.   De Natura Stirpium libri Tres. Basel, 1537.
Folio, 18th century calf gilt. Wheldon 129-957 1974 £275

RUEL, J.   De Natura Stirpium Libri Tres. Basel, 1537.
Folio, 18th century calf gilt, rubbed, second edition. Wheldon 131-1193
1974 £275

RUFFINI, JOHN   The Paragreens on a Visit. Edinburgh, 1856.
8vo., orig. blue cloth, plates, first edition. Ximenes 35-89 1974 $25

RUFFNER, W. H.   A Report on Washington Territory. New York,
1889. Folding map, cloth. Jenkins 61-2587 1974 $15

RUGG, H. HODSON   Observations on London Milk. London, n.d.
12mo., orig. printed wrappers, second edition. Ximenes 35-90 1974 $15

RUGGIERI, F.   Studio d'Architettura Civile. Florence, 1722-24.
2 vols. in 1, folio, contemporary calf, worn, large crisp clean copy, plates.
Quaritch 940-550 1974 £120

RUGGLE, GEORGE   Ignoramus. 1630. 8vo., contemporary vellum,
has 3 last blank leaves, inner margins wormed, engraved frontispiece. Thomas
32-189 1974 £35

RUGGLE, GEORGE   Ignoramus. Londini, 1630. 12mo., gilt,
contemporary mottled calf, first edition. Dawsons PM 252-842 1974 £110

RUHNKENIUS, DAVID   Opuscula Ruhnkeniana. London, 1807. 8vo.,
red morocco with gilt fillets, richly gilt tooled spine. Schumann 499-100 1974
sFr 85

RULE, MARTIN   The Life and Times of St. Anselm. 1883.
2 vols., orig. cloth. Howes 185-920 1974 £8

RULE, MARTIN   The Missal of St. Augustine's Abbey. 1896.
Roy. 8vo., plates, scarce. Howes 186-2059 1974 £16.50

RULES and Regulations for the Control and Management of the Financial
Department of the Constabulary Force of Ireland. Dublin, 1837. 12mo., orig.
cloth, fine, first edition. Ximenes 33-327 1974 $22.50

RULES and Regulations for the Sword Exercise of the Cavalry; to which is added,
The Review Exercise. Boston, n.d. (1802). First American edition, engraved
plates. Ximenes 36-149 1974 $70

THE RULES and Regulations of the Franklin Fire Society, Instituted at Boston,
March 21, 1792. Boston, 1792. 12mo., unbound. Gurney 66-160 1974 £8

RULES for the Management and Cleaning of the Rifle Musket, Model 1863.
Washington, 1863. 12mo., text illus., covers soiled, interior bit browned with
age, else fine, scarce. Current BW9-355 1974 $27.50

RULES, Orders, and Forms of Proceedings of the House of Commons of Canada.
Ottawa, 1868. Bi-lingual. Hood's 104-607 1974 $40

RULHIERE, CLAUDE C. DE   Histoire, ou Anecdotes sur la Revolution de Russie. Paris, 1797. 8vo., contemporary calf, gilt, first edition. Hammond 201-
461 1974 £18

RUMFORD, SIR BENJAMIN THOMPSON, COUNT   An Enquiry Concerning the
Nature of Heat, and the Mode of Its Communication. London, 1804. 4to.,
boards, plates. Gurney 66-161 1974 £35

RUMFORD, BENJAMIN THOMPSON, COUNT   Essays. London, 1796. 8vo.,
fine, orig. boards, uncut, first edition. Dawsons PM 247-253 1974 £15

RUMFORD, SIR BENJAMIN THOMPSON, COUNT   Essays, Political, Economical
and Philosophical. London, 1800-02. 8vo., 3 vols., old calf, worn. Gurney
66-162 1974 £35

RUMFORD, BENJAMIN THOMPSON, COUNT   Experimental Essays. Dublin,
1796. Boards, plates, third edition. Hammond 201-270 1974 £28.50

RUMFORD, SIR BENJAMIN THOMPSON, COUNT   Philosophical Papers.
Together with Letters to Several Persons on Subjects Connected with Science and
Useful Improvement. Vol. 1. London, 1802. 8vo., old calf, worn, folding
plates, first edition. Gurney 66-163 1974 £35

RUMFORD, BENJAMIN THOMPSON, COUNT   The Complete Works. Boston,
1870 (-1875). Orig. green cloth gilt, 4 vols., illus. Dawsons PM 245-650
1974 £50

RUMILLY, R.   Sir Wilfrid Laurier. Paris, 1931. Card cover,
pages yellowed. Hood's 102-258 1974 $10

RUMPF, G. E.   Herbarium Amboinense. Amsterdam, 1741-55.
Folio, contemporary mottled paper boards, plates. Wheldon 130-67 1974 £1,000

RUMPF, G. E.   Herbarium Amboinense. Amsterdam, 1747-55.
7 vols., folio, contemporary mottled paper boards, engraved plates, complete
copy, rare. Wheldon 128-1308 1973 £1,000

RUMPLER, T.   Die Sukkulenten. Berlin, 1892. 8vo., cloth.
Wheldon 131-1691 1974 £7.50

RUNDELL, MARIA ELIZA   A New System of Domestic Cookery. London,
1811. 8vo., boards, plates, new edition. Hammond 201-174 1974 £30

RUNDELL, MARIA ELIZA   A New System of Domestic Cookery. 1815.
8vo., plates, rebacked, new edition. Quaritch 939-228 1974 £37.50

RUNDELL, MARIA ELIZA   A New System of Domestic Cookery. London,
1818. 8vo., cloth, plates, new edition. Hammond 201-175 1974 £25

RUNDELL, MARIA ELIZABETH   A New System of Domestic Cookery. Halifax,
1860. Orig. cloth, plates, rebacked. Covent 55-696 1974 £8.50

RUNTING, E. G. V.   Practical Chiropody. St. Louis, 1927. Second
edition. Rittenhouse 46-570 1974 $10

RUNYON, DAMON   Omnibus: Guys and Dolls, Money from Home,
and Blue Plate Special. Sun Dial, 1944. 505p. Austin 54-877 1973 $8.50

RUNYON, DAMON   Runyon a la Carte. Lippincott. 192p.
Austin 54-878 1973 $6.50

RUNYON, DAMON   Short Tales. Somerset, 1946. 435p. Austin
54-879 1973 $7.50

RUNYON, DAMON   Trials and Other Tribulations. Lippincott,
1947. 285p. Austin 54-880 1973 $8.50

RUPERT OF DEUTZ   De Divinis Officiis Libri XII. Cologne, 1526.
First edition, woodcut device on title by Woensam, wormholes, else excellent,
folio, modern old style calf. Thomas 32-260 1974 £100

RUBERT OF DEUTZ   In XII. Prophetas Minores, Commentariorum
Libri XXXII. (Cologne), 1527. First edition, folio, modern old style calf.
Thomas 32-261 1974 £100

RUPP, FREDERICK A.   John Montcalm, Heretic. Reading, 1908.
Rittenhouse 46-571 1974 $10

RUPP, I. DANIEL   A Collection of Thirty Thousand Names of
Immigrants in Pennsylvania. 1856. Rebacked, orig. edition. Austin 57-572
1974 $95

RUPP, I. DANIEL   History of Lancaster County. Lancaster, 1844.
8vo., orig. bindings, first edition. Butterfield 8-508 1974 $40

RUPP, I. DANIEL   History of Northampton, Lehigh, Monroe,
Carbon and Schuykill Counties, Pennsylvania. Harrisburg, 1845. Ballinger
1-305 1974 $40

RUPP, I. DANIEL   History of the Counties of Berks and Lebanon.
Lancaster, 1844. 8vo., orig. bindings, first edition. Butterfield 8-507 1974
$60

RUPPIN, ARTHUR   Der Aufbau des Landes Israel. Berlin, 1919.
Austin 62-551 1974 $27.50

RUSCELLI, GIROLAMO   Precetti Della Militia Moderna. 1583. Small 4to., woodcuts, modern boards. Zeitlin 235-193 1974 $75

RUSCHENBERGER, W. S. W.   Elements of Conchology. Philadelphia, 1844. Leather-backed boards, first edition. Hayman 57-664 1974 $10

RUSCONI, G. A.   I Dieci Libri d'Architettura di Gio: Antonio Rusconi. Venice, 1660. Folio, old dark morocco, gilt, clean crisp copy, second edition. Quaritch 940-551 1974 £185

RUSH, BENJAMIN   Essays. Philadelphia, 1806. Crown 8vo., full antique mottled calf. Broadhurst 23-1266 1974 £40

RUSH, BENJAMIN   Essays, Literary, Moral and Philosophical. Philadelphia, 1806. Second edition with additions, crown 8vo., newly bound full antique mottled calf, panelled back, leather labe, tooled blind on covers, fine. Broadhurst 24-1295 1974 £40

RUSH, JAMES   Philosophy of the Human Voice. Lippincott, 1855. Austin 51-812 1973 $17.50

RUSH, RICHARD   Memoranda of a Residence at the Court of London . . . From 1819 to 1825, Including the Negotiations on the Oregon Question. Philadelphia, 1845. Three quarter calf, first edition. Jenkins 61-2303 1974 $20

RUSINOL, SANTIAGO   Jardins d'Espanya. Barcelona, 1903. Folio, three quarter leather, rubbed, plates. Minters 37-256 1973 $35

RUSINOL, SANTIAGO   Jardins d'Espanya. (Barcelona, 1914). Small folio, portfolio, plates. Wheldon 129-1528 1974 £5

RUSKAY, SOPHIE   Horsecars and Cobblestones. 1948. 240p., illus. Austin 62-552 1974 $10

RUSKIN, JOHN   Ariadne Florentina. 1873-76. 6 vols. and appx., sewn, wood and metal engravings. Allen 216-1541 1974 $15

RUSKIN, JOHN   The Art of England: Lectures Fiven at Oxford. 1887. Second edition, full vellum, spine & sides panelled in gilt, gilt top, morocco labels, very nice copy. Covent 51-1602 1973 £8.50

RUSKIN, JOHN   Cambridge School of Art: Mr. Ruskin's Inaugural Address. Cambridge, 1858. Nice copy, scarce, first edition. Covent 51-1606 1973 £12.50

RUSKIN, JOHN   The Crown of Wild Olive. London, 1866. 8vo., orig. cloth gilt, inscription presentation, second edition. Dawsons PM 247-254 1974 £30

RUSKIN, JOHN   The Ethics of the Dust. London, 1866. 8vo., orig. violet cloth, foxed, first edition. Ximenes 35-91 1974 $15

RUSKIN, JOHN   Introduction to "German Popular Stories". n.d. Plates, nice copy, front hinge weak, ads at end. Covent 51-1612 1973 £8.40

RUSKIN, JOHN   The King of the Golden River. 1932. Roy 8vo., full limp vellum, signed, limited edition. Broadhurst 23-166 1974 £70

RUSKIN, JOHN   The King of the Golden River. London, 1932. No. 90 of edition limited to 575 signed copies, covers slightly yellowed around the edges, box somewhat darkened, near mint, orig. tissue wrapper, illus. by Arthur Rackham. Ross 87-474 1974 $150

RUSKIN, JOHN   The King of the Golden River; or, the Black Brothers: A Legend of Stiria. London, 1851. 4to., orig. glazed boards, illus. by Richard Doyle, rubbed, internally fine. MacManus 224-382 1974 $80

RUSKIN, JOHN   The King of the Golden River. 1932. Roy. 8vo., full limp vellum, illus. & color plates by Arthur Rackham, mint, one of 410 copies signed by author. Broadhurst 24-842 1974 £70

RUSKIN, JOHN   Lectures on Architecture and Painting. London, 1854. 8vo., orig. cloth, plates, first edition. Ximenes 35-92 1974 $25

RUSKIN, JOHN   Lectures on Architecture and Painting. 1854. Orig. brown cloth, plates, illus., first edition. Marsden 39-400 1974 £18

RUSKIN, JOHN   Lectures on Architecture and Painting. 1854. Orig. cloth, plates. Covent 55-1262 1974 £21

RUSKIN, JOHN   Lectures on Architecture and Painting, Delivered at Edinburgh in November, 1853. 1854. Small 8vo., plates, cloth, first edition. Quaritch 940-231 1974 £9

RUSKIN, JOHN   Lectures on Art. Oxford, 1870. 8vo., half parchment, fine, first edition. Dawsons PM 252-844 1974 £10

RUSKIN, JOHN   Lectures on Art. Oxford, 1870. 8vo., orig. cloth, worn, first edition. Bow Windows 62-783 1974 £15

RUSKIN, JOHN   Lectures on Art. Oxford, 1870. Inscription, very good copy, first edition. Covent 51-1603 1973 £15

RUSKIN, JOHN   Lectures on Art Delivered Before the University of Oxford in Hilary Term, 1870. Oxford, 1870. Orig. purple cloth, spine faded, first edition, very good copy. MacManus 224-383 1974 $35

RUSKIN, JOHN   Letters to Charles Eliot Norton. 1905. 2 vols., plates. Allen 216-1542 1974 $10

RUSKIN, JOHN   Modern Painters. London, 1856-60. Large 8vo., illus., contemporary calf, fine, first edition. Dawsons PM 250-69 1974 £35

RUSKIN, JOHN   Modern Painters. 1903. 6 vols., 8vo., plates, woodcuts, half calf, gilt, fourth edition. Quaritch 940-233 1974 £21

RUSKIN, JOHN   Notes by Mr. Ruskin on His Drawings by J. M. W. Turner, Exhibited at the Fine Art Society's Galleries, March 1878. 1878. Nice copy, slight pencil scoring, wrappers. Covent 51-1604 1973 £7.50

RUSKIN, JOHN   Notes on Samuel Prout and William Hunt. 1880. Folio, plates, half leather, gilt. Quaritch 940-232 1974 £30

RUSKIN, JOHN   On the Nature of Gothic Architecture. 1854. Orig. wrappers, frontispiece. Covent 55-1264 1974 £8.50

RUSKIN, JOHN   The Oxford Museum. 1859. Engraved frontis., folding plan, text illus., orig. patterned cloth, spine faded, very nice copy, ads at end, rare, first edition. Covent 51-1613 1973 £15.75

RUSKIN, JOHN   The Poems. 1891. 2 vols., crown 8vo., full navy calf gilt, first edition. Howes 185-409 1974 £8.50

RUSKIN, JOHN   Ruskin on Music. 1894. Frontispiece, fine. Covent 55-1265 1974 £8.50

RUSKIN, JOHN   The Seven Lamps of Architecture. 1880. Small 4to., plates, handmade paper, orig. boards. Bow Windows 62-786 1974 £6.50

RUSKIN, JOHN   The Seven Lamps of Architecture. 1890. 8vo., orig. cloth, corners worn, light damp stain on frontispiece. Bow Windows 66-596 1974 £5

RUSKIN, JOHN   The Stones of Venice. 1851. 3 vols., roy. 8vo., contemporary half red morocco, gillus., first edition. Thomas 30-135 1973 £40

RUSKIN, JOHN   The Stones of Venice. 1893. 3 vols., full blue morocco, gilt, plates, fifth edition. Marsden 39-403 1974 £12

RUSKIN, JOHN   The Two Paths. London, 1859. 8vo., illus., contemporary calf, rubbed, first edition. Dawsons PM 252-846 1974 £8

RUSKIN, JOHN   Ulric the Farm Servant. Orpington, 1888. 8vo., three quarter morocco, first edition. Goodspeed's 578-306 1974 $12.50

RUSKIN, JOHN   Unto This Last. Hammersmith, 1907. 8vo., orig. vellum backed boards, limited. Bow Windows 62-275 1974 £48

RUSKIN, JOHN   The Works. London, 1903-12. 39 vols., large 8vo., plates, illus., orig. morocco, uncut. Dawsons PM 252-847 1974 £675

RUSKIN, JOHN   The Works of. London & New York, 1903.
39 vols., 8vo., plates, fine, dark blue cloth, collected library edition. Dawsons
PM 252-1101 1974 £550

RUSLING, JAMES F.   The Great West and Pacific Coast. New York,
(1877). 8vo., orig. bindings. Butterfield 8-719 1974 $25

RUSNEL, P. DE   Le Mercure Indien. Paris, 1672. Crown 4to.,
13 parts in 1 vol., old French calf gilt. Smith 193-125 1973 £30

RUSPOLI, IPPOLITO   Avanzi e Ricordi del Monte Palatino Tratti dal
Vero e Posti in Litografia. (Rome, 1846). Oblong 4to., cloth boards, fine.
Traylen 79-568 1973 £30

RUSS, K.   Einheimische Stubenvogel. Magdeburg, 1913.
8vo., cloth, plates. Wheldon 130-613 1974 £10

RUSS, K.   The Speaking Parrots. 1884. 8vo., orig. dec.
cloth, gilt, plates, scarce. Wheldon 130-612 1974 £10

RUSSELL, A.   The Natural History of Aleppo. 1756. 4to.,
contemporary calf, plates, first edition. Wheldon 130-308 1974 £70

RUSSELL, A.   The Natural History of Aleppo. 1794. 4to.,
2 vols., contemporary calf, rebacked, plates, second edition. Wheldon 130-309
1974 £80

RUSSELL, BERTRAND   The Analysis of Mind. 1921. Faded, first
edition. Howes 185-1977 1974 £5

RUSSELL, BERTRAND   A Critical Exposition of the Philosophy of
Leibniz. Cambridge, 1900. 8vo., orig. cloth, fine, first edition.   Ximenes
35-93 1974 $60

RUSSELL, BERTRAND   An Essay on the Foundations of Geometry.
Cambridge, 1897. Demy 8vo., first edition, very good copy, orig. cloth.
Broadhurst 24-1296 1974 £25

RUSSELL, BERTRAND   Freedom and Organization. 1934. Bookplate,
English first edition. Covent 56-1121 1974 £10.50

RUSSELL, BERTRAND   Mysticism and Logic. 1918. Faded, first
edition. Covent 55-1272 1974 £12.50

RUSSELL, BERTRAND   Mysticism and Logic. 1929. Orig. edition.
Austin 61-866 1974 $10

RUSSELL, BERTRAND   On Education. 1926. Fine, dust wrapper,
English first edition. Covent 56-1125 1974 £10

RUSSELL, BERTRAND   Our Knowledge of the External World. 1926.
Book-plate, fine, revised edition. Covent 55-1273 1974 £5.25

RUSSELL, BERTRAND   Philosophical Essays. 1910. First edition, demy
8vo., publisher's presentation copy, orig. cloth, fine. Broadhurst 24-1297 1974
£10

RUSSELL, BERTRAND   Philosophical Essays. 1910. 8vo., orig. cloth,
first edition. Broadhurst 23-914 1974 £12

RUSSELL, BERTRAND   The Philosophy of Pacificism. n.d. Wrappers,
foxed. Covent 55-1274 1974 £21

RUSSELL, BERTRAND   The Practice and Theory of Bolshevism. 1920.
Cloth-backed boards, English first edition. Covent 56-1126 1974 £6.30

RUSSELL, BERTRAND   Skeptical Essays. 1928. First American
edition. Austin 61-873 1974 $10

RUSSELL, BERTRAND   War. n.d. Fine, wrappers, English first edition. Covent 56-1127 1974 £10

RUSSELL, C. E.   English Mezzotint Portraits and Their States
from the Invention of Mezzotinting Until the Early Part of the 19th Century.
1926. 2 vols., imp. 8vo., imp. 4to., half pigskin, fine, limited. Quaritch
940-234 1974 £75

RUSSELL, CHARLES M.   Good Medicine. Garden City, c. 1929. 4to.,
orig. binding, moderately worn d.w. Wilson 63-147 1974 $10

RUSSELL, CHARLES M.   Good Medicine, Memories of the Real West.
(1930). Orig. cloth, plates, first edition. Putnam 126-341 1974 $18

RUSSELL, CHARLES M.   Memories of Old Montana. Pasadena,
(1945). Cloth, dust jacket, mint, frontispiece. Bradley 35-326 1974 $10

RUSSELL, DORA   Children. New York, 1933. First American
edition. Covent 55-1392 1974 £7.50

RUSSELL, DORA   The Right to be Happy. 1927. English first
edition. Covent 56-2025 1974 £5.25

RUSSELL, E. S.   Form and Function. 1916. 8vo., cloth, scarce.
Wheldon 130-370 1974 £7.50

RUSSELL, GEORGE   Enchantment and Other Poems by A. E.
New York, 1930. 8vo., quarter cloth boards, limited edition. Emerald 50-853
1974 £12.50

RUSSELL, GEORGE WILLIAM   The Divine Vision and Other Poems. London,
1904. First edition, near mint, lacking d.w., orig. binding. Ross 86-2 1974
$20

RUSSELL, GEORGE WILLIAM   The Earth Breath and Other Poems. 1897.
Boards, foxing, scarce, first American edition. Covent 55-5 1974 £15

RUSSELL, GEORGE WILLIAM   The Interpreters. London, 1922. Lacking d.w.,
orig. binding, very nice copy. Ross 86-3 $12

RUSSELL, GEORGE WILLIAM   Voices of the Stones. London, 1925. Penciled
name on free fly, back cover very lightly worn, near fine, orig. binding. Ross
86-4 1974 $10

RUSSELL, J.   The History of the War Between the United States
and Great Britain. Hartford, 1815. First edition, full calf, expert repairs, foxed.
Jenkins 61-2564 1974 $37.50

RUSSELL, JOHN   Don Carlos. 1822. 8vo., contemporary half
calf, first edition. Hill 126-215 1974 £7.50

RUSSELL, JOHN   Essays and Sketches of Life and Character.
London, 1821. 8vo., later calf, second edition. Ximenes 35-94 1974 $15

RUSSELL, JOHN   The Life of William Lord Russell. London,
1819. 4to., foxing, inscription, contemporary half calf, rubbed, first edition.
Bow Windows 62-790 1974 £20

RUSSELL, JOHN   The Nun of Arrouca. London, 1822. 8vo.,
tree calf, gilt, morocco labels, first edition. Ximenes 35-95 1974 $75

RUSSELL, JOHN   The Red Mark and Other Stories. New York,
1919. Fine, wom, dust wrapper, first U.S. edition. Covent 56-343 1974 £35

RUSSELL, JOHN   A Tour in Germany. Edinburgh, 1825. 12mo.,
2 vols., half calf, second edition. Hill 126-230 1974 £16

RUSSELL, M. C.   Stars, A Fairy Tale. London, 1928. Signed,
numbered. Hood's 104-785 1974 $10

RUSSELL, OSBORNE   Journal of a Trapper: or, Nine Years in the
Rocky Mountains, 1834-1843. Boise, 1921. Second edition enlarged. Jenkins
61-2309 1974 $42.50

RUSSELL, P.   An Account of Indian Serpents. 1796.
Imp. folio, new half morocco, plates, rare. Wheldon 131-103 1974 £250

RUSSELL, PATRICK   A Treatise of the Plague. London, 1791. Large
4to., contemporary calf, first edition. Dawsons PM 249-430 1974 £95

RUSSELL, RICHARD   De Tabe Glandulari. Oxford, 1750. 8vo.,
red morocco, gilt, fine, first edition. Dawsons PM 249-431 1974 £40

RUSSELL, RICHARD   De Tabe Glandulari. Oxford, 1750. 8vo.,
recent half calf, plates, first edition. Bow Windows 66-598 1974 £48

RUSSELL, RICHARD   A Dissertation Concerning the Use of Sea Water
in Diseases. Oxford, 1753. 8vo., contemporary calf, second edition. Dawsons
PM 249-432 1974 £32

RUSSELL, RICHARD   A Dissertation on the Use of Sea Water in the Diseases of the Glands. London, 1760. Small 8vo., contemporary calf, fourth edition. Schumann 35-416 1974 $135

RUSSELL, W. H.   Canada: Its Defences, Condition, and Resources. New York & Boston, 1865. Worn spine. Hood's 103-557 1974 $15

RUSSELL, W. H.   My Diary North and South. Boston, New York & Toronto, 1863. Orig. linen binding, faded. Hood's 103-558 1974 $12.50

RUSSELL, W. H.   The War: From the Landing at Gallipoli to the Death of Lord Raglan. 1855. 8vo., orig. cloth. Bow Windows 66-599 1974 £8.50

RUSSELL, W. CLARK   The Emigrant Ship. Cassell, 1893. Austin 62-549 1974 $10

RUSSELL, W. CLARK   A Strange Voyage. 1886. English first edition. Covent 56-1130 1974 £5.25

RUSSELL, WILLIAM   The History of America, From Its Discovery By Columbus to the Conclusion of the Late War. London, 1778. 2 vols., orig. mottled card covers, engravings. Hood's 103-559 1974 $900

RUSSELL, WILLIAM   Recollections of a Detective Police-Officer. 1856. 8vo., contemporary half calf, labels, rare, first edition. Howes 186-394 1974 £10

RUSSELL, WILLIAM H.   The Civil War in America. Boston, (1861). Orig. printed wrappers, scarce. Hayman 57-101 1974 $12.50

THE RUSSIAN Jew in the U. S. 1905. 403p., orig. ed. Austin 62-44 1974 $12.50

RUST, ALBERT D.   Record of the Rust Family . . . Descendants of Henry Rust, Who Settled in Hingham, Mass., 1634-1635. Waco, 1891. Shaken, orig. binding. Butterfield 10-272 1974 $37.50

RUTH, FRANCIS J.   The Life and Work of. Plymouth, 1888. Cloth. Hayman 57-394 1974 $10

RUTHERFORD, ANWORTH   Squawberry Canyon. 1932. Morocco, gilt top, illus. by Harry Pierce, numbered, signed by author, plastic dust wrapper, slip case, first edition. Dykes 22-118 1973 $20

RUTHERFORD, ERNEST   Radiations from Radioactive Substances. Cambridge, 1930. 8vo., orig. green cloth, illus., plates, first edition. Dawsons PM 245-652 1974 £16

RUTHERFORD, ERNEST   Radioactive Substances and their Radiations. Cambridge, 1913. 8vo., orig. green cloth, gilt, plates, first edition. Dawsons PM 245-651 1974 £18

RUTHERFORD, ERNEST   Radioactive Substances and their Radiations. Cambridge, 1913. 8vo., orig. cloth, first edition. Schumann 35-418 1974 $85

RUTHERFORD, ERNEST   Radio-Activity. Cambridge, 1904. 8vo., orig. cloth, first edition. Gilhofer 61-70 1974 sFr. 750

RUTHERFORD, ERNEST   Radio-Activity. Cambridge, 1904. 8vo., orig. cloth. fine. first edition. Schumann 35-417 1974 $175

RUTHERFORD, ERNEST   The Radioactivity of Thorium Compounds. (London, 1902). 2 vols., 8vo., foxing, orig. printed wrappers. Bow Windows 62-791 1974 £250

RUTHERFORD, MARK   The Autobiography Of. 1881. 8vo., 2 vols., rebound, half red morocco, gilt, inscribed, scarce, first edition. Rota 190-786 1974 £25

RUTHERFORD, MARK   Catherine Furze. 1893. 8vo., 2 vols., orig. brown cloth, gilt, unopened, fine, first edition. Rota 190-787 1974 £35

RUTHERFORTH, THOMAS   Ordo Institutionum Physicarum in Private Lectionibus. 1743. 4to., contemporary calf, gilt, plates, first edition. Dawsons PM 245-653 1974 £35

RUTHERFORTH, THOMAS   Ordo Institutionum Physicarum in Privatis Lectionibus. 1756. 4to., modern half calf, gilt, fine, uncut, second edition. Dawsons PM 245-654 1974 £25

RUTHERFORTH, THOMAS   A System of Natural Philosophy. Cambridge, 1748. 2 vols., large 4to., contemporary calf, worn, plates, first edition. Schuman 37-225 1974 $125

RUTHERFURD, SAM   A Survey of the Spiritual Antichrist. 1648. Small 4to., contemporary sheep, bookplate. Thomas 28-103 1972 £21

RUTLEDGE, JOHN   A Defence Against Calumny. (Newport), 1803. 8vo., orig. bindings. Butterfield 8-575 1974 $20

RUTTER, J.   Delineations of the North Western Division of the County of Somerset. Shaftesbury & London, 1829. 8vo., plates, calf. Quaritch 939-541 1974 £25

RUTTER, JOAN   Here's Flowers. 1937. 8vo., orig. cloth, illus., rubbed. Marsden 39-335 1974 £5.50

RUTTER, O.   The Dragon of Kinabalu. London, (n.d.). 8vo., uncut, orig. cloth, dust wrapper. Bow Windows 62-792 1974 £5

RUTTLEDGE, HUGH   Everest 1933. 1934. Roy 8vo., orig. cloth, first edition. Broadhurst 23-1705 1974 £5

RUTTLEDGE, HUGH   Everest: The Unfinished Adventure. 1937. Plates, folding maps, first edition, super roy. 8vo., frayed d.w., orig. cloth, fine. Broadhurst 24-1672 1974 £8

RUTTY, JOHN   Materia Medica Antiqua & Nova. Rotterdam, 1775. 4to., marbled boards, calf, rubbed. Thomas 28-270 1972 £21

RUTTY, JOHN   Materia Medica Antiqua & Nova, Repurgata and Illustrata. Rotterdam, 1775. 4to., marbled boards, calf spine, joints cracked almost breaking. Thomas 32-327 1974 £21

RUYON, DAMON   A Slight Case of Murder. 1935. 73p., paper. Austin 51-811 1973 $7.50

RYAN, JAMES   The Differential and Integral Calculus. New York, 1828. 8vo., plates, orig. boards, uncut, first edition. Zeitlin 235-194 1974 $45

RYAN, THOMAS   Recollections of an Old Musician. Dutton, 1899. Austin 51-814 1973 $7.50

RYCAUT, PAUL   The Present State of the Ottoman Empire. London, 1668. Folio, old calf, rebacked, plates, second edition. Traylen 79-535 1973 £80

RYE, E. C.   British Beetles. 1890. 8vo., cloth, plates, second edition. Wheldon 131-850 1974 £5

RYE, W.   Records and Record Searching. 1897. 8vo., cloth, revised second edition. Quaritch 939-744 1974 £6

RYERSON, EGERTON   First Lessons In Christian Morals. Toronto, 1871. Staining. Hood's 103-263 1974 $30

RYERSON, EGERTON   First Lessons On Agriculture. Toronto, 1870. Foxing, first edition. Hood's 103-345 1974 $15

RYGG, A. N.   Norwegians in New York. (1941). Cloth, illus. Putnam 126-360 1974 $15

RYGG, A. N.   Norwegians in New York. Brooklyn, 1941. Illus. Austin 57-575 1974 $22.50

RYLAND, J. E.   Life and Correspondence of John Foster. 1846. 2 vols., new buckram. Allen 216-613 1974 $12.50

RYLANDS, GEORGE H. W.   Words and Poetry. 1928. First edition. Covent 55-1419 1974 £10.50

RYLANDS, GEORGE H. W.   Words and Poetry. London, 1928. Nice copy, scarce, first edition, orig. cloth. Crane 7-297 1974 £5

RYLEY, E.   All About Kitty Cat. New York, 1927. 24mo., color plates. Frohnsdorff 16-26 1974 $5

RYMER, T.   Foedera, Conventiones, Literae, et Cujuscunque Generis Acta Publica. 1739-45. 10 vols., folio, plates, buckram. Quaritch 939-229 1974 £400

S

S., C. L. J.   Intricate Paths. London, 1876. 8vo., orig. maroon cloth, first edition. Ximenes 35-97 1974 $17.50

S., L. D.   Le Chant de la Sainte Eglise. 1913. Quarter roan. Howes 185-1483 1974 £5

SAALFELD, EDMUND   Lectures On Cosmetic Treatment. New York, n.d. Second edition. Rittenhouse 46-573 1974 $15

SAARINEN, ELIEL   The City. New York, (1943). Grey cloth. Dawson's 424-237 1974 $30

SAARINEN, ELIEL   The City: Its Growth – Its Decay – Its Future. New York, 1943. 4to., cloth, illus, diagrams. Minters 37-567 1973 $28

SAARINEN, ELIEL   Search for Form. New York, 1948. Biblo & Tannen 213-392 1973 $15

SABARTES, JAIME   Picasso. New York, 1948. 1st ed., illus. Biblo & Tannen 214-425 1974 $10

SABATINI, RAFAEL   The Historical Nights' Entertainment. (1919-1938). 8vo., 3 vols., orig. cloth, first edition. Rota 189-749 1974 £5

SABBATINI, LUIGI ANTONIO   La Vera Idea delle Musicali Numeriche Signature. Venice, 1799. 4to., contemporary colored boards, leather back, worn, fine, very rare. Harper 213-131 1973 $285

SABIN, JOSEPH   Monogram and Alphabet Album. New York, 1871. 8vo., cloth, rebacked, plates. Kraus B8-375 1974 $37.50

SABINE, ROBERT   The Electric Telegraph. 1867. Diagrams, English first edition. Covent 56-1155 1974 £45

SACCARDO, P. A.   La Botanica in Italia. Venice, 1895-1901. 4to., 2 vols., cloth. Wheldon 129-188 1974 £20

SACCARDO, P. A.   Chromotaxia seu Nomenclator Colorum. Padua, 1894. 8vo., boards, plates, scarce, second edition. Wheldon 131-179 1974 £5

SACCHI-PLATINA, BARTOLOMEO DE
Please turn to
PLATINA, BARTOLOMEO DE SACCHI

SACCO, GIUSEPPE POMPEIO   Medicina Theorico-Practica ad Saniorem Saeculi Mentem Centenis. Parma, 1686. Large 4to., contemporary vellum, first edition. Schuman 37-226 1974 $195

SACHAR, ABRAM LEON   Sufferance is the Badge. Knopf, 1939. Austin 62-754 1974 $10

SACHEVERELL, HENRY   The Political Union. London, 1710. Disbound, trimmed not cropped, mild uniform edge discoloration. Wilson 63-601A 1974 $20

SACHEVERELL, HENRY   The Tryal of. 1710. Folio, old calf. Quaritch 939-488 1974 £25

SACHEVERELL, W.   An Account of the Isle of Man. 1702. Small 8vo., old calf, rebacked. Quaritch 939-394 1974 £50

SACHS, CURT   World History of the Dance. New York, 1937. Biblo & Tannen 210-954 1973 $10

SACHS, FERDINAND GUSTAV JULIUS VON   Lectures on the Physiology of Plants. Oxford, 1887. Roy. 8vo., orig. half morocco, text figures. Wheldon 128-1159 1973 £10

SACHS, FERDINAND GUSTAV JULIUS VON   Lectures on the Physiology of Plants. Oxford, 1887. 8vo., orig. half morocco, woodcuts. Wheldon 131-1194 1974 £10

SACHS, FERDINAND GUSTAV JULIUS VON   Textbook of Botany. Oxford, 1882. Roy. 8vo., half morocco, second edition. Wheldon 130-1051 1974 £10

SACHS, MAURICE   Alias. Paris, 1935. 12mo., orig. wrapper, uncut, first edition. L. Goldschmidt 42-359 1974 $12.50

SACKUR, ERNST   Die Cluniacenser in Ihrer Kirchlichen und Allgemeingeschichtlichen Wirksamkeit. 1892-94. 2 vols. in 1, thick 8vo., buckram, scarce. Howes 185-1619 1974 £18

SACKVILLE, GEORGE   The Trial Of. London, (1760). 8vo., modern green marbled boards, calf, first edition. Dawsons PM 251-401 1974 £35

SACKVILLE-WEST, EDWARD   The Rescue. 1945. One of 850 copies, plates, gilt top, very nice copy, first edition. Covent 51-1631 1973 £6.30

SACKVILLE-WEST, R. W.   Historical Notices of the Parish of Withyham In the County of Sussex. London & Tunbridge Wells, 1857. 4to., woodcuts, orig. cloth, plates. Traylen 79-398 1973 £12

SACKVILLE-WEST, VICTORIA   Andrew Marvell. 1929. Dust wrapper, near mint, boards. Covent 55-1278 1974 £5.25

SALLUSTIUS CRISPUS, GAIUS   De Coniuratione Catalinae. 1560. Old marbled boards, morocco spine. Thomas 30-115 1973 £20

SACKVILLE-WEST, VICTORIA   The Dark Island. Garden City, 1936. Orig. binding, first edition, one large tear in d.w., fine, heavy dec. paper wrapper. Ross 87-483 1974 $12.50

SACKVILLE-WEST, VICTORIA   The Edwardians. London, 1930. First trade edition, lacking d.w., bookplate, orig. binding, heavy dec. paper wrapper, fine. Ross 87-485 1974 $20

SACKVILLE-WEST, VICTORIA   The Edwardians. London, 1930. No. 48 of edition limited to 125 copies, signed, lacking d.w., unusually fine, tight copy, orig. binding, protected by heavy dec. paper wrapper. Ross 87-484 1974 $40

SACKVILLE-WEST, VICTORIA   Family History. 1932. Fine. Covent 51-2554 1973 £5.25

SACKVILLE-WEST, VICTORIA   Family History. London, 1932. Orig. binding, first edition, lacking d.w., spine somewhat faded & spotted, very nice. Ross 87-486 1974 $15

SACKVILLE-WEST, VICTORIA   Knole and the Sackvilles. London, 1922. Orig. binding, lacking d.w., covers worn & somewhat faded, two illus. pages loose, heavy dec. paper wrapper, first edition, good working copy. Ross 87-488 1974 $12.50

SACKVILLE-WEST, VICTORIA   Orchard and Vineyard. London, 1921. Orig. binding, first edition, some staining, good copy, printed copy of poem "December Night" laid in. Ross 87-490 1974 $10

SACKVILLE-WEST, VICTORIA   Collected Poems. 1933. Quarter vellum, fine, signed. Covent 55-1279 1974 £15

SACRAMENTO County in the Heart of California. Sacramento, (1915). 12mo., wrapper. Saddleback 14-258 1974 $12.50

SACRAMENTO Valley, California. San Francisco, (1911). 8vo., wrapper, 62 pages. Saddleback 14-259 1974 $12.50

SACY, ANTOINE-ISAAC SILVESTRE DE   Bibliotheque. Paris, 1842-47. 3 vols., 8vo., contemporary cloth, rubbed. Dawsons PM 10-534 1974 £20

SADLEIR, MICHAEL   Excursions in Victorian Bibliography. 1922. Fine, first edition. Covent 51-245 1973 £14

SADLEIR, MICHAEL   Excursions in Victorian Bibliography. London, 1922. 8vo., orig. cloth, dust wrapper. Dawsons PM 10-537 1974 £45

SADLEIR, MICHAEL   Excursions in Victorian Bibliography. London, 1922. 8vo., orig. cloth, dust wrapper. Dawsons PM 252-849 1974 £30

SADLEIR, MICHAEL   Thyrza. 8vo., numbered, intialled, fine. Ximenes 35-98 1974 $40

SADLEIR, T. U.   Georgian Mansions in Ireland. 1915. 4to., orig. illus. buckram, plates, first edition. Bow Windows 64-672 1974 £42.50

SADLER, H.   History and Records of the Lodge of Emulation.
London, 1906. 8vo., illus., orig. cloth, foxing. Bow Windows 62-348 1974
£6.50

SADLER, M. T. H.   Hyssop. 1915. Faded, first edition. Covent
55-1282 1974 £7.50

SADLER, MICHAEL THOMAS   Ireland. London, 1829. 8vo., quarter cloth
boards, worn, uncut, second edition. Emerald 50-860 1974 £15

SADLER, MICHAEL THOMAS   The Law of Population. London, 1830.
2 vols., 8vo., orig. cloth, fine, first edition. Dawsons PM 247-255 1974 £85

SADLER, RALPH   Letters & Negotiations Of. 1720. New
buckram, rubber stamp. Allen 213-1939 1973 $20

SADLER, RALPH   The State Papers and Letters of. Edinburgh,
1809. 2 vols., 4to., orig. half cloth, labels, plates, illus., best edition.
Howes 186-1194 1974 £25

SADLIER, MRS. J.   Con O'Regan or Emigrant Life in the New World.
Sadlier, 1885. Austin 62-755 1974 $27.50

SADOLETO, JACOPO   Epistolarum Libri Sexdecim. Cologne, 1554.
8vo., contemporary blind stamped pigskin over wooden boards, very fine copy.
Schafer 10-109 1974 sFr 800

SAENGER, GERNART   Today's Refugees, Tomorrow's Citizens.
Harper, 1941. Austin 62-555 1974 $10

SAENGER, GERNART   Today's Refugees, Tomorrows Citizens. 1941.
286 pages. Austin 57-577 1974 $10

SAFFORD, WILLIAM H.   The Life of Harman Blennerhassett. Chillicothe,
1850. Frontis. lithograph, ex-library, backstrip chipped, first edition. Butterfield 10-477 1974 $7.50

SAFFORD, WILLIAM H.   The Life of Harman Blennerhassett. Cincinnati,
1853. Cloth. Hayman 57-666 1974 $20

SAGE, ELIZABETH   A Study of Costume. Scribner, 1926.
Austin 51-815 1973 $8.50

SAGRA, RAMON DE LA   Histoire Physique, Politique et Naturelle de
l'Ile de Cuba. Paris, 1840. 2 vols., folio & 8vo., half morocco, plates.
Wheldon 131-519 1974 £40

SAGRI, NICOLO   Ragionamenti Sopra le Varieta. 1574. Small
4to., woodcuts, wrappers. Zeitlin 235-195 1974 $225

SAHLBERG, J.   Ofversigt af Finlands och den Skandinaviska
Halfons Cicadariae. 1871. 8vo., plates. Wheldon 128-790 1973 £5

SAIGE, G.   Documents Historiques Relatifs Aux
Seigneuries de Menton. 1909. 4to., boards. Allen 213-1757 1973 $15

SAINT, LAWRENCE B.   Stained Glass of the Middle Ages in England
& France. 1913. Illus. in colour. Eaton Music-670 1973 £5

SAINT-AMANT, PIERRE CHARLES DE   Voyages en Californie et dans l'Oregon.
Paris, 1854. Thick 8vo., orig. printed wrappers, fine, first edition. Ximenes
35-99 1974 $150

SAINT-GAUDENS, HOMER   The American Artist and His Times. New
York, 1941. 4to., cloth, plates. Minters 37-33 1973 $22

ST. GEORGE, HENRY   Historical and Heraldic Commonplace Book.
(c.1700). Folio, contemporary vellum. Quaritch 939-745 1974 £120

SAINT-GEORGES DE BOUHELIER   La Tragedie du Nouveau Christ. Paris,
1901. 12mo., contemporary three quarter cloth, orig. wrapper, uncut, first
edition. L. Goldschmidt 42-361 1974 $12.50

SAINT HENRY, SISTER M.   Nativism in Pennsylvania with Particular
Regard to its Effect on Politics and Education. Philadelphia, 1936. 47p.
Austin 62-756 1974 $17.50

ST. JOHN, BAYLE   Two Year's Residence in a Levantine Family.
London, 1850. 8vo., orig. rose cloth, fine, first edition. Ximenes 35-100
1974 $27.50

ST. JOHN, C.   Wild Sports and Natural History of the Highlands.
1919. Roy 8vo., buckram, plates. Wheldon 130-310 1974 £7.50

ST. JOHN, C.   Wild Sports and Natural History of the Highlands.
1927. 8vo., cloth, illus. Wheldon 130-311 1974 £5

ST. JOHN, C. E.   Revision of Rowland's Preliminary Table of
Solar Spectrum Wave-Lengths. 1928. 4to., orig. printed wrappers. Bow
Windows 64-673 1974 £10

ST. JOHN, CHRISTOPHER   Ellen Terry and Bernard Shaw. New York,
1931. First edition, no. 582 of edition limited to 3,000 copies, some fading,
orig. binding, inscription, near fine. Ross 87-531 1974 $15

SAINT JOHN, H. C.   Notes and Sketches from the Wild Coasts of
Nipon. 1880. 8vo., cloth, illus. Wheldon 131-391 1974 £7.50

SAINT JOHN, HENRY, VISCOUNT BOLINGBROKE
Please turn to
BOLINGBROKE, HENRY ST. JOHN 1678-1751

SAINT JOHN, OLIVER   Speech. London, 1640. 4to., calf antique,
fine, first edition. Dawsons PM 251-402 1974 £85

ST. JOHN, OLIVER   The Speech or Declaration. London, 1641.
Small 4to., disbound, first edition. Dawsons PM 247-256 1974 £45

THE ST. Lawrence Basin, The Interoceanic Water Routes and the Interior of the
United States. N. P., 1853. Huge folding map in color, some damage to folds.
Jenkins 61-2396 1974 $15

ST. MARS, F.   On Nature's Trail, A Wonder Book of the Wild.
Toronto, 1912. Illus. Hood's 104-453 1974 $12.50

SAINT MARTIN, M. J. DE   L'Art de Faire des Armes. Vienna, 1804. Orig.
marbled boards, rebacked, plates. Dawson's 424-117 1974 $100

SAINT-NON, RICHARD DE   Recueil de Griffonnis. (Paris, ca., 1780).
Large folio, marbled boards, vellum back. Marlborough 70-25 1974 £375

SAINT-NON, RICHARD DE   Voyage Pittoresque ou Description des Royaumes
de Naples et de Sicile. Paris, 1781-1786. 4 vols. in 5, imp. folio, plates,
half morocco, gilt, rubbed, first edition. Quaritch 940-235 1974 £1,650

SAINT PIERRE, JACQUES HENRI BERNARDIN DE   Paul and Virginia. 1798.
Fine engraved plates, fourth edition, small square 8vo., orig. boards, spine trifle
rubbed, good copy. George's 610-640 1973 £5

SAINT-PIERRE, JACQUES HENRI BERNARDIN DE   Paul and Virginia. New
York, 1805. 12mo., contemporary tree calf, vignettes. Ximenes 35-102 1974
$15

SAINT-PIERRE, JACQUES HENRI BERNARDIN DE   Romans, Contes et Opuscules.
Paris, 1834. 2 vols., 12mo., contemporary maroon morocco, gilt, illus.
L. Goldschmidt 42-114 1974 $130

SAINT-PIERRE, JACQUES HENRI BERNARDIN DE   Voyages of Amasis. Boston,
1795. 12mo., modern three quarter morocco, first edition. Ximenes 35-103 1974
$35

SAINT-PIERRE, T.   The Americans and Canada in 1837-38.
Montreal, 1897. Orig. paper covers, cloth spine, signed by Saint-Pierre, no.
198 of limited edition of 200. Hood's 102-577 1974 $55

SAINT-REAL, CESAR VISCHARD DE   Oeuvres Melees. Paris, 1689. 12mo.,
contemporary calf, gilt back, spine worn, woodcut device on title. Bow Windows
66-604 1974 £12.50

SAINT-SIMON, LOUIS DE ROUVROY DE   Memoires Complets et Authentiques
sur le Siecle de Louis XIV et Regence. Paris, 1856. 20 vols., half contemporary
speckled calf, gilt, leather labels. Smith 194-568 1974 £40

SAINT VALIER, JEAN BAPTISTE DE LA CROIX CHEVRIERES DE   Catechisme du
Diocese de Quebec. Paris, 1702. 12mo., old sprinkled vellum, water stained,
first edition, rare. Quaritch 933-183 1973 £225

ST. YVES, CHARLES   A New Treatise of the Diseases of the Eyes. London, 1741. 8vo., contemporary calf, first edition in English. Dawsons PM 249-433 1974 £85

SAINT ANDREW'S SOCIETY OF THE STATE OF NEW YORK   Historical Sketch of. New York, 1856. Spine chipped. Jenkins 61-1881 1974 $15

ST. FRANCIS of Assisi. 1922. Small 4to., limp vellum with ties, illus. Hammond 201-751 1974 £120

ST. MARK's la Basilica di San Marco In Venezia, Illus. Nella Storia e Nell' Arte da Scrittori Veneziani Sotto la Direzione di C. Boito. 1888-92. Folio, limp vellum, plates, illus. Allen 213-1845 1973 $30

SAINT Nicholas, an Illustrated Magazine for Boys and Girls. New York, 1923. Biblo & Tannen 213-804 1973 $22.50

ST. NICHOLAS Book of Plays and Operettas. Century, 1916. Illus. Austin 51-819 1973 $8.50

SAINTE-BEUVE, CHARLES AUGUSTIN   Catalogue des Livres et Curieux Composant la Bibliotheque de M. Sainte-Beuve. Paris, 1870. Small 8vo., orig. wrapper, uncut. L. Goldschmidt 42-179 1974 $17.50

SAINTE-BEUVE, CHARLES AUGUSTIN   Causeries du Lundi. Paris, c. 1875. 15 vols., small 8vo., contemporary tree calf, gilt. Howes 185-414 1974 £21

SAINTE-BEUVE, CHARLES AUGUSTIN   Causeries du Lundi. Paris, 1928-32. 15 vols., 12mo., orig. wrapper. L. Goldschmidt 42-364 1974 $30

SAINTE-BEUVE, CHARLES AUGUSTIN   Port-Royal. Paris, 1867-71. 7 vols., crown 8vo., contemporary half morocco, revised third edition. Howes 185-415 1974 £12.50

SAINTE-BEUVE, CHARLES AUGUSTIN   Port-Royal. Paris, 1926-32. 7 tomes in 10 vols., roy. 8vo., three quarter hard grain morocco, gilt, uncut, numbered, limited edition. L. Goldschmidt 42-365 1974 $75

SAINTE-BEUVE, CHARLES AUGUSTIN   Portraits Litteraires. Paris, 1882-78-76. 5 vols., contemporary morocco backed marbled boards, gilt. Smith 193-449 1973 £6

SAINTE-MARTHE, DENYS DE   Histoire de S. Gregoire le Grand. 1697. Crown 4to., half calf, rebacked, stains. Howes 185-1230 1974 £20

SAINTINE, X. B.   Le Chemin des Ecoliers. Paris, 1861. Roy. 8vo., orig. half hard grain morocco, gilt, first edition. L. Goldschmidt 42-367 1974 $100

SAINTSBURY, GEORGE   Corrected Impressions. 1895. 8vo., orig. cloth, first edition. Rota 190-563 1974 £15

SAINTSBURY, GEORGE   A History of English Criticism. (1911). Austin 61-880 1974 $10

SAINTSBURY, GEORGE   A History of English Prosody. London, 1906-10. 3 vols., 8vo., fine, orig. cloth, first edition. Dawsons PM 252-851 1974 £22

SAINTSBURY, GEORGE   A Last Scrap Book. 1924. One of 250 large paper copies signed by author, buckram backed vellum, very good copy, first edition. Covent 51-1634 1973 £5.25

SAINTSBURY, GEORGE   Loci Critici. 1903. 439 pages. Austin 61-881 1974 $12.50

SAINTSBURY, GEORGE   A Scrap Book. 1922. Small 4to., buckram-backed boards, signed, English first edition. Covent 56-1140 1974 £10.50

SAINTSBURY, GEORGE   A Scrap Book. London, 1922-24. 3 vols., 8vo., uncut, orig. cloth, dust wrappers, first editions. Bow Windows 62-797 1974 £10.50

SAINTSBURY, GEORGE   A Short History of English Literature. (1898). Austin 61-882 1974 $10

SAKLATWALLA, J. E.   Omar Khayyam as a Mystic. Bombay, 1928. 12mo., wrappers, portrait. Covent 55-1162 1974 £12.50

SAKURAI, TADAYOSHI   Human Bullets. Boston & New York, 1907. Scarce, torn dust jacket, fine. Ballinger 1-42 1974 $17

SALA, GEORGE AUGUSTUS   Paris Herself Again In 1878-89. 2 vols., orig. dec. cloth, plates, illus. Covent 55-1284 1974 £12.50

SALA, GEORGE AUGUSTUS   Things I Have Seen and People I Have Known. London, 1894. 2 vols., 8vo., orig. cloth, fine, first edition. Ximenes 35-104 1974 $35

SALA, GEORGE AUGUSTUS   The Thorough Good Cook. New York, 1896. Heavy boards, gilt, faded, first edition. Covent 55-697 1974 $25

SALA, GEORGE AUGUSTUS   A Trip to Barbary By a Roundabout Route. London, 1866. 8vo., orig. cloth, first edition. Ximenes 35-105 1974 $20

SALA, GEORGE AUGUSTUS   Twice Round the Clock. 1862. Orig. patterned cloth, portrait, English first edition. Covent 56-2028 1974 £10.50

SALAMAN, MALCOLM C.   Old English Mezzotints. London, 1910. 4to., orig. wrappers, plates. Dawsons PM 10-538 1974 £5

SALAMAN, MALCOLM C.   The Woodcut of To-Day at Home and Abroad. 1927. Roy 8vo., patterned cloth, English first edition. Covent 56-1502 1974 £7.50

SALE, CHARLES   The Specialist. St. Louis, 1929. 12mo., limp lea., sgd. Biblo & Tannen 213-596 1973 $8.50

SALE, EDITH TUNIS   Colonial Interiors. New York, 1930. Blue cloth. Dawson's 424-222 1974 $40

SALE, EDITH TUNIS   Interiors of Virginia Houses of Colonial Times. Richmond, 1927. Illus., orig. plates, first and only edition, 8vo., spine faded, minor cover soiling, interior perfect. Current BW9-438 1974 $40

SALE, EDITH TUNIS   Interiors of Virginia Houses of Colonial Times. Richmond, 1927. First edition, orig. plates, marbled end papers, very good, orig. binding. Wilson 63-115 1974 $30

THE SALEM Belle: A Tale of 1692. Boston, 1842. 12mo., orig. cloth, spine bit faded, first edition, fine. MacManus 224-384 1974 $25

SALET, PIERRE   Omar Khayyam. Paris, 1927. Wrappers, first edition. Covent 55-1161 1974 £7.50

SALISBURY, W.   Hints Addressed to Proprietors of Orchards. 1816. 8vo., orig. boards, rebacked, uncut, plates. Wheldon 130-1487 1974 £28

THE SALISBURY Spelling-Book, With Historical and Moral Extracts from the New Testament, Questions and Answers on the Extracts, Lessons in Religion. Salisbury, 1809. Twelfth edition, small woodcuts, 12mo., orig. leather backed boards, small holes in spine, internally fine. George's 610-641 1973 £10.50

SALLUSTIUS CRISPUS, GAIUS   De Coniuratione Catalinae. 1509. 19th century russia gilt, stains, rubbed. Thomas 30-19 1973 £70

SALLUSTIUS CRISPUS, GAIUS   De Coniuratione Cataline. Venice, 1509. Small 8vo., vellum, stained throughout, slight worming, tall sound working copy. Thomas 32-214 1974 £60

SALLUSTIUS CRISPUS, GAIUS   The Conspiracy of Catiline and the War of Jugurtha. London & New York, 1924. Limited to 1025 copies, 8vo., red paper boards, cloth shelf back, binding scuffed, interior fine, orig. prospectus included. Current BW9-600 1974 $12.50

SALLUSTIUS CRISPUS, GAIUS   Salustio Cathilinario, y Iugurta. Antwerp, 1554. 12mo., 19th century calf, worn. Harper 213-132 1973 $195

SALMASIUS, CLAUDE   Claudii Salamasii ad Johannem Miltonum Responsio. Londini, 1660. 12mo., old boards, morocco label. Bow Windows 62-802 1974 £85

SALMASIUS, CLAUDE   Defensio Regia Pro Carolo I. 1650. 12mo., contemporary vellum, rare. Bow Windows 62-803 1974 £65

SALMI, MARIO   L'Abbazia di Pomposa. 1936. Folio, illus.
Allen 213-1759 1973 $35

SALMON, ANDRE   Creances 1905-1910. Paris, 1926. 12mo.,
orig. wrapper, uncut, first edition. L. Goldschmidt 42-368 1974 $15

SALMON, JOSEPH WHITTINGHAM   Moral Reflections in Verse. 1796.
8vo., orig. boards, inscribed, fine, first edition. Ximenes 35-107 1974 $100

SALMON, NATHANIEL   History of Hertfordshire. 1728. Folio, old
panelled calf, rebacked. Quaritch 939-389 1974 £45

SALMON, NATHANIEL   The History of Hertfordshire. London, 1728.
Folio, contemporary calf, gilt, leather label, first edition. Traylen 79-337
1973 £35

SALMON, THOMAS   Modern History. London, 1739. 4to., 3 vols.,
contemporary calf, gilt, second London edition. Dawsons PM 251-330 1974
£165

SALMON, THOMAS   Modern History. London, 1744-1746. Folio,
3 vols., contemporary panelled calf, third edition. Dawsons PM 251-331 1974
£175

SALMON, THOMAS   A Review of the History of England. London, 17-
22. 8vo., contemporary calf. Hammond 201-462 1974 £12

SALMON, WILLIAM   Botanologia. 1710. Folio, modern boards,
calf back, woodcuts. Wheldon 131-1822 1974 £180

SALMON, WILLIAM   Polygraphice. 1685. Old calf, plates, worn,
soiled, fifth edition. Thomas 28-43 1972 £12

SALM-REIFFERSCHEID-DYCK, J.   Cacteae in Horto Dyckensi Cultae Anno
1849. Bonn, 1850. 8vo., new cloth, scarce. Wheldon 131-1694 1974 £20

SALOPIAN Shreds and Patches. Shrewsbury, 1874-81. 4 vols., 4to., illus.,
wrappers. Quaritch 939-535 1974 £10

SALTER, J. W.   A Monograph of the British Trilobites from the
Cambrian, Silurian and Devonian Formations. 1864-83. 4to., half calf,
plates. Wheldon 131-1074 1974 £15

SALTONSTALL, W.   Ports of Piscataqua. Portsmouth, 1941. Large
4to., linen, illus., fine. Putman 126-82 1974 $12.75

SALUSTE DU BARTAS, GUILLAUME DE
Please turn to
DU BARTAS, GUILLAUME DE SALUSTE

SALVANDY, NARCISSE ACHILLE DE   Paris, Nantes et la Session. Paris,
1832. 8vo., contemporary half lemon calf, gilt. L. Goldschmidt 42-369
1974 $15

SALVERSON, L.   Lord of the Silver Dragon. Toronto, 1927.
Illus. Hood's 103-506 1974 $12.50

SALVIN, F. H.   Falconry in the British Isles. 1873. 8vo., orig.
cloth, plates, second edition. Bow Windows 64-234 1974 £320

SAMINSKY, LAZARE   Music of our Day. New York, 1939. Biblo &
Tannen 214-911 1974 $7.50

SAMMES, AYLETT   Britannia Antiqua Illustrata. London, 1676.
Folio, old calf, map. Quaritch 939-232 1974 £15

SAMOUELLE, GEORGE   The Entomologist's Useful Compendium. 1819.
8vo., old calf, rebacked, plates. Bow Windows 64-235 1974 £16

SAMPSON, G. V.   Statistical Survey of the County of Londonderry.
Dublin, 1802. 8vo., plates, modern half antique calf, gilt. Emerald 50-862
1974 £30

SAMPSON, GEORGE   The Concise Cambridge History of English
Literature. 1941. Orig., unrevised edition. Austin 61-884 1974 $10

SAMPSON, LILLA BRIGGS   The Sampson Family. Baltimore, (c.1914).
12mo., cloth. Saddleback 14-790 1974 $25

SAMPSON, THOMAS   Electrotint. London, 1842. 8vo., orig. stiff
printed wrappers, plates, fine, scarce, first edition. Ximenes 35-110 1974 $90

SAMS, CONWAY WHITTLE   The Conquest of Virginia: The Forest Primeval.
1916. First edition, orig. cloth, fine, med. 8vo., illus. Broadhurst 24-1673
1974 £15

SAMS, WILLIAM   A Tour Through Paris. London, n.d. Folio,
plates, contemporary half morocco, gilt. Marlborough 70-36 1974 £210

SAMUEL, SIGMUND   The Seven Years War in Canada, 1756-1763.
Toronto, 1934. Illus., inscribed & signed by author. Hood's 102-119 1974 $45

SAMUELS, MAURICE VICTOR   The Florentines. Brentano, 1904. Austin 51-
816 1973 $10

SAMUELS, MARICE VICTOR   The Great Hatred. Knopf, 1940. Austin 62-
558 1974 $7.50

SAMUEL, MAURICE VICTOR   Jews on Approval. Liveright, 1932. Austin
62-559 1974 $12.50

SAMUELS, MAURICE VICTOR   You Gentiles. Harcourt, 1924. Austin 62-561
1974 $7.50

SAN Diego, the Beautiful. San Diego, c. 1915. Folio, wrapper, hand colored
illus. Jenkins 61-396 1974 $12.50

SAN DIEGO, California, City and County. San Diego, (1919). 8vo., wrapper.
Saddleback 14-261 1974 $10

SAN DIEGO Yesterdays: Being Sketches of Incidents in the Indian, Spanish,
Mexican and American History of. San Diego, (c.1921). 12mo., quarter cloth.
Saddleback 14-262 1974 $15

SAN Francisco, the Queen City. San Francisco, c. 1910. Folio, wrapper, illus.
Jenkins 61-400 1974 $11

SANBORN, FRANKLIN BENJAMIN   Henry D. Thoreau. Houghton, 1882.
324 pages. Austin 54-883 1973 $7.50

SANBORN, FRANKLIN BENJAMIN   Recollections of Seventy Years. Boston,
1909. 2 vols., orig. binding. Butterfield 10-478 1974 $17.50

SANBORN, FRANKLIN BENJAMIN   Thoreau the Poet-Naturalist. Boston,
1902. Orig. cloth backed boards, morocco label, one of 250 copies, very fine,
best edition. MacManus 224-439 1974 $50

SANBORN, KATE   The Wit of Women. Funk and Wagnall, 1885.
215p. Austin 54-884 1973 $17.50

SANCHEZ, A. N. RIBEIRO   Examen Historique sur l'Apparition. (Paris),
1774. 12mo., stitched, uncut. Gurney 64-193 1974 £15

SANCHO, IGNATIUS   Letters of the Late. 1782. 8vo., 2 vols., contemporary calf, gilt, frontispiece, fine. Hill 126-232 1974 £50

SAND, GEORGE   Letters of George Sand. London, 1886.
3 vols., bdg. torn on one. Biblo & Tannen 213-805 1973 $17.50

SAND, MAURICE   The History of the Harlequinade. 1915. 8vo.,
2 vols., plates, cloth. Quaritch 936-538 1974 £20

SAND, MAURICE   Plays for Marionettes. French, 1931.
Austin 51-817 1973 $8.50

SANDAY, W.   Studies In the Synoptic Problem. 1911. 8vo.,
orig. cloth, frontispiece. Howes 185-1623 1974 £5

SANDBURG, CARL   Abraham Lincoln, The Prairie Years. New
York, (1926). Photos, cartoons, sketches, maps, fourth printing, 2 vols., 8vo.,
publisher's box near mint, d.j. Current BW9-378 1974 $35

SANDBURG, CARL   Abraham Lincoln: The War Years. New York,
1939-40. 4 vols., fine. Jenkins 61-1376 1974 $35

SANDBURG, CARL   Chicago Poems. New York, 1916. Dark green
cloth, first edition. Dawson's 424-299 1974 $50

SANDBURG, CARL   Chicago Poems. New York, 1916. Orig.
cloth, first edition, with first page of publisher's ads at back, fine. MacManus
224-385 1974 $27.50

SANDBURG, CARL   Chicago Poems. New York, 1916. First U.S.
edition, covers faded & somewhat marked, booklabel, very good copy. Covent
51-3255 1973 £20

SANDBURG, CARL   Cornhuskers. New York, 1918. Boards, fine,
first edition, first issue. Dawson's 424-300 1974 $40

SANDBURG, CARL   Good Morning, America. New York, 1928.
First edition, 8vo., fine, author's signature card laid in. Current BW9-273 1974
$20

SANDBURG, CARL   Good Morning, America. New York, 1928.
Third printing, signed by author, small spots on front cover, orig. binding. Butterfield 10-479 1974 $10

SANDBURG, CARL   Mary Lincoln, Wife and Widow. New York,
(1932). Tan cloth. Putman 126-23 1974 $10

SANDBURG, CARL   Remembrance Rock. New York, 1948. 1st reg.
ed., sgd. by author. Jacobs 24-125 1974 $10

SANDBURG, CARL   Rootabaga Stories. New York, 1922. Lacking
d.w., orig. binding, illus., owner's name in ink on free fly, front hinge tender,
nice. Ross 87-503 1974 $60

SANDBURG, CARL   Smoke and Steel. New York, 1920. 1st ed.,
spine torn. Biblo & Tannen 214-768 1974 $12.50

SANDBY, PAUL   A Collection of His Etched Work. 1747-1758.
Folio, contemporary marbled boards. Marlborough 70-22 1974 £450

SANDEAU, JULES   Sacs et Parchemins. Paris, 1851. 2 vols.,
12mo., orig. wrapper, uncut. L. Goldschmidt 42-372 1974 $17.50

SANDEMAN, JOHN G.   The Sandeman Genealogy. Edinburgh, 1895.
4to., blue morocco gilt, rubbed. Howes 186-1649 1974 £10.50

SANDERS, ALVIN HOWARD   A History of the Percheron Horse. Chicago, 1917.
12mo., cloth, illus., first edition. Putman 126-15 1974 $17

SANDERS, B. H.   Emily Murphy, Crusader. Toronto, 1945.
Photographs. Hood's 103-232 1974 $12.50

SANDERS, J.   The Select Florist. Derby, 1829. Small 8vo.,
orig. boards. Wheldon 131-1568 1974 £10

SANDERS, JACQUIN   Freak Show. Little, Brown, 1954. 276p.
Austin 51-818 1973 $8.50

SANDERS, WILLIAM BLISS   Half-Timbered Houses and Carved Oak
Furniture of the 16th & 17th Centuries. London, 1894. Folio, plates, orig.
cloth, foxing, worn. Bow Windows 62-804 1974 £6.50

SANDERS, WILLIAM BLISS   Half Timbered Houses and Carved Oak Furniture.
1894. Folio, half red morocco, ex-library. Marsden 37-431 1974 £6

SANDERSON, GEORGE P.   Thirteen Years Among the Wild Beasts of India.
Edinburgh, 1912. 8vo., orig. dec. cloth, plates. Wheldon 129-298 1974 £5

SANDERSON, JOHN   The American in Paris. Philadelphia, 1839.
2 vols., 12mo., orig. cloth, printed paper labels. Ximenes 35-111 1974 $12.50

SANDERUS, ANTOINE   Chorographia Sacra Brabantiae. The Hague,
1726-27. 3 vols., engravings, folio, contemporary calf, gilt backs, splendid
large paper copy. Schumann 499-101 1974 sFr 11,000

SANDFORD   The Amorous Poem entitled Hero & Leander.
1933. Buckram, engravings, limited edition. Marsden 37-432 1974 £21

SANDFORD, F.   The History of the Coronation of . . . James II.
1687. Folio, plates, contemporary mottled calf. Quaritch 939-746 1974 £90

SANDHAM, ELIZABETH   Juliania. 1800. First edition, half title, orig.
boards, 12mo., rare, lacking large portion of upper cover, engraved frontispiece.
George's 610-642 1973 £8

SANDON, H.   The Composition and Distribution of the Protozon
Fauna of the Soil. 1927. 8vo., cloth, scarce. Wheldon 130-888 1974 £5

SANDYS, CHARLES   Consuetudines Kanciae. 1851. Full calf,
gilt, bookplate. Howes 186-2060 1974 £10

SANDYS, GEORGE   Anglorum Speculum. 1684. Crown 8vo., contemporary calf, rebacked, first edition. Broadhurst 23-1268 1974 £45

SANDYS, GEORGE   Anglorum Speculum, or the Worthies of England,
in Church and State. 1684. First edition, crown 8vo., contemporary calf,
rebacked, fine, complete with half title & ads. Broadhurst 24-1320 1974 £45

SANDYS, GEORGE   Sandys Travells. London, 1670. Folio, early
19th century calf gilt, leather label, sixth edition. Traylen 79-570 1973 £68

SANFORD, J. L.   Studies and Illustrations of the Great Rebellion.
London, 1858. 8vo., contemporary calf, gilt, foxed. Bow Windows 62-806
1974 £8.50

SANFORD, M. M. (Mrs)   A Visit to El-Fay-Gno-Land. New York,
1879. 1st ed. Biblo & Tannen 210-751 1973 $17.50

SANGER, WILLIAM W.   The History of Prostitution. New York, 1859.
8vo., first edition. Rinsland 58-93 1974 $15

SANNAZARO, JACOPO   Arcadia. Milan, 1509. 4to., 18th century
mottled calf, very rare. Schumann 499-103 1974 sFr 1,050

SANNAZARO, JACOPO   Arcadia. 1514. Blue stained calf gilt, faded,
first Aldine edition. Thomas 30-28 1973 £65

SANNAZARO, JACOPO   Opera Omnia Latine Scripta. 1535. Vellum,
blue morocco labels, stains, first collected edition. Thomas 30-73 1973 £40

SANSAY, LEONOARA   Secret History. Philadelphia, 1808. 12mo.,
contemporary sheep, rare, first edition. Ximenes 35-112 1974 $175

SANSON, NICHOLAS D'ABBEVILLE   Atlas Nouveau. (1692)-1696. Large
folio, contemporary panelled calf. Bow Windows 64-675 1974 £4,500

SANSOVINO, FRANCESCO   L'Historia di Casa Orsina. 1565. Small folio,
contemporary calf, gilt, first edition. Zeitlin 235-197 1974 $325

SANTAYANA, GEORGE   Character and Opinion in the United States.
Scribner, 1921. 233p., orig. hard cover ed. Austin 54-885 1973 $12.50

SANTAYANA, GEORGE   Dialogues in Limbo. Scribner, 1925. 193p.,
orig. ed. Austin 54-886 1973 $12.50

SANTAYANA, GEORGE   Dominations and Powers. Scribner, 1951.
481p., orig. ed. Austin 54-887 1973 $8.25

SANTAYANA, GEORGE   Interpretations of Poetry and Religion. New
York, 1900. 12mo., cloth, back faded, first edition. Goodspeed's 578-310
1974 $10

SANTAYANA, GEORGE   The Last Puritan. London, 1935. Orig.
binding, first edition, covers lightly worn, very nice. Ross 87-506 1974 $10

SANTAYANA, GEORGE   The Last Puritan. Scribner, 1936. 602p.
Austin 54-888 1973 $5

SANTAYANA, GEORGE   The Last Puritan. New York, 1936. Cloth,
dust wrapper, first edition. Dawson's 424-301 1974 $10

SANTAYANA, GEORGE   Little Essays. Scribner, 1921. 290p., orig.
ed. Austin 54-897 1973 $10

SANTAYANA, GEORGE   My Host the World (Vol. 3 Persons and Places)
Scribner. 149p. Austin 54-889 1973 $7.50

SANTAYANA, GEORGE   Persons and Places. Scribner, 1944. 262p.
Austin 54-890 1973 $4.75

SANTAYANA, GEORGE　　The Philosophy of Santayana. Scribner, 1936. 587p. Austin 54-896 1973 $12.50

SANTAYANA, GEORGE　　Poems. Scribner, 1925. 140p., orig. ed. Austin 54-891 1973 $12.50

SANTAYANA, GEORGE　　The Realm of Essence. Scribner, 1927. 183p., orig. ed. Austin 54-892 1973 $22.50

SANTAYANA, GEORGE　　Scepticism and Animal Faith. Scribner, 1923. 314p., lst ed. Austin 54-893 1973 $22.50

SANTAYANA, GEORGE　　Soliloquies in England. Scribner, 1923. 264p., orig. hard cover ed. Austin 54-894 1973 $12.50

SANTAYANA, GEORGE　　Some Tums of Thought in Modern Philosophy. New York, 1933. Biblo & Tannen 213-992 1973 $6.50

SANTAYANA, GEORGE　　Winds of Doctrine. Dent, 1914. 215p., orig. ed. Austin 54-895 1973 $12.50

SANTAYANA, GEORGE　　The Works of. New York, 1936-40. 15 vols., orig. cloth backed boards, paper labels, Triton edition, one of 940 sets, fine, signed by author. MacManus 224-386 1974 $250

SANTOS, FRANCISCO DE LOS　　Description of the Royal Palace, and Monastery of St. Lawrence, Called the Escurial. 1760. 4to., rebound in half calf, gilt, plates. Quaritch 940-552 1974 £75

SANUTO, LIVIO　　Le Rapina di Proserpina. Venice, 1551. First edition, with final blank, some headlines shaved, small 8vo., 18th century colored dec. boards, the Landau copy with bookplate. Thomas 32-152 1974 £55

SANUTUS, PETRUS AURELIUS　　Soli Deo Honor et Gloria. 1543. Small 4to., quarter calf. Thomas 30-79 1973 £30

SAPPHO　　The Poems of. London, 1924. Small crown 4to., orig. parchment backed boards, uncut, handmade paper, limited. Bow Windows 62-807 1974 £7.50

SAPPINGTON, JOHN　　The Theory and Treatment of Fevers. Arrow Rock, 1844. Tan calf. Putnam 126-200 1974 $22

SARCEY, F.　　Comediens et Comediennes. Paris, 1884. 8vo., full green morocco, little rubbed, gilt spine, engraved plates. Bow Windows 66-606 1974 £10.50

SARFATTI, MARGHERITA G.　　Le Opere di Gaetano Previati dell' Associazione Nazionale fra Mutilati ed Invalidi di Guerra. Milan, 1927. 4to., wrapper, plates. Minters 37-203 1973 $26

SARGEAUNT, JOHN　　Westminster Verses. London, (1922). Small 8vo., portrait, orig. parchment boards, limited. Bow Windows 62-1038 1974 £8

SARGENT, EPES　　Velasco. New York, 1839. 12mo., orig. violet cloth, faded, first published edition. Ximenes 35-113 1974 $25

SARGENT, GEORGE H.　　A Busted Bibliophile and His Books. Boston, 1928. 12mo., boards, cloth back, paper label, first edition. Goodspeed's 578-508 1974 $15

SARGENT, JOHN　　The Mine. 1785. 4to., modern calf-backed boards, first edition. Quaritch 936-211 1974 £25

SARGENT, JOHN SINGER　　A Catalogue of the Memorial Exhibition of the Works of. Boston, 1925. First edition, small 4to., full page illus., bottom of front cover stained, interior fine. Current BW9-598 1974 $18.75

SARGENT, LUCIUS MANLIUS　　Dealings with the Dead. Boston, 1856. 2 vols., review copy inscribed by publisher, orig. binding. Butterfield 10-482 1974 $35

SARGENT, LUCIUS MANLIUS　　The Stage-Coach. Boston, 1838. 12mo., orig. cloth, first edition, very minor foxing. MacManus 224-387 1974 $40

SARGENT, WINTHROP　　Boston. Boston, 1803. 12mo., sewn as issued, uncut, corrected enlarged second edition. Goodspeed's 578-311 1974 $15

SAROYAN, WILLIAM　　Adventures of Wesley Jackson. Harcourt, 1946. 285p. Austin 54-899 1973 $6

SAROYAN, WILLIAM　　The Adventures of Wesley Jackson. Faber, Faber, 1947. 336p., English ed. Austin 54-898 1973 $6

SAROYAN, WILLIAM　　Boys and Girls Together. Harcourt, 1963. 153p. Austin 54-900 1973 $4

SAROYAN, WILLIAM　　The Cave Dwellers. Putnam. 187p. Austin 54-901 1973 $10

SAROYAN, WILLIAM　　The Daring Young Man on the Flying Trapeze. Random, 1934. 270p. Austin 54-902 1973 $7.50

SAROYAN, WILLIAM　　The Daring Young Man on the Flying Trapeze and Other Stories. New York, 1934. First edition, orig. binding, d.w. somewhat darkened on spine, fine copy. Ross 87-509 1974 $40

SAROYAN, WILLIAM　　Dear Baby. Harcourt, 1944. 115p. Austin 54-903 1973 $6.50

SAROYAN, WILLIAM　　The Human Comedy. New York, 1943. First edition, illus., d.w. chipped & torn at back, orig. binding, internally near mint. Ross 87-510 1974 $15

SAROYAN, WILLIAM　　The Human Comedy. Harcourt, Brace, 1943. 291p., orig. ed., illus. Austin 54-904 1973 $5

SAROYAN, WILLIAM　　Little Children. Harcourt, Brace, 1937. 243p. Austin 54-905 1973 $8.50

SAROYAN, WILLIAM　　Love, Here Is My Heart. Modern Age, 1938. 145p., paper. Austin 54-906 1973 $8.50

SAROYAN, WILLIAM　　Love, Here Is My Hat. New York, 1938. First edition, stiff paper covers & wrappers, scarce, fine. Ross 87-511 1974 $12.50

SAROYAN, WILLIAM　　My Name Is Aram. Harcourt, 1940. 220p., orig. illus. ed. Austin 54-907 1973 $6

SAROYAN, WILLIAM　　My Name is Aram. New York, 1940. Illus., first edition, orig. binding, d.w. somewhat chipped, fine. Ross 87-512 1974 $10

SAROYAN, WILLIAM　　One Day In the Afternoon of the World. Harcourt, Brace, 1964. 245p. Austin 54-908 1973 $7.50

SAROYAN, WILLIAM　　Papa You're Crazy. Little, Brown, 1956. 165p. Austin 54-909 1973 $7.50

SAROYAN, WILLIAM　　Rock Wagram. Doubleday, 1951. 301p. Austin 54-910 1973 $6.50

SAROYAN, WILLIAM　　Short Drive, Sweet Chariot. Phaedra, 1966. 133p., hard cover ed. Austin 54-911 1973 $7.50

SARPI, PAOLO　　Father Paul of Beneficiary Matters. 1730. New buckram. Allen 213-1761 1973 $12.50

SARRATT, J. H.　　A New Treatise on the Game of Chess. London, 1821. 8vo., 2 vols., contemporary half calf, gilt, first edition. Hammond 201-89 1974 £12.50

SARRE, FRIEDRICH　　Islamic Bookbindings. (1923). Imp. 4to., plates, illus., buckram, limited. Quaritch 940-608 1974 £50

SARS, G. O.　　Carcinologiske Bidrag til Norges Fauna. Christiania, 1870-79. 3 parts in 1 vol., 4to., half calf, plates, library stamp, scarce. Wheldon 128-922 1973 £15

SARS, G. O.　　On Some Remarkable Forms of Animal Life. 1875. 4to., half cloth, plates. Wheldon 129-793 1974 £7.50

SARTIRO, ENRICO C.　　Social and Religious Life of Italians in America. 1918. Orig. ed. Austin 62-563 1974 $10

SARTORIO, ARISTIDE   Sibilla. Milano, (1923). Large 4to., boards, signed. Rich Summer-92 1974 $50

SARTORY, A.   Champignons Parasites. (Paris, 1920-24). 8vo., cloth, plates. Wheldon 129-1334 1974 £12

SARTORY, A.   Compendium Hymenomycetum. Paris, 1922-23. Plates, wrappers. Wheldon 129-1337 1974 £10

SARTORY, A.   Guide Pratique. Paris, n.d. 8vo., cloth, plates. Wheldon 129-1335 1974 £5

SARTORY, A.   Les Mycoses Pulmonaires. Paris, 1923. Roy 8vo., buckram, plates. Wheldon 129-1336 1974 £7.50

SARTRE, JEAN-PAUL   L'Etre et le Neant. Paris, 1943. 8vo., orig. printed wrappers, very fine, first edition. Gilhofer 61-100 1974 sFr. 450

SASS, J. E.   Elements of Botanical Microtechnique. New York, 1940. 8vo., cloth, scarce. Wheldon 131-1195 1974 £5

SASSOON, SIEGFRIED   The Daffodil Murderer. 1913. First edition, demy 8vo., paper printed wrapper, exceptionally fine copy, scarce. Broadhurst 24-846 1974 £40

SASSOON, SIEGFRIED   The Flower-Show Match and Other Pieces. London, 1941. Orig. binding, first edition, owner's name in ink on fly, fine, dust wrapper. Ross 87-514 1974 $12.50

SASSOON, SIEGFRIED   The Heart's Journey. London, 1928. First English ordinary edition, orig. binding, lacking d.w., unusually fine, tight copy. Ross 87-515 1974 $12.50

SASSOON, SIEGFRIED   The Heart's Journey. New York, 1927. Linen-backed boards, fine, signed, first U.S. edition. Covent 56-1146 1974 £21

SASSOON, SIEGFRIED   The Heart's Journey. New York & London, 1927. Med. 8vo., boards, cloth spine, mint, d.w., limited to 590 copies, signed by author, on rag paper. Broadhurst 24-848 1974 £45

SASSOON, SIEGFRIED   The Heart's Journey. New York, 1927. First edition, limited to 590 numbered copies, signed by author, very nice copy, d.w., scarce, orig. cloth. Crane 7-282 1974 £40

SASSOON, SIEGFRIED   In Sicily. 1930. 8vo., orig. cloth, first edition. Rota 189-766 1974 £10

SASSOON, SIEFGRIED   Memoirs of a Fox-Hunting Man. London, 1928. 8vo., orig. cloth, presentation inscription, first English edition. Dawsons PM 252-852 1974 £16

SASSOON, SIEGFRIED   Memoirs of a Fox-Hunting Man. 1928. Near fine, English first edition. Covent 56-1147 1974 £25

SASSOON, SIEGFRIED   Memoirs of a Fox-Hunting Man. London, 1928. No. 99 of edition limited to 260 copies on English hand made paper, slight staining inside covers, orig. binding, signed, fine. Ross 87-516 1974 $65

SASSOON, SIEGFRIED   Memoirs of a Fox-Hunting Man. London, 1929. First illus. edition, limited to 300 numbered copies, handmade paper, signed by author and artist, orig. dec. parchment boards, two corners bumped, nice copy. Crane 7-283 1974 £40

SASSOON, SIEGFRIED   Memoirs of a Fox Hunting Man. 1929. Illus., nice copy, first edition. Covent 51-1640 1973 £7.50

SASSOON, SIEGFRIED   Memoirs of an Infantry Officer. 1930. 8vo., buckram, gilt, first edition. Quaritch 936-539 1974 £20

SASSOON, SIEGFRIED   Memoirs of an Infantry Officer. 1930. Fine, torn & defective d.w., first edition. Covent 51-1642 1973 £5.25

SASSOON, SIEGFRIED   Memoirs of an Infantry Officer. London, 1930. 8vo., orig. buckram, signed, first edition. Dawsons PM 252-853 1974 £25

SASSOON, SIEGFRIED   The Old Century and Seven More Years. London, 1938. First edition, orig. binding, lacking d.w., fine. Ross 87-517 1974 $15

SASSOON, SIEGFRIED   The Old Huntsman and Other Poems. London, 1917. First edition, first issue, with errata slip pasted in, rubbed & somewhat torn d.w., small splatter stains, orig. binding, chip out of bottom front cover, internally fine. Ross 87-518 1974 $65

SASSOON, SIEGFRIED   Poems. 1931. Boards, fine, first edition. Covent 51-1645 1973 £6.30

SASSOON, SIEGFRIED   Poems by Pinchbeck Lyre. 1931. First edition, crown 8vo., mint, orig. tissue wrapper. Broadhurst 24-850 1974 £12

SASSOON, SIEGFRIED   The Redeemer. Cambridge, 1916. 8vo., un-bound, first edition. Quaritch 936-540 1974 £50

SASSOON, SIEGFRIED   Rhymed Ruminations. London, (1940). 12mo., cloth. Goodspeed's 578-312 1974 $12.50

SASSOON, SIEGFRIED   The Road to Ruin. 1933. Demy 8vo., mint, d.w., first edition, orig. cloth. Broadhurst 24-851 1974 £6

SASSOON, SIEGFRIED   The Road to Ruin. London, 1933. First edition, spine slightly worn, unusually nice copy, d.w., crimson paper boards. Crane 7-284 1974 £6

SASSOON, SIEGFRIED   Satirical Poems. 1926. First edition, crown 8vo., orig. cloth, fine. Broadhurst 24-847 1974 £10

SASSOON, SIEGFRIED   Sherston's Progress. (1936). 8vo., orig. buck-ram, fine, signed, first edition. Bow Windows 64-676 1974 £12

SASSOON, SIEGFRIED   To My Mother. London, 1928. Orig. boards, first edition, one of 500 numbered copies, signed by author, fine. MacManus 224-388 1974 $25

SASSOON, SIEGFRIED   Vigils. London, 1935. First English ordinary edition, lacking d.w., orig. binding, spine slightly faded, fine. Ross 87-520 1974 $15

SASSOON, SIEGFRIED   The War Poems. 1919. Spine faded & frayed, very good copy, first edition. Covent 51-1648 1973 £8.50

SASSOON, SIEGFRIED   The Weald of Youth. (1942). 8vo., orig. cloth, portrait, inscription on fly, dust wrapper, first English edition. Bow Windows 66-608 1974 £5.15

SATGE, OSCAR DE   Pages from the Journal of a Queensland Squatter. 1901. 8vo., cloth, maps, illus., inscribed by author. Bow Windows 66-609 1974 £12

SATGE ST. JEAN, CAROLINE DE   The Cave of the Huguenots. Bath, n.d. 8vo., orig. cloth, plates, gilt, first edition. Ximenes 35-114 1974 $10

THE SATYR of Titus Petronius Arbiter. London, 1694. 2 parts in 1 vol., 8vo., contemporary panelled calf, first English edition. Dawsons PM 252-781 1974 £145

SAUL, EDWARD   An Historical and Philosophical Account of the Barometer. London, 1730. 8vo., nineteenth century half shagreen, first edition. Schumann 35-421 1974 $110

SAULNIER, GILBERT   The Love and Armes of the Greke Princes. London, 1640. Folio, contemporary calf, fine, first English edition. Dawsons PM 252-854 1974 £170

SAUMIERES, JACQUES LANGLADE   New Memoirs and Characters of the Two Great Brothers. London, 1693. 8vo., contemporary sheep, first edition in English. Dawsons PM 251-134 1974 £65

SAUNDERS, CHARLES FRANCIS   The Southern Sierras of California. London, 1924. Blue cloth, illus., fine, first English edition. Bradley 35-50 1974 $12

SAUNDERS, DANIEL   A Journal of the Travels and Sufferings of. Salem, 1794. 12mo., contemporary calf, first edition. Ximenes 35-120 1974 $90

SAUNDERS, EDWARD   The Hemiptera Heteroptera of the British Islands. 1892. 8vo., orig. cloth, plates. Bow Windows 64-783 1974 £45

SAUNDERS, EDWARD   The Hymenoptera Aculeata of the British Islands. 1896. 8vo., orig. cloth, plates. Bow Windows 64-784 1974 £50

SAUNDERS, EDWARD   Synopsis of British Heterogyna and Fossorial Hymenoptera. 1880-84. 8vo., half calf, plates. Wheldon 130-787 1974 £7.50

SAUNDERS, H.   Manual of British Birds. 1927. 8vo., cloth, third edition. Wheldon 129-524 1974 £5

SAUNDERS, HENRY S.   Parodies on Walt Whitman. New York, 1923. lst ed. Biblo & Tannen 214-778 1974 $7.50

SAUNDERS, JOHN MONK   Wings. 1927. 249p., illus. Austin 51-821 1973 $7.50

SAUNDERS, M.   Lincolnshire in 1836. Lincoln, 1836. 8vo., contemporary calf, corners worn, rebacked, engraved plates, illus., some foxing. Bow Windows 66-610 1974 £45

SAUNDERS, MARSHALL   Beautiful Joe, an Autobiography. 1894. Spine rubbed. Allen 216-1556 1974 $12.50

SAUNDERS, O. E.   English Illumination. Florence, (1928). 2 vols., 4to., half green morocco. Quaritch 939-233 1974 £110

SAUNDERS, RICHARD   The Astrological Judgment and Practice of Physick. London, 1677. 8vo., contemporary calf, first edition. Schumann 35-422 1974 $145

SAUNDERS, WILLIAM   An Answer to the Observations of Mr. Geach, and to the Cursory Remarks of Mr. Alcock, on Dr. Baker's Essay on the Endemial Colic of Devonshire. London, 1767. 8vo., boards, slightly wormed. Gurney 66-164 1974 £12

SAUNDERS, WILLIAM WILSON   Mycological Illustrations. 1871-72. Parts 1 & 2 in 1 vol., imp. 8vo., half morocco, extremely rare. Wheldon 131-1463 1974 £45

SAUNDERS, WILLIAM WILSON   Mycological Illustrations. 1871-72. Roy. 8vo., cloth. Wheldon 129-1339 1974 £45

SAUNDERSON, NICHOLAS   The Elements of Algebra. Cambridge, 1740. 4to., 2 vols., contemporary calf, plates, first edition. Dawsons PM 245-655 1974 £45

SAURAT, DENIS   Gods of the People. London, 1947. Biblo & Tannen 213-993 1973 $9.50

SAUSSURE, HORACE BENEDICT DE   Essais sur l'Hygrometrie. 1783. 4to., contemporary continental boards, gilt, fine, first edition. Dawsons PM 245-656 1974 £65

SAUSSURE, HORACE BENEDICT DE   Essais sur l'Hygrometrie. 1783. 8vo., orig. Grench marbled boards, fine, plates, second edition. Dawsons PM 245-657 1974 £44

SAUSSURE, HORACE BENEDICT, DE   Essais sur l'Hygrometrie. 1783. 8vo., plates, wrappers, uncut. Zeitlin 235-198 1974 $100

SAUSSURE, HORACE BENEDICT DE   Melanges Hymenopterologiques. Geneva, 1877-78. 4to., plates. Wheldon 129-675 1974 £7.50

SAUVAGEAU, C.   Four Papers on Marine Algae. 1929-36. 8vo., wrappers. Wheldon 131-1464 1974 £5

SAUVAGEOT, C.   Palais, Chateaux, Hotels et Maisons de France du XVe au XVIIIe Siecle. Paris, 1867. 4 vols., folio, plates, half red morocco. Quaritch 940-553 1974 £40

SAUVAGES DE LA CROIX, FRANCOIS BOISSIER DE   Memoires sur l'Education des Vers a Soie. Nimes, 1778. 8vo., contemporary marbled calf. Schumann 35-423 1974 $125

SAUVAGES DE LA CROIX, FRANCOIS BOISSIER DE   Nosologia Methodica Sistens Morborum Classes. Amsterdam, 1768. 2 vols., 4to., old calf, new cloth backs. Schuman 37-228 1974 $95

SAVAGE, EDWARD   Police Records and Recollections. Boston, 1865. Rubbed, excellent. Rinsland 58-77 1974 $17

SAVAGE, HENRY   Richard Middleton: A Biography. 1922. Illus., front hinge little cracked, else fine, first edition. Covent 51-1268 1973 £5.25

SAVAGE, I. O.   A History of Republic County, Kansas. Beloit, 1901. 8vo., cloth. Saddleback 14-433 1974 $45

SAVAGE, JOHN   Horace to Scaeva. London, 1730. 8vo., wrappers, uncut, first edition. Dawsons PM 252-855 1974 £55

SAVAGE, SARAH   Advice to a Young Woman at Service. New York, 1823. 12mo., disbound, first edition. Ximenes 35-122 1974 $10

SAVAGE, RICHARD   The Progress of a Divine. London, 1735. Folio, quarter morocco, scarce, first edition. Ximenes 35-121 1974 $175

SAVAGE, WILLIAM   Practical Hints on Decorative Printing. London, 1822. Marbled boards, calf, frontispiece, illus. Dawson's 424-136 1974 $650

SAVAGE-LANDOR, A. HENRY   Across Unknown South America. 1913. Imp. 8vo., 2 vols., first edition, orig. cloth, fine, maps, coloured plates, illus. by author. Broadhurst 24-1674 1974 £15

SAVAGE-LANDOR, A. HENRY   Across Unknown South America. 1913. Imperial 8vo., 2 vols., orig. cloth, first edition. Broadhurst 23-1706 1974 £15

SAVERY, THOMAS   The Miners Friend. London, 1702. 8vo., fine, tall copy, contemporary panelled morocco, first edition. Traylen 79-268 1973 £900

SAVERY, THOMAS   Navigation Improv'd. London, 1698. 4to., full blue morocco by Sangorski & Sutcliffe, orig. edition, rare, engravings. Kraus 137-72 1974 $2,500

SAVIGNY, JOHN H.   A Treatise on the Use and Management of a Razor. London, (1786). Small 8vo., disbound. Goodspeed's 578-313 1974 $15

SAVIGNY, R.   Resume de l'Histoire du Costume en France. Paris, 1867. Presentation, red leather, fine, illus. Ballinger 1-249 1974 $15

SAVILE, GEORGE, MARQUIS OF HALIFAX
Please turn to
HALIFAX, GEORGE SAVILE, MARQUIS OF

SAVILE, H.   Rerum Anglicanum Scriptores Post Bedam Praecipui. 1596. Folio, old calf. Quaritch 939-234 1974 £70

SAVILLE, JOHN FAUCIT   The Miller's Maid. French, ca. 1849. Austin 51-822 1973 $6.50

SAVILLE-KENT, WILLIAM
Please turn to
KENT, WILLIAM SAVILLE

SAVO, JIMMY   Little World, Hello! S & S, 1947. 181p. Austin 51-823 1973 $6

SAVONAROLA, GIROLAMO   Devoti Discorsi Sopra Alcuni Detti de la Sacra Scrittura. Venice, 1556. 8vo., vellum, fine, gilt, woodcut. Harper 213-137 1973 $115

SAVONAROLA, GIROLAMO   Exposizione Sopra l'Ave Maria. Florence, c. 1495. Small 4to., vellum. Thomas 28-309 1972 £160

SAVONAROLA, GIROLAMO   Prediche Quadragesimale Sopra Amos Propheta. Venice, 1539. Very thick 8vo., full green morocco, gilt, fine. Harper 213-135 1973 $125

SAVONAROLA, GIROLAMO   Prediche Sopra Alquanti Salmi. Venice, 1544. 8vo., old vellum, woodcut, staining. Harper 213-136 1973 $65

SAVONAROLA, GIROLAMO   De Simplicitate Vitae Christianae. Venice, 1533. 8vo., boards, fine. Harper 213-134 1973 $125

SAVONAROLA, GIROLAMO   Operetta Sopra e Dieci Comandamenti di Dio. Florence, 1508. 4to., boards, woodcuts, very fine. Harper 213-133 1973 $400

SAVONAROLA, GIROLAMO   Opus Eximium, Adversus Divinatricem Astronomiam. Florence, 1582. 8vo., contemporary limp vellum. Harper 213-138 1973 $95

SAVORY, GERALD   George and Margaret. 1937. Austin 51-824 1973 $7.50

SAWARD, B. C.   Decorative Painting. n.d. Illus., first edition. Covent 55-122 1974 £5.25

SAWARD, B. C.   Decorative Painting. n.d. Orig. dec. cloth, English first edition. Covent 56-1503 1974 £21

SAWER, J. C.   Odorographia, a Natural History of Raw Materials and Drugs Used in the Perfume Industry Including Aromatics Used in Flavouring. 1894. 8vo., cloth, very scarce. Wheldon 131-1796 1974 £15

SAWER, J. C.   Rhodologia. Brighton, 1894. 8vo., orig. wrappers. Wheldon 130-1454 1974 £7.50

SAWYER, ANNA   Poems on Various Subjects. Birmingham, 1801. 8vo., contemporary half calf, first edition. Dawsons PM 252-856 1974 £38

SAWYER, CHARLES J.   English Books 1475-1900. 1927. 8vo., 2 vols., orig. cloth, illus. Broadhurst 23-461 1974 £25

SAWYER, CHARLES J.   English Books, 1475-1900. 1927. 2 vols., 8vo., buckram, illus., limited. Howes 185-835 1974 £35

SAWYER, CHARLES J.   English Books 1475-1900. Westminster, 1927. 2 vols., 8vo., orig. cloth, fine, limited, first edition. Dawsons PM 10-541 1974 £46

SAWYER, EDMUND   Memorials of Affairs of State. 1725. 3 vols., folio, contemporary panelled calf, sole edition. Howes 186-1319 1974 £45

SAWYER, EUGENE T.   History of Santa Clara County, California. Los Angeles, 1922. 4to., three quarter leather, illus. Saddleback 14-274 1974 $100

SAWER, J. CH   Odorographia. London, 1892-1894. 8vo., 2 vols., orig. brown blind-stamped cloth, illus., presentation copy, first edition. Dawsons PM 245-658 1974 £120

SAWYER, LEMUEL   Printz Hall; A Record of New Sweden. Philadelphia, 1839. 2 vols., orig. cloth, ends of spines worn, first edition, some foxing. MacManus 224-389 1974 $100

SAWYER, MOSES H.   Lieutenant Colborn. Portland, 1861. 12mo., orig. cloth, first edition. Ximenes 35-123 1974 $25

SAWYER, RUTH   The Way of the Storyteller. Viking, 1942. Austin 51-825 1973 $7.50

SAXBY, HENRY   The British Customs. London, 1757. 8vo., contemporary speckled calf, first edition. Dawsons PM 247-257 1974 £20

SAXE, JOHN GODFREY   Selections from the Poems Of. Boston & New York, 1905. 8vo., fine, vignette. Ballinger 1-44 1974 $15

SAXE, MAURICE, COMTE DE   Reveries. 1757. 4to., plates, half dark calf, stains. Howes 186-1758 1974 £30

SAXE, MAURICE, COMTE DE   Reveries. London, 1757. 4to., contemporary calf, gilt, first English edition. Hammond 201-621 1974 £48

SAXON, LYLE   Lafitte the Pirate. New York - London, (1930). 8vo., orig. bindings, first edition. Butterfield 8-193 1974 $12.50

SAXON, LYLE   Old Louisiana. New York - London, (1929). 8vo., orig. bindings, illus., inscribed, first edition. Butterfield 8-194 1974 $15

SAY, JEAN BAPTISTE   De l'Angleterre et Des Anglais. Londres & Paris, 1816. 8vo., modern boards. Dawsons PM 247-258 1974 £30

SAY, JEAN-BAPTISTE   Catechisme d'Economie Politique. Paris, 1821. 8vo., half calf, second edition. Dawsons PM 247-259 1974 £30

SAY, JEAN-BAPTISTE   Catechisme d'Economie Politique. Paris, 1826. 8vo., quarter morocco, third edition. Dawsons PM 247-260 1974 £20

SAY, T.   The Complete Writings on the Entomology of North America. New York, 1859. Part 2, 8vo., orig. wrappers, worn. Wheldon 128-792 1973 £5

SAYCE, A. H.   The Egypt of the Hebrews and Herodotos. London, 1902. Biblo & Tannen 213-932 1973 $12.50

SAYER, R.   The Compleat Drawing-Master. 1766. 4to., plates, modern half calf, orig. drab wrappers. Quaritch 940-236 1974 £90

SAYERS, G. F.   The Handbook of Tanganyika. London, 1930. 8vo., maps, charts, illus., orig. cloth, fine, first issue. Bow Windows 62-809 1974 £8.50

SAYERS, I.   The Foundling-Chapel Brawl. London, 1804. 4to., orig. wrappers, presentation, inscribed. Dawsons PM 252-857 1974 £25

SAYERS, DOROTHY L.   Busman's Honeymoon. 1937. 8vo., orig. cloth, first edition. Rota 190-348 1974 £6

SAYERS, DOROTHY L.   Gaudy Night. New York, 1936. Biblo & Tannen 210-519 1973 $10

SAYERS, DOROTHY L.   Hangman's Holiday. New York, 1933. 1st ed. Biblo & Tannen 210-520 1973 $12.50

SAYERS, DOROTHY L.   The Documents in the Case. 1930. English first edition. Covent 56-345 1974 £7.50

SAYERS, JAMES   Elijah's Mantle. London, 1807. 8vo., modern boards, first edition. Ximenes 35-125 1974 $20

SAYERS, JAMES   An Etched Caricature. (London), 1783. Folio. Ximenes 35-127 1974 $20

SAYERS, JAMES   The Uti Possidetis. London, 1807. 8vo., modern boards, first edition. Ximenes 35-126 1974 $20

SAYLER, OLIVER   The Russian Theatre Under the Revolution. 1920. Illus., first U. S. edition, small nick in spine, inscription, nice copy. Covent 51-1816 1973 £10.50

SAYLER, OLIVER M.   Revolt in the Arts. New York, 1930. First U. S. edition, fine copy, torn d.w. Covent 51-2106 1973 £21

SAYLIN, GEORGE J.   An Issue On the Occasion of the Twenty-Fifth Anniversary of the Jewish National Fund. Los Angeles, 1927. 8vo., wrapper. Saddleback 14-275 1974 $10

SAYRE, JOEL   Hizzoner the Mayor. Day, 1933. 288p. Austin 54-912 1973 $6.50

SAYRE, JOEL   Rackety Rax. Knopf, 1932. 147p. Austin 54-913 1973 $6.50

SCADDING, HENRY   Cabot's Head. Toronto, 1892. Hood's 103-673 1974 $10

SCADDING, HENRY   Early Notices of Toronto. Toronto, 1865. Marbled board, linen spine. Hood's 102-633 1974 $25

SCADDING, HENRY   Jubilee Of the Diocese of Toronto, 1839-1889. Toronto, 1890. Hood's 103-267 1974 $20

SCADDING, HENRY   Surveyor-General Holland. Toronto, 1896. Marbled boards. Hood's 103-233 1974 $15

SCALE, B.   An Hibernian Atlas. 1798. 4to., half calf, maps, plates. Quaritch 939-630 1974 £150

SCALETTA, CARLO CESARE   Scuola Mecanico-Speculativo Practica. 1711. Small folio, plates, modern half vellum, gilt, rare, first edition. Zeitlin 235-199 1974 $275

SCALETTA, CARLO CESARE   Scuola Mecanico. 1745. Folio, gilt, eighteenth century half morocco, plates, first Venetian edition. Dawsons PM 245-659 1974 £55

SCALIGER, JOSEPH   Scaligeriana. 1666. Calf. Allen 213-1763 1973 $17.50

SCARBOROUGH, DOROTHY   A Song Catcher in Southern Mountains American Folk Songs of British Ancestry. New York, 1937. 8vo., orig. bindings. Butterfield 8-15 1974 $15

SCARPA, ANTONIO   Degli Aneurismi. Florence, 1845. 8vo., contemporary half shagreen. Schumann 35-425 1974 $110

SCARPA, ANTONIO   A Memoir On the Congenital Club Feet of Children. London, 1818. 4to., contemporary calf, plates, first English edition. Schuman 37-229 1974 $110

SCARPA, ANTONIO   De Penitiori Ossium Structura Commentarius. 1800. 8vo., wrappers, uncut, plates. Dawsons PM 249-439 1974 £36

SCARPA, ANTONIO   Saggio di Osservazioni e d'Esperienze sulle. Venice, 1802. 8vo., contemporary calf-backed boards. Schumann 35-424 1974 $110

SCARPA, ANTONIO   Tabulae Nevrologicae. Pavia, 1794. Folio, contemporary half calf, plates, very rare first edition. Gilhofer 61-27 1974 sFr. 4,800

SCARPA, ANTONIO   Tabulae Neurologicae. 1794. Large folio, 19th century boards, first edition. Dawsons PM 249-438 1974 £585

SCARPA, ANTONIO   A Treatise on Aneurism. Edinburgh, 1819. 8vo., contemporary purple calf, gilt. Dawsons PM 249-441 1974 £45

SCARPA, ANTONIO   A Treatise on Hernia. Edinburgh and London, 1814. 8vo., modern half calf, fine, first edition in English. Dawsons PM 249-440 1974 £55

SCARRON, PAUL   The Comic Romance of Monsieur Scarron. London, 1775. 2 vols., 8vo., contemporary calf, first English edition. Dawsons PM 252-858 1974 £60

SCARRON, PAUL   The Comical Romance and Other Tales. 1892. 2 vols., plates, limited. Howes 185-419 1974 £5.50

SCARRON, PAUL   Le Jodelet ou le Me. Paris, 1648. 4to., modern red leather, red slipcase, third edition. Schumann 499-104 1974 sFr 360

SCARRON, PAUL   Le Virgile Travesty en vers Burlesques. Paris, 1655. 6 parts in 1 vol., 12mo., full green levant morocco, gilt. L. Goldschmidt 42-115 1974 $160

SCARRON, PAUL   The Whole Comical Works of. London, 1700. 8vo., late 19th century half calf, first edition. Ximenes 35-128 1974 $150

SCARRON, PAUL   The Whole Comical Works. London, 1712. 8vo., mid 19th century half calf, third edition. Ximenes 35-129 1974 $60

SCARRON, PAUL   Les Oeuvres. Paris, 1715-20. 10 vols., 12mo., contemporary brown calf, gilt. L. Goldschmidt 42-116 1974 $360

SCAWEN, WILFRED   The Love Lyrics and Songs of Proteus. Kelmscott Press, 1892. Small 4to., limp vellum, silk ties, uncut, limited to 300 copies, golden type in red & black, fine. Broadhurst 24-1015 1974 £175

SCENES in China, Exhibiting the Manners, Customs, Diversions and Singular Peculiarities of the Chinese. London, (c. 1820). Engraved plates, 12mo., orig. boards, roan spine. George's 610-644 1973 £10

SCENES in Crater Lake National Park, America's Scenic Wonder. Crater Lake, c. 1900. Small folio, pict. wrapper, hand colored illus. Jenkins 61-2093 1974 $12.50

SCENES in Glacier National Park. N. P., c. 1925. Small folio, wrapper, hand colored illus. Jenkins 61-1753 1974 $10

SCENES in Glacier National Park: The Top of the Continent. Brooklyn, c. 1910. Wrapper, small folio, hand coloured photos. Jenkins 61-1754 1974 $10

SCHABOL, J. R.   La Pratique de Jardinage. Paris, 1770. 2 vols., 8vo., contemporary mottled sheep, plates, first edition. Wheldon 131-1569 1974 £30

SCHACHNER, NATHAN   The Price of Liberty. 1948. Austin 62-566 1974 $8.50

SCHACHT, H.   Die Pflanzenzelle. Berlin, 1852. Roy. 8vo., orig. boards, worn, plates, scarce, first edition. Wheldon 128-1160 1973 £10

SCHACHT, H.   The Microscope. 1855. 8vo., cloth, second edition. Wheldon 129-99 1974 £7.50

SCHACHT, ROLAND   Henri Matisse. Dresden, 1922. 4to., boards, illus. Minters 37-107 1973 $22

SCHAEFER, H.   Catalonien in Malerischer, Architectonischer und Antiquarischer Beziehung. Leipzig & Darmstadt, (c. 1840). Roy. folio, boards, cloth spine, plates. Quaritch 940-797 1974 £12

SCHAEFFER, J.   Russula-Monographie. 1933-34. 8vo., cloth, 2 vols., plates. Wheldon 129-1340 1974 £10

SCHAEFFER, JACOB CHRISTIAN   Die Armpolypen in den Sussen Wassern um Regensburg. Regensburg, 1754. Small 4to., sewed, plates, scarce. Wheldon 131-948 1974 £10

SCHAEFFER, LUTHER M.   Sketches of Travels in South America, Mexico, and California. New York, 1860. Jenkins 61-2321 1974 $12.50

SCHAERER, L. E.   Enumeratio Critica Lichenum Europaeorum. Bern, 1850. 8vo., cloth, coloured plates, scarce. Wheldon 128-1419 1973 £10

SCHAFER, H.   Die Kunst des Alten Orients. Berlin, 1925. Roy. 8vo., plates, half morocco, first edition. Quaritch 940-353 1974 £10

SCHAFF, PHILIP   History of the Christian Church. Edinburgh, 1884-93. 10 vols., orig. cloth, revised edition. Howes 185-1630 1974 £25

SCHAFF, PHILIP   A History of the Creeds of Christendom. 1877. 3 vols., large 8vo., orig. cloth, scarce. Howes 185-1631 1974 £25

SCHAFFER, JACOB CHRISTIAN   Der Afterholzbock in Einem Sendschreiben Beschrieben. Regensburg, 1763. 4to., plate, second edition. Wheldon 131-852 1974 £5

SCHAFFER, JACOB CHRISTIAN   Der Weichschaalige Cronen und Kaeulenkafer. Regensburg, 1763. 4to., plate, rare, second edition. Wheldon 131-853 1974 £5

SCHAFFER, JACOB CHRISTIAN   Das Zwiefalter Oder Afterjungferchen. Regensburg, 1763. 4to., plate, second edition. Wheldon 131-851 1974 £7.50

SCHANZ, PAUL   A Christian Apology. Dublin & New York, 1891-92. 3 vols. Howes 185-1632 1974 £5.50

SCARBOROUGH'S Road Map and Motor Guide to Indiana. Indianapolis, (1914). Wrappers, folding map. Hayman 59-306 1974 $10

SCATTERING BRANCHES. 1940. Wrappers, English first edition. Covent 56-1386 1974 £21

SCHARF, J. THOMAS   History of Philadelphia 1609-1884. Philadelphia, 1884. Large thick 4to., 3 vols., orig. cloth, gilt. Butterfield 8-555 1974 $75

SCHAUFFLER, ROBERT HAVEN   Brahms, the Unknown. New York, 1936. Biblo & Tannen 214-819 1974 $8.50

SCHAUFFLER, ROBERT HAVEN   Scum of the Earth. 1912. 58 pages. Austin 57-594 1974 $10

SCHEDEL, HARTMANN   Liber Chronicarum. (Nuremberg, 1493). Folio, woodcut, old russia, rebacked, inscriptions, slipcase, first edition. Dawsons PM 250-70 1974 £8500

SCHEEBEN, MATTHIAS J.   Handbuch der Katholischen Dogmatik. 1925.
4 vols., thick large 8vo., orig. cloth. Howes 185-1633 1974 £15

SCHEELE, CARL WILHELM   Chemical Observations and Experiments on Air
and Fire. London, 1780. 8vo., contemporary paper-covered boards, rare, first
edition. Dawsons PM 245-660 1974 £525

SCHEERBART, PAUL   Munchhausen und Clarissa. Berlin, 1906.
8vo., cloth. Minters 37-485 1973 $20

SCHEFER, LEOPOLD   Albert Durer. New York, 1862. 12mo.
Biblo & Tannen 210-126 1973 $10

SCHEINER, CHRISTOPHER   Oculus Hoc Est. 1652. 4to., modern full
brown morocco, gilt. Dawsons PM 249-442 1974 £145

SCHEIWILLER, GIOVANNI   Arturo Tosi. Milan, 1942. Folio, cloth,
plates. Minters 37-212 1973 $24

SCHEIWILLER, GIOVANNI   Pompeo Borra. Milan, (1941). Large 4to.,
boards, cloth spine, limited edition. Minters 37-177 1973 $18.50

SCHEIWILLER, GIOVANNI   Pompeo Borra. Milan, (1941). Inscribed.
Minters 37-177A 1973 $20

SCHELLE, E.   Handbuch der Kakteenkultur. Stuttgart, 1907.
8vo., cloth, illus. Wheldon 131-1695 1974 £7.50

SCHELLE, E.   Kakteen, Kurzbeschreibung Nebst Angaben
Uber die Kultur der Gegenwartig im Handel Befindlichen Arten und Formen.
Tubingen, 1926. 8vo., cloth, illus. Wheldon 131-1696 1974 £5

SCHELLENBERG, H. C.   Die Brandpilze der Schweiz. Bern, 1911. Roy
8vo., half cloth. Wheldon 129-1341 1974 £5

SCHELLING, F. E.   Elizabethan Drama, 1558-1642. 1908. 2 vols.,
top of one spine repaired. Allen 216-1843 1974 $15

SCHENCK, ELIZABETH HUBBELL   A History of Fairfield. New York, 1889,
1905. 8vo., brown cloth, 2 vols., gilt, scarce, fine. Butterfield 8-93 1974
$65

SCHENCK VON GRAFENBERG, J.   Observationum Medicarum Rararum,
Novorum, Admirabilium, et Monstrosarum. 1596. 8vo., 2 vols. in 1, first
editions, contemporary blind stamped vellum. Gurney 66-165 1974 £65

SCHENK, A.   Handbuch der Botanik. Breslau, 1879-90.
8vo., half morocco, worn. Wheldon 129-960 1974 £7.50

SCHEREMETEW, S. D.   Die Waffensammlung des Grafen S. D.
Scheremetew in St. Petersburg. 1897. Folio, plates. Allen 213-1766
1973 $45

SCHERER, C.   Das Furstenberger Porzellan. Berlin, 1909.
4to., boards. Quaritch 940-660 1974 £28

SCHERMERHORN, E. W.   Malta of the Knights. (1929). 8vo., orig.
cloth, worn. Bow Windows 64-677 1974 £9.75

SCHERMERHORN, R. A.   These Our People. Heath, 1949. Austin
62-572 1974 $10

SCHERZ, JOHANN GEORG   Glossarium Germanicum Medii Aevi.
Strassburg, 1781-84. 2 vols., green half calf of the late 19th century, beautiful
copy, orig. edition. Schumann 499-105 1974 sFr 450

SCHERZER, KARL   Narrative of the Circumnavigation of the
Globe by the Austrian Frigate Novarra. 1861-63. 3 vols., 8vo., half calf,
folding map, illus., slight spotting, first English edition. Bow Windows 66-612
1974 £75

SCHEUCHZER, JOHANN JAKOB   Herbarium Diluvianum Collectum. Leyden,
1723. Folio, contemporary boards, frontispiece, plates, fine. Schafer 8-171
1973 sFr. 1,200

SCHIFFNER, V.   Die Hepaticae der Flora von Buitenzorg. Leyden, 1900. Roy 8vo., buckram. Wheldon 130-1346 1974 £5.50

SCHILDKRAUT, JOSEPH   My Father and I. Viking, 1959. 246p., illus.
Austin 51-827 1973 $7.50

SCHILLER, JOHANN CHRISTOPH FRIEDRICH VON   Sammtliche Werke. 1844.
10 vols., full English tree calf gilt, fine, labels. Howes 186-397 1974 £35

SCHILLER, JOHANN CHRISTOPH FRIEDRICH VON   The Robbers. London,
1795. 8vo., modern boards, second edition. Dawsons PM 252-859 1974 £15

SCHILLER, JOHANN CHRISTOPH FRIEDRICH VON   Gedichte. Leipzig,
1908. Orig. black calf, 2 X 1 1/4. Gregory 44-457 1974 $28.50

SCHILLER, JOHANN CHRISTOPH FRIEDRICH VON   Sammtliche Werke.
Stuttgart und Tuningen, 1828. 12 vols., contemporary leather backed marbled
boards, gilt, rubbed. Smith 194-569 1974 £8.50

SCHILLINGS, C. G.   In Wildest Africa. 1907. 2 vols., roy. 8vo.,
illus., cloth. Wheldon 128-231 1973 £7.50

SCHILLINGS, C. G.   With Flashlight and Rifle. 1906. 2 vols.,
roy. 8vo., cloth, illus. Wheldon 131-392 1974 £15

SCHIMPER, A. F. W.   Plant Geography. Oxford, 1903. Roy 8vo.,
orig. half morocco, illus., maps. Wheldon 129-961 1974 £20

SCHIMPER, A. F. W.   Plant-Geography Upon a Physiological Basis.
Oxford, 1903. Thick med. 8vo., quarter morocco, collotypes, illus., maps,
inscribed presentation copy. Broadhurst 24-1156 1974 £30

SCHINZ, H.   Festschrift Hans Schinz. Zurich, 1928.
8vo., wrappers, plates. Wheldon 131-1196 1974 £6

SCHINZ, H.   Flora der Schweiz, Teil 1 Exkursions-Flora.
Zurich, 1923. Crown 8vo., boards, fourth revised edition. Wheldon 131-1354
1974 £7.50

SCHIODTE, J. C.   De Metamorphosi Eleutheratorum Observationes.
Kjobenhavn, 1876-1883. 8vo., orig. cloth, plates. Bow Windows 64-241 1974
£7.50

SCHIOLER, E. L. T. L.   Danmarks Fugle. Copenhagen, 1925-31.
3 vols., folio, orig. half vellum, plates, map. Wheldon 131-104 1974 £165

SCHIRO, GEORGE   Americans by Choice. 1940. Illus., 183
pages. Austin 57-596 1974 $17.50

SCHKUHR, C.   Histoire des Carex ou Laiches. Leipzig, 1802.
Small 4to., new half morocco, plates, rare. Wheldon 131-1197 1974 £45

SCHKUHR, C.   Histoire des Carex ou Laiches. Leipzig, 1802.
Small 4to., new half morocco. Wheldon 129-962 1974 £45

SCHLAGINTWEIT, A.   Neue Untersuchungen Uber die Physikalische
Geographie und die Geologie der Alpen. Leipzig, 1854. 2 vols., 4to. &
folio, half morocco, plates, extremely scarce. Wheldon 131-1076 1974 £70

SCHLAGINTWEIT, A.   Neue Untersuchungen uber die Physikalische
Geographie und die Geologie der Alpen. Leipzig, 1854. Folio, orig.
wrappers, plates. Wheldon 131-1077 1974 £30

SCHLEGEL, AUGUSTUS WILLIAM   Course of Lectures on Dramatic Art and
Literature. 1833. 442p., orig. ed. Austin 51-828 1973 $6.25

SCHLEGEL, H.   Abbildungen neuer oder unvollstandig. Dusseldorf, 1837-44. Imperial 4to., new quarter morocco, plates. Wheldon 129-41
1974 £100

SCHLEGEL, HERMANN   Natuurlijke Historie van Nederland. Amsterdam, 1870. 8vo., half morocco, plates, scarce. Wheldon 130-421 1974 £15

SCHLEIDEN, MATTHIAS JACOB   Grundzuge der Wissenschaftlichen Botanik.
Leipzig, 1842-43. 2 vols., 8vo., contemporary boards, rubbed, very rare
first edition. Gilhofer 61-44 1974 sFr. 1,600

SCHLEIDEN, MATTHIAS JACOB   Grundzuge der Wissenschaftlichen Botanik.
Leipzig, 1861. 8vo., new cloth, fourth edition. Wheldon 129-963 1974 £25

SCHLEIN, MIRIAM   When Will the World Be Mine? New York, 1953. 4to., lithographs, lst ed. Frohnsdorff 16-201 1974 $7.50

SCHLESINGER, MAX   Saunterings In and About London. 1854. Illus. with engravings. Austin 61-887 1974 $12.50

SCHLICH, W.   Manual of Forestry. 1895-97. 8vo., 5 vols., cloth, plates, first edition. Wheldon 130-1570 1974 £7.50

SCHLICH, W.   Manual of Forestry. 1906-11. 5 vols., 8vo., cloth, plates, text-figures. Wheldon 128-1624 1973 £10

SCHLIEMANN, HENRY   Troja. New York, 1884. Biblo & Tannen 213-130 1973 $32.50

SCHLOMANN, ALFRED   Illustrierte Technische Worterbucher. Berlin, (1932). 8vo., grey cloth gilt, illus., first edition. Dawsons PM 245-662 1974 £9

SCHLOTHEIM, E. F. VON   Beschreibung Merkwurdiger Krauter-Abdrucke und Pflanzen-Versteinerungen. Gotha, 1804. Folio, old half calf, plates, very rare. Wheldon 128-1042 1973 £50

SCHLOTHEIM, E. F. VON   Die Petrefactenkunde auf Ihrem Jetzigen Standpunkt. 1820-23. 2 vols., 8vo. and 4to., cloth, very rare. Wheldon 128-1043 1973 £75

SCHLUGA, J. B.   Primae Lineae Cognitionis Insectorum. Vienna, 1767. 8vo., boards, plates, rare. Wheldon 131-854 1974 £10

SCHLUMBERGER, GUSTAVE   Le Siege, la Prise et le Sac de Constantinople par les Turcs en 1453. Paris, 1915. Half crimson morocco gilt, plates, scarce. Howes 186-663 1974 $8.50

SCHMALZ, JOHN BARNES   Nuggets from King Solomon's Mine. Newton, Mass., 1908. 12mo., suede bdg., worn. Biblo & Tannen 213-920 1973 $12.50

SCHMARDA, L. K.   Zur Naturgeschichte Aegyptens. Vienna, 1854. 4to., boards, plates, rare. Wheldon 130-891 1974 £5

SCHMECKEBIER, LAURENCE   John Steuart Curry's Pageant of America. New York, 1943. Colour plates, illus., signed, mint, orig. binding. Ross 86-33 1974 $15

SCHMID, C. VON   Marie, ou la Corbeille de Fleurs. Tours, 1852. 12mo., orig. boards, rubbed, engraved frontis. George's 610-648 1973 £5

SCHMIDT, A.   Shakespeare-Lexicon. 1874. 2 vols., ex-library. Allen 216-2178 1974 $25

SCHMIDT, ADOLF   Atlas der Diatomaceen-Kunde. Leipzig, 1885-1944. Atlas 4to., half morocco, worn, plates, orig. wrappers. Bow Windows 64-242 1974 £520

SCHMIDT, ADOLF   Atlas der Diatomaceenkunde. (1885-1944). 4to., in 5 loose leaf binders. Wheldon 128-1421 1973 £90

SCHMIDT, MASTER FRANZ   A Hangman's Diary. London, 1928. Biblo & Tannen 210-521 1973 $8.50

SCHMIDT, R.   Das Porzellan als Kunstwerk und Kulturspiegel. Munchen, (1925). 8vo., illus., orig. boards, morocco label, worn. Bow Windows 62-811 1974 £5.50

SCHMIDT, VON DANIEL   Das Allgemeine ABC Buchstabier und Lesebuch. Lancaster, 1824. Woodcuts, boards. Rinsland 58-906 1974 $75

SCHMIED, F. L.   Paysages Mediterraneens. Paris, 1933. Mid-blue morocco, illus., slipcase, signed. Dawson's 424-57 1974 $950

SCHMIED, F. L.   Le Tapis de Prieres. 1938. Roy. 4to., plates, unbound in dec. paper wrapper, cloth backed case. Quaritch 940-237 1974 £30

SCHMIEDEKNECHT, OTTO   Die Hymenopteren Mitteleuropas. Jena, 1907. 8vo., orig. cloth. Bow Windows 64-243 1974 £6.50

SCHMITZ, ROBERT   The Piano Works of Claude Debussy. New York, 1950. Biblo & Tannen 214-834 1974 $9.50

SCHNEIDER, C. K.   Illustriertes Handworterbuch der Botanik. Leipzig, 1917. Roy 8vo., boards, second edition. Wheldon 130-1053 1974 £8.50

SCHNEIDER, GEORGE   The Book of Choice Ferns. 1892-94. 4to., 3 vols., orig. cloth, plates, scarce. Wheldon 130-1455 1974 £35

SCHNEIDER, GEORGE   The Book of Choice Ferns. 1892-94. 3 vols. in 5, 4to., orig. dec. cloth, plates. Wheldon 131-1570 1974 £35

SCHNEIDER, GEORGE   Choice Ferns for Amateurs. 1905. 8vo., cloth, scarce. Wheldon 131-1571 1974 £5

THE SCHNEIDERMAN Case. New York, 1943. 46 pages. Austin 57-597 1974 $10

THE SCHNEIDERMAN Case. New York, 1943. Austin 62-575 1974 $10

SCHNITZLER, ARTHUR   Hands Around. 1929. Austin 51-829 1973 $6.50

SCHNOENBERNER, FRANZ   Confessions of a European Intellectual. Macmillan, 1946. Austin 62-576 1974 $10

SCHNURER, GUSTAVE   L'Eglise et la Civlisation au Moyen Age. Paris, 1933-38. 3 vols., buckram. Howes 185-1636 1974 £18

SCHOENAICH, CHRISTOPH OTTO VON   Arminius. 1764. Small 8vo., 2 vols., contemporary calf. Hill 126-233 1974 £35

SCHOENBERNER, FRANZ   The Inside Story of an Outsider. Macmillan, 1949. Austin 62-577 1974 $10

SCHOENLEIN, J. L.   Allgemeine und Specielle Pathologie und Therapie. 1839. 8vo., 4 vols., wrappers, uncut. Gurney 64-194 1974 £15

SCHOENLEIN, J. L.   Allgemeine und Specielle Pathologie und Therphie. (St. Gallen), 1841. 8vo., 4 vols. in 2, old boards, portrait. Gurney 66-166 1974 £25

SCHOEPF, J. D.   Materia Medica Americana Potissimum Regni Vegetabilis. Erlangen, 1787. 8vo., half morocco, first edition, rare. Gurney 66-167 1974 £850

SCHOEPF, J. D.   Materia Medica Americana Potissimum Regni Vegetabilis. Cincinnati, 1903. Small 4to., new cloth. Wheldon 128-1693 1973 £20

SCHOEPF, J. D.   Materia Medica Americana Potissimum Regni Vegetabilis. Cincinnati, 1903. Small 4to., new cloth. Wheldon 130-1623 1974 £20

SCHOFIELD, WILLIAM HENRY   Mythical Bards and the Life of William Wallace. 1920. Austin 61-889 1974 $17.50

SCHOLES, P. A.   The Puritans and Music in England and New England. London, 1934. Orig. ed., illus. Biblo & Tannen 214-914 1974 $10

SCHOLTE, LEONORA R.   A Stranger in a Strange Land. Eerdmans, 1942. Austin 62-579 1974 $12.50

SCHOLZ, BENJAMIN   Anfangsgrunde der Physik. Vienna, 1816. 8vo., orig. wrappers, plates, first edition. Schumann 35-427 1974 $95

SCHONGAUER, MARTIN   Katalog der Kupferstiche Martin Schongauers. Vienna, 1925. 4to., plates, sewed. Quaritch 940-238 1974 £60

SCHONHEINTZ, JACOB   Apologia Astrologie. Nuremberg, 1502. 4to., boards, leather spine, large woodcut, first edition, Georg Tannstetter's copy. Kraus 137-73 1974 $1250

SCHONICHEN, GEORG   Den Achtbarn vnd Hochgelerten zu Leypsck. (Eilenburg, 1523). Small 4to., modern half vellum, rare. Schafer 8-139 1973 sFr. 600

SCHONLAND, S.   Materials for a Critical Revision of
Crassulaceae. Cape Town, 1929. 4to., cloth. Wheldon 131-1697 1974 £5

SCHONLEIN, JOHANN LUCAS   Allgemeine und Specielle Pathologie und
Therapie. Leipzig, 1839. 4 parts in 2 vols., 8vo., contemporary leather
backed boards. Schuman 37-230 1974 $65

SCHOOLCRAFT, HENRY ROWE   Narrative of an Expedition. New York,
1834. 8vo., orig. cloth, first edition. Ximenes 35-130 1974 $125

SCHOOLCRAFT, HENRY ROWE   Report of the Secretary of the Interior
Communicating...A Report on the State of Indian Statistics. Washington, 1854.
Jenkins 61-1174 1974 $10

SCHOOLEY, JOHN C.   A Process of Obtaining a Dry Cold Current of
Air from Ice, and Its Different Applications. Cincinnati, 1855. 8vo., orig.
beige printed wrappers, very good copy, wood engraved illus., first edition.
Ximenes 37-189 1974 $35

SCHOOLING, W.   The Governor and Company of Adventurers
of England Trading Into Hudson's Bay, 1670-1920. London, 1920. Card cover,
illus., presentation. Hood's 103-822 1974 $22.50

SCHOOTEN, FRANZ VAN   Exercitationvm Mathematicarvm Libri Quinque.
(1657). Small 4to., contemporary calf, first edition. Zeitlin 235-201 1974
$385

SCHOOTEN, FRANZ VAN   De Organica Conicarum Sectionum in Plano
Descriptione. Leiden, 1646. 4to., limp vellum, first edition. Dawsons PM
245-664 1974 £110

SCHOTT, CASPAR   Anatomia Physico-Hydrostatica Fontium. 1663.
8vo., contemporary vellum, plates, first edition. Dawsons PM 245-667 1974 £90

SCHOTT, CASPAR   Cursus Mathematicus. 1661. Folio, contemporary calf, plates, first edition. Dawsons PM 245-666 1974 £85

SCHOTT, CASPAR   loco-Seriorum Naturae et Artis. N.P., n.d.
4to., seventeenth century calf, plates, first edition. Dawsons PM 245-668 1974
£145

SCHOTT, CASPAR   Mechanica Hydraulico-Pnevmatica. 1657. 4to.,
contemporary vellum, plates, first edition, first issue. Dawsons PM 245-665 1974
£385

SCHOTT, CASPAR   Mechanica Hydraulico-Pneumatica. Wurzburg,
1657. Small 4to., old calf, rebacked, woodcuts, plates, first edition, first
issue. Traylen 79-269 1973 £220

SCHOTT, CASPAR   Technica Curiosa. (Wurzburg), 1664. Thick
4to., frontispiece, plates, contemporary vellum over boards, gilt, superb
copy, first edition. Schafer 8-172 1973 sFr. 3,200

SCHOUTEN, GAUTIER   Voyage Aux Indies Orientales, 1658-65.
Rouen, 1725. 2 vols., 12mo., old calf, rebacked. Thomas 28-333 1972 £50

SCHOUTEN, GAUTIER   Voyage Aux Indies Orientales, 1658-65. 1725.
2 vols., 12mo., old calf, rebacked, generally clean and sound, plates, portrait.
Thomas 32-348 1974 £50

SCHOUTEN, WILLEM CORNELISZ   lournael ofte Beschryvinghe van de
Won-Derlijcke Reyse. Amsterdam, 1619. 4to., boards, maps, plates, very
fine, unrecorded edition. Harper 213-139 1973 $1200

SCHOY, A.   L'Art Architectural, Decoratif, Industriel et
Somptuaire de l'Epoque Louis XVI. Liege & Paris, 1868. 2 vols., roy. folio,
plates, contemporary quarter morocco, scarce. Quaritch 940-475 1974 £56

SCHRADER, FRANK C.   Preliminary Report on the Cape Nome Gold
Region, Alaska. Washington, 1900. Plates, folding maps, fine. Jenkins
61-97 1974 $18.50

SCHRADER, FREDERICK   The Germans in the Making of America.
1924. 274 pages. Austin 57-603 1974 $12.50

SCHRADER, JUSTUS   Observationes et Historiae Omnes. Amsterdam,
1674. 12mo., contemporary vellum. Dawsons PM 249-240 1974 £135

SCHRAM, DOMINIC   Institutiones Theologiae Mysticae. Augsburg,
1777. 2 vols., crown 8vo., contemporary mottled sheep, labels. Howes
185-1637 1974 £8.50

SCHREIBEN VON Tartarischen Kranckheiten. (1563). 8vo., vellum, first edition. Dawsons PM 249-392 1974 £265

SCHREIBER, CHARLOTTE   Journals. London, 1911. lst ed., 2 vols.,
orig. dec. cl., illus. with plates. Jacobs 24-126 1974 $100

SCHREIBER, CHARLOTTE   Journals. London, 1911. 2 vols., large thick
8vo., illus., excellent copy, orig. cloth. Gregory 44-266 1974 $90

SCHREIBER, CHARLOTTE   Lady Charlotte Schreiber's Journals. 1911.
2 vols., imp. 8vo., plates, buckram. Quaritch 940-662 1974 £50

SCHREINER, OLIVE   Dreams. 1891. Portrait, orig. dec. cloth,
gilt top, fine, first edition. Covent 51-1653 1973 £8.50

SCHREINER, OLIVE   Dreams. 1891. Orig. cloth, worn, first
edition. Rota 188-820 1974 £7.50

SCHREINER, OLIVE   Dreams. London, 1901. Cloth, first edition.
Dawson's 424-302 1974 $20

SCHREINER, OLIVE   Trooper Peter Halket of Mashonaland. 1897.
8vo., orig. cloth, frontispiece, covers marked, uncut, first edition. Bow
Windows 66-614 1974 £12.50

SCHREINER, OLIVE   Undine. New York, 1928. Cloth, illus., first
edition. Dawson's 424-303 1974 $12.50

SCHRIEKE, B.   Alien Americans. Viking, 1936. 208p.
Austin 62-580 1974 $10

SCHRIEKE, B.   Alien Americans. 1936. 208 pages. Austin
57-599 1974 $10

SCHRODER, C.   Die Insekten Mitteleuropas. Stuttgart, 1914.
Roy 8vo., orig. half cloth, plates. Wheldon 130-789 1974 £5

SCHROEDER, ERIC   Persian Miniatures in the Fogg Museum of Art.
Cambridge, 1942. 4to., plates. Biblo & Tannen 214-396 1974 $42.50

SCHROEDER, THEODORE   "Obscene" Literature and Constitutional Law.
1911. Austin 51-830 1973 $17.50

SCHROEDER VAN DER KOLK, JACOB L. C.   On the Minute Structure and
Functions of the Spinal Cord and Medulla Oblongata. London, 1859. 8vo., orig.
brown cloth, gilt, first editions. Dawsons PM 249-444 1974 £8

SCHROETER, C.   Das Pflanzenleben der Alpen. Zurich, 1908.
Roy 8vo., orig. half morocco, plates. Wheldon 129-1119 1974 £6

SCHROETER, J.   Die Pilze Schlesiens. Breslau, 1889-1908.
Roy 8vo., 2 vols., half cloth. Wheldon 129-1343 1974 £30

SCHROETER, J. H.   Aphroditographische Fragmente, zur Genauern
Kenntniss des Planeten Venus. Helmstedt, 1796. 4to., old boards, folding
plates, first edition. Gurney 66-168 1974 £65

SCHROT, MARTIN   Wappenbuch des Heiligen Romischen Reichs.
Munchen, 1580. Folio, contemporary pigskin, wooden boards, woodcuts,
excellent condition, first complete edition. Harper 213-140 1973 $1100

SCHUBERT, GOTTHILF HEINRICH VON   Lehrbuch der Sternkunde fur Schulen.
Munich, 1832. 12mo., contemporary boards. Schuman 37-231 1974 $50

SCHUBERT, GOTTHILF HEINRICH VON   Naturgeschichte der Vogel. Esslingen,
1882. Small folio, orig. cloth backed dec. boards, eighth edition. Wheldon
129-526 1974 £25

SCHUH, FRANZ   Pathologie und Therapie der Pseudoplasmen.
1854. 8vo., old half calf, rebacked. Dawsons PM 249-445 1974 £8

SCHULBERG, BUDD   The Disenchanted. Random, 1959. 113p.,
illus. Austin 51-831 1973 $7.50

SCHULBERG, BUDD   A Face in the Crowd. Random, 1957.
Austin 51-832 1973 $10

SCHULLIAN, D. M.   A Catalogue of Incunabula and Manuscripts.
New York, (n.d.). 8vo., orig. cloth, illus. Bow Windows 62-815 1974
£8.50

SCHULTE, J. E.   Erfelijkheid en Eugenetiek. Haarlem, 1938-39.
2 vols., roy. 8vo., cloth, plates. Wheldon 131-180 1974 £5

SCHULZ, E. D.   Cactus Culture. New York, 1942. 8vo.,
cloth, plates, revised edition. Wheldon 131-1698 1974 £5

SCHULZ, K.   Die Flechtenvegetation der Mark Brandenburg.
Berlin, 1931. 8vo., wrappers. Wheldon 131-1465 1974 £5

SCHULZ, P. F. F.   Unsere Zierpflanzen. Leipzig, 1909. 8vo.,
plates, cloth. Wheldon 131-1572 1974 £5

SCHULZE, R. E.   Amerikanische Hexactinelliden nach dem
Materiale der Albatross-Expedition. Jena, 1899. 2 vols., 4to., orig. wrappers,
atlas of plates. Wheldon 128-925 1973 £7.50

SCHULZE, R. E.   Hexactinelliden des Indischen Oceanes.
Berlin, 1894-1900. 3 parts, 4to., wrappers, plates. Wheldon 128-926 1973
£7.50

SCHULZE-GAEVERNITZ, G. VON   The Cotton Trade in England and on the Continent. Manchester and London, 1895. 8vo., orig. cloth. Hammond 201-814
1974 £8

SCHUMANN, KARL   Bluhende Kakteen. 1900-1921. 4to., orig.
cloth, 3 vols. Bow Windows 64-244 1974 £135

SCHUMANN, KARL   Bluhende Kakteen. Neudamm, 1900-21.
3 vols., roy. 4to., new buckram, plates, rare, complete set. Wheldon
131-105 1974 £150

SCHUMANN, KARL   Gesamtbeschreibung der Kakteen. Neudamm,
1903. Roy. 8vo., cloth, second edition. Wheldon 131-1699 1974 £38

SCHUMANN, KARL   Verzeichnis der . . . Kakteen, mit Einem
Genauen Litteraturnachweis. Neudamm, 1897. 8vo., boards. Wheldon
131-1701 1974 £5

SCHUR, P. J. F.   Enumeratio Plantarum Transsilvaniae. Vienna,
1866. 8vo., buckram, rare. Wheldon 128-1309 1973 £10

SCHURIG, MARTIN   Spermatologia Historico-Medica. 1720. 4to.,
old German half vellum, worn, first edition. Dawsons PM 249-446 1974 £135

SCHURZ, CARL   Henry Clay. Boston, c. 1899. 2 vols., green
cloth, Standard Library edition, tissue guards. Wilson 63-171 1974 $10

SCHUTZ, L. THOMAS-LEXIKON   Sammlung, Uebersetzung u. Erklaerung
der in Saemtlichen Werken Vorkommenden Kunstausdruecke. 1895. Half calf.
Allen 213-1814 1973 $15

SCHWAB, WILLIAM H.   Four Centuries of Fine Books & Manuscripts,
Cat. 5. New York, (1942). Illus. Current BW9-493B 1974 $8

SCHWARTZ, JACOB   1100 Obscure Points. 1931. First edition,
8vo., orig. cloth, limited to 666 copies. Sawyer 293-60 1974 £12.50

SCHWARTZ, JACOB   The Writings of Alfred E. Coppard: A
Bibliography. 1931. Limited to 650 numbered copies, signed by Coppard, very
fine, inscription, first edition. Covent 51-463 1973 £6

SCHWENKE, F.   Designs for Decorative Furniture and Modern
Chamber-Arrangement. London, 1882. Folio, quarter morocco, worn, plates.
Bow Windows 62-816 1974 £22

SCHWENKE, PAUL   Die Turkenbulle Pabst Calixtus III. Berlin,
1911. Roy. 8vo., orig. printed wrappers. Kraus B8-376 1974 $18.50

SCHWERD, FRIEDRICH MAGNUS   Die Beugungserscheinungen. 1835. 4to.,
orig. printed boards, plates, presentation copy, first edition. Dawsons PM 245-
669 1974 £48

SCHWERDT, C. F. G. R.   Hunting, Hawking, Shooting. 1928-37.
4 vols., roy. 4to., half morocco, plates. Quaritch 939-235 1974 £675

SCHWOB, MARCEL   La Croisade des Enfants. Paris, 1896. Dec.
paper wrappers, one of 500 copies, spine chipped, nice for fragile book, edition
de Mercure de France. Ross 87-522 1974 $10

SCHWOB, MARCEL   Le Liver de Monelle. Paris, 1897. Paper
covers, spine slightly chipped, fine for fragile book, edition de Mercure de France.
Ross 87-523 1974 $10

SCHWOB, RENE   Une Melodie Silencieuse. Paris, 1929.
8vo., wrapper, drawing. Minters 37-79 1973 $25

SCHYRLAEUS DE RHEITA, ANTONIO MARIA   Oculus Enoch et Eliae. Antwerp,
1645. Folio, contemporary stained vellum, plates, first edition. Dawsons PM
245-670 1974 £450

SCILLA, A.   De Corporibus Marinis Lapidescentibus. Rome,
1759. 4to., half calf, plates. Wheldon 129-863 1974 £18

SCILT, JOANNES   Thesaurus Teutonicarum, Ecclesiasticarum,
Civilium, Litterariarum. 1728-27-28. 3 vols., thick folio, contemporary calf,
plates, worn. Howes 186-1202 1974 £75

SCLATER, PHILIP LUTLEY   Argentine Ornithology. 1888-89. Roy 8vo.,
2 vols., half maroon morocco, plates, rare, limited edition. Wheldon 130-68
1974 £485

SCLATER, PHILIP LUTLEY   A Monograph of the Birds Forming the Tanagrine
Genus Calliste. 1857(-1858). 8vo., half red morocco, plates, very rare.
Wheldon 131-106 1974 £1,000

SCLATER, PHILIP LUTLEY   A Monograph of the Jacamars and Puff-Birds.
1879-82. Roy 4to., contemporary half morocco, fine. Broadhurst 23-1179 1974
£775

SCLATER, PHILIP LUTLEY   A Monograph of the Jacamars and Puff-Birds.
London, (1879-82). Roy. 8vo., full morocco, gilt, plates, rare. Traylen
79-112 1973 £700

SCLATER, PHILIP LUTLEY   A Monograph of the Jacamars and Puff-Birds.
1879-1822. 7 parts, roy. 4to., orig. printed wrappers, uncut, limited, rare.
Wheldon 131-107 1974 £1,175

SCLATER, PHILIP LUTLEY   On Recent Advances in Our Knowledge of the
Geographical Distribution of Birds. 1891. 8vo. Wheldon 131-693 1974 £5

SCLATER, WILLIAM   An Exposition With Notes Upon the First and
Second Epistles to the Thessalonians. 1630-32. Thick small 4to., old calf.
Thomas 28-104 1972 £30

SCLATER, WILLIAM LUTLEY   The Geography of Mammals. 1899. 8vo.,
cloth, scarce. Wheldon 129-399 1974 £10

SCLATER, WILLIAM LUTLEY   Systema Avium Aethiopicarum. 1924-30. 8vo.,
2 vols., wrappers. Wheldon 130-615 1974 £7.50

SCLATER, WILLIAM LUTLEY   Systema Avium Aethiopicarum. 1924-30.
2 vols., 8vo., cloth. Wheldon 131-694 1974 £15

SCORER, A. G.   The Entomologist's Log-Book and Dictionary
of the Life Histories and Food Plants of the British Macro-Lepidoptera. 1913.
8vo., cloth, scarce. Wheldon 131-855 1974 £5

SCORESBY, WILLIAM   An Account of the Arctic Regions, With a
History and Description of the Northern Whale-Fishery. Edinburgh, 1820. First
edition, 2 vols., engravings, leather, spine & corners rebound in leather, folding
plates & charts in perfect condition. Hood's 102-72 1974 $200

SCORESBY, WILLIAM   Journal of a Voyage to the Northern Whale
Fishery. Edinburgh, 1823. Full leather, rebound, plates, maps, fine.
Hood's 103-83 1974 $125

SCORESBY, WILLIAM   My Father: Being Records of the Adventurous
Life of the Late William Scoresby, Esq. of Whitby. 1851. First edition, crown
8vo., very good copy, contemporary name on fly, scarce. Broadhurst 24-1677
1974 £6

SCOT, MICHAEL   Liber Phisionomie. Venice, 1508. 4to.,
dark morocco, gilt. Traylen 79-270 1973 £160

SCOT, REGINALD   A Perfite Platforme of a Hoppe Garden.
London, 1576. Thin 8vo., full morocco gilt, fine, woodcuts, second edition.
Traylen 79-54 1973 £200

THE SCOTCH – Irish in America. 1889. 210 pages. Austin 57-600 1974
$17.50

SCOTCH-IRISH in America, Proceedings of the Scotch-Irish Congress at Columbia,
Tennesse, May 1889. Cincinnati, 1889. Emerald 50-864 1974 £6

SCOTCH-IRISH in America, Proceedings and Adresses of the Third Congress.
Nashville, 1891. Demy 8vo., portrait. Emerald 50-865 1974 £6

THE SCOTH-IRISH of Northampton County, Pennsylvania. N. P., 1926. Illus.
Jenkins 61-2174 1974 $18.50

SCOTISH Elegiac Verses. Edinburgh, 1842. 8vo., cloth, leather label, uncut,
first edition. Dawsons PM 252-860 1974 £30

SCOTT, A. W.   Australian Lepidoptera. 1864. Folio, plates,
modern buckram backed boards. Wheldon 129-678 1974 £30

SCOTT, ALLEN M.   Chronicles of the Great Rebellion from the
Beginning of the Same Until the Fall of Vicksburg. Cincinnati, 1864. Cloth.
Hayman 59-120 1974 $10

SCOTT, A. MACCALLUM   Winston Churchill in Peace and War. 1916.
Covers slightly faded, name in pencil on endpaper, very good copy, first edition.
Covent 51-401 1973 £17.50

SCOTT, CYRIL   Music. London, 1933. 1st ed. Biblo & Tannen
214-915 1974 $7.50

SCOTT, D. C.   The Spirit of Canada. Toronto, 1939. Card
cover, illus. Hood's 103-162 1974 $20

SCOTT, D. H.   Studies in Fossil Botany. 1920-23. 2 vols.,
8vo., orig. cloth, orig. printing, third edition. Wheldon 128-1044 1973 £6.50

SCOTT, DELAWARE W.   Christianity and the Jew. 1914. Austin
62-581 1974 $12.50

SCOTT, DIXON   Men of Letters. 1923. 313 pages. Austin
61-890 1974 $10

SCOTT, EPHRAIM   "Church Union" and the Presbyterian Church In
Canada. Montreal, 1928. Hood's 104-323 1974 $10

SCOTT, FRANK J.   The Art of Beautifying Suburban Home Grounds.
New York, 1870. Small 4to., plates, first edition, fine crisp copy, virtually
new green gilt cloth. Butterfield 10-64 1974 $100

SCOTT, FREDERIC GEORGE   The Unnamed Lake, and Other Poems. Toronto,
1897. Ex-library. Hood's 104-787 1974 $15

SCOTT, G. R.   Phallic Worship. 1941. 8vo., plates, illus.,
orig. cloth, dust wrapper, limited. Bow Windows 62-818 1974 £8.50

SCOTT, GEORGE GILBERT   An Essay on the History of English Church
Architecture Prior to the Separation of England from the Roman Obedience.
1881. 4to., cloth, rebacked, plates. Quaritch 940-554 1974 £65

SCOTT, HELENUS   The Adventures of a Rupee. London, 1782.
12mo., contemporary calf, top of spine worn, front hinge tender, second edition.
Ximenes 36-172 1974 $50

SCOTT, JAMES   The Guardian Angel. New York, 1859.
12mo., orig. cloth, first edition. Ximenes 35-134 1974 $15

SCOTT, JOB   Journal of. Wilmington, 1797. Contemporary
leather. Jenkins 61-2328 1974 $30

SCOTT, JOB   Journal of. New York, 1797. Contemporary
leather, worn. Jenkins 61-2329 1974 $35

SCOTT, JOHN   Poetical Works. 1786. 8vo., contemporary tree
calf, gilt, frontispiece, second edition. Quaritch 936-17 1974 £35

SCOTT, JOHN   Story of the 32nd Iowa Infantry Volunteers. 18-
96. 8vo., cloth, illus. Putman 126-62 1974 $60

SCOTT, LEADER   The Cathedral Builders. 1899. Rubbed, illus.
Covent 55-72 1974 £21

SCOTT, LEADER   Cathedral Builders. 1899. Plates. Allen
213-1770 1973 $12.50

SCOTT, MICHAEL   The Cruise of the Midge. Edinburgh and London,
1836. 8vo., 2 vols., orig. dark green fine-diaper cloth, gilt, first edition. Hammond 201-324 1974 £30

SCOTT, MICHAEL   The Cruise of the Midge. Edinburgh, 1836.
2 vols., 8vo., orig. cloth, first edition. Ximenes 35-135 1974 $40

SCOTT, MICHAEL   Tom Cringle's Log. 1833. First edition, 2 vols.,
f'cap. 8vo., full marbled calf, panelled backs, richly tooled gilt, leather labels,
very fine. Broadhurst 24-861 1974 £35

SCOTT, MICHAEL   Tom Cringle's Log. Edinburgh and London, 1834.
8vo., 2 vols., orig. maroon fine-diaper grain cloth, gilt, second edition. Hammond 201-325 1974 £22

SCOTT, PETER   A Bird in the Bush. London, 1936. 4to., orig.
cloth, gilt, illus., first edition. Hammond 201-672 1974 £30

SCOTT, PETER   Morning Flight. (1936). 4to., cloth, illus.
Wheldon 131-695 1974 £7.50

SCOTT, PETER   Morning Flight. 1936. 4to., cloth, coloured
and other plates, scarce, first ordinary edition. Wheldon 128-557 1973 £7.50

SCOTT, PETER   Wild Chorus. 1939. 4to., orig. cloth, plates.
Wheldon 130-616 1974 £10

SCOTT, PETER   Wild Chorus. (1939). 4to., cloth, plares.
Wheldon 131-696 1974 £7.50

SCOTT, PETER   Wild Chorus. London, 1939. 4to., orig. cloth,
gilt, plates, illus., first edition. Hammond 201-671 1974 £10

SCOTT, R. W.   Recollections of Bytown. Ottawa, n.d.
Signed. Hood's 104-728 1974 $40

SCOTT, R. W.   Recollections of Bytown, Some Incidents in the
History of Ottawa, ca. 1911. Card cover, signed. Hood's 102-634 1974 $40

SCOTT, ROBERT FALCON   Scott's Last Expedition. 1913. 2 vols., 8vo.,
orig. cloth, coloured plates, illus, maps, slight foxing, second edition. Bow
Windows 66-617 1974 £12.50

SCOTT, ROBERT FALCON   Scott's Last Expedition. 1913. 2 vols., roy.
8vo., coloured and photogravure plates, illus., maps, orig. cloth, fine.
Broadhurst 24-1679 1974 £15

SCOTT, SARAH   The History of Cornelia. London, 1750.
12mo., contemporary calf, first edition. Ximenes 35-136 1974 $275

SCOTT, SUTTON S.   Southbooke. Columbus, 1880. Cloth. Hayman
57-220 1974 $12.50

SCOTT, T. A.   The British Parasitic Copepoda. 1913. 2 vols.,
8vo., cloth, plates (some coloured), very scarce, orig. printing. Wheldon
128-928 1973 £15

SCOTT, T. A.   The British Parasitic Copepoda. 1913. 8vo.,
2 vols., cloth, plates, scarce. Wheldon 130-892 1974 £15

SCOTT, T. W.   The Story of the Flying Machines. (1918).
Small 8vo., orig. wrappers, illus., slightly worn, extremely scarce. Sawyer
293-1 1974 £12.50

SCOTT, THOMAS   Aphorismes of State. 1624. Small 4to.,
disbound, first edition. Ximenes 35-137 1974 $65

SCOTT, THOMAS   Mock-Marriage. 1696. Sewn. Allen
216-1949 1974 $75

SCOTT, THOMAS   Newes from Pernassvs. 1622. Small 4to.,
modern quarter calf, fine, scarce, first edition. Dawsons PM 252-1102 1974
£140

SCOTT, THOMAS   The Second Part of Vox Populi. 1624. Small
4to., modern quarter calf, rare, second edition. Dawsons PM 252-1104 1974
£125

SCOTT, THOMAS   A Speech Made in the Lower House of
Parliament. (London), 1621. Small 4to., disbound, first edition. Ximenes
35-138 1974 $20

SCOTT, THOMAS   Vox Popvli Vox Dei. (N.P., n.d.). Small
4to., 19th century russia, fine, first collected edition. Dawsons PM 252-1103
1974 £150

SCOTT, WALTER   Anne of Geierstein; or The Maiden of the Mist.
London, 1829. 3 vols., 8vo, orig. boards with green cloth shelf back, bindings
very worn & dulled, text clear with no foxing. Current BW9-274 1974 $32.50

SCOTT, WALTER   Ballads and Lyrical Pieces. Baltimore, 1811.
18mo., orig. bindings. Butterfield 8-218 1974 $12.50

SCOTT, WALTER   Ballads and Lyrical Pieces. Baltimore, 1811.
2 vols. in 1, 12mo., contemporary calf, worn. Ximenes 35-139 1974 $15

SCOTT, WALTER   The Border Antiquities of England and Scotland.
1814-17. 2 vols., folio, plates, half calf. Quaritch 939-236 1974 £30

SCOTT, WALTER   Description of the Regalia of Scotland.
Edinburgh, 1854. 12mo., orig. wrappers, scarce. Ximenes 35-140 1974 $10

SCOTT, WALTER   The Field of Waterloo. Edinburgh, 1815. 8vo.,
orig. brown paper wrapper, uncut, rare, first edition. Quaritch 936-541 1974
£25

SCOTT, WALTER   Halidon Hill. Edinburgh, 1822. 8vo.,
contemporary straight-grained morocco, first edition. Ximenes 35-141 1974
$150

SCOTT, WALTER   The Journal of Sir Walter Scott. New York,
1891. Biblo & Tannen 210-913 1973 $7.50

SCOTT, WALTER   The Lady of the Lake. Glasgow, (1905). Orig.
tartan silk binding, leather label, 2 X 1 1/4. Gregory 44-458 1974 $17.50

SCOTT, WALTER   Letters On Demonology and Witchcraft. London,
1830. Frontispiece, first edition. Rittenhouse 46-578 1974 $50

SCOTT, WALTER   The Letters, 1787-1832. 1932. 12 vols., orig.
cloth gilt, very scarce, Centenary edition. Howes 185-420 1974 £110

SCOTT, WALTER   Lord of the Isles, a Poem. 1815. 4to.,
half calf, one joint cracked the other broken, first edition. Allen 216-1567 1974
$25

SCOTT, WALTER   Marmion: Tale of Flodden Field. 1808. 4to.,
half calf, joint cracked, first edition. Allen 216-1568 1974 $25

SCOTT, WALTER   Marmion; A Tale of Flodden Field. Philadelphia,
1809. First American edition, 16mo. Current BW9-275 1974 $12

SCOTT, WALTER   Marmion. Edinburgh, 1855. Contemporary
morocco, gilt, plates. Smith 194-745 1974 £7.50

SCOTT, WALTER   New Love Poems. Oxford, 1932. Orig.
parchment backed marbled boards, limited. Howes 185-423 1974 £5.50

SCOTT, WALTER   Novels. 1912. 24 vols., crown 8vo., orig.
limp maroon lambskin, fine. Howes 185-422 1974 £18

SCOTT, WALTER   The Pirate. Edinburgh, 1822. Contemporary
cloth, 3 vols., labels., English first edition. Covent 56-1161 1974 £10.50

SCOTT, WALTER   Poetical Works of. Edinburgh, 1823. 10 vols.,
12mo., contemporary diced calf, some joints cracked, frontispieces, plate.
Bow Windows 66-618 1974 £12

SCOTT, WALTER   The Poetical Works. Edinburgh, 1823.
10 vols., 12mo., contemporary morocco gilt. Dawsons PM 252-862 1974 £60

SCOTT, WALTER   The Poetical Works. Edinburgh, 1825.
10 vols., 8vo., contemporary calf. Dawsons PM 252-863 1974 £50

SCOTT, WALTER   The Poetical Works of. London, 1904. 8vo.,
frontispiece, contemporary tree calf, gilt. Bow Windows 62-820 1974 £6

SCOTT, WALTER   The Poetical Works. Edinburgh, 1874. Thick
roy. 8vo., contemporary blue levant morocco, gilt, raised band's, plates.
Smith 194-327 1974 £8.50

SCOTT, WALTER   The Private Letter Books of. 1930. Illus.
Austin 61-893 1974 $15

SCOTT, WALTER   The Vision of Don Roderick. Edinburgh and
London, 1811. 4to., modern half calf, first public edition. Dawsons PM 252-
861 1974 £25

SCOTT, WALTER   The Vision of Don Roderick. Edinburgh, 1811.
4to., old half calf, first published edition, second issue. Ximenes 35-142
1974 $12.50

SCOTT, WALTER   Waverley. Edinburgh, 1814. 3 vols., 12mo.,
contemporary half calf and marbled boards, spines gilt, very good condition,
cloth folding case, rare, first edition. Ximenes 37-191 1974 $400

SCOTT, WALTER   Waverley Novels. Edinburgh, 1829-33. Contemporary dark green straight-grained morocco, gilt, 48 vols., plates. Hammond
201-356 1974 £950

SCOTT, WALTER   Waverley Novels. Edinburgh, 1829-33.
48 vols., small 8vo., contemporary half dark green morocco, gilt. Howes
186-399 1974 £60

SCOTT, WALTER   The Waverley Novels. Edinburgh, 1829-33.
50 vols., 12mo., plates, contemporary half calf, first colleceted & revised
edition. Dawsons PM 252-1105 1974 £150

SCOTT, WALTER   Waverley Novels. Edinburgh, 1832.
65 vols., 8vo., contemporary light-blue half calf gilt, labels. Dawsons PM
252-864 1974 £240

SCOTT, WALTER   Waverley Novels. Edinburgh, 1862-63.
25 vols. in 13, crown 8vo., contemporary half morocco gilt. Howes 185-424
1974 £40

SCOTT, WALTER   The Waverley Novels. 1898-1900. 8vo.,
green half calf, 24 vols., illus. Bow Windows 64-678 1974 £54

SCOTT, WALTER SIDNEY   The Georgian Theatre. Westhouse, 1946.
Austin 51-833 1973 $8.50

SCOTT, WALTER SIDNEY   Harriet & Mary. 1944. 4to., frontispiece,
orig. quarter morocco, limited. Bow Windows 62-382 1974 £35

SCOTT, WALTER SIDNEY   Harriet & Mary. London, 1944. 4to., orig.
full morocco, fine, first edition. Dawsons PM 252-887 1974 £125

SCOTT, WILLIAM   The Beauties of the Border. 1821. 12mo.,
orig. cloth, plates, worn, first edition. Ximenes 35-143 1974 $20

SCOTT, WILLIAM   Scott's New Lessons In Reading and Speaking.
To Which are Prefixed the Elements of Gesture. Philadelphia, 1816. Old calf,
worn, red label, plates. Butterfield 10-483 1974 $25

SCOTT, WILLIAM BELL   Autobiographical Notes of His Life, and Notices of His Artistic and Poetic Circle of Friends, 1830-82.   1895.   2 vols., plates. Allen 216-1574 1974 $17.50

SCOTT, WILLIAM BELL   History and Practice of the Fine and Ornamental Arts.   1867.   Illus., rebound, revised second edition.   Covent 55-123 1974 £8.50

SCOTT-ELLIOTT, G. F.   The Flora of Dumfriesshire.   Dumfries, 1896. 8vo., cloth, folding map, scarce.   Wheldon 128-1218 1973 £5

SCOTUS, MICHAEL
Please turn to
SCOTT, MICHAEL

SCOUGAL, HENRY   The Works Of.   Glasgow, 1765.   Small 8vo., contemporary calf.   Hill 126-236 1974 £12.50

SCREWS and Screw-Making, With a Chapter on the Milling Machine.   1891. Illus., scarce.   Covent 55-1434 1974 £12.50

SCRIPPS, JOHN LOCKE   Life of Abraham Lincoln.   (Chicago, 1860). Sewed as issued, rare, first issue.   Hayman 59-361 1974 $650

SCRIPTORES Historiae Augustae.   1661.   New buckram.   Allen 213-1941 1973 $12.50

SCRIPTORES Rei Militaris.   (Rome, 1494).   5 parts in 1 vol., 4to., old vellum, fine complete copy, second edition.   Harper 213-142 1973 $875

SCRIVE, G.   Relation Medico-Chirurgicale.   London, 1857. 8vo., quarter shagreen.   Gurney 64-195 1974 £15

SCROPE, G. P.   The Geology and Extinct Volcanos of Central France.   1858.   8vo., cloth, plates, second edition.   Wheldon 131-1078 1974 £15

SCROPE, WILLIAM   The Art of Deer-Stalking.   1839.   Roy. 8vo., old calf, plates, best & new edition.   Quaritch 939-674 1974 £42.50

SCROPE, WILLIAM   Days and Nights of Salmon Fishing in the Tweed. London, 1898.   4to., 3/4 lea. and marbled bds., gilt, illus.   Jacobs 24-134 1974 $30

SCRUGGS, WILLIAM L.   The Colombian and Venezuelan Republics, With Notes on Other Parts of Central and South America.   Boston, 1905.   New edition, 8vo., presentation copy, uncut, illus., fold out colored maps, very good. Current BW9-605 1974 $20

SCUDDER, HORACE E.   Boston Town.   Boston, (1881).   8vo., orig. bindings, illus., fine.   Butterfield 8-29 1974 $15

SCUDDER, S. H.   Nomenclator Zoologicus.   Washington, 1882. 2 parts in 1 vol., 8vo., cloth, very scarce.   Wheldon 128-294 1973 £18

SEABROOK, W. B.   The Magic Island.   London, (1929).   8vo., illus., orig. cloth, worn.   Bow Windows 62-822 1974 £5.50

SEA-COALE, Char-Coale, and Small-Coale.   1643.   Small 4to., brown levant morocco gilt, rare.   Quaritch 939-238 1974 £300

SEAGER, H. W.   Natural History in Shakespeare's Time.   1896. 8vo., cloth, scarce.   Wheldon 130-192 1974 £7.50

SEAGER, H. W.   Natural History in Shakespeare's Time.   1896. 8vo., cloth, text-figures, scarce.   Wheldon 128-129 1973 £7.50

SEALE, R. F.   The Geognosy of the Island St. Helena.   1834. Oblong folio, modern boards, morocco, plates.   Wheldon 129-864 1974 £45

SEALSFIELD, CHARLES   Cabin Book.   1871.   Binding worn, spotted, lacks last flyleaf, plates.   Allen 216-1300 1974 $10

SEARLE, M.   Turnpikes and Toll-Bars.   (1930).   2 vols., 4to., plates, illus., half morocco, limited.   Quaritch 939-222 1974 £50

SEARLE, RONALD   Co-operation in a University Town.   (1939). Orig. cloth, illus., fine, first edition.   Rota 188-822 1974 £5

SEARLE, T.   Sir William Schwenk Gilbert.   London, 1931. Plates, illus., crown 4to., orig. cloth, text fine.   Forster 98-299 1974 £4.50

SEARS, CLARA ENDICOTT   Highlights Among the Hudson River Artists. Boston, 1947.   Sm. 4to., lst ed., illus.   Biblo & Tannen 213-410 1973 $12.50

SEASHORE, CARL E.   Psychology of Music.   New York, 1938.   Illus. Biblo & Tannen 214-916 1974 $7.50

SEATTLE: The Gateway to Alaska.   Seattle, c. 1910.   Small folio, wrappers, photos.   Jenkins 61-2592 1974 $12.50

SEATTLE: Gateway to Alaska and the Orient.   Seattle, c. 1910.   Wrappers, illus.   Jenkins 61-2591 1974 $10

SEATTLE: The Seaport of Success.   Seattle, (1914).   Small folio, wrappers, photos.   Jenkins 61-2593 1974 $12.50

SEATTLE.   Seattle, c. 1909.   Small folio, wrappers, illus.   Jenkins 61-2588 1974 $12.50

SEAVER, G.   Edward Wilson.   1937.   8vo., cloth, illus., plates.   Wheldon 130-193 1974 £5

SEBASTIANI, A.   Florae Romanae Prodromus.   Rome, 1818. 8vo., new cloth, plates.   Wheldon 130-1208 1974 £10

SEBASTIANI, A.   Florae Romanae Prodromus.   Rome, 1818.   8vo., new cloth, engraved plates.   Wheldon 128-1310 1973 £10

SEBASTIANI, A.   Florae Romanae Prodromus.   Rome, 1818. 8vo., half calf, folding engraved plates.   Wheldon 128-1311 1973 £12

SEBOTH, J.   Alpine Plants Painted from Nature.   (1879-80). 4 vols., small 4to., orig. half leather, worn, coloured frontispieces, coloured plates.   Wheldon 128-1534 1973 £12

SEBRIGHT, J. S.   Observations upon Hawking.   1828.   8vo., modern boards.   Wheldon 129-527 1974 £35

SECCOMBE, THOMAS   The Age of Johnson.   London, 1912.   12mo. Biblo & Tannen 213-784 1973 $8.50

THE SECOND BOOK of the Rhymers' Club.   1894.   8vo., orig. cloth, bookplate, scarce, first edition.   Rota 189-36 1974 £45

THE SECOND Century of Creepy Stories.   London, n.d.   Biblo & Tannen 210-688 1973 $12.50

THE SECOND Century of Detective Stories.   London, n.d.   Biblo & Tannen 210-421 1973 $12.50

SECOND Manifeste du Surrealisme.   Paris, 1930.   4to., uncut pages, paper bound.   Covent 51-1658 1973 £15

THE SECOND Studdy Dogs Portfolio.   London, 1922.   Folio, 16 color plates. Frohnsdorff 16-118 1974 $20

THE SECRET History of Arlus and Odolphus.   (London), 1710.   8vo., wrappers, first edition.   Ximenes 33-22 1974 $150

THE SECRET History of the Green Room.   1792.   2 vols., sound but amateur rexine.   Thomas 32-197 1974 £15

SECRET Memoirs of the Late Mr. Duncan Campbel.   London, 1732.   8vo., gilt, contemporary calf, first edition.   Ximenes 33-23 1974 $150

SECRET Passions--Shakespeare Novels.   1844.   3 vols.   Austin 51-853 1973 $17.50

SECRETAN, E.   Catalogue de Tableaux Anciens et Modernes, Aquarelles et Dessins, et Objects d'Art Formant la Celebre Collection de M. E. Secretan dont la Vente en a Lieu a Paris.   Paris, 1889.   2 vols., folio, red half morocco, limited, edition de luxe.   Quaritch 940-798 1974 £15

SECRETS MERVEILLEUX de la Magie Naturelle et Cabalistique du Petit Albert. 1754. 12mo., plates, contemporary mottled sheep, gilt. Dawsons PM 245-17 1974 £45

SECUNDUS, JOANNES   Kisses. London, 1790. 8vo., contemporary half calf, fourth edition. Ximenes 35-144 1974 $12.50

SEDDON, JAMES A.   Information Relative to the Act to Provide and Organize a General Staff. Richmond, 1864. Jenkins 61-673 1974 $12.50

SEDGWICK, ADAM   The Life and Letters of. Cambridge, 1890. 2 vols., 8vo., cloth, plates. Wheldon 128-130 1973 £10

SEDGWICK, ADAM   Peripatus. 1895 and 1899. Frontispiece, orig. cloth, 2 vols. Bow Windows 64-245 1974 £6.50

SEDGWICK, ADAM   A Student's Text-book of Zoology. (1905). 8vo., cloth. Wheldon 129-350 1974 £5

SEDGWICK, ADAM   A Students Text-Book of Zoology. 1927, 1905, 1927. 8vo., 3 vols., cloth. Wheldon 130-371 1974 £15

SEDGWICK, ADAM   A Student's Text-Book of Zoology. 1927-32. 3 vols., 8vo., cloth, scarce. Wheldon 131-457 1974 £15

SEDGWICK, ADAM   A Student's Text-Book of Zoology. 1905. Vol. 2, 8vo., cloth. Wheldon 131-458 1974 £5

SEDGWICK, CATHERINE MARIA   Hope Leslie. London, 1830. 3 vols., 12mo., orig. quarter cloth, rare, first English edition. Ximenes 35-145 1974 $175

SEDGWICK, CATHERINE MARIA   Hope Leslie. New York, 1842. 2 vols., 12mo., orig. cloth, fine, second edition. Ximenes 35-146 1974 $35

SEDGWICK, CATHERINE MARIA   Letters from Abroad to Kindred at Home. New York, 1841. 2 vols., 12mo., cloth, inscribed by author, bindings worn, first edition. Goodspeed's 578-317 1974 $25

SEDGWICK, CATHERINE MARIA   The Linwoods. London, 1835. 3 vols., 12mo., later half calf, scarce, first English edition. Ximenes 35-148 1974 $100

SEDGWICK, CATHERINE MARIA   Tales and Sketches. New York, 1844. 12mo., orig. cloth, first edition. Ximenes 35-149 1974 $27.50

SEDGWICK, HENRY DWIGHT   France. Boston, 1929. Biblo & Tannen 213-704 1973 $7

SEDGWICK, HENRY DWIGHT   Pro Vita Monastica. Boston, 1922. 1st ed. Biblo & Tannen 210-799 1973 $7.50

SEDGWICK, SUSAN ANNE   Walter Thornley. New York, 1859. 12mo., orig. cloth, first edition. Ximenes 35-150 1974 $12.50

SEDLEY, CHARLES   Antony and Cleopatra. London, 1696. Small 4to., disbound, second edition. Ximenes 35-151 1974 $45

SEDLEY, CHARLES   Bellamira. London, 1687. Small 4to., disbound, first edition. Ximenes 35-152 1974 $125

SEDLEY, CHARLES   The Faro Table. 1931. Linen-backed boards, English first edition. Covent 56-1162 1974 £5.25

SEDLEY, CHARLES   The Mulberry-Garden. London, 1675. Small 4to., disbound, second edition. Ximenes 35-153 1974 $40

SEE, R. R. M.   English Pastels. 1911. Mounted plates (some in colour), demy 8vo., cream parchment boards, uncut, covers little dust stained, fine, limited to 750 copies. Broadhurst 24-185 1974 £16

SEEBAK, FRIEDRICH   Holderlin-Bibliographie. Munchen, 1922. Wrappers, first German edition. Covent 55-844 1974 £8

SEEBOHM, FREDERIC   The Oxford Reformers. 1913. Revised third edition. Howes 185-1641 1974 £5

SEEBOHM, FREDERIC   The Tribal System in Wales. 1904. 8vo., orig. cloth. Broadhurst 23-1539 1974 £5.50

SEEBOHM, HENRY   The Birds of Siberia. 1901. 8vo., orig. cloth, scarce. Wheldon 130-618 1974 £20

SEEBOHM, HENRY   The Birds of the Japanese Empire. 1890. Roy 8vo., orig. cloth. Wheldon 129-528 1974 £30

SEEBOHM, HENRY   The Birds of the Japanese Empire. 1890. Roy. 8vo., orig. cloth, very scarce. Wheldon 131-700 1974 £45

SEEBOHM, HENRY   Coloured Figures of the Eggs of British Birds. 1896. Roy. 8vo., cloth, plates. Wheldon 131-702 1974 £20

SEEBOHM, HENRY   The Geographical Distribution of the Family Charadriidae. (1881). Roy 4to., half green morocco, plates. Wheldon 130-70 1974 £450

SEEBOHM, HENRY   The Geographical Distribution of the Family Charadriidae. (1888). Roy 4to., orig. green cloth, plates, scarce. Wheldon 130-69 1974 £250

SEEBOHM, HENRY   A History of British Birds. London, 1883-85. 4to., 4 vols., contemporary green half morocco, gilt, illus., plates, first edition. Hammond 201-673 1974 £24

SEEBHOM, HENRY   A History of British Birds. 1883-85. 4 vols., roy. 8vo., half calf, plates. Wheldon 131-701 1974 £22

SEEBOHM, HENRY   Siberia In Asia. 1882. 8vo., orig. cloth, illus. Wheldon 131-393 1974 £10

SEEBOHM, HENRY   Siberia in Europe. 1880. 8vo., half morocco, map. Wheldon 129-301 1974 £7.50

SEEBOHM, HUGH E.   The Picture of Kebes the Theban. 1906. Square 12mo., boards, fine, partly unopened copy, only 50 copies printed. Covent 51-658 1973 £45

SEEGER, ALAN   Poems. New York, 1917. Very nice copy, scarce. Covent 51-1659 1973 £12.60

SEEING Lancaster County from a Trolley Window. Lancaster, (1910). 4to., photo illus., pictorial wrapper. Butterfield 10-514 1974 $10

SEELEY, L. B.   Mrs. Thrale: Afterwards Mrs. Piozzi. n.d. Illus. Austin 61-894 1974 $12.50

SEEMAN, B.   Flora Vitiensis. 1865-73. 4to., half calf, plates, rare. Wheldon 130-71 1974 £750

SEGALAS, MME ANAIS   Les Oiseaux de Passage. Paris, 1837. 8vo., three quarter blue hard grain morocco, gilt, uncut, first edition. L. Goldschmidt 42-375 1974 $35

SEGNERI, PAOLO   Quaresimale. 1679. Folio, 19th century half calf, label, first edition. Howes 185-1642 1974 £25

SEGNERI, PAOLO   The Quaresimale. 1863-69. 3 vols. in 1, thick 8vo., rebound, cloth. Howes 185-1643 1974 £5.50

SEGNERI, PAOLO   Le Quietiste. Paris, 1687. 12mo., half red morocco, rubbed, first French edition. Ximenes 35-155 1974 $15

SEGSWORTH, W. E.   Retraining Canada's Disabled Soliders. Ottawa, 1920. Hood's 104-135 1974 $10

SEGUIN, L. G.   Scenes & Characters from the Works of George Eliot. 1888. 4to., plates. Allen 216-532 1974 $15

SEGUY, E.   Code Universel des Couleurs. Paris, 1936. 8vo., orig. cloth, plates. Wheldon 129-102 1974 £5

SEGUY, E.   Les Moustiques de l'Afrique Mineure. Paris, 1924. 8vo., sewed, plates, maps. Wheldon 129-679 1974 £5

SEIFRIZ, W.   Protoplasm. New York, 1936. 8vo., cloth.
Wheldon 131-181 1974 £7.50

SEILHAMER, G.O.   The Bard Family. Chambersburg, 1908.
8vo., cloth, limited. Saddleback 14-774 1974 $25

SEITZ, A.   Les Macrolepidopteres de la Region Palearctique
Vol. 2, Bombycides et Sphingides Palearctiques. Stuttgart, 1913. 2 vols.,
4to., publisher's half morocco, coloured plates, French edition. Wheldon
128-795 1973 £40

SEITZ, A.   Les Macrolepidopteres de la Region Palearctique. Stuttgart, 1913. 4to., 2 vols., half morocco. Wheldon 130-790 1974
£40

SEITZ, A.   Les Macrolepidopteres du Globe. Paris, 1909-
28. 4to., 2 vols., new buckram, plates. Wheldon 130-792 1974 £95

SEITZ, A.   Les Macrolepidopteres du Globe. Stuttgart,
1914. 4to., 2 vols., orig. half morocco, plates. Wheldon 130-791 1974 £40

SEITZ, A.   Les Macrolepidopteres du Globe, Vol. 3,
Noctuides Palearctiques. Stuttgart, 1914. 2 vols., 4to., orig. half morocco,
coloured plates, French edition. Wheldon 128-796 1973 £40

SEITZ, A.   Les Macrolepidopteres du Globe, Vol. 13,
Diurnes Ethiopiens. Paris, 1909-28. 2 vols., 4to., new buckram. Wheldon
128-797 1973 £95

SEITZ, DON CARLOS   Joseph Pulitizer. New York, 1924. First
edition, orig. binding. Wilson 63-342 1974 $12.50

SEIZ, JOHANN C.   Het Derde Jubeljaar der Uitgevondene
Boekdrukkonst, Behelzende Een Beknopt Historis Verhaal Van de Uitvinding der
Edele Boekdrukkonst. Harlem, 1740. Old vellum, full page engravings. Kraus
B8-300 1974 $40

SELBY, CHARLES   Boats At Dawn. Taylor, 1849. Austin 51-834
1973 $6.50

SELBY, CHARLES   The Married Rake. French, n.d. Austin
51-835 1973 $6.50

SELBY, CHARLES   The New Footman. French, 1855. Austin
51-836 1973 $6.50

SELBY, CHARLES   Robert Macaire. Taylor, 1843. Austin
51-837 1973 $6.50

SELBY, CHARLES   The Unfinished Gentleman. ca. 1840.
Austin 51-838 1973 $6.50

SELBY, CHARLES   The Widow's Victim. Taylor, 1847.
Austin 51-839 1973 $6.50

SELBY, PRIDEAUX JOHN   A History of British Forest-Trees. 1842. 8vo.,
orig. wrappers. Wheldon 129-1629 1974 £7.50

SELBY, PRIDEAUX JOHN   A History of British Forest Trees. London, 1842.
8vo., contemporary calf, gilt, illus. Hammond 201-674 1974 £9.50

SELBY, PRIDEAUX JOHN   Illustrations of British Ornithology. Edinburgh,
1833. 8vo., 2 vols., contemporary half green calf. Wheldon 129-529 1974
£10

SELBY, PRIDEAUX JOHN   Illustrations of British Ornithology. 1841.
2 vols., double elphant folio, half green morocco gilt, rubbed, plates.
Wheldon 131-108 1974 £6,000

SELBY, PRIDEAUX JOHN   Illustrations of British Ornithology.
Edinburgh, 1833. 2 vols., 8vo., contemporary half green calf, scarce.
Wheldon 131-703 1974 £15

SELBY, PRIDEAUX JOHN   The Natural History of Pigeons. Edinburgh,
1835. 8vo., orig. cloth, plates. Smith 194-792 1974 £8.50

SELDEN, JOHN   The Table Talk. 1856. Second edition.
Austin 61-895 1974 $12.50

SELDEN, JOHN   Titles of Honor. London, 1614. Small 4to.,
half calf. Quaritch 939-747 1974 £40

SELDEN, JOHN   Titles of Honor. London, 1672. Small folio,
old calf, woodcuts, third & best edition. Quaritch 939-748 1974 £21

SELDEN, JOHN 1584-1654   Opera Omnia. 1726. 3 vols. in 6, folio,
contemporary calf, gilt. Quaritch 939-239 1974 £100

SELDEN, JOHN 1584-1654   The Reverse of Back-Face of the English Janus.
1682. Folio, old style half calf. Quaritch 939-240 1974 £15

SELDEN, JOHN 1584-1654   Two Treatises. London, 1683. Folio, old calf,
rebacked. Quaritch 939-241 1974 £30

SELDEN, SAMUEL   Stage Scenery and Lighting. 1936. 435p.,
rev. ed. Austin 51-840 1973 $7.50

SELDES, GILBERT   Movies for the Millions. 1937. Frontispiece,
faded, plates. Covent 55-411 1974 £7.50

SELDES, GILBERT   The Seven Lively Arts. 1924. First U. S.
edition, illus., one of 300 copies bound in Javanese Batik, signed by author,
cloth backed boards, spine label torn, near fine. Covent 51-1660 1973 £20

A SELECT and Impartial Account of the Lives, Behaviour and Dying Words, of the
Most Remarkable Convicts, from the Year 1700 down to the Present Time. London,
1760. 2 vols., 12mo., quarter calf and marbled boards, very good, folding
engraved frontis. Ximenes 36-61 1974 $75

SELECTED Articles on Censorship of the Theatre and Moving Pictures. Wilson,
1931. 385p. Austin 51-74 1973 $12.50

SELECTED Articles on Immigration. Wilson, 1915. Austin 62-527 1974 $15

SELECTED Views of Emporia. Emporia, c. 1895. Illus. Jenkins 61-1282 1974
$10

SELECTED Views of Los Angeles and Vicinity. (Los Angeles), c. 1900. Small
folio, photos, wrapper. Jenkins 61-411 1974 $12.50

SELECTED Views of Portland. Portland, 1912. Small folio, wrapper, photos.
Jenkins 61-2094 1974 $10

SELECTED Views, Oriental Limited Route. N. P., c. 1900. Small folio,
wrappers, hand colored. Jenkins 61-2594 1974 $12.50

SELECTIONS from the Family Papers Preserved at Caldwell. Glasgow, 1854.
2 parts in 3 vols., 4to., buckram, orig. edition. Quaritch 939-650 1974 £25

SELFRIDGE, H. GORDON   The Romance of Commerce. 1918. Thick
8vo., foxed, first edition. Howes 186-1570 1974 £5

SELFRIDGE, THOMAS O.   A Correct Statement of the Whole Preliminary
Controversy. Charlestown, 1807. Plain blue wrappers, uncut, first edition.
Bradley 35-390 1974 $40

SELFRIDGE, THOMAS O.   Trial of. Boston, (1806). Orig. boards, worn,
foxed, first edition. Bradley 35-391 1974 $40

SELIGMAN, G. SAVILLE   Domestic Needlework. (1926). Folio, fine,
plates, dust wrapper. Quaritch 940-772 1974 £95

SELIGMANN, LEOPOLD   Die Sammlung Dr. Leopold Seligmann, Koln.
Berlin, 1930. Large folio, plates, cloth. Quaritch 940-354 1974 £10

SELKIRK, JAMES   Recollections of Ceylon. London, 1844.
8vo., orig. cloth, fine, first edition. Ximenes 35-157 1974 $75

SELL, JESSE C.   Twentieth Century History of Altoona and Blair
County, Pennsylvania. Chicago, 1911. 4to., leather. Saddleback 14-678
1974 $75

SELLAR, ROBERT   The Narrative of Gordon Sellar Who Emigrated
to Canada in 1825. Huntington, 1915. Hood's 103-508 1974 $20

SELLARDS, E. H.   The Geology of Texas, Vol. 1, Stratigraphy.
1932. 8vo., cloth, plates, folding coloured map. Wheldon 128-1045 1973 £5

SELLER, ABEDNIGO   The Antiquities of Palmyra. London, 1696.
8vo., quarter calf antique, gilt, first edition. Hammond 201-998 1974 £36

SELLERY, G. C.   Medieval Foundations of Western Civilization.
1929. Allen 213-1777 1973 $10

SELMI, FRANCESCO   Manuale dell'Arte d'Indorate. Reggio, 1844.
12mo., wrappers, first edition. Gurney 64-196 1974 £7.50

SELNECKER, NIKOLAUS   Evangeliorum et Epistolarum Omnium Quae
Dominicis et Festis Diebus in Ecclesia Christi Proponi Solent. Frankfort, 1575.
2 parts in 1 vol., thick 8vo., contemporary pigskin over wooden boards, illus.,
first edition. Schafer 8-140 1973 sFr. 900

SELOUR, E.   Bird Life Glimpses. 1905. Crown 8vo., cloth,
plates. Wheldon 131-704 1974 £7.50

SELOUR, E.   Bird Watching. 1901. 8vo., orig. parchment
gilt. Wheldon 130-619 1974 £10

SELOUR, E.   Bird Watching. 1901. 8vo., orig. parchment
gilt, illus., hand made paper, numbered, limited. Wheldon 128-561 1973 £10

SELOUS, FREDERICK COURTENEY   Life of. 1919. 8vo., cloth, plates.
Wheldon 130-194 1974 £5

SELOUS, FREDERICK COURTENEY   Travel and Adventure In South East Africa.
1893. Crown 4to., plates, orig. buckram gilt, first edition. Smith 194-585
1974 £10

SELVA, DOMENICO   Esposizione delle Communi. 1761. Small 8vo.,
plates, half contemporary calf, gilt, boards, fine, first edition. Zeitlin 235-203
1974 $195

SELWYN, A.   Moral Fairy Tales. (c. 1830). Lithograph
plates, engravings, 12mo., orig. boards, roan spine, slightly rubbed, early
stitching defective. George's 610-655 1973 £5

SELWYN, C. E.   Rhyming Snapshots of an Idle Fellow. Toronto,
1924. Hood's 103-750 1974 $15

SELYS LONGCHAMPS, E. DE   Collections Zoologiques Catalogue. Brussels,
1908. 4to., wrappers, coloured plates, text-figures. Wheldon 128-798 1973
£8

SELYS-LONGCHAMPS, E. DE   Etudes de Micro-Mammalogie. Paris, 1839.
8vo., orig. wrappers, plates, scarce. Wheldon 130-422 1974 £7.50

SELZ, JEAN   Maurice de Vlaminck. New York, n.d.
4to., color plates. Biblo & Tannen 214-557 1974 $15

SEMELAIGNE, RENE   Les Pioniers de la Psychiatrie Francaise Avant
et Apres Pinel. Paris, 1930. Large 8vo., 2 vols., quarter cloth. Gurney 66-169
1974 £15

SEMPILL, HUGH   De Mathematicis Disciplinis. 1635. Folio, contemporary mottled calf, first edition. Schumann 35-428 1974 $175

SEMPILL, HUGH   A Short Address to the Public. London, 1793.
8vo., modern boards. Dawsons PM 251-403 1974 £15

SEMPILL, ROBERT   Sempill Ballates. 1872. New buckram, blind
stamp. Allen 216-1847 1974 $10

SEMRAU, MAX   Die Kunst der Barockzeit und des Rokoko.
Esslingen, 1913. Illus. Biblo & Tannen 214-500 1974 $20

SENAC, JEAN BAPTISTE   Traite de la Structure du Coeur. Paris, 1749.
4to., 2 vols., contemporary French mottled calf, first edition. Dawsons PM
249-447 1974 £400

SENAC, JEAN BAPTISTE   Traite de la Structure de Coeur, de son Action,
et de les Maladies. Paris, 1749. Folding engraved plates, 2 vols. in one, 4to.,
contemporary calf, rebacked, first edition, fine. Broadhurst 24-1321 1974 £300

SENAULT, LE PERE JEAN FRANCOIS   De l'Usage des Passions. (Leyden,) 1643.
12mo., contemporary limp vellum. Schumann 35-429 1974 $75

SENEBIER, JEAN   Memoires sur l'Influence de l'Air et de Diverses
Substances Gazeuses dans la Germination de Differentes Graines. Geneva, 1801.
8vo., quarter parchment, first edition. Gurney 66-170 1974 £25

SENEBIER, PIERRE   Traite d'Arithmetique. 1774. 4to., orig. boards,
uncut, foxed, rare. Zeitlin 235-204 1974 $75

SENECA, LUCIUS ANNAEUS   De Benifizii Tradotto in Volgar Fiorentino
da Messer Benedetto Varchi. Firenze, 1554. Small 4to., paper boards, remains
of old wrappers on title, morocco labels. Bow Windows 66-619 1974 £30

SENECA, LUCIUS ANNAEUS   His Tenne Tragedies. 1927. 2 vols. Allen
213-964 1973 $15

SENECA, LUCIUS ANNAEUS   Opera Quae Extant. Amsterdam, 1672. 3 vols.,
8vo., contemporary calf, panelled backs, raised bands, tooled borders, leather &
metal clasps, engraved ex libris C. W. Count of Nostitz, fine, rare. Broadhurst
24-862 1974 £100

SENECA, LUCIUS ANNAEUS   Seneca's Morals Abstracted. London, 1679.
8vo., contemporary mottled calf, first edition. Dawsons PM 252-866 1974
£90

SENECA, LUCIUS ANNAEUS   Seneca's Morals by Way of Abstract. 1696.
8vo., frontis., old mottled calf, rebacked, sixth edition. Bow Windows 62-824
1974 £8.50

SENECA, LUCIUS ANNAEUS   The Workes. London, 1614. Folio, gilt,
contemporary calf, first English edition. Dawsons PM 252-865 1974 £145

SENEX, J.   The Roads Through England Delineated. 1757.
Oblong small 4to., limp leather, worn. Quaritch 939-223 1974 £100

SENIOR, NASSAU WILLIAM   Journals . . . . Relating to Ireland. London,
1868. 2 vols., orig. cloth, second edition. Emerald 50-867 1974 £15

SENN, LOUIS   Recherches Anatomico-Pathologiques sur la Meni-
ngite Aigue des Enfans. Paris, 1825. 8vo., contemporary boards, first edition.
Schumann 35-430 1974 $85

SENNETT, MACK   King of Comedy. Doubleday, 1954. 284p.,
illus. Austin 51-841 1973 $10

SENOUR, F.   Major General William T. Sherman and His
Campaigns. Chicago, 1865. Orig. cloth, fine, frontispiece, first edition.
Bradley 35-91 1974 $40

SENSINI, GUIDO   Studi di Scienze Sociali. Rome, 1932. Roy.
8vo., orig. wrappers. Howes 186-1573 1974 £5

SENTENCIAS   Primera Parte de las Sentencias. Coimbra,
1554. Small 4to., full red morocco, gilt, rare, complete, very fine. Harper
213-143 1973 $1250

LES SEPT Peches Capitaux. Paris, 1926. 4to., orig. wrapper, orig. etchings,
limited edition. Minters 37-72 1973 $500

SEQUEIRA, EDUARDO   A Beira Mar. Porto, 1889. Orig. wrappers,
boards, plates, illus. Dawson's 424-118 1974 $50

SEQUEL to the Second Book of Lessons, for the Use of Schools. Toronto, 1860.
Orig. binding. Hood's 102-430 1974 $15

SERAO, F.   Neapolitanae Scientiarum Academiae. De
Vesuvii Conflagratione quae Mense Majo Anno MDCCXXXVII Accidit. Naples,
1738. 4to., contemporary vellum, folding plates, rare, first edition. Wheldon
128-1046 1973 £35

A SERIOUS Appeal to the Wisdom and Patriotism of the Legislature of the State of
New York; On the Subject of a Canal Communication Between the Great Western
Lakes and the Tide Waters of the Hudson. N. P., 1816. 8vo., disbound, very
scarce, first edition. Ximenes 37-74 1974 $85

SERLING, ROD   Patterns. 1957. Austin 51-842 1973 $8.50

SERLIO, SEBASTIANO   De Architectura Libri Quinque. Venice, 1568-59. Folio, 18th century mottled calf, rebacked, illus., second issue of the first Latin edition. Quaritch 940-555 1974 £400

SERLIO, SEBASTIANO   Von der Architectur Funff Bucher. Basel, 1609. Large folio, woodcut illus., contemporary vellum over boards, very good copy, first complete German edition. Schafer 8-97 1973 sFr. 3,600

SERLIO, SEBASTIANO   Von der Architectur Funff Bucher . . . Jetzundt sum Ersten aus dem Italienischen und Niederlandischen. Basel, 1609. Large folio, woodcut illus., contemporary vellum over boards, very good copy, first complete German edition, second issue. Schafer 10-91 1974 sFr 3,600

SERNA SANTANDER, CARLOS ANTONIO DE LA   Dictionnaire Bibliographique Choisie du Quinzieme Siecle. Brussels, 1805-07. 3 vols., 8vo., orig. boards, foxed. Dawsons PM 10-546 1974 £40

SERRES, OLIVER DE   The Perfect Use of Silk-Wormes, and Their Benefit. 1607. 2 parts, first English edition, full page woodcuts, small 4to., contemporary dark brown mottled calf, panelled back, complete with two final blanks at end, fine. Broadhurst 24-1160 1974 £600

SERRISTORI, LUIGI   Sopra Le Macchine-A-Vapore Saggio. 1816. Small 8vo., plates, modern boards. Zeitlin 235-205 1974 $75

SERVETUS, MICHAEL   Dialogorum de Trinitate Libri duo. (Regensberg, c. 1721). 8vo., old red morocco, worn, rebacked, second edition. Gurney 66-171 1974 £120

SERVETUS, MICHAEL   Syruporum Universa Ratio, ad Galeni Censuram Diligenter Expolita. Lyons, 1547. Small 8vo., modern pigskin, new edition. Kraus 137-74 1974 $650

SERVICE, JAMES   Metrical Legends of Northumberland. 1834. 12mo., orig. quarter cloth, first edition. Ximenes 35-159 1974 $22.50

SERVICE, JAMES   Metrical Legends of Northumberland. Alnwick, 1834. Orig. boards, bookplate. Dawson's 424-49 1974 $30

SERVICE, ROBERT   Complete Poems. New York, (1940). Hood's 103-751 1974 $12.50

SERVOS, L. C.   Frontenac and The Maid of the Mist. Emmaus, 1938. Signed, second edition. Hood's 104-578 1974 $12.50

SESSE, JOSE DE   Libro de la Cosmographia Universal del Mundo. Saragossa, 1619. 4to., vellum, first edition. Schuman 37-233 1974 $300

SESSIONS, F. C.   From Yellowstone Park to Alaska. 1890. Orig. cloth, illus., first edition. Putnam 126-265 1974 $10

SETH-SMITH, DAVID   Parrakeets. (1902-)1903. Roy 8vo., new half red morocco, plates. Wheldon 129-42 1974 £75

SETH-SMITH, DAVID   Parrakeets. London, 1903. Cloth, plates, illus., first edition. Dawson's 424-319 1974 $100

SETH-SMITH, DAVID   Parrakeets. 1903. Roy. 8vo., half morocco, plates. Wheldon 131-109 1974 £185

SETHE, KURT   Urkunden der 18. Leipzig, 1914. Biblo & Tannen 213-934 1973 $12.50

SETON, ERNEST THOMPSON   Animal Heroes. New York, 1905. Dec. green cloth, gilt, mint, first edition. Bradley 35-333 1974 $25

SETON, ERNEST THOMPSON   Bannertail. New York, 1922. Brown cloth, gilt, pictorial label, signed, fine, first edition. Bradley 35-334 1974 $25

SETON, ERNEST THOMPSON   The Biography of a Grizzly. New York, 1900. Dec. cloth, drawings, first edition. Bradley 35-339 1974 $20

SETON, ERNEST THOMPSON   Great Historic Animals. New York, 1937. Pictorial cloth, dust jacket, fine, plates, first edition. Bradley 35-335 1974 $20

SETON, ERNEST THOMPSON   Lives of the Hunted. New York, 1901. Dec. green cloth, d.j., mint, first edition. Bradley 35-340 1974 $30

SETON, ERNEST THOMPSON   Lives of the Hunted. New York, 1901. First edition, fine, pictorial green cloth. Bradley 35-341 1974 $15

SETON, ERNEST THOMPSON   Lives of the Hunted. New York, 1901. Orig. binding, backstrip faded. Butterfield 10-484 1974 $12.50

SETON, ERNEST THOMPSON   Monarch the Big Bear of Tallac. New York, 1904. Cloth, pictorial label, fine, first edition. Bradley 35-336 1974 $10

SETON, ERNEST THOMPSON   The Trail of the Sandhill Stag. London, 1899. First impression, coloured frontis., drawings, soft cover. Hood's 102-542 1974 $17.50

SETON, ERNEST THOMPSON   Two Little Savages. New York, 1903. Dec. light blue cloth, drawings, first edition. Bradley 35-337 1974 $20

SETON, ERNEST THOMPSON   Woodmyth & Fable. New York, 1905. Dec. red cloth, illus., fine, first edition. Bradley 35-338 1974 $10

SETON-WATSON, R. W.   A History of the Czechs and Slovaks. 1943. Maps. Howes 186-1203 1974 £5

SETTIMELLI, EMILIO   La Critica di B. Croce. Bologna, 1912. 8vo., worn covers, foxed. Minters 37-392 1973 $30

SETTLE, ELKANAH   Absalom Senior. London, 1682. Folio, uncut, marbled wrappers, first edition. Dawsons PM 252-867 1974 £195

SETTLE, ELKANAH   The Character of a Popish Successour. London, 1681. Small folio, disbound, first edition. Dawsons PM 251-517 1974 £20

SETTLE, ELKANAH   The Character of a Popish Successour. London, 1681. Folio, first edition. Ximenes 35-160 1974 $25

SETTLE, ELKANAH   Azaria and Hushai. London, 1682. 4to., blue paper wrappers, first edition. Dawsons PM 252-868 1974 £65

SETTLE, ELKANAH   The Fairy-Queen. London, 1692. 4to., modern half morocco, first edition. Dawsons PM 252-869 1974 £125

SETTLE, ELKANAH   The Heir of Morocco. London, 1694. 4to., modern boards, second edition. Dawsons PM 252-870 1974 £60

SEVEN Coloured Lithographs of Russian Uniforms. Brown pigskin, gilt, plates. Bow Windows 62-210 1974 £110

SEVEN Xmas Eves, Being the Romance of a Social Revolution. Philadelphia, 1894. 8vo., many illus., dec. brown cloth, cover slightly soiled, interior fine. Current BW9-16 1974 $12

SEVERANCE, FRANK H.   An Old Frontier of France. New York, 1917. Portraits, maps. Hood's 103-788 1974 $60

SEVERINUS, MARCUS AURELIUS   De Efficaci Medicina Libri III. Frankfurt, 1682. Folio, contemporary vellum, illus. Schumann 35-431 1974 $145

SEVESTRE, A.   Dictionnaire de Patrologie. Paris, 1865-52-64. 5 vols., roy. 8vo., half buckram. Howes 185-1646 1974 £25

SEVIGNE, MARIE (DE RABUTIN CHANTAL) MARQUISE DE   Lettres. Paris, 1862-68. 14 vols., 8vo. and 4to., three quarter levant morocco, gilt, uncut. L. Goldschmidt 42-117 1974 $200

SEVIGNE, MARIE (DE RABUTIN CHANTAL) MARQUISE DE   Letters from the Marchioness de Sevigne to Her Daughter, the Countess de Grignan. 1927. 10 vols., crown 8vo., top edges gilt, others uncut, some foxing, else fine, orig. cloth, limited to 1,000 copies. Broadhurst 24-446 1974 £15

SEVIGNE, MARIE (DE RABUTIN CHANTAL) MARQUISE DE   Recueil des Lettres. Paris, 1754. 8 vols., small 12mo., contemporary marbled calf, gilt, morocco back labels. L. Goldschmidt 42-118 1974 $140

SEVIGNE, MARIE (DE RABUTIN CHANTAL) MARQUISE DE   Letters from the Marchioness de Sevigne to her Daughter the Countess de Grignan. 1927. Small 8vo., 10 vols., cloth. Quaritch 936-544 1974 £10

SEVIGNE, MARIE (DE RABUTIN CHANTAL) MARQUISE DE   Letters from. 1927. Crown 8vo., 10 vols., orig. cloth, uncut, limited. Broadhurst 23-462 1974 £15

SEWALL, JONATHAN MITCHELL   Miscellaneous Poems. Portsmouth, 1801. 12mo., contemporary sheep, rare, first edition. Ximenes 35-161 1974 $125

SEWARD, ALBERT CHARLES   Plant Life Through the Ages. Cambridge, (1933), 1941. 8vo., cloth, figures, second edition. Wheldon 128-1162 1973 £6

SEWARD, ALBERT CHARLES   Plant Life Through the Ages. Cambridge, 1931. 8vo., cloth, illus., scarce. Wheldon 130-1054 1974 £7.50

SEWARD, ALBERT CHARLES   Plant Life through the Ages. Cambridge, 1931. Roy 8vo., cloth, illus. Wheldon 129-964 1974 £15

SEWARD, ALBERT CHARLES   Plant Life Through the Ages. 1941. 8vo., cloth, second edition. Wheldon 131-1198 1974 £6

SEWARD, ANNA   Elegy on Captain Cook. London, 1780. 4to., disbound, first edition. Ximenes 37-190 1974 $65

SEWARD, ANNA   Letters of. Edinburgh, 1811. 8vo., orig. boards, rebacked, plates, first edition. Hammond 201-327 1974 £35

SEWARD, WILLIAM H.   The Works of William H. Seward. New York, 1972. 5 vols. Biblo & Tannen 213-95 1973 $60

SEWEL, WILLIAM   The History of the Rise, Increase and Progress of the Christian People called Quakers. 1722. Folio, quarter calf, first English edition. Hill 126-239 1974 £18

SEWELL, ANNA   Black Beauty. (n.d.). Illus. in colour by Cecil Aldin, covers little rubbed. Bow Windows 66-6 1974 £10.50

SEWELL, ELIZABETH MISSING   Laneton Parsonage. 1846-48-49. First edition of parts 2 & 3, second edition of part 1, together 3 parts in 1 vol., stout 12mo., new red buckram. George's 610-658 1973 £7.50

SEWELL, MRS.   Mother's Las Words. London, (c. 1890). 8vo., full page full color pictures, dec. front cover, rebacked, very fine. Current BW9-123 1974 $22.50

SEX Mythology, Including an Account of the Masculine Cross. 1895. Orig. buckram backed boards. Smith 193-795 1973 £5

SEYER, SAMUEL   Memoirs Historical and Topographical of Bristol. Bristol, (1821). 2 vols. in 1, 4to., plates, half calf gilt. Quaritch 939-366 1974 £50

SEYER, SAMUEL   Memoirs Historical and Topographical of Bristol. Bristol, 1821-23. 2 vols., thick 4to., contemporary half morocco gilt, plates, staining. Howes 186-2009 1974 £60

SEYMOUR, A. B.   Host Index of the Fungi of North America. Cambridge, 1929. Small 4to., orig. buckram. Wheldon 129-1345 1974 £15

SEYMOUR, CHARLES   The Intimate Papers of Colonel House Arranged as a Narrative. Boston, 1926. 2 vols. Jenkins 61-1080 1974 $10

SEYMOUR, CHARLES, JR.   Masterpieces of Sculpture from the National Gallery of Art. New York, 1949. 4to., plates. Biblo & Tannen 214-495 1973 $27.50

SEYMOUR, EDWARD ADOLPHUS   A Treatise in Which the Elementary Properties of the Ellipse are Deduced. London, 1842. 8vo., contemporary blue calf, gilt, first edition. Dawsons PM 245-671 1974 £25

SEYMOUR, R.   The School Master Abroad. 1834. Oblong folio, half morocco, gilt, plates, orig. front wrapper, rare, first edition. Quaritch 940-239 1974 £250

SEYMOUR, ROBERT   Humorous Sketches. 1878. New buckram, blind stamp. Allen 216-823 1974 $25

SEYMOUR, WILLIAM W.   Cross In Tradition, History & Art. 1898. 4to., plates. Allen 213-1780 1973 $20

SEYNES, J. DE   Recherches Pour Servir. Paris, 1874-88. 4to., cloth, plates. Wheldon 129-1346 1974 £20

SEYNES, J. DE   Recherches Pour Servir a l'Histoire Naturelle des Vegetaux Inferieurs. Paris, 1874-88. 3 parts in 1 vol., 4to., cloth, plates, scarce. Wheldon 131-1466 1974 £20

SFORTUNATI, GIOVANNI   Nuovo Lume Libro de Arithmetica. (1545). 4to., modern vellum, fine. Dawsons PM 245-672 1974 £135

SFORZA, MUTIUS   Hymnorum Libri Tres. Rome, 1593. Has both blanks, old vellum, little worn, lacks ties. Thomas 32-262 1974 £50

SGRILLI, B. S.   Descrizione e Studi dell' Insigne. Florence, 1733. Folio, boards, gilt, plates. Broadhurst 23-194 1974 £90

SGUARIO, EUSEBIO   Dell'Elettricismo. Venice, 1746. 8vo., contemporary vellum, gilt. Dawsons PM 245-673 1974 £40

SHACHTMAN, MAX   Sacco and Vanzetti. New York, 1927. Orig. pictorial wrappers, scarce, first edition. Bradley 35-329 1974 $50

SHACKLEFORD, ANN   The Modern Art of Cookery Improved. London, 1767. 12mo., contemporary calf, rare, first edition. Ximenes 35-162 1974 $225

SHACKLETON, ERNEST   The Heart of the Antarctic. 1909. Roy 8vo., orig. cloth, 2 vols., illus., plates, scarce. Wheldon 130-313 1974 £20

SHACKLETON, ERNEST   South: The Story of Shackleton's Last Expedition. 1919. Plates, first edition, roy. 8vo., half dark green morocco, panelled back, fine. Broadhurst 24-1681 1974 £12

SHACKLETON, ERNEST   South. The Story of Shackleton's Last Expedition 1914-1917. New York, 1920. Illus., diagrams, first edition, 8vo., colored frontis., large colored folding map, fine. Current BW9-452 1974 $18

SHADWELL, C. L.   The Paradise of Dante Alighieri. 1915. 8vo., orig. cloth, some spotting. Bow Windows 66-165 1974 £5

SHADWELL, THOMAS   The Amorous Bigotte. London, 1690. 4to., full polished calf, first edition. Ximenes 35-163 1974 $175

SHADWELL, THOMAS   The Lancashire-Witches. London, 1682. 4to., full polished calf, gilt, fine, first edition. Ximenes 35-164 1974 $275

SHADWELL, THOMAS   The Scowrers. London, 1691. 4to., disbound, first edition. Ximenes 35-165 1974 $150

SHADWELL, THOMAS   The Complete Works. 1927. 4to., 5 vols., cloth, limited numbered edition. Hammond 201-328 1974 £45

SHADWELL, THOMAS   The Complete Works of. London, 1927. 5 vols., orig. buckram, uncut, fine, limited edition. Dawsons PM 252-871 1974 £50

SHADWELL, THOMAS   The Works of. Fortune Press, 1927. 5 vols., crown 4to., half morocco, uncut, fine, scarce, one of 90 copies on Kelmscott unbleached hand made paper, signed by editor. Broadhurst 24-978 1974 £130

SHAIRP, JOHN CAMPBELL   Aspects of Poetry. 1882. Orig. edition. Austin 61-896 1974 $12.50

SHAIRP, JOHN CAMPBELL   On Poetic Interpretation of Nature. 1878. 279 pages. Austin 61-897 1974 $10

SHAKESPEARE, EDWARD O.   Report On Cholera In Europe and India. Washington, 1890. Rittenhouse 46-584 1974 $25

SHAKESPEARE, WILLIAM   As You Like It. Philadelphia, 1890. Roy. 8vo., orig. cloth gilt, fine. Howes 185-433 1974 £9.50

SHAKESPEARE, WILLIAM   Cassell's Illustrated Shakespeare. n.d.
3 vols., 4to., illus., half contemporary calf gilt. Smith 193-149 1973 £6.50

SHAKESPEARE, WILLIAM   A Collection of Poems. London, (1709-10).
2 vols. in 1, 8vo., 19th century calf. Dawsons PM 252-877 1974 £150

SHAKESPEARE, WILLIAM   The Comedies, Histories and Tragedies.
New York, 1939-40. Ltd. to 1,950 sets, 37 vols. Biblo & Tannen 210-762
1973 $300

SHAKESPEARE, WILLIAM   The Tragedy of Coriolanus. Hammersmith,
1914. Full vellum. Dawson's 424-64 1974 $250

SHAKESPEARE, WILLIAM   Dramatic Works. London, 1826. 12mo., India
paper ed., calf bdg. worn and broken. Biblo & Tannen 214-764 1974 $12.50

SHAKESPEARE, WILLIAM   Dramatic Works. 1838. Austin 51-847
1973 $17.50

SHAKESPEARE, WILLIAM   The Dramatic Works of William Shakespeare.
Harper, 1829. 2 vols., engravings. Austin 51-849 1973 $25

SHAKESPEARE, WILLIAM   The Dramatick Writings of. 1788. 20 vols.,
12mo., contemporary half sheep, labels. Howes 185-431 1974 £35

SHAKESPEARE, WILLIAM   Ein Sommernachts-Traum. Munich, 1878. Red
cloth, gilt. Dawson's 424-119 1974 $50

SHAKESPEARE, WILLIAM   Hamlet. 1903. 136p., illus. Austin 51-911
1973 $10

SHAKESPEARE, WILLIAM   Hamlet. Doubleday, 1947. Austin 51-846
1973 $7.50

SHAKESPEARE, WILLIAM   The Historie of Henrie the Fourth. London,
(c.1880). 2 vols., 4to., vellum, full brown morocco gilt. Dawsons PM
252-872 1974 £180

SHAKESPEARE, WILLIAM   The History of King Lear. 1729. Small 8vo.,
nineteenth century cloth. Quaritch 936-212 1974 £10

SHAKESPEARE, WILLIAM   The Tragedie of Julius Caesar. Hammersmith,
Doves Press, 1913. Limited edition, printed in red and black, 8vo., limp vellum,
uncut, as issued, fine copy, limited to 200 copies. Sawyer 293-129 1974 £150

SHAKESPEARE, WILLIAM   Lucrece. Doves Press, 1915. Printed in red
and black, 8vo., orig. limp vellum, fine, limited to 175 copies on paper. Sawyer
293-128 1974 £75

SHAKESPEARE, WILLIAM   The Merchant of Venice. Glasgow, (1904).
Orig. tan suede, 2 1/8 X 1 3/8. Gregory 44-459 1974 £12.50

SHAKESPEARE, WILLIAM   The Merry Wives of Windsor. New York, 1910.
Large 8vo., orig. binding, tipped in color plates, small split top of backstrip.
Wilson 63-568 1974 $17.75

SHAKESPEARE, WILLIAM   The Merry Wives of Windsor. London, 1910.
4to., orig. cloth, gilt, plates. Hammond 201-498 1974 £7.50

SHAKESPEARE, WILLIAM   A Midsummer Night's Dream. 1908. 4to.,
orig. cloth gilt, plates, first edition. Howes 185-393 1974 £35

SHAKESPEARE, WILLIAM   Mr. William Shakespeares Comedies, Histories,
and Tragedies. London, 1632. Folio, modern vellum, morocco label, second
folio edition. Dawsons PM 252-874 1974 £1600

SHAKESPEARE, WILLIAM   Mr. William Shakespeare's Comedies, Histories,
and Tragedies. London, 1685. Folio, 18th century speckled calf, fourth
edition. Dawsons PM 252-875 1974 £3250

SHAKESPEARE, WILLIAM   Mr. William Shakespear's Comedies, Histories,
and Tragedies. London, 1785. Folio, contemporary mottled calf, half morocco
box, fine, fourth edition. Dawsons PM 250-72 1974 £4500

SHAKESPEARE, WILLIAM   Mr. William Shakespeare's Comedies, Histories,
and Tragedies. Methuen, 1910. Folio, boards, unopened. Quaritch 936-546
1974 £70

SHAKESPEARE, WILLIAM   Mr. William Shakespeare's. Mifflin, 1911.
6 vols. Austin 51-850 1973 $37.50

SHAKESPEARE, WILLIAM   Mr. William Shakespeare's. Yale Univ.,
1955. Austin 51-845 1973 $14.75

SHAKESPEARE, WILLIAM   The Philosophy of W. Shakespeare. 1857.
Austin 51-851 1973 $10

SHAKESPEARE, WILLIAM   The Plays Of. n.d. 4to., orig. designed
cloth, illus. Smith 193-152. 1973 £5.50

SHAKESPEARE, WILLIAM   The Plays of. London, 1765. 8 vols., 8vo.,
speckled calf, frontispiece, first edition. Dawsons PM 252-555 1974 £180

SHAKESPEARE, WILLIAM   The Plays of. London, 1773. 10 vols.,
contemporary speckled calf, gilt tooling on spines, morocco labels, third edition,
fine set, with all half title and frontispiece portrait in vol. 1. MacManus
224-390 1974 $200

SHAKESPEARE, WILLIAM   The Plays. London, 1773. 10 vols., 8vo.,
contemporary speckled calf, gilt. Dawsons PM 252-556 1974 £65

SHAKESPEARE, WILLIAM   The Plays. London, 1778. 10 vols., 8vo.,
contemporary tree calf, second edition. Dawsons PM 252-557 1974 £85

SHAKESPEARE, WILLIAM   The Plays. 1803. 21 vols., large 8vo., worn,
contemporary sprinkled calf, first variorum edition. Howes 186-404 1974 £55

SHAKESPEARE, WILLIAM   Plays. c.1865. 3 vols., thick roy. 8vo.,
half crimson morocco gilt. Howes 185-432 1974 £15

SHAKESPEARE, WILLIAM   The Poems of. Kelmscott Press, 1893. Printed
in golden type in red & black, 8vo., full limp vellum, silk ties, uncut, limited
to 500 copies. Broadhurst 24-1018 1974 £225

SHAKESPEARE, WILLIAM   The Poems of. Hammersmith, 1893. 8vo.,
orig. limp vellum, fine. Dawsons PM 252-878 1974 £250

SHAKESPEARE, WILLIAM   The Poems of William Shakespeare. New
York, 1941. 2 vols., folio. Biblo & Tannen 210-763 1973 $50

SHAKESPEARE, WILLIAM   Romeo & Juliet. 1936. Fine, illus. Covent
55-894 1974 £12.50

SHAKESPEARE, WILLIAM   Tragedy of Romeo and Juliet. New York,
1935. 4to., illus. Biblo & Tannen 210-740 1973 $7.50

SHAKESPEARE, WILLIAM   Shakespeare Memorial 1564-1864. Lond., 1864.
Austin 51-852 1973 $17.50

SHAKESPEARE, WILLIAM   Songs. London, 1905. Red morocco, gilt,
fine, 2 3/4 X 2 1/2. Gregory 44-460 1974 £22.50

SHAKESPEARE, WILLIAM   Sonnets. New York, 1941. Biblo & Tannen
210-739 1973 $7.50

SHAKESPEARE, WILLIAM   The Tempest. London, 1690. Small 4to.,
disbound. Ximenes 35-166 1974 $125

SHAKESPEARE, WILLIAM   The Tempest. London, 1901. Sm. 4to.
Biblo & Tannen 210-153 1973 $17.50

SHAKESPEARE, WILLIAM   La Tempete. Paris, n.d. 4to., full crushed
morocco gilt, plates, foxing. Covent 55-885 1974 £15

SHAKESPEARE, WILLIAM   Twelfth Night. 1932. Small folio, limited,
half-niger morocco. Dawsons PM 252-873 1974 £110

SHAKESPEARE, WILLIAM   Twenty-Five Sonnets. 1921. Orig. buckram
backed boards, limited. Howes 185-442 1974 £5

SHAKESPEARE, WILLIAM   Venus and Adonis. Oxford, 1905. 4to.,
modern cloth. Ximenes 35-167 1974 $50

SHAKESPEARE, WILLIAM   The Winter's Tale. Lippincott, 1898.
Orig. ed. Austin 51-848 1973 $17.50

SHAKESPEARE, WILLIAM   The Complete Works Of. n.d. 3 vols., 4to.,
half contemporary calf gilt, illus. Smith 193-150 1973 £6

SHAKESPEARE, WILLIAM   The Works Of. n.d. 3 vols. of 4, 4to.,
plates, contemporary brown morocco, imperial edition. Smith 193-154 1973
£15

SHAKESPEARE, WILLIAM   The Works Of. n.d. 4 vols., 4to., plates,
orig. cloth. Smith 193-151 1973 £10

SHAKESPEARE, WILLIAM   The Works of. 1733. 7 vols., calf, gilt,
labels, rubbed. Howes 185-430 1974 £115

SHAKESPEARE, WILLIAM   Works. 1844. 8 vols., demy 8vo., full
brown calf, gilt, labels, rubbed. Howes 186-405 1974 £40

SHAKESPEARE, WILLIAM   Works. Liverpool, 1846. 3 vols., roy. 8vo.,
half green morocco gilt, foxing, plates, illus. Howes 186-406 1974 £21

SHAKESPEARE, WILLIAM   The Complete Works Of. 1869. Illus. with
engravings. Austin 61-899 1974 $27.50

SHAKESPEARE, WILLIAM   The Works Of. 1891-1893. 9 vols., large
demy 8vo., orig. cloth gilt. Smith 194-235 1974 £9

SHAKESPEARE, WILLIAM   The Works. London & New York, 1894-95.
9 vols., large 8vo., contemporary crushed morocco gilt, second & third editions.
Dawsons PM 252-876 1974 £120

SHAKESPEARE, WILLIAM   Works. 1899. Small 8vo., 10 vols., cloth,
Eversley edition. Quaritch 936-545 1974 £12

SHAKESPEARE, WILLIAM   The Complete Works of. Garden City, 1936.
Cambridge edition text, illus., orig. binding. Wilson 63-567 1974 $12.50

A SHAKESPEARE Bibliography. London. 7 vols., 4to., cloth. Dawsons PM
11-694 1974 £116

SHAKESPEARE and His Friends--Shakespeare Novels. 1838. 3 vols. Austin
51-854 1973 $17.50

SHAKESPEARE'S England. Oxford, 1916. 2 vols., thick large 8vo., plates,
first edition. Howes 186-1205 1974 £8.50

SHAKESPEARIANA. London, 1779. 2 vols., 8vo., 19th century half calf,
gilt, first edition. Ximenes 35-168 1974 $65

SHALLENBERGER, MRS. E. H.   Stark County and Its Pioneers. Cambridge,
1876. Cloth, very scarce. Hayman 59-272 1974 $65

THE SHANACHIE. Dublin, 1906-7. 8vo., orig. cloth, uncut, plates, fine,
scarce. Broadhurst 23-918 1974 £50

SHANKS, EDWARD   The Island of Youth and Other Poems. 1921.
Buckram, fine, unopened, English first edition. Covent 56-1165 1974 £7.50

SHANKS, EDWARD   The Queen of China and Other Poems. 1919.
Boards, English first edition. Covent 56-1166 1974 £8.50

SHAPLAND, H. P.   The Practical Decoration of Furniture. 1926.
4to., 2 vols., plates, English first edition. Covent 56-1656 1974 £15

SHAPLAND, H. P.   The Practical Decoration of Furniture. 1926-
27. 3 vols., plates. Marsden 39-412 1974 £10

SHARKEY, MARY AGNES   The New Jersey Sisters of Charity. Longmans,
Green, 1933. 3 vols., illus. Austin 62-587 1974 $37.50

SHARKEY, MARY AGNES   The New Jersey Sisters of Charity. 1933.
3 vols., illus. Austin 57-611 1974 $37.50

SHARLIP, WILLIAM   Adult Immigrant Education. Macmillan, 1925.
Austin 62-588 1974 $10

SHARLIP, WILLIAM   Adult Immigrant Education. 1925.
317 pages. Austin 57-612 1974 $10

SHARP, CUTHBERT   A History of Hartlepool. Durham, 1816.
8vo., old half calf, worn, uncut. Ximenes 35-169 1974 $65

SHARP, EVELYN   The Child's Christmas. London, (1906). 4to.,
orig. cloth, gilt, dust-wrapper, plates, illus. Hammond 201-497 1974 £5

SHARP, GRANVILLE   Remarks Concerning the Encroachments on the
Thames. 1771. Small 8vo., modern boards. Quaritch 939-261 1974 £30

SHARP, GRANVILLE   Remarks on the Opinions of Some of the Most
Celebrated Writers on Crown Law. 1773. Small 8vo., modern boards, first edition.
Quaritch 939-242 1974 £50

SHARP, GREGORY   An Arguement in Defence of Christianity.
London, 1755-62. 2 vols. in 1, 8vo., contemporary calf, first edition.
Ximenes 35-170 1974 $35

SHARP, GREGORY   The Origin and Structure of the Greek Tongue.
London, 1777. 8vo., contemporary calf, plates, second edition. Ximenes
35-171 1974 $35

SHARP, LUKE PSEUD.
Please turn to
BARR, ROBERT

SHARP, R. FARQUHARSON   A Dictionary of English Authors Biographical
and Bibliographical. 1897. Very good copy, full buckram, first edition.
Covent 51-2182 1973 £10.50

SHARP, SAMUEL   A Treatise on the Operations of Surgery. London,
1739. 8vo., eighteenth century panelled calf, first edition. Schumann 35-433
1974 $175

SHARP, THOMAS   A Dissertation on the Pageants. Coventry,
1825. 4to., plates, cloth. Quaritch 939-572 1974 £17.50

SHARP, WILLIAM   The Writings of Fiona Macleod. London,
1931. 7 vols., 8vo., dust jacket, pocket edition. Emerald 50-870 1974 £10

SHARPE, CHARLES KIRKPATRICK   A Historical Account of the Belief in
Witchcraft in Scotland. Glasgow, 1884. Crown 8vo., orig. edition. Howes
186-1928 1974 £6.50

SHARPE, EDWARD   Britaines Busse. London, 1615. 4to., modern
half morocco, first edition. Dawsons PM 247-261 1974 £95

SHARPE, MARY F.   Plain Facts for Future Citizens. Am. Book Co.
240p., illus. Austin 62-589 1974 $8.50

SHARPE, REGINALD R.   London and the Kingdom. 1894-95. 3 vols.,
orig. green cloth gilt, plates. Howes 186-2140 1974 £9

SHARPE, RICHARD BOWDLER   A Handbook to the Birds of Great Britain. 1896-
97. 4 vols., 8vo., cloth, plates. Wheldon 131-706 1974 £10

SHARPE, RICHARD BOWDLER   Hand-List of the Genera and Species of Birds.
1899-1912. 8vo., cloth. Wheldon 130-621 1974 £25

SHARPE, RICHARD BOWDLER   A Monograph of the Hirundinidae. 1885-94.
4to., 2 vols., orig. cloth. Broadhurst 23-1184 1974 £800

SHARPE, RICHARD BOWLDER   A Monograph of Hirumdinidae or Family of
Swallows. 1885-94. 2 vols., med. 4to., binder's cloth, uncut, hand coloured
plates, maps, bound from orig. parts all wrappers preserved, fine. Broadhurst
24-1162 1974 £1,150

SHARPE, RICHARD BOWDLER   The Zoology of the Afghan Demlimitation
Commission. Birds. (c. 1890). 4to., stitched, coloured plates. Sawyer
293-242 1974 £28

SHARPE, WILLIAM   Diagnosis and Treatment of Brain Injuries With
and Without a Fracture of the Skull. Philadelphia, 1920. Rittenhouse 46-731
1974 $25

SHARPHAM, EDWARD   Cupid's Whirligig. 1926. Linen-backed boards,
English first edition. Covent 56-531 1974 £7.50

SHARPIES, A.   Diseases and Pests of the Rubber Tree. 1936.
8vo., cloth, scarce. Wheldon 129-1666 1974 £7.50

SHARROCK, ROBERT   The History of the Propagation and Improvement
of Vegetables by the Concurrence of Art and Nature. Oxford, 1660. F'cap 8vo.,
newly bound in full brown calf, fine, complete with ads at end. Broadhurst
24-1163 1974 £75

SHAW, BYAM   Legendary Ballads. 1908. Plates, faded.
Covent 55-1351 1974 £6.50

SHAW, GEORGE   General Zoology. 1803-04. Vols. 4 & 5,
2 vols., roy. 8vo., russia, gilt, plates. Wheldon 131-768 1974 £25

SHAW, GEORGE   A Manual of Electro-Metallurgy. London,
1844. 8vo., orig. cloth, fine, second edition. Ximenes 35-172 1974 $22.50

SHAW, GEORGE BERNARD   The Apple Cart. London, 1930. Light foxing,
d.w., fine, orig. binding. Ross 86-406 1974 $10

SHAW, GEORGE BERNARD   The Apple Cart. London, 1930. 12mo.,
cloth, dust jacket, fine, first edition. Goodspeed's 578-319 1974 $15

SHAW, GEORGE BERNARD   The Art of Rehearsal. 1928. Austin 51-856
1973 $6.50

SHAW, GEORGE BERNARD   The Art of Rehearsal. New York, 1928. Wrappers, first U.S. edition. Covent 56-2034 1974 £15

SHAW, GEORGE BERNARD   The Arts League of Service Annual. 1921-22.
Wrappers, fine, scarce, first edition. Rota 188-829 1974 £5

SHAW, GEORGE BERNARD   Aspects of Wilde. 1938. 8vo., orig. cloth,
second edition. Broadhurst 23-927 1974 £6

SHAW, GEORGE BERNARD   Augustus Does His Bit. (1916). 8vo., orig.
buff wrappers, fine, first edition. Rota 190-876 1974 £60

SHAW, GEORGE BERNARD   Back to Methuselah. 1921. First edition, crown
8vo., mint, slightly frayed d.w., orig. cloth. Broadhurst 24-871 1974 £8

SHAW, GEORGE BERNARD   Cashel Byron's Profession. 1886. Roy 8vo.,
orig. wrapper, first edition. Quaritch 936-567 1974 £30

SHAW, GEORGE BERNARD   Cashel Byron's Profession. 1906. Austin 51-
858 1973 $7.50

SHAW, GEORGE BERNARD   The Complete Plays of. (1931). 8vo., orig.
cloth, inscription on half-title, first edition. Bow Windows 66-622 1974 £7.50

SHAW, GEORGE BERNARD   Dramatic Opinions & Essays. New York,
1906. 2 vols., first edition, orig. binding, name in ink on free fly, spine labels
slightly soiled, very nice copy. Ross 87-524 1974 $30

SHAW, GEORGE BERNARD   Ellen Terry and Bernard Shaw. 1931. 8vo.,
orig. green cloth, uncut, first limited edition. Bow Windows 62-828 1974 £25

SHAW, GEORGE BERNARD   Everybody's Political What's What? London,
1944. 8vo., orig. cloth, fine, first edition. Dawsons PM 252-881 1974 £145

SHAW, GEORGE BERNARD   Everybody's Political What's What? London,
1944. 8vo., orig. cloth, first edition. Dawsons PM 247-262 1974 £10

SHAW, GEORGE BERNARD   Fabian Essays in Socialism. 1889. Ex-library,
slightly worn and shaken, first edition, second issue. Allen 216-1582 1974 £10

SHAW, GEORGE BERNARD   Fabian Essays in Socialism. 1889. 8vo., dec.
cloth, signature, first edition. Quaritch 936-568 1974 £20

SHAW, GEORGE BERNARD   Fabian Essays In Socialism. n.d. Orig.
designed cloth. Smith 194-521 1974 £12

SHAW, GEORGE BERNARD   Heartbreak House. 1919. Austin 51-862
1973 $8.50

SHAW, GEORGE BERNARD   Heartbreak House. 1919. 8vo., orig. cloth,
inscribed, first edition. Rota 190-877 1974 £75

SHAW, GEORGE BERNARD   How to Settle the Irish Question. 1917. 8vo.,
orig. wrapper, first edition. Quaritch 936-569 1974 £16

SHAW, GEORGE BERNARD   The Inca of Perusalem. 1915. First edition,
proof copy, f'cap. 8vo., orig. blue grey paper wrapper printed "Rough Proof-
Unpublished", mint, loosely inserted is list of Cast of Play authographed by all
the Performers. Broadhurst 24-868 1974 £130

SHAW, GEORGE BERNARD   The Intelligent Woman's Guide to Socialism and
Capitalism. London, 1928. Lacking d.w., orig. binding, fine. Ross 86-408
1974 $15

SHAW, GEORGE BERNARD   The Intelligent Woman's Guide to Socialism
and Capitalism. London, 1928. 8vo., orig. cloth, inscription, first edition.
Dawsons PM 252-882 1974 £75

SHAW, GEORGE BERNARD   The Intelligent Woman's Guide to Socialism
and Capitalism. London, 1928. Orig. binding, first edition, lacking d.w.,
spine slightly loosened, very nice. Ross 87-525 1974 $15

SHAW, GEORGE BERNARD   The Irrational Knot. 1905. Austin 51-864
1973 $8.50

SHAW, GEORGE BERNARD   The Irrational Knot. London, 1905. Orig.
binding, first edition, front hinge tender, light foxing, covers lightly worn, nice.
Ross 87-526 1974 $12.50

SHAW, GEORGE BERNARD   The Irrational Knot. 1905. First edition,
crown 8vo., orig. cloth, fine. Broadhurst 24-865 1974 £8

SHAW, GEORGE BERNARD   The Irrational Knot. 1909. Near fine, first
edition. Covent 55-1354 1974 £5.25

SHAW, GEORGE BERNARD   John Bull's Other Island and Major Barbara:
Also How He Lied to Her Husband. London, 1907. First edition, first issue,
inscription in unknown hand, fine, orig. binding. Ross 87-527 1974 $25

SHAW, GEORGE BERNARD   Letters Of. 1927. 8vo., orig. cloth, uncut,
mint, first edition. Broadhurst 23-923 1974 £40

SHAW, GEORGE BERNARD   Letters of . . . to Miss Alma Murray. Edinburgh,
1927. First edition, demy 8vo., sewn, paper printed wrapper, uncut, mint,
limited to 30 copies. Broadhurst 24-876 1974 £45

SHAW, GEORGE BERNARD   London Music 1888-89. 1937. Austin 51-859
1973 $8.50

SHAW, GEORGE BERNARD   Love Among the Artists. Chicago, 1900. Small
8vo., rebound, green buckram, gilt, first edition. Quaritch 936-570 1974 £18

SHAW, GEORGE BERNARD   Love Among the Artists. Chicago, 1900. Crown
8vo., orig. cloth, scarce, first edition. Broadhurst 23-920 1974 £10

SHAW, GEORGE BERNARD   Love Among the Artists. 1907. Austin 51-865
1973 $8.50

SHAW, GEORGE BERNARD   Man and Superman. 1903. First edition, crown
8vo., spine slightly faded, orig. cloth. Broadhurst 24-864 1974 £12

SHAW, GEORGE BERNARD   Man and Superman. 1907. Austin 51-866
1973 $8.50

SHAW, GEORGE BERNARD   Man and Superman. Leipzig, 1913. First
edition, wrappers, very good copy. Covent 51-1672 1973 £5.25

SHAW, GEORGE BERNARD   Man and Superman. 1947. Austin 51-867
1973 $7.50

SHAW, GEORGE BERNARD   The Man of Destiny. 1910. Austin 51-868
1973 $8.50

SHAW, GEORGE BERNARD   Misalliance, the Dark Lady of the Sonnets and
Fanny's First Play. 1914. Austin 51-869 1973 $8.50

SHAW, GEORGE BERNARD   Misalliance: The Dark Lady of the Sonnets,
Fanny's First Play. 1914. First edition, crown 8vo., mint, d.w., orig. cloth.
Broadhurst 24-866 1974 £8

SHAW, GEORGE BERNARD   The Need for Expert Opinion in Sexual Reform. 1930. Plates, English first edition. Covent 56-1168 1974 £8.50

SHAW, GEORGE BERNARD   On Going to Church. Boston, 1905. First U. S. edition, very nice copy. Covent 51-1673 1973 £10.50

SHAW, GEORGE BERNARD   Peace Conference Hints. London, 1919. Orig. binding, unusually nice copy. Ross 86-410 1974 $15

SHAW, GEORGE BERNARD   The Perfect Wagnerite. 1909. Austin 51-870 1973 $7.50

SHAW, GEORGE BERNARD   The Perfect Wagnerite. Leipzig, 1913. Orig. red cloth. Covent 55-1132 1974 £5.25

SHAW, GEORGE BERNARD   Plays Pleasant and Unpleasant. 1898. Crown 8vo., orig. cloth, 2 vols., first edition. Broadhurst 23-919 1974 £15

SHAW, GEORGE BERNARD   Plays Pleasant and Unpleasant. 1910. 2 vols. Austin 51-871 1973 $12.50

SHAW, GEORGE BERNARD   Prefaces. Constable, 1934. Roy 8vo., cloth, orig. edition. Quaritch 936-571 1974 £4

SHAW, GEORGE BERNARD   Press Cuttings. London, 1909. First edition, gray wrappers, front & back covers separated from vol. and badly chipped, not a collector's copy. Ross 87-530 1974 $10

SHAW, GEORGE BERNARD   The Quintessence of Ibsenism. 1891. Bookplate, very good copy, gilt top, first edition. Covent 51-1677 1973 £12.50

SHAW, GEORGE BERNARD   The Quintessence of Ibsenism. London, 1913. Second edition, bookplate, photo of G. B. S. pasted in, lacking d.w., nice, orig. binding. Ross 86-411 1974 $10

SHAW, GEORGE BERNARD   The Quintessence of Ibsenism. 1925. Austin 51-872 1973 $7.50

SHAW, GEORGE BERNARD   Ruskin's Politics. 1921. Linen backed boards, very fine unopened copy, tissue wrappers, first edition. Covent 51-1678 1973 £7.50

SHAW, GEORGE BERNARD   Ruskin's Politics. 1921. Linen backed boards, very fine unopened copy, tissue wrappers, first edition. Covent 51-1618 1973 £7.50

SHAW, GEORGE BERNARD   Saint Joan. London, 1924. Covers protected by light glassine wrapper, unopened, nice. Ross 86-413 1974 $20

SHAW, GEORGE BERNARD   Saint Joan: A Chroncile Play in Six Scenes and an Epilogue. London, 1924. 12mo., orig. cloth, first edition, fine, dust jacket, tipped-in is letter from Herbert Ashley to Shaw, in the lower margin Shaw has written reply. MacManus 224-393 1974 $130

SHAW, GEORGE BERNARD   The Sanity of Art. 1908. 8vo., orig. paper wrappers, first edition. Bow Windows 64-682 1974 £7.50

SHAW, GEORGE BERNARD   Selected Passages from the Works Of. 1912. 8vo., orig. cloth, first edition. Rota 190-875 1974 £25

SHAW, GEORGE BERNARD   Shaw Gives Himself Away. 1939. Roy 8vo., morocco, leather, uncut. Broadhurst 23-1056 1974 £100

SHAW, GEORGE BERNARD   Tales from Bernard Shaw. (London, 1929). Quarter vellum, boards, uncut, illus., limited, first edition. Bow Windows 62-831 1974 £10.50

SHAW, GEORGE BERNARD   Three Plays for Puritans. 1900. Austin 51-874 1973 $7.50

SHAW, GEORGE BERNARD   Three Plays for Puritans. 1901. First edition, crown 8vo., binding discoloured, owner's label on fly, orig. cloth. Broadhurst 24-863 1974 £8

SHAW, GEORGE BERNARD   Translations and Tomfooleries. 1926. Austin 51-876 1973 $8.50

SHAW, GEORGE BERNARD   An Unsocial Socialist. London, 1884. 12 parts in 2 vols., 8vo., orig. cloth, first edition. Dawsons PM 252-883 1974 £110

SHAW, GEORGE BERNARD   An Unsocial Socialist. 1900. Orig. edition. Austin 51-877 1973 $7.25

SHAW, GEORGE BERNARD   An Unsocial Socialist. New York, 1905. First U. S. edition, very nice copy. Covent 51-2565 1973 £6.50

SHAW, GEORGE BERNARD   The Works Of. 1930. Roy 8vo., 33 vols., orig. cloth, uncut, limited edition. Broadhurst 23-924 1974 £200

SHAW, GEORGE BERNARD   The Complete Plays of. London, 1931. Thick 8vo., orig. cloth, dust jacket, first edition, tipped-in is T.L.s. from the Director of the British Empire Film Institute to Shaw, with reply in bottom margin from Shaw. MacManus 224-392 1974 $140

SHAW, GEORGE BERNARD   Collected Works. 1930-38. 30 vols., large 8vo., limited library edition. Howes 185-443 1974 £95

SHAW, GEORGE BERNARD   The Works of. 1930. 33 vols., complete, roy. 8vo., uncut, mint, dust wrappers, limited to 1000 numbered sets. Broadhurst 24-877 1974 £200

SHAW, GEORGE BERNARD   The Works. London, 1930-38. 33 vols., large 8vo., orig. cloth, limited, fine. Dawsons PM 252-885 1974 £400

SHAW, GEORGE BERNARD   Complete Works. 1930-38. Gilt tops, 33 vols., English first edition. Covent 56-2035 1974 £350

SHAW, H.   The History and Antiquities of the Chapel at Luton Park. 1829. Folio, orig. half leather, label, plates. Quaritch 939-296 1974 £32

SHAW, HENRY   A Book of Sundry Draughtes. London, 1848. 8vo., contemporary half vellum, plates, first edition. Ximenes 35-173 1974 $30

SHAW, HENRY   Dresses and Decorations of the Middle Ages. 1843. 2 vols., quarter morocco, worn at corners, colour-printed. Eaton Music-673 1973 £60

SHAW, HENRY   Dresses and Decorations of the Middle Ages. London, 1843. 4to., 2 vols., modern half blue buckram, gilt, first edition. Dawsons PM 251-336 1974 £100

SHAW, HENRY   Dresses and Dcorations of the Middle Ages. Pickering, 1843. 2 vols., imp. 8vo., plates, woodcuts, full diced russia, gilt, leother labels, first edition. Quaritch 940-476 1974 £150

SHAW, HENRY   Specimens of Ancient Furniture Drawn from Existing Authorities. Pickering, 1836. 4to., plates, cloth, roan spine, worn. Quaritch 940-584 1974 £25

SHAW, IRWIN   The Assassin. Random, 1946. Austin 51-881 1973 $12.50

SHAW, IRWIN   The Assassin. New York, 1946. 1st ed. Biblo & Tannen 214-769 1974 $9.50

SHAW, IRWIN   The Gentle People. Random, 1939. 212p. Austin 51-882 1973 $12.50

SHAW, IRWIN   Sailor Off the Bremen and other Stories. New York, 1939. 1st ed. Biblo & Tannen 210-800 1973 $10

SHAW, J.   Cimelia Physica. (1796). Imp. folio, plates, modern half morocco gilt antique, plates, rare. Wheldon 131-112 1974 £2,250

SHAW, LLOYD   Cowboy Dances. Caldwell, 1939. Photos, diagrams, orig. binding, worn d.w. Wilson 63-148 1974 $12.50

SHAW, LOUISA   The Isle of the Deathless. London, 1850. 12mo., orig. cloth, first edition. Ximenes 35-174 1974 $12.50

SHAW, SIMEON   The Chemistry of the Natural and Artificial Heterogenous Compounds, Used in Manufacturing Porcelain, Glass and Pottery. 1837. Thick 8vo., cloth, calf spine, rubbed, very scarce, limited. Quaritch 940-663 1974 £45

SHAW, SIMEON   The History and Antiquities of Staffordshire. 1798-1801. 2 vols., folio, old half morocco. Quaritch 939-551 1974 £185

SHAW, SIMEON   History of the Staffordshire Potteries. 1829. 12mo., half calf, gilt, bookplate, rare. Bow Windows 62-832 1974 £75

SHAW, SIMEON   History of the Staffordshire Potteries. 1829. Small 8vo., half morocco, rare, first edition. Quaritch 939-552 1974 £60

SHAW, SIMEON   History of the Staffordshire Potteries. 1900. 8vo., cloth. Quaritch 939-553 1974 £18

SHAW, W.   Notes on the Thadou Kukis. 1929. 8vo., map, orig. cloth, plates, illus. Bow Windows 64-247 1974 £8.50

SHAW, WILLIAM   An Analysis of the Gaelic Langauge. 1778-79. Contemporary half calf, boards. Broadhurst 23-1269 1974 £60

SHAW, WILLIAM A.   A History of the English Church During the Civil Wars and Under the Commonwealth, 1640-1660. 1900. 2 vols., scarce. Howes 185-1648 1974 £14

SHAW-SPARROW, W.   Frank Brangwyn and His Work. 1910. Small 4to., coloured and collotype plates, tips of corners rubbed, top edges gilt, other edges untrimmed. Bow Windows 66-77 1974 £18.50

SHAY, FRANK   Deep Sea Shanties. 1925. 4to., illus., orig. cloth backed boards, d.w. Smith 193-157 1973 £5

SHEA, JOHN   Perils of the Ocean and Wilderness. 1856. Orig. cloth, first edition. Putnam 126-342 1974 $18

SHEA, JOHN GILMARY   The Cross and the Flag. 1900. Austin 62-590 1974 $47.50

SHEA, JOHN GILMARY   The Fallen Brave. New York, 1861. 4to., marbled boards and leather. Butterfield 10-184 1974 $15

SHEA, JOHN GILMARY   Pope-Day in America. N.P., 1888. First edition, 8vo., new wrappers, unique, fine. Current BW9-602 1974 $22.50

SHEARIN, HUBERT GIBSON   The Expression of Purpose Old English Prose. 1903. Ex-library, sturdy library binding, folded tables. Austin 61-905 1974 $27.50

SHEAVYN, P.   The Literary Profession in the Elizabethan Age. Manchester, 1909. 8vo., orig. cloth, faded. Bow Windows 62-833 1974 £6.50

SHEBBEARE, JOHN   Letters on the English Nation. London, 1755. 2 vols., 8vo., contemporary calf, first edition. Ximenes 35-175 1974 $90

SHEBBEARE, JOHN   A Third Letter to the People of England. London, 1756. 8vo., modern quarter calf, first edition. Dawsons PM 252-886 1974 £20

SHEBBEARE, JOHN   A Fourth Letter to the People of England. London, 1756. 8vo., half calf, first edition. Dawsons PM 247-263 1974 £36

SHEDD, WILLIAM B.   Italian Population in New York. 1934. Austin 62-591 1974 $7.50

SHEDDEN, THOMAS   An Essay on the Infinite. London & Cambridge, n.d. 8vo., orig. cloth, fine, first edition. Ximenes 35-176 1974 $15

A SHEED & Ward Anthology. 1931-37. 3 vols., first edition. Covent 51-99 1973 £6.30

SHEENAN, J. EASTMAN   Plastic Surgery of the Orbit. New York, 1927. 4to., orig. green cloth, fine, first edition. Dawsons PM 249-449 1974 £25

SHEFFIELD, JOHN   Observations on the Manufactures, Trade and Present State of Ireland. London, 1785. 8vo., modern boards. Dawsons PM 247-264 1974 £15

SHEFFIELD, JOHN   The Works. 1723. 4to., 2 vols., contemporary calf, gilt. Hill 126-242 1974 £30

SHEFFIELD UNIVERSITY   Experimental Researches and Reports Published by the Department of Glass Technology. Sheffield, 1919-42. 24 vols., 8vo., plates, sewed as issued. Quaritch 940-619 1974 £35

SHELFORD, R. W. C.   A Naturalist in Borneo. (1916). 8vo., cloth, plates, portrait, very scarce. Wheldon 128-232 1973 £12

SHELFORD, VICTOR E.   Naturalist's Guide to the Americas. Baltimore, 1926. First edition, maps, semi-flex leather, bookplate. Wilson 63-47 1974 $12.75

SHELLEY, F.   Legends of Gems. New York, 1895. Small 8vo., half morocco, portrait. Quaritch 940-477 1974 £20

SHELLEY, GEORGE ERNEST   The Birds of Africa. 1896-1905. 4 vols., small 4to., cloth, plates, rare. Wheldon 131-111 1974 £250

SHELLEY, GEORGE ERNEST   A Monograph of the Nectariniidae. 1876-80. Roy. 4to., full red morocco, gilt, plates, rare. Wheldon 131-110 1974 £2,800

SHELLEY, HENRY C.   The Life and Letters of Edward Young. 1914. Plates, spine trifle spotted, very good copy, first edition. Covent 51-2076 1973 £5.25

SHELLEY, MARY WOLLSTONECRAFT GODWIN   Tales and Stories. London, 1891. First edition, inner hinges split. Biblo & Tannen 210-666 1973 $30

SHELLEY, PERCY BYSSHE   An Address to the People on the Death of Princess Charlotte. N.P., n.d. 8vo., cloth slipcase. Ximenes 35-179 1974 $225

SHELLEY, PERCY BYSSHE   Adonais. London, (1927). 4to., inscribed, orig. parchment boards. Bow Windows 62-676 1974 £5

SHELLEY, PERCY BYSSHE   The Cenci. London, 1819. First edition, 8vo., blue morocco, gilt line borders, presentation copy from author, inscribed, brown morocco backed slip in case, T. Jeffn. Hogg's copy with his handwriting on blank leaf in front. Sawyer 293-265 1974 £2,850

SHELLEY, PERCY BYSSHE   The Cenci. New York, 1903. Roy. 8vo., orig. boards, uncut, limited. Howes 185-158 1974 £18

SHELLEY, PERCY BYSSHE   Hellas. 1822. 8vo., speckled calf, gilt, first edition. Quaritch 936-573 1974 £150

SHELLEY, PERCY BYSSHE   Hellas. 1886. Portrait, orig. boards, rubbed. Covent 55-1361 1974 £10.50

SHELLEY, PERCY BYSSHE   Letters from Percy Bysshe Shelley to Elizabeth Hitchener. 1908. Small 8vo., cloth. Quaritch 936-574 1974 £6

SHELLEY, PERCY BYSSHE   The Lyrical Poems and Translations. 1918. One of 250 numbered copies on large paper, full vellum, gilt. Covent 51-2333 1973 £30

SHELLEY, PERCY BYSSHE   Miscellaneous Poems. London, 1826. 12mo., orig. boards, paper label, frontispiece. Ximenes 35-180 1974 $70

SHELLEY, PERCY BYSSHE   The Poems. 1901. 3 vols., buckram, English first edition. Covent 56-2096 1974 £110

SHELLEY, PERCY BYSSHE   Poetical Works. 1882. 8vo., 4 vols., plates, light blue levant morocco, gilt. Quaritch 936-575 1974 £50

SHELLEY, PERCY BYSSHE   Poetical Works. 1892. Imp. 8vo., orig. cloth, fine. Broadhurst 24-299 1974 £25

SHELLEY, PERCY BYSSHE   Poetical Works. 1889. Very good copy, new edition, portrait. Covent 51-1691 1973 £6.30

SHELLEY, PERCY BYSSHE   Poetical Works. c.1900. Full maroon levant morocco, gilt. Howes 186-417 1974 £5

SHELLEY, PERCY BYSSHE   Posthumous Poems. London, 1824. 8vo., full morocco, gilt, first edition. Ximenes 35-181 1974 $175

SHELLEY, PERCY BYSSHE   Queen Mab. (London, 1829). 8vo., cloth, G. E. Woodberry's copy. Goodspeed's 578-320 1974 $25

SHELLEY, PERCY BYSSHE   Selected Poems of. Hammersmith, 1914. Small 4to., limp vellum, paper wrappers, limited. Bow Windows 62-276 1974 £175

SHELLEY, PERCY BYSSHE   The Sensitive Plant. c.1900. 4to., orig. vellum, gilt, illus. Howes 185-400 1974 £18

SHELLEY, PERCY BYSSHE   Shelley's Lost Letters to Harriet. 1930. Near fine, numbered, signed, hand made paper. Covent 55-1362 1974 £7.50

SHELLEY, PERCY BYSSHE   Shelley Memorials. London, 1859. 8vo., orig. cloth, first edition. Ximenes 35-182 1974 $45

SHELLEY, PERCY BYSSHE   The Works of. London, 1880. 8 vols., 8vo., illus., orig. cloth, inscription, faded. Bow Windows 62-834 1974 £52.50

SHELTON, LOUISE   Beautiful Gardens in America. New York, 1924. 4to. Biblo & Tannen 210-204 1973 $15

SHELTON, WILLIAM HENRY   The History of the Salmagundi Club. (New York), 1927. Cloth, illus., signed. Bradley 35-278 1974 $20

SHEM TOV IBN SHEM TOV   Sefer Ha'emunot. Ferrara, 1556. First edition, small 4to., cloth backed boards, ownership stamp of S. Zuckermann. Thomas 32-59 1974 £275

SHENSTON, THOMAS S.   The Oxford Gazetteer. Hamilton, 1852. Fine, signed by author. Hood's 102-635 1974 $110

SHENSTON, THOMAS S.   The Oxford Gazetteer. Hamilton, 1852. Fine, signed. Hood's 104-729 1974 $110

SHENSTONE, WILLIAM   The Works in Verse and Prose. London, 1764. 2 vols., 8vo., contemporary calf, first edition. Dawsons PM 252-888 1974 £45

SHENTON, EDWARD   The Gray Beginning. Philadelphia, 1924. Inscribed by author, first copy sold, orig. binding. Butterfield 10-453 1974 $12.50

SHEPARD, THOMAS   The Parable of the Ten Virgins Opened and Applied. 1695. Small folio, modern calf, soiled. Thomas 28-32 1972 £30

SHEPARD, THOMAS   The Sincere Convert. London, 1669. Contemporary sheep. Smith 194-186 1974 £15

SHEPARD, THOMAS   Theses Sabbaticae. London, 1650. 3 vols. in 1, contemporary calf, rebacked, browned, worn. Smith 194-185 1974 £18

SHEPHERD, DANIEL   Saratoga. New York & Boston, 1856. 12mo., orig. blue green cloth, first edition. Ximenes 35-183 1974 $12.50

SHEPHERD, MAJOR W.   Prairie Experiences in Handling Cattle and Sheep. London, 1884. 1st ed., 8 plates, orig. cl. Jacobs 24-29 1974 $60

SHEPHERD, RICHARD HERNE   The Bibliography of Swinburne. London, 1884. One of 25 numbered copies, very good, rebound in blue wrappers, first edition. Covent 51-1786 1973 £10

SHEPHERD, RICHARD HERNE   The Bibliography of Thackeray. London, n.d. 8vo., orig. blue green cloth, fine, first edition. Ximenes 35-339 1974 $15

SHEPHERD, RICHARD HERNE   Tennysoniana. 1866. First edition, title label chipped. Covent 51-1810 1973 £15

SHEPHERD, RICHARD HERNE   Tennysoniana. London, 1866. 8vo., uncut, full green morocco, gilt, first edition. Ximenes 35-184 1974 $75

SHEPHERD, RICHARD HERNE   Translations from Charles Baudelaire. Pickering, 1879. 8vo., orig. cloth, signed, first edition, third issue. Rota 189-793 1974 £12

SHEPHERD, THOMAS H.   Metropolitan Improvements. 1827-29. 2 vols., 4to., half calf, plates, foxing. Quaritch 939-470 1974 £180

SHEPHERD, THOMAS H.   Metropolitan Improvements. London, 1829. 4to., 2 vols., contemporary purple morocco gilt, first edition. Dawsons PM 251-92 1974 £130

SHEPHERD, THOMAS H.   Modern Athens! 1829. 4to., plates, illus., half morocco. Quaritch 939-675 1974 £80

SHEPHERD, THOMAS JAMES   History of the First Presbyterian Church. N.P., 1882. 8vo., orig. bindings, plates. Butterfield 8-556 1974 $10

THE SHEPHERDESS of the Alps. London, n.d. 12mo., stitched, dog-eared. Ximenes 33-24 1974 $20

SHEPPARD, EDGAR   Memorials of St. James's Palace. 1894. 2 vols., orig. cloth gilt, plates, illus. Howes 186-2141 1974 £5.50

SHEPPARD, ETHEL   The Sun-Worshippers. 1910. 8vo., orig. cloth, first edition. Rota 190-859 1974 £5

SHEPPARD, G. C.   My Northern Exposure. New York, London, 1922. Illus. Hood's 102-543 1974 $10

SHERATON, T.   The Cabinet-Maker and Upholsterer's Drawing Book. 1895. 4to., plates, cloth, gilt, facsimile reprint of the third edition. Quaritch 940-586 1974 £22

SHERBORN, C. D.   Index Animalium, Sectio Prima 1758-1800. Sectio Secunda, 1801-1850. 1902-33. 9 vols., roy. 8vo., buckram. Wheldon 128-131 1973 £60

SHERBURNE, ANDREW   Memoirs Of. Utica, 1828. 12mo., contemporary sheep, gilt, first edition. Dawsons PM 251-136 1974 £30

SHERBURNE, JOHN   The Life and Character of John Paul Jones. New York, 1851. Portrait frontispiece, foxed, spine chipped, orig. cloth, tight copy. Jenkins 61-1246 1974 $15

SHERER, JOSEPH MOYLE   Tales of the Wars of Our Times. London, 1829. 2 vols., 8vo., contemporary half morocco, first edition. Ximenes 35-185 1974 $70

SHERIDAN, CHARLES   Observations on the Doctrine. London, 1779. 8vo., modern boards, second edition. Dawsons PM 247-266 1974 £15

SHERIDAN, CHARLES FRANCIS   A History of the Late Revolution in Sweden. Dublin, 1778. 8vo., contemporary calf, first edition. Ximenes 35-186 1974 $30

SHERIDAN, FRANCES   The History of Nourjahad. London, 1767. 12mo., contemporary calf, rubbed, first edition. Ximenes 35-187 1974 $100

SHERIDAN, PAUL   Late and Early Joys At the Players Theatre. 1952. Austin 51-883 1973 $10

SHERIDAN, PHILIP H.   Personal Memoirs of. New York, 1888. Cloth. Hayman 57-676 1974 $10

SHERIDAN, RICHARD BRINSLEY   The Critic. London, 1781. 8vo., old sprinkled calf, first edition. Goodspeed's 578-325 1974 $35

SHERIDAN, RICHARD BRINSLEY   The Critic. Dublin, 1781. 12mo., disbound, first Dublin edition. Ximenes 35-188 1974 $25

SHERIDAN, RICHARD BRINSLEY   Dramatic Works. 1883. 3 vols., limp leather worn, on Holland paper, limited edition. Allen 216-2058 1974 $10

SHERIDAN, RICHARD BRINSLEY   The Duenna. London, 1794. 8vo., red morocco gilt, first authorised edition. Bow Windows 62-835 1974 £95

SHERIDAN, RICHARD BRINSLEY   Pizarro. London, 1799. 8vo., uncut, cloth box, first edition. Dawsons PM 252-889 1974 £130

SHERIDAN, RICHARD BRINSLEY   The Plays of Richard B. Sheridan. London, 1900. Biblo & Tannen 213-815 1973 $9.50

SHERIDAN, RICHARD BRINSLEY   The Rivals. 1775. 8vo., morocco extra, gilt, first edition. Quaritch 936-213 1974 £70

SHERIDAN, RICHARD BRINSLEY   The School for Scandal. n.d. 4to., half levant morocco, gilt, English first edition. Covent 56-1842 1974 £12.50

SHERIDAN, RICHARD BRINSELY   Sheridaniana. 1826. New buckram, rubber stamp, portrait stained. Allen 216-2285 1974 $10

SHERIDAN, RICHARD BRINSLEY   The Speech. Birmingham, (1802). 8vo., faded purple cloth, uncut, first editions. Dawsons PM 251-476 1974 £30

SHERIDAN, RICHARD BRINSLEY   The Speech of. London, (n.d.). 8vo., modern boards. Dawsons PM 247-265 1974 £15

SHERIDAN, RICHARD BRINSLEY   Speeches of. 1816. 5 vols., 8vo., half calf, gilt tooled spines, portrait, morocco labels, marbled sides, fine. Bow Windows 66-625 1974 £52

SHERIDAN, RICHARD BRINSLEY   Speeches of the Late Right Honourable Richard Brinsley Sheridan. 8vo., contemporary half calf, worn, 5 vols., first edition. Bow Windows 64-685 1974 £28

SHERIDAN, RICHARD BRINSLEY   A Trip to Scarborough. London, 1781. 8vo., calf antique, first edition. Dawsons PM 252-890 1974 £125

SHERIDAN, RICHARD BRINSLEY   A Trip to Scarborough. Dublin, 1781. 12mo., disbound, first Dublin edition. Ximenes 35-189 1974 $25

SHERIDAN, RICHARD BRINSLEY   Works. 1821. 8vo., 2 vols., orig. boards, uncut. Quaritch 936-576 1974 £35

SHERIDAN, THOMAS   British Education. Dublin, 1756. 12mo., contemporary calf, fine, first Dublin edition. Hill 126-90 1974 £35

SHERIDAN, THOMAS   A Course of Lectures on Elocution. London, 1762. 4to., contemporary marbled stiff wrappers, first edition. Ximenes 35-190 1974 $90

SHERIDAN, THOMAS   A Dissertation on the Causes of the Difficulties, Which Occur, In Learning the English Tongue. London, 1762. 4to., modern wrappers, rare, second edition. Ximenes 37-192 1974 $65

SHERINGHAM, ROBERT   De Anglorum Gentis Origine Disceptatio. 1670. 8vo., old calf, Cholmondeley library plate. Bow Windows 66-626 1974 £18

SHERLOCK, MARTIN   Letters on Several Subjects. Dublin, 1781. 2 vols. in 1, 12mo., contemporary calf, first Irish edition. Ximenes 35-191 1974 $20

SHERLOCK, WILLIAM   A Letter to a Friend. London, 1692. Small 4to., disbound, first edition. Ximenes 35-192 1974 $15

SHERLOCK, WILLIAM   A Vindication of the Case of Allegiance. London, 1691. Small 4to., disbound, first edition. Ximenes 35-193 1974 $10

SHERMAN, L. A.   What is Shakespeare? New York, 1912. Small 8vo., half maroon calf, gilt. Quaritch 936-564 1974 £6

SHERRIFF, R. C.   Badger's Green. 1930. Quarter vellum, signed, first edition. Rota 188-834 1974 £6

SHERRIFF, R. C.   Journey's End. London, 1930. 12mo., cloth, vellum back, authographed by authors, first edition. Goodspeed's 578-326 1974 $10

SHERRIFF, R. C.   Journey's End. 1930. Crown 8vo., orig. cloth, uncut, limited, first edition. Howes 185-446 1974 £5.50

SHERRIFF, R. C.   St. Helena. Stokes, 1934. Austin 51-884 1973 $7.50

SHERWIN, HENRY   Mathematical Tables. London, 1717. 8vo., contemporary panelled calf, first edition. Dawsons PM 245-674 1974 £40

SHERWOOD, JOHN D.   The Comic History of the United States. Fields, Osgood, 1870. 549p., illus. Austin 54-915 1973 $10

SHERWOOD, MRS.
Please turn to
SHERWOOD, MRS. MARY MARTHA (BUTT)

SHERWOOD, MRS. HENRY
Please turn to
SHERWOOD, MRS. MARY MARTHA (BUTT)

SHERWOOD, MARGARET   Undercurrents of Influence in English Romantic Poetry. 1934. Allen 216-1482 1974 $10

SHERWOOD, MARY   The Orphans of Normandy. London, 1822. 12mo., contemporary half calf, first edition. Ximenes 35-194 1974 $35

SHERWOOD, MRS. MARY MARTHA (BUTT)   Ermina. 1831. First edition, engraved frontis., woodcuts, 12mo., orig. boards, roan spine, worn, stitching weak. George's 610-661 1973 £6

SHERWOOD, MRS. MARY MARTHA (BUTT)   History of Henry Milner. 1831-37. 4 parts in 3 vols. as issued, 12mo., contemporary cloth, trifle rubbed. George's 610-664 1973 £7.50

SHERWOOD, MRS. MARY MARTHA (BUTT)   History of John Marten, a Sequel to the Life of Henry Milner. 1844. First edition, some foxing in text, 12mo., orig. cloth lower cover stained, hinges sprung. George's 610-665 1973 £5

SHERWOOD, MRS. MARY MARTHA (BUTT)   The History of the Fairchild Family. 1839-47. 3 vols., contemporary cloth, frontis., first & thirteenth editions. Smith 194-762 1974 £50

SHERWOOD, MRS. MARY MARTHA (BUTT)   The History of the Fairchild Family. London, 1854. Small 8vo., 3 vols., orig. cloth. Hammond 201-329 1974 £6.50

SHERWOOD, MRS. MARY MARTHA (BUTT)   The Welsh Cottage. Wellington, 1820. Engraved frontis., 12mo., grained calf, spine gilt, first edition. George's 610-680 1973 £10.50

SHERWOOD, ROBERT EDMUND   Here We Are Again. Bobbs, Merrill, 1926. Austin 51-885 1973 $8.50

SHERWOOD, ROBERT EDMUND   Here We Are Again. Indianapolis, 1926. Biblo & Tannen 213-874 1973 $15

SHERWOOD, ROBERT EMMET   There Shall Be No Night. Scribner, 1940. Austin 51-886 1973 $6

SHERWOOD, MRS. ROSINA (EMMET) 1854-   Pretty Peggy and Other Ballads. New York, 1880. 4to., glazed pictorial boards, cloth spine, illus., first edition. Frohnsdorff 16-310 1974 $20

SHERWOOD, MRS. ROSINA (EMMET) 1854-   Pretty Peggy and Other Ballads. London, c. 1880. 4to., glazed pictorial boards, cloth spine, illus. Frohnsdorff 16-309 1974 $20

SHERWOOD, "UNCLE" BOB   Hold Yer Hosses. Macmillan, n.d. 361p., illus. Austin 54-914 1973 $10

SHESTOV, LEON   Penultimate Words. Boston, 1916. First American edition. Covent 55-1128 1974 £5.50

SHIEL, M. P.   The Best Short Stories of M. P. Shiel. London, 1948. 1st ed. Biblo & Tannen 210-667 1973 $10

SHIEL, M. P.   The Bible Against Protestantism and for Catholicity. Boston, (1846). Ex-library. Austin 57-616 1974 $12.50

SHIEL, M. P.   How the Old Woman Got Home. 1928. Austin 61-907 1974 $12.50

SHIEL, M. P.   The Invisible Voices. 1936. First American edition. Austin 61-908 1974 $12.50

SHIEL, M. P.   The Pale Ape and Other Pulses. London, n.d. Biblo & Tannen 210-668 1973 $15

SHIEL, M. P.   The Strand Magazine. 1894. Orig. cloth, bookplate, first edition. Rota 188-838 1974 £5

SHIEL, M. P.   The Yellow Danger. 1898. Orig. cloth, worn, first edition. Rota 188-836 1974 £10

SHIEL, M. P.   The Yellow Wave. 1905. Orig. cloth, first edition, first issue, inscribed. Rota 188-837 1974 £25

SHIELD, WILLIAM   The Woodman. 1791. Oblong roy. 8vo., contemporary boards, calf rebacked. Quaritch 940-825 1974 £80

SHIELDS, GEORGE O.   The Big Game of North America. Chicago & New York, 1890. First edition, thick 8vo., illus., dec. cloth, good. Current BW9-155 1974 $32.50

SHILLITOE, THOMAS   Journal of the Life, Labours and Travels of. 1839. 2 vols., full contemporary calf. Howes 185-1650 1974 £10

SHIPMAN, DOROTHY   Stardust & Holly, Poems & Songs of Christmas. New York, 1932. First edition, 16mo., very good. Current BW9-78 1974 $16.50

SHIPMAN, LOUIS EVANS   Three Comedies. Macmillan, 1923. 334p. Austin 51-887 1973 $7.50

SHIPMAN, LOUIS EVANS   The True Adventures of a Play. Kennerley, 1914. 182p., illus. Austin 51-888 1973 $7.50

SHIPTON, JAMES   Pharmacopoeiae Collegii Regalis Londini. London, 1699. 12mo., contemporary calf. Gurney 64-198 1974 £32

SHIRAS, GEORGE   Hunting Wild Life With Camera and Flashlight. Washington, (1935). Photos, 2 vols., 8vo., fine. Current BW9-197 1974 $17.50

SHIRAS, GEORGE   Hunting Wild Life With Camera and Flashlight. Washington, 1936. 2 vols., second edition. Hood's 103-380 1974 $35

SHIRE, WILLIAM   A Familiar Discourse or Dialogue Concerning the Mine-Adventure. London, 1700. 8vo., fine, contemporary panelled calf, first edition. Dawsons PM 247-268 1974 £130

SHIRLEY, EVELYN PHILIP   Noble and Gentle Men of England. 1860. Small 4to., half morocco gilt, second edition. Quaritch 939-749 1974 £12.50

SHIRLEY, EVELYN PHILIP   The Noble and Gentle Men of England. Westminster, 1866. Small 4to., contemporary half morocco, gilt, third edition. Hammond 201-446 1974 £12

SHIRLEY, HENRY   The Martyr'd Souldier. London, 1638. 4to., 19th century half calf, first edition. Dawsons PM 252-892 1974 £220

SHIRLEY, JAMES   The Coronation. London, 1640. Small 4to., disbound, very good copy, first edition. Ximenes 37-193 1974 $275

SHIRLEY, JOHN   The Accomplished Ladies Rich Closet of Rarities. 1687. 12mo., half calf, frayed. Quaritch 939-243 1974 £120

SHIRLEY, JOHN   The Most Delectable History of Reynard the Fox. London, 1694. 4to., old russia gilt, book-plate. Dawsons PM 252-893 1974 £190

SHIRLEY, RALPH   Occultists and Mystics of All Ages. London, 1920. Rittenhouse 46-587 1974 $10

SHIRLEY Temple Story Book. 1935. 106p., illus. Austin 51-955 1973 $12.50

SHIRLEY, WILLIAM   Edward the Black Prince. London, 1750. 8vo., modern boards, first edition. Dawsons PM 252-894 1974 £15

SHIRREFS, ANDREW   Poems. Edinburgh, 1790. 8vo., portrait, contemporary calf, gilt, first edition. Ximenes 35-195 1974 $40

SHOBERL, FREDERIC   Natural History of Quadrupeds. C., 1843. Small 8vo., orig. brown cloth, gilt, second edition. Hammond 201-140 1974 £6

SHOEMAKER, HENRY W.   Penn's Grandest Cavern. Altoona, 1916. 8vo., orig. bindings, wrapper, signed. Butterfield 8-512 1974 $10

SHOOK, J. B.   Shook's Guide for Swine, Poultry and Stock Breeders. Circleville, 1885. Cloth. Hayman 59-505 1974 $10

SHORB, S. CAMPBELL   "The Primeval Dignity of Man". San Francisco, 1867. Rittenhouse 46-589 1974 $12.50

SHORT, BERNARD   The Harbinger to the Cottage Harmonist. Belfast, (1829). 8vo., orig. boards. Emerald 50-879 1974 £12.50

SHORT, ERNEST   Sixty Years On the Theatre. 1951. 402p., illus. Austin 51-889 1973 $10

SHORT, THOMAS   Discourses. London, 1750. 8vo., worn, contemporary sheep, first edition. Ximenes 35-196 1974 $125

SHORT Observations on the Right Hon. Edmund Burke's Reflections. London, 1790. 8vo., modern boards. Dawsons PM 247-269 1974 £15

A SHORT Vocabulary in the Language of the Seneca Nation. London, 1818. 8vo., disbound, rare, first edition. Ximenes 35-158 1974 $125

SHORTER, CLEMENT KING   Charlotte Bronte and Her Circle. 1896. 8vo., orig. cloth, illus., first edition. Rota 190-887 1974 £5

SHORTER, CLEMENT KING   Immortal Memories. 1907. Orig. linen, English first edition. Covent 56-1885 1974 £5.25

SHORTER, CLEMENT KING   The Life and Works of the Sisters Bronte. 1900. 7 vols., illus. Austin 61-142 1974 $67.50

SHORTER Lyrics of the Twentieth Century, 1900-1922. 1922. One of 200 copies, numbered on large paper, cloth backed boards, gilt top, very nice, first edition. Covent 51-100 1973 £8.40

SHORTHORN Breeders' Guide. London, 1924. 4to., pictorial cloth, illus, maps. Putnam 126-283 1974 $10

SHORTHOUSE, JOSEPH HENRY   ALS. 12mo., fine. Ximenes 35-197 1974 $35

SHORTRIDGE, G. C.   The Mammals of South West Africa. 1934. 2 vols., roy. 8vo., cloth, maps. Wheldon 128-349 1973 £30

SHORTRIDGE, G. C.   The Mammals of South West Africa. 1934. Roy 8vo., 2 vols., cloth, plates. Wheldon 130-423 1974 £30

SHORTT, W. T. P.   Sylva Antiqua Iscana, Numismatica. Exeter and London, n.d. 8vo., orig. green cloth, gilt. Dawsons PM 251-67 1974 £10

SHOVE, FREDEGOND   Daybreak. 1922. Orig. patterned boards, English first edition. Covent 56-637 1974 £21

SHOWELL, C.   Shakespeare's Avon from Source to Severn. Birmingham, 1901. 4to., drawings, half vellum, limited edition. Smith 194-293 1974 £6

SHOWERMAN, GRANT   Eternal Rome. 1924. 2 vols., plates. Allen 213-931 1973 $10

SHRIDHARANI, K.   My India My America. Duell, 1941. Austin 62-592 1974 $10

SHRIVER, WILLIAM P.   Immigrant Forces, Factors in the New Democracy. 1913. 277p., paper. Austin 62-593 1974 $7.50

SHRUBSOLE, WILLIAM   The History and Antiquities of Rochester. Rochester, 1772. Small 8vo., plates, half calf, rebound, first edition. Howes 186-2062 1974 £25

SHUCKFORD, SAMUEL   The Sacred and Prophane History of the World Connected. 1731. 8vo., 2 vols., contemporary panelled calf, second edition. Hill 126-243 1974 £10.50

SHUFFELDT, R. W.   Studies of the Human Form. Philadelphia, 1908. 4to., orig. buckram gilt, photographs, first edition. Smith 193-96 1973 £6

SHULL, J. M.   Rainbow Fragments. New York, 1931. 8vo.,
cloth, coloured and plain illus., scarce. Wheldon 128-1535 1973 £5

SHULL, J. M.   Rainbow Fragments. New York, 1931. 8vo.,
cloth, illus., scarce. Wheldon 131-1573 1974 £5

SHULMAN, IRVING   Harlow. Geis, 1964. Austin 51-890 1973
$7.50

SHUNSEN, O-OKA   Ehon Kara Kurenai, 'Picture Book Chinese
Crimson'. (1737). 3 vols., illus., orig. covers, rare. Quaritch 940-419
1974 £150

SHURCLIFF, SIDNEY N.   Jungle Islands. New York, 1930. Imp. 8vo.,
orig. cloth, coloured and other plates, drawings, maps. Sawyer 293-248 1974
£10

SHURLOCK, MANWARING   Tiles from Chertsey Abbey Surrey. London,
1885. Folio, half calf, orig. wrappers, plates. Traylen 79-391 1973 £15

SHUTE, JOSIAS   Sarah and Hagar. 1649. Folio, contemporary
sheep, rubbed. Howes 185-1651 1974 £15

SHUTE, NEVIL   Kindling. New York, 1938. Inscription,
faded, first American edition. Covent 55-1371 1974 £6.50

SIAMESE Tales. 1796. Engraved frontis., roughly hand coloured, some text
damp stained, 12mo., contemporary calf, spine rubbed, joints broken. George's
610-682 1973 £10

THE SIAMESE Tales. London, 1796. 12mo., contemporary sheep, frontispiece,
first edition. Ximenes 33-25 1974 $90

SIBBALD, ROBERT   Scotia Illustrative. Edinburgh, 1683-84. Folio,
contemporary calf, rebacked, first edition. Dawsons PM 251-68 1974 £100

SIBBALD, ROBERT   Scotia Illustrata Sive Prodromus Historiae
Naturalis in Quo Regionis Natura. Edinburgh, 1684. Folio, contemporary calf,
plates, presentation. Traylen 79-385 1973 £180

SIBLY, E.   Magazine of Natural History. (?1794-96).
Vols. 1 & 2, 8vo., calf, engraved frontispieces. Wheldon 131-182 1974 £15

SIBLY, E.   An Universal System of Natural History. (180-).
8vo., contemporary diced calf gilt, plates, second edition. Wheldon 130-133
1974 £15

SIBREE, J.   A Naturalist in Madagascar. 1915. 8vo.,
orig. cloth, maps, illus., scarce. Wheldon 128-234 1973 £12

SIBREE, J.   A Naturalist in Madagascar. 1915. 8vo.,
orig. cloth, illus., scarce. Wheldon 129-304 1974 £10

SIBSON, FRANCIS   Collected Works of. 1881. 4 vols., 8vo.,
plates, figures, charts, some foxing. Bow Windows 66-628 1974 £12

SIBSON, FRANCIS   Collected Works. London, 1881. 4 vols.,
8vo., orig. cloth, unopened, first edition. Schuman 37-234 1974 $95

SICARD, ROCH-AMBROISE   Cours d'Instruction D'un Sourd-Muet de Naissance. 1799. 8vo., half calf, gilt, first edition. Dawsons PM 249-450 1974
£90

SICHEL, WALTER   Bolingbroke and his Times. 1901-02. 2 vols.,
orig. buckram gilt, scarce, orig. edition. Howes 186-626 1974 £15

SICHEL, WALTER   Sheridan. 1909. 2 vols., plates, ex-library.
Allen 216-2060 1974 $15

SICHEL, WALTER   Sheridan from New and Original Material.
1909. 2 vols., med. 8vo., top edges gilt, others uncut, first edition, illus., orig.
cloth, exceptionally fine copy. Broadhurst 24-463 1974 £6

SICHEL, WALTER   Sterne, A Study to Which Is Added the Journal
to Stella. 1910. Plates, dull covers. Covent 55-1410 1974 £10.50

SICKERT, WALTER   Reproductions of Paintings and Drawings. 1919.
Crown 4to., half red calf, scarce, inscribed. Broadhurst 23-195 1974 £25

SIDDONS, HENRY   Time's a Tell-Tale. London, 1807. 8vo.,
modern boards, first edition. Dawsons PM 252-895 1974 £15

SIDEWALKS of America. Bobbs, Merrill, 1954. 605p. Austin 54-156 1973 $15

SIDEY, JAMES ARCHIBALD   Remollescences of a Medical Student.
Edinburgh, 1886. 4to., orig. cloth, fine, first edition. Ximenes 35-198
1974 $15

SIDGWICK, HENRY   Collection of the Works. 1887-1906. 9 vols.,
orig. cloth. Howes 185-1996 1974 £35

SIDNEY, E.   Blights of the Wheat. (1846). 16mo., orig.
cloth. Wheldon 129-1667 1974 £15

SIDNEY, HENRY   Diary of the Times of Charles II. 1843.
2 vols., full polished calf gilt, labels. Howes 186-1213 1974 £12.50

SIDNEY, MARGARET PSEUD.
Please turn to
LOTHROP, HARRIET MULFORD STONE

SIDNEY, PHILIP   Astrophel and Stella. Nonesuch Press, 1931.
Med. 8vo., boards, dec. wrapper, uncut, orig. board slip in case, fine, limited
to 725 copies, on Van Gelder paper. Broadhurst 24-1029 1974 £20

SIDNEY, PHILIP   Astrophel and Stella. 1931. 8vo., boards,
dec. wrapper, uncut, limited edition. Broadhurst 23-1068 1974 £20

SIDNEY, PHILIP   Complete Poems. 1877. 3 vols., ex-library,
lower portion stained. Allen 216-1848 1974 $20

SIDNEY, PHILIP   The Defence of Poesy. 1810. 4to., old half
calf. Hill 126-244 1974 £16

SIDONIUS   Oeuvres. 1835. 3 vols., sewn. Allen
213-1944 1973 $15

SIEBOLD, ELIAS VON   Annalen der Klinischen Schule. 1805. 8vo.,
old boards. Gurney 64-199 1974 £25

SIEBOLD, PHILLIPP FRANZ DE   Fauna Japonica. Leyden, (1842)-1850.
Folio, new half red morocco, gilt, plates, rare, orig. issue. Wheldon 131-113
1974 £1,250

UN SIECLE de Modes Feminines 1794-1894. 1896. Small 8vo., dec. boards.
Quaritch 940-730 1974 £10

SIEDENBURG, J.   The American Painter, W. H. Singer, Jr.
Buffa, 1928. 4to., boards, cloth spine, limited edition. Minters 37-34
1973 $20

THE SIEGE of Carlaverock. 1828. 4to., frontispiece, calf gilt. Quaritch
939-708 1974 £30

SIEMENS, C. WILLIAM   The Electro-Magnetic Practical System of Units.
London, 1882. 8vo., stitched as issued, inscribed. Dawsons PM 245-675 1974
£6

SIENA SCHOOL   Pictures of the School of Siena and Examples of
the Minor Arts of the City. 1904. Roy. 4to., plates, buckram. Quaritch
940-241 1974 £25

SIENKIEWICZ, HENRY K.   After Bread. Fenno, 1897. Austin 62-594
1974 $8.50

SIEPMAN, CHARLES   Radio Television and Society. Oxford, 1950.
Austin 51-891 1973 $7.50

SIERRA, G. MARTINEZ   The Cradle Song. Dutton, 1931. Austin
51-892 1973 $8.50

SIEVEKING, LANCELOT DE GIBERNE   Stampede. 1924. Stained cover, d.w.,
illus. Covent 55-391 1974 £9.50

SIEVWRIGHT, COLIN   The Sough O' the Shuttle. Dundee, 1866.
8vo., orig. cloth, fine, first edition. Ximenes 35-199 1974 $30

SIEWERT, H.　　　　　　Storche, Erlebnisse mit dem Schwarzen und Weissen Storch. Berlin, 1932. 8vo., cloth, map, photographic illus., inscription. Wheldon 128-564 1973 £7.50

SIFFERATH, N. L.　　　　A Short Compendium of the Catechism for the Indians, With the Approbation of the Rt. Rev. Frederic Baraga. Buffalo, 1869. Wrappers, fine. Hayman 59-603 1974 $65

SIGAUD DE LA FOND, JEAN RENE　Traite de l'Electricite. Paris, 1771. 12mo., contemporary French calf, gilt, plates, first edition. Dawsons PM 245-676 1974 £65

SIGAUD DE LA FOND, JOSEPH AIGNAN　Description et Usage d'un Cabinet de Physique Experimentale. Paris, 1775. 2 vols., 8vo., contemporary calf, gilt, plates, first edition. Schuman 37-236 1974 $365

SIGHART, JOACHIM　　　Albert the Great of the Order of Friar-Preachers. 1876. Ownership stamps. Howes 185-898 1974 £5

I SIGNAD Juletid. En Julbok for Barn. Rock Hill, (c. 1930). 12mo., pictorial front cover bit soiled, illus., near fine. Current BW9-21 1974 $9

SIGNOT, JACQUES　　　La Totale et Vraie Description de tous les Passaiges. Paris, 1518. Contemporary limp vellum. Schumann 499-106 1974 sFr 3,750

SIGORGNE, PIERRE　　　Institutions Newtoniennes. Paris, 1769. 8vo., contemporary mottled calf, plates. Schumann 35-355 1974 $165

SIGOURNEY, LYDIA HOWARD HUNTLEY　Letters to Mothers. Hartford, 1838. 12mo., orig. purple cloth, foxed, first edition. Ximenes 35-200 1974 $25

SIGOURNEY, LYDIA HOWARD HUNTLEY　Lucy Howard's Journal. New York, 1858. 8vo., orig. green cloth, first edition. Ximenes 35-201 1974 $10

SIGOURNEY, LYDIA HOWARD HUNTLEY　Moral Pieces, in Prose and Verse. Hartford, 1815. Contemporary half roan, first edition, very good. MacManus 224-394 1974 $60

SIGOURNEY, LYDIA HOWARD HUNTLEY　On the Death of Miss Sarah Russ. Hartford, 1822. 8vo., first edition. Ximenes 35-202 1974 $100

SIGOURNEY, LYDIA HOWARD HUNTLEY　Pocahontas. New York, 1841. 12mo., orig. brown cloth, foxing, first edition. Ximenes 35-204 1974 $12

SIGOURNEY, LYDIA HOWARD HUNTLEY　Poems for Children. Hartford, 1836. Square 12mo., orig. cloth, scarce, first edition. Ximenes 35-205 1974 $27.50

SIGOURNEY, LYDIA HOWARD HUNTLEY　Sketch of Connecticut. Hartford, 1824. 12mo., old half morocco, inscribed, first edition. Ximenes 35-206 1974 $15

SIGOURNEY, LYDIA HOWARD HUNTLEY　Sketches. Philadelphia, 1834. 12mo., orig. brown cloth, foxing, frontis., first edition. Ximenes 35-207 1974 $17.50

SIGUENZA Y GONGORA, DON CARLOS DE　The Mercurio Volante. Los Angeles, 1932. Limited to 635 numbered copies. Jenkins 61-1856 1974 $37.50

SIGURJONSSON, J.　　　Loftur. 1939. Roy. 8vo., wood engravings, orig. morocco backed boards, gilt, fine, limited edition. Smith 193-410 1973 £15

SIGURJONSSON, J.　　　Loftur. 1939. 8vo., orig. morocco backed boards, gilt, wood engravings, limited edition. Smith 194-522 1974 £10.50

SILCOCK, ARNOLD　　　Introduction to Chinese Art and History. New York, 1948. Illus. Biblo & Tannen 214-397 1974 $12.50

SILIUS ITALICUS, TIBERIUS CATIUS ASCONIUS　De Bello Punico Secundo XVII Libri Nuper Diligentissime Castigati. Venice, 1523. Small 8vo., old vellum, new label, armorial bookplate, only Aldine edition. Thomas 32-215 1974 £40

SILIUS ITALICUS, TIBERIUS CATIUS ASCONIUS　De Bello Punico Secundo. 1523. Late 18th century red straight grain morocco gilt, raised bands. Thomas 30-64 1973 £60

SILIUS ITALICUS, TIBERIUS CATIUS ASCONIUS　De Bello Punico Secundo. 1523. 18th century mottled calf, gilt, stains. Thomas 30-65 1973 £40

SILLAR, DAVID　　　　Poems. Kilmarnock, 1789. 8vo., later half calf, first edition. Ximenes 35-208 1974 $175

SILLMAN, LEONARD　　　Here Lies Leonard Sillman. Citadel, 1959. Austin 51-893 1973 $7.50

SILONE, IGNAZIO　　　And He Hid Himself. Harper, 1946. 126p. Austin 51-894 1973 $8.50

SILTZER, FRANK　　　　Newmarket. London, 1923. Biblo & Tannen 213-1017 1973 $27.50

SILTZER, FRANK　　　The Story of British Sporting Prints. (1925). 8vo., plates, orig. cloth, worn. Quaritch 940-242 1974 £40

SILURIENSIS, LEOLINUS　　The Anatomy of Tobacco. London, 1884. 1st ed., vellum, 1/2 morocco slipcase. Biblo & Tannen 210-768 1973 $40

SILVA, I. F. DA　　　Diccionario Bibliographico Portuguez . . . Applicaveis a Portugal e ao Brazil. Lisbon, 1883-5. Vols. 10-13, illus., med. 8vo., lacking 6 wrappers. Forster 98-81 1974 £6

SILVA TAROUCA, E.　　　Unsere Freiland-Stauden. Vienna, 1913. Roy. 8vo., cloth, coloured plates, text-figures. Wheldon 128-1626 1973 £5

SILVER, A. P.　　　　Farm-Cottage, Camp and Canoe In Maritime Canada. London, (1908). Illus. Hood's 103-189 1974 $10

SILVERSMITHS' Work of European Origin. 1901. Roy. 4to., plates, buckram. Quaritch 940-687 1974 £45

SILVESTRE, JOSEPH-BALTHASAR　Paleographie Universelle. Paris, 1841. 4 vols., full page plates colored by hand, atlas folio, contemporary three quarter red morocco, gilt backs, from the library of Prince Vorontsov, with armorial bookplates. Kraus B8-241 1974 $750

SILVESTRE DE SACY, A. I.　　Grammaire Arabe. Paris, 1831. 2 vols., thick large 8 vo., green half calf, plates, second edition. Harper 213-144 1973 $125

SILVEUS, W. A.　　　Grasses. San Antonio, 1942. Illus., orig. cl., ltd. to 800 copies. Jacobs 24-30 1974 $15

SIM, FRANCES M.　　　Robert Browning: Mystic and Artist. n.d. Austin 61-911 1974 $10

SIMA, MICHEL　　　　Faces of Modern Art. New York, 1959. 4to., color plates. Biblo & Tannen 210-334 1973 $27.50

SIME, S. H.　　　　The Butterfly. 1899. Half calf, English first edition. Covent 56-718 1974 £10

SIMEON, OF DURHAM　　Libellus de Exordio Atque Procursu Dunhelmensis Ecclesiae. 1732. 8vo., contemporary calf. Quaritch 939-245 1974 £17.50

SIMIENOWICZ, CASIMIR　　The Great Art of Artillery. London, 1792. Folio, contemporary marbled boards, fine, first edition in English. Dawsons PM 251-404 1974 £235

SIMKBOVITCH, NATASHA　Merry Christmas! New York, 1943. First collected edition, folio, colored dec. paper board covers & endpapers, full color illus., interior very good. Current BW9-77 1974 $17.50

SIMKHOVITCH, MARY KINGSBURY　Neighborhood. Norton 1938. 301p., illus. Austin 62-595 1974 $10

SIMMONDS, FLORENCE　　Modern Art. New York, 1908. 2 vols., 4to., illus. Jacobs 24-49 1974 $40

SIMMONS, ALFRED　　　Old England and New Zealand. 1879. 8vo., orig. cloth, coloured folding map, some spotting. Bow Windows 66-631 1974 £10

SIMMONS, C.　　　A Laconic Manual and Brief Remarker. Toronto, 1853. Sixth edition. Hood's 104-56 1974 $25

SIMMS, FREDERICK WALTER   Practical Tunnelling. London, 1844. 4to., contemporary publisher's morocco, plates, inscribed. Hammond 201-956 1974 £48

SIMMS, FREDERIC WALTER   Public Works of Great Britain. 1838. Large folio, green half morocco gilt, illus., plates. Hammond 201-946 1974 £175

SIMMS, FREDERICK WALTER   Public Works of Great Britain. 1838. Folio, plates, foxing, half morocco. Quaritch 939-90 1974 £185

SIMMS, FREDERICK WALTER   A Treatise on the Principles and Practice of Levelling. London, 1866. 8vo., orig. cloth, plates, fifth edition. Hammond 201-955 1974 £10.50

SIMMS, FREDERICK WALTER   A Treatise of the Principles and Practice of Levelling. 1884. Imp. 8vo., orig. cloth, plates, seventh edition. Covent 55-1237 1974 £15

SIMMS, JEPTHA ROOT   The American Spy. Albany, 1857. 8vo., orig. printed wrappers, second edition. Ximenes 35-209 1974 $27.50

SIMMS, P. M.   The Bible in America. New York, 1936. 8vo., cloth, illus., first edition. Putman 126-41 1974 $11

SIMMS, RUPERT   Bibliotheca Staffordiensis. Lichfield, 1894. 4to., orig. cloth, uncut, rubbed. Dawsons PM 10-578 1974 £80

SIMMS, RUPERT   Bibliotheca Staffordiensis. Lichfield, 1894. Roy. 4to., orig. cloth, limited edition. Quaritch 939-554 1974 £25

SIMMS, WILLIAM GILMORE   Guy Rivers. New York, 1834. 2 vols., 12mo., orig. blue cloth, labels, first edition. Ximenes 35-210 1974 $275

SIMMS, WILLIAM GILMORE   The Partisan: A Tale of the Revolution. New York, 1835. 2 vols., orig. cloth, worn, paper labels, first edition, some foxing, very good set. MacManus 224-395 1974 $100

SIMMS, WILLIAM GILMORE   A Supplement to the Plays of William Shakespeare. Philadelphia, 1855. 8vo., orig. red cloth, second edition. Ximenes 35-211 1974 $17.50

SIMON, CONSTANCE   English Furniture Designers. 1905. Roy 8vo., plates, English first edition. Covent 56-1657 1974 £12.50

SIMON, J. FRANZ   Animal Chemistry. London, 1845(-1846). 8vo., 2 vols., orig. green cloth. Dawsons PM 249-451 1974 £18

SIMON, J. FRANZ   Handbuch der Angewandten Medizinischen. Berlin, 1840-42. 8vo., 2 vols., old boards, first edition. Gurney 64-200 1974 £15

SIMON, J. FRANZ   Handbuch der Angewandten Medizinischen Chemie. Berlin, 1840-42. 8vo., 2 vols., old baords, plates, first edition. Gurney 66-172 1974 £15

SIMON, JOHN   A Physiological Essay On the Thymus Gland. London, 1845. Large 4to., orig. cloth, illus., first edition. Schuman 37-237 1974 $120

SIMON, JOHN K. C. B.   English Sanitary Institutions. London, 1890. 8vo., orig. cloth, first edition. Schumann 35-435 1974 $125

SIMON, OLIVER   Printing Of To-Day. London, 1928. 4to., orig. cloth backed dec. boards. Dawsons PM 10-558 1974 £18

SIMON, RICHARD   A Critical History of the Text of the New Testament. London, 1689. 2 parts in 1 vol., 4to., half old 19th century morocco. Smith 194-187 1974 £18.50

SIMONDS, J. B.   A Practical Treatise on Variola Ovina or Small Pox in Sheep. 1848. 8vo., orig. cloth, coloured plates. Wheldon 128-1661 1973 £10

SIMONDS, J. B.   A Practical Treatise on Variola Ovina or Small Pox in Sheep. 1848. 8vo., orig. cloth, plates. Wheldon 131-1797 1974 £10

SIMONIN, L.   Les Pierres, Esquisses Mineralogiques. Paris, 1869. Roy. 8vo., half morocco, coloured plates, nice copy, scarce. Wheldon 128-1048 1973 £7.50

SIMONS, HI   George Grosz. Chicago, 1921. 8vo., wrapper, scarce, plates. Minters 37-346 1973 $28

SIMPSON, E. BLANTYRE   Robert Louis Stevenson's Edinburgh Days. 1914. Illus. Austin 61-913 1974 $12.50

SIMPSON, EDWIN   The Dramatic Unities in the Present Day. London, 1874. 8vo., orig. cloth, first edition. Ximenes 35-212 1974 $15

SIMPSON, G. G.   The Principles of Classification. New York, 1945. Roy 8vo., wrappers. Wheldon 129-401 1974 £7

SIMPSON, J. PALGRAVE   Daddy Hardacre. French, 1857. Austin 51-895 1973 $6.50

SIMPSON, JAMES Y.   Antiquarian Notices of Syphilis in Scotland. Edinburgh, (1862). 8vo., boards, roan spine, first edition. Broadhurst 23-1272 1974 £35

SIMPSON, JAMES Y.   Antiquarian Notices of Syphilis in Scotland. Edinburgh, (1862). First edition, demy 8vo., bords, roan spine, presentation copy from author, fine. Broadhurst 24-1325 1974 £35

SIMPSON, JAMES Y.   Physicians and Physics. Edinburgh, 1856. 8vo., orig. cloth, first edition. Broadhurst 23-1271 1974 £55

SIMPSON, JAMES Y.   Physicians and Physics: Three Addresses. Edinburgh, 1856. First edition, demy 8vo., inscribed presentation copy, fine, orig. cloth. Broadhurst 24-1324 1974 £55

SIMPSON, JOHN HOPE   The Refugee Problem. 1939. Diagrams, maps. Austin 57-621 1974 $37.50

SIMPSON, JOHN HOPE   The Refugee Problem. Oxford, 1939. 637p. Austin 62-597 1974 $37.50

SIMPSON, SAMUEL L.   The Golden-Gated West Songs and Poems. Philadelphia and London, 1910. Gilt top, lst ed. Dykes 24-70 1974 $10

SIMPSON, THOMAS   Essays. 1740, 43 and 57. 4to., contemporary calf, first editions. Broadhurst 23-1273 1974 £50

SIMPSON, THOMAS   Select Exercises for Young Proficients in the Mathematicks. London, 1752. 8vo., contemporary sheep, rebacked, first edition. Dawsons PM 245-677 1974 £25

SIMPSON, WILLIAM   The Seat of War in the East. Colnaghi, 1855-56. 2 vols. in 1, roy. folio, plates, half red morocco, gilt. Quaritch 940-243 1974 £2,500

SIMROCK, M. KARL   Remarks of M. Karl Simrock on the Plots of Shakespeare Plays. 1850. Austin 51-896 1973 $15

SIMS, G. R.   Living London. 1901-03. 3 vols., 4to., illus., engravings, half roan gilt. Smith 194-267 1974 £10

SIMS, GEORGE R.   Dagonet Abroad. 1895. Orig. dec. cloth gilt, faded. Covent 55-1374 1974 £7.50

SIMS, GEORGE R.   Once Upon a Christmas Time. 1898. Dec. cloth gilt, faded, plates. Covent 55-1375 1974 £7.50

SIMS, GEORGE R.   Two London Fairies. 1906. Orig. pictorial cloth. Covent 55-1376 1974 £6.30

SIMS, R.   Manual for the Geologist, Topographer, etc. 1861. New buckram, second edition. Allen 213-1540B 1973 $12.50

SIMSON, ROBERT   Apollonii Pergaei Locorum Planorum. Glasgow, 1749. First edition, 4to., old calf, fine. Broadhurst 24-1327 1974 £40

SINCLAIR, GEORGE   Hortus Gramineus Woburnensis. 1824. Roy. 8vo., half calf, coloured plates, scarce, second edition. Wheldon 128-1662 1973 £20

SINCLAIR, GEORGE   Hortus Gramineus Woburnensis. 1824. Roy 8vo., new half green morocco, uncut, plates. Wheldon 129-43 1974 £30

SINCLAIR, GEORGE   Hortus Gramineus Wobumensis. 1826. Roy
8vo., half calf, plates, third edition.   Wheldon 130-1597 1974 £22

SINCLAIR, GEORGE   Hortus Gramineus Wobumensis. 1826. Roy.
8vo., new cloth, plates.   Wheldon 131-1574 1974 £18

SINCLAIR, GEORGE   Hortus Gramineus Wobumensis. (circa, 1849).
8vo., orig. cloth, plates.   Wheldon 130-1598 1974 £12

SINCLAIR, JAMES   History of Short-Horn Cattle. 1907. 8vo.,
orig. half calf, plates, scarce.   Wheldon 129-402 1974 £20

SINCLAIR, JAMES   History of Short-Horn Cattle. 1907. 8vo.,
new half calf, plates.   Wheldon 131-520 1974 £20

SINCLAIR, JOHN   The Code of Agriculture. London, 1817.
8vo., plates, 19th century cloth, first edition.   Dawsons PM 247-270 1974 £45

SINCLAIR, JOHN   The Code of Agriculture. 1832. 8vo., orig.
cloth, plates, fifth edition.   Wheldon 130-1599 1974 £6

SINCLAIR, JOSEPH   Wasteland. Harper, 1946.   Austin 62-599
1974 $6.50

SINCLAIR, UPTON   Dragon Harvest. New York, 1945. First
printing, orig. binding.   Butterfield 10-488E 1974 $7.50

SINCLAIR, UPTON   The Goslings. Pasadena, (1924). Pictorial
wrapper, first edition.   Butterfield 10-487 1974 $20

SINCLAIR, UPTON   How I Got Licked and Why. 1935. Illus.
Covent 55-1377 1974 £6.50

SINCLAIR, UPTON   The Jungle. 1906. Lettering on spine rubbed,
first edition.   Allen 216-1305 1974 $12.50

SINCLAIR, UPTON   The Jungle. New York, 1906. 12mo., cloth,
fine, first edition.   Goodspeed's 578-327 1974 $15

SINCLAIR, UPTON   The Lie Factory Starts. Los Angeles, n.d.
Wrappers.   Dawson's 424-304 1974 $10

SINCLAIR, UPTON   Love's Pilgrimage. New York, (1911). Red
boards, rubbed.   Dawson's 424-345 1974 $22.50

SINCLAIR, UPTON   Manassas. New York, 1904. Orig. cloth,
first edition, upper hinge cracked, otherwise fine.   MacManus 224-397 1974 $30

SINCLAIR, UPTON   Money Writes. New York, 1927. 1st ed.
Biblo & Tannen 210-801 1973 $10

SINCLAIR, UPTON   The Profits of Religion. Pasadena, 1918.
First American edition.   Covent 55-1379 1974 £7.50

SINDING, PAUL C.   History of Scandinavia. 1866. Maps,
ninth edition.   Austin 57-624 1974 $20

SINEL, JOSEPH   A Book of American Trademarks. New York,
1924. No. 1033 of edition limited to 2050 copies, on imported Japanese paper,
mint, unopened copy, badly split box, orig. binding.   Ross 86-34 1974 $30

SINGER, CHARLES   From Magic to Science. 1928. Roy. 8vo.,
orig. cloth, plates.   Smith 194-936 1974 £8.50

SINGER, KURT   The Danny Kaye Story. Nelson, 1958.
Austin 51-897 1973 $6.50

SINGER, MAX   La Teinture Moderne. 1875. Marbled boards.
Dawson's 424-238 1974 $75

SINGER, SAMUEL WELLER   Deux Dialogues sur la Peinture. Londres,
1811. 18mo., orig. boards, inscribed, first edition.   Ximenes 35-213 1974 $60

SINGER, SAMUEL WELLER   The Text of Shakespeare. 1853. 8vo., cloth.
Hill 126-241 1974 £21

SINGH, BHAWANI   Travel Pictures. 1912. 4to., orig.
parchment backed boards, illus., photo. portrait coloured by hand, signed by
author, top edges gilt, other edges uncut.   Bow Windows 66-632 1974 £18.50

SINGLETON, ESTHER   Dutch and Flemish Furniture. 1907. Imp.
8vo., frontispiece, plates, cloth.   Quaritch 940-588 1974 £6

SINGLETON, ESTHER   Furniture. 1913. Illus., cloth, uncut.
Covent 55-485 1974 £6.50

SINGLETON, ESTHER   The Furniture of Our American Forefathers.
1901. 2 vols., imp. 8vo., illus., boards, vellum backs.   Quaritch 940-587
1974 £40

SINGLETON, ESTHER   The Shakespeare Garden. 1922. Illus., orig.
edition.   Austin 61-914 1974 $12.50

SINGLETON, ESTHER   The Shakespeare Garden. 1923. 8vo., cloth,
illus., scarce.   Wheldon 130-196 1974 £7.50

SINGLETON, ESTHER   The Story of the White House. New York, 1907.
8vo., 2 vols., orig. bindings, plates.   Butterfield 8-686 1974 $15

SINIBALDI, GIOVANNI BENEDETTO   Geneanthropeiae Sive de Hominis Generatione. 1642. Folio, contemporary mottled calf, gilt, first edition.   Dawsons
PM 249-452 1974 £235

SINISTRARI, LOUIS MARIE D'AMENO   De La Demonialite et des Animaux
Incubes et Succubes. Paris, 1876. 12mo., contemporary half calf, rubbed,
second edition.   Bow Windows 62-839 1974 £6.50

SINN Fein Rebellion Handbook. Dublin, 1916. 8vo., wrappers, illus., first
issue.   Emerald 50-887 1974 £12.50

SINNETT, MRS. PERCY   A Story About a Christmas in the 17th Century.
London, 1846. First edition, 12mo., full page full color illus., spine faded with
some chipping and wear, orig. green covers intact, interior very good.   Current
BW9-79 1974 $40

SIRIGATTUS, FRANCISCUS   De Ortu et Occasu Signorum. Lyons, 1536.
Small 4to., new calf, stains.   Thomas 32-307 1974 £35

SIRINGO, CHARLES   Riata and Spurs. Boston, 1927. Illus.,
brown-stamped dec. tan cloth, scarce, first edition, first issue.   Bradley 35-345
1974 $60

SISLER, W. J.   Peaceful Invasion. Winnipeg, 1944.   Hood's
102-431 1974 $12.50

SISMONDI, JEAN CHARLES LEONARD SIMONDE DE   Histoire des Francais.
Brussels, 1836-44. 21 vols., demy 8vo., contemporary calf.   Howes 186-1217
1974 £50

SISMONDI, JEAN CHARLES LEONARD SIMONDE DE   Historical View of the
Literature of the South of Europe. 1853. 2 vols., 8vo., contemporary calf,
fourth edition.   Bow Windows 66-633 1974 £7.50

SITIUS, FRANCESCO   Dianoia Astronomica, Optica, Physica, Qua
Syderei Nuncii Rumor de Quatuor Planetis. Venice, 1611. Small 4to., vellum,
first edition.   Schumann 500-8 1974 sFr 6,000

SITWELL, EDITH   Alexander Pope. London, 1930. First ordinary
edition, d.w. faded & somewhat tattered, very nice, orig. binding.   Ross 86-414
1974 $15

SITWELL, EDITH   Alexander Pope. London, 1930. Cloth, illus.,
uncut, signed, limited edition.   Dawson's 424-305 1974 $50

SITWELL, EDITH   Bucolic Comedies. London, 1923. First edition,
spine faded, very nice, orig. binding.   Ross 86-415 1974 $25

SITWELL, EDITH   Clowns' Houses. Oxford, 1918. Dec. wrappers,
cover almost detached, nice copy of fragile book, press clippings laid in, first
edition.   Covent 51-1699 1973 £15.75

SITWELL, EDITH   Clowns' Houses. Oxford, 1918. Orig. dec.
wrappers, English first edition.   Covent 56-1181 1974 £28.50

SITWELL, EDITH   The Collected Poems. London, 1930. 8vo.,
orig. cloth, signed, first edition.   Dawsons PM 252-897 1974 £30

SITWELL, EDITH   The Collected Poems Of. London, 1930.
Orig. buckram, dust jacket, very fine, boxed, autographed, limited, first
edition.   Jenkins 48-436 1973 $85

SITWELL, EDITH   Collected Poems. 1930. Book-label, fine, English first edition. Covent 56-1182 1974 £7.50

SITWELL, EDITH   Facade. Kennington, 1922. Frontis., red paper boards, no. 62 of edition limited to 150 copies, spine partially separated, signed. Ross 86-418 1974 $175

SITWELL, EDITH   Five Poems. London, 1928. 4to., cinnamon coloured morocco, signed, limited, first edition. Bow Windows 62-840 1974 £360

SITWELL, EDITH   Gold Coast Customs. London, 1929. 8vo., orig. black cloth, first edition. Dawsons PM 252-896 1974 £18

SITWELL, EDITH   Cold Coast Customs. London, 1929. Frontis., newspaper review pasted in, covers somewhat worn & spotted, penciled name on free fly, nice copy. Ross 86-419 1974 $17.50

SITWELL, EDITH   Jan Barston, 1719-1746. London, 1931. Large paper edition, no. 49 of 250 copies, signed, lacking d.w., fine, orig. binding. Ross 86-420 1974 $35

SITWELL, EDITH   The Mother and Other Poems. Oxford, 1915. 8vo., quarter morocco, wrappers, rare, first edition. Rota 189-804 1974 £100

SITWELL, EDITH   The Mother and Other Poems. 1915. Small 8vo., orig. brown paper wrapper, first edition. Quaritch 936-578 1974 £75

SITWELL, EDITH   Poetry and Criticism. 1925. Wrappers, English first edition. Covent 56-1184 1974 £10

SITWELL, EDITH   Poetry and Criticism. 1925. Very good copy, wrappers, first edition. Covent 51-1700 1973 £8.50

SITWELL, EDITH   Rustic Elegies. 1927. Small 8vo., portrait, first edition. Howes 185-451 1974 £8.50

SITWELL, EDITH   Rustic Elegies. 1927. Orig. cloth, dust wrapper, inscription, first edition. Rota 188-842 1974 £5

SITWELL, EDITH   Rustic Elegies. New York, 1927. 8vo., orig. cloth, frontispiece, inscription, first American edition. Bow Windows 62-841 1974 £24

SITWELL, EDITH   Rustic Elegies. New York, 1927. Frontis., first U. S. edition, nice copy. Covent 51-1701 1973 £10

SITWELL, EDITH   The Sleeping Beauty. 1924. Fine copy, d.w., first edition, uncommon in d.w. Covent 51-1702 1973 £12.60

SITWELL, EDITH   The Sleeping Beauty. 1924. Dust wrapper, presentation copy, inscribed, English first edition. Covent 56-1186 1974 £25

SITWELL, EDITH   The Song of the Cold. London, 1945. D.w. slightly chipped, near mint, orig. binding. Ross 86-422 1974 $10

SITWELL, EDITH   Street Songs. London, 1942. First edition, lacking d.w., fine, orig. binding. Ross 86-423 1974 $20

SITWELL, EDITH   Troy Park. 1925. Dull covers, first edition. Covent 55-1381 1974 £8.50

SITWELL, EDITH   Twentieth Century Harlequinade and Other Poems. Oxford, 1916. Covers somewhat faded, one page carelessly opened, good copy, first edition. Covent 51-1704 1973 £42.50

SITWELL, EDITH   Wheels, Fourth Cycle. Oxford, 1919. Near fine copy, corners slightly bumped, orig. binding. Ross 86-424 1974 $35

SITWELL, EDITH   Wheels: A Third Cycle. Oxford, 1918. Nice copy, cloth backed pictorial boards, first edition. Covent 51-1703 1973 £12

SITWELL, EDITH   The Wooden Pegasus. Oxford, 1920. Cloth-backed boards, unopened, English first edition. Covent 56-2040 1974 £35

SITWELL, EDITH   The Wooden Pegasus. Oxford, 1920. Pink paper boards, d.w., name in ink on fly, scarce, fine. Ross 86-425 1974 $75

SITWELL, GEORGE RERESBY   Tales of My Native Village. 1933. Small 4to., illus. Covent 55-1382 1974 £15

SITWELL, GEORGE RERESBY   Tales of My Native Village. 1933. Crown 4to., orig. boards, illus., first edition. Howes 185-453 1974 £7.50

SITWELL, OSBERT   All At Sea. 1927. Torn and defective d.w., first edition. Covent 51-1709 1973 £6.30

SITWELL, OSBERT   Argonaut and Juggernaut. 1919. Very nice copy, first edition. Covent 51-1705 1973 £12.50

SITWELL, OSBERT   Argonaut and Juggernaut. London, 1919. First edition, one of 1000 copies, inscription by author, spine darkened, spine label worn, nice only. Ross 86-426 1974 $75

SITWELL, OSBERT   Autobiographies. 1945. 5 vols., plates, illus., orig. buckram. Smith 194-523 1974 £5

SITWELL, OSBERT   Dumb Animals. London, 1930. Inscribed by author, lacking d.w., unusually fine, bright copy, orig. binding. Ross 86-428 1974 $60

SITWELL, OSBERT   England Reclaimed. 1927. Fine, first edition. Howes 185-454 1974 £8.50

SITWELL, OSBERT   The Man Who Lost Himself. 1930. Orig. edition. Austin 61-919 1974 $10

SITWELL, OSBERT   Mrs. Kimber. 1937. Drawings, one of 500 copies, nice copy, worn d.w., first edition. Covent 51-1707 1973 £10.50

SITWELL, OSBERT   Out of the Flame. London, 1923. Frontis., sculpture portrait, inscribed by author, d.w. somewhat chipped & worn, fine, orig. binding, first edition. Ross 86-429 1974 $75

SITWELL, OSBERT   The People's Album of London Statues. 1928. 4to., signature, fine, first edition. Rota 188-843 1974 £6

SITWELL, OSBERT   The True Story of Dick Whittington. 1945. Crown 8vo., fine, first edition. Howes 185-456 1974 £10

SITWELL, SACHEVERELL   The Cyder Feast. 1927. Buckram, unopened, numbered, signed, fine. Covent 55-1383 1974 £15

SITWELL, SACHEVERELL   The Cyder Feast and Other Poems. New York, 1927. 8vo., orig. patterned boards, first American edition. Bow Windows 64-687 1974 £7.50

SITWELL, SACHEVERELL   Collected Poems. 1936. Pencil scoring throughout, very good copy, first edition. Covent 51-1711 1973 £6

SITWELL, SACHEVERELL   Conversation Pieces. (1936). 4to., orig. cloth, illus., some coloured, first edition, second issue. Bow Windows 66-635 1974 £12

SITWELL, SACHEVERELL   Conversation Pieces. 1936. Small 4to., plates, illus., inscription, first edition. Howes 186-425 1974 £10

SITWELL, SACHEVERELL   Dear Miss Heber. 1936. Plates, nice copy, first edition. Covent 51-1716 1973 £5.25

SITWELL, SACHEVERELL   Grand Tour. 1935. 8vo., orig. cloth, wrappers, first edition. Rota 189-824 1974 £5

SITWELL, SACHEVERELL   The Hundred and One Harlequins. 1922. Worn, English first edition. Covent 56-1193 1974 £21

SITWELL, SACHEVERELL   Maurentania: Warrior, Man and Woman, a Journey Through North Africa. 1940. First edition, uncorrected proof copy, orig. printed wrappers, very good copy. Crane 7-286 1974 £6

SITWELL, SACHEVERELL   Narrative Pictures. 1937. Crown 4to., plates, first edition. Howes 186-426 1974 £10

SITWELL, SACHEVERELL   Old Fashioned Flowers. 1939. Roy. 8vo., cloth, coloured plates, scarce first edition. Wheldon 128-1536 1973 £5.50

SITWELL, SACHEVERELL   The Thirteenth Caesar. 1924. Fine, first edition. Howes 185-457 1974 £8.50

SITWELL, SACHEVERELL   La Vie Parisienne. 1937. Orig. cloth, inscribed, first edition. Rota 188-846 1974 £15

SIX Etchings from Nature by G. Gabrielli. n.d. Oblong folio, new cloth boards. Emerald 50-253 1974 £15

SIX Hundred Dollars a Year, A Wife's Effort at Low Living, Under High Prices. Boston, 1867. 16mo., orig. binding. Butterfield 10-18 1974 $10

SIX Old Plays, On Which Shakespeare Founded His. 1779. 2 vols. in 1, back strip loose, joints cracked, contemporary half calf, internally very clean sound copy, bookplate, first edition. Covent 51-1665 1973 £21

THE SIXPENNY Miscellany. London, 1726. 8vo., modern half calf, scarce, first edition. Dawsons PM 252-899 1974 £80

SIXTUS IV   A Fragment, Comprising the Last Nine Leaves of "De Sanguine Christi . . . De Potentia dei. 1473. 4to., old half calf, marbled sides, worn, small worm hole through lower margins. Bow Windows 66-636 1974 £65

SJOSTEDT, Y.   Wissenschaftliche Ergebnisse der Schwedischen Zoologischen Expedition Nach dem Kilimandjaro. Stockholm, 1910. 3 vols., 4to., orig. boards, plates, scarce. Wheldon 128-235 1973 £31

SKEEL, EMILY ELLSWORTH FORD   Mason Locke Weems, His Works and Ways . . . Letters, 1784-1825. New York, 1929. Small 4to., vols. 2 and 3 only. Butterfield 10-31 1974 $75

SKELTON, JOHN   The Crookit Meg. London, 1880. 8vo., orig. pictorial cloth, first edition. Ximenes 35-214 1974 $20

SKELTON, JOHN   Mary Stuart. 1898. 4to., contemporary dark green calf, coloured frontispiece, illus., limited, second edition. Bow Windows 66-837 1974 £16

SKELTON, JOHN   Poems. London, 1924. First edition, one of 780 numbered copies, slight pencilling, very nice copy, scarce, orig. cloth. Crane 7-142 1974 £12

SKELTON, JOSEPH   Skelton's Engraved Illustrations. Oxford, 1823. Folio, frontis., plates, buckram. Quaritch 939-525 1974 £25

SKELTON, JOSEPH   Skelton's Engraved Illustrations. Oxford, 1823. Folio, plates, buckram. Quaritch 939-524 1974 £35

SKELTON, JOSEPH   Skelton's Etchings of the Antiquities of Bristol. (1825). Roy. 4to., plates, buckram. Quaritch 939-367 1974 £15

SKELTON, PHILIP   Deism Revealed. 1751. 12mo., 2 vols., contemporary calf, second edition. Hill 126-245 1974 £13.50

SKENE, ALEXANDER J. C.   Treatise On the Diseases of Women. New York. 1889. Rittenhouse 46-588 1974 $10

SKENE, J.   Series of Sketches of Existing Localities Alluded to in Waverley Novels, Etched from Original Drawings. 1829. Half morocco, plates. Allen 216-1572 1974 $17.50

SKENE, W. F.   The Four Ancient Books of Wales. Edinburgh, 1868. 2 vols., thick 8vo., orig. cloth, plates, scarce. Howes 186-1219 1974 £21

SKENE, W. F.   The Highlanders of Scotland. 1837. 2 vols., 12mo., half calf, some finger marks and stains. Bow Windows 66-638 1974 £15

SKETCHES from Nature. London, 1779. 4to., disbound, first edition. Ximenes 35-119 1974 $75

SKETCHES of Beautiful Salt Lake City, Utah. Salt Lake City, 1938. Small folio, wrappers. Jenkins 61-2480 1974 $20

SKETCHES of Newport and Its Vicinity; With Notices Respecting the History, Settlement and Geography of Rhode Island. New York, 1842. Engravings, 12mo., spine repaired, else fine. Current BW9-431 1974 $20

SKETCHLEY, W.   The Cocker. 1814. 8vo., illus., plates, green levant morocco gilt. Quaritch 939-247 1974 £160

SKEY, FREDERIC C.   Operative Surgery. Philadelphia, 1851. Orig. binding, illus., light marginal damp stain, measurable edge wear, dull. Wilson 63-381 1974 $15

SKINNER, CORNELIA OTIS   Nuts in May. Dodd, Mead, 1950. 188p., illus. Austin 54-917 1973 $6

SKINNER, JOHN   Amusements of Leisure Hours. Edinburgh, 1809. 12mo., modern boards, first edition. Ximenes 35-216 1974 $25

SKINNER, MAUD   One Man In His Time. Univ. of Penn., 1938. Austin 51-901 1973 $12.50

SKINNER, OTIS   Footlights and Spotlights. Bobbs, Merrill, 1924. Austin 51-902 1973 $12.50

SKINNER, THOMAS   The Life of General Monk. 1723. 8vo., contemporary panelled calf, first edition. Quaritch 936-157 1974 £10

SKODA, JOSEPH   Abhandlung Uber Perkussion und Auskultation. Vienna, 1854. 8vo., contemporary half cloth. Dawsons PM 249-453 1974 £30

SKOTTOWE, AUGUSTINE   The Life of Shakespeare. London, 1824. 2 vols., 8vo., contemporary half calf, first edition. Dawsons PM 252-880 1974 £10

SKRINE, H.   A General Account of All the Rivers of Note. 1801. 8vo., maps, half calf. Quaritch 939-849 1974 £20

SLADE, DANIEL DENISON   Diptheria. Philadelphia, 1864. Rittenhouse 46-591 1974 $12.50

SLADE, WILLIAM   Vermont State Papers. Middlebury, 1823. Old calf, leather label. Butterfield 10-519 1974 $50

THE SLANG Dictionary: Etymological Historical and Anecdotal. 1894. 382 pages. Austin 61-920 1974 $17.50

SLARE, FREDERICK   Experiments and Observations Upon Oriental and Other Bezoar-Stones. London, 1715. 8vo., half calf, first edition. Schumann 35-438 1974 $110

SLATER, JOHN HERBERT   Book Plates and Their Value. London, 1898. 8vo., orig. cloth, uncut, first edition. Dawsons PM 10-564 1974 £8

SLATER, JOHN HERBERT   Engravings and Their Value. 1900. Thick crown 8vo., plates, orig. cloth gilt, revised third edition. Smith 194-74 1974 £6.50

SLATTER, H.   Views of All the Colleges. Oxford, (1824). Oblong 12mo., half calf. Quaritch 939-526 1974 £70

SLATTER, J.   Some Notes of the History of the Parish of Whitchurch, Oxon 1895. Orig. cloth gilt, frontispiece, first edition. Smith 194-274 1974 £5

SLATYER, WILLIAM   The Psalmes of David. (London), 1643. 12mo., early 19th century calf, rubbed, gilt, first edition. Traylen 79-186 1973 £105

SLAUGHTER, PHILIP   A History of St. Mark's Parish, Culpeper County, Viriginia, With Notes of Old Churches and Old Families. (Baltimore), 1877. Cloth, scarce first edition, complete with folding map & errata slip, author's presentation inscription. Hayman 59-646 1974 $32.50

SLAUSON, ALLAN   A Check List of American Newspapers in the Library of Congress. Washington, 1901. Cloth. Jenkins 61-1952 1974 $12.50

SLAVS In California. Oakland, Cal., 1937. 137p., illus. Austin 62-585 1974 $27.50

SLEBOS, J. C.   Grondslagen voor Aesthetiek en Stijl. Amsterdam, 1939. 4to., cloth, plates, illus. Minters 37-569 1973 $42.50

SLEEPER, JOHN SHERBURNE   Mark Rowland. Boston, 1867. 8vo., orig. purple cloth, worn, first edition. Ximenes 35-217 1974 $10

THE SLEEPING and the Dead. Chicago, 1947. Biblo & Tannen 210-591 1973 $15

THE SLEEPY Lagoon Case. Los Angeles, 1942. 30 pages, pamphlet. Austin 57-453 1974 $10

SLEIGH, BERNARD   Witchcraft. Berkeley Heights, 1934. Very scarce, woodcuts, limited edition. Ballinger 1-202 1974 $50

SLEZER, JOHN   Theatrum Scotiae. London, 1693. Folio, contemporary sprinkled calf, gilt, fine, first edition. Dawsons PM 251-99 1974 £1,350

SLOAN, EDWIN PLUMMER   The Thyroid. Springfield, 1936. Rittenhouse 46-592 1974 $15

SLONIM, MARC   Russian Theatre. World, 1961. Austin 51-903 1973 $10

SMALE, M.   Diseases and Injuries of the Teeth. London, 1901. 8vo., diagrams, orig. cloth, revised second edition. Bow Windows 62-843 1974 £12

SMALL, HENRY BEAUMONT   The Canadian Handbook and Tourist's Guide. Montreal, 1866. Illus. Hood's 103-36 1974 $50

SMALL, HENRY BEAUMONT   Chronicles of Canada. Ottawa, 1868. Paper cover. Hood's 104-659 1974 $60

SMALL, HENRY BEAUMONT   Chronicles of Canada. Ottawa, 1868. Paper cover, spine taped, handwritten letter from Small included. Hood's 102-578 1974 $60

SMALL, JOHN W.   Scottish Market Crosses. 1900. 4to., faded. Allen 213-1789 1973 $15

SMALL, JOHN W.   Scottish Woodwork of the 16th and 17th Centuries. Stirling, (1878). Folio, plates, cloth. Quaritch 940-589 1974 £5

SMALL Rain Upon the Tender Herb. London. Sixth edition, full red roan, 1 1/4 X 1. Gregory 44-461 1974 $20

SMALL Rain Upon the Tender Herb. Thirteenth edition, 1 3/8 X 1, full red morocco, gilt, silver clasp. Gregory 44-462 1974 $40

SMALL Rain Upon the Tender Herb. (c. 1840). Eighteenth edition, full black morocco, 1 1/4 X 1. Gregory 44-463 1974 $18.50

SMALL Rain Upon the Tender Herb. Twentieth edition, full red roan, fine, matching solander case, 1 1/4 X 1. Gregory 44-464 1974 $25

SMALL Rain Upon the Tender Herb. London. Fourteenth edition, 1 1/4 X 1, full red morocco, fine. Gregory 44-465 1974 $20.

SMALL Rain Upon the Tender Herb. Sixteenth edition, 1 1/4 X 1, full dark green morocco, wallet flap, excellent. Gregory 44-466 1974 $10

SMALL Rain Upon the Tender Herb. Seventeenth edition, 1 1/4 X 1, full brown morocco, wallet flap, bit rubbed. Gregory 44-467 1974 $8.50

SMALL Rain Upon the Tender Herb. Twenty seventh edition, 1 1/4 X 1, full black morocco, wallet flap. Gregory 44-468 1974 $8.50

SMALL Rain Upon the Tender Herb. Twenty ninth edition, 1 1/4 X 1, full red morocco, inscription. Gregory 44-469 1974 $10

SMALL Rain Upon the Tender Herb. Thirty ninth edition, 1 1/4 X 1, full red roan. Gregory 44-470 1974 $8.50

THE SMALL Years. Cambridge, 1930. First edition, orig. binding, fine, dust wrapper. Ross 87-146 1974 $12.50

SMARAGDUS, ARDO   Opera Omnia ex Variis Editionibus Primum In Unum Collecta. Paris, 1865. Roy. 8vo., half vellum, morocco label. Howes 185-1655 1974 £6.50

SMART, JOHN   Tables of Interest, Discount, Annuities. London, 1726. 4to., contemporary panelled calf, fine, first edition. Dawsons PM 247-272 1974 £30

SMEATON, JOHN   Experimental Enquiry Concerning the Natural Powers of Wind and Water to Turn Mills. . . 1794. 8vo., contemporary boards, rebacked, uncut, folding tables & plates, first edition. Bow Windows 66-639 1974 £60

SMEATON, JOHN   The Report of . . .: Drainage of the North Level of the Fens. (1768). 4to., orig. wrappers, first edition. Hammond 201-851 1974 £35

SMEATON, JOHN   Reports of the late John Smeaton. London, 1812. 4to., 3 vols., orig. boards, rebacked, plates, first edition. Hammond 201-947 1974 £185

SMEATON, JOHN   A Review of Several Matters. (Edinburgh), 1768. 4to., half calf, first edition. Gurney 64-201 1974 £35

SMEDLEY, CAROLINE ANNE   Ladies Manual of Practical Hydropathy. London, (1878). 8vo., orig. cloth, gilt, sixteenth edition. Hammond 201-592 1974 £9.50

SMEDLEY, FRANK E.   The Fortunes of the Colville Family. London, 1853. 8vo., orig. dec. cloth, first edition. Ximenes 35-215 1974 $22.50

SMEDLEY, JOHN   Practical Hydropathy. London, (1860). 8vo., orig. cloth, gilt, illus., third edition. Hammond 201-593 1974 £7.50

SMEDLEY, JOHN   Practical Hydropathy. London, (1877). 8vo., orig. cloth, gilt, fifteenth edition. Hammond 201-594 1974 £5

SMEE, ALFRED   Instinct and Reason. 1850. Large 8vo., orig. cloth. Hill 126-247 1974 £10.50

SMELLIE, G.   Memoir of the Rev. John Bayne, D. D., of Galt. Toronto, 1871. Blank fly leaf removed. Hood's 102-260 1974 $12

SMELLIE, WILLIAM   The Philosophy of Natural History. Dublin, 1790. 2 vols., 8vo., contemporary tree calf, spines gilt, morocco labels, first Irish edition. Ximenes 37-194 1974 $90

SMET, PIERRE JEAN DE   Western Missions and Missionaries. New York, 1863. Portrait, orig. cloth, first edition in English, inscribed and signed by author. Jenkins 61-2361 1974 $175

SMETHAM, JAMES   Letters. 1892. 2 vols., portrait, orig. cloth, first & second editions. Marsden 39-418 1974 £15

SMILES, SAMUEL   The Huguenots. 1867. 448 pages, orig. edition. Austin 57-629 1974 $12.50

SMILES, SAMUEL   Josiah Wedgwood. 1894. Crown 8vo., orig. cloth. Broadhurst 23-198 1974 £8

SMILES, SAMUEL   Josiah Wedgwood. London, 1894. 8vo., gilt, cloth, first edition. Hammond 201-993 1974 £7.50

SMILES, SAMUEL   A Publisher and His Friends. 1891. 2 vols., thick 8vo., portrait. Howes 185-773 1974 £8.50

SMILES, SAMUEL   Robert Dick, Baker of Thurso, Geologist and Botanist. 1878. First edition, crown 8vo., etched portrait, illus., orig. cloth, fine. Broadhurst 24-1166 1974 £8

SMILES, SAMUEL   Self-Help. London, 1859. 8vo., orig. red cloth, first edition. Dawsons PM 250-71 1974 £95

SMITH   The Heraldry of Smith Being a Collection of the Arms Borne by. 1870. 4to., plates, cloth. Quaritch 939-750 1974 £10

SMILLIE, JAMES   Mount Auburn. New York, 1847. 4to., cloth, illus. Saddleback 14-494 1974 $10

SMITH, A. C.   The Monk and the Dancer. New York, 1909. 12mo., boards, cloth back, badly worn copy, first edition. Goodspeed's 578-329 1974 $10

SMITH, A. D.   Old Fuss and Feathers: The Life and Exploits
of Lt. Gen. Winfield Scott.   New York, 1937. Scarce. Jenkins 61-1608
1974 $17.50

SMITH, A. D.   Old Fuss and Feathers: The Life and Exploits
of Lt. Gen. Winfield Scott.   New York, 1937. Jenkins 61-2331 1974 $17.50

SMITH, A. GORDON   A Short History of Medieval England. London,
1925. 12mo. Biblo & Tannen 214-659 1974 $7.50

SMITH, A. L.   A Monograph of the British Lichens. 1918-26.
8vo., cloth, 2 vols., plates, second edition. Wheldon 129-1419 1974 £25

SMITH, ADAM   Essays On Philosophical Subjects. London,
1795. 4to., old half calf, leather label, rubbed, first edition. Traylen 79-187
1973 £230

SMITH, ADAM   Essays on Philosophical Subjects . . . To Which
is Prefixed an Account of the Life and Writings of the Author. 1795. First
edition, demy 4to., full antique style calf by Bayntun, panelled back, raised bands,
leather label, uncut, fine, scarce. Broadhurst 24-1328 1974 £200

SMITH, ADAM   An Inquiry Into the Nature and Causes of the
Wealth of Nations. London, 1776. 2 vols., 4to., contemporary speckled calf,
first edition. Dawsons PM 252-1106 1974 £2100

SMITH, ADAM   An Inquiry Into the Nature and Causes of the
Wealth of Nations. 1778. 2 vols., 4to., contemporary tree calf, rebacked,
second edition. Bow Windows 66-640 1974 £560

SMITH, ADAM   An Inquiry into the Nature and Causes of
the Wealth of Nations. 1809. 3 vols., contemporary calf, rubbed. Heffer
35-282 1973 £25

SMITH, ADAM   An Inquiry into the Nature and Causes of the
Wealth of Nations. London, 1819. 8vo., 3 vols., orig. boards. Hammond 201-
269 1974 £22

SMITH, ADAM   An Inquiry into the Nature and Causes of the
Wealth of Nations. Oxford, 1869. 8vo., orig. cloth. Broadhurst 23-1274
1974 £6

SMITH, ADAM   The Theory of Moral Sentiments. 1792. 8vo.,
2 vols., contemporary tree calf, bookplates, seventh edition. Hill 126-248 1974
£18

SMITH, ADAM   Works. 1812-11. 5 vols., half black calf
gilt, first & only collected edition. Howes 186-1580 1974 £65

SMITH, ALBERT   The Adventures of Mr. Ledbury and his Friend
Jack Johnson. London, 1886. Roy 8vo., orig. cloth, gilt, plates. Hammond
201-490 1974 £9

SMITH, ALBERT   The Wassail-Bowl. London, 1843. 2 vols.,
12mo., orig. cloth, illus., first edition. Dawsons PM 252-900 1974 £18

SMITH, ALBERT   Wild Oats and Dead Leaves. London, 1860.
8vo., orig. dec. cloth, first edition. Ximenes 35-220 1974 $22.50

SMITH, ALEXANDER   Poems. Boston, 1853. 188 pages. Austin
61-921 1974 $10

SMITH, B. E.   The Century Cyclopedia of Names. London &
New York, 1904. 4to., three quarter contemporary black morocco gilt. Smith
193-298 1973 £5

SMITH, BERTHA W.   The Writing Art. 1931. 277 pages. Austin
61-922 1974 $10

SMITH, BERTHA H.   Yosemite Legends. San Francisco, c. 1904.
Illus., tissue guards, bookplate, orig. binding. Wilson 63-151 1974 $10

SMITH, C. H.   An Introduction to the Mammalia. Edinburgh,
1842. Post 8vo., half morocco, plates. Wheldon 131-521 1974 £15

SMITH, C. W.   Oriental Ornithology. 1829. Oblong folio,
orig. wrappers, plates. Wheldon 131-115 1974 £200

SMITH, CEDRIC ELLSWORTH   The Yellow Book. 1928. 413 pages, illus.
Austin 61-1098 1974 $12.50

SMITH, CHARLES H.   Jacksonville, Board of Trade, Jacksonville,
Florida. Jacksonville, 1902. 8vo., cloth. Saddleback 14-350 1974 $17.50

SMITH, CHARLES 1715?-1762   The Ancient and Present State of the County
and City of Waterford. 8vo., reprint. Emerald 50-888 1974 £5.50

SMITH, CHARLES HAMILTON   The Ancient Costume of Great Britain and
Ireland. Folio, plates, half morocco, improved edition. Quaritch 939-248
1974 £180

SMITH, CHARLES ROACH   The Antiquities of Richborough. London, 1850.
4to., modern half yellow morocco, gilt, collected edition. Dawsons PM 251-
69 1974 £80

SMITH, CHARLES ROACH   Collectanea Antiqua, Etchings and Notices of
Ancient Remains. 1848-80. 7 vols., 8vo., half calf, plates. Quaritch 939-
249 1974 £30

SMITH, CHARLES ROACH   Retrospections, Social and Archaeological.
1883-1891. 8vo., orig. cloth, 3 vols., first edition. Bow Windows 64-690
1974 £15

SMITH, CHARLOTTE   Elegiac Sonnets. Worcester, 1795. 12mo.,
contemporary sheep, worn, plates. Ximenes 35-221 1974 $75

SMITH, CHARLOTTE   Ethelinde. 1789. 5 vols., half calf, spines
badly torn, text fine, first edition. Allen 216-2062 1974 $75

SMITH, CHARLES W.   Pacific Northwest Americana. New York,
1921. Jenkins 61-2110 1974 $20

SMITH, CLARK ASHTON   The Second Interment. New York, 1933.
Orig. pictorial wrappers, illus. Covent 55-653 1974 $5.25

SMITH, CLARK ASHTON   The Star-Treader. San Francisco, 1912. Dec.
boards, gilt, fine, first American edition. Covent 55-1388 1974 $25

SMITH, D. A.   At the Forks of the Grand. (Paris, n.d.).
Hood's 104-733 1974 $17.50

SMITH, DAVID WILLIAM   A Gazeteer of the Province of Upper Canada.
New York, 1813. Orig. marbled boards, rare, first edition. Bradley 35-56
1974 $100

SMITH, DAVID WILLIAM   A Short Topographical Description of His
Majesty's Province of Upper Canada. London, 1799. Three quarter leather,
marbled boards. Hood's 104-734 1974 $200

SMITH, EDGAR F.   Chemistry In Old Philadelphia. Philadelphia,
1919. Rittenhouse 46-594 1974 $10

SMITH, EDMUND   Phaedra and Hippolitus. London, (n.d.).
4to., modern half calf, second edition. Dawsons PM 252-901 1974 £85

SMITH, ELBERT H.   Me-ka-tai-me-she-kia-kiak. New York, 1849.
8vo., gilt cloth. Butterfield 8-157 1974 $25

SMITH, ELIZABETH   The Complete Housewife. London, 1773.
8vo., old calf, rebacked, frontispiece, plates. Traylen 79-216 1973 £40

SMITH, ELIZABETH   Memoirs of Frederick and Margaret Klopstock.
1808. 8vo., old calf, worn, first edition. Bow Windows 64-691 1974 £6.50

SMITH, ELIZABETH ELTON   The Three Eras of Woman's Life. London,
1836. 3 vols., small 8vo., contemporary green half calf, first edition. Dawsons
PM 252-902 1974 £15

SMITH, ERNEST ASHTON   Allegheny College – A Century of Education.
Meadville, 1916. Fine. Ballinger 1-314 1974 $15

SMITH, ERNEST BRAMAH   English Farming and Why I Turned It Up. London,
1894. Stiff wrappers, unusually fresh copy, scarce. Ross 86-75 1974 $50

SMITH, ERNEST BRAMAH   English Farming and Why I Turned It Up. 1894.
Orig. cloth, wrappers, first edition. Rota 188-118 1974 £5

SMITH, ERNEST BRAMAH   Kai Lung Unrolls His Mat. 1928. First edition, crown 8vo., very fine copy, orig. cloth. Broadhurst 24-573 1974 £5

SMITH, ERNEST BRAMAH   Kai Lung's Golden Hours. 1922. Crown 8vo., very fine copy, first edition. Broadhurst 24-572 1974 £5

SMITH, ERNEST BRAMAH   Kai Lung's Golden Hours. London, 1924. No. 17 of edition limited to 250 copies, signed, near mint, orig. binding. Ross 86-76 1974 $30

SMITH, ERNEST BRAMAH   Kai Lung's Golden Hours. 1924. Small 4to., linen backed boards, English first edition. Covent 56-173 1974 £15.75

SMITH, ERNEST BRAMAH   Kin Weng and the Miraculous Tusk. 1941. Light gray boards, fine. Ross 86-77 1974 $15

SMITH, ERNEST BRAMAH   The Moon of Much Gladness Related by Kai Lung. 1932. First edition, crown 8vo., very fine, orig. cloth. Broadhurst 24-574 1974 £5

SMITH, ERNEST BRAMAH   The Transmutation of Ling. 1911. 4to., orig. cloth, plates, first edition. Rota 189-153 1974 £7.50

SMITH, ERNEST BRAMAH   The Wallet of Kai Lung. 1900. 8vo., orig. pictorial cloth, d.w., fine, scarce, first edition. Quaritch 936-316 1974 £20

SMITH, ERNEST BRAMAH   The Wallet of Kai Lung. 1923. Linen backed boards, signed, English first edition. Covent 56-174 1974 £15.75

SMITH, F.   Catalogue of Hymenopterous Insects. 1853-59. 12mo., wrappers, plates, scarce. Wheldon 129-682 1974 £20

SMITH, F.   Catalogue of Hymenopterous Insects In the Collection of the British Museum. 1853-59. 7 parts, 12mo., wrappers, plates, very scarce. Wheldon 131-856 1974 £20

SMITH, F.   Catalogue of Hymenopterous Insects in the Collection of the British Museum. 1853-59. 7 parts in 2 vols., new cloth, plates, very scarce. Wheldon 128-803 1973 £15

SMITH, FRANCIS G.   A Manual of Auscultation and Percussion. Philadelphia, 1845. Rittenhouse 46-43 1974 $15

SMITH, FRANCIS HOPKINSON   The Arm-Chair at the Inn. New York, 1912. Illus., first edition, 8vo., some rubbing at extremities, else very good. Current BW9-276 1974 $8.50

SMITH, FRANCIS HOPKINSON   Gondola Days. Boston, 1897. First edition. Biblo & Tannen 210-802 1973 $8.50

SMITH, FRANCIS HOPKINSON   In Thackeray's London. New York, 1913. First edition, large 8vo., illus. by author, fine. Current BW9-277 1974 $27.50

SMITH, FRANCIS HOPKINSON   The Other Fellow. Boston & New York, 1899. Presentation copy, signed, rubbed. Ballinger 1-41 1974 $11

SMITH, FRANCIS HOPKINSON   Colonel Carter's Christmas. New York, 1903. Illus., first edition, 12mo., full page full color illus. Current BW9-80 1974 $15

SMITH, FRANK M.   San Francisco Vigilance Committee of '56 With Some Interesting Sketches of Events Succeeding 1846. San Francisco, 1883. Jenkins 61-418 1974 $45

SMITH, FREDERICK   The Early History of Veterinary Literature and Its British Development. London, 1924-33. 3 vols., large 8vo., orig. cloth, fine, first book form edition. Dawsons PM 10-568 1974 £30

SMITH, G.   Essays on the Construction of Cottages Suited for the Dwellings of the Labouring Classes. Glasgow, 1834. 8vo., plates, orig. cloth, printed label. Quaritch 940-556 1974 £12

SMITH, G.   A Naturalist In Tasmania. 1909. 8vo., cloth, plates. Wheldon 131-395 1974 £10

SMITH, G. W.   History of Illinois. Chicago, 1927. 4to., illus., cloth, 6 vols., fine. Putnam 126-155 1974 $65

SMITH, G. ELLIOT   Egyptian Mummies. 1924. 4to., orig. buckram gilt, plates, first edition. Smith 193-43 1973 £10

SMITH, G. ELLIOT   Elephants and Ethnologists. 1924. Small 4to., illus., orig. cloth backed boards, first edition. Bow Windows 64-250 1974 £12

SMITH, G. M.   Cryptogamic Botany. New York, 1938. 8vo., cloth, 2 vols. Wheldon 129-1422 1974 £5

SMITH, G. M.   Phytoplankton of the Inland Lakes of Wisconsin. Madison, 1924. Roy 8vo., cloth, plates. Wheldon 129-1421 1974 £7.50

SMITH, G. M.   Phytoplankton of the Inland Lakes of Wisconsin. Madison, 1920-24. 8vo., 2 vols., cloth, plates. Wheldon 129-1420 1974 £15

SMITH, GEORGE   A Compleat Body of Distilling. 1749. 8vo., contemporary sheep, fine, frontispiece. Hill 126-249 1974 £65

SMITH, GABRIEL   The Laboratory. London, 1799. 8vo., 2 vols., contemporary tree calf, rebacked, gilt, plates, sixth edition. Hammond 201-949 1974 £40

SMITH, GEORGE 1871-   The Oldest London Bookshop. London, 1928. Plates, demy 4to., orig. linen, slightly dust soiled, signed presentation copy from Smith. Forster 98-158 1974 £10

SMITH, GERTRUDE   The Arabella and Araminta Stories. Boston, 1895. 4to., dec. cloth, little spotted, dec. endpapers, fine illus., first edition. Frohnsdorff 15-183 1974 $50

SMITH, GOLDWIN   The Civil War in America. 1866. Crown 8vo., limp cloth. Broadhurst 23-1708 1974 £6

SMITH, GOLDWIN   Reminiscences. New York, 1910. Hood's 102-261 1974 $10

SMITH, H. M.   Historical Sketches of Old Vincennes. 1903. 12mo., cloth, illus., worn, second edition. Putnam 126-174 1974 $15

SMITH, H. ALLEN   The Age of the Tail. Brown, 1955. 159p., illus. Austin 54-918 1973 $6.50

SMITH, H. ALLEN   The Complete Practical Joker. Doubleday, 1953. 320p. Austin 54-919 1973 $6.50

SMITH, H. ALLEN   Desert Island Decameron. 1945. Illus. Austin 54-920 1973 $6.50

SMITH, H. ALLEN   Don't Get Perconel with a Chicken, Little, Brown, 1959. 132p. Austin 54-921 1973 $6

SMITH, H. ALLEN   How to Write Without Knowing Nothing. Little, Brown, 1961. 179p. Austin 54-922 1973 $7.50

SMITH, H. ALLEN   Larks in the Popcorn. Doubleday, 1948. 256p., illus. Austin 54-923 1973 $6.50

SMITH, H. ALLEN   Let the Crabgrass Grow. Geis, 1960. 256p., illus. Austin 54-924 1973 $6.50

SMITH, H. ALLEN   Lo, the Former Egyptian. Doubleday, 1947. 212p., illus. Austin 54-925 1973 $6.50

SMITH, H. ALLEN   Lost in the Horse Latitudes. Blakiston, 1946. 223p., illus. Austin 54-926 1973 $6

SMITH, H. ALLEN   Low Man on a Totem Pole. Doubleday, Doran, 1941. Austin 54-927 1973 $6

SMITH, H. ALLEN   Mr. Kleins Kampf. Stackpole, 1939. 202p., illus. Austin 54-928 1973 $7.50

SMITH, H. ALLEN   Mister Zip. Doubleday, 1952. 252p. Austin 54-929 1973 $6.50

SMITH, H. ALLEN   People Named Smith. Doubleday, n.d. 255p., illus. Austin 54-930 1973 $6

SMITH, H. ALLEN   The Pig in the Barber Shop. Little, Brown,
1958. 316p. Austin 54-931 1973 $6.50

SMITH, H. ALLEN   The Rebel Yell. Doubleday, 1954. 124p.,
illus. Austin 54-932 1973 $6

SMITH, H. ALLEN   Rhubarb. Doubleday, 1946. 301p., illus.
Austin 54-933 1973 $6

SMITH, H. ALLEN   Robert Gair. Dial, 1939. 118p. Austin
54-934 1973 $7.50

SMITH, H. ALLEN   A Short History of Fingers. Little, Brown,
1943. 301p., illus. Austin 54-935 1973 $6

SMITH, H. ALLEN   Son of Rhubarb. Trident, 1967. 275p., illus.
Austin 54-936 1973 $6.50

SMITH, H. ALLEN   Three Men on Third. Doubleday, 1951.
250p., illus. Austin 54-943 1973 $6.50

SMITH, H. ALLEN   To Hell in a Hand-Basket. Doubleday, 1962.
341p. Austin 54-937 1973 $7.50

SMITH, H. ALLEN   Two-Thirds of a Coconut Tree. Little, Brown,
1963. 369p., illus. Austin 54-938 1973 $6.50

SMITH, H. ALLEN   Waikiki Beachnik. Little, Brown, 1960.
308p., illus. Austin 54-939 1973 $6

SMITH, H. ALLEN   We Went Thataway. Doubleday, 1949. 256p.,
illus. Austin 54-940 1973 $6.50

SMITH, H. ALLEN   The World, the Flesh and H. Allen Smith.
Hanover, 1954. 301p. Austin 54-942 1973 $8.50

SMITH, H. ALLEN   Write Me a Poem Baby. Little, Brown, 1956.
142p. Austin 54-941 1973 $6

SMITH, HAROLD CLIFFORD   Buckingham Palace. 1930. Roy. 4to., orig.
cloth, plates, presentation, limited edition. Broadhurst 23-200 1974 £25

SMITH, HAROLD CLIFFORD   Buckingham Palace. 1930. Super roy. 4to.,
coloured and plain plates, mint, orig. board box, presentation edition, limited
to 750 copies on hand made paper. Broadhurst 24-189 1974 £25

SMITH, HAROLD CLIFFORD   Buckingham Palace. (1930). Roy. 4to.,
plates, cloth, dust wrapper. Quaritch 940-478 1974 £9

SMITH, HAROLD CLIFFORD   Buckingham Palace. (1931). 4to., illus.,
orig. cloth, coloured and other plates, spine faded. Bow Windows 66-644 1974
£8.50

SMITH, HORACE   Amarynthus. London, 1821. 8vo., orig.
boards, inscribed presentation, scarce, first edition. Ximenes 35-222 1974 $75

SMITH, HORACE   Brambletye House. London, 1826. 3 vols.,
8vo., orig. boards, labels, first edition. Ximenes 35-223 1974 $100

SMITH, HORACE   Gale Middleton. Philadelphia, 1834. 2 vols.,
12mo., orig. quarter cloth, first American edition. Ximenes 35-224 1974 $10

SMITH, HORACE   The New Forest. London, 1829. 12mo., 3 vols.,
contemporary half calf, gilt, first edition. Hammond 201-330 1974 $15

SMITH, HORACE   Rejected Addresses. Boston, 1841. Third
American edition. Austin 61-924 1974 $12.50

SMITH, HUGH   A Treatise on the Use and Abuse of Mineral Waters.
London, 1780. 8vo., boards, fourth edition. Hammond 201-595 1974 £7.50

SMITH, J. C.   Catalogue of First Portion of the Collection of
Mezzotinto Engravings. 1887. Frontispiece, rare. Marsden 39-419 1974 £15

SMITH, J. E. A.   The History of Pittsfield. Springfield, 1876.
Large 8vo., orig. bindings, ex-library. Butterfield 8-269 1974 $35

SMITH, J. F.   Digest of Reported Cases: Supreme Court of
Judicature for Ontario and Supreme and Exchequer Courts of Canada. Toronto,
1887. Three quarter leather. Hood's 104-624 1974 $30

SMITH, J. H.   Historical Sketch of the County of Wentworth and
the Head of the Lake. Hamilton, 1897. Leather, marbled endpapers, illus.
Hood's 102-636 1974 $35

SMITH, J. R.   Bibliotheca Cantiana. London, 1837. 8vo.,
orig. cloth, inscription, rubbed, plates. Bow Windows 62-847 1974 £25

SMITH, J. T.   Antiquities of Westminster. 1807-(1809).
2 vols. in 1, imp. 4to., contemporary russia gilt. Quaritch 939-489 1974 £90

SMITH, JAMES   Rejected Addresses. London, 1812. 12mo.,
contemporary half calf, first edition. Dawsons PM 252-903 1974 £45

SMITH, JAMES EDWARD   The English Flora. (1828-30). 8vo., buckram,
second edition. Wheldon 129-1018 1974 £12

SMITH, JAMES EDWARD   Exotic Botany. 1804-05 (-1808). 2 vols. in
1, 8vo., new half morocco, gilt, library stamp. Wheldon 128-1537 1973 £200

SMITH, JAMES EDWARD   Flora Britannica. 1800-04. 8vo., wrappers.
Wheldon 129-1017 1974 £10

SMITH, JAMES EDWARD   Gleanings of Botany. (1791-92). Small folio,
new half calf. Wheldon 129-44 1974 £185

SMITH, JAMES EDWARD   A Grammar of Botany. 1821. 8vo., plates,
contemporary calf. Wheldon 131-1200 1974 £5

SMITH, JAMES EDWARD   An Introduction to Physiological and
Systematical Botany. 1809. 8vo., calf, plates, second edition. Wheldon
131-1201 1974 £5

SMITH, JAMES EDWARD   Introductory Discourse On the Rise and Progress
of Natural History Delivered by the President, April 8, 1788. (1791). 4to.,
modern boards. Wheldon 131-183 1974 £20

SMITH, JAMES EDWARD   Plantarum Icones Hactenus Ineditae. 1789-91.
3 vols., folio, modern cloth & unbound in loose leaves, engraved plates, rare.
Wheldon 128-1164 1973 £35

SMITH, JAMES EDWARD   Spicilegium Botanicum. (1791-92). 2 parts
in 1 vol., small folio, new half calf, plates, very rare. Wheldon 131-116
1974 £185

SMITH, JAMES ELIBANK   Mercury's Letters on Science. London, (1853).
Small 8vo., orig. glazed green printed wrappers, first edition. Dawsons PM 245-
680 1974 £15

SMITH, JOHN   Irish Diamonds. London, 1847. 12mo.,
orig. cloth, worn, plates, first edition. Ximenes 35-227 1974 $15

SMITH, JOHN   Monograph of the Stalactites and Stalagmites of the
Cleaves Cove. London, 1894. 4to., orig. cloth, gilt, plates, first edition. Hammond 201-390 1974 £10

SMITH, JOHN 1580-1631   The Generall Historie of Virginia, New England,
and the Summer Isles. London, 1627. Small folio, contemporary calf, rare, fine,
first edition. Dawsons PM 250-73 1974 £6850

SMITH, JOHN 1580-1631   Select Discourses. London, 1660. Small 4to.,
old calf, first edition. Ximenes 35-225 1974 $200

SMITH, JOHN 1630-1670   The Pourtract of Old Age. London, 1694. Small
8vo., contemporary calf, second edition. Schumann 35-441 1974 $210

SMITH, JOHN 1662-1717   Poems Upon Several Occasions. London, 1713.
8vo., contemporary panelled calf, scarce, first edition. Ximenes 35-226 1974
$175

SMITH, JOHN fl. 1673-1680   Horological Dialogues. London, 1675. 12mo.,
contemporary dark blue morocco, gilt, rebacked, first edition. Dawsons PM 245-
681 1974 £300

SMITH, JOHN 1752-1809   The Newhampshire Latin Grammar. Boston, 1812.
8vo., orig. binding, third edition. Butterfield 8-360 1974 $10

SMITH, JOHN 1798-1888   A Dictionary of Popular Names of the Plants
Which Furnish the Natural and Acquired Wants of Man. 1882. 8vo., cloth, scarce.
Wheldon 129-1668 1974 £7.50

SMITH, JOHN 1798-1888   Ferns, British and Foreign. (1866). 8vo., cloth,
scarce. Wheldon 129-1423 1974 £5

SMITH, JOHN CHALONER   British Mezzotinto Portraits. London, 1884.
4 vols., 4to., orig. cloth, plates. Dawsons PM 10-570 1974 £95

SMITH, JOSEPH   Bibliotheca Smithiana. Venice, 1755. 4to.,
new half calf, marbled boards, fine. Dawsons PM 10-571 1974 £120

SMITH, JOSEPH, 1805-1844   Book of Mormon
Please turn to
BOOK of Mormon

SMITH, JOSEPH EMERSON   Oakridge. Boston, 1875. 12mo., orig.
cloth, first edition. Ximenes 35-228 1974 $12.50

SMITH, JUSTIN HARVEY   Troubadours at Home. 1899. 2 vols., half
morocco. Allen 213-1790 1973 $25

SMITH, JUSTIN HARVEY   The War With Mexico. New York, 1919.
2 vols., fine set. Jenkins 61-1609 1974 $75

SMITH, KATE   Living In a Great Big Way. 1938. 208p.
Austin 51-904 1973 $7.50

SMITH, LANGDON   Evolution. Boston, 1909. Illus., orig.
binding. Butterfield 10-489 1974 $12.50

SMITH, LOGAN PEARSALL   Treasury of English Prose. 1921. Ex-library.
Austin 61-925 1974 $10

SMITH, LUCY   Biographical Sketches of Joseph Smith. 1853.
Full green morocco, gilt. Dawson's 424-346 1974 $250

SMITH, MATTHEW   Memoirs of Secret Service. London, 1699.
8vo., contemporary calf, gilt, first edition. Ximenes 35-229 1974 $275

SMITH, MATTHEW H.   Twenty Years Among the Bulls and Bears of Wall
Street. Hartford, 1870. Cloth, scarce, first edition. Hayman 57-685 1974 $15

SMITH, NATHAN   Practical Essay on Typhous Fever. New York,
1824. Orig. boards, worn. Rittenhouse 46-595 1974 $25

SMITH, PERCY J.   Lettering. 1936. Roy. 8vo., illus., dust
wrapper, fine, first edition. Howes 185-841 1974 £5.75

SMITH, R.   A Wonder of Wonders. London, 1662. 4to.,
19th century half calf, rare. Dawsons PM 252-904 1974 £165

SMITH, R.   Court Cookery. 1725. 8vo., contemporary
calf, second edition. Quaritch 939-250 1974 £75

SMITH, R. A.   A Centenary of Science in Manchester. 1883.
8vo., orig. cloth, little worn, scarce. Wheldon 128-132 1973 £10

SMITH, R. C.   The Familiar Astrologer. 1831. Thick 8vo.,
contemporary calf, plates, first edition. Howes 186-1933 1974 £21

SMITH, R. F.   Doniphan County, Kansas. (Troy), 1868.
8vo., cloth. Saddleback 14-434 1974 $125

SMITH, R. BOSWORTH   Life of Lord Lawrence. 1885. 2 vols.,
portraits, maps. Howes 186-941 1974 £5.25

SMITH, RALPH D.   The History of Guilford, Connecticut. Albany,
1877. 8vo., cloth. Saddleback 14-337 1974 $35

SMITH, ROBERT   A Compleat System of Opticks. Cambridge, 17-
38. 4to., 2 vols., red quarter calf, uncut, plates, first edition. Dawsons PM
245-682 1974 £95

SMITH, ROBERT   A Compleat System of Opticks in Four Books.
Cambridge, 1738. 2 vols., 4to., old calf, gilt, leather labels. Traylen
79-271 1973 £95

SMITH, ROBERT   Harmonics. 1749. 8vo., plates, contemporary
calf, gilt, rare, first edition. Zeitlin 235-206 1974 $150

SMITH, ROBERT   Robert Smith's Address to the People of the United
States. Baltimore, 1811. 12mo., first edition. Ximenes 35-230 1974 $50

SMITH, ROBERT   The Universal Directory for Taking Alive and Des-
troying Rats. London, 1786. 8vo., half calf, gilt, plates, third edition. Hammond 201-999 1974 £21

SMITH, ROBERT PAUL   And Another Thing. Norton, 1959. 110p.
Austin 54-944 1973 $6

SMITH, ROBERT PAUL   Crank. Norton, 1962. 154p. Austin 54-945
1973 $6

SMITH, ROBERT PAUL   The Time and the Place. S & S, 1952. 245p.
Austin 54-946 1973 $7.50

SMITH, ROBERT PAUL   Where He Went. Viking, 1958. Austin
54-947 1973 $12.50

SMITH, SAMUEL   The Provincial Statutes of Upper Canada.
York, 1818. Contemporary hard cover binding, foxing. Hood's 103-690 1974
$150

SMITH, S. R.   The Story of Wyoming Valley. Kingston,
1906. 12mo., cloth, presentation. Saddleback 14-679 1974 $25

SMITH, SEBA   Way Down East; or, Portraitures of Yankee
Life. New York, 1854. Orig. cloth, ends of spine rubbed, first edition, very
good copy. MacManus 224-398 1974 $30

SMITH, STEVIE   Over the Frontier. London, 1938. First edition,
extremely fine copy, d.w., orig. cloth, scarce. Crane 7-288 1974 £10

SMITH, SYDNEY   Essays: Social and Political. n.d. 1st and
2nd series in 1 vol. Austin 61-926 1974 $10

SMITH, SYDNEY   The Works of. 1848. 3 vols., 8vo., half
calf, rebacked, corners worn, portrait, library stamps, fourth edition. Bow
Windows 66-645 1974 £22

SMITH, T. R.   Poetica Erotica. New York, 1921. 3 vols.,
boards, gilt. Rich Summer-94 1974 $27.50

SMITH, THOMAS   The Common-Wealth of England. London, n.d.
12mo., modern olive morocco, gilt. Dawsons PM 251-338 1974 £45

SMITH, THOMAS   An Essay on the Theory of Money and Exchange.
London & Edinburgh, 1811. 8vo., modern boards, paper label. Dawsons PM
247-273 1974 £35

SMITH, THOMAS   De Graecae Ecclesiae Hodierno Statu
Epistola. 1698. New buckram. Allen 213-724 1973 $12.50

SMITH, THOMAS CHARLTON   Rude Rhymes. Dublin, 1817. 8vo., orig.
boards, label, uncut, scarce, first edition. Ximenes 35-231 1974 $27.50

SMITH, THOMAS L.   History of the Town of Windham. Portland,
1873. 8vo., cloth. Saddleback 14-464 1974 $12.50

SMITH, THORNE   Biltmore Oswald. Stokes, 1918. 87p., illus.
Austin 54-948 1973 $17.50

SMITH, THORNE   The Bishop's Jaegers. Doubleday, Doran,
1932. 311p., illus. Austin 54-949 1973 $6.50

SMITH, THORNE   Did She Fall. Cosmopolitan Book Co., 1930.
286p. Austin 54-950 1973 $6.50

SMITH, THORNE   Dream's End. McBride, 1933. 342p. Austin
54-951 1973 $10

SMITH, THORNE   The Night Life of the Gods. Doubleday, Doran, 1931. 311p. Austin 54-953 1973 $6.50

SMITH, THORNE   The Passionate Witch. Doubleday, Doran, n.d. 267p., illus. Austin 54-952 1973 $6.50

SMITH, THORNE   Rain in the Doorway. Doubleday, Doran, 1933. 304p., illus. Austin 54-954 1973 $6.50

SMITH, THORNE   Skin and Bones. Doubleday, Doran, 1933. 306p., illus. Austin 54-955 1973 $7.50

SMITH, THORNE   The Stray Lamb. Heinemann, Long., 1930. 313p. Austin 54-956 1973 $7.50

SMITH, THORNE   Topper. Literary Guild, 1935. 292p. Austin 54-957 1973 $6

SMITH, THORNE   Topper Takes a Trip. Doubleday, Doran, 1932. 325p., illus. Austin 54-958 1973 $6.50

SMITH, THORNE   Turnabout. Doubleday, Doran, 1931. 312p. Austin 54-959 1973 $6.50

SMITH, W. G.   Building the Nation. Toronto, 1922. Map, 202 pages. Hood's 104-326 1974 $10

SMITH, W. RAMSAY   Myths and Legends of the Australian Aboriginals. New York, n.d. Biblo & Tannen 213-132 1973 $12.50

SMITH, WILLIAM   A Delineation of the Strata of England and Wales. 1815. Large folio, contemporary half calf, label, fine, plates, first edition. Dawsons PM 250-74 1974 £2750

SMITH, WILLIAM   A True, Short, Impartial Relation. (London), 1664. Small 4to., disbound, first edition. Ximenes 35-232 1974 $27.50

SMITH, WILLIAM   Observations on the Utility, Form and Management of Water Meadows. Norwich, 1806. 8vo., orig. boards. Wheldon 129-865 1974 £50

SMITH, WILLIAM d. 1673   Balm from Gilead. 1675. Small folio, calf, inscription. Thomas 28-102 1972 £25

SMITH, WILLIAM 1727-1803   The Charge Given by Sir William Smith. London, 1682. Folio, wrapper, first edition. Hammond 201-189 1974 £6

SMITH, WILLIAM 1727-1803   Discourses on Public Occasions in America. London, 1762. 8vo., contemporary morocco, fine, second edition. Ximenes 35-233 1974 $250

SMITH, WILLIAM 1727-1803   Eulogium on Benjamin Franklin...Before the American Philosophical Society. Philadelphia, 1792. Sewn, foxed, first printing. Jenkins 61-903 1974 $40

SMITH, WILLIAM 1727-1803   An Oration in Memory of General Montgomery. Philadelphia, 1776. 8vo., disbound, first edition. Ximenes 35-234 1974 $75

SMITH, WILLIAM 1808-1857   A Synopsis of the British Diatomaceae. 1853-56. 2 vols., roy. 8vo., modern half cloth, plates (some coloured), very scarce. Wheldon 128-1424 1973 £18

SMITH, WILLIAM 1813-93   A Dictionary of Christian Antiquities. 1875-80. 2 vols., thick 8vo., half calf, orig. edition. Howes 185-1657 1974 £15

SMITH, WILLIAM 1813-1893   A Dictionary of Christian Biography, Literature, Sects, and Doctrines. 1877-87. 4 vols., thick 8vo., half calf, orig. edition. Howes 185-1658 1974 £45

SMITH, WILLIAM 1813-1893   Dictionary of Greek and Roman Biography and Mythology. 1880. 3 vols., buckram. Allen 213-982 1973 $50

SMITH, WILLIAM 1813-1893   Dictionary of Greek and Roman Antiquities. 1890-91. 2 vols., new buckram, third edition. Allen 213-981 1973 $35

SMITH, WILLIAM 1859-   History of Canada. Quebec, 1815. 2 vols., contemporary binding, marbled boards, gilt, excellent. Hood's 104-660 1974 $450

SMITH, WILLIAM 1859-   Political Leaders of Upper Canada. Toronto, 1931. Hood's 104-57 1974 $22.50

SMITH, WILLIAM 1859-   Political Leaders of Upper Canada. Toronto, 1931. Hood's 102-45 1974 $22.50

SMITH, WILLIAM ABBOTTS   On Human Entozoa. London, 1863. 8vo., orig. brown cloth. Dawsons PM 249-454 1974 £12

SMITH, WILLIAM HENRY   Bacon and Shakespeare. 1858. Second edition, covers worn, very good copy, wrappers. Covent 51-1666 1973 £15.15

SMITH, WILLIAM RUDOLPH   The History of Wisconsin. Madison, 1854. 2 vols., orig. cloth, first edition. Bradley 35-410 1974 $60

SMITH, WILLIAM RUDOLPH   The History of Wisconsin. Madison, 1854. 8vo., orig. gilt stamped cloth, fine. Butterfield 8-737 1974 $25

SMITH, WILLIAM RUDOLPH   Incidents of a Journey from Pennsylvania to Wisconsin Territory in 1837. Chicago, 1927. Limited to 115 copies, very fine copy. Jenkins 61-2365 1974 $42.50

SMITH, WILLIAM WYE   Poems. Toronto, 1888. Inscribed, signed. Hood's 104-791 1974 $12.50

SMITH, WINEHELL   Lightnin'. French, 1918. Austin 51-905 1973 $7.50

SMITH'S Directory for Reading & Neighbourhood. Reading, 1875. Contemporary cloth, orig. wrappers. Smith 194-253 1974 £6.50

SMITH-DAMPIER, J. L.   Carthusian Worthies. Oxford, 1940. Howes 185-462 1974 £6.50

SMITHHANDERS, ERNST   Land Und Leute in Nordamerika. Berlin, 1926. Austin 62-603 1974 $27.50

SMOKING and Smokers. London, 1851. 8vo., orig. cloth, gilt, illus., first edition. Hammond 201-1001 1974 £9

SMOLLETT, TOBIAS GEORGE   The Adventures of Peregrine Pickle. London, 1776. 4 vols., 12mo., contemporary tree calf, spines gilt, bit rubbed, frontis., very good copy, sixth edition. Ximenes 37-195 1974 $45

SMOLLETT, TOBIAS GEORGE   Adventures of Peregrine Pickle. (1929). Illus., complete in 1 vol. Austin 61-927 1974 $10

SMOLLETT, TOBIAS GEORGE   The Adventures of Roderick Random. London, 1748. 2 vols., 12mo., contemporary calf, fine, second edition. Ximenes 35-238 1974 $150

SMOLLETT, TOBIAS GEORGE   The Expedition of Humphry Clinker. London, 1771. 3 vols., 12mo., contemporary calf-backed boards, morocco labels, first edition, first issue. Dawsons PM 252-905 1974 £350

SMOLLETT, TOBIAS GEORGE   The Expedition of Humphry Clinker. London, 1771. 3 vols., 12mo., contemporary calf, bit worn, armorial bookplate of Thomas Fletcher, second edition. Ximenes 37-196 1974 $75

SMOLLETT, TOBIAS GEORGE   The History and Adventures of an Atom. London, 1769. 2 vols., 12mo., contemporary calf, first edition. Ximenes 35-239 1974 $275

SMOLLETT, TOBIAS GEORGE   The History of England. Edinburgh, Glasgow and London, 1818. 8vo., 5 vols., contemporary calf, gilt. Dawsons PM 251-339 1974 £28

SMOLLETT, TOBIAS GEORGE   The History of England from the Revolution in 1688, to the Death of George II. 1810-1811. 6 vols., 8vo., contemporary half calf, engravings on copper and wood, joints broken, some covers detached. Bow Windows 66-646 1974 £7.50

SMOLLETT, TOBIAS GEORGE   The History of England, from the Revolution to the Death of George II. 1812. 5 vols., contemporary diced calf, gilt. Howes 186-1223 1974 £25

SMOLLETT, TOBIAS GEORGE   Travels Through France and Italy. 1766. 8vo., 2 vols., contemporary calf, first edition. Quaritch 936-216 1974 £80

SMOLLETT, TOBIAS GEORGE Works, With Memoirs of His Life. 1797.
8 vols., half calf, blind stamp on titles. Allen 216-R 1974 $50

SMOLLETT, TOBIAS GEORGE Miscellaneous Works. Bohn, 1858. 3 vols.,
plates, contemporary half crimson morocco. Howes 186-427 1974 £6.50

SMUCKER, S. M. Arctic Explorations and Discoveries During the
19th Century. New York, 1857. Foxing, staining, worn. Hood's 103-85
1974 $17.50

SMYTH, HENRY DE WOLF Atomic Energy for Military Purposes.
Princeton, 1945. Printed wrappers, illus., first trade edition. Bradley 35-349
1974 $75

SMYTH, SIR JAMES CARMICHAEL Precis of the Wars in Canada, 1755-1814.
London, 1862. Hood's 102-93 1974 $75

SMYTH, SIR JAMES CARMICHAEL Precis of the Wars in Canada, 1755-1814.
London, 1862. Hood's 104-102 1974 $75

SMYTH, MARY W. Biblical Quotations In Middle English
Literature Before 1350. 1911. Ex-library, sturdy library binding, orig. edition.
Austin 61-928 1974 $12.50

SMYTH, NEWMAN Passing Protestantism and Coming Catholicism.
Scribners, 1912. Austin 62-604 1974 $7.50

SMYTH, WILLIAM HENRY The Life and Services of Captain Philip Beaver.
London, 1829. 8vo., orig. boards, fine, first edition. Ximenes 35-240 1974 $45

SMYTH, WILLIAM HENRY Nautical Observations. 1840. 8vo., orig.
cloth, scarce. Broadhurst 23-1543 1974 £15

SMYTHIES, B. E. Birds of Burma. Rangoon, 1940. Roy. 8vo.,
orig. cloth, folding map, coloured plates, good copy, extremely scarce, orig.
edition. Wheldon 128-566 1973 £50

SMYTH'S Penny Almanac for 1894. 8vo., unbound, 6 items. Emerald 50-42
1974 £20

SNEAD-COX, J. G. The Life of Cardinal Vaughan. 1910. 2 vols.,
thick 8vo., plates. Howes 185-1741 1974 £6.50

SNELGRAVE, WILLIAM A New Account of Some Parts of Guinea.
London, 1734. 8vo., contemporary calf, first edition. Ximenes 35-241
1974 $300

SNELGROVE, L. E. The Introduction of Queen Bees. Bleadon,
1943. 8vo., cloth, plates, second edition. Wheldon 129-723 1974 £5

SNELGROVE, L. E. The Introduction of Queen Bees. Bleadon,
1943. 8vo., cloth, plates. Wheldon 131-858 1974 £5

SNELGROVE, L. E. Swarming. (1934). 8vo., cloth. Wheldon
219-722 1974 £5

SNELGROVE, L. E. Swarming. 1935. 8vo., cloth, second edition.
Wheldon 130-796 1974 £5

SNELGROVE, L. E. Swarming, Its Control and Prevention.
Weston-Super-Mare, (1943). 8vo., cloth, frontispiece. Wheldon 131-859
1974 £5

SNELL, HENRY JAMES Practical Instructions in Enamel Painting on Glass.
London, n.d. 8vo., orig. cloth, gilt, illus. Hammond 201-948 1974 £7

SNELL, WILLEBRORD Cyclometricus. 1621. 4to., modern half tan
morocco, fine, first edition. Zeitlin 235-208 1974 $750

SNELL, WILLEBRORD Tiphys Batavus. 1624. Small 4to., half mottled
calf, gilt, fine, rare, first edition. Zeitlin 235-210 1974 $650

SNELLEN VAN VOLLENHOVEN, S. C. Essai d'Une Faune Entomologique de
l'Archipel Indo-Neerlandais, Monographies 1 - 3. The Hague, 1863-68. 3 vols.,
4to., wrappers, coloured plates, rare. Wheldon 128-804 1973 £25

SNELLEN VAN VOLLENHOVEN, S. C. Essai d'Une Faune Entomologique de
l'Archipel Indo-Neerlandais, Monographies 1 - 3. The Hague, 1863-68.
3 vols. in 1, 4to., half morocco, coloured plates, rare. Wheldon 128-805
1973 £30

SNIDER, C. H. J. The Glorious "Shannon's" Old Blue Duster and
Other Faded Flags of Fadeless Fame. Toronto, 1923. Illus. Hood's 103-560
1974 $17.50

SNIDER, C. H. J. The Glorious "Shannon's" Old Blue Duster and
Other Faded Flags of Fadeless Fame. Toronto, 1923. Illus. Hood's 104-837
1974 $17.50

SNODGRASS, R. E. Anatomy and Physiology of the Honeybee.
New York, 1925. 8vo., cloth, scarce. Wheldon 129-724 1974 £7.50

SNOW, CHARLES PERCY Richard Aldington. n.d. Portrait, fine, scarce,
wrappers. Covent 51-2567 1973 £10.50

SNOW, EDWARD ROWE Famous New England Lighthouses. Boston,
1945. First edition, orig. binding. Wilson 63-59 1974 $10

SNOW, EDWARD ROWE The Romance of Boston Bay. Boston, 1944.
Illus. Jenkins 61-1533 1974 $10

SNOW, JACK The Magical Mimics In Oz. Chicago, 1946.
Sm. 4to., 1st ed. Frohnsdorff 16-87 1974 $15

SNOWDEN, JAMES ROSS A Description of the Medals of Washington.
Philadelphia, 1861. 4to., facsimile engravings, orig. binding. Butterfield 10-
517 1974 $65

SNOWDEN, MARY ROSS The Uninvited Christmas Guest and Other Stories.
Pittsburg, 1914. First edition, 12mo., autographed presentation copy, back cover
and part of spine water damaged, some staining on page tops of contents, else good.
Current BW9-81 1974 $9.75

SNOWDEN, RICHARD The History of North and South America. Philadelphia, 1818. New cloth, rebound. Hayman 57-686 1974 $10

SOBEL, BERNARD The Theatre Handbook & Digest of Plays. 1940.
First U. S. edition, fine, presentation inscription by editor. Covent 51-1817
1973 £8.40

SOBOL, LOUIS The Longest Street. Crown. 448p., illus.
Austin 51-906 1973 $8.50

SOBOLEW, D. Mittel-Devon des Kielce-Sandomir-Gebirges.
St. Petersburg, 1909. 8vo., plates. Wheldon 129-867 1974 £5

SOBY, JAMES T. Twentieth-Century Italian Art. New York,
1949. Sm. 4to., illus. sgd. Biblo & Tannen 214-507 1974 $27.50

SOBY, JAMES T. Twentieth-Century Italian Art. New York,
1949. 143 plates, 5 in color. Biblo & Tannen 214-508 1974 $15

SOCIAL Harmony. A Collection of the Most Esteemed and Celebrated Glees,
Catches, Canzonets, Rounds, Canons, etc., by the Most Eminent Composers.
n.d. New Binding, brown cloth. Eaton Music-524 1973 £5

SOCIETA INTERNAZIONALE DI MICROBIOLOGIA Bolletino, Sezzione
Italiana. Milan, 1929-39. Vols. 1 - 11 No. 6, 8vo., parts as issued. Wheldon
128-64 1973 £18

SOCIETE ROYALE DES ANTIQUARIES DU NORD Atlas de l'Archeologie du
Nord Representant des Echantillons de l'Age de Bronze et l'Age der Fer.
Copenhagen, 1857. Folio, contemporary boards, cloth spine, plates. Quaritch
940-355 1974 £9

SOCIETY OF INDUSTRIAL ENGINEERS U. S. Industrial Design, 1949-1950.
New York, 1949. 4to., illus. Biblo & Tannen 210-124 1973 $17.50

SOEMMERRING, DETMAR WILHELM De Oculorum Hominis Anamaliumque Sectione Horizontali Commentatio. Gottingen, 1818. Folio, orig. wrappers, first
edition. Schumann 35-443 1974 $125

SOEMMERRING, SAMUEL THOMAS Abbildungen des Menschlichen Auges.
Frankfurt, 1801. Folio, contemporary boards, plates, first edition. Schumann 35-
444 1974 $95

SOEMMERRING, SAMUEL THOMAS   Icones Organorum Humanorum Olfactus. Frankfurt, 1810. Folio, modern half cloth, orig. boards, first Latin edition. Schumann 35-445 1974 $165

SOEMMERING, SAMUEL THOMAS   Uber den Saft, Welcher aus den Nerven Wieder Eingesaugt Wird. Landshut, 1811. 8vo., orig. boards, first edition in German. Schuman 37-239 1974 $95

SOKOLSKY, GEORGE   We Jews. Doubleday, Doran, 1935. Austin 62-605 1974 $10

SOLANO DE LUQUE, FRANCISCO   Observaciones Sobre el Pulso. Madrid, 1787. 8vo., contemporary calf. Schumann 35-446 1974 $115

SOLDAN, W. G.   Geschichte der Hexenprozesse. Munich, (1911). 8vo., 2 vols., morocco-backed boards. Schumann 35-447 1974 $145

A SOLEMN Appeal to the Citizens of Great Britain and Ireland Upon the Present Emergency. London, 1788. 8vo., disbound, first edition. Ximenes 35-25 1974 $15

SOLIS, ANTONIO DE   Istoria Della Conquista del Messico. Firenze, 1709. Large thick quarto, first Italian edition. Jenkins 61-2366 1974 $45

SOLIS-COHEN, S.   Pharmacotherapeutics, Materia Medica and Drug Action. New York & London, 1928. 8vo., orig. cloth, first edition. Gurney 66-173 1974 £12.50

SOLLAS, W. J.   The Age of the Earth and Other Geological Studies. 1905. 8vo., cloth, gilt, illus., first edition. Hammond 201-391 1974 £5

SOLLAS, W. J.   Ancient Hunters and Their Modern Representatives. 1911. Orig. buckram gilt, plates. Smith 193-44 1973 £5

SOLLERIUS, JOANNES BAPTISTA   Acta S. Rumoldi, Episcopi et Martyris, Apostoli et Patroni Mechliniensium. Antwerp, 1718. Folio, contemporary calf gilt, plates. Howes 185-1616 1974 £15

SOLMS-LAUBACH, H.   Fossil Botany. Oxford, 1891. 8vo., orig. half morocco, illus. Wheldon 130-969 1974 £15

SOLON, LOUIS MARC EMMANUEL   The Art of the English Potter. 1885. Illus., revised second edition. Covent 55-487 1974 £8.50

SOLON, LOUIS MARC EMMANUEL   A History and Description of Italian Majolica. London, (1907). 8vo., orig. cloth, plates, illus., limited. Bow Windows 62-850 1974 £28

SOLON, LOUIS MARC EMMANUEL   A History of the Old French Faience. London, 1903. 8vo., plates, illus., browned, orig. cloth, limited. Bow Windows 62-851 1974 £16

SOLON, LOUIS MARC EMMANUEL   Sale Catalogue of the Pottery and Porcelain in the Collection of. 1912. 4to., plates, buckram, scarce. Quaritch 940-664 1974 £11

SOLVYNS, B.   The Costume of Hindostan . . . 1798 and 1799. 1804. Folio, plates, half red morocco. Quaritch 940-737 1974 £150

SOMAIZE, ANTOINE BAUDEAU DE   Le Dictionnaire des Precieuses. Paris, 1856. 2 vols., 12mo., cloth, uncut. L. Goldschmidt 42-119 1974 $25

SOMARE, ENRICO   Exhibition of Italian 19th Century Paintings. New York, 1949. 4to., color plates. Biblo & Tannen 214-226 1974 $32.50

SOME Events of Boston and Its Neighbors. Boston, 1917. First edition, 8vo., illus., pristine. Current BW9-391 1974 $10

SOME Experiences of Boss Neff in the Texas and Oklahoma Panhandle. Amarillo, 1941. 1st ed., illus. Dykes 24-146 1974 $40

SOME Feudal Lords and their Seals. 1904. 3 vols., roy. 4to., cloth, illus. Quaritch 939-716 1974 £20

SOME Interesting Boston Events. Boston, 1916. First edition, 8vo., illus., except for small crack at top of spine it is mint. Current BW9-392 1974 $10

SOME NEW Letters and Writings of Lafcadio Hearn. Tokyo, 1925. Cloth, frontispiece. Dawson's 424-273 1974 $25

SOME of the Contributions of Italy and Her Sons to Civilization and American Life. 1933, n.p. Austin 62-131 1974 $12.50

SOMERS   A Collection of Scarce and Valuable Tracts. 1809-15. 13 vols., 4to., plates, half morocco, second & best edition. Quaritch 939-251 1974 £180

SOMERSET, EDWARD MARQUIS OF WORCESTER Please turn to WORCESTER, EDWARD SOMERSET

SOMERSET, G. A.   Day After the Fair. French, 1827. 33p. Austin 51-907 1973 $6.50

SOMERVELL, THOMAS HOWARD   After Everest: The Experiences of a Mountaineer and Medical Missionary. 1936. Plates, maps, first edition, orig. cloth, med. 8vo., fine. Broadhurst 24-1685 1974 £5

SOMERVILLE, D. M. M. C.   Ski-Running. 1904. 8vo., orig. boards, plates, illus. Bow Windows 66-650 1974 £5

SOMERVILLE, E.   In Mr. Knox's Country. 1915. Crown 8vo., orig. green cloth, illus., first edition. Howes 185-463 1974 £7.50

SOMERVILLE, MARY   Mechanism of the Heavens. London, 1831. 8vo., cloth, first edition. Dawsons PM 245-685 1974 £13

SOMERVILLE, WILLIAM   The Chace. 1735. 4to., contemporary sprinkled calf, rebacked, first edition. Quaritch 936-218 1974 £65

SOMERVILLE, WILLIAM   The Chase. London, 1735. 8vo., later half calf, first octavo edition. Ximenes 35-242 1974 $35

SOMERVILLE, WILLIAM   The Chase. Dublin, 1766. 12mo., disbound. Ximenes 35-243 1974 $10

SOMERVILLE, WILLIAM   The Chase. Bulmer, 1796. 4to., new boards, woodcuts, water stained. Quaritch 940-25 1974 £35

SOMERVILLE, WILLIAM   The Chase. London, 1796. Small 8vo., new edition, contemporary half calf. Hammond 201-331 1974 £9

SOMERVILLE, WILLIAM   The Chase. London, 1800. Small 8vo., cloth, gilt, plates, new edition. Hammond 201-332 1974 £7.50

SOMERVILLE, WILLIAM   The Chase. London, 1802. Full Calf, gilt, blindstamped. Dawson's 424-50 1974 $85

SOMERVILE, WILLIAM   The Chase. London, 1817. Small 8vo., contemporary half calf, plates, illus. Hammond 201-333 1974 £10

SOMERVILLE, WILLIAM   On the Diuretic Properties of the Pyrola Umbellata. London, 1814. 8vo., modern boards. Dawsons PM 249-455 1974 £9

SOMMARIO DELLE vite de Gl'Imperatori Romani. 1637. 4to., disbound, illus. Dawsons PM 251-178 1974 £10

SOMMER, OSKAR   The Arthurian Romances, Vulgate Version. Washington, 1908-16. 1st ed., uncut, 4to., 7 vols. Biblo & Tannen 214-586 1974 $200

SOMMERFELD, ARNOLD   Atombau und Spektrallinien. Braunschweig, 1919. 8vo., illus., orig. printed wrappers, first edition. Gilhofer 61-84 1974 sFr. 300

SOMMERVILLE, WILLIAM   Hobbinol, Field Sports, and the Bowling Green. London, 1813. Marbled boards, unopened, calf. Dawsons 424-120 1974 $70

SOMNER, WILLIAM   The Antiquities of Canterbury. London, 1703. Folio, contemporary diced russia, fine, second edition. Dawsons PM 251-70 1974 £85

SOMNER, WILLIAM   A Treatise of Gavelkind. 1660. Small 4to., contemporary sheep, rebacked. Howes 186-2063 1974 £25

SOMNER, WILLIAM   A Treatise of Gavelkind. 1726. Crown 4to., contemporary calf, second edition. Howes 186-2064 1974 £40

THE SONG of Roland. New York, 1938. Biblo & Tannen 210-741 1973 $10

A SONGBOOK for Socialists. n.d. (c. 1885). Very good copy, wrappers, first edition. Covent 51-1727 1973 £7.50

SONGS of the South. Doubleday, Page, 1913. 333p., 3rd ed. Austin 54-248 1973 $12.50

THE SONGSTER'S Companion. Brattleborough, 1815. 12mo., contemporary sheep, rubbed, foxed. Ximenes 35-247 1974 $27.50

SONNECK, OSCAR GEORGE T.   Early Opera in America. New York, 1915. First edition, illus. Biblo & Tannen 214-919 1974 $10

SONNECK, OSCAR GEORGE T.   Report on "The Star-Spangled Banner", "Hail Columbia", "America" and "Yankee Doodle". Washington, 1909. Plates, 8vo., back cover spotted, interior fine. Current BW9-437 1974 $20

SONNENSCHEIN, WILLIAM SWAN   The Best Books. London, 1910-35. 6 vols., 4to., orig. boards, third edition. Dawsons PM 10-573 1974 £70

SONNERAT, PIERRE   Voyage a la Nouvelle Guinee. Paris, 1776. 4to., contemporary calf, plates, leather label, first edition. Traylen 79-538 1973 £160

SONNERAT, PIERRE   Voyage a la Nouvelle Guinee. Paris, 1776. 4to., modern half calf antique style, engraved plates, rare. Wheldon 128-237 1973 £140

SONNERAT, PIERRE   Voyage Aux Indes Orientales et a la Chine. Paris, 1782. 2 vols., 4to., contemporary calf, plates, leather labels, first edition. Traylen 79-537 1973 £125

SONNERAT, PIERRE   Voyage Aux Indes Orientales et la Chine. Paris, 1782. 3 vols., plates, old half calf, worn, first 8vo. edition. Bow Windows 62-852 1974 £125

SONS OF ITALY   Will You Guide Me? New York, n.d., ca. 1923. 20p., illus. Austin 62-287 1974 $12.50

THE SONS of the Sires; a History of the Rise, Progress and Destiny of the American Party. Philadelphia, 1855. First edition, orig. binding, corner wear, backstrip edges measurably worn. Wilson 63-154 1974 $20

THE SONS of the Sires: A History of the Rise, Progress, and Destiny of the American Party . . . to Which is Added a Review of the Letter of Henry A. Wise Against the Know-Nothings. Philadelphia, 1855. Foxed. Jenkins 61-1324 1974 $25

SOPHOCLES   Sophoclis Aiax Flagellifer. Lyon, 1550. 8vo., old boards, gilt leather back, label, first edition. Harper 213-145 1973 $325

SOPHOCLES   Sophoclis Tragoediae Septem. 1786. 2 vols., 4to., old calf, gilt, rebacked. Bow Windows 62-853 1974 £15.50

SOPHOCLES   Tragedies. Oxford, 1849. Austin 51-908 1973 $6.50

SOREL, ALBERT   L'Europe et la Revolution Francaise. Paris, 1913-18. 8 vols., large 8vo., cloth. Howes 186-1225 1974 £32

SORELLI, GUIDO   The Nun of Florence. 1840. Orig. blind stamped cloth, faded, first edition. Howes 185-465 1974 £6.50

SORENSON, ALFRED   History of Omaha from the Pioneer Days to the Present Time. Omaha, 1889. Cloth, fine. Hayman 57-693 1974 $17.50

SOTHEBY, WILLIAM   The Georgics of Virgil. London, 1800. 8vo., contemporary calf, gilt, first edition. Ximenes 35-248 1974 $35

SOTHEBY, WILLIAM   A Tour Through Parts of Wales. 1794. 4to., plates, contemporary marbled boards, uncut. Quaritch 939-695 1974 £55

SOTHEBY, FIRM, AUCTIONEERS, LONDON   Catalogue of the Renowned Collection of Western Manuscripts, the Property of A. Chester Beatty, Esq. London, 1932-33. 2 vols., plates. Kraus B8-38 1974 $125

SOTHEBY, FIRM, AUCTIONEERS, LONDON   Lord Taunton Heirlooms. 1920. Plates. Kraus B8-248 1974 $15

SOTHEBY, FIRM, AUCTIONEERS, LONDON   The Stourhead Heirlooms. 1883. Half red morocco, board loose. Kraus B8-245 1974 $125

SOTHERN, EDWARD H.   Julia Marlowe's Story. Rinehart, 1954. Austin 51-909 1973 $6.50

SOTHERN, EDWARD H.   The Melancholy Tale of Me. Scribner, 1916. Austin 51-910 1973 $7.50

SOUBIES, ALBERT   Histoire de la Musique en Russia. Paris, 1898. Book plate, inscription, English first edition. Covent 56-975 1974 £5.25

SOUBIES, ALBERT   Historie de la Musique en Russie. Paris, 1898. Orig. dec. cloth, illus., English first edition. Covent 56-1954 1974 £5.25

SOULIE, FREDERIC   Confession Generale. Paris, 1857. 2 vols., 8vo., contemporary half cherry red sheep, gilt. L. Goldschmidt 42-376 1974 $15

SOULIE, GEORGE   Strange Stories from the Lodge of Leisures. London, 1913. 12mo., 1st ed. Biblo & Tannen 210-670 1973 $15

SOUPAULT, PHILIPPE   Lurcat. Paris, 1928. Large 4to., wrappers, limited edition. Minters 37-103 1973 $24

SOUPAULT, PHILIPPE   Souvenirs de James Joyce. Algiers, 1943. Portraits, English first edition. Covent 56-759 1974 £65

SOUPAULT, PHILIPPE   William Blake. 1928. Illus., fine, English first edition. Covent 56-156 1974 £12.50

SOUSA, JOHN PHILIP   The Fifth String. London, 1903. Illus., first English edition, 8vo., plum gilt dec. cloth with minor spots, bookplate, very good, presentation from author. Current BW9-278 1974 $30

SOUSELY, CLARENCE   Tales by the Tramp. Chicago, ca. 1910. Biblo & Tannen 213-817 1973 $12.50

SOUTH, RICHARD   Catalogue of the Collection of Palaearctic Butterflies. 1902. 4to., orig. cloth, portrait, plates. Bow Windows 64-253 1974 £8.50

SOUTH, ROBERT   Sermons Preached Upon Several Occasions. Oxford, 1842. 5 vols., full buff calf, gilt, fine, best edition. Howes 185-1659 1974 £28

SOUTH AFRICAN PHILOSOPHICAL SOCIETY   Transactions. Cape Town, 1878-1909. Vols. 1 - 18, 8vo. and roy. 8vo., cloth, very scarce. Wheldon 128-67 1973 £100

THE SOUTH Bend Fugitive Slave Case, Involving the Right to a Writ of Habeas Corpus. New York, 1851. Wrapper. Butterfield 10-113 1974 $7.50

SOUTH Carolina and Arkansas: Papers and Proceedings. Washington, 1868. Jenkins 61-161 1974 $12.50

SOUTHACK, JOHN   The Life of. N.P., 1809. 8vo., contemporary half calf, rare, first edition. Ximenes 35-253 1974 $150

SOUTHALL, J. E.   Wales and her Language. Newport, 1892. 8vo., orig. cloth. Broadhurst 23-1544 1974 £5

SOUTHALL, JAMES P. C.   Mirrors, Prisms and Lenses. New York, 1923. 8vo., dark green cloth, gilt, illus., second edition. Dawsons PM 245-686 1974 £6

SOUTHERN, TERRY   Candy. Putnam, 1964. 224p. Austin 54-961 1973 $6.50

SOUTHERN Lights and Shadows. Harper, 1907. 288p. Austin 54-567 1973 $6.50

SOUTHERN Table Book: A New Selection of Arithmetical Tables . . . For the Use of Schools. Charleston, 1857. 24mo., wrapper. Butterfield 10-67 1974 $10

SOUTHERN WHALE FISHERY COMPANY   Abstract Reports From the Comissioner of . . . to the Directors. London, 1850. 8vo., orig. grey printed wrappers, folding map, very scarce, first edition. Ximenes 37-157 1974 $60

THE SOUTHERN Zion's Songster. Raleigh, 1864. 16mo., orig. buff printed wrappers, somewhat chipped, very scarce. Ximenes 36-55 1974 $80

SOUTHERNE, THOMAS   The Fatal Marriage. London, 1694. 4to., calf antique, first edition. Dawsons PM 252-906 1974 £130

SOUTHEY, ROBERT   All for Love. London, 1829. 8vo., orig. green cloth, label, frontispiece, first edition. Ximenes 35-254 1974 $35

SOUTHEY, ROBERT   All for Love. London, 1829. 8vo., orig. cloth, paper label, first edition. Dawsons PM 252-907 1974 £25

SOUTHEY, ROBERT   The Book of the Church. 1825. 2 vols., full half calf, gilt, morocco labels. Howes 185-1660 1974 £10

SOUTHEY, ROBERT   Common Place Book. 1849. 416 pages. Austin 61-930 1974 $17.50

SOUTHEY, ROBERT   Commonplace Book. 1850-51. 4 vols., new buckram, blind stamp, second edition. Allen 216-1605 1974 $30

SOUTHEY, ROBERT   The Doctor. 1836. 2 vols. in 1. Austin 61-931 1974 $10

SOUTHEY, ROBERT   Essays, Moral and Political. London, 1832. 2 vols., 8vo., orig. quarter cloth and boards, printed paper labels, very good copy, scarce, first edition. Ximenes 37-197 1974 $65

SOUTHEY, ROBERT   The Expedition of Orsua. Philadelphia, 1821. 12mo., orig. boards, orange paper backstrip, printed paper label, first American edition. Ximenes 37-198 1974 $45

SOUTHEY, ROBERT   Expedition of Orsua: and Crimes of Aguirre. Philadelphia, 1821. Boards, spine, worn, foxed. Allen 216-2066 1974 $12.50

SOUTHEY, ROBERT   Joan of Arc. London, 1806. 2 vols., 12mo., contemporary mottled calf, gilt, third edition. Ximenes 35-255 1974 $45

SOUTHEY, ROBERT   The Life of Nelson. London, 1813. 2 vols., 8vo., orig. boards, rare, first edition. Ximenes 35-256 1974 $175

SOUTHEY, ROBERT   Omniana, or Horae Otiosiores. 1812. 2 vols., new buckram, blind stamp, first edition. Allen 216-1609 1974 $25

SOUTHEY, ROBERT   The Poetical Works of. London, 1837-38. 10 vols., small 8vo., frontispieces, contemporary gilt framed calf, morocco labels, faded. Bow Windows 62-856 1974 £40

SOUTHEY, ROBERT   Southey's Common-Place Book. 1876. 4 vols., thick 8vo., orig. green cloth. Howes 185-466 1974 £18.50

SOUTHEY, ROBERT   A Tale of Paraguay. London, 1825. 12mo., contemporary half calf, first edition. Ximenes 35-257 1974 $45

SOUTHGATE, FRANK   Wildfowl & Waders. (1940). Crown 4to., orig. cloth, book plate. Bow Windows 64-255 1974 £9.50

SOUTHWICK, GEORGE J.   Jokes Without Whiskers. Chicago, 1904. 95p. Austin 54-962 1973 $7.50

SOUTHWICK, GEORGE J.   Southwicks Monologues. Chicago, 1903. 96p., paper. Austin 54-963 1973 $7.50

SOUTHWICK, SOLOMON   Address Deliverd. Albany, 1821. 8vo., disbound, first edition. Ximenes 35-258 1974 $17.50

SOUVARINE, BORIS   Stalin. c.1937. Roy. 8vo., scarce. Howes 186-1584 1974 £7.50

SOUVENIR Historical Book Issued in Connection With the Sesqui-Centennial Celebration of Huntingdon County, Pennsylvania. (Huntingdon), 1937. 4to., wrapper. Saddleback 14-671 1974 $10

SOUVESTRE, E.   Tryphina la Jolie Jean Rouge-Gorge. (c. 1840). 8vo., colored pictorial boards, color plates. Gregory 44-59 1974 $15

SOUVIROS, GUILLAUME   Traicte de la Dysenterie. 1574. 12mo., modern red crushed morocco, gilt. Dawsons PM 249-456 1974 £385

SOVA, ANTONIN   Balada O Jednom Cloveku a Jeho Radostech. Prague, n.d. Large 4to., wrappers, illus., plates. Minters 37-250 1973 $25

SOVER, BARTHOLOMEW   Curvi ac Recti Proportio. 1630. 4to., contemporary English blindruled calf, fine, first edition. Dawsons PM 245-687 1974 £56

SOWERBY, A. DE C.   A Sportsman's Miscellany. 1917. 8vo., illus., cloth, scarce. Wheldon 128-238 1973 £10

SOWERBY, GEORGE BRETTINGHAM   Illustrated Index of British Shells. 1887. Roy. 8vo., orig. red cloth, plates, scarce, second edition. Wheldon 130-835 1974 £30

SOWERBY, GEORGE BRETTINGHAM   Popular British Conchology. 1854. Post 8vo., orig. dec. cloth, gilt, hand coloured plates by author, scarce. Wheldon 128-855 1973 £10

SOWERBY, GEORGE BRETTINGHAM   Popular British Conchology. 1854. Post 8vo., orig. dec. cloth, gilt, plates. Wheldon 131-907 1974 £10

SOWERBY, GITHA   Yesterday's Children. 1908. 4to., orig. red cloth, gilt, fine, plates, illus. Hammond 201-143 1974 £6

SOWERBY, J. G.   Afternoon Tea. C., 1880. 4to., orig. printed boards, dustwrapper, illus. Hammond 201-144 1974 £7.50

SOWERBY, JAMES   English Botany. London, 1790-1814. 8vo., 36 vols., green half morocco, gilt, plates, first edition. Hammond 201-676 1974 £795

SOWERBY, JAMES   English Botany. 1790-1814. 8vo., contemporary calf, plates. Wheldon 129-45 1974 £550

SOWERBY, JAMES   English Botany. 1790-1814. 8vo., contemporary half calf, plates. Wheldon 130-1110 1974 £500

SOWERBY, JAMES   English Botany. 1790-1866. 8vo., new buckram. Wheldon 130-1109 1974 £700

SOWERBY, JAMES   English Botany. (1832-) 1835-40. 7 vols., 8vo., modern cloth, uncut, hand-coloured plates. Wheldon 128-1221 1973 £60

SOWERBY, JAMES   English Botany. (1832-) 1835-46. 8vo., contemporary half green morocco, plates, second edition. Wheldon 130-1111 1974 £300

SOWERBY, JAMES   English Botany. (1847-) 1849-51. 4 vols., 8vo., orig. cloth, rare, hand-coloured plates, third edition. Wheldon 128-1222 1973 £25

SOWERBY, JAMES   The Mineral Conchology of Great Britain. 1812-29(-1846). 8vo., buckram, plates. Wheldon 129-868 1974 £300

SOWERBY, JAMES   The Mineral Conchology of Great Britain. 1812-29. 6 vols., 8vo., buckram, plates. Wheldon 131-1080 1974 £300

SOWERBY, JOHN EDWARD   British Wild Flowers. 1894 or 1914. Roy. 8vo., cloth, hand-coloured plates. Wheldon 128-1223 1973 £15

SOWERBY, JOHN EDWARD   British Wild Flowers. 1914. Roy. 8vo., publisher's cloth, hand-coloured plates & frontispiece. Wheldon 128-1224 1973 £15

SOWERBY, JOHN EDWARD   British Wild Flowers. London, 1876. Roy 8vo., orig. cloth, gilt, illus., new edition. Hammond 201-678 1974 £30

SOWERBY, JOHN EDWARD   British Wild Flowers. 1876. Roy. 8vo., orig. cloth, plates. Wheldon 130-1112 1974 £20

SOWERBY, JOHN EDWARD   British Wild Flowers. 1914. Roy 8vo., cloth, plates. Wheldon 130-1113 1974 £15

SOWERBY, JOHN EDWARD   British Wild Flowers. 1863. 8vo., contemporary half morocco gilt, plates. Wheldon 129-1019 1974 £25

SOWERBY, JOHN EDWARD   British Wild Flowers. 1914. Roy. 8vo., pbulisher's Cloth, plates. Wheldon 131-1243 1974 £15

SOWERBY, JOHN EDWARD   British Poisonous Plants. London, 1861. 8vo., orig. cloth, gilt, plates, second edition. Hammond 201-677 1974 £20

SOWERBY, JOHN EDWARD   British Wild Flowers. London, 1860. 8vo., plates, calf gilt, leather label, first edition. Traylen 79-57 1973 £12

SOWERBY, JOHN EDWARD   British Wild Flowers. London, 1914. Roy. 8vo., cloth, frontispiece, plates. Traylen 79-58 1973 £9

SOWERBY, JOHN EDWARD   The Ferns of Great Britain. 1855-56. Roy 8vo., orig. cloth. Wheldon 129-1424 1974 £10

SOWERBY, JOHN EDWARD   The Ferns of Great Britain. 1855. 8vo., orig. cloth, plates. Wheldon 131-1468 1974 £5

SOWERBY, JOHN EDWARD   The Grasses of Great Britain. London, (1857). Roy 8vo., orig. cloth, gilt, plates. Hammond 201-679 1974 £27.50

SOWTER, JOHN   The Way to Be Wise and Wealthy. London, 1755. 8vo., plate, paper wrappers. Dawsons PM 247-275 1974 £15

SPAFFORD, HORATIO GATES   Some Cursory Observations on the Ordinary Construction of Wheel-Carriages. Albany, 1815. 8vo., old wrappers, first edition, very good copy, very uncommon. Ximenes 36-173 1974 $85

SPAIN and Spanish America in the Libraries of the University of California: A Catalogue of Books. Berkeley, 1928. 2 vols. Jenkins 61-2394 1974 $125

SPALDING, J. T.   A Bibliographical Account of the Works Relating to English Topography. Exeter, 1912-13. 5 vols., large 8vo., orig. quarter imitation vellum, cloth, uncut. Dawsons PM 10-575 1974 £210

SPALDING, JOSEPH   Spider Island. French, 1942. Austin 51-913 1973 $7.50

SPALDING, WALTER R.   Music. Boston, 1939. Biblo & Tannen 214-921 1974 $12.50

SPALDING, WILLIAM A.   History and Reminiscences, Los Angeles City and County, California. Los Angeles, (1931). 3 vols., 4to., cloth. Saddleback 14-286 1974 $37.50

SPALDING CLUB   A Series of the Publications from the Commencement. Aberdeen, 1841-54. 25 vols., 4to., cloth, plates. Quaritch 939-676 1974 £180

SPALLANZANI, LAZZARO   De Fenomeni Della Circolazione. Modena, 17-73. 8vo., orig. limp boards, first edition. Schumann 35-448 1974 $260

SPALLANZANI, LAZZARO   Experiences Pour Servir a l'Histoire des Animaux et des Plantes. Geneva, 1785. 8vo., contemporary marbled calf, first edition in French. Schumann 35-449 1974 $125

SPALLANZANI, LAZZARO   Experiences sur la Digestion. 1783. 8vo., contemporary half calf, first edition in French. Dawsons PM 249-457 1974 £45

SPALLANZANI, LAZARO   Experiences sur la Digestion de l'Homme et de Differentes Especes d'Animaux. Geneva, 1783. 8vo., contemporary calf, first edition in French. Schuman 37-240 1974 $225

SPALLANZANI, LAZZARO   Experiments upon the Circulation of the Blood. London, 1801. 8vo., modern half calf, first edition in English. Dawsons PM 249-458 1974 £85

SPALLANZANI, LAZZARO   Memorie su la Respirazione. 1803. 8vo., contemporary half calf, first edition. Dawsons PM 249-459 1974 £110

SPALLANZANI, LAZZARO   Viaggi alle Due Sicilie. Pavia, 1792-7. 8vo., 6 vols., orig. pasteboards, first edition. Gurney 64-202 1974 £125

SPALLANZANI, LAZZARO   Viaggi alle Due Sicilie e in Alcune Parti Dell' Appennino. Pavia, 1792-7. 8vo., 6 vols., orig. pasteboards, uncut, first edition, fine. Gurney 66-174 1974 £125

SPALTEHOLZ, WERNER   Hand Atlas of Human Anatomy. Philadelphia, n.d. 3 vols. Rittenhouse 46-597 1974 $15

SPANGENBERG, JOHANN   Margarita Theologica, Praecipuos Locos Doctrinae Christianae. Basel, 1544. 8vo., wrappers. Schumann 499-107 1974 sFr 540

SPANISH Art, an Introductory Review of Architecture, Painting, Sculpture, Textiles, Ceramics, Woodwork, Metalwork. 1927. 4to., cloth, illus. Eaton Music-674 1973 £20

SPARE, AUSTIN OSMAN   Anathema of Zos. (London), 1927. 4to., illus., drawing, frontispiece, paper wrappers. Bow Windows 62-857 1974 £28

SPARE, AUSTIN OSMAN   The Focus of Life. 1921. Frontispiece, illus., plates, cloth back, boards. Marsden 39-424 1974 £10

SPARGO, JOHN   The Jew and American Ideals. 1921. 148 pages. Austin 57-633 1974 $10

SPARKES, J. C. L.   Wild Flowers in Art and Nature. (1894). 4to., cloth, plates, scarce. Wheldon 129-1020 1974 £5

SPARKS, EDWIN EARLE   The English Settlement in Illinois. Cedar Rapids, 1907. Purple cloth, limited edition. Putnam 126-157 1974 $18

SPARLING, H. HALLIDAY   Irish Minstrelsy: Being a Selection of Irish Songs, Lyrics and Ballads. n.d. Frontis., spine darkened, nice copy, half buckram dec. boards. Covent 51-2103 1973 £10.50

SPARLING, H. HALLIDAY   The Kelmscott Press and William Morris. London, 1924. 8vo., plates, orig. boards, uncut. Dawsons PM 10-333 1974 £35

SPARRMAN, ANDERS   Tal, om Den Tilvaxt Och Nytta, Som Vetenskaperne I Allmanhet, Sardeles Natural-Historien. Stockholm, 1778. 8vo., modern cloth, uncut, very rare. Wheldon 131-185 1974 £60

SPARRMAN, ANDERS   A Voyage Round the World With Captain James Cook. 1944. Folio, frontispiece, morocco backed marbled boards, limited. Bow Windows 62-383 1974 £105

SPARRMAN, ANDERS   A Voyage Round the World With Captain James Cook in H. M. S. Resolution. Golden Cockerel Press, 1944. Limited to 350 copies, map, woodcuts, folio, orig. green buckram gilt, morocco label, top edges gilt, others uncut, fine, scarce. Sawyer 293-152 1974 £125

SPARROW, WALTER SHAW   Advertising and British Art. 1924. 4to., plates, illus., orig. boards, cloth spine. Quaritch 940-479 1974 £38

SPARROW, WALTER SHAW   Angling in British Art Through Five Centuries. 1923. 4to., illus., orig. cloth, good copy. Quaritch 940-246 1974 £20

SPARROW, WALTER SHAW   British Sporting Artists from Barlow to Herring. 1922. 4to., illus., orig. cloth gilt. Quaritch 940-245 1974 £45

SPARROW, WALTER SHAW   George Stubbs & Ben Marshall. 1929. 4to., half calf, leather label, plates. Quaritch 940-247 1974 £60

SPARROW, WALTER SHAW   George Stubbs and Ben Marshall. London, 1929. 4to., worn, plates. Traylen 79-292 1973 £12

SPARROW, WALTER SHAW   Henry Alken. 1927. Roy. 4to., plates, cloth, rubbed. Quaritch 940-6 1974 £28

SPARROW, WALTER SHAW   Prints and Drawings By Frank Brangwyn With Some Other Phases of His Art. London, 1919. Large 4to., cloth, illus., plates. Minters 37-492 1973 $18.50

SPEARS, JOHN R.   A History of the Mississippi Valley. New York, 1903. Cloth, illus. Hayman 57-694 1974 $12.50

SPECIMEN of a New Jest Book. London, 1810. 8vo., disbound, scarce, first edition. Ximenes 33-394 1974 $50

SPECIMENS OF Printing Types. New York, 1882, 1883, 1884 and 1885. Brown cloth, vignettes. Dawson's 424-143 1974 $350

THE SPECTATOR. London, 1747. 8 vols., old mottled calf, gilt. Jacobs 24-128 1974 $35

THE SPECTATOR. London, 1775. 8 vols., 8vo., foxing, contemporary tree calf, worn. Bow Windows 62-859 1974 £15

THE SPECTATOR. 1898. 8vo., 8 vols., buckram, portraits, first edition. Quaritch 936-579 1974 £60

SPECTATOR'S Gallery. 1933. Dull covers, signature. Covent 55-53 1974 £5.25

SPEECE, CONRAD   The Mountaineer. Staunton, 1823. 12mo., contemporary sheep, scarce, third edition. Ximenes 35-259 1974 $50

THE SPEECHES of Mr. Sheridan, Mr. Fox, Mr. Burke, Mr. Pitt, Major Scott, Mr. Beaufoy, etc. London, 1787. 8vo., modern boards. Dawsons PM 247-267 1974 £15

SPEECHLY, W.   A Treatise on the Culture of the Pine Apple. York, 1779. Roy 8vo., modern half calf, uncut, plates, rare, first edition. Wheldon 130-1488 1974 £35

SPEED, J.   Wales, Pembrok Shire, Glamorgan Shire, Mounmouth Shire. 1627. Maps. Quaritch 939-696 1974 £30

SPEED, SAMUEL   Fragmenta Carceris. London, 1674. Small 4to., diced russia, rare, first edition. Ximenes 35-260 1974 $250

SPEEDY, TOM   The Natural History of Sport in Scotland with Rod and Gun. Edinburgh and London, 1920. Small crown 4to., orig. cloth, illus., first edition. Bow Windows 64-256 1974 £12

SPEIDELL, JOHN   A Breefe Treatise of Sphaericall Triangles. London, 1627. 4to., contemporary limp vellum, fine, first edition. Dawsons PM 245-689 1974 £325

SPEIDELL, JOHN   A Geometricall Extraction. London, 1617. 4to., new boards, second edition. Dawsons PM 245-688 1974 £20

SPEIGHT, HAROLD E. B.   Life and Writings of John Bunyan. 1928. Austin 61-933 1974 $10

SPEKE, JOHN HANNING   Journal of the Discovery of the Source of the Nile. 1863. Thick demy 8vo., plates, illus., orig. cloth gilt. Smith 194-528 1974 £55

THE SPELLING-BOOK: A Companion to the Readers. Toronto, 1867. Spine mended, cover faded. Hood's 102-433 1974 $15

SPELMAN, HENRY   De Non Termerandis Ecclesiis, Churches Not to Be Violated. 1646. 3 works in 1 vol., small 4to., 19th century half calf. Howes 185-1661 1974 £35

SPELMAN, HENRY   The English Works. 1723. Folio, label, contemporary sprinkled calf, first collected edition. Quaritch 939-252 1974 £30

SPELMAN, HENRY   The History and Fate of Sacrilege. 1895. Thick 8vo., scarce, fourth edition. Howes 185-1662 1974 £5

SPELMAN, HENRY   Relation of Virginia 1609. London, 1872. Small 4to., orig. bindings, wrapper, uncut, unopened, limited edition. Butterfield 8-679 1974 $12.50

SPENCE, BEN W.   Prohibition in Canada. 1918. Wrappers, English first edition. Covent 56-211 1974 £5.25

SPENCE, JOSEPH   Anecdotes, Observations and Characters, of Books and Men. 1820. 8vo., orig. boards, first edition. Quaritch 936-580 1974 £40

SPENCE, JOSEPH   A Parallel. 1758. 8vo., contemporary calf, book-plate, first edition. Dawsons PM 252-908 1974 £85

SPENCE, LEWIS   A Dictionary of Medieval Romance and Romance Writers. London, (1913). Med. 8vo., orig. cloth. Forster 98-83 1974 £6

SPENCE, LEWIS   A Dictionary of Medieval Romance and Romance Writers. 1913. Thick 8vo., faded. Howes 186-1937 1974 £6.50

SPENCER, BALDWIN   Native Tribes of the Northern Territory of Australia. 1914. Roy. 8vo., orig. buckram, plates, first edition. Smith 193-468 1973 £15

SPENCER, C.   Compton Castle. (1856-61). 2 items in 1 vol., 4to., half morocco, plate, label. Quaritch 939-342 1974 £5

SPENCER, D. A.   The Cinema To-Day. 1939. Illus. Covent 55-412 1974 £7.50

SPENCER, HENRY   Men That Are Gone from the Households of Darlington. Darlington, (1862). 8vo., foxing, contemporary half sheep, rubbed. Bow Windows 62-860 1974 £10

SPENCER, HERBERT   Education: Intellectual, Moral and Physical. (1861). 8vo., orig. cloth, uncut, first edition. Hill 126-91 1974 £20

SPENCER, J. W. W.   The Duration of Niagara Falls and the History of the Great Lakes. New York, 1895. Illus., endpapers & part of covers stained. Hood's 102-637 1974 $15

SPENCER, J. W. W.   The Falls of Niagara. Ottawa, 1907. 8vo., folding map, plates, text-figures. Wheldon 128-1051 1973 £10

SPENCER, J. W. W.   The Falls of Niagara. Ottawa, 1907. 8vo., plates, frontispiece. Wheldon 131-1081 1974 £10

SPENCER, JOHN   A Discourse Concerning Prodigies. London, 1665. 8vo., contemporary sheep, second edition. Dawsons PM 252-909 1974 £35

SPENCER, JOHN   A Discovrse of Divers Petitions. London, 1461. 4to., contemporary morocco, gilt, morocco label, first edition. Dawsons PM 252-910 1974 £535

SPENCER, JOHN   Things New and Old. London, 1658. Folio, new calf antique, first edition. Dawsons PM 252-911 1974 £100

SPENCER, JOSEPH WILLIAM WINTHROP   The Duration of Niagara Falls and the History of the Great Lakes. New York, 1895. Illus. Hood's 104-736 1974 $15

SPENCER, L. J.   The World's Minerals. 1911. 8vo., cloth, coloured plates. Wheldon 128-1050 1973 £5

SPENCER, THEODORE   Studies in Metaphysical Poetry. 1939. Fine, wrappers, first American edition. Covent 55-1023 1974 £7.50

SPENCER, WALTER T.   Forty Years in My Bookshop. 1923. Plates, illus., orig. cloth, first edition. Marsden 39-427 1974 £8

SPENCER, WALTER G.   Diseases of the Tongue. London, 1931. 8vo., orig. red cloth, gilt. Dawsons PM 249-460 1974 £6

SPENDER, J. A.   Life of Herbert Henry Asquith. 1932. 2 vols., large 8vo., plates. Howes 186-577 1974 £7.50

SPENDER, J. A.   The Life of Sir Henry Campbell-Bannerman. (1923). 2 vols., thick 8vo., plates. Howes 186-680 1974 £7.50

SPENDER, JOHN KENT   Therapeutic Means for the Relief of Pain. London, 1874. Rittenhouse 46-598 1974 $10

SPENDER, STEPHEN   The Destructive Element. 1935. Spine little faded, fine copy, d.w., scarce. Covent 51-2572 1973 £10.50

SPENDER, STEPHEN   Forward from Liberalism. London, 1937. Orig. binding, Left Book Club edition not for sale to public, name in ink on fly, some dust staining, nice tight copy. Ross 87-533 1974 $12.50

SPENDER, STEPHEN   Forward from Liberalism. London, 1937. Limp cloth, some dust staining of covers, unusually fine, tight copy. Ross 86-433 1974 $12.50

SPENDER, STEPHEN   Poems. 1933. 8vo., orig. cloth, scarce, first edition. Rota 189-827 1974 £10

SPENDER, STEPHEN   Poems Of. 1934. Orig. edition. Austin 61-935 1974 $10

SPENGLER, OSWALD   The Decline of the West. (1926). Orig. cloth, first English edition. Rota 188-857 1974 £8

SPENSER, EDMUND   Colin Clovts Come Home Again. London, 1595. Small 4to., early 19th century russia, fine, first edition. Dawsons PM 252-912 1974 £1500

SPENSER, EDMUND   Complaints. London, 1591. 4to., full crushed crimson levant, rare, fine, first edition. Dawsons PM 252-913 1974 £1550

SPENSER, EDMUND   The Faerie Queen. (London), 1617. Folio, full red morocco, covers panelled in blind and gilt, woodcut illus., third folio edition. Ximenes 37-200 1974 $250

SPENSER, EDMUND   The Faerie Queene. 1751. 4to., 2 vols., full contemporary crimson calf, English first edition. Covent 56-2049 1974 £225

SPENSER, EDMUND   The Fairy Queen. 1758. 2 vols., plates, contemporary calf. Smith 193-128 1973 £10

SPENSER, EDMUND   Faerie Queen. 1758. 2 vols., new buckram. Allen 216-1857 1974 $35

SPENSER, EDMUND   The Faerie Queene. London, 1758-59. 4 vols., 8vo., contemporary tree calf, first edition. Ximenes 35-262 1974 $75

SPENSER, EDMUND   The Faerie Queene, with, Minor Poems. 1923-25. 2 vols., roy. folio, hand made paper, pigskin sides, morocco backs, antique style, uncut, fine, limited, printed in red, black and blue. Sawyer 293-48 1974 £850

SPENSER, EDMUND   The Faerie Queene. Cambridge, 1909. 2 vols., folio, orig. canvas backed boards, uncut, limited, hand made paper. Bow Windows 66-653 1974 £48

SPENSER, EDMUND   The Faerie Queen, and Minor Poems. Ashedene Press, 1923 & 1925. 2 vols., printed in red & black, folio, ivory vellum sides, brown cowhide panelled backs, uncut, limited to 180 copies, fine. Broadhurst 24-974 1974 £550

SPENSER, EDMUND   The Faerie Queen and Minor Poems. 1923 and 25. Folio, ivory vellum, brown cowhide, panelled backs, uncut, limited edition. Broadhurst 23-991 1974 £550

SPENSER, EDMUND   The Shepheardes Calendar. 1896. Royal 8vo., holland-backed boards, illus. Hammond 201-738 1974 £200

SPENSER, EDMUND   Spenser's Minor Poems. 1925. Folio, uncut, orig. boards, fine, limited edition. Dawsons PM 252-914 1974 £320

SPENSER, EDMUND   The Work of. London, 1715. 6 vols., 12mo., contemporary panelled calf, first edition. Ximenes 35-261 1974 $100

SPENSER, EDMUND   The Works Of. 1715. 6 vols., 8vo., plates, contemporary calf gilt. Smith 194-188 1974 £9

SPENSER, EDMUND   Works. 1873. 8vo., 5 vols., half green morocco, gilt. Quaritch 936-581 1974 £55

SPERONI, SPERONE   Dialoghi. 1544. 19th century calf gilt. Thomas 30-81 1973 £40

SPEWAK, BELLA   Boy Meets Girl and Spring Song. 1946. Austin 51-914 1973 $8.50

SPEWAK, BELLA   By 3 Angels. Random, 1953. Austin 51-916 1973 $7.50

SPEWAK, BELLA   Clear All Wires. French, 1932. Austin 51-915 1973 $6.50

SPICER, A. DYKES   The Paper Trade. 1907. 8vo., orig. cloth, illus., first edition. Rota 190-735 1974 £5

SPIELMANN, MARION HARRY   Hugh Thomson. 1931. 4to., orig. cloth, illus., plates. Broadhurst 23-489 1974 £8

SPIELMANN, MARION HARRY   Hugh Thomson: His Art, His Letters, His Humour and His Charm. 1931. Coloured & plain plates, text illus., small 4to., bookplate, nice copy, first edition. Covent 51-1844 1973 £8.50

SPIELMANN, MARION HARRY   Kate Greenaway. 1905. Thick crown 4to., illus., plates, orig. buckram gilt, limited. Howes 185-206 1974 £165

SPIERA, AMBROSIUS DE   Quadragesimale de Floribus Sapientiae. Venice, 1485. 4to., old boards, vellum back, waterstains, fine, large copy. Harper 213-146 1973 £625

SPILLER, BURTON L.   Firelight. New York, The Derrydale Press, (1937). First edition, limited to 950 numbered copies, very fine, illus. Current BW9-165 1974 $65

SPILLER, BURTON L.   Grouse Feathers. New York, 1935. 4to., orig. dec. cl., illus., ltd. to 950 copies. Jacobs 24-32 1974 $40

SPILSBURY, JOHN   A Collection of 50 Prints from Antique Gems. c. 1784. Large 8vo., green morocco, slightly worn. Eaton Music-675 1973 £20

SPINDLER, KARL   The Mystery of the Casement Ship. Berlin, (1931). 8vo., cloth boards. Emerald 50-892 1974 £7

SPINGARN, J. E.   Critical Essays of the 17th Century. 1908-09. Frontis., 3 vols., full plum calf, labels, gilt prize stamp on upper covers, very nice set. Covent 51-2437 1973 £22.50

SPINOZA, BENEDICT   Opera Quae Supersunt Omnia. 1802-03. 2 vols., contemporary calf, rubbed, rebacked, cover detached, library stamp. Bow Windows 66-654 1974 £76

THE SPIRIT of Irish Wit, or Post-Chaise Companion. London, 1812. 8vo., full calf, frontispiece, rebacked. Emerald 50-14 1974 £12

SPITTA, E. J.   Microscopy. 1920. 8vo., cloth, plates, third edition. Wheldon 129-105 1974 £7.50

SPITTA, PHILLIP   The Life of Bach. 1899. 8vo., orig. cloth, 3 vols., first edition. Broadhurst 23-206 1974 £25

SPIVAK, JOHN L.   Shrine of the Silver Dollar. 1940. 180p., illus. Austin 62-745 1974 $6.50

SPLAN, JOHN   Life with the Trotters. Chicago, 1889. Brown buckram, leather label, first edition. Bradley 35-352 1974 $20

SPOEHR, H. A.   Photosynthesis. New York, 1926. 8vo., cloth. Wheldon 129-965 1974 £5

SPOFFORD, HARRIET ELIZABETH PRESCOTT   Sir Rohan's Ghost. Boston, 1860. 12mo., orig. grey cloth, uncut, worn. Bow Windows 62-861 1974 £9

SPOONER, C. E.   Narrow Gauge Railways. 1879. Folding plates, demy 8vo., very fine copy, orig. cloth. Broadhurst 24-1329 1974 £35

SPORER, PATRITIUS   Theologiae Moralis Super Decalogum. Venice, 1716. 3 vols. in 2, folio, contemporary vellum. Howes 185-1664 1974 £15

THE SPORTSMAN'S Dictionary. 1778. 4to., contemporary calf, engraved plates. Wheldon 128-69 1973 £35

SPOTTISWOODE, JOHN   The History of the Church of Scotland. 1655. Folio, half buckram, first edition. Howes 185-1665 1974 £35

SPRAGUE, BEATRICE PUTNAM   Uxbridge, Year By Year, 1727-1927. Woonsocket, 1927. 8vo., cloth. Saddleback 14-496 1974 $10

SPRAGUE, JOHN T.   Electricity. London, 1875. 8vo., orig. maroon cloth, gilt. Dawsons PM 245-690 1974 £5

SPRANGE, J.   The Tunbridge Wells Guide. 1801. 8vo., orig. sprinkled calf. Broadhurst 23-1545 1974 £10

SPRAT, THOMAS   The History of the Royal Society of London. London, 1702. 4to., contemporary panelled calf, rebacked, second edition. Dawsons PM 245-691 1974 £45

SPRAT, THOMAS   A True Account and Declaration of the Horrid Conspiracy Against the Late King. Folio, contemporary calf, rubbed, rebacked. Thomas 28-202 1972 £27

SPRENGER, JAKOB   Der Hexenhammer. Berlin, 1923. Rittenhouse 46-600 1974 $10

SPRIGGE, S. SQUIRE   Physic and Fiction. (1921). Inscription, marked covers. Covent 55-1024 1974 £15.75

SPRINGFIELD. Springfield, 1904. Wrapper, illus. Jenkins 61-1544 1974 $12.50

THE SPRINGFIELD Almanac, Directory and Business Advertiser for 1845. Springfield, 1845. 8vo., orig. printed wrappers, frayed and soiled, very scarce, first printing. Ximenes 37-138 1974 $45

SPROGLE, HOWARD O.   The Philadelphia Police Past and Present. Philadelphia, 1887. Thick 8vo., illus., full leather, gilt, rubbed. Rinsland 58-89 1974 $35

SPRY, W.   The British Coleoptera Delineated. 1861. 8vo., half morocco, plates, very scarce. Wheldon 131-117 1974 £50

SPRY, W. J. J.   The Cruise of Her Majesty's Ship "Challenger". 1877. 8vo., orig. cloth. Broadhurst 23-1710 1974 £8

SPULER, A.   Die Schmetterlinge Europas. Struttgart, 1908-10. 4to., orig. cloth. Wheldon 129-686 1974 £50

SPURR, GEORGE G.   The Land of Gold. Boston, 1881. Orig. pictorial red cloth, first edition. Bradley 35-353 1974 $20

SPURR, J. E.   Geology of the Yukon Gold District, Alaska. Washington, 1898. Paper cover, illus., maps. Hood's 103-381 1974 $17.50

SPYRRI, J.   The Shirley Temple Edition of Heidi. Random, n.d. 252p., illus. Austin 51-960 1973 $10

SQUAIR, J.   The Townships of Darlington and Clarke. Toronto, 1927. Map, plates. Hood's 103-675 1974 $75

SQUAIR, JOHN   John Seath and the School System of Ontario. Toronto, 1920. Card cover, some pages browned. Hood's 102-434 1974 $7.50

SQUIER, EPHRAIM GEORGE   Nicaragua, Its People, Scenery, Monuments and the Proposed Interoceanic Canal. New York, 1852. 2 vols., rebacked, plates, maps. Jenkins 61-1954 1974 $30

SQUIRE, J. C.   Collected Parodies. London, n.d. (1921). First edition, orig. binding, spine faded, back hinge tender, unopened, internally near mint. Ross 87-534 1974 $12.50

SQUIRE, J. C.   Life and Letters. 1921. Orig. edition. Austin 61-936 1974 $10

SQUIRE, J. C.   The Survival of the Fittest and Other Poems. London, 1916. Orange paper covers, presentation inscription by author to Stanley Unwin, covers darkened, nice. Ross 87-535 1974 $15

SQUIRE, L.   Wildfowling with a Camera. 1938. 4to., cloth, plates, fine. Wheldon 130-624 1974 £7.50

SQUIRE, WILLIAM   The Unreasonableness of the Romanists. London, 1670. 8vo., contemporary calf, first edition. Ximenes 35-266 1974 $35

SQUIRES CLUB   The Squires' Club, Inc. 1938. 62p., illus. Austin 62-288 1974 $12.50

STACE, MACHELL   An Alphabetical Catalogue of An Extensive Collection of the Writings of Daniel De Foe. 1830. Cloth, portrait. Howes 185-656 1974 £5

STACKHOUSE, J.   Nereis Britannica. (1795-)1801. Folio, uncut, modern quarter morocco, plates. Wheldon 129-46 1974 £150

STAFFORD, JEAN   Boston Adventure. New York, (1944). Orig. printed wrappers, first edition, advance proof copy, fine. MacManus 224-399 1974 $37.50

STAFFORD, THOMAS   Pacata Hibernia. London, 1633. Folio, half calf, portraits, maps. Quaritch 939-631 1974 £60

STAFFORD, THOMAS   Pacata Hibernia. Dublin, 1820. 2 vols. in 1, roy. 8vo., buckram, second edition. Quartich 939-632 1974 £18

STAFFORD, THOMAS   Pacata Hibernia. Dublin, 1820. 2 vols., new cloth, illus., second edition. Emerald 50-894 1974 £25

STAIG, R. A.   The Fabrician Types of Insects in the Hunterian Collection at Glasgow University, Coleoptera. Cambridge, 1931-40. 2 vols., parts 1 & 2, 8vo., cloth, plates. Wheldon 131-861 1974 £7.50

STAINER, C. L.   Jonson and Drummond Their Conversations. 1925. 8vo., orig. boards, dust wrapper. Bow Windows 66-655 1974 £6.25

STAINTON, H. T.   British Butterflies and Moths. 1867. Post 8vo., cloth, plates. Wheldon 130-803 1974 £5

STAINTON, H. T.   A Manual of British Butterflies and Moths. 1857-59. 2 vols., 8vo., half calf, scarce. Wheldon 128-810 1973 £7.50

STAINTON, H. T.   A Manual of British Butterflies and Moths. 1857-59. 2 vols., 8vo., cloth, scarce. Wheldon 131-862 1974 £7.50

STAINTON, H. T.   The Natural History of the Tineina. 1855-73. 13 vols., 8vo., orig. cloth, coloured plates, scarce. Wheldon 128-809 1973 £50

STAINTON, H. T.   The Natural History of the Tineina. 1855-73. 8vo., 13 vols., orig. cloth, plates, scarce. Wheldon 130-802 1974 £50

STALPART VANDER WIEL, CORNELIS   Observationum Rariorum Medic. Leyden, 1687. Small 8vo., boards, first edition. Schumann 35-451 1974 $95

STAMPION DE JONGHE, JOHAN J.   Algebra Ofte Nieuwe Stel-Regel. 1639. 4to., contemporary vellum, gilt. Zeitlin 235-211 1974 $225

STAN, ANISOARA   They Crossed Mountains and Oceans. 1947. 388p., illus. Austin 62-607 1974 $12.50

STANARD, MARY NEWTON   The Dreamer, A Romantic Rendering of the Life-Story of Edgar Allan Poe. Richmond, 1909. First edition, 8vo., limited to 1000 copies, very scarce, presentation copy from author. Current BW9-267 1974 $30

STANCARI, VITTORIO FRANCESCO   Schedae Mathematicae. Bologna, 1713. 4to., contemporary red morocco, gilt, fine, first edition. Dawsons PM 245-692 1974 £30

STANDISH, ARTHUR   The Commons Complaint. London, 1611. 4to., modern wrappers, first edition. Dawsons PM 247-276 1974 £250

STANDISH, J.   Practical Hints on Planting Ornamental Trees. 1852. Small 8vo., orig. cloth.   Wheldon 131-1753 1974 £10

STANDLEY, P. C.   Flora of Yucatan. 1930. 8vo., half morocco. Wheldon 129-1120 1974 £5

STANFIELD, C.   Stanfield's Coast Scenery. 1836. 4to., cloth back, boards, plates.   Quaritch 939-253 1974 £45

STANGE, EDWARD F.   Japanese Colour Prints. London, 1910. First edition, 12mo., plates, very good.   Current BW9-552 1974 $18

STANHOPE, B. S.   The Church Plate of the County of Hereford. 1903. 4to., plates, cloth.   Quaritch 939-384 1974 £12.50

STANHOPE, LADY HESTER LUCY   A New Light on Her Life and Love Affairs. London, 1913.   Biblo & Tannen 213-705 1973 $8.50

STANHOPE, PHILIP DORMER
Please turn to
CHESTERFIELD, PHILIP DORMER STANHOPE

STANHOPE, PHILIP HENRY   Life of William Pitt. 1861. 4 vols., crown 8vo., orig. cloth, portraits.   Howes 186-1132 1974 £18

STANLEY, ARTHUR PENRHYN   Historical Memorials of Westminster Abbey. London, 1868. Illus., binding worn.   Biblo & Tannen 213-706 1973 $12.50

STANLEY, ARTHUR PENRHYN   Letters and Verses. 1895. Buckram, gilt, rebound, first edition.   Howes 185-1668 1974 £5.50

STANLEY, ARTHUR PENRHYN   Sinai and Palestine. 1873. 8vo., prize calf, gilt, maps.   Bow Windows 64-697 1974 £5.75

STANLEY, EDWARD   Before and After Waterloo Letters from. London, 1907. 8vo., plates, orig. cloth, illus., gilt, faded.   Bow Windows 62-865 1974 £5.75

STANLEY, EDWARD   A Familiar History of Birds. London, 1865. Small 8vo., contemporary polished calf, gilt, illus., new edition.   Hammond 201-680 1974 £6.50

STANLEY, HENRY MORTON   The American Testimonial Banquet to. 1890. 8vo., calf, rebacked, upper cover embossed, scarce.   Sawyer 293-12 1974 £42

STANLEY, HENRY MORTON   Autobiography. 1909. Map, illus., orig. edition.   Austin 57-636 1974 $12.50

STANLEY, HENRY MORTON   The Congo and the Founding Of Its Free State. 1886. 2 vols., thick demy 8vo., plates, illus., orig. pictorial buckram. Smith 194-580 1974 £10

STANLEY, REVA   The Archer of Paradise. Caldwell, 1937. Pictorial cloth, illus., dust jacket, first edition.   Bradley 35-258 1974 $16

STANLEY, REVA   A Biography of Parley P. Pratt. Caldwell, 1937. Orig. cloth, illus., first edition.   Putnam 126-319 1974 $17

STANLEY, THOMAS   The History of Philosophy. London, 1687. Folio, contemporary mottled calf, first collected edition.   Ximenes 35-269 1974 $175

STANLEY, THOMAS   The History of Philosophy. 1701. Folio, contemporary calf, rebacked, third edition.   Howes 185-2003 1974 £35

STANNIUS, H.   Handbuch der Anatomie der Wirbelthiere. Berlin, 1854. 8vo., cloth, second edition.   Wheldon 129-595 1974 £7.50

STANNIUS, F. H.   Zwei Reihen Physiologischer Versuche. Rostock, 1851. 8vo., boards, presentation inscription.   Gurney 64-203 1974 £60

STANNIUS, HERMANN   Beitrage zur Kenntniss der Amerikanischen Manati's. Rostock, 1846. 4to., boards, plates.   Gurney 66-175 £15

STANNUS, MRS. GRAYDON   Old Irish Glass. 1931. 4to., plates, English first edition.   Covent 56-1658 1974 £10

STANSBURY, ARTHUR J.   Trail of the Rev. Albert Barnes, Before the Synod of Philadelphia, 1835. New York, 1836. Orig. binding.   Butterfield 10-299 1974 $15

STANSBURY, HOWARD   Exploration and Survey of the Valley of the Great Salt Lake of Utah. Philadelphia, 1852. 8vo., orig. bindings, plates, fine. Butterfield 8-638 1974 $20

STANTON, G. SMITH   When the Wildwood was in Flower. New York, 1909. Mint copy.   Jenkins 61-2397 1974 $65

STANTON, RICHARD   A Menology of England and Wales. 1887. Thick 8vo., scarce.   Howes 185-1670 1974 £7.75

STAPFER, P.   Shakespeare et l'Antiquite. 1879-80. Half calf worn.   Allen 216-2183 1974 $10

STAPLEDON, OLAF   Sirius. 1944. Fine, English first edition. Covent 56-2051 1974 £5.25

STAPYLTON, MARTIN   Letters to the Most Noble the Marquis of Lansdowne. London, 1828. 8vo., boards, presentation copy, first edition.   Hammond 201-190 1974 £38.50

THE STAR of Saville. 1935. 8vo., full black morocco, uncut, limited edition. Broadhurst 23-1051 1974 £100

STARK, A. C.   The Fauna of South Africa. 1900-06. 8vo., 4 vols., orig. green cloth, rare.   Wheldon 130-625 1974 £300

STARK, FREYA   Letters from Syria. 1942. Orig. cloth, fine, dust wrapper, first edition.   Rota 188-858 1974 £5

STARK, J.   Elements of Natural History. Edinburgh, 1828. 2 vols., 8vo., new cloth, plates, library stamps, scarce.   Wheldon 129-295 1973 £15

STARK, J.   Elements of Natural History. Edinburgh, 1828. 2 vols., 8vo., new cloth, plates.   Wheldon 131-459 1974 £15

STARK, J.   Scenery of the Rivers of Norfolk. Norwich & London, 1834. Roy. folio, half red morocco, plates.   Quaritch 939-499 1974 £120

STARK, R. M.   A Popular History of British Mosses. 1860. Small 8vo., orig. cloth, plates, second edition.   Wheldon 131-1469 1974 £5

STARKE, R. G.   The Lord of Lanoraie. Montreal, 1898. Illus. Hood's 104-793 1974 $15

STARKEY, GEORGE   Secrets Reveal'd. London, 1669. 8vo., contemporary calf.   Gurney 64-204 1974 £115

STARKEY, JAMES   The Dublin Magazine. 1935-40. 4 vols., 4to., wrappers.   Emerald 50-775 1974 £5

STARKEY, JAMES   Poems. Dublin, 1912. Portrait, first edition, crown 8vo., uncut, orig. cloth, fine, poem written in author's hand on fly. Broadhurst 24-829 1974 £25

STARKEY, WILLIAM   Poems. Dublin, 1938. First edition, portrait, crown 8vo., orig. cloth, fine.   Broadhurst 24-830 1974 £6

STARR, RICHARD F. S.   Indus Valley Painted Pottery. Princeton, 1941. 1st ed., illus.   Biblo & Tannen 214-399 1974 $15

STARRETT, VINCENT   The Blue Door. New York, 1930. 8vo., orig. cloth, first edition.   Rota 190-352 1974 £6

STARRETT, VINCENT   Persons from Porlock and Other Interruptions. Chicago, 1938. 8vo., orig. copy, signed, fine, first edition.   Rota 190-918 1974 £5

STAS, JEAN SERVAIS   Nouvelles Recherches sur les Lois des Proportions Chimiques. Brussels, 1863. Large 4to., orig. pictured boards, cloth back, rubbed, illus., first separate edition.   Schuman 37-241 1974 $250

STATE Military Rendezvous of the Connecticut National Guard at Niantic, Connecticut. Waterbury, c. 1898. Boards, photos. Jenkins 61-702 1974 $12.50

STATE Necessity Considered as a Question of Law. London, 1766. 8vo., modern boards. Dawsons PM 247-282 1974 £20

STATE Street Events, A Brief Account of Divers Notable Persons and Sundry Stirring Events Having to do With the History of This Ancient Street. Boston, 1916. First edition, 8vo., illus., very fine. Current BW9-393 1974 $12.50

STATEMENT of Principles of the Hammersmith Socialist Society. 1890. Very good copy, first edition. Covent 51-1728 1973 £9.50

STATEMENT of the Claim of Robert Wilson . . . . . in Relation to the Barony of Berners. 1832. Folio, orig. boards. Howes 186-1619 1974 £5

STATEMENT of the Disposition of Some of the Bodies of Deceased Union Soldiers and Prisoners of War Whose Remains Have Been Removed to National Cemeteries in the Southern and Western States. Washington, 1868. Wrapper. Jenkins 61-2399 1974 $15

STATEMENT of the Disposition of Some of the Bodies of Deceased Union Soldiers and Prisoners of War Whose Remains Have Been Removed to National Cemeteries in the Southern and Western States. Washington, 1868. Wrapper. Jenkins 61-2398 1974 $17.50

STATEMENT of the Disposition of Some of the Bodies of Deceased Union Soldiers and Prisoners of War Whose Remains Have Been Removed to National Cemeteries in the Southern and Western States. Washington, 1869. Wrapper. Jenkins 61-2400 1974 $15

STATIONER'S COMPANY   A Transcript of the Registers of the Worshipful Company of Stationers, from 1640-1708 A.D. 1913-14. 3 vols., folio, roan spines, top edges gilt. Thomas 32-291 1974 £150

STATISTICAL SOCIETY   Catalogue of the Library. 1884. Imp. 8vo., orig. cloth, frayed spine. Howes 185-844 1974 £7.50

STATIUS, PUBLIUS PAPINIUS   Sylvarum Libri Quinque. 1502. Late 18th century vellum gilt, morocco labels, first Aldine edition. Thomas 30-12 1973 £100

STATIUS, PUBLIUS PAPINUS   Sylvarum Libri Quinque. Venice, 1502. First Aldine edition, few stains, quite good copy, old vellum, armorial bookplate of Holland House. Thomas 32-216 1974 £100

STATUTA Civilia Civitatis Bononiae. (Bologna, 1475.) Folio, old boards, leather back, stains, large complete copy, fine. Harper 213-147 1973 $4500

STATUTES of the Corporation of the Orphan Hospital and Workhouse at Edinburgh. To Which is Prefixed an Account of the said Hospital from its Establishment in 1733. Edinburgh, 1777. 12mo., disbound, last page dustsoiled. Gurney 66-176 1974 £7.50

STAUDINGER, O.   Exotische Schmetterlinge in Systematischer Reihenfolge mit Berücksichtigung Neuer Arten. Furth, (1884-) 1888. 2 vols., imp. 4to., orig. dec. cloth, coloured plates, good condition. Wheldon 128-812 1973 £75

STAUDINGER, O. AND LANGHANS, H.   Exotische Schmetterlinge. 1888-92. Folio, 3 vols., orig. cloth, plates, rare. Wheldon 130-75 1974 £150

STAVELEY, E. F.   British Insects. 1871. 8vo., orig. cloth, rebacked, plates, Wheldon 131-863 1974 £5

STAVELEY, E. F.   British Spiders. 1866. Crown 8vo., cloth, plain and coloured plates. Wheldon 128-929 1973 £5

STAVELEY, E. F.   British Spiders. 1866. Crown 8vo., cloth, plates. Wheldon 131-949 1974 £5

STEARNS, CHARLES   The Ladies' Philosophy of Love. Leominster, 1797. 8vo., contemporary half calf, first edition. Ximenes 35-270 1974 $50

STEARNS, CHARLES W.   Shakespeare's Medical Knowledge. New York, 1865. Small 8vo., contemporary tree calf. Schumann 35-432 1974 $65

STEARNS, FRANK PRESTON   Sketches from Concord and Appledore. New York, 1895. Plates, orig. dec. cloth, gilt, first U.S. edition. Covent 56-861 1974 £10.50

STEARNS, M.   Along the Trail. 1936. Illus. Hood's 103-190 1974 $10

STEBBING, E. P.   "Collected Papers. Forestry, Agriculture and General Subjects 1905-07. 1905-07. Vol. 2, roy. 8vo., half leather. Wheldon 131-1754 1974 £7.50

STEBBING, E. P.   Indian Forest Insects. 1914. Crown 4to., orig. cloth, plates, scarce. Wheldon 129-688 1974 £20

STEBBING, E. P.   Jungle by-ways in India. 1911. 8vo., cloth, illus., second edition. Wheldon 129-305 1974 £5

STEBBING, HENRY   The Christian in Palestine. n.d. (c. 1850). Engraved plates, demy 4to., contemporary red morocco, panelled back, richly tooled gilt, attractive copy. Broadhurst 24-1687 1974 £50

STEDMAN, ARTHUR   Short Biographies of American Authors Represented in "A Library of American Literature". New York, 1890. 8vo., cloth, signed by author. Goodspeed's 578-532 1974 $10

STEDMAN, CHARLES   The History of the Origin, Progress, and Termination of the American War. London, 1794. 4to., new half calf, maps, first edition. Traylen 79-497 1973 £225

STEDMAN, EDMUND CLARENCE   American Anthology. 1900. Top of spine pulled, spine darkened. Allen 216-1618 1974 $10

STEDMAN, EDMUND CLARENCE   Mater Coronata. Boston, 1901. Fine, uncut, unopened, dust jacket. Ballinger 1-46 1974 $10

STEDMAN, EDMUND CLARENCE   Poems Now First Collected. Boston, 1897. 12mo., cloth, paper label, uncut, first edition. Goodspeed's 578-332 1974 $25

STEEDMAN, CHARLES J.   Bucking the Sagebrush. New York and London, 1904. Gilt top, 1st ed. Dykes 24-246 1974 $85

STEEDMAN, CHARLES J.   Bucking the Sagebrush. New York, 1904. Orig. cloth, illus., dust wrapper, fine, rare, first edition. Bradley 35-354 1974 $100

STEEGMULLER, FRANCIS   French Follies and Other Follies. Reynal, 1946. 174p. Austin 54-964 1973 $7.50

STEEL, FLORA ANNIE   English Fairy Tales. 1918. Illus. by Arthur Rackham, one of 500 copies, numbered, signed by artist, coloured plates, 4to., orig. parchment, top edges gilt, others uncut. George's 610-838 1973 £75

STEELE, ANDREW   The Natural and Agricultural History of Peat-Moss. Edinburgh, 1826. 8vo., orig. boards, first edition. Hammond 201-50 1974 £14.50

STEELE, JAMES W.   Frontier Army Sketches. 1883. Ex-library, second edition. Allen 216-1306 1974 $10

STEELE, JAMES W.   Old Californian Days. Chicago, 1889. Gray cloth, gilt, illus., first edition. Bradley 35-51 1974 $23

STEELE, JAMES W.   Old Californian Days. Chicago, 1893. Illus. Jenkins 61-433 1974 $10

STEELE, RICHARD   The Christian Hero. London, 1701. 8vo., orig. calf. Rich Summer-95 1974 $60

STEELE, RICHARD   The Crisis. Edinburgh, 1714. 8vo., disbound. Dawsons PM 247-283 1974 £10

STEELE, RICHARD   The Crisis. London, 1714. 4to., disbound, first edition, second issue. Dawsons PM 251-340 1974 £20

STEELE, RICHARD   The Crisis. London, 1714. 4to., disbound, first edition, second issue. Ximenes 35-271 1974 $35

STEELE, RICHARD   The Funeral. London, 1702. Small 4to., disbound, first edition. Ximenes 35-272 1974 $45

STEELE, RICHARD   The Guardian. London, 1714. 2 vols., 8vo., contemporary calf, gilt, first edition. Ximenes 35-273 1974 $80

STEELE, RICHARD   The Lover. London, 1715. 12mo., rebacked, contemporary calf, first collected edition. Ximenes 35-274 1974 $55

STEELE, RICHARD   The Perverse Widow. New York, 1909. 16mo., 3 mounted color plates; 1st ed. Frohnsdorff 16-23 1974 $5

STEELE, RICHARD   Poetical Miscellanies. London, 1714. 8vo., contemporary calf, gilt, label, first edition. Dawsons PM 252-916 1974 £160

STEELE, ROBERT   The Earliest English Music Printing. London, 1903. 4to., plates, contemporary half morocco gilt. Dawsons PM 10-580 1974 £21

STEELE, ROBERT   Mediaeval Lore. 1893. Book-plate, buckram. Covent 55-1120 1974 £25

STEELE, RUFUS   Mustangs of the Mesa. Hollywood, 1941. 1st ed., inner hinges reinforced, a few hand-colored illus. Dykes 24-119 1974 $12.50

STEELE, WILBUR DANIEL   Diamond Wedding. Doubleday, n.d. 309p. Austin 54-965 1973 $7.50

STEELE, WILBUR DANIEL   Full Cargo. Doubleday, 1951. 369p. Austin 54-966 1973 $10

STEELE, WILBUR DANIEL   That Girl From Memphis. Doubleday, Doran, 1945. 470p. Austin 54-968 1973 $6

STEELE, WILBUR DANIEL   The Way to the Gold. Doubleday, 1955. 375p. Austin 54-967 1973 $8.50

STEELE, ZADOCK   The Indian Captive. Montpelier, 1818. 16mo., contemporary calf, worn. Butterfield 8-654 1974 $35

STEELEY, B.   Stowe. London, 1766. 8vo., calf antique, plates. Ximenes 35-154 1974 $125

STEELMAN, SAMUEL   History of Hollywood Lodge No. 355, F. & A. M. Hollywood, (1945). 12mo., cloth. Saddleback 14-288 1974 $10

STEEN, MARGUERITE   William Nicholson. London, 1943. 8vo., cloth, illus. Minters 37-161 1973 $16

STEENSTRUP, JOHANNES JEPETUS SMITH   Om Fortplantning og Udvikling Gjennem Vexlende Generationsraekker. Copenhagen, 1842. 4to, plates, new buckram. Wheldon 131-460 1974 £50

STEENSTRUP, JOHANNES JEPETUS SMITH   On the Alternation of Generations. 1845. 8vo., cloth, plates, scarce. Wheldon 131-461 1974 £7.50

STEENSTRUP, JOHANNES JEPETUS SMITH   Undersogelser Over Hermaphroditis-mens. 1845. 4to., boards, worn. Dawsons PM 249-462 1974 £8

STEENSTRUP, JOHANNES JEPETUS SMITH   Undersogelser over Hermaphroditis-mens. Copenhagen, 1845. 4to., boards, first edition. Gurney 64-206 1974 £25

STEERE, EDWARD   Swahili Tales. London, 1889. Biblo & Tannen 214-583 1974 $10

STEERWELL, J.   The Little Traveller. London, (c. 1830). 16mo., color plates, tan boards. Gregory 44-59A 1974 $35

STEFAN, PAUL   Oskar Kokoschka: Dramen und Bilder. Leipzig, 1913. 4to., boards, cloth spine, plates, scarce first edition. Minters 37-464 1973 $75

STEFANSSON, E.   Here is Alaska. New York, 1943. Photos. Hood's 102-75 1974 $12.50

STEFANSSON, E.   Within the Circel: Portrait of the Arctic. New York, 1945. Maps. Hood's 102-76 1974 $10

STEIN, A.   Serindia. Oxford, 1921. Thick 4to., 5 vols., orig. brown buckram, illus. Bow Windows 64-699 1974 £385

STEIN, ELIAS   Nouvel Essai sur le Jeu des Echecs. 1789. 8vo., old boards, cloth spine, rare, first edition. Bow Windows 66-656 1974 £11

STEIN, GERTRUDE   Americans d'Amerique; Paris, 1933. One of 2200 numbered copies, presentation copy, inscribed by author & translator, very nice copy, dusty wrappers. Covent 51-2573 1973 £40

STEIN, GERTRUDE   The Autobiography of Alice B. Toklas. London, 1933. First English edition, illus., d.w. slightly browned, mint, additional protective heavy dec. paper wrapper, orig. binding. Ross 87-536 1974 $40

STEIN, GERTRUDE   The Autobiography of Alice B. Toklas. London, 1933. Illus., d.w. slightly browned, mint, additional protective heavy dec. paper wrapper. Ross 86-437 1974 $40

STEIN, GERTRUDE   The Autobiography of Alice B. Toklas. New York, 1933. Plates, English first edition. Covent 56-1200 1974 £5.25

STEIN, GERTRUDE   Autobiographie d'Alice Toklas. Paris, 1934. Wrappers, fine, presentation copy, first French edition. Covent 56-1201 1974 £45

STEIN, GERTRUDE   Composition as Explanation. 1926. 8vo., orig. cloth, first edition. Rota 189-832 1974 £15

STEIN, GERTRUDE   Composition as Explanation. London, 1926. Boards, first edition. Dawson's 424-306 1974 $30

STEIN, GERTRUDE   An Elucidation. N.P., 1927. 12mo., orig. printed wrappers. Ximenes 35-275 1974 $60

STEIN, GERTRUDE   Geography and Plays. Boston, 1922. First U. S. edition, fine, cloth backed boards. Covent 51-1743 1973 £15.75

STEIN, GERTRUDE   How to Write. Paris, 1931. Edition limited to 1000 copies, covers and spine lightly worn & soiled, very nice copy, orig. binding. Ross 86-439 1974 $60

STEIN, GERTRUDE   How to Write. Paris, 1931. 8vo., orig. cloth, scarce, first edition. Rota 190-920 1974 £21

STEIN, GERTRUDE   Operas and Plays. Paris, 1932. Orig. wrappers, English first edition. Covent 56-1203 1974 £42.50

STEIN, GERTRUDE   Picasso. Paris, 1938. First French edition, fine, wrappers. Covent 51-1745 1973 £25

STEIN, GERTRUDE   Picasso. 1938. Rebound, full buckram, first French edition. Covent 56-1204 1974 £8.50

STEIN, GERTRUDE   A Village: Are You Ready Yet Not Yet. Paris, 1928. One of 100 copies, numbered & signed by author & illus., 4to., wrappers, perfect copy, lithographs. Covent 51-3256 1973 £195

STEIN, GERTRUDE   Wars I Have Seen. Boston, 1945. 8vo., orig. cloth, dust wrapper, first English edition. Rota 189-833 1974 $5

STEIN D' ALTENSTEIN, I.   Armorial des Alliances de la Noblesse de Belgique. 1880. Folio, plates, full morocco. Allen 213-1793 1973 $50

STEINBECK, JOHN   Bombs Away. New York, 1942. First printing, d.j., orig. binding. Butterfield 10-493 1974 $12.50

STEINBECK, JOHN   Burning Bright. Viking, 1950. Austin 51-920 1973 $10

STEINBECK, JOHN   Cup of Gold. Collier, 1936. 269p. Austin 54-969 1973 $7.50

STEINBECK, JOHN   Cup of Gold. New York, (1936). Stained d.j., orig. binding. Butterfield 10-495 1974 $7.50

STEINBECK, JOHN   Des Souris et des Hommes. Paris, 1939. First French edition, one of 35 numbered copies on alfa, fine, wrappers. Covent 51-1747 1973 £35

STEINBECK, JOHN   The Forgotten Village. New York, 1941. 4to., d.j. with fragment lacking, bottom covers stained, first edition, photos. Butterfield 10-496 1974 $10

STEINBECK, JOHN   The Grapes of Wrath. New York, 1939. Orig. cloth, few very light stains, first edition, about fine, slightly worn dust jacket. MacManus 224-401 1974 $60

STEINBECK, JOHN   The Long Valley. New York, 1938. 8vo., orig. cloth, first edition. Rota 189-836 1974 £7.50

STEINBECK, JOHN   The Long Valley. Viking, 1939. 303p., orig. ed. Austin 54-971 1973 $6.50

STEINBECK, JOHN   Of Mice and Men. New York, 1937. 8vo., orig. cloth, first edition, first issue. Rota 189-835 1974 £8.50

STEINBECK, JOHN   Once There Was a War. Viking, 1958. 233p. Austin 54-970 1973 $7.50

STEINBERG, MILTON   A Partisan Guide to the Jewish Problem. Bobbs-Merrill, 1945. Austin 62-610 1974 $7.50

STEINBERG, SAUL   All in Line. New York, 1945. First U. S. edition, 4to., covers little marked, very good copy. Covent 51-2577 1973 £5

STEINER, EDWARD A.   Against the Current. 1920. 230 pages. Austin 57-638 1974 $10

STEINER, EDWARD A.   The Broken Wall. Revell, 1911. 219p., illus. Austin 62-611 1974 $12.50

STEINER, EDWARD A.   The Making of a Great Race. Revell, 1929. Austin 62-612 1974 $12.50

STEINER, GIUSEPPE   La Chitarra del Fante. Piacenza, 1920. 8vo., wrapper, second edition. Minters 37-440 1973 $27.50

STEINER, JACOB   Die Geometrischen Konstructionen Ausgefuhrt Mittelst der Geraden Linie und Eines Festen Kreises. Berlin, 1833. 8vo., half cloth, folding tables, first edition. Gilhofer 61-38 1974 sFr. 700

STEINER, JACOB   Gesammelte Werke. 1881-1882. Tall 8vo., 2 vols., plates, orig. printed wrappers, unopened, uncut. Zeitlin 235-212 1974 $120

STEINER, PAULA   Lovis Corinth, dem Ostpreussen. Ludwig, 1925. 8vo., boards, plates. Minters 37-452 1973 $18

STEININGER, J.   Geognostische Studien am Mittelrheine. Mainz, 1819. 8vo., half calf, library stamp. Wheldon 128-1054 1973 £10

STEINMATZ, ANDREW   History of the Jesuits. 1848. 8vo., full contemporary calf, gilt, first edition. Broadhurst 23-1276 1974 £30

STEINMATZ, ANDREW   History of the Jesuits: From the Foundation of Their Society to its Suppression by Pope XIV. 1848. Engraved portraits, first edition, 3 vols., demy 8vo., full contemporary light brown calf, panelled backs, richly tooled gilt, marbled edges, fine. Broadhurst 24-1330 1974 £30

STEINMETZ, ANDREW   The Gaming Table. 1870. 2 vols., gilt, contemporary half green calf. Howes 186-204 1974 £12.50

STEINMETZ, ANDREW   Japan and Her People. London, 1859. 8vo., orig. dec. cloth, illus., first edition. Ximenes 35-276 1974 $17.50

STEINMETZ, CHARLES P.   American and the New Epoch. Harper, 1916. Austin 62-613 1974 $6.50

STEINWAY & SONS   Portraits of Musical Celebrities. New York, 1929. Biblo & Tannen 213-887 1973 $9.50

STELL, I.   The Hastings Guide. 1804. Contemporary half calf, plates, foxing, map. Howes 186-2202 1974 £18

STELLING-DEKKER, N. M.   Die Hefesammlung des Centraalbureau. Amsterdam, 1931. Roy 8vo., buckram. Wheldon 129-1355 1974 £15

STELLUTI, FRANCESCO   Persio. Rome, 1630. 4to., contemporary speckled calf, gilt, first edition. Dawsons PM 245-693 1974 £285

STELLY, J. A.   Arcana Hortensia. Constantz, 1718. 12mo., boards. Wheldon 129-1536 1974 £10

STELZLE, CHARLES   A Son of the Bowery. Doran, 1926. 335p. Austin 62-614 1974 $7.50

STENDHAL
Please turn to
BEYLE, MARIE HENRI

STENERSEN, ROLF   Edvard Munch. Oslo, 1945. 4to., wrappers, soiled, illus., plates. Minters 37-224 1973 $18

STENHOUSE, T. B. H.   The Rocky Mountain Saints. New York, 1873. 3/4 lea., illus. Biblo & Tannen 213-62 1973 $32.50

STENNET, J.   An Exact Account of Two Real Dreams. London, 1725. 8vo., boards. Schumann 35-452 1974 $65

STEP, E.   Toadstools and Mushrooms of the Countryside. (1913). Post 8vo., cloth, plates. Wheldon 131-1470 1974 £5

STEPHANUS, CAROLUS
Please turn to
ESTIENNE, CHARLES

STEPHANUS, HENRICUS
Please turn to
ESTIENNE, HENRI

STEPHANUS OF BYZANTIUM   De Urbibus. 1502. Folio, 18th century vellum, gilt, morocco labels. Thomas 30-14 1973 £275

STEPHEN, A. G. A.   Private Schools in Canada, A Handbook of Boys' Schools Which are Members of the Canadian Headmasters' Association. Toronto, 1938. Ex-library. Hood's 102-435 1974 $7.50

STEPHEN, GEORGE   The Adventures of a Gentleman in Search of a Horse. London, 1836. 16mo., gilt cloth. Frohnsdorff 16-253 1974 $15

STEPHEN, JAMES   The Dangers of the Country. London, 1807. Marbled boards, worn. Dawson's 424-201 1974 $20

STEPHEN, JAMES   Observations on the Speech of the Hon. John Randolph. New York, 1806. Cloth. Dawson's 424-200 1974 $20

STEPHEN, JAMES   The Speech of. London, 1809. 8vo., wrappers, first edition. Dawsons PM 251-484 1974 £22

STEPHEN, JAMES   War in Disguise. 1806. Marbled boards, gilt, third edition. Dawson's 424-199 1974 $20

STEPHEN, JAMES F.   Horae Sabbaticae. London, 1892. 3 vols., 8vo., orig. cloth, fine, first edition. Ximenes 35-277 1974 $27.50

STEPHEN, LESLIE   History of English Thought In the 18th Century. 1902. 2 vols., orig. cloth, third edition. Howes 185-2005 1974 £8.50

STEPHEN, LESLIE   History of English Thought in the Eighteenth Century. New York & London, 1902. 2 vols., 8vo., orig. cloth, third edition. Bow Windows 62-867 1974 £10

STEPHEN, LESLIE   Sketches from Cambridge. 1865. Orig. cloth, bookplate, English first edition. Covent 56-2054 1974 £35

STEPHEN, LESLIE   Studies of a Biographer. 1910. 4 vols., crown 8vo. Howes 185-472 1974 £12

STEPHENS, ALEXANDER H.   A Constitutional View of the Late War Between the States. Philadelphia, (1868-1870). 2 vols., orig. brown cloth, gilt, frontispiece, first edition. Bradley 35-92 1974 $60

STEPHENS, ALEXANDER H.   Speech on the State of the Union. Washington, 1847. Orig. address leaf made out and signed by Stephens. Jenkins 61-1610 1974 $22.50

STEPHENS, ANN S.   Fashion and Famine. New York, 1854. 12mo., orig. green cloth, first edition. Ximenes 35-278 1974 $15

STEPHENS, ANN S.   The Rejected Wife. Philadelphia, n.d. 12mo., orig. cloth, first edition. Ximenes 35-279 1974 $25

STEPHENS, ARCHIBALD JOHN   The Book of Common Prayer. Dublin, 1849-50. 3 vols., orig. cloth. Howes 185-990 1974 $7.50

STEPHENS, FREDERICK   Notes on a Collection of Drawings and Wood-cuts by Thomas Bewick. London, 1881. Cloth, plates, inscribed, presentation copy. Dawson's 424-32 1974 $75

STEPHENS, FREDERICK G.   James Clarke Hook. (1882). Etchings, plates, illus., disbound. Marsden 37-263 1974 £8

STEPHENS, G. W.   The St. Lawrence Waterway Project. Montreal, 1930. Large folding maps. Hood's 102-779 1974 $17.50

STEPHENS, HENRY   The Book of the Farm. Edinburgh & London, 1889-91. 3 vols., 8vo., plates, illus., orig. cloth. Bow Windows 62-868 1974 £12.50

STEPHENS, J. F.   A Manual of British Coleoptera. 1839. 8vo., orig. cloth. Bow Windows 64-258 1974 £4.50

STEPHENS, JAMES   Collected Poems. 1926. Quarter parchment-vellum, fine, signed, English first edition. Covent 56-1206 1974 £27.50

STEPHENS, JAMES   The Crock of Gold. London, 1912. Orig. cloth, rubbed, first edition, good copy. MacManus 224-402 1974 $75

STEPHENS, JAMES   The Crock of Gold. 1921. Faded, worn, English first edition. Covent 56-1207 1974 £12.50

STEPHENS, JAMES   The Demi-Gods. 1914. Blind stamped 'Presentation Copy' on title page, else fine, first edition. Covent 51-1755 1973 £10

STEPHENS, JAMES   Etched in Moonlight. New York, 1928. Med. 8vo., boards, linen spine, paper printed label, uncut, spine slightly browned, else mint, orig. publisher's slip-in-case, limited to 750 copies, numbered & signed by author. Broadhurst 24-896 1974 £15

STEPHENS, JAMES   Etched in Moonlight. 1928. Fine, dust wrapper, English first edition. Covent 56-2055 1974 £6.50

STEPHENS, JAMES   Five New Poems. 1913. Wrappers, fine, English first edition. Covent 56-2056 1974 £5.25

STEPHENS, JAMES   Five New Poems. 1913. First edition, demy 8vo., paper printed wrapper, cover slightly split, very fine. Broadhurst 24-895 1974 £5

STEPHENS, JAMES   Five New Poems. 1913. Fine, English first edition. Covent 56-1208 1974 £10

STEPHENS, JAMES   Green Branches. New York, 1916. Orig. parchment-backed boards, first American edition, one of 500 copies, fine copy. MacManus 224-403 1974 $35

STEPHENS, JAMES   Harmonium. New York, 1923. First edition, cloth, lacking d.w., owner's inscription, unusually fine, tight copy, heavy dec. paper wrapper. Ross 86-442 1974 $75

STEPHENS, JAMES   Irish Fairy Tales. London, 1920. Illus. by Arthur Rackham, lacking d.w., ink inscription, very nice, scarce, orig. binding. Ross 86-441 1974 $135

STEPHENS, JAMES   Irish Fairy Tales. 1920. Crown 4to., plates, orig. buckram gilt. Smith 193-399 1973 £12

STEPHENS, JAMES   Irish Fairy Tales. 1920. Small 4to., orig. cloth gilt, plates, first edition. Howes 185-394 1974 £25

STEPHENS, JAMES   Kings and the Moon. London, 1938. 8vo., cloth boards, first edition. Emerald 50-898 1974 £5

STEPHENS, JAMES   Reincarnations. 1918. Dust wrapper, fine, unopened. Covent 55-1409 1974 £10.50

STEPHENS, W. R. W.   A History of the English Church. 1901-1910. 9 vols., complete set. Howes 185-1674 1974 £45

STEPHENS, W. R. W.   St. John Chrysostom. 1883. 472 pages. Howes 185-1305 1974 £5

STEPHENS, WILLIAM   Hamilton. Toronto, 1871. Second edition. Hood's 103-753 1974 $17.50

STEPHENSON, HENRY THEW   The Elizabethan People. New York, 1910. Inner hinges split. Biblo & Tannen 213-707 1973 $7.50

STEPHENSON, HENRY THEW   The Study of Shakespeare. 1915. Small 8vo., full green calf, gilt, plates. Quaritch 936-565 1974 £7

STEPHENSON, JOHN   Medical Botany. (1827)-1831). 8vo., 4 vols., blue cloth binding, plates. Bow Windows 64-259 1974 £88

STEPHENSON, JOHN   Medical Zoology and Mineralogy. 1838. Roy 8vo., contemporary half roan, plates. Wheldon 130-1624 1974 £100

STEPHENSON, MILL   A List of Monumental Brasses In Surrey. n.d. Thick demy 8vo., plates, illus., binders buckram. Smith 194-281 1974 £5

STEPHENSON, ROBERT   Description of the Patent Locomotive Steam Engine. London, 1838. 4to., boards, presentation copy, inscribed. Hammond 201-919 1974 £65

STEPHENSON, TERRY E.   Caminos Viejos. Santa Ana, 1930. 8vo., cloth, limited. Saddleback 14-289 1974 $50

STEPHENSON, TERRY E.   Shadows of Old Saddleback. Santa Ana, 1931. 8vo., quarter leather, rebacked, morocco. Saddleback 14-290 1974 $50

STEPHENSON, TERRY E.   Shadows of Old Saddleback. Santa Ana, 1931. 8vo., quarter cloth, rebacked. Saddleback 14-291 1974 $40

STEPHENSON, W. H.   A History of the South. Large 8vo., cloth, fine, 9 vols. Putnam 126-253 1974 $60

STEPHENSON, BLAKE & CO. LTD.   Printing Types: Borders, Initials etc. Sheffield, 1924. Plates, demy 8vo., good copy, orig. cloth. Broadhurst 24-472 1974 £12

STEPNEY, GEORGE   An Essay. Dublin, 1701. 4to., uncut, stitched as issued. Dawsons PM 251-485 1974 £12

STERLAND, W. J.   Descriptive List of the Birds of Nottinghamshire. Mansfield, 1879. 8vo., orig. cloth. Wheldon 130-626 1974 £5

STERLING, ADA   A Belle of the Fifties, Memoirs of Mrs. Clay. New York, 1905. 8vo., orig. cloth, illus. Putnam 126-235 1974 $10

STERLING, ADA   The Jew and Civilization. 1924. 330p. Austin 62-616 1974 $7.50

STERLING, WILSON   Quarter-Centennial History of the University of Kansas. Topeka, 1891. 16mo., cloth. Saddleback 14-435 1974 $10

STERNE, LAURENCE   Letters of. London, 1775. 3 vols., 8vo., contemporary calf, first edition. Dawsons PM 252-917 1974 £165

STERNE, LAURENCE   Laurence Sterne's Letter to the Rev. Mr. Blake. St. Louis, 1915. 4to., boards, first edition. Goodspeed's 578-331 1974 $15

STERNE, LAURENCE   Second Journal to Eliza. 1929. Orig. cloth, fine, first edition. Rota 188-861 1974 £5

STERNE, LAURENCE   A Sentimental Journey through France and Italy. London, 1768. Small 8vo., contemporary calf, gilt, first edition. Hammond 201-334 1974 £110

STERNE, LAURENCE   A Sentimental Journey through France and Italy. 1768. Small 8vo., contemporary calf, rebacked, frontispiece, first edition. Quaritch 936-224 1974 £140

STERNE, LAURENCE   A Sentimental Journey through France and Italy. 1768. 12mo., contemporary calf, 2 vols., rebacked, second edition. Quaritch 936-225 1974 £35

STERNE, LAURENCE   A Sentimental Journey through France and Italy. London, 1792. 8vo., contemporary sprinkled calf, plates. Hammond 201-335 1974 £10

STERNE, LAURENCE   A Sentimental Journey Through France and Italy. 1897. Unusually fine copy, gilt design on upper board, illus., first edition. Covent 51-1581 1973 £10

STERNE, LAURENCE   A Sentimental Journey Through France and Italy. 1910. 4to., orig. cloth, coloured plates, slight spotting. Bow Windows 66-657 1974 £10

STERNE, LAURENCE   A Sentimental Journey Through France and Italy. 1910. 4to., orig. buckram gilt, limited. Howes 185-473 1974 £7.50

STERNE, LAURENCE   A Sentimental Journey Through France and Italy. 1926. Illus., nice edition. Austin 61-941 1974 $12.50

STERNE, LAURENCE   A Sentimental Journey Through France & Italy. 1927. Orig. cloth, illus. Marsden 37-531 1974 £5

STERNE, LAURENCE   The Works. Harrisburgh, 1804-05. 5 vols., 12mo., contemporary tree calf, spines gilt, morocco labels, good copy, rare, second American collected edition. Ximenes 37-201 1974 $125

STERNE, LAURENCE   Works, With Life of the Author. 1885. 4 vols., plates, new buckram, blind stamp, illus. by. Thomas Stothard. Allen 216-2068 1974 $25

STETSON, CHARLOTTE PERKINS   Women and Economics. Boston, 1900. Orig. binding. Butterfield 10-541 1974 $10

STETTINER, RICHARD   Die Illustrierten Prudentius Handschriften. Berlin, 1905. Folio, plates, half blue cloth (plate vol. only). Kraus B8-257 1974 $250

STEUART, HENRY   The Planter's Guide. Edinburgh, 1828. Large 8vo., orig. boards, uncut, plates, second edition. Traylen 79-59 1973 £6

STEUART, HENRY   The Planter's Guide. Edinburgh, 1828. Demy 8vo., contemporary half calf, marbled boards, plates foxed. Broadhurst 24-1172 1974 £5

STEUDEL, E. G.   Nomenclator Botanicus. Stuttgart, 1841. 4to., new buckram, second edition. Wheldon 129-967 1974 £15

STEVENS, ASHTON   Actorviews. Covici, McGee, 1923. 324p., illus. Austin 51-921 1973 $10

STEVENS, C. A.   Berdan's United States Sharpshooters in the Army of the Potomac, 1861-65. St. Paul, 1892. Scarce, illus., orig. binding. Butterfield 10-185 1974 $40

STEVENS, DANIEL G.   The First Hundred Years of the American Baptist Publication Society. Philadelphia, (1924). 8vo., cloth. Goodspeed's 578-533 1974 $10

STEVENS, F. L.   The Fungi Which Cause Plant Disease. New York, 1913. Roy 8vo., cloth. Wheldon 129-1357 1974 £10

STEVENS, F. L.   Plant Disease Fungi. New York, 1925. 8vo., cloth. Wheldon 129-1356 1974 £5

STEVENS, GEORGE ALEXANDER   The Birth-Day of Folly, an Heroi-Comical Poem. London, 1755. 4to., disbound, very scarce, first edition. Ximenes 37-203 1974 $75

STEVENS, HAZARD   The Life of Issaac Ingalls Stevens by His Son. 1900. 2 vols., scarce, illus., orig. binding. Butterfield 10-186 1974 $50

STEVENS, HENRY   Recollections of Mr. James Lenox of New York and Formation of His Library. 1886. Large paper copy, new buckram. Allen 216-190 1974 $10

STEVENS, HENRY   Recollections of Mr. James Lenox of New York. London, 1887. 12mo., plates, orig. half cloth, uncut. Dawsons PM 10-582 1974 £7

STEVENS, JOHN H.   Personal Recollections of Minnesota and Its People. Minneapolis, 1890. 8vo., cloth. Saddleback 14-522 1974 $25

STEVENS, PAUL   Fables. Montreal, 1857. 8vo., orig. printed wrappers, first edition. Ximenes 35-280 1974 $20

STEVENS, WILLIAM   Observation on the Healthy and Diseased Properties of the Blood. London, 1832. 8vo., half calf, first edition. Schumann 35-453 1974 $65

STEVENS, WILLIAM   Observations on the Healthy and Diseased Properties of the Blood. 1832. 8vo., contemporary calf, gilt spine, neatly rebacked, slight foxing, first edition. Bow Windows 66-658 1974 £15.50

STEVENS, WILLIAM O.   The Cross In the Life and Literature of the Anglo-Saxons. 1904. Ex-library, sturdy library binding, orig. edition. Austin 61-942 1974 $10

STEVENSON, ALEXANDER F.   The Battle of Stone's River. Boston, 1884. Orig. blue cloth, scarce, worn, first edition. Bradley 35-426 1974 $32

STEVENSON, BURTON   Stevenson's Book of Quotations. 1938. Thick roy. 8vo., buckram, revised third edition. Howes 185-385 1974 £6.50

STEVENSON, DAVID   Fifty Years on the London and North Western Railway. 1891. 8vo., orig. cloth, first edition. Broadhurst 23-1277 1974 £12

STEVENSON, DAVID   The Principles and Practice of Canal and River Engineering. Edinburgh, 1872. Roy 8vo., orig. cloth, gilt, plates, illus., second edition. Hammond 201-865 1974 £25

STEVENSON, H.   The Birds of Norfolk. 1866-90. 3 vols., 8vo., orig. cloth, portrait, plain and coloured plates, scarce. Wheldon 128-568 1973 £10

STEVENSON, J.   Hymenomycetes Britannici. 1886. 2 vols., 8vo., cloth, woodcuts, scarce. Wheldon 128-1427 1973 £10

STEVENSON, J.   Hymenomycetes Britannici: British Fungi. 1886. 2 vols., 8vo., cloth, woodcuts, scarce. Wheldon 131-1471 1974 £10

STEVENSON, J.   Mycologia Scotica. Edinburgh, 1879. 8vo., cloth, scarce. Wheldon 131-1472 1974 £7.50

STEVENSON, J. H.   Heraldry in Scotland. Glasgow, 1914. Crown 4to., 2 vols., half vellum, uncut, limited edition. Broadhurst 23-1278 1974 £40

STEVENSON, JOHN   Two Centuries of Life in Down. Belfast, 1920. 8vo., cloth boards. Emerald 50-900 1974 £6.50

STEVENSON, ROBERT LOUIS   Across the Plains. London, 1892. 8vo., orig. buckram boards, first edition. Ximenes 35-281 1974 $15

STEVENSON, ROBERT LOUIS   The Ebb-Tide. London, 1894. Orig. pictorial cloth, first edition, bookplate of John Stuart Groves and another, about fine. MacManus 224-404A 1974 $25

STEVENSON, ROBERT LOUIS   Edinburgh. London, 1879. Etchings by A. Brunet-Debaines, folio, orig. cloth gilt, bit rubbed, first edition, fine copy, Jermone Kern's copy with his bookplate. MacManus 224-405 1974 $110

STEVENSON, ROBERT LOUIS   Catriona. London, 1893. Orig. blue buckram, first edition, very good copy. MacManus 224-404 1974 $25

STEVENSON, ROBERT LOUIS   A Child's Garden of Verses. London, 1885. 12mo., blue cloth, gilt, top edge gilt, fine copy, scarce first edition, first issue. Frohnsdorff 15-158 1974 $250

STEVENSON, ROBERT LOUIS   A Child's Garden of Verses. London, 1885. 12mo., blue cloth, gilt, bevelled edges, top edge gilt, marginal repair to title, very good copy, first edition, second issue. Frohnsdorff 15-159 1974 $125

STEVENSON, ROBERT LOUIS   Island Nights' Entertainments. London, 1893. Orig. pictorial cloth, somewhat rubbed, upper hinges shaky, first English edition, very good copy. MacManus 224-406 1974 $25

STEVENSON, ROBERT LOUIS   Island Nights' Entertainments. 1893. 8vo., orig. cloth, illus., first edition. Bow Windows 66-659 1974 £12.50

STEVENSON, ROBERT LOUIS   Island Night's Entertainments. 1893. Orig. blue-green pictorial cloth gilt, plates. Howes 186-434 1974 £6.50

STEVENSON, ROBERT LOUIS   Kidnapped, Being Memoirs of the Adventures of David Balfour in the Year 1751. London, 1886. Orig. red cloth, small stain on spine, first issue, with following readings: p. 40 "business", p. 64 "nine", p. 101 "Islands", with folding map, upper hinge bit shaky, else fine copy. MacManus 224-407 1974 $50

STEVENSON, ROBERT LOUIS   A Lowden Sabbath Morn. 1898. Illus. Austin 61-945 1974 $12.50

STEVENSON, ROBERT LOUIS   More New Arabian Nights. 1885. Orig. cloth, faded. Covent 55-1414 1974 £10

STEVENSON, ROBERT LOUIS   More New Arabian Nights. 1885. 8vo., orig. cloth, scarce, gilt, first edition. Rota 190-924 1974 £5

STEVENSON, ROBERT LOUIS   Novels, Tales, Letters and Miscellanies Of. 1920. 25 vols. Austin 61-946 1974 $47.50

STEVENSON, ROBERT LOUIS   Poems and Ballads. New York, 1896. 1st Amer. ed. Biblo & Tannen 213-604 1973 $10

STEVENSON, ROBERT LOUIS   Prayers Written at Vailima. 1910. 4to., orig. white boards. Smith 193-682 1973 £5.50

STEVENSON, ROBERT LOUIS   Prayers Written at Vailima. London, 1910. 4to., orig. boards, uncut, top edges gilt, reproduction of the illuminated manuscript by Alberto Sangorski. Kraus B8-405 1974 $50

STEVENSON, ROBERT LOUIS   Prayers Written at Vailma. London, 1928. 8vo., white paper boards, soiled, interior mint, reproductions of illuminations. Current BW9-279 1974 $22.50

STEVENSON, ROBERT LOUIS   The Silverado Squatters. 1883. 8vo., dark blue cloth, first edition. Rota 190-923 1974 £8.50

STEVENSON, ROBERT LOUIS   The Strange Case of Dr. Jekyll and Mr. Hyde With Other Fables. 1896. Bookplate, fine copy, first edition. Covent 51-1760 1973 £8.50

STEVENSON, ROBERT LOUIS   Tales and Fantasies. London, 1904. 1st ed. Biblo & Tannen 210-674 1973 $22.50

STEVENSON, ROBERT LOUIS   Treasure Island. New York, 1911. First edition, pres. copy. Biblo & Tannen 210-171 1973 $25

STEVENSON, ROBERT LOUIS   Treasure Island. 1927. 4to., full vellum, morocco label, plates, English first edition. Covent 56-691 1974 £225

STEVENSON, ROBERT LOUIS   Treasure Island. New York, Limited Editions Club, 1941. Limited edition, coloured plates and illus., roy. 8vo., orig. flex. cloth, fine. Sawyer 293-204 1974 $40

STEVENSON, ROBERT LOUIS   Three Short Poems. London, 1898. Orig. paper over boards, first edition, no. 8 of 30 copies, fine. MacManus 224-408 1974 $75

STEVENSON, ROBERT LOUIS   Vailima Letters. 1895. One of 125 numbered copies on hand made paper, portraits, buckram, gilt top, covers faded, very good copy, first edition. Covent 51-1761 1973 £14

STEVENSON, ROBERT LOUIS   Virginibus Puerisque. London, 1881. 12mo., cloth, back faded, covers trifle soiled, Augustine Birrell's copy with his bookplate, first edition. Goodspeed's 578-340 1974 $25

STEVENSON, ROBERT LOUIS   Virginibus Puerisque and Other Prayers. 1881. Orig. cloth, scarce, first edition. Rota 188-862 1974 £25

STEVENSON, ROBERT LOUIS   Weir of Hermiston. London, 1896. 8vo., orig. buckram, foxing, first published edition. Bow Windows 62-870 1974 £9.50

STEVENSON, ROBERT LOUIS   Weir of Hermiston. London, 1896. Orig. blue buckram, first published edition, bookplate, very fine copy. MacManus 224-409 1974 $25

STEVENSON, ROBERT LOUIS   Works. 1900-10. Crown 8vo., black buckram. Howes 186-432 1974 £12

STEVENSON, ROBERT LOUIS   The Works of. New York, c. 1920. 10 vols., blue cloth, paper labels, good. Current BW9-280 1974 $20

STEVENSON, ROBERT LOUIS   Works. 1922-23. Vailima edition, 26 vols., med. 8vo., buckram, top edges gilt, others uncut, fine. Broadhurst 24-1715 1974 £80

STEVENSON, ROBERT LOUIS   The Works. London, 1922-23. 26 vols., 8vo., plates, orig. buckram, illus., gilt. Dawsons PM 252-918 1974 £96

STEVENSON, ROBERT LOUIS   Works. 1924. 35 vols., complete, orig. dec. leather gilt, gilt tops, very nice set. Covent 51-3257 1973 £45

STEVENSON, ROBERT LOUIS   The Wrong Box. 1889. Crown 8vo., orig. scarlet cloth, spotted, first edition. Howes 186-438 1974 £7.50

STEVIN, SIMON   Les Oeuvres Mathematiques . . . ou Sont Inserees les Memoires Mathematiques. Leiden, 1634. 6 parts in 1 vol., with rare correction leaf to p. 529 laid in, woodcut diagrams, folio, contemporary calf, rebacked, with the Earl Fitzwilliam's Bookplate, best & most complete edition. Kraus 137-79 1974 $1,450

STEWARD, AUSTIN   Twenty-Two Years a Slave and Forty Years a Freeman. Rochester, 1857. First edition, orig. binding. Butterfield 10-114 1974 $50

STEWART, BASIL   Japanese Colour-Prints and the Subjects They Illustrate. 1920. Small 4to., half morocco, rubbed, plates, scarce. Quaritch 940-420 1974 £50

STEWART, BASIL   Subjects Portrayed in Japanese Colour-Prints. 1922. Crown 4to., orig. cloth, uncut. Broadhurst 23-208 1974 £80

STEWART, C. J.   A Catalogue of the Library Collected By Miss Richardson Currer. London, 1833. Large 8vo., marbled boards, second edition. Dawsons PM 10-583 1974 £70

STEWART, CECIL   Topiary. n.d. Small 4to., half buckram, fine, English first edition. Covent 56-532 1974 £15.75

STEWART, CHARLES SAMUEL   Sketches of Society In Great Britain and Ireland. Philadelphia, 1834. 2 vols., 12mo., orig. violet cloth, labels, first edition. Ximenes 35-282 1974 $30

STEWART, DUGALD   An Account of the Life and Writings of William Robertson. 1801. 8vo., contemporary mottled calf, gilt. Hill 126-228 1974 £16

STEWART, DUGALD   Philosophical Essays. Edinburgh, 1810. 4to., contemporary calf, gilt, first edition. Ximenes 35-283 1974 $125

STEWART, DUNCAN   A Short Historical and Genealogical Account of the Royal Family of Scotland. Edinburgh, 1739. Crown 4to., contemporary panelled calf, rebacked. Howes 186-1653 1974 £12.50

STEWART, FRANCES ANNE   A Journal of Three Months' Tour. (London,) 1843. 12mo., orig. cloth, plates, first editon. Ximenes 35-284 1974 $12.50

STEWART, JEAN   Poetry in France and England. 1931. Fine, English first edition. Covent 56-1805 1974 £3.50

STEWART, JOHN   The Life and Adventures of the Celebrated Walking Stewart. London, 1822. 8vo., later cloth, scarce, first edition. Ximenes 35-285 1974 $25

STEWART, RANDALL   Nathaniel Hawthorne. Yale Univ., 1948. 279p., orig. ed. Austin 54-972 1973 $12.50

STEWART, S. A.   A Flora of the North-East of Ireland. 1888. Crown 8vo., cloth. Wheldon 128-1225 1973 £5

STIANSEN, P.   History of the Norwegian Baptists in America. Cloth, illus., fine. Putnam 126-359 1974 $15

STIDGER, O. P.   Commentary on Proposed Immigration and Exclusion Law. San Francisco, 1913. Austin 62-618 1974 $12.50

STIELTJES, G. J.   Handleiding Tot de Kennis der Verschillende. 1832. 8vo., contemporary half calf, first edition. Dawsons PM 251-405 1974 £35

STIGAND, C. M.   The Game of British East Africa. 1913. 4to., cloth, plates, second edition. Wheldon 129-403 1974 £25

STIGAND, WILLIAM   The Life Work, and Opinions of Heinrich Heine. 1875. 2 vols., contemporary half calf, gilt, first edition. Howes 185-216 1974 £12

STILES, HELEN E.   Pottery of the Ancients. New York, 1938. Biblo & Tannen 214-94 1974 $10

STILES, HENRY R.   A History of the City of Brooklyn. Brooklyn, 1867. 2 vols., fine, maps. Ballinger 1-316 1974 $50

STILL, A. T.   Autobiography of Kirksville. 1897. Orig. cloth, signed, first edition. Putnam 126-206 1974 $22.50

STILL, GEORGE FREDERICK   The History of Paediatrics. London, 1931. 8vo., orig. green cloth, first edition. Dawsons PM 249-463 1974 £20

STILLE, CHARLES J.   The Life and Services of Joel R. Poinsett. Philadelphia, 1888. Wrapper, chipped. Jenkins 61-2203 1974 $35

STILLE, CHARLES J.   Memorial of the Great Central Fair for the U. S. Sanitary Commission. Philadelphia, 1864. First edition, 4to., illus., orig. binding, bevelled edges. Wilson 63-97 1974 $35

STILLINGFLEET, BENJAMIN   Miscellaneous Tracts Relating to Natural History. London, 1791. 8vo., contemporary tree calf, rebacked, plates, fourth edition. Hammond 201-681 1974 £12.50

STILLINGFLEET, EDWARD   Irenicum. 1661. Small 4to., contemporary calf, worn, first edition. Howes 185-1676 1974 £75

STILLINGFLEET, EDWARD   Origines Britannicae. Oxford, 1842. 2 vols., orig. cloth, printed labels, best edition. Howes 185-1677 1974 £10

STILLINGFLEET, EDWARD   Six Sermons. 1669. Crown 8vo., rubbed, contemporary calf, first edition. Howes 185-1678 1974 £18

STIMSON, DOROTHY   Scientists and Amateurs. New York, 1948. Biblo & Tannen 213-868 1973 $9.50

STIMSON, E.   The Cholera Beacon. London, 1937. Card cover. Hood's 103-676 1974 $15

STIMSON, E. R.   History of the Separation of Church and State In Canada. Toronto, 1887. Second edition. Hood's 104-327 1974 $20

STIRLING, EDWARD   The Bloomer Costume or the Figure of Fun. Taylor, ca. 1850. Austin 51-923 1973 $6.50

STIRLING, EDWARD   The Buffalo Girls. London, n.d. 16mo., disbound, frontispiece, first edition. Ximenes 35-286 1974 $12.50

STIRLING, EDWARD   Mrs. Caudles Curtain Lecture. French, 1845. Austin 51-922 1973 $6.50

STIRLING, JAMES   Methodus Differentialis. London, 1753. 4to., old half sheep. Gurney 64-207 1974 £30

STIRLING, JAMES   Methodus Differentialis. London, 1753. 4to., old half sheep, rubbed. Gurney 66-177 1974 £30

STIRLING, PATRICK J.   The Australian and Californian Gold Discoveries, and Their Probable Consequences. Edinburgh, 1853. Folding chart, first edition, crown 8vo., uncut, unopened, spine dulled & little worn, scarce, orig. cloth. Broadhurst 24-1688 1974 £15

STIRLING-MAXWELL, WILLIAM   Don John of Austria. 1883. 2 vols., thick roy. 8vo., orig. cloth, engravings. Howes 186-962 1974 £9.50

STIRLING-MAXWELL, WILLIAM   Don John of Austria. London, 1883. 2 vols., large 8vo., orig. cloth, library stamp, engravings. Bow Windows 62-873 1974 £8.50

STIRRUP, THOMAS   The Description and Use of the Universall Quadrat. London, 1655. Small 4to., contemporary calf, rebacked, plates, fine, first edition. Traylen 79-272 1973 £175

STISTED, GEORGIANA M.   The True Life of Capt. Sir Richard Burton. 1896. Crown 8vo., orig. buckram, portrait, first edition. Howes 185-53 1974 £5.25

STITH, WILLIAM   The History of the First Discovery and Settlement of Virginia. New York, 1865. One of 50 copies, large paper, uncut, top edges gilt, printed for Joseph Sabin and initialled by him. Jenkins 61-2551 1974 $75

STOCCHETTI, FELICE   Ragionamenti . . . Intorno Alla Pressione Dell' Aria. 1705. 4to., contemporary vellum, first edition. Dawsons PM 245-695 1974 £35

STOCK, JOSEPH   The Book of Job. 1805. 4to., contemporary half calf. Hill 126-253 1974 £15

STOCK, NELLY   Miss Weeton; Journal of a Governess, 1807-11. 1936-39. 2 vols. Allen 216-1627 1974 $15

STOCKDALE, JOHN JOSEPH   The History of the Inquisitions. London, 1810. 4to., modern boards, first edition. Dawsons PM 251-518 1974 £18

STOCKDALE, PERCIVAL   The Poet. London, 1773. 4to., disbound. Ximenes 35-287 1974 $75

STOCKTON, FRANCIS RICHARD   The Adventures of Captain Horn. Scribner, 1875. 404 pages, orig. edition. Austin 54-973 1973 $7.50

STOCKTON, FRANCIS RICHARD   The Associate Hermits. Harper, 1899. Illus., 257 pages, orig. edition. Austin 54-974 1973 $10

STOCKTON, FRANCIS RICHARD   Buccaneers and Pirates of Our Coasts. New York, 1898. 12mo., cloth, first edition. Goodspeed's 578-345 1974 $10

STOCKTON, FRANCIS RICHARD   Captain Chap. 1897. Orig. pictorial cloth, English first edition. Covent 56-1211 1974 $8.50

STOCKTON, FRANCIS RICHARD   The Captain's Toll Gate. Appleton, 1903. 359 pages, illus., orig. edition. Austin 54-975 1973 $10

STOCKTON, FRANCIS RICHARD   The Casting Away of Mrs. Lecks and Mrs. Aleshine. New York, (1886). Orig. cloth, first state, with signature numbers present, clippings about the book pasted in, fine, boxed. MacManus 224-412 1974 $65

STOCKTON, FRANCIS RICHARD   The Girl at Cobhurst. 1898. Orig. edition. Austin 54-976 1973 $7.50

STOCKTON, FRANCIS RICHARD   The Great Stone of Sardis. 1898. Illus., very good copy, orig. pictorial cloth, first edition. Covent 51-1765 1973 £10.50

STOCKTON, FRANCIS RICHARD   A Jolly Friendship. New York, 1880. Orig. cloth, first edition, very fine copy. MacManus 224-413 1974 $50

STOCKTON, FRANCIS RICHARD   The Lady, or the Tiger? And Other Stories. New York, 1884. Orig. cloth, ends of spine rubbed, first edition, very good copy, boxed. MacManus 224-414 1974 $85

STOCKTON, FRANCIS RICHARD   The Lady or the Tiger? New York, 1884. 12mo., cloth, little rubbed. Goodspeed's 578-343 1974 $15

STOCKTON, FRANCIS RICHARD   Mrs. Cliff's Yacht. Scribner, 1896. 314 pages, illus., orig. edition. Austin 54-977 1973 $7.50

STODDARD, DAYTON   Lord Broadway. Funk, 1941. 368p., illus. Austin 51-924 1973 $10

STODDART, J.   Remarks on Local Scenery and Manners in Scotland. 1801. 2 vols., roy. 8vo., old calf, plates. Quaritch 939-677 1974 £35

STODDARD, LOTHROP   The Revolt Against Civilization. 1950. Austin 62-619 1974 $6.50

STODDARD, LOTHROP   Social Classes in Post-War Europe. Scribner, 1925. Austin 62-620 1974 $10

STOEFFLER, JOHANNES   In Procli Diadochi. Tubingen, 1534. Folio, late 16th century Italian vellum, recased, woodcut diagrams, fine, first edition. Harper 213-148 1973 $1,200

STOEFFLER, JOHANNES   Procli Diadochi. (1534). Folio, modern half calf, labels, gilt. Zeitlin 235-215 1974 $350

STOKER, BRAM   Dracula. Westminster, 1897. 8vo., uncut, orig. yellow cloth, first edition. Dawsons PM 252-919 1974 £60

STOKER, BRAM   Dracula's Guest. New York, 1937. Biblo & Tannen 210-675 1973 $10

STOKER, BRAM   A Glimpse of America: A Lecture Given at the London Institution Dec. 1, 1885. 1886. Backstrip split, wrappers torn at edges, darkened & detached, else very good copy, first edition. Covent 51-1768 1973 £12.50

STOKER, BRAM   The Lady of the Shroud. London, 1909. Biblo & Tannen 210-676 1973 $15

STOKER, BRAM   The Lair of the White Worm. London, 1911. 1st ed., inner hinge split. Biblo & Tannen 210-677 1973 $20

STOKER, BRAM   The Mystery of the Sea. New York, 1904. Biblo & Tannen 210-678 1973 $10

STOKER, BRAM   Personal Reminiscences of Henry Irving. Macmillan, 1906. 385p., orig. ed. Austin 51-925 1973 $14

STOKER, BRAM   Personal Reminiscences of Henry Irving. 1906. 2 vols., plates, orig. cloth, orig. edition. Howes 186-460 1974 £6

STOKER, BRAM   The Shoulder of Shasta. 1895. Faded, first edition. Covent 55-1416 1974 £12.50

STOKER, BRAM   The Snake's Pass. New York, 1890. 1st ed. Biblo & Tannen 210-679 1973 $75

STOKER, BRAM   The Watter's Mou. Westminster, 1895. Biblo & Tannen 210-680 1973 $22.50

STOKES, CHARLES   Round About the Rockies. Toronto, 1923. Photographs, plates. Hood's 104-877 1974 $15

STOKES, GEORGE GABRIEL   Mathematical and Physical Papers. Cambridge, 1880-1905. 8vo., 5 vols., orig. cloth, portraits. Gurney 66-178 1974 £48

STOKES, I. N. PHELPS   American Historical Prints, Early Views of American Cities. New York, 1933. 8vo., cloth, orig. edition. Goodspeed's 578-534 1974 $25

STOKES, LESLIE   Oscar Wilde. Random, 1938. Austin 51-926 1973 $7.50

STOKES, M.   Early Christian Architecture in Ireland. 1878. Imp. 8vo., plates, cloth, woodcuts. Quaritch 939-633 1974 £22.50

STOKES, RICHARD L.   Benedict Arnold. Putnam, 1941. 137p. Austin 51-927 1973 $8.50

STOKES, WHITLEY   Archiv Fur Celtische Lexikographie. Halle, 1904. 2 vols., roy. 8vo., half vellum. Emerald 50-906 1974 $25

STOKES, WILLIAM   A Treatise on the Diagnosis and Treatment of Diseases of the Chest. Dublin, 1837. 8vo., contemporary blue half calf, first edition. Dawsons PM 249-466 1974 £90

STOKES, WILLIAM   A Treatise on the Diagnosis and Treatment of Diseases of the Chest. Dublin, 1837. 1st ed., 3/4 mod. calf and patterned bds., gilt spine. Jacobs 24-157 1974 $300

STOLBERG, BENJAMIN   Tailor's Progress. Doubleday, 1944. Austin 62-621 1974 $7.50

STOLL, CASPAR   Representation Exactement Coloriee d'Apres Nature des Cigales. Amsterdam, 1788. Large 4to., boards, copperplates, very fine. Harper 213-149 1973 $450

STOLL, ELMER EDGAR   From Shakespeare to Joyce. 1944. Ex-library. Austin 61-949 1974 $12.50

STOLL, MAXIMILIAN   Praelectiones in Diversos Morbos Chronicos. Vienna, 1788-1789. 8vo., contemporary half calf, worn, first edition. Schumann 35-454 1974 $110

STOLZ, F.   Lateinische Grammatik. 1900. New buckram. Allen 213-1007 1973 $12.50

STONE, EDMUND   Analise des Infiniment Petits. Paris, 1735. 4to., contemporary sheep, gilt, plates. Dawsons PM 245-696 1974 £20

STONE, EDWIN M.   History of Beverly. Boston, 1843. 12mo., orig. cloth, foxing, first edition. Ximenes 35-288 1974 $25

STONE, ELIZABETH ARNOLD   Unita County: Its Place in History. Laramie, 1924. 8vo., cloth. Saddleback 14-772 1974 $50

STONE, FRED   Rolling Stone. New York, 1945. Biblo & Tannen 213-905 1973 $8.50

STONE, J. M.   The History of Mary I, Queen of England. 1901. Plates, ex-library, scarce. Howes 186-1060 1974 £5.25

STONE, JAMES   The Complete Baker. Salisbury, (1770). First edition, 8vo., disbound, small wormhole through lower margins but not affecting text, good copy, rare. Sawyer 293-270 1974 £52

STONE, JAMES EDWARD   Register of the Charlestown Men in the Service During the Civil War. Boston, 1919. Wrapper. Butterfield 10-378 1974 $10

STONE, JOHN HURFORD   Copies of Original Letters Recently Written by Persons in Paris to Dr. Priestley. London, 1798. 8vo., cockerell boards, cloth back. Dawsons PM 245-616 1974 £10

STONE, LIVINGSTON   Domesticated Trout. Charlestown, 1877. 8vo., frontis., text illus., gilt dec. green cloth, very good, third revised & enlarged edition. Current BW9-199 1974 $15

STONE, MELVILLE E.   "M. E. S." His Book. New York, 1918. Cloth, illus., paper label, first edition. Bradley 35-359 1974 $20

STONE, THOMAS   General View of the Agriculture of the County of Bedford With Observations On the Means of Improvement. 1794. 4to., modern boards. Wheldon 128-1665 1973 £7.50

STONE, THOMAS T.   Sketches of Oxford County. Portland, 1830. 12mo., orig. quarter roan and boards, very scarce, first edition. Ximenes 37-204 1974 $75

STONE, W.   American Animals. New York, 1902. Crown 4to., buckram, plates. Wheldon 131-523 1974 £7.50

STONE, W.   American Animals. New York, 1922. Biblo & Tannen 213-854 1973 $10

STONE, MRS. WILLIAM LANGSHAWE   The Cotton Lord. London, 1842. 2 vols., 12mo., half calf, first edition. Dawsons PM 252-920 1974 £60

STONE, WILLIAM HALE   Twenty-Four Years a Cowboy and Ranchman. (1905). Illus., stiff printed wrappers, rare, first edition. Bradley 35-360 1974 $3600

STONE, WILLIAM LEETE   Life of Joseph Brant. New York, 1838. First edition, 2 vols. Biblo & Tannen 213-40 1973 $115

STONE, WILLIAM LEETE   The Poetry and History of Wyoming. New York, 1844. 8vo., orig. bindings, second edition. Butterfield 8-515 1974 $30

STONE, WILLIAM LEETE   Ups and Downs in the Life of a Distressed Gentleman. New York, 1836. 12mo., orig. cloth, faded, first edition. Ximenes 35-289 1974 $40

STONEHOUSE, JOHN HARRISON   London, 1931. 5 parts, with prospectus, 8vo., orig. green printed wrappers, matching cardboard case, fine. Ximenes 36-74 1974 $35

STONEY, GEORGE J.   On the Cause of Double Lines and of Equidistant Satellites in the Spectra of Gases. Dublin, 1891. 4to., 1st ed., orig. wraps. Jacobs 24-166 1974 $75

STONHAM, CHARLES   The Birds of the British Islands. 1906-1911. 4to., 5 vols., orig. wrappers, plates. Bow Windows 64-262 1974 £14

STOOPNAGLE, LEMUEL Q.   You Wouldn't Know Me From Adam. Whittlsey, 1944. Austin 51-928 1973 $6.50

STOPES, MARIE CARMICHAEL   A Banned Play. 1926. Presentation copy, inscribed, English first edition. Covent 56-2059 1974 £15

STOPES, MARIE CARMICHAEL   Contraception. 1923. Orig. cloth, plates. Smith 194-531 1974 £5

STOPES, MARIE CARMICHAEL   Contraception, Its Theory, History and Practice. London, 1923. 8vo., orig. cloth, plates, first edition. Gurney 66-179 1974 £15

STOPES, MARIE CARMICHAEL   Married Love. n.d. 8vo., orig. cloth, presentation copy, inscribed, limited edition. Broadhurst 23-1280 1974 £6

STOPFORD, FRANCIS   The Romance of the Jewel. 1920. 4to., orig. quarter leather, gilt boards, plates. Covent 55-934 1974 £35

STORCK, ANTHONY   An Essay of the Medicinal Nature of Hemlock. Edinburgh, 1762. 8vo., contemporary calf, first edition. Schumann 35-455 1974 $145

STORCK, ANTHONY   An Essay on the Medicinal Nature of Hemlock; to which is annexed, A Necessary Supplement on the Subject. Edinburgh, 1762. 12mo., contemporary calf, bit rubbed, second edition, 2 parts. Ximenes 36-174 1974 $40

STORER, JAMES SARGANT   Antiquarian and Topographical Cabinet. London, 1807-11. 8vo., 10 vols., contemporary diced russia, first edition. Dawsons PM 251-71 1974 £175

STORER, JAMES SARGANT   Delineations Graphic and Descriptive of Fountains' Abbey in the West Riding County of York. Ripon, (n.d.). 4to., nineteenth century embossed cloth, spine faded, plates, vignette illus., bookplate. Bow Windows 66-661 1974 £28

STORER, JAMES SARGANT   History and Antiquities of the Cathedral Churches of Great Britain. 1816-19. 4 vols., roy. 8vo., contemporary roan backs, plates. Marsden 39-431 1974 £18

STORIES About Mortimer. 1830. Full page engravings hand coloured, small square 8vo., contemporary cloth, spine faded. George's 610-695 1973 £6

STORIES of Old Daniel. 1810. Second edition, engraved frontis., some slight browning, 12mo., contemporary tree calf, trifle rubbed, joint broken. George's 610-697 1973 £7.50

STORIES Selected from the History of Scotland. 1825. Third edition, engraved plates, 12mo., orig. ptd. boards, roan spine, slightly rubbed. George's 610-704 1973 £7.50

STORR, RAYNER   Concordantia ad Quatuor Libros Latine Scriptos De Imitatione Christi. 1911. Scarce. Howes 185-897 1974 £7

STORRS, JOHN WHITING   Poems. Ansona, conn., 1887. 325p. Austin 54-978 1973 $17.50

STORRS, RONALD   Orientations. 1937. 8vo., orig. cloth, illus., first edition. Rota 190-612 1974 £6.50

STORY, ISAAC   A Parnassian Shop. Boston, 1801. 8vo., contemporary tree calf, first edition. Ximenes 35-291 1974 $70

STORY, ROBERT H.   William Carstares. 1874. Orig. cloth, portrait, scarce. Howes 186-691 1974 £5.50

STORY, SOMMERVILLE   The Sculptures of Rodin. New York, 1949. Folio, 115 plates. Biblo & Tannen 214-491 1974 $22.50

THE STORY of a Round Loaf. 1868. 4to., orig. dec. cloth, gilt. Hammond 201-115 1974 £7.50

THE STORY of Shipping. n.d. 4to., illus., plates, contemporary red morocco gilt, limited edition. Smith 193-699 1973 £5

STORY of the Bluenose. Lunenburg, 1933. Card cover, signed. Hood's 102-214 1974 $20

STOSCH, P. DE   Pierres Antiques Gravees, sur Lesquelles les Graveurs ont mis leurs Noms. Amsterdam, 1724. Large folio, contemporary calf, plates, fine. Quaritch 940-356 1974 £60

STOTHERT, WILLIAM   A Narrative of the Principal Events of the Campaigns of 1809, 1810 and 1811, in Spain and Portugal. 1812. 8vo., grey paper boards, label on spine, uncut, folding map. Bow Windows 66-662 1974 £45

STOTSENBURG, JOHN H.   An Impartial Study of the Shakespeare Title. Louisville, 1904. First edition. Austin 61-950 1974 $27.50

STOUT, REX   Rue Morgue No. 1. New York, 1946. 1st ed. Biblo & Tannen 210-532 1973 $9.50

STOW, JOHN   A Survey of London. London, 1598. 4to., old vellum, first edition. Dawsons PM 251-72 1974 £350

STOW, JOHN   A Survey of London. London, 1603. 4to., calf, front cover detached, second edition. Goodspeed's 578-347 1974 $125

STOW, JOHN   A Survey of the Cities of London and Westminster. 1720. 2 vols., folio, plates, contemporary calf, rebacked, fifth edition. Quaritch 939-850 1974 £300 ·

STOW, JOHN   A Survey of the Cities of London and Westminster. London, 1720. 2 vols., folio, full tan morocco gilt, rubbed, fine, plates. Traylen 79-366 1973 £220

STOWE, HARRIET BEECHER   The Key to Uncle Tom's Cabin. n.d. Orig. cloth, English first edition. Covent 56-2061 1974 £10.50

STOWE, HARRIET BEECHER   The Key of Uncle Tom's Cabin. (1853). Orig. patterned cloth, cover faded, upper joint partly split, very good copy, first edition. Covent 51-1769 1973 £6.30

STOWE, HARRIET BEECHER   Minister's Wooing. 1859. Spine worn, first edition. Allen 216-1628 1974 $10

STOWE, HARRIET BEECHER   Uncle Tom's Cabin. 1852. Half calf gilt, wood engravings, first English edition. Smith 193-411 1973 £10

STOWE, HARRIET BEECHER   Uncle Tom's Cabin. London, 1852. 8vo., dark blue half morocco, gilt, illus., first English edition.   Hammond 201-336 1974 £25

STOWE, HARRIET BEECHER   Uncle Tom's Cabin. London, 1852. Orig. wrappers, illus., uncut, first English edition.   Dawsons PM 252-921 1974 £150

STOWE, HARRIET BEECHER   Uncle Tom's Cabin. Boston, 1852. 2 vols., 8vo., plates, orig. pictorial cloth, gilt, first edition, first issue.   Dawsons PM 250-75 1974 £1150

STOWE, HARRIET BEECHER   Uncle Tom's Cabin. Boston, 1852. 2 vols., three quarter brown morocco, first edition, fine, full page illus.   Schumannn 499-110 1974 sFr 1,800

STOWE: A Description of the Magnificent House and Gardens.   Buckingham, 1780. 8vo., contemporary sheep, rebacked, new edition.   Wheldon 131-1578 1974 £40

STRABO   Geographicorum Commentarii. Basel, 1523. Contemporary limp vellum, very fine, woodcut title borders.   Schumann 499-111 1974 sFr 2,500

STRABO   Rerum Geographicarum Libri Septemdecim. Basel, 1571. Thick folio, contemporary limp vellum, maps, fine, early edition.   Harper 213-150 1973 $750

STRABO   De Situ Orbis. 1516. Small folio, calf backed boards, stains, first edition.   Thomas 30-34 1973 £25

STRACHAN, JOHN   An Introduction to Early Welsh. Manchester, 1909. 8vo., orig. cloth, scarce.   Broadhurst 23-1555 1974 £6

STRACHAN, JOHN   A Letter to the Congregation of St. James' Church, York, U. Canada, Occasioned by the Hon. John Elsley's Publication of the Bishop of Strasbourg's Observations. York, 1834. Orig. mottled card covers re-spined and cornered.   Hood's 102-309 1974 $60

STRACHAN, JOHN   A Letter to the Congregation of St. James' Church, York. York, 1834. Orig. mottled card covers.   Hood's 104-328 1974 $60

STRACHAN-DAVIDSON, JAMES LEIGH   Cicero and the Fall of the Roman Republic. London, 1925. Illus.   Biblo & Tannen 214-604 1974 $7.50

STRACHAN-DAVIDSON, JAMES LEIGH   Problems of the Roman Criminal Law. Oxford, 1912. 2 vols.   Biblo & Tannen 214-661 1974 $32.50

STRACHEY, LYTTON   Elizabeth and Essex. 1928. Dust wrapper, buckram, plates, fine.   Covent 55-1417 1974 £5.25

STRACHEY, LYTTON   Elizabeth and Essex. London, 1928. First edition, very nice copy, presentation inscription to Roger Senhouse from author, orig. cloth, neatly tipped in post card from Strachey to Senhouse.   Crane 7-296 1974 £50

STRACHEY, LYTTON   Portraits in Miniature. London, 1921. 8vo., orig. cloth, dust wrapper, fine, first edition.   Ximenes 35-293 1974 $15

STRACHEY, LYTTON   Portraits in Miniature. 1931. Orig. buckram, first edition.   Howes 185-476 1974 £5

STRACHEY, MARJORIE   Savitri and Other Women. 1920. First edition. Covent 55-1420 1974 £8.50

STRACHEY, RAY   The Cause. 1928. Plates, English first edition. Covent 56-2141 1974 £12.50

STRAIGHT, MICHAEL   Trial By Television. Beacon, 1954. 282p., illus. Austin 51-929 1973 $10

STRAKER, C.   Instructions in the Art of Lithography. London, 1867. Orig. cloth, rebacked, plates.   Dawson's 424-137 1974 $300

STRANG, D.   The Printing of Etchings and Engravings. 1930. 8vo., illus., cloth, scarce.   Quaritch 940-248 1974 £8

STRANG, LEWIS C.   Famous Prima Donnas. Page, 1900. 270p., illus. Austin 51-930 1973 $8.50

STRANGE, MICHAEL   Who Tells Me True. Scribner, 1940. 396p., illus. Austin 51-931 1973 $10

STRANGE, R.   A Descriptive Catalogue of a Collection of Pictures, Selected from the Roman, Florentine, Lombard . . . Flemish, French and Spanish Schools. 1769. Small 8vo., half calf.   Quaritch 940-250 1974 £18

STRANGE, RICHARD   The Life and Gests of S. Thomas Cantilupe. (Ghent), 1674. Small 8vo., contemporary vellum, leather label, first edition. Traylen 79-188 1973 £85

STRANGE, T. A.   English Furniture, Decoration, Woodwork and Allied Arts. n.d. (c. 1910). Demy 4to., leather spine, spine rubbed, illus., fine. Broadhurst 24-199 1974 £12

STRANGE Ports of Call. New York, 1948. lst ed.   Biblo & Tannen 210-592 1973 $15

THE STRANGER'S Guide in Brighton. Brighton, (1847). 12mo., half polished calf, gilt, frontis., illus.   Beeleigh 18-456 1974 £6

THE STRANGER'S Guide in Brighton. Brighton, (1852). 12mo., half calf, gilt, lithographed views.   Beeleigh 18-457 1974 £5.50

STRAPAROLA, GIOVANNI FRANCESCO   The Most Delectable Nights of. Paris, 1906. 2 vols., 8vo., orig. cloth, coloured plates, illus., limited.   Bow Windows 66-664 1974 £10.50

STRASBURGER, EDUARD ADOLF   Ueber Zellbildung und Zelltheilung. Jena, 1875. 8vo., half cloth, plates, rebacked, first edition.   Gilhofer 61-61 1974 sFr. 400

STRASBURGER, G.   Ueber den Bau und das Wachsthum der Zellhaute. Jena, 1882. 8vo., half calf, plates.   Wheldon 128-1169 1973 £5

STRATFORD, E.   An Essay on the True Interests and Resources of the Empire. London, 1783. 8vo., modern boards.   Dawsons PM 247-284 1974 £15

STRATHESK, JOHN   Bits from Blinkbonny. Edinburgh, 1882. 8vo., orig. cloth, worn, second edition.   Bow Windows 64-712 1974 £7.50

STRATON, C. R.   Survey of the Lands of William, First Earl of Pembroke, Transcribed from Vellum Rolls in the Possession of the Earl of Pembroke and Montgomery. 1909. 2 vols., 4to., half brown hardgrain morocco, plates, top edges gilt.   Thomas 32-290 1974 £85

STRATTON, A.   The English Interior. 1920. Large 4to., plates. Eaton Music-676 1973 £10

STRATTON, CLARENCE   Theatron. Holt, 1928. 303p., illus. Austin 51-932 1973 $17.50

STRATTON, R. B.   Captivity of the Oatman Girls. San Francisco, 1857. 12mo., orig. brown cloth, illus., revised second edition.   Ximenes 35-294 1974 $225

STRATTON-PORTER, GENE   The Song of the Cardinal. Indianapolis, 1903. lst ed., illus., bdg. rubbed.   Biblo & Tannen 213-605 1973 $10

STRAUS, OSCAR S.   Under Four Administrations. Houghton, 1922. Austin 62-624 1974 $7.50

STRAUS, RALPH   John Baskerville, a Memoir. Cambridge, 1907. 4to., cloth, uncut, fine, limited.   Dawsons PM 10-26 1974 £33

STRAUS, ROGER   Liberty and Democracy. Willett, Clark, 1939. Austin 62-625 1974 $7.50

STRAUSS, DAVID FRIEDRICH   Das Leben Jesu Kritisch Bearbeitet. Tubingen, 1835-36. 2 vols., 8vo., contemporary half calf, gilt, rubbed, fine, first edition.   Gilhofer 61-40 1974 sFr. 1,000

STRAUSS, DAVID FRIEDRICH   Ulrich von Hutten. Leipzig, 1914. Roy. 8vo., orig. calf. Schuman 37-127 1974 $95

STRAUSS, JOHANN   Oeuvres Choisies de Johann, Joseph & Edouard Strauss. Paris, 1874. 3 vols., cloth, corners broken, first collected works. Eaton Music-525 1973 £10

STRAUSS, MAX   Kunstschatze der Sammlung Dr. Max Strauss in Wien. Vienna, 1920. 4to., plates, full leather, gilt, limited. Quaritch 940-800 1974 £20

STREET, GEORGE EDMUND   Brick and Marble in the Middle Ages. London, 1855. 8vo., orig. cloth, illus., first edition. Ximenes 35-296 1974 $22.50

STREETER, BURNETT HILLMAN   The Chained Library. London, 1931. 4to., orig. cloth, illus., fine, plates. Dawsons PM 10-586 1974 £40

STREETER, D. W.   An Arctic Rodeo. New York, 1929. Illus., map. Hood's 102-78 1974 $7.50

STREHLNECK, E. A.   Chinese Pictorial Art. Shanghai, 1914. 4to., orig. patterned silk, inscribed, English first edition. Covent 56-1509 1974 £48

STRELE, KARL   Die Technik des Kolorirens. Welmar, 1869. Boards, cloth, third edition. Dawson's 424-240 1974 $25

STRICKLAND, AGNES   Lives of the Queens of England. 1841-48. 12 vols., crown 8vo., contemporary half morocco gilt, second edition. Howes 186-1240 1974 £30

STRICKLAND, AGNES   Lives of the Queens of Scotland. 1850-59. 8 vols., crown 8vo., half morocco, first edition. Howes 186-1241 1974 £35

STRICKLAND, AGNES   The Moos-House. (1823). Revised new edition, with half title, engraved plates, 12mo., contemporary roan backed boards. George's 610-708 1973 £5

STRICKLAND, AGNES   Tales of the School-Room. (c. 1835). First edition, hand coloured lithograph frontis., 12mo., orig. embossed cloth. George's 610-709 1973 £5

STRICKLAND, AGNES   The Use of Sight. (1824). First edition, 12mo., orig. boards, morocco spine, copperplates. George's 610-710 1973 £10

STRICKLAND, SAMUEL   Twenty-Seven Years in Canada West. 1853. 2 vols., 8vo., orig. cloth, some spotting and stains, first edition. Bow Windows 66-666 1974 £78

STRICKLER, HARRY M.   Massanutten Settled by the Pennsylvania Pilgrim, 1726. N.P., c.1924. 8vo., wrapper. Saddleback 14-745 1974 $12.50

STRINDBERG, AUGUST   Breviaire Alchimique. Paris, c. 1912. Portrait, wrappers, covers detached & torn, sewing weak, very good copy. Covent 51-1770 1973 £5.25

STRINGER, ARTHUR   Hephaestus. Toronto, 1903. Mended spine. Hood's 104-795 1974 $10

STROBELBERGER, JOHANN STEPHAN   De Dentium Podagra. Leipzig, 1630. 12mo., contemporary calf, first edition. Schumann 35-457 1974 $475

STRODE, WILLIAM   The Floating Island. London, 1655. 4to., modern boards, first edition. Dawsons PM 252-922 1974 £115

STRONG, MRS. ARTHUR   Roman Sculpture from Augustus to Constantine. 1907. 8vo., orig. cloth, plates, inscription, spine faded. Bow Windows 66-667 1974 £5

STRONG, GEORGE A.   The Song of Milgenwater. Cincinnati, 1856. 12mo., half morocco, first edition. Ximenes 35-297 1974 $17.50

STRONG, LEONARD ALFRED GEORGE   Difficult Love. Oxford, 1927. Orig. cloth, bookplate, first edition. Rota 188-871 1974 £5

STRONG, LEONARD ALFRED GEORGE   March Evening and Other Verses. 1932. One of 100 numbered copies, signed by author, presentation copy, very good copy, wrappers, first edition. Covent 51-1775 1973 £7.50

STRONG, MOSES M.   History of the Terr. of Wisconsin. Madison, 1885. Orig. cloth. Putnam 126-353 1974 $30

STRONGCASTLE, C.   An Essay to Prevent the Exportation of Wool. London, 1742. 8vo., orig. wrappers, fine. Quaritch 939-290 1974 £20

STROTHER, EDWARD   Criticon Febrium. London, 1716. 8vo., contemporary panelled calf, first edition. Schumann 35-458 1974 $110

STROTHER, EDWARD   An Essay on Sickness and Health. London, 1725. 8vo., contemporary panelled calf, first edition. Gurney 64-208 1974 £20

STROTHER, EDWARD   An Essay on Sickness and Health. London, 1725. 8vo., contemporary panelled calf, first edition. Gurney 66-180 1974 £20

STROZZI, TITUS VESPASIANUS   Poemata. 1513. 2 parts in 1 vol., early 19th century dark blue straight grain morocco gilt, raised bands, first edition. Thomas 30-26 1973 £100

STRUNSKY, SIMEON   No Mean City. New York, 1944. 1st ed. Biblo & Tannen 213-80 1973 $7.50

STRUTT, JACOB GEORGE   Sylva Britannica. (1830). Imperial 8vo., half morocco, plates. Wheldon 130-1574 1974 £25

STRUTT, JACOB GEORGE   Sylva Britannica. (1830). Imp. 8vo., half morocco, gilt, plates. Wheldon 131-1755 1974 £25

STRUTT, JOSEPH   A Complete View of the Dress and Habits of the People of England. 1842. 2 vols., roy. 4to., half morocco, plates. Quaritch 939-255 1974 £85

STRUTT, JOSEPH   A Complete View of the Dress and Habits of the People of England. 1796-99. 2 vols., 4to., plates, contemporary diced russia, rebacked in calf, labels. Quaritch 940-738 1974 £120

STRUTT, JOSEPH   The Regal and Ecclesiastical Antiquities of England. 1773. 4to., russia, first edition. Quaritch 939-256 1974 £9

STRUVE, BURCARD GOTTHELF   Bibliotheca Philosophica in Suas Classes. Jena, 1728. 8vo., contemporary calf, fourth edition. Dawsons PM 10-588 1974 £15

STRUVE, CHRISTIAN AUGUSTUS   Asthenology: or, the Art of Preserving Feeble Life. London, 1801. 8vo., contemporary half calf, first edition in English. Schuman 37-242 1974 $95

STRYKER, WILLIAM S.   Official Register of the Officers and Men of New Jersey in the Revolutionary War. Trenton, 1872. Tall thick 8vo., orig. binding. Butterfield 10-437 1974 $75

STRYPE, JOHN   Historical Collections of the Life and Acts Of. 1728. 8vo., contemporary panelled calf, second edition. Hill 126-254 1974 £8.50

STRYPE, JOHN   The Life and Acts of Matthew Parker. 1711. Folio, contemporary calf, rebacked, first edition. Howes 185-1529 1974 £28

STRYPE, JOHN   The Life and Acts of Matthew Parker. 1711. Folio, contemporary calf, browning. Smith 194-532 1974 £7.50

STRYPE, JOHN   Memorials of Thomas Cranmer. 1694. Folio, contemporary panelled calf, illus., first edition. Howes 185-1090 1974 £28

STRYPE, JOHN   Memorials of Thomas Cranmer. 1848-54. 3 vols. in 4, orig. cloth, best edition. Howes 185-1091 1974 £20

STUART, ANDREW   Genealogical History of the Stewarts. 1798. 4to., orig. boards, rebacked, uncut. Howes 186-1654 1974 £12.50

STUART, ANDREW   Letters. London, 1773. 4to., contemporary tree calf, first edition. Dawsons PM 251-341 1974 £20

STUART, DANIEL   Peace and Reform. London, 1794. 8vo., first edition. Dawsons PM 247-286 1974 £15

STUART, JAMES   Poems. Belfast, 1811. 8vo., contemporary half calf, first edition. Ximenes 35-298 1974 $35

STUART, JAMES   Poems on Various Subjects. Belfast, 1811. 8vo., half calf. Emerald 50-912 1974 £10

STUART, JAMES   Three Years in North America. Edinburgh, 1833. 2 vols., 8vo., orig. boards, uncut, third edition. Bow Windows 62-18 1974 £10

STUART, RUTH MC ENERY   Daddy do-Funny's Wisdom Jingles. New York, 1913. lst ed., author's sgd. pres., illus. Biblo & Tannen 210-752 1973 $32.50

STUART-WORTLEY, EMMELINE CHARLOTTE ELIZABETH MANNERS   Travels in the United States, 1849-50. New York, 1851. Ex-library, orig. cloth. Jenkins 61-2693 1974 $17.50

STUBBE, HENRY   A Censure Upon Certain Passages Contained In the History of the Royal Society as Being Destructive to the Established Religion of England. Oxford, 1671. 2 works in 1 vol., 4to., quarter calf. Traylen 79-273 1973 £135

STUBBS, C. W.   Cambridge and Its Story. 1912. 4to., orig. cloth, illus., lithographs, slight foxing. Bow Windows 66-668 1974 £6.50

STUBBS, WILLIAM   The Constitutional History of England. 1874-78. 3 vols., thick crown 8vo., rebound, cloth. Howes 186-1245 1974 £10

STUBBS, WILLIAM   The Constitutional History of England In Its Origin & Development. Oxford, 1880. 3 vols., contemporary tree calf gilt. Smith 193-636 1973 £6

STUBBS, WILLIAM   Historical Introductions to the Rolls Series. 1902. Scarce, orig. & best edition. Howes 186-1246 1974 £6.50

STUDER, JACOB H.   Columbus, Ohio. Columbus, 1873. 12mo., cloth, illus. Saddleback 14-628 1974 $15

STUDIES of Flowers. c. 1880-90. 2 vols., 4to., half roan, coloured plates. Wheldon 128-1540 1973 £70

THE STUDIO. 1907. Half green morocco, gilt, illus. Marsden 37-470 1974 £7

STUKELEY, WILLIAM   The Medallic History of Marcus Aurelius Valerius. 1757-59. 4to., antique calf, boards, first edition. Broadhurst 23-1283 1974 £45

STUKELEY, WILLIAM   The Medallic History of Marcus Aurelius Valerius Carausius, Emperor in Britain. 1757-59. Engraved plates, first edition, 2 vols. in 1, 4to., newly bound antique calf by Bayntun, panelled back marbled boards, fine. Broadhurst 24-1333 1974 £50

STURGE-MOORE, THOMAS
Please turn to
MOORE, THOMAS STURGE

STURGEON, T.   Without Sorcery. N.P., 1948. lst ed. Biblo & Tannen 210-681 1973 $20

STURGEON, WILLIAM   Scientific Researches. 1850. Large 4to., orig. cloth, gilt, first edition. Dawsons PM 245-698 1974 £65

STURGES, PRESTON   Strictly Dishonorable. Liveright, 1929. Austin 51-933 1973 $8.50

STURGIS, B. B.   Field Book of Birds of the Panama Canal Zone. New York, 1928. Post 8vo., cloth, scarce. Wheldon 129-330 1974 £5

STURGIS, WILLIAM   The Oregon Question. Boston, 1845. 8vo., wrapper. Butterfield 8-461 1974 $25

STURLASON, SNORRE   Heimskringla. Cambridge, 1932. Roy. 8vo., orig. buckram gilt, plates, best English edition. Howes 185-215 1974 £9

STURM, J.   Flora von Deutschland. Stuttgart, 1900-07. 12mo., orig. cloth, plates. Wheldon 129-1123 1974 £35

STURM, J.   Flora Von Deutschland in Abbildungen Nach der Natur. Stuttgart, 1900-07. 15 vols., 12mo., orig. cloth, plates, second edition. Wheldon 131-1357 1974 £35

STURM, JOHANN CHRISTOPH   Mathesis Enucleata. London, 1700. 8vo., contemporary panelled calf, first edition in English. Schumann 35-459 1974 $175

STURM, JOHANN CHRISTOPH   Praelectiones Academicae. Frankfurt and Leipzig, 1722. 4to., contemporary calf, rebacked. Dawsons PM 245-699 1974 £25

STURMY, SAMUEL   The Mariner's Magazine. London, 1669. 7 books & addenda in 1 vol., engraved portrait frontispiece, engraved folding plates, folio, contemporary calf, woodcuts, first issue, first edition, very fine copy. Kraus 137-80 1974 $3,400

STURMY, SAMUEL   The Mariner's Magazine, Stor'd With These Mathematical Arts. London, 1684. 7 books and addenda in 1 vol., Folio, contemporary calf, fine, revised third edition, engraved plates, woodcuts. Kraus 137-81 1974 $875

STUTTERS, PERCIVAL   How Percival Caught the Python. How Percival Caught the Tiger. (New York), 1836-37. 2 vols., square 24mo., cloth and boards, color illus., very good copies. Frohnsdorff 16-452 1974 $30

STUYT, JAN   Jan Stuyt, Architect, Den Haag. Zoug, 1933. 8vo., cloth spine, plates. Minters 37-572 1973 $25

SUAREZ DE RIBERA, FRANCISCO   Cirurgia Methodica Chymica Reformada. Madrid, 1722. 4to., contemporary calf, rubbed, first edition. Schuman 37-243 1974 $95

SUBLIGNY, ADRIEN THOMAS PERDOU DE   The Mock-Clelia. London, 1678. 8vo., modern quarter calf, first English edition. Dawsons PM 252-923 1974 £115

SUCKLING, G. W.   Movable Kidney. Birmingham, 1909. 8vo., orig. red cloth, gilt, second edition. Dawsons PM 249-467 1974 £8

SUCKLING, JOHN   Fragmenta Avrea. London, 1646. 8vo., sprinkled calf gilt, fine, first edition. Dawsons PM 252-924 1974 £375

SUCKLING, JOHN   The Works. London, 1709. 8vo., full blue morocco, gilt, portrait, some foxing, large copy. Ximenes 37-205 1974 $40

SUCKLING, JOHN   Works. 1719. 12mo., contemporary calf, portrait. Quaritch 936-226 1974 £25

SUDERMANN, HERMANN   Roses. Scribner, 1909. Austin 51-934 1973 $7.50

SUDHOFF, KARL   Bibliographia Paracelsica. Berlin, 1894-98. 2 vols. in 1, thick 8vo., cloth, lacks 3rd vol. Kraus b8-190 1974 $65

SUE, EUGENE   The Mysteries of Paris. London, 1845. Roy. 8vo., illus., three quarter red calf, marbled boards, fine. Current BW9-608 1974 $32.50

SUE, EUGENE   The Mysteries of Paris. 1845-46. 3 vols., roy. 8vo., half crimson morocco gilt. Howes 185-478 1974 £21

SUE, EUGENE   De Rohan. 1845. Orig. cloth gilt, illus., English first edition. Covent 56-1217 1974 £10.50

SUE, EUGENE   Les Sept Peches Capitaux. Amsterdam, 1847-48. 6 tomes in 3 vols., 16mo., contemporary half cloth. L. Goldschmidt 42-385 1974 $15

SUE, EUGENE   The Wandering Jew. London, 1844. 3 vols., 8vo., orig. cloth, plates, first English edition. Ximenes 35-299 1974 $20

SUE, EUGENE   The Works of. (N.P., n.d.). 10 vols., 8vo., frontispieces, plates, orig. cloth, faded. Bow Windows 62-882 1974 £12.50

SUESS, E.   Das Antlitz der Erde. Vienna and Leipzig,
1888-1909. Imperial 8vo., half morocco, plates. Wheldon 130-974 1974 £45

SUESS, E.   La Face de la Terre. Paris, 1897-1918. 8vo.,
5 vols., brown cloth binding, maps, illus. Bow Windows 64-264 1974 £48

SUESS, E.   Das Antlitz der Erde. Vienna and Leipzig,
1888-1909. 4 vols., imp. 8vo., half morocco neat, maps, plates (some coloured).
Wheldon 128-1056 1973 £45

SUESS, E.   The Face of the Earth. Oxford, 1904-24.
Roy 8vo., 5 vols., cloth, plates. Wheldon 129-869 1974 £40

SUETONIUS, GAIUS TRANQUILLUS   History of the Twelve Caesars. 1899.
2 vols., square 8vo., orig. buckram backed boards, gilt. Howes 186-495 1974
£8.50

SUETONIUS, GAIUS TRANQUILLUS   De Vita Duodecim Caesarum Libri XII.
Strassburg, 1520. Small 4to., modern quarter vellum, lacks second leaf, else
complete, clean and sound. Thomas 32-265 1974 £36

SUFFLING, E. R.   Epitaphia: 1300 British Epitaphs. 1909. Orig.
cloth gilt, fine, scarce, first edition. Covent 51-2322 1973 £7.50

SUFFOLK Green Books. Ipswich, 1894-1828. 13 vols., dampstains. Howes
186-2190 1974 £35

SUGDEN, ALAN VICTOR   A History of English Wallpaper. London,
(1925). Folio, color plates, fine, d.w., orig. cloth. Gregory 44-286 1974
$150

SUKENOBU: Ehon, Shinobu-Gusa: Picture Book ' The Hare's Foot Fern'.
(1750). 3 vols. in 1 complete, illus., orig. embossed covers, buckram slip case.
Quaritch 940-421 1974 £60

SUKENOBU: Ehon Hana, Momiji 'Picture Book Flowers and Autumn Leaves'.
(1770). 3 vols. in 1 complete, illus., orig. grey covers with green bands, worn.
Quaritch 940-422 1974 £60

SULIVAN, RICHARD J.   Tour Through Parts of England, Scotland and
Wales in 1778. 1785. 2 vols., new buckram, rubber stamp, second edition.
Allen 216-893 1974 $25

SULLIVAN, A.   Aviation in Canada, 1917-1918. Toronto,
1919. Photos, rebound in black fabric. Hood's 102-122 1974 $25

SULLIVAN, EDMUND J.   Rosalynde; Euphues Golden Legacie. 1902.
One of 100 copies, numbered & signed by artist, plates, boards, bookplate, nice
copy. Covent 51-2581 1973 £15

SULLIVAN, EDWARD D.   The Fabulous Wilson Mizner. Henkle, 1935.
Austin 51-935 1973 $12.50

SULLIVAN, FRANK   A Rock In Every Snowball. Little, Brown,
1946. 220p. Austin 54-979 1973 $7.50

SULLIVAN, MRS. FREDERICK   Tales of the Peerage and the Peasantry.
London, 1835. 3 vols., 8vo., orig. boards, green morocco, first edition.
Ximenes 35-301 1974 $55

SULLIVAN, GERALD E.   The Story of Englewood. Englewood, c.1924.
12mo., cloth. Saddleback 14-396 1974 $15

SULLIVAN, MARK   Our Times 1900-1925. New York & London,
1935. 6 vols., deluxe edition, blue white & gilt cloth, limited to 570 sets,
inscribed in vol. 1 by author, bookplates, glassine wrappers, very fine. Butterfield 10-503 1974 $85

SULLIVAN, MARK   Our Times. New York, 1926-1935. 6 vols.,
lst eds., illus. Jacobs 24-33 1974 $40

SULLIVAN, ROBERT   A Dictionary of Derivations. 1875. 304 pages.
Austin 61-953 1974 $12.50

SULLIVAN, W. F.   History of Mr. Rightway and His Pupils. 1816.
First edition, engraved plates, 12mo., orig. boards, roan spine, soiled & trifle
rubbed. George's 610-711 1973 £5

SULLY, HENRY   Observations. 1828. 8vo., contemporary half
calf, fine. Dawsons PM 249-468 1974 £22

SULLY, MAXIMILIEN DE BETHUNE   The Memoirs of the Duke of Sully. London,
1810. 8vo., 5 vols., contemporary diced calf, gilt, new edition. Hammond 201-
463 1974 £12

SULLY, MAXIMILIEN DE BETHUNE   Memoirs Translated from the French.
1810. 5 vols., large 8vo., contemporary half calf, new revised edition. Howes
186-1247 1974 £18.50

SULLY-PRUDHOMME, R. F.   Poesies. Paris, (1883)-1897. 8vo., 4 vols.,
blue niger quarter morocco. Bow Windows 64-714 1974 £15

SULZER, JOHANN GEORGE   Allgemeine Theorie der Schonen Kunste.
Leipzig, 1773-75. 8vo., contemporary marbled calf, gilt back rubbed, illus.,
fine copy, second impression of first edition. Schumann 499-112 1974 sFr 790

SUM Nung Au-Young. New York, 1930. Portrait, dust wrapper, presentation,
inscribed, limited, fine. Covent 55-398 1974 £15

SUMMERS, MONTAGUE   Demoniality. London, n.d. (1927). Limited to
1290 copies, this is no. 38 of only 90 printed on Arnold unbleached handmade
paper, full vellum, signed by Summers, near mint, unopened, very rare. Ross
86-443 1974 £140

SUMMERS, MONTAGUE   The Discovery of Witches. 1928. Frontis.,
wrappers, bookplate, very nice copy, scarce, first edition. Covent 51-1778
1973 £7.50

SUMMERS, MONTAGUE   The Grimoire. (1936). Crown 8vo.,
frontispiece, first edition. Howes 186-440 1974 £5.50

SUMMERS, MONTAGUE   The Grimoire and Other Supernatural Stories.
London, n.d. Biblo & Tannen 210-682 1973 $15

SUMMERS, MONTAGUE   The History of Witchcraft and Demonology.
1926. Plates, name on fly, very good copy. Covent 51-2515 1973 £10.50

SUMMERS, MONTAGUE   The Vampire. 1928. Plates, corners bumped,
very good copy. Covent 51-2516 1973 £10.50

SUMMERS, MONTAGUE   The Vampire in Europe. 1929. Plates, covers
somewhat faded, very good copy. Covent 51-2517 1973 £8.50

SUMMERS, MONTAGUE   The Werewolf. 1933. Plates, fine, slightly
worn d.w. Covent 51-2518 1973 £12.60

SUMMERS, MONTAGUE   The Works of Thomas Shadwell. 1927. Crown
4to., half morocco, uncut, fine, scarce, signed. Broadhurst 23-996 1974 £140

SUMNER, CHARLES   Speech on the Cession of Russian America to
the United States. Washington, 1867. No map. Jenkins 61-105 1974 $20

SUN NEWSPAPERS   Casual Essays of The Sun. New York, 1905.
First edition, 8vo., fine condition. Current BW9-84 1974 $40

SUNDERLAND, CHARLES SPENCER, 3RD EARL 1674-1722   Bibliotheca
Sunderlandiana. London, 1881-83. 6 vols., orig. printed wrappers, some corners
chipped off. Kraus B8-258 1974 $38.50

THE SUPERNATURAL Omnibus. New York, 1932. Biblo & Tannen 210-683
1973 $10

SUPERVIELLE, JULES   Gravitations. Paris, 1925. 12mo., orig.
wrapper, uncut, first edition. L. Goldschmidt 42-386 1974 $12.50

SUPPIGER, A. E.   Picturesque Gold, Silver and Copper Mining
in Yavapai County, Arizona. 1903. Oblong 8vo., cloth. Saddleback 14-10
1974 $25

SUR les Pas De Marthe et de Marie. Montreal, 1929. Handsome leather binding.
Hood's 102-743 1974 $12.50

Sur Les Pas de Marthe et de Marie. Montreal, 1929. Leather binding. Hood's
104-329 1974 $12.50

SURREY Archaeological Collections. 1858-1965. 64 vols., 8vo., plates, cloth. Quaritch 939-563 1974 £300

SURTEES, ROBERT SMITH   The Analysis of the Hunting Field. 1846. Roy. 8vo., crushed red levant morocco, plates, first edition, second issue. Quaritch 939-851 1974 £175

SURTEES, ROBERT SMITH   Ask Mamma. (1858). Orig. pictorial cloth gilt, plates, English first edition. Covent 56-1222 1974 £45

SURTEES, ROBERT SMITH   "Ask Mamma." 1858. Full mottled calf, gilt, foxing, first illus. edition. Howes 186-441 1974 £30

SURTEES, ROBERT SMITH   Handley Cross. (1854). Orig. pictorial cloth gilt, plates, first illus. edition. Covent 56-1223 1974 £45

SURTEES, ROBERT SMITH   The Hunting Tours of Surtees. Edinburgh, 1927. 8vo., illus., plates, orig. dec. cloth. Bow Windows 62-883 1974 £7.50

SURTEES, ROBERT SMITH   Jorrock's Jaunts and Jollities. 1843. 8vo., orig. green cloth, plates, second edition, second issue. Quaritch 939-852 1974 £500

SURTEES, ROBERT SMITH   Jorrocks's Jaunts and Jollities. (1901). Imp. 8vo., illus., cloth, plates. Quaritch 939-257 1974 £25

SURTEES, ROBERT SMITH   Mr. Facey Romford's Hounds. (1865). Orig. pictorial cloth gilt, English first edition. Covent 56-1224 1974 £45

SURTEES, ROBERT SMITH   Mr. Sponge's Sporting Tour. (1853). Orig. pictorial cloth gilt, English first edition. Covent 56-1225 1974 £45

SURTEES, ROBERT SMITH   Mr. Sponge's Sporting Tour. London, (1853). Modern half morocco, illus., first edition, second issue, colored plates in fine state, lacks half-title and ads at rear. MacManus 224-417 1974 £50

SURTEES, ROBERT SMITH   Mr. Sponge's Sporting Tour. London, 1853. 8vo., contemporary half calf, gilt, illus., first edition. Dawsons PM 252-925 1974 £55

SURTEES, ROBERT SMITH   Plain or Ringlets. 1860. Orig. pictorial cloth gilt, English first edition. Covent 56-1226 1974 £45

SURVEY of International Affairs. 1925-41. 20 vols., roy. 8vo., maps. Howes 186-1248 1974 £100

THE SUSQUEHANA Synod of the Evangelical Lutheran Church in the U. S. 1917. 340p., illus. Austin 62-393 1974 $17.50

SUTCLIFF, ROBERT   Travels In Some Parts of North America, 1804, 1805, and 1806. York, 1811. Leather, plates, worn. Hood's 103-561 1974 $250

SUTER, H.   Manual of the New Zealand Mollusca. 1913-15. 2 vols., 8vo. and 4to., cloth, plates, scarce. Wheldon 129-857 1973 £25

SUTHERLAND, ABBY A.   Talks With Girls. Philadelphia, 1915. First edition, 8vo. Current BW9-85 1974 $8.50

SUTHERLAND, ALEXANDER   Macrimmon. 1823. 12mo., 4 vols., contemporary half calf, fine. Hill 126-200 1974 £60

SUTHERLAND, ALEXANDER   A Summer Ramble in the North Highlands. Edinburgh, 1825. 12mo., orig. boards, first edition. Ximenes 35-300 1974 $22.50

SUTHERLAND, JAMES   The Adventures of an Elephant Hunter. London, 1912. 8vo., illus., signature, orig. cloth, first edition. Bow Windows 62-893 1974 £6.50

SUTHERLAND, THOMAS JEFFERSON   A Letter to Her Majesty the Queen, With Letters to Lord Durham, Lord Glenelg, and Sir George Arthur. To Which is Added an Appendix Embracing a Report of the Testimony Taken on the Trial of the Writer by a Court Martial at Noronto in Upper Canada. Albany, 1841. Cloth. Hood's 102-579 1974 $250

SUTHERLAND, THOMAS JEFFERSON   A Letter to Her Majesty the Queen, With Letters to Lord Durham, Lord Glenelg and Sir George Arthur. Albany, 1841. Cloth. Hood's 104-661 1974 $250

SUTHERLAND, W.   Handbook of Hardy Herbaceous and Alpine Flowers. 1871. Crown 8vo., orig. cloth. Wheldon 130-1457 1974 £5

SUTPHEN, W. G. VAN T.   The Golfer's Alphabet. New York, 1898. Square 4to., pict. boards, cloth spine, lst ed., illus., with two orig. pen-and-ink drawings. Frohnsdorff 16-348 1974 $100

SUTTON, DENYS   American Painting. London, 1948. Sm. 4to., 48 plates. Biblo & Tannen 213-418 1973 $7.50

SUTTON, FRED E.   Hands Up: Stories of Six-Gun Fighters of the Old Wild West. Indianapolis, 1927. Jenkins 61-2414 1974 $40

SUTTON, JOHN D.   History of Braxton County and Central West Virginia. Sutton, 1919. Cloth, slightly rubbed. Hayman 59-673 1974 $50

SVEDENSTIERNA, ERIC THOMAS   Nagra Underrattelser om Engelska Jernhand-teringen. Stockholm, 1813. 8vo., contemporary Swedish half calf, gilt, fine, first edition. Dawsons PM 245-700 1974 £25

SVEVO, ITALO   As A Man Grows Older. 1932. English first edition. Covent 56-1227 1974 £6.30

SVININE, PAUL   Sketch of the Life of General Moreau. New York, 1814. 12mo., contemporary half morocco. Ximenes 35-302 1974 $15

SWAIN, E. G.   The Stoneground Ghost Tales. Cambridge, 1912. lst ed. Biblo & Tannen 210-684 1973 $15

SWAINSON, C.   A Handbook of Weather Folk-Lore. Edinburgh and London, 1873. 8vo., quarter calf, rebacked. Hammond 201-682 1974 £8.50

SWAINSON, WILLIAM   Animals in Menageries. 1838. Post 8vo., half calf, worn, scarce. Wheldon 130-372 1974 £10

SWAINSON, WILLIAM   Exotic Conchology. 1834 (-1835). 4to., contemporary half calf, hand-coloured lithographed plates. Wheldon 128-858 1973 £75

SWAINSON, WILLIAM   A Preliminary Discourse on the Study of Natural History. 1834. Post 8vo., cloth. Wheldon 129-192 1974 £10

SWAINSON, WILLIAM   A Selection of the Birds of Brazil and Mexico. 1841. Roy 8vo., contemporary half calf, plates. Wheldon 130-77 1974 £1,100

SWAINSON, WILLIAM   Taxidermy. (1840). Post 8vo., cloth, scarce. Wheldon 130-199 1974 £10

SWAINSON, WILLIAM   Zoological Illustrations. 1820-33. 8vo., 2 vols., new half morocco gilt, plates, rare. Wheldon 130-76 1974 £250

SWAINSON, WILLIAM   Zoological Illustrations, the Complete Section on Birds. 1820-33. 2 vols., 8vo., new half morocco gilt, hand-coloured plates, rare. Wheldon 128-570 1973 £250

SWAMMERDAM, JAN   The Book of Nature or the History of Insects. 1758. Folio, contemporary calf, engraved plates. Wheldon 128-814 1973 £200

SWAMMERDAM, JAN   Bybel der Natuure, of Histoire der Insecten-Biblia Naturae, sive Historia Insectorum. Leyden, 1737-38. 2 vols. in 3, newly bound in half calf, antique style, engraved plates, nice copy, first collected edition. Wheldon 128-813 1973 £225

SWAMMERDAM, JAN   Histoire Generale des Insectes. Utrecht, 1685. 4to., new half calf antique, plates. Wheldon 131-864 1974 £80

SWAMMERDAM, JAN   Miraculum Naturae Sive Uteri Muliebris Fabrica. 1679. Small 4to. Rittenhouse 46-603 1974 $155

SWAN, JOSEPH   A Demonstration of the Nerves of the Human Body. London, 1834. 4to., orig. cloth, second edition. Dawsons PM 249-469 1974 £25

SWANN, H. KIRKE   A Monograph of the Birds of Prey. 1924-45.
4to., 2 vols., new half red morocco, plates, limited edition. Wheldon 130-78
1974 £135

SWANN, H. KIRKE   Nature in Acadie. 1895. 8vo., cloth.
Wheldon 130-315 1974 £5

SWANN, H. KIRKE   A Synopsis of the Accipitres. 1922. 8vo.,
buckram, second edition. Wheldon 130-631 1974 £10

SWANZY, H. B.   Some Account of the Family of Hassard. 1903.
8vo., orig. wrappers, illus. Bow Windows 64-541 1974 £7.50

SWAYNE, H. G. C.   Through the Highlands of Siberia. London,
1904. 1st ed. Biblo & Tannen 213-708 1973 $25

SWAYNE, JOHN   The Register of. Belfast, 1935. 8vo., cloth.
Howes 185-1685 1974 £5

SWAYSLAND, EDWARD J. C. Boot and Shoe Design and Manufacture.
1905. 4to., plates, orig. quarter red morocco. Howes 186-1576 1974 £14

SWAYSLAND, W.   Familiar Wild Birds. 1903. Contemporary half
morocco, illus., plates. Wheldon 130-632 1974 £7.50

SWEDENBORG, EMANUEL   The Beauties Of. 1824. 8vo., orig. boards.
Hill 126-256 1974 £17.50

SWEDENBORG, EMANUEL   A Compendium of the Theological Writings
of. London, 1875. 8vo., orig. cloth, rubbed, label. Bow Windows 62-894
1974 £5

SWEDENBORG, EMANUEL   The Doctrine of the New Jerusalem.
Philadelphia, 1815. 12mo., orig. boards, worn, first American edition. Ximenes
35-304 1974 $45

SWEDENBORG, EMANUEL   Opera Philosophica et Mineralia. Dresden,
1734. 3 vols., illus., plates, folio, contemporary calf, backs richly gilt,
complete, extremely rare, from the Prince Liechtenstein Library. Kraus 137-82
1974 $1,250

THE SWEDISH Intelligencer. London, 1632. Small 4to., disbound,
frontispiece, first edition. Ximenes 35-303 1974 $20

SWEDISH-AMERICAN LINE   The Will to Succeed. Stockholm, 1948.
Austin 62-629 1974 $12.50

SWEENEY, JAMES JOHNSON   African Negro Art. New York, 1935.
1st ed., illus., scarce. Biblo & Tannen 213-280 1973 $17.50

SWEENEY, JAMES JOHNSON   Joan Miro. New York, 1941. 4to.,
boards, illus., plates. Minters 37-357 1973 $18

SWEET, ALEX. E.   On a Mexican Mustang. Hartford, 1883. 8vo.,
orig. bindings, illus., fine, first edition. Butterfield 8-631 1974 $45

SWEET, ROBERT   The British Flower Garden. 1823-33. Roy 8vo.,
5 vols., contemporary half calf, plates, fine. Wheldon 130-79 1974 £720

SWEET, ROBERT   The British Flower Garden. 1823-38. 7 vols.,
roy. 8vo., half calf, plates. Wheldon 131-119 1974 £900

SWEET, ROBERT   The British Warblers. 1823(-32). Roy. 8vo.,
half parchment, plates, rare. Wheldon 131-121 1974 £150

SWEET, ROBERT   Cistineae. 1825-1830. 8vo., orig. cloth,
half morocco, plates. Bow Windows 64-265 1974 £120

SWEET, ROBERT   Cistineae. 1825-30. Roy. 8vo., printed
paper wrappers, uncut, half morocco book box, very rare, plates. Wheldon
131-120 1974 £300

SWEET, ROBERT   The Natural Order of Cistus. London,
1825-30. Thick roy. 8vo., plates, foxed. Traylen 79-60 1973 £105

SWEETING, W. D.   Original Papers Relating to Northamptonshire.
1881. Small 8vo., cloth, plates, wrappers. Quaritch 939-505 1974 £5

SWEN, EARL G.   A Bibliography of Virginia. Richmond, 1916.
Part 1, 8vo., wrappers. Kraus B8-259 1974 $15

SWETTENHAM, FRANK   Arabella in Africa. 1925. Plates, covers
faded, very good copy. Covent 51-2612 1973 £6.50

SWIFT, EDMUND L.   The Life and Acts of St. Patrick. Dublin,
1809. 8vo., half calf. Emerald 50-920 1974 £5

SWIFT, JANET H. M.   The Passion Play of Oberammergau. 1930.
Austin 51-937 1973 $7.50

SWIFT, JONATHAN   A Complete Collection of Genteel and Ingenious
Conversation. London, 1738. 8vo., contemporary calf, rubbed, first edition.
Dawsons PM 252-926 1974 £95

SWIFT, JONATHAN   A Complete Collection of Genteel and
Ingenious Conversation. London, 1738. 8vo., contemporary calf, gilt, fine,
first edition. Ximenes 35-305 1974 $225

SWIFT, JONATHAN   A Complete Collection of Genteel and Ingenious
Conversation. 1738. 8vo., contemporary calf, rebacked, first edition. Quaritch 936-227 1974 £65

SWIFT, JONATHAN   The Conduct of the Allies. 1712. 8vo., cloth,
first edition. Quaritch 936-228 1974 £35

SWIFT, JONATHAN   Directions to Servants in General. London,
1745. 8vo., modern red leather, fine, first London edition. Dawsons PM
252-927 1974 £175

SWIFT, JONATHAN   Gulliver's Travels. 1909. Med. 4to., orig.
cream dec. buckram, top edges gilt, others uncut, ties, limited to 750 copies,
numbered & signed by artist, coloured plates, illus. by Arthur Rackham, fine,
Broadhurst 24-841 1974 £135

SWIFT, JONATHAN   Gulliver's Travels. 1940. Illus. with
engravings. Austin 61-956 1974 $10

SWIFT, JONATHAN   Gullivers Reise ins Land der Riesen. Berlin,
1922. Large 4to., illus., orig. red morocco. Marlborough 70-48 1974 £275

SWIFT, JONATHAN   The Hibernian Patriot. 1730. 8vo., half modern calf, new edition. Quaritch 936-229 1974 £45

SWIFT, JONATHAN   The History of the Athenian Society. London,
(n.d.). Folio, contemporary panelled calf, fine, first edition. Dawsons PM
252-932 1974 £550

SWIFT, JONATHAN   History of the Four Last Years of the Queen.
1758. 8vo., contemporary calf, first edition. Quaritch 936-230 1974 £30

SWIFT, JONATHAN   The History of the Four Last Years of the Queen.
London, 1758. 8vo., contemporary calf, gilt, first edition. Dawsons PM
252-928 1974 £50

SWIFT, JONATHAN   The History of the Last Four Years of the Queen.
London, 1758. 8vo., contemporary calf, gilt, first edition. Hammond 201-338
1974 £32

SWIFT, JONATHAN   The History of the Four Last Years of the Queen.
London, 1758. 8vo., full morocco, stained, first edition. Bow Windows
62-895 1974 £45

SWIFT, JONATHAN   The Intelligencer. 1729. 8vo., half calf, first
London edition. Quaritch 936-231 1974 £80

SWIFT, JONATHAN   Miscellanies in Prose and Verse. London,
1711. Contemporary sprinkled calf, morocco label, first edition. Dawsons PM
252-929 1974 £70

SWIFT, JONATHAN   Miscellaneous Works. London, 1720. 8vo.,
modern calf, stains. Dawsons PM 252-930 1974 £140

SWIFT, JONATHAN   A New Journey to Paris. 1711. 8vo., half
brown calf, scarce, first edition. Quaritch 936-232 1974 £80

SWIFT, JONATHAN   On Poetry. Dublin, 1733. Folio, disbound,
first edition. Ximenes 35-306 1974 $175

SWIFT, JONATHAN   Part of the Seventh Epistle of the First Book of
Horace. London, 1713. Small 4to., early 18th century wrappers, first edition.
Ximenes 35-307 1974 $150

SWIFT, JONATHAN   The Poetical Works of. Edinburgh, 1778.
4 vols., 12mo., green calf, gilt. Emerald 50-921 1974 £10

SWIFT, JONATHAN   Poetical Works Of. 1854. 3 vols. Austin
61-957 1974 $22.50

SWIFT, JONATHAN   A Proposal for Correcting, Improving and Ascer-
taining the English Tongue. 1712. 8vo., rebound, first edition. Quaritch 936-
233 1974 £80

SWIFT, JONATHAN   The Publick Spirit of the Whigs. 1714. 4to.,
modern boards, fine, unopened, first edition. Quaritch 936-234 1974 £110

SWIFT, JONATHAN   Remarks on the Life and Writings of Dr.
Jonathan Swift. 1752. Second edition corrected, portrait, calf, fair copy.
Thomas 32-195 1974 £8.50

SWIFT, JONATHAN   Remarks On the Life and Writings Of. 1752.
Calf, portrait, corrected second edition. Thomas 28-255 1972 £8.50

SWIFT, JONATHAN   Remarks on the Life and Writings of. London,
1752. 8vo., frontispiece, contemporary calf, gilt, first London edition. Bow
Windows 62-896 1974 £40

SWIFT, JONATHAN   A Tale of a Tub. London, 1704. 8vo.,
contemporary panelled calf, rebacked, second edition. Ximenes 35-308 1974
$165

SWIFT, JONATHAN   A Tale of a Tub. 1724. 12mo., contemporary
calf, plates, sixth edition. Hill 126-258 1974 £21

SWIFT, JONATHAN   Travels into Several Remote Nations of the World.
1726. 8vo., 2 vols., full red morocco, gilt, first edition. Quaritch 936-238
1974 £350

SWIFT, JONATHAN   Travels into Several Remote Nations of the
World. First edition, engraved portrait, maps, plans, 4 parts in 2 vols., small
8vo., modern calf, slightly brown and finger stained in places, good copy, rare.
Sawyer 293-271 1974 £340

SWIFT, JONATHAN   Travels into Several Remote Nations of the World.
1726-27. 8vo., full crimson levant morocco, gilt. Hammond 201-339 1974 £185

SWIFT, JONATHAN   Travels into Several Remote Nations of the World.
1727. 8vo., 2 vols., contemporary calf, gilt, second edition. Quaritch 936-
239 1974 £140

SWIFT, JONATHAN   Travels into Several Remote Nations of the World.
1727(1728). 12mo., 2 vols., contemporary calf, rebacked. Quaritch 936-240
1974 £90

SWIFT, JONATHAN   Travels Into Several Remote Nations of the World.
Glasgow, 1764. 12mo., old calf, rebacked. Hill 126-259 1974 £8.50

SWIFT, JONATHAN   Verses on the Death of. London, 1739. 8vo.,
modern boards, fourth edition. Dawsons PM 252-931 1974 £15

SWIFT, JONATHAN   The Works. 1760-65. 17 vols., crown 8vo.,
contemporary calf, plates. Howes 185-480 1974 £35

SWIFT, LINDSAY   The Massachusetts Election Sermons. Cambridge,
1897. 4to., orig. wrappers, uncut. Kraus B8-260 1974 $10

SWIFT, THEOPHILUS   The Touch-Stone of Truth. Dublin, 1811.
8vo., boards, third edition. Emerald 50-925 1974 £5

SWINBURNE, ALGERNON CHARLES   An Appeal to England Against the
Execution of the Condemned Fenians. Manchester, 1867. 8vo., orig. wrappers,
uncut, cloth folder, fine copy. Sawyer 293-287 1974 £80

SWINBURNE, ALGERNON CHARLES   Astrophel and Other Poems. 1894.
8vo., orig. cloth, owner's name label, first edition. Bow Windows 66-682 1974
£5

SWINBURNE, ALGERNON CHARLES   Atalanta in Calydon. London, 1923.
Small 4to., vellum, uncut. Bow Windows 62-898 1974 £8.50

SWINBURNE, ALGERNON CHARLES   Atalanta in Calydon. 1930. Small
4to., white buckram, gilt, fine. Covent 55-1425 1974 £7.50

SWINBURNE, ALGERNON CHARLES   Auguste Vacquerie. Paris, 1875.
8vo., orig. wrappers, scarce, first edition. Ximenes 35-310 1974 $40

SWINBURNE, ALGERNON CHARLES   The Ballad of Bulgarie. 1893. Limited
to 25 copies, 8vo., plain orange wrappers, as issued, preserved in cloth folder,
fine copy. Sawyer 293-272 1974 £120

SWINBURNE, ALGERNON CHARLES   A Century of Roundels. 1892. 8vo.,
orig. cloth, third edition. Bow Windows 64-719 1974 £6.50

SWINBURNE, ALGERNON CHARLES   Chastelard. New York, 1866. 8vo.,
orig. brown cloth, fine, first edition. Ximenes 35-311 1974 $20

SWINBURNE, ALGERNON CHARLES   Dolores. Hotten, 1867 (not after 1896).
8vo., red calf gilt, slight stain on half title, good copy, scarce. Sawyer
293-288 1974 £80

SWINBURNE, ALGERNON CHARLES   The Duke of Gandia. London, 1908.
8vo., orig. cloth, gilt, first edition. Hammond 201-340 1974 £7.50

SWINBURNE, ALGERNON CHARLES   Erechtheus. 1894. 8vo., orig. cloth,
new edition. Bow Windows 64-721 1974 £8.75

SWINBURNE, ALGERNON CHARLES   Les Fleurs du Mal and Other Studies.
1913. Crown 8vo., orig. boards, uncut, limited. Broadhurst 23-946 1974 £50

SWINBURNE, ALGERNON CHARLES   Les Fleurs du Mal and Other Studies.
1913. Crown 8vo., orig. printed boards, uncut, limited to 32 copies, inscribed
presentation copy. Broadhurst 24-898 1974 £40

SWINBURNE, ALGERNON CHARLES   Letters. (London), 1913. 8vo.,
modern cloth, orig. wrappers, first edition. Ximenes 35-312 1974 $25

SWINBURNE, ALGERNON CHARLES   Letters from. 1915. Crown 8vo., orig.
boards, uncut, limited. Broadhurst 23-947 1974 £50

SWINBURNE, ALGERNON CHARLES   Letters from. 1915. Orig. cloth.
Broadhurst 23-948 1974 £50

SWINBURNE, ALGERNON CHARLES   Letters to the Press. 1912. Crown 8vo.,
uncut, boards, limited edition. Broadhurst 23-945 1974 £30

SWINBURNE, ALGERNON CHARLES   Letters. 1919. 2 vols., new buckram.
Allen 216-1636 1974 $12.50

SWINBURNE, ALGERNON CHARLES   Letters from. 1915. Frontispiece, crown
8vo., orig. boards, uncut, inscribed presentation copy from Thomas J. Wise.
Broadhurst 24-900 1974 £40

SWINBURNE, ALGERNON CHARLES   Letters from . . . to Richard Monckton
and Other Correspondents. 1915. Frontispiece, crown 8vo., orig. boards, uncut,
limited to 20 copies, fine, inscribed presentation copy from Thomas J. Wise.
Broadhurst 24-899 1974 £40

SWINBURNE, ALGERNON CHARLES   Letters to Edward Dowden and Other
Correspondents. 1914. Limited edition, 8vo., dark blue half calf gilt, orig.
wrappers preserved, good copy, limited to 20 copies. Sawyer 293-289 1974 £58

SWINBURNE, ALGERNON CHARLES   Letters to Sir Edward Lytton-Bulwer and
Other Correspondents. 1913. Limited to 20 copies, 8vo., orig. blue wrappers,
unopened, preserved in cloth folder, brown stain on wrappers, good copy, with
bookplate of Clement K. Shorter. Sawyer 293-290 1974 £62

SWINBURNE, ALGERNON CHARLES   Letters to the Press. 1912. Crown
8vo., boards, uncut, limited to 32 copies, from the Library of Oliver Brett with
bookplate. Broadhurst 24-897 1974 £25

SWINBURNE, ALGERNON CHARLES   Lucretia Borgia. 1942. Folio, orig.
cloth, limited edition. Broadhurst 23-1008 1974 £50

SWINBURNE, ALGERNON CHARLES   Lucretia Borgia.   Golden Cockerel
Press, 1942. Folio, uncut, illus., limited to 350 copies, orig. cloth, fine.
Broadhurst 24-986 1974 £50

SWINBURNE, ALGERNON CHARLES   Miscellanies. 1886. Cover spotted,
top of spine slightly torn, first edition. Allen 216-1637 1974 $10

SWINBURNE, ALGERNON CHARLES   Notes on Poems and Reviews. London,
1866. 8vo., full morocco, gilt, first edition. Ximenes 35-313 1974 $125

SWINBURNE, ALGERNON CHARLES   Ode on the Proclamation of the French
Republic; Sept. 4th, 1870. 1870. Wrappers, cover faded, nice copy, largely
unopened, first edition. Covent 51-1783 1973 £5.25

SWINBURNE, ALGERNON CHARLES   Poems. 1904. 6 vols. Allen 216-1638
1974 $35

SWINBURNE, ALGERNON CHARLES   The Poems. 1905-12. 11 vols., orig.
navy buckram gilt. Howes 185-483 1974 £30

SWINBURNE, ALGERNON CHARLES   Poems and Ballads. London, 1866.
Near fine copy, orig. cloth, armorial bookplate, second issue of first edition, ads
inserted at beginning in correct order, extremely scarce. Covent 51-1784 1973
£110

SWINBURNE, ALGERNON CHARLES   The Poems. 1904. Half levant morocco,
gilt, 6 vols., English first edition. Covent 56-2065 1974 £75

SWINBURNE, ALGERNON CHARLES   Poems and Ballads. 1890-89. Vols.
1-2, half calf, badly rubbed. Allen 216-1639 1974 $10

SWINBURNE, ALGERNON CHARLES   Shakespeare. 1909. 83 pages.
Austin 61-958 1974 $10

SWINBURNE, ALGERNON CHARLES   A Song of Italy. 1867. Unopened,
fine. Covent 55-1427 1974 £7.50

SWINBURNE, ALGERNON CHARLES   Songs Before Sunrise. 1909. 4to.,
orig. vellum backed boards, gilt, limited edition. Smith 193-414 1973 £7.50

SWINBURNE, ALGERNON CHARLES   A Song of Italy. 1867. Orig. blue cloth,
inscription, first edition. Howes 186-444 1974 £7.50

SWINBURNE, ALGERNON CHARLES   Songs of Two Nations. 1893. 8vo.,
orig. cloth, second edition. Bow Windows 64-722 1974 £8.50

SWINBURNE, ALGERNON CHARLES   The Spring Tide of Life. 1918. Illus.
by Arthur Rackham, very nice copy, first edition. Covent 51-1548 1973 £10

SWINBURNE, ALGERNON CHARLES   The Springtide of Life. 1918. Crown
4to., plates, first edition. Marsden 37-382 1974 £8

SWINBURNE, ALGERNON CHARLES   Swinburne's Proof Sheets and American
First Editions. Cambridge, 1920. 8vo., orig. cloth. Broadhurst 23-949 1974
£6

SWINBURNE, ALGERNON CHARLES   Under the Microscope. 1899. Rebacked
in buckram, limited edition. Allen 216-1640 1974 $10

SWINBURNE, ALGERNON CHARLES   William Blake. 1868. Orig. blue
cloth, plates, second edition. Covent 55-225 1974 £30

SWINBURNE, ALGERNON CHARLES   The Collected Poetical Works of.
London, 1919-20. 6 vols., 8vo., orig. cloth. Bow Windows 62-899 1974
$12.50

SWINBURNE, HENRY   Travels In the Two Sicilies, 1777-1780.
London, 1783. 2 vols., thick 4to., contemporary polished tree calf, leather
labels, plates, first edition. Traylen 79-572 1973 £45

SWINDELL, LARRY   Spencer Tracy. World, 1969. Austin 51-938
1973 $7.50

SWINEY, G. C.   Historical Records. London, 1893. Orig. red
cloth, plates, illus. Dawson's 424-123 1974 £35

SWINNERTON, FRANK   The Georgian Scene. New York, 1934.
Biblo & Tannen 210-923 1973 $7.50

SWINNERTON, FRANK   R. L. Stevenson. New York, 1923. 1st Amer.
ed. Biblo & Tannen 214-772 1974 $9.50

SWINNERTON, FRANK   Young Felix. New York, 1923. 1st Amer. ed.,
author's sgd. pres. Biblo & Tannen 214-773 1974 $10

SWINTON, A. H.   Insect Variety. (1881). 8vo., orig. cloth-
backed boards, plates. Wheldon 130-806 1974 £7.50

SWIRE, HERBERT   The Voyage of the Challenger. Golden Cockerel
Press, 1938. Plates in colour, drawings, 2 vols., folio, uncut, slip-in-case,
limited to 307 copies, on Van Gelder paper, fine. Broadhurst 24-985 1974 £150

THE SWISS in the United States. Madison, 1940. Illus., 153 pages. Austin
57-662 1974 $17.50

SYDENHAM, THOMAS   Medecine Pratique de Sydenham. Paris, 1774.
8vo., contemporary mottled calf, gilt, first edition in French. Dawsons PM
249-472 1974 £35

SYDENHAM, THOMAS   Opera Universa. London, 1685. 4 parts in 1
vol., 8vo., contemporary calf, worn. Schuman 37-244 1974 $125

SYDENHAM, THOMAS   The Whole Works Of. London, 1697. 8vo.,
modern quarter calf, second edition. Dawsons PM 249-470 1974 £90

SYDENHAM, THOMAS   The Whole Works Of. London, 1705. 8vo.,
modern quarter calf, fourth edition. Dawsons PM 249-471 1974 £70

SYDOW, ECKART VON   Die Deutsche Expressionistische Kultur und
Malerei. Berlin, 1920. Boards, plates. Minters 37-487 1973 $25

SYDOW, ECKART VON   Die Deutsche Expressionistische Kultur und
Malerei. Berlin, 1920. Small 4to., orig. patterned boards, plates. Covent
55-639 1974 £45

SYDOW, P.   Monographia Uredinearum. Leipzig, 1904-
24. 4 vols., roy. 8vo., cloth, plates, rare. Wheldon 128-1430 1973 £75

SYERS, R.   The History of Everton. Liverpool, 1830.
8vo., contemporary half calf, plates. Bow Windows 64-723 1974 £4.75

SYKES, ARTHUR ASHLEY   An Enquiry into the Meaning of Demonjacks.
London, 1737. 2 vols. in 1, 8vo., contemporary calf, gilt, second edition.
Ximenes 35-315 1974 $40

SYKES, JOHN   Local Records. Newcastle, 1824. 8vo., modern half calf, labels, first edition. Dawsons PM 251-73 1974 £35

SYKES, NORMAN   Church and State In England In the XVIII th
Century. 1934. Scarce. Howes 185-1686 1974 £6.50

SYLVESTER, NATHANIEL BARTLETT   Historical Sketches of Northern New York
and the Adirondack Wilderness. Troy, 1877. Nice copy, first edition. Butterfield 10-504 1974 $30

SYLVESTER, NATHANIEL BARTLETT   Historical Sketches of Northern New York
and Adirondack Wilderness. Troy, 1877. Orig. cloth, first edition. Putman
126-87 1974 $22

SYLVIUS, FRANCISCUS   Opera Medica. Utrecht & Amsterdam, 1695.
Thick 4to., contemporary half vellum, rubbed. Schuman 37-245 1974 $145

SYLVIUS, JACQUES   Livre de la Generation de Lhomme. Paris,
1559. Small 8vo., dark blue morocco, gilt. Dawsons PM 249-473 1974 £325

SYLVIUS, JACOBUS, OF AMIENS
Please turn to
DU BOIS, JACQUES

Caution: Many Sylvius, Jacobus
Caution: Du Bois often edited Galen, etc., and was not the author of such works.

SYME, PATRICK   Werner's Nomenclature of Coloures.
Edinburgh, 1821. Second edition, colours on engraved plates, orig. drab boards,
paper label, uncut, fine copy, rare. Sawyer 293-34A 1974 £75

SYMMONS, EDWARD   A Vindication of King Charles. 1648.
Small 4to., old calf, worn, stains. Thomas 28-204 1972 £8.50

SYMONDS, JOHN ADDINGTON   Essays. London, 1893. Biblo & Tannen
210-924 1973 $15

SYMONDS, JOHN ADDINGTON   In the Key of Blue. 1893. White buckram,
signed, gilt. Marsden 37-395 1974 £25

SYMONDS, JOHN ADDINGTON   In the Key of Blue and other Prose Essays.
London, 1896. Biblo & Tannen 213-819 1973 $8

SYMONDS, JOHN ADDINGTON   An Introduction to the Study of Dante.
London, 1899. Biblo & Tannen 210-925 1973 $10

SYMONDS, JOHN ADDINGTON   The Life of Michelangelo Buonarroti.
London, 1893. First edition, 2 vols., etched portrait and 50 reproductions. Biblo
& Tannen 210-245 1973 $17.50

SYMONDS, JOHN ADDINGTON   The Life of Michelangelo Buonarroti. 1893.
2 vols., gilt, portrait, English first edition. Covent 56-60 1974 £27.50

SYMONDS, JOHN ADDINGTON   Many Moods. 1878. Orig. cloth,
book-plate. Covent 55-1428 1974 £7.50

SYMONDS, JOHN ADDINGTON   Many Moods. London, 1917. Biblo &
Tannen 213-820 1973 $9.50

SYMONDS, JOHN ADDINGTON   New and Old. 1880. Spine faded, English first edition. Covent 56-1231 1974 £10.50

SYMONDS, JOHN ADDINGTON   New and Old. London, 1917. Biblo &
Tannen 213-821 1973 $9.50

SYMONDS, JOHN ADDINGTON   A Problem in Greek Ethics. London, 1901.
Ltd. to 100 copies. Biblo & Tannen 213-482 1973 $12.50

SYMONDS, JOHN ADDINGTON   Renaissance In Italy. 1897-98. 7 vols.,
orig. buckram, gilt. Smith 194-117 1974 £8.50

SYMONDS, JOHN ADDINGTON   Sir Philip Sidney. London, 1886. Biblo &
Tannen 213-816 1973 $6.50

SYMONDS, JOHN ADDINGTON   Sketches and Studies in Italy and Greece.
London, 1900. 3 vols. Biblo & Tannen 213-822 1973 $17.50

SYMONDS, JOHN ADDINGTON   Sketches in Italy and Greece. London,
1874. 8vo., orig. cloth, fine, first edition. Ximenes 35-316 1974 $17.50

SYMONDS, JOHN ADDINGTON   Sketches in Italy and Greece. London,
1874. 1st ed. Biblo & Tannen 213-823 1973 $15

SYMONDS, JOHN ADDINGTON   Walt Whitman: A Study. 1893. Plates,
small 4to., gilt top, first edition. Covent 51-1976 1973 £6

SYMONDS, MARY   Needlework Through the Ages. 1928. Thick
roy. 8vo., mint, coloured and plain plates, orig. cloth. Broadhurst 24-205
1974 £75

SYMONDS, MARY   Needlework Through the Ages. 1928. Thick
roy. 4to., plates, quarter vellum, gilt, fine, scarce. Quaritch 940-773 1974
£105

SYMONDS, ROBERT WEMYSS   English Furniture. 1929. Roy. 4to., orig.
cloth, illus. Broadhurst 23-212 1974 £36

SYMONDS, ROBERT WEMYSS   English Furniture from Charles II to George II.
1929. Roy. 4to., plates, illus., cloth, gilt, presentation copy, limited edition.
Quaritch 940-591 1974 £45

SYMONDS, ROBERT WEMYSS   Masterpieces of English Furniture and Clocks.
(1940). 4to., plates, illus., cloth. Quaritch 940-592 1974 £35

SYMONDS, ROBERT WEMYSS   Old English Walnut and Lacquer Furniture.
1923. 4to., plates, cloth. Quaritch 940-590 1974 £14

SYMONDS, ROBERT WEMYSS   The Present State of Old English Furniture. 1921.
Photos., cloth. Eaton Music-678 1973 £10

SYMONDS, ROBERT WEMYSS   The Present State of Old English Furniture.
London, 1927. 4to., plates, orig. cloth, rubbed. Bow Windows 62-900 1974
£7.50

SYMONDS, ROBERT WEMYSS   The Present State of Old English Furniture.
1927. 4to., plates, English first edition. Covent 56-1660 1974 £7.50

SYMONS, ALPHONSE JAMES ALBERT   Emin: The Governor of Equatoria.
1928. One of 300 numbered copies, cloth backed boards, nice copy, first edition.
Covent 51-1793 1973 £5.25

SYMONS, ALPHONSE JAMES ALBERT   Frederick Baron Corvo. London, 1927.
Small 4to., full blue morocco, uncut, first edition. Dawsons PM 252-936 1974
£600

SYMONS, ALPHONSE JAMES ALBERT   The Quest for Corvo. 1934. First
edition, demy 8vo., mint, d.w., orig. cloth. Broadhurst 24-599 1974 £16

SYMONS, ARTHUR   Aubrey Beardsley. Paris, 1906. Cloth backed
boards, plates, English first edition. Covent 56-1549 1974 £5.25

SYMONS, ARTHUR   Colour Studies In Paris. 1918. Illus., orig.
edition. Austin 61-961 1974 $12.50

SYMONS, ARTHUR   Figures of Several Centuries. 1916. Buckram,
gilt top, very good copy, first edition. Covent 51-1791 1973 £7.50

SYMONS, ARTHUR   From Catullus; Chiefly Concerning Lesbia.
1924. One of 200 copies, numbered & signed by author, 4to., very good copy.
Covent 51-2582 1973 £12.50

SYMONS, ARTHUR   London. 1909. 8vo., orig. cloth, fine, first
edition. Rota 189-850 1974 £7.50

SYMONS, ARTHUR   Marcel Proust: An English Tribute. 1923.
Presentation copy, inscribed by Symons, one of 150 numbered copies on large
paper, quarter vellum, nice copy. Covent 51-2583 1973 £25

SYMONS, ARTHUR   Notes on Joseph Conrad, With Some Unpublished
Letters. London, 1925. First edition, mint, unopened, glassine wrapper.
Ross 87-130 1974 £12.50

SYMONS, ARTHUR   Notes on Joseph Conrad. 1926. Frontis.,
one of 250 numbered copies on hand made paper, signed by author, fine, buckram
backed boards, with some unpublished letters from Conrad. Covent 51-451
1973 £8.40

SYMONS, A. J. A.   A Bibliographical Catalogue of the First Loan
Exhibition of Books and Manuscripts, 1922. 1922. Orig. buckram backed
boards, labels, limited. Howes 185-847 1974 £7.50

SYMONS, J.   The Battle of Queenston Heights. Toronto,
1859. Light card cover, frontis., small map. Hood's 102-124 1974 $50

SYMONS, J.   The Battle of Queenston Heights. Toronto,
1859. Frontispiece, map. Hood's 104-141 1974 $50

SYMONS, JULIAN   Confusions about X. (1939). 8vo., orig. cloth,
dust wrapper, fine, first edition. Rota 189-570 1974 £10

A SYMPOSIUM on Andre Furuseth. New Bedford, Mass, n.d., ca. 1948. 233p.,
illus. Austin 62-188 1974 $17.50

SYMPSON, A.   A Short, Easy and Effectual Method to Prevent
the Running of Wool. London, 1741. 8vo., orig. wrappers. Quaritch
939-281 1974 £18

SYNGE, EDWARD   A Collection of Pamphlets. London, 1927-36.
6 items in 1 vol. Emerald 50-926 1974 £25

SYNGE, JOHN MILLINGTON   The Aran Islands. Dublin, 1907. 8vo.,
cloth boards, first edition. Emerald 50-927 1974 £15

SYNGE, JOHN MILLINGTON   The Aran Islands. Dublin, 1911. 8vo., illus., rubbed. Emerald 50-928 1974 £6

SYNGE, JOHN MILLINGTON   Four Plays. Dublin, 1911. Fine, English first edition. Covent 56-1234 1974 £7.50

SYNGE, JOHN MILLINGTON   Four Plays. Dublin, 1911. Upper cover trifle marked, else fine. Covent 51-1795 1973 £6.30

SYNGE, JOHN MILLINGTON   In Wicklow, West Kerry and Connemara. Dublin, 1911. Buckram, English first edition. Covent 56-2067 1974 £25

SYNGE, JOHN MILLINGTON   Poems and Translations. 1909. One of 250 copies, nice copy, cloth backed boards. Covent 51-1796 1973 £45

SYNGE, JOHN MILLINGTON   The Shadow of the Glen and Riders to the Sea. 1905. Orig. cloth, wrappers. Rota 188-876 1974 £25

SYNGE, JOHN MILLINGTON   The Shadow of the Glen and Riders to the Sea. London, 1905. Very good copy, somewhat torn & dusty wrappers, first edition. Covent 51-1797 1973 £10.50

SYNGE, JOHN MILLINGTON   The Tinker's Wedding. Dublin, 1907. Bookplate, very good copy. Covent 51-1798 1973 £5.25

SYNGE, JOHN MILLINGTON   The Tinker's Wedding. Luce, 1911. 52 pages. Austin 51-940 1973 $6.50

SYNGE, JOHN MILLINGTON   The Works. Dublin, 1910. 4 vols., 8vo., orig. cloth, first collected edition. Dawsons PM 252-937 1974 £48

SYNGE, JOHN MILLINGTON   The Works of. Dublin, 1910. 8vo., 4 vols., orig. cloth, first collected edition. Bow Windows 64-724 1974 £36

SYNGE, JOHN MILLINGTON   Complete Works. Random, 1935. 625 pages. Austin 51-939 1973 $6.50

SYPHER, J. R.   History of the Pennsylvania Reserve Corps. Lancaster, 1865. 8vo., full calf. Butterfield 8-471 1974 $25

SZYK, ARTHUR   The New Order. New York, 1941. Sm. 4to. Biblo & Tannen 214-59 1974 $10

T

T., E. S.   The Staff Surgeon.   London, 1865.   Foxing. Hood's 104-581 1974 $25

T., E. S.   The Staff Surgeon; or, Life in England and Canada.   London, 1865.   1 vol., slight foxing.   Hood's 102-544 1974 $25

T. E. ZELL & CO.   A Guide to the City of Chicago.   Chicago, 18-68.   16mo., cloth, fine.   Putman 126-111 1974 $30

TABARANT, A.   Le Vrai Visage de Retif de la Bretonne.   Paris, 1936.   12mo., orig. wrapper.   L. Goldschmidt 42-107 1974 $10

TABARRANI, PIETRO   Observationes Anatomicae.   Lucca, 1753. 8vo., stiff wrappers, plates.   Schuman 37-246 1974 $165

TABARIN   Oeuvres Completes.   Paris, 1858.   2 vols., small 12mo., cloth, uncut.   L. Goldschmidt 42-120 1974 $20

TABER, EDWARD MARTIN   Stowe Notes, Letters and Verses.   Boston, 1913.   8vo., orig. cloth, plates.   Bow Windows 64-725 1974 £5

TACITUS, GAIUS CORNELIUS   The Annales of.   London, 1605.   Small folio, seventeenth century calf, gilt, third edition.   Dawsons PM 252-938 1974 £65

TACITUS, GAIUS CORNELIUS   The Annales.   London, 1622.   Small folio, contemporary calf, rebacked.   Dawsons PM 252-939 1974 £52

TACITUS, GAIUS CORNELIUS   The Annales.   1622.   Small folio, quarter calf, worn, fifth collected edition.   Thomas 28-205 1972 £15.75

TACITUS, GAIUS CORNELIUS   Cornelii Taciti de Vita et Moribus Julii Agricolae Liber.   Doves Press, 1900.   8vo., orig. limp vellum, fine, limited to 225 copies on paper.   Sawyer 293-130 1974 £75

TACITUS, GAIUS CORNELIUS   The Ende of Nero and Beginning of Galba.   1591.   Folio, old blind stamped calf, rebacked, first edition.   Dawsons PM 251-342 1974 £190

TACITUS, GAIUS CORNELIUS   Opera.   1534.   Eighteenth century red morocco gilt, rebacked, bookplate.   Thomas 30-71 1973 £50

TACITUS, GAIUS CORNELIUS   Les Oeuvres de G. Cornelius Tacitus.   Paris, 1582.   Folio, 17th century tan calf, gilt, first edition.   L. Goldschmidt 42-121 1974 $130

TACITUS, GAIUS CORNELIUS   Cpera.   Leyden, 1621.   32mo., vellum, first Elzevir edition.   Goodspeed's 578-352 1974 $15

TACITUS, GAIUS CORNELIUS   Opera Quae Supersunt.   1753.   4 vols., new buckram, stained text.   Allen 213-1031 1973 $17.50

TACITUS, GAIUS CORNELIUS   The Works of.   1793.   4 vols., 4to., folding engraved maps, contemporary tree calf, joints broken.   Bow Windows 66-684 1974 £16

TACQUET, ANDREAS   Elementa Euclidea Geometriae.   1744-1749. 8vo., contemporary vellum.   Zeitlin 235-73 1974 $95

TACQUET, ANDREAS   Elementa Geometriae Planae ac Solidae.   1672. Small 8vo., contemporary calf, plates.   Zeitlin 235-216 1974 $45

TAFT, DONALD   Human Migration.   1936.   590 pages. Austin 57-664 1974 $10

TAFT, ROBERT   Artists and Illustrators of the Old West, 1850-1900.   New York, 1853.   Mint.   Jenkins 61-2419 1974 $12.50

TAFT, WILLIAM HOWARD   Popular Government.   New Haven, 1914. Signed.   Jenkins 48-388 1973 $75

TAGER, ALEXANDER B.   The Decay of Czarism.   1935.   297p. Austin 62-630 1974 $15

TAGGARD, GENEVIEVE   The Life and Mind of Emily Dickinson.   New York, 1930.   Orig. boards, paper label, first edition, one of 200 numbered copies, signed by author.   MacManus 224-128 1974 $27.50

TAGLIENTE, GIOVANNI ANTONIO   Lo Presente Libro Insegna la Vera Arte Delo.   Venice, 1547.   Small 4to., limp vellum, fine.   Dawsons PM 10-592 1974 £350

TAGORE, RABINDRANATH
Please turn to
RAVINDRANATHA, THAKURA

TAILHADE, LAURENT   Omar Khayyam et les Poisons de l'Intelligence. Paris, 1905.   Wrappers, worn.   Covent 55-1163 1974 £10

TAILLANDIER, ALPHONSE   Proces d'Estienne Dolet, Imprimeur et Libraire a Lyon, 1543-46.   Paris, 1836.   Small 8vo., brown half morocco, gilt back, heavy papier verge.   Kraus B8-310 1974 $58.50

TAINE, HIPPOLYTE   Philosophie de l'Art.   Paris, 1865.   12mo., half morocco, gilt, orig. wrapper, first edition.   L. Goldschmidt 42-390 1974 $25

TAINE, HIPPOLYTE   Voyage aux Pyrenees.   Paris, 1860.   8vo., half red hard grain morocco, gilt, woodcuts illus., third edition.   L. Goldschmidt 42-388 1974 $75

TAINE, HIPPOLYTE   Voyage en Italie.   Paris, 1866.   2 vols., 8vo., three quarter morocco, gilt, uncut, first edition.   L. Goldschmidt 42-389 1974 $50

TAIT, JOHN   Poetical Legends.   London, 1776.   4to., disbound, very good copy, first edition.   Ximenes 37-206 1974 $150

TAIT, R. H.   Newfoundland.   New York, 1939.   Hood's 103-191 1974 $17.50

TALASSI, ANGELO   L'Olmo Abbattuto.   Lisbon, 1795.   8vo., contemporary mottled calf, first edition.   Ximenes 35-319 1974 $12

TALBOT, EDWARD ALLEN   Five Years' Residence in the Canadas.   London, 1824.   2 vols., rebound, boards, browned.   Hood's 103-677 1974 $250

TALBOT, FREDERIC ARTHUR AMBROSE   Lightships and Light-Houses.   Philadelphia, 1813.   8vo., pictorial cloth, ex-library, first edition.   Putman 126-46 1974 $15

TALBOT, FREDERIC ARTHUR AMBROSE   Moving Pictures, How They are Made and Worked.   Philadelphia, London, 1912.   Illus., orig. binding.   Butterfield 10-427 1974 $25

TALBOT, M. D.   A Letter To the Rev. William Palmer.   1841-42. Cloth, presentation, inscribed.   Howes 185-1688 1974 £5

TALBOT, STAR   The Marvellous Book.   Shanghai, 1930.   Roy. 4to., plates, rubbed, very scarce.   Quaritch 940-423 1974 £48

THE TALE OF Beowulf.   1895.   4to., limp vellum with ties.   Hammond 201-735 1974 £215

THE TALE of the Emperor Coustans and of Over Sea.   Kelmscott Press, 1894. Woodcut titles, borders and initials, printed in red and black, 16mo., orig. Holland backed boards, uncut, fine, limited to 525 copies on paper.   Sawyer 293-188 1974 £95

THE TALE OF the Emperor Coustans and of Over Sea.   1894.   12mo., holland-backed boards.   Hammond 201-732 1974 £65

TALES, Comic, Instructive & Amusing.   1808.   2 vols., contemporary calf gilt, plates, foxing.   Smith 193-300 1973 £7.50

TALES for Youth. 1797. 16mo., later calf, faded, some soiling and ink scoring. George's 610-717 1973 £7.50

TALFOURD, FRANCIS   Shylock. French, ca. 1850. Austin 51-943 1973 $7.50

TALFOURD, THOMAS NOON   The Athenian Captive. London, 1838. 8vo., disbound, first edition. Ximenes 35-320 1974 $10

TALFOURD, THOMAS NOON   Ion: A Tragedy in Five Acts. London, (1835). 8vo., cloth, front cover detached, first edition. Goodspeed's 578-368 1974 $10

TALFOURD, THOMAS NOON   Ion. London, (1835). Large 8vo., orig. purple cloth, second private edition. Dawsons PM 252-940 1974 £25

TALFOURD, THOMAS NOON   Ion. London, 1836. 8vo., boards, first published edition. Dawsons PM 252-941 1974 £12

TALFOURD, THOMAS NOON   The Letters of Charles Lamb, With a Sketch of His Life. London, 1837. 2 vols., orig. cloth, spines faded, first edition, with the half-titles, fine set, half morocco slipcase. MacManus 224-270 1974 $105

TALFOURD, THOMAS NOON   Memoirs of Charles Lamb. 1892. Portraits, English first edition. Covent 56-782 1974 £10

TALLEYRAND, CHARLES MAURICE DE   Bibliotheca Splendidissima. London, 1816. 8vo., marbled boards, contemporary half calf. Dawsons PM 10-593 1974 £65

TALMAN, JAMES J.   Travel in Ontario Before the Coming of the Railway. 1933. Vol. 28. Hood's 102-780 1974 $7.50

TAMBIMUTTU, M. J.   Poetry in Wartime. London, 1942. First edition, very nice copy, orig. cloth, neat name on fly. Crane 7-6 1974 £5

THE TAME Goldfinch; or, The Unfortunate Neglect. Philadelphia, 1808. 12mo., orig. blue marbled paper covers, first edition, some off-setting from the first plate, plates, fine copy. MacManus 224-261 1974 $45

TANAKA, S.   Figures and Descriptions of the Fishes of Japan. Tokyo, (1935). Vols. 1 - 30 in 1 vol., roy. 8vo., orig. half leather, plates, second edition. Wheldon 128-662 1973 £18

TANDY, JAMES N.   The Trial Of. Dublin, 1792. 8vo., modern boards. Dawsons PM 251-343 1974 £12

TANNENBAUM, SAMUEL A.   The Handwriting of the Renaissance. New York, 1930. 8vo., cloth. Goodspeed's 578-537 1974 $10

TANNER, H. C.   The Lobby from Thurlow Weed's Time. Albany, c. 1888. Orig. binding, light edge wear. Wilson 63-251 1974 $10

TANNER, HENRY   English Interior Woodwork of the XVI, XVII, and XVII th Centuries. 1902. Folio, plates. Marsden 37-475 1974 £10

TANNER, HENRY   Old English Doorways. London, 1903. Small 4to., plates, illus., inscription, orig. cloth, faded. Bow Windows 62-903 1974 £5.25

TANNER, J. T.   The Ivory-Billed Woodpecker. New York, 1942. Roy. 8vo., orig. wrappers, text-figures, plates. Wheldon 128-573 1973 £5

TANNER, JOHN   The Hidden Treasures of the Art of Physick. London, 1659. Small thick 8vo., contemporary calf, worn, stains, first edition. Traylen 79-274 1973 £150

TANNER, THOMAS   Notitia Monastica. 1744. Folio, plates, contemporary panelled calf, second edition. Howes 185-1690 1974 £35

TANNER, THOMAS HAWKES   A Practical Treatise On the Diseases of Infancy and Childhood. Philadelphia, 1866. Second American edition. Rittenhouse 46-605 1974 $9

TANQUEREL DES PLANCHES, LOUIS JEAN CHARLES MARIE   Traite des Maladies de Plomb ou Saturnines. Paris, 1839. 8vo., 2 vols., contemporary boards, first edition. Schumann 35-461 1974 $145

TANSLEY, ARTHUR GEORGE   The British Islands and Their Vegetation. Cambridge, 1939. Thick crown 4to., plates, orig. buckram gilt. Smith 193-24 1973 £5

TANSLEY, ARTHUR GEORGE   The British Islands and Their Vegetation. Cambridge, 1939. Roy. 8vo., cloth, plates, orig. issue. Wheldon 128-1226 1973 £10

TAPPAN, DAVID   A Sermon Preached Before His Excellency John Hancock, Esq. Boston, 1792. Disbound. Bradley 35-365 1974 $20

TARAVAL, SIGISMUNDO   The Indian Uprising in Lower California, 1734-1737. Los Angeles, 1931. Limited to 665 copies. Jenkins 61-449 1974 $35

TARAVAL, SIGISMUNDO   The Indian Uprising in Lower California, 1734-1737. Los Angeles, 1931. Limited to 635 numbered copies, boards, vellum back. Jenkins 61-438 1974 $60

TARBELL, IDA M.   The Life of Abraham Lincoln. 1904. 2 vols., plates, fine, gilt tops, first edition. Covent 51-1135 1973 £6

TARBELL, IDA M.   The Life of Elbert H. Gary. New York and London, 1925. Orig. binding. Butterfield 10-505 1974 $15

TARDIEU, AMBROISE AUGUSTE   Etude Medico-Legale sur la Folie. Paris, 1872. Foxing. Rittenhouse 46-606 1974 $26

TARDIF, G.   Le Livre de l'Art de Fauconnerie et des Chiens de Chasse. Paris, 1882. 2 vols. in 1, post 8vo., half calf, scarce, limited edition. Wheldon 128-574 1973 £12

TARDIF, J.   Methode Theorique et Pratique de Plain-Chant. 1883. Roy. 8vo., cloth, stained. Howes 185-1484 1974 £7.50

TARGIONI TOZZETTI, GIOVANNI   Notizie degli Aggrandimenti delle Scienze Fisiche. 1780. 4to., half vellum, boards, labels. Zeitlin 235-217 1974 $385

TARGIONI-TOZZETTI, GIOVANNI   Notizie sulla Storia della Scienze Fisiche. 1852. Folio, modern marbled boards, white vellum, fine, unopened, uncut. Zeitlin 235-218 1974 $275

TARIF Parisien de Composition Typographique Elabore par la Comission Patronale de 1878. Paris, n.d. 16mo., orig. printed wrappers. Kraus B8-377 1974 $12

TARKINGTON, BOOTH   Alice Adams. New York, 1921. Orig. cloth, illus., inscribed copy, about fine, first issue, with "I can't see you why don't wear . . . " p. 419. MacManus 224-420 1974 $25

TARKINGTON, BOOTH   Beasley's Christmas Party. New York, 1909. First edition, 12mo., colored illus., cover dull, interior fine. Current BW9-86 1974 $17.50

TARKINGTON, BOOTH   Beasley's Christmas Party. New York, 1909. First edition, 8vo., colored text illus., colored frontis., mint, d.j. Current BW9-87 1974 $28.50

TARKINGTON, BOOTH   Claire Ambler. New York, 1928. Boards, first U.S. edition. Covent 56-1237 1974 £10.50

TARKINGTON, BOOTH   Claire Ambler. New York, 1928. Special edition, signed by author & publisher's, some soiling on white covers, else perfect. Current BW9-281 1974 $42.50

TARKINGTON, BOOTH   The Midlander. Garden City, 1932. Signed, numbered, rubbed, first edition. Ballinger 1-208 1974 $15

TARKINGTON, BOOTH   Penrod. New York, 1914. Orig. blue mesh cloth, first issue with this binding, very fine copy. MacManus 224-421 1974 $40

TARKINGTON, BOOTH   Penrod. New York, 1914. 12mo., cloth, unusually clean copy, first edition, first issue. Goodspeed's 578-369 1974 $50

TARKINGTON, BOOTH   Some Old Portraits. New York, 1939. Orig. cloth, first edition, one of 247 numbered copies, signed by author, boxed, very fine. MacManus 224-422 1974 $35

TARLETON, BANASTRE   A History of the Campaigns of 1780 and 1781, in the Southern Provinces of North America. London, 1787. 4to., tree calf, first edition, handsome copy, folding maps. Butterfield 10-506 1974 $450

TARLETON, BANASTRE   A History of the Campaigns of 1780 and 1781 in the Southern Provinces of North America. London, 1787. 4to., modern half calf, uncut. Traylen 79-498 1973 £190

TARN, W. W.   The Treasure of the Isle of Mist. New York, (1934). 8vo., illus. by Robert Lawson, very good copy, frayed d.j. Frohnsdorff 16-487 1974 $10

TASSIS, AUGUSTE   Guide du Correcteur ou Complement des Grammaires et des Lexiques. Paris, n.d. (c. 1885?). 8vo., orig. printed wrappers, tenth edition. Kraus B8-379 1974 $18

TASSIS, AUGUSTE   Guide du Correcteur ou Complement des Grammaires et des Lexiques. Paris, n.d. (after 1877). Small 8vo., orig. printed wrappers, half leather, eighth edition. Kraus B8-378 1974 $20

TASSO, TORQUATO   Discorsi . . . Dell' Arte Poetica. Venice, 1587. Small 4to., old limp vellum, fine, orig. edition. Harper 213-151 1973 $375

TASSO, TORQUATO   Jerusalem Delivree. Paris, 1774. 12mo., contemporary morocco, gilt spines, engraved frontis. Schumann 499-113 1974 sFr 140

TASTU, A.   Album Poetique des Jeunes Personnes. Paris, 1854. 8vo., foxing, contemporary diaper cloth, gilt. Bow Windows 62-904 1974 £8

TATE, ALFRED O.   Edison's Open Door. New York, 1938. Biblo & Tannen 213-859 1973 $8.50

TATE, ALLEN   Reason in Madness. New York, 1941. 8vo., orig. cloth, first edition. Rota 189-854 1974 £5

TATE, ALLEN   Stonewall Jackson. New York, 1928. 8vo., orig. cloth, inscription, first edition. Rota 189-852 1974 £8.50

TATE, ALLEN   The Vigil of Venus. n.d. 8vo., orig. cloth, fine, first edition. Ximenes 35-322 1974 $40

TATE, NAHUM   A Poem Upon Tea. London, 1702. 8vo., modern boards, scarce, second edition. Dawsons PM 252-942 1974 £55

TATTERSALL, C. E. C.   A History of British Carpets from the Introduction of the Craft Until the Present Day. 1934. Roy. 4to., plates, illus., cloth. Quaritch 940-774 1974 £21

TAUBMAN, HOWARD   Music On My Beat. 1943. Austin 51-945 1973 $7.50

TAULER, JOHANN   Sermons. Paris, 1855. 2 vols., half calf. Howes 185-1693 1974 £5.50

TAUNTON, ETHELRED L.   The English Black Monks of St. Benedict. 1897. 2 vols., scarce. Howes 185-1694 1974 £8.50

TAUNTON, ETHELRED L.   The History of the Jesuits In England. 1901. Plates, soiled, scarce. Howes 185-1695 1974 £5

TAUNTON, Massachusetts. Taunton, 1889. Embossed boards, photographs. Jenkins 61-1546 1974 $12.50

TAVENOR-PERRY, J.   Dinanderie. 1910. 4to., plates, illus., English first edition. Covent 56-1511 1974 £20

TAVERNE, ANTOINE DE LA   Journal de la Paix d'Arras. Paris, 1651. 12mo., contemporary brown calf, gilt. L. Goldschmidt 42-122 1974 $25

TAVERN ANECDOTES. (1825). Small 8vo., orig. boards, uncut, frontispiece. Hill 126-292 1974 £12.50

TAVERNER, P. A.   Birds of Eastern Canada. Ottawa, 1922. Roy 8vo., orig. printed boards, plates, second edition. Wheldon 130-633 1974 £7.50

TAVERNER, P. A.   Birds of Western Canada. Ottawa, 1926. Thick 8vo., printed wrapper, plates, illus. Hammond 201-683 1974 £10.50

TAVERNER, P. A.   Birds of Western Canada. Ottawa, 1926. Roy. 8vo., orig. wrappers, coloured plates, text-figures, very scarce first edition. Wheldon 128-575 1973 £6

TAVERNER, P. A.   Birds of Western Canada. Ottawa, 1928. Roy 8vo., orig. cloth. Wheldon 129-531 1974 £7.50

TAWARA, SUNAO   Das Reizleitungssystem des Saugetierherzens. Jena, 1906. Large 8vo., half calf, label, very fine, first edition. Schafer 8-175 1973 sFr. 300

TAYLERSON, A. W. F.   The Revolver 1818-1914. London. 3 vols., illus., cloth. Dawsons PM 11-739 1974 £13.50

TAYLOR   Practical Hints to Young Females on the Duties of a Wife. London, 1816. 12mo., frontispiece, old diced calf, worn, inscription, sixth edition. Bow Windows 62-907 1974 £7.50

TAYLOR, A.   Birds of a County Palatine Being a Camera Record of Birds Found Infrequently for the Most Part in the County of Lancaster. 1913. 4to., cloth, illus. Wheldon 131-709 1974 £7.50

TAYLOR, A. A.   The Great Revival at Norwalk, Ohio. Cleveland, 1873. Printed wrappers. Hayman 57-398 1974 $10

TAYLOR, ALFRED E.   The Faith of a Moralist. 1930. 2 vols., orig. cloth, first edition. Howes 185-2011 1974 £7.50

TAYLOR, ALFRED E.   The Problem of Conduct. 1901. Scarce, first edition. Howes 185-2012 1974 £5.75

TAYLOR, ALFRED SWAINE   On Poisons. London, 1848. 8vo., old half calf, first edition. Gurney 64-211 1974 £15

TAYLOR, ALFRED SWAINE   On Poisons, in Relation to Medical Jurisprudence and Medicine. London, 1848. 8vo., old half calf, first edition. Gurney 66-182 1974 £15

TAYLOR, AMOS   The Genuine Experience and Dying Address of Mrs. Dolly Taylor. 1796. 12mo., early wrappers, rare, fourth edition. Ximenes 35-323 1974 $100

TAYLOR, ARTHUR   The Glory of Regality. 1820. 8vo., modern marbled boards, bookplate. Quaritch 939-751 1974 £15

TAYLOR, BAYARD   The Echo Club and Other Literary Diversions. Boston, 1876. 16mo. Biblo & Tannen 213-825 1973 $8.50

TAYLOR, BAYARD   El Dorado: or, Adventures in the Path of Empire. London, 1850. 2 vols., colored plates, slight chipping, else very nice set. Jenkins 61-2422 1974 $100

TAYLOR, BERT LESTON   A Penny Whistle. Knopf, 1921. 130p. Austin 54-980 1973 $7.50

TAYLOR, BERT LESTON   The So-Called Human Race. Knopf, 1922. 330p. Austin 54-981 1973 $7.50

TAYLOR, CHARLES H.   Builder of The Boston Globe. N.p., 1923. Biblo & Tannen 213-826 1973 $9.50

TAYLOR, CONYNGHAM C.   Toronto "Called Back", from 1888 to 1847. Toronto, 1888. Illus., inscribed, map, revised edition. Hood's 104-62 1974 $30

TAYLOR, DEEMS   A Treasury of Gilbert & Sullivan. New York, 1941. 1st ed., 4to., illus. Biblo & Tannen 214-850 1974 $9.50

TAYLOR, EMMA FLOWER   Dickens Tea-party. Watertown, NY, 1913. Folio, colored plates, ltd. to 100 copies, sgd. Biblo & Tannen 214-774 1974 $37.50

TAYLOR, F.   The Hon. Thomas D'Arcy McGee. Montreal, 1868. Orig. binding. Hood's 103-238 1974 $35

TAYLOR, FENNINGS   The Last Three Bishops Appointed by the Crown. London, 1870. Faded, inscribed. Hood's 103-272 1974 $15

TAYLOR, FITCH W.   A Voyage Round the World . . . In the United States Frigate Columbia . . . Including . . . the Visit . . . to China During the Opium Difficulties at Canton. New Haven and New York, 1844. 2 vols. in 1, third edition, colored frontis., backstrip chipped. Butterfield 10-507 1974 $20

TAYLOR, FITCH W.   A Voyage Round the World . . . In the United States Frigate "Columbia". New Haven & New York, 1847. 2 vols. in 1, illus., foxing. Hood's 104-917 1974 $25

TAYLOR, FRANCIS HENRY   The Taste of Angels. Boston, 1948. 1st ed. Biblo & Tannen 210-347 1973 $15

TAYLOR, FREDERICK WINSLOW   The Principles of Scientific Management. New York and London, 1911. 8vo., orig. red cloth, gilt, first published edition. Dawsons PM 245-704 1974 £145

TAYLOR, GEORGE   A History of the Rise, Progress and Suppression of the Rebellion. Dublin, 1828. Small 8vo., half calf, new edition. Quaritch 939-635 1974 £10

TAYLOR, GEORGE   A History of the Rise . . . . of the Rebellion in the County of Wexford. Dublin, 1829. 8vo., new cloth boards. Emerald 50-931 1974 £7.50

TAYLOR, GEORGE   Maps of the Roads of Ireland. 1778. Roy 8vo., orig. cloth, board, first edition. Broadhurst 23-1558 1974 £120

TAYLOR, GEORGE   Maps of the Roads of Ireland. 1778. Roy. 8vo., contemporary panelled calf, first edition. Quaritch 939-636 1974 £50

TAYLOR, H. V.   The Apples of England. 1936. Roy. 8vo., cloth, illus. Wheldon 131-1581 1974 £5

TAYLOR, HENRY   Historic Notices. 1883. 8vo., boards, uncut, illus. Broadhurst 23-1559 1974 £5

TAYLOR, HENRY   St. Clement's Eve. London, 1862. 8vo., orig. purple cloth, inscribed, first edition. Ximenes 35-324 1974 $15

TAYLOR, HENRY   The Virgin Widow. 1850. Orig. cloth, first edition, inscribed from author to William Allingham. Thomas 32-156 1974 £12

TAYLOR, IDA SCOTT   Baby's Book. London, ca. 1901. 4to., padded silk covers with hand-colored floral decoration and gilt-lettered. All edges gilt; illus. Frohnsdorff 16-128 1974 $15

TAYLOR, ISAAC   Scenes of British Wealth. London, 1823. 12mo., orig. roan-backed printed red boards, plates, first edition. Hammond 201-145 1974 £24

TAYLOR, J.   Geological Essays. 1864-67. 8vo., half morocco, rubbed. Broadhurst 23-1560 1974 £12

TAYLOR, J.   A Medical Treatise of the Virtues of Fir-Hill Well, Illustrated with Selected Cases. Aberdeen, 1800. Disbound. Thomas 32-329 1974 £10.50

TAYLOR, J. BAYARD   Views A-Foot. London, 1847. 2 vols., 12mo., orig. cloth, first English edition. Ximenes 35-325 1974 $15

TAYLOR, J. BAYARD   Views Afoot. New York, 1847. 2 parts in 1 vol., rebound in buckram. Wilson 63-573 1974 $15

TAYLOR, J. BAYARD   A Visit to India, China and Japan. New York, 1855. 8vo., orig. cloth, faded, first edition. Ximenes 35-326 1974 $10

TAYLOR, J. E.   Flowers. 1878. 8vo., orig. dec. cloth, plates. Wheldon 130-1062 1974 £5

TAYLOR, J. E.   Flowers, Their Origin, Shapes, Perfumes and Colours. London, 1878. Colored figures, woodcuts, orig. cloth, 8vo. Gregory 44-287 1974 $8.75

TAYLOR, J. E.   Our Island-Continent. 1886. Post 8vo., orig. dec. cloth, scarce. Wheldon 130-317 1974 £12

TAYLOR, J. P.   Cardinal Facts of Canadian History. Toronto, 1899. Hood's 102-48 1974 $20

TAYLOR, JAMES   A Farewell Sermon by the Rev. John Taylord Delivered in Deerfield at the Time of His Dismissal . . . 1806. Greenfield, 1806. Wrapper. Jenkins 61-703 1974 $12

TAYLOR, JANE   City Scenes, or a Peep into London. 1828. Engraved plates, 12mo., orig. boards, roan spine, trifle rubbed, plates & some text rather heavily browned. George's 610-726 1973 £10

TAYLOR, JANE   Display, a Tale for Young People. 1815. First edition, contemporary inscription, engraved frontis., 12mo., new red buckram. George's 610-724 1973 £15

TAYLOR, JANE   Display, a Tale for Young People. 1815. Third edition, half title, engraved frontis., 12mo., grained calf, slightly rubbed. George's 610-725 1973 £5.25

TAYLOR, JANE   Little Anne and Other Poems. n.d. 4to., orig. quarter cloth, boards. Hammond 201-119 1974 £17.50

TAYLOR, JANE   Little Ann and Other Poems. London, n.d. Illus. by Kate Greenaway, 8vo., some cover soiling, very good. Current BW9-118 1974 $32.50

TAYLOR, JANE   Meddlesome Matty and Other Poems. 1925. Cloth-backed pictorial boards, inscription, English first edition. Covent 56-1187 1974 £8.50

TAYLOR, JANE   Rhymes for the Nursery. 1806. First edition, lacks 1 leaf of text, 12mo., orig. half roan, corners worn, board sides, very rare. George's 610-729 1973 £35

TAYLOR, JANE   Rhymes for the Nursery. Boston, (1837). Square 16mo., cloth with orig. paper label, lacking front free endpaper, very good copy, hand colored engravings, rare edition. Frohnsdorff 15-165 1974 $150

TAYLOR, JEFFERYS   A Month in London. 1832. First edition, plates, frontis., 12mo., contemporary quarter roan, cloth sides. George's 610-732 1973 £6

TAYLOR, JEREMY   Ductor Dubitantium. 1696. Folio, old calf, engraved portrait, rebacked, fourth edition. Bow Windows 66-688 1974 £28

TAYLOR, JEREMY   The Great Exemplar of Sanctity and Holy Life. 1649. Small 4to., contemporary calf, rebacked, first edition. Bow Windows 62-906 1974 £27.50

TAYLOR, JEREMY   Rule and Exercises of Holy Dying. 1693. Old calf, engraved plate, sixteenth edition. Allen 216-1956 1974 $10

TAYLOR, JEREMY   The Rule and Exercises of Holy Living. London, 1840. Small 8vo., contemporary roan, gilt. Hammond 201-722 1974 £6

TAYLOR, JEREMY   The Whole Works. London, 1839. 15 vols., 8vo., full calf, third edition. Traylen 79-189 1973 £10

TAYLOR, JEREMY   The Whole Works. 1847-54. 10 vols., thick 8vo., orig. cloth, best edition. Howes 185-1696 1974 £65

TAYLOR, JEREMY   The Worthy Communicant. 1683. Small 8vo., contemporary calf, stains. Howes 185-1697 1974 £21

TAYLOR, JOHN   All the Workes of. London, 1630. Folio, illus., green morocco gilt, first edition. Dawsons PM 252-944 1974 £320

TAYLOR, JOHN   Canadian Handbook and Tourist's Guide. Montreal, 1867. Orig. boards, illus. Hood's 103-163 1974 £50

TAYLOR, JOHN 1757-1832   Monsieur Tonson. London, 1830. 12mo., illus., orig. wrappers, first edition. Dawsons PM 252-943 1974 £12

TAYLOR, MEADOWS   Tara. Edinburgh & London, 1863. 3 vols., 8vo., contemporary calf, first edition. Dawsons PM 252-945 1974 £90

TAYLOR, MICHAEL   A Sexagesimal Table. London, 1780. Large 4to., modern half calf, gilt, first edition. Dawsons PM 245-705 1974 £35

TAYLOR, N.   Flora of the Vicinity of New York. New York, 1915. Roy. 8vo., wrappers, plates. Wheldon 128-1313 1973 £5

TAYLOR, RICHARD   Destruction and Reconstruction. New York, 1879. 1st ed. Biblo & Tannen 213-26 1973 $25

TAYLOR, RICHARD   Te Ika A Maui. London, 1870. 8vo., illus., plates, polished calf, morocco label, second edition. Bow Windows 62-908 1974 £45

TAYLOR, RICHARD COWLING   Two Reports on the Coal Lands, Mines and Improvements of the Dauphin and Susquehanna Coal Company and of the Geological Examinations. Philadelphia, 1840. 8vo., orig. boards, maps, scarce. Wheldon 131-1084 1974 £10

TAYLOR, ROBERT LEWIS   Professor Fodorski. Doubleday. 250p. Austin 54-982 1973 $6.50

TAYLOR, ROBERT LEWIS   W. C. Fields. New York, 1949. 1st ed. Biblo & Tannen 210-944 1973 $7.50

TAYLOR, ROSEMARY   Ghost Town Bonanza. Drowell, 1954. 248p. Austin 54-983 1973 $6.50

TAYLOR, ROSEMARY   Haren Scare'm. Crowell, 1951. 246p., illus. Austin 54-984 1973 $6.50

TAYLOR, ROSEMARY   Ridin' the Rainbow. Whittlesey, 1944. 271p., illus. Austin 54-985 1973 $6

TAYLOR, ROSS MC LAURY   Brazos. Indianapolis, (1938). Blue-green cloth, fine, first edition. Bradley 35-379 1974 $10

TAYLOR, S.   The History of Gavel-Kind. London, 1663. 4to., old calf, rebacked. Quaritch 939-415 1974 £50

TAYLOR, SAMUEL   Angling In All Its Branches. 1800. 8vo., half calf, morocco label, cloth sides, some spotting. Bow Windows 66-690 1974 £18

TAYLOR, SAMUEL   An Essay Intended to Establish a Standard for a Universal System of Stenography. Albany, (1810). Plates, marbled boards and leather, first U. S. edition. Butterfield 10-486 1974 $45

TAYLOR, SAMUEL   The Happy Time. Random, 1950. Austin 51-950 1973 $7.50

TAYLOR, T. P.   The Bottle. Taylor, 1847. Austin 51-953 1973 $7.50

TAYLOR, THOMAS   The Eleusinian and Bacchic Mysteries. New York, 1891. Illus., orig. cl., gilt. Jacobs 24-173 1974 $25

TAYLOR, THOMAS   Sallust on the Gods and the World. London, 1793. Full stamped calf, gilt, marbled edges. Jacobs 24-175 1974 $25

TAYLOR, THOMAS WARDLAW   Historical Sketch of Saint James Square Presbyterian Congregation, Toronto, 1853-1903. Toronto, n.d. Illus. Hood's 103-273 1974 $12.50

TAYLOR, THOMAS WARDLAW   The Public Statutes Relating to the Presbyterian Church in Canada. Winnipeg, 1897. Card cover, second edition. Hood's 103-274 1974 $12.50

TAYLOR, TOM   The Autobiography and Memoirs of Benjamin Robert Haydon, 1786-1846. 1926. 2 vols., fine, plates. Covent 51-2383 1973 £12.50

TAYLOR, TOM   The Fools Revenge. Ca. 1865. Austin 51-952 1973 $10

TAYLOR, TOM   Life of Benjamin Robert Haydon. London, 1853. 3 vols., 8vo., orig. rose cloth, first edition. Ximenes 35-327 1974 $45

TAYLOR, TOM   To Oblige Benson. French, ca. 1854. Austin 51-954 1973 $6.50

TAYLOR, UNA   Nets for the Wind. 1896. Title vignette, orig. dec. cloth, spine faded, very good copy, first edition. Covent 51-1804 1973 £5.25

TAYLOR, W. H.   Canadian Seasons. Toronto, 1913. Inscribed. Hood's 104-797 1974 $10

TAYLOR, WILLIAM   Historic Survey of German Poetry. 1828-30. 3 vols., contemporary half green morocco, rubbed, first edition. Howes 186-447 1974 £45

TAYLOR, WILLIAM   Seven Years Street Preaching in San Francisco. New York, c. 1856. Joints split, light foxing & marginal damp stain, orig. binding. Wilson 63-126 1974 $10

TAYLOR, WILLIAM COOKE   Life and Times of Sir Robert Peel. (1846-51). 4 vols., contemporary diced calf gilt. Howes 186-1128 1974 £18

TCHAIKOVSKY, MODESTE   The Life and Letters of Peter Ilich Tchaikovsky. 1906. Plates, English first edition. Covent 56-1956 1974 £7.50

TCHEMERZINE, AVENIR   Bibliographie d'Editions Originales et Rares d'Auteurs Francais. Paris, 1927-33. 10 vols., 8vo., illus., quarter sheep, marbled boards. Dawsons PM 10-597 1974 £370

TCHIHATCHEFF, P. DE   Asie Mineure. Paris, 1866. Atlas 4to., cloth backed boards, plates. Bow Windows 64-169 1974 £15

TEA, EVA   Giacomo Boni Nella Vita del Suo Tempo. Milan, 1932. 2 vols., 8vo., wrappers, soiled covers. Minters 37-176 1973 $25

TEALE, THOMAS P.   Brooklyn City Directory and Annual Advertiser, 1848-49. Brooklyn, 1848. 12mo., quarter cloth. Saddleback 14-593 1974 $20

TEALE, THOMAS PRIDGIN   Dangers to Health. London and Leeds, 1879. 8vo., orig. dec. cloth, gilt, plates, first edition. Hammond 201-957 1974 £6

TEALE, THOMAS PRIDGIN   On Amputation. London, 1858. 8vo., orig. cloth, first edition. Gurney 64-212 1974 £15

TEALE, WILLIAM HENRY   Lives of English Laymen. 1842. 8vo., orig. cloth, presentation, inscribed. Covent 55-1430 1974 £5.25

TEALL, J. J. H.   British Petrography. Birmingham, 1886 (-1888). Imp. 8vo., half morocco, coloured plates. Wheldon 128-1058 1973 £20

TEALL, J. J. H.   British Petrography. Birmingham, 1886(-1888). Imperial 8vo., half morocco, 2 vols., plates. Wheldon 130-975 1974 £25

TEASDALE, SARA   Stars To-Night. New York, 1930. Orig. cloth backed boards, paper label, first edition, one of 150 copies signed by author, illus. & signed by Dorothy P. Lathrop, very good. MacManus 224-423 1974 $30

TECTON, ARCHITECTS   Planned A.R.P. Based On the Investigation of Structural Protection Against Air Attack In the Metro. Borough of Finsbury. Westminster, 1939. 4to., cloth, illus., plates, scarce. Minters 37-573 1973 $27.50

TEDESCHI, NICCOLO, ABP. OF PALERMO   Super Libros Decretalium. Venice, 1477. 2 parts in 1 vol., folio, early 18th century calf, gilt, rubbed, foxing, fine. Harper 213-115 1973 $1500

TEGETMEIER, WILLIAM BERNHARD   Pheasants, Their Natural History and Practical Management. 1911. 8vo., cloth, coloured and plain plates, scarce, fifth edition. Wheldon 128-576 1973 £10

TEGETMEIER, WILLIAM BERNHARD   Pigeons. 1868. Imp. 8vo., new half calf, woodcuts, plates. Wheldon 129-532 1974 £25

TEGETMEIER, WILLIAM BERNHARD   Pigeons: Their Structure, Varieties, Habits and Management. 1868. Coloured engravings, illus., imp. 8vo., contemporary half calf, binding rubbed, frontispiece lightly foxed. Broadhurst 24-1174 1974 £25

TEICHMEYER, HERMANN FRIEDERICH   Elementa Anthropologiae. 1719. 4to., modern half calf. Dawsons PM 249-476 1974 £30

TEICHMEYER, HERMANN FRIEDERICH   Institvtiones Medicinae Legalis vel Forensis. 1723. 4to., modern half calf, first edition. Dawsons PM 249-477 1974 £55

TEILLERS, J. W.   Ethnographica in het Museum van het Bataviaasch Genootschap van Kunsten en Wetenschappen te Batavia. Holland, 1910. Parts 1-12 complete, plates, super roy. 4to., text in English & Dutch, orig. folder, fine. Broadhurst 24-209 1974 £5

TELEVISION and Radio in American Life. Wilson, 1953. Austin 51-6-6 1973 $7.50

TELLER, DANIEL W.   The History of Ridgefield. Danbury, 1878. 8vo., orig. bindings. Butterfield 8-95 1974 $20

TEMMINCK, COENRAAD JACOB   Manuel d'Ornithologie. Paris, 1820-40. 8vo., contemporary half leather, 4 vols., second edition. Wheldon 129-533 1974 £30

TEMMINCK, COENRAAD JACOB   Manuel d'Ornithologie. Paris, 1820-40. 4 vols., 8vo., contemporary half leather, scarce, second edition. Wheldon 131-710 1974 £30

TEMMINCK, COENRAAD JACOB   Verhandelingen Over de Natuurlijke Geschiedenis der Nederlandsche Overzeesche Bezittingen. Leyden, 1839-45. 3 vols. in 5, folio, buckram, plates. Wheldon 131-122 1974 £900

TEMPERLEY, HAROLD   A Century of Diplomatic Blue Books. Cambridge, 1938. Large 8vo., orig. cloth, first edition. Dawsons PM 10-598 1974 £6

TEMPERLEY, HAROLD   A History of the Peace Conference of Paris. 1920-24. 6 vols., roy. 8vo., orig. edition. Howes 186-1252 1974 £32.50

TEMPESTA, A.   The Four Evangelists. Manchester & London, 1873. 4to., plates, contemporary gilt framed calf, label, rebacked. Bow Windows 62-909 1974 £12

TEMPLE, JOSIAH HOWARD   History of North Brookfield. (Boston), 1887. 8vo., orig. bindings. Butterfield 8-271 1974 $25

TEMPLE, WILLIAM   Memoirs of What Past in Christendom. 1692. Small 8vo., contemporary calf, gilt, second edition. Howes 186-1254 1974 £32.50

TEMPLE, WILLIAM   Miscellanies. Glasgow, 1761. 12mo., contemporary calf. Hill 126-260 1974 £12.50

TEMPLE Bar. 1861-84. 68 vols., thick 8vo., cloth, stained. Howes 186-448 1974 £145

TEMPLETON, WILLIAM   The Millwright and Engineer's Pocket Companion. London, 1874. Small 8vo., orig. cloth, illus. Hammond 201-958 1974 £6

TEMPLETON-ARMSTRONG, I.   The Old Vice and the New Chivalry. Toronto, 1884. Illus. Hood's 102-352 1974 $12.50

TEMPLIN, H.   Fergus, the Story of a Little Town. Fergus, 1933. Signed, illus. Hood's 103-678 1974 $35

TEMPSKY, G. F. VON MITLA   A Narrative. London, 1838. Red cloth, gilt, plates, first edition. Dawson's 424-124 1974 $175

TEN Lithographic Drawings of Scenery In the Vicinity of the Lakes. 1826. Oblong folio, contemporary morocco backed marbled boards. Smith 193-195 1973 £20

TENDE, GASPARD DE   An Account of Poland. London, 1698. 8vo., contemporary panelled calf, browned, fine. Traylen 79-573 1973 £75

TENENBAUM, JOSEPH   Peace for the Jews. 1945. Austin 62-757 1974 $10

TENENBAUM, JOSEPH   Races, Nations and Jews. Bloch, 1934. Austin 62-634 1974 $10

TENISON, E. M.   Elizabethan England. 1937. Crown 4to., illus., plates, stained. Howes 186-1255 1974 £8.50

TENNANT, J.   A Stratigraphical List of British Fossils. 1847. 12mo., cloth, rebacked. Wheldon 130-976 1974 £5

TENNANT, PAMELA   The Children and the Pictures. London & New York, 1907. 8vo., cloth, plates, first edition. Frohnsdorff 15-182 1974 $15

TENNANT, STEPHEN   The Story of Felix Littlejohn. n.d. Roy 8vo., fine, illus., presentation copy, inscribed, English first edition. Covent 56-720 1974 £15

TENNENT, JAMES EMERSON   Sketches of the Natural History of Ceylon. 1861 or 1868. Crown 8vo., orig. cloth, plates, frontis., text-figures. Wheldon 128-240 1973 £10

TENNENT, JAMES EMERSON   Sketches of the Natural History of Ceylon. 1861 or 1868. Crown 8vo., orig. cloth, plates. Wheldon 130-318 1974 £10

TENNERONI, ANNIBALE   Inizii di Antiche Poesie Italiane Religiose e Morali. Florence, 1909. Large 8vo., orig. printed wrappers, unopened. Kraus B8-262 1974 $25

TENNESSEE   Public Acts of the State of Tennessee, Passed at the Extra Session of the 33rd General Assembly, April, 1861. Nashville, 1861. Boards. Jenkins 61-2433 1974 $35

TENNEY, TABITHA   Female Quixotism. Boston, 1841. 3 vols., 12mo., orig. purple cloth, fifth & last edition. Ximenes 35-329 1974 $17.50

TENNYSON, ALFRED   Alfred Lord Tennyson: A Memoir By His Son. 1897. 2 vols., illus. Austin 61-965 1974 $17.50

TENNYSON, ALFRED   Enoch Arden. 1864. Spine very worn, contents very fine, first published edition. Allen 216-1650 1974 $22.50

TENNYSON, ALFRED   Enoch Arden. London, 1864. Orig. cloth, first edition. Dawson's 424-307 1974 $40

TENNYSON, ALFRED   Enoch Arden. London, 1864. Spine slightly faded, very nice copy, ads at front, first edition. Covent 51-1806 1973 £21

TENNYSON, ALFRED   Enoch Arden, Etc. London, 1864. First edition, backstrip torn but intact, good copy, orig. binding. Ross 86-444 1974 $17.50

TENNYSON, ALFRED   The Foresters. London, 1892. 8vo., orig. cloth, bookplate, first English edition. Bow Windows 62-910 1974 £6.50

TENNYSON, ALFRED   Guinevere. 1867. Folio, orig. green cloth gilt, plates. Howes 185-134 1974 £7.50

TENNYSON, ALFRED   Harold. Osgood, 1877. Austin 51-962 1973 $7.50

TENNYSON, ALFRED Idylls of the King. (n.d.). 8vo., orig. cloth, plates, faded. Bow Windows 64-729 1974 £5.50

TENNYSON, ALFRED Idylls of the King. 1859. Small 8vo., orig. blind stamped cloth, faded. Howes 185-490 1974 £12.50

TENNYSON, ALFRED Idylls of the King. London, 1859. 12mo., cloth, back hinge broken, very clean copy, first edition. Goodspeed's 578-371 1974 $25

TENNYSON, ALFRED In Memoriam. Limited to 125 copies in special binding, small folio, gold thonged limp vellum, gilt title and device, gold end papers, uncut, top edges gilt, slip case, fine, scarce. Sawyer 293-240 1974 £85

TENNYSON, ALFRED In Memorium. London, 1850. 8vo., uncut, orig. cloth covers, rubbed, first edition. Ballinger 1-215 1974 $35

TENNYSON, ALFRED In Memoriam. London, 1859. Eighth edition, ink inscription, full green leather. Ross 86-445 1974 $25

TENNYSON, ALFRED In Memoriam. 1885. Crown 8vo., full levant morocco, uncut, limited edition. Broadhurst 23-882 1974 £20

TENNYSON, ALFRED In Memoriam. 1899. Small 8vo., dark green crushed levant morocco gilt, raised bands. Thomas 28-145 1972 £50

TENNYSON, ALFRED In Memoriam. 1914. Cloth-backed boards, English first edition. Covent 56-1239 1974 £8.50

TENNYSON, ALFRED In Memoriam. 1933. Extra roy. 8vo., dec. boards, uncut, unopened, limited. Broadhurst 23-1072 1974 £15

TENNYSON, ALFRED In Memoriam. Nonesuch Press, 1933. Extra roy. 8vo., dec. boards, paper printed label, uncut, unopened, limited to 2000 copies, fine. Broadhurst 24-1033 1974 £15

TENNYSON, ALFRED In Memoriam. 1933. Imp. 8vo., orig. gilt boards, uncut, unopened, limited edition. Howes 185-353 1974 £15

TENNYSON, ALFRED Locksley Hall. 1886. 8vo., orig. cloth, bookplate, first edition. Bow Windows 64-730 1974 £6

TENNYSON, ALFRED Locksley Hall Sixty Years After and the Promise of May. London, 1886. Probably first issue, inked name, spine slightly faded, fine bright copy, orig. binding. Ross 86-446 1974 $17.50

TENNYSON, ALFRED The Lover's Tale. 1879. 8vo., bookplate, English first edition. Covent 56-2069 1974 £5

TENNYSON, ALFRED Maud. 1893. 8vo., limp vellum with ties. Hammond 201-728 1974 £110

TENNYSON, ALFRED Maud and Other Poems. London, 1855. Orig. cloth, nice copy, inscription, ads at front, first edition. Covent 51-1808 1973 £21

TENNYSON, ALFRED Maud, and Other Poems. 1855. Small 8vo., orig. blind stamped cloth, first edition. Howes 186-451 1974 £12.50

TENNYSON, ALFRED Poems. London, 1830. Full green morocco, first edition. Dawson's 424-308 1974 $60

TENNYSON, ALFRED Poems. (c., 1851). 8vo., contemporary morocco, frontispiece, foxing. Bow Windows 64-731 1974 £5.75

TENNYSON, ALFRED Poems. London, 1851. Small 8vo., 2 vols., contemporary crimson morocco, gilt, seventh edition. Hammond 201-355 1974 £44

TENNYSON, ALFRED Poetic and Dramatic Works. 1919. 7 vols., plates, large paper edition. Allen 216-2291 1974 $35

TENNYSON, ALFRED Poetical and Dramatic Works. 1914. Thick f'cap 4to., good copy, tear in cloth of front hinge, orig. cloth. Broadhurst 24-300 1974 £25

TENNYSON, ALFRED Poetical Works. London, n.d. Portrait, tree calf, gilt, fine, 2 1/4 X 1 7/8. Gregory 44-471 1974 $18.50

TENNYSON, ALFRED Queen Mary. London, 1875. First edition, first issue, with misprint p. 126, library plate, covers lightly worn, very nice, tight copy, orig. binding. Ross 86-447 1974 $10

TENNYSON, ALFRED Queen Mary. 1875. 12mo., full contemporary morocco, gilt, English first edition. Covent 56-2070 1974 £8.50

TENNYSON, ALFRED Queen Mary. 1875. 8vo., orig. cloth, first edition. Bow Windows 64-732 1974 £7.50

TENNYSON, ALFRED Seven Poems & Two Translations. Hammersmith, 1902. 8vo., limp vellum, limited. Bow Windows 62-277 1974 £55

TENNYSON, ALFRED Works. 1877. 7 vols., med. 8vo., full dark green morocco, panelled backs, raised bands, tooled gilt, all edges gilt, fine. Broadhurst 24-1716 1974 £60

TENNYSON, ALFRED Works. 1877. Orig. quarter morocco, gilt, 7 vols., English first edition. Covent 56-2071 1974 £27.50

TENNYSON, ALFRED Complete Poems and Plays. 1906. 5 vols. in 2, crown 8vo., half levant morocco gilt. Howes 186-449 1974 £10

TENNYSON, FREDERICK Days and Hours. London, 1854. 8vo., orig. dec. cloth, label, first edition. Bow Windows 62-911 1974 £30

TENNYSON, HALLAM Jack and the Bean-Stalk. 1886. First edition, drawings, cover little stained, very good copy. Covent 51-337 1973 £5.25

TERENCE
Please turn to
TERENTIUS AFER, PUBLIUS

TERENTIUS AFER, PUBLIUS Comoediae. Basle, 1519. Small 4to., back repaired, contemporary blind stamped pigskin over boards, manuscript annotations. Schafer 10-111 1974 sFr 1,100

TERENTIUS AFER, PUBLIUS Comoediae. Paris, 1528. 12mo., vellum. Thomas 28-311 1972 £30

TERENTIUS AFER, PUBLIUS Comoediae. Paris, 1528. 12mo., vellum, slightly loose, complete, but lacks (2?) leaves at end, small hole punched in first few leaves. Thomas 32-266 1974 £30

TERENTIUS AFER, PUBLIUS Comoediae. Paris, 1552. First edition, first issue with colophon dated 1551, Folio, reversed calf, armorial bookplate of Wakefield Grammar School, clean sound copy. Thomas 32-267 1974 £80

TERENTIUS AFER, PUBLIUS Comedie, Vita. 1563. Vellum gilt, morocco labels. Thomas 30-118 1973 £12

TERENTIUS AFER, PUBLIUS Comoediae. Paris, 1642. Folio, frontis., gilt, contemporary marbled calf, worn, fine. Harper 213-153 1973 $425

TERENTIUS AFER, PUBLIUS Comoediae. Birmingham, 1772. Large 4to., russia, rebacked, gilt tooled spine, library stamps. Thomas 32-275 1974 £35

TERENTIUS AFER, PUBLIUS The Comedies of... 1900. 2 vols., 8vo., bookplate, paper backed boards, uncut. Dawsons PM 252-946 1974 £15

TERENTIUS AFER, PUBLIUS Le Comedie Volgari. 1546. Vellum. Thomas 30-89 1973 £25

TERENTIUS AFER, PUBLIUS The Plays of. London, 1927. 8vo., very fine, soiled d.j. Current BW9-610 1974 $18

TERENTIUS AFER, PUBLIUS   Phormio. Deventer, 1518. Small 4to., half morocco, fine, unrecorded edition. Harper 213-152 1973 $950

TERENTIUS AFER, PUBLIUS   Terence in English. London, 1614. Small 4to., contemporary vellum, fourth edition. Ximenes 35-331 1974 $85

TERES, T.   Richard in Cyprus. London, n.d. 8vo., wrappers, first edition. Ximenes 35-332 1974 $27.50

TERHUNE, ALBERT PAYSON   The Story of Damon and Pythias. 307p., illus. Austin 51-963 1973 $7.50

TERRANEO, LORENZO   De Glandulis Universim, et Speciatim ad Urethram Virilem Novis. Leiden, 1729. 8vo., boards, folding plates. Gurney 66-183 1974 £25

TERRINGTON, WILLIAM   Cooling Cups and Dainty Drinks. London and New York, 1870. 8vo., orig. cloth, gilt, first edition. Hammond 201-176 1974 £10

TERRY, CHARLES   New Zealand. 1842. 8vo., orig. cloth, plates, frontispiece, first edition. Bow Windows 64-734 1974 £110

TESAURO, EMMANUEL   Italia Sotto I Barbari. 1691. Small 8vo., French red morocco gilt. Thomas 28-144 1972 £12.50

TESKEY, ADELINE M.   Where the Sugar Maple Grows. Toronto, 1901. Illus., soft leather. Hood's 102-353 1974 $10

TESKEY, ADELINE M.   Where the Sugar Maple Grows. Toronto, 1901. Leather, illus., fold stamping. Hood's 104-503 1974 $10

THE TESTAMENT of the Twelve Prophets. Glasgow, 1684. Small 8vo., old calf, worn. Thomas 28-105 1972 £25

TESTE, ALPHONSE   A Practical Manual of Animal Magnetism. 1843. 8vo., orig. cloth, some foxing, covers worn. Bow Windows 66-692 1974 £7.25

TEUFFEL, WILHELM SIGISMUND   Geschichte der Roemischen Literatur. 1916-13. 3 vols. Allen 213-1100 1973 $22.50

TEUFFEL, WIHELM SIGISMUND   A History of Roman Literature. London, 1873. 2 vols., orig. edition. Biblo & Tannen 214-665 1974 $27.50

TEXAS HISTORICAL RECORDS SURVEY   Inventory of the Hood County Archives of Texas. San Antonio, 1940. Wrappers. Hayman 59-620 1974 $12.50

TEXAS HISTORICAL RECORDS SURVEY   Inventory of the Jackson County Archives of Texas. Jackson County, 1940. Wrappers, scarce. Hayman 59-622 1974 $15

TEXAS HISTORICAL RECORDS SURVEY   Inventory of the Marion County Archives of Texas. San Antonio, 1940. Wrappers. Hayman 59-623 1974 $12.50

TEXAS HISTORICAL RECORDS SURVEY   Inventory of the Mills County Archives of Texas. San Antonio, 1940. Wrappers. Hayman 59-625 1974 $12.50

TEXAS HISTORICAL RECORDS SURVEY   Inventory of the Sabine County Archives of Texas. San Antonio, 1939. Wrappers. Hayman 59-628 1974 $15

THE TEXT BOOK of Advanced Freemasonry. 1873. 8vo., orig. cloth, English first edition. Covent 56-487 1974 £5

THACHER, JAMES   The American Orchardist. Boston, 1822. 8vo., orig. boards, rare, first edition. Wheldon 130-1489 1974 £50

THACKERAY, WILLIAM MAKEPEACE   The Adventures of Philip. 1862. 3 vols., crown 8vo., full calf gilt, fine, first edition. Howes 185-493 1974 £38

THACKERAY, WILLIAM MAKEPEACE   Ballads. Boston, 1856. First American edition, 8vo., very good. Current BW9-282 1974 $22.50

THACKERAY, WILLIAM MAKEPEACE   Denis Duval. New York, 1867. 8vo., orig. printed wrappers, illus., fine. Ximenes 35-333 1974 $10

THACKERAY, WILLIAM MAKEPEACE   Denis Duval. 1867. Crown 8vo., half crimson levant morocco gilt, first edition. Howes 185-494 1974 £25

THACKERAY, WILLIAM MAKEPEACE   Doctor Birch and His Young Friends. London, 1849. 4to., orig. pink glazed boards, rubbed, first edition, vignette title-page, plates colored, very good copy, boxed. MacManus 224-425 1974 $75

THACKERAY, WILLIAM MAKEPEACE   Doctor Birch and His Young Friends. 1849. Small 4to., contemporary half calf gilt, plates, first edition. Howes 185-495 1974 £30

THACKERAY, WILLIAM MAKEPEACE   An Essay on the Genius of George Cruikshank. (London), 1840. 8vo., half morocco, gilt, illus., plates, very good copy, first edition. Ximenes 37-207 1974 $75

THACKERAY, WILLIAM MAKEPEACE   The History of Henry Esmond. London, 1852. 3 vols., 8vo., orig. cloth, uncut, fine, first edition. Dawsons PM 252-947 1974 £150

THACKERAY, WILLIAM MAKEPEACE   The History of Pendennis. London, 1849. 2 vols., 8vo., orig. blue blind-stamped cloth, illus., first edition. Dawsons PM .252-948 1974 £23

THACKERAY, WILLIAM MAKEPEACE   The History of Pendennis. 1849-50. 2 vols., full calf gilt, illus., first edition. Howes 185-496 1974 £30

THACKERAY, WILLIAM MAKEPEACE   The History of Pendennis. 1849-50. 2 vols. in 1, thick 8vo., half crimson levant morocco, gilt, plates, foxing. Howes 186-453 1974 £25

THACKERAY, WILLIAM MAKEPEACE   The History of Pendennis. London, 1849-50. 2 vols., 8vo., old half calf, rubbed, first edition. Goodspeed's 578-372 1974 $25

THACKERAY, WILLIAM MAKEPEACE   History of Pendennis. 1849-50. 2 vols., half calf, worn, plates, first edition in book form. Allen 216-1659 1974 $45

THACKERAY, WILLIAM MAKEPEACE   The History of Samuel Titmarsh and the Great Hoggarty Diamond. 1849. Crown 8vo., half levant morocco, gilt, first edition. Howes 185-497 1974 £26

THACKERAY, WILLIAM MAKEPEACE   The History of Samuel Titmarsh and the Great Hoggarty Diamond. London, 1849. Orig. glazed boards, ends of spine chipped, joints worn, first edition, plates somewhat spotted, half-morocco slip case. MacManus 224-426 1974 $75

THACKERAY, WILLIAM MAKEPEACE   The History of Samuel Titmarsh and The Great Hoggarty Diamond. London, 1902. First edition. Biblo & Tannen 210-167 1973 $10

THACKERAY, WILLIAM MAKEPEACE   Irish Sketch Book. New York, 1847. Orig. wrappers, signed by author on cover. Allen 216-1660 1974 $20

THACKERAY, WILLIAM MAKEPEACE   The Kickleburys on the Rhine. London, 1850. Small 4to., orig. pink glazed boards, hinges cracked, some rubbing, first edition, colored plates, very clean internally, half morocco slipcase. MacManus 224-427 1974 $100

THACKERAY, WILLIAM MAKEPEACE   Miscellaneous Works of. London, 1840-68. 8 vols., 8vo., green half calf, rubbed. Bow Windows 62-916 1974 £22.50

THACKERY, WILLIAM MAKEPEACE   Mr. Brown's Letter to a Young Man About Town. Cambridge, 1901. Numbered, uncut, unopened, fine. Ballinger 1-48 1974 $15

THACKERAY, WILLIAM MAKEPEACE   The Newcomes. n.d. illus., boxed, fine. Austin 61-966 1974 $10

THACKERAY, WILLIAM MAKEPEACE   The Newcomes. New York, 1855. 2 vols. in 1, half calf, rubbed. Allen 216-1661 1974 $12.50

THACKERAY, WILLIAM MAKEPEACE   The Newcomes Memoirs. London, 1853-55. Orig. wrappers, illus., slip-case, fine, first edition. Dawsons PM 252-949 1974 £260

THACKERAY, WILLIAM MAKEPEACE   Notes of a Journey from Cornhill. London, 1846. 8vo., orig. red cloth, illus., fine. Ximenes 35-334 1974 $60

THACKERAY, WILLIAM MAKEPEACE   The Orphan of Pimlico. London, 1876. Large 4to., orig. cloth, illus., first edition. Dawsons PM 252-950 1974 £30

THACKERAY, WILLIAM MAKEPEACE   Our Annual Execution. Philadelphia, 1902. 12mo., watered silk, first separate edition. Goodspeed's 578-373 1974 $15

THACKERAY, WILLIAM MAKEPEACE   "Our Street." London, 1848. 4to., orig. pink glazed boards, hinges cracked, first issue, plates colored by author, covers bit soiled, very good copy, morocco backed box. MacManus 224-429 1974 $100

THACKERAY, WILLIAM MAKEPEACE   Mrs. Perkin's Ball. London, 1847. Orig. glazed boards, somewhat rubbed, first issue with no letterpress under the plate facing the title, colored plabes, very good copy, boxed. MacManus 224-428 1974 $80

THACKERAY, WILLIAM MAKEPEACE   Rebecca and Rowena. London, 1850. 4to., orig. pink glazed boards, rubbed, first edition, colored plates, very good copy of fragile book, boxed. MacManus 224-430 1974 $80

THACKERAY, WILLIAM MAKEPEACE   The Rose and the Ring; or, The History of Prince Giglio and Prince Bulbo. London, 1855. Modern half vellum, leather label, first edition, plates, woodcuts, fine, boxed. MacManus 224-431 1974 $80

THACKERAY, WILLIAM MAKEPEACE   Roundabout Papers. London, 1863. 8vo., orig. purple cloth, illus., first edition. Ximenes 35-335 1974 $22.50

THACKERAY, WILLIAM MAKEPEACE   The Second Funeral of Napoleon. London, 1841. Square 12mo., plates, orig. wrappers, rare, first edition. Dawsons PM 252-951 1974 £250

THACKERY, WILLIAM MAKEPEACE   Some Family Letters. Cambridge, 1911. Fine, unopened, uncut. Ballinger 1-49 1974 $15

THACKERAY, WILLIAM MAKEPEACE   Thackerayana. 1875. Orig. pictorial cloth gilt, English first edition. Covent 56-1240 1974 £15

THACKERAY, WILLIAM MAKEPEACE   Unpublished Verses. London, 1899. Orig. yellow printed wrappers, stitched, first edition, one of 25 numbered copies, laid-in is a signature of Thackeray, elaborately dec. red morocco slipcase, fine. MacManus 224-432 1974 $85

THACKERAY, WILLIAM MAKEPEACE   Vanity Fair. 1848. Thick 8vo., full polished tree calf, plates, first edition. Howes 185-498 1974 $50

THACKERAY, WILLIAM MAKEPEACE   Vanity Fair. Cambridge, 1865. 3 vols., 8vo., orig. cloth, illus., fine. Ximenes 35-336 1974 $27.50

THACKERAY, WILLIAM MAKEPEACE   Vanity Fair. Oxford, 1931. 2 vols., large 8vo., cloth-backed dec. boards, illus. Covent 55-877 1974 £40

THACKERAY, WILLIAM MAKEPEACE   The Virginians. 1857-59. First edition in the orig. 24 parts, earliest issue, engraved plates, woodcuts by author, 8vo., orig. yellow printed wrappers, uncut, with advertisements and slips, green cloth box, fine copy. Sawyer 293-273 1974 £235

THACKERAY, WILLIAM MAKEPEACE   The Virginians. London, 1858-59. 2 vols., 8vo., orig. blue cloth, first book edition. Ximenes 35-337 1974 $30

THACKERAY, WILLIAM MAKEPEACE   The Virginians. London, 1858-59. Orig. wrappers, cloth box, first edition. Dawsons PM 252-952 1974 £250

THACKERAY, WILLIAM MAKEPEACE   The Virginians. 1858-59. 2 vols., full calf gilt, illus., first edition. Howes 185-499 1974 £28

THACKERAY, WILLIAM MAKEPEACE   Works. 1869-86. 24 vols., 8vo., half blue levant morocco, spines gilt, orig. illus. by author, fine set, best library edition. Sawyer 293-274 1974 £290

THACKERAY, WILLIAM MAKEPEACE   The Works of. 1874. 12 vols., 8vo., contemporary half calf, gilt backs, morocco labels, marbled sides, illus. Bow Windows 66-693 1974 £44

THACKERAY, WILLIAM MAKEPEACE   Works. 1877. 12 vols., crown 8vo., contemporary half morocco gilt. Howes 185-491 1974 £45

THACKERAY, WILLIAM MAKEPEACE   The Works of. London, 1883-86. 26 vols., 8vo., illus., orig. cloth, rubbed. Bow Windows 62-914 1974 £14

THACKERAY, WILLIAM MAKEPEACE   The Works Of. 1894-6. 8vo., 13 vols., half morocco, illus., frontispieces. Bow Windows 64-735 1974 £68

THACKERAY, WILLIAM MAKEPEACE   Collected Works. 1911. 20 vols., roy. 8vo., orig. cloth gilt, illus., limited. Howes 185-492 1974 £50

THACKERAY, WILLIAM MAKEPEACE   Collection of the Works of. London, 1877-82. 12 vols., 8vo., contemporary half morocco, illus., inscription, frontispieces. Bow Windows 62-915 1974 £45

THAULER, JOANNES   Opera Omnia. Paris, 1623. Small 4to., contemporary calf, rubbed. Smith 194-189 1974 £10

THAXTER, CELIA   Among the Isles of Shoals. Boston, 1882. 16mo., cloth, presentation copy with inscription in author's hand, seventh edition. Goodspeed's 578-374 1974 $15

THAYER, WILLIAM SYDNEY   Osler and Other Papers. Baltimore, 1931. Rittenhouse 46-610 1974 $15

THEATRE '63. Random House, 1953. 564p. Austin 51-182 1973 $10

THEODORETUS   Dialogi tres Contra Haereses. Rome, 1547. 4to., old boards, leather back, worn, inscription, fine, first edition. Harper 213-154 1973 $485

THEOPHILUS   An Essay Upon Various Arts. 1847. 8vo., orig. cloth, very scarce. Quaritch 940-252 1974 £35

THEOPHRASTUS   Traite des Pierres de Theophraste Traduit du Grec. Paris, 1754. 12mo., contemporary mottled calf. Quaritch 940-480 1974 £25

THESAURUS of Humor. Crown, 1940. 605p. Austin 54-735 1973 $10

THALBITZER, S.   Emotion and Insanity. London, 1926. 8vo., orig. green cloth, gilt, first edition in English. Dawsons PM 249-478 1974 £6

THAYER, WILLIAM M.   Marvels of the New West. Norwich, 1888. Illus., pict. cloth. Jenkins 61-2445 1974 $12.50

THAYLER, ABBOT H.   Abbot H. Thayler Memorial Exhibition - 1922. New York, 1922. Paper boards, glassine wrappers, fine. Ballinger 1-50 1974 $17.50

THEINER, A.   Histoire des Deux Concordats de la Republic Francaise et de la Republic Cisalpine. Paris, 1869. 3 parts in 2 vols., roy. 8vo., cloth. Howes 186-1256 1974 £18

THEINER, A.   Vetera Monumenta Hibernorum et Scotorum Historiam Illustratia. Rome, 1864. Folio, cloth. Howes 186-1257 1974 £38

THEIR Husband's Wives. Harper, 1907. 18lp. Austin 54-568 1973 $6.50

THELLER, E. A.   Canada In 1837-38. Philadelphia, 1841. 2 vols., worn, staining. Hood's 103-562 1974 $150

THEOBALD, F. V.   An Account of British Flies. 1892. 8vo., cloth, plates. Wheldon 129-689 1974 £5

THEOBALD, W. Descriptive Catalogue of the Reptiles of British India. Calcutta, 1876. 8vo., contemporary half calf. Wheldon 129-598 1974 £7.50

THEOCRITUS The Idyllia, Epigrams and Fragments of Theocritus, Bion and Moschus, With the Elegies of Tyrtaeus. Exeter, 1786. 4to., later half calf, spine gilt, very good copy, outer edges uncut, first edition. Ximenes 37-181 1974 $45

THEOCRITUS Theocritus, Bion and Moschus. 1922. Limited edition, coloured plates, 2 vols., 4to., orig. holland backed boards, paper labels, dust wrappers, top edges gilt, others uncut, fine, limited to 500 copies on hand made paper. Sawyer 293-142 1974 £120

THEOCRITUS The Idyls of Theocritus, Bion and Moschus. 1922. 4to., 2 vols., linen backed boards, English first edition. Covent 56-694 1974 £125

THEOCRITUS The Idylls of. 1925. 4to., clothbacked boards, English first edition. Covent 56-1268 1974 £5.25

THEOPHYLACTUS, ARCHBISHOP OF ACHRIDA Enarrationes in Epistolas. Rome, 1477. Folio, half leather, large copy. Harper 213-155 1973 $750

THEOSOPHY in Ireland. 1925-48. 71 issues, orig. wrappers. Emerald 50-776 1974 £35

THESE THINGS the Poets Said. 1935. Cloth-backed boards, fine, limited edition. Covent 56-1020 1974 £75

THE THESPIAN Dictionary. 1802. Small 8vo., old quarter calf, portraits, first edition. Hill 126-265 1974 £28

THEURIET, A. Nos Oiseaux. Paris, 1887. Imp. 8vo., full crushed levant morocco, woodcuts, slip case, limited edition de luxe. Quaritch 940-253 1974 £350

THIBAULT, GIRARD Academie de l'Espee. 1628. Large folio, 18th century marbled boards, gilt, first edition. Marlborough 70-10 1974 £1,850

THIERRY, AMADEE Histoire de la Gaule Sous la Domination Romaine. 1878. 2 vols. in 1, new buckram. Allen 213-1106 1973 $15

THIERRY, AMADEE Recueil d'Escaliers en Pierre, Charpente, Menuiserie et en Fonte a l'Usage des Ouvriers en Batiments. Paris, 1838. 4to., plates, contemporary boards. Quaritch 940-559 1974 £24

THIERS, ADOLPHE 1797-1877 Histoire du Consulat et de l'Empire. Paris, 1845-62. 20 vols., contemporary quarter morocco, marbled boards, plates, fine, first edition. Howes 186-1258 1974 £38

THIERS, ADOLPHE 1797-1877 De la Propriete. Paris, 1848. 8vo., gilt, half contemporary polished sheep, first edition. L. Goldschmidt 42-394 1974 $37.50

THIERS, ADOLPHE 1797-1877 Histoire de la Revolution Francaise. Paris, 1865-80. 10 vols., 8vo., quarter morocco, gilt on spines, plates, Denham Court bookplate. Bow Windows 66-694 1974 £18

THIERS, ADOLPHE 1797-1877 La Monarchie de 1830. Paris, 1831. 8vo., orig. boards, first edition. L. Goldschmidt 42-393 1974 $50

THILLAYE, L. J. S. Essai sur l'Emploi Medical de l'Electricite. Paris, 1803. 8vo., orig. wrappers, uncut, unopened. Gurney 64-214 1974 £20

THIS QUARTER. Monte Carlo, 1927. Orig. wrappers, blue cloth boards, gilt. Rota 188-533 1974 £7.50

THOM, ADAM The Claims of the Oregon Territory Considered. London, 1844. Sewn, rare. Jenkins 61-2099 1974 $37.50

THOM, CHARLES The Aspergilli. 1926. 8vo., cloth, scarce. Wheldon 129-1359 1974 £5

THOM, CHARLES The Penicillia. 1930. Roy 8vo., cloth. Wheldon 129-1360 1974 £5

THOM, CHARLES Telegraphic Connections. New York, 1892. Oblong 8vo., orig. green cloth, ex-library. Zeitlin 235-219 1974 $37.50

THOMA, LUDWIG Moral. Knopf, 1916. Austin 51-964 1973 $6.50

THOMAS A KEMPIS Imitatio Christi
Please turn to
IMITATIO CHRISTI

THOMAS A KEMPIS 1380-1471 The Christian's Pattern. 1742. Contemporary calf, rubbed, plates. Howes 185-895 1974 £8.50

THOMAS A KEMPIS 1380-1471 The Christian's Pattern. London, 1759. 8vo., frontis., contemporary calf, rebacked, engravings. Bow Windows 62-12 1974 £8.50

THOMAS AQUINAS Indices Auctoritatum Omniumque Rerum Notabilium Occurrentium in Summa Theologiae. Rome, c.1930. Thick roy. 8vo., cloth. Howes 185-1712 1974 £7.50

THOMAS AQUINAS In Tres Psalterii Primos Nocturnos. Venice, 1505. Small folio, old calf, worn. Thomas 30-141 1973 £40

THOMAS AQUINAS Summa Theologica. Paris, 1864. 4 vols., roy. 8vo., half morocco, mottled boards. Traylen 79-165 1973 £12

THOMAS AQUINAS Summa Theologica. 1872-82. 4 vols., half calf. Allen 213-1810 1973 $25

THOMAS AQUINAS Summa Theologica. Paris, 1887-89. 5 vols., roy. 8vo., half vellum. Howes 185-1714 1974 £15

THOMAS AQUINAS Summa Totius Theologiae. Rome, 1619. Small 8vo., French red morocco gilt. Thomas 28-146 1972 £30

THOMAS, ANNIE Eyre of Blendon. London, 1881. 3 vols., library labels, rubber stamps, very good copy, rebound in black cloth, first edition. Covent 51-1897 1973 £10.50

THOMAS, AUGUSTUS The Print of My Remembrance. Scribner, 1922. Austin 51-967 1973 $8.50

THOMAS, B. Deutsche Plattnerkunst. Munich, (1944). Roy. 8vo., plates, boards. Quaritch 940-704 1974 £8

THOMAS, BERTHRAM Arabia Felix. 1932. 397 pages, illus., map. Austin 61-573 1974 $17.50

THOMAS, DAVID Y. Arkansas and Its People. New York, 1930. 4 vols., 4to., cloth. Saddleback 14-18 1974 $70

THOMAS, DYLAN Deaths and Entrances. 1946. Orig. cloth, fine, first edition. Rota 188-885 1974 £21

THOMAS, DYLAN 18 Poems. 1934. Orig. cloth, first edition, second issue. Rota 188-883 1974 £55

THOMAS, DYLAN The Map of Love. 1939. Orig. cloth, first edition, first issue. Rota 188-884 1974 £40

THOMAS, DYLAN The Map of Love. 1939. First edition, crown 8vo., mint, d.w., first issue in fine grained mauve cloth. Broadhurst 24-902 1974 £28

THOMAS, DYLAN New Poems. 1943. Limp wrappers. Allen 216-1671 1974 $10

THOMAS, DYLAN Portrait of the Author as a Young Dog. London, 1940. First edition, spine & some edges of covers faded, nice copy, scarce, orig. cloth. Crane 7-298 1974 £30

THOMAS, DYLAN Portrait of the Artist as a Young Dog. 1940. 8vo., orig. cloth, first edition. Rota 190-942 1974 £18

THOMAS, DYLAN   Twenty-Five Poems. London, 1936. 8vo., orig. boards, first edition. Dawsons PM 252-954 1974 £70

THOMAS, DYLAN   Twenty-Five Poems. 1936. 8vo., orig. cloth, first edition. Rota 189-855 1974 £50

THOMAS, DYLAN   Twenty-Five Poems. 1936. Grey boards, fine, only 730 copies printed, first edition. Covent 51-1826 1973 £30

THOMAS, DYLAN   Twenty-Five Poems. 1936. Crown 8vo., boards, first edition, very fine copy. Broadhurst 24-901 1974 £45

THOMAS, DYLAN   Two Poems. Oxford, 1935. Fine, wrappers, English first edition. Covent 56-2080 1974 £6.30

THOMAS, DYLAN   Two Poems. 1936. English first edition. Covent 56-1249 1974 £15

THOMAS, E.   Scoliastes de Virgile. 1880. Sewn. Allen 213-1169 1973 $10

THOMAS, E. CREWDSON   History of the Schoolmen. 1941. Thick 8vo., scarce. Howes 185-2014 1974 £5.50

THOMAS, E. S.   Reminiscences of the Last Sixty-Five Years. Hartford, 1840. 2 vols., new half black morocco, marbled boards, first edition. Bradley 35-283 1974 $60

THOMAS, EDWARD   An Annual of New Poetry. 1917. First edition, demy 8vo., boards, uncut, very good copy. Broadhurst 24-916 1974 £20

THOMAS, EDWARD   British Butterflies and Other Insects. London, 1908. First edition, covers worn, front hinge loosening, nice copy, illus. in color. Ross 87-541 1974 $15

THOMAS, EDWARD   Chosen Essays. 1926. Crown 4to., buckram, uncut, faded, limited edition. Broadhurst 23-1034 1974 £20

THOMAS, EDWARD   Chosen Essays. 1926. 4to., buckram, gilt, illus. Hammond 201-755 1974 £50

THOMAS, EDWARD   Cloud Castle and Other Papers. 1922. First edition, demy 8vo., very fine, first issue, with spine lettered in gilt, orig. cloth. Broadhurst 24-918 1974 £12

THOMAS, EDWARD   Cloud Castle and Other Papers. 1922. First edition, demy 8vo., orig. cloth, fine, second issue, spine lettered in black. Broadhurst 24-919 1974 £6

THOMAS, EDWARD   Cloud Castle, and Other Papers. 1922. Half title & title trifle foxed, unusually fine crisp copy, faded d.w., scarce in this condition. Covent 51-2591 1973 £10

THOMAS, EDWARD   Collected Poems. 1920. Demy 8vo., boards, cloth spine, uncut, limited, one of 100 copies, printed on Japan paper. Broadhurst 24-917 1974 £32

THOMAS, EDWARD   Feminine Influence on the Poets. 1910. 8vo., orig. cloth, first edition. Rota 190-943 1974 £12

THOMAS, EDWARD   George Borrow. 1912. Orig. violet cloth gilt, plates, scarce, first edition. Howes 186-472 1974 £18

THOMAS, EDWARD   The Happy-Go-Lucky Morgans. n.d. Covers little stained, name on fly, variant issue with title page undated but integral, without frontis. and ads, scarce title in any state. Covent 51-1833 1973 £17.50

THOMAS, E.   The Icknield Way. 1913. Orig. pictorial cloth gilt, illus., plates. Smith 194-535 1974 £7

THOMAS, EDWARD   The Icknield Way. 1916. First edition, med. 8vo., orig. cloth, fine, first edition, coloured frontispiece, illus. Broadhurst 24-915 1974 £12

THOMAS, EDWARD   In Pursuit of Spring. 1914. Plates, English first edition. Covent 56-2083 1974 £7.50

THOMAS, EDWARD   In Pursuit of Spring. 1914. First edition, plates, med. 8vo., orig. cloth, fine. Broadhurst 24-914 1974 £12

THOMAS, EDWARD   The Isle of Wight. 1911. Plates, pictorial boards, English first edition. Covent 56-1252 1974 £6.30

THOMAS, EDWARD   The Last Sheaf. 1928. First edition, crown 8vo., fine, soiled d.w., orig. cloth. Broadhurst 24-920 1974 £7

THOMAS, EDWARD   Light and Twilight. 1911. First edition, f'cap. 8vo., orig. cloth, fine. Broadhurst 24-912 1974 £7

THOMAS, EDWARD   Maurice Maeterlinck. London, 1911. Orig. binding, spine faded, first edition, bookplate, nice copy. Ross 87-542 1974 $15

THOMAS, EDWARD   A Pocket Book of Poems and Songs for the Open Air. 1929. 334 pages. Austin 61-967 1974 $10

THOMAS, EDWARD   Poems. London, 1917. Frontis. portrait, orig. drab boards, presentation inscription, beautiful copy, first edition. Covent 51-1834 1973 £35

THOMAS, EDWARD   Richard Jefferies: His Life and Work. 1909. Plates, gilt top, very good copy, first edition. Covent 51-1836 1973 £5.25

THOMAS, EDWARD   Richard Jefferies, His Life and Work. 1909. Plates, map. Covent 55-1445 1974 £7.50

THOMAS, EDWARD   Selected Poems. Newtown, 1927. First edition, limited to 275 numbered copies, printed in black & red, tall 8vo., yellow buckram, very nice copy. Crane 7-301 1974 £60

THOMAS, EDWARD   Selected Poems. 1927. 8vo., buckram, gilt. Hammond 201-758 1974 £50

THOMAS, EDWARD   Some British Birds. London, 1908. Orig. binding, first edition, illus. in color, spine faded, name in ink on fly, corners somewhat rubbed, very nice. Ross 87-543 1974 $15

THOMAS, EDWARD   The South Country. 1909. Near fine, first edition. Covent 55-1446 1974 £6.30

THOMAS EDWARD   The Woodland Life. 1897. Crown 8vo., first edition, very fine, mostly unopened, orig. cloth. Broadhurst 24-911 1974 £90

THOMAS, ELIZABETH   The Metamorphosis of the Town. London, 1730. 8vo., modern calf, very rare, very good copy, first edition. Ximenes 37-210 1974 $175

THOMAS, ELIZABETH   Purity of Heart. 1817. 12mo., orig. boards, uncut, second edition. Hill 126-201 1974 £40

THOMAS, GILBERT   How to Enjoy Detective Fiction. London, 1947. 1st ed. Biblo & Tannen 210-533 1973 $10

THOMAS, H.   The Ancient Remains, Antiquities, and Recent Improvements, of the City of London. London, 1830. 2 vols., 8vo., gilt, contemporary half roan, marbled boards. Bow Windows 62-936 1974 £20

THOMAS, HELEN   As It Was. London, 1926. 8vo., orig. orange cloth, dust wrapper, first edition, first issue. Dawsons PM 252-956 1974 £20

THOMAS, HELEN   As It Was. 1926. First edition, crown 8vo., mint, d.w., first issue, scarce, orig. cloth. Broadhurst 24-921 1974 £12

THOMAS, HELEN   As It Was. New York, 1926. 12mo., cloth, first edition. Goodspeed's 578-376 1974 $10

THOMAS, HELEN   World Without End. 1931. Fine, worn, dust wrapper, English first edition. Covent 56-1254 1974 £6.30

THOMAS, HENRY   Early Spanish Bookbindings. London, 1939. 4to., plates, orig. cloth-backed boards, fine. Dawsons PM 10-601 1974 £10

THOMAS, ISAIAH   The History of Printing In America. Worcester, 1810. 2 vols., 8vo., contemporary sheep, plates, first edition. Dawsons PM 10-602 1974 £105

THOMAS, JEAN   Ballad Makin' in the Mountains of Kentucky. New York, (1939). Cloth. Hayman 59-344 1974 $12.50

THOMAS, LOWELL   The First World Flight. Boston, 1925. Illus., limited to 575 numbered copies, autographed by narrators and Thomas, boxed. Jenkins 61-2446 1974 $125

THOMAS, MAUDE   Dress Cutting and Making for the County Council and other Technical Classes Tailor System. London, c., 1890. 8vo., cloth. Hammond 201-961 1974 £7.50

THOMAS, NORMAN   What Socialism Is and Is Not. Chicago, 1932. Four page booklet. Bradley 35-380 1974 $50

THOMAS, ROBERT BAILEY   The Farmer's Almanack . . . For the Year of Our Lord, 1838. Boston, 1838. 16mo., woodcuts, fine, new wrappers. Current BW9-446 1974 $12

THOMAS, W.   A Survey of the Cathedral-Church of Worcester. 1737. 4to., contemporary calf, illus. Quaritch 939-586 1974 £12.50

THOMAS, WILLIAM I.   The Polish Peasant in Europe and America. 1918. Orig. edition. Austin 57-666A 1974 $12.50

THOMAS, WILLIAM I.   The Polish Peasant in Europe and America. 1918. Orig. edition. Austin 57-666 1974 $12.50

THOMAS OF ELMHAM   Historia Monasterii S. Augustini Cantuariensis. 1858. Thick roy. 8vo., orig. half roan, worn. Howes 186-1182 1974 £9

THOMAS, TOBYAS   The Life of the Late Famous Comedian, Jo Hayns. London, 1701. 8vo., polished calf, rare, first edition. Ximenes 35-341 1974 $450

THOMAS-STANFORD, CHARLES   Early Editions of Euclid's Elements. London, 1926. 4to., orig. holland-backed boards. Dawsons PM 10-603 1974 £32

THOMASSIN, LOUIS   Dictionnaire de Discipline Ecclesiastique Ou Traite du Gouvernement de l'Eglise. Paris, 1856. 2 vols., thick roy. 8vo., half maroon calf, rubbed. Howes 185-1720 1974 £5.50

THOME, JAMES A.   Emancipation in the West Indies. New York, 1838. Orig. boards, cloth, first edition. Bradley 35-347 1974 $40

THOME, JAMES A.   Emancipation in the West Indies. New York, 1838. 1st ed., orig. bds. Jacobs 24-31 1974 $40

THOME, WILHELMUS   De Corneae Transplantatione. Bonn, (1834). 4to., orig. wrappers, plates. Schumann 35-462 1974 $85

THOMPSON, ALAN R.   The Anatomy of Drama. Univ. of Calif., 1946. Austin 51-968 1973 $10

THOMPSON, ARTHUR R.   Nature by Day. 1932. Small crown 4to., 2 vols., frontispiece. Bow Windows 64-270 1974 £4.50

THOMPSON, ARTHUR R.   Nature by Night. 1931. Roy 8vo., orig. dec. cloth, illus. Wheldon 129-308 1974 £5

THOMPSON, SIR BENJAMIN, COUNT RUMFORD
Please turn to
RUMFORD, SIR BENJAMIN THOMPSON, COUNT

THOMPSON, CHARLES JOHN SAMUEL   The Mystery and Lure of Perfume. Philadelphia, (1927). Plates, illus., three quarter morocco, first American edition. Bradley 35-436 1974 $20

THOMPSON, CHARLES JOHN SAMUEL   Poison Mysteries in History, Romance and Crime. Philadelphia, 1924. Biblo & Tannen 210-534 1973 $12.50

THOMPSON, CHARLES JOHN SAMUEL   The Quacks of Old London. London, New York & Paris, 1928. Rittenhouse 46-612 1974 $25

THOMPSON, DANIEL PIERCE   Gaut Gurley. Boston, 1857. 12mo., orig. brown cloth, worn, first edition. Ximenes 35-342 1974 $12.50

THOMPSON, DANIEL PIERCE   Gaut Gurley. 1860. Allen 216-1673 1974 $12.50

THOMPSON, DANIEL PIERCE   May Martin. Montpelier, 1835. 18mo., contemporary half calf, first edition. Ximenes 35-343 1974 $300

THOMPSON, D'ARCY WENTWORTH   On Growth and Form. Cambridge, 1917. 8vo., cloth, illus., first edition. Schuman 37-247 1974 $95

THOMPSON, D'ARCY WENTWORTH   On Growth and Form. Cambridge, 1942. 8vo., orig. cloth, d.j., nice copy, revised second edition. Wheldon 131-188 1974 £15

THOMPSON, DAVID   History of the Late War, Between Great Britain and the United States . . . To Which is Added an Appendix, Containing Public Documents. 1832. 16mo., neatly rebound, very scarce, some corners and edges of text pages professionally repaired. Butterfield 10-522 1974 $100

THOMPSON, DOROTHY   Once On Christmas. London, 1938. Small 16mo., d.j. with tears, book mint, illus. Current BW9-88 1974 $8.75

THOMPSON, EDWARD   The Fair Quaker. London, 1773. 8vo., modern boards, first edition. Dawsons PM 252-957 1974 £15

THOMPSON, EDWARD MAUNDE   English Illuminated Manuscripts. London, 1895. Boards, vellum, uncut, limited edition. Dawson's 424-351 1974 $60

THOMPSON, EDWARD MAUNDE   An Introduction to Greek and Latin Palaeography. Oxford, 1912. Dark blue cloth, gilt, plates. Dawson's 424-352 1974 $80

THOMPSON, ELBERT N. S.   The Controversy Between the Puritans and the Stage. 1903. Ex-library. Austin 61-968 1974 $10

THOMPSON, ELEANOR S.   Training Girls for Art Vocations. Toronto, 1935. Inscribed and signed by author. Hood's 102-170 1974 $12.50

THOMPSON, ELEANOR S.   Training Girls for Art Vocations. Toronto, 1935. Inscribed, signed. Hood's 104-179 1974 $12.50

THOMPSON, ERNEST SETON
Please turn to
SETON, ERNEST THOMPSON

THOMPSON, FRANCIS   Health and Holiness. London, 1905. 12mo., orig. printed wrappers, first edition. Ximenes 35-344 1974 $10

THOMPSON, FRANCIS   Poems Of. 1932. Ex-library. Austin 61-969 1974 $12.50

THOMPSON, FRANCIS   Saint Ignatius Loyola. 1909. Illus., very good copy, first edition. Covent 51-1843 1973 £15

THOMPSON, FRANCIS   Shelley. 1909. 8vo., buckram, English first edition. Covent 56-1256 1974 £15.75

THOMPSON, FRANCIS   Une Antienne de la Terre. Paris, 1920. Small 4to., wrappers, unopened, English first edition. Covent 56-1255 1974 £21

THOMPSON, FRANCIS   The Works Of. 1913. 8vo., 3 vols., orig. cloth, signature, first edition. Rota 189-864 1974 £7.50

THOMPSON, FRANCIS   The Works. London, (1913). 3 vols., 8vo., orig. cloth gilt, fine, first collected edition. Dawsons PM 252-958 1974 £15

THOMPSON, FRANK V.   Schooling of the Immigrant. Harper, 1920. Austin 62-635 1974 $12.50

THOMPSON, FRANK V.   Schooling of the Immigrant. 1920. 408 pages, ex-library. Austin 57-668 1974 $12.50

THOMPSON, G. A.   Coonah-Town Comedy. Chicago, 1903. 111p., illus., paper. Austin 54-986 1973 $10

THOMPSON, GEORGE   A Description of the Royal Palace and Monastery of St. Laurence. London, 1760. 2 parts in 1 vol., 4to., contemporary half calf, plates. Traylen 79-574 1973 £25

THOMPSON, GEORGE   Prison Life and Reflections. Oberlin, 1847. 3 parts in 1 vol., orig. cloth, first edition. Bradley 35-381 1974 $150

THOMPSON, GEORGE   Travels and Adventures in Southern Africa. London, 1827. 4to., contemporary russia, illus., first edition. Ximenes 35-345 1974 $275

THOMPSON, HAROLD W.   Body, Boots and Britches. Lippincott, 1939. Orig. hard cover edition. Austin 54-987 1973 $10

THOMPSON, HENRY YEATES   Illustrations from One Hundred Manuscripts in the Library of. London, 1916. Vol. 6, plates, large 4to., cloth, one of 120 copies. Kraus B8-264 1974 $58

THOMPSON, J. H.   Jubilee History of Thorold Township and Town. Thorold, 1897-98. Worn cover. Hood's 103-680 1974 $25

THOMPSON, J. M.   The Witchery of Archery. Pinehurst, (1928). Pictorial cloth, fine. Putnam 126-238 1974 $20

THOMPSON, JAMES   Note on Professor Faraday's Recent Experiments on 'Regelation'. (N.P., n.d.) 8vo., plain wrappers, sewn. Zeitlin 235-79 1974 $35

THOMPSON, JOSEPH P.   Man in Genesis and in Geology. New York, 1870. Cloth covers stained. Butterfield 10-511 1974 $12.50

THOMPSON, MARY P.   Landmarks in Ancient Dover, New Hampshire. Durham, 1892. 8vo., map, cloth. Saddleback 14-551 1974 $12.50

THOMPSON, NATHANIEL   A Collection of 86 Loyal Poems. 1685. Modern calf, second edition. Thomas 32-198 1974 £105

THOMPSON, R. L.   Webster County History -- Folklore from the Earliest Times to the Present. Webster Springs, 1942. Illus., woodcuts, dust jacket, wrappers, type set by hand, only 500 copies printed. Hayman 59-676 1974 $25

THOMPSON, RICHARD W.   Recollections of Sixteen Presidents from Washington to Lincoln. Indianapolis, 1894. 2 vols., illus., untrimmed. Jenkins 61-1377 1974 $12.50

THOMPSON, ROBERT   The Gardener's Assistant. (1859). Roy. 8vo., half calf, plates, scarce orig. issue. Wheldon 131-1582 1974 £5

THOMPSON, ROBERT   The Gardener's Assistant. 1892. 4to., plates, orig. cloth, illus. Bow Windows 64-271 1974 £12.50

THOMPSON, ROBERT   The Gardener's Assistant. 1905. 6 vols., imp. 8vo., plates, orig. cloth. Smith 193-25 1973 £5.50

THOMPSON, RUTH PLUMLY   Captain Salt In Oz. Chicago, 1936. Sm. 4to., cloth. Frohnsdorff 16-86 1974 $8.50

THOMPSON, RUTH PLUMLY   The Lost King of Oz. Chicago, 1925. Sm. 4to., orig. cloth, 12 color plates; 1st ed., illus. Frohnsdorff 16-91 1974 $35

THOMPSON, RUTH PLUMLY   Ozoplaning With the Wizard of Oz. Chicago, 1939. Sm. 4to., illus. Frohnsdorff 16-88 1974 $9

THOMPSON, SAMUEL   Reminiscences Of a Canadian Pioneer For the last Fifty Years. Toronto, 1884. Hood's 103-239 1974 $50

THOMPSON, SLASON   Eugene Field. Scribner, 1901. 2 vols., 346p., 349p. Austin 54-988 1973 $12.50

THOMPSON, T. S.   Thompson's Coast Pilot for the Upper Lakes. Detroit, 1896. Orig. card covers, rebacked, mended. Hood's 102-781 1974 $25

THOMPSON, WADDY   Recollections of Mexico. New York, 1846. Cover chipped, text stained, first edition. Jenkins 61-2447 1974 $22.50

THOMPSON, WADDY   Recollections of Mexico. New York, 1846. First edition, cloth, light foxing. Hayman 59-631 1974 $20

THOMS, HERBERT   Classical Contributions to Obstetrics and Gynecology. Springfield, 1935. Rittenhouse 46-613 1974 $15

THOMS, W. J.   Early English Prose Romances. (n.d.). 8vo., orig. cloth, slight foxing, covers faded, revised new edition. Bow Windows 66-696 1974 £6

THOMSON   Dialogues in a Library. London, 1797. 8vo., contemporary calf, first edition. Ximenes 35-347 1974 $25

THOMSON, C. L.   A Short History of Canada. London, n.d. Hood's 103-563 1974 $15

THOMSON, CHARLES WYVILLE   The Voyage of the Challenger. 1877. 2 vols., 8vo., orig. cloth, plates. Wheldon 131-327 1974 £30

THOMSON, CHARLES WYVILLE   The Voyage of the "Challenger". London, 1877. 2 vols., roy. 8vo., full calf, rebacked, leather labels, plates, first edition. Traylen 79-440 1973 £30

THOMSON, CHARLES WYVILLE   The Voyage of the Challenger. 1938. Folio, orig. cloth, uncut, 2 vols., limited edition. Broadhurst 23-1003 1974 £145

THOMSON, DAVID CROAL   Life and Labours of Hablot K. Browne. 1884. 4to., orig. pictorial cloth, English first edition. Covent 56-179 1974 £45

THOMSON, DAVID CROAL   The Water Colour Drawings of Thomas Bewick. London, 1930. Cloth, gilt, illus. Dawson's 424-51 1974 $50

THOMSON, G. M.   The Ferns and Fern Allies of New Zealand. Melbourne and Dunedin, 1882. 8vo., cloth, plates, scarce. Wheldon 130-1354 1974 £5

THOMSON, GEORGE   Misochumias Eleschthe. London, 1671. 8vo., quarter morocco, rare, first edition. Ximenes 35-348 1974 $325

THOMSON, GLADYS SCOTT   The Russells in Bloomsbury, 1669-1771. 1940. Plates, first edition. Covent 55-839 1974 £5.25

THOMSON, H. DOUGLAS   The Mystery Book. London, 1934. Biblo & Tannen 210-684 1973 $12.50

THOMSON, IGNATIUS   The Patriot's Monitor for Vermont. Randolph, 1810. 8vo., orig. bindings. Butterfield 8-667 1974 $15

THOMSON, J. ARTHUR   The Wonder of Life. London, 1929. Orig. binding, tipped in color plates on inserted colored stock, printed tissue guards, text illus., bookplate. Wilson 63-405 1974 $10

THOMSON, JAMES   Antient and Modern Italy Compared. 1735. 4to., disbound, first edition. Quaritch 936-244 1974 £15

THOMSON, JAMES 1700-1748   Alfred. 1740. 8vo., cloth, first edition. Quaritch 936-245 1974 £40

THOMSON, JAMES 1700-1748   The Castle of Indolence. London, 1748. 4to., contemporary calf gilt, first edition. Dawsons PM 252-959 1974 £75

THOMSON, JAMES 1700-1748   A Criticism on the New Sophonisba. London, 1730. 8vo., modern boards, first edition. Dawsons PM 252-965 1974 £15

THOMSON, JAMES 1700-1748   A Defence of the New Sophonisba.   London, 1730. 8vo., modern boards, first edition.   Dawsons PM 252-966 1974 £20

THOMSON, JAMES 1700-1748   Edward and Eleonora. 1739. 8vo., cloth, first edition.   Quaritch 936-243 1974 £18

THOMSON, JAMES 1700-1748   Edward and Eleonora.   London, 1739. 8vo., modern boards, fine, first edition.   Dawsons PM 252-960 1974 £15

THOMSON, JAMES 1700-1748   Edward and Eleonora.   London, 1739. 8vo., modern boards, fine, first edition.   Dawsons PM 252-960 1974 £15

THOMSON, JAMES 1700-1748   A Poem to the Memory of the Right Honourable The Lord Talbot.   London, 1737. 8vo., modern boards, first edition.   Dawsons PM 252-961 1974 £15

THOMSON, JAMES 1700-1748   The Seasons.   London, 1730. 4to., fine, plates, contemporary calf, first collected edition.   Dawsons PM 252-962 1974 £65

THOMSON, JAMES 1700-1748   The Seasons.   London, 1730. 4to., plates, contemporary panelled calf, first collected edition.   Ximenes 35-349 1974 £90

THOMSON, JAMES 1700-1748   Seasons. 1802.   New buckram, frontis., engraved plates, new edition.   Allen 216-2076 1974 $15

THOMSON, JAMES 1700-1748   The Seasons.   London, 1807. Folio, rubbed, plates, contemporary half morocco and marbled boards.   Jacobs 24-129 1974 $60

THOMSON, JAMES 1700-1748   The Seasons. 1859.   Illus., 228 pages.   Austin 61-972 1974 $10

THOMSON, JAMES 1700-1748   The Seasons. 1927.   Roy. 8vo., illus., orig. marbled cloth, label, limited numbered edition.   Howes 186-340 1974 £8.50

THOMSON, JAMES 1700-1748   Tancred and Sigismunda.   London, 1745. 8vo., modern boards, first edition.   Dawsons PM 252-963 1974 £15

THOMSON, JAMES 1700-1748   The Tragedy of Sophonisba.   London, 1730. 8vo., modern boards, first edition.   Dawsons PM 252-964 1974 £25

THOMSON, JAMES 1828-1897   Arcana Naturae ou Recueil d'Histoire Naturelle.   Paris, 1859. Folio, quarter morocco, plates, frontis., very scarce.   Wheldon 131-865 1974 £60

THOMSON, JAMES 1828-1897   Musee Scientifique.   Paris, 1860. Roy. 8vo., coloured plates.   Wheldon 128-818 1973 £5

THOMSON, JAMES 1828-1897   Physis, Recueil d'Histoire Naturelle.   Paris, 1867. Vols. 1-2 in 6 parts, roy. 8vo., wrappers.   Wheldon 128-817 1973 £6

THOMSON, JAMES 1834-1882   The City of Dreadful Night. 1880.   Inscription, very nice copy, first edition.   Covent 51-1845 1973 £25

THOMSON, JAMES 1700-1748   Poetical Works of. 1854. 2 vols.   Austin 61-971 1974 $15

THOMSON, JAMES 1834-1882   The Poetical Works of. 1895. 8vo., 2 vols., orig. cloth.   Bow Windows 64-737 1974 £5.50

THOMSON, JAMES 1834-1882   Shelley. 1884.   Boards, gilt label, rebound, numbered, signed.   Covent 55-1447 1974 £7.50

THOMSON, JAMES 1834-1882   Vane's Story.   London, 1881. 8vo., orig. cloth, uncut, first edition.   Dawsons PM 252-967 1974 £15

THOMSON, JAMES 1834-1882   Vane's Story, Weddah and Om-El-Bonain, and Other Poems. 1881.   Very nice copy, inscribed, first edition.   Covent 51-1846 1973 £6

THOMSON, JOHN   A New General Atlas.   Edinburgh, 1817. Large folio, contemporary calf, gilt.   Broadhurst 23-1608 1974 £375

THOMSON, JOHN   A New General Atlas.   Edinburgh, 1817. Large folio, contemporary calf, panelled back, double page maps in colour, very fine copy.   Broadhurst 24-1574 1974 £375

THOMSON, JOHN   Tables of Interest.   Edinburgh & London, 1776. 8vo., contemporary sheep, label.   Dawsons PM 247-287 1974 £15

THOMSON, JOSEPH JOHN   Applications of Dynamics to Physics and Chemistry.   London, 1888. 8vo., orig. cloth, gilt, first edition.   Dawsons PM 245-708 1974 £20

THOMSON, JOSEPH JOHN   Conduction of Electricity through Gases.   Cambridge, 1903. 8vo., orig. green cloth, first edition.   Dawsons PM 245-712 1974 £25

THOMSON, JOSEPH JOHN   Conduction of Electricity Through Gases.   Cambridge, 1903. 8vo., orig. green cloth, worn, first edition.   Dawsons PM 250-76 1974 £25

THOMSON, JOSEPH JOHN   Conduction of Electricity through Gases.   Cambridge, 1928-1933. Orig. cloth, 2 vols., gilt, third edition.   Dawsons PM 245-713 1974 £10

THOMSON, JOSEPH JOHN   Electricity and Matter.   London, 1904. 8vo., orig. cloth, first edition.   Dawsons PM 245-714 1974 £10

THOMSON, JOSEPH JOHN   Electricity and Matter. 1911. 8vo., blue cloth.   Dawsons PM 245-715 1974 £6

THOMSON, JOSEPH JOHN   The Electron in Chemistry.   Philadelphia, 1923. Large 8vo., orig. red cloth, gilt, first edition.   Dawsons PM 245-716 1974 £12

THOMSON, JOSEPH JOHN   Elements of the Matehmatical Theory of Electricity and Magnetism.   Cambridge, 1895. 8vo., orig. green cloth, first edition.   Dawsons PM 245-710 1974 £12

THOMSON, JOSEPH JOHN   Elements of the Mathematical Theory of Electricity and Magnetism.   Cambridge, 1904. 8vo., orig. green cloth, gilt, illus., third edition.   Dawsons PM 245-711 1974 £7

THOMSON, JOSEPH JOHN   Rays of Positive Electricity.   London, 1921. 8vo., orig. blue cloth, plates, second edition.   Dawsons PM 245-718 1974 £10

THOMSON, JOSEPH JOHN   Recollections and Reflections.   London, 1936. 8vo., blue cloth, gilt, plates, first edition.   Dawsons PM 245-719 1974 £9

THOMSON, KATHARINE   Rosabel.   London, 1835. 3 vols., 12mo., half calf, gilt, first edition.   Dawsons PM 252-968 1974 £50

THOMSON, MORTIMER NEAL   Doesticks' Tormentor.   N.P., 1855. 12mo., disbound, somewhat soiled, first edition.   Ximenes 37-211 1974 $25

THOMSON, RICHARD   An Historical Essay on the Magna Charta. 1829.   Contemporary half calf.   Howes 186-1262 1974 £8.50

THOMSON, RICHARD   A Lecture on Some of the Most Characteristic Features of Illuminated Manuscripts.   London, 1857. Roy 8vo., cloth, gilt.   Hammond 201-1000 1974 £18.50

THOMSON, ROBERT DUNDAS   Experimental Researches on the Food of Animals. 1846. 8vo., contemporary half calf, boards, first edition.   Broadhurst 23-1285 1974 £10

THOMSON, SPENCER   Wild Flowers. 1859. 12mo., orig. cloth gilt, plates, nice bright copy, fourth edition.   Wheldon 131-1244 1974 £5

THOMSON, THOMAS   The History of Chemistry.   London, 1830-31. Small 8vo., 2 vols., contemporary half calf, gilt, first edition.   Dawsons PM 245-721 1974 £50

THOMSON, THOMAS   History of the Royal Society.   London, 1812. 4to., old cloth, first edition.   Gurney 64-215 1974 £35

THOMSON, THOMAS   History of the Royal Society, from Its Institution to the end of the 18th Century. London, 1812. 4to., old cloth, first edition. Gurney 66-185 1974 £35

THOMSON, THOMAS   An Outline of the Sciences of Heat and Electricity. London and Edinburgh, 1830. 8vo., contemporary speckled calf, rebacked, illus., first edition. Dawsons PM 245-720 1974 £16

THOMSON, VIRGIL   The State of Music. New York, 1939. 1st ed. Biblo & Tannen 214-926 1974 $9.50

THOMSON, W. G.   A History of Tapestry. 1930. Large 8vo., illus., cloth, revised edition. Dawsons PM 11-752 1974 £10

THOMSON, WILLIAM   A Practical Treatise on the Cultivation of the Grape Vine. London and Edinburgh, 1862. 8vo., orig. cloth, gilt, illus., second edition. Hammond 201-684 1974 £11

THOMSON, WILLIAM   Travels in Europe, Asia, and Africa. Dublin, n.d. 2 vols., 8vo., contemporary calf, third edition. Ximenes 35-350 1974 $45

THONNELIEUR, JULES   Catalogue de la Bibliotheque Orientale de feu M. Jules Thonnelier. Paris, 1880. Large 8vo., half cloth, orig. wrappers bound in. Kraus B8-265 1974 $32.50

THORBURN, ARCHIBALD   British Birds. 1915-16. 4 vols., roy. 4to., orig. red buckram, coloured plates, first edition. Wheldon 128-579 1973 £90

THORBURN, ARCHIBALD   British Birds. London, 1916. 4 vols., 4to., faded, plates, first & second editions. Traylen 79-113 1973 £150

THORBURN, ARCHIBALD   British Birds. 1916. 4 vols., roy. 4to., orig. red buckram, coloured plates. Wheldon 128-580 1973 £85

THORBURN, ARCHIBALD   British Birds. 1917-18. Roy 4to., 4 vols., orig. cloth. Broadhurst 23-1189 1974 £130

THORBURN, ARCHIBALD   British Birds. 1917-18. 4 vols., imp. 4to., orig. red cloth, plates, second & third editions. Wheldon 131-123 1974 £200

THORBURN, ARCHIBALD   British Birds. 1925-26. 8vo., 4 vols., orig. red cloth, new edition. Wheldon 129-536 1974 £25

THORBURN, ARCHIBALD   British Birds. 1925-1926,1933. 8vo., 4 vols., orig. red cloth, new edition. Wheldon 129-537 1974 £20

THORBURN, ARCHIBALD   British Birds. 1931-26. 4 vols., 8vo., plates, new edition. Traylen 79-114 1973 £150

THORBURN, ARCHIBALD   British Mammals. 1920. Roy 4to., 2 vols., new half red morocco gilt. Wheldon 129-404 1974 £200

THORBURN, ARCHIBALD   British Mammals. 1920. 2 vols. in 1, roy. 4to., publisher's blue cloth, dust jacket, coloured plates. Wheldon 128-354 1973 £150

THORBURN, ARCHIBALD   Game Birds and Wild Fowl of Great Britain and Ireland. 1923. Imp. 4to., newly rebound, red buckram, coloured plates. Wheldon 128-581 1973 £150

THORBURN, ARCHIBALD   Games Birds and Wild-Fowl of Great Britain and Ireland. 1923. Imp. 4to., half red morocco gilt, plates, scarce, nice copy. Wheldon 131-124 1974 £250

THORBURN, ARCHIBALD   A Naturalist's Sketch Book. London, 1919. 4to., orig. buckram, gilt, plates, first edition. Hammond 201-685 1974 £85

THORBURN, GRANT   Life and Writings. New York, 1851. 276 pages. Austin 57-669 1974 $27.50

THORDEMAN, B.   Armour from the Battle of Wisby. Stockholm, 1939. 2 vols., 4to., plates, illus., canvas. Quaritch 940-705 1974 £30

THOREAU, HENRY DAVID   Cape Cod. Boston & New York, 1896. 2 vols., orig. dec. cloth, spines bit faded, first illus. edition, bookplates. MacManus 224-433 1974 $30

THOREAU, HENRY DAVID   Letters to Various Persons. Boston, 1865. Orig. cloth, first edition, very good copy. MacManus 224-434 1974 $50

THOREAU, HENRY DAVID   Letters to Various Persons. Boston, 1865. 8vo., orig. purple cloth, fine, first edition. Ximenes 35-351 1974 $75

THOREAU, HENRY DAVID   Of Friendship. Cambridge, 1901. One of 500 numbered copies, narrow 12mo., gilt dec. covers, full red morocco, fine. Current BW9-284 1974 $55

THOREAU, HENRY DAVID   Walden. Boston & New York, 1897. 2 vols., orig. dec. cloth, spines faded, photogravures, bookplate, fine. MacManus 224-435 1974 $35

THOREAU, HENRY DAVID   Walden, or Life in the Woods. 1927. Woodcuts, one of 100 numbered copies on handmade paper, plates on Japanese vellum, signed by artist, extra signed engraving laid in, nice copy, vellum backed cloth, first edition. Covent 51-1848 1973 £35

THOREAU, HENRY DAVID   Walden, or Life in the Woods. Boston, 1936. Boards, slipcase, illus., fine. Dawson's 424-78 1974 $50

THOREAU, HENRY DAVID   A Week on the Concord and Merrimack Rivers. Boston & Cambridge, 1849. Orig. cloth, rebacked, orig. spine laid-down, first edition, internally fine & clean, boxed. MacManus 224-436 1974 $750

THOREAU, HENRY DAVID   The Writings of. Boston & New York, 1906. 20 vols., orig. cloth, paper labels, the Walden edition, one of 200 copies, very fine set, many photos. MacManus 224-437 1974 $300

THOREAU, HENRY DAVID   A Yankee in Canada, With Anti-Slavery and Reform Papers. Boston, 1866. Orig. cloth, ends of spine worn, hinges crudely strengthened, first edition, good copy. MacManus 224-438 1974 $55

THORELL, T.   Descriptive Catalogue of the Spiders of Burma. 1895. 8vo., cloth. Wheldon 131-951 1974 £12

THORESBY, RALPH   Ducatus Leodiensis. London, 1715. Folio, full calf, gilt, illus., first edition. Dawsons PM 251-74 1974 £85

THORESBY, RALPH   Ducatus Leodiensis. 1816. Folio, new buckram, second edition. Allen 213-1823 1973 $50

THORIUS, RAPHAEL   Hymnus Tabaci. London, 1651. Small 8vo., nineteenth century English calf, gilt, first editions in English. Schumann 35-464 1974 $165

THORLEY, JOHN   Melissologia. 1744. 8vo., contemporary calf, rebacked, scarce, first edition. Broadhurst 23-1190 1974 £52

THORNBURY, WALTER   Historical and Legendary Ballads and Songs. 1876. 4to., plates, illus., orig. cloth. Smith 194-749 1974 £5

THORNBURY, WALTER   Old and New London. London, n.d. 6 vols., roy. 8vo., soiled, engravings. Traylen 79-367 1973 £10

THORNBURY, WALTER   Old and New London. (1897-98). 6 vols., illus., water-stained. Austin 61-973 1974 $75

THORNDALE, THERESA   Sketches and Stories of the Lake Erie Islands. Sandusky, 1898. Cloth, faded, inner hinges reglued. Hayman 59-634 1974 $12.50

THORNDIKE, EDWARD L.   Educational Psychology. New York, 1919. 8vo., orig. blue cloth. Dawsons PM 249-479 1974 £12.50

THORNDIKE, HERBERT   Theological Works. Oxford, 1844-56. 6 vols. in 10, orig. cloth. Howes 185-1721 1974 £35

THORNDYKE, RUSSELL   Doctor Syn. 1915. English first edition. Covent 56-442 1974 £8.50

THORNE, WILLIAM   Chronicle of Saint Augustine's Abbey.
1934. Thick 8vo., illus. House 186-2065 1974 £10

THORNHILL, JOHN BENSLEY   British Columbia in the Making, 1913. London,
1913. Illus., maps. Hood's 104-878 1974 $12.50

THORNTON, ARTHUR   The X Rays. Bradford, 1896. 12mo., orig.
wrappers. Gurney 64-216 1974 £18

THORNTON, J. QUINN   Memorial Praying for the Establishment of a
Territorial Government in Oregon. Washington, 1848. Jenkins 61-2100 1974
$15

THORNTON, R. H.   American Glossary. 1912. 2 vols. Allen
216-1420 1974 $15

THORNTON, ROBERT JOHN   Botanical Extracts. 1810. 3 vols., folio,
plates, contemporary straight-grain morocco gilt, rubbed. Wheldon 131-1206
1974 £75

THORNTON, ROBERT JOHN   Botanical Extracts. 1810. Folio, 2 vols. in 3,
plates, straight grained red morocco, gilt panelled. Bow Windows 64-273 1974
£48

THORNTON, ROBERT JOHN   Elementary Botanical Plates Illustrative of the
Science of Botany. 1810. Folio, contemporary half calf, plates. Wheldon
131-1205 1974 £75

THORNTON, ROBERT JOHN   A Family Herbal. 1814. 8vo., half calf, portrait, woodcuts, second edition. Wheldon 130-1625 1974 £20

THORNTON, ROBERT JOHN   A Family Herbal. London, 1814. Full calf,
rebacked, illus. Dawson's 424-52 1974 $100

THORNTON, ROBERT JOHN   A New Family Herbal. 1810. Roy. 8vo.,
contemporary half red morocco gilt, rubbed, inscribed presentation copy, first
edition. Quaritch 940-21 1974 £100

THORNTON, ROBERT JOHN   A New Family Herbal. 1810. Quarter scored
calf gilt, somewhat rubbed but sound, woodcuts. Thomas 32-317 1974 £30

THORNTON, ROBERT JOHN   A New Family Herbal. London, 1810. 8vo.,
contemporary half calf, gilt, illus., first edition. Hammond 201-472 1974 £25

THORNTON, ROBERT JOHN   A New Family Herbal. 1810. Quarter
scored calf gilt, rubbed. Thomas 28-271 1972 £30

THORNTON, ROBERT JOHN   New Illustrations of the Sexual System of
Carolus Von Linnaeus . . . and the Temple of Flora or Garden of Nature.
(1799-)1807. 3 parts in 2 vols., atlas folio, contemporary blue straight grain
morocco, gilt, plates. Wheldon 131-125 1974 £4,750

THORNTON, ROBERT JOHN   Temple of Flora. 1812. Imp. 4to., modern
three quarter brown morocco, gilt, plates. Wheldon 130-82 1974 £675

THORNTON, T.   A Sporting Tour Through the Northern Parts of
England. 1804. 4to., buckram, plates. Quaritch 939-263 1974 £30

THORP, JOSEPH   Eric Gill. 1929. 4to., plates, cloth. Quaritch 936-392 1974 £30

THORP, N. HOWARD   Tales of the Chuck Wagon. (Santa Fe, 1926).
Stiff pictorial wrappers, fine, first edition. Bradley 35-382 1974 $10

THORPE, BENJAMIN   Diplomatarium Anglicum Aevi Saxonici.
1865. Cloth, scarce. Howes 186-1263 1974 £8.50

THORPE, BENJAMIN   Diplomatarium Anglicum Aevi Saxonici.
1865. 8vo., calf, leather labels. Quaritch 939-264 1974 £10.50

THORPE, FRANCIS NEWTON   William Pepper, M. D. Philadelphia, 1904.
Soiled and weak cover. Rittenhouse 46-617 1974 $25

THORPE, JOHN   Registrum Roffense. 1769. Thick folio,
half calf, portrait. Howes 186-2066 1974 £68

THORPE, JOHN   Registrum Roffense. London, 1769. Folio,
modern polished half calf, gilt. Dawsons PM 251-75 1974 £135

THORPE. NIELS   Peter Nielsen's Story. Minnesota, 1949.
Austin 62-637 1974 $10

THORPE, WILLIAM ARNOLD   English and Irish Glass. 1927. Roy. 8vo.,
plates, cloth. Quaritch 940-620 1974 £10

THORPE, WILLIAM ARNOLD   A History of English and Irish Glass. 1929.
2 vols., imp. 8vo., frontispiece, plates, cloth, orig. edition. Quaritch
940-621 1974 £65

THORY, CLAUDE ANTOINE   Monographie ou Histoire Naturelle du Genre
Groseillier. Paris, 1829. 8vo., orig. printed wrappers, rebacked, uncut, rare,
plates. Wheldon 130-1490 1974 £85

THORY, CLAUDE ANTOINE   Monographie ou Histoire Naturelle du Genre
Groseillier. Paris, 1829. 8vo., orig. printed wrappers, uncut, plates, very
scarce. Wheldon 131-126 1974 £75

THOU, JACQUE-AUGUSTE DE   Historie Universelle. Londres, 1734.
16 vols., crown 4to., contemporary russia, gilt, morocco labels, first edition.
Howes 186-1264 1974 £90

THOUGHT Control in U.S.A. 1947. Austin 51-821 1973 $17.50

THOUVENAL, PIERRE   Traite sur le Climat de l'Italie. Verona, 1797.
8vo., 4 vols., orig. wrappers, first edition. Gumey 64-217 1974 £18

THE THREE Chances. London, 1858. 3 vols., 8vo., orig. purple blue cloth,
gilt, uncut, first edition. Dawsons PM 252-969 1974 £95

THREE Letters to a Member of the Honurable House of Commons, from a Country
Farmer, Concerning the Prices of Provisions. London, 1766. 8vo., blue paper
wrappers. Dawsons PM 247-288 1974 £10

A THREEFOLD Cord, or Precept, Promises and Prayer. London, (c. 1850). Full
olive green morocco, covers fully gold stamped, all edges gilt, inscription, fine,
2 7/8 X 2 1/4. Gregory 44-472 1974 $40

THRILLERS. New York, 1929. 1st ed. Biblo & Tannen 210-550 1973 $10

THRING, G. HERBERT   The Marketing of Literary Property. 1933.
Faded. Covent 55-1356 1974 £5

THROUGH The Southwest Along the Santa Fe. Kansas City, c. 1895. Oblong
folio, views in color. Jenkins 61-1857 1974 $15

THRUM, THOMAS G.   Hawaiian Almanac and Annual for 1876.
Honolulu, 1875. Green prt. wrapper, small portion of top right edge missing.
Jenkins 61-1036 1974 $25

THRUSTON, MALACHIA   De Respirationis Usu Primario, Diatriba. Leyden,
1671. 12mo., old calf. Schumann 35-465 1974 $95

THUCYDIDES. 1930. Folio, full white pig-skin, panelled back, gilt, uncut,
limited edition. Broadhurst 23-992 1974 £450

THUCYDIDES   De Bello Peloponnesiaco Libri Octo.
Amstelaedami, 1731. Folio, contemporary russia, gilt panelled covers, maps,
engraved frontispiece, skillfully rebacked. Bow Windows 66-700 1974 £48

THUCYDIDES   History. 1829. 3 vols., illus. Allen
213-1114 1973 $10

THUCYDIDES   History of the Peoloponnesian War. 1900.
2 vols., second revised edition. Allen 213-1116 1973 $12.50

THUCYDIDES   History of the Peleponnesian War. 1930.
Finely printed in red and black, hand made paper, folio, white pigskin, gilt title
on spine, uncut, fine, limited to 250 copies. Sawyer 293-49 1974 £750

THUCYDIDES   History of the Peloponnesian War. Chelsea, 1930. Folio, vellum, orig. brown calf, fine. Dawsons PM 250-78 1974 £4500

THUCYDIDES   History of the Peloponnesian War. Chelsea, 1930. Folio, uncut, orig. pigskin. Dawsons PM 252-970 1974 £650

THUILLIER, JEAN LOUIS   Flore des Environs de Paris ou Distribution Methodique des Plantes. 1785-90. Post 8vo., boards, rare. Wheldon 130-1212 1974 £15

THUMB Autograph Book, With Gems of Thought from Classical Authors. Glasgow, n.d. Full black morocco, 2 1/4 X 1 7/8. Gregory 44-473 1974 $35

THUNBERG, CARL PETER   Flora Japonica Sistens Plantas. Tokyo, 1933. 8vo., orig. half cloth, plates. Wheldon 130-1213 1974 £30

THURBER, JAMES   Alarms and Diversions. Harper, 1957. 367p., 1st ed. Austin 54-993 1973 $7.50

THURBER, JAMES   Alarms and Diversions. Harper, 1957. 367p., illus. Austin 54-994 1973 $5

THURBER, JAMES   The Beast In Me. Harcourt, Brace, 1948. 340p., illus., 1st ed. Austin 54-995 1973 $8.50

THURBER, JAMES   Fables For Our Time and Famous Poems Illustrated. Harper, 1940. 124p., illus., 1st ed. Austin 54-996 1973 $10

THURBER, JAMES   Fables for Our Time and Famous Poems. 1940. Illus., dust wrapper, fine. Covent 55-1450 1974 £7.50

THURBER, JAMES   Further Fables For Our Time. S & S, 1956. 174p., illus. Austin 54-997 1973 $5

THURBER, JAMES   Further Fables For Our Time. Simon, Schuster, 1956. 174p., illus., 1st ed. Austin 54-998 1973 $7.50

THURBER, JAMES   Is Sex Necessary. Harper, 1929. 197p., illus., orig. ed. Austin 54-1008 1973 $6

THURBER, JAMES   Is Sex Necessary? Harper, Row, 1957. 190p., illus. Austin 54-1009 1973 $5

THURBER, JAMES   The Last Flower. Harper, 1939. Orig. hard cover ed., illus. Austin 54-1000 1973 $6.50

THURBER, JAMES   The Male Animal. Random, 1940. 202p., illus. Austin 51-969 1973 $7.50

THURBER, JAMES   The Male Animal. French, 1941. Austin 51-970 1973 $6.50

THURBER, JAMES   Men, Women and Dogs. New York, 1943. 8vo., cloth. Minters 37-43 1973 $10

THURBER, JAMES   Men, Women and Dogs. Harcourt, Brace, 1943. 199p. Austin 54-1001 1973 $8.50

THURBER, JAMES   The Middle Aged Man On the Flying Trapeze. Harper, 1935. 226p., illus. Austin 54-1002 1973 $8.50

THURBER, JAMES   My Life and Hard Times. Harper, 1933. 153p., illus., orig. ed. Austin 54-1003 1973 $6

THURBER, JAMES   The Owl In the Attic. Harper, 1931. 151p., illus. Austin 54-999 1973 $7.50

THURBER, JAMES   Thurber Country. S & S 1973. 276p., illus. Austin 54-1004 1973 $5

THURBER, JAMES   Thurber's Dogs. S & S, 1955. 294p., illus., 1st ed. Austin 54-1005 1973 $8.50

THURBER, JAMES   The White Deer. Harcourt, Brace. 113p., illus. Austin 54-1006 1973 $5

THURBER, JAMES   The Wonderful "O". S & S 1957. 72p., illus., 1st ed. Austin 54-1007 1973 $7.50

THURLOW, EDWARD HOVEL   Arcita and Palamon. London, 1822. 8vo., contemporary russia, inscribed, first edition. Ximenes 35-352 1974 $25

THURMANN, J.   Lethea Bruntrutana. 1861-64. 4to., buckram, plates. Wheldon 128-1059 1973 £15

THURSTON, HERBERT   The Holy Year of Jubilee. 1900. Plates, illus. Howes 185-1722 1974 £7.50

THURSTON, LORRIN A.   A Hand-Book on the Annexation of Hawaii. St. Joseph, 1898. 12mo., wrapper, maps. Saddleback 14-354 1974 $20

THURTLE, FRANCES   Ashford Rectory. 1818. Second edition, 12mo., half roan, engraved frontis., little light foxing. George's 610-741 1973 £5

THURTLE, FRANCES   Ashford Rectory. 1818. Second edition, 12mo., later boards, cloth spine, edges uncut, engraved frontis. George's 610-742 1973 £5

THURTLE, FRANCES   History of France, from the Earliest Periods to the Second Return of Louis XVIII to the Throne of His Ancestors. 1818. 12mo., contemporary calf, engraved frontis., title foxed, second edition. George's 610-745 1973 £5

THURTLE, FRANCES   Popular Voyages and Travels, Throughout the Continents and Islands of Asia, Africa, and America. 1820. Coloured aquatint frontis., plates, 12mo., half calf, ex-libris copy. George's 610-746 1973 £10

THURTLE, FRANCES   The Young Travellers. 1816. Second edition, engraved frontis., ink stain on title, 12mo., new blue buckram. George's 610-747 1973 £5

THWAITES, REUBEN GOLD   Afloat on the Ohio. Chicago, 1897. 8vo., orig. bindings. Butterfield 8-440 1974 $15

THWAITES, REUBEN GOLD   The Colonies, 1492-1750. New York, 1898. Maps. Hood's 103-564 1974 $25

THYARD, PONTUS DE   Douze Fables de Fleuves ou Fontaines. Paris, 1585. 12mo., vellum, first edition, first issue, near pristine, extremely rare. Schumann 499-114 1974 sFr 14,000

THYLMANN, KARL   Bonaventura. Weimar, 1915. Limited to 50 copies on Japanese vellum, orig. lithographs, signed by Thylmann, large 8vo., green levant morocco gilt, top edges gilt, slip in case, fine copy. Sawyer 293-275 1974 £45

THYRAEUS, PETRUS, S. J.   De Variis tam Spirituum. Cologne, 1593. 4to., contemporary limp vellum, first edition. Schumann 35-466 1974 $110

TIBB, R. CAMPBELL   Leaders of Men, Types and Principles of Success . . . In the Lives of Prominent Canadian and American Men. Toronto & Chicago, 1904. Illus. Hood's 102-51 1974 $17.50

TIBB, R. CAMPBELL   Leaders of Men, Types and Principles of Success . . . In the Lives of Prominent Canadian and American Men. Toronto & Chicago, 1904. Illus. Hood's 104-63 1974 $17.50

TIBBLE, J. W.   John Clare, a Life. London, 1932. First edition, spine faded, orig. cloth, nice copy. Crane 7-44 1974 £5

TIBULLUS, ALBIUS   Poetical Trans. of Elegies, & Poems of Sulpicia. 1759. 2 vols. in 1, new buckram. Allen 213-1122 1973 $15

TIBULLUS, ALNINO   Quae Exstant, Ad Fidem Veterum Membranarum. Amsterdam, 1708. 4to., contemp. blind-stamped vellum, lea. label. Jacobs 24-176 1974 $35

TICKELL, JOHN   The History of the Town and County of Kingston upon Hull. Hull, 1796. Large 4to., half calf, boards. Dawsons PM 251-76 1974 £50

TICKELL, R. E.   The Vale of Nantgwilt. 1894. Oblong folio, orig. cloth, scarce. Broadhurst 23-1563 1974 £30

TICKELL, RICHARD   Anticipation. London, 1779. 8vo., sewn as issued, very good copy, entirely uncut, first edition. Ximenes 37-212 1974 $50

TICKELL, RICHARD   An English Green Box. London, 1779. 8vo., disbound, first edition. Ximenes 35-354 1974 $15

TICKNOR, CAROLINE   Amiable Autocrat. Schuman, 1947. 470p. Austin 54-1014 1973 $10

TICKNOR, CAROLINE   Hawthorne and His Publisher. Houghton, 1913. 339p., orig. ed. Austin 54-1013 1973 $12.50

TICKNOR, GEORGE   History of Spanish Literature. Boston, 1864. 3 vols., 8vo., later half calf, third edition. Ximenes 35-355 1974 $12.50

TICKNOR, GEORGE   The Life of William Hickling Prescott. Boston, 1864. 1st ed., orig. full mor., with inscription from subject's son. Jacobs 24-34 1974 $85

TIDAL Harbours Commission First Report. 1845. Folio, orig. wrappers, 230 pages. Howes 186-1764 1974 £7.50

TIDD, THOMAS   Considerations on the Use and Properties of the Pneumatic Machine. London, 1754. 4to., wrappers. Zeitlin 235-221 1974 $45

TIDY, GORDON   A Little About Leech. 1931. Separately mounted plates, small 4to., very good copy, lacking one plate, first edition. Covent 51-1114 1973 £6

TIDY, GORDON   A Little About Leech. 1931. Fine, illus., English first edition. Covent 56-819 1974 £12.50

TIEDEMANN, FRIEDRICH   Anatomie des Fischherzens. Landshut, 1809. 4to., old boards, uncut, plates, first edition. Gurney 66-186 1974 £25

TIEDEMANN, FRIEDRICH   The Anatomy of the Foetal Brain. Edinburgh, 1826. 8vo., orig. boards, plates, first edition in English. Schumann 35-467 1974 $135

TIEMANN AND COMPANY   The American Armamentarium Chirurgicum. New York, 1879. Illus. Rittenhouse 46-618 1974 $15

TIETZE, HANS   The Drawings of the Venetian Painters of the 15th and 16th Centuries. New York, (1944). 4to., plates, cloth, limited. Quaritch 940-255 1974 £135

TIETZE, HANS   Paintings and Drawings. New York, 1948. Illus. Biblo & Tannen 214-528 1974 $17.50

TIGNY, F. M. G. T.   Histoire Naturelle des Insectes. Paris, 1830. 10 vols., small 8vo., contemporary half calf, plates, very scarce. Wheldon 131-869 1974 £50

TILDEN, M.   History of Stephenson County. Chicago, 1880. Part leather, fine. Putnam 126-158 1974 $70

TILDEN, WILLIAM A.   Chemical Discovery and Invention in the Twentieth Century. 1922. 8vo., cloth, gilt, illus., plates. Hammond 201-962 1974 £6

TILDEN, WILLIAM A.   Famous Chemists, the Men and Their Work. 1921. Label, illus. Covent 55-1328 1974 £5.25

TILGHMAN, ZOE AGNES STRATTON   Outlaw Days. Oklahoma City, 1926. Illus., wrapper, scarce. Jenkins 61-2448 1974 $17.50

TILLOTSON, JOHN   The Works. 1728. 3 vols., folio, portrait, contemporary panelled calf. Howes 185-1723 1974 £21

TILLSON, CHRISTIANA HOLMES   A Woman's Story of Pioneer Illinois. Chicago, 1919. 12mo., orig. cloth, second edition. Ximenes 35-356 1974 $12

TILTON, WARREN   Trifleton Papers. Boston, 1856. 8vo., orig. cloth, first edition. Ximenes 35-357 1974 $10

TILTON, THEODORE   Sonnets to the Memory of Frederick Douglass. Paris, 1895. Wrapper. Butterfield 10-115 1974 $10

TILT'S Miniature Almanack, 1842. Orig. light olive cloth, 2 1/4 X 1 1/4. Gregory 44-474 1974 $22.50

TILT'S Miniature Almanack, 1843. Orig. light olive cloth, 2 1/4 X 1 1/4. Gregory 44-475 1974 $22.50

TILT'S Miniature Almanack, 1845. Orig. light olive cloth, very slightly mottled, 2 1/4 X 1 1/4. Gregory 44-476 1974 $22.50

TILT'S Minature Almanack for 1847. Full red morocco, 2 3/8 X 1 1/4, gilt, fine. Gregory 44-477 1974 $40

TILT'S Miniature Almanack for 1853. Orig. olive cloth, mottled, 2 1/4 X 1 1/4. Gregory 44-478 1974 $22.50

TIMBERLAKE, CRAIG   The Bishop of Broadway. 1954. Austin 51-971 1973 $15

TIMBERLAKE, HENRY   A Trve and Strange Discourse of the Trauailes of Two English Pilgrimes. London, 1609. Small 4to., black morocco, gilt, first edition. Traylen 79-539 1973 £280

TIMBS, JOHN 1801-1875   Abbeys, Castles and Ancient Halls of England and Wales. London, (n.d.). 3 vols., 8vo., plates, inscription, orig. cloth, rubbed. Bow Windows 62-939 1974 £6.50

TIMBS, JOHN 1801-1875   A Century of Anecdore, 1760-1860. 1864. 2 vols., half leather, marbelized boards, ex-library. Austin 61-974 1974 $17.50

TIMPERLEY, C. H.   The Printers' Manual. London, 1838. 8vo., contemporary half morocco, first edition. Dawsons PM 10-606 1974 £40

TIMPSON, THOMAS   Church History of Kent from the Earlies Period to the Year MDCCCLVIII. 1859. Crown 8vo., orig. cloth, frayed. Howes 186-2067 1974 £5.50

TINDAL, WILLIAM   The History and Antiquities of the Abbey and Borough of Evesham. Evesham, 1794. 4to., half calf, plates. Quaritch 939-587 1974 £30

TINDALL, WILLIAM YORK   D. H. Lawrence and Susan His Cow. 1939. First edition. Austin 61-975 1974 $10

TINGRY, PIERRE FRANCOIS   The Painter and Varnisher's Guide. London, 18-16. 8vo., boards, plates, uncut, second edition. Dawsons PM 245-722 1974 £15

TINKER, CHAUNCY BREWSTER   The Translations of Beowulf. 1903. Ex-library, sturdy library binding, orig. edition. Austin 61-976 1974 $10

TINKER, EDWARD LAROCQUE   Old New Orleans. New York, 1931. 4 vols., first edition. Jenkins 61-1414 1974 $30

TINKHAM, GEORGE H.   History of San Joaquin County, California. Los Angeles, 1923. 4to., three quarter leather. Saddleback 14-304 1974 $125

TIPPETTS, KATHERINE BELL   Prince Arengzeba, A Romance of Lake George. New York, (1892). Orig. binding. Butterfield 10-19 1974 $15

TIPPING, HENRY AVRAY   English Furniture of the Cabriole Period. 1922. Small 4to., plates, cloth, signed. Quaritch 940-594 1974 £8

TIPPING, HENRY AVRAY   Grinling Gibbons and the Woodwork of His Age. 1914. White buckram, frontispiece, boards. Marsden 39-180 1974 £22

TIPPLE, BERTRAND M.   Alien Rome. Washington, D. C., 1924. 226 pages. Austin 57-670 1974 $12.50

TIRANTI, JOHN   A Collection of Antique Vases, Tripods, Candelabra. London, 1921. Orig. binding, plates. Covent 55-488 1974 £7.50

TIRRELL, ALBERT J.   The Trial of... Boston, n.d. 8vo., sewn, very good copy, woodcut portrait, first edition. Ximenes 37-54 1974 $45

TISCHLER, G.   Allgemeine Pflanzenkaryologie. Berlin, 1921-22. Roy. 8vo., buckram, text-figures. Wheldon 128-1171 1973 £18

TISSANDIER, GASTON   L'Heliogravure; Son Histoire et ses Procedes, ses Applications a l'Imprimerie et a la Librairie. Paris, 1874. 4to., orig. printed wrappers. Kraus B8-366 1974 $20

TISSOT, CLEMENT JOSEPH   Gymnastique Medicinale et Chirurgicale. Paris, 1780. 12mo., contemporary calf-backed boards, first edition. Schumann 35-468 1974 $65

TISSOT, C. U. D.   Unleitung fur Den Gemeinen Mann. Frankfurt, 1770. 18th century bookplate. Rittenhouse 46-619 1974 $25

TISSOT, J. JAMES   The Life of Our Saviour Jesus Christ. New York, 1903. 3 vols., plates, dec. cloth gilt. Marsden 39-451 1974 £12

TISSOT, M.   L'Onanisme. Lavsanne, 1769. Paper covers, dog-eared, fourth edition. Rittenhouse 46-620 1974 $50

TISSOT, SIMON ANDRE   De la Sante des Gens de Lettres. 1768. Small 8vo., contemporary calf. Dawsons PM 249-480 1974 £16

TITIAN   The Venetian School. 1915. 4to., plates, buckram. Quaritch 940-256 1974 £25

TITIAN   Zeichnungen des Titian. Berlin, 1924. 4to., plates, half blue morocco, gilt. Quaritch 940-257 1974 £58

TITUS, MRS. FRANCES W.   Narrative of Sojourner Truth. Battle Creek, 1878. Frontis. portrait, orig. brown and gilt cloth, fine. Butterfield 10-116 1974 $45

TIZAC, H. D'A. DE   Les Animaux dans l'Art Chinois. (1923). Folio, plates, unbound in orig. portfolio. Quaritch 940-424 1974 £16

TOALDO, GIUSEPPE   Dell Uso de Conduttori Metallici. 1774. 4to., marbled boards, first edition. Zeitlin 235-222 1974 $95

TOALDO, GIUSEPPE   Della Vera Influenza. 1770. 4to., contemporary boards, uncut, first edition. Zeitlin 235-223 1974 $125

TOBALDUCCI, CLAUDIO   Delli Dialogi della Qvantita. 1588. 4to., old limp boards, uncut. Zeitlin 235-224 1974 $225

TOBIN, JOHN   The Honey Moon. London, 1805. 8vo., modern boards, first edition. Dawsons PM 252-972 1974 £15

TOCQUEVILLE, ALEXIS DE   Democracy in America. Cambridge, 1862. 2 vols. Biblo & Tannen 213-98 1973 $17.50

TODA Y GUELL, EDUARDO   Bibliografia Espanola de Cerdena. Madrid, 1890. 4to., unbound. Kraus B8-266 1974 $12.50

TODARO, A.   Relazione sui Cotoni Coltivati nel R. Orto Botanico di Palermo nell Anno. Palermo, 1877. Folio, orig. wrappers, coloured plate. Wheldon 128-1667 1973 £5

TODARO, A.   Relazione sulla Cultura dei Cotoni. Rome, 1877-78. Roy 8vo and folio, half morocco and orig. boards, 2 vols., plates. Wheldon 129-1670 1974 £25

TODD, H. C.   A Manual of Ortheopy. York, 1833. Fourth edition. Hood's 102-437 1974 $75

TODD, H. G.   Armory and Lineages of Canada. New York, 1913. Hood's 102-52 1974 $45

TODD, H. J.   The History of the College of Bonhommes. 1823. Imp. folio, half morocco, second edition. Quaritch 939-312 1974 £50

TODD, JOHN   The Sunset Land. 1870. 321p. Austin 62-638 1974 $15

TODD, W. E. C.   The Birds of the Santa Marta Region of Colombia. 1922. 8vo., half morocco, plates. Wheldon 131-712 1974 £18

TODD, WILLIAM B.   Edmund Burke. London. 8vo., illus., cloth. Dawsons PM 252-96 1974 £6.30

TODE, H. J.   Fungi Mecklenburgenses Selecti. 1790-91. Small 4to., half calf, plates. Wheldon 129-1362 1974 £50

TODHUNTER, ISAAC   Researches in the Calculus of Variations. London and Cambridge, 1871. 8vo., orig. green cloth, gilt, first edition. Dawsons PM 245-723 1974 £15

TOLAND, JOHN   Amyntor. London, 1699. 8vo., label, contemporary mottled calf, first edition. Dawsons PM 252-710 1974 £50

TOLEDO, FRANCISCO   In Sacrosanctum Loannis Evangelium Commentarii. Cologne, 1599. 2 parts in 1 vol., folio, old blind-panelled calf. Howes 185-1727 1974 £15

TOLENTINO, RAOUL   Illustrated Catalogue of Gothic and Renaissance Italian and French Art Gathered By. 1924. Roy. 8vo., plates, boards, printed wrapper. Quaritch 940-803 1974 £10

TOLET, FRANCOIS   A Treatise on Lithotomy. London, 1683. Small 8vo., modern marbled boards, first English edition. Dawsons PM 249-481 1974 £95

TOLKIEN, JOHN RONALD REUEL   Beowulf. 1936. Wrappers, very fine, first edition. Covent 55-1454 1974 £21

TOLKIEN, JOHN RONALD REUEL   Beowulf: The Monsters and the Critics. 1936. Wrappers, fine, first edition. Covent 51-1853 1973 £12.50

TOLKIEN, JOHN RONALD REUEL   The Hobbit. 1937. First edition, crown 8vo., fine, d.w., illus., first issue with 'Dodgson' incorrectly spelt on d.w., orig. cloth. Broadhurst 24-923 1974 £50

TOLKIEN, JOHN RONALD REUEL   Sir Gawain and the Green Knight. Oxford, 1925. First edition, good copy, heavy pencilling, very scarce, orig. cloth. Crane 7-302 1974 £25

TOLKIEN, JOHN RONALD REUEL   Sir Gawain and the Green Knight. Oxford, 1925. Crown 8vo., orig. cloth. Broadhurst 23-952 1974 £10

TOLKOWSKY, SAMUEL   Hesperides. 1938. 8vo., cloth, text-figures, plates, scarce. Wheldon 128-1668 1973 £20

TOLKOWSKY, SAMUEL   Hesperides. 1938. 8vo., cloth, plates, scarce. Wheldon 130-1491 1974 £20

TOLLARD   Traite des Vegetaux Qui Composent l'Agriculture de l'Empire Francais ou Catalogue Francais et Latin des Vegetaux dont on Trouve Desindividus et des Graines . . . Paris, 1805. 8vo., half calf, worn, rare. Wheldon 131-1798 1974 £25

TOLLEMACHE, S.   British Trees. 1901. Roy 8vo., cloth, plates. Wheldon 130-1576 1974 £10

TOLLER, ERNST   Blind Man's Buff. 1938. Fine, English first edition. Covent 56-1258 1974 £2.50

TOLLER, ERNST   Letters from Prison. 1936. Plates, dust wrapper, English first edition. Covent 56-2089 1974 £5.25

TOLLER, ERNEST   No More Peace. Farrar, Rinehart, 1937. Austin 51-973 1973 $10

TOLLER, ERNST   Seven Plays. 1935. Fine, English first edition. Covent 56-1257 1974 £7.50

TOLLER, SAMUEL   The Law of Executors and Administrators. 1806. Contemporary calf, enlarged second edition. Howes 186-997 1974 £7.50

TOLLINGTON, R. B.   Clement of Alexandria: A Study in Christian Liberalism. 1914. 2 vols., med. 8vo., plates, orig. cloth, fine. Broadhurst 24-1337 1974 £6

TOLPUDDLE MARTYRS. 1934. 4to., orig. cloth, plates, illus. Broadhurst 23-1286 1974 £6

TOLSTOI, ALEKSEI KONSTANTINOVICH   The Death of Ivan the Terrible. 1926. Austin 51-974 1973 $10

TOLSTOY, LEO NICOLAEVICH   The Autobiography of Countess Sophie Tolstoi. 1922. Boards, bookplate. Covent 55-1455 1974 £12.50

TOLSTOY, LEV NICOLAEVICH   The Living Corpse. Brown, 1916. Austin 51-975 1973 $7.50

TOLSTOY, LEV NICOLAEVICH   The Complete Works of. London, (1904). 24 vols., 8vo., illus., orig. cloth. Dawsons PM 252-973 1974 £70

THE TOMAHAWK. London. 3 vols., 4to., orig. green cloth, morocco labels, plates, gilt. Dawsons PM 252-974 1974 £60

TOMES, ROBERT   The War With the South, A History of the Great American Rebellion. New York, 1862. 3 vols., illus., foxing, fine, steel engravings. Ballinger 1-320 1974 $35

TOMIOKA, KENZO   The Tokwaan-Kokyo-Zuroku or Ancient Chinese Mirrors from the Collection of. Kyoto, 1924. Large folio, plates, native silk binding. Quaritch 940-425 1974 £32

TOMKINS, C.   A Tour of the Isle of Wight. 1796. 2 vols. in 1, 4to., half calf, plates. Quaritch 939-379 1974 £130

TOMKINSON, G. S.   A Select Bibliography of the Principal Modern Presses Public and Private. London, 1928. 4to., orig. cloth-backed boards, fine. Dawsons PM 10-608 1974 £40

TOMKINSON, J. W.   Hokusai Master of the Japanese Ukiyo-ye School of Painting. (1904). Roy. 4to., half morocco, rubbed, scarce, plates. Quaritch 940-401 1974 £40

TOMLINS, F. G.   A Brief View of the English Drama. 1840. Austin 51-976 1973 $8.50

TOMLINSON, HENRY MAJOR   All Our Yesterdays. 1930. Some foxing, very good copy, first edition, first issue. Covent 51-1856 1973 £5.25

TOMLINSON, HENRY MAJOR   All Our Yesterdays. 1930. Buckram, signed, English first edition. Covent 56-1259 1974 £5

TOMLINSON, HENRY MAJOR   All Our Yesterdays. 1930. 8vo., orig. cloth, signed, first edition. Rota 190-948 1974 £7.50

TOMLINSON, HENRY MAJOR   All Our Yesterdays. London, 1930. First trade edition, first issue, with error running head p. 67, inscription by author, d.w. lightly worn, fine, orig. binding. Ross 87-545 1974 $35

TOMLINSON, HENRY MAJOR   All Our Yesterdays. London, 1930. Orig. binding, frontispiece portrait, no. 387 of edition limited to 1,025 copies, signed, mint in box. Ross 87-544 1974 $20

TOMLINSON, HENRY MAJOR   Below London Bridge. London, 1934. Orig. binding, photos, d.w. lightly chipped & soiled, fine. Ross 87-546 1974 $15

TOMLINSON, HENRY MAJOR   Gallion's Reach. London, 1927. Orig. binding, first edition, some foxing, fine, d.w. Ross 87-548 1974 $10

TOMLINSON, HENRY MAJOR   Gallion's Reach. New York, 1927. 8vo., cloth backed boards, plates, signed. Rich Summer-100 1974 $22.50

TOMLINSON, HENRY MAJOR   Illusion: 1915. New York, 1928. Blue boards, real first edition, slight fading of spine, fine, protective wrapper. Ross 87-550 1974 $15

TOMLINSON, HENRY MAJOR   Illusion. 1915. 12mo., boards, cloth back, publisher's box, very fine, first edition. Goodspeed's 578-382 1974 $15

TOMLINSON, HENRY MAJOR   An Illustrated Catalogue of Rare Books on the East Indies and a Letter to a Friend. 1932. No. 133 of edition limited to 165 copies, orig. black cloth and yellow boards, unopened, very fine. Ross 87-551 1974 $20

TOMLINSON, HENRY MAJOR   London River. London, 1921. First edition. Biblo & Tannen 210-805 1973 $10

TOMLINSON, HENRY MAJOR   London River. London, 1921. Orig. binding, frontispiece, light foxing, d.w. slightly chipped, first edition, fine. Ross 87-552 1974 $10

TOMLINSON, HENRY MAJOR   Norman Douglas. London, 1931. No. 32 of edition limited to 260 copies, orig. binding, signed, corners somewhat dented, fine. Ross 87-553 1974 $15

TOMLINSON, HENRY MAJOR   Out of Soundings. London, 1931. 8vo., orig. cloth, illus., limited, slipcase, first edition. Bow Windows 62-941 1974 £5

TOMLINSON, HENRY MAJOR   Out of Soundings. London, 1931. No. 270 of edition limited to 275 copies, signed by author, illus., protective glassine wrapper slightly torn, fine, tight copy. Ross 87-554 1974 $30

TOMLINSON, HENRY MAJOR   The Sea and the Jungle. 1912. First edition, frontis., 8vo., orig. cloth, fine, scarce. Sawyer 293-276 1974 £16.50

TOMLINSON, HENRY MAJOR   The Sea and the Jungle. London, 1930. Woodcuts, no. 414 of edition limited to 515 copies, hand made paper, signed, new edition, bookplate, d.w. darkened & slightly chipped, very nice. Ross 87-555 1974 $25

TOMLINSON, HENRY MAJOR   The Snows of Helicon. 1933. 8vo., orig. cloth, cellophane d.w., slipcase, signed limited edition. Bow Windows 66-703 1974 £8.50

TOMLINSON, HENRY MAJOR   Waiting for Daylight. London, 1922. First edition, dust staining on spine of d.w., internally fine. Ross 87-556 1974 $15

TOMLINSON, HENRY MAJOR   Waiting for Daylight. New York, 1922. First printing of American edition, no. 870 of edition limited to 2,100 copies, bookplate, fine, protective glassine wrapper. Ross 87-557 1974 $25

TOMLINSON, W. W.   The North Eastern Railway. Newcastle, (1914). Thick 4to., orig. cloth, gilt, plates, illus., first edition. Hammond 201-933 1974 £25

TOMPKINS, DANIEL D.   Address of the Albany Republican Corresponding Committee. N.P., n.d. 8vo., disbound, first edition. Ximenes 35-359 1974 $10

TOMS, EDWARD   The Accomplish'd Maid. London, 1767. 8vo., modern boards, first edition. Dawsons PM 252-975 1974 £15

TOMSON, GRAHAM R.   Ballads of the North Countrie. n.d. 442 pages. Austin 61-977 1974 $10

TONER, JOSEPH MEREDITH   The Medical Men of the Revolution. Philadelphia, 1876. Detached boards. Rittenhouse 46-621 1974 $75

TONG, W.   An Account of the Life and Death of the Late Reverend Mr. Matthew Henry. 1716. Contemporary panelled calf, rubbed, dust soiled. Smith 194-191 1974 £5

TOOKE, JOHN HORNE   The Diversions of Purley. 1829. 2 vols., new library binding, new revised edition.   Austin 61-978 1974 $37.50

TOOKE, JOHN HORNE   Diversions of Purley. 1860. 739 pages. Austin 61-979 1974 $27.50

TOOKE, WILLIAM   The Life of Catharine II. Philadelphia, 1802. 2 vols., 8vo., orig. boards, fine, first American edition.   Ximenes 35-360 1974 $35

TOPFFER, RODOLPHE   Les Amours de Mr. Vieix Bois. Impr. de Aubert & Cie. (Paris?, c. 1839). Oblong 8vo., orig. half calf, rubbed, good copy.   Quaritch 940-258 1974 £60

TOPHAM, EDWARD   The Fool. London, 1786. 8vo., modern boards, first edition.   Dawsons PM 252-976 1974 £15

TOPINARD, PAUL   Anthropology. London, 1894. 8vo., orig. blue cloth, first edition in English.   Dawsons PM 249-482 1974 £11

TOPPING, C. W.   Canadian Penal Institutions. Toronto, 1929. Card cover.   Hood's 104-664 1974 $12.50

TORELLI, GIUSEPPE   Scala de' Meriti a Capo d'Anno. Verona, 1751. Small 8vo., contemporary wrappers, first edition.   Schuman 37-248 1974 $85

TORONTO ART GALLERY   Catalogue of Memorial Exhibitions of the Work of Clarence Gagnon and J. W. Beatty. Toronto, 1942. Card cover, illus., some coloured.   Hood's 102-131 1974 $7.50

TORRE, GIOVANNI MARIA DELLA   Scienza della Natura Generale. 1750. 4to., 2 vols., orig. boards, ex-library.   Zeitlin 235-225 1974 $250

TORRENTINUS, HERMANNUS   Elucidarius Carminum et Historiarum. Strassburg, 1510. Small 4to., boards, waterstains.   Harper 213-156 1973 $375

TORREY, BRADFORD   Spring Notes from Tennessee. Boston – New York, 1896. 8vo., orig. bindings.   Butterfield 8-615 1974 $15

TORRIANO, PIERO   Carlo Carra. Milan, 1942. Folio, cloth, foxed, plates.   Minters 37-384 1973 $22

TORRIANO, PIERO   Primo Conti. Florence, 1941. Small folio, cloth, plates, limited edition.   Minters 37-391 1973 $30

TORRICELLI, EVANGELISTA   Lezioni Accademiche. Florence, 1715. 4to., contemporary vellum, frontispiece, first edition.   Gilhofer 61-15 1974 sFr. 1,600

TORTI, FRANCISCO   Ad Criticam Dissertationem. Modena, 1715. 4to., quarter vellum, uncut, first edition.   Gurney 64-218 1974 £20

TORY, GEOFFROY   Aediloquium. Cracow, 1539. 4to., marbled boards, rare, very good copy.   Harper 213-157 1973 $1250

TORSELLINO, ORAZIO   The History of Our B. Lady of Loreto. N.P., 1608. 8vo., 18th century calf, gilt, morocco labels, first English edition, second issue.   Dawsons PM 252-977 1974 £135

TORTORI, E.   Genesi Organizzazione e Metamorfosi degli Infusori. Florence, 1895. 4to., orig. boards, plates, scarce.   Wheldon 130-897 1974 £70

TOSI & BECCHIO   Altars, Tabernacles & Sepulchral Monuments of 14th & 15th Centuries Existing at Rome. 1843. Folio, plates, new buckram.   Allen 213-1829 1973 $25

TOTIVS Theologicae Veritatis. 1580. 16mo., old calf, stains, worn.   Bow Windows 62-193 1974 £15

TOUCHET, JAMES 3RD EARL OF CASTLEHAVEN
Please turn to
CASTLEHAVEN, JAMES TOUCHET, 3RD EARL OF

TOUJOURS de l'Amour. Brussels, (1799). Narrow 16mo., color plates, orig. black morocco.   Gregory 44-299 1974 $55

TOULMIN, J.   The History of the Town of Taunton. Taunton, 1791. 4to., plates, modern boards, first edition.   Quaritch 939-543 1974 £15

TOULMIN, J.   The History of the Town of Taunton. Taunton, 1822. Roy. 8vo., orig. boards, new edition.   Quaritch 939-544 1974 £17.50

TOULMIN, CAMILLA   Lays & Legends. 1845. Grey cloth, illus. Eaton Music-679 1973 £10

TOUMANOFF, C.   Las Tiques. Saigon, 1944. Roy 8vo., sewed, plates, scarce.   Wheldon 130-899 1974 £7.50

TOUMANOFF, C.   Les Tiques de l'Indochine. Saigon, 1944. Roy. 8vo., sewed, plates, scarce.   Wheldon 128-819 1973 £7.50

TOUNLEY, H.   English Woodlands and Their Story. 1910. 8vo., cloth.   Wheldon 129-1632 1974 £5

TOURGEE, ALBION W.   An Appeal to Caesar. New York, 1884. Cloth, slightly rubbed, first edition.   Hayman 59-637 1974 $12.50

TOURGEE, ALBION W.   An Appeal to Caesar. 1884. Orig. cloth, scarce, first edition.   Putnam 126-231 1974 $10

THE TOURIST in Wales. n.d. (c. 1840). 4to., contemporary half calf, panelled back, engraved plates, marbled boards, fine.   Broadhurst 24-1544 1974 £75

TOURNEFORT, JOSEPH PITTON DE   Elemens de Botanique. Lyon, 1797. 6 vols., 8vo., contemporary calf gilt, plates.   Wheldon 131-1208 1974 £50

TOURNEFORT, JOSEPH PITTON DE   Histoire des Plantes. Paris, 1698. 8vo., contemporary calf gilt.   Wheldon 129-1129 1974 £35

TOURNEFORT, JOSEPH PITTON DE   Histoire des Plantes qui Naissent aux Environs de Paris. Paris, 1698. 8vo., contemporary calf, rare first edition. Wheldon 128-1695 1973 £35

TOURNEFORT, JOSEPH PITTON DE   Institutiones Rei Herbariae. Paris, 1719. 3 vols., 4to., contemporary calf, worn, plates, scarce, third edition. Wheldon 131-1207 1974 £75

TOURNEFORT, JOSEPH PITTON DE   Relation d'un Voyage du Levant. Lyons, 1717. 3 vols., 8vo., contemporary calf, plates.   Schuman 37-249 1974 $175

TOURNEFORT, JOSEPH PITTON DE   A Voyage Into the Levant. London, 1741. 3 vols., 8vo., contemporary calf, leather labels, plates, fine.   Traylen 79-540 1973 £68

TOURNEUR, CYRIL   The Atheist's Tragedy. London, 1611. 8vo., disbound, scarce, third edition.   Ximenes 35-361 1974 $17.50

TOUSSAINT, F. V.   Manners. London, 1752. 12mo., worn, contemporary calf, third edition.   Bow Windows 62-943 1974 £25

TOUSSAINT, FRANZ   Sakountala. Paris, 1922. 16mo. Biblo & Tannen 210-1016 1973 $9.50

TOUSSAINT-LUCA, A.   Guillaume Apollinaire. Paris, 1920. 8vo., wrappers.   Minters 37-262 1973 $60

TOUSSENEL, ALPHONSE   L'Esprit des Betes. Paris, (1868). Roy. 8vo., half green hard grain morocco, gilt, illus.   L. Goldschmidt 42-397 1974 $40

TOUT, OTIS B.   The First Thirty Years, 1901-1930. San Diego, 1931. 4to., cloth, illus.   Saddleback 14-306 1974 $65

TOUT, T. F.   Chapters in the Administrative History of Mediaeval England. 1920-33. 6 vols., 8vo., plates, cloth, orig. edition. Quaritch 939-266 1974 £35

TOUT, T. F.   The Place of the Reign of Edward II in English History. Manchester, 1914. Large 8vo., cloth, rebound, scarce. Howes 186-1266 1974 £8.50

TOUZEAU, J.   The Rise and Progress of Liverpool. Liverpool, 1910. Roy 8vo., 2 vols., orig. cloth. Broadhurst 23-1566 1974 £7.50

TOW, J. S.   The Real Chinese in America. Academy Press, 1923. Austin 62-641 1974 $12.50

TOWGOOD, MICAJAH   An Essay Towards Attaining a True Idea of Character. London, 1764. 2 vols. in 1, 8vo., later half morocco, gilt, first editions. Ximenes 35-362 1974 $30

TOWLE, J.   A Grammar of Astronomy. Philadelphia, 1825. Plates, leather, worn, foxing. Rinsland 58-912 1974 $50

TOWNSEND, CHARLES WENDELL   The Birds of Essex County. Cambridge, 1905. 4to., orig. cloth, scarce. Wheldon 130-638 1974 £7.50

TOWNSEND, CHARLES WENDELL   Captain Cartwright and His Labrador Journal. Boston, 1911. Photographs, map, illus. Hood's 103-192 1974 $45

TOWNSEND, EDWARD W.   "Chimmie Fadden." New York, 1895. 1st ed. Biblo & Tannen 210-806 1973 $10

TOWNSEND, EDWARD W.   Chimmie Fadden. Lovell, Coryell, 1895. 346p., illus. Austin 54-1015 1973 $10

TOWNSEND, G.   The Oedipis Romanus. 1819. 8vo., uncut, orig. boards. Hill 126-269 1974 £17.50

TOWNSEND, GEORGE ALFRED   The Life, Crime, and Capture of John Wilkes Booth. New York, (1865). Pictorial wrappers, frontispiece, scarce. Putman 126-20 1974 $55

TOWNSEND, RICHARD H.   Original Poems. Baltimore, 1809. 12mo., contemporary quarter roan, first edition. Ximenes 35-364 1974 $30

TOWNSEND, W. J.   A New History of Methodism. 1909. 2 vols., thick roy. 8vo., plates. Howes 185-1729 1974 £6.50

TOWNSEND, W. CHARLES   Memoirs of the House of Commons. 1844. 2 vols., full polished calf, fine, second edition. Howes 186-1267 1974 £15

TOWNSHEND, C. V. F.   The Military Life of Field-Marshal George. Toronto, 1907. Illus. Hood's 103-240 1974 $40

TOWNSHEND, THOMAS   Considerations. 1793. 8vo., modern boards, uncut. Dawsons PM 251-344 1974 £20

TOWNSHEND, THOMAS   Poems. London, 1796. 8vo., half calf, first edition. Ximenes 35-365 1974 $40

TOWNSON, R.   Travels in Hungary. 1797. 4to., old half calf, weak joints, folding coloured map, plates. Wheldon 128-241 1973 £40

THE TOY-SHOP. 1830. New edition revised, frontis., woodcuts, 12mo., orig. boards, roan spine, rubbed, ads at end. George's 610-752 1973 £6.50

TRACY, W. P.   Men Who Made St. Joseph "The City Worth While". St. Joseph, (c.1919). Oblong 8vo., leather. Saddleback 14-532 1974 $35

TRAHARD, PIERRE   La Jeunesse de Prosper Merimee. Paris, 1925. Wrappers, 2 vols., illus., English first edition. Covent 56-932 1974 £15

TRAIL, J. W. H.   A Memorial Volume. Aberdeen, 1923. 8vo., cloth, plates. Wheldon 131-1245 1974 £5

TRAILL, CATHARINE PARR   Afar In the Forest. London, 1873. Plates, illus., mended spine. Hood's 103-512 1974 $50

TRAILL, CATHERINE PARR   Canadian Wild Flowers. Montreal, 1868. Rare first edition, rebound, lithographs. Hood's 102-171 1974 $250

TRAILL, H. D.   Social England. 1894-97. 6 vols., one vol. slightly spotted. Allen 216-1688 1974 $50

TRAIN, ARTHUR   Page Mr. Tutt. New York, 1926. 8vo., orig. cloth, first edition. Rota 190-360 1974 £6

TRAIN, GEORGE FRANCIS   Spread-Eagleism. New York, 1859. Cloth, little foxed, nice copy. Hayman 59-638 1974 $20

TRAITE EXPERIMENTAL Analytique et Pratique de la Pousse des Terres. Paris, 1808. 4to., old calf, gilt, plates. Zeitlin 235-149 1974 $37.50

TRANSCRIPTS Made from the Patent and Close Rolls . . . . in the Sixteenth Century. (c.1575). Roy. 8vo., half calf. Quaritch 939-193 1974 £120

TRANSITION. New York, 1936. Wrappers, orig. cloth. Rota 188-534 1974 £5

TRANSITION. New York, 1937. Wrappers, orig. cloth. Rota 188-535 1974 £5

TRANSPORTATION London, 1835. Orig. boards, paper label, worn, faded. Dawson's 424-309 1974 $200

TRAPP, JOSEPH   Peace. London, 1713. 8vo., modern boards, second edition. Dawsons PM 252-978 1974 £20

TRAPP, MARIA AUGUSTA   The Story of the Trapp Family Singers. Lippincott, 1949. 309p., illus. Austin 62-643 1974 $6.50

TRATADO Sobre os Meyos da Preservacao da Peste, Mandado Fazer por Ordem de sua Magestade. Lisbon, 1748. 8vo., old boards. Gurney 66-187 1974 £15

TRAVELERS in Time. New York, 1947. 1st ed. Biblo & Tannen 210-673 1973 $12.50

THE TRAVELLERS New Guide Through Ireland. Dublin, 1815. 8vo., plates, map, rebacked. Emerald 50-941 1974 £20

TRAVELS in Cashmere, Little Tibet, and Central Asia. New York, 1874. 1st ed. Biblo & Tannen 213-937 1973 $12.50

TRAVEN, B.   The Bridge in the Jungle. New York, 1938. 1st Amer. ed. Biblo & Tannen 213-608 1973 $12.50

TRAVEN, B.   The Death Ship. 1934. 8vo., orig. cloth, scarce, first English edition. Rota 189-874 1974 £6.50

TRAVERS, BENJAMIN   Observations on the Pathology of Venereal Affections. London, 1830. 8vo., orig. boards, rebacked, first edition. Gurney 66-188 1974 £16

TRAVERS, M. W.   The Discovery of Rare Gases. London, 1928. 4to., blue boards, illus., first edition. Dawsons PM 245-724 1974 £10

A TREASURY of American Prints. New York, 1939. 4to. Biblo & Tannen 210-107 1973 $8.50

A TREASURY of Art Masterpieces. New York, 1939. 4to., color plates, 1st ed. Biblo & Tannen 210-108 1973 $17.50

A TREASURY of Humorous Poetry. Estes, 1902. 407p., illus., orig. ed. Austin 54-601 1973 $10

A TREASURY of Plays for Children. Little, Brown, 1921. Austin 51-666 1973 $6.50

TREATISE On Mensuration for the Use of Schools. Toronto, 1854. Hood's 104-415 1974 $20

TREATIES Of the United States With the Indians. c.1837. 8vo., foxing, rebound. Rinsland 58-963 1974 $50

A TREATISE on the Management of Foreign and British Birds in Captivity. Hertford, 1936. 8vo., orig. cloth, scarce, second edition. Wheldon 130-443 1974 £12

TREATY, Laws and Rules Governing the Admission of Chinese. 1917, 1920. Austin 62-92 1974 $22.50

TREATY of Peace, Good Correspondence & Neutrality in America. 1686. Small 4to., full polished calf, first English edition. Ximenes 35-369 1974 $275

TREDGOLD, THOMAS   Elementary Principles of Carpentry. 1853. 4to., plates, orig. cloth, rebacked, recased. Quaritch 940-560 1974 £30

TREDGOLD, THOMAS   Practical Essay on the Strength of Cast Iron. London, 1824. 8vo., orig. boards, uncut, fine, plates. Dawsons PM 245-725 1974 £40

TREDGOLD, THOMAS   A Practical Treatise on Rail-Roads and Carriages. London, 1825. 8vo., orig. boards, plates, first edition. Hammond 201-922 1974 £75

TREDGOLD, THOMAS   Principles of Warming and Ventilating Public Buildings. London, 1824. 8vo., orig. boards, fine, uncut, illus., second edition. Zeitlin 235-226 1974 $87.50

TREDGOLD, THOMAS   The Steam Engine. London, 1827. 4to., contemporary calf, gilt, plates, first edition. Hammond 201-980 1974 £65

TREDGOLD, THOMAS   Tracts on Hydraulics. London, 1836. 8vo., orig. cloth, gilt, plates, second edition. Dawsons PM 245-726 1974 £15

TREDWELL, DANIEL M.   Monograph on Privately Illustrated Books. 1892. 4to., slightly worn. Allen 216-207 1974 $10

TREGELLAS, WALTER H.   Cornish Worthies. 1884. 2 vols. Austin 61-981 1974 $47.50

TREITSCHKE, HEINRICH VON   History of Germany in the 19th Century. 1915. 7 vols., thick 8vo., orig. edition. Howes 186-1270 1974 £46

TRELAWNY, EDWARD JOHN   Adventures of a Younger Son. London, 1831. 3 vols., 12mo., orig. blue boards, gilt, first edition. Dawsons PM 252-979 1974 £60

TRELAWNY, EDWARD JOHN   Recollections of the Last Days of Shelley and Byron. London, 1858. 8vo., orig. cloth, first edition. Ximenes 35-370 1974 $45

TRELAWNY, EDWARD JOHN   Records of Shelley, Byron and the Author. London, 1878. 2 vols., 8vo., orig. black cloth, scarce. Ximenes 35-371 1974 $60

TRELEASE, W.   The Yucceae. 1902. 8vo., cloth, plates. Wheldon 131-1704 1974 £7.50

TREMAINE, C. M.   New York's First Music Week. New York, 1920. Author's sgd. pres. Biblo & Tannen 214-927 1974 $12.50

TREMAINE, MARIE   Early Printing in Canada. Vienna, 1934. Wrappers. Dawson's 424-173 1974 $12.50

TREMBLAY, ERNEST   Riel; Reponse a Monsieur J. A. Chapleau. St. Hyacinthe, 1885. Contemporary mottled boards, linen spine. Hood's 102-834 1974 $35

TREMBLAY, J. C.   Les Noces d'Argent Episcopales de Sa Grandeur Mgr. M. T. Labrecque. Chicoutimi, 1917. Illus., faded. Hood's 103-278 1974 $10

TRENCH, RICHARD CHEVENIX   On the Study of Words. London, 1851. 8vo., orig. cloth, first edition. Ximenes 35-372 1974 $20

TRENCH, W. STEUART   Realities of Irish Life. 1868. 8vo., illus., contemporary half calf, first edition. Bow Windows 64-739 1974 £8.50

TRENCHARD, JOHN   An Argument, Shewing, That a Standing Army Is Inconsistent. London, 1697. Small 4to., disbound, first edition. Ximenes 35-373 1974 $45

TRENCHARD, JOHN   A Discourse of Standing Armies. London, 1722. 8vo., boards, first edition. Hammond 201-623 1974 £5.50

TRENT, SPI M.   My Cousin, Will Rogers. New York, 1938. lst ed., illus. Biblo & Tannen 213-828 1973 $7.50

TRESSAN, LOUIS ELIZABETH DE LA VERGNE DE BROUSSIN   Essai sur le Fluide Electrique. Paris, 1786. 8vo., 2 vols., contemporary calf, gilt, first edition. Dawsons PM 245-727 1974 £75

TRESSAN, LOUIS ELISABETH DE LA VERGNE DE BROUSSIN   Roland l'Amoureux, de Matheo-Maris Boyardo. Paris, 1796. 2 parts in 1, small 12mo., lemon polished calf, gilt, illus. L. Goldschmidt 42-123 1974 $25

TRETIAKOV, S.   Roar China. International, n.d. 89p. Austin 51-977 1973 $7.50

TREVELYAN, GEORGE MACAULEY   Sir George Otto Trevelyan, a Memoir. London, 1932. Biblo & Tannen 213-710 1973 $10

TREVELYAN, GEORGE MAC AULAY   Sir George Otto Trevelyan. 1932. Illus. Austin 61-983 1974 $10

TREVELYAN, GEORGE OTTO   The American Revolution. New York, 1899 and 1903. 3 vols. Jenkins 61-2459 1974 $14.50

TREVELYAN, GEORGE OTTO   The Ladies in Parliament. Cambridge, 1869. Orig. cloth, bookplate. Covent 55-1469 1974 £5.25

TREVELYAN, MARY CAROLINE   William the III and the Defence of Holland. 1930. Plates, maps. Howes 186-1312 1974 £5

TREW, CHRISTOPHER JACOB   Plantae Selectae. Nuremberg, 1750-73. Imp. folio, half morocco, plates. Wheldon 129-1710 1974 £2,750

TRI-MOUNTAIN; or, The Early History of Boston. Philadelphia, (c. 1850). 16mo., plates, orig. green cloth, front inner hinge sprung, ends of spine & edges worn, else good. Current BW9-143 1974 $28.50

TRIAL, Life and Execution of Anton Probst. Philadelphia, (1866). Printed tan wrappers, fine, unopened, first edition. Bradley 35-392 1974 $40

TRIANA, J.   Nouvelles Etudes sur les Quinquinas. Paris, 1870. Folio, orig. half cloth, plates, rare. Wheldon 128-1172 1973 £25

TRIANA, J.   Nouvelles Etudes Sur les Quinquinas. Paris, 1870. Folio, orig. half cloth, plates, rare. Wheldon 130-1063 1974 £25

A TRIBUTE to the Belgian King and People. (1914). 4to., illus., orig. cloth, fine. Bow Windows 62-536 1974 £6

TRICASSE, PATRICE   Tricassi Cerasariensis Mantvani Enarratio Pvlcherrima Principiorum Chyromantiae. 1560. Small 4to., illus., calf antique. Bow Windows 62-946 1974 £70

TRIGGS, HARRY INIGO   The Art of Garden Design in Italy. 1906. Folio, buckram, plates, plans, text figures. Wheldon 128-1541 1973 £12

TRIGGS, HARRY INIGO   The Art of Garden Design in Italy. 1906. Folio, buckram, plates. Wheldon 131-1584 1974 £20

TRIGGS, HARRY INIGO   Garden Craft in Europe. London, n.d. (c.1913). 4to., illus., top edge gilt, bookplate, lacks front free blank, orig. binding. Wilson 63-325 1974 $15

TRIGGS, HARRY INIGO   Some Architectural Works of Inigo Jones. 1901. New cloth, drawings, illus. Eaton Music-680 1973 £20

TRIMBLE, W. COPELAND   The Historical Record of the 27th Inniskilling Regiment. London, 1876. 8vo., plates, illus., scarce. Emerald 50-942 1974 £10

TRIMEN, H.   Flora of Middlesex. 1869. Crown 8vo., cloth, coloured map. Wheldon 128-1227 1973 £7.50

TRIMEN, H.   Flora of Middlesex. 1869. Crown 8vo.,
cloth, map. Wheldon 131-1246 1974 £7.50

TRIMMER, MRS.   The Charity School Spelling Book. 1818. 12mo.,
boards, new edition. Hammond 201-147 1974 £5

TRIMMER, MRS.   The Charity School Spelling Book. 1818. 12mo.,
boards, new edition. Hammond 201-148 1974 £5

TRIMMER, K.   Flora of Norfolk. 1866. Crown 8vo., cloth,
scarce. Wheldon 128-1228 1973 £5

TRIMMER, MARY   A Natural History of the Most Remarkable
Quadrupeds, Birds, Fishes, Serpents, Reptiles, and Insects. 1826. Woodcuts,
2 vols., 16mo., full calf, leather labels. George's 610-755 1973 £15

TRIMMER, SARAH   Companion to the Book of Common Prayer of the
Church of England. 1791. First edition, 12mo., half calf, gilt. George's
610-756 1973 £5.25

TRIMMER, SARAH   Fabulous Histories. 1821. Woodcut vignette,
title almost detached, 12mo., half calf, 13th edition. George's 610-758 1973
£5

TRIMMER, SARAH   Series of Prints, Designed to Illustrate the
Scripture History. 1828. 12mo., contemporary sheep, rubbed, copperplates.
George's 610-762 1973 £5.25

TRIP, TOM   The History of Giles Gingerbread: A Little Boy,
Who Lived Upon Learning. York, n.d. (c. 1820). 24mo., orig. printed wrappers,
woodcuts, very good copy. Frohnsdorff 16-436 1974 $50

TRIP, TOMMY   Natural History of Four-Footed Beasts. Glasgow,
1802. Woodcuts, half green morocco. Gregory 44-56 1974 $95

TRIPP, ALONZO   The Fisher Boy. Boston, 1857. 12mo., orig.
grey cloth, first edition. Ximenes 35-374 1974 $17.50

TRIPP, F. E.   British Mosses. 1888. 2 vols., roy. 8vo.,
half green calf, nice copy, new edition. Wheldon 128-1431 1973 £10

TRIPP, F. E.   British Mosses, Their Homes, Aspects,
Structure and Uses. 1874. 2 vols., roy. 8vo., orig. cloth, plates. Wheldon
131-1474 1974 £20

TRISSINO, GIOVANNI GIORGIO   La Italia Liberata da Gotthi del Trissino.
(Venice, 1548). 3 vols. in 1, 18th century mottled calf, gilt spine, worn and
repaired but sound. Thomas 32-269 1974 £80

TRISTAN DE SAINT-AMANT, J.   Commentaires Historiques. 1635. Folio,
plates, vellum. Allen 213-1129 1973 $35

TRISTRAM, H. B.   The Land of Israel. London, 1876. 8vo.,
maps, plates, orig. cloth, third edition. Bow Windows 62-947 1974 £5.50

TRISTRAM, H. B.   Natural History of the Bible. 1889. 8vo.,
orig. cloth. Wheldon 129-194 1974 £5

TRISTRAM, WILLIAM OUTRAM   Coaching Days and Coaching Ways. 1888.
4to., orig. green cloth, gilt, illus., first edition. Howes 186-479 1974 £21

TRISTRAM, WILLIAM OUTRAM   Coaching Days and Coaching Ways. 1893.
Crown 8vo., orig. plain cloth, illus., first edition. Howes 185-528 1974 £5

TRISTRAM, WILLIAM OUTRAM   Moated Houses. (1910). 8vo., orig. cloth,
plates, illus. Bow Windows 66-708 1974 £5

TRITES, W. B.   The Gypsy. Nice, (c.1926). Wrappers,
presentation inscription, first edition. Rota 188-892 1974 £5

TRITHEIM, JOHANN   Liber de Scriptoribus Ecclesiasticis. Basle,
1494. Small folio, 18th century calf, rebacked, first edition. Dawsons PM
250-77 1974 £1850

TRIVISANO, G. BATTISTA   Visione. Genova, 1568. 4to., marbled
boards, fine. Harper 213-158 1973 $375

TROEDSSON, G. T.   On the Middle and Upper Ordovician Faunas of
Northern Greenland. Copenhagen, 1926-29. 2 parts in 1 vol., roy. 8vo.,
buckram, plates. Wheldon 128-1061 1973 £7.50

TROELTSCH, ANTON FRIEDRICH VON   The Surgical Diseases of the Ear. London, 1874. 8vo., orig. cloth, gilt, second edition. Dawsons PM 249-483
1974 £8

TROELTSCH, ERNST   The Social Teaching of the Christian Churches.
1931. 2 vols., roy. 8vo. Howes 185-1731 1974 £8.50

TROGUS POMPEIUS
Please turn to
JUSTINUS, MARCUS JUNIANUS

TROJA, MICHELE   De Novorum Ossium. Paris, 1775. 12mo., contemporary wrappers, uncut, first edition. Schumann 35-471 1974 $175

TROLLOPE, ANDREW   An Inventory of the Church Plate of
Leicestershire. 1890. 2 vols., 4to., illus. Howes 186-2079 1974 £10.75

TROLLOPE, ANTHONY   An Autobiography. Edinburgh & London,
1883. 2 vols., 8vo., orig. cloth, half calf, first edition. Dawsons PM
252-980 1974 £30

TROLLOPE, ANTHONY   An Autobiography. Edinburgh, 1883. 2 vols.,
frontis., name on half title, very good copy. Covent 51-1864 1973 £21

TROLLOPE, ANTHONY   An Autobiography. Edinburgh, 1883.
8vo., orig. plum cloth, first edition. Ximenes 35-375 1974 $40

TROLLOPE, ANTHONY   Ayala's Angel. 1881. First edition, no half
titles required, 3 vols., 8vo., green morocco gilt, fine set, bookplate of the Earl
of Carysfort in each vol. Sawyer 293-277 1974 £175

TROLLOPE, ANTHONY   Ayala's Angel. London, 1881. 3 vols.,
8vo., orig. orange dec. cloth, first edition. Ximenes 35-376 1974 $175

TROLLOPE, ANTHONY   Can You Forgive Her? London, 1864.
2 vols., 8vo., cloth, first edition. Goodspeed's 578-386 1974 $50

TROLLOPE, ANTHONY   Can You Forgive Her? 1866. 2 vols., illus.,
second edition, leather title labels torn, bookplates, contents very good, full
calf, raised panelled spine gilt. Covent 51-1865 1973 £10

TROLLOPE, ANTHONY   The Claverings. London, 1867. 2 vols., 8vo.,
orig. green cloth, uncut, first edition. Dawsons PM 252-981 1974 £80

TROLLOPE, ANTHONY   An Editor's Tales. London, 1870. 8vo.,
orig. cloth, gilt, first edition. Dawsons PM 252-982 1974 £40

TROLLOPE, ANTHONY   An Eye for an Eye. London, 1879. 2 vols.,
8vo., orig. cloth, first edition. Dawsons PM 252-983 1974 £60

TROLLOPE, ANTHONY   The Golden Lion of Granpere. London, 1872.
8vo., orig. brown cloth, first edition. Dawsons PM 252-984 1974 £44

TROLLOPE, ANTHONY   He Knew He Was Right. London, 1869.
2 vols., 8vo., plates, orig. blind-stamped cloth, first edition. Dawsons PM
252-985 1974 £70

TROLLOPE, ANTHONY   How the "Mastiffs" Went to Iceland. London,
1878. 4to., orig. cloth, plates. Dawsons PM 252-986 1974 £120

TROLLOPE, ANTHONY   How the "Mastiffs" Went to Iceland. 1878.
First edition, demy 4to., presentation copy inscribed by author's son, colour map,
mounted photos, lithographs, very fine, rare, orig. cloth. Broadhurst 24-924
1974 £120

TROLLOPE, ANTHONY   Hunting Sketches. London, 1865. 8vo.,
orig. cloth, half calf, first edition. Dawsons PM 252-987 1974 £30

TROLLOPE, ANTHONY   Is He Popenjoy? London, 1878. 3 vols.,
8vo., orig. brown cloth, first edition. Dawsons PM 252-988 1974 £70

TROLLOPE, ANTHONY   John Caldigate. London, 1879. 3 vols.,
8vo., orig. cloth, first edition. Dawsons PM 252-989 1974 £60

TROLLOPE, ANTHONY   The Last Chronicle of Barset. London, 1867.
8vo., plates, orig. cloth, first edition, first issue. Dawsons PM 252-991
1974 £100

TROLLOPE, ANTHONY   The Last Chronicle of Barset. New York,
1867. 8vo., orig. green cloth, illus., first American edition. Ximenes
35-377 1974 $25

TROLLOPE, ANTHONY   The Last Chronicle of Barset. London, 1867.
8vo., 2 vols., half crimson morocco, gilt, plates, illus., first edition. Hammond
201-341 1974 £48

TROLLOPE, ANTHONY   The Landleaguers. London, 1883. 3 vols.,
8vo., orig. green cloth, first edition. Dawsons PM 252-990 1974 £60

TROLLOPE, ANTHONY   The Life of Cicero. 1880. 2 vols., first
edition, first issue, unusually fine unopened copy. Covent 51-1866 1973 £40

TROLLOPE, ANTHONY   Miss MacKenzie. London, 1865. 2 vols.,
8vo., orig. cloth, first edition, second issue. Dawsons PM 252-992 1974 £100

TROLLOPE, ANTHONY   New Zealand. 1874. Orig. dec. cloth, map.
Covent 55-1474 1974 £35

TROLLOPE, ANTHONY   An Old Man's Love. London & Edinburgh,
1884. 2 vols., 8vo., orig. cloth. Dawsons PM 252-993 1974 £85

TROLLOPE, ANTHONY   An Old Man's Love. Edinburgh, 1884.
2 vols., 8vo., orig. cloth, first edition. Ximenes 35-378 1974 $45

TROLLOPE, ANTHONY   Orley Farm. 1862. 2 vols., plates,
contemporary half green calf gilt, first edition. Howes 186-489 1974 £40

TROLLOPE, ANTHONY   Orley Farm. London, 1862. 2 vols., 8vo.,
cloth, resewn, backs faded, illus. by J. E. Millais, first edition. Goodspeed's
578-385 1974 $75

TROLLOPE, ANTHONY   Orley Farm. London, 1862. 2 vols., 8vo.,
half calf, illus. by J. E. Millais, first issue. Goodspeed's 578-384 1974 $75

TROLLOPE, ANTHONY   Orley Farm. London, 1862. 2 vols., 8vo.,
orig. cloth, first book edition. Ximenes 35-379 1974 $27.50

TROLLOPE, ANTHONY   Phineas Finn. New York, 1868. 8vo., orig.
brown cloth, fine, first American edition. Ximenes 35-380 1974 $75

TROLLOPE, ANTHONY   The Prime Minster. London, 1876. 4 vols.,
8vo., orig. cloth, rubbed, first edition. Dawsons PM 252-995 1974 £120

TROLLOPE, ANTHONY   South Africa. London, 1878. 2 vols., 8vo.,
orig. scarlet cloth, first edition. Dawsons PM 252-996 1974 £130

TROLLOPE, ANTHONY   Travelling Sketches. London, 1866. 8vo.,
orig. red cloth, fine, first edition. Ximenes 35-381 1974 $45

TROLLOPE, ANTHONY   Orley Farm. London, 1862. 2 vols., 8vo.,
orig. cloth, first edition. Dawsons PM 252-994 1974 £85

TROLLOPE, ANTHONY   Travelling Sketches. London, 1866. 8vo.,
orig. red cloth, gilt, first edition. Dawsons PM 252-997 1974 £36

TROLLOPE, ANTHONY   The Vicar of Bullhampton. London, 1870.
8vo., contemporary half calf, plates, first edition. Dawsons PM 252-998
1974 £35

TROLLOPE, ANTHONY   The Way We Live Now. London, 1875.
2 vols., 8vo., orig. cloth, plates, first edition. Dawsons PM 252-999 1974
£85

TROLLOPE, FRANCES   The Barnabys in America. London, 1843.
3 vols., 12mo., contemporary morocco, first edition. Dawsons PM 252-1001
1974 £55

TROLLOPE, FRANCES   Domestic Manners of the Americans. London,
1832. 2 vols., 8vo., plates, orig. cloth, first edition. Dawsons PM 252-1002
1974 £70

TROLLOPE, FRANCES   Domestic Manners of the Americans. New
York, 1949. Biblo & Tannen 213-100 1973 $12.50

TROLLOPE, FRANCES   Life and Adventures of Michael Armstrong, the
Factory Boy. 1840. Old calf, etched plates, foxed, one joint cracked, first
book edition. Allen 216-1691 1974 $50

TROLLOPE, FRANCES   The Vicar of Wrexhill. London, 1837.
3 vols., 8vo., orig. boards, plates, first edition. Dawsons PM 252-1003
1974 £85

TROLLOPE, THOMAS ADOLPHUS   A Summer in Brittany. 1840. 2 vols., fine,
contemporary half calf, plates, labels. Covent 55-1476 1974 £65

TROLLOPE, WILLIAM   The Iliad of Homer. London, 1836. 8vo.,
contemporary diced calf, second edition. Bow Windows 62-948 1974 £5.75

TROLLOPE, THOMAS ADOLPHUS   A Summer in Western France. London,
1841. 2 vols., 8vo., morocco gilt, plates, first edition. Dawsons PM 252-1004
1974 £25

TRONCHIN, THEODORE   De Colica Pictonum. Geneva, 1757. 8vo.,
disbound, first edition. Schuman 37-250 1974 $85

TROTSKY, LEON   The History of the Russian Revolution. 1934.
Near fine. Covent 55-1477 1974 £7.50

TROTSKY, LEON   My Life: The Rise & Fall of a Dictator. 1930.
Very good copy, portrait, first edition. Covent 51-1867 1973 £8.50

TROTTER, B.   A Horseman and the West. Toronto, 1925.
Hood's 104-879 1974 $25

TROTTER, JOHN B.   Memoirs of the Latter Years of Charles James
Fox. 1811. Orig. boards, label, uncut. Howes 186-826 1974 £7.50

TROUSSEAU, ARMAND   Clinque Medicale de l'Motel-Dieu de Paris.
Paris, 1861. 2 vols., 8vo., half morocco, first edition. Schuman 37-251
1974 $95

TROUSSEAU, ARMAND   Clinique Medicale. Paris, 1861(-1862). 8vo.,
2 vols., nineteenth century half calf, rebacked, first edition. Dawsons PM
249-484 1974 £65

TROUSSEAU, ARMAND   Lectures on Clinical Medicine. 1868-1872.
8vo., 5 vols., orig. cloth gilt, first edition in English. Dawsons PM 249-485
1974 £16

TROWBRIDGE, JOHN TOWNSEND   Ironthorpe. Boston, 1855. 12mo.,
orig. cloth, first edition. Ximenes 35-382 1974 $15

TRUBNER, NICOLAS   Trubner's Bibliographical Guide to American
Literature. 1859. Ex-library. Allen 216-208 1974 $15

THE TRUE Principles of the Revolution. London, 1741. 8vo., contemporary black
half morocco. Dawsons PM 251-347 1974 £10

A TRUE Relation of the Treaty and Ratification of the Marriage. N.P., n.d.
4to., modern boards, first edition. Dawsons PM 251-348 1974 £20

TRUEMAN, D.   Cottage Poems. 1848. 12mo., scarce,
contemporary sheep, worn, first edition. Ximenes 35-384 1974 $22.50

TRUESDELL, EDWARD D.   Birth Fractures and Epiphyseal Dislocations.
New York, 1917. Rittenhouse 46-624 1974 $12.50

TRUFFAUT, G.   Les Ennemis des Plantes Cultivees. Paris, 1912.
Roy 8vo., half morocco, plates. Wheldon 129-1672 1974 £5

TRUFFLE Eater. n.d. Orig. pictorial boards, worn, illus. Covent 55-1177 1974 £7.50

TRUITT, CHARLES J. Historic Salisbury, Maryland. Garden City, (c.1932). 12mo., cloth, Bicentennial edition. Saddleback 14-468 1974 $15

TRUMAN, BEN C. Missions of California. Los Angeles, 1903. Pict. wrapper. Jenkins 61-443 1974 $12.50

TRUMBLE, A. Sword & Scimetar. 1886. 4to., plates, illus., new buckram. Allen 213-1830 1973 $25

TRUMBULL, H. CLAY The Knightly Soldier, a Biography of Major Henry Ward Camp. Philadelphia, 1872. Illus., orig. binding. Wilson 63-364 1974 $12.50

TRUMBULL, JOHN McFingal. London, 1776. 8vo., wrappers, first English edition. Ximenes 35-385 1974 $125

TRUMBULL, JOHN McFingal. Hartford, 1782. Orig. paper boards, first complete edition. Ballinger 1-217 1974 $45

TRUMBULL, JOHN M'Fingal. Boston, 1799. 12mo., fine, contemporary green morocco. Ximenes 35-386 1974 $15

TRUMBULL, JOHN M'Fingal. (Augusta), 1813. 12mo., orig. printed boards. Ximenes 35-388 1974 $15

TRUMBULL, JOHN The Progress of Dulness. 1801. 12mo., contemporary quarter sheep, third collected edition. Ximenes 35-389 1974 $27.50

TRUSLER, JOHN Hogarth Moralized. London, 1831. Half contemporary morocco gilt, plates, engravings, complete edition. Smith 194-99 1974 £5

TRUSLER, JOHN The Works of William Hogarth. London, n.d. 4to., 2 vols., green half morocco, gilt, plates. Hammond 201-485 1974 £36

TRY Again: A Farce in Two Acts. London, 1790. 8vo., modern boards, first edition. Dawsons PM 252-1005 1974 £15

TRYON, G. W. Guide to the Study of Helices. Index to the Helices. Philadelphia, 1894-95. 2 vols., 8vo., half calf. Wheldon 131-909 1974 £15

TRYON, G. W. Structural and Systematic Conchology. Philadelphia, 1882-84. 8vo., orig. cloth, plates. Wheldon 130-837 1974 £30

TRYON, G. W. Structural and Systematic Conchology. Philadelphia, 1882-84. 3 vols. in 1, 8vo., orig. cloth, plates, map. Wheldon 128-859 1973 £30

TSCHIRCH, A. Anatomischer Atlas. Leipzig, 1900. 8vo., orig. half morocco. Wheldon 129-1697 1974 £15

TUBEUF, K. VON Diseases of Plants. 1897. Roy 8vo., cloth. Wheldon 129-1363 1974 £7.50

TUBEUF, K. VON Monographie der Mistel. Muncih, 1923. Imp. 8vo., cloth, plates, maps, scarce. Wheldon 131-1209 1974 £10

TUCK, RUTH Not With the Fist. Narcourt, Brace, 1946. Austin 62-644 1974 $12.50

TUCKER, A. G. C. Ornithologia Danmoniensis. 1809. 4to., orig. wrappers, plates, rare. Wheldon 131-714 1974 £30

TUCKER, A. G. C. Ornithologia Danmoniensis. 1809. 4to., orig. wrappers, plates. Wheldon 129-538 1974 £30

TUCKER, ELIZABETH S. A Cup of Tea. New York, 1892. Oblong 4to., cloth spine, glazed pict. boards, 1st ed., spine ends and cover edges worn. Frohnsdorff 16-295 1974 $35

TUCKER, EMMA CURTISS The Later Version of the Wycliffite Epistle to the Romans, Compared with the Latin Original. 1914. Ex-library, sturdy library binding. Austin 61-987 1974 $27.50

TUCKER, GEORGE "Fashion." 1858. 8vo., orig. wrappers, scarce, first edition. Ximenes 35-390 1974 $75

TUCKER, JAMES The Reformed Roman or Oriental Baths. Dublin, 1860. 8vo., boards, first edition. Hammond 201-596 1974 £6

TUCKER, JOSIAH A Brief Essay on the Advantages and Disadvantages which Respectively Attend France and Great Britain. London, 1787. 8vo., marbled wrappers. Hammond 201-271 1974 £14

TUCKER, JOSIAH A Brief Essay on the Advantages & Disadvantages . . . France and Great Britain, With Regard to Trade. London, 1787. 8vo., modern boards. Dawsons PM 247-293 1974 £15

TUCKER, JOSIAH An Essay on the Advantages and Disadvantages Which Respectively Attend France and Great Britain. Glasgow, 1756. 12mo., contemporary calf, gilt, fourth edition. Hammond 201-272 1974 £12.50

TUCKER, JOSIAH Four Letters on Important National Subjects. Glocester, 1783. 8vo., modern boards, first edition. Dawsons PM 247-291 1974 £40

TUCKER, JOSIAH Four Tracts. Glocester, 1774. 8vo., old half calf, first edition. Dawsons PM 247-289 1974 £65

TUCKER, JOSIAH Reflections on the Expediency of a Law. London, 1751. 8vo., modern boards, first edition. Dawsons PM 251-519 1974 £10

TUCKER, JOSIAH Reflections on the Present Matters in Dispute Between Great Britain and Ireland. London, 1785. 8vo., modern boards. Dawsons PM 247-292 1974 £15

TUCKER, JOSIAH A Series of Answers to Certain Popular Objections. Gloucester, 1776. 8vo., wrappers, first edition. Dawsons PM 247-290 1974 £45

TUCKER, MA (Mrs.) Life of Mark M. Pomeroy. Carleton, 1868. 230p. Austin 54-1016 1973 $15

TUCKER, NATHANIEL BEVERLEY The Partisan Leader. N.P., 1856. 2 vols., 12mo., three quarter morocco, rare first edition. Ximenes 35-391 1974 $450

TUCKER, ST. GEORGE The Devoted Bride. Philadelphia, (1864). Cloth. Hayman 57-228 1974 $25

TUCKER, ST. GEORGE A Dissertation on Slavery. Philadelphia, 1796. 8vo., contemporary wrappers, uncut, first edition. Dawsons PM 247-294 1974 £150

TUCKER, ST. GEORGE Hansford. Richmond, 1857. 8vo., orig. cloth, first edition. Ximenes 35-392 1974 $20

TUCKER, SOPHIE Some of These Days. N.P., 1945. Author's sgd. pres. Biblo & Tannen 210-959 1973 $7.50

TUCKER, SOPHIE Some of These Days. 1945. Austin 51-978 1973 $6

TUCKER, SOPHIE Some of These Days. Garden City, 1945. Signed, first edition. Ballinger 1-321 1974 $15

TUCKER, T. G. Life in the Roman World of Nero and St. Paul. New York, 1924. Biblo & Tannen 214-666 1974 $12.50

TUCKER, W. B. Laurentian Tales. Montreal, 1922. Inscribed, illus. by photos. Hood's 102-671 1974 $7.50

TUCKERMAN, CHARLES K. International Obligations. Athens, 1868. 8vo., orig. wrappers, first edition. Ximenes 35-393 1974 $15

TUCKEY, JAMES KINGSTON Narrative of an Expedition to Explore the River Zaire. London, 1818. 4to., contemporary straight grained morocco, gilt, map, first edition. Bow Windows 62-949 1974 £100

TUCKEY, JAMES KINGSTON   Narrative of an Expedition to Explore the River Zaire...; to which is added, The Journal of Prof. Smith, and an Appendix.   1818. 4to., newly rebound in half calf antique style, plates, good copy, scarce.   Wheldon 128-242 1973 £50

TUDOR, WILLIAM   Gebel Teir.   Boston, 1829.   12mo., orig. boards, paper label, first edition.   Ximenes 35-394 1974 $50

TUDOR-CRAIG, ALGERNON   Armorial Porcelain of the 18th Century.   1925. Plates in colour, illus., med. 4to., top edges gilt, others uncut, scarce, orig. cloth, fine, limited to 1000 copies.   Broadhurst 24-213 1974 £45

TUDOR-CRAIG, ALGERNON   Armorial Porcelain of the Eighteen Century. 1925.   4to., orig. cloth, uncut, scarce, limited edition.   Broadhurst 23-220 1974 £45

TUER, ANDREW WHITE   Bartolozzi and His Works.   New York, (1881-82).   2 vols., 4to., orig. vellum gilt, illus., fine, plates, first edition. Dawsons PM 10-25 1974 £30

TUER, ANDREW WHITE   Bartolozzi and His Work.   1881.   2 vols., demy 4to., full parchment, engravings, top edges gilt, others uncut, fine.   Broadhurst 24-214 1974 £21

TUER, ANDREW WHITE   History of the Horn-Book.   London, 1896. 2 vols., 4to., illus., orig. vellum gilt, scarce, first edition.   Dawsons PM 10-611 1974 £225

TUER, ANDREW WHITE   Old London Street Cries and the Cries of To-Day With Heaps of Quaint Cuts.   London, 1885.   16mo., hand colored frontis., illus. Frohnsdorff 16-246 1974 $22.50

TUER, ANDREW WHITE   Pages and Pictures from Forgotten Childrens Books.   London, 1898-99.   Orig. cloth gilt, uncut, illus., first edition. Dawsons PM 10-612 1974 £10

TUER, ANDREW WHITE   Pages and Pictures from Forgotten Children's Books.   1898-99.   Crown 8vo., inner hinges sprung, good copy.   George's 610-767 1973 £10.50

TUER, ANDREW WHITE   Pages and Pictures from Forgotten Children's Books. 1898-89.   Crown 8vo., orig. cloth gilt, scarce.   Howes 185-859 1974 £15

TUER, ANDREW WHITE   Stories from Old-Fashioned Children's Books. 1899-1900.   Crown 8vo., orig. cloth, gilt, trifle rubbed.   George's 610-769 1973 £10.50

TUKE, DANIEL HACK   Geist und Korper.   Jena, 1888.   8vo., contemporary German boards.   Dawsons PM 249-486 1974 £6

TUKE, JOHN   General View of the Agriculture of the North Riding of Yorkshire.   London, 1800.   8vo., orig. wrappers, illus.   Hammond 201-54 1974 £30

TUKE, SAMUEL   The Adventures of Five Hours.   London, 1704. Small 4to., disbound, fourth edition.   Ximenes 35-395 1974 $20

TUKE, SAMUEL   Description of the Retreat . . . for Insane Persons of the Society of Friends.   York, 1813.   8vo., half morocco, first edition.   Schumann 35-472 1974 $585

TULASNE, L. R.   Selecta Fungorum Carpologia of the Brothers. Oxford, 1931.   Imperial 4to., illus., 3 vols.   Bow Windows 64-278 1974 £30

TULASNE, L. R.   Selecta Fungorum Carpologia.   Oxford, 1931. 4to., cloth, 3 vols., plates.   Wheldon 129-1364 1974 £25

TULASNE, L. R.   Selecta Fungorum Carpologia.   Oxford, 1931. 4to., 3 vols., calf, plates.   Wheldon 130-1355 1974 £30

TULASNE, L. R.   Selecta Fungorum Carpologia.   Oxford, 1931. 3 vols., 4to., cloth, plates.   Wheldon 131-1475 1974 £25

TULL, JETHRO   The Horse Hoeing Husbandry.   Dublin, 1733. 8vo., contemporary calf, plates.   Bow Windows 64-279 1974 £65

TULL, JETHRO   The Horse-Hoing Husbandry.   London, 1740. Folio, contemporary calf, label, fine, first & second editions.   Dawsons PM 247-295 1974 £140

TULL, JETHRO   Horse Hoeing Husbandry.   1751.   8vo., contemporary calf, plates.   Bow Windows 64-280 1974 £60

TULL, JETHRO   The New Horse-Hoing Husbandry.   London, 1733.   Small folio, contemporary calf, morocco label, fine, plates, first enlarged edition.   Dawsons PM 250-79 1974 £350

TULLBERG, T.   Zoologiska Studien.   Uppsala, 1907.   4to., plates.   Wheldon 131-463 1974 £5

TUNK, OLIVER P.   An Awful Alphabet.   New York, 1898.   8vo., full page illus., covers soiled, hinges & binding weak, shaken.   Current BW9-104 1974 $7.50

TUNSTALL, M.   Ornithologia Britannica.   1771.   Folio, contemporary marbled paper wrappers.   Wheldon 129-539 1974 £20

TUNSTALL, M.   Ornithologia Britannica.   1771.   Folio, contemporary marbled paper wrappers, very rare.   Wheldon 131-715 1974 £20

TUNSTALL, WILLIAM   Ballads.   London, 1716.   8vo., modern boards, first edition.   Dawsons PM 252-1006 1974 £40

TUPPER, CHARLES   Recollections of Sixty Years In Canada. London, Toronto, 1914.   Frontispiece, plates, inscribed.   Hood's 103-241 1974 $35

TUPPER, F. B.   The History of Guernsey and Its Bailiwick. Guernsey, 1854.   8vo., morocco gilt.   Quaritch 939-328 1974 £20

TURBERVILLE, A. S.   Johnson's England: An Accout of the Life and Manners of His Age.   Oxford, 1933.   2 vols., illus., demy 8vo., orig. cloth, fine.   Broadhurst 24-1340 1974 £6

TURBERVILLE, T. C.   Worcestershire in Nineteenth Century.   1852. 8vo., orig. cloth, covers dull.   Bow Windows 66-709 1974 £7.50

TURGENEV, IVAN   Liza.   1869.   2 vols., orig. patterned cloth. Covent 55-1478 1974 £35

TURGENEV, IVAN   Liza.   London, 1869.   2 vols., 8vo., orig. blind stamped cloth, presentation inscription, first English edition.   Dawsons PM 252-1007 1974 £75

TURMEL, JOSEPH   Histoire des Dogmes.   Paris, 1931-36.   5 vols., roy. 8vo., orig. wrappers.   Howes 185-1732 1974 £18

TURNBELL, MARTIN   Poetry and Crisis.   1938.   Boards, fine, faded d.w., first edition.   Covent 51-1870 1973 £8.50

TURNBULL, GEORGE   A Treatise on Ancient Painting.   1740.   Roy. folio, plates, contemporary mottled calf, rebacked.   Quaritch 940-260 1974 £30

TURNBULL, JOHN   A Voyage Round the World, In the Years 1800-04.   London, 1805.   3 vols., small 8vo., old half calf, leather labels, first edition.   Traylen 79-441 1973 £90

TURNBULL, JOHN D.   Rudolph.   Boston, 1807.   12mo., first edition. Ximenes 35-396 1974 $90

TURNBULL, ROBERT J.   A Visit to the Philadelphia Prison.   London, 1797.   8vo., orig. bindings, sewed.   Butterfield 8-559 1974 $20

TURNBULL, W. P.   Birds of East Lothian.   Philadelphia, (1863). Roy 8vo., contemporary half morocco.   Wheldon 129-540 1974 £25

TURNBULL, W. P.   The Birds of East Lothian and a Portion of the Adjoining Counties.   Glasgow, 1867.   4to., orig. half green roan, lithographs, hand-coloured frontispiece, inserted presentation slip, limited large paper edition.   Wheldon 128-585 1973 £50

TURNBULL, W. P.   The Birds of East Lothian. Glasgow, 1867. Roy 8vo., orig. half green roan, presentation copy, second edition. Wheldon 130-642 1974 £30

TURNBULL, W. P.   The Birds of East Lothian and a Portion of the Adjoining Counties. Glasgow, 1867. Roy. 8vo., orig. half roan, second edition. Wheldon 131-716 1974 £25

TURNELL, MARTIN   Poetry and Crisis. 1938. Boards, dust wrapper, English first edition. Covent 56-857 1974 £10

TURNER, ARLIN   Hawthorne As Editor. Louisiana State Univ., 1941. 290p., orig. ed. Austin 54-1017 1973 $17.50

TURNER, CUTHBERT HAMILTON   The Oldest Manuscript of the Vulgate Gospels. 1931. Plates. Howes 185-1733 1974 £7.50

TURNER, D.   The Botanist's Guide Through England and Wales. 1805. 2 vols., 8vo., orig. boards, uncut, rare. Wheldon 131-1247 1974 £25

TURNER, D.   The Botanist's Guide. 1805. Crown 8vo., orig. boards, 2 vols., uncut. Wheldon 129-1023 1974 £25

TURNER, D. K.   History of the Neshaminy Presbyterian Church. Philadelphia, 1876. 8vo., orig. bindings, plates. Butterfield 8-518 1974 $20

TURNER, DANIEL   A Short History of the Westminster Forum. London, 1781. 2 vols., 8vo., contemporary calf, first edition. Ximenes 35-397 1974 $80

TURNER, DAWSON   Account of a Tour in Normandy. 1820. 2 vols. in 1, 8vo., contemporary half calf, neatly rebacked, etched plates, illus., armorial bookplate of Sir Frederick Pollock. Bow Windows 66-710 1974 £62.50

TURNER, DAWSON   Muscologia Hibernica Spicilegium. Yarmouth, 1804. Crown 8vo., contemporary half calf, plates, very scarce. Wheldon 131-1476 1974 £35

TURNER, EDWARD   Elements of Chemistry. Philadelphia, 1840. Thick 8vo., contemporary sprinkled calf, gilt. Zeitlin 235-300 1974 $25

TURNER, EDWARD RAYMOND   Ireland and England in the Past and at the Present. New York, 1919. 8vo., cloth boards. Emerald 50-945 1974 £8

TURNER, G.   An Inquiry into the Revenue, Credit and Commerce of France. London, 1742. 8vo., modern boards, first edition. Dawsons PM 247-296 1974 £40

TURNER, J. H.   Yorkshire Notes and Queries. 1888-94. 8vo., half morocco, illus. Broadhurst 23-1568 1974 £50

TURNER, J. KELLY   History of Edgecombe County, North Carolina. Raleigh, 1920. 8vo., cloth. Saddleback 14-607 1974 $25

TURNER, JAMES   Pallas Armata. London, 1683. Folio, contemporary calf, gilt, first edition. Dawsons PM 251-406 1974 £75

TURNER, JOSEPH MALLORD WILLIAM   The Harbours of England. (1856). Orig. red cloth gilt, plates. Quaritch 939=268 1974 £120

TURNER, JOSEPH MALLORD WILLIAM   Liber Fluviorum. 1853. Imp. 8vo., plates, contemporary green morocco, gilt, large paper. Quaritch 940-262 1974 £65

TURNER, JOSEPH MALLORD WILLIAM   Notes by Mr. Ruskin on His Collection of Drawings. 1878. 4to., quarter roan, plates, map, minor stains, cloth sides, uncut. Bow Windows 66-597 1974 £65

TURNER, JOSEPH MALLORD WILLIAM   River Scenery. 1827. 4to., clean copy, contemporary half calf, engravings. Quaritch 940-263 1974 £150

TURNER, JOSEPH MALLORD WILLIAM   The Turner Gallery. 1875. Large folio, contemporary half crimson morocco, gilt, plates. Hammond 201-500 1974 £28.50

TURNER, JOSEPH MALLORD WILLIAM   A Complete Inventory of the Drawings of the Turner Bequest. 1909. Orig. cloth, worn. Marsden 37-487 1974 £5

TURNER, JOSEPH MALLORD WILLIAM   Picturesque Views on the Southern Coast of England. 1826. 2 vols. in 1, 4to., contemporary citron morocco, plates, gilt. Quaritch 939-267 1974 £175

TURNER, JOSEPH MALLORD WILLIAM   The Rivers of France. 1837. Roy. 8vo., plates, contemporary cloth, gilt. Smith 193-687 1973 £9

TURNER, MARGARET   The Gentle Shepherd. 1790. 8vo., early speckled calf, first edition. Quaritch 936-203 1974 £20

TURNER, S.   The History of the Anglo-Saxons from the Earliest Period to the Norman Conquest. 1836. 3 vols., 8vo., cloth bound, folding map, sixth edition. Bow Windows 66-711 1974 £18

TURNER, THOMAS   A Practical Treatise on the Arterial System. London, 1825. 8vo., orig. boards, unopened, first edition. Schumann 35-473 1974 $85

TURNER, WILLIAM   The Ceramics of Swansea and Natgarw. 1897. Crown 4to., plates, some in colour, fine, orig. cloth. Broadhurst 24-215 1974 £30

TURNER, WILLIAM   The Ceramics of Swansea and Nantgarw. 1897. Small 4to., illus., cloth. Quaritch 939-697 1974 £28

TURNER, WILLIAM   The Ceramics of Swansea and Nantgarw. 1897. Crown 4to., orig. cloth. Broadhurst 23-221 1974 £35

TURNER, WILLIAM   Transfer Printing on Enamels, Porcelain and Pottery. London and New York, 1907. Dark green cloth, plates. Dawson's 424-241 1974 $40

TURNER, WILLIAM d. 1568   Libellus de re Herbaria Novus. 1877. 4to., orig. boards. Wheldon 129-1024 1974 £15

TURNER, WILLIAM d. 1568   The Names of Herbes. 1881. 8vo., wrappers, scarce. Wheldon 130-1627 1974 £5

TURNER, WILLIAM 1761-1859   An Address to Parents. 1792. 12mo., orig. cloth. Bow Windows 64-740 1974 £15

TURNER, WILLIAM 1832-   Report on the Human Skeletons. Edinburgh, 1884-86. Large 8vo., 2 parts in 1 vol., plates, orig. wrappers, buckram. Bow Windows 64-281 1974 £6.75

TURNER-TURNER, J.   The Giant Fish of Florida. 1902. Crown 4to., binding slightly faded, orig. cloth. Broadhurst 24-1176 1974 £10

TURNEY, CATHERINE   My Dear Children. Random, 1940. 193p., illus. Austin 51-979 1973 $7.50

TURNLEY, JOSEPH   Popery in Power. 1850. 394 pages, illus. Austin 57-673 1974 $15

TURNOR, HATTON   Astra Castra. London, 1865. 4to., quarter calf, gilt, plates, illus. Hammond 201-981 1974 £48

TURPIN, J. P. P.   Observations sur la Famille des Cactees. Paris, 1830. 8vo., wrappers, plates. Wheldon 131-1705 1974 £10

TURRETTINO, F.   Institutio Theologia Elencticae. 1696. 4 vols., contemporary vellum, foxing. Smith 194-192 1974 £25

TURSELIN, HORACE   De Vita Francisci Xaverii, Libri Sex. 1597. Small 8vo., old vellum, second edition. Howes 185-1175 1974 £8.50

TURTON, M. CONWAY   Cassiar. Toronto, 1934. Hood's 103-826 1974 $20

TURTON, WILLIAM   British Fauna. Swansea, 1807. 12mo., modern boards, uncut, rare. Wheldon 131-396 1974 £15

TURTON, WILLIAM   Conchylia Insularum Britannicarum. Leicester, n.d. 4to., new quarter calf, plates. Wheldon 130-838 1974 £50

TURTON, WILLIAM   A Manual of the Land and Fresh-Water Shells of the British Islands. 1831. Crown 8vo., orig. cloth, worn, plates. Wheldon 130-839 1974 £5

TURTON, WILLIAM   A Manual of the Land and Fresh-Water Shells of the British Islands. 1840. Post 8vo., cloth, coloured plates, new edition. Wheldon 128-862 1973 £7.50

TURTON, WILLIAM   A Manual of the Land and Fresh-Water Shells of the British Islands. 1831. Crown 8vo., orig. cloth, hand-coloured plates. Wheldon 128-861 1973 £5

TURTON, WILLIAM   A Manual of the Land and Fresh-Water Shells of the British Islands. 1840. 8vo., cloth, plates, scarce. Wheldon 131-910 1974 £7.50

TURTON, WILLIAM   Manual of the Land and Fresh Water Shells of the British Islands. 1857. Crown 8vo., cloth. Wheldon 129-754 1974 £5

TURZAK, C.   Benjamin Franklin. (1935). 4to., orig. cloth, illus., signed by artist, limited, first edition. Bow Windows 66-713 1974 £12.50

TUSSER, THOMAS   Five Hundred Points of Good Husbandry. 1663. Printed in black letter, 8vo., old calf, very good copy, scarce. Broadhurst 24-1177 1974 £50

TUSSER, THOMAS   Five Hundred Points of Good Husbandry. 1812. Quarter calf, boards. Broadhurst 23-1192 1974 £20

TUSSER, THOMAS   Five Hundred Points of Good Husbandry. London, 1931. 4to., orig. reversed calf, gilt. Hammond 201-51 1974 £38

TUSSER, THOMAS   Tusser Redivivus. 1710. 8vo., contemporary calf, scarce. Broadhurst 23-1191 1974 £55

TUTHILL, LOUISA CAROLINA   The Belle, the Blue and the Bigot. Providence, 1844. 12mo., orig. cloth, worn, first edition. Ximenes 35-398 1974 $20

TUTT, J. W.   British Noctuae and Their Varieties. 1891-92. 4 vols., 8vo., cloth, scarce. Wheldon 128-820 1973 £5

TUTT, J. W.   British Noctuae and Their Varieties. 1891-92. 4 vols., 8vo., cloth, scarce. Wheldon 131-871 1974 £10

TUTT, J. W.   A Natural History of the British Lepidoptera. 1899-1914. 8vo., 9 vols., orig. cloth. Wheldon 129-691 1974 £35

TUTTLE, CHARLES RICHARD   Our North Land. Toronto, 1885. Rebound, maps, engravings. Hood's 102-835 1974 $25

TUTTLE, CHARLES RICHARD   Short History of the Dominion of Canada from 1500-1878. Boston, 1878. Engravings. Hood's 104-666 1974 $17.50

TUTTLE, SAMUEL L.   A History of the Presbyterian Church. New York, 1855. 8vo., orig. bindings, illus. Butterfield 8-378 1974 $10

TWAIN, MARK, PSEUD.
Please turn to
CLEMENS, SAMUEL LANGHORNE

TWEED, JOHN   Popular Observations on Regimen and Diet. Chelmsford, (1820). 8vo., orig. boards, uncut. Hill 126-279 1974 £12.50

TWEEDDALE, ARTHUR   Ornithological Works. 1881. 4to., half morocco, plates, rare. Wheldon 130-83 1974 £220

TWELVE One Act Plays. Longman's, 1926. 326p. Austin 51-286 1973 $10

29 NON-ROYALTY Mystery Plays. Greenberg, 1945. 318p. Austin 51-456 1973 $8.50

TWENTY-ONE Welsh Gipsy Folk-Tales. 1933. Crown 4to., sheepskin, uncut, gilt, limited edition. Broadhurst 23-1048 1974 £50

TWENTY-TWO Strange Stories. Glasgow, n.d. (ca. 1945). 1st ed. Biblo & Tannen 210-606 1973 $12.50

TWENTY-TWO Years' Work of the Hampton Normal and Agricultural Institue. Hampton, 1893. Ex-library, maps, orig. binding. Butterfield 10-118 1974 $25

TWICE A YEAR. New York, 1941. 8vo., orig. cloth, dust wrapper, torn, first edition. Rota 189-42 1974 £5

TWICHELL, JOSEPH W.   Some Old Puritan Love-Letters: John and Margaret Winthrop, 1618-1638. New York, 1893. Top edge gilt. Jenkins 61-1547 1974 $10

TWINING, ELIZABETH   Illustrations of the Natural Orders of Plants. London, 1868. Tall 8vo., color plates, quarter green morocco. Gregory 44-300 1974 $135

TWINING, THOMAS   Travels in America. New York, 1894. 16mo. Biblo & Tannen 213-101 1973 $10

TWISDEN, JOHN RAMSKILL   The Family of Twysden. 1939. Thick 8vo., plates, stained. Howes 186-1656 1974 £5

TWISS, TRAVERS   The Oregon Question Examined. London, 1846. 8vo., first edition. Traylen 79-499 1973 £60

TWISSE, WILLIAM   A Treatise of Mr. Cottons. London, 1646. Small 4to., contemporary calf, first edition. Ximenes 35-399 1974 $125

TWO Papers On the Subject of Taxing the British Colonies in America. London, 1767. 8vo., modern half cloth, scarce, first edition. Ximenes 35-268 1974 $150

TWO Years of Harriman, Tennessee. New York, (1892). 12mo., cloth. Saddleback 14-697 1974 $15

TWOPENY, WILLIAM   English Metal Work. 1904. 4to., buckram gilt, English first edition. Covent 56-1662 1974 £15

TWYSDEN, ROGER   Historiae Anglicanae Scriptores X. (1652). Half calf. Allen 213-1835 1973 $15

TYAS, ROBERT   Flowers and Heraldry. London, 1851. 12mo., color plates, orig. cloth. Gregory 44-301 1974 $40

TYAS, ROBERT   The Sentiment of Flowers. London, 1836. 12mo., orig. green morocco, gilt, plates. Hammond 201-687 1974 £10

TYERMAN, L.   The Life and Times of John Wesley. 1890. 3 vols., frontispieces. Howes 185-1771 1974 £9.50

TYERMAN, L.   The Life of George Whitefield. 1876-77. 2 vols., thick 8vo., portraits, scarce. Howes 185-1778 1974 £8.50

TYLER, LYON GARDINER   The Cradle of the Republic: Jamestown and James River. Richmond, 1906. Jenkins 61-2542 1974 $10

TYLER, MOSES COIT   A History of American Literature during the Colonial Period. New York, 1898. 2 vols. in 1. Biblo & Tannen 210-927 1973 $8

TYLER, MOSES COIT   A History of American Literature. New York, 1878. 2 vols., 8vo., orig. brick cloth, first edition. Ximenes 35-400 1974 $25

TYLER, MOSES COIT   A History of American Literature. New York, 1879. 2 vols., orig. binding. Butterfield 10-515 1974 $25

TYLER, MOSES COIT   Literary History of the American Revolution, 1763-83. 1898. 2 vols. Allen 216-1696 1974 $10

TYLER, PARKER   Classics of the Foreign Film. Citadel, 1962. Austin 51-980 1973 $12.50

TYLER, PARKER   Magic and Myth of the Movies. Holt, 1947. Austin 51-982 1973 $7.50

TYNAN, KATHERINE
Please turn to
HINKSON, KATHERINE TYNAN

TYNAN, PATRICK   The Irish National Invincibles and Their Times.
New York, 1894. 8vo., illus., cloth boards. Emerald 50-951 1974 £7.50

TYNDALL, JOHN   Contributions to Molecular Physics in the
Domain of Radiant Heat. 1872. 8vo., orig. cloth, plates, some spotting,
bookplate, first edition. Bow Windows 66-716 1974 £14.50

TYNDALL, JOHN   Contributions to Molecular Physics in the Domain
of Radiant Heat. London, 1872. 8vo., contemporary maroon cloth, gilt, first
edition. Dawsons PM 245-729 1974 £20

TYNDALL, JOHN   Essays On the Floating-Matter of the Air in
Relation to Putrefaction and Infection. London, 1881. 8vo., orig. red cloth,
gilt, first edition. Gilhofer 61-63 1974 sFr. 350

TYNDALL, JOHN   The Glaciers of the Alps. 1896. 8vo.,
cloth, frontispiece. Wheldon 131-1086 1974 £5

TYNDALL, JOHN   Hours of Exercise in the Alps. 1871. Demy
8vo., plates, orig. cloth, fine. Broadhurst 24-1690 1974 £12

TYNDALL, JOHN   Mountaineering in 1861. 1862. Orig. cloth,
plates. Smith 193-417 1973 £9.50

TYNDALL, JOHN   Notes on a Course of Nine Lectures on Light.
London, 1870. Small 8vo., cloth, gilt, first edition. Hammond 201-983 1974
£6.50

TYNDALL, JOHN   Sound. London, 1867. 8vo., orig. blue cloth,
gilt, illus., first edition. Dawsons PM 245-728 1974 £7

TYNDALL, JOHN   Sound. 1869. 8vo., contemporary morocco,
portrait, slight foxing, presentation label, second edition. Bow Windows 66-719
1974 £6

TYPOTIUS, JACOBUS   Symbola Divina & Humana Pontificum Imperatorum
Regum. Frankfurt, 1642. 3 parts in 1 vol., folio, old calf, worn, 18th century
rebacking, plates. Quaritch 940-265 1974 £60

TYRELL, G. N. M.   Science and Psychical Phenomena. New York,
1938. Biblo & Tannen 210-987 1973 $12.50

TYRRELL, JOSEPH BURR   The Gold of the Klondike. 1912. Card cover,
plates. Hood's 102-80 1974 $10

TYRRELL, R. V.   The Correspondence of M. Tullius Cicero. 1904-
1933. 8vo., 6 vols., orig. cloth. Broadhurst 23-513 1974 £10

TYRWHITT, R. ST. JOHN   A Handbook of Pictorial Art. 1875. Illus.,
rubbed, second edition. Covent 55-129 1974 £21

TYSON, EDWARD   Orang-Outang, Sive Homo Silvestris.
London, 1699. 4to., plates, contemporary mottled calf, bookplate, first edition.
Dawsons PM 250-80 1974 £2150

TYSON, EDWARD   Orang-Outang, Sive Homo Sylvestris. London,
1699. 4to., modern quarter calf, first edition. Dawsons PM 249-487 1974
£1,250

TYSON, PHILIP T.   Information in Relation to the Geology and
Topography of California. Washington, 1850. Folding maps & plates, scarce.
Jenkins 61-444 1974 $18.50

TYSSOT DE PATOT, SIMON   Voyages et Avantures de Jacques Masse.
Bourdeaux, 1710. 12mo., contemporary calf, first edition. Ximenes 35-407
1974 $70

TYTLER, ALEXANDER FRASER   Essay on the Principles of Translation. London,
1791. 8vo., contemporary calf, first edition. Ximenes 35-408 1974 $60

TYTLER, PATRICK FRASER   History of Scotland. Edinburgh, 1841-50.
10 vols., 8vo., cloth, gilt. Quaritch 939-678 1974 £12.50

TYTLER, PATRICK FRASER   Life of Sir Walter Raleigh. Edinburgh, 1833.
Thick 12mo., full contemporary calf gilt, illus., second edition. Howes
186-1151 1974 £7.50

TZARA, TRISTAN   Original Holograph Poem. 1943. Single sheet,
mounted, signed, 11 lines, English first edition. Covent 56-1221 1974 £125

U

UBALDINI, PETRUCCIO   Le Vite Delle Donne Illustri. Londra, 1591. Small 4to., mottled calf, worn. Thomas 28-207 1972 £25

UBALDINI, PETRUCCIO   Le Vite Delle Donne Illustri. Londra, 1591. Lacks second title and leaf of index, inner margin of title little worn, else good, small 4to., mottled calf, bit worn but sound. Thomas 32-141 1974 £25

UBERTINUS DE CASALI   Arbor Vitae Crucifixae Jesu. Venice, 1485. Small folio, 17th century calf, gilt, worn. Thomas 30-146 1973 £75

UDO, ARCHIBISHOP OF MAGDEBURG   Hystoria Horrenda Terribilisque Nimis. Basel, c. 1472. 4to., boards, first separate edition, fine, large copy. Schumann 499-115 1974 sFr 7,500

UELAND, ANDREAS   Recollections of an Immigrant. 1929. 262 pages. Austin 57-674 1974 $10

UEXKULL, J. VON   Theoretical Biology. 1926. 8vo., cloth. Wheldon 129-109 1974 £7.50

UHDE, WILHELM   The Impressionists. Vienna, 1937. Folio, plates, lst ed. Biblo & Tannen 214-539 1974 $15

UHLENBECK, C. C.   A New Series of Blackfoot Texts from the Southern Peigans Blackfoot Reservation, Teton Co., Montana. Amsterdam, 1912. Paper cover. Hood's 102-479 1974 $40

ULANOV, BARRY   The Incredible Crosby. McGraw, Hill, 1948. Austin 51-984 1973 $8.50

ULLYETT, H.   Rambles of a Naturalist Round Folkestone. Folkestone, 1880. Post 8vo., orig. cloth. Wheldon 130-319 1974 £5

ULVESTAD, MARTIN   Norge I Amerika. Minneapolis, 1901. 624p. Austin 62-649 1974 $37.50

UNAMUNO, P. L. M.   Enumeracion y Distribucion Geographica de las Esferopsidales. Madrid, 1933. Roy 8vo., sewed. Wheldon 130-1357 1974 £5

UNAMUNO, P. L. M.   Enumeracion y Distribucion Geografica de los Ascomicetos. Madrid, 1941. Roy 8vo., orig. wrappers. Wheldon 130-1358 1974 £5

UNCANNY Tales. London, 1916. 12mo., lst ed. Biblo & Tannen 210-551 1973 $17.50

UNCLE Henry. New York, 1922. lst ed. Biblo & Tannen 210-716 1973 $7.50

UNCLE John's Story of Bob, the Squirrel. Philadelphia, 1849. 12mo., plates, orig. quarter cloth, pictorial boards. Ximenes 33-425 1974 $30

UNDERHILL, D. C.   Underhill's New Table-Book: or, Tables of Arithmetic Made Easier. New York, 1846. 24mo., wrapper. Butterfield 10-68 1974 $7.50

UNDERHILL, JOHN G.   Spanish Literature In the England of the Tudors. New York, 1899. 8vo., orig. cloth gilt. Dawsons PM 10-616 1974 £6

UNDERHILL, REUBEN L.   From Cowhides to Golden Fleece. Stanford, 1939. Jenkins 61-445 1974 $20

UNDERWOOD, MICHAEL   A Treatise on the Diseases of Children. London, 1784. Small 8vo., half calf, gilt, first edition. Dawsons PM 249-488 1974 £350

UNGER, F.   Iconographia Plantarum Fossilium. Vienna, 1853. Folio, cloth, coloured plates. Wheldon 128-1062 1973 £12

UNGNAD, ARTHUR   Selected Babylonian Business and Legal Documents of the Hammurabi Period. Leiden, 1907. Biblo & Tannen 213-938 1973 $12.50

THE UNION: or Select Scots and English Poems. Edinburgh, 1753. 8vo., contemporary sprinkled calf, label, first edition, first issue. Dawsons PM 252-1008 1974 £52

UNION LEAGUE OF PHILADELPHIA   Chronicles of . . . 1862-1902. Philadelphia, 1902. Illus., hinges cracked internally, orig. binding. Wilson 63-255 1974 $12.75

THE UNITED EMPIRE LOYALISTS' ASSOCIATION   Annual Transactions, 1898-1926. 2 vols., leather. Hood's 102-854 1974 $225

UNITED KINGDOM FOREIGN CAGE-BIRD SOCIETY   Reports, a Series From Sept. 1890 to May 1895. (1893)-95. 1 vol., 8vo., cloth. Wheldon 131-717 1974 £5

UNITED STATES - BUREAU OF THE CENSUS   Transportation By Water, 1906. Washington, 1908. Hood's 102-784 1974 $17.50

UNITED STATES - GEOLOGICAL SURVEY   The San Francisco Earthquake and Fire . . . 1906 . . . Their Effects on Structures and Structural Materials. Washington, 1907. Plates, wrapper, front loose. Butterfield 10-481 1974 $10

UNITED STATES - SECREATARY OF WAR   Report of . . . Showing the Contracts Made Under the Authority of That Dept. During the Year 1848. (Washington), (1849). Disbound. Wilson 63-34 1974 $10

UNITED STATES - SENATE   Hearings Before the Committee on Public Lands and Surveys United States Senate Pursuant to . . . Resolutions Providing for an Investigation. Washington, 1924. 3 vols., finely bound, grained blue cloth, black morocco, marbled edges. Butterfield 10-337 1974 $65

UNITED STATES - SENATE   Preliminary Report on the Inland Waterways Commission. Washington, 1908. Large folding maps, three quarter leather. Hood's 102-785 1974 $10

THE UNITED States Almanac. Philadelphia, 1828. Wrapper, folded chart. Butterfield 10-516 1974 $50

THE UNITED States Biographical Dictionary and Portrait Gallery of Eminent and Self-Made Men. Chicago, 1877. 4to., leather 698 pages. Saddleback 14-767 1974 $20

U. S. CAMERA. New York, 1943. Large 4to., cloth, profusely illus. Minters 37-620 1973 $20

UNITED STATES DEPARTMENT OF AGRICULTURE   North American Fauna, No. 7, The Death Valley Expedition, Part 2. Washington, 1893. 8vo., cloth, plates. Wheldon 131-384 1974 £12

UNITED STATES - PATENT OFFICE   Catalogue of the Library of. Washington, 1878. Jenkins 61-476 1974 $17.50

U. S. TREASURY DEPARTMENT   Annual Report and Statements of the Chief of the Bureau of Statistics on the Foreign Commerce and Navigation, Immigration and Tonnage of the U. S. for the Fiscal Year Ending June 30, 1885. Austin 62-652 1974 $17.50

UNITED STATES - WAR DEPARTMENT   Abstract of Infantry, Including Exercises Manoeuvres of Light-Infantry and Riflemen. Boston, 1830. Orig. calf. Jenkins 61-4 1974 $45

UNITED STATES - WAR DEPARTMENT   Army Regulations, Revised...Auxillary and Reserve Force Circulars, Issued by Order of the Secretary of State for War. 1874. Contemporary half calf, rubbed. Bow Windows 66-17 1974 £8.50

THE UNITY of Italy. Putnam, 1871. 197p. Austin 62-292 1974 $67.50

THE UNIVERSITY of Alabama. Tuskaloosa, c. 1900. Folio, wrapper, photos. Jenkins 61-34 1974 $12.50

University of Chicago. Chicago, 1921. Wrapper, hand colored. Jenkins 61-1128 1974 $10

THE UNOFFICIAL Palace of New York: A Tribute to the Waldorf-Astoria. New York, 1939. Ballinger 1-298 1974 $12.50

UNONIUS, GUSTOF   Minnen Fran en s Juttonarig Vistelse i. Nordvestra Amerika. 1862. 2 vols., 8vo., orig. cloth, plates, second edition. Ximenes 35-413 1974 $85

UNWIN, GEORGE   The Gilds and Companies of London. (1925). 8vo., orig. cloth, plates, illus. Bow Windows 66-721 1974 £6.50

UNWIN, J. D.   Hopousia. 1940. Portrait, fine, first edition. Covent 55-873 1974 £12.50

UPDIKE, DANIEL BERKELEY   Printing Types. Cambridge, 1922. 1st ed., bdgs. worn, 2 vols. Biblo & Tannen 213-444 1973 $17.50

UPHAM, CHARLES W.   Salem Witchcraft. Boston, 1867. 2 vols., 1st ed., illus. Jacobs 24-35 1974 $65

UPTON, BERTHA   The Golliwoog in Holland. (1904). First edition, full page coloured and tinted text illus., oblong 4to., orig. cloth backed coloured pictorial boards, stitching little loose. George's 610-770 1973 £6

UPTON, BERTHA   The Golliwogg's Desert Island. (1906). Full page coloured illus., tinted text illus., oblong 4to., orig. cloth backed coloured pictorial boards, fine copy, apparently first edition. George's 610-774 1973 £10.50

UPTON, GEORGE P.   The Standard Symphonies. Chicago, 1889. Biblo & Tannen 214-928 1974 $7.50

UPTON, JOHN   Remarks on Three Plays of Benjamin Jonson. London, 1749. 8vo., disbound, first edition. Ximenes 37-213 1974 $100

UPTON, WILLIAM TREAT   Anthony Philip Heinrich, a 19th Century Composer in America. New York, 1939. 1st ed., illus. spine faded. Biblo & Tannen 214-858 1974 $12.50

UPWARD, ALLEN   The Accused Princess. 1900. Orig. pictorial cloth, English first edition. Covent 56-1274 1974 £6.30

URBANA and Champaign County. Urbana, (1942). Cloth, cover lightly soiled. Hayman 59-430 1974 $10

URE, ANDREW   A Dictionary of Chemistry. 1828. 8vo., half calf, plates, third edition. Bow Windows 64-743 1974 £8.50

URE, ANDREW   Recent Improvements in Arts, Manufactures, and Mines. London, 1846. 8vo., orig. cloth, gilt, uncut, illus. Dawsons PM 245-734 1974 £10

URE, G. P.   The Handbook of Toronto. Toronto, 1858. Foxing. Hood's 103-42 1974 $45

URFE, HONORE D'   Astrea. London, 1657-58. 3 vols., folio, early mottled calf, first edition. Ximenes 35-414 1974 $175

URNSHIBARA, YOSHIJIRO   Ten Woodcuts Cut and Printed in Colour After Design by Frank Brangwyn. 1924. Mounted plates in colour, some signed by artist, roy. 4to., dec. boards, cloth spine, limited to 270 copies, fine. Broadhurst 24-216 1974 £20

THE USEFUL Family Herbal. London, 1754. 8vo., contemporary calf, plates, scarce, first edition. Ximenes 35-28 1974 $60

USSHER, JAMES   Annales Veteris et Novi Testamenti. Geneva, 1722. Thick folio, old calf, boards. Howes 185-1739 1974 £7.50

USSHER, JAMES   An Answer to a Challenge Made by a Jesuite in Ireland. London, 1631. 5 items in 1 vol., small 4to., contemporary calf. Emerald 50-957 1974 £55

USSHER, JAMES   Veterum Epistolarum Sylloge. Dublin, 1632. 4to., contemporary sheep, first edition. Dawsons PM 251-352 1974 £25

USSHER, JAMES   Veterum Epistolarum Hibernicarum Sylloge. Dublin, 1632. Small 4to., old polished calf, first edition. Quaritch 939-637 1974 £30

USSHER, R. J.   The Birds of Ireland. 1900. 8vo., orig. cloth, maps, plates. Wheldon 129-541 1974 £7.50

USSHER, W. A. E.   Geology of Country Around Plymouth and Liskeard. 1907. 8vo. Wheldon 131-1087 1974 £7.50

UTAH   Acts, Resolutions and Memorials Passed by the Legislative Assembly of the Territory of Utah. Great Salt Lake City, 1863. Orig. printed wrappers, near mint copy. Jenkins 61-2465 1974 $60

UTAH   Indian Depredations in Utah: Memorial of the Legislative Assembly of Utah Territory. Washington, 1869. Charts. Jenkins 61-2471 1974 $12.50

UTAH   Memorial of Citizens of Utah Against the Admission of That Territory as a State. Washington, 1872. Jenkins 61-2472 1974 $12.50

UTAH   Report of the Governor of. Washington, 1889. Ptd. wrapper. Jenkins 61-2475 1974 $12.50

UTAH   Report of the Governor of. Washington, 1890. Ptd. wrapper. Jenkins 61-2476 1974 $12.50

UTAH   Report of the Governor of. Washington, 1891. Ptd. wrapper. Jenkins 61-2477 1974 $12.50

UTAH   Report of the Governor of. Washington, 1892. Ptd. wrapper. Jenkins 61-2478 1974 $13.50

UTAH   Report of the Governor of. Washington, 1893. Ptd. wrapper. Jenkins 61-2479 1974 $12.50

UTAH COMMISSION   Special Report of. Washington, 1884. Wrapper. Jenkins 61-2483 1974 $10

UTHMAN IBN UMAR   Al-Kafiya. (Rome, 1592). 4to., vellum, gilt, rare, fine, first edition. Harper 213-159 1973 $1750

UTLEY, HENRY M.   Michigan as a Province, Territory and State. (New York), 1906. 4 vols., maroon linen cloth, illus., fine. Putnam 126-195 1974 $40

UTLEY, HENRY M.   Michigan as a Province, Territory and State. New York, 1906. 4 vols., 8vo., cloth. Saddleback 14-509 1974 $55

UTTERSON, EDWARD VERNON   Select Pieces of Early Popular Poetry. London, 1817. 2 vols., 8vo., orig. boards, limited, first edition. Ximenes 35-416 1974 $65

UTTLEY, W. V.   A History of Kitchener, Ontario. Kitchener, 1937. Inscribed, illus., fading. Hood's 103-691 1974 $45

UVAROFF, ALEXIS   Oeuvres Posthumes. (Moscow, 1890). Roy. folio, plates, boards, leather spine, rare. Quaritch 940-358 1974 £15

UWINS, DAVID   A Treatise on Those Disorders of the Brain and Nervous System. London, 1833. 8vo., orig. boards, rebacked, uncut, first edition. Dawsons PM 249-489 1974 £55

UZANNE, LOUIS OCTAVE   The Book-Hunter in Paris. 1895. Illus. Howes 185-863 1974 £5

UZANNE, LOUIS OCTAVE   The Fan. 1884. Roy. 8vo., full powder blue gilt morocco, illus. Quaritch 940-739 1974 £30

UZANNE, LOUIS OCTAVE   La Femme a Paris. Paris, 1894. 4to., full red morocco, illus. Jacobs 24-132 1974 $30

UZANNE, LOUIS OCTAVE   The French Bookbinders of the 18th Century. Chicago, 1904. 4to., plates, boards, buckram back. Quaritch 940-610 1974 £60

UZANNE, LOUIS OCTAVE   La Reliure Moderne Artistique et Fantaisiste. Paris, 1887. Engraved frontis., plates, brown three quarter morocco, top edges gilt, others uncut, marbled endpapers. Kraus B8-268 1974 $65

V

VACHER, M.   Les Races Bovines en France.   Paris, 1900.
Folio, orig. portfolio, scarce.   Wheldon 131-525 1974 £10

VAIL, J. P. A.   Vail's Poughkeepsie City Directory for 1875-
1876. Poughkeepsie, c.1875. 8vo., quarter leather. Saddleback 14-594
1974 $15

VAILE, P. A.   Modern Dennis. New York, 1915. Biblo &
Tannen 213-1019 1973 $9.50

VAILLANT, GEORGE C.   Artists and Craftsmen in Ancient Central
America. New York, 1935. 4to., illus. Biblo & Tannen 214-253 1974 $7.50

VAILLANT, S.   Botanicon Parisiense. Leyden and Amsterdam,
1727. Folio, contemporary calf, plates. Wheldon 129-1130 1974 £120

VAILLANT, S.   Botanicon Parisiense. Leyden & Amsterdam,
1727. Folio, contemporary calf, plates. Wheldon 131-1359 1974 £150

VAJDA, ERNEST   Fata Morgana. Doubleday, Page, 1924.
Austin 51-986 1973 $8.50

VALE, EUGENE   The Technique of Screenplay Writing.
'944. Austin 51-985 1973 $10

VALE, ROBERT B.   Wings, Fur & Shot. New York & Harrisburg,
1936. First edition, 8vo., colored frontis., full page drawings, uncut, near mint.
Current BW9-200 1974 $16

VALE AND Other Poems. New York, 1931. Dust wrapper, first U. S. edition.
Covent 56-4 1974 £10.50

VALENTINI, DOMINICUS   Oratio de Scientiarvm et Vniversitatvm Vtilitate.
1741. Tall 4to., contemporary boards. Zeitlin 235-227 1974 $85

VALENTINI, GEORG WILHELM VON   Military Reflections on Turkey.
London, 1828. 8vo., orig. cloth, first English edition. Ximenes 35-418
1974 $15

VALENTYN, FRANCOIS   Oud en Nieuw Oost-Indien. Dordrecht &
Amsterdam, 1724-26. 5 vols. in 8, folio, contemporary calf, gilt, plates,
first edition. Traylen 79-541 1973 £950

VALERI, FRANCESCO MALAGUZZI   La Corte di Lodovico il Moro. Milano,
1917. Large 4to., gilt, signed. Rich Summer-103 1974 $35

VALERIUS, FLACCUS   Setini Balbic Argonavti Cu. 1702. 12mo.,
contemporary vellum, foxing. Smith 194-193 1974 £5

VALERIUS MAXIMUS   Dictorum et Factorum Memorabilium Libri
Novem. 1502-03. Early 19th century dark green morocco gilt, first Aldine
edition, second issue. Thomas 30-13 1973 £100

VALERIUS MAXIMUS   Dictorum. & Factorum Memorabilium Libri
Novem. Strassburg, 1514. Small 4to., old calf, raised bands, gilt, stains.
Thomas 28-312 1972 £30

VALERIUS MAXIMUS   Factorum et Dictorum Memorabilium Libri IX.
1888. Torn spine. Allen 213-1957 1973 £10

VALERY, PAUL   Album de vers Anciens. Paris, 1920. Small
4to., orig. wrapper, limited, first edition. L. Goldschmidt 42-398 1974 $40

VALERY, PAUL   Une Conquete Methodique. Paris, 1925. 8vo.,
orig. cloth, wrappers, first edition. Rota 189-878 1974 £5

VALERY, PAUL   Eupalinos, or the Architect. 1932. One of
250 copies, signed by author, orig. white buckram gilt, very nice copy. Covent
51-2597 1973 £15

VALERY, PAUL   Introduction to the Method of Leonardo da Vinci.
1929. 4to., patterned boards, fine, first English edition. Rota 189-879 1974
£10

VALERY, PAUL   La Jeune Parque. Paris, 1917. 4to., wrappers,
first French edition. Covent 56-2097 1974 £35

VALERY, PAUL   Le Serpent. 1924. One of 525 numbered copies,
near fine, first edition. Covent 51-643 1973 £18.50

VALETTE, A.   Manuel Pratique de Lithographie. Lyon,
1891. 8vo., boards, lithographic plates. Kraus B8-269 1974 $35

VALK, G.   Comitatus Northumbria Vernacule
Northumberland. (Amsterdam, c.1720). Map. Quaritch 939-510 1974 £40

VALK, G.   Ducatus Eboracensis. (Amsterdam, c.1720).
Map. Quaritch 939-605 1974 £40

VALK, G.   Ducatus Eboracensis Pars Orientalis.
(Amsterdam, c.1720). Map. Quaritch 939-606 1974 £50

VALK, G.   Glocestria Ducatus, cum Monumethensi
Comitatu. (Amsterdam, c.1720). Map. Quaritch 939-269 1974 £50

VALK, G.   Oxonium Comitatus Vulgo Oxford Shire.
(Amsterdam, c. 1720). Map. Quaritch 939-527 1974 £50

VALLANCE, AYMER   Old Crosses and Lychgates. (1920). 8vo.,
orig. cloth, illus. Bow Windows 66-722 1974 £6.50

VALLANCE, AYMER   William Morris: His Art, His Writings and His
Public Life. 1897. Very good copy, first edition, illus. Covent 51-1326
1973 £30

VALLANDIGHAM, EDWARD NOBLE   Delaware and the Eastern Shore. Philadelphia - London, 1922. 8vo., illus., orig. bindings, fine, dust jacket. Butterfield 8-109 1974 $30

VALLE, G. DELLA   Storia del Duomo di Orvieto. Rome, 1791.
Roy. 4to., contemporary boards, leather spine. Quaritch 940-561 1974 £9

VALLE, PIETRO DELLA   Viaggi. Rome, 1650-58-63. 4 parts in 3
vols., late 17th century or early 18th century calf, gilt, first editions. Harper
213-160 1973 $1250

VALLEE, A.   Un Biologiste Canadien, Michael Sarrazin,
1659-1735. Quebec, 1927. Hood's 104-285 1974 $15

VALLEE, RUDY   Vagabond Dreams Come True. Dutton, 1930.
Austin 51-987 1973 $6

VALLENTIN, ANTONINA   Leonardo da Vinci: The Tragic Pursuit of
Perfection. New York, 1938. Colored illus., orig. binding, spine somewhat
faded, near mint in d.w. Ross 87-201 1974 $10

VALLENTIN, E. F.   Illustrations of the Flowering Plants and Ferns of
the Falkland Islands. 1921. Small 4to., cloth. Wheldon 129-1131 1974 £30

VALLERY-RADOT, RENE   The Life of Pasteur. 1902. 8vo., 2 vols., orig.
issue, cloth. Wheldon 131-241 1974 £10

VALLERY-RADOT, RENE   Louis Pasteur. London, 1885. 8vo., orig.
cloth, uncut, first edition in English. Dawsons PM 249-398 1974 £6

VALLES, JULES   Des Mots . . . Paris, 1920. 12mo., orig.
wrapper, first edition. L. Goldschmidt 42-404 1974 $10

VALLESIUS, FRANCISCUS   Commentarius in Quartum. 1591. 4to., contemporary vellum. Dawsons PM 245-735 1974 £65

VALLET, L.   A Travers l'Europe. Paris, 1893. Roy. 4to.,
plates, half morocco, orig. pict. wrapper. Quaritch 940-740 1974 £54

VALLEY of the Upper Maumee River. Madison, 1889. 2 vols., half leather.
Hayman 59-283 1974 $50

THE VALLEY of Wyoming: The Romance of Its History and Its Poetry. New York,
1866. 8vo., orig. bindings. Butterfield 8-520 1974 $15

VALLIANT, GEORGE C.   Indian Arts in North America. New York,
1939. 1st ed., col. frontis., illus., 4to. Jacobs 24-36 1974 $40

VALLIANT, GEORGE C.   Indian Arts in North America. New York,
1939. 4to., 1st ed., dw., illus. Biblo & Tannen 213-281 1973 $52.50

VALLIERE, JEAN FLORENT DE 1667-1759　Catalogue des Livres de la Bibliotheque de Feu. 1783. 3 vols., contemporary calf gilt, rubbed, morocco labels. Thomas 30-133 1973 £55

VALOR Beneficiorum. London, 1695. 12mo., contemporary calf, frontispiece. Quaritch 939-270 1974 £35

VALROGER, L. DE　Les Celtes, La Gaule Celtique. 1879. Buckram. Allen 213-1839 1973 $10

VALSALVA, ANTONIO MARIA　De Aure Humana Tractatus. Utrecht, 1717. 4to., half calf. Schumann 35-476 1974 $165

VALUE, VICTOR　Experience Consulted. Philadelphia, 1832. 12mo., orig. wrappers, fine, first edition. Ximenes 35-419 1974 $45

VALVERDE DI HAMUSCO, GIOVANNI　La Anatomia del Corpo Humano. 1586. Folio, contemporary limp vellum. Dawsons PM 249-490 1974 £650

VAN BOEHN　Miniatures and Silhouettes. London, 1926. Coloured & plain illus., inner hinge tender, orig. cloth, 8vo. Gregory 44-278 1974 $15

VANBRUGH, JOHN　Plays. London, 1759. 2 vols., 12mo., contemporary calf, fifth collected edition. Ximenes 35-420 1974 $60

VANBRUGH, JOHN　Plays. 1893. 2 vols., ex-library, tops of spines frayed. Allen 216-2079 1974 $25

VANBRUGH, JOHN　The Provok'd Husband. London, 1728. 8vo., marbled boards, first edition. Dawsons PM 252-1009 1974 £60

VANBRUGH, JOHN　The Provok'd Husband. 1760. 12mo., contemporary vellum, frontispiece. Hill 126-216 1974 £8.50

VANBRUGH, JOHN　The Relapse. London, 1698. Small 4to., disbound, second edition. Ximenes 35-421 1974 $25

VANBRUGH, JOHN　The Complete Works. 1927-28. 4 vols., 4to., orig. buckram backed boards, plates, limited edition. Dawsons PM 252-1010 1974 £95

VANBRUGH, JOHN　The Complete Works of. 1927. Crown 4to., 4 vols., boards, uncut, limited edition. Broadhurst 23-1063 1974 £40

VANBRUGH, JOHN　The Complete Works of. Nonesuch Press, 1927. 4 vols., crown 4to., boards, linen spines, paper printed labels, uncut, slight uniform fading, limited to 1300 sets. Broadhurst 24-1024 1974 £45

VAN BUREN, MARTIN　Mexico – Texas – Canada: Message Transmitting Information. Washington, 1838. Jenkins 61-2489 1974 $37.50

VAN BUREN, WILLIAM HOLME　Lectures On Diseases of the Rectum Delivered at the Bellevue Hospital Medical College. New York, 1870. Rittenhouse 46-630 1974 $10

VANDAS, C.　Reliquiae Formanekianae. Brunn, 1909. 8vo., wrappers. Wheldon 128-1314 1973 £10

VANDAS, C.　Reliquiae Formanekianae. Brunn, 1909. 8vo., wrappers. Wheldon 130-1215 1974 £10

VANDENHOFF, GEORGE　Leaves From an Actor's Note-Book. London, 1860. 12mo., orig. cloth, fine, first edition. Ximenes 35-423 1974 $22.50

VANDERBILT African Expedition 1934 Zoological Results. Philadelphia, 1937. Parts 1 - 6, roy. 8vo., morocco, plates. Wheldon 131-398 1974 £5

VAN DER ELST, JOSEPH　The Last Flowering of the Middle Ages. New York, 1945. 4to., color and b&w plates. Biblo & Tannen 210-93 1973 $14.50

VAN DER HEYDEN, HERMANN　Speedy Help for Rich and Poor. London, 1653. 12mo., panelled calf antique, second edition in English. Dawsons PM 249-491 1974 £385

VAN DERVEER, HELEN R.　Little Sallie Mandy. Philadelphia, (1924). 16mo., boards, cloth spine, full color plates, very good copy, orig. dust jacket. Frohnsdorff 16-511 1974 $15

VAN DERVEER, HELEN R.　Little Sallie Mandy. Philadelphia, (1924). 16mo., boards, cloth spine, full color plates, very good. Frohnsdorff 16-512 1974 $10

VANDER-VILIUS, AELIUS F.　De Naturalum Rerum Scientia Oratio. 1592. 8vo., modern boards, fine. Current BW9-614A 1974 $40

VAN DER WEYDEN, ROGIER　Paintings from The Escorial and the Prado. New York, 1946. Folio, color plates. Biblo & Tannen 214-542 1974 $15

VAN DER WEYDEN, ROGIER　Pieta. New York, n.d. 4to., color plates. Biblo & Tannen 214-543 1974 $15

VAN DE WATER, FREDERIC F.　Glory-Hunter, a Life of General Custer. Indianapolis, (1934). First edition, cloth. Hayman 59-642 1974 $25

VAN DE WATER, FREDERIC F.　Rudyard Kipling's Vermont Feud. New York, 1937. Biblo & Tannen 213-829 1973 $7.50

VANDIER, JACQUES　La Religion Egyptienne. Paris, 1949. Frayed wraps. Biblo & Tannen 213-939 1973 $7.50

VAN DINE, S. S.　The Dragon Murder Case. New York, 1933. lst ed., fine copy. Biblo & Tannen 213-529 1973 $15

VANDOR, PAUL E.　History of Fresno County, California. Los Angeles, 1919. 2 vols., 8vo., cloth, illus. Saddleback 14-308 1974 $125

VAN DOREN, CARL　Benjamin Franklin. New York, 1938. 3 vols., orig. cloth, plates, fine, first edition. Bradley 35-430 1974 $35

VAN DOREN, CARL　Mutiny in January. New York, 1943. Illus., blind-stamped blue cloth, first edition. Bradley 35-11 1974 $12.50

VAN DRUTEN, JOHN　Bell, Book and Candle. Random, 1948. Austin 51-988 1973 $7.50

VAN DRUTEN, JOHN　The Distaff Side. 1933. 144p., paper. Austin 51-989 1973 $6.50

VAN DRUTEN, JOHN　There's Always Juliet. French, 1932. 176p. Austin 51-991 1973 $7.50

VAN DRUTEN, JOHN　Young Woodley. Simon, Schuster, 1925. Austin 51-992 1973 $7.50

VAN DUSEN, ELIZABETH K.　Picturesque Porto Rico. 1927. 291 pages, illus. Austin 57-677 1974 $10

VAN DYK, HENRY STOE　The Gondola. London, 1827. 12mo., green half morocco gilt, first edition. Dawsons PM 252-1011 1974 £25

VAN DYKE, HENRY　The Builders and Other Poems. New York, 1897. 12mo., orig. half vellum, first edition. Ximenes 35-424 1974 $17.50

VAN DYKE, HENRY　The Lost Word, A Christmas Legend of Long Ago. New York, 1898. First edition, 12mo., full page gravures, minor spots on covers, else perfect. Current BW9-90 1974 $16.50

VAN DYKE, JOHN C.　The Grand Canyon of the Colorado. New York, 1920. Pictorial cloth, illus., gilt, first edition. Bradley 35-155 1974 $20

VAN DYKE, JOSEPH S.　Popery. Philadelphia, 1877. 304 pages. Austin 57-678 1974 $12.50

VAN DYKE, PAUL　Catherine de Medicis. 1923. 2 vols. Allen 213-1363 1973 $10

VANEL, CHARLES　The Royal Mistresses of France. London, 1695. 8vo., later calf, scarce, first English edition. Ximenes 35-425 1974 $125

VAN EVERY, DALE   Charles Lindbergh. New York, 1927. 1st ed.
Biblo & Tannen 213-645 1973 $9.50

VAN EVERY, EDWARD   Sins of America. Stokes, 1931. 299p.
Austin 54-1019 1973 $15

VAN EYCK, H.   Hubert et Jean Van Eyck. Brussels, 1910.
4to., plates, half leather. Quaritch 940-266 1974 £35

VAN GORDON, S.   Rough Life on the Frontier. Chicago, (1903).
Orig. cloth, illus, almost mint. Putnam 126-348 1974 $10

VAN HOESEN, H. B.   Bibliography, Practical, Enumerative,
Historical. 1928. Allen 216-210 1974 $15

VANHUMBEEK, P. J.   Epreuve des Filets de la Fonderie en
Characteres. . . Brussels, n.d. (c. 1835). 8vo., orig. printed wrappers.
Kraus B8-384 1974 $50

VANINI, LUCILIO   Amphitheatrvm Aeternae Providentiae. 1615.
Small 8vo., old panelled calf, gilt. Zeitlin 235-228 1974 $475

VAN LAER, A. J. F.   Minutes of the Court of Fort Orange and
Beverwyck, 1652-1656. Albany, 1920. Vol. 1. Jenkins 61-1934 1974 $12.50

VAN LEEUWEN, W. M.   Treubia Recueil De Travaux Zoologiques.
Holland, 1928. 8vo., orig. printed wrappers. Bow Windows 64-284 1974 £3.50

VAN LOON, HENDRIK WILLEM   Life and Times of Pieter Stuyvesant. New
York, 1928. Illus. Jenkins 61-1935 1974 $12.50

VAN LOON, HENDRIK WILLEM   Report to Saint Peter. New York, 1947.
1st ed., illus. Biblo & Tannen 210-808 1973 $7.50

VAN RENSSELAER, MRS. JOHN KING
Please turn to
VAN RENSSELAER, MAY (KING)

VAN RENSSELAER, MAY (KING)   New Yorkers of the XIX Century. New
York, c. 1897. Boards. Saddleback 14-595 1974 $35

VANS, HUGH   Some Observations on the Scheme Projected
for Emitting 60000 1. Boston, 1738. 8vo., modern wrappers, rare, first edition.
Ximenes 35-426 1974 $325

VANSITTART, NICHOLAS   Substance of Two Speeches. London, 1811.
8vo., orig. wrappers, fine, uncut, first edition. Ximenes 35-427 1974 $50

VANSITTART, ROBERT   The Singing Caravan. 1932. Imperial 8vo.,
brown toned sheepskin, gilt, uncut, limited edition. Broadhurst 23-1044 1974
£30

VAN THIENEN, FRITHJOF   Jan Vermeer of Delft. New York, 1949.
Sm. 4to., color plates. Biblo & Tannen 214-554 1974 $10

VAN TIEGHEM, P.   Traite de Botanique. Paris, 1891. 2 vols.,
8vo., half calf, text-figures, second edition. Wheldon 128-1173 1973 £10

VANUXEM, LARDNER   Geology of New York. Albany, 1842. 4to.,
engraved vignette, torn. Bow Windows 64-285 1974 £8

VAN VALZAH, WILLIAM W.   The Diseases of the Stomach. Philadelphia,
1898. Rittenhouse 46-631 1974 $10

VAN VECHTEN, CARL   Music After the Great War and Other Studies.
New York, 1915. First U. S. edition, very good copy. Covent 51-1885 1973
£35

VAN VECHTEN, CARL   Red: Papers on Musical Subjects. 1925. First
U. S. edition, signed presentation copy, very good, bookplate. Covent 51-1887
1973 £5.25

VAN VECHTEN, CARL   The Tiger in the House. 1921. Very good copy,
inscription, illus., first edition. Covent 51-1888 1973 £10.50

VAN VOORHIS, JOHN S.   The Old and New Monongahela. Pittsburgh,
1893. 8vo., orig. bindings, portrait. Butterfield 8-521 1974 $25

VAN WATERS, GEORGE   The Poetical Geography . . . To Which are
Added the Rules of Arithmetic in Rhyme. Cincinnati, 1851. 8vo., wrappers, bit
chipped at edges & soiled, woodcuts. Current BW9-345 1974 $45

VAN WYCK, FREDERICK   Hours With Old Engravers. Boston, 1936.
Ltd. to 150 copies. Biblo & Tannen 210-309 1973 $15

VAN WYCK, FREDERICK   Select Patents of New York Towns. Boston,
1938. Illus., limited to 125 copies for private distribution only, presentation
copy. Jenkins 61-1937 1974 $17.50

VARDOULAKIS, MARY   Gold in the Streets. 1945. 255 pages.
Austin 57-679 1974 $10

VARENIUS, BERNHARD   Cosmography and Geography, In Two Parts.
London, 1693. Folio, contemporary calf, leather label, illus. Traylen
79-442 1973 £535

VARENIUS, BERNHARD   Geographia Generalis. Cambridge, 1681.
8vo., contemporary calf, plates, second edition. Schuman 37-189 1974 $110

VARENIUS, BERNHARD   Geographia Generalis. Amsterdam, 1650.
Small thick 12mo., contemporary vellum, diagrams, first edition. Schuman 37-
254 1974 $175

VARESI, GILDA   Enter Madame. Putnam, 1921. Austin
51-993 1973 $6.50

VARIGNON, PIERRE   Nouvelle Mecanique ou Statique. Paris, 1725.
4to., 2 vols., contemporary sprinkled calf. Zeitlin 235-229 1974 $250

VARIGNON, PIERRE   Projet d'une nouvelle Mechanique. Paris, 1687.
4to., contemporary sprinkled calf, gilt. Zeitlin 235-230 1974 $375

VARRO, MARCUS TERENTIUS   Operum Quae Exstant. 1601. 16mo.,
vellum. Allen 213-1135 1973 $15

VARTHEMA, LUDOVICO DE   Itinerario de Lvdovico de Varthema Bolognese
Nello Egitto. Venice, n.d. Small 8vo., dark green morocco, gilt. Traylen
79-443 1973 £220

VASARI, GIORGIO   Lives of the Most Eminent Painters, Sculptors
and Architects. 1912-15. 10 vols., imp. 8vo., plates, orig. buckram, gilt.
Quaritch 940-267 1974 £250

VASEY, G.   Delineations of the Ox Tribe. 1851. 8vo.,
orig. cloth. Wheldon 129-405 1974 £20

VASI, GIUSEPPE   Della Magnificenze di Roma Antica e Moderna.
Rome, 1747-1761. Small oblong folio, contemporary vellum. Marlborough 70-
23 1974 £700

VASILIEV, A. A.   History of the Byzantine Empire. Madison,
1928-29. 1st ed., 2 vols. Biblo & Tannen 214-667 1974 $17.50

VASILIEV, A. V.   Space, Time, Motion. New York, 1924. First
U.S. edition. Covent 56-1128 1974 $25

VATICAN - BIBLIOTECA - VATICANA   Codices Manuscripti Palatini Graeci
Bibliothecae Vaticanae. 1885. 4to., sewn. Allen 213-1141 1973 $12.50

VATICAN - BIBLIOTECA - VATICANA   Codices Palatini Latini. 1886. 4to.,
sewn. Allen 213-1142 1973 $15

VAUGHAN, E. M. C.   Pinafore Pictures and Rhymes. (c. 1875).
Full page chromolithographs, imp. 8vo., orig. cloth, gilt. George's 610-780
1973 £5

VAUGHAN, HENRY   The Best of Both Worlds. 1918. Orig.
patterned boards, very nice copy. Covent 51-2526 1973 £15

VAUGHAN, HENRY   Poems. 1924. 8vo., dec. boards, uncut,
limited edition. Broadhurst 23-1033 1974 £30

VAUGHAN, HENRY   Poems. 1924. 8vo., cloth backed figured
boards, limited edition. Dawsons PM 252-1012 1974 £45

VAUGHAN, JOHN   The Wild-flowers of Selborne and Other
Papers. London, 1906. Biblo & Tannen 213-855 1973 $9.50

VAUGHAN, R. B.   Life & Labours of St. Thomas Aquinas. 1871.
2 vols., new buckram. Allen 213-1816 1973 $25

VAUGHAN, THOMAS   The Hotel. London, n.d. 8vo., disbound,
second edition. Ximenes 35-428 1974 $15

VAUMORIERE, PIERRE ORTIGUE   The Art of Pleasing in Conversation.
London, 1736. 2 vols., 12mo., contemporary calf, gilt, fine, first edition.
Ximenes 35-429 1974 $90

VAUVENARGUES, LUC DE CLAPIERS DE   Introduction a la Connaissance de
l'Esprit Humain. Paris, 1746. 12mo., contemporary calf, gilt, morocco label,
first edition. L. Goldschmidt 42-124 1974 $300

VAUVENARGUES, LUC DE CLAPIERS DE   Oeuvres Morales. Paris, 1874.
3 vols., small 12mo., contemporary red long grain morocco, gilt, uncut.
L. Goldschmidt 42-125 1974 $27.50

VAUX, FREDERIC W.   Rambles in the Pyrenees. London, 1838.
8vo., orig. dark green cloth, first edition. Ximenes 35-430 1974 $25

VAYSSE DE VILLIERS, REGIS J. F.   Itineraire Descriptif ou Description
Routiere. Paris, 1816-21. 5 vols., contemporary half calf, map, labels.
Howes 186-1278 1974 £15

VEALE, E.   Jack the Giant. Philadelphia, 1896. 8vo.,
mint copy, illus. Frohnsdorff 16-233 1974 $20

VEALE, E.   The Jolly Chinee. Philadelphia, 1897. 8vo.,
mint copy, illus. Frohnsdorff 16-234 1974 $20

VECCHI, OMERO   Poeti Allo Specchio. 1926. Small 8vo.,
wrapper. Minters 37-396 1973 $22.50

VECHTEN, CARL VAN
Please turn to
VAN VECHTEN, CARL

VEDDER, EDWARD B.   Syphilis and Public Health. Philadelphia,
1918. Rittenhouse 46-633 1974 $10

VEDDER, ELIHU   Digressions of V Written for His Own Fun and
That of His Friends. Boston & New York, 1910. Fine. Ballinger 1-53
1974 $15

VEDDER, ELIHU   Digressions, Written for His Own Fun and That
of His Friends. 1910. 4to., plates, ex-library. Allen 216-1700 1974 $12.50

VEENDORP, H.   Hortus Academicus Lugduno Batavus. Harlem,
1938. Roy 8vo., buckram, illus. Wheldon 129-195 1974 £10

VEGA, GARCILASO DE LA
Please turn to
GARCILASO DE LA VEGA

VEGETIUS, FLAVIUS RENATUS   De Re Militari. Rome, 1494. Small 4to.,
vellum, dec. woodcut initials. Thomas 32-272 1974 £425

VEGETIUS, FLAVIUS RENATUS   Veteres de Re Militari Scriptores Quotquot
Extant. 1670. 3 parts in 2 vols., contemporary calf. Howes 186-1766 1974
£21

VEILLER, BAYARD   The Fun I've Had. 1941. Austin 51-994
1973 $7.50

VEITCH, JAMES H.   Hortus Veitchii. 1906. Imperial 8vo., orig.
cloth, scarce. Broadhurst 23-1193 1974 £50

VEITCH, JAMES H.   Hortus Veitchii. 1906. Imp. 8vo., orig. half
morocco, plates, nice copy, very scarce. Wheldon 131-1585 1974 £35

VEITCH, JAMES H.   A Manual of the Coniferae. 1881. Roy. 8vo.,
orig. cloth gilt, frontis., illus. Wheldon 128-1630 1973 £5

VEITCH, JAMES H.   Manual of the Coniferae. 1900. Roy 8vo.,
cloth, scarce. Wheldon 130-1577 1974 £10

VEJDOVSKY, F.   Neue Untersuchungen. Prague, 1907. Imperial
4to., linsen, plates. Wheldon 129-110 1974 £15

VEJDOVSKY, F.   Neue Untersuchungen Uber die Reifung und
Befruchtung. Prague, 1907. Imp. 4to., modern calf, plates, rare. Wheldon
131-189 1974 £15

VELAND, ANDREAS   Recollections of an Immigrant. Minton,
1929. Austin 62-648 1974 $10

VELASQUEZ, DIEGO   Diego Velasquez und Sein Jahrhundert. Bonn,
1922-23. 2 vols., roy. 8vo., plates, half leather. Quaritch 940-268 1974
£28

VELENOVSKY, J.   Ceske Houby. Prague, 1920-22. 8vo., orig.
wrappers. Wheldon 129-1367 1974 £10

VELENOVSKY, J.   Ceske Houby. Prague, 1920-22. Roy 8vo.,
cloth, 2 vols. Wheldon 129-1368 1974 £15

VELENOVSKY, J.   Ceske Houby. Prague, 1920-22. 2 vols.,
roy. 8vo., cloth. Wheldon 131-1477 1974 £15

VELENOVSKY, J.   Monographia Discomycetum Bohemiae. Prague,
1934. Roy 8vo., half morocco, plates. Wheldon 129-1366 1974 £25

VELENOVSKY, J.   Novitates Mycologicae. Prague, 1939. Roy
8vo., buckram. Wheldon 129-1369 1974 £5

VELPEAU, ALFRED ARMAND LOUIS MARIE   Embryologie ou Ovologie Humaine.
Brussels, 1834. Large folio, contemporary limp boards, first Belgian edition.
Schumann 35-477 1974 $145

VELPEAU, ALFRED ARMAND LOUIS MARIE   Lecons Orales de Clinique
Chirurgicale. Paris, 1840(-1841). 8vo., 3 vols., contemporary half calf, first
edition. Dawsons PM 249-492 1974 £38

VELPEAU, ALFRED ARMAND LOUIS MARIE   Traite des Maladies du Sein et de la
Region Mammaire. Paris, 1854. 8vo., quarter shagreen, slightly rubbed,
coloured plates, first edition. Gurney 66-189 1974 £26

VELPEAU, ALFRED ARMAND LOUIS MARIE   A Treatise on the Diseases of the
Breast and Mammary Region. London, 1856. 8vo., orig. green cloth, uncut,
first edition in English. Dawsons PM 249-493 1974 £24

VENEGAS, MIGUEL   A Natural and Civil History of California.
London, 1759. 2 vols., 8vo., old calf gilt, leather labels, first edition.
Traylen 79-500 1973 £300

VENEL, A. J.   Essai sur la Sante et sur l'Education. Yverdon,
1776. 8vo., contemporary calf, first edition. Gurney 64-220 1974 £20

VENERONI, GIOVANI   The Complete Italian Master. London, 1795.
12mo., contemporary sheep. Ximenes 35-431 1974 $25

VENETTE, NICOLAS   L'Art de Tailler les Arbres Fruitiers. Paris,
1683. Small 8vo., contemporary vellum, woodcut plates. Wheldon 131-1758
1974 £120

VENETTE, NICOLAS   Traite des Pierres Qui s'engendrent dans les Terres
and dan les Animaux. Amsterdam, 1701. 12mo., half calf, gilt, plates, first edition. Hammond 201-553 1974 £65

VENN, JOHN   Biographical History of Gonville and Caius
College. 1897-1901. 3 vols., roy. 8vo., orig. cloth, plates. Howes
186-1987 1974 £20

VENN, JOHN   The Principles of Empirical Or Inductive
Knowledge. 1907. Thick 8vo., ex-library, second & best edition. Howes
185-2032 1974 £6

VENNER, THOMAS   Via Recta ad Vitam Longam. London, 1638.
8vo., contemporary calf, rebacked. Gurney 64-221 1974 £45

VENNER, TOBIAS   Via Recta ad Vitam Longam. London, 1628.
2 parts in 1 vol., 4to., old calf, worn. Schuman 37-255 1974 $210

VENNER, TOBIAS   Via Recta ad Vitam Longam. London, 1660.
4to., contemporary sheep, gilt. Dawsons PM 249-494 1974 £110

VENNING, M. A.   Rudiments of Conchology. 1830-37. Small 8vo., contemporary morocco, plates. Wheldon 131-911 1974 £7.50

VENNING, RALPH   Milke and Honey. London, 1653. 8vo., contemporary black morocco, first edition. Ximenes 35-432 1974 $120

VENTENAT, E. P.   Description des Plantes Nouvelles et peu Connues. Paris, 1800(-1802). Imperial 4to., contemporary leather-backed boards, plates, rare. Wheldon 130-84 1974 £300

VENTURI, A.   Studi dal Vero Attraverso la Raccolte Artistiche d'Europa. Milan, 1927. Roy. 8vo., cloth, gilt, illus. Quaritch 940-270 1974 £10

VENTURI, GIOVANNI BATTISTA   Recherches Experimentales. Paris, (1797). 8vo., orig. blue wrappers, uncut, unopened, first edition. Dawsons PM 245-737 1974 £75

VENTURI, LIONELLO   Italian Painters of Today. New York, 1959. 4to., illus. Biblo & Tannen 214-550 1974 $40

VENTURI, LIONELLO   Marc Chagall. New York, 1945. Sm. 4to., ltd. ed. Biblo & Tannen 214-70 1974 $67.50

VENUTI, RIDOLFINO   Accurata E Succinta Descrizione Topographica Della Antichita di Roma. Rome, 1824. 2 vols., 4to., contemporary Italian red morocco gilt, labels, plates. Thomas 28-332 1972 £95

VERBIEST, FERDINAND   A Newly Made Collection of Astronomical Instruments. Peking, c. 1668. 2 vols., large woodcuts, on soft thin China paper, folio, orig. brown paper wrappers, half leather case, Nicolas Freret's copy. Kraus 137-83 1974 $18,000

VERBUM Sempiternum. London, 1849. Blind tooled brown leather, half clasp missing, else fine, 2 1/4 X 1 7/8. Gregory 44-479 1974 $60

VERDOORN, F.   Manual of Pteridology. The Hague, 1938. Roy 8vo., cloth, illus., scarce. Wheldon 130-1362 1974 £12.50

VERELST, HENRY   A View of the Rise, Progress, and Present State of the English Government in Bengal. London, 1772. 4to., 2 parts in 1 vol., buckram, gilt, first edition. Dawsons PM 247-297 1974 £35

VERGA, GIOVANNI   Little Novels of Sicily. Oxford, 1925. Covers, faded, English first edition. Covent 56-808 1974 £7.50

VERGILIUS, POLYDORUS   Anglicae Historiae Libri Vigintiseptem. Basle, 1570. Folio, old vellum, staining. Thomas 28-208 1972 £25

VERGILIUS, POLYDORUS   De Inventibus Rerum Libri Viii. Amsterdam, 1671. 12mo., engraved frontispiece, contemporary vellum, Prince Liechtenstein's copy. Kraus B8-385 1974 $45

VERGILIUS, POLYDORUS   A Pleasant and Compendious History of the First Inventers and Instituters of the Most Famous Arts... London, 1686. 12mo., half calf, rebacked. Hammond 201-985 1974 £75

VERGILIUS MARO, PUBLIUS   Bucolica et Georgica. 1774. Morocco, rubbed, plates, foxing. Allen 213-1159 1973 $35

VERGILIUS MARO, PUBLIUS   Bucolica, Georgica et Aeneis. Birmingham, 1766. Contemporary vellum gilt, plates. Smith 193-102 1973 £10

VERGILIUS MARO, PUBLIUS   L'Eneide. Paris, 1648. 4to., contemporary calf gilt, worn, illus., first edition. Harper 213-167 1973 $250

VERGILIUS MARO, PUBLIUS   The Georgics of Virgil. London, 1871. 8vo., orig. cloth, presentation, first edition. Dawsons PM 252-1017 1974 £35

VERGILIUS MARO, PUBLIUS   The Passion of Dido for Aeneas. London, 1658. 8vo., contemporary sheep, fine, rare, first edition. Dawsons PM 252-1018 1974 £750

VERGILIUS MARO, PUBLIUS   Servius. In Vergilii Carmina Commentarii. 1878-1902. Vols. 1-3 only in 6 vols., new buckram. Allen 213-1168 1973 $70

VERGILIUS MARO, PUBLIUS   Opera. 1830-41. 5 vols., half calf. Allen 213-1152 1973 $35

VERHAAL dat de Ambassadeurs van Siam Aan Haar Koning Gedaan Hebben. Batavia, 1688. Orig. edition, small 4to., half calf, uncut. Kraus B8-414 1974 $575

VERHAEREN, EMILE   James Ensor. Brussels, 1908. 4to., plates, wrapper. Minters 37-247 1973 $42

VERHEYEN, PHILIPPE   Corporis Humani Anatomiae. Brussels, 1710. 2 parts in 1 vol., thick 4to., contemporary calf, plates. Schuman 37-256 1974 $95

VERINI, UGOLINO   De Illustratione Urbis Florentiae Libri Tres. Paris, 1583. Folio, contemporary limp vellum, first edition. Harper 213-161 1973 $475

LE VERITABLE Riel Tel Que Depeint Dans les Lettres de sa Grandeur Mgr. Grandin . . . Suivi D'Extraits des Mandements de nos Seigneurs les Eveques Concernant l'Agitation Riel. Montreal, 1887. Contemporary mottled boards, linen spine. Hood's 102-836 1974 $110

LE VERITABLE Riel tel Que Depeint Dans des Lettres de sa Grandeur Mgr. Grandin. Montreal, 1887. Contemporary mottled boards. Hood's 104-667 1974 $110

VERLAINE, PAUL   Fetes Galantes. Paris, 1928. Edition limited to 375 copies, etched plates, 4to., dark blue morocco, gilt line borders, orig. wrappers, preserved, half morocco wrapper and slip-in case, very fine copy. Sawyer 293-71 1974 £750

VERLAINE, PAUL   Fetes Galantes. 1944. One of 30 copies on papier Goldflake, half calf, fine. Covent 51-2279 1973 £25

VERLAINE, PAUL   Fetes Galantes. 1944. One of 30 copies printed on "Papier Goldflake", 8vo., half dark blue leather, fine copy. Sawyer 293-114 1974 £55

VERLAINE, PAUL   Hommage a Verlaine. Paris, 1910. Square 8vo., contemporary half hard grain morocco, gilt. L. Goldschmidt 42-406 1974 $35

VERLAINE, PAUL   Poesies Completes. Paris, 1923-26. 6 (of 7) vols., small 4to., orig. wrapper, uncut. L. Goldschmidt 42-405 1974 $60

VERLOT, B.   Les Plantes Alpines. Paris, 1873. Roy. 8vo., orig. half morocco, coloured plates. Wheldon 128-1543 1973 £7.50

VER MEHR, J. L.   Checkered Life. Bancroft, 1877. Austin 62-656 1974 $17.50

VERMIGLI, PIETRO MARTIRE   The Common Places. 1583. Folio, 19th century half sheep, label. Thomas 28-107 1972 £75

VERMIGLI, PIETRO MARTIRE   Dialogus de Utraque in Christo Natura. Zurich, 1575. 8vo., old manuscript vellum, very rare. Harper 213-162 1973 $350

VERNE, JULES   Adrift in the Pacific. 1889. 8vo., orig. pictorial cloth, plates, gilt. Hammond 201-149 1974 £5

VERNE, JULES   De la Terre a la Lune. Paris, (1865). Small 8vo., contemporary read half leather, gilt back, firs issue of orig. edition, with the errata leaf, very rare. Schafer 10-149 1974 sFr 1,500

VERNE, JULES   From the Earth to the Moon. 1883. Engraved plates, orig. dec. cloth gilt, Author's Illus. Edition, nice copy. Covent 51-1892 1973 £6.30

VERNE, JULES   Le Tour de Monde en Quatre-Vingt Jours; toghether with, Le Docteur Ox. Paris, c. 1880. 2 works in 1 vol., frontispieces, engraved text illus., roy. 8vo., contemporary half green morocco, little foxing, very nice copy. Covent 51-1893 1973 £10

VERNER, W.   My Life Among the Wild Birds in Spain. 1909. Roy 8vo., cloth, illus., plates. Wheldon 129-543 1974 £15

VERNEUIL, E. DE   Description des Fossiles du Neocomien Supertieur de Utrillas et ses Environs. Le Mans, 1868. 4to., orig. wrappers, plates. Wheldon 131-1088 1974 £5

VERNEY, FRANCES P.   Memoirs. 1892-99. 8vo., 4 vols., orig. cloth,
gilt. Broadhurst 23-1287 1974 £42

VERNEY, FRANCES P.   Memoirs of the Verney Family. 1892-99.
4 vols., half crushed morocco, plates, illus., fine, orig. & best edition. Howes
186-1285 1974 £52

VERNEY, FRANCES P.   Memoirs of the Verney Family. 1892-99.
Plates, 4 vols., med. 8vo., orig. cloth, illus., fine. Broadhurst 24-1342 1974
£45

VERNEY, FRANCES P.   Memoirs of the Verney Family During the Civil
War. London, 1892-99. 6 vols., 8vo., illus., book-plate, orig. cloth. Bow
Windows 62-957 1974 £48

VERNON, WILLIAM WARREN   Readings on the Inferno. 1906-09. 6 vols.,
thick crown 8vo., plates, faded, second edition. Howes 186-126 1974 £20

VERNON-HARCOURT, L. F.   A Treatise on Rivers and Canals. Oxford, 1882.
8vo., 2 vols., orig. cloth gilt, plates, first edition. Hammond 201-866 1974
£10.50

VERNULZ, NICOLAS DE   Rhetorum Collegii Porcensis Inclytate
Academiae Lovanensis Orationes. 1663. 16mo., old calf. Allen 213-1848
1973 $10

VERREN, ANTOINE   Livre des Prieres Publiques de l'Administration
des Sacrements et des Autres rites et Ceremonies de l'Eglise. Paris, 1856. 12mo.,
brown cloth gilt. Harper 213-163 1973 $35

VERSES On Mans Mortalitie. 1925. Thin 8vo., orig. wrappers, foxed,
woodcuts. Howes 185-429 1974 £7.50

VERSTEGEN, RICHARD Fl. 1565-1620   A Restivtion of Decayed Intelligence.
London, 1634. 4to., contemporary calf, rebacked. Dawsons PM 251-65 1974
£35

VERTES, MARCEL   Art and Fashion. New York, 1944. 4to.,
plates. Biblo & Tannen 210-101 1973 $15

VERTOT, RENE AUBERT DE   Histoire des Chevaliers Hospitaliers de S.
Jean de Jerusalem. 1726. 4 vols., calf, plates. Allen 213-1849 1973 $100

VERTOT, RENE AUBERT DE   History of Knights Hospitallers of St. John of
Jerusalem. 1757. 5 vols., 16mo., calf. Allen 213-1850 1973 $25

VERTOT, RENE AUBERT DE   Revolutions de Portugal. Paris, 1768. 12mo.,
contemporary French mottled calf, gilt, plate, fine. Bow Windows 62-960 1974
£10.50

VERZOCCHI, GIUSEPPE   Il Lavoro. Milan, 1950. 4to., color plates.
Biblo & Tannen 214-555 1974 $57.50

VESALIUS, ANDREAS   Opera Omnia Anatomica et Chirurgica Cura
Hermanni Boerhaave & Bernhardi Siegfried Albini. Leiden, 1725. Folio, orig.
leather, rebound. Rittenhouse 46-634 1974 $850

VESEY-FITZGERALD, B.   A Book of British Waders. 1939. 8vo., cloth.
Wheldon 130-644 1974 £5

VESLING, JOHANN   The Anatomy of the Body of Man. London,
1653. Small folio, contemporary calf, first edition in English. Dawsons PM
249-495 1974 £450

VESLING, JOHANN   Syntagma Anatomicum. 1666. 4to., contemporary calf, gilt. Dawsons PM 249-496 1974 £90

VETUSTA Monumenta. 1747-1906. 7 vols., roy. folio, half green morocco
gilt, wrappers, plates. Quaritch 939-35 1974 £550

VIAGGI Fatti da Vinetia, alla Tana, in Persia, in India, et in Constantinopoli.
1543. Old vellum gilt, morocco labels, first edition. Thomas 30-80 1973 £60

VIAU, THEOPHILE DE   Les Oeuvres de Theophile. Paris, 1660.
2 tomes in 1 vol., 12mo., full crimson morocco, gilt. L. Goldschmidt 42-126
1974 $400

VIBERT, J. G.   La Comedie en Peinture. 1902. 2 vols., roy.
4to., illus., half calf, orig. wrappers. Quaritch 940-271 1974 £35

VICKERS, A.   Phycologia Barbadensis. Paris, 1908. 4to.,
orig. half cloth, plates, scarce, limited edition. Wheldon 130-1363 1974 £50

VICKERS, ROY   The Exploits of Fidelity Dove. n.d. Bookplate,
scarce, English first edition. Covent 56-1276 1974 £55

VICKERY, SUKEY   Emily Hamilton. Worcester, 1803. 12mo.,
contemporary tree calf, gilt, first edition. Ximenes 35-433 1974 $225

VICTOR, BENJAMIN   An Epistle to Sir Richard Steele. London,
1722. 8vo., disbound, very rare, second edition. Ximenes 37-214 1974
$175

VICTOR, BENJAMIN   The Widow of the Wood. London, 1755.
12mo., contemporary calf, worn, first edition. Ximenes 35-434 1974 $125

VICTOR, BENJAMIN   The Widow of the Wood. London, 1755.
12mo., contemporary half calf, rubbed, first edition. Dawsons PM 252-1013
1974 £75

VICTOR, ORVILLE J.   The History, Civil, Political and Military, of
the Southern Rebellion. New York, (1861). 4to., 2 vols., orig. binding.
Butterfield 10-187 1974 $15

VICTOR, SEXTUS AURELIUS   Historiae Romanae Breviarium. 1670. Vellum.
Allen 213-1148 1973 $10

VICTOR Book of Operas. New York, 1949. Biblo & Tannen 214-929 1974 $10

VICTORIA, QUEEN   The Letters. 1907-32. 9 vols., large 8vo.,
plates, orig. cloth gilt, orig. & best edition. Howes 186-1287 1974 £45

VICTORIA, QUEEN   The Letters of Queen Victoria. London, 1908.
12mo., 3 vols., illus. Biblo & Tannen 213-713 1973 $20

VICTORIA & ALBERT MUSEUM. SCHREIBER COLLECTION   Catalogue of
English Porcelain, Earthenware, Enamels and Glass Collected by Charles Schreiber
and Lady C. E. Schreiber and Presented to the Victoria and Albert Museum in 1884.
1924-30. 3 vols., imp. 8vo., plates, cloth, rubbed, wrappers. Quaritch 940-661
1974 £30

VICTORIA AND ALBERT MUSEUM, SOUTH KENSINGTON   Dickens Exhibition,
March to October, 1912. Med. 8vo., half vellum, orig. wrappers bound in,
bookplate. Forster 98-74 1974 £3

VICTORIA County History. 1914. Imp. 8vo., plates, maps, orig. edition.
Howes 186-2017 1974 £15

VICTORIA History of the County of Lincoln. 1906. Folio, vol. 2. Traylen
79-349 1973 £15

VICTORIA History of the County of Surrey. London, 1902-05. Vols. 1 & 2
only, small folio, full red morocco, uncut. Traylen 79-392 1973 £25

VICTORIA Miniature Almanack & Fashionable Remembrancer for 1872. London.
2 1/2 X 1 5/8, orig. red morocco. Gregory 44-481 1974 $65

VICTORIA Miniature Almanack for 1858. Full red morocco, 2 7/8 X 1 1/4,
wallet flap. Gregory 44-480 1974 $25

VIDA DE San Felipe de Jesus Protomartir de Japon y Patron de su Patria Mexico.
Mexico, n.d. (1801). 8vo., contemporary tree calf, first edition, fine, rare.
Ximenes 36-148 1974 $275

VIDAL, EMERIC ESSEX   Picturesque Illustrations of Buenos Ayres &
Monte Video. Buenos Ayres, 1943. Orig. pictorial wrappers, plates. Smith
194-596 1974 £20

VIDAL, GORE   Visit to a Small Planet. Little, Brown, 1956.
Austin 51-997 1973 $7.50

VIDAL Y SOLER, S.   Revision de Plantas Vasculares Filipinas. Manila, 1886. Roy 8vo., half calf, plates, scarce. Wheldon 129-1132 1974 £25

VIDALIN, AUGUSTE   Le Souverain ou du Gouvernement d'Apres
l'Esprit des Institutions. Paris, 1830. 8vo., contemporary cherry red calf, gilt,
mint. L. Goldschmidt 42-407 1974 $75

LE VIE de N. S. Jesus-Christ Ecrite Par Les Qualtre Evangelistes Coordonnee. Paris, 1853. 2 vols. in 1, plates, contemporary French red morocco, gilt. Smith 194-559 1974 £15

VIELLES Chansons Por Les Petits Enfants. Paris, n.d. (c. 1900). Square 8vo., d.j. soiled & torn, profusely illus. in color, very fine. Current BW9-146 1974 $18.75

VIENNAE Avstriae Vrbis Nobilissime a Sultano Saleymano Immanissimo Turcarum Tyranno Immenso cum Exercitu Obsessae Historia. Augsburg, 1530. Small 4to., modern half calf, gilt, fine. Schafer 8-141 1973 sFr. 1,200

VIEUSSENS, RAYMOND   Experiences et Reflexions sur la Structure. Paris, 1755. 12mo., old half calf, worn, first edition. Gurney 64-222 1974 £25

VIEUSSENS, RAYMOND   Experiences et Reflexions sur la Structure et l'Usage des Visceres; Suivies d'une Explication Physico-Mechanique de la Pluspart des Maladies. Paris, 1755. 12mo., old half calf, worn, first edition. Gurney 66-190 1974 £25

VIEWS of Fortress Monroe and Vicinity. Old Point Comfort, 1896. Boards, photos. Jenkins 61-2553 1974 $10

VIEWS of Oswego and Vicinity. Oswego, 1886. 12mo., fold out, wrappers, photos. Jenkins 61-1938 1974 $10

VIEWS of the St. Lawrence. c. 1870-80. Orig. cloth gilt, plates. Smith 193-479 1973 £9.50

VIGENERE, BLAISE DE   Les Commentaires de Jules Cesar des Guerres de la Gaule. Chouet, 1594. Small 8vo., contemporary calf, gilt, third edition. L. Goldschmidt 42-127 1974 $45

THE VIGIL of Venus. Golden Cockerel Press, 1939. Limited to 100 copies on hand made paper, Latin text and English Translation of facing pages, engravings, 4to., citron levant morocco, cloth slipcase, good copy. Sawyer 293-150 1974 £175

VIGGIANI, ANGELO   Lo Schermo. Venice, 1575. 4to., full red morocco, gilt, copperplates, fine. Harper 213-164 1974 $525

VIGNE, GODFREY T.   Six Months In America. London, 1832. Rebound, plates, leather spine. Hood's 103-565 1974 $175

VIGNOLA, GIACOMO BAROZZI   Le Due Regole della Prospettiva Pratica. Rome, 1611. Folio, woodcuts, contemporary limp vellum. Quaritch 940-562 1974 £350

VIGNOLA, GIACOMO BAROZZI   Il Cinque di Architettura et Agiumtade Lopere. Venice, (n.d., ?159-). Folio, engraved plates, uncut, unpressed, unbound, title page and last page somewhat soiled. Thomas 32-14 1974 £45

VIGNY, ALFRED DE   Cinq-Mars . . . an Historical Romance. 1847. 8vo., contemporary cloth. Hill 126-202 1974 £8.50

VIGNY, ALFRED DE   Cinq-Mars, ou Une Conjuration sous Louis XIII. Paris, 1829. 4 vols. in 2, 12mo., contemporary quarter calf, gilt spines, some spotting. Bow Windows 66-724 1974 £6

VIGNY, ALFRED DE   Poesies Completes. Paris, 1841. 12mo., contemporary half calf, gilt. L. Goldschmidt 42-411 1974 £17.50

VIGO, GIOVANNI DE   Practica in Arte Chrurgica Copiosa. 1518. 4to., contemporary French calf. Dawsons PM 249-497 1974 £285

VIGO, GIOVANNI DE   Practica jo de Vigo Copiosa in Arte Chirurgica. Venice, 1520. Small folio, modern limp boards, wormholes. Thomas 32-331 1974 £35

VILAPLANA, ANTONIO RUIZ   Burgos Justice. 1938. Dust wrapper, faded covers. Covent 55-1395 1974 £6.30

VILDRAC, CHARLES   Seize Reproductions d'Apres les Tableaux de Henri-Matisse. Paris, 1922. Folio, plates. Minters 37-108 1973 $20

VILES, E.   The Fratemitye of Vacabondes. 1869-71. Roy 8vo., half morocco, gilt, illus. Hammond 201-342 1974 £10.50

THE VILLAGE: A Collection of Interesting Narratives. New York, 1839. Marbled boards, illus., revised. Hood's 104-918 1974 $25

VILLARS, D.   Memoire sur la Construction et l'Usage du Microscope. Strasburg & Paris, 1806. 8vo., half calf, folding plate. Wheldon 128-71 1973 £10

VILLIERS, ALAN   Whalers of the Midnight Sun. New York, 1934. Woodcuts. Rinsland 58-55 1974 $12.50

VILLIERS, WILLIAM   A Letter to Miss F--d. London, 1761. 8vo., disbound, first edition. Ximenes 35-435 1974 $45

VILLIERS DE L'ISLE-ADAM, COMTE DE   L'Amour Supreme. Paris, 1886. 12mo., contemporary half cloth, orig. wrapper, uncut, first edition. L. Goldschmidt 42-408 1974 $20

VILLIERS DE L'ISLE-ADAM, COMTE DE   Histoires Insolites. Paris, 1888. 12mo., half cloth, orig. wrapper, uncut, first edition. L. Goldschmidt 42-409 1974 $40

VILLIERS DE L'ISLE-ADAM, COMTE DE   La Revolte. Paris, 1870. 8vo., orig. wrapper, first edition. L. Goldschmidt 42-410 1974 $17.50

VILLIERS-STUART, C. M.   Gardens of the Great Mughals. 1913. 8vo., cloth, plates. Wheldon 129-1544 1974 £7.50

VILLIERS-STUART, C. M.   Spanish Gardens. 1929. Roy 8vo., cloth, plates. Wheldon 129-1543 1974 £7.50

VILLON, FRANCOIS   The Complete Works of. New York, 1928. Illus., limited to 960 copies, signed by the translator, thick 8vo., 2 vols., red cloth, contents near mint, d.j.'s rubbed with some tears. Current BW9-288 1974 $27.50

VILLON, FRANCOIS   Les Oeuvres. Paris, n.d. 16mo., full red morocco, gilt, rare, fine, complete copy. Harper 213-165 1973 $4750

VILLON, FRANCOIS   Oeuvres. Paris, 1923. 3 vols., 8vo., orig. wrapper. L. Goldschmidt 42-129 1974 $55

VILLON, FRANCOIS   The Testaments. 1924. Frontispiece, boards, English first edition. Covent 56-1277 1974 £5

VILMORIN-ANDRIEUX   The Vegetable Garden. 1905. 8vo., orig. cloth. Bow Windows 64-286 1974 £7.50

VILMORIN-ANDRIEUX et Cie, Les Plantes Potageres. Paris, 1904. Roy. 8vo., cloth, text-figures, third edition. Wheldon 128-1544 1973 £5

VINALL, JOHN   The Labour of the Righteous and Their Rest. 1818. Cloth. Howes 185-1745 1974 £5

VINCENS, F.   Recherches Organogeniques. Paris, 1917. 8vo., cloth, plates. Wheldon 129-1373 1974 £5

VINCENT, BENJAMIN   Haydn's Dictionary of Dates. New York, 1883. Biblo & Tannen 213-680 1973 $17.50

VINCENT, FRANCIS   A History of the State of Delaware. Philadelphia, 1870. 8vo., orig. bindings, fine. Butterfield 8-110 1974 $55

VINCENT, GEORGE E.   Rough Rider. Akron, 1899. 12mo., orig. cloth, illus., first edition. Ximenes 35-436 1974 $10

VINCENT, J. B.   Essai sur l'Histoire de l'Imprimerie en Belgique, 'Depuis le 15me Jusqu a la fin du 18m3 Siecle. Brussels, 1867. 8vo., orig. printed wrappers. Kraus B8-386 1974 $30

VINCENT, KITTY   Sugar and Spice. 1926. Plates, dust wrapper, English first edition. Covent 56-721 1974 £5.25

VINCENT, L.   Elenchus Tabularum Pinacothecarum, Atque Nonnullorum Cimeliorum in Gazophylacio. Harlem, 1719. 4to., modern calf, uncut, engraved plates, rare. Wheldon 128-72 1973 £30

VINCENT, L.   Elenchus Tabularum Pinacothecarum, Atque Nonnullorum Cimeliorum in Gazophylacio. Harlem, 1719. 4to., modern calf, uncut, plates, rare. Wheldon 131-190 1974 £30

VINCENT, LEON H.   DeWitte Miller: A Bibliographical Sketch.
Cambridge, 1912. Fine. Ballinger 1-55 1974 $12.50

VINCENT, WILLIAM   A Plain and Succienct Narrative. London, 1780.
8vo., modern boards. Dawsons PM 251-355 1974 £10

VINCENT DE BEAUVAIS   The Mirror of the World. (Westminster, 1481).
Small folio, 18th century panelled calf, illus., fine, first English edition.
Dawsons PM 252-1016 1974 £36,000

VINCENT Van Gogh...a Bibliography. New York, 1942. Poor copy, damp
stained, text clean. Biblo & Tannen 213-446 1973 $15

VINCENTIUS BELLOVACENSIS
Please turn to
VINCENT DE BEAUVAIS

VINES, SHERARD   The Course of English Classicism. London,
1930. 12mo., lst ed. Biblo & Tannen 210-930 1973 $8.50

VINET, ALEXANDRE   Histoire de la Litterature Francaise au
Dix-Huitieme Siecle. Paris, 1853. 2 vols., 8vo., contemporary half cherry
red polished calf, gilt. L. Goldschmidt 42-412 1974 $15

VINING, C.   Bigwigs, Canadians Wise and Otherwise.
Toronto, 1935. Illus. Hood's 104-184 1974 $22.50

VINNEN, ARNOLD   In Quatuor Libros Institutionum Imperialium
Commentarius Academicus et Forensis. 1793. 2 vols. in 1, boards, torn spine.
Allen 213-578 1973 $15

VINSON, MARIBEL Y.   Primer of Figure Skating. New York, 1938.
Biblo & Tannen 213-1020 1973 $8.50

VIOLET, P.   Traite en Forme de Lettre Contre la Nouvelle
Rhabdomance. 1694. 12mo., contemporary calf, rebacked, gilt, first edition.
Dawsons PM 245-738 1974 £45

VIOLLET-LE-DUC, EUGENE E.   Ancien Theatre Francois ou Collection des
Ouvrages Dramatiques les Plus Remarquables Depuis les Mysteres Jusqu'a Corneille.
Paris, 1854-57. 10 vols., 12mo., red jansenist morocco, gilt. L. Goldschmidt
42-128 1974 $225

VIOLLET-LE-DUC, EUGENE E.   Dictionnaire Raisonne du Mobilier Francais
de l'Epoque Carlo-Vingienne a la Renaissance. 1873-74. 6 vols., 8vo., quarter
dark red morocco, gilt, plates, illus. Quaritch 940-483 1974 £68

VIOLLET-LE-DUC, EUGENE E.   Habitations Modernes. Paris, 1875-77. Folio,
2 vols., contemporary blue boards, plates. Dawsons PM 251-100 1974 £75

VIRCHOW, RUDOLF   Briefe an Seine Eltern. Berlin, 1906. 8vo.,
plates, orig. blue cloth, very fine, first edition. Schafer 8-174 1973 sFr. 100

VIRCHOW, RUDOLF   Cellular Pathology. London, 1860. 8vo.,
modem buckram, untrimmed, fine, first edition in English. Dawsons PM 249-
499 1974 £140

VIRCHOW, RUDOLF   Die Cellularpathologie. Berlin, 1858. 8vo.,
orig. brown cloth, boards, first edition. Dawsons PM 249-498 1974 £625

VIRCHOW, RUDOLF   Die Cellularpathologie. Berlin, 1858. 8vo.,
illus., orig. cloth, worn, orig. boards, fine, rare, first edition. Dawsons PM
250-81 1974 £625

VIRCHOW, RUDOLF   Die Einheitsbestrebungen in Der
Wissenschaftlichen Medicin. Berlin, 1849. 8vo., orig. printed wrappers, very
fine, uncut, first edition. Schafer 8-173 1973 sFr. 160

VIRCHOW, RUDOLF   Handbuch der Speciellen Pathologie und Therapie.
Erlangen, 1854. 8vo., contemporary cloth-backed boards, fine, first edition.
Schumann 35-481 1974 $75

VIRCHOW, RUDOLF   Handbuch der Specieleen Pathologie und Therapie.
Erlangen, 1855. 8vo., contemporary half cloth, fine, first edition. Schumann
35-480 1974 $75

VIRCHOW, RUDOLF   Ueber Einige Merkmale Nieder Menschenrassen
am Schadel. Berlin, 1875. Large 4to., orig. pictorial boards, first edition.
Schumann 35-479 1974 $125

VIRDUNG OF HASSFURT, JOHANN   Nova Medicinae Methodus, Nunc
Primum & Condita & Aedita, ex Mathematica Ratione Morbos Curandi. Ettlingen,
1532. Small 4to., woodcuts, modern half vellum, good copy, some marginal
waterstains, first edition. Schafer 10-142 1974 sFr 1,600

VIRGIL
Please turn to
VERGILIUS MARO, PUBLIUS

VIRGIL, POLYDORE
Please turn to
VERGILIUS, POLYDORUS

VIRGINIA   Acts of the General Assembly of the State of
Virginia, Passed in 1861. Richmond, 1861. Orig. half calf. Jenkins 61-2518
1974 $25

VIRGINIA   Acts of the General Assembly of the State of
Virginia, Passed in 1861-62. Richmond, 1862. Jenkins 61-2519 1974 $25

VIRGINIA   Acts of the General Assembly of the State of
Virginia, Passed at Session of 1863-64. Richmond. Jenkins 61-2520 1974
$22.50

VIRGINIA   The New Constitution of Virginia, With the
Amended Bill of Rights as Adopted by the Reform Convention of 1850-51 and
Amended by the Convention of 1860-61. Richmond, 1861. Jenkins 61-2537
1974 $25

THE VIRGINIA Planter's Almanac for the Year of Our Lord 1806. Richmond,
n.d. 12mo., disbound, rare, good copy. Ximenes 37-3 1974 $40

VIRMAITRE, CHARLES   Les Maisons Comiques. Paris, 1868. 12mo.,
contemporary half red sheep. L. Goldschmidt 42-413 1974 $15

VISCHER-MERIAN, K.   Henman Sevogel Von Basel und sein Geschlecht.
1880. Folio, plates. Allen 213-1779 1973 $20

VISCONTI, ENNIO QUIRINO   Le Opere. Milan, 1818-37. 15 vols. in 14,
8vo. and roy. 8vo., plates, contemporary vellum gilt, morocco labels.
Quaritch 940-359 1974 £350

VISIAK, E. H.   Flints and Flashes. 1911. English first edition.
Covent 56-2099 1974 £5.25

VISIAK. E. H.   The Haunted Island. 1910. Dust wrapper, fine,
English first edition. Covent 56-1278 1974 £5.25

VISIGOTHIC LAWS   Forus Antiquus Gothorum Regum Hispaniae.
Madrid, 1600. Thick folio, contemporary limp vellum, complete copy, rare.
Harper 213-168 1973 $950

A VISIT to London, Containing a Description of the Principal Curiosities in the
Brithish Metropolis. 1805. First edition, copperplates, 12mo., orig. boards,
roan spine. George's 610-784 1973 £20

A VISIT to London, Containing a Description of the Principal Curiosities in the
British Metropolis. (c. 1820). Copperplates, new edition, 12mo., contemporary
roan backed boards. George's 610-785 1973 £10.50

THE VISITATION of the County of Gloucester Begun by Thomas May. 1884.
Imperial 8vo., orig. cloth. Broadhurst 23-1385 1974 £10

VISITATIONS of Berkshire. 1840. Folio, leather label, boards. Quaritch
939-773 1974 £30

VISITATIONS of the County of Devon. Exeter, (1895). 4to., half morocco
gilt. Quaritch 939-760 1974 £32.50

VISITS to the Aviary, for the Instruction of Youth. 1800. Engraved frontispiece,
12mo., orig. boards, leather spine worn. George's 610-786 1973 £10

VISMES, A. P. J.   Nouvelles Recherches sur l'Origine et la Desti-
nation des Pyramides d'Egypte. Paris, 1812. 8vo., 19th century half crimson
morocco, gilt, first edition. Dawsons PM 251-78 1974 £65

VISSCHER, WILLIAM LIGHTFOOT   "Black Mammy." Cheyenne, 1885.
8vo., orig. brown pictorial cloth, fine, first edition. Ximenes 35-437 1974
$90

VITAL Records of Norwich, Connecticut, 1659-1848. Hartford, 1913. Jenkins
61-706 1974 $10

VITELLI, GIOVANNI   A Treatise on the Formation, Cultivation and
Development of the Voice. (185-). 8vo., orig. printed wrappers, signed. Hill
126-182 1974 £8.50

VITRIARIUS, PHIL   Institutiones Juris Naturae. 1711. Small
8vo., contemporary vellum, gilt. Bow Windows 62-962 1974 £18

VITRUVIUS POLLIO, MARCUS   De Architectura. Amsterdam, 1649. 4 parts
in 1 vol., small folio, 18th century calf, worn, woodcuts. Thomas 28-44
1972 £25

VITRUVIUS POLLIO, MARCUS   De Architectura. Amsterdam, 1649. 4 parts
in 1 vol., small folio, 18th century calf, little worn head and spine, but sound.
Thomas 32-15 1974 £25

VITRUVIUS POLLIO, MARCUS   De Architectura Libri Decem. Venice, 1567.
Folio, illus., old limp vellum, crisp copy. Quaritch 940-563 1974 £350

VIVES, JUAN LUIS   De l'Ufficio del Marito. Venice, 1546.
8vo., contemporary limp vellum, fine, first Italian translation. Harper 213-170
1973 $285

VIVES, JUAN LUIS   Sacrum Diurnum de Sudore Iesu Christi. Lyon,
1532. 8vo., boards, very rare, very good copy. Harper 213-169 1973 $750

VIVIANI, VINCENZIO   Discorso al Serenissimo Cosimo III. 1687. 4to.,
boards, uncut, fine, first edition. Dawsons PM 245-739 1974 £85

VIZETELLY, ERNEST A.   With Zola in England. 1899. Orig. pictorial
cloth, portraits. Covent 55-1573 1974 £10.50

VLACQ, ADRIAEN   Trigonometria Artificialis. 1633. Folio, contemporary calf, rare, first edition. Zeitlin 235-232 1974 $500

VLACQ, ADRIAEN   Trigonometria Artificialis. 1633. Folio, contemporary green undressed calf, rebacked, gilt, first edition. Dawsons PM 245-
740 1974 £200

VLEKKE, B. H. M.   Nusantara. Massachusetts, 1943. 8vo.,
maps, inscription, orig. cloth, first edition. Bow Windows 62-963 1974 £7.50

VLIET, MINA A.   History of the Early Life and Business Interests
of the Village and Township of Leslie, Michigan. Leslie, 1914. 12mo., cloth.
Saddleback 14-510 1974 $15

VOCHS   Opusculum Praeclarum de Omni Pestilentia.
1537. 8vo., underlining. Rittenhouse 46-635 1974 $135

VOGELSTEIN, JULIE   Von Franzoesischer Buchmalerei. Muncih,
1914. Half cloth, plates. Kraus B8-272 1974 $36

VOGT, CECILE   Etude sur la Myelinisation des Hemispheres
Cererbraux. Paris & Leipzig, 1900. 8vo., orig. wrappers, illus., first edition.
Gurney 66-191 1974 £10

VOGT, FRIEDRICN   Geschichte der Deutschen Litterar Von den
Altesten Zeiten bis Zur Gegenwart. Leipzig & Vienna, 1897. 4to., plates,
illus., blue binders cloth. Dawsons PM 10-622 1974 £7

VOIART, ANNE ELISE   La Vierge d'Arduene. Paris, 1822. 8vo.,
half cloth, leather label, uncut, orig. wrapper. L. Goldschmidt 42-414
1974 $20

VOIGT, JOHANN HENRICH   Der Kunstgunstigen Einfalt Mathematischer.
Hamburg, 1668. 4to., unbound, sewn. Zeitlin 235-233 1974 $175

VOISIN, A.   Catalogue Methodique de la Bibliotheque de
l'Universite de Gand . . . Jurisprudence. Ghent, 1839. Engraved frontispiece,
8vo., unbound, waterstains. Kraus B8-273 1974 $15

VOISIN, JOSEPH DE   Theologia Ivdaeorum Sive Opus. Paris, 1647.
4to., contemporary vellum, gilt, woodcut, first edition. Bow Windows 62-964
1974 £22

VOITURE, VINCENT DE   Letters of Affaires, Love and Courtship.
London, 1657. 12mo., full morocco, gilt, first English edition. Dawsons PM
252-1019 1974 £95

VOLCKAMER, J. G.   Flora Noribergensis. Nuremberg, 1700. 4to.,
contemporary vellum, plates, rare. Wheldon 130-1217 1974 £70

VOLNEY, CONSTANTIN FRANCOIS CHASSEBOEUF   Tableau de Climat du
Sol des Etats-Unis d'Amerique. Paris, 1803. 8vo., 2 vols., contemporary tree
calf, gilt, fine, first edition. Gurney 66-192 1974 £63

VOLNEY, CONSTANTIN FRANCCOIS CHASSEBOEUF   Tableau du Climat et du
Sol des Etats-Unis d'Amerique. Paris, 1825. 8vo., buckram, uncut, folding
maps, second edition. Gurney 66-193 1974 £25

VOLNEY, CONSTANTIN FRANCOIS CHASSEBOEUF   Travels Through Egypt
and Syria. New York, 1798. 2 vols., 8vo., contemporary calf, first American
edition. Ximenes 35-438 1974 $40

VOLTA, ALESSANDRO   Le Opere de Alessandro Volta. 1918-23. 4to.,
2 vols., rebound, half morocco, plates. Dawsons PM 245-744 1974 £20

VOLTA, ALESSANDRO   Sulla Formazione Della Grandine. 1824. 8vo.,
orig. printed wrappers, uncut, first separate edition. Dawsons PM 245-743 1974
£18

VOLTAIRE, FRANCOIS MARIE AROUET DE   Candide. New York, 1928.
Folio, orig. pictorial cloth, illus. by Rockwell Kent, first edition, one of 1,470
numbered copies, signed by the artist, fine. MacManus 224-265 1974 $30

VOLTAIRE, FRANCOIS MARIE AROUET DE   Elemens de la Philosophie de
Neuton. Amsterdam, 1738. 8vo., contemporary green morocco, gilt borders,
half morocco slipcase, first edition, splendid copy, binding by Derome, engraved
plates, diagrams, from the libraries of Robert Samuel Turner and Louis Olry-
Roederer. Kraus 137-67 1974 $2,500

VOLTAIRE, FRANCOIS MARIE AROUET DE   The Ignorant Philosopher. 1767.
8vo., contemporary calf, first English edition. Quaritch 936-248 1974 £30

VOLTAIRE, FRANCOIS-MARIE AROUET DE   Letters Concerning the English Nation. London, 1733. 8vo., contemporary panelled calf, fine, first edition. Dawsons PM 245-570 1974 £135

VOLTAIRE, FRANCOIS MARIE AROUET DE   Letters Concerning the English
Nation. London, 1733. 8vo., contemporary calf, fine, rare, first edition in
English. Harper 213-171 1973 $285

VOLTAIRE, FRANCOIS MARIE AROUET DE   The Philosophical Dictionary.
1765. 8vo., contemporary sheep, first edition in English. Hill 126-280 1974
£48

VOLTAIRE, FRANCOIS MARIE AROUET DE   Poesies. Paris, (c. 1825). Orig.
green printed wrappers, fine, 2 3/4 X 1 3/4. Gregory 44-482 1974 $65

VOLTAIRE, FRANCOIS MARIE AROUET DE   The Princess of Babylon. 1927.
One of 1500 copies, vellum backed boards, gilt top, illus., very nice copy, first
edition. Covent 51-1368 1973 £5.25

VOLTAIRE, FRANCOIS MARIE AROUET DE   The Princess of Babylon. New York,
1928. Ltd. ed., uncut & unopened. Biblo & Tannen 213-610 1973 $8.50

VOLTAIRE, FRANCOIS MARIE AROUET DE   The Whole Prose Romances of
Voltaire. 1900. 3 vols., quarter leather, gilt, fine, etchings. Covent 55-1491
1974 £45

VON BEAUST, FRIEDRICH FERDINAND   Memoirs of. London, 1887. 2 vols.,
orig. binding. Wilson 63-604 1974 $10

VON BOEHN, MAX   Dolls and Puppets. 1932. Plates, illus., worn,
dust wrapper, English first edition. Covent 56-358 1974 £32.50

VON HUBL, ARTHUR FREIHERRN   Three-Colour Photography. London, 1915.
Red cloth, illus. Dawson's 424-327 1974 $45

VON MACH, EDMUND   Greek Sculpture.   Boston, 1903. Plates, cloth gilt, English first edition.   Covent 56-1517 1974 £6.50

VONSACHER-MASOCH, L.   Venus In Furs.   New York, 1928. Numbered, illus.   Rinsland 58-76 1974 $32

VON ZEDTWITZ, BARONESS   The Double Doctrine of the Church of Rome. New York, 1906.   Austin 62-659 1974 $8.50

VOORHELM, GEORGE   Traite sur la Jacinte.   Haarlem, 1773. 8vo., old quarter blue morocco, plates, fine, rare, third edition.   Traylen 79-61 1973 £35

VORAGINE, JACOBUS
Please turn to
JACOBUS DE VARAGINE

VORONOFF, SERGE   Rejuvenation by Grafting.   (1925). 8vo., cloth, gilt, plates.   Dawsons PM 249-501 1974 £10

VOSMAER, G. C. J.   Bibliography of Sponges.   Cambridge, 1928. 8vo., cloth, scarce.   Wheldon 130-201 1974 £5

VOSMAER, G. C. J.   The Sponges of the Bay of Naples.   The Hague, 1933-35. 2 vols., 4to., cloth & portfolio, plates.   Wheldon 131-956 1974 £30

VOSS, GERHARD JOHN   Rhetorices Contractae.   1672. Old calf, torn spine.   Allen 213-1175 1973 $25

VOSS, JOHANN HEINRICH   Mythologische Briefe.   1827. 2 vols. in 1, foxed.   Allen 213-1176 1973 $10

VOSSIUS, GERARD JOHANN   De Quatvor Artibvs Poplaribvs.   Amsterdam, 1660. 4to., contemporary calf, rebacked.   Dawsons PM 245-745 1974 £65

VOSSIUS, GERARD JOHANN   Historiae de Controversiis Quas Pelagius Elsque Reliquiae Moverunt.   1618. Small 4to., half 19th century calf.   Smith 194-195 1974 £30

VOSSIUS, GERARD JOHANN   Historiae de Controversisu.   Amstelodumi, 1655. Small 4to., old vellum, waterstain.   Smith 194-148 1974 £35

VOSSIUS, ISAAC   De Lucis Natura et Proprietate.   Amsterdam, 1662. 4to., half calf, first edition.   Schumann 35-482 1974 $165

VOSTER, ELIAS   A Treatise on Arithmetic.   Limerick, 1835. 8vo., half leather.   Emerald 50-549 1974 £12

VOULLIEME, ERNST   Der Buchdruck Kolns Bis Zum Ende des Funfzehnten Jahrhunderts.   Bonn, 1903. 8vo., orig. cloth, rubbed, first edition. Dawsons PM 10-624 1974 £26

VOULLIEME, ERNST   Die Deutschen Drucker des Funezehnten Jahrhunderts.   Berlin, 1922. Small folio, dec. boards, morocco label, second edition.   Dawsons PM 10-625 1974 £34

VOX Angliae.   London, 1682. Folio, disbound, browned, first edition. Dawsons PM 252-1021 1974 £25

VOYAGE Autour du Monde Sur la Corvette la Coquille Pendent les Annees 1822-25.   Paris, 1826-30. 3 vols., 4to., roy. folio, half calf, plates, rare. Wheldon 131-33 1974 £850

VREELAND, FRANK   Foremost Films of 1938.   Pitman, 1939. Austin 51-999 1973 $15

VRIES, ABRAHAM DE   Arguments des Allemands en Faveur de Leur Pretention a l'Invention de l'Imprimerie, ou Examen Critique de l'Ouvrage de A. E. Umbreit . . . Traduit du Hollandais.   The Hague, 1845. Large 8vo., orig. printed wrappers.   Kraus B8-388 1974 $30

VRIES, ABRAHAM DE   Bewijsgronden der Duitschers voor Hunne Aanspraak op de Uitvinding der Boekdrukkunst.   The Hague, 1844. Tall 8vo., orig. printed board (loose).   Kraus B8-387 1974 $20

VRIES, ABRAHAM DE   Eclaircissemens sur l'Histoire de l'Invention de l'Imprimerie . . . Traduit du Hollandais.   The Hague, 1843. 8vo., half leather. Kraus B8-389 1974 $28

VRIES, HUGO DE   Die Mutationstheorie.   Leipzig, 1901-03. 2 vols., roy. 8vo., half cloth, joints worn, coloured plates.   Wheldon 128-1174 £75

VRIES, HUGO DE   Die Mutationstheorie.   Leipzig, 1901-03. 8vo., 2 vols., half morocco, plates, first edition.   Dawsons PM 245-228 1974 £150

VRIES, HUGO DE   Die Mutationstheorie.   Leipzig, 1901(-03). 8vo., 2 vols., brown buckram, plates, first edition.   Dawsons PM 249-139 1974 £150

VRIES, HUGO DE   Die Mutationstheorie.   Leipzig, 1901-03. Roy 8vo., 2 vols., new cloth.   Wheldon 129-972 1974 £75

VRIES, HUGO DE   Die Mutationstheorie.   Leipzig, 1901-03. 2 vols., roy. 8vo., new cloth, plates.   Wheldon 131-1210 1974 £100

VRIES, HUGO DE   The Mutation Theory.   London, 1910-11. 2 vols., 8vo., orig. cloth, plates, illus.   Schuman 37-257 1974 $75

VRIES, HUGO DE   Species & Varieties.   Chicago & London, 1906. Thick demy 8vo., orig. cloth, second edition.   Smith 194-817 1974 £10

VRIES, SCATO DE   Il Breviario Grimani.   Leiden, 1906. Vols. 6-8, large folio, colored & other plates, unbound, in yellow slipcases.   Kraus B8-275 1974 $150

VYNER, ROBERT T.   Notitia Venatica.   1910. 2 vols., imp. 8vo., orig. pictorial cloth, plates, revised & enlarged edition.   Howes 186-497 1974 £20

VYNER, ROBERT T.   Notitia Venatica.   (1910). 2 vols., roy. 8vo., cloth, new revised edition.   Quaritch 939-271 1974 £30

VYNNE, HAROLD R.   The Woman That's Good.   Chicago, (1900). Cloth.   Hayman 57-229 1974 $10

W

W., E. Journal of a Governess. 1823. Engraved frontis., list of subscribers, oblong small 8vo., orig. wrappers, spine defective, lacks label. George's 610-417 1973 £5

W., G. Brief Memories of Niagara. London, n.d. Illus. Hood's 103-692 1974 $30

WAALS, J. D. VAN DER Over de Continuiteit van den Gas. Leiden, 1873. 8vo., orig. cloth, first edition. Gurney 64-223 1974 £90

WACHSBERGER, A. Martin Elsaesser: Bauten und Entwurfe aus den Jahren 1924-1932. Berlin, 1933. Large 4to., soiled cloth, illus., plates, ex-library. Minters 37-524 1973 $28

WACHTLER, HANS Die Blutezeit der Griechischen Kunst im Spiegel der Reliessarkophage. Leipzig, 1910. 12mo., illus. Biblo & Tannen 213-484 1973 $7.50

WADDELL, HELEN The Abbe Prevost. 1933. Quarter vellum, signed, English first edition. Covent 56-1279 1974 £6.30

WADDING, LUKE Epitome Annalium. 1662. Vol. 1 only, new buckram, stained text, foxed. Allen 213-1857 1973 $22.50

WADDINGTON, SAMUEL Arthur Hugh Clough: A Monograph. 1883. Hinges weak, name on title, very good copy, first edition. Covent 51-409 1973 £5.25

WADE, BLANCHE ELIZABETH Ant Ventures. Chicago & New York, (1924). 8vo., cloth, pictorial paste-label, illus. by Harrison Cady, very good copy, first edition. Frohnsdorff 15-11 1974 $10

WADE, BLANCHE ELIZABETH Ant Ventures. Chicago, 1924. 8vo., illus. Frohnsdorff 16-157 1974 $15

WADE, JOHN PETER A Paper On the Presentation and Treatment of the Disorders of Seamen and Soldiers in Bengal. London, 1793. 8vo., contemporary speckled calf, first edition. Schuman 37-258 1974 $65

WADE, MASON Parkman, Francis...Heroic Historian. New York, 1942. 1st ed. Biblo & Tannen 213-82 1973 $15

WADE, W. M. Walks in Oxford. Oxford, n.d. Full contemporary calf, 2 vols., plates, English first edition. Covent 56-2090 1974 £35

WADMORE, JAMES FOSTER Some Account of the Worshipful Company of Skinners. 1902. Roy. 8vo., plates. Howes 186-1444 1974 £8.50

WAGENKNECHT, EDWARD Cavalcade of the English Novel. 1943. Orig. unrevised edition. Austin 61-988 1974 $10

THE WAGGON of Life and Other Lyrics by Russian Poets of the 19th Century. London, 1947. Ltd. ed. Biblo & Tannen 214-744 1974 $15

WAGGONER, HYATT H. Hawthorne. Harvard, 1955. 264p., orig. ed. Austin 54-1021 1973 $8.50

WAGLER, J. G. Monographia Psittacorum. Munich, (1832). 4to., contemporary boards, rare. Wheldon 128-589 1973 £25

WAGNER, R. Icones Physiologicae. Leipzig, 1839. Folio, illus., plates. Wheldon 129-353 1974 £7.50

WAGNER, RICHARD The Authentic Librettos of the Wagner Operas. New York, 1938. Biblo & Tannen 210-960 1973 $9.50

WAGNER, RICHARD Richard Wagner in seinen Briefen. Stuttgart, 1907. Square 8vo., cloth gilt, English first edition. Covent 56-1957 1974 £7.50

WAGNER, RICHARD The Ring of the Niblung. 1911-12. 2 vols., 4to., plates, orig. buckram. Howes 185-395 1974 £45

WAGNER, RICHARD Tristan and Isolde. (1861). Folio, half green morocco, nice copy, first edition. Quaritch 940-826 1974 £140

WAHLENBERG, C. Flora Svecica Enumerans Plantes Svecica Indigenes. Uppsala, 1824-26. 2 vols., 8vo., contemporary half calf, worn. Wheldon 128-1316 1973 £18

WAHLENBERG, C. Flora Upsaliensis. Upsala, 1820. 8vo., modern boards, calf back antique style, map, rare. Wheldon 128-1315 1973 £30

WAHLENBERG, G. Flora Upsaliensis. Upsala, 1820. 8vo., calf, rebacked, rare. Wheldon 130-1218 1974 £38

WAHLENBERG, G. De Vegetatione et Climate in Helvetia Septentrionali. Zurich, 1813. 8vo., new cloth. Wheldon 130-1219 1974 £18

WAINWRIGHT, JOHN W. The Medical and Surgical Knowledge of William Shakespeare. New York, 1907. Signed. Rittenhouse 46-636 1974 $25

WAIT, BENJAMIN Letters from Van Dieman's Land. Buffalo, 1843. 8vo., orig. quarter calf, first edition. Ximenes 35-439 1974 $250

WAIT, W. E. Manual of the Birds of Ceylon. 1925. 4to., cloth, plates, map, scarce. Wheldon 128-590 1973 £10

WAIT, W. E. Manual of the Birds of Ceylon. 1925. 4to., cloth, plates, scarce. Wheldon 130-645 1974 £12

WAIT, W. E. Manual of the Birds of Ceylon. Colombo, 1931. Roy. 8vo., orig. cloth, map, scarce, second edition. Wheldon 128-591 1973 £7.50

WAITE, ARTHUR EDWARD The Book of Black Magic and of Pacts. Chicago, 1940. Roy. 8vo., plates, illus. Howes 186-1950 1974 £7.50

WAITE, ARTHUR EDWARD Lives of Alchemystical Philosophers. London, 1888. 8vo., orig. cloth. Schuman 37-259 1974 $90

WAITE, ARTHUR EDWARD A New Encyclopaedia of Freemasonry. (c.1921) 2 vols., orig. cloth, plates, illus., new revised edition. Bow Windows 66-731 1974 £9.50

WAITE, ARTHUR EDWARD The Real History of the Rosicrucians. London, 1887. First edition, uncut, backstrip edges quite worn. Wilson 63-51 1974 $37.50

WAITE, ARTHUR EDWARD Studies in Mysticism and Certain Aspects of the Secret Tradition. 1906. Demy 8vo., orig. cloth, fine. Broadhurst 24-1343 1974 £6

WAITE, J. M. Lessons in Sabre, Singlestick, Sabre and Bayonet, and Sword Feasts. London, c., 1880. 8vo., orig. cloth, gilt, illus. Hammond 201-624 1974 £12

WAKE, W. A Practical Discourse Concerning Swearing. 1696. Small 8vo., contemporary sprinkled calf. Quaritch 939-272 1974 £30

WAKEFIELD, H. R. The Clock Strikes Twelve. Sauk City, 1946. 1st ed., ltd. Biblo & Tannen 210-685 1973 $30

WAKEFIELD, H. R. Imagine a Man in a Box. New York, 1931. Biblo & Tannen 210-686 1973 $15

WAKEFIELD, H. R. They Return at Evening. 1928. English first edition. Covent 56-1753 1974 £5.25

WAKEFIELD, PRISCILLA An Introduction to Botany in a Series of Familiar Letters. 1807. 12mo., contemporary red straight-grain morocco, nice copy, hand-coloured plates, fifth edition. Wheldon 128-1175 1973 £7.50

WAKEFIELD, PRISCILLA An Introduction to Botany. 1831. 8vo., orig. boards, plates, tenth edition. Wheldon 131-1211 1974 £7.50

WAKEFIELD, PRISCILLA An Introduction to the Natural History and Classification of Insects. London, 1816. 12mo., orig. green cloth, trifle worn, hand colored plates, first edition. Ximenes 37-215 1974 $50

WAKEFIELD, PRISCILLA The Juvenille Travellers. 1808. Sixth edition, lacks half title and map, 12mo., contemporary calf, ads at end. George's 610-788 1973 £5

WAKEFIELD, PRISCILLA   The Juvenille Travellers. 1813. Ninth edition, folding coloured map, 12mo., contemporary half calf, rubbed. George's 610-789 1973 £7.50

WAKEFIELD, SHERMAN D.   How Lincoln Became President, The Part Played by Bloomington, Illinois and Certain of Its Citizens in Preparing Him for the Presidency and Securing His Nomination and Election. New York, 1936. First edition, limited to 650 numbered copies signed by author, d.j., 8vo., book mint, letter about book loosely laid in. Current BW9-439 1974 $42.50

WAKELEY, ANDREW   The Mariner's Compass Rectified. London, 1763. Woodcuts. Rinsland 58-51 1974 $150

WAKSMAN, S. A.   Enzymes. 1926. 8vo., cloth. Wheldon 129-114 1974 £7.50

WAKSMAN, S. A.   Enzymes, Properties, Distribution, Methods and Applications. 1926. 8vo., cloth. Wheldon 131-191 1974 £7.50

WAKSMAN, S. A.   Humus, Origin, Chemical Composition and Importance in Nature. (Baltimore), 1936. 8vo., cloth, figures, scarce. Wheldon 128-1176 1973 £7.50

WAKSMAN, S. A.   Principles of Soil Microbiology. 1927. 8vo., cloth. Wheldon 129-113 1974 £7.50

WALCOT, CHARLES   A Good Fellow. French, 1856. Austin 51-1001 1973 $6.50

WALCOT, CHARLES   Hiawatha. French, 1856. Austin 51-1002 1973 $8.50

WALCOT, CHARLES   Nothing To Nurse. French, 1857. Austin 51-1003 1973 $6.50

WALCOT, CHARLES   One Coat For Two Suits. French, 1857. Austin 51-1004 1973 $6.50

WALCOTT, CHARLES DOOLITTLE   Paleontology of the Eureka District. Washington, 1884. 8vo., orig. bindings, plates, presentation inscription. Butterfield 8-335 1974 $15

WALD, LILLIAN D.   Windows on Henry Street. Little, Brown, 1934. Austin 62-662 1974 $10

WALDO, FREDERICK   Captain Lightfoot. Topsfield, 1926. Orig. binding, illus., fine, d.w. Wilson 63-60 1974 $15

WALDO, FREDERICK   Down the Mackenzie Through the Great Lone Land. New York, 1923. Illus. Hood's 104-882 1974 $15

WALDRON, FRANCIS GODOLPHIN   Heigho for a Husband! London, 1794. 8vo., modern boards, first edition. Dawsons PM 252-1022 1974 £15

WALDRON, WILLIAM WATSON   Pocahontas. New York, 1841. 12mo., orig. green cloth, inscribed, first edition. Ximenes 35-440 1974 $17.50

WALDSCHMIDT, J. J.   Advice to a Physician. London, 1695. 12mo., old calf, rebacked. Traylen 79-275 1973 £50

WALEY, ARTHUR   The Analects of Confucius. 1938. Some foxing, very good copy, torn d.w., first edition. Covent 51-1908 1973 £5.25

WALEY, ARTHUR   The Book of Songs. 1937. Covers dusty, very good copy, in remains of d.w., first edition. Covent 51-1909 1973 £6.30

WALEY, ARTHUR   A Hundred and Seventy Chinese Poems. 1918. Linen backed boards, spine chafed, name on fly, very good copy, scarce, first edition. Covent 51-1910 1973 £8.40

WALEY, ARTHUR   An Introduction to the Study of Chinese Painting. 1923. 4to., plates, cloth orig. & best edition. Quaritch 940-427 1974 £35

WALEY, ARTHUR   The Poet Li Po. 1919. Wrappers, corner crumpled, else nice copy, scarce, first edition. Covent 51-1904 1973 £6.30

WALEY, ARTHUR   Three Ways of Thought in Ancient China. 1939. Name on fly, very good copy, torn d.w., first edition. Covent 51-1905 1973 £5.25

WALEY, ARTHUR   The Year Book of Oriental Art and Culture. London, 1925. Folio, 2 vols., vol. 1 text, vol. 2 plates portfolio, orig. cloth. Gregory 44-165 1974 $18.50

WALKE, H.   Naval Scenes and Reminiscences of the Civil War. New York, 1877. Large 8vo., illus., diagrams, orig. binding. Butterfield 10-188 1974 $27.50

WALKER, A.   Remarks Made in a Tour from London to the Lakes of Westmoreland and Cumberland in the Summer of MDCCXCI . . . to Which is Annexed, a Sketch of the Police, Religions, Arts, and Agriculture of France, Made in an Excursion to Paris in MDCCLXXXV. 1792. First edition, demy 8vo., full mottled calf by Fazakerley, raised bands, entirely uncut, fine, complete with rare portrait mounted to size. Broadhurst 24-1554 1974 £35

WALKER, ADAM   Analysis of a Course of Lectures in Natural and Experimental Philosophy. (London, c., 1800). 8vo., cloth, tenth edition. Gurney 64-224 1974 £8

WALKER, ADAM   Analysis of a Course of Lectures in Natural and Experimental Philosophy. (London, c. 1800). 8vo., tenth edition, cloth. Gurney 66-194 1974 £8

WALKER, ALEXANDER   The Celluloid Sacrifice. Hawthorn, 1966. Austin 51-1005 1973 $10

WALKER, ALEXANDER   Intermarriage. London, 1838. 8vo., orig. cloth, uncut, first edition. Dawsons PM 249-502 1974 £30

WALKER, CHARLES   Authentick Memoirs of . . . . Sally Salisbury. London, 1723. 8vo., frontispiece, modern boards, first edition. Dawsons PM 252-1023 1974 £30

WALKER, CHARLOTTE ABELL   Under a Lucky Star. New York, 1901. Biblo & Tannen 213-922 1973 $8.50

WALKER, E. S.   History of the Springfield Baptist Assoc. 1881. Cloth. Putnam 126-151 1974 $22.50

WALKER, EDWARD   Historical Discourses upon Several Occasions. 1705. Folio, contemporary calf. Quaritch 936-249 1974 £15

WALKER, EDWARD   Terrestial and Cosmical Magnetism. Cambridge, 1866. 8vo., orig. red cloth, uncut, first edition. Dawsons PM 245-746 1974 £7

WALKER, ELMER   A Thoroughbred Tramp. Rossiter, 1914. 95p., illus., paper. Austin 54-1022 1973 $7.50

WALKER, F.   Catalogue of Specimens of Dermaptera Saltatoria. 1869-71. 5 vols. in 2, new cloth. Wheldon 131-875 1974 £38

WALKER, F.   Catalogue of Specimens of Dermaptera Saltatoria in the Collection of the British Museum. 1869-71. 5 vols. in 2, 8vo., new cloth. Wheldon 128-822 1973 £38

WALKER, F.   Catalogue of the Specimens of Blattariae. 1868. 8vo., new cloth, rare. Wheldon 129-695 1974 £7.50

WALKER, F.   Catalogue of the Specimens of Heteropterous Hemiptera. 1867-73. 8vo., new cloth. Wheldon 129-693 1974 £55

WALKER, F.   Catalogue of the Specimens of Heteropterous Hemiptera in the Collection of the British Museum. 1867-73. 8 vols. in 3, 8vo., new cloth, very rare. Wheldon 131-876 1974 £55

WALKER, F.   Catalogue of the Specimens of Neuropterous Insects. 1852-53. 12mo., new cloth. Wheldon 129-694 1974 £17

WALKER, F.   Insecta Britannica: Diptera. 1851-56. 3 vols., 8vo., cloth, ex-library, clean and sound. Wheldon 128-823 1973 £5

WALKER, F.   List of the Specimens of Lepidopterous Insects in the Collection of the British Museum. 1854-66. 35 parts in 12 vols., 12mo., new cloth. Wheldon 131-874 1974 £75

WALKER, G. G.　　　The Honourable Artillery Company in the Great War. 1930. 8vo., orig. cloth, dust wrapper. Bow Windows 64-744 1974 £5

WALKER, GEORGE　　　The Voyages and Cruises of Commodore Walker. London, 1760. 2 vols., small 8vo., contemporary calf gilt, leather labels, fine, first edition. Traylen 79-444 1973 £300

WALKER, J.　　　The Armorial Bearings. Newcastle, 1824. 8vo., modern boards, cloth back. Quaritch 939-752 1974 £20

WALKER, J.　　　Geological Map of England, Wales and Part of Scotland. 1835. Roy 8vo., orig. cloth case. Wheldon 129-873 1974 £50

WALKER, J.　　　Great American Paintings from Smibert to Bellows, 1729-1924. New York, 1943. 4to., plates, 1st ed. Biblo & Tannen 210-397 1973 $15

WALKER, J.　　　Liverpool and Manchester Railway. Liverpool, 1829. 8vo., library stamp, scarce. Quaritch 939-91 1974 £95

WALKER, J. H.　　　A Scotsman in Canada. London, 1935. Cover faded. Hood's 104-286 1974 $12.50

WALKER, JAMES B.　　　Experiences of Pioneer Life in the Early Settlements and Cities of the West. Chicago, 1881. Cloth. Hayman 59-650 1974 $35

WALKER, JOHN　　　Elements of Elocution. Boston, 1810. Portrait, engraved charts, old calf, leather label, rubbed but sound, first U. S. edition. Butterfield 10-520 1974 $15

WALKER, JOHN　　　Folk Medicine in Modern Egypt. London, 1934. Biblo & Tannen 210-1019 1973 $15

WALKER, JONATHAN　　　Trial and Imprisonment of. Boston, 1845. 8vo., orig. black cloth, first edition. Ximenes 35-441 1974 $45

WALKER, OBADIAH　　　Of Benefits of Our Saviour, Jesus Christ, to Mankind. 1680. Calf covers worn and detached. Allen 216-1960 1974 $40

WALKER, OBADIAH　　　Of Education. Oxford, 1673. 12mo., contemporary calf, second edition. Ximenes 35-442 1974 $75

WALKER, THOMAS　　　A Review of Some of the Political Events. London, 1794. 8vo., disbound, first edition. Ximenes 35-443 1974 $22.50

WALKER, THOMAS A.　　　The Severn Tunnel: Its Construction and Difficulties, 1872-1887. 1888. Engraved portraits, first edition, roy. 8vo., binder's cloth, leather label, fine. Broadhurst 24-1556 1974 £20

WALKER, THOMAS A.　　　The Severn Tunnel. 1888. First edition, med. 8vo., binder's cloth, very good copy, portraits on steel, sketches, plans. Broadhurst 24-1344 1974 £20

WALKINGAME, F.　　　The Tutor's Assistant. Montreal, 1841. Hood's 104-417 1974 $25

WALKLEY, T.　　　A Catalogue of the Dukes, Marquesses, Earles, Viscounts, Barons. London, 1642. Small 8vo., contemporary sheep. Quaritch 939-753 1974 £25

WALKLEY, T.　　　A New Catalogue of the Dukes, Marquesses, Earls, Viscounts, Barons. London, 1652. Small 8vo., old calf. Quaritch 939-754 1974 £12.50

THE WALKING Statue. (N.P., n.d.). 4to., modern boards. Dawsons PM 252-1024 1974 £8

WALL, F.　　　A Monograph of the Sea Snakes. Calcutta, 1909. 4to., orig. wrappers, plates, text-figures. Wheldon 128-666 1973 £7.50

WALL, MARTIN　　　Clinical Observations on the Use of Opium in Low Fevers. Oxford, 1786. 8vo., disbound. Gurney 64-225 1974 £16

WALL, SARAH E.　　　Orange Grove. Worcester, 1866. 12mo., orig. dark brown cloth, first edition. Ximenes 35-444 1974 $15

WALL, WILLIAM　　　The History of Infant Baptism. Oxford, 1844. 4 vols., full calf gilt, best edition. Howes 185-1754 1974 £18

WALLACE, ALFRED RUSSELL　　　Darwinism. London, 1889. 8vo., portrait, map, illus., orig. cloth, second edition. Bow Windows 62-237 1974 £5.75

WALLACE, ALFRED RUSSELL　　　Darwinism. (1899). 8vo., cloth, portrait, map. Wheldon 131-294 1974 £5

WALLACE, ALFRED RUSSELL　　　Darwinism, an Exposition of the Theory of Natural Selection, With Some Of Its Applications. (1889). 8vo., cloth, portrait, map, text figures. Wheldon 128-96 1973 £5

WALLACE, ALFRED RUSSELL　　　Geographical Distribution of Animals. 1876. 2 vols., large 8vo., plates, orig. cloth gilt. Smith 193-424 1973 £10

WALLACE, ALFRED RUSSELL　　　The Geographical Distribution of Animals. 1876. 8vo., 2 vols., calf gilt, plates, maps. Wheldon 129-354 1974 £45

WALLACE, ALFRED RUSSELL　　　Die Geographische Verbreitung der Thiere. Dresden, 1876. 8vo., 2 vols., half leather, worn, plates. Wheldon 130-374 1974 £10

WALLACE, ALFRED RUSSELL　　　Island Life. 1880. 8vo., orig. cloth, maps, illus. Wheldon 129-115 1974 £30

WALLACE, ALFRED RUSSELL　　　The Malay Archipelago. 1867. 8vo., 2 vols., orig. green cloth, illus., second edition. Wheldon 130-322 1974 £10

WALLACE, ALFRED RUSSELL　　　The Malay Archipelago. 1869. 2 vols., 8vo., rebound in green cloth, maps, illus., very scarce first edition. Wheldon 128-245 1973 £35

WALLACE, ALFRED RUSSELL　　　The Malay Archipelago. 1869. 2 vols., 8vo., orig. cloth, maps, illus., good clean copy, second edition. Wheldon 128-246 1973 £22

WALLACE, ALFRED RUSSELL　　　The Malay Archipelago. 1890. 8vo., cloth, plates. Wheldon 129-310 1974 £5

WALLACE, ALFRED RUSSELL　　　A Narrative of Travels on the Amazon and Rio Negro. 1889. Post 8vo., cloth. Wheldon 129-311 1974 £5

WALLACE, ALFRED RUSSELL　　　A Narrative of Travels on the Amazon and Rio Negro. 1889. 8vo., cloth, plates, second edition. Wheldon 131-399 1974 £10

WALLACE, ALFRED RUSSELL　　　A Narrative of Travels. 1892. 8vo., prize calf, gilt, plates. Wheldon 130-323 1974 £7.50

WALLACE, ALFRED RUSSELL　　　Natural Selection and Tropical Nature. 1891. 8vo., cloth, new edition. Wheldon 128-73 1973 £7.50

WALLACE, ALFRED RUSSEL　　　The World of Life. 1910. Plates, illus., inscribed, English first edition. Covent 56-1156A 1974 £21

WALLACE, D. MAC KENZIE　　　Russia. 1877. 2 vols., 8vo., orig. cloth, folding maps, covers soiled, third edition. Bow Windows 66-733 1974 £5.50

WALLACE, EDGAR　　　The Devil Man. 1931. Dust wrapper, frayed, English first edition. Covent 56-2103 1974 £5.25

WALLACE, EDGAR　　　The Feathered Serpent. New York, 1928. First American edition. Covent 55-1494 1974 £5.25

WALLACE, EDGAR　　　Kitchener's Army and the Territorial Forces. n.d. 4to., dec. cloth gilt, fine, English first edition. Covent 56-1285 1974 £12.50

WALLACE, EDGAR　　　Kitchener's Army and the Territorial Forces. n.d. 4to., half morocco gilt, English first edition. Covent 56-1284 1974 £15

WALLACE, EGLANTINE　　　The Ton. 1788. 8vo., cloth. Quaritch 936-251 1974 £5

WALLACE, F. W.　　　Blue Water. Toronto, 1935. Ex-library. Hood's 104-582 1974 $10

WALLACE, F. W.　　In the Wake of the Wind-Ships.　London, (1927). 8vo., illus., map, orig. cloth.　Bow Windows 62-966 1974 £5.75

WALLACE, JOSEPH　　Sketch of the Life and Public Services of Edward D. Barker.　Springfield, 1870. 8vo., orig. blue cloth, first edition. Ximenes 35-445 1974 $15

WALLACE, LEW　　The Fair God.　Boston, 1873. 8vo., orig. violet cloth, first edition.　Ximenes 35-446 1974 $20

WALLACE, LEW　　The Prince of India.　New York, 1893. 2 vols., 12mo., orig. blue cloth, first edition, first issue.　Ximenes 35-447 1974 $12

WALLACE, ROBERT　　A Dissertation on the Numbers of Mankind, in Ancient and Modern Times.　Edinburgh, 1809. Revised & corrected second edition, demy 8vo., contemporary mottled calf, fine.　Broadhurst 24-1345 1974 £10

WALLACE, W. S.　　A History of the University of Toronto.　Toronto, 1927. Hood's 102-439 1974 $35

WALLACE, W. S.　　The Memoirs of the Rt. Hon. Sir George Foster. Toronto, 1933. Illus.　Hood's 102-266 1974 $15

WALLACE, W. S.　　Notes on Military Writing for English-Canadian Soldiers.　Toronto, 1943.　Hood's 102-127 1974 $10

WALLACE, WILFIRD　　Life of St. Edmund of Canterbury.　1893. Plates, scarce.　Howes 185-1133 1974 £7.50

WALLACE, WILLIAM　　Lectures and Essays On Natural Theology and Ethics.　1898. Thick 8vo., portrait.　Howes 185-2034 1974 £5

WALLACE Collection Catalogues: Pictures and Drawings.　1920. 8vo., orig. cloth, illus.　Bow Windows 66-732 1974 £12

WALLACH, IRA　　Gutenberg's Folly.　Abelard, Schuman, 1954. 160p., illus.　Austin 54-1023 1973 $6.50

WALLACH, IRA　　Hopaglong Freud.　Schuman, 1951. 119p., illus.　Austin 54-1024 1973 $6.50

WALLACH, IRA　　Muscle Beach.　Little, Brown, 1959. 236p. Austin 54-1025 1973 $6

WALLACK, LESTER　　Memories of 50 Years.　Scribner, 1889. Austin 51-1008 1973 $6.50

WALLEN, WILLIAM　　The History and Antiquities of the Round Church at Little Maplestead.　1836. 8vo., rebacked, orig. cloth, woodcut illus., plates.　Bow Windows 66-734 1974 £8.50

WALLENBERG, J. K.　　The Place-Names of Kent.　1934. Large 8vo., orig. wrappers.　Howes 186-2069 1974 £5.50

WALLER, EDMUND　　Instructions to a Painter.　London, 1666. Folio, half calf, first complete edition.　Dawsons PM 252-1026 1974 £125

WALLER, EDMUND　　Poems.　London, 1693. 8vo., modern boards, sixth edition.　Dawsons PM 252-1027 1974 £30

WALLER, EDMUND　　Poems.　1711. 8vo., contemporary panelled calf, eighth edition.　Quaritch 936-252 1974 £10

WALLER, EDMUND　　The Second Part of Mr. Waller's Poems. London, 1690. Small 8vo., contemporary mottled calf, first edition.　Dawsons PM 252-1028 1974 £120

WALLER, WILLIAM　　Vindication of the Character and Conduct of. 1793. Orig. marbled boards, label, sole edition.　Howes 186-1292 1974 £10

WALLERIUS, J.　　Systema Mineralogicum Quocorpora Mineralia in Classes.　Stockholm, 1772-75. 2 vols., 8vo., contemporary boards, neatly rebacked in calf, plate.　Wheldon 128-1063 1973 £35

WALLETT, WILLIAM FREDERICK　　The Queen's Jester.　1870. 8vo., orig. dec. cloth, portrait.　Hill 126-282 1974 £5.50

WALLING, H. F.　　Tackabury's Atlas of the Dominion of Canada. Montreal, Toronto, & London, 1875. Mended spine.　Hood's 103-44 1974 $75

WALLIS, A.　　The Pottery and Porcelain of Derbyshire. 1870. 8vo., half leather, scarce, second edition.　Quaritch 939-340 1974 £12

WALLIS, HENRY　　Notes on Some Early Persian Lustre Vases.　1885-89. Folio, contemporary half morocco, gilt, illus., plates, first edition.　Hammond 201-1003 1974 £48

WALLROTH, G. F. W.　　Schedulae Criticae de Plantis Florae Halensis Selectis Corollarium Novum.　Halle, 1822. 8vo., cloth, plates, scarce. Wheldon 128-1317 1973 £12

WALN, ROBERT　　American Bards.　Philadelphia, 1820. 12mo., disbound, first edition.　Goodspeed's 578-399 1974 $10

WALPOLE, HORACE, EARL OF OXFORD 1717-1797　Anecdotes of Painting in England.　1765. 4to., 4 vols., contemporary russia, gilt, plates, second edition. Quaritch 936-253 1974 £55

WALPOLE, HORACE, EARL OF OXFORD 1717-1797　Anecdotes Told Me by Lady Denbigh.　1932. Cloth backed boards, English first edition.　Covent 56-1287 1974 £10

WALPOLE, HORACE, EARL OF OXFORD 1717-1797　A Catalogue of the Classic Contents of Strawberry Hill Collected By.　London, 1842. 4to., orig. printed wrappers, first edition.　Dawsons PM 10-629 1974 £56

WALPOLE, HORACE, EARL OF OXFORD 1717-1797　A Catalogue of the Classic Contents of Strawberry Hill.　London, 1842. 4to., contemporary gilt framed vellum, illus.　Dawsons PM 252-1030 1974 £70

WALPOLE, HORACE, EARL OF OXFORD 1717-1797　A Catalogue of the Royal and Nobel Authors of England.　London, 1759. 2 vols., 8vo., contemporary calf, second edition.　Ximenes 35-448 1974 $35

WALPOLE, HORACE, EARL OF OXFORD 1717-1797　A Catalogue of the Royal and Nobel Authors of England.　London, 1796. 8vo., contemporary calf, fine, new edition.　Dawsons PM 10-630 1974 £18

WALPOLE, HORACE, EARL OF OXFORD 1717-1797　Correspondence. London, 1937. 2 vols., 8vo., blue cloth, plates.　Dawsons PM 252-1031 1974 £7

WALPOLE, HORACE, EARL OF OXFORD 1717-1797　Journal of the Printing Office at Strawberry Hill.　1923. 4to., parchment back, limited.　Quaritch 939-473 1974 £25

WALPOLE, HORACE, EARL OF OXFORD 1717-1797　The Letter of Horace Walpole.　1906. 9 vols., steel portraits.　Austin 61-989 1974 $95

WALPOLE, HORACE, EARL OF OXFORD 1717-1797　The Letters.　1840. 6 vols., portraits, orig. cloth, plates, worn.　Howes 186-499 1974 £7.50

WALPOLE, HORACE, EARL OF OXFORD 1717-1797　Letters From.　1818. 4to., contemporary half calf, marbled boards, first edition.　Broadhurst 23-517 1974 £20

WALPOLE, HORACE, EARL OF OXFORD 1717-1797　Letters from...to George Montague, 1736-1770, Now first Published from the Originals.　1818. Roy. 4to., contemporary half calf, marbled boards, first edition, fine.　Broadhurst 24-494 1974 £20

WALPOLE, HORACE, EARL OF OXFORD 1717-1797　Letters...to George Montagu.　1818. Large 4to., contemporary calf, gilt, first edition.　Hill 126-283 1974 £21

WALPOLE, HORACE, EARL OF OXFORD 1717-1797　The Magpie and Her Brood.　(1764). 4to., first edition.　Ximenes 35-449 1974 $200

WALPOLE, HORACE, EARL OF OXFORD 1717-1797　Memories of the Last Ten Years of the Reign of the George the Second.　1822. Large 4to., 2 vols., orig. boards, rebacked, uncut, first edition.　Hill 126-284 1974 £25

WALPOLE, HORACE, EARL OF OXFORD 1717-1797　Memoris of the Reign of King George III.　1894. 4 vols., paper brittle.　Allen 216-2080 1974 $15

WALPOLE, HORACE, EARL OF OXFORD 1717-1797   The Mysterious Mother.
London, 1791. 8vo., contemporary tree calf, third edition. Dawsons PM 252-
1029 1974 £24

WALPOLE, HORACE, EARL OF OXFORD 1717-1797   Private Correspondence.
1820. 4 vols., half calf. Allen 216-t 1974 $20

WALPOLE, HORATIO   The Convention Vindicated. London, 1739.
8vo., paper wrappers, first edition. Dawsons PM 247-299 1974 £20

WALPOLE, HORATIO   The Grand Question. London, 1739. 8vo.,
disbound, first edition. Dawsons PM 247-298 1974 £16

WALPOLE, ROBERT   Aedes Walpolianae. 1747. Contemporary
panelled calf, front cover detached, engraved title, folding plates. Eaton
Music-683 1973 £40

WALPOLE, ROBERT   The Life of. London, 1731. 8vo., disbound,
first edition. Ximenes 35-451 1974 $22.50

WALPOLE, ROBERT   Memoirs of the Life and Administration of.
1816. 4 vols., contemporary calf gilt. Howes 186-1293 1974 £20

WALPOLE, ROBERT   A Short History of Parliament. 1713. 8vo.,
cloth, uncut. Quaritch 936-254 1974 £18

WALPOLE, ROBERT   Some General Considerations Concerning the
Alteration and Improvement of Publick Revenues. 1733. 8vo., modern boards,
roan back. Quaritch 939-273 1974 £15

WALPOLE-BOND, J.   A History of Sussex Birds. 1938. Small 4to.,
3 vols., buckram, scarce. Wheldon 130-646 1974 £35

WALSH, JAMES JOSEPH   History of Medicine In New York. New York,
1919. 5 vols., illus. Rittenhouse 46-638 1974 $65

WALSH, JAMES JOSEPH   History of Medicine In New York. New
York, 1919. 5 vols., 8vo., orig. cloth, illus., first edition. Schuman 37-260
1974 $110

WALSH, JAMES JOSEPH   What Civilization Owes to Italy. 1923.
Austin 62-664 1974 $10

WALSH, JOHN BENN   Astronomy and Geology Compared. London, 18-
71. 8vo., orig. blue cloth, gilt, fine. Dawsons PM 245-748 1974 £10

WALSH, RICHARD J.   Adventures of Marco Polo Edited for the Modern
Reader. New York, 1948. 1st ed., illus. Frohnsdorff 16-7 1974 $15

WALSH, ROBERT   The American Review of History and Politics.
Philadelphia, 1811-12. Vol. 1, three quarter calf, worn, foxed. Jenkins
61-2562 1974 $35

WALSH, ROBERT   An Appeal From the Judgements of Great Britain
Respecting the U.S.A. Philadelphia, 1819. Leather, marbled boards, signed,
presentation. Rinsland 58-98 1974 $37

WALSH, ROBERT   A Letter on the Genius and Dispositions of the
French Government. London, 1810. 8vo., half calf, rebacked. Dawsons PM
247-300 1974 £12

WALSH, THOMAS   The World's Great Catholic Poetry. 1932.
584 pages. Austin 61-991 1974 $10

WALSH, WILLIAM   A Dialogue Concerning Women. London,
1691. 8vo., contemporary mottled calf, first edition. Ximenes 35-452 1974
$275

WALSH, WILLIAM   Works. 1736. New buckram, rubber stamp.
Allen 216-1961 1974 $10

WALSHE, E. H.   Cedar Creek, a Tale of Canadian Life.
Toronto, n.d. Illus. Hood's 103-515 1974 $10

WALSHE, WALTER HAYLE   The Nature and Treatment of Cancer. London,
1846. 8vo., orig. cloth, gilt, first edition. Hammond 201-554 1974 £6.50

WALSINGHAM, CHARLOTTE   O'er Moor and Fen. Philadelphia, 1876.
Orig. cloth, somewhat worn, first edition. MacManus 224-443 1974 $25

WALSINGHAM, LORD   Fauna Hawaiiensis. Microlepidoptera.
Cambridge, 1907. 4to., wrappers, plates. Wheldon 131-877 1974 £10

WALSINGHAM, THOMAS   Historia Brevis. London, 1574. Folio, calf
antique, fine, first edition. Dawsons PM 251-356 1974 £140

WALTER, H.   Einfurung im die Allgemeine Pflanzengeographie
Deutschlands. Jena, 1927. Roy. 8vo., buckram, text-figures, coloured folding
maps. Wheldon 128-1318 1973 £5

WALTER, JOHN   Flights of Fancy. Small 4to., half calf,
unpublished. Dawsons PM 252-1033 1974 £225

WALTER, RICHARD   A Voyage Round the World, In the Years
1740-44 By George Anson. London, 1767. 4to., old calf, rebacked, gilt,
leather label, plates, twelfth edition. Traylen 79-413 1973 £52

WALTER, T.   Flora Caroliniana. 1788. 8vo., modern half
calf, plate. Wheldon 129-1134 1974 £350

WALTER, T.   Flora Caroliniana, Secundum Systema
Vegetabilium Perillustris Linnaei Digesta. 1788. 8vo., modern calf antique.
Wheldon 131-1361 1974 £350

WALTER, THOMAS   The Grounds and Rules of Musick Explained.
Boston, 1746. Oblong 8vo., contemporary blindstamped calf, rubbed but sound,
fourth edition. Ximenes 37-216 1974 $750

WALTER, WILLIAM BICKER   Sukey. Baltimore. 1821. 8vo., disbound,
inscribed, presentation. Ximenes 35-454 1974 $20

WALTER, WILLIAM BICKER   Sukey. Boston, 1821. 8vo., orig. printed
wrappers, fine, first edition. Ximenes 35-453 1974 $45

WALTERS, H. B.   The Art of the Greeks. (1906). 8vo., orig.
cloth, plates, illus., some foxing. Bow Windows 66-735 1974 £6.50

WALTERS, H. B.   Catalogue of Bronzes, Greek, Roman and
Etruscan, in the Department of Greek and Roman Antiquities. 1899. 4to.,
plates, illus., cloth. Quaritch 940-300 1974 £21

WALTERS, H. B.   Catalogue of the Silver Plate. London, 1921.
4to., plates, illus., fine, orig. cloth. Bow Windows 62-969 1974 £14

WALTERS, H. B.   Slect Bronzes, Greek, Roman and Etruscan in
the Department of Antiquities. Quaritch 940-301 1974 £25

WALTERS, HENRY   Incunabula Typographica. Baltimore, 1906.
4to., orig. embossed calf, fine. Dawsons PM 10-634 1974 £45

WALTERS, JOHN   A Dissertation on the Welsh Language. 1771.
8vo., contemporary calf, scarce, first edition. Ximenes 35-455 1974 $60

WALTERS, RAYMOND   The Bethlehem Bach Choir. 1918.
290 pages. Austin 57-687 1974 $12.50

WALTHER, JOHANN   Epitaphium Des Ehrwirdigen Herrn und Vaters
Martini Luthers. Wittenberg, 1546. 4to., boards, woodcut, very rare first
edition. Harper 213-208 1973 $575

WALTON, EVANGELINE   Witch House. Sauk City, 1945. 1st ed., ltd.
Biblo & Tannen 210-688 1973 $15

WALTON, IZAAK   The Compleat Angler. Frowde, n.d. Portrait,
illus., orig. limp red roan, fine, 2 1/4 X 1 3/4. Gregory 44-484 1974 $20

WALTON, IZAAK   The Complete Angler. London, 1760. 8vo., full
dark green morocco, gilt, illus., plates, first Hawkins edition. Hammond 201-77
1974 £85

WALTON, IZAAK   The Complete Angler. London, 1808. 8vo.,
contemporary morocco, gilt, illus., plates, seventh edition. Hammond 201-78
1974 £60

WALTON, IZAAK   The Complete Angler. London, 1808. Thick
4to., green morocco gilt, plates, engravings, morocco-backed case. Traylen
79-295 1973 £325

WALTON, IZAAK   The Complete Angler. London, 1869. Small
8vo., cloth, gilt. Hammond 201-76 1974 £5

WALTON, IZAAK   Compleat Angler. 1897. 4to., many illus.
Allen 216-1962 1974 $15

WALTON, IZAAK   The Compleat Angler. 1902. 2 vols., 8vo.,
plates, illus., half levant morocco. Quaritch 939-274 1974 £35

WALTON, IZAAK   Compleat Angler. 1925. 4to., coloured plates.
Allen 216-1963 1974 $12.50

WALTON, IZAAK   The Complete Angler. London, 1925. 8vo.,
vellum, etchings, uncut, orig. cloth. Bow Windows 62-971 1974 £8.50

WALTON, IZAAK   The Compleat Angler. Boston, 1928. Limited
to 600 copies, 12mo., green and blue pictorial paper covered boards, cloth spine,
mint, publisher's box rubbed. Current BW9-615 1974 $48.50

WALTON, IZAAK   The Compleat Angler. London, 1931. No.
533 of edition limited to 775 signed copies, spine slightly darkened, glassine
wrapper missing, mint, perfect box, illus. by Arthur Rackham. Ross 87-475 1974
$250

WALTON, IZAAK   The Life of Dr. Sanderson. London, 1676.
8vo., calf, worn, frontispiece, first edition. Ximenes 35-456 1974 $25

WALTON, IZAAK   The Life of Dr. Sanderson. London, 1678.
8vo., half calf, spine gilt, frontispiece portrait engraved, first edition. Ximenes
37-217 1974 $65

WALTON, IZAAK   The Lives of Dr. John Donne. York, 1807.
8vo., contemporary diced calf, rebacked, portraits, plate, second edition.
Bow Windows 66-736 1974 £7.50

WALTON, IZAAK   The Lives of Dr. John Donne, Sir Henry
Wotton, Richard Hooker. Boston, 1860. Biblo & Tannen 213-834 1973 $12.50

WALTON, THOMAS   Steel Ships. London, 1908. Roy 8vo., orig.
cloth, gilt, illus., plates, fourth edition. Hammond 201-706 1974 £16

WALWORTH, MANSFIELD TRACY Warwick. New York, 1869. 12mo.,
orig. brick red cloth, first edition. Ximenes 35-457 1974 $17.50

WAMPEN, H. F.   Anthropometry. (1864). 4to., plates, cloth.
Quaritch 940-741 1974 £10

WANDELL, SAMUEL H.   Aaron Burr. New York, 1925. Cloth, 2 vols.
Hayman 57-728 1974 $12.50

WANDREI, DONALD   The Web of Easter Island. Sauk City, 1948.
1st ed., ltd. Biblo & Tannen 210-690 1973 $17.50

WANLEY, HUMFREY   Antiquae Lituraturae Septentrionalis Liber
Alter. Oxford, 1703-05. 2 parts in 1 vol., folio, new half calf. Dawsons
PM 10-635 1974 £45

WANLEY, NATHANIEL   The Wonders of the Little World. 1806. Large
8vo., 2 vols., contemporary calf, frontispiece, plates, new edition. Hill 126-
286 1974 £15

THE WAR Illustrated. London, 1914-18. 8 vols., 4to., illus. Traylen
79-159 1973 £10

WAR PICTURES by British Artists. 1943. Post 8vo., wrappers, English first edition. Covent 56-1519 1974 £10.50

WAR! War! War! n.d., 1940. 292p., paper. Austin 62-94 1974 $10

WARBURTON, THE REVEREND   Julian. 1751. 8vo., contemporary speckled
calf, rebacked, second edition. Bow Windows 66-737 1974 £10

WARBURTON, ELIOT   Memoirs of Horace Walpole and His
Contemporaries. 1852. 2 vols., ex-library. Austin 61-990 1974 $27.50

WARBURTON, J.   History of the City of Dublin. 1818. 2 vols.,
4to., plates, half calf. Quaritch 939-638 1974 £35

WARBURTON, ROWLAND EYLES EGERTON   Hunting Songs and Ballads.
London, 1846. 4to., illus., 19th century half morocco, first edition. Dawsons
PM 252-1034 1974 £35

WARBURTON, WILLIAM   A Critical and Philosophical Enquiry. London,
1727. 12mo., contemporary panelled sprinkled calf, first edition. Dawsons PM
251-357 1974 £140

WARD, A. C.   Twentieth – Century Literature 1901-1940.
1940. Ex-library, revised & enlarged seventh edition. Austin 61-994 1974 $10

WARD, A. W.   The Cambridge History of English Literature.
New York, c. 1907-17. 14 vols., orig. binding, top edges gilt, fine, clean set.
Wilson 63-576 1974 $50

WARD, A. W.   The Cambridge History of English Literature.
1933. 15 vols. Austin 61-995 1974 $75

WARD, A. W.   A History of Dramatic Literature. 1899.
3 vols., froyed, best edition. Howes 185-543 1974 $12.50

WARD, ARTEMUS   Complete Works. Chatto, Windus, 1865.
518p. Austin 54-1026 1973 $17.50

WARD, BERNARD   The Dawn Of the Catholic Revival in England.
1909. 2 vols., thick 8vo., plates, orig. edition. Howes 185-1755 1974 £12.50

WARD, C. W.   The American Carnation. New York, 1903.
8vo., illus., half calf, English first edition. Covent 56-643 1974 £18

WARD, CATHERINE G.   The Cottage on the Cliff. London, n.d.
Thick 8vo., contemporary half calf, frontispiece. Ximenes 35-460 1974 $25

WARD, CATHERINE G.   The Rose of Claremont. London, 1820.
2 vols., 8vo., contemporary tree calf, plates, first edition. Ximenes 35-461
1974 $35

WARD, CHRISTOPHER   The Dutch and Swedes on the Delaware. Philadelphia, 1930. 8vo., orig. bindings. Butterfield 8-111 1974 $15

WARD, ELIZABETH STUART PHELPS 1844-1911   The Madonna of the Tubs.
Boston, 1887. First edition, illus., beveled edges. Wilson 63-577 1974 $15

WARD, ERIC   A Book of Make-Up. French, 1930. 98p.
Austin 51-1010 1973 $7.50

WARD, H. B.   Fresh Water Biology. New York, 1918. 8vo.,
cloth. Wheldon 130-267 1974 £10

WARD, H. C.   Wild Flowers of Switzerland. 1883. Imp.
4to., orig. cloth, coloured plates, frontispiece. Wheldon 128-1319 1973 £12

WARD, H. C.   Wild Flowers of Switzerland. 1883. Imperial
4to., orig. cloth, plates. Wheldon 130-1220 1974 £12

WARD, MRS. H. D.
Please turn to
WARD, ELIZABETH STUART PHELPS 1844-1911

WARD, H. M.   Trees. Cambridge, 1904-09. Crown 8vo.,
cloth, scarce. Wheldon 129-1637 1974 £7.50

WARD, MRS. HUMPHREY
Please turn to
WARD, MARY AUGUSTA ARNOLD

WARD, J. C.   The Geology of the Northern Part of the English
Lake District. 1876. Roy. 8vo., good copy, orig. cloth. Broadhurst 24-1560
1974 £8

WARD, JAMES W.   Woman. A Poem Read Before the Graduating
Class of the Female College of Ohio at Their Commencement Exercies, July 17,
1852. Cincinnati, 1852. 12mo., limp cloth, first edition.   Goodspeed's
578-389 1974 $10

WARD, JOHN   A Compendium of Algebra. London, 1724. 8vo.,
contemporary panelled calf, second edition.   Dawsons PM 245-749 1974 £8

WARD, JOHN   New Zealand. London, 1842. 8vo., fine,
first edition.   Ximenes 35-464 1974 $75

WARD, JOHN   The Young Mathematician's Guide. London, 17-
13. 8vo., contemporary panelled calf, second edition.   Hammond 201-986 1974
£15

WARD, JOHN   The Young Mathematician's Guide. London, 17-
28. 8vo., contemporary panelled calf, gilt, illus., fifth edition.   Hammond 201-
987 1974 £12.50

WARD, JOHN   The Young Mathematician's Guide. London, 17-
52. 8vo., modern half calf, ninth edition.   Dawsons PM 245-750 1974 £20

WARD, L.   Forty Years of 'Spy'. London, (n.d.). 8vo.,
illus., inscription, orig. cloth, faded.   Bow Windows 62-973 1974 £5

WARD, L. B.   Father Charles E. Coughlin. Tower, 1933.
Austin 62-746 1974 $8.50

WARD, MAISIE   Gilbert Keith Chesterton. 1943. Illus.
Austin 61-230 1974 $12.50

WARD, MAISIE   Wilfred Marks and the Transition. 1937.
Ex-library.   Austin 61-997 1974 $15

WARD, MAISIE   The Wilfrid Wards and the Transition. 1934.
Ex-library.   Austin 61-996 1974 $12.50

WARD, MARY AUGUSTA ARNOLD   Fenwick's Career. London, 1906. 2 vols.,
illus., limited to 250 numbered copies, signed.   Jacobs 24-130 1974 $90

WARD, MARY AUGUSTA ARNOLD   Helbeck of Bannisdale. London, 1898.
8vo., orig. dark green cloth, first edition.   Ximenes 35-463 1974 $17.50

WARD, MARY AUGUSTA ARNOLD   The History of David Grieve. London,
1892. 3 vols., 8vo., orig. cloth, first edition.   Dawsons PM 252-1035 1974
£95

WARD, MILTON   Poems. Plymouth, 1826. 12mo., orig. grey
boards, worn, scarce, first edition.   Ximenes 35-465 1974 $65

WARD, R.   Records of Big Game. 1928. Roy. 8vo.,
cloth, illus., ninth edition.   Wheldon 128-356 1973 £6

WARD, RICHARD   The Life of the Learned and Pious Dr. Henry More.
1710. 8vo., nineteenth century red morocco, gilt.   Hill 126-288 1974 £21

WARD, ROBERT   Animadversions of Warre. London, 1639.
Folio, contemporary calf, rebacked, woodcuts, plates, good copy, first edition.
Traylen 79-160 1973 £125

WARD, ROBERT ARTHUR   A Treatise on Investments. 1852. Orig. cloth,
bookplate, second edition.   Covent 56-400 1974 £6.50

WARD, ROBERT D.   The Immigration Problem. 1904.   Austin
62-667 1974 $8.50

WARD, ROBERT PLUMER   De Vere. London, 1827. 4 vols., 12mo.,
contemporary half morocco, first edition.   Dawsons PM 252-1036 1974 £20

WARD, ROBERT PLUMER   Tremaine. 1825. 3 vols., crown 8vo.,
full calf gilt, labels, first edition.   Howes 186-502 1974 £37.50

WARD, ROBERT PLUMER   Tremaine. London, 1825. 3 vols., 8vo.,
orig. boards, first edition.   Dawsons PM 252-1037 1974 £40

WARD, ROLAND   A Naturalist's Life Study in the Art of
Taxidermy. London, 1913. 4to., illus., orig. cloth, rubbed.   Bow Windows
62-974 1974 £12

WARD, SETH   Idea Trigonometriae Demonstratae. 1654. 4to.,
contemporary sheep, rebacked, first edition.   Dawsons PM 245-751 1974 £135

WARD, SETH   Vindiciae Academiarum. Oxford, 1654. 4to.,
old half calf.   Gurney 64-227 1974 £80

WARD, THOMAS   England's Reformation. London, 1715. Contemporary calf, 2 vols., rebacked.   Dawson's 424-334 1974 $100

WARD, THOMAS   Errata of the Protestant Bible. 1847.
Ex-library, library binding.   Austin 57-689 1974 $17.50

WARD, THOMAS   Errata of the Protestant Bible. Sadler, 1847.
Austin 62-668 1974 $17.50

WARD, WILFRED PHILIP 1856-1916   The Life and Times of Cardinal Wiseman.
1900. 2 vols., crown 8vo., portraits.   Howes 185-1789 1974 £5.50

WARD, WILFRED PHILIP 1856-1916   The Life of John Henry Cardinal Newman.
1913. 2 vols., thick 8vo., dust soiled.   Howes 185-1498 1974 £8.50

WARD, WILLIAM   The Early Schools of Naugatuck. Naugatuck,
c.1906. 12mo., cloth, illus.   Saddleback 14-338 1974 $10

WARD, WILLIAM   A View of the History, Literature, and
Mythology of the Hindoos. London, 1822. 3 vols., 8vo., half green leather,
gilt, new edition.   Traylen 79-542 1973 £12

WARD, WILLIAM TILLEARD   Practical Observations on Distortions of the
Spine, Chest, and Limbs; Together with, Remarks on Paralytic and Other Diseases
Connected with Impaired or Defective Motion. London, 1822. 8vo., orig.
boards, uncut, first edition.   Gurney 66-195 1974 £15

WARDE, FREDERIC   Printers Ornaments. 1928. Orig. cloth.
Broadhurst 23-524 1974 £15

WARDE, FREDERIC   Printers Ornaments. 1928. 4to., orig. cloth,
uncut, limited edition.   Broadhurst 23-523 1974 £21

WARDE, FREDERIC   Printers Ornaments Applied to the Composition of
Decorative Borders, Panels and Patterns. 1928. Orig. cloth, fine, ordinary edition.
Broadhurst 24-499 1974 £15

WARDE, FREDERIC   Printers Ornaments, Applied to the Composition
of Decorative Borders. 1928. 4to., orig. cloth gilt, ordinary edition.   Howes
185-875 1974 £7.50

WARDE, FREDERIC   Printers Ornaments, Applied to the Composition
of Decorative Borders. 1928. 4to., orig. buckram gilt, special limited edition.
Howes 185-874 1974 £16.50

WARDE, FREDERIC   Printers Ornaments Applied to the Composition of
Decorative Borders, Panels and Patterns. 1928. Med. 4to., mint, uncut, limited,
hand made paper, edition de luxe.   Broadhurst 24-498 1974 £21

WARDEN, DAVID BAILLIE   A Statistical, Political, and Historical Account
of the United States of North America. London, 1819. 8vo., 3 vols., new half
calf, orig. marbled boards, first edition.   Dawsons PM 251-358 1974 £95

WARDEN, WILLIAM   Letters Written on Board His Majesty's Ship the
Northumberland and at St. Helena. Brussels, 1817. Full contemp. calf, rebacked.
Jacobs 24-164 1974 $25

WARDLE, T.   Kashmir. 1904. 8vo., morocco, presentation
copy.   Wheldon 131-400 1974 £10

WARDROP, JAMES   History of James Mitchell, a Boy Born Blind and
Deaf. London, 1813. Large 4to., half calf, very rare, only edition.   Schuman
37-261 1974 $110

WARE, EUGENE F.   The Indian War of 1864 Being a Fragment of the
Early History of Kansas, Nebraska, Colorado, and Wyoming. Topeka, 1911.
Illus., first edition, very nice copy.   Jenkins 61-2567 1974 $87.50

WARE, ISAAC   A Complete Body of Architecture. 1756.
Roy. folio, half calf antique, illus., plates.   Quaritch 940-564 1974 £92

WARE, JAMES   The Whole Works. Dublin, 1739-46. 3 vols.
in 2, folio, plates, buckram.   Quaritch 939-639 1974 £60

WARE, WILLIAM   Letters of Lucius M. Piso. New York, 1837.
2 vols., 12mo., orig. boards, fine, first edition. Ximenes 35-466 1974 $45

WARE, WILLIAM   Probus. New York, 1838. 2 vols., 12mo.,
orig. cloth, fine, first edition. Ximenes 35-467 1974 $35

WARE, WILLIAM   Zenobia. London, 1838. 2 vols., 12mo.,
contemporary calf, first English edition. Ximenes 35-468 1974 $25

WARE, WILLIAM   Zenobia. New York, 1848. 2 vols., 12mo.,
orig. dark brown cloth, fine, seventh edition. Ximenes 35-469 1974 $17.50

WARE, WILLIAM R.   The American Vignola. Scranton, c., 1906.
4to., blue cloth, plates, illus., second edition. Rich Summer-9 1974 $8.50

WARFIELD, CATHERINE ANN   The Wife of Leon. New York, 1844.
12mo., orig. boards, foxed, first edition. Ximenes 35-470 1974 $20

WARING, DOROTHY   American Defender. Speller, 1935.
267p., illus. Austin 62-669 1974 $8.50

WARING, J. B.   Masterpieces of Industrial Art. 3 vols.,
folio, illus., rubbed, fine. Covent 55-130 1974 £175

WARING, JANET   Early American Wall Stencils. New York, n.d.
Dust wrapper, fine, plates. Dawson's 424-243 1974 $50

WARING, JOHN BURLEY   Masterpieces of Industrial Art and Sculpture at
the International Exhibition, 1862. 1863. 3 vols., folio, plates, full morocco
gilt, worn, recased. Quaritch 940-484 1974 £120

WARLOCK, PETER   Songs of the Gardens. 1925. One of 875
numbered copies, parchment binding, very nice copy, first edition. Covent
51-1367 1973 £12.50

WARMING, E.   Lehrbuch der Okologischen. Berlin, 1902.
Roy 8vo., cloth, second edition. Wheldon 129-973 1974 £5

WARMING, E.   Oecology of Plants. Oxford, 1909. Roy.
8vo., cloth, scarce. Wheldon 128-1177 1973 £10

WARMING, E.   Oecology of Plants. Oxford, 1909. Roy 8vo.,
cloth, scarce. Wheldon 130-1067 1974 £10

WARNE, FRANK JULIAN   The Immigrant Invasion. 1913. 336 pages,
illus. Austin 57-691 1974 $15

WARNE, FRANK JULIAN   The Immigrant Invasion. Dodd, Mead, 1913.
336p., illus. Austin 62-670 1974 $15

WARNE, FRANK JULIAN   The Tide of Immigration. 1916. 387 pages.
Austin 57-692 1974 $10

WARNER, ANNA BARTLETT   Dollars and Cents. New York, 1852. 2 vols.,
12mo., orig. cloth, first edition. Dawsons PM 252-1038 1974 $30

WARNER, CHARLES DUDLEY   My Summer in a Garden. Boston, 1871.
12mo., orig. green cloth, first edition. Ximenes 35-471 1974 $12.50

WARNER, CHARLES DUDLEY   My Summer in a Garden. Boston, (1912).
Orig. cloth, illus., fine. Bradley 35-397 1974 $25

WARNER, G. T.   Harrow In Prose & Verse. (c.1913). 4to.,
plates, orig. cloth, gilt. Bow Windows 62-975 1974 £10

WARNER, J. J.   An Historical Sketch of Los Angeles County,
California. Los Angeles, 1936. 8vo., quarter cloth. Saddleback 14-310
1974 $12.50

WARNER, LANGDON   The Craft of the Japanese Sculptor. New
York, 1936. 4to., plates. Biblo & Tannen 214-401 1974 $27.50

WARNER, R.   Antiquitates Culinariae. 1791. 4to., worn,
plates, roxburghe. Quaritch 939-275 1974 £50

WARNER, R.   An Illustration of the Roman Antiquities
Discovered at Bath. Bath, 1797. 4to., cloth back. Quaritch 939-545
1974 £12

WARNER, REX   Poems. 1937. Fine, first edition, scarce.
Covent 51-1914 1973 £10.50

WARNER, RICHARD   An Attempt to Ascertain the Situation of the
Ancient Clausentum. 1792. 4to., old wrappers. Hill 126-289 1974 £13.50

WARNER, RICHARD   A Letter to David Garrick. London, 1768. 8vo.,
half calf, gilt, first edition. Hammond 201-343 1974 £17.50

WARNER, RICHARD   A Letter to David Garrick. London, 1768.
8vo., contemporary half calf, first edition. Ximenes 35-472 1974 $80

WARNER, RICHARD   Topographical Remarks. 1793. 2 vols., rebound,
modern three quarter calf, fine, English first edition. Covent 56-1264 1974 £55

WARNER, ROBERT   Select Orchidaceous Plants. 1862-65 & 1865-
75. Folio, 2 vols., plates, orig. cloth. Bow Windows 64-288 1974 £620

WARNER, SUSAN BOGERT   The Hills of the Shatemuc. New York,
1856. 12mo., orig. cloth, first edition. Ximenes 35-473 1974 $10

WARNER, SUSAN BOGERT   Say and Seal. London, 1860. 8vo., orig.
black cloth, plates, frontispiece, fine, first edition. Ximenes 35-474 1974 $30

WARNER, SYLVIA TOWNSEND   A Moral Ending and Other Stories. London,
1931. First edition, limited to 500 numbered copies, signed by author, tall 8vo.,
fine, orig. cloth. Crane 7-305 1974 £7.50

WARNER, SYLVIA TOWNSEND   Summer Will Show. New York, 1936. Nice
copy, frayed d.w., inscribed by author, first edition, orig. cloth. Crane
7-306 1974 £8.50

WARR, G. FINDEN   Dynamics. London, 1851. 8vo., orig. cloth,
first edition. Dawsons PM 245-753 1974 £8

WARREN, CHARLES   The Supreme Court in United States History.
Boston, 1923. First edition, 3 vols., orig. binding. Wilson 63-257 1974 $45

WARREN, G. W.   The History of the Bunker Hill Monument
Association. Boston, 1877. Brown cloth, gilt, illus., fine, engravings.
Rinsland 58-909 1974 $35

WARREN, JANE S.   The Morning Star. Boston, (1860). 16mo.,
orig. bindings. Butterfield 8-137 1974 $15

WARREN, JOHN COLLINS   Address Before the American Medical Association
at the Anniversary Meeting in Cincinnati, May 8, 1850. Boston, 1850.
Stains. Rittenhouse 46-640 1974 $10

WARREN, JOHN COLLINS   Etherization. Boston, 1848. Small 8vo., orig.
brown cloth, first edition. Dawsons PM 249-503 1974 £135

WARREN, JONATHAN MASON   Surgical Observations. Boston, 1867. 8vo.,
orig. mauve cloth, uncut, unopened, first edition. Dawsons PM 249-504 1974
£90

WARREN, SAMUEL   Passages from the Diary of a Late Physician.
New York, 1832. 3 vols. Rittenhouse 46-644 1974 $10

WARREN, SAMUEL   Passages from the Diary of a Late Physician.
New York, 1834. 3 vols., rebacked. Rittenhouse 46-642 1974 $50

WARREN, SAMUEL   Passages From the Diary of a Late Physician.
New York, 1857. 3 vols., vol. 3 cover loose. Rittenhouse 46-643 1974 $22.50

WARREN, SAMUEL   Ten Thousand-A-Year. Edinburgh & London,
1841. 3 vols., 8vo., orig. blind-stamped cloth, first English edition. Dawsons
PM 252-1039 1974 $25

WARRINGTON, W.   History of Wales. 1786. 4to., foxing,
half calf. Quaritch 939-698 1974 £15

WARRINGTON, WILLIAM   The History of Wales. Brecon, 1823. 8vo.,
2 vols., orig. boards, uncut, plates. Broadhurst 23-1590 1974 £6

WARTON, JOSEPH   An Essay. 1806. 2 vols., frontispieces,
full contemporary calf, rebacked, fifth edition. Howes 186-368 1974 £16

WARTON, JOSEPH   An Essay on the Writings and Genius of Pope.
London, 1756. 8vo., 19th century half morocco gilt, first edition.   Dawsons
PM 252-1040 1974 £60

WARTON, T.   Essays on Gothic Architecture.   1800. 8vo.,
plates, contemporary tree calf, large copy.   Quaritch 940-565 1974 £18

WARTON, T.   The History and Antiquities of Winchester.
Winchester, 1773. 2 vols., small 8vo., plates.   Quaritch 939-380 1974 £12

WARTON, THOMAS   The History of English Poetry.   1774-78-81.
4to., 3 vols., old green mottled calf, gilt, first edition.   Hill 126-290 1974
£60

WARTON, THOMAS   Observations on the Faerie Queene of
Spenser.   London, 1754. 8vo., contemporary calf, bit rubbed but sound, good
copy, first edition.   Ximenes 37-218 1974 $125

WARTON, THOMAS   Observations on the "Fairy Queen" of Spencer.
London, 1762. 2 vols., 8vo., contemporary calf, gilt, second edition.   Ximenes
35-475 1974 $125

WARWICK, F. W.   Experiments In Physics.   New York, 1939.
Illus., faded spine, fine.   Ballinger 1-325 1974 $17.50

WARWICK BROS. AND RUTTER LIMITED   The Story of the Busines, 1848-1923.
(Toronto, 1923).   Boxed, presentation copy signed by Rutter.   Hood's 102-398
1974 $15

WASHBURN, ANDREW   Documents in the Case of . . . Late of the 14th
Regiment Mass. Volunteers.   N. P., n.d. (c. 1863).   Stitched.   Wilson 63-365
1974 $10

WASHBURN, EMORY   Topographical and Historical Sketches of the
Town of Leicester.   Worcester, 1826. 8vo., orig. wrappers, fine, first edition.
Ximenes 35-476 1974 $22.50

WASHBURN, E. W.   Studies in Early English Literature.   New York,
1882.   Biblo & Tannen 210-932 1973 $8.50

WASHBURN, HENRY T.   Genealogy and Other Writings of.   (Watertown,
n.d., c. 1926).   Cloth, light underlining in pencil.   Hayman 59-658 1974 $10

WASHINGTON, BUSHROD   Reports of Cases Argued and Determined in the
Court of Appeals of Virginia.   Richmond, 1798. 2 vols., repaired, foxed.
Jenkins 61-2554 1974 $45

WASHINGTON, GEORGE   Autographed Letters and Documents of..., Now
in Rhode Island Collections.   Providence, 1932.   First edition, 8vo., mint, except
for minor foxing on title page.   Current BW9-439a 1974 $12.50

WASHINGTON, GEORGE   Letters from His Excellency George Washington
to Arthur Young, and Sir John Sinclair, Containing an Account of His
Husbandry.   Alexandria, 1803. 8vo., orig. blue boards, orig. condition,
scarce, fine copy, first American edition.   Ximenes 37-219 1974 $100

WASHINGTON, GEORGE   A Message of the President . . . To Congress,
Relative to France and Great Britain; Delivered, Dec. 5, 1793.   Philadelphia,
1795.   Full leather.   Butterfield 10-523 1974 $125

WASHINGTON-METCALFE, THOMAS   The Santa Anna Trilogy.   1931-32-33.
3 vols., presentation copies, inscribed by author, vols. 1 & 3 fine in slightly worn
dust wrappers.   Covent 51-1917 1973 £12.50

WASHINGTON: Photographs in Black.   New York, 1889.   Stiff wrapper, illus.
Jenkins 61-790 1974 $12.50

WASHINGTON NATIONAL GALLERY OF ART   Masterpieces of Painting from the
National Gallery of Art.   Washington, 1945.   Folio, full page color plates.
Biblo & Tannen 210-61 1973 $20

WASHINGTON and Jefferson College, Washington, Pennsylvania.   Harrisburg,
1902.   Boards, photos.   Jenkins 61-2189 1974 $12.50

WASSERSCHLEBEN, F. W. H.   Die Bussordnungen der Abendlandischen Kirche.
1851.   Buckram, damp-stained, scarce.   Howes 185-1763 1974 £10

WATELET, CLAUDE HENRI   Silvic.   Londres, 1743.   Small 8vo., 19th
century half hard grain morocco, gilt.   L. Goldschmidt 42-136 1974 $45

WATERBURY, Connecticut.   Waterbury, 1889.   Wrapper, photographs.   Jenkins
61-707 1974 $12.50

WATERHOUSE, EDWARD   A Discourse and Defence of Arms and Armory.
London, 1660.   Small 8vo., russia gilt.   Quaritch 939-755 1974 £35

WATERHOUSE, EDWARD   A Short Narrative of the Late Dreadful Fire
In London.   1667.   Modern brown crushed levant morocco.   Thomas 28-210
1972 £45

WATERHOUSE, RUPERT   A Case of Suprarenal Apoplexy.   1911.   Large
8vo., green cloth.   Dawsons PM 249-505 1974 £10

WATERMAN, C.   Flora's Lexicon.   Boston, 1852.   Rebacked,
orig. back laid on, 8vo.   Gregory 44-306 1974 $35

WATERS, FRANK   The Colorado.   New York, Toronto, 1946.
Ist ed., illus.   Dykes 24-201 1974 $20

WATERS, THOMAS   The Recollections of a Policeman.   Boston,
1856.   Orig. dec. cloth, gilt, first U.S. edition.   Covent 56-345A 1974 £65

WATERS, THOMAS FRANKLIN   Publications of the Ipswich Historical Society
VII.   1900.   Second edition, portrait, 4to.   Butterfield 10-380 1974 $10

WATERS, THOMAS FRANKLIN   A Sketch of the Life of John Winthrop.   (Cambridge), 1899. 4to., orig. bindings.   Butterfield 8-273 1974 $15

WATERSON, MRS. R. C.   Adelaide Phillipps.   Williams, 1883. 170p.,
illus.   Austin 51-1013 1973 $7.50

WATKIN, E. W.   Alderman Cobden of Manchester.   1891.   Crown
4to., parchment spince, uncut.   Broadhurst 23-1591 1974 £8

WATKIN, I.   Oswestry.   1920. 8vo., orig. cloth, illus.
Broadhurst 23-1592 1974 £5

WATKINS, C. T.   A Portable Cyclopaedia.   London, 1810.   12mo.,
old calf, rebacked.   Gumey 64-228 1974 £20

WATKINS, C. T.   A Portable Cyclopaedia.   London, 1810.   12mo.,
old calf, rebacked, plates, apparently orig. edition and only edition.   Gurney
66-196 1974 £20

WATKINS, J.   An Essay Towards a History of Bideford in the
County of Devon.   1792. 8vo., modern boards.   Quaritch 939-343 1974 £10

WATKINS, JOHN   Memoirs of . . . . the Right Honorable Richard
Brinsley Sheridan.   London, 1817. 2 parts in 1 vol., 4to., contemporary green
half calf, first edition.   Dawsons PM.252-891 1974 £30

WATKINS, JOHN ELFRETH   Famous Mysteries.   Philadelphia, 1919.
Biblo & Tannen 210-540 1973 $10

WATKINS, MAURICE   Chicago.   Knopf, 1927.   Austin 51-1000
1973 $8.50

WATLING, T.   Drawings of Australian Birds.   (1923).   Small
4to., plates.   Wheldon 130-646A 1974 £5

WATNEY, VERNON J.   Cornbury and the Forest of Wychwood.   1910.
Folio, plates, niger morocco, gilt.   Quaritch 939-528 1974 £25

WATSON, A. D.   Love and the Universe.   Toronto, 1913.
Inscribed.   Hood's 103-757 1974 $10

WATSON, ARTHUR C.   The Long Harpoon.   New Bedford, 1929.   Cloth,
scarce, pen and ink sketches.   Hayman 59-662 1974 $12.50

WATSON, GOODWIN   Action for Unity.   Harper, 1947.   Austin
62-672 1974 $10

WATSON, H. C.   The New Botanist's Guide.   1835-37.   Crown
8vo., cloth, 2 vols.   Wheldon 129-1026 1974 £12

WATSON, H. C.   Topographical Botany. 1873-74. 2 vols.,
8vo., half calf. Wheldon 131-1250 1974 £7.50

WATSON, HENRY HOUGH   On Detecting the Presence of Arsenic. Manchester, 1842. 8vo., wrapper, inscribed. Hammond 201-988 1974 £6.50

WATSON, HENRY HOUGH   On the Relative Attractions of Sulphuric Acid for
Water. Manchester, 1842. 8vo., boards, inscribed. Hammond 201-989 1974
£6.50

WATSON, J. F.   Index to Native and Scientific Names of
Indian and Other Eastern Economic Plants and Products. 1868. Roy. 8vo.,
sewed, scarce. Wheldon 128-1670 1973 £7.50

WATSON, JAMES   The History of the Art of Printing. Edinburgh,
1713. Small 8vo., contemporary blind panelled calf. Dawsons PM 10-637
1974 £550

WATSON, PETER WILLIAM   Dendrologia Britannica. 1825. 2 vols.,
8vo., contemporary half calf, plates, rare. Wheldon 131-128 1974 £400

WATSON, RICHARD   Chemical Essays. London, 1800. Small 8vo.,
contemporary calf, labels, fine, 5 vols., seventh edition. Dawsons PM 245-755
1974 £28

WATSON, ROBERT   Crime. (1895). Orig. pictorial cloth, illus.,
English first edition. Covent 56-270 1974 £12.50

WATSON, ROBERT   The History of the Reign of Philip the II.
Dublin, 1777. 2 vols., contemporary calf. Howes 186-1299 1974 £7.50

WATSON, ROBERT   The History of the Reign of Philip the Second,
King of Spain. 1779. 3 vols., 8vo., contemporary calf, hinges cracked, worn,
third edition. Bow Windows 66-740 1974 £7.50

WATSON, THOMAS   Canadian Crystals. Toronto, 1901. 1st ed.
Biblo & Tannen 210-815 1973 $10

WATSON, W.   Cactus Culture for Amateurs. 1889. 8vo.,
cloth. Wheldon 131-1706 1974 £5

WATSON, W.   Orchids. 1893. 8vo., orig. cloth, plates
(some coloured), scarce, revised second edition. Wheldon 128-1578 1973 £7.50

WATSON, W.   Orchids. 1903. 8vo., orig. cloth, gilt,
illus., plates, scarce. Wheldon 129-1589 1974 £20

WATSON, W.   Orchids: Their Culture and Management. 1903.
8vo., orig. cloth gilt, scarce, plates, new edition. Wheldon 131-1637 1974
£20

WATSON, WILLIAM   Experiments and Observations. London, 1746.
8vo., quarter calf, boards. Gurney 64-229 1974 £48

WATSON, WILLIAM   The Poems Of. 1905. 2 vols. Austin
61-999 1974 $12.50

WATSON, WILLIAM   The Purple East. (London), 1896. Small
4to., orig. wrappers, rare, first edition. Ximenes 35-480 1974 £70

WATSON, WILLIAM   Wordworth's Grave and Other Poems. 1891.
Austin 61-1000 1974 $10

WATT, G.   Dictionary of the Economic Products of India.
London and Calcutta, 1889-96. 8vo., orig. half calf. Wheldon 129-1678
1974 £160

WATT, JAMES   Correspondence of. London and Edinburgh, 1846.
8vo., modern boards, uncut, first edition. Dawsons PM 245-757 1974 £25

WATT, ROBERT   Bibliotheca Britannica. 1824. 4 vols., 4to.,
calf, rubbed, rebacked in buckram. Allen 216-211 1974 $75

WATTS, ISAAC   The Glory of Christ as God-Man Display'd.
London, 1746. 2 vols. in 1, 8vo., contemporary calf, first edition. Ximenes
35-481 1974 $50

WATTS, ISAAC   Horae Lyricae. Poems. London, 1706.
8vo., contemporary panelled calf, first edition. Ximenes 35-482 1974 $175

WATTS, ISAAC   An Humble Attempt Toward the Revival of
Practical Religion Among Christians. London, 1735. 12mo., contemporary
calf, second edition. Ximenes 35-483 1974 $22.50

WATTS, ISAAC   An Humble Attempt Towards the Revival of
Practical Religion Among Christians. London, 1742. 12mo., contemporary
calf, third edition. Ximenes 35-484 1974 $15

WATTS, ISAAC   Hymns. 1834. Small 8vo., quarter dark
green roan, gilt. Thomas 28-319 1972 £15.75

WATTS, ISAAC   The Improvement of the Mind. London,
1741. 8vo., contemporary calf, first edition. Ximenes 35-485 1974 $75

WATTS, ISAAC   The Improvement of the Mind. London, 1743.
8vo., contemporary calf, rubbed, second edition. Schuman 37-262 1974 $75

WATTS, ISAAC   The Psalms of David. Sutton, 1808. 16mo.,
old calf, worn. Butterfield 8-279 1974 $10

WATTS, ISAAC   The Psalms of David Imitated. Worcester,
1786. 8vo., contemporary calf, inscribed. Ximenes 35-486 1974 $100

WATTS, ISAAC   Reliquiae Juveniles. London, 1734. 12mo.,
contemporary calf, gilt, scarce, first edition. Ximenes 35-487 1974 $100

WATTS, ISAAC   Reliquiae Juveniles. London, 1737. 12mo.,
contemporary calf, second edition. Ximenes 35-488 1974 $75

WAUGH, ALEC   The Loom of Youth. 1917. Crown 8vo.,
orig. cloth, scarce, first edition. Howes 186-504 1974 £7.50

WAUGH, ARTHUR 1866-   A Hundred Years of Publishing. 1930. 8vo.,
orig. cloth, portraits. Broadhurst 23-526 1974 £6

WAUGH, EDWIN   Works. Manchester, 1881-83. Roy 8vo., quarter roan. Broadhurst 23-1595 1974 £20

WAUGH, EVELYN   Black Mischief. London, 1932. 8vo., orig.
cloth, illus., limited, signed, first large paper edition. Bow Windows 62-978
1974 £65

WAUGH, EVELYN   Black Mischief. 1932. First edition, orig.
cloth, crown 8vo., fine. Broadhurst 24-927 1974 £10

WAUGH, EVELYN   Black Mischief. 1932. 8vo., orig. cloth, first
edition. Rota 190-971 1974 £7

WAUGH, EVELYN   Black Mischief. 1932. Crown 8vo., orig.
cloth, map, first edition. Howes 185-547 1974 £10

WAUGH, EVELYN   Black Michief. 1932. Crown 8vo., orig. cloth,
first edition. Broadhurst 23-955 1974 £12

WAUGH, EVELYN   Black Mischief. 1932. One of 250 copies on
large paper, numbered & signed by author, drawings, violet cloth gilt, spine
faded, very nice copy. Covent 51-2603 1973 £55

WAUGH, EVELYN   Brideshead Revisited. Boston, 1945. 8vo.,
orig. cloth, first American edition. Rota 189-911 1974 £5

WAUGH, EVELYN   Brideshead Revisited. 1945. Dust wrapper,
fine, first edition. Howes 186-505 1974 £12.50

WAUGH, EVELYN   Edmund Campion. 1935. One of 50 copies
numbered for private distribution, presentation copy, inscribed from author, nice
copy, buckram, bookplate. Covent 51-2604 1973 £110

WAUGH, EVELYN   A Handful of Dust. 1934. First U. S.
edition, spine faded and discoloured at base, signature. Covent 51-1924 1973
£6.50

WAUGH, EVELYN   Ninety-Two Days. 1934. Plates, folding map,
fine, slightly worn d.w., first edition. Covent 51-1933 1973 £22.50

WAUGH, EVELYN   Ninety-Two Days. 1934. Plates, fine, map, dust wrapper. Covent 55-1499 1974 £42.50

WAUGH, EVELYN   Put Out More Flags. London, 1942. First edition, very nice copy, inscription on fly, orig. cloth. Crane 7-307 1974 £6

WAUGH, EVELYN   Robbery Under Law. 1939. Blue cloth, fine, scarce, first edition, first issue. Covent 55-1501 1974 £30

WAUGH, EVELYN   Rossetti, His Life and Works. 1928. Orig. cloth, illus., second edition. Marsden 39-390 1974 £5.25

WAUGH, EVELYN   Scoop. 1938. Bookplate, English first edition. Covent 56-1294 1974 £10

WAUGH, EVELYN   Scoop. 1938. First edition, crown 8vo., orig. cloth, fine. Broadhurst 24-928 1974 £12

WAUGH, EVELYN   Vile Bodies. 1930. First edition, crown 8vo., fine, d.w., orig. cloth, inscribed presentation copy from author. Broadhurst 24-926 1974 £40

WAUGH, EVELYN   Waugh in Abyssinia. 1936. Presentation copy, inscribed from author, fine, bookplate. Covent 51-2611 1973 £45

WAUGH, EVELYN   Work Suspended. 1942. Crown 8vo., dust wrapper, scarce, first edition. Howes 186-509 1974 £18

WAUGH, W. T.   James Wolfe, Man and Soldier. Toronto, 1928. Maps, illus. Hood's 103-243 1974 $25

WAWN, WILLIAM T.   The South Sea Islanders and the Queensland Labour Trade. London, 1893. First edition, 8vo., illus., maps, back hinge weak, some light foxing. Current BW9-606 1974 £40

WAWRA, HEINRICH   Botanische Ergebnisse. Vienna, 1866. Folio, plates, orig. boards, worn. Bow Windows 64-289 1974 £98

WAWRA, HEINRICH   Botanische Ergebnisse der Reiser Seiner. Vienna, 1866. Folio, orig. stamped brown morocco, plates, scarce. Wheldon 130-86 1974 £120

WAY, ARTHUR S.   The Lay of the Nibelung Men. Cambridge, 1911. 8vo., orig. quarter cloth. Bow Windows 62-979 1974 £7.50

WAYBURN, NED   The Art of Stage Dancing. 1925. Austin 51-1014 1973 $12.50

WAYLAND, FRANCIS   The Elements of Political Economy. New York, 1837. 8vo., orig. patterned cloth, first edition. Ximenes 35-489 1974 $50

WEALE, W. H. L.   Bibliographia Liturgica. London, 1928. 8vo., orig. cloth. Dawsons PM 10-638 1974 £24

WEALE, W. H. I.   Catalogus Missalium Ritus Latini ab Anno M.CCCC.LXXIV. 1928. Mint. Thomas 32-74 1974 £21

WEATHERS, J.   Beautiful Bulbous Plants for the Open Air. n.d. 8vo., cloth, coloured plates. Wheldon 128-1546 1973 £5

WEATHERS, J.   A Practical Guide to Garden Plants. 1901. 8vo., orig. cloth. Bow Windows 64-290 1974 £5

WEAVER, EMILY P.   Old Quebec. Toronto, 1907. Dec. cloth, illus. Hood's 103-789 1974 $12.50

WEAVER, EMILY P.   The Story of the Counties of Ontario. Toronto, 1913. Illus., map, foxed. Hood's 103-693 1974 $20

WEAVER, GEORGE H.   Beginnings of Medical Education In and Near Chicago. Chicago, 1925. Boards, library stamp. Rittenhouse 46-647 1974 $10

WEAVER, J. E.   Plant Ecology. New York, 1938. 8vo., cloth, second edition. Wheldon 129-974 1974 £5

WEAVER, L.   English Leadwork, Its Art and History. 1909. 4to., illus. Eaton Music-687 1973 £15

WEAVER, L.   The House and Its Equipment. (c. 1922). Crown 4to., orig. cloth, illus., covers little rubbed. Bow Windows 66-741 1974 £5

WEAVER, L.   Small Country Houses of To-day. (n.d.). 4to., frontispiece, illus., orig. cloth. Bow Windows 64-748 1974 £8.50

WEAVER, L.   Small Country Houses of Today. 1922. 2 vols., cloth, revised third edition. Eaton Music-686 1973 £10

WEAVER, RAYMOND M.   Herman Melville. New York, 1921. Plates, faded. Covent 55-1096 1974 £8.50

WEAVER, THOMAS   Plantagenets Tragicall Story. London, 1649. 8vo., contemporary calf, first edition. Ximenes 35-490 1974 $300

WEAVER, WILLIAM D.   Catalogue of the Wheeler Gift of Books. New York, 1909. 2 vols., 8vo., orig. cloth. Dawsons PM 10-639 1974 £35

WEAVER, WILLIAM D.   Catalogue of the Wheeler Gift of Books, Pamphlets and Periodicals in the Library of the American Institute of Electrical Engineers. New York, 1909. 2 vols., 8vo., cloth, fine copy. Goodspeed's 578-548 1974 $50

WEBB, A. P.   A Bibliography of the Works of Thomas Hardy, 1865-1915. London, 1916. First edition, very nice copy, scarce, orig. cloth. Crane 7-128 1974 £10

WEBB, A. P.   A Bibliography of the Works of Thomas Hardy, 1865-1915. 1916. Illus., near fine, first edition. Covent 51-871 1973 £12.50

WEBB, ASTON   London of the Future. London, (1921). Crown 4to., plates, plans, diagrams, orig. buckram. Forster 97-291 1974 £3

WEBB, CHARLES HENRY   John Paul's Book. Hartford & Chicago, 1874. Thick 8vo., orig. cloth, first edition. Ximenes 35-491 1974 $10

WEBB, DANIEL   An Inquiry into the Beauties of Painting. 1760. Small 8vo. Eaton Music-688 1973 £10

WEBB, DANIEL   Remarks on the Beauties of Poetry. London, 1762. 8vo., half calf antique, first edition. Ximenes 35-492 1974 $85

WEBB, DANIEL   Remarks on the Beauties of Poetry. 1762. 8vo., orig. wrappers, uncut. Hill 126-291 1974 £48

WEBB, E. A.   The History of Chislehurst. London, 1899. Thick 4to., orig. buckram, worn, plates, maps. Traylen 79-341 1973 £8

WEBB, E. A.   The Records of St. Bartholomew's Priory and of the Church and Parish. 1921. 2 vols., thick roy. 8vo., plates, illus., presentation. Howes 186-2150 1974 £16

WEBB, FRANCIS   Poems. Salisbury, 1790. 4to., old half calf, worn, scarce, first edition. Ximenes 35-493 1974 $50

WEBB, FRANCIS   Somerset. London, 1811. 4to., orig. plain wrappers, fine, first edition. Ximenes 35-494 1974 $25

WEBB, J.   A Vindication of Stone-Heng Restored. London, 1665. Folio, illus., old calf. Quaritch 939-579 1974 £90

WEBB, J. J.   Industrial Dublin Since 1698 and the Silk Industry. Dublin, 1913. 8vo., cloth boards. Emerald 50-975 1974 £6

WEBB, MARY GLADYS   The Golden Arrow. London, 1916. 8vo., orig. cloth, first edition. Dawsons PM 252-1042 1974 £35

WEBB, MARY GLADYS   Gone to Earth. London, 1917. 8vo., orig. cloth, fine, first edition. Dawsons PM 252-1043 1974 £35

WEBB, MARY GLADYS   Gone to Earth. 1917. Very good copy, first edition. Covent 51-1943 1973 £15

WEBB, MARY GLADYS   Seven for a Secret. London, 1922. 8vo., orig. green cloth, first edition. Dawsons PM 252-1044 1974 £30

WEBB, P. B.   Elogio di Filippo Barker Webb Scritto da Filippo Paralatore. Florence, 1856. 4to., full calf. Wheldon 131-251 1974 £10

WEBB, P. B.   Histoire Naturelle des Iles Canaries. Paris, 1836-44. Imp. 4to., cloth. Wheldon 131-401 1974 £40

WEBB, P. B.   Iter Hispaniense. Paris, 1838. 8vo., boards, rare. Wheldon 129-1135 1974 £5

WEBB, PHILIP CARTERET   An Account of a Copper Table. London, 1760. 4to., boards, illus. Hammond 201-1004 1974 £10

WEBB, SIDNEY   A Constitution for the Socialist Commonwealth of Great Britain. c. 1920. Stiff wrappers, upper wrapper partly raised from board, else very good, first edition. Covent 51-1944 1973 £10

WEBB, SIDNEY   The History of Trade Unionism. 1920. Boards, English first edition. Covent 56-2109 1974 £7.50

WEBB, SIDNEY   The Prevention of Destitution. n.d. Orig. wrappers, browned, special edition. Covent 55-1503 1974 £5.25

WEBB, THOMAS S.   The Freemason's Monitor. Salem, 1816. Leather, worn. Hayman 57-740 1974 $15

WEBB, W. L.   Brief Biography and Popular Account of the Unparalleled Discoveries of T. J. 1913. Frontispiece, illus., orig. covers. Covent 55-1330 1974 £9.50

WEBB, W. L.   The Centennial History of Independence, Missouri. N.P., 1927. 12mo., cloth. Saddleback 14-534 1974 $17.50

WEBB, WALTER PRESCOTT   Divided We Stand: The Crisis of a Frontierless Democracy. New York, 1937. Jenkins 61-2614 1974 $17.50

WEBB, WALTER PRESCOTT   The Great Plains. Boston, (1931). Jenkins 61-2610 1974 $20

WEBB, WALTER PRESCOTT   The Texas Rangers. Boston - New York, (1935). 8vo., orig. bindings, fine, dust jacket. Butterfield 8-632 1974 $10

WEBB, WALTER PRESCOTT   The Texas Rangers. New York, 1935. Special edition, limited to 205 copies, autographed, half calf, boxed, very fine, partly uncut. Jenkins 61-2612 1974 $285

WEBB, WALTER PRESCOTT   The Texas Rangers: A Century of Frontier Defense. Boston, 1935. Illus., first edition, first issue. Jenkins 61-2618 1974 $32.50

WEBB, WILFRED MARK   The Heritage of Dress. 1912. Illus., faded, new revised edition. Covent 55-531 1974 £5

WEBBER, C. H.   Old Naumkeag. Salem, 1877. 8vo., orig. bindings. Butterfield 8-274 1974 $10

WEBBER, SAMUEL   The Case of. (c.1740). Folio. Quaritch 939-292 1974 £20

WEBBER, SAMUEL   Logan, an Indian Tale. Cambridge, 1821. 12mo., modern cloth, uncut, first edition. Ximenes 35-495 1974 $40

WEBBER, SAMUEL   A Short Account of the State of Our Woolen Manufactories. London, 1739. 8vo., modern boards, fine, first edition. Dawsons PM 247-301 1974 £30

WEBER, ADOLF   Wirtschaftspolitik. Munich, 1932-33. 2 vols., cloth. Howes 186-1601 1974 £7.50

WEBER, CARL J.   In Thomas Hardy's Workshop. Waterville, 1934. Wrappers, fine. Covent 55-811 1974 £5.25

WEBER, CARL J.   Thanks to the Censor. 1932. Austin 51-1015 1973 $7.50

WEBER, ERNST HEINRICH   Wellenlehre auf Experimente Gegrundet. Leipzig, 1825. 8vo., contemporary boards. Zeitlin 235-236 1974 $725

WEBER, FREDERICK PARKES   Aspects of Death and Correlated Aspects of Life in Art. 1922. Thick 8vo., orig. buckram, illus., scarce, fourth & best edition. Howes 186-1955 1974 £15.50

WEBER, JOHANN CARL W.   Die Alpen Pflanzen Deutschlands und der Schweiz. Munich, 1880. 4 vols., post 8vo., cloth, plates, scarce, fourth edition. Wheldon 131-1362 1974 £50

WEBER, M.   The Fishes of the Indo-Australian Archipelago. Leiden, 1911-13. Vols. 1 and 2, 8vo., orig. cloth, rare orig. issues. Wheldon 128-667 1973 £25

WEBER, MAX   Retrospective Exhibition. New York, 1949. Biblo & Tannen 210-151 1973 $7.50

WEBER, V. F.   "Ko-Ji Ho-ten." Paris, 1923. 2 vols., folio plates, cloth, morocco backs, gilt, orig. & best edition. Quaritch 940-428 1974 £150

WEBER, WILHELM   Elektrodynamische Maassbestimmungen. Leipzig, 1864. 4to., orig. printed wrappers, first edition. Zeitlin 235-235 1974 $175

WEBER, WILHELM   Zur Galvanometrie. Gottingen, 1862. 4to., old boards. Gurney 66-197 1974 £25

WEBERBAUER, A.   El Mundo Vegetal de los Andes Peruanos. Lima, 1945. Roy. 8vo., plates. Wheldon 131-1363 1974 £20

WEBSTER, A. D.   Tree Wounds and Diseases, Their Prevention and Treatment. 1916. 8vo., cloth, plates. Wheldon 131-1761 1974 £5

WEBSTER, BENJAMIN   The Golden Farmer. Taylor, 1847. 38p. Austin 51-1016 1973 $6.50

WEBSTER, BENJAMIN   Highways and Byways. French, 1831. Austin 51-1017 1973 $6.50

WEBSTER, CHARLES A.   The Church Plate. Cork, 1909. 4to., illus., cloth, unopened. Quaritch 939-640 1974 £8

WEBSTER, CHARLES A.   The Church Plate of the Diocese of Cork, Cloyne and Ross. Cork, 1909. 4to., illus., fine. Emerald 50-976 1974 £5

WEBSTER, DANIEL   Mr. Webster's Address at the Laying of the Corner Stone of the Addition to the Capitol, July 4, 1851. Washington, 1851. Print. wrappers, inscribed by Amos Tuck. Wilson 63-53 1974 $10

WEBSTER, DANIEL   Mr. Webster's Speech at Marshfield, Mass. . . . Sept 1, 1848 . . . and His Speech On the Oregon Bill . . . Deliverd in the U. S. Senate, August 12, 1848. Boston, 1848. Disbound, sewn. Wilson 63-261 1974 $10

WEBSTER, DANIEL   Mr. Webster's Speech on the Greek Revolution. Washington City, 1824. First edition, 8vo., some interior foxing, recovered in new blue gray wrappers. Current BW9-440 1974 $12.50

WEBSTER, DANIEL   Mr. Webster's Speech on the President's Protest . . . Delivered in the Senate of the U. S. May 7, 1834. Washington, 1834. Folded, stitched as issued, uncut, light edge fraying, some foxing. Wilson 63-262 1974 $10

WEBSTER, DANIEL   Report Upon the Constitutional Rights. (Boston), 1821. 8vo., fine, uncut, first edition. Ximenes 35-496 1974 $25

WEBSTER, DANIEL   Speech at the Laying of the Cornerstone of the Addition to the Capitol. Washington, 1851. New half morocco, orig. wrapper bound in. Jenkins 61-791 1974 $15

WEBSTER, DANIEL   Speech Before the New York Historical Society. New York, 1852. New half morocco, orig. wrapper bound in. Jenkins 61-1940 1974 $17.50

WEBSTER, DANIEL   Speech Before the New York Historical Society.
New York, 1852. New half morocco, orig. wrapper bound in.   Jenkins 61-2623
1974 $17.50

WEBSTER, DANIEL   Speech in Answer to Mr. Calhoun.   Washington,
1838. New half morocco.   Jenkins 61-2624 1974 $19.50

WEBSTER, DANIEL   Speech on Renewing the Charter of the Bank of
the U. S. Washington, 1832. New half morocco.   Jenkins 61-2625 1974 $15

WEBSTER, DANIEL   Texas: A Report Upon the Subject of the
Relations Between the U. S. and the Republic of Texas. Washington, 1842.
Jenkins 61-2627 1974 $27.50

WEBSTER, DANIEL   The Treaty of Washington of 1842.   Washington,
1846. New half morocco.   Jenkins 61-2619 1974 $15

WEBSTER, DANIEL   The Works Of.   Large 8vo., 6 vols., green cloth,
fine. Putman 126-53 1974 $26

WEBSTER, JOHN   The Dramatic Works of.   London, 1857.
4 vols., small 8vo., half morocco, rubbed. Bow Windows 62-980 1974 £28

WEBSTER, JOHN   The Dramatic Works.   London, 1857. 4 vols.,
8vo., orig. cloth, first edition. Dawsons PM 252-1045 1974 £40

WEBSTER, JOHN   The Duchess of Malfi.   London, 1945. Orig.
lithographs, line drawings, signed by Michael Ayrton, tall 8vo., one corner
bumped, extremely nice copy, d.w., scarce, orig. cloth. Crane 7-15 1974 £25

WEBSTER, JOHN   Metallographia.   London, 1671. Small 4to.,
old panelled calf, rebacked. Traylen 79-276 1973 £105

WEBSTER, JOHN   The Complete Works of.   1927. 4 vols., 8vo.,
orig. cloth. Bow Windows 66-742 1974 £48

WEBSTER, JOHN CLARENCE   Acadia at the End of the 17th Century. St.
John, 1934. Heavy card cover, small line maps. Hood's 102-215 1974 $22.50

WEBSTER, JOHN CLARENCE   Journals of Beausejour.   1937. Card cover.
Hood's 102-216 1974 $40

WEBSTER, JOHN CLARENCE   The Seige of Beausejour in 1755. St. John,
1936. Card cover. Hood's 102-217 1974 $30

WEBSTER, JOHN CLARENCE   The Siege of Beausejour in 1755. St. John,
1936. Hood's 104-235 1974 $30

WEBSTER, JOHN CLARENCE   Wolfe and the Artists. Toronto, 1930. Limited
to 500 copies. Hood's 102-173 1974 $45

WEBSTER, JOHN CLARENCE   Wolfe and the Artists. Toronto, 1930. Limited
edition. Hood's 104-186 1974 $45

WEBSTER, MARGARET   Shakespeare Without Tears. 1942. Austin
51-1018 1973 $10

WEBSTER, NOAH   An American Dictionary of the English Language.
New York, 1828. 4to., 2 vols., half morocco, first edition. Bow Windows 64-
749 1974 £90

WEBSTER, NOAH   The American Spelling Book. Wells River, 1843.
8vo., orig. boards, worn. Butterfield 8-669 1974 $15

WEBSTER, NOAH   The Prompter; or, A Commentary on Common
Sayings and Subjects, Which are Full of Common Sense. Boston, 1797. 18mo.,
rebound, buckram. Butterfield 10-524 1974 $25

WEBSTER, NOAH   Secret Societies and Subversive Movements.
1924. 8vo., orig. cloth. Bow Windows 64-750 1974 £4.50

WEBSTER, WILLIAM   The Consequences of Trade. London, 1740.
8vo., disbound, uncut, third edition. Dawsons PM 247-302 1974 £10

WECHSBERG, JOSEPH   Red Plush and Black Velvet. 1961. Austin
51-1019 1973 $7.50

WEDDELL, ALEXANDER W.   Richmond Virginia in Old Prints, 1737-1887.
Richmond, 1932. Small folio, limited edition, unopened, illus., large folding
maps, very fine copy. Jenkins 61-2555 1974 $85

WEDEL, GEORG WOLFGANG   Pathologia Medica Dogmatica.   Jena, 1692.
4to., old vellum, first editions. Schumann 35-483 1974 $85

WEDGWOOD, G. R.   The History of the Tea-Cup.   c., 1875. 12mo.,
cloth, gilt, illus. Hammond 201-895 1974 £9.50

WEDL, CARL   Rudiments of Pathological Histology.   London,
1855. 8vo., orig. green cloth, uncut. Dawsons PM 249-506 1974 £20

WEED, THURLOW   The Facts Stated on the Morgan Abduction.
Chicago, 1882. Wrapper. Butterfield 10-59 1974 $20

WEEDON, L. L.   The Land of Long Ago.   London, n.d. (c. 1890).
Oblong 4to., pictorial boards, cloth spine, stand up three dimensional plates,
pen & ink illus. by E. Stuart Hardy. Frohnsdorff 16-591 1974 $150

WEEKLEY, ERNEST   Something About Words. 1935. Ex-library.
Austin 61-1005 1974 $10

WEEKLY Tables of Births and Deaths Registered in London. 1847-49. 3 vols.,
4to., boards, cloth backs. Quaritch 939-203 1974 £20

WEEMS, MASON LOCKE   The Life of George Washington; With Curious
Anecdotes. Philadelphia, 1808. 16mo., engraved portrait, old boards, leather
back, worn but sound. Butterfield 10-525 1974 $45

WEEVER, JOHN   Ancient Funerall Monuments. London, 1631.
Small folio, contemporary speckled calf, first edition. Dawsons PM 251-79
1974 £85

WEHDE, ALBERT   Since Leaving Home. 1923. 575p. Austin
62-673 1974 $12.50

WEHLE, HARRY B.   American Miniatures, 1730-1850. Garden
City, (1937). 4to., orig. binding, d.j. Butterfield 10-23 1974 $15

WEHLE, HARRY B.   American Miniatures, 1730-1850. New York,
(1937). 4to., portraits, fine, orig. cloth, d.w. Gregory 44-310 1974 $20

WEHLE, HARRY B.   A Catalogue of Italian, Spanish and Byzantine
Paintings. New York, 1940. Ltd. ed., illus. Biblo & Tannen 214-239 1974
$10

WEHMEYER, L. E.   The Genus Diaporthe. Ann Arbor, 1933. 4to.,
cloth, plates. Wheldon 129-975 1974 £12

WEIDMANN, JOHANN PETER   De Necrosi Ossium. Frankfurt, 1793. Large
folio, contemporary calf-backed boards, first edition. Schumann 35-484 1974
$175

WEIGEL, OSWALD   Katalog Einer Sammlung Illuminirter
Manuscripte und Miniaturen auf Einzelblaettern. Leipzig, 1898. Wrappers,
color plates. Kraus B8-278 1974 $35

WEINBERGER, BERNHARD WOLF   Dental Bibliography. New York, 1929.
Second edition. Rittenhouse 46-648 1974 $30

WEINER, ED   Damon Runyon Story. Longman, 1948. 258p.
Austin 54-882 1973 $7.50

WEINGARTEN, JOHANN JACOB   Fursten-Spiegel / Oder Monarchia des
Hochloblichen Ertz-Hauses Oesterreich. Prague, 1673. 2 vols. in 1, small
folio, blind stamped contemporary pigskin over wooden boards, only edition.
Schumann 499-118 1974 sFr 500

WEINSTEIN, GREGORY   The Ardent Eighties and After. 1947. 242p.,
illus. Austin 62-674 1974 $12.50

WEIR, F. G.   Scugog and Its Environs. Port Perry, 1927.
Hood's 103-694 1974 $25

WEIR, G. M.   Survey of Nursing Education In Canada.
Toronto, 1932. Card cover. Hood's 103-611 1974 $25

WEIR, HARRISON   Our Poultry and All About Them. 1902. 2 vols., 4to., plates, half contemporary morocco gilt. Smith 193-761 1973 £20

WEIR, JAMES   The Winter Lodge: or, Vow Fulfilled. Philadelphia, 1854. Orig. cloth, first edition, foxed throughout. MacManus 224-445 1974 $37.50

WEIR, L. H.   Parks . . . A Manual of Municipal and County Parks. New York, 1928. First edition, 2 vols., 4to., photos, plans, bookplate, orig. binding. Wilson 63-326 1974 $32.50

WEIR, W.   Sixty Years in Canada. Montreal, 1903. Hood's 104-743 1974 $15

WEISBACH, W.   Impressionismus, Ein Problem der Malerei in Der Antike und Neuzeit. Berlin, 1910-11. 2 vols. in 1, large 8vo., plates, illus., half morocco, orig. wrappers. Quaritch 940-272 1974 £15

WEISGAL, MEYER W.   Theodor Herzl. Brooklyn, 1929. 218p. Austin 62-758 1974 $17.50

WEISMANN, AUGUST FRIEDRICH LEOPOLD   Essays Upon Heredity and Kindred Biological Problems. 1891-92. 2 vols., 8vo., cloth. Wheldon 131-194 1974 £7.50

WEISMANN, AUGUST FRIEDRICH LEOPOLD   Essays Upon Heredity and Kindred Biological Problems. Oxford, 1891(-1892). 8vo., 2 vols., orig. cloth, gilt, uncut, unopened, second edition in English. Dawsons PM 249-507 1974 £18

WEISMANN, AUGUST FRIEDRICH LEOPOLD   The Evolution Theory. 1904. Roy. 8vo., 2 vols., orig. cloth, plates. Wheldon 129-116 1974 £30

WEISMANN, AUGUST FRIEDRICH LEOPOLD   The Evolution Theory. 1904. 2 vols., roy. 8vo., orig. cloth, plates. Wheldon 131-192 1974 £30

WEISMANN, AUGUST FRIEDRICH LEOPOLD   The Germ-Plasm. 1893. 8vo., cloth, scarce. Wheldon 131-195 1974 £15

WEISMANN, AUGUST FRIEDRICH LEOPOLD   Das Keimplasma. Jena, 1892. 8vo., illus., orig. printed wrappers, very crisp, unopened, first edition. Gilhofer 61-66 1974 sFr. 500

WEISMANN, AUGUST FRIEDRICH LEOPOLD   A Translation of Essays Upon Heredity and Kindred Biological Problems. 1889-92. 8vo., 12mo., 2 vols., buckram. Gurney 64-230 1974 £20

WEISMANN, AUGUST FRIEDRICH LEOPOLD   Vortrage Uber Descendenztheorie. Jena, 1902. 2 vols. in 1, 8vo., new cloth, coloured plates, first edition. Wheldon 128-74 1973 £25

WEISMANN, AUGUST FRIEDRICH LEOPOLD   Vortrage Uber Deszendenz-Theorie. Jena, 1913. 2 vols. in 1, roy. 8vo., plates, third edition. Wheldon 131-193 1974 £10

WEISS, EMIL RUDOLPH   E. R. Weiss zum funfzigsten Geburtstage. Leipzig, (1925). Boards, vellum back, bookplates. Dawson's 424-178 1974 $185

WEISS, FERI FELIX   The Sieve. Boston, 1921. Ex-library, illus. Austin 57-693 1974 $10

WEISS, FERI FELIX   The Sieve. Boston, 1921. 307p., illus. Austin 62-676 1974 $10

WEISS, SARA   Decimon Huydas, a Romance of Mars. Rochester, 1906. Cloth. Hayman 57-231 1974 $12.50

WEISS, TRUDE   The Light-Hearted Student. 1930. Book-label. Covent 55-261 1974 £8.50

WEISSMANN, ADOLF   Die Primadonna. Berlin, 1920. Orig. cloth-backed pictorial boards, English first edition. Covent 56-977 1974 £15

WEIZMANN, CHAIM   Trial and Error. 1949. 2 vols., orig. ed. Austin 62-675 1974 $12.50

WELCH, CHARLES   Modern History of the City of London. 1896. Large 4to., half maroon morocco, illus., plates, special edition. Howes 186-2151 1974 £18

WELCH, DENTON   In Youth Is Pleasure. 1944. Frontispiece, fine, dust wrapper. Covent 55-1505 1974 £10.50

WELCH, DENTON   In Youth is Pleasure. 1944. Crown 8vo., orig. cloth, first edition. Broadhurst 23-963 1974 £12

WELCH, DENTON   In Youth is Pleasure. 1944. First edition, crown 8vo., fine, d.w., orig. cloth. Broadhurst 24-934 1974 £12

WELCH, DENTON   Maiden Voyage. 1943. Crown 8vo., orig. cloth, first edition. Broadhurst 23-962 1974 £20

WELCH, DENTON   Maiden Voyage. 1943. First edition, crown 8vo., mint, d.w., orig. cloth. Broadhurst 24-933 1974 £20

WELCH, F. G.   That Convention. New York, 1872. 1st ed., spine torn, good used; scarce. Biblo & Tannen 213-831 1973 $20

WELCH, SAMUEL M.   Home History. Buffalo, 1891. 8vo., cloth, 423 pages. Saddleback 14-596 1974 $15

WELCH, W. E.   The Oklahoma Spirit of '17. Oklahoma City, 1920. 8vo., cloth, 445 pages. Saddleback 14-641 1974 $17.50

WELCH, WILLIAM HENRY   Adaptation in Pathological Processes. 1897. 8vo., contemporary half calf. Dawsons PM 249-508 1974 £8

WELCH, WILLIAM HENRY   Contributions to the Science of Medicine. Baltimore, 1900. Cover loose. Rittenhouse 46-649 1974 $35

WELCH, WILLIAM HENRY   The Eightieth Birthday of William H. Welch. New York, 1930. Rittenhouse 46-650 1974 $20

WELCH, WILLIAM HENRY   In Honour of. Baltimore, 1910. Uncut, like new. Rittenhouse 46-651 1974 $15

WELCH, WILLIAM HENRY   Papers and Addresses. Baltimore, 1920. Large 8vo., 3 vols., orig. green cloth, fine, first edition. Dawsons PM 249-509 1974 £60

WELCKER, ADAIR   A Voyage With Death. Oakland, 1878. 16mo., orig. wrappers, scarce, first edition. Ximenes 35-497 1974 $22.50

WELD, CHARLES RICHARD   A History of the Royal Society. 1848. 8vo., 2 vols., polished calf, illus., plates. Bow Windows 64-751 1974 £42

WELD, CHARLES RICHARD   A History of the Royal Society. London, 1848. 8vo., 2 vols., orig. cloth, illus., first edition. Schumann 35-486 1974 $110

WELD, ISAAC   Illustrations of the Scenery of Killarney and the Surrounding Country. 1812. 8vo., contemporary gilt framed calf, plates, maps, upper joint cracking. Bow Windows 66-743 1974 £36

WELD, ISAAC   Travels Through the States of North America and the Provinces of Upper and Lower Canada, 1795-97. London, 1799. Map, illus., orig. marbled boards, excellent. Hood's 103-567 1974 $350

WELDON, ANTHONY   The Court and Character of King James. 1650. Small 8vo., sheep, stains. Thomas 28-211 1972 £18

WELLBELOVED, ROBERT   A Treatise on the Law Relating to Highways. 1829. Thick 8vo., rebound, buckram. Howes 186-1456 1974 £10

WELLER, CARL HEINRICH   Die Krankheiten des Menschlichen Auges. Berlin, 1826. 8vo., modern half calf. Dawsons PM 249-510 1974 £15

WELLER, HENRY   Marriage on Earth. Grand Rapids, 1849. 12mo., orig. wrappers, fine, first edition. Ximenes 35-498 1974 $22.50

WELLES, C. M.   Three Years Wanderings Around the World. Hartford, 1864. 8vo., orig. bindings, engravings. Butterfield 8-56 1974 $12.50

WELLESLEY, DOROTHY   Letters on Poetry from W. B. Yeats to Dorothy Wellesley. Oxford, 1940. Orig. binding, first edition, slightly rumpled d.w.,

WELLESLEY, DOROTHY   Letters On Poetry from W. B. Yeats to Dorothy Wellesley. 1940. Slightly rumpled d.w., near mint, orig. binding. Ross 86-490 1974 $15

WELLING, JAMES CLARKE   Addresses, Lectures, and Other Papers. Cambridge, 1903. Wilson 63-264 1974 $12.50

WELLMAN, RITA   Victoria Royal: The Flowering of a Style. 1939. Illus. Austin 61-1006 1974 $10

WELLNER, GEORG   Die Flugmaschinen. 1910. Tall 8vo., orig. half black buckram, gilt. Zeitlin 235-237 1974 $97.50

WELLS, A. J.   San Bernardino County, California. San Francisco, (1909). 8vo., wrapper, soiled. Saddleback 14-312 1974 $17.50

WELLS, CAROLYN   The Omnibus Fleming Stone. Burt, 1923. Austin 54-1029 1973 $10

WELLS, CAROLYN   The Rest of My Life. Lippincott, 1937. 295p. Austin 54-1030 1973 $6

WELLS, CAROLYN   The Rubaiyat of Bridge. New York, 1909. 12mo., 1st ed., illus. Biblo & Tannen 213-611 1973 $7.50

WELLS, CAROLYN   A Satire Anthology. Scribner, 1905. 369p. Austin 54-1031 1973 $8.50

WELLS, CAROLYN   Such Nonsense. Doran, 1918. 249p., illus. Austin 54-1032 1973 $10

WELLS, CAROLYN   A Whimsey Anthology. 1906. 288 pages. Austin 61-1007 1974 $10

WELLS, CHARLES   Joseph and His Brethren. 1908. 12mo., cloth gilt, fine, English first edition. Covent 56-1107 1974 £5.25

WELLS, CHARLES JEREMIAH   Stories After Nature. London, 1891. 8vo., orig. cloth, uncut. Dawsons PM 252-1046 1974 £8

WELLS, DANIEL WHITE   A History of Hatfield. Springfield, (1910). 8vo., orig. bindings. Butterfield 8-275 1974 $35

WELLS, EDWARD   The Young Gentleman's Astronomy, Chronology, and Dialling. London, 1718. 8vo., modern half calf, second edition. Dawsons PM 245-759 1974 £25

WELLS, ELIAB HORATIO   Beneath the Star of Bethlehem. New York and Washington, 1907. Gilt dec. cloth. Dykes 24-71 1974 $15

WELLS, GEOFFREY H.   The Works of H. G. Wells, 1887-1925. 1926. Buckram. Howes 185-879 1974 £12.50

WELLS, HERBERT GEORGE   Christina Alberta's Father. 1925. 8vo., orig. cloth, inscribed, first edition. Rota 189-928 1974 £8

WELLS, HERBERT GEORGE   Experiment in Autobiography. 1934. 2 vols., illus., fine, dust wrappers, first edition. Rota 188-923 1974 £5

WELLS, HERBERT GEORGE   Experiment in Autobiography. 1934. 2 vols., plates, faded. Covent 55-1508 1974 £5.25

WELLS, HERBERT GEORGE   First & Last Things. 1908. First edition. Howes 186-515 1974 £5

WELLS, HERBERT GEORGE   Floor Games. 1911. Square 8vo., orig. pictorial cloth, plates, English first edition. Covent 56-1300 1974 £15

WELLS, HERBERT GEORGE   The History of Mr. Polly. 1910. Frontispiece, rubbed. Covent 55-1510 1974 £8.50

WELLS, HERBERT GEORGE   In Memory of Amy Catherine Wells. (1927). Wrappers, English first edition. Covent 56-1302 1974 £12.50

WELLS, HERBERT GEORGE   In the Days of the Comet. London, 1906. 8vo., orig. cloth, fine, first edition. Dawsons PM 252-1047 1974 £8

WELLS, HERBERT GEORGE   In the Fourth Year: Anticipations of a World Peace. 1918. Austin 61-1017 1974 $10

WELLS, HERBERT GEORGE   The Invisible Man. London, 1897. 8vo., orig. red cloth, first edition. Dawsons PM 252-1048 1974 £26

WELLS, HERBERT GEORGE   Joan and Peter. 1918. Edges of text spotted, very good copy, slightly frayed & soiled d.w., first edition, scarce. Covent 51-1947 1973 £10.50

WELLS, HERBERT GEORGE   Kipps, the Story of a Simple Soul. 1905. Crown 8vo., orig. green cloth, gilt, first edition. Howes 186-516 1974 £7.50

WELLS, HERBERT GEORGE   Man Who Could Work Miracles. Macmillan, 1936. Austin 51-1023 1973 $10

WELLS, HERBERT GEORGE   Mr. Britling Sees it Through. 1916. First edition. Howes 186-518 1974 £5

WELLS, HERBERT GEORGE   The New Machiavelli. New York, 1910. Inscribed, first American edition. Covent 55-1215 1974 £25

WELLS, HERBERT GEORGE   The Outline of History. London, 1920. 2 vols., 4to., illus., orig. cloth, faded, first bound edition. Bow Windows 62-982 1974 £6.50

WELLS, HERBERT GEORGE   The Outlook for Homo Sapiens. 1942. First edition, 8vo., orig. cloth, fine in dust wrapper, with an A.L.s. from the author to Lady Swettenham. Sawyer 293-282 1974 £38

WELLS, HERBERT GEORGE   The Passionate Friends. 1913. Dust wrapper, fine, first edition. Howes 186-519 1974 £5

WELLS, HERBERT GEORGE   The Problem of the Troublesome Collaborator. 1930. 2 vols., orig. boards, English first edition. Covent 56-1306 1974 £55

WELLS, HERBERT GEORGE   Russia in the Shadows. (1920). Plates, d.w., fine, first edition. Howes 186-521 1974 £5

WELLS, HERBERT GEORGE   The Science of Life. 1931. Imp. 8vo., cloth, illus. Wheldon 131-197 1974 £6

WELLS, HERBERT GEORGE   The Science of Life. 1931. 2 vols. Austin 61-1028 1974 $12.50

WELLS, HERBERT GEORGE   The Sea Lady. London, 1902. 8vo., orig. red cloth, first English edition. Dawsons PM 252-1049 1974 £16

WELLS, HERBERT GEORGE   Select Conversations With an Uncle. 1895. Small 8vo., silken cloth, scarce, first edition. Howes 186-523 1974 £21

WELLS, HERBERT GEORGE   Select Conversations with an Uncle. London & New York, 1895. Small 8vo., orig. silver cloth, fine, first edition. Dawsons PM 252-1050 1974 £40

WELLS, HERBERT GEORGE   The Soul of a Bishop. 1917. Orig. cloth, presentation inscription, first edition. Rota 188-920 1974 £8

WELLS, HERBERT GEORGE   Star-Begotten. 1937. 217 pages. Austin 61-1032 1974 $10

WELLS, HERBERT GEORGE   The Stolen Bacillus. London, 1895. 8vo., orig. cloth, uncut, fine, first edition. Dawsons PM 252-1051 1974 £20

WELLS, HERBERT GEORGE   Tales of Space and Time. London & New York, 1900. 8vo., orig. cloth, first edition. Dawsons PM 252-1052 1974 £20

WELLS, HERBERT GEORGE   The War in the Air. 1908. Orig. blue cloth, plates. Howes 186-528 1974 £21

WELLS, HERBERT GEORGE   The Wheels of Chance. 1896. Illus., orig. dec. cloth, gilt top, nice copy, first edition. Covent 51-1949 1973 £10

WELLS, HERBERT GEORGE   The Wonderful Visit. 1895. 8vo., orig. cloth, pencilled notes, bookplate, first edition. Bow Windows 66-744 1974 £18.50

WELLS, HERBERT GEORGE   The Works. London, 1924-27. 28 vols., large 8vo., orig. cloth, limited. Dawsons PM 252-1053 1974 £375

WELLS, HERBERT GEORGE   Works of. London, 1933. 12 vols., 8vo., orig. cloth. Bow Windows 62-984 1974 £8.50

WELLS, JAMES M.   The Chisolm Massacre. Chicago, 1877. 8vo., orig. bindings. Butterfield 8-308 1974 $45

WELLS, JAMES M.   The Chisolm Massacre: A Picture of "Home Rule" in Mississippi. Washington, 1878. Ex-library. Jenkins 61-1698 1974 $12.50

WELLS, JOHN A.   Rifle Shots at Past and Passing Events. Philadelphia, n.d. 8vo., quarter cloth, orig. wrappers, first edition. Ximenes 35-500 1974 $17.50

WELLS, JOHN EDWIN   Manual of Writings in Middle English, 1040-1440. 1926. Allen 216-1861 1974 $25

WELLS, JOHN EDWIN   A Manual of the Writings In Middle English 1050-1400. 1916. Orig. edition. Austin 61-1040 1974 $19.75

WELLS, LAURA JAY   The Jay Family of La Rochelle and New York Province and State. New York, 1938. Wrapper, illus., limited edition. Jenkins 61-1941 1974 $10

WELLS, OLIVER   An Anthology of the Younger Poets. Philadelphia, 1932. Orig. cloth backed boards, paper label, first edition, one of 500 numbered copies, bookplate removed, otherwise as new. MacManus 224-159 1974 $35

WELLS, T. SPENCER   A Lecture on the Revival of the Turkish, or Ancient Roman Bath. London, c., 1860. 8vo., boards, inscribed, presentation copy. Hammond 201-600 1974 £5.50

WELLS, WILLIAM CHARLES   An Essay on Dew. London, 1814. 8vo., orig. boards, slipcase, rare, first edition. Zeitlin 235-238 1974 $550

WELLS, WILLIAM CHARLES   Two Essays. 1818. 8vo., new half calf. Wheldon 129-118 1974 £120

WELLS, WILLIAM CHARLES   Two Essays: One Upon Single Vision With Two Eyes: The Other On Dew. 1818. 8vo., new half calf. Wheldon 131-198 1974 £120

WELSER, MARCUS   Opera Historica et Philologica. Nurnberg, 1682. Thick folio, contemporary calf, worn, internally fine, first collected edition. Harper 213-173 1973 $395

WELSH, CHARLES   Coloured Books for Children. London, 1887. 16mo., wrappers, binding broken. Goodspeed's 578-550 1974 $10

WELTY, EUDORA   Delta Wedding. New York, 1946. 1st ed. Biblo & Tannen 213-612 1973 $10

WELWITSCH, F.   Catalogue of the African Plants Collected in 1853-61. 1896-1901. 2 vols. in 6 parts, 8vo., boards, cloth backs, scarce. Wheldon 128-1320 1973 £25

WELZL, J.   Thirty Years in the Golden North. New York, 1932. Hood's 102-82 1974 $7.50

WENDEHACK, CLIFFORD CHARLES   Golf & Country Clubs. New York, 1929. Large 4to., cloth covers, soiled, plates. Minters 37-579 1973 $16

WENDELL, BARRETT   A Literary History of America. New York, 1901. Biblo & Tannen 210-933 1973 $7.50

WENDELL, BARRETT   The Temper of the Seventeenth Century In English Literature. 1904. Ex-library, orig. edition. Austin 61-1041 1974 $10

WENING, R.   Thailand. New York, n.d. 4to. Biblo & Tannen 210-294 1973 $12.50

WENINGER, F. X.   Protestantism and Infidelity. 1862. Ex-library. Austin 57-694 1974 $12.50

WENINGER, F. X.   Protestantism and Infidelity. Sadlier, 1862. Austin 62-677 1974 $12.50

WENTWORTH, JOHN   The Wentworth Genealogy: English and American. Boston, 1878. 3 vols., cloth, spines faded, else nice. Hayman 59-211 1974 $50

WENTWORTH, T.   The Office and Dutie of Executors. London, 1641. Small 8vo., old sheep, third edition. Quaritch 939-277 1974 £10

WENZEL, JOSEPH   De Penitiori Structura Cerebri Hominis et Brutorum. Tubingen, 1812. Large folio, contemporary boards, first edition. Schumann 35-487 1974 $175

WENZEL, JOSEPH   Observations sur le Cervelt. Paris, 1811. 8vo., contemporary wrappers, plates, first edition in French. Schuman 37-263 1974 $95

WERDERMANN, E.   Bluhende Kakteen und Andere Sukkulente Pflanzen Neudamm, 1930-38. Parts 1 - 38, 4to., orig. portfolios, plates. Wheldon 131-1708 1974 £85

WERFEL, FRANZ   Goat Song. Doubleday, 1926. Austin 51-1025 1973 $8.50

WERFEL, FRANZ   Juarez and Maximilian. S & S, 1926. Austin 51-1026 1973 $7.50

WERICH, J. L.   Pioneer Hunters of the Kankakee. 1920. Cloth, illus., fine. Putnam 126-180 1974 $15

WERNER, ABRAHAM GOTTLOB   New Theory of the Formation of Veins. Edinburgh, 1809. 8vo., new half morocco, uncut. Wheldon 129-876 1974 £60

WERNER, ABRAHAM GOTTLOB   Traite des Caracteres Exterieurs des Fossiles. Dijon, 1790. 8vo., contemporary calf, rebacked. Wheldon 131-1089 1974 £45

WERNER, ABRAHAM GOTTLOB   Traite des Caracteres Exterieurs des Fossiles. 1790. 8vo., contemporary calf. Wheldon 129-874 1974 £45

WERNER, ABRAHAM GOTTLOB   A Treatise on the External Characters of Fossils. Dublin, 1805. 8vo., contemporary half calf, rare. Wheldon 130-979 1974 £70

WERNER, J. C.   Atlas des Oiseaux d'Europe. (1826-)1842. 8vo., 3 vols., half calf. Wheldon 129-49 1974 £250

WERNER, JOHANN   Canones Sicvt Brevissimi. 1546. Small 4to., modern vellum, first edition. Zeitlin 235-239 1974 $150

WERTENBAKER, THOMAS J.   Virginia under the Stuarts 1607-1688. Princeton-London, 1914. 8vo., orig. bindings. Butterfield 8-682 1974 $15

WERTH, LEON   Bonnard. Paris, 1923. 4to., wrappers, illus. Minters 37-51B 1973 $25

WERTH, LEON   Bonnard. Paris, 1923. Wrappers. Minters 37-51A 1973 $26

WERTH, LEON   Bonnard. Paris, 1923. 4to., half leather, boards, orig. wrappers, rubbed, plates, illus. Minters 37-51 1973 $36

WERTHEIM, E.   The Technique of Vagino-Peritoneal Operations. London, 1907. Rittenhouse 46-653 1974 $15

WESLEY, JOHN   Collection of Hymns By. 1811. 12mo., polished calf antique. Bow Windows 64-753 1974 £10.50

WESLEY, JOHN   Extract of Count Zinzendore's Discourses on the Redemption of Man by the Death of Christ. New Castle-Upon-Tyne, 1744. Half 19th century morocco, rubbed. Smith 194-197 1974 £15

WESLEY, JOHN   An Extract of the Christian's Pattern. 1741. 12mo., contemporary calf gilt, rebacked, rubbed. Smith 194-198 1974 £20

WESLEY, JOHN   Primitive Physic. London, n.d. 12mo., cloth. Schumann 35-488 1974 $75

WESLEY, JOHN   A Treatise On Justification. Bristol, 1765. 12mo., contemporary calf, worn. Smith 194-199 1974 £5

WEST, G. S.   A Comparative Study of Dominant Phanerogamic and Higher Cryptogamie Flora of Aquatic Habit. 1905-10. 2 Parts, 8vo., plates. Wheldon 128-1229 1973 £5

WEST, G. S.   A Comparative Study of Dominant Phanerogamic and High Cryptogamic Flora of Aquatic Habit. 1905-10. 8vo., plates. Wheldon 130-1117 1974 £5

WEST, G. S.   A Treatise on the British Freshwater Algae.
1927. 8vo., wrappers. Wheldon 129-1429 1974 £7.50

WEST, G. S.   A Treatise on the British Freshwater Algae.
Cambridge, (1927). 8vo., cloth. Wheldon 131-1478 1974 £7.50

WEST, GILBERT   A Canto of the Fairy Queen. London, 1739.
Folio, quarter calf, first edition. Ximenes 35-502 1974 $50

WEST, JANE   Miscellaneous Poetry. London, 1786.
4to., old half calf, first edition. Ximenes 35-503 1974 $80

WEST, JANE   The Refusal. 1810. 12mo., 3 vols., orig.
boards, orig. paper labels, first edition. Broadhurst 23-964 1974 £45

WEST, JANE   The Refusal. 1810. 3 vols., 12mo., orig.
boards, orig. paper printed labels, bindings rubbed, first edition, complete with
half titles. Broadhurst 24-935 1974 £50

WEST, JOHN   The Substance of a Journal During a Residence
at the Red River Colony, British North America. 1824. 8vo., contemporary
half calf, uncut, frontispiece, some damp stains. Bow Windows 66-746 1974
£24

WEST, JOHN C.   A Texan In Search of a Fight. Waco, 1901.
Inscribed. Jenkins 48-493 1973 $85

WEST, JOHN C.   A Texan in Search of a Fight. Waco, 1901.
Inscribed and signed by author, with adv. leaflet & leaflet about Mrs. West
tipped in, rare. Jenkins 61-2641 1974 $85

WEST, KENYON   The Laureates of England. 1895. Illus. edition.
Austin 61-1042 1974 $10

WEST, L. SACKVILLE   Knole House. 1906. F'cap 4to., binding good,
text fine, coloured and plain plates, orig. cloth. Broadhurst 24-220 1974 £5

WEST, LEVON   Making an Etching. London, 1932. Boards,
cloth, illus. Dawson's 424-138 1974 $30

WEST, MAE   Diamond Lil. Caxton, 1939. 256p. Austin
54-1033 1973 $10

WEST, REBECCA   D. H. Lawrence. London, 1930. Name in
ink on free fly, covers lightly worn, very nice, orig. binding. Ross 86-308
1974 $20

WEST, REBECCA   Elegy. New York, 1930. Buckram, browned,
bookplate, numbered, signed. Covent 55-989 1974 £27.50

WEST, RICHARD   Skallagram. New York, 1925. Numbered.
Ballinger 1-43 1974 $15

WEST, THOMAS   The Antiquities of Furness. 1774. 4to.,
map, plates, modern boards. Quaritch 939-423 1974 £16

WEST, THOMAS   A Guide to the Lakes In Cumberland. Kendal,
1821. 8vo., contemporary half pink calf, leather label. Traylen 79-344
1973 £30

WEST Baden Springs. French Lick, 1907. Wrapper, illus. Jenkins 61-1162
1974 $12

WESTALL, RICHARD   Victories of the Duke of Wfllington. London,
1819. Folio, royal blue half morocco gilt, first edition. Dawsons PM 251-409
1974 £150

WESTALL, WILLIAM   Great Britain Illustrated. 1830. 4to., cloth,
morocco back, rubbed. Quaritch 939-278 1974 £95

WESTALL, WILLIAM   Great Britain Illustrated. London, 1830. Rebound, boards. Dawson's 424-125 1974 $100

WESTALL, WILLIAM   Illustrations to Lord Byron. n.d. Engravings
dated 1819, contemporary fine binding. Eaton Music-689 1973 £5

WESTALL, WILLIAM   Picturesque Tour of the River Thames. 1828.
First edition, large folding engraved maps, coloured aquatint views, coloured
vignettes, roy. 4to., red straight grained morocco, gilt floral borders, spine
richly gilt tooled, buckram box, slight offsets on plates, fine tall copy. Sawyer
293-113 1974 £1,350

WESTAWAY, F. W.   Obessions and Convictions of the Human
Intellect. London, (1938). 8vo., plates, illus., orig. cloth, first edition.
Bow Windows 62-986 1974 £5.50

WESTBY-GIBSON, J.   Bibliography of Shorthand. 1887. Ex-library.
Allen 216-212 1974 $25

WESTCHESTER INDEPENDENT POLITICAL CLUB, INC. Westchester Independent
Political Club: Souvenir Journal. 1935. 76p., illus. Austin 62-290 1974
$27.50

WESTCOTT, EDWARD N.   David Harum. New York, 1900. First illus.
edition, limited to 750 copies, 8vo. Current BW9-289 1974 $25

WESTEN, WALTER V-ZUR   Reklamekunst, Aus Zwei Jahr Tausenden.
Berlin, 1925. Illus. Covent 55-131 1974 £45

WESTERMARCK, EDWARD   The History of Human Marriage. 1894.
Second edition. Howes 186-1957 £7.50

WESTERMARCK, EDWARD   The Origin and Development of the Moral
Ideas. 1906. 2 vols., thick 8vo., scarce. Howes 186-1958 1974 £14

THE WESTERN Garland. N.P., (Newcastle?), n.d. (c. 1760). 12mo., later
half roan, very scarce. Ximenes 36-48 1974 $75

THE WESTERN "Patriot" for the Year 1838. Canton, (1837). Pict. wrappers.
Hayman 59-15 1974 $20

WESTHOFEN, W.   The Forth Bridge. 1890. Super roy 4to., limp
cloth, illus. Broadhurst 23-1229 1974 £10

WESTLAKE, H. F.   Westminster Abbey. 1923. 2 vols., folio,
plates, illus., half canvas. Quaritch 939-490 1974 £17.50

WESTMACOTT, CHARLES MOLLOY   Fitzalleyne of Berkeley. London, 1825.
2 vols., 8vo., orig. boards, first edition. Dawsons PM 252-1054 1974 £80

WESTON, JESSIE L.   From Ritual to Romance. Cambridge, 1920.
First edition, good copy, some worming to hinges, sound working copy, scarce,
orig. cloth. Crane 7-309 1974 £7

WESTON, JESSIE L.   The Three Days' Tournament. 1902. Cloth
backed boards, unopened, inscription. Covent 55-1026 1974 £5.25

WESTON, MARIA D.   Kate Felton. Boston, 1859. 12mo., orig.
violet cloth, frontispiece, first edition. Ximenes 35-507 1974 $15

WESTPHAL, KARL GEORG HEINRICH   Rathgeber fur alle Diejenigen,
Welche au Hamorrhoiden in Geringerem Oder Hoherem Grade Leiden. Leipzig,
1827. 12mo., contemporary boards, first edition. Schuman 37-264 1974 $50

WESTPHALIUS, JOHANNES CASPAR   Pathologia Daemoniaca. Leipzig, 1707.
4to., modem half calf. Dawsons PM 249-511 1974 £23

WESTREENEN DE TIELLANDT, BARON DE   Rapport sur les Recherches,
Relatives a l'Invention Premiere et a l'Usage le Plus Ancien de l'Imprimerie
Stereotype. The Hague, 1833. Large folding plates, unopened. Kraus B8-391
1974 $45

WESTWOOD, JOHN OBADIAH   Arcana Entomologica. (1841)-1845. 2 vols.,
roy. 8vo., orig. cloth, hand colored plates. Wheldon 128-825 1973 £65

WESTWOOD, JOHN OBADIAH   Arcana Entomologica. 1841-45. 2 vols.,
roy. 8vo., new half morocco, plates, rare, complete copy. Wheldon 131-879
1974 £120

WESTWOOD, JOHN OBADIAH   British Moths and Their Transformations.
London, 1849. 4to., 2 vols., contemporary half morocco, gilt plates. Hammond
201-689 1974 £75

WESTWOOD, JOHN OBADIAH   Catalogue of Orthopterous Insects in the Collection of the British Museum, Part 1, Phasmidae. 1859. 4to., orig. cloth, plates, rare, foxed. Wheldon 131-880 1974 £15

WESTWOOD, JOHN OBADIAH   An Introduction to the Modern Classification of Insects. 1839-40. 2 vols., 8vo., cloth, worn, frontispiece. Wheldon 131-881 1974 £5

WESTWOOD, JOHN OBADIAH   Polaeographia Sacra Pictoria. 1845. 4to., contemporary half morocco, plates, rubbed. Howes 185-881 1974 £60

WESTWOOD, T.   Bibliotheca Piscatoria. 1883. First edition, gilt top, bookplate, nice copy. Covent 51-247 1973 £16.50

WETHERALD, E.   The House of the Trees. Boston, New York & Toronto, 1895. Hood's 103-758 1974 $12.50

WETHERBEE, JOHN   A Brief Sketch of Colorado Territory. Boston, 1863. 8vo., orig. wrappers, first edition. Ximenes 35-508 1974 $650

WETHERED, H. N.   A Short History of Gardens. 1933. 8vo., cloth, illus., scarce. Wheldon 129-196 1974 £5

WETHERED, H. N.   A Short History of Gardens. 1933. 8vo., cloth, illus. Wheldon 131-252 1974 £5

WETHERED, NEWTON   From Giotto to John. London, 1926. Illus. Biblo & Tannen 214-562 1974 $8.50

WETHERED, NEWTON   Mediaeval Craftsmanship and the Modern Amateur. 1923. Illus. Covent 55-1101 1974 £12.50

WETMORE, ALPHONSO   Gazetteer of the State of Missouri. St. Louis, 1837. 8vo., orig. cloth, paper label, first edition. Ximenes 35-509 1974 $125

WETMORE, HELEN CODY   Last of the Great Scouts. Chicago and Duluth, (1899). 8vo., orig. bindings, illus. Butterfield 8-721 1974 $12.50

WETMORE, HELEN CODY   Last of the Great Scouts. London, 1903. 8vo., orig. bindings, illus., second London edition. Butterfield 8-722 1974 $10

WETMORE, PROSPER MONTGOMERY   Lexington. New York, 1830. 8vo., orig. half morocco, rubbed, first edition. Ximenes 35-510 1974 $17.50

WETTERWALD, X.   Blatt, und Sprossbildung Bei Euphorbien und Cacteen. Halle, 1889. 4to., plates. Wheldon 131-1709 1974 £5

WETTON, G. N.   Wetton's Guide-Book to Northampton and Its Vicinity. Northampton, 1849. Small 8vo., orig. morocco gilt, worn, illus., plates. Traylen 79-371 1973 £10

WETTSTEIN, R. R. VON   Vegetationsbilder aus Sudbrasilien. Leipzig, 1904. Roy. 8vo., orig. portfolio, coloured and other plates. Wheldon 128-1321 1973 £10

WEYGANDT, CORNELIUS   Irish Plays and Playwrights. Boston & New York, (1913). Orig. cloth, first edition, inscribed copy, fine. MacManus 224-446 1974 $40

WEYGANDT, CORNELIUS   The Red Hills. Philadelphia, 1929. 8vo., orig. bindings, first edition. Butterfield 8-526 1974 $10

WEYMAN, STANLEY   A Gentleman of France. London, 1893. 3 vols., 8vo., orig. cloth, fine, first edition. Ximenes 35-511 1974 $225

WHALL, C. W.   Stained Glass Work. London, 1905. Illus., bdg. and edges stained. Biblo & Tannen 214-266 1974 $8.50

WHARTON, EDITH   The Buccaneers. Appleton, 1938. 371 pages. Austin 54-1034 1973 $7.50

WHARTON, EDITH   The Children. Appleton, 1928. 346p. Austin 54-1035 1973 $6

WHARTON, EDITH   Crucial Instances. Scribner, 1901. 242p. Austin 54-1036 1973 $10

WHARTON, EDITH   Crucial Instances. Scribner, 1909. 242p. Austin 54-1037 1973 $7.50

WHARTON, EDITH   Crucial Instances and Sanctuary. Scribner, 1914. 356p. Austin 54-1038 1973 $8.50

WHARTON, EDITH   The Custom of the Country. Scribner, 1913. 594p. Austin 54-1040 1973 $4.75

WHARTON, EDITH   The Custom of the Country. Scribner, 1913. 594p., 1st ed. Austin 54-1039 1973 $7.50

WHARTON, EDITH   The Decoration of Houses. New York, 1902. Orig. binding, front hinge tender, lacking d.w., owner's name in ink on fly, nice copy, protected by heavy dec. paper wrapper. Ross 87-573 1974 $15

WHARTON, EDITH   The Descent of Man and Other Stories and Madame de Tryemes. Scribner, 1914. 395p. Austin 54-1041 1973 $8.50

WHARTON, EDITH   Ethan Frome. New York, 1922. Limited edition, one of 2,000 copies, ex-library, stamp inside both covers, nice, orig. binding. Ross 87-574 1974 $12.50

WHARTON, EDITH   French Ways and Their Meaning. Appleton, 1919. 149p. Austin 54-1042 1973 $12.50

WHARTON, EDITH   The Fruit of the Tree. Scribner, 1907. 633p., illus., orig. ed. Austin 54-1043 1973 $7.50

WHARTON, EDITH   Ghosts. New York, 1937. 1st ed. Biblo & Tannen 210-692 1973 $15

WHARTON, EDITH   The Greater Inclination. New York, 1899. First U. S. edition, dec. boards, gilt top, scarce, exceptionally fine copy. Covent 51-1955 1973 £37.50

WHARTON, EDITH   The Hermit and the Wild Woman. Scribner, 1908. 279p. Austin 54-1044 1973 $12.50

WHARTON, EDITH   Hudson River Bracketed. Appleton, 1929. 560p. Austin 54-1045 1973 $3.75

WHARTON, EDITH   Italian Villas and Their Gardens. New York, 1904. 4to., 1st ed. Biblo & Tannen 210-161 1973 $50

WHARTON, EDITH   The Mother's Recoin Pense. Appleton, 1925. 342p. Austin 54-1051 1973 $4.75

WHARTON, EDITH   A Motor-Flight Through France. Scribner, 1908. 201p., illus. Austin 54-1046 1973 $8.50

WHARTON, EDITH   Old New York--False Dawn (40's). Appleton, 1924. 143p. Austin 54-1047 1973 $3.50

WHARTON, EDITH   Old New York--New Year's Day (70's). Appleton, 1924. 160p. Austin 54-1050 1973 $3.50

WHARTON, EDITH   Old New York--The Old Maid (50's). Appleton, 1924. 191p. Austin 54-1048 1973 $3.50

WHARTON, EDITH   Old New York--The Spark (60's). Appleton, 1924. 109p. Austin 54-1049 1973 $3.50

WHARTON, EDITH   The Reef. New York, 1912. 1st ed. Biblo & Tannen 210-817 1973 $7.50

WHARTON, EDITH   A Son at the Front. Appleton, 1923. 426p. Austin 54-1052 1973 $4.75

WHARTON, EDITH   Tales of Men and Ghosts. New York, 1910. 1st ed. Biblo & Tannen 210-693 1973 $17.50

WHARTON, EDITH   Twilight Sleep. Appleton, 1927. 373p. Austin 54-1053 1973 $4.75

WHARTON, EDITH   The Valley of Decision. Scribner, 1902. 656p. Austin 54-1055 1973 $7.50

WHARTON, EDITH   The Valley of Decision. Scribner, 1902.
Orig. 2 vol. ed. Austin 54-1054 1973 $12.50

WHARTON, EDITH   The World Over. Appleton, 1936. 308p.
Austin 54-1056 1973 $10

WHARTON, GRACE   Literature of Society. 1862. 2 vols., half
morocco. Allen 216-1713 1974 $12.50

WHARTON, J. L.   Hydrographical Surveying. 1909. Illus., new
& enlarged edition. Covent 55-1331 1974 £6.50

WHATELY, ROGER   The Silver Streak. 1935. 268p., illus.
Austin 51-1027 1973 $12.50

WHATLEY, GEORGE   A Letter to the Lords and Commons of Great Britain in Parliament Assembled. 1742. 8vo., cloth. Quaritch 936-255 1974 £18

WHEATLEY, HENRY B.   Prices of Books. London, 1898. 8vo., orig.
cloth. Dawsons PM 10-649 1974 £5

WHEATLEY, HENRY B.   The Story of London. London, 1904. 12mo.,
illus. Biblo & Tannen 213-471 1973 $10

WHEATLEY, HENRY BENJAMIN   How to Make an Index. London, 1902. 12mo.,
orig. green cloth, uncut. Dawsons PM 10-647 1974 £5

WHEATLEY, HENRY BENJAMIN   Samuel Pepys and the World He Lived In.
1895. Allen 216-1942a 1974 $15

WHEELER, EDWARD S.   Scheyichibi and the Strand. Philadelphia, 1876.
8vo., orig. bindings, engravings. Butterfield 8-381 1974 $25

WHEELER, W. M.   The Social Insects. 1928. 8vo., cloth, illus.,
very scarce. Wheldon 131-882 1974 £10

WHEELS of Progress, a Story of the Development of Toronto and Its Public Transportation Services. Toronto, 1944. Hood's 102-786 1974 $12.50

WHEILDON, WILLIAM WILDER   Letters from Nahant, Historical, Descriptive
and Miscellaneous. Charlestown, 1842. 16mo., pictorial wrapper. Butterfield
10-381 1974 $15

WHELDON, J. A.   The Flora of West Lancashire. 1907. 8vo.,
cloth, plates, scarce. Wheldon 129-1027 1974 £10

WHELER, R. B.   History and Antiquities of Stratford-Upon-
Avon. Stratford-Upon-Avon, (1806). Small 8vo., half calf, plates. Quaritch
939-573 1974 £15

WHEN CHURCHYARDS Yawn. 1931. Roy 8vo., English first edition. Covent
56-1754 1974 £5.25

WHIFFEN, MARCUS   Stuart and Georgian Churches. London, 1948.
Biblo & Tannen 214-36 1974 $7.50

WHILT, JAMES W.   Mountain Memories. n.p., 1925. 12mo.,
author's sgd. pres. Biblo & Tannen 213-832 1973 $7.50

WHINCOP, THOMAS   Scanderbeg. 1747. 8vo., contemporary calf,
plates, first edition. Quaritch 936-256 1974 £30

WHIPPLE, LEON   Our Ancient Liberties. Wilson, 1927.
153p., orig. ed. Austin 62-678 1974 $8.50

WHIPPLE, MAURINE   This is the Place. New York, 1945. Illus.,
cloth, fine, dust jacket, first edition, first issue. Bradley 35-393 1974 $10

WHIPS & Scorpions, Specimens of Modern Satiric Verse 1914-1931. 1932. Fine
copy, d.w., orig. cloth, first edition. Crane 7-7 1974 £6

WHISHAW, FRANCIS   The Railways of Great Britain and Ireland. 1840.
4to., half calf, gilt, plates, first edition. Hammond 201-923 1974 £48

WHISTLER, JAMES ABBOTT MCNEILL   Catalogue of Etchings by. New York,
1902. One of 135 numbered copies, cloth backed boards, some foxing, very good
copy. Covent 51-1958 1973 £6.30

WHISTLER, JAMES ABBOTT MC NEILL   The International Society of Sculptors,
Painters and Engravers, Memorial Exhibition of the Works of...in the New Gallery,
Regent St., London, 22 Feb. - 15 April, 1905. Large paper edition, cloth spine,
de Luxe edition. Eaton Music-691 1973 £10

WHISTLER, LAURENCE   The Burning-Glass. 1941. Wrappers, fine,
signed, numbered. Covent 55-1527 1974 £35

WHISTLER, LAURENCE   Manuscript. n.d. Folio, orig. cloth. Broadhurst 23-683 1974 £45

WHISTLER, REX   Fairy Tales and Legends. 1935. Dec. cloth
gilt, booklabel, illus., English first edition. Covent 56-724 1974 £35

WHISTLER, REX   Fairy Tales and Legends by Hans Andersen.
1935. Dec. cloth, illus., first edition. Marsden 37-524 1974 £10

WHISTON, WILLIAM   An Account of a Surprizing Meteor. London, 17-
16. 8vo., calf antique, first edition. Dawsons PM 245-761 1974 £95

WHISTON, WILLIAM   Astronomical Principles of Religion, Natural and
Reveal'd. 1717. 8vo., contemporary panelled calf, fine, plates. Hill 126-295
1974 £52

WHISTON, WILLIAM   The Longitude Discovered by the Eclipses, Occul-
tations, and Conjunctions of Jupiter's Planets. London, 1738. 8vo., calf antique,
first edition. Dawsons PM 245-762 1974 £195

WHISTON, WILLIAM   A New Theory of the Earth. London, 1696. 8vo.,
contemporary mottled calf, gilt, plates, first edition. Dawsons PM 245-760 1974
£175

WHITACRE, JOSEPH A.   Marshall County in the World War 1917-18.
(Marshalltown), 1919. 8vo., cloth. Saddleback 14-417 1974 $15

WHITAKER, J.   Notes on the Birds of Nottinghamshire. Nottinghamshire, 1907. 8vo., cloth, plates. Wheldon 130-647 1974 £7.50

WHITAKER, JOHN   The Course of Hannibal over the Alps Ascertained.
London, 1794. 8vo., 2 vols., contemporary calf, gilt, first edition. Hammond
201-464 1974 £18

WHITAKER, JOHN   History of Manchester. 1771-75. 2 vols.,
4to., plates, half morocco. Quaritch 939-424 1974 £35

WHITAKER, JOHN   The History of Manchester. London, 1771-1775.
4to., 2 vols., contemporary quarter calf, rebacked, uncut, fine, first edition.
Dawsons PM 251-81 1974 £60

WHITAKER, JOSEPH, F. Z. S.   A Descriptive List of the Deer-Parks and
Paddocks of England. 1892. 8vo., plates, cloth. Quaritch 939-279 1974 £8

WHITAKER, JOSEPH ISAAC SPADAFORA   The Birds of Tunisia. 1905. 2 vols.,
roy. 8vo., orig. cloth, gilt tops, hand coloured plates, numbered, limited.
Wheldon 128-596 1973 £140

WHITAKER, JOSEPH ISAAC SPADAFORA   The Birds of Tunisia. 1905. 2 vols.,
roy. 8vo., orig. half green morocco, gilt, plates, fine, scarce, limited. Wheldon
131-129 1974 £210

WHITAKER, THOMAS DUNHAM   An History of Richmondshire. 1823.
2 vols., folio, recently bound in half calf, engraved plates, slight foxing, illus.
Bow Windows 66-747 1974 £130

WHITAKER, THOMAS DUNHAM   Loidis and Elmete. Leeds & Wakefield,
1816. 2 vols., folio, brown morocco gilt, plates. Traylen 79-412 1973 £68

WHITAKER, WILLIAM   Geology of London and Part of the Thames Valley.
1889. 2 vols., 8vo., cloth. Wheldon 128-1065 1973 £10

WHITAKER, WILLIAM   Geology of London and of Part of the Thames
Valley. 1889. 2 vols., 8vo., cloth. Wheldon 131-1090 1974 £10

WHITAKER, WILLIAM   Memoirs of the Geological Survey. London, 18-
89. 8vo., 2 vols., orig. cloth, gilt, illus. Hammond 201-393 1974 £16

WHITCHER, FRANCES M.   The Widow Bedott Papers. Hurst, n.d. 228p.
Austin 54-1057 1973 $6.50

WHITCOMB, ROYDEN P.   First History of Bayonne, New Jersey.
Bayonne, 1904. 12mo., cloth. Saddleback 14-558 1974 $12.50

WHITE, A.   The Stapeliae. Pasadena, 1933. Roy. 8vo.,
cloth, frontispiece, first edition. Wheldon 131-1710 1974 £10

WHITE, A. V.   Report to International Joint Commission Relating
to Official Reference re Lake of the Woods Levels. Washington, 1916. 2 vols.,
plates. Hood's 102-787 1974 $17.50

WHITE, C.   An Account of the Regular Gradation in Man,
and In Different Animals and Vegetables. 1799. 4to., half calf, plates, rare.
Wheldon 128-75 1973 £60

WHITE, CAROLINE LOUISA   Aelfric: A New Study of His Life and Writings.
1898. Ex-library, sturdy library binding, orig. edition. Austin 61-1043
1974 $10

WHITE, CHARLES   A Treatise On the Management of Pregnant and
Lying-In Women. London, 1777. 8vo., contemporary calf, revised second
edition. Schuman 37-265 1974 $135

WHITE, CHARLES E.   The Bungalow Book. New York, 1923.
Drawings by author, d.j., orig. binding. Butterfield 10-65 1974 $10

WHITE, CHARLES T.   Lincoln the Athlete and Other Stories. New
York, 1930. Limited to 150 copies, inscribed by author, orig. binding. Butterfield 10-354 1974 $35

WHITE, E. B.   Quo Vadimus. Harper, 1939. 219p. Austin
54-1058 1973 $7.50

WHITE, E. B.   The Wild Flag. Houghton, Mifflin, 1946.
188p. Austin 54-1059 1973 $5

WHITE, GILBERT   A Nature Calendar by Gilbert White. 1911.
Folio, cloth, on Italian hand-made paper, numbered, signed by editor, limited
edition. Wheldon 128-249 1973 £10

WHITE, GILBERT   The Natural History and Antiquities of Selborne.
London, 1789. 4to., marbled calf gilt, plates, leather labels, first edition.
Traylen 79-123 1973 £180

WHITE, GILBERT   The Natural History and Antiquities of
Selborne. 1837. 8vo., cloth, text-figures. Wheldon 128-248 1973 £7.50

WHITE, GILBERT   Natural History and Antiquities of Selborne.
1880. 8vo., orig. cloth. Bow Windows 64-294 1974 $7.50

WHITE, GILBERT   The Natural History and Antiquities of Selborne.
1900. 4to., 2 vols., orig. vellum, plates, rare, limited edition. Wheldon 130-
85 1974 £90

WHITE, GILBERT   The Natural History and Antiquities of Selborne
and a Garden Kalendar. London, 1900. 4to., 2 vols., orig. parchment, gilt,
plates. Hammond 201-690 1974 £55

WHITE, GILBERT   The Natural History and Antiquities of Selborne
in the County of Southampton. 1813. 4to., contemporary red morocco gilt,
plates, nice copy, scarce. Wheldon 128-247 1973 £35

WHITE, GILBERT   The Natural History and Antiquities of Selborne
in the County of Southampton. London, 1911. 4to., orig. cloth, gilt, plates.
Hammond 201-478 1974 £8

WHITE, GILBERT   The Natural History of Selborne. 1789. Crown
4to., full morocco, gilt, uncut, first edition. Broadhurst 23-1196 1974 £350

WHITE, GILBERT   The Natural History of Selborne. 1789. Crown
4to., full dark green morocco by Douglas Cockerell, panelled back, raised
bands, choice copy, uncut, engraved plates. Broadhurst 24-1180 1974 £375

WHITE, GILBERT   The Natural History of Selborne. 1825. 8vo.,
2 vols., modern boards. Wheldon 130-325 1974 £15

WHITE, GILBERT   The Natural History of Selborne. 1887.
Austin 61-1044 1974 $10

WHITE, GILBERT   The Natural History of Selborne. 1900. Roy
8vo., buckram. Wheldon 130-326 1974 £5

WHITE, GILBERT   The Natural History of Selborne. 1929. Roy.
8vo., canvas backed boards, d.j. Wheldon 129-313 1974 £10

WHITE, GILBERT   The Works in Natural History. 1802. 8vo.,
2 vols., contemporary half morocco gilt. Wheldon 129-312 1974 £20

WHITE, GILBERT   The Works in Natural History. 1802. 2 vols.,
8vo., contemporary calf, plates, second edition. Wheldon 131-402 1974 £30

WHITE, GILBERT   The Works i.. Natural History of. 1802.
2 vols. in 1, 8vo., new half calf antique style, plates (2 coloured). Wheldon
128-250 1973 £20

WHITE, GILBERT   The Writings Of. 1938. Roy 8vo., 2 vols.,
orig. cloth, limited edition. Broadhurst 23-1079 1974 £60

WHITE, GLEESON   Ballads and Rondeaus. 1888. Austin 61-1045
1974 $12.50

WHITE, GLEESON   Book-Song. 1893. Austin 61-1046 1974
$12.50

WHITE, GLEESON   English Illustration "The Sixties", 1855-70.
1897. 4to, new buckram, plates. Allen 216-1719 1974 $30

WHITE, GLEESON   English Illustration 'The Sixties'. 1855-70.
Roy 8vo., orig. cloth, uncut. Broadhurst 23-225 1974 £30

WHITE, GLEESON   Master-Painters of Britain. Birmingham,
1910. Orig. cloth, illus. Marsden 37-525 1974 £6

WHITE, HENRY KIRKE   Poetical Works of Henry Kirke White. 1854.
Austin 61-1047 1974 $12.50

WHITE, J.   The Introduction to Fauna Calpensis. 1913.
8vo., boards, illus. Wheldon 130-329 1974 £5

WHITE, J. W.   The Flora of Bristol. Bristol, 1912. 8vo.,
cloth, plates, scarce. Wheldon 129-1028 1974 £12

WHITE, J. W.   The Flora of Bristol. Bristol, 1912. 8vo.,
cloth, plates, scarce. Wheldon 131-1251 1974 £12

WHITE, J. W.   Verse of Greek Comedy. 1912. Worn spine.
Allen 213-1197 1973 $12.50

WHITE, JAMES   A Compendium of Cattle Medicine.
Philadelphia, 1823. Foxing, loose front cover. Rittenhouse 46-658 1974 $15

WHITE, JAMES   A Compendium of Cattle Medicine.
Philadelphia, 1823. Foxing, very loose front cover. Rittenhouse 46-658
1974 $15

WHITE, JAMES   A New Century of Inventions. Manchester,
1822. 4to., contemporary calf, rebacked, plates, rare. Traylen 79-278 1973
£110

WHITE, JAMES   Ninth Report of the Geographic Board of
Canada, 1910. Ottawa, 1910. Maps. Hood's 103-46 1974 $40

WHITE, JAMES   Original Letters. London, 1796. 12mo.,
maroon morocco, gilt, first edition. Ximenes 35-512 1974 $150

WHITE, JAMES   Original Letters. London, 1797. 12mo., early
half calf, frontis., second edition. Ximenes 35-513 1974 $225

WHITE, JAMES   A Treatise on Veterinary Medicine. 1808-9.
12mo., 2 vols., orig. boards, rebacked, plates. Hammond 201-55 1974 £12.50

WHITE, JAMES C.   The Autonomic Nervous System. New York,
1941. Second edition. Rittenhouse 46-660 1974 $17.50

WHITE, JAMES W.   Dental Materia Medica. Philadelphia, 1868.
12mo., illus. Rittenhouse 46-661 1974 $20

WHITE, JOHN   Arts Treasury. London, (n.d.). Goodspeed's
578-400 1974 $25

WHITE, L. E.   English Sacred Poetry of the Olden Time.
1864. Dec. green cloth, gilt. Marsden 39-498 1974 £6

WHITE, MRS. K.   A Narrative of the Life of K. White. 1809.
12mo., contemporary sheep, rare, first edition. Ximenes 35-514 1974 $400

WHITE, OWEN P.   The Autobiography of a Durable Sinner. New
York, 1942. First edition, cured issue. Jenkins 61-2647 1974 $25

WHITE, OWEN P.   Lead and Likker. New York, 1932. Scarce.
Jenkins 61-2648 1974 $20

WHITE, PAUL W.   News On the Air. Harcourt, Brace, 1947.
Austin 51-1028 1973 $8.50

WHITE, RAY B.   Infallable Popes. 1929. 128 pages, illus.
Austin 57-697 1974 $10

WHITE, STEWART EDWARD   Arizona Nights. New York, 1907. 1st ed.,
illus. Dykes 24-55 1974 $40

WHITE, T. H.   England Have My Bones. 1936. First American
edition. Austin 61-1049 1974 $10

WHITE, T. H.   Gone to Ground. 1935. Presentation copy,
inscribed, English first edition. Covent 56-1316 1974 £35

WHITE, T. H.   The Sword in the Stone. 1938. Very nice
crisp copy. Covent 51-2614 1973 £7

WHITE, T. H.   The Sword in the Stone. 1938. Presentation
copy, inscribed from author, with drawing in pen by him, covers marked, nice
copy, worn d.w., first edition. Covent 51-1968 1973 £30

WHITE, THOMAS   The Battle of Britain and Other Poems.
Montreal, 1945. Unopened. Hood's 104-804 1974 $15

WHITE, THOMAS   De Mvndo Dialogi Tres Qvibvs Materia.
1642. 4to., contemporary sheep, misbound, bookplate, stains. Bow Windows
62-992 1974 £66

WHITE, THOMAS   De Mvndo Dialogi Tres Ovibvs Materia. 1642.
4to., old calf, gilt. Zeitlin 235-240 1974 $750

WHITE, W. L.   They Were Expendable. Austin 51-1029 1973
$7.50

WHITE, WALTER   A July Holiday in Saxony. London, 1857.
8vo., orig. cloth, fine, first edition. Ximenes 35-516 1974 $12

WHITE, WILLIAM   History, Gazetteer and Directory of Devonshire.
1850. 12mo., contemporary calf, coloured map, rubbed. Bow Windows
66-748 1974 £25

WHITE and Franconia Mountains. Woodstock, c. 1890. Boards, photographs.
Jenkins 61-1822 1974 $12.50

THE WHITE Book of the City of London. 1861. Large square 8vo., orig. cloth.
Howes 186-2123 1974 £8.50

WHITEHEAD, ALFRED NORTH   The Concept of Nature. 1920. Near fine.
Covent 55-1531 1974 £7.50

WHITEHEAD, ALFRED NORTH   The Concept of Nature. Cambridge, 1920. 8vo.,
orig. cloth, gilt, fine, first edition. Dawsons PM 245-763 1974 £7

WHITEHEAD, ALFRED NORTH   Principia Mathematica. Cambridge, 1925-27.
3 vols., roy. 8vo., vol. 1 very good, vols. 2 & 3 fine, orig. cloth, second edition.
Broadhurst 24-1351 1974 £32

WHITEHEAD, ALFRED NORTH   Process and Reality. 1929. English first edition. Covent 56-2115 1974 £15

WHITEHEAD, ALFRED NORTH   Science and the Modern World. 1926. English
first edition. Covent 56-2116 1974 £7.50

WHITEHEAD, ALFRED NORTH   Symbolism. 1928. Dust wrapper, English first
edition. Covent 56-1318 1974 £5.25

WHITEHEAD, C. E.   The Camp-Fires of the Everglades. Edinburgh,
1891. Roy. 8vo., orig. cloth, frontispiece, plates, vignettes, top edge gilt,
other edges uncut, nice clean copy, very scarce. Wheldon 128-251 1973 £12

WHITEHEAD, GEORGE   Bernard Shaw Explained. Watts, 1925.
Austin 51-1032 1973 $8.50

WHITEHEAD, J.   Exploration of Mount Kina Balu. 1893. Folio,
orig. green cloth gilt, plates, scarce. Wheldon 130-330 1974 £120

WHITEHEAD, PAUL   The History of an Old Lady and Her Family.
London, 1754. 8vo., recent quarter morocco, first edition. Ximenes 35-517
1974 $125

WHITEHEAD, PAUL   Manners. London, 1739. Folio, disbound,
first edition, first issue. Ximenes 35-518 1974 $50

WHITEHEAD, T. H.   Geology of Southern Part of South Staffordshire.
1927. 8vo., cloth. Wheldon 130-980 1974 £5

WHITEHEAD, T. H.   Geology of Southern Part of South Staffordshire
Coalfield. 1927. 8vo., cloth. Wheldon 128-1066 1973 £5

WHITEHEAD, WILLIAM   Creusa. London, 1754. 8vo., modern boards,
first edition. Dawsons PM 252-1056 1974 £15

WHITEHEAD, WILLIAM   An Essay on Ridicule. London, 1743. Folio,
disbound, first edition. Ximenes 35-519 1974 $65

WHITEHEAD, WILLIAM   The Roman Father. London, 1750. 8vo.,
modern boards, second edition. Dawsons PM 252-1057 1974 £12

WHITEHEAD, WILLIAM   The Roman Father. 1750. 8vo., leather, first
edition. Quaritch 936-257 1974 £10

WHITEHEAD, WILLIAM   The School for Lovers. London, 1762. 8vo.,
modern boards, first edition. Dawsons PM 252-1058 1974 £15

WHITEHEAD, WILLIAM   The School for Lovers. 1762. 8vo., cloth, first
edition. Quaritch 936-258 1974 £9

WHITEHEAD, WILLIAM 1715-1785   A Trip to Scotland. 1770. 8vo., cloth,
first edition. Quaritch 936-259 1974 £9

WHITEHILL, A.   Royal Nursery ABC Book. (c. 1840). Frontis.,
plate, small wood engravings, some hand coloured, small 8vo., full mottled calf,
little pencil scoring. George's 610-812 1973 £5.50

WHITEHURST, J.   An Inquiry Into the Original State and Formation
of the Earth. 1786. 4to., half calf, portrait, plates, second edition. Wheldon
128-1067 1973 £50

WHITELOCK, BULSTRODE   Memorials of the English Affairs. 1682.
Folio, stains, first edition. Howes 186-1307 1974 £36

WHITELOCK, BULSTRODE   Monarchy. London, 1679. 12mo., speckled
calf, worn. Dawsons PM 251-360 1974 £30

WHITEMAN, PAUL   Jazz. New York, 1926. Illus., first edition,
fine, d.j., orig. binding. Butterfield 10-322 1974 $20

WHITFIELD, CHRISTOPHER   Together and Alone. Golden Cockerel Press,
1945. Engravings, roy. 8vo., quarter white morocco, top edges gilt, others uncut,
one of 100 copies, signed by author and artist. Broadhurst 24-993 1974 £25

WHITING, M. H.   Faith White's Letter Book. Boston, n.d.
12mo., orig. green cloth, first edition. Ximenes 35-520 1974 $12.50

WHITING, ROBERT R.   A Ball of Yarn, Its Unwinding. San Francisco
and New York, 1907. Full page color illus., yellow dec. paper board covers,
first book edition, 8vo. Current BW9-617 1974 $22

WHITLEY, WILLIAM T.   Art in England. 1930. Roy 8vo., buckram,
plates, English first edition. Covent 56-1521 1974 £8.50

WHITLEY, WILLIAM T.   Gilbert Stuart. Cambridge, 1932. 4to.,
7 portraits. Biblo & Tannen 214-513 1974 $11

WHITLOCK, RICHARD   Observations on the Present Manners of the
English. London, 1654. 8vo., contemporary sheep, rebacked, first edition.
Dawsons PM 252-1059 1974 £285

WHITLOCK, RICHARD   Zootomia. London, 1654. 8vo., contemporary
sheep, frontispiece. Quaritch 939-280 1974 £300

WHITLOCK, RICHARD   Zootomia, or, Observations On the Present
Manners of the English. London, 1654. Small 8vo., old calf, rebacked, first
edition. Schuman 37-266 1974 $165

WHITLOCKE, BULSTRODE   Memorials of the English Affairs. London, 1709.
Folio, contemporary panelled calf. Dawsons PM 251-359 1974 £25

WHITMAN, ALFRED   Charles Turner. 1907. Orig. cloth, plates,
gilt, rubbed. Marsden 37-486 1974 £6

WHITMAN, ALFRED   Samuel William Reynolds. 1903. Orig.
cloth, plates, gilt. Marsden 37-393 1974 £6

WHITMAN, C. O.   The Behaviour of Pigeons. Washington, 1919.
4to., orig. cloth. Wheldon 130-648 1974 £15

WHITMAN, NARCISSA PRENTISS   The Coming of the White Women. Portland,
1937. 8vo., cloth. Saddleback 14-661 1974 $15

WHITMAN, WALT   An American Primer. Boston, 1904. Orig.
quarter-parchment, spine darkened, first edition, one of 500 copies, fine.
MacManus 224-447 1974 $30

WHITMAN, WALT   As a Strong Bird on Pinions Free. Washington,
1872. 8vo., orig. green cloth, nice copy, first edition. Ximenes 37-221
1974 $100

WHITMAN, WALT   Franklin Evans of the Inebriate. New York,
1929. Orig. cloth, paper label, limited to 700 copies, fine. MacManus
224-448 1974 $27.50

WHITMAN, WALT   Leaves of Grass. Brooklyn, 1855. 4to.,
orig. green cloth, inscriptions, plate, fine, first edition, first issue. Dawsons
PM 250-82 1974 £5500

WHITMAN, WALT   Leaves of Grass. Boston, 1860-61. Orig.
embossed cloth, third edition, frontispiece tinted, about fine. MacManus
224-449 1974 $75

WHITMAN, WALT   Leaves of Grass. Boston, (1879). Orig.
cloth, faded, portrait, inscribed. Covent 55-1533 1974 £10

WHITMAN, WALT   Leaves of Grass. 1882. Rebacked. Allen
216-1722 1974 $15

WHITMAN, WALT   Leaves of Grass. Philadelphia, 1894. Quarter
morocco, new edition. Covent 56-1319 1974 £25

WHITMAN, WALT   Not Meagre, Latent Boughs Alone. N.P.,
n.d. 12mo., inscription. Ximenes 35-521 1974 $75

WHITMAN, WALT   November Boughs. Philadelphia, 1888. Orig.
cloth, first edition, fine copy. MacManus 224-450 1974 $60

WHITMAN, WALT   November Boughs. 1889. Portrait, faded,
English first edition. Covent 56-1320 1974 £25

WHITMAN, WALT   Specimen Days and Collect. Glasgow, 1883.
Frontis., fine copy. Covent 51-1969 1973 £12.50

WHITMAN, WALT   Specimen Days in America. London, 1887.
12mo. Biblo & Tannen 214-777 1974 $15

WHITMAN, WALT   The Wound Dresser. Boston, 1898. Orig.
cloth, first printing, with 1897 copyright notice, fine. MacManus 224-451
1974 $55

WHITMAN'S Print-Collector's Handbook. 1918. Illus., uncut, sixth edition.
Covent 55-491 1974 £8.50

WHITMORE, W. H.   The Heraldic Journal. Boston, 1865. Illus.,
orig. cl. Jacobs 24-147 1974 $25

WHITNAH, JOSEPH C.   The City That Grew From a Rancho. Richmond,
c.1944. 8vo., cloth. Saddleback 14-313 1974 $15

WHITNEY, A. D. T.   Mother Goose for Grown Folks. New York,
1860. 8vo., orig. green cloth, first edition. Ximenes 35-522 1974 $12.50

WHITNEY, A. D. T.   Real Folks. Boston, 1872. 8vo., orig.
green cloth, illus., fine, first edition. Ximenes 35-523 1974 $10

WHITNEY, A. D. T.   Zerub Throop's Experiment. Boston, n.d.
8vo., orig. green cloth, first edition. Ximenes 35-524 1974 $12

WHITNEY, J. PARKER   Reminiscences of a Sportsman. New York, 1906.
8vo., orig. bindings, inscribed. Butterfield 8-57 1974 $15

WHITNEY, PETER   The History of the County of Worcester, In the
Commonwealth of Massachusetts. Worcester, 1793. Large 8vo., leather.
Saddleback 14-497 1974 $45

WHITNEY, RUTH   Liverpool Centennial, 1830-1930. (Liverpool),
1930. 12mo., wrapper. Saddleback 14-598 1974 $10

WHITTAKER, EDMUND TAYLOR   A History of the Theories of Aether and Electricity. Dublin and London, 1910. 8vo., green cloth, presentation copy, first
edition. Dawsons PM 245-765 1974 £10

WHITTAKER, FREDERICK   A Complete Life of Gen. George A. Custer.
New York, 1876. Jenkins 61-735 1974 $17.50

WHITTIE, JOHN   An Exact Diary of the Late Expedition Of. London, 1689. 4to., contemporary boards, first edition. Dawsons PM 251-361
1974 £70

WHITTIER, JOHN GREENLEAF   Ballads. London, 1844. 16mo., orig.
green morocco, gilt, first edition. Ximenes 35-525 1974 $150

WHITTIER, JOHN GREENLEAF   Leaves from Margaret Smith's Journal.
Boston, 1849. 8vo., orig. cloth, first edition. Ximenes 35-526 1974 $17.50

WHITTIER, JOHN GREENLEAF   Leaves from Margaret Smith's Journal in the
Province of Massachusetts Bay, 1678-79. Boston, 1849. Orig. cloth, chipped
at ends of spine & along joints, first edition, with the 2 leaves of ads, internally
very clean. MacManus 224-452 1974 $40

WHITTIER, JOHN GREENLEAF   Moll Pitcher. Boston, 1832. 8vo., orig.
plain wrappers. Ximenes 35-527 1974 $10

WHITTIER, JOHN GREENLEAF   A Sabbath Scene. Boston, 1854. 12mo.,
orig. wrappers, first separate edition. Ximenes 35-528 1974 $17.50

WHITTIER, JOHN GREENLEAF   Songs of the Free, and Hyms of Christian Freedom.
Boston, 1836. 12mo., publisher's sheep, first edition. Goodspeed's 578-403
1974 $15

WHITTIER, JOHN GREENLEAF   The Stranger in Lowell. Boston, 1845.
Modern quarter morocco, first edition, lacks the first leaf (blank?), some
spotting, small waterstain. MacManus 224-453 1974 $65

WHITTIER, JOHN GREENLEAF   The Vision' of Echard and Other Poems. Boston,
1878. First edition, 12mo., nice bright copy, very fine. Current BW9-292
1974 $14.50

WHITTIER, JOHN GREENLEAF   Poetical Works. Oxford, 1910. Thick crown
8vo., tree calf gilt. Howes 185-177 1974 £18.50

WHITTINGHAM, CHARLES   A Collection of 7 Works in 29 Volumes. London,
1803-10. 8vo., half straight-grained morocco, gilt, boards, plates. Hammond
201-1006 1974 £165

WHITTINTON, ROBERT   Editio cum Interpretamento Francisci Nigri
Diomedes de Accentu in Pedestri Oratione. 1519. Small 4to., quarter calf,
two armorial bookplates, Part 2 only, signature of William Herbert. Thomas
32-274 1974 £600

WHITTOCK, NATHANIEL   The Oxford Drawing Book. (c.1830). Oblong 4to., orig. boards, rebacked in calf, new and improved edition. Quaritch 940-273 1974 £50

WHITTOCK, NATHANIEL   A Topographical and Historical Description of the University and City of Oxford. Oxford, n.d. 4to., unbound, plates. Traylen 79-379 1973 £12.50

WHITTON, F. E.   Wolfe and North America. London, 1929. Maps, illus. Hood's 103-568 1974 $20

WHITTY, MICHAEL JAMES   Tales of Irish Life. London, 1824. 2 vols., 8vo., half calf, boards, worn. Emerald 50-983 1974 £12

WHITWELL, ST.   On Warming and Ventilating Houses and Buildings. Cambridge, 1834. 4to., modern half morocco. Zeitlin 235-241 1974 $87.50

WHITWORTH, CHARLES   An Account of Russia. 1758. 8vo., early 19th century calf, gilt, first edition. Ximenes 35-529 1974 $225

WHYMPER, EDWARD   The Ascent of the Matterhorn. 1880. Illus., first edition, demy 8vo., very good copy, orig. cloth. Broadsides 24-1696 1974 £10

WHYMPER, EDWARD   Scrambles Amongst the Alps in the Years 1860-69. 1893. Illus., maps, demy 8vo., binder's leather, fourth edition, fine. Broadhurst 24-1698 1974 £15

WHYMPER, EDWARD   Travels Amongst the Great Andes of the Equator. 1892. Illus., maps, demy 8vo., fully bound in tree calf, panelled back, gilt borders, edges gilt, very fine copy. Broadhurst 24-1697 1974 £15

WHYMPER, EDWARD   Travels Amongst the Great Andes of the Equator. 1892. 8vo., cloth, plates, text-figures, maps. Wheldon 128-252 1973 £7.50

WHYTE, FREDERIC   Actors of the Century. 1898. Roy. 8vo., cloth gilt, portraits. Covent 55-1441 1974 £10.50

WHYTE, ROBERT B.   Robert Barbour Whyte. Edinburgh, 1918. Crown 8vo., plates. Howes 186-535 1974 £5.50

WHYTE, SAMUEL   The Shamrock. Dublin, 1772. 4to., contemporary full calf. Emerald 50-984 1974 £45

WHYTE, SAMUEL   A Shamrock. Dublin, 1772. 4to., contemporary sheep, first edition. Ximenes 35-530 1974 $150

WHYTE, WILLIAM FOOTE   Street Corner Society. 1943. Orig. unrevised edition. Austin 57-698 1974 $10

WHYTE-MELVILLE, GEORGE JOHN   Black but Comely. London, 1879. 8vo., 3 vols., orig. cloth, first edition. Dawsons PM 252-1060 1974 £18

WHYTE-MELVILLE, GEORGE JOHN   Black but Comely. London, 1879. 3 vols., 8vo., orig. grey cloth, first edition. Ximenes 35-531 1974 $30

WHYTE-MELVILLE, GEORGE JOHN   General Bounce. London, 1855. 2 vols., 8vo., orig. tan cloth, first edition. Ximenes 35-532 1974 $30

WHYTE-MELVILLE, GEORGE JOHN   Holmby House. London, 1860. 2 vols., 8vo., orig. cloth, first edition. Ximenes 35-533 1974 $27.50

WHYTE-MELVILLE, GEORGE JOHN   M. or N. London, 1869. 2 vols., 8vo., orig. orange-brown cloth, first edition. Ximenes 35-534 1974 $25

WICKENDEN, WILLIAM   Poems. Cambridge, 1823. 12mo., old diced calf, first edition. Ximenes 35-535 1974 $15

WICKERSHAM, JAMES   Old Yukon. Washington, 1938. 8vo., cloth. Saddleback 14-3 1974 $12.50

WICKERSHAM, JAMES   Old Yukon. Washington, 1938. Orig. blue cloth, illus., scarce, presentation, first edition. Bradley 35-9 1974 $34

WICKERSHAM, JAMES   Old Yukon Tales -- Trails -- and Trials. Washington, D.C., 1938. 8vo., orig. bindings. Butterfield 8-13 1974 $20

WICKES, FRANCES G.   The Inner World of Man. New York, 1948. Biblo & Tannen 213-1002 1973 $9.50

WICKES, STEPHEN   Sepulture. Philadelphia, 1884. Rittenhouse 46-664 1974 $10

WICKHAM, HARVEY   The Impuritans. 1929. Portraits, English first edition. Covent 56-1887 1974 £10.50

WICKLIFFE, HENRY   Rappo-Mania Overthrown. Boston, 1853. 12mo., orig. wrappers, first edition. Ximenes 35-536 1974 $40

WICKSTEED, JOSEPH H.   Blake's Innocence and Experience. London, 1928. 1st ed., plates. Biblo & Tannen 213-728 1973 $15

WICTENHAGENS, ERNST   Geschichte der Kunst. Eklingen, 1919. Biblo & Tannen 214-565 1974 $17.50

WIDDEMER, MARGARET   A Tree with a Bird In It. New York, 1922. Author's sgd. pres. Biblo & Tannen 210-818 1973 $7.50

WIDEFORD, WILLIAM   Ob Nichts Anzunemen sey, Dan Was Klar in Der Hayligen Geschrifft ist. (Augsburg), 1524. Small 4to., modern half vellum over boards, woodcut title border, very fine, very rare. Schafer 8-142 1973 sFr. 1,200

WIDENER, JOSEPH   The Joseph Widener Collection, Tapestries at Lynnewood Hall, Elkins Park, Pennsylvania. Philadelphia, 1932. Folio, cloth, plates, limited. Quaritch 940-776 1974 £35

WIDJINDIWINI-MASINAIGAN. Wikwemikong, 1913. Cloth. Hayman 59-280 1974 $10

WIDTSOE, JOHN A.   In the Gospel Net. Salt Lake City, 1942. Austin 62-682 1974 $12.50

WIEDEBURG, JOHANN BERNHARD   Mathesis Biblica Septem Speciminibus Comprehensa. 1730. Contemporary boards, uncut, first edition. Dawsons PM 245-767 1974 £15

WIEDERSHEIM, ROBERT   Elements of the Comparative Anatomy of Vertebrates. London, 1886. 8vo., orig. cloth, illus., author's signed presentation inscription. Gurney 66-198 1974 £20

WIEDERSHEIM, ROBERT   Elements of the Comparative Anatomy of Vertebrates. 1897. 8vo., cloth, second edition. Wheldon 130-376 1974 £7.50

WIELAND, CHRISTOPH M.   The Adventures of Don Sylvio de Rosalva. 1904. Half blue calf gilt, rare. Howes 185-556 1974 £6.50

WIENER, LEO   Commentary to the Germanic Laws and Medieval Documents. Cambridge, Mass., 1915. Biblo & Tannen 214-670 1974 $15

WIENER, LOUIS 1912-   Hand-Made Jewelry. New York, 1948. Biblo & Tannen 214-290 1974 $7.50

WIERNIK, PETER   History of the Jews in America. 1931. Revised, enlarged, second edition. Austin 57-701 1974 $10

WIGAND, JUSTUS HEINRICH   Die Geburt des Menschen. Berlin, 1820. Thick 8vo., boards, plates, first edition. Schumann 35-489 1974 $95

WIGGIN, JAMES BARTLETT   The Wild Artist in Boston. Boston, 1888. Orig. cloth, first edition. MacManus 224-454 1974 $25

WIGGIN, KATE DOUGLAS   The Bird's Christmas Carol. Boston, 1892. 12mo., full page illus., spine bit soiled, else very good. Current BW9-94 1974 $8.50

WIGGIN, KATE DOUGLAS   Penelope's Progress. Boston & New York, 1898. Very fine. Ballinger 1-63 1974 $10

WIGGIN, KATE DOUGLAS   Penelope's Progress. Boston & New York, 1898. Orig. tartan cloth, first edition, with 12 line poem in author's hand on a fly-leaf, signed, hinges tracked. MacManus 224-455 1974 $50

WIGGIN, KATE DOUGLAS   Rebecca of Sunnybrook Farm. 1903. 8vo., orig. cloth, first English edition. Rota 190-986 1974 £5

WIGGIN, KATE DOUGLAS   Rebecca of Sunnybrook Farm. Boston & New York, 1903. Orig. illus. cloth, first state with the type of publisher's imprint at foot of spine measuring 1/16" high, fine. MacManus 224-456 1974 $30

WIGGIN, KATE DOUGLAS   Rebecca of Sunnybrook Farm. Boston & New York, 1903. Orig. illus. cloth, first state, very fine, pasted-in the inside of upper cover is a short letter from author to seeker of her autograph. MacManus 224-457 1974 $75

WIGGIN, KATE DOUGLAS   The Romance of a Christmas Card. Boston, 1916. First edition, 8vo., colored frontis., fine, color illus. Current BW9-93 1974 $8.75

WIGGIN, KATE DOUGLAS   The Shirley Temple Edition of Rebecca of Sunnybrook Farm. Random, n.d. Austin 51-961 1973 $10

WIGGIN, KATE DOUGLAS   Timothy's Quest. London, 1895. 8vo., orig. linen cloth, frontis. Bow Windows 62-997 1974 £7.50

WIGGLESWORTH, MICHAEL   Meat Out of the Eater. Boston, 1717. Fifth edition, old calf, sound, 18mo. Butterfield 10-29 1974 $125

WIGHT, CLARISSA   A Copy of Writings. Sangerfield, 1820. 8vo., orig. wrappers, first edition. Ximenes 35-537 1974 $22.50

WIGHT, FANNY   Nellie's Christmas Eve. New York, (c. 1890). 8vo., full page full color illus., pictorial colored front wrapper, rebacked, fine. Current BW9-95 1974 $27.50

WIGHT, ROBERT   General Index of the Plants Described and Figured in Dr. Wight's Work Entitled "Icones Plantarum Indiae Orientalis". 1921. 4to., wrappers. Wheldon 131-1366 1974 £7.50

WIGHT, ROBERT   Icones Plantarum Indiae Orientalis. Madras, 1840-53. 4to., 6 vols., modern cloth, plates. Wheldon 129-1136 1974 £250

WIGHT, ROBERT   Icones Plantarum Indiae Orientalis. Madras, 1840-53. 6 vols., 4to., modern cloth, rare, plates, complete copy, orig. issue. Wheldon 131-1364 1974 £250

WIGHT, ROBERT   Illustrations of Indian Botany or Figures Illustrative of Each of the Natural Orders of Indian Plants. Madras, (1838-) 40. 2 vols., 8vo., half calf, hand-coloured plates. Wheldon 128-1323 1973 £150

WIGHT, ROBERT   Illustrations of Indian Botany. Madras, 1840-50. 2 vols., 4to., half morocco, gilt, plates, rare. Traylen 79-64 1973 £245

WIGHT, ROBERT   Illustrations of Indian Botany. Madras, (1838-)1840-50. 2 vols., 4to., contemporary half green morocco, plates, very rare. Wheldon 131-130 1974 £575

WIGHT, ROBERT   Illustrations of Indian Botany or Figures Illustrative of Each of the Natural Orders of Indian Plants. Madras, (1838-) 1840. 2 vols., 4to., half calf, plates. Wheldon 131-1365 1974 £150

WIGHT, ROBERT   Spicilegium Neilgherrense. Madras, (1846-)1851. 2 vols., 4to., modern half green morocco, plates. Wheldon 131-131 1974 £300

WIGHT, ROBERT   Spicilegium Neilgherrense. (1846) and 1851. 4to., 2 vols., orig. cloth. Broadhurst 23-1197 1974 £350

WIGHT, ROBERT   Spicilegium Neilgherrense. Madras, (1846) and 1851. Hand coloured plates, 2 vols., 4to., orig. cloth, fine. Broadhurst 24-1181 1974 £375

WIGHT, THOMAS   A History of the People Called Quakers. 1811. 8vo., contemporary calf, fourth edition. Quaritch 939-641 1974 £25

WIGHT, THOMAS   A History of the Rise and Progress of the People Called Quakers In Ireland, 1653-1700. Dublin, 1751. Small 4to., old calf, stains. Thomas 28-212 1972 £15

WIGHTMAN, ORRIN SAGE   The Diary of an American Physician in the Russian Revolution, 1917. New York, 1928. Rittenhouse 46-665 1974 $15

WIGHTWICK, GEORGE   Hints to Young Architects. 1860. 8vo., orig. cloth, woodcuts, scarce, second issue. Quaritch 940-568 1974 £8

WIGHTWICK, GEORGE   The Palace of Architecture. 1840. Roy. 8vo., plates, illus., half calf, scarce. Quaritch 940-567 1974 £12

WILBERFORCE, WILLIAM   A Letter on the Abolition of the Slave Trade. London, 1807. 8vo., contemporary half calf, gilt, first edition. Dawsons PM 250-83 1974 £200

WILBERFORCE, WILLIAM   A Practical View of the Prevailing Religious System of Professed Christians. London, 1797. 8vo., contemporary panelled calf, rebacked, first edition. Ximenes 35-538 1974 $100

WILBUR, JAMES BENJAMIN   Ira Allen Founder of Vermont 1751-1814. Boston – New York, 1928. 8vo., 2 vols., orig. bindings, dust jacket. Butterfield 8-655 1974 $17.50

WILBUR, JENNIE AURELIA   Songs of the West. Chicago, 1866. 12mo., orig. violet cloth, first edition. Ximenes 35-539 1974 $35

WILCOCKE, SAMUEL HULL   A Narrative of Occurrences in the Indian Coutries of North America. London, 1817. Spine mended. Hood's 102-837 1974 $175

WILCOCKE, SAMUEL HULL   A Narrative of Occurrences in the Indian Countries of North America. London, 1817. Mended spine. Hood's 104-669 1974 $175

WILCOX, ALANSON   A History of the Disciples of Christ in Ohio. Cincinnati, (1918). Cloth, scarce. Hayman 57-607 1974 $12.50

WILCOX, ELLA WHEELER   Collected Poems. London, 1917. 3 vols., 8vo., orig. morocco gilt. Dawsons PM 252-1061 1974 £10

WILCOX, MARRION   Senora Villena and Gray: An Oldhaven Romance. New York, 1887. 2 vols. in 1, orig. cloth, first edition. MacManus 224-458 1974 $25

WILDE, HAGAR   Guest In the House. French, 1940. Austin 51-1033 1973 $6.50

WILDE, JANE FRANCESCA, (ELGEE) LADY 1826-1896   Social Studies. London, 1893. 8vo., cloth boards, faded, scarce. Emerald 50-985 1974 £9

WILDE, JANE FRANCESCA, (ELGEE) LADY 1826-1896   Social Studies. 1893. Cover partly faded, booklabel, very good copy, first edition. Covent 51-1980 1973 £8.40

WILDE, OSCAR   Autograph Letter. Signed. Dawson's 424-312 1974 $150

WILDE, OSCAR   The Ballad of Reading Gaol. New York, 1903. Japan vellum. Ballinger 1-225 1974 $17.50

WILDE, OSCAR   The Ballad of Reading Gaol. New York, 1919. Very good copy, detached & somewhat browned wrappers. Covent 51-1981 1973 £6.30

WILDE, OSCAR   De Profundis. Paris, 1905. First French edition, fine, wrappers. Covent 51-1982 1973 £10.50

WILDE, OSCAR   De Profundis. 1905. English first edition. Covent 56-2118 1974 £12.50

WILDE, OSCAR   De Profundis. London, 1905. 8vo., orig. blue cloth, fine, first edition. Dawsons PM 252-1062 1974 £28

WILDE, OSCAR   Essays, Criticisms and Reviews. London, 1901. 4to., wrappers, first pirated edition. Dawsons PM 252-1063 1974 £30

WILDE, OSCAR   Five Poems. 1895. Fine, English first edition. Covent 56-1324 1974 £10

WILDE, OSCAR   A Florentine Tragedy. 1908. Austin 51-1034 1973 $8.50

WILDE, OSCAR   For Love of the King. (1922). Limited first edition, 8vo., orig. white buckram gilt, top edges gilt, others uncut, scarce. Sawyer 293-286 1974 £48

WILDE, OSCAR   The Happy Prince and Other Tales. London, 1888. Orig. printed boards, some rubbing, first edition, illus. by Walter Crane, frontispiece loose, good copy of fragile book. MacManus 224-459 1974 $100

WILDE, OSCAR   The Happy Prince and Other Tales. London, 1888. Large 8vo., 1st ed., illus. Frohnsdorff 16-241 1974 $135

WILDE, OSCAR   The Happy Prince & Other Tales. 1910. Crown 4to., illus., orig. limp boards. Smith 194-722 1974 £10

WILDE, OSCAR   The Harlot's House. 1929. Illus., 102 pages. Austin 61-1053 1974 $12.50

WILDE, OSCAR   A House of Pomegranates. London, 1915. 4to., 16 color plates, spine torn. Biblo & Tannen 210-159 1973 $10

WILDE, OSCAR   An Ideal Husband. 1899. Cloth gilt, faded. Covent 55-1537 1974 £15

WILDE, OSCAR   An Ideal Husband. 1899. Covers slightly faded, first edition, very good copy. Covent 51-1985 1973 £40

WILDE, OSCAR   The Importance of Being Earnest. 1899. Nice copy, first edition. Covent 51-1986 1973 £45

WILDE, OSCAR   The Importance of Being Earnest. 1910. Orig. cloth, presentation inscription, limited edition. Smith 193-162 1973 £5

WILDE, OSCAR   Impressions of America. Sunderland, 1906. Edition limited to 500 copies, wrappers, internally fine, scarce. Ross 86-458 1974 $40

WILDE, OSCAR   Intentions. 1891. Very good copy, first edition. Covent 51-1987 1973 £20

WILDE, OSCAR   Lady Windermere's Fan. 1893. Very good copy, first edition. Covent 51-1988 1973 £25

WILDE, OSCAR   Lady Windermere's Fan. Paris, 1903. 8vo., orig. cloth, first edition. Rota 189-956 1974 £5

WILDE, OSCAR   Letters to the Sphinx. 1930. Limited to 275 numbered copies, signed by Adad Leverson, spine darkened, very good copy, first edition. Covent 51-1989 1973 £15

WILDE, OSCAR   The Picture of Dorain Gray. n.d. Orig. boards, gilt, rubbed. Smith 194-542 1974 £8.50

WILDE, OSCAR   The Picture of Dorian Gray. 1890. Orig. grey boards, English first edition. Covent 56-2119 1974 £15

WILDE, OSCAR   The Picture of Dorian Gray. London, (1891). Orig. parchment backed boards, few scratches on spine, first edition, fine copy. MacManus 224-460 1974 $85

WILDE, OSCAR   The Picture of Dorian Gray. 1891. 4to., orig. grey bevelled boards, very good uncut copy, first limited edition. Bow Windows 66-749 1974 £165

WILDE, OSCAR   The Picture of Dorian Gray. Paris, 1913. Biblo & Tannen 213-833 1973 $7.50

WILDE, OSCAR   The Plays of. Boston, 1905. 2 vols., very good. Covent 51-1990 1973 £6.30

WILDE, OSCAR   Poemes en Prose. Paris, 1906. Orig. wrappers, quarter cloth slip-case, fine. Covent 55-1538 1974 £32.50

WILDE, OSCAR   Poems. Boston, 1882. Very nice copy, orig. cloth. Covent 51-1991 1973 £10.50

WILDE, OSCAR   Poems in Prose. Portland, 1906. 12mo., orig. dec. gilt wrappers, near mint. Covent 55-1539 1974 $17.50

WILDE, OSCAR   Poems in Prose, and Private Letters. 1919. Wrappers, spine defective, leaves browned throughout, very good copy, first edition. Covent 51-1992 1973 £5.25

WILDE, OSCAR   Poems Of. 1908. 353 pages. Austin 61-1055 1974 $10

WILDE, OSCAR   The Portrait of Mr. W. H. (n.d.). 8vo., orig. paper wrappers, frayed, limited. Bow Windows 62-994 1974 £16.50

WILDE, OSCAR   The Portrait of Mr. W. H. (London), n.d. 4to., orig. wrappers, first separate edition. Ximenes 35-540 1974 $45

WILDE, OSCAR   The Portrait of Mr. W. H. New York, 1921. Frontis., first U. S. edition, one of 1000 numbered copies, very fine, damaged slipcase. Covent 51-1993 1973 £10.50

WILDE, OSCAR   Rose-Leaf and Apple-Leaf. London, 1904. 8vo., orig. printed wrappers, fine. Ximenes 35-541 1974 $45

WILDE, OSCAR   Salome. Paris & Londres, 1893. Half morocco, orig. printed wrappers bound-in, first edition, wrappers a bit faded, fine copy. MacManus 224-461 1974 $100

WILDE, OSCAR   Salome. Berlin, 1905. Very good copy, faded and slightly detached wrappers. Covent 51-1994 1973 £5

WILDE, OSCAR   Salome. Boston, 1907. Drawings, back cover lightly worn, fine, scarce, orig. binding. Ross 86-459 1974 $40

WILDE, OSCAR   Salome. Paris, 1922. Plates, browned, fine. Covent 55-1540 1974 £35

WILDE, OSCAR   Sixteen Letters. 1930. One of 550 numbered copies, frontis., gilt top, cover little soiled, very good copy, first edition. Covent 51-1997 1973 £6

WILDE, OSCAR   Sixteen Letters. 1930. One of 550 copies, this copy out of series, plates, gilt top, bookplate, fine, frontis. portrait, first edition. Covent 51-1996 1973 £12.60

WILDE, OSCAR   Sixteen Letters from. London, 1930. 8vo., orig. pink cloth, illus., bookplate, first edition. Bow Windows 62-995 1974 £15

WILDE, OSCAR   The Soul of Man Under Socialism. London, 1904. No. 176 of edition limited to 250 copies, brown paper wrappers, pirated edition, remarkably fine, near mint. Ross 86-461 1974 $30

WILDE, OSCAR   Three Times Tried. (1912). English first edition. Covent 56-2124 1974 £15.75

WILDE, OSCAR   La Vie de Prison en Angleterre. Paris, 1906. Wrappers, unopened. Covent 55-1541 1974 £6

WILDE, OSCAR   A Woman of No Importance. 1894. Very good copy, first edition, rare. Covent 51-1999 1973 £30

WILDE, PERCIVAL   The Craftsmanship of the One-Act Play. Crown, 1951. Austin 51-1035 1973 $12.50

WILDEMAN, E. DE   Icones Selectae Horti Thenensis. Brussels, 1899-1909. Roy 8vo., 6 vols., plates. Wheldon 129-1546 1974 £10

WILDEMAN, E. DE   Icones Selectae Horti Thenensis. Brussels, 1899-1909. Vols. 1 - 6, roy. 8vo., in parts as issued, plates, scarce. Wheldon 131-1587 1974 £10

WILDEMAN, E. DE   Plantae Novae Vel Minus Cognitae ex Herbario Horti Thenensis. Brussels, 1904-10. 10 parts, roy. 8vo., orig. wrappers, scarce. Wheldon 131-1588 1974 £5

WILDER, DWIGHT   Life and Letters of. Boston, 1891. 8vo., orig. cloth. Putman 126-69 1974 $12.50

WILDER, MARSHALL P.   The Sunny Side of the Street. New York, 1905. 1st ed., inner hinges split. Biblo & Tannen 213-906 1973 $7.50

WILDER, THORNTON   The Angel that Troubled the Waters. New York, 1928. 8vo., boards, little worn, autographed, first edition. Goodspeed's 578-395 1974 $10

WILDER, THORNTON   The Bridge of San Luis Rey. New York, 1927. Illus., first edition, very fine. MacManus 224-463 1974 $65

WILDER, THORNTON   The Cabala. New York, 1926. Orig. cloth backed boards, first edition, fine. MacManus 224-464 1974 $85

WILDER, THORNTON   The Happy Journey. French, 1934. 24p. Austin 51-1036 1973 $8.50

WILDER, THORNTON   The Long Christmas Dinner and Other Plays in One Act. New Haven, 1931. Orig. parchment backed boards, first edition, one of 525 numbered copies, signed by author, bookplate of John Stuart Groves, boxed, very fine. MacManus 224-465 1974 $25

WILDER, THORNTON   The Long Christmas Dinner and Other Plays in One Act. New York, 1931. Orig. cloth, first trade edition, presentation copy from author, fine, somewhat worn dust jacket. MacManus 224-466 1974 $25

WILDER, THORNTON   The Merchant of Yonkers. New York & London, 1939. First edition, orig. binding, d.j. Butterfield 10-531 1974 $25

WILDER, THORNTON   The Woman of Andros. New York, 1930. Orig. cloth, first edition, contemporary presentation inscription from author, fine. MacManus 224-467 1974 $25

WILDER, THORNTON   The Woman of Andros. New York, 1930. First edition, 12mo., presentation copy from author, spine & top of covers faded, else fine. Current BW9-294 1974 $35

WILDMAN, THOMAS   A Treatise on the Management of Bees. 1768. 4to., plates, contemporary half calf, first edition. Howes 186-1607 1974 £30

WILDMAN, THOMAS   A Treatise on the Management of Bees. 1778. 8vo., contemporary boards uncut, scarce. Wheldon 129-725 1974 £20

WILDRIDGE, THOMAS TINDALL   The Grotesque in Church Art. 1899. 4to., plates, illus., numbered. Covent 55-132 1974 £20

WILDRIDGE, THOMAS TINDALL   Northumbria. 1888. Plates, new buckram. Allen 213-1869 1973 $15

WILENSKI, R. H.   Outline of English Painting. New York, 1948. Illus. Biblo & Tannen 214-566 1974 $9.50

WILKES, JOHN   A Complete Collection of the Genuine Papers, Letters, etc., in the case of. 1769. Small 8vo., contemporary calf, rebacked, ex-library. Quaritch 936-260 1974 £30

WILKES, JOHN   English Liberty. (1769). Folio, early boards, first edition. Quaritch 936-262 1974 £60

WILKES, JOHN   Essay on Woman. 1764. Small 8vo., late polished calf. Quaritch 936-261 1974 £60

WILKIE, FRANC B.   Davenport. Past and Present. Davenport, 1858. 8vo., cloth. Saddleback 14-418 1974 $35

WILKINS, EARNEST P.   The Favourite Localities of the Tourist. London and Isle of Wight, 1860. Roy 8vo., orig. cloth, plates, first edition. Hammond 201-394 1974 £25

WILKINS, EDWARD G. P.   My Wife's Mirror. French, 1856. Austin 51-1037 1973 $7.50

WILKINS, GEORGE   The Convert. 1826. 8vo., orig. boards, uncut. Hill 126-297 1974 $25

WILKINS, JOHN   The Discovery of a New World. London, 1640. 8vo., old half calf. Dawsons PM 245-768 1974 £220

WILKINS, JOHN   A Discovery of a New World. London, 1684. 8vo., nineteenth century half calf, gilt, fourth edition. Dawsons PM 245-769 1974 £120

WILKINS, JOHN   The Discovery of a World in the Moone. London, 1638. Small 8vo., contemporary black calf, repaired, first edition, woodcut diagrams, engraved bookplate of G. W. F. Gregor. Kraus 137-86 1974 $850

WILKINS, JOHN   An Essay Towards a Real Character. London, 16-68. Folio, contemporary calf, fine, plates, first edition. Dawsons PM 245-770 1974 £135

WILKINS, JOHN   An Essay Towards a Real Character. London, 1668. 2 works in .1 vol., folio, new polished calf, rare, first edition. Schuman 37-267 1974 $250

WILKINS, JOHN   Mathematical Magick. London, 1680. 8vo., contemporary calf, rebacked, illus., third edition. Dawsons PM 245-771 1974 £60

WILKINS, JOHN   Mathematical Magick. London, 1691. 8vo., contemporary calf, illus., fourth edition. Hammond 201-995 1974 £75

WILKINS, JOHN   Of the Principles and Duties of Natural Religion. London, 1710. 8vo., contemporary panelled calf, sixth edition. Traylen 79-192 1973 £6

WILKINSON, E. S.   Shanghai Birds. Shanghai, 1929. Roy 8vo., cloth, plates, scarce. Wheldon 130-650 1974 £20

WILKINSON, GEORGE THEODORE   An Authentic History of the Cato Street Conspiracy. London, c., 1820. 8vo., contemporary half calf, gilt, plates. Hammond 201-194 1974 £12.50

WILKINSON, J. GARDNER   The Manners and Customs of the Ancient Egyptians. London, 1878. 8vo., 3 vols., brown half calf, gilt, boards, new edition. Dawsons PM 251-80 1974 £55

WILKINSON, J. GARDNER   On Colour and On the Necessity for a General Diffusion of Taste Among all Classes. 1858. 8vo., plates, woodcuts, rebacked, contemporary calf. Quaritch 940-274 1974 £25

WILKINSON, JOSEPH   Select Views in Cumberland, Westmoreland and Lancashire. Ackermann, 1821. Engraved plates, roy. folio, orig. quarter morocco, rebacked, fine. Broadhurst 24-1568 1974 £75

WILKINSON, LOUIS UMFREVILLE   The Buffoon. New York, 1916. First U.S. edition, very good copy, very scarce. Covent 51-1492 1973 £27.50

WILKINSON, MARGUERITE   New Voices. New York, 1920. lst ed. Biblo & Tannen 210-938 1973 $7.50

WILKINSON, TATE   Memoirs of His Own Life. York, 1790. 4 vols., 12mo., orig. wrappers, fine, rare, first edition. Ximenes 35-543 1974 $400

WILKS, GEORGE   The Barons of the Cinque Ports. 1892. Crown 4to., orig. cloth gilt, frontispiece. Howes 186-2071 1974 £7.50

WILKS, THOMAS E.   Bamboozing. Taylor, 1842. Austin 51-1038 1973 $6.50

WILKS, THOMAS E.   Captain's Not a Miss. French, 1836. Austin 51-1039 1973 $6.50

WILKS, THOMAS E.   The Crown Prince. French, ca. 1840. Austin 51-1040 1973 $6.50

WILLARD, DANIEL E.   The Story of the Prairies. Chicago - New York, (1907). 8vo., orig. bindings, illus., inscribed. Butterfield 8-410 1974 $20

WILLARD, EMMA   An Address to the Public. Middlebury, 1819. Wrappers, rebacked, second edition. Dawson's 424-347 1974 $100

WILLCOX, ORLANDO BOLIVAR   Shoepac Recollections. New York, 1856. 12mo., orig. green cloth, first edition. Ximenes 35-545 1974 $25

WILLCOX, WALTER T.   The Historical Records of the Fifth Royal Irish Lancers. 1908. 4to., orig. buckram gilt, plates, scarce. Howes 186-1772A 1974 £18

WILLETT, EDWARD   Letters Addressed to Mrs. Bellamy. 1785. 8vo., unbound, scarce. Hill 126-266 1974 £65

WILLETT, EDWARD   True Blue. New York, n.d. 8vo., first edition. Ximenes 35-546 1974 $15

WILLETTE, A.   Madeleine Monologue et 9 Dessins. Paris, 1920. 4to., wrappers, disbound, soiled, limited edition. Minters 37-146 1973 $40

WILLIAM, HENRY   A Letter. N.P., n.d. Small folio, first printing. Ximenes 35-547 1974 $50

WILLIAM, PRINCE OF SWEDEN   Wild African Animals I Have Known. London, (1923). 4to., illus., orig. cloth, first edition. Bow Windows 62-998 1974 £7.50

WILLIAM V. WILLIS AND COMPANY   Catalog - Surgical Instruments. Philadelphia, 1917. Cloth. Rittenhouse 46-699 1974 $10

WILLIAMS, A.   Drops from the Fountain. London, 1834. Full black morocco, blind tooled, fine, 3 1/8 X 2 1/4. Gregory 44-485 1974 $32.50

WILLIAMS, ALFRED M.   Sam Houston and the War of Independence in Texas. New York, 1893. 1st ed., maps. Jacobs 24-37 1974 $25

WILLIAMS, ARCHIBALD   Conquering the Air. New York, c. 1928. Revised and enlarged edition, illus., orig. binding. Wilson 63-461 1974 $10

WILLIAMS, BASIL   Erskine Childers. 1926. Wrappers. Covent 55-395 1974 £12.50

WILLIAMS, BENJAMIN SAMUEL   Choice Stove and Greenhouse Flowering Plants Comprising Descriptions of Upwards of 1,100 Species and Varieties. 1873. Crown 8vo., cloth, plates, scarce, second edition. Wheldon 131-1590 1974 £5

WILLIAMS, BENJAMIN SAMUEL   Choice Stove and Greenhouse Ornamental Leaved Plants. 1876. Orig. cloth, plates, foxed, second edition. Smith 194-22 1974 £5

WILLIAMS, BENJAMIN SAMUEL   Choice Stove and Greenhouse Ornamental Leaved Plants. 1876. 8vo., cloth, plates, scarce, second edition. Wheldon 131-1589 1974 £5

WILLIAMS, BENJAMIN SAMUEL   The Orchid Grower's Manual. 1877. Crown 8vo., orig. cloth, illus., fifth edition. Wheldon 129-1592 1974 £5

WILLIAMS, BENJAMIN SAMUEL   The Orchid Grower's Manual. 1894. Roy. 8vo., orig. dec. cloth, illus., seventh edition. Wheldon 129-1591 1974 £15

WILLIAMS, BENJAMIN SAMUEL   Select Ferns and Lycopods. London, 1868. 8vo., cloth, gilt, plates, illus. Hammond 201-691 1974 £6

WILLIAMS, BLANCHE COLTON   George Eliot: A Biography. 1936. Illus. Austin 61-1057 1974 $15

WILLIAMS, C. B.   The Migration of Butterflies. Edinburgh, 1930. 8vo., orig. cloth. Bow Windows 64-298 1974 £5

WILLIAMS, CATHERINE R.   Fall River, an Authentic Narrative. Boston, 1833. 12mo., boards, cloth back, paper label, first edition. Goodspeed's 578-396 1974 $10

WILLIAMS, CHARLES   Bacon. London, 1933. First edition, very good copy, inscribed by author, orig. cloth. Crane 7-315 1974 £25

WILLIAMS, CHARLES   He Came Down From Heaven. 1938. Orig. cloth, dust wrapper, signature, first edition. Rota 188-933 1974 £10

WILLIAMS, CHARLES   James 1. London, 1934. First edition, very good copy, inscribed by author, orig. cloth. Crane 7-316 1974 £25

WILLIAMS, CHARLES   Many Dimensions. 1931. English first edition. Covent 56-1337 1974 £5.25

WILLIAMS, CHARLES   Poetry at Present. Oxford, 1930. Near fine, first edition, scarce. Covent 51-2004 1973 £10.50

WILLIAMS, CHARLES   A Short Life of Shakespeare. Oxford, 1933. Orig. cloth, scarce, first edition. Rota 188-935 1974 £5

WILLIAMS, CHARLES   Thomas Cranmer of Canterbury. 1936. Near fine, inscribed, presentation. Covent 55-1546 1974 £21

WILLIAMS, CHARLES   Three Plays. 1931. Presentation, inscribed, cloth-backed pictorial boards, near fine. Covent 55-1547 1974 £30

WILLIAMS, CHARLES   To Michal. 1944. 4to., orig. cloth, fine, first edition. Rota 188-934 1974 £10

WILLIAMS, CHARLES   War in Heaven. 1930. Bookplate, very good copy, first edition. Covent 51-2005 1973 £6

WILLIAMS, CHARLES   Windows of Night. n.d. Publisher's compliments slip tipped in, very good copy, first edition. Covent 51-2006 1973 £8.50

WILLIAMS, CHARLES   Witchcraft. London, 1941. First edition, very nice copy, orig. cloth, scarce. Crane 7-317 1974 £8

WILLIAMS, CHARLES HANBURY   The Foundling Hospital. London, 1743. 8vo., modern boards, first edition. Dawsons PM 252-1065 1974 £10

WILLIAMS, CHARLES HANBURY   The Works. London, 1822. 3 vols., 8vo., contemporary speckled calf, gilt. Dawsons PM 252-1066 1974 £12.50

WILLIAMS, CHARLES HANBURY   Works. 1822. 3 vols., buckram, ex-library, bindings not uniform. Allen 216-2083 1974 $25

WILLIAMS, CHARLES JAMES BLASIUS   Principles of Medicine. London, 1843. 8vo., orig. cloth, rebacked, first edition. Dawsons PM 249-512 1974 £14

WILLIAMS, CHARLES THEODORE   Pulmonary Consumption. London, 1871. 8vo., modern quarter calf, uncut, first edition. Dawsons PM 249-513 1974 £24

WILLIAMS, D.   The History of Monmouthshire. 1796. 4to., plates, half calf. Quaritch 939-699 1974 £100

WILLIAMS, D. E.   The Life and Correspondence of Sir Thomas Lawrence. London, 1831. 2 vols., 8vo., orig. cloth, first edition. Ximenes 35-548 1974 $27.50

WILLIAMS, E.   Iolo Manuscripts. 1848. New buckram, blind stamp. Allen 216-1863 1974 $25

WILLIAMS, EDWIN   The Presidents of the United States. New York, 1849. Cloth. Hayman 57-756 1974 $15

WILLIAMS, ELIEZER   English Works, With Memoir. 1840. Buckram, ex-library. Allen 213-1872 1973 $12.50

WILLIAMS, EMLYN   Night Must Fall. French, 1935. Austin 51-1041 1973 $6

WILLIAMS, F. N.   Prodromus Florae Britannicae. Brentford, 1901-12. Parts 1 - 10, 8vo. Wheldon 131-1252 1974 £5

WILLIAMS, F. S.   The Midland Railway. London, 1877. Roy 8vo., orig. cloth, gilt, illus., third edition. Hammond 201-932 1974 £15

WILLIAMS, GOMER   History of the Liverpool Privateers and Letters of Marque With an Account of the Liverpool Slave Trade. 1897. First edition, med. 8vo., frontispiece, fine, orig. cloth. Broadhurst 24-1570 1974 £25

WILLIAMS, H. L.   Modernizing Old Houses. New York, 1948. Sm. 4to., illus. Biblo & Tannen 213-157 1973 $9.50

WILLIAMS, H. W.   Select Views In Greece. 1829. 2 vols., illus., plates, new buckram. Allen 213-1203 1973 $50

WILLIAMS, H. W.   Select Views of Greece With Classical Illustrations. 1829. 2 vols. in 1, 4to., full red morocco, engraved plates, some foxing. Bow Windows 66-751 1974 £110

WILLIAMS, HAROLD   Book Clubs & Printing Societies of Great
Britain and Ireland. London, 1929. 8vo., orig. figured cloth, limited edition.
Goodspeed's 578-551 1974 $50

WILLIAMS, HELEN E.   Spinning Wheels and Homespun. Toronto, 1923.
Illus. Hood's 102-747 1974 $7.50

WILLIAMS, HELEN MARIA   A Narrative of the Events Which Have Taken
Place in France. London, 1815. 8vo., orig. grey boards, fine, first edition.
Ximenes 35-549 1974 $40

WILLIAMS, HENRY W.   History of St. Louis. St. Louis, 1854. 8vo.,
orig. cloth, rebound, rare. Putnam 126-201 1974 $250

WILLIAMS, IOLO   Points in Eighteenth-Century Verse. London,
& New York, 1934. 8vo., orig. boards. Dawsons PM 10-653 1974 £38

WILLIAMS, J.   The Natural History of the Mineral Kingdom.
Edinburgh, 1789. 2 vols., 8vo., buckram. Wheldon 128-1068 1973 £28

WILLIAMS, J.   A Treatise on the Medicinal Virtues of the
Mineral Waters of the German Spa. 1773. Old calf, spine worn, covers
detached, joints breaking, quite fair within. Thomas 32-332 1974 £12.50

WILLIAMS, J. B.   A Guide to the Printed Materials for English
Social and Economic History. New York, 1926. 2 vols., 8vo., cloth.
Dawsons PM 11-802 1974 $17.50

WILLIAMS, J. FLETCHER   A History of the City of Saint Paul, and of the
County of Ramsey, Minnesota. St. Paul, 1876. 8vo., cloth. Saddleback
14-523 1974 $25

WILLIAMS, JESSE LYNCH   The Art of Playwriting. Univ. of Penn., 1928.
Austin 51-1042 1973 $7.50

WILLIAMS, JOHN   Dr. John Williams' Last Legacy. New York,
1827. 12mo., contemporary mottled calf. Ximenes 35-550 1974 $45

WILLIAMS, JOHN   A Narrative of Missionary Enterprises in the
South Sea. London, 1837. 8vo., illus., plates, frontispiece, foxing,
contemporary half calf, worn. Bow Windows 62-1000 1974 £24

WILLIAMS, JOHN S.   History of the Invasion and Capture of
Washington, and of the Events Which Preceded and Followed. New York, 1857.
Ex-library, map. Jenkins 61-792 1974 $15

WILLIAMS, JOSEPH   Narrative of a Tour from the State of Indiana
to the Oregon Territory in the Years, 1841-42. New York, 1921. Cloth.
Jenkins 61-2652 1974 $35

WILLIAMS, JOSEPH   Narrative of a Tour from the State of Indiana to
the Oregon Territory. New York, 1921. 8vo., orig. cloth, second edition.
Ximenes 35-551 1974 $20

WILLIAMS, M. B.   Jasper National Park. Ottawa, 1928. Illus.
Hood's 104-884 1974 $12.50

WILLIAMS, M. B.   Through the Heart of the Rockies and Selkirks.
Ottawa, 1921. Illus., map. Hood's 104-885 1974 $10

WILLIAMS, NORMAN P.   The Ideas of the Fall and of the Original Sin.
1927. Faded, scarce. Howes 185-1783 1974 £6.50

WILLIAMS, OSCAR   New Poems, 1940. New York, 1941. First
U. S. edition, cover slightly soiled, very good copy. Covent 51-79 1973 £7.50

WILLIAMS, OSCAR   That's All That Matters. New York, 1945.
1st ed. Biblo & Tannen 210-819 1973 $10

WILLIAMS, R.   The History and Antiquities of the Town of Aber-
conway. 1839. 8vo., orig. boards, first edition. Broadhurst 23-1601 1974 £6

WILLIAMS, ROBERT FOLKESTONE   Shakespeare and His Friends.
Philadelphia, 1839. 3 vols., 12mo., orig. quarter cloth, fine, first American
edition. Ximenes 35-552 1974 $65

WILLIAMS, ROBERT FOLKESTONE   The Youth of Shakespeare. Paris, 1839.
8vo., contemporary half calf, first Paris edition. Ximenes 35-553 1974 $30

WILLIAMS, ROGER   Experiments of Spiritual Life and Health, and
Their Preservatives. Providence, 1863. Loose wrapper. Jenkins 61-2653
1974 $15

WILLIAMS, S. WELLS   The Middle Kingdom. New York, 1901.
2 vols., illus., very fine. Ballinger 1-327 1974 $12.50

WILLIAMS, SAMUEL   The Natural and Civil History of Vermont.
Burlington, 1809. Enlarged edition of Vol. 2, full calf, foxed. Jenkins 61-2513
1974 $20

WILLIAMS, SAMUEL   The Natural and Civil History of Vermont. Burlington, 1809. 8vo., 2 vols., old calf, labels, second edition. Butterfield 8-
656 1974 $50

WILLIAMS, T. H.   Picturesque Excursions in Devonshire and
Cornwall. 1804. Roy. 8vo., half calf, plates. Quaritch 939-344 1974 £60

WILLIAMS, TENNESSEE   The Roman Spring of Mrs. Stone. New York,
1950. 1st ed. Biblo & Tannen 210-820 1973 $17.50

WILLIAMS, TENNESSEE   The Vengeance of Nicrotis. Chicago, 1928.
Pictorial wrappers, English first edition. Covent 56-1341 1974 £35

WILLIAMS, W.   Golwg ar Deyrnas Crist. 1799. Small 8vo.,
half calf. Quaritch 939-700 1974 £35

WILLIAMS, WALTER   The Press Congress of the World of Hawaii.
Columbia, 1922. Illus. with photos. Jenkins 61-1042 1974 $17.50

WILLIAMS, WILLIAM   Occult Physick. London, (1660). 8vo., contemporary calf, first edition. Dawsons PM 249-514 1974 £250

WILLIAMS, WILLIAM CARLOS   The Great American Novel. Paris, 1923.
Orig. cloth backed boards, some sun-darkening, first edition, limited to 300
numbered copies, lacks the label on spine, fine copy. MacManus 224-474
1974 $200

WILLIAMS, WILLIAM CARLOS   In the American Grain. New York, 1925.
First U. S. edition, good copy, leaves slightly stained at edges throughout.
Covent 51-2013 1973 £10.50

WILLIAMS, WILLIAM CARLOS   In the Money. White Mule - Part 2. Norfolk,
(1940). Orig. cloth, spine faded, first edition, advance copy. MacManus
224-475 1974 $35

WILLIAMS, WILLIAM CARLOS   Spring and All. 1923. First edition, faded
blue wrappers, rare, booklabel of Shakespeare & co. Covent 51-2014 1973 £55

WILLIAMS-ELLIS, A.   An Anatomy of Poetry. Oxford, c., 1922.
Cloth-backed boards, English first edition. Covent 56-859 1974 £5

WILLIAMSON, C. W.   History of Western Ohio and Auglaize County.
Columbus, 1905. One half leather, scarce. Hayman 57-537 1974 $60

WILLIAMSON, DAVID B.   Illustrated Life, Services, Martyrdom, and Funeral of Abraham Lincoln. Philadelphia, (1865). Cloth. Hayman 57-459 1974
$12.50

WILLIAMSON, GEORGE   Memorials of the Lineage, Early Life, Education,
and Development of the Genius of James Watt. Greenock, 1856. First edition,
crown 4to., binder's cloth little rubbed, text & plates fine, tinted lithographs,
engraved portraits. Broadhurst 24-1353 1974 £22

WILLIAMSON, GEORGE CHARLES   The Book of Famille Rose. 1927. 4to.,
gilt, plates, buckram, limited. Quaritch 940-667 1974 £110

WILLIAMSON, GEORGE CHARLES   The Book of Ivory. 1938. 8vo., cloth,
plates. Quaritch 940-485 1974 £15

WILLIAMSON, GEORGE CHARLES   Curious Survivals. 1923. Plates, first
edition, demy 8vo., very good copy, inscribed by author, orig. cloth. Broadhurst
24-224 1974 £8

WILLIAMSON, GEORGE CHARLES   The History of Portrait Miniatures. 1904.
2 vols., folio, plates, half red morocco, gilt. Quaritch 940-275 1974 £135

WILLIAMSON, GEORGE CHARLES   The History of Portrait Miniatures. 1904.
2 vols., folio, buckram, gilt, limited edition. Quaritch 940-276 1974 £36

WILLIAMSON, GEORGE CHARLES   Memoirs in Miniature. 1933. First edition, demy 8vo., fine, d.w., orig. cloth, signed and inscribed by author. Broadhurst 24-226 1974 £8

WILLIAMSON, GEORGE CHARLES   Murray Marks and His Friends. 1919. Illus., first edition, demy 8vo., uncut, fine, d.w., signed by author, orig. cloth. Broadhurst 24-223 1974 £8

WILLIAMSON, GEORGE CHARLES   Stories of an Expert. 1925. Frontis., illus. Covent 55-492 1974 £6.50

WILLIAMSON, GEORGE CHARLES   Stories of an Expert. 1925. Coloured frontis., plain plates, first edition, 8vo., very good copy, orig. cloth, long presentation inscription in author's hand. Broadhurst 24-225 1974 £8

WILLIAMSON, HAMILTON   Little Elephant. (New York, 1930). Square 8vo., pictorial boards, illus. by Berta and Elmer Hader, very good copy, orig. d.j. Frohnsdorff 16-409 1974 $10

WILLIAMSON, HENRY   Devon Holiday. London, 1935. First edition, green buckram boards, rather mottled and faded, nice copy, scarce. Crane 7-325 1974 £7.50

WILLIAMSON, HENRY   The Flax of Dreams. 1936. First edition, crown 8vo., orig. cloth, fine. Broadhurst 24-936 1974 £5

WILLIAMSON, HENRY   The Flax of Dream. London, 1936. First collected edition, revised, nice copy, frayed d.w., orig. cloth. Crane 7-326 1974 £6

WILLIAMSON, HENRY   Genius of Friendship: T. E. Lawrence. 1941. Dent in upper cover, very good copy, d.w., first edition. Covent 51-1109 1973 £7.50

WILLIAMSON, HENRY   The Gold Falcon, or, The Haggard of Love. London, 1933. First edition, nice copy, inscription on fly, scarce, orig. cloth. Crane 7-323 1974 £7.50

WILLIAMSON, HENRY   The Linhay on the Downs. 1929. Extra crown 8vo., boards, uncut, limited, first edition. Broadhurst 23-966 1974 £6

WILLIAMSON, HENRY   The Lone Swallows. 1922. Orig. cloth backed boards, printed label, first edition. Howes 185-558 1974 £7.50

WILLIAMSON, HENRY   The Old Stag. New York, 1927. First American edition, pictorial boards, good copy, bookplate. Crane 7-320 1974 £5

WILLIAMSON, HENRY   On Foot in Devon. London, 1933. First edition, very nice copy, d.w., orig. cloth, scarce. Crane 7-324 1974 £7.50

WILLIAMSON, HENRY   The Pathway. 1933. Crown 8vo., fine, dust wrapper, new edition. Howes 185-559 1974 £15

WILLIAMSON, HENRY   Salar the Salmon. 1935. Crown 8vo., orig. cloth, first edition. Broadhurst 23-971 1974 £8

WILLIAMSON, HENRY   Salar the Salmon. 1935. Dust wrapper, fine. Covent 55-1550 1974 £8.50

WILLIAMSON, HENRY   Salar the Salmon. 1936. 8vo., orig. cloth, illus., plates, first edition. Broadhurst 23-972 1974 £6

WILLIAMSON, HENRY   Salar the Salmon. 1936. Coloured plates, first illus. edition, proof copy, demy 8vo., paper printed wrapper, cover slightly dust stained. Broadhurst 24-937 1974 £6

WILLIAMSON, HENRY   The Star-Born. 1933. 8vo., paper wrapper, label, first edition. Broadhurst 23-970 1974 £5

WILLIAMSON, HENRY   The Star-Born. London, 1933. First edition, wood engravings, first issue, nice copy, bookplate, orig. cloth. Crane 7-322 1974 £10

WILLIAMSON, HENRY   The Village Book. (1930). 8vo., orig. vellum backed cloth, sides faded, signed by author, first limited edition. Bow Windows 66-753 1974 £10

WILLIAMSON, JAMES A.   The Voyages of the Cabots and the English Discovery of North America Under Henry VII and Henry VIII. London, 1929. Small 4to., limited to 1051 copies on Japan vellum, maps, orig. prospectus laid in, vellum back soiled, blue cloth, fine. Current BW9-444 1974 $35

WILLIAMSON, JAMES A.   The Voyages of the Cabots and the English Discovery of North America Under Henry VII and Henry VIII. London, 1929. 4to., parchment backed boards, uncut, limited edition. Traylen 79-503 1973 £28

WILLIAMSON, THAMES   Hunky. 1929. Austin 62-683 1974 $7.50

WILLIAMSON, W. C.   A Monograph on the Morphology and Histology of Stigmaria Ficoides. 1887. 4to., half calf, plates. Wheldon 131-1091 1974 £10

WILLIAMSON, W. C.   On the Recent Foraminifera of Great Britain. 1858. Folio, boards, tinted plates. Wheldon 128-932 1973 £10

WILLIAMSON, W. C.   On the Recent Foraminifera of Great Britain. 1858. Folio, buckram, plates. Wheldon 129-798 1974 £10

WILLIS, B.   East African Plateaus and Rift Valleys. Washington, 1936. 4to., orig. limp boards, plates. Wheldon 131-1092 1974 £10

WILLIS, B.   Survey of St. Asaph. Wrexham, 1801. 2 vols., 8vo., speckled calf, portrait. Quaritch 939-702 1974 £20

WILLIS, B.   A Survey of the Cathedral Church of St. Asaph. 1720. 8vo., russia, gilt, first edition. Quaritch 939-701 1974 £30

WILLIS, GEORGE L.   History of Shelby County. 1929. 8vo., cloth, illus., fine, first edition. Putnam 126-245 1974 $22

WILLIS, IRENE COOPER   The Authorship of Wuthering Heights. London, 1936. First edition, nice copy, d.w., orig. cloth, inscription on fly. Crane 7-135 1974 £6

WILLIS, J.   Canadian Boards at Work. Toronto, 1941. Hood's 102-399 1974 $10

WILLIS, J.   Canadian Boards At Work. Toronto, 1941. Hood's 104-383 1974 $10

WILLIS, J. C.   A Dictionary of the Flowering Plants and Ferns. Cambridge, 1925. Crown 8vo., cloth, rebacked, fifth edition. Wheldon 131-1212 1974 £7.50

WILLIS, LAULII   The Story of Laulii. San Francisco, 1889. 8vo., orig. dec. cloth, illus., fine, first edition. Ximenes 35-554 1974 $12.50

WILLIS, NATHANIEL PARKER   Al'Abri. New York, 1839. 12mo., orig. violet cloth, foxing, paper label, first edition. Ximenes 35-555 1974 $20

WILLIS, NATHANIEL PARKER   Canadian Scenery. London, 1842. 2 vols., full morocco, plates, gilt, fine. Hood's 103-166 1974 $800

WILLIS, NATHANIEL PARKER   Canadian Scenery. London, 1842. 2 vols., leather, marbled boards, plates, foxing, first edition. Hood's 104-188 1974 $650

WILLIS, NATHANIEL PARKER   Fun-Jottings. Auburn, 1853. 12mo., orig. green cloth, first edition. Ximenes 35-556 1974 $10

WILLIS, NATHANIEL PARKER   Fun Jottings. Alden, Beardsley, 1853. 371p. Austin 54-1060 1973 $17.50

WILLIS, NATHANIEL PARKER   Inklings of Adventure. New York, 1836. 12mo., orig. violet cloth, first edition. Ximenes 35-557 1974 $70

WILLIS, NATHANIEL PARKER   Melanie and Other Poems. New York, 1837. 12mo., orig. patterned cloth, first American edition, frontis. portrait, bright copy. MacManus 224-476 1974 $25

WILLIS, NATHANIEL PARKER   Poem Delivered Before the Society of United Brothers, at Brown University, With Other Poems. New York, 1831. Orig. cloth, paper label on spine chipped, first edition, scarce. MacManus 224-477 1974 $35

WILLIS, NATHANIEL PARKER   Poems. Baird, 1855. 410p., illus. Austin 54-1061 1973 $12.50

WILLIS, NATHANIEL PARKER   The Prose Writing of Nathaniel Parker Willis. Scribner, 1885. 365p., orig. ed. Austin 54-1062 1973 $10

WILLIS, NATHANIEL PARKER   The Rag-Bag. New York, 1855. 12mo., orig. cloth, inscribed, presentation, first edition. Ximenes 35-560 1974 $12.50

WILLIS, NATHANIEL PARKER   Sketches. Boston, 1827. Orig. cloth backed boards, paper label on spine defective, first edition, presentation copy from author. MacManus 224-478 1974 $65

WILLIS, NATHANIEL PARKER   Sketches. Boston, 1827-29. 2 vols. in 1, 8vo., contemporary half calf, first editions. Ximenes 35-561 1974 $50

WILLIS, NATHANIEL PARKER   Trenton Falls, Picturesque and Descriptive. New York, 1862. Spine chipped. Jenkins 61-1943 1974 $22.50

WILLIS, NATHANIEL PARKER   Trenton Falls, Picturesque and Descriptive. New York, 1865. Jenkins 61-1944 1974 $12.50

WILLIS, R.   Architectural History of Chichester Cathedral. Chichester, 1861. 4to., foxing, contemporary half morocco, rubbed. Bow Windows 62-1002 1974 £9.50

WILLIS, R.   The Architectural History of the University of Cambridge. Cambridge, 1886. 4 vols., roy. 8vo., plates, illus., buckram. Quaritch 939-325 1974 £65

WILLIS, THOMAS   Affectionum Quae Dicuntur Hystericae et Hypochondriacae Pathologia Spasmodica Vindicata, Contra Responsionem Epistolarum Nathanael Highmori, M.D. Leiden, 1671. 12mo., quarter vellum, folding plates. Gurney 66-199 1974 £45

WILLIS, THOMAS   Opera Omnia. Geneva, 1676. Thick 8vo., contemporary vellum, plates, first edition. Schumann 35-490 1974 $275

WILLIS, THOMAS   Pathologiae Cerebri, et Nervosi Generis Specimen. Amsterdam, 1668. 12mo., quarter vellum, engraved portrait, first Dutch edition. Gurney 66-200 1974 £60

WILLIS, THOMAS   The Remaining Medical Works. London, 1683. Folio, contemporary calf, plates. Gurney 64-233 1974 £285

WILLISON, J.   Sir George Parkin; a Biography. London, 1929. Ex-library. Hood's 102-267 1974 $10

WILLISON, JOHN   The Afflicted Man's Companion. Philadelphia, 1849. New edition. Rittenhouse 46-667 1974 $10

WILLIUS, F. A.   Cardiac Classics. St. Louis, 1941. Small tears on spine, very good. Rittenhouse 46-668 1974 $25

WILLKOMM, M.   Bilder-Atlas des Pflanzenreichs. Esslingen, (1887). Folio, half calf, gilt. Wheldon 130-1069 1974 £10

WILLMOTT, ELLEN   The Genus Rosa. 1910-1914. 4to., 2 vols., dark green niger half morocco, buckram sides, uncut, plates. Bow Windows 64-299 1974 £365

WILLMOTT, ELLEN   The Genus Rosa. 1914. Folio, 2 vols., quarter morocco, uncut, fine. Broadhurst 23-1198 1974 £240

WILLMOTT, ELLEN   The Genus Rosa. 1914. Folio, half green calf, gilt, 2 vols. Wheldon 129-50 1974 £300

WILLMOTT, ELLEN   The Genus Rosa. 1914. 2 vols., folio, half green calf, gilt, plates. Wheldon 131-132 1974 £300

WILLMOTT, ELLEN   Warley Garden in Spring and Summer. 1909. Folio, boards, plates. Wheldon 131-1591 1974 £5

WILLMOTT, R. A.   The Poems of Oliver Goldsmith. Routledge, 1877. Large demy 8vo., plates, orig. blue cloth, new edition. Smith 194-724 1974 £7

WILLMOTT, R. A.   The Poets of the 19th Century. 1866. Orig. cloth, engravings, rubbed. Smith 194-750 1974 £5

WILLOUGHBY, B.   Gentlemen Unafraid. New York, London, 1929. Illus. Hood's 102-84 1974 $7.50

WILLOUGHBY, FRANCIS   Ornithologiae Libri Tres. London, 1676. Large folio, contemporary calf, gilt, plates, presentation, first edition. Traylen 79-116 1973 £600

WILLOUGHBY, VERA   A Sentimental Journey Through France & Italy. 1927. Illus., orig. cloth, first edition. Rota 188-939 1974 £6

WILLS, ALFRED   "The Eagle's Nest" in the Valley of Sixt. London, 1860. 8vo., orig. cloth, first edition. Ximenes 35-562 1974 $27.50

WILLS, HELEN   Tennis. New York & London, 1928. First edition, orig. binding, d.j., illus. by author. Butterfield 10-508 1974 $17.50

WILLS, L. J.   The Physiographical Evolution of Britain. 1929. 8vo., cloth, plates. Wheldon 130-981 1974 £5

WILLS, NATHANIEL PARKER   Poem Delivered Before the Society of United Brothers. New York, 1831. 8vo., orig. cloth, first edition. Ximenes 35-559 1974 $22.50

WILLSHIRE, W. H.   An Introduction to the Study & Collection of Ancient Prints. London, 1874. 8vo., contemporary quarter roan, frontispiece. Bow Windows 62-1004 1974 £6

WILLSON, BECKLES   America's Ambassadors to England. 1928. Portraits, scarce. Howes 186-1315 1974 £6

WILLSON, BECKLES   America's Ambassadors to France. 1928. Thick 8vo., portraits, orig. edition. Howes 186-1316 1974 £6

WILLSON, BECKLES   In the Ypres Salient: The Story of a Fortnight's Canadian Fighting, June 2-16, 1916. London, 1916. Card cover, photos, maps. Hood's 102-127 1974 $7.50

WILLSON, BECKLES   Nova Scotia, the Province That Has Been Passed By. Toronto, n.d. Illus., revised edition. Hood's 104-236 1974 $17.50

WILLSTATTER, R.   Untersuchungen Uber Chlorophyll, Methoden und Ergebnisse. Berlin, 1913. 8vo., half cloth, plates, text-figures. Wheldon 128-1180 1973 £5

WILLUGHBY, FRANCIS   Ornithological Libri Tres. 1676. Folio, contemporary calf, plates. Wheldon 131-133 1974 £450

WILLUGHBY, FRANCIS   The Ornithology Of. 1678. Small folio, contemporary calf, rebacked, fine. Broadhurst 23-1199 1974 £200

WILLUGHBY, FRANCIS   The Ornithology of. 1678. Folio, engraved plates, contemporary calf. Wheldon 128-597 1973 £225

WILLUGHBY, FRANCIS   The Ornithology Of. 1678. Folio, full calf, plates. Wheldon 130-651 1974 £240

WILLUGHBY, FRANCIS   The Ornithology of Francis Willughby. 1678. Folio, contemporary calf, plates. Wheldon 131-723 1974 £225

WILLYAMS, COOPER   A Voyage to the Mediterranian in His Majesty's Ship Swiftsure. 1802. Folio, contemporary diced russia, gilt borders, coloured plates, rebacked calf, contrasting leather labels, extremely fine, very scarce large paper edition. Broadhurst 24-1700 1974 £450

WILMER, JOHN   The Case of John Wilmore Truly and Impartially Related. London, 1682. Folio, full calf gilt, leather labels, fine, first edition. Traylen 79-504 1973 £425

WILMORE, A. C.   History of the White River Conference United Brethren Church. Dayton, 1925. Large 8vo., cloth, illus., fine. Putnam 126-177 1974 $15

WILMOT, JOHN EARL OF ROCHESTER
Please turn to
ROCHESTER, JOHN WILMOT, EARL OF

WILSON, ALEXANDER   American Ornithology. Edinburgh, 1831. 12mo., orig. cloth, 4 vols. Wheldon 129-1712 1974 £20

WILSON, ALEXANDER   American Ornithology. Edinburgh, 1831.
4 vols., 12mo., orig. cloth, scarce. Wheldon 131-724 1974 £20

WILSON, ALEXANDER   American Ornithology. 1832. Frontis., 3 vols.,
contemporary straw weave calf. Bow Windows 64-300 1974 £68

WILSON, ALEXANDER   American Ornithology. 1876. 3 vols., 8vo.,
orig. half morocco, colour printed plates, scarce, foxed. Wheldon 128-599
1973 £65

WILSON, ALEXANDER   The Foresters. West Chester, 1838. 16mo.,
contemporary sheep, some foxing, very good copy, third edition. Ximenes
37-222 1974 £60

WILSON, AMOS   The Sweets of Solitude! Boston, 1821.
12mo., orig. wrappers, fine, rare, first edition. Ximenes 35-563 1974 $150

WILSON, ARCHIBALD   Manuscript Relating to Pauperism and Poor
Law. c.1840. 8vo., cloth boards, slip case. Emerald 50-583 1974 £20

WILSON, ARNOLD T.   Loyalties. 1936. 2 vols., roy. 8vo., plates,
maps, soiled, scarce. Howes 186-1317 1974 £8

WILSON, BENJAMIN   An Account of Experiments. London, 1778.
4to., disbound, plates, first edition. Zeitlin 235-242 1974 $75

WILSON, BENJAMIN   An Essay Towards an Explication of the Phaenomena of Electricity. London, 1746. 8vo., contemporary polished calf, first edition. Schumann 35-356 1974 $165

WILSON, CARROLL A.   Familiar "Small College" Quotations. (New
York, 1933). 8vo., wrappers, presentation inscription by author. Goodspeed's
578-552 1974 $10

WILSON, D. P.   Life of the Shore and Shallow Sea. 1935.
Roy. 8vo., orig. cloth, coloured plate, photographs, scarce, orig. issue.
Wheldon 128-167 1973 £5

WILSON, DANIEL   Chatterton: A Biographical Study. 1869.
Orig. purple cloth, covers faded, nice copy, first edition. Covent 51-387 1973
£5.25

WILSON, DANIEL   Prehistoric Annals of Scotland. 1863.
2 vols., second edition. Allen 213-1874 1973 $12.50

WILSON, E. A.   Penny Plain, Two-Pence Coloured. London,
1932. 4to., illus. plain & coloured, orig. cloth. Gregory 44-317 1974 $47.50

WILSON, E. A.   Vertebrata. 1907. Plates. Wheldon
131-527 1974 £5

WILSON, E. H.   The Cherries of Japan. Cambridge, 1916.
8vo., cloth, plates, scarce. Wheldon 130-1463 1974 £7.50

WILSON, EDMUND   A Book of Princeton Verse 1916. Princeton,
1916. 12mo., cloth, trifle spotted, fine copy, first edition. Goodspeed's
578-407 1974 $25

WILSON, EDMUND   The Boys in the Back Room. San Francisco,
1941. Orig. cloth backed boards, paper label, first edition, very good copy.
MacManus 224-479 1974 $30

WILSON, EDMUND   To the Finland Station. New York, 1940.
1st ed. Biblo & Tannen 213-719 1973 $12.50

WILSON, EDMUND   The Undertaker's Garland. New York, 1922.
First U. S. edition, very good copy, scarce. Covent 51-2020 1973 £15.75

WILSON, EDWIN BIDWELL   Vector Analysis. New Haven, 1913. Blue cloth
gilt, second edition. Dawsons PM 245-772 1974 £8

WILSON, ERNEST HENRY   China, Mother of Gardens. Boston, (1929).
Excellent copy, 8vo., orig. cloth. Gregory 44-318 1974 $35

WILSON, ERNEST HENRY   If I Were to Make a Garden. Boston, (1931).
4to., illus., fine, orig. cloth. Gregory 44-318A 1974 $16.50

WILSON, ERNEST HENRY   The Romance of Our Trees. Garden City, 1920.
First edition, limited to 1000 numbered copies, bookplate, front inner hinge cracked,
edge wear, orig. binding. Wilson 63-328 1974 $12.75

WILSON, FRANCIS   The Eugene Field I Knew. 1898. Half vellum,
limited to 12 copies, first edition. Allen 216-585 1974 $15

WILSON, FRANCIS   John Wilkes Booth. Boston, 1929. 8vo., cloth,
illus., first edition. Putman 126-18 1974 $15

WILSON, FRANCIS   Joseph Jefferson. New York, 1906. Illus.,
one of 160 numbered and sgd. copies. Jacobs 24-131 1974 $25

WILSON, FRED TAYLOR   Our Constitution and its Makers. New York,
1937. Biblo & Tannen 213-103 1973 $8.50

WILSON, FREDERICK COLLINS   Short Poems. London, 1863. 12mo., orig.
blue cloth, presentation, first edition. Ximenes 35-564 1974 $12.50

WILSON, G. J. N.   Early History of Jackson County. (Atlanta),
1914. Orig. red cloth, faded, second edition. Putnam 126-241 1974 $20

WILSON, GEORGE   Cyril. Leeds, 1834. 8vo., early green
binder's cloth, scarce, first edition. Ximenes 37-223 1974 $27.50

WILSON, H. H.   Ariana Antiqua. London, 1841. 4to., orig.
cloth, plates. Hammond 201-1008 1974 £18

WILSON, H. W.   Battleships in Action. London, (n.d.).
2 vols., 8vo., illus., orig. cloth, diagrams, first edition. Bow Windows
62-1006 1974 £10

WILSON, H. W.   With the Flag to Pretoria. 1900-1901. 4to.,
2 vols., orig. cloth, illus. Bow Windows 64-755 1974 £8.50

WILSON, H. W.   With the Flag to Pretoria. 1900-02. 4 vols.,
4to., orig. half roan, illus. Bow Windows 66-754 1974 £12.50

WILSON, H. W.   With the Flag to Pretoria. London, 1900-02.
4 vols., 4to., illus., rubbed, orig. half roan. Bow Windows 62-1007 1974
£14

WILSON, HARRIETTE   Memoirs. London, (n.d.). 4 vols. in 2, 8vo.,
orig. boards, plates, paper labels. Dawsons PM 252-1067 1974 £80

WILSON, HARRIETTE   Memoirs. 1929. Thick crown 8vo., half
morocco. Howes 185-560 1974 £5

WILSON, HARRIETTE   The Memoirs of Harriette Wilson. London,
1924. Cloth, gilt, limited edition. Dawson's 424-348 1974 $25

WILSON, HARRY LEON   Bunker Beam. Doubleday, Page, 1912. 307p.,
illus., orig. ed. Austin 54-1063 1973 $7.50

WILSON, HARRY LEON   Cousin Jane. Cosmopolitan, 1925. 388p.
Austin 54-1064 1973 $7.50

WILSON, HARRY LEON   Lone Tree. Cosmopolitan, 1929. 331p.
Austin 54-1065 1973 $7.50

WILSON, HARRY LEON   Oh, Doctor. Cosmopolitan, 1923. 384p.,
illus. Austin 54-1066 1973 $6.50

WILSON, HARRY LEON   Professor How Could You! Cosmopolitan, 1924.
340p. Austin 54-1067 1973 $6.50

WILSON, HARRY LEON   Ruggles, Bunker and Merton. Doubleday,
Doran, 1935. Austin 54-1068 1973 $17.50

WILSON, HARRY LEON   Ruggles of Red Gap. Doubleday, Page, 1915.
371p., illus. Austin 54-1069 1973 $6.50

WILSON, HARRY LEON   The Wrong Twin. Doubleday, Page, 1921.
361p., illus. Austin 54-1070 1973 $7.50

WILSON, HENRY   History of the Rise and Fall of the Slave Power in
America. (1877). Large 8vo., 3 vols., cloth, worn. Putnam 126-233 1974
$48

WILSON, HENRY　　Wonderful Characters. London, 1830. Illus. with engraved ports., 3/4 calf. Jacobs 24-167 1974 $35

WILSON, J.　　A Synopsis of British Plants. 1744. 8vo., contemporary calf, plates, rare. Wheldon 130-1118 1974 £20

WILSON, J.　　A Synopsis of British Plants In Mr. Ray's Method. Newcastle-Upon-Tyne, 1744. 8vo., contemporary calf, plates. Wheldon 131-1253 1974 £25

WILSON, JAMES　　Illustrations of Zoology. 1831. Folio, half morocco, gilt. Broadhurst 23-1200 1974 £525

WILSON, JAMES　　Lectures on the Structure and Physiology of the Parts Composing the Skeleton. London, 1820. 8vo., contemporary half calf, first edition. Dawsons PM 249-516 1974 £20

WILSON, JAMES　　A Missionary Voyage to the Southern Pacific Ocean. London, 1799. 4to., contemporary calf, rebacked, plates. Traylen 79-555 1973 £50

WILSON, JAMES 1861-　　The Evolution of British Cattle. 1909. 8vo., cloth, faded, illus., scarce. Wheldon 129-406 1974 £5

WILSON, JASPER　　A Letter, Commercial and Political. London, 1793. 8vo., modern boards. Dawsons PM 247-303 1974 £10

WILSON, JOHN　　The City of the Plague and Other Poems. Edinburgh, 1817. 8vo., contemporary red half morocco, second edition. Bow Windows 64-756 1974 £5.50

WILSON, JOHN　　A Familiar Treatise On Cutaneous Diseases. London, 1813. 8vo., old boards, new three quarter cloth, first edition. Schuman 37-268 1974 $95

WILSON, JOHN　　Noctes Ambrosianae. Redfield, (1854). 5 vols. Austin 61-1062 1974 $47.50

WILSON, JOHN　　The Recreations of Christopher North. Edinburgh, 1842. 3 vols., 8vo., orig. cloth, first edition. Ximenes 35-565 1974 $30

WILSON, JOHN A.　　Adventures of Alf. Wilson. Toledo, 1880. New cloth, first edition, scarce, rebound. Hayman 59-123 1974 $20

WILSON, JOHN A.　　Adventures of Alf. Wilson. Toledo, 1880. Orig. cloth, fine, first edition. Hayman 57-108 1974 $27.50

WILSON, JOHN HAROLD　　The Court Wits of the Restoration. Princeton, 1948. Biblo & Tannen 210-940 1973 $8.50

WILSON, LOUIS R.　　The University Library, Its Organization, Administration and Functions. Chicago, 1945. Cloth, diagrams, charts. Kraus B8-280 1974 $16.50

WILSON, MONA　　The Life of William Blake. 1932. Frontispiece, fine. Covent 55-226 1974 £6.50

WILSON, NICHOLS FIELD　　Adventures in Business. Buena Park, 1944. 4to., cloth. Saddleback 14-316 1974 $25

WILSON, OWEN S.　　The Larvae of the British Lepidoptera. 1880. Plates, English first edition. Covent 56-983 1974 £52.50

WILSON, OWEN S.　　The Larvae of the British Lepidoptera and Their Food Plants. 1880. Roy. 8vo., modern half calf, plates. Wheldon 131-883 1974 £25

WILSON, RICHARD ALBERT　　The Miraculous Birth of Language. 1942. Austin 61-1065 1974 $10

WILSON, ROBERT A.　　Mexico and Its Religion. New York, 1855. 8vo., orig. brown cloth, fine, first edition. Ximenes 35-566 1974 $25

WILSON, RUFUS R.　　Lincoln in Caricature. Elmira, 1945. Folio, maroon cloth, signed, limited edition. Putman 126-26 1974 $18

WILSON, S. B.　　Aves Hawaiienses. 1890-99. Roy 4to., map, contemporary half levant morocco, gilt. Wheldon 129-51 1974 £1,000

WILSON, SARAH　　A Visit to Grove Cottage for the Entertainment and Instruction of Children. (London), 1823. 16mo., orig. printed boards, roan spine gilt, engraved title, engravings on plates, very good copy, first edition. Frohnsdorff 15-173 1974 $45

WILSON, THOMAS　　The Knowledge and Practice of Christianity Made Easy. 1787. Small 8vo., calf, rebacked. Thomas 28-33 1972 £8.50

WILSON, THOMAS　　Works. Oxford, 1847-63. 7 vols. in 8, orig. cloth, best edition. Howes 185-1785 1974 £50

WILSON, W. R.　　Records of a Route Through France and Italy. 1835. 8vo., half antique calf, first edition. Broadhurst 23-1719 1974 £10

WILSON, W. R.　　Records of a Route Through France and Italy; With Sketches of Catholicism. 1835. Engraved plates, first edition, demy 8vo., half calf antique, fine. Broadhurst 24-1701 1974 £10

WILTON, MARY MARGARET (STANLEY) EGERTON, COUNTESS OF d. 1858 The Art of Needle-Work from the Earliest Ages. 1840. 8vo., orig. cloth, fine, first edition. Quaritch 940-777 1974 £20

WILTSHIRE Archaeological and Natural History Magazine. 1854-96. 28 vols., half green calf, plates, illus., scarce. Howes 186-2224 1974 £100

WILTSHIRE Archaeological and Natural History Society Magazine. 1854-1925. 42 vols., 8vo., plates, illus., half calf gilt. Quaritch 939-580 1974 £100

WINANS, WALTER　　The Art of Revolver Shooting. New York & London, 1901. Imp. 8vo., orig. cloth, inscribed presentation. Howes 186-1676 1974 £18

WINANS, WALTER　　The Sporting Rifle. New York & London, 1908. Imp. 8vo., orig. cloth, illus., first edition. Howes 186-1677 1974 £15

WINARICKY, CHARLES　　Jean Gutenberg, ne en 1412 a Kuttenberg en Boheme . . . Inventeur de l'Imprimerie a Mayence en 1450. Brussels, 1847. Small 8vo., orig. printed wrappers, bound in half leather, gilt leather labels. Kraus B8-393 1974 $45

WINCHELL, ALEXANDER　　Preadamites. Chicago, 1886. 8vo., orig. cloth, illus., fourth edition. Schuman 37-269 1974 $50

WINCHELL, ALEXANDER　　Sketches of Creation. New York, 1870. 12mo., orig. cloth, illus., first edition. Schuman 37-270 1974 $95

WINCHESTER, C.　　Aerial Photography. London, 1928. Crown 4to., illus., orig. cloth, first edition. Bow Windows 62-1008 1974 £5.85

WINCHESTER, C. T.　　An Old Castle. New York, 1922. 1st ed. Biblo & Tannen 210-941 1973 $7.50

WINCHESTER, ELHANAN　　The Process and Empire of Christ. Brattleboro, 1805. 12mo., contemporary tree calf, first edition. Ximenes 35-567 1974 $40

WINCKELMANN, J. J.　　Monumenti Antichi Inediti. Rome, 1821. 3 vols., roy. folio, plates, contemporary quarter calf, gilt, worn. Quaritch 940-361 1974 £98

WINCKELMANN, J. J.　　Winckelmann und Seine Zeitgenossen. Leipzig, 1923. 3 vols., roy. 8vo., half vellum, leather label. Quaritch 940-362 1974 £18

WINCKELMANN, JOHN　　History of Ancient Art Among the Greeks. 1880. 4 vols. in 2, plates. Allen 213-1206 1973 $20

WINDELBAND, WILHEIM　　A History of Philosophy. New York, 1893. Roy. 8vo., orig. cloth. Howes 185-2043 1974 £5

WINDELER, B. C.　　Elimus. Paris, 1923. Cloth-backed boards, numbered, fine. Covent 55-1449 1974 £30

WINDHAM, WILLIAM　　Speeches in Parliament. 1812. 3 vols., half calf gilt, labels, portrait. Howes 186-1318 1974 £14.50

WINDLER, PETER JOHANN　　Tentamina de Causa Electricitatis. 1747. 4to., modern half vellum, first edition. Zeitlin 235-243 1974 $85

WINDSOR, J.   Flora Cravonensis. Manchester, 1873. Post 8vo., orig. cloth, inscribed, scarce. Wheldon 128-1232 1973 £7.50

WINES, J. M.   Hoosier Happenings. Kansas City, (1926). Wrappers. Hayman 59-310 1974 $10

WINFIELD, C.   History of Hudson County. 1874. Part leather. Putman 126-84 1974 $30

WING, FRANK   The Fotygraft Album. Reilly, Britton. Illus. Austin 54-1071 1973 $7.50

WING, VINCENT   Astronomia Instaurata. London, 1656. Folio, contemporary calf, rebacked, first edition. Dawsons PM 245-774 1974 £150

WINGATE, EDMUND   Arithmetick. London, 1668. 8vo., contemporary calf, fourth edition. Gurney 64-234 1974 £25

WINGATE, EDMUND   Mr. Wingate's Arithmetick. London, 1699. 8vo., contemporary panelled calf. Dawsons PM 245-775 1974 £20

WINGATE, EDMUND   Tabulae Logarithmicae. London, 1633. Small 8vo., calf, rebacked, diagrams. Traylen 79-279 1973 £45

WINKLEMAN, GRACE   Provo, Pioneer Mormon City. Portland, c.1942. 12mo., cloth. Saddleback 14-733 1974 $15

WINKELMANN, ABBE   Reflections on the Painting and Sculpture of the Greeks. 1765. 8vo. Eaton Music-694 1973 £15

WINKLER, H.   Untersuchungen uber Pfropfbastarde. Jena, 1912. 8vo., cloth. Wheldon 130-1070 1974 £7.50

WINSHIP, GEORGE PARKER   Gutenberg to Plantin. Cambridge, 1926. Dark blue cloth, illus. Dawson's 424-180 1974 $15

WINSHIP, GEORGE PARKER   Notes on a Reprint of the New-England Primer Improved for the Year 1777. Cambridge, (1922). 32mo., wrappers, presentation inscription by author. Goodspeed's 578-553 1974 $10

WINSHIP, GEORGE PARKER   William Caxton and His Work. Berkeley, 1937. Blue cloth. Dawson's 424-181 1974 $25

WINSLOW, C.-E. A.   The Life of Hermann M. Biggs. Philadelphia, 1929. Illus. Rittenhouse 46-669 1974 $20

WINSLOW, HORATIO   Into Thin Air. 1928. English first edition. Covent 56-443 1974 £15

WINSLOW, JAMES BENIGNUS   An Anatomical Exposition of the Structure of the Human Body. London, 1776. Large 4to., contemporary calf, rebacked, fifth edition. Schumann 35-491 1974 $165

WINSLOW, KENELM   Veterinary Materia Medica and Therapeutics. New York, 1905. Revised third edition. Rittenhouse 46-670 1974 $10

WINSTANLEY, WILLIAM   The Honour of the Taylors. London, 1687. Small 4to., early 19th century blindstamped calf, rare. Ximenes 35-568 1974 $475

WINSTON, STEPHEN   G. B. S. 90. Dodd, Mead, 1946. Austin 51-880 1973 $10

WINSTON, STEPHEN   The Quintessence of G. B. S. 1949. 404p. Austin 51-879 1973 $8.50

WINTER, KEITH   The Shining Hour. French, 1935. Austin 51-1047 1973 $7.50

WINTER, WILLIAM   Life and Art of Richard Mansfield, With Selections from His Letters. 1910. 2 vols., plates. Allen 216-2134 1974 $15

WINTER, WILLIAM   The Poems of William Winter. New York, 1909. Special ltd. ed. on Japan vellum, ltd. to 150 copies, sgd. Biblo & Tannen 210-822 1973 $52.50

WINTER, WILLIAM   Shadows of the Stage. Macmillan, 1892. Orig. ed. Austin 51-1048 1973 $7.50

WINTER, WILLIAM   Shadows of the Stage--2nd Series. Macmillan, 1893. Austin 51-1049 1973 $7.50

WINTER, WILLIAM   Shakespeare's England. Macmillan, 1892. Austin 51-1050 1973 $6

WINTER, WILLIAM   The Trip to England. Osgood, 1880. Austin 51-1051 1973 $10

WINTER, WILLIAM   Wallet of Time. 1913. 2 vols., plates. Allen 216-2197 1974 $17.50

WINTHROP, THEODORE   The Canoe and the Saddle. Boston, 1863. 8vo., orig. bindings, first edition. Butterfield 8-464 1974 $25

WINTHROP, THEODORE   Cecil Dreeme. Boston, 1861. 8vo., orig. brown cloth, first edition. Ximenes 35-569 1974 $12.50

WINTHROP, THEODORE   John Brent. Boston, 1862. 12mo., orig. brown cloth, stains, first edition. Ximenes 35-570 1974 $17.50

WINTLE, E. D.   The Birds of Montreal. Montreal, 1896. Hood's 103-388 1974 $12.50

WINTON, JOHN G.   Modern Steam Practice and Engineering. London, 1884. Thick 8vo., contemporary half morocco, plates, illus. Hammond 201-996 1974 £12

WINWAR, FRANCES   Oscar Wilde and the Yellow Nineties. New York, 1940. Biblo & Tannen 210-937 1973 $7.50

WIRSUNG, CHRISTOPHER   The General Practise of Physicke. London, 1617. Thick folio, half calf, rubbed, third edition in English. Schuman 37-271 1974 $350

WIRSUNG, CHRISTOPHER   The General Practice of Physicke. London, 1617. Folio, contemporary speckled calf, rebacked, third edition in English. Dawsons PM 249-518 1974 £290

WIRSUNG, CHRISTOPHER   Ein Newes Artzney Buch. 1572. Folio, contemporary blind-tooled pigskin, boards, second edition. Dawsons PM 249-517 1974 £300

WIRT, ELIZABETH W. G.   Flora's Dictionary. 1830. 4to., buckram, interleaved with vari-colored paper. Allen 216-1736 1974 $10

THE WISDOM of China and India. New York, 1942. Biblo & Tannen 213-943 1973 $8.50

THE WISDOM of Jesus. 1932. Folio, orange limp vellum, slip-case, fine. Hammond 201-752 1974 £450

THE WISDOM of Jesus. Ashendene Press, 1932. Printed in red & black, 4to., limp orange vellum, silk ties, uncut, orig. board slip-in-case, one of 328 copies, fine. Broadhurst 24-976 1974 £375

THE WISDOM of Jesus. 1932. 4to., limp orange vellum, uncut, orig. board. Broadhurst 23-993 1974 £300

WISE, HUGH D.   Tigers of the Sea. New York, The Derrydale Press, 1937. Illus., green cloth badly faded, inner hinge loose, else good, limited to 950 copies. Current BW9-174 1974 $27.50

WISE, ISAAC M.   Reminiscences. 1901. 367 pages. Austin 57-703 1974 $15

WISE, JAMES W.   Mr. Smith Meet Mr. Cohen. Reynal, 1940. Austin 62-686 1974 $7.50

WISE, JAMES WATERMAN   Liberalizing Liberal Judaism. Macmillan, 1924. Austin 62-685 1974 $7.50

WISE, JOHN   A System of Aeronautics. Philadelphia, 1850. 8vo., plates, orig. cloth, gilt, rubbed, good copy, first edition. Gilhofer 61-46 1974 sFr. 1,200

WISE, JOHN S.   A Treatise on American Citizenship. Thompson, 1906. Austin 62-687 1974 $8.50

WISE, STEPHEN S.   As I See It. 1944. Austin 62-688 1974 $6.50

WISE, STEPHEN S.   Challenging Years. Putnam, 1949. Austin 62-689 1974 $8.50

WISE, T. A.   History of Paganism In Caldeonia. 1884. 4to., new buckram. Allen 213-1876 1973 £15

WISE, THOMAS JAMES   The Ashley Library. 1895. Drawings, very good copy, wrappers, very scarce, first edition, punctured throughout with pin pricks. Covent 51-2022 1973 £25

WISE, THOMAS JAMES   The Ashley Library. London, 1936. Vol. 11 of 11, 4to., cloth, one of 200 copies. Kraus B8-281 1974 $45

WISE, THOMAS JAMES   A Bibliography of the Writings in Prose and Verse of Elizabeth Barrett Browning. London, 1918. 4to., orig. boards, uncut. Dawsons PM 10-89 1974 £65

WISE, THOMAS JAMES   A Bibliography of the Writings in Prose and Verse of Elizabeth Barrett Browning. London, 1918. 4to., orig. printed boards, fine, presentation inscription. Dawsons PM 252-86 1974 £65

WISE, THOMAS JAMES   A Bibliography of the Writings of Joseph Conrad. London, 1921. 8vo., orig. boards, worn, revised second edition. Dawsons PM 10-133 1974 £18

WISE, THOMAS JAMES   A Bibliography of the Writings of Joseph Conrad. London, 1921. 8vo., orig. boards, second edition. Dawsons PM 252-175 1974 £18

WISE, THOMAS JAMES   A Bibliography of the Writings of Walter Savage Landor. London, 1919. Small 4to., orig. cloth-backed boards, uncut. Dawsons PM 10-348 1974 £25

WISE, THOMAS JAMES   A Bibliography of the Writings of Walter Savage Landor. London, 1919. Small 4to., orig. cloth-backed boards, signed, presentation. Dawsons PM 252-636 1974 £25

WISE, THOMAS JAMES   Carmen Saeculare. 1887. 8vo., orig. stiff wrappers, gilt. Quaritch 936-584 1974 £70

WISE, THOMAS JAMES   A Dryden Library. London, 1930. Limited to 160 copies on antique paper, plates, crown 4to., orig. buckram, author's bookplate and presentation inscription. Forster 98-106 1974 £52

WISE, THOMAS JAMES   Letters of Thomas J. Wise to John Henry Wrenn. New York, 1944. 8vo., plates, orig. cloth. Dawsons PM 10-655 1974 £15

WISE, THOMAS JAMES   Letters to John Henry Wrenn. 1944. Plates. Allen 216-215 1974 $17.50

WISE, THOMAS JAMES   A Shelley Library. London, 1924. 4to., orig. buckram gilt, plates, fine, first edition. Dawsons PM 10-554 1974 £40

WISE, THOMAS JAMES   War in Samoa. 1893. 8vo., orig. wrappers. Quaritch 936-583 1974 £65

WISEMAN, NICHOLAS   Recollections of the Last Four Popes and of Rome in Their Times. 1858. Half calf, first edition. Howes 185-1788 1974 £5

WISEMAN, NICHOLAS   Twelve Lectures on the Connexion between Science and Revealed Religion. London, 1836. 8vo., contemporary diced calf, gilt, fine, labels, first edition. Dawsons PM 245-776 1974 £25

WISEMAN, NICHOLAS   Two Letters. Rome, 1835. 8vo., disbound, rare, first edition. Ximenes 35-577 1974 $50

WISEMAN, RICHARD   Several Chirurgical Treatises. London, 1686. Folio, contemporary mottled calf, rebacked, fine, second edition. Dawsons PM 249-519 1974 £225

WISEMAN, RICHARD   Severall Chirurgicall Treatises. London, 1676. Folio, contemporary calf, worn, first edition. Schumann 35-492 1974 $475

WISLIZENUS, F. A.   A Journey to the Rocky Mountains in the Year 1839. St. Louis, 1912. Folding map, 500 copies. Jenkins 61-2686 1974 $85

WISSLER, CLARK   The American Indian. New York, 1922. Orig. binding, illus., maps, second edition. Wilson 63-377 1974 $20

WISTAR, ISAAC JONES   Autobiography. Philadelphia, 1937. Folded mpa, 4to., d.j., orig. binding. Butterfield 10-533 1974 $37.50

WISTER, OWEN   A Journey in Search of Christmas. New York, 1904. First edition, 12mo., full page illus. by Frederic Remington, dec. front cover, spine slightly faded, very fine. Current BW9-96 1974 $38.50

WITHER, GEORGE   Campo-Musae. London, 1643. 8vo., contemporary panelled calf, second edition. Dawsons PM 252-1073 1974 £210

WITHER, GEORGE   Hallelujah. 1857. 8vo., half morocco, portrait. Bow Windows 64-758 1974 £8.50

WITHER, GEORGE   Hymns and Songs of the Church. London, 1856. Small 8vo., portrait, half morocco. Bow Windows 62-1010 1974 £9.50

WITHER, GEORGE   Ivvenilia. London, 1626. Green morocco, gilt, first edition, second issue. Dawsons PM 252-1074 1974 £320

WITHERBY, H. F.   A Practical Handbook of British Birds. 1919-24. 2 vols., 8vo., cloth, plates. Wheldon 131-725 1974 £20

WITHERING, WILLIAM   A Botanical Arrangement of British Plants. Birmingham, 1787-92. 8vo., 3 vols., modern boards, plates, scarce, second edition. Wheldon 130-1119 1974 £35

WITHERING, WILLIAM   An Arrangement of British Plants. Birmingham, 1796. 8vo., 4 vols., contemporary boards, uncut, third edition. Wheldon 129-1030 1974 £18

WITHERING, WILLIAM   An Arrangement of British Plants. 1801. 8vo., 4 vols., half morocco, fourth edition. Wheldon 129-1031 1974 £15

WITHERING, WILLIAM   An Arrangement of British Plants. 1818. 4 vols., 8vo., half green calf, engraved plates, sixth edition. Wheldon 128-1233 1973 £12

WITHERING, WILLIAM   An Arrangement of British Plants. London, 1830. 8vo., 4 vols., orig. cloth, plates. Hammond 201-692 1974 £12

WITHERING, WILLIAM   A Botanical Arrangement of British Plants. 1830. 8vo., 4 vols., half calf, plates, seventh edition. Wheldon 130-1120 1974 £12

WITHERING, WILLIAM   The Miscellaneous Tracts. London, 1822. 2 vols., 8vo., new half calf, leather labels. Traylen 79-280 1973 £200

WITHERING, WILLIAM   A Systematic Arrangement of British Plants. 1801. 4 vols., 8vo., half morocco, plates, fourth edition. Wheldon 131-1254 1974 £15

WITHERING, WILLIAM   A Systematic Arrangement of British Plants. 1818. 4 vols., 8vo., half green calf, plates, sixth edition. Wheldon 131-1255 1974 £12

WITHERS, ALEXANDER S.   Chronicles of Border Warfare. Clarksburg, 1831. 8vo., contemporary calf, first edition. Butterfield 8-727 1974 $150

WITHERS, PHILIP   Nemesis, or a Letter to Alfred. (London, 1789). Small 4to., disbound, first edition. Ximenes 35-578 1974 $35

WITHERS, ROBERT   A Description of the Grand Signor's Seraglio. London, 1650. Small 8vo., contemporary calf, rebacked, first edition. Traylen 79-543 1973 £48

WITHERS, W.   The Acacia Tree, Robinia Pseudo-Acacia. 1842. 8vo., cloth. Wheldon 128-1633 1973 £7.50

WITHERS, W.   The Acacia Tree, Robinia Pseudo-Acacia, Its Growth, Qualities and Uses. 1842. 8vo., orig. cloth. Wheldon 131-1764 1974 £7.50

WITHERS, W. B.   The History of Ballarat. 1887. Orig. cloth, plates, second edition. Smith 194-598 1974 £20

WITHIE, J. "The Names and Armes of them that Hath beene Aldermen." 1878. 12mo., plates, cloth back. Quaritch 939-756 1974 £5

WITHINGTON, ANTOINETTE Hawaiian Tapestry. New York, 1937. First edition, inscribed, signed & dated by author. Jenkins 61-1043 1974 $25

WITHROW, O. C. J. The Romance of the Canadian National Exhibition. Toronto, 1936. Hood's 102-55 1974 $10

WITHROW, O. C. J. The Romance of the Canadian National Exhibition. Toronto, 1936. Hood's 104-67 1974 $10

WITTE, E. T. Een keur van Bloemheesters. Leyden, (190-). Small 4to., orig. cloth, plates. Wheldon 129-1641 1974 £5

WITTE, E. T. Een keur van Vaste-Planten. Leyden, 1900. Small 4to., cloth, plates. Wheldon 129-1550 1974 £10

WITTKE, C. A History of Canada. Toronto, 1941. Maps, fifth edition. Hood's 103-570 1974 $25

WITTSTEIN, G. C. Anleitung zur Chemischen. Nordingen, 1868. 8vo., half morocco. Wheldon 129-978 1974 £5

WODDERBORNIUS, JOHANNES Quatuor Problematum Quae Martinus Horky Contra Nuntium Siderum de Quatuor Planetis Disputanda Proposuit. Padua, 1610. Tan morocco, gilt line borders, with exlibris of Pietro Ginori Conti, first edition. Schumann 500-6 1974 sFr 28,000

WODEHOUSE, P. G. Fish Preferred. 1929. First American edition. Austin 61-1069 1974 $10

WODEHOUSE, P. G. A Gentleman of Leisure. 1910. Dust wrapper, English first edition. Covent 56-1348 1974 £7.50

WODEHOUSE, P. G. Mike, A Public School Story. 1909. Plates, orig. pictorial cloth, English first edition. Covent 56-2140 1974 £12.50

WODEHOUSE, P. G. Nothing But Wodehouse. Garden City, (1932). Austin 61-1079 1974 $10

WODROW, ROBERT A History of the Sufferings of the Church of Scotland from the Restoration to the Revolution. Glasgow, 1828-30. 4 vols., contemporary half calf, labels. Howes 185-1790 1974 £15

WODSON, HARRY M. The Whirlpool: Scenes from Toronto Police Court. Toronto, 1917. Illus. Hood's 102-356 1974 $12.50

WOILLEZ L'Orpheline de Moscou ou le Jeune Institutrice. 1856. Full morocco gilt, illus., fine, twelfth edition. Bradley 35-58 1974 £5.25

WOLF, EDMUND JACOB Lutherans in America. 1889. 544 pages, illus. Austin 57-707 1974 $12.50

WOLF, EDMUND JACOB Lutherans in America. Hill, 1889. 544p., illus. Austin 62-691 1974 $12.50

WOLF, FRANCES NATHAN Four Generations. 1939. 192 pages. Austin 57-708 1974 $17.50

WOLF, JOSEPH Feathered Favourites. London, 1854. 4to., orig. cloth gilt, plates. Wheldon 130-653 1974 £40

WOLF, JOSEPH The Life and Habits of Wild Animals. 1874. Folio, orig. parchment backed boards, plates. Bow Windows 64-302 1974 £20

WOLF, JOSEPH The Life of Joseph Wolf, Animal Painter. 1895. 8vo., cloth, plates. Wheldon 131-254 1974 £15

WOLF, JOSEPH Naturgeschichte der Vogel Deutschlands in Getreuen Abbildungen und Beschreibungen. Nuremberg, (?1812-21). Imp. folio, contemporary calf, hand coloured plates, rare. Wheldon 128-602 1973 £2,500

WOLF, JOSEPH The Poets of the Woods, Twelve Pictures of English Song Birds. London, 1853. Crown 4to., contemporary full red morocco gilt, plates. Wheldon 131-134 1974 £40

WOLF, PAUL Stadtebau, Das Formproblem der Stadt in Vergangenheit und Zukunft. Leipzig, n.d. 4to., boards, illus. Minters 37-580 1973 $30

WOLF, V. The Waves. 1931. 8vo., orig. cloth, dust wrapper, lightly foxed, first edition. Bow Windows 66-757 1974 £33

WOLFE, BERTRAM D. Diego Rivera, His Life and Times. New York, 1939. 1st ed. dw. Biblo & Tannen 213-388 1973 $17.50

WOLFE, F. How to Identify Oriental Rugs. London, (1931). 4to., plates, illus., orig. cloth. Bow Windows 62-1011 1974 £15

WOLFE, HUMBERT The Blind Rose. 1929. Ex-library, first American edition. Austin 61-1090 1974 $10

WOLFE, HUMBERT Requiem. 1927. Ex-library, first American edition. Austin 61-1089 1974 $10

WOLFE, HUMBERT The Silent Knight. 1937. Austin 51-1054 1973 $7.50

WOLFE, THEODORE F. Literary Shrines. 1895. Plates, orig. cloth, gilt, spine faded, else very good, first edition. Covent 51-2098 1973 £5.25

WOLFE, THOMAS Look Homeward Angel. New York, 1929. Orig. cloth, spine duller, first edition, with Scribner Press seal on copyright page, about fine. MacManus 224-480 1974 $50

WOLFE, THOMAS Of Time and the River. New York, 1935. Orig. cloth, first edition, about fine, somewhat worn dust jacket. MacManus 224-481 1974 $32.50

WOLFE, THOMAS Of Time and the River. New York, 1935. First edition, 8vo., book fine, d.j. little creased. Current BW9-296 1974 $35

WOLFE, THOMAS The Web and the Rock. New York, 1939. Orig. cloth, worn, first edition. Rota 188-949 1974 £8.50

WOLFE, THOMAS You Can't Go Home Again. New York, 1940. 1st ed. Biblo & Tannen 210-823 1973 $10

WOLFE, THOMAS You Can't Go Home Again. New York, (1940). Reprint, d.j., orig. binding. Butterfield 10-535 1974 $10

WOLFE, WELLINGTON C. Men of California. San Francisco, c.1901. 8vo., leather. Saddleback 14-317 1974 $15

WOLFERSTAN, BERTRAM The Catholic Church In China From 1860-1907. 1909. Scarce, map. Howes 185-1791 1974 £5

WOLFRADT, WILLI George Grosz. Leipzig, 1921. 8vo., cloth spine, boards, plates. Minters 37-347 1973 $12.50

WOLFSON, VICTOR Excursion. Random, 1937. Austin 51-1055 1973 $7.50

WOLLASTON, T. Catalogue of Coleopterous Insects of Madeira. 1857. 8vo., new cloth, plate. Wheldon 131-884 1974 £7.50

WOLLASTON, WILLIAM The Religion of Nature Delineated. London, 1725. 4to., contemporary panelled calf. Ximenes 33-49 1974 $75

WOLLEY, JOHN Ootheca Wolleyana. 1864-1907. Half morocco, gilt, orig. wrappers, fine. Broadhurst 23-1201 1974 £80

WOLLEY-DOD, A. H. Flora of Sussex. Hastings, 1937. Thick 8vo., illus., maps, scarce, orig. edition. Howes 186-2213 1974 £8.50

WOLLSTONECRAFT, MARY 1759-1797 Please turn to GODWIN, MARY (WOLLSTONECRAFT)

WOLLSTONECRAFT, MARY 1797-1851 Please turn to SHELLEY, MARY WOLLSTONECRAFT GODWIN

WOLSELEY, CHARLES   The Unreasonableness of Atheism Made Manifest. London, 1669-70. 8vo., early panelled calf, first & second editions.   Ximenes 35-579 1974 $90

WOLTERBEEK, PIETER   Catalogue d'une Tres-Belle Collection d'Estampes. Amsterdam, 1845. Contemporary half cloth.   Kraus B8-282 1974 $60

WOMANS Worth. 8vo., contemporary limp vellum gilt, stained, worn. Dawsons PM 252-1078 1974 £550

WOMEN'S VOCIES. 1887. Orig. pictorial cloth gilt, rubbed, book-plate. Covent 55-57 1974 £12

THE WONDERFUL History of Dame Trot and Her Pig. London, 1883. 4to., pictorial boards, cloth spine, illus., 1st ed. Frohnsdorff 16-264 1974 $60

WOOD, ANTHONY   Athenae Oxonienses. London, 1691. Folio, modem half morocco, gilt, first edition in English. Dawsons PM 251-141 1974 £90

WOOD, C. A.   The Fundus Oculi of Birds. Chicago, 1917. Roy. 4to., cloth, coloured plates, text-figures, scarce. Wheldon 128-603 1973 £10

WOOD, C. A.   The Fundus Oculi of Birds. Chicago, 1917. Roy. 4to., cloth, plates. Wheldon 131-726 1974 £10

WOOD, CATHERINE M.   Palomar, from Tepee to Telescope. N.P., c.1937. 8vo., cloth. Saddleback 14-319 1974 $10

WOOD, CHARLES ERSKINE   Heavenly Discourse. Vanguard, 1928. 344p., orig. ed., illus. Austin 54-1072 1973 $4.50

WOOD, ESTHER   Dante Gabriel Rossetti and the Pre-Raphaelite Movement. 1894. Plates, parchment back, scarce, presentation inscription. Marsden 39-391 1974 £10

WOOD, FERNANDO   A Biography of. (New York, c.1856). 8vo., orig. yellow printed wrappers, first edition. Ximenes 35-580 1974 $15

WOOD, FREDERIC J.   The Turnpikes of New England. Boston, 1919. Tall 4to., orig. bindings. Butterfield 8-349 1974 $25

WOOD, GEORGE   Peter Schlemihl in America. Philadelphia, 1848. 8vo., orig. brown cloth, worn, first edition. Ximenes 35-581 1974 $17.50

WOOD, H. T.   Report of the Committee on Leather for Book-binding. 1905. 4to., orig. cloth, plates. Bow Windows 64-454 1974 £6.50

WOOD, HENRY J.   The Gentle Art of Singing. 1927. First edition, 4 vols., roy. 4to., half cloth, board sides, very good set, first edition, inscribed presentation copy from author. Broadhurst 24-227 1974 £12.50

WOOD, J. G.   The Common Objects of the Sea Shore. n.d. Orig. blue cloth, wood engravings. Smith 193-764 1973 £5

WOOD, J. G.   Insects at Home. 1876 or 1892. 8vo., cloth, plates. Wheldon 129-696 1974 £5

WOOD, J. G.   Insects at Home. 1883. 8vo., prize morocco gilt, plates, illus. Wheldon 129-697 1974 £7.50

WOOD, J. W.   Pasadena, California, Historical and Personal. N.P., 1917. 8vo., cloth, illus. Saddleback 14-320 1974 $25

WOOD, LESLIE   Romance of the Movies. Heinemann, 1937. Austin 51-1058 1973 $7.50

WOOD, LESLIE   The Romance of the Movies. 1937. Dust wrapper, fine, illus. Covent 55-413 1974 £7.50

WOOD, N.   British Song Birds. 1836. Post 8vo., cloth. Wheldon 128-604 1973 £7.50

WOOD, NICHOLAS   A Practical Treatise on Rail-Roads, and Interior Communication in General. London, 1825. 8vo., orig. boards, rebacked, plates, first edition. Hammond 201-924 1974 £48

WOOD, RALPH   The Pennsylvania Germans. Princeton, 1942. First edition, orig. binding, signed by Richard H. Shryock. Wilson 63-106 1974 $12.75

WOOD, S.   Report of the Expedition to the Pembina Settlement and the Condition of Affairs on the Northwestern Frontier of the Territory of Minnesota. Washington, 1850. Large folding map. Jenkins 61-1680 1974 $17.50

WOOD, S. V.   A Monograph of the Crag Mollusca. 1848-74. 4to., 3 vols., cloth. Wheldon 129-877 1974 £30

WOOD, S. V.   A Monograph of the Crag Mollusca. 1848-82. 3 vols., 4to., half calf, plates, complete copy, scarce. Wheldon 131-1093 1974 £60

WOOD, T. W.   Curiosities of Ornithology. Croombridge, (1871). 8vo., orig. cloth gilt, colour printed plates, scarce. Wheldon 128-605 1973 £10

WOOD, T. W.   Curiosities of Ornithology. Groombridge, (1871). 8vo., orig. cloth gilt, plates, scarce. Wheldon 131-727 1974 £20

WOOD, W.   Illustrations of the Linnean Genera of Insects. London, 1821. 2 vols., 8vo., contemporary panelled calf, plates, leather labels, first edition. Traylen 79-75 1973 £35

WOOD, W.   Index Entomologicus. London, 1839. Roy. 8vo., new half calf, old cloth sides, plates. Traylen 79-74 1973 £30

WOOD, W.   Index Entomologicus. 1854. Roy. 8vo., half green morocco, plates. Wheldon 131-135 1974 £40

WOOD, W.   Index Testaceologicus. 1818. 8vo., new cloth, coloured plates, first edition. Wheldon 128-865 1973 £10

WOOD, W.   Index Testaceologicus. 1825-28. 8vo., old half calf, rebacked, plates, rare. Wheldon 131-912 1974 £30

WOOD, W.   Index Testaceologicus. 1828. 8vo., new cloth, plates, second edition. Wheldon 131-913 1974 £7.50

WOOD, W.   Index Testaceologicus. 1856. Roy. 8vo., orig. half green morocco gilt, hand coloured plates. Wheldon 128-867 1973 £30

WOOD, W.   Zoography. 1807. Roy. 8vo., orig. boards, vignettes, plates, uncut, large paper. Wheldon 128-296 1973 £30

WOOD, W.   Zoography. 1807. Roy. 8vo., orig. boards, uncut, plates. Wheldon 131-465 1974 £30

WOOD, WALES W.   A History of the Ninety-Fifth Regiment Illinois Infantry Volunteers. Chicago, 1865. Cloth, ex-library, first edition. Bradley 35-93 1974 $24

WOOD, WILLIAM   The Fight For Canada. Boston, 1906. Maps, portraits. Hood's 103-130 1974 $25

WOOD, WILLIAM   Flag and Fleet. Toronto, 1919. Inscription, illus. Hood's 103-131 1974 $15

WOOD, WILLIAM   General Conchology. London, 1835. 8vo., half green morocco, gilt, plates, second edition. Hammond 201-693 1974 £60

WOOD, WILLIAM   The Storied Province of Quebec, Past and Present. Toronto, 1931. 4 vols., leather spines and corners, marbled boards. Hood's 102-748 1974 $85

WOOD, WILLIAM B.   Personal Recollections of the Stage. Philadelphia, 1855. Biblo & Tannen 213-907 1973 $10

WOOD JONES, F.   The External Characters of Pouch Embryos of Marsupials. 1920-24. 9 parts in 1 vol., 8vo., cloth, text-figures, plates. Wheldon 128-359 1973 £5

WOOD-MARTIN, W. G.   The Lake Dwellings of Ireland.   Dublin,
1886. Roy. 8vo., cloth boards, illus. Emerald 50-990 1974 £26

WOODBERRY, GEORGE E.   Nathaniel Hawthorne. Houghton, 1902.
302p., orig. ed. Austin 54-1073 1973 $7.50

WOODBERRY, GEORGE E.   North Shore Watch. (Cambridge), 1883.
8vo., orig. morocco, first edition. Goodspeed's 578-410 1974 $25

WOODBERRY, GEORGE E.   The Northshore Watch. (Boston), 1883. 8vo.,
boards, paper label, uncut, presentation copy inscribed by author, first edition.
Goodspeed's 578-409 1974 $25

WOODBRIDGE, ELIZABETH   The Drama. 1898. Austin 51-1056 1973 $10

WOODBRIDGE, ELIZABETH   Studies In Jonson's Comedy. 1898. Ex-library,
sturdy library binding, orig. edition. Austin 61-1092 1974 $10

WOODBRIDGE, WILLIAM   An Address Delivered By Request. Detroit,
1849. 8vo., orig. wrappers, fine, first edition. Ximenes 35-583 1974 $27.50

WOODBRIDGE, WILLIAM C.   Rudiments of Geography. Hartford, 1830.
Thirteenth edition, without atlas, some staining, cover worn. Hood's 102-441
1974 $30

WOODFALL, WILLIAM   An Impartial Sketch of the Debate in the House
of Commons of Ireland. London, 1785. 8vo., modern boards. Dawsons PM
247-304 1974 £15

WOODFALL, WILLIAM   Sir Thomas Overbury. London, 1777. 8vo.,
disbound, first edition. Ximenes 35-584 1974 $40

WOODFORD, SAMUEL   A Paraphrase Upon the Psalms of David.
1678. Old calf gilt, worn, corrected second edition. Thomas 28-108 1972 £25

WOODHEAD, ABRAHAM   Church Government. Oxford, 1687. Small
4to., contemporary calf, first edition. Ximenes 35-585 1974 $40

WOODHEAD, ABRAHAM   A Discourse of the Necessity of Church-Guides.
(London), 1675. Small 4to., contemporary calf, first edition. Ximenes 35-586
1974 $60

WOODHOUSE, L. G. O.   The Butterfly Fauna of Ceylon. Colombo,
1942. 4to., orig. binding, coloured plates and plain plates, map, rare, orig.
limited issue. Wheldon 128-828 1973 £15

WOODHOUSE, L. G. O.   The Butterfly Fauna of Ceylon. Colombo,
1942. 4to., orig. binding, plates. Wheldon 130-811 1974 £25

WOODLEY, GEORGE   The Church Yard. London, 1808. 12mo.,
contemporary calf, first edition. Ximenes 35-587 1974 $35

WOODLOCK, THOMAS F.   The Catholic Pattern. S & S, 1942. 201p.
Austin 62-694 1974 $8.50

WOODMAN, A. J.   Picturesque Alaska. Boston, 1889. Pict.
cloth, illus. Jenkins 61-110 1974 $11.50

WOODMAN, HENRY   The History of Valley Forge. Oaks, 1921. 8vo.,
cloth, illus. Putman 126-44 1974 $20

WOODRING, W. P.   Geology of the Republic of Haiti.
Port-au-Prince, 1924. 8vo., wrappers, plates, maps, scarce. Wheldon
128-1069 1973 £10

WOODRING, W. P.   Geology of the Republic of Haiti. 1924. 8vo.,
wrappers, plates, scarce. Wheldon 130-982 1974 £10

WOODROFFE, PAUL   The Tempest. 1903. Dec. cloth gilt, illus.,
plates, faded. Marsden 37-540 1974 £5

WOODROOFFE, SOPHIA   Lethe and Other Poems. London, 1844.
8vo., orig. cloth, first edition. Ximenes 35-588 1974 $12.50

WOODS, H.   An Introductory Lecture on the Study of
Zoology . . . Delivered at the Literary and Scientific Institution Bath on Nov.
28, 1825. Bath, 1825. 8vo., modern boards, rare. Wheldon 128-297 1973
£10

WOODS, H.   A Monograph of the Fossil Macrurous Crustacea
of England. 1925-31. 7 parts, 4to., plates. Wheldon 131-1095 1974 £10

WOODS, J.   The Tourist's Flora. 1850. 8vo., cloth, plate,
scarce. Wheldon 128-1325 1973 £7.50

WOODS, J.   The Tourist's Flora. 1850. 8vo., cloth, plates,
scarce. Wheldon 130-1221 1974 £7.50

WOODS, RALPH   Pilgrim Places in North America. Longmans,
1939. Austin 62-695 1974 $10

WOODS, S. D.   Lights and Shadows of Life on the Pacific
Coast. New York, 1910. 12mo., cloth. Saddleback 14-324 1974 $10

WOOD'S Illustrated Natural History. 1866. New edition, with Thomas Hardy's
presentation inscription to his sister, covers somewhat worn, contents loose, very
good. Covent 51-873 1973 £30

WOODWARD, A. S.   A Catalogue of British Fossil Vertebrata. 1890.
8vo., cloth, scarce. Wheldon 131-1097 1974 £5

WOODWARD, A. S.   The Fossil Fishes of the Hawkesbury Series at
Gosford. Sydney, 1890. 4to., boards, plates. Wheldon 128-1070 1973 £10

WOODWARD, A. S.   The Fossil Fishes of the Hawkesbury Series at
Gosford. Sydney, 1890. 4to., boards, plates. Wheldon 131-1096 1974 £10

WOODWARD, ALICE B.   The Peter Pan Picture Book. London, 1911.
4to., 28 color plates. Frohnsdorff 16-77 1974 $15

WOODWARD, B. B.   Catalogue of British Species of Pisidium. 1913.
8vo., cloth, plates, scarce. Wheldon 129-757 1974 £5

WOODWARD, E. M.   Our Campaigns. Chicago, (1865). Cloth.
Hayman 57-99 1974 $12.50

WOODWARD, H.   A Monograph of the British Carboniferous
Trilobites. 1883-84. 4to., half calf, plates. Wheldon 131-1098 1974 £10

WOODWARD, H.   A Monograph of the British Fossil Crustacea
Belonging to the Order Merostomata. 1866-78. 4to., half calf, plates.
Wheldon 131-1099 1974 £15

WOODWARD, HENRY   A Letter from. London, 1752. 8vo., uncut,
fine, second edition. Ximenes 35-589 1974 $75

WOODWARD, HORACE B.   Geology of East Somerset and the Bristol Coal
Fields. 1876. 8vo., orig. cloth back. Quaritch 939-546 1974 £12

WOODWARD, HORACE B.   The Geology of England and Wales. 1876. 8vo.,
cloth, illus., frontispiece, first edition. Hammond 201-395 1974 £7

WOODWARD, HORACE B.   The Geology of England and Wales. 1887.
8vo., cloth, second edition. Wheldon 130-983 1974 £5

WOODWARD, HORACE B.   History of the Geological Society of London.
1907. 8vo., cloth, illus., portraits. Wheldon 131-218 1974 £10

WOODWARD, J.   An Account of the Societies for Reformation of
Manners. 1699. 8vo., old calf, rebacked. Quaritch 939-493 1974 £40

WOODWARD, R. B.   Natal Birds. Pietermaritzburg, 1899. 8vo.,
cloth, scarce. Wheldon 130-654 1974 £30

WOODWARD, S.   A Synoptical Table of British Organic Remains.
1830. 4to., orig. cloth, scarce. Wheldon 130-984 1974 £10

WOODWARD, S. P.   A Manual of the Mollusca. 1851-56. 8vo.,
orig. cloth, plates, first edition. Wheldon 130-845 1974 £5

WOODWARD, S. P.   A Manual of the Mollusca. 1851-56. 8vo.,
limp morocco, worn, plates, frontispiece. Wheldon 131-914 1974 £7.50

WOODWARD, S. P.   A Manual of the Mollusca. (1880). 8vo.,
cloth, plates. Wheldon 130-846 1974 £10

WOODWARD, S. P.   A Manual of the Mollusca. 1880 or 1910. 8vo.,
cloth, plates, frontispiece, fourth edition. Wheldon 128-868 1973 £7.50

WOODWARD, W. H.   Catalogue of a Collection of Pottery Belonging
To. 1928. 4to., plates, half vellum, limited edition. Quaritch 940-668
1974 £7

WOODWORTH, JOHN   The Battle of Plattsburgh. Montpelier, 1819.
12mo., orig. wrappers, scarce, first edition. Ximenes 35-590 1974 $80

WOODWORTH, JOHN   Reminiscences of Troy. Albany, 1853. 8vo.,
wrappers. Saddleback 14-601 1974 $15

WOOLCOTT, ALEXANDER   The Dark Tower. Random, 1934. Austin
51-1057 1973 $10

WOOLEY, C. LEONARD   Ur of the Chaldees. New York, 1930. 12mo.,
illus. Biblo & Tannen 210-1021 1973 $7.50

WOOLF, LEONARD   Fear and Politics. 1925. 8vo., orig. cloth,
wrappers, first edition. Rota 190-992 1974 £12

WOOLF, LEONARD   Fear and Politics. 1925. Dec. wrappers,
booklabel, scarce, some foxing. Covent 51-2622 1973 £12.50

WOOLF, LEONARD   Imperialism and Civilization. 1933. Wrapper,
foxing, new edition. Covent 56-1353 1974 £12.50

WOOLF, LEONARD   The Village in the Jungle. London, 1913.
First edition, covers stained, good copy, very scarce. Crane 7-334 1974 £12

WOOLF, LEONARD   The Village in the Jungle. 1925. Dust wrapper, second edition. Covent 56-1354 1974 £21

WOOLF, VIRGINIA   Between the Acts. New York, 1941. First
American edition, fine, d.w., orig. binding, heavy dec. paper wrapper. Ross
86-463 1974 $20

WOOLF, VIRGINIA   Between the Acts. 1941. First edition, crown
8vo., fine, d.w., orig. cloth. Broadhurst 24-951 1974 £20

WOOLF, VIRGINIA   The Common Reader. London, 1925. White
boards, gray cloth spine, first edition, first issue, lacking d.w., owners
inscription in ink on fly, fine, heavy dec. paper wrapper. Ross 87-575 1974
$50

WOOLF, VIRGINIA   The Common Reader. 1925-32. 2 vols.,
dust wrapper, first edition. Howes 186-541 1974 £30

WOOLF, VIRGINIA   The Common Reader, Second Series. 1932.
First edition, demy 8vo., orig. cloth, fine. Broadhurst 24-946 1974 £8

WOOLF, VIRGINIA   The Common Reader, Second Series. London,
1932. Lacking d.w., spine faded, very good copy, orig. binding. Ross 86-465
1974 $20

WOOLF, VIRGINIA   The Common Reader, Second Series. London,
1932. Clipping of Isabel Paterson's essay on author and Leonard Woolf's reply
laid in, d.w. very slightly chipped, mint, heavy protective paper wrapper.
Ross 87-576 1974 $45

WOOLF, VIRGINIA   The Death of the Moth and Other Essays. 1942.
8vo., orig. cloth. Bow Windows 64-760 1974 £4.50

WOOLF, VIRGINIA   The Death of the Moth and Other Essays.
1942. 8vo., inscription, orig. cloth, first edition, second impression. Bow
Windows 62-1014 1974 £7.50

WOOLF, VIRGINIA   The Death of the Moth and Other Essays. 1942.
Demy 8vo., orig. cloth, fine, first edition. Broadhurst 24-952 1974 £8

WOOLF, VIRGINIA   The Death of the Moth and Other Essays.
London, 1942. Tight, pristine copy, protected by heavy dec. paper wrapper, orig.
binding. Ross 86-466 1974 $55

WOOLF, VIRGINIA   Entre les Actes. Algiers, 1944. One of 120
numbered copies on velin, rare edition, wrappers, very fine, unopened. Covent
51-2029 1973 £40

WOOLF, VIRGINIA   Flush: A Biography. 1933. Frontispiece, first
edition, demy 8vo., bookplate, orig. cloth. Broadhurst 24-948 1974 £8

WOOLF, VIRGINIA   Flush, A Biography. London, 1933. First
edition, lacking d.w., fine, orig. binding, heavy dec. paper wrapper. Ross
86-467 1974 $20

WOOLF, VIRGINIA   A Haunted House and Other Short Stories.
1943. First edition, crown 8vo., fine, d.w., orig. cloth. Broadhurst 24-953
1974 £12

WOOLF, VIRGINIA   A Haunted House and Other Short Stories.
London, 1943. Pristine, d.w., orig. binding, protective dec. paper wrapper.
Ross 86-468 1974 $55

WOOLF, VIRGINIA   A Haunted House and Other Short Stories.
1944. 8vo., orig. cloth, dust wrappers. Bow Windows 64-761 1974 £7.50

WOOLF, VIRGINIA   A Letter to a Young Poet. London, 1932.
Pristine, orig. paper wrappers & heavy protective dec. paper wrapper. Ross
86-469 1974 $25

WOOLF, VIRGINIA   Monday or Tuesday. London, 1921. Woodcut
illus., Saxon Sydney-Turner's copy with his name in ink on fly, lacking d.w.,
very fine, heavy protective dec. paper wrapper, orig. binding, first edition.
Ross 87-581 1974 $100

WOOLF, VIRGINIA   Mrs. Dalloway. New York, 1925. First
American edition. Lacking d.w., back cover slightly stained, very nice copy,
orig. binding. Ross 86-471 1974 $45

WOOLF, VIRGINIA   Night and Day. Duckworth, 1919. Bookplate,
English first edition. Covent 56-2143 1974 £21

WOOLF, VIRGINIA   On Being Ill. London, 1930. No. 23 of
edition limited to 250 copies, signed, pristine, very scarce, d.w., orig. binding,
heavy dec. paper wrapper. Ross 86-473 1974 $300

WOOLF, VIRGINIA   Orlando, a Biography. New York, 1928.
First limited edition, no. 117 of 861 copies on pure rag paper, lacking d.w.,
near mint, protective heavy dec. paper wrapper. Ross 87-582 1974 $100

WOOLF, VIRGINIA   Roger Fry. London, 1940. Lacking d.w., orig.
binding, fine, heavy protective dec. paper wrapper. Ross 86-474 1974 $40

WOOLF, VIRGINIA   A Room of One's Own. 1929. First edition,
post 8vo., orig. cloth, fine. Broadhurst 24-944 1974 £12

WOOLF, VIRGINIA   A Room of One's Own. London, 1929. Lacking
d.w., else fine tight copy, orig. binding, first edition, protected by heavy dec.
paper wrapper. Ross 87-584 1974 $50

WOOLF, VIRGINIA   Stavrogin's Confession. Richmond, 1922.
8vo., full blue cloth, first English edition. Rota 190-995 1974 £15

WOOLF, VIRGINIA   Street Haunting. San Francisco, 1930. Orig.
binding, no. 377 of edition limited to 500 copies, signed, spine lightly faded,
mint, orig. box, scarce. Ross 87-585 1974 $175

WOOLF, VIRGINIA   Three Guineas. 1938. First edition, crown
8vo., fine, d.w., orig. cloth. Broadhurst 24-950 1974 £12

WOOLF, VIRGINIA   Three Guineas. London, 1938. Mint, d.w.,
orig. binding, heavy dec. paper wrapper. Ross 86-475 1974 $50

WOOLF, VIRGINIA   To the Lighthouse. 1927. First edition, crown
8vo., slight spotting of fore-edge, else fine, orig. cloth. Broadhurst 24-943
1974 £35

WOOLF, VIRIGINA   To the Lighthouse. London, 1927. 8vo.,
orig. blue cloth, first edition. Dawsons PM 252-1079 1974 £35

WOOLF, VIRGINIA   To the Lighthouse. London, 1927. Fine, orig.
binding, Saxton Sydney Turner's copy with his name in ink on fly, lacking d.w.,
fine, protective heavy dec. paper wrapper. Ross 86-476 1974 $150

WOOLF, VIRGINIA   Walter Sickert. London, 1934. 16mo., wrappers, soiled cover. Minters 37-165 1973 $12

WOOLF, VIRGINIA   The Waves. 1931. First edition, crown 8vo., fine, orig. cloth. Broadhurst 24-945 1974 £30

WOOLF, VIRGINIA   The Waves. London, 1931. First edition, but for lack of d.w. this copy would be mint, orig. binding. Ross 86-477 1974 $75

WOOLF, VIGINIA   The Waves. London, 1931. Orig. binding, d.w. slightly chipped, heavy dec. paper wrapper, scarce in d.w. Ross 87-586 1974 $75

WOOLF, VIRGINIA   The Years. New York, n.d. Faded, wrappers, English first edition. Covent 56-2144 1974 £5

WOOLF, VIRGINIA   The Years. 1937. Thick crown 8vo., orig. cloth, dust wrapper, first edition. Howes 186-542 1974 £15

WOOLF, VIRGINIA   The Years. 1937. First edition, crown 8vo., orig. cloth, fine. Broadhurst 24-949 1974 £20

WOOLF, VIRGINIA   The Years. 1937. Dust wrapper, fine, English first edition. Covent 56-1356 1974 £25

WOOLF, VIRGINIA   The Years. London, 1937. Mint, d.w., orig. binding, heavy dec. paper wrapper. Ross 86-479 1974 $55

WOOLLCOMBE, WILLIAM   Remarks on the Frequency and Fatality of Different Diseases. London, 1808. 8vo., contemporary mottled calf, only edition. Schumann 35-493 1974 $85

WOOLLCOTT, ALEXANDER   While Rome Burns. New York, 1934. 8vo., orig. cloth, first edition. Rota 190-996 1974 £5

WOOLLCOTT, ALEXANDER   While Rome Burns. New York, 1934. Orig. cloth, first edition, one of 500 numbered copies, signed by author, boxed, fine. MacManus 224-482 1974 $27.50

WOOLMAN, JOHN   A Journal of the Life and Travels of...in the Service of the Gospel. (London, 1901). 16mo., orig. vellum, one of 250 numbered copies, woodcut frontis., printed in red and black, fine. MacManus 224-154 1974 $65

WOOLNER, THOMAS   Pygmalion. 1881. Orig. cloth, scarce, first edition. Rota 188-951 1974 £10

WOON, BASIL   The Real Sarah Bernhardt. Boni, Liveright, 1924. Austin 51-1059 1973 $7.50

WOOSTER, D.   Alpine Plants. 1874. 2 vols., roy. 8vo., orig. blue cloth, coloured plates, scarce. Wheldon 128-1548 1973 £22

WOOSTER, D.   Alpine Plants. 1874. 2 vols., roy. 8vo., orig. blue cloth, scarce, plates. Wheldon 131-1593 1974 £50

WOOTON, ELMER OTTIS   Flora of New Mexico. Washington, 1915. 8vo., orig. wrappers, rare. Wheldon 131-1368 1974 £15

WOOTTON, A. C.   Chronicles of Pharmacy. London, 1910. 8vo., orig. red cloth, gilt, first edition. Dawsons PM 249-520 1974 £45

WORCESTER, EDWARD SOMERSET   A Century of the Names and Scantlings of Such Inventions, as at Present I Can Call to Mind to Have Tried and Perfected. London, 1663. 12mo., contemporary morocco, repaired, engraved bookplate of John Byng, Without the supplement. Kraus 137-77 1974 $950

WORCESTER, EDWARD SOMERSET   A Century of the Names and Scantlings of Such Inventions, as At Present I Can Call to Mind to Have Tried and Perfected. London, 1663. 12mo., contemporary calf, rebacked, first edition, with the rare supplement. Kraus 137-76 1974 $1,250

WORCESTER, EDWARD SOMERSET   A Century of the Names and Scantlings of Such Inventions. London, 1663. 12mo., contemporary calf, first edition. Dawsons PM 245-777 1974 £110

WORCESTER, NOAH   A Solemn Review of the Custom of War. Philadelphia, 1815. 12mo., sewn as issued. Ximenes 35-591 1974 $15

WORDSWORTH, CHRISTOPHER   Greece. 1882. Thick sup. roy. 8vo., orig. designed buckram, plates. Smith 193-484 1973 £9.50

WORDSWORTH, CHRISTOPHER   Greece. 1853. Crown 4to., maps, contemporary dark green gilt tooled morocco, new edition. Smith 193-483 1973 £20

WORDSWORTH, CHRISTOPHER   Greece, Pictorial, Descriptive and Historical. London, 1840. Gilt, marbled boards, plates. Dawson's 424-126 1974 $50

WORDSWORTH, CHRISTOPHER   Greece: Pictorial, Descriptive, and Historical. 1882. Med. 8vo., orig. cloth, fine, illus. Broadhurst 24-1702 1974 £15

WORDSWORTH, CHRISTOPHER   Memoirs of William Wordsworth. London, 1851. 2 vols., illus., very good copy, rebacked, orig. cloth, with autograph slip of Mrs. Wordsworth laid in. Covent 51-2625 1973 £10.50

WORDSWORTH, CHRISTOPHER   Who Wrote Eikon Bazilikh? London, 1824. 8vo., contemporary half calf, rubbed. Dawsons PM 10-658 1974 £5

WORDSWORTH, CHRISTOPHER 1848-   The Old Service Books of the English Church. 1904. Plates, orig. buckram, gilt. Smith 193-849 1973 £7.50

WORDSWORTH, J.   Fragments & Specimens of Early Latin. 1874. New buckram. Allen 213-1210 1973 $15

WORDSWORTH, WILLIAM   A Decade of Years. 1911. 8vo., limp vellum, slip-case, fine, presentation copy. Hammond 201-748 1974 £120

WORDSWORTH, WILLIAM   A Decade of Years. 1911. 4to., full limp vellum, uncut. Broadhurst 23-994 1974 £150

WORDSWOTH, WILLIAM   The Deserted Cottage. London, 1859. Illus., 8vo., large brown fox marks affecting about 48 pages, engravings, full green blind tooled leather heavily scuffed & worn. Current BW9-298 1974 $10

WORDSWORTH, WILLIAM   Our English Lakes, Mountains, and Waterfalls. 1864. 8vo., orig. dec. cloth gilt, illus. Quaritch 939-293 1974 £75

WORDSWORTH, WILLIAM   Poems. London, 1807. 2 vols., 12mo., orig. grey-blue boards, first edition. Dawsons PM 252-1080 1974 £280

WORDSWORTH, WILLIAM   Poems. 1911. Demy 4to., orig. cloth, fine. Broadhurst 24-301 1974 £25

WORDSWORTH, WILLIAM   Poetical Works. 1840. 6 vols., 8vo., full tan polished calf, gilt. Howes 186-544 1974 £20

WORDSWORTH, WILLIAM   Poetical Works. 1840-37. 6 vols., small 8vo., orig. cloth, portrait. Howes 185-563 1974 £7.50

WORDSWORTH, WILLIAM   Poetical Works. London, 1849. Small 8vo., 7 vols., contemporary polished calf, gilt, new and revised edition. Hammond 201-344 1974 £21

WORDSWORTH, WILLIAM   The Poetical Works. London, 1857. 6 vols., 8vo., orig. cloth, frontispiece. Ximenes 35-592 1974 $35

WORDSWORTH, WILLIAM   Poetical Works. 1887. Vols. 1-8, buckram, ex-library. Allen 216-1747 1974 $35

WORDSWORTH, WILLIAM   The Poetical Works Of. 1892. 7 vols. Austin 61-1093 1974 $47.50

WORDSWORTH, WILLIAM   The Prelude. Boston, 1888. Biblo & Tannen 213-835 1973 $7.50

WORDSWORTH, WILLIAM   The Prelude, or Growth of a Poet's Mind. 1850. First edition, demy 8vo., contemporary half morocco, panelled back, gilt rules, marbled boards, edges marbled, complete with half title, fine. Broadhurst 24-960 1974 £21

WORDSWORTH, WILLIAM   The Prelude, or Growth of a Poet's Mind. London, 1850. 8vo., orig. violet cloth, spine faded, very nice copy, first edition. Ximenes 37-225 1974 $90

WORDSWORTH, WILLIAM   The Prelude or Growth of a Poet's Mind. 1926. Portrait, cover somewhat stained, very good, first edition. Covent 51-2042 1973 £5.25

WORDSWORTH, WILLIAM   Prose Works. 1876. 3 vols., new buckram, rubber stamp. Allen 216-1748 1974 $50

WORDSWORTH, WILLIAM   The Recluse. 1891. One of 50 copies on hand made paper, boards, edges untrimmed, very good copy. Covent 51-2043 1973 £8.50

WORDSWORTH, WILLIAM   The Waggoner. London, 1819. 8vo., orig. wrappers, paper label, first edition. Ximenes 35-593 1974 $75

WORDSWORTH, WILLIAM   Yarrow Revisited. 1835. Rebound, leather label, cloth, foxing. Covent 55-1562 1974 £20

WORDSWORTH, WILLIAM   Yarrow Revisited. Boston, 1836. 8vo., orig. green cloth, second American edition. Ximenes 35-594 1974 $10

WORKMAN, HERBERT B.   John Wyclif. 1926. 2 vols., plates, orig. & best edition. Howes 185-1794 1974 £12.50

THE WORKS of Armand de Bourbon, Prince of Conti. 1711. 8vo., contemporary calf, frontispiece, first English edition. Hill 126-64 1974 £12.50

THE WORKS of the British Poets. 1808. Sharpe's Elegant edition, beautiful engravings, 12mo., 103 vols. in 44, 11 vols. in 5 with supplement, together 49 vols., contemporary dark blue straight grained morocco, with gilt, good library set, complete. Sawyer 293-76 1974 £260

THE WORKS of the English Poets. 1810. 8vo., 21 vols., contemporary russia, gilt. Quaritch 936-519 1974 £65

THE WORKS of the Most Celebrated Minor Poets. 1749 and 1750. Contemporary calf, 3 vols., first edition. Quaritch 936-156 1974 £70

THE WORLD for the Year One Thousand Seven Hundred and Fifty Three. London, 1755. 3 vols., folio, contemporary marbled boards, first edition. Dawsons PM 252-1083 1974 £55

THE WORLD of Adventure. (1891). 6 vols., crown 4to., illus., plates, orig. pictorial cloth gilt. Howes 186-286 1974 £8.50

THE WORLD'S Fair. London, (1851). Orig. blue cloth, gilt, illus., inscription, bookplate. Dawson's 424-218 1974 $100

WORLIDGE, JOHN   Systema Agriculturae. 1675. Folio, woodcuts, contemporary calf, rebacked, second edition. Wheldon 131-1800 1974 £90

WORLIDGE, JOHN   Systemata Agriculturae. 1681. Folio, contemporary calf, rebacked, third & best edition. Howes 186-1612 1974 £65

WORLIDGE, THOMAS   A Select Collection of Drawings From Curious Antique Gems. 1768. 2 vols. in 1, 4to., large paper, plates, contemporary red straight-grained morocco, gilt. Quaritch 940-486 1974 £65

WORNUM, R. N.   Some Account of the Life and Works of Hans Holbein. 1867. 8vo., orig. cloth, portrait, illus., some foxing, inscribed by author. Bow Windows 66-350 1974 £8.50

WORRINGER, W.   Die Altdeutsche Buchillustration. 1912. Illus. Allen 213-1878 1973 $10

WORSLEY, RICHARD   Museum Worsleyanum. 1794. 2 vols., imp. folio, half green morocco, gilt, leather labels, uncut, engravings. Quaritch 940-363 1974 £250

WORSLEY, T. C.   Barbarians and Philistines. (1940). Orig. cloth, inscribed, first edition. Rota 188-952 1974 £5

WORSTER, BENJAMIN   A Compendious and Methodical Account of the Principles of Natural Philosophy. London, 1722. 8vo., contemporary panelled calf, rebacked, first edition. Schumann 35-357 1974 $175

WORTHAM, LOUIS J.   A History of Texas. Forth Worth, 1924. 5 vols., 8vo., three quarter leather, presentation. Saddleback 14-719 1974 $90

WORTHINGTON, A. M.   A Study of Splashes. 1908. Fine, illus. Covent 55-1332 1974 £15

WORTHINGTON, E. B.   Science in Africa. 1938. 8vo., cloth, maps, plates, scarce. Wheldon 129-316 1974 £5

WORTLEY, EMMELINE CHARLOTTE ELIZABETH MANNERS STUART-
Please turn to
STUART-WORTLEY, EMMELINE CHARLOTTE ELIZABETH MANNERS

WOTTON, WILLIAM   Reflections Upon Ancient and Modern Learning. London, 1694. 8vo., contemporary mottled calf, first edition. Ximenes 35-595 1974 $150

WOTY, WILLIAM   The Shrubs of Parnassus. London, 1760. 12mo., contemporary sheep, first edition. Dawsons PM 252-1084 1974 £35

WOTY, WILLIAM   The Shrubs of Parnassus. London, 1760. 12mo., contemporary calf, first edition. Ximenes 35-596 1974 $175

WOUK, HERMAN   The City Boy. 1948. Austin 62-697 1974 $6

WOUWERUS, JOANNES   Dies Aestiva. Oxford, 1636. 12mo., calf antique, first edition. Ximenes 35-597 1974 $35

WRANGELL, FERDINAND   Narrative of An Expedition to the Polar Sea. New York, 1841. 12mo., orig. cloth, first American edition. Ximenes 35-598 1974 $20

WRANGHAM, FRANCIS   The English Portion of the Library of. 1826. Edition limited to 70 copies, woodcuts, 8vo., dark blue morocco gilt, floral border gilt tooled on centre panels, fine copy, rare. Sawyer 293-61 1974 £145

WRATISLAW, THEODORE   Algernon Charles Swinburne: A Study. 1900. Frontis., portrait, with remains of bookplate, very good copy, first edition. Covent 51-1788 1973 £6.50

WRAXALL, NATHANIEL WILLIAM   Historical and Posthumous Memoirs. 1772-84. 1884. 5 vols., rebacked, one joint cracked. Allen 216-2084 1974 $25

WRAXALL, NATHANIEL WILLIAM   Historical Memoirs of My Own Time. 1815. 2 vols., contemporary half olive morocco gilt, first edition. Howes 186-1324 1974 £15

WRAXALL, NATHANIEL WILLIAM   Memoirs of the Courts of Berlin. London, 1799. 2 vols., 8vo., contemporary half calf, first edition. Ximenes 35-599 1974 £27.50

WREN, C. P.   Odd--But Even So. Philadelphia, 1942. 1st ed. Biblo & Tannen 210-695 1973 $10

WREN, PERCIVAL CHRISTOPHER   Beau Geste. London, (1927). Orig. buckram, gilt, fine, slipcase, autographed, specail limited edition. Jenkins 48-548 1973 $50

WREN SOCIETY   The Transactions. Oxford, 1924-43. 20 vols., 4to., buckram backs, boards, drawings. Marsden 39-518 1974 £325

WRIGHT, ABRAHAM   Delitiae Delitiarum Sive Epigrammatum ex Optimis Quibusq. Oxford, 1637. 12mo., early calf, first edition. Ximenes 35-600 1974 $90

WRIGHT, AKINS   A History of the Principal and Most Distinguished Martyrs in the Different Ages of the World. Cincinnati, 1829. Leather, little worn, light internal dampstains. Hayman 59-438 1974 $15

WRIGHT, ANDREW   Court-Hand Restored. 1846. Small 4to., orig. cloth, rebacked, plates, eighth edition. Howes 185-887 1974 £6.50

WRIGHT, ARNOLD   Parliament: Past and Present. n.d. (c. 1910). Profusely illus., 2 vols., demy 4to., good copy, orig. cloth. Broadhurst 24-1359 1974 £5

WRIGHT, AUSTIN TAPPAN   Islandia. New York, (1942). Cloth, dust wrapper, first edition. Dawson's 424-313 1974 $30

WRIGHT, C. T. HAGBERG   Subject-Index of the London Library. London, 1909-23. 2 vols., 4to., orig. cloth gilt, library stamps. Dawsons PM 10-369 1974 £15

WRIGHT, CONSTANCE   Silver Collar Boy. London, 1934. First edition, very good copy, illus., orig. cloth. Crane 7-313 1974 £5

WRIGHT, E. P.   Spicilegia Biologica. 1870. 8vo., plates, orig. wrappers. Wheldon 128-76 1973 £5

WRIGHT, FRANCES   Altorf. Philadelphia, 1819. 12mo., disbound, first edition. Ximenes 35-601 1974 $125

WRIGHT, FRANCES   Altorf, a Tragedy. Philadelphia, 1819. 12mo., sewn as issued, first edition, unbound, fine. MacManus 224-483 1974 $100

WRIGHT, FRANK LLOYD   The Future of Architecture. New York, n.d. Plates, small 4to., new edition. Covent 56-1424 1974 £5.25

WRIGHT, FRANK LLOYD   An Organic Architecture. London, 1939. Crown 4to., plates, orig. cloth, first edition. Smith 193-55 1973 £8

WRIGHT, FRANK LLOYD   When Democracy Builds. Chicago, (1945). Cloth, dust wrapper, illus., first edition. Dawson's 424-242 1974 $30

WRIGHT, GEORGE NEWENHAM   The Chinese Empire Illustrated. n.d. 2 vols., 4to., plates, orig. cloth, foxing. Smith 194-604 1974 £9.50

WRIGHT, GEORGE NEWENHAM   Lancashire. (1843). 4to., plates, orig. cloth, gilt, fine. Quaritch 939-425 1974 £65

WRIGHT, GEORGE NEWENHAM   Lancashire. (1845). 2 vols., 4to., gilt, contemporary half green morocco, portraits. Quaritch 939-426 1974 £90

WRIGHT, GEORGE NEWENHAM   The Rhine, Italy and Greece. c. 1840. 4to., plates. Allen 213-1211 1973 $15

WRIGHT, GEORGE NEWENHAM   The Shores and Islands of the Mediterranean. n.d. (1840). Demy 4to., contemporary half morocco, few plates slightly spotted, binding little rubbed, else fine clean copy. Broadhurst 24-1703 1974 £60

WRIGHT, H. G.   The Fruit Grower's Guide. (1892). 4to., orig. dec. cloth, plates. Wheldon 130-1495 1974 £40

WRIGHT, H. G.   The Fruit-Growers Guide. (1924). 2 vols., roy. 8vo., cloth, plates, new revised edition. Wheldon 131-1594 1974 £7.50

WRIGHT, HELEN MARTHA   The First Presbyterian Congregation Mendham. Jersey City, 1939. 8vo., 2 vols., orig. bindings. Butterfield 8-382 1974 $10

WRIGHT, HENRIETTA   Little Folk in Green. New York, 1883. Biblo & Tannen 210-753 1973 $12.50

WRIGHT, ISAAC   The East Side. Toledo, (1894). Cloth, scarce, inner hinges little cracked, owner's inscription. Hayman 59-479 1974 $10

WRIGHT, J.   All Clear, Canada! Toronto, 1944. Illus. Hood's 103-518 1974 $10

WRIGHT, MRS. J.   The Globe Prepared for Man. C., 1855. Small 8vo., orig. cloth, gilt, second edition. Hammond 201-396 1974 £6

WRIGHT, J. C.   In the Good Old Times. c.1900. Orig. cloth, presentation, inscribed. Howes 186-1965 1974 £5

WRIGHT, J. C.   The Story of the Brontes. 1925. Fine, English first edition. Covent 56-1583 1974 £5.25

WRIGHT, J. F. C.   Slava Bohu, The Story of the Dukhobors. New York & Toronto, 1940. Hood's 104-887 1974 $27.50

WRIGHT, J. W.   Colorado in Color and Song. Denver, 1899. Oblong 4to., unpaginated, colored views with tissue guards. Butterfield 10-200 1974 $25

WRIGHT, JAMES   The History and Antiquities of the County of Rutland. London, 1684. Folio, contemporary panelled calf, rebacked, fine, first edition. Dawsons PM 251-83 1974 £120

WRIGHT, JAMES   History and Antiquities of the County of Rutland. London, 1684. Folio, illus., buckram. Quaritch 939-530 1974 £20

WRIGHT, JAMES   Observations Upon the Important Object of Preserving Wheat and Other Grains from Vermin. London, 1796. 4to., fine, contemporary streaked calf, first edition. Dawsons PM 247-305 1974 £50

WRIGHT, JOHN   The American Negociator. London, 1761. 8vo., contemporary calf, scarce, first edition. Ximenes 35-603 1974 $200

WRIGHT, JOHN   A Compleat History of the Late War. London, 1765. 2 vols. in 1, 8vo., old calf, gilt, leather label, plates. Traylen 79-505 1973 £75

WRIGHT, JOHN MICHAEL   An Account of His Excellence Roger Earl of Castlemaine's. London, 1688. Folio, contemporary calf, first edition. Ximenes 35-602 1974 $450

WRIGHT, JOSEPH   The English Dialect Dictionary. 1898-1905. 6 vols., thick 4to., cloth, rebacked, orig. edition. Howes 185-108 1974 £35

WRIGHT, JOSEPH   The English Dialect Dictionary. Oxford, 1898-1905. 4to., 6 vols., orig. cloth. Bow Windows 64-763 1974 £75

WRIGHT, LEWIS   The Brahma Fowl. 1870. Crown 8vo., cloth, text-figures, coloured plates. Wheldon 128-606 1973 £5

WRIGHT, LEWIS   The Illustrated Book of Poultry. London, 1890. Green morocco, plates, new edition. Dawson's 424-127 1974 $95

WRIGHT, LEWIS   Optical Projection. London, 1891. 8vo., signature, orig. cloth, foxing, stains. Bow Windows 62-1018 1974 £6

WRIGHT, LEWIS   The Practical Poultry Keeper. London, 1897. Color plates, engravings, 8vo., orig. cloth. Gregory 44-322 1974 $18.50

WRIGHT, M.   Svenska Faglar. Stockholm, 1927-29. 3 vols., imp. 4to., orig. half calf, plates. Wheldon 131-136 1974 £165

WRIGHT, M.   Svenska Foglar Efter Naturen. Stockholm, 1917-29. 3 vols., in 105 parts, imp. 4to., orig. wrappers, coloured plates. Wheldon 128-607 1973 £120

WRIGHT, ORVILLE   The Wright Brothers Aeroplane. New York, 1908. Wrappers, photographs. Covent 55-149 1974 £12.50

WRIGHT, PERCY   Spaniards and Spanish Bull Fights. Newcastle-upon-Tyne, 1887. Rear cover scored, front cover slightly marked, very good, wrappers, first edition. Covent 51-307 1973 £5

WRIGHT, RICHARD   Native Son. New York, 1940. Fine, dust wrapper, first U.S. edition. Covent 56-2146 1974 £12.60

WRIGHT, RICHARDSON   Grandfather was Queer. Lippincott, 1939. 358p., illus., orig. ed. Austin 54-1074 1973 $7.50

WRIGHT, RICHARDSON LITTLE 1887-   House and Garden's Portfolio. New York, 1937. Small folio, orig. boards. Wheldon 129-1552 1974 £15

WRIGHT, RICHARDSON LITTLE 1887-   House and Garden's Portfolio of Twenty-Five Flower Prints. New York, 1937. Small folio, orig. boards. Wheldon 131-1595 1974 £15

WRIGHT, ROBERT MARR   Dodge City. N.P., (1913). Cloth, rare, first edition. Hayman 57-772 1974 $50

WRIGHT, ROBERT MARR   Dodge City. (Wichita, 1913). Pictorial green cloth, frontispiece, first edition. Bradley 35-212 1974 $120

WRIGHT, S. FOWLER   The Throne of Saturn. Sauk City, 1949. 1st ed., ltd. Biblo & Tannen 210-696 1973 $18.50

WRIGHT, SOLOMON ALEXANDER   My Rambles as East Texas Cowboy, Hunter, Fisherman, Tie-cutter. Austin, 1942. Dec. cloth, fine, dust wrapper, first edition. Dykes 22-211 1973 $20

WRIGHT, T.   Life of William Cowper. 1892. Plates, new buckram. Allen 216-2000 1974 $17.50

WRIGHT, T.   Political Poems & Songs Relating to English History. 1859. 2 vols., 4to., half calf, ex-library. Allen 213-1879 1973 $25

WRIGHT, T.　　　　　　　Three Chapters Of Letters Relating to Suppression of Monasteries. 1843. New buckram. Allen 213-1331 1973 $12.50

WRIGHT, T.　　　　　　　Uriconium. 1872. Roy. 8vo., cloth, illus., frontispiece. Quaritch 939-536 1974 £8

WRIGHT, THOMAS　　　　The Anglo-Latin Satirical Poets and Epigrammatists of the 12th Century. 1872. Orig. half cloth. Howes 186-1183 1974 £5

WRIGHT, THOMAS　　　　The Female Vertuoso's. London, 1693. Small 4to., modern red half morocco, first edition. Dawsons PM 252-1085 1974 £175

WRIGHT, THOMAS　　　　The Homes of Other Days. 1871. 8vo., orig. cloth, foxing, covers worn. Bow Windows 66-758 1974 £5.25

WRIGHT, THOMAS　　　　Louthiana. 1748. 4to., contemporary calf, illus., plates, first edition. Bow Windows 64-764 1974 £55

WRIGHT, THOMAS　　　　Louthiana. London, 1748. 4to., contemporary half calf, gilt, first edition. Dawsons PM 251-84 1974 £60

WRIGHT, THOMAS　　　　Narratives of Sorcery and Magic. New York, 1852. Cloth. Hayman 57-773 1974 $15

WRIGHT, W.　　　　　　Grotesque Architecture. 1802. 8vo., orig. wrappers, plates, uncut, frontispiece, new edition. Quaritch 940-571 1974 £60

WRIGHT, W. B.　　　　　The Quanternary Ice Age. 1937. Plates, illus., maps. Smith 194-940 1974 £5

WRIGHT, W. B.　　　　　The Quaternary Ice Age. 1937. 8vo., cloth, plates, scarce. Wheldon 130-985 1974 £7.50

WRIGHT, W. P.　　　　　Cassell's Dictionary of Practical Gardening. n.d. 2 vols., 4to., plates, half contemporary morocco, gilt. Smith 193-27 1973 £12

WRIGHT, WILLIAM　　　The Brontes in Ireland. London, 1894. 8vo., half leather, gilt, third edition. Emerald 50-992 1974 £7.50

WRIGHT, WILLIAM　　　History of the Big Bonanza. Hartford - San Francisco, 1876. 8vo., orig. bindings, worn. Butterfield 8-336 1974 $35

WRIGHT, WILLIAM LORD　　Photoplay Writing. Falk, 1922. Austin 51-1061 1973 $10

WRIGLEY, M.　　　　　　Studies of Trees and Flowers. (1911). Roy 8vo., cloth. Wheldon 129-1033 1974 £7.50

WRIGLEY, M.　　　　　　Studies of Trees and Flowers. (1911). Roy. 8vo., cloth. Wheldon 131-1214 1974 £7.50

WRIGLEY'S Hotel Directory: Hotels, Resorts and Tours. Vancouver, 1930. Illus. Hood's 104-69 1974 $17.50

WRONG, GEORGE M.　　　Canada and the American Revolution. Toronto, 1935. Hood's 103-571 1974 $25

WRONG, GEORGE M.　　　The Canadians. New York, 1938. 1st ed., illus. Biblo & Tannen 213-21 1973 $10

WRONG, GEORGE M.　　　The Chronicles of Canada. Toronto, 1915-16. 32 vols., leather, excellent. Hood's 103-845 1974 $175

WRONG, GEORGE M.　　　The Fall of Canada. Oxford, 1914. Illus. Hood's 103-792 1974 $35

WRONG, GEORGE M.　　　Louisbourg in 1745. Toronto, 1897. Hood's 104-238 1974 $30

WRONG, GEORGE M.　　　The Rise and Fall of New France. New York, 1928. 2 vols., maps. Hood's 103-793 1974 $55

WROTH, LAWRENCE C.　　A History of Printing in Colonial Maryland. Baltimore, 1922. 4to., fine, cloth. Dawsons PM 10-659 1974 £50

WU, G. D.　　　　　　　Prehistoric Pottery in China. London, (1938). Crown 4to., illus., orig. cloth. Bow Windows 62-1019 1974 £10.50

WUNDERBAHRLICHER Bericht Von Einem Jueden aus Jerusalem Buertig. Leiden, 1645. Small 4to., paper wrappers. Schumann 499-117 1974 sFr 1,200

WUNDERLICH, C. A.　　　Geschichte der Medicin. Stuttgart, 1859. 8vo., old boards. Gurney 64-235 1974 £15

WUNDT, WILHELM MAX　　Essays. Leipzig, c. 1920. 8vo., orig. cloth. Howes 185-2047 1974 £5.50

WUNDT, WILHELM MAX　　Grundzuge der Physiologischen Psychologie. Leipzig, 1874. Large 8vo., contemporary half cloth, rare, first edition. Ximenes 35-604 1974 $700

WUNDT, WILHELM MAX　　Grundzuge der Physiologischen Psychologie. Leipzig, 1874. Large 8vo., contemporary half cloth, browned, first edition. Schafer 8-176 1973 sFr. 1,600

WUNDT, WILHELM MAX　　Grundzuge der Physiologischen Psychologie. Leipzig, 1874. 8vo., illus., contemporary half cloth, worn, very rare first edition. Gilhofer 61-59 1974 sFr. 2,500

WUORINEN, JOHN H.　　　The Finns on the Delaware. 1938. Map, orig. edition. Austin 57-711 1974 $10

WURALT, L. VON　　　　Die Zeitalter der Entdeckungen, der Renaissance und der Glaubenskaempfe. 1941. 4to., plates. Allen 213-1661 1973 $12.50

WURDZ, GIDEON　　　　The Foolish Dictionary. Grosset, Dunlap, 1904. n.p., illus. Austin 54-1075 1973 $7.50

WURSTISEN, CHRISTIAN　　Germaniaw Historicorum Illustrium. Frankfurt, 1585. Full contemporary blind-stamped pigskin, 2 vols. Dawson's 424-335 1974 $400

WYATT, MATTHEW DIGBY　　The Industrial Arts of the 19th Century. 1851-53. 2 vols. in 3, roy. folio, contemporary crimson morocco, good copy. Quaritch 940-487 1974 £400

WYATT, MATTHEW DIGBY　　Industrail Arts of the Nineteenth Century. 1851-53. Folio, 2 vols., half morocco, plates. Broadhurst 23-229 1974 £110

WYATT, THOMAS　　　　A Manual of Conchology. 1838. 8vo., orig. cloth, plates. Bow Windows 64-303 1974 £28

WYATT, W.　　　　　　Contributions to the Flora and Fauna of Repton. 1881. 8vo., cloth, scarce, second edition. Wheldon 129-318 1974 £5

WYCHE, RICHARD T.　　　Some Great Stories and How To Tell Them. Newson, 1912. Austin 51-1062 1973 $6

WYCHERLEY, WILLIAM　　Miscellany Poems. 1704. First edition, f'cap. folio, fine contemporary sprinkled calf, panelled back, raised bands, skifully rebacked, first issue, very fine unpressed copy. Broadhurst 24-961 1974 £220

WYCHERLEY, WILLIAM　　Miscellany Poems. London, 1704. Folio, fine, panelled calf, first edition. Dawsons PM 252-1086 1974 £300

WYCHERLEY, WILLIAM　　Works. London, 1713. 8vo., contemporary panelled calf, hinges worn, first collected edition. Goodspeed's 578-411 1974 $50

WYCHERLEY, WILLIAM　　The Complete Works. Soho, 1924. 4 vols., 4to., orig. buckram-backed boards, uncut, limited edition. Dawsons PM 252-1087 1974 £55

WYER, HENRY S.　　　　Nantucket in Picture and Verse. Nantucket, 1892. Boards, illus. Jenkins 61-1552 1974 $20

WYETH, N. C.　　　　　The Wyeths. Boston, 197-. Illus by the author. Dykes 24-56 1974 $17.50

WYETH, S. D.   Sacred History; The Earlies Republic in the
World. Philadelphia, (1863). Orig. cloth, 2 1/8 X 1 7/8. Gregory 44-487
1974 $30

WYLD, JAMES   A New General Atlas of Modern Geography.
(c., 1835). Large 4to., modern half calf, maps. Bow Windows 64-765 1974
£330

WYLIE, ELINOR   Angles and Earthly Creatures. New York,
1929. Orig. cloth, first edition, one of 200 numbered copies, fine, slightly
worn dust jacket, boxed. MacManus 224-484 1974 $27.50

WYLIE, ELINOR   Collected Poems. New York, 1932. Orig.
cloth backed boards, paper label, first edition, one of 210 numbered copies,
signed by editor, as new, slightly worn box. MacManus 224-485 1974 $35

WYLIE, ELINOR   Jennifer Lorn, A Sedate Extravaganza. 1924.
Dust wrapper, English first edition. Covent 56-1358 1974 £5.25

WYLIE, MAX   Best Broadcasts of 1939. McGraw, Hill, 1940.
Austin 51-1064 1973 $12.50

WYLIE, MAX   Radio Writing. 1939. 550p., illus. Austin
51-1063 1973 $10

WYLIE, PHILIP   Babes and Sucklings. Knopf, 1929. 300p.
Austin 54-1076 1973 $7.50

WYLIE, PHILIP   An Essay On Morals. Rinehart, 1947. 204p.
Austin 54-1077 1973 $6.50

WYLIE, PHILIP   The Innocent Ambassadors. Rinehart, 1957.
384p. Austin 54-1078 1973 $6.50

WYLIE, W. W.   Yellowstone National Park. Kansas City, 1882.
16mo., orig. bindings, illus. Butterfield 8-746 1974 $10

WYLLIE, BERTIE   Sheffield Plate. (1913). 8vo., plates, cloth.
Quaritch 940-692 1974 £5

WYNDHAM, GEORGE   Life and Letters. n.d. 2 vols. Allen
216-1763 1974 $12.50

WYNDHAM, HENRY P.   The Diary of the Late George Bubb
Dodington. London, 1809. 8vo., contemporary half calf, worn, fourth edition.
Bow Windows 62-264 1974 £7.50

WYNNE, WILLIAM   The Life of Sir Leoline Jenkins. 1724. 2 vols.,
folio, contemporary panelled calf, sole edition. Howes 186-961 1974 £65

WYON, FREDERICK W.   The History of Great Britain. 1876. 2 vols.,
cloth, rebound, scarce. Howes 186-1326 1974 £12.50

WYTFLIET, CORNELIUS   Histoire Universelle des Indes Occidentales et
Orientales. Douai, 1611. Small folio, contemporary limp vellum, maps, rare.
Harper 213-174 1974 $3000

XYZ

X, DR. JACOBUS, PSEUD. Untrodden Fields of Anthropology. New York, n.d. 2 vols. in 1. Rittenhouse 46-365 1974 $25

X, DR. JACOBUS, PSEUD. Untrodden Fields of Anthropology. Paris, 1896. 2 vols., three quarter crushed levant morocco gilt, very scarce, limited. Smith 193-784 1973 £15

XENIDES, J. P. The Greeks in America. Doran, n.d. 160p. Austin 62-699 1974 $12.50

XENOPHON The Whole Works of. London, 1831. 8vo., contemporary half roan, rubbed. Bow Windows 62-1020 1974 £6

XIMENES, LEONARDO I sei Primi Element i della Geometria Piana. Venice, 1752. 8vo., contemporary vellum, first ediion. Ximenes 35-611 1974 $300

XIMENES, LEONARDO Piano di Operazioni Idrauliche. (1782). 4to., contemporary half calf, rare. Zeitlin 235-244 1974 $150

XIMENES, LEONARDO Teoria e Pratica delle Resistenze. 1782. 4to., contemporary half mottled calf, gilt, rare, first edition. Zeitlin 235-245 1974 $150

Y CYMMRODOR. 1881-1928. 16 vols., illus., orig. wrappers. Howes 186-1853 1974 £12.50

YAIR, JAMES The Staple Contract. Edinburgh, 1776. 8vo., contemporary half calf. Dawsons PM 247-306 1974 £10

YALE UNIVERSITY The Edward B. Greene Collection of Engraved Portraits and Portrait Drawings at Yale University. New Haven, 1942. Roy. 4to., cloth, plates, limited. Quaritch 940-282 1974 £8

YAMASHINA, Y. A Natural History of Japanese Birds. Tokyo, 1933-41. Roy 8vo., 2 vols., orig. cloth. Wheldon 130-657 1974 £25

YANKOFF, PETER D. Peter Menikoff. Cokesbury, 1928. 294p. Austin 62-701 1974 $12.50

YARRELL, WILLIAM A History of British Birds. (1837-),1843-56. 8vo., 3 vols., calf. Wheldon 130-658 1974 £50

YARRELL, WILLIAM A History of British Birds. 1843. 3 vols., imp. 8vo., half green levant morocco, gilt, wood-engravings. Wheldon 131-137 1974 £195

YARRELL, WILLIAM A History of British Birds. 1843. First edition, 3 vols., contemporary full calf, panelled back, all edges gilt, wood engravings, fine. Broadhurst 24-1183 1974 £20

YARRELL, WILLIAM A History of British Birds. 1845. 3 vols., 8vo., orig. cloth, scarce, wood engravings, second edition. Wheldon 131-728 1974 £20

YARRELL, WILLIAM A History of British Birds. 1856. 3 vols., 8vo., orig. cloth, wood engravings, third edition. Wheldon 128-608 1973 £10

YARRELL, WILLIAM A History of British Birds. 1871-85. 4 vols., 8vo., orig. cloth, wood engravings, fourth edition. Wheldon 128-609 1973 £16

YARRELL, WILLIAM A History of British Birds. 1871-85. 4 vols., half red morocco, panelled backs, gilt tops, wood engravings, fourth edition. Wheldon 128-610 1973 £20

YARRELL, WILLIAM A History of British Fishes. 1836-39. 3 vols., 8vo., orig. cloth, woodcuts. Wheldon 131-777 1974 £20

YARRELL, WILLIAM A History of British Fishes. 1841. 2 vols., 8vo., orig. cloth, wood-engravings, second edition. Wheldon 128-664 1973 £12

YARRELL, WILLIAM A History of British Fishes. 1841. 2 vols., 8vo., contemporary full green morocco, gilt, wood engravings, second edition. Wheldon 131-779 1974 £25

YARRELL, WILLIAM On the Growth of the Salmon in Fresh Water. 1839. Oblong folio, orig. wrappers, plates, rare. Wheldon 131-778 1974 £30

YARRELL, WILLIAM On the Growth of the Salmon in Fresh Water. 1839. Oblong folio, orig. wrappers, scarce. Wheldon 130-720 1974 £30

YATES, EDMUND Mr. Thackeray, Mr. Yates, and the Garrick Club. (London), 1859. 8vo., old wrappers, first edition. Ximenes 35-612 1974 $125

YEATES, G. K. A Bird Lover's Britain. 1937. 4to., cloth, plates, scarce. Wheldon 129-551 1974 £5

YEATS, JOHN BUTLER Further Letters of. Dublin, 1920. Orig. cloth, first edition. Rota 188-953 1974 £30

YEATS, JOHN BUTLER Passages from the Letters of. Dundrum, 1917. 8vo., orig. quarter canvas, signed by author, limited edition. Bow Windows 66-159 1974 £60

YEATS, WILLIAM BUTLER The Abbey Row. Dublin, (1907). 4to., orig. dec. wrappers. Quaritch 936-596 1974 £40

YEATS, WILLIAM BUTLER Autobiographies. 1926. Orig. buckram, plates, first collected edition. Smith 194-547 1974 £5

YEATS, WILLIAM BUTLER Autobiographies. 1926. Buckram, fine, d.w., portraits, English first edition. Covent 56-1362 1974 £45

YEATS, WILLIAM BUTLER Autobiographies. 1926. Orig. cloth, illus., portrait, faded, first edition. Howes 186-546 1974 £12.50

YEATS, WILLIAM BUTLER Autobiographies. 1926. 8vo., orig. cloth, illus., first edition. Rota 189-982 1974 £6.50

YEATS, WILLIAM BUTLER Autobiographies. 1927. New edition. Austin 61-1095 1974 $12.50

YEATS, WILLIAM BUTLER Autobiographies: Reveries Over Childhood and Youth & The Trembling of the Veil. New York, 1927. Plates, very good copy, new edition. Covent 51-2054 1973 £8.40

YEATS, WILLIAM BUTLER Autobiographies: Reveries Over Childhood and Youth and the Trembling of the Veil. New York, 1927. Fine, orig. binding. Ross 86-480 1974 $45

YEATS, WILLIAM BUTLER A Book of Irish Verse. 1895. Nice copy. Covent 55-1567 1974 £12.50

YEATS, WILLIAM BUTLER A Book of Irish Verse. 1895. English first edition. Covent 56-1363 1974 £21

YEATS, WILLIAM BUTLER A Book of Irish Verse. London, 1900. 8vo., uncut, revised edition. Emerald 50-1008 1974 £5

YEATS, WILLIAM BUTLER The Bounty of Sweden. Dublin, 1925. Orig. binding, lacking d.w., some darkening, very good copy, one of 400 copies. Ross 87-588 1974 $75

YEATS, WILLIAM BUTLER The Bounty of Sweden. Dublin, 1925. 8vo., orig. linen backed boards, limited, first edition. Bow Windows 62-223 1974 £42

YEATS, WILLIAM BUTLER The Bounty of Sweden: A Meditation, and a Lecture Delivered Before the Royal Swedish Academy and Certain Notes. Dublin, 1925. Orig. cloth backed boards, paper label, first edition, one of 400 copies, fine. MacManus 224-486 1974 $100

YEATS, WILLIAM BUTLER The Cat and the Moon and Certain Other Poems. Dublin, 1924. One of 500 copies, unopened, lacking d.w., orig. binding. Ross 86-481 1974 $120

YEATS, WILLIAM BUTLER The Cat and the Moon and Certain Poems. Dublin, 1924. 4to., orig. boards, uncut, limited edition. Dawsons PM 252-1088 1974 £45

YEATS, WILLIAM BUTLER The Celtic Twilight. 1893. 8vo., orig. green cloth, first edition, first issue. Howes 185-565 1974 £50

YEATS, WILLIAM BUTLER   The Celtic Twilight. 1902. Orig. dec. cloth, portrait, English first edition.   Covent 56-1364 1974 £20

YEATS, WILLIAM BUTLER   The Countess Kathleen and Various Legends and Lyrics. 1892. 8vo., orig. parchment backed boards, spine and covers dull, first edition.   Bow Windows 66-761 1974 £50

YEATS, WILLIAM BUTLER   Cutting of an Agate. 1912. Top of spine missing, first edition.   Allen 216-896 1974 $15

YEATS, WILLIAM BUTLER   The Cutting of an Agate. 1919. Gilt, fine, English first edition.   Covent 56-1365 1974 £28

YEATS, WILLIAM BUTLER   The Cutting of an Agate. 1919. Cover stained, very good copy, first edition.   Covent 51-2056 1973 £8.40

YEATS, WILLIAM BUTLER   The Cutting of an Agate. 1919. Small 8vo., cloth, first edition.   Quaritch 936-588 1974 £15

YEATS, WILLIAM BUTLER   The Cutting of an Agate. 1919. 8vo., orig. cloth, dust wrapper, first edition.   Bow Windows 66-762 1974 £45

YEATS, WILLIAM BUTLER   The Death of Synge and Other Passages from an Old Diary. Dublin, 1928. Orig. binding, one of 400 copies, unopened, mint, orig. tissue wrapper.   Ross 87-592 1974 $120

YEATS, WILLIAM BUTLER   Dramatis Personae: 1896-1902. London, 1936. Frontis. portrait, near mint, d.w., orig. binding.   Ross 86-484 1974 $45

YEATS, WILLIAM BUTLER   Dramatis Personae. Dublin, 1935. 8vo., orig. linen backed boards, first edition.   Bow Windows 62-224 1974 £42

YEATS, WILLIAM BUTLER   Dramatis Personae. Dublin, 1935. 8vo., orig. cloth, fine, first edition.   Rota 189-984 1974 £50

YEATS, WILLIAM BUTLER   Dramatis Personae. Dublin, 1935. One of 400 copies, mint, orig. tissue wrapper.   Ross 86-483 1974 $135

YEATS, WILLIAM BUTLER   Dramatis Personae. 1936. Cloth backed boards, plates, English first edition.   Covent 56-1366 1974 £25

YEATS, WILLIAM BUTLER   Dramatis Personae. London, 1936. Orig. binding, first English collected edition, spine lightly soiled, very nice.   Ross 87-593 1974 $25

YEATS, WILLIAM BUTLER   Early Poems and Stories. 1925. Orig. cloth, first edition.   Rota 188-960 1974 £7.50

YEATS, WILLIAM BUTLER   Early Poems and Stories. 1925. First edition, orig. cloth, spine slightly faded.   Broadhurst 24-968 1974 £8

YEATS, WILLIAM BUTLER   Early Poems and Stories. 1925. Crown 8vo., orig. cloth, uncut, unopened, first edition.   Broadhurst 23-985 1974 £20

YEATS, WILLIAM BUTLER   Early Poems and Stories. 1925. Orig. cloth, faded, first edition.   Broadhurst 23-986 1974 £8

YEATS, WILLIAM BUTLER   Early Poems and Stories. London, 1925. 8vo., orig. cloth, faded.   Bow Windows 62-1021 1974 £18

YEATS, WILLIAM BUTLER   Early Poems and Stories. 1925. First edition, crown 8vo., uncut, unopened, mint, d.w., orig. cloth.   Broadhurst 24-967 1974 £20

YEATS, WILLIAM BUTLER   Early Poems and Stories. London, 1925. First edition, orig. binding, lacking d.w., fine.   Ross 87-594 1974 $65

YEATS, WILLIAM BUTLER   Early Poems and Stories. New York, 1925. 8vo., paper boards, blue cloth, signed, limited edition.   Emerald 50-1004 1974 £35

YEATS, WILLIAM BUTLER   Essays. London, 1924. 8vo., cloth boards. Emerald 50-1003 1974 £5

YEATS, WILLIAM BUTLER   Estrangement. Dublin, 1926. Orig. binding, first edition, one of 300 copies, lacking d.w., unopened, fine.   Ross 87-595 1974 $90

YEATS, WILLIAM BUTLER   Estrangement. Dublin, 1926. One of 300 copies, lacking d.w., unopened, fine.   Ross 86-487 1974 $95

YEATS, WILLIAM BUTLER   Estrangement: Being Some Fifty Thoughts from a Diary Kept by . . . in the Year 1909. Dublin, 1926. Orig. cloth backed boards, paper label, first edition, one of 300 copies, fine.   MacManus 224-487 1974 $100

YEATS, WILLIAM BUTLER   Fairy & Folk Tales of the Irish Peasantry. n.d. Orig. cloth.   Smith 193-800 1973 £8

YEATS, WILLIAM BUTLER   Fairy and Folk Tales of the Irish Peasantry. London, 1888. 8vo., dark blue cloth, label, first edition.   Emerald 50-998 1974 £20

YEATS, WILLIAM BUTLER   Fairy and Folk Tales of the Irish Peasantry. 1888. Small 8vo., orig. cloth, fine, first edition.   Quaritch 936-589 1974 £45

YEATS, WILLIAM BUTLER   Fairy anf Folk Tales of the Irish Peasantry. London, 1888. Crown 8vo., orig. cloth, first edition.   Hammond 201-346 1974 £40

YEATS, WILLIAM BUTLER   Fairy and Folk Tales of the Irish Peasantry. c. 1900. Crown 8vo., orig. green cloth gilt, early edition.   Howes 186-550 1974 £12

YEATS, WILLIAM BUTLER   The First Annual Volume of Beltaine. London, n.d. 8vo., orig. boards, fine, label, scarce.   Ximenes 35-613 1974 $175

YEATS, WILLIAM BUTLER   Florence Farr, Bernard Shaw and W. B. Yeats. Dublin, 1941. Orig. cloth, first edition.   Rota 188-963 1974 £35

YEATS, WILLIAM BUTLER   Four Years. Dundrum, 1921. Orig. cloth, first edition.   Rota 188-958 1974 £35

YEATS, WILLIAM BUTLER   Four Years. Dundrum, 1921. 8vo., orig. holland backed boards, illus., woodcut, first edition.   Bow Windows 62-220 1974 £40

YEATS, WILLIAM BUTLER   A Full Moon in March. 1935. Extra crown 8vo., orig. cloth, first edition.   Broadhurst 23-989 1974 £25

YEATS, WILLIAM BUTLER   A Full Moon in March. 1935. First edition, extra crown 8vo., mint, d.w., orig. cloth.   Broadhurst 24-970 1974 £25

YEATS, WILLIAM BUTLER   The Green Helment and Other Poems. New York, 1912. First American edition, owner's name in ink, lacking d.w., nice, orig. binding.   Ross 86-489 1974 $20

YEATS, WILLIAM BUTLER   The Herne's Egg. 1938. Orig. cloth, first edition.   Rota 188-962 1974 £10

YEATS, WILLIAM BUTLER   The Herne's Egg, and Other Plays. New York, 1938. First U. S. edition, fine, d.w.   Covent 51-2059 1973 £8.40

YEATS, WILLIAM BUTLER   If I Were Four-and-Twenty. Dublin, 1940. 8vo., orig. linen backed blue boards, woodcut, first edition.   Bow Windows 62-221 1974 £56

YEATS, WILLIAM BUTLER   If I Were Four and Twenty. Dublin, 1940. No. 12 of 450 copies, unopened, orig. binding, near mint, tissue wrapper.   Ross 87-597 1974 $110

YEATS, WILLIAM BUTLER   Irish Love Songs. 1902. First edition, f'cap. 8vo., boards, parchment spine, uncut, inscribed presentation copy, fine.   Broadhurst 24-963 1974 £20

YEATS, WILLIAM BUTLER   The King of the Great Clock Tower, Commentaries and Poems. Dublin, 1934. One of 400 copies, inscription, very good copy.   Covent 51-2060 1973 £40

YEATS, WILLIAM BUTLER   The Land of Hearts Desire. San Francisco, 1926. 8vo., cloth backed boards, limited edition.   Emerald 50-1005 1974 £25

YEATS, WILLIAM BUTLER   Last Poems and Plays. 1940. First edition, demy 8vo., mint, d.w., orig. cloth.   Broadhurst 24-971 1974 £15

YEATS, WILLIAM BUTLER   Later Poems. London, 1922. 8vo., orig. cloth, bookplate, inscriptions, first edition. Bow Windows 62-1022 1974 £35

YEATS, WILLIAM BUTLER   Later Poems. 1922. Spine faded, English first edition. Covent 56-1367 1974 £25

YEATS, WILLIAM BUTLER   Letters to the New Island. Cambridge, 1934. 8vo., orig. cloth, portrait, dust wrapper, first edition. Bow Windows 66-763 1974 £48

YEATS, WILLIAM BUTLER   Love's Bitter-Sweet. Dublin, 1925. 8vo., orig. linen backed boards, limited. Bow Windows 62-222 1974 £24

YEATS, WILLIAM BUTLER   Michael Robartes and the Dancer. Dundrum, 1920. Orig. cloth, first edition. Rota 188-957 1974 £32

YEATS, WILLIAM BUTLER   October Blast. Dublin, 1927. 8vo., orig. linen backed boards, limited, first edition. Bow Windows 62-225 1974 £42

YEATS, WILLIAM BUTLER   On the Boiler. Dublin, 1939. 4to., printed wrappers, mint. Ross 87-600 1974 $65

YEATS, WILLIAM BUTLER   On the Broiler. Dublin, (1939). Small 4to., wrappers, fine, first edition. Rota 189-985 1974 £15

YEATS, WILLIAM BUTLER   The Oxford Book of Modern Verse, 1892-1935. Oxford, 1936. First issue, bookplate, fine, orig. binding. Ross 86-491 1974 $40

YEATS, WILLIAM BUTLER   The Oxford Book of Modern Verse. 1936. Orig. cloth, bookplate, faded, first edition. Rota 188-965 1974 £5

YEATS, WILLIAM BUTLER   The Oxford Book of Modern Verse. 1936. Orig. cloth, faded, fine, first edition. Rota 188-966 1974 £7.50

YEATS, WILLIAM BUTLER   A Packet for Ezra Pound. Dublin, 1929. Orig. linen backed boards, label, fine. Howes 186-547 1974 £35

YEATS, WILLIAM BUTLER   Pages from a Diary. Dublin, 1944. 8vo., orig. quarter canvas, limited edition. Bow Windows 66-160 1974 £45

YEATS, WILLIAM BUTLER   Per Amica Silentia Lunae. 1918. Inscribed, English first edition. Covent 56-1368 1974 £55

YEATS, WILLIAM BUTLER   Per Amica Silentia Lunae. 1918. Gilt dec. cover, English first edition. Covent 56-1369 1974 £15

YEATS, WILLIAM BUTLER   Per Amica Silentia Lunae. 1918. Orig. cloth, faded, first edition. Rota 188-955 1974 £22

YEATS, WILLIAM BUTLER   Per Amica Silentia Lunae. London, 1918. Review copy, first edition, orig. binding, slightly torn d.w., fine. Ross 86-492 1974 $70

YEATS, WILLIAM BUTLER   Plays and Controversies. 1923. Inscribed, very good copy perserved in specially made new slip case, some pencil annotations, hinges weak, first edition. Covent 51-2062 1973 £42.50

YEATS, WILLIAM BUTLER   Plays for an Irish Theatre. London, 1911. 8vo., buckram backed boards, rubbed. Emerald 50-1001 1974 £20

YEATS, WILLIAM BUTLER   Plays for an Irish Theatre. 1911. Cloth backed boards, English first edition. Covent 56-1370 1974 £35

YEATS, WILLIAM BUTLER   Plays for an Irish Theatre. London and Stratford-upon-Avon, 1911. First edition, drawings, specially bound green patterned boards and three quarter dark green calf & corners, nice copy. Ross 86-493 1974 $65

YEATS, WILLIAM BUTLER   Plays for an Irish Theatre. London and Stratford-upon-Avon, 1911. First edition, drawings, specially bound in green patterned boards and three quarter dark green calf and corners, dust-stained and somewhat spotted, fine. Ross 87-601 1974 $65

YEATS, WILLIAM BUTLER   Poems. 1899. Orig. cloth worn, second English edition. Rota 188-954 1974 £8

YEATS, WILLIAM BUTLER   Poems. 1904. 8vo., orig. cloth gilt, fourth English edition. Quaritch 936-586 1974 £15

YEATS, WILLIAM BUTLER   Poems. London, 1908. 8vo., dec. cloth, gilt, rubbed. Emerald 50-1000 1974 £10

YEATS, WILLIAM BUTLER   Poems. London, (1913). 8vo., portrait, orig. cloth, gilt, uncut. Bow Windows 62-1023 1974 £6

YEATS, WILLIAM BUTLER   Poems. (1924). 8vo., orig. cloth, portrait. Bow Windows 64-767 1974 £5.50

YEATS, WILLIAM BUTLER   The Poems of William Blake. 1893. 12mo., gilt pictorial cloth, gilt, first edition. Quaritch 936-587 1974 £7

YEATS, WILLIAM BUTLER   The Poems of William Blake. 1893. Post 8vo., vellum, uncut, scarce, first edition. Broadhurst 23-980 1974 £60

YEATS, WILLIAM BUTLER   The Poems of William Blake. 1893. 8vo., quarter vellum, orig. cloth, rare, first edition. Rota 189-989 1974 £65

YEATS, WILLIAM BUTLER   Responsibilities. Churchtown, 1914. 8vo., orig. linen backed boards, first edition. Bow Windows 62-226 1974 £55

YEATS, WILLIAM BUTLER   Responsibilities and Other Poems. 1916. First edition, crown 8vo., orig. cloth, fine. Broadhurst 24-966 1974 £16

YEATS, WILLIAM BUTLER   Responsibilities. 1916. English first edition. Covent 56-1374 1974 £32.50

YEATS, WILLIAM BUTLER   Responsibilities and Other Poems. 1916. Crown 8vo., orig. cloth, first edition. Broadhurst 23-983 1974 £17

YEATS, WILLIAM BUTLER   Responsibilities and Other Poems. 1916. 8vo., orig. cloth, first edition. Rota 189-981 1974 £20

YEATS, WILLIAM BUTLER   Responsibilities and Other Poems. 1916. Small 8vo., orig. cloth, gilt, first edition. Quaritch 936-590 1974 £25

YEATS, WILLIAM BUTLER   Responsibilities: Poems and a Play. Dundrum, 1914. First edition, demy 8vo., boards, linen spine, uncut, one of 400 copies, fine. Broadhurst 24-965 1974 £45

YEATS, WILLIAM BUTLER   Reveries Over Childhood and Youth. London, 1916. 8vo., stains, frontispiece. Emerald 50-1002 1974 £6

YEATS, WILLIAM BUTLER   Reveries Over Childhood and Youth. 1916. Small 8vo., cloth, portraits, first published edition. Quaritch 936-591 1974 £20

YEATS, WILLIAM BUTLER   The Second Book of the Rhymers' Club. 1894. Square small 8vo., orig. cloth, first edition. Quaritch 936-592 1974 £50

YEATS, WILLIAM BUTLER   The Secret Rose. London, 1897. 8vo., illus., dec. cloth, rubbed. Emerald 50-999 1974 £20

YEATS, WILLIAM BUTLER   The Secret Rose. New York, 1897. Orig. dec. cloth gilt, plates, first U.S. edition. Covent 56-1375 1974 £32.50

YEATS, WILLIAM BUTLER   The Secret Rose. 1897. 8vo., orig. cloth, illus., first edition. Rota 189-979 1974 £50

YEATS, WILLIAM BUTLER   Selected Poems. 1929. Dec. cloth, d.w., English first edition. Covent 56-1376 1974 £35

YEATS, WILLIAM BUTLER   Seven Poems and a Fragment. Dundrum, 1922. Orig. cloth, first edition. Rota 188-959 1974 £35

YEATS, WILLIAM BUTLER   The Shadow Waters. 1900. First edition, f'cap. 4to., very good copy, orig. cloth. Broadhurst 24-962 1974 £30

YEATS, WILLIAM BUTLER   The Shadow Waters. 1900. 4to., orig. cloth, first edition. Broadhurst 23-981 1974 £30

YEATS, WILLIAM BUTLER   The Shadowy Waters. 1900. Roy. 8vo., orig. cloth gilt, first edition. Howes 185-566 1974 £35

YEATS, WILLIAM BUTLER   The Shadowy Waters.   London, 1900. 8vo.,
orig. dark blue ribbed cloth, gilt, uncut, first edition.   Bow Windows 62-1039
1974 £50

YEATS, WILLIAM BUTLER   The Shadowy Waters.   1907. Wrappers, first
Acting edition.   Covent 56-2147 1974 £15.75

YEATS, WILLIAM BUTLER   The Shadowy Waters.   1907. First Acting
edition, very good copy in wrappers.   Covent 51-2063 1973 £8.50

YEATS, WILLIAM BUTLER   The Shadowy Waters.   1911. Second edition,
back faded, very good copy.   Covent 51-2064 1973 £6

YEATS, WILLIAM BUTLER   Stories from Carleton. n.d. 8vo., dark green
cloth, first edition.   Rota 189-990 1974 £7.50

YEATS, WILLIAM BUTLER   Stories of Red Hanrahan.   Dundrum, 1904.
Linen backed boards, English first edition.   Covent 56-1377 1974 £85

YEATS, WILLIAM BUTLER   Stories of Red Hanrahan.   Dundrum, 1904.
8vo., orig. cloth, first edition.   Rota 189-980 1974 £45

YEATS, WILLIAM BUTLER   Stories of Red Hanrahan and the Secret Rose.
1927. 8vo., red cloth, illus., plates, first edition.   Bow Windows 66-765
1974 £25

YEATS, WILLIAM BUTLER   Stories of Red Hanrahan and the Secret Rose.
1927. Orig. pictorial cloth gilt, English first edition.   Covent 56-1378 1974 £21

YEATS, WILLIAM BUTLER   The Tables of the Law, and the Adoration of the
Magi. Stratford, 1914. No. 107 of 510 copies, second published edition, near
mint, unopened.   Ross 86-494 1974 $20

YEATS, WILLIAM BUTLER   Three Things.   London, n.d. (1929). Drawings,
mint, orig. binding.   Ross 86-496 1974 $7.50

YEATS, WILLIAM BUTLER   Three Things.   1929. 8vo., boards, signed,
limited edition.   Quaritch 936-593 1974 £18

YEATS, WILLIAM BUTLER   A Vision.   1925. 8vo., boards, parchment back,
fine, dust wrapper, plates, signed, limited, first edition.   Quaritch 936-594 1974
£70

YEATS, WILLIAM BUTLER   A Vision.   1937. Orig. buckram backed
designed boards, plates.   Smith 193-425 1973 £8.50

YEATS, WILLIAM BUTLER   The Wanderings of Oisin and Other Poems.   1889.
8vo., orig. cloth, rare, first edition, first issue.   Rota 189-978 1974 £250

YEATS, WILLIAM BUTLER   The Well of the Saints.   London, 1905.
Small 8vo., orig. cloth-backed boards, first edition.   Bow Windows 62-1024
1974 £27.50

YEATS, WILLIAM BUTLER   Wheels and Butterflies.   1934. Crown 8vo., orig.
cloth, first edition.   Broadhurst 23-988 1974 £14

YEATS, WILLIAM BUTLER   Wheels and Butterflies.   1934. First edition,
crown 8vo., orig. cloth, fine.   Broadhurst 24-969 1974 £14

YEATS, WILLIAM BUTLER   Wheels and Butterflies.   1934. Orig. cloth,
scarce, first edition.   Rota 188-961 1974 £15

YEATS, WILLIAM BUTLER   Wheels and Butterflies.   1934. Crown 8vo.,
dust wrapper, fine.   Howes 186-549 1974 £22.50

YEATS, WILLIAM BUTLER   Wheels and Butterflies.   New York, 1935.
Dust wrapper, first U.S. edition.   Covent 56-2148 1974 £17.50

YEATS, WILLIAM BUTLER   Where There Is Nothing.   1903. Small 8vo.,
boards, first English edition.   Quaritch 936-595 1974 £15

YEATS, WILLIAM BUTLER   Where There is Nothing.   New York, 1903.
Orig. parchment paper wrappers, first American public edition, one of 100
numbered copies on Japanese vellum, dust jacket, fine.   MacManus 224-488
1974 $110

YEATS, WILLIAM BUTLER   The Wild Swans at Coole.   1919. Faded,
English first edition.   Covent 56-1380 1974 £20

YEATS, WILLIAM BUTLER   The Wild Swans at Coole.   1919. Orig. cloth,
bookplate, first edition.   Rota 188-956 1974 £25

YEATS, WILLIAM BUTLER   The Winding Stair.   New York, 1929. Cloth
gilt, labels, English first edition.   Covent 56-1381 1974 £75

YEATS, WILLIAM BUTLER   The Winding Stair and Other Poems.   1933. Orig.
dec. cloth, fine, English first edition.   Covent 56-1382 1974 £35

YEATS, WILLIAM BUTLER   The Winding Stair and Other Poems.   1933.
8vo., orig. cloth.   Bow Windows 64-768 1974 £6

YEATS, WILLIAM BUTLER   The Winding Stair and Other Poems.   London,
1933. 8vo., orig. cloth, first edition.   Bow Windows 62-1025 1974 £18.50

YEATS, WILLIAM BUTLER   The Winding Stair and Other Poems.   London,
1933. First English edition, inscription in ink, owner's name on title pages, good
copy.   Ross 86-495 1974 $55

YEATS, WILLIAM BUTLER   The Winding Stair and Other Poems.   London,
1933. First English edition, orig. binding, fine, d.w., light pencilling in margins.
Ross 87-604 1974 $60

YEATS, WILLIAM BUTLER   Poems.   1904. Orig. full dec. cloth gilt,
portrait, signed, English first edition.   Covent 56-1371 1974 £65

YEATS, WILLIAM BUTLER   Poems.   1906. Dec. gilt spine, fine, English
first edition.   Covent 56-1373 1974 £35

YEATS, WILLIAM BUTLER   Collected Works in Verse and Prose.   1908.
8 vols., demy 8vo., parchment spines, top edges gilt, others uncut, mint, limited
to 1060 copies.   Broadhurst 24-964 1974 £220

YEATS, WILLIAM BUTLER   The Collected Works.   London, 1908. 8 vols.,
quarter vellum, one of 250 sets of the 1060 printed which were taken over by
Chapman & Hall, with their imprint at foot of title page, fine to near mint, scarce,
covers unwarped.   Ross 86-482 1974 $750

YEATS, WILLIAM BUTLER   The Collected Works.   Stratford-on-Avon,
1908. 8 vols., large 8vo., orig. quarter parchment, uncut, fine.   Dawsons PM
252-1089 1974 £340

YEATS, WILLIAM BUTLER   Collected Works in Verse and Prose.   1908.
8vo., 8 vols., parchment spines, uncut, mint.   Broadhurst 23-982 1974 £250

YEATS, WILLIAM BUTLER   Collected Works.   Stratford, 1908. 8vo., 8
vols., cloth, gilt, fine.   Quaritch 936-585 1974 £300

YEATS, WILLIAM BUTLER   Poems.   1909. Frontis., portrait, English first
edition.   Covent 56-1372 1974 £35

YEATS, WILLIAM BUTLER   The Collected Poems.   1933. Crown 8vo., orig.
cloth, faded, first edition.   Broadhurst 23-987 1974 £8

YEATS, WILLIAM BUTLER   The Collected Poems Of.   1939. 8vo., orig.
cloth.   Bow Windows 64-766 1974 £4.50

YECHIEL BEN YEKHTIEL   Ma'lot Ha'midot.   Cremona, 1556. First
edition, cloth backed boards, sound copy.   Thomas 32-64 1974 £300

YEDAIAH BEN ABRAHAM OF BEZIERS   Bechinot Olam.   Grodno, 1798. Cloth
backed boards, lacks last leaf, some margins cut close.   Thomas 32-61 1974 £20

YEDAIAH BEN ABRAHAM OF BEZIERS   Bechinot Olam.   Warsaw, 1884. Calf
backed boards.   Thomas 32-62 1974 £8

YEIGH, F.   Ontario's Parliament Buildings.   Toronto,
1893. Illus.   Hood's 103-696 1974 $10

THE YELLOW Book.   1894. Illus., darkened spine.   Rota 188-536 1974
£5

THE YELLOW Book, Vol. 1, April, 1894. Small 4to., illus., orig. yellow buckram. Smith 193-426 1973 £7

THE YELLOW Book, Vol. 2, July, 1894. Small 4to., illus., orig. yellow buckram. Smith 193-427 1973 £7

YELLOWSTONE in Photo Color. St. Paul, c. 1918. Color photographs in folder. Jenkins 61-2720 1974 $15

YEMENIZ, N.			Catalogue de la Bibliotheque de M. N. Yemeniz. Paris, 1867. Large 8vo., cloth, orig. wrappers. Dawsons PM 10-661 1974 £28

YEOMAN, THOMAS			The Report of . . . Drainage of the North Level of the Fens. (1769). 4to., orig. wrappers, first edition. Hammond 201-852 1974 £18

YERKES, R. M.			Almost Human. (1925). 8vo., cloth, illus. Wheldon 129-407 1974 £5

YERKES, R. M.			A Collection of 17 Zoological Papers. 1899-1914. 8vo., cloth. Wheldon 129-355 1974 £7.50

YETTS, W. P.			The George Eumorfopoulos Collection, Catalogue of the Chinese and Corean Bronzes, Sculpture, Jades, Jewellery and Miscellaneous Objects. 1932. Folio, plates, cloth, good copy, limited edition. Quaritch 940-389 1974 £50

YEZIERSKA, ANZIA			Arrogant Begger. 1927. 279 pages. Austin 57-716 1974 $12.50

YEZIERSKA, ANZIA			Arrogant Beggar. Doubleday, Doran, 1927. Austin 62-704 1974 $12.50

YEZIERSKA, ANZIA			Bread Givers. 1925. 297 pages. Austin 57-717 1974 $12.50

YEZIERSKA, ANZIA			Bread Givers. Doubleday, 1925. 297p., limited 1st ed. (500 copies), signed by author. Austin 62-705 1974 $17.50

YOKOHAMA Guide Book. (Yokohama, 1908). Orig. binding, illus., English and Japanese text. Wilson 63-607 1974 $12.50

YONGE, CHARLOTTE MARY		The Dove in the Eagle's Nest. London, 1866. 2 vols., 8vo., orig. cloth, first edition. Ximenes 35-614 1974 $25

YONGE, CHARLOTTE MARY		The Heir of Redclyffe. London, 1897. 8vo., illus., orig. cloth, foxing, signature. Bow Windows 62-1026 1974 £5.75

YONGE, CHARLOTTE MARY		History of Christian Names. London, 1863. 2 vols., first edition. Austin 61-1099 1974 $37.50

YONGE, CHARLOTTE MARY		History of Christian Names. 1863. 2 vols., half contemporary green morocco gilt, foxed. Smith 194-549 1974 £6

YONGE, CHARLOTTE MARY		The Lances of Lynwood. London, 1855. 8vo., orig. cloth, plates, first edition. Ximenes 35-615 1974 $35

YONGE, CHARLOTTE MARY		Womankind. London, 1877. Orig. green cloth, gilt. Dawson's 424-349 1974 $25

YONGE, NORMAN B.			The Still Small Voice. London, 1860. 8vo., orig. blue cloth, first edition. Ximenes 35-616 1974 $12.50

YORICK, PSEUD.
Please turn to
STERNE, LAURENCE

YORKE, PHILIP			The Royal Tribes of Wales. Wrexham, 1799. 4to., contemporary calf, rebacked, foxing and stains, frontispiece, plates. Bow Windows 66-766 1974 £14

YORKE, PHILIP			The Royal Tribes of Wales. Wrexham, 1799. 4to., contemporary tree calf gilt. Quaritch 939-703 1974 £40

YORKE, PHILIP			The Royal Tribes of Wales. 1799 and 1802. 4to., contemporary half morocco, boards. Broadhurst 23-1605 1974 £40

YORKE, PHILIP			The Royal Tribes of Wales to Which is Added an Account of the Fifteen Tribes of North Wales. Liverpool, 1887. Demy 4to., portraits, orig. cloth, fine. Broadhurst 24-1571 1974 £15

YOUNG, A. H.			The Parish Register of Kingston, Upper Canada, 1785-1811. Kingson, 1921. Maps, illus. Hood's 103-697 1974 $20

YOUNG, A. H.			The War Book of Upper Canada College, Toronto. Toronto, 1923. Illus. Hood's 104-142 1974 $27.50

YOUNG, ALFRED			Catholic and Protestant Countries Compared. 1845. Austin 62-708 1974 $8.50

YOUNG, ANDREW			Thirty One Poems. 1922. One of 200 copies, fine, unopened. Covent 51-2075 1973 £10

YOUNG, ARTHUR			Annals of Agriculture and Other Useful Arts. 1784-92. 17 vols., 8vo., calf backs. Quaritch 939-294 1974 £45

YOUNG, ARTHUR			Annals of Agriculture. 1790-92. 8vo., plates, contemporary speckled calf, first edition. Dawsons PM 247-311 1974 £120

YOUNG, ARTHUR			Autobiography, With Selections from His Correspondence. 1898. Plates, new buckram. Allen 216-2085 1974 $12.50

YOUNG, ARTHUR			A Course of Experimental Agriculture. London, 1770. 2 vols., 4to., contemporary calf, first edition. Dawsons PM 247-309 1974 £95

YOUNG, ARTHUR			The Expediency of a Free Exportation of Corn. London, 1770. 8vo., disbound, first edition. Ximenes 35-617 1974 $40

YOUNG, ARTHUR			The Farmer's Calender. 1805. 8vo., plates, contemporary calf, sixth edition. Wheldon 131-1801 1974 £20

YOUNG, ARTHUR			The Farmer's Tour through the East of England. London, 1771. 8vo., 4 vols., contemporary calf, gilt, plates, first edition. Hammond 201-58 1974 £145

YOUNG, ARTHUR			The Farmer's Calendar. 1805. 8vo., contemporary calf, plates. Wheldon 129-1679 1974 £20

YOUNG, ARTHUR			Letters Concerning the Present State of the French Nation. London, 1769. 8vo., contemporary calf, first edition. Dawsons PM 247-308 1974 £65

YOUNG, ARTHUR			Rural Oeconomy. 1770. 8vo., contemporary calf, gilt, first edition. Hammond 201-59 1974 £65

YOUNG, ARTHUR			Rural Oeconomy. London, 1770. 8vo., contemporary calf, first edition. Dawsons PM 247-310 1974 £80

YOUNG, ARTHUR			Rural Oeconomy. 1773. Contemporary calf, rubbed, second edition. Howes 186-1613 1974 £38

YOUNG, ARTHUR			A Six Months Tour Through the North of England. Dublin, 1770. 3 vols., 8vo., plates, contemporary calf. Quaritch 939-295 1974 £50

YOUNG, ARTHUR			Six Months Tour Through the North of England. 1770. Engraved plates, first edition, 4 vols., 8vo., full contemporary, raised bands, leather title labels, vol. 1 uniformly rebacked, complete with ads at end of vol. 1. Broadhurst 24-1572 1974 £72

YOUNG, ARTHUR			A Six Months Tour Through the North of England. London, 1771. 4 vols., 8vo., contemporary sprinkled calf, plates, worn, second edition. Traylen 79-312 1973 £48

YOUNG, ARTHUR			A Six Weeks Tour. London, 1768. 8vo., illus., contemporary calf, first edition. Dawsons PM 247-307 1974 £90

YOUNG, ARTHUR			A Six Weeks Tour. London, 1768. 8vo., illus., contemporary calf, signatures, first edition. Dawsons PM 250-85 1974 £90

YOUNG, ARTHUR			A Tour in Ireland. 1780. 2 vols., plates, contemporary calf backed boards, morocco labels, second edition. Howes 186-1614 1974 £42

YOUNG, ARTHUR   Travels, During the Years 1787, 1788, 1789. 1792-94. 2 vols., 4to., contemporary calf gilt, first & second editions. Dawsons PM 247-312 1974 £90

YOUNG, BARBARA   This Man from Lebanon. New York, 1945. 1st ed.   Biblo & Tannen 210-729 1973 $10

YOUNG, BESS M.   Animals We Know. New York, 1927. 16mo. Frohnsdorff 16-53 1974 $7.50

YOUNG, DAL   Apologia Pro Oscar Wilde. (1895). Wrappers, English first edition. Covent 56-1335 1974 £12.60

YOUNG, DAL   Apologia Pro Oscar Wilde. (1895). Wrappers, English first edition. Covent 56-2125 1974 £12.50

YOUNG, DONALD   American Minority Peoples. 1932. 621 pages. Austin 57-719 1974 $12.50

YOUNG, DONALD   American Minority Peoples. Harper, 1932. Austin 62-707 1974 $12.50

YOUNG, E.   The Centaur not Fabulous. 1755. 8vo., contemporary calf, rebacked, frontispiece, first edition.   Quaritch 936-264 1974 £50

YOUNG, E. HILTON   A Bird in the Bush. 1936. 4to., plates, illus., English first edition. Covent 56-1841 1974 £25

YOUNG, EDWARD   The Complaint. Hartford, 1824. Old calf. Biblo & Tannen 213-836 1973 $10

YOUNG, EDWARD   Conjectures on Original Composition. London, 1759. 8vo., disbound, scarce, second edition.   Ximenes 35-618 1974 $100

YOUNG, EDWARD   Night Thoughts, on Life, Death, and Immortality. London, 1801. Small 8vo., contemporary blue straight-grained morocco, gilt, fine, plates.   Hammond 201-347 1974 £10

YOUNG, EDWARD   A Poem on the Last Day. Oxford, 1713. 8vo., disbound, first edition.   Dawsons PM 252-1090 1974 £45

YOUNG, EDWARD   The Universal Passion. London, 1725. Folio, disbound, first edition. Ximenes 35-619 1974 $90

YOUNG, FILSON   Christopher Columbus and the New World of His Discovery. London, 1906. 2 vols., foxed. Jenkins 61-570 1974 $10

YOUNG, FILSON   Letters from Solitude. London, 1912. 8vo., orig. cloth, inscribed, first edition. Dawsons PM 252-1091 1974 £15

YOUNG, FILSON   With the Battle Cruisers. 1921. Thick roy. 8vo., illus., frontispiece. Howes 186-1775 1974 £5

YOUNG, FRANK H.   Technique of Advertising Layout. New York, 1947. 4to.   Biblo & Tannen 210-4 1973 $12.50

YOUNG, G. A.   A Descriptive Sketch of the Geology, and Economic Minerals of Canada. Ottawa, 1909. Plates, maps, ex-library. Hood's 103-389 1974 $10

YOUNG, G. A.   Geology and Economic Minerals of Canada. Ottawa, 1926. Illus., maps.   Hood's 104-461 1974 $15

YOUNG, G. F.   The Medici.   New York, 1923. 8vo., 2 vols., orig. cloth.   Broadhurst 23-230 1974 £8

YOUNG, GEORGE   Extracts from a Geological Survey of the Yorkshire Coast.   (c., 1840). Small 4to., contemporary straight-grained morocco, rebacked, gilt.   Hammond 201-397 1974 £50

YOUNG, GEORGE   A Geological Survey of the Yorkshire Coast. Whitby, 1822. 4to., calf back, plates. Wheldon 129-879 1974 £50

YOUNG, GEORGE   A Geological Survey of the Yorkshire Coast. Whitby, 1822. 4to., rebound in boards, calf antique back, plates, rare, first edition. Wheldon 131-1100 1974 £50

YOUNG, GEORGE   A Geological Survey of the Yorkshire Coast. 1822. 4to., orig. boards, plates, first edition.   Hammond 201-398 1974 £55

YOUNG, GEORGE   A History of Whitby and Streoneshalh Abbey. Whitby, 1817. 2 vols., 8vo., contemporary half calf, plates, folding map, rubbed.   Bow Windows 66-767 1974 £55

YOUNG, H. H.   Conversations Between the Rabbi of the Boarding House.   St. Paul, 1893.   Austin 57-720 1974 $17.50

YOUNG, HARRY   Hard Knocks. Portland, 1915. Brown cloth, marbled boards, illus., scarce, inscription. Bradley 35-416 1974 $80

YOUNG, HUGH H.   Young's Practice of Urology.   Philadelphia, 1926. 2 vols.   Rittenhouse 46-672 1974 $35

YOUNG, J.   The Origin of the Ocean Mail Steamers Between Liverpool and the St. Lawrence and the Advantages of the Northern Route. Montreal, 1877. Paper cover.   Hood's 102-788 1974 $40

YOUNG, J. R.   An Elementary Treatise on Algebra.   1839. 8vo., contemporary sheep. Bow Windows 64-770 1974 £6

YOUNG, J. R.   On the Theory and Solution of Algebraical Equations.   1835. 8vo., contemporary sheep.   Bow Windows 64-771 1974 £5.75

YOUNG, JOHN C.   An Address Delivered Before the Union Literary Soc. of Miami University at Its 13th Annual Celebration, August 8, 1838. Oxford, 1838.   Orig. yellow print. wrapper.   Wilson 63-145 1974 $10

YOUNG, MARIA JULIA   Memoirs of Mrs. Crouch. 1806. Small 8vo., 2 vols., half green morocco, gilt.   Quaritch 936-598 1974 £35

YOUNG, MARIA JULIA   Memoirs of Mrs. Crouch. London, 1806. 2 vols., 12mo., orig. boards, scarce, first edition. Ximenes 35-620 1974 $125

YOUNG, MURDO   Antonia. 1818. Small 8vo., orig. boards, first edition.   Quaritch 936-599 1974 £55

YOUNG, ROBERT   The Poetical Works of.   Londonderry, 1863. 8vo., cloth boards. Emerald 50-1012 1974 £5

YOUNG, ROBERT M.   Belfast and the Province of Ulster.   Brighton, 1909. 4to., illus., roan backed linen boards. Emerald 50-1015 1974 £22

YOUNG, ROBERT M.   Historical Notices of Old Belfast.   Belfast, 1896. 4to., illus., frontispiece.   Emerald 50-1014 1974 £7.50

YOUNG, ROBERT M.   The Town Book of the Corporation of Belfast. Belfast, 1892. 8vo., cloth boards.   Emerald 50-1013 1974 £10

YOUNG, ROLAND   Thorne Smith, His Life and Times. Doubleday, Doran, 1934. 32p., illus., paper.   Austin 54-960 1973 $12.50

YOUNG, THOMAS   A Course of Lectures on Natural Philosophy and the Mechanical Arts. London, 1807. 2 vols., 4to., contemporary half calf, plates, fine, very rare first edition.   Gilhofer 61-30 1974 sFr. 4,400

YOUNG, THOMAS   An Essay on Humanity to Animals.   London, 1822. 8vo., orig. wrappers, fine, third edition.   Ximenes 35-621 1974 $27.50

YOUNG, WILLIAM P.   A Ford Dealer's Twenty Year Ride, the Joy Ride, the Sleigh Ride and Rough Ride . . . From Company Profits to Dealer Losses. N. P., 1932. Orig. binding.   Butterfield 10-75 1974 $15

THE YOUNG Christian's Pocket Book.   London, 1857.   Orig. black stamped olive cloth, 2 3/4 X 2 1/4.   Gregory 44-488 1974 $18.50

THE YOUNG WOMAN'S Companion.   Manchester, 1811. 8vo., contemporary calf, plates, first edition.   Hammond 201-177 1974 £35

YOUNGMAN, W. E.   Gleanings from Western Prairies.   Cambridge, 1882.   Blue cloth, illus., first edition.   Bradley 35-417 1974 $40

THE YOUTH of Shakespeare. 1839. 3 vols. Austin 51-855 1973 $17.50

YUILLE, ROBERT   Short Mongolian Grammar. (Selenginsk, 1838).
Contemporary printed boards, 4to., orig. edition. Kraus B8-415 1974 $675

YULE, HENRY   The Book of Sir Marco Polo. 1875. 2 vols.,
med. 8vo., best edition, illus., orig. cloth, fine. Broadhurst 24-1704 1974 £22

YZENDOORN, REGINALD   History of the Catholic Mission in the Hawaiian
Islands. Honolulu, 1927. 8vo., cloth. Saddleback 14-355 1974 $25

ZABRISKIE, GEORGE A.   A Little About Washington Irving. 1945.
Dec. cloth, dec. end sheets, illus., fine first separate edition. Dykes 22-130
1973 $12.50

ZABRISKIE, GEORGE A.   A Little About Washington Irving. 1945.
Illus., lst ed. Dykes 24-72 1974 $12.50

ZABRISKIE, GEORGE A.   Ships' Figureheads in and about New York.
'946. Illus., lst ed. Dykes 24-73 1974 $17.50

ZACCHIAS, PAOLO   De Mali Hipochondriaci. Rome, 1639. 8vo.,
old limp vellum, first edition. Gurney 64-236 1974 £75

ZACCHIAS, PAOLO   Quaestiones Medico-Legales. 1657. Folio,
old calf. Gurney 64-237 1974 £50

ZACCONE, PIERRE   Nouveau Langage des Fleurs. Paris, 1856.
Orig. yellow wrappers, color plates, 8vo. Gregory 44-323 1974 $20

ZAHALON, JACOB   Ozar Ha-Hayyimm. 1683. Small folio, orig.
paper boards, worn. Dawsons PM 249-521 1974 £320

ZAHN, JOHANNES   Specula Physico-Mathematico-Historica.
Nuremberg, 1696. 3 vols. in 2, folio, plates, contemporary blind stamped
pigskin, fine. Traylen 79-282 1973 £235

ZAMOYSKI, JAN   Oratio. Paris, 1573. 4to., marbled boards,
red morocco back, rare, fine, first and only edition. Harper 213-175 1973
$525

ZAMOYSKI, JAN   De Senatu Romano Libri duo. Venice, 1563.
4to., marbled boards, red morocco back, fine, very rare, first edition. Harper
213-176 1973 $525

ZANDER, K.   Rassegeflugel. Berlin, (1914-25). Roy. 8vo.,
orig. portfolio, plates. Wheldon 131-729 1974 £25

ZANGWILL, ISRAEL   The Celibates Club. Macmillan, 1905.
Austin 62-709 1974 $8.50

ZANGWILL, ISRAEL   Children of the Ghetto. Macmillan, 1926.
Austin 62-711 1974 $8.50

ZANGWILL, ISRAEL   Dreamers of the Ghetto. Harper, 1899.
Austin 62-710 1974 $7.50

ZANGWILL, ISRAEL   The Forcing House. Macmillan, 1922. 278p.
Austin 51-1067 1973 $8.50

ZANGWILL, ISRAEL   The Master. Harper, 1895. 523p., illus.
Austin 62-713 1974 $8.50

ZANGWILL, ISRAEL   The Melting Pot. Heinemann, 1914. 216p.
Austin 62-714 1974 $8.50

ZANGWILL, ISRAEL   The Next Religion. Macmillan, 1912. 194p.
Austin 51-1069 1973 $7.50

ZANGWILL, ISRAEL   Now and Forever. McBride, 1925. 156p.
Austin 62-715 1974 $10

ZANGWILL, ISRAEL   Selected Works. 1938. 3 vols. in 1, orig.
edition. Austin 57-724 1974 $21.25

ZANGWILL, ISRAEL   Selected Works. 1938. 3 vols in one, orig.
ed. Austin 62-716 1974 $21.25

ZANGWILL, ISRAEL   Speeches, Articles, and Letters of. London,
1937. 8vo., orig. cloth, first edition. Bow Windows 62-522 1974 £5

ZANGWILL, ISRAEL   They That Walk in Darkness. Philadelphia, 1899.
First edition. Biblo & Tannen 213-615 1973 $15

ZANGWILL, ISRAEL   Too Much Money. Macmillan, 1925. 102p.
Austin 51-1070 1973 $7.50

ZANGWILL, ISRAEL   The Voice of Jerusalem. London, 1920.
8vo., orig. cloth. Bow Windows 62-523 1974 £6

ZANGWILL, ISRAEL   The Voice of Jerusalem. 1921. 368 pages.
Austin 57-725 1974 $10

ZANGWILL, ISRAEL   The Voice of Jerusalem. Macmillan, 1921.
Austin 62-717 1974 $10

ZANGWILL, ISRAEL   The War God. Heinemann, 1914. 164p.
Austin 62-718 1974 $10

ZANGWILL, ISRAEL   Without Prejudice. Century, 1896. 384p.
Austin 62-719 1974 $7.50

ZANI, P.   Materiali per Servire alla Storia dell' Origine e
de' Progressi dell' Incisione in Rame e in Legno. Parma, 1802. 8vo., plates,
contemporary speckled calf. Quaritch 940-283 1974 £30

ZANOTTI, FRANCESCO MARIA   Della Forza de'Corpi. 1752. Small 4to.,
half vellum, gilt, ex-library, first edition. Zeitlin 235-246 1974 $75

ZANUCK, DARRYL F.   Noah's Ark. Grosset and Dunlap, 1928.
Austin 51-1068 1973 $10

ZASHCHITA RASTEUIIOT VREDITELI   Bulletin du Bureau Permanent des
Congres Entomo-Phytopathologiques de Russie. Leningrad, 1924-29. Vols. 1-6
in 3 vols., roy. 8vo., half cloth. Wheldon 131-885 1974 £20

ZATTA, ANTONIO   Atlante Novissimo. 1779-85. Folio, 4 vols.,
contemporary vellum backed boards, maps, fine. Bow Windows 64-773 1974
£2,750

ZECH, JULIUS   Tafelin der Additions. Leipzig, 1849. Small
4to., orig. black cloth, first edition. Zeitlin 235-247 1974 $47.50

ZEILLER, R.   Vegetaux Fossiles du Terrain Houiller de la
France. Paris, 1880. 2 vols., 4to., wrappers. Wheldon 131-1101 1974 £10

ZEITLIN, IDA   Skazki. 1926. Roy. 8vo., illus., plates,
orig. buckram gilt. Howes 186-1968 1974 £7.75

ZEITSCHRIFT der Gesellschaft fur Erdkunde zu Berlin. Berlin, 1928. Roy. 8vo.,
cloth, plates. Wheldon 131-1102 1974 £5

ZELLER, H.   Feldblumen aus Dem Heilingen Land. Basel,
1875. 4to., orig. boards, colour printed plates, first edition. Wheldon 128-1327
1973 £10

ZELLER, H.   Feldblumen aus Dem Heiligen Land. Basel,
1875. 4to., orig. boards, plates, first edition. Wheldon 130-1222 1974 £10

ZELLER, H.   Wild Flowers of the Holy Land. 1876. 4to.,
orig. cloth, plates, second edition. Wheldon 129-1137 1974 £15

ZELLER, P. C.   Beitrage zur Kenntniss. Vienna, 1872-75.
8vo., plates. Wheldon 129-698 1974 £5

ZELLNER, J.   Chemie der Hoheren Pilze. Leipzig, 1907.
8vo., buckram. Wheldon 129-1378 1974 £7.50

ZENE Artzney. Mainz, 1532. 4to., modern wrappers, cloth case, extremely
rare, second edition. Schuman 37-273 1974 $3500

ZERVOS, C.   Die Kunst Kataloniens, Baukunst, Plastik,
Malerei, vom 10. Bis Zum 15. Jahrhundert. Vienna, 1937. Folio, illus.,
canvas. Quaritch 940-364 1974 £10

ZEVIANI, GIOVANNI VERARDO   Del Flato a Favore del' Ipocondriaci. Verona, 1761. 4to., orig. limp boards, second edition. Schuman 37-274 1974 $65

ZIEBER, EUGENE   Hearaldry in America. Philadelphia, 1909. Illus., gilt dec. cloth, fine copy, second edition. Wilson 63-26 1974 $40

ZIEGLER, H. E.   Lehrbuch der Vergleichenden. 1902. Roy 8vo., cloth, plate. Wheldon 129-602 1974 £5

ZIEGLER, J. L.   An Authentic History of Donegal Presbyterian Church. Mount Joy, (1902). 8vo., orig. bindings, plates. Butterfield 8-528 1974 $17.50

ZIGROSSER, CARL   Six Centuries of Fine Prints. New York, 1937. Sm. 4to., illus., bdg. slightly soiled. Biblo & Tannen 213-385 1973 $17.50

ZILBOORG, GREGORY   The Medical Man and the Witch During the Renaissance. Baltimore, 1935. Library stamp. Rittenhouse 46-673 1974 $15

ZIMMERMAN, GODFREY   Autobiography. London, 1852. 8vo., orig. blue cloth, frontispiece, first edition. Ximenes 35-622 1974 $10

ZIMMERMANN, E. A. W.   A Political Survey of the Present State of Europe. 1787. 8vo., contemporary quarter calf, uncut, fine, first edition. Hill 126-300 1974 £18

ZINCKE, F. BARHAM   Egypt of the Pharaos and of the Khedive. Orig. cloth, rubbed, second edition. Covent 56-405 1974 £6.50

ZINCKE, F. BARHAM   A Month in Switzerland. London, 1873. 8vo., orig. green cloth, first edition. Ximenes 35-623 1974 $15

ZINKEISEN, DORIS   Designing for the Stage. n.d. Small 4to., cloth-backed boards, illus., English first edition. Covent 56-2078 1974 £6.30

ZINN, JOHANN GOTTFRIED   Descriptio Anatomica Ocvli Hvmani Iconibvs Illvstrata. 1755. 4to., boards, first edition. Dawsons PM 249-522 1974 £265

ZIONIST ORGANIZATION OF AMERICA   The American War Congress and Zionism. 1919. Austin 62-722 1974 $17.50

ZIPF, GEORGE KINGSLEY   National Unity and Disunity. 1941. 408p. Austin 62-723 1974 $17.50

ZIRKLE, C.   The Beginnings of Plant Hybridization. Philadelphia, 1936. Roy. 8vo., cloth, plates. Wheldon 131-255 1974 £5

ZISKIND SEGAL RASHKOW   Tavi Le'zikaron. Breslau, 1831. Text trifle spotted, else clean and sound, cloth backed boards. Thomas 32-63 1974 £5

ZITTEL, K. A.   Handbuch der Palaeontologie. Munich, 1876-93. 5 vols., roy. 8vo., half cloth, scarce, complete set. Wheldon 131-1104 1974 £50

ZITTEL, K. A.   Text-Book of Paleontology. 1913-32. 8vo., 3 vols., cloth, second edition. Wheldon 130-986 1974 £15

ZITTEL, K. A.   Traite de Palaeontologie. Paris, 1883-94. 4 vols., roy. 8vo., orig. wrappers. Wheldon 131-1105 1974 £30

ZITTEL, K. A.   Traite de Paleontologie. Paris, 1883-94. Roy 8vo., orig. wrappers, 4 vols. Wheldon 129-880 1974 £30

ZITTEL, K. A.   Traite de Paleontologie. Paris, Munich and Leipzig, 1891. Roy 8vo., wrappers. Wheldon 129-881 1974 £7.50

ZOBEL, JOHANN GEORG   Beschreibung einer Flaechen-Berechnung- und Theilungs-Maschine. Munich, 1815. 4to., orig. dec. boards, plates, fine, first edition. Dawsons PM 245-781 1974 £20

ZOLA, EMILE   L'Argent. Paris, 1891. 12mo., three quarter cloth, uncut, orig. wrapper, first edition. L. Goldschmidt 42-415 1974 $130

ZOLA, EMILE   L'Assommoir. London, 1928. Orig. boards, paper label, fine, boxed, signed, specail limited edition. Jenkins 48-558 1973 $40

ZOLA, EMILE   Le Docteur Pascal. Paris, 1893. 12mo., full cloth a la Bradel, uncut, orig. wrapper, first edition. L. Goldschmidt 42-416 1974 $140

ZOLA, EMILE   The Fortune of the Rougons. Paris, n.d. Wrappers, suppressed English edition. Covent 56-1390 1974 £7.50

ZOLA, EMILE   La Joie de Vivre. Paris, 1884. 12mo., contemporary cloth, uncut, orig. wrapper, first edition. L. Goldschmidt 42-417 1974 $150

ZOLA, EMILE   Lettre a la Jeunesse. Paris, 1897. 8vo., orig. wrapper, first edition. L. Goldschmidt 42-418 1974 $20

ZOLA, EMILE   Lourdes, les Trois Villes I. Paris, 1894. 12mo., full purple cloth, orig. wrapper, uncut, faded, first edition. L. Goldschmidt 42-419 1974 $125

ZOLA, EMILE   Nana. Paris, 1882. Large 8vo., leather label, contemporary full cloth, first illus. edition. L. Goldschmidt 42-420 1974 $180

ZOLA, EMILE   Les Quatre Evangiles. Paris, 1901. 2 vols., 8vo., half cloth, orig. wrapper, excellent copy, first edition. L. Goldschmidt 42-421 1974 $160

ZOLA, EMILE   Les Quatre Evangiles. Paris, 1903. 2 vols., 8vo., half cloth, orig. wrapper, uncut, excellent copy, first edition. L. Goldschmidt 42-422 1974 $150

ZOLA, EMILE   Les Trois Villes. Paris, 1896. 12mo., three quarter calf, gilt, orig. wrapper, first edition. L. Goldschmidt 42-423 1974 $125

ZOLA, EMILE   Le Voeu d'Une Morte. Paris, 1889. 12mo., half green cloth, orig. wrapper, uncut. L. Goldschmidt 42-424 1974 $17.50

ZOLLERS, GEORGE D.   Thrilling Incidents on Sea and Land. Mount Morris, 1892. Cloth. Hayman 57-777 1974 $10

ZONCA, VITTORIO   Novo Teatro di Machine. 1656. Small folio, contemporary paper boards, uncut. Zeitlin 235-248 1974 $975

ZONCA, VITTORIO   Novo Teatro di Machine et Edificii per Varie et Sicure Operationi. Padua, 1656. Folio, engravings, stains, contemporary vellum over thin boards, good copy. Schafer 8-177 1973 sFr. 3,000

ZOOLOGICAL SOCIETY OF LONDON   The Gardens and Menagerie of the Zoological Society Delineated. 1830-31. 2 vols., 8vo., new cloth, library stamp, scarce. Wheldon 128-298 1973 £10

THE ZOOLOGIST. 1843-1916. 74 vols., 8vo., uniform red cloth, bookplate. Wheldon 131-469 1974 £250

ZOPF, W.   Die Pilze. Breslau, 1890. 8vo., half morocco, rubbed. Wheldon 131-1480 1974 £10

ZOTTOLI, ANGELO   Cursus Literature Sinicae. 1879-82. 5 vols., thick 8vo., half calf, stained. Howes 186-1970 1974 £45

ZOUCH, THOMAS   The Life of Izaak Walton. 1823. Large paper copy, portrait frontispiece, text illus., extra illus. with early engravings, 4to., dark green levant morocco gilt, fine copy. Sawyer 293-281 1974 £95

ZOUCH, THOMAS   Memoirs of the Life and Writings of Sir Philip Sidney. (York & London), 1808. 4to., contemporary calf, gilt, first edition. Ximenes 35-624 1974 $75

ZOUCH, THOMAS   Memoirs of Life and Writings of Sir Philip
Sidney. 1809. 4to., new buckram, second edition. Allen 216-1854 1974 $15

ZUCCHI, NICOLO   Optica Philosophia Experimentis. 1652. 4to.,
old vellum, gilt. Zeitlin 235-249 1974 $250

ZUCKER, A. E.   Ibsen, the Master Builder. Holt, 1929.
Austin 51-1074 1973 $12.50

ZUCKER, A. F.   The Chinese Theater. 1925. Buckram-backed
patterned boards, fine, English first edition. Covent 56-725 1974 £50

ZUCKERMAN, NATHAN   The Wine of Violence. 1947. 362p. Austin
62-724 1974 $15

ZUJOVIC, J. M.   Les Roches des Cordilleres. Paris, 1884. 4to.,
boards, plates. Wheldon 131-1106 1974 £7.50

THE ZURICH Letters. 1842-45. 2 vols., thick 8vo., orig. cloth, worn.
Howes 185-1537 1974 £10

ZWEIG, STEFAN   Deux Grands Romanciers du XIXe Siecle.
Paris, 1927. First French edition, presentation copy inscribed, wrappers, spine
faded. Covent 51-2086 1973 £5

ZWEIG, STEFAN   The Old-Book Peddlar and Other Tales for
Bibliophiles. Chicago, 1937. 16mo., boards, presentation copy. Goodspeed's
578-555 1974 $10

ZYCHA, H.   Kryptogamen Flora der Mark Brandenburg:
Band VIa Pilze II, Mucorineae. Leipzig, 1935. 8vo., buckram, extremely
rare orig. printing. Wheldon 131-1481 1974 £15

ZYCHA, H.   Kryptogamenflora der Mark Brandenburg. Leipzig, 1935. 8vo., buckram. Wheldon 129-1379 1974 £15

ZYL, JOHANNES VAN   Theatrum Machinarum Universale. 1734. Folio,
contemporary half calf, fine, rare, plates, first edition. Dawsons PM 245-782
1974 £530